International Directory of

COMPANY HISTORIES

CONTENTS

Preface . . . . page vii
List of Abbreviations ix

Company Histories

Alberta Energy Company Ltd. 3
Allied Irish Banks, plc 7
AltaVista Company 11
Altera Corporation 14
American Biltrite Inc. 19
American Foods Group 23
Angelica Corporation 28
Applica Incorporated 32
Ashanti Goldfields Company Limited 37
AsiaInfo Holdings, Inc. 41
Assisted Living Concepts, Inc. 45
At Home Corporation 48
Atlanta National League Baseball Club, Inc. 52
Atmos Energy Corporation 56
Baker & Taylor Corporation 59
Bertelsmann A.G. 63
Bingham Dana LLP 68
Boral Limited 72
Borders Group, Inc. 77
Boyd Gaming Corporation 80
British Airways PLC 83
Bull S.A. 89
Cahners Business Information 92
Casual Corner Group, Inc. 96
Catalina Lighting, Inc. 99
Central Japan Railway Company 103
Cinram International, Inc. 107
Companhia Vale do Rio Doce 111
Comverse Technology, Inc. 115
ContiGroup Companies, Inc. 119
Costco Wholesale Corporation 123
Cravath, Swaine & Moore 126
CTB International Corporation 129
Dawson Holdings PLC 132
Dechert 135
Dover Downs Entertainment, Inc. 139
DreamWorks SKG 142
Du Pareil au Même 147
Electronics for Imaging, Inc. 150
Enbridge Inc. 154
EZCORP Inc. 159
Fedders Corporation 162
Fender Musical Instruments Company 168
Fox Entertainment Group, Inc. 173
Franklin Electric Company, Inc. 177
GEAC Computer Corporation Ltd. 181
Gerresheimer Glas AG 186
Givaudan SA 190
Goss Holdings, Inc. 194
GrandVision S.A. 198
Grey Wolf, Inc. 201
Griffin Land & Nurseries, Inc. 204
Grolier Incorporated 207
Guinness/UDV 212
The Hain Celestial Group, Inc. 217
Harmonic Inc. 221
Harrah's Entertainment, Inc. 224
Hasbro, Inc. 229
International Creative Management, Inc. . . . 235
IONA Technologies plc 238
James Beattie plc 242
J.C. Penney Company, Inc. 245
Juniper Networks, Inc. 251
Kimberly-Clark Corporation 256
Kinko's, Inc. 261
Lincare Holdings Inc. 265
Loblaw Companies Limited 268

Lynch Corporation 273
MAXIMUS, Inc. 277
Minolta Co., Ltd. 281
National Presto Industries, Inc. 286
OfficeMax, Inc. 291
Peebles Inc. 296
Pepper Hamilton LLP 300
Plum Creek Timber Company, Inc. 304
Randstad Holding n.v. 307
RF Micro Devices, Inc. 311
River Oaks Furniture, Inc. 314
Robert Bosch GmbH 317
Rockford Corporation 322
Rockwell Automation 326
Ross Stores, Inc. 332
Rowan Companies, Inc. 336
Rural Cellular Corporation 340
The Sage Group 343
St. Jude Medical, Inc. 347
Samsonite Corporation 353
SAP AG 358
Sawtek Inc. 364
SED International Holdings, Inc. 367
Shells Seafood Restaurants, Inc. 370
Skis Rossignol S.A. 373
SmartForce PLC 377
Smithfield Foods, Inc. 381
The Sports Authority, Inc. 385
Stearns, Inc. 389
Stone Manufacturing Company 392
Swinerton Inc. 397
Taittinger S.A. 401
Tattered Cover Book Store 406
TBWA\Chiat\Day 410
Telecom Italia S.p.A. 415
Terra Lycos, Inc. 420
The 3DO Company 426
TV Guide, Inc. 431
Vail Resorts, Inc. 435
Veit Companies 440
Verizon Communications 443
Vinci 450
Waters Corporation 453
Wells-Gardner Electronics Corporation 458
White Wave 462
Wipro Limited 465
WMC, Limited 469
Working Assets Funding Service 473

Index to Companies 477
Index to Industries 663
Geographic Index 697
Notes on Contributors 727

PREFACE

The St. James Press series *The International Directory of Company Histories (IDCH)* is intended for reference use by students, business people, librarians, historians, economists, investors, job candidates, and others who seek to learn more about the historical development of the world's most important companies. To date, *IDCH* has covered over 5,250 companies in 43 volumes.

Inclusion Criteria

Most companies chosen for inclusion in *IDCH* have achieved a minimum of US$25 million in annual sales and are leading influences in their industries or geographical locations. Companies may be publicly held, private, or nonprofit. State-owned companies that are important in their industries and that may operate much like public or private companies also are included. Wholly owned subsidiaries and divisions are profiled if they meet the requirements for inclusion. Entries on companies that have had major changes since they were last profiled may be selected for updating.

The *IDCH* series highlights 10% private and nonprofit companies, and features updated entries on approximately 45 companies per volume.

Entry Format

Each entry begins with the company's legal name, the address of its headquarters, its telephone, toll-free, and fax numbers, and its web site. A statement of public, private, state, or parent ownership follows. A company with a legal name in both English and the language of its headquarters country is listed by the English name, with the native-language name in parentheses.

The company's founding or earliest incorporation date, the number of employees, and the most recent available sales figures follow. Sales figures are given in local currencies with equivalents in U.S. dollars. For some private companies, sales figures are estimates and indicated by the abbreviation *est.* The entry lists the exchanges on which a company's stock is traded and its ticker symbol, as well as the company's NAIC codes.

Entries generally contain a *Company Perspectives* box which provides a short summary of the company's mission, goals, and ideals, a *Key Dates* box highlighting milestones in the company's history, lists of *Principal Subsidiaries, Principal Divisions, Principal Operating Units, Principal Competitors,* and articles for *Further Reading.*

American spelling is used throughout *IDCH*, and the word "billion" is used in its U.S. sense of one thousand million.

Sources

Entries have been compiled from publicly accessible sources both in print and on the Internet such as general and academic periodicals, books, annual reports, and material supplied by the companies themselves.

Cumulative Indexes

IDCH contains three indexes: the **Index to Companies**, which provides an alphabetical index to companies discussed in the text as well as to companies profiled, the **Index to Industries**, which allows researchers to locate companies by their principal industry, and the **Geographic Index**, which lists companies alphabetically by the country of their headquarters. The indexes are cumulative and specific instructions for using them are found immediately preceding each index.

Suggestions Welcome

Comments and suggestions from users of *IDCH* on any aspect of the product as well as suggestions for companies to be included or updated are cordially invited. Please write:

The Editor
International Directory of Company Histories
St. James Press
27500 Drake Rd.
Farmington Hills, Michigan 48331-3535

ABBREVIATIONS FOR FORMS OF COMPANY INCORPORATION

A.B.	Aktiebolaget (Sweden)
A.G.	Aktiengesellschaft (Germany, Switzerland)
A.S.	Aksjeselskap (Denmark, Norway)
A.S.	Atieselskab (Denmark)
A.Ş.	Anomin Şirket (Turkey)
B.V.	Besloten Vennootschap met beperkte, Aansprakelijkheid (The Netherlands)
Co.	Company (United Kingdom, United States)
Corp.	Corporation (United States)
G.I.E.	Groupement d'Intérêt Economique (France)
GmbH	Gesellschaft mit beschränkter Haftung (Germany)
H.B.	Handelsbolaget (Sweden)
Inc.	Incorporated (United States)
KGaA	Kommanditgesellschaft auf Aktien (Germany)
K.K.	Kabushiki Kaisha (Japan)
LLC	Limited Liability Company (Middle East)
Ltd.	Limited (Canada, Japan, United Kingdom, United States)
N.V.	Naamloze Vennootschap (The Netherlands)
OY	Osakeyhtiöt (Finland)
PLC	Public Limited Company (United Kingdom)
PTY.	Proprietary (Australia, Hong Kong, South Africa)
S.A.	Société Anonyme (Belgium, France, Switzerland)
SpA	Società per Azioni (Italy)

ABBREVIATIONS FOR CURRENCY

$	United States dollar
£	United Kingdom pound
¥	Japanese yen
A$	Australian dollar
AED	United Arab Emirates dirham
B	Thai baht
B	Venezuelan bolivar
BFr	Belgian franc
C$	Canadian dollar
CHF	Switzerland franc
COL	Colombian peso
Cr	Brazilian cruzado
CZK	Czech Republic koruny
DA	Algerian dinar
Dfl	Netherlands florin
DKr	Danish krone
DM	German mark
E£	Egyptian pound
Esc	Portuguese escudo
EUR	Euro dollars
FFr	French franc
Fmk	Finnish markka
GRD	Greek drachma
HK$	Hong Kong dollar
HUF	Hungarian forint
IR£	Irish pound
K	Zambian kwacha
KD	Kuwaiti dinar
L	Italian lira
LuxFr	Luxembourgian franc
M$	Malaysian ringgit
N	Nigerian naira
Nfl	Netherlands florin
NIS	Israeli new shekel
NKr	Norwegian krone
NT$	Taiwanese dollar
NZ$	New Zealand dollar
P	Philippine peso
PLN	Polish zloty
Pta	Spanish peseta
R	Brazilian real
R	South African rand
RMB	Chinese renminbi
RO	Omani rial
Rp	Indonesian rupiah
Rs	Indian rupee
Ru	Russian ruble
S$	Singapore dollar
Sch	Austrian schilling
SFr	Swiss franc
SKr	Swedish krona
SRls	Saudi Arabian riyal
W	Korean won
W	South Korean won

Alberta Energy Company Ltd.

#3900, 421-7 Avenue S.W.
Calgary, Alberta T2P 4K9
Canada
Telephone: (403) 266-8111
Fax: (403) 266-8154
Web site: http://www.aec.ca
Public Company
Incorporated: 1973
Employees: 1,173
Sales: $2,200 million (2000)
Stock Exchanges: Toronto New York
Ticker Symbol: AOG
NAIC: 211111 Crude Petroleum and Natural Gas Extraction

Alberta Energy Company Ltd. is the largest Canadian-based producer of North American gas and the largest North American independent gas storage operator. The company's total assets exceeded $50 million as of December 31, 2000. Alberta Energy Company's primary activities involve oil and natural gas exploration, development and production, and the ownership and operation of petroleum pipeline systems. The company's activities are focused on three ''growth platforms:'' the Western Canada Growth Platform, the United States Rocky Mountains Growth Platform, and the Ecuador Growth Platform. In December 1995, Alberta Energy Company Ltd. paid $1.1 billion to acquire Conwest Exploration Company Ltd., one of the most prominent oil and gas exploration firms in North America. The transaction immediately propelled Alberta Energy to the top of the oil and gas industry, increasing its market capitalization to $2.2 billion. The merger was a boon to Alberta Energy, and increased its exploration land by 56 percent, natural gas reserves by 49 percent, conventional oil reserves by 84 percent, gas production by 55 percent, and conventional oil production by 96 percent. In 1995, Alberta Energy sold its non-oil and gas assets. During the following five years, Alberta Energy doubled production of oil and natural gas liquids and expanded midstream business. The company's late 1990's and early twenty-first century ventures led it to become the largest foreign oil producer in Ecuador and a significant gas producer in the Rocky Mountain area of the United States.

Early History

At the height of the OPEC oil embargo during the early 1970s, the government of the province of Alberta, Canada, decided to initiate a capital investment program to lessen the dependence on foreign oil. The government organized a group of managers and executives from the oil and gas exploration industry and proposed to form a new company that would be operated on a for-profit basis by non-government personnel. The concept of forming a new oil and gas exploration firm was attractive to a number of the businessmen approached by the Alberta provincial government, and they agreed to organize and manage the company, despite some reservations expressed regarding the volatility of the industry at that time.

Initially, Alberta Energy focused on gas exploration and production as well as conventional oil exploration and production. Operating almost exclusively in the province of Alberta, the company purchased extensive tracts of land in the Berland River area of west-central Alberta and the region around East Peace River Arch, both with potentially high reserves of oil and gas. During the mid- and late-1970s, management decided to diversify its activities to provide a more stable cash flow for company operations, and the company entered the lumber industry to produce fiberboard for the commercial market.

In the early 1980s, however, with the fear of another oil embargo receding into the past, the deregulation of the natural gas industry in Canada, and the highly protectionist attitude of the United States in the area of forest products, the company's revenues began to plummet. Yet, the talent and dogged persistence of the company's management team guided it through these trying years. Management successfully renegotiated Alberta Energy Company's gas contracts, established more sensitive market pricing, and confirmed long-term purchasing agreements. As the price for a barrel of crude oil fell, it was offset by the concurrent lower price for petroleum land purchase, and company management began to acquire ever-larger tracts of

Key Dates:

1973: Company is incorporated.
1975: Company sells shares publicly.
1986: Company establishes pipeline division.
1989: Company begins construction of Vancouver Island Natural Gas Pipeline.
1994: Alberta Government completes divestiture of company shares and company becomes fully privatized.
1995: Company acquires Conwest Exploration Company Ltd.
1999: Company acquires Pacalta Resources Ltd. and begins oil exploration in Oriente Basin (Ecuador/Colombia).
2000: Company acquires McMurry Oil Company and begins expansion into the Rocky Mountain area of United States.
2001: Express Pipeline adds connection in Montana and opens new U.S. markets for Alberta oil.

land in Alberta for exploration and development. In addition, the provincial government of Alberta declared a royalty holiday for new oil production, thereby boosting the profits of new oil discovered by the company during this time. Finally, management implemented a restructuring program that reduced the company's operating expenses by consolidating the responsibilities of staff members, requiring longer work hours of its employees, and initiating a cost-cutting strategy for all oil and gas exploration.

Growth and Expansion in the Late 1980s

The restructuring strategy implemented by Alberta Energy Company's management team was successful beyond its expectations. From 1982 to 1986, the average daily western Canadian gas production at the company increased from 193 to 252 million cubic feet. The average daily western Canadian conventional oil production from 1982 to 1986 increased from 346 to 4,613 barrels. The company's oil and natural gas landholdings during the period shot up from 2.8 million to 3.2 million acres. By 1986, the company held interest in 2,960 producing gas wells and 265 producing oil wells, almost all of them located in Alberta. Also during this time, the company acquired the following: Chieftain Development Company, Ltd., a firm involved in the international gas and oil exploration industry; Pan-Alberta Gas Ltd., one of Canada's leading natural gas marketers; and Blue Ridge Lumber Ltd., a softwood lumber plant that Alberta Energy management turned into a leading medium density fiberboard manufacturing operation.

In 1986, the company established a separate operating division for its burgeoning pipeline operation. Earlier, the company had commissioned the building of the Alberta Sands Oil Pipeline, a 270-mile pipeline that delivered oil from a plant located at Fort McMurray to the Edmonton area, where it was distributed to local refineries. Another pipeline, the Cold Lake Heavy Oil Pipeline, provided a transportation network for heavy oil blends from the Primrose/Cold Lake area to Edmonton. The final system to be incorporated into the company's pipeline operating division was the Alberta ethane-gathering network, which collected ethane from natural gas processing plants within Alberta and transported it to storage caverns located near Fort Saskatchewan.

By 1989, Alberta Energy Company owned more than six million acres of exploratory and development landholdings in Alberta, Saskatchewan, British Columbia, and Beaufort, and ranked as one of the top 10 companies in total reserves and in oil and gas production levels in the Western Canadian Sedimentary Basin. One of the major areas of exploration during this time was the Waskahigan/Karr/Gold Creek in west-central Alberta. The company held 330,000 acres of land in the area, which included four exploratory wells and 10 development wells. Alberta Energy Company reported 100 billion cubic feet of natural gas reserves and 3.6 million barrels of oil and natural gas liquids in its landholdings. Within a year, management projected that production levels would surpass 18 million cubic feet of gas and 600 barrels of natural gas liquids. Although prices for gas declined by four percent, sales of synthetic and conventional oil increased by more than 20 percent and production was at record levels.

During the same year, Alberta Energy Company, through its 50 percent share in the Pacific Coast Energy Corporation, successfully negotiated with both the Canadian government and the British Columbia provincial government to begin construction of the Vancouver Island Natural Gas Pipeline. With a price tag of more than $280 million, the pipeline would deliver natural gas to Vancouver Island and southwestern British Columbia. Alberta Energy also had an interest in the Iroquois Gas Transmission System, which stretched from Iroquois, Ontario to Long Island, New York. In addition to these new developments, the company completed a major renovation and expansion of its Cold Lake Heavy Oil Pipeline, which operated from northeastern Alberta to Edmonton. One of the innovative aspects of this renovation program included state-of-the-art variable speed pump technology. The company's operation of all the pipeline systems under its control was one of the safest in Canada, and for the third straight year there had been no lost-time mishap.

In the two other sectors of the company's activities, development occurred rapidly. The Blue Ridge Lumber operation reported record shipments of both lumber and medium density fiberboard in 1989, with a high volume of chips sales adding to the firm's profitability. Under Alberta Energy management, Blue Ridge Lumber Ltd. was committed to extensive and continuous reforestation programs, resulting in nearly 8,000 acres of the company's landholdings being seeded for regeneration. The company's petrochemicals divisions, having experienced a short period of depressed prices for nitrogen fertilizer at the beginning of the year, began to see prices rise as the year went on. In its first full year of operating within the continental United States, Alberta Energy Company had established ammonium nitrate subsidiaries in Borger, Texas, in Beatrice, Nebraska, in Early, Iowa, and in Leal, North Dakota.

Development During the 1990s

In the early 1990s, a severe and widespread economic downturn spread throughout Canada, yet Alberta Energy Company weathered these conditions with remarkable success. In 1992, natural gas sales, measured in cubic feet per day, increased by ten percent, and oil and natural gas liquid sales increased by 12 percent. Because of the company's astute management, especially in the areas of oil and gas production and lumber operations, net earnings rose an impressive 206 percent. Much of this increase was due to strict cost controls, which resulted in a nominal increase of only one percent in operating expenses for 1992. For example, the company's funding and development costs were drastically reduced during the early 1990s. From 1988 to 1990, exploration and development costs amounted to $15.20 per barrel; by 1992, exploration and development costs amounted to $6.40 per barrel.

In 1992, the sources of Alberta Energy Company's operating income were a combination of natural gas, conventional oil, lumber, and pipeline revenues. Surprisingly, during this time, the largest generator of revenue was the company's strong pipeline operation. In 1992, Alberta Energy Company wholly owned and operated approximately 820 miles of crude oil pipelines and had a one-third interest in a highly successful 550-mile methane gathering system in the province of Alberta. In addition, the company still owned a one-half interest in a natural gas pipeline to Vancouver Island. To expand its activities in this area and continue to reduce operating costs, the company began negotiating with a potential Japanese partner to commercialize its "transoil" technology, an innovative technique that uses water to pipeline heavy oil, rather than the traditional oil-based diluent.

1995 was one of the best years for Alberta Energy Company. The company's exploration and development program, the largest to date in more than ten years, resulted in 235 new wells, including 44 that were explorational and 191 that were developmental, with an astounding success rate of 84 percent. Conventional oil production during 1995 increased by 36 percent primarily as a result of new drilling success at the company's Suffield and Ogsten sites. Total liquids production increased by a total of 15 percent, more than 42,000 barrels per day. Although the company maintained and expanded its pipeline network throughout Alberta, as well as other smaller investments, management decided to sell the forest products and lumber operation and its associated fiberboard manufacturing facilities. This allowed Alberta Energy Company to lessen its debt and to garner its financial resources for long-range opportunities.

A major transaction in the company's history, however, involved the acquisition of Conwest Exploration Company Limited for $1.1 billion. One of the most prominent and successful oil and gas exploration companies in North America, Conwest was primarily operating in the West Peace River Arch region of Alberta province. The merger, a friendly transaction, created the second largest publicly traded oil and gas exploration company on the Canadian stock exchanges. More important, the merger dramatically increased Alberta Energy Company's exploration land, natural gas reserves, conventional oil reserves, gas production, and conventional oil production. With the acquisition of Conwest, the company's stock price shot up 22 percent during 1995.

Given the volatility of the oil and gas exploration industry, Alberta Energy Company's purchase of Conwest and its assets provided the long-term stability that management sought. Having sold all of its non-oil and gas business, the company was ready, and possessed the resources, to focus exclusively on oil and gas exploration, processing, pipelines and gas storage.

Into the New Millennium

The company's expansion following the mid-nineties focused primarily on the development of gas and oil in Western Canada, the Rocky Mountain region of the United States, and Ecuador.

The Western Canada exploration and development involved expansion of oil and gas reserves in northeast British Columbia and the western Alberta foothills, thermal recovery of oil at Foster Creek in northeast Alberta, and oil sands development through the Syncrude Joint Venture near Fort McMurray in northeast Alberta.

In the United States, the company focused on the Jonah gas field in Wyoming, and the Mamm Creek gas field in Colorado. In June 2000, Alberta Energy Company Oil & Gas (USA) Inc., a subsidiary of Alberta Energy Company, established the U.S. Rockies Growth Platform through the acquisition of all shares of McMurry Oil Company and other private interests. In February 2001, Alberta Energy Company Oil & Gas (USA) acquired all shares of Ballard Petroleum. Ballard's principal properties were in the Mamm Creek field in the Piceance Basin of Colorado.

Alberta Energy Company was also involved in oil exploration and development in the Oriente Basin, a rainforest area in the northeastern corner of Ecuador bordering Colombia. The Ecuador Growth Platform was established in May 1999 with the acquisition of all outstanding common shares of Pacalta Resources Ltd. Alberta Energy Company positioned its Ecuadorian ventures to act as a catalyst for its vision of building a "Global Super-Independent." In February 2001, Alberta Energy Company became part of an agreement with the Government of Ecuador to construct a new 450,000-barrel-per-day export pipeline.

The company also explored new resource pools in 2000, including locations in the Arctic, off Australia's northwest coast, along Africa's west coast, and in the Caspian Sea off Azerbaijan. In 2001, the company scheduled appraisal and exploration wells in these and other locations. In addition, the company had interests in the development of a 1.3 million acre natural gas site in the Alaska Foothills and Mackenzie Delta and on Alaska's North Slope. The company planned to double production by the year 2004 based upon existing assets.

Pipelines continued to be a significant sector of Alberta Energy Company's business. In the year 2000, The company owned or co-owned several pipelines within Alberta as well as the U.S. Rocky Mountains, the U.S. Midwest, and South America. Alberta Energy Company owned and operated natural gas storage facilities in Alberta, California, and Oklahoma. By the turn of the century, Alberta Energy Company was the largest independent gas storage operator in North America. During the year 2000, Alberta Energy Company acquired a remaining 30 percent interest in Alberta Energy Company Pipelines, L.P., and acquired a 50 percent interest in the Express Pipeline System not already owned. The company also formed the Cold Lake Pipeline Limited Partnership and negotiated long-term commitment contracts with four major producers.

During 2000, Alberta Energy Company oil reserves increased by 27 percent, its reserve life index increased to 17 years, and fourth-quarter profits increased sevenfold. The company set records in annual earnings and cash flow during the quarter, and reported a net income of $306 million with 141 million common shares outstanding held by 40,000 shareholders. Eighty percent of the company's shares were held by major institutional investors.

Principal Subsidiaries

Alberta Energy Company Oil and Gas Partnership; Alberta Energy Company Oil Sands, L.P.; Alberta Energy Company Oil Sands Limited Partnership; Alberta Energy Company Overseas Resources Ltd.; Alberta Energy Company Global Holdings (Bermuda) Ltd.; Alberta Energy International Ltd.; Alberta Energy Company Argentina S.A.; City Investing Company Limited; City Oriente Limited; Alberta Energy Company Pipelines, L.P.; Alberta Oil Sands Pipeline Ltd.; Alberta Energy Company West Ltd.; Alberta Energy Company Liquidity Management Hungary Limited Liability Company; Alenco Inc.; Alberta Energy Company Express Holdings Inc.; Express Pipeline Partnership; Platte Pipe Line Company; Alberta Energy Company Oil and Gas (USA) Inc.; McMurry Oil Company; Fort Collins Consolidated Royalties, Inc.; Green River Pipeline Limited Liability Company; Jonah Gas Gathering Company; Wild Goose Storage Inc.; Express Pipeline Limited Partnership; Marquest Limited Partnership.

Further Reading

''Alberta Energy Company Eyes Expanding Gas Storage,'' *The Oil Daily,* April 16, 2001, v.51.

''Alberta Energy Company Purchases Manchester Gas Storage,'' *Gas Processors Report,* April 2, 2001.

''Alberta Energy Company,'' *Petroleum Economist,* November 2000, v.67 p. 51.

''Alberta Energy Says It Is Buying Ballard Petroleum,'' *The New York Times,* January 19, 2001, p. C3.

''Calgary's Alberta Energy Company Buys Into U.S. Company,'' *Gas Processors Report,* March 19, 2001.

Carlisle, Tamsin, ''Mergers in Canada Heat Up as Prices for Energy Soar,'' *The Wall Street Journal,* January 19, 2001, p. A13.

''First-Quarter 2001 Marked by Multiple Records for Canada's E&P Firms,'' *The Oil Daily,* May 23, 2001, p. 51.

Nguyen, Lily, ''Alberta Energy Company triples profit, boosts dividend,'' *Globe & Mail* (Toronto, Canada), April 19, 2001, p. B7.

Toal, A. Brian, ''Long-Distance Runner.'' Alberta Energy Company Ltd. President Gwyn Morgan Transforming Company into Global Conglomerate,'' *Oil and Gas Investor,* October 2000, v. 20, p. 43.

Tyson, Ray, ''Canada's Aggressive Alberta Energy Sees More Deals in Arctic,'' *Platt's Oilgram News,* October 4, 2000, v. 78, p. 1.

—Thomas Derdak
—update: Elizabeth Shé

Allied Irish Banks, plc

Bank Centre
P.O. Box 452
Ballsbridge
Dublin 4
Ireland
Telephone: (353) 1-660-0311
Fax: (353) 1-660-9137
Web site: http://www.aibgroup.com

Public Company
Incorporated: 1966 as Allied Irish Banks Limited
Employees: 31,000
Total Assets: EUR 79,688 million (2000)
Stock Exchanges: Dublin London New York
Ticker Symbol: AIB
NAIC: 522110 Commercial Banking

Allied Irish Banks, plc (AIB) is the largest bank in Ireland, and its significant investments in the United States, Great Britain, and Europe make it important internationally. As the largest private sector employer in Ireland and the second largest public company, it is difficult to overstate AIB's importance on its home turf: 40 percent of the banked population there are customers. The company's assets are valued at approximately EUR 80 billion, making it one of the world's 200 largest banks and placing it among the *Financial Times* 500 top Global Companies.

Origins

As the three points in the company's old logo suggest, Allied Irish Banks Limited was formed in 1966 as an amalgamation of three banks: the Royal Bank of Ireland Ltd. (founded 1836), the Provincial Bank of Ireland Ltd. (founded 1825), and the Cork-based Munster and Leinster Bank Ltd. (founded in 1885 to take over the failed Munster Bank). Munster and Leinster Bank was the largest of the three independent banks remaining in Ireland and contributed more than half of the shares of the new holding company. (The heritage of these banks could be traced back even further; Munster and Leinster's holdings included those of a private bank dating to the days of William of Orange.) The banks, when combined, provided thorough coverage of the island, both geographically and economically. Altogether, their combined assets were worth £250 million. After operating in a type of loose "Trinity" arrangement, in 1968 the banks began to trade as one company. This integration was fully completed in 1972.

Many industries in the British Isles faced consolidation during the 1960s. For the Irish banking industry, this reduction in numbers first affected the numerous private banks. *The Economist* reported the island had a thousand branch offices to serve less than five million people; it was felt that fewer, larger banks would be able to provide more modern and efficient service (the bank employees union, which had held a strike just before AIB's creation, was another factor).

Both Allied Irish Banks and its slightly larger rival, the Bank of Ireland, entered this phase of consolidation under pressure from North American competitors, which first entered the Irish market in 1965, beginning with First National City Bank. Both the Bank of Ireland and AIB began offering new services and forming international strategic alliances; AIB showed itself to be more dedicated to merchant and industrial banking. In a March 1968 company statement, Chairman Edmond M.R. O'Driscoll reported on a newly formed alliance between AIB and Toronto-Dominion Bank, strengthening AIB's international stance. At the same time, a recently devalued pound stimulated growth on the home front.

AIB continued to standardize its three families of branch offices, which in 1971 numbered 281 in the Irish Republic and 46 in Northern Ireland; only 11 branches had been closed after the merger. During this time, several subsidiaries specialized in various areas of business finance: the Hire-Purchase Company of Ireland and its Northern Ireland counterpart (brought to the group by the Munster and Leinster Bank); Mercantile Credit Co. of Ireland (a hire-purchase bank in which Provincial Bank had a 40 percent stake); Allied Irish Leasing Ltd, which financed industrial expansion; and the Allied Irish Investment Corporation, a merchant bank formed in association with Hambros Bank, Toronto-Dominion, and the Irish Life Assurance Company. In 1967, the group boasted assets of £318

Company Perspectives:

AIB, wherever we operate, will be the leading Irish banking group, creating superior value for our customers and shareholders. Our success will be determined by: the level of customer satisfaction; the return to our shareholders; the contribution of individuals and teams; our performance as a good corporate citizen.

million. The late 1960s were booming years for Irish industry, one of the fastest growing in Europe, and for AIB.

Changes in the 1970s

In the early 1970s, Allied Irish Banks, which formerly derived income only from interest on loans, began charging fees for services, such as 5p per transaction and 5p per £100 withdrawal of cash. The competitive situation inspired the new way of doing business.

Wages accounted for three-fourths of a bank's costs; in the 1970s, bank employees, among the most highly paid workers in the country, lobbied for increases in salaries. The Irish Bank Officials Association, spurred by staff alienation after the merger, called a devastating, eight-month strike in 1970, which sent customers scrambling to the smaller, nonassociated banks. Two other strikes were called during the decade. As Mary Campbell reported in *The Banker*, ''[The Union's] strength is reflected . . . in the incredible facts that these banks cannot employ married women or take on new staff (except in certain specialized cases) who are 21 years of age; starting salaries are the same at all ages.'' To make matters more expensive, the banks often sent promising staff members to earn an M.B.A. Both AIB and the Bank of Ireland succeeded in reforming staff grades in 1989, resulting in some cost savings and better utilization of specially skilled employees without significant layoffs. As AIB Chief Executive Gerald Scanlan told The Banker: ''We're no longer paying people IR £24,000 for an IR £8,000 job.'' At the same time, AIB continued to fight for longer hours; its Irish branches were open only half the hours of its American ones.

A common language and a history of Irish immigration made America an attractive overseas market. AIB's first New York branch opened in 1978, specializing in serving companies from the British Isles. In 1983, AIB Group invested in a 43 percent share of America's First Maryland Bancorp, with its 1820s roots making it even more venerable than the original three Allied Irish Banks. After increasing its stake in First Maryland to 49.7 percent in 1988, AIB offered to buy the rest of the shares and, by March 1989, the company had, for a total investment of US $522 million. At the end of 1991, AIB's subsidiary First Maryland Bancorp bought The York Bank and Trust Company, entering AIB in the southern Pennsylvania market. First Maryland Bancorp offered credit cards through another subsidiary, First Omni Bank NA.

AIB restructured itself in 1986. It became a stockbroker in 1987 with the opening of Allied Irish Securities, a few weeks before the market collapsed on infamous Black Monday. Two years later, after agreeing to buy Ireland's second largest stockbroker, Goodbody James Capel (the Bank of Ireland owned 49 percent of the largest, J&E Davy), it formed the Capital Markets division to manage all of its treasury, international, corporate banking, and investment banking operations. Insurance and stock brokering interested both AIB and its chief rival.

Expansion in the 1990s

Early in 1991, AIB merged with TSB Northern Ireland plc. The company's operations in Northern Ireland, known as First Trust Bank, numbered nearly 100 branches with 1,400 employees. Although AIB spent much effort in developing its successful overseas business, it (like the Bank of Ireland) seemed to fare best in its home territory. This is largely because of the Irish economy, which performed relatively well, with a less intense downturn early in the 1990s than that of Britain, where AIB also had a long-established presence. In 1992, Allied Irish lost IR £26 million in Britain; the next year it succeeded in reclaiming a profit of IR £7 million. Unfortunately, Ireland, quite dependent on England for trade, suffered its own recession a couple of years later, enduring high unemployment and high interest rates.

In the mid-1990s, Ireland accounted for just under half of the group's income and the United States accounted for about 30 percent. Besides its subsidiary First Maryland Bancorp, the group maintained an AIB branch in New York City. Other locations included Brussels, the Cayman Islands, the Channel Islands, Frankfurt, and the Isle of Man. In addition, the company obtained a 16.3 percent shareholding (worth about IR £13 million) in the Polish bank Wielkopolski Bank Kredytowy. AIB had been advising the 63-branch bank since 1991. Neither AIB nor the Bank of Ireland appeared especially optimistic about continental prospects, with the exception of Eastern Europe. In 1994, AIB bid for the state-owned Budapest Bank; AIB would later concentrate its Eastern European expansion efforts on Polish markets alone.

The Pacific Rim was also an important venue. By the late-1980s, offices were operational in Singapore, Sidney, and Tokyo. In 1995, the company's partnership with Phillip Securities in Singapore was mirrored by a new Malaysian partnership involving both Phillip and Grand Care. Both ventures shared the name Allied Phillip Capital Management and offered investment management services in the emerging Pacific market.

AIB earned admiration for its innovative management and quality assurance practices. In the late 1980s, it implemented an ''action learning'' program to set management priorities in the large and evolving market in Great Britain. Although Ireland, with a population (3.5 million) not much larger than South Carolina's, seemed to provide only limited opportunities for growth, Allied Irish Banks was one of the few foreign banks to expand successfully into the United States. Its conservative approach, cultivated in light of its size and regional origins, seemed sure to offer similar returns in the future. AIB's balance sheet remained healthy as the company continued to orchestrate its international growth, in its reserved manner, while also maintaining its loyal domestic customer base. Its three main divisions, AIB Banking, USA, and Capital Markets, gained strength and vitality.

The United States division continued to expand throughout the Mid-Atlantic region through strategic acquisitions and in-

Key Dates:

1966: Company is founded upon the alliance of Royal Bank of Ireland, Provincial Bank of Ireland Ltd., and Munster & Leinster Bank.
1970: Company introduces banking services in Great Britain.
1972: Company adopts the name Allied Irish Banks, plc.
1978: Opens first American branch in New York.
1987: Company offers stockbroker services with the opening of Allied Irish Securities.
1989: Company acquires full ownership of First Maryland Bancorp, forms Capital Markets division.
1991: Acquires TSB Bank Northern Ireland, creating First Trust Bank.
1997: Acquires majority ownership of Poland's Wielkopolski Bank Kredytowy.
1999: First Maryland Bancorp and mid-Atlantic holdings renamed Allfirst Financial Inc. Acquires majority ownership of Poland's Bank Zachodni. Secures option to buy up to 25 percent of Keppel Tatlee Bank (KTL).
2001: Bank Zachodni WBK forms by merger of two Polish subsidiaries.

vestments of First Maryland Bancorp, and by the late 1990s, had added National Bank of Maryland, Dauphin Deposit Corporation, The York Bank, Farmers Bank, Bank of Pennsylvania, and Valley bank to the family. The acquisition of Dauphin Deposit in 1997 transformed First Maryland Bancorp into one of America's top 50 banks. In 1999, the entire Mid-Atlantic group was renamed Allfirst Financial Inc and given a new logo; by 2000, Allfirst's assets climbed to US $18.4 billion. AIB's own brand operations, located in New York, Philadelphia, Los Angeles, Chicago, and San Francisco, reported a net income of US $184.4 million in 2000, representing a 7 percent increase from 1999. AIB added to its portfolio Community Counseling Service Co., a privately-owned consulting firm to the not-for-profit (NFP) sector, to complement its existing array of financial services already dedicated to non-profit organizations. In all, the United States division profits grew 10 percent in 2000.

The Capital Markets division, comprised of three main units, Corporate Banking, Investment Banking, and Treasury and International, also enjoyed steady profits. In 1999, AIB secured the rights to acquire a 24.9 percent equity stake in Singapore-based Keppel Tatlee Bank Limited (KTL), an alliance that would enhance the positioning of both AIB and KTL as key players in Singapore's financial market; AIB's private banking and treasury operations in Singapore were sold to KTL as well.

Pacing Itself in the New Millenium

In preparation for the 2002 conversion to the European Monetary Unit (EMU), AIB invested heavily in systems development, communications, and education programs, and began offering Euro-based banking services well in advance. While Ireland enjoyed a more buoyant economy than most of its European neighbors, the combination of a somewhat decelerated European market and the imminent arrival of a single currency fueled speculation of cross-border mergers that would affect banks throughout Europe.

Profits from AIB's Banking division grew 19 percent in 2000, with retail and commercial outlets numbering 300 in Ireland, 70 in Northern Ireland, and 35 in Great Britain. In addition to its traditional services, AIB also offered online banking services, including home mortgaging. Banking services in the UK focused on small to medium sized business and professional markets as the company successfully endeavored to cultivate long-lasting relationships with its customers. In 2000, AIB paid Eur 114.33 million to the Irish Revenue Commissioners to settle its portion of a banking scandal involving falsified nonresident savings accounts that enabled account holders to avoid paying the Deposit Interest Retention Tax, which was otherwise collected from resident account holders. Other Irish banks were implicated as well; the scandal was not confined to AIB.

A fourth division was formed in the late 1990s to support AIB's Eastern European interests and specifically, its investments in Poland's banking sector. In 1996, AIB acquired an additional 20 percent interest in Wielkopolski Bank Kredytowy; by 1997, AIB had attained majority (60.14 percent) ownership. Allied Irish also acquired majority ownership (80 percent) of a second Polish bank, Bank Zachodni S.A. in 1999. AIB's banking operations in Poland gained momentum with the merger of Wielkopolski Bank Kredytowy and Bank Zachodni, which, when completed in June 2001, established Bank Zachodni WBK as the fifth largest bank in Poland. AIB retained majority (70.5 percent) holding of the newly formed bank. As one of the largest banks quoted on the Warsaw Stock Exchange, Bank Zachodni WBK would be attractive to both domestic and international investors as it streamlined and expanded banking services to meet traditional and high-tech customer needs in an emerging market.

As an increasingly international company, over half of its profits and assets in 2000 were either made or held outside the Republic of Ireland. With a domestic economy stronger than the European average, AIB eagerly anticipated achieving growth projections and continued to thrive amid increasing competition and rising costs from accelerating business programs, technology, and e-business services. Its commitment to customer satisfaction and conservative approach to expansion enabled the company to maintain its healthy balance sheet and deliver long-term shareholder value. Although limited geographically, AIB's domestic presence remained a strong and steadfast anchor to its international operations. Boasting over five million retail, corporate and commercial customers, AIB found itself consistently winning consumer accolades, such as the "Best Business Bank in Great Britain," and steadily advancing in the *Financial Times* rankings of Europe's largest companies.

Principal Subsidiaries

AIB Capital Markets-Corporate Finance Ltd.; AIB Custodial Services; AIB European Investments Ltd.; AIB Finance & Leasing; AIB Fund Management Ltd.; AIB International Consultants Ltd.; AIB International Financial Services Ltd.; AIB Investment Services Ltd.; AIB Securities Services Ltd.; Allied Irish Capital Management Ltd.; Ark Life Assurance Company

Ltd.; CICM Ltd.; Goodbody Stockbrokers; AIB Bank Ltd. (Great Britain); AIB Bank (Channel Islands) Ltd. (Great Britain); AIB Bank (Isle of Man) Ltd. (Great Britain); AIB Fund Managers (Channel Islands) Ltd. (Great Britain); AIB Investment Managers Ltd. (Great Britain); AIB Trust Company (Isle of Man) Ltd. (Great Britain); AIB Trust Company (Jersey) Ltd. (Great Britain); AIB Unit Trust Managers Ltd. (Great Britain); AIB Investment Managers Ltd. (Northern Ireland); First Trust Bank (Northern Ireland); AIB Bank Ltd. (Belgium); AIB Bank Ltd. (Germany); Bank Zachodni WBK (70.5%)(Poland);AIB Bank Ltd. (Singapore); Allied Irish Banks (United States); Allfirst Financial Inc. (United States).

Principal Divisions

AIB Bank; USA Division; AIB Capital Markets; Poland Division.

Principal Operating Units

Republic of Ireland; Northern Ireland; Great Britain; Group Treasury and International; Investment Banking; Corporate Banking.

Principal Competitors

Bank of Ireland; Barclays PLC (UK); Lloyds TSB Group plc (UK).

Further Reading

AIB Group Public Affairs, *The AIB Group*, Dublin: AIB Group, 1995.
''AIB Advances Merger Plans,'' *The Banker*, November 2000, p. 52.
''AIB Takes Stake in Singapore Bank,'' *The Banker*, June 1999, p. 15.
''AIB's Allied Front,'' *Euromoney*, June 2000, p. 224.
Arnold, Wayne, ''Allied Irish Bank's Move into Singapore Seen as Mixed Benefit,'' *New York Times*, June 18, 1999, p. 3.
——, ''Bank Bid is in Line with Singapore's Goals,'' *New York Times*, June 13, 2001, p. W1.
''Banks Face Squeeze on Profits,'' *The Banker*, February 1979, pp. 87–92.
Barrow, G.L., *The Emergence of the Irish Banking System 1820–1845*, New York: Gill and Macmillan, 1975.
Bee, Robert N., ''Buying into a US Bank: The Allied Irish Experience,'' *The Banker*, July 1986, pp. 32–35.
Blanden, Michael, ''Back to the Home Turf,'' *The Banker*, February 1990, pp. 61–62.
——, ''Celtic Tiger on the Prowl,'' *The Banker*, February 1995, pp. 35–38.
——, ''Green, Green Grass of Home,'' *The Banker*, February 1992, pp. 19+.
——, ''Victim of Its Success,'' *The Banker*, March 2000, pp. 40–41.
Bourke, Kevin J., ''Implementing a Marketing Action: A Programme for AIB Group,'' *Long Range Planning*, December 1992.
Bray, Nicholas, ''Allied Irish Banks Looking To Resume International Expansion Begun in '80s,'' *Wall Street Journal*, February 3, 1995, p. B6.
——, ''Analysts Point to Bank of Ireland, A.I.B. as Top Choices Among European Stocks,'' *Wall Street Journal*, May 16, 1994, p. A11.
Brown, John Murray, ''Market Focus: Banks and Builders Buoy Dublin,'' *Financial Times*, June 5, 2001.
''Business Buzz: Coming Cash Tsunami,'' *The Banker*, July 6, 2000, p. 1.
Campbell, Mary, ''Irish Banking Today,'' *The Banker*, November 1972, pp. 1388–94.
''First Maryland Getting New Brand,'' *Bank Advertising News*, March 8, 1999, pp. 1, 17.
Gilbart, James William, *The History of Banking in Ireland*, London: Longman, 1836.
Kimbell, Lucy, and Grog Smosarski, ''Wielkopolski Grows with Polish Economy,'' *Central European*, April 1994, p. 37.
Leighton, Oonagh, ''Good Crack at Poland,'' *Central European*, February 1999, pp. 17–20.
McRae, Hamish, ''Irish Banks Consolidate,'' *The Banker*, August 1968, pp. 707–13.
Murphy, Paul, ''Gloves Off and Come Out Fighting,'' *The Banker*, February 1989, pp. 43–48.
——, ''Seconds Out, Round One,'' *The Banker*, February 1988, pp. 42–49.
Murphy, Seamus, ''Irish Banks Dragged Through the DIRT,'' *European Banker*, January 2000, p. 2.
''New Head Sought for WBK,'' *Finance East Europe*, May 12, 1995, p. 8.
O'Hara, Terrence H., ''Perpetual To Sell Credit Card Unit to Irish Bankers,'' *Washington Business Journal*, April 1, 1991, p. 4.
Panday, Mark, ''Irish Banks Set Priority Markets,'' *Euromoney*, July 1989, pp. 99–100.
''Ready for a New Brew,'' *The Banker*, February 1993, pp. 13–16.
Seekings, David, ''Allied Irish Banks in Britain: Organisational and Business Development Through Action Learning,'' *Leadership and Organization Development Journal*, 1987, pp. 26–31.
Shapiro, Stacy, ''Irish Government Takes Control of Insurer,'' *Business Insurance*, March 25, 1985.
''Small Is Beautiful,'' *Euromoney*, January 1990, pp. 29, 32.
Spender, Barnabas, ''De Buitleir Sees an Allied Vision,'' *International Tax Review*, July/August 1993, pp. 44–46.
Stewart, Kathryn, ''Corporate Identity: A Strategic Marketing Issue,'' *International Journal of Bank Marketing*, 1991, pp. 32–39.
Thackray, John, ''Curate's Egg for Foreign Bankers,'' *Euromoney*, November 1989, pp. 121–37.
''The Second Group,'' *The Economist*, August 27, 1966, pp. 848–49.
Webb, Sara, ''Allied Irish Gets Right to Buy Stake in Singapore Bank,'' *Wall Street Journal*, June 3, 1999, p. A23.
Wills, Gordon, ''What Manager Doesn't Study at Home?'' *European Journal of Marketing*, 25, no. 4, 1991, pp. 128–32.
Wilson, Brian, ''Organisation and Business Development Through Action Learning,'' *International Journal of Bank Marketing*, 1988, pp. 57–66.

—Frederick C. Ingram
—update: Suzanne P. Selvaggi

AltaVista Company

1070 Arastradero Road
Palo Alto, California 94304
U.S.A.
Telephone: (650) 320-7700
Fax: (650) 320-7720
Web site: http://www.altavista.com

Private Company
Incorporated: 1995
Employees: 635
Sales: $73.6 million (1999)
NAIC: 514191 On-Line Information Services

Billing itself as ''the premier knowledge resource on the Internet,'' AltaVista Company is responsible for creating the first full-text, searchable database of the World Wide Web. The company's eponymous search technology may be likened to a vast road map that spans the entire Internet, providing users with immediate access to what many consider the richest, most relevant information in electronic format, from web pages and shopping to up-to-the-minute news, live audio and video, and countless other resources. AltaVista is majority-owned by CMGI, Inc. and headquartered in Palo Alto, California. The company also has offices in San Mateo and Irvine, California, as well as Chicago, New York, and London.

Progenitor: Digital Equipment Corporation (1957–95)

AltaVista Company is the progeny of Digital Equipment Corporation (DEC). Founded in 1957 by MIT engineers Kenneth Olsen and Harlan Anderson, DEC created the first interactive computer, called the PDP-1, in 1960. Three years later, the fifth-generation version, the PDP-5, was released and given the moniker ''the minicomputer.'' DEC's revenues and profits grew an average of 30 percent annually for the next 20 years.

In 1974, the company entered the computer network arena when it introduced digital network architecture (DNA) in order to connect its computers to local area networks (LANs) and wide-area networks (WANs), creating DECnet Phase I. This was followed by DEC engineer Gordon Bell's creation of a line of computers more powerful than the PDPs. Known as VAX, the first one, called the VAX-11/780, was released in 1977. Two years later, Olsen committed billions of dollars to expand the VAX computer line utilizing entirely DEC-manufactured components. Focusing on the large commercial market, products such as the VAX 6000 mini, released in 1984, as well as an extended DECnet, helped the company's sales and earnings soar in the mid-1980s.

But in the 1990s, the company suffered. Slow both in realizing the increasing importance of UNIX and in joining the open personal computer market, DEC reported its first-ever quarterly loss in 1990 and a net fiscal loss for 1991. Olsen stepped down from his post by 1992, replaced by Robert Palmer, who instituted a massive restructuring. More than 60,000 employees were laid off and numerous manufacturing plants were shut down in an effort to resuscitate the failing giant.

With Palmer at the helm, the company began a quick turnaround. Japanese giant Mitsubishi agreed to manufacture DEC's Alpha chip in 1993; DEC sold its RDB database software operations to Oracle in 1994; and DEC and Raytheon together created a multimillion-dollar joint venture to upgrade the onboard computers for the U.S. Navy's E-2C Hawkeye aircraft.

Then, in 1995, the company developed the AltaVista Internet search engine, ''which was designed to index every word on the Web.'' The search engine was released in December of that year and a subsidiary company was created to operate this promising new business.

Stacking the DEC in 1995: Web Indexing and Searching with AltaVista

According to AltaVista's web site, ''Big ideas, excellent equipment, and a fascination with keeping track of information'' were all part of the reason for AltaVista's creation at DEC's Research lab in Palo Alto. ''During the spring of 1995, three DEC scientists were discussing Digital's new Alpha 8400 computers over lunch. These computers held the promise to run

Company Perspectives:

AltaVista's venerable brand has been built from our core philosophy to help users unlock the potential of the Internet. That's how the trust and loyalty of AltaVista's users have made us the leading provider of search results in the world. Our founding promise to the global Internet community remains to span the Web in the widest possible spectrum to access, organize and present the most relevant content to users. And through our excellence in search and our selectiveness with strategic partnerships, AltaVista's objective Web-wide perspective is reflected in every product and service we create. Since our inception in 1995, AltaVista has been dedicated to unlocking the potential of the Internet. Unlike other so-called portals which try to control user views by pre-selecting search results, our founders instilled in us an ethic of objectivity which guides our approach in everything we do. That's why our proven technology has succeeded more than any other in delivering relevant content to worldwide markets. For Web novices and enthusiasts alike, AltaVista can be considered the one true portal through which objective Web-wide access will remain our first priority. Today, AltaVista delivers the ultimate Internet experience with the integration of content, commerce and community platforms, creating a broad range of highly distinctive products and services for our users and partners.

existing database software up to 100 times faster than any competing hardware. In the midst of this conversation, our researchers devised an idea to store every word of every page on the entire Internet in a searchable index, then leverage the Alpha 8400 to create a fast, objective way to extract relevant information from this massive body of knowledge.''

The name AltaVista came from employees who had been viewing a partially erased lab board. ''The word 'Alto' (of Palo Alto) was juxtaposed beside the word 'vista' and someone called out, 'How about AltoVista!' '' This led to the slightly modified appellation AltaVista, or ''the view from above.'' In December 1995, the first searchable full-text database of the World Wide Web, now called AltaVista, was released. The following year, DEC toyed with the idea of taking AltaVista public either as a partially owned subsidiary or as a complete spinoff, but decided instead to retain full ownership.

In February 1997, AltaVista provided the first multilingual search capability on the Internet. A year later, the company's web site achieved record traffic and substantial ad revenue growth. Later that year, in May, the company provided the first-ever, single web search tool for Chinese, Japanese, and Korean users.

Hit the DEC: The Demise of a Giant, 1997–98

Unfortunately for DEC, the creation of AltaVista was not enough to save itself, and it seemed to be a classic case of too little, too late. In 1997, DEC sold its printing systems business to Virginia-based Genicom. Also that year, Digital sued Intel, accusing the latter of utilizing patented technology governing branch management (used to speed up a computer chip) to develop the Pentium microprocessor. Intel, of course, countersued, accusing DEC of violating 14 Intel patents. To settle the litigation, DEC sold its semiconductor production operations to Intel in 1998, and the $625 million deal received approval from the Federal Trade Commission with the condition that DEC make its Alpha technology available to such Intel rivals as Advanced Micro Devices (AMD) and International Business Machines (IBM).

It was the death-knell for the 41-year-old computer giant. In June 1998, Compaq Computer Corporation paid approximately $9 billion to acquire DEC. Palmer stepped down and the company was completely absorbed into Compaq. Digital Equipment Corporation, a world leader in implementing and supporting networked business solutions, was gone.

Compaq acquired DEC in order to improve its customer services battle against Dell. Immediately, the company chose AltaVista as the primary default search engine for the Compaq Presario line of desktop PCs and began altering AltaVista to make it more user-friendly. By January 1999, AltaVista Company was restructured as a wholly owned subsidiary of Compaq, and Rod Schrock was named the president and CEO of the new entity, serving in that position until October 2000.

Over the next six months—while Compaq acquired Shopping.com, a leading online retailer of products and services, and Zip2, the leading provider of Internet platform solutions for media companies and local e-commerce merchants, both of which were integrated into AltaVista—AltaVista launched AltaVista.de, its German site. AltaVista also set a new strategy in motion with the introduction of robust services for web-savvy users, such as Enhanced AltaVista Search (offering the Internet's first web index freshness guarantee and new multimedia search capabilities); the AltaVista Microportal (the world's first microportal, a personalized desktop window to premier AltaVista services); and Shopping.com (adding seven superstores within the first Ultrastore concept, which carried with it the Internet's first 125 percent satisfaction guarantee).

Compaq, like DEC, considered taking AltaVista public in early 1999 in order to compete with such rivals as Yahoo! and Lycos, but decided against it. Instead, in August 1999, CMGI, Inc.—a leading Internet incubator representing a network of 70 established and emerging companies—acquired a majority (83 percent) ownership in AltaVista from Compaq in exchange for $2.7 billion in stock and cash (representing a 16.4 percent stake in CMGI, as well as $220 million over three years). CMGI also decided against taking AltaVista public, canceling the pending IPO in early 2000.

Late in 1999, AltaVista entered the Internet service provider (ISP) arena by becoming the first leading Internet brand to provide nationwide dial-up free Internet access (supported by advertising), signing up 500,000 users within the first three months, an unprecedented Internet event. A few months later, AltaVista unveiled a dramatic new media and commerce network of services. Besides AltaVista Search (which was, at the time, the Web's most powerful and comprehensive guide), the company attempted to diversify into the Internet portal arena with the launch of AltaVista Live! and the expansion of its local portals service through 40 new web sites. By mid-2000, how-

Key Dates:

1957: Digital Equipment Corporation (DEC) is founded.
1995: DEC creates AltaVista search engine and organizes the business as a subsidiary company.
1998: DEC and AltaVista are acquired by Compaq Computer Corporation.
1999: CMGI, Inc. acquires 83 percent of AltaVista.
2000: AltaVista acquires Raging Bull, Inc.

ever, the company realized that these latest moves were misguided, and it canned the ISP and portals thrust, quickly returning to its core competencies of technology and search engines.

Following a strategic growth strategy, from late 1999 through late 2000, AltaVista began debuting foreign sites for Ireland, the United Kingdom, Sweden, France, The Netherlands, Italy, Denmark, Spain, India, and Australia. The India site alone covered more than 1.25 million pages of the Internet, making it the largest index of Indian web sites in the world.

In February 2000, AltaVista launched new Image, Audio, and Video search centers, creating the most extensive multimedia library on the Web to date. In November of that year, the company was awarded four more search technology patents, bringing the total number up to 38. By the end of 2000, the AltaVista web site was drawing more than 19 million visitors per month. The company had also, for a reported $160 million, acquired Raging Bull, Inc., which operated a financial information web site that competed with such heavyweights as Motley Fool and TheStreet.com. However, the following year Raging Bull was sold to Terra Lycos, Inc. In a highly volatile and costly business environment, AltaVista clearly had its hands full simply doing what it had done best since its inception: providing state-of-the-art Internet searching amidst a still growing field of feisty competitors.

Principal Competitors

AOL Time Warner Inc.; Microsoft Corporation; At Home Corporation; Yahoo! Terra Lycos, Inc.; Google; About.com; Deja.com; Disney Internet; GoTo.com; Inktomi Corporation; MyWay.com; theglobe.com.

Further Reading

Astor, David, ''Gist Makes Deal,'' *Editor & Publisher*, September 4, 1999, p. 42.

Auerbach, Jon G., ''AltaVista Says CMGI Position May Bar Deals,'' *Wall Street Journal*, February 17, 2000, p. B10.

Darwin, Jennifer, ''Compaq Plans AltaVista Spin-Off; Names Schrock As Chief Executive,'' *Houston Business Journal*, January 29, 1999, p. 4A.

Deck, Stewart, ''AltaVista Stake Sold to CMGI for $2.3B,'' *Computerworld*, July 5, 1999, p. 20.

DuBois, Grant, ''AltaVista to Offer New Power Search,'' *eWEEK*, August 1, 2000, http://www.zdnet.com/eweek/stories/general/0,11011,2610525,00.html.

Essex, David, ''Helping Content Sites Make Money; CrossCommerce Automates Merchandising for Sites Lacking e-Commerce Infrastructure,'' *Computerworld*, May 8, 2000, p. 86.

Fass, Allison, ''AltaVista to Sell Its Own Ads,'' *New York Times*, August 9, 2000, p. C6.

Gardner, Dana, ''Lycos, AltaVista Juice Up Their Portals: Companies Look to Spur Online Retail Sales,'' *InfoWorld*, October 25, 1999, p. 10.

Harris, Donna, ''Cars.com Teams with AltaVista,'' *Automotive News*, July 31, 2000, p. 39.

Hechinger, John, ''AltaVista to Cut One-Fourth of Staff, Refocus Business,'' *Wall Street Journal*, September 18, 2000, p. B4.

Holson, Laura M., ''Chief Quits at AltaVista,'' *New York Times*, October 20, 2000, p. C4.

Izarek, Stephanie, ''And the Search Goes On: AltaVista Goes Wireless with Raging Search Unplugged,'' *Fox News.com*, August 23, 2000, http://www.foxnews.com/vtech/082300/raging.sml.

Linnett, Richard, ''Wieden's Black Eye,'' *ADWEEK Eastern Edition*, February 14, 2000, p. 44.

Long, Timothy, ''AltaVista's IPO: Playing the Waiting Game,'' *Computer Reseller News*, September 11, 2000, p. 16.

Mickey, Bill, ''And You, Sir, Are No Simple Searcher,'' *Online*, May 2000, p. 6.

Mullins, Robert, ''Don't Cry Over Dot-Com Layoffs: New Jobs Are Dime a Dozen,'' *Business Journal*, June 9, 2000, p. 16.

Niccolai, James, ''AltaVista Offers Slicker Translations,'' *PC World .com*, June 15, 2000, http://www.pcworld.com/news/article.asp?aid=17196.

Notess, Greg R., ''AltaVista,'' *Online*, May 2000, p. 16.

Rapoza, Jim, ''AltaVista Pushes the Search Envelope—Updated Engine Lets Companies Extend Searches to Databases; Search Management Improves,'' *PC Week*, April 24, 2000, p. 30.

Ray, Eric J. and Deborah S., and Richard Seltzer, *AltaVista Search Revolution*, 2nd ed., New York: McGraw-Hill, 1998, 400 p.

Rosa, Jerry, ''No Shortage of Shortfalls—Shaky Outlook Spreads Beyond Services Sector,'' *Computer Reseller News*, September 25, 2000, p. 6.

Rosier, Ben, ''AltaVista to Back UK Site with £6M Drive,'' *Marketing*, December 9, 1999, p. 11.

Sherman, Chris, ''New Web Map Reveals Previously Unseen 'Bow-Tie' Organizational Structure,'' *Information Today*, July 2000, p. 56.

Simpson, Glenn R., and Andrea Petersen, ''AltaVista, Kozmo Distance Themselves from DoubleClick Over Privacy Worries,'' *Wall Street Journal*, March 1, 2000, p. A3.

Sirapyan, Nancy, ''AltaVista,'' *PC Magazine*, December 5, 2000, p. 187.

Smith, Aaron, ''AltaVista Lays-Off 225 to Streamline for IPO,'' *IPO Reporter*, September 25, 2000, p. ITEM00269005.

Sorkin, Andrew Ross, ''British Internet Access,'' *New York Times*, March 7, 2000, p. C4.

Vijayan, Jaikumar, ''Portals Gear Up for Holiday Season; 'Portal' Sites Add Shopping, Other Services,'' *Computerworld*, November 1, 1999, p. 28.

Williamson, Debra Aho, ''AltaVista Paints 'Smarter' Pose to Focus Brand; The Challenge: Major Campaign Moves the Needle, but IPO-Bound Portal Has Yet to Hit Profitability,'' *Advertising Age*, March 13, 2000, p. 62.

Zeichick, Alan, ''Network Applications—Finders, Seekers—AltaVista's Search Engine Indexes an Enterprise's Shared Data Resources,'' *InternetWeek*, July 24, 2000, p. 37.

—Daryl F. Mallett

Altera Corporation

2610 Orchard Parkway
San Jose, California 95134
U.S.A.
Telephone: (408) 894-7000
Toll Free: (800) 767-3753
Fax: (408) 828-0463
Web site: http://www.altera.com

Public Company
Incorporated: 1984
Employees: 1,945
Sales: $1.38 billion (2000)
Stock Exchanges: NASDAQ
Ticker Symbol: ALTR
NAIC: 334413 Semiconductors & Related Device Manufacturing

Altera Corporation is a leading maker of high-density programmable logic devices (PLDs), based on metal-oxide semiconductor technology (CMOS). These logic chips are circuits used in a variety of devices to produce electrical signals. The specific technology associated with programmable logic chips requires less power than other chips, and is more efficient than custom logic chips, reducing development time and time-to-market. Altera's products are sold to makers of communications, computer, and industrial equipment. By 2000, Altera was selling its range of products to over 13,000 customers worldwide. The company has distributors in all European and major Asian markets; and by the end of 2000, exports accounted for 43 percent of Altera's sales. In addition to PLDs, Altera also creates software to help customers program standard integrated circuits.

Birth of the Erasable, Reprogrammable Chip

Altera began in 1983 under the guidance of Rodney Smith—a British applications engineer and then Fairchild Semiconductor manager. Joining Smith as founding members were four others with considerable semiconductor industry experience: Robert Hartmann, James Sansbury, Paul Newhagen, and Michael Magranet. The name ''Altera'' was introduced in 1984, standing for the word ''alterable.'' That year, the company introduced its first generation of chips.

Altera's sales strategy, from the beginning, has been to offer a range of standard programmable parts for the IBM PC AT with inexpensive development tools, allowing customers to self-design and program custom logic circuits that meet their specific needs. This strategy was formulated to meet the industry need created by the delay associated with custom chips, due to the high percentage of silicon designs that require revision toward the end of the design cycle. With erasable, reprogrammable chips, revision can proceed immediately and repeatedly until all design bugs have been eliminated. A relationship with Intel Corp. began in August 1984, when the companies agreed to swap certain designs. In 1985, Intel began to market a group of Altera's logic microchips.

1988: Altera Goes Public

In 1988, Altera went public, and calendar sales for the year reached $38 million. The company also purchased a minority interest in Cypress Semiconductor's wafer fabrication facility (fab), and introduced a new generation of chips. The company launched the industry's first erasable programmable logic device (EPLD), which provided a complete interface to the PS2's Micro Channel Bus. This new device allowed vendors to save time and board space. New EPLD programming software—usable on IBM PC AT and compatible computers—accompanied the device. Later that year, Altera came forth with another innovation, MAX (multiple-array matrix), a new architecture for ultraviolet erasable programmable logic devices that doubled the timing and quadrupled the density of previous AND/OR EPLD arrays. The new devices presented up to 5,000 gates, system speeds of up to 40 MHz, and over 200,000 unique programmable elements. Because the structure of the new PLDs differed so much from previous PLD devices, which used the AND/OR architecture, Altera offered a tool-kit addition to quicken the learning curve for designers. The package, which was workable on IBM Personal Computer ATs and compatibles, contained a graphics-design editor, a design-processing

Company Perspectives:

Altera's mission is to be a preeminent supplier of programmable silicon solutions to the electronics industry through product leadership, excellent value, and superior quality and service.

engine, a timing simulator, and programming software modules, all controlled by a supervisor task-control module.

Altera's key competitor, Xilinx, introduced similar technology in 1988. No longer was Altera alone in its market niche of programmable logic. Altera's relationship with Xilinx would be a heated rivalry over the coming years.

Altera Expands into Japan

The U.S. semiconductor market during the 1980s was dominated by five large companies: Advanced Micro Devices, Inc., Intel Corp., Motorola, Inc., National Semiconductor Corp., and Texas Instruments, Inc. However, companies such as Altera and Xilinx were seen as formidable ''upstarts.'' Altera consistently ranked among the top five public semiconductor companies in the categories of net profits and gross margins (with margins reaching an impressive 60 percent). The company had been able to carve a niche due to specialization, focusing on top-notch design of PLDs, and spending its research and design budget on new product development. In 1989, sales rose 55 percent to $59 million, with $11 million net.

Looking primarily to Japan, Altera stepped up its overseas sales techniques in 1989. Lacking a Japanese office or distributor, the company hired two distributors with unique entrepreneurial approaches to aggressively promote Altera's product line to the Japanese market. The majority of Japanese sales were handled by JMC, a nine-year-old company led by Haruki Kamiyama. Kamiyama, the youngest member of a Japanese trade delegation that visited the U.S. around this time, was an entrepreneur committed to selling U.S. technology in Japan. Altera's other Japanese distributor, Paltek, focused primarily on market development. Because almost all semiconductor business in Japan goes through distributors (as opposed to the United States, where 75 percent of business is done directly with customers), these two distributors were key to Altera's 1989 growth in Japanese business. By 1990, 15 percent of the company's business was due to sales in Japan.

Sales in 1990 were $78.3 million, a 33 percent increase, with net income of $13.4 million. In June of that year, Altera made its first cash investment in a fab. The company invested $7.4 million in Cypress Semiconductor's Round Rock, Texas facility. In exchange they received guaranteed IC production capability, a portion of the fab's CMOS capacity, access to next-generation products whenever they come on-line, and the right to purchase up to 20 percent of the fab over time. Cypress received the rights to Altera's next generation of MAX products (Altera was already producing Cypress's line of programmable logic devices, SRAMs, and other products). Altera President Rodney Smith told Computer Design that the production purchasing option with Cypress would save Altera approximately $30 million in construction costs over sharing production with another vendor. Although Altera had never before entered into this type of relationship with a fab, the company already had exchange and foundry agreements with Intel, Texas Instruments, and Sharp. These arrangements enabled the company to continue producing state-of-the-art chips with no production facilities.

Altera's partners also benefit from these relationships. For example, Texas Instruments used Altera's erasable programmable logic chip to design a compact, high-resolution video camera that was flexible enough to be used under different lighting systems, and for uses ranging from closed-circuit security to industrial inspection and monitoring systems. The chip proved a low-cost, high-yield option.

In 1991, another new chip generation was introduced. The Max 7000 family of ultraviolet-erasable programmable logic devices provided between 4,000 and 40,000 gates, increasing up to five times the capacity of previous high-density programmable chips. Sales surpassed the $100 million mark, reaching $106.9 million, with net income of $17.8 million.

Challenges During the 1990s

The year 1992 included the development of another new chip generation, as well as a series of challenges for Altera. The slowdown of Japanese business caused by overseas economic conditions, as well as competitive pricing by rival companies, led Altera to drop its chip prices. A drop in sales brought the company down to $101.5 million, with net income of only $11.5 million. The crisis was short-lived, however; sales in Japan increased by 87 percent in 1993. At this time, Altera's Japanese sales accounted for about 20 percent of business, with NEC serving as the company's largest customer, and Matsushita, Sony, Mitsubishi Electric, and Toshiba among the company's biggest clients. Altera's Japanese-bound chips primarily serviced two types of products: telecommunications equipment, including digital telephone exchanges and cellular telephone base stations; and professional audio visual equipment, such as portable camcorders. Also in 1992, a class action lawsuit was filed against Altera. It included some current and former officers and directors. The suit alleged violations of federal security laws, and was settled out of court in July 1994.

Overall 1993 revenues surged to $140.3 million, with an 84 percent increase in net income to $21.2 million. That year, the company also invented a system to protect delicate leads from ruin during burn-in and test processes, as well as after customer purchase. The device also reduced time-to-market by facilitating programming and prototyping. The company also developed two compatible sockets, one for use on PC boards and the other for programming EPLDs in carriers.

As new products aged, manufacturing costs went down, and Altera was able to drop prices on its products over time. In 1993, such a discount was passed on to Altera's customers, with 30 percent price cuts on the volume-driven FLEX 8000 family of PLDs. At the end of 1993, Altera and Xilinx each introduced Pentium-compatible products, seeking to migrate programmable array logic (PAL) markets toward programmable logic device solutions. Altera's product targeted the high-density macrocell portion of the PLD business, while Xilinx's was aimed at the low-

Key Dates:

1983: Altera is founded by Robert Hartmann, Michael Magranet, Paul Newhagen, and Jim Sansbury; British applications engineer Rodney Smith joins later in 1983 as chairman, president, and CEO.
1988: The company goes public; sales for the year reach $38 million.
1989: Altera establishes a Japanese market for its products, which helps to push sales up 55 percent over the previous year.
1992: A class action lawsuit is filed against Altera, alleging violations of Federal security laws.
1993: Japanese sales account for 20 percent of Altera's business.
1994: The class action lawsuit is settled out of court; Altera purchases Intel's programmable logic device (PLD) business.
1996: Altera brings to market the industry's largest capacity chip—the 10K100, which has 10 million transistors.
2000: Altera acquires Northwest Logic, a privately held company that provides system design services; John Daane replaces Rodney Smith as Altera's CEO; the company rolls out the Excalibaur family of embedded processor solutions.
2001: Altera forges a partnership with Nuvation Labs Corporation, a leading engineering design firm.

density segment. Altera also released the MAX 7000E family of complex PLDs, which featured architectural improvements of circuit performance of complex PLDs, as well as enhanced routability and usability features. At this time, Altera was the number three volume manufacturer of programmable CMOS logic devices, with a 15 percent market share. Ahead of Altera was Advanced Micro Devices, and in the number one position was competitor Xilinx, Inc., with a 24 percent share.

For Altera, 1994 was a year characterized by new product innovations and an ongoing effort to beat the competition with presence in new market segments. Seeking to gain a lead, Altera increased its market share to 20 percent in 1994 with the purchase of Intel's PLD business, for about $50 million in cash and stock. In addition, the Intel acquisition delivered new customers and 15 new products to Altera. Further, Altera established itself as a programmable logic vendor, supporting Microsoft's Windows NT operating system by releasing MAX PLUS II version 4.0, representing a shift to the fully 32-bit software environment. MAX PLUS II incorporates VHDL, a very-high-speed integrated circuit hardware description language synthesis. This VHDL standard was promoted when eleven companies joined to form Analog VHDL International (AVI), an industry group that helped develop the IEEE 1076.1 standard (the analog extension of VHDL.)

Altera Battles Xilinx

Altera also made a first step into the reconfigurable hardware products market in 1994. The company introduced a high-capacity programmable logic add-in board for PCs—the Reconfigurable Interconnect Peripheral Processor (RIPP 10). This ISA bus board supports up to 100,000 gates of reconfigurable logic, allowing up to eight Altera FLEX 8188 devices. The company also put forth the industry's highest density single-die device, the 16,000-gate EPF51500 PLD, which was immediately followed by Xilinx's introduction of a 25,000-gate device. In April, the company introduced the largest capacity PLD on the market and the first off-the-shelf PLD/MCM—the 50,000-gate PLD multichip module PEF8050M, targeted at the ASIC prototyping market, as well as imaging applications and reconfigurable hardware products (RHPs).

Altera and Xilinx continued to race each other for introduction of industry-leading products. In June 1994, both companies came forth with products moving their devices to an unprecedented five-nanosecond pin-to-pin delay time range. Xilinx targeted new markets with faster speed devices, while Altera's EPM7032 was aimed at applications requiring logic integration in systems with next-generation microprocessors. In July, Altera made its first overtures to the military market, offering four PLDs as military standard compliant. Although defense spending was decreasing, a new emphasis on upgrading existing programs made design engineers receptive to off-the-shelf solutions to integrate system features into smaller board space, while keeping design costs low. As add-in card designers began to look toward PCI-compliant PLDs, Xilinx and Altera both claimed to introduce the industry's first programmable logic devices that were fully compliant with the Peripheral Component Interconnect (PCI) specification.

In August 1994, competitor Advanced Micro Devices filed a suit against Altera. AMD charged Altera with violating six of AMD's programmable logic device technology patents. Altera followed with a countersuit, stating that AMD infringed upon at least two, and perhaps as many as six, of Altera's PLD patents. The case would be decided against AMD in 1996. Another suit had been initiated against Altera by Xilinx in June 1993, also regarding patent infringement. Altera filed a separate suit against Xilinx and the case continued to boomerang with multiple countersuits probing the company patents over the next couple of years. In 1994, Xilinx continued to lead the CMOS PLD market with a 29 percent share, while Altera retained 18 percent, followed by AMD with 16 percent.

Another innovation in the MAX family, the MAX 9000 architecture, was introduced in October 1994. The 9000 family more than doubled the density of currently available EPLDs, reaching system speeds of up to 80Mhz, and increasing cell utilization. Sales in 1994 neared $200,000, with almost 50 percent of revenues derived from foreign sales. Data communications and telecom customers comprised about 44 percent of sales. The $58 million increase in sales over 1993 represented the largest one-year increase in Altera's history. International semiconductor shipments reached $100 billion, along with sales of CMOS PLDs (the newly preferred method for implementing logic design).

In 1995, Altera came out with its MAX 9000 family of erasable PLDs. After a 30 percent drop in the price of the MAX 7000 family of erasable PLDs, the company's sales burst to more than twice the previous year's, reaching an incredible $401.6 million, with $86.9 million in net income. By this time,

Altera had 881 employees, as compared to 370 just five years earlier. Also in 1995, Altera and Xilinx announced that their chips could service the lucrative $3 billion DSP semiconductor market, competing with dedicated and general-purpose DSP chips. Altera introduced Flexible Logic Element matrix (FLEX) 10,000, another programmable logic architecture which sent the market over the 100,000 gate barrier. The device was created with what Altera called a ''sea of programmable bits'' architecture, using the embedded/standard logic block combination.

The company put a new face on an old model in 1995, augmenting the three-year-old MAX 7000 line with the MAX 7000S family. This new line of CPLDs was based on a new 0.5 micron, triple-layer metal process developed with Altera's foundry partners. Since its introduction in 1992 when it generated $5 million in sales, the MAX 7000 had grown to an $80 million sales product by 1994, making it Altera's most successful CPLD line. Also in 1995, while industry reports bemoaned longer lead times in the field programmable gate array (FPGA) market, Altera announced that it had reduced lead times for two devices—the 12,000-gate EPF81188A and 16,000-gate EPF81500A—from 20 weeks to 10 weeks.

Altera and Xilinx once again were neck-and-neck in their announcements of industry landmark products, with Xilinx's introduction of the industry's fastest FPGA and Altera's announcement of the highest gate count FPGA shipped in volume.

Partnerships in the 1990s

Joining six intellectual property providers, Altera launched the Altera Megafunctions Partners Program (AMPP) in August 1995. Megafunctions are hardware description language (HDL)-based designs of system-level functions that may be compiled in MAX-PLUS II software and targeted to Altera's device architectures. This new alliance was charged with the development of synthesizable function blocks for Altera's PLDs. The five other partners in AMPP—Eureka Technology, CAST Inc., RAVIcad, Silicon Engineering, and Advacel—were provided with access to Altera's 21,000 design seats.

In another partnership development, Altera entered into a U.S. joint venture wafer fabrication site with foundry partner Taiwan Semiconductor Manufacturing Corp. (TSMC). The site was located in Camas, Washington. The agreement caused TSMC to displace Sharp as Altera's biggest wafer supplier. Later, the companies were joined by Analog Devices and Integrated Silicon Solutions, Inc., forming a joint venture company named WaferTech.

The industry's largest capacity chip was introduced by Altera in 1996. The 10K100 capacity chip contains 10 million transistors. Also that year, the company unveiled MegaCore and OpenCore, software programs that allowed engineers to evaluate MegaCore functions prior to licensing them. A major industry slowdown in computers led to downsizing, and Altera was no exception. An oversupply of inventory and reduction of chip demand led to revenue decline during the year's first quarter, and the company cut its workforce by 11 percent in June, eliminating about 100 positions. At the same time, the company authorized the repurchase of up to two million company shares.

Forging a new union, Altera joined Synopsis in a five-year agreement to jointly develop and market designer tools to support complex programmable logic devices (CPLDs). The partnership targeted two market segments: second wave designers changing to HDL-based designs for CPLDs and FPGAs, and gate array designers migrating to programmable logic for designs with gate densities of 100,000 or less.

Altera Sees a Bright Future

In 1983, Altera brought a new idea to the market, introducing the reprogrammable logic device. Today that innovation is a billion-dollar industry, bustling with competition. Altera's niche is, and always has been, its emphasis on new-product development, through an investment in research and development over production. By the latter half of the 1990s, the PLD market had swelled to over $2 billion in sales, and Altera stood as one of the industry's leaders due to the complexity of its chips. The company's success was fueled by its long-time emphasis on research and development over production, as well as its close customer relationships. At the end of 1998, Altera employed a staff of 1,208, and had $154 million in net income and $654 million in net revenue. Still, the competition was always knocking on Altera's door. In 1998, Altera held a wafer thin edge over its archrival Xilinx Inc.—31.5 percent vs. 30.3 percent—in the market for programmable logic chips, according to Dataquest Inc.

Altera and Xilinx have been in a turf war for years, and while their products may seem similar, the inter-workings of the two companies are reported to be vastly different. Altera is known in the industry as having a traditional, top-down management style, whereas Xilinx terms its management as ''consensus style,'' in which decision-making is decentralized and delegated to the rank and file as much as possible to encourage employee innovation. Altera's CEO Rodney Smith describes his management style as demanding but fair. ''We ask a lot of people, but we give a lot in return,'' Smith said in a 1999 article for the trade journal *Electronic Business*. He pointed that Altera offers a profit sharing and bonus plan, which is unique from others in that it is divided equally among employees regardless of position.

As the 1990s came to a close, a new competitor immerged from the pack to chase after Altera and Xilinx's dominance of the PLD marketplace. Lattice Semiconductor of Hillsboro, Oregon, became a third-place vendor with 20 percent of an estimated $2.5-billion PLD market by acquiring Vantis Corp. in April 1999. The three companies now accounted for 80 percent of all sales of PLDs, according to the market research firm IC Insights.

The year 2000 was marked by Altera's record profits and rapid-fire product introduction pace. Most significantly, Altera launched the Excalibur family of embedded processor solutions, which included a range of high-density programmable logic devices with embedded processors. Altera extolled this new product line as creating true system-on-a-programmable-chip (SOPC) solutions for its customers and giving the company a foundation for future growth. Also in 2000, John Daane took over Rodney Smith's role as Altera's CEO and president. Smith stayed on as the Chairman of the Board. In a letter to shareholders published in Altera's 2000 annual report, Daane regarded the year as a milestone for the company's long-term goal of capturing the SOPC market. He commented, ''Our real competition in this area includes other types of devices, particularly application-specific integrated circuits (ASICs) and application-specific standard products (ASSPs). With the products introduced during 2000, we can now offer a broader range of PLD-based solutions that were previously only possible with ASICs and ASSPs, while adding the benefits of programmability—increased flexibility, the ability to easily differentiate a design, and faster time-to-market.'' Profits and revenues continued to reach new heights in 2000. Revenue grew 65 percent to $1.38 billion, while income from continuing operations increased 76 percent to $394 million.

As the PLD industry grows and reshapes itself with each new technological advancement, Altera continues to look for ways to stay on top. In September of 2000, Altera acquired Northwest Logic, a privately held company specializing in telecommunications, data communications, and embedded processor systems design. Terms of the agreement were not disclosed, but the acquisition was herald by Altera as its latest strategy to ''invest in leading-edge capabilities that enhance its ability to provide solutions to customers.'' Continuing with that formula the following year, the company forged a partnership with Nuvation Labs Corporation. Altera is banking on Nuvation's reputation as a leading Silicon Valley engineering design firm to give them an advantage over their competitors in offering faster time-to-market delivery of complex PLDs.

With the Semiconductor Industry Association predicting that the market for programmable logic devices will reach $4.5 billion by 2002, the competitive atmosphere for PLD market share is fierce. Established companies like Altera are always mindful of innovative upstarts that may bump them from their status as a top-tier semiconductor company. Altera will also continue to battle with old foes like Xilinx, which recently initiated another legal confrontation with Altera when it asked the U.S. International Trade Commission for an injunction that has the potential to jeopardize the U.S. sales of several major Altera products. Altera dismissed this latest round of legal maneuvering as ''saber rattling.'' To be successful in the long-term, Altera's goal is to create even more robust devices, while continuing its long-standing business practice of being fabless (not owning fabrication facilities) and serving three primary segments: communications, electronic data processing, and industrial applications.

Principal Competitors

Lattice Semiconductor; Xilinx.

Further Reading

''Altera's new CEO approaches difficult position with optimism,'' *Electronic Buyers News*, December 11, 2000, pg. 18.

''Altera buys Northwest Logic,'' *Electronic Engineering Times*, October 2, 2000, pg. 81.

''Altera to Cut Employment 11%,'' *Wall Street Journal*, June 26, 1996, p. B6.

''Altera 2Q Sales up 26%, Net 24%,'' *Electronic News*, July 22, 1996, p. 16.

Arnold, Bill, ''Slugfest,'' *Electronic Business*, August 25, 1999, pg. 76.

Case, John, ''Intimate Relations,'' *Inc.*, August 1990, pp. 64–72.

Cohen, Sarah, ''Washington Fab Venture Lures 2 More,'' *Electronic News*, July 1, 1996, p. 6.

DeTar, Jim, ''Altera, Partners Launch PLD Program,'' *Electronic News*, August 14, 1995, p. 49.

Keating, Peter, ''Coming off the Ropes, These Techs Pack Punch,'' *Money*, December 1996, pp. 76–78.

Lammers, David, ''Next-gen architecture aims to take PLDs to system level—Altera plants stake in ASIC turf with Raphael,'' *Electronic Engineering Times*, August 31, 1998, pg. 18.

Lineback, J. Robert, ''Altera's Speedy Way to Tailor Add-Ons to IBM's PS2,'' *Electronics*, February 18, 1988, pp. 99–102.

Mayer, John H., ''Altera Buys into Cypress Fab Capability,'' *Computer Design*, June 18, 1990, p. 34.

Matsumoto, Craig, ''Xilinx asks ITC to ban some Altera products,'' *Electronic Engineering Times*, December 11, 2000, pg. 4.

Rice, Valerie, ''Where They Are Now: 1987's Superstars Revisited,'' *Electronic Business*, September 4, 1989, pp. 35–38.

——, ''Breaking into Japan: Small U.S. Companies Find Success in a Demanding Market,'' *Electronic Business*, November 27, 1989, pp. 60–62.

Souza, Crista, ''Chip Makers Tout Customizable Socs: Altera Rolls Out Mercury, a PLD Hybrid That Leaves Room for Integration,'' *Electronic Buyers News*,'' February 19, 2001, pg. 28.

''Trial Prospects Grow for Xilinx, Altera,'' *Electronic News*, December 12, 1994, p. 65.

Wiegner, Kathleen K., ''Roll-Your-Own Chips,'' *Forbes*, October 1, 1990, pp. 242–244.

''Xilinx, Altera Tout Faster, Larger Programmable Devices,'' *Electronic News*, October 16, 1995, pp. 52–53.

—Heidi Feldman
—update: Suzanne L. Rowe

American Biltrite Inc.

57 River Street
Wellesley Hills, Massachusetts 02481-2097
U.S.A.
Telephone: (781) 237-6655
Fax: (781) 237-6880
Web site: http://www.ambilt.com

Public Company
Incorporated: 1954 as American Biltrite Rubber Company
Employees: 3,040
Sales: $420.37 million (2000)
Stock Exchanges: American
Ticker Symbol: ABL
NAIC: 326192 Resilient Floor Covering Manufacturing; 322222 Coated and Laminated Paper Manufacturing; 326299 All Other Rubber Product Manufacturing; 339914 Costume Jewelry and Novelty Manufacturing; 321918 Other Millwork (Including Flooring)

American Biltrite Inc. is a leading producer of adhesive-coated, pressure-sensitive papers and films, pressure-sensitive tapes and adhesive products, and floor coverings. The latter operations are conducted principally, and indirectly, through the company's 55 percent controlling stake in Mercerville, New Jersey-based Congoleum Corporation, one of North America's largest makers of resilient vinyl flooring for the residential and commercial markets. American Biltrite also controls nearly 95 percent of K&M Associates L.P., a national supplier of costume jewelry and related accessories based in Providence, Rhode Island.

American Biltrite began as a small family-owned enterprise when Miah Marcus and Frank Bernstein jointly founded the Ewell Rubber Company in 1908. The business partnership established between Marcus and Bernstein that year marked the beginning of a close association between their two families, one that would unite generations of their descendants for decades to come. Together, the Marcus and Bernstein families led the company through its formative decades and into maturity, developing it into a recognized world leader in its field through expansion and diversification, as each successive generation assumed the reins of command first held by Miah Marcus and Frank Bernstein. The legacy of Marcus-Bernstein leadership lasted 74 years, spanning two world wars, a decade-long depression, and sweeping technological advancements in the industry. Then, after the two families decided to go their separate ways, their dissociation gave birth to an entirely new company, American Biltrite Inc. of the 1990s and early 21st century. For the Marcus family, who continued to control American Biltrite into the 21st century, much was owed to the early efforts of their forefather, Miah Marcus, and his business associate, Frank Bernstein.

The First 50 Years

When Miah Marcus and Frank Bernstein started Ewell Rubber in 1908, they joined one of the oldest industries in the United States, a business that traced its roots to the first shoemakers in the American Colonies. Although Marcus and Bernstein were not cobblers, they were closely involved with the cobblers of their time, having established Ewell Rubber as a manufacturer of rubber heels and soles for the shoe rebuilding industry. In this business, Ewell Rubber and its descendant companies would remain for the decades to follow, developing into the largest producer of its kind in the world.

The company did not take long to begin its long climb to the top of its industry, recording encouraging success from the beginning of its corporate life. By 1910, two years after its founding, Ewell Rubber's business was brisk enough to warrant the addition of a second manufacturing facility, known as Panther Rubber Mfg. Co., in Stoughton, Massachusetts. The company's next defining move occurred in 1913, when Marcus and Bernstein established a Canadian division. The foray into Canada marked a signal year in the young company's development, when it extended its presence beyond U.S. borders for the first time and secured a foothold in markets that would contribute revenue for the remainder of the century. Next, another manufacturing facility was established in Chelsea, Massachusetts, in 1917, adding a fourth facet to the company's scope of operations as it neared the conclusion of its first decade of existence.

Key Dates:

1908: Miah Marcus and Frank Bernstein found the Ewell Rubber Company, making rubber heels and soles for shoes.
1913: A Canadian division is established.
1917: Company expands into the production of rubber flooring.
1951: Company changes its name to American Biltrite Rubber Company.
1956: Boston Woven Hose & Rubber, maker of industrial rubber products, is acquired.
1959: American Biltrite goes public.
1961: Bonafide Mills, Inc., a maker of vinyl-asbestos and asphalt coverings, is acquired.
1982. Company is split apart: Biltrite Corporation, controlled by the Bernstein family, takes over the domestic footwear operations; American Biltrite Inc., controlled by the Marcus family, takes over the floor covering, tape products, and Canadian businesses.
1983: American Biltrite acquires 50 percent of K&M Associates, national supplier of costume jewelry.
1986: Ideal Tape Co. is acquired.
1993: Company's floor tile business is merged with the vinyl sheet flooring business of Congoleum Corporation; this new entity retains the Congoleum name yet is 44 percent owned by American Biltrite.
1995: Congoleum completes an initial public offering of its stock, resulting in American Biltrite gaining majority voting control over Congoleum; American Biltrite gains majority control of K&M.
2000: Janus Flooring Corporation, a Canadian producer of prefinished solid hardwood flooring, is acquired.

The division in Chelsea, originally named the Panco Rubber Company, was dedicated to the production of heels and soles, as were the other two U.S. facilities in Stoughton and Trenton. In 1932, the Chelsea and Stoughton operations were renamed the Panther Panco Rubber Company, a corporate title that would endure until 1951, when the company became known as American Biltrite Rubber Company.

During these first decades of growth, the company entered into a new business, that of flooring materials, which, along with rubber heel and sole production, established its existence during the years of Marcus-Bernstein leadership and constituted the basis of American Biltrite's business after the departure of the Bernstein family. In 1917, when the Chelsea plant was built, the production facility at Trenton, the birthplace of the company, was expanded and revamped to produce Amtico Rubber Flooring, giving birth to the American Tile and Rubber Company. From the production of rubber floorings, the company later established additional facilities to manufacture vinyl floorings, eventually becoming the world's largest producer of floorings made with both materials. Driven by the business generated by its two product lines, footwear materials and flooring materials, the company persevered through the 1930s, withstanding the debilitative effects of the Great Depression, and entered the 1940s, as the United States geared itself for the entry into World War II.

During the war, the Amtico manufacturing facilities were converted to produce shoe soles for the U.S. Marine Corps and the U.S. Navy. The production plants at Chelsea and Stoughton also did their part to aid the war effort, supplying the armed forces with heels, soles, and raincoats.

The conclusion of international hostilities and the beginning of the 1950s ushered in a decade of prolific, unprecedented growth for the Marcus-Bernstein-controlled company, the last decade in which the concern operated out of the public spotlight. As if to signal the arrival of exponential growth and the ascension to global leadership in its markets, the company changed its name in 1951, adopting the corporate title "American Biltrite Rubber Company." Under this banner, American Biltrite moved forward during the 1950s, recording resolute growth as the postwar rebirth of the nation's economy invigorated manufacturing industries across the country. Between 1954 and 1959, American Biltrite enjoyed uninterrupted sales and earnings growth, recording during the six-year period a 151 percent increase in annual sales and a prodigious 745 percent leap in net income. On the heels of this impressive upswing in sales and earnings, American Biltrite became a publicly traded company, making its initial stock offering in April 1959 as it concluded its first 50 years of business.

1960s Expansion

The energetic climb of sales and earnings came to a halt in 1960, but the setback was only temporary, engendered by start-up costs incurred from an ambitious expansion program launched by the company as the decade began. The expansion program became the largest in American Biltrite's history by the time it was concluded, bolstering the company's already solid and world-recognized market position. Before the benefits of the expansion program were realized, American Biltrite's annual sales volume exceeded $70 million and its market dominance already had been established. The company ranked as the largest producer of rubber soling material in the world, one of the four largest manufacturers of rubber heels, and one of the two largest producers of solid vinyl and rubber floor coverings. Footwear and floorings, however, represented only part of American Biltrite's manufacturing scope. Buttressing its stalwart market leadership in these two business areas was the company's involvement in a host of other markets, giving it a balanced customer base. Of American Biltrite's total sales volume at the beginning of the 1960s, 40 percent was generated by the company's industrial rubber and miscellaneous products division, which manufactured a variety of products for the oil and automotive industries. Another 25 percent of sales was derived from the production of transmission and conveyor belts for the construction, mining, textile, automotive, air conditioning, agricultural, and aviation industries. All told, the company was registering enviable success in each of its business areas as the 1960s began. Moreover, as the decade unfolded American Biltrite improved itself on all fronts, strengthening each segment of its operations through aggressive expansion and strategic acquisitions.

The expansion program began in 1960 with the acquisition of National Shoe Products Corp., a distributor of shoe supplies to manufacturers. With the distribution area of its Biltrite footwear products line broadened by the addition of National Shoe Products, American Biltrite next strengthened its floor coverings business, acquiring a vinyl-asbestos and asphalt coverings manufacturer, Bonafide Mills, Inc., in 1961 and doubling the production capacity of its Amtico Rubber Flooring division in Trenton, New Jersey, in 1962. Two new manufacturing plants began operation in 1962 as well, a shoe and heel facility in Ripley, Mississippi, and a pressure hose manufacturing facility in Hohenwald, Tennessee. Additional expansion efforts were completed at the company's chemical production plant in Wilmington, Massachusetts, and its Sherbrooke plant in Quebec, which provided American Biltrite with its first Canadian facilities for manufacturing vinyl asbestos and asphalt tile. By the end of 1963, manufacturing square footage had increased roughly 50 percent. Growth continued in the years following, making the 1960s as productive as the 1950s.

By 1967, sales had nearly doubled from the total recorded at the beginning of the decade, reaching $142 million. Of total sales during the late 1960s, one-third was generated by Amtico Rubber Flooring and the solid vinyl and asbestos tile flooring it manufactured. Still a leader in its field, Amtico Rubber Flooring's product line was broadened in 1967 with the acquisition of Dalton, Georgia-based Noxon Mills, Inc., a manufacturer of various types of carpeting. Montreal-based Consolidated Carpet Mfg., Ltd. was purchased the following year, adding another carpeting concern to the company's fold and aiding in its push to become a major carpet producer. Two other divisions rounded out the rest of American Biltrite's operations: Biltrite Footwear, the world's largest producer of shoe soling materials, which widened its lead in 1967 with the acquisition of Cat's Paw Rubber Company, and a relatively new division, Boston Woven Hose & Rubber.

Boston Woven Hose & Rubber had been acquired in 1956, midway through American Biltrite's six-year period of vigorous growth during the decade, ranking the company as a leader in the production of industrial rubber products such as rubber and plastic bases, conveyor belts, and transmission belts. Within this division was the synthetic turf and sports surface department, which was regarded by industry observers as perhaps the most promising area of American Biltrite's business during the late 1960s. Two new products introduced during the late 1960s by this department, Uni-Turf and Poly-Turf, were marketed in relatively new niches in the broadly defined flooring materials market. Uni-Turf, soon after its introduction, had been used at several major tennis tournaments, and Poly-Turf, a synthetic grass that could withstand cleated shoes, had scored encouraging initial success as a surface for outdoor playgrounds and baseball and football stadiums.

1982 Reorganization

The wide-ranging business interests that composed American Biltrite's operations provided steady, consistent growth as the company entered the 1970s, the last decade of Marcus-Bernstein leadership and the last decade the company's business mix would be as diverse. In 1982, the Marcus and Bernstein families, who each owned 37.5 percent of American Biltrite, signed a definitive agreement to divide into two separate corporations. At the time they declined to provide a reason for the split. From 1982 forward, there would be two companies that shared the roots of American Biltrite: Biltrite Corporation, which comprised the domestic footwear business formerly belonging to American Biltrite, and American Biltrite Inc., consisting of the floor covering, tape products, and Canadian businesses formerly owned by American Biltrite. After seven decades of close cooperation, the two families had severed the ties that linked them together, with the Bernsteins assuming 75 percent control of Biltrite Corporation and the Marcuses controlling 75 percent of American Biltrite Inc. The remaining 25 percent of each company was sold to the public.

In the wake of the 1982 spinoff, American Biltrite underwent several years of dramatic change. In June 1983, Marcus-led management steered American Biltrite in a new direction, acquiring a 50 percent interest in K&M Associates, a national jewelry supplier that sold costume jewelry to large retail chains such as Sears and Wal-Mart. Although the acquisition of a jewelry supplier took the company in a decidedly different direction, the 50 percent stake in K&M Associates proved to be a boon to American Biltrite's profitability. By 1985, the profits gleaned from K&M Associates' business activities were contributing more than half of American Biltrite's total earnings, buoying the company's stature as it sought to redefine itself following the 1982 reorganization.

In addition to developing entirely new business interests, American Biltrite also focused on strengthening its more traditional business interests, such as building a $4 million vinyl floor tile manufacturing facility at its Amtico Rubber Flooring division's plant in Trenton, New Jersey, in late 1985. The following year, the company completed its most defining move in its new, modern era, acquiring Ideal Tape Co. from Chelsea Industries for $9.3 million. A manufacturer of pressure-sensitive tape for the footwear, computer, and heating, ventilating, and air conditioning (HVAC) industries, Ideal Tape would become one of the primary engines driving American Biltrite's growth during the late 1980s and into the 1990s. With manufacturing plants in Massachusetts, Missouri, and Belgium, Ideal Tape also increased American Biltrite's global presence and, combined with the marketing strength of the company's Canadian footwear division, enabled American Biltrite to secure a more entrenched position in Canada in particular.

In the four years since the Bernsteins and Marcuses had divided their assets, American Biltrite had made tremendous strides. Revenues had more than doubled since the 1982 split, rising to $110.1 million, and the company's earnings had recorded a robust jump, soaring to $3.1 million from a deficit in 1982.

Adding Congoleum in the 1990s

American Biltrite continued to expand its customer base and product lines during the late 1980s and into the 1990s, building its growth on the development of its pressure-sensitive and adhesive tape products. In 1993 the company completed the formation of a joint venture with Congoleum Corporation that combined its floor tile business with Congoleum's principal business of producing sheet vinyl flooring, creating an entity that retained the name Congoleum Corporation yet was 44 percent owned by American Biltrite. The original Congoleum company had a history dating back to Nairn Linoleum Co., which was founded in 1886. The Congoleum brand itself was introduced in 1924.

As American Biltrite entered the mid-1990s, the company was enjoying substantial growth, with its two primary divisions achieving high levels of performance. In 1994, American Biltrite's tape products division recorded a 28 percent increase in sales, the largest in the division's history. The company's Ideal Tape division also recorded a banner year, increasing its sales 18 percent, the biggest gain in its history. As American Biltrite prepared for the late 1990s and the future, its international business was growing rapidly, particularly in the Far East and in Australia, where the company served markets through its Singapore-based operation, American Biltrite Far East, Inc.

A February 1995 public offering of Congoleum stock altered American Biltrite's relationship with that entity. American Biltrite continued to own 44 percent of the common stock of Congoleum but gained 57 percent of the voting shares, giving American Biltrite majority voting control. Prior to the offering, American Biltrite had been treating Congoleum as a joint venture, but with the offering it now consolidated the accounts of Congoleum with its own. Consequently, American Biltrite saw its revenues skyrocket from $106.1 million in 1994 to $404.5 million in 1995. Nearly 69 percent of overall revenues now stemmed from Congoleum. Also in 1995 American Biltrite gained majority control of K&M Associates, and with the purchase of an additional 11.75 percent stake in 1996, it held an 82.25 percent partnership interest in K&M by year-end 1996.

The following year, the two businesses that comprised the company's tape operations, Tape Products (Moorestown, New Jersey) and Ideal Tape (Lowell, Massachusetts), were combined into a new division called Tape Products/Ideal Division, which was based in Moorestown. The move was designed to promote greater efficiency and coordination among the various product lines, as well as to enhance profitability. After several years in the red, K&M returned to profitability in 1997 thanks in part to the addition of the entire Kmart chain to its list of customers and to the launch of a new line of products bearing the name of supermodel Kathy Ireland, which were initially distributed through about 500 Kmart stores. K&M now distributed its products to more than 3,900 stores.

From 1998 through 2000, overall revenues at American Biltrite were flat, despite steady increases in sales in the company's tape products, jewelry, and Canadian segments. At Congoleum, however, revenues fell from $258.3 million in 1998 to $226.3 million in 2000. There were a number of reasons for this decline, including a highly competitive pricing environment; a steady decline in the shipment of manufactured housing units, which constituted one of Congoleum's prime markets; and the increasing popularity of hard surface products, such as wood flooring. With the additional challenge of sharply rising raw material costs, Congoleum fell into the red in 2000. Results that year also reflected a $7.7 million special charge taken by Congoleum for a major change in national distributors, from L.D. Brinkman & Co. to Mohawk Industries. American Biltrite, therefore, reported that its earnings before income taxes and other items fell from $20.1 million in 1999 to $2.9 million in 2000.

Steps were being taken at the turn of the millennium to turn Congoleum's fortunes around. Responding to the rapid growth in the wood flooring category, Congoleum introduced a wood laminate line in 1999, and American Biltrite acquired Janus Flooring Corporation in October 2000 for C$4.5 million. Based in Toronto, Canada, Janus was a producer of prefinished solid hardwood flooring. Also in 2000, Congoleum made its largest introduction of new products in company history. With its tape products, jewelry, and Canadian segments performing well, American Biltrite faced a bright future in the early 21st century provided that Congoleum could be placed back on the right track.

Principal Subsidiaries

American Biltrite (Canada) Ltd.; American Biltrite Far East, Inc.; American Biltrite Sales Corporation; Majestic Jewelry, Inc.; Ocean State Jewelry, Inc.; Aimpar, Inc.; ABTRE, Inc.; Ideal Tape Co., Inc.; American Biltrite Intellectual Properties, Inc.; K & M Trading (H.K.) Limited (Hong Kong); Congoleum Corporation (55%); ABItalia, Inc.; Abimex, LLC; ABIcan, Ltd. (Canada); Janus Flooring Corporation (Canada).

Principal Divisions

Tape Products.

Principal Competitors

Armstrong Holdings, Inc.; Dal-Tile International Inc.; Shaw Industries, Inc.; Minnesota Mining and Manufacturing Company; Avery Dennison Corporation; Du Pont Kansai Automotive Coatings Co.; Ivex Packaging Corporation; R Tape Corporation; VPI, LLC; AAi FosterGrant; Monet Inc.; Victoria Creations Inc.; B.F. Goodrich Company; Biltrite Corporation; West America Rubber Company.

Further Reading

''American Biltrite,'' *Rubber World,* July 1986, p. 5.

''American Biltrite Board Clears Accord to Split Firm into Two Companies,'' *Wall Street Journal,* May 26, 1982, p. 41.

''American Biltrite Closing Two Plants,'' *Barron's,* November 17, 1980, p. 51.

''American Biltrite Rubber,'' *Financial World,* December 27, 1972, p. 16.

''American Biltrite Rubber,'' *Wall Street Transcript,* July 8, 1968, p. 13,793.

''American Biltrite Rubber Results Snap Back from a Modest Decline,'' *Barron's,* September 30, 1963, p. 22.

''American Biltrite Signs Accord to Split into Two Concerns,'' *Wall Street Journal,* August 12, 1982, p. 5.

''Flashier Than It Looks,'' *Forbes,* September 9, 1985, p. 158.

Maturi, Richard J., ''Tape Measure,'' *Barron's,* May 11, 1987, p. 64.

Nicholson, Sy, ''American Biltrite Has Many Facets for Continued Growth,'' *Investment Dealers' Digest,* 1961, p. 32.

Rolland, Louis J., ''Biltrite on the Amex,'' *Financial World,* December 11, 1963, p. 21.

—Jeffrey L. Covell
—update: David E. Salamie

AMERICAN FOODS GROUP

American Foods Group

544 Acme St.
P.O. Box 8547
Green Bay, Wisconsin 54308
U.S.A.
Telephone: (920) 437-6330
Fax: (920) 436-6466
Web site: http://www.americanfoodsgroup.com

Private Company
Incorporated: 1975
Employees: 1450 (2000 est.)
Sales: $580 million (2000 est.)
NAIC: 311612 Meat Processed from Carcasses; 484230 Specialized Freight (except Used Goods) Trucking, Long Distance; 511199 All Other Publishers

A bona fide Green Bay packer, Wisconsin's American Foods Group is a mid-sized, privately-owned meat packing and processing company. It is the 18th-largest meatpacker in the United States, primarily handling the slaughtering and packing of cattle. The company also produces value-added beef and processed pork products to meet particular customer demands. Going beyond the normal commodity-boxed beef and ground beef marketed under its own labels, American Foods offers case-ready ground beef in a variety of sizes, fat-content levels and packaging, and private labeling options for major retail and food service accounts. The company also launched the Ackerman & Cooke catalog division in 1999, which offers premium meat products via direct mail and the Internet. In addition, American Foods operates cold storage and distribution facilities. And along with the beef, processed pork, and catalog divisions, American Foods continues to remain competitive with its new transportation division, which manages a fleet of refrigerated trucks to deliver the company's goods.

Early Years

Although the American Foods Group later came to be known as the largest meatpacking center east of the Mississippi, it was a small operation until about 1985. In 1971, Paul Schanno and Roger Miller bought the Endlich Packing Company in Green Bay, renaming it Green Bay Dressed Beef. They grew the operation from about 35 to 40 head per day to about 150 head per day by January of 1975. The partners bought another slaughterhouse, Huron Dressed Beef, in 1974, and as soon as it began operating in 1975, established the American Foods Group. The company remained a slaughterhouse-only business until 1978. Then it expanded to also include a boning operation, which lasted only for a few years. In 1980, Schanno passed away and Miller then assumed full control of the American Foods Group. Production had grown steadily to about 800 to 900 head per day by the time Miller sold the American Foods Group to the company's attorney, Carl Kuehne, in 1985.

Going Beyond Meatpacking

Many would agree that the competitive edge of American Foods is synonymous with the leadership of Carl Kuehne. After practicing law for about 20 years, Kuehne bought American Foods in Green Bay in 1985. For him, it marked a return to a profession that spans several generations of family members. For the company, it marked a new era in expansion and innovation. Kuehne was instrumental in redirecting American Foods so that it would grow beyond its humble meatpacking focus. Originally composed of two slaughter and processing plants, American Foods grew to become a $600 million dollar company of four plants, two distribution/cold storage centers, a trucking company, and a print and online catalog company.

As past chairman of the American Meat Institute, Kuehne was already attuned to subtle shifts, or opportunities, in the meat business. As head of American Foods, he stimulated product development in an effort to increase retail and food service accounts. He re-engineered the company's infrastructure, honing a team-selling system not often employed in the meat industry. He greatly increased the size of the company. Under his direction, the company embraced the meat industry's case-ready trend early in 1991, providing pre-packaged, labeled, and priced products to retailers from the Wisconsin and Ohio plants before many of their competitors. Employment at American Foods increased to more than 1,700 employees, and the firm made it on the Fortune 500

Company Perspectives:

Our goal is to know and understand the customer needs for both product and services, and to deliver consistent products that meet and exceed our customers' needs and expectations.

list of the largest privately held companies in the country. Since 1985, the corporate objectives were to add value by further processing various beef products and to acquire related businesses that would complement its operation.

Innovation and Expansion Throughout the 1990s

The early 1990s marked a time when food processing companies saw company consolidations, budget cutbacks, and stiff competition, which forced many to make tough decisions about how to continue to attract new markets, as well as increase efficiency and production. It was clear that some form of expansion and flexibility was necessary to survive. ''Food processing plants have to do more. They must feature quick, adaptable plants or processing lines that enable quick changeovers and can accommodate several products,'' observed Mike Pehanich, a publisher and editor of *Food Plant Strategies*, in a statement to *Plant Sites and Parks Magazine*. American Foods was more than up for the challenge.

But while many companies relocated to rural plants for cheaper land and labor, less stringent environmental regulations, and financial incentives from communities bidding against each other, more companies in the meat industry chose to expand by consolidating into bigger plants. In fact, for decades, the meat industry has shown this trend: In the 1990s, it was roughly ten times more concentrated geographically than in the early 1960s, while the processed meats industry is nearly three times as concentrated.

American Foods found that it was more cost-effective to expand and refit existing plants, and look to its already well trained workers for efficiencies and production-line innovations. Twenty-five million dollars was spent in the mid-1990s to ready the Mitchell, Huron, and Green Bay plants for value-added production. And demand for products was so high that some facilities were expanded more than once to keep up. The Mitchell, South Dakota, cooked-foods facility was remodeled to allow the option of two more smokehouses. The expansion of its beef processing plant in Green Bay, Wisconsin, cost between \$8 million to \$10 million and increased the plant's payroll by about \$200 million. In 1994, the company moved its Golden Valley-based sales office of 32 employees to the nearby headquarters in Green Bay.

Charles Merrick, chief administrative officer of American Foods, explained to *Plant Sites and Parks Magazine* how labor skills were a major factor in deciding to expand the Green Bay beef plant: ''If we had moved, we would have lost skilled, trained employees. In a start up, it takes about one to two years to get the efficiency in your labor force. For example, in our industry, it's important that the worker get all the meat off the bone. New guys might damage meat when doing this, reducing their efficiency. While the labor force can physically be replenished in about six months, it's the lack of experience that hurts operations.''

The efficiencies gained by the plant expansions allowed American Foods to increase output, with ground beef production increasing to more than 30 percent by mid-1994 to late 1995. The redesigned facilities also gave the American Foods Group a lot of flexibility to cut orders to specification, a service that put the company ahead of many others and attracted many demanding customers who sought special cuts in custom packaging. And in another effort to improve customer responsiveness, Kuehne launched a shipping line in 1996. America's Service Line was successful, within two months, in bottom-line profit. The fleet not only managed a 98-percent on-time delivery rate, but also provided customers the value-added service of back hauling their vegetables and cheeses.

With the Internet presenting many opportunities for conducting business online, traditional ''brick and mortar'' retailers increasingly turned to e-commerce ventures to help improve sales during the 1990s. E-tailers, as they were often called, soon saw meat-tailers join their ranks. In December of 1999, American Foods launched Ackerman & Cooke, an Internet and catalog sales division named after Kuehne's European ancestors, who were also well known for their expertise in raising, butchering, and transporting cattle and meat. The new division was an exciting way to expand the company's core business of wholesaling to supermarkets and restaurants to also include direct sales to individual consumers.

''Styled after the old-world butcher shop of long ago,'' as the company's Web site states, the online catalog offers an appealing way to get fresh, quality meats cut to order, wrapped in butcher paper, sealed in air-tight packaging, placed inside custom cold packs, and shipped right away. Other products available through the catalog include candies, chocolates, and cakes.

Another e-commerce opportunity presented itself to American Foods in April of 2000. FoodUSA.com, a Madison-based Internet start-up, began to bring together meat producers and buyers on the Internet in a process designed to reduce costs and create new selling opportunities for the nation's \$100 billion meat and poultry industry. With the start-up showing lots of promise in its first two months in business, raking in \$500,000 in revenue, American Foods tested it out as a selling opportunity on a limited basis. But less than one year after the dot-com's debut, it went out of business. Most analysts believe that it was no coincidence that the demise of FoodUSA.com came soon after the emergence of a competitor site, Provision X, backed by meat industry giants including IBP, Tyson Foods, Smithfield Foods, Cargill's Excel, Gold Kist, and Farmland Industries. American Foods has so far not taken part in this other e-commerce opportunity, which may be as well, since the new venture attracted the attention of antitrust officials at the U.S. Justice Department. Even though this e-commerce venture did not pay off, American Foods continued to stand by its traditional sales force.

Labor Issues in Mid to Late 1990s

The plant expansions and new emphasis on efficiency and flexibility proved largely successful for American Foods, but

Key Dates:

1975: American Foods Group is established.
1985: Carl Kuehne acquires American Foods Group.
1994: Sales office moves from Golden Valley to Green Bay headquarters.
1995: Beef division takes on major expansion efforts.
1996: A number of employees arrested for falsified immigration documents.
1997: Huron pork plant sold to competitor Smithfield Foods.
1999: American Foods Group launched catalog and Internet division.
2000: 1.1 million pounds of beef recalled due to E. coli scare.
2001: Kuehne recognized for community leadership.

not without some controversy. In the meat industry, narrow margins, along with the relentless goal of slaughtering and processing in faster and better ways, have significant repercussions for employee wages and conditions. While margins in the meat industry were already quite low—meatpacking typically saw a 1-percent margin, while meat processing usually saw a 2 percent margin—American Foods aggressively pursued steady growth with a target of 3 percent return. ''During the 1970s and 1980s, when oligopolies were emerging in the processing of beef, pork, chicken, and among other types of fish, workers' wages declined, while productivity and work-related injuries increased,'' according to Michael Broadway, in the book *Any Way You Cut It: Meat Processing and Small-Town America.* According to the Occupational Safety and Health Administration (OSHA), meat-processing jobs are among the most hazardous in America. The U.S. Department of Labor's 1992 study on the topic found that in 1990, the probability of incurring an injury in a meatpacking plant was three times higher than for manufacturing workers as a whole.

Still, American Foods recognized that safety was a critical condition of work and could point to relatively positive statistics when it comes to work-related injuries: Even though the employee count grew by 50 percent from 1992 to 1995, for example, total injuries went down 4 percent. In addition, total loss-time injury went down 24 percent; lost days due to injury went down 52 percent; late duty days due to injury went down 23 percent; repetitive trauma cases went down 10 percent; and total lost-time illness went down 44 percent. Such conditions are, no doubt, a credit to the employee cooperation and the safety orientation program that covers a range of safety topics, including personal protective equipment, hazardous communication, forklift safety, and emergency evacuation procedures. As a result of such work safety improvements, the company received the American Meat Institute's Award of Commendation in 1996.

The company's steady growth and outstanding safety record may have attracted more than it bargained for. In August of 1996, American Foods was publicly embarrassed by the discovery that illegal immigrants, apparently eager to find better work and earn higher wages, managed to obtain work at the company. Agents from the Immigration and Naturalization Service, along with Green Bay police, arrested 77 Mexican men and women working with false papers at the Green Bay dressed beef plant and took them to the Mexican border. Although Kuehne explained that the company did everything correctly and legally to verify worker documentation, while making every effort to avoid discriminatory practices, the arrests brought national attention to the not-so-uncommon presence of illegal immigrant workers in the meat industry.

Even though American Foods' expansion and labor management efforts seemed to have been handled fairly well overall, job security for many people working for American Foods became far from reliable in 1997: Three years after investing $10 million dollars in its Huron, South Dakota pork plant, American Foods sold the plant to competitor Smithfield Foods, which had no intention of maintaining the hog operation. ''With the hog slaughtering industry beset by virtually unprecedented hog prices, and in view of other economic conditions, we opted to sell this facility to Smithfield Foods,'' explained Kuehne to the Associated Press. In fact, there was an untimely 46 percent drop in hog production in South Dakota at about the time the plant was renovated to increase its capacity by 40 percent in 1994. In addition, the controversy over corporate hog production in South Dakota and a petition drive to ban it were factors in the decision to sell the plant. As a result, 850 people were laid off, and a class-action lawsuit immediately ensued charging that the company failed to give employees proper notice of the plant's shutdown. The parties reached a settlement of $2 million, which averaged about $1,400 per worker after subtracting 33 percent of the settlement funds for legal fees.

Despite such labor management challenges, American Foods managed to steadily increase employee morale overall, and establish community-building programs that improve many aspects of employees lives. In May of 2001, Kuehne was recognized for his 15 years of business leadership and community-based projects. It was clear from the start that Kuehne and the company were working to give something back to the diverse worker community that includes people from 25 countries. As the company evolved from commodity to value-added sales in the early 1990s, communication became key to the company's work culture. Regular meetings, rap sessions, and multi-departmental teamwork energized workers. Turnover rates reduced from 100 percent each year to as low as 35 percent. The company partnered with Neighborhood Housing Services to offer loans to employees so they can buy homes. Kuehne launched numerous innovative programs to attract and retain employees, including participation in the Employer-Assisted Homeownership Program with Neighborhood Housing Services. The program offered forgivable loans for down payment and closing costs to purchase a home. American Foods also offered pre-natal care for pregnant employees, education assistance for employees, and scholarships for employees' children.

Successes and Challenges in the New Millennium

Early on in the new millennium, it became clear that American Foods' early focus on flexibility and custom orders paid off. Retailers were looking for ways to cut more and more labor out of their operations, shifting more packaging responsibilities to their suppliers. For meat companies, this meant case-ready products in a variety of specifications. Without a doubt, case-ready meat products became the next, hot trend in the meat industry, a trend that the company had already embraced during the previous 10 years. The company's largest customer and strongest partner, for example, is a national retailer that sells more meat than American Foods can hope to produce; however, the company is so responsive to the retailer's needs that the partnership thrives. ''When the retailer indicated an interest in case-ready ground beef, we found a label application in England that suited the needs of their marketplace. Now we're in a position to supply in excess of 250,000 pounds of case-ready ground beef each week for them, all prepackaged and prepriced with their label,'' explains Kuehne to *Meat & Poultry* magazine.

No doubt, American Foods' expansion and efficiency efforts throughout the 1990s, and its customer-direct catalog efforts, put the company in a good position to meet the millennium's increasingly customer-focused, value-added trends. But consumers expected even more convenience in the forms they find appealing. So American Foods took on additional innovative investments—from building new facilities in Ohio and Wisconsin in 2000 to developing even more custom packaging and labeling. The company came to offer retailers a wide range of label brands to choose from: American Foods Group, Sheboygan Sausage Company, Green Bay Dressed Beef, Dakota Supreme, Dakota Valley, Golden Prairie, Iowa Pork, Server's Choice, Wisconsin Beef Industries, Smokrest, Americas Meals, and Black Angus Reserve.

The future of case-ready products, and American Foods' investment in it looks bright: About 7.5 percent of all fresh ground beef was sold in case-ready form during 1999, according to research conducted by *Cattle Buyers Weekly*. That rose to 15 percent early in 2000, and may have gone beyond that by the year's end. Case-ready ground beef is expected to account for at least 50 percent of all fresh ground beef sales by 2003. And although case-ready beef cuts will be slower to grow, sales doubled from 2.5 percent in 1999 to 5 percent in 2000, and are expected to double again in 2001 to 10 percent. Better still, projections for 2003 are at 20 percent.

Perhaps a victim of its own success, American Foods was unfortunately faced with a widely publicized E. coli scandal in December 2000. When several people became ill from beef tainted with the E. coli virus, investigators traced the source of the meat to American Foods, although it did not become clear when the contamination occurred in the supply chain, according to the *Saint Paul Pioneer Press*. As a precautionary measure, the company issued a 1.1 million pound beef recall and lawsuits ensued. The company did not expect sales to be hurt, in a year when more than 70 recalls were issued, with 18 of them involving E. coli. Since then, the company has stepped up efforts to ensure that its beef products are safe.

While many other companies in the meat industry scramble to retool for the new millennium, American Foods seemed well poised to meet the challenges, as it continued to respond quickly to the demands of new and changing markets. And with a continued focus on value-added products and developing stronger ties with retailers, consumers, and employees, the Green Bay packer promised to succeed even more.

Principal Subsidiaries

Dakota Cold Storage; America's Service Lines; American Foods—Mitchell (Dakota Pork Industries); American Foods—Sharonville; American Foods—Green Bay (Green Bay Dressed Beef); American Foods Specialties; Ackerman & Cooke (catalog).

Principal Competitors

Atlantic Premium Brands; Colorado Prime; ConAgra Foods; Farmland Industries; Hormel; IBP; Moyer Packing; Packerland; Smithfield Foods; Stock Yards Packing; Wolverine Packing

Further Reading

''American Foods Group Acquires Dawson-Baker Packing Co and Will Rename the Affiliate America's Beef Co LLC: Dawson Has Yearly Sales of $42 mil,'' *National Provisioner*, August 1998.

''American Foods Group Issues Voluntary Recall,'' *PR Newswire Association*, December 4, 2000.

''American Foods Group Launches Catalog and Internet Division,'' *Business Wire*, December 14, 1999.

''American Foods Will Close Office,'' *Star Tribune Metro Edition* (Minneapolis, MN), October 24, 1994, p. 9D.

''Beef,'' 2000 State of the Industry Report Supplement, *National Provisioner*, August 2000, p. 30.

''Companies Answer Dakota Pork Workers' Lawsuit,'' *Associated Press Newswires*, September 7, 1997.

''Dakota Pork Plant Sold to Smithfield Foods,'' *Associated Press Newswires*, August 1, 1997.

''Dakota Pork Will Likely Pay Off Fired Workers,'' *Associated Press Newswires*, January 1, 1999.

Daley, Dave, ''INS Arrests 77 at Green Bay Meat Plant,'' *Milwaukee Journal Sentinel*, August 21, 1996.

Daykin, Tom, ''Green Bay Packer Selling Fresh Beef and Pork on the Web,'' *Milwaukee Journal Sentinel Final*, December 15, 1999, p. 7.

——, ''Meat Producers, Buyers Will Meet Online,'' *Milwaukee Journal Sentinel Final*, April 10, 2000, p. 15D.

——, ''CEO Says Recalled Beef Won't Hurt Green Bay, Wis,-Based Meat Packer,'' *Milwaukee Journal Sentinel Final*, December 7, 2000.

DiLorenzo, Jim, ''Green Bay Dressed Beef Plans to Expand its 127,000-sq-ft Plant by Another 27,000 sq ft in 11/95,'' *National Provisioner*, October 1995, p. 26.

Dolan, Thomas G., ''Special Report: Packaging: Trends and Traits'' *National Provisioner*, January 2001.

Drabenstott, Mark, Mark Henry, and Kristin Mitchell, ''Where Have All the Packing Plants Gone? The New Meat Geography in rural America.'' *Economic Review—Federal Reserve Bank of Kansas City*, Third Quarter 1999, pp. 65–82.

Egerstrom, Lee, ''American Foods Group Issues Voluntary Recall,'' *Saint Paul Pioneer Press*, December 5, 2000.

Gallo-Torres, Julia M., ''Food for Thought,'' *Plant Sites & Parks Magazine*, September/October 1997.

Gants, Rebecca, ''American Foods Group,'' *Meat & Poultry*, July 1, 1997.

''Kuehne to Receive Free Enterprise Award,'' *The Green Bay News-Chronicle*, May 2001.

Majeski, Tom, ''Wisconsin Meatpacker Offers Financial Aid to Those Ailing from E. Coli,'' *Saint Paul Pioneer Press*, December 13, 2000.

——, ''Scientists Trace E. Coli to Green Bay, Wis. Meatpacker,'' *Saint Paul Pioneer Press*, December 16, 2000.

Petrak, Lynn, ''Rewriting the Rules,'' 2000 State of the Industry Report Supplement, August 2000, *National Provisioner*, pp. 64–69.

Phelps, Nathan, ''Kuehne's Leadership Recognized,'' *Green Bay Press-Gazette*, May 2001.

''Pork,'' 2000 State of the Industry Report Supplement, August 2000, *National Provisioner*, p. 44.

''Recalls of Tainted Meat Not Working, Attorney Says,'' *PR Newswire Association*, December 5, 2000.

''Refrigerated and Frozen Processed Meat and Poultry Products are Winning Over Consumers,'' *Refrigerated & Frozen Foods*, November 1995.

''Sausage,'' 2000 State of the Industry Report Supplement, August 2000, *National Provisioner*, 2000 State of the Industry Report Supplement, August 2000, p. 48.

Stull, Donald D., Michael J. Broadway, and David Griffith, Eds. *Any Way You Cut It: Meat Processing and Small-Town America,* Lawrence: University of Kansas Press, 1995.

''Wisconsin-based Packer Seeking Partners as Investors,'' *The Associated Press State & Local Wire*, May 19, 1999.

—Heidi Wrightsman

Angelica Corporation

424 South Woods Mill Road
Chesterfield, Missouri 63017
U.S.A.
Telephone: (314) 854-3800
Fax: (314) 854-3890
Web site: http://www.angelica.com

Public Company
Incorporated: 1904 (as Angelica Jacket Company)
Employees: 6,760
Sales: $458.6 million (2000)
Stock Exchanges: New York
Ticker Symbol: AGL
NAIC: 812990 All Other Personal Services; 812331 Linen Supply; 812320 Drycleaning and Laundry Services (except Coin-Operated); 448190 Other Clothing Stores

Angelica Corporation is a major manufacturer and retailer of uniforms to service businesses and their employees in the United States. It also rents and launders linens and other textiles, primarily to the U.S. healthcare industry. The company operates in three business segments: Textile Services (which provides laundry and rental services primarily to the healthcare sector); Manufacturing and Marketing (which makes and sells uniforms and business apparel to the healthcare, hospitality, and other service industries); and Life Retail Stores (which sells uniforms and shoes, primarily to individual healthcare professionals).

1878–1903: Origins

From its entrepreneurial beginnings in the late 19th century, Angelica established itself as a trendsetter, a characteristic that would describe the company more than a century later when it ranked as a dominant uniform apparel manufacturer and marketer. The company evolved from a fledgling upstart into a diversified, multinational concern by developing styles that became standard attire for service industry employees. Success in one market spawned entry into another, eventually creating a multifaceted company with a chain of retail stores, a textile rental and laundry service business, and uniform apparel lines in a host of markets. However, it all began with one garment—the company's first original creation—a cook's uniform sewn by the wife of railroad chef, Cherubino Angelica, in St. Louis, Missouri, in 1878. From this first uniform, scores of original, trendsetting designs followed, making the Angelica label a pervasive fixture in the American workplace.

The cook's uniform created by Angelica's wife was distinctly different from his usual chef's attire, and unlike the garments worn by other cooks in St. Louis and, presumably, anywhere else. The white hat was tall, resembling a crown with a pillow seated on top. The white coat was double-breasted, cloth buttons sewn to the sides, with two reversible layers of cloth in front to protect the wearer from direct heat and spattering grease. The cuffs, split on the sides, functioned as potholders when turned down. Although the white chef's uniform tailored by Cherubino Angelica's wife would become a ubiquitous, traditional garment worn by chefs a century later, in 1878 it was distinctly new and quickly drew comments from other railroad chefs, who were intrigued by its design and functionality. Cherubino Angelica attracted enough attention with his novel uniform to leave his job with the railroad and start his own company, an entrepreneurial venture that marked the beginning of Angelica Corporation's existence.

With his wife supplying the uniforms, Cherubino Angelica began soliciting orders from cooks for outfits identical to the one he had modeled while working as a cook himself, recording sufficient success to keep his small business afloat. By the 1890s, the Angelica family business had reached a respectable level of prominence, having created the uniforms worn by the glamorous Harvey Girls, the waitresses who worked at the Fred Harvey Restaurants located in train stations across the nation. In 1897, while *en route* to his native Italy, Cherubino Angelica was killed in the shipwreck of the S.S. Burgoyne off the coast of Newfoundland, leaving a firmly established business that was nearing its twentieth year of operation.

1903–45: Diversification

Following Angelica's death, the company continued under the control of the Angelica family. In the early years of the new

Company Perspectives:

To attract and maintain superior associates who are committed to building a results-oriented culture by providing customers with quality products and services in a timely fashion which will, consequently, add value over the long term for our shareholders.

century, the Angelica family business diversified for the first time when it began competing in the nascent linen supply industry; then, in 1903, after 25 years of stewarding the company, the Angelicas sold their small enterprise to Alfred J. Levy. Levy paid $2,500 for the company and its six sewing machines; he then recruited his brother Mont, a recent graduate of the University of Michigan, to join him in managing the business.

Together, the Levy brothers endeavored to transform the image of uniforms from a ''Badge of Servility'' to a ''Mark of Service,'' as their early advertising proclaimed, and toward this objective the pair were successful, at least in promoting greater attention to the garments worn by workers in the service industry. After incorporating their company as Angelica Jacket Company in 1904, the brothers expanded their production capabilities, amassing 32 sewing machines by 1910, when Angelica Jacket's roster of customers included employers in the hotel industry, the restaurant industry, the food processing industry, and the railroad industry. By this point, the innovative tradition first established by Cherubino Angelica's wife had remained alive within the company under the tutelage of the Levy brothers. Angelica Jacket had pioneered bandettes, tea aprons, and large wrap-around aprons worn by waitresses, and had promoted the adoption of white jackets instead of black coats for waiters.

A decade later, still pressing for the elimination of black mohair coats for waiters, which the company rightly charged were unsanitary because they were not washable, Angelica Jacket launched a campaign to promote its washable white uniforms with the slogan, ''Sliding to Success on a Cake of White Soap.'' Two years later, in 1922, the company embraced a full spectrum of colors, offering for the first time a line of garments in fast-dyed colors and made from synthetic fibers. Concurrent with the introduction of this lively panoply of uniforms, the company opened an office and warehouse in New York City, as the breadth of its operations expanded.

As business grew and the demand for uniforms intensified, Angelica Jacket's marketing and distribution reach extended with the establishment of warehouses in Chicago in 1928 and in Los Angeles in 1932. With operations spread across country, Angelica Jacket moved forward through the 1930s, its progress fueled by the momentum generated by more than a half century of business. However, by the beginning of the 1940s, events outside of the company's control precipitated sweeping changes throughout its operations, bringing its traditional business shuddering to a temporary halt. By 1941, the United States was at war, bringing to a formal end the decade-long Depression and ushering in a period of sacrifice and concerted action by the American people and by American businesses. At Angelica Jacket, the manufacturing and marketing of uniforms gave way to a different product line, as the company did what it could to contribute to the war effort. During the war years, Angelica Jacket ranked as one of the largest manufacturers of combat jackets for the armed forces and served as a supplier for the Red Cross. On the domestic front, the company designed a line of uniforms called ''Plantswear'' for women thrust into manufacturing jobs previously held nearly exclusively by men.

1945–58: Growth

After the conclusion of the Second World War, when annual sales for the company reached $3.5 million, Angelica Jacket faced the postwar years with renewed vigor, its sights set on fulfilling ambitious plans. Embodying this irrepressible optimism was the company's new objective: ''to have our label on the back of every uniform used in the country.'' Though an unrealistic goal, the proclamation motivated employees and management to pursue the unattainable, giving the company the driving spirit to capitalize on the unprecedented prosperity to come in the decades ahead. In the late 1940s, the company strengthened its position in one of the markets that would enable it to take advantage of the lucrative economic times ahead when it bolstered its involvement in the health care industry. For years, Angelica Jacket had manufactured and marketed a line of hospital staff uniforms, but beginning in 1949 its participation in the growing health care market was entrenched with the introduction of a line of patient and operating apparel, foreshadowing its foray into the production of specialized protective apparel for contaminant-free environments 15 years later.

The 1950s, 1960s, and 1970s witnessed the explosive growth of service industries in the United States, a phenomenon that had a definitive effect on the magnitude of Angelica Jacket. More service personnel meant a greater need for uniforms and, not surprisingly, a greater demand for Angelica Jacket's line of men's and women's washable service apparel. The company broadened its marketing scope during the maturation of the service industries to include a variety of occupations, but it did so with a different corporate title. In 1950, as it prepared to meet the mounting apparel needs of service industry employers across the country, the company changed its name from Angelica Jacket Company to Angelica Uniform Company, then moved forward, expanding its manufacturing capabilities and increasing the ranks of its production personnel for the bright future ahead.

1958–90: Acquisitions

By the end of the 1950s, Angelica Uniform was a publicly-traded company, having made its initial public offering in 1958, when seven factories, eight warehouses, and 1,000 company employees comprised the growing Angelica empire. As the company entered the 1960s, with annual sales exceeding $10 million, it was regarded as the largest manufacturer of men's and women's washable service apparel for hospitals, restaurants and hotels. Angelica Uniform's enviable industry ranking became more domineering during the decade as it diversified its business, evolving into a well-rounded concern supported by burgeoning markets. The company entered the textile rental field in 1961, began production of protective apparel for ''clean room'' environments in 1964, then made several pivotal moves in 1965 to respond to the changing nature of its industry.

Key Dates:

1904: The company is incorporated as Angelica Jacket Company.
1922: The company introduces for the first time in the U.S. colored uniforms for waitresses. The company opens offices and a warehouse in New York City.
1941: Angelica Jacket converts to war production, manufacturing combat jackets for soldiers and uniforms for the women who fill manufacturing jobs at home.
1949: Angelica Jacket expands its healthcare business, supplementing its manufacture of uniforms with a line of patient and operating room apparel.
1950: The company's name is changed to Angelica Uniform Company.
1958: Angelica Uniform goes public.
1961: The company enters the textile rental business.
1965: The company enters retail sales of its uniforms by acquiring a mail order business and establishing its first Life Uniform retail shops. It also strengthens its healthcare textile line through acquisition.
1967: The company changes its name to Angelica Corporation.
1982: Angelica embarks on an acquisitions strategy over the next 12 years, designed primarily to bolster its hospital service business.
1991: Recession initiates a period of little or no growth.
1993: Cost cutting in the health care industry further harms Angelica's performance.
1999: Sale of the company is investigated, but quickly abandoned.
2000: Company reports increased earnings due primarily to cost savings.

By the mid-1960s, workers in the service industries were required with increasing frequency to furnish their own uniforms, a shift in the composition of the company's customer base that Angelica Uniform's management sought to mirror by acquiring James G. Fast Company, a Chicago mail order firm, and by entering the retail uniform business with the opening of the company's first Life Uniform Shop. Concurrent with these two signal moves, both of which were made in 1965, Angelica Uniform acquired Kansas City White Goods Company, strengthening its textile product line for health care institutions, and crossed U.S. borders for the first time with the acquisition of a uniform company in Canada. On the heels of these important additions to the company's range of operations, Angelica Uniform Company changed its name in 1967 to Angelica Corporation.

In 1968 Angelica returned to diversifying its interests, acquiring the California-based Environmentals Incorporated, a provider of laundry and linen services to hospitals and other health care institutions. Angelica's involvement in the medical market, which dated back more than 20 years by this point, was fast becoming the primary engine driving the company's growth, as hospitals and other health care institutions increasingly sought outside laundry and linen service assistance. Newly constructed hospitals were no longer outfitted with laundry facilities, while older hospitals turned to companies like Angelica to realize significant cost savings, providing a substantial boost to Angelica's business.

Although Angelica's strong position in the medical market represented its most promising avenue of growth as the 1970s neared, the company's other businesses by no means remained idle. Angelica's international involvement in uniform production was deepened in 1970 with the acquisition of Whitewear Manufacturing Company, a Canadian manufacturer of uniforms. Its retail business—the operation of a chain of retail stores stocking uniforms and shoes—had recorded explosive growth, giving the company 100 Life Uniform Shops by 1973. Annual sales by this point had more than doubled since the name change in 1967, eclipsing $80 million during the early years of the 1970s. By the mid-1970s, Angelica's involvement in the medical market was propelling the company, accounting for more than half of the company's total sales for the first time in its history. As annual sales reached and then surpassed the $100 million mark during the latter half of the 1970s, the company's three primary business segments were each recording resolute growth. The company's Life Uniform Shops, with more than 150 units located in nearly every major U.S. city, had quickly become the largest specialty uniform chain in the nation. Its uniform business, after a century of development, was widely regarded as a venerable giant by industry observers, and its growing presence in the health care market buoyed prospects for the future, fueling optimism as Angelica entered the 1980s.

During the early 1980s, Angelica was the market leader in each of its three business segments: the rental of textile and garment services, the manufacture and marketing of uniforms, and the operation of a national chain of specialty apparel retail stores. Its linen rental business for the health care industry continued to be regarded as the company's major growth vehicle, helping Angelica generate more than $200 million a year in total sales by 1982. In the decade ahead, the company relied heavily on strengthening its resources through acquisitions, absorbing, in seven separate transactions between 1982 and the end of the decade, rental service facilities in Texas, Arizona, California, Connecticut, Pennsylvania, New Jersey, and Rhode Island. Annual sales swelled as a result, increasing from roughly $200 million at the beginning of the decade to nearly $330 million by the decade's conclusion.

1990–Present: Challenges

During the early 1990s, Angelica acquired a substantial number of laundry facilities in Florida through its purchase of Service Control Corp. It also established a presence overseas with its 1991 and 1994 acquisitions of uniform companies based in England.

At the same time, the company began to encounter external circumstances that hindered its continued ability to grow. The recession of the early 1990s adversely affected its revenues, beginning in 1991 when sales of uniforms both to its service industry customers and to its individual retail customers either declined or remained flat. Sales of its dominant (about half of revenue) hospital rental and laundry services nevertheless increased, due to the company's previous acquisitions and the addition of several new hospital customers.

By 1993, major changes in hospital operations began to affect the company's revenue. The Clinton Administration began to work on its major proposal to reform the U.S. healthcare system. At the same time, managed care emerged as a major influence on payments for health services. Both developments pressured all players in the industry to reduce costs. For Angelica, this meant that fewer patients were entering hospitals and that those who did enter stayed for less time. Consequently, the need for linens declined as did demand for the company's rental and laundry services.

As late as 1994, *Money* suggested that these cost-cutting pressures might help Angelica, which could launder linens more efficiently and cheaply than could individual hospitals. Hospitals did outsource their laundry services, but that did not help Angelica. The industry was fragmented, and Angelica saw its revenues decline, as it was forced to compete with companies charging lower prices for the same services. It had to decrease its prices or lose customers.

In 1997, after about five years of declines in revenues, profits and the stock price, the annual shareholders meeting voted to elect all directors annually and to eliminate the directors' and officers' golden parachutes. A proposal to explore the sale of the company was defeated. Two months later the CEO resigned.

The new CEO spent about 18 months trying to cut costs and raise prices. When these efforts were unsuccessful in improving the company's performance, he hired an investment firm to investigate other options for improving shareholder value, including a sale of the firm. Six months later, after approaching 160 domestic and foreign potential purchasers, Angelica halted the initiative. No company offered what the company considered a fair price.

As it entered the twenty-first Century, Angelica confronted the same problems that had afflicted it during the previous decade. Hospitals were still cutting costs, and competition was still formidable. The company had adopted some new strategies to improve its performance. It sold some poorly performing U.S. facilities as well as its United Kingdom acquisitions. It contracted about 60 percent of its manufacturing operations to companies in Mexico, Central America, and the Far East as a means of cutting costs. It cut its dividend by two-thirds in order to preserve operating capital. It also had some success in attracting new hospitals as customers for its laundry and rental services.

These measures improved Angelica's performance, at least temporarily. Revenues from the dominant textile services division continued a slow decline, but reductions in costs allowed the division to show an increase in earnings in 2000. But, manufacturing and marketing and Life Retail Stores showed little improvement.

In May 2001, the company again reported poor performance, as increased revenues were more than offset by increased costs, especially energy expenses. Competition in a fragmented industry, the consequent inability to maintain pricing at levels allowing the company to maintain margins, and increasing costs combined to keep the company in the weak position it had been in for the previous decade.

Principal Subsidiaries

Angelica Realty Co.; Angelica Textile Services, Inc; Angelica International Ltd.; Southern Service Company; Industrias Textiles El Curu (Costa Rica).

Principal Divisions

Textile Services; Manufacturing and Marketing; Retail Sales.

Principal Competitors

ARAMARK; Casual Male; Cintas; G&K Services; Healthcare Services; Sodexho; SSI Surgical Services; Steiner; Superior Uniform Group; UniFirst.

Further Reading

''Angelica Corp.,'' *Wall Street Journal*, November 2, 1990, p. B3.

''Angelica Corporation,'' *The Wall Street Transcript*, June 17, 1985, p. 78, 273.

''Angelica Corp.'s Young Is Named Chief Executive,'' *Wall Street Journal*, May 24, 1989, p. B13.

''Angelica Unit Suffers Loss in Operating Profit, Sales,'' *St. Louis Post-Dispatch*, March 12, 1997, p. 7C.

Conrad, Lee, ''Angelica Stock at 52-Week Low, Profit Shrinks,'' *St. Louis Business Journal*, October 28, 1996, p. 12A.

''Hospital Cost Cutting Could Cure Angelica,'' *Money*, October 1994, p. 71.

Manning, Margie, ''Cintas Potential Buyer for St. Louis Textile Company,'' *Business Courier Serving Cincinnati-Northern Kentucky*, November 19, 1999, p. 5.

——, ''Hubble Scraps Mission to Sell Angelica, Alters Course,'' *St. Louis Business Journal*, May 1, 2000, p. 7.

Miller, Patricia, ''Angelica to Pay Down Debt, Fund Acquisitions with Loan,'' *St. Louis Business Journal*, July 4, 1991, p. 19A.

''Profitable Fields,'' *Financial World*, December 22, 1965, p. 14.

''Recession Hurts Angelica,'' *St. Louis Post-Dispatch*, May 19, 1993, p. 5B.

Roney, William C., ''Angelica Corporation,'' *The Wall Street Transcript*, November 29, 1982, pp. 67, 873.

Stroud, Jerri, ''Angelica CEO Gives Up Post: Young Will Stay On, Loewe Returns,'' *St. Louis Post-Dispatch*, August 2, 1997, p. 24.

Tucci, Linda, ''Angelica Turnaround Gets Boost from Catalog, Internet,'' *St. Louis Business Journal*, September 4, 2000, p. 3A.

——, ''Shareholder Seeks Sale of Angelica As Earnings Plunge, Stock Dives,'' *St. Louis Business Journal*, September 6, 1999, p. 12A.

Willatt, Norris, ''No Washday Blues,'' *Barron's*, September 27, 1963, p. 5.

''Women's Apparel a Growth Field,'' *Financial World*, March 1, 1961, p. 7.

—Jeffrey L. Covell
—update: Anne L. Potter

Applica Incorporated

5980 Miami Lakes Drive
Miami Lakes, Florida 33014
U.S.A.
Telephone: (305) 362-2611
Fax: (305) 364-0502
Web site: http://www.applicainc.com

Public Company
Incorporated: 1963 as Save-Way Barber and Beauty Supply, Inc.
Employees: 17,000
Sales: $749 million (2000)
Stock Exchanges: New York
Ticker Symbol: APN
NAIC: 335211 Electric Housewares and Household Fan Manufacturing; 335221 Household Cooking Appliance Manufacturing; 421620 Electrical Appliance, Television, and Radio Set Wholesalers; 335228 Other Major Household Appliance Manufacturing

Applica Incorporated is a manufacturer and marketer of a wide range of branded, licensed, and private-label small household appliances, mostly in North America, Latin America, and the Caribbean. Through its operating subsidiary, Applica Consumer Products, Inc., the company markets products under licensed brand names such as Black & Decker. Under the Windmere name, Applica also designs and markets kitchen and seasonal products at discount prices. The company manufactures and distributes hair care appliances to the professional salon industry, personal care products, home environment products, and pet care products, such as the computerized LitterMaid cat litter box. In June 1998, Applica acquired Black & Decker's Household Products Group, which designs kitchen and clothing-care appliances under Black & Decker licenses, and markets these products to retailers and distributors in North and Latin America. Within the United States, Applica holds leading market share in several product categories, such as toaster ovens and irons. Previously known as Windmere-Durable Holdings, Applica changed its name in May 2000.

Early History

Applica was founded in 1963 by Belvin Friedson, a longtime operator of five barber colleges in downtown Miami. With an initial capital investment of $45,000, the former college dropout launched Save-Way Barber and Beauty Supply, Inc., selling various hair-care products on a cash-and-carry discount basis to both professional shop owners and consumers. In 1964, Friedson opened his first store in North Miami Beach and generated $2 million in sales, quickly taking advantage of the contacts he had developed during his career in the barber and beauty shop industry. In his fourth year of operating the company, Friedson took it public to raise funds for his rapidly expanding business. The $450,000 generated from the initial public offering of common stock not only stood as a visible sign of the promise shown by the young company, but it provided the capital for product diversification. Backed by this financial support, Save-Way's early success continued in the late 1960s as Friedson began marketing women's wigs and hairpieces nationwide.

With the new decade came the first serious test for the company. The market for beauty and barber supplies virtually dried up, forcing Friedson to focus on a new market. In 1972 he switched to the product line that would soon become the company's backbone: hair dryers, curlers, and other personal care accessories. That same year, he enlisted the services of Durable, a Chinese manufacturing company that would later become a subsidiary, to supply Save-Way with appliances. Friedson established the Windmere Products division to handle the distribution of the new product line.

The new strategy showed early signs of success. By 1975, revenues had grown to $9 million. Save-Way had landed its most important sales contract to date, entering into an agreement with Eckerd Drugs, a nationally known retailer that would remain one of its largest customers through the 1990s.

During the mid-1970s, the Windmere division quickly rose to the forefront of the company. Friedson's son David took over as the division's national sales manager in 1976, after he dropped out of college. Under his direction, Windmere sales increased five-fold over the next eight years, jumping to $35

Company Perspectives:

Applica Incorporated aims to be a premiere marketer and manufacturer of consumer appliances that provide product solutions to help consumers through their day.

million in 1983, which represented 70 percent of revenue for the entire company.

The rapid expansion of Windmere products was fueled primarily by what Toni Mack of Forbes has called an ''unabashed copycat'' strategy. Instead of developing its own products, the company attempted to reproduce gadgets that others had made successful. For instance, when an industry leader such as Bristol-Myers' Clairol was successful with an innovative curling iron or hair roller set, Windmere would quickly join forces with Durable to produce a replica of the product at a considerably lower cost. Taking advantage of cheap labor costs in Durable's Hong Kong factories, Windmere was able to pass the savings along to its customers and become the low-cost producer in the industry. Durable became a 50 percent joint partner in 1979.

Explosive Growth in the 1980s

Having completed a second public offering that raised an additional $1 million, the company entered the 1980s with a sound balance sheet and momentum from a year that saw revenues increase by 50 percent to $41.8 million and net profit more than double to $4.6 million. Such rapid growth, however, was temporarily checked in the early 1980s by a shortage of labor in the company's Hong Kong factories that made getting products out the door on time a difficult task. To fix the chronic problem, Friedson and Durable established manufacturing operations in China, where labor was abundant and half as costly. Although the decision proved to be sound in the long run, immediate gains were negated by high set-up costs that resulted in three years of slow growth.

A new marketing strategy would serve as another catalyst for the company's strong growth in the mid-1980s. Having adopted the corporate name Windmere in 1983, making Save-Way Industries Inc. a division, the company attempted to increase its presence in the hair care products market and jump-start its profit margins through an aggressive mail-in rebate campaign. Hair dryers and curling irons, for instance, were advertised at an outrageously low ''final cost''—usually below $5 and sometimes even free. Consumers had only to follow the rebate form correctly and mail it in with their coupon and sales receipt to take advantage of the savings. Although the company would, of course, lose money on consumers who were so diligent, Friedson wagered that most would not, after leaving the store, take the time to follow the correct procedure.

Friedson's views on human nature proved correct; on average, only one out of every four buyers went to the trouble to claim the rebate money. And the cost of paying off that 25 percent, according to Friedson, did not come close to offsetting the increase in sales volume—at no additional cost—that the rebates generated. One product alone, the VIP Pro hair dryer, advertised at just $4.88 after rebate, netted a profit of $6.5 million. This was a large contribution to a 30 percent climb in total earnings in 1983.

Although this rebate gimmick provided a needed boost during a down period in the personal care appliance market, it could not sustain long-term growth. That would depend on the company's ability to add reputable brand names to its product base through acquisition, while at the same time adapting rapidly to the trends in the volatile hair-care appliance industry.

To meet the first of these two marketing objectives, Windmere acquired a 44 percent interest in Extron International Inc. in 1983 and the remaining 56 percent the following year. The purchase of the Texas-based private corporation gave Windmere the licensing rights to the trade names Faberge, Brut, and Grand Finale.

Six months after signing the deal, Windmere acquired an exclusive license to market four lines of Ronson electric shavers and other small consumer appliances. By June 1984, the company had contracted Japanese and Austrian firms to manufacture rotary electric and rechargeable razors and was selling them by as much as $20 less than the competition. Six months later, Windmere controlled five percent of the national electric razor market. Licensing established product names such as these proved a more cost-effective strategy for expanding the company. Not only did the company save on research and development expenses, but it did not have to invest heavily in the expensive advertising campaigns needed to introduce a new product to the market.

Much of the company's growth in the mid- and late 1980s, however, was the direct result of the strong performance of its own products. From its earliest days, the company had attempted to develop the Windmere product line by introducing products used in beauty salons to the general public. In the 1970s, for instance, Windmere began manufacturing and selling a pistol-grip hairdryer based on a model from its professional line. The company tried to make the same profitable transition a decade later with a product designed to make hair wavy, known as the Crimper. Although retailers initially showed little interest in the hair-crimper when it was introduced in 1987, once it became popular in trend-setting Hollywood, it became a huge success. A similar type of curling iron called the Waver was introduced that same year, along with the Clothes Shaver, a device that removed fuzz and fabric pills from clothing. Both products helped to give Windmere instant brand recognition, something it had struggled 12 years to achieve.

As young women across the country snatched up the newfangled curling irons in hopes of achieving the ''in'' look, Windmere revenues and profits soared to record levels. By 1987, the performance of the company had exploded to record-breaking levels. Sales climbed to $145 million and earnings had risen to $11.9 million, which represented increases of 54 percent and 120 percent, respectively, from the previous year. The momentum from these new products led the company to another year of torrid growth in 1988, as sales rose to $193 million and earnings more than doubled to $32.6 million. Meanwhile, its stock jumped from $11 a share to a high of $27 per share.

Key Dates:

1963: Save-Way Barber and Beauty Supply founded by Belvin Friedson as a wholesale and retail supplier.
1964: Friedson opens first retail store in Miami.
1968: Company completes its initial public offering.
1975: Company lands its first wholesale supply contract with retailer Eckerd Drugs.
1976: David Friedson becomes Windmere's national sales manager.
1979: Japanese manufacturer Durable becomes a joint partner.
1984: Unfair competition and patent infringement lawsuit is initiated against the company by competitor Philips Electronics.
1988: The 180 retail barber and beauty supply store chain is sold for $23 million.
1989: Company shares become listed on the New York Stock Exchange.
1992: Company wins $57 million settlement with Philips.
1998: Company purchased the Black & Decker Household Products Group for $315 million.
1999: Windmere-Durable Holdings consolidated its sales, marketing, and product development business into a single division.
2000: Windmere changed name to Applica Inc.
2001: Applica extended its trademark license agreement with the Black & Decker Corporation through December 2006.

Late 1980s Setbacks

Although most outward signs suggested that Windmere had finally arrived as a major player in the personal appliances industry, a number of obstacles surfaced in the late 1980s that brought growth to a near standstill. In May 1989, the first sign of trouble appeared. Sales of hot products such as the Crimper fell victim to changing fashion trends, leading to an 11 percent decline in earnings and an alarming build-up of inventory. Moreover, products designed to fill the void performed poorly, exacerbating the problem. And in November, Friedson sold $2.9 million worth of company stock shortly before another quarter of disappointing financial results was released. As Windmere stock plummeted, revenues, which had been predicted by some analysts to exceed $285 million, dipped to $178 million and earnings fell to $7.6 million.

Perhaps the most serious threat to the stability of the company, however, came from China (the site for 90 percent of Windmere's manufacturing operations) and the 30-cents-an-hour labor that made the company the low-cost producer in the industry. In June 1989, a series of student-led protests and period of political unrest temporarily slowed down production and jeopardized the future of Windmere's manufacturing operations. Although the turmoil in China directly affected the company for only four to six weeks, it posed a serious threat to the company's debt financing. With virtually all of the company's manufacturing factories based within the tumultuous area of the violence in Tiananmen Square, the financial community viewed Windmere too much of a risk. For the next three years, the company would be forced to take out unsecured loans on a 60- to 90-day basis.

Early 1990s Recovery

Windmere's downward spiral continued into the new decade. It failed to come up with a new premier product that could pick up the slack left by declining sales of the Crimper, the Waver, and the Clothes Shaver. The company's entrance into the health-related products industry, through the introduction of an electric rotary toothbrush called PlakTrak, did not live up to the high expectations suggested by a $3 million advertising campaign. Furthermore, an ongoing unfair competition and patent infringement lawsuit brought by Philips Electronics regarding a rotary electric shaver manufactured by Izumi Products and sold by Windmere, initiated in 1984, continued to divert much-needed resources and energy from the development of a viable management strategy for renewal.

In 1990, however, Windmere emerged from the lawsuit victorious and was awarded an $86.9 million judgment. Two years later, the company collected $57 million as part of a full settlement from Philips. The decision not only gave the company a financial shot in the arm—a net gain of $29 million after legal fees, taxes, and other expenses—but it enabled Friedson and his managerial team to focus on reshaping the business. n May 1997, Windmere paid Izumi Products $4.5 million, effectively removing itself as a party to the Japanese manufacturer's suit against Windmere and Philips Electronics, which claimed that the settlement between Windmere and Philips took place without Izumi's consent and was therefore unfair.

Between the time of the decision and the time of the final settlement in 1992, Windmere devoted its attention primarily to reorganization and restructuring. The company cut costs at its Durable manufacturing facilities, reducing the break-even point by more than one-third, largely by reducing its work force by 30 percent, down to 7,000. At the same time, the company worked to reduce its inventories and tighten up its balance sheet. Not only did the company trim its inventories by more than 16 percent, but it used the money from the lawsuit to pay off debts.

A favorable decision by the U.S. government to retain China's status as a most favored nation added to the positive momentum of the lawsuit. If duties had been imposed, Windmere would have had to raise prices and most likely would have lost its advantage over such competitors as Conair, Bristol-Myers Squibb, and Helen of Troy. These companies manufactured in Costa Rica or bought from the Far East, locations that all had higher labor and manufacturing costs.

The Mid-1990s Renewal

As Windmere celebrated its 30th anniversary in 1993, it showed several visible signs of renewed financial health. Total revenues, for the second straight year, approached the record levels of 1988. More significant, the company attained the strongest financial position in its history, with $146 million in equity, $25 million in cash, and virtually no debt. An aggressive television and print campaign to support new lines of hair and curling irons, combined with completely redesigned packaging, represented the company's renewed commitment to its core business. The following year, the company strengthened its presence by acquiring the licensing rights to the Helene Curtis Salon Selectives brand name for a line of personal hair care appliances. This opened the way for a new line of hair dryers, curling irons, hair setters, combs, and brushes.

As Windmere entered the second half of the 1990s, it looked to distance itself further from the 1990–1991 decline and regain the respect of its stockholders and the financial community. While continuing to improve the efficiency of its operations, the company also hoped to develop a gadget that would do for the 1990s what the Crimper and the Clothes Shaver did for the 1980s. In a June 1996 meeting with shareholders, Friedson unveiled one of the leading candidates: the LitterMaid, a computerized cat box billed as the ''pooper scooper'' for the Internet Age. Friedson planned an extensive marketing campaign, including infomercials and adding specialty retailers to market the company's latest gadget to the 65 million cat owners in the United States. Since LitterMaid was introduced in 1997, more than 1.5 million cats and their owners have enjoyed this product, which uses infrared signals to activate an automatic raking system to keep litter clean and virtually odor free. In late 2000, Applica relaunched the brand with a new logo, redesigned packaging, and designed an improved Web site and an updated infomercial to capitalize on the momentum.

Brand-Building and Millennial Marketing

In the late 1990s, brands were big business in the kitchenware industry. In January 1997, Windmere bought the rights to the Farberware name. Also that year, through partners Salton, Inc., and NewTech Electronic Industries, Inc., the company signed agreements with Kmart to become a supplier of a wide range of small electrical appliance and consumer electronics under the White-Westinghouse brand name. In July 1999, CBS Corp. and White Consolidated Industries, Inc., settled a dispute over the Westinghouse trademark, allowing both Salton, Inc., and Windmere to continue to use the White-Westinghouse name.

For more than two years, Windmere searched for a high-profile brand it could champion. In June 1998, Black and Decker agreed to sell its household products division to Windmere-Durable Holdings for $315 million. As part of its acquisition of the Black & Decker Household Products Group in June 1998, Applica licensed the Black & Decker brand in North America, Central America, South America (except Brazil), and the Caribbean for specific household appliances. Black and Decker would keep lighting and cleaning products, such as the Dustbuster cordless vacuum. The licensing agreement was subject to renewal if desired by both companies. In July 2001, Applica extended its trademark license agreement with the Black & Decker Corporation through December 2006. Applica's early renewal was partially motivated by its intent to use the Black & Decker brand on the first product being developed under a strategic alliance with a yet-to-be announced package-goods firm.

In December 1999, Windmere-Durable Holdings consolidated its sales, marketing, and product development business into a single division called the Consumer Product Group, headed by Mike Michienzi. The reorganization combined the company's Household Products Group and Windmere Corporation into one entity, based in Shelton, Conn. Michienzi now oversaw all Windmere's small electrics brands and personal care, professional care, Jerdon, and LittleMaid divisions. Until this point, the parent company operated Windmere and Household Products as separate entities. Windmere's Miami headquarters would now house back-office functions, such as financial and supply-line operations. The company consolidated operations at its plants in China and Mexico, and integrated its back-office operations in Miami.

The millennial year was a significant one for the company, which changed its name to Applica Incorporated in May 2000. The word ''Applica'' comes from the English word ''appliance'' and the Latin word ''plicare,'' which means to fold into one unified whole. At the beginning of 2000, the company recorded $700 million a year in sales and planned to extend the Black & Decker name to seasonal products such as air conditioners, heaters, humidifiers, and fans. Product innovation was a key piece of Applica's overall strategy, and the company debuted 40 new products at the industry Housewares Show, including countertop coffeemakers—a category that Black & Decker had vacated. At this juncture, the company's five-year strategy included plans to capitalize on the growing personal care market, estimated at $1 billion annually. Applica, which sold primarily through mass market and drug channels, was seeking alternative distribution channels for its wares. Meanwhile, Applica developed a dual-brand strategy that positioned the Black and Decker line as the premiere brand, while Windmere appliances served consumers at bargain price points. Eager to launch new product categories, Applica developed rice cookers, grills, griddles, waffle makers, and irons. The company was taking steps to be a leader in small appliances and a player on the global stage. New Black & Decker kitchen products on the horizon included the Smart Brew coffeemaker line, which included a perfect-pour feature, tying in with Applica's strategy to link the brand with innovative, solution-oriented products.

Meanwhile, the company was also building upon retail brands through partnerships with companies such as Starbucks and Target. In mid-2000, Applica added the Black & Decker slow cooker to the housewares collection launched the previous year by famed architect Michael Graves at discount chain Target, which rounded out its products in the collection. Around this time, Kmart expanded its merchandise of Applica-manufactured Black & Decker small electric products, a line that now included products made exclusively for Kmart. The retailer stated an intention to become a destination for Black & Decker small electrics, which now contributed 60 percent of Applica's annual revenue. In November 2000, amid much industry speculation, Applica entered a joint production-development deal with an unnamed packaged goods firm, with the first product to be unveiled by 2002. (Because of a confidentiality agreement, Applica has not been allowed to name the partner until the release of the first product.)

Although Applica's fourth-quarter 2000 bottom line declined because of the slower economy and higher raw material costs, the company managed to lower its inventory levels and cut debt. The company remained ambitious, with a goal of 50 percent market share in each category in which it competes. Looking at how the company can continue to grow, Applica knows it must develop innovations for products that serve an eternal purpose. ''A toaster still makes toast. A can opener still opens cans,'' Michienzi said in the April 9, 2001 edition of *HFN*. ''How do you get people to spend more for those products?''

Principal Subsidiaries

Applica Consumer Products, Inc.; Belson Products; Durable Electrical Metal Factory, Ltd.; Jerdon Products; NewTech Electronic Industries.

Principal Competitors

Philips; Salton; Sunbeam; Hamilton-Beach/Proctor-Silex.

Further Reading

DeGeorge, Gail, ''Windmere Tries to Comb Out the Kinks,'' *Business Week*, July 24, 1989, p. 44.

Fields, Gregg, ''Florida-Based Windmere Has High Hopes for Self-Cleaning Cat Box,'' *Miami Herald*, June 14, 1996.

Fogarty, Fred E., ''Work Is a Family Affair for Windmere Executive,'' *South Florida Business Journal*, June 22, 1987, p. 28.

Hagy, James R., ''Windmere to Wall Street: Take Us Back,'' *Florida Trend*, June 1992, pp. 29–32.

Lieber, Ed. ''Small Electrics, Exclusive Perks,'' *HFN*, Nov. 27, 2000, p. 1.

Lieber, Ed. ''Speculation Heats Up Over Identity of Applica's New Partner,'' *HFN*, Nov. 27, 2000, p. 43.

Mack, Toni, ''Rebate Madness,'' Forbes, February 13, 1984, p. 76.

Murray, Shanon D. ''Black & Decker Selling Division,'' *The Baltimore Sun*, May 12, 1998, p. 1C.

Oakes, David L., ''New Windmere President Carves Own Niche,'' *South Florida Business Journal*, February 11, 1985, p. 3.

Phillips, Dana, ''Under Heat, Windmere Stock Turns On,'' *South Florida Business Journal*, April 5, 1996, p. 1A.

Porter, Thyra, ''Windmere Eyes Whole House with Black & Decker Brand,'' *HFN*, Jan. 17, 2000, p. 66.

Porter, Thyra, ''Windmere Reorganizes Management,'' *HFN*, Dec. 20, 1999, p. 1.

Quail, Jennifer, ''New-Product Growth Is Applica's Number-One Goal,'' *HFN*, April 9, 2001.

Seemuth, Mike, ''Florida's CEOs: Life at the Top,'' *Florida Trend*, June 1994, pp. 50–54.

Thau, Barbara, ''Windmere to Tackle New Categories,'' HFN, March 20, 2000.

Thau, Barbara, ''Chicago Connection: The Retail Data Base: Kitchenware,'' *HFN*, Dec. 13, 1999, p. 57.

Turner, Alison, ''Windmere Rally More Than Hot Air,'' *South Florida Business Journal*, July 23, 1993, pp. 1, 18–29.

Werner, Holly M. ''Windmere to Pay $4.5 M to Izumi in Settlement,'' *HFN*, May 19, 1997, p. 57.

—Jason Gallman
—update: Michelle Feder

Ashanti Goldfields Company Limited

Gold House
Patrice Lumumba Road
P.O. Box 2665
Accra
Ghana
Telephone: (233 21) 77 2190
Fax: (233 22) 77 5947
Web site: http://www.ashantigold.com

Public Company
Incorporated: 1897 as Ashanti Goldfields Corporation, Ltd.
Employees: 10,429 (2000 est.)
Sales: $582.2 million (2000 est.)
Stock Exchanges: New York London Ghana Zimbabwe Australia Toronto
Ticker Symbol: ASL (New York); ASN (London); AGC (Ghana); Ashanti (Zimbabwe); AHA (Australia); AHD.U (Toronto)
NAIC: 212221 Gold Ore Mining

Over a century after its incorporation, Ashanti Goldfields Company Limited of Accra, Ghana, remains one of the largest producers of gold in the world, achieving an annual gold production of 1.74 million ounces in 2000. It is also Ghana's largest earner of foreign funds and the only mining operation on the New York and London stock exchanges run by black Africans. Originally operating with a single mine—the Obuasi mine in Ghana's Ashanti region that gives the company its name—Ashanti has in recent years expanded aggressively throughout Africa and now operates seven mines in Ghana, Zimbabwe, Guinea, and Tanzania. The company also maintains 25 active exploration projects in six African countries and about 20 outside the continent. Ashanti's most productive mine is Obuasi, which, despite over 100 years of continuous operation, is still one of the top-producing mines in the world and the largest mine in Africa outside South Africa. Conscious of its success on an often volatile and troubled continent, Ashanti prides itself in its relationships with local authorities and traditional political and social institutions in the African countries where it operates. The company has assisted local communities with infrastructure projects such as roadways, water and electricity access, and education.

Early Days

The rich goldfields in the Ashanti region of what is now Ghana were controlled by the powerful Asante (Ashanti) state as far back as the 17th century. The British colonization of Ghana in 1874 and the ensuing Ashanti wars brought a large number of Europeans to the area, and soldiers and travelers spread the word about the region's legendary gold reserves—''you could pick up gold as you would potatoes,'' reported one traveler. Widespread interest opened the region for large-scale commercial gold production. In 1890, Joseph E. Ellis and Chief Joseph E. Biney, Fatwe merchants from Africa's Cape Coast, and their accountant Joseph P. Brown negotiated mining concessions for 100 square miles in the Obuasi District. There they opened the Ellis Mine and introduced modern industrial mining techniques to the area. The Ellis mine operated for five years, then the partners sold the concession to Edwin Arthur Smith of the London-based firm Smith and Cade. With the overthrow of the Ashanti king in 1896, the Ashanti protectorate was brought directly under British control, and Cade was given approval to mine the region.

On June 11, 1897, Cade listed the Ashanti Goldfields Corporation Ltd. on the London Stock Exchange and set up operations at Obuasi on December 24 of that same year. The technique of adit mining—wherein a horizontal passage is dug from the earth's surface into the mine—proscribed by mining engineer John Daw tapped into the most immediately accessible ore in the hills around Obuasi and yielded initially impressive results. The Obuasi mine yielded 2,544 ounces of gold in its first year of operation and 4,673 ounces the second year. This early success, coupled with the devastation of the South African gold trade during the Boer War (1899–1902), fed Ashanti's rapid growth that continued until the uprising of the Ashanti people against British rule in 1900.

Company Perspectives:

Ashanti's Mission is to build an African gold mining and exploration company to international standards of excellence, managed predominantly by Africans. Ashanti aims to pursue growth for the benefit of our shareholders, employees and the nations where we operate.

Into the Twentieth Century

The impact of the anti-colonial conflict on Ashanti was devastating. Work was halted, mines became run-down and collapsed due to lack of upkeep. However, the good relations maintained by Daw and Cade with their local employees ensured the safety of the European staff during the hostilities. After the end of the conflict—despite the arrival of the railway line—Ashanti continued to suffer. Output did not return to previous levels, leading to shareholder skepticism over Daw's mining techniques. Edwin Cade died in 1903, leading to a further devaluation of shares. In 1905, an independent assessment of Ashanti operations was carried out by chemist W.R. Feldtmann and mining engineer J.A. MacTear. They criticized Daw's adit mining approach, declaring that the easily reachable ore was nearly exhausted, and that the hills around Obuasi did not contain the rich reefs (veins of ore) once believed. Daw resigned in 1906, and Feldtmann took over as consulting engineer.

Under Feldtmann, Ashanti underwent a period where output was slowed to allow for a change in mining techniques. Shallow adit mining was discontinued in favor of shaft mining in which a vertical tunnel is dug deep into the ground. To accommodate these new techniques, the company's profits were directed into new equipment. Feldtmann also developed more efficient methods of treating gold ore once it was mined. The discovery of an exceptionally rich ore deposit in 1908 brought fruit to Feldtmann's efforts, and Ashanti's success increased until the advent of World War I forced cutbacks in operations.

After the war, Ashanti saw a yearly increase in gold output. Significant discoveries in 1937 of gold along the Obuasi fissure and other locations gave rise to a time of great optimism at Ashanti. The company made plans for major expansions and budgeted for increased output. These plans were cut short by the dawn of World War II, which had a disastrous effect on the entire African gold mining industry. Most mines in the Gold Coast region were shut down for the duration of the war, but a few profitable operations—including Ashanti—were kept open on a ''care and maintenance'' basis, making do with aging and obsolete equipment.

Postwar Turbulence

The end of World War II saw a short surge in the African gold industry (often referred to as the ''jungle boom''), but that growth was short-lived. The industry had been cut off from foreign investment since 1942, and many mines that had opened shortly after the war found that they could not sustain themselves, and quickly closed. Ashanti was one of only four operations on the Gold Coast that remained open during this time and was the largest and most profitable. At this time, Ashanti was led by its autocratic chairman General Sir Edward Spears, who lived abroad and visited the company's operations only infrequently, treating it, according to Ashanti's company history, as ''a personal fiefdom.''

During Spears' leadership, the government of Ghana underwent rapid changes. In 1957, the British Parliament granted Ghana its independence, and Kwame Nkrumah became the country's first prime minister. In 1960, a new constitution was drafted, and the country became the Republic of Ghana, with Nkrumah as its president. Nkrumah proved to be an increasingly dictatorial leader, limiting freedom of action, imprisoning his critics, and finally introducing a one-party system in 1964. He nationalized five of Ghana's six producing gold mines (all but Ashanti), and granted Spears favorable land leases for Ashanti in exchange for derisory royalties. Nkrumah was deposed by the National Liberation Council (NLC) in 1966. The NLC soon began to question the contribution of mining operations such as Ashanti to the local economy and appeared to threaten the favorable land lease options Spears had enjoyed under Nkrumah. In response, Spears threatened to flood the mines. The Ghanaian government then ordered the commissioner of mines and energy to seek new investors for its mining industry, including the Ashanti Goldfields.

The Lonrho Years

Fortunately, Lonrho (London and Rhodesia Mining and Land Company—now Lonmin) already had an interest in acquiring the company, and the government quickly welcomed the takeover. Lonrho acquired Ashanti in 1968 for £3 million (US$2.1 million) in stock, promising to preserve Ashanti as a separate entity. Ashanti was delisted from the London Stock Exchange, and Lonrho offered the Ghanaian government a 20 percent interest in the company in exchange for a 50-year extension on its land leases. The government would also have an option to buy another 20 percent of the company for £1 (US$.70) per share. In response to the sentiment in Ghana that Ashanti had not been growing quickly enough to meet the country's currency needs, Lonrho also promised to increase the mine capacity from 45,000 to 80,000 tons of ore per month. Spears was invited to join the Lonrho board. He retained the title of chairman, but, after expressing much dissatisfaction with the increased government involvement with Ashanti, resigned in 1971.

The Lonrho years were marked by turmoil. Violence between police and miners at the March 1969 strike killed three and wounded 28, and another strike in 1970 closed the mine for a week. A coup in 1972 once again forced a change in government, and the new administration, led by Ignatius Archeampong, demanded government ''participation'' in all mining companies and acquired 55 percent of Ashanti shares. The company was ordered to change its name to the Ashanti Goldfields Company and relocate its headquarters to Accra from London.

As part of their ''participation'' in Ashanti's operations, the government appointed Lloyd A.K. Quashie, a geologist and mining expert, to Ashanti's board of directors as deputy managing director. Under his direction, the company began efforts to improve conditions for local workers, and instituted a program to decrease the percentage of ''expatriate positions''—positions held by non-Africans. The program sent ''promising

Key Dates:

1897: Ashanti Goldfields Corporation, Ltd. is incorporated in London and the Ashanti mine begins operation.
1906: W.R. Feldtmann becomes consulting engineer and reforms mining techniques.
1914: World War I forces production cutbacks.
1937: General Sir Edward Spears becomes chairman.
1966: The new National Liberation Council orders search for new investors for company.
1968: Company acquired by Lonrho of London.
1972: New government acquires 55 percent of company's shares.
1985: Company receives £159 million loan for expansion from the International Finance Corporation.
1986: Sam E. Jonah becomes company chief executive.
1994: Company listed on London and Ghana stock exchanges.
1996: Company listed on New York Stock Exchange.
2000: Company's seventh mine, Geita, opens in Tanzania.

young Ghanaians'' to universities abroad, with the idea that they would return to work for the company, supplanting the expatriates. One of the first recipients of these educational opportunities was Sam E. Jonah, who attended Exeter's Camborne School of Mines in Cornwall, England, and the Imperial College of Science and Technology in London and later became the CEO of Ashanti.

Despite the turbulent times, Ashanti continued to prosper, reaching a peak production level of 533,000 ounces in 1972. Unfortunately, by that time, many ore deposits had been exhausted. This depletion, combined with the loss of foreign exchange and a high tax bill led to another decline through the seventies. The company was unable to expand its interests, invest in new plants, or even replace outdated equipment. Annual production fell to 232,000 ounces in 1980. Profits continued to fall, and in 1982, the company experienced the first operating loss in its history.

A New Beginning

It took another governmental shift to turn the company's fortunes around. In 1981, the Provisional National Defence Council, led by Jerry Rawlings, took control. At first, the new government's socialist ideology seemed to spell even more trouble for the Ashanti. But by 1983, the government realized that outside capital would be needed to achieve its goal of rebuilding Ghana's economy, so the political stance shifted to welcome a more free-market philosophy. Its Economic Recovery Program, backed by the International Monetary Fund (IMF), the World Bank, and Western aid donors aimed to rehabilitate Ghana's major export earners, and Ashanti was one of its major beneficiaries. In 1985, Ashanti was granted a £159 million (US$111 million) IMF loan, and the new Minerals and Mining Law allowed Ashanti to keep 45 percent of its export earnings.

With this fresh infusion of capital, Ashanti was ready for an ambitious program of expansion and modernization. In 1986, the company's first Ghanaian CEO, Sam Jonah, was appointed. He embarked on a major overhaul of company operations. While the company's headquarters had been in Accra for twelve years, much of the planning and budgeting was still carried out by consultants in the London office. Jonah transferred these duties to Ghana, keeping the staff geographically close to the mine site. Communications between management and line workers was improved, wages for mine workers were raised, and the company began the community renewal plan that is now a hallmark of all its operations throughout Africa. Ashanti purchased new equipment for mining surface oxides and commissioned a heap leach (a low-cost method of extracting ores) facility in 1990, and the company built an oxide treatment plant in 1991. This project established the Obuasi mine as the largest surface mining operation in Africa and the mine as a whole became one of the top five in the world. Gold production reached record highs, increasing by 25 percent. Loans from the International Finance Corporation (IFC) helped the company launch its Ashanti Mines Expansion Program, allowing it to take advantage of highly profitable, lower grade underground gold resources.

Growth and Renewal

Holder of the majority of Ashanti shares, the Ghanaian government in 1994 announced its plan to sell 17.9 million shares—a full half of its 55 percent stake—in a share flotation on the London and Ghana stock exchanges. The company reserved 1.2 million shares exclusively for Ghanaians, and each of Ashanti's employees received five free shares. In 1996, Ashanti became the first African-operated company to list on the New York Stock Exchange. The capital raised by these two flotations (the London IPO alone was worth $454 million) allowed the company to pay its debts to the IFC and begin its expansion in Ghana and in other African nations. By the end of the 1990s, in addition to the original mine in Obuasi, Ashanti operated the Ayanfuri, Bibiani, and Iduapriem mines in Ghana, the Siguiri mine in Guinea, and the Freda-Rebecca Mine in Zimbabwe. The nineties also saw Ashanti expanding its links with the communities where its mines are located. Beginning in 1990–91, the company supplied water resources such as hand pumps, boreholes, and hand-dug wells for the Obuasi township and 137 smaller villages and townships. Ashanti also undertook projects to bring electricity to villages without it and to build schools for the families of its staff.

Into the New Millennium

A well-publicized crisis at the end of the nineties nearly spelled disaster for the company. The price of gold rose dramatically in September of 1999. The company had outstanding hedge contracts, and the rise in gold price exposed the company to possible margin calls on these contracts. Ashanti's credit lines were frozen. The freeze resulted in a shortfall of capital, which put in danger the completion of the Geita mine in Tanzania, slated for opening in 2000. Ashanti successfully resolved these problems, however, by negotiating a period of margin-free trading and a $100 million bridge facility to finance completion of the Geita mine. Geita opened in August of 2000, three months ahead of schedule, and was the largest gold mine in Tanzania.

Ashanti reported a gold production of 1.74 million ounces for the year 2000—a record for the company, despite its recent difficulties and the cessation of surface mining operations at Obuasi. In 2001, the company's future plans included further expansion in Africa, including operations in the Ivory Coast and the Congo. In his remarks at the Indaba Conference in Cape Town, South Africa, in February 2001, Jonah acknowledged the difficulties of the past and expressed pride in the company's recovery. ''We were able to keep focus, despite some particularly choppy waters,'' he said. ''And I am confident we can continue to do so as we train our eyes further out into the future.''

Principal Subsidiaries

Ashanti Goldfields (Ayanfuri) Limited; Ashanti Goldfields (Bibiani) Limited; Ghanaian-Australian Goldfields Limited (80%); Société Ashanti Goldfields de Guinee S.A. (Guinea) (85%); Ashanti Goldfields Tanzania Limited (Tanzania); Ashanti Goldfields Zimbabwe Limited (Zimbabwe); Ashanti Treasury Services Limited (Isle of Man).

Principal Competitors

Barrick Gold Corporation; Newmont Mining Corporation; Placer Dome, Inc.

Further Reading

''African Privitisation: Golden Shares,'' *The Economist,* March 19, 1994, p. 96.

''Anglo's Long Trek North,'' *The Economist,* November 2, 1996, p. 69.

''Ashanti Goldfields Becomes First African Company to List on New York Stock Exchange,'' *Jet,* March 18, 1996, p. 46.

''Ashanti Record,'' *Mining Journal,* February 9, 2001, p. 111.

''Ashanti's Geita Pours First Gold,'' *American Metal Market,* June 14, 2000, p. 6.

Ayensu, Edward S., *Ashanti Gold: The African Legacy of the World's Most Precious Metal,* Accra, Ghana: Ashanti Goldfields Company Limited, 1997.

Barnabas, Thondhlana, ''Investors Warm to Ashanti,'' *African Business,* July/August 1997, p. 28.

Bowman, Louise, ''Pits-Tops,'' *Project Finance,* February 2001, pp. 52–53.

Cozens, Claire, ''Ashanti First out of Africa,'' *Corporate Finance,* December 1995, p. 41.

Cronjé, Suzanne, Margaret Ling, and Gillian Cronjé, *The Lonrho Connections: A Multinational and Its Politics in Africa,* Encino, Calif.: Bellwether Books, 1976.

De Giorgio, Emmanuelle Moors, ''Ashanti—The Full Story,'' *African Business,* December 1999, pp. 34–36.

''Ghana,'' *Microsoft Encarta Encyclopedia,* Redmond, Wash.: Microsoft Corporation, 1999.

''Gold,'' *Microsoft Encarta Encyclopedia,* Redmond, Wash.: Microsoft Corporation, 1999.

Gordon-Walker, Rupert, ''Rich Pickings or Fool's Gold?'' *Euromoney,* May 1996, p. 22.

McGeary, Johanna, and Marguerite Michaels, ''Africa Rising: Hope on the Continent,'' *Time,* March 30, 1998, pp. 34–45.

Olivier, Charles, ''Ashanti Breaks Free from IFC,'' *Corporate Finance,* August 1995, p. 4.

Picker, Ida, ''Sam Jonah of Ashanti Goldfields Co.: A Glittering Success Story in Sub-Saharan Africa,'' *Institutional Investor,* June 1996, p. 29.

''President Praises Sam Jonah,'' *Africa News Service,* August 14, 2000.

Winfred, Arthur, Jr., Dennis Doverspike, and James E. Kuthy, ''Striking Gold through a Deep-Level Organizational Intervention in Ghana's Mining Industry,'' *International Journal of Organizational Analysis,* April 1996, pp. 175–186.

—Lisa Whipple

AsiaInfo Holdings, Inc.

4/F, Zhongdian Information Tower
No.6 Zhongguancun South Street
Beijing, China
Telephone: +(86) 10-6250-1658
Fax: +(86) 10-6250-1893
Web site: http://www.asiainfo.com

Public Company
Incorporated: 1993
Employees: 650 (2000)
Sales: $176.1 million (2000 est.)
Stock Exchanges: NASDAQ
Ticker Symbol: ASIA
NAIC: 541511 Custom Computer Programming Services; 511210 Software Publishers; 541512 Computer System Design Services

Less than a decade after its incorporation, AsiaInfo Holdings, Inc. has grown from its humble beginnings as a small venture in Dallas, Texas to the leading provider of software products and Internet infrastructure systems in China. The Beijing-based company is divided into two main business units. Its Network Solutions business caters to Chinese telecommunications service providers. AsiaInfo has built most of mainland China's Internet infrastructure and has pioneered the way for much of China's burgeoning Internet and telecommunications industry. The company is known for designing and building China's first national commercial Internet backbone (a main Internet line that carries data to smaller sub-networks), its first provincial Internet backbone, its first WAN (Wide Area Network) providing public services, and its first network system providing nationwide roaming capability. Its other core area of business is Software Products. AsiaInfo has developed messaging and e-mail programs and billing and customer management software for Internet service providers and continues to develop proprietary software for Internet and telecommunications companies. The management team of AsiaInfo consists of native-born Chinese, and most have studied abroad and returned to ''work for China.'' This image has helped the company in its dealings with the central Chinese government—AsiaInfo is the first Internet company to receive official approval from the Chinese Securities Regulatory Commission to list abroad.

Early Inspiration

AsiaInfo was founded in 1993 by Edward Tian and James Ding, two Chinese-born academics who had studied in the United States. Tian came to the United States in 1987 to earn a Ph.D. in Natural Resources Management at Texas Tech University. When he heard a 1993 speech by Vice President Al Gore on the information superhighway, Tian's direction began to shift from academics to entrepreneurship. He wanted to somehow bring Internet connectivity to China. ''We were starved for information,'' Tian told *Wired* magazine in 1999. ''The Internet could give Chinese children access. From an isolated province, they could visit the Louvre or any library in the world.'' He began writing articles about the Internet for Chinese journals and began e-mail discussion groups for expatriate technology professionals. Later in 1993 he teamed up with his acquaintance James Ding, who had recently moved to Dallas after earning his Master's degree in Information Science from the University of California at Los Angeles and graduating from the Executive Program at Hass Business School at UC Berkeley. Ding was also driven by a loyalty to his homeland. ''You see how big the difference is between the U.S. and your home country,'' he told *The Industry Standard* in 2000. ''And you want to be able to do something to help. It's not a comfortable thing to say, 'OK, now I'm living my life in the United States. I'm just going to forget about China.' ''

While Tian and Ding's ultimate ambition lay in China, they wanted to prove they could run a successful company in the United States first. They approached Tian's business mentor, Louis Lau, a U.S.-born Chinese-American who supported their vision of a wired China. He loaned the pair $50,000 to begin their venture. Tian and Ding started AsiaInfo as a service that sold research on Chinese markets to U.S. companies. They also founded *AsiaInfo Daily News*, which translated Chinese news into English for American readers. While they ran the business

Company Perspectives:

AsiaInfo's mission is to be the leading China-based company providing world-class software products and network solutions that enable its customers to build, maintain, operate, and continuously improve their Internet and communications infrastructure. To fulfill this mission, AsiaInfo combines this advanced knowledge of cutting-edge technologies, best practice management, and thorough understanding of China's unique operating environment to strive to stay ahead of domestic and international competition and to meet its customers' highest expectations.

in the United States, Ding and Tian also made trips to China to promote the Internet in academic and political arenas.

Return to China

In 1995, Tian and Ding moved to Beijing, China, to set up operations. (AsiaInfo still maintains an office in the United States and, while its headquarters are in Beijing, the company remains a U.S. incorporated company.) Initially, they worked as consultants to other companies, developing information systems software. Soon they were hired by Sprint, who had made an early entry into China and had received a commission from the Chinese government to design and build a prototype commercial Internet network. AsiaInfo and Sprint worked together until the government asked for bids on a contract to build ChinaNet, the first national Internet backbone. Sprint and AsiaInfo dissolved their relationship and competed for the contract. Thanks in part to the close relationship that Tian had created with the Ministry of Post and Telecommunications (now the Ministry of Informational Industry), AsiaInfo secured the $8 million contract in November 1995.

Internet Explosion

Prior to 1993, all telecommunications industry in China was under the control of the government. After that year, the government took steps to reform the industry, and, as a result, the years between 1994 and 1998 saw a tremendous surge in the growth of the Internet in China. The rate of installed fixed lines tripled in those four years. In 1994, there were approximately 50,000 Internet users in China. By 1997, there were 620,000, and by mid-1998, that number had risen astonishingly to 1.2 million. AsiaInfo grew in sync with this explosion, and its business helped the industry expand. At the end of 1995 the company began work on ChinaNet. While such ''backbones'' depend on cable and wires, AsiaInfo's contribution to ChinaNet was not the physical infrastructure—this was built by China Telecom. Instead, AsiaInfo designed the network and determined the number of servers to attach. Their work required over $4 million in imported equipment, including Sun SPARCstations and Cisco routers. The result was the primary commercial Internet system for all of China.

More success soon followed. In 1996 AsiaInfo signed an agreement with the Shanghai Post and Telecom Administration Bureau to build Shanghai Online, a municipal public information network, and began construction of the China Financial Data Communication Network, a national network linking major financial institutions across China. It was soon apparent that the company needed an infusion of cash to grow, and Tian and Ding approached Bo Feng, one of the first venture capitalists in China. Feng, who was only 26 years old at the time, saw great potential in AsiaInfo and its hope for China's future. ''I'm not interested in a company if it only has a great product,'' he told *Wired* magazine in 1999. ''I'm not interested in a body without a soul.''

At that time Feng did not have his own fund, so he approached contacts in the United States and Hong Kong. One meeting in particular illustrated the infancy of the Internet in China. During their conversation, a potential investor asked Feng and Tian, ''What's the Internet?'' Tian gave the man a comprehensive description of the Internet and AsiaInfo's place within it. The man, whose investments included bacon fat and pork sides, responded, ''Aha! Now I understand. You are a plumber.'' Eventually, AsiaInfo was able to round up $18 million from investors such as Warburg Pincus, ChinaVest, Fidelity Investment Company, and Sandy Robertson.

The next two years saw further growth for the company. In 1997 AsiaInfo entered the Internet software market with two network management software products, AIOBS and AINexus. Also that year, the company won the contract from China Telecom to build a nationwide narrowband Internet access network known as 169.net. Additionally, Fidelity Investment Company chose AsiaInfo as one of the world's most promising companies for investment. In 1998 the company promoted the concept of Carrier Class IP which became the industry standard in China. AsiaInfo also installed its new e-mail software, AIMailCenter, at 21cn.com, China's largest Internet portal. The company made two strategic acquisitions that year: a 40 percent controlling interest in Guangdong Wayngying, a company that provided systems integration services and software products in China's Guangdong province, and a full acquisition of AI Zhejiang, a producer of wireless customer management and billing software.

Surviving Rapid Changes 1998–99

By 1998, AsiaInfo had designed 90 percent of China's Internet infrastructure and was growing 200 percent a year. Tian and Ding's technical expertise was legendary, but they were less knowledgeable about how businesses worked. All the earnings AsiaInfo took in were immediately spent on expansion, and the company had almost no cash. The venture capital firm Warburg Pincus invested an additional $11 million in AsiaInfo, with the condition that the company hire a professional CFO. Tian and Ding recruited Han Ying, Hewlett-Packard's China operations controller. Han immediately got the company a $5 million bridge loan, and she dramatically reduced the time it took the company to get paid from six to three months.

Also in 1998 the company opened an office in Santa Clara, California. This new office—AsiaInfo Holdings, Inc. became the sole owner of the company, even though the headquarters—AsiaInfo Technologies (China) Co. Ltd.—remained in China. ''We operate 100 percent in China, but because China does not have a modern legal system, we decided on this structure,'' Tian

Key Dates:

1993: Company is founded by Edward Tian and James Ding and incorporates in Dallas, Texas.
1995: AsiaInfo relocates to Beijing, China and wins the contract to build ChinaNet.
1996: The company begins construction of the China Financial Data Communication Network.
1997: AsiaInfo wins the contract to build 169.net, a nationwide narrowband Internet access network.
1998: Company opens an office in Santa Clara, California, and hires Han Ying as CFO to manage rapid earnings.
1999: Edward Tian leaves AsiaInfo for the telecommunications firm China Netcom.
2000: AsiaInfo has an initial public offering (IPO) on NASDAQ and raises $127 million; the company divides into two business units: Network Solutions and Software Products; the company engineers CNCNet, a high-speed IP backbone for 17 Chinese cities.

told *Global Tech Ventures* in 1998. In 2000 Ding further explained the dual office approach to CNN, ''It's very important because the positioning of AsiaInfo is to build a bridge between China's Internet infrastructure and the United States' technology. . . . Our U.S. office has a very important role in . . . helping to bridge both countries to promote the business for both countries.''

In 1999, Edward Tian was invited to become the president and CEO of state-run China Netcom, the third-largest telecommunications company in China. Tian left AsiaInfo that year, but remained one of the company's largest shareholders. James Ding became CEO of AsiaInfo upon Tian's departure. Although AsiaInfo went on to do business with China Netcom, the company did not enjoy a special advantage due to its former leader's new position. ''We had a mutual understanding that AsiaInfo was not going to take advantage of Edward's position [at China Netcom],'' Ding told *Virtual China* in 2000. China Netcom went on to build the country's most advanced telecommunications network—in only 16 months.

A New Century

In December 1999, AsiaInfo filed a registration statement for an initial public offering on the NASDAQ of up to $50 million of its common stock. On March 3, 2000 the company announced the IPO. Five million shares were offered at an initial price of $24. The IPO raised $127 million, its shares rising 315 percent on the first day of trading alone.

The new century also saw a shift in direction for AsiaInfo. Although the company had a virtual monopoly on the telecommunications systems integration market in China, this business was not very profitable. As CEO, Ding began to focus more on the company's software and Internet service businesses, where margins were better. AsiaInfo was restructured into two business units: Network Solutions and Software Products. At first this shift was seen as risky, because software was a relatively unproven part of AsiaInfo's operations. But skeptics were soon proved wrong. ''They're demonstrating that it's a viable business now,'' James Chang, an analyst for Credit Suisse First Boston told *The Asian Wall Street Journal Weekly* in 2001. In August 2000 China Unicom launched a nationwide IP network that used AsiaInfo's software programs AIOBSv5 and AIMailCenter. By the third quarter of 2000, software represented about 37 percent of AsiaInfo's net revenue—an increase of 16 percent from the previous year. The company turned a profit for the first time in the second quarter of 2000.

Its success as a software company did not inspire AsiaInfo to abandon the networking business that had made it so successful in the mid-1990s. In January 2000 China Netcom hired AsiaInfo to engineer a high-speed IP backbone for 17 cities in southern and eastern China, known as CNCNet. In March China Unicom contracted with the company to expand its VoIP (Voice over IP) network to an additional 300 cities nationwide. And in September China Mobile contracted AsiaInfo to engineer a national IP backbone connecting the country's 31 provincial capitals.

Despite the wildly fluctuating stock market of 2000–01, and a decrease in capital spending in China for telecommunications interests, AsiaInfo continued to flourish. In 2001 the company posted a net income of $2.6 million on revenue that rose 45 percent to $17 million. Plans for the future included continuing to build the software business so as to be able to develop products for new telecommunications services soon to be available in China such as wireless messaging, wireless data, long distance via VoIP, and unified messaging. ''We have the first-mover advantage,'' James Ding predicted to Dow Jones Newswires in 2001. ''In the next few years, we're still going to maintain our dominant position in the Internet and software spectrum.''

Principal Divisions

Software Products; Network Solutions.

Principal Subsidiaries

AsiaInfo Technologies; Guangdong Wangying Information Technology (40%); Zhejiang AsiaInfo Telecommunciations Technology; MarSec Holdings (75%).

Principal Competitors

ASPAC Communications; New Tel; UTStarcom.

Further Reading

''Analysts See an AsiaInfo Age,'' *The Asian Wall Street Journal Weekly*, May 14, 2001, pp. 1–2.
''AsiaInfo Acquires New Software Client after Successful Delivery of Network Solutions,'' *China Telecom*, October 2000, p. 6.
''AsiaInfo Expands Position in Wireless Market with Multiple Contract Wins from China Mobile,'' *China Telecom*, June 2001, p. 13.
''AsiaInfo Eyes GEM on Top of NASDAQ Listing,'' *South China Morning Post*, May 2, 2001, p. 4.
''AsiaInfo Holdings Inc.,'' *The New York Times*, February 28, 2000, p. C6.

''AsiaInfo Holdings, Inc. Announces Initial Public Offering,'' *Business Wire*, posted March 3, 2000, http://www.businesswire.com.

''AsiaInfo Holdings, Inc. Files Registration Statement for Initial Public Offering, Use of the Ticker Symbol ASIA Proposed but Not Yet Approved by NASDAQ,'' *Business Wire*, posted December 23, 1999, http://www.businesswire.com.

''AsiaInfo Holdings to Build China Post Billing System,'' *Asia Pulse*, posted June 22, 2001, http://www.asiapulse.com.

''AsiaInfo Holdings to Supply Hebei Telecom with Software Products,'' *Asia Pulse*, posted February 12, 2001, http://www.asiapulse.com.

''AsiaInfo Makes Strategic Investment in Intrinsic Technology,'' *Asia Pulse*, posted May 9, 2001 http://www.asiapulse.com.

''AsiaInfo Offers Rare China Play in Net Sector,'' *Wall Street Journal*, January 24, 2000, p. 9.

''AsiaInfo Posts Profit, Revenue Skyrockets,'' *123Jump*, June 8, 2001.

''AsiaInfo Sells First Internet Data Center Billing Software to China NetCom,'' *China Telecom*, October 2000, p. 7.

''AsiaInfo's Network Management Software Selected for Liaoning Telecom Provincial Network Expansion,'' *China Telecom*, June 2001, p. 17.

''AsiaInfo Software Selected by Sichuan Broadcasting and Television Network Ltd. for Cable Internet Project,'' *Cableoptics Newsletter*, December 2000, pp. 7-8.

''AsiaInfo Taps into Outsourcing Market,'' *Asiainfo Daily China News*, December 12, 2000 p. 1.

''AsiaInfo to Provide Network Services to Shanghai Online,'' *Asia Pulse*, posted January 16, 2001 http://www.asiapulse.com.

''AsiaInfo Wins Two Software Contracts from China Telecom,'' *Asia Pulse*, posted July 27, 2001 http://www.asiapulse.com.

Chang, Leslie, ''IPO Promises Entry into China's Internet,'' *Wall Street Journal*, January 24, 2000, p. A21.

——, ''Rare China Play Offered,'' *The Asian Wall Street Journal Weekly*, January 31, 2000, p. 18.

''China Mobile Selects AsiaInfo to Build National Backbone Covering All of the 31 Provinces,'' *China Telecom*, October 2000, p. 7.

Elstein, Aaron, ''ASIA Net Surge Is Mistake, IPO Mix-up Sends Toll Road Stock Soaring,'' *The Asian Wall Street Journal Weekly*, January 10, 2000, p. 14.

——, ''Confused Traders Find Wrong ASIA in IPO Geography,'' *Wall Street Journal*, January 6, 2000, p. C23.

Icon Group International, *Asiainfo Holdings, Inc.: International Competitive Benchmarks and Financial Gap Analysis*, San Diego: Icon Group International, October 2000.

''Intrinsic Deal Could Spur Overseas Growth,'' *The Asian Wall Street Journal Weekly*, May 14, 2001, p. 3.

''Jilin Mobile Signs Contract with AsiaInfo for Messaging Products and Services,'' *China Telecom*, December 2000, p. 6.

''Jitong, AsiaInfo Unit Signs Security Service Pact,'' *Asiainfo Daily China News*, June 14, 2001, p. 1.

Mufson, Steven, ''The Entrepreneur and the Net: Helping China Leap Forward,'' *International Herald Tribune*, June 17, 1998, p. 2.

——, ''The Information Highway: From Texas to Beijing,'' *The Washington Post*, June 16, 1998, p. A1.

Ng, Eric, ''New Firms to Reap Windfall by Using New Technology,'' *South China Morning Post*, April 10, 2000, p. 3.

Richardson, Karen, ''SG Asset's Tech Fund Looks Back to Get Ahead,'' *The Asian Wall Street Journal Weekly*, May 21, 2001, p. 26.

Sender, Henny, ''As Good as It Gets,'' *Far Eastern Economic Review*, June 29, 2000, pp. 66–67.

Sheff, David, ''He's Got Guanxi!,'' *Wired*, February 1999.

—Lisa Whipple

Assisted Living Concepts, Inc.

11835 NE Glenn Widing Dr., Bldg. E
Portland, Oregon 97220-9057
U.S.A.
Telephone: (503) 252-6233
Fax: (503) 252-6597
Web site: http://www.alcco.com

Public Company
Incorporated: 1994
Employees: 3,613
Sales: $139.4 million (2000)
Stock Exchanges: American
Ticker Symbol: ALF
NAIC: 623311 Continuing Care Retirement Communities; 62311 Nursing Care Facilities; 621999 All Other Miscellaneous Ambulatory Health Care Services

Assisted Living Concepts, Inc. owns, leases, and develops free-standing assisted living residences for moderate income older adults who need assistance with the activities of daily living, such as bathing, dressing, and shopping. Its facilities are designed to allow residents to ''age in place''—to maintain a fairly independent lifestyle as long as possible while being able to take advantage of healthcare services as needed. The company builds its residences primarily in rural and suburban communities with populations ranging from 10,000 to 40,000. In addition to housing, the company provides personal care, support services, and nursing services according to the individual needs of its residents and as permitted by state regulation. While the company receives 80 percent of its revenues from private pay sources, it also participates in Medicaid waiver programs.

Capturing a Profitable Market Niche: 1982–93

When her elderly mother complained about living in a nursing home in the early 1980s, Keren Brown Wilson did more than feel guilty or speak with the staff. Wilson, a West Virginia coal miner's daughter, helped pioneer the idea for what was to become a new industry: assisted living facilities.

To be sure, although she had never taken a business course or headed a major company, Wilson was prepared for the job. Her idea was the expression not just of filial duty, but of years of professional experience. Wilson had completed a Ph.D. in urban affairs and gerontology at Portland State University, earning a fellowship at a time when the federal government was channeling individuals into careers in gerontology. Later, she consulted on privately funded assisted living projects, and worked in the field of public policy for the aging in a dozen states.

Wilson became convinced, as she described it in a 1997 *Oregonian* article, that ''we were on the wrong path'' in providing care for the aging. ''Everything we knew, academically, every bit of theory was not being carried out in practice.'' The elderly were being denied independence, privacy, dignity and control—all crucial ingredients to longevity and prolonged quality of life. ''They had no control over their environment. They had no control over their care. They had no control over decision making.''

Beginning in 1982, Wilson went to work to finance her first assisted living facility, despite resistance from bankers and bureaucrats. At the time, nursing homes were not homes, but healthcare holding tanks, where the top priorities were patient safety and 24-hour nursing care for people considered too ill to care for themselves. Unlocked doors and kitchenettes in small individual apartments—the things Wilson foresaw including in her facility—meant danger, not independence. ''Conventional lenders thought the product was too different to be sellable,'' she was quoted as saying in a 1997 *Oregonian* article. ''They said, 'That's not how it's done.' '' Fortunately, she was able to secure financing to build apartments for the elderly under an Oregon bond program for senior housing. With $900,000 in the bank, Wilson applied to a different state agency and received a license to provide residential care. Park Place Living Center, the resulting 112-unit development for the elderly, in Tigard, Oregon, a suburb of Portland, provided radical innovations, such as private apartments with kitchens and locking doors, along with staff to help residents perform daily living activities, such as eating, bathing, and shopping.

Three years later in 1985, Wilson convinced Richard Ladd, who ran the Oregon Senior and Disabled Services Division

> **Company Perspectives:**
>
> *To provide affordable, quality housing and services which reflect and support independence, dignity, choice, privacy, and individuality in meeting the needs and preferences of all tenants in a home-like setting.*

until 1992, to conduct a Medicaid demonstration project in assisted living. Ladd, who had laughed at Wilson's idea back when she first proposed it, was so impressed with the practice of assisted living after touring Park Place that he arranged for permission to let 20 Medicaid patients move into Wilson's second facility, Regency Park Living Center. In 1986, Oregon permanently amended its rules to allow any qualified Medicaid patient to receive care in an assisted living facility instead of a nursing home.

Spinoff in 1994

By 1994, assisted living was an acknowledged new industry that was attracting imitators and gaining attention on Wall Street—close to a $15 billion industry overall. Wilson's Concepts in Community Living, Inc. (CCL), which had incorporated in 1988, drew the attention of Peter Sidoti, senior equity analyst at NatWest Securities and Andre Dimitriadis, former executive at Beverly Enterprises and American Medical International. The two men approached Wilson with the idea of forming the first publicly traded assisted living company. Wilson resigned from CCL, leaving her husband, Michael DeShane, to run the company's consulting business, and Assisted Living took shape as a CCL spinoff in November 1994. The fledgling public company had six residences in operation and 1994 revenues of $2.1 million. It netted approximately $18.5 million in its initial public offering of two million common shares, putting the proceeds toward buying one residence and leasing another.

By 1995, Assisted Living had six facilities in Oregon, ten in Texas, and three in Washington. The company lost money that year, as expected—$575,000 on revenues of $4 million—but finished 1996 in the black with a total profit of $149,000 on revenues of $19 million. By the end of 1996, Assisted Living had more than 50 licensed assisted living facilities in six states—Washington, Oregon, Idaho, Texas, Ohio, and New Jersey—and more under construction. These out-of-state residences, part of Assisted Living's national expansion program, undertaken with Chicago-based Walken Development Co., added 65 facilities to the company's total in Indiana, Ohio, South Carolina, New Jersey, and Georgia from 1996 to 1999.

Even as it grew, Assisted Living continued to seek to serve the low-end of the private pay assisted living market, as had its predecessor agency, CCL. Costs to the resident averaged $1,600 a month, about 65 percent of the average nursing home rate. The company focused on states where Medicaid paid for assisted living or waivers were pending so that once residents had spent down to Medicaid eligibility they could remain at Assisted Living facilities, or ''age in place.''

Assisted Living placed a premium on keeping costs sufficiently low to make a niche for itself among the lower-end private pay residents and so that residences could operate profitably even if all revenues were derived through Medicaid reimbursements. To hold costs down to $55,000 to $70,000 per new unit, the company typically built in smaller towns, which it perceived as an underserved market, and looked for residential, rather than commercial, locations to minimize on raw land costs. Its facilities were all small—in the 25-to-50 unit range—and single story to avoid the necessity of elevators or stairs. There were no common spaces, such as private dining rooms and exercise rooms, and the laundry room available to residents doubled as the facility laundry during off hours. Over the years, Assisted Living developed a standard architectural plan that varied only in finishes by region. It avoided dual occupancy designs to eliminate management time spent pairing roommates and mediating situations when individuals did not get along. Most of the company's development was outsourced, with fixed prices and ''not to exceed'' bidding the rule.

On the operating side, Assisted Living instituted three practices. Its ''universal workers'' were trained to perform multiple tasks, such as personal care, housekeeping, food services, laundry, and medical assistance, which enabled them to schedule other tasks during slow times, while simultaneously ensuring residents' continuity of care. Building small enabled the company to eliminate middle managers. Cluster management, the construction of grouped facilities, allowed it to achieve economies of scale in such areas as maintenance.

In 1997, Assisted Living began to acquire other assisted living companies, the first of which was Carriage House Assisted Living of Nebraska. Shortly thereafter, it acquired Home and Community Care, Inc. (HCI) and merged both companies' operations to add home health and hospice services to the company's offerings. In anticipation of the merger, the company reorganized its executive ranks; HCI's chief executive, William McBride, replaced Wilson as Assisted Living's CEO, and Wilson became president and COO of the company. In addition, Assisted Living also formed a subsidiary to manage health, hospice, and durable medical equipment operations. A second stock offering was held in 1997 to finance purchases. The company saw a 157 percent jump in revenue to $49 million that year, and income skyrocketed to $4.21 million.

By the end of 1998, Assisted Living owned and operated 173 residences in 15 states. The company closed its home healthcare operations and reached an agreement in November to be purchased by American Retirement Corporation (ARC), a company that concentrated on affluent residents in urban markets, for $242 million, The transaction would have created one of the largest housing and healthcare service providers in the United States. Then trouble struck; the deal with ARC fell through when auditors questioned Assisted Living's accounting methods.

Legal Woes and Changes Within the Industry: Late 1990s–2000s

According to the auditors, the way in which Assisted Living accounted for loss reimbursements from its joint ventures made what were loans look like income. As a result, two years of losses had become two years of profits. In February, Assisted Living reduced its income for 1997 by $1.6 million and its

Key Dates:

1982: Keren Brown Wilson secures funding for her first assisted living facility.
1988: Concepts in Community Living is incorporated.
1994: Assisted Living Concepts, Inc. is organized as a spinoff from Concepts in Community Living.
1997: Assisted Living acquires Carriage House Assisted Living and Home and Community Care (HCI); HCI's chief executive, William McBride, replaces Wilson as Assisted Living's head.
1998: An audit forces Assisted Living to recalculate past earnings.
1999: Wilson replaces McBride as president and chief executive in March; the American Stock Exchange halts trading in Assisted Living's stock in April.
2000: Assisted Living agrees to a $30 million settlement in order to avoid a class-action suit; Wilson is replaced by William James Nicol.

income for the first nine months of 1998 by $3.4 million. In the wake of this recalculation, Assisted Living's stock plunged to less than half its former value, and shareholders filed a securities fraud class-action lawsuit. Wilson replaced McBride as president and CEO in March 1999, the month Assisted Living said it would also restate its 1996 earnings. In April 1999, the American Stock Exchange halted trading in Assisted Living's stock when the company missed its 15-day deadline for filing reports with the Securities and Exchange Commission. Trading stopped at a little less than $3 a share, significantly down from the stock's December 1997 high of $22.

Meanwhile the trend in senior housing moved from rapid to modest expansion in 1998 and 1999, in part because of the strained availability of capital and because expansion had led to a housing oversupply. Critics began to accuse public assisted living companies, such as Assisted Living, of being more interested in meeting Wall Street's high growth-and-earnings expectations than in serving clientele. They said that facilities were accepting seniors who should really have been in nursing homes where they would have received better care. Assisted Living was not immune to such charges. In 1998, investigators temporarily banned new residents from two Assisted Living homes in Oregon after they discovered several instances of seriously substandard care; the Vancouver, Washington facility was charged with endangering residents by disregarding physicians' orders. It remained open, but under state monitoring. In Oregon at the time, assisted living centers were required to meet the needs of residents on a 24-hour basis, but there was no mandate governing level of staffing. Further, while the state required a week of training to become a facility administrator, it did not screen for unqualified applicants.

However, in spite of its legal troubles and net losses—almost $29 million in 1999—Assisted Living continued on a growth curve, ranked eighth in the *Business Journal of Portland's* list of the 100 fastest-growing companies, based on revenue growth from 1996 to 1999. In 2000, Assisted Living agreed to a $30 million settlement in order to avoid litigating the class-action suit filed by investors. In October, Wilson stepped down as president and chief executive, replaced by William James Nicol, a longtime healthcare industry professional.

By the year 2000, assisted living companies nationwide provided housing to as many as a million people. Despite its popularity, the industry was experiencing growing pains and struggling to fulfill its dual mission of providing autonomy and quality managed care. But with the number of Americans over age 65 certain to nearly double to almost 70 million by 2030, the future of assisted living seemed assured. Publicly traded assisted living operators accounted for about 10 percent of all assisted living units in the United States and about 35 percent of all freestanding assisted living facilities of more than 30 units in 2001. According to Wilson in an article that appeared in the *Oregonian* in May 2001, assisted living companies were undergoing a period of transition in which they "have to act more adult. . . . Those who don't learn how to manage what they've developed to deal with ongoing problems and do it efficiently won't be in business."

Principal Subsidiaries

Assisted Living Concepts Services.

Principal Competitors

Alterra Healthcare Corporation; American Retirement Corporation; Beverly Enterprises, Inc.; Brookdale Living Communities; Life Care Centers; Sun Healthcare Group Inc.; Sunrise Assisted Living.

Further Reading

"Assisted Living Captures Profitable Market Niche," *Modern Healthcare*, May 8, 1995, p. 72.
Gamzon, Mel, "Back to Basics," *National Real Estate Investor*, March 15, 2000, p. 85.
"Making Senior Housing Affordable," *Journal of Property Management*, July/August 1997, p. 29.
Mayes, Steve, "Assisted Living Offers Elderly Autonomy and Care," *Oregonian*, May 23, 2000, p. A1.
Smith, Ray A., "Assisted-Living Firms Grapple with Oversupply—Construction Falls Sharply and Operators Offer Incentives to Fill Space," *Wall Street Journal*, April 18, 2001, p. B12.
Woodward, Steve, "Assisted Living Expands Reach into Health Care with Triple Play," *Oregonian*, September 10, 1997, p. F1.
——, "Proving Conventional Wisdom Wrong," *Oregonian*, June 22, 1997, p. R4.

—Carrie Rothburd

At Home Corporation

450 Broadway Street
Redwood City, California 94063
U.S.A.
Telephone: (650) 556-5000
Fax: (650) 556-5100
Web site: http://www.home.net

Public Company
Incorporated: 1999
Employees: 2,987
Sales: $616.37 million (2000)
Stock Exchanges: NASDAQ
Ticker Symbol: ATHM
NAIC: 541519 Other Computer Related Services; 514191 On-Line Information Services; 51121 Software Publishers

At Home Corporation, doing business as Excite@Home, is the leading broadband Internet service provider (ISP) as well as the fifth largest paid ISP in the United States. The company is the result of the January 1999 merger between Excite, Inc. and @Home Network, at the time the largest Internet-related merger ever. The Redwood City, California-based company boasts more than three million subscribers, annual revenues surpassing $600 million, and numerous subsidiaries, affiliates, and partners. In mid-2001 telecommunications powerhouse AT&T Corp. still retained a 74 percent voting stake and 23 percent equity interest in At Home, which was showing signs of financial weakness.

At Home Network: 1995–98

In May 1995, The At Home Network (@Home) was founded by TCI International Inc., with funds from venture capital giant Kleiner Perkins, in order to grow its Internet business. The company's founding CEO was William Randolph Hearst III, former editor of the *San Francisco Examiner* and grandson of the famous media baron. The following year, Comcast Corporation and Cox Communications Inc. also assumed stakes in the company.

@Home quickly became successful by providing interactive services to homes and businesses through its own network architecture, as well as through a myriad of transport options, including telecom circuits and the cable industry's hybrid-fiber coaxial (HFC) infrastructure. Essentially, the company created a parallel Internet of its own. The cable connection provided users with significant speed increases over conventional dial-up Internet access, and the company's national, multi-megabit backbone allowed for unique content offerings that went far beyond then contemporary web experiences. @Home was not simply a connection to the already overloaded Internet. Instead, @Home used advanced network technology to enable connections up to a hundred times faster than traditional telephone modems. In addition, The @Home Network provided a high level of network management and customer support, complemented by multimedia content tailored to the network's high bandwidth capabilities. The @Home Network was well differentiated from other Internet connectivity solutions by its high-speed, performance-engineered network, and its full-featured service offerings.

Early in 1996, Hearst stepped up to become vice-chairman of the company and @Home brought in former Silicon Graphics Chief Operating Officer Thomas Jermoluk as its new CEO. In April 1997, Canada's top two cable providers, Rogers Communications Inc. and Shaw Communications Inc., became partners in the venture, and the company announced a Canadian-based cable modem service. The following month, after spending in excess of $38 million since its inception to develop its services, At Home filed to go public. The initial public offering occurred in July, and the company sold nine million shares and raised $94.5 million.

By January 1998, @Home boasted 50,000 subscribers, a number which would double by April. During that year, @Home partnered with U.K.-based telecom operator ComTel Ltd. to create a British @Home service; with Intel Corporation to announce a Netherlands-based cable modem service; with Sumitomo Group for a Japan-based service; and with Cable &

Company Perspectives:

Excite@Home's drive to be the best broadband online service provider in the world centers on combining compelling online content, personalization, and tight navigational services with the distribution power of its extensive broadband infrastructure. The Company's goal is to continue to provide suites of advanced interactive services that capture the imagination, deliver the sheer power of the Internet, and reinforce their commitment to their customers.

Wireless Optus Limited for an Australia-based service. Also in 1998, the company built a new corporate campus. In June of that year, the company went retail and held a North American shopping mall tour to promote the company and its services.

Excite Inc.: 1993–98

Excite Inc. was founded, according to it own company history, by "six burrito-loving Stanford grads sitting in a garage on Lockwood Drive in Cupertino, CA. It was their penchant for cheap Mexican cuisine that set the stage for the idea that ultimately led to the creation of Architext Software," later incorporated into Excite, Inc. as Excite Search. For as the six founders—Mark Van Haren, Ryan McIntyre, Ben Lutch, Joe Kraus, Graham Spencer, and Martin Reinfried—sat in Rosita's Taqueria in Redwood City on the evening of February 28, 1993, the idea came to them: Create a software tool to manage the vast amount of information available on the Internet. "We knew that we didn't want to work for any big company," explained then president Kraus to *Red Herring* magazine in early 1995. "We wanted to work together and do something entrepreneurial." The five computer programmers and one political science major set off at once for the Stanford library to research the best way in which to fill the information search-and-retrieval void. While simultaneously holding down income-producing jobs, the five programmers agreed upon their plan of attack, got busy at their Sun workstations, "and the political science major—Joe Kraus—cut off several inches of hair and became 'Phone Boy.' "

Armed with a software product and business named Architext that combined search-and-retrieval with automatic hypertext linking, subject-grouping, and automatic abstracting, Phone Boy began calling all up and down Sand Hill Road, the haven of West Coast venture capital firms. Response was initially negative. Architext even received a letter of rejection from a company to whom they had never sent a proposal! It was not until more than a year and a half after the landmark evening in Rosita's, in December 1994, that the entrepreneurs would hit paydirt. It arrived in the form of venture capital giant Kleiner Perkins Caulfield & Byers (KPCB), along with Institutional Venture Partners. Chief supporter Vinod Khosla of KPCB even provided the fledgling company with a badly needed $4,000 hard disk drive. "We just met the man and he bought us a hard drive. That went a long way," explained Kraus. And thus it began—the guys were off into the world of business plans, contracts, and the reality of turning over increasing amounts of control to their benefactors.

In October 1995, Architext launched the Excite suite of services at www.excite.com, and the company gained momentum quickly. Exclusive distribution agreements were signed with Microsoft Network and Netscape. The company officially changed its name to Excite, Inc., and went public in April 1996 with an initial public offering of two million shares at $17 per share. By the time the dust cleared that month, the company had grown to 65 employees, was housed in a 19,000-square-foot office in Mountain View, California, and had hired veteran media mogul George Bell to be its CEO. Architext had blossomed into a serious technology concern, with business cards, letterhead, and bottles of Odwalla-brand juice seemingly everywhere.

In 1996, Excite experienced a number of milestones. The company grew from 13 advertisers under contract at the end of January to some 370 by the end of the year. Revenues soared from $145,000 to over $14 million. In addition, experienced senior-level management, from an incredible list of established companies, was now in place. In addition, the company acquired two search-and-navigation competitors, Magellan and WebCrawler. Excite also launched its first national advertising campaign to the sound of Jimi Hendrix's "Are You Experienced?" and introduced several new products, including Excite City.Net, Excite Live!, ExciteSeeing Tours, and Excite NewsTracker, as well as Excite 2.0, an updated version of its original product.

The following year also witnessed some major events for the company as well. Two were nearly simultaneous: the early April consolidation and move to a new 88,000-square-foot facility in Redwood City, California—right down the street from the original birthplace of the company, Rosita's—and the launch of *Excite 3.0*, which featured Excite Channels, formerly code-named "Purple Haze." Excite's employees numbered around 200, and the Odwalla intake soared to some 2,000 bottles per month.

Excite@Home: 1999

In January 1999, The @Home Network announced a merger with Excite, Inc. By April, @Home boasted 500,000 subscribers and announced a Japan-based cable modem joint venture service. By the time the $7.2 billion deal closed in May 1999, At Home Corporation represented the largest-ever Internet merger. The combined company became the self-proclaimed "leader in broadband focused on the global deployment of consumer and commercial broadband services." With stars in its corporate eyes, @Home built a new Internet backbone with the capacity to hold five million users.

The company grew by leaps and bounds following the merger. In May, the Netherlands-based @Home service finally opened for business, followed by announcements for Australia-based and Germany-based joint venture services in June and September, respectively. By the end of 1999, the combined company, now operating as Excite@Home, touted one million cable modem subscribers worldwide. Excite CEO George Bell came aboard the new company as president, and its holdings included the Enliven Business Unit (formed in 1996) and MatchLogic Inc. (a targeted marketing services company, also formed in 1996).

Key Dates:

1993: Excite, Inc. is founded as Architext.
1995: @Home Network is founded.
1996: Architext changes its name to Excite, Inc., and goes public in April 1996 with an initial public offering of two million shares at $17 per share.
1997: @Home is taken public in July.
1999: Some 500,000 households now subscribe to the @Home service; @Home and Excite merge to form At Home Corporation, doing business as Excite@Home.
2001: At Home faces liquidity problems, low stock price levels, and the pending termination of agreements with Cox Communications and Comcast Cable.

AT&T Corp. gained a stake in the company when it acquired TCI in 1999. The acquisition was important to the telecommunications giant because it now had a foothold in direct-home cable conduits, which was further expanded when AT&T acquired MediaOne Internet Services, making AT&T the largest cable provider in the United States. AT&T rattled its saber in the sheath, making noises about splitting up Excite@Home, but partner Cox Communications nixed the idea.

Instead, the company continued to make acquisitions, purchasing Full Force Systems Inc. for approximately $1.7 million in cash and stock and online advertising firm Narrative Communications Corp. for $93.8 million in stock in December 1998. The company acquired e-commerce firm iMall Inc., for $425 million in stock, and Webshots Corporation, for 2.1 million shares of stock in October 1999. Two months later the company acquired, for $780 million in cash and stock, Bluemountain.com, the online branch of greeting card phenomenon Blue Mountain Arts Inc.

Jermoluk moved up to chairman in early 2000, giving up the CEO position to Bell, who eventually also became chairman. In February of that year, the company acquired Kendara Inc. for 1.5 million shares of stock. In April 2000, the company expanded into digital subscriber line (DSL) services, adding nearly 15.3 million households to its broadband footprint. The following month, Excite@Home featured 1.5 million broadband subscribers, had 123 million Excite pages viewed, had 21 cable affiliate relationships and one DSL relationship, and passed 87 million homes with its cables. The company also entered into a joint venture with Dow Jones & Company to create Work.com, Inc., a business portal.

Also during that year, the company extended its distribution agreements with cable partners AT&T, Cox, and Comcast and had reached affiliate agreements with numerous other cable companies across North America, including Cablevision Systems, Century Communications, Charter Communications, Cogeco Cable, Garden State Cable, Insight Communications, InterMedia Partners, Jones Intercable, Midcontinent Cable, Prime Cable, Rogers Cablesystems, Shaw Communications, Suburban, and Videon CableSystems. As AT&T leveraged to expand its voting stake in the company, Cox and Comcast agreed to give up their board seats and their veto rights, leaving AT&T with a controlling stake in the company. Also in 2000, the company announced plans to combine its international operations with Chello, a broadband ISP controlled by United Pan-Europe Communications.

Following on the heels of a third quarter 2000 loss of $668.7 million, Bell announced his decision to step down as CEO as soon as a successor could be found, but would remain chairman at least through 2001. The future of the company was further clouded by late August 2001, when reports surfaced that both Cox and Comcast planned to terminate their distribution agreements with At Home, effective June 2002. By this time the company was clearly showing signs of financial strain, and shares of its stock were trading at a mere $0.40.

Principal Subsidiaries

At Home Network Solutions, Inc. (46%); At Home Network Australia Pty Ltd. (50%); At Home Japan Limited (43%); Bluemountain.com; Excite Asia Pacific Pty Ltd. (50%); Excite Canada (50%); Excite Espana (Spain); Excite Italia (Italy; 50%); Excite Japan (50%); Excite UK Limited (50%); Full Force; iMall; MatchLogic; Narrative; Webshots; Work.com, Inc.

Principal Competitors

AOL Time Warner Inc.; Microsoft Corporation; Adelphia Communications Corp.; AltaVista Company; Yahoo! Inc.; Covad Communications Group; Disney Internet; EarthLink, Inc.; High Speed Access; Hughes Electronics Corporation; Mediacom Communications; Prodigy Communications Corporation; PSINet; SBC Communications Inc.; SoftNet; UUNET; Verizon Communications Inc.; WorldCom, Inc.

Further Reading

Alpert, Bill, "Relaxing @Home: A Cable-Modem Company Fixes Its Y2002 Problem," *Barron's*, April 3, 2000, p. 14.
"AT&T Doesn't Feel 'At Home' Providing Content for the Internet," *Telecommunications Reports*, October 4, 1999, p. 16.
"AT&T Reaffirms Its Commitment to Excite@Home As Cable ISP," *Telecommunications Reports*, August 16, 1999, p. 17.
Avalos, George, "AT&T Purchase of Tele-Communications Inc. Lifts Cable Industry," *Knight-Ridder/Tribune Business News*, July 15, 1998, p. OKRB98196026.
Bonisteel, Steven, "At Home Says Major Investors Putting Squeeze On," *Newsbytes,* August 27, 2001.
"CEO Sells $25M in Stock," *Washington Business Journal*, December 10, 1999, p. 38.
Cowley, Stacy, "Cox, Comcast Bail on Excite@Home," *Industry Standard,* August, 31, 2001.
"Earnings Roundup," *InternetWeek*, April 19, 1999, p. 7.
"Excite@Home: Rebound@Hand?" *Business Week*, November 29, 1999, p. 152.
"Excite@Home Growth Surge," *New York Times*, August 24, 2000, p. C10.
"Excite At Home Posts Wider Period Loss But Beats Forecasts," *Wall Street Journal*, July 20, 2000, p. B20.
Hazelwood, Sara, "Silicon Valley Well-Represented in Annual Technology Survey," *Business Journal*, November 19, 1999, p. 21.
Heim, Sarah J., "Excite Introduces New Instant Messaging App.," *MEDIAWEEK*, September 25, 2000, p. 68.

Higgins, John M., "Cablevision Gets a Piece of @Home," *Broadcasting & Cable*, October 6, 1997, p. 20.

Hostetler, Michele, and Brooke Shelby Biggs, "Net's Influence Spreading Throughout Valley," *Business Journal*, May 6, 1996, p. 1.

Hwang, Diana, "Intelligent Agents Seek Place on Web," *Computer Reseller News*, February 12, 1996, p. 75.

Kuchinskas, Susan, "Excite@Home's Decision," *ADWEEK Eastern Edition*, November 29, 1999, p. 57.

Loftus, Peter, "Top Web Firms Are Expected to Weather Weakness in Online Ads," *Wall Street Journal*, July 10, 2000, p. B13.

Mangalindan, Mylene, "Excite@Home Adds Subscribers But Posts $668.7 Million Net Loss," *Wall Street Journal*, October 25, 2000, p. B2.

Mermigas, Diane, "Business Briefs," *Electronic Media*, October 25, 1999, p. 14.

Nadile, Lisa, "Search Firms Rev Up Offerings for the Web," *PC Week*, March 11, 1996, p. 46.

Notess, Greg R., "Searching Beyond Text: Multimedia Search Tools," *Online*, November 2000, p. 63.

Sacharow, Anya, "Plans for WebCrawler," *ADWEEK Eastern Edition*, February 23, 1998, p. 28.

Siegel, Alan, and Andrew Zolli, "Portal Envy; Viewpoint: Internet Portals Lack Strong Branding, Risking Audience and Ad Dollars," *Advertising Age*, May 10, 1999, p. 50.

Taylor, Kathy, "Search for Tomorrow: Three Internet Search Engines Are Set to Start Selling Stock; Are They Investments in the Future or the Past?" *MEDIAWEEK*, April 1, 1996, p. 31.

Tedesco, Richard, "@Home Ventures Outside for Capital," *Broadcasting & Cable*, April 21, 1997, p. 62.

Tillett, L. Scott, "Dotcoms Get More Personal," *InternetWeek*, April 24, 2000, p. 35.

—Daryl F. Mallett

Atlanta National League Baseball Club, Inc.

755 Hank Aaron Drive
Atlanta, Georgia 30315
U.S.A.
Telephone: (404) 522-7630
Fax: (404) 614-1391
Web site: http://www.atlantabraves.com

Wholly Owned Subsidiary of Time Warner, Inc.
Founded: 1871 as Boston Red Stockings
Employees: 100+
Sales: $155.2 million (1999)
NAIC: 711211 Sports Teams and Clubs

The Atlanta National League Baseball Club, Inc., better known as the Atlanta Braves, is the oldest professional baseball team in continuous operation. Previously at home in Boston and Milwaukee, the Braves are located in Atlanta where owner and media mogul Ted Turner has dubbed them "America's Team." After more than a hundred years of intermittent success, the Braves under Turner's ownership have become one of the most successful franchises in Major League Baseball, proving to be a consistent winner throughout the 1990s and into the 21st century.

Origins

The Braves were originally the Red Stockings of Boston, the direct descendants of the first openly professional baseball team, the Cincinnati Red Stockings, which from 1869 to 1870 toured the country taking on all comers. When the team returned to amateur status, Harry Wright, the player-manager, took some teammates as well as the club nickname to Boston to play in the newly formed National Association, the first professional sports league in the country. The Red Stockings won four pennants during the five-year history of the National Association. However, the team lost some of its best players to the newly formed National League in 1876, and then opted to join the league that remains in operation today.

Boston had another run of successful clubs in the 1890s, playing under the name "Beaneaters." A new rival major league, the American League, started play in 1901. It created a Boston franchise that not only took one of the Beaneaters' best players, Jimmy Collins, it eventually appropriated the club's old nickname, becoming the Red Sox in 1909, and quickly began to lure away its fans as well. The Beaneaters helped to accelerate the process by fielding a succession of poor clubs and changing managers on a regular basis. The team also changed names, becoming the Doves in 1906 after two brothers, George and John Dovey, bought the team. In 1910 the franchise was sold to a syndicate headed by William Hepburn Russell and became known as the "Rustlers." Following Russell's death in 1911, the team was sold to James Gaffney who had ties to the New York City political machine, Tammany Hall. Tammany, named after a Delaware Indian chief, referred to its leaders as "Chiefs." It seemed appropriate to call Gaffney's players the "Braves," a name that would follow the club to Milwaukee and Atlanta.

The "Miracle" of 1914

After 14 years without contending for a league pennant, the Braves began the 1914 season with renewed hope, but the team lost 18 of its first 22 games and was mired in last place by July 4, the traditional halfway point in the baseball season. Boston then began an historic comeback, climbing steadily through the standings, and within five weeks overtook the New York Giants for first place. The club would go on to win the pennant by 10 ½ games, then defeat the highly favored Philadelphia A's in the World Series. It would become forever known in baseball lore as the "Miracle Braves" of 1914.

Many of the key games late in the regular season, as well as the World Series, were played in Fenway Park, the home of the cross-town rival Red Sox. The Braves' ballpark, the South End Grounds, had been originally built in 1876 but was too small to accommodate the number of fans who now wanted to watch the team. In August of 1915 the Braves opened a new facility, Braves Field, the last in a wave of concrete-and-steel ballparks that ushered in baseball's modern era. Gaffney, who enjoyed the action of an inside-the-park home run, had the field designed to suit his tastes. The distances from home plate to the outfield seem incredible by today's standards. Down the foul lines the walls were 402 feet away; to dead center the distance was 550 feet.

Key Dates:

1876: Boston Red Stockings franchise joins National League.
1901: American League Red Sox begin play in Boston, threatening franchise fan base.
1914: "Miracle Braves" win franchise's first World Series.
1948: Braves make last World Series appearance as a Boston franchise.
1953: Braves move to Milwaukee.
1957: Braves win second World Series.
1966: Braves move to Atlanta.
1976: Ted Turner purchases Braves.
1995: Braves win third World Series.
1996: Braves become part of Time Warner, remaining under Turner's control; Braves begin play in Turner Field.

Braves Field was also the largest ballpark in terms of seating capacity. On its opening day it held more than 40,000 fans, then the largest crowd to ever watch a baseball game. The Red Sox would borrow the park for the 1915 and 1916 World Series, making it three consecutive years that a team would eschew the home field advantage in favor of increased attendance.

Ownership Changes and Season Slumps

Unfortunately for the Braves, the miracle season of 1914 and the opening of a new ballpark in 1915 would not begin a period of renewed prosperity. The team would soon tumble to the bottom of the standings, and the Red Sox would solidify a hold on the loyalty of Boston's baseball fans. New ownership took over the Braves in 1918, but the New York group headed by George Washington Grant only added to the team's decline. Fans who worried that Grant was too close to John McGraw, the New York Giants' manager, seemed justified after a series of trades between the two teams clearly favored the Giants.

Following a season in which they lost one hundred games, the Braves again changed ownership in 1923. The new owner, Judge Emil Fuchs, brought in legendary pitcher Christy Mathewson to run the team, but the Braves continued to lose. It was little consolation that the Red Sox were suffering a similar fate. They were trading their best players, most notably Babe Ruth, to another New York team, the Yankees. Both the Braves and the Red Sox endured poor attendance during a period when, overall, baseball was enjoying a golden era of prosperity.

By 1935, in the midst of a national depression, Fuchs was in such dire financial shape that he made plans to install a dog racing track in the outfield of Braves Field, a concept that the National League rejected. Fuchs then turned to an aging star in hopes that he could stimulate ticket sales. That player was Babe Ruth, but years of hard living had finally caught up to the Babe. He was overweight and unable to shake an assortment of nagging injuries. He had a few bright moments, however, such as a three-home run game in Pittsburgh, but essentially Ruth was just a shadow of his former self, and he retired before the end of the season. The 1935 Braves would lose 115 games, the worst record of a National League team for the century, eclipsing even the woeful 1962 expansion New York Mets.

After Fuchs stepped down as president of the club, the partners of the franchise reorganized and chose Bob Quinn to run the team. The first thing he did was to conduct a fan poll for a new nickname. As the Boston Bees for the next six seasons, the team would do no better in the standings. A new group of investors from the Boston construction industry, headed by Lou Perini, bought the team and restored the Braves nickname. Perini also insisted that better days lay ahead for the franchise.

The Braves began to turn around with the hiring of manager Billy Southworth, lured away from St. Louis, where he had led the Cardinals to three pennants in six years. In 1946 Southworth's Braves won 81 games, finishing 15½ games out of first place. The following season the team won 86 games, only eight games behind the pennant winners. In 1948 Southworth would lead the Braves to their first World Series appearance in over 30 years. Although the Braves lost to the Cleveland Indians in six games, the club still enjoyed a hugely successful year. The Braves drew 1.45 million in attendance and turned a robust profit. As had happened following the 1914 season, however, prosperity seemed to be short-lived for the franchise. Dependent on too many aging veteran ballplayers, the Braves began to drop in the standings, finishing fourth the next three years, with attendance slipping as well. When the team finished 1952 in seventh place, 32 games out of first, only 281,000 fans had attended Braves Field. Less than a mile away in Fenway Park, the Red Sox drew well over a million. Braves' management lost almost $600,000, and the newspapers were reporting rumors that Perini was looking to move the franchise to another city. The leading candidate was Milwaukee.

The 1953 Move to Milwaukee

Milwaukee was home to the Brewers, the Braves' minor league affiliate, and had just built a stadium in hopes of gaining a major league team. The St. Louis Browns, who like the Braves were the second team in a two-team town, were known to be eager to move to Milwaukee. Perini was able to block the move because of the Brewers connection to the Braves, but because he had promised the city to not stand in the way of Milwaukee getting a major league team, he put himself in an awkward position. Publicly he still held out hope to Boston that the Braves would give its fans two more years to support the team. During spring training the team appeared ready to open the season in Boston, then the *Sporting News* reported that the Braves would move to Milwaukee before the season opened. The next day Perini held a news conference to confirm the story. The franchise would now be known as the Milwaukee Braves. It would be the first realignment in Major League Baseball in over 50 years, and would lead to more teams changing cities in the next few seasons.

Milwaukee welcomed their new big league team with enthusiasm. The Braves led baseball in attendance for 1953, drawing more than 1.8 million fans. The next year they became only the third team to break the two million barrier, drawing almost twice as many fans as the next leading National League franchise. The Braves would draw more than two million for three more years in succession. The team also began to build a contending ballclub. After a second place finish in 1956, the Braves won the National League pennant in 1957 and squared off against the New York Yankees in the World Series. A Game 7 victory brought the franchise its second World Series title.

Although the Braves would again win the National League Pennant in 1958, home attendance dipped below the two million mark. The team again met the Yankees in the World Series, this time losing in seven. The following season featured a tight pennant race, yet attendance continued to drop. When the Braves and Dodgers finished the season in a tie that forced a three-game playoff, only 20,000 fans attended the first game of the playoff, which the Braves lost.

The love affair between Milwaukee and the Braves had clearly lost its passion. Although the Braves continued to be a winning team, over the next several seasons they never seriously contended for the National League pennant. In 1962 the Braves failed to draw more than a million fans for the first time since moving to Milwaukee, netting only 766,921 in attendance. A Chicago-based syndicate headed by William Bartholomay bought the team, and was soon denying rumors that the Braves were planning to move once again, this time to Atlanta. Milwaukee area officials were not pleased, and animosity between the team's management and the local government would escalate over the next two seasons. The Braves were accused of intentionally playing to lose ball games in 1964, supposedly to embarrass the city. Team president John McHale threatened to sue Milwaukee County Chairman Eugene Grobschmidt for slander. When it seemed apparent that the Braves were preparing to leave for Atlanta in 1965, Milwaukee County filed suit in hopes of keeping the franchise, accusing the team of antitrust violations. After the Braves countersued, the county board rejected a $500,000 cash settlement that would have allowed the Braves to immediately leave for Atlanta.

The 1965 season was played under a cloud, as the team's management and elected officials continued to fight in the newspapers as well as in court. The Braves played relatively well, finishing ten games over .500, but 11 games out of first place. Attendance collapsed, falling to 555,000. The situation in Milwaukee was obviously untenable, and ownership decided to simply relocate to Atlanta for the following season and allow the pending lawsuit of the city to run its course. A circuit judge then ruled that the Braves had violated Wisconsin's antitrust laws: the National League either had to find a new team for the city or return the Braves within a month. After the league won an appeal to the state supreme court, the matter went to the U.S. Supreme Court, which decided not to hear the case. The Braves, which had started in the Northeast and moved to the Midwest, were now a southern team, owned by the Atlanta-LaSalle Corporation based in Chicago.

As had Milwaukee, Atlanta embraced the newcomers. The Braves drew more than 1.5 million in the first season. In 1969 the team won a division title, losing to the Mets in the League Championship Series. Then the Braves began to slide in the standings, and as a result attendance suffered. What had happened to the franchise in Milwaukee appeared to be replicating itself in Atlanta. After five seasons of drawing more than a million, the Braves dipped below the mark in 1972, attracting little more than 750,000 fans. By 1975 attendance would drop to 534,672, a total less than what the Braves had drawn in their final, lame-duck season in Milwaukee ten years earlier. Again there were rumors of the franchise relocating, either to Denver or Toronto. At the very least, the owners were looking to sell the franchise. The club found a local suitor who had been televising Braves' games for the past three seasons. That man was Ted Turner.

1976: Ted Turner and "America's Team"

Turner inherited a billboard company from his father, then in 1970 purchased a low-powered Atlanta UHF station that featured old movies and television reruns. The Braves' television contract with WSB, an NBC affiliate, paid the club $200,000 a year to broadcast twenty road games. In need of programming, Turner offered $600,000 for five years to broadcast sixty games each season. In need of cash, ownership accepted, even though much of Atlanta was unable to clearly receive Turner's station. Turner then created a Braves television network by making his station available to a number of Southern markets by microwave transmission. The Braves were quickly becoming a regional team, and Turner's station was escaping its local confines.

When Turner decided to deliver his station to cable systems nationwide by satellite, thus turning it into a "superstation," securing the rights to the Braves became paramount. For that reason he bought the team for $11 million on January 6, 1976. As Turner's WTBS became available to viewers around the country, the Braves would acquire a national following, prompting Turner to declare them "America's Team." Meanwhile, Turner tried every promotional angle he could think of to increase attendance. His best gimmick, perhaps, was playing the role of folk hero: the champion of the little guy who was tired of seeing the local ballclub get kicked around. Attendance began to rise even though the team continued to struggle on the field.

Turner was a controversial owner. He upset Major League Baseball when he decided to manage his team for a day. When he openly tampered with a free agent player, Gary Matthews, Turner was suspended for the 1977 season and prohibited from exercising any control in the management of the team. When he was reinstated, Turner would exert less day-to-day influence on the Braves, preoccupied with founding an all-news cable station, which would become known as CNN, as well as other media ventures. Still, Turner was committed to making the Braves a winning franchise, both for the sake of his hometown and the television ratings that would determine the ad rates WTBS could charge.

Although the Braves finished last in their division from 1976 to 1979, the club was retooling its management and improving player talent. By 1982 the Braves would win a division championship. Although the team would again sink in the standings and attendance would be spotty, there was no doubt that Turner was committed to making the Braves a perennial winner. Following three straight last place finishes, the franchise turned the corner in 1991. Featuring a solid pitching staff, the franchise would play in the World Series for the first time in over 30 years. Although it lost to the Minnesota Twins in seven games, the Atlanta Braves served notice to the rest of baseball that the club was now able to live up to the inflated aspirations of its colorful owner.

Pitching and a minor league system stocked with talent became the hallmarks of the Braves in the 1990s. Although the team would win only one World Series, 1995, it would appear in four others and win its division title every year from 1991 through 2000, with the exception of 1994 when a players' strike brought the season to an abrupt close. No other team in baseball won as consistently as the Braves during this period. In 1992 the team drew three million fans for the first time in franchise history.

When Turner sold Turner Broadcasting to Time Warner the team became part of the media giant, but remained under Turner's control. In 1996 the team was able to use the Atlanta Olympics as a way to replace aging Atlanta-Fulton County Stadium. Braves management and the Atlanta Committee for the Olympic Games worked together to build the Olympic stadium so that when the games were over, the structure could be converted into a new baseball park. Less than eight months after the closing ceremonies for the Olympics, the Braves had a new home, Turner Field. A new facility for a winning ballclub added greatly to the worth of the franchise. The team that Ted Turner had bought for $11 million in 1976 was estimated by *Forbes* to be worth $348 million by May 2000.

Principal Competitors

New York Mets; Florida Marlins; Philadelphia Phillies; Montreal Expos.

Further Reading

Bibb, Porter, *It Ain't as Easy as It Looks: Ted Turner's Amazing Story,* New York: Crown Publishers, 1993.

Goldberg, Robert, and Gerald Jay Goldberg, *Citizen Turner,* Orlando: Harcourt Brace & Company, 1995.

Klapisch, Bob, and Pete Van Wieren, *The Braves: An Illustrated History of America's Team,* Atlanta: Turner Publishing, 1995.

Ritter, Lawrence, *Lost Ballparks,* New York: Penguin Books, 1992.

Thorn et al., *Total Baseball,* Kingston, N.Y.: Total Sports, 1999.

—Ed Dinger

Atmos Energy Corporation

3 Lincoln Centre, Suite 1800
5430 LBJ Freeway
Dallas, Texas 75240
U.S.A.
Telephone: (972) 934-9277
Fax: (972) 855-3075
Web site: http://www.atmosenergy.com
Public Company
Incorporated: 1983
Employees: 2,062
Sales: $850.2 million (2000)
Stock Exchanges: New York
Ticker Symbol: ATO
NAIC: 22121 Natural Gas Distribution

Atmos Energy Corporation, headquartered in Dallas, Texas, prides itself on being the country's most efficient provider of natural gas. It is a major utility-holding company with operations in 13 states. Nationally, it ranks fifth among gas distribution companies. It conducts most of its out-of-state business through its major subsidiaries or divisions, which operate in Kentucky as Western Kentucky Gas Company; in Louisiana as Trans Louisiana Gas Company; in Colorado, Kansas, and parts of Missouri as Greeley Gas Company; and in Georgia, Illinois, Iowa, other parts of Missouri, South Carolina, Tennessee, and Virginia as United Cities Gas Company. In its home state of Texas, it runs its natural gas distribution operation under its older name, Energas Company. Atmos also has a propane distribution subsidiary, United Cities Propane Inc., which sells propane in Kentucky, North Carolina, Tennessee, and Virginia. In partnership with three other utilities, Atmos also formed US Propane, which itself partnered with a leading propane distributor, Heritage Propane. In addition to its retail and wholesale propane distribution operations, Atmos has other nonutility businesses. It sells natural gas to West Texas agriculture and industrial customers, owns a 45 percent interest in a natural gas services company, and stores natural gas. In all, Atmos provides natural and propane gas to over one million customers.

1906–23: Amarillo Gas Starts Up and Connects to the Great Panhandle Gas Field

Atmos Energy traces its origins back to 1906, when brothers J.C. and Frank Storm of Kirksville, Missouri, got wind of the need for a gas plant in Amarillo, Texas. Although the Storms would later claim that Amarillo did not seem like a promising place to start a business, they decided to take a chance, hoping that Amarillo would grow into more than just a cattle trail junction. They formed the Amarillo Gas Company and began laying pipe under the town's streets, not a terribly difficult task considering the fact that none of them were paved.

The Storms manufactured gas from coke and oil, unaware that Amarillo lay only 20 miles from one of the world's largest natural gas deposits, the great Panhandle gas field, which was not discovered until 1918, when another predecessor of Atmos, the Amarillo Oil Company, began drilling there. Amarillo Gas made a pipeline connection to the field in 1920.

1924–53: Amarillo Gas Becomes Part of Southwestern Development Company

In 1924, Southwestern Development Company acquired both Amarillo Oil and Amarillo Gas. Southwestern also started other gas distribution companies. By 1927, in its search for new markets, it put a pipeline under construction to extend its service to West Texas, all the way to Midland and Odessa.

Despite having to contend with the economic problems caused by the Dust Bowl drought and the Great Depression, Southwestern Development continued to grow in the 1930s. In 1933, it was one of the country's first gas distributors to inject an odor additive to its gas, an important safety measure that in 1937 became mandatory throughout Texas.

Through the war years of the early 1940s, Southwestern's customer base grew steadily. By 1945, it was serving about 53,000 people and businesses. At the war's end, a population boom started that by 1950 had nearly doubled the company's number of customers. With the start up of new families, gas appliances became increasingly popular, encouraging home economists to provide such services as cooking demonstrations in ''blue flame'' kitchens in the company offices.

Company Perspectives:

As our industry changes, we will continue to lead the way—but we'll never give up that hometown touch you've come to expect. Our one million + customers have always known that being an Atmos customer means you get dependable, efficient service when you need it. We know that your time is as important as ours and do our best to perform service tasks as quickly as possible. When you contact us, you can depend on a prompt and personal response. So, even though we are one of the largest gas distribution companies in the United States, you will feel like our most important customer.

1954–80: Consolidation and Continued Expansion

By 1954, Southwestern had consolidated all its diverse gas distribution businesses under the name Pioneer Natural Gas Company. The reorganized company faced excellent prospects for accelerated sales. For one thing, natural gas was a bargain commodity, and for another, its use was expanding. Notably, during the 1950s and 1960s, farmers in the Panhandle region of Texas, too often devastated by drought, turned to irrigation farming in increasing numbers. They used the inexpensive and readily available gas to power engines for pumping water from underground aquifers and circulating it through irrigation pipes and ditches. In those two decades, the farmers' need for gas greatly helped Pioneer's sales. Annually, during dry summer months, the company sold up to 50 billion cubic feet of natural gas, more than it sold for the winter heating of its customers' homes.

In 1958, Pioneer acquired the Empire Southern Gas Company, again expanding its customer base. Then, during the 1960s, its success also prompted Pioneer to diversify beyond its production and utility operations. Among other things, it started coal and uranium mining, heavy machine production, and tire retreading operations. In all, the parent company added 13 subsidiaries, some of which were closed down when they failed to operate at an acceptable profit margin. Included in these was Trans State Tire Company, which Pioneer bought in 1969 and sold off a year and a half later.

Pioneer's diversification continued into the 1970s. In 1973, it still owned and operated ten subsidiaries. Notably, after the energy crunch that started in 1971, Pioneer began bolstering its exploration operations, and over the next ten years, riding the oil boom, turned itself into a billion-dollar corporation.

1981–87: Pioneer Forms Energas Company and Spins It Off to Prosper on Its Own

As part of a restructuring move, in 1981 Pioneer formed Energas Company, its natural gas distribution subsidiary, and two years later spun it off as an independent company, one that Pioneer's managers did not expect to survive on its own. Charles Vaughan, Energas' first president, had other expectations, however. He was determined to make the operation grow. Ironically, when the oil bubble burst in the mid-1980s, it was Pioneer that did not survive intact. It was absorbed in a merger, while, despite the odds, Energas not only survived but seemed to thrive on economic adversity.

In 1986, Energas began a period of significant expansion when it acquired the Trans Louisiana Gas Company (TransLa), a company originally formed in 1928 as Gulf Public Service Company.

Gulf Public had become part of a Louisiana utility company that had earlier started out in Alexandria, Louisiana, as an ice manufacturer and distributor. Through acquisitions and mergers, TransLa had increased the geographical range of its customer base to stretch from Monroe in the northern part of Louisiana to Franklin in the southern part.

Initially, Energas made history by attempting a hostile takeover of TransLa, the first such attempt in the industry. However, when TransLa was placed on the block by its own board, the buyout by Energas became amicable enough. Its acquisition added 69,000 Louisiana residents and businesses to Energas's customer base. The purchase also prompted the company to move its corporate headquarters to Dallas, a more centralized location.

In the following year, 1987, Energas acquired Western Kentucky Gas Company (WKG), an outfit that, in 1934, had began providing natural gas for about 2,200 customers. At the time of its acquisition by Energas, WKG's customer base had grown to almost 150,000. It was serving Kentucky communities in the higher growth regions of the state. It also serviced a number of major industrial customers, including aluminum plants and food processors as well as the only Corvette plant in the world. The assets of WKG included those of two other companies: Western Kentucky Gas Resources and Dixie Irrigation. These became wholly owned subsidiaries of Energas.

1988–2001: Energas Becomes Atmos Energy and Continues to Expand

In 1988, Energas changed its name to Atmos, a name selected on the strength of the fact that it came from a Greek word meaning "gases in the atmosphere." The name also seemed to connote energy. In any case, as Atmos Energy Corporation, the newly organized company began trading on the New York Stock Exchange. As part of the change, Energas Company was reorganized as an unincorporated division of Atmos. In the same year, Dixie Irrigation, which came to Energas with its acquisition of WKG, changed its name to WKI, Inc., but two years later was dissolved.

Atmos continued its dynamic growth into and through the 1990s. In 1993, it purchased the Greeley Gas Company, then privately owned by the Schlessman family. Greeley had been founded in 1902 in Greeley, Colorado. Like Amarillo Gas, until gas was piped in from the Texas Panhandle in the 1930s, it initially distributed manufactured gas for homes and such public conveniences as street lamps. In 1944, Gerald Schlessman acquired the company and began expanding its operations by purchasing several smaller companies. At the time of its transfer to Atmos, Greeley had almost 100,000 customers in Colorado, Kansas, and Missouri. Included in its customer base were residents and businesses in fast growing regions like Colorado's ski and resort towns of Durango and Steamboat Springs.

In July of 1997, Atmos reached a major milestone when it acquired its millionth customer. That mark came from its merger

Key Dates:

1906: J.C. and Frank Storm found the Amarillo Gas Company, forerunner of Atmos Energy.
1918: Amarillo Oil Company drills first natural gas well in the great Panhandle gas field.
1924: Amarillo Gas Company and Amarillo Oil Company are acquired by Southwestern Development Company.
1953: Southwestern's various gas distribution businesses are consolidated as Pioneer Natural Gas Company.
1981: Pioneer Corporation names its natural gas distribution division Energas Company.
1983: Energas is spun off as an independent, publicly held gas distribution company.
1986: Company acquires Trans Louisiana Gas Company.
1987: Company acquires Western Kentucky Gas Company.
1988: Energas changes name to Atmos Energy and begins trading on the New York Stock Exchange.
1993: Atmos Energy acquires Greeley Gas Company.
1997: Atmos merges with United Cities Gas Company.

with the United Cities Gas Company of Brentwood, Tennessee. United Cities was founded in 1929 as a butane air manufacturer and distributor, operating plants in 17 cities. It had grown through various acquisitions, eventually expanding its operations into ten states. In 1996, the year before its purchase by Atmos, United Cities had revenues of $353.4 million and reported a net income of $17.2 million. As a division of Atmos, United Cities reduced its range to eight states, but by the decade's end it accounted for about 250,000 homes and businesses in Atmos's customer base, distributing natural gas in over 375 cities and towns in midwestern and southeastern states.

By 1998, Atmos had grown into the 12th largest natural gas utility in the country, but not without some "painful side effects." Up through 1996, the company's business strategy had been to operate each of its acquired companies, many of which lacked advanced technology, as separate business units. In time, that policy proved very inefficient, particularly when the company tried to link them in its expanding network. Many of the companies had incompatible computer systems that often made customer information retrieval difficult if not impossible. None of them even had identical billing systems.

To improve service and cut overhead, Atmos sought to create uniform and consistent procedures for conducting its business. Accordingly, it phased in some new programs, starting with a fresh customer service initiative (CSI). The CSI consisted of several projects, including the creation of a centralized customer support center, the implementation of hand-held meter reading devices and mobile data terminals for in-field service, and the development of a new customer information system (CIS) with the infrastructure to support it. The implementation of these new initiatives quickly cut operation expenses and increased Atmos's net earnings. Until Atoms created its centralized call center in Amarillo, it had relied on more than 100 unconnected local service offices to conduct its business, an inefficient system at best.

Atmos continued its growth into the start of the new century. In April 2000, it arranged to purchase two Louisiana natural gas LDCs (local distribution companies) from Citizens Utilities, paying approximately $375 million. The two companies, Louisiana Gas Service of Harvey, Louisiana, and LGS Natural Gas, its intrastate pipeline affiliate, added about 279,000 customers in the New Orleans and Monroe areas of the state.

Atmos's growth and consolidations strategies also involved some select divestitures and partnering agreements. Among other moves taken in 2000, Atmos sold the assets of a natural gas distribution system serving around 5,100 customers in the Gaffney, South Carolina, area to Piedmont Natural Gas.

However, the company's focus in 2000 was on growth. Besides its purchases in Louisiana, it acquired some smaller companies. Among others, it purchased the Missouri gas distribution assets of Southwestern Energy Co. The assets were part of Associated Natural Gas Co., a division of Arkansas Western Gas Co., Southwestern's utility subsidiary. The acquisition brought 48,000 additional residential, commercial, and industrial consumers into Atmos's customer base. In exchange for 1.4 million shares of its common stock, worth about $33.3 million, Atmos also purchased the remaining 55 percent interest in Houston-based Woodward Marketing L.L.C., a natural gas services company in which Atmos already owned a 45 percent interest. Altogether, the additions increased Atmos's customer base to 1.4 million, making it the fifth largest pure gas utility in the United States. Atmos also became the largest natural gas utility in Louisiana.

Principal Subsidiaries

Energas Company; Greeley Gas Company; Trans Louisiana Gas Company; UCG Energy Corp.; United Cities Gas Company; Western Kentucky Gas Company.

Principal Competitors

Southern Union Company; TXU Corp.; UtiliCorp United Inc.; Xcel Energy Inc.

Further Reading

Byrne, Harlan S., "Atmos Energy Corp," *Barron's*, January 22, 1990, p. 47.
"Energas to Change Name to Atmos Energy Corp.," *Wall Street Journal*, September 22, 1988, p. 10E.
Goodman, Charles, "Customer Service Initiatives Help Atmos Energy's Growth," *Pipeline & Gas Journal*, November 1998, p. 28.
Molis, Jim, "Dallas' Atmos Energy to Buy Tennessee's United Cities Gas Co.," *Knight-Ridder/Tribune Business News*, July 26, 1996.
Rohloff, Greg, "Atmos Energy Seeks More Acquisitions, CEO Says," *Knight-Ridder/Tribune Business News*, February 17, 1998.
——, "West Texas Gas Utility Requests 12.5 Percent Rate Hike," *Knight-Ridder/Tribune News*, August 11, 1999.
Shook, Barbara, "Atmos Energy Adds 2 LDCs to Network," *Oil Daily*, April 17, 2000.
"Texas Adds More CNG Retail Stations, While GM Unveils Gas-Fueled Vehicles," *Oil Daily*, November 26, 1991, p. 5.
"Utility Integrates Various SCADA Systems into One," *Pipeline & Gas Journal*, February 1999, p. 28.

—John W. Fiero

Baker & Taylor Corporation

2709 Water Ridge Parkway
Charlotte, North Carolina 28217
U.S.A.
Telephone: (704) 357-3500
Toll Free: (800) 775-1800
Fax: (704) 329-9105
Web site: http://www.btol.com

Private Company
Incorporated: 1992 as Baker & Taylor, Inc.
Employees: 2,800
Sales: $1.13 billion (2000 est.)
NAIC: 422920 Book, Periodical, and Newspaper Wholesalers; 421990 Other Miscellaneous Durable Goods Wholesalers; 323117 Books Printing; 514191 On-Line Information Services

Baker & Taylor Corporation is the leading book supplier to libraries and the No. 2 book supplier in the United States. Baker & Taylor ships more than 1 million ISBNs (titles) each year. The company maintains one of the largest in-stock book, video, and music inventories in the United States, with an estimated 385,000 titles in inventory and more than 1.5 million available for order. The company has three divisions. Its institutional arm distributes books, tapes, calendars, CDs, DVDs, and videos to about 28,000 schools and libraries worldwide. Its retail division supplies approximately 20,000 brick-and-mortar and Internet retailers, including Amazon.com and independent booksellers. The Informata.com unit is Baker & Taylor's business-to-business e-commerce division, which distributes electronic content, licenses database services, and creates Internet portals. The investment firm The Carlyle Group and its affiliates own 85 percent of Baker & Taylor; management, employees, and other private investors own the rest.

19th Century Origins

Baker & Taylor was founded by David Robinson and B.B. Barber in 1828, beginning its corporate life as a small bindery and subscription book publisher in Hartford, Connecticut. A short time later, Robinson and Barber opened a bookstore to distribute their own books and other publishers' books. After establishing a solid position in Hartford, the two businessmen moved their flourishing concern to New York City in 1835. During the ensuing years, the focus of the company's business shifted from publishing its own books toward distributing other publishers' books. The company was relying on the latter to fuel its growth by the time its ownership was passed to the two men whose names would become synonymous with book distribution in the 20th century. In 1885, exactly 50 years after the relocation from Hartford to New York City, James S. Baker and Nelson Taylor purchased the company founded by Robinson and Barber, lending their surnames to a concern that would bear the Baker & Taylor name for more than the next century.

In terms of business focus, James Baker and Nelson Taylor did not alter the direction of the business they acquired from Robinson and Barber until 1912, when they abandoned publishing entirely and instead directed the company toward wholesaling. In the decades ahead, Baker & Taylor would establish itself as a prodigious competitor in its new business, becoming a familiar name to librarians and bookstore owners across the country who purchased books from the venerable wholesaler. In 1958 Baker & Taylor was purchased by *Parents Magazine*, remaining under its control until W.R. Grace & Co. acquired the company in 1970, beginning a period in the company's history that insiders would later characterize as difficult years.

1970s and 1980s: W.R. Grace & Co. at the Helm

When Baker & Taylor joined the W.R. Grace & Co. fold, it became sibling to a host of other businesses that operated under the expansive corporate umbrella of the diversified conglomerate. W.R. Grace & Co.'s corporate reach was broad, including a wide range of business interests that ran the gamut from Baker & Taylor's book wholesaling business, to the manufacture of oil rigs, to the marketing of bull semen. Positioned within this eclectic array of businesses, Baker & Taylor, to a certain degree, was lost in the mix. The company struggled to assert itself amid its parent company's diverse business interests, but as the years of W.R. Grace & Co.'s ownership wore on, its business began

Company Perspectives:

Baker & Taylor is a leading full-line distributor of books, videos, and music products to Internet and traditional retailers and to library customers. We also provide our customers with value-added proprietary data products and customized management and outsourcing services. We have been in business over 170 years and have developed long-term relationships with our customers and with the major book publishers, movie studios, and record labels.

to suffer. Librarians, who had relied on and trusted the Baker & Taylor name for more than a century, began to reassess their opinion of the book wholesaler, and, as a result, the company gradually developed a reputation among its customers for inconsistent service. Changes were needed, but it would be years before Baker & Taylor's management could direct the company as they saw fit and enter into a new era without the influence of W.R. Grace & Co.

Gerald G. Garbacz witnessed the effects of W.R. Grace & Co.'s ownership of Baker & Taylor firsthand, joining the book wholesaler in 1974, four years after its acquisition by the diversified conglomerate. By 1980 Garbacz had risen to the position of president, a post that provided him with a revealing vantage point from which to evaluate the company's operation under W.R. Grace & Co. Garbacz would later say during an interview with *Library Journal* that W.R. Grace & Co.'s management ''placed a great deal of emphasis on short-term financial performance with very little emphasis on the development of markets and human resources,'' chiding the parent company's approach to sustaining Baker & Taylor's long-term vitality. In spite of the damage done to the book wholesaler's reputation during the 1970s and 1980s, however, there were some positive aspects to W.R. Grace & Co.'s 22-year reign of control. During this time, Baker & Taylor became a more diversified business, gaining, through acquisitions engineered by W.R. Grace & Co., two new facets to its long-established business of wholesaling all types of books: computer software and videocassette distribution arenas. With the addition of these sister businesses, the foundation for the future Baker & Taylor, Inc. was created, engendering the well-rounded information and entertainment concern that existed in the 1990s.

Baker & Taylor Video's roots extended back to 1975 when Chicago-based Sound Unlimited was founded. The company, which lengthened its name in 1979 to Sound Video Unlimited, operated as a regional wholesaler of videocassettes. Before being acquired, the company helped pioneer the distribution of videocassette programming in VHS and BETA formats, along with another videocassette distribution company, VTR Incorporated, which was purchased by W.R. Grace & Co. in 1986. Sound Video Unlimited and VTR were then merged, forming Baker & Taylor Video, the largest full-line videocassette distributor in the United States. The establishment of Baker & Taylor Video in 1986 coincided with the acquisition of SoftKat, a computer software distribution firm founded in 1983 during the early years of the personal computer industry. Personal computers, in subsequent years, would become ubiquitous fixtures in homes and offices, while the demand for videocassettes would burgeon as well, giving Baker & Taylor Books two solid counterparts within W.R. Grace & Co.'s corporate structure.

The years spent under W.R. Grace & Co.'s management strengthened Baker & Taylor's business in other areas, particularly in international markets. Although Baker & Taylor had crossed U.S. borders just before its acquisition by W.R. Grace & Co., operating its distribution activities in foreign countries through offices in Somerville, New Jersey, the company's international business was bolstered considerably while under the ownership of W.R. Grace & Co. Sales offices were opened in Australia and Japan in 1983 and 1986, respectively. Then, following the 1989 acquisition of Feffer & Simons, which operated as an international publishers' representative, Baker & Taylor International, Ltd. was formed, providing Baker & Taylor Books with a corporate conduit to extend its wholesaling services to international markets.

The formal establishment of an international division in 1989, coupled with the acquisition of videocassette and computer software distribution companies, made Baker & Taylor a diversified competitor in the distribution business, certainly more so than when the company was first acquired by W.R. Grace & Co. in 1970. But its diversity also incited the harshest criticism of W.R. Grace & Co.'s management by Baker & Taylor executives. Garbacz cited W.R. Grace & Co.'s central failure as the company's decision to operate the Baker & Taylor businesses as separate entities, reflecting to a *Library Journal* reporter that ''there was a very large element of uncertainty under Grace; they didn't want the various units of B&T working together as closely as [Baker & Taylor management] wanted.'' This point was reiterated by another Baker & Taylor executive, who told *Publishers Weekly*, ''When we were owned by Grace, all three divisions operated as very separate, very independent companies with little or no interaction.''

1992: W.R. Grace & Co. Divestiture

For those disenchanted with the manner in which the Baker & Taylor businesses were managed under the auspices of W.R. Grace & Co., welcome news arrived in November 1991 when the diversified conglomerate announced its intention to sell its Baker & Taylor subsidiaries. Several months after the announcement, in early 1992 ownership of the Baker & Taylor businesses was passed to a group of Baker & Taylor management and The Carlyle Group, a private, Washington, D.C.-based merchant banking and investment firm whose specialty was acquiring businesses from large conglomerates. Like W.R. Grace & Co., The Carlyle Groups's business interests were diverse, including companies involved in real estate, airline catering, chemicals, aerospace, and commercial and military aircraft manufacturing. Unlike W.R. Grace & Co., however, Carlyle's management of the Baker & Taylor businesses met with the approval of Garbacz and his management team, ushering in the beginning of a new era for both Garbacz and Baker & Taylor.

The acquisition of the various Baker & Taylor businesses by Carlyle also engendered the formation of Baker & Taylor, Inc., which was organized in March 1992 as a holding company for Baker & Taylor Books, its distribution divisions, Video and SoftKat, and Baker & Taylor International, Ltd. Leading the

Key Dates:

1828: Baker & Taylor is founded as a small bindery and subscription book publisher in Hartford, Connecticut.
1835: David Robinson and B.B. Barber move the firm to New York City.
1885: James S. Baker and Nelson Taylor purchase the company.
1912: The company discontinues publishing to concentrate on wholesaling.
1958: *Parents Magazine* acquires the company.
1970: W.R. Grace & Co. purchases Baker & Taylor.
1986: Baker & Taylor Video, the largest full-line videocassette distributor in the U.S. is formed.
1989: Baker & Taylor International, Ltd. is created to extend wholesaling services internationally.
1991: Ownership is passed on to a set of Baker & Taylor managers and affiliates of The Carlyle Group.
1993: Baker & Taylor Entertainment is established as a supplier of videocassettes and music recordings in cassettes and CDs.
1999: The company creates on-demand publishing division Replica Books.
2000: Baker & Taylor launches an e-commerce division Informata.com; and the company settles with the Department of Justice a lawsuit alleging Baker & Taylor of overcharging school districts, libraries, and the government.

newly formed Baker & Taylor, Inc. during its first year of business was Gerald G. Garbacz, who was named chairman and chief executive officer of the company, in addition to his duties as the top executive of Baker & Taylor Books. Under Garbacz's stewardship, the Baker & Taylor units were governed in a decidedly more concerted manner than during the W.R. Grace & Co. years. The company's corporate culture was revamped and its focus was altered, transforming Baker & Taylor into an information and entertainment services firm rather than a company purely focused on distribution. As part of these changes, Baker & Taylor's software division, SoftKat, underwent a name change in 1992, becoming Baker & Taylor Software. The following year, Baker & Taylor Software, which dealt in educational and entertainment computer software, was combined with Baker & Taylor Video, a supplier of videocassettes and music recordings in both cassette and compact disc formats, to form Baker & Taylor Entertainment.

When Baker & Taylor employees reported for work on May 16, 1994, they heard surprising news. Chicago-based Follett Corp., a distributor of books, textbooks, and computer software to the school library market, had announced its intention to acquire The Carlyle Group's 92 percent stake in Baker & Taylor, Inc., setting the stage for another new era in the company's history. With three divisions that operated in business areas similar to those of Baker & Taylor and another three divisions involved in markets not served by Baker & Taylor, Follett struck industry pundits as a good match for the units composing Baker & Taylor, Inc. This acquisition would combine the $800 million in annual sales generated by Baker & Taylor, Inc. with Follett's $650 million in annual sales. Negotiations between family-owned Follett and The Carlyle Group were conducted throughout the rest of May, continuing into June, but were called off in the middle of the month after several weeks of discussions failed to yield a final agreement between the two companies.

In the wake of the aborted sale, The Carlyle Group announced that it would return to supporting Baker & Taylor's long-term strategy of upgrading its systems and achieving greater efficiencies through the consolidation of the company's operations, but the majority owner of the book, entertainment, and software distributor did make one important change. Slightly more than a week after the Follett deal fell through, The Carlyle Group executives ordered sweeping changes in Baker & Taylor's top management, replacing Garbacz, who officially resigned as chairman and chief executive officer of the company, with three individuals, Patrick Gross, Joseph Wright, and Craig Richards. With Garbacz gone, it was up to Gross and Wright, who jointly served as the company's chairman, and Richards, who was named chief executive officer, to lead Baker & Taylor through its new era, as the venerable company moved toward its third century of business.

Turn of the Millennium: The Internet Age

Baker & Taylor profited from its early relationship with Amazon.com, in which it provided books and a broad database of available books to the Internet retailer. In 1996 as online bookselling was becoming more widespread, Baker & Taylor and its main competitor, Ingram Book Co., a unit of Ingram Industries, were creating computer programs that would allow booksellers to link their Web sites to the distributors' extensive database of books. The distributors' programs would become available to booksellers the following year.

In November 1998 an announcement came that rocked the book business: Barnes & Noble was planning to buy the biggest book distributor, Ingram Book Group of Nashville, for $600 million. Barnes & Noble's bid for Ingram would give the retailer access to a broad, nationwide distribution system that could boost the retailer's disappointing Internet operation. The American Booksellers Association, which represented 3,400 independent booksellers, opposed the merger. The January 4, 1999 issue of *Mergers & Acquisitions Report* predicted that Amazon.com and Borders would bid for privately held Baker & Taylor—the only large competitor to the Ingram Book Group. But in June 1999 Barnes & Noble called off the takeover.

Meanwhile, Baker & Taylor's business grew by 20 percent to about $1 billion in 1998. In May 1999 B&T revealed the most aggressive expansion in its 171-year history, including plans to enlarge service centers in Georgia, Illinois, Nevada, and New Jersey by more than 650,000 square feet. These plans reportedly were in place before the Barnes & Noble/Ingram merger agreement had been announced. Also in 1999, the trend of on-demand publishing gained traction in the industry, thanks to faster and cheaper technology. Baker & Taylor's Replica Books, the on-demand division of Baker & Taylor Books, gathered other publishers' backlists and bought rights to out-of-print titles, instead of seeking unpublished works for its on-demand projects. Replica Books works with authors and publishers to keep books in print, prolonging the life of a book. Today, each title is kept in an electronic database, and the books are printed on a high-speed printer and bound in hardcover or paperback.

With the "Internet Revolution" at full speed, in April 1999, Baker & Taylor entered a relationship with VarsityBooks.com, an upstart company that would sell college textbooks over the Internet. CEO Eric J. Kuhn had cold-called James Ulsamer, president of the retail division of Baker & Taylor. Having succeeded with horizon-expanding Amazon.com, Ulsamer decided to take a chance on VarsityBooks, and Baker & Taylor agreed to warehouse the books, process orders, and ship books for the Internet retailer. The relationship with Baker & Taylor gave the newcomer credibility. But like many dot-com disappointments, VarsityBooks was unable to sustain its stock value, and in January 2001 the company was delisted from the NASDAQ.

Baker & Taylor had attempted to go public in late 1999, but a public offering was never completed, which the company attributed to soft market conditions. In the summer of 2000, to focus on business-to-business opportunities in the Internet-driven market, Baker & Taylor launched a new e-commerce business, Informata.com. The division would concentrate on electronic content, database operations, and the creation of Internet portals to host fulfillment services for vendors. Its first portal, TheLibraryPlace.com, sold a variety of products for librarians, including books, music, movies, furniture, and equipment. In the fall of 2000 the American Booksellers Association launched Booksense.com, the e-commerce wing of the organization's family of independent-bookseller Web sites, using Baker & Taylor's Title Source Database, which at the time contained 2.2. million books.

In August 2000 Baker & Taylor and its former parent company, W.R. Grace & Co. reached a settlement with the Department of Justice, which had filed suit against the library supplier for overcharging school districts, libraries, and the government. The suit alleged that as early as 1980, Baker & Taylor's trade books, intended for a general readership, were wrongly classified as non-trade titles to institutions. As a result, the libraries received smaller discounts, while full-trade discounts on the same books were given to retailers. The two companies paid a total of $15.5 million to 18 states in the lawsuit, with proceeds going to state library systems. Baker & Taylor and W.R. Grace Co. denied the claims.

In January 2001 Craig Richards, CEO of both Baker & Taylor and Informata, left the company. The January 22, 2001, issue of *Publishers Weekly* speculated that Richards' departure was associated with his inability to find a buyer for Baker & Taylor at a price palatable to the wholesaler's parent holding company, The Carlyle Group. Gary Rautenstrauch, Baker & Taylor's chief operating officer, succeeded Craig Richards as president. In June 2001, continuing to build its retail division, the company entered an agreement with Alibris.com, the used, rare, and out-of-print online bookstore, whereby the retailer would list its titles online with Baker & Taylor's Title Source II. The deal allows librarians looking for out-of-print, out-of-stock, or rare books to link directly from the wholesaler's bibliographic records to listings on the Alibris Web site, where orders can be fulfilled. Around this time, Baker & Taylor joined with Gaylord Information Systems to provide improved electronic data interchange (EDI) ordering in Polaris, GIS's library automation system. The new interface allows Polaris customers to do online collection development, ordering, and acquisitions through Baker & Taylor.

Principal Subsidiaries

Baker & Taylor, Inc.; Professional Media Services Corp.; YBP Library Services.

Principal Competitors

Ingram Book Co.

Further Reading

Annichiarico, Mark, "Baker & Taylor's Coup de Grace," *Library Journal,* September 15, 1993, p. 44.

"Baker & Taylor Expected to Provide Distribution for ABA Web Site," *Book Publishing Report,* March 22, 1999.

"Book Vendors Settle Claims of Defrauding Government," *The San Francisco Chronicle,* August 3, 2000, p. A2.

Breen, Peter, "Fulfilling Dreams," *Chain Store Age Executive,* May 1999, p. 244.

"Climbing Quickly," *Business Journal of New Jersey,* September 1989, pp. 46, 53–54.

"Garbacz Departs as B&T Revamps Top Management," *Publishers Weekly,* July 4, 1994, p. 10.

Irwin, Neil, "Varsity Group's Tough Test," *The Washington Post,* January 29, 2001, p. E1.

Marks, John, "Book 'Trust' Goes Bust," *U.S. News & World Report,* June 14, 1999, p. 45.

Milliot, Jim, "Follett Corp. the Likely Buyer of Baker & Taylor," *Publishers Weekly,* May 23, 1994, p. 26.

Milliot, Jim, and Ed Nawotka, "Richards Resigns at B&T," *Publishers Weekly,* January 22, 2001, p. 169.

O'Brien, Maureen, "B&T Sale Finalized; Reorganized as Solo Corp.," *Publishers Weekly,* March 30, 1992, p. 8.

Paige, Earl, "Baker & Taylor Settles in at Simi," *Billboard,* June 26, 1993, p. 67.

Peaff, George, "On the Fast Track," *Business Journal of New Jersey,* September 1989, p. 43.

"Projected Sales of Baker & Taylor to Follett Corp. Called Off," *Publishers Weekly,* June 27, 1994, p. 13.

Reid, Calvin, and Jim Milliot, "B&T Debuts Portal," *Publishers Weekly,* July 31, 2000, p. 10.

Rosen, Judith, "BookSense.com Boots Up," *Publishers Weekly,* September 18, 2000, p. 31.

Seideman, Tony, "B&T to Simplify Ordering of Multimedia Products," *Publishers Weekly,* August 1, 1994, p. 10.

St. Lifer, Evan, "Follett Ready to Finalize Deal for Baker & Taylor," *Library Journal,* June 15, 1994, p. 12.

Stuart, Scott, "Might Amazon Be Lurking for Ingram?" *Mergers and Acquisitions Report,* January 4, 1999.

"The Deal Is Off," *Book Publishing Report,* June 7, 1999.

Walt, Kathy, "Texas to Get Share of $15.5 Million," *The Houston Chronicle,* August 3, 2000, p. 27.

—Jeffrey L. Covell
—update: Michelle Feder

Bertelsmann A.G.

Carl-Bertelsmann-Strasse 270
D-33311 Gütersloh
Germany
Telephone: +49-52-41-80-0
Fax: +49-52-41-751-66
Web site: http://www.bertelsmann.com

Private Company
Incorporated: 1835 as Bertelsmann Verlag
Employees: 82,200
Sales: EUR 20.04 billion (2001)
NAIC: 511130 Book Publishers; 334612 Prerecorded Compact Disc (Except Software), Tape, and Record Production; 511120 Periodical Publishers

Bertelsmann A.G. is one of the world's largest media conglomerates, encompassing subsidiaries that span music, broadcasting, print, and the Internet. With operations in 60 countries, primarily in Europe and North America, Bertelsmann is active in these main areas: magazine and newspaper publishing; book publishing; book and music clubs; entertainment businesses in music, television, and multimedia; media e-commerce; and industrial businesses in printing, paper production, and other media-related fields. Among its several hundred worldwide subsidiaries, the best-known operations include Gruner + Jahr, publisher of magazines in Europe and the United States; Random House, Inc., the world's largest book and publishing company; and such record labels as RCA Music Group, Arista, BMG Ariola, and BMG Japan, which jointly make up BMG.

19th Century Origins

The company was founded as a family business in the middle of the 19th century and had already grown to a considerable size before World War II. The significant expansion phase of the company, however, only began after the German currency reform of 1948, when Reinhard Mohn succeeded with the Bertelsmann book club (the Lesering) in introducing a revolutionary form of direct sales to the traditional German publishing market. Bertelsmann grew into an international force on the back of this great success. In 2001, 17.3 percent of Bertelsmann's share capital was in the hands of the Mohn family; 25.1 percent was held by Belgian financier Albert Frere's Groupe Bruxelles Lambert; and 57.6 percent of the capital stock was held by the Bertelsmann Foundation, established in 1977 by Reinhard Mohn with the intention to take over the Mohn family's share in Bertelsmann and appoint the company's management.

Although a multiple media giant by the turn of the 21st century, the company began in 1835 as a small publisher of evangelical hymn books and devotional pamphlets in Pietist eastern Westphalia, where its headquarters have remained, resisting any suggestions of transferring to Hamburg or Munich. The founder of the company was Carl Bertelsmann, who was born in Gütersloh in 1791, two years after the French Revolution. His father died before he was two years old. His mother was to find him an apprenticeship in a bookbinder's business as she had done for his elder brother. However, to avoid conscription into Napoleon's Russian army, Carl Bertelsmann went traveling along the route from Berlin to Upper Silesia. After Napoleon's defeat and exile, Carl Bertelsmann returned to his hometown in 1815, then upon his brother's death in 1819, was able to set up his own bookbinder shop in his hometown.

''The little Bertelsmann from Gütersloh,'' as he was known in the area, soon found a place in the Pietist movement that shaped the eastern Westphalian community, and discovered that it particularly needed hymnbooks for its services. Gradually Bertelsmann's bookbinding business became a book-printing business as well, and then developed into a full publishing house. Bertelsmann dedicated himself to working industriously for his company, which, while small, expanded rapidly. By the time of his death, it employed 14 people.

When Carl Bertelsmann died in 1850, he left behind a wife and son and a considerable fortune. He had laid the foundations for the company's subsequent development, but he was not there to witness the success of the firm's bestseller, the *Missionsharfe* (*Missionary Harp*), a hymnbook of which two million copies were printed. The first edition appeared in 1853. By this time Bertelsmann was publishing not only Christian literature, but also historical and philological books, as well as novels. It

Company Perspectives:

Bertelsmann is an international media corporation. We provide information, education, and entertainment around the globe. The ultimate purpose of our community is to contribute to the advancement of society. We strive to be leaders in the markets in which we operate. Our joint efforts focus on creative content, customer relations, and strong return on capital. We want to ensure motivating and fair working conditions. We commit ourselves to the continuity and progress of our corporation.

ran its own printing press as before. Heinrich Bertelsmann, who inherited the business from his father, was able, as a result, to build on a very wide foundation that prevented his company from remaining a small publisher of denominational literature.

The printing and publishing house grew considerably in the second generation, thanks in part to the acquisition of other publishing houses that could not hold their own against competition in the market. This tradition of buying up weaker competitors to modernize them and thus make them competitive once more is a policy that Bertelsmann still pursues. By the time Heinrich Bertelsmann died in 1887, his 60 employees had moved into a brand-new building.

The company consequently came under the ownership of the Mohn family in its third generation, after Heinrich Bertelsmann's only child, Friederike Bertelsmann, married Johannes Mohn in 1881. Johannes Mohn was a minister's son from the Westerwald who had learned about the book trade under Heinrich Bertelsmann. Although without personal means and an outsider in Gütersloh, Mohn immediately took on the responsibilities of the business after his father-in-law's death, showing considerable talent in its management. In particular, he expanded the printing side so that book production could be increased steadily without incurring outside costs.

For this conservative company, with its strong allegiance to throne and church, the German defeat in World War I and the consequent revolution, bringing about the kaiser's abdication, was a painful break with the past. Disheartened by events, the 65-year-old Johannes Mohn passed on the responsibility for the business to his son Heinrich, only 26 years old at the time. Like his great-grandfather, grandfather, and father before him, Heinrich Mohn had had the best possible theoretical and practical training for his career as a publisher. Bad health and hard times would, however, prevent him from enjoying his position to the full.

Surviving World War II

Before the war, Johannes Mohn had already had a taxable income of 100,000 marks a year. He was a millionaire. Despite the family wealth, the Gütersloh printing and publishing house was almost forced to close, not long after Heinrich Mohn had taken it over, because of the effects of galloping inflation in Germany in 1923. For the first time in the company's history, no new employees were taken on, while valued staff had to be laid off. Scarcely had this crisis been overcome when an even greater world economic crisis broke out in 1930.

Heinrich Mohn countered these difficulties and the Third Reich with the help of his Christian convictions. Like his predecessors he was extremely close to the Evangelical Church and in particular to the part of that church, the Bekennende Kirche, or German Confessional Church, which stood by its faith in God in opposition to Hitler. At the same time Mohn was successfully trading with the German air force, which he supplied with millions of cheap books and pamphlets. When World War II began in 1939, roughly 400 printers, typesetters, and publishers worked for Bertelsmann in Gütersloh. The company had a turnover of 8.1 million reichsmarks in 1941 and by this time had far outstripped its German competitors.

The Nazi authorities, however, disapproved of the company's publication of religious texts and after the war began, Mohn's right to print these works was removed. His printing works were provided with less and less paper by the authorities, making it increasingly difficult to operate. When the British forces bombed Gütersloh in March 1945, most of the company's buildings were destroyed. Although a few of the expensive printing machines remained intact so that the business was able to continue, the company's future looked uncertain because Heinrich Mohn's health was failing.

Good fortune came to Bertelsmann's aid, when Reinhard Mohn returned home from a prisoner-of-war camp earlier than his elder but less-gifted brother, Sigbert Mohn. Neither was to have inherited the company originally, but when the eldest of the four brothers was killed on the sixth day of the war, the position fell to Sigbert. Since Sigbert returned from the Russian prisoner-of-war camp later in 1949, his younger brother Reinhard took charge of affairs in Gütersloh in 1947.

After his school-leaving exams at the Evangelical Foundation Grammar School in Gütersloh, Reinhard Mohn had wanted to become an aeronautical engineer, but when the war broke out, he was called up to join the German Africa Corps under General Erwin Rommel. After Reinhard was injured, he was taken prisoner by the American troops.

After his return to Gütersloh, Reinhard Mohn took the company helm with determination. When the West Germans suddenly stopped buying books after Germany's adoption of the deutsche mark in 1948, the young publisher made a daring decision. Instead of hoping for better times like the other publishers of the day, in 1950 he invited the West German retail booksellers to form the Lesering together with Bertelsmann. For a small sum, any reader could become a member of this book club. In return, the reader would receive a certain number of books from C. Bertelsmann Verlag every year.

There had already been book clubs in Germany. What was new about the Bertelsmann Lesering, however, was that the "corner bookshops" were made partners by the publishing house. With this type of direct sales the bookshops also profited, whereas previous book clubs had only created undesirable competition. Nevertheless there were still those who were critical. Many bookshop owners who did not acquire any Lesering members and consequently did not benefit from the club felt threatened. They were afraid that the Bertelsmann Lesering would take away their customers, but these fears proved to be exaggerated. In fact, the Bertelsmann Lesering won many people over to buying

Key Dates:

1835: Carl Bertelsmann starts the company, specializing in the publication of hymnbooks and devotional pamphlets.
1850: Carl Bertelsmann dies and his son, Heinrich Bertelsmann assumes leadership of the company.
1887: With Heinrich Bertelsmann's death, the company comes under control of the Mohn family.
1945: Most of the company's buildings are destroyed by British bombing raids.
1950: Reinhard Mohn introduces the hugely successful Lesering, the first Bertelsmann book club.
1962: Bertelsmann takes its first step abroad, founding a book club in Spain.
1969: Continuing to expand into various media, Bertelsmann enters the magazine business by purchasing a stake in the Hamburg publishing house Gruner + Jahr.
1979: During 1979–1980 Bertelsmann expands into the U.S. market by acquiring Arista records and Bantam Books.
1986: The RCA label and Doubleday publishers are purchased, and Bantam Doubleday Dell publishing group is incorporated.
1987: The company's global music businesses are combined to form Bertelsmann Music Group (BMG).
1998: Bertelsmann takes over Random House, merging it with Bantam Doubleday Dell to create Random House, Inc.
2000: Europe's biggest television group, the RTL Group becomes Bertelsmann's first complete corporate division to go public, and is listed on the London stock exchange.

books who previously had not dared to go into bookshops for fear of their lack of education being exposed.

The Bertelsmann Lesering proved highly successful. It gave the Gütersloh printing and publishing house two decisive advantages over its competitors: a certain guarantee of purchases of its own books and the high-capacity use of its printing presses. These two factors combined to make Bertelsmann's turnover soar in the 1950s. Company turnover doubled each year between 1951 and 1953, going from DM7 million to DM30 million. This was a far greater turnover than that of any other book publisher in West Germany. In 1956–57, Bertelsmann was to break the DM100 million barrier. By 1973, Reinhard Mohn saw the figure reach DM1 billion. At the end of this 22-year period, the company employed a workforce of 11,000 at Gütersloh and elsewhere as opposed to the original 500 workers in 1951.

Postwar Success

The success of the company could not be explained by the Bertelsmann Lesering alone. Two additional decisions implemented by Reinhard Mohn were to be of great significance. The first, born from necessity, was to cover the company's enormous need for capital; Mohn made his employees shareholders, but without voting rights. This and other socially minded actions made the Gütersloh office, far from West Germany's glittering metropolis, a greatly envied workplace. Mohn's second decision was to branch out from books and invest in modern media such as records, magazines, and television to keep pace with changing consumer demands.

These changes all took place with breathtaking speed in the 1950s, 1960s, and 1970s. Most successful was the acquisition of a stake in the Hamburg publishing company Gruner + Jahr, which was gradually built up to a 74.9 percent shareholding in 1976. Not only did the Hamburg sister company bring in excellent results, owing to good management, but it also helped Bertelsmann achieve wider acceptance in the media world following a long period during which the Westphalian family business had been regarded as rather provincial.

The principle behind Bertelsmann's acquisitions was always the same. Reinhard Mohn bought firms that were active in related fields of business and which could be purchased relatively cheaply because of problems they could not solve themselves. He would place a couple of trusted colleagues in leading posts and leave them to work hard on their own. Delegation of responsibility and decentralization of business were his beliefs. For ambitious managers who valued a certain degree of independence, it was and remained a challenge. By 1994 Bertelsmann consisted of around 300 profit centers, which operated virtually independently from one another and were coordinated from the group's headquarters in Gütersloh.

Business Expansion Abroad

During the end of the 1960s, Bertelsmann reached the limits of its growth within the German-speaking world. Mohn decided to expand the business abroad. The first step was to introduce Bertelsmann's Lesering to Spain, with all the other sectors of operation—from the printing works to the book and magazine publishing companies—following at short intervals. As a result, turnover rose to DM5.5 billion by 1980 and the number of employees rose to 30,000 worldwide. Bertelsmann transformed into a public limited company because of the colossal growth in its capital requirements, prepared to leap to the top of the media world league.

In 1981 after more than 30 years at the head of the company, Mohn moved from being chairman of the company to being chairman of the supervisory board. For the first time in Bertelsmann's history, Mohn left the operational running of the company to a manager who was not a member of the family. In taking this step he instituted a ruling which he applied to all members of the board and to himself and which would become company policy at Bertelsmann: employees may not remain in their jobs past 60 years of age.

Under its new boss Dr. Mark Wössner (a former assistant to Mohn, who had made his way to the top beginning in the late 1960s in the printing and industrial plant sectors), Bertelsmann AG held the position of the leading media group in the world for a time in the mid-1980s (until Time and Warner merged in 1989). This leadership role was made possible by several acquisitions in the United States, which stretched the Westphalian company to the limits of its capacity. Between 1985 and 1986 Bertelsmann acquired the publishing group Doubleday-Dell and turned the music section of RCA into the BMG (Bertelsmann Music Group). It was a massive package, for which Wössner paid more than US$800 million. This show of strength catapulted Bertelsmann AG's world turnover above DM9 billion, with the group employing more than 40,000 people worldwide.

Bertelsmann also looked to Eastern Europe, where possibilities had been revealed by the fall of the Berlin Wall and the Eastern Bloc. With world turnover of DM13.3 billion in 1989–90, Bertelsmann AG was well equipped to make the most of these developments. In 1990 alone, Bertelsmann spent DM1 billion in the newly opened eastern Germany, by starting a book club, buying the largest regional newspaper there, and acquiring in a joint deal with Maxwell, the publisher of Berlin's leading daily newspaper.

The company's major moves into the U.S. market did not immediately pay off. In 1992, for instance, 21 percent of Bertelsmann's sales originated in the United States, but only about 10 percent of its profits. But it was the acquisition of the New York publisher Random House in 1998, the largest investment in corporate history that finally catapulted the United States into the position of being Bertelsmann's largest market, garnering 33.8 percent of the company's revenues by 2000. Random House was merged with Bertelsmann's Bantam Doubleday Dell to create the behemoth new publishing company dubbed Random House, Inc. With a stable of respected and popular authors including John Updike, Toni Morrison, Michael Crichton, and John Grisham, Random House, Inc. became the largest book publisher in the Anglophile world.

By the mid-1990s, in the area of multimedia, BMG Entertainment decided that rather than making acquisitions or developing products and services on its own, it would follow a strategy of partnering with the world's most innovative software developers. The earliest significant computer technology venture was BMG's partnership with the leading American online service provider, America Online, to set up online services in Germany, France, and England. Bertelsmann financed the 50–50 venture with US$100 million and also gained a 5 percent stake in America Online (AOL) with an additional US$50 million investment. This early bet on AOL, suggested to Bertelsmann's management board by Thomas Middlehoff, then head of corporate development, turned out to be a goldmine. It also boosted Middlehoff's reputation for forward-thinking, winning him the position of CEO of Bertelsmann in 1998. As AOL's CEO Steve Case told *Business Week* in November, 2000, this early gamble showed Middlehoff could "provide the leadership necessary to bring Bertelsmann into the Internet Century." When AOL merged with Bertelsmann's competitor Time Warner in 2000, Bertelsmann had no choice but to cut its alliance with AOL, but the sale of its 5 percent stake in AOL and 50 percent stake in AOL Europe brought Bertelsmann more than US $7 billion.

However, all was not rosy for Bertelsmann at the beginning of the new millennium. The Bertelsmann Music Group struggled despite having a banner year in 2000, with BMG artists, such as Carlos Santana, winning 24 Grammy Awards. The studio, featuring staple acts like Whitney Houston and the Dave Matthews Band, pulled in a 4.7 percent return on sales for the year. But with a dearth of new recordings, and a shake-up in management, BMG struggled to stay in the black. The music business in general also perceived a threat from Internet Web sites that allowed users to share digital music files for free, a practice the studios perceived as copyright infringement and cutting into profits. The most successful of these sites Napster, with over 50 million users, came specifically under fire in 2000 as five major recording studios, including Bertelsmann, sued the file-sharing upstart. But in late 2000, Thomas Middlehoff shocked the other studios by offering Napster a $60 million "loan" to help it create a secure technology that would allow users to pay to trade music, in order to not violate copyright laws. In return, if Napster delivered, Bertelsmann would drop its lawsuit. Middlehoff told *BuinessWeek Online*, "If we didn't do anything, the music industry would die."

In 2001, despite the struggling BMG, the downward spiral of the popularity of its mainstay book clubs, the shakiness of various dot-com investments, and drops in print advertising in the Gruner + Jahr magazine division, Bertelsmann was not in trouble financially. The company was nearly debt-free, boasted a 15 percent sales growth in the previous year, and sat on US $13 billion in cash (much from the sale of its stake in AOL), which was ripe for new investments.

In a bold move in Februrary 2001, Bertelsmann acquired an additional 30 percent stake in RTL Group, Europe's biggest television company (with annual sales of about $4 billion), giving it a 67 percent majority stake. Acquiring the 30 percent stake from Groupe Bruxelles Lambert, Bertelsmann offered a 25 percent stake of its holdings in return. This move sent the message that Bertelsmann was prepared to deal with the repercussions of Groupe Bruxelles Lambert selling its stake in the company a few years down the line, making Bertelsmann a publicly listed company for the first time in the company's long history. But by taking control of RTL, and developing a relationship with Napster, Bertelsmann was paving the way to take a major part in the future of file-sharing of TV and video content on the Internet. By reinventing itself for the digital world, Bertelsmann seemed willing to take chances in order to maintain and better its already enviable position in the media industry.

Principal Subsidiaries

Random House, Inc. (New York); Random House Group (London); Plaza & Janés (Barcelona); Verlagsgruppe Random House (Munich); Gruner + Jahr (Hamburg; 74.9%); Prisma Presse (Paris; 74.9%); Gruner + Jahr USA (New York; 74.9%); Brown Printing (Waseca; 74.9%); BMG Music (New York); BMG Ariola (Munich); BMG Japan (Tokyo); Sonopress (Gütersloh); RTL Television (Cologne); RTL Radio (Paris); Pearson TV (London); UFA Sports (Hamburg); Springer Verlag (Berlin & Heidelberg; 86.5%); MOHN Media (Gütersloh); Maul-Belser (Nuremberg; 75%); Bertelsmann Services Group (Gütersloh); BCA (London); Bookspan (New York; 50%); Barnes & Noble.com (New York; 40%); bol.com AG (London, Munich).

Principal Divisions

Bertelsmann AG; Random House; Gruner + Jahr AG; BMG; RTL Group; Bertelsmann Arvato AG; DirectGroup Bertelsmann; BertelsmannSpringer; Bertelsmann in the USA.

Principal Competitors

AOL Time Warner; Axel Springer; Walt Disney.

Further Reading

Barnet, Richard J., and John Cavanagh, *Global Dreams: Imperial Corporations and the New World Order,* New York: Simon & Schuster, 1994, p. 480.

''Bertelsmann Gets Bigger,'' *Business Week,* April 15, 1996, p. 65.

''Bertelsmann: The Media Company that Makes Murdoch's Empire Look Small,'' *Economist,* April 9, 1988.

Clark, Thomas, Clausen, Sven, and Harding, James, ''Bertelsmann Plans Shake-up,'' *Financial Times,* June 4, 2001.

''Coming to America: The Sequel: Bertelsmann,'' *Economist,* November 16, 1991, p. 90.

Edmondson, Gail, and Patrick Oster, ''Waltz of the Media Giants,'' *Business Week,* September 12, 1994.

Ewing, Jack, ''Bertelsmann: A New Net Powerhouse?'' BusinessWeek Online, posted November 13, 2000, http://www.businessweek.com.

——, ''Bertelsmann: Building a Video Napster,'' BusinessWeek Online, posted February 5, 2001, http://www.businessweek.com.

——, ''Bertelsmann's Time of Trials,'' BusinessWeek Online, posted May 28, 2001, http://www.businessweek.com.

''Ich Bin ein Amerikaner,'' *Economist,* June 18, 1994, pp. 69–71.

Landler, Mark, ''An Overnight Success—after Six Years,'' *Business Week,* April 19, 1993, pp. 52, 54.

Lottman, Herbert R., ''Beyond Books at Bertelsmann: The World's Biggest Book Publisher Has Many Other Irons in the Fire, at Home and Abroad,'' *Publishers Weekly,* January 23, 1995, p. 17.

Morais, Richard C., ''The Latest U.S. Media Giant Isn't Even American,'' *Forbes,* April 25, 1988, p. 70.

Picaper, Jean-Paul, ''Bertelsmann: le Géant Allemand de l'Edition,'' *Le Figaro,* February 20, 1989.

Schifrin, Matthew, ''The Betriebsergebnis Factor,'' *Forbes,* May 23, 1994, pp. 118–124.

Studemann, Frederick, ''Europe's Great Communicator,'' *International Management,* September 1992, pp. 34–37.

—Dirk Bavendamm
—translated from the German by Philippe A. Barbour
—updates: David E. Salamie, Linda M. Gwilym

Bingham Dana LLP

150 Federal Street
Boston, Massachusetts 02110
U.S.A.
Telephone: (617) 951-8000
Fax: (617) 951-8736
Web site: http://www.bingham.com

Limited Liability Partnership
Founded: 1891 as Carver & Blodgett
Employees: 1,140
Sales: $208.37 million (2000)
NAIC: 54111 Offices of Lawyers

Bingham Dana LLP is one of the largest law firms in the United States. Begun as a small Boston partnership focused on its admiralty and banking practice, Bingham Dana is a full-service law firm whose 500 lawyers practice in a wide range of legal specialties, from real estate, antitrust, and intellectual property to litigation, financial transactions, and mergers and acquisitions. Its bankruptcy practice was ranked the fourth largest in the United States, according to the February 15, 2001 issue of *Turnarounds and Workouts*. Bingham Dana is a great example of the consolidation trend in the legal profession, for its mergers in the late 1990s and early 2000s effectively doubled its number of lawyers and its annual revenues. It also is a pioneer in developing diversified nonlegal businesses; it created two subsidiaries and a joint venture to provide a variety of business, financial, investment, and related consulting services. Bingham Dana's lawyers represent clients in many nations and thus play important roles in international trends such as privatization, the globalized economy, and the high-technology online revolution.

Origins and Early Practice: 1891–1945

In 1891 Eugene P. Carver and Edward E. Blodgett started the partnership of Carver & Blodgett to serve maritime interests in Boston and other Atlantic ports. The son of a ship captain, Carver graduated from Boston University's law school in 1882 and had a solo corporate practice for several years. Blodgett graduated from Harvard Law School in 1889 and married Carver's daughter before the two men formed their partnership.

With international trade booming, the new partnership had plenty of admiralty or maritime work. An early client was the Boston Tow Boat Company. In 1899 the firm argued in the U.S. Supreme Court over damages after a Canadian schooner sank from a collision with an American steamship. In the 1890s the firm also started a banking practice by serving the Massachusetts National Bank, later renamed The First National Bank of Boston and then just Bank of Boston.

By the 1920s the partnership had accumulated so many records that it began throwing out many of its historical files, which made it more difficult for future historian David Grayson Allen to write a firm history.

When the firm's core admiralty work and its overall revenues declined in the 1930s amid the Great Depression, it decided to merge with another Boston partnership. Thus in 1933 it merged with Pillsbury, Dana, Young & Moulton, which had been started in 1919 by Samuel H. Pillsbury and Ripley L. Dana. The merger created a new partnership with a strengthened banking practice, but the goal to create a broad-based general law firm was not realized until after World War II.

The Post-World War II Years

In the late 1940s and 1950s, Bingham Dana's main client was First National Bank of Boston. In 1956 and 1957 it assisted First National when it tried to expand by acquiring the Granite Trust Company of Quincy, Massachusetts, but the state government passed a law prohibiting it. However, in the 1960s an amended Bank Holding Company Act passed by Congress allowed First National and other national banks to expand and diversify. Bingham Dana also helped the bank start new lines of credit as the American economy boomed and also assisted the bank's subsidiaries in Europe, South America, and the Caribbean.

Meanwhile, Bingham Dana's admiralty practice continued to decline, in part due to the industry's general downturn and New York law firms gaining much of this practice. However, the firm

> ### Company Perspectives:
>
> *Bingham Dana gets it done. Helping our clients prosper in this dynamic and challenging environment is the mission of Bingham Dana: more than 500 attorneys who understand that business judgment is an essential component of sound legal advice, that imagination can be just as important as intelligence—and that markets and opportunities don't wait for lawyers.*

entered new but related areas as environmental regulations and technological changes impacted the maritime industry.

The firm's modest corporate practice was set back in 1950 when long-term client Lever Brothers moved from Cambridge to New York. In spite of that loss, Bingham Dana increased in size to become Boston's fourth largest law firm in 1960.

In the 1960s Bingham Dana became more specialized when it organized banking, corporate, litigation, tax, and trusts and estates as its five departments. It also added many more associates, who helped the firm finally develop into a full-service law firm, a goal it had sought since the 1930s.

The law firm's main growth area in the 1970s and early 1980s was litigation. Several experts at the time said a litigation explosion was damaging the American justice system, although others disagreed. In any case, Bingham Dana grew from lawsuits in which it represented corporations, among them mutual fund companies being sued by stockholders.

In 1971 the firm represented the *Boston Globe* during the much publicized controversy over the Pentagon Papers that described the United States' role in Vietnam since the late 1940s. The federal government wanted to stop newspapers from publishing the damaging report, but the U.S. Supreme Court ruled against the government.

In 1978 Bingham Dana represented The First National Bank of Boston and other clients in a case that overturned a Massachusetts state law prohibiting corporations from spending money on certain political issues. The U.S. Supreme Court ruling that corporations had a First Amendment right to express their political views ''affected electoral campaign spending statutes in about 31 states,'' according to historian David Grayson Allen.

Bingham Dana & Gould in 1989 started a family practice as a section of its probate department. However, this department, with just 14 lawyers, remained one of the smaller specialties of the law firm. That was fairly typical for large law firms that served mostly corporate clients.

Meanwhile, the firm added new offices as it grew to serve its clients' needs. This was part of a general transformation of large law firms that in the late 20th century became much larger and adopted business methods previously unused. For example, firms increasingly recruited experienced lawyers from competitors in what was called lateral hiring. Some firms began using public relations and marketing experts, while others employed outside consultants to advise them on a wide range of difficult issues ranging from firm management to retaining associates.

The Firm in the 1990s and Beyond

When the firm's centennial history was published in 1991, it had more than 225 lawyers based in five offices. David Grayson Allen, also the author of a history of Price Waterhouse, wrote that the law firm's culture focused on maintaining ''a firm of independent lawyers pursuing their own work.'' He quoted a former managing partner who said he seldom made ''command decisions.'' Another partner noted that Bingham Dana's success in the late 20th century was based on being ''a bunch of basically uncontrollable individuals.'' Of course, the firm's lawyers worked together on complex legal matters, but the emphasis remained on individualism and the entrepreneurial spirit.

John C. Larrabee, the former head of Bingham Dana's fiduciary services department, in 1999 was found guilty of six counts of securities fraud for his insider trading. In 1995 Larrabee told a stockbroker that Bank of Boston Corporation, a long-term Bingham Dana client, was about to announce its acquisition of BayBanks Inc.

In the late 1990s BankBoston Corporation used Bingham Dana and other law firms to significantly expand its presence in Argentina, Brazil, and other Latin American nations. The bank planned that by 2001 about one-third of its revenue would come from its investments in those areas.

Bingham Dana in 2000 represented Raytheon when it arranged $4.75 billion in financing through a combination of bonds and bank debt. It also helped Biomatrix Inc., a New Jersey pharmaceutical company, win a libel suit against three individuals who had used the Internet to charge that Biomatrix was headed by a Nazi and was killing people with its arthritis product. Since over 100 similar cases had been settled out of court, this was the first time a court ruled that such online comments were libelous.

Like other major law firms, Bingham Dana played an important role in the globalized economy. For example, its project development and finance group helped develop electrical and infrastructure projects in many nations by serving clients like the U.S. Department of Energy, the Export-Import Bank of the United States, Energy Investors Funds, El Paso Energy Corporation, and the Overseas Private Investment Corporation.

Under the leadership of Jay Zimmerman, elected managing partner in 1995, Bingham Dana made several major changes. First, in 1999 it merged with the 55 lawyers of Hartford, Connecticut's Hebb & Gitlin, which had expertise in financial restructuring and insolvency. Ed Hebb and Richard A. Gitlin had founded their partnership 25 years earlier. Before the merger, the Indonesian government had chosen Hebb & Gitlin to help it resolve its $80 billion in corporate debt, a project that involved at least 170 companies. After the merger effective July 1, 1999, Bingham Dana opened a Singapore office to deal with the Indonesian enterprise and other overseas work.

Bingham Dana in 1999 also began two nonlegal businesses. Bingham Consulting Group LLC, a wholly owned subsidiary, was started to help companies deal with government agencies and the media when complex public policy issues were involved. It was headed by Stephen E. Merrill, a former New Hampshire governor.

Key Dates:

1891: Partnership of Carver & Blodgett begins in Boston.
1907: Firm is renamed Blodgett, Jones & Burnham after Carver leaves to form his own firm.
1913: Practice now known as Blodgett, Jones, Burnham & Bingham.
1930: Burnham, Bingham, Gould & Murphy is chosen as the firm's new name.
1933: Merger leads to the new firm name of Burnham, Bingham, Pillsbury, Dana & Gould.
1937: Partnership is renamed Bingham, Dana & Gould.
1973: Firm's London office is started.
1981: Washington, D.C. office is established.
1991: Firm opens a new office in Hartford, Connecticut.
1997: Firm acquires Marks & Murase's Japanese Practice Group and its Los Angeles and New York offices and also changes its name to Bingham Dana LLP.
1999: Firm merges with Hartford's Hebb & Gitlin and then opens its Singapore office.
2001: Bingham Dana launches its first international advertising program; in May, it merges with New York City's Richards & O'Neil LLP.

The other nonlegal business started in 1999 was Bingham Legg Advisers LLC. According to the Bingham Dana web site, the new joint venture with investment firm Legg Mason ''marks the first time that a major law firm has partnered with a global investment firm to offer a full range of investment and trust administration services to high net-worth individuals.'' With the huge baby boom generation aging, many financial services companies began or increased their estate and trust services. ''Estate planning is where the money is, and what people are concerned about,'' said Raymond A. Mason, chair and CEO of Baltimore's Legg Mason Inc. in the February 2000 *USBanker*. Bingham Legg Advisers by early 2001 managed client assets worth about $2 billion.

In March 2001 Bingham Dana created its third nonlegal business, a wholly owned subsidiary called Bingham Strategic Advisors LLC that offered businesses guidance on mergers and acquisitions (M&A), restructurings, and joint ventures. For example, it furnished M&A advice to the Jean R. Yawkey Trust when it sold its controlling share of the Boston Red Sox and also to the Sumitomo Bakelite Company when it purchased Occidental Chemical's Durez Division.

Bingham Dana on May 1, 2001 merged with the New York City firm of Richards & O'Neil LLP. The addition of 75 lawyers brought Bingham Dana's totals to about 500 lawyers and its New York office to over 125 lawyers. On its web site, Bingham Dana Managing Partner Jay S. Zimmerman said, ''Richards & O'Neil is one of the best midsized firms in New York, with a sophisticated corporate transactional practice. Their corporate, real estate, litigation and Asian practice groups will fit exceptionally well with our existing practice areas.''

Accompanying its rapid growth, Bingham Dana in February 2001 began its initial international advertising program in several major publications, including the *Wall Street Journal*, the *Boston Globe*, the *Hartford Courant*, the *Lawyer* in London, the *Daily Deal*, *Boston Business Journal*, and the *Economist*. Such professional advertising was virtually unheard of just a generation earlier.

Bingham Dana's expansion was mirrored in its financial performance. According to the *American Lawyer*'s surveys of the nation's 100 largest law firms, in 1997 Bingham Dana had annual revenue of $106 million, which placed it 88th on the list. In 1998 it improved to 82nd with $133 million in gross revenue. Its 1999 revenue of $161.5 million earned it a ranking of 81st. Then in 2000 the firm reported annual revenue of $208.37 million, almost double what it had been just three years earlier.

Bingham Dana and several other large law firms grew by leaps and bounds in the 1990s and in the new millennium. The best example was London's Clifford Chance, which mushroomed to about 3,000 lawyers by merging with New York City and German law firms. Consolidation seemed to be the name of the game, as big firms acquired small or midsized firms in a reflection of what was happening with their corporate clients.

The obvious question was how far this consolidation trend would go. The increasing size of law firms brought serious challenges, the main one being the management and integration of a more diverse lawyer base. Such internal matters, as well as competition from other law firms and big accounting firms with their tax lawyers, rapidly changing economic and political systems, and new technology gave Bingham Dana plenty to deal with in the years ahead.

Principal Subsidiaries

Bingham Consulting Group LLC; Bingham Strategic Advisers LLC; Bingham Legg Advisers LLC.

Principal Operating Units

Banking and Finance Group; Commercial Technology Group; Employee Benefits Group; Entrepreneurial Services Group; Environmental Group; European Practice Group; Financial Restructuring; Institutional Finance Practice; Intellectual Property Group; International Group; International Trade Group; Investment Management Group; Japanese Practice Group; Latin American Practice Group; Grupo Latinoamericano; Mergers and Acquisitions Group; Project and Structured Finance; Public Policy Group; Real Estate Group; Sports, Entertainment and Media Group; Antitrust/Franchise Group; Regulatory and Litigation Services for Broker-Dealers; General Litigation Matters; Internal Investigations Group; Labor and Employment; Project Finance and Construction Litigation; Securities Litigation Group; Technology and Intellectual Property Litigation; Business Regulation and White Collar Defense Practice Group; Estate Planning Group; Tax.

Principal Competitors

Hale and Dorr LLP; Ropes & Gray; Skadden, Arps, Slate, Meagher & Flom.

Further Reading

Allen, David Grayson, *Bingham, Dana & Gould: A Centennial History,* Boston: Bingham, Dana & Gould, 1991.

''Biomatrix Prevails in Online Libel Suit Against 3 Individuals,'' *Wall Street Journal*, August 3, 2000, p. C19.

Huber, Peter W., *Liability: The Legal Revolution and Its Consequences,* New York: Basic Books, Inc., Publishers, 1988.

''Larrabee Is Convicted of Securities Fraud in Bank of Boston Case,'' *Wall Street Journal*, November 24, 1999, p. B14.

''Litigation Explosion Undermines Justice,'' *USA Today*, August 10, 1984, p. 14A.

McReynolds, Rebecca, ''Brokers Reach for Trust Business,'' *USBanker*, February 2000, pp. 44–47.

Pollock, Ellen Joan, and Alecia Swasy, ''Myerson & Kuhn Seeks Chapter 11 Status,'' *Wall Street Journal*, December 28, 1989, p. 1.

''Raytheon Raises $4.75 Billion,'' *Airfinance Journal*, April 2000, p. 24.

Spiess, Gary, ''Expanding in Latin America,'' *International Financial Law Review*, September 1998, p. 72.

Weems, Christopher, ''Bingham Dana, Legg Mason Put Union of Law, Finance into Practice,'' *Trusts & Estates*, January 2000, p. 72.

—David M. Walden

Boral Limited

Level 39
AMP Centre
50 Bridge Street
Sydney, New South Wales 2000
Australia
Telephone: (02) 9220-6300
Fax: (02) 9233-6605
Web site: http://www.boral.com.au

Public Company
Incorporated: 1946 as Bitumen and Oil Refineries (Australia) Limited
Employees: 13,500
Sales: A$4.03 billion ($1.51 billion) (2000)
Stock Exchanges: Australia
Ticker Symbol: BLD
NAIC: 212321 Construction Sand and Gravel Mining; 324121 Asphalt Paving Mixture and Block Manufacturing; 327121 Brick and Structural Clay Tile Manufacturing; 327310 Cement Manufacturing; 327320 Ready-Mix Concrete Manufacturing; 327331 Concrete Block and Brick Manufacturing; 327420 Gypsum Product Manufacturing

Founded as an oil-refining company shortly after the conclusion of World War II, Boral Limited later divorced itself from its initial interests, diversified into a wide range of resource and material fields, and is today one of Australia's largest manufacturers of building and construction materials. During the 1990s Boral expanded operations in the United States and Asia, but domestic operations still account for about 80 percent of overall revenues. The company, through a number of subsidiaries, is involved in quarrying, timber operations, and masonry, as well as the production of bricks, roofing tiles, cement, concrete, and asphalt.

Early Years: Focusing on Oil Refining

Boral, originally known as Bitumen and Oil Refineries (Australia) Limited, was incorporated in 1946. The new company was assisted financially by California Texas Oil Company, whose Australian subsidiary, Caltex, purchased 40 percent of the initial stock. Caltex also agreed to provide the new company with a 25-year supply of crude oil and technical assistance for three years. In return, Bitumen and Oil guaranteed Caltex a supply of refinery byproducts.

An entrepreneurial promoter named David Craig became the company's first chairman, and Elton Griffin was named chief executive. Griffin was an accountant by trade and maintained board positions with several other Australian companies, including the City Mutual Life Assurance Society and Email Limited.

T.G. Murray, another founding director, succeeded Craig as chairman in 1947. Murray also served as board chairman for the City Mutual Life Assurance Society, where Griffin was a director, and was a board member of other major Australian companies.

Bitumen and Oil stock, issued in early 1946, represented the 60 percent of the company that Caltex did not own. Initially the stock did well on the market as a result of widespread interest in the new corporation. The stock soon fell victim to nose-diving prices, before leveling off once production began in late 1948.

When production finally commenced, it was on Botany Bay, New South Wales, at a new plant on land in Matraville, leased from the Australian government. Despite difficulties in obtaining permission to construct the facility on the Botany Bay parcel, near Sydney, construction schedules stayed on course.

By 1949 Bitumen and Oil's prospects were good. Chairman Murray told stockholders that year that increased government-sanctioned roadwork should benefit the company, though the cost of interstate transport and the limited supply of steel for drums could hinder profits. The company closed out its first full year of production with a net profit of A$40,747.

Bitumen and Oil steadily increased production through the mid-1950s. In 1954 the company embarked on its first major expansion, and Queensland Oil Refineries—later known as Boral Resources (Queensland)—was founded. Activities of the new operation included processing semirefined oil received from Matraville into heavy fuel oil and bitumen.

Company Perspectives:

The new Boral has great strengths on which to build its future. We are a resource-based company with large, strategically located reserves; we have built leading market positions in most of our markets; and developed strong relationships with a broad range of longstanding customers, based on decades of reliable delivery of quality products.

After several years of divestment and restructuring, new Boral's assets are robust and competitive; and the company's management team and people are experienced and committed to generating higher returns from their businesses.

With these advantages and a much stronger financial position, new Boral is well placed to move forward as a focused, value-driven building and construction materials supplier operating in Australia and increasingly overseas.

The company entered the field of petroleum tars that same year, with the purchase of a minority interest in Petroleum and Chemical Corporation, which provided an outlet for refinery byproducts. The acquisition of a smaller company, W.B. Constructions, during this same time gave Bitumen and Oil a base for the manufacture and distribution of emulsion and tars in the states of New South Wales and Victoria.

Diversifying in the 1960s

Bitumen and Oil made a number of acquisitions during the early 1960s, which set the way for expansion in some areas and capital gains in others through the sale of new assets. In 1961 a controlling interest was purchased in Petroleum and Chemical Corporation. That same year Bitumen and Oil targeted Huddart Parker, a shipping group, for its first major takeover. Bitumen and Oil sold some of Huddart Parker's assets shortly after the successful acquisition, but picked up bargaining power within the oil industry, having secured markets to store heavy fuel and diesel oil.

During this time the company also expanded bituminous operations in Victoria, with the formation of Reid Brothers & Carr Proprietary, an asphalt-manufacturing company owned jointly by Reids Quarries and Bitumen and Oil. Fowler Road Construction Proprietary was also purchased and later became the spray division of Boral Resources (Victoria). Bituminous surfacing operations were then extended into South Australia through the purchase of an interest in Bitumax Proprietary, which later became a wholly owned subsidiary.

In 1963 Bitumen and Oil acquired Mt. Lyell Investments, primarily because of its large interest in the fertilizer industry. Mt. Lyell soon was sold, after plans to manufacture fertilizer from refinery byproducts fell through because of unforeseen high costs.

Early in 1964 the Gas Supply Company was acquired, which included gas plants in Victoria, New South Wales, and Queensland. The Victorian operations were later sold. The Norman J. Hurll Group was acquired later that year, and went on to form an integral part of the Bitumen and Oil subsidiary Gas Group. During this same time the company also purchased a majority interest in Mt. Lyell Mining and Railway, a tin manufacturing company. Company officials later decided to abandon the tin field, and the mining company was sold for capital gain.

A 1964 decision to diversify into construction resources was the highlight of the period. This diversification marked the beginning of a shift in corporate focus. Two large quarry groups were purchased in 1964, paving the way for restructuring and ultimately representing two major building blocks in the formation of the Boral of the early 21st century.

The two groups purchased—Albion and Reid—were consolidated under the name Albion Reid Proprietary, which later became the subsidiary Boral Resources (Victoria) Proprietary. Activities of smaller quarrying companies—including Carr Fowler, Reid Brothers & Carr, and Dammann Asphalt—were then incorporated into the interests of Albion Reid.

On November 19, 1963, the company adopted the name Boral Limited, which was an acronym for Bitumen and Oil Refineries (Australia) Limited. The new name signified the company's move away from its original core business, oil refining. With the formation of the Albion Reid group, Boral had entered the premixed-concrete industry in South Australia. Operations were later expanded to include quarrying, and the subsidiary became known as Boral Resources (South Australia) Proprietary. In 1966 Boral acquired its third major quarry company, Bayview, rounding out the group that was then Boral's foundation.

Boral's acquisitions were put on hold for the next three years while company operations were consolidated. In April 1967 John O'Neill was named a company director and later that year was appointed chairman, following the retirement of T.G. Murray. O'Neill, a director of the City Mutual Life Assurance Society, brought a background to Boral that included the law, banking, oil exploration, and insurance.

1970s: Exiting from Oil Refining, Expanding in Building and Construction

Boral merged its oil interests with the French-based Total in 1969. Boral's previous attempts to provide larger coverage of the retail petroleum market and acquire an assured crude oil supply had been less than successful. In a major reorganization spanning the next two years, Boral sold its remaining oil interests to Total and completely separated itself from its original field.

With oil refining behind it, Boral became increasingly committed to expansion in the building and construction industries. Early acquisitions spurred by this new direction included Warringah Brick in New South Wales, Brittains Bricks in Queensland, and Steel Mills Limited—later Boral Steel Limited—operating in New South Wales and Queensland.

Boral continued expansion into the brick field in the early 1970s, with the purchase of Glen Iris Bricks, later known as Boral Bricks (Victoria). Meanwhile, the company acquired a trio of concrete-masonry-block companies, including Besser Vibrapac of Queensland, Jaywoth Industries in New South Wales, and Hollostone, operating in Victoria and South Australia.

Key Dates:

1946: Bitumen and Oil Refineries (Australia) Limited is incorporated as an oil-refining firm.
1963: Company is renamed Boral Limited.
1964: Diversification into construction materials begins.
1969: Boral merges its oil refining operations into a joint venture with Total, then exits entirely from oil refining two years later.
1976: Cyclone Company, a maker of fencing, prefab building, window frames, and other products, is acquired.
1979: Company enters U.S. market through purchase of partial interest in California Tile.
1980: Merry Group, a U.S. clay brick maker, is acquired.
1982: BMI Limited, a major Australian construction materials group, is purchased.
1987: Blue Circle Southern Cement Limited, the largest cement maker in Australia, is acquired.
1993: Manufacturing division is spun off as Azon Limited; Sagasco Holdings, a gas firm, is acquired.
1997: Natural gas distribution operations are spun off to shareholders as Envestra Limited.
2000: Through a demerger, the energy operations are separated from the building and construction materials operations, which form the core of the new Boral.

Boral also expanded into the field of gas and asphalt early in the decade with the acquisition of Brisbane Gas Company, which became Gas Corporation of Queensland, and asphalt operations from Esso.

In 1973 Elton Griffin retired as CEO and was succeeded by Eric J. Neal. Neal, a ten-year veteran of the company, had served in various managerial roles before replacing Griffin. The new CEO was quick to direct other diversification moves, and in 1976 Boral purchased Cyclone Company of Australia, which became Boral Cyclone. The acquisition brought Boral into the fields of fencing, materials-handling equipment, prefabricated buildings, aluminum window frames and shower screens, wire screen cloth, and hand tools.

Peter Finley was named Boral's fourth chairman in 1976. Finley, a chartered accountant, would in 1990 become vice-chairman of the National Australia Bank and chairman of Email Limited, a company of which Elton Griffin had once been a board member.

In 1978 Boral Cyclone purchased the Melwire Group, whose operations included woven-wire conveyor belts, wire screens for heavy industry, and other woven-wire products. Melwire later acquired Mounts Wire Industries, a New Zealand company with similar operations. That same year Boral took over its first mining interest and a major gypsum producer, Australian Gypsum Industries. The subsidiary Boral Bricks Proprietary also acquired Albury Brickworks and Pacific Brick Proprietary about the same time. Meanwhile, Boral was also establishing its presence in the United States, with the 1979 purchase of a partial interest in California Tile, a concrete-tile-manufacturing company based near Los Angeles (the remaining interest was purchased in 1980).

1980s: Further Acquisitions at Home and Abroad

Boral entered the 1980s joining a growing number of major Australian industrial suppliers diversifying into energy. Under an agreement with Esso Exploration and Production Australia, Boral began oil and gas exploration in Queensland's Galilee Basin in 1980. A few years later Boral acquired a 37 percent stake in the Oil Company of Australia (OCA), a Queensland-based gas exploration company. A subsequent purchase of additional interest in the oil company made OCA an 85 percent-owned subsidiary.

In 1982 the takeover of BMI Limited of Australia was completed, giving Boral full control over a major construction materials group. BMI's interests were complementary to those of Boral, and included operations in concrete, asphalt, and bricks, as well as timber, a new area for the company.

Expansion and diversification led to increasing sales, and by 1983 the company passed A$1 billion in sales for the first time. The 1980 acquisition of the Augusta, Georgia-based Merry Group, the third largest manufacturer of clay bricks in the United States, made Boral the fourth largest brick manufacturer in the world. Once under Boral's wing, the Merry Group went on to acquire brickworks in Maryland, Oklahoma, Texas, Virginia, and South Carolina.

In 1985 Boral purchased Johns Perry, an Australian company involved in heavy engineering, ropes and strappings, and lifts and escalators. The following year the Edenhall Group of the United Kingdom was acquired.

In order to safeguard its cement supply, Boral bought Blue Circle Southern Cement Limited, in 1987. The A$630 million acquisition was Boral's costliest takeover ever. Blue Circle, Australia's largest cement manufacturer, also had interests in coal and limestone. The purchase of Blue Circle and certain U.S. interests helped push Boral's sales over A$2 billion in 1987; the company posted A$2.37 billion in sales, more than double 1983's figures.

Also in 1987, Eric Neal retired as CEO. Neal had played a key role in Boral's expansion in the Pacific, the United States, and the United Kingdom. Neal was succeeded by Bruce R. Kean. Kean, who had joined Boral in 1968, had served as general manager of the company's energy group and later headed up a number of building-products, manufacturing, and overseas operations. Kean picked up where Neal left off, continuing expansion drives in the United States and Australia. The new CEO also led Boral into continental Europe. Acquisitions there included two clay-brick and tile operations and a limestone and gravel processing plant in West Germany, as well as two Dutch brick manufacturers.

During the late 1980s a handful of Australian companies agreed to be bought out by Boral, which led to further expansion into the tool manufacturing field. These acquisitions included the Bell quarrying concrete, asphalt, and tire business, based in Western Australia; Patience & Nicholson, a cutting-tool company; Trojan, a shovel and hand tool maker; the concrete and masonry manufacturing company Calsil Limited; and a window manufacturing company, Dowell Australia Limited.

Acquisition activity also picked up in the United States in the late 1980s, where Boral acquired Fontana Asphalt, a major southern California asphalt supplier and quarry operator. Other U.S. acquisitions in the late 1980s included Blair Paving and Vernon Paving; another southern California asphalt manufacturer; and U.S. Tile Company, a clay-roofing-tile manufacturer.

Struggles and Restructuring in the 1990s

Boral entered the 1990s on a wave of rising revenues, having posted annual profit increases for 19 consecutive years. Despite the spate of overseas endeavors, better than 80 percent of Boral's activities remained in its home country. The economic downturn of the early 1990s hit Boral hard, given the company's exposure to the cyclical housing market. For the fiscal year ending in June 1991, the company's annual profits failed to increase over the previous year, the first time that had happened in 20 years. Boral also cut its dividend for the first time in 43 years. Profits fell further still in 1992.

In December 1991 Mobil veteran Jim Leslie succeeded Finley as chairman of Boral. One of the first major moves under his chairmanship was the bolstering of timber operations through the purchase of Pacific Dunlop's forestry products division for A$158 million. This move made Boral the leading hardwood timber producer in Australia, with operations added in New South Wales and Tasmania. The Leslie era was also noted for an increased concentration on Boral's core building products and energy businesses. To that end a hodgepodge of manufacturing operations outside the two core areas were spun off as Azon Limited in 1993. Seeking to increase the company's energy operations as a counter to the cyclical building industry, Leslie and Kean launched a takeover bid of Sagasco Holdings, which operated South Australia's suburban gas network and held various production assets. Following some resistance from Sagasco and its major shareholders, Boral succeeded by increasing its bid to A$816 million. Shortly after the completion of this deal in late 1993, Tony Berg took over as managing director from the retiring Kean. Berg, with a background in investment banking, was a former head of Australia's Macquarie Bank. In November 1994 Leslie was succeeded as chairman by Peter Cottrell, who had been on the Boral board of directors since 1992.

Under Berg's leadership, Boral aimed to be one of the world's leaders in building and construction and to be a major player in the Australian energy sector, focusing particularly on production and distribution of natural gas. Most of the remaining operations outside of these areas were soon divested. For example, in 1995 Boral sold its elevator business to Otis Elevator Co. of the United States. Although there were no acquisitions completed on the scale of the Sagasco purchase, Boral did gain the leading position in the U.S. brick market through the 1995 purchases of Bickerstaff Clay Products Company and Isenhour Brick and Tile Company. In addition to bricks, Boral's U.S. operations also focused on tiles, fly ash, and plasterboard. The other major overseas push came in Asia, where the company concentrated on plasterboard and premixed concrete activities in Indonesia, Malaysia, and China. In 1994 Boral began work on the first plasterboard factory in Indonesia and purchased the only plasterboard producer in Malaysia, Wembley Gypsum Products Sdn Bhd. Boral entered the rapidly opening Chinese market for the first time in 1995 when it established a joint venture with a local firm to construct the first plasterboard factory in Shanghai.

Net income dropped nearly in half for the fiscal year ending in June 1996 as Boral was buffeted by another downturn in the housing and construction markets. Seeking to cut its debt load, Boral in July 1997 spun off its natural gas distribution operations to shareholders as a new company called Envestra Limited, a move that gained the company A$899 million. Boral's net debt to equity ratio was thereby reduced to only 25 percent. Other businesses deemed noncore were sold off as well, including the North American gypsum and German tile operations.

Early 21st Century: Newly Focused via Demerger

With the company's financial performance lagging behind that of its main building and construction material rivals, its share price depressed, and the Asian financial crisis hurting the company's operations in that region, Berg and Boral were under continuous pressure in the late 1990s from shareholders and the investment community. Many analysts advocated a company breakup into separate building and energy firms. In October 1999 Boral announced just such plans, with a demerger completed in February 2000. For various reasons, it was actually the building and construction materials business that was demerged from Boral. The old Boral, consisting of the energy operations, was renamed Origin Energy Limited, and the demerged entity took on the Boral Limited name.

With the completion of the demerger, Berg left the company, and Rod Pearse took over as managing director. Pearse had been hired by Berg in 1994 to head the construction materials division. A number of noncore operations were divested in the first several months following the demerger in order to reduce a newly enlarged debt load. Among these were the European brick operations, Boral Tyres, a woodchip operation in Tasmania, and the windows extrusion business. Boral also restructured its troubled Asian activities, in particular through the June 2000 establishment of an Asia-wide plasterboard joint venture with Lafarge, a French building materials firm. The venture, called Lafarge Boral Gypsum in Asia Ltd., was initially 26.7 percent owned by Boral, but the company committed to increasing that ownership to 50 percent within three years by financing new projects. By 2001, with the Australian housing and construction markets beginning to recover and Boral's financial state improving as well, Pearse began looking for acquisitions to further strengthen the company's position. In mid-2001 Boral completed the A$70 million purchase of Concrete Pty Limited, a privately held concrete maker based in Sydney. The market responded positively to the move, indicating that the new Boral might very well face a much brighter future than its dismal decade of the 1990s.

Principal Subsidiaries

Erinbrook Pty Ltd.; Hi-Quality Concrete Industries Pty Ltd.; Blue Circle Southern Cement Pty Ltd.; BCSC Gypsum Investments Pty Ltd.; BCSC Investments Pty Ltd.

Principal Divisions

Australian Construction Materials; Cement; Clay & Concrete Products; Plasterboard; Timber; Boral USA.

Principal Competitors

CSR Limited; Fletcher Building Limited; Holcim Ltd.; James Hardie Industries Limited; CRH plc; RMC Group plc; Aggregate Industries plc; Ube-Mitsubishi Cement Corporation.

Further Reading

Beeby, Melanie, "Double Your Money: Berg Still Haunted by His Vision," *Australian Financial Review,* September 3, 1998.

"Boral Rounds Recession Mark and Heads for Renewed Growth," *Rydge's,* October 1983, pp. 34+.

"Bottom Heavy Management for a Better Bottom Line at Boral," *Rydge's,* March 1986, pp. 42+.

Boyd, Tony, "How Boral Cemented Its Asian Future," *Australian Financial Review,* August 28, 1995, p. 24.

Brief History of Boral Limited, Sydney: Boral Limited, 1989.

Craig, Duncan, "Boral Puts Its Foot on the Gas," *Australian Financial Review,* September 13, 1996, p. 48.

Ferguson, Adele, "What Went Wrong at Boral," *Business Review Weekly,* July 22, 1996, p. 20.

Howarth, Ian, "For $800M, Boral Takes Sagasco: Now Watch the Changes," *Australian Financial Review,* October 15, 1993.

Hoyle, Simon, "Restructuring Has Delivered the Goods, Declares Boral," *Australian Financial Review,* September 4, 1997, p. 21.

Hughes, Anthony, "Back to the ACCC: Boral Bids for Rival," *Sydney Morning Herald,* June 5, 2001, p. 25.

——, "Boral Down, Will Keep Promise to Grow in US," *Sydney Morning Herald,* February 15, 2001, p. 26.

——, "Boral's Losing Energy," *Sydney Morning Herald,* December 20, 1999, p. 31.

——, "It's Official: A Split Decision," *Sydney Morning Herald,* October 21, 1999, p. 25.

King, Stephanie, *From the Ground Up: Boral's First 50 Years,* Sydney: State Library of New South Wales Press, 1996, 104 p.

Kitney, Damon, "Boral's Building Blocks Cut for Expansion," *Australian Financial Review,* September 4, 2000, p. 20.

——, "Building Blocks Start Falling into Place at Boral," *Australian Financial Review,* March 19, 2001, p. 5.

Light, Deborah, "How Neal Charts the Course at Boral," *Business Review Weekly,* March 14, 1986, p. 14.

Maley, Karen, "Up and Down: Tony Berg's Career Path," *Australian Financial Review,* October 23, 1999, p. 30.

Mclachlan, Colin, and Brook Turner, "Boral Dividend Cut: The First in 43 Years," *Australian Financial Review,* September 3, 1991.

Pearse, Rod, "Boral's New Top Gun Ready for Tough Role," *Australian Financial Review,* December 6, 1999, p. 22.

Rennie, Philip, "Sir Eric Shows 'em How," *Rydge's,* May 1984, pp. 42+.

Ries, Ivor, "A Tense Time for Tony Berg," *Australian Financial Review,* November 14, 1998, p. 27.

Sevior, John, "A 'Gleaming New Direction' for Boral," *Sydney Morning Herald,* October 21, 1993, p. 25.

Sykes, Trevor, "Hard Men at the Top Ran a Tough Ship," *Australian Financial Review,* October 21, 1999, p. 27.

Syvret, Paul, "Boral's New Chief Has Eye on Asia," *Australian Financial Review,* August 30, 1993, p. 18.

Tabakoff, Nick, "Boral Makes Maiden Investment in China," *Australian Financial Review,* August 21, 1995, p. 19.

Tait, Nikki, "Bosses at Boral Build a Dynamic Image," *Financial Times,* October 21, 1993, p. 32.

West, Michael, "Berg: Surgeon or Grim Reaper?," *Sydney Morning Herald,* July 15, 1996, p. 37.

—Roger W. Rouland
—update: David E. Salamie

Borders Group, Inc.

100 Phoenix Dr.
Ann Arbor, Michigan 48108
U.S.A.
Telephone: (734) 477-1100
Fax: (734) 477-1965
Web site: http://www.bordersgroup.com

Public Company
Incorporated: Borders Group incorporated 1994
Employees: 30,000
Sales: $3.27 billion (2001)
Stock Exchanges: New York
Ticker Symbol: BGP
NAIC: 451211 Book Stores; 45122 Prerecorded Tape, Compact Disc and Record Stores; 551112 Offices of Other Holding Companies

Borders Group Incorporated is the second of the three largest bookstore chains in the United States, based on sales and number of stores. It is the fastest-growing bookstore chain. It operates 354 superstores under the name Borders Books and Music. The superstores feature books as well as special events, including live music, story times, and appearances by artists and authors. The Borders Group subsidiary, Waldenbooks, leads all other book companies in the world in the mall-based book business. Waldenbooks operates stores in over 862 malls and airports. In addition, Borders Group's efforts at international expansion has led to the establishment of Borders bookstores in the United Kingdom, Australia, Singapore, New Zealand, and Puerto Rico. Borders Group, Inc. also has 32 bookstores in the United Kingdom operating under the name Books Etc.

Early History

Borders Group, Inc. came into existence following the spin-off from its parent Kmart Corporation in May 1995. However, the Borders name dates back over two decades. Borders began as an independent used bookstore in Ann Arbor, Michigan. The shop was founded in 1971 by Louis and Tom Borders. Serving the bustling academic community of the University of Michigan and Ann Arbor's smaller colleges, the store held its own and became a popular neighborhood hangout. Within the next several years, the Borders brothers opened two more bookstores in Michigan, one in Atlanta, and another in Indianapolis. In addition, Louis and Tom started a wholesaling business they called BIS (Book Inventory Systems), which experienced healthy growth.

Toying with the idea of a ''superstore,'' the brothers opened their first prototype large-scale retail store in 1985. Its success and the rise of similar competing stores set the retail book industry on its ear. The superstore model shifted sales from small, indoor-mall-based chain stores and independent booksellers to the new chain superstores. By 1988, with their five Midwest bookstores and BIS's bustling service numbering 14 bookstore clients, the brothers' enterprise was bringing in a net income of $1.9 million from sales of $32.3 million. But the brothers wanted to expand in a big way.

To achieve their dream of taking the Borders name national, Louis and Tom put their faith in a young man named Robert DiRomualdo. DiRomualdo had a Harvard MBA, and was a graduate of the Drexel Institute of Technology. DiRomualdo had worked his way through several merchandising and marketing positions at Acme Markets and Little General Stores before becoming president and chief executive of Hickory Farms, the prominent food shop chain.

When DiRomualdo joined the Borders brothers' enterprise in 1988, the industry was ripe for the kind of expansion Louis and Tom had hoped for. The late 1980s and early 1990s were a time of unprecedented growth for book retailers. Industry sales mushroomed from $59 million in sales for the top two superstore chains with only 31 units in 1989, to nearly $1.4 billion by 1994 from 350 units; this represented an astounding 87 percent compound annual rate. Taking advantage of these circumstances, DiRomualdo, who was named president and chief executive in 1989, opened 14 new stores in the next three years. Within a few short years, DiRomualdo had turned Borders into a household name in the Midwest, and analysts considered Borders the premier book superstore chain of the 1990s.

Company Perspectives:

The goal of Borders Group, Inc. is to be the best-loved provider of books, music, video and other entertainment, as well as educational and informational products and services. Borders strives to be the world leader in selection, service, innovation, ambiance, community involvement, and shareholder value.

National Status

By 1992, Borders had quadrupled its size and was beginning the complicated process of going public. Around the same time, the retailer attracted the attention of the huge Kmart Corporation, which had bought Waldenbooks in 1984 and was looking to expand its book retailing segment even further. In October of 1992, Louis and Tom Borders sold their business (though they remained investors), and Borders became a wholly owned subsidiary of Kmart. Sales from Borders' operations for 1993 reached $224.8 million, a 15.8 percent increase in net sales over the previous year. Several changes were implemented in 1993, including modernized cash registers, a human resources department, formal training programs for employees, and the introduction of music to the stores' stock.

In August 1994, Borders and sibling Waldenbooks formed a new company called Borders Group, Inc., with plans to eventually break free from Kmart. DiRomualdo joined with George Mrkonic, who ran Kmart's specialty stores division for four years (which included Builders Square, The Sports Authority, Pay Less Drug Stores, Waldenbooks, Borders, Kmart's in-store Reader's Market shops and others) and had jumped over to the Group in November. He had helped shape the company into a mechanized book and music mecca. By the end of the year, Borders had acquired five CD Superstores and one Planet Music outlet. The company went on to add four Planet stores and 32 new Borders superstores.

The Group's overall sales for 1994 reached $1.5 billion. With what some analysts have called the industry's most sophisticated computer inventory management and sales system, Borders not only possessed the highest sales-per-foot ratio in the industry, but was able to track popular titles by selling season. Borders had identified as many as 55 separately defined seasonal patterns and programmed these into the computer system to keep better track of seasonal and regular bestselling titles, and to help maintain a supply of such titles with little or no interruption in prospective sales.

Though Kmart's ownership of Borders (and Waldenbooks) was to end with the formation of the Borders Group, Inc., finances were settled with the proceeds of a public offering of the new company's stock in May 1995. Two months later, Borders announced it would purchase Kmart's 13 percent stock share. DiRomualdo was installed as chairman and chief executive, while Mrkonic became vice-chairman and president. After a one-time write-off of $182 million, the Borders Group announced second quarter (1994) sales of nearly $364 million, representing an 11.7 percent gain over the previous year's posted sales of $327 million.

Though Borders' transition from small retailer to national chain wasn't completely smooth, many long-time employees remained with the company and were rewarded for their loyalty by generous benefits worked out during the Kmart acquisition. One sore point arose in 1994 with the proposed closure of Louis and Tom's original Borders store in Ann Arbor, set for relocation into an old department store building. Not only was the new store slated to be a Borders Books & Music (the previous was books-only), but its spacious 45,000-square foot interior (four times the size of the original) could in no way maintain the homey atmosphere of the first Borders book shop, despite the added benefits of much more space and extras like the popular new espresso bars.

Nevertheless, Borders new format was obviously giving customers what they wanted and needed. In addition to its unique, state of the-art inventory and ordering system, Borders' employee base was another of its major boons; most employees were full-time and college-educated, and all were tested for their knowledge of literature and music prior to hiring. Additionally, the bookstore chain prided itself on first-rate customer service, offering patrons a wide range of services, from locating out-of-print titles to community activities like children's storytelling hours and poetry readings.

Rounding out Borders' offerings were growing varieties of alternative educational and informational media, from videos to CD-ROMs, a relaxing and comfortable environment that encouraged customers to linger, and the ubiquitous espresso bars. An industry-first that was quickly copied by competitors, Borders' espresso bars grew from a store add-on and overhead cost to a $20 million profit per year venture. In 1995, 82 of the company's 88 superstores had espresso bars, and all new stores were scheduled to have them.

The Borders superstore prototype in 1996 was 30,000 square feet of space, substantially larger than major competitor Barnes & Noble's megastore. Averaging 128,000 book titles and about 57,000 prerecorded music titles at an initial cost of $2.6 million, most Borders superstores became profitable within 12 months of business. Since the majority of Borders' superstores were built following the early 1990s, the company's success by 1996 had been swift and immediate.

Revenue figures for year-end 1995 were just shy of $1.6 billion for the Borders Group as a whole, with Borders Books & Music stores contributing over $622.6 million (a 63.4 percent increase over 1994's sales). The superstores contributed a healthy 39.6 percent slice of the Group's overall sales, a welcome and expected 12.2 percent increase from their share in 1994. Sales in 1996 reached more than $2 billion, with Borders' superstores division hitting $950 million.

Second only to Barnes & Noble in sales, industry analysts chose Borders' superstores over Barnes & Noble as having a better variety of products, and most expected the bookseller to overtake its rival in the near future. Additionally, Borders planned to take advantage of Waldenbooks' status as a cash cow to finance expansion across the nation. Scheduled to open between 30 and 35 new Borders superstores in 1996 and to continue the trend (from 35 to 40 new superstores per year) until the end of the 1990s, Borders hoped to not only prove its mettle but to become the country's top book-retailing chain.

Key Dates:

1971: Original Borders bookstore is founded by Louis and Tom Borders.
1985: Prototype superstore opens.
1992: Borders becomes subsidiary of Kmart.
1994: Borders and Waldenbooks merge and form Borders Group, Inc.
1995: Company purchases Borders stock held by Kmart; Borders Group, Inc. makes initial public offering.
1996: Company closes more than 100 Waldenbooks locations; focuses on superstore development.
1997: Borders Online, Inc. created to establish electronic sales operations; stores open in United Kingdom and Singapore.
1998: Company launches Borders.com Web site.
1999: Management begins aggressive expansion and opens more stores in England, Australia, and New Zealand.
2001: Company teams with Amazon.com to launch a co-branded Web site.

Late 1990s and Early 2000s

The late 1990s and early 2000s posed significant challenges to the book industry, in general, and Borders Group specifically. Stock prices were down, online businesses suffered losses, and shareholders questioned Borders management. Independent booksellers went to court with charges that the big chains had made unfair deals with publishers, thus discouraging competition. Borders was ordered to pay the American Booksellers Association (ABA) a settlement of $2.5 million in June 2001.

Financially, the year 2000 was a gloomy one for book retailers. Borders Group, Inc. stock price dipped 28.1 percent during the year, though sales and earnings during the last quarter increased 18 percent and were up 9.9 percent for the year. Annual sales at superstores increased 14 percent over the previous year.

The Company's Web site, Borders.com, launched in 1998, was the big loser for the Company. Though sales were up in the fourth quarter, total annual sales were down $27.4 million. The site posted losses in the fourth quarter of both 1999 and 2000, with an annual loss of $18.4 million for the year 2000. Borders became an online bookseller later than its major, already well-established, competitors. Business losses were also attributed to a general retreat in the industry from discounting online purchases, and subsidizing book sales by selling below operating costs. As Borders and other online sellers stopped discounting and offering other incentives to purchasers, online sales were reduced substantially. Borders Group, Inc. closed the doors on its online store and turned it over to Amazon.com in April 2001. Amazon.com planned to provide inventory, content, and customer service for the new Borders.com, and Borders Group planned activities to boost sales for the site.

In December 2000, Borders management faced heavy criticism from shareholders Alan and Barry Lafer, who controlled approximately two percent of the Company shares. The Lafer brothers had previously asked the Company to consider strategic options, including a possible sale of Borders Group, Inc. The Lafers accusations were fueled by the Company's slow growth during the previous fiscal year. During summer 2000, Merrill Lynch had been hired to evaluate the options. Subsequently, the Company resolved to remain independent. In renewed criticism, the Lafers charged that the half-time employment contracts of top executives weakened the Company's management capabilities. Part-time management leads to part-time results, they claimed.

The Lafer brothers also accused management of errors in handling the Company's online expansion and the acquisition of the retail toy store, All Wound Up. The Company had acquired All Wound Up in March 1999 and, by January 2001, planned to discontinue its operations.

In March 2001, Borders announced that Greg Josefowicz, the president and chief executive, would become chairman at the end of the year, replacing Robert DiRomualdo.

After the realignment of online commitments and internal review of options and management, Borders Group's strategy in the new millennium was to continue growth and increase profitability by focusing primarily on its superstores and continuing to develop mall and kiosk bookstores.

Principal Subsidiaries

Borders, Inc.; Waldenbooks.

Principal Competitors

Barnes & Noble; Books-A-Million; Amazon.com.

Further Reading

''Amazon.com and Borders to Relaunch Borders.Com,'' *EFE World News Service*, April 11, 2001.
''Barnes and Noble and Borders Group to Pay American Booksellers Association settlement,'' *Chain Store Executive with Shopping Center Age*, June 2001, p. 24.
''Borders Group,'' *Billboard*, January 20, 2001, p. 71.
''Borders Group,'' *Billboard*, March 31, 2001, p. 55.
''Borders Group, Inc. Announces Year-End Results,'' *PR Newswire*, March 11, 1996, p. 311.
''Borders Group, Inc.: Booking Profits,'' *United States Equity Research: Retailing*, June 22, 1995.
''Kmart Sells Remaining 13% Stake in Borders Group,'' *New York Times*, August 17, 1995, p. C3.
McKenna, John F. and Buchanan, Robert F., ''Strategic Assessment: Borders Group, Inc.,'' *NatWest Securities*, October 9, 1995.
Milliot, Jim, ''Chain Sales Rise 9% to $7.2 Billion,'' *Publishers Weekly*, April 2, 2001 p. 9.
——, ''Industry Stocks Stumbled in 2000,'' *Publishers Weekly*, January 8, 2001, p. 10.
Mutter, John, ''Beyond Borders: Trimming Walden,'' *Publishers Weekly*, February 7, 1994, pp. 28–32.
''Taking over Borders.com,'' *Display & Design Ideas*, May 2001, p. 10.

—Taryn Benbow Pfalzgraf
—update: Elizabeth Shé

Boyd Gaming Corporation

2950 South Industrial Road
Las Vegas, Nevada 89109
U.S.A.
Telephone: (702) 792-7200
Fax: (702) 792-7313
Web site: http://www.boydgaming.com

Public Company
Incorporated: 1975 as The Boyd Group
Employees: 14,000
Sales: $1.08 billion (2000)
Stock Exchanges: New York
Ticker Symbol: BYD
NAIC: 72112 Casino Hotels; 551112 Offices of Other Holding Companies; 71329 Other Gambling Industries (pt)

Boyd Gaming Corporation is a multi-jurisdictional gaming company with properties in Nevada, Louisiana, Indiana, Mississippi, and Illinois. In Nevada, Boyd Gaming owns casino and hotel facilities on the Las Vegas Strip, in downtown Las Vegas, and on the Boulder Strip. Properties in the greater Las Vegas area include the Stardust Resort and Casino, Sam's Town Hotel and Gambling Hall, the Eldorado Casino, the Jokers Wild Casino, the California Hotel and Casino, the Fremont Hotel and Casino, and the Main Street Station Casino, Brewery and Hotel. In Louisiana, Boyd Gaming operates the Treasure Chest Casino and Delta Downs Racetrack. In Indiana, the company operates the Blue Chip Casino. In Mississippi, the company operates Sam's Town Hotel and Gambling Hall in Tunica County. In Illinois, the company operates the Par-A-Dice Hotel and Casino. Through a joint venture with MGM Mirage, Boyd Gaming is developing a $1 billion hotel casino in Atlantic City, New Jersey. Named The Borgata, the gaming and entertainment complex is scheduled to open in 2003. Boyd Gaming also owns a travel agency named Vacations-Hawaii, which provides chartered flights to Las Vegas as part of exclusive packages to the company's hotel casinos in Las Vegas.

Origins

The Boyd name in Las Vegas was established by the family's patriarch, Sam Boyd. As a youth during the 1920s, Boyd helped support his mother and siblings by working at the Long Beach Amusement Park in California. Without a father to support the family, the Boyds relied on the income earned by Sam at the amusement park's carnival games to survive. The family's financial prospects improved dramatically after Sam Boyd moved to Las Vegas, but few acquaintances could have guessed that his arrival in Las Vegas marked the beginning of a multibillion-dollar gambling empire bearing the Boyd name.

Boyd moved to Las Vegas in September 1941 with $80 to his name. His modest bankroll—the financial foundation of Boyd Gaming—soon grew, however. Boyd immersed himself in the area's burgeoning gambling scene, gaining the practical experience he would later use to operate his own casinos. He first found employment as a dealer, before rising through the ranks of Las Vegas's employment hierarchy. Boyd was promoted to pit boss, then to shift supervisor, saving his money as he learned the operational aspects of casino management. Eventually, he saved enough money to buy an interest in the Sahara Hotel, giving him the financial leverage to pursue his ambitions. Next, Boyd became a general manager and partner at The Mint located in downtown Las Vegas, his last position before moving into casino ownership outright.

The California Opens in 1975

From the outset, Boyd's fiefdom of casinos involved his son, William Boyd. William Boyd was a practicing attorney in 1962 when he and his father purchased the Eldorado Club in Henderson, Nevada, located southeast of Las Vegas. Although the Eldorado Club represented the first instance that the father-and-son team joined forces in the casino business, the acquisition did not represent the formal beginnings of the Boyds' hotel and gaming enterprise. That moment, according to the company's reckoning, did not arrive until a dozen years later. In 1973, William Boyd quit his law practice to join his father on a full-time basis, two years before the pair unveiled what became regarded as Boyd Gaming's first property. In 1975, The California Hotel and Casino opened in downtown Las Vegas, marking

Company Perspectives:

We, as members of Boyd Gaming Corporation, operate with only the highest degree of integrity, and rely on the competence and friendliness of each person in our organization to provide entertainment and service to satisfy our customers' wants. Through teamwork, we strive to maximize shareholder value, to be among the leading companies in our industry and to provide opportunities for all while we support and enhance our communities.

the inaugural year of The Boyd Group, the direct predecessor to Boyd Gaming Corporation.

The California occupied 15.5 acres in downtown Las Vegas. The hotel, after expansion, contained nearly 800 guest rooms, while the casino, comprising 36,000 square feet of gaming space, featured 35 table games and 1,100 slot machines. Included within the hotel and casino complex were five restaurants and a recreational vehicle park capable of serving 95 vehicles, the only such facility in downtown Las Vegas. It was a fitting flagship property for the Boyds, a sizeable anchor for the stable of gaming complexes that would follow in its wake. After registering success with The California, the Boyds moved into largely uncharted territory, helping to create a third major gaming area in the greater Las Vegas region. Construction of Sam's Town Las Vegas began on 13 acres of desert at the intersection of Nellis Boulevard and Boulder Highway. The hotel and casino dwarfed The California, securing the Boyds' presence along what would become known as the Boulder Strip. Sam's Town opened in 1979, comprising a 648-room hotel and an approximately 130,000-square-foot casino with 12 restaurants. It was the first gaming resort to cater to local residents. Like The California, Sam's Town predominantly featured slot machines because slot machine wagering ranked as the most consistently profitable segment of the casino entertainment business.

The tenth anniversary of The California's grand opening was marked by the addition of two more Boyd hotel and gaming properties. In 1985, the company added its first casino on the Las Vegas Strip, the Stardust Resort and Casino, a hotel with more than 1,500 rooms and a gaming area measuring roughly 75,000 square feet. The Boyd Group also acquired the Fremont Hotel and Casino in 1985. Located in downtown Las Vegas, the Fremont consisted of a 450-room hotel and a 36,000-square-foot casino.

Aggressive Expansion During the 1990s

The addition of the Stardust and the Fremont gave the Boyds a total of four properties—the size of their company until the early 1990s. The pace of expansion accelerated during the 1990s, as the number of Boyd-operated properties nearly tripled during a six-year period. The beginning of this new, more ambitious era coincided with the end of another era. In 1993, Sam Boyd passed away, leaving behind a company set to record substantial physical growth. William Boyd, serving as chairman and chief executive officer, spearheaded the expansion, greatly increasing the company's geographic scope as state gambling restrictions eased.

Before shaping his company into a multi-jurisdictional operator, Boyd fleshed out the company's presence in Nevada. On the Boulder Strip, where the company's western-theme Sam's Town Hotel and Gambling Hall had helped establish a new major gaming area in Nevada, Boyd added two new properties, the Eldorado Casino and the Joker's Wild Casino. Neither of the two additions to the Boyd Group's portfolio included hotel operations, a first for the company. The Eldorado Casino, situated on four acres in downtown Henderson, was the smallest of the company properties, a distinction it would hold for the remainder of the 1990s. The gaming space measured 16,000 square feet, filled with 600 slot machines and 11 table games. As with the original Eldorado Club acquired in 1962, the Eldorado Casino drew its business primarily from Henderson residents. The Joker's Wild, situated on 13 acres of company-owned land on the Boulder Strip, contained 22,500 square feet of gaming space, featuring 625 slot machines, 11 table games, a restaurant, a sports bar, and an entertainment lounge. The facility drew the bulk of its business from local residents and from visitors to Las Vegas arriving via the Boulder Highway.

The third facility acquired in 1993 joined the company's fold in December. For $16.5 million, the company purchased the Main Street Station Casino, Brewery and Hotel, located in downtown Las Vegas. Closed at the time of its acquisition by the Boyd Group, the Main Street property underwent two years of renovation and expansion before opening in November 1996. At the property's grand opening, guests found a 406-room hotel, a restaurant, a café, a brew pub, and 28,500 square feet of gaming space, featuring 905 slot machines and 22 table games.

Moving Beyond Nevada: 1994

In 1994, the Boyd Group, renamed Boyd Gaming Corporation, took its first steps outside Nevada. In May, the company exported its western-theme hotel casino concept to Mississippi, opening a Sam's Town in Tunica County, Mississippi, roughly 25 miles south of Memphis, Tennessee. Featuring a 200-room hotel, a 92,000-square-foot casino, and four restaurants in its original incarnation, the property was within a 200-mile radius of a population of roughly three million adults, including residents of Nashville, Tennessee; Jackson, Mississippi; and Little Rock, Arkansas. A little more than six months after the hotel casino opened, an $18 million expansion project added 308 guest rooms, a swimming pool, and a recreational area, testifying to the property's success in Mississippi's dockside gambling market. Less than two years later, in 1996, the property was expanded again. A 350-room hotel tower was constructed, a 1,000-space parking garage was added, and the facility's gaming space was increased to 75,000 square feet.

Boyd Gaming moved into another market in 1994, investing in Treasure Chest Casino, a riverboat operation located on Lake Pontchartrain in Kenner, Louisiana, near the New Orleans International Airport. Boyd Gaming acquired a 15 percent interest in Treasure Chest and managed the property, which was modeled after an 18th-century Victorian-era, paddle-wheel riverboat. Capable of serving 1,750 customers, the Treasure Chest housed 24,000 square feet of gaming space and, after an $11 million expansion project in January 1996, featured an entertainment complex. In October 1997, Boyd Gaming assumed full ownership over the property, purchasing the 85 percent interest it did

Key Dates:

1941: Sam Boyd moves to Las Vegas.
1962: Boyd and his son William acquire the Eldorado Club.
1975: Boyd Gaming's first property, The California Hotel and Casino, opens.
1979: Sam's Town Hotel and Gambling Hall opens on the Boulder Strip.
1985: The Stardust Resort and Casino and the Fremont Hotel and Casino become Boyd Gaming properties.
1994: Boyd Gaming opens a hotel casino in Mississippi, its first property outside of Nevada.
1998: Company signs a joint venture agreement with Mirage Resorts (later MGM Mirage) to develop and own The Borgata, an Atlantic City hotel casino complex scheduled for completion in 2003.
2001: Delta Downs Racetrack is acquired.

not already own. Also in 1994, the company signed a management agreement to manage the Silver Star Resort and Casino, a casino located on tribal lands owned by the Mississippi Band of Choctaw Indians. Boyd Gaming began managing the Silver Star when the facility opened in July 1994, signing a seven-year agreement with the Choctaw. An expansion project completed during the late 1990s added a 505-room hotel to the property, which contained 90,000 square feet of gaming space. Boyd Gaming terminated its management contract before it was set to expire, ending its association with the Silver Star in January 2000.

Boyd Gaming's accelerated pace of expansion continued into 1995, resulting in one strategic acquisition and one miscue. The company's efforts to expand its gaming empire rarely failed, but in 1995 the company recorded a notable mistake. In September, the $70 million Sam's Town Kansas City opened, but after further investment, the property failed to meet expectations. Roughly three years later, in July 1998, the casino was closed. On a more positive note, the company added a new subsidiary in 1995, acquiring Vacations-Hawaii, a 43-year-old travel agency located on the Hawaiian Islands. Within six months of its affiliation with Boyd Gaming, Vacations-Hawaii began offering discounted nonstop charter service to Las Vegas that included exclusive vacation packages to Boyd Gaming's hotel casinos in the Las Vegas area. Initially, the charter service was offered twice per week, but in 1996 the schedule was increased to include six nonstop flights per week.

During the latter half of the 1990s, Boyd Gaming pursued expansion at a more leisurely pace, but the additions to the company's portfolio of properties were significant, nevertheless. In December 1996, another riverboat casino was acquired, the Par-A-Dice Riverboat Casino in East Peoria, Illinois. Located along the Illinois River, the casino, which originally opened in 1991, contained 33,000 square feet of gaming space and sat adjacent to the Par-A-Dice Hotel, a 208-room, full-service hotel.

The company's next significant move occurred in July 1998, when it signed a joint venture agreement with Mirage Resorts, Incorporated (which merged with MGM Grand in 2000 to become MGM Mirage). The two companies agreed to jointly develop and own a casino hotel entertainment complex in Atlantic City, New Jersey. The project—later named The Borgata—was enormous, evolving into a 40-story, $1 billion hotel casino with 2,010 guest rooms and 120,000 square feet of gaming space. The groundbreaking ceremony for the development was held in September 2000, with construction expected to be completed in time for The Borgata's grand opening in 2003.

The preparatory work required to turn The Borgata development into a reality was immense, but Boyd and his executive management team did not shy from pursuing other acquisition candidates. In November 1999, the company added its 12th property by acquiring the Blue Chip Casino, a riverboat casino in Michigan City, Indiana. Opened in 1997, the three-deck Blue Chip contained 37,000 square feet of gaming space and two restaurants, existing as one of five casino riverboats authorized to operate in Indiana along Lake Michigan.

The expected completion of The Borgata in 2003 promised to conclude a remarkable ten-year period of growth for Boyd Gaming. The company had entered 1993 with four properties to its name before embarking on an aggressive expansion campaign that tripled the number of its holdings by the decade's conclusion and increased its annual revenues to more than $2 billion by 2000. As the completion of The Borgata neared, the company continued to demonstrate a willingness to expand further. In May 2001, Boyd Gaming acquired the Delta Downs Racetrack, adding a new dimension to the company's gaming operations. Located near Vinton, Louisiana, Delta Downs was eligible under Louisiana law to operate slot machines, prompting Boyd Gaming to file for licenses to begin casino operations at the racetrack. With further acquisitions expected, the company pressed ahead, intent on making Boyd Gaming a national leader in the gaming industry.

Principal Subsidiaries

California Hotel and Casino Inc.; Boyd Tunica, Inc.; Boyd Kenner, Inc.; Boyd Louisiana L.L.C.; Boyd Mississippi, Inc.; Par-A-Dice Gaming Corporation; East Peoria Hotel, Inc.; Vacations-Hawaii; Boyd Atlantic City, Inc.

Principal Competitors

MGM Mirage; Mandalay Resort Group; Park Place Entertainment Corporation; Harrah's Entertainment, Inc.

Further Reading

''Boyd Gaming Receives License Approval from Louisiana State Racing Commission,'' *PR Newswire,* May 15, 2001, p. 36.
Kaberline, Brian, ''Sam's Town All Dressed Up with No Time to Open,'' *Kansas City Business Journal,* August 18, 1995, p. 3.
Kostelni, Natalie, ''Hitting the Jackpot,'' *Philadelphia Business Journal,* February 2, 2001, p. 12.
''Mirage, Boyd to Build Casino-Hotel,'' *Travel Weekly,* July 8, 1996, p. 24.
''Sam's Town Opens in Miss.,'' *Travel Weekly,* July 18, 1994, p. 66.

—Jeffrey L. Covell

British Airways PLC

Waterside, PO Box 365
Harmondsworth
Middlesex UB7 0GB
England
Telephone: (44) 20 8562 4444
Toll Free: (800) 247-9297 (U.S. only)
Fax: (44) 20 8759 4314
Web site: http://www.britishairways.com

Public Company
Incorporated: 1924 as Imperial Air Transportation, Ltd.
Employees: 65,157
Sales: £9.278 billion (US $13.151 billion) (2001)
Stock Exchanges: London New York Frankfurt Munich
Ticker Symbol: BAY (London); BAB (New York)
NAIC: 481111 Scheduled Passenger Air Transportation; 481112 Scheduled Freight Air Transportation; 56152 Tour Operators

British Airways PLC is the largest international airline in the world. It is based at Heathrow Airport in London, the busiest international airport in the world, and has a global flight network through partners such as American Airlines in the United States and Qantas in Australia. As the United Kingdom's sole global network carrier, it transports 36 million passengers a year to approximately 268 destinations and 97 countries.

Early History: Linking the British Empire

British Airways' earliest predecessor was Aircraft Transport & Travel, Ltd., founded in 1916. On August 25, 1919 this company inaugurated the world's first scheduled international air service with a converted de Havilland 4A day bomber leaving Hounslow (later Heathrow) Airport for London and also Le Bourget in Paris. Eight days later another company, Handley Page Transport, Ltd., started a cross-channel service between London's Cricklewood Field and both Paris and Brussels.

That same year Britain's advisory committee for civil aviation proposed plans for establishing a world airline network linking Britain with Canada, India, South Africa, Australia, and New Zealand. Because airplanes capable of crossing wide stretches of water were not yet available, the committee recommended that first priority be given to a route to India and be operated by a state-assisted private enterprise.

Progress was made quickly. Before the end of the year the British government was operating a service to Karachi and had established a network of 43 Royal Air Force (RAF) landing strips throughout Africa to the Cape of Good Hope. Meanwhile, strong competition from subsidized foreign airline companies had forced many of the private British air carriers out of business. By March 1921 all British airline companies had suspended their operations. The government intervened with a pledge to keep the British companies flying, using its own form of subsidization.

In January 1923 Parliament appointed the Civil Air Transport Subsidies Committee to form a single British international air carrier from existing companies. On March 31, 1924 Daimler Airway, British Marine Air Navigation, Instone Air Line, and Handley Page merged to become Imperial Air Transport.

In 1925 Imperial Airways operated a number of European routes while it surveyed a route across the Arabian desert from Cairo to Basra in present-day Iraq. The airline was faced with a number of problems on this route. The desert was featureless, making it easy to get lost. Water stops and meteorological and radio stations were difficult to maintain. Basra was a major terminal on the route to India. However, on January 7, 1927 the Persian government forbade Britain the use of its airspace, blocking all flights to India. Negotiations reopened this airspace two years later, but not before generating a demand for longer range aircraft.

Passengers flying to India flew from London via Paris to Basel, where they boarded a train for Genoa. Next, a flying boat took them on to Alexandria, where they flew in stages to Karachi. The passage to India, previously three weeks by sea, had been reduced to one week by air.

Imperial Airways' service to Calcutta was established in July 1933, to Rangoon in September, and to Singapore in December. In January of the following year, Australia's

Company Perspectives:

British Airways is all about bringing people together, and taking them wherever they want to go. This applies as much to our employees as the 36 million people who travel with us every year. The travel industry is notoriously competitive, and we have certainly had our share of challenges over the past few years. We believe we now have a firm strategy in place that gives us good cause for optimism going forward.

Queensland and Northern Territories Air Service (Qantas) inaugurated a route linking Singapore with Brisbane. The passage to Australia could be completed in 12½ days.

A commercial service through Africa was opened in 1931 with flying boats linking Cairo with Mwanza on Lake Victoria. In April 1933 the route was extended to Cape Town, the trip from London taking 10½ days. An east-west trans-African route from Khartoum in the Sudan to Kano in northern Nigeria was established in February 1936. This route completed a world network that linked nearly all the countries of the British Empire.

The primary source of revenue on the network was not from transporting passengers but mail. Nevertheless, an increase in demand for more passenger seating and cargo space generated a need for larger airplanes. Britain's primary supplier of flying boats, the Short Company, developed a new model designated the C-class, with 24 seats and weighing 18 tons. Since it had an increased range and flew 145 miles per hour, it was able to simply bypass ''politically difficult areas.'' The Short C-class went into service in October 1936. A year later Imperial Airways made its first trans-Atlantic crossing with a flying boat equipped with extra fuel tanks. It was Pan Am, however, that first scheduled a regular trans-Atlantic service, employing more sophisticated and updated Boeing airplanes.

World War II and Nationalization

Imperial Airways was formed with the intention of being Britain's ''chosen instrument'' for overseas air service. On its European services, however, Imperial was competing with the British Continental airline and an aggressive newcomer called British Airways, which had been created in October 1935 by the merger of three smaller airline companies. Three months later the company acquired a fleet of Lockheed 10 Electras, which were the fastest airplanes available. The competition from British Airways threatened the ''chosen instrument'' so much that in November 1937 a Parliamentary committee proposed the nationalization and merger of Imperial and British Airways. When the reorganization was completed on November 24, 1939, the British Overseas Airways Corporation (BOAC) was formed.

The creation of BOAC was overshadowed by the declaration of war on Germany the previous September. The Secretary of State for Air assumed control of all British air services, including BOAC. Within a year Italy had entered the war and France had fallen. Britain's air routes through Europe had been eliminated. British flying boats, however, continued to ferry personnel and war cargo between London and West Africa with an intermediate stop at Lisbon in neutral Portugal. The air link to Khartoum maintained Britain's connection to the ''Horseshoe Route,'' from Cape Town through East Africa, Arabia, India, and Singapore to Australia. When Malaysia and Singapore were invaded by the Japanese, BOAC and Qantas opened a nonstop service between Ceylon and Perth in western Australia. BOAC transported ball bearings from neutral Sweden using a route that was dangerously exposed to the German Luftwaffe. BOAC also operated a service for returning flight crews to North America after they delivered American- and Canadian-built aircraft to the Royal Air Force.

When the war ended, BOAC had a fleet of 160 aircraft and an aerial network that covered 54,000 miles. The South American destinations of BOAC were assigned to a new state-owned airline, British South American Airways (BSAA), in March 1946. Similarly, the European services were turned over to British European Airways (BEA) in August 1946. After the war, Britain reestablished its overseas services to the nations of its empire. Some of the nations that had recently gained their independence from Britain received advice (and often finance) from BOAC.

In order to remain competitive with the American airline companies, BOAC purchased Lockheed Constellations, the most advanced commercial aircraft of the day. They later added Boeing 377 Stratocruisers and Canadair Argonauts (modified DC-4s). BEA operated generally smaller airplanes and more frequent flights between the British Isles and Continental Europe. In 1948 it joined other Allied airline companies in the airlift to Berlin during the Soviet blockade.

Fleet Strategies: From the Comet to the Concorde

Following a series of equipment failures at BSAA, the Civil Aviation ministry declared that the company should reemerge with BOAC. On July 30, 1949, BSAA was absorbed by BOAC. Even though its passenger load had steadily increased, BOAC accumulated a debt of £32 million in the five years from 1946 to 1951. Much of this was due to ''recapitalization,'' or purchasing new equipment, including the British-built Handley Page Hermes and de Havilland's DH Comet 1, the world's first jetliners.

In January 1954 one of BOAC's Comets exploded near Elba in the Mediterranean. Another Comet crashed near Naples only 16 days after an investigation of the first crash was concluded. As a result, the Comet's certificate of airworthiness was withdrawn. An investigation determined that the Comet's pressurized cabin was inadequately designed to withstand low-air pressures at altitudes over 25,000 feet. When the airplane reached that altitude it simply exploded. The cabin was strengthened and the jet reintroduced in 1958 as the DH Comet 4.

The company was forced to purchase propeller-driven DC-7s to cover equipment shortages when delivery of its Britannia turboprops was delayed in 1956. When the Comet reentered service in 1958, BOAC found itself with two undesirable fleets of aircraft, which were later sold at a loss of £51 million.

South American operations were suspended in 1954 when the Comet was taken out of service. Operation of the route with shorter range aircraft was too costly. At the insistence of Argen-

Key Dates:

1916: Predecessor Aircraft Transport & Travel Ltd. is founded.
1919: The company inaugurates the world's first scheduled international air service.
1933: Service to India and Singapore is established.
1935: British Airways is formed by the merger of three smaller airline companies.
1939: British Airways and Imperial Airways are merged and nationalized to form British Overseas Airways Corporation (BOAC).
1949: British South American Airways (BSAA) is absorbed by BOAC.
1958: The first successful jet trans-Atlantic service is completed.
1962: BOAC and Air France agree to commit funds to build a supersonic transport (SST).
1967: BOAC establishes its second around-the-world route.
1974: The company is reorganized under the ''British Airways'' name.
1976: British Airways and Air France simultaneously inaugurate the first SST Concordes into service.
1987: British Airways is privatized.
1987: British Airways acquires British Caledonian (BCal).
1988: British Airways forms a marketing alliance with United Airlines that collapses two years later.
1992: British Airways purchases 44 percent of USAir Inc.
1997: The company sells its stake in USAir Inc.
1998: ''Oneworld'' global alliance is launched between British Airways, American Airlines, Qantas, Canadian Airlines, and Cathay Pacific—a group that eventually grows to eight members.
2000: British Airways' London Eye observation wheel opens; 3 million people ride the wheel in its first year of operation.

tina and Brazil, which claimed Britain had ''lost interest'' in South America, the routes were reopened in 1960. That same year the first of 15 Boeing 707 jetliners was delivered to BOAC.

British European Airways used a wide variety of aircraft for its operations and remained a good customer for British aircraft manufacturers. In 1964 the company accepted delivery of the first de Havilland Trident 1, a three-engine airliner capable of speeds up to 600 miles per hour. A few years later, when the company expressed an interest in purchasing a mixed fleet of Boeing 727s and 737s, it was instructed by the government to ''buy British'' instead. BEA complied, ordering BAC-111s and improved versions of the Trident.

BOAC's cargo traffic was growing at an annual rate of 27 percent. Nevertheless, a sudden and unexplained drop in passenger traffic during 1961 left many of the world's airline companies with ''excess capacity,'' or too many empty seats to fly profitably. At the end of the fiscal year BOAC's accumulated deficit had grown to £64 million. The losses, however, were underwritten by the British government, which could not allow its flag carrier to go bankrupt.

BOAC and Air France agreed to commit funds to build a supersonic transport (SST) in 1962. In June the company became associated with the Cunard Steamship Company. A new company, BOAC-Cunard Ltd., was placed in charge of the trans-Atlantic air services in an attempt to capture a larger portion of the American travel markets.

The British government published a ''White Paper'' (a statement of government policy) that recommended a drastic reorganization of BOAC. In response, the company's chairman, Sir Matthew Slattery, and the managing director, Sir Basil Smallpiece, resigned. Britain's minister for aviation appointed Sir Giles Guthrie as the new chairman and chief executive officer. Under Sir Giles Guthrie BOAC suspended its unprofitable services and rescheduled its equipment purchases and debt payments. After the financial situation had improved, the company continued to purchase new equipment and expand its flight network. In April of 1967 BOAC established its second around-the-world route and opened a new cargo terminal at Heathrow.

The company's sister airline, BEA, had been paying close attention to consumer marketing for vacationers. In 1967 the company created a division called BEA Airtours Ltd., offering complete travel packages to a number of vacation spots. In May 1969 BOAC opened a passage to Japan via the North Pole. The route was shortened even farther when the Soviet Union granted BOAC landing rights in Moscow and a Siberian airlane to Tokyo.

On March 31, 1972, after six years of record profits, BOAC announced that it no longer owed any money to the government. Later, on July 17, following several recommendations on further reorganization of the state-owned airline companies, management of BEA and BOAC were coordinated under a new government agency called the British Airways Group. On April 1, 1974 the two companies were merged and renamed British Airways. A second reorganization of the internal management structure occurred in 1977.

The first British Airways' Concorde was introduced in 1976. Jointly manufactured by British Aerospace and the French firm Aerospatiale, the supersonic Concorde was capable of carrying 100 passengers at the speed of 1,350 miles per hour at an altitude of 55,000 feet. A seven-hour flight from New York to London was cut nearly in half the time by the Concorde. British Airways employed additional Concordes on a number of international services, most notably London-Singapore, which was temporarily suspended through 1978 due to ''political difficulties.''

Road to Privatization in the 1980s

In 1980 Prime Minister Margaret Thatcher appointed Lord (John) King as the new chairman of British Airways. His stated assignment was to prepare the airline for privatization (sale to private stockholders). Lord King's first move was to adopt aggressive ''American-style'' marketing and management philosophies. As a result, he initiated a massive campaign to scale down the company and reduce costs. Additional unprofitable air services were terminated, and a staff reduction (begun under Lord King's predecessor, Roy Watts) was continued. A British Airways official told *Business Week* magazine, ''we had too many staff but couldn't get rid of them because of the unions.'' In order to utilize the excess labor, the company was forced to remain large. Lord King established a better relationship with labor, which had become more agreeable to layoffs and revisions of work rules. In three years the workforce was reduced from 60,000 to 38,000 without a strike.

On July 11, 1983, no fewer than 50 senior executives were fired. The company's chief executive officer, Colin Marshall, hired in their place a team of younger executives (mostly with non-airline business backgrounds). The new executive staff initiated a series of programs to improve punctuality and service at the airline, whose BA acronym stood in many customers' minds for "Bloody Awful." They hired Landor Associates, a successful San Francisco-based design firm with considerable experience with airlines, to develop an entirely new image for British Airways. The result was controversial. The British Airways coat of arms and portion of the Union Jack on the airplane's tail fin was bound to upset the more politically temperamental countries of the third world, which the company served. The familiar "Speedbird" logo, which harkened back to the days of Imperial Airways, was removed despite employee petitions to retain it.

British Airways also recognized a need to replace older airplanes in its fleet with more modern and efficient equipment. The company's Lockheed TriStars were sold to the RAF for conversion into tankers, and the BAC-111s were sold because they would violate new noise regulations. British Airways leased a number of airplanes until new purchases could be made after the privatization.

The company was plagued by its decision to retain separate European and overseas divisions. The result was a perpetuation of the previous management regimes of BEA and BOAC. To rectify this problem the operation was further divided into eight regional groups involved in three different businesses: cargo, charter, and tours. Each of the eight groups was given increased autonomy and responsibility for its business and profitability.

The Laker Airways Skytrain, an initially successful cut-rate trans-Atlantic airline, was forced to close down due to what its chairman, Freddie Laker, claimed was a coordinated attack by a number of airlines to drive the company into bankruptcy. Laker charged the companies, which included British Airways, with violations of antitrust laws. He later settled out of court for £48 million, but in a subsequent civil suit British Airways was also required to issue travel coupons to passengers who claimed they were hurt by the collapse of Laker Airways.

Ironically, in the mid-1980s the company began advocating the deregulation of European airlines in the belief that it could compete more effectively than its rivals. Air France and Lufthansa in particular were reluctant to participate, claiming that deregulation would endanger the delicate market balance which took so many years to establish.

In 1985 British Airways was made a public limited company, but its stock was retained by the government until such time that it could be offered to the public. The privatization of British Airways (which was limited to a 51 percent sale) was delayed by a number of problems. The company's chief domestic rival, British Caledonian, opposed British Airways' privatization, claiming that the company already controlled 80 percent of the domestic market and was too large to compete against. But British Airways' most significant obstacle to privatization involved reducing the debt that it accumulated during the 1970s, and increasing the company's profitability. In February 1987 the privatization was finally consummated when 720.2 million shares of British Airways stock were sold to the public for one billion pounds (US $1.47 billion).

Poised for International Growth: Acquisitions and Alliances

British Caledonian, or BCal, was formed in 1970 through the merger of Caledonian Airways and British United Airways. For many years, BCal was British Airways' only large domestic competitor, fighting vigorously under the direction of Sir Adam Thompson for more favorable operating rights from the British government. When Britain's Civil Aviation Authority recommended the reallocation of British Airways routes to BCal in 1984, Lord King threatened to resign. Instead, British Airways was instructed to trade its profitable Middle East routes for some of BCal's less profitable Latin American destinations. The Middle Eastern routes became much less popular during 1986 as a result of regional tensions and falling oil prices. BCal, which had been generating a fair profit, started to lose money and was faced with bankruptcy.

In July 1987 British Airways acquired BCal for £237 million in stock. The new airline had almost 200 aircraft, and by combining British Airways' 560,000-kilometer-route structure with BCal's unduplicated 110,000-kilometer network, now formed one of the largest airline companies in the world. Several smaller independent British airline companies unsuccessfully challenged the BA/BCal merger on the grounds that the new company would dominate both London's Heathrow and Gatwick Airports, forcing them to relocate to the less accessible and underdeveloped field at Stansted.

With its dominance of the home market secure for the time being, British Airways aggressively expanded in Europe, North America, and the Pacific Rim over the next several years, aiming to become a global airline. Its first foray into the lucrative U.S. market came in 1988 when it formed a marketing alliance with United Airlines designed to feed customers from one carrier to the other and vice versa. This partnership set the pattern for British Airways' expansion—it would not be based on forming new airlines outside England or acquiring them, but rather through strategic alliances. Nevertheless, this first partnership collapsed a little more than two years later when United became a direct competitor to British Airways once it had gained access to Heathrow in 1991, along with American Airlines. The two strongest airlines in the United States had purchased the Heathrow rights from the floundering Pan Am and TWA, immediately increasing competition in British Airways' home market.

While the alliance with United was still operating, British Airways suffered losses in Europe in 1990 and 1991 because of the Gulf crisis in the Middle East. Shortly after, in July 1991, it entered into an alliance with Aeroflot in Russia to create a new airline called Air Russia. After several false starts over the next few years, this venture never got off the ground. Additional proposed alliances failed for assorted other reasons. Officials from British Airways and KLM Royal Dutch Airlines held merger discussions in 1991 and 1992, but talks broke down over the valuation of the two firms. Later in 1992 British Airways attempted to purchase 44 percent of USAir Inc. for $750 million. American, United, and Delta Air Lines (the U.S. "Big Three") vigorously lobbied against the deal and demanded enhanced access to the British market if the deal was to be approved by the U.S. government. In December the USAir purchase was blocked.

That same month the first in a string of alliances was struck when the airline paid £450 million for 25 percent of Qantas, the Australia-based international airline. British Airways next acquired a 49.9 percent stake in the leading French independent carrier TAT European Airlines, and later launched a start-up in Germany called Deutsche BA with 49 percent ownership. Through these alliances, British Airways enhanced its position in the Pacific Rim and Europe. It now refocused its attention across the Atlantic where it restructured an offer for a piece of USAir into a $400 million purchase of 25 percent of the company. This alliance received U.S. government approval. The government also approved a code-sharing arrangement that enabled the partners to offer their customers a seamless operation when they use both airlines to reach their destination.

While all this dealmaking was going on abroad, British Airways faced an embarrassing and potentially costly fight at home with Richard Branson's upstart Virgin Atlantic Airlines. Since starting operations in the early 1980s, Virgin had made some inroads against British Airways primarily by focusing on customer service, something "Bloody Awful" BA had neglected for years. Branson filed suit against British Airways in 1991 alleging that British Airways had smeared Branson and his airline and conducted "dirty tricks" such as spreading rumors about Virgin's insolvency. In 1993 the suit was settled out of court with British Airways offering a public apology and paying £500,000 to Branson and £110,000 to Virgin. The case also led to the resignation of Lord King. Second-in-command Colin Marshall took over as chairman. Further litigation followed between the two rivals, most seriously a $1 billion antitrust suit brought by Virgin in the United States. Various suits damaged British Airways' reputation and led to comments such as the following from the *Economist:* "BA now looks . . . like an anxious, overbearing giant trying to squash a feisty little rival."

With its Virgin difficulties continuing, British Airways' overseas partners suffered huge losses: in 1993 Qantas lost $271 million, while in 1994 TAT lost $60 million and USAir lost $350 million. The situation at USAir was so grim that British Airways declared that they would hold back an additional $450 million investment in the firm until the carrier reestablished itself in the black. The alliance continued to deteriorate and in pursuit of more promising partnerships, British Airways eventually sold its stakes in USAir in 1997.

As it approached the long-awaited 1997 deregulation of the European airline industry, British Airways was on solid ground. In the process of becoming one of the largest airlines in the world, it had also managed to remain one of the most profitable.

In mid-1996 British Airways announced plans for a broad alliance with American Airlines. Under this plan, the two carriers would coordinate schedules and pricing, code-share (sell seats) and more importantly, share profits and revenues. Together they submitted a joint application to the U.S. Department of Transportation requesting approval of the proposed venture and granting antitrust immunity. Their plan was vehemently attacked by competitors on the basis that it would permit the two airlines to monopolize cross-Atlantic traffic between Heathrow and the U.S. Both airlines had, in fact, previously refused to relinquish takeoff and landing slots at Heathrow; combined, they would control 85 percent of the peak takeoff slots in the largest single aviation market in the world. Intermittent negotiations and attempts to secure antitrust immunity continued into 2001, with both airlines struggling to agree on terms more conducive to an "open skies" agreement between the two countries. Competitors United Airlines and Lufthansa had already secured antitrust immunity and had prospered from "open skies" between the U.S. and Germany. Air France and Delta Airlines now threatened to beat British Airways and American to the punch.

Separately, the "Oneworld" alliance formed in 1998 by British Airways and a group of others eventually became one of the most successful. Officially launched in February 1999 by British Airways, American Airlines, Qantas, Canadian Airlines, and Cathay Pacific, it provided an interchangeable network for frequent fliers to claim rewards. The group eventually grew to eight members and 23 affiliates by 2001, and collectively served more than 200 million passengers in 133 countries with 566 destinations.

British Airways continued to expand its network through a combination of new routes, code-sharing agreements, and franchise partnerships with both domestic and international carriers. By 2001 it had acquired CityFlyer Express and British Regional Airlines Group (BRAL), and a 9 percent stake in Spain's Iberia Airlines.

On the Brink: Preparing for Industry Consolidation and a Global Future

Starting in the mid-1990s, British Airways began investing in advanced information technologies to build a "virtual airline" to expedite ticketing, scheduling, and customer service functions. It also began outsourcing "non-core" operations that had been previously overstaffed—ground transport services, in-flight catering, and heavy-engine maintenance—to reduce costs and allow the company to refocus squarely on operating its air network. The outsourcing measures frustrated industrial relations and failed to significantly reduce employee numbers. Further, industry analysts speculated that the airline would be more vulnerable to an economic downturn because it would no longer have secondary sources of revenue to offset the accompanying downturn in air travel revenues. Not surprisingly, when the air travel market slowed in 1998, British Airways' net profits of $330 million dropped precipitously to $34 million.

Declining profitability during the late 1990s led the airline to concentrate on the premium market for business travelers. By combining fleet and network changes, it could increase the number of business passengers, lower costs, and cater to a more profitable section of the market.

Tapped for the role of chief executive in May 2000, Rod Eddington set out to reduce exposure in unprofitable and non-core areas, selling stakes in Air Liberté and even placing its own no-frills carrier, Go (launched only in 1998), on the market. Plans to build Gatwick into a second international hub were abandoned. Instead, unprofitable routes were suspended and key longhaul routes were relocated to Heathrow. Smaller aircraft, specifically Boeing 777s, would replace the older, larger aircraft and play a major role in a new fleet strategy. With bigger business travel sections, each new aircraft could seat a greater number of premium business travelers and help cut excess capacity. It was anticipated that by 2002 more than half of British Airways' fleet would consist of Boeing 777s.

In an effort to create a more appealing environment for its premium business travelers, British Airways invested in costly product and service enhancements. These included passenger seats that expanded into six-foot flat beds for in-flight sleeping; new state-of-the-art, in-flight entertainment; and modernized airport lounges with an upscale look and feel.

A veteran of Cathay Pacific and Ansett, Eddington's approach improved both operations and morale. During his first year, the airline faced a number of adversities. Following a tragic Air France Concorde accident in Paris in 2000, British Airways' entire Concorde fleet was grounded. In addition, foot-and-mouth disease caused a serious decline in travel and tourism in England, and rising oil prices doubled fuel prices.

A small highlight of 2000, the British Airways London Eye observation wheel opened in London. The London Eye, billed as the world's highest observation wheel, offers passengers panoramic views of the city from 450 feet above the river Thames. During the wheel's first year of operation, 3 million people rode.

By early 2001, the British Airways fleet and product strategy appeared to be working. Two positive trends had emerged: premium business traffic was on the rise and costs were on the decline. Pretax profits in 2000–2001 amounted to £145 million, a marked improvement over the previous year's £5 million. The impact of the U.S. economic slowdown remained to be determined, though, and the airline faced difficult conditions in both passenger and cargo markets. British Airways' fleet of seven Concordes was expected to return to service after a full year of safety modifications and further comfort upgrades. However, the terrorist attacks in New York City and Washington, D.C., in September 2001, added new levels of financial stress and uncertainty to the travel and airline industries.

European airlines found themselves on the brink of momentous change in 2001. The potential for industry-wide consolidation had begun to fuel discussions of cross-border alliances—even cross-border mergers—that would be necessary to survive the ensuing instability. British Airways was certain to take aggressive action in staking a claim. In June 2001, it resumed talks with KLM for a £5 billion merger between the two, which could create the world's third-largest airline. Chief Executive Eddington vowed to continue pressing European regulatory authorities to allow the cross-border consolidation process, declaring ''[Consolidation] is a lengthy process (it took 30 years in the United States), but it is both inevitable and necessary if we're to develop our position in the long-term. And I intend that British Airways will be in the vanguard of that process.''

Principal Subsidiaries

Air Miles Travel Promotions Ltd.; BA & AA Holdings Ltd. (90.0%); Bedford Associates Inc.; Britair Holdings Ltd.; British Airways Capital Ltd. (89.0%); British Airways (European Operations at Gatwick) Ltd.; British Airways Finance B.V.; British Airways Holdings Ltd.; British Airways Holidays Ltd.; British Airways Maintenance Cardiff Ltd.; British Airways Regional Ltd.; British Airways Travel Shops Ltd.; British Asia Airways Ltd.; CityFlyer Express Ltd.; Deutsche BA Luftfahrgesellschaft GmbH; Go Fly Limited; Speedbird Insurance Company Ltd.; The Plimsoll Line Ltd.; World Network Services Pvt Ltd.; Concorde International Travel Pty Ltd. (50.0%).

Principal Competitors

Deutsche Lufthansa AG; Societe Air France; American Airlines; KLM Royal Dutch Airlines; Singapore Airlines Limited; Scandinavian Airlines System; Swissair Group; Japan Airlines Company, Ltd.; UAL Corporation (United Airlines); Virgin Atlantic Airways Limited.

Further Reading

''Antitrust Implications: The British Airways-American Airlines Alliance,'' U.S. Senate Subcommittee on Antitrust, Business Rights, and Competition of the Committee on the Judiciary, 105th Congress, 1st session, April 22, 1997, p. 342.

Banks, Howard, *The Rise and Fall of Freddie Laker*, London: Faber, 1982, p. 155.

Campbell-Smith, Duncan, *The British Airways Story: Struggle for Take-Off*, London: Hodder and Stoughton, 1986, p. 327.

Corke, Alison, *British Airways: The Path to Profitability*, New York: St. Martin's Press, 1986, p. 145.

Doganis, Rigas, *The Airline Business in the Twenty-First Century*, New York: Routledge, 2001, p. 256.

Done, Kevin, ''BA and American Joint Venture Plan Faces Criticism,'' *Financial Times*, July 23, 2001, p. 14.

Done, Kevin, and Mark Odell, ''BA and American Under Pressure on Joint Venture,'' *Financial Times, posted* July 30, 2001, http://www.newsft.com.

Dwyer, Paula, ''Air Raid: British Air's Bold Global Push,'' *Business Week,* August 24, 1992, pp. 54–60.

Dwyer, Paula, and Keith L. Alexander, ''Sky Anxiety: Faltering Partners Are Shaking British Airways' Strategy of Global Alliances,'' *Business Week,* March 21, 1994, p. 38.

Gurassa, Charles, ''BA Stood for Bloody Awful,'' *Across the Board,* January 1995, pp. 55–56.

Kindel, Stephen, ''Economies of Scope,'' *Financial World,* September 14, 1993, pp. 42–43.

Lynn, Matthew, ''Battle of the Atlantic,'' *Management Today,* November 1991, p. 48.

Palmer, Jay, ''The British Are Coming: By Slashing Costs, Selling Comfort and Forging Alliances, British Airways Has Made Itself a Contender in the Battle to Rule the Skies,'' *Barron's,* December 12, 1994, pp. 29–34.

Penrose, Harald, *Wings Across the World: An Illustrated History of British Airways*, London: Cassell, 1980, p. 304.

Simensen, Ivar M., ''BA, KLM Seen Back in Merger Talks,'' *Financial Times MarketWatch*, posted June 10, 2001, http://www.newsft.com.

Wada, Isae, ''Going Global: BA Chief Executive Outlines Carrier's Expansion Plans,'' *Travel Weekly,* September 6, 1990, pp. 1–3.

''We Are Flying into Turbulence,'' *Economist,* March 4, 1995, pp. 64–66.

—updates: David E. Salamie, Suzanne Selvaggi

Bull S.A.

68, route de Versailles
78430 Louveciennes
France
Telephone: (+33) 1-39-66-60-60
Fax: (+33) 1-39-66-60-62
Web site: http://www.bull.com

Public Company
Incorporated: 1933 as Compagnie des Machines Bull
Employees: 17,209
Sales: EUR 3.24 billion ($2.83 billion) (2000)
Stock Exchanges: Euronext Paris Dusseldorf Frankfurt
Ticker Symbol: BUL
NAIC: 541511 Custom Computer Programming Services; 541513 Computer Facilities Management Services; 541512 Computer Systems Design Services.

Bull S.A., once France's spearhead to counter the global computing dominance of IBM, is redefining itself for the 21st century as a streamlined information technology (IT) services and systems integration company. Since its restructuring, begun at the end of 2000, Bull has reorganized along two primary, autonomous businesses: Integris, its services arm, accounting for 49 percent of the company's 2000 annual sales of EUR 3.24 billion; and Bull Infrastructure & Systems, inheriting the company's background in servers and other computer and IT infrastructure systems, which generated 30 percent of sales. In February 2001, the company surprised the computer industry by selling off its pioneering smart-card division, CP8, to Schlumberger for $325 million. More than 80 percent of Bull's sales come from its European base, with 40 percent of total sales generated in France alone. Despite several decades of operations in the United States, the North American market added only 7 percent of the company's sales in 2000. Bull is led by CEO and Chairman Guy de Panafieu. The company's major shareholders include the French government, France Telecom, NEC, and Motorola.

Computing Pioneer in the 1930s

The origins of Bull lie in the need of insurance companies to process their voluminous data quickly. In 1919 a young Norwegian engineer named Fredrik Rosing Bull invented a counting and sorting machine for his employer, the Store-brand Insurance Company of Oslo. The machine used punch cards to tabulate figures at a rate which, though slow by modern standards, far exceeded the output of Storebrand's best secretaries. Bull did not live to enjoy the fruits of his ingenuity, dying in 1925 at the age of 43. Several years later the employee of a French bank, Georges Vieillard, was asked to develop a better adding machine. He discovered that the patents to Bull's tabulator were held by a Norwegian cancer clinic. Vieillard bought the patents for about $4,000—though he continued to pay royalties for many years—and subsequently founded a Paris company to develop and market the Bull machines. Vieillard quickly ran out of money and turned for help to his punch card supplier, Papeteries Aussedat. The latter was owned by the Callies family, who promptly formed a joint venture with Vieillard called Compagnie des Machines Bull. By 1935 Bull had launched its first significant line, the 150 series of tabulators, and thus found itself locked in a struggle with the French subsidiary of IBM.

For the remainder of the 1930s Bull grew at a modest rate. Most of its customers were banks, nearly all of them French. The company's real expansion came only after World War II had spurred the French scientific community to develop a rudimentary computing machine. Bull seized on this technology immediately after the war, forming alliances with Olivetti and Exacta in Italy and West Germany to develop the computer's business and military potential. In 1951 the company introduced the world's first germanium-diode computer, the Gamma 3, and its sales began a swift climb from $1.5 million in 1950 to $92 million in 1963. By the mid-1950s Bull had wrested 50 percent of the French market from IBM. It opened sales centers across Europe and in Latin America and became a source of considerable pride for the French business community. Bull even exported computer parts to the United States under the Remington Rand name, further proof that the company had earned its skyrocketing stock value. At decade's end, with George Vieillard still managing the firm and the Callies family supplying capital strength, Bull's future appeared assured.

In retrospect, however, it is clear that the company made a significant blunder in 1956. Responding to IBM's introduction of new technology, Bull outlined plans for a new, very large,

Company Perspectives:

"As an IT solutions company, we at Bull help our customers to become even more efficient and productive through the use of advanced information technology. We help them to reach new frontiers in operational performance and excellence and we help them to work faster and better to meet the challenges of the net economy."

—Guy de Panafieu, chairman and CEO

very fast computer to be available by 1960, and called for that reason the Gamma 60. In effect, IBM had raised the ante, and Bull eagerly matched the pot, its confidence high after a run of record-setting profits. Bull, however, had reached the limit of resources—the Gamma 60 was slow in development, late in delivery, and plagued by a series of mechanical flaws.

By 1962, with IBM's surge continuing unabated, Bull began to feel a profit squeeze. Realizing that international competition demanded international cooperation, the company signed long-term R&D agreements with Honeywell, NEC, and RCA; but these were no immediate help, and by late 1963 Bull's situation was grave. That year the company lost $25 million and could hope to save itself only by merging with a wealthy suitor. General Electric (GE), which coveted Bull's computer experience and worldwide marketing base, offered to buy into the ailing company.

French President Charles de Gaulle forbade the deal, however, because Bull was crucial to the development of French nuclear weapons and therefore could not be tied to any foreign powers. For a precarious year Gaullist nationalism strove with capitalist reality, but the issue was never really in doubt: to compete with IBM, Bull needed the financial muscle and knowhow that GE could offer. In 1964 GE paid $43 million for its 66 percent of the partnership, the French government created a separate company for military research, and together GE and Bull—minus the ousted Callies family—set out to battle IBM.

New Owners for the 1970s

IBM proved to be more than a match for the new partners, and GE's computer venture lasted only a few years. By the end of the 1960s, though Bull-GE was finally showing a profit, the U.S. partner had lost its stomach for the endless struggle with IBM and sold all seven of its computer manufacturing plants to Honeywell. The purchase changed Bull's name once again, this time to Honeywell Bull (HB). The new marriage lasted a bit longer and was somewhat more successful than the Bull-GE association. Honeywell was the second largest computer-maker in the United States, and with its technical experience and financial support was able to raise HB's sales to about $500 million in 1974. At that time the company controlled 17.3 percent of the French computer market, behind IBM but well ahead of relative newcomer Compagnie Internationale de l'Informatique (Cii). The latter had been hastily assembled in 1966 by de Gaulle in response to GE's purchase of Bull, and by the mid-1970s it was apparent that the government wanted to unite France's two native computer companies. In 1976 the merger was effected, with the French state owning 53 percent of the newly christened Cii-HB, and Honeywell the remaining 47 percent.

At this juncture, Cii-HB was still predominantly a mainframe manufacturer and had trouble posting profits. In 1980 sales hit $1.3 billion but net income remained a slim $29 million, and in the following year the company lost money. Honeywell was therefore perhaps not greatly disturbed to learn in 1981 that its share of Cii-HB had become the target of President François Mitterand's new Socialist government. Mitterand wanted to make Cii-HB a fully nationalized concern, and in 1981 signed a contract calling for a gradual buyout of Honeywell's stake in the consortium. Honeywell and the again-renamed Compagnie des Machines Bull would continue to share research and development, however, along with their longstanding partner NEC. Bull surprised most observers by announcing that it was committed to a program of worldwide acquisitions designed to strengthen its microcomputer and office products divisions.

As new Chairman Jacques Stern had predicted, Bull climbed out of the red by 1985 and continued its aggressive tactics. With NEC supplying the processors for a new line of mainframes—the DPS9—and the Bull Questar and Micral lines providing office equipment and microcomputer solutions, the French company soon emerged as a well-rounded international computer maker. Bull still lacked a major opening to the U.S. market, for which reason in 1987 it hooked up with its old partners in a new venture, the Massachusetts-based Honeywell Bull.

Bull acquired 42.5 percent of Honeywell's $1.85 billion computer business at the same time that NEC bought 15 percent, and Honeywell kept 42.5 percent for itself. The deal signaled Honeywell's retreat from the IBM battleground, emphasized the following year when Bull bought up another 22.6 percent of the joint venture and renamed it Bull HN Information Systems. Groupe Bull Chairman Stern thus found himself with a two-headed corporation. Bull HN operated in the United States and Bull S.A., out of Paris; in 1989 Groupe Bull further solidified its U.S. base with the $1.4 billion purchase of Zenith's microcomputer interests, Zenith Data Systems. The resulting firm was truly a worldwide consortium. Two years later, Bull took full control of Bull HN.

Restructuring: 1990s–2000s

Profits again dipped and then disappeared in 1989. Francis Lorentz, elected chairman and CEO in 1989, attempted to bring his company's goals into focus. Even with the government's help—Mitterand had fed Bull over $1 billion in capital between 1983 and 1990—Bull proved unable to continue selling everything from micros to mainframes, and slipped into a long period of losses that ended only in 1995. By 1991, the company was forced to turn to the French government, which provided Bull with a nearly FFr 10 billion rescue package.

By then, Lorentz had been ousted, eventually replaced by Jean-Marie Descarpentries, who led the company on a vast streamlining effort beginning in 1993. In that year, the company bought a nearly 20 percent share in Packard Bell, then transferred its Zenith Data Systems to the fast-growing desktop PC company. By 1995, Bull's streamlining effort—which included

Key Dates:

1921: Fredrik Rosing Bull invents punch card-based adding and sorting machine.
1933: Paul Vieillard acquires Bull patents and founds Compagnie des Machines Bull.
1935: Company launches the Bull 150 line of tabulators.
1951: Company introduces first germanium-diode computer, the Gammer 3.
1964: GE acquires 66 percent of Bull.
1966: French government creates Compagnie Internationale de l'Informatique (Cii).
1969: Honeywell acquires Bull, which is renamed Honeywell Bull.
1976: Honeywell Bull merges with Cii, leaving the French state in control of 53 percent of the newly christened Cii-HB, and Honeywell, the remaining 47 percent.
1979: Cii-HB develops first smart-card technology.
1982: French government, led by François Mitterand, completes buyout of Bull, which reverts to its original name.
1989: Company acquires Zenith Data Systems (ZDS), the microcomputer business of Zenith, for $1.4 billion.
1993: Company acquires 20 percent of Packard Bell.
1998: Compagnie des Machines Bull changes name to Bull S.A.
2001: Bull sells its smart-card division, CP8, to Schlumberger for $325 million.

cutting much of the company's bloated organization, including reducing its number of Parisian facilities from 25 to just five offices—enabled it to eke out a small profit.

Meanwhile, Bull had continued to launch innovative products, including its DCM architecture, introduced in 1991 and serving as the basis for its OpenMaster integrated systems and network management software; and Escala, the first server built around the PowerPC processor, launched in 1994. That year also saw the release of a CMOS featuring 4.7 million transistors, and leading the way to the introduction of the first fifth-generation CMOS-based mainframe computer in 1997. By then, the company had also introduced a Unix-based mainframe, Sagister.

Descarpentries stepped down in 1997, replaced by Guy de Panafieu as CEO and chairman. Panafieu quickly launched Bull on a new restructuring as the company moved closer to becoming a market specialist. Bull now launched a new investment campaign, solidifying its operations as it focused more tightly on services, servers, and software. At the same time, the company began shedding employees. Yet in 1998, Bull added a new unit, the smart card operations of NBS Technology, and then transferred its software development arm to the United States. That year, also, the company shortened its name to Bull S.A.

Its new restructuring proved costly for the company as Bull saw its profits once again wiped out. By the end of its 1999 fiscal year, the company's losses had mounted to EUR 288 million. Losses continued into 2000, once again topping the EUR 200 million mark. Nonetheless, the company was coming closer to achieving a new corporate identity, which was revealed near the end of the 2000 year. At that time, Bull announced its decision to regroup its operations into two autonomous business units, a services arm, named Integris, and an infrastructure and systems integration wing, Bull Infrastructure & Systems. Bull quickly moved to beef up its newly defined core operations, launching a new subsidiary, Evidian, for the development of e-business security systems software, and acquiring Osis, a specialist consultancy with expertise in systems and telecommunications, and Italy's Arcanet, that country's leading developer of software for the telecommunications industry.

Not all of Bull's reorganization moves were greeted with enthusiasm. Its February 2001 sale of its CP8 smart-card division to Schlumberger for $325 million helped raise the company's cash flow, but also attracted criticism from some industry observers. As one analyst told the *International Herald Tribune:* ''It's the beginning of the end for Bull. They used to sell noncore assets; now they're selling their crown jewel.'' Whether Bull's refocus was to become the end of an era or the beginning of a new future, the company continued to make its mark on computing history into the new century.

Principal Subsidiaries

Bull S.A. (97.5%); OGIC; SOFOM; European Computer Industry Research Centre (Germany; 33.3%); Evidian; Bull International NV (Netherlands); Bull HN Information Systems Inc. (U.S.A.).

Principal Operating Units

Integris; Bull Infrastructure & Systems.

Principal Competitors

Accenture Ltd.; Acer Inc.; Atos Origin; Cap Gemini Ernst & Young; CMG plc; Compaq Computer Corporation; Computer Associates International, Inc.; Computer Sciences Corporation; Dell Computer Corporation; Electronic Data Systems Corporation; Finsiel S.p.A.; Fujitsu Limited; Gateway, Inc.; Getronics NV; GFI Informatique SA; International Business Machines Corporation; International Computers Limited; Logic Plc; NEC Corporation; Sema Group; Siemens AG; Sopra SA; Group Steria SCA; Sun Microsystems Inc.; Toshiba Corporation; Unilog SA; Unisys Corporation.

Further Reading

Brandel, Mary, ''Left for Dead: But They're Still ALIVE!'' *Computerworld*, November 7, 1994.
Connell, James, ''Bull Gets a Bid,'' *International Herald Tribune*, January 4, 2001.
''Facts and Figures,'' Paris: Groupe Bull, 1989.
Floren, Paul, ''France's Bull to Move Software Unit to US,'' *International Herald Tribune*, February 14, 1998.
''Machines Bull's Computer Crisis,'' *Fortune*, July 1964.
''Schlumberger to Buy Bull's Smart Card Unit for $325 Million,'' *Semiconductor Business News*, February 9, 2001.

—Jonathan Martin
—update: M.L. Cohen

Cahners Business Information

350 Hudson Street, 4th Floor
New York, New York 10014
U.S.A.
Telephone: (212) 519-7700
Fax: (212) 519-3768
Web site: http://www.cahners.com

Wholly Owned Subsidiary of Reed Elsevier plc
Incorporated: 1998
Employees: 6,000
Sales: $900 million (2000 est.)
NAIC: 511120 Periodical Publishers; 514191 On-Line Information Services

Cahners Business Information publishes trade, or ''business-to-business,'' magazines serving the media, manufacturing, electronics, construction, and retail industries. Cahners Business publishes more than 135 magazines, bearing titles such as *Variety*, *Broadcasting & Cable*, *Construction Equipment*, *Hotel & Travel Index*, *Publishers Weekly*, and *Pharmaceutical Laboratory*. The company also publishes information and marketing solutions through more than 125 webzines and web portals. A member of the London-based Reed Elsevier plc group, Cahners Business complements its print and online publications with an extensive roster of directories, research, and direct-marketing lists.

Origins

Cahners Business was formed in 1998, its birth created by the combination of three companies—Cahners Publications, Chilton Publications, and Reed Travel Group—owned by the nearly $6 billion-in-sales Anglo-Dutch conglomerate Reed Elsevier plc. The history of the Cahners name stretches back well before 1998, however, as do the histories of Chilton and Reed Travel.

Of the three companies, Chilton Publications is the eldest, formed in 1904 by two partners who owned a printing operation and published a bicycle parts magazine. The partners chose the name Chilton from a passenger list of the 1620 voyage of the *Mayflower,* one of their first printing jobs. Through the years, Chilton Publications developed into a major publisher of do-it-yourself manuals, automotive guides, and specialty business publications such as *American Metal Market* and *Motor Age*.

Reed Travel traces its roots to 1928, when Elwood Ingledue created the first hotel referral system. He published 70 hotel brochures, each bearing the name *Hotel Informant,* which were displayed on racks in hotel lobbies in California. Following the success of the *Hotel Informant*, Ingledue published the *Hotel Index* and the *Travel Index* in 1929. The two titles were later merged, creating the *Hotel & Travel Index*, which proved to be an indispensable aid to travel agents across the globe. The *Hotel & Travel Index* was acquired by Ziff Davis during the latter half of the 1960s, one of a series of acquisitions he completed during the period. Combined, Davis's acquisitions formed The Travel Group, which was later acquired by publishing magnate Rupert Murdoch. In 1989, Murdoch sold the group to Reed International, the English half of Reed Elsevier plc.

Cahners Publications, distinct from Cahners Business, got its start shortly after the end of World War II. The company's first magazine, *The Palletizer* (renamed *Modern Materials Handling*), was started by Norman Cahners. Cahners and an ex-U.S. Navy ordnance officer named Saul Goldweitz developed Cahners Publications into a formidable trade magazine publisher and trade show management company, achieving enviable success during the 1960s, when the trade magazine industry was expanding rapidly. Cahners Publications developed a reputation as one of the first niche publishing firms, emerging as a pioneer in the publication of magazines with sharply focused, specialty subject matters. The trade magazines, which were distributed according to a system known as ''controlled circulation,'' subsisted entirely on revenue derived from advertisers.

All three of the companies that came together to form Cahners Business experienced a number of changes in ownership. Cahners Publications began as an independent company before London-based Reed International acquired a 29 percent stake in the company in 1970. By 1977, Cahners Publications was a wholly owned subsidiary of Reed International. After changing hands from Ziff Davis to Rupert Murdoch, the Travel Group joined Reed International in 1989, operating under the

Company Perspectives:

Cahners' purpose is to provide essential business information to our markets. We deliver this information in the form that is most effective for business people to use in making business decisions. The quality and timeliness of this information allow us to forge strong relationships with readers and users. These relationships make us a powerful marketing partner with our advertisers. Balancing short-term profits with longer-term shareholder value, we are committed to growing our business. We strive to establish values, practices and policies that make us the preferred employer in our industry. We strive to create a business environment that allows us to offer unparalleled service to our customers.

same corporate umbrella as Cahners Publications. Chilton Publications fell under the stewardship of several parent companies, beginning with the American Broadcasting Corporation before being sold to Capital Cities and then later to Walt Disney Company. The merger of the three companies occurred under the direction of a new parent company, created in 1993.

Formation of Reed Elsevier: 1993

In 1993, Reed International and a Dutch company named Elsevier NV created a joint venture company named Reed Elsevier plc. As part of Reed International, Cahners Publications and the Reed Travel Group became part of the new company, although each business operated separately. Under the Anglo-Dutch management of Reed Elsevier, Cahners Publications was instructed to complete a number of divestitures. In 1995 the Reed Elsevier subsidiary sold its consumer magazines—14 titles, including such names as *Modern Bride* and *Sail*—for an estimated $160 million. Reed Elsevier's vice-president of finance explained the reasoning behind Cahners Publications' withdrawal from the consumer sector, remarking in a December 1998 interview with *Folio*, ''We made the decision to exit all cyclical consumer markets and put those proceeds into higher margin science, professional, and business titles.''

Roughly a year after Cahners Publications exited the consumer magazine market, the company gained the leader who would oversee the merger of the three Cahners Business companies. In May 1996, Bruce Barnet was appointed president and chief executive officer of Cahners Publications. Oddly, given the company's recent withdrawal from the consumer sector, Barnet's career was steeped in consumer magazine publishing. He had spent 22 years at Time Inc., serving, during one period, as president of Time Asia. Barnet left the Time organization in 1990, becoming president of Riordan Publishing, then president and chief executive officer of Cowles Enthusiast Media. Barnet's selection as president and chief executive officer of Cahners Publications represented his first job in trade publishing.

Barnet's first major task at Cahners Publications was a formidable one. In September 1997, Cahners Publications acquired Radnor, Pennsylvania-based Chilton Publications, paying ABC Inc., a subsidiary of Walt Disney Company, $447 million. At the time of the acquisition, Cahners Publications published 90 titles and Chilton Publications published 39 magazines, covering subjects related to the automotive, jewelry, eye care, entertainment, manufacturing, and food industries. Barnet was charged with integrating Chilton Publications' magazines and its research operations, Chilton Marketing Research Co., into the Cahners Publications organization, but first a name change was deemed in order. Reed Elsevier executives were keen to establish the name of their company in the United States, prompting them to christen the combination of Chilton Publications and Cahners Publications as Reed Elsevier Business Information.

The new corporate banner did not fly for long. Barnet disliked the new name, expressly because the Reed Elsevier name was relatively unknown in the United States. The Cahners name, however, enjoyed widespread recognition among readers and, perhaps most important, among advertisers. Barnet convinced his superiors at the London offices of Reed Elsevier to capitalize on the Cahners cachet, resulting in the switch to Cahners Business Information as the company's corporate title in March 1998.

Debut of Cahners Business Information: 1998

By the time Reed Elsevier executives had settled on a new name—after reportedly sifting through more than 2,000 names—Reed Travel Group had joined the fold. In September 1997, the same month the Chilton Publications acquisition was completed, Reed Travel Group became mired in a scandal involving the fraudulent over-reporting of circulation figures for its magazines, according to *Folio.* In response, Reed Elsevier, as the group's parent company, put Reed Travel under Barnet's control in January 1998, at which time the business was renamed Cahners Travel Group.

Against the backdrop of acquisitions, mergers, and restructuring efforts, Barnet applied himself to the difficult task of integrating Chilton Publications into Cahners Business. From late 1997 through 1998, Barnet completed a number of divestitures. In November 1997, the first group of magazines was sold to the Washington Post Company. The sale involved the company's 24-title computer group, which included trade journals such as *Reseller Management* and *Government Computer News.* The motivation behind the divestitures echoed the reasoning offered by Reed Elsevier officials in 1995. ''The concept was to emphasize and prioritize markets,'' Barnet told *Folio* in December 1998. ''In doing so,'' he continued, ''we had to readjust portfolios and eliminate those titles not worth investing in.'' Along with the divestitures came additions to Cahners Business' library of magazine titles. The company acquired *Gifts & Decorative Accessories* and *Playthings*, among others, and started several new publications on its own, such as *Pharmaceutical Laboratory* and *Digital TV.* The company also launched a host of web sites in a bid to bolster its online presence. The most ambitious web site was Manufacturing Marketplace, which contained content culled from 26 titles. In all, the company launched 14 new properties in 1997 and 1998, giving it an approximate total of 130 magazine titles, 140 web sites, and hundreds of directories and newsletters.

Cahners Business entered the last year of the decade as a company generating nearly $1 billion in annual revenue. By all measures, the company ranked as an industry giant, but the

Key Dates:

1904: Chilton Publications is formed.
1928: Predecessor to Reed Travel Group is formed when Elwood Ingledue launches the *Hotel Informant.*
1946: Cahners Publications launches its first magazine.
1977: Reed International completes acquisition of Cahners Publications.
1989: Rupert Murdoch sells a group of travel magazines to Reed International, forming Reed Travel Group.
1993: Reed Elsevier plc is formed.
1997: Cahners Publications acquires Chilton Publications.
1998: Cahners Business Information, comprising Cahners Publications, Chilton Publications, and Reed Travel Group, is formed.
2000: Marc Teren is appointed chief executive officer of Cahners Business.

1990s ended on a sour note primarily because of problems stemming from the acquisition of Chilton. Critics claimed Cahners Business had paid too much for the publisher. Other industry experts noted that Barnet had failed to integrate Chilton Publications' operations into Cahners Business. Some observers pointed to the uneasy relationship between the English and Dutch halves of Reed Elsevier as one cause for Cahners Business' anemic financial performance. Tension between the two sides had existed, according to numerous reports, since the joint-venture company was created in 1993, which, the pundits claimed, disabled Barnet's efforts to effectively manage Cahners Business.

Whatever the cause, there was little doubt as to the existence of a problem. Sales had flattened, leading to a 45 percent decline in operating profit during the first half of 1999 compared to the same period in 1998. In September 1999, Barnet resigned, leaving after a five-week period in which 400 jobs were eliminated. According to the business press, it was unclear whether Barnet was forced to resign or the decision was his; Reed Elsevier offered little public explanation. In a brief statement to the press, Reed Elsevier said Barnet left ''to pursue other investment and business opportunities.'' As part of the layoffs, 100 jobs were eliminated at the company's Radnor office, the home of Chilton Publications. Another 100 employees were asked to transfer to other locations, as the company relocated the production of 11 magazines, moving them from Radnor to offices across the country. Several titles were sold as well, including agreements to sell *Review of Optometry*, *Review of Ophthalmology*, and *Eyewear* in August 1999, and *Energy User News* the following month.

In the wake of Barnet's departure, Bruce Nairn, who had recently been appointed chief operating officer, took over as acting chief executive officer. A search was begun for a new, permanent chief executive officer, ending in January 2000 when Cahners Business announced it had hired Marc Teren. Before joining Cahners Business, Teren worked at Walt Disney Company, where he had general management responsibilities for Disney Interactive. After leaving the Disney organization, Teren served as chief executive officer of washingtonpost.newsweek.com, the new media arm of the Washington Post Co. His experience earned him the reputation of an Internet savvy executive, a talent that was sorely needed at Cahners Business. The company had been slow to embrace the Internet, according to some observers, and the selection of Teren suggested the realization of such a shortcoming.

With Teren at the helm, an era that officially began in February 2000, Cahners Business adopted a more focused, Internet-oriented approach to publishing. Two acquisitions early in Teren's tenure signaled the company's new strategy. The smaller of the two acquisitions was completed in June 2000, when Cahners Business purchased an application service provider and web site design firm named eLogic Corp. for $79 million. In March 2000, one month after Teren joined Cahners Business, the company purchased $126-million-in-sales, Atlanta, Georgia-based CMD Group for approximately $300 million. A publishing and data business, CMD Group provided project, product, and cost data to the construction industry in North America, Australia, and Scandinavia. The company published more than 100 regional editions of construction market data, as well as a directory of more than 20,000 architectural firms called ProFile, which published in print and on the Internet.

The addition of eLogic and CMD Group, among other acquisitions, strengthened Cahners Business' presence as an Internet company. Divestitures completed during the same period sharpened the company's strategic focus. Teren reorganized the company into three units of specialization, each with its own president who was responsible for roughly $300 million worth of business. The three areas of focus were manufacturing/electronics, media, and construction/retail. As part of this reorganization, certain divestitures were made, shedding the company of businesses that did not fit into the new structure. In January 2001, a group of food and industrial publications was sold, followed by two groups of automotive titles in March 2001.

As Teren guided Cahners Business into the first decade of the 21st century, he focused on the company's core brands and their relation to the Internet. In an interview with *ADWEEK Eastern Edition* on May 7, 2001, Teren said: ''The most important thing that was happening on the Internet was not about the revenue but the perception that on the Internet, with that distribution vehicle, someone else's brand position was more relevant to readers and advertisers than the trusted brands that we owned. It was the usurping of that position that accelerated all our investment levels.'' Looking ahead, further acquisitions were expected, as Teren strove to make Cahners Business the number one or number two publisher in each of its markets.

Principal Subsidiaries

A.F. Lewis and Company Inc.; Cahners New Product Information; Daily Variety Ltd.; TRACOM Corp.

Principal Competitors

PRIMEDIA, Inc.; VNU USA Inc.; Advance Publications, Inc.; Crain Communication Inc.

Further Reading

Adams, Mark, "The Big 3," *ADWEEK Eastern Edition,* May 7, 2001, p. SR8.

Bishop, Todd, "Cahners in Midst of Companywide Reorder," *Philadelphia Business Journal,* August 27, 1999, p. 4.

"Cahners to Acquire CMD Group for $299.5 Million," *Business Publisher,* March 31, 2000, p. 1.

Callahan, Sean, "Cahners CEO Exits Company Amid Restructuring," *Business Marketing,* October 1, 1999, p. 4.

Freeman, Laurie, "Reed Elsevier Reinstates Cahners Name, Publisher Sees Strength in Original Brand After Weighing Alternatives," *Business Marketing,* March 1998, p. 3.

Harvey, Mary, "Why Marc Teren Matters," *Folio: The Magazine for Magazine Management,* September 2000, p. 32.

Holliday, Heather, "Cahners Cuts Another 101 Jobs," *Folio: The Magazine for Magazine Management,* October 1999, p. 22.

Kostelni, Natalie, "Chilton Deal Near," *Philadelphia Business Journal,* January 21, 2000, p. 8.

Russell, Anne M., "Cahners: The Fast-Moving Company," *Folio: The Magazine for Magazine Management,* December 1998, p. 32.

—Jeffrey L. Covell

CASUAL CORNER®

Casual Corner Group, Inc.

100 Phoenix Avenue
Enfield, Connecticut 06083-1700
U.S.A.
Telephone: (860) 741-0771
Toll Free: (800) 662-8042
Fax: (860) 745-9714
Web site: http://www.casualcornergroup.com

Private Company
Incorporated: 1950
Employees: 9,000
Sales: $808 million (2000 est.)
NAIC: 44812 Women's Clothing Stores

Casual Corner Group, Inc. operates approximately 950 clothing stores for women in 45 states. Primarily based in malls, the company's stores include the flagship Casual Corner chain as well as Petite Sophisticate, August Max Woman, and Casual Corner Annex. Casual Corner Group is owned and managed by President and CEO Claudio Del Vecchio, whose family controls Luxottica Group, the Italian eyeglass manufacturer.

Humble Beginnings: 1950s

On April 1, 1950, partners Charles E. Carples and Stanley W. Vogel opened the first Casual Corner on 14 LaSalle Road, West Hartford, Connecticut. The partners borrowed $5,000 each and furnished the store with poles, beams, and nets from old tobacco barns. Their 750-square-foot store had a sales staff of two—the founders' wives. After three months the store lost its entire staff due to pregnancies.

Casual Corner's founding arose from the strong relationship between Carples and Vogel. Their friendship went back to their youth—they grew up together on the same street in Hartford, Connecticut, and attended the same public schools. After World War II both men returned to the area. Carples entered the women's clothing industry working for Sage-Allen; Vogel entered the same industry working for Brown-Thomson. Although the friends enjoyed the work they felt there had to be a better way of being in business. They wanted to start a company that would be friendly and fun—one that would make employees look forward to coming to work.

Carples and Vogel saw an opportunity in the way the country was changing. Suburbs were springing up. Dress was becoming less formal. Yet, in the 1950s, a women's clothing shop meant a dress store. Any sportswear was found in the large department stores. Specialty shops did not exist. Consequently, Carples and Vogel founded Casual Corner as one of the first sportswear stores for women.

The partners planned to attract 50 percent of their business from working women, 30 percent from college students, and the rest from what they called country club women. Vogel said the store began in an era when women could not wear pants in most places, Bermuda shorts did not exist, and the concept of paired blouse and skirt was relatively new. Also unusual for the era was Casual Corner's allowing women to browse and try on clothes. In most stores blouses were kept behind glass and there were no dressing rooms. The store name was chosen partially to convey the less formal, more friendly nature of both the shopping experience and the clothes.

The personality of Casual Corner was captured in a poem that appeared near the front door of each store in the 1950s: "Come in and browse and tarry and chat/ Casual Corner is meant just for that/ Come in and leisurely look awhile/ And find here what's good and fine in style/ And if you wish your business we'll tend/ Come in as a stranger—leave as a friend."

By 1951 Carples and Vogel were successful enough to open a second store in Springfield, Massachusetts. Further expansion during the early years occurred in Providence, Boston, Worcester, Syracuse, and Rochester. In the early years Carples and Vogel discovered another store called Casual Corner based in Washington, D.C. The D.C. store had started the same week as Carples and Vogel's store and 85 percent of the merchandise was the same. The discovery led not to a legal challenge but to the formation of the Casual Corner Association, one of the nation's earliest retailing cooperatives.

Carples and Vogel gave store employees some unusual benefits for the time period. Employees who stayed with the com-

Company Perspectives:

Simply put, our customer comes first. At Casual Corner Group, we pride ourselves on understanding her changing needs, and we make it our number one priority to ensure her shopping experience is enjoyable and rewarding. When a customer visits our store, we do everything possible to treat her with respect, consideration and incomparable personal attention. Her continued satisfaction with Casual Corner Group is essential to our growth . . . and to our success.

pany for three years received 10 percent of their salary in a retirement fund that was vested from day one.

In the business partnership, Carples handled the real estate and operations, while Vogel made the merchandise and retailing decisions. Two decades after founding the company they still shared a large office in the company's Springfield, Massachusetts headquarters.

1960s–70s: Mall-Driven Success

Casual Corner was among the first U.S. retail companies to buy product from the Far East. In the late 1960s the company bought sweaters, T-shirts, and sportswear from Hong Kong. During that decade Casual Corner became a store for junior women.

Through Carples's initiative, the company became an early convert to the shopping centers or malls that sprouted up outside core cities in the late 1960s and early 1970s. About 1966 Casual Corner opened a store in the Framingham (Massachusetts) Shoppers World. The following year the company anchored a Cincinnati, Ohio mall, Tri-County Shopping Center.

During their department store days Carples and Vogel had witnessed the power of advertising. They used both newspaper advertising and direct mail to build Casual Corner sales. A Dalmatian became the store mascot. Carples thought the dog with spots reinforced the fun image the store sought to convey. Through the years the Dalmatian changed from a long, skinny, upright dog leaning against a lamp post to what Carples called a ''Dalmatian pig,'' a short, stubby animal on all fours with round spots.

Acquisition by U.S. Shoe

In 1970 U.S. Shoe bought Casual Corner. Under Chairman Philip Barach, U.S. Shoe wanted to expand its shoe sales through a specialty retail chain. But selling shoes at Casual Corner did not work at that time because specialty stores were not set up to house large assortments or provide the technical expertise of shoe sales experts.

Two vital elements U.S. Shoe brought to Casual Corner were sound managerial skills and the funds required for major expansion. The new owner planned to expand Casual Corner by about 15 stores a year. Carples and Vogel were placed on the board of U.S. Shoe and Stan Rutstein, the Casual Corner general merchandising manager, became president of the store chain.

By 1971 Casual Corner had about 700 employees in a chain of 32 ''sportswear emporiums.'' Large chain stores were difficult to manage in this pre-computerized era. When Carples and Vogel installed point-of-sale computerized registers in the early 1970s other retailers came to corporate headquarters to examine how the system operated. Each store was polled every night via telephone lines. The day's sales results were downloaded and a sales report printed.

During the 1970s Casual Corner continually expanded. It built a large warehouse in Enfield, Connecticut, and offered a Casual Corner credit card. By the end of the decade, what had been a chain of 16 stores in the early 1960s had grown to 352 stores.

1980: Formation of Women's Specialty Retailing Group

In sheer store numbers, the heyday for Casual Corner ran from the mid-1970s through the mid-1980s when the chain grew to 1,800 stores. By 1980 the company had become one of the nation's most successful specialty retailers and wanted to expand its reach to different market segments. Traditionally, the store had targeted women ages 25 to 45. In 1980, the company opened the Caren Charles chain for more conservative women, ages 35 to 55. It also formed Antics, a store for juniors or younger women.

In 1982 Casual Corner acquired Ups and Downs, a women's specialty store with some 200 outlets, and merged the nine Antics stores into it. That year the company purchased Petite Sophisticate of Cincinnati, a store for women 5 feet, 4 inches and shorter.

U.S. Shoe felt there were now too many store divisions for one executive to oversee. It thus formed the Women's Specialty Retailing Group (WSRG) and named a president for each division. The divisions reported to WSRG Chief Executive Officer Noel Davidson.

Petite Sophisticate showed particularly encouraging success. During President Fred Skurow's 13-year reign, Petite Sophisticate grew to more than 450 stores. However, WSRG was not immune to failure. A ''test'' division for women's accessories called Cabaret opened during the 1980s but soon closed.

In 1986 Davidson added a division for large sizes called Sophisticated Women. August Max, which had been kept separate from WSRG for about eight years, was then put under Davidson's control. Three years later he merged the two and the name became August Max Woman.

About this time another U.S. Shoe division, a discount women's clothing business in Washington, was not doing well. In 1990 that business was put under the WSRG umbrella. Under the name Career Image, the stores were moved by Davidson into outlet malls which were just starting at the time. By 2000 that division, renamed Casual Corner Annex, had more than 250 stores nationwide.

Signs of Struggle: Mid-1980s to Mid-1990s

By the middle of the 1980s Casual Corner showed signs of struggle. Some industry observers felt the chain did not have a

Key Dates:

1950: Company is founded in West Hartford, Connecticut.
1970: U.S. Shoe Corporation purchases the company.
1980: Casual Corner operates under U.S. Shoe's newly created Women's Specialty Retailing Group (WSRG).
1995: Luxottica Group buys U.S. Shoe in May; WSRG becomes autonomous and is renamed Casual Corner Group, Inc. in October.
2000: Company opens 21,000-square-foot flagship store in New York City.

strong enough appeal to any segment of the market. In 1991 the U.S. Shoe board removed Barach in favor of his heir apparent, Bannus Hudson. Hudson had a strong marketing background and wanted Casual Corner to become more of a marketing-driven company. He hired Mike Searles away from Kids ''R'' Us to run Casual Corner.

''This was not a business that could be fixed by tinkering with a strategy here or there. There were just too many problems cutting through the company. Drastic action was needed,'' said Barry Bryant, a retail analyst at Lardenburg Thalmann & Co., in the March 1994 issue of *Stores*.

Searles said Petite Sophisticate and Career Image were Casual Corner's only healthy divisions. In 1993–94 he reshaped the WSRG subsidiaries into a leaner, centralized, synergistic operation. He focused Casual Corner on one particular market—business women from 25 to 45. By moving the company from individual brand management to cross-brand management he greatly decreased payroll and added efficiencies. Rather than having five brand managers traveling to one city to serve five different divisions, Searles had one manager for all stores in the geographic region.

But, while these and other expense reductions saved close to $40 million on an annual basis, Searles was not successful. His inability to solidify a differentiated product strategy resulted in losses of $50 million in 1993 and $100 million in 1994.

1995: New Owner, Luxottica

Attracted by the profitable LensCrafters subsidiary of U.S. Shoe, Luxottica Group, a world leader in eyewear, bought a struggling U.S. Shoe in October 1995. Luxottica CEO and President Claudio Del Vecchio, son of Luxottica Chairman Leonardo Del Vecchio, sold the shoe business but kept the women's clothing operations. In October 1995 WSRG was transformed into Casual Corner Group, Inc.

Del Vecchio replaced Searles with Leopoldo Borzino and began to set up a vertically integrated organization similar to Luxottica. Under this strategy the company would design, manufacture, and retail its own product. After a year Del Vecchio took over the Casual Corner presidency himself and determined that Casual Corner could not manufacture its own product profitably.

Del Vecchio opened a fashion office in Milan and hired a chief merchandising officer. Two production teams were formed—one in the Enfield, Connecticut office and another in Hong Kong. He cut the New York-based staff by about 50 percent, invested in a new distribution center in Enfield, and put money into management information systems. Del Vecchio also developed a new superstore concept to bring two or more of the company's brands under one roof. Older Casual Corners usually were about 4,500 square feet, but the new stores were to be 6,000 to 10,000 square feet in size. Del Vecchio's ability to take the company private, invest heavily in the infrastructure, and build an efficient organization allowed the company to remain in business.

Under Del Vecchio the company announced a signature collection called ''collectibles.'' Collectibles were affordable seasonless separates in black and navy that could be combined in multiple ways and give customers the feel of a much larger wardrobe. By 1999 Casual Corner had returned to profitability.

In July 2000 Del Vecchio announced the opening of the company's web site. ''Our desire,'' he said, ''is to provide a dynamic e-commerce environment and superior customer service along with the capabilities to create a more personalized purchase experience to help drive sales and traffic through our various retail stores.''

Throughout 2000 Casual Corner sold moderate and higher priced women's clothing from more than 300 mainly mall-based shops in about 45 states. It also sold under the names Petite Sophisticate (300 locations; sizes 0–14); August Max Woman (90 locations; sizes 12–26) and Casual Corner Annex (250 locations).

The September 2000 opening of a new 22,000-square-foot flagship store, on 3rd Avenue in New York City, gave Casual Corner Group another hold on its claim as one of the largest and oldest specialty retail chains in the United States.

Principal Competitors

AnnTaylor Stores Corporation; Christopher & Banks Corporation; Federated Department Stores Inc.; The May Department Stores Company; The Talbots, Inc.

Further Reading

''Casual Corner Group: Celebrating 50 Years in Style,'' Enfield, Conn.: Casual Corner Group, Inc., 2000.

''Casual Corner Group to Implement the Complete E.piphany Solution As Key Component of the Company's Click-and-Mortar Strategy,'' *PR Newswire,* July 13, 2000.

Jenkes, Roberta, ''How to Succeed in Business and Still Be Best of Friends,'' *West Hartford News*, April 22, 1971, p. 1.

Kroll, Luisa, ''The Son Also Rises,'' *Forbes*, September 17, 2001, pp. 126–28.

Reda, Susan, ''Rx for WSRG: Clean Sweep,'' *Stores*, March 1994.

—Chris John Amorosino

Catalina Lighting, Inc.

18191 North West 68th Avenue
Hialeah, Florida 33015
U.S.A.
Telephone: (305) 558-4777
Toll Free: (800) 966-7074
Fax: (305) 558-3024
Web site: http://www.catalinaltg.com

Public Company
Incorporated: 1974
Employees: 3,800
Sales: $202.6 million (2000)
Stock Exchanges: New York
Ticker Symbol: LTG
NAIC: 335121 Residential Electric Lighting Fixture Manufacturing; 335122 Commercial, Industrial, and Institutional Electric Lighting Fixture Manufacturing

Florida-based Catalina Lighting, Inc., designs, manufactures, imports, and distributes an extensive line of lighting fixtures and lamps under a variety of brand names, notably Westinghouse, but also Catalina, Dana, Illuminada, and Meridian. As an original equipment manufacturer, it also makes privately-labeled products for high sales-volume customers, including major retail chains. Altogether, Catalina sells over 15 million items per year, mostly in the United States. Its products are merchandised by a wide range of retailers, including home centers, warehouse clubs, discount department stores, and hardware outlets. The company also sells products abroad, principally in Europe and Canada, but also in Mexico, other Latin American countries, Asia, and Australia. Catalina operates a 475,000 square foot distribution center in Tupelo, Mississippi, plus warehouses in Toronto and Mexico City. It also owns a manufacturing subsidiary, Go-Gro Industries, Ltd., which is based in Hong Kong but has its production facilities in Guangdong Province, China. The subsidiary, which manufactures about 40 percent of Catalina's product line, exports its lamps and fixtures both to distributors and retailers in Europe and to Catalina's subsidiaries and customers in Canada and the United States. The remaining 60 percent of Catalina's sold products are made by independent suppliers in China. In 2000, Catalina also acquired Ring Ltd., a U.K. manufacturer of automotive replacement parts as well as lighting products for trains and buses. Catalina's largest customers are Home Depot and Wal-Mart, which, between them, account for about 32 percent of the company's total sales.

1980–89: Origins and Growth

David Moss, Catalina Lighting, Inc.'s founder, started the company in 1980 as Moss Manufacturing, a ceiling fan manufacturing business. Some accounts trace Catalina's origin back to1974, when Moss started up a firm to represent other equipment manufacturers. That forerunner, incorporated in Florida in 1974, is technically the seminal company on which Catalina Lighting was built, although that first firm failed before Moss started again in the ceiling fan business.

In an innovative move in 1985 that helped build his maverick reputation, Moss began importing low-cost lighting fixtures from Far Eastern manufacturers. Throughout the 1980s, Moss would routinely spend over 200 days a year in China and other Far East countries. He knew that he could cut manufacturing costs by using overseas factories and workers, bringing prices on popular but cost prohibitive products down to affordable levels for average-income Americans. The key was selling huge lots of such fixtures to large store chains, making everything from coach lanterns to track lighting and portable lamps available at 40 to 50 percent below the market price on comparable items produced by other manufacturers.

Moss renamed his company Catalina Lighting in 1987 and in the next year took it public, with an initial public offering of common stock at $3.50 per share. By that time, Catalina had become a favorite with home-improvement merchandisers, thanks to the fact that the company's price competitive-products were boxed in eye-catching, colorful cartons that attracted customers wandering around floor to ceiling shelving filled with unattractive, cardboard-brown boxes.

In August 1989, Moss resigned as Catalina's chairman, president, CEO, and director. He believed that the time had come for

Company Perspectives:

At Catalina Lighting we are dedicated to providing today's best value in lighting products, whether decorative or functional in nature. Our knowledge and resources enable us to deliver true lighting excellence. Whether it's basic lighting products, or those on the cutting edge of style and technology, Catalina Lighting is committed to being the lighting supplier of choice. And we'll continue to do so by providing the latest in lighting products, supported by our dedication to complete customer satisfaction.

him to turn the active leadership of the company over to others. He also indicated that his 260 days on the road in Asia the previous year had contributed to a sense of burn-out and that he simply wanted to slow down. Under the terms of his resignation, Moss agreed to serve a five-year term as a company consultant in international marketing and product development. At the time he stepped down, Moss owned about 1.3 million shares of Catalina's stock, or approximately 25 percent. He was replaced as CEO and president by John Browder, president of Catalina's Dallas-based subsidiary, Christina Lighting Inc. Browder had joined Catalina in July 1988, after his own ceiling fan company, Unitex, was bought by Catalina. David Friedson, president and CEO of Windmere Corp., which owned 17.9 percent of Catalina, succeeded to Catalina's chairmanship. Dean Rappaport served as vice-president and COO, while Robert Hersh was executive vice-president.

Moss left Catalina on very solid footing. In its second-quarter report for the period ending March 31, 1989, Catalina listed assets of $22.19 million. It had also built a solid customer base, including such major chains as Home Depot, Kmart, Pay n' Pak, Grossman's, and Hand Andy. Nevertheless, because Moss had been the energetic force behind the company, his resignation led to considerable speculation about Catalina's future. For some industry watchers, the company had been what Brian Major, writing in *HFD-The Weekly Home Furnishing Newspaper*, termed "a one-man show." Doubts arose about its impending purchase of Dana Imports, a Boston-based supplier of functional lighting and desk lamps with annual revenues of about $9 million. As it turned out, the transition was smooth enough, and the deal with Dana went through without a hitch.

1990–95: A Completely Imported Line Begets Foreign Manufacturing

By 1990, Catalina, with revenues of $55 million, ranked third behind its lighting supply competitors, Thomas Industries, with $74 million in sales, and Dynasty Classics, with $65 million in sales. However, Catalina's executives were predicting that it would soon lead the pack. It was a new kind of lighting supplier: a well-financed public company in a position to provide complete lighting programs to high-volume retail chains. It was also rapidly expanding its product line, which ran the gamut between coach lanterns and desk lamps. Moreover, although not unique, it was one of the few companies in the industry with no domestic plants. Its complete line was imported.

In the summer of 1990, Catalina introduced a line of outdoor lanterns and chandeliers for the lighting showroom market, a segment of the industry that it had not previously tried to crack. Including in its new offerings were the Illuminada line, which included coach and post lanterns exported from Italy. Catalina was also redesigning some of its product packaging, and had begun building a new 350,000 square foot distribution center near Dallas. Its success could be measured by the increased space given its products in the country's biggest home-improvement outlets and mass-merchandise and warehouse clubs.

In 1991, in an internal shake-up, Catalina terminated Browder. Robert Hersh replaced him as president and CEO. Browder, the company alleged, had broken securities laws and had to be fired, but the move resulted in a legal battle when Browder sued Catlina for his wrongful termination and, to the company's embarrassment, eventually won his suit in court.

Catalina's success in the 1990s continued to be based on its manufacture and distribution of derivative or knock-off items. In 1994, as cited in a July 25 *Fortune* article, "Companies to Watch," Hersh, tongue in cheek, described the company as "co-originators," thereafter cheerfully admitting that the term was the equivalent of "copycats." For years, Catalina modeled many of its fixtures on high-ticket items found in lighting showrooms, manufacturing and selling imitations of those items at much lower prices through such large home-center and department store chains as Home Depot and Kmart. The strategy entailed legal risks, including patent infringement suits.

In 1994, Catalina made two strategic decisions, one of which was to buy its own manufacturing plant in China; the other was to build a domestic factory in Mississippi. The first of these decisions turned out well. In August 1994, Catalina purchased Go-Gro Industries of Hong Kong, a decorative residential lighting manufacturer. In the deal, Catalina paid $7.5 million in cash and 750,000 shares of its common stock.

Go-Gro, which maintained production facilities in Shenzhen Province, China, had about 2,500 employees. At the time, more than 50% of its sales were made in Europe, and it was producing revenues of $38 million. The acquisition brought the promise of fulfilling Catalina's expansion plans, which called for broadening its markets, establishing a presence both in China's domestic marketplace and those of other countries. Go-Gro would prove to be a wise investment for the company.

Not so its venture in Mississippi. Started in 1994, the Meridian factory was built to produce a line of portable lighting products and decorative table lamps. The company created the line to be marketed in home centers, office superstores, and mass merchant outlets. Although plans called for production to start almost immediately, the Meridian plant did not reach its full operational capacity until 1996. By that time, the domestic lighting market had softened considerably, with a serious drop in the demand for table lamps, and it was soon clear that the facility was turning into a costly white elephant.

Challenges in the Late 1990s

The market downswing of the mid-1990s compelled Catalina to take some belt tightening moves and to streamline its operation for greater efficiency. Looking for ways to save, at the beginning

Key Dates:

1974: David Moss starts up a manufacturers' representative firm.
1980: Moss founds Moss Manufacturing, a ceiling fan supplier.
1985: Moss starts importing lighting fixtures.
1987: Moss renames company Catalina Lighting.
1988: Catalina Lighting goes public.
1989: Moss leaves company and is succeeded by John Browder as president and CEO; Catalina acquires Dana Imports.
1994: Catlina purchases Go-Gro Industries.
1996: Company enters licensing agreement with Westinghouse.
1997: Catalina is required to recall halogen torchiere-style floor lamps and closes Mississippi plant.
1999: Catalina licenses GE's fluorescent torchiere technology.
2000: Company acquires Ring plc, a British competitor.

of 1996, the company closed its warehouses in Boston and Carrollton, Texas. It also began building a new 475,000 square-foot facility in Baldwin, Mississippi, near Tupelo, in which two of its distribution operations would be consolidated and streamlined through the use of full, computerized automation.

In what perhaps was an inevitable turn because of its ''co-origination,'' Catalina was hit with four patent infringement suits in 1996, brought by Black and Decker Corp. after Catalina started selling a line of hands-free, flexible flashlights based on B & D's popular SnakeLight. Catalina's Portable Hugger and its variations sold for less than the comparable B & D items, prompting B & D to bring its suits against the company. In a 1997 settlement agreement, Catalina had to pay Black and Decker $1 million and refrain from the further manufacture and sale of all its patent-infringing products. At about the same time, Browder won his lawsuit against Catalina in a jury trial and was awarded damages of around $1.1 million for past salary losses and another $400,000 for lost stock options.

Those settlements and other problems led to Catalina's net loss of $3.1 million in 1997, despite the fact that its revenues had reached a decade high of $197.0 million. It was the first time that the company had gone into the red since 1991. The principal cause was not litigation, however; it was the cost of operating the unprofitable Meridian plant. By 1996, when the plant finally went on line, the market for table lamps had taken a negative shift and turned the enterprise into a poor gamble. Facing the fact that the same kind of products could be made both more cheaply and easily in the Orient, Catalina decided to close down the Meridian operation and lease out the facility. According to CEO Hersh, quoted in a September 26, 1997 article in the *South Florida Business Journal*, for two years the Meridian plant had ''sucked away'' the company's earnings at the rate of ''$400,000 to $500,000 a quarter.'' Also in 1997, the company also was hit with a product safety recall imposed by the Consumer Product Safety Commission on halogen torchiere-style floor lamps after it was found that the lamps posed definite fire hazzards. As a group, Catalina and nine other manufacturers took financial hits when 40 million such lamps were ordered off the market.

Catalina survived the bad year, however, and returned to profitability in 1998, despite the fact that its total revenues fell by over $35 million. Although its net income, at $1.1 million, barely put it back in the black, it was at least a turnaround. The closing of the Meridian plant had reduced Catalina's costs by downsizing its operations and reducing its personnel from 3,225 in 1997 to 2,815 in 1998, a 12.7 percent cut. Moreover, with most of its problems in the past, Catalina's prospects seemed good; in fact, its revenues over the next two years would continue to grow, producing respectable if not noteworthy profits.

1999 and Beyond: Continued Growth Through Product Development and Acquisition

Some of Catalina's gains towards the end of the decade came from new products that commanded a wider market margin than the halogen torchiere lamps, which, with their novelty worn thin, were losing popularity and suffering a rapidly narrowing market margin. Also, the company continued its rollout of products under the Westinghouse brand, which it had been developing since 1996.

By 2000, the company's sales had reached $202.6 million, rising above its previously high of $197 million attained in 1997. Its workforce had also grown above that of 1997, reaching 3,600. The company also positioned itself to fend off any takeover attempts by renewing its stockholder rights plan, a type of plan sometimes called an anti-takeover defense. Under its terms, potential buyers of the company would have to offer a fair price to all stockholders.

Despite the increased revenues, Catalina's net income in 2000 dropped to $2.8 million or $0.37 a share, down from $6.5 million and $0.80 a share in 1999. The downturn was partly the result of actions taken by management that imposed charges that lowered pretax earnings by $1.3 million. To offset further profit-draining costs and improve its customer service, in September 2000 the company completed plans to shutdown its Boston office and consolidate its activities in Miami.

Still, Catalina remained upbeat and bent on expansion, not just through new product development but also through acquisition. Its chief end-of-the decade move was its purchase of Ring PLC, a British competitor that took Catalina into some new market segments. Ring, for which Catalina paid $33.8 million in July 2000, manufactures both automotive and home lighting as well as fixtures for trains and buses. If things went as planned, the purchase would give Catalina an enhanced image in its European markets and help grow its annual revenues considerably.

Principal Subsidiaries

Go-Gro Industries, Ltd. (Hong Kong); Ring Ltd. (U.K.).

Principal Competitors

Cooper Industries, Inc.; General Electric Company; The Genlyte Group Incorporated; Holophane Corporation; Juno Lighting, Inc.; Koninklijke Philips Electronics N.V.

Further Reading

"Catalina Lighting Acquires Go-Gro," *HFD—The Weekly Home Furnishings Newspaper*, August 15, 1994, p. 25.

"Catalina Settles B&D Suits," *HFN—The Weekly Newspaper for the Home Furnishing Network*, March 10, 1997, p. 22.

Garau, Rebecca, "Green Light for Growth; Catalina Seen Making Huge Strides in '98," *HFN—The Weekly Newspaper for the Home Furnishing Network*, October 27, 1997, p. 13.

Labate, John, "Companies to Watch," *Fortune*, July 25, 1994, p. 233.

Major, Brian, "Catalina Refutes Forecasts: Proves It Can Survive Without Former Chairman," *HFD—The Weekly Home Furnishings Newspaper*, December 18, 1989, p. 29.

——, "Wither Catalina after Moss? Industry Debates His Effect on Business, Next Move," *HFD—The Weekly Home Furnishings Newspaper*, August 21, 1989, p. 23.

Meyer, Nancy, "Catalina in the Black," *HFN—The Weekly Newspaper for the Home Furnishing*, May 11, 1998, p. 46.

——, "Catalina Leaner, More Focused," *HFN—The Weekly Newspaper for the Home Furnishing*, July 10, 1995, p. 1.

——, "Catalina's Tuneup," *HFN—The Weekly Newspaper for the Home Furnishing Network*, October 21, 1996, p. 13.

Moss, David, "Program Selling Sparks Catalina," *HFD—The Weekly Home Furnishings Newspaper*, August 6, 1990, p. 32.

—John W. Fiero

Central Japan Railway Company

JR Central Towers
1-1-4, Meieki,
Nakamura-ku, Nagoya, 450-6101
Japan
Telephone: +81-3-3274-9727
Fax: +81-3-5255-6780
Web site: http://www.jr-central.co.jp/

Public Company
Incorporated: 1987 as Central Japanese Railway Company
Employees: 23,564
Sales: ¥ 1.33 trillion (US$11.33 billion) (2001 est.)
Stock Exchange: Tokyo
Ticker Symbol: 9022
NAIC: 482111 Line-Haul Railroads; 721110 Hotels (except Casino Hotels) and Motels; 531120 Lessors of Nonresidential Buildings (except Miniwarehouses)

The Central Japan Railway Company is one of seven firms created as a result of the break-up of the Japanese National Railway (JNR), a state-controlled agency that maintained a near monopoly over all railway business in Japan from its inception in 1949 to its dissolution in 1987. Known as JR Central, or more commonly as JR Tokai (the region of the Japanese island, Honshu, where JR Central operates), the Central Japan Railway Company is built around its highly profitable Tokaido Shinkansen (bullet train) line, which connects metropolitan Tokyo with Osaka to the southwest and accounts for 80 percent of JR Tokai's total revenue. The company has also expanded into varied enterprises, including real estate and hotel management.

701–1906: Establishment of the Tokaido Line and Government-Controlled Railway

The history of JR Tokai officially begins in 1987, but a more complete overview of the company includes a brief overview of the development of the rail industry in Japan. In 701 A.D., the Taiho Code divided Japan into five capital provinces connected by seven main roadways. The Tokaido was the main road connecting Edo (now Tokyo) to the old capital, Kyoto. By the start of the 17th century, known as the Edo Period, the Tokaido highway had become the most important road in Japan. The "53 stages of the Tokaido" became part of Japanese lore over subsequent centuries as the highway evolved into the 300-mile Tokaido railway line in 1889.

During the latter half of the 19th century, Japan began to fully embrace rail travel and freight transport. In 1870, construction of a national railway system began, and in 1872 the Emperor sat in attendance for the opening of Japan's first steam-driven line between Tokyo and Yokohama. Passage of the Railway Nationalization Act of 1906 initiated an official state-run railway agency. This act allowed the Japanese government to purchase all the main railway lines that connected regions within Japan while leaving the feeder lines, lines that served local communities and their needs, to private enterprise. The government would maintain control of the main lines for the following 80 years.

1949–64: Japanese National Railway and the Birth of the Bullet Train

In 1949, the Japanese National Railway, a centralized agency designed to maintain all lines owned by the government, was established. It quickly became apparent that an upgrade in service was necessary during the era of high economic growth in the country during the 1950s. Increasing numbers of people needed to traverse the island of Honshu, specifically the area between Tokyo and Osaka. In 1956, the Tokaido Line Augmentation Survey Board was created as part of the JNR, and within two years, research and development of the bullet train (Shinkansen) began. The Shinkansen would almost immediately become the foundation of Japanese railway travel and, in many ways, of the entire Japanese economy.

October 1, 1964, stands as one of the most important dates in the socio-economic history of Japan during the latter half of the 20th century. On that day, the first Shinkansen line, the Tokaido, was completed. The event coincided with the start (two weeks later) of the Tokyo Olympic games, the first to be

Company Perspectives:

The company strives to contribute to community development by adhering to sound management principles; provide modern, friendly, and reliable services; and establish a cheerful, fresh, and active corporate culture.

held in Asia. It would be 17 years before a comparable bullet-train system was completed anywhere else in the world.

1964–87: Massive Debt in the JNR

The following 20 years represented a period of extreme contrasts for JNR. The Shinkansen system was revolutionizing travel both in Japan and abroad and quickly became the most popular form of travel in the nation. The JNR, however, was not experiencing a corresponding economic boom. On the contrary, it was during this period that the agency began to accrue huge debts. The Japanese economy expanded sharply during the 1970s and with it a trend toward increased automobile ownership and air transport. This contributed to a decline in both passenger and freight railway business. According to Fumitoshi Mizutani, associate professor in the Graduate School of Business Administration at Kobe University, JNR controlled over half of all passenger and freight movement in Japan in 1955. By 1985, however, the company's share of passenger travel fell by roughly 17 percent while their share of freight transport plummeted to barely 5 percent of total freight movement. Although JNR continued to innovate, rolling out the second generation of Shinkansen, the series 100, the company was spiraling deeply into debt.

JNR's troubles had several contributing factors. The company struggled to maintain centralized control over railway operations on all four of Japan's islands. A strong railway union which deeply mistrusted management, the bureaucracy of a public ownership system that made quick decision making impossible even for seemingly small affairs, and a lack of economic competition all added to economic woes and a gradual loss of public faith in the efficiency of JNR. Once the company's debt began to accumulate, it grew exponentially. By the 1980s, the debt had risen to ¥37.1 trillion ($275 billion), and it was clear that a major overhaul was necessary.

1987–2000: Breakup of the JNR and Creation of the Central Japan Railway Company

The ceremonial end of the JNR is described by Paul Noguchi: ''In a public ceremony at midnight on April 1, 1987, the president of the JNR, dressed in an engineer's uniform, rode a C-56 steam locomotive into Tokyo and blew the whistle that signaled the end of the 115-year-old national railways. This ceremony marked the closing of the industry that was once regarded as the symbol and backbone of Japan's modernization.'' The JNR had been dissolved, and in its place stood seven new companies and two new government agencies. The Central Japan Railway Company (JR Tokai) was one of the three Honshu JR's (along with JR East and JR West) and served the Tokai region of Honshu, connecting the northeast to the southwest. In addition, three new JR passenger companies were created, one for each of the smaller islands. One of the most significant developments was the creation of JR Freight, which removed the burden of freight transportation management from the passenger JRs, leaving them to focus predominantly on providing passenger services and solidifying their economic base by diversifying into other fields.

Perhaps the most significant development in the dissolution of JNR, however, was the creation of the Japan National Railway Settlement Corporation (JNRSC), a state agency that held all of the stock in the seven companies. The formation of the JNRSC attempted to address the public's lack of faith in the JNR and the fear that no one would be interested to invest in the new companies. (As of 2001, the JNRSC controlled 39.5 percent of JR Tokai's stock.) The JNRSC also inherited ¥25.5 trillion ($212.5 billion) of the JNR's total ¥37.1 trillion ($275 billion) debt to allow each new company a relatively clean financial start. JR Tokai inherited roughly ¥2 trillion ($16.6 billion) of the debt. In addition, the Shinkansen Holding Corporation (SHC) was formed to maintain control of the highly profitable Shinkansen lines and lease them to the new companies. The Tokaido Shinkansen line was leased to JR Tokai, and, when the SHC was disbanded in 1991, JR Tokai purchased the line for ¥5.1 trillion ($42.5 billion). This price was significantly higher than any of the other Shinkansen lines, but with good reason: The Tokaido Shinkansen connected the Shinkansen lines of JR East to the lines of JR West and represented one of the most lucrative businesses in all of Japan.

The purchase of the Tokaido line also pushed JR Tokai into debt deeper than any of the other JR firms. In 1997, when the government amended its plans to liquidate JNR debt (which had grown by more than ¥2 trillion in 10 years) by making the JR firms shoulder a larger percentage of the whole, JR Tokai stood to suffer the most. Though the series 300 Shinkansen trains had lowered travel time (and thereby increased the potential number of passengers per day) and JR Tokai had diversified into dining services, a tour group company, and hotel and department store subsidiaries, the debt accumulated from JNR and the purchase of the Tokaido line continued to drain the company's resources. Nonetheless, in 1994, JR Tokai began construction of what would become its home offices, the JR Central Towers building in Nagoya, the heart of the Tokai region. Upon its completion in 2000, the Towers stood as the largest building in Japan.

The following year marked a first for a JR firm, and one that JR Tokai would rather forget. A 17-year-old boy caught his fingers in an electronic train door at a station along the Tokaido line. No one noticed. As he tried to yank his fingers from the door, the train began to move and the boy was dragged off the platform to his death. In 2001, JR Tokai was found liable for damages and forced to pay almost ¥50 million ($400,000) to the boy's parents. It was the first fatality for which a JR company was found liable in the 30-year history of the Shinkansen.

In 1997, JR Tokai became the third JR firm (following JRs East and West) to be listed on the Tokyo Stock Exchange. This year also marked the completion of the Yamanashi Linear Test Line, an 18.4-km (11.5-mile) track designed to assist in railway research. Two years later JR Tokai signed a franchise contract

Key Dates:

1870: Construction begins on Japan's first railway line.
1881: The Nippon Railway Company becomes Japan's first private railway.
1889: The three hundred mile long Tokaido line is constructed.
1906: Japanese government passes the Railway Nationalization Act.
1949: Japan National Railway (JNR) established.
1964: The first high-speed "bullet train" line, the Tokaido Shinkansen, is completed between Tokyo and Osaka.
1987: JNR, wracked with ¥37.1 trillion ($275 billion) in debt, privatizes into 7 companies, including Central Japan Railway (JR Tokai).
1991: JR Tokai purchases Tokaido Shinkansen line for ¥5.1 trillion ($42.5 billion).
1992: Company establishes JR Tokai Hotels Co., Ltd. Establishes JR Tokai Department Store Co., Ltd.
1994: Company establishes JR Central Building Co. Ltd. and construction on JR Central Towers begins.
2000: Nagoya JR Central Towers building opens as the largest building in Japan. Wholly owned real estate subsidiary established. Tokaido Shinkansen receives two awards for world technological achievements: the Electric Engineering Milestones prize, becoming the third Japanese winner of the prize; and the Landmarks in Mechanical Engineering award, the first Japanese winner.
2001: JR Tokai pays almost ¥50 million ($400,000) after a Japanese court finds the company responsible in the 1995 death of a teen whose fingers were trapped in an automatic train door.

with Marriott International Inc., the United States hotel chain, to open a Marriott hotel in the Nagoya JR Central Towers.

In 1999 the 700 series of Shinkansen (known as Dr. Yellow) was completed. The 700 series was the first to explicitly focus on environmental concerns, such as the reduction of energy consumption by lowering air drag and a new system of regenerative brakes that recycle electrical power. Power consumption of the series 700 was almost 10 percent lower than that of the series 300.

The New Century

As the twentieth century ended, JR Tokai clearly had its sights set on the future. Primary among its goals was to clean up its debt. To this end, in 2000 JR Tokai and JR West sold their cumulative shares of Japan Telecom (10.2 percent of the total stock) to British cellular phone operator Vodafone Group PLC for ¥280 billion ($233.4 million). JR Tokai said it planned to apply its portion of these proceeds to debt relief.

Another significant development in 2000 was the opening of the JR Central Towers building, which comprised the central railway hub station in Nagoya, business offices, a Marriott hotel, and a department store. In its first day of business, nearly 230,000 customers visited JR Nagoya Takashimaya department store and spent ¥550 million ($4.6 million).

Also at this time, a new type of train was in development in Japan. Magnetic Levitation (Maglev) trains represented the successor technology to the Shinkansen trains. Although in the 1980s the debt of JNR forced Japan to drastically reduce its R&D budget and enabled France to develop the world's fastest trains, the Maglev system represented a concerted attempt to return Japan to the top. Some observers have stated that the Dr. Yellow trains, and others like them in the world, represent the most advanced systems possible using traditional "wheels-on-tracks" technology. The new Maglev trains move beyond this system by utilizing magnets that lift the train off its tracks and thereby almost entirely eliminate friction between wheel and track.

At the dawn of the 21st century, Central Japan Railway Company remained one of the most significant companies in Japan. It owned the Tokaido railway line, the most fabled transportation route in Japan. The company had evolved itself into a diversified organization with businesses that moved beyond rail transport to include real estate, department store, and hotel management. With the opening of the largest building in Japan, JR Central Towers, in 2000, the sale of significant holdings, and the development of new technologies, JR Tokai was aimed squarely at alleviating the debt accrued from the JNR and the purchase of the Tokaido Shinkansen railway line. As the company continued to establish itself as a powerful player in Japanese and international economic circles, it worked to solidify profit through both diversification and maintenance of some of Japan's most important socioeconomic legacies.

Principal Subsidiaries

JR Central Building Co., Ltd.; Shinsho Technos Co. Ltd. (22%); JR Tokai Hotels Co., Ltd.; JR Tokai Takashimaya Co., Ltd.(59%); Shizuoka Terminal Hotel Co., Ltd. (77%); JR Tokai Bus Co., Ltd.; Shin Yokohama Station Development Co., Ltd.; Nagoya Terminal Building Co., Ltd. (51%); Tokai Kiosk Co., Ltd. (90%); J Diner Tokai Co., Ltd.; Passenger Service Co., Ltd.; JR Tokai Tours Co., Ltd. (70%); Nagoya Station Development Co., Ltd.; JR Tokai Construction Co., Ltd.; Chuo Liunen Supply Co., Ltd. (78%); Nippon Kikai Hosen Co., Ltd. (73%); JR Tokai Shoji Co., Ltd. (70%); Tokai Kotsu Kikai Co., Ltd. (51%); JR Tokai Agency Co., Ltd. (90%); JR Tokai Kansai Development Co., Ltd.

Principal Competitors

East Japan Railway Company; West Japan Railway Company; Keihin Electric Express Railway.

Further Reading

"Doubts Grow About Rail Privatization in Japan as Government Alters Terms," *Euroweek*, December 19, 1997, p. 10.
"Focus: Japan Reconstructs," *Far Eastern Economic Review*, June 16, 1988.
Hara, Nobuko, "JR East Puts Privatization Back on Track," *Euromoney*, November 1993, p. 67.

Ishikawa, Tatsujiro, and Mitsuhide Imashiro, *The Privatisation of Japanese National Railways: Railway Management, Market, and Policy*, London: Athlone Press, 1998.

"JNR Settlement To Be Disbanded Next Thurs.," *Jiji Press English News Service*, October 16, 1998.

"JR Companies Reject LDP Plan on JNR Debt Disposal," *Jiji Press English News Service*, February 18, 1998.

"JR Tokai to Set Up Real Estate Unit in March," *Jiji Press English News Service*, February 26, 2001.

"Magnetic Attraction: A Modern High-Speed Train Gathers a Head of Steam," *Far Eastern Economic Review*, February 11, 1988.

"Marriott Hotel to Open in Nagoya in 2000," *Jiji Press English News Service*, March 9, 1999.

Ministry of Transport, Railway Bureau, ed., *Issues and Achievements in the Five Years Since the Japan National Railways Reform*, Tokyo: Japan Transport Economics Research Center, 1992.

Mizutani, F., "An Assessment of the Japan Railway Companies Since Privatization: Performance, Local Rail Service and Debts," *Transport Reviews,* vol. 19, no. 2, pp. 117–139.

Mizutani, F., and K. Nakamura, "Privatization of the Japan National Railway: Overview of Performance Changes," *International Journal of Transport Economics* vol.24, no.1, pp. 75–99.

Noguchi, Paul H., *Delayed Departures, Overdue Arrivals: Industrial Familialism and the Japanese National Railways*, Honolulu: University of Hawaii Press, 1990.

"Only JR Tokai Sees Higher FY '97 Sales among 7 JR Firms," *Jiji Press English News Service*, May 26, 1998.

Polinder, Douglas W., "Rails in the Rising Sun" *Trains*, May 1990, pp. 32–40.

Sakita, Masami, "Restructuring of the Japanese National Railways: Review and Analysis," *Transportation Quarterly*, January 1989.

Shimbun, Mainichi, "JR Tokai Pays up for Shinkansen Death," *Mainichi Daily News*, March 9, 2001.

"Shinkansen Stranded After JR Let Trains Run," *Yomiuri Shimbun/Daily Yomiuri*, September 16, 2000.

Steiner, Robert, "Tokyo Hits a Wall with Economic Plans: Schedule for Privatizations Is Thrown Off by Drop in Japanese Stock Prices," *Wall Street Journal*, June 28, 1995.

Watanabe, Susumu, "Restructuring of the Japanese National Railways: Implications for Labour," *International Labour Review*, 1994, p. 89.

—Jerod L. Allen

Cinram International, Inc.

2255 Markham Rd.
Toronto, Ontario M1B 2W3
Canada
Telephone: (416) 298-8190
Fax: (416) 298-0612
Web site: http://www.cinram.com

Public Company
Incorporated: 1969 as Cinram Ltd.
Employees: 3,600
Sales: C$652.3 million (2000)
Stock Exchanges: Toronto
Ticker Symbol: CRW
NAIC: 334612 Prerecorded Compact Disc (Except Software), Tape, and Record Reproducing; 334611 Software Reproducing; 51212 Motion Picture and Video Distribution; 42199 Other Miscellaneous Durable Goods Wholesalers

Cinram International, Inc. is one of the world's leading independent manufacturers of prerecorded video- and audiocassettes, compact discs (CDs), CD-ROMs, and DVDs. Cinram also distributes videos and has stakes in several companies that offer media content online. Major customers of the firm include Twentieth Century Fox Home Entertainment, Polygram, Universal Music, and Sony. Based in Toronto, Canada, the publicly held Cinram operates through a number of subsidiaries in North America and Europe.

Early Years

Cinram was founded in 1969 by Isidore Philosophe, a Lebanese immigrant, and Samuel Sokoloff in Montreal to manufacture prerecorded 8-track tape cartridges and audiocassettes. The company's name was derived from a combination of the words cinema, radio, and music. During the mid-1970s Cinram expanded its ability to produce cassettes, which were beginning to replace the bulkier, lower-fidelity 8-tracks as the consumer format of choice. Injection molding equipment was also purchased to enable the manufacturing of cassette shells in-house.

In 1979 Cinram moved its operations to Toronto, putting it closer to the home base of many of its clients. At this time the firm further expanded its cassette manufacturing capabilities, and added a new plant to make vinyl records, giving it the ability to produce the full range of prerecorded music formats in use at the time.

Manufacturing capacity was again increased with the purchase of automated cassette-making equipment during the early 1980s, a period which saw the company experience dramatic growth in orders for both cassettes and records. In 1985 Cinram purchased the manufacturing operations of Quality Records, one of Canada's leading music companies. Quality then contracted with Cinram for production of its records and tapes.

Public Offering, Move into CD Production: 1986–93

By the early 1980s the compact disc had arrived as a music format, and all indications were that it would become a major new source of revenue for the industry. To acquire the capital needed to put a CD manufacturing facility into operation, Cinram made a public stock offering in March 1986. The following year the firm built a CD plant, which shipped its first orders by late fall. Cinram reported earnings of C$3.4 million for the year on sales of C$29.1 million.

In 1988 the company acquired Praxis Technologies Corp., a financially troubled maker of CDs. A favorable tax write-off was derived in the bargain. Late in the year Cinram signed a contract with CBS Canada to take over manufacture of CDs and vinyl records for that company. Cinram's move into CDs was proving to be a timely one, as orders for vinyl discs were dropping steeply while CDs were going through the roof. Soon sales of audiocassettes also began to fall off as the CD became the dominant prerecorded music format. With this in mind, Cinram established Nobler Technologies, Inc. in Boston, Massachusetts, to design and build automated CD manufacturing equipment. Nobler serviced both Cinram and outside clients. A second U.S. subsidiary was added in 1990 when Cinram purchased the PRC Tape Company of Richmond, Indiana. PRC, later renamed Cinram, Inc., was one of the largest independent audiocassette duplicators in the United States, with a workforce of 500.

Company Perspectives:

Our customers' success is our success. We are a leader by providing our customers with what they want, when they want it, how they want it, and at the right price.

Cinram's vinyl record output had now slowed to a trickle, and in 1991 the firm mothballed production of this venerable audio format. The company began manufacturing prerecorded videocassettes during the same year, producing them at the Richmond and Toronto factories. Plans were also announced for production of digital audiocassettes and laser videodiscs, which were both then expected to become popular consumer formats. The company's revenues and earnings for 1991 were more than double the figure of 1987, standing at C$67.8 million and C$8.5 million, respectively.

In 1993 Cinram purchased Nelson Vending Technologies Ltd. for C$4 million. Nelson had been formed in the mid-1980s to assemble a chain of video vending machines in Canada. This once-promising concept had not caught on with the public, however, and Nelson was limping along with 16 employees and 200 machines by the time Cinram acquired it. As had been the case with Praxis, Cinram's interest was as much in the favorable tax write-offs as it was in the video vending concept, due to Nelson's C$36 million in tax losses. Cinram also saw appeal in Nelson's advanced computer tracking system, which it hoped to adapt to its own purposes. Despite Nelson's marginal status, Cinram continued to run the company, which had recently acquired the more successful video vending chain Video Cube, Inc. After the acquisition, the latter firm's management was put in charge of the entire operation. In hopes of stirring up business, the company was renamed The Amazing Video Network, and the ability to sell videotapes was added to the machines. The year 1993 also saw Cinram subsidiary Nobler Technologies begin shipping CD-making machinery to China in the first phase of a multimillion-dollar deal.

International Expansion: 1994–97

The recently enacted North American Free Trade Agreement (NAFTA) gave Cinram new opportunities to grow, and in 1994 the company established a joint venture with Auriga-Aurex S.A. de C.V. of Mexico to build a CD plant in Mexico City. Cinram's investment was C$10 million. The same year the company also bought a small maker of interactive advertising kiosks for retail stores, Sierra Creative Communications, Inc. Sierra's kiosks used CD-ROMs which were made by Cinram.

In 1995 Cinram expanded to Europe with the acquisition of two leading French videocassette duplication companies, Duplication France S.A. and Video Pouce S.A. The deals were valued at C$4.5 million and C$1.5 million, respectively. Both companies were losing money at the time Cinram purchased them. That same year also saw a C$24 million acquisition on Cinram's home turf, that of Agincourt Productions Ltd., a division of Baton Broadcasting Inc. Agincourt, which operated under the name AP Video International, produced prerecorded videotapes in Canada for major movie studios.

The following year Cinram reached an agreement to buy the CD-manufacturing operations of an American company, Disc Manufacturing, Inc. (DMI), for US$80 million. DMI operated plants in Huntsville, Alabama, and Anaheim, California, which produced 200 million discs per year, including a sizable number of CD-ROMs. The new plants doubled Cinram's CD output. Shortly after this purchase Cinram got into the nascent DVD business when it formed a joint DVD-authoring venture with Pacific Ocean Post, a digital post-production company based in Santa Monica, California. DVDs, primarily used for video, held seven times as much data as CDs and could be produced at Cinram's CD manufacturing facilities.

Cinram was now receiving a great deal of attention from investors, and they boosted the company's stock price to more than C$27 by March 1996, up from just C$12 a year earlier. Revenues for the year were C$340.7 million, nearly five times the amount reported half a decade earlier. Profits were a healthy C$31.2 million. The company was also flush with capital from two special warrant issues, the most recent of which had raised more than C$100 million.

At the end of 1996 Cinram reached an agreement with Videoprint, Ltd. to purchase its videotape duplication and distribution operations for C$14.7 million. Videoprint, headquartered in the United Kingdom, gave Cinram additional presence in the European market. The company continued to broaden its European holdings in 1997 with acquisition of most of the videocassette duplication assets of Grupo Condor S.L. of Spain, which consisted of two manufacturing facilities that could produce 25 million tapes per year. These were later consolidated into a single site in Zaragoza, Spain, and renamed Cinram España S.A.

Cinram also reached agreements with two top entertainment corporations during the year to acquire some of their manufacturing operations in Europe. In the Netherlands, the company purchased video- and audiotape maker Polygram Manufacturing and Distribution Centres B.V. from Polygram N.V. Cinram subsequently reached an agreement to manufacture the bulk of Polygram's prerecorded tapes around the world. A similar deal was struck with Sony Music Entertainment (U.K.) Limited to take over Sony's British videocassette duplication operations, and then to manufacture tapes for Sony Music and sister company Columbia Tri-Star Home Video in the United Kingdom. During 1997 Cinram also changed its name to reflect the company's global reach, becoming Cinram International, Inc.

Music Industry Downturn, Evaporating Profits: 1998–2001

The company's streak of upward stock price growth hit a rough spot in early 1998 when a quarterly earnings report came up short of analyst predictions. The share price quickly dropped by 15 percent, then continued to slide throughout the year. Cinram's earnings were being hurt by the sluggish sales of music recordings and videos, which were seeing few hits at the time. Investors were also skittish because of the growing popularity of the MP3 digital recording format, which was increasingly being used to trade music over the Internet. The long-term impact on prerecorded CD and tape sales was not yet clear, but it offered the potential of disaster for Cinram, as well as the music industry at

Key Dates:

1969: Cinram Ltd. is founded in Montreal to make prerecorded tapes.
1979: Operations are moved to Toronto.
1985: Company purchases Quality Records' manufacturing unit.
1986: Initial public offering raises funds to build Cinram's first compact disc (CD) plant.
1987: CD factory opens, begins shipping orders.
1989: Nobler Technologies, Inc. is formed to design and build CD-making equipment.
1990: Richmond, Indiana-based PRC Tape Company is acquired and becomes company's first U.S. manufacturing site.
1991: Cinram ceases making vinyl records, begins to produce videocassettes.
1993: Nelson Vending Technologies is acquired and renamed The Amazing Video Network.
1994: Joint venture is formed in Mexico with Auriga-Aurex to manufacture CDs.
1995: Cinram purchases two French videotape makers and Canadian firm AP Video.
1996: Company agrees to buy U.S. CD maker DMI and U.K. tape manufacturer Videoprint.
1997: Company purchases tape and videocassette duplication arms of Dutch Polygram and British Sony, respectively; changes name to Cinram International, Inc.
2000: Cinram signs major videotape, DVD manufacturing, and distribution deal with Fox Home Entertainment.

large. Despite these troubles, *Forbes* still ranked Cinram one of the 100 best small companies in the world, an honor which the firm had received for several years running.

To address investor concerns, the company reached a deal with Internet music provider MP3.com in November 1999 in which the latter purchased 1.5 million shares of Cinram stock at C$13 each. Customers would be able to select a set of songs for a custom CD of their own creation on MP3.com's web site, and Cinram would manufacture and ship it within two days. Cinram also acquired a stake in U.S.-based Internet software and music distribution company Broadcast Software Corp. These forward-looking moves did not halt the company's stock slide, however, and the share price dropped below the C$5 mark by early 2000.

During the summer of 2000 a major agreement was reached with Twentieth Century Fox Home Entertainment to designate Cinram the exclusive manufacturer and distributor of that firm's VHS tapes in North America, followed a short time later by a similar pact regarding DVDs. The deal was estimated to be worth more than C$750 million over five years. To handle the increased production this would require, Cinram began an 800,000-square-foot expansion of its Huntsville, Alabama plant.

The year 2000 also saw the company purchase another CD plant in Louviers, France, from Universal Manufacturing and Logistics, which was capable of producing 110 million discs per year. The deal included a pact with Universal Music Ltd. to manufacture that company's CDs in Europe. Cinram acquired a French DVD authoring firm in Paris around this time as well.

Still trying to come to grips with the protracted sales slump, in December 2000 Cinram announced a C$48 million restructuring which included layoffs at all of its facilities worldwide and the closing of its Anaheim, California CD plant. When the final figures were released for the year, the company had lost C$28 million on revenues of more than C$652 million. The red ink was attributed to a combination of the continuing lack of pop music hits, a spike in raw material costs, the impact of such online music trading services as Napster, and the strong sales of home CD-burners. At the company's spring 2001 annual meeting, founder and CEO Philosophe vowed to stick with Cinram's core strategy through the industry's continuing period of uncertainty. He noted that Cinram's increasing emphasis on distribution was proving to be a good addition to the company's portfolio of services, and predicted a return to profitability.

After a stunning run of success during most of the 1990s, Cinram was dealing with a lengthy revenue slump by tightening its belt while continuing to look to the future. With seasoned management in place, and the full potential of DVD not yet realized, it looked to be a strong candidate for survival during the ongoing industry shakeout.

Principal Subsidiaries

Video Centre; The Amazing Video Network; Cinram España S.A. (Spain); Cinram, Inc. (U.S.A.); Cinram Latinoamericana S.A.de C.V. (Mexico); Cinram Europe (U.K.); Cinram France; Cinram Audio Discs (France); Cinram U.K. Ltd.; Cinram Nederland B.V. (Netherlands).

Principal Competitors

Thomson Multimedia; QCA, Inc.; Metatec International, Inc.; WEA Manufacturing; DOCdata N.V.; G.T.C. Transcontinental Group Ltd.

Further Reading

Brieger, Peter, ''Money-Losing Cinram Sticks with Strategy,'' *National Post*, June 14, 2001, p. C6.

——, ''Will Cinram Survive Recording Shakeout?,'' *National Post*, March 29, 2001, p. D3.

Enchin, Harvey, ''Cinram Buys Arm of Quality,'' *Globe and Mail*, November 5, 1985, p. B2.

Hasselback, Drew, ''Cinram Well Prepared for High-Tech DVD Revolution,'' *Financial Post*, April 22, 1999, p. 31.

Mahood, Casey, ''Can Canada Compete? CD Maker Spins Its Way to Success,'' *Globe and Mail*, December 5, 1991, p. B1.

McArthur, Keith, ''Cinram May Climb Charts Again,'' *Globe and Mail*, December 23, 1999, p. B14.

Miles, Stephen, ''Cinram Still Has DVD Ace Up Its Sleeve,'' *National Post*, March 19, 1999, p. D3.

Northfield, Stephen, ''Cinram's Shares Pause After Lucrative Climb,'' *Globe and Mail*, April 1, 1997, p. B12.

——, ''Cinram Tuned in to Multimedia Trends,'' *Globe and Mail*, March 7, 1996, p. B14.

Olunyk, Zena, ''Cinram Rides High on Cutting Edge of Technology,'' *Financial Post*, February 7, 1997, p. 21.

O'Reilly, Tom, "Replication Doom & Gloom Forecast," *Tape-Disc Business*, January 1, 2001, p. 63.

Paddon, David, "Cinram to Cut Jobs, Trim Costs in 2001 Following Weak Sales of CDs, CD-ROMs," *Canadian Press*, December 22, 2000.

Simons, Andrew, "Cinram Closes Anaheim Plant, Lays Off 300," *Orange County Business Journal*, May 28, 2001, p. 3.

Stinson, Marian, "Cinram Stock Boosted by News of Fox Deal," *Globe and Mail*, June 15, 2001, p. B19.

Waldie, Paul, "Video Rental Machines a Challenge for Cinram," *Financial Post*, June 26, 1993, p. 10.

Weinberg, Paul, "The Next Relic: Cinram Became a Success Making Prerecorded CDs and Tapes; Will the Internet Make Those Hard Media Obsolete?," *Globe and Mail*, October 29, 1999, p. 186.

—Frank Uhle

Companhia Vale do Rio Doce

Avenida Graca Aranha 26
PO Box 2414
20005 Rio de Janeiro
Brazil
Telephone: (+55) 21-272-4477
Fax: (+55) 21-272-4611
Web site: http://www.cvrd.com.br

Public Company
Incorporated: 1942
Employees: 11,442 (2000)
Sales: $5,034 million (2000)
Stock Exchanges: New York, BOVESPA
Ticker Symbol: RIO/\, VALE5
NAIC: 212210 Iron Ore Mining; 212299 All Other Metal Ore Mining; 212221 Gold Ore Mining; 212222 Silver Ore Mining; 482111 Line-Haul Railroads; 483111 Deep Sea Freight Transportation

Companhia Vale do Rio Doce (CVRD) is the world's largest producer and exporter of iron ore and the largest diversified mining company in the Americas. Starting from two integrated mine-railroad-port systems, CVRD grew to become a symbol of Brazil's industrial prowess over the course of the second half of the twentieth century. With a network of railways, ports and shipping lines to move the millions of tons of ore it produces each year, CVRD is truly a multi-faceted industrial jewel that remains a source of pride for Brazilians.

To fully understand the history behind CVRD, one must look at the economic and geo-political environment of Brazil over the last 50 years. Beginning centuries before the founding of CVRD, explorers had traveled Brazil's remote Doce River Valley in search of gold and other precious natural resources. In 1891, Brazil's first Republican Constitution dramatically altered the nation's mining regulations to allow landowners the rights to mineral reserves found on their property. However, the law allowed the underground mineral reserves to be worked by foreign-owned companies. At that time, geological explorations began to reveal abundant supplies of iron concentrated in the rich earth of the remote Minas Gerais state, where three billion tons of the ore lay buried. Huge mining companies in France, the United Kingdom, the United States and Belgium swiftly purchased many of these iron-ore beds at well below market value. In 1919, United States entrepreneur Percival Farquhar purchased the Itabira Iron Ore Company from its British founders. With the help of his other company, the Vitoria-Minas Railroad, Farquhar planned to build a monopoly in Brazilian iron ore production and exports.

The Early Years: 1940s

In the 1930s, Brazil was facing a major economic and political crisis. The outcome of that year's presidential election was challenged by a political-military insurrection, with power ultimately handed to Getulio Vargas. The so-called 1930 Revolution and Brazil's newest leader championed a movement toward nationalism. The Vargas years (1930–1945) in Brazil are characterized by the creation of a powerful interventionist federal government, and this sentiment applied to the nation's valuable supply of mineral reserves. Political concerns arose over the growing foreign ownership of mines at this time. In a conciliatory gesture, Farquhar and other mine owners ''Brazilianized'' the Itabira Iron Ore Company, splitting it into Companhia Brasileria de Mineracao and Itabira Mineracao.

As Vargas tightened his political control over Brazil, he began to focus on a pro-development philosophy. The Vargas regime pushed for a transition from an agricultural economy to an industrialist one in Brazil.

In 1940, Vargas sought to establish capital-intensive national industries, with emphasis on steel, electricity, transportation and weaponry. With World War II now in full swing, Europe and its allies had a growing need for iron ore. Mineral-rich Brazil used this to its advantage, garnering favors from the Allied nations. The Washington Agreements were signed in March 1942 by Brazil, the United Kingdom and the United States, defining the bases for establishing iron ore production and export in Brazil. Vargas obtained a $45 million EXIMBANK loan from the United States to establish the first major steel-producing plant in Latin America, Companhia Si-

Company Perspectives:

Companhia Vale do Rio Doce (CVRD) is the largest diversified mining company of the Americas. In addition to iron ore, it has significant interests in aluminum, steel, manganese, pulp and paper, gold, copper, kaolin, potash and other natural resources. It is a major logistics player in Brazil, owning and operating railroads, maritime terminals and a shipping company.

derugica Nacional (CSN). The Washington Agreements also called for the transfer of United Kingdom-owned Itabira Mines to the Brazilian government along with the Vitoria-Minas Railroad. In exchange, Brazil declared war against the Third Reich. Vargas also obtained another $14 million loan from the US EXIMBANK to purchase machinery and equipment.

On June 1, 1942, Vargas created the Companhia Vale do Rio Doce (CVRD), in accordance with the Washington Agreements, and began fulfilling his plan to modernize the Brazilian economy.

1950s–60s: Reaching Carajas

CVRD was originally designed to provide raw materials for CSN. In 1949, the company was supplying 80 percent of Brazil's iron ore exports. By this time Vargas had been out of power for four years, but he was elected to the presidency again in 1951. Vargas quickly resumed his industrialization plan for Brazil and in 1952 created the National Bank for Economic Development (BNDE) to finance industrial pursuits. It was also this year that the Brazilian government took over definitive control of CVRD operations.

By that time, an aging Vargas realized his political clout was waning and he began losing favor among the Brazilian industrial elite. Besides his creation in 1953 of Petrobas, a government-owned oil monopoly, the last years of Vargas' rule were lacking in industrial-based achievements. Political rivals and rumors of corruption began to plague Vargas, who committed suicide in the presidential palace in 1954. A new president, Juscelino Kubitschek, advocated many of the same modernization ideas of Vargas, but his equally ambitious plan involved a triangulated strategy between the Brazilian state-owned companies, private Brazilian firms, and European and American nationals. With the Kubitshcek plan underway, the late 1950s proved to be the most productive in Brazil's history.

In 1959, CVRD inaugurated the Paul Wharf at the Port of Vitoria with the start-up of regular exports of fines and run-of-mine ores. Later, the company incorporated its own shipping arm, Vale do Rio Doce Navegacao SA—Docenave, which has grown to become one of the top 10 shipping companies in the world. The company's first long-term iron ore supply contracts were also signed in 1962. Five years later, CVRD incorporated another important subsidiary, Florestas Rio Doce (FRDSA). CVRD reached another important milestone that year. By 1967, the company ranked among the six largest export companies in the world.

In 1968, CVRD employee Jose Eduardo Machado, a geologist with the Ore Prospecting Center, reached Carajas, or Amazonia, for the first time. Geological surveys would later prove that Carajas held the world's largest iron ore reserves, more than 18 billion tons. The next year, the first CVRD palletizing plant was inaugurated at Tubarao, Espirito Santo State.

1970s–80s: Building a Conglomerate

CVRD continued to incorporate numerous subsidiaries during the next two decades. The company, in association with US Steel, incorporated the Amazonia Mineracao SA mining company in 1970. The next year it incorporated a prospecting subsidiary, Rio Doce Geologia e Mineracao—Decegeo. The company absorbed $82 million in investments over the next seven years as it completed the widest ranging geological survey ever carried out in Brazil. It was through this prospecting drive that CVRD discovered 35 new deposits of 11 different minerals in 13 Brazilian states. In 1973, CVRD incorporated the Celulose Nipo-Brasileria XA-CENIBRA pulp mill and Companhia Italo-Brasileria de Pelotizacao-Itabrasco palletizing plant (with CVRD owning 50.9 percent and with Italy's Finsider International owning the balance).

Four additional subsidiaries were incorporated in 1974. A pelletizing plant, Companhia Nipo-Brasileira de Pelotizacao-Nibrasco, was set up as a joint venture with a group of Japanese steel mills headed by Nippon Steel that year. Companhia Hispano-Brasileira de Pelotizacao, another pelletizing plant, was set up by CVRD with Spain's Ensidesa. Aluminio Brasileiro SA-Albras was incorporated as a joint venture aluminum production company by CVRD and Nippon Amazon Aluminium to produce primary aluminum. Mineracao Rio do Norte—MRN, a multinational mining consortium set up to work bauxite deposits along the Trombetas River, Para State, was incorporated in 1974 as well.

In 1975, CVRD became the world's largest iron ore exporter, a title the company still holds, with 16 percent of the seaborn market for this product. By 1976, the company was bringing in export revenues of $717 million through its products and became Brazil's leading foreign exchange earnings generator. Two more mining subsidiaries were incorporated that year: Minas da Serra Geral—MSG and Urucum Mineracao SA, a mining company set up to work the Urucum and Jacadigo manganese reserves near Corumba, Mato Grosso State. In 1977, CVRD was awarded exclusive mining rights for Carajas. Just as it had done with the Vitoria-Minas railroad, CVRD began constructing an integrated mine-railroad-port system to accommodate the ore mined from Carajas. In 1978, CVRD began work on the Carajas Railroad.

CVRD incorporated another aluminum subsidiary in 1978 called Alumina do Norte do Brasil. The early 1980s saw several more start-ups for CVRD. Valesul Aluminio SA and Minas Serra Geral, mining iron ore, began operating in 1982. The next year, CVRD started operations at the Coaling Terminal in Ponta de Tubarao and at the Timbopeba Iron Ore Mining Project. In 1984, CVRD started gold production at Fazenda Brasileiro in Bahia State.

In 1985, CVRD inaugurated the Carajas Iron Ore Project. That year the company used local and foreign capital to start operations at Eletrovale, Nova Era in Minas Gerais State. In

Key Dates:

1942: CVRD is incorporated as a federally owned company.
1952: Brazilian government takes control of CVRD operations.
1962: Company incorporates shipping arm—Vale do Rio Doce Navagacao-Docenave.
1968: A CVRD geologist reaches Carajas (Amazonia) for the first time, site of the world's largest iron ore reserves.
1975: CVRD becomes the world's largest iron ore exporter.
1977: CVRD is awarded exclusive mining rights to Carajas.
1995: CVRD is included in Brazil's National Privatization Program.
1997: CVRD is privatized.
1999: Ambassador Jorio Dauster is appointed new CEO.
2000: Company is listed on New York Stock Exchange.

1987, CVRD incorporated Bahia Sul Celulose, in association with Companhia Suzano de Papel e Celulose, to produce bleached eucalyptus pulp.

1990s and Beyond: Privatization on the Horizon

By the late 1980s, political and economic turmoil in Brazil prompted Constitutional reform efforts in the Congress. After decades of military rule, democracy came to the forefront with the drafting of the new Constitution in October 1988. Among the elements of the so-called Citizenship Constitution were limits on presidential terms and enhanced voting rights for citizens. Some argued the document gave the government too many responsibilities, while imposing undesirable restrictions on foreign investors. But Brazil was in the midst of an economic crisis during these years, and citizens were ready for new solutions that were not explored during the years of military rule. One effect of the constitutional changes was that a more negative attitude developed toward the state monopolies held in energy and mining, and it was this shift in attitude that paved the way toward the eventual privatization of these industries.

During the years that led to the privatization of CVRD, the company acquired stakes in a number of steel and pulp mills. In 1992, CVRD started operations at its Bahia Sul Celulose pulp mill, and it inaugurated the Capitao Eduardo—Costa Lacerda branch line in Minas Gerais State, linking the Vitoria-Minas Railroad to the Federal Railroad Network (RFFSA). The new 46-kilometer stretch of track sped the outflow of products from the cerrado savannas while significantly reducing freight costs. On June 10, CVRD signed its first management contract with the Brazilian government, its majority stakeholder.

In 1993, CVRD purchased a stake in steel-maker Companhia Siderurgica Nacional (CSN), which likewise held a small share in CVRD. That year, CVRD became the leading gold producer in Latin America with 12 tons per year. In 1994, the company announced record iron ore sales of 101 million tons. The 1995 acquisition of stock control of SEAS, a manganese iron ore plant in France, opened up fresh prospects for CVRD products on the European market.

The Brazilian government's $45 billion plan for privatization soon extended to its prized industrial conglomerate. CVRD was included in Brazil's National Privatization Program by Decree No. 1,510 on June 1, 1995, but the road to privatization would not be a smooth one. For the last 50 years, the state had directly intervened in the Brazilian economy by running its largest industrial companies, including CVRD. Once the task of modernization was nearly complete, it was time for private enterprise to take over to improve the efficiency of the economy. With Brazil then accounting for 40 percent of Latin America's economy as a whole, this was a significant undertaking. Given Brazil's history, it looked as if attracting foreign investors would remain a challenge.

The sale of CVRD was considered controversial because, unlike other state-owned companies, it was profitable and well-managed. By early 1997, President Fernando Henrique Cardosa had planned to sell the government's 51 percent of CVRD for an estimated $5 billion. A year earlier, CVRD had signed its first private sector partnership agreement with Southern Star Resources Ltd, an American company, to work the gold deposits. Still, progress toward privatization was slow in order to ensure public support.

After weeks of worker-led protests outside the Rio de Janeiro stock exchange and court-ordered delays, a Brazilian consortium led by CSN emerged as the winner of the privatization auction for CVRD in May 1997. CSN bid $3.4 billion for 41.73 percent of the common shares held by the Brazilian government, with a premium of 19.99 percent over the asking price. The consortium also included four Brazilian pension funds, Banco Opportunity and NationsBank of the United States. CSN, which was itself privatized in 1993, shocked investors by winning the CVRD prize. Although CSN was Brazil's largest steel maker, two more powerful Brazilian consortiums were considered the likely winners of the auction. CSN was under the direction of Benjamin Steinbruch, who was 43 and considered to be a relative upstart in the Brazilian business community, but CVRD's iron ore business, transportation network and other business assets made Steinbruch's company an overnight giant in the steel industry.

In 1998, CVRD reported its best-ever financial performance with profits of 1,029 billion Reals, a new record for private companies in Brazil. That same year, CVRD produced record iron ore output at Carajas of 45.8 million tons. CVRD remained under the leadership of Steinbruch as chairman and CEO until 1999, when former ambassador Jorio Dauster was appointed the new CEO of the company. Dauster took on a complex shareholder structure and a cumbersome group of non-core businesses when he inherited the helm. The company began divesting non-core assets in order to revive interest in CVRD stock, which had begun to lose value since privatization.

In 2000, CVRD began to focus on its core businesses of mining and logistics. The company looked to sell off its pulp and paper assets along with non-core assets in its steel and transportation sectors. In early 2001, CVRD sold its interest in

Bahia Sul as a first step toward withdrawing from the pulp and paper industry, and in March of that year the company sold its 10.3 percent stake in CSN. Expansion also remained an important goal that year, with CVRD planning to develop five more copper mines in Carajas. The company also looked to diversify in order to decrease its reliance on iron ore revenues, which in 2001 comprised up to 60 percent of group sales. Dauster announced plans in 2001 to expand CVRD's low-level alumina, aluminum and bauxite base to build stronger alternate sources of revenue. The company also began forming Valepontocom and other Internet ventures to develop an e-commerce business. In 2001, CVRD began developing portals related to its mining and logistics businesses.

Principal Subsidiaries

Ferrous: Urucum Mineracao SA; Mineracao Mato Grosso; S/A Min. Trindade SAMITRI; RDME; SIBRA; CPFL; NORPEL—Pelotizacao do Norte SA. Non Ferrous: Docegeo; 24 Mining Companies; Para Pigmentos; Brazil Kaolin Company Ltd. Logistics: TVV—Terminal de Vila Velha SA; Docenave; Navedoce; Seamar. Holdings: Aluvale; Florestas Rio Doce; Celmar; Valepontocom; Solostrata S/A; Multistrata S/A. Energy: vale Do Rio Doce Energia SA. Others Abroad: Rio Doce International; Rio Doce Asia; Rio Doce Europa Servicos e Comercio; Rio Doce International Finance; Itabira Internacional Servicos e Comercio; Itabira Rio Docia Company Ltd ITACO; Rio Doce America; Rio Doce Ltd; CVRD Overseas; CVRD Finance.

Principal Competitors

Anglo American; BHP; Rio Tinto plc.

Further Reading

''A Sorry State,'' *Economist*, March 27, 1999, p. 9.

Barham, John, ''Shaping Up for the Struggle of the Titans: Interview Jorio Dauster: Recasting the Mining Group Will Tax All the Ex-diplomat's Skills,'' *Financial Times*, July 8, 1999, p. 12.

Colitt, Raymond, ''Vexed Question of Ownership: A Tangled Web of Cross-shareholdings Bedevils the Future of Brazil's Iron and Steel Industry,'' *Financial Times*, May 15, 2000.

De Lima, Paulo-Tarso Flecha, ''Liberalism versus Nationalism: The Prodevelopment Ideology in Recent Brazilian Political History (1930—1997),'' *Presidential Studies Quarterly*, June 1999 p. 370.

Dolan, Kerry A., ''Resurgent Brazil,'' *Forbes*, June 2, 1997 p. 116.

Dyer, Geoff, ''CVRD Kicks Off Disposals With Bahia Sul Sale,'' *Financial Times*, February 23, 2001.

Katz, Ian, ''Look Who's Buying Up Brazil's Crown Jewels,'' *Business Week*, June 2, 1997, p. 130B.

''Nerves of Steel in Brazil,'' *Economist*, May 10, 1997, p. 64.

Oppenheimer, Andres, and Ellison, Katherine, ''Latin America for Sale? Awaiting the Broader Shift to Private Enterprise, Latin America Frets Over Pitfalls of the Past,'' *Miami Herald*, August 17, 1996, p. A1.

Osava, Mario, ''Government Claims Victory in Battle Over Privatization,'' *Interpress Service*, May 7, 1997.

''The Iron Chancellor,'' *Economist*, January 17, 1998, p. 63.

Wang, Michael, ''CVRD Mulling Plans to Beat Brazil Energy Woes,'' *Dow Jones Newswires*, May 8, 2001.

—update: Rebecca Rayko Cason

Comverse Technology, Inc.

170 Crossways Park Drive
Woodbury, New York 11797
U.S.A.
Telephone: (516) 677-7200
Fax: (516) 677-7355
Web site: http://www.cmvt.com

Public Company
Incorporated: 1984
Employees: 6,400
Sales: $1.2 billion (2000)
Stock Exchanges: NASDAQ
Ticker Symbol: CMVT
NAIC: 541512 Computer Systems Design Services; 33418 Printed Circuit Assembly; 33429 Other Communications Equipment Manufacturer; 514191 On-Line Information Services; 511210 Software Publishers

Founded in 1984, Comverse Technology, Inc. quickly grew to be a leader in multimedia messaging communications systems, namely mobile mailboxes for wireless networks. With over 370 customers in more than 100 countries, Comverse provides voice mail, fax and messaging services to most of the world's largest telecommunications companies. Comverse sells its products through an international sales force and found success early by securing a multimillion-dollar contract with the German government. The contract gave Comverse recognition as a contender in the new wireless voice mail messaging market. Today, Comverse continues to stay on top by offering a wide range of updated features, options, and variations on its systems and by developing new technologies for the communications field. Even with the slowdown in the tech sector during 2000 and 2001, Comverse has been able to post record revenues.

A Pioneer of Wireless Voice Mail Systems During the Early 1980s

Kobi Alexander founded Comverse Technology in 1984. A native of Israel, Alexander had studied economics in Tel Aviv before moving to New York in the early 1980s. He enrolled at New York University, but also found a job as an investment banker at Shearson Lehman. Alexander worked full-time at Shearson and earned his Masters of Business Administration at night. Alexander had always wanted to run his own business, but he did not expect an opportunity to arise so early. In 1982, Alexander met Boaz Misholi, an Israeli engineer who had an idea for a business venture. ''The week after I met him, I resigned from Shearson,'' Alexander recalled in the June 18, 1990, Newsday. ''I always knew I wanted to have my own company.''

Misholi's idea was to develop a voice and fax messaging system that would allow customers to store, process, access, and transmit information from any telephone or fax machine. The system would offer a far more comprehensive alternative to answering machines and other rudimentary gear available at the time. Misholi and Alexander recruited some engineers to help them develop the system. They also moved to their native Israel, where the national government was awarding subsidies to high-technology start-up companies.

In Israel, Alexander and Misholi operated their venture as Efrat Future Technology Ltd. It took the company just a few years to design and develop a marketable messaging system. Alexander and Misholi worked with the development team in Israel for two years. Joining them was Alexander's brother-in-law, Yechiam Yemini, who served as the company's chief scientist. In 1984, Alexander, Yemini, and Misholi moved back to New York to begin laying the groundwork for an infrastructure through which they could market their product once it was ready to sell.

The three partners set up a company in Woodbury, New York, called Comverse (a fusion of ''communication'' and ''versatility''). In fact, that enterprise became the parent company of Israel-based, Efrat Future Technology, Ltd. Comverse was incorporated in New York in 1984. The company generated sales of a few million dollars annually during its first three full years of operations. Net losses during the period were only slightly less than the company's sales volume because of expenses related to marketing and ongoing research and development. To raise additional investment capital, Comverse went public on the NASDAQ in 1986.

Company Perspectives:

Comverse is dedicated to the development and delivery of a broad range of multimedia network-based infrastructure, systems, applications and services, all designed to offer the user a personalized communications experience for network, cable, or Internet service providers. Committed to delivering market solutions that inspire the world, Comverse leverages global leadership and a successful heritage in network-based enhanced services, offering our customers the ability to deliver unprecedented access to communication, content, commerce, and community.

The product that Comverse began marketing in the late 1980s looked like a simple box. Inside the case, though, was a complex multimicroprocessor computer. The computer, when hooked to a customer's telephone line, was capable of performing a number of information-management functions related to voice and fax messaging, as well as call processing. For example, it could store incoming and outgoing messages for different people in personal ''mailboxes.'' Although similar products were on the market at the time, Comverse claimed to be the first company to integrate voice, fax, and call processing functions into a single system.

Securing Exclusive Partnerships in the Late 1980s

Misholi served as president and chief executive of Comverse in 1986 and 1987. In 1988, he resigned to pursue other interests; he later became a professor of computer science at Columbia University. Alexander stepped up to assume the helm, still aided by Yemini. Alexander realized that, because his tiny company was participating in an industry dominated by such telecommunications technology giants as AT&T, he would have to devise a savvy marketing strategy if he wanted to compete successfully. To that end, he decided early to target the international market, particularly in Europe. With the European economic unification scheduled for 1992, Alexander reasoned, Comverse could benefit by developing an early lead in its niche on that continent.

Specifically, Alexander and fellow executives succeeded during the late 1980s in securing exclusive relationships with several of the top equipment distributors in Europe. Between 1987 and 1990, Comverse signed marketing agreements with six large European distributors who had already established cozy relationships with governments and major equipment buyers. Those agreements gave Comverse an edge over larger rivals, because the distributors often learned of potential deals before Comverse or its rivals. That allowed Comverse to begin pushing its product early in the decision-making process. Among the companies that had agreed to distribute Comverse systems were Ascom Gfeller (Switzerland), GPT (United Kingdom and Australia), Voice Data Systems (Holland), and Oki (Japan).

Nokia Data Systems, an electronics products distributor based in Helsinki, Finland, became the sixth major distributor to sign up with Comverse in the late 1980s. Nokia Data was a member of the $5 billion Nokia Group, the world's largest manufacturer of mobile phones and cable machines. The agreement was important for Comverse because it made the company Nokia's exclusive provider of messaging equipment. Nokia enjoyed a close relationship with the Finnish national telephone company and provided Comverse with a strong link to parts of Europe and the Soviet Bloc that were relatively inaccessible through other marketing channels. Indeed, Comverse was banking on such emerging regions as the former Eastern Bloc to drive industry growth in the long-term.

Comverse's European Marketing Strategy into the 1990s

Comverse found a winning formula when it targeted Europe for its sales expansion. In 1990, the company landed a lucrative German government contract worth $10 million. The German post office, or Deutsch Bundespost, was accepting bids to supply messaging systems for German cellular telephone users. Competing for the contract were such telecommunications and computer giants as AT&T, Hewlett-Packard, the Netherlands' Alcatel, and Germany-based Siemens. Comverse was aided in the bidding process by Ascom Gfeller, a large Swiss distributor with which it had signed an agreement in the late 1980s. The giant contract—by far the largest ever captured by Comverse—gave the company instant recognition as a contender in the market for messaging systems.

The system that Comverse had developed during the 1980s and agreed to supply to the Deutsch Bundespost was dubbed the ''Trilogue.'' The product allowed callers who failed to connect with a cellular phone user to leave a message in the user's ''mailbox'' for later voice or fax retrieval, or remote paging. By the time it secured the Deutsch Bundespost contract, Comverse had sold only about 300 Trilogue systems, mostly in the United States. The German government, though, planned to install enough Trilogue systems to create 100,000 mailboxes for cellular phone customers.

Before the German contract, Comverse employed about 150 people, roughly 40 of whom were located at Comverse's New York headquarters; the rest were in Israel. The company performed most of its research, development and manufacturing in Israel, then assembled, marketed and distributed the systems from its New York offices. Most of the equipment was shipped to Europe. In fact, the percentage of its products shipped overseas had grown from ten percent in 1987 to about 80 percent by 1990. Comverse's United States sales were mostly to domestic telephone companies, particularly the wireless divisions of the Regional Bell Operating Companies and independent cellular companies like PacTel and McCaw.

A Small Company Grows Bigger During the Early 1990s

Largely in response to the German deal, but also because of subsequent contracts, Comverse began adding staff and beefing up operations in the early 1990s. Sales increased to nearly $16 million in 1990 and then to more than $21 million in 1991. After posting its first positive net income in 1989 (of $380,000), Comverse's profit rose to nearly $3 million in 1991. Augmenting growth in sales of its proven Trilogue systems, Comverse was developing and marketing other technologies. In 1990, for instance, it started selling a product called FaxLogue,

Key Dates:

1984: Israel native Kobi Alexander, along with Yechiam Yemini and Boaz Misholi, form Comverse Technology.
1986: Comverse goes public.
1990: The German government awards Comverse a $10 million contract to supply messaging systems.
1991: Sales reach $21 million with profits at nearly $3 million.
1992: Comverse purchases Startel Corporation, a leading supplier of transaction processing systems; the company also enters into a partnership with AT&T to provide multilingual voice processing systems.
1997: The company acquires Boston Technology in a merger deal, after which Comverse becomes one of the biggest makers of telephone voice processing equipment.
1999: Comverse acquires Amarex Technology, Inc., a privately held software development company; the company purchases Intouch Systems, Inc., maker of speech recognition software.
2000: Comverse acquires the Israeli startup Exalink for $480 million in stock; the company also buys Loronix Information Systems, Inc.

a Trilogue add-on system that provided a wide range of options for sending, receiving, and storing facsimile messages. The technology was first implemented by US West Communications, a Regional Bell Operating Company.

A series of developments during the early 1990s combined to rapidly boost Comverse's revenue and profit. In 1991, for example, Comverse agreed to purchase (in 1992) the assets of Startel Corp., which became a subsidiary of Comverse. Based in Irvine, California, Startel Corp. was a leading supplier of transaction processing systems used mostly by the telephone answering service industry, hospitals, and corporate message centers. The acquisition brought important new technology to Comverse's research and development lab and gave it access to a new segment of the market.

Likewise, Comverse scored a big victory late in 1992 when it reached an agreement with global communications giant AT&T for that company to offer Comverse's multilingual voice-processing system to corporate customers and telecommunications providers outside of the United States. The deal was a huge boon for Comverse because it represented an endorsement of its technology by the communications industry leader. The agreement gave AT&T the right to market Comverse's Trilogue and newer Trilogue Infinity products. Among the systems' newer features was a ''virtual telephone'' feature that allowed residents in developing countries to have a telephone number without actually owning a telephone or paying for a separate line.

Rapid Expansion in the Mid-1990s

In addition to marketing successes, Comverse continued to profit from the development and introduction of cutting-edge technology. By the mid-1990s, its Trilogue systems featured a number of sophisticated features. For example, newer Trilogue units incorporated multilingual speech recognition that allowed users to control their messaging functions by speaking commands in their native language. Other complex functions allowed Comverse's gear to support a variety of protocols and equipment and to minimize communication costs and maximize the efficiency of information flow.

As important as advances in Comverse's core Trilogue product division were, the company also found success in a different line of technology called AudioDisk. Comverse had developed AudioDisk in the late 1980s and started marketing it in the early 1990s. It assumed a much lower public profile than Trilogue, however, because the AudioDisk systems were marketed primarily to police and intelligence organizations. Therefore, the company was comparatively discreet about sales of the units. AudioDisk systems enabled police and intelligence gatherers, as well as public health, safety, and financial institutions, a much-improved alternative to wire-tapping, which traditionally relied on reel-to-reel tape. AudioDisk used digital technology to simultaneously monitor hundreds of telephone and fax lines and retrieve data instantly. Although it had received much less public attention than the Trilogue line, AudioDisk systems accounted for about 50 percent of Comverse's total revenue base in 1993. Furthermore, growth prospects were favorable. Sales gains in the AudioDisk division amplified hefty gains in Trilogue shipments driven largely by rapid international growth from Asia to Europe.

Comverse reaped the benefits of rapid expansion during the mid-1990s. Its sales rose to $37.5 million in 1992 before more than doubling in 1993, while net income increased to nearly $15 million. Then, in 1994, Comverse boosted revenues more than 40 percent to $98.84 million. But, even with yearly increases in revenues and profits, the company continued to look for ways to improve upon itself. It also faced tough competition from Octel Communications, which at the time was the industry leader of messaging services. When word came out that Octel would be purchased by telecommunications giant Lucent Technologies, Comverse needed to find a way to remain competitive. In August 1997, it secured a deal to merge with Boston Technology, headquartered in Wakefield, Massachusetts. Previously, Comverse had been primarily marketing its services to digital cellular phone or wireless companies, Boston Technology specialized in supplying voice mail, fax and messaging services to traditional wire-based telephone companies. The merger allowed Comverse to now offer its services to both wireless and wireline companies and gave Comverse clout, as it became one of the largest makers of messaging systems in the world. Boston Technology's operations were combined with Comverse's Network Systems division and Francis Girard, president and CEO of Boston Technology, became president and CEO of the Network Systems division, while Kobi Alexander continued in his current position of chairman, president and CEO of Comverse.

Comverse Takes the Lead in Voice Messaging by 2000

By the end of the 1990s, Comverse stood as the market share leader of wireless voice messaging systems with revenues reaching $1.2 billion and a customer list that included telecommunications giants Sprint PCS and Vodafone in Europe. But the company was also in danger of becoming a one-hit wonder. After 15 years in business, Comverse derived a whopping 73 percent of its revenues from essentially just one product—mobile mailboxes. Critics of Comverse point out that since its breakthrough voice mail system, the company has offered little else in the way of innovative products. Aware of the criticism, Comverse began a business strategy in the late 1990s and early 2000s to acquire companies with promising technologies of their own. For example, in March of 2000, Comverse signed an agreement to acquire Loronix Information Systems, Inc., a leading developer of software-based digital video recording, networking and live Internet video streaming technology. Management decided to run Loronix from its existing facility in Durango, Colorado, as a subsidiary of Comverse. The company quickly followed up that transaction with the purchase of an Israeli start-up company Exalink for $480 million in stock. Comverse hoped Exalink, like Loronix, would help it expand into the high-speed 3G video streaming technology arena and capture more sales to cell phone companies that had begun to outfit their networks with this much ballyhooed new technology.

Prior to acquiring Loronix and Exalink, Comverse bought Amarex Technology, Inc., a privately held software development company in March 1999. In August of that same year, Comverse purchased InTouch Systems, Inc., maker of speech recognition software. InTouch, based in Cambridge, Massachusetts, perfected the industry standard for natural language speech application interface based on continuous, speaker-independent, large-vocabulary speech recognition technology. Called InFlection, it gives subscribes the capability to dial, check email and even surf the net through voice commands. Subscribers may also have email and fax messages read to them over the phone. Commenting on the acquisition in a press release, Kobi Alexander, chairman, president, and CEO of Comverse, recognized the benefit and need for voice-activated services. ''The increasing need to reduce the complexity of communications, as well as the growing focus on safety issues relating to using wireless handsets while driving are fueling the demand for a single, easy-to-use voice-based interface to network-based services,'' Alexander pointed out. ''The integration of InTouch's state-of-the-art voice technology applications and middleware with Comverse's wide portfolio of advanced messaging and information services positions Comverse to expand its leadership in enhanced services even further by providing our customers with leading-edge voice activated services.''

As of 2001, Comverse Technology Inc. divided its products and services into five primary business groups. Comverse Network Systems sells the company's Access NP and Trilogue Infinity enhanced services platforms to wireless, wireline, and Internet companies. Through the Comverse Infosys division, the company offers the Audiodisk line of multimedia digital monitoring systems to law enforcement and intelligence agencies. The Ulticom division is a leading provider of network signaling software for wireless, wireline, and Internet communication services and was formerly known as DGM&S Telecom. Startel is Comverse's provider of integrated voice, data and networking software, which is used by telephone answering services, governments, universities and healthcare organizations. Comverse's star*home division delivers enhanced roaming messaging services to subscribers worldwide.

With Comverse's current rapid expansion through acquisitions, chances are good the company will add more divisions and product lines in an effort to keep its technology competitive and to retain its leadership in the marketplace.

Principal Competitors

Lucent Technologies; Nortel Technologies

Principal Subsidiaries and Divisions

Comverse Network Systems; Comverse Infosys; Loronix Information Systems; star*home; Startel; Ulticom.

Further Reading

''$2 Million Order for Comverse,'' *Israel Business Today*, April 7, 1995, p. 12.

''AT&T Using Comverse Technology System,'' *LI Business News*, May 30, 1994, p. 43.

Alexander, Kobi, ''Comverse Technology Announces 1994 Results,'' *Business Wire*, posted March 22, 1995, http://www.businesswire.com.

Bernstein, James, ''Big Catch for Small Fry,'' *Newsday*, May 18, 1990, p. 47.

——, ''High-Tech David Beats out Goliaths,'' *Newsday*, June 18, 1990, Section 3, p. 5.

Berry, Don M., Alexander, Kobi, et al., ''Comverse Technology Inc. Enters into Definitive Agreement to Acquire Startel Corp.,'' *Business Wire*, posted October 18, 1991, http://www.businesswire.com.

''Best Comverse Profits Ever,'' *Israel Business Today*, May 21, 1993, p. 5.

Citrano, Virginia, ''Telecom Contracts Spur N.Y. Exporters,'' *Crain's New York Business*, March 8, 1993, p. 17.

''Contract Signed by Comverse, US West,'' *Business News*, March 12, 1990, p. 13.

Demery, Paul, ''Sales Calls Ringing for Telecom Exports,'' *Business News*, January 22, 1990, p. 3(2).

Labate, John, ''Comverse Technology,'' *Fortune*, May 17, 1993, p. 102.

Machlis, Avi, ''Comverse Acquires Israeli Start-up,'' *Financial Times*, London Edition, July 6, 2000, p. 34.

McDonald, Michael, ''Message for Comverse Is Diversification,'' *Crain's New York Business*, March 26, 2001, p. 14.

Smithberg, Kristen, ''Boston Technology Joins Comverse in Merger Deal,'' *RCR Radio Communications Report*, August 25, 1997, p. 22.

''Record Quarter at Comverse,'' *LI Business News*, December 4, 1989, p. 6.

Wax, Alan J., ''Comverse, AT&T Connect,'' *Newsday*, October 7, 1992, p. A37.

—Dave Mote
—update: Suzanne L. Rowe

ContiGroup Companies, Inc.

277 Park Avenue
New York, New York 10172
U.S.A.
Telephone: (212) 207-5100
Fax: (212) 207-2910
Web site: http://www.contigroup.com

Private Company
Incorporated: 1921
Employees: 13,500 (2000)
Sales: $15 billion (2000)
NAIC: 422510 Grain and Field Bean Wholesalers; 31111 Animal Food Manufacturing; 311611 Animal (Except Poultry) Slaughtering; 311615 Poultry Processing

Formerly Continental Grain, ContiGroup Companies, Inc. is a world leader in integrated pork and poultry production, cattle feeding, and agriculture. Founded in 1813 as a commodity trading business in Belgium, ContiGroup was the second largest grain exporter in the United States until it sold the commodity marketing side of its business to Gargill—the largest U.S. grain exporter—in 1999. After the sale, the company changed its name from Continental Grain to ContiGroup and focused principally on meat proteins. Since the shift in focus, ContiGroup has become the second largest integrated pork producer in the United States. It operates 12 poultry plants in the southeastern U.S., runs one of the world's largest cattle feeding operations, and operates one of the largest shrimp farms in Ecuador. The company also has interests in animal feed, flour milling, and aquaculture in China, Latin America, and the Caribbean. ContiGroup owns 78 percent of the publicly traded finance company ContiFinancial (which was under bankruptcy in 2001), and operates an investment business, ContiInvestments.

A Family Tradition

In 1994, Paul J. Fribourg was named president and chief operating officer of Continental Grain, representing the sixth generation of the Fribourg family to enter the company's highest echelon of management. Concurrent with Paul Fribourg's promotion, his father, Michel Fribourg, made room for his second-born son in Continental's executive management hierarchy by moving aside to become the company's chairman emeritus, a position he held until his death in 2001. Michel Fribourg's stepping-down marked the gradual transfer of power from one Fribourg to another in a chain of command that stretched back nearly two centuries. It was Michel Fribourg's great-great-grandfather, Simon Fribourg, who founded the commodity trading business in his native Belgium in 1813. Fribourg's business was nearly two decades old when the industrial revolution commenced, forever changing the face of Europe and creating fertile ground for Simon Fribourg's commodity business.

European Origins

That Simon Fribourg founded his business before this monumental shift from an agrarian Europe to an industrial one was propitious. In the coming half century, Europe would experience unprecedented scientific progress and social change, engendering significant and wide-ranging developments in industry, commerce, and trade that brought vast new wealth to western European countries. Before the century was through, an extensive system of railways, under construction in Belgium by the 1850s, would not only significantly increase the speed of shipping goods, but it would also cut the cost of transportation in half. The methods by which these goods were produced changed as well, as small-scale craft industries and guilds gave way to the age of mechanization and full-fledged manufacturing plants. With the proliferation of these modern, heavy industries came large towns and cities and the emergence of a new class of citizens able to survive and prosper through the manipulation of capital rather than by owning land or tending to it.

As the effects of this industrial revolution spread, a society and marketplace for Fribourg and his business were made immeasurably stronger, buttressed by the advent of a middle class, the development of railroads, and the emergence of large urban and industrial centers. The effects of the forces that created this new Europe would enable Fribourg and his descendants to flourish in a world of commerce that, as the industrial revolution took firm root in Europe then spread elsewhere, witnessed the

Company Perspectives:

Drawing on nearly two centuries of innovation and achievement, ContiGroup Companies brings together some of the strongest, most experienced operations in international agribusiness, and ranks as a major supplier of nutritional protein to people around the world. CGC is one of the world's largest cattle feeders; the sixth-largest integrated poultry producer in the United States; and, through its interest in Premium Standard Farms, the nation's second-largest integrated pork producer. The company is also a leader in aquaculture and flour milling, and one of the largest animal feed and poultry producers in China.

rise of merchants, manufacturers, bankers, and commodity traders like Fribourg.

Before Europe was transformed by the industrial revolution, Simon Fribourg operated exclusively in Belgium, maintaining his company as a domestic commodity trading business. Simon then gave control of the company to his son, Michel Fribourg. Under Michel Fribourg's watch, the family business would make a significant move beyond Belgium's borders, as the currents of the industrial revolution reverberated from their origin in Britain to reshape three continental countries in particular: Germany, France, and Belgium.

Although many of the changes taking place during the century pointed toward industrial progress, rapid advances in agricultural methods occurred as well, leading to more abundant crops and occasional surpluses of food. Steam-plows and steam-threshers were becoming more and more common by the 1840s, replacing the tedious and millennia-old method of tilling and harvesting by hand. By the time these new agricultural implements were emerging in substantial numbers, investments by the Belgian aristocracy stimulated the growth of heavy industries in the valleys of the Meuse and Sambre.

Despite these early technological gains, the Irish potato disease of 1845 and 1846 had repercussive effects on the European mainland, leading to a grave shortage of wheat that doubled prices in western Europe in the late 1840s. Food riots erupted in Italy, France, Germany, and Belgium, and a financial crisis erupted after banks exhausted stocks of gold to pay for wheat. To exacerbate the situation, a severe drought crippled Belgian agriculture in 1848. In the midst of this tumult, Michel Fribourg made a fateful decision that forever changed the future course of his family's business. In 1848, Fribourg traded several trunks of gold for the as yet untapped market of Ukrainian wheat, which he in turn sold to his hungry fellow Belgians. This event signaled the beginning of the rise of the Fribourg family fortune.

In the coming years, the tides of change moved in a favorable direction for the Fribourg family, particularly as it began to operate as an import and export commodity trading business. Although industrial output had doubled in Europe in the 35 years spanning Simon Fribourg's founding of the business and the decision by his son to purchase Ukrainian wheat, free trade in the region continued to be stymied by a complicated web of tariffs and import restrictions. However, this web began to unravel slowly, just prior to Michel Fribourg's foray into Ukrainian wheat, making the second half of the 19th century a much more hospitable environment for the family business. As with the industrial revolution itself, Britain led the way toward the easing of tariffs and import restrictions, repealing the Corn Laws in 1846 and removing regulations which hampered wheat imports. Other European countries followed suit, enabling the Fribourg enterprise to expand and prosper; by the end of the century it had become a grain trading empire.

Nearly all of the changes that made the nineteenth century a signal era in modern history also made countries highly dependent on traded grain. As the twentieth century approached, the company's position as a premier commodity trader put the Fribourg empire at the crest of the remarkable period of commercial growth that would affect the entire world. The same industrial, social, and scientific advances that had swept through Europe were, by the turn of the century, raging in the United States, a country with tremendously vast agricultural potential. Accompanying this shift from east to west, particularly in terms of agricultural production, Russia, which had become Europe's primary grain supplier in the nineteenth century, ceased to serve as such after World War I, creating a new market for the Fribourg family to broker their commodity services.

American Venture

To capitalize on this limitless new market, the Fribourg family business, at that time led by Jules and Rene Fribourg, established its first U.S. office in Chicago in 1921. That same year, the company was reorganized as Continental Grain Company. Continental Grain strengthened its U.S. presence in 1930, when it leased a Galveston terminal from Southern Pacific Railroad. Interestingly, the Great Depression served Continental Grain well, for it enabled the company to purchase existing U.S. grain facilities at bargain prices. During the decade-long financial slide, Continental Grain purchased U.S. grain elevators across the country, obtaining facilities in such key locations as Kansas City, Kansas; Nashville, Tennessee; and Toledo, Ohio. By the end of the decade and after less than 20 years in the United States, the company had established both a sophisticated grain network and a stable and growing business in North America.

The outbreak of World War II in 1939 not only signaled the coming of hostilities that would stretch across the globe, but it also portended flight from Belgium for the Fribourg family. When the Germans captured Belgium in 1940, the Fribourgs were forced to flee their homeland and emigrate to the United States, where they continued to run their successful agricultural commodities business. Among the family members in this abrupt emigration was Michel Fribourg, named after his great-grandfather who had established the firm foundation for Continental Grain's subsequent success.

Postwar Leadership

After his father's death in 1944, Michel Fribourg, then 31 years old, assumed control of what had become a $300-million family enterprise. Ultimately, Michel would prove to be one of the company's most capable leaders, preparing Continental Grain for a modern global economy most notably through the

Key Dates:

1813: Company founded in Belgium by Simon Fribourg.
1921: Company reorganized as Continental Grain, opens first U.S. operation in Chicago.
1940: Fribourg family flees Belgium for U.S.
1944: Michel Fribourg becomes head of company.
1965: Company purchases Allied Mills, Inc.
1984: Donald Staheli becomes company president.
1988: Michel Fribourg steps down as CEO, Donald Staheli assumes the post.
1991: Company enters grain venture with Scoular.
1994: Paul Fribourg becomes company president.
1996: Company takes ContiFinancial public; company forms ContiInvestments.
1997: Paul Fribourg becomes CEO.
1998: Company buys 51 percent stake in Premium Standard Farms.
1999: Company sells commodity marketing business, changes name to ContiGroup.
2000: ContiFinancial declares bankruptcy.
2001: Michel Fribourg dies.

diversification of the company's business network into the production of beef, pork, and poultry products and the broadening of their business scope to include feed and flour milling and financial services. Michel Fribourg also achieved considerable success in geographically increasing the scope of Continental Grain's operations by expanding them into more than 50 countries, which served customers in more than 100 countries.

The strides achieved by Michel Fribourg during the postwar period were momentous, particularly through two of his most noteworthy achievements, one of which bore a striking resemblance to the greatest achievement recorded by his great-grandfather and namesake. Through the negotiating efforts of Michel Fribourg in the 1960s, Continental Grain hammered out a historic grain trade agreement with the former Soviet Union, becoming the first company to export American grain to the United States' cold war adversary. This lucrative trade agreement was followed a decade later by a similar deal with China, and Continental Grain became the first company to export American grain to that country.

Against the backdrop of these two significant trade agreements, Continental Grain embarked on an aggressive acquisition program during the 1960s and 1970s, purchasing Allied Mills, Inc., a feed mill concern, in 1965, and absorbing numerous agricultural and transport businesses. These acquisitions, part of Michel Fribourg's diversification drive, brought together several notable properties under Continental Grain's corporate umbrella, including feedlots in Texas, an English soybean producer, a bakery, and the agricultural products unit of Quaker Oats.

Entering the 1980s, Continental Grain narrowed the scope of its operations, divesting itself of its banking units and its commodities. The agricultural bust of the 1980s, however, resulted in the company's once again diversifying its operations by forming a number of financial units, most notably ContiFinancial. By the middle of the decade, the company was generating an estimated $14 billion in annual sales, up from roughly $5 billion a decade earlier, a prodigious sales volume recorded as the company underwent managerial changes of an unprecedented nature. One of the architects of the company's success during this period was Donald Staheli, who had joined the Allied Mills unit in 1969 and who eventually became president of Continental Grain in 1984. Four years later, when Michel Fribourg relinquished his chief executive post, Staheli became Continental Grain's chief executive, the first non-Fribourg to hold such a position in the company's 175-year history.

However, this historic shift in power only lasted a few years before a new Fribourg embraced the family legacy. Paul Fribourg, son of Michel, had spent his entire career at Continental Grain after his graduation from Amherst College in 1976. He joined the company's Chicago office in the mid-1970s, beginning as a grain merchandiser and then climbing up the corporate ladder as so many Fribourg's had done before him. By the late 1980s, Paul Fribourg was exercising his own influence on the company, realigning its international grain and oilseeds operations to create Continental Grain's World Grain and Oilseeds Processing Group, a division that he headed. Paul assumed his place in the Fribourg family legacy in 1994 when he was named president of Continental Grain. Fribourg ultimately succeeded Staheli as chairman and CEO in 1997.

Growth in the 1990s

As it had for decades, Continental Grain operated during the 1990s as the second largest grain and related commodities company in the world. Although sales were essentially flat during the first half of the decade, remaining static at an estimated $15 billion, the company maintained its firm economic foundation and continued to grow. In 1991, the company entered a grain-selling venture with the agricultural giant Scoular. ContiFinancial, the company's mortgage and home equity unit, had grown vigorously through the 80s and 90s, and in 1996 Continental Grain offered 16% of ContiFinancial shares to the public. The company formed ContiInvestments in 1997, an investment unit focused on securities, real estate, and private equity. Also in 1997, the company purchased the Campbell Soup poultry processing business, and in 1998 it bought a 51 percent share of Premium Standard Farms, a pork producer and processor.

Turn-of-the-Century Change

Continental Grain's increased interest in meat processing, as evidenced by its Campbell Soup and Premium Standard acquisitions, marked a significant change in focus for the company. In late 1998, Continental sought to sell its commodity marketing group to Cargill, Inc., the world's largest grain handler. Until that point, Cargill had been the company's principal competitor. The deal was held up for over eight months while the U.S. Department of Justice (DOJ) investigated the transaction for possible anti-competitive practices. In July 1999, the DOJ approved a modified version of the sale in which certain grain facilities had to be divested, and the transaction was completed quickly. The company changed its name to ContiGroup Companies, Inc., and focused its subsequent operations on its financial and animal protein units.

In 2000, ContiFinancial succumbed to a variety of unfavorable economic factors—Asian and Russian economic crises, unstable capital markets—that had plagued it since 1998. After unsuccessfully seeking a buyer, ContiFinancial filed for chapter 11 bankruptcy. Despite this setback, ContiGroup thrived under its new focus. In 2000, the company sold its U.S. Animal Nutrition Division to Ridely, Inc. for $37 million, and an acquisition of the Lundy Packing Company doubled the processing capacity of its Premium Standard division. The company reached sales of $10 billion in 2000. This optimistic start to the twenty-first century was tempered with sadness at the death of Michel Fribourg on April 10, 2001. The chairman emeritus was 87 years old.

Principal Subsidiaries

ContiBeef LLC; Premium Standard; ContiLatin; Asian Industries; ContiChem-LPG; ContiInvestments.

Principal Competitors

Cactus Feeders; Smithfield Foods; Tyson Foods.

Further Reading

''3 Million-Share Offer Set for Contifinancial,'' *American Banker*, August 29, 1997, p. 5.

Byrne, Harlan S., ''Land of Plenty,'' *Wall Street Journal*, October 18, 1973, p. 1.

Cocheo, Steve, ''Tractors, Combines, Feed . . . And Credit,'' *ABA Banking Journal*, New York, November, 1995, p. 56.

''Commodity Concern to Sell Marine Assets to CSX Unit,'' *The Wall Street Journal,* September 18, 1995, p. C16.

''Continental Grain Co.,'' *The Wall Street Journal,* July 17, 1997, p. B5.

''Continental Grain Co.,'' *The Wall Street Journal,* March 21, 1997, p. B12.

''Continental Grain Company Loads Historic Corn Shipment,'' *Milling & Baking News*, May 18, 1993, p. 29.

''Continental Grain Lumbers through Market,'' *Bank Loan Report*, September 14, 1992.

''Continental Grain Makes Announcement,'' *Business Wire*, October 8, 1998, p. 1078.

''Continental Grain May Buy Georgia Poultry Operations,'' *The Wall Street Journal,* March 4, 1997, p. B4.

''Continental Grain Sets Venture,'' *The Wall Street Journal,* February 23, 1995, p. A6.

''Continental Grain to Settle Iraq Fraud Case,'' *The New York Times,* November 26, 1996, v146 p. C6.

''Continental's Coup,'' *Newsweek*, February 3, 1964, p. 65.

Cornfeld, Richard S., ''Case Serves as Good Example of Shifting Legal Landscape,'' *Feedstuffs*, August 9, 1999, pp. 8–9.

Cullen, Jennifer Felser and Denise Lopez, ''New York Area's Top Privately Held Companies,'' *Crain's New York Business*, November 25, 1996, p. 23.

''DuPont-Continental Grain Link,'' *The Wall Street Journal,* March 18, 1996, p. C22.

Einhorn, Cheryl Strauss, ''Commodities Corner: Double Trouble?'' *Barron's*, November 16, 1998, p. MW14.

''Feed Maker is Expanding,'' *The New York Times*, February 29, 2000, p. C25.

Fluke, Cecily J., and Robert J. Sherwood, ''Private Ways,'' *Forbes*, New York, November 30, 1998, pp. 197, 274.

''Good Neighbors Can Still Get Sued,'' *Successful Farming*, September 2000, p. 16.

Hayenga, Marvin, and Robert Wisner, ''Study Evaluates Cargill's Purchase of Continental Grain's Grain Business,'' *Feedstuffs*, February 8, 1999, pp. 5–11.

Kafka, Peter, ''The Big Five,'' *Forbes*, November 30, 1998, p. 200.

Kichen, Steve, and Tina Russo McCarthy, ''Private Business,'' *Forbes*, New York, December 4, 1995, p. 170.

Kilman, Scott, and Joseph B. Cahill, ''Cargill to Buy Grain Assets from Its Rival,'' *The Wall Street Journal,* November 11, 1998, p. A10.

Kilman, Scott, and Steven Lipin, ''Cargill in Talks to Buy Rival's Grain Assets, Continental Grain Co. Deal Could Raise Concerns of Antitrust Regulators,'' *The Wall Street Journal* November 10, 1998, p. A3.

Kilman, Scott, ''Continental Grain Co. No Longer Lives by Bread Alone: New CEO Fribourg Deals with Loans, Chicken, and Need to Share Power,'' *The Wall Street Journal*, May 21, 1997, p. B6.

Kilman, Scott, ''Continental Grain Enters the Business of Meatpacking,'' *The Wall Street Journal,* January 7, 1998, p.A10.

Kilman, Scott, ''Continental Grain to Give CEO's Post to Paul Fribourg of Owning Family,'' *The Wall Street Journal*, April 1, 1997, p. B9.

Krebs, Candace, ''Is Marital Bliss Leading to Public Discord?'' *Agri Marketing*, March 2001, pp. 38–40.

Lavinia, Robert J., ''Continental Grain—Tosco Joint Venture Launched,'' *PR Newswire*, October 30, 1992, p. 1.

''Michel Fribourg (Obituary),'' *Feedstuffs*, April 23, 2001, p. 17.

''Michel Fribourg,'' *Forbes*, October 26, 1987, p. 154.

Muirhead, Sarah, ''ContiGroup to Sell Animal Nutrition Business,'' *Feedstuffs*, October 11, 1999, p. 1.

Muirhead, Sarah, ''DOJ Approves Cargill-Continental Deal,'' *Feedstuffs*, July 12, 1999, pp. 1–2.

Myerson, Allen R., ''Cargill Set to Buy Main Unit of Continental Grain, Its Chief Rival,'' *The New York Times,* November 11, 1998, p. C1.

''Rising Complaints Over Cargill/Continental Deal,'' *Agra Europe*, November 20, 1998, p. M/4.

Schwartz, John, ''Michel Fribourg, 87, Trader Who Opened Soviet Market,'' *The New York Times*, April 12, 2001, p. C17.

''Shh . . . Hedging Going On!,'' *Forbes*, November 1, 1976, p. 47.

''U.S. Gives Approval to Cargill Acquisition,'' *The New York Times,* July 9, 1999, p. C8.

Vail, Bruce, ''Continental Grain Realigns Shipping Units,'' *American Shipper*, September 1994, p. 23.

Wilke, John R., ''U.S. Demands Cargill Sell-Offs for Continental Buyout Approval,'' *The Wall Street Journal*, June 9, 1999, p. A4.

''Zimmerman of Salomon to Join Continental Grain,'' *The Wall Street Journal,* April 12, 1996, pB2.

Zuckerman, Laurence, ''Executive-Suite Shifts at Continental Grain,'' *New York Times*, July 1, 1994, p. D3.

Zwerdling, Daniel, ''Down on the Farm, the Seeds of Bad Policy Yield a Crop of Failure,'' *The Progressive*, September, 1983, pp.18–23.

—Jeffrey L. Covell
—update: Lisa Whipple

Costco Wholesale Corporation

999 Lake Drive
Issaquah, Washington 98027
U.S.A.
Telephone: (425) 313-8100
Fax: (425) 313-8103
Web site: http://www.costco.com

Public Company
Incorporated: 1983
Employees: 90,000 (full- and part-time)
Sales: $34.14 billion (2001)
Stock Exchange: NASDAQ
Ticker Symbol: COST
NAIC: 452910 Warehouse Clubs and Superstores

Are you in the market for a summer-camp-sized tub of peanut butter? Or perhaps a lifetime supply of panty liners? Maybe you are tantalized by one of the shiny new wheelbarrows stacked high to the ceiling or can't resist the outrageously cheap DVD player? But more than likely, you, like many of the other Costco customers, will at least buy an industrial-sized package of toilet paper, the consistently number-one selling item at Costco Wholesale Corporation's hugely popular discount-shopping warehouses.

Costco Wholesale Corporation operates a chain of membership warehouses that sell a wide variety of name-brand products, as well as the company's own Kirkland Signature brand of products, at discount prices to businesses and individuals who are members of selected employee groups. The membership warehouse-club concept emerged in the early 1980s and has become a huge industry, crossing into international markets. With 360 warehouses, located in the United States, Canada, Mexico, Japan, Taiwan, Korea, and the United Kingdom, Costco Wholesale Corporation is the largest and most profitable chain of its kind.

1980s Beginnings

In September 1983 Costco's first warehouse opened in Seattle, Washington. At this time, warehouse outlets had long existed, but the concept of a wholesale club was relatively new and promising. Dubbed ''buyers' clubs'' and begun in 1976, these warehouses were wholesalers that required shoppers to become members and pay an annual membership fee. The membership fee helped reduce already-low overhead, so that items could be sold at an average of 9 percent over cost from the manufacturer. At the time Costco was formed, membership warehouses were primarily a West Coast phenomenon. However since then, their popularity has spread throughout the United States, across the borders to Canada and Mexico, and beyond to many other countries.

From the company's inception, Jeffrey H. Brotman has served as chairman of Costco, and James D. Sinegal has been president. While Sinegal had a background in membership warehouses and retail chains (having been mentored by Sol Price, the founder of Fed Mart and Price Club), Brotman was an executive of an oil exploration company and cofounder of a group that operated a chain of apparel stores. In 1985 Costco became a publicly owned company, and in 1993, Costco merged with Price Club to become Price/Costco, Inc. In August 1999, the company reincorporated and changed its name to Costco Wholesale Corporation.

Increased Sales and New Marketing Concepts

Since 1984 Costco has had to increase the size of their shopping carts four times. Their customers spend an average of $95 a visit, a rate that has been steady over the years. But with some savvy stocking practices, including being the first membership warehouse to offer an expanding fresh-food section (featuring a bakery, refrigerated produce area, fresh meats, and seafood), people are visiting Costco more often. In 1995 customers visited an average of once every three weeks, but by 1999, they were returning every ten days. With more and more frequently returning customers, as well as the company's constant expansion into new markets with warehouses opening every year, Costco saw its sales earnings grow by a rate of 6 percent a year from 1995 to 2000.

Costco has three membership levels, ranging in price from $35 to $100 a year (in the U.S.): Business, Gold Star (individ-

Company Perspectives:

Costco is able to offer lower prices and better values by eliminating virtually all the frills and costs historically associated with conventional wholesalers and retailers, including salespeople, fancy buildings, delivery, billing and accounts receivable. We run a tight operation with extremely low overhead which enables us to pass on dramatic savings to our members.

ual), and Executive. Any business or store with a retail sales license is qualified for a Business membership ($45 a year), allowing these customers to shop for resale or business use. Business members (numbering 4.1 million in 2000) can also buy goods for private use, and the membership includes a spouse card. The member also has the option of buying up to six additional membership cards ($35 each) for associates or partners in the business (with a transferable company card being another option).

Gold Card memberships ($45 annual fee) are available to individuals in selected occupations or groups, and is also open to those who do not own a business. These memberships include the same wholesale prices offered to business members. Annual fees are fully refunded if members are not satisfied.

The third membership level, Executive ($100 annual fee), has all the perks of the other memberships, and other benefits. Members can purchase additional services such as auto and homeowner insurance, long-distance services, and mortgage services, as well as discounted business services such as health insurance and merchant credit card processing at vastly reduced rates. Executive members also get a 2 percent annual reward on most of their purchases. An additional perk for Executive and Business members is special opening hours, beyond the regular member shopping hours.

Discount-Shopping Warehouse Strategy Changes and Expands

Costco's strategy is to offer high-quality, brand-name merchandise at prices below those of traditional wholesalers, discount retailers, and supermarkets. To achieve this, Costco buys nearly all of its merchandise at volume discounts from manufacturers, rather than distributors, and stock is usually shipped directly to selling warehouses to minimize freight costs. Warehouses are often on industrial sites or in other areas where property costs are at a minimum, and stocked items are placed directly onto the selling floor or are still stacked on their pallets, reducing handling and stocking labor. The number of sales and service employees is also minimal, with a large percentage of the employees holding part-time status. Warehouses are almost entirely self-service, from finding and buying items, to loading them into a customer's vehicle.

Despite having warehouses that span three acres, and piles of merchandise stacked to the ceiling, Costco only carries 4,000 carefully chosen products at a time. Compared to a grocery store, that has an average of 40,000 products, or a Wal-Mart Supercenter, that has as many as 125,000 items, Costco's stock selection may seem relatively spare. However, the fewer products makes for easier inventory and tracking of prices. Three-quarters of the items are ''basic'' products like batteries, laundry detergent, or instant noodles. But then there are the ''high-end'' name-brand products, from exclusive trendsetters such as Ralph Lauren, or Nike, or Waterford, which may be stocked at Costco one day, and then gone the next day. With the complete lack of advertising (with expenditures reserved only for new warehouse openings), the sudden and seemingly random appearance of ultra-cheap name-brand products keeps the customers returning for fear of missing a good deal. Word of mouth and savings do the rest. The company manages to keep its sale prices at 14 percent above the product's cost or less. Striving for high volume, not high margins keeps profits high. In 1999, Costco's individual warehouses were pulling in an average of $91 million per year.

The company also has its own line of products, released under the Costco label of Kirkland Signature. In the constant quest to better prices, the company decided to start making products themselves. ''We sell a six-pack of Kodak 200-speed film for $21.99,'' CEO Sinegal told *Fortune* magazine in 1999, ''Then we have our own [private-label brand] for $6.99. How can you not provide that value for your customers? That doesn't mean we want to get rid of Kodak. But at some point, a vendor's going to realize that option is open. And it does create leverage for us.'' The company also taps factories around the world to produce items that are dead-ringers in look and quality of name-brand products (such as popular clothing brands), and sells them at even lower cut-rate prices than the name brands. In 1999, roughly 12 percent of Costco's products were released marked with the Kirkland name.

Costco has an extremely generous return policy on its products sold, garnering trust and loyalty in its customers. Costco is so confident in their products, they have a ''return-anything-at-anytime'' guarantee. *Fortune* magazine, profiling the ''cult of Costco'' in 1999, highlighted the ''diamond guarantee,'' where Costco promised to pay a member $100 if a stone was appraised for less than double the Costco price. Buying diamonds at Costco? You bet. At times, they often experienced waiting lists for Costco's $20,000 engagement rings. Having such upscale items on sale in a warehouse next to stacks of printer paper or a year's supply of cat food may seem odd, but Costco tends to attract middle- and upper-middle-class customers, those who are ''noticeably more bourgeois, . . . some of the most over-educated, overemployed hoarders,'' according to *Fortune*.

Over the years, Costco has added departments, expanding beyond just the traditional discount warehouse offerings. Extremely successful is the fresh-food department, which includes meat, bakery, deli, and produce. A large majority of the stores also feature a pharmacy, an optical-dispensing center, one-hour photo services, a food court, and the ever-popular and cheap hot-dog stands.

By the year 2001, 125 of the U.S. Costco stores also featured gas stations with cut-rate prices. The trend of selling gas at discount superstores was repeated by chains such as Wal-Mart and Sam's Club, competing with traditional gas stations, and cutting into the market. According to Reuters, these so-called ''hypermarkets'' (including Costco) contributed to an at least

Key Dates:

1983: Costco opens its first warehouse in Seattle, Washington.
1985: Costco becomes a publicly owned company.
1993: Price Club, a major wholesale club competitor, merges with Costco to form Price/Costco, Inc.
1998: The Costco.com Web site is launched.
1999: Costco reincorporates and changes its name to Costco Wholesale Corporation.
2001: Costco introduces the B2B (Business to Business) Web site.

one-cent decline in U.S. retail gasoline profits from 1997 to 2001, from 13.6 to 12.4 cents a gallon. ''Gasoline wars are becoming more frequent as a result of the growing share of these big competitors,'' Holly Tuminello, Vice-President of the Petroleum Marketers Association of American (PMAA) told Reuters in July 2001. ''That's because they are willing to use gasoline as a loss-leader to attract people to their other products.'' In 2001 the ''hypermarket'' gasoline sales accounted for roughly 3.5 percent of U.S. gasoline sales (or more than 12.6 million gallons a day), but that amount was expected to grow to 16 percent by 2005 as the various superstore chains continued to expand their services to meet the demand.

Surviving 21st-Century Challenges

With a bull run of over six years straight of profit-earning increases, Costco experienced an unexpected decline in earnings in the first half of 2001. Much of this was beyond the company's control, as the West Coast of the U.S. suffered from an energy crisis that sent energy prices skyrocketing. The state of California, where fully one-fourth of Costco's warehouses were located, experienced some of the worst of the crisis, as rolling blackouts became a concern. ''Energy prices in California will certainly impact Costco more than another national retailer,'' David Schick, an analyst at Robinson-Humphrey, told the *New York Times* in June 2001, ''It costs more to operate in California, and they have an awful lot of operations in California.'' The company responded to the crisis by equipping California stores with backup generators to keep refrigeration units running in case of blackouts, turning down air-conditioning, and designing new warehouses with as many skylights as building codes permit to allow the company to turn off lights during the day.

Though the energy crisis was much to blame for the slide in profits, there were several other factors that contributed. The economy was in a slowdown, decreasing overall retail sales. Plus the company was dramatically expanding, having already opened 27 new warehouses that fiscal year (a 90 percent spending jump), bringing the total to 360 warehouses in the U.S., Canada, Mexico, the United Kingdom, Korea, Taiwan, and Japan. Also, the profits couldn't match the year-earlier profits that were driven much by Y2K-related buying.

Despite the slowdown, Costco sales (in stores open at least a year) rose 5 percent in 2001, a crucial statistic in the industry. Revenue from membership fees (which had been increased the previous year) increased 23 percent, and Costco continued to maintain an impressive 86 percent renewal rate in memberships, the highest in the industry. The company had about 16 million active members and over 35 million cardholders.

In addition to its already existing e-commerce Web site for members, Costco.com (that had been launched in 1998), Costco officially launched the ''B2B'' (Business to Business) portion of their online shopping Web site in April 2001. This new feature allowed businesses in the U.S. to order products online for delivery, with some areas (Seattle, Los Angeles, and San Francisco) having the option of next-business-day local delivery from the Costco fleet. By further branching into e-commerce, and with plans to continue the company's expansion at the rate of 40 new warehouses a year, Costco continued its rapid growth with no slowdown in sight.

Principal Competitors

BJs Wholesale Club; Kmart; Wal-Mart; Target.

Further Reading

Branch, Shelly, ''Inside the Cult of Costco,'' *Fortune*, September 6, 1999.
''Expansion Costs Blamed for Costco's 13% Decline in Earnings,'' *The New York Times*, June 1, 2001, p. C4.
''Gas Stations Facing Threat from Superstores,'' *Reuters,* posted July 17, 2001, http://www.reuters.com.
Nelson, Robert T., ''Costco Profit Slides 12% as Energy Dims Earnings,'' *The Seattle Times*, June 1, 2001, p. C1.
——, ''Slowdown Trips Ws Costco's Bull Run,'' *The Seattle Times*, March 9, 2001, p. C1.

—Carol I. Keely
—update: Linda M. Gwilym

Cravath, Swaine & Moore

825 Eighth Avenue
New York, New York 10019-7475
U.S.A.
Telephone: (212) 474-1000
Fax: (212) 474-3700
Web site: http://www.cravath.com

Partnership
Founded: 1819 as the solo practice of Richard M. Blatchford
Employees: 900 (1998)
Sales: $350 million (1999)
NAIC: 54111 Offices of Lawyers

Cravath, Swaine & Moore is one of the world's largest and most prominent law firms. Its heritage includes partners such as William H. Seward, one of the founders of the Republican Party who served as President Lincoln's secretary of the State Department. In the early 20th century, Paul Cravath created a modern institutional law firm using what became known as the ''Cravath system'' that many other large law firms have emulated. Cravath, Swaine & Moore represents many large corporations all over the world in financial transactions, mergers, acquisitions, tax concerns, and other matters. It also has been involved in many high-profile cases. For example, it successfully defended IBM in antitrust lawsuits that lasted from 1969 to 1982 and represented the Federal Deposit Insurance Corporation in its case against Michael Milken. The Cravath firm consistently ranks as one of the top Wall Street law firms based on its size, profitability, and its long-term reputation for high-quality legal services. Although the firm has branch offices in London and Hong Kong, the large majority of its attorneys work out of the home office in New York City. The Cravath firm is a good example of an influential law firm that has expanded internationally without opening branch offices all over the world.

The Predecessor Firms from 1819–1906

In 1819 Richard M. Blatchford began his solo practice in New York City. In the upstate New York town of Auburn, Elijah Miller retired as a judge and then formed a partnership with young William H. Seward in 1823. Both Blatchford and Seward had graduated from Union College and contended against Andrew Jackson's Democratic Party, so they had close ties from the beginning.

In 1826 the Bank of England chose Blatchford as its financial agent and counsel in the United States, which brought in many clients over the next 40 years. About the same time, Blatchford became the counsel to the second Bank of the United States. After that bank's charter expired in 1836, Blatchford became the receiver for some state banks that failed in the Panic of 1837. The Auburn firm merged into the New York City firm in 1854. From 1841 to 1858 the Blatchford firm and then the merged firm were heavily involved in litigation involving the American Trust & Banking Company.

William H. Seward was the most famous of the law firm's early attorneys. He was elected governor of New York in 1838, helped found the Republican Party, and in 1856 and 1860 tried in vain to gain his party's presidential nomination. During the Civil War, he served as Lincoln's secretary of the State Department, a connection that helped his law firm gain the famous Pinkerton security agency as a long-term client. Among his most famous acts on behalf of the United States during this time was the purchase of Alaska from Russia in 1867, which was mockingly referred to by the American public at the time as ''Seward's Folly.''

After the Civil War, the law firm represented various clients in litigation resulting from the conflict. Some of its postwar clients were railroads, including the Mobile & Ohio and the Pennsylvania Central, that became involved in litigation as the industry consolidated. During the depression that started in 1873, the law firm first contacted J. & W. Seligman & Co., a bank that later became a long-term client that financed railroads. Additionally, in the late 1800s the firm gained more corporations as clients. For example, it helped incorporate the American Tobacco Company in 1890 and represented that company when it acquired smaller businesses on its way to becoming one of the few big corporations in the South.

Company Perspectives:

Our hallmark is the quality of our practice. We are not, and will never try to be, the largest law firm measured by number of lawyers. Instead, our goal is to be the firm of choice for clients with the most interesting and challenging transactions and cases. For men and women as they begin their legal careers, it is exciting to learn to be a lawyer by working on these important and news-breaking matters.

The Early Cravath Firm: 1906–45

Following the trend of other large law firms around the turn of the century, ''litigation became something of a stepchild in the office'' wrote Robert Swaine in his firm history. ''None of the partners had much enthusiasm for litigation other than that involving corporate reorganization or financial transactions.'' The firm's clients from 1913 to 1920 included American Hide & Leather, California Packing, Columbia Gas & Electric, Communipaw Steel, Green Fuel Economizer, Hoboken Land & Improvement, International Harvester, New York Talking Machine and affiliated Chicago Talking Machine, James H. Rhodes & Company, and Royal Dutch-Shell Group subsidiaries in the United States. Work for Price, Waterhouse & Company led to the Cravath firm becoming counsel to the American Institute of Accountants.

After World War I, Paul Cravath continued to build his law firm but also became more involved in civic and community affairs. For example, he was a director of the New York Symphony Society, the Metropolitan Opera, and the Juilliard School of Music, and was a founder of the Council on Foreign Relations when it was started in 1921. However, Paul Cravath's main contribution to the legal profession occurred in the early 20th century when he began some innovative changes that not only transformed his law firm but also other large law firms. The so-called ''Cravath system'' included hiring new law school graduates, training them as associates, and, after several years, allowing the best to become partners. Lockstep compensation was the norm, with partner earnings based primarily on seniority in the firm. Although lateral hiring of experienced lawyers from other firms occurred occasionally, most growth of the big law firms relied on this system of recruiting, internal training, and loyalty to the firm.

The Securities and Exchange Commission (SEC) and new banking and union laws led to more demands for legal services in the 1930s. In his firm history, Robert T. Swaine explained what had happened in the 1920s and 1930s. ''The expansion of personnel and the tendency toward specialization, which began in the larger offices of New York and other cities in the early 1920s accelerated during the boom, and, with little hesitation at the 1929 market collapse, continued as depression-induced bankruptcies and New Deal agencies engulfed business and created such demands on the profession that competent legal assistance was at a premium.''

During the late 1930s, based on listings in the *Martindale-Hubbell Law Directory,* Cravath, de Gersdorff, Swaine & Wood at that time had 18 partners and an undisclosed number of associates. Described by Ferdinand Lundberg as a ''law factory'' that could ''grind out standardized legal advice, documents, and services,'' Cravath served Ford Motor Company, Bethlehem Steel Corporation, and the Chicago, Milwaukee and St. Paul Railroads. From 1928 to 1944 the Cravath law firm worked on 16 railroad reorganizations or receiverships, a continuation of work it had started back in 1875. In 1935 the Chemical Bank & Trust Company chose the firm as its general counsel for its trust departments. The law firm also served chemical and drug companies such as American Cyanamid and Hoffman-La Roche, and its most important newspaper and magazine client starting in 1928 was Time Inc.

Considerable work for the Cravath firm came from securities issues. For example, it represented Kuhn, Loeb & Co.; Bancamerica-Blair Corporation; J. & W. Seligman & Co.; and Union Securities Corporation on securities and bonds issued in the 1930s and early 1940s for General American Tank Car, Armour of Delaware, Consolidated Oil, Douglas Aircraft, General American Transportation, Polaroid, International Business Machines, Coca-Cola Company, Pacific Gas & Electric, and many railroads and other businesses listed in Swaine's book.

The Cravath firm grew in the 1920s, with new offices started in Washington, D.C. and Paris. However, the Paris office closed in 1934 during the depression, and the Washington office also was later closed. In 1944 the firm consisted of 72 lawyers and 118 clerical workers.

Post-World War II Practice

By 1948 the Cravath firm had expanded to 97 lawyers and 166 staff. Economic growth in the 1950s brought even more expansion. To meet client expectations, Cravath lawyers worked very long hours. In 1958, Hoyt A. Moore, the firm's oldest active partner in the 1950s, said in *Fortune* magazine that he did not need any extra help. ''That's silly. No one is under pressure. There wasn't a light on when I left at two o'clock this morning.'' Similar work patterns continued in the decades ahead at the Cravath firm and some other big law firms.

Cravath, Swaine & Moore was ranked as Wall Street's second biggest law firm, based on the total number of lawyers. As of December 1957, Cravath included 116 lawyers, and only Shearman & Sterling & Wright with 125 lawyers was larger.

One of Cravath's notable achievements after World War II was helping IBM withstand a series of antitrust lawsuits that threatened its breakup. Initiated by the federal government in 1969, the case was finally ended in 1982 when the government admitted that its case was ''without merit.'' Cravath also helped IBM prevail during those years in lawsuits filed by Memorex Corporation, Telex Corporation, Control Data, Greyhound Computer Corporation, California Computer Products, and Transamerica. ''The Cravath approach in IBM has become the model for complex litigation at nearly every other major firm,'' concluded James B. Stewart in *The Partners: Inside America's Most Powerful Law Firms.*

To represent IBM, the Cravath firm sent as many as 80 attorneys to work at IBM's offices in White Plains, New York, near its corporate headquarters. Associates laboring for three or four years on the case sometimes became discouraged and left

Key Dates:

1819: The Blatchford law firm is started in New York City.
1823: The partnership of Miller & Seward is formed in Auburn, New York.
1854: The two law firms merge to create Blatchford, Seward & Griswold in New York City.
1885: The firm adopts the name of Seward, Da Costa & Guthrie.
1893: The partnership becomes Seward, Guthrie, Morawetz & Steele.
1901: The partnership adopts the new name of Guthrie, Cravath & Henderson.
1913: Cravath & Henderson is formed.
1920: The partnership is renamed Cravath, Henderson, Leffingwell & de Gersdorff.
1924: The law firm opens a branch office in Washington, D.C.
1928: Cravath, de Gersdorff, Swaine & Wood becomes the new partnership name.
1944: On March 1 the name of Cravath, Swaine & Moore is adopted.
1994: The firm opens its Hong Kong office.

the firm. ''The loss of associates was far in excess of normal turnover because of dissatisfaction with the narrow experience,'' wrote Erwin Cherovsky in 1991. Although the law firm gained about $20 million a year in revenues, it was forced to hire outside attorneys, so-called lateral hires, in a move contrary to its firm culture. Cherovsky concluded, ''the long, arduous litigation placed a severe strain on Cravath and the institutional basis of its organization.''

In addition to the IBM case, the firm handled other high-profile suits. In the 1970s the Cravath firm successfully defended CBS when it was sued for libel by General William Westmoreland, the head of the U.S. Army in Vietnam. It also helped Royal Dutch/Shell Group successfully defend itself against antitrust allegations.

The firm grew from 263 attorneys in 1986 to 305 in 1990. Its gross revenues also increased, from $119 million in 1986 to $213 million in 1989. According to surveys in *The American Lawyer,* the Cravath firm in 1988 and 1989 led the nation in profits per partner with $1.6 million and $1.8 million respectively.

The Firm in the 1990s and Beyond

In the 1990s big law firms grew even larger, in part because of the growth of their multinational corporate clients and an increasingly globalized economy stimulated by declining trade barriers from agreements such as the North American Free Trade Agreement. However, law firms disagreed on how to provide services for the growing number of cross-border business deals. A few like London's Clifford Chance chose to create a global firm by consolidating with other law firms, resulting in numerous offices worldwide. On the other hand, the Cravath firm and most New York law firms chose to work with local lawyers in joint ventures without creating so many international offices. In 2000 the Cravath firm maintained just two small foreign offices in London and Hong Kong and said it planned no new branches. Cravath's London branch included lawyers who practiced only United States law, while Clifford Chance and some American law firms in London had attorneys qualified in both American and British law.

That lack of foreign offices did not seem to dent Cravath's international growth. In fact, in 1998 most of Cravath's work in mergers and acquisitions was with overseas clients. In the 1990s Cravath assisted in major mergers, including WorldCom acquiring MCI, the Conrail/Norfolk/CSX deal, the AT&T/Lucent transaction, Boeing's acquisition of McDonnell, the Westinghouse/Infinity deal, and the merger between Morgan Stanley and Dean Witter. In 1999 the Cravath law firm ranked as the world's seventh largest merger/acquisition law firm, with a total of 97 deals worth $451.3 billion.

According to *The American Lawyer's* annual listing of America's largest law firms, the Cravath law firm was ranked number 20 based on its 1999 gross revenue of $350 million. It was also ranked third in the nation for its 1999 profits per equity partner of $2.1 million, and one of the ''Winners of the Nineties'' from its 37-percent growth in profits per partner since 1990. With its historic record of excellence combined with this recent performance, Cravath, Swaine & Moore seemed well prepared to compete in the rapidly changing globalized economy of the new millennium.

Principal Competitors

Davis Polk & Wardwell; Simpson Thacher & Bartlett; Sullivan & Cromwell; Cleary, Gottlieb, Steen & Hamilton; Wachtell, Lipton, Rosen & Katz.

Further Reading

''The Battle of the Atlantic,'' *Economist,* February 26, 2000.
Cherovsky, Erwin, *The Guide to New York Law Firms,* New York: St. Martin's Press, 1991.
Klaw, Spencer, ''The Wall Street Lawyers,'' *Fortune,* February 1958, pp. 140+.
Kurson, Ken, ''The New Mergermania,'' *Esquire,* August 1, 1998.
Lundberg, Ferdinand, ''The Law Factories: Brains of the Status Quo,'' *Harper's Magazine,* July 1939, pp. 180–92.
McNatt, Robert, ''Top 10 M&A Law Firms,'' *Business Week,* February 28, 2000, p. 6.
Malkani, Sheila V., and Michael F. Walsh, eds., ''Cravath, Swaine & Moore,'' in *The Insider's Guide to Law Firms,* 2d ed., Boulder, Colo.: Mobius Press, 1994.
Mannix, Rob, ''Inside US Firms in London,'' *International Financial Law Review,* August 1999, pp. 35–39.
Stewart, James B., *The Partners: Inside America's Most Powerful Law Firms,* New York: Simon and Schuster, 1983.
Swaine, Robert T., *The Cravath Firm and Its Predecessors, 1819–1947,* 3 Vols, New York: Cravath, Swaine, 1948.
Watson, Thomas J., Jr., and Peter Petre, *Father Son & Co.: My Life at IBM and Beyond,* New York: Bantam Books, 1990.

—David M. Walden

CTB International Corporation

State Road 15 North
P.O. Box 2000
Milford, Indiana 46542
U.S.A
Telephone: (219) 658-4101
Fax: (219) 658-3471
Web site: http://www.ctbinc.com

Public Company
Incorporated: 1952 as Chore-Time Equipment Inc.
Employees: 1,200
Sales: $259.11 million (2000)
Stock Exchanges: NASDAQ
Ticker Symbol: CTBC
NAIC: 332311 Prefabricated Metal Building and Component Manufacturing; 333922 Conveyor and Conveying Equipment Manufacturing

CTB International Corporation is a leading producer of equipment used by the grain, poultry, swine, and egg production industries. The company's main products include feed and grain storage bins, automated feeding, watering, and ventilation systems, and commercial egg laying and handling systems. Marketed under the trade names Chore-Time, Brock, Fancom, Roxell, Sibley, and Staco, CTB's products are sold in more than 90 countries around the world through a network of more than 1,000 distributors. The company maintains facilities in the United States, Europe, and Latin America.

1950s: A Better Way of Feeding Chickens

The forerunner to CTB International was founded in 1952 by a 42-year-old entrepreneur named Howard S. Brembeck. A native of northern Indiana, Brembeck entered the University of Chicago in 1929, with plans to major in economics. By the end of his freshman year, however, the United States was held immobile by the grip of the Depression. The Urbana, Indiana, bank in which the Brembeck family had its money deposited had collapsed, taking with it the family's savings.

Dropping out of college, Brembeck returned home and took a $5-a-week apprenticeship with Cyclone Manufacturing. Cyclone was a maker of chicken seed throwers—canvas bags with hand cranks that farmers used to scatter the feed around the barnyard. Under the tutelage of Cyclone's owner and Brembeck's second cousin D.E. Speicher, Brembeck learned about virtually every aspect of the manufacturing business—from materials purchasing, to product design, to sales.

By 1944, he had become the general manager of Cyclone. When he was offered a high-paying executive position with a farm-implement distributor in Alliance, Ohio, he left Indiana and moved his young family to the neighboring state. Eight years later, however, Brembeck was tired of working for someone else. Quitting his job, he began working in his home, experimenting with a new and better kind of chicken feeder. He named his fledgling manufacturing business Chore-Time Equipment.

In 1954, Brembeck moved his business back to Indiana, renting a run-down garage near the small town of Milford to manufacture his product. By 1955, his three-year-old business had sales of more than $100,000. He was not entirely satisfied with the feeding device, however. ''I still thought there had to be a more efficient way to feed chickens,'' he explained in an August 2000 interview with the *Indianapolis Star*. By the end of the 1950s, he had invented a more complicated feeding system: a motorized auger that carried feed from the storage gin to the feeder, and that could go up, down, and around corners. It was this device that set his business on the path to success.

As sales of the motorized feeding device increased, Chore-Time continued to grow and to develop new products to serve the poultry and livestock industries. In 1957, Brembeck began manufacturing small hopper bins for the bulk storage of feed. He formed a separate company—Brock Manufacturing Inc.—to handle this new business.

1960–80s: Continued Growth

In 1967, Brembeck partnered with another businessman, Forrest Ramser, to establish Roxell, N.V. Based in Belgium, Roxell was to serve as the European arm of Chore-Time,

Company Perspectives:

The company's goals are: 1. To make systems for the care of poultry and livestock, and feed and grain storage and handling systems that users consider the best in the world. 2. To do such an outstanding job of selling and servicing our products that users will prefer our products to all others. 3. To create a working environment that gives employees the opportunity to develop their best selves and do their best work. 4. To develop alert, progressive management in all areas. 5. To build a business dedicated to: EXCELLENCE IN ALL THINGS.

manufacturing and marketing a line of feeding and storage equipment similar to that of Chore-Time.

In 1976, Brembeck restructured his businesses, merging Chore-Time Equipment and Brock Manufacturing into a single corporation: CTB Inc. The company retained Chore-Time and Brock as trade names, however, continuing to market products under the increasingly well-known brands. That same year, Brembeck's daughter, Caryl, joined CTB's board of directors.

CTB's European operation, Roxell, was spun off from the company in 1985, coming under separate ownership. Also in 1985, CTB formed a new subsidiary: CTB Vinyl Products. The new company, which evolved from CTB's manufacture of vinyl products for agricultural use, manufactured residential and commercial vinyl products such as fencing and decking materials.

The late 1980s saw another member of the Brembeck family join CTB. In 1988, Brembeck's grandson, Chris Chocola, became an employee of the family business, soon attaining the rank of general manager of CTB's Brock division.

Early to Mid-1990s: A Flurry of Changes

At the beginning of the 1990s, CTB had sales of more than $100 million. In June 1992, the company established a South American office, production facility, and warehouse in Uruguay. The new office was to be a home base for CTB's plans to broaden its market in Argentina, Brazil, Paraguay, and Uruguay. A few years after establishing its Uruguay plant, the company incorporated Chore-Time Brock Ltda. in Brazil, to serve the Brazilian market. Also in the early 1990s, the company boosted the capacity of its domestic operations, expanding both its Chore-Time plant and its Brock plant in Milford.

In July 1993, Chris Chocola became executive vice-president of CTB, and the following March he was named the company's CEO. In 1995, the 85-year-old Howard Brembeck retired, and without its founder, early in the following year, CTB was acquired by American Securities Capital Partners, L.P., a New York-based private investment firm. American Securities' managing director, Michael Fisch, became the chairman of CTB's board of directors. The Chocola family—Brembeck's daughter and her son—retained a minority stake in the company, and Chris Chocola remained as the company's president and CEO.

Under its new ownership, CTB began to expand and diversify more rapidly, making two significant acquisitions in 1997. The first of these acquisitions was Fancom Holding B.V., a Netherlands-based maker of climate-control and software systems used in the poultry and livestock industries. The second acquisition was the grain systems division of Butler Manufacturing Co., a Kansas City, Missouri-based producer of commercial and agricultural grain bins. Butler's primary market was in the western grain belt, while CTB's grain bin business was stronger in the east. In addition, Butler's bins were of different sizes and shapes than CTB's line. Therefore, the purchase served to approximately double the size of the company's grain bin business, and to strengthen its presence in terms of both geography and product lines. CTB paid a total of $41.6 million for the Fancom and Butler acquisitions, which had a combined total of almost $70 million in sales in 1996. And at the same time it was working to finalize its acquisitions, CTB shed a division that fit less tightly with is agricultural focus. The company sold CTB Vinyl Products to Royal Group Technologies Ltd.

In August 1997, just a few months after finalizing its Butler and Fancom acquisitions, CTB went public, selling five million shares on the NASDAQ and raising $70 million in the offering. The shares sold represented less than 40 percent of the total number of shares; American Securities continued to own a controlling interest—approximately 39 percent—in the company.

CTB used its IPO proceeds to pay off debt associated with the Fancom and Butler acquisitions and then embarked on a course of rapid growth, fueled largely by further acquisitions. In February 1998, CTB entered into a joint venture with Rota Industria de Maquinas Agricolas, a Brazilian manufacturing company. The new enterprise, christened Rota Brock Ltda., produced commercial grain storage silos, feed bins, and grain and seed handling equipment.

Late 1990s: Downturn and Restructuring

More growth was soon to follow. In April 1998, CTB announced that it had agreed to purchase Sibley Industries, of Anderson, Missouri. Sibley, which had been in business since 1928, was manufacturer of poultry brooders, heaters for poultry and livestock, and livestock handling equipment. In June, CTB announced its plan to acquire STACO, Inc., a Shaefferstown, Pennsylvania manufacturer of feeders and other equipment for the swine-raising industry. And in January 1999, the company re-acquired Roxell N.V., the Belgium-based company that Howard Brembeck had started in 1967 and sold in 1985. Roxell, by that time, had sales of $41 million, net income of $1.9 million, and facilities in Arkansas and Brazil, as well as Belgium.

The late 1990s were difficult for CTB, however. The Asian economic crisis sent ripples through many of the company's markets and made an especially serious impact on its operations in Brazil. By early 1999, Brazilian economic conditions forced CTB to dissolve its newly formed Rota Brock Ltda, before it even began manufacturing. Things were not going especially well for CTB at home, either. In the fall of 1998, the U.S. hog industry suffered a major downturn, with prices dropping lower than they had been in decades. This was followed by a softening in the egg market in 1999. The combination of domestic and foreign circumstances resulted in damage to CTB's bottom line. In 1998, the company experienced a 34 percent decline in net income. Although earnings improved slightly in 1999, they still fell below the company's expectations.

Key Dates:

1952: Howard Brembeck forms Chore-Time Equipment Inc. to manufacture and sell poultry feeders.
1957: Brembeck forms Brock Manufacturing Inc. to produce feed storage bins for poultry and livestock farms.
1976: Chore-Time and Brock are merged into one company: CTB Inc.
1995: Brembeck retires from CTB.
1996: The company is acquired by American Securities Capital Partners, L.P.
1997: CTB goes public, changing its name to CTB International; acquires Fancom Holdings and grain division of Butler Manufacturing.
1998: Company acquires Sibley Industries and STACO, Inc.
1999: Company acquires Roxell N.V.; restructures organization.

In March 1999, Chris Chocola retired the offices of CTB president and CEO, becoming the company's board chairman. His replacement was Victor Mancinelli, a veteran of the agricultural manufacturing industry. Mancinelli had served since 1992 as executive vice-president and chief operating office for Gehl Company, a manufacturer of construction and agricultural equipment used by dairy and livestock farmers.

The shift in leadership was not the only change afoot at CTB as 1999 unfolded. In November of that year, the company announced that it was restructuring its organization to streamline operations, improve efficiency, and reduce cost. As part of the reorganization, CTB cut its Milford, Indiana, staff by 12 percent for a projected annual reduction in payroll expenses of $2.1 million. The company also modified its plant layouts, introduced new manufacturing techniques, and organized into business units in order to dedicate employees to consistently serving specific customer groups. Once the reorganization was complete, the company was organized into three groups: the protein group (devoted to the production of pork, poultry, and eggs), the grain group, and the international group.

CTB's streamlining efforts paid off in 2000. The company saw four quarters of improvement, and ended the year with $13 million in net earnings—up $2.8 million from the previous year, despite the fact that sales for the year actually decreased by $13.5 million. Even so, the company continued to tweak its operations to enhance cost savings. In December 2000, it restructured its Netherlands-based Fancom subsidiary to reduce staffing by nearly 20 percent and to consolidate two of the subsidiary's facilities. It also made further cost-cutting adjustments at its Milford location and at various other operating units.

The company also began to grow its product line again. In November 2000, it purchased patents, trademarks, and trade names for a line of products manufactured and marketed by ABC Industries. ABC's product lines included dry bulk handling equipment and dust-control devices. The specific products acquired by CTB included bin sweeps for use in grain bin unloading, a dust-control product used in grain and industrial receiving facilities, and a line of bucket elevators and conveyors used to move grain. CTB planned to begin producing these new products through its Brock division.

2001 and Beyond

CTB continued to face significant challenges as it looked to the future. The domestic market for poultry had begun to soften in late 2000 and continued to be slow into the first quarter of 2001. Not only did this affect the company's protein group, but caused a trickle-down effect for the grain division as well. As a result, CTB reported first quarter 2001 declines in both sales and net income, as compared to first quarter 2000.

Despite difficult market conditions, CTB remained optimistic about its prospects for the future. In a presentation compiled in the spring of 2001, the company listed five major initiatives in its long-range growth strategy. They included: 1) becoming a best cost manufacturer through greater operational efficiency, improved productivity, and reduced expenses; 2) maintaining a product-driven focus through a commitment to product leadership and the introduction of innovative new products; 3) achieve a greater global presence by expanding its presence in key markets; 4) strengthening itself through acquisition, with the goal of greater product line diversity and distributor presence; and 5) leveraging financial strength by growing sales and earnings.

The company believed that the factors driving its future growth would be primarily population growth, increasing demand for animal protein, and the need for greater production efficiency in the markets it served. In fact, one could almost sum up CTB's confidence in its future success with the first two lines of its formal business strategy: "People Gotta Eat. It's A Fact of Life."

Principal Subsidiaries

Chore-Time Brock B.V (Netherlands); Chore-Time Hog Production Systems; Chore-Time Ltda. (Brazil); Fancom B.V. (Netherlands); Roxell, Inc.; Roxell N.V. (Belgium); Sibley Industries, Inc.

Principal Divisions

Chore-Time/Brock International; Brock Grain & Feed Systems; Chore-Time Egg Production Systems.

Principal Operating Units

Protein Group; Grain Group; International Group.

Principal Competitors

GSI Group Inc.; Gehl Company.

Further Reading

Frazier, Lynne McKenna, "CTB's Buying, Selling Shows Its Ag Focus," *Fort Wayne News-Sentinel*, May 5, 1997, p. 3B.
Key, Peter, "Farm Supplier Emerging from Shell," *Indianapolis Star-News*, September 1, 1997, Bus. Sec., p. 1.
"Power Trio," *Business People Magazine*, May 1, 1997, p. 47.
Shaw, Bill, "A Disarming Fellow," *Indianapolis Star*, August 30, 2000, p. E1.

—Shawna Brynildssen

Dawson Holdings PLC

AMP House, 9th Floor
Dingwall Road
Croydon CR0 9XA
United Kingdom
Telephone: 44 20 8667 0770
Fax: 44 20 8774 3010
Web site: http://www.dawson.co.uk

Public Company
Incorporated: 1891
Employees: 3,393
Sales: £626.6 million (2000)
Stock Exchanges: London
Ticker Symbol: DWN
NAIC: 42292 Book, Periodical, and Newspaper Wholesalers; 54187 Advertising Material Distribution Services; 54189 Other Services Related to Advertising; 56142 Telephone Call Centers

Dawson Holdings PLC operates the third largest newspaper distribution company in the United Kingdom, Surridge Dawson Ltd. Other Dawson subsidiaries distribute books, magazines, travel brochures, and inflight reading materials, and offer marketing and telephone call-center services. The publicly traded company sold off its library services and academic journal subscription fulfillment subsidiaries in 1999.

Early Years

Dawson Holdings traces its beginnings to the year 1809, when William Dawson established a bookselling and newspaper distribution business in the city of London. Finding a ready market, Dawson soon began distributing London papers to outlying provincial areas. In the beginning the newspapers were transported on horseback, but in 1825 Dawson began shipping them via coach. William Dawson's family continued to run the business through much of the 19th century, until 1891 when the Sampson Low publishing organization took control of the firm. Following the transfer the company was formally incorporated.

In 1895 Dawson opened a new branch in London to deliver papers to businesses and government agencies. Over the next several decades the company broadened its geographic reach, opening wholesale offices in Cardiff, Wales, and Exeter and Leicester, England. These were later joined by others, including branches in Brighton and Barnstaple. In 1921 the firm also opened a branch in Paris named Messageries Dawson SA.

In 1934 the company's wholesale newspaper business was merged with that of P.W.J. Surridge & Sons, Ltd. to form Surridge Dawson & Co. Ltd., which continued to serve London and outlying areas. The combined firm moved its headquarters at this time to a larger space on Blackfriars Road in London. Over the next few years Surridge Dawson acquired several other news wholesalers in Southampton, Folkestone, Littlehampton, and Southend. Dawson also continued to operate its book wholesaling operation during this time, which specialized in servicing libraries.

Surviving the Blitz: 1940s–50s

World War II affected Surridge Dawson dramatically, with the Blackfriars Road facility bombed on several occasions. To continue to serve its customers, the company arranged to transfer operations to several temporary locations, including the Daily Mirror building. The firm weathered the hostilities, and following the war its business picked up, such that larger quarters were soon required.

During the 1950s Surridge Dawson opened more branches in Boston, Chatham, Hitchin, Skegness, and Wicanton. The latter incorporated a printing company, later named the Surdaw Press, which Surridge Dawson used for its own printing needs. Expansion continued during the early 1960s through a series of acquisitions. In 1963 Abel Heywood & Son, Ltd. of Manchester was purchased, giving the firm one of northwest England's three largest wholesale agencies. Surridge Dawson subsequently expanded further in this region, buying eight more smaller companies, as well as five others in the rest of the United Kingdom. British newspaper wholesalers also undertook their first major ''rationalization,'' in which geographic territories were divided between the competing firms.

Company Perspectives:

Dawson Holdings will provide quality logistic and marketing support services that meet the real needs of all our customers. This objective will be achieved by the effective utilisation of the skill set and knowledge base of all our employees and by continual focus on understanding our customers' needs. We will achieve industry benchmark levels of efficiency by the effective use of technology, the elimination of duplication and waste, and the application of process improvement techniques. We will maximize our shareholder value by a complete dedication to the achievement of our corporate objectives and delivery of sustained real growth.

Focusing on Provincial News Distribution: Mid-1960s–80s

By the mid-1960s newspaper wholesaling in the city of London had become a difficult business to make a profit in. In an attempt to remain viable, Surridge Dawson merged its London operations with George Vickers of Brixton to form Surridge Vickers Ltd. Cost-cutting efforts were made, but the venture remained a money-loser and Surridge Dawson subsequently withdrew from the London market to concentrate on its regional operations.

During the 1970s and 1980s Surridge Dawson continued to acquire other small newspaper wholesale companies. During this period the company shifted its distribution from the by now standard rail transport to trucks. Surridge Dawson also took on considerably more Sunday newspapers than it had before.

In 1985 Dawson Holdings acquired McGregor Subscription, Inc. of the United States, a library services firm. Dawson also added to its book distribution business through the 1991 acquisition of Bumpus, Haldane & Maxwell Ltd.'s book wholesaling operations. The company had by now begun offering online services to businesses and libraries in the United Kingdom, France, and Spain through its Dawson Europe Ltd. subsidiary. In 1993 Dawson Europe won a contract to market OCLC's FirstSearch online news and journal database to its European customers.

The following year Dawson purchased a major U.S.-based library subscription firm, The Faxon Company, Inc., for £9.4 million. The acquisition made Dawson the second largest library subscription fulfillment company in the world, with some 36,000 customers around the globe. Faxon subsidiaries acquired included Faxon Canada and the Turner Subscription Agency. Dawson also bought a Spanish company, Madrid-based Libreria Ciencia Industria (LCI), during the year.

Going Public: 1995

In June 1995 Dawson began selling shares on the London Stock Exchange's newly formed Alternative Investment Market. The price of the stock quadrupled over the succeeding 18 months as the firm reported consistent profits and rising dividends. In the summer of 1996 Dawson Holdings acquired the remaining 57.5 percent of Surridge Dawson, making it a full-fledged subsidiary. The company paid approximately £15.4 million to buy out P.W.J. Surridge. The deal made Dawson Holdings the U.K.'s third largest newspaper distribution company, with 14 percent of the market.

In 1997 Dawson launched three online information services in the United States for library customers, including Information Quest, which offered eight million table-of-contents entries from more than 12,000 international journals. Access to the abstracts or full text of the articles was available for a fee via several delivery methods. During the year Dawson also purchased the news wholesaling operations of British newspaper and magazine distributor Johnsons News for £32 million. Johnsons was the fourth largest company in the British news distribution marketplace, with six news depots in the south of England, and its operations were folded into the existing Surridge Dawson system.

Difficulties integrating Faxon into the company forced Dawson to forecast a downturn in earnings from its library services business in early 1998, and the stock price quickly lost more than 15 percent of its valuation. That year also saw the firm settle a lawsuit that had arisen out of the Faxon acquisition with several of the latter firm's vendors. The out-of-court settlement was for a reported £5 million.

In the summer of 1999 Surridge Dawson completed a new "superhouse" distribution facility in London, Premier Park, which consolidated the operations of several smaller locations. It was reportedly the largest news distribution site in the United Kingdom, handling 500,000 papers that were destined for 2,000 newsagents around London, which the firm had resumed servicing in the years since its late 1960s withdrawal. Surridge Dawson was also operating 17 other news distribution depots around the United Kingdom. Immediately following Premier Park's opening, problems surfaced that resulted in delayed or cancelled deliveries. Surridge Dawson issued a public apology and also made a payment to the Newsagents Federation to salve the wounds of unhappy vendors.

Sale of Information Services Group: 1999

Dawson's 1994 acquisition of Faxon had not been entirely successful, partially because Faxon brought its own difficulties into the equation, and partly because the library services market was becoming difficult to draw a profit from. As a result, Dawson's bottom line was taking a continuing hit, so in the fall of 1999 the company reached a deal to sell off its entire Information Services Group for £34 million. The buyer was RoweCom, Inc., a Cambridge, Massachusetts-based library services firm run by a former owner of Faxon. Dawson units sold included Dawson Information Quest, Dawson UK, Faxon Canada, Ltd., Faxon Company, Inc., and Turner Subscription. The company continued to offer book distribution services to libraries in the United Kingdom and Europe.

Following the sale, Dawson acquired BFG Holdings, Ltd. Group, which operated four travel brochure distribution and telephone call center businesses. Soon after, four companies owned by Johnsons Group, Ltd. were also purchased. These included Johnsons Inflight News, which supplied reading materials to airline lounges, planes, and Eurostar trains; Johnsons Services News, a supplier of magazines to armed services bases; Johnsons Sporting News, which serviced British betting

Key Dates:

1809: William Dawson forms a bookselling and newspaper distribution firm in London.
1891: Business is purchased by Sampson Low publishing organization and incorporated.
1934: Surridge Dawson & Co. is formed as a joint venture with P.W.J. Surridge & Sons.
1940–45: Company offices are bombed during World War II, forcing a move to temporary quarters.
1950s–60s: Company expands via opening of new branches and acquisition of smaller distributors.
1967: Surridge Dawson exits London newspaper distribution business.
1994: Library service provider Faxon Company is acquired.
1995: Dawson Holdings goes public.
1996: Remaining portion of Surridge Dawson is purchased from P.W.J. Surridge.
1997: News wholesaling arm of Johnsons News is purchased for £32 million.
1999: Dawson exits library services market with the sale of Faxon Company and purchases travel-related publishers Johnsons Inflight and BFG Holdings.

shops; and Johnsons Subscriptions, a subscription fulfillment and marketing services firm. The BFG and Johnsons deals were valued at £12.4 million and £14.3 million, respectively.

The acquisitions continued in 2000, with additional complementary companies brought into the fold, including Martini Airport Services and Bridge Marketing Support Services. Bridge was merged into the BFG businesses, now known collectively as Dawson Media Services, while Martini was placed with Johnsons Inflight into the division called Dawson Media Direct. Marketing services offered by Dawson companies included point-of-sale advertisement placement and checking, mailing and multifaxing, mail-order fulfillment, designing and printing, and database management.

The year 2000 was a difficult one for the company. A U.S.-based software firm Dawson had formed, EOSi, proved unprofitable and was sold to the latter's management. A battle between the top news distributors also erupted, after market leader W.H. Smith announced plans to create a national magazine distribution network, leapfrogging the regional, ''rationalized'' one that existed. Both Surridge Dawson and John Menzies, the number two firm, threatened to take Smith to court, and a major newspaper publisher also announced it would withdraw many of its titles from Smith if the plan went through. Though some large retailers were in favor of the national network, smaller independents and publishers both expressed fears that a large number of independent news agents would fold if the present system was changed, serving to decrease overall news and magazine sales in the end. After a few stormy months, Smith announced it was looking for a buyer for its distribution arm, and the attempted realignment was shelved.

Dawson's library book sales division was proving to be a bright spot for the company, however, with the successful introduction of a new web-based ordering service, enterBooks.com, proving both profitable and efficient operationally. Introduced in December 1999, it was followed by enterProfile.com in 2001, which enhanced and added to the enterBooks system. The book division had grown to include four subsidiaries by 2001, located in France, England, Spain, and the United States. In addition to distributing books, Spanish arm Dawson España offered other library services including management and accounting systems, while Quality Books in the United States was a major distributor of small press book titles, videos, and audio recordings on informational and educational topics.

Approaching the end of its second century in business, Dawson Holdings was continuing to grow and change as it worked to improve its bottom line. Attempts to find additional sources of revenue were ongoing, with the acquisitions of BFG Holdings and the Johnsons companies providing new directions for the company to pursue.

Principal Subsidiaries

Surridge Dawson Ltd.; Quality Books, Inc. (U.S.A.); Dawson España (Spain); Dawson France (France); Dawson Books UK; BFG Holdings, Ltd.; Johnsons Inflight News; Johnsons Sporting News; Services News; Johnsons Subscriptions; Martini Airport Services; Worldwide Magazine Distribution; Bridge Marketing Support Services.

Principal Competitors

W.H. Smith PLC; John Menzies PLC; Lagardère SCA; Baker & Taylor Corporation.

Further Reading

''Battle of the Newsagents: Publishers, Wholesalers and Retailers Are Locked in a Battle Over Newspaper Distribution,'' *Economist*, December 2, 2000.

Cole, Robert, ''Dawson's Pounds 26M Deals Boost Network,'' *Times of London*, December 15, 1999, p. 4M.

Comet, William, ''Pounds 32M Dawson Deal a Wholesale Winner,'' *Daily Mail*, December 3, 1997, p. 61.

''Dawson Holdings: H2 Operating Margins Below H1,'' *Dow Jones International News*, September 20, 2000.

''Dawson in Pounds 15M Bid for Surridge,'' *Daily Telegraph London*, May 26, 1996, p. 1.

''Dawson Shares Down Sharply After Profit Warning,'' *Dow Jones International News*, January 7, 1998.

Doran, James, ''John Menzies Aiming to Scoop Top Spot in Newspaper Distribution,'' *Scotsman*, September 7, 1997, p. B1.

''Faxon's Latest Suitor Wins Their Hand,'' *Information Today*, October 1, 1994, p. 1.

Garside, Julie, ''Smith's UK Deal Is Hit by Mirror Move,'' *Sunday Herald*, December 3, 2000, p. 3.

Gresser, Charis, ''Booming Dawson Hits Pounds 21 a Share,'' *Daily Telegraph London*, December 19, 1996, p. 29.

''RoweCom to Acquire Dawson Information Services Group,'' *Online Libraries & Microcomputers*, October 1, 1999.

''SD Says Sorry for That Rocky Ride,'' *Grocer*, November 13, 1999.

Stevenson, Tom, ''Dawson Storms to Treble Profits,'' *Independent-London*, December 19, 1996, p. 20.

—Frank Uhle

Dechert

4000 Bell Atlantic Tower, 1717 Arch Street
Philadelphia, Pennsylvania 19103-2793
U.S.A.
Telephone: (215) 994-4000
Fax: (215) 994-2222
Web site: http://www.dechert.com

Partnership
Founded: 1875 as Mac Veagh & Bispham
Employees: 1,703
Sales: $284.5 million (2000)
NAIC: 54111 Offices of Lawyers

Dechert is one of the largest international law firms, especially after a major merger in 2000. It maintains offices in Philadelphia; London; Boston; New York City; Brussels; Harrisburg, Pennsylvania; Hartford, Connecticut; Newport Beach, California; Paris; Princeton, New Jersey; Luxembourg; and Washington, D.C. Dechert provides legal counsel in a wide range of specialties, from banking, taxation, and antitrust to intellectual property, biotechnology, litigation, and employment law. Dechert's 700 lawyers serve large multinational companies, small startup firms, nonprofit groups, government agencies, and individuals. Its predecessor firms represented the Pennsylvania Railroad and Getty Oil Company, among others. Contemporary clients include Aetna, Pfizer, US Airways, the Investment Funds Institute of Canada, Nomura Capital, The British Retail Consortium, Gerber Products Company, Internet Capital Group, CNN, and Comcast Corporation. Francis Biddle and U.S. Senators Arlen Specter and Joseph Clark were three prominent Dechert partners.

Origins of the First Predecessor Firm: 1875–99

The first predecessor of Dechert began in 1875 when Wayne Mac Veagh and George Tucker Bispham started a partnership. Mac Veagh had graduated from Yale in 1853 and then studied as an apprentice in a law firm before joining the bar in 1856. After the Civil War, Mac Veagh served as the U.S. minister to Turkey and on an Indian commission.

Meanwhile, Bispham graduated from the University of Pennsylvania in 1858 and in 1861 graduated from the Law Department of the University of Pennsylvania and was admitted to the bar. In 1874 he wrote *Principles of Equity*, an important legal textbook for the next several decades.

Although both Mac Veagh and Bispham brought their own clients to the new partnership, in 1877 the firm marked a major turning point when Mac Veagh was named general counsel and solicitor for the Pennsylvania Railroad's Philadelphia District. Thus began about a century of service to one of the nation's largest railroads.

In the late 1800s the partnership gained other clients, including The Philadelphia Saving Fund Society, the Pennsylvania Fire Insurance Company, and the Westmoreland Coal Company. Bispham in 1889 joined the Board of Managers of the Girard Trust Company, one of the firm's long-term clients.

A leading member of the Republican Party, Mac Veagh in 1877 headed the commission that led to the compromise resolving the 1876 Hayes-Tilden presidential election dispute that originated in Louisiana. As President Garfield's attorney general, Mac Veagh indicted the president's assassin. Bispham in 1884 became a law professor at the University of Pennsylvania, so both partners distinguished themselves outside their law firm practice.

In his history of the Dechert law firm, Robert V. Massey, Jr., said Bispham's most significant litigation occurred when he defended the Pennsylvania Railroad after several homeowners charged that the railroad's operations decreased their property values. The Pennsylvania Supreme Court ruled in favor of the railroad, and the plaintiff's appeal to the U.S. Supreme Court failed.

A Developing Practice: 1900–45

In addition to the Pennsylvania Railroad, the Philadelphia law firm served a variety of banks and insurance and coal companies in the early 20th century. Following the 1908 collapse of part of the Phoenix Bridge Company's bridge across the St. Lawrence River, the company used the law firm to defend itself against lawsuits.

Company Perspectives:

Dechert is a multipractice, international law firm committed to providing the highest level of legal representation to our clients. Our more than 700 lawyers across 11 U.S. and European offices work collaboratively with clients to recognize business opportunities and challenges and to help them achieve their business goals. We creatively build on our legal experience and industry knowledge to deliver the smart, solid results our clients seek.

Dechert supports the varied and international interests and growth of our clients. We offer services in more than 30 practice areas and industry concentrations to fit the unique scope and complexity of clients' legal needs.

Name partner John Hampton Barnes served as president of the Chestnut Street Realty Company, a subsidiary of the Girard Trust Company. The realty company owned Philadelphia's Morris Building, which was the law firm's home from 1910 to 1942. In the late 1930s a firm lawyer was appointed to represent the Philadelphia Transportation Company when it faced a series of lawsuits.

Name partner Francis Biddle became quite well known in the first half of the 20th century. While remaining with the first predecessor law firm from 1916 to 1939, he often served in major government positions. He became an assistant U.S. attorney in 1922. In the mid-1930s he served as the chair of the National Labor Board and was instrumental in the origins of the 1935 National Labor Relations Act or Wagner Act that led to a huge increase in the percentage of American workers in unions. During World War II, he served as President Roosevelt's attorney general.

During the depression of the 1930s, the law firm represented its long-term client Pennsylvania Railroad in a number of lawsuits. Those were Pennsylvania Railroad's peak years. According to the June 1936 issue of *Fortune* magazine, the railroad's 100,000 employees were 10 percent of that industry's workforce. The Pennsylvania Railroad also was one of the four railroads in the famous board game Monopoly that Parker Brothers patented during the Great Depression.

The Second Predecessor Firm and the 1942 Merger

When World War II began, the first predecessor firm, then known as Barnes, Myers & Price, lost most of its lawyers due to military or government service. With just two or three lawyers left, it decided to merge with Dechert, Smith & Clark, another small partnership in Philadelphia.

Robert Dechert and Curtis Bok had formed the second predecessor firm in 1930. After graduating from the University of Pennsylvania in 1916, Dechert served as an Army officer during World War I and then graduated from the University of Pennsylvania Law School in 1921. After working for his father's law firm, he became the vice-president and counsel of The Penn Mutual Life Insurance Company. Dechert remained the head of Penn Mutual's legal department after forming his partnership with Curtis Bok. When the two predecessor firms merged in 1942, the Barnes firm moved to the larger facilities in the Packard Building where the predecessor Dechert firm had its offices.

The Post-World War II Years

After World War II ended, the merged Dechert firm became more specialized, a typical development for such law firms. In 1946, for the first time, it formally created four practice groups: taxation, litigation, fiduciary, and business and corporate law. Its business practice of advising corporate clients on how to deal with the government's increasing laws and regulations expanded, while its litigation practice declined in comparison.

Robert Dechert headed his firm's taxation practice and was chosen as the president of both the Association of Life Insurance Counsel and the Insurance Federation of Pennsylvania. Dechert also served as counsel and trustee to the American College of Life Underwriters.

In 1946 the firm's 28 lawyers made it Philadelphia's second largest law firm behind Morgan, Lewis & Bockius with 36 lawyers. In 1955 the growing Dechert firm with 39 lawyers moved its offices to Penn Center. In 1954 the firm hired its first full-time female associate, but it was not until 1973 that a woman became a Dechert partner.

In the 1960s Carroll Robbins Wetzel, a member of the Dechert firm since 1931, made major contributions in the banking law field. In 1962 he played a key role in writing a report for the U.S. Comptroller of the Currency concerning proposed changes in the National Banking Act. In 1966 and 1967 Wetzel served as chairman of the American Bar Association's Banking and Business Section.

To mark the firm's centennial, in 1975 it published a book on its history written by retired partner Robert V. Massey, Jr. Unfortunately, Massey seldom even mentioned who the firm's clients were over the previous 100 years. In his preface Massey explained that he included little such information ''to avoid dulling the reader's interest.''

The Dechert law firm in the early 1980s represented Getty Oil Company, which had been started back in the 1930s by J. Paul Getty. On January 6, 1984 Getty Oil signed an agreement to be acquired by Texaco for $10.2 billion. However, that acquisition led to a major legal battle when Pennzoil filed a lawsuit for $15 billion in damages from Texaco for interfering in its planned takeover of Getty Oil. In November 1985 a Texas state court's ruling for Pennzoil awarded the company $10.53 billion. In April 1987 Texaco filed for Chapter 11 bankruptcy protection. Dechert Price & Rhoads in May 1987 represented several former Getty directors when they issued a formal statement saying they had never agreed to merge with Pennzoil. Robert Lenzner in his 1985 book about J. Paul Getty described the merger and litigation that pitted Getty descendants against each other, but he did not mention the role of the Dechert law firm, a fairly common omission in business histories.

Practice in the 1990s and the New Millennium

Dechert Price & Rhoads expanded its international practice in 1995 by opening an office in Paris. Since law firms from outside of the European Union were allowed to open a French

Key Dates:

1875: Mac Veagh & Bispham is formed in Philadelphia.
1894: Bispham, Wintersteen & Barnes becomes the new partnership after Mac Veagh leaves.
1906: Wintersteen, Barnes & Brinton is the firm's new name.
1917: Firm is renamed Barnes & Brinton.
1923: Barnes, Biddle & Morris is established.
1928: Barnes, Brinton & Biddle becomes the firm's new name.
1929: Barnes, Biddle & Myers is the new name.
1930: Dechert & Bok, the second predecessor firm, is founded.
1932: Dechert, Bok & Smith is the new name.
1934: Dechert, Bok, Smith & Clark becomes the new name.
1936: Dechert, Smith & Clark is the new name.
1939: First predecessor firm is renamed Barnes, Myers & Price after Biddle leaves.
1942: Two predecessor firms merge to become Barnes, Dechert, Price & Smith.
1946: Merged firm's new name becomes Barnes, Dechert, Price, Smith & Clark.
1948: Partnership becomes known as Barnes, Dechert, Price, Myers & Clark.
1952: Barnes, Dechert, Price, Myers & Rhoads is the new name.
1961: Firm is renamed Dechert Price & Rhoads after Myers retires.
1968: Firm opens its Brussels office.
1969: Harrisburg, Pennsylvania, and Washington, D.C. offices are established.
1972: London office is launched.
1980: Partnership opens its new office in New York City.
1987: Boston and Princeton, New Jersey offices are opened.
1994: Dechert firm forms an alliance with London's Titmuss Sainer & Webb, which is renamed Titmuss Sainer Dechert.
1995: Firm opens its Paris office.
1996: Firm's office in Hartford, Connecticut is started.
2000: Dechert Price & Rhoads merges with London's Titmuss Sainer Dechert to become Dechert.

office only by associating with a French lawyer, Dechert's office was officially a correspondent office. Its goal was to serve non-French corporations operating in France and other European nations.

In 1996 Dechert Price & Rhoads attempted to strengthen its Washington, D.C. office when it hired veteran litigator Leonard Garment. The firm's goal was to increase its access and influence in Congress and other parts of the federal government, for Garment had a long history of government involvement, from being a crisis manager in the Middle East, Wounded Knee, and Watergate episodes to representing Reagan officials in the Iran-Contra scandal and Judge Robert Bork when he was appointed but not confirmed to the U.S. Supreme Court. By early 1998 Garment had gained some business for the firm, completed his memoirs, and then left Dechert. However, he filed an age discrimination lawsuit against the firm that was settled out of court in 1999.

The Garment case illustrated relatively new developments in the legal profession. First, lawyers now sued other lawyers, an unheard of event a generation ago. It also showed changing expectations of senior lawyers. "It isn't a learned profession any more that values sagacity and experience," said Stanley Brand, a Garment attorney in the Dechert lawsuit, in the *Wall Street Journal* on January 4, 2000. On the other hand, Joel Henning, senior vice-president of legal consulting firm Hildebrandt International, said, "Knowledge and wisdom and insight are all well and good, but there are tremendous expenses, and very demanding clients."

Meanwhile, the Dechert firm teamed up with Pepper, Hamilton & Scheetz, another large Philadelphia law firm, to cooperate in training young associates. Writer Amy Stevens commented that, "Such camaraderie was once unheard of for competing law firms." This development was fueled by clients' unwillingness to pay their outside law firms for training new associates.

In the 1990s Dechert's intellectual property lawyers annually issued a report on trademark trends. Not surprisingly, its April 2001 report on trends in 2000 said that dot-com trademark applications had declined rapidly as Internet companies struggled in the stock market.

Dechert Price & Rhoads's clients in the late 1990s included some of the largest U.S. corporations, namely Philip Morris Companies, Sun Company, Crown Cork & Seal, Campbell Soup, AmeriSource Health, Baxter International, American Stores, and VF Corporation.

In the late 1990s Dechert Price & Rhoads's gross revenue increased, but its relative standing declined in the *American Lawyer*'s annual rankings of the nation's 100 largest law firms. In 1997 the firm's gross revenue of $160.5 million placed it at number 54. In 1998 it had $171.5 million in gross revenue and a number 59 ranking, which fell to number 60 based on its 1999 gross revenue of $197 million.

In 1994 Dechert Price & Rhoads had formed an alliance with the London law firm Titmuss Sainer & Webb, which then changed its name to Titmuss Sainer Dechert. The London firm served as legal adviser to The British Retail Consortium. According to Dechert's web site, the firm repeatedly had "been voted number one in the country by the Legal 500 (the clients' leading guide to U.K. law firms) for its advice to the retail sector."

After six years of the alliance, the two firms merged in 2000 to create a unified partnership called, simply, Dechert that by 2001 included 700 lawyers in 12 worldwide offices. This merger was part of an international trend in which law firms consolidated into much larger megafirms. For example, London's Clifford Chance merged in 2000 with a New York City firm and a German firm to form the world's largest law practice with about 3,000 lawyers. The consolidation trend exemplified by mergers of American and British law firms was part of a worldwide phenomenon in which businesses of all kinds joined forces.

At the start of new millennium, Dechert faced numerous challenges as political, economic, and social changes occurred rapidly all over the world. New technologies usually required legal systems to play catch-up. Trading alliances impacted exports and imports by multinational corporations and smaller companies. The Internet economy still in its infancy continued to be important. Lawyers debated the wisdom of multipractice partnerships, how to retain young associates lured by larger salaries at other firms, and how to attract and retain more minority and female lawyers. Dechert lawyers needed to deal with these and many more complex issues to succeed in the years ahead.

Principal Operating Units

Antitrust; Bankruptcy and Reorganization; Business and Technology; Complex Commercial Litigation; Corporate and Securities; Criminal, Government Investigations and Civil Fraud; Employee Benefits and Executive Compensation; Environmental Law; Federal Tax; Financial Services; Government Affairs; Health Law; Immigration; Intellectual Property; International Business; International Trade; Labor and Employment; Latin America; Media Law; Mergers and Acquisitions; Privacy Law; Private Client; Product Liability and Mass Tort; Real Estate and Mortgage Finance; Securities Litigation and Enforcement; Securitization; State and Local Tax; Tax-Exempt Organizations.

Principal Competitors

Pepper Hamilton; Morgan, Lewis & Bockius; Skadden, Arps, Slate, Meagher & Flom.

Further Reading

Chartrand, Sabra, "Requests for New Trademarks by Internet Companies Have Fallen As the Market Has Slowed," *New York Times*, May 7, 2001, p. 2.

"Dechert Partners Approve Transatlantic Merger; Firm Banks on Success Following Six-Year Alliance," *PR Newswire*, June 26, 2000, p. 1.

Lenzner, Robert, *The Great Getty: The Life and Loves of J. Paul Getty—The Richest Man in the World,* New York: Crown Publishers, Inc., 1985.

Massey, Robert V., Jr., *Dechert Price & Rhoads: A Law Firm Centennial 1975,* Philadelphia: Dechert Price & Rhoads, 1975.

"Paris Move for Dechert," *International Financial Law Review*, June 1995, p. 3.

Petzinger, Thomas, Jr., "Ex-Getty Directors Defend Their Acts in Texaco-Pennzoil Takeover Contest," *Wall Street Journal*, p. 1.

Schmitt, Richard B., "Storied Lawyer, in His Twilight, Sues His Firms," *Wall Street Journal*, January 4, 2000, p. B1.

Shook, Barbara, "Ex-Getty Directors Say No Pennzoil Deal Made," *Houston Chronicle*, May 27, 1987, p. 1.

——, "Pact Called Not Binding in Getty-Pennzoil Talks," *Houston Chronicle*, September 27, 1985, p. 2.

Stevens, Amy, "Lawyers and Clients: Rival Firms Discover the Benefits of Training Young Lawyers Jointly," *Wall Street Journal*, December 11, 1995, p. B8.

Tagliabue, John, "International Merger Wave Catches Europe's Law Firms," *New York Times*, August 4, 2000, p. C3.

—David M. Walden

Dover Downs Entertainment, Inc.

1131 North DuPont Highway
Dover, Delaware 19903
U.S.A.
Telephone: (302) 674-4600
Fax: (302) 734-3124
Web site: http://www.doverdowns.com
Public Company
Incorporated: 1967 as Dover Downs, Inc.
Employees: 932
Sales: $245.87 million (2000)
Stock Exchanges: New York
Ticker Symbol: DVD
NAIC: 711212 Racetracks

Dover Downs Entertainment, Inc. operates six tracks for motorsports racing, including Dover Downs International Speedway in Delaware, Grand Prix Association of Long Beach in California, Gateway International Raceway in Madison, Illinois, and Memphis Motorsports Park, Nashville Speedway USA, and Nashville Superspeedway USA in Tennessee. Dover Downs International Raceway also has live harness horse racing and offers wagering on simulcast horse races and more than 1,500 slot machines. The late chairman John Rollins's family owns about 48 percent of the company, yet controls 67 percent of the voting power.

Attracting Sanctioned Auto Racing

Construction began on Dover Downs International in 1968; it was built as a multipurpose facility for both motor and horse racing. Motorsports christened the track with a NASCAR (National Association for Stock Car Auto Racing) Winston Cup race on July 6, 1969, which was won by legendary driver Richard Petty. The track, one mile in length, soon became known as "The Monster Mile." In 1971, NASCAR formatted Winston Cup races at two per track a year. This, plus the NASCAR Busch Series races that take place the day before Winston Cup races, fueled further growth at Dover Downs.

Dover Downs added dates from the Indy Racing League in 1998 and 1999 and NASCAR Craftsman Truck Series events in September of 2000. MBNA America Bank, a major Delaware corporation, held the title sponsorship to all motorsport racing events at Dover Downs. The track had a seating capacity of 133,000 reserved seats, allowing the track to attract more fans at one time than any other professional sporting event from New York to Washington, D.C.

Harness Racing Highs and Lows

Harness racing began at Dover Downs on November 10, 1969. The popularity and profits from harness racing grew tremendously in the beginning, due in part to Sunday pari-mutuel racing during the winter months. Dover Downs also hosted thoroughbred racing in the early 1970s. From the mid-1970s through the mid-1980s, harness racing at Dover Downs became less significant. The draw of competition and casinos in New Jersey was cutting into the public's gaming dollars. In response to such competition, Dover Downs introduced simulcast racing of both harness and thoroughbred racing, which helped to lure customers back in the early 1990s.

In order to keep harness racing alive at the track, Dover Downs followed the national trend of adding slots to its facility. By 1998, slots accounted for $112.8 million of its $141 million in revenue. In comparison, Dover Downs revenue was $14 million in 1994, before slots were added.

Adding Slots

Faced with increasing competition in the form of live and simulcast racing, lotteries, and the casinos in Atlantic City, Dover Downs lobbied the state of Delaware to add slot machines to its facility. In 1994 the state passed the Delaware Horse Racing Redevelopment Act, which allowed for a maximum of 2,000 slot machines at Dover Downs. The slot machines were supervised by the Delaware State Lottery and the monies were divided between the state, the track, and horseracing purses. Dover Downs Slots opened on December 29, 1995, with 500 slot machines. Several expansions had increased the number of machines to the maximum of 2,000 by the year 2000.

Company Perspectives:

The company's mission is to exceed customer expectations by providing a great entertainment experience with friendly, courteous, and timely service; to provide employees with challenging and exciting opportunities in an environment where teamwork and mutual respect are paramount; to contribute to the growth of the community by providing economic stimulus, employment opportunities, and active support; to provide shareholders with exceptional returns on their investments, emphasizing growth and long-term value.

With the opening of Dover Downs Slots, and the money added to harness racing purses because of it, the track was able to offer bigger purses and, in turn, attract higher quality racing. By 2000, Dover Downs was one of the top-paying harness tracks in the country and over 400 other racing facilities around the United States were simulcasting Dover Downs's races, bringing in more betting dollars.

Popularity of Auto Racing in the 1990s

In the 1990s, NASCAR gained in popularity and was on the edge of mainstream success. With more races and venues scheduled and a new multibillion-dollar television contract with FOX and NBC, NASCAR—and its affiliates—were posting more gains. Publicly traded racing related stocks were declining in the late 1990s; however, Dover Downs was poised to reap the benefits of NASCAR's growing popularity.

A report by Credit Suisse First Boston (CSFB) noted that track operators were involved in sponsorship deals and media access, all of which provided steady gains and growth potential. Racing related companies enjoyed growing returns, due to the stability of the sport sanctioning bodies, and sales generated on a predictable recurring basis. Track operators would share in the $2.4 billion six-year television deal that began in 2001 and in the $10 to $25 million generated from Internet and international fees.

The CSFB report also stated that the Winston Cup Series had 17 of the 20 largest spectator sports in 1999. In 2000, coverage rose to 17 markets in the United States and rose again in 2000 to 19, with the Chicago and Kansas City markets added.

NASCAR scrambled to take advantage of the sport's popularity. Once confined to tracks in the South, in the 1990s NASCAR added events in Las Vegas, Texas, California, Chicago, and Kansas City. Traditionally, each track had two Winston Cup races each year. To accommodate new tracks, NASCAR began taking away one date from some tracks and awarding them to the new tracks. Each June, the middle of the racing season, rumors circulated as NASCAR began to set the schedule for the following year. Owners of older tracks feared losing one—or even both—of their Winston Cup dates.

By 2001, Dover Downs was one of 13 tracks that still held two Winston Cup dates. To keep with growing demands and to hold onto dates, racetracks continually made improvements in seating, luxury, and concessions. Due to prep time before a race and breakdown afterwards, it was tough for track operators to use a racetrack for anything other than their NASCAR races. Dover Downs was one of the few, with the harness racing and the addition of slots, to utilize a multipurpose facility. Seating capacity at Dover Downs was 145,000.

The Winston Cup Series was not the only auto racing event offered at Dover Downs. The track also hosted the Busch Series and Craftsman Truck Series. The Winston Cup Series saw a 97 percent growth in attendance, going from 3.3 million fans in 1990 to 6.5 million fans in 1999. Dover Downs pushed hard to make the Busch Series racing stand on its own, with higher purses and its own stars, making it an attractive package for network programming and more revenue.

NASCAR looked to expand in the Northeast, specifically the lucrative New York-area market. Plans were to build a track in New Jersey or New York. While some felt a track in the New York area would pull fans from Dover Downs, the company maintained they get fans from across the country and there were enough fans to support Dover Downs and a track in the New York vicinity.

Adding New Tracks in the 1990s

On January 2, 1998, Dover Downs acquired Nashville Speedway USA, a banked oval racetrack just over one-half mile long. Located in the Tennessee State Fair Grounds, the track was one of the oldest in the United States, having held its first auto race in 1904. Nashville Speedway hosted one of the most successful NASCAR Weekly Racing Series on Saturday nights. Between 1957 and 1984, Nashville Speedway hosted NASCAR Winston Cup races, and eventually hosted the Busch Series, Craftsman Truck Series, NASCAR Slim Jim All Pro Series, the ASA AC Delco Series (American Speed Association), and the Southern All Star Racing Series.

Dover Downs acquired the Grand Prix Association of Long Beach, Inc. in July 1998. The Grand Prix Association hosted the Grand Prix of Long Beach, a race through the streets of Long Beach, California. The race was sanctioned by CART (Championship Auto Racing Teams). In the acquisition of the Grand Prix Association of Long Beach, Dover Downs also received St. Louis Raceway Park and Memphis Motorsports Park.

Memphis Motorsports Park was long used for minor races. When Grand Prix acquired the track, it put over $13 million in improvements, making Memphis one of the few multi-use racetracks in the country. It could host drag racing, off-road events, and amateur nights. The completion of a three-quarter-mile track allowed Memphis to compete for a Busch Series event, elevating its status. The track had a capacity of 28,000 and 13 corporate suites. In 1998 Memphis hosted a Craftsman Truck Series event and in 1999 hosted the Busch Series Sam's Town 250. Dover Downs planned to invest more money in the track to bring seating capacity to 88,000.

Dover Downs pumped some $10 million in improvements to the St. Louis Raceway Park, known as "the swamp" because of its terrible conditions. By 1999 the track was renamed Gateway International Raceway, and boasted new grandstands, a suite tower, a new foundation, outside lights, restrooms, and concession stands. Gateway attracted a Busch Series and Craftsman Truck Series race, plus an Indy Racing Northern Light Series

Key Dates:

1968: Construction begins on a multipurpose track in Dover, Delaware.
1969: Dover Downs hosts first Winston Cup race and runs its first harness race.
1995: Dover Downs opens slots.
1996: Company goes public.
1998: Dover Downs hosts first Indy Racing League event; acquires Nashville Speedway USA; acquires Grand Prix Association of Long Beach, Inc.
1999: Dover Downs breaks ground on the Nashville Superspeedway, as well as the Dover Downs Hotel and Conference Center.

race. The work at the track was completed in 2000, with a seating capacity of 120,000, a sufficient enough capacity to attract a Winston Cup date.

Nashville Superspeedway had its inaugural season in 2001. Dover Downs broke ground on the property in July 1999. The facility has a 1.33-mile superspeedway and when completed will have a short track, oval dirt track, a drag strip, and a road course. Nashville hosts races from Indy Racing Northern Light League, Busch Series, Craftsman Truck, ARCA (Automobile Racing Club of America) RE/MAX Series, and the USAC (United States Auto Club) Coors Light Silver Bullet series. The first race scheduled was a Busch Series event on April 14, 2001.

2000 and Beyond

Dover Downs broke ground in December 1999 on a new hotel and conference complex in Dover. The opening was planned for January 2002 for the first phase, which would have 232 rooms, a ballroom and concert hall, and a fine dining restaurant. The second phase of the hotel would add 250 rooms. When completed, the hotel would have 12 suites and almost all rooms would have a view of the track.

The completed hotel and conference center, in addition to slots and continual improvements to the Dover Downs track, should allow the company to hold onto two dates from the Winston Cup Series for some time to come. Pushing to elevate the Busch Series will add profits to Dover Downs, as well as the other tracks the company owns.

The improvements to the Dover Downs track helped attract horse racing fans, and the purses offered, along with the revenue from slots, would allow the company to continue to attract high-quality races. Acquiring and building new tracks in new markets allowed Dover Downs to add revenue through smaller series auto racing. Especially at the new Nashville Superspeedway, Dover Downs hoped to be in the forefront as NASCAR looked to add dates in nontraditional areas.

Principal Subsidiaries

Dover Downs, Inc.; Dover Downs International Speedway, Inc.; Dover Downs Properties, Inc.; Nashville Speedway USA, Inc.; Grand Prix Association of Long Beach, Inc.; Gateway International Motorsports Corporation, Inc.; Gateway International Services Corporation, Inc.; Memphis International Motorsports Corporation, Inc.; Motorsports Services Corporation of Memphis, Inc.

Principal Competitors

Richmond International Raceway; Pocono International Raceway; Nazareth Speedway; Atlanta Motor Speedway; Talladega Superspeedway; California Speedway; Indianapolis Motor Speedway; Kansas Speedway; Harrington Raceway; Delaware Park; Rosecroft Raceway; Philadelphia Park; Garden State Park; The Meadowlands.

Further Reading

Fleischman, Bill, ''NASCAR Struggles to Accommodate Demand,'' *Philadelphia Daily News,* June 16, 2000.
Garrity, Brian, ''Motorsports Business Preparing to Accelerate on Wall Street,'' *Amusement Business,* October 2, 2000, p. 24.
Ghosh, Chandrani, ''Mint Juleps and One-Armed Bandits,'' *Forbes,* August 9, 1999, p. 53.
Hollahan, Terry, ''Motorsports Park Revving Up,'' *Memphis Business Journal,* October 1, 1999, p. 1.
Kloeckner, Rod, ''Madison, Ill., Raceway's Growth Startles Owner,'' *Belleville News-Democrat,* April 2, 1999.
Minch, Morgan, ''NASCAR Race Poised for Further Success,'' *Memphis Business Journal,* October 20, 2000, p. 9.
Mooradian, Don, ''NASCAR Attendance Doubles During Past Decade,'' *Amusement Business,* June 5, 2000, p. 23.
Most, Doug, ''Developers Consider Meadlowlands for NASCAR Racetrack,'' *Record,* December 9, 1999.
''Sponsors, Merchandisers on the Fast Tract From Pit Row to Wall Street,'' *Automotive Marketing,* March 1999, p. 14.
Yue, Lorene, ''Motor-Sport Stocks Race Ahead,'' *Detroit Free Press,* June 7, 1999.

—Lisa Musolf Karl

DreamWorks SKG

1000 Flower Street
Glendale, California 91201
U.S.A.
Telephone: (818) 733-7000
Fax: (818) 733-9918
Web site: http://www.dreamworks.com

Private Company
Incorporated: 1994
Employees: 1,500 (2000)
Sales: $1,242 million (est.2000)
NAIC: 512110 Motion Picture and Video Production; 512120 Motion Picture and Video Distribution; 512240 Sound Recording Studios; 512220 Integrated Record Production/Distribution

Founded in 1994 by entertainment moguls Steven Spielberg, Jeffrey Katzenberg, and David Geffen, DreamWorks SKG is a private entertainment company that produces and distributes popular films, music, and television shows. The acclaimed film director and producer Spielberg mainly oversees the live-action movies for DreamWorks (which has included *Saving Private Ryan* and *Gladiator*), while former Disney-executive and animation guru Katzenberg focuses on the company's animated film efforts (which includes *The Prince of Egypt* and *Shrek*), and recording industry maven Geffen produces DreamWorks' film soundtracks and albums for popular artists (including Nelly Furtado and Henry Rollins). The prime-time *Spin City* and *The Job* are among the many television shows that the company also produces. The company initially aimed to develop an even broader entertainment offering, with its short-lived DreamWorks Interactive division, to include PC and console-based games (*The Lost World: Jurassic Park* and *Medal of Honor*, among others), a chain of cutting-edge video game centers (the now-Sega/Universal-run GameWorks), and an interactive Web site to showcase and exchange new and emerging digital entertainment (the now-less-impressive Pop.com). Since pulling out of those ventures, DreamWorks SKG has focused on its core strengths and has proven to be a major player in the entertainment business, especially amid the 2001 success of the computer-animated feature film, *Shrek*, which is arguably on a par with similar efforts by archrival The Walt Disney Company .

Three Entertainment Moguls Unite

It was no coincidence that the ''S,'' ''K,'' and ''G'' in DreamWorks SKG are the first letters of the last names of the company's chief partners. One of the most powerful people in entertainment, Spielberg is responsible for many of the most successful films in history, as director of *Jaws* (1975), *Close Encounters of the Third Kind* (1977), *Raiders of the Lost Ark* (1981), *E.T., The Extra-Terrestrial* (1982), *Jurassic Park* (1993), *Schindler's List* (1993), *Twister* (1996), and *Saving Private Ryan* (1998). He also was a producer or executive producer for dozens of other blockbuster live-action and animated films, including *Back to the Future* (1985), *Who Framed Roger Rabbit* (1988), *An American Tail: Fievel Goes West* (1991), *Men in Black* (1997), and *Deep Impact* (1998). Spielberg's live-action and animation talents also traveled to network, cable, and syndicated television shows, producing and directing several shows including the *Tiny Toon Adventures* animated series (1990–current) and *Amazing Stories* (1985–1987).

Before co-founding DreamWorks, Katzenberg made a name for himself as an executive in the entertainment business, most notably as Chairman of The Walt Disney Studios from 1984 to 1994. He was responsible for the production, marketing, and distribution of all Disney filmed entertainment including motion pictures, television, cable, syndication, home video and interactive entertainment. Under his direction, Disney's studios created some of its most successful films, including *Good Morning Vietnam*, *Pretty Woman*, *The Little Mermaid*, *Beauty and the Beast* (the first animated feature to be nominated for the Best Picture Oscar), *Aladdin*, and *The Lion King* (the highest domestic grossing animated film of all time at $313 million). Citing differences with then fellow Disney executive Michael Eisner, Katzenberg left the Magic Kingdom and almost immediately joined Spielberg and Geffen to found DreamWorks. The departure would later prove to be an unclean break, as Katzenberg would find himself to be in a long, high-profile battle to cash in on a bonus he held was owed to him by Disney.

Company Perspectives:

Steven Spielberg, Jeffrey Katzenberg, and David Geffen launched DreamWorks SKG in October 1994. Their vision was to create an artist-friendly studio to develop, produce, and distribute superior film and music entertainment that would inspire and delight audiences worldwide. DreamWorks SKG is now a leading producer of live-action motion pictures, animated feature films, network, syndicated and cable television programming, home video and DVD entertainment, and consumer products.

By the time Geffen helped found DreamWorks, he was already head of his own empire in the music business. Geffen Records was one of the largest record labels in the industry, the crowning achievement of his three decades in the corporate rock world. He is credited with guiding the careers of 1970s big-name acts including Crosby, Stills, Nash and Young; Jackson Browne; and the Eagles. When he founded Geffen Records in 1980, he was able to immediately sign Elton John, Donna Summer, and Neil Young, the first in a long list of notable popular music artists, which also included Guns N' Roses, Aerosmith, Cher, Sonic Youth, and Nirvana.

The Early Years, A Shaky Start: 1994–97

Spielberg, Katzenberg, and Geffen each brought their unique strengths, experiences and talent to DreamWorks, and each would appropriately head the company's core businesses: live-action movies, animated movies, and music, respectively. With $2 billion to start with, and a host of impressive high-tech partnerships, DreamWorks was one of the most exciting companies to watch from the outset. By 1995, Microsoft had invested $30 million in DreamWorks to co-develop interactive games, which spawned a new division, DreamWorks Interactive. Paul Allen showed even greater interest, investing about $500 million for a stake in the new company. Even though Spielberg, Katzenberg, and Geffen would bring so much to their shared ''Dream,'' many initially wondered whether it would be true to its name and actually ''Work.'' Indeed, industry insiders were baffled by the company's shaky start.

In 1997, DreamWorks turned out its first movie, *The Peacemaker*, with George Clooney and Nicole Kidman, but it was considered to be far from a success, reaching only $12 million during its opening weekend. But, what followed was a string of much more successful movies: *Mouse Hunt* (Nathan Lane), *Amistad* (with Morgan Freeman and Anthony Hopkins), *Small Soldiers* (with the voice of Tommy Lee Jones), *Paulie* (with Gena Rowlands, Cheech Marin, and Buddy Hackett), and *Deep Impact* (with Robert Duvall and Morgan Freeman). *Amistad*, which came out in 1996, was Spielberg's first directorial project for DreamWorks. On the animated film front, DreamWorks joined with PDI in 1996 to co-produce original computer-generated feature films, including *Antz*, which was completed in 1998, just weeks ahead of Disney's own insect-themed animation film, *A Bug's Life*. Katzenberg also landed for DreamWorks the rights to *Chicken Run*, a promising Claymation project that was in development by Oscar-winning Aardman Animations. The film would later become a hit in 2000.

DreamWorks's music subsidiary was originally named DreamWorks SKG Music, with DreamWorks Records and SKG Records as separate labels—the first, for soundtracks and specialty recordings, and the second, for individual recording artists and bands. The first artist signed to SKG Records was George Michael, whose album in 1996 turned out to be much less successful than expected. But, when DreamWorks struck an unusual joint-venture pact with Rykodisc to cover two of Morphine's next albums, it seemed the company's music business was headed in the right direction. The band was already playing in college radio stations all over, heading top-10 lists, and winning prestigious awards such as the Boston Music Awards in 1995 and 1996.

Aside from its movie and music core, DreamWorks explored other entertainment channels. DreamWorks TV turned out its first shows for ABC, *High Incident* and *Champs*. These two turned out to be unsuccessful, but the studio followed up in 1996 with the high-profile *Ink* for CBS, starring Ted Danson, which lasted one full season. In September 1996, DreamWorks also debuted *Spin City* for ABC, starring Michael J. Fox, which turned out to be DreamWorks' most successful television show. At the time, however, DreamWorks was still stunned when their plans for a syndicated show with Maury Povich and Connie Chung fell through.

In April 1996, DreamWorks, Sega, and Universal founded Sega GameWorks, a chain of electronic game centers in Seattle, Las Vegas, Ontario, California, and other cities. It was no surprise that Spielberg would get into the game business, being an avid gamer himself. With cutting-edge games, a club-like atmosphere, and slick merchandising, the chain was well received amid lots of initial fanfare. That same year, DreamWorks' biggest-selling game was *Goosebumps: Escape from Horrorland*, a first-person perspective, animated adventure game based on the R.L. Stine children's books and TV series.

A Turning Point: 1998

DreamWorks began to outgrow its shaky start and turn out critically acclaimed, successful films. *Deep Impact* was released in early 1998, and was DreamWorks' highest-grossing film, at an impressive $350.9 million worldwide, which was split with co-producer Paramount Pictures. Later, *Saving Private Ryan* would not only become the year's highest grossing film, at $216 million, but it would also bring in several Oscar awards, including Best Picture and Best Director for Spielberg. Even though the opening weekend sales for *Antz* was about half of the Disney film, the DreamWorks project, headed by Katzenberg, would be the first one of many to seriously challenge Disney's position as head of the animation kingdom. Not only did *Antz* open in theaters weeks before Disney's *A Bug's Life*, it also managed to make $70 million, making it the most successful non-Disney animated film at the time.

Released during the holiday season, *The Prince of Egypt* proved to be a blockbuster as well. It was DreamWorks' first animation film that was created completely in-house. To help promote its new Biblical movie, DreamWorks landed a unique

Key Dates:

1994: DreamWorks SKG is founded.
1995: Company joins with Microsoft to create DreamWorks Interactive.
1996: Company forms special-effects venture PDI/DreamWorks.
1997: *The Peacemaker* debuts as DreamWorks' first feature film.
1998: *Saving Private Ryan* and *The Prince of Egypt* become the company's first major successes.
1999: Company pulls out of Playa Vista studio development.
2000: DreamWorks Interactive sold to Electronic Arts. DreamWorks purchases a majority stake in PDI.
2001: Computer-animated feature film *Shrek* puts company's animation on par with Disney's.

deal with Wal-Mart, in which the retailer would sell special gift packs that included commemorative tickets (good at any theater in the country), a collector's edition book, a limited edition lithograph, and a collector's edition CD set. Even *Small Soldiers* earned the studio in the neighborhood of $10 million dollars, despite its disappointing $46 million gross. Every bit helped, as it turned out that DreamWorks finished the year with the highest average gross per film of all the major studios. The company's total box office gross for the year reached a high of $473 million.

Chaos Amid Continued Success: 1999

Spielberg, Katzenberg, and Geffen had been planning for years to build a state-of-the-art studio to serve as the central home for the company, which was scattered all over the Los Angeles area. By November 1998, they bought about 47 acres of land just west of Los Angeles for $20 million, the focal point for a larger 1,100-acre development for high-tech companies, new housing, and a man-made lake. The entertainment moguls were surely not the only ones excited about this prospect. At least 50,000 new jobs were forecasted around this development project, reason enough for the local government to pledge tens of millions of dollars in tax breaks. The proposed studio would have been the first new studio built in the Los Angeles area in the 70 years since Warner Brothers built their Burbank studio, but it wasn't meant to be.

The Wetlands Action Network, Southwest Center, and CalPIRG filed a lawsuit against DreamWorks, citing their concerns about the studio's plans to develop on the last significant wetland in the Los Angeles basin. The media-savvy protestors also arranged sit-ins and demonstrations at movie premieres, proving to be a significant problem for DreamWorks. Later in 1999, DreamWorks pulled out of the development project, which they claim was due to financial reasons. DreamWorks has since remained a decentralized network of facilities around Los Angeles, with even the Glendale animation studios located too cozily next to studios of rival Disney.

Despite the company's inability to find a new home, 1999 proved to be another good year for DreamWorks, with Oscar-winning Best Picture of 1999, *American Beauty* (with Kevin Spacey), *Galaxy Quest* (with Tim Allen), *Forces of Nature* (with Sandra Bullock and Ben Affleck), *The Haunting* (with Liam Neeson), and *What Lies Beneath* (with Harrison Ford and Michelle Pfeifer). The home video rental release of *Saving Private Ryan*, released mid-year, became 1999's most successful rental release. Still riding high on the wave of the war film's success, DreamWorks secured a deal with NBC to launch the animated *Semper Fi*, which would draw from resources used in making *Saving Private Ryan*, including Spielberg as executive producer. DreamWorks closed its television animation unit, however. The company would instead look to possible partnerships with Fox and Nickelodeon for future animated shows for television.

The company celebrated its fifth anniversary in October 1999, looking back at an impressive series of projects, including fourteen feature films, several television shows, and more than 40 record releases. That same month, DreamWorks joined forces with Imagine Entertainment to create the Internet entertainment company, Pop.com. Funded by Paul Allen's Vulcan Ventures, Inc., the ambitious equal partnership was set up to develop a Web site that would produce and broadcast original Internet-only programming. It was hoped to offer a mix of live action and animation shorts, video-on-demand and live events, and non-linear interactive features and games. Unfortunately, the site folded 11 months later, amid the dot-com shakeout and failed attempts to sell the site to Atom Films or to merge it with IFILM.

Films Remain Priority: 2000

In early 2000, DreamWorks moved to refocus its efforts on live-action and animated films. DreamWorks Interactive was sold to Electronic Arts, a company that was fast on the move to become the leader of Internet-based gaming. (It had just partnered with America Online to create and deliver online games and interactive entertainment for AOL properties). DreamWorks then purchased a majority stake in the special effects and animation leader PDI. The company also stepped up its television program development efforts, to include two new, half-hour shows—one called *The Job*, starring Denis Leary, and the other called *Freaks and Geeks*. Also in the television line-up were 12 hours of miniseries programming for the HBO *Band of Brothers*, and the 20-hour *Taken* for Sci-Fi Channel. The Emmy award-winning *Spin City* continued to be a major success for DreamWorks, even after Michael J. Fox left and was replaced by Charlie Sheen. The show entered syndication in the fall, having brought in an estimated $2.5 to $3 million per segment. According to Katzenberg and Fox executive Dan McDermott, it was enough to cover the division's operating costs and ensure profitability.

In an effort to jumpstart another of DreamWorks' non-film ventures, this time the music division, DreamWorks Records began offering a new service on its Web site to attract new talent to the label. With the new service, unsigned music artists could submit their music clips to the label via the Web site. Geffen's part of the DreamWorks empire could have probably used the extra momentum. Despite having an impressive array of critically acclaimed artists signed to the label, DreamWorks Records had not managed to generate impressive record sales. In 1999, the label had only three albums that earned industry distinctions for sales. One artist, Papa Roach, made the top-10 charts in 2000, which to industry analysts, was not enough. But, the label's head of new media, Jed Simon insisted, "The rest of the industry is more of a singles-driven business. We still believe in artist development and feel that ultimately will be the winning strategy."

By mid-2000, DreamWorks already managed to top its 1998 total gross of $473 million, with $475 million. This was also a year marked with 5 Oscar awards and $336 million for *American Beauty*, strong box office debuts for *Gladiator* (at $32.7 million) and the claymation film *Chicken Run* ($17.5 million), $67 million from *Road Trip*, and a $30 million opening weekend for *What Lies Beneath*. Three of DreamWorks' year-2000 films grossed more than $100 million for the year (*American Beauty*, *Gladiator*, and *Chicken Run*).

2001 and Beyond

Despite Spielberg's personal zeal for gaming, DreamWorks shed its stake in the GameWorks business, further honing in on its core film strengths. In another strategic move, DreamWorks secured a five-year extension on its distribution deal with Universal Studios. The pact granted Universal the enviable international distribution rights to live action and animated DreamWorks features and worldwide home video, as well as music distribution rights. "This is an extremely important and significant milestone for DreamWorks," Katzenberg said. "With this deal we have very much secured DreamWorks' future capital needs for the next two to three years in what is going to be a difficult, demanding and turbulent debt marketplace." Days after the lucrative deal, DreamWorks struck yet another one, this time with Turner Broadcasting Systems. The precedent-setting theatrical output deal, combined with an earlier 1998 syndication agreement between the two companies, gave TBS access to nearly all of DreamWorks' titles released from 1997 to 2007, and rights to titles as far out as 2015. In exchange, DreamWorks would get $350 to $450 million dollars, depending on the final box office revenue.

But, if it seemed that DreamWorks was wrestling with financial troubles, the additional blockbuster successes of *Gladiator* and *Shrek* would put such worries to rest. In March, Oscar awards went to yet another DreamWorks project—this time, for *Gladiator*. The film won for Best Picture, Best Actor (Russell Crowe), and other categories, for a total of five awards. By the end of the 2001 summer, DreamWorks' new animated feature film reached an estimated $261 million gross, dwarfing all other releases earlier in the year, including Disney's animated movie, *Atlantis,* and even DreamWorks' Spielberg co-production with Warner Brothers Studios, *A.I.* The Oscar-worthy *Shrek* firmly established DreamWorks' position as a major force in the feature animation business.

Principal Competitors

Alliance Atlantis Communications; AOL Time Warner; Artisan Entertainment; Carsey-Werner; Fox Entertainment; Lions Gate Entertainment; Lucasfilm; MGM; Pixar; Sony; Universal Studios; Viacom; The Walt Disney Company.

Principal Subsidiaries

DreamWorks Records; DreamWorks Digital.

Further Reading

Adalian, Josef, "D'Works TV Gets Busy," *Daily Variety*, January 10, 2000, p. 1.

Bart, Peter, "Amblin Along with the Three Faces of Steve," *Variety*, August 18, 1997.

Cox, Dan, "D'Works Feat of Clay," *Variety*, December 4, 1997, p. 1.

Diorio, Carl, and Cathy Dunkley, "Dream Dollars: U Extends Distribution Pact for Five Years," *Daily Variety*, April 17, 2001, pp. 1.

"DreamWorks and Imagine Go Digital," [Company Press Release], October 25, 1999.

"DreamWorks Forces Theaters' Hands," *Mr. Showbiz*, posted March 24, 1999, http://www.mrshowbiz.com.

"DreamWorks' *Prince*ly Deal," *Mr. Showbiz*, posted October 30, 1998, http://www.mrshowbiz.com.

"DreamWorks Sheds GameWorks," *Los Angeles Business Journal*, February 12, 2001.

"DreamWorks Television Launches Olympic Web Site," *Business Wire*, posted July 18, 1996, http://businesswire.com.

Duke, Paul, "D'Works: What Lies Beneath?" *Variety*, July 24, 2000, p. 1.

Duke, Paul, and Carl Diorio, "Dream Quirks: Biz Plan Seems Iffy," *Variety*, July 26, 2000, p. 1.

Dunphy, Laura, "Struggling Record Label at DreamWorks Turns to Net," *Los Angeles Business Journal*, July 3, 2000.

Errico, Marcus, "DreamWorks Scraps Dream Studio," *E! Online News*, posted July 1, 1999, http://www.eonline.com.

Farmer, Melanie Austria, "Electronic Arts to Buy DreamWorks, Microsoft Venture," *CNET News.com,* posted February 24, 2000, http://www.cnet.com.

Fleming, Michael, "D'Works' 'Sember Fi' Hits the Beach at NBC," *Daily Variety*, September 30, 1999, p. 1.

Gelmis, Joseph, "The Game Plan for DreamWorks," *Newsday*, September 24, 1997, p. C04.

Gennusa, Chris, "DreamWorks at 5: Still Pushing Ahead—After Growing Pains, It's a Mini-Major," *The Hollywood Reporter*, October 21, 1999.

"Gladiator Axes Scream 3 Record," *Mr. Showbiz*, posted May 9, 2000, http://www.mrshowbiz.com.

"Gladiator Wins the Crowd," *Mr. Showbiz*, posted May 7, 2000, http://www.mrshowbiz.com.

Grove, Martin, "Looking Back at Summer's Hits and Misses," *The Hollywood Reporter*, August 31, 2001.

Grover, Ronald, "What Burst Pop.com's Bubble?" *BusinessWeek Online*, posted September 25, 2000, http://www.businessweek.com.

Harlow, John, "How the DVD Saved Hollywood," *Sunday Times (London)*, August 19, 2001.

Hindes, Andrew, " 'Antz Colony' Cranks It Up: DreamWorks Becoming a Success," *Variety*, October 19, 1998.

"Interview with Steve Hickner, Co-Director, *The Prince of Egypt*," *VFXPro*, posted December 18, 1998, http://www.vfxpro.com.

"Katzenberg Settlement Revealed," *Mr. Showbiz*, posted July 8, 1999, http://www.mrshowbiz.com.

Kurutz, Steve, "AMG Biography: David Geffen," *All Music Guide*, accessed October 1, 2001, http://www.allmusic.com.

McConville, Jim, "DreamWorks Pics to Turner: TBS Will Pay Up to $450 million in Precedent-Setting Deal," *The Hollywood Reporter*, April 25, 2001.

"Mo Ostin, Lenny Waronker & Michael Ostin Named to Head DreamWorks SKG Music," *PR Newswire*, posted October 5, 1995, http://prnewswire.com.

Natale, Richard, and Jack Matthews, "DreamWorks on Cloud 9 with 'Shrek,' Studio Becomes Disney's Peer," *Daily News (New York)*, June 19, 2001, p. 37.

"Production to Begin in September on 'Taken,' 20-Hour Miniseries Event from Sci-Fi Channel, Steven Spielberg, and DreamWorks

Television,'' *Business Wire*, posted July 12, 2001, http://businesswire.com.

Rice, Lynette, ''D'Works Closes Animated TV Unit, Feature Division Absorbs Direct-to-Video Arm in Retooling,'' *The Hollywood Reporter*, March 9, 1999.

Rich, Laura, ''Mickey Mouse's Worst Nightmare,'' *The Industry Standard Magazine*, May 14, 2001.

Robischon, Noah, ''Intelligence Community: A Guide to the ''A.I.'' Web game—Its Creators Tell EW.com All You Need to Know About Playing the Hot New Cyber-Mystery,'' *Entertainment Weekly's EW.com*, posted July 2, 2001, http://www.ew.com/ew.

Sandler, Adam, ''D'Works Takes Double Dose of Morphine,'' *Variety*, December 19, 1996.

''*Spin City* Wins Time Period in Adults 18–34 and Retains 96% of Adults 18–49 Audience From Lead-In, According to Fast National Ratings Information Provided By Nielson Media Research,'' *PR Newswire*, posted November 30, 2000, http://www.prnewswire.com.

Spring, Greg, ''DreamWorks Down, But Not Out of TV, Eyes Next Big Thing,'' *Electronic Media*, June 16, 1997, p. 3.

''Steven Spielberg Sets First DreamWorks Project,'' *Mr. Showbiz*, posted November 7, 1996, http://www.mrshowbiz.com.

''Steven Spielberg's *Saving Private Ryan* Becomes No. 1 Rental Title of All Time: American Audiences Respond to Award-Winning WWII Drama During Memorial Day Weekend,'' *Business Wire*, posted June 4, 1999, http://businesswire.com.

Waller, Don, ''Diskery Slow to Get Rolling,'' *Variety*, July 24, 2000, pp. 69.

''Woody Migrates to DreamWorks,'' *Mr. Showbiz*, posted March 30, 2000, http://www.mrshowbiz.go.com.

—Heidi Wrightsman

Du Pareil au Même

Zone Industrielle Villemilan
18 Avenue Ampère
F-91320 Wissous
France
Telephone: (+33) 1-69-81-46-46
Fax: (+33) 1-69-81-46-00
Web site: http://www.dpam.com

Public Company
Incorporated: 1982 as C'Mauve
Employees: 1,108
Sales: EUR 150.1 million ($140 million) (2000)
Stock Exchanges: Euronext Paris
Ticker Symbol: DPA
NAIC: 448150 Clothing Accessories Stores; 448130 Children's and Infants' Clothing Stores; 315291 Infants' Cut and Sew Apparel Manufacturing; 448210 Shoe Stores

France's Du Pareil au Même (DPAM) wants to dress the world's kids. The Wissous-based company has captured one of the largest shares of the French infant and children's clothing market, offering high-quality, fashionable garments at low prices. Nearly all of the company's success has been built on word-of-mouth advertising. The company's publicity budget remains among the smallest in the business. DPAM also does not manufacture its own clothing designs, but instead subcontracts production to manufacturers in lower-cost areas such as India, China, Taiwan, and Malaysia. The company engages in a policy of rapid product turnover, eschewing the typical seasonal base of the retail clothing market to turn out as many as 2,400 new clothing items each year. Few DPAM garment styles remain for long in the company's chain of more than 100 company-owned French stores and 45 international stores, including 17 company-owned subsidiary stores, in 20 countries. The rapid turnover of styles helps to encourage shoppers to overcome any reluctance to purchase an item immediately—the style might not be in the store the next time the customer returns. As such, DPAM has gained one of the highest sales-per-square-meter ratios in the French market. Since the late 1990s, DPAM has pursued growth along two strategic paths: the first, the continued expansion of the company's own and franchised stores on the international market. The second, the continued rollout of new yet related retail concepts. These include the DPAM Bébé retail chain of infant furniture and accessories, also present as ''corner'' shops within the larger DPAM retail concept. While the company has had less success pursuing the adolescent market—which has shown a preference for name-brand goods over DPAM's inhouse designs, DPAM is hoping to translate its DPAM Enfant touch to the children's shoe market, launching DPAM Chaussures as an independent and ''corner'' shop concept in 2000. Founder Simon Benharrous continues to help guide the company's design activity. Presiding over day-to-day management and future expansion is Bernard Denet. DPAM is traded on the Euronext Paris Stock Exchange. Investment house Argos Soditic owns a majority share of the company.

Something Else Entirely in the 1980s

Simon Benharrous entered the garment manufacturing business with a background as a costume maker for France's theater and movie industry. Benharrous launched his own company, C'Mauve, in 1982, with the idea of creating a unique line of children's fashions. The market for children's clothing in France was rather small, dominated by just a few well-known and somewhat old-fashioned brands. Benharrous sought to shake up the market with brightly colored, contemporary designs.

Benharrous soon turned to the creation of his own retail concept to distribute his clothing designs. In 1986, he launched a new retail store brand, ''Tout Autre Chose,'' translatable as ''Something Else Entirely.'' By the end of that year, Benharrous's company had opened four Tout Autre Chose stores in Paris.

Parisian parents snapped up Benharrous's designs and Benharrous quickly discovered that word-of-mouth advertising was enough to fill his stores and empty the clothing racks. By 1988, Benharrous was ready to expand outside of the French capital and begin to conquer the provincial markets. In that year, the company opened its first store in Lyon. A year later, the company's sales had grown to nearly FFr 60 million.

Key Dates:

1982: Simon Benharrous creates children's clothing firm C'Mauve.
1986: Benharrous launches a new brand and retail store, Tout Autre Chose.
1988: First store outside of Paris is opened.
1990: Benharrous changes Tout Autre Chose brand/store name to Du Pareil au Même.
1993: C'Mauve absorbs Du Pareil au Même.
1994: Company launches new brands/retail stores, including Serelou, DPAM Maison, and ''Fais-moi une place dans ton armoire.''
1995: Corporation officially changes its name to Du Pareil au Même and is listed on the Paris bourse.
1997: Franchise openings in Switzerland and Portugal are completed.
1998: Simon Benharrous sells shares to investment house Argos Soditic; Bernard Denet becomes CEO.
1999: Company acquires DPAM Suisse; distribution agreement with Itochu (Japan) is signed; company launches e-commerce web site.
2000: DPAM enters markets in Spain and Italy.
2001: Company launches DPAM Chaussures in order to gain a foothold in the children's shoe market.

Yet Benharrous's dreams of future growth of the Tout Autre Chose retail chain were interrupted in 1990 when the company discovered that the brand had already been claimed by a manufacturer of ready-to-wear clothing. This setback, however, only seemed to inspire Benharrous, who quickly invented a new brand name: ''Du Pareil au Même,'' translatable as ''From the Similar to the Same.'' The new name seemed to inspire Benharrous's customers as well and quickly became one of the fastest-growing retail chains in France in the early 1990s.

Benharrous's playful and colorful designs were matched by a strong retail concept. Among the leading factors for the chain's success was its policy of avoiding the traditional seasonal base for its clothing factors, in which stores introduced new lines of clothing designs just four times a year. Instead, DPAM, as the chain was quickly nicknamed by its customers, rolled out new designs on a nearly continual basis. Stores received new clothing items nearly every day, and the company launched as many as 2,400 new designs each year.

DPAM's customers learned that they could expect to find something new with every visit to the store. To encourage customer purchases, DPAM rarely kept its designs in stores for more than two weeks. At the same time, the company, willing to accept lower margins than many of its competitors, offered its clothing for prices as much as 40 percent lower than other children's clothing sellers. Yet the company remained committed to quality, avoiding synthetic fibers in favor of primarily natural materials. DPAM also carefully chose its locations, sticking to France's downtown centers, rather than moving out to the growing numbers of suburban shopping centers. The DPAM formula proved successful even during the long crisis that marked the French economy during the first half of the decade.

Benharrous's company, still known as C'Mauve, changed its status to a limited liability company in 1990. In 1993, C'Mauve absorbed the Du Pareil au Même brand name before the company changed its name to its flagship brand in 1995 in concert with the company's listing on the Paris stock exchange.

By the time of its introduction on the stock exchange, DPAM had grown to a chain of more than 40 stores, with 380 employees, and an average of 20,000 customers per day paying an average of FFr 225 per visit. With some 7 percent of the French children's clothing market, DPAM had also achieved one of the domestic industry's highest annual sales-per-square-meter rates, some FFr 143,000. Annual sales had topped FFr 370 million in 1994. The stock exchange listing reduced Benharrous's ownership to just over 86 percent of the company.

By then, Benharrous hoped to reproduce the success of the company's original clothing line, now dubbed DPAM Enfant, into three new brand concepts. The first was called DPAM Maison, (DPAM Home) and featured infant furniture and accessory items. The second was called Sérelou, French slang for ''it's heavy,'' and was geared toward the adolescent market. The third was geared to the adult market, and was called ''Fais-moi une place dans ton armoire'' (''give me a place in your dresser''). Neither of the latter two brands took off—in the case of Sérelou, for example, DPAM had not taken into account the growing penchant of the ten-year-old and older set for name brands. DPAM Maison, which grew into a separate retail concept, remained nonetheless a minor part of the growing DPAM empire.

International Growth for the 21st Century

Benharrous faced a different kind of problem in 1996 when the company's auditor refused to certify its first annual report as a public company. The dispute over the method of accounting for inventory led the company to publish its inaugural report as uncertified. DPAM was to face official investigation into the matter, which remained unresolved at the turn of the century. Meanwhile, DPAM continued to mark its successful growth throughout France, and revealed its intention to boost its retail business to as many as 100 stores by the end of the decade.

DPAM also began plotting its international expansion. Among the first countries to receive the company's attention were Japan and Israel. Instead of opening stores under its own direction, DPAM conferred development in these countries to local distributors through a master franchise program. The company was particularly interested in the Japanese market, and hoped to develop a network of more than 50 stores through its franchise holder. Yet DPAM also dreamed of reproducing its success in France on the international market by extending its portfolio of company-held stores.

Moving abroad proved more difficult than expanding at home. While DPAM's own-store network grew to 86 stores by 1997 and then to 93 stores by the end of 1998, all but two of these were in France. Meanwhile, its international development had barely taken off. By the end of 1998, DPAM was present in 17 countries, ranging from Saudi Arabia to Iceland and Brazil, but for the most part its operations were limited to just one or two franchised stores in each country. The company had begun a tentative expansion, opening its own branches in Portugal and

Switzerland. But in these markets too DPAM proceeded only slowly, with just two Portuguese stores and four Swiss stores at the end of 1999.

In 1998, Simon Benharrous announced his intention to sell off his holding in the company to a new company, Kokanee, set up by the investment house Argos Soditic France to acquire DPAM. The sale netted Benharrous nearly FFr 350 million; the company's founder remained to guide its designs. Argos Soditic brought in Bernard Denet, who had worked previously for Lacoste, to oversee DPAM's further growth. DPAM's new majority shareholder affirmed its interest in DPAM's development, stating to *Les Echos* that the acquisition was "a change for continuation. We are not raiders. We are here for an industrial cycle, that is, roughly five years."

Denet took up the mandate to continue to expand the company's French presence, renovate its stores, and especially step up the international expansion of its successful DPAM brand. At home, meanwhile, Denet sought to improve the company's margins, by reducing its stock levels and streamlining its logistics systems, but also by reducing the level of its employee turnover through higher salaries and other incentives. These measures helped to boost DPAM's sales to more than FFr 820 million (EUR 125.3 million) and also helped the company eliminate its net debt and instead build a strong treasury with which to continue its expansion.

The company stepped up its foreign store openings through 1999. That year marked a number of important developments, such as an agreement with Japan's Itochu to place DPAM corner shops in that company's 30 Ito Yokado stores. The company now boosted its target in Japan to as many as 100 DPAM stores and boutique shops. The company also took over the four-store DPAM Suisse franchise company and began to target an aggressive expansion drive in that country, expecting to reach 15 company-owned stores and as many as 25 stores throughout Switzerland.

Meanwhile, DPAM was forced to take stock of its other brands. An attempt was made to revive the flagging Sérelou concept, which had never quite taken off with France's prepubescent set. After renaming the brand and chain SRL, the company announced its decision to close these stores by August 2000. A less dramatic fate was in store for DPAM Maison, which instead was renamed as the clearer DPAM Bébé. The company announced its intention to bring DPAM Bébé corners into its DPAM Enfant stores as well. DPAM also began developing a new concept to extend its operations beyond clothing and into footwear.

The arrival of Swedish clothing giant H&M in France in 1999 gave the company new impetus to step up its international growth. The year 2000 marked a turning point for the France-focused group as it created new subsidiaries to bring it into neighboring Italy and Spain, while also adding new stores in Portugal. If international sales represented less than 5 percent of total company sales at the end of the century, DPAM now announced its intention to boost the part of foreign operations to as much as 50 percent of total group sales by 2005. At the same time, DPAM turned to the extra-national market when it launched its own e-commerce-capable web site in 1999. That site performed strongly from the start, and by 2000 was breaking even, with sales of FFr 1.5 million. The company expected its web site sales to top FFr 3 million by the end of 2001. Importantly, half of its online sales were coming from the international market, with growing numbers of orders arriving from the United States and Canada, markets where DPAM was not yet physically present.

After shutting its SRL retail stores, DPAM opened its newest retail concept, DPAM Chaussures, with the intention to bring to children's shoes what it had brought to children's clothing. If the company had not been able to prove its appeal to the adult and adolescent clothing markets, its newest retail brand, which brought the company's quality and strong designs with the same commitment to low prices, was expected to become a strong player in the French—and perhaps global—children's market.

Principal Subsidiaries

DPAM Suisse; DPAM Italia; DPAM Portugal; DPAM Espagne.

Principal Competitors

Auchan Group; Etam Developpement; Galeries Lafayette; H&M Hennes & Mauritz AB; Jacardi SA; Laura Ashley Holdings plc; Mothercare plc; Pinault-Printemps-Redoute S.A.; SMOBY SA; Toys "R" Us, Inc.

Further Reading

Arlinian, Ariane, "Du Pareil au Même dans la cour des grands," *Capital*, August 1999, p. 36.

Hamou, Nathalie, "Du Pareil au Même prend pied dans la chaussure," *La Tribune*, March 27, 2000.

Lecoeur, Xavier, "DPAM veut restaurer sa rentabilité en 2001," *Les Echos*, March 29, 2001, p. 18.

—M.L. Cohen

Electronics for Imaging, Inc.

303 Velocity Way
Foster City, California 9440
U.S.A.
Telephone: (650) 357-3500
Toll Free: (800) 568-1917
Fax: (650) 357-3231
Web site: http://www.efi.com

Public Company
Incorporated: 1989
Employees: 896
Sales: $588.4 million (2000)
Stock Exchanges: NASDAQ
Ticker Symbol: EFII
NAIC: 334611 Software Reproducing; 511210 Software Publishers; 334119 Other Computer Peripheral Equipment Manufacturing

Electronics for Imaging, Inc. (EFI) designs and sells hardware and software that support high-quality, low-cost color printing in office environments. The company has established itself as a global leader in its niche since its inception in 1989. Through strong overseas sales, strategic acquisitions, and the introduction of new technology, EFI has been achieving impressive growth throughout the 1990s and into the new century.

Company Origins Up to 1989

Electronics for Imaging (EFI) was founded in 1989 by 51-year-old Efraim ''Efi'' Arazi, a native of Israel. By the time he established EFI, Arazi had already developed a reputation as a pioneer and visionary in the computer graphics industry through his founding and leadership of Scitex Corporation Ltd. Arazi earned an engineering degree in the 1960s at the Massachusetts Institute of Technology (MIT), where he was also exposed to computers. After graduating, Arazi remained in the United States for a few years and helped NASA develop an early version digital camera. He then returned to Israel and, in 1968, started the company that became Scitex.

During the 1970s and 1980s Arazi built Scitex into a leading developer and manufacturer of graphic design and publishing hardware. Importantly, Scitex is credited with pioneering the electronic color imaging process in 1968, as well as with numerous related breakthroughs in the succeeding two decades. By the late 1980s, Scitex was known as a world leader in computerized color printing. The company's products were used to generate high-quality, prepress, computerized color images that were printed using conventional ''long-run'' printing techniques. Before Arazi left Scitex, the company was generating revenues approaching $600 million annually and had sold more than $1.5 billion worth of equipment.

In 1988, Arazi walked away from his chief executive post at Scitex, despite the company's surging sales and profits, and started a new company that he dubbed Electronics for Imaging, or EFI, as he nicknamed it. Arazi's plan for EFI was to explore a new sphere of the color imaging industry that had been mostly untapped until that time. ''While CEO of Scitex, I began to see an opening for color software, but discovered there was no way to do it within a $600 million company,'' he said in 1993 in the *San Francisco Business Times.* ''You don't use a Boeing 747 to go shooting at flies,'' Arazi wryly observed.

Arazi's specific plan was to develop a relatively low-cost, easy-to-use system that would allow users to process and print high-quality graphics, including photo images, in a low-technology environment. Prior to the late 1980s, high-quality color processing and printing was done only on expensive equipment, like that developed by Scitex, and typically by graphics professionals. The potential for a major shift in computerized color graphics printing technology began to emerge in the mid-1980s. During that time, such major copier manufacturers as Canon, Kodak, and Minolta began developing and introducing machines that were capable of generating high-quality color copies for the mass market. The price of that technology declined rapidly in the late 1980s, putting it within reach of many small and midsize companies.

Arazi wanted to initiate a revolution in color desktop publishing similar to the one caused by the black-and-white desktop laser printer. Those systems, introduced in the 1980s, made it possible for individuals to generate black-and-white text and

Company Perspectives:

EFI's greatest strength is its spirit of innovation. This spirit is fueled by the creativity of Fiery users and the ideas of our employees. From our intuitive and universal Fiery user interface to our advanced ColorWise editing software, EFI technology creates workflow efficiencies by making copiers and printers invaluable extensions of the desktop computer. These extensions do more than simply print a document. They empower you to quickly and easily express yourself in eye-catching presentations, personalized proposals and more. The only limit is your imagination.

graphics that would have been created just a few years earlier only on expensive, professional, ''offset'' printing equipment. Rather than develop separate color imaging and printing machines that were the color equivalents of desktop laser printers, however, Arazi realized that all he needed to do was develop software that would allow a desktop computer or workstation to communicate with advanced color copiers. Users could then use their desktop computers and peripherals to print professional looking color images on their copiers.

Top-Notch Team and Pioneering Research Fuels Success in the Early 1990s

Arazi's new enterprise hardly resembled the classic startup venture on a shoestring budget. Aside from access to his personal hoard of cash, Arazi had connections to numerous sources of investment capital. For example, Scitex became a major investor in the company, and EFI was able to get $10.1 million in startup cash in the form of advances on products and sublicenses from copier manufacturers. Indeed, the copier manufacturers eagerly supported Arazi's effort because they realized that his planned system could vastly increase the market for their products. Support from outside sources allowed EFI to show revenues of $3.7 million during its first two years, despite the lack of a salable product.

EFI also differed from the typical startup in that its management ranks were packed with heavy-hitting talent. Experienced veterans on EFI's team included principal scientist Dr. Yigal Accad and director of research Dr. Jacob Aizikowitz, both of whom had worked for Arazi at Scitex. Among other members were: Liz Bond, a former director at Adobe Systems; Donald McKinney, a former vice-president at Silicon Graphics; and David Izuka, a previous WordStar International executive and software industry veteran. In addition to its own staff, EFI benefited from links with researchers at MIT.

The association with MIT was important because it provided the technological foundation upon which EFI would build its first product. EFI became the exclusive licensee of the W.F. Schreiber U.S. Patent 4,500,919. Issued in 1989 and effective for seven years, that patent was the result of eight years and $4 million worth of research conducted at MIT. The outcome of that research and development effort was the first layman-oriented, color preprinting, device-independent technology. A total of four Ph.D. and 12 masters degrees were awarded to researchers who contributed to the project. The chief advantage of the technology was that it brought under control the multiple variables that made it difficult to reproduce color images: lighting, inks, paper, and computer input devices, among others.

EFI's development team scrambled during 1989 and 1990 to build marketable products based on technology related to the patent. It started out focusing on four products: the Eport Color Server, a system that would move color between different desktop publishing and printing devices; the Fiery Controller, a device that would allow color copiers to function as color computer printers; Cachet, a software product that would allow desktop publishers to preview and manipulate color images; and the Color Receiver, which would effectively link desktop publishing and commercial printing systems. EFI planned to license and sell its technology and products to various software, hardware, and copier manufacturing companies.

Innovative Product Development and an IPO During the1990s

EFI introduced the Fiery color server, its first product, in 1991. The Fiery server was a box that housed hardware and software. The box could be used to link a personal computer—Macintosh or IBM compatible—and a high-grade color copier to manipulate and generate four-color, offset-quality reproductions. A major technological advantage of the product was that it offered, for the first time on a nonprofessional system, WYSIWYG—what-you-see-is-what-you-get—functionality, meaning that the printer produced a true reproduction of the computerized image users viewed on their screens.

The Fiery system was a landmark device and represented the start of a transformation in color printing, enabling users for the first time to print short runs of high-quality color images at reasonable prices. Traditional offset color printers, in contrast, had to produce hundreds or thousands of images to achieve price efficiency. The Fiery system was capable of producing a color document or image for roughly 35 cents a page, whereas the first page printed by a conventional offset system effectively cost $2,000 due to laborious fixed equipment and set up costs. Furthermore, because the technology was new, the price differential between Fiery and color offset printing was expected to increase throughout the mid- and late 1990s.

With its licensing and distribution programs already in place, EFI was able to capitalize quickly on demand for its Fiery system. The company generated sales of $16.43 million and net income of $618,000 in 1991, its first year of product sales. Those figures rose to $53.7 million and $2.18 million, respectively, in 1992. In an effort to sustain that momentum, Arazi decided to generate investment capital in 1992 by taking EFI public. Although his plan was criticized by some analysts who believed that the company's short profit history would minimize cash flow from the sale, the October 1992 offering brought nearly $40 million to EFI.

In 1993 EFI was greeted with a deluge of orders for its Fiery systems from such companies as Canon, Xerox, Kodak, and Agfa (of Belgium), which put the systems in the hands of companies that owned or leased their color copying equipment. The Fiery units were priced between $20,000 and $38,000,

Key Dates:

1989: EFI is founded by Efraim ''Efi'' Arazi.
1991: The company's first Fiery print server is introduced; European offices open.
1995: Avida is named president and CEO.
1996: Company reaches milestone 50,000 cumulative Fiery servers installed worldwide.
1997: EFI acquires Pipeline Associates, Inc.; company enters digital black-and-white market; 100,000 cumulative Fiery servers installed worldwide.
1999: EFI introduces eBeam, an appliance for capturing whiteboard images using Web-based technology; Guy Gecht becomes president; company acquires Management Graphics and its EDOX Document Servers.
2000: Gecht is named CEO; Splash Technology is acquired; Velocity workflow software is launched; over 700,000 cumulative EFI print controllers installed worldwide.
2001: Company acquires the Publishing Solutions Group of Dutch IT specialists FAIR bv.

depending on printing speed and other features. In addition, by 1993 EFI was beginning to introduce other products from its development pipeline. Early in the year it began selling its Cachet software, which allowed a computer user to scan a photograph into the computer and manipulate the image for printing. That shrink-wrapped product sold for $500 to $600.

Strong demand allowed EFI to boost revenues to $89.5 million in 1993 and net income to nearly $8 million. The company's stock price jumped to $24 going into 1994 and then to nearly $30 later in the year. However, the price subsequently fell to the mid-$20s on speculation that the company's sales would slide early in 1995. That speculation was caused partly by EFI's intent to introduce a new, less expensive line of Fiery controller systems. Some observers believed that the company was trying to dump its inventory before it brought out the new line, thereby artificially raising its stock price. Those critics were undoubtedly surprised when EFI sales and profits continued to surge.

EFI's sales rose more than 40 percent in 1994 to $130 million, and net income increased to a record $21.3 million. Management seemed determined to repeat those impressive gains in 1995. Importantly, the company began selling its new Fiery XJ product line, which was a line of three-color controller products, each shaped like a different-sized rectangular tower and offering progressively advanced features. EFI executed a pivotal agreement with Canon for that company to market, sell, and service EFI's Fiery XJ products under the Canon brand name. That announcement and other positive developments pushed EFI's stock price past $50 by mid-1995.

By 1995 EFI had shipped more than 20,000 Fiery systems. That figure would rise to more than 50,000 by 1996. Sales surpassed $190 million for the 1995 year and were growing rapidly early in 1996 with units being shipped throughout the United States, Europe, and Japan. In 1994, Arazi relinquished his role as president and CEO but remained as chairman of the board while going on to found another new business venture, Imedia Corporation. Arazi was succeeded as president and CEO by 32-year-old Dan Avida, a talented computer engineer who had joined EFI in 1989.

Under Avida's direction, EFI doubled the cumulative number of Fiery controllers sold to a total of more than 100,000 by the end of 1996. In the last few years of the decade, EFI expanded its product offerings and business ventures. In 1999 alone, EFI produced more than 45 new or enhanced products, including its Web-based whiteboard-capturing technology, called eBeam. Also during that year, former vice president and general manager of the Fiery Servers Division, Guy Gecht, took over as EFI president. In January 2000, Gecht assumed the role of CEO, while Chief Operating Officer Fred Rosenzweig was appointed president. Under Gecht's and Rosenzweig's leadership, EFI continued strong growth through acquisitions, original equipment manufacturer (OEM) partnering, and new product development.

Into the Twenty-First Century

Introduced in 1999, EFI's eBeam appliance, which was designed to capture notes off any surface (such as a whiteboard) and transfer them to a computer, established the company's foray into Web-based technology. The eBeam's pen-like sleeves fit over standard whiteboard markers (or other markers) and transmit data to receivers that are mounted to the top of the whiteboard or presentation easel. The material captured by the eBeam can then be transferred to a computer or broadcast over the Internet using its built-in Web technology. The product sold for about $600.

In 2001, EFI introduced its ImagePort accessory, which worked with the eBeam and the growing arena of Personal Digital Assistants (PDAs). With ImagePort, data captured by the eBeam can be downloaded to a PDA or a printer without going through a computer by using ImagePort's infrared technology.

In addition to the eBeam, EFI new offerings included color servers and custom-made technology for the established Fiery product line. Their two new server platforms, Fiery Z4 (for agency and graphic arts) and Fiery X4 (corporate servers), performed two to three times as fast as their predecessors and featured many enhancements. Fiery color servers also stood on their own for the first time, working with color copiers and printers and establishing the basis for partnerships with companies such as Canon, Toshiba, Epson, Ricoh, Xerox, and Minolta.

In addition to those new products, the company designed a platform for digital black-and-white printing with its Fiery X2 controller. Designed to work with the Minolta Di620 black-and-white printer and copier, the Fiery X2 turned monochrome printing into a fast-paced, networked document-creation process. The server also worked with Java-enabled technology to allow users to control printing through the Internet or Intranet. These innovations boosted EFI's revenues for 1999 to $571 million. In 2000 revenues increased to more than $588 million, based on 50 new product introductions.

However, EFI was not focused only on new products during the latter part of the 1990s. The company also launched their

Professional Services division, including EFI Academy, which provided training and coursework in computer graphics generation and management, including several personalized classes. During this time, acquisitions became a significant aspect of the company's growth strategy. The first of these occurred in 1997 when EFI took over Pipeline Associates, Inc. In 1999 the company acquired Management Graphics, Inc., a Minneapolis company, developer of the EDOX line of digital color document servers. In 2000 EFI acquired Splash Technology Holdings, a company had sued EFI for copyright infringement less than a year earlier. And in 2001, the buying continued as EFI acquired Dutch-based FAIR's Publishing Solution Group, whose variable data printing applications, which enable custom document processing, were a key asset.

EFI's vision for the future included more widespread use of color in a greater range of documents. The Internet continued to play a big part in the company's growth model. EFI had invested more than $200 million in research and development; the goal of the company into 2001 and beyond was to improve the color document printing process and to establish easy, effective means of communication through its printing tools and software.

Principal Competitors

Imation Corporation; Scitex Corporation Ltd; Interlink Electronics, Inc.; ScanSoft, Inc.; Colorbus.

Further Reading

Abelson, Reed, "Leapfrogger," *Forbes,* October 28, 1991, p. 203.

Carlsen, Clifford, "EFI-vescence: Success Bubbles for 'Computer King of Color'," *San Francisco Business Times,* August 20, 1993, p. 8A.

——, "Firm Pushes Color-Image Revolution," *San Francisco Business Times,* September 3, 1990, p. 1.

Davis, Gil, and Liz Bond, "Profile of Electronics for Imaging," *Business Wire,* June 1, 1990.

"Electronics for Imaging Acquires Fair's Publishing Solutions Group," *Creativepro.com,* posted February 26, 2001, http://www.creativepro.com/front/home.

"Electronics for Imaging Acquires Fair's Publishing Solutions Group; Variable Data Printing Applications a Key Asset," *Forbes.com,* posted February 26, 2001, http://www.forbes.com.

"Electronics for Imaging Closes Splash Acquisition," *San Francisco Business Times,* posted October 24, 2000, http://sanfrancisco.bcentral.com/sanfrancisco.

"E.F.I. Opens Center in Israel," *Israel Business Today,* January 1, 1993, p. 4.

Hevenor, Keith, "Guy Gecht," *Electronic Publishing,* December 1999.

Labate, John, "Electronics for Imaging," *Fortune,* June 28, 1993, p. 107.

Levy, Lawrence, "Scitex Executive Named President of Electronics for Imaging Europe," *Business Wire,* April 7, 1994.

"Mr. Color; Dan Avida, Head of Electronics for Imaging, Hopes the Company's Fiery Product Will Help Make Black and White Printing Obsolete," *Forbes,* December 4, 1995, p. 270.

"New eBeam ImagePort from EFI Syncs with Handheld Devices: Whiteboard System a First for PDAs," *Forbes.com,* February 22, 2001.

"Record Revenues for EFI," *Israel Business Today,* October 23, 1992, p. 11.

Serwer, Andrew E., "America's Fastest Growing Companies," *Fortune,* August 8, 1994.

Weber, Merril, "EFI the 'If Only' Story of the Year," *Israel Business Today,* April 21, 1995, p. 14.

—Dave Mote
—update: Kerri DeVault

Enbridge Inc.

3000 Fifth Ave. Place
425 1st St. Southwest
Calgary, Alberta T2P 3L8
Canada
Telephone: (403) 231-3900
Toll Free: (800) 481-2804
Fax: (403) 231-3920
Web site: http://www.enbridge.com

Public Company
Incorporated: 1949 as Interprovincial Pipe Line Co.
Employees: 5,500
Sales: $1.96 billion (2000)
Stock Exchanges: NASDAQ Toronto
Ticker Symbols: ENBR; ENB
NAIC: 48611 Pipeline Transportation of Crude Oil; 48621 Pipeline Transportation of Natural Gas; 48699 All Other Pipeline Transportation; 22121 Natural Gas Distribution; 221122 Electric Power Distribution; 221111 Hydroelectric Power Generation; 221112 Fossil Fuel Electric Power Generation; 221113 Nuclear Electric Power Generation; 221119 Other Electric Power Generation; 221121 Electric Bulk Power Transmission and Control

Calgary-based Enbridge Inc. is a North American leader in energy transportation, distribution, and related services. As a transporter of energy, Enbridge operates the world's longest crude oil and liquids pipeline system in Canada and the United States. As a distributor of energy, Enbridge owns and operates Canada's largest natural gas distribution company (through its 1994 acquisition of Consumers' Gas), and plays a role in generating and distributing electricity. In addition, Enbridge provides retail energy products and services to a growing number of Canadian and U.S. markets.

Development of Interprovincial Pipe Line: Late 1940s

Enbridge's energy transportation business originated with the Imperial Oil Company Limited's development of the Leduc oil fields in Alberta in the late 1940s. After the Leduc discovery in 1947 and the even larger Redwater discovery in 1948, Alberta's oil producers suddenly developed the capacity to produce far more crude oil than the refinery in Edmonton could handle. The need for pipelines as the only economical means of moving crude oil quickly arose.

Pipelines were largely nonexistent in Canada in the 1940s, with only 418 miles of oil pipeline in operation throughout the entire country in 1947. Unlike the U.S. oil industry, the Canadian counterpart had grown chaotically, often subject to outside competition and control. Imperial Oil itself provided an example of this. It had been formed from the merger of 16 producing and refining companies in 1880 to fend off U.S. competitors and to gain economies of scale. In 1899, it had become an affiliate of Standard Oil and was almost totally dependent upon imported crude oil by 1947.

After the 1947 Leduc discovery, Imperial Oil envisioned a 450-mile oil line from Edmonton southeast to Regina. In order to construct and operate this pipeline, which would traverse more than one province, Imperial Oil applied to the federal government to incorporate Interprovincial Pipe Line Co. in 1949 as the first permanent link between Canada's rich western reserves and the energy markets of North America. Then Minister of Transport Lionel Chevrier introduced a bill, closely patterned after the Railway Act, for the creation of The Pipe Lines Act of Canada. The bill received wide support from all parties, and was passed into law in late April 1949. It incorporated five pipeline companies—Interprovincial Pipe Line, Westcoast Transmission Company, Trans-Northern Pipe Line Company, Western Pipes Company, and British American Pipe Line Company. In June, the federal Board of Transport Commissioners authorized Interprovincial to build its 450-mile pipeline, and the first crude oil and liquids pipeline from Edmonton to Regina was completed later that year.

All of the original officers of the new pipeline company were past officers of Imperial. Many had had pipelining experience in South America as part of the parent company's International Petroleum operations in Peru and its Tropical Oil operations in Colombia. As a result, they brought with them years of pipeline laying knowledge and had a vision for Interprovincial. Even while proceeding with the approved line, the company had its engineering group at work on design and feasibility studies for a

Company Perspectives:

Enbridge will go beyond all others to deliver energy and related services to North American and international customers. This common vision bonds the many different but related businesses of the corporation together in a unified purpose. A number of themes are embedded in the vision statement to reflect the values and qualities that distinguish us from all others.

We are a service business. We deliver energy through long distance transportation and local distribution and provide complementary energy services such as marketing of energy and related products and services. We have a sense of competitive excellence. We will distinguish ourselves from peers and competitors with the quality, reliability and responsiveness of our service. We demonstrate a sense of agility and innovation. We will extend ourselves beyond traditional boundaries and approaches to develop services that best meet our customers' needs. We are customer-focused. Our success will be measured by our customers and how they see us surpassing others in meeting their needs. We have a global reach. We will serve customers in Canada, the United States and internationally.

much longer system from Edmonton to the head of Lake Superior, from which point the crude could be moved by tanker during the summer shipping season to refineries in the southeastern Ontario port of Sarnia. By the summer of 1949, Imperial had decided to extend the pipeline to Superior, Wisconsin. In August, Lakehead Pipe Line Company Inc. was incorporated as a wholly owned subsidiary of Interprovincial, in charge of constructing and operating the U.S. portion of the pipeline system. In September, the Canadian Board of Transport Commissioners approved the 340-mile extension of Interprovincial's planned system from Regina to Gretna on the Manitoba-U.S. border. Lakehead Pipe Line would handle the section of the pipeline from Gretna to Superior, 360 miles away, and, possibly, later to Chicago.

The decision to terminate the IPL line at Superior rather than keeping it within Canada raised a storm of political protest among those with strong nationalist sympathies who questioned the financial reasons behind the move. However, Commerce Minister C.D. Howe, at the October opening ceremony for the pipeline, countered that the IPL line would stop a drag on the economy of at least $150 million a year that was being spent on foreign crude.

In fact, the route IPL's line traversed was 120 miles shorter and considerably less expensive than an all-Canadian alternative, and was thus more quickly built. The "fastest pipe in the West" was completed between the spring and fall of 1950, about 1,130 miles of line laid in 150 days with the capacity to store about 800,000 barrels in Edmonton and another 150,000 at Superior. The first Canadian oil reached Superior two months later, in early December.

Pipe Line Expansion: 1950s–60s

The years from 1951 to 1957 were a time of rapid growth at IPL. The number of employees doubled, system capacity quadrupled, and movement of oil through the pipeline—throughput—quintupled. For the first full year of operation, profits were a healthy $3.4 million on operating revenues of $14.5 million. Before the line was even in operation, in fact, additional capacity was required. The system of winter storage of crude at Superior alternating with summer shipments to Sarnia proved inadequate to handle the growing volume of oil.

Throughout the next two decades, there was continuous expansion and growth of the IPL system. Beginning in 1951 and 1952, workers undertook the initial looping of the IPL system, laying 100 miles of line beside the original in sections between Regina and the U.S. border crossing at Gretna. In 1953, IPL's stock was listed on the Toronto and Montreal stock exchanges, and additional looping was done along the line between Edmonton and Superior. The terminal planned for Superior was scrapped in favor of extending the system across Wisconsin and Michigan to Sarnia by laying two lines made of steel underwater across the Straits of Mackinac between Lakes Huron and Michigan, a technological first. The year 1953 also marked the entry of a second oil pipeline venture, the Trans Mountain Oil Pipe Line Company, to ship Alberta crude to distant markets west.

Looping between Edmonton and Superior continued yearly to provide increased capacity. By 1955, the first year in which IPL did not undertake major construction, the system's capacity had grown to 217,000 barrels per day on the Edmonton-Regina section, 193,000 between Regina and Gretna, 163,000 between Gretna and Superior, and 147,000 between Superior and Sarnia. In 1956, another 156-mile extension from Sarnia to the outskirts of Toronto increased the main line of the IPL system to 1,930 miles, with an additional 92-mile spur to Buffalo, New York. IPL now owned and operated the longest crude oil pipeline in the world. Five types of crude moved through the system, shipped in "batches" to suit customers' needs for different types of crude. Throughput passed the 1,000-billion barrel mark, and the company still continued to grow despite a second half of the year slowdown in the wake of the Suez crisis.

The years from 1958 to 1965 saw a major reshaping of the North American oil business and IPL's role within it. Governments became a more dominant force in the industry. Growing fleets of "supertankers" now carried cheap, abundant Middle Eastern oil to consumers following the Suez crisis. The real cost of oil declined after allowing for inflation. Although the pace of expansion slowed, the company's operations continued to grow more complex. This growth and complexity accelerated the trend toward automation, which involved a combination of remote control, computerization, and electrification of diesel-powered pumping stations. At the same time, the Royal Commission on Energy recommended the creation of a comprehensive energy policy, and, in 1958, created the National Energy Board (NEB). As envisioned in the royal commission report and the government's 1959 legislation, the principal role of this body was to advise the government on energy policies and oversee their implementation. The NEB ended forever the laissez-faire regulatory attitude that had prevailed in Canada under the Board of Transport Commissioners.

Between 1966 and 1973, IPL roughly doubled its capacity, throughput, revenues, and earnings. Oil consumption had been growing at a rate of 7 percent annually since the end of World War II. By 1967, IPL was moving crude to refineries in Ontario,

Key Dates:

1848: Consumers' Gas Company begins to distribute gas to Toronto's street lamps.
1880: Imperial Oil Company is formed.
1949: Imperial Oil applies to the Canadian government to incorporate the Interprovincial Pipe Line Co. (IPL).
1950: Company completes its first pipeline and delivers oil to Superior, Wisconsin.
1953: Company's stock is listed on the Toronto and Montreal stock exchanges.
1956: IPL owns and operates the longest crude oil pipeline in the world.
1969: IPL completes its Chicago Loop, beginning deliveries to Chicago a year later.
1976: Company's Montreal pipeline begins delivery of oil.
1986: Company acquires Home Oil.
1994: Company, now named IPL Energy, acquires Consumers' Gas, which is later organized as the subsidiary Enbridge Consumers Gas.
1998: Company changes name to Enbridge Inc.

Buffalo, Detroit, Toledo, and other points in the United States and required yet more delivery capacity for markets east of Superior. U.S. demand for Canadian crude was higher than expected and, for the first time, IPL could not meet refiners' requirements despite the fact that it increased capacity by 100,000 barrels per day.

Management sought the solution to capacity shortfall in a new line east from Superior to Chicago and from Chicago to Sarnia. The expansion made Canadian oil accessible for the first time to the big Chicago refinery center, which consumed oil at the rate of nearly 700,000 barrels a day. The system as envisioned would be one of the world's largest to transmit crude oil: from Edmonton to Superior, it would include three separate lines; from Superior east, there would be two lines, one through the Straits of Mackinac and a second through Chicago.

American independent oil producers protested the growing volume of Canadian oil, which undersold U.S. crude at refineries in the Great Lakes region. Nevertheless, an informal agreement between the Canadian and U.S. governments resulted in the January 1968 presidential permit allowing construction of the Chicago loop, which was completed in 1969. This agreement, however, limited Canadian oil deliveries to U.S. refineries east of the Rocky Mountains to an annual increase of 27,000 barrels a day during a three-year term, and prohibited deliveries into the Chicago area until 1970. Following the opening of the Chicago market, deliveries increased in 1970 by 16 percent, bringing total throughput to about 900,000 barrels per day.

The Energy Crisis of the 1970s

When OPEC raised prices in 1971 and began to ship refined products for the first time, about 85 percent of the oil and gas production and 99 percent of the oil refining in Canada was in the hands of foreign corporations, according to T.C. Douglas, head of the New Democratic Party. In early 1972, OPEC again raised its prices upward for Arab crude, and that year, IPL's average deliveries exceeded one million barrels a day. In 1973, when OPEC prices jumped again from about $2.50 to $12 per barrel, U.S. demand for Canadian crude grew so much that IPL and Lakehead began operating at full capacity. As a result, in March the NEB instituted industry regulation, imposing an export tax on Canadian crude to equal the prevailing price of crude in Chicago. This change marked the beginning of increased governmental involvement in the oil industry. Prime Minister Trudeau's government, in favor of energy "self-reliance," sought to guarantee a market in Canada for Canadian oil "at a level sufficient to ensure the development of . . . Canadian sources of supply." Specifically, this meant the government supported "security of supply," which translated into the extension of a pipeline from Sarnia to Montreal. IPL began to prepare its application to the NEB for the new pipeline in late 1973.

The mid-1970s seemed to mark the end of an era of expansion at IPL and Lakehead. In response to higher oil prices, consumers' rate of increase in consumption of oil products, which had been growing 7 percent annually for decades, dropped by one half. Cars, industrial plants, and furnaces became more energy-efficient. New natural gas distribution networks and hydroelectric, coal-fired, and nuclear power stations came into being. In addition, forces of environmentalism, nationalism, and socialism converged to inform the government's intervention in the affairs of the oil industry following the Arab oil embargo of 1973. Prime Minister Trudeau asked the oil industry to temporarily freeze prices. Subsequent uncertainties about environmental regulations slowed project growth and led to the 1977 shelving of some projects. In 1975, after a full year of hearings, IPL was issued a certificate of public convenience and necessity for the Montreal pipeline, and a deficiency agreement, which said that the government would make up earnings shortfalls whenever the operating revenue in a given year failed to meet the costs of the extension. The new pipeline first delivered oil in June 1976 and reached its planned delivery level of 250,000 barrels per day in December.

In 1977, there was an upsurge in heavy oil production in Canada as OPEC prices again rose by almost a dollar. The late 1978 overthrow of the Shah of Iran reduced world oil supplies and led to a staggering rise in the price of light crude from about $13 to $32 in 1979. Eastern Canadian refineries exceeded pipeline capacity by 100,000 barrels per day, turning around the throughput decline of the mid-1970s. Higher prices spurred new exploration efforts industry-wide and encouraged development of new technologies for enhancing recovery from old wells.

Meanwhile, in 1978, after two years of public hearings on tariffs, IPL was placed under direct rate regulation by the NEB. Tariffs were designed to reduce revenues by approximately 5 percent for the Canadian system, excluding the Montreal extension. The government also limited oil exports to the midwestern United States. On the American side, in 1977, the newly created Federal Energy Regulatory Commission took over regulation of Lakehead operations.

Diversification and Deregulation in the 1980s

IPL entered the 1980s feeling considerably uncertain about the future of its east-west pipeline operations. After several years of record earnings, profits in 1980 decreased 12 percent due to lower throughput and increased operating costs, the first such decline since 1974. Demand for refined oil products was flat throughout the first half of the 1980s. To compensate, the company sought two ways to continue its growth and increase share values: by expanding its pipeline operations and by diversifying non-pipeline investments. Refineries underwent modifications so they could accept increased volumes of heavy crude. Greater quantities of natural gas liquids and refined products were shipped through the IPL-LPL system to meet greater demand.

Industry fluctuations notwithstanding, the company's growth continued unabated. In 1983, IPL undertook construction of the Norman Wells pipeline, the first crude oil line to be built in the far north since World War II, followed by a massive expansion of its mainline system. IPL established Interprovincial Pipe Line (NW) Limited, a new, wholly owned subsidiary to build and operate the new pipeline. It also took over part ownership of the IPL Tower, an Edmonton landmark. In 1982, the government instituted policies to subsidize tanker transportation from Montreal and incentives to export surplus heavy oil to the states. As a result, there was an upsurge in deliveries in the second half of 1982. A decline in U.S. oil production also created market opportunities for Canadian crude.

By 1981, IPL was looking seriously for diversification options. After several aborted attempts, it joined with Amoco, Anschutz, and Union Pacific and invested in Frontier Pipeline Company, laying pipeline from northeastern Utah to Casper, Wyoming, in 1983. Then in 1986, Imperial Oil, which still owned 33 percent of IPL, approached the company with a plan to exchange shares with Hiram Walker, the Canadian liquor, gas, and oil conglomerate that owned Home Oil. IPL became Hiram Walker's largest shareholder and vice versa. Later in 1986, IPL exchanged its shares in Hiram Walker for ownership of all the shares of Home Oil and created a new corporate identity, Interhome Energy Inc. Two more name changes followed; the company became Interprovincial Pipe Line Inc. in 1991 and IPL Energy Inc. in 1994. In 1993, IPL relocated the company's corporate office from Toronto to Calgary to better serve its two operating units, its pipeline business in Edmonton and its oil business in Calgary.

Energy Integration in the 1990s

Meanwhile, inside IPL, another shift was occurring. The first generation of IPL employees, those who had built the company since the 1950s, were leaving or nearing retirement. At the same time, the national election of a Progressive Conservative government in the early 1980s led to the removal of export restrictions on Canadian oil and set the stage for price deregulation of the Canadian oil business beginning in 1985. Special incentives by provincial governments in 1983 and 1984 began to revive light oil productivity on the prairies. The company initiated a three-phase expansion plan to build capacity and handle the increase in heavy oil shipments, and enjoyed record earnings for the fifth consecutive year in 1985. Then, in 1986, before the Canadian petroleum industry had fully integrated the effects of deregulation, world oil prices plummeted to less than half their 1985 levels. Notwithstanding this slump, the company went on to complete the second phase of capacity expansion in 1987.

Another shift was going on throughout the broader energy industry as well, that of convergence, or the integration of the crude oil, natural gas, and electrical power segments in North America. As late as 1993, IPL represented a single line of business, a crude oil pipeline system. Then, in 1994, IPL acquired most of the shares of Consumers' Gas, the largest natural gas utility in Canada and the premier natural gas distributor to metropolitan Toronto, parts of eastern Ontario, Quebec, and New York state. IPL acquired the remaining shares of Consumers' in 1996, and Consumers' Gas became a wholly owned subsidiary of the company. In 1997, IPL launched a new subsidiary, Consumersfirst, opening the first of five retail stores that sold natural gas and electric products and services to customers. Throughout the late 1990s, IPL engaged in a number of projects to develop and/or operate gas pipelines to serve Quebec, New Brunswick, Ontario, and New York. The Alliance Pipeline project, begun in partnership with 16 other Alberta companies in 1999, would deliver natural gas from British Columbia to the Chicago hub when complete, while the proposed Vector pipeline would link Chicago with the more eastern markets of Ontario and New York. The Transmaritime Project, undertaken in association with TransCanada PipeLines, consisted of the plan to ship Sable Island, Nova Scotia gas to Canadian and northeastern U.S. markets. IPL also acquired an interest in AltaGas Services, a Calgary-based natural gas company in 1999. During the same period it purchased the electric utility of the city of Cornwall, Ontario.

The company continued to build its core infrastructure in crude oil throughout the second half of the 1990s as well. In 1995, it completed phase one of its System Expansion Program (SEP I) plan, embarked on SEP II, and acquired several strategic feeder pipelines. In 1998, it began its Terrace Phase I Expansion Program to increase heavy crude oil capacity in the Midwest. It also purchased an interest in the Chicap Pipeline, which ran oil from the Gulf Coast to Chicago and brought its capacity to 2.2 million barrels per day. In 1999, it completed construction of its Athabasca Pipeline from the oilsands deposits of northeastern Alberta to its main crude oil pipeline system. Several other of IPL's ventures in the 1990s expanded its scope geographically. In 1995, in its first international venture, it embarked on developing OCENSA, a new Colombian pipeline, along with TransCanada PipeLines. Four years later, it announced an agreement to acquire an interest in the Jose crude oil terminal and shipping facility located in Venezuela.

The company's profits reflected its steady growth throughout the 1990s—from \$81 million in 1993 to \$180 million in 1996, and then gradually upward to \$288 million in 1999. IPL, which now had two business units, Energy Transportation and Energy Distribution, changed its name again in 1998 to Enbridge Inc. The name, which was an elision of "energy" and "bridge," was meant to signify "the connection the company will make with energy customers around the world" and to transform a family of companies into "one company with one vision."

Enbridge looked to the future with a vision of moving into the additional utilities of electricity and water. The owner of the world's longest crude oil and petroleum liquids pipeline system in the Western Hemisphere hoped one day soon to become a one-stop shop for a variety of energy consumer needs.

Principal Subsidiaries

Enbridge Pipelines Inc.; Enbridge Technology Inc.; Enbridge Consumers Gas; Lakehead Pipe Line Partners, L.P. (U.S.A.; 14.5%); Enbridge Midcoast Energy, Inc. (U.S.A.); Noverco Inc. (32%); Enbridge Gas New Brunswick; Enbridge International Inc.

Principal Competitors

Foothills Pipe Lines Ltd.; Irving Oil Ltd.; TransCanada PipeLines Ltd.; Westcoast Energy Inc.

Further Reading

''Athabasca Pipeline to Handle Growing Oilsands Production,'' *Oil & Gas Journal*, April 26, 1999, p. 60.

Bott, Bob, *Mileposts: The Story of the World's Longest Petroleum Pipeline*, Toronto: Interprovincial Pipe Line Company, 1989.

''Enbridge's Gradual Shift into Gas,'' *Gas Processors Report*, August 23, 1999.

Gray, Earle, *The Great Canadian Oil Patch*, Toronto: Maclean-Hunter Limited, 1970, pp. 133–50.

McCarten, James, ''Enbridge Poised to Reap Rewards of Electric Deregulation,'' *Canadian Press Newswire*, November 25, 1998.

A Tradition of Service: The Story of Consumers' Gas, Toronto: Consumers' Gas Company Ltd., 1993.

—Carrie Rothburd

EZCORP Inc.

1901 Capital Parkway
Austin, Texas 78746
U.S.A.
Telephone: (512) 314-3400
Fax: (512) 314-3404
Web site: http://www.ezcorp.com

Public Company
Incorporated: 1989
Employees: 2,100
Sales: $197.4 million (2000)
Stock Exchanges: NASDAQ
Ticker Symbol: EZPW
NAIC: 522298 All Other Nondepositing Credit Intermediation

Owning and operating some 300 pawnshops under the name EZPAWN, EZCORP Inc. is the second largest pawnshop company in the country. The stores provide loans to customers who present property of value as collateral. EZPAWN stores accept pre-owned goods, such as, jewelry, sporting goods, and consumer electronics, in lieu of loan redemption and then sells those goods at approximately 70 percent of retail value. EZPAWN stores are located primarily in the south, including Texas, where the company owns nearly 200 stores, as well as Colorado, Oklahoma, and Indiana. The company also owns a large interest in Albemarie and Bond Holdings, a pawnshop operator in the United Kingdom.

1970s Origins and Rapid Momentum

Courtland L. Logue, Jr., opened his first pawn shop in Austin, Texas, in 1974. Employed as an accountant, Logue was inspired by the success of his father's friend, who operated a pawn shop in Dallas. The store turned a good profit and required little effort, and Logue decided that, with hard work, he could be even more successful in the pawn business. The first EZPAWN was indeed a success, and eventually Logue was overseeing a chain; over the next 15 years he would open one new store a year. Logue located these stores near large grocery stores in lower-middle income communities rather than in impoverished neighborhoods, as was typical of the time. Operating under the banner EZPAWN or U-Pawn-It, the stores tended to be free standing or strip center stores, each with 3,000 square feet, approximately half storage and half retail space. Seeking to counter the stereotype of pawn shops as dingy or seedy, Logue distinguished his stores with vibrant blue awnings on the exterior and clean, bright, interiors, thus attracting more shoppers and making them comfortable.

Corporate reorganization and further expansion followed when the company was able to obtain $10 million in capital investment in May 1989. With 16 stores in business, Logue formed a corporate umbrella, Transamerica Pawn Holdings, which purchased the loosely organized EZPAWN stores. Over the next 18 months Transamerica acquired or opened 41 additional stores throughout Texas. Investment per store averaged $192,000, excluding real estate, with each store becoming profitable in three to six months.

By the end of fiscal 1991 (September 30), the company's annual revenues had reached $23.8 million and net income was at $1.2 million. The retail business, the sale of goods forfeited in lieu of loan repayment, accounted for 54 percent of total revenues and 24 percent of net revenues (total revenues less cost of goods sold). The stores' merchandise consisted primarily of jewelry, at 50 percent of retail sales, as well as consumer electronics, tools, musical instruments, and firearms. Because pawn loans were based on 20 to 65 percent of estimated resale value of the property, EZPAWN sold the goods at below market value. The service charges made on loans to sellers accounted for 46 percent of the company's total revenues and 76 percent of net revenues in 1991. EZPAWN charged approximately 20 percent per month, or 240 percent per annum for loans up to $108, in accordance with state law, and less for loans of higher incremental amounts. Loan amounts averaged between $60 and $70.

Transamerica adopted the name EZCORP Inc. in December 1991, in conjunction with its initial public offering of stock on the NASDAQ exchange. Shares in EZCORP were offered at $9.75 each, and the sale netted $25 million for working capital and continued expansion. With 66 stores in operation, the company planned to open or purchase 40 additional stores in 1992

Company Perspectives:

EZPAWN offers instant cash loans and bargains in 300+ stores in 12 states. EZPAWN is the second largest pawnship chain in America. Convenient, clean, bright stores with friendly EZPAWN associates will help you get an instant cash loan or find that perfect bargain.

and 50 stores in 1993, expanding in existing markets or into adjacent markets. A secondary offering of stock in March 1992, at $16.50 per share, raised an additional $26.4 million.

With renewed capital, the company began a vigorous expansion program. During 1992 EZCORP opened 25 pawnshops and acquired another 45 existing shops, bringing the total number to 127 stores. Moreover, the company expanded outside Texas for the first time, with six stores in Oklahoma; 11 stores in Mississippi; two each in Colorado, Alabama, and Tennessee; and one in Arkansas. In its home state of Texas, the company's total number of stores reached 103, with an EZCORP presence in Houston, Corpus Christi, Dallas, and San Antonio. Store expansion more than doubled revenues and net income. Strategies for growth at store level included improved profitability through cost controls, attracting new customers, and focus on the retail business, adding a line of new jewelry to its pre-owned merchandise.

EZCORP continued its fast pace of growth the following year, increasing its outlets by 25 new units and 34 acquired units, for a company wide total of 186 units. The company added 30 stores in Texas, three in Oklahoma, eight in Colorado, nine in Alabama; and five in Tennessee; EZPAWN entered the pawnshop market in Georgia with four stores in the Atlanta area. Total revenue and net income more than doubled again, to $108.6 million and $6.1 million, respectively.

By 1993 the company's financial performance was strong, given the maturity of its stores as well as the greater number of them. EZCORP also improved operations through loan analysis, additions to its internal audit staff which adjusted store level controls, and investment in a retail inventory management system. Retail sales also improved with gross profit margins at 25 percent in 1993 and a 131 percent increase in revenues to $63.8 million. EZCORP attributed improvements to same store sales growth, the addition of new jewelry, and fewer wholesale purchases. The company reduced the prices on old inventory and sold slow-moving gold and silver jewelry as scrap metal to clear out retail display space for higher profit goods. In November 1993, EZCORP centralized jewelry cleaning and refurbishment at a new 8,100 square foot processing center. The company prepared to build on its successful retail sales with advertising and promotion of its new and pre-owned jewelry.

Mid-1990s: Management Changes and Financial Challenges

The company continued to grow at a fast pace in late 1993 and in 1994, establishing 48 new stores and acquiring six stores. The company entered the Indiana market for the first time with nine stores. In existing markets EZCORP added seven new stores in Georgia, 20 new stores in Texas, one in Arkansas, three in Alabama, and ten in Colorado. Despite, or perhaps because of, such rapid growth, net income fell due to several charges, including management recruitment and relocation, inventory markdown and clearance pricing, and inventory evaluation. Also, EZCORP reworked its method of estimating the accrual of pawn service charges, on a loan-by-loan basis, resulting in lower estimates. Logue's new jewelry program proved to be the biggest problem, resulting in a $5 million loss in fiscal 1991 alone. As a result of the slowdown and financial struggles, the board of directors decided to make some radical changes, forcing Logue to resign and replacing him with Vincent Lambiase as CEO and President.

EZCORP reorganized the executive office with personnel particularly adept at handling a large chain of stores. Lambiase created three executive-level positions: chief financial officer, vice-president of operations, and vice-president of marketing and merchandising. He also decentralized certain controls and decision-making responsibilities to the store level, while store managers reported to regional managers. EZCORP used computer technology to facilitate management, with a new point-of-sale computer system and management information systems that allowed regional and central managers to obtain real-time data from individual store systems.

While *Fortune* magazine named EZCORP one of America's Fastest-Growing Companies for 1995, the pace of EZCORP's growth slowed as it closed or consolidated unprofitable stores. EZCORP closed six stores in Texas, one in Oklahoma, two in Mississippi, and two in Georgia. Nevertheless, the company opened three new stores in Louisiana (two in New Orleans) and one store in Florida, entering those markets for the first time, and added five stores in Colorado, 12 in Indiana (primarily in the Indianapolis area), and one in Alabama. These stores tended to be larger than the company's older units, with 2,000 square feet of retail selling space and 4,000 square feet of storage and administrative space. Each store operated with a store manager, an assistant manager, and three to four sales representatives. Investment for newly established stores averaged $450,000 each for the first year, for inventory, pawn loans, property, and equipment, and $250,000 for each acquired store.

Still, such impressive growth belied financial problems, and eventually the company's struggles became public knowledge. EZCORP's stock value dropped from $28 in 1993 to approximately $4 in 1995, as net losses of $15.8 million were reported. To immediately address its problems, EZCORP moved to scrap its jewelry program and refine its lending practices. The latter was achieved by instituting management incentive programs to improve lending practices, loan redemption rates, and inventory turnover at an acceptable rate of cash return. Improvements to EZCORP's loan portfolio resulted in a lower inventory of unredeemed goods and better quality forfeited merchandise. A new inventory reserve methodology refined merchandise valuation, more closely matching the loan amounts to potential sale prices and profit margins.

EZCORP continued to open new stores but also closed stores that did not meet certain performance standards. At the end 1995 the company closed an additional 18 stores. At the start of 1996 EZCORP operated 245 stores in 11 states: 147 in Texas; 24 in Colorado; 21 in Indiana; 15 in Alabama; nine in Mississippi; nine in Georgia; eight in Oklahoma; seven in Tennessee; three in Louisiana; one in Arkansas; and one in Florida.

Key Dates:

1974: Courtland Logue, Jr., establishes an EZPAWN store in Austin.
1989: Reincorporation ensues with the help of $10 million capital investment.
1991: A name change to EZCORP accompanies initial public offering of stock.
1992: 70 stores are established or acquired.
1994: New management and restructuring addresses problems of growth.
1995: 245 stores are in operation in ten states.
1998: Prosperous economy leads to slowdown in pawn industry.
2000: Company initiates payday loan advance service in Texas.

To provide another outlet for excess jewelry inventory, EZCORP opened two JewelryLand Outlet stores in Atlanta in September 1996. The 1,500-square-foot stores resembled typical mall jewelry stores but operated like the retail end of a pawnshop. At 60 to 70 percent of actual value, jewelry prices ranged from $10 to $5,000. The company expected to draw a customer base similar to those realized at discounters such as Target and Wal-Mart.

Economic Prosperity in Late 1990s Proves Bad for Pawnshops

EZCORP rebounded from its mid-1990s financial difficulties. In 1998, the company closed only one store, acquired three stores, and established 35 new stores, for a total of 286 stores in operation. EZCORP entered three new markets, California, with six stores in Sacramento, and Las Vegas and Raleigh-Durham, with three stores each. Same store growth improved with a higher average loan rate of $70 and higher loan redemption, at 80 percent. During fiscal 1998 net income reached $9.2 million on $197.4 million in total revenues.

However, the gains EZCORP made in between 1996 and 1998 were offset as the U.S. economy improved, and the demand for collateral-based, high interest loans declined. Profitability suffered as the company made fewer loans; the volume increases declined from 17 to 13 percent between 1998 and 1999. Profit margins on merchandise decreased as well, from 16 percent in 1998 to 12 percent in 1999. Still, EZCORP celebrated a milestone as its 300th store opened in November 1998; by the end of the following year, the company would boast a chain of 334 stores.

The company attempted to reach a wider audience through the Internet with EZPAWN.com. The web site offered over 400,000 items for sale, but was intended primarily to sell its preowned, one-of-a-kind jewelry. A ''virtual-photo jewelry tray'' contained similar styles of jewelry for display upon request at the web site. The site taught consumers to look at the gram weight of gold jewelry, helping them to understand the difference in valuation of jewelry. EZPAWN.com was the first pawnshop to be listed on shop@aol, an online shopping destination, and was located in that site's Jewelry and Watches Department.

In August 2000 Joseph Rotunda, after five months as COO, became CEO at EZCORP, while Lambiase became vice-chairman of the board. Rotunda brought experience from Thorn Americas, where he oversaw impressive growth of the Rent-A-Center, Remco, and U-Can-Rent stores, which increased from a total of 700 to 1,400 stores. CEO Rotunda began a restructuring program to reduce debt and overhead expenses. EZCORP closed 37 stores in 2000, reducing the chain to 299 units in 12 states, and planned to close another 17 stores. Fiscal 2000 saw a net loss of $32.6 million. Rotunda attempted to improve profitability by changing lending guidelines, adjusting interest rates, and reinstating lending on hunting rifles. He hoped to improve operations through a new management compensation plan, employee training, and a new program of standards for operation.

Moreover, EZCORP sought to offset the decline in demand for pawnshop loans by offering payday loan advances. While many people no longer needed to pawn belongings to make ends meet, a good economy made consumer spending escalate; perceiving a need to supplement the cash available to them between paychecks, consumers flocked to check-cashing service centers, which offered loans whereby a personal check covered the amount of the loan plus interest until the customer's next payday. Customers tended to be steady workers who occasionally needed extra money between paychecks. EZCORP began to test offer the service at stores in Texas in late 2000 and planned to extend the service to its pawnshops nationwide in 2001. As the economy began to slump in 2001, EZCORP could also perhaps expect its pawn facilities to realize greater revenues.

Principal Subsidiaries

EZPAWN Colorado, Inc.; EZPAWN Indiana, Inc.; EZPAWN Oklahoma, Inc; Texas EZPAWN Management, Inc.; EZCORP International Inc.

Principal Competitors

Cash America International, Inc.; First Cash Financial Services, Inc.; PawnMart, Inc.

Further Reading

Auster, Bruce, ''The Pawn of a New Era is Upon Us,'' *U.S. News & World Report,* December 8, 1997, p. 64.
''EZCORP,'' *Chain Store Age Executive with Shopping Center Age,* December 1992, p. 50.
''Joe Rotunda Named President and COO of EZCORP, Inc.,'' *PR Newswire,* April 7, 2000, p. 1,026.
''Major Pawnshop Operator Opens Two Jewelry Outlets,'' *Atlanta Constitution,* September 21, 1996, p. 2E.
Nguyen, Hang, ''Dallas-Area Pawnshops Offer Payday Advances as Good Economy Cuts Business,'' *Knight-Ridder/Tribune Business News,* August 23, 2000.
Nulty, Peter, ''Serial Entrepreneur: Tips From a Man who Started 28 Businesses,'' *Fortune,* July 10, 1995, p. 182.
Pletz, John, ''Strong Economy Makes Business Difficult for Pawnshops,'' *Austin American-Statesman,* August 24, 1999.
Scott, Dave, ''Pawnshops Multiply Despite Seedy Image,'' *Dallas Business Journal,* June 26, 1992, p. 1.
Sparks, Debra, ''Buddy, Can You Spare a Dime,'' *Financial World,* September 16, 1996, p. 16.

—Mary Tradii

Fedders Corporation

Westgate Corporate Center
505 Martinsville Road
P.O. Box 813
Liberty Corner, New Jersey 07938
U.S.A.
Telephone: (908) 604-8686
Toll Free: (800) 345-4494
Fax: (908) 604-0715
Web site: http://www.fedders.com

Public Company
Incorporated: 1913 as Fedders Manufacturing Co., Inc.
Employees: 3,420
Sales: $409.8 million (2000)
Stock Exchanges: New York Boston Philadelphia Midwest Pacific
Ticker Symbol: FJA FJC
NAIC: 334413 Semiconductors & Related Device Manufacturing; 333415 Air-conditioning and Warm Air Heating Equipment and Commercial and Industrial Refrigeration Equipment

Fedders Corporation is the largest U.S. manufacturer of room air conditioners, primarily for the residential market. Its sales and earnings in this business have fluctuated considerably, partly because of the unpredictability of North American summer weather and partly because of the cyclical nature of the recession-prone housing market. To increase its market base, Fedders has expanded into Asia and the Middle East, bringing its cooling products to millions in sweltering cities. Fedders has also employed an ambitious international strategic acquisition and joint venture program to reposition itself as a leader in a broad variety of air treatment businesses, including air cleaners, humidifiers, dehumidifiers, and thermal technology products, extending its reach beyond its traditional customers and markets.

Before Air Conditioners, 1890s–1940s

Fedders began as a metalworking shop started by Theodore C. Fedders in 1896 in Buffalo, New York. At first it made milk cans and kerosene tanks for Standard Oil Co. and bread pans for National Biscuit Co. Shortly after the turn of the century Buffalo became the home of such automobile makers as Pierce-Arrow and the Thomas Five. Fedders converted his plant to making radiators for these models and, in time, other automobile makers as well. During World War I the company also made radiators for airplanes, and, in addition, it manufactured appliances for heating and electrical refrigeration. In 1924 Fedders had net income of $241,000 on sales of $3.2 million. It went public in December 1926, offering 50,000 nonvoting shares at $25 a share.

Fedders's stock was caught in the great 1929 Wall Street crash, sinking to $3 a share from a high that year of $50. The company lost money the following four years, with sales falling by half between 1931 and 1933, when they reached a low of $1.8 million. In 1934, however, sales nearly doubled, and Fedders became profitable again, as it was during the successive years of the decade. Westinghouse Electric Corp. began distributing the company's refrigerator coils and accessories in 1936. Three years later Fedders erected a $200,000 plant in Owosso, Michigan, to produce radiators closer to the auto factories. Net sales reached nearly $6 million in 1940, and net income was $270,000. That year the company had branch offices in seven cities.

Fedders's sales reached $9.1 million, with net income of $386,000, in 1941, but the subsequent halt to automobile manufacturing because of World War II cut deeply into the business, and the company sold the Owosso plant in 1942. Although Fedders received contracts to make links and clips for machine-gun belts and Garand-rifle bullets, in 1944 it earned only $15,498 on sales of $5.7 million. Before the company could retool for the postwar period, the Fedders family decided to sell a majority interest in the firm to Frank J. Quigan, Inc. This private company, the world's leading manufacturer of handbag frames, was based in the New York City borough of Queens. Frank J. Quigan, chairman of the board, became board chairman of the renamed Fedders-Quigan Corp., and Salvatore Giordano, president of Quigan, became president of Fedders-Quigan. There was no formal merger of the two companies, however, until 1949.

Air-Conditioning Pioneer, 1940s–1960s

In 1947, Fedders-Quigan moved aggressively into the manufacture of newly introduced room air conditioners and two years

Company Perspectives:

We at Fedders Corporation are pledged to make our products and services the standard of excellence around the globe. Fedders will accomplish this objective by providing to our customers and fellow employees defect-free products and services, on time, every time, at competitive prices. We will fully understand the requirements of our customers and will strive to comply with them at all times. The result of our actions will be products and services which meet or exceed our customers' standards for performance, delivery, reliability, and excellence.

later also began to market under its own name the electric water coolers it had been manufacturing for Cordley & Hayes since 1932. Besides Queens and Buffalo, it operated plants in Trenton and Newark, New Jersey. Sales shot up from $11.6 million in 1946 to $33.6 million in 1950, while profits rose from $905,000 to nearly $2 million in this period. The number of employees rose to about 3,000. In 1951, however, Quigan reportedly began speculating in the company's stock and wound up owing Giordano about $500,000. Quigan resigned from the company in order to vacate the court judgments for this amount that Giordano had secured. Giordano, who had joined Quigan as a $16-a-week floor boy in 1927, became chairman as well as president of Fedders-Quigan in 1952.

By the mid-1950s well over a million room air conditioners were being sold each year in the United States. In 1955 Fedders-Quigan sold 120,000 of these units under the Fedders name, far more than any other company, and also made air conditioners for the Whirlpool-Seeger Corp. and the Crosley division of Avco Manufacturing Corp. Almost 15,000 small stores were selling Fedders units in 1956. The company also was making heaters, radiators, and radiator cores for Chrysler Corporation automobiles and home radiators, convectors, and hot-water boilers. In 1956 it began making year-round central air conditioners for five- and six-room ranch-style houses. It also was turning out thousands of women's handbag frames a year, a business it maintained, Giordano said, out of sentiment. He held more than 10 percent of the company's common stock in 1956.

Giordano was a great believer in offering junkets to Fedders-Quigan's dealers and distributors as an incentive to push the product. During the 1950s dealers who had bought 45 Fedders air conditioners were flown by the company for a weeklong all-expenses-paid vacation at a Florida beach resort, and those who doubled the number were entitled to take their wives along. A distributor with ten eligible dealers was entitled to come along himself. In the fall of 1953 more than 500 people made the trip to the Hollywood Beach Hotel. By 1960 some ''super'' sales representatives were earning enough points for two overseas trips a year. That fall a crowd of 4,000 spent a week at Grand Bahama Island, while nearly 1,000 vacationed in Paris, and the ''supersalesmen'' spent ten days in Israel.

Fedders-Quigan, which shortened its name to Fedders in 1958, peaked in sales at $70.7 million in fiscal 1957 (the year ended August 31, 1957), when it earned $3.6 million. After two relatively poor years it earned a record $4.5 million on net sales of $68.8 million in fiscal 1960. From 1955 to 1960 the national dollar volume in manufacturing and installing air-conditioning equipment rose by more than 50 percent, but Fedders had to share the market with a growing number of competitors: more than 50 in all. Increasingly Fedders began to focus its hopes on central residential systems. It also had organized a subsidiary, Fedders Financial Corp., to finance wholesale purchases of Fedders air-conditioning equipment.

Diversification and Expansion, 1960s–70s

By 1964 Fedders was stagnating, both its sales and profits having slipped from the 1960 levels. On the plus side, finances were sound, despite a long-term debt of $8.6 million, and dividends had been paid each year since 1945. However, management began casting around for additions to its existing products: air conditioners; automobile radiators, heater cores, and oil coolers (still principally for Chrysler); and heat-transfer equipment, including convectors, condensors, evaporators, and dehumidifiers. (The manufacture of frames for women's handbags and pocketbooks was discontinued in 1966.)

A decision was made to diversify into home appliances in 1964, when Fedders signed a five-year contract with the Franklin Appliance division of Studebaker Industries. Under the agreement Studebaker would manufacture a full line of home appliances under the Fedders name, to be sold by Fedders' network of 77 distributors and 15,000 dealers. Fedders introduced a 15-model line of its own manufactured home appliances in 1967. As a result, company sales increased from $62.3 million in fiscal 1966 to $88.9 million in fiscal 1967, and net income from $1.2 million to $4.6 million. In 1966 Fedders vacated its leased Newark plant, erecting a large facility for the manufacture of air conditioners at Edison, New Jersey, where it also established corporate headquarters.

Fedders expanded its home appliance operations by purchasing Borg-Warner Corporation's Norge division in 1968 for about $45 million in cash, stock, and notes. Chicago-based Norge, which had sales of $114 million in 1967, was making a full line of laundry equipment such as washers and dryers, as well as air conditioners and kitchen ranges. Included in its operations were nearly 3,400 franchised ''Norge Village'' coin-operated, self-service laundry and dry-cleaning units, containing 20 to 50 machines each.

The expanded Fedders was an industry giant with 9,000 employees in fiscal 1970, when it had net sales of $295.8 million and net income of $15.6 million. It was still the largest producer of room air conditioners but saw greater growth potential for engineered central air-conditioning systems, not only in homes but also in industrial plants, hospitals, schools, and mass transportation systems. Fedders expanded its stake in this business sector by purchasing Climatrol Industries, Inc., a manufacturer of unitary central air-conditioning systems, in 1970 for $27.7 million worth of stock. During this period a share of Fedders' stock rose from a low of $3 to as high as $50. To finance its expansion, however, Fedders had raised its long-term debt to $60 million by the end of fiscal 1970.

Nine Consecutive Losses, 1970s–80s

After a record fiscal 1971, in which it earned nearly $17 million on income of $346.6 million, Fedders fell on hard times.

Key Dates:

1896: Fedders begins as metalworking shop in Buffalo, New York.
1924: The company, primarily manufacturing automobile and airplane radiators, has a net income of $241,000 on sales of $3.2 million.
1926: Fedders goes public.
1947: Fedders begins manufacturing a new consumer product: the room air conditioner.
1949: Fedders and the private company Frank J. Quigan, Inc. formally merge.
1960: Net sales of the company's room air conditioners peak at $68.8 million.
1964: Fedders looks to diversify, signing an agreement with Franklin Appliance to manufacture a full line of home appliances.
1968: Fedders acquires Borg-Warner Corporation's Norge division.
1970: The company is the largest producer of room air conditioners, but expands into other markets with the acquisition of Climatrol Industries, Inc.
1976: Fedders purchases Chrysler Corporation's unprofitable Airtemp division.
1980: The company ends its fiscal year with continued losses due to a shrinking domestic market for room air conditioners and a recession in the U.S. economy.
1985: Fedders becomes profitable again, resuming the payment of dividends which it had suspended since 1974.
1987: Fedders spins off its compressor and automotive-components division into a company named NYCOR, Inc.
1988: Salvatore Giordano, Jr., succeeds his father as CEO of both Fedders and NYCOR.
1991: Fedders acquires the Emerson Quiet Kool brand from The Jepson Corp.
1993: The company begins exporting air conditioners to Asia and the Middle East.
1994: Corporate headquarters move to Liberty Corner, New Jersey.
1998: Fedders and Bosch-Siemens Havsgerate GmbH enter into a 50–50 joint venture to manufacture room air conditioners in Spain.
1999: Trion, Inc., producer of humidification systems and Envirco HEPA filtration systems for cleanroom manufacturing, is acquired.
2000: Fedders buys ABB Koppel, Inc., a leading air conditioner manufacturer in the Philippines, and Sun Manufacturing, Inc., manufacturer of specialized air-conditioning equipment used in the telecommunications industry.
2001: Fedders begins a 10-year licensing agreement to produce room air-conditioning units under the Maytag name; acquires Polenz GmbH, a distributor of air treatment products in Germany.

Fiscal 1972 ended with lower earnings and profits due to a seven-and-a-half-month strike at the Edison plant. Business failed to reach the record 1971 level in fiscal 1973. The Arab oil embargo imposed in late 1973 touched off an energy crisis, resulting in sharply higher electricity costs, a national recession, and the collapse of the housing market. In fiscal 1974 Fedders lost $10.5 million and dropped its line of manufactured ranges and refrigerators. The company, in fiscal 1975 (the year ended October 31, 1975), lost nearly $12 million on disastrously low income of $170.2 million—less than half the 1971 total.

Fedders could take some consolation in the fact that it was not the only company in its industry suffering the downturn in market conditions, for between 1970 and 1975 national shipments of room air conditioners fell from nearly six million to fewer than three million. Accordingly, Fedders raised its commitment to central air-conditioning systems by purchasing the domestic assets of Chrysler Corporation's unprofitable Airtemp division in 1976 for about $58.5 million in cash, notes, and stock. Airtemp was producing air-conditioning systems up to 1,100 tons, compared with Fedders' top limit of 200 tons. Fedders ended the fiscal year with a profit of $249,000 on sales of $291.3 million, but it lost money on continuing operations.

Fedders downsized itself in early 1979 by selling the Norge division, which accounted for 22 percent of its fiscal 1978 sales, to Magic Chef Inc. The very modest purchase price of about $13.3 million in cash and notes indicated that Norge, which had only five percent of the laundry-machine market, was performing poorly. The Norge plant in Effingham, Illinois, was converted to the manufacture of room air conditioners. Fedders ended fiscal 1979 with a catastrophic loss of $36.5 million on income of $176.8 million and lost nearly $29 million more the following year on revenue of only $137.9 million. By the end of fiscal 1980 it had divested itself of the Fedders Refrigeration Co., which made freezers.

The severe recession of the early 1980s compounded Fedders' woes. In 1982 it recorded its ninth consecutive loss (in terms of continuing operations) and, based on its long-term-debenture debt of $66.6 million, had a negative net worth of $42.8 million. In 1983 it put on the market its three central air-conditioning businesses, which had lost $37.8 million the previous fiscal year, and also placed on the block its 90-acre Edison office and manufacturing complex. There was no buyer for the businesses (which still had sales of $12.4 million in 1984), so their assets had to be sold off piecemeal with the Edison real estate. These properties fetched a total of $42.6 million during 1984 and 1985 and left Fedders with three businesses: room air conditioners under the Airtemp, Climatrol, and Fedders brands, made in Effingham; rotary compressors for powering air conditioners, manufactured in Frederick, Maryland; and replacement radiators, heaters, and additional components for the automotive aftermarket, still being made in Buffalo. Corporate headquarters were moved to Peapack, New Jersey.

Renewed Prosperity in the 1980s

Fedders became profitable again in 1983, when it earned (after discounting extraordinary credits) $1.4 million on drastically reduced income of $80.8 million. The next two years were even better, and in 1985 the company resumed paying dividends, which it had omitted since 1974. Its share of the domestic room air conditioner market almost doubled between 1984 and 1986, to 16 percent. Although Fedders also found a profitable market in many parts of the world that wanted air-conditioning, installing central systems with ducts in those markets was not easy.

In 1987 Fedders spun off the compressor and automotive-components divisions into a company named NYCOR, Inc. This company remained under Fedders management and was initially located at Fedders's corporate headquarters. In 1989 NYCOR sold its compressor subsidiary, Rotorex Corp., back to Fedders for about $45 million in cash and the assumption of $49.5 million in Rotorex debt. It sold the automotive-components business (FEDCO) in 1990 and became for a time a shell company with a pile of cash. Salvatore Giordano, Jr., succeeded his father as chief executive officer of both Fedders and NYCOR in 1988. His 78-year-old father remained chairman of the board.

By the end of the decade Fedders was once again riding high, finishing 1989 with a record $367.6 million in net sales and record net income of $23.7 million. Its share of the North American market for residential room air conditioners had grown from eight percent in 1982 to about 30 percent. To handle its increased business Fedders had acquired additional manufacturing facilities in Tennessee and Ontario, modernized its largest manufacturing plant (at Effingham), and established an international subsidiary. It was marketing its air conditioners under the Tempair name and private labels as well as under the Fedders, Airtemp, and Climatrol brands. The acquisition from General Electric Co. of a Columbia, Tennessee, facility in 1988 for $17.3 million made Fedders the only high-volume producer in the world of plastic-cabinet window air conditioners. Among North American manufacturers of room air conditioners, only Fedders was making its own rotary compressors, which were in short supply. The company's long-term debt had declined to $53.9 million.

Roller-Coaster Ride During the 1990s

However, as the 1990s dawned, Fedders was again headed downward. In fiscal 1990, which ended with a cool summer, it lost $15.6 million—the first of four consecutive years of losses—on net sales of only $241.4 million. Despite this poor year, in January 1991 the company acquired the Emerson Quiet Kool brand from The Jepson Corporation for $56 million in cash plus the assumption of certain liabilities. This left Fedders, according to columnist Dan Dorfman in April 1991, with no cash, a $170-million debt, and the imminent prospect of bankruptcy—all at a time of huge unsold inventories of air conditioners.

The nadir of Fedders' plight was fiscal 1992, when it lost $24.9 million on revenues of $192 million. During that year it sold Rotorex back to NYCOR for $72.8 million and closed the Emerson Quiet Kool plant in Woodbridge, New Jersey, plus another facility in Dover, New Jersey. The company lost another $1.8 million in fiscal 1993 on net sales of $158.6 million. The sale to NYCOR, however, helped Fedders reduce its long-term debt from $173 million to $25 million by May 1993, and it took aim at the international market to decrease its dependence on the vagaries of summer weather in North America.

Exports had made up only 7.6 percent of Fedders's sales in fiscal 1992 and were limited to the Americas. In 1993, however, the company focused on Southeast Asia, the sweltering Middle East, and the southern part of China, notorious for its ''Oven Cities.'' A Fedders Asia subsidiary was created in 1994, and the following year this unit entered into a $24-million, 60–40 percent Fedders Xinle joint venture with China's Ningbo Air Conditioner Factory to manufacture air conditioners at this facility. Initial production was 200,000 units a year, with Fedders hoping to increase the level to 500,000 by 1999. Much of the output was to be exported to such countries as Japan and India.

Domestic business also picked up, with three consecutive hot summers, at least in some areas, from 1993 through 1995. Sales were also helped by the company's ability to meet the just-in-time demands of such retailers as Wal-Mart, Best Buy, and Home Depot, who were increasingly vital to Fedders' sales. Net sales shot up to $231.5 million in fiscal 1994 and $316.5 million in fiscal 1995, while net income—aided by tax-loss carryovers from previous years—was $21 million and $29.5 million, respectively. In 1995 Fedders paid its first cash dividend since 1991 and, at the end of the year, decided to reintegrate itself with NYCOR, which lost $7.8 million on sales of $32.9 million in 1995. The merger was accomplished in 1996. Fedders ended the fiscal year with record sales of $371.8 million and record net income of $31.2 million.

In 1995 Fedders was manufacturing room air conditioners, primarily for the residential market, in models ranging in capacity from 5,000 to 40,000 BTUs. These were made and marketed under the Fedders, Airtemp, and Emerson Quiet Kool brands and also under private labels. Its manufacturing facilities were in Effingham, Illinois, and Columbia, Tennessee. In 1994 Fedders moved its corporate headquarters to Liberty Corner, New Jersey. Fedders North America had its headquarters in Whitehouse, New Jersey, and a new subsidiary of Fedders International, Inc., Fedders Asia, Pte., moved into Singapore quarters.

Rotorex was manufacturing compressors and pump assemblies, chiefly for Fedders' air conditioners, in Frederick, Maryland. Materials Electronic Products Corp. (''Melcor''), a business acquired by NYCOR in 1992 for $14.9 million, was manufacturing solid-state heat-pump modules performing the same cooling and heating functions as freon-based compressors and absorption refrigerators in Trenton, New Jersey, and near Lawrence Township, New Jersey. These products, sold under the trademark FRIGICHIP, were primarily being used in portable beverage coolers and refrigerators; laboratory, scientific, medical, and restaurant equipment; and telecommunications and computer equipment.

In 1995 the Giordano family owned about 15 percent of Fedders' Class A (nonvoting) common stock and about 95 percent of Class B (nontradable but voting) common stock. The company's long-term debt was $14.4 million in early 1996.

An Expanding Global Presence During the Late 1990s

An abnormally cool summer in North America in 1996 was blamed for a sharp decline in U.S. sales of room air conditioners and larger than normal end-of-season inventories at the retail level. Consequently, Fedders experienced a downturn in revenues the following year. For its 1997 fiscal year ending August 31, the company posted net earnings of $18.8 million, down 39.8 percent from its 1996 fiscal year earnings of $31.2 million. To guard against further declines, the company implemented a business strategy to diversify revenues, income, and profits through an ambitious acquisition and restructuring effort.

In January 1998, Fedders shifted more of its air conditioner production to China and increased its practice of outsourcing components. At the same time it reorganized its corporate structure, closing three offices, laying off employees, and moving its North American sales, marketing, service, and administrative support functions to Effingham, Illinois. Additionally, the company looked at increasing its international presence. By 1998, the overseas market for room air conditioners was reported to be five times larger than U.S. unit demand (20 million units vs. 4 million units) and nearly 15 times the U.S dollar volume. More importantly, international markets presented better long-term growth potential.

While other companies struggled, Fedders actually benefited from the Asian economic crisis of 1997. The fallout from the crisis resulted in lowered prices for components Fedders purchased from Asian manufacturers in following years, helping the company to boost its bottom line. According to Fedders' CEO Sal Giordano, Jr., the Asian situation had ''positive implications for Fedders for both the short and long term.''

Strategic Acquisitions and Alliances for the New Millennium

At the close of the 1990s, Fedders continued pursing strategic acquisitions and alliances to support growth in new and existing markets. In August 1999, Fedders transferred production of pumps for compressors from the United States to Taiwan and China, enabling the company to reduce operating costs at its automated compressor assembly operation in Maryland. Next, Trion, Inc. was acquired in November 1999. Trion's electronic air cleaners, industrial and residential humidification systems, and Envirco HEPA filtration systems for cleanroom manufacturing substantially expanded Fedders' presence in the air treatment industry. In January 2000 Fedders bought ABB Koppel, Inc., a leading air conditioner manufacturer in the Philippines (renamed Fedders Koppel, Inc.). The company quickly followed up that acquisition with its purchase of Sun Manufacturing, Inc., a leading manufacturer of specialized air-conditioning equipment used in the telecommunications industry. In November 2000, Fedders' subsidiary, Melcor Corporation, acquired Eubank Manufacturing, Inc. of Longview, Texas, maker of cooling systems used to control the environment in cellular tower transmission equipment rooms. ''Eubank is a strategic acquisition that strengthens our push into the telecom equipment cooling market,'' reported Fedders CEO, Sal Giordano, Jr. The company's strategy to diversify revenues seemed to be paying off. Fedders' sales for 2000 hit a record high of $409.8 million, while earnings before interest, taxes, depreciation, and amortization soared to $58.8 million.

But even a company with sizzling sales figures must continue to plan for the future. Looking at strengthening its leadership position in the North American room air-conditioning market, Fedders entered into a ten-year licensing agreement with the Maytag Corporation. In 2001, Fedders held the exclusive rights to produce air conditioners under the Maytag brand to be sold to consumers in the United States, Canada, and Mexico. Both Fedders and Maytag worked together to aggressively promote the new line, with the joint goal of obtaining significant market share within the first five years. In addition to the Maytag name, Fedders consumer products such as air conditioners, humidifiers, dehumidifiers, and electronic air purifiers, are marketed globally under the Emerson Quiet Kool, Airtemp, Trion, Koppel, and Herrmidifier brands, as well as under private labels.

In March 2001, the company acquired Polenz GmbH, a distributor of air treatment products in Germany, and announced plans to construct a research and development facility and a production plant in China, further expanding its international presence. A restructuring plan announced in April 2001 organized the company into four principal operating units: Fedders Unitary Products, Fedders Appliances, Fedders Engineered Products, and Fedders International. That same year, joint ventures were announced with Quanzhou Hua Yu in China to manufacture thermoelectric modules, which are used to precisely control temperatures in applications such as fiber-optic communications and biotechnology, and with Voltas in India to produce room air conditioners.

Principal Operating Units

Fedders Unitary Products; Fedders Appliances; Fedders Engineered Products; Fedders International (Singapore).

Principal Subsidiaries

Sun Air Conditioning; Eubank Manufacturing Enterprises; Melcor Corporation; Envirco; Fedders North America; Trion, Inc.; Herrmidifier; Fedders Koppel (Phillipines); Polenz GmbH (Germany); Trion Ltd. (U.K.)

Principal Competitors

Matsushita; Toshiba; Whirlpool.

Further Reading

Abelson, Reed, ''Companies to Watch,'' *Fortune,* September 11, 1989, p. 152.

Alexander, Louis, ''Airlifts for Private Industry,'' *Flying,* January 1961, pp. 44, 70.

Beatty, Gerry, ''Fedders-Maytag Room Air Tie-In: Will Consumers Buy the Value?'' *HFN: The Weekly Newspaper for the Home Furnishing Network,* June 5, 2000, p. 53.

''Chrysler Sells Airtemp Assets to Fedders Corp.,'' *Wall Street Journal,* February 24, 1976, p. 3.

Cuff, Daniel F., ''Fedders Chief Finds Use for Spinoff's Nest Egg,'' *New York Times,* November 5, 1990, p. D4.

Doherty, Ed, ''Welcome to a Long, Hot Summer,'' *Financial World,* August 31, 1983, pp. 28–29.

Dorfman, Dan, ''Fedders Getting Cool Reception,'' *USA Today,* April 12, 1991, p. B3.

''Fedders,'' *Wall Street Transcript,* August 12, 1968, pp. 14029–30.

''Fedders Acquires Borg-Warner's Norge Division,'' *Wall Street Journal,* July 3, 1968, p. 2.

''Fedders Corp.,'' *Wall Street Transcript,* August 19, 1968, p. 14162.

——, *Wall Street Transcript,* December 28, 1987, p. 87845.

''Fedders Corporation,'' *Wall Street Transcript,* December 4, 1989, p. 95582.
——, *Wall Street Transcript,* March 12, 1990, p. 96605.
''Fedders Enjoys a Brisk Rebound from Strike-Dampened Showing,'' *Barron's,* July 20, 1964, p. 18.
''Fedders-Quigan Gets a Break,'' *Business Week,* December 8, 1951, pp. 114–16.
Kimelman, John, ''Company Watch,'' *Financial World,* November 22, 1994, p. 18.
Lazo, Shirley A., ''Payouts Heat Up at Fedders,'' *Barron's,* July 3, 1995, p. 38.
''Magic Chef Buys Unit of Fedders for $13.3 Million,'' *Wall Street Journal,* February 13, 1979, p. 17.
''Management Brief: Keeping Cool in China,'' *Economist,* April 6, 1996, pp. 73–74.
O'Brian, Bridget, ''Fedders Insiders Selling Shares This Summer,'' *Wall Street Journal,* August 9, 1995, pp. C1, C13.
Pine, Michael C., ''Fedders: Straw Hats in Summer?'' *Financial World,* August 12, 1996, p. 20.
Savona, Dave, ''Global Go-Getters,'' *International Business,* May 1993, p. 22.
Sullivan, Barbara, ''Torrid Weather Warmly Received in Effingham,'' *Chicago Tribune,* July 24, 1995, pp. 1, 3.
''We Got Razzle-Dazzle,'' *Forbes,* November 1, 1973, p. 45.
''Why Everybody Likes a Prize Trip,'' *Business Week,* November 21, 1953, pp. 56–57.
Zipser, Alfred R., ''Air Conditioners in Heavy Demand,'' *New York Times,* June 3, 1956, pp. 1, 9.

—Robert Halasz
—update: Suzanne L. Rowe

Fender Musical Instruments Company

7975 North Hayden Road
Scottsdale, Arizona 85258
U.S.A.
Telephone: (480) 596-9690
Fax: (480) 596-1384
Web site: http://www.fender.com

Private Company
Incorporated: 1959
Employees: 1000 (est.)
Sales: $280 million (2000)
NAIC: 339992 Musical Instrument Manufacturing; 334310 Audio & Video Equipment Manufacturing

Fender Musical Instruments Company is the leading maker of solid-body electric guitars with an estimated 50 percent of the U.S. market. The company, which markets products under several brand names, including Fender, Guild, Sunn, Floyd Rose, Rodriguez, and Squier, produces an estimated 1,000 guitars a day in more than 100 different colors and finishes. In addition to its own guitars, which are manufactured in the U.S., Mexico, Japan, China, and Korea, Fender is the sole North American distributor for the prestigious Rodriguez line of Spanish guitars, and manufactures a wide variety of mass-produced and custom-made amplifiers and audio equipment. Its classic Telecaster and Stratocaster guitars have been mainstays of popular music almost since their inception, played by guitarists from Buddy Holly to Ritchie Blackmore to Eric Clapton to Kurt Cobain.

Clarence Leo Fender, born in 1909 near Anaheim, California, never learned to play the guitar, but the company he started in 1943, which would become the Fender Musical Instruments Company, and the guitars and amplifiers he designed changed the course of popular music. Fender's reputation for producing quality amplifiers and electric guitars was already established in country music when rock and roll began to sweep the nation in the late 1950s and early 1960s. When early rock stars, including Buddy Holly, Jimi Hendrix, Eric Clapton, and The Beatles, began playing Fender's brightly colored guitars and basses, the company's success was ensured.

The Early Years

Fender began tinkering with radios in 1922, and by the time he graduated from high school in 1928, he was operating an amateur "ham" radio station. He was also building amplifiers and public-address systems, and from 1930 until 1938, he supplemented his income as a California civil-service accountant by renting his homemade equipment for dances, political rallies, and baseball games. In 1938, he opened a repair shop, Fender's Radio Service, in Fullerton, California. The shop also sold phonographs and repaired amplifiers.

In the early 1940s Fender teamed up with Clayton "Doc" Kauffman, then a professional violinist and lap-steel guitarist, to design a phonograph record-changer. They sold their design for $5,000 and formed K&F Manufacturing. In 1943 K&F Manufacturing developed a new pickup for electric guitars in which the strings passed through the magnetic coil. K&F filed for a patent on the pickup in 1944, which was granted in 1948. Fender later said that K&F built its first guitar to test the new pickup.

By 1945, Fender and Kauffman, working out of a shack behind the radio-repair shop, were manufacturing amplifiers and lap-model Hawaiian steel guitars, which were sold as sets. Fender wanted to expand the business, taking advantage of the fact that many musical instrument companies had gone out of business during World War II, but Kauffman was worried about going into debt.

Fender told *BAM* magazine, "It cost a lot of money to get into large-scale production, and the 1930s depression was still fresh in Kauffman's mind, so he didn't want to get involved. He had a ranch or farm in Oklahoma, and he was afraid if we got over-extended on credit he might lose it. He thought he'd better pull out while he had a full skin." Kauffman told much the same story to *Guitar Player* magazine, "I got scared of the business. . . . I didn't have much faith in guitars, and I asked Leo to buy out my half of the business." Fender agreed to trade Kauffman a small press punch for his share of K&F Manufacturing.

In 1946 Fender renamed the business the Fender Electric Instruments Company. That same year, he signed an agreement with Radio & Television Equipment Company (Radio-Tel) of

Company Perspectives:

Fender Musical Instruments Corporation has been an American icon for over 50 years. In that time, Fender's contribution to the evolving sound of contemporary music has been global and continuous. By introducing the first commercially viable solid-body electric guitar, the first electric bass, and countless classic amplifiers, Fender musical instruments have left their mark on jazz, blues, country, rock, and many other styles of popular music.

Santa Ana, California, which had been supplying parts for his repair shop, to be sole distributor for Fender amplifiers and guitars. Fender also turned over operation of his repair shop to Dale Hyatt, so he could concentrate on making musical instruments. By 1949, Fender amplifiers and guitars were firmly entrenched in the country music industry.

The 1950s Telecaster

In the spring of 1950 the Fender Electric Instruments Company introduced a single-pickup, solid-body electric guitar, which it called the Esquire. The company started taking orders for the Esquire, but before Fender could start full production, the guitar had been redesigned as a dual-pickup solid-body called the Broadcaster. The Broadcaster was renamed the Telecaster in 1951 because of a conflict with Gretsch Broadkaster drums. Although it was sometimes derided as a ''canoe paddle,'' because of its plain solid-ash body and screwed-on fretted maple neck, the Telecaster became the first commercially successful solid-body electric guitar.

Other guitar makers had created solid-body electric guitars as early as the mid-1930s, and in his book, *Fender: The Inside Story,* Forrest White, former vice-president and production manager for the Fender Electric Instruments Company, traces the concept of the Telecaster to a guitar that a part-time guitar maker in southern California, Paul Bigsby, created in 1947 for Merle Travis.

Fender supplied amplifiers for the Saturday night ''Cliffe Stone Show'' in Placentia, California, and there seems little doubt that Fender would have seen Travis play his custom-designed electric guitar on the show. In 1979 Travis wrote in the *JEMF Quarterly* that he loaned his guitar to Fender for a week to make a copy, and he argued for years that he, not Fender, should be considered the father of the solid-body electric guitar.

Despite the dispute, in 1951 Fender received a patent for ''a new, original, and ornamental design for a guitar,'' and it was Fender who popularized the electric, solid-body guitar; both the Gibson Les Paul, itself a classic, and Fender's own Stratocaster were inspired by the Telecaster design. In *American Guitars: An Illustrated History,* Tom Wheeler, former consulting editor for *Guitar Player* magazine, calls Fender ''the Henry Ford of electric guitars and the Telecaster . . . his Model T.'' With the success of the Telecaster, which sold for $189.50, Fender closed his repair shop to devote all his energy to designing and manufacturing musical instruments, which by late 1951 also included the first electric bass. By the late 1960s the Telecaster and its descendants would revolutionize the performance and recording of popular music—and aside from the Stratocaster, Fender himself would be hard-pressed to follow his own act. As his friend Alvino Rey put it, ''Everyone thought his first guitar was his best, but no one would tell him that.''

Before long, however, Leo Fender became unhappy with his distribution arrangement with Radio-Tel, which seemed content to focus its marketing efforts on Fender's amplifiers and lap-steel guitars. In his book, White quotes his former employer: ''During this time, they (Radio-Tel) didn't sell hardly any of our (solid-body) guitars. [The guitars] just sat there in this garage, and termites got into them and ate through the bodies. We never found out about the termites until dealers started calling us about holes in the guitars. We ended up taking back 500 guitars and had to burn them all.''

In 1953, Leo Fender formed Fender Sales, Inc., to take over distribution from Radio-Tel. Surprisingly, his partners in the venture were, or had been affiliated with Radio-Tel, including Donald Randall, former sales manager who became president of the distribution company, and Charles Hayes, a former salesman. The third partner was F.C. Hall, who owned Radio-Tel. Later that year, Hall purchased the Electro String Instrument Corporation from founder Adolph Rickenbacker, placing himself in the position of being both Fender's competitor and partner. When Hayes died in an automobile accident in 1955, Fender and Randall bought his interest in Fender Sales from his widow and ousted Hall. Fender and Randall each then owned 50 percent of the distribution company, although Fender continued to own 100 percent of Fender Electric Instruments.

In 1954 Fender Electric Instruments introduced the Stratocaster. While the Telecaster may have looked like a canoe paddle, Tony Bacon and Paul Day, authors of *The Fender Book*, describe the Stratocaster as ''in some ways [owing] more to contemporary automobile design than traditional guitar forms, especially in the flowing, sensual curves of that beautifully proportioned, timeless body.'' The Stratocaster also included a built-in vibrato and came in a variety of Du Pont car colors. Although the Stratocaster took a while to catch on—the year of its introduction, it barely outsold the older Telecaster—it became the most popular and most copied solid-body electric guitar ever made. It was also the guitar that would make Fender Electric Instruments worth millions of dollars and make Leo Fender an icon among rock musicians.

Building on the phenomenal success of the Stratocaster, Fender Electric Instruments introduced a line of less expensive guitars and amplifiers in 1955. The ''studio instruments'' were branded with the name ''White,'' a tribute to Fender's production manager, Forrest White. Fender also attempted to transcend the top of the line with his Jazzmaster guitar design; unfortunately, it never really caught on. The company also introduced a three-quarter-sized solid-body guitar in 1955, an electric mandolin in 1957, a short-lived electric violin in 1958, and its first acoustic guitars in 1964. Fender dabbled briefly with brass instruments, buying a horn company and introducing the Hayes brand in 1954. However, the horn business, like the White brand, was abandoned a year later. Fender Electric Instruments, which had fewer than 15 employees in 1947, had more than 100 employees by the time it incorporated in 1959.

1938: Clarence Leo Fender opens Fender's Radio Service in Fullerton, California.
1943: Fender, with business partner Clayton Kauffman, designs a new pickup for electric guitars.
1946: Fender, now the company's sole proprietor, renames the company Fender Electric Instruments Company.
1948: Patent is granted to Fender and Kauffman's electric guitar pickup.
1951: Fender introduces the Telecaster guitar, for which the company receives a patent.
1954: Fender introduces the Stratocaster guitar, which becomes the most popular solid-body electric guitar ever made.
1959: Fender Electric Instruments incorporates.
1965: Fender is acquired by CBS for $13 million.
1981: William Schultz is named president of the Fender division.
1982: Schultz reorganizes Fender, producing only top-of-the-line, classic models in America.
1985: Fender division sold by CBS to a management company headed by Schultz. Company's name changed to Fender Musical Instruments.
1985: All U.S. production of Fender guitars ceases.
1986: Schultz opens new plant in Corona, California, producing American Standard Telecasters and Stratocasters and custom guitars.
1987: Fender acquires Sunn, an amplifier company.
1991: Company headquarters is moved to Scottsdale, Arizona and facilities are opened in Mexico, China, and Korea.
1995: Fender acquires Guild Guitar Company.
2001: Fender lays off 59 of 800 production workers from its Corona facility.
2001: Fender debuts the CyberTwin amplifier.2001: Fender awards construction contract for new headquarters in Scottsdale.

The CBS Years

In 1964 Leo Fender, then 55, became ill and offered to sell Fender Electric Instruments to Randall, still his partner in Fender Sales, for $1.5 million. At the time, the company was producing 1,500 amplifiers, electric guitars, acoustic guitars, and other instruments per week, and was the largest exporter of musical instruments in the United States. Fender Electric Instruments employed 600 people, 500 of them in manufacturing.

Randall lacked the resources to purchase the company himself but agreed to find another buyer. After talking with several companies, including the Baldwin Piano & Organ Co., Randall negotiated a deal with the Columbia Broadcasting System. On Jan. 5, 1965, CBS announced that a subsidiary, Columbia Records Distribution Corp., had purchased Fender Electric Instruments and Fender Sales for $13 million. The press release noted, "The Fender guitar is considered the outstanding instrument of its type by both professional musicians and amateurs." The new Columbia Records division was known initially as Fender CBS, but that was changed to CBS Musical Instruments in 1966, as it acquired other companies, including Steinway & Sons and flute maker Gemeinhardt Co.

CBS began making changes almost immediately. Fender Electric Instruments had expanded haphazardly over the past 20 years until it occupied 29 buildings scattered throughout Fullerton. To consolidate operations, CBS announced plans to build a 120,000-square-foot, $1.3 million facility, complete with a dust-free air-filtering system. The building was completed in 1966. CBS also began sending efficiency experts to Fullerton to analyze how the former Fender Electric Instruments Company operated. White, who had been responsible for production since 1954, commented in his book, "We had been invaded by a horde of 'know-it-all CBS experts' at both Fender Sales and the factory."

Demoted from vice-president to plant manager with the takeover, White quit less than two years later in a dispute over the quality of an amplifier that CBS planned to introduce. He wrote, "I asked all of my key personnel to come to the conference room. I told them that I had too much respect for Leo to have any part in building something that was not worthy of having his name associated with it."

Many other longtime Fender employees also believed that quality was declining, as CBS cut back on product lines and produced few new models. Randall, who had become vice-president and general manager under CBS, left the company in 1969 but apparently more because of corporate politics than a concern over quality. White quotes him as saying, "Everybody at CBS was climbing the corporate ladder, stepping on everyone else's fingers as they climbed up. There was a tremendous amount of infighting." However, despite the management upheaval and concerns over quality, sales at CBS Musical Instruments almost tripled from $20 million in 1971 to nearly $60 million in 1981.

Meanwhile, Leo Fender had been retained by CBS as a consultant in research and development from 1965 until 1970, although according to White, CBS executives made fun of his ideas. In 1972 Fender's consulting business, CLF Research, began manufacturing stringed instruments for Tri-Sonics, Inc., a company formed by White and Tom Walker, a former district manager at Fender Sales. Tri-Sonics changed its name briefly to Musitek, short for Music Technology, before finally settling on Music Man, Inc., in 1974. Fender was named vice-president in 1974 and became president in 1975. The company was sold in 1984.

In 1980 Leo Fender and George Fullerton, another longtime Fender Musical Instruments employee who quit CBS, formed G&L Inc. to market instruments made by CLF. G&L originally stood for George and Leo, but when Fullerton sold out in 1986, receptionists began answering the telephone, "Guitars by Leo." The company was sold after Fender's death in 1991.

Post-CBS

By the early 1980s Japanese competition was beginning to affect the bottom line at CBS Musical Instruments. CBS tried shifting some of its manufacturing to Korea to reduce tooling costs, but that experiment was abandoned by the end of the year because of poor quality. CBS also recruited three top executives from Yamaha Musical Instruments. John McLaren was hired to head up CBS Musical Instruments, William Schultz was hired as president of the Fender division, and Dan Smith was named director of marketing for electric guitars.

In *The Fender Book,* Tony Bacon and Paul Day, quote Smith: ''We were brought in to kind of turn the reputation of Fender around, and to get it so it was making money again. It was starting to lose money, and at that point in time everybody hated Fender. We thought we knew how bad it was. We took for granted that they could make Stratocasters and Telecasters the way they used to make them, but we were wrong. So many things had changed in the plant.''

In 1982 Schultz virtually shut down U.S. production of Fender guitars, focusing instead on reissuing limited editions of top-of-the-line, ''classic'' Fender guitars from pre-CBS days. Schultz also formed a joint venture, Fender Japan, with two Japanese distributors, Kanda Shokai and Yamano Music. Fuji Gen-Gakki, which made Ibanez brand instruments, was licensed to manufacture Fender guitars, which were sold only in Japan. Fuji Gen-Gakki also manufactured lower-priced, vintage Fender guitars under the Squire Series brand name. The Squire Series originally was intended for the Japanese and European market, but export to the U.S. market began in 1983.

A year later, with CBS a potential takeover target, the company began soliciting offers for its Fender Musical Instruments division. Among the companies expressing interest were the International Music Co. and Kaman Music Corporation, which manufactured Ovation guitars. In the end, however, CBS offered to sell to a management group headed by Schultz for $12.5 million. The sale was completed in March 1985, and the company name was changed to Fender Musical Instruments.

According to *Forbes*, the management group borrowed $9 million and CBS took back a note for $2.5 million, which gave Fender Musical Instruments about $11 in debt for every $1 in equity. Making matters worse, the sale did not include the production facilities in Fullerton, which CBS sold separately. As a result, Schultz, chairman of the company, was forced to halt all U.S. production of Fender guitars, and only Japanese-made instruments were listed in the 1985 catalog. Schultz also slashed employment at Fender Musical Instruments from 800 to about 90 workers, mostly in research and design.

To begin rebuilding the company, Schultz created the Fender Custom Shop in Corona, California, which produced about five models for a Vintage reissue series and began offering free or discounted guitars to rock music stars. In return, the musicians agreed to appear in Fender Musical Instruments advertisements. In 1986, Fender Musical Instruments introduced the American Standards model Stratocaster and Telecaster guitars. By 1996, the Corona plant, which also produced the company's amplifiers and speakers, employed about 600. Schultz, who moved company headquarters to Scottsdale, Arizona, in 1991, also opened guitar-manufacturing facilities in Mexico, China, and Korea.

In addition, Fender opened its Amp Custom Shop in Scottsdale in 1992. This enabled Fender to provide custom amplifiers along with custom guitars to its higher-profile and professional customers. Six years later, in 1998, Fender reintroduced the Sunn line of amplifiers to the marketplace. Fender had acquired this legendary company, whose products had been endorsed by the Who, the Rolling Stones, and Jimi Hendrix, in 1987. Schultz saw great potential for growth in the amplifier and speaker market, telling *Forbes* in 1996, ''We're going to build people's confidence [in sound equipment] as we did in rebuilding the guitar line.'' In 2001, Fender debuted its CyberTwin amplifier, which attempted to combine the classic and the modern by allowing musicians a wide range of sound options, including emulation of old-fashioned tube amplifiers, using actual tubes combined with digital processing in an entirely new configuration.

Fender also expanded its operations into the acoustic market, importing guitars from manufacturers in Southeast Asia. More significantly, the company became the North American distributor for Manuel Rodriguez guitars. These guitars, handmade in Spain by the Rodriguez family since 1905, are widely recognized as among the highest-quality acoustic guitars in the world, regularly retailing in the thousands of dollars.

In 1995, Fender acquired the Guild Guitar Company, a Rhode Island-based manufacturer of handmade electric and acoustic guitars that were played by Keith Richards, Eric Clapton, Jerry Garcia, Brian May, and Richie Havens. Although Fender kept Guild's Westerly, RI plant open, the company shifted the guitar manufacturing to its Corona plant. Fender spokesman Morgan Ringwalk cited the more ideal climatic conditions in southern California, telling the New London, Connecticut *Day* that ''Wood is a touchy material to work with, and being close to the ocean in Westerly really messes with it. Getting a consistent product is very tough.'' Guild foreman Gilbert Diaz questioned that decision, pointing out that Guild had made top-of-the-line guitars in Rhode Island for years, ocean humidity and all. A Guild Custom Shop was also opened in Nashville. In 1998, DeArmond guitars were introduced under the Guild name. Manufactured in Korea, with the pickups installed at the Corona plant, the DeArmond line was designed with affordability in mind.

In 1995 the company sold 1.1 million guitars, with sales across the industry growing an average of 10 percent a year. To keep pace with Fender's growing sales volume, in 1998 the company opened a new facility on Corona. Built on a new 19-acre site, the $20 million, state-of-the-art plant covered 177,000 square feet and produced all of Fender's American-made guitars, with a capacity of over 350 a day. The facility was designed with California's rigorous air-quality standards in mind; the company claimed that the plant's air emissions were 95 percent clean, and South Coast Air Quality Management District spokesman Larry Watkins called Fender's air quality control ''a dynamite system.'' With the Fender Custom Shop on the same site, and the Amp Custom Shop moved from Scottsdale to Corona, all of Fender's U.S. manufacturing was consolidated in one place. As senior vice-president of operations Doug Mills told the Riverside, California *Press-Enterprise*, ''Southern California is the home of rock and roll.''

William Mendello, then president of Fender Musical Instruments, told *Forbes* in 1996 that he estimated the value of the company at about $250 million if it went public. Revenues for the closely held company were estimated at $160 million. In 2000, Fender's reported revenue reached $280 million, and the company name maintained prominence among musicians, with regular reviews in *Guitar Player* magazine and an entire Web site (http://www.tdpri.com) devoted to discussion of the Fender Telecaster.

A slowing economy brought a wave of hard times to Fender in 2001. In June the company laid off 59 out of 800 production workers from its flagship Corona facility, the first layoff at the plant since Schultz's acquisition of Fender in 1985. Still, heading into the new millennium, Fender has held fast to the optimism that saw it through its frequently tumultuous 50-year history. Schultz stated that the layoff was temporary, and expected Fender's production to increase with the Christmas shopping season and, over the longer term, a recovering economy. In March 2001, the company awarded a contract for construction of a new headquarters in Scottsdale, from which to direct its worldwide operation.

Principal Subsidiaries

Guild; Sunn; Floyd Rose; Squier.

Principal Competitors

Gibson; Kaman Music Corporation; Yamaha Musical Instruments.

Further Reading

Bacon, Tony, *50 Years of Fender: Half a Century of the Greatest Electric Guitars*, San Francisco: Miller Freeman, Inc., 2000.

Bacon, Tony, and Paul Day, *The Fender Book*, San Francisco: Miller Freeman, Inc., 1992.

Berkman, Leslie, ''Fender Dismisses Workers,'' *The Press-Enterprise*, June 14, 2001, p. C01.

——, ''Fender in Tune with New Corona Plant,'' *The Press-Enterprise*, July 17, 1998, p. G01.

Costanza, Michael, ''Guitar Factory to Leave Westerly, R.I. for Southern California,'' *The Day*, June 28, 2001.

Johnson, R. Colin, ''CyberTwin Architecture Eschews Use of Digital Signal Processor to Emulate Tubes,'' *Electronic Engineering Times*, June 11, 2001, p. 81.

Matzer, Marla, ''Playing Solo,'' *Forbes*, March 25, 1996, pp. 80–81.

McAuliffe, Don, ''Fender to Expand Corona Guitar Production,'' *The Press-Enterprise*, November 8, 1996, p. C01.

McCollum, Brian, ''Album Celebrates 50 Years of Fender Guitars,'' *Tacoma News Tribune*, December 14, 1996, p. SL2.

Padgett, Mike, ''Money in Music,'' *The Business Journal*, March 23, 2001, p. 24.

Smith, Richard, *Fender: The Sound Heard 'Round the World*, Fullerton, CA: Garfish, 1995.

——, ''Fenderology: The Birth of the Tele, Strat & Jazzmaster,'' *Guitar Player*, August 1996, p. 85.

——, ''Fifty Years of Fender, 1946–1996,'' Fender Musical Instruments (press release), 1996.

——, ''The Twang Heard 'Round the World: A History of Fender's Fabulous Telecaster,'' *Guitar Player*, May 1998, p.66.

Wheeler, Tom, *American Guitars: An Illustrated History*, New York: Harper Perennial, 1992.

White, Forrest, *Fender: The Inside Story*, San Francisco: Miller Freeman, Inc., 1994.

—Dean Boyer
—update: Heidi Wrightsman

Fox Entertainment Group, Inc.

Web site: http://www.fox.com
Public Company
Incorporated: 1998
Employees: 12,000
Sales: $8,589.0 million (2000)
Stock Exchanges: New York
Ticker Symbol: FOX
NAIC: 512110 Motion Picture and Video Production; 512120 Motion Picture and Video Distribution; 513120 Television Broadcasting; 513210 Cable Networks; 551112 Offices of Other Holding Companies

Fox Entertainment Group is one of the world's biggest players in the entertainment business. Its main components consist of Fox Broadcasting Company, which comprises the Fox television network of 29 television stations; Fox Cable Networks, comprising several cable networks; Fox Filmed Entertainment, including Twentieth Century Fox film studios, television, and animation divisions; the FOX News Channel; and Fox Sports Enterprises, which consists of holdings in the Los Angeles Staples Center and ownership of the Los Angeles Dodgers. Among its best-known productions are the television series *The Simpsons*, *The X-Files*, and *Ally McBeal*; the films *The Grapes of Wrath* (1940), *South Pacific* (1958), *The Sound of Music* (1965), *Star Wars* (1977), and *Titanic* (1997); and special-interest programming, such as Fox Kids shows and live racing events. The company's smaller holdings include the National Geographic and golf cable channels, interests in the New York Knicks, the Fox Sports World Español channel, and Telecine, a pay-television service in Brazil.

1904 to the Great Depression: The Early Years Under William Fox

In 1904 a Hungarian immigrant named William Fox (originally Wilhelm Fried) bought a New York nickelodeon for $1,600 and built the failing business into a successful entertainment company, eventually owning 25 theaters in New York. After teaming up with B.S. Moss and Sol Brill to open the Greater New York Film Rental Company, he formed the Box Office Attraction Company in 1913 to produce films, which were in huge demand and short supply at the time.

By 1915, Fox had consolidated operations into the Fox Film Corporation, moved the company to Los Angeles, and embarked on a movie-making career. Within a few years, Fox had established his studio as a major supplier of films around the world. At the end of the decade, his company was producing 50 films a year and was worth nearly $200 million.

The company continued to prosper throughout the 1920s, producing movies, creating a chain of elegant movie palaces in cities around the country, and pioneering sound-on-film technology in newsreels and feature films. However, circumstances changed during the 1930s. Although some of film's best-known movie stars (Henry Fonda, John Wayne, Loretta Young), were introduced during this decade, the Great Depression hampered the fledgling film industry just as it did the rest of the U.S. Fox had borrowed heavily to finance the technology and equipment his new industry and innovations demanded, and now he could not pay back the millions he owed. He struggled to save his company but had to sell his shares.

In 1936, the Fox Film Corporation merged with Twentieth Century Pictures, creating Twentieth Century Fox. That same year, William Fox was forced to declare bankruptcy. Although he planned to return to the movie business, he never did. He was injured in a car crash, convicted on tampering charges, spent six months in jail for bribing a judge, and spent his remaining years battling ill health until he died in 1952 of heart failure.

The 1940s Through the 1970s: New Life as Twentieth Century Fox

During the 1940s and 1950s, Twentieth Century Fox once again became financially solvent and began producing movie hits. Although the political and social upheaval of the 1960s resulted in many sober and experimental films, Twentieth Century Fox continued to win over audiences with hits such as *The Sound of Music* and *Doctor Dolittle*. It also did well with television productions during this period.

Company Perspectives:

It is the daily dedication and professionalism of the thousands of Fox employees that fuel our Company's greatness. It is their work, often done under enormous creative pressure and time constraints, that gives life to our Company and enjoyment to our millions of customers. Our focus in the coming years must be to direct this huge pool of energy toward an even better future: better products and services, deeper connections with our customers, new and more lucrative sources of revenue and, most importantly, sustained growth for our shareholders.

After some success in the early 1970s with the movies *M*A*S*H*, *Patton*, and *The French Connection*, the company enjoyed during the latter part of the decade one of its most lucrative periods when special-effects films hit the screen. *Star Wars*, the twice-rejected sci-fi flick of newcomer George Lucas, was Fox's financial boon of the era. Although the studio spent more than three times its original budget on the film, it collected more than $200 million in ticket sales worldwide to more than make up for its investment.

The 1980s: News Corp. Creates a Television Network

In 1981 oilman Marvin Davis bought Twentieth Century Fox for $722 million, and a few years later, Rupert Murdoch's News Corporation, Ltd. purchased 50 percent of the company from Davis. In 1985 News Corp. purchased the remainder of the company for $575 million. Although Fox continued its success with action films and blockbuster dramas during the 1980s and 1990s, Murdoch envisioned a media company that encompassed a television network with programming seven nights a week to compete with ABC, NBC, and CBS. However, News Corp. was riddled with $675 million in debt at the time and many observers were skeptical that Murdoch's proposition was viable. Nevertheless, Murdoch bought six television stations from communications company Metromedia and established the Fox Broadcasting Company (FBC).

In the first two years, FBC lost $136 million, but was being broadcast on more than 100 affiliate stations across the country. Its first show, *The Late Show Starring Joan Rivers*, was cancelled after just a few months following controversy surrounding the antics on the show. However, *Married with Children*, FBC's next experiment, proved an adequate success and the cornerstone of its limited programming at the time. This program helped established the network's major demographic: 18 to 34-year-old viewers.

Sticking to this demographic proved a wise choice for FBC. In 1990, the company made its first profit, following the success of a prime-time animated show called *The Simpsons*. Continuing to cater to its target audience, FBC succeeded with shows such as *In Living Color* and *America's Most Wanted*. FBC also benefited from their programming innovation of initiating new series in August. By releasing new shows in August, Fox was able to steal viewers from the other networks, which were following industry tradition and airing re-runs at this time of year.

Fox Broadcasting Company created a stir in 1993 when it spent $1.6 billion for a four-year package for the rights to broadcast NFL football, outbidding CBS and establishing itself as a major sports network. Analysts predicted the company would lose money in the sports arena, but by 1995 Fox was talking about developing its own sports network to compete with ESPN. Through a joint venture with Tele-Communications Inc., Fox purchased a 50 percent interest in Liberty Media, a TCI division that owned 15 regional sporting networks. These network affiliates combined with the rest of Fox's sports ventures to form a new company called Fox Sports.

By now Fox had 22 regional cable networks that aired 14 major-league baseball teams, 15 NBA teams, 11 NHL teams, and a handful of college sports broadcasts. The company's vision was to cater to local sports enthusiasts by offering local programming tailored to the area it served. Fox followed each of its sports broadcasts with two hours of sports news.

The Mid-1990s: The Fourth Network Comes of Age

Despite its many successes, Fox struggled to establish its identity in the mid-1990s. At this point, the company still delivered its programming via satellite to a few affiliate stations, most of which broadcast on UHF. Murdoch was eager to replace these affiliates with VHF affiliates and thus reach a much broader audience.

In 1994, News Corp. struck the deal that began Fox's ascent to major network standing. The company bought New World Communications Group, Inc. for 2.5 billion, giving Fox 10 new stations, increasing its total to 20. Fox was now assured of reaching 40 percent of all television-viewing households.

In 1995, Fox branched out into children's programming, forming a partnership with Saban Entertainment, Inc. to launch children's channels around the world. The two companies consolidated in 1996 into Fox Children's Network, which became the number one children's programming service in the U.S. In addition to Fox's television broadcasts, its Fox Kids Countdown radio show was broadcast on more than 180 stations, and its quarterly kids magazine had 13 million readers per issue.

In late 1996, Fox spent $100 million to launch its own 24-hour cable news station. Four years later, after overcoming obstacles to get cable providers to carry the network, Fox had the fastest-growing news channel, equaled CNN's ratings, and reached 54 million viewers with broadcasts that were admittedly conservative and employed newscasters who strayed from the stoicism of the mainstream networks.

When Fox celebrated its tenth anniversary as a broadcast medium in 1997, it was divided into the Fox Group, Fox Television Group, and Fox Entertainment. The company also had something of a reputation for delivering trashy television. That reputation and a significant drop in ratings for its most popular show, *The X-Files*, indicated it was time for another change. In 1998, the Fox Entertainment Group was formed to comprise all the company's television, sports, and movie divisions. Analysts and investors welcomed the change, as it would put the business on a par with other media moguls, such as Disney and Time-Warner. News Corp. followed the renaming by selling 13.4 percent of the Fox Entertainment Group's shares

Key Dates:

1904: William Fox buys a New York City nickelodeon.
1913: Fox's Box Office Attraction Company begins making movies.
1915: Fox Film Corporation established.
1930: William Fox forced to sell his shares of the business due to heavy personal and corporate debt.
1935: Fox Film Corporation merges with Twentieth Century Pictures.
1981: Marvin Davis buys Twentieth Century Fox.
1985: Rupert Murdoch's News Corporation, Ltd. buys Twentieth Century Fox.
1986: Fox Broadcasting Company (FBC) established.
1993: Fox purchases rights to broadcast NFL football.
1994: News Corporation, Ltd. buys New World Communications Group.
1995: Fox forms a partnership with Saban Entertainment, Inc.
1996: Fox News Channel (FNC) is founded.
1997: Fox buys International Family Entertainment.
1998: Fox Entertainment Group is founded and undertakes its first public offering.
1999: The company buys out half of Liberty Media's remaining holdings in Fox Sports.
2000: Cable networks consolidated into Fox Cable Networks. Fox News Channel is launched.

in an initial public offering in 1998. After the offering, which raised $2.8 billion, making it one of the largest offerings in American history, News Corp. owned about 80 percent of the new company.

Fox Entertainment Group also continued its cable interests. In 1999, the company bought out half of Liberty Media's remaining holdings in Fox Sports for $1.425 billion; this allowed it to consolidate the sports and cable interests into one entity. Fox still remained strong as the leader in global filmed entertainment with a 20 percent share of the viewing audience. The news and sports stations had more than 40 million and 62 million subscribers, respectively.

Fox Entertainment Group's plans for the future focused on maintaining its 18 to 34 demographic and continuing its success as a fourth major network television channel and movie producer, making more blockbuster movies, expanding its cable services, producing hit television shows, and preserving its sports and news interests.

Principal Subsidiaries

Fox Broadcasting Company; Fox Filmed Entertainment; Los Angeles Dodgers, Inc.; New York Knickerbockers; New York Rangers.

Principal Operating Units

Fox Broadcasting Company; Fox Cable Networks; Fox Filmed Entertainment; Fox News Channel; Fox Sports Enterprises.

Principal Competitors

AOL Time Warner; Carsey-Werner; DreamWorks SKG; Liberty Media; MGM; NBC; Sony Pictures Entertainment; Universal Studios; USA Networks; Viacom; Walt Disney; ABC; UPN; CBS.

Further Reading

Byrne, Bridget, "Hounded Herzog Quits Fox," *E!online*, March 22, 2000.

Byrne, Harlan S., "The Empire Builder: Rupert Murdoch Loves Media Companies and Debt," *Barron's National Business and Financial Weekly*, Dec 8, 1986.

Cerone, Daniel, "Fox Vows to Treat NFL With 'Reverence'," *Los Angeles Times*, January 15, 1994, p. F15.

Cho, Joshua, "Murdoch's Fox Entertainment Tones Down IPO Offer," *Cable World*, October 12, 1998 p. 14.

Collins, L., "News to Form $32b Fox Group," *The Courier-Mail* (Brisbane, Australia), July 1, 1998, p. 39.

Farache, Emily, "Fox's Golden Guy Tarnished," *E!online*, November 16, 1999.

"Fox and New Regency Sign Groundbreaking Deal" *Business Wire*, September 8, 1997.

Freeman, Michael and Consoli, John, "Reality Hits Peter Roth," *Mediaweek*, November 23, 1998, pp. 12–13.

Graham, Jefferson, "Sandy Grushow Gets the Last Laugh," *USA Today*, June 26, 1997, p. 3D.

Gray, Verne, "Show by Show: Fox News Channel, MSNBC," *Mediaweek*, March 17, 1997, p. CR10.

Hofmeister, Sallie, "Fox, TCI Expected to Form Sports Network," *Los Angeles Times*, October 31, 1995

Katz, Ephraim, *The Film Encyclopedia*. New York: Harper Perennial, pp. 1382–83.

King, Susan, "How *Cleopatra* Nearly Sank Fox," *Los Angeles Times*, April 3, 2001 p. F-3.

Ledbetter, James, "Fox Gets Healthy (But Keeps Smoking)," *The Industry Standard*, March 27, 1999.

Littleton, Cynthia, "News Corp. Builds Syndication Muscle," *Broadcasting and Cable*, July 22, 1996, p. 7.

——, "Twentieth Begins New World Takeover," *Broadcasting and Cable*, October 21, 1996, p. 44.

Littleton, Cynthia, and Lynette Rice, "Matoian Out, Roth in at Fox," *Broadcasting and Cable*, September 9, 1996, p. 15.

"Marvin Davis' Script for 20th Century Fox," *Business Week*, April 19, 1982.

Martzke, Rudy, "Fox Sports Set to Rival ESPN," *USA Today*, November 1, 1995, p. 2C.

McAdams, Deborah D., "Fox Maneuvers for NASCAR Net," *Broadcasting & Cable*, May 22, 2000, p. 40.

McClellan, Steve, "News Corp. Sells Less to Public," *Broadcasting and Cable*, October 12, 1998, p. 53.

——, "SRO for Fox IPO," *Broadcasting and Cable*, November 16, 1998, p. 4.

Miller, Ron, "Ouster of Fox President Lucie Salhany Wasn't Unexpected," *Knight-Ridder/Tribune News Service*, July 8, 1994.

"News Corp. Unites Fox Sports," *Television Digest*, April 12, 1999.

Plotz, David, "Fox News Channel," *Slate Magazine*, posted November 22, 2000, http://slate.msn.com.

Rice, Lynette, "10 Years from Wannabe to Big Four," *Broadcasting and Cable*, September 22, 1997, pp. 36–38.

——, "Hill Named FBC Chairman," *Broadcasting and Cable*, September 8, 1997, p. 30.

Schlosser, Joe, "Fox's Split Personality," *Broadcasting and Cable*, May 29, 2000, pp. 18–22.

——, "Fox to Kick Reality 'Heroin'," *Broadcasting and Cable*, December 13, 1999, p. 6.

Schmuckler, Eric, ''Fox Flips Top Execs Again,'' *Mediaweek*, October 3, 1994, p. 3.

Sharkey, Betsy, ''Changing the Face of Fox,'' *Mediaweek*, November 20, 1995, p. 22.

——, ''Fox Wants a Bigger Broom,'' *Mediaweek*, July 27, 1998, pp. 2–3.

Shister, Gail, ''Fox to Dump 'Reality Specials' for Sitcoms and Dramas,'' *News-Times Online Edition*, posted January 14, 2000, http://www.newstimes.com.

Stroud, Michael and Schlosser, Joe, ''Fox Seeks Off-Cable Hit in Herzog,'' *Broadcasting and Cable*, November 23, 1998, pp.10–14.

Tedesco, Richard, ''CNNfn, MSNBC, Stream after Fox,'' *Broadcasting and Cable*, March 17, 1997, p. 106.

—Kerri DeVault

Franklin Electric Company, Inc.

400 East Spring Street
Bluffton, Indiana 46714
U.S.A.
Telephone: (219) 824-2900
Fax: (219) 824-2909
Web site: http://www.franklin-electric.com

Public Company
Incorporated: 1946
Employees: 2,802
Sales: $325.7 million (2000)
Stock Exchanges: NASDAQ
Ticker Symbol: FELE
NAIC: 335312 Motor and Generator Manufacturing; 335314 Relay and Industrial Control Manufacturing; 333911 Pump and Pumping Equipment Manufacturing; 333913 Measuring and Dispensing Pump Manufacturing

Franklin Electric Inc. of Blufton, Indiana, is the world's leading producer of submersible motors, which are used primarily for pumping systems in water wells, underground diesel and gasoline storage, and wastewater systems. The company produces a wide range of submersible electric motors and other specialty electric motors, for the commercial, industrial and original equipment manufacturer (OEM) markets. Franklin's other specialty motors are used the world over in products such as gasoline dispensers, paint sprayers, electric hoists, livestock feeding systems, explosion-proof vapor exhaust fans and ice cream machines. Franklin has over 2,800 employees at facilities in more than 15 countries.

1940s Origins

The Franklin Electric Company was founded in Blufton, Indiana, by E.J. (Ed) Schaefer and T.W. (Wayne) Kehoe. Schaefer and Kehoe, then both in their 40s, were already successful electrical engineers who believed they could make a go of manufacturing small electric motors on a mass scale. With their wives as their business partners, and less than $20,000 in start-up capital, Schaefer and Kehoe started the company in November 1944. From the very beginning the two engineers had their sights set on serving a nation-wide market, and hence they were reluctant to name the new firm after themselves. Instead they christened the concern after Benjamin Franklin, whom they considered the country's first electrical engineer, because of his early experiments with electromagnetism.

From the beginning, Schaefer and Kehoe planned that Franklin would specialize in designing products for the specific needs of individual customers. As they were getting started, however, World War II was at its peak and there was virtually no civilian market for electrical motors. Despite that formidable hurdle, its first customer got Franklin off to a running start. Less than three months after it was founded, Franklin received a contract from the U.S. government to produce lightweight electric generators to power the radio equipment used by paratroopers and other assault troops. Over the next four months Franklin sold $228,219 in generators to the Army Signal Corps. The military contract kept the young company very busy. In fact, the Army was Franklin's *only* customer during 1945. In August 1945, however, World War II ended. When the Army's orders to Franklin abruptly stopped, the company had to learn to cope with a peacetime economy.

Franklin Electric formally incorporated in 1946 and began designing and manufacturing fractional horsepower motors that could be used in homes, to pump in water for drinking and washing, or pump water out of flooded basements. It was a time when returning GIs were causing a boom in new home building. The motors were a hit. Sales in 1947 reached nearly $1.7 million and earned Franklin profits of about a quarter of a million dollars.

In 1950, the company introduced its breakthrough product. It had been in development for most of the late 1940s and once it had been perfected it set Franklin on the course it would follow into the new millennium. Called its greatest achievement by Franklin itself, the invention was an electric motor that was fully-submersible. It was designed to function under water, in particular to operate pumps. Unlike Franklin's earlier pump motors, the new submersibles were more quiet, more resistant to freezing,

Company Perspectives:

Mr. Edward Schaefer, Franklin's founder, believed in the ability of ordinary individuals to do extraordinary things. He understood that imagination, commitment, and persistence can open doors into worlds filled with opportunity. Over the years Franklin people have had the courage to open many such doors, and as we begin the 21st century, we are pledged to build on this Franklin heritage. We are confident we are prepared to meet the challenges of the future and to extend the Franklin record of achievement for many years to come.

smaller, easier to install and had a much higher pumping capacity. Another critical improvement was that the new submersible pumps could operate at a depth of 100 feet. They could recover water from much deeper in the earth than the conventional pumps of the day. Grateful customers included communities who had lost water supplies because their water tables had dropped so low. The pumps also made possible settlement of areas with naturally low water tables for the first time. The motors proved to be highly versatile and eventually their application was expanded to include gasoline pumps, commercial air conditioning units, crude oil recovery and deep-sea use.

Fortunes Rise in the 1950s with a New Submersible Pump

Franklin's submersible pumps were an immediate success. Before long they were the company's leading product, the basis of its growing product line. An innovative variation for homeowners was the Submatic sump pump. Introduced in 1951, the Submatic was sealed in a special stainless steel casing. The casing was designed to sense when water was rising and to turn on the motor automatically. Not only was an external float switch no longer needed to detect flooding, the motor could be also mounted out of sight beneath floor level. The Submatic became one of Franklin's most successful products. By the 1980s, homeowners made up about half of the customer base for Franklin submersible motors, with commercial and agricultural customers making up the other half.

By late 1952 Franklin had about 500 employees turning out over 1,000 motors every day. The company continued to grow steadily through the 1950s. Nationwide sales reached $12 million in 1959.

The company went public that same year, its stock opening at $18 a share. As the Franklin product line continued to diversify in the 1960s, sales continued to climb. Around this time Franklin served its northernmost customer when one of its 3HP submersible motors was sent first to the U.S. Army Polar Research Center at Thule, Greenland, and from there on to a research base near the North Pole. The site was so remote that delivery had to be made by a parachute drop to scientists camped on the ground. In May 1966, founder and board member Wayne Kehoe passed away.

Submersible motors were firmly established by the 1960s and in 1966 a new model was introduced. That same year, Franklin's one millionth submersible motor was produced at the Siloam Springs, Arkansas, plant. Franklin was not the country's only producer of such motors. By mid-decade, however, Franklin had produced more than four times as many submersible motors as any other company. On an annual basis its output exceeded all its competitors put together.

The mid-1960s saw the introduction of a brand new line of Franklin products. Specialized gearmotors developed by the company were marketed successfully to makers of conveyors, business machines, and other commercial and industrial equipment. At the same time, Franklin introduced a system of automatic packaging equipment for supermarkets which could wrap and label various sized packages of fresh meat at a rate of 35 per minute. It food packaging products were so successful, that Franklin expanded the line in 1968 by purchasing J.B Dove & Sons, Inc, the maker of a broad line of packaging equipment. A second such acquisition, Battle Creek Packaging Machines, Inc., made in 1969, added 30 more wrapping machines to Franklin's line.

By the mid-1960s it was clear that Franklin motors could be used to pump more than just water. In 1967, Franklin and Gould Pumps, Inc. made a deal to sell oil pumping systems and to consolidate production and marketing of motors and pumps needed for oil wells under one roof. The two companies formed Oil Dynamics, a joint venture, that specialized in secondary oil recovery systems. The venture was a highly successful one. Thirty years later, in November 1994, Franklin would buy an additional 47 percent of Oil Dynamic shares, increasing its control in the firm to 97 percent; by October 1997 Franklin would sell Oil Dynamics to Baker Hughes Inc. for approximately $31.5 million in cash.

Franklin introduced its ''Sea-Mersibles'' line in 1968. These were general purpose submersible motors for undersea use. Recognizing the importance of this field to its business, a year later the company established the independent Oceanology Engineering Department. Franklin manufactured its five-millionth fractional horsepower motor in 1969, and one year later was listed among *Fortune*'s top 1,000 manufacturing firms in the United States.

Expansion at Home and Globally in the 1970s

Franklin Electric passed a number of milestones in 1972. Its submersible motor production topped 2 million. Its main plant at Blufton, Indiana, was enlarged by 74,000 square feet. It booked record sales of more than $64 million. It acquired a 200,000 square foot facility in Jacksonville, Arkansas, from the Singer Company, and the plant in Siloam Springs was doubled in size.

The 1970s also saw an expansion of Franklin's overseas activities. The company had established its first foreign presence as early as 1962 when it set up a plant in Dandenong, Victoria, Australia, a venture in which Franklin had a 50 percent holding. A year afterwards it established its first wholly-owned subsidiary, Franklin Electric of Canada; in 1965 Franklin Electric Europa GmbH, a wholly-owned subsidiary located in Wittlich, West Germany, was formed. In the early-1960s foreign sales accounted for barely three percent of Franklin's total business. By 1969, however, the percentage had grown nearly

Key Dates:

1944: E.J. Schaefer and T.W. Kehoe found Franklin Electric Company.
1950: Franklin develops the first practical submersible motor.
1951: The Submatic sump pump is introduced.
1962: Franklin establishes its first foreign venture in Australia.
1963: Franklin founds its first fully-owned, foreign subsidiary, Franklin Electric of Canada.
1964: Franklin diversifies into food packaging equipment.
1965: Franklin Electric Europa GmbH is founded.
1966: Franklin manufactures its one millionth submersible motor.
1967: Oil Dynamics, Inc is founded as a joint venture with Gould Pumps, Inc.
1969: Franklin produces its five millionth fractional horsepower motor.
1970: *Fortune* ranks Franklin in top 1000 manufacturing companies in the U.S.
1980: Franklin produces its ten millionth fractional motor.
1982: The Amazing Little Switch, an inexpensive solid state switch, goes into production.
1991: Founder E.J. Schaefer passes away.
1994: Franklin acquires a 97 percent interest in Oil Dynamics, Inc.
1997: Franklin sells Oil Dynamics, Inc. to Baker Hughes, Inc.

fourfold. In 1972, at a time when exports from South Africa were being severely curtailed by international sanctions, Franklin Electric South Africa Pty, another wholly-owned subsidiary, was formed in Johannesburg. Another subsidiary, Franklin Electric do Brasil, Ltd., was formed around this time. It marketed and later also manufactured Franklin products for the Latin American market. Canadian business was increasing rapidly. Franklin acquired Control Company of Canada in 1973, and a year later expanded its facilities in Strathroy Ontario by 67,000 feet. 1983 saw the opening of Franklin's first Mexican plant, a submersible motor facility in Monterrey, Mexico.

Franklin's sales grew by leaps and bounds through the 1970s. It expanded its Blufton plant a second time in 1975, adding 50,000 square feet. It brought out major new products including the four-inch Super Stainless, the industry's only fully submersible motor in a stainless steel casing. In 1976 the company recorded new sales highs, driven by demand for electric motors for home heating and electricity that was increasing so rapidly the company could hardly keep up. The demand continued through the end of the decade. In 1980 Franklin purchased a factory in Wilburton, Oklahoma, that was three-quarters the size of the home facility in Blufton. The same year the ten-millionth Franklin fractional motor rolled out of the Blufton plant.

The Challenging 1980s

By 1982, however, the boom times had begun to wane rapidly catching Franklin with large back stocks of inventory. The company was forced to initiate belt-tightening measures. In April it announced plans to close four of its domestic plants temporarily, a move that affected a full two-thirds of the company's total workforce. Within six months, the company was operating at only 50 percent capacity, according to president Conrad J. Balentine, and sales were down 19 percent from a year earlier. The situation did not take a turn for the better until 1983 when a midwestern heat wave and drought created a new demand for motors for air conditioning units and motors that could be used to drill for and pump water.

General Electric added to Franklin's woes in 1982, when the gigantic competitor brought suit, claiming that former GE employees had revealed company secrets after being hired by Franklin. GE alleged that the purloined information had enabled Franklin to trim millions of dollars from the cost of manufacturing its fractional horsepower motors. The damages GE sought were never publicized, and the suit dragged out for a year before the two companies eventually reached an out of court settlement of which the details were never revealed.

The doldrums experienced by the motor industry were offset by the fruits of Franklin's research and development (R&D) activities. In 1982 it brought out the electrical industry's first cheap, dependable solid state switch, of which its straightforward name said it all: the Amazing Little Switch. Called the most outstanding innovation in electric motors in over 30 years, tests showed it could perform without failure for more than 15 million starts against less than one million for older centrifugal switches. The Amazing Little Switch was first put to use in motors for swimming pools and spas and in airless paint sprayers. Another Franklin innovation was the Subtrol, a control device with a built-in microprocessor capable of detecting 15 potential problems in underwater motors and pumps. The Subtrol was especially attractive to users of large pumping systems, such as municipal waterworks and wastewater facilities and operators of large agricultural irrigation systems, for whom breakdowns could be costly and time-consuming. By 1985 Franklin had completed the development of a submerged pump that was operated by solar energy. The new product was seen as a boon to Third World villages that did not have supplies of electricity as well as to ranchers in remote areas who needed to pump water for livestock.

In 1988, Franklin Electric approved a recapitalization plan. Public holders, the company pension plan, management shareholders, and the Schaefer family all received additional shares for each share already held. Public holders received a cash bonus as well. The purpose of the plan was to avoid any hostile takeover attempts that might result from the high estate taxes that could accrue upon the death of its founder, CEO, and principal shareholder Edward Schaefer, then 87 years old. Edward Schaefer passed away in 1991.

The 1990s and Beyond

By the 1990s a full one-third of Franklin's sales were from foreign markets. In 1991 it added a distribution center to its European headquarters in Germany to be positioned for the new European Union and the newly opened markets in Eastern Europe. It moved into the Asian market for the first time as well. Subsidiaries were established in Mexico and Australia. Its oil pumps brought Franklin substantial business in de-sovietized Russia. Eventually it also established a Netherlands holding company and a European trading company.

Franklin's submersible motor line continued to expand until the end of the 1990s, into new applications such as mine dewatering and geothermal heating. Franklin's Engineered Motor Products Division developed an Integrated Motor Drive System that promised to be widely accepted. It combined sensor technology and electronic control into a so-called "smart motor" with a wide range of uses.

Given the company's role as the leader in submersible motors, as well as its healthy balance sheet, analysts regarded the future of Franklin Electric as solid. Its commitment to "aggressive, but thoughtful global expansion," according to company literature, promised greater market share for the company, particularly in Europe and the Middle East.

Principal Subsidiaries

Franklin Electric Europa GmbH; Franklin Electric of Canada; Franklin Electric do Brasil, Ltd.; Franklin Electric (International) Pty. Ltd. (Australia); Franklin Electric South Africa Proprietary Ltd.; Motores Franklin S.A. de C.V. (Mexico); FE Petro, Inc.

Principal Divisions

Submersible Motors; Fueling Systems; Industrial Motors; Electronics.

Principal Competitors

A.O. Smith Corporation; Baldar Electric Company; Lincoln Electric Company; MagneTek Inc.; Owosso Corporation; Regal-Beloit Corporation.

Further Reading

Culbertson, Katie, "Franklin Pumps Along Through Acquisitions," *Indianapolis Business Journal,* May 22, 2000, p. B19.

"Firm Proposes a Revamping That Includes Major Payout," *Wall Street Journal*, December 20, 1988.

"Franklin Electric Co. Settles Suit With GE," *Wall Street Journal*, January 2, 1984.

"GE Says Secrets Stolen by Two Former Staffers," *Washington Post*, December 24, 1982.

Metz, Robert, "Motor Maker Recommended," *New York Times*, November 10, 1981.

"Ownership Control of Oil Dynamics Transferred to Franklin Electric," *PR Newswire*, November 28, 1994.

"Recapitalization, Conversion Approved by Shareholders," *Wall Street Journal*, August 28, 1989.

"Solar Pumping," *Industry Week*, February 18, 1985.

—Gerald E. Brennan

GEAC Computer Corporation Ltd.

Yonge Corporate Centre
4100 Yonge Street, 6th Floor
Toronto, Ontario, M2P 2B5
Canada
Telephone: (416) 642-1960
Fax: (416) 642-1961
Web site: http://www.geac.com

Public Company
Incorporated: 1971
Employees: 6,000
Sales: C$990.1 million (US$669 million)(2000)
Stock Exchanges: Toronto
Ticker Symbol: GAC
NAIC: 511210 Software Publishers

Canada-based GEAC Computer Corporation Ltd. is one of the top five global suppliers of the software and systems solutions known as ERP, or mission critical Enterprise Resource Planning. The company provides ERP applications for financial administration, human resources, manufacturing, distribution, customer relationship management (CRM), and supply chain management (SCM). The company was founded in 1971 to develop and market software for online batch processing, primarily to financial institutions, libraries, and academic institutions. During the 1990s the company embarked on an aggressive acquisition strategy and expanded into a wide range of vertical markets, including newspaper publishing, health care, hospitality, property management, and others. Its 1999 acquisition of JBA Holdings PLC doubled the size of the company and transformed GEAC into a leading provider of ERP software.

Software for Libraries and Financial Institutions: 1970s–80s

GEAC was founded in 1971 in Markham, Ontario, by Robert Isserstedt and R. Angus German. In its first year the company broke even on sales of $200,000. It sold software for online processing on existing computers that were built for batch processing. By 1976 GEAC's software had become too sophisticated for existing computers, so the company began offering its own online computer hardware.

GEAC introduced its first library automation product, the GEAC Library Information System (GLIS) in 1977. The GLIS system proved popular with medium-size and larger academic libraries in North America and elsewhere. It ran on minicomputers manufactured by GEAC and was marketed as a preconfigured turnkey combination of hardware and software. GLIS was initially limited to circulation control, with online catalog access and acquisitions capabilities added later.

In 1980 Charles Williams became president and CEO of GEAC. Under Williams, the company specialized in financial and library applications and was focused on niche markets. Major customers included the Royal Bank of Canada, the University of Waterloo, and York University in Toronto. GEAC was listed on the Toronto Stock Exchange in May 1983 at C$15.75 a share. The company's stock rose 42.9 percent in 1983 to end the year at C$22.50. In its April 1984 review of high-tech companies, *Canadian Business* called GEAC "a quality company, well managed and strong on marketing."

For fiscal 1984 GEAC reported sales of C$61.4 million, up from C$48 million in fiscal 1983 and C$35.6 million in fiscal 1982. Moreover, the company had been profitable every year since 1972, showing a C$6 million profit in 1984. In 1984 the French National Library in Paris awarded GEAC a C$2 million contract to automate its library catalog. The company also won a C$1.4 million contract from the Smithsonian Institution to computerize the catalog of its vast collection. During 1984 GEAC led the library automation industry in new system installations. By mid-1985 GEAC had offices in the United States, United Kingdom, the Netherlands, Ireland, France, and Australia.

However, GEAC began experiencing financial difficulties in the mid-1980s and was in receivership from late 1986 through early 1987. The company posted substantial losses in 1987 and 1988. Its poor financial performance was attributed to an unsuccessful expansion into the U.S. banking market as well as to unfavorable developments in the Canadian banking industry. During this period the company's library automation business

Company Perspectives:

GEAC is among the world's largest suppliers of mission critical e-Business Enterprise Resource Planning (ERP) software and systems solutions to corporations around the globe. Operating globally with more than 10,000 businesses relying on our ERP systems every business day, GEAC is an important and integral component of the emerging e-business world.

reportedly remained profitable, but uncertainty about the company's long-term financial stability led to a downturn in new GLIS installations, especially in the United States.

To help ease its financial woes, GEAC obtained $20 million in financing from Helix Investments Ltd., a Toronto-based venture capital firm. Stephen Sadler became GEAC's chief financial officer (CFO) in September 1987, and with his help GEAC returned to profitability in fiscal 1989 ending April 30. The company acquired new library automation software, called Advance, through the acquisition of Advanced Libraries and Information Inc., which developed the software, for C$3 million. Advance software became available from GEAC in late 1989. The following year Sadler was named GEAC's CEO.

Aggressive Acquisition Strategy: 1990–95

At the end of 1992 GEAC strengthened its position in the library automation market by acquiring CLSI Inc., which had subsidiaries in Canada, France, the Netherlands, and the United Kingdom. CLSI was the first company to commercialize a minicomputer-based circulation control system and was one of the best-known library automation vendors. CLSI had two product lines: the LIBS 100 system, which was introduced in the mid-1970s, and a second-generation library automation system called LIBS 100plus that was introduced in June 1992. At the time of GEAC's acquisition of CLSI, more than 50 customers had signed up for the LIBS 100plus upgrade. GEAC paid C$13.5 million for CLSI.

Observers noted that the two companies were complementary in several ways. CLSI was strong in the public library market, while GEAC had focused on academic libraries. CLSI had an effective circulation module that complemented GEAC's serials and cataloging modules. The library automation systems of both companies were Unix-based. Following the acquisition GEAC developed a transparent interface between the two systems and renamed the LIBS 100plus system Plus. GEAC continued to service and support GLIS and LIBS 100 installations, but the company stopped developing or actively marketing the older systems.

By 1993 GEAC had Advance, its integrated online library system, installed in 48 North American locations as well as at additional international locations. The system included Acquisitions, Authority Control, Cataloging, Circulation, Materials Booking, OPAC (online public access catalog), Serials, and other modules. The system also included optional gateways and interfaces for electronic ordering, online databases, and electronic bulletin boards. GEAC had development centers in Canada, the United States, the United Kingdom, France, Australia, and New Zealand, with operations in ten countries covering North America, Europe, and the Pacific Rim. In addition GEAC marketed and supported CLSI's LIBS 100 system installations. In April 1993 GEAC acquired Computer Library Services International (Australia) Pty Limited of Melbourne, Australia, which distributed LIBS 100 products to Australian libraries and provided CD-ROM network solutions and database subscriptions there. For fiscal 1993 ending April 30 GEAC reported revenues of C$102.7 and its cash reserves exceeded C$40 million.

As of early 1994 the Advance library automation system was installed in 110 libraries worldwide, the Plus system was in approximately 70 libraries, and there were some 135 GLIS installations and 690 installations of the CLSI LIBS 100 system. Including library consortium participants, GEAC systems automated the operations of more than 2,500 libraries, making GEAC's the largest worldwide installed base.

During the first half of the 1990s GEAC made several other acquisitions. In 1992 the company acquired McDonnell Douglas Information Systems Canada, a vendor of computer products and services for specialized applications. In 1993 alone GEAC acquired: Mentat Computer Systems Pty. Ltd., an Australian developer of manufacturing software; Concord Management Systems Inc., a Florida-based developer of software for construction companies; MAI Ltd. and Tekserv Computer Services, both located in the United Kingdom; NBI Canada Inc., a Toronto-based reseller of network products; New Tech Hospitality Systems Ltd., an Australian developer of hotel management software; Claymore Systems Group, a developer of Unix-based software for real estate and property management applications; ECI Computer Inc., a California-based developer of computer systems for hotels and convention centers; Nisus Development & Technology, an acquisition that included software to manage golf course pro shops; Datamark International Ltd. of New Zealand and its subsidiary, Dmark International Pty. Ltd. of Australia, both of which developed software for manufacturing companies. These acquisitions were expected to help GEAC maintain a 20–30 percent annual growth rate. The acquisitions shared the characteristic of developing Unix-based products.

In 1994 GEAC acquired Collier-Jackson, Inc., which provided business automation systems to newspapers, from CompuServe, Inc., for an undisclosed amount. Headquartered in Tampa, Florida, Collier-Jackson had about 1,000 customers with some 2,500 different computer software applications in place. CompuServe, then a subsidiary of H&R Block Inc., had originally acquired Collier-Jackson in 1987. The acquisition was expected to enable GEAC to expand its offering in existing markets and take the company into new markets. Following the acquisition, Collier-Jackson was renamed GEAC/Collier-Jackson. The company changed its orientation from mainframe-based solutions to software applications that could be used in a PC-based client/server environment.

Under the leadership of CEO Stephen Sadler, GEAC emerged as a leading Canadian software company. Over the course of five years Sadler oversaw more than 20 acquisitions, many of them financially troubled companies acquired at bargain prices. The acquisitions, along with Sadler's talent for cost-cutting, drove GEAC's revenues and increased the com-

Key Dates:

1971: GEAC Computer Corporation Ltd. is founded in Markham, Ontario.
1977: GEAC introduces its first library automation product, the GEAC Library Information System (GLIS).
1983: GEAC becomes a public company, with stock trading on the Toronto Stock Exchange.
1992: GEAC acquires library automation vendor CLSI Inc.
1996: GEAC acquires Dun & Bradstreet Software Inc.
1997: GEAC receives the Editor's Choice Award from *Software Magazine.*
1999: GEAC acquires JBA Holdings PLC for C$205.5 million.

pany's profits. For fiscal 1994 GEAC reported record revenue of C$152 million. The acquisitions enabled GEAC to diversify into a wide range of markets, including construction, property management, manufacturing, distribution, newspapers, financial institutions, libraries, hotels, and clubs. In 1996 Sadler became GEAC's vice-chairman.

Continued Growth: 1996–99

William Nelson was GEAC's chairman and CEO when the company announced it would acquire Dun & Bradstreet Software Inc. (DBS) in October 1996 for $191 million. Headquartered in Atlanta, Georgia, DBS was formed in 1990 through the merger of Management Science of America Inc. and McCormack & Dodge Corp. At the beginning of 1996 Dun & Bradstreet Corp. announced it would split into three companies and sell DBS, which had annual revenue of some $350 million. In mid-1996 venture capital firm Bain Capital Inc. signed a letter of intent to purchase DBS for $210 million, but the deal fell through. GEAC agreed to purchase DBS for $150 million in cash and $41.25 million in 18-month term notes.

GEAC was attracted to DBS's large base of mainframe users as well as the growth of its client/server business. DBS had two main software product lines: SmartStream, a line of business client/server applications, and MainStream, a line of software applications for mainframe users. Following the acquisition, GEAC split DBS into two divisions: GEAC SmartStream for client/server software and GEAC MainStream for mainframe applications.

In April 1997 GEAC held its first user group conference since acquiring DBS, at which it outlined a new business plan. The company was reorganized into separate divisions focusing on client/server applications and mainframe applications. The company planned to focus on human resources and financial applications and abandon manufacturing applications. GEAC also planned to focus on critical vertical markets, including financial services, health care, business services, and the public sector.

Following its purchase of DBS, GEAC continued to make other, smaller acquisitions in 1997. Among the companies it acquired was Comp-Tech Inc., a California-based network systems integrator with a client base of more than 170 customers and annual revenue of some $2 million. This acquisition was part of GEAC's strategy to increase its customer service coverage to include not only conventional maintenance but also network expertise, remote connection services, and on-site help desk capabilities. GEAC expanded its customer service offerings by acquiring Florida Computer & Network (FCN) of Fort Lauderdale, Florida. FCN was a network systems integrator with more than 500 customers and annual revenue of approximately $1.3 million. GEAC also acquired the AMS Group located in Sudbury, Ontario, to strengthen its Customer Service Division. The Northern Ontario company had more than 2,000 customers and annual revenue of approximately C$8.5 million. AMS provided sales and service for several manufacturers' products, networking and connectivity solutions, CAD (computer-assisted design) services, and computer training and education courses.

GEAC strengthened its position in Australia with the acquisition in January 1997 of FGH Decision Support Systems Pty. Ltd. of Sydney, Australia. FGH was a major supplier of service management software for manufacturing, distribution, and service industries and had more than 800 customers throughout Australia, South Africa, and the United Kingdom. During the year GEAC enjoyed several major sales in the Asia-Pacific region, adding such new customers as the New Zealand Department for Courts, Bank Danamon of Indonesia, the Royal Australian Air Force, and the International Broadcasting Corporation of Thailand.

In mid-1997 GEAC was selected by *Software Magazine* as one of 13 software companies to receive its Editor's Choice Awards. "GEAC is notable for management's bold moves which have created one of the software industry's largest vendors and a company to watch," noted the magazine. As a result of GEAC's acquisition of DBS, the company's revenue jumped from C$205 million in 1996 to C$381.2 million in 1997 ending April 30. Income from operations rose from C$40.6 million in 1996 to C$57.5 million in 1997, but the company reported a net loss of C$71.1 million for 1997 compared to net income of C$35.6 million in 1996. The 1997 loss was the result of a one-time charge of $121.4 million for expenses associated with software, goodwill, inventory, and fixed assets. GEAC returned to profitability in 1998, as revenue increased 70 percent to C$646.4 million and net income reached C$168.7 million, further strengthening GEAC's cash position and allowing it to pursue more acquisitions.

GEAC continued to acquire smaller companies in 1998. In January it acquired Princeton Network Systems Inc. (PNS), a computer services provider based in South Plainfield, New Jersey. PNS had annual revenue of approximately $4 million. In December GEAC acquired TWG Technologies Inc., which was based in Vancouver, British Columbia, and had annual revenues of approximately C$3 million. TWG was a provider of NT Server and Unix networked computer system integration and support services to large and mid-sized companies. Both acquisitions strengthened GEAC's Customer Service Division, which was renamed the Networks and Technical Services Division.

A larger acquisition involved Remanco International, Inc., a leading supplier of restaurant computer systems with annual revenue of C$20 million. Remanco developed one of the first point-of-sale computer systems for restaurants in 1976. The acquisition strengthened GEAC's position in the hospitality industry and added a valuable distribution channel for GEAC's point-of-sale products.

In Australia GEAC acquired Cruickshank Technology Pty. Ltd., a leading supplier of maintenance management software with more than 1,100 sites worldwide. Cruickshank had annual revenues of approximately C$4 million. Its principal product line was the MAINPAC maintenance management solution, a system used to manage company assets in a wide range of industries. GEAC also acquired Stowe Computing Australia Pty. Ltd. and Stowe Computing NZ (New Zealand) Ltd. With annual revenue of A$10 million, Stowe provided municipal government and library management software in Australia and New Zealand. Its customers included some of the region's largest municipal governments.

GEAC's largest acquisition of 1998 involved Interealty Corp., based in Vienna, Virginia. Interealty had annual revenue equaling some C$100 million and was a well-known supplier of real estate information systems to the residential brokerage market in North America. It provided software and services to the Multiple Listing Services (MLS) and various regional real estate boards, reaching some 300,000 real estate professionals. Interealty also built and managed web sites for major real estate brokerage firms. The acquisition enabled GEAC to enter a new vertical market with significant market share.

During 1998 GEAC enjoyed large-scale sales of its library software in Europe. New customers included the Amsterdam Public Library, Blois Public Library, and the National Library of France. In the insurance and banking markets, GEAC added Microsoft to its FastApps program. FastApps provided a rapid implementation solution to mid-market insurance and banking organizations.

GEAC also implemented its web strategy in 1998 by introducing CyberStream Human Resources. CyberStream was the brand name given to GEAC's suite of self-service web applications that could be accessed from a browser-based interface. CyberStream Procurement was also available, and other web-based applications were in development. CyberStream applications were designed to serve the needs of two types of users: the occasional, self-service user who wanted to interact with the system without learning the full system and without maintaining programs on their desktop, and the transaction-intensive user who needed the full power of the SmartStream system through a web environment.

In September 1998 GEAC combined its Enterprise Server and SmartStream Divisions to form the GEAC SmartEnterprise Solutions Division. The new division would deliver a comprehensive, cohesive enterprise strategy to customers, allowing them to leverage their current investments while benefiting from new technology advancements. GEAC recognized that its customers wanted integrated enterprise solutions that combined the power of the mainframe with the flexibility of client/server computing. In May 1999 the SmartEnterprise Solutions Division announced a new web-based portal, Net Foundations, that organizations could deploy to access all server-based and back office GEAC applications across an enterprise. Net Foundations provided customers with a single point of access from any location or device.

Becoming a Leading ERP Software Vendor: 1999–2000

For fiscal 1999 ending April 30, GEAC reported revenue of C$783.0 million, operating income of C$184.4 million, and a net loss of C$111.6 million due to a fourth quarter charge of C$268.9 million for write downs and restructuring charges. Before the end of the fiscal year, GEAC announced a change in leadership, naming Douglas G. Bergeron as GEAC's CEO and president. Bergeron was most recently Group CEO at SunGard Brokerage Systems Group. As part of the planned management transition, William Nelson, who turned 65 in 1999, would continue as chairman of the board. Stephen Sadler, former vice-chairman, also retired that year.

In September 1999 GEAC completed an acquisition that would transform the company into a leading provider of enterprise resource planning (ERP) solutions. It acquired British-based JBA Holdings PLC for C$205.5 million. JBA was one of the world's largest mid-market ERP software companies. Its 1998 revenue exceeded C$500 million, and the company serviced more than 4,500 customers in more than 50 countries in industries such as food and beverage, apparel, automotive supply, and electronics. Following the acquisition, GEAC's projected annual revenue would exceed C$1.3 billion for the combined companies, which would have more than 30,000 customers and 6,000 employees. GEAC claimed it would be the fourth largest ERP software company in the world after SAP, Oracle Corp., and PeopleSoft Inc.

JBA became GEAC's ERP division, with former JBA CEO Ken Briddon as its head. The JBA name and its products and services would remain unchanged. Its main ERP product line was System 21 for mid-size companies running IBM's AS/400 mainframe. System 21 was completely web-enabled, gave companies the ability to launch themselves as e-businesses, and ran on GEAC's @ctive enterprise technology. Following the acquisition GEAC and IBM formed a strategic alliance to provide comprehensive e-business solutions. The alliance gave GEAC access to new customers and revenue opportunities.

Other acquisitions completed in 1999 included the Australian-based Cybergraphic Systems Ltd. for C$16 million. With annual revenue of approximately C$22 million, Cybergraphic was an international provider of integrated information management solutions for editorial, advertising, pagination, and Internet functions of the publishing industry. Its customers included major newspaper groups such as Hollinger, Knight-Ridder, News Corp. and the Fairfax Group. GEAC also acquired the financial and human resources management systems business of Clarus Corporation. Based in Atlanta, Georgia, Clarus had 1998 revenue of more than $40 million and some 300 North American customers.

For fiscal 2000 GEAC reported a 26.5 percent increase in revenues to C$990.1 million (US$669 million). Net income was C$49.1 million. President and CEO Douglas Bergeron noted that GEAC was on track to reach C$2 billion in revenues over the next three years. The company's strategy was to build a "branded global business from a highly fragmented marketplace," according to Bergeron. GEAC completed 11 acquisitions in fiscal 2000.

Acquisitions completed between January 2000 and the end of April 2000 included the real estate unit of GTE Enterprise Initiatives, Inc., a subsidiary of GTE Corp. that provided Multiple Listing Systems (MLS) for the real estate industry. This unit, with annual revenue of C$19 million, would be merged with GEAC's Interealty division headquartered in Vienna, Virginia. GEAC also acquired the remaining 49 percent of JBA s.r.o., an Eastern European distributor of System 21 software and solutions. Another European acquisition involved Denmark's RunTime, which provided e-Customer Relationship Management (eCRM) solutions to the apparel, footwear, and textile industries. GEAC also expanded its Publishing Systems division by acquiring Gazette Technologies from Gazette Communications, Inc. Gazette's key product was MarketInfo, a software suite used by newspapers to provide demographic analyses of specific newspaper markets.

In May 2000 GEAC entered the application services provider (ASP) market by launching Pyramaz as a wholly owned subsidiary. Pyramaz specialized in ERP e-business infrastructure solutions and other e-business services. GEAC would offer Pyramaz solutions as an option to all of its more than 10,000 ERP customers. Customers could reduce the cost of ownership by utilizing Pyramaz's ASP services. Pyramaz e-Purchase was the first integrated solution offered by the ASP, with Business Intelligence applications and eCRM solutions to follow.

In July 2000 GEAC sold its SmartStream Banking Systems (SBS) business for C$160 million to an investor group led by European venture capital firm 3i. For fiscal 2000 SBS had generated C$23 million in revenue. In May GEAC had purchased SBS's main competitor, Management Data GmbH, which more than doubled the size of SBS's business. The sale of SBS was part of GEAC's strategy to "unlock the value" that existed in its non-core vertical market businesses. In March 2000 the company had spun off Interealty.com as a wholly-owned subsidiary.

Toward the end of 2000 GEAC underwent another change in senior management. In October Douglas Bergeron resigned as president and CEO, as well as from the board of directors. Chairman William Nelson was appointed interim CEO. John Caldwell was elected to the board of directors and named interim president and COO. Caldwell subsequently became GEAC's president and CEO. He was previously president and CEO of CAE Inc., a Canadian technology company that specialized in commercial and military flight simulation. Nelson was replaced by Charles S. Jones as the company's non-executive chairman of the board.

Looking ahead for 2001 and beyond, GEAC was strongly positioned in the ERP market for mid-size companies and ranks as the fifth-largest ERP software company in the world. During 2000 the company demonstrated its commitment to increase shareholder value, reduce overall debt, and improve the firm's financial position by divesting its banking systems business, which it considered a non-core vertical market. Having acquired more than 40 companies and products from 1990 through 2000, GEAC remains committed to growth through the selective acquisition of mature application software companies with substantial revenues.

Principal Subsidiaries

Interealty.com; Pyramaz.

Principal Divisions

SmartEnterprise Solutions; Publishing Systems; Hotel Systems; Library Systems; Network and Technical Services; Restaurant Systems.

Principal Competitors

J.D. Edwards & Co.; SAP; Lawson Software; Oracle Corp.; PeopleSoft Inc.

Further Reading

Cibbarelli, Pamela R., "Cibbarelli's Surveys: User Ratings of GEAC's Advance Software," *Computers in Libraries,* September 1993, p. 63.

Cimino, Daniela, "DBS Joins GEAC," *Software Magazine,* December 1996, p. 28.

"Dun and Who?," *Computerworld,* November 18, 1996, p. 53.

Gaughan, Thomas M., "GEAC Complements Itself by Purchasing CLSI," *American Libraries,* January 1993, p. 9.

"GEAC Computer Gobbles up Remanco," *Nation's Restaurant News,* June 29, 1998, p. 41.

Kalawsky, Keith, "Soft Selloff," *Canadian Business,* August 21, 2000, p. 9.

Kerstetter, Jim, "Sybase Relationship Could Be D&B's Achilles' Heel," *PC Week,* November 4, 1996, p. 27.

Lee, Betty, "High-Tech Investing," *Canadian Business,* April 1984, p. 131.

Martin, Jim, "GEAC Acquires JBA," *Midrange Systems,* November 8, 1999, p. 1.

"New Owner GEAC Splits up D&B Software Divisions," *PC Week,* November 25, 1996, p. 27.

Rosenberg, Jim, "Collier-Jackson Sold to Canadian Firm," *Editor & Publisher,* August 13, 1994, p. 30.

——, "System Vendors' Industry Outlook," *Editor & Publisher,* February 7, 2000, p. 33.

Roy, Piali, "How to Grow & Prosper," *Canadian Business,* Summer 1996, p. 54.

Saffady, William, "Integrated Library Systems for Microcomputers and Mainframes: A Vendor Study, Part 2," *Library Technology Reports,* March-April 1994, p. 157.

Silburt, David, "Hitting the Books," *Canadian Business,* July 1985, p. 18.

Vadlamudi, Pardhu, "Dun & Bradstreet Software Gets New Owner," *InfoWorld,* October 28, 1996, p. 19.

"The VAR Wire," *VARbusiness,* April 26, 1999, p. 9.

Weston, Randy, "GEAC to Focus on Financial, Human Resources Apps," *Computerworld,* April 7, 1997, p. 12.

——, "Transfer of Ownership Makes D&B Users Wary," *Computerworld,* October 28, 1996, p. 16.

Williams, Kathy, and James Hart, "Collier-Jackson Shifts Its Vision," *Management Accounting (USA),* October 1994, p. 22.

—David P. Bianco

Gerresheimer Glas AG

Mörsenbroicher Weg 191
D-40470 Düsseldorf
Germany
Telephone: (49) (211) 6181-0
Fax: (49) (211) 6181-295
Web site: http://www.gerresheimer.com

Public Company
Incorporated: 1864
Employees: 6,100
Sales: DM 1.47 billion ($750 million) (1999)
Stock Exchanges: Frankfurt/Main Dusseldorf Hamburg Berlin
Ticker Symbol: GERG.F
NAIC: 327213 Glass Container Manufacturing; 327212 Other Pressed and Blown Glass and Glassware Manufacturing

Gerresheimer Glas AG, headquartered in Germany, is the leading manufacturer in both Europe and the United States of packaging systems for the pharmaceutical, laboratory, and cosmetic industries. The company's product range includes high-quality specialty glass, such as small glass containers and glass tubes, as well as plastic packaging products for the medical sector. Gerresheimer Glas operates 19 production companies in seven countries—including the United States, Poland, Belgium, the United Kingdom, France, and Italy. About 73 percent of the total sales of Gerresheimer Glas are generated outside Germany. About two-thirds of all Gerresheimer Glas employees work abroad. Formerly owned by German power giant VIAG, Gerresheimer Glas was sold to the investment bank Investcorp in the spring of 2000.

1860s Origins of World's Largest Glass Bottle Factory

Ferdinand Heye, the founder of Gerresheimer Glas, grew up in a merchant family in Bremen, Germany. Early in the 19th century, his parents bought shares in the Glashütte Schauenstein, a glass factory in Obernkirchen at the river Weser, and later invested in two more glass factories. At the beginning of the 1860s, Ferdinand Heye purchased a property in Gerresheim near Dusseldorf where all the necessary ingredients for glassmaking were available: sand, soda ash, limestone, and coal. In 1864, Ferdinand Heye founded his own glass manufacturing business. One year later, the first glassworks started operation with twelve glassblowers. Only two years later, a third glassworks started production in Gerresheim, and in 1871, Ferdinand Heye's factory operated six altogether. In that same year, the Gerresheimer Glas factory produced 7.8 million bottles, placing it in the top echelons of German glass manufacturers.

In the middle of the 19th century glassmaking technology was still in its early stages. Several hundred kilograms of each raw material were put together in a ''harbor,'' a huge pot furnace where they were heated and melted together. Glassblowers took small amounts of the fluid glass mass out of the furnace and shaped them into bottles by blowing into their glassmaker's pipe—an iron pipe that was about 1.2 meters long and about 10 millimeters wide. The glassblowers owned their own pipes, whose length varied depending on the size of the bottle to be made. The fire that heated the furnaces was hard to control so that melting and glassblowing alternated in irregular cycles with many interruptions. A new technology developed by German engineer Friedrich Siemens was introduced in 1874 that made a regular 24-hour production cycle possible. The melting process began at noon and glassmaking started between four and five o'clock in the morning. In 1881, new tank furnaces were introduced at Ferdinand Heye's factory that allowed a continuous production cycle without interruptions. The glass mixture traveled through three zones inside the oven while melting, and the uninterrupted flow of material was supported by continuously feeding the ovens and removing glass mass.

The fact that Ferdinand Heye set up shop at a railroad station near the river Rhine was crucial to his success in the market. The first major customers of the Gerresheimer Glas factory were vineyards along the Rhine and Mosel rivers who converted their packaging from pitchers and casks to glass bottles. Germany's economic upswing after the founding of the German empire in 1871 resulted in increased demand for quality wines,

Company Perspectives:

Wherever You May Be. *The Gerresheimer group is a worldwide network with 19 production facilities. We are expanding our international activities and pursue single-mindedly the "global approach." We are never far away and are prepared to meet your demands—oriented towards quality, service and efficiency.*

sparkling wine, and liquor. Improved technologies for brewing and preserving beer fueled shipments of bottled beer in the 1880s. Another emerging market was the rising number of German bottlers of mineral water who also switched over from clay jugs to glass bottles. Every owner of a mineral water spring used his own bottles with an individual design and the bottler's identifying mark molded into the glass. In 1875, Ferdinand Heye took a trip to Breslau in East Prussia to speak at a meeting of German mineral spring water owners. He convinced them to use a uniform shaped bottle and stick a paper label on the front with all the necessary information which made it possible for them to reuse any kind of mineral water bottle. As a result the production process for the bottles could be standardized at the Gerresheimer Glas factory.

However, the dynamic growth of production capacity at Gerresheim called for an expansion into new markets. In 1882, the first glass bottles made in Gerresheim were shipped overseas. Only five years later half of the factory's total output was shipped up the Rhine river to other countries. Continuous expansion and modernization fueled the company's further growth. Only twenty years after it was founded, the Gerresheimer Glas factory was the world's biggest manufacturer of glass bottles. In 1886 the factory's output amounted to 45 million bottles a year.

A Nomadic Profession Settles in Gerresheim in the 1880s

Because of the factory's dynamic growth, Ferdinand Heye was under pressure to find enough skilled glassblowers to meet demand. At that time, being a glassblower meant living the life of a nomad, following the glassworks around the country. Glassworks depended on charcoal for melting the glass ingredients, so they moved from one forest to the next until they ran out of wood again. Experienced glassblowers were sought after and well-paid professionals because the level of their skill determined the quantity and quality of the bottles they made. Always in search of better opportunities, these workers did not maintain a high degree of loyalty to single employers.

The first glassblowers for Heye's factory came from the area around the river Weser and later from other German glassmaking centers such as Thuringia and Prussia. However, the introduction of the new glass melting tubs in 1881 increased the demand for more glassblowers significantly, and Heye had to turn eastward to find them. To attract glassblowers from far away places such as East Prussia, Poland, the Baltic States, the Netherlands, and even Russia to his factory, Heye offered them free housing. To accommodate his work force the entrepreneur invested in several apartment buildings which soon developed into a small suburb. The apartments had special features such as soundproof bedrooms without windows to make it as easy as possible for the workers to sleep at any given time. This was important because the work regimen was dictated by the factory's production cycles. Whenever a batch of glass in a furnace was ready for blowing, messengers were sent to the workers to wake them up for their next ten-hour shift. After two ten-hour shifts, work at the melting tub was interrupted for four hours.

To keep his glassblowers happy Heye expanded their benefits package far beyond anything that was common at that time. Known for their interest in music, socializing, sports, and education, Heye provided his glassblowers with a huge "Volksgarten," including a music pavilion. A gymnasium, a swimming pool, and several rooms that could be used for educational events were added later. As early as 1867, Ferdinand Heye had a health insurance program for his workers. In 1882 he added a pension fund and accident insurance. The glassblowers' wives and daughters were also offered jobs at the glass factory, such as making bottle caps, as well as work that could be done either in their own homes, such as sewing sacks for packaging bottles, or at a nearby textile factory. Tuition for school children of employees of the Gerresheimer Glas factory was also paid by the company.

As a consequence of the glass factory's dynamic growth, the population of Gerresheim grew sevenfold between 1864 and 1900. The number of workers at Ferdinand Heye's company more than tripled within ten years, from about 500 in 1880 to 1,700 a decade later. During that same period of time, the factory's output also increased more than threefold, from 14 million to over 47 million. Around 1900, about half of the 11,500 Gerresheim inhabitants were directly or indirectly connected with Ferdinand Heye's glass factory. To secure future growth, Ferdinand Heye transformed the family business into a stock company in 1888. It was now called the Actien-Gesellschaft der Gerresheimer Glashüttenwerke, vorm. Ferd. Heye. The founder retained 80 percent of the share capital. Only seven months later, on July 26, 1889, Ferdinand Heye died.

A Single Machine Changes Everything in 1907

After Ferdinand Heye's death, Hermann Heye, at age 23 the oldest of the founder's five sons, took over the family business. He had learned glassmaking from scratch and was well prepared for his new responsibilities. Within a short period of time Hermann Heye earned a reputation in Germany and abroad.

At the beginning of the 1890s, Gerresheimer Glas bottles were shipped to every continent, including England and the United States, the bases of the company's main competitors. After the end of the Spanish-American War, Gerresheimer Glas bottles were exported again to Latin America, mainly Havana and Puerto Rico. By the end of the century, Gerresheimer glass bottles were even being shipped to West India to be filled with rum. After the turn of the century, a wave of consolidation transformed the European glassmaking industry. Smaller glassworks lost ground because of their lower productivity. Glassblowers left them and went to work for the bigger factories, which in turn were taken over by the market leaders. Its new company structure served Gerresheimer Glas well because it

Key Dates:

1864: Ferdinand Heye starts his own business with 12 glassblowers.
1886: Ferdinand Heye is the world's largest glass bottle maker.
1907: First contacts with world market leader Owens and the operation of the first Owens glassblowing machine in Europe.
1959: Owens-Illinois, Inc. acquires 50.1 percent of Gerresheimer Glas shares.
1987: Gerresheimer Glas buys glass tubes makers in Germany, Italy, and the United Kingdom.
1990: German VIAG concern becomes majority shareholder of Gerresheimer Glas.
1994: The company acquires American glassmaker OI Kimble FTS Inc.
2000: Investment bank Investcorp agrees to take over Gerresheimer Glas in a $200 million deal.

provided the necessary capital to secure its leading position in the market. Between 1894 and 1904, Gerresheimer Glas acquired ten additional glass factories. In 1904, Gerresheimer Glas started the production of wired glass, which became popular in construction as translucent building material for railroad stations and halls.

Hermann Heye also played a major role in the introduction of a breakthrough technology to his company. As early as 1902, the production cycle at Gerresheimer Glas had been changed to three shifts. In 1907 Heye traveled to a trade show in Manchester, England, where the Owens machine, an American invention, was being shown in Europe for the first time. The new machine was able to produce 16,000 glass bottles a day—as much as 75 glassblowers were able to make in a day's work. Realizing the potential for his industry Heye, acquired an option for a license on the patent for the European market. However, he was not able to finance this endeavor on his own. To raise the money he had to win other European glass container makers over to his idea. His efforts resulted in the founding of an industry association of European glass bottle manufacturers—the Europäischer Verband der Flaschenfabriken. The new organization led by Heye was finally able to acquire the patent. In May 1908 the first Owens machine in Europe started production at Gerresheimer Glas.

To avoid extensive layoffs, Heye negotiated with Owens, by that time the world market leader of glass containers, to introduce the new machines only gradually into Europe. Even during World War I, Owens kept the agreement although it was encouraged by England to breach it. By 1925, all glass bottles at Gerresheimer Glas were made by Owens machines.

A New Era of Expansion Begins in 1932

Gerresheimer Glas survived the hard times of World War I and the economic depression of the 1920s. In 1932 Gerresheimer Glas took over Glashütte Achern, another German glass manufacturer which was located near the vineyards of southern Germany. Another acquisition followed in 1940 when Gerresheimer Glas bought a 50-percent share in Glashütte Budenheim, located near Mainz, another center of German wine country. One year later, another company was bought in Bavarian Amberg, not far from the large number of Bavarian breweries.

Hermann Heye died in the same year World War II broke out. Production came to a complete halt at the end of the war, but Gerresheimer Glas started making flat glass and glass containers again at the end of 1945. New technical manager Leo Breuer launched a modernization program in 1946, resulting, among other things, in the introduction of new gob-forming machines and the erection of two new furnaces with a melting area of 1,650 square feet and a batch house where the glass mass could be mixed, weighed, and handled automatically. By 1958 the Owens machines had been replaced by the new rotating R7-machines and IS-multiple-section-machines. In the same year a new plant was built in Oldenburg in northern Germany. Altogether by 1958, the Gerresheimer Glas group operated six glass production facilities.

1959 marked the year when Gerresheimer Glas lost its independence. In that year one of the company's main competitors, American company Owens-Illinois, Inc., acquired 50.1 percent of the capital of Gerresheimer Glas, which was upgraded to 75.7 percent three years later. In 1960 a technical assistance agreement was signed with the parent company which gave Gerresheimer Glas access to Owen's technical know-how. To meet the ever-growing goals for glass output, Gerresheimer Glas began hiring workers from abroad once again. By 1971, 27 percent of the company's work force came from outside Germany.

During the 1960s, Gerresheimer Glas increased its core market and expanded into new fields. New glass containers were introduced for baby food and instant products. Gerresheimer Glas also expanded into plastic container and corrugated carton boxes through its new subsidiaries Gerro Plastik and Gerro Karton, expanding its scope to become a packaging materials group. In the 1970s and 1980s Gerresheimer Glas secured a leading position in the market for glass containers. In 1971, the company took over Lohr-based Spessarter Hohlglaswerke, a firm that specialized in small containers; it also took over pipe-glass manufacturer Bünder Glas GmbH in 1987 and glass container maker Glashüttenwerke Holzminden GmbH & Co., and glass tubes producer Fritz GmbH & Co. in 1989.

Coping with Globalization in the 1990s

At the beginning of the 1990s Gerresheimer Glas changed owners. The company was taken over by German energy conglomerate VIAG, which bought 51 percent of its shares. During the 1990s Gerresheimer Glas focused on its core business and set its sights on international expansion. In 1991, the company acquired the German leader in the specialty glass market—Tettauer Glashüttenwerke AG. Two years later the plastic and carton manufacturing subsidiaries were sold. In 1995 Gerresheimer Glas acquired Gebrüder Stoevesandt AG, another leading German glass container manufacturer specializing in products for the beverage and food industry.

International expansion began in 1994 with the acquisition of OI Kimble FTS Inc., an American manufacturer of glass tubes. Three years later Gerresheimer Glas bought a 60-percent share in Belgian glassworks Nouvelles Verreries de Momignies S.A., a manufacturer of glass containers for perfume and cosmetics. Another acquisition that year was a 61.53-percent share in Polish glass and plastic container manufacturer Boleslawiek Fabryka Materalów Medycznych Polfa Spolka Akcyjna, a company that specialized in packaging solutions for pharmaceuticals and other health care products. Through American company Kimble USA Inc., Gerresheimer Glas was also involved in Enbosa, a joint venture with Mexican Vitro S.A., to set up a new subsidiary for making glass containers for the pharmaceutical industry in Argentina.

In August 1999 Gerresheimer Glas took another major strategic step. In order to be able to completely focus on the fast growing markets for pharmaceutical, laboratory, and cosmetics packaging systems, the company sold its standard glass container business for the food and beverage industry. When German power conglomerates VIAG and VEBA decided to merge in 1999 to form Germany's largest energy supplier, Gerresheimer Glas went on sale again. In spring 2000, the investment bank Investcorp based in Bahrain signed an agreement with VIAG to take over a 72.96 percent-stake for $206 million. Based on the booming global pharmaceutical industry, Investcorp expected Gerresheimer Glas to grow further.

Principal Subsidiaries

Spessart Glas GmbH; Gerro Plast GmbH Kunststoffartikel; Tettauer Glashüttenwerke AG; Bünder Glas GmbH; Fritz GmbH & Co. KG; Nouvelles Verreries de Momignies S.A. (Belgium; 60%); FBG Trident Ltd. (United Kingdom); Kimble Italiana S.p.A. (Italy); Verretubex S.A. (France); The Anchor Glass Company Ltd. (United Kingdom); Kimble USA Inc.; Boleslawiek Fabryka Materialów Medycznych ''Polfa'' S.A. (Poland, 99.8%).

Principal Competitors

Schott Glas; Pilkington plc; Cristaleria Espanola SA; Compagnie de Saint-Gobain; Owens-Illinois, Inc.

Further Reading

100 Jahre Gerresheimer Glas, Dusseldorf-Gerresheim, Germany: A.G. der Gerresheimer Glashüttenwerke, vorm. Ferd. Heye, 1964.

Gross, Herbert, *Die Zukunft der Glaspackung*, Dusseldorf, Germany: Econ Verlag GmbH, 1964.

''Innovations in Glass,'' *BUSINESS*, September 1997.

''Investcorp Eyes Glass Acquisition,'' *MEED: Middle East Economic Digest*, April 21, 2000, p. 6.

—Evelyn Hauser

Givaudan SA

5, Chemin de la Parfumerie
1214 Vernier
Switzerland
Telephone: (41) 22 780 9111
Fax: (41) 22 780 9150
Web site: http://www.givaudan.com

Public Company
Incorporated: 1895
Employees: 5,075 (2000)
Sales: $1.31 billion (2000 est.)
Stock Exchanges: Swiss Munich NASDAQ NM
Ticker Symbol: GIVN (Swiss); 938427 (Munich); GVDBF (NASDAQ NM)
NAIC: 311942 Spice and Extract Manufacturing; 325199 All Other Basic Organic Chemical Manufacturing

A company whose historical roots date back to the beginnings of the modern flavor and fragrance industry in the late eighteenth century, Givaudan SA of Vernier, Switzerland is one of the leading creators of fragrances and flavors in the world with sales that reached $1.31 billion in 2000. Givaudan became a public company when it was spun off from its parent company, the pharmaceutical giant Roche in 2000. Givaudan produces flavor and fragrance compounds for a variety of products; its Cincinnati-based flavor division supplies the ''taste'' in food products ranging from soft drinks to soups, and its fragrance division headquartered in Switzerland provides the aroma in perfumes and personal care and household products. More than 30 percent of women's fine perfumes, including Poison by Christian Dior, Obsession by Calvin Klein, and Opium by Yves Saint Laurent, owe their signature scents to Givaudan's fragrance scientists. While Givaudan's corporate headquarters are in Switzerland, it maintains factories and operating facilities in over thirty countries. A leader in technical innovation since its founding, Givaudan devotes over $98 million per year on research and development and has twice won Fragrance Foundation Awards for technological breakthroughs.

Pioneers in Perfumery

Givaudan was founded as a Zurich perfume factory in 1895 by brothers Leon and Xavier Givaudan. In 1898, after a local bakery complained that the perfume production was hurting sales—fumes from the factory made the bread smell like violets—the brothers moved operations across the Rhone to Vernier near Switzerland.

The industry of perfume-making was undergoing a major change at this time. The first synthetic fragrance, coumarin (the scent of new-mown hay), had been produced in 1868. Prior to this time all perfumes had to be distilled directly from natural ingredients. This process was expensive and time-consuming. As many as 8,000 rose or jasmine blossoms were needed to create one gram of essential oil, meaning that commercial perfumes were only available to the wealthy. During the next 20 years, many other synthetic scents, including musk, vanilla, and violet, were produced. Many fragrance houses saw the new synthetics as a threat, calling them a ''corrupting influence'' on the art of perfumery. The Givaudan brothers, however, saw great opportunity in synthetics. Synthetics could be produced at a much lower cost than natural essential oils. The Givaudans sought to enlarge the market for synthetic perfume chemicals by producing them inexpensively and on a much larger scale than had previously been possible. They invested their early profits in increasing their research facilities, and Givaudan became one of the pioneers in commercial production of fragrance ingredients that would become industry staples such as synthetic musks, phenyl ethyl alcohol, and ionones. Givaudan was also among the first companies that promoted the use of fragrance in cosmetics and soaps.

Givaudan's focus on synthetic fragrance ingredients did not diminish the importance of natural perfumes in their business. The company blended natural and synthetic ingredients to widely expand its palette of scents, and it focused much of its energy on locating exotic natural scents all over the world to be duplicated in the Givaudan laboratories. This practice would remain a focus for Givaudan throughout the life of the company, and would drive later technological advances. Dr. Ernest Geurter, the company's vice president and technical director in the years preceding World War II, himself traveled all over the world in pursuit of indigenous oils and fragrances.

Company Perspectives:

At Givaudan, we believe that undisputed leadership in flavours and fragrances depends on creating what we call "sensory advantage" for our customers. Creating sensory advantage depends on our ability to bring together nature, creativity, science, technology, and business. To do this, our company has defined three core values:

Customer Focus—Our commitment to customer service comes first and foremost. We continually strive to leverage our global capabilities, bringing superior benefits to all of our customers.

Sense of Urgency—To be the undisputed leader means we constantly challenge ourselves, creating and nurturing a performance-driven company culture that also embraces openness and creativity.

Ambitious Innovation—Innovation means more than investing heavily in research and development to come up with new molecules and ingredients; it also means envisioning bold new concepts in manufacturing, marketing, delivery and more. In short, it means innovating throughout every aspect of our industry and exploiting those innovations for the benefit of all our customers worldwide.

International Expansion

Givaudan thrived during the years between the turn of the century and the First World War. Synthetics had become widely accepted in all fragrance markets, and manufactured perfume became available to the general public for the first time. The growth enjoyed by the company sparked its international expansion, and Givaudan opened a factory in Lyon, France in 1917. In 1924, Givaudan branched out into the United States with the opening of its plant in the Delwanna section of Clifton, New Jersey. The Delwanna/Clifton facility became Givaudan's major manufacturer, and the years between 1924 and 1948 saw a significant increase in the company's output. In that period, the company's production of synthetic aromatics for fragrance and flavors grew from 2 million pounds to 20 million pounds per year.

A School for Perfumers

In 1946, to ensure qualified personnel for the future, Givaudan opened its own perfume school in Grasse in southern France, becoming the only fragrance company in the world to possess such a facility. Graduates of the Givaudan school were required to identify 2,800 synthetic odors and 140 natural ones at the end of a three- to five-year course of study. In 2001, the school was the oldest perfumery school in the world, and the company estimated that one out of three fragrances existing in the world had been created by Givaudan-trained perfumers.

The Roche Acquisition

The company continued to grow throughout the 1940s, 50s, and into the early 60s, opening factories in Whyteleaf, England, Sao Paolo, Brasil, and Sant Celoni, Spain. In 1963, Givaudan was acquired by Roche, a Swiss pharmaceutical company best known for the drugs Valium and Librium. The Givaudan acquisition was part of Roche's expansion into new markets such as chemical, perfume, and diagnostic instruments. The following year, Roche continued its expansion into the perfume market by acquiring Roure, a French perfume concern famous for developing the first "designer" fragrance ("Shocking" for Elsa Schiaparelli).

As a subsidiary of Roche, Givaudan continued to grow, opening facilities and acquiring concerns throughout the world, including the chemical company ICMESA (Industrie Chimiche Meda Societa Azionaria) in Seveso, Italy near Milan in 1969. In the mid-seventies, Givaudan developed its Headspace technology, which allowed perfumers to capture living smells in the laboratory without touching the source of the scent. Headspace technology would become an industry standard for over twenty years, with all major fragrance houses developing their own versions.

Disaster in Seveso

Seven years after becoming a subsidiary of Givaudan, the ICMESA Seveso factory was the site of an infamous environmental accident that would plague the company for years to come. On July 10, 1976, an explosion in the factory released a cloud of hazardous gases into the air. The cloud contained dioxin, a highly toxic chemical known to cause cancer, birth defects, and extensive kidney, liver, and lung damage. One thousand acres surrounding the factory were contaminated. Damages totaled over $78 million; hundreds of people were evacuated and thousands of animals died from eating exposed food. The Roche company history reports that "From the beginning Roche and Givaudan [made] every effort to redress the damage done," but later reports faulted both the company and government officials for delaying action. According to *Business Week* in October of 1976, while the company cordoned off part of the factory immediately after the disaster, no announcement regarding the danger was made for a full week. Full scale evacuation of the affected population did not begin until two weeks following the accident. Investigations and court proceedings would continue for over 18 years following the disaster, and Roche, Givaudan, and ICMESA would end up paying over 19 billion lira in damages in court-ordered judgments and out-of-court settlements. The disaster sparked fears about dioxin at Givaudan's New Jersey plant, but an inspection conducted by the Environmental Protection Agency in 1983 found no traces of the toxin at the factory or in the surrounding community.

Givaudan in the Nineties

The early 1990s saw Givaudan joining forces with some of the world's oldest fragrance and flavor houses. In 1990, Givaudan merged with Fritzche, Dodge & Olcott, a perfume house established in 1796. In 1991, Roche combined its subsidiary Roure (established in 1820) with Givaudan, forming Givaudan Roure. The company would bear this name throughout the decade.

The 1990s were a decade of tremendous technical innovation for Givaudan Roure. In 1994, in an effort to keep up with the growing flavor demand, the company opened a new flavor manufacturing facility in Hanover, New Jersey. At its opening, the facility was heralded as the most technically advanced in the industry. The plant was fully-automated and featured a custom-

Key Dates:

1895: Company founded by Leon and Xavier Givaudan in Zürich, Switzerland.
1898: Company builds chemical factory in Vernier, Geneva.
1917: Factory in Lyon, France, is built.
1924: Facility opens in Clifton, NJ.
1946: Givaudan opens its own perfume school.
1950: Company opens factories in UK and Brazil.
1960: Company opens factory in Spain.
1963: Pharmaceutical company Roche acquires Givaudan.
1964: Roche acquires Roure.
1976: Accident at Icmesa (a subsidiary of Givaudan) plant in Seveso, Italy, contaminates surrounding areas with dioxin and other chemicals.
1989: Givaudan acquires Reidel-Arom.
1990: Givaudan acquires Fritzche, Dodge & Olcott.
1991: Company is merged with Roure, forming Givaudan Roure.
1995: Shanghai Givaudan Roure Ltd. founded in Shanghai.
1997: Company acquires Tastemaker.
2000: Roche spins-off Givaudan Roure as Givaudan SA, company listed on Swiss Stock exchange.

built compounding facility run by a ''paperless'' environment. In the past, formulators would read orders from a batch printout, then manually retrieve the raw materials needed to fill the order. With the new compounding system, operators could simply input the materials and amounts, and the machine would fill the order automatically. In 1995, Givaudan Roure introduced a new sunscreen agent, Parsol 1789, the first organic material to provide protection against both short and long UVA rays.

Givaudan Roure developed its revolutionary technology Scent Trek in 1996, earning the Fragrance Foundation's first Fifi Innovation Technology of the Year Award. Scent Trek expanded the capabilities of the older Headspace technology by allowing perfume scientists to gather scents from plants and flowers outside the laboratory. The new technology was a boon for perfumers and ecologists alike. A much wider variety of scents was now available, as scientists could now extract scent from plants that could not be grown in a laboratory. Scent Trek extracted the essence of a plant without killing it, allowing for the capture of endangered rainforest scents. Scent Trek could also reproduce non-plant-based scents and undetected compounds of scents, called ''notes,'' to add complexity to perfumes. For example, when Givaudan created the Michael Jordan cologne Bijan, it used Scent Trek to sample notes from Jordan's favorite golf course, a leather baseball glove, and a Costa Rican beach.

1997 saw Givaudan Roure further expanding its flavor market with its merger with the US flavor company Tastemaster. Givaudan Roure acquired Tastemaster for $1.1 billion, and moved its flavor operations to Tastemaster's headquarters in Cincinnati. The merger gave the company 14.4 percent of the United States flavor market, and Givaudan Roure became the global leader in the flavors market. The acquisition was the first in a series of reorganization steps the company took that year, which included the closing of the manufacturing plant in Clifton, New Jersey operated by the company for nearly 50 years.

Independence

In December 1999, Roche announced its intention to spin off its flavors and fragrance interests and focus on its pharmaceutical business. The subsidiary Givaudan Roure became Givaudan SA and began trading on the Zurich Stock Exchange on June 8, 2000. The spin off left the basic structure of the Givaudan intact, and the company continued the rapid growth and development it had enjoyed as a Roche subsidiary. In August 2000, Givaudan opened a new factory in Bangalore, India, which doubled the company's existing production capabilities, and in November of that year, the company opened a new Sensory and Technology Centre in Shanghai.

In keeping with its tradition of exploring new technologies, in December 2000 Givaudan acquired a minority stake in the United States company DigiScents—which developed the use of scents on the Internet and in computer games—becoming its exclusive perfume supplier. In 2001, Givaudan earned a second Fifi award for technological innovation—this time for the Virtual Aroma Synthesizer, which allows for scent composition and modification via computer. In the past, a perfumer would compose a formula for a scent based on a customer's description, submit it to the laboratory to have a sample made, then deliver the sample to the customer at a later time. Any adjustments to the scent had to undergo the same time-consuming process, and since scent is difficult to translate into language, a perfume often had to undergo many adjustments before the customer was satisfied. The VAS allowed the perfumer and customer to sit down together to compose and manipulate scents in real time.

At Givaudan's annual shareholder's meeting in May 2001, the company's chairman, Dr. Henri B. Meier expressed optimism about Givaudan's continued growth as a business and as a technological pioneer. He spoke about the direction of Givaudan's technology development efforts: research in microbiology, and attempts to understand how the human sense organs break down flavors and scents and deliver them to the brain. While the company's overriding goal was to be the undisputed world leader in the fragrance and flavors market, Dr. Meier noted that future acquisitions must bring added value to the company. He cautioned shareholders, ''size at the expense of profit is not our ambition.''

Principal Divisions

Givaudan Fragrances Corp.; Givaudan Flavors Corp.

Principal Operating Units

Givaudan do Brasila Ltda. (Brazil); Shanghai Givaudan Ltd. (China); Givaudan France SA; Givaudan Singapore Pte. Ltd.; Givaudan Dübendorf Ltd. (Switzerland); Givaudan Flavors Corp. (USA); Givaudan Fragrances Corp. (USA).

Principal Competitors

International Fragrances & Flavors; Quest International; Firmenich.

Further Reading

Bedoukian, Paul Z., *Perfumery and Flavoring Synthetics,* Amsterdam: Elsevier, 1967.

Born, Pete, "Givaudan-Roure's Jean Amic's Farewell," *WWD*, March 6, 1998, p. 10.

Bruce, Gain, "A Bittersweet Wind Brings Concern," *Chemical Week*, December 3, 1997, pp. 34–36.

Chadderon, Lisa, "The Sweet Smell of Success," *Fast Company*, April 1998, p. 144.

Collings, Richard, "Givaudan Puts SEI in Charge of Fund," *Investment Management Weekly*, January 1, 2001, p. 3.

Cornwell, Rupert, "Seveso Trial Opens Amid Doubt about Waste," *Financial Times,* April 19, 1983, p. 2.

Davis, Don, "Spinoff for Givaudan," *Global Cosmetic Industry*, August 2000, p. 15.

Ennen, Steve, "A New Identity for Sensectinnati," *Food Processing*, January 2001, p. 48.

"European Report: Givaudan Launches into Scented Sites with American Digiscents Group," *European Report*, December 20, 2000, p. 1.

Floreno, Anthony, "Executive Q & A," *Chemical Market Reporter*, May 11, 1998, pp. 14–15.

——, "F & F Financial Results Show There's Growth in Industry," *Chemical Market Reporter*, January 26, 1998, p. 17.

——, "F & F Industry in Flux as Major Players Regroup," *Chemical Market Reporter*, April 14, 1997, pp. 4, 24.

——, "Givaudan Refocuses Vision on its Way to F & F Top Spot," *Chemical Market Reporter*, October 13, 1997, p. 28.

——, "Givaudan Reorganizes after Tastemaker Buy," *Chemical Market Reporter*, June 23, 1997, pp. 3, 22.

——, "Givaudan Shows Signs of Strength," *Chemical Marketing Reporter*, September 23, 1996, p. 7.

——, "Givaudan-Roure Announces Global Frag Restructuring," *Chemical Market Reporter*, April 6, 1998, p. 27.

——, "Headspace Methods Go Where Perfumers Haven't Gone Before," *Chemical Marketing Reporter*, May 13, 1996, p. 31.

"Former Givaudan CEO Faces 4-Month Jail Term," *WWD*, May 28, 1999, p. 12.

"Fragrance Maker Banks on SSA's BPCS," *Asia Computer Weekly*, July 20, 1998, p. 1.

"French Court Weighs Tainted Talc," *Chemical Week,* October 31, 1979. p. 22.

Gajilan, Arlyn Tobias, Bill Vourvoulias, and Beth Kwon, "Making Scents," *Newsweek*, July 13, 1998, p. 10.

Gallagher, Matthew, "Givaudan-Roure Opens High Tech Flavor Facility," *Chemical Marketing Reporter*, June 13, 1994, p. 30.

"Givaudan Consolidates Business, with New Site at Mount Olive, N.J.," *Chemical Market Reporter*, May 15, 2000, p. 33.

"Givaudan Corporation said today that it 'is pleased to report' . . . that the . . . EPA has found no traces of dioxin . . . [at] its Clifton N.J. plant," *PR Newswire Association, Inc.*, June 24, 1983.

"Givaudan May Give the Swiss a Miss," *Soap, Perfumery, and Cosmetics*, December 2000, p. 3.

"Givaudan Roure and Tastemaker Join Forces," *Dairy Foods*, August 1997, p. 48.

"Givaudan Roure Split," *Global Cosmetic Industry*, July 2000, p. 12.

"Givaudan Senses New Future Scents," *Cosmetics International*, November 25, 2000, p. 6.

Givaudan-Delawanna, Inc., *The Givaudan Index: Specifications of Synthetics and Isolates for Perfumery,* New York: Givaudan-Delawanna, Inc., 1949.

"Givaudan's Amic Planning to Retire," *WWD*, October 3, 1997, p. 9.

Goldemberg, Robert L., "Green Tea and Other Goodies," *Drug & Cosmetic Industry*, September 1994, p. 58.

Hasbach, Ann, "Process Attains 97 Percent Odor Removal," *Pollution Engineering*, May 1998, pp. 55–56.

Hume, Claudia, "Roche to Spin off Givaudan, Focus on Pharmaceuticals," *Chemical Week*, December 15, 1999, p. 11.

"India: Linc Scents Gains from Swiss Deal," *Businessline*, June 19, 1999, p. 1.

Landau, Peter, "Givaudan Roure Breaks Ground for New Manufacturing Plant," *Chemical Market Reporter*, August 31, 1998, p. 18.

Landau, Peter, "Roche Holdings to Spin off Givaudan-Roure F & F Entity," *Chemical Market Reporter*, December 13, 1999, p. 28.

"Major Reorganization at Givaudan Roure," *DCI*, November 1997, p. 6.

Mitchell, James K., "Seveso: A Paradoxical Classic Disaster," in *The Long Road to Recovery: Community Responses to Industrial Disaster,* Tokyo: United Nations University Press, 1996.

Molaro, Regina, "Givaudan's New Look," *Global Cosmetic Industry*, October 2000, p. 10.

Morris, Edwin, *Scents of Time: Perfume from Ancient Egypt to the 21st Century,* Boston: Bulfinch Press, 2000.

Naude, Alice, "Personal Care '95: Shades of Difference," *Chemical Marketing Reporter*, May 8, 1995, p. SR8.

Newman, Cathy, *Perfume: The Art and Science of Scent,* Washington DC: National Geographic Society, 1998.

Pillivuyt, Ghislaine, Pauline Mercier, and Doris Jakubec, *The Art of Perfume in the 18th Century—Les Flacons de la Séduction,* Paris: La Biblioteque des Arts, 1986.

"Probers Detail Dioxin Damage," *Chemical Week,* August 9, 1978, p. 20.

Sfiligoj, Eric, "The New Givaudan Roure: A Matter of Tastemaker," *Beverage World*, August 15, 1997, p. 88.

Snowden, Lynn, "Scent Trek," *Harper's Bazaar*, February 1996, pp. 80–81.

"Swiss Chemical Company Agrees to Out-of-Court Settlement," *Associated Press,* March 25, 1980.

"The Costly Aftermath of a Poison Cloud," *Business Week,* October 11, 1976, p. 32.

"The Experience of Three Scents of Inspiration," *Cosmetics International*, January 10, 2000, p. 3.

Topfer, Kurt, "Prestige Fragrances a Draw with Men in US Marketplace," *Chemical Marketing Reporter*, August 10, 1992, p. 5.

"U.S. Hexachlorophene Curbs Will Hit Hard at 3 Firms, Have Little Effect on Others," *Wall Street Journal*, September 25, 1972, p. 4.

Wicks, John, "Perfume Industry Expects Steady Growth," *Financial Times,* March 15, 1983, p. V.

Wilkinson, Stephanie, "Hands-on PC Training Works for Firm's Execs," *PC Week*, May 1, 1989, p. 59.

Young, Vicki, and Pete Born, "Givaudan Sets IPO on Zurich Exchange," *WWD*, June 8, 2000 p. 11.

—Lisa Whipple

Goss Holdings, Inc.

700 Oakmont Lane
Westmont, Illinois 60559-5546
U.S.A.
Telephone: (630) 850-5600
Fax: (630) 850-6310
Web site: http://www.gossgraphic.com

Private Company
Incorporated: 1885 as Goss Printing Press Company
Employees: 2,500
Sales: $600 million (2000 est.)
NAIC: 333293 Printing Machinery and Equipment Manufacturing

Goss Holdings, Inc., through its Goss Graphic Systems subsidiary, brings the written word in myriad form to readers around the world. Dominating North America's manufacture and distribution of web offset printing, Goss presses are the backbone of many internationally renowned newspapers including the *Chicago Tribune, Los Angeles Times, Miami Herald, New York Times, USA Today, Wall Street Journal,* the United Kingdom's *Financial Times,* Brazil's *Zero Hora,* China's *People's Daily,* Japan's *Yomiuri Shimbun,* and Norway's *Adresseavisen.* Additionally, Goss is a major force in the production of advertising inserts, controlling nearly three-quarters of that market. In 2000, the company emerged from Chapter 11 bankruptcy protection, battered though by no means beaten.

In the Beginning: 1885–92

Four years after the 1871 fire that devastated Chicago, a small printing company was established by brothers Samuel and Frederick Goss, and their primary financial backer, Jacob Walser, who provided working capital of $100,000 for the startup. Two others played a role in the formation of the company, Benjamin Babcock, who published periodicals locally, and attorney David Alland, who was representing Babcock's wife (who contributed $25,000 to the newly chartered company). The basis for the company was to design, build, and sell printing presses, and the Goss brothers had already built their first prototype, called the ''Clipper,'' a variation on a two-color printing press. Sam and Fred had found a way for the press to print on both sides of paper simultaneously by reversing one of its cylinders.

Though the small company secured orders for the Clipper press, its first few years were fraught with problems, including a fire that destroyed the manufacturing site and damaged two presses. Fred, Sam, and Jacob were undeterred and moved to new office and manufacturing space at the corner of Clinton Street and Jackson Boulevard. By this time, the Babcocks and David Alland had sold their shares back to Walser and the Gosses, and another person had come to Chicago to join the fledgling company. William ''Peanuts'' Goss, who also worked in the printing business, joined his older brothers and became Goss Printing Press Company's general superintendent, with Fred continuing in sales, Sam as chief designer, and Jacob as president and treasurer.

Within the next few years, Goss made a name for itself in the evolving printing industry, which had long been dominated by three companies: R. Hoe & Company, Walter Scott & Company, and Duplex Printing Press Company. Though the company's chief rivals were located outside Illinois, each had an office in Chicago and had secured prominent clients within the city. After weathering its first four years, Goss initiated plans to move to a larger facility in 1889. The next year the company bought 20,000 square feet of land on Rebecca Street (later Sixteenth Street) and built a two-story structure with ample room for manufacturing and management offices. The company officially began operation at 335–351 Rebecca Street in 1891, and remained there for the next six decades (which included 11 subsequent renovations and additions).

By 1892 Goss was gaining respect in the printing press business, but an inventor named Joseph L. Firm would soon give the company the impetus needed to best its competitors. Firm had been working on a new press for years and had received little support or respect from the industry; in fact, he was ignored and maligned. But Fred thought otherwise and invited Firm to Chicago to meet with Sam and Jacob. The Goss company then offered Firm ten annual payments of $2,500 for the rights and title to his invention, as well as a 10 percent royalty from any and all presses resulting from his original design. Firm's two-deck design became the basis for the Goss

Company Perspectives:

At Goss Graphic Systems, we aspire to be valued by our customers as true business partners, providing superior products and services that not only meet but anticipate their needs.

We constantly seek out the best talent, the freshest ideas, and the newest technologies to assure that our customers have a competitive edge. And we assure the highest quality in every product, part and service we deliver.

Straightline Newspaper Perfecting Press, which debuted in 1892. The Straightline press was faster and better designed than traditional presses and many newspaper producers took notice. But less than a year after the Straightlines were built and sold, Walter Scott's presses were rumored to have the same straight-lined design and had been attracting big sales.

Patents and Their Worth: 1893 to 1910

In 1893 the World's Columbian Exposition was held in Chicago and both the Clipper and Straightline presses were exhibited alongside rival machinery, including presses from Walter Scott & Company. Both Goss presses were award winners, testament to the young company's growing foothold in the industry. Yet part of Goss Printing Press Company's future was riding on the legal status of a Scott press, allegedly an imitation of a Goss Straightline press. Because Firm had patented his design, the Gosses and Walser felt they had the law on their side. They first wrote to Walter Scott, asking him to desist from using the trademarked technology, hoping to settle the matter outside the courts. After no favorable response or resolution, attorney Charles Pickard was hired to file a patent infringement suit against Scott in New Jersey federal court. The suit, filed in 1895, was resolved two years later when the judge sided with Scott, believing the newer press innovations were a natural progression of design and not from the patented work of Joseph Firm.

Disheartened, the Gosses and Walser were nevertheless determined to appeal, despite increasing financial hardship. Another of the Goss company's competitors, R. Hoe & Company, had jumped into the fray with an offer after the initial court proceedings went against Goss—Hoe's management offered to buy Firm's patent rights. Though certainly in need of funds, but still believing the validity of their claims would be upheld in court, the Gosses and Walser declined to sell outright, but did approve licensing rights for $125,000 to Hoe & Company. The cash infusion helped defray costs, legal and otherwise, but as the courtroom wrangling continued, Goss employees and shareholders began to have doubts about the company's fate. Then Hoe tendered an offer to acquire the company, and believing Goss Printing Press Company's future was in serious jeopardy, its principals decided to sell for $1.5 million.

Luckily for Goss and to the detriment of both Scott and Hoe, the U.S. Court of Appeals in Philadelphia overturned the lower court's decision and found in favor of Goss. The opinion reaffirmed that the press improvements were indeed from Firm's trademarked designs, and ordered Walter Scott & Company to not only stop manufacturing such presses but to give Goss a financial statement and restitution for all sales and profits made from the pirated innovations. The Goss brothers and Walser were thrilled with the ruling and thankful that Hoe & Company had found their selling price too steep—they now set out to prove to the printing industry just how valuable their company and its products could be.

By 1897 there were 125 variations of the Straightline press in use; ten of these were sold to printers in Canada, and another was sold to Cuba. Customers gave glowing testimonials and salesman Fred was quick to use them to sell presses to new clients throughout North America and beyond. Among the newspapers printed on Goss Straightline presses were Providence, Rhode Island's *Evening and Sunday Telegram,* the *Kansas City* (Missouri) *World, Chicago Journal, Detroit Free Press,* and *New York Tribune.* The next year the company scored its first major overseas order, selling and installing a Straightline press for Dublin's *Irish Daily Independent.* This was followed by a sale in Glasgow, Scotland, and similar receptions as Goss presses were introduced to the European continent. Within the next several years international demand from the United Kingdom, Australia, Chile, France, Holland, Italy, New Zealand, South Africa, and other countries grew at such a fast pace that Goss opened a manufacturing plant in Middlesex, England, in 1910 under the name of the Goss Printing Press Company of England, Limited.

Unprecedented Growth: 1911–28

While Goss Printing Press Company continued designing presses and improving them, the company had earned a reputation for excellence as Straightline presses became the pride of newspaper producers. Many Goss clients were so fond of their presses that the machines were prominently featured in their product advertisements, essentially giving Goss free advertising. Yet the company was shaken by the successive deaths of William in 1912, Jacob in 1913, and Fred in 1914. As the Chicago-based operation tried to cope with the deaths, the U.K. operation was falling apart. Despite some wartime manufacturing in early World War I, the Goss Printing Press Company of England suffered from poor management and the building and land were sold in 1916.

Throughout this dark period, the company carried on, in part due to Joseph Walser, Jacob's son, who had taken over for William in production and engineering. New presses and industry firsts were introduced, including the Flying Cam folder, the Semi-Rotary Press, and the "Comet"; then the company turned to producing gun mounts for the Navy after the U.S. entered World War I in 1917. After the war ended, Goss received a letter of commendation in 1918 from Franklin D. Roosevelt, then the assistant Secretary of the Navy. This year also marked the retirement of Sam Goss from the company.

The original founders of Goss Printing Press Company were now gone. Albert "Bert" Eddy, selected by Sam Goss as his successor, was running the company when the *Chicago Tribune*'s Robert McCormack chose Goss presses to revitalize his newspaper's production. The results were stellar and the basis for a long and prosperous relationship for both parties. Sales and profits were excellent, yet trouble loomed on the horizon and arrived after Joseph Walser's death in January 1921. For the next several years the board of directors was controlled by

Key Dates:

1885: Goss Printing Press Company is officially chartered in Chicago, Illinois, by Fred and Sam Goss, and Jacob Walser.
1891: New manufacturing facility on Rebecca Street opens.
1898: Company completes its first major European sale, to Dublin's *Irish Independent Press.*
1910: Goss opens its first international plant, in Middlesex, England.
1912: William "Peanuts" Goss dies; Joseph Walser joins company.
1913: Jacob Walser dies.
1914: Fred Goss dies.
1916: Middlesex plant is closed and sold.
1922: Sam Goss, last of the original founders, dies.
1957: Following a merger, company is renamed Miehle-Goss-Dexter Inc.
1969: Another merger, with North American Rockwell, leads to the new name MGD Graphics Systems.
1985: Goss business celebrates its centennial.
1996: Rockwell sells off the MGD Graphics Systems division to a New York investment firm, which retains a controlling interest; company is renamed Goss Graphic Systems, Inc.
1999: Company files for bankruptcy protection and reorganization.
2000: Goss emerges from Chapter 11 protection with strong sales.

Eddy, and discord grew among some of the company's management and Goss and Walser heirs. Three young men, however, came to the fore—Robert "Hook" Corbett, Joseph Riggs, and Curtis Crafts—and each had a profound effect on the company's future.

The Great Depression and Beyond: 1929–59

Though Bert Eddy had believed 1929 would be a great year for Goss, the collapse of Wall Street and the onset of the Great Depression put the company in peril. Corbett, Riggs, and Crafts bristled under Eddy's leadership, particularly his refusal to allow the building of a new prototype designed by Crafts or to consider moving to a single-story premises outside of Chicago. The three younger men eventually prevailed and scaled back Eddy's influence, only to find Goss sitting idle in 1933 with neither orders nor repair work to generate badly needed funds. Yet the inauguration of Franklin Roosevelt and implementation of his New Deal policies helped stabilize the printing industry, enough so that Crafts built his newfangled "anti-friction" press. The success or failure of the Anti-Friction Press meant either the resurgence of Goss or its demise; luckily for everyone involved the new press was a hit.

In addition to Crafts' accomplishment, Goss further reestablished itself in England where the company slowly rebuilt its reputation after selling off its Middlesex plant. After buying and renovating the printing operations of Joseph Foster & Sons outside London, Goss-Foster Limited was in business. Like its antecedent, the U.K. operation ran into problems, primarily personality conflicts and organizational disarray; also like its forerunner, another world war turned production to armaments. The same occurred in the Chicago manufacturing plant, when Goss once again worked on weaponry for the U.S. Navy.

After the conclusion of World War II, Goss went back to printing press design and the latest technological coup came with the introduction of the Goss Headliner Press, hailed by many as the "Press of the Future." The 18-ton Headliner presses were soon put into service at the nearby *Chicago Tribune,* and became the press of choice for many in the industry. Soon Goss management heard that rival Duplex Press Company, based in Battle Creek, Michigan, had fallen on hard times after completing wartime production and was nearing bankruptcy. Desperately in need of additional manufacturing space, Goss made a successful offer for Duplex and moved production of smaller press units to the Michigan facility.

In the 1950s the company continued expanding both domestically and overseas; the Battle Creek facility had been sold and operations moved to a 20-acre stretch of land in Cicero, Illinois, outside Chicago. Among the growing who's who of clients printing their newspapers on Goss equipment were the Birmingham, Alabama's *News* and *Age-Herald,* Minneapolis, Minnesota's *Star-Journal* and *Tribune,* the New York *Daily News, Chicago Tribune, Chicago Sun-Times,* and both the *Melbourne Herald* and the *Sydney Sun* in Australia. The company's good fortunes, however, had drawbacks as well: there were internal squabbles over stock, including some members' insistence on a public offering, and the growing fear that an outsider could acquire enough stock for a takeover attempt. To save Goss from being swallowed by a company with no interest other than profit, it was merged with another like-minded leader in the industry and renamed Miehle-Goss-Dexter, Inc. in 1957.

After the Merger: 1960s

Miehle-Goss-Dexter Inc. (MGD) became the world's largest manufacturer of printing presses and graphic arts equipment. During the 1960s came the company's first web offset press, the Suburban, developed at a new plant in Rockford, Illinois. The first Suburban order came from the *St. Louis Daily Record,* and others soon followed. The popularity of the web offset presses pushed Headliner presses somewhat into the background, though they were still in widespread use and had lured in more big-name clients, including the *New York Times*. Demand for the offset presses, though, was swift and plans were quickly underway to build a huge plant in Cedar Rapids, Iowa. The new $7 million manufacturing facility began filling orders in 1965 for newspaper producers in the United States, Canada, Europe, and South America.

Miehle-Goss-Dexter's next innovation was a fully-automated magazine press, first ordered by *Reader's Digest* and capable of printing up to 140 pages at a time. While MGD was thriving in the last years of the 1960s, even having made it onto the *Fortune* 500 list of top industrial companies at number 461, old foes had failed: both Walter Scott & Company and R. Hoe & Company had succumbed to hard times and had been swallowed by Wood Industries. Sales for MGD in 1968 had reached $154 million, and the company was riding high enough to once again find itself ripe for a merger or an outright acquisition.

Just such a scenario surfaced in 1968 when North American Rockwell, the aerospace and automotive company, indicated its interest in MGD. The initial discussions went nowhere until Rockwell executives announced they had bought up a considerable amount of MGD stock and were prepared to offer $31 a share to acquire a controlling interest. MGD management was surprised and dismayed; they had no thoughts of merging or being taken over and suddenly several other suitors came out of the woodwork to acquire the company. In 1969 MGD's board finally relented and chose Rockwell, which had upped its share price and seemed, at least to some, the lesser of the evils trying to corral the company. The merger's good news was the deep pockets Rockwell had available for expansion; Miehle-Goss-Dexter was reborn as MGD Graphics Systems of North American Rockwell.

Part of Rockwell: 1970s–80s

After the merger, the new division had its ups and downs, as did Rockwell. In 1973 North American Rockwell became Rockwell International to better represent its evolving global presence, and two years later was embroiled in a messy strike by members of the International Association of Machinists and Aerospace Workers, which precipitated the sale of the Cicero plant and leasing part of the premises back to Rockwell. Despite minor setbacks, the MGD Graphics division carried on, making improvements on its many presses and keeping such influential customers as the *New York Tribune* happy.

In 1982 and again in 1985 the division was restructured, segmenting into newspaper, commercial, and international units. Technology was also pushed to the forefront, and CAD/CAM (computer-aided design and computer-aided manufacturing) had been introduced. The first machine produced using the CAD/CAM system was the Headliner Offset, which was quickly assimilated into the industry and the first installed in Gainesville, Florida, to produce the *Gainesville Sun* (owned by the *New York Times)* and then put into use by the *Los Angeles Times* and London's *Daily Telegraph.* Nearby *Chicago Tribune,* one of the Goss company's longtime customers, built a state-of-the-art facility called the Freedom Center, equipped with over $77 million worth of offset printers bought from MGD. Several other world-renowned papers, including the *Wall Street Journal* and the new *USA Today,* were also printed on MGD machinery.

Reversals & Renewals: 1990s and Beyond

The MGD Graphics Systems division, though never exactly homogeneous with the rest of Rockwell International's operations, coexisted to mutual profit until the mid-1990s when rumors began circulating about the division's falling sales. The rumors were never confirmed, however, and 1995 year-end revenues seemed healthy at $700 million, with an operating profit of $66 million. Yet at the January 1996 Newspaper Association of America's Publishers Convention, Rockwell publicly announced its intention to sell off the graphics division for $600 million to a New York investment firm created by Stonington Partners Inc., which would own a controlling interest. The small company founded by Sam and Fred Goss and Jacob Walser was back: not only in name as Goss Graphic Systems, Inc., but as an independent company once again.

In 1997 Goss brought out the first printing press combining the old and the new—using conventional offset lithography with digital imaging. This press, called ADOPT/CP (Advanced Digital Offset Printing Technologies/Concept Press) was the next in the Goss company's long line of technological firsts and was expected to set another standard for the industry. Yet in the late 1990s all was not smooth sailing, despite its roster of loyal customers and leading edge technology. The venerable company filed for Chapter 11 protection in 1999 and restructured to save the Goss name.

Like a cat with nine lives, Goss Graphic Systems emerged from bankruptcy protection and began clawing its way back to the top. The company's stellar reputation in both production and service withstood its precarious financial position and the orders continued to come in. Its difficulties were actually a testament to the durability of its own products; its presses lasted so long the only reason clients replaced them was for new technological advances, and older presses were usually sold and kept in use elsewhere. Given that replacement of a press generally ran every quarter-century, repeat business in the printing industry was rather slow. Nevertheless, by the end of 2000, Goss had announced solid financial results, including higher orders both domestically and overseas (including orders for newspaper production in Korea, Puerto Rico, and Turkey), as well as increases in cash flow and margins. Goss Graphic Systems, once again, was in good shape and poised to lead the industry in the next century.

Principal Subsidiaries

Goss Graphic Systems, Inc.

Principal Competitors

Baldwin Technology Company, Inc.; Koenig & Bauer-Albert A.G.; MAN Roland A.G.; Mitsubishi Heavy Industries, Ltd.; Pamarco Technologies.

Further Reading

Gaines, Sally, "Lenders, Shareholders Accept Goss Chapter 11 Reorganization," *Chicago Tribune,* July 31, 1999, p. 2.

Kogan, Herman, *Proud of the Past, Committed to the Future,* Chicago: Mobium Press, 1985, 172 p.

Rosenberg, Jim, "Rockwell Sells Graphic Systems," *Editor & Publisher,* May 4, 1996, p. 34.

"Trade Commission Acts, Foreign Pressmakers Face Duties," *Chicago Tribune,* August 22, 1996, p. 3.

Young, David, "Printing Press Unit in Buyout Goss to Re-Emerge As Stand-Alone Firm," *Chicago Tribune,* May 1, 1996, p. 1.

——, Rockwell Seeks Midwest Base," *Chicago Tribune,* January 14, 1999, p. 3.

Ziemba, Stanley, "Goss Printing Press Re Emerges," *Chicago Tribune,* October 18, 1996, p. 1.

—Nelson Rhodes

GrandVision S.A.

Tour Utopia, Cedex 3810
92071 Paris La Défense
France
Telephone: (+33) 1-47-67-59-00
Fax: (+33) 01-47-67-59-05
Web site: http://www.grandvision.com

Public Company
Incorporated: 1981 as Fotofast
Employees: 10,000
Sales: EUR 851 million ($995 million)(2000)
Stock Exchanges: Euronext Paris
Ticker Symbol: 5297.PA
NAIC: 446130 Optical Goods Stores

France's GrandVision S.A. is Europe's leading retail optical services and retail photographic services group. The company operates six chains of retail stores under two major divisions. GrandVision's retail photographic services division operates the store chains Photo Service and Photo Station. Based primarily in France, these stores represent 30 percent of the company's total sales. Photo Service is France's leading one-hour photograph developing service, a sector the company pioneered in that country. With store sizes averaging 100 square meters, including developing lab, the 215-strong Photo Service chain represents sales of more than EUR 140 million per year.

Photo Station is the company's discount photography services chain, with stores averaging just 50 square meters. Photo Station operates 212 stores in France, Switzerland, and Luxembourg and contributes some EUR 90 million to GrandVision's annual sales. The company's fastest growing division is its retail optical services division, which operates under four main brands: the flagship Grand Optical, U.K.-based Vision Express, Générale d'Optique, and Solaris. The company's high-end brand, Grand Optical represents a network of 64 retail stores in France, and in other countries, including Switzerland and Italy. The typical Grand Optical store is 300 square meters, although the company has been rolling out a 1,000-square-foot-plus 'megastore' concept in locations such as the prestigious Champs d'Elysées. Grand Optical provides more than EUR 125 million per year in sales.

Générale d'Optique is GrandVision's discount eyewear chain, with 104 stores generating more than EUR 90 million per year. Solaris, the most recent of the company-launched brands is a fast-growing chain of sunglasses specialists, with 27 stores in 2000 with an average size of 50 square meters per store. Vision Express, acquired by GrandVision in 1997, is a network of 103 optical stores located in the United Kingdom and Ireland. The company has been refitting its U.K. operations to align more closely with the Grand Optical concept, and the United Kingdom now represents the company's fastest growth market, posting more than EUR 180 million in annual sales per year.

The company is also present in a number of other foreign markets, including Belgium, Luxembourg, Spain, Portugal, Switzerland, Poland, Czech Republic, Latvia, Lithuania, and Argentina. Grouped under its International Optical Branch, these operations oversee more than 100 stores and contributed more than EUR 65 million in sales in 1999. Traded on the Euronext Paris exchange, GrandVision is led by co-founders and co-chairmen Daniel Abittan and Michael Likierman.

The Fast Track to Success in the 1980s

England's Michael Likierman came to France in the late 1970s in order to launch the Habitat retail chain in that country. There he met Daniel Abittan, then with Price-Waterhouse. On a trip to the United States, the pair discovered a new type of photo developing machine that allowed photographs to be developed in just one hour. Abittan and Likierman decided to introduce the one-hour photo concept in France and brought over their first developing machine. The pair launched their own company, Fotofast, in 1981. The Paris-based company quickly built up a network of film collection depots, many of which were located in the Parisian Metro; films were brought to the company's central laboratory for developing.

Service became the company's hallmark, comprising not only a convenient one-hour service, but also a reputation as one of the best service providers in a country where the words "service" and "retail" were rarely found in the same sentence.

Company Perspectives:

The company's mission is to develop new retailing concepts that provide outstanding service to our customers, personal fulfillment to our staff and a fair return to our shareholders.

Fotofast was immediately successful and led Likierman and Abittan to expand the concept. In 1982, the company added developing machines to the retail stores themselves, choosing shopping malls for its new locations. Two years later, the company's commitment to high-quality service was incorporated into its name, when the company opened its first Photo Service store. Shortly thereafter, the company changed its name as well. In 1985, all of the company's stores were rebranded as Photo Service.

The company's success inspired a raft of competitors. Photo Service acquired one of these, the eight-store chain Photo Hall launched by appliance retailer Darty, in 1986. By the late 1980s, Abittan and Likierman were looking for new retail territory to conquer. The pair made a three-day new trip to the United States in 1988 to search for fresh opportunities. That trip, marked by misfortune at the onset, would help bring the company new potential and profit. Arriving in New York City, Abittan broke his glasses. Extremely nearsighted, he was about to cancel the trip, reasoning that three days was too short a time to have a new pair of glasses made for him. That was when Abittan and Likierman discovered LensCrafters.

Launched by Dean Butler in the early 1980s, LensCrafters was the first eye wear retailer to offer a one-hour eyeglass dispensing service. In the mid-decade, Butler sold his company to U.S. Shoe Corporation and then left that company in 1988 in order to found a new company, operating on a similar concept, in Australia and the United Kingdom. Butler's new company was called Vision Express.

Meanwhile, Abittan and Likierman had found their new retail niche. After a year of preparation, the pair opened its first Grand Optical store in the Belle-Epine shopping center near Paris in May 1989. Featuring its own laboratory and equipment, Grand Optical represented a new revolution in the French retail market, offering quality eyeglasses, mounted in designer frames, in just one hour. The company had started from scratch, targeting a high-end market, adding in the company's tested service formula. As Abittan explained to *L'Expansion*, the company ''invented a market by bringing the machines into the store, and in order to that we had to manufacturer the equipment on a reduced scale. We brought the glass craftsman back into the store.''

The company had initially grown only modestly, with plans to add a second store after its testing the Grand Optical format for its first year. However, the first store met with such success that Abittan and Likierman quickly made arrangements to roll out new stores. By the end of its first year, there were five Grand Optical stores in operation. The company took on a new name, Groupe Projets Services (GPS), placing Photo Service as a GPS subsidiary. GPS ended 1989 with sales of FFr 15 million.

Market Leader during the 1990s

By mid-1990, GPS had doubled the number of its Grand Optical stores, while continuing to build up its Photo Service and Photo Hall chains. Underscoring its high-end focus, Grand Optical opened a new flagship store on Paris's Champs Elysées. Grand Optical rapidly overtook the company's photography wing. Photo Service had grown to 103 stores by the end of 1993. Yet, Grand Optical, with 34 stores by the end of the 1993, was quickly overtaking Photo Service. By 1994, Grand Optical represented the largest part of GPS's sales. The company changed its name to Grand Optical Photoservice (GOP) in 1993.

The company's other photography business, Photo Hall, was less successful. In 1993, GOP began developing new concepts, opening nine PhotoPoints stores, a network of film collection depots attached to the Photo Hall chain. By the end of 1994, however, GOP had sold off its Photo Hall chain. More successful was the launch of a discount eye wear chain, Générale d'Optique, which opened two pilot stores in 1993. The new chain was meant to counter increasing competition, as a number of supermarkets and hypermarkets began adding discount optical departments, and other competitors, such as Tati Optic and Alain Aflelou, were attracting price-conscious consumers. Générale d'Optique enabled the company to compete for this consumer segment, while Grand Optical maintained its higher-end business.

In 1994, GOP went public, listing on the Paris Bourse's secondary market. The listing, which reduced founders Abittan and Likierman's holding to under 28 percent of the company's shares, with 34 percent of voting rights, was made in order to finance the company's ambitious expansion program. From 115 Photo Service stores and 44 Grand Optical stores at the end of 1994, GOP wanted to build the former to 200 stores and the latter to 70 to 100 stores by decade's end. The success of GOP since the creation of Grand Optical suggested that the company was not being too ambitious; from just FFr 15 million in sales in 1989, the company had grown to more than FFr 1 billion by the end of 1994.

The 50th Grand Optical store opened in 1995. In that year, GOP made its first move internationally, entering the Spanish market. That expansion was to prove an expensive one, however. The success of its Générale d'Optique pilot stores had meanwhile encouraged the company to officially launch the chain. GOP quickly built up Générale d'Optique, which had 50 stores by the end of 1996. Meanwhile, after abandoning Photo Hall, GOP continued an opportunity to extend its retail photography operations from the one-hour format to a discount photo format. That opportunity came in 1995, when the company acquired the Photo Station chain. With prices significantly lower than competitors, Photo Station quickly captured a leading share of the photographic services market.

After testing a new store format in 1995, GOP launched Solaris, a small boutique concept specializing in sunglasses, the following year. Also in 1996 the company's new store openings gained pace, seeing 13 new Grand Opticals, 12 new Générale d'Optique stores, five new Photo Stations. The company continued to build all of its retail chains in France. Yet an increasingly crowded competitive landscape led it to look beyond France's borders for future growth.

Key Dates:

1981: Fotofast is established in Paris, offering one-hour photo developing.
1984: Company is renamed Photo Service.
1989: Company introduces one-hour eyeglasses dispensing in Paris and changes its name to Groupe Projets Services.
1991: A Grand Optical store opens on the Champs Elysées.
1993: Company is again renamed, Grand Optical Photoservice.
1994: Company goes public on the Paris exchange.
1996: The Solaris store format is introduced.
1997: Company acquires Vision Express and is renamed GrandVision.
1998: A restructuring leads to the creation of the International Optical Branch.
2000: GrandVision launches its megastore format.

Organic expansion in Spain had proved costly to implement and slow to build toward critical mass for the company. Instead, for its next major international move, GOP launched a friendly takeover of the United Kingdom's Vision Express. Likierman and Vision Express founder Dean Butler had met some years earlier and had already discussed the possibility of joining the two companies. The acquisition of Vision Express, in the form of a stock swap, was valued at FFr 1.46 billion and was to weigh heavily on the company's financial books. Yet it created Europe's leading opticians group, with more than FFr 5 billion in annual sales. The acquisition also gave the company a new name, GrandVision SA, as the company moved its listing on the Paris Bourse's monthly settlements market and then onto its main board.

The stock market, however, was less enthusiastic about the acquisition, especially its short-term effects on GrandVision's profits, and GrandVision quickly slumped. In response, the company restructured its optical operations, creating three divisions—France, England, and International—in 1998, as well as creating a new division, International Optical Branch, to oversee its growing international operations. GrandVision stepped up its store openings that same year, opening more than 70 stores in France, and nearly 30 in the United Kingdom and elsewhere. The company also embarked on a redevelopment of the Vision Express chain, which now began to adopt elements from the company's Grand Optical format. Where Vision Express had emphasized price, the U.K. branch now focused on raising its quality of service and product range. The repositioning of the company's Vision Express operations, which also included a 100-store strong franchised operation, was to take more than two years but provided the desired results: by 2000, GrandVision's U.K. operations were driving its sales growth.

The company continued to invest in its retail chains as the decade and century drew to a close. Photo Station jumped to more than 200 stores in 1999. Photo Service, which had topped 200 stores by 1997, now turned to conquer the Internet as GrandVision seized opportunities offered by the growing implantation of digital cameras. Meanwhile, Grand Optical rolled out a new "megastore" concept featuring more than 1,000 square feet of selling space, at its Champs Elysées flagship store; two more megastores were to open in 2000. That year, Générale d'Optique celebrated the opening of its 100th branch. As a whole, the company opened some 120 stores in 2000 alone, 20 more than the company had originally forecast.

International Growth into the Next Century

As the company entered the 21st century, its focus turned to fueling its international growth. The company had begun adding new markets, including Belgium in 1998; the Vision Express acquisition had also brought it stores in more than 20 countries. GrandVision exited a number of these countries, such as Russia, Sweden, the Philippines, and Germany. Instead, GrandVision turned toward such countries as Italy, Spain, Portugal, and a number of eastern European countries where it was slowly building the market pressure to achieve profitability. In 1999, the company created its GrandVision International Supply subsidiary, which functioned as a central buying facility for all of its optical chains. Entering 2001, with revenues rising to over EUR 851 million, GrandVision announced an agreement with French rival Optic 2000 to form a partnership for their lens and glasses frame purchasing. The joint-venture was expected to handle a purchasing budget of nearly EUR 700 million, providing a significant savings.

Principal Subsidiaries

Grand Optical; Solaris; Vision Express (U.K.); Photo Service; Photo Station; Générale d'Optique; GrandVision International Supply.

Principal Competitors

Auchan S.A.; Carrefour S.A.; De Rigo S.p.A.

Further Reading

Briançon, Pierre, et. al., "Trophée de la decennie," *L'Expansion*, September 23, 1999.
Chevallard, Lucile, "La groupe d'optique et de photo GrandVision poursuit son redressement," *Les Echos*, September 8, 2000, p. 30.
De Linares, Jacqueline, "La spectaculaire ascension de GrandVision," *Nouvel Observateur*, October 15, 1999.
"GrandVision s'allie à Optic 2000 pour ses achats d'optiques," *Les Echos*, January 31, 2001.
"Michael Likierman—GrandVision Group SA," *Wall Street Transcript*, November 6, 2000.
Price, Christopher, "Eyes Focus on the Big Picture," *Financial Times*, September 2, 1997.

—M.L. Cohen

Grey Wolf, Inc.

10370 Richmond Avenue, Suite 600
Houston, Texas 77042
U.S.A.
Telephone: (713) 435-6100
Fax: (713) 435-6170
Web site: http://www.gwdrilling.com

Public Company
Incorporated: 1980 as DI Industries Inc.
Employees: 2,500
Sales: $269 million (2000)
Stock Exchanges: American
Ticker Symbol: GW
NAIC: 213111 Drilling Oil and Gas Wells

Grey Wolf, Inc., formerly DI Industries, is a Houston-based company that does onshore contract drilling, principally for natural gas. In its domestic operations, it uses a fleet of 120 drilling rigs. For years it operated drilling rigs overseas, but in 1998, in Venezuela, it shut down the last five rigs in its international operations. The company currently concentrates its operations on four regions: South Texas; the Gulf Coast (Louisiana and Texas); Ark-La-Tex (southern Arkansas, northern Louisiana, and northeastern Texas); and southern Mississippi and Alabama. Although reeling from slumping oil and gas prices in the late 1990s, which forced the company to sell off some of its nonessential assets and cut its work force, Grey Wolf has started a strong recovery. The company has also entered a new drilling market, the Rocky Mountains, through a drilling contract with Burlington Resources.

1980–89: Origins, the Oil Bust, and Overseas Opportunities

The company that emerged as Grey Wolf, Inc. in 1997, started out as DI Industries in 1980, an oil and gas exploration and production company founded by Max Dillard. The son of a drilling contractor, Dillard had entered the industry contracting business in 1969 and had worked his way up from the bottom.

In 1985, in response to growing demand for drilling rigs, DI Industries established Drillers, Inc., a subsidiary specializing in oil and gas contract drilling. It was bad timing. The domestic oil industry went into a tailspin at about the same time, compelling DI to make some major adjustments to the depressed market conditions. In 1986, the company only had 16 drilling rigs. Its business had also turned topsy-turvy. Early on, it had generated 90 percent of its revenues from oil and gas drilling and exploration and only ten percent from industrial work; then, all of a sudden, industrial work accounted for 80 percent of its business and all of its profits. To stay alive, DI took on turnkey jobs and diversified. In the process, it bid on some high-risk assignments, including, for example, drilling wells on the Strategic Petroleum Reserve at Choctaw Bayou in Louisiana, which required boring into salt domes, a dangerous enterprise.

DI also started taking contracts for work abroad, in South and Central America, where, over the next few years, it began drilling operations in Argentina, El Salvador, Mexico, Guatemala, and Venezuela. Although there was a general global slowdown in the petroleum industry, most producing areas in the world were not hit as severely as those in the United States.

1990–2000: Tough Times, Restructuring, and Turning the Corner

Times turned ever tougher for DI in the 1990s, a decade in which the whole petroleum industry continued to reel from slumping or static oil prices, although for DI it started out on a positive note. Its revenues in 1990 jumped to $58 million, close to doubling the $32.5 million from the previous year. However, only in 1990 and 1997 did the company record net profits. That of 1990 was minimal ($1.8 million), and that of 1997 ($10.2 million) was tied to the purchase of the Grey Wolf Drilling Company, whose name DI then adopted as its own. The next year, 1998, despite its record-setting revenue production of $241.0 million, the company suffered a net loss of $83.2 million.

Efforts to sustain the company's growth never really abated, however. DI started out the decade with a zero debt service, which encouraged expansion even in the face of the industry's stagnation. In 1990 it was planning to construct a new rig yard

Company Perspectives:

As a supplier of land drilling services, our business depends on the level of drilling activity by oil and gas exploration and production companies operating in the geographic markets where we operate. The number of wells they choose to drill is strongly influenced by past trends in oil and gas prices, current prices, and their outlook for future oil and gas prices within those geographic markets. Low oil and gas prices, or the perception among oil and gas companies that future prices are likely to decline, can materially and adversely affect us in many ways, including: our revenues, cash flows and earnings; the fair market value of our rig fleet; our ability to maintain or increase our borrowing capacity; our ability to obtain additional capital to finance our business and make acquisitions, and the cost of that capital; and our ability to retain skilled rig personnel who we would need in the event of a upturn in the demand for our services.

to house big-hole drilling equipment it had purchased from Baker-Hughes in 1988. Also, after a public offering raised $15 million in new funds, DI bought a pair of oilfield rig-up supply yards from Rigs-R-Us, paying just over $1 million for the Houston and Odessa, Texas sites. DI wanted the yards to help its Alamo Machine and Tool subsidiary, an oilfield equipment supplier. It also bought the drilling assets of the Michigan-based James Bigard Drilling Co. The equipment, acquired for a little over $5 million in cash, included 12 rigs plus a trucking company with a 26-vehicle fleet, and some casing tools. The purchase pushed DI's rig count to 95.

During the next year, the demand for onshore rigs was again growing. With the industry seemingly on the road to recovery, DI increased its rig count to 100 by acquiring six rigs and some operational equipment from Woolf & McGee Inc. of Tyler, Texas. The price, paid half in cash and half in stock, was $3.4 million.

DI relied on a wider geographic distribution of its rigs to compensate for problems at specific sites, including not just a downturn in demand but such other factors as the weather. For example, in 1991, high rainfall in Louisiana and South Texas caused serious difficulties. DI was able to make up for the slowdowns by securing work-over contracts in Montana and Utah and by increasing its activity in Latin America, where there was a booming energy market in the early 1990s. The company began moving its idle, excess drilling rigs into markets in both Central and South America, including Argentina and Venezuela.

However, an increasing debt load, stiffer competition, and diminishing demands continued to take a big toll. After founder and CEO Max Dillard resigned in 1995, the company began cutting free assets that were not producing sufficient income. In the following year, attempting to rebound from 1995's heavy losses, DI Industries entered a complex merger with an unnamed private investment affiliate of New York-based Somerset Capital Partners and R.T. Oliver Inc., Land Rig Acquisition Corp., and two other unnamed parties. Under the terms of the agreement, DI was to issue up to 80 million shares of its common stock, or about two-thirds of its outstanding stock, retaining a 33 percent interest and majority control of the firm. In the deal, DI acquired 14 deep-well drilling rigs from the R.T. Oliver and Land Rig Acquisition.

Starting in 1996, DI also sold off all its oil and gas producing properties in South and Central America except those in Venezuela, and it also withdrew from some domestic, non-core markets, deliberately narrowing its focus. To replace Dillard, DI also brought Thomas P. Richards over from his post as senior vice-president in charge of worldwide operations for Diamond Offshore Drilling, Inc. Richards, a 54 year-old industry veteran, who had started out as a roughneck to help pay college expenses, had won considerable respect for his ability to bring together good management teams. According to Steve Webster, CEO of R&B Falcon Corp., and one involved in the recapitalization of DI, Richards "completely changed the character of the company in a short period of about 18 months."

Some help came in the form of a promising resurgence in the petroleum industry, which again increased demand for rigs. With Richards at the helm, DI began an aggressive expansion program, adding around 100 rigs in its fewer, more concentrated markets. The acquisitions started in 1996. First, in exchange for 5.5 million shares of its common stock, DI got all the south Texas operational assets of Mesa Drilling Inc. These included six diesel electric drilling rigs, three of which were in operation, and three of which were cold stacked but ready to be added to DI's Gulf Coast division. Then, towards the end of the year, for about $26 million, DI purchased all the land rigs and related equipment of Diamond Offshore Drilling Inc.

Early in 1997, DI bought Flournoy Drilling Company, an Alice, Texas-based outfit whose assets included 13 drilling rigs, 17 rig-hauling trucks, and yard and office facilities near Corpus Christi, Texas. The $38.9 million deal included an exchange of 12.4 million shares of DI's common stock plus a $800,000 outlay to retire Flournoy's debt.

A major purchase followed in March of the same year, when, for $61.6 million in cash and 14 million shares of stock, DI acquired Grey Wolf Drilling Co. (GWDC). That company, a Gulf coast drilling contractor, brought both its name and 18 rigs when the two companies merged, and the deal increased DI's domestic rig count to 67. GWDC was nearly 100 years old, having been led since 1978 by James K.B. Nelson, a graduate of Texas A&M University and longtime veteran of the drilling industry. Nelson would retire his positions as president and CEO of GWDC and retain a seat on the board of directors of the newly formed Grey Wolf Inc. The newly configured Grey Wolf continued to be led by CEO and President Richards.

GWDC was DI's fifth acquisition since its reorganization under Richards. The company had spent over $100 million to acquire 65 rigs, bringing its total count to 108 land rigs and five under labor contracts. And the acquisitions continued. In August 1997, it bought six idle land rigs and associated equipment from Cactus Drilling Co., at a cost of $23.7 million. The purchase increased Grey Wolf's total land rig fleet to 121, 29 of which were in its inventory of cold-stacked rigs needing refurbishing.

Key Dates:

1980: Max M. Dillard founds DI Industries.
1985: DI becomes a holding company for Drillers Inc. subsidiary.
1986: Company begins drilling operations in Central and South America.
1988: Company purchases big-hole drilling equipment from Baker-Hughes Inc.
1994: DI expands drilling operations in Argentina, Venezuela, and Mexico with the help of a loan from a Norwegian bank.
1995: Founder Max Dillard retires and is succeeded by Thomas P. Richards.
1997: Company purchases Grey Wolf Drilling Company; DI holding company changes its corporate name to Grey Wolf, Inc.
2000: Company inks contract with Burlington Resources, entering the Rocky Mountain market.

In 1998, for $56.4 million, the company also bought Murco Drilling Corporation. Murco, a Louisiana company, owned ten rigs operating in Louisiana and adjacent states. However, 1998 was not shaping up as a good year. Oil prices again slumped and the demand for land rigs once more dropped, forcing Grey Wolf to take some new belt-tightening measures. It reduced its work force, sold additional non-core assets, and ended its drilling in Venezuela, its last overseas operation. Still, even in the worst of the industry downswings, Grey Wolf looked for core-focused options that could help it recover from the negative impact of the faltering market.

Although losses continued through most of 2000, a break came in October of that year. The company signed a two-year, $11.6 million contract with Burlington Resources for the use of its ultra-deep drilling rig. That opened a new market for Grey Wolf: the Rocky Mountains. Furthermore, in February 2001, the company reported that in the fourth quarter of 2000, ending in December, it netted $5 million from $82.3 million in revenue. That was a major improvement over the same quarter from 1999, when, with revenues of $51.8 million, Grey Wolf went in the red by $8.1 million, bringing its net loss for the fiscal year to $41.3 million. According to Richards, it was the best quarter in the company's history and represented the upturn that the company had been looking for. The company still recorded a net loss of $9 million for fiscal 2000, but its revenues had climbed a whopping 82.7 percent, up to $269.0 million from $172.4 million in 1998. More important, the hoped for turnaround had started. Richards noted that the whole energy industry would continue to benefit from OPEC's spigot tightening, which between 1986 and 2001 had reduced excess world oil capacity from 14 million to just 8 million barrels. Richards believed 2001 would see the return of Grey Wolf to profitability. With the price of natural gas climbing to record highs through the winter of 2000–2001, it seemed to be a fairly safe prediction, at least in the short run.

Principal Subsidiaries

Drillers Inc.

Principal Divisions

Ark-La-Tex; Gulf Coast; South Texas.

Principal Competitors

Nabors Industries, Inc.; Pride International, Inc.; Rowan Companies, Inc.; Precision Drilling Corporation; Parker Drilling Company.

Further Reading

De Rouffignac, Ann, ''Knowing the Drill: Tom Richards Rose from Roughneck to become CEO of Grey Wolf,'' *Houston Business Journal*, March 13, 1998, p. 16.

''DI Shifting Rig Focus to Latin America,'' *Oil and Gas Journal*, October 24, 1994, p. 34.

''DI Slates Merger, Gets Cash Infusion in Effort to Bounce Back from Losses,'' *Oil Daily*, April 22, 1996, p. 7.

Fan, Aliza, ''DI Send Excess Drilling Rigs to Latin America,'' *Oil Daily*, October 17, 1994, p. 1.

Fletcher, Sam, ''Grey Wolf Sees Red, Slates Charges, Cutbacks,'' *Oil Daily*, February 18, 1999.

——, ''Land Drillers Plan to Wait out Low Oil Prices,'' *Oil Daily*, April 27, 1998.

''Grey Wolf, Inc. Announces Adoption of a Shareholder Rights Plan,'' *PR Newswire*, September 21, 1998.

''Grey Wolf, Inc. Announces Election of Thomas P. Richards as Chairman of the Board,'' *PR Newswire*, November 10, 1998.

Hogan, Rick, ''DI Industries to Acquire Grey Wolf in Deal Worth More Than $100 million,'' *Oil Daily*, 47 (March 12, 1997), p. 1.

McNamara, Victoria, ''DI Acquisition Raises Rig Count to 100,'' *Houston Business Journal*, June 10, 1991, p. 9.

McNamara, Victoria, ''DI Inc. Planning Construction of a New Rig Yard,'' *Houston Business Journal*, February 19, 1990, p. 7.

O'Connor, Terry, ''Grey Wolf Is Back in Black,'' *Daily Advertiser* (Lafayette, La.), February 15, 2001, p. D1.

Starr, Spencer, ''US-Based Driller Grey Wolf Exits International Markets,'' *Platt's Oilgram News*, February 17, 1999, p. 1.

Weeden, Scott L., ''Driller Inc. Attacks 'High Risks' During Wait for the Return of Growth Market,'' *Oil Daily*, August 26, 1986, p. 5.

—John W. Fiero

Griffin Land & Nurseries, Inc.

One Rockefeller Plaza
New York, New York 10020
U.S.A.
Telephone: (212) 218-7910
Fax: (212) 218-7917

Public Company
Incorporated: 1979 as Culbro Land Resources, Inc.
Employees: 353 (1999)
Sales: $62.9 million (1999)
Stock Exchanges: NASDAQ
Ticker Symbol: GRIF
NAIC: 531210 Offices of Real Estate Agents and Brokers; 42293 Flower, Nursery Stock, and Florists' Supplies Wholesalers

Griffin Land & Nurseries, Inc. is a spin-off from the Culbro Corporation, which in 1997 decided to separate its holdings into tobacco and nontobacco related businesses. The former became General Cigar Holdings, and the latter Griffin Land & Nurseries. Operating out of its offices in New York City, Griffin is divided into two subsidiaries. Imperial Nurseries sells containerized plants (mostly azaleas and rhododendron) to garden store chains, retail and wholesale nurseries, as well as landscapers. Imperial distributes its plants through its seven wholesale centers located in Connecticut, Maryland, Ohio, Pennsylvania, and Virginia. A second subsidiary, Griffin Land, manages the company's many real estate holdings, the bulk of which are located in Connecticut. The company also owns approximately one-third of Centaur Communications, a British publisher of business magazines that includes *Marketing Week* and *New Media Age.* Through Centaur, Griffin also controls an interest in Linguaphone Group, a designer and distributor of language teaching materials. The Cullman family, known for its long ties to the tobacco industry, owns 48 percent of Griffin.

The Cullman Family Comes to America in 1848

The roots of Griffin Land & Nurseries reach back to the mid-19th century when a German wine merchant named Ferdinand Kullmann immigrated to the United States and changed his name to Cullman. In addition to his wine business, he is supposed to have made and sold cigars. Ferdinand's son Joseph became involved in the tobacco business as a teenager, going to work for a New York City merchant who bought and sold leaf tobacco. His son, also named Joseph, continued the family connection with tobacco after he graduated from college in 1904. He traveled throughout the United States and the world, buying tobacco seeds, leaf, and wrapper tobacco. Cigars consist of cut tobacco filler pressed inside rolled-up wrapper leaf. Because it requires a variety of properties, wrapper tobacco is the most expensive leaf. It should be strong, yet silky in texture, even in color, flavorful, and burn properly. Despite his father's misgivings, young Joseph Cullman wanted to grow wrapper tobacco in the Connecticut River Valley. Connecticut broadleaf, a maduro-style (very dark) wrapper tobacco, was already being grown there. Joseph tried growing Havana seed in the fertile soil, and the result was a lighter wrapper that proved to be extremely popular with customers. The Cullmans quickly became one of the largest growers of tobacco in Connecticut and acquired land that would one day become the bulk of the property held by Griffin Land & Nurseries.

Tobacco became king in a corridor that ran from Windsor, Connecticut, to Hadley, Massachusetts, with wrapper tobacco grown on 12,000 acres of land and binder tobacco grown on an additional 30,000 acres. The Cullman family business, known as Cullman Brothers, expanded its holdings in the area by buying smaller farms and in 1960 added more Connecticut land when it acquired General Cigar Company. The deal also allowed Cullman Brothers to move into manufacturing and distribution. Diversification would become a necessity in the late 1960s when the business was greatly changed by the introduction of homogenized leaf, a man-made cigar wrapper that consisted of tobacco by-products. The demand for natural wrapping tobacco began to drop precipitously.

Continuing to increase its holdings, Cullman Brothers bought the Connecticut-based American Sumatra Tobacco Company in 1969. As part of the transaction, Cullman Brothers received Imperial Nurseries, a 200-acre business that Cullman Brothers would dramatically expand to 1,500 acres, as the need for land on which to cultivate tobacco continued to fall. Unlike

Key Dates:

1960: Cullman Brothers adds to Connecticut land holdings with purchase of General Cigar Company.
1969: Cullman Brothers acquires Imperial Nurseries through purchase of Sumatra Tobacco Company.
1995: Bid for General Cigar division of Culbro Corporation prompts division of Culbro businesses.
1997: Griffin Land & Nurseries becomes an independent business.
1998: Company is accepted for listing on the NASDAQ.

many tobacco companies that sold off their holdings, Cullman Brothers opted to put their 5,500 acres of Connecticut land to different use.

Becoming known as Culbro Corporation in 1976, the family business created a division called Culbro Land Resources in 1977 in order to develop its land holdings. The entity created the Griffin Center, a 600-acre complex in Windsor, Connecticut, featuring 700,000 square feet of offices and a million square feet of research and development and light industrial space. Major tenants included CIGNA Group and Hartford Insurance. Adjacent to the Bradley International Airport, Culbro Land built another 600-acre park called Hazelwood Business Center, later changed to the New England Tradeport. In 1988 the company made an entry into residential development when it began infrastructure work at a 152-acre site called Walden Woods. Forty-five homes were eventually built and sold before the company discontinued the enterprise.

Culbro's nontobacco business concerns included Centaur Communications, as well as the Eli Witt Company, a wholesale-distributor that primarily served the southeastern United States. By 1987 tobacco sales contributed only nine percent of Culbro's total revenues. Despite efforts to diversify, the company saw the price of its stock remain stagnant. What no one could foresee was that cigar smoking would enjoy a rebirth of popularity in the 1990s and prompt renewed attention to Culbro's tobacco interests.

Renewed Popularity of Cigars Leads to Griffin Spin-Off

In 1995 Tabacalera, a Spanish tobacco monopoly, offered $100 million for a 50 percent stake in the General Cigar division of Culbro. Alerted to the changing climate in cigar smoking, CEO Edgar Cullman, Jr., declined the offer, deciding instead to reinvigorate the company's original business, in particular its premium, high margin cigars that included the Macanudo and Partagas labels. In May 1996 Cullman opened a cigar lounge in Manhattan called Club Macanudo, which became extremely popular and profitable. He then began to consider a major acquisition in the cigar business, a transaction that might necessitate a public offering of Culbro stock. In order to receive the highest net dollars from an offering, it was felt that Culbro would be better served as a ''pure play'' cigar company. As a result Cullman decided to split Culbro into two public companies that would operate independently. The tobacco business would belong to General Cigar Holdings and all nontobacco business would go to a new entity called Griffin Land & Nurseries. The split went into effect on February 27, 1997. Culbro shareholders received equal shares of Griffin stock at no cost, tax-free.

Management for Griffin Land & Nurseries came from the ranks of Culbro. Although Edgar Cullman was chairman of the board, day-to-day operations were run by Frederick M. Danziger, named president and chief executive officer. Danziger, a Culbro director since 1975, had been involved in the company's real estate operations in the early 1980s. Richard L. Wyckoff remained president of Imperial Nurseries, a post he had held since 1991. Although it was not installing an entirely new management team, Griffin was starting many support operations from scratch, and for a period of time would have to depend upon General Cigar for financial and administrative services. General Cigar also held a lease on approximately 500 acres of Griffin land in Connecticut, should conditions warrant an expansion in the cultivation of tobacco; but the two companies quickly began to lead their separate existences.

Griffin's commercial real estate land holdings included 3,335 acres in Connecticut, 432 acres in Massachusetts, and 15 acres in Florida. Nursery real estate included 712 acres in Connecticut, 1,046 acres in Florida, 26 acres in Pennsylvania, 16 acres in Virginia, 28 acres in Ohio, and 20 acres in Maryland. The smaller parcels were the sites of Imperial Nurseries' seven sales and service centers that each included a warehouse and office facility and several acres of nursery stock. The book value of the company's undeveloped land holdings, located primarily in Connecticut, was approximately $12 million.

Griffin inherited some problems as well. Before the Culbro split, Eli Witt had filed for bankruptcy in November 1996, and Griffin was obligated to indemnify General Cigar for any liabilities, in particular unsecured creditors that had formed a committee to inquire about the asset transfer to Griffin. The matter was eventually settled when a sale of Eli Witt to the H.T. Hackney Co. was completed.

The value of some of Griffin's property located in Simsbury, Connecticut, was also compromised by the presence of the pesticide chlorodane. Until the company's plan to reduce chlorodane contamination was approved by local authorities, and the work completed, Griffin would be unable to develop the property. Griffin faced other obstacles in utilizing its real estate. The majority of Connecticut land holdings were located in the northwest quadrant of Hartford, where the company's ability to develop the land to its best use was subject to material zoning and other regulatory restrictions. Furthermore, the Hartford area had in recent years suffered a loss of employment in the defense and insurance industries, which depressed the local real estate market.

Aside from the problems that the company inherited from the Culbro split, and which it assumed would ultimately be overcome, Griffin also faced natural forces that would simply remain a constant. The nursery business was seasonal, with the bulk of sales coming in the spring and dependent on how weather disrupted construction projects that used its plants for landscaping. Because the company's containerized plants were maintained for as long as five years before they were mature enough to be sold, predicting future demand was paramount—

and exceedingly difficult. To lessen risk, Imperial Nurseries decided to increase its production of perennials, which have a shorter growing cycle. The division also began to terminate its involvement in field-grown plants, opting instead to outsource to other growers.

Griffin Begins First Full Year of Operations in 1998

In 1998, the company's first full year in operation, Griffin posted net sales of $51,231,000 and a net income of $121,000. In April the company was accepted for listing by the NASDAQ Stock Market; previously stock had been traded on the OTC Bulletin Board. The Eli Witt matter was also resolved, freeing Griffin from further liability. Imperial Nurseries enjoyed strong sales during the fall, which contributed greatly to the company's final results for the year. During the second quarter, Griffin Land completed construction on a 98,000-square-foot warehouse in the company's New England Tradeport. By the end of the year the facility was fully leased, and the company began construction on an additional 100,000-square-foot warehouse to be located nearby. Occupancy at Griffin Center South was also increased to 95 percent by the end of 1998. The company's equity investments were adversely affected by losses at Linguaphone but more than compensated for by positive results from Centaur. Griffin also increased its ownership in Centaur, purchasing an additional 500,000 shares of common stock to total 35 percent of Centaur's outstanding common stock.

In 1999 both of Griffin's subsidiaries showed marked improvement over the previous year's results. The company reported a net income of $2.47 million on net sales of $62.94 million. Much of the increase in the operating results for Griffin Land was due to the sale of undeveloped land for approximately $1 million. In addition, the division's new 98,000-square-foot warehouse in the New England Tradeport was fully leased for the entire year. The construction of 100,000 square feet of additional warehouse space was also completed during the course of 1999, but was not yet leased. In August Griffin completed an agreement that provided it with a $20 million line of revolving credit to provide working capital for both of its divisions.

In November 1999 Griffin Land announced it had filed an application to build a planned residential community on some of its land in Simsbury, Connecticut, to be called "Meadowood." The company hoped to build 640 homes on 363 acres, ranging in price from under $130,000 (deemed "affordable" by Connecticut statutory provisions) to over $500,000. Plans called for over one-third of the acres to be devoted to open space, with walking trails and room for a soccer field and little league field. Residents would have access to meeting houses, pools, as well as tennis and basketball courts. The company also made an effort to satisfy environmental concerns about the area, in particular the remediation of residual pesticide use from previous agricultural use.

Griffin entered 2000 with the goal of making significant improvements to both sides of its business. Imperial Nurseries looked to open a new wholesale center in Somerset, New Jersey, subject to municipal approval. The division planned to make improvements to a Florida farm operation by building additional loading docks, renovating customer service facilities, and increasing irrigation capacity to cultivate previously unused land. The operation looked to faster growing plants as well as different soil mixes to help increase profitability.

Griffin Land planned to continue its efforts in residential development, as well as on the industrial side by adding buildings to both Griffin Center South and New England Tradeport. In July the division announced a major agreement with JDS Uniphase Corporation to build a 165,000-square-foot facility on a 65-acre parcel in Windsor, Connecticut, with the possibility of two additional buildings of 150,000 square feet each.

In little more than three years, the spin-off corporation had made a successful transition from a collection of tobacco company interests to a viable independent operation.

Principal Subsidiaries

Griffin Land; Imperial Nurseries.

Further Reading

"Bankruptcy-Law Protection Is Filed for Eli Witt Co," *Wall Street Journal,* November 13, 1996, p. B4.

Fioravante, Janice, "Smokin'!" *Chief Executive,* October 1997, p. 26.

Hall, Ken, "Tobacco No Longer King in Connecticut Valley," *Across the Board,* September 19, 1986, p. 18.

Porter, John W., "Culbro Land Resources Lights Up Office Market North of Hartford," *Across the Board,* March 4, 1988, p. 20.

—Ed Dinger

Grolier Incorporated

90 Old Sherman Turnpike
Danbury, Connecticut 06810
U.S.A.
Telephone: (203) 797-3500
Fax: (203) 797-3197
Web site: http://www.publishing.grolier.com

Private Company
Wholly Owned Subsidiary of Scholastic
Incorporated: 1936 as The Grolier Society, Inc.
Employees: 2000
Sales: $380 million (2001)
NAIC: 511130 Book Publishers; 511140 Database and Directory Publishers

Grolier Incorporated is a leading publisher of reference books and multimedia reference products in the United States, and, under its Children's Press and Franklin Watts imprints, is the country's major publisher of children's nonfiction. The company is a wholly owned subsidiary of children's book publisher Scholastic, which purchased it from the French media conglomerate Lagardère in 2000. Grolier publishes encyclopedias, children's books, reference sets, educational materials, and electronic products. The company's best-known titles include *Encyclopedia Americana* and the *New Book of Knowledge,* a children's encyclopedia. Grolier's electronic products include the *Guinness Multimedia Disc of Records* and the *Grolier Multimedia Encyclopedia.* The company also manages direct-to-home and e-commerce children's book clubs which ranks include three million active customers. By company estimates, half of all American children participate in a Grolier book club by the time they reach kindergarten.

Early History

The company originated with the Grolier Society founded in 1895 by a group of Boston scholars. Named after Jean Grolier, a designer and collector of French Renaissance books, the Society produced deluxe editions and memoirs in elegant bindings and sold them on a subscription basis. The Society was incorporated as a business under the name The Grolier Society, Inc. on May 22, 1936, under the laws of Delaware after being purchased by one of the Society's top salespeople, Fred Murphy. In 1960 the company changed its name to Grolier Incorporated. Soon after purchasing the Society, Murphy acquired *Encyclopedia Americana,* which became one of Grolier's major products. Under Murphy, Grolier became a sales-oriented company. He divided it into discrete businesses, giving managers wide leeway to run their divisions and instituting an incentive plan providing division managers a percentage of sales and profits generated by their respective operations. The incentive plan helped to boost company morale and productivity as individuals could earn substantial money, while being given the freedom to run their areas with minimum interference.

In the beginning Grolier worked much like a finance company, operating largely on installment sales. The company might borrow money, for example, at 4.5 percent and receive 12 or 15 percent in return on its installment accounts. Due to rapid expansion, by the late 1960s and early 1970s Grolier became the largest hardcover publisher of encyclopedias and reference books in the United States, earning about $317 million in sales. In 1969, the 74-year old publicly owned company recorded higher sales for the 30th consecutive year and held about 30 percent of the total encyclopedia market.

In the same year the company purchased Scarecrow Press in Metuchen, New Jersey, a supplier of catalogs, anthologies, and other specialized publications to libraries and schools; and Haddon Bindery, Inc. of Camden, New Jersey, a provider of binder facilities for Grolier's single-volume publications. Western Wood Mfg., acquired in 1967, produced bookcases for Grolier's major multivolume sets. Grolier's juvenile book division also included the subsidiary Franklin Watts, Inc., a publisher of children's books. The company further pursued the educational market through another subsidiary, Grolier Educational Corporation.

While Grolier published the popular 30-volume *Encyclopedia Americana,* its bestseller was the 20-volume *Book of Knowledge,* which gained wide acceptance as a basic reference work for children in middle elementary grades. Other Grolier products included the 50-volume set of the *World's Greatest Clas-*

Company Perspectives:

Grolier is the leader in direct-to-home and e-commerce book clubs for children ages five and under, offering such well-known brands as Dr. Seuss, Barbie, and Disney. Grolier is also the leading online and print publisher of children's reference products—including Encyclopedia Americana, *the* New Book of Knowledge, *and* Nueva enciclopedia Cumbre, *a Spanish-language encyclopedia sold primarily to U.S. school libraries. Grolier has established itself as the major publisher of nonfiction children's books in the United States under the imprints of Children's Press and Franklin Watts, selling to both libraries and the consumer market.*

sics, the 20-volume *Encyclopedia International,* the 20-volume *American Peoples Encyclopedia,* the 10-volume *Grolier Universal Encyclopedia,* the 10-volume *Book of Art,* the *Book of Popular Science,* the *Encyclopedia Canadiana,* and several other encyclopedias, yearbooks, and references in French, Spanish, and Japanese. In 1969 the company's subsidiary Grolier International sold these products in 40 foreign countries. Most of its revenues came from door-to-door sales by 7,000 salespeople on commission. Grolier also operated a mail-order business, accounting in 1968 for about 26 percent of the company's net income.

Hard Times During the 1960s and 1970s

Despite these early successes and sound products, in the 1960s and early 1970s Grolier embarked on misguided diversification and expansion programs. The company borrowed heavily, becoming over-leveraged while diversifying into mostly unrelated areas, including trailer parks, water-skiing manufacturing, trailer manufacturing, woodworking products, vending machines, and South American publishing. In 1973 Grolier wrote off three of its domestic subsidiaries—water-skiing manufacturing, vending-machine financing, and bookbinding—for $5 million. Two years later Grolier ended its mobile-home operations, writing off another $11.9 million. In the 1960s Grolier also expanded into the fast-growing foreign encyclopedia market, an expansion that proved to be ill-advised. By 1976 company losses included special charges of $25.4 million for divesting 23 foreign operations in 15 countries. In the same year steep foreign exchange losses hit the company, amounting to $23.2 million. As a result of these missteps, between 1973 and 1976 Grolier lost nearly $160 million, about $77.8 million in 1976 alone. These losses, which showed a consolidated negative net loss of $45.5 million, prompted the New York Stock Exchange to delist the company.

During this period Grolier also saw its share of the U.S. encyclopedia market slip by 15 percent, stemming largely from the industry's image of slick, fast-talking door-to door salespeople and high prices of encyclopedias at $300 to $500 a set. The industry's tarnished image was to some extent justified. In 1972 a complaint filed with the U.S. Federal Trade Commission (FTC) accused Grolier of fraudulent and deceptive practices in door-to-door and other sales techniques, recruitment of personnel, and debt collection. Encyclopedia Britannica and about 30 other companies were found to have engaged in similar practices. In 1976 an administrative law judge upheld the major provisions of the Grolier FTC complaint. Grolier appealed the decision to the FTC's five-member commission, which one year later unanimously sustained the 1976 decision. Grolier was ordered, therefore, to cease and desist all deceptive practices, and to ensure that the company's sales force properly represent the company's products.

At the same time that Grolier faced financial difficulties, its two major competitors for the encyclopedia market, Field Enterprises Educational Corporation and Encyclopedia Britannica, were experiencing substantial growth. The profitability of both companies resulted primarily from expansion into the same overseas markets that Grolier found unmanageable. While Grolier lost money in these markets, Encyclopedia Britannica alone had expanded into 150 countries, finding the foreign business enormously profitable.

1970s: Management Shifts and Impending Bankruptcy

In 1976 under duress from creditors, the company's board of directors demanded a change in management. Disagreement between members of the board and inside management (some had inherited substantial stock in the company) resulted in the selection of Robert B. Clarke to salvage the firm. Clarke was a longtime company insider who joined Grolier in 1949 as a shipping clerk. He rose through middle management before taking charge in 1967 of Grolier Enterprises, the company's profitable mail-order business. Three years after becoming division president, for tax reasons, he relocated operations to Danbury, Connecticut, from the company's New York headquarters on Lexington Avenue. Clarke had a reputation for financial discipline, and at the time of his selection, he was working on evaluating the profitability of Grolier's various businesses.

Upon becoming company president on October 23, 1976, Clarke moved quickly to reorganize the company and keep creditors at bay. Grolier was already in default to several banks for more than $220 million. He relocated the corporate headquarters to Connecticut, where the local corporate court would be more sympathetic to Grolier's financial plight than the courts in New York. To restore the company's finances, he pulled out of losing ventures, cut staff, and hastily implemented cost- and cash-flow controls. He hired the investment firm Goldman Sachs to evaluate the company's financial viability. He also hired Harvey Miller, a bankruptcy expert of Weil, Gotshal to examine the bankruptcy angle. Clarke's concern was how bankruptcy would affect company relations with suppliers and manufacturers, and whether it would ruin Grolier's credit supply. Clarke was also worried that Grolier's subsidiary businesses would have to follow the parent company into bankruptcy. He knew that if Grolier declared bankruptcy, creditors would petition the courts for the liquidation of all assets, including the subsidiary businesses. Nevertheless, if one of Grolier's subsidiaries could pay creditors more than they would otherwise receive through wholesale liquidation, the courts would likely protect the business.

As a result, Grolier crafted a strategy of avoiding bankruptcy by using its most profitable subsidiary, the mail-order division,

Key Dates:

1895: Grolier Society is founded in Boston.
1936: Company is incorporated as The Grolier Society, Inc.
1960: Company is renamed Grolier Incorporated.
1967: Company acquires Western Wood Mfg.
1969: Company acquires Scarecrow Press and Haddon Bindery.
1972: FTC complaint is filed against company alleging deceptive practices in door-to-door sales and other areas.
1976: Grolier is delisted on the New York Stock Exchange; Robert B. Clarke becomes company president.
1977: FTC issues cease and desist order regarding the company's alleged deceptive sales and other practices.
1978: In addition to door-to-door sales, Grolier begins a telemarketing campaign to sell encyclopedias and other books.
1982: Grolier Electronic Publishing is formed.
1986: Grolier introduces the first electronic encyclopedia, *Academic American Encyclopedia.*
1988: The company is acquired by Hachette, a subsidiary of Lagardère, in hostile takeover.
1990: Grolier is massively restructured; William C. Johnson becomes CEO.
1995: The company consolidates Children's Press and Franklin Watts subsidiaries.
1996: Grolier files an $8 million lawsuit against Dorling Kindersley (DK) Publishing, citing unfair competition and interference.
1998: The company settles lawsuit with DK Publishing.
1999: Lagardère puts Grolier up for sale.
2000: Grolier is acquired by Scholastic.

to carry the entire company and pay off creditors. The subsidiary placed all of Grolier's purchase and manufacturing orders, and paid suppliers and creditors from its own money. Nevertheless, Grolier's position was precarious at best. If creditors either severed its credit line or tightened the terms, the company would be put out of business. To avoid this scenario, the company courted its creditors, assuring them of payment and managing to assuage the concerns of 23 lending institutions to which Grolier owed substantial sums.

At the same time Clarke maintained the support of Grolier's board of directors and launched other strategies to return the company to profitability. In 1977 he negotiated a restructuring agreement with the banks to give Grolier time to reorganize and set out to expand the company's market for encyclopedias. Despite criticism that the market lacked growth opportunity, Grolier nevertheless increased its door-to-door encyclopedia sales. In 1978 Clarke pursued telephone sales, a strategy that proved more profitable than traditional door-to-door sales. The company's use of telephone sales to reach a vast market yielded $43 million for its encyclopedias and other book products in just three years. Grolier began its telemarketing campaign by renting space in downtown Danbury, Connecticut, and hiring six women to make telephone calls. The company also developed a computer databank including the names of millions of individuals who either owed Grolier money or were buying one of its products. By expanding its market, increasing sales, and finally earning profits, Grolier managed to offset its debt payments.

In 1978 Grolier also launched a $1.3 million direct-mail and television advertising campaign, representing another dramatic departure from its traditional door-to-door sales program. The campaign advertised the popular children's encyclopedia the *New Book of Knowledge* to the consumer using three direct-mail packages targeting 1.8 million U.S. families and two weeks' worth of television commercials in 28 prime mail-order television markets. At the same time Grolier tried to enhance the marketability of the 20-volume set by reducing its price by 39 percent. The *Book of Knowledge* was first published in 1908 and then completely revised in 1966. In an interview, Grolier president and Chief Executive Officer, Robert Clarke, stated that the advertising program amounted to the largest marketing campaign ever for a multivolume set in the mail-order publishing field. The campaign stemmed from marketing analysis showing declining encyclopedia sales due to consumer discontent over high prices, dislike of door-to-door salespeople, and parental uncertainty of whether their children would make use of the reference books.

Despite Clarke's aggressive capital restructuring program, by 1983 the company continued to have difficulties. Grolier still owed 23 lending institutions $96 million. In lieu of payment in full, the banks agreed to receive $36 million in cash plus a combination of common and preferred stock and warrants worth more than $16 million. Clarke raised the cash through an $82 million bond issue, spending part of it to retire $35 million in Swiss notes. Although free of the banks and the Swiss, Grolier's load of public debt amounted to over half its total capital. Nevertheless, in 1982 the company formed a successful new subsidiary, Grolier Electronic Publishing, which in 1986 introduced the first encyclopedia in electronic format on compact-disc read-only memory (CD-ROM) under the name Academic American Encyclopedia. The company also introduced the product on laser videodisc. Grolier produced both products, containing the encyclopedia's entire nine-million-word text on a single disc, with Activenture Corporation, an expert in optical disc storage technology in Monterey, California. The products, establishing Grolier as the preeminent leader in the field, brought the company closer to realizing its plans of a disc-based encyclopedia encompassing audio, video, and software applications. In addition, the products positioned the company well for future developments in the expanding market for electronic information.

Grolier Regains Financial Health in the 1980s

By the late 1980s Grolier reestablished its financial footing as a leading worldwide publisher and distributor of encyclopedias, children's books, reference sets, and educational materials. In 1987, the company also marketed health information after acquiring Krames Communications, a major direct distributor of health and medical publication materials. In addition to Grolier's operations as a primary producer and distributor of electronic publishing products and services, its other businesses included photo-finishing services, educational toys, play equipment, and classroom furniture for children. The company sold these products in the U.S., Canada, and in 20 other countries through its operations in Mexico, Italy, Australia, the United Kingdom, and the Philippines.

The company's direct-marketing operations constituted its principal means of sales. Grolier began direct marketing by selling annual supplements that updated previously sold encyclopedia or reference sets. The company considerably expanded these operations both internally and through new acquisitions. Most of its direct-marketing sales in the U.S. and Canada came from direct-mail advertising using pamphlets, brochures, and specialty catalogs. The company continued its telemarketing program, selling certain products using trained telephone sales representatives. Under its direct-marketing system, Grolier also marketed children's and other books through book clubs, including the Beginner Reader's Program, Disney's Wonderful World of Reading, the Popular Science Book Club, and Outdoor Life Book Club.

Hostile Takeover and the Early 1990s

In 1988 soon after returning to profitability, Grolier became a hostile takeover target. Although profitable, the company's comparatively small size made it vulnerable in an era of massive leveraged buyouts, mergers, acquisitions, hostile takeovers, and corporate restructurings. In 1986 Lewis Rabinowitz, head of the investment firm R. Lewis Securities, Inc., anticipated the buyout by purchasing large sums of Grolier stock on behalf of his wealthy clients. Rabinowitz believed Grolier's book niche would appeal to large publishers seeking to expand their markets. Grolier's allure also lay in its extensive direct-marketing organization, providing access to upscale, education-oriented young families with children. Rabinowitz's prediction proved correct in 1988 when Hachette, France's largest communications company, offered $415 million in an unsolicited bid. In a prepared statement, Clarke responded that Grolier management would recommend to the board that the company pursue a course that would maximize shareholder value.

Despite public statements of a friendly offer, Hachette filed suit against Grolier in federal court in Manhattan. Hachette challenged Grolier's ''poison pill'' approach, adopted in 1986, making its acquisition enormously expensive unless approved by the company's board of directors. Hachette's suit also challenged Delaware's takeover statute, allowing corporations to impose difficult conditions on businesses pursuing acquisitions. In 1987, Hachette, owner of newspaper, film, television, radio, printing, and retailing operations, had $3 billion in sales, nearly one-third of these from its book publishing operation. That same year, Grolier had sales of $424 million.

In April 1988 Grolier's poison pill approach and Delaware registration failed to ward off Hachette's $450 million hostile takeover. Shortly after in 1990, Hachette made sweeping changes in Grolier's top management. Clarke was replaced by William C. Johnson as Grolier CEO, ending Clarke's 40-year career as a loyal company insider. Hachette removed other longtime executives, including Howard B. Graham, executive vice-president of Grolier Incorporated and president of Grolier International; and Jonathan N. Gillet, president of Franklin Watts, the adult and juvenile trade subsidiary.

After becoming CEO, Johnson divested several subsidiaries to focus on Grolier's core publishing businesses. He sold the company's educational toy maker, Childcraft Education, to Walt Disney for $52 million, and in 1992, sold Krames Communications to K-III Holdings. He subsequently reorganized Grolier's operations under four main divisions, including the direct-marketing group, the publishing group, reference group, and the international group. Under each operation, Johnson appointed a senior executive to run the divisions. As a result of the reorganization, Grolier's operations generated returns on sales of 10 percent with revenues of $385 million in 1991. After the direct-marketing division, the publishing group represented Grolier's largest operation with 440 employees and approximately 20 percent of total company sales. The publishing group targeted the school and library market as its core business. In 1992 the division had about 20 percent of the U.S. market for juvenile and young adult books and reference books for the school and library market. In a restructuring move, the division sought to eliminate competitive marketing between its various units by redirecting their sales strategies to differing segments of the library market. The publishing group consisted of Children's Press, Grolier Educational Corporation, Franklin Watts, Orchard Books, and Scarecrow Press.

Post-Restructuring in the 1990s

Grolier quickly became a profitable U.S. affiliate of Hachette, a subsidiary of France's third-largest business empire, Largardère. Hachette's management predicted a brighter future for Grolier after years of financial struggle. In 1994 Peter D. Nalle was named chief operating officer in charge of publishing and reference operations. Nalle was previously president of Simon & Schuster's professional information group, and earlier, president and CEO of J.B. Lippincott Co. His appointment was expected to enable Grolier to move more aggressively into key markets. In 1995 Grolier further streamlined operations by consolidating its Children's Press and Franklin Watts children's book publishing subsidiaries into the company's Danbury, Connecticut headquarters. The consolidation resulted from management analysis of Grolier's long-term competitive position. As a result of this analysis, the company also sold educational publisher Scarecrow Press to University Press, and expanded its electronic publishing division, Grolier Electronic Publishing (GEP). GEP subsequently enhanced its multimedia activity through a strategic alliance with Metro-Goldwyn-Mayer, enabling the development and distribution of interactive multimedia games worldwide. In the late 1990s Grolier continued to increase its focus on electronic publishing and multimedia. Among the titles the company introduced on CD-ROM were Prehistoria, an encyclopedia of prehistoric facts, and a 30-volume Encyclopedia Americana. In 1996, the company launched Grolier Online, a subscription-based Internet educational portal aimed at schools and public libraries.

Also in 1996 three key editors at Grolier's imprint Orchard Books, Orchard president Neal Porter and senior editors Richard Jackson and Melanie Kroupa, left the company to join Dorling Kindersley (DK) Publishing to launch a new fiction imprint for that company. The defection prompted Grolier to file an $8 million unfair competition lawsuit against DK, alleging that DK had lured away the editors and was attempting to sign authors and book titles still under contract to Grolier. DK vigorously denied the charges. Finally in July of 1997, the two companies came to an agreement that settled the lawsuit. DK agreed to pay Grolier an undisclosed sum of money, and the two companies announced plans to collaborate on electronic publishing ventures.

New Owner for a New Century

In 1999 Grolier's parent company Lagardère announced that it was putting Grolier up for sale. At the time of the offer, company officials said that their asking price of $400 to 500 million was not ''realistic,'' but apparently, they underestimated Grolier's value. In 2000, children's book publisher Scholastic acquired the company for $400 million. The acquisition was considered by industry experts to be a perfect match. Grolier's main areas of operations complemented Scholastics existing businesses well: Grolier's Kid's Clubs and Interactive units targeted children up to age five; Scholastic's similar programs focused on ages 6–12. At the time of the deal Scholastic predicted that acquiring Grolier would increase its annual operating income by $30 million. The deal resulted in the elimination of approximately 300 positions at Grolier, primarily in telemarketing and customer service. In 2001 Grolier's operations were still located in Danbury, Connecticut, but some industry experts speculated that Scholastic might consolidate operations in New York.

Principal Divisions

Kid's Clubs; Interactive; International; Publishing.

Principal Competitors

Encyclopaedia Britannica; Golden Books; PRIMEDIA.

Further Reading

''Consolidation Continued in 2000 in Educational Software Industry,'' *Electronic Education Report*, January 17, 2001.

''DK Rejects Grolier's Claims of Interference,'' *Publishers Weekly*, November 11, 1996, p. 16.

''Fears Confirmed for 50 Grolier Employees Axed by Scholastic,'' *BP Report*, July 24, 2000.

Fields, Howard, ''Clarke Retires among Top Shake-up at Grolier,'' *Publishers Weekly,* February 10, 1989, p. 14.

Frederick, Heather Vogel, ''Phil Friedman: Grolier Pioneers the E-frontier,'' *Publishers Weekly*, December 18, 2000, p. 48.

''FTC Rules against Grolier on Unfair Practices,'' *Publishers Weekly,* April 17, 1978, pp. 24–26.

''Grolier Boosts Scholastic's Q2 Revenue, Scholastic Splits Stock 2 for 1,'' *Electronic Education Report*, January 17, 2001.

''Grolier Electronic Publishing Changes Its Name to Grolier Interactive Inc.,'' *Information Today*, March 1996, p. 37.

''Grolier Interactive Launches CD-ROM Reference Suite,'' *Information Today*, January 1999, pp. 31, 36.

''Grolier: Its Encyclopedias Are Best Sellers,'' *Financial World,* August 6, 1969, p. 12.

''Grolier Launches School Edition of 2000, Multimedia Encyclopedia,'' *Information Today*, January 2000, p. 42.

''Grolier Publishing Embracing Technology to Spur Growth,'' *Publishers Weekly*, September 21, 1998, p. 12.

''Grolier Vows to Expand Orchard,'' *Publishers Weekly*, September 9, 1996, p. 18.

Hatch, Denny, ''Grolier: The Early Days,'' *Target Marketing, Philadelphia,* October 1999, pp. 112, 121.

''How Grolier Lost $13 a Share,'' *Business Week,* April 4, 1977, p. 31.

''How Grolier Turned Around,'' *Publishers Weekly,* April 30, 1982, pp. 26–27.

Lottman, Herbert R., ''French Plan to Sell Grolier,'' *Publishers Weekly*, November 29, 1999, p. 21.

Marcial Gene G., ''Why Grolier Looks Ripe for the Picking,'' *Business Week,* November 3, 1986, p. 128.

Milliot, Jim, ''Grolier Moving Children's Press, Watts to Danbury,'' *Publishers Weekly,* March 20, 1995, p. 18.

——, ''Robinson: Grolier Will Boost Scholastic Profits,'' *Publishers Weekly*, April 24, 2000, p. 12.

——, ''Scholastic Agrees to Acquire Grolier,'' *Publishers Weekly*, April 17, 2000, p.9.

——, ''Scholastic Has Record Year and Begins Grolier Integration,'' *Publishers Weekly*, July 24, 2000, p. 9.

——, ''Scholastic Reports Solid Gains,'' *Publishers Weekly*, March 19, 2001, p. 10.

——, ''Scholastic Sales Surge Continues,'' *Publishers Weekly*, January 1, 2001, p. 19.

Orr, Alicia, ''Direct Marketer of the Year,'' *Target Marketing, Philadelphia,* October 1999, pp. 94–108.

Parr, Jann, ''Waiting for New Hardware,'' *Forbes,* November 17, 1986, p. 262.

''Perpetual Comeback,'' *Forbes,* December 5, 1983, pp. 259, 262.

''PLWeb Turbo Chosen for Encyclopedia Americana Online,'' *Information Today*, June 1997, p. 59.

Reddish, Jeannette M., ''People of the Financial World,'' *Financial World,* February 15, 1978, p. 4.

Reid, Calvin, ''Grolier,'' *Publishers Weekly,* March 25, 1996, p.18.

——, ''Grolier, DK Settle $8 Million Tampering Lawsuit,'' *Publishers Weekly*, July 14, 1997, p. 10.

——, ''Grolier Files $8 Million Suit Challenging DK Hiring,'' *Publishers Weekly*, November 4, 1996, p. 45.

——, ''Grolier Looks Ahead after Divestitures, Reorganization,'' *Publishers Weekly,* March 16, 1992, pp. 9–10.

——, ''Wilson Named to Head Orchard, Ruling on Preliminary Injunction,'' *Publishers Weekly*, November 25, 1996, p. 48.

Reuter, Madalynne, ed., ''News of the Week: Hachette Launches Bid of $415 Million for Grolier,'' *Publishers Weekly,* March 25, 1988, p. 10.

——, ''The Week: Grolier Unveils Unusual Selling Tactics for the New Book of Knowledge,'' *Publishers Weekly,* January 23, 1978, p. 287.

Rogers, Michael, ''Scholastic to Acquire Grolier Inc.,'' *Library Journal*, June 1, 2000, p. 28.

Rose, Mattyew, and Nikhil Deogun, ''Scholastic Corp. is Nearing Agreement to Buy Grolier for About $400 Million,'' *The Wall Street Journal,* April 13, 2000, p. B4.

''Scholastic Adds E- Encyclopedias, Door to New Market with Grolier,'' *Educational Marketer*, May 1, 2000.

''Scholastic-Grolier Combo Will Take Children from Cradle to Middle School,'' *BP Report*, April 24, 2000.

''Scholastic Is Planning to Buy Grolier,'' *The New York Times,* April 15, 2000, p. B3.

Sorkin, Andrew Ross, ''Dorling Kindersly and Orchard Books Settle Battle over Editors,'' *The New York Times,* July 21, 1997, p. C9.

Spain, Tom, ''Grolier Encyclopedia to Bow in New Formats,'' *Publishers Weekly,* August 16, 1985, p. 18.

Wagner, Susan, ''Judge Upholds FTC Complaint against Grolier,'' *Publishers Weekly,* November 22, 1976, pp. 19–20.

—Bruce P. Montgomery
—update: Lisa Whipple

Guinness/UDV

Park Royal Brewery
London NW10 7RR
United Kingdom
Telephone: (44) 20 8965 7700
Fax: (44) 20 8965 1882
Web site: http://www.guinness.ie

Wholly owned subsidiary of Diageo, Inc.
Incorporated: 1886
Employees: 24,691
Sales: £7,117 million (US $10,793 million)(2000)
NAIC: 312120 Breweries; 312140 Distilleries; 312130 Wineries

The dark creamy stout brewed by Guinness for more than two centuries is a product that is regarded as synonymous with the drinking habits of the Irish. Yet, Guinness stout is now purchased in many foreign countries. Through ingenious marketing strategies and adept management, Guinness has achieved the status of a multi-national corporation. Their success, however, has had to overcome several obstacles and pitfalls along the way.

Guinness Beginnings

In 1759 Arthur Guinness, an experienced brewer, leased an old brewery at James Gate in Dublin. Besides renting the brewery Guinness signed an unusual 9,000-year lease for a mill, a storehouse, a stable, a house, and two malthouses. As it turned out, he did not require so long a lease; in just four years, significant quantities of ale and table beer were emerging from the new workplace.

Soon after the brewery was in full operation, Arthur Guinness began to establish a reputation in both business and civic affairs. The company secured an active trade with pubs in towns surrounding Dublin and also became one of the largest employers in the city. As a vocal participant in public life, Guinness supported such diverse issues as penal reform, parliamentary reform, and the discouragement of dueling. Although a Protestant, he strongly supported the claims of the Irish Catholic majority for equality.

The business nearly came to an abrupt end in 1775, when a dispute over water rights erupted into a heated exchange between Guinness and the mayor's emissaries. The argument centered around the City Corporation's decision to fill in the channel that provided the brewery with water. When the sheriff's men appeared at James Gate, Guinness grabbed a pickaxe from a workman and with a good deal of "improper language" ordered them to leave. For fear of escalating violence, the parties to the dispute finally settled by means of a tenant agreement.

In 1761, Arthur Guinness married Olivia Whitmore. Of the 21 children born to them only 10 survived. Their eldest son, Hosea, became a clergyman. Consequently, after the founder's death in 1803, the thriving company was passed on to the second son, Arthur, who, like his father, soon became active in both civic and political affairs. He served in the Farming Society of Ireland, the Dublin Society, the Meath Hospital, and the Dublin Chamber of Commerce. Most importantly, as an elected director in the Bank of Ireland, he played a significant role in settling currency issues. In politics, Arthur adhered to his father's beliefs by advocating the claims of the religious majority.

From the very beginning of his career, it appears that Arthur's main concern was not so much in managing the company as in pursuing his banking interests. Nonetheless, brewery records indicate that from the end of the Napoleonic Wars to the end of the Great Famine in 1850, the company's production output increased by 50%. For this reason, Arthur is often credited with making the Guinness fortune.

Trade to England Begins

A great deal of that success, of course, can be attributed to Arthur Guinness's decision to shift most of the firm's trade from Ireland to England. Yet, the growth of Guinness was a result not only of management's business acumen and the firm's financial strength, but also of the myths surrounding the beverage. From its earliest days, Guinness stout was considered a nutritional beverage and promoter of virility. Although the company was once accused of mashing Protestant Bibles and Methodist hymn

Key Dates:

1759: Arthur Guinness takes over a small brewery in St. James Gate on the outskirts of Dublin and brews ales and porters.
1769: Guinness Brewery's first export is 54 barrels of Guinness porter shipped to England.
1799: Guinness focuses production exclusively on porter, later called stout.
1821: The company's first brew of Extra Superior porter, now known as the standard pint of Guinness.
1840: Extra Superior porter accounts for 82% of the company's exports.
1886: Guinness becomes the first major brewery to be floated on the London Stock Exchange. By this date, the St. James brewery had become the largest brewery in the world, producing 1.2 million barrels a year.
1920: Guinness production reaches 3 million barrels a year.
1936: Guinness' first overseas brewery, the Park Royal Brewery opens in London.
1955: Guinness Book of World Records conceived by Guinness managing director Hugh Beaver.
1961: Launch of Guinness draught.
1981: First non-family member, Ernest Saunders, takes over Guinness as chief executive officer.
1986: Guinness acquires Distillers Company of Scotland for £2.6 billion.
1987: Saunders asked to resign amid a stock manipulation controversy surrounding the Distillers Company acquisition.
1989: Guinness draught in cans is launched.
1997: Guinness and Grand Metropolitan undertake $19 billion merger to form Diageo.
1999: Guinness draught in bottles is launched.
2000: Guinness and UDV are combined to form Guinness/UDV.

books into the brew in order to force ingestion of anti-Papal doctrine, Britain's leading medical journal during the mid-19th century claimed the drink was ''. . . one of the best cordials not included in the pharmacopoeia.'' This notion formed the basis of the company's advertisement campaign of 1929, which suggested that drinking Guinness could lead to the development of ''strong muscles,'' ''enriched blood,'' and the alleviation of ''exhausted nerves.'' Somewhat surprisingly, this tradition still continues in Britain: the national health insurance system underwrites the purchase of Guinness for nursing mothers.

When Arthur died in 1855, his son, Benjamin Lee, assumed control of the company. Fifty-seven years old at the time, he had already worked for nearly 30 years at the brewery. During his tenure as head of the firm, the James Gate facility became the pre-eminent porter brewery in the world. Following the tradition of his family, he was also intimately involved in civic affairs. He was awarded a baronetcy in 1867 for his contributions to the restoration of St. Patrick's Cathedral and other services; he died a year later.

Although Benjamin Lee Guinness, in his will, divided the responsibility for running the firm equally between his two sons, Edward Cecil and Arthur Edward, Edward soon emerged as the more astute of the two. The younger of the brothers, he was said to be an energetic yet excitable man. His decisions were controversial and, apparently, overwhelming: after eight years Arthur decided to leave the brewing business, and the partnership was dissolved.

In the tradition of his family, Edward became a leading figure in both civic affairs and in English social life. After his marriage to his cousin Adelaide, he seems to have ''arrived,'' and the young couple circulated freely in elite circles. Among the many dignitaries entertained at their opulent 23,000 acre estate in Suffolk was King Edward VII.

Edward Guinness's wealth, prestige, influence, and mainly his philanthropies eventually earned him the title of Lord Iveagh. He drew heavily from the family fortune to contribute to worthy causes. He established the Iveagh Trust to provide basic necessities for 950 indigent families. He donated money for the continuing restoration of St. Patrick's Cathedral. He was, as well, recognized as an enlightened employer, ahead of his time in providing pension plans, health services, and housing for his employees.

Guinness Goes Public, Opens Second Brewery

In 1886, Guinness became a public company, its shares traded on the London exchange (Dublin, at that time lacked its own exchange). The company raised six million pounds on its shares, and embarked on an ambitious period of expansion in Ireland, England, and abroad. Guinness's unique brewing process ensured that the quality of the produce would not be impaired by long voyages to foreign markets. By the 1920's, Guinness had reached the shores of East and West Africa and the Caribbean.

In 1927, leadership of the company passed to the next generation. The second Lord Iveagh is recognized primarily for his role in creating a modern brewery at Park Royal in London, built to service the company's growing business in southeast England. The facility became operational in 1936, and it is there that Guinness Extra and Draught Guinness were first brewed for the British market. By 1974, production at this plant exceeded that at James Gate by 100 percent.

Construction of the Park Royal facility was completed under the supervision of a civil engineer, Hugh E.C. Beaver. He formed a close association with managing director C.J. Newbold, yet turned down Newbold's invitation to join the Guinness board of directors. After World War II Lord Iveagh personally asked Beaver to join the company as assistant managing director—and, this time, Beaver accepted. When Newbold died in the late 1940s, Beaver assumed the position of managing director. He is credited with modernizing the company's operations, introducing new management and research policies, increasing exports, and diversifying the company's product base. On his initiative the company was officially divided into Guinness Ireland and Guinness U.K. (control of both concerns remains with a central board of directors).

Beaver was also a strong advocate of generating new ideas through ''brainstorming sessions.'' One now-famous product to emerge from these meetings was Harp lager. When Britons began taking their holidays abroad during the 1950's, they returned home with a new taste for chilled lager. Beaver sensed this changing preference, and during one of the "brainstorming sessions" company executives decided that Guinness should become the first local firm to market its own lager. Named for the harp on the label of Guinness's traditional product, Harp lager soon became the most successful product in the growing British lager market.

The Company Branches Out

Beaver is also recognized as the founder of the extraordinarily successful publication, *Guinness Book of World Records.* Initially created as something of a company lark, the book has been such a success, throughout the world, that it is now a company tradition. The *Guinness Book of World Records* now sells some five million copies in 13 different languages.

Beaver, now Sir Hugh, retired in 1960, but throughout the next decade Guinness continued to expand—notably abroad, in countries with warm climates. Consistent with this strategy, the company constructed new breweries in Nigeria and Malaysia—then, a second and third brewery in Nigeria, as well as breweries in Cameroon, Ghana, and Jamaica. Guinness also developed a new product during this period, Irish Ale, which was exported to France and Britain. To offset the declining market for stout, the company began to diversify into pharmaceuticals, confectionary, and plastics, as well as other beverages.

Although both sales and earnings per share had doubled between 1965 and 1971, Guinness entered the 1970's confronting a number of problems. Compared to those of its competitors, the company's shares sold at modest prices, largely because Guinness operated outside the tiedhouse system (the five largest brewers owned and operated most of the country's 100,000 pubs), and investors felt the other breweries had the advantage for growth. The London financial community reasoned that Guinness was at a disadvantage because the company had to absorb the added costs of retailing.

There were also problems at the James Gate brewery. The Park Royal facility continued to outproduce the older Dublin site, and the company and its employees' union reached an agreement whereby the James Gate work force would be reduced by nearly one half. This solution temporarily solved the problem of decreasing profits at the James Gate facility and allowed operations to continue at the highly esteemed landmark facility. By 1976, however, the cost-cutting plan was seen to have achieved less than had been expected.

The company's diversification efforts were also, during this period, less than stellar; in the event, the company had gone on a purchasing spree in which 270 companies, producing a wide variety of products from baby bibs to car polish, had been acquired, and many of these companies were operating in deficit.

Even in the base brewing business, Guinness had its share of troubles. Its witty advertisements certainly appealed to the middle class but ignored the working class that provided the bulk of Guinness's custom. A new product, designed to combine the tastes of stout and ale, was a three-million-pound mistake. The Guinness share price continued to decline.

Ernest Saunders Takes Over

To remedy the situation, Guinness executives called in the first non-family professional manager to take over leadership of the company. The sixth Lord Iveagh, as well as numerous Guinness relations, remained on the board, but Ernest Saunders, a former executive at J. Walter Thompson and Nestlé, stepped in as chief executive officer.

Saunders saw his first task as reducing the company's disparate holdings. He sold 160 companies. The companies that remained were all retail businesses. He then reduced the work force and brought in a new management team to develop and market the company's products. He made a large investment in increased and more eclectic advertising. He made cunning acquisitions in specialty foods, publishing, and retailing (including the 7 Eleven convenience stores). Brewing, according to Saunders, would in the future comprise only half of Guinness's total volume. Financial analysts, and the City of London in general, were pleased with Saunders's efforts. The Guinness share price began noticeably to climb.

By mid-1985, Saunders seemed to have conquered. During his tenure the company's profits had tripled, its share price increased four-fold. He had accomplished a dazzling takeover of Distillers Company (Dewar's White Label, Johnnie Walker, and Gordon's). That Guinness could—and would—pay £2.5 billion for a company twice its size surprised many industry analysts, yet Saunders's wish to create a multi-national company on the scale of Nestlé seemed to justify the expense. There were rumors that Saunders might be honored with a knighthood.

Within a matter of months, however, there were other kinds of rumors in the City—rumors concerning Saunders's methods in making the Distillers acquisition. In order to make possible the Distillers takeover, Saunders, with two of his fellow directors, allegedly had orchestrated an international scheme to provoke the sale of Guinness shares, thus raise their value and make possible the acquisition. Outside investors were indemnified in various ways against any losses incurred in purchasing huge numbers of Guinness shares. Bank Leu in Switzerland purchased Guinness shares, with the understanding that the company would eventually buy them back. In return, Guinness deposited $75 million (in a non–interest-earning account) with the bank. The bank's chairman happened to be Saunders's ex-boss at Nestlé and a Guinness board member. Ivan F. Boesky, the American arbitrageur who has now admitted to "insider trading" in numerous deals, has been cited as the primary source of information about the Distillers takeover. Boesky is himself believed to have played a large role in the takeover; Guinness made a $100 million investment in a limited partnership run by Boesky only one month after Boesky had made significant purchases of Guinness shares. Boesky is now believed to have been only the tip of the iceberg, only one of various international investors who bought Guinness shares in an effort to increase their value. The company's auditors have discovered some $38 million worth of invoices for "services" rendered by various international investors during the takeover.

The charges, if true, were extremely serious—and, obviously a violation of British company laws. Starting in late 1986, events moved quickly. In December of that year, the British

Trade and Industry Department instigated an investigation of Guinness. In January 1987, the Guinness board of directors asked for Saunders's resignation, and subsequently, in March, brought legal action against Saunders and one of his fellow directors, John Ward. In May, the British government brought charges of fraud against Saunders: the claim was that Saunders knowingly destroyed evidence during the Trade and Industry Department investigation. Throughout these events, Saunders continued to deny all charges brought against him.

New CEO Moves Guinness Out of Further Demise

The Guinness share price tumbled as a result of the continuing scandal. To prevent any further decline, Anthony Tennant, Guinness's new chief executive officer, announced a plan to sell the company's subsidiary businesses and to concentrate solely on brewing. Clares Equipment, a manufacturer of shopping equipment, was sold for £28.5 million as a start. Over the next 3 years, the company acquired Buckley's Brewery PLC, All Brand Importers, Schenley Canada, J. Cawsey, and their Canadian beer distributor, Rymax Corp. They also bought 24 percent of H Moet Hennessy Louis Vuitton (LVMH), a French cognac, champagne, and perfume maker. In 1991, Guinness purchased 99.3 percent of La Cruz de Campo SA, a Spanish beer maker. It was the largest foreign investment in Spain's history.

In a 1990 trial, Ernest Saunders and three other executives were convicted of theft and false accounting. Saunders served nine months of a 2.5-year sentence, released early due to health concerns. Guinness put the scandal behind them when they agreed to pay Argyll 92 million pounds in 1991.

Sir Anthony Tennant retired in 1992. The next few years found Guinness continuing to purchase spirits, wine, and beer companies, and rearranging the holdings it already had. International expansion continued as well, as Guinness moved into Australia, Mexico, Venezuela, Spain, and the U.S. In 1994, Guinness and LVMH reorganized to discontinue Guinness' involvement in LVMH's perfume and luggage lines.

Saunders and the Guinness scandal once again made news in 1994, when the European Commission of Human Rights ruled that Saunders did not receive a fair trial in 1990. The fraud convictions moved to an appeals court. The court upheld the earlier convictions. Three of the defendants (not Saunders) continued to fight their convictions, and in January 2001 the case was once again referred to the Court of Appeal.

The year 1997, was pivotal for the company as Guinness joined forces with Grand Metropolitan, who produced the brands Smirnoff, Baileys, and J&B. By combining the spirits parts of both businesses, the new parent company, Diageo, created United Distiller & Vintners. One of the 10 largest mergers in history, the company comprised Guinness Brewing Worldwide; Grand Met wines; Moet Hennessy; Jose Cuervo; Stolichnaya; plus Pillsbury and Burger King, to name a few. Now the company had its hands in more than 200 countries and had 180 bottling facilities. In 2000, Diageo combined all its alcoholic business units to form the present-day Guinness/UDV.

Expansion wasn't the only venture going on in Guinness headquarters. In the mid-1990s, the company faced a plateau in sales as alcoholic purchases waned and markets faced economic difficulties. To counter this, the company marketed Guinness in two different ways: They started putting Guinness in a can, and they beefed up the "Irish pub" popularity. The Guinness-in-a-can was a novel concept due to Guinness' "smoothifier," a plastic device in the cans that created the same experience as a keg-pulled beer. The company also struggled to overcome Guinness' image as a dark, heavy, unhealthy beer choice. They also helped new pubs create a "Guinness experience" by participating in the designs from the furniture to the food. At this time, Guinness was also fortunate to tap into the popularity of single-malt drinks by offering more scotches than any other distiller.

The early part of the new century brought more expansion to Guinness/UDV (with the purchase of Seagram's, for example) and some ventures into the wine business with a new organization headed by Raymond S. Chadwick of Seagram. The company hit some bumps, too, as Guinness once again fell in popularity with younger generations who felt it represented their parents' drinks. A strike at breweries in Dublin, Kilkenny, Waterford, and Dundalk halted production for a day in February 2001. Later that year, the company closed its production facility at Dundalk, laying off 140 people. To combat these struggles, Guinness increased its marketing efforts, rearranged its senior executive teams, and continued to distribute and develop new alcoholic beverages well into 2001.

Principal Subsidiaries

Arthur Guinness Son & Co. (Great Britain) Ltd.; Arthur Guinness Son & Co. (Belfast) Ltd.; Irish Bonding Co. Ltd. (N. Ireland); Croft Inns Ltd. (N. Ireland); Martin the Newsagent plc; Guinness Enterprises Ltd.; Clares Equipment Ltd.; R. Gordon Drummond Ltd. (Scotland); Lavells Ltd.; The Harp Lager Co. Ltd.; Guinness Ireland Ltd.; Arthur Guinness Son & Co. (Dublin); Guinness Group Sales; Harp Ireland Ltd.; Irish Ale Breweries Ltd.; Murtagh Properties Ltd.; Meadow Meats Ltd.; Guinness Overseas Ltd.; Guinness Exports Ltd.; Guinness Malaysia Berhad (Malaysia); Guinness Cameroun SA (Cameroon); Guinness-Harp Corp. (U.S.A.); Arthur Bell & Sons plc; The Distillers Co. plc; The Champneys Group Ltd.; Neighborhood Stores plc; Richter Brothers Inc.

Principal Competitors

Adolph Coors; Allied Domecq; Anheuser-Busch; Asahi Breweries; Bacardi; Bass Brewers; Boston Beer; Brauerei Beck; Brown-Forman; Carlsberg; Constellation Brands; Danone; Foster's Brewing Gallo; Heineken; Interbrew; Kendall-Jackson; Kirin; Miller Brewing; Molson; Pernod Ricard; Remy Cointreau; Robert Mondavi; S&P; Scottish & Newcastle; South African Breweries; Suntory; V&S.

Further Reading

Ashworth, Jon, "Guinness Case Appeal," *The Times* (Britain), January 3, 2001.

——, "Guinness Trial Trio Seek UK Ruling," *The Times* (Britain), January 4, 2001.

Banks, Howard, "We'll Provide the Shillelaghs," *Forbes*, April 8, 1996, p. 68.

"The Business of Guinness," *Marketing*, December 4, 1997, p. 27.

Curtis, James, "Can Guinness Keep Ahead?" *Marketing*, March 5, 1998, p. 14.

''Grand Met and Guinness: About as Big as It Gets,'' *Beverage World*, June 15, 1997, p. 14.

Grose, Thomas K. ''Erin Go Lager,'' *U.S. News & World Report*, March 19, 2001, p. 41.

''Guilty in the Guinness Trial,'' *The Economist*, September 1, 1990, p. 13.

''The Guinness Affair, Bitter End,'' *The Economist*, November 29, 1997, p. 89.

Guinness, Jonathan, *Requiem for a Family Business*, New York: Macmillan, 1997.

''The Guinness Scandal,'' *The Economist*, July 1, 1989, p. 74.

''Guinness UDV North America Names Seagram Executives as Leadership Team for New Integrated Wines Company,'' *Business Wire*, posted July 6, 2001, http://www.businesswire.com.

Holland, Kelley, ''Grand Met and Guinness Tie One On,'' *Business Week*, May 26, 1997 p. 62.

''How Guinness Adopted a Careline Strategy,'' *Marketing*, August 27, 1998, p. 12.

Jackson, Michael, ''The New Muscle in the Industry,'' *Forbes*, November 25, 1991, p. S4.

Kay, William, ''More Trouble Brewing: Guinness Scandal Leads to Criminal Charges,'' *Barron's National Business and Financial Weekly*, May 18, 1987, p. 44.

Kennedy, Dominic, ''I Just Told a White Lie,'' *The Times* (Britain), January 30, 2001.

Khermouch, Gerry, ''UDV Streamlines,'' *Brandweek*, July 13, 1998, p. 13.

MacDonald, Lauries, ''Guinness Puts Pub in a Can,'' *Beverage World*, January 31, 1992, p. 10.

MaGee, Audrey, ''Sacked Guinness Workers Get Free Beer for a Decade,'' *The Times* (Britain), June 1, 2001.

Maland, Oliver, ''The Guinness Case,'' *Campaign*, July 31, 1998, p. 19.

Maling, Nick, ''Guinness Axes Failing Enigma,'' *Marketing Week*, December 10, 1998, p. 4.

McLuhan, Robert, ''Guinness Aims for New Fans,'' *Marketing*, July 2, 1998, p. 23.

Mills, Kevin, ''The Big Pint Is Getting Bigger,'' *Irish Business News*, March 16, 1998.

Nolan, Alexis, ''On Top of the World,'' *Supply Management*, February 18, 1999, p. 24.

Prince, Greg W. ''Planet Guinness,'' *Beverage World*, September 1994, p. 41.

Sherrid, Pamela, ''Britain's Business Elite Takes a Fall,'' *U.S. News & World Report*, February 2, 1987, p. 47.

''Stout Fellows,'' *The Economist*, June 9, 1990, p. 66.

Stroud, Michael, ''Guinness' Record,'' *Broadcasting & Cable*, August 10, 1998, p. 44.

Walsh, Dominic, ''Guinness Strike May Cost Diageo Millions,'' *The Times* (Britain), April 13, 2001.

Weever, Patrick, ''Guinness, A Loud Report,'' *Sunday Telegraph*, November 9, 1997, p. 5.

—update: Kerri DeVault

The Hain Celestial Group, Inc.

50 Charles Lindbergh Boulevard
Uniondale, New York 11553
U.S.A.
Telephone: (516) 237-6200
Fax: (516) 237-6240
Web site: http://www.hain-celestial.com

Public Company
Incorporated: 1926 as Hain Pure Foods Co.
Employees: 940
Sales: $412.9 million (2001)
Stock Exchanges: NASDAQ
Ticker Symbol: HAIN
NAIC: 311920 Coffee and Tea Manufacturing; 311411 Frozen Fruit, Juice, and Vegetable Manufacturing; 311412 Frozen Specialty Food Manufacturing; 311423 Dried and Dehydrated Food Manufacturing; 311812 Commercial Bakeries; 311821 Cookie and Cracker Manufacturing; 311823 Dry Pasta Manufacturing; 311830 Tortilla Manufacturing; 311919 Other Snack Food Manufacturing; 311999 All Other Miscellaneous Food Manufacturing

The Hain Celestial Group, Inc. manufactures, markets, distributes and sells natural, organic, medically directed (sugar-free and low-salt), snack and weight management food products, many of which are the top in their categories. Among the company's many well-known brands are: Arrowhead Mills (grains), DeBoles (pasta), Estee (diabetic foods), Hain Pure Foods (rice cakes and cooking oils), Health Valley (natural soups, snacks, chili, cereal, and baked goods), Kineret (frozen kosher foods), Westsoy (soy-based drinks), Terra Chips (vegetable snacks), and most notably, Celestial Seasonings (specialty teas). Formerly the Hain Food Group, the Uniondale, New York-based company changed its name to The Hain Celestial Group when it acquired Celestial Seasonings in 2000. H.J. Heinz owns nearly 20 percent of the company.

From Carrots to Oils and Beyond: 1926–94

Hain Pure Food Company was founded in 1926 in Stockton, California, by Harold Hain, who was originally interested in marketing carrot juice. The company grew well beyond its humble beverage beginnings to become one of North America's oldest and most prominent natural food businesses, known for selling a range of foods that are minimally processed, mostly or completely free of artificial ingredients, preservatives, and other non-naturally-occurring chemicals, and are near to their whole natural state as possible. In 1955, the company introduced its Hollywood line of vegetable cooking oils. With the debut of Hain Yogurt Chips in the early 1970s, Hain began developing diet and health snacks. By 1983, the company was offering more than 300 natural and health food items. The company's products found their place all over: in supermarkets, health food stores, and specialty shops throughout the United States and abroad in countries such as Austria, England, Germany, and Japan.

The small but promising natural food company was bought and sold through many larger companies throughout the 1980s and into the early 1990s before it could develop and grow significantly. Hain Pure Food was acquired by Ogden Corp. in 1981, and was again sold in 1986 to IC Industries Inc., which assigned Hain Pure Food to its Pet, Inc. specialty foods subsidiary. In 1991 the former IC Industries, which had become Whitman Corp., spun off Pet, which became an independent company. Pet sold Hain in 1993 to focus on its core businesses. The buyer, in April 1994, was Kineret Acquisition Corp., a specialty foods company based in Jericho, New York, that paid $22 million in cash and stock for the operation. At long last, Hain's latest parent company would prove to be loyal, under the steady leadership of Irwin Simon, a former career executive in the food industry whose mission was to buy specialty food companies that were mismanaged or not realizing their potential, including those selling natural, low-fat, or ethnic foods. At this time, Hain was marketing even more natural food products, including the Hollywood line of specialty cooking oils, carrot juice, mayonnaise, and margarine, and had sales of about $50 million a year.

Company Perspectives:

We have always emphasized that our success is built on four key strengths: our brands, our people, our strategy, and our financial performance. In the past, our commitment to this recipe resulted in achievements of which we are very proud. And, we are excited about our prospects for the future, as we continue toward our objective of becoming a billion-dollar company.

Flourishing Under Strong Leadership: 1994–97

The Hain acquisition ''made us a major player in the natural-food industry,'' Simon said. ''It allowed me to hire a different level of people, and from a company standpoint, it allowed me to be able to participate in certain advertising and promotions and upgrade systems.'' Simon immediately began to focus on one of Hain's most successful product lines, its all-natural rice cakes, which accounted for about 40 percent of Hain's sales. Simon repackaged the line in brightly colored, resealable cardboard cartons, introduced rice cake snack bars, and marketed Mini Munchies, a new line of bite-size rice cakes in several flavors, including ''strawberry cheesecake.'' Although Quaker Oats dominated this market, Simon did not let the food giant faze him. ''People always ask me, 'Doesn't Quaker frighten you?' '' he told a Forbes reporter in 1996. ''But every time I see Quaker ads on TV I just shout, 'Yeah!' They're growing the category.''

Simon moved his company to Uniondale in August 1994 and changed its name to Hain Food Group four months later. In fiscal 1994 (the year ended June 30, 1994), the company reported a loss of $502,000 on sales of $15 million. But, it also came up with 24 new products to market. With the completion of the Hain acquisition, revenues rose to $58.1 million in fiscal 1995. The company moved into the black that year, with $2.4 million in net income. Hain raised $7.6 million in 1994 from the conversion of warrants to common stock in connection with the company's initial public offering. The funds were used to retire a $7.9 million loan.

In late 1995 Hain Food Group purchased Estee Corp., a deficit-ridden producer of sugar-free and low-sodium products for persons on medically directed diets, including diabetics, and other health-conscious consumers, for $11.3 million. Simon immediately closed the company's New Jersey plant, dismissing 180 employees and contracting production to a Canadian firm. Hain's acquisitions continued in 1996, when Simon purchased Growing Healthy Inc., a fledgling baby food company, and Harry's Premium Snacks, a potato chip and pretzel maker.

During fiscal 1996, the company had revenues of $68.6 million and earnings of $2.1 million, and it upped the number of its food products to 250. Simon was running a very lean operation, with only 43 employees, by farming out manufacturing and distribution. Nevertheless, when sales declined to $65.4 million in fiscal 1997, a drop that was attributed in large part to a $10.5 million sales fall-off for Hain's rice cakes, net income fell to $1.1 million. That year, the company marketed 71 new products.

In March 1997, Hain reached an agreement to manufacture, market, and sell soups, snacks, and other food products of Weight Watchers Gourmet Food Co., a subsidiary of H.J. Heinz Co., with the products to continue to be sold under the Weight Watchers name. These 60-odd products were the dry and refrigerated goods that had generated only $17 million in sales for Weight Watchers in 1996 but at one time had done $100 million a year in business before becoming ''lost within the Heinz infrastructure,'' according to Simon. Under the five-year agreement, Weight Watchers would receive royalties and a share of the profits. This transaction made Hain, according to one of its executives, the nation's leading marketer of foods sold to dieters and other consumers with special medical needs. Hain repackaged the line to connect it more closely to Weight Watchers ''1-2-3 Success'' theme and added 30 new products.

Hain Food Group's next major acquisition, in October 1997, was that of Westbrae Natural, Inc., a California-based company with sales of nearly $38 million the previous year, for $23.5 million in cash. Westbrae's leading product was soy milk. The purchase allowed Hain to strengthen its presence in natural food stores, where Westbrae averaged 250 to 300 stockkeeping units (SKUs). Following the transaction, Hain's product line reached 1,000 SKUs spanning 13 brand lines. Other 1997 acquisitions included Alba Foods, a Heinz line of dry milk products, and Boston Popcorn Co., a snack food firm. Having sold the manufacturing facilities of its acquisitions, Hain now was dealing with a network of 95 co-packers. Simon was named 1997 Entrepreneur of the Year by Ernst & Young; he was also named one of *Business Week*'s Best Entrepreneurs of the Year.

Going Public and Maturing: 1997–99

Hain Food Group made a new public offering of 2.5 million shares of common stock at $9 a share in December 1997. The proceeds of about $21 million were used to pay down debt, which was $16.6 million in mid-1998. In large part because of the Westbrae acquisition, net sales rose to $104.3 million in fiscal 1998. Net income increased to a record $3.3 million, inspiring the price of the stock to rise as high as $28.625 a share in the summer of 1998. One of the company's supporters was billionaire George Soros, whose Soros Fund Management bought a 16 percent stake in early 1997 and still owned nearly 10 percent in October 1998. White Rock, a Texas corporation and limited partnership, owned 20.1 percent. Simon held 10.7 percent of the shares.

In April 1998, Hain Food Group announced that it had agreed to acquire four closely held natural foods businesses for $60 million, plus the assumption of about $20 million in debt, from Shansby Group, a San Francisco investment company, and other owners. These firms were Arrowhead Mills Inc., DeBoles Nutritional Foods Inc., Dana Alexander Inc., and Garden of Eatin' Inc. The acquisition was completed in July 1998.

By this time Simon, who had a five-year plan to increase company sales to $500 million by 2002, was paying more attention to promoting Hain Food Group products among consumers rather than merely distributors and retailers. The company had become involved in a number of promotional campaigns, including ones involving Weight Watchers, the American Diabetic Association, schools, and several cancer groups. ''As we move into the 21st century,'' he told a reporter, ''there is more awareness about nutrition and healthy foods. . . .

Key Dates:

1926: Hain Pure Food Company is founded.
1955: Company introduces Hollywood vegetable oils.
1994: Hain is acquired by Kineret Acquisition Corp.
1998: Company begins alliance with Heinz.
2000: Company acquires Celestial Seasonings and becomes The Hain Celestial Group.
2001: International expansion includes purchase of Yves Veggie Cuisine.

We see the market (for better-for-you foods) growing drastically.'' Accordingly, Hain, in the latter half of 1998, introduced Chicken Broth and Noodles with Echinacea, Country Vegetable with Echinacea, Creamy Split Pea with St. John's Wort, and Chunky Tomato with St. John's Wort. These products were described on their labels as ''herbal supplements,'' rather than soup, probably because dietary supplements were subject to less government regulation than were foods.

In addition to its Hain and Westbrae lines of natural food products, Hain Food Group's products, in mid-1998, consisted of the Hollywood Foods line, the Estee and Featherweight lines of sugar-free and low-sodium products, kosher frozen foods under the Kineret and Kosherific labels, the licensed Weight Watchers products, and about 40 snack food items under the Boston Popcorn and Harry's Original names. The additions from the July 1998 acquisitions consisted of 360 ready-to-eat grains, nut butters, and nutritional oils produced by Arrowhead Mills and DeBoles, about 48 natural food vegetable chip items by Terra Chips, and a variety of tortilla chip products from Garden of Eatin'. Nondairy drinks accounted for about 19 percent of Hain's fiscal 1998 net sales.

Also by June 1998, Hain entered into a license agreement with food giant Heinz to market and sell its Earth's Best baby food products to natural food stores. The venture did so well that, by the end of 1999, Hain had purchased the trademarks for the product line and secured the option to grow the product line itself. That same year, Heinz moved to tap into the growing natural foods market, by making a $100 million investment in Hain, which represented a 19.5 percent stake. During this fruitful time with Heinz, Hain continued to make strategic acquisitions and join company with yet another food giant: In December, 1998, Hain bought Nile Spice soup and meal cup from The Quaker Oats Company, and, in May 1999, Hain acquired NNG (Natural Nutrition Group, Inc.), an organic food manufacturer that marketed its products under the Health Valley, Breadshop's and Sahara brands. Sales for fiscal 1998 grew 97.5 percent, as the company continued to flourish.

Merging with Celestial and Forging On: The New Millennium

In May 2000, Hain acquired Celestial Seasonings, the largest manufacturer and marketer of herbal teas in the United States, which had introduced roughly 50 tea varieties throughout the world. Chiefly responsible for creating the herb tea industry in the United States, Celestial Seasonings was founded by Mo Siegel and Wyck Hay, who introduced the country's consumers to colorfully packaged, decaffeinated herb teas that offered ''soothing teas for a nervous world.'' During the mid-1990s, Celestial Seasonings controlled an estimated 51 percent of the herb tea market. By the time of the acquisition by Hain, Celestial Seasonings had reached $109.8 million in revenue for 1999. Together, Hain and Celestial Seasonings became the largest natural foods company in the United States, and was renamed The Hain Celestial Group. In fiscal 2000, sales reached $404 million, and promised to be even greater in the future with Celestial Seasonings in the mix. According to Simon, ''The transaction combines Hain, with its experience in selling to specialty natural foods markets, and Celestial Seasonings, which has great expertise in successfully reaching the retail mass market.''

In 2001, Hain Celestial sought to grow its international markets by engaging in key acquisitions and ventures, to help grow its brand presence and distributions channels abroad. It bought Netherlands-based Fruit Chips, maker of Gaston's fruit, vegetable, and potato chips, and then changed its name to Terra Chips to grow the Terra brand in Europe. In June of that same year, the company acquired Vancouver, Canada-based Yves Veggie Cuisine, Inc., a manufacturer and distributor of meat- and cheese-alternative food products that are made instead with soy protein. Hain Celestial could take advantage of the Canadian company's extensive and established infrastructure, sales force, and distribution network. Soon after that acquisition, Hain Celestial announced a join-venture with Grupo Siro, Spain's largest snack company, to further expand its distribution channels in Europe.

Principal Subsidiaries

AMI Operating, Inc.; Arrowhead Mills, Inc.; Celestial Seasonings; Dana Alexander, Inc.; DeBoles; Nutritional Foods, Inc.; Earth's Best; Garden of Eatin', Inc.; Hain Pure Food Co., Inc.; Harry's Premium Snacks; Health Valley Company; Kineret Foods Corp.; Little Bear Organic Foods, Inc.; Natural Nutrition Group, Inc.; Terra Chips B.V.; Westbrae Natural Foods, Inc.; Westbrae Natural, Inc.; Yves Veggies Cuisine, Inc.

Principal Competitors

The B. Manischewitz Company; Bestfoods; Campbell Soup; ConAgra Foods; Frito-Lay; Galaxy Nutritional Foods; Gardenburger; General Mills; Guiltless Gourmet; Kellogg; Kraft Foods; Nestlé; Proctor & Gamble; Quaker Oats; Tofutti Brands.

Further Reading

Ain, Stewart, ''A Dynamo in the Food Marketing Arena,'' *New York Times*, April 12, 1998, Sec. 14 (*Long Island Weekly*), p. 2.
Anderson, Duncan Maxwell, ''Free At Last,'' *Success*, July/August 1995, p. 14.
Atchinson, Sandra D., ''An Herbal Tea Party Gets a Bitter Response,'' *Business Week*, June 20, 1988, p. 52.
——, ''Kraft Is Celestial Seasonings' Cup of Tea,'' *Business Week*, July 28, 1986, p. 73.
——, ''Why Celestial Seasonings Wasn't Kraft's Cup of Tea,'' *Business Week*, May 8, 1989, p. 76.
Davids, Meryl, ''Healthy Harvest,'' *Chief Executive*, May 1998, p. 25.

Dwyer, Steve, ''Hain's 'Natural' High,'' *Prepared Foods*, April 1998, pp. 12–13, 15–16.

''Hain Celestial Expands European Snack Business Through Grupo Siro Venture and Introduction of New Terra Products,'' *PR Newswire*, posted August 1, 2001, http://www.prnewswire.com.

''The Hain Celestial Group and H.J. Heinz Company Plan New Beverage Initiative,'' *The Beverage Network*, posted August 27, 2000, http://www.bevnet.com.

''Hain Food Seals 4-Store Acquisition,'' *Newsday*, July 2, 1998, p. A60.

''Heinz Increases Share in Hain Celestial,'' *Pittsburgh Business Times*, June 12, 2000.

''Hitting Bottom,'' *Inc.*, March 1994, p. 36.

Locke, Tom, ''A Taste for Success: Mo Siegel Trusts His Tastebuds in Running Celestial Seasonings,'' *Denver Business Journal*, July 30, 1993, p. 3A.

——, ''Celestial Seasonings Plans Public Offering,'' *Denver Business Journal*, June 4, 1993, p. 1.

Miller, Hilary S., ''Celestial Seasonings Takes Aim at RTD Tea—Again,'' *Supermarket News*, July 24, 1995, p. 30.

Nagle, Claire, ''It's High Time for Tea Tours,'' *Colorado Business Magazine*, March 1994, p. 66.

''Natural Foods Superpower Emerges from Hain Food-Celestial Merger,'' *Boulder County Business Report*, March 2000.

Plank, Dave, ''Hain and Celestial Merger Goes 1, 2, 3,'' *Boulder County Business Report*, April 2000.

''Quality and Taste Spur Hain Snack Line Growth,'' *Snack Food*, March 1983, pp. 20–22.

Sandberg, Lisa, ''Natural Food Industry Gears Up for Youth Market,'' *The National Post (Canada)*, November 22, 2000, p. B4.

Shaw, Hollie, ''Hain Gobbles Yves Veggie-Soy-based 'Meat' Goods: U.S. Natural Food Giant Buys Vancouver Company,'' *Financial Post*, June 12, 2001.

Siegel, Jennifer and Mo Siegel, with Jordan Simon, *Celestial Seasonings' Cookbook: Cooking with Tea*, New York: Park Lane Press, 1996.

Siegel, Mo, and Nancy Burke, *Celestial Seasonings' Herbs for Health and Happiness: All You Need to Know*, Alexandria, VA: Time-Life Books, 1999.

Siklos, Richard, ''Real Men Do Eat Niche,'' *Financial Post*, October 16, 1997, p. 12.

Steers, Stuart, ''Celestial Explores Retail: Herbal Tea Firm Seeks Partner,'' *Denver Business Journal*, May 5, 1995, p. 1A.

Studnick, Alison, ''Ricequake,'' *Food & Beverage Marketing*, January 1995, pp. 26–7.

Sugarman, Carole, ''Magic Bullets,'' *Washington Post*, October 21, 1998, p. E1.

Tascarella, Patty, ''Heinz Puts on a New Baby Face,'' *Pittsburgh Business Times*, June 5, 1998, p. 1.

Waters, Jennifer, ''Growing Healthy Leftovers for Sale,'' *Minneapolis-St. Paul City Business*, May 3, 1996, p. 1.

Wolf, Chris, ''Celestial Merger Brings Enterprise Clout, Consolidation, Responsibility,'' *The Boulder County Business Report*, April 2000.

Woods, Bob, ''Healthy Appetite,'' *Food & Beverage Marketing*, May 1998, p. 8.

Wooley, Scott, ''The Slipstream Strategy,'' *Forbes*, October 7, 1996, pp. 78, 80.

''Yves Veggie Cuisine, the Leading Fresh Meat Analog Company, Merges with Hain Celestial,'' *Canada NewsWire*, posted June 11, 2001, http://www.newswire.ca.

—Robert Halasz (Hain),
Jeffrey L. Covell (Celestial Seasonings)
—update: Heidi Wrightsman

Harmonic Inc.

549 Baltic Way
Sunnyvale, California 94089
U.S.A.
Telephone: (408) 542-2500
Toll Free: (800) 788-1330
Fax: (408) 542-2510
Web site: http://www.harmonicinc.com

Public Company
Incorporated: 1988 as Harmonic Lightwaves, Inc.
Employees: 925
Sales: $184.1 million (1999)
Stock Exchanges: NASDAQ
Ticker Symbol: HLIT
NAIC: 334220 Radio and Television Broadcasting and Wireless Communications Equipment Manufacturing

Harmonic Inc., formerly Harmonic Lightwaves, Inc., provides a range of products and solutions that enable satellite, wireless, fiber, and cable television companies to offer interactive services. The company is organized into two divisions, the Broadband Access Networks Division and the Convergent Systems Division. In addition, the company has a research and development subsidiary located in Israel. Its Broadband Access Networks Division provides optical networking products that enable the delivery of interactive services in networks originally designed for one-way cable transmission. Its Convergent Systems Division develops solutions for operators to maximize the capacity of their broadband networks through advanced compression, processing, and multiplexing technology. In May 2000 Harmonic completed its acquisition of DiviCom, a provider of open solutions for digital television, from C-Cube Microsystems, Inc. for $1.7 billion.

Developed Broadband Solutions for Cable TV Systems, 1988–94

The company was founded in 1988 as Harmonic Lightwaves, Inc. in Sunnyvale, California. One of the founders was Moshe Nazarathy, the company's vice-president of research and later senior vice-president, general manager of the company's Israel R&D Center. Prior to cofounding Harmonic Lightwaves, he served as principal scientist at Hewlett-Packard's Photonics and Instruments Laboratory.

In November 1988 Anthony Ley was named president and CEO. He had spent 25 years at Schlumberger Ltd., both in Europe and the United States. Schlumberger was a multibillion dollar oil exploration and industrial aviation corporation based in England. It owned Fairchild Semiconductor Corp. from 1983 to 1985; during that period Ley was vice-president of research and engineering at Fairchild's Palo Alto location. Ley, who was born in London, England, has advanced mechanical engineering degrees from Cambridge University in England and from the Massachusetts Institute of Technology. He became a consultant in 1985 and was hired by Harmonic Lightwaves in 1988, first as a consultant, then as president and CEO. He would add the title of chairman of the board in 1995.

When Ley joined the company it was involved in fiber-optic measurement projects. Over the next decade he would guide Harmonic Lightwaves in the emerging market of fiber optics for cable television. The company's first product was introduced in 1992, the high-power YAGLink transmitter. At the time of its introduction, it was the industry's highest powered laser transmitter for broadband video services. YAGLink enabled cable operators to enjoy substantial savings by consolidating their headends, which receive and process content from a variety of sources. Following YAGLink, Harmonic introduced a complementary suite of standards-based, high-performance optical transmission platforms capable of delivering both broadcast and two-way interactive services.

In 1994 Harmonic added the PWRLink DFB laser transmitter to its product line. This transmitter provided operators with a variety of transmission technologies. In 1995 the company introduced the MAXLink 1550 nm transmission system, which could reach farther than the PWRLink 1310 nm DFB laser transmitter.

Expanded Product Line Through Internal Growth and Acquisitions, 1995–2000

Harmonic Lightwaves went public in 1995 with an initial public offering of 2.6 million shares priced at $6.75 a share. For

Company Perspectives:

Harmonic is a leading provider of innovative broadband solutions that deliver video, voice and data to communications providers around the world. Harmonic's technically advanced fiber-optic, digital video and IP [Internet protocol] data delivery systems enable network operators to provide a range of interactive and advanced digital services that include high-speed Internet access, telephony, digital video, HDTV, video and audio streaming, and video-on-demand.

the year the company reported revenue of $39.2 million and net income of $4.1 million. It had about 230 employees. Over the next five years the company would see its revenue grow dramatically, rising to $60.9 million in 1996, $74.4 million in 1997, $83.9 million in 1998, and $184.1 million in 1999. The company would report a profit in four of the next five years; a net loss of $21.5 million in 1998, which included a $14 million acquisition charge for in-process research and development, was followed by a profit of $23.7 million in 1999.

In 1997 Harmonic introduced the industry's first scaleable node, the PWRBlazer, which could be reconfigured to support a growing demand for bandwidth. In January 1998 Harmonic acquired New Media Communications Ltd., which was renamed Harmonic Data Systems Ltd., for $17.6 million in stock. This acquisition allowed Harmonic to expand its products to include high-speed data delivery software and hardware. New Media Communications Ltd. was a privately held Israeli developmental company with 15 employees.

In 1998 the company introduced METROLink, the cable industry's first DWDM (dense wave division multiplexing) system, which allowed operators to dramatically increase the two-way bandwidth capacity of their networks. During the year it also introduced the TRANSend digital headend, a platform for encoding, compressing, multiplexing, and modulating digital signals prior to transmission over broadband networks. Sales for 1998 rose 13 percent to $83.9 million, compared to $74.4 million in 1997. The growth was attributed mainly to the sale of new products, including TRANSend digital headend products, METROLink DWDM systems, and PWRBlazer scaleable nodes. Also, domestic customers began to spend more in the second half of 1998.

At the end of 1999 the company had 454 employees. During the year sales to AT&T accounted for 41 percent of revenue, compared to 17 percent in 1998. Over the past three years sales to customers outside the United States had declined from 59 percent in 1997 to 30 percent in 1999. Sales in 1999 increased 119 percent to $184.1 million, compared to $83.9 million in 1998. The increase was attributed primarily to higher unit sales of METROLink DWDM systems and PWRBlazer scaleable nodes, which began volume shipment in mid-1998. The company's domestic and international customers also increased their spending during 1999. Domestic sales rose 172 percent, mainly due to increased shipments to AT&T. International sales were up 51 percent on higher shipments to Canada and the United Kingdom. During the year Harmonic raised $58.3 million through a secondary public stock offering.

In May 2000 Harmonic completed its acquisition of DiviCom, the leading provider of high-quality standards-based digital video, audio, and data products and systems for satellite, wireless, fiber, and cable companies. DiviCom's products and systems enabled its customers to deliver digital video, audio, and data over a variety of networks. The acquisition of an open solutions provider for digital video gave Harmonic the resources to expand its penetration into satellite, wireless, telecommunications, and other emerging markets for broadband communications. DiviCom was acquired from C-Cube Microsystems, Inc. for $1.7 billion, in a complex merger that resulted in C-Cube Microsystems continuing independently as purely a semiconductor company.

Another acquisition was completed in July 2000. Harmonic issued about 284,000 shares to acquire privately held Cogent Technologies, Inc. of Santa Cruz, California. Cogent was a developer of MPEG-2 technology for digital television.

Harmonic is Organized into Two Divisions

Harmonic organized into two divisions, the Broadband Access Networks Division and the Convergent Systems Division. Its Broadband Access Networks Division provides optical networking products that enable the delivery of interactive services in networks originally designed for one-way cable transmission. The division's principal product lines are optical transmitters, optical nodes, and data gateways. The firm's three principal lines of optical transmitters are designed to dramatically increase the bandwidth capacity of existing Hybrid Fiber Coax (HFC) cable networks for the delivery of services that require two-way communication. Harmonic's METROLink DWDM system, first introduced in 1998, allows operators to increase the two-way bandwidth capacity of their networks without expensive system upgrades. METROLink enables operators to provide narrowcast services directly from the headend and eliminates the need to put costly and complex equipment in multiple hubs. Harmonic's 1550 nm MAXLink transmission system, introduced in 1995, provides a cost-effective solution for various applications and architectures, including long haul applications that are beyond the reach of 1310 nm transmitters. MAXLink is also used with fiber-deep architectures that utilize high-power optical amplifiers. The company's third line of optical transmitters is PWRLink, a family of 1310 nm DFB laser transmitters that were first introduced in 1994.

Harmonic's scaleable optical node platform, PWRBlazer, was first introduced in 1997. It provides operators with a range of transmission technologies for fiber-rich network architectures. The scaleable nodes can be reconfigured at any time to support growing demand for bandwidth in HFC networks. They can also meet the need for smaller node sizes resulting from large-scale deployment of interactive services, including high-speed Internet access, telephony, and video-on-demand.

A key element of Harmonic's strategy has been to develop products, or data gateways, that enable operators to introduce new broadband services. In 2000 the company introduced the world's first NODE CMTS, a new transmission technology for

Key Dates:

1988: Company is founded in California as Harmonic Lightwaves, Inc.
1998: Company acquires New Media Communications Ltd., which becomes Harmonic Data Systems Ltd.
2000: Harmonic acquires DiviCom business unit, a provider of open solutions for digital television, from C-Cube Microsystems, Inc. for $1.7 billion.

HFC access networks. By placing the CMTS in the node, NODEcmts provides Ethernet-over-HFC capability, resulting in significantly increased upstream IP data capacity, which gives operators an advanced tool for delivering interactive services to their customers. Another data gateway developed by Harmonic is called InterSect, which is an interactive set-top box controller that provides digital cable television operators with the ability to deliver TCP/IP traffic to set-top boxes.

Harmonic's Convergent Systems Division develops solutions for operators to maximize the capacity of their broadband networks through advanced compression, processing, and multiplexing technology. Its principal product lines include encoders, multiplexing and stream processing products, and high-speed data delivery software and hardware technology. Harmonic's TRANSend digital headend platform, first introduced in 1997, includes a range of products for encoding, compressing, multiplexing, and modulating digital signals prior to transmission over broadband networks. The company's CyberStream product line, which was introduced in 1998 following the acquisition of New Media Communications Ltd., enables Internet access and high-speed data delivery primarily over satellite or wireless networks to residential and business subscribers.

Principal Divisions

Broadband Access Networks Division; Convergent Systems Division.

Principal Subsidiaries

Harmonic Data Systems Ltd. (Israel).

Principal Competitors

ADC Telecommunications, Inc.; ANTEC Corp.; General Instrument Corp. (subsidiary of Motorola, Inc.); Philips Electronics North America Corp.; Scientific-Atlanta, Inc.; Lucent Technologies, Inc.; Broadlogic, Inc.; SkyStream Corp.; Hybrid Networks, Inc.; SAGEM.

Further Reading

Anderson, Karen, and Glen Dickson, "TCI Provides Internet Access with MetroLink," *Broadcasting & Cable,* September 7, 1998, p. 53.

Barrett, Larry, "Riding a Wave of Success," *Business Journal,* December 23, 1996, p. 14.

"DiviCom Merges with Harmonic," *Electronic News,* May 8, 2000, p. 10.

Guzzo, Maria, "Seven Law Firms File Suit over Harmonic's Plunge in Stock," *Business Journal,* July 7, 2000, p. 12.

"Harmonic Acquires C-Cube Business," *Business Journal,* November 26, 1999, p. 21.

"Harmonic Lightwaves," *Television Digest,* April 24, 1995, p. 6.

Kerschbaumer, Ken, "Harmonic Launches SatBox Access," *Broadcasting & Cable,* May 22, 2000, p. 47.

—David P. Bianco

Harrah's Entertainment, Inc.

1023 Cherry Road
Memphis, Tennessee 38117-5423
U.S.A.
Telephone: (901) 762-8600
Toll Free: (800) eHARRAH
Fax: (901) 762-8637
Web site: http://www.harrahs.com

Public Company
Incorporated: 1971 as Harrah's
Employees: 40,000
Sales: $3.5 billion (2000)
Stock Exchanges: New York
Ticker Symbol: HET
NAIC: 72112 Casino Hotels; 71321 Casinos

Tracing its roots to a small Reno bingo parlor, Harrah's Entertainment, Inc. is one of the most recognized names in the casino gaming business. Operating under the Harrah's, Rio, and Showboat brand names, Harrah's maintains casinos in markets across the United States. Harrah's prides itself in providing excellent customer service and in bringing technological innovation to the gaming industry. Instead of building new hotel-casino complexes like many of its competitors, Harrah's has concentrated on a successful strategy of brand identification and a customer rewards program that helps drive business to Harrah's casinos across the country.

The Early Years

William Fisk Harrah was the son of a Venice, California, lawyer and real estate operator who also had served as mayor of this seaside community. The senior Harrah went bankrupt during the Depression and was left with only one asset: a leased building on the honky-tonk Venice pier jutting into the Pacific Ocean. Here he operated a nickel-and-dime game of dubious legality, loosely based on bingo, in which players sat in a circle and rolled marbles toward a number. After Bill Harrah was caught cheating on a college chemistry exam in 1930, he went to work running the game and soon concluded he could do better than his father, who sold it to him for $500. He got rid of the shills his father had hired, refurbished the premises, and grossed as much as $50,000 a year.

In the wake of a state crackdown on gambling, Harrah moved in 1937 to Reno, Nevada, where gambling had been legalized six years earlier. There he bought a bingo parlor that was located too far from the action and failed in three months. In 1939, however, he reopened in the two-block gambling heart of Reno. Three years later he opened a casino, equipping it with a blackjack and a craps table and 20 slot machines.

The enterprise flourished during the free-spending World War II years, and in 1946 Harrah's Club opened in quarters that had been expanded by the purchase of neighboring properties. Harrah added roulette to the card and dice tables and served liquor to the players. His spotlessly clean, glass-fronted, plush-carpeted casino was a contrast to the rough frontier-type betting parlors of the time and was the first to be lined with one-way mirrors so as to oversee the dealers and cashiers handling the chips and cash. By 1948 the gross annual revenue of Harrah's Club was more than $1.5 million and its net profit, after taxes, was about $100,000. This was just the start, for when Harrah swore off alcohol in 1952 (after almost losing his life driving while drunk), he turned his attention from hell-raising to a more highly focused passion for profit.

The Reno and Lake Tahoe Casino-Hotels, 1955–70

In 1955 Harrah bought a dingy casino—housed in a Quonset hut—on the southern shore of Lake Tahoe, just east of the California state line, for $500,000. He built a false front around it and reopened it as Harrah's Tahoe. Four years later he relocated the casino across the highway, in the world's largest single structure devoted to gambling. The new casino was a highly integrated operation that included a ten-acre parking lot and an 850-seat theater-restaurant stocked with star entertainers. Blizzards habitually buried the area each winter, but Harrah assembled a fleet of snowplows to clear the mountain roads, which were doubled in width at his own expense. Not averse to the low-budget trade, he established a vast bus net-

Company Perspectives:

The vision of Harrah's Entertainment is to offer exciting environments and to become legendary at creating smiles, laughter, and lasting memories with every guest we entertain. The company's mission is to build lasting relationships and create a great time, every time—guaranteed—by delivering comfort, action, a shot to win, and hospitality (C.A.S.H.) to the max through enthusiastic, highly trained, friendly, attentive and empowered employees who have pledged to provide unsurpassed entertainment and service to every guest.

work to bring in customers from 31 California cities and even opened a child-care center for gambling parents to park their offspring. The Lake Tahoe casino was said to have turned a profit of more than $1 million in its first year.

The annual gross from Harrah's two casinos was estimated at $40 million in 1961, and four years later William Harrah was described as the world's biggest gambling operator. With 2,500 employees, he was the largest employer in Nevada except for the Atomic Energy Commission. A lover of fast cars, he established Rolls Royce, Ferrari, and Jeep dealerships and assembled the world's largest automobile collection, which the Internal Revenue Service allowed him to write off as a business expense.

With both his casinos booming and no inclination to take on the competition in Las Vegas, Harrah next turned to the hotel business. He constructed the highest building in Reno, a 24-story hotel across the street from his casino. Completed in 1968, it cost about $7 million. Next he erected a luxurious 18-story hotel, which opened in 1973, on his Lake Tahoe property. Every room came with a view of the lake and two marble-finished bathrooms.

Public Company in the 1970s

In part to finance these ventures and support his lifestyle (he was married six times), Harrah took his company public in 1971, raising $4 million after taxes and expenses by offering 13 percent of the stock at $16 per share. No Wall Street firm would handle the offering, but it was oversubscribed, and within a year the stock had soared to $71 per share. Overcoming the financial sector's misgivings about the gambling industry, Harrah's became, in 1973, the first casino company listed on the New York Stock Exchange.

Harrah's net sales increased from $77.9 million in 1970 to $195.6 million in 1979, and net income grew from a low of $4.3 million in 1971 to a record $16.9 million in 1978. One securities analyst called Harrah's the most tightly controlled and best-managed casino company in the world. Its two casinos, operating around-the-clock every day of the year, accounted for about 10 percent of Nevada's gambling volume. Games of chance now included baccarat, poker, and keno, as well as the roulette, blackjack, craps, and bingo tables and 3,733 slot machines. The 1,600 seats at the theater-restaurants in Reno and Lake Tahoe were filled nearly every night. The two hotels enjoyed a 92 percent occupancy rate. Nearly 250,000 customers came every year by bus, leading Harrah's president to acknowledge, ''We are the Safeway of the industry.''

By the late 1970s, however, Harrah's was beginning to encounter difficulties from the opening of competing hotel-casinos in Reno and environmental constraints on further development in the Lake Tahoe area. The company scrapped plans to open a new Reno hotel-casino just across the street from the existing one and a combination hotel-casino and theme park just outside the city. When Harrah died in 1978, he left his heirs almost six million shares of stock in his company, but no cash to pay estate taxes of $35 million or a $13 million debt to a Reno bank.

Holiday Inns Subsidiary in the 1980s

At this point a buyer for Harrah's emerged in the unlikely form of family-oriented Holiday Inns, Inc., a Memphis-based company previously run by pious Baptists opposed to gambling. Even before Harrah's death, however, Holiday Inns executive Michael Rose was seeking his participation in a joint venture in Atlantic City, New Jersey, where gambling had been legalized in 1977. The company bought, in 1979, a stake in a casino adjacent to the Holiday Inn on the Las Vegas Strip. It was renamed Holiday Casino and, later, Harrah's Las Vegas. Holiday Inns also announced plans to build two casino-hotels in Atlantic City. In February 1980 the company acquired Harrah's, which was still about 70 percent owned by William Harrah's estate, for $310 million in cash and notes. Rose, who became chief executive officer of Holiday Inns the next year, sold most of Harrah's 1,400 automobiles for $100 million and gave the rest to a Reno museum.

Now a wholly owned subsidiary of Holiday Inns, Harrah's became the operator of a casino opened in 1980 on marshland a mile and a half north of Atlantic City's boardwalk and named Harrah's Marina Hotel Casino. It had 506 guest rooms, a casino with capacity for 6,300 patrons, and an array of other spaces, including restaurants and bars, a Broadway-sized theater, conference and meeting rooms, a high-rise garage for 2,100 cars, and a ''fun'' center for children and teenagers. A 264-suite tower was added later. Harrah's Marina (later renamed Harrah's Atlantic City) proved to be the most consistently profitable casino in Atlantic City. In 1985, for example, the facility earned $48.8 million before taxes, by far the best performance of any of the 11 Atlantic City casinos.

In 1984, Harrah's opened, in partnership with real estate developer Donald J. Trump, the tallest building on the Atlantic City boardwalk, the 39-story Harrah's Trump Plaza hotel and casino. The joint venture, built by the Trump Organization on Trump land but with Harrah's money, collapsed in acrimony when the competing Trump's Castle made its debut the following year right across the street from Harrah's Marina. In 1986 Trump bought Harrah's half-share in Trump Plaza (Harrah's name had been removed) for $59.1 million.

Despite acrimonious ventures on the East Coast, Harrah's pursued developments out west. Harrah's opened Bill's Lake Tahoe Casino in 1987 on a 2.1-acre site adjacent to Harrah's Lake Tahoe. The following year Harrah's Laughlin was opened in Laughlin, Nevada, on a natural cove on the Colorado River,

Key Dates:

1937: William Harrah moves his small-time casino operations from California to Reno, Nevada.
1946: The posh, full-service Harrah's Club opens, the first casino in the country to use one-way mirrors to oversee dealers.
1948: Gross annual revenue of Harrah's exceeds $1.5 million.
1955: Harrah's Tahoe opens.
1961: Annual gross from Harrah's two casinos is estimated at $40 million.
1971: Harrah's goes public, offering 13 percent of the stock at $16 per share.
1973: Harrah's becomes first casino company to be listed on the New York Stock Exchange.
1978: William Harrah dies.
1980: Holiday Inns, Inc. acquires Harrah's for $310 million; opens the highly successful Harrah's Marina Hotel Casino in Atlantic City.
1989: The holding company Promus is created, which becomes the parent firm of Harrah's.
1991: Harrah's relocates headquarters from Reno to Memphis.
1993: Harrah's establishes a riverboat casinos division, taking advantage of new forms of legalized gambling, expanding its operations into many states.
1995: Promus divides itself into two, creating separate public corporations for its lodging and gaming operations; the latter becoming Harrah's Entertainment.
1998: Harrah's acquires Showboat, Inc. for $1.2 billion in stock and debt; it also takes over the casino Sam's Town in Missouri.
1999: Harrah's and the Rio Hotel and Casino merge.
2000: Harrah's completes its acquisition of Players International, Inc., acquiring three properties.
2001: Harrah's announces plans to acquire Harveys Casino Resorts.

with 464 hotel rooms and 26,500 square feet of casino space. Late in 1988 a second Laughlin hotel tower was completed.

Headlong Expansion in the 1990s

In 1989 Holiday Corp., formerly Holiday Inns, became the Promus Cos., Inc.. The following year Rose sold the Holiday Inns hotel chain to Bass PLC of Great Britain for $2.23 billion. Holiday shares were then converted, on a one-for-one basis, to Promus shares, with Holiday's Embassy Suites, Hampton Inn, and Homewood Suites hotel divisions remaining as Promus units. Harrah's continued to thrive as the company's casino-entertainment division and in 1991 relocated its headquarters from Reno to Memphis, Tennessee.

Casino gambling had been legal only in Nevada and New Jersey until 1989, but between 1989 and 1996 it was legalized in some form in 21 additional states. In 1993 Harrah's established a new division for riverboat casinos and opened the first of these facilities along the Illinois River in Joliet, Illinois. A second Joliet floating casino opened the following year. Also during 1993–95 Harrah's established riverboat casinos along the Mississippi River in Vicksburg and Tunica, Mississippi, the Red River at Shreveport, Louisiana, and along the Missouri River in North Kansas City, Missouri. A second Tunica riverboat opened in 1996.

Harrah's also continued to create or acquire land-based casinos in the 1990s. Eagle Gaming, L.P., one-sixth owned by Harrah's, opened casinos in the Colorado historic mining towns of Central City and Black Hawk in 1993. Harrah's managed them for a fee. In addition, in 1992 Harrah's announced the creation of a new division for casinos on Indian lands. Congress had, in 1988, passed a law legalizing games of chance on Indian reservations in any state where such games were allowed for churches, temples, and veterans and other groups. By August 1993 no less than 73 tribes in 19 states were offering or would soon be offering full-scale casino gambling. Harrah's Ak-Chin, near Phoenix, opened in December 1994. A year later the Upper Skagit Indians and Harrah's opened a casino entertainment complex about 70 miles north of Seattle.

On February 1, 1996, Harrah's celebrated the grand opening of its first international casino entertainment complex, Sky City Casino in Auckland, New Zealand. This property consisted of 45,000 square feet of casino space and was also to include a hotel, theater, and 1,076-foot tower. The company, which held a 20 percent share in the joint venture, was to manage it for a fee.

An embarrassment for Harrah's was the failure of Harrah's Casino New Orleans, which was owned by Harrah's Jazz Co., a partnership in which a subsidiary of Harrah's Entertainment held a 47-percent interest. On the edge of the French Quarter, this temporary casino (a permanent one was under construction which would open a few years later) opened in 1995 but closed in nine weeks, grossing less than half of its projected $33 million a month and causing the partnership to file for bankruptcy. Harrah's Entertainment wrote off $93.5 million of losses in the failed venture but was not responsible for Harrah's Jazz Co.'s $435-million junk bond debt.

In late 1995 Harrah's and Players International, Inc. broke ground on a joint riverboat casino entertainment complex in Maryland Heights, Missouri, a suburb of St. Louis. Each company was to operate two boats, connected by a shoreside entertainment mall anchored by a 291-room hotel managed by Harrah's. During 1995 Harrah's also announced plans for major expansions of its Las Vegas and Atlantic City casino properties, including the addition of a hotel tower and additional casino space. Construction of a $78-million expansion of Harrah's North Kansas City also began that year.

In 1995, the Promus Cos. divided into two separate corporations, with the casino division becoming Harrah's Entertainment, Inc. and the hotel division Promus Hotels Corp. Rose remained chairman of both companies. By the end of February 1996, Harrah's offered 16 casinos with 592,500 square feet of space, 16,377 slot machines, 898 table games, 63 restaurants, and 21,905 parking spaces. There were 5,736 hotel rooms at the end of 1995. Gaming volume came to $20.6 billion that year, compared with $8.5 billion in 1991. Harrah's long-term debt was $753.7 million in 1995.

The riverboat division was Harrah's most lucrative in 1995, accounting for 43 percent of its $354 million operating profit, followed by Atlantic City (22 percent), Southern Nevada (18 percent), and Northern Nevada (16 percent). Of Harrah's $1.55 billion in revenues that year, the riverboat operations accounted for 38 percent, followed by Atlantic City (22 percent), Northern Nevada (20 percent), and Southern Nevada (19 percent). Net income was $78.8 million.

A key marketing tool was the Harrah's Gold Card, accepted at each Harrah's property. Its database included, in 1994, 3.2 million cardholders and 3.1 million potential cardholders who had stayed at a Harrah's property or played in one of the casinos. In addition to enabling the company to follow trends in play and the popularity of certain games, the gold card was used to gather information on guests for marketing purposes and to reward them, based on volume of play.

Placing a Winning Bet at the Turn of a New Century

As the 1990s drew to a close, Las Vegas saw an unprecedented growth in billion-dollar destination properties. Opulent, themed mega-casinos such as the Venetian, Mandalay Bay, Monte Carlo, and Bellagio opened to rave reviews. But while the trend toward building big from the ground up captured the imagination of many in the gaming industry, Harrah's focused on expanding its brand identification and acquiring existing properties, big and small. In a letter to shareholders, Harrah's chairman and CEO Phillip Satre explained, ''building such facilities is not the most efficient method of sustaining revenue and earnings growth or return on investment because new casinos alone do not translate into long-term customer satisfaction.''

So instead of expending billions to build something new, Harrah's concentrated on a buyout formula that seemed like a safe bet. In 1998 Harrah's bought Showboat, Inc. for $1.2 billion in stock and debt. It also acquired Sam's Town, a struggling casino in Missouri. Then in 1999 Harrah's and the Rio Hotel and Casino merged, allowing Harrah's to align itself with one of the first large destination properties in Vegas.

With the acquisition of these properties and the continued profitable partnerships with Indian gaming casinos scattered across the country, Harrah's developed what no other gaming company had before: brand recognition. To further drive the Harrah's name into the American gaming psyche, the company launched Total Gold, building on the success of its Gold Card program. This nationwide brand loyalty program allowed gamblers to earn points by making excursions to smaller facilities, such as the riverboat casino in Joliet or East Chicago, and redeeming them as discounts on trips to Harrah's more well-known, larger properties, such as those in Vegas and Atlantic City. In April 2000, the Total Gold program became Total Rewards, an expanded three-tiered rewards system, giving Harrah's even more ways to track customers' play and offer incentives.

Also aiding Harrah's brand recognition campaign was the 1999 decision by the U.S. Supreme Court to lift a ban on gambling advertising that featured people inside casinos. After the ruling, Harrah's hit the airwaves in nine cities with two ads showing the joys of playing slot machines. The spots end with the tagline, ''You know you gotta get to Harrah's, oh yeah.'' In an article for *Advertising Age* magazine Harrah's vice-president of brand management Amanda Totaro notes that the campaign's focus on people gambling is the result of market research data indicating that consumers visit Harrah's for the thrill of the game, regardless if they win or lose.

By the year 2000, Harrah's had grown from a single bingo parlor into a national powerhouse, operating 21 casinos in 17 U.S. markets. Moreover, half of the U.S. population now lived within a three-hour drive of a Harrah's owned or managed property. And in an industry that many characterized as mature, Harrah's continued to see increases in revenues. Company-wide revenues grew 15 percent in 2000, to $3.5 billion. Part of that growth was aided by Harrah's acquisition of Players International, Inc. in March 2000. All three of the properties were expected to assume the Harrah's name by the end of 2001. Also, in April of 2001 the company announced plans to buy Harveys Casino Resorts from Colony Capital Investors, III, L.P., for $625 million. As part of the purchase agreement, Harrah's Entertainment will acquire Harveys Resort in Lake Tahoe, Harveys Casino Hotel and Bluffs Run Casino in Council Bluffs, Iowa, and Harveys Wagon Wheel Hotel-Casino in Central City, Colorado. ''The Harveys properties are an excellent complement to our existing geographic network of casino locations and will allow us to further expand the revenue and earnings capabilities of our industry-leading customer-loyalty program, Total Rewards,'' said Phil Satre.

While overall the future looked bright for Harrah's, the company experienced some setbacks in recent years. The Las Vegas Rio property took a huge hit in payoffs made to gamblers at its table games for the year 2000. Harrah's calls this bad luck, ''unusually low table-game hold percentages'' and ''unsatisfactory entertainment results.'' Management reports that it has taken steps to correct the problem by reducing betting and credit limits. Meanwhile, Harrah's New Orleans continued to be plagued with problems in 2000 and 2001. JCC Holding Company, the casino's primary owner, filed for bankruptcy. Harrah's Entertainment owns 43 percent of JCC and is trying to reorganize the structure so the casino can remain viable. But the plan must be approved by the Louisiana legislature, which so far has not taken kindly to the Harrah's gaming presence in the Big Easy. It remains to be seen if Harrah's can beat the odds on this one.

Principal Subsidiaries

Aster Insurance Ltd. (Bermuda); Harrah's Operating Co., Inc.

Principal Competitors

MGM Mirage; Park Place Entertainment; Trump Hotels and Casinos.

Further Reading

Berger, Meyer, ''The Gay Gamblers of Reno,'' *Saturday Evening Post,* July 10, 1948, pp. 22–23, 74, 76, 78.

Bukro, Gary, ''The Christmas Tree Is in the Mail, Really,'' *Chicago Tribune,* November 23, 1995, pp. 1, 4.

Davis, Wendy, ''Harrah's Ads Accentuate the Positive,'' *Advertising Age,* March 19, 2001, p. 49.

Getmanikow, George, ''Holiday Inns Discards Family Image for Stake in Gambling Industry,'' *Wall Street Journal,* January 11, 1980, pp. 1, 31.

''Harrah's Says It Will Acquire Harveys Casino Resorts,'' *The New York Times,* April 25, 2001, p. C4.

Hughlett, Mike, ''Analysts See Rosy Future for Harrah's Parent,'' *New Orleans Times-Picayune,* December 17, 1995, p. F3.

Johnston, David, *Temples of Chance,* New York: Doubleday, 1992.

Land, Barbara, and Myrick Land, *A Short History of Reno,* Reno and Las Vegas: University of Nevada Press, 1995.

Mandel, Leon, and William Fisk, *Harrah,* New York: Doubleday, 1982.

McDowell, Edwin, ''Promus Proposes to Divide Its Units into Two Companies,'' *New York Times,* January 31, 1995, pp. D1, D7.

Monroe, Keith, ''The New Gambling King and the Social Scientists,'' *Harper's Magazine,* January 1962, pp. 35–41.

''Taking the Risk Out of Gambling,'' *Time,* November 21, 1977, p. 78.

''The Big Easy's Bad Bet,'' *Fortune,* December 8, 1997, p. 162.

''The Last Harrah,'' *Forbes,* October 16, 1978, p. 66.

''The Legacy of William Harrah,'' *Harrah's People,* Spring 1995, pp. 4–11.

''The Two Faces of Bill,'' *Forbes,* July 1, 1972, pp. 39, 41.

Wernick, Robert, ''The World's Biggest Gambler,'' *Saturday Evening Post,* February 13, 1965, pp. 27–32.

—Robert Halasz
—update: Suzanne L. Rowe

Hasbro, Inc.

1027 Newport Avenue
Pawtucket, Rhode Island 02862-1059
U.S.A.
Telephone: (401) 431-TOYS (8697)
Toll Free: (800) 255-5516
Fax: (401) 431-8535
Web site: http://www.hasbro.com

Public Company
Incorporated: 1926 as Hassenfeld Brothers Inc.
Employees: 8,900
Sales: $3.79 billion (2000)
Stock Exchanges: New York London
Ticker Symbol: HAS
NAIC: 339931 Doll and Stuffed Toy Manufacturing; 339932 Game, Toy, and Children's Vehicle Manufacturing; 511210 Software Publishers

Truly successful toy companies do not just make toys; they manufacture popular culture. Hasbro, Inc., which is the second largest toy maker in the world, behind only Mattel, Inc., certainly fits that description. From America's Action Hero to a plastic anthropomorphized potato to vehicles that transform into robots to the largest bird in the world, Hasbro toys are instantly recognized by millions of Americans. Hasbro makes G.I. Joe, Mr. Potato Head, and Transformers, and owns licenses for Sesame Street characters. Thanks to numerous acquisitions in the 1980s and 1990s, it also makes Playskool and Romper Room preschool toys, Tonka trucks, Kenner's Nerf toys, and Cabbage Patch Kids (by way of Coleco). Hasbro has become dominant in the area of board games and puzzles through its ownership of Milton Bradley (maker of Scrabble and Parcheesi) and Parker Brothers (maker of Monopoly). Into the late 1990s and early 21st century, Hasbro has continued to acquire popular brands, adding Pokémon game cards with their procurement of Wizards of the Coast and reacquiring the license to toys developed from Disney Studios movie releases.

Early History from 1923 to the 1930s

Hasbro traces its origin to an enterprise founded in Providence, Rhode Island, in 1923 by Henry, Hilal, and Herman Hassenfeld, brothers who had emigrated to the United States from Poland. The Hassenfeld brothers engaged in the textile remnant business, selling cloth leftovers. By the mid-1920s they were using the remnants to make hat liners and pencil-box covers. After realizing the popularity of the covers, they soon began making the boxes themselves with eight employees—all family members. In 1926 the company incorporated under the name Hassenfeld Brothers Inc.

Hilal Hassenfeld became involved in other textile ventures, and Henry took control of the new company. Although a paternalistic employer, Henry Hassenfeld was also a tough and shrewd businessman. During the Great Depression—with 150 employees in 1929 and 200 employees in 1930—Hassenfeld Brothers commanded annual sales of $500,000 from sales of pencil boxes and cloth zipper pouches filled with school supplies. At that point, however, the company's pencil supplier decided to raise its prices and sell its own boxes at prices lower than Hassenfeld's. Henry Hassenfeld responded with a vow to enter the pencil business himself, and in 1935 Hassenfeld Brothers began manufacturing pencils. This product line would provide the company with a steady source of revenue for the next 45 years.

Transformation to Toy Manufacturing from the 1930s to 1960

During the late 1930s the Hassenfeld Brothers began to manufacture toys, an extension of the company's line of school supplies. Initial offerings included medical sets for junior nurses and doctors and modeling clay. During World War II Henry's younger son, Merrill Hassenfeld, acted on a customer's suggestion to make and market a junior air raid warden kit, which came complete with flashlights and toy gas masks.

By 1942, as demand for school supplies tapered off, the company had become primarily a toy company, although it continued its large, profitable pencil business. Hilal Hassenfeld died in 1943, at which point Henry Hassenfeld became CEO and his son Merrill Hassenfeld became president. Also during

Company Perspectives:

The company's focus will be on building a strong global business and further strengthening its presence in the children's and family leisure time and entertainment industry. Hasbro is well poised to leverage its incredible portfolio of classic brands globally, regionally and locally, and aims to achieve this goal with an increased emphasis on global brand marketing and product development, complemented by coordinated regional and local marketing and sales activity.

World War II, the company ventured into plastics, but was forced, due to labor shortages, to reduce employment to 75.

After the war Merrill Hassenfeld began marketing a girls makeup kit after seeing his four-year-old daughter play with candy as though it were lipstick and rouge. In 1952, the company introduced its still-classic Mr. Potato Head, the first toy to be advertised on television. In 1954 Hassenfeld became a major licensee for Disney characters. By 1960, revenues hit $12 million, and Hassenfeld Brothers had become one of the largest private toy companies in the nation.

Turbulent Times During the 1960s and 1970s

Henry Hassenfeld died in 1960. Merrill Hassenfeld then assumed full control of the parent company, while his older brother Harold Hassenfeld, continued to run the pencil making operations. Merrill Hassenfeld's succession was logical given his interest and expertise in the toy business, but it also marked the beginning of an intramural rivalry between the two sides of the company. Harold Hassenfeld would come to resent the fact that the pencil business received a lower percentage of capital investment even though it was a steadier performer and accounted for a higher percentage of profits than toys.

In 1961 Hassenfeld Brothers (Canada) Ltd., now Hasbro Canada Inc., was founded. Hassenfeld Brothers seemed to defy the vagaries of the toy business in the early 1960s when it introduced what would become one of its most famous and successful product lines. According to author Marvin Kaye in *A Toy Is Born,* the company conceived G.I. Joe in 1963 when a licensing agent suggested a merchandise tie-in with a television program about the U.S. Marine Corps called ''The Lieutenant.'' The company liked the idea of a military doll, but did not want to pin its fate on a TV show that might prove short-lived; so, it went ahead and created its own concept, and in 1964 Hassenfeld unleashed G.I. Joe, a 12-inch ''action figure'' with articulated joints. In its first two years, G.I. Joe brought in between $35 and $40 million and accounted for nearly two-thirds of the company's total sales.

The company changed its name to Hasbro Industries, Inc. in 1968—it had sold its toys under the Hasbro trade name for some time—and went public. Only a small portion of Hasbro stock went on the open market, however; the majority stake remained in the hands of the Hassenfeld family. At the same time, Hasbro decided that it could no longer ignore the public's growing disapproval of war toys, which was fueled by disillusionment with the Vietnam War. In 1969 G.I. Joe, still the company's leading moneymaker, was repackaged in a less militaristic ''adventure'' motif, with a different range of accessories. Also in 1969, the company acquired Burt Claster Enterprises, the Baltimore, Maryland-based television production company responsible for the popular ''Romper Room'' show for preschoolers. Burt Claster Enterprises had also begun to manufacture a line of ''Romper Room'' toys. Nevertheless, a month-long Teamsters strike and troubles with Far Eastern suppliers hurt Hasbro in 1969, and the company posted a $1 million loss for the year.

The 1960s ended on a turbulent note for Hasbro, providing a foretaste of the decade to come. In 1970 Hasbro decided that it had to diversify, and it opened a chain of nursery schools franchised under the ''Romper Room'' name. The company hoped to take advantage of President Richard M. Nixon's Family Assistance Plan, which subsidized day care for working mothers. Running the preschools was a very big mistake. Merrill Hassenfeld's son, Alan Hassenfeld, told the *Wall Street Journal,* ''We'd get phone calls saying, 'We can't find one of the kids.' The whole company would stop.'' Within five years Hasbro had left the day care business. Another ill-fated diversification move was Hasbro's line of Galloping Gourmet cookware, which sought to capitalize on a contemporary television cooking show of the same name. That venture literally fell apart when termites ate salad bowls stacked in a warehouse.

In addition, two products from Hasbro's 1970 line turned into public relations disasters: Javelin Darts were declared unsafe by the government, and Hypo-Squirt, a water gun shaped like a hypodermic needle, was dubbed by the press a ''junior junkie'' kit. Both products were promptly removed from the market. The continuing success of ''Romper Room'' and its related toy line proved to be a bright spot for Hasbro, although the company came under fire from the citizens group Action for Children's Television, which accused the program of becoming an advertising vehicle for toys.

In 1974 Merrill Hassenfeld became CEO of Hasbro, while his son, Stephen D. Hassenfeld, became president. Hasbro regained its profitability but floundered once again later in the decade. Poor cash flow accounted for some of the problems, but the company's underlying mistake was casting its net too far and too wide in an effort to compensate for G.I. Joe's declining popularity. Hasbro discontinued G.I. Joe in 1975 because of the rising price of plastic. By 1977—the year Hasbro acquired Peanuts cartoon characters licensing rights—the company suffered $2.5 million in losses and carried a heavy debt. The financial situation became serious enough that Hasbro's bankers forced it to suspend dividend payments in early 1979. The toy division's poor performance fueled Harold Hassenfeld's resentment that the Empire Pencil subsidiary continued to receive a smaller proportion of capital spending to profits than did the toy division. The dam threatened to burst in 1979 when Merrill Hassenfeld died at age 61. Stephen Hassenfeld was chairman Merrill Hassenfeld's heir apparent, but Harold Hassenfeld refused to recognize Stephen Hassenfeld's authority.

The feud was resolved in 1980, when Hasbro spun off Empire Pencil, which had become the nation's largest pencil maker, and Harold exchanged his Hasbro shares for shares of the new company. At the same time, Stephen Hassenfeld became the toy company's CEO and chairman of the board, and

Key Dates:

1923: Polish immigrant brothers Henry and Hilal Hassenfeld found a textile remnant business in Providence, Rhode Island.
1926: Hassenfeld Brothers Inc. is incorporated; company begins making pencil boxes and cloth zipper pouches.
1935: Hassenfeld Brothers begins manufacturing pencils, one of its stalwart revenue sources until 1980.
1943: Hilal Hassenfeld dies. Henry becomes CEO while Henry's son, Merrill, is named president of Hassenfeld Brothers. The company expands its product line to include toys, such as paint sets, wax crayons, and doctor and nurse kits.
1952: Mr. Potato Head, the first toy to be advertised on television, is introduced.
1954: Hassenfeld Brothers becomes a major licensee of Disney characters.
1961: Hassenfeld Brothers (Canada) Ltd. is founded.
1964: G.I. Joe is introduced; the popular action figure accounts for nearly two-thirds of the company's total revenue in its first two years.
1968: Hassenfeld Brothers Inc. changes its name to Hasbro Industries, Inc. The company goes public with a small portion of stock; the rest remains with the Hassenfeld family.
1969: Company acquires Romper Room Inc. (now Claster Enterprises Inc.) television production company.
1974: Merrill Hassenfeld becomes CEO; his son, Stephen D. Hassenfeld, becomes president.
1975: G.I. Joe is discontinued due to rising price of plastic.
1979: Merrill Hassenfeld dies.
1980: Empire Pencils, the nation's largest pencil maker, separates from Hasbro. Stephen Hassenfeld becomes CEO and chairman of the board of Hasbro.
1982: G.I. Joe is reintroduced.
1983: Hasbro purchases assets from Warner Communication's Knickerbocker Toy Company, including Raggedy Ann and Raggedy Andy.
1984: Alan Hassenfeld becomes president of Hasbro. The company acquires the Milton Bradley Company and its subsidiary Playskool; company is renamed Hasbro Bradley Incorporated. The Hasbro Children's Foundation is established to help needy children throughout the world.
1985: Hasbro unites its four subsidiaries—Hasbro Toys, Milton Bradley, Playskool, and Playskool Baby—under the name Hasbro, Inc.
1989: Hasbro acquires Coleco Industries, makers of Cabbage Patch Kids. Stephen Hassenfeld dies. His brother, Alan Hassenfeld, becomes chairman of the board and chief executive officer.
1991: Hasbro acquires Tonka Corporation, including Kenner Products and Parker Brothers divisions. Tonka Trucks, Monopoly, Nerf, Easy-Bake Oven, Clue, and Play-Doh are among the many products acquired. Operations are established in Greece, Hungary, and Mexico.
1992: Company acquires Nomura Toys Ltd. of Japan, and the controlling interest to Palmyra, a toy distributor in Southeast Asia.
1994: Hasbro acquires Games division of John Waddington PLC, makers of Pictionary.
1995: Company acquires the Laramie Corporation, makers of SuperSoaker brand water guns. Hasbro creates new division within company, Hasbro Interactive, which releases CD-ROM versions of board games such as Monopoly and Scrabble, and other popular toys, including Tonka and Mr. Potato Head.
1997: Company acquires licensing rights to three new Star Wars prequels for almost $600 million and over 7 percent of Hasbro stock.
1998: Hasbro acquires Tiger Electronics, makers of Furby, and also acquires the license to Teletubbies.
1999: Company acquires Wizards of the Coast, makers of Pokémon, Magic: The Gathering, and Dungeons and Dragons game cards.
2001: Hasbro sells Hasbro Interactive and Games.com, an interactive gaming Web site, to Infogrames Entertainment. The company closes plants in Cincinnati, San Francisco, and Napa.

dedicated himself to turning Hasbro around. Where it had once been overextended, the company slashed its product line by one-third between 1978 and 1981, while its annual number of new products was cut by one-half. Hasbro also refocused on simpler toys, such as Mr. Potato Head—products that were inexpensive to make, could be sold at lower prices, and had longer life cycles. This conservative philosophy precluded Hasbro from entering the hot new field of electronic games, as did the fact that it could not spare the cash to develop such toys. The decision to stay out of the market was vindicated in the early 1980s when the electronics boom turned bust and shook out many competitors.

Perhaps the most important event in Hasbro's revival was the 1982 return of G.I. Joe. The U.S. political climate at the time made military toys popular again, and G.I. Joe was reintroduced as an antiterrorist commando, complete with a cast of comrades and exotic villains, whose personalities were sculpted with the help of Marvel Comics. Two years later, Hasbro introduced its highly successful Transformers line—toy vehicles and guns that could be reconfigured into toy robots. Transformers were tied into a children's animated TV series and proved so popular that *People* magazine asked Stephen Hassenfeld to pose with them for a cover photo.

Major Acquisitions Mark the 1980s

In 1983 Hasbro acquired GLENCO Infant Items, a manufacturer of infant products and the world's largest bib producer. Hasbro also sold about 37 percent of its own stock to Warner Communications in exchange for cash and Warner's struggling Knickerbocker Toy Company subsidiary, which made Raggedy Ann and Raggedy Andy dolls. The new Warner holdings did not threaten the company's autonomy, however; the shares were put into a voting trust controlled by the Hassenfeld brothers and other Hasbro executives. In 1984 Stephen Hassenfeld turned over the position of president to his brother, Alan, while remaining CEO and chairman.

In the early 1980s Hasbro was the nation's sixth best-selling toy maker, with revenues of $225.4 million and $15.2 million in profits. Flush with newfound strength, in 1984 it acquired Milton Bradley, the nation's fifth best-selling toy maker, and second only to General Mills's Parker Brothers subsidiary in production of board games and puzzles. Milton Bradley had been founded by a Springfield, Massachusetts, lithographer who set up shop in 1860 and immediately turned out a popular reproduction of a portrait of presidential candidate Abraham Lincoln. Bradley's portrait, however, showed Lincoln clean-shaven, so when Lincoln grew his beard, sales fell off. Looking for a way to stay in business, Bradley invented and produced a board game called The Checkered Game of Life, a distant precursor of a popular Milton Bradley game, The Game of Life, which was introduced in 1960. The game's success convinced Bradley to stay in the game business. During the Civil War he produced a lightweight packet of board games for the amusement of Union troops. The company incorporated in 1882.

During the late 19th century, Milton Bradley (MB) relied mostly on such favorites as chess and checkers and traditional European games. During the 20th century, however, the company designed and marketed more original games, sometimes with great success. During the Depression, a Milton Bradley financial game called Easy Money became popular. In the 1950s, Milton Bradley pioneered games with tie-ins to television shows—Concentration was an early favorite. In 1968 MB acquired Chicago-based Playskool Manufacturing, which was noted for its preschool toys. Among Milton Bradley's later successes was the ''body action'' classic Twister, which was published in 1971 and became a popular prop with talk show hosts for a while after Johnny Carson challenged Eva Gabor to a go-around on ''The Tonight Show.''

In 1984, however, Milton Bradley had found itself in an uncertain financial position after fending off a hostile takeover from British conglomerate Hanson Trust. In the wake of that failed bid, several unidentified parties bought up large blocks of MB stock, fueling speculation that another takeover attempt was imminent. Finally, in May 1984, MB agreed to be acquired by Hasbro for $360 million. MB's strength in board games and puzzles complemented Hasbro's plastic toys and stuffed animals. Milton Bradley's Playskool subsidiary provided a solid preschool line including classics such as Lincoln Logs and ABC blocks. The new Hasbro Bradley Incorporated immediately challenged Mattel's position as the nation's leading toy maker. In 1985 Hasbro Bradley became Hasbro, Inc.

If Hasbro's and Milton Bradley's product lines merged well, their chief executives did not. Stephen Hassenfeld became president and CEO of Hasbro Bradley, with Milton Bradley chief James Shea, Jr., becoming chairman. After only a few months, however, Shea resigned. Stephen himself became chairman, with brother Alan Hassenfeld replacing him as president.

Hasbro surpassed Mattel to become the largest toy company in the world in the mid-1980s. Having done so, it then attempted to dethrone Mattel's Barbie, queen of the fashion doll market. In 1986 Hasbro introduced Jem, a fashion doll given the dual identity of business woman/record producer and purple-haired rock musician. While Jem posted strong initial sales, her popularity quickly faded and she was retired the following year. In 1988 the company brought out Maxie, a blonde doll scaled to match Barbie in size so that she could wear Barbie clothing and accessories. Maxie lasted twice as long as Jem and was discontinued in 1990.

In 1989 Hasbro acquired bankrupt rival Coleco Industries, owners of the Cabbage Patch Dolls, for $85 million. The Coleco acquisition proved to be Stephen Hassenfeld's final business achievement. In 1989, he died at age 47, having converted the relatively modest toy company that his grandfather had founded into a juggernaut at the top of its industry with 1989 sales of $1.41 billion, a huge increase over the $104 million figure of the year he took over.

Acquisitions Continue During the 1990s

A new and more challenging era began when 41-year-old Alan Hassenfeld became chairman and CEO of Hasbro. The younger Hassenfeld continued the acquisition trend of the 1980s, as Hasbro acquired Tonka Corporation in 1991 for $486 million. With the deal, Hasbro added not only the Tonka line of toy trucks but also Tonka's Parker Brothers unit, the maker of Monopoly, and Kenner Products, which featured Batman figures and the Strawberry Shortcake doll. The Parker Brothers unit was merged into Hasbro's already strong Milton Bradley division. Hasbro took a $59 million charge in 1991 to cover costs of consolidating the Tonka acquisition and restructuring overall operations.

In the late 1980s, Alan Hassenfeld had spearheaded an effort to increase Hasbro's international sales, primarily by taking toys that failed in the U.S. market and remarketing them overseas at prices as high as four times their original prices. He had helped increase international sales from $268 million in 1985 to $433 million in 1988. So it was not surprising that as chairman he would push to increase Hasbro's international presence. He did just that in 1991, establishing operations in Greece, Hungary, and Mexico.

It was the Far East, however, which Hassenfeld saw as a critical market for Hasbro to develop. He gained two more distribution channels there in 1992 by purchasing Nomura Toys Ltd., based in Japan, and buying a majority stake in Palmyra, a Southeast Asian toy distributor. Thanks to these efforts, by 1995, Hasbro's international sales had reached $1.28 billion, which represented almost 45 percent of total sales, a significant increase over the 22 percent figure of 1985. More than 46 percent of the company's operating profit was attributable to operations outside the United States in 1995. One international setback came in 1993 when Hasbro lost out to arch-rival Mattel in a bid for J.W. Spear, a U.K.-based maker of games.

While international results were improving, Hasbro began to show some weaknesses on the domestic front. Much of the growth since 1980 had come from the company's various acquisitions, along with Hasbro's largely successful efforts to leverage the new assets it gained through the deals. Many new product development activities, on the other hand, were not as successful, with the exception of product lines developed to tie in with the movie *Jurassic Park* and the popular children's television show "Barney." As a result, domestic sales stagnated in the early 1990s, and actually fell from $1.67 billion in 1993 to $1.58 billion in 1995. And worldwide sales showed much slower growth as well. From 1991, the year of the Tonka acquisition, to 1995, sales increased only 33.5 percent, with half of the increase occurring in 1992 alone. To help improve the company's domestic performance, a reorganization was completed in 1994 that merged the Hasbro Toy, Playskool, Playskool Baby, Kenner, and Kid Dimension units into a new Hasbro Toy Group. Meanwhile, in 1993 Mattel acquired Fisher-Price and soon thereafter regained the number one spot in the toy industry.

Also contributing to Hasbro's challenges in the 1990s was its belated struggle to enter the market for electronic games. Eventually, in 1992, the company began development of a mass market virtual reality game system. Although such a system was successfully developed, it was judged too expensive for the mass market and the project was abandoned in 1995, resulting in a charge of $31.1 million. In 1993, Hasbro bought a 15-percent stake in Virgin Interactive Entertainment, a producer of game software for Sega and Nintendo systems, with the intention of developing software based on Hasbro toys and games. Two years later, however, Hasbro dissolved the partnership and sold its stake.

A more promising venture began in 1995 with the establishment of Hasbro Interactive and the release of its first product that same year, a CD-ROM version of Monopoly. More than 180,000 units were sold in the first eight weeks following its release. Additional titles to be released in 1996 included Risk, Battleship, and Playskool-brand games.

In 1995, Mattel approached Hasbro about a possible merger of the two largest toy companies in the world. Negotiations took place in secret over the course of several months until the Hasbro board early in 1996 unanimously turned down a $5.2 billion merger proposal that would have given Hasbro stockholders a 73 percent premium over the then-current selling price. Hasbro officials expressed doubts that the merger could pass antitrust challenges and wanted a large up-front payment to help the company's performance during what would have likely been a lengthy antitrust review and to protect itself against the possibility that the merger would collapse. Mattel officials, on the other hand, maintained that the merger would have had little difficulty gaining approval, but backed away—and did not initiate a hostile takeover—when Hasbro waged a vigorous media campaign emphasizing the possible negative ramifications of such a mega-merger. Also clouding the deal was an ongoing Federal Trade Commission investigation into alleged exclusionary policies between toy manufacturers and toy retailers, involving most notably the Toys "R" Us chain.

Having maintained its independence, Hasbro adopted a multipronged strategy for reinvigorating its performance as the turn of the century approached. Its strategies included leveraging its well-known brands in new ways; stepping up efforts to market electronic versions of established games, particularly through the Hasbro Interactive initiative; continuing to grow internationally; and bolstering new product development primarily through media tie-ins. Already planned for 1997 were several promising film tie-in prospects, including the movies *Jurassic Park 2, Batman and Robin,* and *Barney's Great Adventure,* as well as the theatrical re-release of *Star Wars.*

As the new millenium approached, Hasbro looked to be moving towards regaining the top spot in the ever more international and multimedia consumer landscape of children's toys and entertainment. In 1995, it acquired the Laramie Corporation, creators of the SuperSoaker line of water guns; within three years it had added Tiger Electronics, makers of Furby and Poo-Chi interactive toys. In the April 16, 1999 issue of the *Wall Street Journal,* Joseph Pereira stated that Furby generated about ten percent of Hasbro's total revenue for the quarter as the "must-have" toy of the 1998 Christmas season. That same year also marked the procurement of Galoob Toys, Inc., makers of MicroMachines. The following year, Hasbro not only acquired Wizards of the Coast, makers of the popular 1999 Christmas children's gift, Pokémon game cards, but they also reaped huge dividends from merchandise associated with the first of three Star Wars prequels, *The Phantom Menace.* The movie broke the single-day take record in its first 24 hours of release and helped influence high sales of the Phantom Menace line of action figures. With two more prequels to be released in the following decade, Star Wars looked to be a continuous source of revenue for Hasbro, justifying the steep price paid for the license in 1997—almost $600 million and a 7.4 percent stake in Hasbro, Inc.

Restructuring for the 21st Century

As the 20th century came to a close, Hasbro seemed prepared to seriously challenge incumbent children's toy leader Mattel. However, precipitous drop-offs in Pokémon and Star Wars merchandise sales and a weak interactive games market led to Hasbro's first negative financial quarter since 1995. Hasbro's software games division, Hasbro Interactive, and their interactive gaming Web site, Games.com, had lost over $100 million in 1999 and in 2000, and for the final quarter of 2000, Hasbro overall posted a net loss of $180 million.

Determined to return to profitability in 2001, Hasbro took decisive action. It sold Hasbro Interactive and Games.com to French video game company Infogrames Entertainment and consolidated its U.S. toy group in Pawtucket, Rhode Island, shutting down plants in Cincinnati, San Francisco, and Napa, reducing its workforce by 850 jobs. The company refocused attention on its core group of brands and more traditional toy lines, including Mr. Potato Head, Monopoly, and G.I. Joe; dedicated itself to expanding these brands and toys beyond their traditional markets; and announced movie licenses with Pixar and Disney, as well as Harry Potter movie tie-in trading cards by Wizards of the Coast. Although Hasbro again reported losses in the first quarter 2001 ($25 million loss on revenues of $463 million), the company persevered in rededicating itself to the brands that have made it into one of the most influential producers of popular culture in the previous century.

Principal Subsidiaries

Galoob Toys, Inc; Tiger Electronics Inc.; Milton Bradley Company.; Playskool, Inc.; Tonka Corporation; Parker Brothers & Co; Nomura Toys Ltd. (Japan); Romper Room Enterprises;

Kenner Products; Wizards of the Coast, Inc; Oddzon Products, Inc.; Laramie Corporation; WowWee, Inc.

Principal Operating Units

Hasbro Games Group; Hasbro Toys Group; Hasbro Canada; Hasbro de Mexico; Hasbro Latin America; Hasbro France; Hasbro Deutschland; Hasbro Italy; Hasbro Spain; Hasbro UK.

Principal Competitors

Mattel; LEGO; Acclaim Entertainment; Applause; Bandai; Electronic Arts; Infogrames, Inc.; JAKKS Pacific; Marvel Enterprises; Nintendo; Ohio Art; Play-By-Play; Playmates; Playmobil; SEGA; Sony; Toymax International; Ty; Vivendi Universal Publishing.

Further Reading

''America's Toy Industry: Nightmare,'' *The Economist,* December 16, 1995, pp. 58, 62.

Barnes, Julian E., ''Hasbro Has Loss as Pokémon Wanes,'' *New York Times,* April 24, 2001, p. 9.

Gaudiosi, John, ''Infogrames Passes Go on Hasbro Buy,'' *Video Business,* December 11, 2000, p. 1.

Goodman, Julie, ''Hasbro Buys Seller of Red-Hot Pokémon,'' *Columbian,* September 10, 1999, p. C2.

Hammonds, Keith H., '' 'Has-Beens' Have Been Very Good to Hasbro,'' *Business Week,* August 5, 1991, pp. 76–77.

''Hasbro Buys Wizards of the Coast; TSR dropped as SF/Fantasy Imprint,'' *Science Fiction Chronicle,* December 1999, p. 5.

''Hasbro Completes Sale of Interactive Business,'' *New York Times,* January 30, 2001, p. C4.

''Hasbro Had Net Loss For Fourth Quarter, Plans More Job Cuts,'' *Wall Street Journal,* February 12, 2001, p. B2.

''Hasbro Shareholders Set Vote on Proposal to Sell,'' *Providence Business News,* April 9, 2001, p. 10.

''Hasbro's Net Soars, Thanks to the Force,'' *New York Times,* July 16, 1999, p. 7.

Jereski, Laura, ''It's Kid Brother's Turn to Keep Hasbro Hot,'' *Business Week,* June 26, 1989, pp. 152, 155.

Kaye, Marvin, *A Toy Is Born,* New York: Stein and Day, 1973.

Kimelman, John, ''No Babe in Toyland,'' *Financial World,* January 4, 1994, pp. 34–36.

Lefton, Terry, ''Da Baum,'' *Brandweek,* February 8, 1999, pp. 32–36.

Michlig, John, *G.I. Joe: The Complete Story of America's Favorite Man of Action,* San Francisco: Chronicle Books, 1998.

Miller, G. Wayne, *Toy Wars: The Epic Struggle Between G.I. Joe, Barbie, and the Companies that Make Them,* New York: Times Books-Random House, 1998.

''Not Toying Around,'' *Forbes,* January 3, 1994, p. 131.

Pasztor, Andy, and Joseph Pereira, ''Hasbro Remains Interested in a Merger with Mattel,'' *Wall Street Journal,* January 29, 1996, pp. A3, A6.

——, Joseph Pereira, and Steven Lipin, ''Hasbro Faces New Struggles Post-Mattel,'' *Wall Street Journal,* February 5, 1996, pp. A3, A4.

Pereira, Joseph, ''Hasbro Posts Gain of 77% in Profit, Topping Forecasts,'' *Wall Street Journal,* April 16, 1999, p. A4.

——, ''Toys: Hasbro Strikes Back—Hot Toys Help It Battle Mattel,'' *Wall Street Journal,* April 15, 1999, p. B1.

Pesek, William, Jr., ''Toy Wars,'' *Barron's,* May 24, 1999, pp. 17–19.

Petrecca, Laura, ''Hasbro Hopes Star Wars Toys Prosper without Sequel,'' *Advertising Age,* March 6, 2000, p. 58.

''Pokémon Parent Shaking Up Family,'' *Spokesman Review,* December 8, 1999, p. A14.

Sansweet, Stephen J., ''Toy Story: Mattel Offers $5 Billion in Unsolicited Bid for Rival Hasbro,'' *Wall Street Journal,* January 25, 1996, pp. A3, A10.

''Toys: Hasbro Hopes Japan's 'Pokémon' Grabs U.S. Children,'' *Wall Street Journal,* May 26, 1998, p. B1.

''With Profits Down, Hasbro to Cut 5% of Its Work Force,'' *New York Times,* October 13, 2000, p. C4.

—Douglas Sun
—updates: David E. Salamie, Jerod L. Allen

International Creative Management, Inc.

8942 Wilshire Boulevard
Beverly Hills, California 90211
U.S.A.
Telephone: (310) 550-4000
Fax: (310) 550-4100

Private Company
Incorporated: 1975
Employees: 650
Sales: $125 million (1998 est.)
NAIC: 71141 Agents and Managers for Artists, Athletes, Entertainers, and Other Public Figures

International Creative Management, Inc. (ICM) is a leading Hollywood talent agency. Emerging from the shadow of Creative Artists Associates, which redefined the industry in the 1980s, ICM's 150 agents represent film stars Mel Gibson and Julia Roberts, the director Francis Ford Coppola, and former British Prime Minister Margaret Thatcher, among others. ICM is the only major talent agency ever to have been publicly owned.

Creative and Famous Origins

ICM was created in 1975 out of an alliance between Creative Management Associates (CMA) and the International Famous Agency (IFA). CMA included in its stable the legendary agent Sam Cohn; IFA had been part of the predecessor to Warner Communications. The new agency, ICM, was part of Josephson International, Inc., a publicly traded company. A period of backstabbing ensued among the various strong personalities making the deals; the chaos gave rival Creative Artists Associates (CAA) time to grow. CAA had also started in 1975, launched by five former employees of show biz giant, the William Morris Agency. Marvin Josephson, who had put together CMA and IFA to form ICM, was meanwhile acquiring a string of unrelated businesses, looking for a jackpot.

Jeffrey Berg, an erudite English major from the University of California at Berkeley, became president of ICM in 1980. His career had started in the proverbial birthplace of many a life in show business, the mailroom. James Wiatt was named president of the agency in 1985. He had joined ICM as a literary agent in the late 1970s after starting with the Frank Cooper Agency in 1976.

The 1980s were profitable for ICM. Like CAA, ICM captured many prime clients after the 1986 death of William Morris leader Stan Kamen, who had been considered Hollywood's top agent. Revenues for ICM were about $56 million in the 1987–1988 fiscal year.

Private in 1988

ICM was taken private in 1988 in a $70 million management buyout. Josephson remained a minority shareholder after the deal; he and the other executives acquired 60 percent of the company's stock. They carried debt of more than $60 million, financed through Chase Manhattan.

In 1989 ICM signed an innovative five-year production agreement with Glinwood Films, a British sales company. The unique arrangement promised to make major motion picture projects available to independent international distributors, while opening an entirely new source of financing for ICM.

By 1990, ICM was at the top of its game. It found work for some of Hollywood's best-paid actors, talents like Mel Gibson, Eddie Murphy, and Arnold Schwarzenegger, who garnered more than $20 million for his role in *Twins* and presumably handed over ten percent of it to ICM. The firm also packaged successful television shows such as *The Simpsons.* ICM reached into several European countries, further geographically than its rivals, as well into more industries, such as theater, book publishing, and network television journalism.

Some insiders said that the agency's very size could work against itself; it was too massive for personnel in the various divisions to be aware of what was going on next door. Others described ICM with a more individualized approach for its clientele. Still, its chairmen at the time, Jeffrey Berg and Guy McElwaine, aimed to make ICM the ''Tiffany'' of the industry within ten years.

ICM created its own international financial services unit in 1991. Frans J. Afman, a pioneering entertainment banker from

Key Dates:

1975: Marvin Josephson forms International Creative Management, Inc. (ICM) out of two talent agencies.
1988: ICM executives take the company private.
1992: ICM leases a new Beverly Hills headquarters building.
1998: James Wiatt leaves ICM; several agents and clients follow.

Credit Lyonnais Nederland, was picked to head the unit. However, he was gone within a couple of years. Also in 1991, ICM acquired the Fair Warning musical talent agency. It represented rock acts such as Metallica. Three years later, ICM acquired Wasted Talent, which represented rock acts U2 and REM. Later, Wasted Talent was merged with Fair Warning to create ICM International.

The Corporate 1990s

During the 1990s, talent agencies saw their roles expand into corporate marketing. After all, according to Berg, they were specialists in optimizing brand equity. Coca-Cola hired Michael Ovitz, head of CAA, to restyle its image. ICM arranged for Visa's sponsorship of the 1990 Paul McCartney U.S. tour.

ICM moved out of West Hollywood and signed a lease on a Beverly Hills headquarters building in June 1992. There was some consolidation among large talent agencies that October. William Morris bought Triad Artists, while InterTalent prepared to fold. At the same time, ICM was undergoing a management buyout. Berg, Wiatt, Cohn, and McElwaine were acquiring Josephson's majority interest.

The new roles of talent agencies eventually produced some clashes. When Credit Lyonnais, which owned Metro-Goldwyn-Mayer, contracted with CAA to help it dispose of some entertainment properties, Berg claimed the deal produced a conflict of interest. Michael Ovitz denied the consulting arrangement gave his agency any special entrée at MGM.

The *Washington Post* reported on the new opportunities being created by new media for talent agencies. Banned from producing movies or network television programs due to the antitrust legacy of MCA Inc. (once the largest talent agency in the United States), they could instead develop video games or other multimedia content. While ICM preferred to remain an agency rather than a producer, Berg did posit the company's expansion into different fields of communications. As the *Los Angeles Times* noted, increasingly sophisticated and lucrative CD-ROM productions were opening new markets for writers, actors, and musicians. This saw ICM and other Hollywood agencies attempting to sell within the computer industry—a vast shift of culture.

As new possibilities arose, ICM negotiated a deal with Random House and Broderbund Software to bring Dr. Seuss to electronic media in 1993. Also, International PCBX Systems Inc. called on ICM to market its audio imaging and data transmission technologies. Additionally, ICM provided celebrity guests for Oldsmobile's Celebrity Circle broadcast on America Online (AOL) beginning in April 1995. Dubbed the first regularly scheduled on-line program, Celebrity Circle, a daily, one-hour program, offered AOL members the chance to ask the star questions.

In the mid-1990s, ICM had 100 agents in Los Angeles and 70 in the New York office, headed by Sam Cohn. In March 1995, ICM fired four LA agents who planned to start their own agency, charging them with trespassing and stealing client files. That same month, pop singer Madonna left CAA for William Morris; four weeks later, she was with ICM. Backstabbing and suspicion were at an all-time high in the talent agency business, reported the *Los Angeles Times,* which blamed the trend on the huge amounts of money stars could command. Over the preceding months, ICM had lost comedic talents such as Billy Crystal and Eddie Murphy to CAA, while gaining director Renny Harlin and actress Goldie Hawn.

When executives Michael Ovitz and Ron Meyer left CAA to become presidents of the Walt Disney Co. and MCA, respectively, several CAA clients jumped ship to join ICM. Sylvester Stallone did so after Meyer had signed him to a $60-million, three-picture contract at MCA.

Stars capable of attracting audiences both in the United States and abroad were most in demand, since two-thirds of a movie's revenues could be made overseas. International markets were growing as U.S. box office receipts stagnated. By 1996, ICM had offices in London and Paris, joint ventures in Madrid and Rome, and was planning to open branches in Hong Kong and Latin America.

ICM was bringing in commissions worth about $115 million a year in the mid-1990s. The company refinanced its debt with Beverly Hills-based City National Bank, avoiding the need to take on another equity partner.

1998 Management Shuffle

The top ranks at ICM were realigned in the fall of 1998, when Wiatt assumed the titles of co-chairman and co-CEO alongside Berg (who retained his traditional titles minus the ''co-'' prefix). At the same time, the firm named Nancy Josephson, a daughter of company founder Marvin Josephson, to the first senior management position (co-president) ever held by a woman at a major talent agency. Nancy Josephson had been an entertainment lawyer in New York City before joining ICM in 1986. She was credited with building the agency's TV business, packaging NBC's wildly successful *Friends* sitcom.

James Wiatt resigned in August 1999, citing differences with Jeff Berg. Wiatt was soon named president of the William Morris Agency, which almost certainly offered him more money than the $1.5 million a year he had been making at ICM, which was still paying down debt from its management buyout. He also reportedly wanted more authority.

Another top agent, David Wirtschafter, left ICM right after Wiatt, and dozens of clients followed. The defections came not long after former CAA head Michael Ovitz, whose tenure at Disney had been short-lived, lured *ER* creator Michael Crichton and comedian Robin Williams to his own management firm,

Artists Management Group (AMG). Wiatt then began an aggressive campaign to attract still more ICM clients and agents to William Morris.

ICM replaced Sam Cohn as head of its New York office with two literary agents in the summer of 1999; however, Cohn remained an agent with the firm. Rival William Morris cut its New York staff in the fall of 1999, a sign of New York's diminishing influence in the film industry. Elaine Goldsmith-Thomas, known for representing Julia Roberts for a dozen years, left ICM in September 2000 to head the New York office of Revolution Studios, a new production venture. Roberts remained with ICM, represented by Jeff Berg.

Principal Subsidiaries

ICM International.

Principal Divisions

Book; Music; News and Business Affairs; Motion Picture; Commercial.

Principal Competitors

Creative Artists Agency; William Morris Agency.

Further Reading

''All Quiet on the ICM Front,'' *Screen Finance,* May 2, 1990.
''And the Winner Is . . . ,'' *Economist,* March 30, 1996, p. 62.
Bates, James, ''Clash of the Hollywood Titans,'' *Los Angeles Times,* April 9, 1993, p. D1.
——, ''ICM Settles on City National for Refinancing,'' *Los Angeles Times,* May 11, 1996, p. D2.
Bates, James and Alan Citron, ''Charges Fly as Two Talent Agencies Clash,'' *Los Angeles Times,* April 3, 1993, p. D1.
Cieply, Michael and Alan Citron, ''ICM Reaches for the Ring,'' *Los Angeles Times,* July 29, 1990, p. D1.
Citron, Alan, ''Big Changes Jolt Talent Industry,'' *Los Angeles Times,* October 19, 1992, p. D1.
——, ''Ex-Insider Is Happy on the Outside,'' *Los Angeles Times,* May 18, 1993, p. D4.
——, ''Major Talent Agency Launches Financing Unit,'' *Los Angeles Times,* July 12, 1991, p. D2.
——, ''Talent Agencies Find Galaxies Beyond Stars,'' *Los Angeles Times,* September 17, 1991, p. D1.
Collins, Scott, ''Hollywood Reporter Fires Writer Who Sued ICM,'' *Los Angeles Times,* December 19, 1995, p. D6.
Dutka, Elaine, ''Stallone Follows Costner, Baldwin Out CAA Door, Signs with ICM,'' *Los Angeles Times,* November 8, 1995, p. D2.
Eller, Claudia, ''Agency Wars: The Cutthroat World of the Talent Business,'' *Los Angeles Times,* April 28, 1995, p. D1.
——, ''Agents Are Casting About in a Torrent of Change,'' *Los Angeles Times,* September 17, 1999, p. C1.
——, ''ICM Shuffle Creates New Executive Team,'' *Los Angeles Times,* October 24, 1998, p. C1.
Eller, Claudia and James Bates, ''ICM Fires Four Top Agents Who Planned to Form Rival Agency,'' *Los Angeles Times,* March 30, 1995, p. D1.
——, ''Talent Exec's Exit Could Spark Industry Frenzy,'' *Los Angeles Times,* August 7, 1999, p. C1.
Eller, Claudia and Sallie Hofmeister, ''ICM Executive Is a Top Talent Among Agents,'' *Los Angeles Times,* November 24, 1998, p. C1.
Harmon, Amy, ''For Multimedia's Emerging Superstars, Are Hollywood Talent Agents the 10 Percent Solution?'' *Los Angeles Times,* June 12, 1994, p. D1.
McDowell, Edwin, ''Buyout May Mean Raises for ICM Talent Agents,'' *New York Times,* May 9, 1988, p. D8.
Parkes, Christopher, ''An Eye on the Big Picture,'' *Financial Times,* November 25, 1996, p. 12.
Schrage, Michael, ''Hollywood Agencies Can Become Stars of the Pop Culture Business,'' *Washington Post,* May 27, 1994, p. F3.
Schuch, Beverly and Donald van de Mark, Interview with Jeff Berg, *Bizz Buzz,* CNNfn, July 9, 1999.
Weinraub, Bernard, ''Agents' Dismissals Signal New York's Fade-Out in Film Business,'' *New York Times,* October 4, 1999, p. C1.
——, ''Ex-Head of Talent Agency Emerges to Lead a Rival,'' *New York Times,* August 10, 1999, p. C2.
——, ''Hitching Stars to His Wagon,'' *New York Times,* June 19, 2000, p. C1.

—Frederick C. Ingram

IONA Technologies plc

The IONA Building
Shelbourne Road
Ballsbridge Dublin 4
Ireland
Telephone: +353-1-637-2000
Toll Free: (800) 672-4948
Fax: +353-1-637-2888
Web site: http://www.iona.com

Public Company
Incorporated: 1991
Employees: 650
Sales: $105 million (1999)
Stock Exchanges: Irish NASDAQ
Ticker Symbol: IONA
NAIC: 511210 Software Publishers

Headquartered in Dublin, Ireland, with a U.S. office in Waltham, Massachusetts, IONA Technologies plc is an established leader in providing middleware based on the CORBA (Common Object Request Broker Architecture) standard. Basically, middleware enables computers using different platforms to communicate with each other. Well-positioned as a middleware leader in e-business, IONA provides services worldwide. In response to the emerging market for enterprise portals, IONA leads the industry with the introduction of its iPortal Suite of servers and middleware for business-to-business e-commerce and enterprise portal applications.

Provider of Low-Cost Middleware: 1991–95

IONA Technologies plc was founded in 1991 in Dublin, Ireland, by Dr. Christopher Horn, Annrai O'Toole, and Dr. Sean Baker, all of whom were associated with Trinity College, Dublin. Horn was the initial developer of Orbix, IONA's basic middleware product, and served as IONA's president, CEO, and chairman from the beginning. From 1984 to 1994 Dr. Horn had served as a lecturer in the computer science department of Trinity College, Dublin, where he was involved in distributed computing. At the time of the company's founding Annrai O'Toole was a research assistant in the computer science department at Trinity College, having earned his M.S. in computer science there in 1991. He would become IONA's chief technology officer. Dr. Sean Baker held a tenured post in Trinity College's computer science department and received his doctorate there. He would become the firm's chief scientific officer.

Baker has written two textbooks on CORBA, a software architecture and specification that allows programs at different locations and developed by different vendors to communicate in a network through an interface broker. CORBA was initially developed by a consortium of vendors through the Object Management Group (OMG), which grew to include more than 500 member companies. CORBA was the standard on which IONA based its middleware products, which enabled companies to integrate their information systems with clients, customers, and the Internet. The OMG's CORBA specifications were first released in 1991.

A key element of CORBA is the object request broker (ORB). In a network of clients and servers on different computers, ORB makes it possible for a client program to request services from a server program without having to understand where the server is in the distributed network or what the interface to the server program looks like. IONA's initial product, Orbix ORB, ran on Microsoft Windows and Windows NT. It also offered support for a range of Unix platforms, including SunOS, Solaris, IRIX, and HP/UX. IONA first introduced Orbix in 1993.

In 1994 SunSoft Inc., a division of Sun Microsystems Inc., acquired a 25 percent minority interest in IONA for $600,000. SunSoft produced an ORB that only operated on Solaris and was a component of DOE (Distributed Objects Everywhere). SunSoft and IONA planned to make their ORBs interoperable. By 1994 the Object Management Group had put forth a standard for building an ORB called CORBA, but it still lacked specifications for communicating between different platforms. Orbix was compliant with version 1.1 of CORBA. At the time IONA had only 12 employees. Although its Orbix had been successfully evaluated, some larger companies remained concerned about IONA's stability, given its small size. The investment

Company Perspectives:

Enterprise portal technology is all about aggregating existing applications and web-enabling businesses, and IONA helps companies do just that. IONA provides industry-leading organizations around the world with complete enterprise portal solutions through the IONA iPortal suite, a comprehensive family of products; our unbiased support for diverse Internet and non-Internet technologies; and our standards-based portal assembly, configuration, and management tools.

from SunSoft gave IONA a strategic backer and added credibility to the firm.

During 1994 companies that produced ORBs were working on developing interoperability between Microsoft's OLE (Object Linking and Embedding) object standard and CORBA. Rather than adopting CORBA, Microsoft was committed to Digital Equipment Corp.'s Common Object Model (COM) as its distributed object standard. In 1994 IONA was working on a beta version of Orbix that would allow developers to integrate Microsoft's OLE with Unix applications. In April 1995 IONA began shipping new versions of Orbix-OLE that allowed developers to create OLE-based applications with Microsoft's Visual Basic or Visual C++ or Powersoft Corp.'s PowerBuilder and to invoke server-based objects via CORBA. Analysts expressed hope that IONA's Orbix-OLE would help bridge the gap that existed between OLE and CORBA. Later in 1995 IONA planned to release Orbix 2.0, which would support CORBA 2.0.

IONA was focused on its core product, Orbix, and committed to the CORBA standard. Its goal was to become a high-volume ORB producer. By mid-1995 it had more than 200 customers for its shrink-wrapped, low-cost products. In June 1995 it signed a $750,000 contract with Boeing's Commercial Airplane Group to supply it with ORB technology. It had also signed third-party deals with companies such as Novell, Visix, Isis, and NobleNet to use its ORB products. By the end of the decade IONA would have more than 3,500 customers, a network of more than 400 system integrators and consulting organizations using its products, and strategic alliances with leading software companies.

With the release of Orbix 2.0 in fall 1995, IONA opened a U.S. office near Cambridge, Massachusetts. Orbix 2.0 enabled Microsoft's OLE to be distributed across networks that were supported by CORBA. For example, a Microsoft Excel spreadsheet could pull data from a variety of sources as needed. For 1995 the company reported revenue of $8.6 million and net income of $2.2 million.

New Products and Strategic Alliances: 1996

Java was another programming language coming into use in the mid-1990s. In 1996 IONA introduced Orbix Java, which would allow Java applets running in a browser client to access the database and transactional services of server applications built around CORBA. Following beta testing in early 1996, Orbix Java shipped later in that year.

In 1996 IONA licensed its ORB technology to Silicon Graphics Inc. It also signed a joint development and licensing agreement with IBM to link Iona's ORB to IBM's Systems Object Model and Distributed Systems Object Model server technologies. By working closely with IONA, IBM could ensure tighter compatibility with ORBs from other companies.

At the Object World East Show in May 1996, IONA demonstrated OrbixTalk, which facilitated event-driven or indirect client/server communications. OrbixTalk linked ORB to a message logging system and provided guaranteed delivery of communications. Later in the year IONA announced product integrations with three other companies: Isis Distributed Systems Inc., NeXT Software Inc., and Persistence Software Inc. The technology partnership with Isis resulted in Orbix + Isis, which added fault tolerance, an important factor in the reliability of a distributed system. Chicago-based Options Clearing Corp. would base its transaction-processing framework on Orbix + Isis. The agreement with NeXT Software would result in linking Orbix with NeXT's architecture for building distributed Web server systems. IONA's partnership with Persistence Software would give Orbix the ability to store and access objects in a relational database.

In October 1996 IONA introduced a beta version of Orbix Web 2.0, which linked Java applets to ORBs. The company also announced it was developing a link to allow interoperability between Microsoft's Distributed Component Object Model (COM) and CORBA. Before the end of the year IONA had separate agreements with BEA Systems Inc. and Transarc to produce transaction management systems using Orbix 2.0.

A Dominant ORB Provider for CORBA: 1997

In January 1997 IONA began shipping its Orbix/Enterprise middleware that would link ORBs and mainframe computers running on OS/390. The product was developed in conjunction with BellSouth Corp.

At Object World East, IONA demonstrated a suite of object-based tools and services for creating transaction-intensive and messaging-oriented systems. Its Orbix/Object Transaction Monitor was an integrated bundle consisting of the Orbix CORBA ORB and Transarc's object-transaction service, CORBA naming and event services, Secure Sockets Layer security, load balancing, tuning, and database connectivity. The suite would enter beta testing in the second quarter. Also introduced at the show were Iona's Orbix 2.2, which included a graphical user interface (GUI) for managing and monitoring applications; the Orbix Internet Inter-ORB Protocol engine; and a beta version of Orbix Trader, an object search engine that searched for objects and services across a distributed system.

During 1997 IONA emerged as the dominant ORB provider in the CORBA market. It had grown to about 420 employees. For 1997 the company had $48.6 million in revenue and $4.8 million in net income, compared to 1996 revenue of $21.2 million and net income of $1.5 million. Its IPO in February 1997 was the fifth largest for NASDAQ, raising some $140 million. At that time Sun Microsystems divested its 25 percent interest in the company for $60 million.

Key Dates:

1991: Company is founded in Dublin, Ireland.
1993: Company introduces its first product, Orbix ORB, an object request broker based on CORBA standards.
1997: IONA goes public with an IPO on the NASDAQ.
2000: Company begins shipping its iPortal Suite for business-to-business electronic commerce.

Later in 1997 IONA announced that its Orbix Wonderwall software would be integrated with Raptor System Inc.'s Eagle firewall. The firewall would allow enterprises to use CORBA-based applications over the Internet without compromising the security of their networks. The firewall would permit the secure transmission of IIOP (Internet Inter-ORB Protocol) packets across the firewall. Up to this point, traditional firewalls had not allowed the transmission of IIOP packets.

Key Agreements: 1998

In late 1997 IONA began a transition from the developer market to the enterprise market. In November 1997 it began shipping its Orbix Object Transaction Monitor (OTM), which included transaction monitoring software from technology partner Transarc. Before the year was over, IONA announced it was negotiating to license Microsoft's COM architecture in order to create technologies that would bridge the gap between COM and CORBA and simplify distributed computing development. By February 1998 Microsoft had licensed its ActiveX core technologies to IONA. The agreement represented something of a truce between Microsoft and those who supported CORBA. It was around this time that Microsoft's Transaction Server (MTS) was gaining momentum after notable improvements following its introduction. As a result, middleware vendors such as IONA would need to make their CORBA-compliant products interoperable with MTS. During 1998 Microsoft would participate in initiatives to bridge the gap between COM and CORBA.

In March 1998 IONA staged its IonaWorld conference in Boston. It announced an agreement with Hewlett-Packard to incorporate IONA's ORB into HP's OpenView network management software. The company also demonstrated Orbix MX, middleware for managing multimedia data—including audio, video, data, and telephony streams—and integrating it with traditional data in an organization's information technology (IT) infrastructure.

In an effort to portray CORBA technology as a mainstream architecture, IONA announced that Hongkong Telecom ordered 100,000 copies of OrbixWeb for use in its set-top boxes. It was just one example of a large-scale system based on CORBA. Since its IPO in February 1997, IONA had progressed in its goal to become a one-stop shop for middleware infrastructure. To its core object middleware and ORBs it had added a number of services for messaging, system management, security, and transaction management.

During 1998 the company was preparing for the release of the new CORBA 3.0 protocol. IONA code-named its next-generation object transaction monitor (OTM) Art. It was expected that the new architecture would enable developers to achieve interoperability with the major competing object models: COM, CORBA, and JavaBeans. After conducting beta testing at 500 sites, IONA released Orbix COMet in July 1998. The product let Windows-based developers create applications that could run in non-Windows environments.

Also during 1998 IONA gained a foothold in the application server market by acquiring unnamed technology from Electronic Data Systems (EDS) for $5 million. The technology would be used to add a layer over the forthcoming next-generation product that was code-named Art. With companies such as IBM, Inprise, and Peerlogic introducing new ORBs, IONA was facing increased competition in its core market. IONA also announced Orbix would be coupled with Symantec Corp.'s Visual Café Enterprise to allow Java developers to create applications and more easily extend them across the enterprise. For 1998 IONA's revenue nearly doubled to $83.6 million. The company reported net income of $7.7 million.

Strengthening for E-Commerce: 1999–2000

Once the Object Management Group released its new CORBA 3.0 specifications at the end of 1998, IONA introduced Orbix 3.0 in early 1999. The new release offered rapid application development capabilities, location transparency and load balancing, Internet security, and integration with applications based on Microsoft's COM specification.

IONA moved to strengthen its support for Java-based application servers by acquiring EJBHome Ltd., a British vendor of Enterprise JavaBeans (EJB). IONA also joined Sun Microsystems' community licensing program for Java. In early 1999 many firms were being cautious about using Java, a relatively new programming language, as the basis of their entire application. However, CORBA-based multiplatform products were beginning to lose market share to Enterprise Java. By March 1999 IONA was offering free downloads of its HomeBase Enterprise JavaBeans toolkit, which it acquired from EJBHome Ltd. The toolkit helped speed the development of EJB component-based applications. Later in 1999 IONA introduced its OrbixHome kit, a development kit designed to generate, integrate, and manage CORBA and EJB components.

At its fall 1999 IONA World user conference in Dublin, IONA announced it would be releasing products for electronic commerce over the next 12 months. The suite of e-commerce products would be released under the name iPortal and would run on top of Orbix. The IONA iPortal Suite would consist of application, integration, and management servers and Orbix 2000. The application server in the suite was an EJB container based on Sun Microsystems' Java 2 platform.

In February 2000 IONA announced it would acquire Watershed Technologies Inc., a developer of Extensible Markup Language (XML) tools and services based in Waltham, Massachusetts, for $13.2 million in cash and stock. IONA planned to incorporate Watershed's technology into its iPortal Web Server. The first components of IONA's iPortal Suite, which was targeted at the business-to-business e-commerce market, began shipping in March 2000, and included Orbix 2000 and the iPortal Application Server. These were followed by the iPortal Integration Server in April and the iPortal Server in June. In July the company's iPortal Application Server received a ''Best of Show'' award at Application Development 2000, an industry event focused on XML- and Java-based technology and processes for building e-business applications.

In May 2000 IONA COO Barry Morris was promoted to CEO, with former CEO Chris Horn continuing as the company's chairman and president. Morris had joined IONA in 1994 and had become COO in April 1999. He had previously worked at Digital Equipment Corp. and Lotus Development Corp.

In June IONA acquired Genesis Development Corp. of West Chester, Pennsylvania, for $24 million in cash and stock. The acquisition added 40 employees; Genesis CEO Jason Matthews became IONA's vice president of worldwide professional services. Genesis provided XML- and Java-based e-business applications for portals and online exchanges primarily in the insurance and financial services markets.

As 2000 drew to a close, IONA was completing its transition from a traditional middleware leader to a competitor in high-level development sectors by introducing a suite of products for e-commerce and enterprise portals. While the company's iPortal Suite was aimed at the business-to-business market, IONA planned to eventually offer products for the business-to-consumer sector. In 2000 the company was reporting record quarter-to-quarter revenue, following record 1999 revenue of $105.4 million and net income of $5.5 million. It appeared the company was successfully expanding into providing products for e-commerce while at the same time maintaining high-volume production of its core middleware products.

Principal Competitors

BEA Systems Inc.; Visigenic Software Inc.; IBM Corp.; Microsoft Corp.; Tibco Finance Technology; Horizon Technology Group PLC; Viador Inc; Hummingbird Communications Ltd.; Oracle Corp.; Sun Microsystems Inc.; Inprise Inc.

Further Reading

Bowen, Ted Smalley, ''Iona Technologies Set to Ship Orbix OTM Software,'' *InfoWorld,* November 17, 1997, p. 15.

Brucken, et al., ''Windows on Iona,'' *Software Magazine,* January 1996, p. 22.

Chappell, David, ''Winner of the CORBA Wars,'' *ENT,* March 24, 1999, p. 14.

Cunningham, Cara, ''Iona Pushes CORBA Efforts,'' *InfoWorld,* March 23, 1998, p. 32.

Gilhooly, Kym, ''Iona Eyes Are Smiling,'' *Software Magazine,* July 1997, p. 115.

Gonsalves, Antone, ''Iona Enters Portal Pursuit,'' *PC Week,* October 25, 1999, p. 25.

——, ''Iona Prepared to Deliver Portal Strategy,'' *PC Week,* March 6, 2000, p. 23.

Haney, Clare, ''Iona Rolls out Web Portal Package,'' *ComputerWorld,* March 13, 2000, p. 26.

——, ''Iona to Ship First Components of B-to-B iPortal Suite,'' *InfoWorld,* March 13, 2000, p. 26.

''Iona Technologies Releases Orbix/Enterprise Link,'' *PC Week,* January 20, 1997, p. 65.

''Irish Green,'' *Forbes,* April 19, 1999, p. 150.

LaMonica, Martin, ''CORBA Middleware Vendors Warm to Java,'' *InfoWorld,* February 5, 1996, p. 45.

——, ''Iona's Orbix Spans CORBA and Visual Basic: Readies Orbix 2.0 for Windows NT,'' *InfoWorld,* October 23, 1995, p. 6.

Lawson, Stephen, ''Iona Offers Internet IIOP Packet Sharing,'' *InfoWorld,* September 8, 1997, p. 21.

Leach, Norvin, ''Iona Tests Windows Edition of Orbix,'' *PC Week,* July 11, 1994, p. 30.

——, ''SunSoft's Stake in Irish Firm Expands Object Broker Options,'' *PC Week,* January 24, 1994, p. 45.

McCowan, Michael, and Jason Pritchard, ''Corba Connection,'' *InformationWeek,* March 17, 1997, p. 1A.

McKay, Niall, ''Competition in CORBA Arena Heats Up,'' *InfoWorld,* June 9, 1997, p. 41.

——, ''Iona Brings Orbix to Multimedia, OpenView,'' *InfoWorld,* March 16, 1998, p. 6.

——, ''Iona Puts Itself in the Middle,'' *InfoWorld,* March 23, 1998, p. 32.

Moeller, Michael, and Antone Gonsalves, ''Iona out to Bridge Gap,'' *PC Week,* December 15, 1997, p. 6.

Patrizio, Andy, ''Iona Package Brings OLE, CORBA Closer,'' *PC Week,* April 24, 1995, p. 27.

Rosen, Michele, ''Iona Touts New Products, Java Support,'' *ENT,* March 24, 1999, p. 16.

Swoyer, Stephen, ''Microsoft Allies with CORBA for Interoperability,'' *ENT,* July 15, 1996, p. 18.

Trott, Bob, and Niall McKay, ''Microsoft Makes Interoperability Strides,'' *InfoWorld,* February 2, 1998, p. 28.

Wirthman, Lisa, ''Iona Stretches Orbit of Orbix,'' *PC Week,* March 24, 1997, p. 69.

Wreden, Nick, ''Iona Looks for Life Beyond Corba,'' *InformationWeek,* April 19, 1999, p. A18.

——, ''Iona Moves to the Enterprise,'' *InformationWeek,* October 20, 1997, p. 134.

—David P. Bianco

Beatties

James Beattie plc

71-80 Victoria Street
Wolverhampton, West Midlands WV1 3PQ
United Kingdom
Telephone: (+44) 1902-422-311
Fax: (+44) 1902-643-355
Web site: http://www.beatties.co.uk

Public Company
Incorporated: 1920 as James Beattie Ltd.
Employees: 1,617
Sales: £106.6 million ($172.2 million) (2000)
Stock Exchanges: London
Ticker Symbol: BTT
NAIC: 45211 Department Stores

James Beattie plc, which operates the Beatties department stores group, one of the leading department store retailers in England's Midlands region, has been adding stores and expanding its existing stores since the late 1990s, building up a park of 12 Beatties stores. With the addition of more than 300,000 square feet of selling space in progress, including more than 107,000 square feet being added to the company's existing stores, Beatties expects to have total selling space of more than 750,000 square feet by the middle of the first decade of the 21st century. The company's home base and flagship store is in the longtime home Wolverhampton, from which chairman Eric Pountain and managing director Chris M.S. Jones oversee operations at the company's existing Northampton, Solihull, Sutton Coldfield, Burton-Upon-Trent, Birkenhead, Worcester, Aylesbury, and Dudley stores. Beatties has built a reputation as an up-market retailer, refusing to enter the discounting contests with competitors during the lean retail years in the United Kingdom during the 1990s. Nonetheless, Beatties remains consistently profitable where its rivals have slumped, keeping to its commitment to high-quality customer service and major brand names. The company continually adds new services and product ranges to its stores, including photography studios, cafes, florist shops, and hair salons. At the same time, Beatties has been attempting to woo over a new generation of shopper, introducing youth-oriented designs and fashions to attract younger shoppers who have long avoided "shopping where their parents shop." Beatties trades on the London Stock Exchange. The company posted nearly £107 million in sales during its 2000 year.

Drapers to Department Store in the 20th Century

James Beattie opened a drapery shop on Wolverhampton's Victoria Street in 1877. Starting with just £300 and working with two assistants, Beattie's shop, then called the Victoria Draper Supply Store, also provided a home for Beattie's assistants. Over the next two decades the store grew into a thriving business. By the end of the 19th century, the store was turning over more than £30,000 per year in sales, with a payroll of some forty employees.

A fire in 1896 destroyed Beattie's business, yet set the stage for the company's expansion into one of the region's most prominent department store chains. Despite suffering losses of up to £10,000 as a result of the fire, Beattie determined to rebuild his business. Instead of building on the company's former Victoria Street site, Beattie relocated across the street—taking up residence in what was to become Beattie's flagship store. The move gave Beattie the opportunity to expand the store.

The larger store proved still more successful than the original store and Beattie soon sought to expand the location again. In 1901, Beattie carried out a new expansion, which marked the end of the company's policy of providing lodging for its employees. With the extra space, Beattie began expanding the store's range of merchandise, and Beattie's began evolving into what was later to become a department store.

James Beattie himself remained in control of his store until his death in 1934, guiding the store's continual expansion as the company acquired adjoining properties. During the 1920s, Beattie reincorporated the store as James Beattie Ltd. After Beattie's death, marking the end of a career spanning nearly 60 years, the next generation of Beatties joined the company in the form of Beattie's grandson. Named after his grandfather, the younger James Beattie was appointed company secretary in 1938 before being named as a joint managing director in 1948. Beattie was to help lead the company's public offering in 1954,

Company Perspectives:

As a department store our main purpose is to provide you with an extensive range of well-chosen, good value merchandise, and to offer this to you in attractive surroundings supported by pleasant and efficient service with complete integrity.

when the company listed on the London Stock Exchange. Despite the public offering, the Beattie family maintained its control of the company's direction through a dual stock setup that enabled them to retain the majority of the company's voting rights. Other stockholders were forced to content themselves with shares providing guaranteed dividends.

The naming of James Beattie to the position of chairman and managing director in 1961 marked the beginning of a new period of growth for Beatties. For nearly 90 years, Beatties had been represented by its single Wolverhampton store. In the 1960s, however, the company began to expand its holdings. The company opened its first branch store in Birkenhead in 1963. This store was joined by two others before the end of the decade, one in Solihull in 1966 and another in Dudley in 1969. Further expansion came in the 1970s when the company opened Beatties department stores in Sutton Coldfield in 1974 and in Northampton in 1975.

New Expansion for the New Century

As the United Kingdom slumped into a long economic recession, starting with the crisis sparked by the Arab Oil Embargo and continuing more or less into the 1990s, Beattie's expansionist moves came to a standstill. Instead, the company focused on improving its existing stores, concentrating on maintaining the stores' attractiveness to their Midlands customers through a number of store extensions and refits. Yet the Beatties stores were finding it increasingly difficult to renew their customer base as a new generation of youth sought the means to set itself apart from their parents—a position that extended to a general avoidance of the somewhat stuffy, service-heavy British department store as exemplified in the hit television comedy *Are You Being Served?*

The retirement of James Beattie in 1987 set the stage for a new period of growth for the company his grandfather had founded more than a century before. Now led by chairman Eric Pountain and managing director Chris Jones, the company began a major renovation of its flagship Wolverhampton store, which, at a cost of more than £3 million, was completed in 1989. The completion of the Wolverhampton renovation, which added, among other features, escalators to the store for the first time, initiated a new period of investment and expansion.

In 1990, the company added its first new store in 15 years when it opened a Beatties department store in Burton-Upon-Trent. Two years later, another new Beatties store appeared in the Midlands retail landscape when the company's four-story Worcester store opened. The company's store holdings swelled to nine with the opening of a Beatties department store in Aylesbury. At the same time, Beattie saw the opportunity to build on its Wolverhampton site, adding an extension to increase its presence on Victoria Street.

Key Dates:

1877: James Beattie opens drapery store in Wolverhampton.
1896: Fire destroys original store; company reopens across the street.
1901: Expansion of store and introduction of department store format.
1920: Company incorporated as limited company.
1934: Founder James Beattie dies and his grandson, also named James Beattie, joins the company.
1948: James Beattie becomes joint managing director.
1954: Company is listed on London Stock Exchange.
1961: James Beattie becomes managing director and chairman.
1963: Company opens second store in Birkenhead.
1987: James Beattie dies.
1989: Company completes £3 million renovation of Wolverhampton store.
1995: Company changes shareholding structure to eliminate two-tiered voting rights.
1998: Beatties announces £12 million renovation plan.

The United Kingdom's deepening economic problems in the early 1990s helped put an end to Beatties' latest growth spurt. By the mid-1990s, the company, which one analyst described as a ''slumbering family company,'' seemed to have returned to bed. Yet, in 1995, the company made a significant change to its shareholding status, ending the long-standing two-tiered voting rights structure that had kept the company's control within the Beattie family. With the Beattie family's agreement, this structure was abandoned and all shares in the company received equal voting rights.

The return to health of the United Kingdom's economy beginning in the mid-1990s sparked a renewal in the company's expansion mood. Beatties, which had refused to follow retail trends toward discounting in order to woo customers, had received praise for weathering the difficulties of the decade. In fact, Beatties had remained profitable and posted steady increases in sales, which topped £90 million in 1996, while many of its discount-eager competitors were struggling and even going under. The company, which had engaged in a number of strict cost control measures to ensure its profitability, began a new investment program in 1998.

At first the company turned to its existing stores, pledging some £12 million in a series of store expansions and store remodelings. The company set its focus on increasing the range of products and services offered in its stores, as well as increasing the number of its brand names. At the same time, Beatties sought to bring young shoppers back to its aisles, increasing its number of youth-oriented designs and fashions, including the hot brand names of the day. By 1999, Beatties could also begin announcing its intention to add new stores to its Midlands department store empire.

Beatties' ambitious expansion program for the turn of the century represented nearly £20 million in investment and called for the opening of three new stores. Among these stores was a 55,000-square-foot store in Huddersfield as anchor tenant in a new shopping mall being built there, and a 90,000-square-foot flagship store in Birmingham, in a site acquired from C&A as the Dutch retailer decided to pull the plug on its struggling U.K. operations. The refitting of the C&A site was expected to cost the company some £6.5 million, but was scheduled to be completed by September 2001, in time to capture a share of the crucial fourth-quarter shopping season. By the end of that year, the company planned to have 11 stores in operation.

By 2000, Beattie was also able to announce the future addition of a 12th store to its growing network. The new store was slated to open as an anchor tenant in the Blackfriars development scheduled for completion in 2004. Meanwhile, Beatties was putting the finishing touches to much of its massive renovation program, completing the refits of its Wolverhampton, Northampton, and Solihull stores by the end of 2000. The renovation and expansion of its Sutton Coldfield store, adding some 30,000 feet, was scheduled for completion in 2002. In all, the company expected to add more than 300,000 square feet of selling space, giving it a park of more than 750,000 square feet of selling space with which to win customers at the start of the new century.

Principal Competitors

Arcadia Group plc; Debenhams plc; Harrods Holdings; House of Fraser plc; Marks and Spencer plc; N Brown Group plc; New Look plc; Next plc; Otto Versand Gmbh & Co.; Selfridges plc.

Further Reading

''Beattie Looks to Expand,'' *Independent*, April 9, 1998, p. 26.

Beyaztas, Binnur, ''James Beattie Stores Line Up 600 New Jobs,'' *Daily Telegraph,* April 8, 1999.

Deshmukh, Anita, ''Store Chain Beats Trend as Sales Rise,'' *Birmingham Post*, September 7, 2000, p. 29.

Finch, Julia, ''Retail Shares Up as Shops Show Recovery Signs,'' *Guardian*, April 8, 1999.

Lissaman, Vicky, ''Tasty Extension at Store,'' *Evening Mail*, September 23, 2000, p. 17.

Morley, Chris, ''Beattie's Superstore Bound for Brum,'' *Evening Mail*, September 6, 2000, p. 1.

—M.L. Cohen

J.C. Penney Company, Inc.

6501 Legacy Drive
Plano, Texas 75024-3698
U.S.A.
Telephone: (972) 431-1000
Toll Free: (800) 953-9421
Fax: (972) 431-1362
Web sites: http://www.jcpenney.net; http://www.jcpenney.com

Public Company
Incorporated: 1913
Employees: 267,000
Sales: $31.85 billion (2001)
Stock Exchanges: New York
Ticker Symbol: JCP
NAIC: 452110 Department Stores; 454110 Electronic Shopping and Mail-Order Houses; 446110 Pharmacies and Drug Stores

With about 1,100 stores in all 50 states as well as Puerto Rico and Mexico, J.C. Penney Company, Inc. (JCPenney) is the second largest department store retailer (trailing Sears, Roebuck and Co.) and the largest catalog merchant in the United States, with licensing agreements for its products throughout the world. The company also runs 49 Renner department stores in Brazil and owns Eckerd Drugstores, one of the largest drugstore chains in the United States, with about 2,600 units in the Southeast, the Northeast, and the Sunbelt. JCPenney boomed in its early days in Western mining towns because it offered all goods at ''one fair price'' and brought fashionable items from the East to remote towns. The company struggled through the 1970s, as upstart companies such as Wal-Mart Stores, Inc. began selling goods at discount prices and longtime rivals such as Sears gave JCPenney tough competition in the hardware and appliance departments. A major reorganization of the company from a mass marketer into a fashion-oriented national department store during the 1980s, along with the relocation of its corporate headquarters from New York to less expensive Texas, put JCPenney in a strong position to compete in the tough retailing climate of the 1990s and early 2000s.

The Golden Rule: 1900–19

James Cash Penney started his first retail store in 1902 in Kemmerer, Wyoming, a small mining town. He was 26 years old and had grown up on a farm near Hamilton, Missouri. Two years after graduating from high school, Penney went to work for a local retailer, J.M. Hale. Penney's health suffered while he was in the Midwest, and his doctor advised him to move to the cooler climate of Colorado. After several ups and downs in Longmont, Colorado, Penney started working for the Golden Rule Mercantile Company, a dry goods retailer founded by T.M. Callahan. Callahan soon promoted young Penney to his Evanston, Wyoming, store to work with one of his partners, Guy Johnson.

Penney put in three years as a salesman, and Callahan and Johnson decided to make him a manager and partner. Penney chose to open his first Golden Rule store in Kemmerer because many of his Evanston customers lived there. The local banker cautioned Penney against opening a ''cash only'' store, as three others had failed in Kemmerer, but Penney did not want to accept mining company scrip or credit. Penney invested his whole savings—$500—and had to borrow $1,500 to be the third partner, with Callahan and Johnson, in the Kemmerer store. Penney's instinct proved correct; the store had $28,898 in sales its first year.

In 1907 Callahan and Johnson dissolved their partnership and Penney bought them out, taking over three stores. He implemented the principles of his former partners and expanded the chain throughout the Rocky Mountains by allowing his store managers to buy a one-third partnership in new stores, provided they had a trained salesperson to take their place as manager at the old store. He established a central buying and accounting office in Salt Lake City, Utah, in 1909, and had 34 stores with more than $2 million in sales by 1912. In 1913, Penney incorporated the company as J.C. Penney Company, Inc. and moved the corporate headquarters to New York City to be closer to manufacturers and suppliers.

Company Perspectives:

Throughout our organization we're making progress in ensuring a common understanding of who we are, the customers we target, and our place in today's competitive landscape. We know that our business is about selling fashion at value prices. Our opportunity is to make sure that we have fashionable, high-quality merchandise at good prices. That's our history, and it is our future.

By 1915 the company had 83 stores and the next year ventured east of the Mississippi River for the first time with stores in Wausau and Watertown, Wisconsin. Penney became chairman of the board in 1917, when the company had 175 stores, and Earl Sams became president. The company continued to open stores at a fast clip. Private label brands were a major reason for the success of the company. Customers liked them because of controlled quality yet cheaper prices than brand names; Penney liked them because he could determine the price and make a higher profit margin. Belle Isle, Ramona, Honor Brand, and Nation Wide were private label names for piece goods, and Big Mac, Waverly, and Lady Lyke were labels on work shirts, men's caps, and lingerie, respectively.

Rapid Growth and Expansion: 1920s–50s

During the next several years, the company's growth was explosive. As Penney's personal wealth increased, so did his charity. Though he had quietly been giving thousands of dollars to local churches and organizations, in 1923 he founded Penney Farms, a 120,000-acre experimental farming area in northern Florida for down-on-their-luck farmers. In 1925 when the company's 674 stores generated sales of $91 million, Penney was again giving some of his good fortune back, this time by establishing the J.C. Penney Foundation to fund a myriad of family-related agencies. The next year, when the company opened an 18-story office and warehouse building in New York, Penney went back to Florida and built the Memorial Home Community, a 60-acre residential tract for retired ministers, church workers, and missionaries, adjacent to Penney Farms.

The 25th anniversary was celebrated in 1927, and founder James Cash Penney declared that the company had a good shot at achieving sales of $1 billion by its 50th anniversary in 1952. The company's managers and executives, who had equity in individual stores they ran or oversaw, traded their ownership for a stake in the company as a whole. In 1929 the company was listed on the New York Stock Exchange. When the Great Depression hit, the company coped by cutting back its inventory and trying to purchase goods at lower prices so it could pass the savings on to customers. The company survived the hard times largely because it had become known for its high quality goods and service, and people turned to JCPenney for the basic items they needed. The company's profits even increased during the Depression; by 1936 sales rose to $250 million, and the number of stores grew to 1,496.

During World War II, the company sold a record number of war bonds through its stores. Materials and merchandise were scarce, yet the company increased its sales to $500 million in 1945. In 1946 Earl Sams was promoted to chairman, with Penney as honorary chairman, and Albert Hughes, a former Utah store manager, was elevated to the presidency. The company—now with 1,602 stores—opened a store in Hampton Village, Missouri, in 1949 in a "drive-in shopping district," a precursor to suburban malls. After only four years as chairman, Earl Sams died in 1950. In an unusual corporate move, J.C. Penney resumed the chairmanship instead of promoting Albert Hughes. A year before its 50th anniversary, the company reached its goal of $1 billion in sales.

In 1954 Penney created the James C. Penney Foundation (its predecessor, the J.C. Penney Foundation, went under during the Depression) to continue his philanthropy, and in 1957 he served as a charter member of the Distributive Education Clubs of America, helped create the Junior Achievement Clubs, and endowed a chair at Westminster College. At the same time, William Batten, a vice-president, conducted an internal study in 1957; the results indicated the company should adapt to changing consumer spending habits, especially by beginning to sell on credit instead of for cash only. The next year, Hughes became chairman and Batten became president. The company issued its first JCPenney card and instituted other changes as a result of the study, including the introduction of major appliances, home electronics, furniture, and sporting goods.

A New Era: 1960–75

In 1962 JCPenney got into the mail-order business for the first time by buying General Merchandise Company, a Wisconsin firm with a discount store operation as well. JCPenney was different from many of its competitors with its late entry into the catalog mail-order business. Other big retailers started in mail-order and then launched into retail stores. JCPenney created the Treasury discount stores from the General Merchandise discount operation. The next year, it mailed its first JCPenney catalog. In eight states, customers could order from the catalog from inside JCPenney stores; a Milwaukee distribution center supplied the goods. The company's first full-line stores, with all the new merchandise lines instituted by President Batten, opened in 1963 in Audubon, New Jersey, and King of Prussia, Pennsylvania. They were prototypes for the JCPenney stores of the next two decades.

The company needed bigger headquarters because it had grown significantly in 38 years; it built a 45-story office in New York in 1964, where the company stayed until its later move to Dallas. At the same time, Batten became the company's fourth chairman and beauty salons, portrait studios, food facilities, and auto service centers were added to full-line stores. Sales topped $3 billion in 1968; in 1969 the company added an Atlanta, Georgia, catalog distribution center and purchased Thrift Drug Company.

Two years later, when James Cash Penney died at age 95, sales for the company he founded hit $5 billion and the catalog business made a profit for the first time. Able to take advantage of the fact that disposable income in the United States was rising faster than inflation, JCPenney reached its highest number of stores in 1973, with 2,053 stores, 300 of which were full-line establishments. Donald Seibert was elected fifth chairman of the board and CEO in 1974, the same year a third catalog distribution center was opened in Columbus, Ohio. The com-

Key Dates:

1902: James Cash Penney opens his first retail store, called the Golden Rule, in Kemmerer, Wyoming.
1913: Penney incorporates his company, consisting of more than 34 stores, as J.C. Penney Company, Inc. and moves the headquarters to New York City.
1929: Company goes public with listing on the New York Stock Exchange.
1958: First JCPenney credit card is issued.
1962: Company enters the mail-order business through the purchase of General Merchandise Company.
1969: Company enters drugstore sector with the purchase of Thrift Drug Company.
1982: Massive reorganization is launched to transform the company from a mass merchant into a national department store.
1988: Headquarters are relocated to Texas.
1990: The Original Arizona Jean Company private brand of clothing is launched.
1997: Company acquires Eckerd Corporation and its 1,750 drugstores for $3.3 billion.
1998: Full-scale launch of jcpenney.com is undertaken.
1999: Credit card operations are sold to GE Capital for $4 billion.

pany offered, and sold, three million shares of common stock in 1975, and Sesame Street joined JCPenney's fold by signing an exclusive licensing agreement for children's wear.

While the company was riding high on these achievements, the recession that began in 1974 took its toll. JCPenney's stock plunged from a high of $51 a share to $17. Earnings dropped from $185.8 million to $125.1 million. Investors believed low-margin items such as appliances were squeezing profits, and that discount and self-service home-center stores were doing a better job than JCPenney in the hardware business. The advent and strong growth of the specialty apparel store also meant tough competition for JCPenney. Like other businesses, JCPenney rebounded and had good growth in 1975, but its executives began to suspect the company needed to be restructured.

1976–85: Mass Merchandiser or Department Store?

Walter Neppl became president in 1976 (Seibert was still chairman), and the company launched its women's fashion program in five markets, designed to help the company compete against specialty stores cropping up in malls. A fourth catalog distribution center, in Lenexa, Kansas, was added in 1978. By then, sales had grown to $10.8 billion, the women's fashion program was introduced in new markets, and a home furnishings line was added. As a fifth distribution center was added in 1979, in Reno, Nevada, the catalog service went nationwide. Sales of the service surpassed $1 billion, making the company the second largest catalog merchandiser in the United States.

To continue expanding the credit policies of the company, JCPenney began accepting Visa in 1979; MasterCard was accepted the next year. The company closed the Treasury discount stores in 1980 because they were unprofitable and decided to focus resources on its JCPenney stores. In 1981, when the company's sales totaled $11.9 billion, JCPenney was the first to sell zero-coupon bonds in domestic public markets. It also reorganized its executive structure around the office of the chairman. Seibert remained chairman, Neppl moved to the new vice-chairmanship, and William Howell was made an executive vice-president. With these officers in place, the company launched a massive reorganization to transform the company from a mass merchant into a national department store. It would take almost a decade to achieve the goals outlined in the JCPenney stores positioning statement, issued in 1982.

The company's first order of business was to expand the fashion programs in men's, women's, and children's departments, and the company divided its stores into two categories, metropolitan (based in regional shopping centers) and geographic (based in smaller communities). A sixth catalog distribution center was also opened in 1982, in Manchester, Connecticut. With the $14 million remodeling of its key store in Atlanta, JCPenney rolled out the prototype of its latest store design. Atlanta was only the beginning. In 1983 JCPenney announced a $1 billion program to give its stores facelifts and rearrange merchandise. Apparel, home furnishings, and leisure lines would be emphasized, and auto service, hard line appliances, paint, hardware, lawn and garden merchandise, and fabrics were phased out. Its big mass merchant competitors, Montgomery Ward and Sears, continued in these lines.

Retail analysts who followed JCPenney called the company's decision difficult but necessary. These lines provided $1.5 billion in annual sales, but were keeping the company from positioning itself as a true department store. In addition, low-margin goods were preventing the company from making its profit potential. In 1983 Howell, who most recently held a vice-chairmanship (along with David R. Gill, who had started with the company back in 1953), was elected the sixth chairman of the board, and David Miller was named president. The company also introduced a communications system for broadcasting directly to its stores using satellite transmissions from headquarters. Merchandise buyers from the home office could show store managers, salespeople, and local buyers what merchandise was available, and the local employees could help select what goods would likely sell in their stores. This gave the company the cost-saving advantages of being centralized, but also allowed it to be sensitive to fashion and seasonal preferences in local markets.

Thrift Drug, long dormant since JCPenney purchased it, scored some big points in 1984, when several major industrial companies became mail-order pharmacy customers. Also in 1984, JCPenney purchased the First National Bank of Harrington, Delaware, and renamed it J.C. Penney National Bank, to assist in credit and financial services. The company began accepting American Express cards as well as Visa, MasterCard, and JCPenney credit cards, and the bank was issuing its own Visas and MasterCards. Thrift Drug celebrated its 50th anniversary in 1985; JCPenney's total year-end sales hit $13.6 billion.

A Dramatic Turnaround: 1986–95

In 1986 JCPenney acquired Units, a chain of stores selling contemporary knitwear and by the next year the company was well on its way to achieving the goals it set forth in 1982. Moving its corporate headquarters to just outside Dallas, Texas, JCPenney was able to cut $60 million from its annual budget although about 1,250 New Yorkers lost their jobs. JCPenney's president, David Miller, added vice-chairman and COO to his titles, and the company began focusing on four major merchandising groups by dividing them into separate business divisions: women's, men's, children's, and home and leisure. By the end of 1986, there were 1,482 JCPenney stores dotting the country, about to undergo a major change. In 1987 the company discontinued sales of home electronics, hard sporting goods, and photo equipment in its stores. The space that became available was then used for women's apparel. Also in the late 1980s, JCPenney opened freestanding furniture stores, called Portfolio, on an experimental basis.

The company's five regional operations were narrowed to four in 1988 to make communication between merchandising divisions and stores easier. The company also launched a massive leveraged employee stock ownership plan (LESOP) in 1988. With its new stance as a national department store focusing on apparel, the company had benefited from its prime regional shopping center space, the most such space of all U.S. retailers. Shoppers at regional malls were there to buy clothes and accessories, not washing machines and paint, and JCPenney was poised to take better advantage of these spending habits. Earnings rebounded as a result, rising from $4.11 per share in 1987 to $5.92 in 1988 from total sales of $14.8 billion.

In 1989 JCPenney was named the exclusive U.S. distributor for Olympic apparel, sold its JCPenney Casualty Insurance Company, and debuted the JCPenney Television Shopping Channel. The company was not, however, immune to the intense competition and promotional atmosphere of late 1989 and early 1990, and earnings slipped slightly to $5.86 per share on sales of $16.1 billion in 1989. In 1990 Miller retired and Vice-Chairman Gill took on the former's responsibilities as COO of JCPenney stores and catalog service. The company also broke ground for its new corporate headquarters in Plano, Texas, just north of Dallas; winnowed its stores down to 1,328 by closing underperforming outlets; and moved away from some of its private labels, focusing instead on major brand names such as Haggar, Healthtex, Jockey, Levi Strauss & Company, Maidenform, Ocean Pacific, Oshkosh, Reebok, Van Heusen, and Warner's. Earnings for 1990 fell to $4.33 per share from overall revenue of nearly $17.4 billion, slowed by the uncertainty over the Persian Gulf and the coming recession.

The next year, the full brunt of the recession and the Gulf War hit consumers and JCPenney rather hard. Retail sales fell from 1990's nearly $16.4 billion to $16.2 billion, but income and per share earnings nosedived (from $577 million to $80 million and from $4.33 to .39 respectively). While the company responded to a shaky economy and adjusted its retail businesses accordingly, its insurance division far outshined other operations with a pretax income surge of 44 percent from 1990's $55 million to $79 million in 1991. To the relief of shareholders and management alike, JCPenney rebounded in 1992 while celebrating its 90th anniversary. After relocating to its new headquarters in Plano, the company was rewarded with replenished catalog sales; record performances from JCPenney Insurance and JCPenney National Bank; retail sales of $18 billion; and a net income hike of $777 million with an ROE leap of 18.6 percent over 1991. Further, James E. Oesterreicher was named president and Gill retired after 39 years with the company.

JCPenney's continued concentration on women—who accounted for 80 percent of apparel sales and on whose behalf each store now allocated up to 41 percent of its space—was paying off. Coupled with a ''contemporary and fashion-forward environment,'' sales rose substantially in 1992 and 1993, due to a revitalized Worthington career collection and the debut and ongoing success of new bath and body products. Another proprietary brand, the Original Arizona Jean Company (begun in 1990), soared in earnings to $400 million from the previous year's $90 million. A hip redesign of the Plain Pockets line, Arizona quickly eclipsed JCPenney's expectations, prompting a slew of additional designs in different sizes and colors. On the heels of these triumphs came a two-for-one stock split in March 1993; a new advertising campaign reflecting the company's invigorated stance (JCPenney—Doing It Right); year-end retail sales just shy of $19 billion (up 5.4 percent); and income of $940 million (up 21 percent) due in part to stronger catalog sales of $3.5 billion (an 11 percent increase).

The next year, 1994, JCPenney was still riding the crest of its Arizona wave and introduced Little Arizona denimwear for toddlers. The continued hoopla over the brand's success had even prompted longtime rival Sears to jump into the proprietary denim fray with its own line, Canyon River Blues. Everyone by now, from consumers to analysts, took note of JCPenney's extraordinary turnaround. Figures for 1994 further demonstrated the company's achievement, with $20.4 billion in retail sales ($800 million from Arizona brandwear), a 6.8 percent comparative store sales increase, and net income topping $1 billion. This year also found Oesterreicher promoted to vice-chairman and CEO, W. Barger Tygart named president, and Howell in his 11th year as chairman.

Late 1990s and Beyond: Struggling, Restructuring, Diversifying

In 1995 JCPenney's recovery lost its momentum, falling short of both its own and analysts' expectations. Retail sales increased only 0.9 percent for the year ($20.6 billion vs. $20.4 billion), income fell from 1994's outstanding $1 billion to $838 million, and comparative store sales experienced a 1.4 percent drop. Accentuating the positive, the company announced that its Gift Registry (introduced in 1994) had already signed up 125,000 registrants (100,000 brides and 25,000 newborns) and planned to hit 250,000 by the end of 1996, while another new venture in home furnishings opened four new stores in 1995 (a Las Vegas store attracted 10,000 patrons on its first day alone) with plans for another 20 locations on the drawing board.

Yet regardless of JCPenney's retail store performance, its lesser known businesses, comprised of its drugstore chain, insurance, and banking services divisions, scored rather well for the year. Thrift Drug, the tenth largest drugstore chain in the nation with 645 stores in 12 states, had sales of nearly $1.9 billion in 1995 (a 20.2 percent increase) and plans for new outlets in North Carolina and New Jersey. The Insurance group, which began reciprocal businesses services in 1990 and moved into Canada in 1992, ran up revenues of $697 million, a 22.1

percent leap from 1994's $571 million; while JCPenney National Bank's revenues grew 21.7 percent from $131 million to $160 million with 470,000 active Visa and MasterCard accounts and receivables of $823 million.

In 1996 the company moved in several directions to regain the footing lost in 1995, including the allocation of $2.1 billion in capital expenditures to open 100 new domestic stores and refurbish 500 more over a three-year period, and the expansion of its international presence through varied licensing agreements. With the drugstore industry entering a period of consolidation, JCPenney faced a choice of selling out or expanding Thrift Drug through acquisitions. The company chose the latter, acquiring Kerr Drug, Fay's, and 200 units from Rite Aid during 1995 and 1996. In February 1997 JCPenney acquired Eckerd Corporation and its 1,750 drugstores for $3.3 billion and began rebranding all of its drugstores under the Eckerd name. JCPenney now ran the fourth largest drugstore chain in the country, with about 2,800 units. For the fiscal year ending in January 1998, drugstore revenues totaled $9.66 billion, nearly one-third of overall company revenues. Other initiatives in 1997 included the sale of the assets of JCPenney National Bank and the reorganization of the company into four operating units: Department Stores and Catalog, Drugstores, Insurance, and International.

JCPenney's department store operations continued to struggle in the late 1990s, burdened by high operating costs and caught in what had developed into a difficult middle market for clothes—a market segment buffeted by competition from discounters such as Wal-Mart and from high-end retailers such as Saks Fifth Avenue. Oesterreicher launched a series of cost-cutting initiatives, including the closure of 75 underperforming stores and the elimination of about 4,900 jobs in 1998. He also implemented a new buying strategy early that year designed to get brand-name fashions into JCPenney stores on a much faster basis. After experimenting with Internet sales as a logical extension of the company's catalog operations, jcpenney.com was transformed into a full-scale sales channel in 1998. Online sales totaled only $15 million that first year but jumped to $102 million for the fiscal year ending in January 2000. The company, meantime, expanded overseas in January 1999 through the $139 million purchase of Renner, a 21-unit department store chain in Brazil. Eckerd was bolstered in March 1999 by the acquisition of the 141-unit New York-based Genovese drugstore chain. Following the rebranding of the acquired stores, there were nearly 2,900 Eckerd outlets.

With the Eckerd unit outperforming the department stores and the company's stock sagging, JCPenney sought ways to unlock the value of its drugstore operations. Plans to issue a tracking stock for Eckerd were first announced in May 1999, but the partial IPO was subsequently canceled three separate times. Needing to reduce debt, JCPenney sold its credit card operations to GE Capital, the financial arm of General Electric Company, for $4 billion in December 1999. That year saw yet another retooling of the department stores aimed at revitalizing their lagging performance. ''Stores-within-a-store'' were set up to highlight eight of JCPenney's top private-label apparel lines, including Original Arizona Jean, St. John's Bay, and Worthington. The company identified two key customer segments, around which it would build its merchandising strategy and advertising campaigns: ''modern spenders,'' primarily consisting of dual-earner households, ages 35 to 54, with up to two children; and ''starting outs,'' consisting of consumers under the age of 35 who were single or just starting a family. It was clear, however, from the results for the fiscal year ending in January 2000 that more drastic measures were needed for a complete turnaround. Although overall net sales increased 6.7 percent to $31.74 billion, department store sales actually fell 8 percent; the sales increase was wholly attributed to Eckerd, which saw its sales increase 20 percent (and Eckerd sales now comprised nearly 40 percent of overall JCPenney sales). Furthermore, net income fell that year to $336 million, a 43 percent decrease over the previous year.

In March 2000 JCPenney launched a $488 million restructuring program aimed at generating annual cost savings of $120 million. By January 2001, the company had closed 48 underperforming department stores as well as nearly 300 Eckerd outlets. In the midst of this latest restructuring, Oesterreicher announced that he planned to retire early. JCPenney then quite unexpectedly went outside the company ranks for his replacement. In September 2000 Allen Questrom was named the eighth chairman and CEO of JCPenney, the first time that an outsider had been tapped for the top position. Questrom had a reputation as a retailing turnaround artist, having previously led both Federated Department Stores, Inc. and Barneys New York Inc. out of bankruptcy. The new leader would be working closely with Vanessa Castagna, who had been hired away from Wal-Mart in 1999 to become chief operating officer of the department store and catalog unit.

In early 2001 Questrom announced that an additional 44 department stores and three catalog outlet centers would be closed and about 5,500 jobs would be cut. With the various charges taken for fiscal 2001, the company reported a net loss of $705 million on sales of $31.85 billion. In February 2001 the company's department stores were converted to centralized merchandising, a move aimed at enabling the company to introduce new fashions faster, present a uniform chainwide image, and cut costs. In June 2001, in another debt-reduction initiative, JCPenney sold its direct marketing services unit, which included the company's insurance operations, to AEGON, N.V. for $1.3 billion. By this time, the company's stock was on the rebound, with investors encouraged by the initial moves made by Questrom and Castagna. Given the depths of the problems at JCPenney and a hidebound corporate culture that was resistant to change, a complete turnaround was neither assured nor in the immediate offing. Questrom estimated that it would take two to five years to transform the company into a competitive force for the 21st century. Thus, as it neared its 100th anniversary in 2002, JCPenney was going through one of the most important periods in its history.

Principal Subsidiaries

Eckerd Corporation; J.C. Penney Funding Corporation; J.C. Penney Properties, Inc.; JCP Realty, Inc.; Thrift Drug, Inc.

Principal Operating Units

Department Stores and Catalog; Eckerd Drugstores.

Principal Competitors

Sears, Roebuck and Co.; Wal-Mart Stores, Inc.; Kmart Corporation; Target Corporation; Kohl's Corporation; Spiegel, Inc.; Otto Versand Gmbh & Co.; Federated Department Stores, Inc.; The May Department Stores Company; Dillard's, Inc.; Nordstrom, Inc.; Saks Incorporated.

Further Reading

Barron, Kelly, "Penney Wise," *Forbes,* September 4, 2000, pp. 72–73.

Beasley, Norman, *Main Street Merchant: The Story of the J.C. Penney Company,* New York: Whittlesey House, [1948], 274 p.

Blumenthal, Karen, "Penney Moves Upscale in Merchandise but Still Has to Convince Public," *Wall Street Journal,* June 7, 1990, p. A1.

Blyskal, Jeff, "Better Slow Than Never," *Forbes,* October 10, 1983, pp. 151+.

Bradford, Stacey L., "Eckerd: Pennies from Hell?," *Financial World,* December 16, 1996, p. 24.

Curry, Mary Elizabeth, *Creating an American Institution: The Merchandising Genius of J.C. Penney,* New York: Garland, 1993, 348 p.

Dunkin, Amy, "The Newly Minted Penney: Where Fashion Rules," *Business Week,* April 17, 1989, pp. 88+.

Forest, Stephanie Anderson, "Can an Outsider Fix J.C. Penney?," *Business Week,* February 12, 2001, pp. 56, 58.

——, "One More Face-Lift for Penney," *Business Week,* March 23, 1998, pp. 86, 88.

——, "A Penney Saved?," *Business Week,* March 29, 1999, pp. 64, 66.

Gilman, Hank, and Steve Weiner, "Penney's Plan to Tap Upscale Market So Far Is Failing to Improve Earnings," *Wall Street Journal,* August 28, 1985.

Gordon, Mitchell, "Back to Basics: That's the Key to the Turnaround at Retailer J.C. Penney," *Barron's,* August 11, 1986, pp. 73+.

Halkias, Maria, "Penney Catalog Still Ranks Number One," *Dallas Morning News,* May 30, 2001, p. 11D.

——, "Penney Closings Detailed: 44 Stores Targeted in Cost-Saving Plan," *Dallas Morning News,* January 26, 2001, p. 1D.

Hazel, Debra, "Pitching Penney into the 21st Century," *Chain Store Age,* January 1997, pp. 51–54, 59.

Helliker, Kevin, "Penney's Catalog Division, Long a Star, Risks Losing Its Luster As Sales Slacken," *Wall Street Journal,* December 24, 1990.

Howell, Debbie, "JCPenney Closings Address Cost Concerns: Store Revival Top Priority," *Discount Store News,* March 6, 2000, pp. 7, 90.

——, "JCPenney Refocuses on Core Customer," *Discount Store News,* June 7, 1999, pp. 7, 168.

"J.C. Penney: Getting More from the Same Space," *Business Week,* August 18, 1975, p. 80.

"J.C. Penney's Fashion Gamble," *Business Week,* January 16, 1978, p. 66.

Jordan, Miriam, "Penney Blends Two Business Cultures: U.S. Retailer Tastes Success in Brazil by Keeping Local Flavor," *Wall Street Journal,* April 5, 2001, p. A15.

Kelly, Mary Ellen, "NAFTA Broadens the Field; Retailers Look Toward Mexico," *Discount Store News,* December 6, 1993, p. 3.

Lettich, Jill, "JCPenney Struggles to Maintain Upscale Image," *Discount Store News,* October 7, 1991, p. 34.

McLoughlin, Bill, "National Chains Build Housewares: Sears, Penney, Ward Mixing in Better Goods," *HFN—The Weekly Newspaper for Home Furnishing Network,* November 18, 1996, p. 1.

"Merchant of Panache: Allen Questrom Must Bring a New Focus and Culture to J.C. Penney," *Chain Store Age,* September 2000, pp. 61–64.

Palmer, Jay, "Back in Vogue? J.C. Penney's Stress," *Barron's,* April 17, 1989, pp. 15+.

Palmieri, Jean E., "JCPenney, Sears Shoot It Out," *Daily News Record,* January 27, 1997, p. 6.

Picard, Diane E., and Alexandra Zissu, "More Signs Christmas Not So Hot As Penney's, Carson's, DH Report Sales," *Women's Wear Daily,* January 3, 1997, p. 2.

Vargo, Julie, and Jean Palmieri, "A Private Label War Grows More Public," *Daily News Record,* February 10, 1997, p. 4.

Weiner, Steve, "Dressed to Kill," *Forbes,* November 2, 1987, pp. 95+.

Zimmerman, Ann, "J.C. Penney Hires Designer CEO for a Turnaround," *Wall Street Journal,* July 28, 2000, p. B1.

—Lisa Collins
—updates: Taryn Benbow-Pfalzgraf, David E. Salamie

Juniper Networks, Inc.

1194 North Mathilda Ave.
Sunnyvale, California 94089
U.S.A.
Telephone: (408) 745-2000
Toll Free: (888) 586-4737
Fax: (408) 745-2100
Web site: http://www.juniper.net

Public Company
Incorporated: 1996
Employees: 1,162
Sales: $673.5 million (2000)
Stock Exchanges: Nasdaq National Market
Ticker Symbol: JNPR
NAIC: 334210 Telephone Apparatus Manufacturing

Juniper Networks, Inc. is a leading supplier of scalable, high-performance Internet Protocol (IP) platforms for the public fiber-optic infrastructure. The company has been rated one of the world's best-managed, fastest-growing companies. Sunnyvale, California-based Juniper introduced the first IP router that was quick enough to clear data congestion on the exponentially growing Internet. The company designs and sells high-end equipment that routes traffic across the largest Internet backbones: giant phone companies and Internet service providers that shoulder the majority of Internet traffic. The company also makes network traffic management software (JUNOS) and offers training, support, and implementation services. Juniper sells directly and indirectly through manufacturers to Internet and telecommunications service providers. In just five years, Juniper has captured one third of the router market, with products geared toward telecommunications service providers, which spend about $70 billion on capital equipment. The company has sustained significant growth where prominent competitor Cisco Systems thwarts most challengers. Having established itself as a niche player, Juniper has more recently expanded its markets from its original focus on the core backbone, with more recent efforts on the network's edge and the emerging mobile IP market. The five-year-old company had one of the most successful initial public offerings in history.

1996 to 1998: Laying the Foundation

Juniper Networks was the creation of computer scientist Pradeep Sindhu, once principal scientist of Xerox's renowned Palo Alto Research Center (PARC), who in 1995 left for a vacation and returned with a concept for a new company that would build reliable, high-performance routers to support the quickly emerging Internet. Sindhu knew that information would soon overtake voice traffic on telephone networks, and the networks would have to keep pace with bandwidth demand. By breaking up data and removing a need for dedicated circuits, routers allowed more traffic and lower costs than switches used by traditional phone networks. Sindhu saw a niche in the $10 billion router market dominated by giant Cisco Systems, which developed routers for phone companies and Internet service providers (ISPs), based on the technology it had used in the corporate market. Sindhu chose the company's name to symbolize the root system of the Juniper tree—quite complex and strikingly strong.

Juniper promised to defeat bottlenecks on the Internet with a product that would move data up to 100 times faster than competing routers. Sindhu started the company in February 1996 with $200,000 in seed money from powerful venture-capital firm Kleiner, Perkins, Caufield & Byers. He hired two other engineers, Bjorn Liencres from Sun Microsystems and Dennis Ferguson from MCI. For business expertise, Sindhu recruited Scott Kriens, co-founder of StrataCom, a leading supplier of switching equipment sold in July 1996 to Cisco for $4.67 billion. The management team included former employees from Bay Networks, Cisco Systems, Silicon Graphics, and 3Com. Sindhu ran the company for the first seven months. Scott Kriens joined Juniper in September as chief executive officer; Sindhu was designated chief technology officer and vice chairman.

The new company received support from Kleiner, Perkins, Caufield & Byers, which invested $2.7 million for a 22 percent stake in the company. To raise money while the company had no products to sell, in September 1996, Juniper sold stakes in

Company Perspectives:

Juniper Networks, our partners and resellers, listen to you, our customers, to deliver the highest quality, industry-leading Internet routing products, services, and solutions that exceed your expectations and earn your trust.

the business to potential customers, a cluster of Cisco competitors that included Ericsson, 3Com, Lucent Technologies, and Nortel Networks. The networking and telecom equipment makers invested $40 million, for a 25 percent stake in the startup.

To best connect billions of potential Internet users, Sindhu wanted to start with new hardware from the ground up. Juniper had a strategy that was unusual for network equipment makers: It outsourced all its manufacturing operations to better use assets, lower production costs, and accelerate time to market–critical for the fast-changing Internet. And the startup harnessed the efficiency of the Internet to streamline operations. From the beginning, Juniper collaborated on designs, linked with outsourcers, and managed inventory via the Web. Juniper established a technology relationship in July 1996 with IBM, to produce all the application-specific integrated circuits (ASICs) designed by Juniper for its Internet platforms. Juniper also partnered with Solectron and Celestica, which manufactured products from the prototype stage to production, and performed material procurement, final assembly, testing, control, and shipment to customers.

In December 1997, Juniper introduced JUNOS, the industry's first operating system designed specifically for the routing and operational needs of the fastest-growing Internet backbone networks. (A backbone is a set of paths that regional networks connect to for long-distance interconnection.) After in-depth testing of JUNOS, in September 1998, Juniper shipped its much-anticipated first product, the M40 router, designed to provide faster, more reliable Internet access and packet delivery. The M40 was capable of forwarding 40 million packets per second, and Juniper promised that this terabit router would deliver traffic up to 10 times quicker than other existing products. The M40 won industry recognition for the best new product, including *PC Magazine UK*'s 1999 Technology Innovation Award. In December, Juniper saw its first quarter of revenue, with sales of $3.8 million. In 1998, Cisco had more than 90 percent market share in the multibillion-dollar core router market, which was growing at light speed. Juniper would start chipping away at Cisco's slice of the market.

1999: Going Global, Going Public

In the bull market of 1999, the heady days of white-hot IPOs, the industry had great expectations for the B-to-B Juniper. New-economy publications called the ''buzzworthy'' start-up a company to watch. During this ''fast company'' year, while the M40 tackled Cisco's market share, Juniper's customer base broadened to more than 50 worldwide. Although the company only had one major product, Juniper was a darling of the telecom-equipment industry since it began. Juniper won accounts with Britain's Cable & Wireless, and MCI WorldCom's UUNet division, becoming a main supplier.

Juniper widened global support though worldwide distributors, including Alcatel of France and Ericsson. It teamed up with Ericsson for a series of strategic agreements to develop and distribute Juniper's IP network technology. Alcatel and Juniper signed an 18-month, $30 million distribution agreement appointing the telecommunications equipment supplier as a reseller.

Meanwhile, Juniper established its European headquarters with an office in the UK. Two months later, the company opened a subsidiary, Juniper Networks K.K., in Japan, the second-largest networking market worldwide. The Tokyo office also supported the sales efforts of Juniper's Japanese distribution partners. In November, Juniper continued its lightning-speed expansion in Asia with the opening of its new regional headquarters in Hong Kong. During this time, M40 routers formed the backbone of a pan-European IP network being built by Iaxis, Inc.

On June 25, 1999, in the heat of the ''dot-com summer,'' Juniper went public. The price per share was $34.00, and 4.8 million shares were offered on the Nasdaq National Market under the trading symbol JNPR. The company had one of the most successful initial public offerings in history. By the end of the first day as a publicly traded company, Juniper's stock rose to $98.88, a 190 percent single-day jump that increased the company's market capitalization to just below $4.9 billion, the highest first-day valuation for a technology company, according to Securities Data Corp. Plus, unlike other new issues, the stock sustained its energy, coasting above $100 for months.

Juniper acquired privately held Layer Five of Palo Alto, California, for $19 million. Founded in 1997, Layer Five was a group of advanced developers of network hardware architectures and related software. Its employees became part of Juniper's engineering organization. Separately, Juniper Networks took a minority investment in New Access Communications of San Jose, California, whose optical distribution technology targeted network service providers. Pradeep Sindhu joined the New Access Communications board of directors.

Juniper announced a three-for-one stock split on November 16, 1999, entitling each stockholder at the close of business on December 31, 1999 to receive two additional shares for every outstanding share of common stock held on the record date. At this time, annual revenue exceeded $100 million, and Juniper reported its first quarter of profitability.

At the end of the year, Juniper launched and began shipping the M20 router, a new class of router for the network's edge. (An edge router is a device that moves formatted information between one or more local area networks [LANs] and a backbone network, using switching technology called ATM (or, asynchronous transfer mode). Englewood, Colorado-based Verio, a high-profile Web-hosting and Internet services company formerly served by Cisco, ordered $7 million of the new routers for its national network, to expand capacity in smaller cities such as Spokane, Washington, and Rochester, New York. The router delivered core-like performance for regional networks and large ISPs faced with the challenge of expanding their networks at the same rate of growth as the Internet core. The new router shared common software, services, and ASIC technology with its predecessor, to serve applications including high-speed access, peering, and hosting.

Key Dates:

1996: Juniper Networks founded by Pradeep Sindhu. The company receives investment capital from Kleiner, Perkins, Caufield & Byers. IBM technology partnership formed.
1997: Management team put in place. The company raises $46 million during corporate investment round. JUNOS operating system ships to customers.
1998: Company ships first product, the M40 Internet backbone router. First quarter revenue is $3.8 million.
1999: Company secures Ericsson investment and OEM agreement. Initial public stock offering generates $63 million. Alcatel signs global distribution agreement. Company announces three-for-one stock split. Iaxis selects M40 router for Pan-European backbone. Hong Kong office opens. Annual revenue exceeds $100 million. Company achieves its first quarter of profitability.
2000: Juniper Networks ships full-performance M160 router. M5 and M10 product platforms launched. Company acquires Micro Magic, Inc.

By the end of fiscal 1999, Juniper's revenue was $102.6 million, up from $3.8 million in 1998. Market share rose from 2.8 percent in 1998 to 14.8 percent in 1999, in spite of fierce competition. The M20 ratcheted up the potential for a second market niche. To keep customers on technology's cutting edge, Juniper delivered four releases of JUNOS throughout the year. At this point, the Internet was changing—it was becoming a multi-service network carrying voice, video, and corporate information, as well as e-mail and e-commerce services. For the next year, Juniper's strategy was to keep investing in research and development, to build a competitive advantage in the Internet infrastructure space, and to expand into the $250 billion optical networking segment.

2000: Whoever Grows the Fastest, Wins

Juniper kicked off the millennium with an acquisition of the Hong Kong-based marketing and sales firm Pacific Advantage (PAL), which bolstered Juniper's sales force and services in Asia. Revving up for the year, Juniper implemented a compensation management package for the company's sales force.

Then, on March 28 came the release of Juniper's long-awaited new router, the M160. ''The M160 is four times faster than the previous product we shipped, which was already faster than anything on the market,'' Kriens told CNNfn. ''In some ways, it's almost staggering, four million phone calls simultaneously supported in one system, three feet tall.'' High-profile customers including UUNet and Cable Wireless purchased the router to upgrade their networks. By a twist of fate, the M160's release date coincided with the news that Cisco, Juniper's primary competitor, surpassed Microsoft to become the most valuable company in the world, with a momentary market capitalization of $560 billion.

Juniper executives disputed an industry notion that the rookie existed primarily as a David to Cisco's Goliath. In *The Industry Standard*, Sindhu emphasized Juniper's niche as the only provider of a router built expressly for the Internet. Through voracious acquisitions, Cisco had evolved as a ''soup-to-nuts'' data-routing generalist, powering everything from B-to-B ISPs to consumer home-networking products. Kriens told CNNfn that Juniper had multiplied equipment capacity by a factor of four without acquisition, and did not plan to grow that way.

On the financial front, a message came loud and clear: At this moment, Internet infrastructure was the hot investment sector. Juniper's stock soared 272 percent this year, *Business Week* reported in its October 2, 2000 issue, even in a shark-infested market. In the second quarter, Juniper nabbed 22 percent of the market for the most powerful routers, while Cisco's piece of the pie dropped to 75 percent, its lowest level in two years, according to market researcher, the Dell'Oro Group. On April 13, 2000, Juniper announced a two-for-one stock split. In ''The Silicon Valley 150,'' *The Mercury News* found in its mid-year review: Juniper made the biggest jump on the list, moving up 54 spots from the previous year to land at number 87. In addition, Juniper's revenues soared 540 percent for the first six months of 2000 compared with the same period in 1999. And the three-year-old company's market capitalization of $50.4 billion was the tenth-highest in the Valley, bested only by behemoths such as Intel, Oracle, and HP (and not surprisingly, Cisco, in the No. 1 spot). In August, Juniper became a component of the Nasdaq 100 Index.

Juniper was also heralded as one of *Forbes* magazine's 20 ''Ramp Champs,'' a list of the world's best-managed, fastest-growing technology companies. Writer Clint Willis noted in the April 3, 2000 publication, ''The firm didn't have a single customer a year and a half ago but since then has seized 13 percent of the high-end router market, which includes many firms thrilled that someone's finally cutting into Cisco's pricing power.'' Kriens and Sindhu received kudos, which continued when Kriens was named Ernst & Young Entrepreneur of the Year.

Previously located in Mountain View, California, Juniper established a new 144,000-square foot corporate headquarters in Sunnyvale, California, which allowed it to consolidate Bay Area locations. The summer also saw a new office open in New Delhi.

In September 2000, Juniper launched the M5 and M10 platforms, a suite that enabled fast bandwidth build-out at the edges of service provider networks, where space and power were limited. The M5 router extended Juniper's core technology to the network's edge, connecting businesses to service providers at high speeds. The M10 delivered routing for service providers in small metropolitan areas. The metropolitan Internet edge routing market was estimated at $1.2 billion in 2000. With Internet traffic doubling every four to six months, a Juniper executive said, the company received a warm reception from large phone companies. Supporting this new product development were 650 Juniper employees, up from 260 in 1999.

At this point, Juniper's routers were four times faster than Cisco's quickest but required only about two-thirds of the electrical power. According to John Shinal in the September 11, 2000 issue of *Business Week*, ''Even though Juniper's biggest machine costs $400,000 on average—twice the price of Cisco's—customers can't get enough of them. That's a rude awakening for Cisco, which didn't need the fastest routers when it was zeroing in on just the corporate market.''

Despite the high barrier to entry, a dozen newcomers promising to revolutionize optical-networking equipment were entering the fray. Where once pundits were describing Juniper as Cisco Junior, now they were wondering which ''newbie'' would become the next Juniper. According to industry lore, one Juniper IP-routing guru used a baseball bat to nail his Cisco resignation to his manager's door. But now he jumped ship, leaving millions in unvested stock options at both companies, to go to Procket, a San Jose startup. In December 2000, Juniper added talent to its team by acquiring Micro Magic, Inc. (MMI), an integrated circuit solutions company, for $260 million. Founded in 1995, MMI had expertise in the tools, methods, and design techniques required to build high-performance circuits. The employees were absorbed into Juniper's engineering organization, to contribute to silicon design.

The worldwide core IP router market was estimated at $2.6 billion during 2000, according to Infonetics Research. Juniper surpassed the industry growth rate to breathtaking extent, with estimated net revenue of $674 million, up 556 percent from 1999. The company's stock gained 122 percent, even as the Nasdaq dropped 39 percent. And a joint venture with Ericsson had Juniper positioning itself in the emerging mobile IP market. Meanwhile, *Business Week* attributed huge efficiencies to Juniper's innovative use of the Internet. In its May 14, 2001 issue, the magazine reported that in 2000, Juniper cashed in a stunning $1.02 million in revenue per employee, vs. $703,529 for Cisco and about $400,000 on average for the communications equipment industry. The magazine forewarned that Juniper would need to lean on the streamlining amid a cooling tech sector. A Juniper executive said in the fall that Juniper controlled 24 percent of the market, while Cisco held about 70 percent. ''But Juniper is fast gaining ground—at the expense of Cisco,'' Salomon Smith Barney analyst Alex Henderson said in *Business Week*'s October 2, 2000 issue. Looking ahead, the analyst was bullish on Juniper, predicting that the company would continue to gain market share into 2001.

2001 and Beyond: Staying Focused

The first quarter saw a battleground between Cisco and Juniper, with a horse race among the high-speed router vendors vying to serve the big carrier networks. Juniper kicked off the year by announcing Q4 net earnings of $60.3 million, or 17 cents per share, beating Wall Street's expectations in spades. On Jan. 31, Cisco introduced a line of products aimed at quelling Juniper's inroads into a longstanding Cisco market. Meanwhile, Juniper and the Optical Networks division of ECI Telecom Ltd. announced that they jointly installed and tested China's first optical Internet using Juniper's routers in Guangdong Province, which planned to invest more than U.S. $400 million in Internet networking over the next five years. Also during this time, Juniper launched a technical certification program for ISP professionals, which was developed in collaboration with customers. At the end of Q1, Juniper had 1,162 employees worldwide.

The economic slowdown that was first perceived as a correction of overvalued technology stocks turned out to be the worst downturn in industry history. During the second quarter, Juniper faced a landscape in which telecommunications customers were investing less in equipment. There were rumors of a price war with Cisco. Also, upstart competitors such as Avici Systems were garnering market share. In April, despite robust earnings, Juniper announced that its 2001 earnings and revenues would fall below Wall Street's expectations. For the full year, Juniper predicted earnings of $.090 to $1.00 per share, below analysts' estimate of $1.05. The next month, Cisco posted its first loss in years and took a $3 billion charge against its own earnings. Pundits pondered Cisco's potentially overextended portfolio.

At a spring industry conference, keynote speaker Kriens predicted consolidation in the telecommunications industry but said that savvy, focused network equipment makers could still profit during the economic lull. Describing this critical juncture in the industry's history, Kriens invoked Winston Churchill: ''This is not the beginning of the end, but the end of the beginning.''

Principal Subsidiaries

Juniper Networks K.K. (Japan); Juniper Networks B.V. (Netherlands); Juniper Networks International Limited (Cayman Islands); Juniper Networks FSC Inc. (Barbados); Juniper Networks U.K. Ltd. (United Kingdom); Juniper Networks GmbH (Germany); Juniper Networks France Sarl (France); Juniper Networks Australia Ltd. (Australia); Juniper Networks Hong Kong Ltd. (Hong Kong); Juniper Networks South Asia Ltd. (Hong Kong); Juniper Networks China Ltd. (Hong Kong); Juniper Networks Canada Inc. (Canada); Juniper Acquisition Corporation; Juniper Networks International, Inc.

Principal Competitors

Cisco Systems.

Further Reading

Ankeny, Jason, ''Juniper's Kriens Calls for Action,'' *Upstart*, posted May 9, 2001, http://www.telecomclick.com.

Black, Jane, ''For Juniper, Single-Mindedness Wins the Race,'' *BusinessWeek Online*, posted February 7, 2001, http://www.businessweek.com.

Bransten, Lisa. ''Juniper Hits Profit Forecast, Lifting Stock'' *The Wall Street Journal*, April 13, 2001, p. B5.

Files, Jennifer, ''Juniper in High-Speed Chase of Cisco,'' *The Mercury News*, posted May 27, 2001, http://www.bayarea.com.

''Juniper Takes Router Lead,'' *CNNfn*, posted March 29, 2000, http://cnnfn.cnn.com.

Key, Angela, ''Juniper: Fresh Competitor? Fresh Meat?'' *Fortune*, May 15, 2000. p. 134.

Korzeniowski, Paul, ''Jumpin' Juniper,'' *Business 2.0*, posted May 15, 2001, http://business2.com.

Krause, Jason, ''10 Optical-Network Startups to Watch,'' *The Industry Standard*, posted September 11, 2000, http://www.thestandard.com.

Krause, Jason, ''Upstart Comes out of the Shadows,'' *The Industry Standard*, posted April 17, 2000, http://www.thestandard.com.

Lai Pai, Uday, ''Juniper Networks Picks Hong Kong for Regional Hub,'' Asia.Internet.com, accessed November 12, 1999, http://asia.internet.com.

La Monica, Paul R., ''Fish Net,'' *Red Herring Magazine*, April 2, 2001.

Malhotra, Priya, ''Juniper Networks Beats Q4 Estimates by Wide Margin,'' *Futures World News*, May 2, 2001.

Marcial, Gene G. ''Why Juniper Has Some Backbone,'' *Business Week*. October 2, 2000, p.35.

Nee, Eric, ''The Ties That Bind,'' *Forbes* 161, April 6, 1998, p. 124.

O'Brien, Chris. ''Forget the Dot.coms: Internet Infrastructure is the Hot Sector,'' *The Mercury News*, posted September 18, 2000, http://www.bayarea.com.

Reinhardt, Andy, ''Nothing Jive About Juniper,'' *Business Week*, September 8, 1997, p. 38.

Serwer, Andy, ''There's Something About Cisco,'' *Fortune*, May 15, 2000, pp. 114–138.

Shinal, John. ''The Upstart That's Eating Cisco's Lunch,'' *Business Week*, Sept. 11, 2000, pp. 84–86.

Stone, Amey, ''Networking Startups: Racers That Can Never Rest,'' *BusinessWeek Online*, posted October 14, 1999, http://www.businessweek.com.

Surowiecki, James, ''The Financial Page: Cisco-holics Anonymous,'' *The New Yorker*, May 21, 2001, pp. 42.

Taylor, Dennis, ''Juniper Networks Leading Red-Hot Pack of Valley IPOs,'' *Silicon Valley/San Jose Business Journal,* July 2, 1999.

''25 Leaders for a Dangerous Time,'' *Business Week,* May 14, 2001, p. EB24.

Willis, Clint, ''Ramp Champs,'' *Forbes ASAP*, April 3, 2000, p. 85.

Wong, Wylie, ''Juniper Chief Still Sees Room for Profit,'' *CNET.com*, posted May 8, 2001, http://www.cnet.com.

—Michelle Feder

Kimberly-Clark Corporation

Kimberly-Clark Corporation

P.O. Box 619100
Dallas, Texas 75261-9100
U.S.A.
Telephone: (972) 281-1200
Fax: (972) 281-1490
Web site: http://www.kimberly-clark.com

Public Company
Incorporated: 1880 as Kimberly & Clark Company
Employees: 66,300 (2000)
Sales: $13.98 billion (2000)
Stock Exchanges: New York Midwest Pacific
Ticker Symbol: KMB
NAIC: 313230 Nonwoven Fabric Mills; 322121 Paper (Except Newsprint) Mills; 322291 Sanitary Paper Product Manufacturing; 339112 Surgical & Medical Instrument Manufacturing

Over 130 years since its founding, Kimberly-Clark Corporation is one of the world's leading producers of tissue, personal care products, and health care products. The company sells its products in 150 countries and maintains manufacturing operations in 41 countries. In addition to its market leaders in tissues and feminine-, child-, and incontinence-care products (which include the brands Huggies, Kotex, Depend, Kleenex), Kimberly-Clark is also a major producer of premium business, correspondence and technical papers. The company is also the market leader in health care products such as facemasks, surgical gowns, and sterilization wrap, and, with its 1999 acquisition of Safeskin, Kimberly-Clark is currently the number one producer of examination gloves in the United States.

Early History

Kimberly, Clark & Company was founded in Neenah, Wisconsin, in 1872 as a partnership of four men: John A. Kimberly, Charles B. Clark, Frank C. Shattuck, and Kimberly's cousin, Havilah Babcock. The company began the first paper mill in Wisconsin. Its initial product was newsprint made from linen and cotton rags. Within six years, the company expanded by acquiring a majority interest in the nearby Atlas paper mill, which converted ground pulpwood into manila wrapping paper. The business was incorporated in 1880 as Kimberly & Clark Company, with John Kimberly as president. In 1889, the company constructed a large pulp- and paper-making complex on the Fox River. The community that grew up around the factory was named Kimberly, in honor of John Kimberly.

Among the company's early innovations was the paper used for rotogravure, a procedure for printing photographs with a rotary press. In 1914, researchers working with bagasse, a pulp by-product of processed sugar cane, produced creped cellulose wadding, or tissue. During World War I, this product, called cellucotton, was used to treat wounds in place of scarce surgical cottons. At that time field nurses also discovered that cellucotton worked well as a disposable feminine napkin. The company later recognized the commercial potential of this application and, in 1920, introduced its Kotex feminine napkin.

In 1924, the company introduced another disposable tissue product, Kleenex, to replace the face towels then used for removing cold cream. A survey showed, however, that consumers preferred to use Kleenex as a disposable handkerchief, prompting the company to alter its marketing strategy entirely. Nationwide advertisements promoting Kleenex for its current use began in 1930, and sales doubled within a year. Uncomfortable marketing such personal-care items as feminine napkins, Kimberly & Clark had created a separate sales company, International Cellucotton Products, which it contracted to manufacture Kotex and Kleenex.

Expansion from 1920s to 1960s

During the 1920s the company built a Canadian pulp mill and power plant called Spruce Falls Power and Paper Company in Kapuskasing, Ontario. In 1925 the company formed what would become Canadian Cellucotton Products Limited, for marketing cellucotton products internationally. The following year Kimberly & Clark, in partnership with the New York Times Company, added a newsprint mill to the Spruce Falls complex and expanded its pulping capacity.

Company Perspectives:

Kimberly-Clark is a leading global manufacturer of tissue, personal care, and health care products with manufacturing facilities in 41 countries and product sales in more than 150. Employing more than 66,000 people worldwide, Kimberly-Clark posted sales of nearly $14 billion in 2000. We are home to some of the world's most trusted and recognized brands—including Kleenex, Kotex, Scott, Depend, Huggies, and Pull-Ups. In 76 countries, our products are No. 1 or No. 2 in market share. Nearly one-fourth of the world's population, or 1.3 billion people, use Kimberly-Clark products each year. We are one of the leading tissue manufacturers in the world and are the second largest household and personal care products company in the U.S. We are a large and diverse community of individuals who trust and respect one another as we work to enhance the quality of life for people around the world. We are motivated to continually deliver superior products and exceed the expectations of our shareholders, our customers, and ourselves.

The company was reorganized and reincorporated in 1928 as Kimberly-Clark Corporation. That same year, as shares of Kimberly-Clark were being traded on the New York and Chicago stock exchanges for the first time, John Kimberly died. He was 90 years old and still president at the time of his death.

In the 1930s, Kimberly-Clark concentrated on marketing its new products. During World War II, the company devoted many of its resources to the war effort. The company also contracted Margaret Buell, creator of the cartoon strip ''Little Lulu,'' to promote Kleenex. Buell and Little Lulu continued to promote Kleenex for Kimberly-Clark into the 1960s.

After the war, Kimberly-Clark initiated a growth program to handle revived consumer product demand. Facilities were built or acquired in Balfour, North Carolina, and Memphis, Tennessee, in 1946, and in Fullerton, California, and New Milford, Connecticut, in the late 1950s. Pulp production at Terrace Bay, Ontario, was launched in 1948, and in 1949 the company, along with a group of investors and newspaper publishers, began the large Coosa River Newsprint Company in Coosa Pines, Alabama. Kimberly-Clark acquired the Michigan-based Munising Paper Company in 1952, Neenah Paper Company in 1956, Peter J. Schweitzer, Inc.—which had mills in France and the United States—in 1957, and the American Envelope Company in 1959. International Cellucotton Products Company formally merged with its parent company in 1955, as did Coosa River Newsprint Company in 1962.

Throughout the 1960s the tampon, first manufactured by Tampax, gained favor among women and ate into Kotex's market share. Kimberly-Clark turned its attention to new products. In 1968 the company introduced Kimbies, a disposable diaper with tape closures. Initial sales were strong despite competition from Procter & Gamble's Pampers. While Kimberly-Clark tended to its diverse operations, however, it failed to keep up with early disposable diaper improvements and market innovations. As a result of continued poor sales and leakage problems, Kimbies were withdrawn from the market in the mid-1970s. Competition in the infant-care product industry caused Kimberly-Clark to reevaluate the balance between its consumer products and lumber and paper products divisions.

Restructuring in the 1970s

Darwin E. Smith, who was elected president of Kimberly-Clark in 1971, took on Procter & Gamble's challenge. Smith decided that to compete properly in consumer product markets Kimberly-Clark had to prune its coated-paper business. Within one year of taking control of the company, Smith initiated changes that included the sale or closure of six paper mills and the sale of more than 300,000 acres of prime northern California land. With cash reserves of more than $250 million, primarily from the land sale, Smith then inaugurated an aggressive research campaign. He assembled a talented research and development team by hiring specialists away from competitors. The company's advertising budget was increased substantially, and plans were made for the construction of additional production facilities.

Marketing was central to Smith's strategy for growth, as Kimberly-Clark emphasized its commitment to consumer products. Research and development efforts enlarged the company's technological base from traditional cellulose fiber-forming technologies to lightweight nonwovens utilizing synthetic fabrics.

A new premium-priced diaper in an hourglass shape with refastenable tapes was introduced in 1978 under the name Huggies. By 1984, Huggies had captured 50 percent of the higher quality disposable diaper market. The sudden popularity of the product caught Kimberly-Clark by surprise, and it was forced to expand production to meet consumer demand.

Diversification in the 1980s

Facial tissue and feminine-care products were also part of Kimberly-Clark's growing consumer product operations. In 1984, it was estimated that the company's Kleenex brand held 50 percent of the tissue market. A chemically-treated virucidal tissue called Avert was test-marketed that same year, but the higher price and limited utility of the product prevented it from gaining widespread popularity. Aimed at health care institutions and at companies as a product to reduce absenteeism, Avert never really got off the ground, and in 1987 Kimberly-Clark decided not to mass market the product.

The 1980, toxic shock syndrome scare caused a slump in tampon sales. Kimberly-Clark began an aggressive advertising campaign on television for Depend incontinence products in the early 1980s. At the time, incontinence products were as unmentionable as feminine-care products had been some 60 years earlier. The promotion resulted in Depend gaining a profitable share of the incontinence products market, and it quickly became the best-selling retail incontinence brand in the United States. In an effort to broaden its position in therapeutic and health care products, Kimberly-Clark acquired Spenco Medical Corporation in Waco, Texas, that same year.

Although sales from primary growth operations—personal-care products—were increasing, approximately 25 percent of

Key Dates:

1872: Company founded as Kimberly, Clark & Company in Neenah, Wisconsin.
1880: Company incorporated as Kimberly & Clark Company.
1920: Company introduces Kotex feminine napkins.
1924: Company introduces Kleenex tissues.
1928: Company reorganized and reincorporated as Kimberly-Clark Corporation.
1942: Company produces M-45 anti-aircraft gun mounts for the Armed Forces in World War II.
1948: Company launches pulp production in Ontario.
1949: Company helps found the Coonsa River Newsprint Company.
1952: Company acquires Munising Paper Company.
1956: Company acquires Neenah Paper Company.
1957: Company acquires Peter J. Schweitzer, Inc.
1959: Company acquires American Envelope Company.
1968: Company enters disposable diaper market with its Kimbies product.
1978: Company introduces Huggies disposable diapers.
1980: Company introduces Depend incontinence products.
1985: Company relocated from Wisconsin to Dallas, Texas.
1995: Company merges with Scott Paper Co.
1997: Company acquires Tecnol Medical Products.
1999: Company acquires Attisholz Holding and Ballard Medical Products.
2000: Company acquires S-K Corporation.
2001: Company introduces Cottonelle Fresh Rollwipes.

Kimberly-Clark's sales continued to come from the pulp, newsprint, and paper businesses. The company further diversified its operations in 1984 by converting its regularly scheduled executive air-shuttle service into a regional commercial airline.

The company's foray into aviation was initiated by the purchase of a six-seat plane in 1948 to shuttle executives between company headquarters in Wisconsin and Kimberly-Clark factories around the country. With six planes in 1969, Smith, then an executive vice-president for finance, suggested that company air travel be converted from a "cost center into a profit center" by offering corporate aircraft maintenance services. K-C Aviation, as the subsidiary was called, later remodeled three DC-9s and in June 1984 initiated flight service between Appleton and Milwaukee, Wisconsin; Boston; and Dallas, Texas. The fledgling airline, operated under the name Midwest Express, got off to a rocky start with a 1985 crash in Milwaukee, planes flying 80 percent empty, and large operating losses. By 1989, however, the operation was in the black, with planes at 66 percent capacity; a $120 million expansion increased the number of destinations to 15 cities and the airline boasted a fleet of 11 DC-9s.

In 1985, stating that the state had a bad climate for business, Smith relocated Kimberly-Clark's headquarters from Wisconsin to Texas. Just before this move Kimberly-Clark was sued by Procter & Gamble, who claimed that Kimberly-Clark had unlawfully infringed on its patented disposable diaper waistband material. Huggies had increased its market share to 31 percent, upsetting Procter & Gamble's Pampers. After nearly two years of litigation, a federal grand jury ruled against Procter & Gamble. Kimberly-Clark enjoyed further successes in its ongoing diaper rivalry with Procter & Gamble later in the decade when it introduced the extremely popular Huggies Pull-Ups disposable training pants in 1989. This product extension helped Kimberly-Clark trim Procter & Gamble's market share lead, as well as propel Huggies into the number one position in the disposable diaper market.

1990s and Beyond

Starting in the late 1980s, Kimberly-Clark began another diversification program—this time geographically, targeting Europe—although the company's largest international growth would come in the early and mid-1990s. To keep the company growing at a healthy pace, Smith began to increase Kimberly-Clark's presence in Europe in 1988. From that year to 1992, the company invested nearly $1 billion in European plants. Although revenues from its European operations increased steadily, the huge investments (totaling $700 million in 1993 alone) and restructuring charges that went along with them began to affect the company's profits. Net income of $435.2 million in 1991 fell to $150.1 million in 1992 before recovering slightly to $231 million in 1993.

Meanwhile, the company further reduced its commodity papers operation in 1991 when it sold Spruce Falls Power and Paper. The following year, Smith, the architect of Kimberly-Clark's restructuring and diversification efforts since 1972, retired as chairman and was succeeded by Wayne R. Sanders. The new chairman had worked his way up the ranks and had spearheaded the risky endeavor of developing Huggies Pull-Ups. The year 1992 also saw the introduction of Huggies Ultra Trim diapers.

Under Sanders's leadership, it appeared as if the company would divest itself completely of its commodity papers roots. Kimberly-Clark announced in late 1994 that it would explore the sale of its North American pulp and newsprint operations. The following year, however, the company decided not to sell because pulp and newsprint prices rose so high it no longer made economic sense to do so. Kimberly-Clark did divest its cigarette papers business in mid-1995 by spinning it off into a company called Schweitzer-Maudit International Inc. after shareholders initiated a proxy fight in 1994, concerned about the potential costs of liability lawsuits against tobacco, which were then beginning to gain strength.

In 1995 Sanders engineered the deal that would usher in a new era for the company: the merger of Kimberly-Clark with the Scott Paper Co. The deal was the logical culmination of Kimberly-Clark's international expansion, since Scott was globally strong and held the number one position in tissue in Europe. The $9.4 billion deal led to a 1995 charge of $1.4 billion for Kimberly-Clark to consolidate the merger, which led to the layoff of 6,000 workers and the sale of several plants. To pass antitrust muster, Kimberly-Clark had to sell the Scotties facial tissue operation, two of four tissue plants in the United States, and its Baby Fresh, Wash-a-Bye Baby, and Kid Fresh brands (which it sold to Procter & Gamble).

The merger with Scott solidified Kimberly-Clark's position as the number two player in the paper products industry and nearly doubled the company's revenues. The merger also marked a change in direction for the company from a focus on low-margin paper and pulp production to higher-profit consumer products. Realizing that its entry into the "diaper wars" with Proctor & Gamble would require streamlined operations, Kimberly-Clark began to divest itself of its pulp and paper manufacturing business in late 1996. The company shut down mills in Alabama, Canada, and Spain. By the end of 1997, pulp production fell to 30 percent of the company's worldwide consumption, down from 80 percent at the beginning of that year.

The company also began to expand its line of professional health care products. In 1997, Kimberly-Clark acquired Tecnol Medical Products, manufacturer of half of all surgical masks used in U.S. hospitals. In 1998, the company restructured its tissue business to consolidate manufacturing operations. The restructuring resulted in the closure of mills, including those in Maine and Wisconsin, and the loss of some 5,000 jobs. In 1999, Kimberly-Clark further divested its pulp business when it sold its Southeast Timberlands, which supplied wood to many of its defunct pulp mills.

In 1999, the company expanded its tissue operations in Europe with its acquisition of the Swiss Company Attisholz. The acquisition nearly tripled Kimberly-Clark's tissue sales in Germany, Switzerland, and Austria. That year, Kimberly-Clark continued its foray into medical and health care products by purchasing Ballard Medical Products, adding such products as respiratory suction catheters, defibrillator pads, and foam-dispensed soap to its line. That acquisition was followed later that year by the purchase of Safeskin, which gave the company the leading spot in the production of disposable surgical gloves.

The turn of the century saw the company continuing its rapid expansion through acquisitions. In 2000, the company grew its Asian markets when it acquired the Taiwanese company S-K Corporation and the Taiwan Scott Paper. In 2001, Kimberly-Clark bought the Italian company Linostar, the second largest diaper manufacturer in Italy. In 2000, the company achieved sales of nearly $14 billion. The annual report for that year reported that in coming years the company would focus on product innovation, strategic acquisitions, and geographic expansion, especially introducing Kimberly-Clark products into countries where they were not currently sold.

Principal Subsidiaries

Avent, Inc.; Ballard Medical Products; Colombiana Kimberly Colpapel S.A. (Colombia; 69%); Hakle-Kimberly Switzerland; Hakle-Kimberly Deutschland; Hogla-Kimberly (Hadera, Israel; 50.1%); Housing Horizons, LLC; Kimberly-Clark Argentina S.A.; Kimberly-Clark a.s. (Czech Republic); Kimberly-Clark Austria Holdings Pty. Ltd.; Kimberly-Clark B.V. (Netherlands); Kimberly-Clark CBG Hygenic Products company Limited (China); Kimberly-Clark Canada Inc.; Kimberly-Clark Central American Holdings (Panama; 81%); Kimberly-Clark de Centro America, S.A. (El Salvador, 81%); Kimberly-Clark Chile (60%); Kimberly-Clark do Brasil Limitada; Kimberly-Clark Ecuador S.A. (69%); Kimberly-Clark Holding Ltd. (United Kingdom); Kimberly-Clark (Hong Kong) Limited; Kimberly-Clark International, S.A. (Panama); Kimberly-Clark Japan Limited; Kimberly-Clark Kenko Industria e Comércio Ltda. (Brazil); Kimberly-Clark Lda. (Portugal); Kimberly-Clark Luxembourg S.A.R.L.; Kimberly-Clark Malaysia Sendirian Berhad; Kimberly-Clark N.V. (Belgium); Kimberly-Clark ooo, (Russia); Kimberly-Clark Paper (Guangzhou) Company Ltd. (China); Kimberly-Clark Paper (Shanghai) Company Ltd. (China); Kimberly-Clark Paraguay, S.A. (92%); Kimberly-Clark Personal Hygienic Products Co., Ltd. (China); Kimberly-Clark Personal Hygienic Products (Nanjinng) Co., Ltd. (China); Kimberly-Clark Peru, S.A. (33%); Kimberly-Clark Philippines Inc. (87%); Kimberly-Clark Poland Sp. z.o.o.; Kimberly-Clark Printing Technology, Inc.; Kimberly-Clark Products (Malaysia) Sdn., Bhd.; Kimberly-Clark Pudumjee Limited (India; 51%); Kimberly-Clark Puerto Rico, Inc. (Delaware); Kimberly-Clark S.L. (Spain); Kimberly-Clark—SID, S.A. (Dominican Republic; 80%); Kimberly-Clark Singapore Pte. Ltd.; Kimberly-Clark S.N.C. (France); Kimberly-Clark Southern Africa (Holdings) (Pty) Ltd. (South Africa; 50% plus one share); Kimberly-Clark S.p.A. (Italy); Kimberly-Clark Technical Paper, Inc.; Kimberly-Clark Thailand Limited; Kimberly-Clark Tissue Company (Pennsylvania); Kimberly-Clark Ukraine LLC; Kimberly-Clark Uruguay, S.A.; Kimberly-Clark Venezuela, C.A. (69%); Kimberly-Clark Vietnam Co., Ltd.; Kimberly-Clark Worldwide, Inc. (Delaware); KIMNICA, S.A. (Nicaragua; 81%); Ovisan Turkey (50.1%); Papeles Absorbentes, S.A. (Guatemala 75%); P.T. Kimberly-Lever Indonesia (50% plus one share); S-K Corporation (Taiwan); Safeskin Corporation (Florida); Scott Paper Company de Costa Rica, S.A. (81%); Scott Paper Company—Honduras, S.A. de C.V. (81%); Scott S.A. (France); Taiwan Scott Paper Corporation; Tecnol, Inc.; YuHan-Kimberly, Limited (South Korea, 70%).

Principal Operating Units

Tissue; Personal Care; Health Care.

Principal Competitors

Georgia-Pacific Corporation; Playtex; Proctor & Gamble.

Further Reading

Benady, David, "Kimberly-Clark Brings in US Chief," *Marketing Week*, July 23, 1998, p. 9.

Byrne, Harlan S., "Keeping the Faith," *Barron's*, December 16, 1996, p. 15.

——, "Paper Profits," *Barron's*, January 10, 2000, p. 20.

——, "Strength Ahead?," *Barron's*, July 28, 1997, p. 13.

Byrne, John A., and Weber, Joseph, "The Shredder: Did CEO Dunlap Save Scott Paper—Or Just Pretty It Up?," *Business Week*, January 15, 1996, pp. 56–61.

Cheverton, Richard E., *The Maverick Way: Profiting from the Power of the Corporate Misfit*, La Palma, CA: Waypoint Books, 2000.

Cody, Harold M., "Consolidation Produces Giants Hoping for Better Performance," *Pulp & Paper*, November 2000, pp. 37–44.

Collins, Glenn, "Kimberly-Clark Plans Split of Stock and Sale of 3 Mills, Stronger Position Sought against P.& G.," *The New York Times*, February 26, 1997, p. C2.

Forest, Stephanie Anderson, and Heidi Dawley, "Pulp Fiction at Kimberly-Clark," *Business Week*, February 23, 1998, p. 90.

Forest, Stephanie Anderson, and Maremont, Mark, ''Kimberly-Clark's European Paper Chase,'' *Business Week*, March 16, 1992, pp. 94, 96.

Frankovich £ Mike, ''Early Intervention,'' *Security Management*, April 2000, pp. 22–24.

Freeman, Laurie, ''Kimberly Holds Its Own Against Giants,'' *Advertising Age*, November 19, 1984.

Glowacki, Jeremy J., ''Kimberly-Clark Corp.: Accelerates Global Expansion with Scott Merger,'' *Pulp & Paper*, December 1995, pp. 34–35.

Goldstein, Alan, ''Learning a New Set of Rules: How Kimberly-Clark Adapted When E-Business Era Arrived,'' *Knight-Ridder/Tribune News Service*, January 10, 2001.

''Gulfstream Buying Kimberly-Clark Aviation Unit,'' *The New York Times*, July 25, 1998, p. B3.

Hackney, Holt, ''Kimberly-Clark: No Escaping a Messy Diaper (Business),'' *Financial World*, April 27, 1993, p. 16.

Ingham, John N., ed., ''Kimberly, John Alfred,'' in *Biographical Dictionary of American Business Leaders, Vol. II*, Westport, Conn.: Greenwood, 1983.

Kaplan -Leiseron, Eva, ''The Maverick Way Profiting From the Power of the Corporate Misfit,'' *Training & Development*, January 2001, p. 66.

''K-C Announces Global Restructuring,'' *Pulp & Paper*, January 1998, p. 23.

''K-C O pts for Recycled, to Shut Mobile Mill,'' *Pulp & Paper*, July 1998, p. 23.

''K-C Takes Cool Approach to its Newest Operating Room Apparel,'' *Health Industry Today*, December 1998, pp. 4–5.

''Kimberly-Clark Acquires Tecnol,'' *The Wall Street Journal*, December 19, 1997, p. B2.

''Kimberly-Clark Awards Options,'' *The New York Times*, October 23, 1997, p. C26.

''Kimberly-Clark Corp.,'' *The New York Times*, April 1, 1997, p. C4.

''Kimberly-Clark Has Plans to Restructure Operations in Europe,'' *The Wall Street Journal*, July 7, 2000, p. A6.

''Kimberly-Clark is Selling 460,000 Acres of Timberland,'' *The New York Times*, June 11, 1999, p. C4.

''Kimberly-Clark Kicks in with Restructuring Plan,'' *PPI*, January 1998, p. 9.

''Kimberly-Clark Plans to Increase Prices 5% for Huggies Diapers,'' *The Wall Street Journal*, April 16, 1998, p. A4.

''Kimberly-Clark Revises Structure,'' *The New York Times*, December 11, 1998, p. C2.

''Kimberly-Clark Selling Southeast Timber,'' *Pulp & Paper*, March 1999, p. 25.

''Kimberly-Clark Snatches Attisholz's Tissue Unit,'' *PPI*, June 1999, p. 15.

''Kimberly-Clark Suit Alleges Infringement of Its Diaper Patents,'' *The Wall Street Journal*, March 21, 2000, p. B8.

''Kimberly-Clark to Acquire Tecnol for 19 Times, Earnings,'' *Weekly Corporate Growth Report*, September 15, 1997.

''Kimberly-Clark to Buy Italian Diaper Manufacturer,'' *The New York Times*, January 25, 2001, p. C4.

''Kimberly-Clark to Close Pulp Mill and Cut 450 Jobs,'' *The New York Times*, May 6, 1998, p. C3.

''Kimberly-Clark to Sell Lines,'' *The Wall Street Journal*, May 19, 1999, p. C27.

''Kimberly-Clark Will Cut Staff 15% in Europe,'' *Wall Street Journal*, January 29, 1996, p. B2.

''Kimberly-Clark—Down the Pan?,'' *Marketing Week*, April 9, 1998, p. 3.

''Kimberly-Clark's Deal for Ballard Expands Industry Acquisition Trend,'' *Health Industry Today*, February 1999, pp. 1, 4.

''Kruger Agrees to Buy Kimberly-Clark Unit for $256.8 Million,'' *The Wall Street Journal*, March 5, 1997, p. B2.

Lenzner, Robert, ''The Battle of the Bottoms,'' *Forbes*, March 24, 1997, pp. 98–103.

Lieber, Ronald B., ''Storytelling: A New Way to Get Close to Your Customer,'' *Fortune*, February 3, 1997, pp. 102–108.

Murray, Matt, ''Kimberly-Clark To Take Charge of $1.4 Billion,'' *Wall Street Journal*, December 14, 1995, pp. A3, A8.

Narisetti, Raju, ''For Sanders, Getting Scott Is Only the Start,'' *Wall Street Journal*, December 5, 1995, pp. B1, B12.

Neff, Jack, ''Kimberly-Clark Finally Reaps Boon from Scott,'' *Advertising Age*, November 8, 1999, p. 24.

Nelson, Emily, ''Kimberly-Clark Posts 7.8% Drop in Net, Lowers Forecast for the Rest of the Year,'' *The Wall Street Journal*, April 24, 2001, p. B8.

Parker-Pope, Tara, ''Contrite, Kimberly-Clark's CEO Promises to Mop Up,'' *The Wall Street Journal*, June 1, 1998, p. B1.

Pearson, John, ''Reforms are Bearing Fruit,'' Business Week, July 8, 1996, p. 86.

''Purchase of Added 5% Stake in Australian Venture is Set,'' *The Wall Street Journal*, May 8, 2001, p. A14.

Richards, Amanda, ''Unite and Conquer,'' *Marketing*, September 18, 1997, pp. 24–25.

Sheridan, John H., ''Going for Growth,'' *Industry Week*, June 9, 1997, pp. 32–44.

Spector, Robert, *Shared Values: A History of Kimberly-Clark*, Lyme, CT: Greenwich Publishing Group, Incorporated, 1997.

Star, Marlene Givant, ''Proxy Fight at Kimberly-Clark: Investors Request Tobacco Spin-Off,'' *Pensions & Investments*, March 6, 1995, pp. 2, 41.

''The Kimberly-Clark Corp to Purchase the Safeskin Corp for 3.19 Times, Revenue,'' *Weekly Corporate Growth Report*, November 29, 1999.

Useem, Jerry, ''Most Admired: Conquering Vertical Limits,'' *Fortune*, February 19, 2001, pp. 84–96.

''Wayne R. Sanders,'' *Business Week*, January 8, 2001, p. 69.

—Carol I. Keeley
—updates: David E. Salamie, Lisa Whipple

Kinko's, Inc.

255 West Stanley Avenue
Ventura, California 93002-8000
U.S.A.
Telephone: (805) 652-4000
Toll Free: (800) 2-Kinkos
Fax: (805) 652-4142
Web site: http://www.kinkos.com

Private Company
Incorporated: 1970 as Kinko's Copies Corp.
Employees: 25,000
Sales: $2,000 million (2000 est.)
NAIC: 514210 Data Processing Services; 561439 Other Business Services (including Copy Shops)

In 1995, Kinko's, Inc. was the leading retail provider of document copying and business services in the world. Kinko's had more than 830 outlets in early 1996, located in every state of the union and four foreign countries—Canada, Japan, South Korea, and the Netherlands. It was providing photocopies, quick printing and finishing services, electronic document distribution and production, mailing services, and time rentals on personal computers, usually at any hour of the day or night. About 145 locations had a special room for conducting videoconferences. A private company, Kinko's does not release its sales figures.

Serving College Campuses in the 1970s

Kinko's Copies Corporation was founded in 1970 by Paul Orfalea, who gave the company the nickname given to him for his curly red hair. Self-described as mechanically inept and dyslexic, he was a ''C'' student at the University of Southern California, from which he graduated in 1971 with a degree in finance. By then Orfalea had observed, ''If you can't fix things and can't read things, then you can't get a job.'' He apparently never looked for one, later telling a Forbes interviewer, ''I'm sort of unemployable. I'm basically a peddler.''

Seeking something to sell, Orfalea fixed his eye one day on the copy machine in the university library. Applying what he had learned from a marketing course that studied product life cycles, he decided, ''This thing here is going to go for a long time.'' With funds from a $5,000 loan in 1969 from the Bank of America, cosigned by his father, he leased an 80-square-foot former hamburger stand in Isla Vista, near the campus of the University of California at Santa Barbara, and rented a small Xerox copier, charging customers four cents a page. He and a few friends also sold about $2,000 a day worth of notebooks and pens out of the makeshift store, wheeling the copier out on the sidewalk when the premises became too crowded. He supplemented his income by going from one dormitory room to another in the evenings, hawking his wares from a knapsack.

When this business proved a success, Orfalea decided to open other stores on other college campuses. Since he did not have funds to finance them and did not want to franchise them, he formed partnerships with owner-operators, retaining a controlling interest in each. These partners were other students who scouted locations along the West Coast, sleeping in their Volkswagen buses or fraternity houses. Publicity consisted of flyers stuffed in mailboxes; orders were taken and delivered personally.

Some of these Kinko's pioneers still were owner-operators many years later. Jim Warren was a surfer who met Orfalea at a keg party and was persuaded to take the enterprise to the Southeast. He and his wife rented a small storefront near the University of Georgia in 1978, where they kept a fire extinguisher handy because the copier they leased tended to burn paper. By 1995 Warren was president of Southeast Kinko's Inc. and a part owner in about 120 Kinko's branches from Delaware to Florida. Tim Stancliffe opened the first Midwest Kinko's in a 175-square-foot space near the University of Colorado. In 1995 he was president of K-Graphics Inc., which owned and operated 90 Kinko's outlets in Colorado, Iowa, Kansas, Michigan, Missouri, Nebraska, New Mexico, South Dakota, and Wisconsin.

By the mid-1970s, Kinko's was providing custom publishing materials for colleges, an innovation extremely popular with college professors. By the end of the decade, the company had

Company Perspectives:

Our primary objective is to take care of our customer. We are proud of our ability to serve him or her in a timely and helpful manner and to provide consistency and high quality at a reasonable price. We develop long-term relationships that promote mutual growth and prosperity. We value initiative, productivity, and loyalty, and we encourage independent thinking and teamwork.

80 stores, averaging 400 square feet in space, located primarily near colleges and universities.

Reaching Out to Small Businesses in the 1980s

By the early 1980s, Kinko's Copies was no longer content simply to copy documents for students. ''At the time, no one was offering a low-end alternative to typesetting in the document duplication market,'' a marketing executive for Kinko's Service Corp., the chain's support arm, told a Computer World reporter in 1987. To exploit this emerging business opportunity, the company began to install typewriters in its shops.

This decision was soon rendered obsolete by the spread of personal computers. Kinko's then considered buying IBM PC clones, but opted for Apple Computer's Macintosh in 1985 because it was easier to use by customers who wanted to create documents without help from Kinko's employees. Another Macintosh advantage was that the documents created could be reproduced on Apple's high-quality LaserWriter printer. By mid-1987 almost one-third of Kinko's roughly 300 outlets were offering desktop publishing services. Kinko's also began selling university-developed educational software for the Macintosh and Apple II computers in 1986.

In 1989 Kinko's Graphics Corporation, operator of about 100 of the chain's copy shops, was slapped with a copyright-infringement lawsuit by eight textbook publishers for copying book segments of as long as 110 pages without permission. A federal judge found the company guilty in 1991 and assessed $1.9 million in damages and court fees. Kinko's Service Corporation then agreed that none of the stores would photocopy textbook anthologies in the future without permission for all copyrighted material.

Kinko's opened its first 24-hours-a-day, seven-days-a-week, outlet in Chicago in 1985. According to the president of Kinko's of Illinois, the company made this decision when people ''started knocking on the glass after hours, begging us to let them in.'' Soon more of Kinko's stores—which numbered 420 at the end of the decade—were operating around the clock to accommodate people who had to produce documents such as manuscripts, screenplays, opera librettos, resumes, posters, fliers, and wedding invitations. A 24-hour Kinko's was installed in the lobby of Chicago's Stouffer Renaissance because foreign executives staying at the hotel wanted to communicate across time zones with headquarters at home.

By mid-1994 almost all Kinko's outlets were open all the time. Manhattan's five stores filled at night with students and business people who rubbed shoulders with punk rockers and anarchists designing, copying, and faxing posters. Each of the five had its own cat as a mascot and dispensed coffee from a machine at no charge.

''Your Branch Office'' in the 1990s

The Kinko's of the 1990s had graduated beyond a low-tech service for college students. The company began opening stores averaging 7,000 square feet in size in suburbs and business areas. These stores aimed to attract small-business owners seeking more advanced document copies, which were sometimes oversized, in color, or bearing sophisticated graphics. In a nationally advertised television campaign begun in 1992, small-business people were urged to use Kinko's as ''your branch office.''

By 1994 Kinko's had added sophisticated color copiers, high-speed, high-volume laser printers, and facsimile machines, leasing rather than buying in order to conserve cash and avoid commitment to equipment that rapidly became outdated. Kinko's shops also began leasing conference rooms. In 1995 only 15 percent of Kinko's sales were still believed to be college-oriented, with large corporations accounting for another 15 percent, miscellaneous community retail use for 10 percent, and small or home-based businesses for 60 percent. The number of Americans estimated to be working from home in 1995 was 40 million, up from about 28 million in 1989. The number of businesses employing between five and 100 persons grew by almost 40 percent between 1980 and 1994. Typically, such customers prepared documents in their offices, then brought them to Kinko's for the professional look made possible only by using quality printing equipment.

In 1993 Kinko's introduced videoconference rooms to 100 of its 725 outlets. Bidding for trade from entrepreneurs, telecommuters, traveling business people, and local representatives of corporations based elsewhere, the company made a huge investment in this new technology. For $150 an hour, customers were offered a room with a large-screen television monitor, a videocassette recorder, a camera with wide-angle and zoom capabilities for focusing on a group or individual, and a device resembling an oversized television remote control. U.S. Sprint provided the equipment and high-speed telephone lines for the voice-picture-data network. Kinko Service Corporation's president said he believed that families might take advantage of a half-price holiday promotion to use such facilities for ''video reunions.''

By 1995 new Kinko's stores were, on average, four times larger than the ones they replaced. This was due in part to the space needed for an ever-increasing inventory of high-end service equipment. (The Xerox 5090 high-speed color-printing machine, for example, nearly filled an entire room.). The company also installed Kinkonet, a system enabling companies to send in orders by computer, with Kinko's distributing the finished product, such as a training manual, to points all over the United States.

A Kinko's outlet typically offered the following services in 1996: full and self-service copying, including four-color copies; desktop publishing, including laser typesetting and printing; onsite Macintosh and IBM computer rentals; office supplies and

Key Dates:

1970: Paul Orfalea opens the first Kinko's in Isla Vista, California.
1975: Kinko's opens its 24th branch.
1979: Kinko's has 80 branches in 28 states.
1985: The first 24-hour Kinko's outlet opens in Chicago.
1989: Kinko's has 420 branches across the country and in Canada.
1991: A Federal judge finds the Kinko's company guilty of copyright infringement in a lawsuit filed by eight textbook publishers.
1992: Kinko's opens international branches in Japan and the Netherlands.
1996: Over 850 Kinko's branches are in operation worldwide.
1999: Kinko's is selected by *Fortune* magazine as one of the 100 best companies to work for in America.
2000: The Internet site, www.Kinkos.com, is launched, creating a new ''clicks-and-mortar'' business division for the company.

stationery; finishing services such as folding, binding, collating, and stapling; custom printing services; facsimile transmission; and mailing, pick-up, and delivery service. FedEx drop boxes were installed in all Kinko's locations. Some outlets also offered one-hour photo service and videoconferencing. Kinko's considered customer service of such importance that each location was being ''mystery shopped'' on a regular basis, with anonymous shoppers grading the store on 29 different points of customer service and store atmosphere.

A New Direction for Kinko's

Even while Kinko's retail niche as a full-service copy shop was secure, new marketplaces were needed if the company wanted to continue to grow and prosper, and especially if Orfalea was to take his company public. During the latter half of the 1990s, Orfalea began shifting Kinko's marketing strategies and re-organizing its corporate structure.

His new business plan called for actively soliciting business from Fortune 500 companies. A newly created outside sales force hit the ground running, knocking on company doors across the county in an effort to bring in new corporate accounts.

In order to raise capital for this expanded growth and to keep outlets outfitted with the latest office technology, Orfalea took a radical step in 1996: selling a one-third stake in the company to Clayton, Dubilier & Rice (CD&R), a New York City-leveraged buyout firm, for $220 million. Up until this time, Orfalea had sole ownership in approximately 110 outlets and a stake in all others, which in essence were joint ventures held in partnership with 130 owner-operators.

The investment by CD&R served as the catalyst for Orfalea to restructure the company. The process began by rolling up what was often described as a ''hodgepodge'' of vastly different partnerships into a single corporate entity and centralizing all management functions at Kinko's headquarters in Ventura, California. Corporate conformity quickly took hold as all Kinko's retail outlets were made to look like each other. The different, sometimes funky, décor of individual outlets was replaced with a uniform appearance; moreover, all Kinko's would offer the same menu of services.

Other changes were less visible, but no less significant. For the first time since its inception in 1970, a board of directors oversaw Kinko's. In mid-1997, Orfalea was replaced as CEO by Joseph Hardin Jr., former president and chief executive of Wal-Mart's Sam's Club. Orfalea remained involved with the company's management, quickly embracing his new duties as the chairman of the board. It required changing his focus from the day-to-day operations to what he describes as ''company ambassador'' responsibilities as Kinko's continued to expand overseas. In a rare interview with *Your Company* magazine, Orfalea reflected on the change as a positive one. ''Now that I'm not as wrapped up inside the business, I can go outside and see the bigger picture. I can observe how Kinko's fits into society and the global economy. Besides trying to figure out what foreign markets we should tap, I can constantly strategize and worry about how viable the organization will be in five years. That's the important stuff.''

Into the Next Century: Sixteen Billion Copies a Year and Counting

As the 1990s came to a close, Kinko's held its own as the world's leading provider of visual communications services, document creation, and copying. In 1999 *Fortune* magazine selected Kinko's as one of the ''100 Best Companies to Work for in America,'' an honor Kinko's would also earn in 2000 and 2001. One of the chief reasons for making the list, according to *Fortune,* was Kinko's philosophy of equality for its employees, such as the fact that each of the 1,000-plus branches shares its profits monthly among its co-workers. The company also received accolades for its efforts to conserve. In addition to using energy-efficient lighting in accordance with the EPA's Green Lights program in nearly all of its U.S. branches, 90 outlets in 10 states are also powered by renewable resources. For example, in the year 2000, six percent of Kinko's energy demand came from renewable energy sources such as solar arrays, windmill farms and geothermal plants.

In order to boost its Internet presence, Kinko's bought a majority stake in Liveprint.com, a small Web company based near Washington D.C., in early 2000. It invested an undisclosed amount in the 65-person Liveprint.com so it could ''bring the power of the Internet to small business and home offices,'' creating what the company likes to call its new ''clicks and mortar business center solution.'' The result is Kinkos.com, the virtual Kinko's, which is hoped to coexist nicely with its physical brethren.

With annual revenues estimated at about $1 billion and 1,100 locations across the United States and worldwide, including branches in Australia, Canada, Japan, the Netherlands, South Korea, and the U.K, many speculate that Kinko's is ready for its next big step: an initial public stock offering. As of May 2001, Kinko's was still a privately held company, but things can change quickly, especially since dot.com IPOs have fallen out of favor with investors. Plans also continue for further branch expansion. CEO Hardin reports that Kinko's is opening about 100 new branches a year. Currently, it is estimated that Kinko's produces 16 billion photocopies a year. That number will surely continue to rise as more of the world becomes hooked on Kinko's 24-hour office services.

Principal Subsidiaries

G & S Corp.; K-Graphics Inc.; Kinko's Graphics Corp.; Kinko's Northwest LP; Kinko's of Illinois; Kinko's Service Corp.; Southeast Kinko's Inc.

Principal Competitors

Copy Max; Kwik Kopy; Mail Boxes; Etc.; Office Depot; Staples

Further Reading

Apodaca, Patrice, ''Kinko's Gambles on High-Tech Services,'' *Los Angeles Times*, October 7, 1994, pp. D2–3.

Beeler, Jeffry, ''Firm Taps Mac for Strategy Move,'' *Computer World*, February 16, 1987, p. 69.

Cox, Meg, ''Kinko's, Publishers Reach Settlement of Copyright Suit,'' *Wall Street Journal*, October 18, 1991, p. B6.

Eisenberg, Daniel, ''Offices By The Hour,'' *Time Magazine*, February 1, 1999.

Fierman, Jaclyn, ''It's 2 A.M.: Let's Go to Work,'' *Fortune*, August 21, 1995, p. 85.

Flynn, Laurie, ''Kinko's Adds Internet Services to Its Copying Business,'' *New York Times*, March 18, 1996, p. D5.

Henry, Shannon, ''Kinko's Makes an Original,'' *The Washington Post*, March 2, 2000, p. E01.

Kempner, Matt, ''Surf's Up for Ever-Changing Kinko's,'' *Atlanta Constitution*, July 6, 1995, p. E1.

Levering, Robert and Moskowitz, Robert, ''The 100 Best Companies to Work For,'' *Fortune*, January 8, 2001, p. 148.

Marchetti, Michele, ''Getting the Kinks Out,'' *Sales and Marketing Management*, March 1997, p. 56.

Moukheiber, Zina, ''I'm Just a Peddler,'' *Forbes*, July 17, 1995, pp. 42–43.

Parker, Penny, ''Partnership Hopes to Copy Success,'' *Denver Post*, May 24, 1995, pp. 1C, 3C.

Szabo, Julia, ''Copy Shop Stitches the Urban Crazy Quilt,'' *New York Times*, July 3, 1994, p. 31.

''The Brains Behind Kinko's: How a Hippie Turned Global Magnate Built a Chain of Office Centers for the Free-Agent Crowd That Vastly Changed the Landscape of Small Business,'' *Your Company*, May 1, 1999, p. 62.

—Robert Halasz
—update: Suzanne L. Rowe

Lincare Holdings Inc.

19337 U.S. 19 North, Suite 500
Clearwater, Florida 33764
U.S.A.
Telephone: (727) 530-7700
Fax: (727) 532-9692
Web site: http://www.lincare.com

Public Company
Incorporated: 1990
Employees: 4,700
Sales: $703 million (2000)
Stock Exchanges: NASDAQ
Ticker Symbol: LNCR
NAIC: 62161 Home Health Care Services; 551112 Offices of Other Holding Companies

Lincare Holdings Inc., based in Clearwater, Florida, is a major provider of oxygen and other respiratory equipment and services to home-care customers in 42 states. In its area of coverage, the company maintains approximately 430 offices, and it continues to expand despite the fact that the 1997 Balanced Budget Act put a cap on Medicare and Medicaid reimbursements on the services it provides, payments which had accounted for approximately 60% of the company's revenue. In addition to providing oxygen, Lincare provides infusion therapy, including palliative care, hydration therapy, chemotherapy, AIDS-related therapies, inhalation therapy, and enteral and parenteral nutritional care; and some home-use medical equipment, including ventilators, wheelchairs, walkers, and hospital beds. The company has established specific programs, with education components as well as therapeutic equipment, including AIM (Asthma Intervention & Management); Pulmonary Rehabilitation; PRO (Positive Respiratory Outcomes); and The HeartSteps Program, primarily designed for patients suffering from CHF (congestive heart failure).

1972–89: Origins and Spin Off

The forerunner of Lincare Holding Inc. was Linde Homecare Medical Systems, which was formed in 1972 as a unit in Union Carbide Corporation's industrial gasses division, or what would later become Praxair. Linde was a name associated with Union Carbide since 1917, when Union Carbide & Carbon Corporation (UCC) was organized from the merger of two chemical producers—National Carbon Company (founded in 1886) and Union Carbide (founded in 1898)—plus Linde Air Products, Prest-O-Lite, and Electro Metallurgical. At the time, Linde Air Products was primarily a producer of oxygen for industrial use.

In the 1980s, Union Carbide ran into some very difficult times. In a partnership arrangement with some indigenous companies, in 1975 it had built a pesticide plant in Bhopal, India. Disaster ensued in 1984, when a storage tank at that facility leaked five tons of poisonous gas, killing more than 3,000 people and leaving 50,000 more with life-long injuries. Partly because the company faced a major liability suit in India, in 1985 it was subjected to a hostile takeover attempt by GAF, a chemicals and roofing materials manufacturer. In order to fend off the attempt, Union Carbide bought back 55 percent of its stock, but in the process went $3 billion into debt. To help retire that immense debt, Union Carbide began selling off some of its holdings, including its battery division (even its Eveready branded products) as well as its agricultural and home and auto products businesses. In 1987, it also spun off Linde Homecare's operations as Lincare Inc., and later, in 1992, it also spun off Praxair, the industrial gasses division to which Linde Homecare had once belonged.

1990–94: The Mixed Blessings of Government Policy and Regulation Changes

In 1990, with the help of investors, Lincare Inc.'s managers bought out the spun-off company, renaming it Lincare Holdings. Specifically, Lincare Holdings was a partnership of two venture capital firms, Dean Witter Capital Corp., and Lincare Inc.'s management. Dean Witter Capital was an affiliate of IPO underwriter Dean Witter Reynolds. The partner-owners took the company public, making an initial public offering in March 1990. The 3.9 million, $14 per share IPO raised $49.2 million, and within ten months, Lincare's stock more than doubled in market value, fluctuating at close to $30 per share.

In December 1992, the company made a second offering of 1.7 million shares at $28.50 per share. By that time, Lincare was

Company Perspectives:

The mission of Lincare is to set standards of excellence for providing respiratory care, infusion therapy and medical equipment to patients in the home. Our company's success, which is characterized by responsiveness and clinical excellence, has been founded on the dedication of our professionals to quality care. Physicians, care givers and patients trust Lincare to provide the quality care they expect and deserve.

providing in-home respiratory therapy from a network of 115 operating centers. Its revenues had also started a rapid rise, and so had its net income. For example, its third quarter net income in September 1992 had risen to almost $4.7 million, up from $936,833 from the same period in the previous year, before the company went public.

Because most of the executives of the newly formed Lincare Holdings had been with the company when it was part of Union Carbide, they had considerable experience and expertise to bring to the task of managing and expanding the company, and analysts attributed much of the company's success in the early and mid-1990s to their sure-handed guidance. Andrew M. Paul, who had served as chairman from 1990, stepped down in 1994, but he remained an active director. James T. Kelly, who had been CEO since 1986 and president since 1987, replaced Paul as chairman. James M. Emanuel, Lincare's CFO, had held that post since 1984. Howard R. Deutsch, who was executive vice-president, general counsel, and board member, proved to be another key figure, credited with overseeing Lincare's aggressive acquisitions strategy.

With the capital raised from it stock offerings and rapid growth in revenue and profits, the company was soon able to embark on its accelerated growth through the acquisition of smaller competitors and entries into new markets. In 1993, along with Abbey and Homedco (which merged as Apria Healthcare Group Inc. in 1995), the industry's other chief operators, Lincare became a principal beneficiary of a costly and complex claims process that the federal government put into effect, one that forced many of Lincare's smaller, mom-and-pop competitors to sell out. The government also reduced the number of insurance companies under contract to process claims from 60 to just four, a move that further discouraged small operators from staying in business. Until these changes came into effect, home oxygen and respiratory services had been dominated by small, $1 million to $3 million operations that Lincare and its chief rival began buying up.

By the summer of 1994, Lincare's centers had grown to 161 operating in 34 states and servicing over 55,000 customers. It had become one of the country's three largest providers of respiratory and other home-care services, and it was poised for even greater growth. Its policy was to purchase existing companies in new market areas rather than open a new Lincare office in a place where its name was unknown. In effect, Lincare treated each purchased company as a small business, customizing operations to fit the specific location of each of its new acquisitions.

The rapid expansion brought Lincare some problems, however. In 1994, after buying a small California company, it briefly came under the scrutiny of the Federal Trade Commission office in San Francisco. Also, because of questionable marketing and administrative services it had provided to a Florida pharmacy between 1989 and 1992, the company came under a 1994 grand jury investigation in Tampa. Although neither of these investigations resulted in serious financial difficulty for Lincare, they were the first in a series of problems that beset the company during the rest of the decade. Another was the mounting possibility that Congress might cut Medicare, something it periodically considered during the Clinton administration. That offered a major threat to Lincare, since, by 1995, Medicare accounted for 60 percent of the company's revenue.

1995 and Beyond: Expansion Despite Challenges

It was in 1995 that Lincare came close to selling out to the Denver-based, home health giant, Coram Healthcare. Lincare agreed to a $1 billion stock swap in April of that year, occasioning analysts to laud it as a very sensible merger that would benefit both companies. Coram was experiencing growing pains of its own, however, and when its debts and losses both mounted, its stock value fell to an unacceptable level. By July the merger value of Coram's stock had fallen to $840 million and, as a result, the parties called the merger deal off.

Despite the fact that in 1996 the company had to pay the federal government $1 million to settle the investigation of the services it had provided the unidentified pharmacy, neither government nor judicial probes nor jettisoned merger plans slowed Lincare down. The company seemed to have an almost uncanny ability to make a strategic move at just the right time. For example, in September 1996, just two days before the American Association of Retired Persons moved its large and lucrative health insurance business to the United Healthcare Group, United had named Lincare as one of its principal service providers. Moreover, Lincare simply continued to expand at a record clip. In 1996, it snapped up another 17 competitors, and in 1997 acquired 24 more. It was also diversifying, something that the scotched merger with Coram would have made easier but that Lincare now had to undertake by itself. By the end of 1996, it was servicing over 105,000 customers in 37 states, and by 1998 the figures had risen to 170,000 customers in 41 states. In 1997, its revenues had reached $443.2 million, with about 90 percent of that coming from delivering oxygen to patients in their homes. Still, because Medicare and Medicaid accounted for about 63 percent of the company's sales, Lincare remained at the mercy of unpredictable, government mandated policy changes, a major risk factor in the health-care industry.

The federal government, which was carefully monitoring that industry because of ever rising health care costs, began new investigations of Lincare in 1998 and 1999, first in California and Oregon and then in Florida. Although the company called such investigations routine and inevitable, the probes provided some bad publicity and somewhat tarnished the company's image. In November 1998, the company was also sued by whistle-blower Kirk Costello, a former employee who charged that the company and its top competitors, Apria Healthcare Inc. and RoTech Inc., habitually gave physicians fraudulent consulting contracts, free equipment, and other kickbacks in return for

Key Dates:

1972: Linde Home Medical Systems is formed as part of Union Carbide's industrial gases division.
1987: Union Carbide spins off Linde Homecare as Lincare Inc., an autonomous affiliate.
1990: Investors help Lincare management buy the company, which is renamed Lincare Holdings, Inc.
1992: Company goes public on the NASDAQ.
1994: Lincare Holdings buys Home Oxygen Plus Equipment and Meridian Medical.
1996: Lincare acquires 17 competitors.
1997: Company purchases an additional 24 competitors.
1998: Federal government scrutiny of Lincare's production plants and billing records.
2000: Federal grand jury begins an investigation of alleged irregularities.

patient referrals for oxygen and other health-care services. No government agency was party to the suit, however.

The success of Lincare in the final years of the twentieth century make such investigations and legal entanglements seem more like petty annoyances than serious setbacks. By July of 2000, just prior to its acquisition of United Medical Inc. of Wynne, Arkansas, Lincare was operating 429 health-care centers in 42 states and servicing over 225,000 customers. The purchase of United Medical brought an additional 42 locations and a $60 million increase in annual revenue, which, at the end of 1999, had already reached $581.8 million, from which the company generated a very healthy net income of $100.7 million—a net profit margin of $17.3 percent. The fact that between 1993 and 1999 Lincare's net profit margin averaged 18.3 percent annually must in part account for the close scrutiny it received and continues to receive from external agencies.

Altogether, in 1999, Lincare purchased the operating assets of 18 local and regional competitors plus the common stock of four other companies. These increased the aggregate total revenues of Lincare by about $61 million. Additionally, in 2000, the company acquired the operating assets of another 15 regional and local competitors, adding about $82 million to its annual revenues. The acquisitions made in the two years brought another 48 centers into Lincare's expanding network.

In truth, at the outset of the new century, the proverbial sky seemed to be Lincare's only limit—unless, of course, the federal government came up with more troublesome obstacles. The company was certainly thriving. In fact, it did even better in 2000 than in 1999, with its gross revenues reaching $702.5 million and its net income almost $116.9 million. Still, the business risks remain real and to a large measure beyond the company's control. The ballooning cost of health care in the United States will undoubtedly lead to new or revised regulations and the continued oversight and scrutiny of health-care providers, including Lincare and its chief competitors.

Principal Competitors

American HomePatient, Inc.; Apria Healthcare Group Inc.; Coram Healthcare Corporation; In Home Health, Inc.; RoTech Medical Corporation; Transworld HealthCare, Inc.

Further Reading

Andelman, Bob, "Lincare Holdings: On a Breath-Taking Acquisitions Trail," *Tampa Bay Business Journal*, August 12, 1994, p. 22.

Hundley, Kris, "Former Manager Files Suit against Clearwater, Fla., Home Oxygen Firm," *Knight-Ridder/Tribune Business News*, November 19, 1998.

——, "United Healthcare-AARP Deal May Benefit Lincare of Clearwater, Fla.," *Knight-Ridder/Tribune Business News*, September 16, 1996.

Silverman, Amy, "Lincare Insiders Start Cashing In," *Tampa Bay Business Journal*, December 18, 1992, p. 1.

——, "Lincare's Shares Jump to New Highs," *Tampa Bay Business Journal*, October 15, 1993, p. 1.

Trigaux, Robert, "Home Respiratory Care Firm Lincare to Settle Federal Inquiry," *Knight-Ridder/Tribune Business News*, October 29, 1996.

—John W. Fiero

Loblaw Companies Limited

22 St. Clair Avenue East
Toronto, Ontario M4T 2S8
Canada
Telephone: (416) 922-8500
Fax: (416) 922-7791
Web site: http://www.loblaw.com

Public Company
Incorporated: 1956
Employees: 114,000
Sales: C$20.1 billion (2000 est.)
Stock Exchanges: Toronto
Ticker Symbol: L
NAIC: 445110 Supermarkets and Other Grocery (except Convenience) Stores; 445210 Meat Markets; 445230 Fruit and Vegetable Markets; 452910 Warehouse Clubs and Superstores

Loblaw Companies Limited is Canada's largest retail and wholesale food retailer, with about 1,000 operations across the country. Founded in 1956, Loblaw focuses on food retailing with the purpose of providing consumers the convenience of one-stop-shopping. The company operates under a number of banners, including Loblaws, No Frills, Maxi, and Zehrs Markets. The company is on the vanguard of private label, also known as generic, brand merchandise. The company's wholesale business serves nearly 12,000 independent stores in Canada. Loblaw Companies Limited is controlled by George Weston Limited, a multinational food-processing and food-retailing company.

1950s and 1960s: Expansion Through Acquisition

The relationship between Loblaws and its parent company, George Weston Limited, began in 1947, when Garfield Weston purchased 26 percent of Loblaws' voting stock. George C. Metcalf advised Weston to purchase Loblaws Groceterias, Ontario's leading food chain. In 1953 Weston acquired a controlling share in Loblaws Groceterias, the namesake company founded by Theodore P. Loblaw, and Metcalf became its president. Loblaw Companies Limited was incorporated in 1956.

Throughout the 1950s and 1960s, Loblaws had a voracious appetite for acquisition. Most notably, the company acquired a controlling interest in the Chicago-based National Tea Co., which made Loblaw Companies Limited the third-largest supermarket company in North America. Most of the C$400 million to purchase the company was borrowed. Piece by piece, Loblaws' parent company, George Weston Limited, acquired a variety of companies, while operating with almost complete secrecy. Metcalf held back information from not just shareholders, but even executives of the company's subsidiaries. Often it was difficult to determine whether Loblaws or Weston owned a subsidiary. The media described the Weston-Loblaws conglomerate of hiding in a "veil of accounting obscurity." Amid such concealment and confusion, financial analysts were hesitant to recommend Loblaws or Weston stock. Metcalf said non-disclosure was a temporary necessity, and in 1966 Weston revealed the breadth of its holdings to the public.

Late 1960s: Disappointing Earnings

The revelation of the company's vast portfolio coincided with internal difficulties. Growth financed by short-term borrowing had caught up with the company as acquisitions delivered disappointing earnings and interest rates peaked. One of Loblaws' profit-making techniques had burdened the company with long-term leases that restricted the company's flexibility. A turning point for Loblaws' parent company came in 1967. Hoping to centralize Loblaws' supermarkets with Weston's supermarkets and baking business (which were competing with each other), Garfield Weston hired an accountant, Keith Dalgish. Rather than streamlining the businesses, Dalgish was forced to focus on financial systems in the face of plummeting sales and profits. Ted Creber became the George Weston Limited president and managing director in 1969, during a time of rising interest rates and labor costs. Through his leadership, the company's orientation shifted from expansion to profitability. Creber launched a restructuring program that laid the foundation for the next generation of Weston-Loblaws executives.

Company Perspectives:

We are a food store first, offering a broad assortment of grocery products, superior perishables, and an ever-evolving and increasing assortment of everyday household nonfood products.

1970s: Restructuring and Recovery

In the early 1970s, Loblaws was on the brink of bankruptcy. In 1971 Dave Nichol and Richard Currie met while working at the Toronto office of McKinsey, an international-management consulting firm. Nichol and Weston had been roommates at the University of Western Ontario. The three had dinner. Weston offered Currie a job with Loblaws, and in July 1972, Weston, at Currie's suggestion, hired Nichol. The threesome rolled up their sleeves and reorganized the company. Currie and Nichol renovated stores, started monthly profit-and-loss statements for each store, and most notably, began analyzing their shelf space and highlighting the importance of category profitability.

In 1972 Garfield Weston's youngest son, 31-year-old Galen Weston, decided to come back to Canada to take over the family food business. He had spent a decade successfully starting and operating a supermarket business in Ireland. During the same year Loblaws hired a design consultant, the Watt Design Group, to help revive its aging stores, which had suffered lost market share through the perception of high prices and poor locations. Watt Design Group developed a "lifestyle retail environment," which eliminated the stores' layout and merchandise mix, while the company's logo and store interiors were redesigned. Through the remodeling process, the company's communications and identity were integrated. At this time, Loblaws focused on produce, to compete with their rival Dominion, which dominated the Toronto meat market. An expanded selection of produce was moved from the back to the front of stores, and large-scale posters of fruit were installed to entice customers. The produce was watered for freshness, and lighting was improved. A communications program was established to voice Loblaws' price position, and a focused internal signage program was implemented. In the revamped stores sales doubled, increasing to C$150,000 to C$200,000 a week.

The campaign was a success and Weston turned to Loblaws' struggling company, the National Tea Co., which had siphoned away profits. In 1970 the chain was the sixth largest in the United States, but by 1973 it had dropped to eleventh and had posted a C$35 million loss. Galen addressed the disaster personally by renting a house in Chicago, where he and operations heavyweight Currie worked to set affairs in order. Galen Weston also pared down the organizational structure of George Weston Limited's food operations, such as Kelly Douglas, to streamline the territorial overlap among the parent company's retail holdings and stem the inefficient use of assets. In the fall of 1976 having spent C$65 million to revive the stores, Loblaws sold 63 National Tea stores to A&P. The divestment of National Tea's assets continued gradually as they became marketable, finishing in 1995 with remaining assets in St. Louis and New Orleans. The net proceeds of the withdrawal exceeded C$1 billion.

That year Loblaws lost C$49 million on sales of C$3billion. Frustrated, Galen Weston appointed Richard J. Currie to the post of president of Loblaws. Currie set an objective of 20 percent return on capital. At this stage the management trio that had saved Loblaws shifted from hands-on to more advisory and planning-oriented roles. Weston moved on to run parent company George Weston Limited after Ted Creber resigned as president. Nichol managed 140 supermarkets as head of Loblaws' Ontario store operations; while as president of Loblaw Companies Limited, Currie became Nichol's supervisor. In 1980, sales soared to C$5 billion with profits of C$46 million. With the company's streamlined organizational chart in place and new promise, Galen Weston proved that although 44 percent publicly owned, at heart George Weston Limited was still a family business.

Before long Nichol established himself as a visionary merchant. Two years into his job as head of the Ontario stores, he achieved his first high-profile product development success with the March 1978 launch of No Name, a line of generic products in bright-yellow packaging with a plain typeface. The inspiration came from Le Carrefour, a French supermarket giant whose Produits Libres (loosely translated as "free products," meaning without marketing or flashy packaging) proved successful. Loblaws' in-store communications simply conveyed that each product was offered at the lowest price possible, teaching consumers to equate "yellow" with "savings." Around this time the company also launched its new discount store model, the No Frills supermarket, where only Loblaws' private-label products and the top national brands were sold. Within four months of the No Name launch, the line had captured nearly ten percent of supermarket sales across the country.

1980s: Revolutionizing Retailing

Having pioneered the use of private labels with the 1970s launch of No Name in the 1980s, Nichol revolutionized food retailing. At Loblaws, Nichol was beginning to focus exclusively on developing house-brand products. In 1981, Loblaw sold more than 300 No Name products. The impact was huge. For example, before Loblaws launched its own generic brand of diapers, Pampers had an 85 percent share of Loblaws' sales. That dropped to 18 percent after Loblaws launched its private-label business.

Generic-brand products can be sold cheaply because they save on advertising and marketing expenses. To this point, Nichols fired Loblaws' advertising agency on the premise that private label saves C$2 million a year. With that money, he built a company television studio and became an advertising maven, with Loblaws becoming one of the first companies to embrace infomercials. Unlike most supermarket industry executives, who generally remain anonymous, Nichol became a household name as the face of Loblaws—responsible for its financial turnaround, Nichol emerged as a company icon. He even wrote his own commercials. Loblaws also used celebrity spokespeople in its advertising, including William Shatner, a Canadian actor who was well known for his role in the television series *Star Trek*.

By 1983 Nichol was developing the first President's Choice products, inspired by the upscale St. Michael's house brand created by United Kingdom retailer Marks & Spencer, PLC.

Key Dates:

1953: George Weston Limited acquires controlling interest in Loblaw. George C. Metcalf becomes president.
1956: Loblaw Companies Limited is incorporated.
1969: Ted Creber becomes president.
1976: Richard J. Currie becomes president.
1978: David Nichol launches No Name line of generic products.
1983: Loblaws launches President's Choice premium house brand.
1989: Loblaws launches a Green brand of environmentally friendly products.
1994: Wal-Mart arrives in Canada.
1998: Merger with Provigo, Inc. for about C$1.74 billion.
2000: John A. Lederer becomes president.

Loblaws' President's Choice brand promised to be better than higher-priced national brands. The packaging featured an upscale design with striking photography that illustrated product benefits. In 1983 inspired by the Los Angeles-based chain Trader Joe's, Nichol launched a newsletter featuring new products and recipes called *Insider's Report*, which by 1986 reached 5 million readers—more than any other Canadian food publication. In 1984 Currie moved Nichol out of store operations and into full-time product development work as president of Loblaws International Merchants.

In this role Nichol flourished as Canada's most famous "food connoisseur" and a marketing wizard. He traveled the world to bring exotic products back to Loblaws, from Italy to shop for espresso to West Germany for sausage. For instance, after he tasted satay sauce at a restaurant in Bali, he put his staff to work replicating and perfecting the sauce in the company's test kitchen. The result, Memories of Szechwan Peanut Sauce & Dressing, has outsold ketchup in some Loblaw stores. Nichol borrowed the "Memories of" slogan, used to name many subsequent sauces, from a restaurant in London called Memories of China. Pundits credited him with the cleverest trend-spotting for his successes in satisfying baby boomers' gastronomic tastes. In addition, he launched The Decadent Chocolate Chip Cookie, which became Canada's most craved cookie. Industry analysts said that amid the growing gap between wealthy shoppers hot for novelty and price-conscious shoppers hungry for value, Nichol helped Loblaws garner brand loyalty from both. Loblaw International Merchants was Nichol's playground and home base for creative new product development. His tenth anniversary cookbook, which included recipes with President's Choice products, was a best-seller.

By 1984 the chain had increased sales by 72 percent—while net earnings jumped by 225 percent. In June 1989 with perfect trend-hunting pitch, Loblaws launched a Green brand of environmentally friendly products that included foam plates, dishwasher detergent, and motor oil. Sales for the Green goods doubled the company's projections. President's Choice gave Loblaws huge marketing muscle because the line transformed Loblaws' stores from traditional retail outlets into something similar to specialty food shops.

Nichol had made Loblaws a private-label powerhouse. In ten years Nichol developed more than 1,700 unique products for the firm. Total private-label sales for Loblaws, including the upscale President's Choice line and its lower price-point generic sibling, the No Name line, were running about C$1.5 billion per year in Canada. More revealing, one out of every three grocery products that Loblaws' shoppers took home were private labels, and in two of the company's chains, private-label sales were pushing 40 percent. These achievements were notable for the North American market, where national brands had long prevailed.

Meanwhile, the mid-1980s found Canada's highly competitive yearly C$32.5 billion grocery business thinking big. In 1986 Loblaws was on the vanguard of the mega-store movement. The company's definition of a mega-store was 80,000 square feet. Traditionally, a good-sized conventional supermarket is 35,000 to 40,000 square feet. In the Toronto metro area, Loblaws had one mega-store in Pickering and one in the works in Burlington. The company acknowledged that the concept entailed some risk (given that it was spending more money on fewer locations), if the site should turn out to be unprofitable. Since the competing Oshawa Group decided to stick with the traditional supermarket format, Loblaws spent C$370 million in 1987 to expand the chain thorough internal building, rather than acquisitions.

End of the Millennium: The Rise of Superstore Shopping

The 1990s saw transition on a number of fronts. After waging war on manufacturers through his private-label programs, Nichol left the company in 1994. He joined Cott Corporation, a Loblaws supplier that revolutionized the market in 1991 when it launched President's Choice Cola in Canada. Loblaws' private label placed Cott on the map and contributed to the Canadian Coca-Cola Limited's C$45 million loss one year later. Nichol's departure raised a question mark about competition posed by his new venture, which had a private-label marketing arm. In the wake of Nichol's departure, Currie merged Intersave, Loblaws' sourcing and purchasing division, with Loblaws International Merchants, Nichol's old department, and created Loblaws Brands Limited to carry on the private-label campaign. By the time Nichol decided to leave, he had shepherded President's Choice into 12 grocery chains in the United States.

Wal-Mart's 1994 arrival in Canada flashed a warning signal for all retailers. In the mid-1990s, Loblaws was busy planning its Canadian expansion amid record sales and earnings. Loblaws had changed from a traditional supermarket chain to a multifaceted food and general merchandise retailer, with a niche of providing a variety of perishable and nonperishable goods. Competition was mounting from specialty fruit and vegetable stores, shopping clubs, and mass-market retail stores. "We're all fighting for our share of the stomach," said Loblaws' vice-president David Williams.

In Patricia Chisholm's article in the November 9, 1998 issue of *Maclean's*, one shopper, a new mother, criticized the massive size of Loblaws by saying, "I went to the big new Loblaws to shop recently and it took me an hour and a half," she said. "I prefer a smaller place where I can be in and out in five minutes, even if it costs more." The new concept, Real Canadian Superstores, started their rollout in late 2000, bringing the largest operations to 160,000 square feet with increased general merchandise lines while keeping food offerings. The debate raged on in Randy Boswell's article in the February 4, 2001 edition of *The Ottawa Citizen,* in which a new 97,000-square-foot store that opened in November 2000 was shown as emblematic of the battle between quaint neighborhood business and big-box behemoths. Loblaws' multi-service outlets, complete with a pharmacy, wine department, dry cleaning, a President's Choice Bank and even fitness centers, became the company's answer to the threat of Wal-Mart. With the Bentonville, Arkansas category killer on the scene, the North American retail market was treacherous. The end of the old-style Loblaws Groceterias and the rise of the one-stop-shopping superstores were sparked by the March 1988 grand opening of a 126,000-square-foot Wal-Mart Supercenter in Washington, Missouri, which leveled its competitors, including a Loblaws-owned National Supermarket. Loblaws has cited the threat of Wal-Mart and other alternative food channels in its negotiations with unions, suggesting that nonunion competitors enjoy lower costs, which can be passed on to customers. The year 2000 brought labor negotiations within the company, resulting in four strikes, all of which were settled.

In November 1998 in a friendly merger valued at about C$1.74 billion Loblaws acquired Provigo, Inc. of Montreal, which had been attractive because Loblaws had a limited presence in Quebec. The Caisse de depot et placement du Québec (the massive provincial fund manager), Provigo's largest shareholder with a 35 percent stake, had squashed two previous attempts by outsiders to gain market share in Quebec's grocery market. In the most well-known instance, Loblaws made a play in 1989 for Steinberg, the once-prominent but then declining Quebec chain. Steinberg was led into bankruptcy by Michel Gauder, who had been bankrolled by the Caisse in a C$1.3 billion purchase. With the Provigo deal, the largest acquisition in the company's history, Loblaws achieved a strong foothold in Quebec at a good price. Afraid of industry consolidation, competitor Metro-Richelieu condemned the merger when it learned about it, right after the announcement of a merger between Toronto's Oshawa Group and Empire Company's Nova Scotia-based Sobeys chain. In the aftermath of the Provigo deal, antitrust regulators forced Loblaws to sell its Loeb chain to Metro-Richelieu to prevent 75 percent control of the local market. In Brenda Branswell's article in the March 27, 2000 issue of *Maclean's*, a shopper wondered if the negative reaction against Loblaws might be nationalistic, provincial, or parochial.

In June 2000 with C$12.9 billion in sales, and 1,116 stores, Loblaws received designation from the trade journal *MMR* as one of the Top 10 world's best mass-market retailers. The criteria included size, sustained sales and earnings growth, global impact, marketing excitement, ambitiously realized expansion plans, and proven success over the long term. Loblaws achieved note for its global reputation as a leader in innovation, particularly in the area of retail technology. Scanners introduced in the 1980s to speed customers through checkouts gave stores the power to analyze the profitability of shelf space to the square inch. This knowledge gave muscle to Nichol's claim that President's Choice, priced below national brands, brought retailers bigger returns.

Since 1998 the President's Choice (PC) label has moved beyond its roots as a product-oriented brand to embrace financial services. The President's Choice Bank, a new subsidiary of Loblaws, developed the PC Financial MasterCard, a no-annual-fee credit card that in March 2001 was launched in British Columbia. The card has a loyalty program through which customers can earn PC points on purchases that are redeemable for free groceries in Loblaw Companies Limited stores. Closer to its roots, in 2001, Loblaws introduced more than 200 President's Choice certified organic products within fresh produce, meat, and grocery items.

In 2000, Loblaw Companies Limited surpassed the C$20 billion sales mark for the first time ever. At the end of the year, the company announced that Richard J. Currie stepped down as president of Loblaw Companies after almost 25 years as president. John A. Lederer was assuming the lead of the management team. At that time, the company was planning to continue its substantial capital investment program, with new retail outlets across Canada; inventory in warehouses and distribution networks and systems; and maintain its reputation for innovation and low-cost operations. Year 2000 sales increased C$1.3 billion, or 7 percent, to C$20.1 billion with healthy growth. In February 2001, George Weston Limited became North America's second biggest bakery with a C$2.7 billion acquisition of Bestfoods Baking Company, which was spun off by the Unilever Group. Weston, the maker of Wonder Bread, outbid Sara Lee Corporation of Chicago. In the spring of 2000, Weston was considering decreasing its 63 percent majority interest in Loblaws by 5 percent to focus more on its baking business.

Principal Subsidiaries

Atlantic Wholesalers Ltd., Sackville, New Brunswick; Fortino's Supermarket Ltd., Hamilton, Ontario; Kelly, Douglas & Company, Limited, Calgary, Alberta; Loblaws Brands Limited; Loblaws Properties Limited, Ontario; Loblaws Quebec Limited; Loblaws, Inc.; Loblaws Supermarkets Limited, Toronto, Ontario; National Grocers Co. Ltd., Toronto, Ontario; President's Choice Bank; Westfair Foods Ltd., Calgary, Alberta; Zehr's Markets, Inc., Cambridge, Ontario.

Principal Competitors

Empire Co. (Sobeys); Metro-Richelieu; Wal-Mart.

Further Reading

Boswell, Randy, "Where Goes the Neighbourhood?," *Ottawa Citizen*, February 4, 2001, p. C5.

Branswell, Brenda, "A Quebec Judge Orders a Supermarket's Demolition," *Maclean's*, March 27, 2000, p. 50.

"Bringing Order to a Billion-Dollar Empire," *Business Week*, September 8, 1975, p. 50.

Burnett, Thane, "What to Do with Leaning Tower of Essa?: Uncertainty Faces Allston Landmark," *Toronto Sun*, May 6, 2001, p. 26.

"Canadian Grocers: Loblaw Anonymous," *Economist,* September 19, 1981, p. 78.

"Cereal Killers," *The Economist,* December 4, 1993, p. 7.

Chisholm, Patricia, ''The Hungry Giants,'' *Maclean's*, November 9, 1998, p. 49.

''Consolidation, Canadian Style,'' *Snack Food & Wholesale Bakery*, February 2001, p. 8.

''Currie Raking in the Dough,'' *Gazette (Montreal),* April 8, 1999, p. C3.

Delean, Paul, ''In the Land of the Giants,'' *Gazette (Montreal)*, March 22, 1999, p. F1.

Delima, Flavian, ''Career Monitor Storytelling Connects People to Their Purpose,'' *Toronto Star*, August 28, 1999.

Deverell, John, ''Firm Eyes $ Billion Price-Display Niche,'' *Toronto Star*, May 28, 1995, p. D5.

——, ''Grocers Shopping Like There's No Tomorrow,'' *Toronto Star*, July 5, 1998, p. D1.

——, ''Loblaw Planning Canadian Expansion,'' *Toronto Star*, April 27, 1995, p. D3.

——, ''Loblaw Pushes Weston Ahead,'' *Toronto Star*, May 8, 1997, p. D2.

''Executive Changes,'' *New York Times Company*, November 15, 2000, p. C10.

''Four Named to Hall of Fame,'' *Toronto Star,* January 25, 1999.

Fox, Linda A., ''The Bread and Butter Wars,'' *Toronto Sun*, November 1, 1998, p. 54.

Foxman, Stuart, ''Megawattage: 30 Years of the Watt Design Group,'' *Strategy*, June 9, 1997, p. 38.

''Grocery Chains Bet Large Size Will Conquer All in Store Wars,'' *Toronto Star*, May 15, 1986, p. E1.

Hemeon, Jade, ''Spotting the Trends,'' *Toronto Star*, October 20, 1991, p. F1.

Hill, Bert, ''Supermarkets Built by Loebs Still Prospering,'' *Ottawa Citizen*, September 27, 1999, p. D3.

Kidd, Kenneth, ''Loblaw to Spend $370 Million in '87 to Expand Chain,'' *Toronto Star*, April 30, 1987, p. E12.

Kim, Soo, ''Weston Aims to Be Major U.S. Baker,'' *Toronto Star*, posted May 9, 2001, http://www.thestar.com.

Kingston, Anne, *The Edible Man: Dave Nichol, President's Choice & the Making of Popular Taste*, McFarland & Associates, Inc, 1995.

''Leon Weinstein, 81, Loblaws President,'' *Toronto Star,* June 1, 1989, p. A10.

''Loblaws Wants More Flexibility from Unions,'' *Toronto Star*, posted May 2, 2001, http://www.thestar.com.

Macissac, Merle, ''One Flew into the Cuckoo's Nest,'' *Canadian Business*, June 1996, p. 104.

Mallick, Heather, ''Dave's Choice: How Dave Nichol Made Us into Low-Rent Gourmets,'' *Toronto Sun*, p. M21.

Maney, Kevin, ''Going for the 'Green,' '' *USA Today*, August 23, 1989, p. 1B.

''MMR Profiles the 10 Best Mass Market Retailers,'' *MMR*, June 26, 2000, p. 55.

''Moving to Quebec,'' *Maclean's,* June 17, 1996, p. 33.

''National Tea's Loss Is A&P's Gain,'' *Business Week,* October 18, 1976, p. 39.

''Passages,'' *Maclean's,* November 23, 1998, p. 28.

Prentice, Michael, ''Grocery Buyers Are Shopping Around,'' *Ottawa Citizen*, July 29, 1997, p. B8.

''Profit Rises at George Weston,'' *Toronto Star*, May 9, 2001.

Quinn, Jennifer, ''George Metcalf, 94, Leader in Life, Business,'' *The Toronto Star*, November 12, 1998, p. D5.

Robin, Laura, ''Coming Soon to a Store Near You.. . .'' *Ottawa Citizen*, November 5, 1997, p. E8.

Shalom, Francois, ''Loblaw Bags Provigo at Last,'' *Gazette*, December 1, 1998, p. E1.

——, ''Loblaw Gets Provigo's Nod,'' *Gazette (Montreal)*, November 17, 1998, p. E1.

Smyth, Julie, ''Cott Cult Leads the Cola Revolution,'' *Scotsman*, December 28, 1994, p. 19.

Spears, John, ''Splurge in Spending Marks Loblaw Push into Combo Stores,'' *Toronto Star*, April 30, 1986, p. C3.

Steed, Judy, ''Dave Nichol: Too Good to Be True?,'' *Toronto Star*, January 23, 1993, p. A1.

——''Memories of Dave Nichol,'' *Ottawa Citizen*, January 31, 1993, p. E4.

Stevenson, Mark, ''Global Gourmet,'' *Canadian Business*, July 1993, p. 22.

——, ''The Hired Hand Waves Goodbye,'' *Canadian Business*, August 1994, p. 12.

Stroud, Jerri, ''Schnucks Excited; Some Worry; Grocery Deal Feeds Debate,'' *St. Louis Post-Dispatch*, March 12, 1995, p. 1E.

Summerfield, Patti, ''Choice Move at Loblaw,'' *Strategy*, October 17, 1994. p. 1.

——, ''Loblaw Tries Loyalty Card in One-Store Test,'' *Strategy*, May 29, 1995, p. 1.

Theoblad, Steven, ''How to Catch a Merger Wave,'' *Toronto Star,* November 19, 1998.

Thompson, Allan, ''Analysts Expect Gaucher Victory in Steinberg War,'' *Toronto Star,* July 25, 1989, p. C3.

Wade Rose, Barbara, ''David Nichol; Super Market Man,'' *Maclean's*, November 3, 1986, p. 6.

'' 'We Just Grew like Topsy, Acquiring Bits and Pieces All over the Place,' '' *Business Week,* September 8, 1975.

''Weston Buys Bestfoods,'' *Maclean's,* March 5, 2001, p. 48.

''Weston Posts Loss,'' *Business Week,* April 11, 1977, p. 40.

Zlomislic, Erica, ''What Went Wrong? Tip Top Repositions Too Far, Too Fast,'' *Strategy*, May 25, 1995, p. 1.

—Michelle Feder

Lynch Corporation

401 Theodore Fremd Avenue
Rye, New York 10580
U.S.A.
Telephone: (914) 921-7601
Fax: (914) 921-6410
Web site: http://www.lynchcorp.com

Public Company
Incorporated: 1928
Employees: 435
Sales: $219.19 million (2000)
Stock Exchanges: American
Ticker Symbol: LGL
NAIC: 333298 All Other Industrial Machinery Manufacturing; 333993 Packaging Machinery Manufacturing; 334419 Other Electronic Component Manufacturing; 322222 Coated and Laminated Paper Manufacturing (pt)

Lynch Corporation is described by its CEO and chairman, well-known money manager Mario Gabelli, as a leveraged buyout (LBO) fund in public form. Since Gabelli gained control of the company in 1985, Lynch has expanded beyond the manufacture of glass-forming machinery and quartz crystals to become a diversified holding company with three main subsidiaries.

Lynch Systems, Inc. continues the company's traditional glass business, designing and producing a broad range of manufacturing equipment used in two primary markets: cathode ray tube (CRT) displays for computer monitors and televisions, and household consumer products such as ovenware, giftware, and tableware. The subsidiary is located in Bainbridge, Georgia, and also has a European presence through Lynch-Amav, a joint venture with a German company that primarily provides engineering services to the glass industry.

Another Lynch subsidiary, Spinnaker Industries, Inc., makes adhesive-backed label stock. With headquarters in Troy, Ohio, Spinnaker Industries itself has three wholly owned subsidiaries: Spinnaker Coating, Inc., Spinnaker Coating-Maine, Inc., and Entoleter, Inc. It is the largest supplier of pressure sensitive postage stamp stock used by the United States Postal Service. The Spinnaker subsidiaries also produce approximately 80 percent of Lynch's total revenues.

The third primary subsidiary, M-tron Industries, Inc., produces crystals that are used primarily in a variety of communications products to control the frequency of signals. Its headquarters is located in Yankton, South Dakota. In recent years, Lynch has also spun off a number of businesses: Lynch Interactive, which acquired the company's telecommunications and broadcast interests along with The Morgan Group, which transports vehicles and mobile homes through a network of independent drivers; Tremont Advisors, providing investment products as well as advisory services; and East/West Communications, holders of five valuable wireless telephone licenses in such areas as Los Angeles and Washington, D.C.

Corporate Ancestry: 1917–70s

The history of the Lynch Corporation can be traced to Anderson, Indiana, and the 1917 foundation of the Lynch Glass Machinery Company, makers of machines to blow glass bottles. Lynch was then incorporated in the state of Indiana in 1928 to acquire Lynch Glass Machinery plus another Anderson business, Dice Machine Company. Lynch then acquired Miller Mold & Manufacturing of Columbus, Ohio, during the 1930s and became involved in producing glass presses. Another major part of today's Lynch Systems also has a long history in the glass industry. Miller Hydro, acquired in 1984, was started in 1914 in Bainbridge, Georgia. Miller Hydro made bottle washers for soft drink and beer producers. That expertise was then transferred to the manufacture of other types of machines, such as case packers, which became the company's main business after the market for bottle washers was eliminated in North America. Over the years, Lynch made a number of other industrial machines, such as butter wrapping machines, ice cream bar machines, and candy bar machines. Even after discontinuing these lines, Lynch was able to make money by providing parts that could be priced at a high margin.

In 1960, Lynch became involved in producing phonographs when it acquired the Symphonic Electronic Corporation. The

> **Company Perspectives:**
>
> *''The Environment I see before us should provide ample opportunity for Lynch to Grow. Declining multiples, especially for basic, 'boring' industrial companies (the kind we love), will create an attractive pool of acquisition candidates; declining interest rates and improved liquidity in the banking and high yield markets will eventually create plenty of financing; and, the new accounting rules on goodwill should help make the fruits of one's efforts look even more rewarding.'' —Mario J. Gabelli, chairman*

company added another division when it acquired Cox Instrument Corporation in 1963. Apparently glass and packing machinery was not a good fit with electronics, because in 1964 the company was forced to cede control to Curtiss-Wright Corp., an aviation and electronics company, which bought $5.5 million in 12-year notes, which could be converted into stock, and warrants to purchase additional shares in Lynch. Potentially Curtiss-Wright would be able to gain 51 percent of Lynch's stock, but it already controlled the board. Under terms of the deal, Curtiss-Wright could nominate seven directors to Lynch's 13-member board.

Although in 1971 and 1972 Symphonic Electronic accounted for 65 percent of Lynch's revenues, it was also the reason the company suffered a net loss of more than $5 million. Management decided to discontinue the operation, selling off its inventory, equipment, and other assets. In 1976 Lynch acquired M-tron Industries for approximately $5.3 million. Unfortunately, the primary market of M-tron's quartz crystals, the CB radio market, suffered an almost immediate setback. The Federal Communications Commission decided to permit CB radios to increase from 23 channels to 40, effecting a change in technology that would reduce the number of needed quartz crystals. Instead of 14, each CB would now only need two or three crystals, resulting in a major reduction in orders for M-Tron. Although Lynch would still report a net profit of $1.4 million on sales of $18.6 million in 1976, the permanent loss of business at M-tron forced the company to take a $2 million write-off in 1977.

Gabelli to the Rescue: 1985

In the early 1980s Lynch sold off its Cox Instrument interests to Ametek, Inc., for approximately $1.65 million, then acquired Miller Hydro for $1.257 million. It was also during this period that Mario Gabelli began to buy the company's stock, which was trading between $6–$10 on the American Stock Exchange. Lynch had originally been listed in 1946 on the New York Curb Exchange, forerunner of the American Stock Exchange (AMEX). Gabelli recognized that Lynch carried potential with little risk and soon bought more than 20 percent of the company for the portfolios he managed. In the meantime, the head of Curtiss-Wright, T. Roland Berner, had taken a major loss buying Western Union stock. When Gabelli learned that Berner intended to sell his 22 percent stake in Lynch, he decided to buy it, rather than face the uncertainty of new ownership. In 1985 the money manager now found himself at the head of a company that, if broken down and liquidated, would realize little more than the $7 million Gabelli had invested in it. It made more sense to try to grow the business and use the corporation as another investment tool. Unlike Warren Buffett, another money manager who found himself as the chief executive of an operating company (textile manufacturer Berkshire Hathaway), which he essentially used as an investment fund, Gabelli opted to buy companies or interests in companies through Lynch.

Gabelli, the son of first generation Italian-American parents, was the quintessential self-made man. Born and raised in the Bronx, where he spoke Italian before learning English, he received a scholarship to Fordham University in New York City. ''As a good Italian boy,'' he said in a *Money* profile, ''you were supposed to be a doctor, a lawyer or an accountant, and accounting seemed practical.'' Aside from being practical, he was also driven to succeed. While maintaining high grades, which would lead to Gabelli graduating summa cum laude in 1965, he also held several school offices and dabbled in business to earn spending money. In addition to caddying he organized student trips to Bermuda and the Caribbean. During a New York blackout, Gabelli sold flashlights out of the trunk of his car.

By the time Gabelli attended the Columbia Graduate School of Business he was already investing in the stock market. It was at Columbia that he would become a firm believer in the theory of value investing, which held that stocks should be valued by what a prospective buyer would be willing to pay for the company. Essentially that meant all of a company's component parts needed to be priced. Gabelli also learned to look for a catalyst, such as the possibility of a takeover, that could then unlock the company's hidden value and result in windfall profits for shareholders. After receiving his M.B.A. at Columbia in 1967, he learned research skills at the Wall Street firm of Loeb Rhoades & Co., where as an analyst he initially covered the auto parts industry and, later, media and broadcasting and conglomerates. When he went to work for William D. Witter Inc. in 1975, Gabelli already enjoyed a reputation as a hard worker and a developing mystique for picking undervalued stocks. It was becoming apparent that he would not be content to remain an analyst much longer. In 1976 Witter was acquired by Drexel Burnham Lambert, and a year later Gabelli decided to strike out on his own, setting up an institutional research boutique operation funded by $100,000 of his own money and a similar amount from outside investors. Contacts he had made at more than 100 institutions allowed Gabelli to survive on research business until his money management company, Gamco, was able to take off. By 1981 he was managing $31 million for 81 accounts. A year later he reached a new level when his pension business signed Honeywell as a client, which opened the door to other major corporations. By the end of the 1980s Gabelli would run a brokerage, as well as three mutual funds. His pension business would manage $2.5 billion for 700 clients. Gabelli was essentially a one-man band, known to work 17-hour days, and still willing to do the nuts and bolts researching. He spent considerable time on the road making some 50 personal visits to companies each year. He was also becoming something of a celebrity, a regular contributor to *Barron's* Roundtable, and an occasional guest on TV business shows. As his funds racked up impressive results, he became known as ''Super Mario,'' an image that helped to bring in even more business.

Key Dates:

1917: Lynch Glass Machinery Company is founded.
1928: Lynch Corporation is incorporated in Indiana.
1964: Curtiss-Wright gains controlling interest in the company.
1985: Money manager Mario Gabelli acquires controlling interest in Lynch.
1986: Gabelli becomes Lynch's chairman and chief executive officer.
1994: Spinnaker Industries, a manufacturer of adhesive-backed materials, is formed as a subsidiary.
1999: Lynch Interactive Corporation is spun off.

Despite being stretched thin by his many commitments, Gabelli became the chairman and chief executive officer of Lynch in 1986, although he tried to delegate most of the day-to-day responsibilities. As a first step in diversifying Lynch's operations, Gabelli raised $23 million for Lynch through convertible bonds. In 1986 he then established Lynch Capital Corporation, a securities brokerage, followed by Lynch Asset Management Company, to which he added the acquisition of Tremont Partners, a Connecticut-based investment management consulting firm. Tremont would then launch a number of investment funds and acquire other money management firms. Gabelli also purchased a 20 percent stake in a Rock Island, Illinois, television station and formed Lynch Entertainment. Furthermore in 1987, he bolstered Lynch's manufacturing segment by acquiring an 83 percent interest in Safety Railway Service corporation, makers of milling machines, heating equipment, and air pollution control equipment. Perhaps of equal attraction was the $3.8 million in cash and marketable securities the company held. Lynch would expand into the service sector in 1988 by acquiring Morgan Drive Away, a transporter of mobile homes and recreational vehicles that would form the basis for The Morgan Group.

In 1989 Gabelli and Lynch moved into the telecommunications sector, establishing Lynch Telephone and buying Western New Mexico Telephone Company. In the next few years, the subsidiary would add other systems, including Inter-Community Telephone, Cuba City Telephone Exchange Company, Belmont Telephone Company, Bretton Woods Telephone Company, and J.B.N. Telephone Company. In 1996 Lynch purchased some 1,400 lines from U.S. West. A year later it acquired Upper Peninsula Telephone Company and spun off East/West Communications. In 1999 Lynch also acquired Iowa's Central Scott Telephone Company.

The Morgan Group added to its Morgan Drive Away business by acquiring the assets of Transamerican Carriers in 1993, followed by Low Transportation, Inc. In 1995 Morgan acquired the assets of Transfer Drivers, Inc., which relocated rental vehicles for customers that included Ryder Systems, Budget Rentals, and Penske Truck Leasing. It also delivered new equipment for customers such as Utilmaster, Grumman Olson, and Bluebird Bus. By 1995 Morgan companies had created a network of 1,800 independent owner-operators with 1,000 part-time drive-away employees. It had 108 offices in 36 states. Furthermore, Morgan Finance provided insurance and financial services to the owner-operators.

Spinnaker Industries arose out of a 1994 reorganization of Safety Railway Service Corporation after Spinnaker Ohio was purchased, which became the Spinnaker Coating subsidiary. Spinnaker Industries was then augmented with purchases that included Brown-Bridge Industries and Alco Standard Corporation. The Spinnaker Coating—Maine subsidiary was created when Brown-Bridge was combined with the acquisition of S.D. Warren Company and its pressure sensitive label stock business. Entoleter, the third Spinnaker Industries subsidiary, had been part of the Spinnaker Ohio acquisition. In 1999 Lynch would opt to focus its attention on the adhesive-backed paper industry, and sold off the industrial tape operations of Spinnaker Industries.

Challenges During the 1990s

In 1990 Gabelli's reputation began to lose some of its luster. His funds posted unprecedented declines and his method of value investing was being called into question, as was his tendency to act as a one-man firm. His connection with Lynch also led to questions about a conflict of interest and subsequent trouble with the Securities and Exchange Commission. Although the SEC did not charge Gabelli or his funds with insider trading, it questioned a 1992 situation in which Lynch securities were traded shortly before financial results were released and Lynch's stock jumped 28 percent in five days. Eventually Gabelli would agree to pay a $100,000 fine to settle the matter, an amount which he characterized as ''Draconian.'' Essentially Gabelli was found to be lax in having appropriate policies in place to guard against insider trading. Gabelli also agreed to allow an independent consultant to review his companies' policies, and announced that his funds would no longer invest in Lynch.

Gabelli's celebrity, which had launched him into the top ranks of money managers, now became something of a burden. Instead of attention and adoration he was receiving scrutiny and criticism. A 1997 *Wall Street Journal* article noted that Gabelli's self-promotion no longer brought in the same number of clients, his funds were no longer producing stellar results, and his method of value investing had simply gone out of style. His energy that had once been portrayed as a strength was now eclipsed by the suggestion that he was not able to build bench strength in his organization. Office intrigue was also aired in public, as infighting was blamed for stalled growth. In particular, Gabelli was accused of locking one of his fund managers out of her office and then withholding pay.

In 1998 Gabelli moved his operations to Rye, New York. Lynch underwent a number of changes that resulted in a reshuffling of businesses, as well as a couple of years of poor earnings. In 1999 Lynch Interactive was spun off, taking with it Lynch's cable television and broadcast television interests, telecommunications operations, as well as The Morgan Group. The company also began the process to spin off Entoleter, which manufactured industrial process equipment and no longer fit in with Spinnaker's emphasis on the adhesive-backed paper label stock business. Troubles with Spinnaker prevented the spinoff from occurring during 2000 and resulted in a restructuring of the business and a cost reduction program. An effort to sell part of M-tron through an initial public offering also failed to materialize.

Lynch showed steady growth in the late 1990s, with its stock showing appreciable gains. The company, which generated revenues of $167 million in 1996, grew sales to more than $219 million in 2000, but the company posted just $85,000 in operating profits in 1999 and a loss of $5 million in 2000. Gabelli appeared to be trying to make Lynch into a traditional public company with a more narrow focus of activity, rather than having it serve as an adjunct to his investment funds, but as long as he was the chairman of the board it would be his name and celebrity that would remain the center of attention.

Principal Subsidiaries

Lynch Systems, Inc.; M-tron Industries, Inc.; Spinnaker Industries, Inc.

Principal Competitors

Avery Dennison Corporation; Bemis Company, Inc.; CTS Corporation; Minnesota Mining & Manufacturing Company; Saronix; Vectron International.

Further Reading

Anderson, Mark H., ''Gabelli Group Settles Charges by SEC That Its Insider-Trading Policy Is Lax,'' *Wall Street Journal,* December 9, 1994, p. B2.

Clements, Jonathan, ''Berkshire Hathaway II?,'' *Forbes,* July 24, 1989, p. 40.

Edgerton, Jerry, ''Money Profile: Value-Oriented Mario Gabelli Still Invests by the Numbers,'' *Money,* August 1986, p. 132.

Robaton, Anna, ''For Gabelli, A Dark Side of Moonlighting: Fund Manager's Other Company Is Underperformer,'' *Crain's New York Business,* June 21, 1999, p. 16.

Rohrer, Julie, ''Cashing in at the Wake,'' *Institutional Investor,* January 1985, p. 67.

——, ''Money Management: What Makes Mario Run?,'' *Institutional Investor,* March 1989, p. 94.

Sandler, Linda, ''Heard on the Street: Gabelli Funds Are Spinning Their Wheels,'' *Wall Street Journal,* July 7, 1997, p. C2.

Sheeran, Lisa R., ''Narrowing the Spread,'' *Inc.,* December 1985, p. 158.

White, James A., '' 'Super Mario' Is Weathering First Setback for His Empire,'' *Wall Street Journal,* February 15, 1991, p. C1.

—Ed Dinger

MAXIMUS, Inc.

11419 Sunset Hills Rd.
Reston, Virginia 20190
U.S.A.
Telephone: (703) 251-8500
Fax: (703) 251-8240
Web site: http://www.maxinc.com

Public Company
Incorporated: 1975
Employees: 4,200
Sales: $399.16 million (2000)
Stock Exchanges: New York
Ticker Symbol: MMS
NAIC: 541611 Administrative Management and General Management Consulting Services

MAXIMUS, Inc. is one of the leading private sector companies that provides program management, information technology, and consulting services to state and local government agencies. Located in Reston, Virginia, MAXIMUS has projects in nearly every state, as well as a number of foreign countries. The company's operations are divided into three groups. The Government Operations Group has grown out of the work that MAXIMUS has chiefly focused on since its founding in 1975: running welfare-to-work projects, managed care enrollment, and other government health and human services programs. The company's Government Consulting Group provides support to government agencies in such areas as information technology, program evaluation, and financial management. The Government Systems Group offers proprietary software and advanced computer systems solutions to public agencies. Since welfare reform legislation passed in 1996, MAXIMUS has dramatically increased its revenues, but not without generating a good deal of controversy. The company received unwanted publicity in Los Angeles, Milwaukee, and especially in New York City, providing ready ammunition for critics who not only question how MAXIMUS does business but attack the very principles that the company espouses.

Turning to the Private Sector: Government in the 1960s

The concept of a private company supporting a government agency was pioneered by Ross Perot and his Electronic Data Systems Corporation (EDS), which was originally created to take over the data processing operations of private businesses. When Congress passed Medicare legislation in 1965, resulting in an enormous amount of paperwork that needed to be processed, the concept was applied to the federal government. Medicare and Medicaid processing proved so lucrative for EDS that within three years it accounted for nearly 25 percent of the company's revenues. By 1977 that amount grew to nearly 40 percent. As a result, Perot would become immensely wealthy and famous enough to twice run for the presidency of the United States.

The founder of MAXIMUS, David V. Mastran, earned an undergraduate degree from West Point in 1965, followed a year later by a master's degree in industrial engineering from Stanford University. He then spent seven years in the air force, including a one-year tour in Vietnam, before returning to school to earn a doctorate in operations research from George Washington University in 1973. He briefly worked at the Pentagon as an air force researcher, then transferred his skills to the old federal Department of Health, Education, and Welfare. He managed contracts and grants and essentially tried to impose discipline on social welfare programs. According to a *Business Week* profile, Mastran was unable to find a private company that understood welfare programs well enough to help the government instill efficiency, and so he decided to quit his position and start a business to fill that need. He told the *Washington Post*, "I decided I couldn't fix this from the inside." In 1975, following a short stint working for the consulting firm of Arthur Young, Mastran founded MAXIMUS with $12,000 and began working alone out of his home. He chose the MAXIMUS name as a reflection of the company's mission: to maximize government efficiency.

The first work for MAXIMUS was a $3,000 contract to assist in the processing of military health-care claims, followed by a $15,000 job in New Hampshire to create statistical profiles of fraudulent Medicaid recipients, but MAXIMUS soon had difficulty with one of its early contracts. Hired by the federal Office of Child Support Enforcement to increase payments by

Company Perspectives:

This company and our success are measured by how we make individual lives better. Time and again, MAXIMUS has continued to deliver on the promise of our mission. Looking ahead, our commitment is just as strong.

deadbeat parents, MAXIMUS developed a system that would target people with high incomes. The agency, however, maintained that the law did not allow for such selectivity and opted not to renew the contract.

Generally MAXIMUS maintained a low profile as it began to collect bigger fees and add employees to handle its mounting workload. In 1984 the company received an important contract from New York City, when it was hired to help reduce welfare fraud. Appalled by the condition of the welfare centers he visited, Mastran began a motivational campaign to improve the morale of welfare workers, awarding cake and trophies to those who were successful at reducing fraud. He said that the experience confirmed his view that a private company was better suited to motivate employees than the government. ''Government workers are not paid on the basis of performance,'' he was quoted as saying. ''I can reward performance; government can't do that.''

In 1988 MAXIMUS signed a major five-year, $49 million contract with Los Angeles County to run its portion of a state welfare-to-work program called GAIN (Greater Avenues for Independence), the first attempt to privatize a welfare system. Rather than just serving in a support capacity, MAXIMUS was essentially replacing government. The company determined whether someone was eligible for welfare, prompting a lawsuit by the Service Employees International Union that contended that only civil service employees had the legal right to make such decisions. Social critics also questioned the inherent conflict of a for-profit company engaged in public work: Would MAXIMUS focus its efforts on the clients that could be more easily placed in jobs, thus padding its success rate at the expense of the people who needed their help the most?

Supporters of MAXIMUS could, at the very least, point to the improved conditions of the welfare environment. Welfare clients, called ''participants'' by MAXIMUS, found softly lit, carpeted, and nicely decorated waiting rooms where they were offered cookies and coffee. Rather than waiting for hours and being subjected to the indifference of receptionists and case workers, they were quickly escorted to private rooms where they could talk to interviewers and watch videos. Moreover, the case managers, handling much less of a workload than their county counterparts, were given an incentive to help clients find work. They received $100 of a $150 bonus paid to MAXIMUS for every client that remained in a job for six months or worked enough to reduce an Aid to Families with Dependent Children (AFDC) grant by at least 50 percent. It was this conflicting view of MAXIMUS, as either innovative savior or calculating opportunist, that would repeatedly surface in the coming years.

By 1990 MAXIMUS was generating $19 million in annual revenues. With state and local governments cutting budgets and increasingly turning to the private sector for help, the company, working in just four states, appeared poised to experience substantial growth. It touted how much money it saved the government, and boasted of its superior computer systems and flexible staff that operated without the hindrance of bureaucratic red tape. Although critics challenged the accuracy of the savings, citing the lack of independent verification, no one could question that MAXIMUS and other private sector companies were now becoming established players.

MAXIMUS experienced a number of problems, however. In 1993 data entry errors in Arizona resulted in the state refunding $250,000 in child support payments. In 1994 Mississippi froze a contract with MAXIMUS when costs actually doubled after the company took over child support collection. Also in 1994 MAXIMUS had problems in West Virginia after it hired a consultant who was a supervisor of a project on which it was bidding. The company claimed that it had been misled by the employee. Although MAXIMUS was never charged with wrongdoing, it decided to withdraw its bid. These problems notwithstanding, MAXIMUS continued to grow. It exceeded $50 million in revenues in 1995, then almost doubled that amount in one year, generating $103.1 million in 1996.

1996 Welfare Reform Legislation Spurs Growth

A watershed moment for MAXIMUS and other private sector program management companies came in August 1996 when President Clinton signed into law the Personal Responsibility and Work Opportunity Act. This welfare reform legislation essentially rewrote the rules. AFDC money was now allocated to states in block grants, and requirements that state or local government agencies be involved in running the program were eliminated. Privatization of welfare-to-work programs funded by federal money was now given a free reign. Wisconsin wasted little time in awarding its business to private contractors. For a number of years its governor, Tommy Thompson, had been granted federal waivers to institute experimental welfare reform programs. Since 1987 when he took office, Thompson claimed that Wisconsin had reduced the number of people on welfare more than the other 49 states combined. In April 1996 he signed a law that would require all able-bodied parents to work in exchange for AFDC money. The program, called Wisconsin Works, or W-2, was put on hold pending federal welfare reform legislation, but as soon as President Clinton signed the bill, the state was quick to act. In September 1996, W-2 went into effect, limiting aid to welfare recipients to two consecutive years or a lifetime total of five years, with the goal of completely eliminating welfare within several years. A year later, MAXIMUS and four nonprofit companies would divide Milwaukee's 24,000 welfare clients.

In 1997 Mastran decided to take MAXIMUS public, prompted, he said, by an offer of more than $100 million from ''a major blue-chip company.'' The $84 million offering, with an initial price of $16 per share, netted Mastran almost $25 million and other executives of the company an additional $20 million. MAXIMUS used the remaining money to fund expansion, making a number of acquisitions in 1998. The company purchased San Antonio-based Spectrum Consulting Group for approximately $19.3 million. Spectrum provided information technology services. MAXIMUS then acquired David M. Griffith & Associates (DMG) of Northbrook, Illinois, for approximately $31.5

Key Dates:

1975: Company is founded.
1984: Contract is signed to help reduce welfare fraud in New York City.
1988: Contract is signed to run state welfare-to-work program in Los Angeles County.
1996: Personal Responsibility and Work Opportunity Act is signed by President Bill Clinton.
1997: Company completes initial public offering of stock.

million. DMG also did consulting work for government agencies, focusing on executive recruiting and human resources planning. The next MAXIMUS acquisition was a $32 million stock swap for Carrera Consulting Group of Sacramento, California, a software provider for government agencies.

Also in 1998, MAXIMUS purchased Phoenix Planning and Evaluation Ltd. out of Rockville, Maryland, for stock worth around $7 million. Phoenix specialized in smart cards and electronic benefits transfer systems that were becoming a popular way for government agencies to distribute payments to clients. Overall, MAXIMUS was filling out its business so that it could offer a full range of services to its government customers. To solidify its cash position and fuel further acquisitions, MAXIMUS made a secondary offering of stock in 1998, selling 4.2 million shares and raising more than $136 million.

Although MAXIMUS was well received by investors, the company came under fire from other circles. In 1997 the company received a $12.4 million contract to manage Connecticut's child-care services for women enrolled in a welfare-to-work program, but quickly experienced problems. After only three months the company was a month late in processing most of the clients' checks to pay for child care, and many welfare recipients had trouble receiving approval for benefits. MAXIMUS upgraded its computer and phone systems and added staff to fix the problems, but when it determined that it would lose $500,000 a month on the contract, the company threatened to terminate the program unless it received more money. The state agreed to increase the contract by an additional $6 million. MAXIMUS maintained that the state had not fully explained the magnitude of the project, but critics contended otherwise. A spokesperson for the Connecticut State Employees Association put it bluntly: ''In terms of service here, they've been abysmal. They underbid, over-promised and they didn't deliver.'' The company's fiercest opponents, state employee unions and welfare advocates, would soon have even more of an opportunity to criticize MAXIMUS.

In Milwaukee, MAXIMUS was hit with a number of Equal Employment Opportunity Commission (EEOC) complaints from former employees who claimed they were passed over for promotions because of race and gender during a restructuring of the company in early 1999. MAXIMUS vigorously denied the charges, which at the very least were a public relations headache, especially since the company was expanding its welfare reform model to Arizona, California, Delaware, and Maryland, as well as being eager to tap into the biggest prize of all, New York City and its pool of 600,000 welfare recipients.

Perhaps even more troubling for the company's reputation to come out of the EEOC complaints was the revelation that its subsidiary MaxStaff Employment Services received the first chance to hire the most qualified job seekers in the W-2 program. Aside from its usual critics, MAXIMUS now had Milwaukee staffing firms denouncing its practices. Former MAXIMUS employees in their EEOC complaints said that the company tested and screened W-2 participants, and those deemed employable—with skills, education, and no criminal record—were set aside for MaxStaff, who would then put them in temp-to-hire positions. Furthermore, the former employees maintained that in some cases MAXIMUS paid MaxStaff to place people. MAXIMUS denied that any money changed hands between MAXIMUS and MaxStaff and characterized the former employees as ''angry with us because they were unable to meet our performance goals.''

Under Fire in New York in 2000

The company's Milwaukee operation led to even more bad press in New York City in 2000 when the city comptroller, Alan Hevesi, questioned a $104 million welfare-to-work contract, renewable for an additional $104 million, that MAXIMUS had been awarded without going through the formal bidding process. Because New York City Mayor Rudolph Giuliani championed the contracts and was running for the U.S. Senate, a situation further complicated by Hevesi's own apparent ambition to seek the mayoralty, MAXIMUS suddenly found itself in the middle of a political imbroglio and under the microscope of the national media. What the press revealed about MAXIMUS, on almost a daily basis, was nothing less than a public relations nightmare.

From the outset it was clear that MAXIMUS, unlike companies that would be invited to bid on the welfare-to-work project, had several months' advance notice. The city's welfare commissioner, Jason A. Turner, had been the architect of Wisconsin's welfare reform and had personal ties to MAXIMUS. A friend of Turner, Tony Kearney, was paid by MAXIMUS but served as a consultant to the city, and was assigned an office on the same floor as Turner. In this role Kearney was able to sit in on meetings with MAXIMUS competitors who were also bidding on welfare-to-work contracts.

To add to the Wisconsin–New York connections, it was revealed that Turner's wife met with the head of the MAXIMUS Wisconsin office, leading to a consulting job for her father. It also became apparent that one of the subcontractors for MAXIMUS named in its proposed contract with New York, who was to receive between 20 and 30 percent of revenues, was run by Richard Schwartz, a former top aide and campaign manager for Giuliani, who had pledged not to accept any consulting contracts with the city. Furthermore, according to Hevesi, MAXIMUS asked to be paid $4,620 for each person placed in a job, but the city bumped the amount to $5,000 per person.

MAXIMUS faced additional problems in Wisconsin, which ordered an independent audit of the company after management admitted that four of its employees, including Kearney, had billed the state for work done elsewhere. The accounting firm hired by the Department of Workforce Development, however, had worked for MAXIMUS from 1997 through 1999, prompting more criticism. Revelations from the state Legislative Audit Bureau were damaging enough to result in Wisconsin withholding or recovering $7.6 million in payments to MAXIMUS. The audit revealed that the company mistakenly billed Wisconsin $51,000 in wages for employees seeking new contracts in other states; spent $196,000 on advertising that instead of explaining the W-2 program to welfare recipients appeared to simply promote MAXIMUS; billed the state $15,741 for a staff party at an expensive resort; paid singer-actress Melba Moore $23,000 to entertain clients and staff; and charged the state for $23,637 for promotional items such as fanny packs and golf balls.

MAXIMUS admitted to some mistakes in judgment but denied any intentional wrongdoing. Eventually the company received its New York contract, albeit drastically cut in size. Nevertheless, it remained a target for critics and politicians, who portrayed MAXIMUS as a company willing to hire local power brokers in order to gain business. As it sought a new contract in Los Angeles, for instance, MAXIMUS hired the former manager in the Los Angeles County welfare office to be its local contract manager. Criticism of its business practices was then used to bolster the arguments of social critics who maintained that the entire privatization of welfare was misguided. No doubt, large numbers of people were removed from the welfare rolls, but was poverty itself being addressed? Or would welfare-to-work simply create a new class of indentured servants? Would children forced into substandard day care facilities, while their mothers now worked at the lowest paying jobs, remain an expense to society for years to come? And finally, were we simply exchanging poor people and corporations as the recipients of the government dole?

Of course MAXIMUS was involved in more areas than just welfare-to-work programs. It continued to expand its services with more than a dozen acquisitions in 1999 and 2000. The company maintained that its goal could be simply expressed in its trademarked slogan: ''Helping Government Serve the People.'' While serving that mission the company was also rewarding its shareholders. In 1998 revenues grew to $233.5 million, then in 1999 to $319.5 million, and in 2000 to $399.2 million with a net profit of $30.5 million. There appeared no reason to believe that those numbers would not continue to grow in the years to come.

Principal Subsidiaries

CCI-MAXIMUS, Inc.; CSI-MAXIMUS, Inc.; DMG-MAXIMUS, Inc.; Strategic Partners International, LLC; UNISON MAXIMUS, Inc.; Valuation Resource Management, Inc.; GovPrograms.com, Inc.

Principal Operating Units

Government Operations; Government Consulting; Government Systems.

Principal Competitors

Accenture Ltd.; Booz-Allen; Electronic Data Systems Corporation; Ernst & Young; PricewaterhouseCoopers.

Further Reading

Bernstein, Nina, ''Company Had Head Start Preparing Bid in Welfare to-Work Program,'' *New York Times,* March 10, 2000, p. B6.

——, ''Squabble Puts Welfare Deals Under the Spotlight in New York,'' *New York Times,* February 22, 2000, p. B1.

Cohen, Adam, ''When Wall Street Runs Welfare,'' *Time,* March 23, 1998, p. 64.

Drew, Christopher, and Eric Lipton, ''2 With Ties to Chief of Welfare Got Jobs with Major Contractor,'' *New York Times,* April 21, 2000, p. A1.

Ehrenreich, Barbara, ''Spinning the Poor into Gold,'' *Harper's,* August 1997, pp. 47–52.

Lueck, Thomas J., ''Hevesi Rejects Largest Pacts for Workfare,'' *New York Times,* March 23, 2000, p. B1.

Maiello, Michael, ''Service Master,'' *Forbes,* April 2, 2001, pp. 121–22.

Mathews, Jay, ''Los Angeles County Tries Free-Enterprise Welfare,'' *Washington Post,* October 17, 1989, p. A3.

——, ''Taking Welfare Private,'' *Newsweek,* June 29, 1992, p. 44.

McCarthy, Sheryl, ''Welfare for Funds and Profit,'' *Ms.,* January/February 1998, pp. 22–27.

Millard, Pete, ''Complaints Mount Against Maximus,'' *Business Journal-Milwaukee,* January 14, 2000, p. 1.

——, ''Lawmakers Lash Out at Maximus,'' *Business Journal-Milwaukee,* August 4, 2000, p. 6.

——, ''Staffing Firms Chafe As Maximus Skims Best Job Prospects,'' *Business Journal-Milwaukee,* January 21, 2000, p. 1.

Rabinovitz, Jonathan, ''Once Under Attack, Company Managing Child Care Benefits Is Promised More Money by States,'' *New York Times,* March 2, 1998, p. B4.

Rotker, Karyn, ''Corporate Welfare for Welfare Corporations,'' *Dollars & Sense,* January 2001, p. 14.

Woellert, Lorraine, ''Maximus Inc: Welfare Privatizer,'' *Business Week,* May 31, 1999, p. 96.

—Ed Dinger

Minolta Co., Ltd.

3-13, Azuchi-machi 2-chome
Chuo-ku, Osaka 541
Japan
Telephone: (06) 6271-2251
Fax: (06) 6266-1010
Web site: http://www.minolta.com

Public Company
Incorporated: 1937 as Chiyoda Kogaku Seiko Kabushiki Kaisha
Employees: 4,881
Sales: ¥482.76 billion (US$4.55 billion) (2000)
Stock Exchanges: Tokyo Osaka Nagoya Frankfurt Düsseldorf
Ticker Symbol: 7753
NAIC: 333315 Photographic and Photocopying Equipment Manufacturing; 333314 Optical Instrument and Lens Manufacturing; 333313 Office Machinery Manufacturing; 334119 Other Computer Peripheral Equipment Manufacturing; 334519 Other Measuring and Controlling Device Manufacturing

Minolta Co., Ltd. is one of Japan's ''big five'' camera makers and a leading manufacturer of digital office equipment, including photocopiers, printers, word processors and other imaging products, radiometric instruments, and planetariums. The company has production facilities in Japan, the United States, Germany, France, Malaysia, China, Hong Kong, and Brazil, and a worldwide marketing network.

1928: Japan-Germany Camera Company Begins to Build Cameras

Minolta Co., Ltd. began modestly in 1928 when 28-year-old Kazuo Tashima agreed to represent his father's import-export company, Tashima Shoten, on a government-backed trade mission to Paris to promote Japanese silk. In Paris, Tashima toured a factory that specialized in high-grade optics, and decided he could produce similar equipment profitably in Japan. Japanese businessmen, including Tashima's father, opposed the idea of producing optical equipment domestically. Unable to start his new venture as a part of Tashima Shoten, Tashima borrowed money from his father's chief clerk and went into business on his own.

Tashima opened shop on November 11, 1928, calling his venture Nichi-Doku Shashinki Shoten (Japan-Germany Camera Company). The name reflected the company's reliance on German technology and expertise. Partners Willy Heilemann, an importer of German items in Kobe, and Billy Neumann, a German engineer with a background in optical instruments, brought state-of-the-art German technology to the new firm. By March 1929, the staff of about 30 was producing one bellows camera, called the Nifcalette, each day—with imported lens and shutter. Within three months, production had grown to 100 cameras a month.

A year later, the Great Depression hit Japan hard, bringing labor strife and strikes. Tashima later referred to his company as ''a small boat which set sail right into the storm.'' Nevertheless, Tashima promoted development of new camera models as the Depression intensified and introduced several models in 1930 and 1931.

A new model introduced in 1933 first carried the Minolta brand name, a name Tashima created to sound like the Japanese word ''minoru-ta,'' which means ripening rice field. The name reminded Tashima of a proverb his mother frequently used, meaning that the more successful one becomes, the more humble one must be: ''The ripest ears of rice bow their heads lowest.'' The name, however, also has a Western meaning, as an acronym for *M*achinery and *In*struments *O*ptica*l* by *Ta*shima.

In 1934, Nichi-Doku Shashinki Shoten began to sell the Minolta Vest, the product that made a reputation for the company. Like other camera companies, Minolta used sheepskin to make a flexible camera bellows. When a shortage of imported sheepskin threatened production, the company developed the first rigid bellows of synthetic resin for the Minolta Vest. The innovation made the Vest easier to focus and less expensive. For the first time, a Minolta product was successful outside of Japan.

The Vest's success made expansion possible. Tashima built new production facilities, including a factory devoted to lens

Company Perspectives:

Looking to the future, Minolta has adopted a new articulation of its corporate mission. First, the Company aims to contribute to the global community by creating ever-greater value and excellence. Responding to the demands of the coming decade, we plan to help build a more abundant society by offering superior products and services and complementing them with additional benefits. Second, Minolta is dedicated to continuously creating and implementing vision-oriented management strategies designed to ensure the Company's ability to maintain the stable development of the Minolta Group into a more vital organization that provides opportunity for individual fulfillment.

production at Sakai. His emphasis on innovation led to the development of the first twin-lens reflex camera in Japan, the Minolta Flex, in 1937. That same year, Tashima reorganized and incorporated the company and renamed it Chiyoda Kogaku Seiko Kabushiki Kaisha (Chiyoda Optics and Fine Engineering Limited) to reflect its broader focus.

Production of Binoculars and Other Optical Products During World War II

In September 1940, Japan joined Germany and Italy in the Tripartite Pact, which divided Asia and Africa into spheres of influence. Japan's domain was to be Southeast Asia. As it became clear that war was ahead, Japanese military planners determined to develop precision optical equipment for range finding, navigation, and bombing aids.

During World War II, when the U.S. military used electronics to track enemy ships and aircraft, the Japanese depended upon optics. Chiyoda Kogaku Seiko produced high-powered binoculars and other optical instruments for wartime use. Demand was so high that it opened the Itami plant in 1942 solely to manufacture optical glass.

Japan ultimately was devastated by the war. One of the primary goals of the Allied occupation forces was the restoration of Japan's economy. Tashima, who was determined to put Minolta back on its feet, had employees dig through the company's bombed-out factories to salvage parts. In 1946, the company produced Japan's first postwar camera, the Semi III.

The Japanese camera industry's major pre-war competitors in Germany had been ruined during wartime bombing. As a result, worldwide markets opened to the Japanese optical industry during the post-war years. The Minolta Semi III was the first camera to be exported after the war with a shipment of 170 cameras in 1947.

Also that year, Chiyoda Kogaku Seiko became the first company to produce coated lenses in Japan, and, in 1948, it began to design and produce a camera to compete with the industry standard, the Leica 35 millimeter. Chiyoda Kogaku Seiko designed a new sand-cast body with interchangeable lenses and a hinged back cover to make film loading easier. The new Minolta 35 included a faster f2.8 lens and more dependable flash photography.

Expanded Exports Starting in Mid-1950s

The company still had to contend with its poor image in overseas markets because the made-in-Japan label still implied goods of inferior quality. However, other Japanese camera firms were changing that perception. Takeshi Mitarai of Canon—then known as Precision Optical—persuaded U.S. occupation forces to stock his cameras in military stores. U.S. servicemen stationed in the East took the cameras home, and Japanese-made cameras soon came to stand for high-quality lenses. That new reputation was reinforced industry-wide when U.S. photographers assigned to the Korean War began to use Nikon cameras; they claimed that their Nikon lenses were superior to the Leicas they were accustomed to using. Chiyoda Kogaku Seiko began exporting to the United States in 1955 through an agreement with the American firm FR Corp. Minolta introduced another breakthrough, the achromatic double-coated lens, in 1956, giving the company entry into the European market beginning late in 1957.

In 1958, Chiyoda Kogaku Seiko put its optical experience to a new use by building its first planetarium. The timing for this venture was propitious: the Soviet Union had launched Sputnik I, the first earth-orbiting artificial satellite, the year before, sparking new interest in space.

Also in 1958, Chiyoda Kogaku Seiko introduced its first single-lens reflex (SLR) camera. The SLR allowed a photographer to see exactly what was being shot through the camera lens by using an angled mirror that reflected the image to the viewer. Previous cameras—called rangefinder cameras—used two lenses, one to take the photo and one for the photographer to look through. When interchangeable lenses came into use in the early 1950s, the rangefinder posed problems: the photographer saw the same image no matter what lens was used, instead of seeing what the camera would actually photograph. The difference between the two images could be substantial. By the mid-1950s, the major Japanese camera companies were developing the more convenient SLRs, and Chiyoda Kogaku Seiko introduced its version, the SR-2, in 1958. Its major competitor was Nikon's SLR, also introduced in 1958, which was recognized as the best of the high-end SLRs on the market.

Chiyoda Kogaku Seiko opened its first overseas subsidiary, Minolta Corporation, in New York City in 1959. The company chose to name the subsidiary Minolta because of the popularity of its Minolta brand name. Shortly thereafter, in mid-1962, Chiyoda Kogaku Seiko changed its own name to Minolta Camera Co., Ltd. Throughout the 1960s, the company continued improving its camera line. It introduced the Uniomat, with a programmed shutter, in 1960, which led to fully programmed autoexposure in the Hi-Matic. In 1962, John Glenn chose the Hi-Matic to take the first photos of earth from space. In 1966, Minolta introduced its longest-running camera line, the SR-T series, which it produced continuously until 1981. These cameras featured through-the-lens light metering, using a patented light compensator to improve exposure in backlit photos. These new products made Minolta more competitive in Europe; so Minolta opened a European subsidiary, Minolta Camera Handelsgesellschaft, in Hamburg in 1965.

Key Dates:

1928: Kazuo Tashima establishes Nichi-Doku Shashinki Shoten (Japan-Germany Camera Company).
1929: The company's first camera, the Nifcalette, is introduced.
1933: The first camera to carry the Minolta brand name is launched.
1937: The company is reorganized and incorporated as Chiyoda Kogaku Seiko Kabushiki Kaisha (Chiyoda Optics and Fine Engineering Limited).
1955: The company begins to export to the United States.
1957: The company begins to export to Europe.
1958: Chiyoda Kogaku Seiko builds its first planetarium.
1959: Minolta Corporation opens in New York City.
1960: The company's first office copier, the Copymaster, is introduced.
1962: The company changes its name to Minolta Camera Co. Ltd.; it enters the data-retrieval field with its 401S microfilm reader-printer.
1977: The company enters the medical equipment market with its fingertip pulse oximeter.
1983: Kazuo Tashima is replaced as president of the company by his son Hideo Tashima and becomes chairman of the board.
1985: Founder Kazuo Tashima dies.
1986: Minolta enters the facsimile machine market.
1987: Honeywell Inc. files a lawsuit against Minolta and other major camera makers.
1993: Hideo Tashima becomes chairman and Osamu Kanaya replaces him as president.
1994: The company name is changed to Minolta Co. Ltd.
1997: Minolta Camera Sales Co. Ltd. and Minolta Business Equipment Trading Co. Ltd are merged to form Minolta Sales Co. Ltd.
1999: Osamu Kanaya is replaced as company president by Yoshikatsu Ota.
2000: Minolta forms a partnership with Konica Corporation.
2001: Minolta sets up a joint venture with Fujitsu.

Diversification in the 1960s and 1970s

More importantly, Minolta diversified. In 1960, the company entered the office copying market—an area that would prove as successful as cameras—when it produced its Copymaster. In 1962, it expanded into the data-retrieval field with the Minolta 401S microfilm reader-printer, and, in 1965, the company opened its Mikawa plant, which produced the Minoltafax 41, the first copier that could reduce document size.

Minolta continued to develop its links with the United States space program, developing the Minolta Space Meter, a state-of-the-art technology for measuring exposures, for the first manned orbit of the moon, the 1968 Apollo 8 mission. The meter was used on nine more Apollo missions, including the mission that landed a man on the moon in 1969.

Minolta developed digital watches, video recorders, and pocket calculators in the 1970s, although not all the company's innovations were successful. In 1975, a Minolta-developed office copier that used a complex, high-resolution technology was launched just as plain-paper copiers took over the industry. The company introduced a single-lens reflex camera using cartridge film in 1976, but despite a $2 million advertising campaign in the U.S., the product was unsuccessful.

Other camera developments were more successful. In 1977, Minolta produced one of the first "smart" cameras. Its XD Series cameras had the first system to override user aperture settings in poor lighting.

Minolta also advanced in other areas. The company entered the field of medical instruments in 1977 with the development of a fingertip pulse oximeter. Its MS-18 Planetarium, built in Tokyo, contained the first fully automated planetarium system, and its new photocopiers produced higher-quality images and included both enlarging and reducing capabilities. These successes were particularly important because the camera market was saturated in Japan, Europe, and the United States.

Redefined Corporate Image in the 1980s

Minolta responded to the changes in its market by redefining itself. It adopted a new logo in 1981 to reflect its broader purpose, and redefined its mission as processing light and images in all types of environments.

In 1983, Tashima, who had run the company since he founded it, relinquished its presidency to his son, Hideo Tashima, and became chairman of the board, the position he held when he died in 1985.

In the 1980s, Minolta made advances in office-automation products, including copiers and a new word processor, but new camera technology brought the company the most attention. In 1985, Minolta unveiled its Maxxum, a SLR 35-millimeter camera with an autofocusing system. The Maxxum became a successful competitor to less-expensive non-SLR cameras, such as Canon's Snappy and AE-1. A U.S. advertising campaign costing more than $15 million, and technological advances that made the Maxxum the European Camera of the Year for 1985, aided its success. The Maxxum challenged Canon's preeminence in the 35-millimeter market, but it was not long before Minolta's Japanese competitors struck back with autofocus cameras of their own. Canon improved on the Maxxum by building the focusing system into the lens itself instead of housing it in the camera body with a mechanical link to the lens, as Minolta had done. Canon's advance made focusing faster, but its camera was more expensive than the Maxxum.

Minolta entered the facsimile machine market with the introduction of several models in 1986. Meanwhile, the company's planetariums became more sophisticated, first in 1984 with the launch of the Infinium—the first single sphere model that used lens projection—then in 1989 with the introduction of the Infinium a, the first planetarium with a swing-type structure. Also developed by Minolta during this period were the first binoculars to offer continuous autofocusing, launched in 1990.

Difficult Times and a Comeback in the 1990s

Minolta suffered through a prolonged downturn in the early 1990s, with a number of developments contributing to its malaise. First, the camera market had become even more competitive in the late 1980s with the introduction of the first 35mm disposable camera, the QuickSnap from Fuji Photo Film, in 1987 and the first super-compact camera, Konica's Big Mini, in 1989. More convenient and less expensive than the bulky, feature-packed cameras offered by Minolta, Canon, and the other major camera makers, the new smaller models quickly caught on, with Fuji seemingly coming out of nowhere to attain the top spot in cameras by 1992. During the same period, video cameras—or camcorders—became increasingly affordable and further eroded the sales of the traditional cameras Minolta specialized in.

A second factor in Minolta's difficulties—although it affected the company's financial results only in 1992—was the lawsuit filed by Honeywell Inc. in 1987 against Minolta. Honeywell had won approval for several patents relating to autofocus technology, which it had intended to use in its own 35mm camera, an effort it abandoned in the mid-1970s. When autofocus SLR cameras gained great popularity in the mid-1980s, Honeywell prepared lawsuits against nearly all the major camera makers. Minolta eventually settled with Honeywell out of court in 1992, agreeing to pay ¥16.9 billion (U.S.$125.1 million) for infringing patent rights. After posting a net loss of ¥2 billion in 1991, Minolta lost ¥36.1 billion in 1992, thanks in part to the settlement.

The third factor in the company's overall decline was the prolonged Japanese recession of the early 1990s, which hurt domestic sales, and the appreciation of the yen, which hurt exports. Minolta's net sales declined for three straight years, starting in 1992. Although the company's losses narrowed each year, Minolta did not return to profitability until 1996. In the midst of these troubled years, Hideo Tashima became chairman in 1993, and Osamu Kanaya, who had served as president and COO of Minolta Corp., replaced Tashima as president.

To turn the company around, Tashima and Kanaya pursued three main objectives: moving production out of Japan to lessen the effects of the strong yen, developing a camera to compete in the compact category, and continuing to diversify the Minolta product line so as to derive a smaller percentage of revenues from cameras. The first objective of moving production overseas began to be implemented in 1992 with the establishment of Minolta Lorraine S.A., based in France. This facility was set up to make toner, lenses, and other components for imaging products; low-end copiers were later added to its assembly lines, with these products sold mostly in the European market. In 1994, production of plain-paper copiers and laser printers began in China through the Shilong Business Equipment Corporation subsidiary. That same year, Minolta entered into two joint ventures in China for the manufacture and sale of cameras and copiers.

In early 1995, Minolta successfully entered the compact camera category with the launch of the Riva Zoom 70W (known in Japan as the CAPIOS and in North America as the Freedom). Minolta also joined the cooperative development effort brought together by Eastman Kodak Co.—the other participants were Fuji, Canon, and Nikon—to create the Advanced Photo System (APS), an effort to revitalize the stagnant still photography market. APS offered easy loading and the ability to select from three photo sizes (4 inch by 6 inch, 4 inch by 7 inch, and a panoramic 4 inch by 10 inch) as pictures are taken. Minolta introduced a full line of APS cameras in early 1996 under the VECTIS brand. The VECTIS line included five compact models and a high-end SLR version that featured five interchangeable lenses. Later in 1996, Minolta launched a children's camera tied to a new animated series.

The company's desire for further diversification was highlighted in mid-1994 by the decision to change the company name to Minolta Co., Ltd., dropping "Camera." The company soon showed a renewed commitment to innovative new product development. In 1995, Minolta launched the BC 3000 book copying system, the first product able to produce high quality copies of bound books. Also in 1995, Minolta added digital cameras to the Minolta product family with the marketing of the RD-175, touted as "one of the smallest and lightest SLR-type digital cameras in the world."

By 1996, Minolta had begun to turn its fortunes around, posting its first profit in five years, and was building on a revitalized reputation for product development and innovation. New products introduced that year included the CF900 multifunction machine, able to copy, scan, and print in full color; and the Infinium aII, bII, and cII planetariums, extensions of the Infinium line and "the world's first projectors to enable planetarium visitors to experience virtual worlds."

2000: A Shift Toward Office Equipment

Recognizing the growing demand for integrated, digital office machines and digital cameras, Minolta stepped up its research and product development work in 1997 by starting a new company in the heart of Silicon Valley. Minolta Systems Laboratory Inc. in San Jose, California, developed software for Minolta's digital-based copiers, laser printers, and cameras. The company also set itself the target of generating 50 percent of sales from digital-related equipment the following year.

Several successful new products helped Minolta work towards that goal, including the Dimage V, a digital camera featuring a unique side-mounted lens that could be rotated 180 degrees and detached. Linked to the camera with a cable, it enabled the photographer to take pictures around a corner, over the top of a crowd or in tight spaces. This family of cameras was expanded in 1998 with the modular EX, offering interchangeable lenses, and the commercial-use RD 3000 SLR a year later. The Dimage name was also carried over into a range of commercial-use film scanners.

However, office machines were rapidly overtaking cameras as the primary focus of Minolta's business. By 2000, office equipment generated nearly 75 percent of sales while cameras were down to about 20 percent.

Production of laser printers had been increased in 1997 with the launch of the PagePro series, marketed as PageWorks in North America. Two years later, Minolta acquired a 51 percent stake in QMS Ltd., an Alabama manufacturer specializing in color laser printers with which it had partnered since 1993. The companies integrated their sales, service, distribution, logistics, marketing and research and development operations to create the Minolta-QMS division, which became a wholly owned subsidiary in 2000.

Through the late 1990s, Minolta had expanded the DiALTA range of digital multifunction office machines and launched several more specialized products, such as the PS7000 digital book scanner, the only machine in the world capable of copying large bound materials up to A2 size, and the VIVID non-contact 3-D digitizers, which were widely used in the production of computer games and graphics, as well as by educators, museums and galleries, architects, engineers, and industrial designers.

Having seen Minolta through the transition, Osamu Kanaya stepped down as president in 1999. He remained on the board as advisor to his successor, Yoshikatsu Ota, who also took the title of representative director.

In the face of increasingly intense global competition, Minolta began a strategy of driving product development and increasing sales by establishing working relationships with other companies. In 2000, Minolta formed an alliance with Konica Corporation, a manufacturer of high-speed digital copiers, to develop office equipment and manufacture Konica's new 'polymerization' toner.

A year later, there followed a joint venture with Fujitsu, Japan's biggest computer maker, to develop and produce advanced color laser printers. F&M Imaging Technology was scheduled to launch its first products in the spring of 2002.

Moving into the 21st century, Minolta was determined to be at the forefront of digital innovation, while also intent on bolstering its reputation as a ''good corporate citizen.'' A five-year plan introduced in 1999 included bringing its major manufacturing plants up to international environmental planning standards, increasing recycling, reducing waste, and making positive contributions to local communities.

Principal Subsidiaries

Minolta Sales Co., Ltd.; Minolta Planetarium Co., Ltd.; Minolta Office System Tokai Co., Ltd.; Minolta Office System Kinki Co., Ltd.; Minolta Office System Tokyo Co, Ltd.; Minolta Office System Kyushu Co. Ltd.; Aoi Camera Co., Ltd.; Sankei Precision Products Co., Ltd.; Toyohashi Precision Products Co., Ltd.; Nara Minolta Seiko Co., Ltd.; Nankai Optical Co., Ltd.; Okayama Minolta Seimitsu Co., Ltd.; Miki Minolta Kogyo Co., Ltd.; Minolta Components Co. Ltd.; MYG Disk Corporation; Minolta Software Laboratory Co. Ltd.; Tokyo Minolta Camera Service Co., Ltd.; Minolta Digital Solution Co., Ltd.; Minolta Logistics Co., Ltd.; Minolta Quality Service Co., Ltd.; Minolta Techno System Co. Ltd.; Minolta-QMS K.K; Minolta Corporation (U.S.A.); Minolta Business Solutions, Inc. (U.S.A.); Minolta Information Systems Inc. (U.S.A.); MINOLTA-QMS Inc. (U.S.A.); Mohawk Marketing Corporation (U.S.A.); Astro-Tec. Mfg., Inc. (U.S.A.); Minolta Systems Laboratory Inc. (U.S.A.); Minolta Advance Technology Inc. (U.S.A.); Minolta Canada Inc.; Minolta Business Equipment (Canada), Ltd.; Minolta Copiadora do Amazonas Ltda. (Brazil); Minolta GmbH (Germany); Minolta Europe GmbH (Germany); Minolta France S.A.; Minolta Lorraine S.A. (France); Minolta (UK) Limited; Minolta (Schweiz) AG (Switzerland); Minolta Austria Gesellschaft mbH; Minolta Camera Benelux B.V. (Netherlands); Minolta-QMS Europe B.V. (Netherlands); Minolta Business Equipment (Belgium) N.V.; Minolta Svenska AB (Sweden); Minolta Business Equipment Sweden AB; Minolta Norway AS; Minolta Italia S.p.A. (Italy); Minolta Portugal Limitada; Minolta Spain S.A.; Minolta Denmark A/S; Minolta Magyarorszag KFT. (Hungary); Minolta Polska sp. z.o.o. (Poland); Minolta spol. sr.o. (Czech Republic); Minolta Slovakia spol. sr.o.; Minolta Romania s.r.l.; UBA Minolta Baltia (Lithuania); Minolta Bulgaria o.o.d.; Minolta Ljubljana d.o.o. (Slovenia); Minolta Zagreb d.o.o. (Croatia); Minolta Beograd d.o.o. (Federal Republic of Yugoslavia); Minolta Ukraine; Minolta International Trading (Shanghai) Co. Ltd. (China); Shanghai Minolta Optical Products Co., Ltd. (China); Wuhan Minolta Wiaic Office Automation Equipments Co., Ltd. (China); Minolta Hong Kong Limited; Minolta Industries (HK) Limited (Hong Kong); Minolta Singapore (PTE) Limited; Minolta Marketing (M) Sdn. Bhd. (Malaysia); Minolta Malaysia Sdn. Bhd.; Minolta Precision Engineering (M) Sdn. Bhd. (Malaysia); Minolta New Zealand Limited; Minolta Business Equipment Australia PTY. Ltd.; Minolta-QMS Australia.

Principal Competitors

Canon; Eastman Kodak; Fuji Photo Film; Xerox.

Further Reading

Bremner, Brian, ''From the Mind of Minolta—Oops, Make that ''Honeywell,'' *Business Week*, February 24, 1992, p. 34.

Hammonds, Keith H., ''Polaroid and Minolta: More Developments Ahead?,'' *Business Week*, July 16, 1990, p. 32.

Kusumoto, Sam, and Edmund P. Murray, *My Bridge to America: Discovering the New World for Minolta*, New York: Dutton, 1989.

''Minolta Through Six Decades,'' *Minolta Messenger*, Number 7, 1988.

Prud'homme, Alex, ''New Believer,'' *Business Month*, August 1990, pp. 44–45.

Knowles, Anne, ''Minolta Acquires Majority Stake in QMS,'' *Zdnet.com*, June 9, 1999, http://www.zdnet.com/eweek/.

Grotta, Daniel, and Sally Wiener Grotta, ''Minolta's RD-175: the Professional's Choice for Electronic Photography,'' *PC Magazine*, May 14, 1996, p. 39.

——, ''Minolta Dimage V,'' *PC Magazine*, February 10, 1998, p. 158.

——, ''Minolta Dimage EX Zoom 1500,'' *PC Magazine*, November 16, 1999, p. 162.

''Minolta Shapes Itself as a 'Digital' Company,'' *Nikkei Weekly*, August 14, 2000.

—Ginger G. Rodriguez
—updates: David E. Salamie, Emma Marl

National Presto Industries, Inc.

3925 N. Hastings Way
Eau Claire, Wisconsin 54703
U.S.A.
Telephone: (715) 839-2121
Toll Free: (800) 877-0441
Fax: (715) 839-2122
Web site: http://www.gopresto.com

Public Company
Incorporated: 1929 as National Pressure Cooking Co.
Employees: 700 (1999)
Sales: $116.6 million (2000)
Stock Exchanges: New York
Ticker Symbol: NPK
NAIC: 335211 Electrical Housewares and Household Fan Manufacturing; 332992 Small Arms Ammunition Manufacturing

National Presto Industries, Inc., based in Eau Claire, Wisconsin, is a leading manufacturer of pressure cookers and small electric kitchen appliances, including the SaladShooter. An aggressive advertiser, National Presto markets its products mainly through national discount chain stores, such as Wal-Mart, Kmart and Target, which account for nearly 80 percent of sales. Although traded on the New York Stock Exchange, the company is essentially family owned. In the 1990s, chairman Melvin Cohen and his daughter, CEO Maryjo Cohen, controlled more than 30 percent of the stock. The company has struggled with declining sales in recent years and is looking to expand into the government defense business as a way to diversify. In March 2001 Presto acquired Amtec, a small munitions plant.

Early 20th-Century Origins

Best known since the 1970s for its innovative, sometimes quirky kitchen gadgets, National Presto can trace its history to the 1905 founding of the Northwestern Iron and Steel Works in Eau Claire, Wisconsin, which made cement mixers. By 1908, however, the company had settled into manufacturing 50-gallon retorts, or steam pressure cookers, for the canning industry. The company also made 30-gallon retorts for hotel use. In 1915, Presto installed an aluminum foundry for manufacturing ten-gallon pressure cookers for home use.

Two years later, the U.S. Department of Agriculture reported that using steam-pressure cookers was the safest way to eliminate the bacteria that cause botulism when canning low-acid foods, including meats and most kinds of vegetables. Business boomed for Northwestern Iron and Steel, whose pressure cookers, sold under the brand name of National, were already well known among home canners. In 1929, the company further capitalized on its cast-aluminum cookware market niche by changing its name to the National Pressure Cooking Co. By 1930, the company's annual net income had surpassed $1 million on revenues of more than $12 million.

Innovations in Pressure Cooking in the 1930s

By 1935, in the midst of the Great Depression, the National Pressure Cooking Co. was selling 60,000 pressure cookers annually, mostly for home canning by farm households. However, these were still miniature versions of the complex, large-scale commercial retorts the company made. Then in the late 1930s, a company engineer, E.H. Wittenberg, developed an easier sealing mechanism with a rubber gasket clamped between upper and lower handles. Wittenberg's ''home-ec seal'' meant that pressure cookers, which provided the fastest as well as the safest method of preparing food, could be used for everyday cooking.

In 1939, the company also introduced the first sauce pan-style pressure cooker for home use, which it marketed under the trade name ''Presto.'' The demand for the new Presto cooker, which became virtually synonymous with pressure cooking, was so great that despite a decade of economic depression in the United States, sales had doubled to $2 million by 1940.

Wartime Production Shake-Up

However, in 1941, as the United States prepared to enter World War II, government restrictions on the use of aluminum in domestic products sharply curtailed production. National Pressure Cooker, which had invested heavily to increase its manufacturing capacity, was forced to lay off most of its employees. Everett R. Hamilton, then president and majority

Company Perspectives:

It is the company's intention to continually provide innovative new products that meet the needs of today's changing lifestyles as well as a wide selection of basic appliances that reflect the image of quality long associated with the Presto name.

owner of the company, managed to land a $3 million government contract to make artillery fuses; but Hamilton died of a heart attack in February 1942, before the conversion to defense work could be completed. An editorial in the Eau Claire Leader noted that Hamilton ''had the satisfaction of knowing that it would be only a matter of months before employees laid off by priorities would be back on the job and that perhaps in the not too distant future the National Pressure Cooker company might be Eau Claire's most important industry.''

However, despite the defense contract, National Pressure Cooker was reportedly on the verge of bankruptcy by the summer of 1942 and unable to meet its payroll. To save the company, Eau Claire businessman Lewis E. Phillips and his brother Jay, bought a controlling interest in the company from Hamilton's widow. The brothers also owned Ed Phillips and Sons, a wholesale distributor of liquor, tobacco, and candy, with operations in Wisconsin and Minnesota. Lewis Phillips became president of National Pressure Cooker and ultimately managed to right the company by negotiating additional government defense contracts. In fact, National Pressure Cooker eventually received five Army and Navy E Awards for its contribution to the war effort, including about 500,000 ''victory pressure canners'' at the request of the Department of Agriculture.

Post-War Diversification

The company resumed production of cookware after the war, introducing a 16-quart canner and a four-quart Presto sauce pan pressure cooker in 1945. The company also acquired the Century Metalcraft Association in Los Angeles, which gave it access to West Coast markets, and the Lakeside Aluminum Co. in Menomonie, Wisconsin.

In 1946, the National Pressure Cooker Co. also formed a subsidiary, the Martin Motors Division, to manufacture outboard motors developed by George W. Martin, a former professional outboard racing champion. The Aluminator, National Pressure Cooker's company newspaper, touted Martin's innovative design, noting that ''this type of motor once in use would give a great new thrill, and unlimited pleasure, to the vast throng of outdoor living people who find so much peace and relaxation on the many waterways of America.'' A year later, the company moved its outboard motor operations and its research and development operations to a 348-acre former government ordnance site near Eau Claire that it had purchased from the War Assets Administration for $350,000. The site became known as Presto, Wisconsin.

However, National Pressure Cooker faced stiff competition in the postwar leisure boating market from Outboard Marine and Manufacturing, the Illinois-based company later known as the Outboard Marine Corporation, which made both the popular Johnson and Evinrude-brand outboard motors. In 1948, Outboard Marine and Manufacturing introduced the first outboard motor with a separate fuel tank and a shift lever that allowed the operator to select forward, reverse, or neutral. Outboard Marine also began manufacturing fiberglass motorboats that were sold through the same network of dealers and distributors that handled Evinrude and Johnson motors. In the early 1950s, National Pressure Cooker filed a complaint with the Federal Trade Commission alleging that Outboard Marine and Manufacturing was pressuring dealers not to carry its Martin outboard motors. The company liquidated the Martin Motor Division in 1954, before the case was resolved.

In 1949, the company also introduced its first electric appliance, a steam iron with the Presto brand name that could use tap water instead of distilled water. By 1950, National Pressure Cooker had introduced the Presto Automatic Dixie-Fryer, a thermostat-controlled deep fryer for home use that presaged many of the company's later innovations. In a ''Talk of the Town'' column in a November 1950 *New Yorker* magazine, company spokesman Russell Bloomberg remarked on the versatility of the deep-fryer: ''The Fryer fills a much needed want for Mrs. Housewife. It does the same work as the expensive commercial kettle. It can take very mediocre leftovers, such as cold mash potatoes and chicken wings, and convert them into delicious croquettes. With it you can glorify corn-meal mush by frying it along with ten per-cent ground-up leftover cheese. Mrs. Housewife can use the fat over and over again, with no interchange of taste. I spent a month frying doughnuts in it eight hours a day, just to determine the absorption of fat. Its entertaining possibilities are endless. Suppose your husband, after a fishing trip, brings home a tiny trout. You can cook it with bread crumbs.''

As the company began introducing more consumer products under the Presto brand name, including an automatic coffee maker, the stockholders voted at the 1953 annual meeting to change the corporate name to National Presto Industries, Inc.

Defense Contracts in the 1950s and 1960s

A few months after changing its name to emphasize its consumer products, National Presto announced that it had signed a multimillion-dollar contract with the U.S. government to produce artillery shells. The company immediately began converting its Eau Claire manufacturing facilities, including the former ordnance plant purchased at the end of World War II, to defense work. The company also announced that its consumer-products division would move to Jackson, Mississippi, where the Century Manufacturing Company subsidiary was building a new facility.

In 1955, National Presto expanded its defense work to include airplane components for the U.S. Air Force. At the time, the company employed about 2,000 defense workers in Eau Claire and about 650 consumer-products workers in Mississippi. In a press release, Phillips noted that the ''new contract represents a diversification of our Eau Claire production, and if all concerned extend their full support, this new contract should aid not only in increasing local employment generally, but in stabilizing our employment at a higher level.''

Key Dates:

1905: The company begins in Eau Claire, Wisconsin, under the name Northwestern Iron and Steel Works.
1915: An aluminum foundry is installed for the specific purpose of manufacturing large-size pressure canners for home use.
1917: The company name is changed to National Pressure Cooker Company.
1939: The first sauce pan-style pressure cooker is introduced and given the trade name ''Presto.''
1942: Brothers Lewis and Jay Phillips buy controlling interest in the company, which is on the verge of bankruptcy since it had to shut down most of its home appliance manufacturing because of the war.
1949: Postwar, the company's sales heat up with the introduction of its first electric steam iron.
1953: The company changes its name to National Presto Industries, Inc., in recognition of its increasing diversification into portable electric housewares.
1958: National Presto introduces the world's first automatic, submersible stainless steel coffee maker.
1969: The company begins trading on the New York Stock Exchange.
1978: National Presto introduces its hot air PopCornNow machine, capitalizing on Americans' more healthful eating habits.
1988: The company brings the enormously popular SaladShooter to market.
1992: National Presto wins its suit against Black & Decker Household Products for patent infringement.
2000: The Pizzazz Pizza Oven is introduced as the company's next great invention for the kitchen.
2001: National Presto purchases Amtec Corporation, a munitions production company.

However, by 1958, the government had cut back sharply on orders for artillery shells, and employment at Presto in Eau Claire had fallen to about 500. Moreover, National Presto's remaining defense workers went out on strike for 60 days in the summer of 1958. When the strike ended, Phillips issued a warning: ''The future of this company in Eau Claire and hence the security of our jobs here, is now almost wholly dependent upon defense contracts awarded by the U.S. Government.''

Phillips' concern was borne out a year later. In 1959, the Army Ordnance Corps abruptly cancelled its contract with National Presto for artillery shells. In a tersely worded statement, Phillips announced, ''This cancellation is indeed an unfortunate turn of events for Presto and its manufacturing employees here at Eau Claire. With little or no notice, this Government decision has forced us completely out of the manufacturing business here in Eau Claire.''

National Presto shut down its defense operations in Eau Claire in 1960, but contracted with the government to maintain the manufacturing equipment in a state of semi-readiness. The tide would soon turn again as the company resumed production of artillery shells in 1964, as U.S. ground troops were being sent to Vietnam. Between 1966 and 1975, National Presto produced more than 92 million 105-millimeter artillery shells. It also produced two million eight-inch artillery shells between 1967 and 1971. At the height of U.S. involvement in Southeast Asia, employment at the defense plant in Eau Claire reached 3,000, a figure that fell off dramatically after the United States withdrew from Vietnam in 1973. The defense plant was again closed in 1980, two years after Phillips' death, but the government continued to contract with National Presto to keep the plant on stand-by through the 1990s. Defense requirements were eventually ceased in 1993, and in the mid-1990s, the company was planning on how best to dispose of the special purpose manufacturing equipment.

Lewis Phillips served as company president until 1960 and chairperson until 1966. An important contributor to his community, he created the Presto Foundation and L.E. Phillips Charities. Upon his death in 1978, Phillips was memorialized in Eau Claire by the numerous educational and health-care facilities that bore his name.

Focus on Consumer Products

While the company's success in defense production through military contracts was erratic, the postwar economy was ripe for new consumer product introductions, as American housewives in particular were encouraged to purchase appliances that would make their lives easier. During the 1950s, Presto's consumer products division had introduced the first in a line of immersible electric cooking appliances. The cookware, including an electric skillet, griddle, and coffee maker, featured a removable ''Master Control'' heat unit, allowing the appliance to be washed safely in water. Over the next dozen years, National Presto also introduced popular models of toasters, egg cookers, hair dryers, and electric toothbrushes. A second manufacturing plant for consumer products was built in Alamogordo, New Mexico, in 1971.

In the mid-1970s, National Presto began introducing kitchen appliances designed for a changing American lifestyle. In 1974 the company produced the PrestoBurger, an electric hamburger cooker that broiled a single patty of meat in less than three minutes. The PrestoBurger was followed by the electric Hot Dogger in 1975, and the Fry Baby, a single-serving, deep fat fryer, in 1976. As Melvin S. Cohen, National Presto's chairman, told Forbes in 1977, ''we were the first in our industry to recognize a fundamental change in American society.'' Cohen referred to demographic changes, noting that ''the Census Bureau says 51% of all U.S. households now consist of singles and doubles, not the traditional family group. They have informal, casual lifestyles and money to spend. Yet everybody designs appliances for that old, traditional 5.8-member family. Well, we started designing for singles and doubles.''

The company continued to expand its product line. Cohen told the Wisconsin Business Journal in 1984: ''Our life-blood is new products. And we must constantly be turning them out and developing new ones. We also recognize that to some extent they're in the nature of yo-yos—that they'll be faddish in nature, they'll enjoy a brief popularity and then virtually disappear from the scene, either by virtue of loss of consumer interest or because it is so widely copied it is no longer attractive.'' While National Presto was unable to guarantee that every one of its products would catch on with consumers—for example, an electric, vibrating hairbrush was a flop—it aggressively tried to defend its successes from copycat competition through patents and litigation.

Competition in the Late 1980s and 1990s

In 1988, National Presto introduced the SaladShooter, an electric slicer/shredder. Hamilton Beach Corp. and Black & Decker Corp. introduced similar products the same year. National Presto, which had patented the mechanical features of its SaladShooter, filed suit against both competitors. Two years later, Hamilton Beach settled by agreeing to destroy its remaining inventory and withdrawing from the slicer/shredder market. In 1992, a federal district court jury found Black & Decker guilty of infringing on National Presto's patent and awarded the company $2.35 million in damages. In 1995, the decision went to the U.S. Court of Appeals, where justices upheld the lower court's finding of patent infringement.

In 1991, National Presto introduced the Tater Twister potato peeler. The same year, the West Bend Co. introduced a similar product. The two companies sued each other, and again National Presto prevailed. In 1993, a federal jury found West Bend guilty of patent infringement and awarded National Presto $230,000 in damages. Indeed, National Presto was becoming a formidable name in the industry. Also in 1993, the Dazey Corp. agreed to withdraw from the deep-fryer market after being sued by National Presto. In the company's 1994 annual report, management noted: "Hopefully, this Company's competitors are now convinced that it will not brook copying, and will aggressively seek injunctive and/or damages relief when infringements occur."

Presto Under Pressure

By the end of 1996, Presto was a small company sitting on a large amount of money, much to the criticism of leading financial analysts. The company had assets of $285.4 million, of which $228 million was in cash, cash equivalents, and marketable securities. Like many companies that go public, National Presto remained under the control of its guiding family members, primarily Lewis Phillip and later, his son-in-law, Melvin Cohen. By 1997, Cohen had been with National Presto for 53 years, starting out as a service manager. He married into the Phillips family, became president of the company in 1954, and later its chairman. His daughter, Maryjo Cohen, took over as the CEO in 1994, and between them, they controlled 30 percent of Presto's stock. Chairman Cohen's conservative views on acquisitions kept the company from pursuing other manufacturing and expansion opportunities. In fact, Presto had a reputation for holding on to its cash reserves for so long, it was said to be "the bank that makes SaladShooter as a sideline." However, CEO Maryjo Cohen defended the company's practice of shying away from acquisitions. In a 1997 article for *Milwaukee Journal Sentinel*, Cohen noted that she didn't think the shareholders were unhappy as Presto was still paying dividends despite sagging sales, and that her company was not one for the investor who wanted a quick run-up in value. At the time of the interview, the company was trading for about $40 a share, down from its high of $82 in 1992.

New products have always been the lifeblood of the company. But without a truly innovative product to add to its current stable of cookers, shooters, and poppers, sales of Presto's small kitchen appliances started to decline, from a high of $128 million in 1992 to $106 million in 1996. Presto needed to find a new product that would ignite sales and assure shareholders that the company was on the right track. To brainstorm ideas, the company used a committee made up of representatives from the manufacturing, sales, and engineering departments, as well as the Cohens. They also actively solicit new product ideas from the public through the company's web site, www.gopresto.com. On its web page, called the "Online Inventor's Kit," Presto walks would-be inventors through the process of submitting product ideas to Presto, which includes completing a nondisclosure form. No data is available as to the number of submissions for new ideas the web page has generated, but as the Internet becomes the way the world, it no doubt will help Presto to stay on top of food and lifestyle trends.

The huge reservoir of cash reserves did allow Presto to weather product failures and slow retail sales. For most of the 1990s, the company had little to cheer about. Besides limited product introductions, Presto had to contend with costly patent infringement litigation, increased competition from other manufacturers and the negative effects of new inventory practices at retailers such as Kmart and Wal-Mart. Presto also lost its government contract in 1992 to maintain its Eau Claire plant in a state of readiness for ammunition manufacturing. Any one of these things might have toppled a less financially secure company, but Presto survived it all.

Still, it was not easy for Cohen to see his company stumble, and he let his displeasure of Presto's performance be known in the 1995 annual report, which featured a flock of sheep on its cover. The caption read: "The trouble with following the herd is stepping in what it leaves behind." The following year Presto found itself behind the pack again, primarily because of two notable product flops. The first, an oversized toaster that would accommodate tall slices of bread created by at-home breadmaking machines, did not even make it to retailers' shelves. Its relatively expensive price kept retailers from ordering it, fearing their customers would not want to shell out more dough for a newfangled toaster. The other product to fizzle that year was the Matchless outdoor barbecue grill. This electric grill seemed like a good option for apartment and condo dwellers, many of whom could not have gas or charcoal grills on their decks. But again price soured sales. Retailing for about $200, it could not compete against other small grills on the market.

Cooking for a New Millenium

For the Christmas season of 1997, the company pinned its hopes on the SaladShooter Mixer Too, a combination vegetable slicer and hand mixer, retailing at about $25. But it was not until the end of the decade and a phenomenon known as "Y2K" that business started to heat up again for Presto.

Sales of pressure cookers took off as the much-publicized Y2K millennium computer bug triggered fears about computer crashes and the breakdown of modern society. (The change of years from 1999 to 2000 was supposed to cause massive computer system failure because many older systems tracked the year by only the last two digits, thereby leaving open the possibility of miscalculating 2000 as 1900 and throwing credit expiration dates, loan due dates, inventories, and many more systems into chaos.) Many people had a renewed interest in canning and preserving foods as a way to survive any calamity Y2K might bring.

Also helping sales was the cache pressure cookers had suddenly acquired with the upscale twenty-something crowd. Flush with dot.com cash, many young professionals were looking to spend less time cooking, yet have all the accoutrements of a well-stocked, gourmet kitchen. Presto answered that call by revamping a number of its pressure cooker units. Don Hoeschen, vice president of sales for National Presto, noted in a 1999 article for *HFN*, a trade journal for small appliance manufactures, that buyers of pressure cookers were interested in more user-friendly features. He wrote, "Generation X wants better-quality, highstyle units. We've addressed that with the buffet handles rather than the stick handles . . . and it's been very successful." Presto saw its sales increase 13.9 percent the first quarter of 1999 to $21.6 million. Earnings grew 16.7 percent to $3.2 million. By the end of the year, Presto posted its annual sales at $114.7 million, a 7 percent increase over 1998.

As the new millenium unfolded, and the world order remained intact, Presto again faced problems in the marketplace and on Wall Street. In May of 2000, it was revealed that Wal-Mart, its largest customer, would drastically cut its purchases of Presto products the following year. The decision was due to Wal-Mart's desire to convert some of its small appliance stock to private-label products purchased from offshore manufactures. Even so, Presto remained optimistic and told shareholders that it hoped to offset the loss with its latest innovation, the Pizzazz revolving pizza oven. This oven, which cooks frozen pizzas in a flash, was touted as ideal for families on the run. Unfortunately, holiday sales of the oven were much lower than expected. Presto executives blamed slow sales on its 15- and 30-second TV ads, explaining that consumers may not have believed their claims of the oven's cooking speed. They also pointed a finger at a softening economy, theorizing that the $89.99 asking price might be tough for some to swallow. However, the company has no plans to pull back from its push of the product, believing there is indeed a market for it.

Presto was dealt another blow at the same time when Target announced that it too would start buying some of its small appliances directly from offshore manufacturers. The loss was estimated to affect about 8 percent of Presto's business with Target. The news was not good on Wall Street. By February 2001, the company was trading at approximately $30 a share, a new low. Worse, Presto was under investigation by the Securities and Exchange Commission, which wanted to know if the company's huge cash reserve made it subject to reporting requirements of the Investment Company Act of 1940.

Presto did find some good news in 2001. In March it purchased Amtec, a small munitions plant. Chairman Melvin Cohen, now in his 80s, explained that the decision to buy Amtec, a privately held manufacturer with about 100 employees, was the first step towards getting back into the defense business. He still feared that in the event of a war, Presto would not be able to make its appliances, as was the case during World War II. With a stake in government defense work, Cohen believes Presto will remain viable and sees this line of business as a way to diversify and expand.

Principal Subsidiaries

Presto Manufacturing Co.; Presto Products Manufacturing Inc.; Jackson Sales and Storage Co.; Canton Sales & Storage Co.; National Holding Investment Co.; National Defense Corp.

Principal Competitors

Sunbeam Products, Inc.; Salton, Inc.; Mirro.

Further Reading

Brammer, Rhonda, "Gizmo King: And National Presto is a Veritable Bank, to Boot," *Barron's*, May 10, 1993, p. 14.

"Court Again Upholds Presto," *HFN: The Weekly Newspaper for the Home Furnishing Network*, September 25, 1995, p. 59.

Gorham, John, "What Would Ben Graham Say?," *Forbes*, September 6, 1999, p. 274.

Hajewski, Doris, "Presto Moves Back into Defense Business," *The Milwaukee Journal Sentinel*, March 1, 2001, p. 1D.

——, "Losing Target Will Drop Sales 8%, Presto Says," *The Milwaukee Journal Sentinel*, February 7, 2001, p. 1D.

——, "Presto Waits to Profit from New Products," *The Milwaukee Journal Sentinel*, September 29, 1997, p. 8.

Hamel, Mark, "National Presto: The Corporate Kitchen Magician," *Wisconsin Business Journal*, December 1984, pp. 20–30.

Lieber, Ed, "Wal-Mart Shift to Private Label Hits National Presto," May 22, 2000, p. 31.

Linquist, Eric, "Empty Plant Awaits Uncle Sam's Call," *Eau Claire Leader-Telegram*, July 19, 1987, p. D1.

"National Presto Industries Plant Humming with Activity with 3,000 Employed in Manufacture of Shells," *Eau Claire Daily Telegram*, March 30, 1968, p. C2.

"National Presto Is Prospering by Thinking Small in Appliances," *Barron's*, August 22, 1977, pp. 30–31.

"Presto Keeps Cash on Hand, Seeks 'Friendly' Acquisition," *Eau Claire Leader-Telegram*, June 19, 1989, p. D1.

"Presto Changeo!," *Financial World*, April 15, 1980, pp. 50–51.

"Presto Grew with Pressure Cooker," *Eau Claire Leader-Telegram*, July 28, 1972, p. E9.

Purpura, Linda M., "B&D, Presto Salad Shootout: File Shredder Patent Suits," *HFN: The Weekly Home Furnishings Newspaper*, June 25, 1990, p. 1.

Rublin, Lauren R., "Pot Full of Cash: National Presto's Beautiful Balance Sheet," *Barron's*, October 24, 1988, pp. 38–42.

"Stock of Eau Claire, Wis., Appliance Maker Falls after Wal-Mart Cuts Orders," *The Milwaukee Journal Sentinel*, May 19, 2000.

"Talk of the Town," *The New Yorker*, November 25, 1950, p. 30.

The History of National Presto Industries, Inc., Eau Claire, Wisc.: National Presto Industries, Inc., 1996.

"Tom Swift And His Electric Hamburger Cooker," *Forbes*, October 15, 1977, p. 112.

"What Took the Steam Out of National Presto," *Business Week*, April 3, 1978, pp. 29–30.

—Dean Boyer
—update: Suzanne Rowe

OfficeMax, Inc.

3605 Warrensville Center Road
Shaker Heights, OH 44122
U.S.A.
Telephone: (216) 921-6900
Fax: (216) 491-4040
Web site: http://www.officemax.com

Public Company
Incorporated: 1988
Employees: 38,489 (2001)
Sales: $5.156 billion (2000)
Stock Exchanges: New York
Stock Symbol: OMX
NAIC: 453210 Office Supplies and Stationary Stores

OfficeMax, Inc. is the third-largest office supply chain in the United States. The company operates nearly 1,000 high-volume, deep-discount "superstores" in 49 states, Puerto Rico, and the US Virgin Islands. In addition to office products, OfficeMax stores also feature CopyMax modules (offering print-for-pay services) and FurnitureMax facilities, which offer office furniture. The company also maintains an e-commerce business (officemax.com), which carries over 20,000 items. Through joint ventures, OfficeMax operates stores in Mexico and Brazil.

OfficeMax started in 1988 as a simple idea. In little more than five years the company bolted to the forefront of the American business supplies industry, posting more than $2 billion in annual sales by 1995 and generating sound profits by 1993. The company achieved that stunning success despite intense competition and an economic recession that began in the late 1980s and lingered throughout the early 1990s. The company's savvy marketing, distribution, management, and financial systems and strategies became models for other superstore retailers in the 1990s.

1988: Humble Beginnings

The OfficeMax concept was hatched by entrepreneurs Michael Feuer and Robert Hurwitz. Feuer, who became the driving force behind the chain's growth, had been nurturing the idea during more than 17 years of service with Fabri-Centers of America, a 600-store retailer in Cleveland. By his early 40s, Feuer had risen to the executive ranks. Still, he was frustrated by his inability to run the company as he believed it should be operated. "At age 42 I was bored and, like many executives, I also suffered from the Frank Sinatra syndrome—I wanted to do it my way," Feuer recalled in September 1993. "I had always claimed that if we could just cut through all the nonsense—for example, the 20 to 25 percent of time most executives spend on CYB (covering your butt)—and do it my way, we could make millions," Feuer observed.

Feuer finally jumped ship and, despite other excellent corporate job offers, decided to start his own enterprise. He and Hurwitz decided that they didn't want to fund the start-up with bank debt or venture capital because they didn't want to forfeit control of the operation. So they scrambled to raise capital from friends and family. They eventually found 50 investors, including several doctors and lawyers, who were willing to contribute a total of $3 million. The sum was paltry compared to other retail start-up businesses at the time, but the pair thought that they could parlay the cash into a winning enterprise.

Feuer and Hurwitz launched their enterprise on April Fool's Day in 1988. On that day, they laid out on a sheet of paper their concept for a new type of office products store. Their goal was to create a large business supplies discount store that was an exciting place to shop, and offered professional and friendly service, as well as prices between 10 and 30 percent less than those found in more traditional office supply retailer shops. The main goal was to bypass all of the middlemen, such as wholesalers and distributors. Achieving that goal, they reasoned, would allow them to effectively replace mom-and-pop office supply stores, much as supermarkets had replaced small grocers years earlier.

OfficeMax was fighting an uphill battle from the start. In May, an office supplies industry trade paper published a list of 15 start-up companies that were trying to crack into the business; OfficeMax was 14th on the list by asset size. The start-up team knew that it had to keep expenditures at an absolute minimum to compete. So Feuer and Hurwitz rented office space in a 500-square-foot brick warehouse that had barely any heat or

Company Perspectives:

OfficeMax provides office goods and services to small and medium-size businesses, home office customers, and individual consumers. The company has almost 1,000 superstores and delivery centers in the United States, on the Internet at OfficeMax.com, via direct mail catalogs, and through a nationwide commercial sales force.

air-conditioning. The space was equipped with a few pieces of cheap office furniture, a coffee machine, and a copier (the copier and coffee machine couldn't be operated at the same time, however, because the fuse would blow). They decided not to invest in a fax machine until it became absolutely necessary.

OfficeMax started out with a skeletal staff of seven people, not including the founders. Their requirements for potential employees were simple: they had to be hard workers with open minds, big hearts, and plenty of enthusiasm. They also had to be willing to work for very little money. Feuer and Hurwitz attracted the workers by promising them part ownership in the company if they stuck with it, and by offering them the chance to go farther, faster, and to have more fun than they had ever had in any other job. From the beginning, Feuer made it clear that OfficeMax would be operated differently from the bureaucracies from which most of the team members had come. There would be no secrets, criticism and praise would be swift and frank, and everyone would cooperate as a team.

Thus, OfficeMax was up-and-running without a single store or any other operation that could bring in any money. The founders hoped that they would be able to get manufacturers to fund their inventory, but they soon found that few big companies were eager to do business with a meager upstart. To overcome such hurdles, the team got together every morning and created a game plan for the day on a blackboard. They flew by the seat of their pants and used every trick they could conjure to get what they needed. Importantly, the company was able to get an unsecured line of credit from a local Cleveland bank. The bank granted the line of credit under one condition: that the founders agree never to use it.

Feuer and Hurwitz were able to take their ''line of credit'' to big suppliers like Xerox and convince them to fund their inventory on credit, sometimes for a full year or more. Indeed, the OfficeMax team learned early that the only way to get the cooperation of potential suppliers was to act as though OfficeMax was much bigger than it really was. They dealt with suppliers as though OfficeMax was a soon-to-be major chain with 20, 50, or even 300 stores going up in the near future, suggesting that if those suppliers wanted to secure a place with OfficeMax tomorrow, they would have to cooperate today. To the founders' surprise, most companies played along. Those that didn't often regretted it, as OfficeMax quickly became the leading customer for many major office equipment and supplies manufacturers.

1988–90: Going from One Store to Thirty in Two Years

Incredibly, OfficeMax opened its first store just 90 days after the founders had created their business blueprint on April Fool's Day. Observers were surprised that the team had managed to find space, hire and train a store staff, and hone a store concept in just three months. But to them it was a simple matter of survival; they had to start generating cash flow so that they could pay their bills. The first OfficeMax was opened on July 5, 1988, at the Golden Gate Shopping Center in the Cleveland area. The only advertising for the grand opening was a newspaper ad two days prior to the store's opening. Nevertheless, the store had sales of $6,400 on its first day.

After only six months in operation, the store was breaking even (before corporate overhead). That feat was accomplished partly as a result of the grueling hours put in by the team. Feuer, for instance, worked at the corporate office from 7:00 a.m. to 7:00 p.m. He would then race home, shower, put on casual clothes, and drive out to the store to observe the customers and employees. When a customer left the store without purchasing anything, Feuer was known to chase him down in the parking lot and ask him if OfficeMax had failed in any way. That type of thinking was later reflected in OfficeMax's intensive customer-satisfaction orientation. For example, the company began requiring that all customer complaints be resolved to the customer's satisfaction within 24 hours.

Enthused by the quick success of the first store, Feuer and Hurwitz hurried back to the original investment group and raised additional capital for expansion. They dumped the cash into an aggressive growth program that, amazingly, had OfficeMax operating 13 stores in Ohio and Michigan less than 12 months after opening the first outlet. Sales had climbed to an impressive rate of $13 million annually and, more important, the stores were operating at a profit. The success was so quick that it worried Feuer, who was convinced that the company's accounting system was messed up and that OfficeMax could easily be teetering on the edge of bankruptcy.

Shortly before OfficeMax had fired up its first store, a similar office superstore venture called Office World had started in Chicago. The business was funded heavily by retailer Montgomery Ward, but despite hefty financial backing, the effort had lost $10 million in the span of a few years. Thus, when Montgomery Ward approached OfficeMax about the possibility of a merger between OfficeMax and Office World, Feuer and Hurwitz were hesitant. They eventually warmed up to the idea, however, and the resulting agreement brought seven new stores to their chain, as well as the resources of several deep-pocketed venture capital firms. OfficeMax, for its part, only had to give up two of the ten seats on its board.

By the summer of 1990, following the Office World merger, OfficeMax was operating a total of 30 stores. After once again going back to its investment group, the company was banking an impressive $33 million in cash. The cost-conscious founders finally decided that it was time to move into a better headquarters facility, one that featured separate men's and women's bathrooms, for example. The rest of the money was put to use funding an aggressive expansion plan that would, the company hoped, add 20 more stores to the chain within a year. Despite healthy gains and a bright future, however, a development in 1990 threatened to quash OfficeMax and its competitors.

Feuer and Hurwitz had perceived the threat years earlier. Finally, their fears were realized when mass discount merchant

Key Dates:

1988: Company founded by Michael Feuer and Robert Hurwitz.
1990: Company merges with Office World; Kmart invests $40 million in OfficeMax.
1991: Kmart purchases 92 percent of outstanding shares and becomes company's owner.
1992: Company purchases Office Warehouse and Bizmart.
1994: Company makes largest IPO in industry history; launches FurnitureMax, CopyMax, and OfficeMax Online.
1995: Second stock offering eliminates Kmart's ownership.
1996: Company opens Mexico City superstore.
1997: Company opens more stores in Mexico and its first store in Japan.
1998: Company opens its first urban-targeted OfficeMax PDQ store and opens stores in Brazil.
2000: Gateway invests $50 million in company and becomes its exclusive computer provider.
2001: HP replaces Gateway as company's computer provider; company closes 50 stores.

Kmart announced plans to roll out an office supplies superstore dubbed Office Square. OfficeMax executives realized that the new venture, backed by Kmart's massive bank account and retailing savvy, could literally crush start-ups like OfficeMax. Feuer and Hurwitz, refusing to ignore the threat, began trying to initiate talks with Kmart. The talks initially centered on an outright purchase of OfficeMax by Kmart. But Feuer and Hurwitz were hesitant to give up control of their company. The two companies finally agreed to a plan whereby Kmart invested $40 million in OfficeMax in return for a 22 percent ownership share.

Early 1990s: Life with Kmart

Fortunately for the founders, Kmart turned out to be OfficeMax's greatest ally, rather than its worst enemy. Feuer and Hurwitz were allowed to maintain total control of the company, and Kmart smartly became a silent financial partner. With its new bankroll, OfficeMax intensified its expansion efforts and quickly met the goals that it had set with Kmart executives. Both companies were so pleased with the arrangement that Kmart decided to up the ante in 1991. It purchased 92 percent of the outstanding shares from the original investors and became the owner of OfficeMax. The net result was that OfficeMax was sitting on a mountain of cash and had virtually no long-term debt. Furthermore, Feuer and Hurwitz were still firmly in control of the company.

The deal couldn't have been sweeter for OfficeMax, which was suddenly positioned to launch a bid to dominate the national business supplies superstore segment. That's exactly what the company did. During the next 18 months the company began opening new OfficeMax outlets at a feverish pitch. More importantly, the company purchased the 46-store Office Warehouse chain and the 105-outlet Bizmart chain, and eventually integrated those stores into the OfficeMax organization. As a result of store additions and acquisitions, OfficeMax was operating 328 stores in 38 states, coast-to-coast, by the end of 1993. Sales for that year climbed to $1.41 billion, from just $245 million in 1991, while net income increased to $1.08 billion (OfficeMax's first positive annual net income).

Although cash was a major ingredient in the company's recipe for growth, its shrewd operating strategy was just as important for success. Indeed, throughout its expansion, OfficeMax maintained its customer focus. It also adapted the format of its stores to capitalize on the huge growth in the small and home-based business markets, which became the dominant industry trend during the early 1990s. In addition, OfficeMax managed to implement cutting-edge information and distribution systems that allowed the top mega-discounters like Kmart and Walmart to thrive. By the mid-1990s, OfficeMax was efficiently operating nearly 400 stores and several distribution centers, and stocking more than 6,000 brand name office products, business machines, computers and related electronic devices, software, and other goods.

With Kmart's financial backing and the OfficeMax team's successful operating strategy, the company sustained its blistering growth rate in 1994. By the end of the year, the company was operating 388 stores in 40 states and Puerto Rico. Importantly, the end of 1994 marked a huge change for the company. Late in that year, its well-heeled parent, Kmart, sold out. Kmart's investors had been pressuring Kmart to sell off its side interests and refocus its resources on the hyper-competitive general merchandise discount industry. Kmart's directors stooped to the pressure and decided to bail out of the OfficeMax venture. OfficeMax completed the largest initial public offering in the history of the retail chain industry when it sold 35.7 million shares at a price of $19 per share, bringing in the $678 million that allowed Kmart to reduce its ownership interest. A subsequent offering in July 1995 entirely eliminated Kmart's ownership share.

Mid-1990s: Going Public Without Kmart

Thus, after growing by leaps and bounds with the help of Kmart, OfficeMax was suddenly on its own again as a publicly held enterprise. For 1994, OfficeMax posted $1.81 billion in sales, $30.4 million of which was netted as income. As Hurwitz had removed himself from day-to-day operations at OfficeMax following the stock sale, Feuer stepped up expansion plans in 1995, hoping to boost OfficeMax's 11 percent share of the U.S. office supplies superstore market. By 1995, OfficeMax became the second largest business superstore in the nation (behind Office Depot), and was gunning for the number one slot.

Meanwhile OfficeMax launched related ventures beginning in 1994, including FurnitureMax, a chain of discount office furniture stores, and CopyMax, a chain of copy-service centers. Both of the new store concepts were designed to be connected to existing OfficeMax stores and to serve as add-on profit centers. In 1995, the company debuted its TriMax stores, which consisted of an OfficeMax superstore flanked by a FurnitureMax and a CopyMax. The company also initiated a computer service called OfficeMax Online, (which later became OfficeMax.com), that was designed to enable customers to purchase OfficeMax products online from their home or office computers.

A period of tremendous expansion for OfficeMax began in 1996. In its annual shareholder's meeting, the company announced a major expansion into Southern California—an area where its rivals, Office Depot and Staples, were already well established. Additionally, the company made its first international foray by opening a superstore in Mexico City with its venture partner Grupo Oprimax. This store was followed by more store openings in Mexico, and the company's success in that country was phenomenal. CEO Feuer told *Discount Merchandiser* in 1998, ''We went in with very modest expectations, but they have been more fully realized than anticipated, The volume in Mexican stores is equal or better than in the US.'' The company also began testing a smaller format store called Office PDQ, aimed at urban markets, and formed a joint venture with Jusco Co., Ltd., to open OfficeMax stores in Japan.

During 1997, Staples and Office Depot attempted a merger that was ultimately blocked by the FTC. While its two main competitors were focused on merger plans and court battles, OfficeMax took the opportunity to expand even further, opening a total of 150 stores in 1997 alone. This growth earned them—for a time—the long-coveted number one position in the market. Despite the large number of openings, the company still suffered a gap in sales numbers. Even though it had the greatest number of stores, the company's sales volume fell below $4 billion in 1997—as compared with Office Depot's $6.7 billion and Staples' $5.2 billion. Feuer attributed the gap to the company's relative youth in the market. He planned to make up the numbers in part by focusing on the copy center portion of the business, which had a very high profit margin. In 1998, the company turned its focus to increasing the productivity of its store base, primarily by reducing its inventory of computers—an area that had been disastrous in terms of profitability.

By 2000, the company had eliminated computers completely, instead forming a partnership with Gateway. Under their agreement, Gateway would install Gateway stores inside OfficeMax superstores. The Gateway operations would be staffed by Gateway employees. Gateway also invested $50 million in OfficeMax. However, the deal was scrapped in 2001, with Hewlett Packard replacing the flagging Gateway as OfficeMax's computer supplier.

The year 2000 was challenging for OfficeMax. The company's profits continued to fail to keep pace with its expansion, and the company underwent a major restructuring—which Feurer called ''deliberate suffering.'' It installed a new integrated computer system and revamped its distribution system, a move that it hoped would ultimately save the company several million dollars a year. It also changed its purchasing policies to be more in line with what its customers actually bought, rather than what vendors provided incentives for it to sell. These measures helped, but in 2001, the company was faced with the decision to close stores. In January of that year, the company announced plans to close 50 stores—resulting in the loss of 1,200 jobs—and take a one-time after-tax charge of $69 million. Despite these troubles, Feuer remained optimistic, telling *Futures World News* in May 2001 that he expected the company's growth rate to accelerate in the third quarter of 2001–02.

Principal Operating Units

FurnitureMax; CopyMax; OfficeMax.com.

Principal Competitors

Buhrmann; Office Depot; Staples.

Further Reading

''As Staples, Office Depot Battle FTC, OfficeMax Expands its Concepts,'' *Discount Store News*, July 7, 1997, p. 80.

Baird, Kristen, ''OfficeMax Plan May Supply 900 More Local Jobs,'' *Crain's Cleveland Business*, July 31, 1995, p. 1.

Bartalos, Greg, '''Til the Cows Come Home,'' *Barron's*, Chicopee, June 11, 2001, p. 35.

''Big Name in Office Game is Diversity,'' *Discount Store News*, August 9, 1999, p. 50.

Brandt, John R., and Michael Feuer, ''Taking It to the MAX: How Did Michael Feuer Take a Start-up Company to $1.5 Billion in Revenue in Just Five Years?,'' *Corporate Cleveland*, September 1993, p. 16.

Cotlier, Moira, ''OfficeMax to Close 50 Stores,'' *Catalog Age*, New Canaan, March 15, 2001, p. 7.

Einhorn, Cheryl Strauss, ''Maximum Markdown,'' *Barron's*, Chicopee, December 18, 2000, pp. 23–24.

Einhorn, Cheryl Strauss, ''Promises Kept,'' *Barron's*, Chicopee, February 5, 2001, p. 14.

Garvey, Martin J., ''Gateway Takes Aim at the Business PC Market,'' *Informationweek*, Manhasset, February 28, 2000, p. 30.

''Gateway to the Future,'' *Discount Merchandiser*, April 2000, p. 23.

Hanover, Dan, ''Honey, I—Shrunk—the Store,'' *Chain Store Age*, January 1999, pp. 40–45.

Harrison, Kimberly P., ''OfficeMax to Launch New Unit: Company to Test Concept of Furniture Showroom,'' *Crain's Cleveland Business*, November 14, 1994, p. 1.

Howes, Daniel, ''Kmart Plans to Sell Rest of Stake in OfficeMax,'' *Detroit News*, June 27, 1995, p. E1.

''HP Replaces Gateway at OfficeMax,'' *Client Server News*, May 21, 2001.

Icon Group International, Inc., Staff, *OfficeMax, Inc.: International Competitive Benchmarks & Financial Gap Analysis*, San Diego: Icon Group International, Incorporated, April 2000.

Icon Group International, Inc., Staff, *OfficeMax, Inc.: Labor Productivity Benchmarks & International Gap Analysis*, San Diego: Icon Group International, Incorporated, April 2000.

Johnson, Jay L., ''OfficeMax: On a Fast Track,'' *Discount Merchandiser*, March 1998, pp. 32–34.

Johnson, Jay L., ''The FTC shuffle: Two Losers, One Winner,'' *Discount Merchandiser*, August 1997, p. 19.

Kemp, Ted, ''Staples Chases Small Biz,'' *Internetweek*, November 13, 2000, p. 11.

King, Angela G., ''OfficeMax Stock Shines for Openers,'' *Detroit News*, November 3, 1994, p. E1.

Liebeck, Laura, ''Staples, OfficeMax Look Abroad,'' *Discount Store News*, January 6, 1997, pp. 6, 88.

Marcial, Gene G., ''Officemax May Be Hunter—or Prey,'' *Business Week*, November 25, 1996, p. 154.

''Market Slows, But Still Grows,'' *DSN Retailing Today*, August 7, 2000, p. 40.

Nottingham, Nancy, ''Office Superstore Opens Today on West End,'' *Billings (Montana) Gazette*, June 15, 1995, p. D5.

''Office Superstore Chains Plan 9 Million Sq. Ft. of New Space in '98,'' *Discount Store News*, March 23, 1998, pp. 6, 67.

''Office Superstore Expansion in High Gear,'' *Discount Store News*, October 20, 1997, pp. 5, 77.

''Office Supply Chains Foresee Continued Expansion,'' *Discount Store News*, July 13, 1998, p. 86.

''OfficeMax Boosts Expansion,'' *Chain Store Age*, November 1996, p. 43.
''OfficeMax Plans California Blitz,'' *Discount Store News*, June 3, 1996, p. 3.
''OfficeMax Reveals Plans at Shareholders Meeting,'' *Discount Store News*, May 25, 1998, p. 3.
''OfficeMax to Close 50 Stores, Cut 1,200 Jobs,'' *Futures World News*, May 7, 2001.
''OfficeMax to Offer On-Line Custom Printing,'' *DSN Retailing Today*, May 21, 2001, p. 6.
Pascale, Moira, ''The Price is Right . . . or is It?,'' *Catalog Age*, New Canaan, February 1999, p. 6.
Radcliff, Deborah, ''Back-to-School.com,'' *Computerworld*, August 23, 1999, p. 40.
Russell, John M., ''OfficeMax Breaks Loose,'' *Small Business News-Cleveland*, September 1994, p. 16.
Shingler, Dan, ''Hurwitz Trading Paper for Pillows,'' *Crain's Cleveland Business*, April 11, 1994, p. 1.
''Speculation over OfficeMax Suitor Points to Staples, Hints at Antitrust,'' *Discount Store News*, October 26, 1998, p. 6.
''Staples to Sell 63 Units to OfficeMax, FTC to Decide on Acquisition,'' *Discount Store News*, April 1, 1997, p. 6.
Swanson, Sandra, ''Office-Supply Vendors to Offer E-learning,'' *Informationweek*, August 21, 2000, p. 40.
Thompson, Chris, ''OfficeMax Sees Profits Stack Up for Pending IPO,'' *Crain's Cleveland Business*, September 12, 1994, p. 3.
Troy, Mike, '''98 Writing Instrument Sales Script Strong Outlook for '99,'' *Discount Store News*, February 22, 1999, pp. 41–44.
——, ''Accessories Rise to Demands of Evolving Office Environs,'' *Discount Store News*, April 5, 1999, pp. 19–20.
——, ''Office Suppliers Scurry to Revamp Financials,'' *Discount Store News*, October 25, 1999, pp. 5, 63.
——, ''OfficeMax is the Biggest, Now It Has to Prove It's the Best,'' *Discount Store News*, November 17, 1997, pp. 31–39.
——, ''OfficeMax Looks for Improvement Before it's Too Late,'' *DSN Retailing Today*, November 6, 2000, pp. 37–38.
——, ''OfficeMax Names Peterson President, Gateway In-Store Pact First Challenge,'' *Discount Store News*, March 6, 2000, pp. 5, 87.
——, ''OfficeMax Reorganizes,'' *DSN Retailing Today*, March 19, 2001, pp. 1, 8.
——, ''OfficeMax Unveils New Prototypes,'' *Discount Store News*, August 10, 1998, pp. 10, 118.
——, ''OfficeMax's Actions Draw Shareholder Lawsuits,'' *DSN Retailing Today*, May 8, 2000, pp. 10, 144.
——, ''Softened Office Supply Market Gives Big Three Cause for Pause,'' *DSN Retailing Today*, April 2, 2001, pp. 8, 74.
——, ''Store Closings Imminent for Office Superstore Channel,'' *DSN Retailing Today*, January 1, 2001, p. 6.
——, ''The Rx That Delivers the Max,'' *Discount Store News*, December 8, 1997, pp. 75–76.

—Dave Mote
—update: Lisa Whipple

Peebles Inc.

1 Peebles Street
South Hill, Virginia 23970-5001
U.S.A.
Telephone: (804) 447-5200
Toll Free: (800) 723-4548
Fax: (804) 447-5453
Web site: http://www.peebles.com

Private Company
Incorporated: 1891 as Peebles & Green
Employees: 3,506
Sales: $306.6 million (2001)
NAIC: 452110 Department Stores; 551112 Offices of Other Holding Companies

With over 120 stores in 15 states, ranging from Missouri to New York, Peebles Inc. is one of the oldest and most successful department store chains in the United States. The company specializes in brand-name and private-label family clothing and home furnishings, but aims to offer its customers a broad array of merchandise priced for average shoppers—the "Ford and Chevrolet" customers, in the words of William S. Peebles, Jr., who served as the firm's vice-president from 1931 to 1973. Indeed, Peebles has carved a distinct market niche that caters to middle-income Americans in small to mid-sized markets located in underserved rural areas and small towns.

Throughout most of its history, Peebles has been a closely associated group of individually managed stores owned and operated by Peebles family members and their friends. "Most of the business," wrote Peebles historian Howard E. Covington, Jr., "was tied up in W.S. Peebles & Co., but all the stores were part of a corporate network [that ultimately consisted of] nearly twenty privately held corporations." By the late 1980s, however, that ceased to be the case. Two leveraged buyouts by Wall Street investors that decade shook up the company's management structure and culminated in a corporate restructuring of the firm to Peebles Inc. in 1992. The company is still privately held, but increasingly has taken on the characteristics of a public concern, disclosing, for example, financial information that had previously gone unreported.

Although disruptive and troubling, especially to a company with more than 100 years' history behind it, these management shake-ups proved remarkably successful, as they established a sound basis for rapid, long-term growth. The number of stores in operation increased by a net of 30 percent from 1990 to 1995, while total sales during that same time period increased by more than 26 percent, from $138.7 million in 1990 to $176 million in 1995. By the mid-1990s Peebles ranked as one of the most profitable retailers in the country, even outperforming retail giant Wal-Mart in gross operating margin.

Local Beginnings, 1890s

Peebles Inc. dates its origins to the establishment of the Peebles and Green clothing store in rural Lawrenceville, Virginia, in 1891. Named after its two founders, William S. Peebles and Arthur S. Green, the store was renamed the Peebles and Purdy Co. in 1907 when Green decided to leave the clothing business to become a food retailer. Peebles took on another business partner, Leonard Purdy, and together the two headed up what Covington described as "one of the major mercantile businesses in Lawrenceville, [then] a thriving county seat community with a population of 2,000."

As the town and surrounding Brunswick County grew, so did Peebles's ambition, and he invested $26,000 of his own money in a new retail business, W.S. Peebles & Company. His cousin, W.B. Mitchell, joined him with a $6,000 investment, signing on as vice-president of the firm. Peebles's four sons also were brought on board, as stockholders and, later, as company officers and executives.

The year was 1923. Four years later, Peebles open a second department store in South Hill, Virginia. In 1929, a third store, in Emporia, Virginia, was added. "By 1930," wrote Covington, "Peebles enterprises were among Lawrenceville's brightest success stories."

Like many companies, the firm suffered during the Great Depression, with retail sales in 1930 dropping to 40 percent of

Company Perspectives:

Peebles will strive to be the specialty department store that its target customers think of and shop at first for popular brands of fashionable apparel, accessories, shoes, and home fashions at popular to moderate price points in a conveniently located store and experience superior customer service, typified by its friendly and helpful sales associates, in a fresh, updated shopping environment.

what they had been the year before. During this period, William S. Peebles died. His eldest son, John Isler Peebles, became company president, only to pass away six months later.

The Next Generation of Leadership, 1930s

Peebles's other sons stepped into the breach, assuming leadership of the company with dedication and commitment. Wesley became president and treasurer, William became vice-president, and Marion became secretary. Under their leadership, Peebles soon recovered from its difficulties. In 1934, stockholders began to receive a dividend on their investment, and bonuses were given out to employees. In 1935, a fourth store was opened (in Clarksville, Virginia), and, two years later, two additional stores in southeast Virginia were opened, making Peebles the largest retail merchandiser in the Lawrenceville area.

During the next 40 years, Peebles expanded steadily throughout the region, adding stores in North Carolina (1938), South Carolina (1950), Delaware (1960), and Maryland (1967). In 1943, it entered into a partnership with businessman E.B. Kimbrell and opened a Peebles-Kimbrell department store in Forest City, North Carolina; this was the first of three highly successful joint ventures between the two companies. Twenty years later, there were 26 Peebles or Peebles-Kimbrell stores in four states.

Throughout this period, Peebles distinguished itself from rival competitors in a number of ways. First, it sought to sidestep competition by locating in small communities of between 10,000 and 30,000 households—places typically not served by such larger department store chains as Sears, Macy's, Levitz, and Kmart. In this way, Peebles usually was able to establish itself as a community's dominant retail department store.

Second, individual store managers were given broad latitude to run their stores as they saw fit, with little or no interference from centralized management—provided, that is, they were profitable, which most were. Merchandising, staffing, training, expansion, customer credit, salaries, and compensation were the responsibility of the individual store managers. This system allowed the stores the flexibility they needed to succeed in distinct and competitive markets.

Postwar Changes

In the aftermath of World War II, however, as the United States' economy witnessed unprecedented growth and prosperity, the old ways of doing business no longer proved adequate, and American business became more centralized and hierarchical. Peebles began to make significant changes, sometimes in anticipation of its need to do so, and other times in response to sudden and painful realities.

For example, in 1952, Peebles began coordinating bulk purchases for the firm's growing number of stores. At the same time, Peebles began promoting itself and its products via direct mail marketing, which was then a novel business practice. In 1956, in Lawrenceville, Virginia, it opened its first "supermarket," also a novel move for the time. In 1958, the company took another dramatic step forward when it opened its first store in a major metropolitan area, in Manassas, Virginia, on the outskirts of suburban Washington, D.C.

The move marked a significant change with past company policy, which had been to open stores in the central business districts of rural America. Such a policy became increasingly difficult to maintain, however, as economic growth bypassed these areas and became concentrated instead in the suburbs surrounding major American cities.

Although the Manassas store quickly became profitable, Peebles did not take immediate steps to build on its success. As late as 1968, in fact, two-thirds of its business still took place in the company's traditional small-town department stores. Peebles was changing, but not fast enough, it seemed, to keep pace with the times. Indeed, many of its stores in older and more rural towns were losing money or barely breaking even. Also, newer stores in metropolitan Washington, D.C., were too few in number for the company to take full advantage of their profitability.

Leveraged Buyout, 1960s

Leadership of the company was split, moreover, between the older generation of Peebles, who sought to stay the course, and the younger generation of Peebles, who were pushing for more rapid change. Wesley Peebles, Jr., son of the president and company secretary, was the main catalyst pushing for change, and, in December 1968, he finally won out, as Peebles began merger discussions with a New York investment-banking firm. Peebles eventually reached an agreement with another firm, and Wesley and his cousins agreed to divide the company.

As a result, Peebles's books were opened up to outside analysis for the first time ever, and the firm was found to be worth close to $3.7 million. After a leveraged buyout was executed, Wesley, Jr., left the day-to-day operations of Peebles, and his cousin Bill (William Peebles III) became defacto chief executive officer (the first in the history of the firm).

Despite its financial strength, Peebles was facing significant challenges. The rise of suburban shopping malls or strip centers and heightened competition from discount retailers like Kmart, Grant's, and Roses were rendering many of its traditional stores obsolete and unprofitable, while the average lead time on a new store was two years. Management turnover was a growing problem, and it was becoming increasingly difficult to find young managers to replace those who were departing.

Progress was slow but steady. In 1972, Peebles began using computers to record, track, monitor, and centralize its system of charge accounts, which previously had been done by individual store managers in hand-written entries. Not long thereafter

Key Dates:

1891: Peebles & Green opens in Lawrenceville, Virginia.
1927: Company opens second store in South Hill, Virginia.
1943: Partnership with E.B. Kimbrell; Peebles-Kimbrell department store opens in Forest City, North Carolina.
1978: Company purchases 8 southern department stores.
1986: Company bought by Investcorp for $77.6 million; opens its first centralized distribution center.
1988: Michael Moorman becomes first non-family CEO.
1989: Leveraged buyout by PaineWebber Inc. for $152 million; National Retail Merchants Association names Bill Peebles "Independent Retailer of the Year."
1992: Company restructures and is renamed Peebles Inc.
1995: Company acquired by PC Retail Holding Co., an affiliate of Kelso & Co.
1996: Company acquires Carlisle Retailers Inc. for $11.5 million.
1998: Company acquires Ira A. Watson Co. for $4.5 million; buys five Thomas & Stone stores from Elder-Beerman Stores Corp.
2000: Company joins Doneger Group, a buying and retail consulting company.
2001: Company owns 124 stores in 15 states; buys Stage department stores in Ohio and Indiana

Peebles moved to a centralized buying and distribution system, which also was made possible through computerization. Still, it was not until 1985 that the firm completed its transition to centralized buying, and it was not until 1988 that all in-house credit operations were done electronically.

In October 1972, Peebles opened a second 30,000-square-foot store, in Waldorf, Maryland, a southeastern suburb of Washington, D.C. A year later, William S. Peebles III, formally replaced his uncle, Wesley S. Peebles, as president. In September 1978, Peebles held its first annual management meeting, and, one month later, the company completed its purchase of eight Southern Department Stores, an established department store chain in Virginia specializing in cosmetics, the purchase of which proved immensely profitable. The company now had 37 stores in four states.

Continued Growth and Modernization, 1980s and 1990s

Thirty-one new locations were added in the 1980s, as the process of modernization continued. Downtown stores in declining or stagnant rural areas were closed, but the conservative management style and close customer contact developed there was maintained in the chain's rapidly growing suburban stores.

In 1984, Peebles joined the prestigious New York-based Frederick Atkins buying office, a move which, according to one former merchandise manager, "put us into the major leagues of retailing." In 1984, Peebles also acquired The Collins Company, a regional department store group based in Charlotte, North Carolina, thereby giving the firm its first locations in America's increasingly popular shopping malls. In 1985, Peebles moved its corporate offices from Lawrenceville to South Hill, Virginia, and, in 1986, opened its first centralized distribution center.

Peebles considered going public in the mid-1980s, but was effectively precluded from doing so by virtue of the fact that, despite real progress at modernizing, it still was a network of interlocking companies rather than a single corporate entity with an exclusive balance sheet. Management worked through this problem and decided that it would be substantially more profitable for them to sell Peebles to the highest bidder than to go public. The firm put itself on the market in June 1986 and was bought out in October of that year by Investcorp, an investment group based in Bahrain, for $77.6 million.

In January 1988, Peebles celebrated $100 million in annual sales. That same year, Mike Moorman became the first non-family member to run the Peebles business. A lifelong company employee who began his career at Peebles as a manager trainee in 1964, Moorman remained CEO well into the next century, despite further shakeups at the firm. In 1989, for instance, Peebles was the beneficiary of an immensely profitable leveraged buyout by an investment group headed by PaineWebber Inc., which paid $152 million for Peebles and its 48 stores in seven states. Also that year the National Retail Merchants Association named Bill Peebles its "Independent Retailer of the Year," in honor of his lifelong service to the industry.

In the 1990s, in an effort to stay ahead of the competition and avert the intense competitive pressures plaguing many other retailers, Peebles modernized and streamlined its operations still further. In 1992, the year it renamed itself Peebles Inc., the company cut the lead time that it needed to open a new store from one to two years to only six weeks. The number of Peebles stores thus grew dramatically in the 1990s, as did the number of states in which they were located. In 1996, Peebles acquired Carlisle Retailers Inc. for $11.5 million, with five stores in northeastern Ohio and two in northwestern Pennsylvania. In 1998, the company acquired Ira A. Watson Co. for $4.5 million, increasing store sites by 25 (up to 110). The same year, Peebles bought five Thomas & Stone stores in Virginia and West Virginia from Elder-Beerman Stores Corp. From 1996 to 2000, Peebles added 47 stores, with 29 new store locations acquired from other retailers, further solidifying the company's strength in its core market.

Entering the Twenty-First Century

By the twenty-first century, Peebles' operated 124 stores in 15 states, including Missouri, Indiana, Kentucky, Tennessee, Alabama, North Carolina, South Carolina, Ohio, West Virginia, Maryland, Pennsylvania, New York, New Jersey, and Delaware, as well as its home state, Virginia. Peebles still operated in smaller than traditional retail markets, but modern technology bonded the stores into a centralized organization. The department stores averaged 30,000 square feet, and were mostly located in strip shopping centers. In 2000, Peebles switched to the Doneger Group buying and retail consulting company when Frederick Atkins went out of business.

Peebles continued to rely on direct mail and newsprint advertising targeted at middle-income families. This policy maintained an emphasis on everyday fair prices instead of a more promotional strategy. Peebles offered name brand clothing and furnishings, such as Liz Claiborne and Ralph Lauren, as well as private label merchandise, which allowed the company to avoid direct price competition. The advertising budget was kept to a minimum, with an average of 2 percent of net sales used for advertising and marketing. Peebles relied on its reputation and credibility with repeat customers rather than big sales or markdowns.

Peebles had key operating advantages, including knowledge of its customer base, the ability to share information between stores, and cost-efficient operations through centralization. By monitoring unit sale information daily by store, Peebles was able to determine and respond to inventory needs immediately.

The Peebles Operating Strategy, Withstanding the Test of Time

Peebles's success relied on several key elements: focus on small markets and deliver value; operate small, flexible stores; tailor fashion to local taste; devote at least 85 percent of time and space to the sales floor by centralizing back office tasks; and adapt to local real estate opportunities.

In 2001, Peebles bought nine Stage department stores in Ohio and Indiana, continuing its expansion strategy. The company developed new locations, acquired existing stores and converted them (similar to Watson's and Carlisle's), and remodeled and relocated older stores. These stores did not follow a standard format or adhere to a cookie-cutter look, but rather were designed for operational efficiency, with flexible inventory management adapted to meet the needs of the individual community. Peebles continued to target communities between 10,000 and 25,000 households.

Peebles has managed to weather the ups and downs of the retail business for over 100 years. Their strategy, and motto, "Great Fashions, Great Prices, Everyday," appears to be working.

Principal Competitors

Ames; Dunlap; Federated; Goody's Family Clothing; J.C. Penney; Kmart; Kohl's; The May Co; Saks Inc.; Sears; Target; TJX; Value City; Wal-Mart.

Further Reading

"Beerman to Sell 8 Stone & Thomas Units," *Daily News Record*, August 3, 1998, p. 5.

Covington, Howard E., Jr., *Peebles: A Retail Tradition Begins Its Second Century*, South Hill, Va.: Peebles Inc., 1993.

"Department Store Revival Planned by Peebles Inc.," *Business First-Columbus*, March 30, 2001, p. A16.

Devere, Randall S., "Peebles to Amend Existing Deal via NatWest," *Bank Loan Report*, September 12, 1994, p.4.

"Doneger Adds Former Clients of Atkins Office," *WWD*, April 24, 2000, p. 14.

"Elder-Beerman Acquires Stone & Thomas Chain," *HFN The Weekly Newspaper for the Home Furnishing Network*, August 3, 1998, p. 4.

"Elder-Beerman Completes Sale of Stone & Thomas," *HFN The Weekly Newspaper for the Home Furnishing Network*, October 5, 1998, p. 4.

Emert, Carol, "The Peebles Choice in Suburban Retailing: Peebles, a 55-unit Chain, Hits the Bigtime in Small Towns," *Daily News Record*, June 30, 1994, p. 16.

Gilligan, Gregory J., "Virginia-Based Peebles Department Store Chain is Bought," *Richmond Times-Dispatch*, June 23, 1995.

Owens, Jennifer, "Peebles Falls into Red in 3d Period: SEC Filing," *Daily News Record*, December 18, 1996, p. 8.

Palmieri, Jane E., "Secondary Markets Give Power to the Peebles; CEO Michael Moorman Plans More Growth Outside the Big Cities," *Daily News Record*, February 10, 1997, p. 26.

"Peebles Dep't Stores to Open Units in Four New Markets," *Daily News Record*, May 26, 1994, p. 11.

"Peebles Earnings More than Double," *Daily News Record*, September 18, 1998, p. 1B.

"Peebles's Earnings Up 16%," *WWD*, May 3, 2000, p. 10.

"Peebles First-Quarter Net Gains 12.9%," *WWD*, June 22, 2000, p. 16.

Reed, Vita, "Peebles Keeps Chain Growing by Sticking to a Simple Plan," *Charlotte Observer*, November 15, 1993, p. 2D.

Richards, Geoffrey, "Peebles Capitalizes on Its Rural Retail Heritage," *Shopping Center World*, June 1995.

Ryan, Thomas J., "Peebles Inc., Ira A. Watson Co. Planning to Merge," *Daily News Record*, May 29, 1998, p. 14.

Ryan, Thomas J., and Melanie Kletter, "Weather, Acquisitions Dampen Third Quarter at Belk, Peebles," *WWD*, December 21, 1998, p. 11.

Stoughton, Stephanie, "Peebles: A Retail Tradition's Next Step," *Virginia-Pilot and the Ledger-Star*, December 26, 1994, pp. 1, 8–9, 11.

Stowe, Michael, "Peebles Chairman Knows Employees, Customers Alike," Roanoke (Virginia) *Times & World News*, September 12, 1993, pp. F1–F2.

——, "Peebles Counters Department Store Moves," Roanoke (Virginia) *Times & World-News*, September 12, 1993, pp. F1–F2.

—John R. Guardiano
—update: Elizabeth Shé

Pepper Hamilton LLP

3000 Two Logan Square
Eighteenth and Arch Streets
Philadelphia, Pennsylvania 19103-2799
U.S.A.
Telephone: (215) 981-4000
Fax: (215) 981-4750
Web site: http://www.pepperlaw.com

Limited Partnership
Founded: 1890 as Henry and Pepper
Employees: about 800 in 1999, including 350 lawyers
Sales: $125.5 million (1999)
NAIC: 54111 Offices of Lawyers

Pepper Hamilton LLP is a full-service law firm based in Philadelphia. As one of the 100 largest law firms in the United States, Pepper Hamilton is instrumental in helping small and large companies and other organizations resolve their legal issues in financial, intellectual property, regulatory, and other practice areas. It also represents American firms in their efforts to expand overseas, and similarly helps foreign firms expand to the United States. Pepper Hamilton maintains branch offices in New York; Detroit; Pittsburgh; Harrisburg, Pennsylvania; Berwyn, Pennsylvania; Cherry Hill, New Jersey; Washington, D.C.; Wilmington, Delaware; Tysons Corner, Virginia; and Princeton, New Jersey.

Origins and Early Decades: 1890–1945

Born in 1867 to an old and distinguished Philadelphia family, George Wharton Pepper is regarded as the founder of Pepper Hamilton. Pepper graduated from the University of Pennsylvania Law School in 1889 and the next year joined the Philadelphia firm of Bayard Henry, a small concern with modest offices on Walnut Street. Like many lawyers of his day, Pepper dealt with a wide range of legal issues, including estates, corporate concerns, and litigation. He would eventually become best known, however, as a constitutional lawyer, though his first case before the Supreme Court in 1894 was unsuccessful. Also in 1894, Pepper accepted a position as the Algernon Sydney Biddle professor of law at his alma mater University of Pennsylvania, a position he would hold for some 15 years. While practicing law, teaching, and serving on the boards of various legal and academic institutions, Pepper also found time to author several law reference books, including the *Digest of Decisions and Encyclopedia of Pennsylvania Law.*

In 1920, Pepper's name was added to the law firm's, now known as Henry, Pepper, Bodine & Pepper. Two years later, Pepper, a prominent Republican, was appointed to the U.S. Senate, filling the unexpired term of Boies Penrose, who died in office. In 1926, the firm's original name partner, Henry, died, and Pepper lost his bid for reelection to the Senate. Thereafter he returned to Philadelphia to focus on the law firm.

During his distinguished career, Pepper argued many cases at the U.S. Supreme Court. He helped convince the Court, for example, that Federal League Baseball should be exempt from the 1890 Sherman Antitrust Act, as professional baseball was not involved in interstate commerce. Pepper also argued successfully in *Myers v. United States* (1926) and *United States v. Smith* (1932), two cases concerning the constitutional authority of the U.S. president.

Pepper's most notable U.S. Supreme Court case occurred in 1936 when the court in *United States v. Butler* declared the 1933 Agricultural Adjustment Act (AAA) to be unconstitutional. (President Franklin Roosevelt had promoted the AAA as part of his New Deal to fight the Depression.) In 1938 Congress passed a modified AAA that created farm subsidies as a long-term program. By 1940, Pepper's firm was known as Pepper, Bodine & Stokes.

Postwar Years

By the early 1950s, George Wharton Pepper had scaled back his involvement in the growing firm. Nevertheless, he continued to serve as chairman and attended weekly meetings, weighing in on philosophical issues and business matters until 1955. He died in 1961 at the age of 94. Among the firm's most important work in the 1950s was its success in the Pierre S. duPont estate case, in which the Pepper firm represented the duPont estate in resolving the issue of in which state duPont had legally resided,

Company Perspectives:

We counsel each client as if it were our only client. We commit our combined skills and experience to solve client problems, exercise objective and independent judgment consistent with the highest ethical standards, join with clients to identify and achieve their objectives, and focus always on adding value with efficiency and enthusiasm. Our most valued resource is our people. We recognize that each individual's success depends on the individual and collective efforts of our colleagues—past, present and future. Accordingly, we value service, trust, interdependence and collegiality.

since he had lived in both Delaware and Pennsylvania. The firm ultimately convinced the taxing authorities in Pennsylvania to end their claim to the estate, subsequently freeing up millions of dollars for charitable purposes.

This case and others were handled by John D.M. Hamilton. Earning a law degree from Northwestern University, Hamilton had served as the speaker of the Kansas House of Representatives and the chairman of the Republican National Committee in the 1930s and 1940s. After retiring from politics, he joined the Pepper firm. In 1950, Hamilton started the law firm's pro bono tradition by representing Harry Gold, a colleague of the infamous Rosenbergs, who had confessed to spying for the Soviet Union. Gold, who had provided the Soviet Union with secrets regarding the U.S. atomic energy program, wanted a lawyer without leftist leanings to represent him. "The court appointed Hamilton, who was about as far from the left as you could get," said Augustus S. Ballard, Gold's co-counsel, quoted in the *Legal Intgelligencer* of January 2000. Gold was ultimately sentenced to prison and released on parole with the help of Hamilton. In 1955, Hamilton took over the position of chairman from Pepper.

In 1954 the Pepper law firm merged with the Philadelphia firm of Evans, Bayard & Frick to create Pepper, Bodine, Frick, Scheetz & Hamilton. The Evans firm had been founded by the prominent attorney John G. Johnson, who had argued 168 cases before the U.S. Supreme Court, including famous antitrust cases defending the sugar industry, the railroads in the Northern Securities Case, the Standard Oil Company, and U.S. Steel Company. Ralph Evans took over the Johnson partnership in 1917 and under his leadership the firm represented The Bell Telephone Company of Pennsylvania, Gimbel Brothers, Lukens Steel Company, N.W. Ayer Advertising Agency, The Curtis Publishing Company, the *Philadelphia Inquirer*, and The Travelers Insurance Company. Francis H. Scheetz was at the helm of the Evans firm when it merged with the Pepper firm in 1954. The merged firm of 35 lawyers moved to the Philadelphia headquarters of one of its clients, The Fidelity Bank.

Another merger ensued in 1960, when the Pepper firm joined with Moffet Frye & Leopold, a firm that had been tapped to help incorporate the Sun Oil Company in 1902. The growing ranks of the firm, now renamed Pepper Hamilton & Scheetz, included Roberta P. McKinney, the firm's first female partner, and a rare occurrence for any law firm at the time. In the early 1960s the firm began representing Westinghouse Electric Corporation, some Westinghouse officers, and the H.K. Porter Company in antitrust cases. According to the Pepper law firm's published history, "These were the first cases involving allegations of price fixing which demonstrated the potential for jail terms for those found in violation of the antitrust laws."

In 1963 Pepper attorney Phil Strubing represented The Curtis Publishing Company when it was sued by Wally Butts, the University of Georgia athletic director, and University of Alabama football coach Bear Bryant. The men sued for libel in the U.S. District Court in Atlanta, Georgia, after *The Saturday Evening Post* published an account of what the two coaches considered a private phone conversation allegedly involving game fixing. The district court ruling for Butts was upheld by the U.S. Supreme Court in *Curtis Publishing v. Butts* (1967). Although Strubing and the firm ultimately lost the case, the firm regarded its work as helping to clarify several issues surrounding libel law.

Also during this time, the Pepper law firm began its product liability practice when it defended the manufacturer of thalidomide, a drug that became well-known for causing serious birth defects. Mergers and acquisitions were another practice area enhanced during this time, particularly through the firm's representation of the Sun Oil Company when it merged with Sunray DX Oil Company.

Firm Expansion and Practice: 1969–89

In 1969, the Pepper law firm moved outside of Philadelphia for the first time, opening branches in Harrisburg, Pennsylvania, and Washington, D.C. Two years later attorney Strubing was named chairman of the firm. The Pepper law firm's expansion in the late 20th century reflected a general upward swing in the legal profession as a whole. Many new laws and government regulations, including the 1964 Civil Rights Act and the environmental protection laws of the 1970s, created a need for more legal assistance. Moreover, the growth of the economy, especially in the 1980s, would lead to company start-ups, particularly in high-tech fields, with the personal computer revolution, further increasing the demand for lawyers.

Meanwhile, the legal profession was transformed by two developments in the 1970s. First, the U.S. Supreme Court ruled that professional associations' restrictions on advertising violated the First Amendment's guarantee of free speech. Advertising thus increased among lawyers and other professionals, sparking increased competition. Second, two new periodicals, *The National Law Journal* and *The American Lawyer* began publishing articles concerning law firm finances and management. This also stimulated competition among the largest law firms, who vied for the best lawyers and began hiring public relations experts.

In the 1970s the Pepper law firm represented Volkswagen, first in product liability litigation in 1973 and then in 1976 when the German manufacturer built a Pennsylvania plant at which to manufacture its VW Rabbit. According to the firm's history, "Volkswagen was the first foreign automobile manufacturer to establish an assembly facility in the United States," so the law

Key Dates:

1890: G.W. Pepper joins the law firm of Bayard Henry in Philadelphia.
1900: The firm is renamed Henry, Pepper, Bodine & Pepper.
1922: Pepper is appointed to the U.S. Senate.
1928: Pepper returns to the law firm.
1954: Hamilton joins the firm, which merges with another Philadelphia firm, becoming Pepper, Bodine, Frick, Scheetz & Hamilton.
1960: Firm merges with Moffett, Frye & Leopold and is renamed Pepper Hamilton & Scheetz.
1969: Firm moves outside of Philadelphia for the first time, with branches in Harrisburg, Pennsylvania, and Washington, D.C.
1979: An office in Detroit is established.
1990: An office in New York City opens.
1992: The firm is restructured, forming a ten-member executive panel.
1997: The firm becomes a limited liability partnership (LLP) and shortly thereafter shortens its name to Pepper & Hamilton LLP.

firm faced several new legal challenges. This occurred after the 1973 Arab oil embargo increased oil prices, which in turn stimulated the demand for fuel efficient cars like the VW Rabbit.

When Strubing retired in the mid-1970s, he was succeeded by Augustus (Gus) Ballard in 1974. Ballard oversaw a greater expansion of the firm's national presence, with offices opening in Detroit in 1979, as well as in Berwyn, Pennsylvania, and Wilmington, Delaware in the 1980s. The firm's first overseas office was established in London in 1987 under the leadership of new chairman John G. Harkins, Jr. Moreover, the firm established an affiliate, called Pepper International Associates, to oversee activities in Chinese trade and investment. (That business consulting operation would end in the mid-1990s.)

The 1970s were also highlighted by several prominent cases for the growing firm. In 1975 it was involved when Congress created Consolidated Rail Corporation (Conrail) as a government-owned entity to take over bankrupt northeastern railroads. In the early 1980s the firm again played a major role when Conrail was privatized and made its initial public offering. These developments started the Pepper law firm's transportation practice that became one of its major areas of emphasis. Following the 1979 accident at the Three Mile Island nuclear power plant in Pennsylvania, the Pepper law firm represented liability insurers against thousands of claims. Class action settlements were reached, but many individual claims were being litigated in the early 1990s. After a November 1980 fire in Las Vegas' MGM Grand Hotel killed 87 people and injured over 1,000 people, the Pepper law firm was one of over 300 firms that got involved. Pepper defended the Taylor Construction Company that had managed the hotel's construction. It succeeded in getting all the federal cases transferred to the Las Vegas district court, employed 15 lawyers and several paralegals to prepare for trial, and then helped negotiate settlements for 99 percent of the plaintiffs. The Pepper firm's history booklet described it as "one of the most interesting, demanding engagements in the firm's history."

In 1986, John G. Harkins, Jr., became chairman of the firm. Under his leadership, the firm continued to expand the scope of its practice and expertise. In 1988 property insurance companies faced multiple lawsuits charging them with antitrust violations involving excessive prices and drastically reduced liability coverage. In response, Aetna Casualty & Surety Company recruited four outside law firms, including Pepper Hamilton & Scheetz. Aetna at the time also used the Philadelphia law firm to defend itself in a Dalkon Shield lawsuit in U.S. District Court in Virginia. The Dalkon Shield was a defective intrauterine birth control device that led to numerous product liability lawsuits and the bankruptcy of its manufacturer, A.H. Robins Company, Inc. of Richmond, Virginia. The Pepper law firm helped resolve these complex lawsuits and made it possible for Robins to be acquired by a pharmaceutical company.

The 1980s was famous for its many corporate mergers and acquisitions, and the Pepper law firm played a role in that trend. For example, in 1980 it "assisted one of the earliest preemptive strikes in corporate takeovers," according to its history booklet. The Pepper firm represented Sun Oil Company, one of at least seven companies that were interested in buying the Texas & Pacific Corporation from the Canadian Seagrams Company. Instead of waiting for the normal methods to occur, Sun Oil with the law firm's help took the initiative and made a preemptive strike by offering Seagrams an attractive price of $2.3 billion, which Seagrams accepted.

In 1988 the Pepper law firm represented the Swiss manufacturer Schindler Holding AG when it acquired the Westinghouse Elevator Company from the Westinghouse Electric Company. Over 60 Pepper lawyers and legal assistants helped in the complex deal.

The 1990s and Beyond

In 1992, Chairman Harkins and Paul A. Cunningham, former managing partner of the Washington, D.C. office, left to form their own firm of Harkins Cunningham. Six other Pepper Hamilton partners also joined the new firm that had offices in Philadelphia and Washington, D.C. At that time, the firm restructured, forming a ten-member executive committee led by an executive partner elected by the firm. Moreover, the firm ventured overseas in 1992, establishing an office in Moscow. The firm's first foray abroad had occurred five years earlier, when it opened a London office.

This focus on a global presence was curtailed in the late 1990s, when offices in Moscow and St. Petersburg were shuttered. Many American law firms had opened offices after the former Soviet Union disintegrated in 1991, but high rents and other factors caused some to withdraw. "Given the uncertainty of the business and political climates, we decided some months ago that it did not make economic sense for us to continue to maintain offices in the region," said Pepper Hamilton Executive Partner James Murray in *East European Business Law* of February 1998. The firm's withdrawal left London as its only international office, and that office was soon closed as well.

Nevertheless, the firm continued to grow, establishing a new office in Pittsburgh in 1995.

Moreover, in an era of numerous law firm mergers and a more globalized economy, Pepper Hamilton formed alliances with two U.K. law firms. In 1995 it signed a nonexclusive agreement to collaborate with Eversheds, a large firm with 12 British offices. Then in 2000 Pepper Hamilton and the U.K. firm McGrigor Donald began a close association to benefit their increasing number of clients with international dealings. Founded in 1792, McGrigor Donald included more than 210 lawyers practicing in Edinburgh, Glasgow, London, Belfast, and Brussels. Effective January 1, 2001, Pepper Hamilton merged with Jamieson Moore Peskin & Spicer of Princeton, New Jersey. Some 20 Jamieson Moore lawyers who worked in land use, government relations, banking, corporate securities, commercial litigation, trusts and estates, and ERISA joined Pepper Hamilton, bringing with them clients such as New Jersey Bankers Association, Janssen Pharmaceutical, and various high-technology firms. Some Jamieson Moore lawyers joined other law firms as the firm founded in 1927 dissolved.

During the late 1990s, the firm became a limited liability partnership (LLP) and shortened its name to Pepper Hamilton LLP. According to the *American Lawyer* roster of the nation's 100 largest law firms, Pepper Hamilton ranked number 91 based on its 1997 gross revenue of $101.5 million. The following year, gross revenues grew to $109 million, though in the face of stiff competition its ranking on the *American Lawyer* list slipped to 99. In 1999 the firm brought in $125.5 million, a 15.1 percent increase over the year before.

As the 21st century began, Pepper Hamilton faced numerous challenges. To remain competitive, Pepper Hamilton offered starting salaries of $100,000 to new law school graduates. Retaining the long-term loyalty of good lawyers was a major goal. Pepper Hamilton's 110-year history and good reputation gave the firm a solid foundation to move ahead.

Principal Competitors

Morgan, Lewis & Bockius; Dechert Price; Skadden, Arps.

Further Reading

Austin, James, ''Pepper Hamilton,'' *Legal Intelligencer*, January 2000.

''Coudert Wins Pepper Hamilton Offices,'' *International Financial Law Review* (London), March 1998, p. 4.

Devine, Jay, ''Partners in Pepper Hamilton to Form Separate Firm,'' *PR Newswire*, September 17, 1992, p. 1.

Friedman, Lawrence M., *Crime and Punishment in American History*, New York: BasicBooks, 1993.

Galanter, M., and T. Palay, *Tournament of Lawyers: The Transformation of the Big Law Firm,* Chicago: University of Chicago Press, 1993.

''Law Firm Update,'' *East European Business Law* (London), February 1998, p. 15.

A Proud Tradition: Pepper Hamilton & Scheetz Since 1890, Philadelphia: Pepper Hamilton & Scheetz, 1994.

Rainey, Doug, ''Pepper, Hamilton Adds Operation in Russia,'' *Delaware Business Review*, October 5, 1992, p. 24.

Stone, Peter H., ''Insurance Companies on the Defense,'' *San Francisco Chronicle*, April 18, 1988, p. B3.

''Watching Brief,'' *International Corporate Law* (London), February 1995, p. 12.

—David M. Walden

Plum Creek Timber Company, Inc.

999 Third Avenue, Suite 2300
Seattle, WA 98104-4096
U.S.A.
Telephone: (206) 467-3600
Toll Free: (800) 858-5347
Web site: http://www.plumcreek.com

Public Company
Incorporated: 1999
Employees: 2,325
Sales: $209.1 million (2000)
Stock Exchange: NYSE
Ticker Symbol: PCL
NAIC: 113310 Logging; 113110 Timber Tract Operations; 321113 Sawmills; 321212 Softwood Veneer and Plywood Manufacturing; 321219 Reconstituted Wood Product Manufacturing; 322110 Pulp Mills; 551112 Offices of Other Holding Companies

Plum Creek Timber is the second-largest owner of private timberlands in the U.S., with 7.9 million acres of land in six states. The company also controls nine wood-product conversion facilities and produces wood-fiber products, such as medium-density fiberboard. Plum Creek Timber is sold through the company's 49 warehouses, located throughout the country. The company is based in Seattle and operates two business segments: the Northern Resources segment consists of lands in Washington, Montana, Idaho, and Maine; the Southern Resources segment encompasses Louisiana and Arkansas. Plum Creek Timber exports 9 percent of its harvested timber.

Late 1800s to 1989: From Railroads to Timber

During the 1800s, an act of Congress gave land to railroad corporations as incentive to build railroads from the Great Lakes region to Puget Sound and the West Coast. Congress intended the land to be sold to settlers. While some of the land was sold and settled, much of it remained in control of the railroads and some was sold to timber companies such as Weyerhaeuser and Boise Cascade.

Then, in 1989, Burlington Resources, Inc. spun off Plum Creek Timber, L.P., which took its name from the Minnesota stream where the first U.S. lumber mill was built. Plum Creek Timber was established as a Master Limited Partnership to take advantage of the elimination of double taxation in the tax code. The company started with more than a million acres of forested land in Washington, Idaho, and Montana.

It was a tough time for a timber company. In early 1990, the spotted owl controversy erupted. The owl's habitat is in forests with trees that are hundreds of years old and 200 feet high or more. These trees make the most valuable timber. Environmentalists sued the U.S. Forest Service to protect the spotted owl, and in 1991 a federal judge issued an injunction against logging in the owl's habitat.

Besides the spotted owl problems, Plum Creek was faced also with criticism for its practice of clear-cutting forests quickly and expansively. Forest conservationists were unhappy with Plum Creek's practice of clearing several square miles at a time, what the conservationists referred to as ''checkerboarding.'' Some groups felt Plum Creek over-logged its land. U.S. Rep. Rod Chandler, R-Wash. called Plum Creek the ''Darth Vader of the state of Washington'' in a Wall Street Journal article in 1990. Subsequently, Plum Creek set out to clean up its reputation and establish a plan of action that would mollify environmentalists, preserve wildlife, and increase value for its business.

Plum Creek matched the U.S. Forest Service's shift in focus from harvesting to multi-use forest management. The company set three goals: To keep live trees at each site, preserve wildlife as much as possible, and retain dead trees (snags), which help maintain the habitat and contribute nutrients to the forest. An example of its efforts was a 10-mile strip of forest that was left at its Cougar Ramp site in Washington in 1993; although hardly a forest, the remaining trees contributed to the overall habitat in terms of shade, seed, and visual appeal.

In 1993, Jerry Franklin, a University of Washington professor and ecosystem analyst, presented ideas on ''kinder, gentler for-

Company Perspectives:

At Plum Creek, our entire company is united in carrying out the key strategies that are central to our future growth: Expanding our asset base with high-quality acquisitions. Managing our lands to maximize their value. Continually improving upon our market-driven, value-added product focus. And leading the industry in environmentally responsible resource management.

estry'' to President Clinton at a timber summit in Portland. Shortly thereafter, Plum Creek hired Franklin as an advisor, and his team developed a program they called ''environmental forestry.'' This involved selective logging, protection of streams and their habitats, and taking into account the aesthetic values of avoiding clear-cuts. Plum Creek reduced clear-cutting to 15 percent in the Northwest and to 10 percent in the Rocky Mountains.

Mid 1990s: Expansion into the Southern and Eastern U.S.

In 1996, Plum Creek acquired 538,000 acres of softwood timberland and three wood products production plants in Louisiana and Arkansas from Riverwood International Corp. The deal increased Plum Creek's timber ownership by 25 percent and diversified its land holdings. As part of the agreement, Plum Creek continued sending pulpwood to Riverwood's Louisiana board mill.

In 1998, Plum Creek purchased 905,000 acres of forests in Maine from South African Pulp and Paper (Sappi) for $180 million. This boosted Plum Creek's acreage to more than 3.3 million acres. The company agreed to supply Sappi's paper facility with fiber from these lands. Environmentalist groups, most notably the Natural Resources Council of Maine, opposed this move. The council speculated that Plum Creek would sell off recreational lands, but Plum Creek vowed that was not their plan.

Ten Years in the Making: The I-90 Land Swap in Washington State

When the government granted lands to the railroads in the 19th century, it granted only every other square mile. When timber companies logged these land parcels, they often left clear-cut areas starkly next to untouched areas. To help remedy this checkerboard effect and to make better use of its land, Plum Creek participated in a land swap with the U.S. Forest Service in Washington State. Ten years in the making, the swap was coined ''The I-90 Land Swap.'' In the deal, Plum Creek traded 42,000 acres of land that paralleled Interstate 90 east of Seattle for 11,500 acres of federal lands in the Cascades plus $4.3 million. Supporters argued that the swap moved private lands to areas where forestry made more sense and created public lands better suited for recreation. As part of the deal, Plum Creek also donated 838 acres to the government and held some lands for possible purchase in the future.

Some environmentalists protested the deal, claiming the swap violated the National Environmental Policy Act, the Endangered Species act, and other laws. Further complicating the matter was the discovery of the protected marbled murrelets on the government's land, which meant that Plum Creek could not harvest 1,000 acres of the land it was to receive. But Plum Creek surprised many in the timber industry with a new tactic: it sued the environmentalists for the right to log. The U.S. Forest Service and five environmental groups were named as defendants in the lawsuit. With the lawsuits pending and protestors staked out in the trees, the swap was in danger. Finally, however, in January 2000, after a settlement had been reached with Plum Creek getting about a third less land in exchange for more cash, the deal was finalized.

1990s and Beyond: An Emphasis on the Environment

In 1994, the American Forest and Paper Association established the Sustainable Forestry Initiative (SFI) to address environmental issues within the forestry industry. Developed by foresters, conservationists, and scientists, the program asked companies to use environmentally sound practices, address the needs of the future, adhere to environmentally responsible guidelines, consider the qualities unique to each area, and continuously improve forest management techniques.

Although Plum Creek had conducted third party audits of its practices in the past, in 1999 it added the SFI guidelines to its policies and completed audits of all its land holdings in compliance with SFI. The audits concluded that Plum Creek protected water quality, improved wood use, used chemicals prudently, and protected special sites.

Some environmental groups questioned the validity of Plum Creek's audits, but the company strived for a good image. It set guidelines, based on SFI, that addressed the impact of roads through Plum Creek lands. In June of 1997, Plum Creek developed a habitat conservation plan for the Bull Trout and worked with the National Marine Fisheries Service to create a Native Fish Habitat Conservation plan. The company set up riparian management practices, one of which was maintaining streams with woody debris. Plum Creek also set up land use, range management, and restoration planning. It created policies at its timber mills and wood plants in an attempt to address wood-fiber recovery, safe workplaces, waste disposal, and air quality.

Turn of the Century: Restructuring and a Major Acquisition

In July 1999 Plum Creek reclassified itself from a Master Limited Partnership to a Real-Estate Investment Trust (REIT). Not only did this have tax and financing advantages, it also separated timberlands from pulp and paper operations. Because pulp and paper operations had been performing poorly during this time, those areas brought down the stock of the entire company. Many timber companies converted these parts of their businesses to REITs in order to preserve their overall stock price and bolster their financials.

But Plum Creek didn't own any paper operations and instead converted the entire company to a REIT, a move not done before by any other company. The goal was to make it easier to raise capital, broaden the company's appeal to investors, and create REIT stocks, which were much more liquid than partner-

Key Dates:

1989: Plum Creek Timber Company, L.P., created when it is spun off from Burlington Resources.
1993: Plum Creek puts in place environmental forestry plans and policies.
1994: The Sustainable Forestry Initiative guidelines are established.
1996: Plum Creek buys 538,000 acres of timber land in Arkansas and Louisiana from Riverwood International Corp.
1997: The company builds a sawmill in Louisiana.
1999: Plum Creek becomes a publicly traded Real Estate Investment Trust (REIT).
2000: The Washington State I-90 Land Swap is completed.
2001: The company sells 44,500 acres of timber lands to Pope Resources. A merger with Georgia-Pacific's The Timber Company is finalized.

ship shares because REIT shares could be made available to individual investors, who were unable to buy into a limited partnership. After the REIT conversion, Plum Creek's previous controlling partner, SPO Partners, decreased ownership to 27 percent.

In September 2000, Plum Creek signed an agreement to merge with The Timber Company, an operating group of Georgia-Pacific Corporation. In October 2001, the merger was completed. The transaction was valued at about $4 billion and added 4.7 million acres of timberland to Plum Creek's holdings, making it the second-largest private timberland owner in the U.S., with more than 7.9 million acres in 19 states. As part of the deal, Plum Creek assumed $1 billion of The Timber Company's debt and agreed to honor a 10-year wood supply agreement between Georgia Pacific and The Timber Company.

Principal Competitors

Alliance Forest Products; Boise Cascade; Deltic Timber; Doman Industries; Fletcher Challenge Forests; Georgia-Pacific Group; International Forest Products; Longview Fibre; Louisiana-Pacific; MAXXAM; Weyerhaeuser; Willamette.

Further Reading

''$180 Million Sale of Maine Woodlands Troubles Environmentalists,'' *Washington Post*, October 7, 1998, p. A22.
Blackman, Ted, ''Plum Creek updates panel, lumber plants in Montana (parts I & II),'' *Wood Technology*, January 1995, p. 30.
Bond, Jeff, ''Timber's Good Guys,'' *Washington CEO*, June 2000.
Carlton, Jim, ''Plum Creek Timber to Purchase Land in the Northeast,'' *The Wall Street Journal*, October 7, 1998, p. B2.
DeSilver, Drew, ''More Timber for Plum Creek,'' *Seattle Times*, July 19, 2000, p. C1.
Didisheim, Pete, and Berk, Judy, Statement from The Natural Resources Council of Maine, October 6, 1998.
Draffan, George, ''Facts about Plum Creek Timber,'' *Railroads and Clearcuts*, September 1999.
Ervin, Keith, ''Plum Creek Sues Activists over Land Swap,'' *Seattle Times*, October 17, 1999, p. B1.
Fisher, Frank, ''Chunk of Maine Forest to be Sold,'' Associated Press, October 6, 1998.
——, ''Sappi Announces Deal to Sell 905,000 Acres of Maine Woods,'' *Boston Globe*, October 6, 1998.
''Forests: The biggest tree sale of all,'' *The Economist*, November 6, 1999.
Knickerbocker, Brad, '' 'New Forestry': A Kinder, Gentler Approach to Logging,'' *Christian Science Monitor*, June 20, 1995, p. 10.
Ludwick, Jim, ''Corporate Shift Will Open Plum Creek to All Investors,'' *The Missoulian*, June 9, 1998.
Mapes, Lynda V. ''Big Timber Swap Hits Snag,'' *Seattle Times*, July 21, 1999, p. A1.
——, ''Land Swap Delights Environmentalists,'' *Seattle Times*, November 4, 1999, p. B2.
——, ''Activists, Company Agree on Land Swap,'' *Seattle Times*, November 3, 1999, p. C1.
McClure, Robert, ''Bird Foils Big Timberland Swap,'' *Seattle Post-Intelligencer*, July 22, 1999, p. B1.
——, ''Partial Buyout Seen As Way Around Problem of Endangered Bird,'' *Seattle Post-Intelligencer*, September 10, 1999, A1.
McCoy, Charles, ''Plum Creek Timber Aiming to Convert Into A REIT, Boosting Acquisition Plans,'' *Wall Street Journal*, June 8, 1998, p. B11E.
Otanez, Andrea, ''Plum Creek Timber, Interior to Sign Pact on Habitat Protection,'' *Seattle Times*, November 28, 2000.
''Plum Creek Completes Acquisition of Central Maine Forestlands,'' *Business Wire*, posted November 12, 1998, http://www.businesswire.com.
''Plum Creek Plans Audits to Verify Forest Management Practices,'' *Wood Technology*, March 1999.
''Plum Creek Timber Company to Merge with Georgia-Pacific Subsidiary,'' *The Forestry Source*, September 2000.
''Plum Creek to Buy Products Unit,'' *Pulp & Paper*, October 1996 pp. 23–25.
''Public's 'Green' Attitudes Force Forest-Sector Changes,'' *Wood Technology*, September 1995.
''The I-90 Land Exchange Is Completed,'' *Seattle Post-Intelligencer*, January 6, 2000.
''Timber Co. Finances Purchase with Private Loan,'' *Corporate Financing Week*, October 12, 1998.
Raeburn, Paul, ''Can This Man Save Our Forests?,'' *Popular Science*, June 1, 1994, pp. 81–88.
Thomas, Tom E. ''Plum Creek's Chainsaw Massacre,'' *Business and Society Review*, Fall 1990.
Thompson, Steve, ''Seeing the Forest for the Trees,'' *Missoula Independent*, May 10, 2001.
Turcotte, Deborah, ''Plum Creek Timber Firm Seeks to Shed 'Evil' Image,'' *Bangor Daily News*, October 8, 1998.
Virgin, Bill, ''Timber Deal Is Struck: Plum Creek to Buy Spinoff Unit of GP,'' *Seattle Post-Intelligencer*, July 19, 2000, p. D1.

—Kerri DeVault

Randstad Holding n.v.

P.O. Box 12600
1100 AP Amsterdam-Zuidoost
The Netherlands
Telephone: +31 20 569 59 11
Fax: +31 20 569 55 20
Web site: http://www.randstadholding.com

Public Company
Incorporated: 1960 as Uitzendbureau Amstelveen
Employees: 15,570
Sales: EUR 5.81 billion (2000)
Stock Exchanges: Amsterdam London
Ticker Symbol: RAND
NAIC: 561320 Temporary Help Services; 561310 Employment Placement Agencies; 561330 Employee Leasing Services; 541612 Human Resources and Executive Search Consulting Services; 561720 Janitorial Services; 541511 Custom Computer Programming Services

Randstad Holding n.v. is a Netherlands-based international provider of staffing and employment services to businesses and institutions. With 2,000 branches in 12 European and North American countries, it is the third largest staffing company in the world and is the market leader in the Netherlands, Germany, and the southeastern United States. In 1996, Randstad was the Official Staffing Sponsor of the 1996 Olympic Games in Atlanta, and filled 16,000 positions. Randstad boasts an average growth rate of 20 percent annually over the past 25 years, and the company reached sales of $5.81 billion in 2000. Randstad placed 244,500 staffing employees worldwide in 2000, over twice the number the company placed five years previously. While Randstad's primary business is employment and staffing, the company also offers cleaning and security services.

Beginnings and Early Success

In 1960, Frits J.D. Goldschmeding was working on a thesis for a master's degree at Amsterdam's Vrije Universiteit. His topic: temporary employment. He subsequently started his own temporary services agency, known as Uitzendbureau, from his dorm room. Soon he had more than three-dozen employees. Goldschmeding is said to have conceived the idea after reading a Citroën annual report.

The company was renamed Randstad Uitzendbureau in 1964. (The Randstad is a very densely populated region in the western Netherlands made up of cities, towns, and villages that encircle an area of woods and lakes.) The next year, the company's first international branch, Interlabor, opened in Belgium. In 1968, new offices in Germany followed. The 32 offices in the three countries brought in more than Nfl 47 million of revenues in 1970. Three years later, Randstad broached the French market.

In 1974, a contract cleaning division was established in Germany. These services were initiated in Belgium the next year, and Belglas was acquired. Contract cleaning services were expanded to the Netherlands in 1976, and Korrekt Gebäudereinigung was acquired in Germany. Randstad cleaned or serviced a variety of different types of sites, including planes, trains, and buildings. According to the company, this revenue source grew consistently because businesses believed in the motivational benefit of a clean working environment while at the same time they preferred to delegate non-core activities. Randstad supported the formation of objective quality standards in the cleaning industry and has proudly displayed its ISO certification in this area since 1992.

In 1978, the corporate name was changed to Randstad Holding n.v. The next year, the company opened its 100th office and achieved a net income of more than Nfl 10 million.

Group revenues surpassed Nfl 500 million in 1980. The decade began with the formation of Randon, the security division, which opened in the Netherlands. Besides guard and surveillance services, Randstad provided a home security alarm system through Randon Meldkamer. The company felt its insistence on professionalism made it attractive to this market.

In 1983, the company continued its expansion in the Dutch staffing market with the purchase of a mid-sized Dutch temporary services agency, Tempo-Team, which specialized in indus-

Company Perspectives:

Employment market expertise is the key element in all services offered by Randstad, facilitating the supply of labor to organizations so they can become more effective and focused. This key expertise also underpins the Group's profile as an attractive and reliable employer able to attract and retain employees. These components can be translated into two core concepts: adaptability and employability.

trial and technical services, as did two other of Randstad's Dutch offices, Werknet and Otter-Westelaken. Belgium followed with training services in 1988, when automation services were added to the company's repertoire in the Netherlands. This profitable venture eventually had six offices. Software and hardware sales to financial, distribution, and transport companies added to the revenues of AICA, the computer services bureau, which also developed accounting systems.

Revenues exceeded Nfl 1 billion in time for the company's 25th anniversary in 1985. Over 1,300 staff and a daily average of 36,000 temporary employees then worked for Randstad's 257 offices in four countries. In addition, Lavold, a cleaning services company, was bought, adding to Randstad's capacity in the Netherlands and Belgium.

Randstad began training cashiers, computer operators, and telemarketers, and other personnel for its Dutch clientele in 1986. The Randstad Training Center consisted of fourteen offices in 1994; Randstad also conducted these activities onsite for client companies.

Offices were opened in Great Britain in 1989, when group revenues exceeded Nfl 2 billion. By 1993, the Randstad Employment there had seven offices. Randstad entered the Spanish market late in 1993, as the one-office firm Randstad Trabajo Temporal.

In the 1990s, Randstad began offering higher-trained technical staff in the Netherlands, Belgium, and Great Britain through nine specialized companies (Randstad Interim Techniek, Randstad Research & Development Services, Inter Techniek, Polydesign Nederland, Polydesign België, Interdesign, Randstad Inter Engineering, Randstad Specialist Engineering, and Technisch Bureau Visser). Randstad's technical services division was active in the machinery, transport equipment, electronics, hospitality, insurance, petroleum, and construction industries, among others.

Industry Liberalization in the 1990s

Since the 1960s, the Netherlands had an ideal environment for temp agencies. In the early 1990s, it was estimated that two percent of Dutch workers were temps, more than four times the ratio found in Germany. A third of all Dutch workers had worked for a temporary services agency at some time in their careers. In 1994, the company had 408 offices overall in the Netherlands.

The challenge for Randstad in Europe, like that for many other companies with international aspirations, was the restrictive attitude of certain governments, particularly Germany, Spain, and especially Italy. In these countries, temporary employment agencies were seen as a threat to the job security of long-term employees. The ''Doppeleinsatz'' requirement in Germany, where Randstad Zeit-Arbeit had 31 offices, mandated temporary agencies provide two successive temporary positions for every worker. After a group of temp agencies filed a complaint with the European Commission in 1992, Spain and Germany liberalized their markets somewhat; the ''Doppeleinsatz'' rule was waived for hard-to-place workers in Germany in 1994, and workers were allowed to work nine months as temporaries, rather than six months. A class action was filed against Italy, ultimately to be decided by the European Court of Justice. In areas where public and private sectors controlled labor supply, Randstad foresaw government agencies focusing on gathering candidates, while temporary agencies concentrated on matching the candidates to the most appropriate jobs. In 1994, legislation was passed allowing Belgians to work as long as six months as temporaries, compared to three months previously. Randstad operated under the names Interlabor Interim, Randstad Interim, and Flex Interim in Belgium.

After determining that many of its clients were seeking long-term solutions, Randstad set up several new programs. Vendor-on-Premise placed a Randstad staffing manager to support company management. Facility Staffing handled large-scale, long-term staffing needs. Outsourcing gave Randstad functional responsibility for an entire department, process, or function. Other solutions were labeled ''Vectoring'' and ''Temp-to-Hire.''

Preparing for a New Century

Randstad termed its processes ''social technology.'' ISO certification gave Randstad the opportunity to highlight its systematic approach. These international quality guidelines, originally applied to manufacturing industries, were extended to service industries in 1992 in the Netherlands. Soon, Randstad had picked up a series of certifications—first as a specialist cleaning company, and later, in 1993, as the first international temporary employment agency to receive the appellation.

In 1994, Randstad operated 780 offices in seven countries, including Belgium, Germany, France, Great Britain, and Spain. Nevertheless, the Netherlands hosted the majority—495—of the company's offices, where it had a 37 percent market share. Thirty-five percent of revenues were earned outside the Netherlands. On an average day, nearly 100,000 people were employed by Randstad. This figure had tripled from 36,000 in 1985. Most (86 percent, or Nfl 3.2 billion in 1994) of the firm's income came from temporary services.

The company's French operations, Flex and Randstad, were integrated in 1994 under the name Randstad Intérim. This move, which reduced the number of offices in France from 94 to 75, resulted in some loss of market share but also more efficiency and greater revenues.

The acquisition of Temp Force in 1993 allowed Randstad entrée into the world's largest temporary services market: the United States. Randstad limited itself exclusively to the Southeast, a region where growth in temporary services consistently exceeded 10 percent annually and in which relatively few

Key Dates:

1960: Company is founded in Amsterdam by Frits J.D. Goldschmeding as Uitzendbureau Amstelveen.
1964: Company is renamed Randstad Uitzendbureau.
1965: Company founds Interlabor Interim in Belgium, its first international venture.
1978: Company is renamed Randstad Holding n.v.
1980: Company enters security market with foundation of Randon in the Netherlands.
1983: Company acquires Uizendbureau Tempo-Team and Lavold.
1990: Company is listed on the Amsterdam Stock Exchange.
1992: Company acquires the Flex Group.
1993: Company starts U.S. operations with the acquisition of Temp Force and Jane Jones.
1996: Company becomes an official sponsor of the Atlanta Olympics, provides 16,000 staffing employees.
1998: Company is listed on the AEX-Optiebeurs; Hans Zwartz succeeds Frits J.D. Goldschmeding as CEO.
2000: Company unveils online employment Web site.
2001: Randstad acquires Strategix Solutions.

worked as temporaries. In spite of Randstad's tradition of hiring workers with higher than average educational backgrounds—more than 60 percent had attended post-secondary schools—they reported no problems regarding worker skills in the South, which had long had a spotty reputation for education. Randstad acquired 12 Atlanta offices with the Temp Force purchase, and instantly became the city's largest temporary employer. Nashville's Jane Jones Enterprises, Tennessee's largest independent staffing service, was bought the same year, giving Randstad a total of 25 offices in the United States. Nearly 40 new offices were opened in the next two years so that by 1995, the company had over 70 offices in the United States. Erik Vonk, a newly hired banker who specialized in mergers and acquisitions, led U.S. operations, which were named Randstad Staffing Services.

As had been its custom elsewhere, the company actively managed its acquisitions in the United States, to the chagrin of many existing managers—fewer than half stayed with the new owner more than two years. A chasm existed in most temporary agencies between recruiting temps and marketing to clients; however, Randstad managers were responsible for both areas. The company also prided itself on its decentralized organization.

Randstad supported its risky American start-up with an audacious marketing strategy. While bidding to supply employees for the 1996 Olympic Games, the company elected to become an official sponsor—an unprecedented position for a staffing service. The challenging contract reportedly gave the company a loss on some of its assignments but allowed it instant name recognition and a chance to display its skills. Part of the job included finding over 4,000 bus drivers for the public transportation system. Despite the widespread problems reported in the press, some difficulties in communication between Randstad and the Atlanta Committee for the Olympic Games, the disaster of the July 27 bombing in the Centennial Olympic Park, the company assembled the largest single peacetime flexible workforce to date and counted the experience as positive for the company. Debra Drew, Randstad's vice president and director of Olympic programs told *Workforce* magazine in 1997 that the company had expected a 30 percent staff "no-show"—employees quitting or skipping work without notice. In fact, only four percent of Randstad's Olympic employees did so. "The opportunity to work at the Games just changed people's lives. In the end, it wasn't just about giving people a job, it was giving them the experience of a lifetime," she said.

The exposure gained by participation in the Olympics seemed to help the company grow. In 1997, the company had reached 1,000 branches in Europe and North America. In 1998, the company expanded its North American operations by acquiring the staffing branch of its competitor AccuStaff, Inc. The $850 million cash deal boosted its American presence and helped the company become one of the industry leaders in the United States. Also that year, founder Frits Goldschmeding stepped down as CEO and was succeeded by Hans Zwarts.

The turn of the century saw further growth for Randstad on both sides of the Atlantic. In 1999, the company enlarged its European operations with its acquisition of Time Power Personal-Dienstleistungen in Germany and Tempo Grup in Spain. However, 2000 saw the company with lower revenues than expected, and that year the company sold its cleaning services company Lavold. In 2001, the company once again expanded its operations in North America with its acquisition of Strategix Solutions . By acquiring Strategix, Randstad increased its locations in the U.S. from 89 to 478, providing the company with offices in 34 states. Randstad planned further growth for the twenty-first century, both organically through existing holdings and through acquisitions. In its 2000 annual report, the company specifically pointed to Germany, Spain, and Italy as promising growth regions.

Principal Subsidiaries

BouwFlex; InterTech; Tempo-Team IT-Flex; Randstad Automatiseringsdiensten; Randstad Interim Kader; Randstad Polytechniek; Randstad Interlabor (Belgium); Randstad Vikar (Denmark); Randstad Interim (France); Randstad Zeit-Arbeit (Germany); Time Power Personal-Dienstleistungen (Germany); Randstad Italia (Italy); Randstad Interim (Luxembourg); Randstad Trabajo Temporal (Spain); Tempo Grup (Spain); Randstad Schweiz (Switzerland); Randstad Employment Bureau (UK); e-staff (US); Excel Temporary Services (US); Modis Professional Services (US); Placers (US); Randstad Staffing Services (US); The Richard Michael Group (US); Tempo Services (US).

Principal Divisions

Randstad Europe; Randstad North America; Yacht; Capac/Hedson; Tempo-Team/Otto-Westelaken Group; Cleaning; Security.

Principal Competitors

Adecco; Spherion; Vedior.

Further Reading

"AccuStaff Inc.," *The Wall Street Journal*, September 17, 1998, p. C20.

"Accustaff to Sell Staffing Unit to Randstad," *The New York Times*, August 29, 1998, p. B4.

"Atlanta's Top 25 Temporary Employment Agencies," *Atlanta Business Chronicle*, January 9, 1998, p. 6B.

"Atlanta's Top 25 Temporary Employment Agencies," *Atlanta Business Chronicle*, March 22, 1996, p. 8B.

Branningan, Martha, "Randstad Holding Agrees to Purchase Division of Accustaff for 850 million," *The Wall Street Journal*, August 28, 1998, p. B4.

Bueno, Jacqueline, "Shortage of Bus Drivers Has Put Organizers of Olympics in a Jam," *The Wall Street Journal*, October 25, 1995, p. 4S.

Coleman, Zach, "Major Acquisition Boosts Randstad's U.S. Plans," *Atlanta Business Chronicle*, September 4, 1998, p. 16A.

DeChant, Meredith, "Atlanta's Top 20 Temporary Employment Agencies," *Atlanta Business Chronicle*, June 23, 1995, p.10B.

DeChant, Meredith, "Atlanta's Top 20 Employment Agencies," *Atlanta Business Chronicle*, June 23, 1995, p. 10B.

DeLavan, Joanne, "Temping Appeals to a Wide Range of Workers," *Atlanta Journal-Constitution*, September 10, 1995.

DeMarco, Edward, "Randstad Will Try to Boost U.S. Temp Use," *Atlanta Business Chronicle*, May 7, 1993, p. 10A.

Dorsey, James M., "Randstad Expects to Post Surge in Profits for 1999," *Wall Street Journal Europe*, January 11, 2000, p. 6.

Flynn, Gillian, "HR's Game Plan for the Olympics," *Personnel Journal*, July 1996, p. 72.

Flynn, Gillian, "The Summer Olympics: An HR Disaster?," *Workforce*, February 1997, pp. 25, 28.

"Frits Goldschmeding, Eredoctor University of Rochester," Amsterdam: Randstad Holding n.v., n.d.

Gelnar, Maaike VeenMartin, "Randstad Lowers Forecasts for 2001 for a Second Time," *Wall Street Journal Europe*, April 26, 2001, p. 4.

Hiday, Jeffrey L., "Temporary Workers Reap Higher Pay, Competition, Changes in Sector Also Boost Benefits," *The Wall Street Journal*, November 8, 1996, p. B14.

Joyner, Tammy, "Atlanta Staff Firm Nears Top of Industry with Acquisition," *Knight-Ridder/Tribune Business News*, August 28, 1998.

Laster, Kasee, "Changes in Temping Industry Varied, But Needed," *Business Ledger*, June 13, 1995, p. 14.

Pousner, Howard, "Welcoming the World," *Atlanta Journal-Constitution*, May 9, 1995.

"Randstad to Buy AccuStaff for $850 Million Cash," *Wall Street Journal Europe*, August 31, 1998, p. 3.

Rose, Robert L. and Martin du Bois, "Temporary-Help Firms Start New Game: Going Global, Far-Flung Networks Are Key Assets As Clients Expand Internationally," *The Wall Street Journal*, May 16, 1996, p. B4.

Salwen, Kevin G., "How a Bold Temp Agency Took Gambles—and Won," *The Wall Street Journal*, July 5, 1995, p. 1S.

Turner, Melissa, "Randstad Signs on as Olympic Sponsor, Will Handle Hiring," *Atlanta Journal-Constitution*, September 8, 1994.

Van de Krol, Ronald, "The Netherlands' Invisible Army," *International Management*, March, 1993, pp. 44–45.

Vance, Nick, "Many Ways to Work Temp," *Atlanta Employment Weekly*, June 18–24, 1995.

—update: Lisa Whipple

RF Micro Devices, Inc.

7628 Thorndike Road
Greensboro, North Carolina 27409-9421
U.S.A.
Telephone: (336) 664-1233
Fax: (336) 931-7454
Web site: http://www.rfmd.com

Public Company
Incorporated: 1991
Employees: 1,100
Sales: $289 million (2000)
Stock Exchanges: NASDAQ
Ticker Symbol: RFMD
NAIC: 334413 Semiconductor and Related Device Manufacturing

RF Micro Devices, Inc. (RFMD) designs, develops, manufactures, and markets radio frequency integrated circuits (RFICs), for wireless communications products and applications. The company's products are included in PCS (personal communications services) or wireless phones, cordless phones, wireless local area networks, wireless local loop handsets, industrial radios, wireless security systems, and remote meter readers. The company designs products using four semiconductor process technologies, two of which are silicon-based and two of which use gallium arsenide (GaAs). Generally, GaAs products offer better electrical performance, while silicon-based products are less expensive. Through the company's registered Optimum Technology Matching, RFMD offers customers a trade-off between performance and cost.

Developing RFIC Products for Wireless: 1991–96

RFMD was founded in 1991 in Greensboro, North Carolina. The three cofounders were Jerry Neal, the firm's marketing executive; William Pratt, the company's first CEO and later chief technology officer; and Powell Seymour, vice-president of operations. All three were former employees of Analog Devices, Inc., a semiconductor manufacturer based in Norwood, Massachusetts. Pratt and Seymour were laid off in 1991 when ADI closed down the new products division they had set up in Greensboro. The two men asked Neal, who was still working for ADI, to help them raise capital for the new venture. Realizing that Pratt's strength was in technology and not management, they hired David Norbury as president and CEO in September 1992. Norbury had 10 years of experience in the semiconductor industry, most recently as president and CEO of Polylythics, Inc., in Santa Clara, California.

From the beginning, the company was focused on designing RFIC products for the commercial wireless market. Within that market RFMD would develop products for a wide range of applications, including cellular and PCS, cordless telephony, industrial radios, wireless local area networks (LANs), wireless local loop (WLL) systems, wireless security, and wireless utility meter reading. The company's products included amplifiers, mixers, attenuators, switches, modulators, demodulators, oscillators, and frequency synthesizers. These would convert, switch, process, and amplify the high-frequency signals that carry information to be transmitted or received by devices for wireless personal communications.

In 1992 TRW Inc., a Cleveland-based space and defense contractor, wanted to license a semiconductor technology called GaAs HBT (gallium arsenide heterojunction bipolar transistor) that it had developed for the federal government. TRW didn't have the resources to commercialize the technology and was looking for a partner. It became interested in RFMD. By 1993 RFMD had produced 16 designs for chips based on TRW's GaAs HBT technology. From 1993 until RFMD built its wafer fabrication plant in 1998, TRW would be a contract manufacturer for RFMD. In 1996 TRW would invest $5 million in RFMD stock for a 10 percent ownership interest in the company.

During the 1990s GaAs semiconductor technology would emerge as an effective alternative or complement to silicon technology in many high-performance RF (radio frequency) applications. Devices with GaAs technology typically operate at much higher speeds than silicon devices, or at the same speeds with lower power consumption. RFMD's GaAs HBT products included power amplifiers and small signal devices that were used in advanced subscriber handsets manufactured by leading original equipment manufacturers (OEMs), includ-

Company Perspectives:

RF Micro Devices possesses an exclusive industry license for gallium arsenide (GaAs) heterojunction bipolar transistor (HBT) technology, a state-of-the-art process technology originally developed for high-level military applications. RF Micro Devices' GaAs HBT components combine quality, reliability, performance and competitive pricing—placing RFMD at the forefront of the RFIC (radio frequency integrated circuits) market. RFMD operates the largest GaAs HBT production facility in the world, and the Company continues to add capacity. By the end of calendar year 2000, it is anticipated that the Company's fabrication facilities will be capable of producing 60,000 wafers annually. Finally, by continuing to recruit design expertise (e.g., high-demand RF engineers and technicians) at its headquarters and remote design centers, the Company is well positioned to leverage new design activity into additional volume production programs. RFMD's design talent encompasses a variety of technologies, including GaAs HBT, Silicon bipolar and BiCMOS, Silicon Germanium and GaAs MESFET.

ing Nokia, LG International Corp., Samsung Co. Ltd., Motorola Inc., Robert Bosch GmbH, NEC Inc., Kyocera International Inc., and LM Ericsson Telephone Co.

In 1993 RFMD was selected by Qualcomm Inc. to provide four integrated circuits (IC) for its new digital cell phones. Over the next four years TRW would have to expand its plant three times in order to keep up with demand, tripling its GaAs HBT production. RFMD's second-largest customer in fiscal 1996 was Cincinnati Microwave, Inc., which was experiencing financial difficulties that eventually led to its bankruptcy. In fiscal 1997 Samsung accounted for 23 percent of RFMD's sales, and Qualcomm was its largest customer, accounting for about 33 percent of RFMD's revenue. When Qualcomm demanded everything RFMD could produce, RFMD balked at the idea of being locked into one customer. As a result, it lost most of Qualcomm's business in fiscal 1998. Other cell phone makers were getting interested in RFMD, and the company picked up Samsung, Nokia, and LG International Corp. as customers.

In June 1996 RFMD expanded its strategic relationship with TRW Inc. TRW provided $25 million in equity and debt financing, including $5 million for 10 percent of RFMD's stock, and became a significant shareholder in RFMD. TRW granted RFMD a technology license to develop products using TRW's patented GaAs HBT technology for commercial wireless communications applications. The alliance with TRW enabled RFMD to realize its goal of constructing a wafer fabrication facility to manufacture products using GaAs HBT technologies developed by TRW. Prior to the completion of the facility in September 1998, TRW supplied RFMD with GaAs wafer products. In June 1998 an additional technology license was granted for MBE process patent rights.

Rapid Growth as a Public Company: 1997–2000

At the end of fiscal 1997, RFMD had 133 employees. Revenue was $28.8 million, and the company reported net income of $1.7 million, compared to fiscal 1996 revenue of $9.5 million and a net loss of $5.2 million. The company's IPO in June 1997 raised $38 million. The money was needed to finance construction of RFMD's wafer fabrication facility. Revenue for fiscal 1998 rose to $45.4 million, with a net loss of $500,000.

As part of RFMD's strategy to expand its line of silicon-based RFICs and maintain or increase the portion of overall revenue attributable to silicon-based products, the company entered into a multiyear agreement with IBM Corp. to use its advanced Blue Logic silicon process technology. RFMD's fiscal 1998 revenue from the sale of silicon-based products was $5.2 million. That figure would increase to $15.0 million in fiscal 1999 and $27.2 million in fiscal 2000. In January 1999 RFMD expanded its relationship with IBM to include access to IBM's silicon germanium foundry services. RFMD subsequently designed and sold products using that technology.

RFMD completed construction of its 64,000-square-foot wafer fabrication facility in Greensboro, North Carolina, in June 1998, and began fabricating its own GaAs HBT wafers there in September. By fiscal 2000 the Greensboro facility would account for $180.5 million in sales, or 62.5 percent of total revenue. The company used two independent foundries to supply silicon-based products and another independent foundry to supply GaAs MESFET devices. RFMD also purchased some GaAs HBT wafers from TRW. Six vendors in Asia and one in the United States were used to package and assemble RFMD's products.

With the company's wafer fabrication facility going into production in September 1998, revenue for fiscal 1999 ending March 27 more than tripled to $152.9 million, and net income was a healthy $19.6 million. Wall Street pushed RFMD's stock price from a high of $13 a share in August 1998 to a high around $95 a share in March 1999. In January the company raised about $116 million through a secondary stock offering. It declared a two-for-one stock split payable on March 31, 1999. Another two-for-one stock split was declared later in the year, payable on August 18, 1999.

During calendar 1999 RFMD opened two design centers, one in Cedar Rapids, Iowa, and one in Scotts Valley, California. In June 1999 it opened a small sales office in the United Kingdom to help serve European customers. RFMD's products were sold through 17 U.S. sales representative firms and 14 firms based outside the United States. In April 2000 the company established a sales and support team in Taiwan.

In June 1999 RFMD created four internal organizations: Digital Cellular, Power Amplifier Products, Silicon Systems, and Custom Products. Each organization would have its own design engineering, marketing, applications engineering, product engineering, production/inventory control, and financial management functions. The reorganization was intended to improve new product development, reduce bureaucracy, and improve service to the company's principal wireless customers, and was necessary to control the company's rapid growth.

RFMD also established an integrated MCM (multichip module) assembly facility in Greensboro to complement its wafer fabrication and testing capability. It was responding to demand from its customers that it develop products that combine one or more integrated circuits with one or more passive components,

Key Dates:

1991: RF Micro Devices, Inc. (RFMD) is founded.
1996: TRW Inc. invests in RFMD.
1997: RFMD goes public with an IPO on the NASDAQ.
1998: RFMD completes construction of its wafer fabrication facility in Greensboro, North Carolina.

such as capacitors, inductors, and resistors, into a stand-alone package, or module. Previously, RFMD had relied on outside vendors for assembling and packaging of these modules. The new MCM assembly facility represented a vertical expansion that required an expertise substantially different from its RFIC fabrication processes.

In September 1999 RFMD began construction of a second, 128,000-square-foot fab facility, dubbed Greensboro II, at a site near its first facility. Maintaining and expanding manufacturing capacity was seen as an important element in the company's continuing success.

As part of RFMD's effort to evaluate markets other than wireless communications, the company expanded its GaAs HBT license arrangement with TRW to include products for commercial coaxial and other nonfiber wire applications. RFMD would begin designing products for those markets, including applications such as cable modems, set-top converter boxes, television tuners, and products for the digital subscriber line (DSL) market.

Revenue for fiscal 2000 ending March 25 rose 89 percent to $289.0 million. Net income increased by about 250 percent to $50.1 million. During the previous 12 months the company's stock had split twice and increased more than fivefold in value. For fiscal 2000 sales to Nokia, the world's largest cell phone maker, were about $169 million, or 59 percent of RFMD's revenue.

The company announced it would expand its original Greensboro fab facility to increase capacity from 35,000 wafers per year to a potential 60,000 wafers per year. In February 2000 RFMD entered into another alliance with Qualcomm Inc. to provide advanced power amplifiers for the CDMA (code-division multiple access) market, one of three wireless telephone transmission technologies.

RFMD grew rapidly, from only 133 employees at the end of fiscal 1997 to 817 employees at the end of fiscal 2000. It faced significant challenges in managing that growth effectively. The company was also in the process of expanding its manufacturing capacity, with a second facility expected to begin production before the end of calendar 2000.

TRW's ownership interest in RFMD, which has fluctuated between 10 percent and 30 percent, has kept RFMD from being a takeover target, among other benefits. Saddled with a huge amount of debt from its $6.6 billion acquisition of a European auto parts maker, TRW has had to sell some of its RFMD stock to raise cash. At the end of fiscal 2000 TRW owned about 18 percent of RFMD's stock.

Principal Divisions

Digital Cellular; Power Amplifier Products; Silicon Systems; Broadband Products; Custom Products.

Principal Competitors

Conexant Systems, Inc.; Fujitsu Ltd.; Hitachi Ltd.; Matsushita Communication Industrial Co.; Philips N.V.; Anadigics; TriQuint Semiconductor Inc.

Further Reading

Andrews, Walter, "IBM, Analog Devices SiGe Deal Spurs GaAs Attack," *Electronic News,* December 13, 1993, p. 52.
Craver, Richard, "Greensboro, N.C.-Based RF Micro Devices Targets Broadband-Wired Services," *Knight-Ridder/Tribune Business News,* August 20, 1999.
Dorsch, Jeff, "RF Micro Devices Sets Up 4 Units," *Electronic News,* June 21, 1999, p. 34.
Gibson, Paul, "Little Powerhouse," *Electronic Business,* February 2000, p. 86.
"IBM, RF Micro Collaboration," *Electronic News,* October 18, 1999, p. 6.
McMillan, Alex Frew, "Chips Are Down," *Business North Carolina,* April 1998, p. 26.
Morrison, Gale, "IBM Silicon Germanium Capacity Is Spotlighted," *Electronic News,* March 30, 1998, p. 16.
Prizinsky, David, "RF Micro Devices Deal to Forward TRW $150 Million," *Crain's Cleveland Business,* February 21, 2000, p. 2.
——, "TRW Begins Asset Sale in Move to Trim Debt," *Crain's Cleveland Business,* May 10, 1999, p. 3.
"Two Greensboro, N.C.-Area Technology Firms Make Statewide 'Fast 50' List," *Knight-Ridder/Tribune Business News,* August 20, 1999.
Veverka, Amber, "Greensboro, N.C.-Based Wireless Supplier Plans Expansion," *Knight-Ridder/Tribune Business News,* July 16, 1999.
Weinberg, Neil, "Swords into Dow Shares," *Forbes,* March 6, 2000, p. 148.

—David P. Bianco

River Oaks Furniture, Inc.

1014 North Gloster Street
Tupelo, Mississippi 38801
U.S.A.
Telephone: (662) 680-5585
Fax: (662) 680-4334
Web site: http://www.riveroaksfurn.com

Private Company
Incorporated: 1987
Employees: 1,800
Sales: $126.3 million (1999 est.)
NAIC: 337121 Upholstered Household Furniture Manufacturing

As its current CEO Thomas A. Dieterich maintains, River Oaks Furniture, Inc., is virtually a new company, one that in April 1999 emerged from the bankrupt ashes of its predecessor of the same name. Although restructured as a private company and reorganized with new personnel, it is in the same business as its forerunner—the design and manufacture of leather, upholstered, and reclining furniture under River Oaks, River Crest, and Gaines brand names. The company sells its furniture to a range of stores, including chain outlets and independent retailers. Its largest customer is Sam's Club, Wal-Mart Stores' wholesale club division. Dieterich and other board members now own part of the company.

1987–89: River Oaks Is Successfully Established

In some ways, a history of River Oaks Furniture involves an account of two different businesses, that of the River Oaks company founded by Stephen L. Simons in 1987, and that of a company with the same name that emerged in 1999 from the bankrupt remains of the first company.

Simons, a former executive with Finger Furniture, incorporated the first business with the River Oaks name in August 1987. He headed a group of six investors, five of whom, including Simons and Thomas Keenum, had previously invested in BenchCraft, a furniture manufacturer located in Blue Mountain, Mississippi, that was later acquired by Masco Corporation and became part of LifeStyle Furnishings International, Ltd. The sixth investor was Lawrence (Larry) Ansin, CEO and sole proprietor of Joan Fabrics, a Massachusetts' fabric manufacturer. He had met Simons in the mid-1970s, when Simons was a furniture buyer for a Texas retailer, and had eventually befriended him.

Simons was CEO of the new company, and Keenum was its secretary and treasurer. Both were on the firm's three-member board of directors. The president was John Nail, a veteran Mississippi furniture manufacturer. River Oaks, then based in an old muffler shop in Fulton, Mississippi, began manufacturing mid-priced leather and upholstered furniture. Its line included chairs, love seats, and sofas, using River Oaks and River Crest trade names.

In March 1988, the company's investors established R-O Realty, Inc., another Mississippi corporation. It was set up to purchase real estate that it would then lease to River Oaks. In that same year, Larry Ansin decided to sell Joan Fabrics. Assuming that its sale would require a noncompetition agreement, he arranged to sell his share of River Oaks' stock to his father, Harold Ansin, for the amount of his original investment.

From the outset, Simons, Keenum, and Nail used their industry contacts to quickly build the company's business. Within just a couple of years, its brands were carried by regional and national furniture chains as well as independent retailers. Expansion inevitably followed.

1990–95: Period of Rapid Growth in Sales Brings River Oaks National Recognition

In 1990, the company opened a new plant in Baldwyn, Mississippi, and within a year, because of booming sales, had to move ahead its plans to increase the size of the facility from 50,000 to 100,000 square feet, more than doubling its sales volume and work force.

Two years later, the company initiated a ''Sofas and More'' merchandising program. To independent retail outlets and furniture chains, it offered room packages consisting of furniture

Company Perspectives:

By improving customer service, consolidating our manufacturing capacity, enhancing our delivery capabilities and our product quality, we have strengthened customer relationships which had suffered as a result of the Company's financial difficulties. As we move forward in the new season, we are pleased to report that the tough decisions are now behind us, putting River Oaks well on track to emerge from the reorganization process as a streamlined, efficient manufacturer tightly focused on servicing our valued customers. Through our renewed commitment to customer service, our customers can rest assured that River Oaks will be here to serve them for many years to come.

from its own lines as well as accessories made by other companies. Included in the accessories were lamps, small tables, rugs, and wall hangings.

In 1993, the company went public and made a successful IPO, but not without some attendant bad press. In that year, Larry Ansin died of an inoperable brain tumor. Harold Ansin and trustees of the Ansin Foundation, established by Larry, filed a complaint against both River Oaks and Simons and Keenum in a U.S. District Court in Massachusetts. In their suit, the plaintiffs claimed that Simons and Keenum had fraudulently induced Harold Ansin to sell his shares in the company ten months before they completed plans to take the company public and make an initial stock offering. The suit maintained that the men had kept their intention to take River Oaks public hidden in a successful effort to encourage Harold Ansin to sell his stock in the company for far less than it would have been worth after the company's IPO. It would take three years for the case to come to trial.

Meanwhile, River Oaks was otherwise faring very well. It got a major helping hand in 1993 when it was named an official supplier to 83 military post exchanges in the United States and at bases overseas. That, with reasonably good market conditions, boosted its revenue from $46.2 million in 1992 to $70.1 million, a 52 percent increase. In fact, River Oaks had recorded very strong revenue gains each year since it started, and was averaging a healthy 50 percent increase each year. It was also adding new accounts at an enviable rate, totaling over 650 active clients by 1993. Its performance that year earned it 69th place in *Business Week* magazine's list of the top small-cap companies in America.

Because of its previous performance, River Oaks put its projected sales for 1994 in the $88 million to $90 million range. In actuality, it revenues rose to $107.8 million, netting the company a $4.5 million profit. It was the company's best year, and one that seemed to justify the expanding steps it had taken, including its 1994 purchase of Gaines Furniture Manufacturing, Inc., located in McKenzie, Tennessee, and the opening of a plant in Compton, California.

Founded in 1952, Gaines was one of the Southeast's leading designers and manufacturers of low- to medium-priced leather and upholstered furniture, including sofas, love seats, chairs, and sectional sofas. Its specialty was leather pieces. Under its CEO, Andrew W. Byrd, Gaines had recorded sales of $33 million in 1993. After acquiring the company, River Oaks added the Gaines line to its own, but it moved that line's production site to Belden, Mississippi.

At its 1994 peak, River Oaks had four plants in Mississippi (River Oaks East) and one in California (River Oaks West), and all were staying busy. There was a downside, however; the company's interest and SG&A (selling, general, and administrative) expenses rose higher than were projected, primarily as a result of phasing out the start-up costs of River Oaks West, incurring sizable goodwill expenses in taking over the Gaines line, and adding new travel and product development costs. Because the industry was about to slump, it was a bad time for River Oaks to increase its debt service.

Initially, the downturn that hit the furniture industry in 1995 did not seem to phase the company. Its sales reached a new high of $143.1 million. However, its debt interest and other increasing costs led to a net profit of just $1.1 million. The company was also beginning to experience some further difficulties that would finally lead to its dissolution. Some of the problems were not recognized at the time, including errant accounting that had led to misstatements in the company's reports filed with the Securities Exchange Commission.

1996–98: Struggling Under Chapter 11 and Reorganizing

In 1996, River Oaks' revenue dropped off by $16.8 million, resulting in a net loss of $1.2 million, the company's first loss since 1990. Moreover, on March 26, 1996, the Ansin suit finally reached the trial phase, and within two weeks the federal district court awarded the complainants compensatory damages of $2.3 million, a judgment affirmed on appeal in 1997. It was not good timing for Simons and River Oaks, for despite the fact *Upholstery Design & Manufacturer* still listed River Oaks as a Top 50 company, the firm was sinking into the red. In 1997, its third-quarter net loss reached $3.9 million, compelling the company to take some drastic steps to stem the flow. It idled its plant in Fulton, consolidated its production with its plant in New Albany, and laid off 100 employees, which cut the company's total workforce to less than 1,500. By then it was clear the company's explosive growth had simply been too incautious, and necessary downsizing had begun.

River Oaks had to turn its focus to its corporate earnings in 1997. It engaged Horne CPA Group of Jackson, Mississippi, to unravel account discrepancies from prior years, discovering in the process that in 1995 its former auditors, Chicago-based BDO Seidman, had made misstatements in company reports. The company then brought a $30 million suit against BDO Seidman for that firm's alleged improprieties. The damage was irreparable, however. Because of the company's liquidity problems and financial and legal entanglements, NASDAQ delisted River Oaks' stock. In March 1998, after further profit margins declines added to the company's woes, River Oaks filed for Chapter 11 protection from creditors in order to reorganize under an acting CEO. The job fell to Len York of New York and Charlotte, North Carolina-based OSNOS & Company, the consulting firm that River Oaks engaged to assist in its reorganization and streamlining. In April 1998, the company received bankruptcy court

Key Dates:

1987: Company is founded by Stephen L. Simons and five other investors.
1992: Company initiates its Sofas and More merchandising program.
1993: River Oaks goes public; trustees of the Ansin Foundation file complaint against the company and two officers in U.S. District Court.
1994: Company acquires Gaines Manufacturing.
1996: Ansin trustees win compensatory damages of $2.3 million.
1998: Simons resigns as CEO; company files voluntary petition under Chapter 11 and retains OSNOS & Company to assist its restructuring as a private entity with the same name.
1999: Thomas A. Dieterich is appointed River Oaks CEO and CFO.

approval of $32.9 million in debtor-in-possession (DIP) financing, provided by New York-headquartered BNY Financial Corp.

Over the remainder of 1998, River Oaks took some severe measures to complete its downsizing and consolidate its operations. It reduced its plants in Baldwyn, Mississippi, and Compton, California, to one each, cutting its work force by another 600. According to York, it also ''made dramatic progress in streamlining its operations, reducing operating costs and enhancing operating efficiencies.'' Among the fatalities were Simons and Nail, who were required to resign and leave the company as a condition of its restructuring.

1999–2001: New Leadership

At the beginning of 1999, Ashley Furniture executive Thomas A. Dieterich was appointed permanent CEO to replace York and head up River Oaks' recovery. Dieterich brought 25 years of experience to the task. At the time of his selection, he was Ashley's vice-president of sales for its upholstery division and had the principal responsibilities of overseeing sales and developing merchandising and marketing strategies. Prior to that he had been a partner in Southern Traditions Furniture Company, and before that had been a sales manager with Jackson Manufacturing Company, an independent sales representative, and a retail furniture store manager.

Dieterich took the view that the ''old company'' was made ''history'' as of April 1, 1998, when the interim executives began River Oaks' emergence from its Chapter 11 ashes. By the time he took the reins, Dieterich claimed that River Oaks had become ''an entirely different company with different employees.'' The old company was simply replaced. The new one, organized as a private Mississippi corporation, was partly owned by Dieterich and existing board members Thomas Keenum, Douglas Jumper, and Don Murphy. In March 1999, it bought the operational assets of the old company, which, for the sell-off, had been restyled as the River Oaks Distribution Company. Included, along with its properties, were its River Oaks name, logos, sign marks, trademarks, unexpired leases, and various executory contracts. Before the sale, Dieterich announced, ''We, along with our creditors, believe the proposed sale is in the best interests of all parties, and ensures that River Oaks will emerge from Chapter 11 as a stronger, more competitive company poised to meet the demands of the upholstered furniture market.'' To insure that it would be leaner and tougher, it continued streamlining its organization, improving its product quality, cutting costs, and improving some of its profit margins. It also relocated its corporate headquarters, moving from Fulton to Tupelo, Mississippi.

Dieterich oversaw several operational upgrades. These included the standardization of two of the company's factories in Mississippi and California, a measure that both cut corporate office expenses and inaugurated systems that used new technology not previously employed. Future plans also called for the implementation of an Internet-based factory and dealer system. About other future directions and prospects, Dieterich remained somewhat guarded, perhaps because the new company still had to deal with past problems, including criminal proceedings against a former executive who, in 2000, was sent to federal prison for embezzling about $1 million from the old company.

Principal Competitors

Furniture Brands International; Klaussner Furniture; La-Z-Boy.

Further Reading

Adamson, Guy, ''River Oaks Names CEO,'' *HFN—The Weekly Newspaper for the Home Furnishing Network*, January 4, 1999, p. 40.

''Court Approves $32.9 Million in Financing for River Oaks; BNY Financial to Provide Financial Assistance for Restructuring,'' *Furniture World Magazine*, April 1998.

''Expansion Project to Double Baldwyn Furniture Industry,'' *Mississippi Business Journal*, June 24, 1991, p. 12.

''River Oaks Files Motion Proposing Sale of All Operational Assets to New Reorganized Company,'' *PR Newswire*, January 18, 1999.

''River Oaks Reaches Agreement with Lender; Will Present Reorganization Plan to Court by December 1998,'' *PR Newswire*, October 14, 1998.

''Thomas A. Dieterich Appointed Chief Executive Officer of River Oaks Furniture,'' *Furniture World Magazine*, February 1999.

—John W. Fiero

BOSCH

Robert Bosch GmbH

Robert-Bosch-Platz 1
Postfach 10 60 50
D-70049 Stuttgart
Germany
Telephone: +(49) 711 811 0
Toll free: (877) 509-5970 (U.S. only)
Fax: +(49) 711 811-6630
Web site: http://www.bosch.com

Private Company
Incorporated: 1886
Employees: 196,880
Sales: DM 61.7 billion (2000)
NAIC: 326122 Plastics Pipe and Pipe Fitting Manufacturing; 326199 All Other Plastics Product Manufacturing; 327112 Vitreous China, Fine Earthenware, and Other Pottery Product Manufacturing; 333991 Power-Driven Hand Tool Manufacturing; 33422 Radio and Television Broadcasting and Wireless Communications Equipment Manufacturing; 336312 Gasoline Engine and Engine Parts Manufacturing; 336322 Other Motor Vehicle Electrical and Electronic Equipment Manufacturing; 33634 Motor Vehicle Brake System Manufacturing; 33635 Motor Vehicle Transmission and Power Train Parts Manufacturing; 334514 Totalizing Fluid Meter and Counting Device Manufacturing; 551112 Offices of Other Holding Companies

One of the ten largest companies in Germany, Robert Bosch GmbH is best known as a worldwide supplier of automotive equipment, with world leadership in fuel injection systems and antilock brakes. The company has also developed into a world leader in various other areas, including communications and radio technology, traffic management systems, power tools, household appliances, thermotechnology, automation technology, and packaging machines. Bosch has operations in more than 50 countries on every continent through its subsidiaries and associated companies. Since 1964, 92 percent of the company has been owned by the Robert Bosch Foundation (the Bosch family owns the remaining 8 percent), which runs the company on the basis of nonprofit principles and uses its share of company profits to fund various philanthropic programs.

Early History

The company was founded in Stuttgart in 1886 by a highly motivated, self-educated electrical engineer named Robert Bosch. More talented as an administrator than as an engineer, Robert Bosch gained a reputation for innovation in industrial relations. He instituted an eight-hour workday (which was uncommon at the time) and paid employees at a higher standard rate in the belief that superior working conditions would encourage better employee performance. Bosch readily acknowledged ability and creativity in his employees, assigning the most talented among them to positions in the most promising areas. He also recognized the need for a diverse, high-quality product line as the most direct means to growth.

Bosch entered the automotive industry in the early 1890s, when the company introduced a hand-crank motor starter. Near the dawn of the 20th century, on the strength of the growing American automobile market, Bosch became the world leader in ignition systems. By 1914, 70 percent of the company's sales were in the United States. The outbreak that year of World War I resulted in an American trade embargo against Germany. Bosch was prevented from doing any more business in the United States and forced to rely solely on European sales under a wartime economy.

When the war ended in 1918 the German economy was in a state of complete disarray. The nation fell into a serious economic depression during the 1920s, which caused many businesses to fail. Bosch, however, managed to remain in business, partly as a result of its diversification and good management. As the economic situation stabilized, public discontent in Germany began to rise. Bosch, which expanded modestly during this period, purchased the radio manufacturer Blaupunkt-Werke in 1933. That same year the Nazis under Adolf Hitler seized power

Company Perspectives:

We want satisfied customers. That is why the highest quality of our products and services is one of our major corporate objectives. This also applies to the quality of the work carried out in our name by our trading partners, and in their sales and service organization. Safe, clean, and economical: these are the guiding principles behind our work to manufacture products and systems which satisfy the ever higher demands with respect to safety, environment, and consumption.

and initiated a new economic order characterized by industrial growth and rearmament.

The company enjoyed several periods of strong growth during the 1930s, primarily due to strong demand from German industry and the military for electronic and mechanical products. The company's growth necessitated a new form of organization, and in 1937 it was incorporated as a private limited company. German military adventurism and territorial expansion precipitated World War II, which again eliminated foreign markets for companies such as Bosch. Robert Bosch died in 1942, during the height of Germany's success in the war, and was succeeded by Hans Walz. As outlined in Robert Bosch's will, ownership of the company eventually in 1964 was to be transferred in large part to the Robert Bosch Foundation, with the balance remaining in the hands of the Bosch family.

Postwar Rebuilding

For Germany, the remainder of the war was characterized by severe shortages of all kinds and extensive war damage. At the end of the war Germany was partitioned into occupied Soviet and Western Powers' zones (later East and West Germany). The more heavily industrialized western zone, where Bosch was located, was in ruins. Bosch reorganized and its factories were rebuilt. The American market, however, remained closed to Bosch after the war, again forcing the company to strengthen its connections with smaller European manufacturers. New efforts were made to develop more advanced products, and by 1949 Bosch perfected a mechanical fuel injection system.

West Germany was ''readmitted'' to the world market system in the early 1950s, during which time Bosch became a major supplier of automotive products to foreign manufacturers. During the 1950s the consumer automobile market experienced strong growth, due this time to an expanding world economy and new levels of prosperity.

Also during the 1950s, Bosch began a cautious program of long-term diversification. For example, household appliances were added to the company's product line in 1952 with the introduction of Bosch kitchen appliances. In 1958 washing machines were added, then dishwashers in 1964. In 1952 Bosch also began to manufacture hydraulic equipment and do-it-yourself power tools.

Hans Walz retired in 1962 after 20 years as the company's chief executive. He was replaced by Hans Merkle, a self-taught and apprenticed engineer and businessman, known for his ability to predict changing market conditions. Merkle recognized pollution control and fuel economy as key factors in future automobile sales. Under Merkle's leadership, Bosch began to devote more of its resources to the development of electronic products, and later produced a new fuel injection system that promoted a smoother running engine and reduced fuel consumption.

Potential competitors of Bosch, including Siemens and Bendix, largely ignored the potential of fuel injection systems while Bosch continually perfected new and better versions. When strict new antipollution regulations were enacted in the United States, automobiles equipped with Bosch fuel injectors, such as the Volkswagen Beetle, became extremely popular. Soon afterward, other European manufacturers, including Daimler-Benz and Volvo, decided to integrate the Bosch system into their product line. When the 1973 OPEC oil crisis caused dramatic increases in the price of petroleum, the highly efficient Bosch fuel injection systems became virtually indispensable.

Expansion and Diversification in the 1970s and 1980s

Throughout the 1970s Bosch made moves to expand its operations overseas, moving into Japan and Malaysia in 1972, Turkey in 1973, and Spain in 1978. By the mid-1970s, Bosch had made strong progress in regaining its prewar market share in the United States. Bosch purchased a plant in Charleston, Virginia, in 1974 to produce fuel injection systems in the United States. The company also acquired a 25 percent share of American Microsystems, a manufacturer of integrated circuitry, and a 9.3 percent stake in Borg-Warner, which was well established in the area of microcircuitry. Bosch planned to apply technologies developed by these two companies to produce even more advanced automotive systems.

The Charleston plant was subsequently expanded three times. Through the late 1970s fuel injection systems, Bosch's primary product, became the most important electronic component to automobile manufacturers. By 1984, nearly half of the cars sold in the U.S. were equipped with fuel injection systems.

In the early 1980s several other manufacturers initiated efforts to reduce Bosch's share of the worldwide automotive components market. Marcus Bierich, who was named chief executive officer of Bosch in 1984, reacted quickly to these threats by expanding the company's product line and diversifying its operations.

One of the most important products to emerge from this new initiative was ABS, the antilock braking system. This device prevented brakes from locking by means of an electronic gauge wired to the brake pedal. In addition to being an important safety feature, it made a number of other wires and cables redundant, allowing physical space for ''cruise control'' and other features. By 1985 the Bosch ABS system was standard on many European automobiles and had also been introduced on American luxury cars. Despite competition in this area from Alfred Teves (a subsidiary of ITT) and Honda, Bosch developed additional facilities to build ABS systems in order to meet the anticipated increased demand.

Following the success of ABS, Bosch was also involved in the development of electronic traction control, which involved

Key Dates:

1886: Company is founded by Robert Bosch in Stuttgart.
1887: Construction of first Bosch low-voltage magneto for stationary gas-driven engines.
1909: First production outside Germany starts in U.S.
1927: Production of fuel injection pumps for diesel engines begins.
1928: First Bosch power tools are introduced.
1933: Production of household appliances begins.
1933: Company purchases Blaupunkt-Werke.
1937: Bosch is incorporated as a private limited company.
1942: Robert Bosch dies and is succeeded by Hans Walz.
1951: Bosch begins developing gasoline injection pumps for vehicle engines.
1952: Bosch begins production of kitchen appliances and do-it-yourself power tools.
1957: Starts production of car transistor radios.
1962: Hans Walz retires as chief executive and is replaced by Hans Merkle.
1978: Company launches the world's first series-produced antilock braking system.
1984: Marcus Bierich is named chief executive officer.
1986: Bosch begins production of its first traction control system.
1989: Bosch introduces the vehicle navigation system.
1989: Company creates the Bosch Telecom Business Sector servicing telecommunications and communications systems.
1995: Company launches an electronic stability program.
2000: Bosch introduces the first electrohydraulic brake system.

sensors to measure wheel speed and adjust the speed as necessary to keep the car under control. Bosch began production of its first traction control system in 1986.

As car features grew more sophisticated, Bosch continued to develop systems to aid the driver. A new device called the digital trip meter calculated the course and direction of a car by measuring heat levels of the terrain and posting a computerized map on the driver's dashboard. In addition to making the driver aware of the most efficient available routes, the meter could also detect traffic jams. The product was introduced in 1989 as the Travelpilot navigation system. A more sophisticated version using CD-ROMs and providing data to the driver via voice and symbols was later introduced in 1995 on Japanese luxury-model vehicles.

Fierce competition and a 1984 metalworkers' strike seriously affected the company's production for several months and weakened its lead over competitors. For virtually the first time, clients were forced to evaluate alternative suppliers.

The 1980s also saw Bosch enter the telecommunications market through the acquisition of or the purchase of stakes in various companies involved in the manufacturing of equipment and the development of systems, including Telefonbau und Normalzeit, a German telecommunications company, and Telenorma, the exclusive supplier of communications systems to Bundespost, the national postal and telecommunications group. In 1989 these various activities were consolidated with the creation of the Bosch Telecom Business Sector.

1990s and Beyond

In addition to expansion into the newly merged areas of former East Germany, Bosch continued to expand internationally in the early 1990s. The opened markets of Eastern Europe were one targeted area, as marketing operations were established in Poland, Hungary, and the Czech Republic in 1992; in Bulgaria, Croatia, Latvia, Russia, Slovenia, Ukraine, and Belarus in 1993; and in Romania in 1994. On the manufacturing side, two Czech Republic-based joint ventures were formed in 1992 to produce automotive equipment. In the Asia-Pacific region, Bosch entered into a joint venture to form Korea Automotive Motor Corp. in South Korea in 1993; was involved in another South Korean joint venture the following year, Korea Mechanics and Electronics Corporation; established a sales company in the Philippines in 1995; and entered into no less than six joint ventures in China also in 1995. Finally, in the United States in 1992, Bosch joined Penske Transportation in setting up a joint venture called Diesel Technology Company to develop and produce injector technology for diesel engines used by heavy-duty commercial vehicles.

Bosch continued to refine its electronic automotive components in the 1990s, introducing the Vehicle Dynamics Control system in 1994, designed to improve the stability of vehicles in critical situations by detecting all rotational movements of the car around its vertical axis. The company also entered into the increasingly lucrative market for airbags through a joint venture with Morton International called United Airbag Systems. Bosch was contributing its expertise in electronic components by developing the triggering devices for side-impact airbags the venture was developing.

Despite continuing its long tradition of innovation, Bosch entered a difficult period in the early 1990s under the combined pressure of depressed markets for automobiles and increased competition. Although known for the high quality of its products, Bosch had also over the years developed a reputation for high prices and inflexibility in its relations with its clients. Automakers were increasingly turning to other cheaper and more cooperative suppliers for parts they used to purchase from Bosch or manufacturing the parts themselves. The latter occurred in 1991 when General Motors suddenly cut in half what was previously a standing order for fuel injection parts. Also contributing to Bosch's difficulties was its telecommunications business which, although profitable and already contributing nearly a quarter of overall sales, was finding it increasingly difficult to compete against the giants of the industry—Siemens, Alcatel, and Northern Telecom.

In response to these challenges, Bosch in late 1991 instituted a cost-cutting program and process improvement initiative, and also cut its workforce by about 8,000. The company continued to struggle, however, as market conditions failed to improve, leading in 1993 to the company's first sales decline since 1967. At the same time, net income fell every year from 1989 to 1993, overall going from DM$626 million in 1989 to DM 426 million in 1993. Further moves were taken in 1993 to turn the company around, including the elimination of 13,000 additional jobs and the institution of team-oriented work groups.

The next two years showed modest improvements for Bosch as sales increased 6.2 percent in 1994 and 4 percent in 1995, while net income increased to DM 512 million in 1994 and DM 550 million in 1995. Even if not completely recovered, the company was feeling healthy enough by early 1996 to make a $1.5 billion acquisition of Allied Signal Inc.'s hydraulic- and antilock-braking business for light vehicles. The purchase enabled Bosch for the first time to provide its customers with complete brake systems, and as one of the world's leaders in the field.

The size of this latest acquisition confirmed Bosch's commitment to its core automotive components business and also raised the question of whether the company might divest itself of some assets in order to invest further in the core. The most likely candidate was the telecommunications technology sector, given its struggle to secure a foothold. Even if it retained its diversified portfolio, Bosch's future, like its past, would certainly be tied most closely to automobile components.

Strategic Growth in the New Millennium

Following the acquisition of Allied Signal's brake operations, Bosch continued to shape its global positioning through strategic acquisitions and divestments. Its acquisitions included Zexel Corporation (known since 2000 as Bosch Automotive Systems Corporation), which strengthened its position as the world's second-largest supplier of automotive components. In 1999 Bosch initiated a sell-off of the majority of its telecommunications and mobile telephone holdings from its Communications Technology division. Considering North America its most important foreign market, Bosch bolstered its U.S. presence with the acquisition of Vermont American Corporation. At this time more Bosch employees worked in the U.S. than anywhere else outside Germany.

Sales continued to increase during the second half of the 1990s, and by 2000 had reached DM 61,717 billion, up 50 percent from 1996. Foreign sales increased steadily as well throughout the decade; in 1992, they accounted for just under half of total global sales; by 2001, they accounted for nearly three-quarters. While sales across the board were up, though, a corresponding increase in profits proved elusive.

By 2000, its largest business lines consisted of fuel injection technology for internal combustion engines (diesel and gasoline), systems for active and passive vehicle safety (antilock braking systems, electronic stability programs), electrical machines (starters, alternators, small-power motors), and mobile communications products (car radios, navigation systems, and driver information systems). Its new electrohydraulic brake system, introduced in 2000, was the first fully electronically controlled braking system.

Bosch's three internal divisions enjoyed growth into 2000. Its Automotive Technology, Industrial Technology, and Consumer Goods and Building Technology divisions respectively generated 71.2 percent, 3.8 percent, and 23.6 percent of the total sales. The surviving components of the Communications Technology division, including security technology, aerospace engineering, and broadband networks, generated 1.4 percent of the total sales.

The success of the Automotive Technology division was primarily driven by strong demand for its diesel direct-injection systems in Western Europe. Sales of antilock braking systems, electronic stability programs, and vehicle navigation systems also increased in 2000. Automotive product lines included gasoline, diesel, chassis, and energy systems; and body and automotive electronics. Through its Blaupunkt-Werke subsidiary, Bosch offered the latest in multimedia gadgets for vehicles (together, they outfitted a Volkswagen minivan with a 20-speaker stereo, twin car phones, and video screens on the backs of all four headrests). Bosch's motto ''Safe-Clean-Economical'' pinpointed their continuing efforts to meet market demand for greater safety and further reduction in fuel consumption and emissions. Despite consistent, strong sales, though, escalating start-up costs for new products and relentless price competition prevented the Automotive Technology division from generating corresponding strong profits.

The Industrial Technology division, which focused on automation and packaging, was bolstered with the acquisition of Mannesmann Rexroth AG in 2001, forming Bosch Rexroth, a wholly owned subsidiary that included industrial hydraulics, pneumatics, assembly and linear technology, electric motors and controls, service and mobile hydraulics. Combined, they targeted a 2001 sales volume of about DM 8 billion.

The Consumer Goods and Building Technology division consisted of Bosch's power tools, household appliances, and thermotechnology, as well as the security technology, aerospace engineering, and broadband networks still in existence from the prior Communications Technology division. Its strong power tool brands, Bosch, Skil, and Dremel, made it a leading global manufacturer of power tools.

Promoting innovation remained a top priority at the company, and Bosch invested heavily in research and development, striving to translate innovative strength into more satisfactory profits. In 2000, it invested nearly DM 4 billion, with nearly three-quarters going to automotive research. In Germany alone, Bosch registered 2,400 patents.

Its domestic workforce of 91,000 in 2000 constituted 46 percent of its worldwide headcount. To meet changing conditions and challenges in the marketplace, Bosch launched an internal improvement program that focused on two main threads: Time to Market and Customer Focus. The company aimed to accelerate and improve internal processes while complementing product quality and delivery fulfillment with improved customer service and orientation. Their program motto, ''BeQIK,'' emphasized quality (Q), innovation (I), and focus on the customer—based on the German spelling of customer (K).

Bosch enjoyed strong growth in a favorable world economy through 2000. Against a backdrop of a slowing economy, it expected slower internal growth and a drop in sales, especially in North America. However, it expected to be pleasantly buoyed through the slowdown by sustained sales of its diesel direct-injection system, the production of other innovative, new products, improved customer relations, and sales generated by its newest acquisition, Rexroth.

Principal Subsidiaries

Blaupunkt GmbH; BSH Bosch und Siemens Hausgeräte GmbH (50%); Bosch Telecom GmbH; BT Magnet-Technologie GmbH (50%); Hawera Probst GmbH; Robert Bosch Fahrzeugelektrik Eisenach GmbH; ZF Lenksysteme GmbH (50%); NV Robert Bosch SA (Belgium); Robert Bosch Produktie NV (Belgium); Robert Bosch A/S (Denmark); Robert Bosch SA (France); Atco-Qualcast Limited (U.K.); Worcester Group plc (U.K.); Robert Bosch SpA (Italy); Robert Bosch BV (Netherlands); Van Doorne's Transmissie BV (Netherlands); Robert Bosch A/S (Norway); Robert Bosch AG (Austria); Blaupunkt Auto-Radio Portugal Lda (Portugal); Vulcano Termo-Domesticos SA (Portugal); Robert Bosch AB (Sweden); Robert Bosch Internationale Beteiligungen AG (Switzerland; 90%); Robert Bosch AG (Switzerland); Scintilla AG (Switzerland; 85%); Robert Bosch Espana SA (Spain); Robert Bosch spol.s.r.o. (Czech Republic); Bosch Diesel spol.s.r.o. (Czech Republic); Bosch Sanayi ve Ticaret AS (Turkey); Robert Bosch Ltda (Brazil); Associated Fuel Pump Systems Corporation (United States; 50%); Automotive Electronic Control Systems, Inc. (United States; 51%); Robert Bosch Corporation (United States); S-B Power Tool Company (United States); Vermont American Corporation (United States); Motor Industries Co. Ltd. (India; 54%); Bosch KK (Japan); Bosch Automotive Systems Corporation (Japan; 51%); Bosch Electronics Corporation (Japan); Korea Automotive Motor Corporation (Korea); Robert Bosch Korea Mechanics & Electronics Ltd. (Korea); Robert Bosch (Malaysia); Robert Bosch (South East Asia; Singapore); Robert Bosch (Australia).

Principal Divisions

Automotive Technology; Industrial Technology; Consumer Goods and Building Technology.

Principal Competitors

Hughes Electronics Corporation; Siemens AG; TRW, Inc.

Further Reading

Blau, John R., ''As Bosch Gets Tougher, Will Customers Get Going?,'' *Electronic Business,* January 8, 1990, pp. 81–85.

Bowley, Graham, ''Bosch Warns on High German Labour Costs,'' *The Financial Times*, May 15, 1997, p. 32.

——, ''Growth Outside Germany Helps Bosch to Treble,'' *The Financial Times*, May 15, 1998, p. 29.

''Braking,'' *Economist,* April 25, 1992, pp. 75–76.

Brooke, Lindsay, ''No Strong Recovery,'' *Automotive Industries,* December 1991, pp. 36–38.

Chew, Edmund, ''Bosch Introduces New Brake System,'' *Automotive News*, November 20, 2000, p. J22.

——, ''Bosch Will Lose Its Grip on Engines,'' *Automotive News,* February 14, 2000, p. 320.

Fuhrman, Peter, ''Euro-Thrash,'' *Forbes,* July 22, 1991, pp. 66–67.

Heuss, Theodor, *Robert Bosch, His Life and Achievements,* New York: Henry Holt, 1994, p. 612.

Higgins, Amy, and Sherri Koucky, ''Bosch and Rexroth Merge,'' *Machine Design*, June 7, 2001, p. 28.

''Knowing Who's Bosch,'' *Economist,* February 27, 1993, p. 61.

Kobe, Gerry, ''Robert Bosch Corp. Automotive Group,'' *Automotive Industries,* February 1990, pp. 69–70.

Lindemann, Michael, ''Subdued Start to Year Leaves Bosch Cautious,'' *The Financial Times*, May 10, 1996, p. 29.

Naj, Amal Kumar, ''Allied Signal Selling Piece of Auto Unit,'' *Wall Street Journal,* March 1, 1996, pp. A3, A4.

''New Cars Are Bursting with Blaupunkt,'' *Design News*, January 17, 2000, p. 29.

Plumb, Stephen E., ''All Quiet on the Eastern Front? Not at Bosch,'' *Ward's Auto World,* July 1993, p. 104.

Reier, Sharon, ''Components: Robert Bosch,'' *Financial World,* April 14, 1992, p. 56.

Schroter, Harm G., ''The German Question, the Unification of Europe, and the European Market Strategies of Germany's Chemical and Electrical Industries, 1900–1992,'' *Business History Review,* Autumn 1993, p. 369.

Simonian, Haig, ''Bosch Chief Hits out at High German Taxes,'' *The Financial Times*, September 11, 1997, p. 40.

——, ''Bosch Predicts Big Sales Rise,'' *The Financial Times*, June 19, 1998, p. 24.

''Success by Stealth,'' *Economist,* July 9, 1988, p. 69.

Way, Arthur, ''A Mark of Respect for German Supplier,'' *Financial Times,* July 12, 1994, p. FTS3.

Whitbread, Colin, ''Bosch Begins to Feel Pain of Slowdown,'' *Automotive News*, May 7, 2001, p. H24.

Wilson, Amy, ''Bosch Sees Chance for Successful Diesel Program,'' *Automotive News*, June 18, 2001 p. B32.

——, ''North America Key Area for Bosch,'' *Automotive News*, March 12, 2001, p. Y24.

—updates: David E. Salamie, Suzanne Selvaggi

Rockford Corporation

546 South Rockford Drive
Tempe, Arizona 85281
U.S.A.
Telephone: (480) 967-3565
Toll Free: (800) 366-2349
Fax: (480) 966-3983
Web site: http://www.rockfordcorp.com

Public Company
Incorporated: 1980
Employees: 515
Sales: $144.6 million (2000)
Stock Exchanges: NASDAQ
Ticker Symbol: ROFO
NAIC: 334310 Audio and Video Equipment Manufacturing

Rockford Corporation designs and manufactures high-performance audio equipment for automobiles and home use. Most of its car audio equipment is sold under Rockford Fosgate brands Punch and Punch POWER, and their primary target market is young men aged 16 to 24. Rockford also produces sound amplifiers; signal processors; source units, such as CD players and AM/FM radios; and speakers, including mid-ranges, full-ranges, tweeters, woofers, and subwoofers (a speaker at least eight inches in diameter for bass frequency output). Rockford's lower-priced line of car audio products are sold through Lightning Audio under the Strike, Storm, and Bolt brands. Home theater products, including state-of-the-art surround sound, are marketed under the Fosgate Audionics brand and professional equipment is sold under the Hafler brand. The company's products are available at over 2,300 independent retailers domestically, at more than 400 Best Buy stores, and through distributors and sales representatives in more than 60 countries.

1970s: Reinventing the Market for Car Audio

The history of the Rockford Corporation can be traced to Fosgate Electronics, a specialty amplifier manufacturer founded by Jim Fosgate, the inventor of the company's first powerful amplifiers. While experimenting with audio technology, Fosgate owned and operated a small company called Pro-Line, in Salt Lake City, which produced radio transmitters and receivers for remote control model airplanes. In his spare time, he worked on his "Frequency Energizer," a circuit that adjusted for loss of high- and low-end audio frequencies as they channeled through to the speakers. Fred Hulan, owner of Audio Mart in Kansas City, encouraged Fosgate, providing him with information obtained in his own work. At the time, Hulan installed state-of-the-art audio equipment, called the Acoust-A-Voice, in homes and theaters. Hulan reported to Fosgate the inefficiencies he found in the system, and Fosgate applied his Frequency Energizer circuit to compensate for loss of high and low tones during sound amplification.

After many late night sessions of experimentation, Fosgate and some audio enthusiast friends developed Fosgate's first audio product for the consumer market. The PR-7000 amplifier integrated the Frequency Energizer into a 30-watt car amplifier using a tape loop. Fosgate demonstrated his amplifier at the Consumer Electronics Show in Chicago in 1973, attaching a $300 price tag. Initially, it proved to be an impossible task to find buyers for such an expensive piece of equipment, especially one for which no source unit with appropriate audio outputs existed.

Then, innovations by Fosgate Electronics, particularly that of the Punch Equalization circuit, introduced a level of car audio quality previously unknown, stimulating the market for high-performance car audio equipment which sold through specialty audio retailers. The company marketed its products under the Punch and Punch POWER brands, the latter being the top-of-the-line audio equipment.

By the late 1970s Fosgate Electronics had developed a base of retailer customers, and Jim Fosgate let the company manage itself while he began experimenting with surround sound technology. However, financial difficulties arose at the company that ultimately resulted in its producing lower quality equipment. Fosgate looked for someone to buy the company so that he would be free to concentrate on new inventions. In 1980 a venture capital company, Camelback Capital Corp., purchased

Company Perspectives:

We are Rockford Corporation! Fanatics about audio. We are the standard of excellence when it comes to sound. We invent new technologies to create innovative products of exceptional quality and performance providing the ultimate sensory experience.

Fosgate Electronics, renaming it Rockford Corporation for the street where the company had been located for almost a decade. At this time the company employed 25 people and recorded just under $1 million in annual sales. In 1982 Robert Pothier, of Camelback Capital, became president of Rockford Corporation.

New Ownership in the 1980s

The immediate issues requiring the attention of the new owners involved the quality of the company's products and development of new products. Engineer John France led the effort by applying Fosgate's technology to new product design. France's innovations included the use of MOSFET (metal oxide semiconductor field effect transistors) power for stable sound quality with small circuitry impedance loads. Rockford engineers made formidable improvements to MOSFET technology, an important aspect of quality sound amplification. France also developed a circuit protector first used in the POWER 1000 amplifier.

The quality of the amplifying technology required the development of new speakers. Specifically, audio dealers were reporting that Rockford Fosgate amplifiers were blowing out speakers, and that no speakers on the market could handle the output. After some research into the best speakers on the market, Rockford decided to design speakers itself. The company looked for a quality speaker manufacturer with whom to form a partnership, choosing Carbonneau of Grand Rapids, Michigan. Rockford Carbonneau (later Rockford Acoustic Designs) began production on high-performance audio speakers in 1985, manufacturing a line of woofers, mid-ranges, and tweeters.

Without the advertising budget of its main competitors Kenwood and Pioneer, Rockford pursued methods of marketing that focused on the audio specialty market. In 1985 Rockford became involved the National Autosound Challenge Association to raise awareness of the new capabilities of car stereo. Company employees participated in co-authoring the judging sheet and rule book for the contest, as well as in determining the standards for winning the Autosound Challenge. Rockford then assisted specialty audio retailers in staging contests.

Rockford formed the Rockford Technical Training Institute in 1986 to educate audio dealers and salespeople about the company's products. Training involved system design, installation, speaker enclosure, and system design with existing components from other manufacturers. Rockford brought customers to Tempe, Arizona, for training, rather than train at audio stores, in order to obtain the participants' undivided attention.

Another strategy for gaining market share involved the acquisition of another pioneer audio electronics company, the David Hafler Company, in 1987. David Hafler had been regarded as the father of high fidelity audio; his 50-watt tube amplifiers amazed audio specialists in 1954. Hafler's first company, Dynaco, began the trend toward amplifier kits from which audio enthusiasts built their own amplifiers. The David Hafler Company, formed in 1979, manufactured high quality amplifiers and preamplifiers prewired or, for $100 less, as kits. In the acquisition of Hafler, Rockford also acquired a subsidiary, Acoustat, a manufacturer of high performance electrostatic loudspeakers and electronics. Under the combined talent of Hafler and Rockford engineering staff, the Hafler brand defined the standard in professional audio technology being used by movie theaters, concert venues, traveling musicians, sound recording studios, and broadcast studios while achieving international acclaim.

Merging the engineering staffs from Rockford and Hafler resulted in new patented technology, including the Trans-nova power amplifier. The amplifier used MOSFETs to add power to voltage current without a gain in noise or distortion. The audio signal's ''gain stages,'' levels of increased power, occurred at shorter intervals and less frequently, providing sound output truer to an the original input than ordinary amplifiers.

New Management and Profitability in the 1990s

While Rockford-Fosgate products gained in quality and popularity, the company continued to struggle financially through the 1980s. Problems included product obsolescence, inventory overstock, and delays in product development. In 1992 Rockford instituted a new management team, including Gary Suttle as president and CEO. Reorganization involved the discontinuation or redesign of product lines which generated little or no profit; implementing new marketing and advertising strategies; improving management information systems; and shortening the product development time from up to 24 months to between six and nine months. Product development increased from seven new product introductions in 1991 to 104 new products in 1999. The company earned a profit in 1994, but investments in infrastructure and employee hiring resulted in losses in 1995 and 1996. Nevertheless, Rockford became profitable in 1997, with net earnings of $1.6 million on sales of $87.4 million.

On a solid financial footing, Rockford sought to expand into new markets through national retailers. In August 1998 the company's merchandise became available through Crutchfield, a national consumer electronics catalog retailer. The following March, Best Buy, the largest volume retailer of consumer electronics, began to offer Rockford Fosgate brand products at its chain of 312 stores. High-performance car audio products fit with Best Buy's strategy to provide a wide range of products to its customers. The electronics merchant stocked eight models of amplifiers and a limited selection of woofers and speakers, making an initial purchase of $4.4 million in merchandise and an additional $10.5 million over the next four months.

The move toward national chain distribution was risky for Rockford, as it potentially alienated specialty audio dealers with whom the company had engaged in business over the long-term. Also, mainstream exposure could have diminished the prestige of the Rockford Fosgate brand name. To compensate for these

Key Dates:

1973: Jim Fosgate introduces the PR-7000 amplifier.
1981: Venture capital firm acquires Fosgate's company and renames it Rockford Corporation.
1985: Company begins to design and manufacture speakers that handle amplifier output.
1987: Company acquires the David Hafler Company.
1992: New management team begins transformation to profitability.
1996: Company is profitable and begins to market CD players.
1999: Best Buy, the consumer electronics giant, starts stocking Rockford Fosgate products.
2000: Rockford goes public and acquires Fosgate Audionics.

risks, Rockford decided to create new brands with lower price points for distribution through Best Buy.

Also during this time, Rockford purchased Lightning Audio, a manufacturer and distributor of car audio accessories. Scott Deley had founded Lightning Audio in 1993 to provide the car audio market with power capacitors which prevented problems of power supply, such as dimming headlights, prompted by high level sound audio.

Other new products in 1999 included six digital amplifiers, a surround sound process for mobile audio, and an MP3 changer which allowed MP3 music downloaded from the Internet to be played in car CD players. Rockford developed the first car amplifier that could be custom designed, in terms of function and visual aesthetic, by the consumer. Under the Hafler brand, the company introduced a new series of light-weight, high-performance amplifiers for use in movie theaters and concerts tours. Also, Rockford launched an Internet web site designed for customer self-service. Using BEA WebLogic Server, the company developed sophisticated software which allowed dealers, sales representatives, and company administrators to track orders and shipments, and review account information.

New products, new sales outlets, and a strong economy fueled growth at Rockford. Revenues increased from $87.6 million in 1998 to $123.9 million in 1999, with Best Buy accounting for 20 percent of sales, at $24.7 million. Net income more than doubled from $2.3 million to $6.5 million in 1999, as the company began to use global sources for raw materials and certain components at competitive rates. Lightning Audio amplifiers and speakers were produced in Korea and China, and a four-year agreement with Hyundai Electronics of Korea involved overseas manufacturing of Rockford-Fosgate brand products in accordance with Rockford specifications.

International sales rose slightly to $18.4 million, as increased sales in Europe compensated for slower sales in Asia and Latin America. Rockford began a transition to one-step distribution in certain overseas markets, using independent sales representatives who sold products direct to retailers on behalf of the company, rather than distributors who purchased products wholesale. This allowed for lower overhead and competitive pricing of its products. The company implemented the change in Canada and Germany in 1999, opening a warehouse and sales office in Germany as well as in Austria the next year.

Growth in the 21st Century

Rockford filed with the Securities and Exchange Commission for an initial public offering of stock in May 1999. Due to poor market conditions, the actual offering did not occur for another year, in April 2000. Rockford sold three million shares at $11 per share, raising $32.5 million for continued research and development, investment in new technologies by other companies, and to pay debt.

Funds from the public offering allowed Rockford to remain on the leading edge of audio equipment, particularly with surround sound technology. Rockford acquired a company co-owned by Jim Fosgate and Charles Wood, Fosgate Audionics. Wood founded Audionics in 1969 and merged with Fosgate Research in 1986. Both companies had been involved in the development of surround sound technology for the home environment. In 1982, the home theater originated with the Audionics Space and Image Composers and Fosgate Research TATE processors, both of which used multi-channel decoders to detect the Dolby Motion Picture Matrix Surround information. Fosgate Audionics used a unique matrix decoder designed by Fosgate to further improve the processor's ability to read hidden information for a fuller account of sound recording, including two-channel stereo recordings, even when an older recording techniques or older recordings were used. The Rockford Fosgate division applied the surround sound technology for the automotive stereo market, utilizing the new circuitry of Dolby ProLogic II technology. The company became the first in the industry to license Dolby Pro Logic Surround Sound Decoder technology. Jim Fosgate and Charles Wood remained at Rockford as engineering consultants.

Rockford also made an important stride in amplifier technology with the Single Terminal Alternating Rail Dual Sampling Topology (STARDUST). STARDUST allowed more amplification power, over 1,000 watts, in a smaller size amplifier and with less usage of current from the charging system. The lower energy consumption, resulted in cooler system operation and, hence, better and more reliable performance. Rockford introduced the technology in new amplification products in early 2000 and was granted a patent on the technology in August.

The company used the complex capabilities of its Internet software to boost sales in 2000. In preparation for a new line of home theater products under the Hafler brand, the company had launched a new web site in August 2000. The Hafler.com web site featured user-friendly system design assistance, including three-dimensional virtual reality applications, to help consumers choose components.

For 2001 Rockford redesigned much of its product line, including the Lightning Audio entry level performance systems and Rockford Fosgate amplifiers and subwoofers. Rockford Fosgate introduced its most powerful, high-performance subwoofer, the Power HX2. Lightning Audio launched two new lines of amplifiers and subwoofers, under the Bolt and Storm brand names, to be sold at over 400 Best Buy stores nationwide.

For the fifth year in a row, Rockford products won several awards at the annual Consumer Electronics Show.

Fosgate Audionics introduced two new amplifiers for the home theater market, FA600.3 and the FA1000.5, feeding 200 watts per channel. The amplifiers utilized a Trans-ana circuitry, an improvement on the Trans-nova technology, but manufactured at a lower cost. The Switch Mode Power Supply (SMPS) technology provided a steady supply of power for those exuberant passages in music and movie soundtracks, allowing the full effect of a rising and descending crescendo to remain intact in the home theater.

In addition to the two amplifiers, Fosgate Audionics' 2001 products included four passive speakers, three powered subwoofers, and two processor components. Marketing focused on custom installation through specialty audio and home theater retailers and independent distributors. The company presumed that Fosgate Electonics' early customers, males age 16 to 24 in the 1970s, would comprise some share of the customer base for its quality home audio products. The Fosgate Audionics line replaced the Hafler brand of home theater products, previously sold over the Internet.

Steady growth continued at Rockford, increasing it share of the car audio market in a period of overall decline in the industry. In 2000 sales reached $144.6 million and net income rose to $8 million. Lightning Audio sales more than tripled to $10 million. International sales grew 26.1 percent, to $23.2 million, with improved economic conditions in Asia and Latin America. In its efforts to implement one-step distribution overseas, the company opened a sales and warehouse subsidiary in Japan in 2001.

Principal Subsidiaries

Fosgate Audionics; Lightning Audio, Inc.; Rockford Foreign Sales Corporation; Rockford GmbH Germany; Rockford Japan.

Principal Competitors

Audiovox Corporation; Blaupunkt; Harman International Industries, Inc.; Kenwood Corporation; Pioneer Corporation; Sony Corporation.

Further Reading

''Best Buy Partners with Rockford Fosgate; High-End Car Audio Lineup Strengthens Best Buy Offerings,'' *PR Newswire*, December 15, 1998.

Gilroy, Amy, ''Rockford Fosgate Dealers Upbeat on Nissan Deal,'' *Twice Mobile Electronics*, February 12, 2001, p. 42.

Gonderinger, Lisa, ''Car Stereo Firm Playing New Tune With IPO,'' May 29, 1999, *Arizona Republic*, May 29, 1999, p. E1.

Hodges, Ralph, ''David Hafler and Audio Civilization,'' *Stereo Review*, March 15, 1985, p. 94.

Latshaw, Jamie, ''New Formats for Media on Wheels,'' *Dealerscope*, April 2000, p. 20.

Mattern, Hal, ''Tempe, AZ-Based Car Stereo Maker's IPO Raises Millions,'' *Arizona Republic*, April 21, 2000.

Shaffer, Kelly, ''Arc de Triomphe,'' *Car Audio*, June 2001, p. 27.

Snover, Doug, ''Car Stereo Maker Wins State Honor Foreign Firms Blasted Out,'' *Arizona Republic*, June 20, 1990, p. 6.

Zimmerman, Ann, ''At Home with Jim Fosgate,'' *Residential Systems*, April 2001, p. 46.

—Mary Tradii

Rockwell Automation

777 East Wisconsin Avenue
Suite 1400
Milwaukee, Wisconsin 53202
U.S.A.
Telephone: (414) 212-5200
Fax: (414) 212-5201
Web site: http://www.rockwell.com

Public Company
Incorporated: 1928 as North American Aviation
Employees: 23,500
Sales: $4.42 billion (2000)
Stock Exchanges: New York Pacific London
Ticker Symbol: ROK
NAIC: 335314 Relay and Industrial Control Manufacturing; 334419 Other Electronic Component Manufacturing; 334290 Other Communications Equipment Manufacturing; 336322 Other Motor Vehicle Electrical and Electronic Equipment Manufacturing; 332991 Ball and Roller Bearing Manufacturing; 333612 Speed Changer, Industrial High-Speed Drive, and Gear Manufacturing; 334513 Instruments and Related Product Manufacturing for Measuring, Displaying, and Controlling Industrial Process Variables; 335312 Motor and Generator Manufacturing

Rockwell Automation, known until mid-2001 as Rockwell International Corporation, specializes in industrial automation products, software, systems, and services. Among the company's offerings are controllers, input/output (I/O) systems, sensors, power transmission components, and network monitoring devices. Main brand names include Rockwell Automation, Allen-Bradley, Rockwell Software, Dodge, and Reliance Electric. Rockwell Automation serves a wide range of industries through a network of 5,600 distributors and agents in 80 countries. The company emerged in the early 21st century as the successor of Rockwell International—which was best known as a major defense and aerospace firm—after the latter made a series of strategic divestments starting in the mid-1990s.

Early History of North American Aviation

Charles Lindbergh's flight across the Atlantic in 1927 generated such interest in aviation that suddenly even small aviation companies were deluged with money from investors. So much capital was made available by investors (almost $1 billion by 1929) that holding companies created hundreds of airlines and airplane manufacturers. Three companies in particular emerged in the late 1920s as the largest aeronautic concerns: the Aviation Corporation of the Americas (Avco), run by Averell Harriman and the Lehman Brothers investment firm; the Boeing/Rentschler consortium known as United Aircraft and Transportation; and North American Aviation, the predecessor of Rockwell International, organized by a New York financier named Clement Keys.

Once the engine manufacturer Pratt & Whitney had secured two airplane manufacturers and a major airline, the United Aircraft consortium, as exclusive customers, Clement Keys recognized that his company needed a similar affiliation if it was to survive. He finalized an arrangement wherein the Wright Engine Company became the exclusive supplier of engines for North American Aviation.

North American's major airline, National Air Transport, was one of 45 aviation companies operated by Keys; the list also included the Curtiss Aeroplane & Motor Company and Wright Engine. Curtiss was a successful manufacturer of such airplanes as the Condor, and Wright manufactured some of the highest quality aircraft engines of the day. North American also owned Eastern Air Lines, the pioneer of air service along the eastern coast of the United States, and Transcontinental Air Transport. These subsidiaries made the parent company's stock even more attractive. Money continued to flow into North American from investor groups, making the original stockholders (Keys among them) extremely wealthy.

The bright future of the aviation companies came to an abrupt end on October 24, 1929, when a financial disaster hit Wall Street. Virtually all stocks were inflated in value and backed only with borrowed funds. When investors realized that the market could no longer support the inflated values of their stock, they flooded brokerage houses with orders to sell. The large number of claims led people, banks, and companies into bankruptcy. The resulting stock market crash brought about a ten-year world depression.

> **Company Perspectives:**
>
> *Through our people and our technology partners, we deliver automation solutions in every industry, on every continent, in most countries of the world.*
>
> *As the world continues to move from the industrial age into the information age, there is a great need for bridges between the two. Rockwell Automation provides those bridges, offering ''smart'' automation products that bring together industrial machines with ''information'' technology for more efficient, flexible, less expensive, and higher quality manufacturing and processing.*

In 1930, North American lost its majority control of National Air Transport to the United Aircraft company. The buy-out provided temporary relief to financially troubled North American, which was purchased by General Motors four years later. General Motors was one of the few companies with capital available to refinance a business that held such promise for the future. General Motors acquired North American in an attempt to diversify, since its own product was not selling well during the Great Depression.

Keys retired from business in 1932 because of ill health, and James Howard Kindelberger, who was with Donald Douglas during development of the DC-1 and DC-2, was made president of North American in 1935. He was trained as an engineer but knew the automotive business so well that his managerial acumen overshadowed his engineering skills.

General Motors, which held a substantial amount of stock in Trans World Airlines, sold its holdings in that company in 1936. In the same year, North American (still a subsidiary of General Motors) sold its Eastern Air Lines unit to the airline's director, Eddie Rickenbacker. The divestiture of airline companies from airplane manufacturers was forced upon the three largest aeronautic conglomerates by Senator Hugo Black, who also advocated the breakup of numerous other monopolies. North American Aviation was no longer an airline company but merely a manufacturer of airplanes and airplane parts.

During World War II, North American manufactured thousands of P-51 Mustangs for the U.S. Army Air Corps. The P-51, one of the last mass-produced piston engine airplanes, saw action in every theater during the war. The company also built the B-25 Mitchell bomber and T-6 Texan trainer. The company built more airplanes for the U.S. military than any other company during the war years. The rapid expansion of the company was financed mostly by the government, which was North American's largest customer.

Defense and Aerospace Contracting in the Postwar Era

When the war ended, North American's military contracts also ended. Like Grumman Corporation, North American opted to avoid entering the competitive commercial airliner market. Instead, the company focused its resources on the development of the next generation of military aircraft, namely, jets. Working from designs and prototypes of jet aircraft captured from the Germans after the war, North American built its first fighter jet, called the F-86 Sabre. Because the Sabre's supersonic wings were developed from German designs, the company saved millions of dollars in research and development costs.

In the years after the war, North American attempted to enter the private airplane market, with a small four-passenger plane called the Navion. However, poor sales of the Navion convinced company management of the futility of entering the private market. In 1947 the design and production rights to the Navion were sold to Ryan Aeronautical.

North American continued to develop new equipment for the military. The company built a number of fighters and trainers for the Navy's aircraft carriers, in addition to a new jet called the F-100 Super Sabre. North American also constructed the first experimental supersonic aircraft, the rocket-powered X-15 and X-70.

When General Motors sold its share of the company in 1948, North American diversified its product line, becoming involved in the development of rockets, guidance systems, and atomic energy. It created Rocketdyne, Autonetics, and Atomics International as new divisions to pursue research in those individual fields. Here again, Rocketdyne was assisted by the Germans; much of its rocket and missile technology was acquired from captured German data.

Kindelberger, who had been promoted to chairperson, and the company's new president, J.L. Atwood, planned the company's diversification before the war ended. They both knew that in order for the company to survive the postwar environment, they would have to prove the company's worth to the government by leading the development of the newest defense systems. The government could then justifiably be asked to fund much of the costly development of any new systems.

The company's greatest success was in its Rocketdyne division, which produced the Thor, Jupiter, Redstone, and Atlas rockets. The research and development of an atomic-powered missile was abandoned when the system was declared impractical and unworkable. Research from the ambitious but ill-fated project was converted for use in the development of nuclear reactors.

When the Soviet Union put Yuri Gagarin into space in 1961, the U.S. space program was jolted into action. North American's Redstone rocket was used to launch Alan Shepard and Virgil Grissom into space during the Mercury space program in 1961. Later, John Glenn was launched into orbit aboard a Mercury spacecraft perched atop an Atlas rocket. North American Aviation enabled the United States to recover its technological edge in the space race with the Soviet Union.

In order to meet President John F. Kennedy's challenge to land a man on the moon before 1970, the National Aeronautics and Space Administration (NASA) contracted North American to build the three-passenger Apollo I space capsule. On January 27, 1967, a flash fire swept through the manned capsule during a ground test. Killed in the accident were Virgil ''Gus'' Grissom, Edward White II, and Roger Chaffee. The astronauts' widows each received $350,000 in a legal settlement, but North American was still harshly criticized. Despite the fact that most of its business involved government contracts, the company suffered severe financial reverses that threatened it with bankruptcy.

Key Dates:

1903: Lynde Bradley and Dr. Stanton Allen create the Compression Rheostat Company.
1904: Lincoln Electric Manufacturing Company, forerunner of Reliance Electric, is founded.
1910: Compression Rheostat is renamed Allen-Bradley Company.
1919: Willard Rockwell founds Wisconsin Parts Company.
1928: North American Aviation is established and soon becomes one of the three largest aeronautic concerns in the country.
1930: Collins Radio Company is founded to build and sell radio transmitters.
1948: North American Aviation begins diversification into rockets, guidance systems, and atomic energy.
1953: Rockwell merges Wisconsin Parts and two other firms to form Rockwell Spring and Axle Company.
1958: Rockwell Spring is renamed Rockwell-Standard.
1967: Rockwell-Standard merges with North American Aviation to form North American Rockwell.
1973: North American Rockwell acquires Collins Radio. Following merger with Rockwell Manufacturing, the company is renamed Rockwell International.
1985: Rockwell acquires Allen-Bradley Company of Milwaukee, thereby entering the industrial automation sector.
1995: Rockwell acquires Reliance Electric.
1996: Graphic systems and defense and aerospace businesses are sold off.
1997: Automotive business is spun off to shareholders as Meritor Automotive Inc.
1998: Company spins off its semiconductor operations to shareholders as Conexant Systems, Inc.
1999: Rockwell relocates to Milwaukee.
2001: Rockwell Collins is spun off to shareholders; Rockwell International changes its name to Rockwell Automation.

Within two months of the accident, North American Aviation was a prime candidate for a takeover.

Late 1960s and 1970s: Emergence of Rockwell International

Rockwell-Standard made a $922 million bid for North American Aviation in March 1967. Rockwell-Standard was established in Wisconsin in 1919 as a manufacturer of truck axles and was initially known as Wisconsin Parts Company. Willard Rockwell was the company founder. Rockwell later took over Timken Detroit Axle and Standard Steel Spring Company, the latter based in Coraopolis, Pennsylvania. In 1953 Rockwell merged these three companies to form Rockwell Spring and Axle Company, which was renamed Rockwell-Standard in 1958. By 1967 Rockwell-Standard was the world's leading producer of mechanical automotive parts, including parts for both light and heavy vehicles, in addition to being a manufacturer of industrial machinery.

Under the terms of the merger, J.L. Atwood, president and chief executive officer of North American, would assume the same duties at the new company, while Colonel Willard Rockwell, of Rockwell-Standard, would serve as chairperson. The merger was delayed for a few months by the Justice Department, which argued that the merger would be anticompetitive. The problems were finally resolved and the smaller Rockwell, with sales of $636 million, took over North American, with sales of $2.37 billion.

Atwood said the merger was ''in furtherance of North American's previously announced objective to diversify its activities into the commercial and industrial sector.'' What the company management really wanted was to improve its public image. Its association with the Apollo space capsule tragedy was never forgotten. The merger with the Rockwell company would recover the reputation of integrity that management thought North American deserved. It was clear that Colonel Rockwell would be firmly in charge of the new company, which was called North American Rockwell.

Rockwell's role in the U.S. space program continued, but the company maintained a low profile. It spent much of its first years after the merger manufacturing car and truck parts, printing presses (following the 1969 acquisition of Miehle-Goss-Dexter), tools, industrial sewing machines, and electronic instruments for flight and navigation. The company devoted much of its resources to the development of space systems, including the enormous Saturn V rocket engines, which launched subsequent Apollo missions to the moon. Later, the company was chosen as the primary contractor for NASA's space shuttles. During this time, it also became NASA's largest contractor, a position it continued to hold into the 1990s.

In 1973 the company acquired Collins Radio Company, which had been founded in 1930 and began selling amateur radio transmitters in 1933. The company developed the first modem in 1955, which was as large as a refrigerator and weighed 700 pounds. Collins became the cornerstone of Rockwell's avionics and communications operations. North American Rockwell also merged in 1973 with the Rockwell Manufacturing Company, a separate company created by Willard Rockwell, Jr. Following this merger, the company changed its name to Rockwell International.

Willard Rockwell, Jr., who took over from his father in 1967, retired in 1979, and Robert Anderson assumed the position of chairperson. Anderson had joined Rockwell in 1968 after he left the Chrysler Corporation. He was named president of Rockwell in 1970 and chief executive officer in 1974. Anderson's background in the automotive business made him a conservative and cautious manager. Generally regarded as an engineer more than as a financial manager, he had a strategy for the company's growth and expansion that was markedly different from that of his predecessor. Anderson himself later remarked, ''it's fair to say that we disagreed on the direction of the company altogether.''

Under the junior Rockwell, the company made some risky acquisitions, stretching its balance sheet to an uncomfortable degree. At one point the company was reportedly losing a million dollars a day. Rockwell was trying to establish the firm's business in high profile consumer markets, such as Admiral television, which Anderson sold in 1974.

Anderson, who was originally hired to smooth the transition of management and resources during the 1967 merger, had little tolerance for the waste usually associated with defense contracts. He introduced the General Motors policy, which required all company divisions to submit profit goals for various production periods. As a result of Anderson's strict management, Rockwell's debt-equity ratio (the company's debt divided by its net worth) fell from 99 percent in 1974 to 50 percent in 1977 and to 9 percent in 1983.

Addition of Industrial Automation in the 1980s

Rockwell had initially planned to build the B-1 bomber, but in 1977 the administration of President Jimmy Carter canceled the program, favoring instead the development of Northrop's stealth bomber. By 1983, however, the Reagan administration had reactivated the B-1 project as part of its ambitious military program. Production of the B-1 bomber was expected to generate a profit of approximately $2 billion a year for Rockwell, but subsequent orders for more of the bombers ceased. Once again, Rockwell and its B-1 were summarily excluded from consideration for the production of the next U.S. strategic bomber. The company still had other defense contracts, however: the MX ''Peacekeeper'' missile (designed to replace the nation's stock of aging minuteman missiles), five space shuttles, and a navigation satellite called Navstar.

Willard Rockwell, Jr., resigned as a consultant to Rockwell in 1984 because of a conflict of interest between the company and a separate concern he founded in 1979 called Astrotech. Astrotech was negotiating to purchase one or more of NASA's space shuttles in the belief that only private enterprise could make shuttle flights profitable.

That venture was indefinitely postponed by the explosion of the space shuttle *Challenger* in January 1986. An investigation of the accident later revealed that one of the booster rockets malfunctioned and caused the rocket to collide with the huge external fuel tank. The resulting explosion decimated the orbiter and killed all seven of its astronauts. A few months later President Ronald Reagan announced the order for a new shuttle from Rockwell to replace the *Challenger.*

Shortly before the accident Rockwell was implicated in a government investigation into illegal overcharges on various government contracts. The company was banned from further contract awards until Anderson himself convinced Air Force Secretary Vernon Orr to reinstate the company in December 1985. Anderson promised to fire senior managers involved in any illegal activities.

In 1985 Anderson oversaw the first major acquisition of his career at Rockwell with the $1.7 billion purchase of the Allen-Bradley Company of Milwaukee. Rockwell was suffering from a decrease in business after the cancellation of the B-1 bomber and the completion of the space shuttles. Allen-Bradley provided Rockwell with steady profits from its operations and helped to reduce the company's dependence on government contracts. Allen-Bradley, a successful manufacturer of industrial automation systems, traced its origins back to 1903, when Lynde Bradley and Dr. Stanton Allen created the Compression Rheostat Company, which adopted the Allen-Bradley name in 1910. A key introduction came in 1920: the ''Bradleystat,'' a rheostat (a resistor that regulates a current) designed for automotive dashboards and radios; sales of the Bradleystat exceeded $1.1 million by 1924. By 1985, Allen-Bradley was the number one maker of industrial automation equipment in North America, with revenues of more than $1 billion.

Robert Anderson retired in 1988, relinquishing control of the company to its president, Donald R. Beall, who had been priming himself for Rockwell's leadership position for a decade. Ten years earlier, in 1978, when Beall was president of Rockwell's electronic division in Dallas, he reportedly spent one evening composing some 14 pages of notes delineating what he would do if given control of Rockwell. He was finally given that opportunity and immediately set himself the task of redefining the company's future.

A principal component of Beall's strategy was to reduce Rockwell's dependence on federal defense contracts and increase its presence in the electronics market. Specifically, this meant an expansion of Rockwell's telecommunications operations and a more significant role for the company's Allen-Bradley subsidiary, which Beall had encouraged Anderson to acquire. To make the company more responsive to customers, Beall granted company managers nearly autonomous control of their operations and then sharply reduced the bureaucratic layers of management that had accumulated over the years. Seven management levels were compressed into three, the company's headquarters staff was cut by more than half, and Rockwell's various businesses were reorganized into four major categories: electronics products, automotive products, a graphics unit (which manufactured high-speed newspaper presses), and aerospace.

Transformative 1990s

In the early 1990s, before Beall could complete his transformation of Rockwell, however, economic conditions soured, sending the national economy into a tailspin and shrouding Beall's efforts to create a more diversified, commercially oriented company. Despite the economic downturn, Beall funneled more than $250 million into Allen-Bradley to create a new generation of factory automation products, which, coupled with the company's commanding presence in the market for high-speed modems (a product of Rockwell's 1973 acquisition of Collins Radio), provided two stable, commercially oriented legs for the company to stand on once economic conditions improved.

When conditions did improve, the fruits of Beall's strategy were unveiled. Government-funded business, which in 1988 had accounted for 50 percent of Rockwell's revenues, contributed only 23 percent to the company's sales total in 1993, a span during which 40,000 government-funded jobs within the company had been eliminated. Conversely, Rockwell's commercial business had grown substantially, fueled by Beall's efforts to expand the company's telecommunication business and bolster Allen-Bradley's market position. By 1994, Rockwell's telecommunications unit was manufacturing 80 percent of all modems in computers and fax machines sold throughout the world, while the company's investment in Allen-Bradley began paying dividends, buoyed by a more favorable economic picture. In early 1994, Allen-Bradley was recording $8.1 million in sales per day, the greatest amount in the company's history and cause for much optimism for Rockwell's future as a more dynamic player in the commercial electronics market.

Rockwell solidified its move into industrial automation in January 1995 with the acquisition of Reliance Electric Co. for $1.6 billion, outbidding General Signal Corporation in a several-months-long takeover battle. The addition of Reliance made industrial automation Rockwell's largest business, accounting for 28 percent of overall revenues in fiscal 1995. Reliance was a producer of electric motors and drives used in factories, making for a strategic fit with Allen-Bradley's factory automation systems. Reliance traced its roots back to the founding in 1904 in Cleveland, Ohio, of Lincoln Electric Manufacturing Company, whose first product was the Type AS DC motor. In 1967 Reliance acquired Dodge Mechanical Company, a firm specializing in gear reducers, mounted bearings, and power transmission components.

In mid-1995 Don H. Davis was named president, with Beall remaining chairman and CEO. Shortly thereafter, Rockwell began a series of moves that dramatically changed the nature of the company. Seeking to focus the company on the potentially higher growth areas of electronics and communications, Beall and Davis began divesting operations outside of these areas. In 1996 Rockwell sold off its graphic systems business to Stonington Partners Inc. for $600 million. Then late in 1996 the company sold its defense and aerospace businesses—its best-known operations—to Boeing for $3.2 billion, one part of an ongoing consolidation of the U.S. defense industry. Following the latter sale, business with the Defense Department and NASA accounted for only 6 percent of Rockwell revenues. A further concentration on core areas came in September 1997 when Rockwell spun off its automotive business to shareholders as Meritor Automotive, Inc.

The divestments left Rockwell with three core businesses: automation, avionics and communications (known as Rockwell Collins), and semiconductors. Rockwell Collins was beefed up in December 1997 through the purchase of the in-flight entertainment business of Hughes-Avicom International, Inc. In early 1998 Beall retired and Davis took over as chairman and CEO.

Davis quickly left his own mark on the company with yet another spinoff. Facing a sluggish and potentially volatile market for semiconductors, Rockwell in December 1998 spun off its semiconductor operations to shareholders as Conexant Systems, Inc. This move also precipitated a shifting of the company headquarters in 1999 from California to Milwaukee, where its industrial automation business was located. Meantime, the company launched a sweeping restructuring of its automation operations in mid-1998 that included the layoff of about 3,000 of the unit's 27,000 employees, the closure of factories and the exit from certain product lines, and special charges of nearly $600 million. Consequently, for the fiscal year ending in September 1998, Rockwell posted a net loss of $437 million on sales of $6.75 billion.

Early 21st Century: Emergence of Rockwell Automation

In the final chapter of the dramatic transformation of Rockwell International, the company spun off Rockwell Collins to shareholders in June 2001. Other than both being in the general field of electronics, the two remaining legs of Rockwell International had little in common, giving impetus to the breakup. Davis remained chairman and CEO of the automation firm, which began operating under the name Rockwell Automation. Just prior to the completion of the spinoff, Rockwell announced plans to cut 1,000 jobs and close one factory in an effort to trim expenses by $100 million in the face of a stagnating U.S. economy. The newly incarnated Rockwell Automation thus began on rather shaky ground, but Davis was confident that his company's business would rebound when the general U.S. industrial sector entered a new period of growth.

Principal Subsidiaries

Allen-Bradley Company, LLC; Reliance Electric Industrial Company.

Principal Operating Units

Rockwell Automation Control Systems; Rockwell Automation Power Systems; Rockwell Electronic Commerce; Rockwell Scientific Company (50%).

Principal Competitors

Siemens AG; UNOVA, Inc.; Honeywell International Inc.; ABB Ltd.; Hitachi, Ltd.; Toshiba Corporation.

Further Reading

Anderson, Robert, *Through Turbulent Times,* New York: Newcomen Society, 1984, 24 p.

Bright, Charles D., *The Jet Makers: The Aerospace Industry from 1945–1972,* Lawrence: Regents Press of Kansas, 1978.

Brinton, James B., "Reborn Rockwell Rolls Toward 2000," *Electronic Business Today,* December 1996, pp. 45–47.

Brousell, David R., "For Rockwell, Breaking Up Is the Thing to Do," *Managing Automation,* January 2001.

Cook, Nick, "Who's Winning the U.S. Combat Airframe Battle?," *Interavia Business and Technology,* May 1994, p. 22.

Deady, Tim, "Rockwell's Earning's Socked by Recession: But Northrop Corp. Is Given a Boost by B-2 Revenues," *Los Angeles Business Journal,* April 22, 1991, p. 8.

Donlon, J.P., "Rockwell Comes in from the Cold (War)," *Chief Executive,* December 1996, pp. 38–41.

"Electronics Fuels Rockwell Net Rise; Sales Up Slightly," *Electronic News,* May 16, 1994, p. 10.

Franson, Paul, "Rockwell Dangerfield: Born Again As an Electronics Company, Rockwell Isn't Getting the Respect It Deserves on Wall Street," *Electronic Business,* March 1998, pp. 36–40, 87.

Lipin, Steven, and Jeff Cole, "Rockwell's Beall Takes Big Step Toward Strategy Goal: CEO's Deal with Boeing Advances Aim of Refashioning His Company," *Wall Street Journal,* August 2, 1996, p. B4.

Lubove, Seth, "New-Tech, Old-Tech," *Forbes,* July 17, 1995, p. 58.

MacKnight, Nigel, *Shuttle,* Osceola, Fla.: Motorbooks International, 1985.

Miller, William H., "Don Beall: Conglomerateer," *Industry Week,* January 22, 1996, pp. 13, 15–16.

Mrozek, Donald J., "The Truman Administration and the Enlistment of the Aviation Industry in Postwar Defense," *Business History Review,* Spring 1974.

Ordonez, Jennifer, and Andy Pasztor, ''Rockwell Will Spin Off Avionics Division in 2001, Retaining the Automation Unit,'' *Wall Street Journal,* December 11, 2000, p. A6.

Perry, Nancy J., ''Getting Out of Rocket Science,'' *Fortune,* April 4, 1994, pp. 101+.

''Rockwell International: Reaching for the Automotive Market Abroad,'' *Business Week,* May 5, 1980, p. 87.

——, ''Rockwell to Spin Off Chip Operations, Cut Work Force,'' *Wall Street Journal,* June 30, 1998, p. B4.

——, ''Rockwell Wins Battle to Buy Reliance Electric,'' *Wall Street Journal,* November 22, 1994, p. A3.

Velocci, Anthony L., Jr., ''Rockwell Collins Granted Autonomy,'' *Aviation Week and Space Technology,* December 18/25, 2000, pp. 15–18.

Wartzman, Rick, ''Rockwell Touts Non-Aerospace Business: Only a Quarter of Its Work Comes from Pentagon,'' *Wall Street Journal,* December 27, 1989.

Weimer, De'Ann, ''Will Rockwell Find Some Roots?,'' *Business Week,* May 10, 1999, pp. 77, 80.

Woolley, Scott, ''This Pasture Looked Greener,'' *Forbes,* October 20, 1997, pp. 294–95.

Wrubel, Robert, ''Cliff Function: Don Beall Is Proving Rockwell's Critics Wrong, There Is Life After the B-1B Bomber,'' *Financial World,* August 8, 1989, p. 30.

—Jeffrey L. Covell
—update: David E. Salamie

Ross Stores, Inc.

8333 Central Avenue
Newark, California 94560-3433
U.S.A.
Telephone: (510) 505-4400
Fax: (510) 505-4169
Web site: http://www.rossstores.com

Public Company
Incorporated: 1957
Employees: 19,800
Sales: $2.71 billion (2000)
Stock Exchanges: NASDAQ
NAIC: 448140 Family Clothing Stores

One of the leading off-price retailers in the United States, Ross Stores, Inc. operates a chain of more than 400 Ross ''Dress for Less'' stores in 17 states. Although Ross operates one of the largest chains of its kind in the country, it reached this stature late in its corporate life. When the chain was purchased in 1982 by a group of investors that included Mervin Morris, founder of the Mervyn's chain, it comprised only six units in the San Francisco Bay area. During the ensuing decade, the chain grew robustly under the stewardship of Stuart Moldaw and Don Rowlett who converted the junior department stores to off-price retail units, the first of their kind in California. During the early 21st century, Ross ''Dress for Less'' stores offered brand and designer name apparel, accessories, and footwear for the entire family, as well as home accessories, at prices 20 percent to 60 percent below the prices charged by competing department stores and specialty shops. Of the 409 stores in operation in early 2001, 167 were located in California, by far the most important market for the company. The second and third largest markets were Texas, with 62 stores, and Florida, with 53.

Origins

The roots of the Ross retail chain stretch back to 1957, when the first Ross junior department store opened. But the first definitive year in the company's history occurred nearly 30 years after its birth. In 1982, the year that separated the two distinct eras in Ross's history, two men with a wealth of experience in the off-price retail industry purchased the Ross enterprise when the chain comprised six junior department stores in the San Francisco Bay area. With these six stores, acquired with the help of venture capital partners, the two entrepreneurs made no mistake about their intentions, quickly developing a retail empire that would boast 107 stores three years later, 156 stores by the end of the 1980s, and nearly 300 stores by the mid-1990s. The orchestrators of this rapid expansion that erased three decades of sleepy growth were Stuart Moldaw and Donald Rowlett.

Stuart Moldaw, who became chairman of Ross following the August 1982 acquisition, was not new to the off-price retail scene. Prior to his involvement with Ross, Moldaw founded Pic-A-Dilly, an off-price retail chain, Country Casuals, and The Athletic Shoe Factory. Rowlett, who was selected as the new president of Ross, was no novice either, having created and developed F.W. Woolworth's off-price subsidiary, J. Brannam, into a 36-unit chain. Together, these two retail veterans had visions of creating a powerful off-price retail chain in an area of the country where the off-price concept was virtually nonexistent. Elsewhere, particularly along the East Coast and in the Midwest, off-price retail stores were enjoying burgeoning popularity during the early 1980s, but in California they were conspicuous by their absence, at least as Moldaw and Rowlett saw it. Considering the pace at which Moldaw and Rowlett expanded the Ross chain shortly after acquiring it, the two were intent on pioneering the concept in California and saturating markets before rival off-price chains recognized the opportunities that existed in the state.

Early 1980s: Moldaw and Rowlett Era

Success was realized from the changes instituted by Moldaw and Rowlett, the first of which was recasting the six-unit chain as a different type of retailer. The two shifted the chain's focus away from its junior orientation to create an off-price format stocking branded apparel for men, women, and children, as well as domestics merchandise, shoes, and accessories at sharply reduced prices. Once the stores were dedicated toward attracting a broader customer base and outfitted with a broader merchandise selection, Moldaw and Rowlett made their second

Company Perspectives:

The Ross formula for growth? Great brands . . . great prices . . . Everyday! Over the next several years, we will continue to focus on and implement that basic strategy. We believe that our strict adherence to this fundamental tenet of the off-price business will be the key factor in our ability to successfully enter new markets and accelerate store growth over the next decade.

decisive move by quickly adding to their store count. Two Ross "Dress for Less" stores were opened in the fall of 1982 and 18 stores the following year, more than tripling the size of Ross in little more than a year.

Much of the physical growth recorded during the first full year of Moldaw's and Rowlett's leadership was accomplished by acquiring existing stores in strip malls and freestanding locations abandoned by other retailers. This acquisition strategy would continue to be used by the company as its geographic scope of operations broadened, severing the chains that had fettered it to northern California for three decades. By the end of 1983, Ross "Dress for Less" stores were situated in southern California and the first store beyond the state's borders—a store in Reno, Nevada—was opened, touching off a march across the map that in a few short years would extend the company's presence from coast to coast.

Early in 1984, plans called for the establishment of 20 stores in California, Arizona, Washington, and Oregon, but by the end of the year Ross had opened twice as many, including stores in Utah, Texas, and Oklahoma. Much of the growth during the year was realized from the acquisition of 15 stores from the Handyman division of Edison Brothers Stores, which added Ross "Dress for Less" stores in Texas and Oklahoma. The Handyman deal, completed in July, was concluded in the same month that Ross's corporate headquarters were moved to a 494,000-square-foot facility in Newark, California, which also served as the company's distribution center.

From this location in Newark, the company's expansion would be plotted into the 1990s, as the number of stores, each stocking a list of brand and designer names that rivaled most department stores and specialty stores, increased exponentially. Though its merchandise compared favorably with the selection offered by department stores and specialty stores, Ross charged substantially less than traditional retailers, selling its merchandise for as much as 60 percent below competitors' prices. The enormous savings to be realized lured customers through Ross' stores, convincing management, in turn, that the only obstacle checking the company's financial growth was the number of stores it operated. More stores meant more revenue and greater profits, so Moldaw and Rowlett focused their efforts on expansion, making an initial public offering of stock in 1985 to help fund the opening of additional stores. At the time of the public offering, there were 107 Ross "Dress for Less" stores, an impressive total given the company's total store count of six three years earlier, and an extensive operating territory the company could call its own. After entering Washington, Utah, Arizona, Texas, and Oklahoma, in 1984, Ross entered new markets in Colorado, Florida, Georgia, New Mexico, and Oregon in 1985. By the end of the year, sales were up an encouraging 79 percent, swelling to $375.9 million.

Mid-1980s Tumble

The company's record-setting growth in 1985, which included the addition of 41 stores, was followed by an equally impressive 1986, when 39 stores were opened and new markets were penetrated in Maryland, North Carolina, and Virginia. By this point, there were 121 Ross "Dress for Less" stores scattered throughout 16 states, 40 percent of which had been open for less than a year. Fueled by this new growth, annual sales shot past the $500 million mark by the end of 1986 and future revenue growth seemed assured as expansion plans were laid for the company's penetration into new markets. In 1986, however, the company suffered its first major setback when it was forced to shutter 25 unprofitable stores located primarily in Texas and Oklahoma, where anemic economic conditions crimped Ross's profits. For the year, Ross reported a crippling $41.4 million loss, $39.4 million of which stemmed from the stores closures in Texas and Oklahoma.

On the heels of this downturn, the company lost one of its two chief architects when Rowlett resigned from the company in 1987. It was not long, however, before Ross gained a new architect to rebuild the company and carry it into the 1990s. Following Rowlett's departure, a company veteran, Norman A. Ferber, who was serving as Ross's executive vice-president of merchandising, marketing, and distribution, was appointed as Ross's president and chief operating officer. Less than a year later, in January 1988, Ferber was also named Ross's chief executive officer, taking charge of the company as it was undergoing a series of changes to quickly restore its profitability.

Responding to the $40 million loss in 1986, Moldaw and Ferber drastically cut back on expansion in 1987, opening only 11 stores and situating those stores in markets where Ross "Dress for Less" stores were already located or in close proximity. The days of adding one new state after another to the company's geographic fold were over. Instead of trying to dot the country with store after store, Ross executives focused their expansion in three principal markets, the West Coast, the Washington area, and Florida, and devoted more time to developing a profitable merchandising strategy. Hoping to rescue their company from the red, company officials eliminated the domestics departments in Ross stores and added cosmetics and fragrance departments. Additionally, executives added "high-end" clothing to Ross's merchandising mix, upgrading their inventory with items such as men's sport coats and women's silk dresses.

By the end of 1987, management could point to positive results. For the year, Ross recorded an $11.5 million gain after the more than $40 million loss the year before. Encouraged by their initial success, Moldaw and Ferber continued to refine Ross's merchandising strategy as the 1980s progressed. By 1989, 95 percent of the company's 140 stores contained full cosmetic and fragrance departments staffed with beauty consultants, one of the new and decidedly upscale features adopted by Ross as it repositioned itself for consistent profitability. In the chasm separating discount stores and traditional department

Key Dates:

1957: First Ross junior department store opens.
1982: Stuart Moldaw and Donald Rowlett purchase the Ross chain, which then consists of six stores in the San Francisco Bay area; the pair begin converting the units to off-price Ross ''Dress for Less'' stores.
1983: Rapid expansion begins with the opening of 18 more stores.
1985: Company goes public to fund further expansion.
1992: Sales surpass the $1 billion mark for the first time.
2000: Company announces plans to add 250 new store locations by the end of 2005.

stores, off-price retailers occupied the middle ground, but as the 1990s neared Moldaw and Ferber were tipping the balance toward the department store end of the scale by adopting the trappings of more upscale retail outlets. Like many off-price chains, Ross had never divided, or ''departmentalized,'' its retail floor space into merchandise categories to any great extent, but as the company entered the 1990s chrome and wood partitions were used with increasing frequency to delineate various departments. Among the other changes reshaping the chain was a refocused inventory strategy, as Ross ''Dress for Less'' stores began stocking less variety of merchandise while bolstering their supply of preferred lines, creating a narrower and deeper inventory for stores to stock.

1990s and Beyond: Steady Expansion

Along with these changes came a renewed commitment to expand the chain. In 1989, when Ross ranked as the third largest off-price retailer in the country, company officials announced plans to open 100 to 150 stores during the ensuing five years. As the early 1990s progressed, the chain went a long way toward achieving this ambitious goal. In 1990, 29 new stores were opened, giving the company a total of 185 stores in 18 states by the end of the year and opening up new markets in Philadelphia and in Boise, Idaho. Another 20 stores were opened the following year, as annual sales jumped from $804 million to $930 million, and another 23 stores were added to the chain in 1992, when sales eclipsed the billion-dollar mark, reaching $1.04 billion.

Upon reaching this milestone, Moldaw and Ferber began test marketing a ''Home Accents'' department, which featured picture frames, china, ceramic ware, and crystal. The concept was introduced in 20 stores early in 1992 and quickly registered sufficient success to warrant its incorporation into other existing Ross ''Dress for Less'' stores. With 223 stores by the end of 1992, the company planned to put Home Accents departments in nearly all of its existing locations before the close of 1993, giving it a high-profit-margin vehicle to fuel its financial growth in the years ahead. By the end of 1995, only ten of the company's 292 stores did not contain Home Accents departments. By this time, yet another new department, Bed and Bath, had been launched in 1994. This department featured bed and bath linens and accessories, and by 1997 the rollout of Bed and Bath had been completed throughout the entire chain. In 1996, meantime, a small line of sporting goods, such as basketballs and handheld weights, were added to Ross stores.

Entering the mid-1990s, Ferber, who was named chairman in 1993, was focusing the chain's growth in existing markets. Twenty stores were opened in 1993, another 32 stores in 1994, and 17 stores in 1995, with each successive wave of openings giving Ross a more entrenched market position. With 292 stores by the end of 1995, Ross was collecting nearly $1.5 million a year in sales, having experienced considerable financial growth during the previous decade. Equally as impressive was the company's profitability, which had been strengthened substantially by the changes adopted in the wake of Ross's mid-1980s debacle. In 1995, the company earned more than $43 million, with the average sales per square foot climbing to $230 from an average of $214 in 1991. That the company recorded this increase during a national recession that crippled many retailers throughout the country boded well for its future, fueling confidence that the ''new'' Ross was well-positioned to reap the rewards of a recovering economy. As the company prepared for the late 1990s, it gained new management to lead it toward its future. Effective September 1996, Michael Balmuth, Ross's executive vice-president of merchandising, became the company's CEO, replacing Ferber, who stayed on as chairman. Balmuth had joined Ross in 1989 as senior vice-president and general merchandise manager.

Under Balmuth's leadership in the late 1990s, Ross continued to steadily grow within its existing markets and further expanded the nonapparel offerings of its stores. In 1997 an additional 17 stores were opened and revenues were just a shade under $2 billion. Average sales per square foot rose to $285, a 24 percent increase over the figure for 1995. Profits reached a record $117.5 million. Store openings increased to 26 in 1998 and 29 in 1999, bringing the store count to 378 by the end of the latter year. Continuing its steady growth, Ross posted revenues of $2.47 billion, profits of $150.1 million, and average sales per square foot of $300 for 1999. The late 1990s saw the company test and then begin a chainwide rollout of Maternity and Fine Jewelry departments. By the end of the 1990s, more than 16 percent of overall revenues were derived from the sale of nonapparel goods. Another key initiative in the late 1990s was an aggressive expansion of the company's buying staff to broaden its market coverage and gain additional opportunities to purchase closeout merchandise.

In 2000, 31 more Ross ''Dress for Less'' stores opened, boosting the number of units to 409. That year the company announced plans to accelerate its pace of expansion, aiming to add about 250 new locations by the end of 2005, or about 50 per year. Another aspect of this new expansion program would be the addition of the company's first new markets since 1994. Ross planned in 2001 and 2002 to reenter the Georgia and North Carolina markets and to enter South Carolina for the first time. Helping to manage this new market initiative was James C. Peters, who was hired as president and chief operating officer of Ross Stores in August 2000. Peters had most recently served as president of U.S. retailing for Staples Inc., the office supplies chain. During the first quarter of 2001 two Ross stores opened in the Atlanta, Georgia, metropolitan area, marking a possible beginning of a new era in the story of steady if unspectacular growth for the company.

Principal Competitors

Wal-Mart Stores, Inc.; The TJX Companies, Inc.; Burlington Coat Factory Warehouse Corporation; Kmart Corporation; Target Corporation; Kohl's Corporation; Goody's Family Clothing, Inc.; Stein Mart, Inc.; The Dress Barn, Inc.; Filene's Basement Corp.; Loehmann's, Inc.; Charming Shoppes, Inc.

Further Reading

''Balmuth Named CEO of Ross Stores,'' *Daily News Record,* June 11, 1995, p. 10.

Clark, Ken, ''Off-Price Apparel Chains Struggle to Keep Up,'' *Chain Store Age,* March 2000, pp. 92, 96.

Emert, Carol, ''Ross Is Dressed for Success,'' *San Francisco Chronicle,* March 19, 1997, p. D1.

Gilbert, Les, ''Ross Doing Well in Coast with Off-Price Format,'' *Footwear News,* July 23, 1984, p. 66.

''Going Public Should Help Ross Reach Coast-to-Coast,'' *Discount Store News,* August 5, 1985, p. 18.

Kahn, Hal, ''Ross Stores Inc. CEO to Resign in September,'' *Knight-Ridder/Tribune Business News,* May 31, 1996.

Krein, Pamela, ''Ross Stores to Close 25 Money-Losing Units in Southwest,'' *Discount Store News,* March 16, 1987, p. 39.

Lau, Gloria, ''Know Thy Customer,'' *Forbes,* July 7, 1997, p. 76.

MacIntosh, Jean, ''Refocused Strategy Puts Off-Pricer Ross Stores Right on the Money,'' *Daily News Record,* October 27, 1988, p. 6.

Meek, Pamela, ''Ross Goes Further Upscale in Prototype,'' *Discount Store News,* September 25, 2989, p. 1.

Paris, Ellen, ''A Touch of Class,'' *Forbes,* February 5, 1990, p. 148.

Radwell, Steven, ''Dayton Hudson Sells Its Four Plum Stores,'' *Daily News Record,* February 22, 1984, p. 1.

Razzano, Rhonda, ''Ross Stores Realigns Mix, Redirects Strategies: Off-Price Recovers from Oil Patch Setback,'' *Chain Store Age Executive with Shopping Center Age,* May 1989, p. 25.

''Ross Unveils Aggressive Plan: 25 New Stores Set for 1994,'' *Discount Store News,* March 7, 1994, p. 6.

Ruben, Howard, ''Ross Stores Plays the Off-Price Game,'' *Daily News Record,* February 14, 1984, p. 10.

Rutberg, Sidney, ''Ross Stores Loss Fails to Chill Optimism,'' *Women's Wear Daily,* June 25, 1987, p. 6.

Strom, Shelly, ''Retailer Plans Expansion,'' *Business Journal,* June 16, 2000, p. 3.

Tanaka, Wendy, ''Ross Is Boss,'' *San Francisco Examiner,* February 7, 1997, p. B1.

Young, Kristin, ''Ross to Open in Atlanta Area,'' *Women's Wear Daily,* March 7, 2001, p. 13.

Young, Vicki M., ''Ross Picks Peters As New President,'' *Women's Wear Daily,* July 17, 2000, p. 23.

—Jeffrey L. Covell
—update: David E. Salamie

Rowan Companies, Inc.

2800 Post Oak Blvd., Suite 5450
Houston, Texas 77056-6196
U.S.A.
Telephone: (713) 621-7800
Fax: (713) 960-7660
Web site: http://www.rowancompanies.com

Public Company
Incorporated: 1924 as Rowan Drilling Company
Employees: 4,742
Sales: $645.95 million (2000)
Stock Exchanges: New York Pacific
Ticker Symbol: RDC
NAIC: 213111 Drilling Oil & Gas Wells; 23493 Industrial Non Building Structure Construction; 481211 Nonscheduled Chartered Passenger Air Transportation

Rowan Companies, Inc. is a leader in domestic and international oil drilling with two subsidiary businesses, Era Aviation and LaTourneau, Inc. that support its primary business. Rowan operates drills in Louisiana, Texas, the Gulf of Mexico, Canada, Alaska, and throughout the world. Era Aviation is a charter airline serving Alaska, the Gulf Coast, and the Western United States. LaTourneau, Inc. manufactures offshore drilling rigs. Since 1924, Rowan has been a leader in the industry and has strengthened its position consistently through decades of work in the oil fields.

Roaring to Life in the 1920s

When brothers Charlie and Arch Rowan had the opportunity to purchase a drilling rig in 1923, they decided to seize the day. Charlie, who had experience in the oil fields with Humble Oil, convinced Arch to join him in the fledgling drilling operation in the now famous oil fields of Corsicana, Texas.

Incorporating in 1924 as Rowan Drilling, the company added to its inventory an additional oil rig, purchased for $5,500. With total capital of $30,000, the brothers set the new rig near the town of Wortham. They hit a gusher in November 1924 that reached 200 feet in the air. The event launched Rowan's business and created an oil boom in the city of Wortham that continued until 1927.

In 1927, the Rowan brothers established a second company, Rowan Oil Company. The newly formed company was to sell the oil produced by Rowan Drilling. Headquartered in Fort Worth, the company did not begin making money until 1928.

Continuing Prosperity in the 1930s

Outside of east Texas, the Great Depression had hold on the rest of the country, but in the oil fields, jobs and oil continued to gush plentifully. In 1933, Rowan Oil Company dissolved. Its older counterpart, Rowan Drilling, was also dissolved but then reborn as a Delaware corporation. Four stockholders—Charlie Rowan, Arch Rowan, A.A. Klein, and Bess Brants—divided the company, with the Rowan brothers retaining the majority of the shares.

Drilling with steam power was state-of-the-art for the 1920s, but by 1935 Rowan was moving ahead of the industry by purchasing its first diesel electric rig. In the late 1930s, the company extended its reach beyond Texas and into the marshland of Louisiana.

Because of an excess flood of oil in the market, the Texas Railroad Commission began regulating the production for oil wells. In response to this regulation, Rowan sued the state agency in a case that eventually went all the way to the U.S. Supreme Court. However, Rowan lost the case (6–3) as the Supreme Court refused to overrule the judgment of a state agency.

Changes in the 1940s

The 1940s brought a new landscape to the world and the oil industry. As the United States entered World War II in 1941, oil production was a key factor in the war effort. Rowan was ready to support the war effort with improved drilling technology. Arch Rowan was a founding member of the Petroleum Industry War Council, an organization that later became the National Petroleum Council.

Company Perspectives:

The careful management of three assets—manpower, machines and money—to create stockholder value. Manpower: we believe that Rowan's personnel policies are the number one factor that sets us apart from our competition. We hire at entry level, train and promote from within, reward competence and loyalty and provide top wages and unequaled job security. Machines: Rowan owns and operates premium equipment. Money: Rowan's financial strategy: first, we plan for the long-term survival of the Company. We plan to meet each and every financial commitment on time and in full—just as we have done since 1923. We do not overcommit during the good times and we do not panic during the bad times.

After the war was over in 1945, Rowan, as well as other oil drilling businesses, experienced difficulties. In 1948, imported oil began to have an impact and exceeded domestic oil for the first time. However, demand increased with a growth in automobile and aircraft use.

In 1948 Rowan Drilling Company split into two companies when Rowan Oil was resurrected. This change was in response to Texas liability law and was designed to protect oil holdings by separating the drilling and leasing operations. Internally, changes were happening as well. To facilitate company communication, Rowan launched *The Rowan Grapevine,* a company magazine for Rowan employees.

By the end of 1948, Rowan had 78 wells—55 in Texas, 12 in New Mexico, and 11 in Louisiana. Accessing rigs in the swamps of Louisiana was challenging, so Rowan purchased a twin-engine Beechcraft airplane in 1948 to fly to those remote locations.

Growth in the 1950s

With 24 rigs in operation in three states, Rowan began the 1950s aggressively. In 1951, Rowan began offering benefits to its employees as well as establishing a joint headquarters in Fort Worth, Texas, for the two companies—Rowan Oil and Rowan Drilling.

Though marsh drilling in Louisiana had been successful, drilling in deep water was new to Rowan, and the company first attempted it in 1954 in the Gulf of Mexico. Despite being plagued by bad weather, Rowan persevered and added a second rig. Helicopters were used to transport crew to the rigs.

In 1955, after 32 years of leadership, Arch and Charlie Rowan retired. Hamilton Rogers became president of Rowan Oil Company, and Gilbert Rowe, who had joined Rowan Drilling in 1944, assumed leadership of that company. That same year, Rowan Drilling built the Rowan building in downtown Fort Worth to serve as its headquarters.

Ten years after being split into two companies, Rowan decided that, though initially beneficial due to Texas liability law, operating two companies was not advantageous to the overall organization. The assets of Rowan Oil Company were sold to Texas Pacific Coal & Oil Company in a $9.6 million deal. The remaining company, Rowan Drilling, extended drilling operations into Mississippi in 1958.

Going Public: 1960s

In 1961, company founder Charlie Rowan died. Tragedy followed in 1962 when Arch Rowan, Jr., died at the age of 32 as the result of burns received during an accidental fire at his home. Arch, Jr., was a member of the board of directors of Rowan Drilling.

With Gilbert Rowe at the helm, significant changes happened in the 1960s. In 1963, the company said goodbye to Fort Worth, its headquarters since 1927, and relocated to Houston, Texas. Rowan extended its drilling operations, continuing to add rigs, including one in Alaska in 1966.

The biggest change for the company occurred on September 6, 1967, when Rowan launched its initial public offering (IPO) of 323,000 shares. The decision to become a public company resulted from the need for more operating capital to fund offshore work and technological advances. Two thirds of the common stock following the IPO was still held by Rowan executives and employees.

As of September 30, 1967, Rowan had assets of $8.7 million. Offshore drilling accounted for 42 percent of contract-drilling revenues and 65 percent of net income from contract operations. The move into drilling further north in Alaska brought increased challenges for Rowan. Not only was the weather frigid and hostile, transportation was a problem for the company. This challenge led to the company's decision in 1967 to purchase ERA Helicopters, Alaska's largest helicopter business. With the companies increased capabilities, drilling contracts increased as well.

Worldwide Exploration and Challenges in the 1970s

A new mobile drilling platform was designed and built to further Rowan's oil drilling efforts. Its first contract operation was located off the eastern coast of Nicaragua in 1970 for Shell. A second mobile drilling platform was built and began work in the Gulf of Mexico. The company obtained contracts, with the help of this new equipment, in Nicaragua, Colombia, Honduras, and Venezuela. In 1972, a year after the business had renamed itself Rowan Companies, CEO Gilbert Rowe retired, with Bob Palmer named as his successor.

In 1973, the Yom Kippur War and ensuing embargo of U.S. oil supplies by the Organization of Petroleum Exporting Countries (OPEC) demonstrated U.S. oil dependence. The embargo caused a perceived shortage of gasoline, and OPEC raised the price of their oil. Also in 1973, Rowan purchased a second airline in Alaska—Merric, Inc. Together with Rowan's subsidiary Era, the company now had 36 helicopters and 12 fixed wing aircraft. The airlines were immediately successful, jumping in revenue by 130 percent to $12.8 million by 1974. In 1978, Era built an aviation center at Anchorage International Airport to house the company's fleet.

Rowan's broadening market continued to expand as Rowan began drilling in the North Sea off the coast of Norway in 1973,

Key Dates:

1923: Charlie Rowan buys first drilling rig.
1924: Charlie and Arch Rowan incorporate Rowan Drilling Company and hit gusher later that year.
1927: A second business, Rowan Oil Company, is incorporated to market Rowan Drilling's output.
1933: Rowan Oil dissolves and Rowan Drilling is rechartered as a Delaware corporation.
1935: Rowan Drilling buys first diesel electric rig.
1948: Company purchases its first airplane.
1955: Arch and Charlie Rowan retire; Gilbert Rowe becomes president of the company.
1967: Rowan becomes a public company and purchases ERA Helicopters (renamed Era Aviation).
1971: Rowan Drilling assumes its present-day name.
1972: Bob Palmer becomes CEO.
1978: Hostile takeover attempt is thwarted.
1993: Company purchases LaTourneau, Inc., a manufacturer of offshore drilling rigs.
2000: Company offers for sale 10.3 million shares of common stock.

with the company's first semi-submersible drilling rig. In 1975, a Rowan drilling tender, or rig-towing ship, was the first to venture through the Suez Canal since Egypt has closed the passageway to shipping in 1967 after the Six-Day War.

The year 1978 brought a threat to Rowan—a hostile takeover was attempted by Chicago Bridge & Iron. CEO Bob Palmer thwarted the attempt by negotiating with another investor, Schlumberger, to buy $1.9 million of the company's stock. Schlumberger became a passive investor in the company. Despite the challenges of the 1970s, Rowan had experienced tremendous growth, doubling in size to 1,550 employees and adding new rigs and contracts in new areas.

Challenges of the 1980s

In 1981, Rowan CEO Bob Palmer was named the top CEO in the offshore drilling industry by the *Wall Street Transcript*. The recognition was made in part because of Palmer's aggressive risk-taking in ordering new cantilever jack-up rigs, calculating that the industry would recover and that there would be a need for the new rigs.

However, demand for oil decreased as alternative fuels such as nuclear energy, coal, and natural gas were meeting energy needs. This, combined with an unsure world oil market, created challenges in the 1980s. The leadership of Rowan made it a point to plan for the future, even during this time, by employing new methods and by building a new type of offshore oil rig. These new oil rigs, "The Gorillas," were 40 percent larger and could work in deeper waters, drilling down to 30,000 feet. The $85 million cost was high, but the new rigs represented the company's future direction.

Both revenues and profits dropped in the early 1980s. Profits dropped from $119.4 million to $21.9 million, and revenues dropped from $401.6 million to $206.5 million during a one-year period from 1982 to 1983.

Rowan stuck with its aggressive plan while initiating cost savings-measures. A London office was opened in 1985 and led by Rowan Vice-President Paul Kelly, who had joined the company in 1982. Revenues began to post an increase in 1985 but profits were still declining for the company. The industry was increasingly unstable.

Two disasters made a mark on Rowan in the late 1980s. The new Gorilla rigs were performing well, but on December 8, 1988, Gorilla I, which was drilling in the North Sea, went down in a storm. The crew was rescued, but the rig was lost at sea. Another disaster called for help from Rowan, as one of Era's helicopters was first on the scene of the *Exxon Valdez* oil spill. The Rowan subsidiary was key in providing transportation for rescuers, government officials, media, scientists, and animal rescue workers. Era's service during the crisis earned it a Certificate of Merit award from the Coast Guard in 1989.

Resurgence in the 1990s and Beyond

In 1990, Rowan posted a profit for the first time in five years, led by the company's aviation business, which provided 38 percent of revenues. In 1991, Rowan purchased KLM Helikopters B.V. from KLM Royal Dutch Airlines to add to its aviation sector. In 1993, the company grew again with the purchase of Marathon-LaTourneau Company from General Cable Corporation. The company had been building Rowan's jack-up rigs for several years and now joined the Rowan family as a subsidiary. LaTourneau also operated a steel mill and manufactured heavy mining equipment.

By 1997, Rowan was reaping the benefits of its aggressive strategies as profits hit a record $147 million on $695 million in revenues. In 1998 and 1999, however, the company experienced a downturn, posting a loss in 1999 of $9.7 million.

Net income rebounded to $70.2 million in 2000. That same year, Rowan purchased two companies, The Ellis Williams Company, Inc. and EWCO, Inc.—manufacturers of mud pumps for drilling. Also, new revenue was raised in a secondary issue of 10.3 million shares of common stock at $24 per share. The aviation division increased revenues by 19 percent in 2000. CEO Bob Palmer, in the 2000 annual report said, "This past year has reinforced my belief that 'the fundamentals of our primary business have never been better.' " As Rowan Companies, Inc. moved to the future, it continued to aggressively develop new drilling rigs and new markets.

Principal Subsidiaries

LaTourneau, Inc.; Era Aviation, Inc.

Principal Competitors

Caterpillar Inc.; Global Marine Inc.; Petroleum Helicopters, Inc.

Further Reading

Kelly, Paul, ''Head Off Train Wreck on Electricity,'' *Houston Chronicle*, August 20, 2000.

Rodengen, Jeffrey L., *The Legend of Rowan,* edited by Alex Lieber and Jon VanZile, Fort Lauderdale: Write Stuff Enterprises, 1998.

Rowan Companies Inc. Grapevine—Fifty Years of Growth, Houston: Rowan Companies, Inc., 1973.

Smith, Robert, ''Gorilla Tactics: Rowan Reaps the Rewards As Drilling Market Resurgence Keeps the Rig Contracts Rolling In,'' *Upstream,* February 2, 2001, p. 20.

—Melissa Rigney Baxter

RURAL CELLULAR CORPORATION

Rural Cellular Corporation

3905 Dakota Street
Alexandria, Minnesota 56308
U.S.A.
Telephone: (320) 762-2000
Fax: (320) 808-2181
Web site: http://www.rccwireless.com

Public Company
Incorporated: 1990
Employees: 1,162
Sales: $356.09 million (2000)
Stock Exchanges: NASDAQ
Ticker Symbol: RCCC
NAIC: 513322 Cellular and Other Wireless Telecommunications

Serving over 500,000 customers (and potentially five million) in 14 states, Rural Cellular Corporation (RCC) is the largest independent wireless company operating in a notably rural setting. RCC markets its products and services under the names Cellular 2000, CellularOne, Keypage, and Unicel. According to company sources, RCC was one of the first cellular services to make a profit, doing so just four years after its founding in 1990. Rural Cellular's corporate history has been one of strategic rapid expansion through acquisition. By concentrating on rural areas with high tourist populations and large numbers of small businesses, RCC has been able to serve large numbers of cellular-equipped urban dwellers roaming within its regions. In 1999 alone, Rural Cellular made 27.7 percent of its revenue off of roaming charges.

Emergence of a Distinctively Rural Wireless Provider: 1990

In 1990, Richard P. Ekstrand organized a merger of five cellular partnerships that held the licenses of 40 rural telephone companies from the northern suburbs of Minneapolis, Minnesota, north to the Canadian border and as far west as Fargo, North Dakota. Ekstrand was looking to leave the fast-paced life of the Twin Cities metropolitan area and decided to look to the central Minnesota lakes region for his respite. Ekstrand, like many other former urbanites, was accustomed to the many conveniences that a large metro area had to offer. Wireless communications was a convenience that Ekstrand believed would play a very important role in rural areas. With long distances separating people and their destinations, rural areas were ripe for supporting the technology needed for a full service wireless industry. In a rural setting, furthermore, having a cellular phone provided citizens an added sense of safety. Amidst miles of infrequently driven highways, where motorists could become stranded, and miles of woodland trails and lakes, where quick assistance could make the difference between a safe and enjoyable vacation and disaster, the need for cellular technology seemed obvious.

One of the most important events in RCC's history occurred when Ekstrand and the board of directors decided to take the company public. By 1996 the company, which began with one employee (Ekstrand as president and CEO), had expanded to 500 employees and was firmly in the black. According to an interview in *smartbizmag.com,* Ekstrand referred to RCC's public offering in the following terms: "Our 1996 IPO of three million shares raised over $30 million gross dollars and enabled us to not only secure our 50% + share of cellular and paging marketing in rural Minnesota and border areas, but it also helped us link up with Wireless Alliance later in the year and begin improving service to our existing customers while we looked for new ones."

Ekstrand appeared to revel in acquisition and, following the initial public offering, one acquisition followed another. RCC's venture into the public arena clearly enabled the company's aggressive expansion and at the same time made it a more competitive provider by increasing its services and enhancing its technology.

Growing Through Acquisition: Mid- to Late 1990s

Immediately following the IPO, RCC began to actively seek new acquisitions and partnerships. Rural Cellular's first public move was to create Wireless Alliance, a partnership with Voice

Company Perspectives:

RCC serves rural areas where tourism, agriculture, and small businesses are prevalent. These areas are adjacent to metropolitan areas or include significant highway corridors. We have acquired companies with histories of strong operating results, superior network infrastructures, similar corporate cultures, and commitment to service excellence.

But RCC's vision reaches beyond the geographic boundaries of our wireless footprint to include technology solutions and customer relationships. RCC is focused on generating sustainable value for our shareholders over the long run by investing in state-of-the-art technologies and tailoring our products and services to meet the needs of customers in each region we serve.

We are convinced that by providing innovative solutions through wireless technologies and maximizing customer satisfaction, RCC will continue to fuel its growth and generate strong financial results.

Stream Wireless, an affiliate of Aerial Communications. A deal was struck with RCC owning 70 percent and Voice Stream Wireless controlling the remaining 30 percent. Through this partnership RCC gained 708,000 POPs (or population served) and PCS (personal communication systems) licenses in the area bordering the Midwest region that was already served by RCC. This move was consistent with Rural Cellular's plan to gain control of areas bordering ones in which it previously owned licenses, enabling the company to increase its service areas to customers already serviced by RCC.

PCS were a growing market in cellular sales and RCC's ability to buy the licenses with the cash flow it earned in the IPO was key to RCC's growth. PCS operated on a specific radio spectrum and were limited by the Federal Communications Commission to include at least six potential broadband PCS providers in each geographically designated service area. The Wireless Alliance deal allowed Rural Cellular to be at least one of the six key players in the upper Midwest.

In 1997 RCC looked eastward and acquired Unity Cellular Systems, Inc. (Unicel) in Maine and the related wireless and microwave licenses from Intercel, Inc. For $85.7 million, RCC once again nearly doubled its population served. In the acquisition RCC bought the licenses of 512,000 POPs. This region covered a large portion of the state of Maine, including five RSAs (rural service areas) and one MSA (metro service area) in Bangor.

In 1998 RCC continued by acquiring Atlantic Cellular, extending its service areas in the northeastern United States. Atlantic Cellular's license areas included parts of Massachusetts, New Hampshire, New York, and Vermont. The purchase price was a reported $262.5 million, a far greater amount than any of RCC's previous dealings. At the time of the purchase, RCC was criticized by some industry analysts for growing too quickly, limiting its cash flow and increasing its company debt to an uncomfortable extent. Atlantic not only added 1.1 million POPs to the RCC network, it also brought with it an established long distance business. Notwithstanding the critics, Rural Cellular Corporation was on its way to becoming a force to be reckoned with in the industry. It now held cellular POPs of 2.2 million and showed no signs of stopping. In the next few years, with other cellular licenses selling quickly and at much higher rates, analysts recognized that RCC had actually obtained a good bargain in its acquisition of Atlantic Cellular.

In August 1998 RCC increased its presence in Maine by acquiring Western Maine Cellular, Inc. Although a relatively small addition by previous standards, Western Maine's service area was adjacent to RCC's existing Maine market, making it a good strategic buy, particularly for its customer service, marketing, and distribution.

With its population served totaling over 2.3 million, RCC in 1999 added RCI Group, Inc., which serviced rural customers under the name Glacial Lakes Cellular 2000 in South Dakota, in a geographic area comprising 6,444 square miles.

Later in 1999, RCC acquired St. Cloud Minnesota Personal Communications Systems (PCS) licenses for $1.6 million, and 13 separate local multi-point distribution system (LMDS) licenses for $7 million, of which the company planned to use a portion ''for testing new products, services and systems.'' RCC saw these licenses as a technology to which every home in the future might subscribe.

By far the most impressive accomplishment during RCC's short history was its acquisition in 2000 of Triton Cellular Partners, L.P. and its affiliates. Triton, with a combined total of 2.3 million POPs, was practically RCC's equal. Triton's properties included 20 rural service areas spread throughout Alabama, Kansas, Mississippi, Oregon, and Washington. The geographic regions in Triton's ownership included approximately 152,000 square miles, many of those areas in market clusters surrounding large cities. In order to finance the $1.24 billion purchase price of Triton, RCC completed a $170 million follow-on offering of common stock and a $165 million preferred stock issue, raising the remainder through a new 1.2 billion line of credit.

Triton's strongest asset was the digital technology it chose to invest in, known as time division multiple access (TDMA). This technology, one of three digital types used, was adopted and certified as standard by the Cellular Telecommunications Industry Association and used nationwide by AT&T Wireless and Southwestern Bell Mobile Systems. TDMA technology allowed the customer to obtain service from both digital and analog systems and because of this Triton benefited from a higher percentage of roaming traffic in its region primarily from customers of AT&T, GTE, and Western Wireless. The wireless customer was required to use a multi-mode phone, but was then able to access service from both a digital network or the more common analog system. The clear advantages to digital technology in the industry were better sound, increased system capacity, and lower costs in adding customers. It was projected that over time the industry would convert completely to digital radio technology.

In June 2000 RCC reached a definitive agreement to acquire Saco River Telegraph and Telephone Company. Saco River provided wireless and independent local exchange carrier (ILEC) services to southern Maine and eastern New Hampshire.

Key Dates:

1990: Rural Cellular Corporation (RCC) is incorporated; Richard P. Ekstrand is named president and CEO.
1996: RCC goes public, buys 70 percent of joint venture Wireless Alliance with Voice Stream Wireless.
1997: Company acquires Unity Cellular Systems Inc. (Unicel) and related cellular and microwave licences from Intercel Incorporated for $85.7 million.
1998: RCC acquires Atlantic Cellular for $262.5 million.
2000: RCC acquires Triton Cellular for $1.24 billion.
2001: Company reportedly seeks a buyer.

The licenses acquired included both those for cellular and personal communication systems (PCS). This purchase included 1.08 million POPs and the territories were contiguous to RCC's existing service areas in the Northeast.

Expanded Services, Innovations, and a Potential Sale: 2000–01

Other new services begun by RCC included a new E911 wireless location system, expanded digital service in the Midwest region, and an increase in packaged services regionwide. In Maine RCC introduced Type Talk, which allowed customers to receive written messages and access the Internet by using cell phones.

In September 2000 RCC teamed up with National Telemanagement Corporation (NTC) to provide seamless nationwide roaming to RCC's prepaid Smartpay Wireless subscribers. Other innovations that RCC incorporated into its services included an agreement with Preferred Voice, Inc. Preferred Voice offered a Safety-Talk service to dial specific parties using hands-free voice recognition.

To manage its service areas, RCC maintained a decentralized approach. Each region was independently controlled, meaning that the local office determined the channels of sales and distribution. This system differed from many other large wireless companies and according to RCC: ''This decentralized management approach emphasizes our local presence and enhances our competitive position.'' RCC believed that customer service was best when management stayed local, and that customer retention was directly related to customer service.

Rural Cellular Corporation, with its aggressive drive for growth and its willingness to partner with other corporations to improve its services, seemed destined to stay at the top of the list of successful rural wireless providers. By mid-2001, however, it was getting so large as to be attractive to companies with nationwide coverage and deeper pockets. A May 2001 *Financial Times* article announced that Rural Cellular was in fact seeking a buyer. Like other expanding rural carriers in an increasingly competitive environment, RCC ''faced declining fees from roaming contracts and costly network upgrades,'' not to mention a staggering $1.7 billion in debt. Possible suitors included AT&T Wireless, Verizon, Alltel, and Western Wireless. Whatever the future of RCC, it could be confidently said that founder Richard Ekstrand's original vision had been impressively realized in a relatively short period of time, so much so that the appellation ''rural'' in 2001 seemed all too quaint and ill-suited to describe a company of such scope and ambition.

Principal Subsidiaries

RCC Holdings, Inc.; Wireless Alliance.

Principal Competitors

AT&T Wireless Services, Inc.; Verizon Communications Inc.; Western Wireless Corporation; United States Cellular; Alltel Corporation; Telepak, Inc.; Airtouch Cellular; Sprint PCS; Powertel Inc.; Voice Stream Wireless Corporation; U.S. West; Nextel Communications; Inc.; Panhandle Telecommunications Systems, Inc.

Further Reading

Goldstein, Tally, ''US Mobile Carrier Seeks Buyer,'' *Financial Times,* May 18, 2001.

Killion, Rick, ''When Your Company Is Ready for Faster Growth It May Be Time for . . . Going Public,'' *www.smartbizmag.com,* June 1999.

Lopez, Ed, ''Safety Debate Could Propel Carrier Revenue,'' *Denver Colorado Weekly,* October 4, 1999.

Niemela, Jennifer, ''Phone Home: Rural Cellular's Small-Town Feel Nets Big-Time Gains,'' *Corporate Report,* April 2000, pp. 52–53.

''Rural Cellular Provides Technology Funds to School,'' *Echo Press,* November 5, 1999, p. A 8.

''Rural Cellular Will Acquire Triton for 1.24 Billion to Double in Size,'' *Investor's Business Daily,* November 9, 1999.

—Susan B. Culligan

The Sage Group

Sage House
Benton Park Road
Newcastle-upon-Tyne
NE7 7LZ
United Kingdom
Telephone: (0191) 255 3000
Toll free: 800 854 3415
Fax: (0191) 255 0308
Web site: http://www.sage.com

Public Company
Incorporated: 1981 as Sage Systems
Employees: 5,000
Sales: £412.2 million (US$602.9 million) (2000)
Stock Exchanges: London
Ticker Symbol: SGE
NAIC: 511210 Software Publishers; 541519 Other Computer Related Services.

Within 20 years The Sage Group plc has grown from its humble roots in the northeast of England to become the world's largest supplier of mainstream personal computer accounting software for small and medium-sized businesses, with more than 2.5 million customers around the globe.

Established in 1981 in Newcastle-upon-Tyne, the company has grown rapidly through business expansion and an aggressive program of acquisitions. The group's companies are market leaders in the United Kingdom, France, Germany, and Portugal, and its products are market leaders in the United States.

Sage started out when David Goldman joined forces with Graham Wylie to begin creating and selling accounting software programs in Newcastle at the dawn of the personal computer age. Goldman, who was born in Sunderland in 1937, took articles in accountancy after leaving school at the age of 16. In 1963 he joined a printing company, Campbell Graphics, and quickly rose to the position of managing director.

With computers becoming increasingly available and affordable in the early 1980s, Goldman became interested in the emerging microcomputer industry. He wanted to computerize the estimating, job costing, and invoicing work of his printing business. In 1981 he linked up with Paul Muller, a visiting American lecturer at nearby Newcastle University, to investigate the idea.

Graham Wylie wrote the first Sage accounting program, to run on the Intertec Super Brain machines with the CP/M operating system, while still a student at the University. Using a government grant, Goldman helped Wylie to develop the program for his printing business.

Goldman, Wylie, Muller, and Phil Lever, a partner in Campbell Graphics, saw the potential for selling the software and hardware to other businesses. They formed a new company, Sage Systems, for that purpose. During the next two years, Goldman and Wylie traveled the United Kingdom demonstrating and selling the integrated systems to customers in the print industry.

This fledgling business was taking up more and more of Goldman's time. So, with the British printing industry in massive upheaval, he decided to close Campbell Graphics and concentrate on Sage. The print industry system was sold off and, with Wylie taking the technical lead, the company used the proceeds to develop a new financial accounting system for small businesses.

The company continued developing and updating the accounting program, making versions to run on the MS-DOS operating system first released on the IBM personal computer in 1981. Sage also began to develop a network of resellers across Britain and built up sales of the software package to about 30 copies a month.

Business Takes Off in 1984

It was in 1984 that the business really took off when Sage took advantage of the launch of Amstrad's PCW computer/word processor. Using the CP/M operating system, this was the first real mass-market machine that made ownership of a computer feasible for small businesses and the home.

The PCW proved to be very popular. Goldman recognized and seized the business opportunity it presented. He pushed

Company Perspectives:

At Sage, we see our business as helping small and medium-sized businesses to automate their business processes and transactions. Our origins are in accounting and payroll software, but today we offer a broad range of integrated business applications, including e-business solutions, CRM (customer relationship management) software, human resource management solutions and time recording and billing products.

Sage to quickly repackage and relaunch its accounting software, and the company formalized and expanded its reseller network. Sales soon leaped up to 300 copies a month, and driven by Goldman's marketing savvy, had reached about 6,000 copies a month by the beginning of 1986.

Over the next three years the steady growth of Sage under the guidance of CEO Goldman continued. By 1989 the company employed 50 people, annual turnover had risen to £9 million and profits were £2 million. In December of that year, Sage was floated on the London Stock Exchange with a market capitalization of £21 million.

Expansion Through Acquisition Begins in 1991

At this time, Sage embarked on an aggressive strategy of expansion to strengthen its position as market leader. It acquired a number of leading software companies in Britain and overseas, beginning with the purchase in May 1991 of a 95.1 percent stake in the American company DacEasy for $18 million. Like Sage, the Dallas, Texas-based company produced low-cost accounting software for smaller businesses. The acquisition opened up markets and distribution outlets outside Britain—most importantly in the United States—for Sage software products.

In 1992 Sage acquired two more overseas companies: Ciel in France, which produced ''entry level'' accounting software for small firms, and Dallas-based TeleMagic, which produced programs for sales support, contact management, and other business activities. At the end of that year, Sage acquired British company Dataform.

Sage was continuing to perform well, despite the global recession of the early 1990s. In 1993 the company recorded an operating profit in the U.K. of £5 million, up 18 percent on the previous year. DacEasy, the main U.S. subsidiary, recorded a 100 percent increase in operating profit to £1.4 million.

Paul Walker was appointed chief executive officer of the company in 1994. He had joined Sage a decade earlier and took the post of finance director in 1987, overseeing the flotation two years later. Goldman became company chairman.

Walker oversaw a significant increase in the pace of acquisitions, with 14 companies being acquired by Sage between 1994 and 2000. In 1994 Sage acquired Multisoft Financial Systems in the U.K., Timeslips Inc in the USA—producer of the industry standard software for time tracking and reporting and billing—which became the Time division, and Saari in France. Another French company, Sybel Informatique, was brought into the fold the following year.

Sage took a short break from acquisitions in 1996, then continued the next year by snapping up KHK, Germany's largest single vendor of PC accounting software, and Carpe Diem in the United States. In early 1998, Sage took over State of the Art, a California-based company producing PC software for mid-sized companies, for $263 million, and so gained an important strategic presence in the U.S. market. Two smaller British companies that made software products for accountants, PACS Holdings and PASE, were also bought that year.

Conversion to The Sage Group Brand in 1997

Sage was working hard to integrate all of these acquired companies and their products into its business, and in 1997 decided to rebrand all of its operations around the world and rename itself The Sage Group. Described by the company as its ''most important development,'' this strategy enabled Sage to present itself as a truly international organization, with a name recognized by customers around the world. From this point, all promotion and marketing emphasized the ''security and reassurance associated with buying from a company with international credibility'' that research had shown was desired by the small and medium-sized businesses that were Sage's customers.

The Sage Group brand embraced the Multisoft operation in the U.K., which was merged into the Sagesoft subsidiary that had Graham Wylie at the helm as managing director, and was launched in France and Germany in 1997. State of the Art in the U.S. was renamed Sage Software Inc. in 1998.

David Goldman retired in 1997, having used his marketing skills, entrepreneurial flair, and strategic vision to lead the company to the point of being a major force in the accountancy and business software industry in Britain, Europe, and the United States. He had seen The Sage Group adopted as the company's global brand, and profits rise to £37.6 million, up 25 percent from 1996, from a turnover of £152.1 million. Michael Jackson, who had been a member of the board of directors since 1984, replaced Goldman as chairman. Another retiree that year was Tom Maxfield, who had been the U.K. sales director since 1984. David Goldman died in 1999.

The next major acquisition by Sage, completed early in 1999, was the takeover of Peachtree Software, based in Atlanta, Georgia, for $145 million. This company gave the group a huge haul of one million customers, providing Sage with a strong presence in the U.S. market for entry-level accounting software for small businesses. Peachtree products complimented the products of the Sage Software subsidiary, which were aimed at larger customers.

Another acquisition in Britain followed within two months. Tetra International brought Sage a range of products suitable for mid-sized customers, further expanding the group's customer base. This company was renamed Sage Enterprise Solutions, and repositioned to provide wide-ranging business support software systems. The purchase in late 1999 of Infologia gave Sage a presence in Portugal.

Key Dates:

1981: Sage Systems established in Newcastle-upon-Tyne, U.K.
1984: Launch of Sage software for Amstrad PCW word processor.
1989: Sage Group plc floats on the London Stock Exchange.
1991: DacEasy in the USA is acquired.
1992: Telemagic (USA), Ciel (France), and Dataform (UK) are acquired.
1994: Paul Walker is appointed chief executive of Sage Group.
1994: Multisoft (UK), Timeslips (USA), and Saari (France) are acquired.
1995: Sybel (France) is acquired.
1997: KHK (Germany) and Prosoft (USA) are acquired.
1997: The Sage Group brand is adopted and launched in France and Germany.
1997: Joint founder David Goldman retires and Michael Jackson becomes chairman.
1998: State of the Art (USA), PACS (UK), and PASE (UK) are acquired.
1999: Sage enters the FTSE 100.
1999: Peachtree (USA), Taxsoft (UK), Tetra (UK), and Infologia (Portugal) are acquired.
1999: E-commerce strategy is launched.
2000: Best Software (USA), Hartley (UK), CSM (UK), and Apex Software (Ireland) are acquired.
2001: TAS Software (UK) and Interact Commerce (USA) are acquired.

Internet Strategy Launched in 1999

By this time Sage was clearly dominant in the market for accountancy software for small and medium-sized businesses in the U.K., France, Germany, and the U.S., and the rapid rise of e-commerce was in full force.

Sage recognized that its customers would want products to help them implement e-commerce. In May 1999 Sage announced the Internet strategy that was to become a core element of its business operations. The group formed a partnership with IBM. Sage's CEO, Paul Walker, told the press the objective was to get all of the group's two million customers hooked up to the Web.

A portal site, www.sage.com, was launched, making a range of products and services accessible to business customers on line, and Sage embarked on a process of integrating IBM e-commerce tools into its products. It also made tools available to customers to create their own web sites free of charge—WebSiteCreator—and sell their products on the web—WebTrader. An acquisition tied to this strategy was French company Ubiquis, bought early in 2000, which provided small businesses with web trading tools.

Chairman Michael Jackson declared in the 1999 annual company report: ''Our ambition is to become a leading marketer of on-line products and services to the small to medium-sized business community.''

The Internet and e-business strategy, recently acquired businesses, and the high demand from customers for Year 2000 compliant software, helped generate a huge surge in turnover and profits. Figures for 1999 showed the group's turnover had increased by 60 percent to £307 million, and pretax profits had grown by 56 percent to £74.3 million. The Sage Group entered the prestigious FTSE 100 share index in September 1999, and enjoyed the accolade of Britain's best performing share price of the 1990s after rising an amazing 28,000 percent over the decade.

In early 2000 Sage substantially expanded its presence in the United States with the acquisition of Reston, Virginia-based Best Software, for $445 million. This added asset management software, including human resources and payroll programs for mid-sized companies, to Sage's modular and integrated range of products.

Sage took a hold in Switzerland in 2000 with the purchase of Sesam, the country's leading supplier of accounting software. Two British companies providing software to accountancy firms, Hartley International and CSM, were added to the Sage family, and within months, another U.K. firm, Adaptus Software, was bought.

The acquisition in May 2000 of Apex Software, which supplied software packages to accountants, gave Sage a strong presence in Ireland. This was followed later in the year by the purchase of another Irish company, Computer Resources, which produced payroll software.

A major initiative introduced at this time to continue driving the Internet strategy was the Sage Developer Program. This program provided external developers with access to the same knowledge base of development data as the group's own researchers and engineers, and enabled them to create complimentary tools and products.

In Britain the group also started building a network of 500 Sage Solutions Centers, providing support, implementation, and training to small and medium-sized businesses that were buying Sage products. Since 1998, the Sage Accountants Club had been offering support and benefits to the important community of professional customers, encouraging them not only to use Sage products themselves, but also to recommend the products to their clients.

In the spring of 2000, the high-tech industry, particularly in the United States where much of the group's expansion had been focused, was hit by a sudden downturn, with many e-commerce companies going out of business and stock prices sinking. However, Sage, which had grown to 5,000 employees around the world, was well placed to weather the storm of these difficult trading conditions, which also included a drop in software sales in the wake of the very high demand for Y2K products, thanks to its solid base of customers and its wide portfolio of products and services.

Through its ongoing acquisitions, Sage had steadily diversified over the course of 20 years from being an unglamorous provider of accountancy software products, to become an international powerhouse in the business software industry. The group's extensive range of products for small and medium-sized businesses offered accounting, payroll, forecasting, job-costing, and personnel management tools. The newer Internet software packages enabled smaller firms to build web sites and trade on line, and offered larger firms more comprehensive e-business tools, including on line catalogues and payment systems. Sage also offered a variety of tools for accountants, including tax management and time management products.

The group's figures for 2000 showed the pace of growth had slowed slightly, but was still strong. Sage's operating profit was up by 40 percent to £111.9 million, from turnover of £412.2 million, which had increased by 34 percent from the previous year.

Chairman Michael Walker said in the annual report, "Our commitment to developing relevant e-business products and services for the SME [small and medium enterprises] market is as strong as ever and, despite the challenging market environment, we invested heavily during the year in the development, marketing and support of our e-business products and services. This investment, we believe, is to the long term benefit of the Group."

As he made clear, Sage had its sights firmly set on continuing its success into the first decade of the 21st century. Through a number of communications efforts, including a £6 million series of 500 seminars across Britain in partnership with companies including Cisco Systems and Compaq, it was taking a strong lead in bringing smaller businesses into the new age of e-commerce.

It was also working on a long-term objective of providing customers with a comprehensive range of business management products and services. To this end, acquisitions continued on both sides of the Atlantic.

Early in 2001, a small British firm, TAS Software, was snapped up. This was quickly followed by the $263 million purchase of Interact Commerce, based in Scottsdale, Arizona. A leading player in the U.S. market for customer relationship management programs targeted at small and medium-sized businesses, Interact gave Sage a strong presence in one of the fastest growing sectors of the business software market.

This purchase increased Sage's invaluable group of registered customers around the world to 2.7 million. While the high-tech industry was still struggling and the group was not immune to the difficulties, Sage's interim 2001 figures showed continued growth. In the six months ending March 31, pretax profits were up 10 percent to £59.3 million, from a turnover of up 13 percent to £229.6 million, supporting the assertions of Sage's senior management team that the group has a bright future.

Principal Subsidiaries

Sage Software Ltd.; Sage Enterprise Solutions; Apex Software Systems Ltd. (Ireland); Sage Software Inc. (USA); Sage US Holdings Inc. (USA); Peachtree Software Inc. (USA); Best Software Inc. (USA); Ciel SA (France); Sage France; Ubiquis SA (France); Sage KHG Software Gmbh & Co. KG (Germany); Softinc Ltd. (Switzerland); Interact Commerce Corporation (USA).

Principal Divisions

Sage Software; Sage Enterprise; Ciel (France); Sage France; Sage KHK (Germany); Sage Spain; Sage Infologia (Portugal), Sesam (Switzerland); Sage Software Inc. (USA); Peachtree Software Inc. (USA); Best Software Inc. (USA); Best Canada; Time Division (USA); Sage Canada; Sage Middle East (UAE); Sage International Asia Pacific (Singapore).

Principal Competitors

Intuit; Lawson Software; Cyborg Systems; Oracle; The Ultimate Software Group; FrontRange Solutions; salesforce.com; Siebel Systems; Epicore Software.

Further Reading

"Analysts Caution as Sage Increases Profits by 10 Percent," *The Journal*, Newcastle-upon-Tyne, May 10, 2001.

Batchelor, Charles, "Sage Rises 28,000 Percent in Decade of Soaring IT Shares," *The Financial Times* (London), December 23, 1999, p. 19.

Bilefsky, Dan, "Sage Makes Internet Link with IBM," *The Financial Times* (London), May 12, 1999. p. 28.

Green-Armytage, Jonathan, "The Traveling Wise Man of Accounting Software," *Computer Weekly* (London), February 6, 1997, p. 152.

Hill, Dee, "British Firm Snares DacEasy for $18m," *Dallas Business Journal*, May 3, 1991, p. 1.

Howle, Amber, "Consolidation in Finance on Tap," *Computer Reseller News*, January 17, 2000, p. 22.

Kady II, Martin, "British Firm to Buy Best for $445m," *Washington Business Journal*, January 14, 2000, p. 7.

Kendall, Rik, "Tapping into the Wisdom of Wylie," *The Journal* (Newcastle-upon-Tyne), March 19, 2001.

Kizabo, Joel, and Andrew Ward, "Rumours put Pressure on Sage," *The Financial Times* (London), July 15, 2000, p. 23.

Reynard, Cherry, and Peter Crush, "Britain's Most Admired Companies," *Management Today* (London), December 2000, p. 63.

"Sage," *Investors Chronicle* (London), April 29, 1994, p. 64.

"Sage Agrees to Acquire Best Software," *Wall Street Journal Europe*, January 13, 200, p. 8.

"Sage Buys Up U.S. Company," *The Journal* (Newcastle-upon-Tyne), March 29, 2001.

"Sage Group in Merger," *Computerworld*, February 9, 1998, p. 53.

"Sage Pays £9.7 Million for TAS Software," *The Journal* (Newcastle-upon-Tyne), February 21, 2001.

Shillingford, Joia, "Sage Up 46 percent and Bullish on Expansion," *The Financial Times* (London), December 7, 2000, p. 32.

"The Sage Group plc Completes Tender Offer for Interact Commerce Corporation," PR Newswire Association, posted May 2, 2001, http://www.prnewswire.com.

Withers, Malcolm, "British Accounting Software Maker Continues Acquisitions," *Evening Standard* (London), February 11, 1999.

—Emma Marl

ST. JUDE MEDICAL

St. Jude Medical, Inc.

One Lillehei Plaza
St. Paul, Minnesota 55117-9983
U.S.A.
Telephone: (651) 483-2000
Toll Free: (800) 328-9634
Fax: (651) 490-4333
Web site: http://www.sjm.com

Public Company
Incorporated: 1976
Employees: 5,000
Sales: $1.17 billion (2000)
Stock Exchanges: New York
Ticker Symbol: STJ
NAIC: 334510 Electromedical and Electrotherapeutic Apparatus Manufacturing; 339112 Surgical and Medical Instrument Manufacturing; 339113 Surgical Appliance and Supplies Manufacturing

St. Jude Medical, Inc. (SJM) is the world's leading maker of mechanical heart valves and serves physicians worldwide with medical devices for cardiovascular applications. Besides heart valves, the firm's other products include pacemakers, implantable cardioverter defibrillators (which are used to treat hearts that beat too fast), and specialty catheters. Based in St. Paul, Minnesota, the company maintains manufacturing operations in Arizona, California, Minnesota, South Carolina, Puerto Rico, Canada, Brazil, and Sweden. SJM sells its products in more than 100 countries worldwide.

Mechanical Heart Valve Origins in the 1970s and 1980s

In 1972, the bileaflet mechanical heart valve was developed at the University of Minnesota. This new valve was made of pyrolytic carbon, a hard, shiny material that did not cause blood clots and could last for years in the human body. St. Jude Medical, Inc. was formed and incorporated in 1976 to further develop, market, and manufacture this valve. The company was founded by Manuel A. Villafana, a businessman who began his career at the helm of Cardiac Pacemakers, Inc., revolutionizing the industry with the innovation of long-lasting lithium batteries. Two years before selling his company to Eli Lilly for $127 million, Villafana formed SJM. (He named the company after the patron saint of lost causes and hospital workers.)

In February 1977, SJM made an initial stock offering at $3.50 per share. In October, the first human implant of the SJM mechanical heart valve took place. Dr. Demetre Nicoloff performed the operation on Helen Heikkinen, a 69-year-old heart patient, at the University of Minnesota Hospital in Minneapolis.

A superb salesman, Villafana convinced so many heart surgeons to try the SJM heart valve that the company was criticized for the emphasis placed on sales in what was supposedly a clinical trial program. The Food and Drug Administration (FDA) became involved, prompting Villafana's departure from the company in 1981. Villafana would later establish Helix Biocore, a competitor company.

In 1982, SJM received approval from the FDA to market its mechanical heart valve in the United States. SJM's profits began to ascend rapidly, rising from $2.3 million in 1982 to $4.3 million in 1983. By 1984, SJM had achieved revenues of almost $35 million and profits of $5.3 million, solely from sales of its mechanical heart valve. Twenty-five percent of the 100,000 artificial valves implanted in diseased hearts that year were SJM valves. As a one-product company with a market value of $41 million, SJM could not afford any threat to the successful manufacturing of that vital product.

A threat did come in 1984, however. The distinctiveness of SJM's heart valve was found in the marriage of a bileaflet design, created by St. Jude engineers, and its anti-blood-clotting carbon skin coating, produced and supplied by CarboMedics, a subsidiary of Intermedics, Inc., a cardiac-pacemaker company. In March 1984, the two companies were unable to reach an agreement on a long-term supply contract and filed countersuits.

The dispute had actually begun shortly after CarboMedics was purchased by Intermedics in 1979. Intermedics's reputation in the field was that of a tough player, and SJM executives

Company Perspectives:

For more than 40 years, innovative technologies and products from St. Jude Medical have given people a "Second Chance" at life.

In 1958, a Swedish business that is now part of St. Jude Medical developed the world's first implantable pacemaker, a device that has improved the quality of life for millions of people with bradycardia. Since 1977, more than one million patients have received our "gold standard" mechanical heart valves, and we are now developing new approaches to coronary bypass surgery. The Company's innovative catheter products have made cardiac procedures more effective. And our implantable defibrillators offer sophisticated technologies unimaginable a few years ago.

These products provide creative approaches to treating cardiac diseases and renewed hope to our many patients. For millions of people around the world, a "Second Chance" has meant the opportunity to graduate from college, get married, climb a mountain, learn to play the guitar, raise a family, ride a bike, become grandparents. It's meant better health, a richer life, and more quality time with loved ones.

At St. Jude Medical, we are proud to be part of our patients' "Second Chances."

began to quietly look for a second-source supplier of the valve's carbon coating. In addition, Villafana had launched a pacemaker-development project, in hopes of diversifying the company. G. Russell Chambers, Intermedics's director, threatened to raise the price of the carbon coating when he learned of the pacemaker project. Pacemaker sales accounted for the majority of Intermedics's profits. Chambers's threat worked; Villafana dropped the pacemaker project.

At the same time, a company called Hemex was formed in 1979, selling a heart valve that was similar to SJM's. Observing that Intermedics officers and directors owned stakes in Hemex and that Chambers's son, Rusty Chambers, was Hemex's chairperson, SJM inferred that Intermedics was behind this new competitor in the valve business.

Although Chambers denied any connection between the companies, SJM's new CEO, LaVerne Rees, was unconvinced. In 1981, Rees directed the company to take the necessary steps toward development of its own carbon coating. When this costly and ambitious project was announced in SJM's 1983 annual report, Chambers was outraged and demanded that SJM halt all research efforts. According to *Business Week,* an SJM consultant then attempted to purchase the carbon formula from an employee of CarboMedics. In 1983, Chambers directed his company to stop supplying SJM with carbon components. The dispute became heated, and court depositions alleged that CarboMedics hired detectives to search SJM garbage cans for stolen trade secrets.

CarboMedics charged SJM with patent infringement, while SJM responded with breach of contract, antitrust, and restraint-of-trade claims. Essentially, SJM alleged that Intermedics sought to achieve a monopoly and to restrain trade in the heart valve business. Each company accused the other of theft of trade secrets and contract violation. In the fall of 1984, SJM's board let Rees go, leaving Chairperson William Hendrickson in command, with Thomas M. Garrett III—the attorney who drafted SJM's articles of incorporation—playing a greater role in advising the company.

The legal battle continued for two years and involved court cases in the United States as well as in Europe. Because CarboMedics refused to supply SJM during this period, SJM ran out of completed valves to sell, forcing doctors and patients to look elsewhere for supplies, and eroding the sales and stock market earnings of both companies. According to *Business Week,* in 1985 SJM produced only about one-third of the 25,000 heart valves it had produced in 1984. Intermedics lost approximately $20 million on an annual basis, and SJM sank from record revenues of $35 million in 1984 to $26 million in 1985. SJM's stock, which had previously been a high-rated investment, plummeted, as did that of CarboMedics. Meanwhile, competitors in the heart valve industry had a field day, as their sales—and their share of the market—increased.

In February 1985, SJM named Lawrence A. Lehmkuhl as its new president and CEO. Lehmkuhl, who had previously served as divisional president at American Hospital Supply Corp., made it his first priority to end the supplier boycott of SJM, which threatened to destroy the company's ability to produce and market its only product. Lehmkuhl was selected not only on the basis of his potential to resolve the dispute, but also as a leader who might broaden the company's product line, eliminating the vulnerability associated with being a one-product company. In September 1985, an agreement was signed by the two companies, allowing SJM to continue its carbon manufacturing research and development efforts and to produce limited quantities of pyrolytic carbon.

In 1986, the first SJM mechanical heart valve produced with the company's own pyrolytic carbon-coated components was implanted in a patient in Germany. SJM augmented its mechanical heart valve business in 1986 when it acquired BioImplant, expanding into tissue heart valves. For several years, however, the company sold the tissue valves only outside of the United States. SJM implemented a two-for-one stock split, tripling its authorized common shares to 30 million. Revenues for 1986 rose to $60.5 million.

Once again, the company demonstrated consistent growth and stock market value. By 1988, SJM was again a favorite pick for investment specialists. Fiscal 1987 had closed with a net profit of $17 million and $1.55 a share, with net income rising 44 percent over the prior year to $71.8 million and sales climbing 19 percent. Furthermore, the company had no debt. In fact, SJM's cash balance was an astonishing $65 million. In an article in *Barron's,* investment specialist Bing Carlin selected SJM as his favorite investment, citing competitor Baxter Travenol's suspension of its heart valves (due to possible malfunction) and the FDA's approval of SJM's new low-cost plant in Puerto Rico as optimistic factors for SJM. Another competitor, Pfizer Inc., also experienced failure with its heart valve. In addition, SJM's decision to sell directly to hospitals, rather than working through distributors, meant that the company would retain more profits. The company achieved revenues of $114 million and $148 million in 1988 and 1989, respectively.

Key Dates:

1976: Manuel A. Villafana founds St. Jude Medical, Inc. to develop, market, and make the bileaflet mechanical heart valve.
1977: Company goes public and begins a clinical trial of the heart valve.
1982: FDA grants approval to SJM for the marketing of the mechanical heart valve.
1994: SJM purchases the cardiac pacing device businesses of Siemens AG.
1996: Daig Corporation, a maker of specialized cardiovascular catheters, is acquired, as are the assets of Telectronics Pacing Systems, Inc. and Medtel.
1997: SJM acquires Ventritex, maker of implantable cardioverter defibrillators.
1999: SJM acquires the Angio-Seal unit of Tyco International Ltd. and Vascular Science, Inc.
2000: FDA approves the Photon DR, SJM's first dual-chamber defibrillator, and the Integrity Micro AutoCapture Pacing System, the world's smallest dual-chamber pacemaker.

Conservatively Expanding in the Early 1990s

In 1990, SJM established its International Division, headquartered in Brussels, Belgium. SJM was still a top-rated pick for investors, and the company's stock was selling at 20 times earnings. Other than the decline in profits in 1985, SJM had demonstrated revenue growth of 30 percent or more each year, with revenues of $175.2 million in 1990, and the company possessed over $150 million in cash. More than 300,000 SJM mechanical heart valves had been put to use.

One reason for SJM's success was that the average age of heart valve recipients had declined. Older patients favored non-mechanical heart valves, which were made of pig tissue and did not require anti-clotting medication. Such tissue valves had an average age of five years, and as the age of heart patients declined, the life expectancy after implant increased. This increased life expectancy created a greater demand for mechanical valves, since tissue valves would have to be replaced through open heart surgery after five years.

In addition, SJM had reached an agreement with CarboMedics, giving SJM the right to make increasing quantities of components until 1998 and to make all parts in-house beginning in 1998. The pricing structure contained within the agreement significantly reduced SJM's costs, in exchange for SJM's commitment to purchase decreasing percentages of carbon components over the next five years. Since the revelation of Baxter Travenol's design flaw, SJM had faced virtually no serious competition. The heart valve market was not large enough to attract major pharmaceutical companies as competitors.

Under the leadership of Lehmkuhl, SJM had begun to make cautious acquisitions. Those acquisitions included a Canadian company that manufactured porcine valves that were sold internationally (while awaiting U.S. FDA approval), a company that made intra-aortic balloon pumps, and a centrifugal pump system. In addition, SJM had expanded its research department, funding vascular graft research. The core of SJM's operations, however, remained its heart valve business. In 1991, SJM received FDA approval for two internally developed products: the BiFlex annuloplasty ring and the sterile aortic valved graft. SJM became the only heart valve manufacturer with two sources for pyrolytic carbon-coated components. Revenues rose again, to $209.8 million in 1991.

After five years with annual earnings growth of 59 percent and an 84 percent rise in shares in 1991, SJM's stock suddenly took another downturn in the summer of 1992. The catalyst was the company's disclosure, on July 1, that second quarter sales and earnings had fallen short of analysts' projections. On July 2, investors pulled $285 million out of SJM, 16 percent of the company's market capitalization.

Lehmkuhl attributed the shortfall to aggressive promotion of tissue valves by two competitors, Medtronic, Inc. and Baxter International Inc. *Barron's* magazine also cited a decline in open heart surgeries in Los Angeles, one of SJM's largest markets, as a negative factor, along with an ''inventory adjustment'' by a Japanese customer and decreased sales in Poland. The shortfall was estimated to be only 2 percent of the domestic market (SJM controlled more than 45 percent of the international market and 60 percent of the U.S. market). Nevertheless, since 95 percent of the company's sales continued to be generated by the heart valve, even that small setback was enough to scare off investors who were wary of the risks of a one-product company.

The result was that SJM's shares, which had been priced at $55.50 in January 1992, dropped dangerously to $27.50. Ironically, sales climbed 3.5 percent over the previous year's second quarter to $57 million, and earnings per share rose from 45 cents to 52 cents. Moreover, the company would close 1992 with another dramatic increase, achieving $239.5 million in revenues.

Seeing competition from tissue valve companies as a major challenge, SJM began to work toward sales of tissue valves in the United States. The company already sold both tissue and mechanical valves in Europe, and in 1992 it formed a partnership with Hancock Jaffe Laboratories to design and market a new bioprosthetic tissue valve in the United States. Also during this time, SJM began construction of a new 65,000-square-foot facility for manufacturing pyrolytic carbon-coated components. The facility would undergo FDA qualifications in 1994 and 1995.

Taking a long-anticipated step toward long-term stability, Lehmkuhl made his first aggressive maneuver toward an acquisition strategy when he hired John Alexander as vice-president for corporate development in July 1992. Alexander had previously spearheaded business development and strategy for Baxter International's diagnostics division. SJM had been criticized for being too conservative with its $300 million cash supply by observers who could not understand why the company did not diversify through acquisitions earlier. Lehmkuhl had been cautious, in part, because any acquisition would initially dilute SJM's tremendous earning power. Healthcare company prices had dropped significantly since the beginning of 1992, and the time was seen as ripe for the beginning of an acquisition strategy.

Ronald Matricaria, formerly an executive with Eli Lilly, replaced Lawrence Lehmkuhl as president and CEO in 1993, while Lehmkuhl remained as company chairperson. Matricaria was known as an aggressive competitor, having built Lilly's cardiac pacemakers unit from a failing business to a world leader. Matricaria breathed new life into the acquisition hunt, giving it the code name ''Project Runner,'' and involving the company's top management in a process of self-examination and assessment. This process focused on identifying SJM's business strengths—the manufacture of implant devices and an intricate knowledge of blood flow and clotting—and applying those strengths to potential areas of acquisition. The company studied 16 medical specialties fields in order to make its decision.

In the spring of 1993, the company signed an exclusive license and supply agreement with Telios Pharmaceuticals, Inc. to utilize Telios's proprietary cell adhesion technology. In August, SJM bought a large minority stake in InControl Inc., a company developing an implantable machine to stop atrial fibrillation (rapid pulsing of the heart's upper chambers). In December, SJM acquired Electromedics, a Colorado maker of blood management and blood conservation equipment and related disposable devices, in a $90 million deal. Yet the industry, according to the *Wall Street Journal,* was ''on the rocks''; as a consequence, SJM's stock suffered.

The decline in market value was attributed to two primary factors: cost cutting by corporations and insurance companies and a looming uncertainty, due to President Clinton's proposed healthcare plan, about the future of medical care. SJM faced other problems as well. The company's tax rate went up by almost five percentage points through the loss of tax benefits from manufacturing in Puerto Rico. Moreover, in September 1993 CarboMedics received approval to sell heart valves in the United States. SJM was not yet ready to promote the improved tissue valve being developed. Instead, the company continued its acquisition strategy, hoping to renew growth through diversification. Revenues continued to rise, with sales of $252.6 million at the end of 1993.

Diversifying More Aggressively in the Mid-to-Late 1990s

In June 1994, SJM announced that it was prepared to make a major acquisition. Project Runner had arrived at its conclusion—SJM would enter the expanding market for cardiac rhythm management. SJM would purchase the cardiac pacing device businesses of Siemens AG—the world's number two maker of pacemakers for slow heartbeats (behind Medtronic)—for more than $500 million. The acquisition, which was completed in September 1994 at a cost of $525 million, launched SJM as a top-tier company in the realm of pacing device manufacturers. Further, SJM more than doubled its sales and tripled its workforce. In 1993, Siemens's cardiac rhythm management business demonstrated more than $350 million in sales and retained 1,300 employees.

The year 1994 brought several new developments in existing products as well. SJM announced the first U.S. implants of its stentless tissue heart valve, previously marketed internationally. It also received FDA approval to market its new collagen-impregnated aortic valved graft in the United States. In addition, the company launched an alliance with Advanced Tissue Sciences to pursue the joint development of tissue engineered heart valves and, under the auspices of The Heart Valve Company (the joint venture between SJM and Hancock Jaffe Laboratories), made its first implant of the new bioprosthetic heart valve at Glenfield Hospital in Leicester, England. Finally, the company made a $12 million equity investment in Endo Vascular Technologies, Inc., a leading company in the development of products to less invasively repair damaged or diseased blood vessels.

Net revenues jumped to $848.1 million by 1995, while net profits stood at $117.1 million, resulting in a 13.8 percent profit margin. The following year the company continued its program of diversification through acquisition. In May 1996 SJM acquired Minnetonka, Minnesota-based Daig Corporation, a maker of specialized cardiovascular catheters, for more than $400 million. During medical procedures, surgeons used Daig catheters as high-tech probes able to maneuver through blood vessels to the heart. One line of Daig catheters were known as electrophysiology catheters and were used, for example, to deliver precise doses of radio-frequency energy into the heart to correct an irregular heartbeat.

In April, St. Jude Medical announced that it would pay about $72 million for Cyberonics Inc., which was based in Webster, Texas, and was developing a pacemaker-like device for the treatment of epilepsy. SJM pulled out of this deal in October 1996, however, just prior to announcing the purchases of Ventritex, Inc. and the cardiac rhythm management assets of Telectronics Pacing Systems, Inc. and Medtel for a total of more than $500 million. In November SJM completed the acquisition of the assets of Telectronics and Medtel from Pacific Dunlop Ltd., an Australian conglomerate, while the purchase of Ventritex closed in May 1997. Ventritex brought St. Jude Medical a significant position in another segment of the cardiovascular device market—implantable cardioverter defibrillators (ICDs). Similar to pacemakers, which generally treat slow heart rates, ICDs are used to correct extremely rapid heart rates. Following completion of the Ventritex acquisition, SJM created a new division, the Cardiac Rhythm Management Division, to encompass the firm's pacemaker operations and those of Ventritex, Telectronics, and Medtel. Also in 1997, the FDA granted approval to SJM's Toronto SPV pig-tissue heart value, which was notable as the first U.S.-approved stentless valve—that is, a valve that does not require plastic or metal frames, called stents, to hold it in place. The valve had been approved for sale in Europe in 1995. These approvals were important since valves made from tissue were gaining in popularity based on studies finding them to be more durable than originally thought, a trend that ran counter to SJM's strength in mechanical valves.

St. Jude Medical had some difficulty digesting the acquisitions of Ventritex and Telectronics. This led to slower-than-expected revenue growth and reduced profits, the latter stemming in part from special acquisition-related charges of $52.9 million in 1996 and $58.7 million in 1997. By 1998, revenues had surpassed the $1 billion mark for the first time, specifically totaling $1.02 billion, while the net profit figure of $129.1 million translated into a 12.7 percent profit margin. Most of the profits, however, were being generated by the mainstay heart valve operations, which now accounted for only about 30 percent of overall revenues. The company also had to contend with a lawsuit filed by rival pacemaker firm Guidant Corporation, which had been spun off from Eli Lilly earlier in the decade. Guidant had sued SJM in November 1996, alleging patent infringement in regard to patents licensed by Guidant to Telectronics in 1994. Essentially, Guidant disputed SJM's claim that it had obtained access to the patents when it acquired Telectronics. In August 2000 an arbitrator ruled that SJM had failed to purchase enough assets from Pacific Dunlop for the patent licenses to be transferred, thereby reviving Guidant's original patent infringement lawsuit against St. Jude Medical, which was scheduled for trial in 2001.

Meanwhile, management changes were taking place at the company, which was feeling pressure from shareholders because of its poor performance compared to such rivals as Medtronic and Guidant. In January 1998 Fred Parks was named president and chief operating officer and appeared headed for the CEO position. But Parks, who had been hired away from EG&G Inc., a Massachusetts-based electronics company, left SJM in March 1999 when Terry L. Shepherd was named president and CEO. Shepherd, who had worked alongside Matricaria at Eli Lilly, had headed SJM's Heart Valve Division. Matricaria remained St. Jude Medical's chairman.

In Shepherd's first year at the helm, St. Jude Medical made two significant acquisitions. In March 1999 the company spent $167 million in cash for the Angio-Seal unit of Tyco International Ltd. Angio-Seal, which was integrated into the Daig Division, produced vascular sealing devices used to help seal the punctures in leg arteries that are created by catheters during angioplasty, a procedure used to clear blockages in heart arteries. SJM in September 1999 acquired Vascular Science Inc. for $80 million in cash and $20 million in milestone payments tied to product development goals. A privately held firm based in St. Paul, Vascular Science was developing a device that would enable surgeons to perform coronary-artery-bypass surgery without using sutures. In connection with these acquisitions, St. Jude Medical in 1999 took charges totaling $115.2 million for purchased in-process research and development and an additional $9.8 million for a restructuring of European operations.

SJM got off to rough start in 2000. In January the company voluntarily recalled some of its mechanical heart valves, after finding that ones that had been coated with an infection-preventing substance called Silzone had a high frequency of blood leakage. About 36,000 of the valves had been implanted since the coating was introduced in 1997. Lawsuits were quickly filed in connection with the potentially defective device, with some of the suits seeking class-action status. St. Jude Medical announced that it would no longer use the Silzone coating. Later in 2000, SJM alerted doctors worldwide about possible problems with several of its pacemaker models. The problems were believed to affect a small number of the pacemakers and involved electronic and mechanical malfunctions. On the brighter side, in late 2000 St. Jude Medical won FDA approval for its first dual-chamber defibrillator, the Photon DR. Dual-chamber ICDs, which worked on both the lower and upper and chambers of the heart, were gaining popularity among doctors at the expense of singer-chamber models, and SJM had been beaten to market in this burgeoning sector by arch-rivals Medtronic and Guidant. Also in late 2000 came FDA approval of SJM's Integrity Micro AutoCapture Pacing System, which was noteworthy for being the world's smallest dual-chamber pacemaker. In January 2001 Daniel J. Starks was named president and COO of St. Jude Medical, having previously headed the Cardiac Rhythm Management Division and thereby playing a key role in the development of the newly approved Photon and Integrity products. Although it continued to face stiff competition from Guidant and Medtronic, and had been embarrassed by the series of revelations concerning defective products, St. Jude Medical appeared to be on the verge of finally realizing the fruits of a rocky diversification program.

Principal Subsidiaries

Pacesetter, Inc.; St. Jude Medical S.C., Inc.; St. Jude Medical Sales Corporation (Barbados); St. Jude Medical Europe, Inc.; St. Jude Medical Canada, Inc.; 151703 Canada, Inc.; St. Jude Medical Hong Kong Ltd.; St. Jude Medical Australia Pty., Ltd.; St. Jude Medical Brasil, Ltda. (Brazil); Medical Telectronics, Ltd. (New Zealand); Daig Corporation; St. Jude Medical Colombia, Ltda.; St. Jude Medical Cardiovascular Group; SJM Europe, Inc.; St. Jude Medical Puerto Rico, Inc.; Pacesetter AB (Sweden); St. Jude Medical Sweden AB; St. Jude Medical Denmark A/S; St. Jude Medical Pacesetter Sales AB (Sweden); St. Jude Medical (Portugal)—Distribuicao de Produtos Medicos, Lda.; St. Jude Medical Export Ges.m.b.H. (Austria); St. Jude Medical Medizintechnik Ges.m.b.H. (Austria); St. Jude Medical Italia S.p.A. (Italy); N.V. St. Jude Medical Belgium, S.A.; St. Jude Medical España, S.A. (Spain); St. Jude Medical France S.A.; St. Jude Medical Finland O/y; St. Jude Medical Sp.zo.o. (Poland); St. Jude Medical GmbH (Germany); St. Jude Medical UK Limited; St. Jude Medical AG (Switzerland).

Principal Divisions

Cardiac Rhythm Management Division; Daig Division; Cardiac Surgery Division.

Principal Competitors

Guidant Corporation; Medtronic, Inc.; Abbott Laboratories; Pfizer Inc.; Johnson & Johnson; Boston Scientific Corporation; Arrow International, Inc.; Baxter International Inc.; ATS Medical, Inc.; C.R. Bard, Inc.; Datascope Corp.

Further Reading

Alexander, Steve, "St. Jude to Buy Houston Company: First Will Spend $84 Million for Cyberonics," *Minneapolis Star Tribune,* April 9, 1996, p. 1D.

——, "The Wait Is Over: St. Jude Announces Big Acquisition," *Minneapolis Star Tribune,* June 29, 1994, p. 1D.

Barker, Robert, "All Heart: Examining a Bitter Corporate Feud," *Barron's,* February 11, 1985, pp. 14–30.

Burton, Thomas M., "St. Jude Medical Agrees to Acquire Ventritex," *Wall Street Journal,* October 24, 1996, p. B4.

——, "St. Jude Medical's CEO to Step Down in the Wake of Disappointing Results," *Wall Street Journal,* March 3, 1999, p. B17.

——, "St. Jude to Buy Siemens Cardiac Pacemaker Lines," *Wall Street Journal,* June 28, 1994, pp. A3, A8.

——, "Some Pacemakers Are Defective, St. Jude Says in Letter to Doctors," *Wall Street Journal,* February 16, 2000, p. B7.

Cochran, Thomas N., "Heartening Prospects," *Barron's,* June 6, 1988, p. 60.

David, Gregory E., "Heart to Heart: Crosstown Rivals Medtronic and St. Jude Fight to Keep the World's Blood Flowing," *Financial World,* September 1, 1994, pp. 22–24.

Dorfman, John R., "St. Jude Medical Shares Will Reap Rewards for Long Term Investors, Some Managers Say," *Wall Street Journal,* January 17, 1994, p. C2.

Fiedler, Terry, "Approval for Defibrillator Puts St. Jude in Big Market," *Minneapolis Star Tribune,* October 31, 2000, p. 1D.

——, "St. Jude Buys Local Firm with New Product," *Minneapolis Star Tribune,* September 10, 1999, p. 1D.

——, "St. Jude Buys Vascular-Seal Company," *Minneapolis Star Tribune,* February 6, 1999, p. 1D.

——, "St. Jude Issues Second Product Warning in Month," *Minneapolis Star Tribune,* February 17, 2000, p. 3D.

——, "St. Jude Makes Some Deals," *Minneapolis Star Tribune,* October 24, 1996, p. 1D.

——, "St. Jude Recalls Valves That Pose Risk of Leak," *Minneapolis Star Tribune,* January 25, 2000, p. 1D.

——, "St. Jude to Restructure, Hire President, COO," *Minneapolis Star Tribune,* May 17, 1997, p. 1D.

Forsyth, Randall W., "Too Good to Last?," *Barron's,* January 6, 1992, p. 35.

Gianturco, Michael, "Go with the Greats," *Forbes,* July 19, 1993.

Matricaria, Ronald A., "Diversification Process Developed at St. Jude," *Minneapolis Star Tribune,* December 26, 1994, p. 3D.

Metzler, Melissa, "One-Time Charges Hurt St. Jude's Bottom Line," *Minneapolis-St. Paul CityBusiness,* July 7, 2000, p. S39.

Miller, James P., "St. Jude Medical to Acquire Daig for $427 Million," *Wall Street Journal,* January 31, 1996, p. B3.

Netzer, Baie, "These Health-Care Stocks Can Prosper Even in the Face of Cost-Cutting," *Money,* July 1990, pp. 55, 58.

Pitzer, Mary J., "The Bad Blood Over a Heart Valve," *Business Week,* May 13, 1985, pp. 141, 144.

St. Anthony, Neal, "Diversification Starting to Pay Off for St. Jude Medical," *Minneapolis Star Tribune,* October 30, 1998, p. 1D.

"St. Jude Agrees to Buy Electromedics in $90 Million Deal," *Wall Street Journal,* December 8, 1993, p. C14.

"St. Jude Medical Picks Lawrence Lehmkuhl As President and Chief," *Wall Street Journal,* February 12, 1985, p. 47.

Twitchell, Evelyn Ellison, "Heartfelt Gains: But Is St. Jude Medical Fully Priced?," *Barron's,* November 20, 2000, p. 56.

Wyatt, Edward A., "The Mugging of St. Jude," *Barron's,* August 31, 1992, pp. 17, 25.

Zipser, Andy, "Heart's Content," *Barron's,* September 3, 1990, p. 34.

——, "Twelve Winning Months," *Barron's,* January 6, 1992, p. 34.

—Heidi Feldman
—update: David E. Salamie

Samsonite Corporation

11200 E. 45th Avenue
Denver, Colorado 80239
U.S.A.
Telephone: (303) 373-2000
Toll free: (800) 262-8282
Fax: (303) 373-6300
Web site: http://www.samsonite.com

Public Company
Incorporated: 1912 as Shwayder Trunk Manufacturing Company
Employees: 7,150
Sales: $783.9 million (2000)
Stock Exchanges: NASDAQ
Ticker Symbol: SAMC
NAIC: 316991 Luggage Manufacturing; 421999 Other Miscellaneous Durable Goods Wholesalers

Samsonite Corporation is the leading manufacturer of luggage in the world and the top seller of luggage in the United States, Europe, and Japan. In addition to its world-renowned Samsonite label, the company also markets the popular American Tourister and Lark brands. Under those names, Samsonite offers a full line of luggage, including softside and hardside suitcases, garment bags, casual bags, business cases, and other travel bags and accessories. Samsonite changed ownership several times during the 1980s and early 1990s before regaining its independence in 1995.

Colorado Origins

Samsonite owes its start to Colorado native Jesse Shwayder. After growing up in the American West during the late 1800s, Shwayder was working in New York as a salesman for the Seward Trunk and Bag Company by his mid-20s. He was making a lot of money, but he missed Colorado and longed to pursue his dream of starting his own business. Thus, Shwayder quit his job when he was 28 and moved back to Denver. Shortly thereafter, on March 10, 1910, he founded the Shwayder Trunk Manufacturing Company with his life's savings of $3,500. With a work force of 10 men, Shwayder began manufacturing what were known as suitcases in a 50-by-125-foot room that he had rented in downtown Denver. The management philosophy he adopted to guide the firm from day one, according to company annals, was the Golden Rule (''Do unto others . . .''), to which Shwayder adhered tenaciously.

Shwayder burned through most of his $3,500 in savings during his first year of business. He was able to borrow money to stay afloat, however, and had soon turned the corner toward profitability. His brother, Maurice, joined him in 1912, and together they traveled throughout the region in an effort to drum up sales and keep the business going. A few years later, Sol Shwayder, a third brother, joined the sales team. Shwayder brothers Ben and Mark also jumped on board in 1923; eventually, Mark worked on sales, Maurice and Ben focused on manufacturing, and Sol became the company's attorney. The brothers incorporated in 1912 and, having outgrown their downtown room, moved to larger offices. By 1917 they were selling $76,000 worth of luggage annually throughout the western United States. To keep up with spiraling demand they built a new three-story manufacturing facility. That new plant would also prove inadequate soon, as mail-order advertising expanded the Shwayder's reach eastward across the United States.

The Shwayders' success was no accident. Indeed, Jesse drew from his work experience in New York to develop a strategy that he would pursue from the start. He realized that he was facing stiff competition from deep-pocketed luggage manufacturers. So, rather than trying to compete with other luggage companies on price, he would differentiate his products by quality and charge as high a price as the market would bear. To reflect the quality and durability of their luggage, the Shwayders named their first products ''Samson,'' after the powerful Biblical character. Indeed, the chief advantage of the cases was that they could take a lot of punishment and were extremely durable. In 1916, in fact, the Shwayders took a picture that would become an advertising coup. The four brothers and their father, Isaac, stood on a plank positioned atop one of their suitcases above the caption, ''Strong enough to stand on.'' Because the five portly Shwayder men weighed more than 1,000 pounds together, the picture was strik-

Company Perspectives:

Alongside lengthy experience, the quality and strength that characterize every aspect of the Samsonite business have created a heritage of success. Remembering past triumphs but always looking ahead, Samsonite maintains a global vision—a vision that will propel the company into the new millennium. The future is a world of travel, of abundant mobility, and Samsonite is ready for this world-on-the-move.

ing and became an excellent promotional and direct-mail advertising gimmick for several years.

Domestic and International Expansion

The Shwayders rolled out their first nationally advertised suitcase in 1918. The premium quality case retailed for $4.95 and was advertised in a window at the famous Macy's department store; the suitcase was displayed with a half-ton of sugar resting on top. Boosted by the success of that and other products, Shwayder Trunk revenues rocketed to $300,000 by 1924. In that year, the brothers moved their operation into a gleaming new 80,000-square-foot factory in south Denver; that plant was gradually expanded to include a total of 500,000 square feet. The plant was organized to operate on an assembly-line basis, and even incorporated a state-of-the art conveyor system to transport products and materials in the plant. The company boasted in its literature that it built suitcases the same way that Ford built automobiles.

Shwayder Trunk's revenues bolted to more than $1 million during the late 1920s and sales, particularly to the eastern United States, exploded. To keep pace with demand, the Shwayders leased an 85,000 square foot factory near Detroit. With that plant up and running, the company seemed almost unstoppable. Unfortunately, the 1929 stock market crash and succeeding Great Depression quashed that perception. Indeed, Shwayder Trunk's shipments plummeted by 50 percent within a few years. The brothers, scrambling to meet payroll and pay their bills, began trying to supplant lost luggage sales by manufacturing products ranging from license plates and card tables to stilts, doggie dinettes, and sandboxes. To reflect the diversification, the brothers changed the name of their company in 1931 to Shwayder Brothers, Inc. Interestingly, the Shwayder's card table sales briefly surpassed luggage shipments during the 1930s.

Despite their setbacks in the luggage industry, the Shwayders continued to improve their luggage and invent new travel products. By the 1930s, in fact, the Denver luggage plant was the most modern of its type in the world. From that plant came innovative Samson luggage with exclusive features such as wood-frame construction, super-strong handles, rayon linings, fiber finishes, and secure locks. Specialty fibre finishes were developed by Shwayder Trunk specifically as a covering for Samson suitcases. In 1939 the company introduced a unique suitcase that Jesse dubbed "Samsonite." The suitcase, which was the predecessor to the popular Samsonite Streamlite line, was covered with sturdy vulcanized fiber that was used with a leather binding. The case's tapered shape was destined to become a classic within the industry.

During the early 1940s Shwayder Trunk's factories were converted to produce war materials. Immediately after the war, however, the Shwayders resumed their luggage and folding furniture business and even managed to sell $7 million worth of goods during their first year of postwar production in 1946. During that and the succeeding few years, the brothers integrated into the facilities all of the manufacturing knowledge that they gleaned during war-time production. That allowed them to introduce precision manufacturing methods and to incorporate advanced new synthetic materials into their products. By 1948, sales had shot up to $13 million. The Shwayders then split the company into two divisions: luggage and steel/folding furniture, with the latter division being headquartered at the Detroit factory. The company even opened a second furniture plant in Pennsylvania in 1949.

Shwayder Trunk again converted its manufacturing facilities for war-time production during the Korean War of the 1950s. Although part of that decade was spent building things like bombs and rocket carriers, the brothers managed to increase their luggage and furniture businesses. For example, they began building specialized carrying cases for everything from musical instruments to advanced electronic equipment. And they started producing vinyl clad material for use in automobile interiors. Importantly, the company introduced the Ultralite luggage line in 1956. That luggage was the first to abandon wood-frame construction in favor of magnesium and injection-molded plastics. Also in 1956, Shwayder Brothers expanded out of the United States with a separate Canadian subsidiary and an export sales department focused on Europe. Meanwhile, the flourishing furniture division was consolidated and relocated to a giant production facility in Tennessee.

During the 1960s, the company introduced a number of new products under the increasingly popular Samsonite brand name. They brought out several new travel and attaché cases, for example, as well as a line of upscale folding furniture and a successful line of metal patio furniture. The brothers changed the name of the company in 1965 to Samsonite Corporation to capitalize on the now renowned Samsonite label. Interestingly, the company introduced LEGO by Samsonite in 1960. The snap-together plastic building blocks for children enjoyed immediate acceptance in the North American marketplace and eventually became one of the most popular toys of all time. The stellar success of LEGO prompted Shwayder Brothers to launch more than 50 new toy items before the early 1970s. Lagging performance of the toy division, however, caused the company to jettison the operation in 1972 and focus on furniture and luggage.

Samsonite's gains during the 1960s were achieved under the guiding hand of founder Jesse Shwayder's son, King. Under King's leadership, Samsonite managed to firmly establish itself as the world's leading manufacturer of molded luggage and attaché cases by the early 1970s. Indeed, the company added manufacturing operations and sales offices throughout Europe and even Japan during the 1960s and enjoyed hefty sales increases in those regions. Having grown to dominate the business luggage markets, Samsonite set its sites on the mush-

Key Dates:

1910: Jesse Shwayder founds Shwayder Trunk Manufacturing Company in Denver, Colorado.
1918: Company introduces its first nationally advertised suitcase.
1939: Unique Samsonite suitcase, predecessor to Samsonite Streamlite line, is introduced.
1956: Revolutionary Ultralite luggage line introduced.
1965: Company adopts the name Samsonite Corporation.
1973: Company is purchased by Beatrice Foods Co.
1995: Samsonite regains independent corporate status.

rooming consumer luggage market. To that end, Samsonite introduced a highly successful line of soft-sided luggage during the late 1960s and early 1970s and even built new factories in Arizona and New Mexico dedicated to manufacturing soft-sided luggage. Samsonite simultaneously acquired companies that gave it leading positions in the markets for personal travel luggage-related products (such as leather toiletries kits), as well as redwood patio and casual furniture.

During the 1970s, Samsonite intensified its global expansion efforts related to luggage. By the early 1970s, the company was already operating facilities in Osaka and Tokyo, Japan, as well as in Holland, Spain, Britain, Belgium, Germany, and other countries. During the mid-1970s, though, the company acquired competitors or initiated operations in new manufacturing facilities in France, Germany, the Netherlands, Belgium, Mexico, and other places. By the mid-1970s, then, the company had achieved a truly global presence and was the leading manufacturer of luggage in the world. The enterprise, which was still headquartered in Denver, was employing a work force of 5,000 and boasted the largest and most advanced production facilities in the luggage and casual furniture industries.

Corporate Carousel

After operating as an independent under the direction of the Shwayder family for more than 60 years, Samsonite was engulfed in the corporate consolidation and buyout binge of the 1970s. In 1973 Samsonite was purchased by corporate giant Beatrice Foods Co. At the time, Beatrice was still garnering about 75 percent of its sales from various food and chemical divisions; but it had 1,000 locations around the world, 8,000 different products, more than 65,000 employees, and was growing rapidly through acquisition. Beatrice planned to allow Samsonite to continue operating as a relatively autonomous company, and to support its expansion efforts financially. Beatrice became the first of several companies that would own and sell Samsonite in the 1970s and through the early 1990s. During that time, Samsonite would effectively jettison its furniture operations and focus its energy on the global luggage industry.

Samsonite continued to grow under the Beatrice umbrella during the late 1970s by expanding globally and introducing new products. Unfortunately, its momentum began to wane. Although the company remained a world leader in its key markets, by the early 1980s Samsonite was losing ground. Lackluster management had left the company with a dearth of new products, despite access to Beatrice's bank account, and Samsonite was rapidly losing its edge and reputation as an industry innovator. In addition, competition from low-cost foreign producers was chipping away at Samsonite's market share. To rectify the situation, Beatrice brought in 47-year-old Malcom Candlish to lead the company. The British-born Candlish was a seasoned consumer products industry executive. Beatrice wanted him to revive the company and put it unquestionably back on top of the luggage industry.

Candlish took the helm in 1983 and immediately began whipping the company into shape. He laid off about 250 workers, initiated aggressive cost-cutting programs, and replaced some of the old guard with new, more aggressive employees. By his own estimate, about half of the company's work force had been replaced by 1989. Candlish also launched a comprehensive study to determine exactly what consumer wanted. That survey lead to the introduction of the ''World's Greatest Garment Bag,'' as described in company promotionals, which became a very successful new product. That bag was followed by a string of new soft- and hard-sided luggage products that served to renew Samsonite's innovation edge. By 1986, Samsonite was generating annual sales of about $300 million (50 percent from overseas operations), controlling about 12 percent of the U.S. luggage market, and rapidly improving.

Like its subsidiary, Beatrice was scurrying during the early and mid-1980s to cut costs and refocus its organization. To that end, it sold Samsonite in 1986 to leveraged buyout king Kholberg, Kravis & Roberts. Then, 15 months later, Kholberg spun off Samsonite and eight other companies into a new company called E-II. Six months later, E-II was bought out by American Brands, which subsequently was purchased by billionaire Meshulam Riklis of Riklis Family Corp. Throughout the buyout melee, Candlish managed to keep his chief executive job and even to improve Samsonite's performance. By 1989, in fact, Samsonite was generating an estimated $430 million in sales worldwide, and Candlish was still working to cut costs and bring out more new products.

As Samsonite continued to post gains in the recession of the late 1980s and early 1990s, its parent company, E-II, floundered and eventually filed for Chapter 11 bankruptcy. ''We like to say we have a sick head and a healthy body,'' said Nick Nell, Samsonite's chief financial officer, in the September 27, 1992, *Denver Post.* Samsonite's revenues leapt up into the $500 million range in 1992 from the sale of approximately ten million pieces of luggage worldwide. Those sales included nearly 70 percent of the hard-sided luggage sold throughout the world, including such nations as Russia, Argentina, and China. By the early 1990s, Samsonite was recognized as a U.S. leader in global marketing.

Following a messy reorganization of E-II, Samsonite emerged as a subsidiary of a new company called Astrum International Corp. Steve Green, former E-II executive, became the new chairman and chief executive of Samsonite. Under his direction, Samsonite continued to grow and to retain its global bent. In 1993 Astrum purchased the American Tourister luggage company to complement Samsonite. That purchase significantly bolstered Samsonite's lead in the domestic luggage market and broadened its scope to include some lower tier segments of the market. The combined operations were generating sales of approximately $600 million annually going into 1994. Samsonite posted record sales in 1994 of $634 million, about $72 million of which was profit.

Independence Reclaimed and Leading the Global Industry

Samsonite regained its independence for the first time since 1973 when Astrum announced early in 1995 that it was going to split into two companies, one of which would be the new publicly held, independent, Denver-based Samsonite Corporation. The new company retained the Samsonite and American Tourister divisions and related operations. Green expected to stay on as head of Samsonite. Besides expanding into new global markets, Green announced his intention to broaden Samsonite's product line to include luggage racks, golf and ski bags, camping gear, and even computer and camera cases.

In 1996, however, Green was replaced by Richard Nicolosi, who promised the board of directors that he'd ''turn a good company into a great one.'' Faced also with the challenge of debt reduction, as the earlier carousel of corporate ownership changes had saddled the company with debt, Nicolosi (protégé of ''Chainsaw'' Al Dunlap, the turnaround master at Scott Paper Co.) began implementing cost-cutting measures. He cut the 8,500 workforce by 1,000, shut down factories in Canada and Mexico, and centralized production lines. To save money, the company pulled out of the industry's annual trade show. The result: debt was reduced by $162 million. Stock prices grew optimistically from $18 to $50.

Nicolosi also planned to raise luggage prices across the board and introduce upscale product lines in the U.S., which had already been selling well in Europe. Domestic sales trailed off, though, as the new hardside line failed to stimulate interest in a consumer market with a preference for its softside or hybrid cousin. While company revenues climbed to $741 million in 1997, this mainly resulted from the cost-cutting measures, and investors became frustrated with unimpressive growth in the U.S.; building sales proved to be far more difficult than cutting costs.

In the late 1990s, under the direction of CEO Luc Van Nevel, Samsonite heavily promoted its premium brands worldwide. It began expanding luxury product lines and opening international flagship stores (in Milan, Brussels, London, Washington, D.C., and Hong Kong) as well as licensing its brand names to other companies, such as Hedgren, Hummer, and Trunk & Co.) for use on travel accessories, leather goods, handbags, clothing, and furniture. Samsonite's non-luggage product line by then included footwear and an Italian-designed travel clothing line.

International expansion also continued, particularly in Asia, with ventures in India, Japan, Singapore, South Korea, Thailand, and China. A hefty 55 percent increase in Asian sales helped fuel the company's revenues, which by fiscal year 2000 reached $767.7 million.

Leading the industry in luggage design, it introduced many popular features of the 1990s—molded suitcases on wheels, suitcases with built-in luggage carts, and full-featured, structured garment bags. Samsonite owned approximately 130 patents in the United States alone, and over 900 patents and design registrations around the world. Its innovative designs continued with hybrid luggage products that combined the ''best'' features of softside and hardside luggage. In 2002, the company planned to introduce a ''G-Force'' computer bag that touted 360 degree protection. Most products were designed at Samsonite's own research, development, and design centers in the United States and Europe; they were produced around the world primarily at 12 company-owned or leased facilities.

In 2001, a corporate restructuring plan announced the closing of its long-time Denver manufacturing facility, which was scheduled to cease production of hardside luggage as it had done for almost a century. While hardside luggage manufacturing would proceed at plants outside the United States, the Denver office would continue to host corporate operations and remain a major distribution point. Even with the closing of its Denver manufacturing facility, Samsonite remained the leading global producer and distributor of hardside luggage.

With over half of its 2001 revenue of $783.9 million generated outside the United States, Samsonite products were available in more than 100 countries and 200 company-owned stores. Softside luggage accounted for nearly half of its sales. Its three brands, Samsonite, American Tourister, and Lark, remained top sellers as the company retained its leading position in North America, Europe, and Asia. The company planned to use its existing assets—strong brands, quality products, and global capabilities—to improve profitability and expand sales, especially in the luxury markets.

Principal Subsidiaries

C.V. Holdings, Inc.; SC Denmark ApS (Denmark); Samsonite Europe N.V. (Belgium); Samsonite S.A. (France); Samsonite Limited (United Kingdom); Samsonite B.V. (Netherlands); Samsonite Ges.m.b.H. (Austria); Samsonite GmbH (Germany); Samsonite Hungaria Borond KFT (Hungary); Samsonite Finanziaria S.r.l. (Italy); Samsonite SpA (60%) (Italy); Samsonite Espana S.A. (Spain); Samsonite AB (Aktiebolag) (Sweden); Samsonite A/S (Denmark); Samsonite AG (Switzerland); Samsonite Slovakia S.r.o. (Slovakia); Samsonite Sp. z o.o. (Poland); Samsonite Finland Oy (Finland); Samsonite CZ spol. s.r.o. (Czech Republic); Samsonite Mauritius Limited (Mauritius); Samsonite India Limited (65%) (India); Samsonite Singapore Pte Ltd (80%) (Singapore); Samsonite Asia Limited (Hong Kong); Samsonite Korea Limited (80%) (Korea); Samsonite Malaysia Sdn Bhd (Malaysia); Samsonite Hong Kong (2000) Limited (Hong Kong); Samsonite Luggage (Ningbo) Co. Ltd. (China); Samsonite Latinoamerica, S.A. de C.V. (Mexico); Samsonite Mexico, S.A. de C.V. (Mexico); Samsonite Comercio E Participacoes Ltda. (Brazil); Samsonite Industrial E Comercial Ltda. (Brazil); Samsonite Canada Inc. (Canada); Samson S.A. de C.V. (Mexico); Samsonite Mercosur Limited (51%) (Bahamas); Samsonite Brasil Ltda. (Brazil); Samsonite Argentina S.A. (Argentina); Arife S.A. (70%) (Argentina); Lonberg Express S.A. (Uruguay); Samsonite Company Stores, Inc.; Samsonite Pacific Ltd.; Direct Marketing Ventures, Inc.; Samsonite Holdings Inc.; Astrum R.E. Corp.; The Samsonite Foundation, Inc. (Non-profit corp.); McGregor II, LLC; Hortex

Incorporated; McGregor China Corp.; Jody Apparel II, LLC; WMI II, LLC.

Principal Operating Units

Samsonite Europe N.V.

Principal Competitors

Brown-Furman Corporation, Land's End Inc., LVMH-Moet Hennessy Louis Vuitton S.A.

Further Reading

Alpert, Bill, ''Stuck in a Suitcase: By Reaching For Growth, Samsonite Irks Its Customers,'' *Barron's*, January 12, 1998, p. 18.

Beirne, Mike, ''Samsonite Bags Celebs to Tout New Soft-Side Luggage Totes,'' *Brandweek*, September 13, 1999, p. 12.

——, ''Samsonite Packs Starck for Saucy Travel Gear, Eyes 'Lifestyle' Badge,'' *Brandweek*, October 9, 2000, p. 6.

DeSalvo, Kathy, ''The Gods of Luggage [and Advertising] Must Be Crazy,'' *SHOOT*, December 18, 1998, p. 14.

''Denver Plant to Be Closed,'' *Wall Street Journal*, February 23, 2001, p. B8.

Elder, Drew, ''Samsonite Bagging Profits With Innovative Products,'' *Denver Post*, September 24, 1992, p. C1.

——, ''Samsonite Ignores Storm,'' *Denver Post*, September 27, 1992, p. 1.

Fannin, Rebecca, ''Samsonite, with TBWA, Readies Global Push,'' *Advertising Age*, February 24, 1997, p. 4.

Geer, John F. Jr., ''Same Old Bag: Can Dick Nicolisi Turn Samsonite Into a Growth Company?,'' *Financial World*, November 1997, p. 36.

Gilbert, Daniela, and Ray Allegrezza, ''Bright Lights, Big Name,'' *Weekly Newspaper for the Home Furnishing Network*, August 4, 1997 p. 15.

Goldstein, Lauren, ''Samsonite Wants to Fill Your Suitcase, Not Just Make It,'' *Fortune*, April 12, 1999, p. 44.

Gray, Ellen, ''Chainsaw Colleague Boosts Samsonite,'' *Colorado Business Magazine*, January 1998, p. 30.

Green, Jeff, ''Development Humming at Samsonite,'' *Brandweek*, September 20, 1999, p. 82.

Kempner, Michael W., ''Astrum International Corp. Announces Spin-Off,'' *PR Newswire*, posted April 24, 1995, http://www.prnewswire.com/.

Lieb, Jeffrey, ''Samsonite to Go Independent,'' *Denver Post*, April 25, 1995, p. C1.

——, ''Samsonite Upbeat on Tourister Deal,'' *Denver Post*, August 5, 1993, p. C2.

O'Neal, Nan, ''Durable Samsonite Chief Vows to Set Industry on Fire,'' *Denver Business Journal*, January 16, 1989, p. 10.

Robinson, Simone, ''Case Study: Samsonite Uses Large Amounts of Polypropylene and ABS at its Belgian Suitcase Facility,'' *European Plastics News*, March 1996, p. 43.

''Samsonite Succeeds in Overseas Markets,'' *Denver Business Journal*, March 24, 2000, p. 23A.

''Samsonite Venture Expected to Curb Fakes,'' *Bangkok Post*, February 6, 2001.

Schifrin, Matthew, ''The Dunlap Effect,'' *Forbes*, March 24, 1997, p. 42.

Skolnik, Rayna, ''The Strength Behind Samsonite,'' *Sales & Marketing Management*, September 1986, p. 40.

The Samsonite Story, Denver: Samsonite Corp., 1973.

—Dave Mote
—update: Suzanne Selvaggi

SAP AG

Neurottstrasse 16
69190 Walldorf
Germany
Telephone: (+49) 6227-7-47474
Fax: (+49) 6227-7-57575
Web site: http://www.sap.com

Public Company
Incorporated: 1976
Employees: 25,218
Sales: DM 5,881 million (2000)
Stock Exchanges: Berlin Bremen Düsseldorf Frankfurt Geneva Hamburg Hanover Munich New York Stuttgart
Ticker Symbol: SAP
NAIC: 511210 Software Publishers; 334611 Software Reproducing; 541512 Computer System Design Services

SAP AG is the third-largest independent software supplier worldwide and the largest producer of standard enterprisewide business applications for the client-server software market. The company's principal business activities are the development and marketing of an integrated line of computer software for over 1,000 predefined business processes, from financial accounting, supply chain management, and business work flow to human resources, sales and distribution, and customer relationship management. The largest software group in Europe, its business software applications are used by over 13,500 companies around the world in such industries as chemicals, high tech, telecommunications, electronics, utilities, oil and gas, banking, insurance, healthcare, pharmaceuticals, consumer products, automotive, and retail. Through its 76 international subsidiaries, led by its U.S. subsidiary SAP America, SAP markets its software and consulting, training, and support services in more than 120 countries.

1970s Founding

SAP AG was founded in 1972 by five German engineers with IBM in Mannheim, Germany; interestingly three of the founders, Hasso Plattner, Dietmar Hopp, and Klaus Tschira, were still with SAP in mid-2001. When an IBM client asked IBM to provide enterprise-wide software to run on its mainframe, the five engineers began writing the program only to be told the assignment was being transferred to another unit. Rather than abandon the project altogether, they left IBM and founded SAP in Walldorf, near Heidelberg. While the company originally took its name from the abbreviation for Systemanalyse und Programmenentwicklung (systems analysis and program development), SAP eventually came to stand for Systeme, Anwendungen, und Produkte in Datenverarbeitung (systems, applications, and products in data processing).

Without the benefit of loans from banks, venture capitalists, or the German government, SAP began fashioning its software business gradually through cash flow generated by an ever-growing stable of customers. Working at night on borrowed computers to land their first contracts, Plattner and colleagues built SAP's client list with German firms in its region, beginning with a German subsidiary of the global chemical company ICI and later adding such major German multinationals as Siemens and BMW.

Operating in a corporate computing climate in which business programs were designed to provide only specific, isolated solutions with no relevance to a company's other applications—let alone any outside company's needs—the idea of a fully integrated software product that could be tailored to any company's business proved a hard sell at first. However, because SAP produced software, a nonlabor-intensive product, it was able to avoid the labor agreements and high costs that plague many German manufacturing start-ups. In 1976 SAP declared itself a GmbH (Gesellschaft mit beschränkter Haftung) corporation, or limited company, and by 1978 it was selling its financial accounting software to 40 corporate customers.

R/2 in the Late 1970s

In 1978 SAP began developing, and the following year released, R/2 (R for "real-time"), a mainframe-based, standard business software suite in which integrated modules for accounting, sales and distribution, and production enabled customers to consolidate their financial and operational data into a

Company Perspectives:

Whether opening up new markets or servicing existing ones, SAP is committed to its tested strategy: concentrating on its core business—developing and selling standard enterprise applications software—and partnering with hardware vendors, software suppliers, technology providers, value-added resellers, and consulting firms.

single database and eliminate costly paperwork and data entry. Because the modules were self-standing, businesses could selectively choose what they needed, which could then be customized to their unique requirements. The promise of real-time integration of mission-critical corporate data, viewable through the spreadsheet-like windows of specialized software, offered the potential for uniform data flow, streamlined business operations, and centralized decision-making.

Relying on word of mouth filtering through the overseas branches of its German customers, SAP soon began selling its software outside Europe. With corporate giants like Dow Chemical and Bayer already running R/2, SAP could rely on the fear of obsolescence of its customers' rivals to sell its software to the major competitors in each industry. Among the large corporations that began to adopt R/2 were du Pont, General Mills, Goodyear Tire and Rubber, Heinz, and Shell Oil, as well as 80 of the 100 largest companies in Germany, such as Hoechst, Daimler Benz, and BASF. By 1991 R/2 had gone through four releases or versions and had established itself as the standard for integrated corporate business software in Europe. By 1994 SAP could claim more than 1,400 R/2 installations worldwide.

R/3 Development in the 1980s

As R/2's potential began to peak in the mid-1980s, Plattner and the company's former employer IBM, announced SAA (system applications architecture), a new technology in which all IBM operating systems and platforms would be fully harmonized so that code written for one product would work with any other. Seeing the ramifications of such a high level of integration for its own products, in 1987 SAP began developing R/3 for use in the decentralized, non-mainframe computing environment known as client-server. In client-server arrangements, data is processed not by a single costly mainframe but by many cheaper networked ''server'' computers, which display their data on flexibly arrangeable PCs called ''clients.''

While R/2 focused on providing data-processing solutions for static, individual functions of business operations, such as inventory tracking or shipping, R/3 was designed to allow a business to view its entire business operation as a single-integrated process in which data entered into any single application in the system would simultaneously be registered in every other application. In theory, a company's entire data network would now be a cohesive, interpretable whole that would enable management to more efficiently allocate resources, develop products, manage inventory, forecast trends, streamline manufacturing processes, and automate routine operations.

R/3 itself consisted of IBM's OS/2 operating system as its ''front end'' or user interface; IBM's DB2 program as its database component; and SAP's own proprietary application component, which was based on AT&T's UNIX operating system because it offered the greatest functionality with other vendors' systems. Thus the three-tiered architecture was created—interface or desktop + database + application—on which all later versions of R/3 would be based.

By 1987 SAP had grown to 450 employees and boasted sales of DM 150 million. And although no less than 27 percent of this was plowed back into research, in 1988 SAP GmbH formally converted itself to a publicly traded Aktiengesellschaft (AG) to raise even more capital for research and development.

SAP had established its first operations outside Germany in the mid-1980s, but it was not until the creation of a Swiss-based subsidiary, SAP International, in the late 1980s that it began the expansion that would make it a truly international player in the global client-server software market.

In 1988 it established SAP America in Philadelphia, staffing it initially with transplanted German managers. SAP executives soon realized, however, that an American team was more likely to be able to maneuver through the idiosyncrasies of the U.S. software market and soon began hiring U.S. professionals. One important result was the abandonment of traditional German business practices in favor of a more American approach: lifting limits, for example, on how much salespeople could earn in commissions and submitting budgets in which fully one-third of all annual resources were devoted to product marketing. Fueled by the release of R/3 in 1992, SAP America began to grow into SAP AG's most profitable subsidiary, expanding from two U.S. offices to 20 between 1992 and 1995.

Introduction of R/3 in the 1990s

After five years in development, R/3 had been launched with the expectation that it would complement R/2's multinational-oriented niche by extending SAP's reach into the mid-sized, less mainframe-dominated business software market. Unexpectedly, however, R/3's release coincided with a growing trend toward corporate downsizing, and even SAP's largest customers began eyeing R/3 as a less labor-intensive replacement for R/2. As a result, in the space of one year (1992–93), the percentage of SAP America's total revenue generated by R/3 catapulted from 5 to 80 percent, and R/2's status as SAP's flagship product dwindled from 95 percent of revenues to only 20 percent. R/3 was suddenly hot, and virtually overnight SAP had translated its reputation as Germany's *wunderfirma* to the global stage.

On the strength of R/3's rocketing sales, by the mid-1990s SAP had traveled from the relative anonymity of 1992 to the business applications vendor of choice for nine of the ten largest U.S. corporations, one-third of the *Fortune* 500, seven of the ten largest *Business Week* Global 1000, and 80 percent of the *Fortune* 100 companies in software, computers, peripherals, and semiconductors. Total sales revenues had nearly tripled between 1991 and 1995 to DM 2.7 billion and had increased 66 percent between 1993 and 1994. Such major corporations as Apple, Chevron, Colgate-Palmolive, Digital Equipment, and Polaroid were jumping on the R/3 bandwagon, and by September 1995 SAP could claim over 1,100 installations of R/3 for companies with $1 billion or more in sales (in addition to 700

Key Dates:

1972: Company is founded in Walldorf, Germany by five German engineers.
1976: SAP declares itself a GmbH corporation (a limited company).
1979: SAP R/2 is launched, a real-time mainframe-based standard business software suite.
1988: Company establishes SAP America in Philadelphia.
1992: SAP R/3 is launched servicing a client-server non-mainframe computing environment.
1994: SAP forms an alliance with Microsoft to integrate SAP software with Microsoft products.
1996: SAP industry-specific applications are introduced.
1999: Company launches an integrated web-enabled platform, mySAP.com.
2001: The company acquires TopTier Software and forms SAP Portals.

R/2 installations), and more than 1,300 installations in smaller companies (with 800 R/2 installations). SAP's share price had in the meantime grown 1,000 percent since its introduction on the German stock exchange in 1988, and by 1996 it ranked as the highest valued company in Germany.

Foreign Markets in the 1990s

Two years into the R/3 boom, SAP's sales to German companies, once its sole market, had fallen to 37 percent; North American sales accounted for one-third of all revenues; and the Asia-Pacific market was expected to reach the same level by the year 2000. With two-thirds of all sales revenues now coming from its foreign subsidiaries, in 1996 SAP relocated most of its marketing operation to its Wayne, Pennsylvania, complex. Between 1992 and 1996, it opened subsidiaries in South Africa, Malaysia, Japan, the Czech Republic, Russia, mainland China, and Mexico among others, and was making R/3 available in 14 foreign languages including Russian, Mandarin Chinese, and Thai.

As SAP's global market share in client-server applications began to climb toward 30 percent, new versions of R/3 were released to enhance customizability, reduce installation time, and extend the number of business processes the product addressed. Version 3.0, released in 1995, offered modules in four basic business areas: financial, sales and distribution, manufacturing and logistics, and human resources. A complete R/3 system involved more than 75 modules, 7,000 tables controlling over 3,000 processes, as many as 17 million lines of code, and an installation time of seven to nine months. While individual modules were priced at about $100,000 each, the total installation tab for the average customer (excluding consultants' fees) amounted to $1 million. Complete installations, however, including software, hardware, and system integration, were known to climb as high as $30 million.

If the corporate world's sudden enthusiasm for the R/3 solution at times resembled a religious conversion, there was never a scarcity of heretical dissent. Some customers began to complain of the extreme complexity of R/3's structure, which forced users to search through several layers of menus before finding the application they wanted to run. Configuring the product to conform to the highly particular needs of corporate clients took months and sometimes over a year to complete, and the third-party consultants hired to guide clients through the installation ordeal often had little practical experience or abandoned customers for more lucrative projects midway through. The rule of thumb that corporations should prepare to spend one dollar on consultants for every dollar spent on software became an object of nostalgia as consultant-to-software expense ratios for R/3 installations rose to four and even ten to one.

As SAP began to enjoy the monolithic status of Microsoft and IBM it was also accused of arrogantly forcing its system on customers who could not use R/3 unless it was modified to conform to their unique business practices. Finally, some corporate information technology managers, taking the dictum: ''You don't get fired for buying SAP'' too close to heart, were convincing their companies to invest in R/3 without examining whether they really needed a system so robust, or whether it would create the efficiencies that would justify its cost.

Competition and Other Challenges

SAP's two major competitors, Oracle Systems (United States) and Baan (the Netherlands), were meanwhile making inroads into SAP's market share. Although Oracle's database product was the program most often used as R/3's database component—making SAP the largest value-added reseller of Oracle products—in 1995 Oracle announced it would overtake SAP as the world's leading provider of industry-specific software within three years. Baan, though dwarfed by SAP in sales and customers, scored major coups in the mid-1990s when both Boeing and German giant Siemens Nixdorf rejected R/3 in favor of Baan's quick-installing business software package. SAP Board Member Henning Kagermann dismissed the setbacks, telling the *Deutsche Presse Agentur*, ''If SAP wins a large order, it's accepted as natural. When we lose a potential customer, immediately it's a big headline.'' SAP management also dispelled the severity of the threat posed by Oracle, pointing out that when in head-to-head competition SAP still won the contract 80 percent of the time.

Two public relations disasters in the mid-1990s suggested not only the extent of the controversy that had begun to surround R/3 but also SAP's savvy in handling criticism. In March 1995 the German business magazine *Wirtschaftswoche* published an article accusing SAP of accepting commissions from hardware vendors for computers sold to SAP customers and quoted several users' disparaging remarks about the expense and installation time required by R/3. As share prices nosedived, SAP lashed back. Its hardware partners unanimously denied any kickback arrangement with SAP, and SAP itself took out a court order on the magazine for inaccuracy and deliberate misquotation and ran four-page ads in major German print outlets in which the article's sources claimed they were misquoted and expressed satisfaction with R/3.

Then, in early 1996 U.S. computer industry analyst Forrester Research published a study in which it argued that SAP's R/3 was based on an obsolete architecture that could not keep pace with the open, nonproprietary architecture increasingly favored by the software industry. SAP, Forrester claimed, knew that R/3 would be obsolete by 1997 and secretly planned to foist a brand-new "object-based" system called R/10 on its customers in 1999, masking its deployment through a series of add-ons to R/3. All SAP customers, Forrester advised, should minimize their dependency on R/3 and prepare "exit strategies" to avoid being trapped into an expensive installation of a new SAP product.

SAP reacted by prematurely releasing quarterly financial figures showing that R/3 sales had not in fact peaked and by vehemently denying that it was planning to abandon R/3. It further vowed to spend DM3 billion on research and development over the next five years and announced plans for new versions of R/3 that reflected its willingness to make the product, which was based on its own proprietary programming language and more open to integration with other vendors' products. SAP, moreover, signaled it was embracing the Internet-driven trend toward "object-oriented" software in which applications could be embedded with other vendors' mini-programs (called "objects" or "applets"). The strategy worked, and Forrester Research was soon announcing that SAP was "leading in the new Internet game."

Holding Ground Through the Late 1990s

In the mid-1990s industry observers agreed that SAP's continued dominance of the client-server business software market rested on its ability to stay ahead of the breathtaking pace of change in the global software market. In the mid-1990s, for example, SAP was directly affected by the rise of the "intranet," a version of the Internet created by companies as in-house data networks, mirroring the structure and appearance of the World Wide Web but protected from the cybersurfing public by so-called firewalls. With the potential to perform many of the same business applications and data-processing features of R/3, such intranets represented a plausible challenge to SAP's market leadership. SAP responded by announcing new features that would turn R/3 into an Internet-capable tool. Using a browser connected to the web, for example, two companies with R/3 installed in their systems could process orders in real time over the Internet, while consumers could order products electronically from a company's online catalog and be confident the order was registered immediately in the company's R/3 system.

SAP's ability to sustain its success also depended on its willingness to continue working, à la Microsoft, with its hundreds of strategic partner firms throughout the computer and services industries. SAP's Platform Partners program, for example, had enabled it to cooperate with computer manufacturers such as Compaq and IBM in tailoring SAP products to new hardware developments. And its partnership program with such Big Six accounting firms as Arthur Andersen and Price Waterhouse had spawned a lucrative new subindustry of R/3 consultants whose institutional independence from SAP enabled it to focus more of its resources on improving its product. Finally, SAP's participation with other software vendors in industry-wide initiatives (such as the Open Application Group) to determine standards for new technologies, demonstrated its willingness to cooperate with potential competitors to ensure the continued functionality and influence of its own products.

Significantly, in 1994 SAP formed an alliance with American software giant Microsoft to make SAP software integrated with such Microsoft products as Windows NT, an operating system for networked computers, and SQL Server, a database product. In 1995 Microsoft returned the favor by selecting R/3 for its global finance and accounting data system.

Sales at SAP continued at a brisk pace, soaring to $3.5 billion in 1997, 44 percent of which was derived from its U.S. operations. With complementary and even competing software firms rushing to plug in their products or components to R/3, SAP had succeeded in establishing its product as the "business backbone." SAP's own staff had by then grown to 17,000 employees.

To rein in R/3's ever-increasing capabilities and complexities, SAP deployed a number of new customer initiatives, including a fast-track program to expedite the sales and installation process, and business units to tailor software packages for specific industries. By 1998, SAP's range of industry-specific applications extended to 17 different sectors including aviation, hospitals, automotive, and the military. Diligent efforts were also made to simplify R/3's complex graphical interface and create a friendlier look and feel.

Despite its wild success with R/3, SAP nearly failed to keep pace with rapid changes in the global software marketplace. By the late 1990s, competitors were starting to build versatile functions into their products to exploit the intensifying "business-to-business" Internet marketplace, and as quickly as SAP had captured the market, it was now coming under fire from vendors, employees, and industry observers who lamented its lack of vision and resistance to change.

New Strategy for the 21st Century

In February 1999 SAP executives arrived at a new strategy to deploy in time for the New Millennium. The result was mySAP.com, a web-enabled platform that combined enterprise resource planning (similar to that of R/3) with a series of specialty business software applications such as supply chain management and customer relationship management. Viewed through a role-based, customized web browser window, mySAP.com applications were developer-friendly and capable of integrating with other vendors' databases, applications, operating systems, and hardware. The new platform also extended to electronic business (e-business) marketplaces and corporate web portals, which further linked partner companies together and enabled them to collaborate and conduct transactions with one another whether they were using SAP or non-SAP applications.

The concept of mySAP.com at first proved unclear to customers, even after a $50 million advertising campaign. When crucial U.S. revenues dropped in the first quarter of 2000, management responded with drastic measures. A reorganization of the company's development staff working on product lines was the first step in transforming an internally focused corporate culture into one more customer-centric and better suited for competition in U.S. markets, where business-to-business Internet sales were predicted to skyrocket to $2.7 trillion by 2004. To ensure that products were developed with maximum customer input, SAP America enlisted 100 customers to help write code.

Further, SAP's entire marketing department was relocated from Germany to Manhattan.

The company's efforts paid off and by the second quarter of 2001, total revenues reached $1.85 billion, an increase of 24 percent from the previous year. Revenues from mySAP.com's customer relationship management software increased to $104 million, a 55 percent jump from the previous quarter. Significantly, revenues from its supply chain management software jumped 46 percent to $150 million, giving SAP a 9 percent share and the lead in the supply chain management arena.

As virtually the only software developer not to issue profit warnings in 2001, SAP's higher-than-expected financial results beat analyst forecasts in an otherwise gloomy technology sector. And contrary to the sluggish economy, as Co-Chief Executive Plattner recognized in a June 2001 interview with *Computing Canada*, "It's a time for opportunity."

In the space of one year, 15,000 customers in SAP's R/3 installed base had transitioned to mySAP.com, with the number of licensed users quadrupling to four million. Anticipating that sales of mySAP.com applications would eventually replace those of R/3, SAP predicted that between 80 to 100 percent of its existing customers would migrate to the new platform by 2006.

A significant contract to outfit Nestle Corporation with mySAP.com specialty applications lent critical weight and authority to the new platform. SAP procured similar contracts with other high-profile companies such as Compaq Computers, Cadbury Schweppes, and Nokia. In addition, a slew of U.S.-based subsidiaries was created to support product development and innovation, including application hosting and third-party technologies.

New alliances also helped to strengthen SAP's venture into e-commerce territory. In one such alliance, SAP joined forces with Commerce One to develop e-marketplaces or online trading exchanges where goods and services could be bought or sold. Following the formation of SAP Portals in 2001, SAP teamed up with Yahoo! to develop customized enterprise portals; SAP further bolstered its strength in the enterprise portal market through its acquisition of TopTier Software.

Through its new mySAP.com platform, particularly its specialty applications in supply chain and customer relationship management, SAP appeared to have successfully positioned itself to capitalize on the flourishing e-business market. By nimbly responding to competitive challenges and technological advances, and learning to better market its products, SAP would no doubt remain a formidable presence in the global business software market.

Principal Subsidiaries

SAP America Inc.; SAP Canada; SAP Japan Co. Ltd.; SAP Asia Pte. Ltd. (Singapore); SAP Hong Kong; SAP Software System Co., Ltd. (Beijing); SAP Australia PTY LTD; SAP Mexico, S.A. DE C.V.; SAP-M GmbH; SAP Retail Solutions GmbH & Co.; SAPMarkets Europe GmbH; Steeb Anwendungssysteme GmbH; SAP CRM Consulting GmbH & Co.; eSAP GmbH & Co.; SAPHosting AG & Co. SAP Learning Solutions GmbH; In-Q-MY Technologies GmbH; DACOS Software Holding GmbH; SAP Retail Solutions; eSAP, SAP CRM Consulting; SAPHosting, SAP GmbH; SAP (UK) Limited, SAP France S.A., (France); SAP (Schweiz) AG (Switzerland); SAP Nederland B.V. (Netherlands); SAP Italia S.p.A. (Italy); SAP Österreich GmbH (Austria); NV SAP Belgium SA, SAP (Spain) SA; SAPSA (PTY) LTD. (South Africa); SAP SA (Sweden); SAP Denmark A/S; SAP (Finland) Oy; SAP (Portugal); SAPSA, SAP CR, spol. s r.o. (Czech Republic); SAP Polska Sp. z.o.o., (Poland); SAP Norge AS, (Norway); SAP Hungary Rendszerek (Hungary); SAP Consult C.I.S. (Russia); SAP Hellas S.A. (Greece); SAP Slovensko s.r.o. (Slovakia); SAP Service and Support Centre (Ireland) Limited; Public Services (PTY) Ltd., (South Africa; 70%); CADRA S.A. (France); SAP-OFEK Ltd. (Israel); SAP Labs (France) S.A.; SAP Systems Integration (Schweiz) AG (Switzerland; 54%); IN-Q-MY Labs Limited (Bulgaria); e-sap.fr, (France); SAP Cyprus Ltd. (Cyprus); SAP Bulgaria Ltd. (Bulgaria); SAP (Nigeria) Ltd.; Ithinqcom (PTY) Ltd., (South Africa; 60%); SAP Ireland Ltd. (Ireland); SAP Consult (Ukraine); SAP Public Services, Inc., Washington, D.C.; TopTier Software, Inc. (USA); SAP Labs, Inc. (USA); SAP Brasil Ltda. (Brazil); SAP Andina Y del Caribe C.A. (Venezuela); SAP Argentina S.A.; SAPMarkets, Inc. (USA); Campbell Software, Inc. (USA); SAP International, Inc. (USA); SAP Properties, Inc. (USA); SAP Investment, Inc. (USA); SAP Korea Limited; SAP India Systems Private Limited; SAP Malaysia SDN. BHD.; SAP Taiwan Co. Ltd.; SAP (Beijing) Software System Co., Ltd. (China); SAP Labs India Private Limited (India); SAP Systems Ltd. (Thailand); SAP Asia, (Indonesia); SAP Philippines, Inc.; SAP New Zealand Limited; SAPMarkets Asia Pacific Solutions Pte. Ltd. (Singapore); SAP India (Holding) Pte. Ltd. (Singapore); SAP Systems Integration AG (54%).

Principal Competitors

Oracle Corporation; PeopleSoft, Inc.; Siebel Systems, Inc.; Baan Company N.V.; i2 Technologies, Inc.

Further Reading

Bartholomew, Doug, "Hasso Plattner: Growing Software's Quiet Giant," *Industry Week*, December 21, 1998, pp. 39–44.
"Can SAP Swim with the Swiftest?," *Business Week*, June 26, 2000, p. 46.
Culp, Eric, and O'Brien Browne, "SAP Contends with Its Own Success," *The European*, July 27, 1998, p. 20.
Edmondson, Gail, "America's Latest Software Success Story Is German," *Business Week*, August 8, 1994, p. 46.
Fondiller, David S., "Client Serving," *Forbes*, July 4, 1994, p. 130.
Hamm, Steve, "All Abooarrrd!: SAP America and SAP AG Gain Momentum," *PC Week*, July 17, 1995, p. A1.
Hilson, Gary, "Latest R/3 Tackles Integration with SAP Web Tools," *Computing Canada*, May 4, 2001, p. 1.
——, "SAP Branches Out to E-Business Market Space," *Computing Canada*, June 29, 2001, pp. 1–2.
"Less Ego, More Success," *Business Week*, July 23, 2001, pp. 56–59.
Lieber, Ronald, "Here Comes SAP," *Fortune*, October 2, 1995.
MacMillan, Michael, "SAP Sees R/3 Ending as Mysap.com Flies," *Computing Canada*, June 23, 2000, p. 1.
McKendrick, Joseph, "SAP Begins to Battle for Midmarket Sector," *Ent*, December 9, 1998, p. 12.
Mitchell, Ian, "Late E-Commerce Start Hits SAP," *Computer Weekly*, July 20, 2000, p. 24.

Nee, Eric, ''Hasso Plattner and Klaus Besier: An Interview with Eric Nee,'' *Upside*, December 1995.

Ricciuti, Mike, and J. William Semich, ''SAP's Client/Server Battle Plan,'' *Datamation*, March 15, 1993, pp. 26–32.

Saltz-Trautman, Peggy, ''Creating an Industry,'' *International Business*, February 1996.

Songini, Marc, ''MySAP Sells Despite Foggy Marketing,'' *Computerworld*, June 25, 2001, p. 24.

Stedman, Craig, ''R/3 Stymies Users,'' *Computerworld*, September 21, 1998, p. 100.

——, ''SAP to Streamline R/3 Interface,'' *Computerworld*, December 14, 1998, p. 20.

Steinmetz, Greg, ''German Firm Grows, Silicon-Valley Style,'' *Wall Street Journal*, April 11, 1995, p. A16.

Stone, Martin, ''ERP Davids Nipping at Goliath SAP's Heels: Study,'' *Computing Canada*, November 2, 1998, pp. 23–26.

Sullivan, Thomas, ''Microsoft, SAP Tie SQL Service 7.0 to R/3,'' *Ent*, September 23, 1998.

Sweat, Jeff, ''ERP: The Corporate Ecosystem,'' *Informationweek*, October 12, 1998, pp. 42–52.

''The Prudent Approach to R/3,'' *The Forrester Report*, April 1996.

Waters, Richard, ''SAP America Faces Up to Challenge of Change,'' *The Financial Times*, June 13, 2001, p. 30.

Zeitz, William A., ''SAP R/3: Dream or Nightmare?,'' *ComputerWorld*, January 29, 1996. p. 101.

—Paul S. Bodine
—update: Suzanne P. Selvaggi

Sawtek Inc.

1818 South Highway 441
Apopka, Florida 32703
P.O. Box 609501
Orlando, Florida 32860
U.S.A.
Telephone: (407) 886-8860
Fax: (407) 886-7061
Web site: http://www.sawtek.com

Public Company
Incorporated: 1979
Employees: 770
Sales: $159.8 million (2000)
Stock Exchanges: NASDAQ
Ticker Symbol: SAWS
NAIC: 33422 Radio and Television Broadcasting and Wireless Communications Equipment Manufacturing; 334419 Other Electronic Component Manufacturing

Sawtek Inc., based in Apopka, Florida (near Orlando), is a manufacturer of custom-designed electronic components, especially devices based on Surface Acoustic Wave (SAW) technology, with an emphasis on the high-end performance spectrum of its government and commercial markets. Its main products are SAW bandpass filters for both Intermediate Frequency (IF) and Radio Frequency (RF) commercial applications in the wireless telecommunication handset and infrastructure markets. Sawtek also makes customized high-performance bandpass filters, resonators, delay lines, and oscillators as well as SAW-based subsystems. The company's products are used in a broad range of microwave and radio frequency systems, including digital CDMA (Code Division Multiple Access) and GSM (Global System for Mobile Communication) telephone systems, digital microwave radios, wireless LANs (Local Area Networks), cable and high-definition television, cordless phones, satellite and defense systems, and chemical sensors. Nearly 75 percent of Sawtek's sales are to the communications industry, and among its major customers are Motorola, Hyundai Electronics, Lucent Technologies, Samsung, and Nokia. Its chemical sensors and related components are sold to pharmaceutical companies and to the government. In addition to it facility in Florida, Sawtek operates a manufacturing plant in San José, Costa Rica (Sawtek S.A.) and a direct sales office in Seoul, South Korea (Sawtek Far East). The company, which went public in 1996, has an employee stock ownership plan (ESOP), and at the start of 2001 its employees held about 21 percent of its stock.

1979–89: Origins and Entering the Commercial Market

Four Texas Instrument (TI) employees, headed by Steve Miller and Neal Tolar, founded Sawtek Inc. in 1979. All of them brought SAW technology experience to the new enterprise, begun for the purpose of providing radar and electronic warfare systems to the U.S. military. Prior to co-founding Sawtek, Miller was manager of TI's SAW Device Engineering and Development Laboratory. He had joined Texas Instruments in 1969. Co-founder Tolar, who joined TI in 1967, was a staff member in that company's RF Technology Group of the Corporate Research Laboratory. Until they stepped down from the day-to-day operations of Sawtek, these two men served in a variety of the company's executive positions: Miller was president from 1979 to 1997 and CEO from 1986 to 1999; Tolar, a director since 1979, served as vice-president of operations and engineering from 1979 to 1995, and senior vice-president and chief technical officer from 1995 to 1999.

Basically, SAW technology involved the production of acoustic waves in solid materials used in signal processing. The technology had only been pioneered in the early 1970s, so it was a relatively new technology with great potential and a wide-open field. In the early years of the company's development, Sawtek relied heavily on government contracts, but by the mid 1980s, because of military budget cuts, Sawtek began shifting its focus to the growing number of commercial applications, something Miller and Tolar had sought to tap into from the very beginning. Although the company was aided by the impact of digital technology on the telecommunications industry, which by then had entered a major period of rapid expansion and fueled Sawtek's own growth, the transition to the commercial sphere was at best gradual, taking over a decade.

Company Perspectives:

Sawtek is a leading global supplier of microelectronic signal processing products based on Surface Acoustic Wave and related technologies. We will leverage our proprietary technical expertise, unmatched customer service, rapid product development capability and superior technical support across the broadest range of products, markets and applications. We will aggressively pursue growth opportunities, utilizing our unique strengths to provide differentiated, value-added products and services that offer a competitive advantage in the eyes of our customers.

1990–96: Gaining Market Share and Aggressive Expansion

In fact, in the early 1990s, the military and aerospace industry continued to account for more than half of the company's revenue. In 1991, for example, 61 percent of its net sales were still made in those market segments. However, by 1996, 85 percent of Sawtek's net sales came from the commercial market sector. In that same five-year period (1991–96), the company's international sales increased from 20 percent of total sales to 54 percent, largely aided by the worldwide growth of wireless telecommunications.

An Employee Stock Ownership Plan (ESOP) was instituted by Sawtek in 1991. The company borrowed $4 million from its commercial bank to lend to the ESOP to finance its acquisition of almost 8.9 million shares of common stock. It borrowed another $1.7 million in 1994, lending it to the ESOP for the purchase of over 1.6 million more shares of common stock

In 1995, Sawtek commenced an aggressive expansion campaign, taking major steps in the next year when it went public, expanded its facility in Florida, added more than 300 employees to its work force, and opened a facility in San Jose, Costa Rica, where, for approximately $1.3 million, it purchased a 31,690 square foot plant. At its 16-acre Apopka site, Sawtek added 33,000 square feet of production space plus an additional 13,000 square feet of office space.

Expansion involved considerable risk taking. Among other things, Sawtek relied very heavily on a small number of major customers. In fiscal 1995, for example, 60 percent of its revenues came from sales to the company's top ten customers—telecommunications equipment manufacturers like Lucent Technologies, Motorola, Nokia, Omnipoint, and Alcatel. The risk was exacerbated by Sawtek's recurring problem of not meeting delivery schedules, causing grumbling among some of its customers who wanted their needs met on time. Still, the company remained profitable, earning $4.1 million on revenues of $31.3 million for the fiscal year ending September 30, 1995, up from revenues of $19.1 million and earnings of $1.7 million the previous year.

The financial story changed the next year. Although the expanded Florida plant and new facility in Costa Rica doubled Sawtek's production capacity and helped increase the company's net sales by 84 percent, Sawtek recorded a $300,000 loss in 1996. The red ink was partly explained by the rise in costs resulting from the company's mounting overhead plus its increased debt retirement burden. Among other things, in the last quarter of 1996, the company began paying a quarterly ESOP compensation expense of about $195,000, representing the remaining payments on a loan secured in 1991 to purchase almost nine million shares of common stock for the ESOP program. To help offset its rising costs, pay off $3 million in bank loans, and finance further growth, the company decided to go public that same year, filing a stock registration statement on March 1, 1996. When it made its initial public offering, Sawtek offered 4.5 million shares of common stock, three million of which were owned by the company and the remainder by stockholding investors, including Miller and Tolar.

1997 and Beyond: Some Challenges But Impressive Financial Gains

The company returned to profitability with a vengeance in 1997, when, with revenues of $82.8 million, it netted an income of $20.8 million and a net profit margin of 25.1 percent. It would do even better over the next three years, turning in a stellar balance-sheet performance despite some bumps in its corporate road.

By 1998, the percentage of Sawtek's revenue generated by government contracts had dropped to just 8 percent. Increasingly, the company depended on both domestic and foreign commercial sales to offset the decline in sales to federal agencies. That shift created a problem in 1998, when a major South Korean buyer reneged on its large orders and Qualcomm Inc. cut back on the production of its Q phones, which used filters made by Sawtek. To offset its production costs, the company shifted its manufacturing to its facility in San Jose.

Despite the temporary setback, Sawtek continued its growth strategy. In 1998, it purchased Microsensor Systems, Inc., a private research and development company based in Bowling Green, Kentucky. Microsensor, acquired in a stock swap agreement, designed and manufactured scientific instruments for the chemical sensor market. The instruments employed polymer-coated SAW devices and other technologies, which suited Sawtek's SAW-based chemical sensor initiative. The acquisition provided Sawtek with an array of new products, an established customer base, and an enhanced technical expertise.

Miller stepped down as Sawtek's CEO in 1999. He was succeed by Gary Monetti, who had been the first college graduate to be hired by Sawtek back in 1979, when the company had only 20 employees. He had followed the advice of his father, which was either to start his own company or join a small one where he could make his mark by helping it grow. It was also in 1999 that Sawtek opened an office in Seoul, South Korea, dubbing the operation Sawtek Far East.

Monetti ran into some serious problems in early and late 2000. In February, the company's common stock again took a nose dive. The plunge was attributed to two causes: alleged insider profit taking (including the sale of stock by several Sawtek executives), and announcements made by Qualcomm indicating that it was developing new CDMA chipsets that

Key Dates:

1979: Steve Miller, Neal Tolar, and two other Texas Instruments employees found Sawtek.
1991: Company institutes Employee Stock Ownership Plan.
1996: Sawtek goes public; company purchases facility in San Jose, Costa Rica.
1998: Company shifts production to its Costa Rican facility; it also acquires Microsensor Systems.
1999: Sawtek establishes Sawtek Far East in Seoul, South Korea; Gary Monetti becomes CEO, replacing Steve Miller, who remains chairman.
2000: Ill health causes Monetti to resign as CEO; he is succeeded by Dr. Kimon Anemogiannis; company completes new production facility in Costa Rica.

would eliminate the need for IF transmit filters and render them obsolete. Later, in December, after Qualcomm released the news that its new Zero Intermediate Frequency technology, radioOne, reduced the size and cost of making CDMA radios, Sawtek's stock fell further, quickly dropping by $11.25 per share to $53.75.

The seesawing performance of Sawtek's stock in 1998 and 2000 did not stop the company from developing new products or continuing its expansion. It did take some damage control steps, however. Among other things, it publicized the fact that the sale of stock by Miller, Tolar, and other executive officers was strictly done in accordance with federal securities laws and basically involved the company's ESOP, not individual profit taking. It also responded to Qualcomm's claims, issuing, among other things, a white paper that it posted to its Internet site. According to Sawtek, the transmit IF filter used by Qualcomm in the past was not a SAW filter to begin with and, in any case, was never provided to Qualcomm in volume. Moreover, the SAW IF filter developed for Qualcomm's new chipset was not, Sawtek claimed, a vital company product. It noted that for the fiscal year ending in September 1999, SAW IF filters accounted for less than 1 percent of Sawtek's total sales.

The company certainly treated its difficulties as if they were a press-made mountain heaped over a factual mole hill and certainly nothing to impede progress. In the summer of 2000, it completed construction of its new, 30,000 square-foot manufacturing facility near San Jose, Costa Rica, doubling its production space in that country. Before the new plant's completion, Sawtek's Costa Rican operations already accounted for over half of the company's revenues and contributed significantly to its reduced tax burden. The new facility was slated to be used primarily for manufacturing a new line of products, including RF filters for digital wireless phones and IF filters for GSM wireless phones. The new plant also expanded Sawtek's work force in Costa Rica to over 250 employees.

The expansion in Costa Rica was Sawtek's last major move under Monetti's watch. In November 2000, ill health forced him to step down from his position as Sawtek's CEO and from the company's board of directors. His successor was Dr. Kimon Anemogiannis, who had been an officer with the company since 1998. He was named both CEO and president. To help with the transition, Monetti stayed on the company payroll as an advisor both to Anemogiannis and the company.

Anemogiannis had first joined Sawtek as director of engineering in 1995. He was named vice president-engineering in 1998 and vice president and COO in 1999. Before his employment at Sawtek, he held a variety of engineering posts at Siemens Matsushita, a SAW component manufacturer based in Munich, Germany. At the time that he moved over to Sawtek, he already had an international reputation as an expert and SAW technology innovator. At Sawtek, he had quickly become the chief force behind the company's strategy of becoming a high-volume, low-cost producer of a wide range of SAW-based components.

The new CEO inherited some problems from his predecessor, including the company's volatile stock, which, as noted, continued on its market roller-coaster ride throughout 2000. However, in February 2001, soon after Anemogiannis took on the president's job, Sawtek announced its pre-production release of its new miniature 5 x 5 mm cellular RF SAW duplexer, a device designed to offer higher performance and greater power handling for CDMA, TDMA (Time Division Multiple Access), and AMPS (Advanced Mobile Phone Service) applications than the miniature SAW duplexers then in use. Its development represented the kind of technological breakthrough that had always helped Sawtek weather the inevitable problems that beset most high tech, rapidly changing industries. The company seemed positioned to continue doing so well into the new century.

Principal Subsidiaries

Microsensor Systems Inc.

Principal Competitors

Allen Telecom Inc.; Dover Corporation; Fujitsu Limited; Microwave Filter Company, Inc.; Powerwave Technologies, Inc.; RF Monolithics, Inc.

Further Reading

Dano, Mike, "Sawtek Stock Impacted by Qualcomm Technology News," *RCR Wireless News*, January 1, 2001, p. 24.
Dillon, Paul, "Fast-Growing Sawtek Going Public," *Orlando Business Journal*, March 8, 1996, p. 1.
Perrault, Mike, "Sawtek Rides Waves Despite Weak Economy," *Orlando Business Journal*, October 11, 1991, p. 12.
"Sawtek Announces August Completion of New Costa Rica Production Facility," *Business Wire*, July 31, 2000.
"Sawtek Announces the Appointment of Kimon Anemogiannis as President and Chief Executive Officer," *Business Wire*, November 14, 2000.
"Sawtek Completes Acquisition of Microsensor Systems, Inc.," *Business Wire*, February 25, 1998.
"Sawtek Introduces the World's Smallest Cellular RF Duplexer for Mobile Phones," *Business Wire*, February 14, 2001.
"Sawtek Responds to Comments in the Financial Press," *Business Wire*, February 18, 2000.

—John W. Fiero

SED International Holdings, Inc.

4916 North Royal Atlanta Drive
Tucker, Georgia 30085
U.S.A.
Telephone: (770) 491-8962
Toll Free: (800) 444-8962
Fax: (800) 329-2733
Web site: http://www.sedonline.com
Public Company
Incorporated: 1980 as Southern Electronics Corporation
Employees: 451
Sales: $609.4 million (2000)
Stock Exchanges: NASDAQ
Ticker Symbol: SECX
NAIC: 421420 Office Equipment Wholesalers; 421430 Computer and Computer Peripheral Equipment and Software Wholesalers

SED International Holdings, Inc., through its wholly owned operating subsidiary SED International, Inc., is a mid-size distributor of computer equipment, cellular phones, and related accessories. It serves more than 30,000 value-added resellers, system builders, e-commerce resellers, dealer-agents, and retailers with a selection of more than 5,000 products, fulfillment services, finance options, and e-commerce solutions. SED serves customers throughout the United States. It began supplying the Latin American market in 1994 through a warehouse in Miami and presently has sales and distribution offices in Brazil, Colombia, Argentina, and Puerto Rico.

A Regional Distributor of Consumer Electronics in the 1980s

Southern Electronics Corp., the predecessor to SED International Holdings, Inc., was formed in the Atlanta, Georgia, metropolitan area in 1980. It distributed consumer electronics products to dealers in the Southeast. One of the founders, Gerald Diamond, was the company's president and treasurer.

Southern Electronics remained privately owned until 1986, when an investor group that included Gerald Diamond bought the company's assets for $14.5 million. In October 1986 Southern Electronics completed its initial public offering (IPO), raising $4.5 million that was used to reduce the company's debt. Investment firm Drexel Burnham Lambert underwrote the stock offering and took a 30 percent interest in the company. The company was organized as a holding company, called Southern Electronics Corp., and a wholly owned operating subsidiary, Southern Electronics Distributors, Inc.

Prior to its IPO, Southern Electronics had been facing stiff competition from retailers in the consumer electronics business. With Gerald Diamond as its CEO, the company decided in 1987 to begin distributing computer hardware and peripheral products, such as printers, modems, monitors, and keyboards. It also began distributing cellular phones. For 1987 Southern Electronics reported a net loss of $770,000.

By the end of the decade Southern Electronics had returned to profitability. It was distributing products to approximately 4,500 small dealers and value-added resellers (VARs) in the Southeast. The company stocked some 2,000 products from about 50 original equipment manufacturers (OEMs), typically smaller companies such as Seagate Technology Inc. and Panasonic Consumer Electronics Co., rather than larger OEMs like IBM and Compaq Computer Corp. About 72 percent of Southern Electronics' revenue came from the sale of computer hardware and peripheral products, with cellular phone sales accounting for 18 percent. For 1990 the company's net income rose 35 percent to $3.6 million, and revenue increased 25 percent to $114 million, compared to 1989. Most of the company's profits were used to reduce its long-term debt.

National and International Expansion, 1990s

For fiscal 1991 ending June 30, Southern Electronics had net income of $4.2 million on revenue of $139 million. It had about 150 employees. Later in calendar 1991 the company had a secondary stock offering of 1.6 million shares to raise more than $17 million. Included in the offering was Drexel Burnham Lambert's 30 percent interest in Southern Electronics. At the time Southern Electronics' stock was traded on a ''bid/ask'' basis rather than on the NASDAQ National Market System. The secondary offering was priced at $11 a share. For 1992–93 the company's stock traded in the $7 to $17 range.

Company Perspectives:

SED International, Inc., founded in 1980, is a leading provider of computer hardware, wireless communications and e-business solutions to channel partners throughout the United States and Latin America. SED International delivers world-class service offerings including flexible financing, end-user fulfillment, web hosting and expert technical support.

It was reported in 1994 that Southern Electronics was for sale. It held negotiations with several suitors and by mid-1995 was in merger talks with networking products distributor GBC Technologies Inc. *Computer Reseller News* characterized GBC as a low-volume, value-added supplier of networking products that typically required technical support. Southern Electronics, on the other hand, favored a high-volume, low-cost strategy and typically did not sell the types of computer products that required technical support. After the heads of the two companies failed to agree on a business plan, merger talks between GBC and Southern Electronics were called off in June 1995.

Southern Electronics began looking to supply the Latin American market in 1994, when it opened a warehouse in Miami. In its first year of selling to the region, Southern Electronics had $14.3 million in sales to Latin America. In 1995 the company acquired Miami-based U.S. Computer of North America Inc. for $13.9 million. U.S. Computer had a sales staff that spoke fluent Spanish and Portuguese, and Latin American sales boomed to $171.5 million in fiscal 1996 ending June 30, which represented 37 percent of Southern Electronics' fiscal 1996 revenue of $468.3 million.

During 1997 Southern Electronics Corp., the parent holding company of Southern Electronics Distributors, Inc., changed its name to SED International Holdings, Inc., and Southern Electronics Distributors, Inc., became SED International, Inc. The name changes reflected the growth of SED's international operations. The acquisition of U.S. Computer gave SED the right to distribute Hewlett-Packard Co. products in much of Latin America. In November 1997 SED extended its Hewlett-Packard distribution into Brazil with the acquisition of Magna Distribuidora Ltda., a Sao Paulo-based distributor, for $1.4 million. SED also opened a sales office and distribution center in Bogota, Colombia, in 1997. For fiscal 1997 SED's sales to Latin America reached $290.7 million, or 45 percent of the company's overall revenue of $646.3 million.

Establishing a presence in Latin America allowed SED to bypass the middlemen that previously had carried its products to the region from Miami. Acquiring local distributors in Latin America also gave SED the ability to take advantage of their local market knowledge and customer relationships. SED established a bonus system to encourage local managers to stay and increase sales after their companies were acquired by SED.

Also in 1997 SED acquired the U.S. assets of failing distributor Globelle Corp. for $13 million. Globelle had acquired distributor GBC Technologies in 1996, but then ran into difficulty integrating its operations. Although Globelle had lost its authorization to distribute products made by IBM Corp. and Seagate Technology, the acquisition gave SED authorization to distribute products made by Hewlett-Packard Co. and 3Com Corp. in the United States. SED also gained Globelle's Memphis warehouse that was electronically integrated with Federal Express Corp., as well as the company's sales office at its Minneapolis headquarters.

The acquisition of Globelle helped boost SED's fiscal 1998 revenue to $892.6 million, although a number of factors resulted in a net loss of $255,000. The loss, which included a $6.2 million fourth quarter loss, was the company's first since 1987. Contributing to the loss were slumping demand in the mass-storage market, which was SED's largest product category, and uncollectible receivables. By 1998 SED had grown to 366 employees. The company had recently increased the number of its warehouses from two to four by opening one in Harrisburg, Pennsylvania, and another in the Los Angeles area. In early 1998 SED unveiled a web site where resellers could order more than 10,000 products. In its first six months SED Online Order Express received orders from about 4,200 resellers.

The year 1999 (fiscal year ending June 30) was difficult financially for SED. A slump in the PC market resulted in pricing pressures in certain product segments, notably lower hard drive prices. In an effort to return to profitability, SED laid off 40 employees—about ten percent of its work force—and consolidated some of its warehouse facilities. It closed a 40,000-square-foot warehouse annex in Atlanta, and it sublet half of a 100,000-square-foot warehouse located in City of Industry, California. To achieve profitability the company also focused on reducing overhead, improving gross margins, and providing better service to its vendors. Also contributing to SED's problems was a weakening Latin American market, including economic turmoil in Brazil where inflation had reached 42 percent. SED continued to expand in Latin America, however, having in December 1998 acquired Intermaco S.R.L., an Argentine-based distributor of Hewlett-Packard products.

Although SED had been assembling nonbranded computers known as ''white boxes'' on a build-to-order basis for several years, it contracted with Solectron Corporation to build the nonbranded systems at Solectron's Atlanta facility. The computers would start at $599 and utilize Intel processors and Microsoft Corp. operating systems.

In spite of its cost-cutting efforts, SED posted a $38.9 million loss for the quarter ending March 31, 1999. Contributing to the loss were the devaluation of Brazil's currency, higher than expected credit losses, and slow-moving product. Other problems included losing authorization to distribute disk drives made by Seagate Technology. Seagate was one of several manufacturers who were reducing the number of their channel partners, a practice that strengthened the larger distributors but hurt mid-size distributors like SED. Latin American sales for the quarter fell by 58 percent, and the company also took a $13.6 million charge related to the value of long-term assets.

For fiscal 1999 ending June 30 SED's revenue declined to $707.6 million, and the company reported a net loss of $37.9 million. The company managed to report a profit for the fourth quarter, as it closed more warehouses and laid off almost 40

Key Dates:

1980: Company is founded as Southern Electronics Corp.
1986: Southern Electronics becomes a public company and has its initial public offering (IPO).
1994: Company opens a warehouse in Miami to serve the Latin American market.
1997: Parent company changes name to SED International Holdings, Inc., and its operating subsidiary becomes SED International, Inc.

percent of its U.S. work force. The company expected to be profitable for fiscal 2000, and in fact earned $1.7 million on revenue of $609.4 million. During the year the company restructured its executive management. Gerald Diamond remained as chairman and CEO. His son, Mark Diamond, was promoted from executive vice-president to president and chief operating officer (COO).

SED's return to profitability in 2000 was attributed to a new domestic strategy and improved sales and profits in Latin America, which was served by SED offices in Brazil, Argentina, Colombia, and Puerto Rico. The new domestic strategy involved focusing on increasing gross profit margins, reducing inventory, increasing inventory turnover, lowering bank borrowings, and reducing credit losses. SED remained optimistic it would also be profitable in 2001, and for the first two quarters of fiscal 2001 the company reported a modest profit. Chairman and CEO Gerald Diamond noted that SED was in the process of changing its product mix, re-evaluating its lines of business, and concentrating on areas of higher potential profit.

Principal Subsidiaries

Magna Distribuidora Ltda. (Brazil); Intermaco S.R.L. (Argentina); SED International de Colombia; SED International do Brasil (Brazil).

Principal Divisions

United States; Latin America.

Principal Competitors

CHS Electronics, Inc.; MCSi, Inc.; Ingram Micro Inc.; Tech Data Corp.; Merisel Inc.; Brightpoint Inc.; Cellstar Corp.

Further Reading

Allison, David, "Short-Term Manager Diamond Turns Southern Around," *Atlanta Business Chronicle,* September 17, 1990, p. 3A.
Campbell, Scott, "Bottom Line: Blames Slumping Hard-Drive Sales," *Computer Reseller News,* August 31, 1998, p. 63.
——, "Reeling from Loss, SED Eyes Return to Profitable Business," *Computer Reseller News,* May 24, 1999, p. 57.
——, "SED: Profitability Road Map," *Computer Reseller News,* November 9, 1998, p. 63.
——, "SED Shuffles Corporate Deck," *Computer Reseller News,* September 28, 1998, p. 79.
——, "SED, Solectron Form White-Box Bond," *Computer Reseller News,* November 16, 1998, p. 260.
——, "Small Distributors Seek New Means of Survival," *Computer Reseller News,* October 11, 1999, p. 67.
Coleman, Zach, "Computer Distributor Finds Gold in Latin America," *Atlanta Business Chronicle,* March 27, 1998, p. 7A.
Green, Stephanie, "SED's 1Q Earnings Up 75 Percent," *Computer Reseller News,* November 22, 1999, p. 60.
Pereira, Pedro, "Current PC Market Slump Could Send the Channel Reeling," *Computer Reseller News,* August 3, 1998, p. 53.
——, "How to Not Succeed in Business Despite Really Trying," *Computer Reseller News,* July 14, 1997, p. 129.
——, "Irreconcilable Differences: GBC, Southern Electronics Terminate Negotiations," *Computer Reseller News,* June 5, 1995, p. 185.
——, "SED Seeks to Shift Globelle Acquisition into High Gear," *Computer Reseller News,* July 14, 1997, p. 130.
"SED Latin America Acquisition," *Computer Reseller News,* December 21, 1998, p. 59.
"SED Projects Bigger 3Q Loss," *Computer Reseller News,* March 22, 1999, p. 6.
Sharpe, Anita, "Drexel Cashing Out of Southern Electronics," *Atlanta Business Chronicle,* November 11, 1991, p. 20.
"Southern Electronics Corp.," *Atlanta Business Chronicle,* December 16, 1991, p. 34A.
"Southern Electronics Corp.," *CDA-Investnet Insiders' Chronicle,* May 10, 1993, p. 11.

—David P. Bianco

Shells Seafood Restaurants, Inc.

16313 North Dale Mabry Highway
Tampa, Florida 33618-1326
U.S.A.
Telephone: (813) 961-0944
Fax: (813) 960-8539
Web site: http://www.shellsseafood.com

Public Company
Incorporated: 1993
Employees: 2,200
Sales: $90.4 million (2000)
Stock Exchanges: Over the Counter (OTC)
Ticker Symbol: SHLL
NAIC: 72211 Full-Service Restaurants; 55112 Offices of Other Holding Companies

Tampa-based Shells Seafood Restaurants, Inc. is the holding company for a chain of full-service, casual-dinning seafood restaurants which operate under the Shells name. As of March 2001, the company operated or managed 39 restaurants, most of which were located in Florida, with others located in Kentucky and Ohio. Maintaining a broad, family and young-adult appeal, the company's restaurants offer moderately priced entrees, including fresh fish, shrimp, oysters, scallops, clams, crab, and lobster plates. They also offer daily specials, an array of appetizers, pasta and other side dishes, and desserts. To assure Shells' name recognition and benefit from customer loyalty, the company developed a prototypical image for its restaurants. They are identified by an exterior name and logo sign and a standardized interior color scheme and design. They are also decorated with tropical island motifs and feature bright colors, cheerful signs, and a casual atmosphere consistent with the company's commitment to promoting a relaxed and fun dining experience. Incorporated in 1993, Shells was reorganized and reincorporated as a public company in1996. Between them, Frederick Adler, chairman, and William Hattaway, former CEO and president, own about 39 percent of the business.

1985–91: Origins and Quick Expansion

Shells Seafood Restaurants Inc. emerged from the startup of a single restaurant in Madeira Beach, Florida, in the mid-1980s. Its founder was Swiss-born John Christen, who had behind him years of restaurant experience. Earlier, starting in 1971, he had built a chain of Brewmaster steak houses, which, by the time he sold it in 1983, had expanded to 13 units, all located in the Tampa Bay area. Brewmaster was one of the first casual-diner's pub-style steak houses. It was also the first Florida restaurant to feature a salad bar. Later, when he relinquished operational control of Shells, Christen would undertake the rebuilding of Brewmaster restaurants, using 1990s variations on his original ideas.

For a year before starting up Shells, under the Café Geneva label, Christen made gourmet salad dressing for grocery chains. Then, in 1985, he launched the Shells chain. He built it as a series of separate Chapter S corporations, all of which paid a management fee to Christen. Under his leadership, the chain began a bold expansion program, both in Florida and beyond. Before the recession began taking its toll in the early 1990s, the chain had grown to 28 restaurants, including units located in Atlanta, Mobile, Charlotte, Nashville, and New York. Outside of Florida, and at some places within, the restaurants struggled for profitability, barely sputtering along, and the economic downturn nationally did not help.

1992–93: Company Falters, Reorganizes, and Downsizes under Hattaway

In January 1992, 14 of the stockholder groups joined together, arranged a collective stock swap, and formed Shells Inc. Their idea was to consolidate the company's management and operations, making it more efficient and profitable. Shells Inc. still lumbered along with a heavy debt load, unable to obtain the funding it needed for further expansion. Moreover, its aggressive efforts to expand into markets outside Florida had proved almost fatal.

William Hattaway, a former executive with Red Lobster, bought into the Shells concept in 1993 and, as president and

Company Perspectives:

We are real seafood. Our mission is to become the favorite seafood restaurant in every neighborhood in which we operate. Real Seafood! A combination of tastes and flavors that takes you back to your last beach-side vacation, seafood that tastes so fresh you feel like you have to wipe the sea salt from your hair and the sand off your deck shoes. The sizzle of a fresh piece of fish being tossed on the grill, the aroma of a platter piled high with freshly steamed shrimp, the taste of real butter mixed with the hot sweet tender taste of king crab legs . . . Real Seafood!

CEO, with a 20 percent stake in the company, led its resurgence out of its financial doldrums. When he took over the reins of Shells, Hattaway brought 16 years of experience to the task and an enviable success rate for developing seafood concepts. At the time of Hattaway's departure from Red Lobster, it was owned by General Mills Restaurant Group and was the largest chain of dinner houses in the United States, with an estimated 625 units open at the end of 1993.

Under Chairman Christen, who stepped down at the end of 1992, later to undertake his revamping of Brewmaster, Shells had begun cutting back on its expansion plans and had also begun a major downsizing, something that Hattaway finished. When he started with Shells in February 1993, he closed three more restaurants, which reduced the size of the company's chain to just 10 restaurants, down from the one-time high of 28, and completely retreated into Florida. Between them, Christen and Hattaway closed down all the company's out-of-state operations and all of the Florida units that were not turning a profit.

Hattaway's plan called for the closing of all the smaller units (under 6,000 square feet) in the Shells chain in order to concentrate on the larger, higher volume restaurants at prime sites. The idea was to hack away the financial deadwood and then rebuild a more streamlined and more profitable chain, which Hattaway almost immediately started to do. The guiding principle was to rebuild as an established neighborhood restaurant with an identifiable name and, at the same time, centralize operational control to achieve a higher degree of efficiency.

Plans made in 1993 called for opening 25 new restaurants over the next two years, mainly in the Tampa, Orlando, and Miami areas. By September 1993, the chain was back up to 15 restaurants; however, two of the restaurants, located in Ocala and New Port Richey, operated under a licensing arrangement and were not owned by the company. As was the customary policy with the company, it continued to lease existing restaurant facilities and convert them into Shells restaurants, at an average conversion cost of about $300,000 per unit. Hattaway planned to take advantage of the fact that the economic slowdown of the late 1980s and early 1990s had left many vacant restaurant sites on the market.

In order to give the company a new identity and make it easier to get financing, Hattaway and his associates formed Shells Seafood Restaurants Inc. It was organized to manage the existing Shells restaurants and develop and manage the new units created under the expansion plans of Hattaway and his executive team. The newly reorganized company was bolstered by fresh venture capital, which allowed Hattaway to reduce Shells' debt by issuing preferred stock to the company's creditors.

1994–99: Going Public Despite Growing Pains

Although projections called for averaging a new opening each month during 1994, the company fell far short of that ambitious mark. It also continued to struggle for profitability. In fiscal 1994, with gross sales of $22.2 million, Shells lost $1.6 million. However, under Hattaway, the company had a renewed energy and improved efficiency. By December 1994, Shells Inc. was completely merged with Shells Seafood Restaurant Inc., technically becoming its subsidiary, and in 1995, although Shells was still in the red, the company's revenue rose to $28.6 million and its net loss dropped to $403,000.

The needed turnaround came in 1996, the year in which the company completed plans to go public and floated a $7.1 million initial public offering (IPO) on the NASDAQ Small-Cap market. By March 1996, just before its IPO, Shells either owned or operated 21 restaurants in Florida, ten of which were in the Tampa Bay area. In its prospectus, as of the end of 1995, the company reported a working capital deficit of $4.7 million, which the IPO was in part designed to offset. Funds raised via the stock sale were slated for opening additional restaurants, remodeling others, reducing debt service, installing point-of-service accounting systems, and providing working capital and corporate funds. The company hoped to obtain enough additional third-party financing to open 12 new restaurants in 1996, some at sites outside Florida. The company not only came close to its growth projections, it climbed into the black for the first time in years, netting a profit of $1.4 million on revenues of $39.8 million, a 39 percent increase over the previous year.

Although at the start of 1997 it had still not ventured beyond Florida, Shells had increased its owned or managed restaurants to 32. It also had plans to open up to another 12 within the year, with a focus on expanding into markets outside Florida. Accordingly, of the nine new restaurants that it did place in operation in 1997, seven were opened in Ohio and Kentucky, states in its targeted Midwest territory. The company's decision to expand into the Midwest markets was made in an effort to diversify and minimize the seasonal impact on the Florida market. Thus Shells continued its expansion in the Midwest the next year, when it opened ten new restaurants in that region, followed by one more in 1999. At the beginning of that year, Shells did close a restaurant, but it was one in Florida, located in the Mall of the Americas in Miami and one of a group-unit of six acquired in 1996.

As did the first attempt to establish Shells outside of Florida, the expansion efforts faltered when several of the restaurants opened in the new Midwest markets failed to establish an adequate customer base to make them profitable. The result was that, in 1999, despite attaining revenues of $95.2 million, the company realized a net income loss of $2.7 million. It was also plagued by a significant drop in the market value of its stock, which between 1997 and 1999 had dropped from a high of $14.75 per share to a low of $2.06.

Key Dates:

1985: John Christen founds Shells Seafood in Madeira Beach, Florida.
1992: Christen steps down as company chairman.
1993: William Hattaway becomes Shells' president and CEO, and the company is incorporated.
1996: Company is reincorporated as a public company and makes initial public offering on NASDAQ.
1997: Shells, seeking new markets, opens first restaurants outside Florida since closure of the last out-of-state units in 1993.
2000: NASDAQ delists Shells, and the company begins trading over the counter; Hattaway resigns as CEO as Midwest expansion strategy fails.
2001: David W. Head is named company president and CEO.

As it had in 1992, in 1999 the company began responding to its bottom-line woes by reining in its expansion. In September, it also began closing down restaurants in its new Midwest market, starting with an underperforming unit in Cincinnati that had just opened in February 1998.

2000 and Beyond: Entering a Retrenchment Period

The company pulled the plug on four more restaurants in 2000: one in Ohio, two in Illinois, and one in Florida. It also stipulated that it was reviewing the performance of its restaurants with an eye to closing more, primarily at locations outside Florida, and it put all plans for new units on hold. It opened none in 2000. Clearly, as it had done almost a decade earlier, the company was actively cutting back towards a core of rock-solid performers. Its principal efforts were going into its well-established Florida units. For example, in the last fiscal quarter of 2000, it completed the remodeling of six of its Florida restaurants. It also undertook some marketing improvements, including the revamping of its menu, which was done in November 2000. The return to a retrenching strategy also led to Hattaway's resignation as CEO—a step he took because he had been the chief architect of the company's nearly disastrous expansion into the Midwest market.

In the first three months of fiscal 2001, the company closed six more restaurants: one in Florida, three in Illinois, and two in Ohio. It also indicated that, as in 2000, it had no plans to open any new restaurants during the entire year. Then, in early April, the company announced that it was planning to shut down 16 more restaurants. It also announced that reorganization plans were also in the works, starting with changes at the top that had already been made. On April 2, Shells had named David W. Head both president and CEO, posts that had remained vacant since Hattaway had stepped down midway through 2000. Just prior to taking the positions with Shells, Head had been serving as president, COO, and partner of Le Carnassier, LLC, a franchisee of Red Robin International. Before that, he had been president and COO of Red River Barbeque and Grill as well as president and CEO of Houlihan's Restaurant Group.

There were also other executive changes, including the election of Phillip R. Chapman to the board chairmanship and a reduction in the administration support staff. Chapman replaced Frederick R. Adler, who stepped down but remained a director, as did Hattaway, who, like Adler, still held a significant share of the Shells ownership.

As the company admitted, fiscal 2000 and the first the quarter of 2001 were difficult periods. The performance of the company's Midwest restaurants fell way short of projected earning goals. Returning to its core business might well mean that Shells would once more completely withdraw from markets outside Florida. It was, in fact, negotiating a transfer of the operational control of its remaining midwestern units to an unaffiliated management business. For 2001 and the immediate beyond, expansion was a buried issue; Shells' focus would be on retrenchment and the revitalization its Florida restaurants.

Principal Competitors

Chefs International, Inc.; Darden Restaurants, Inc.; Flanigan's Enterprises, Inc.; Landry's Seafood Restaurants, Inc.

Further Reading

Clancy, Carole, "Shells Cooks Up Plans for $7M IPO," *Tampa Bay Business Journal*, March 8, 1996, p. 1.

Hayes, Jack, "Christen Updates Brewmaster for '90s," *Nation's Restaurant News*, April 24, 1995, p. 7.

——, "Rough Waters Send Shells to Regroup in Fla.," *Nation's Restaurant News*, March 28, 1994, p. 7.

Hundley, Kris, "Tampa-Based Shells Seafood Restaurants Inc. Back in the Swim of Profits," *Knight-Ridder/Tribune Business News*, February 12, 1997.

Peters, James, "Shells Fishes for Growth, Focuses on Florida after Midwest Expansion Stalls," *Nation's Restaurant News*, May 7, 2001, p. 8.

Smith, Katherine S., "Shells Ready for Florida Expansion," *Tampa Bay Business Journal*, September 10, 1993, p. 1.

—John W. Fiero

Skis Rossignol S.A.

B.P. 329
38509 Voiron Cedex
France
Telephone: (76) 66-65-65
Fax: (76) 65-67-51
Web site: http://www.skisrossignol.com

Public Company
Incorporated: 1972
Employees: 2,700
Sales: EUR 430 million (2001)
Stock Exchanges: Euronext Paris
Ticker Symbol: SR
NAIC: 339920 Sporting and Athletic Goods Manufacturing; 421910 Sporting and Recreational Goods and Supplies Wholesalers; 315228 Men's and Boy's Cut and Sew Other Outerwear Manufacturing; 315239 Women's and Girl's Cut and Sew Other Outerwear Manufacturing

Skis Rossignol S.A. is one of the world's premier manufacturers of ski equipment. Headquartered in Voiron, a small town in southeastern France, the company was among the first to make skis in France and was an early leader in ski technology and design. Its skis, for example, were used in the 1936 Winter Olympics, the first to include alpine ski events, and have since been worn by numerous Olympic and World Cup champions. By 2000, almost 40 percent of all downhill skis sold throughout the world were manufactured by Rossignol. The company's major markets are in Europe, Japan, and the United States. Since the 1970s, the company has diversified into new areas of ski equipment, first adding the manufacture of cross-country skis, then ski boots, poles, snowboards, bindings, accessories, and apparel. Rossignol also manufactures tennis rackets and golf clubs. While most of its products are sold under the Rossignol brand name, the company has expanded through the purchase of existing brands, such as Lange (boots) and Dynastar (skis).

1907: Sport Skiing Is Born in the French Alps

For thousands of years, skiing was a practical means of transportation in snowbound regions. In early Scandinavia, for example, hunters and soldiers used skis during the winter months. But it was not until the 20th century that skiing began to develop as a sport. Early events focused on cross-country skiing, but as skiers developed techniques, most notably the telemark turn, downhill events started. Compared with modern equipment, skis of this era were heavy and long, made of solid wood and measuring between eight and 14 feet.

Sport skiing first took hold in the vicinity of Grenoble, a town in the French Alps not far from the Italian border. Early sport skiers used equipment that was manufactured in Scandinavia, though these skis were not designed for conditions in the French Alps, which tended to be steeper and icier than slopes in Scandinavia. The military ski school in Briançon, southeast of Grenoble, introduced the first French-made downhill skis in 1906. By the next year, sport skiing was booming in France. Numerous ski events were held in the Alps, and French artisans joined in the production of skis to meet the demand. These new skis were generally made of ash, pine, or larch—woods chosen for their flexibility and resilience.

During this time, Abel Rossignol, a skiing enthusiast and wood craftsman, was the head of a wood turnery in Voiron, a town just northeast of Grenoble. The turnery, founded in 1901, produced wooden articles for the textile industry. In 1907, Rossignol decided to make his own pair of downhill skis, for which he used solid wood protected by a light-colored varnish. His skis took first prize in a contest sponsored by the Touring Club of France, and in 1911, bolstered by his success, Rossignol established a ''skis and sleds'' division of his company. Rossignol continued to make solid-wood skis for the next three decades with production reaching several hundred skis per year.

In the 1930s, France emerged as a skiing power, led by Emile Allais. At the 1936 Winter Olympics, held at Garmisch-Partenkirchen, Germany, Allais won the bronze medal in the alpine combined, and the following year at the world championships, he won the gold medal in all three alpine events, earning the title ''champion of the world.'' All his medals were won on

Company Perspectives:

Rossignol's wish is simple: to share with you our passion for the wonderful world of winter sports.

Rossignol skis. During this time, Allais codified his method of ski instruction, published in the book *Ski Français*.

In 1936 Rossignol hired Allais as its technical adviser and official tester, a position Allais used to help the company design some of the world's most advanced skis. The primary weakness of the company's skis was their solid-wood construction. Unless the wood had a uniform grain, for example, the ski would tend to warp during production, and even good solid-wood skis would begin to lose their shape with age. Some of Rossignol's competitors had already found a solution—a laminated, or layered, construction similar to plywood, with wood grains running in different directions—which made a lighter, more durable wooden ski. By using different types of wood and various patterns of lamination, manufacturers could determine the ski's flexibility and resilience. Although Rossignol did not originate this method, the company's first laminated ski, the Olympic 41, was an advance in design. Developed in 1941, the ski met with great success after World War II, carrying such racers as Henri Oreiller (1948) and Ottmar Schneider (1952) to Olympic victories. Production of the ski at Rossignol's Voiron factory rocketed to several thousand per year by 1951.

1950s: Metal Skis Are Introduced

Laminated skis presented problems with maintenance and durability. Like all wooden skis, they absorbed water and were easily damaged, and to slide smoothly across the snow, they needed to be waxed regularly. Some manufacturers began to experiment with other materials, especially metal. Metal skis would prove to be more durable, more resilient, and faster than wooden skis. The first successful metal ski was made by American aviation engineer Howard Head. Using the sandwich-type design found on aircraft, Head placed two strips of aluminum (at the top and bottom of the ski) around a plywood core, added a plastic bottom, and attached an exceptionally hard metal edge to improve control. Head skis were an immediate hit, especially among recreational skiers, when they were introduced in the early 1950s.

Allais, who tested an early pair of Head skis in the United States, was impressed with their handling in soft snow and powder, but he found them "totally unsuited" for the hard-packed snow of competitive skiing. Even so, he brought several pairs of Head skis back to France, where he and Rossignol started working to come up with their own design. One of Rossignol's first metal skis, the Allais 60, earned worldwide attention when Frenchman Jean Vuarnet wore a pair when he won the men's downhill event at the 1960 Winter Olympics, held at Squaw Valley, California. The Allais 60 was the first metal ski used to win an Olympic gold medal. Allais later observed that the ski's "characteristics, notably its ability to grip [the snow], were much superior to the wooden skis still used during this time." Despite such early success, the Allais 60 and other metal skis would prove to be merely a bridge in the transition from wooden skis to those made from fiberglass and other synthetic materials, which were both lighter and more resilient than wood or metal.

At the same time that Rossignol was embarking on a program to develop new technology, the company was undergoing significant change. In the mid-1950s, Rossignol was organized into two main activities: ski manufacture and the production of wooden articles for the textile industry. The textile industry was in decline, putting a severe financial strain on Rossignol. In order to save the company, Allais approached his friend Laurent Boix-Vives, a 29-year-old French businessman, who was the owner of Société des Téléskis de Moriond, a small ski-lift company in Courchevel, a town northeast of Grenoble. Boix-Vives agreed to purchase Rossignol for $50,000. One of his first decisions, in 1956, was to drop the company's textile operations (Rossignol's original line of business) and to focus solely on ski production. Under Boix-Vives's guidance, as gérant (managing director, 1956–1960) and then as président-directeur général (from 1960), the company was transformed from a small factory producing several thousand skis per year to a multinational corporation with subsidiaries in several countries. By 1972, when the company was incorporated as Skis Rossignol S.A., Rossignol had become the world's best-selling brand of ski, a position it continued to hold into the next century.

Rossignol's phenomenal growth was aided by several external factors, including the increased popularity of skiing in the 1960s and 1970s, especially in the United States. In 1973, Rossignol established a subsidiary in the United States, Rossignol Ski Company, Inc., in Williston, Vermont, and manufactured skis in that state from 1973 to 1984. Rossignol also gained market share through its investment in research and development, which allowed it to manufacture some of the most advanced ski equipment in the world.

Rossignol's first truly successful fiberglass ski was the Strato, introduced in the mid-1960s. It was actually made of a complex layering of various materials, including a plastic called acrylonitrile butadien styrene (ABS), which formed the top layer and the side walls of the ski. The Strato, like previous Rossignol skis, proved popular among world-class racers. At the 1968 Winter Olympics, held in Grenoble (near the Voiron factory), the Strato was worn by five medalists, including Canadian Nancy Greene, winner of the giant slalom. By this time, the company also was producing skis under the name Dynastar, a brand it bought in 1967.

1970s: Technological Evolution Continues

In the early 1970s, Rossignol introduced its first skis made without any wood. These featured a light-density polyurethane core, which not only was cheaper than wood but also made the ski more comfortable. Rossignol's racing skis, including the ROC and the ST, featured the polyurethane core and, as expected, performed exceptionally well in international competition. For example, at the 1976 Olympic games at Innsbruck, Austria, Rossignol's plastic-core skis were worn by six medalists, twice as many as the nearest competing brand.

Over the next two decades, Rossignol spent millions of dollars refining the design of its plastic-based skis. Performance

Key Dates:

1907: Abel Rossignol sets up a small company in Voiron specializing in wooden items for the textile industry and envisions its first all-wood alpine skis.
1911: Rossignol creates a skis branch in his company.
1942: Rossignol patents the first laminated wood ski.
1956: With the textiles market shrinking, Laurent Boix-Vives takes over Skis Rossignol and concentrates the company's efforts on the more lucrative ski business.
1957: The first metallic ski is developed.
1961: A fiberglass ski is developed. Rossignol products are launched in foreign markets.
1972: Rossignol becomes the world leader for ski manufacturing.
1977: The company launches its first range of products in the summer sports field.
1989: Rossignol acquires the Lange company, a leader in ski boots for racing.
1993: Rossignol acquires the Look company, which is famous for ski bindings.
1995–1998: The company becomes the world leader in manufacturing of winter sports equipment and enters the promising markets of snowboards, parabolic skis, and in-line skates.
2000: Rossignol launches a line of winter sports apparel in Europe and the United States.

and comfort were enhanced, for example, by Rossignol's patented Vibration Absorbing System (VAS), introduced in 1981. Made with an inner layer of steel wire and other materials, VAS was designed to reduce harmful vibration, while preserving vibration that improved ski performance and speed. In 1984, a complementary ''external'' VAS was introduced, comprising a light alloy stress plate attached to the top of the ski. Another notable improvement was the ''Rossitop,'' introduced in 1992, which was an eight-millimeter-thick layer of transparent plastic that protected the ski's cosmetics.

Also important to the company's success was its decision to produce other types of ski equipment. Its first major diversification was in 1971, when the company introduced a Rossignol brand of cross-country skis. These skis, manufactured in Sweden, were made entirely of wood, as were many cross-country skis at the time. But in 1974 the Voiron factory began making a fiberglass model. Cross-country skiing grew increasingly popular during the 1970s, and in 1976, Rossignol established a cross-country division. In 1987, it introduced its ''System Concept'' line of cross-country skis, boots, and bindings, which were specifically designed to work together. That year, Rossignol also developed an air-injection method that produced exceptionally lightweight, durable cross-country skis.

1980s: Diversification Begins

Though Rossignol was the world's largest manufacturer of downhill skis, the company did not have a line of downhill ski boots until 1989, when it purchased Lange, a leading brand of ski boots since 1965. Rossignol gained much from Lange's existing research and development program. In the 1980s, Lange had been working on a compromise between the two most popular types of ski boots. The first—pioneered by Lange's founder Bob Lange of Dubuque, Iowa—was an all-plastic boot fitted with a series of buckles across the front. Exceptionally stiff, this boot efficiently translated body movement to the ski and was especially popular among competitive racers. The second, introduced in the early 1970s, was an all-plastic rear-entry model, in which the back of the boot hinged off to provide easy access for the foot. The rear-entry boot was more convenient and comfortable than front-buckle models, though its performance was generally regarded as inferior. The compromise, introduced in 1989 under both the Lange and Rossignol brand names, was the MID line of ski boots. These were front-buckle boots with a unique hinge system that allowed the top to open wider, thus making them easier to put on. The traditional front-buckle design continued to be used for many Rossignol and Lange boots, especially for high-performance models.

1990s: Remaining Competitive

As early as 1991, Rossignol was testing prototypes of a new downhill ski binding, which was the only major piece of ski equipment it did not yet manufacture. It soon became clear, however, that developing and marketing a new binding would be more expensive than buying an existing brand. Thus, in 1994 Rossignol purchased two well-known brands of ski bindings, Look and Geze, and began to sell bindings under the Rossignol and Look brand names. By the end of the 1990s, the company had solidified about 25 percent of the world market in ski bindings.

By the early 1990s, Rossignol was also making a variety of other ski equipment, including ski poles and accessories such as bags, gloves, socks, shirts, sweaters, and hats. By this time, the company had diversified outside the ski industry. In 1977, it had introduced a line of Rossignol tennis rackets, and, in 1990, Rossignol Ski Company purchased Roger Cleveland Golf Company of Paramount, California.

In the 1990s, a number of variables, such as changes in worldwide snow conditions, economic recessions (especially in Japan), and exchange-rate fluctuations between the French franc and the currencies of its major markets caused a sharp decline in Rossignol's sales. At the time this industry-wide crisis occurred, Rossignol generated more than 80 percent of its sales outside of France. Declining skis sales during the 1990s can also be attributed to the explosion of interest in new and extreme winter sports, especially snowboarding, which appealed greatly to the youth market. Rossignol entered this market by purchasing already-established snowboarding companies such as Original Sin and Emery (purchased in 1999). Rossignol restructured in 1998 and outfitted its Spanish factory to become the industry's largest producer of snowboards.

By the mid-90s, after several years of declining sales of downhill skis (industry sales had dropped 40 percent), the development of parabolic (or shaped skis) revitalized the industry. The shaped skis had a slim hourglass shape, narrow in the middle with a fat tip and a wide tail. This allowed for more stability not only for beginners, but for advanced skiers as well. Rossignol looked to Olympic champion Picabo Street to design its Peak skis, which were bestsellers in the late 1990s. According to *Time* magazine, by 1998 (only four years after their introduction by Elan-Monark) parabolic skis accounted for more than 80 percent of alpine ski sales, and had increased overall ski sales from the previous year by a whopping 82 percent.

Fashionable apparel (especially for snowboarders) became a huge moneymaker in the late 1990s for winter sports clothing manufacturers. After several years of conducting worldwide focus groups on consumer's opinions, Rossignol showed its first line of name-brand winter sports apparel in 2000. While the clothing designs were still under development in 1997, Jeanne-Marie Gund, vice president of communications and advertising, told *WWD* magazine, ''The big message is that the line isn't developed by a bunch of office designers sitting in front of computers all day. We're talking to snowboarders who are using our products 200 days a year.''

By the end of the 20th century, Skis Rossignol S.A. was the world's dominant manufacturer of ski equipment. In 2000, the company sold about 1.2 million pairs of Rossignol and Dynastar alpine skis, or nearly 40 percent of the world's ski category, putting them far ahead of their numerous competitors, such as Head, K2, Elan, Atomic, Salomon, and Pre. The company also had yearly sales in 2000 of some 720,000 pairs of boots (Rossignol and Lange), 900,000 pairs of ski bindings (Rossignol and Look), 91,000 pairs of cross-country skis (Rossignol), and 180,000 snowboards (several brands).

Despite the ever-changing winter sports equipment marketplace, Skis Rossignol S.A. has maintained it dominance. As the world's leading producer of skis, Rossignol has enjoyed almost universal name recognition among skiers—a brand familiarity that has helped the company launch into new lucrative winter sports. The Rossignol name, prominently marked on skis and other equipment, can be seen on almost any ski slope in the world. Many ski shops rent the company's products, thus introducing a large number of potential customers to the Rossignol brands. Its reputation for quality also has been maintained through the sponsorship of top skiers and snowboarders, many of whom have won Olympic and World Cup races, as well as other international competitions using Rossignol equipment.

Principal Divisions

Alpine Skiing, Snowboard, Nordic, Roller Skates and Tennis, Golf, Textiles and Collections.

Principal Subsidiaries

Skis Dynastar S.A. (France); Look Fixations S.A.; Emery S.A.; Lange International S.A. (Switzerland); Rossignol Lange SpA (Italy); Rossignol Ski Poles SpA (Italy); Rossignol Ski AG (Switzerland); Rossignol Ski Deutschland GmbH (Germany); Skis Rossignol de Espana S.A. (Spain); Rossignol Ski Company, Inc. (U.S.); Roger Cleveland Golf Company (U.S.).

Principal Competitors

adidas-Salomon; K2; Rollerblade; Burton Snowboards.

Further Reading

Bays, Ted, *Nine Thousand Years of Skis: Norwegian Wood to French Plastic*, Ishpeming, Mich.: National Ski Hall of Fame, 1990.

Beilinson, Jerry, ''Rossignol: Race Support Pays Off in Olympics,'' *Skiing Trade News*, April 1992, p. 6.

Feitelberg, Rosemary, ''Activewear Veterans: Comeback Kids,'' *WWD*, July 3, 1997, p. 8.

——, ''Winter Sports Gets a Lift,'' WWD, February 1, 2001, p. 6.

Frey, Eric, ''Sunshine For Ski Makers,'' *The Financial Times*, February 7, 2001, p. 36.

''Going Downhill: Rossignol's Image Takes a Spill,'' *Time*, February 23, 1987, p. 68.

Marchant, Valerie, ''The Cool Shapes for Skiing,'' *Time*, Dec 28, 1997, p. 114.

Meader, Cliff, ''In 95: Look to Dynastar, Geze to Rossi,'' *Skiing Trade News*, October 1994, p. 12.

——, ''Second Year Is First Year for Full Rossi Boot Line,'' *Skiing Trade News*, March 1990, p. 40.

''France's Ski Industry: No Business like Snow Business,'' *The Economist*, March 3, 1990, p. 65.

Pachod, Patrick, ''Laurent Boix-Vives Discloses Rossignol's Future Path,'' *Skiing Trade News*, February 1991, p. 19.

Regard sur 50 ans d'innovation dans le ski, Voiron, France: Skis Rossignol S.A., 1993.

''Skis Rossignol: Company Report,'' FT Analysis Report, Thomson Financial Networks Inc., 1993.

Tanler, Bill, ''Ski Production Turns to the Fewer, the Bigger,'' *Skiing Trade News*, October 1993, p. 30.

—Thomas Riggs
—update: Linda M. Gwilym

SmartForce PLC

900 Chesapeake Drive
Redwood City, California 94063
U.S.A.
Telephone: (888) 395-0014
Fax: (888) 395-0015
Web site: http://www.smartforce.com

Public Company
Incorporated: 1984
Employees: 1,684 (est.)
Sales: $168.2 million (2000 est.)
Stock Exchanges: NASDAQ
Ticker Symbol: SMTF
NAIC: 611710 Educational Support Services

Based in Redwood City, California, SmartForce PLC is the largest online training company in the world. The company develops and sells interactive, Web-based educational and training courses that are designed to enrich and empower a company's employees, customers, suppliers, distributors and other business partners. Course offerings help develop knowledge and skills in a variety of subjects, including information technology (IT), business and some professional trades. SmartForce also complements its courses with an online mentoring program, online seminars, training assessment tools, and administrative and reporting tools. And with its latest e-learning technology, the company makes it easy for clients to use SmartForce software to create courses. Clients include 2,500 of the world's largest companies, government agencies and other organizations, with most of its business derived from U.S.-based multinationals. The company has operations in 35 countries and courseware translated into several languages. SmartForce is the first and only profitable, publicly-traded company devoted to online training, and, in 2000, ranked among the top one percent of the world's best performing companies, as rated by Deloitte Touche Tohmatsu.

Irish Beginnings

SmartForce was established as CBT Systems and based in Dublin, Ireland. Founded in 1984 by Pat McDonagh and stockbroker Dermot Desmond, CBT Systems was one of the pioneers among Irish software firms expanding overseas. McDonagh was a primary schoolteacher in the early 1970s, and later sold encyclopedias and worked in sales with Rank Xerox and ICL. After working for Deltax, a U.S. education software company, he took out a $15,000 loan to set up CBT Systems. Desmond left the company one year after it was founded. McDonagh stayed on, and 12 years later, made $45 million after CBT Systems debuted on the NASDAQ.

CBT Systems counted on businesses seeking alternatives to classroom-based instruction for their workforce training needs. As companies become more global, time and location constraints make deploying only classroom-based training less feasible. As a result, companies were increasingly opting for computer-based training for employees. Although CBT Systems originally developed video-based training for IBM mainframe environments, it quickly shifted its focus to client-server technologies and steadily built its business on packaged educational software on diskettes and CD-ROMs. Courseware topics at the time covered information technology (IT) subjects such as back-office technical certification and desktop applications training. In the 1980s, CBT Systems could rely on developing courseware strictly for an IT audience, because IT professionals adopted computer-based training early. When computer-based training became more prevalent, the company expanded its curriculum to cover non-IT topics.

Phenomenal Growth and Expansion

CBT Systems had focused on serving Irish companies until 1987, when Bill McCabe joined the company and helped it expand its business to Britain and the United States. During his tenure as Chief Executive Officer, CBT Systems grew into the largest interactive educational software company in the world. In 1992, the company's sales totaled $6.1 million. That went up to $8.8 million the next year, and in 1994, sales had already reached $19.3 million. During that period, the company moved

Company Perspectives:

At SmartForce—formerly CBT Systems—we've made a name for ourselves as the largest e-learning company in the world today, leading the professional education market into the Internet Age through e-learning—a fundamentally faster and better way to learn. Changing our company's name to SmartForce was a dramatic step taken to demonstrate to our customers and the industry our continual commitment to helping organizations create a smarter workforce—essentially a ''smart force'' that thrives in the new economy. Simply put, SmartForce is nothing short of the reinvention of learning for the Internet Age, with e-learning empowering individual learners and enabling enterprises to gain a competitive advantage in today's ever-changing business world.

from a loss of $410,000 to profits of $2.67 million. Amid such positive developments, the company went public on NASDAQ in April 1995, making it the first Irish technology company to take this path.

By 1995, 70 percent of CBT System's business came from the U.S. Soon after it went public, CBT Systems went on to secure its position in the U.S. market with a handful of major deals and moving its headquarters to Redwood City, California. It signed its first agreement with Microsoft Corporation, to develop interactive, educational software for the Microsoft Certified Professional (MCP) program. Also, the company signed a contract with Manpower, Inc., the world's largest staffing organization at the time, to provide 160 interactive educational training courses for its technical services employees. Another major deal was signed with Oracle to design and develop courseware for the Oracle Developer and Database Administrator Curricula.

By the mid-1990s, CBT Systems had moved into networked offerings and some forms of Web-based training. In December 1996, CBT Systems launched CBT Web, which enabled customers to deploy CBT System's entire library of interactive training software titles over a corporate intranet. This marked the first time that users were not limited to a local area network and could access CBT System's courseware from anywhere in the world. Also, CBT Systems acquired scholars.com, which was the leader in Internet-based training, having developed an innovative mentoring service that made learning advisors accessible by students 12 hours each day, seven days per week, via online chats, e-mail, and newsgroups.

In late 1996, McCabe stepped down as CEO, but remained chairman of CBT System's board of directors. Ex-Apple Computer executive James Buckley took over as CEO, and by 1997, CBT Systems had secured 11 strategic partnership agreements with software groups and had nearly doubled its research and development efforts. In the first quarter of 1997, CBT Systems created an education sales group to address the growing training and education needs in universities, community colleges, and primary and secondary schools. In 1998, Buckley replaced McCabe as chairman of the board of directors, and Greg Priest was named CEO. CBT Systems had acquired Knowledge Well, a company that was a leader in developing interactive educational software for non-IT business and education subjects.

Though CBT Systems had made significant investments to try to capture non-IT markets, it did not lose any ground in the corporate IT market. Corporations were expected to pour an estimated $21.5 billion into technical training in 1998, according to International Data Corp (IDC). By 1998, CBT Systems had expanded internationally by acquiring its distributors in Germany, Canada, Australia, the Middle East, India, Belgium, Luxembourg, and the Netherlands. CBT System's most popular IT courseware was delivered in 191 foreign language versions, primarily French and German. The company added Japanese, Portuguese, Italian, and Spanish to its portfolio of translated titles. Overall, more than 300 titles were translated into various languages.

Redefining a Company—and an Industry

By the end of 1998, CBT Systems had established itself as the world leader in computer-based training, but during 1999, it needed to do much more to secure its leadership. CBT Systems extended its market reach, and increased its course offerings and launched a bold new Web-based training solution.

In May 1999, CBT Systems launched CBTNow, an e-commerce catalog of more than 900 course titles. Individuals were now able to directly purchase course titles. In that same month, CBT Systems launched cbt.community, an innovative, Web-based virtual community, rich in up-to-the-minute educational resources and information, in which learners can interact with each other and with experts in real time. In October 1999, CBT Systems changed its name to SmartForce, signifying another major pioneering shift—this time, to a completely Web-based subscription business. The flagship product was called My SmartForce, a completely Web-based, SmartForce-hosted environment that clients could access via the Internet at smartforce.com.

Developed from scratch, the new e-learning solution was designed to incorporate all the benefits of Web-based training and classroom methods. My SmartForce was conceived as an online destination for workers to go for all of their knowledge needs, and offered a seamless package of learning activities that covered four major learning categories: instruction, collaboration, practice and assessment. Instructional activities included courses, seminars, workshops, articles and white papers. Students could collaborate by accessing live workshops and seminars, meetings, virtual classrooms, one-on-one mentoring sessions, informal chats, threaded discussions and e-mail interaction. Students could apply what they had learned by participating in workshops, task-based simulations, strategy exercises, business modeling simulations and situational exercises. A number of assessment tools were made available: performance-based assessments, proficiency assessments, exam preparation tests, online certification tools and secure e-testing. One of the major, new offerings through My SmartForce was one-to-one online mentoring. About 200 mentors were available to students around the clock to help them set up courses, solve problems, motivate them, and make suggestions. By the end of 2000, the company had moved nearly all of its course offerings to the new platform.

The company's shift to the new My SmartForce e-learning solution signified how technology, content, and services were

Key Dates:

1984: CBT Systems is founded in Dublin, Ireland.
1987: New CEO Bill McCabe begins the company's global expansion.
1995: CBT Systems debuts on NASDAQ.
1996: The company launches CBT Web for corporate intranets.
1999: CBT Systems becomes SmartForce and launches its flagship Web-based solution.
2000: SmartForce launches e3 technology for customizable Web-based training.
2000: Company achieves profitability ahead of schedule.
2001: SmartForce signs 100th million-dollar agreement.

equally key to SmartForce's robust solutions and continued success—it was the successful manifestation of a trend toward highly manageable component-style approaches to learning, with the Web as key to the delivery. The speed and remarkably sophisticated nature of SmartForce's transformation could easily be attributed to the size and agility of its research and development operation. Although SmartForce moved its headquarters to the United States, research and development remained in Dublin. With more than 500 content development professionals on staff, the facility was the largest in-house courseware development center in the world. Led by educational instructors, each team consisted of expert instructional designers, writers, editors, and information systems specialists.

Although SmartForce's bread-and-butter subjects had always been IT-oriented, which still made up about 80 percent of all its subject areas, it also expanded into other critical areas such as business, soft skills, and some professional trades, such as engineering, accounting, and law. Tom Barron, of *Learning Circuits* observed, "In many ways, the success of IT e-learning has paved the way for this broader adoption of technology for non-technical skills. Having proved its worth to many CEOs in 'upskilling' technical staff quickly, more executives are approving wider rollouts of the learning medium to non-technical staff. And as technical staff increasingly find themselves in roles that call for business knowledge, they, too, become targets for soft-skills training." Some of the non-technical business topics that SmartForce came to offer were project management, interpersonal skills, sales training, and other forms of employee orientation. By forging new alliances with business simulation developer Strategic Management Group (SMG) in 2000 and classroom-based soft-skills provider Provant in 2001, SmartForce was poised to offer even more learning modules for non-technical skills development.

SmartForce's Asia-Pacific general manager, Brian Kelly, explains that the company is looking to grow well beyond its IT roots: "We're dipping our toes into the healthcare industry now, too, at least in the U.S. healthcare and banking and finance are massive untapped markets for training. Same with e-business—we're going in there in a big way at the moment. Obviously, there's a huge demand." SmartForce launched its e-Business product portfolio in November 2000. The broadest and most comprehensive set of its e-Learning offerings, SmartForce's e-business portfolio was designed to help companies transform their traditional businesses into e-businesses. It covers both the technical and the business aspects of Internet marketing, e-procurement, e-CRM, Internet security, enterprise applications development, Internetworking, Web site design, and Web development.

By November 2000, SmartForce unveiled the next-generation "e3" technology that would drive the e-learning solution in a way that was faster and completely customizable. Now, not only did SmartForce launch a customizable product that could offer almost everything a person could need at work, it also offered it in a way so that clients did not have to invest in the SmartForce infrastructure, or in the risky venture of integrating online learning courses with their own intranets.

SmartForce's shift to Web-based training wasn't easy—the company reported losses in the first three quarters of 2000. However, many believe it was a short-term adjustment, because SmartForce reached profitability in the fourth quarter of 2000, one quarter ahead of schedule. Also by that year's end, the company had a backlog of business totaling $357 million. Developing networked and Web-based courses proved to be a good move for SmartForce—by 2001, roughly 60 percent of its clients put SmartForce's courses on their intranets. And it might have been only the beginning of a significant trend. In 2000, industry publication *IDC* estimated that $19.5 billion was spent on corporate training, with roughly 11 percent going to Web-based training. And of the $29.3 billion that was projected to be spent on training in 2003, an estimated 40 percent was expected to be Web-based. SmartForce led and enabled this trend by quickly developing powerful tools that make e-learning cost-effective, convenient, and easy to use.

Principal Competitors

Aris; Canterbury Consulting; click2learn.com; DigitalThink; Docent Inc; EarthWeb; Educational Video Conferencing; Element K; Futuremedia; Global Knowledge; Harcourt General; kenexa; Knowledge Universe; Learn2.com; Learning Tree; MindLeaders.com; New Horizons Worldwide; O'Reilly & Associates; ProsoftTraining; SkillSoft; VCampus.

Further Reading

Barron, Tom, "Trend Watch: E-Learning Goes Soft," *Learning Circuits*, January, 2001.

——, "Trend Watch: New Price Models of E-Learning," *Learning Circuits*, October, 2000.

Bass, Jeremy, "SmartForce Sets Fast Learning Pace," *Financial Review*, February 7, 2001.

Brown, Judy, "Training in Bite-Size Pieces Can Save Big Chunks of Time," *eWeek*, May 9, 2001.

Carlton, Jim and Don Clark, "Teaching Tech Pays Off for Training Firms: Companies are Pumping Billions into Technical Training," *The Ottawa Citizen*, March 5, 1998, p. G7.

"CBT Expands to Succeed in New Markets," *The Irish Times*, July 14, 1995, p. 15.

"CBT Names Ex Apple Boss as President," *The Irish Times*, August 27, 1996, p. 15.

"CBT Systems," *Microsoft Office User Specialist Newsletter*, August 1, 1998.

Dobbs, Kevin, ''What Price is Right? Looking for Solid, Bottom-Line Price Comparisons Among E-Learning Vendors? Forget About It,'' *OnlineLearning*, March 2001.

Dutton, Gail, ''Web Conferences Go Far to Save on Travel, Training,'' *Government Computer News*, February 5, 2001.

Emery, Gail Repsher, ''Job Training Expenditures Dropped in '99,'' *Washington Technology*, April 16, 2001, p. 38.

Faden, Mike, ''Get Ready for New Training Push: E-Business: Courses Teach Underlying Concepts to a Wide Cross-Section of Employees,'' *InformationWeek*, November 13, 2000.

Fister, Sarah, ''A Hub for Learning: Will Web-Based Training Sites Be Replaced by Knowledge Hubs for Specific Audiences?,'' *Inside Technology Training*, January 2000.

——, ''Getting a Good Start: Even the Best Web-Based Training Program Can Fail If Learners Aren't Prepared for the Experience,'' *OnlineLearning*, March 2000.

Fox, Loren, ''A Quick Study in E-Learning: SmartForce's New Web-Based Model Is Not Yet the Teacher's Pet,'' *Business 2.0*, March 26, 2001.

Goodridge, Elisabeth, ''Online-Training Market Sees More Consolidation,'' *InformationWeek*, April 16, 2001.

Guthrie, Peter, ''A Learning Experience: Staff Training Comes to the Desktop,'' *Business 2.0*, February 10, 2001.

Keena, Colm, ''Four Class Action Suits Issued in US Against CBT, Company Refuses Comment,'' *The Irish Times*, October 6, 1998, p. 17.

MacCarthaigh, Sean, ''CBT Executives Step Down After Share Collapse, Former Chairman and Chief Executive Bill McCabe Returns,'' *The Irish Times*, October 2, 1998, p. 50.

Margolis, Jason, ''SmartForce Leads Net-Based Learning,'' *CBS MarketWatch*, March 13, 2001.

McGrath, Brendan, ''Irish Software Group's Flotation in US Proves a Resounding Success,'' *The Irish Times*, April 15, 1995, p. 14.

Mingall, Sandra, ''Great Course, But Will They Bite?,'' *e-Xchange*, February 5, 2001.

Murdoch, Bill, ''Is Takeover a Good or Bad Deal for CBT?,'' *The Irish Times*, June 14, 1999, p. 24.

O'Dea, Clare,''Software Entrepreneur with Roots in the Land,'' *The Irish Times*, March 11, 2000.

Oliver, Emmet, ''Focus on Education Helps Boost Profits at Irish-Based Firm,'' *The Irish Times*, October 23, 1997, p. 19.

''Pioneer Among Software Firms,'' *The Irish Times*, September 29, 1998, p. 16.

Rosenberg, Marc Jeffrey, *E-Learning: Strategies for Delivering Knowledge in the Digital Age*, New York: McGraw Hill, 2001.

—Heidi Wrightsman

Smithfield Foods, Inc.

200 Commerce Street
Smithfield, Virginia 23430
U.S.A.
Telephone: (757) 365-3000
Fax: (757) 365-3017
Web site: http://www.smithfieldfoods.com

Public Company
Incorporated: 1936 as Smithfield Packing Company
Employees: 36,000
Sales: $5.15 billion (2000)
Stock Exchanges: New York
Ticker Symbol: SFD
NAIC: 112210 Hog and Pig Farming; 112990 All Other Animal Production

Smithfield Foods, Inc. is the world's largest pork processor, with fiscal 2000 production of 6 billion pounds of fresh pork and processed meats. It is also the world's largest hog producer (almost 12 million hogs annually). As a holding company, Smithfield Foods conducts its business through two groups, the meat-processing group and the hog-production group, each made up of a number of subsidiaries. In addition to North Carolina, where it operates the world's largest hog-processing operation, the company operates industrial pig farms in ten states. Known as a leader in vertically integrated pork processing since 1987, Smithfield raises, slaughters, and processes meat. Its line of hams, hot dogs, bacon, sausage, and deli and luncheon meats is marketed wholesale, under private labels, and under such brand-name labels as Smithfield, Esskay, Gwaltney, Luter's, Jamestown, and Patrick Cudahy. Beginning in 1998 Smithfield expands beyond the United States with acquisitions in Canada, France, and Poland.

1936 to 1969: All in the Family

Many would agree that Smithfield's competitive edge is synonymous with the leadership of chief executive officer Joseph W. Luter III. After reclaiming in 1975 what was his own company, Luter had ushered Smithfield into the high-tech age by acquiring companies, forging partnerships, reducing overhead, and instituting capital improvements to boost efficiency. More importantly, he had elevated Smithfield to the elite ranks of those *Fortune* 500 companies offering the highest total returns to investors.

Since colonial times the small town of Smithfield, Virginia, had been known for its quality hams. Even today, under Virginia law, a ham may only be marketed as a "genuine Smithfield" if it has been cured for six months within the confines of the town. One such marketer, family owned Gwaltney Packing, was the employer of Luter's father and grandfather during the 1930s. In 1936 these two decided to establish their own ham business and succeeded in raising $10,000 from local investors. They opened across the street from Gwaltney and built their small private company into a multimillion-dollar entity.

When Luter's father died suddenly of a heart attack in 1962, Luter, near graduation from college, shelved his plans to attend law school and returned to oversee the business. Seven years later the company, with annual revenues of $35 million, had attracted the interest of Washington, D.C.-based Liberty Equities Corp., a small conglomerate. Luter sold the family company for $20 million but was retained as manager. After being summarily dismissed by the new owners six months later, Luter promptly launched a second career in real-estate development.

Mid-1970s to the Mid-1980s: From Bankrupt to First Billion

The packing plant, now operating as Smithfield Foods, Inc., fattened itself through non-pork acquisitions and unnecessary staff expansion. By the mid-1970s Smithfield was floundering along with Liberty Equities and Luter saw an opportunity to repurchase the company at a fraction of its worth. Because of actions taken by the Securities and Exchange Commission, Liberty had essentially reduced itself to Smithfield Foods, a failing $100 million pork-processing and fish wholesale business, further hampered by a nonproductive chain of 27 seafood restaurants. Price inflation throughout the food industry, as well

Company Perspectives:

Smithfield Foods now owns roughly 50 percent of the hogs we slaughter and raises additional hogs, which we do not process, that are marketed under long-term contracts to other companies. We realize a number of benefits by vertically controlling such a substantial portion of our raw materials. By controlling half our hog supply, our processing operations are ensured of a consistent, high-quality source of raw materials for many of the company's fresh and processed meat products. Continued volume gains in processed meats are helping to further one of our most important goals: creating a balance between fresh and processed meats that maximizes that value from all of our cuts.

as poor management, had severely affected the company; its debt had risen to $17 million while net worth had plummeted to $1 million. Creditors were demanding a management change and Luter agreed to a salary and stock options package that encouraged turnaround. As one analyst in a 1988 *Financial World* article claimed, ''Essentially, Joe Luter got the company back for ten cents on the dollar.''

Luter quickly reduced Smithfield's debt by selling the non-pork operations. He achieved profitability within seven months by slashing nearly $2 million in overhead through the elimination of middle managers and via sharp reductions in data-processing costs. Thus streamlined and firmly back in the meat business, Smithfield began to expand through acquisition. In 1978 it purchased a plant in Kinston, North Carolina. In 1981 Smithfield snatched up Gwaltney (at 35 cents on the dollar) for $34 million. Luter derived special satisfaction from this acquisition because not only had Gwaltney been a longtime competitor, it had also succumbed to the trappings of conglomerate spending under ITT Corp. Luter continued to seek out and buy at bargain rates other underperforming pork companies throughout the 1980s. These included Hancock's Country Hams, Patrick Cudahy Incorporated, and Schluderberg-Kurdle Co. (renamed Esskay, Inc.). By 1988 annual revenues had skyrocketed to $864 million, well within striking range of the billion-dollar mark.

1987 to 1992: Consistent and Predictable Growth

In 1987, in a particularly prescient move, Luter launched a 50–50 partnership with Carroll's Foods, the country's fifth-largest pork producer. Strategically located in North Carolina—within single-day transportation to half the U.S. population—Smithfield-Carroll's had helped the company lessen its dependence on Midwest hog farmers, the traditional source for the pork-packing industry. Coupled with hogs supplied by East Coast giant Murphy Family Farms, the partnership-generated pigs helped to account for 50 percent of Smithfield's annual requirements. In addition to saving on high-transportation costs, Luter also benefited from lower weight loss during shipment, thereby enhancing his product line's quality and marketability.

According to Sharon Reier, ''What is remarkable about Luter's resurrection of Smithfield is that he did it in an industry plagued by plant overcapacity and a flat consumption pattern in pork product over the past ten years, and dominated by large, well-heeled conglomerates that could subsidize poor margins in meat-packing operations with profits from other divisions.'' Of course, even Luter's Midas touch had little control over four-year cycles in hog prices, which directly affected the company's profitability. When prices are high, more pigs are raised and the eventual oversupply results in falling prices and undersupply—a true indicator of a high-risk commodity business. As a consequence of this predictable cycle, net income for Smithfield totaled $7 million in 1990 but rose sharply to nearly $29 million in 1991. Net income for 1992 began cycling downward again to $21 million.

Out of necessity, Smithfield was forced to take a long-term view of earnings performance through compound growth rates. In the 1991 letter to shareholders it explained, ''an analysis of the Company's performance over the last 16 years provides some enlightening results. When the 16 years are divided into four, four-year segments, the Company's earnings fall into a consistent and predictable growth pattern. . . . The Company's sales, net income and net income per share have shown compound growth rates of 14 percent, 31 percent, and 33 percent, respectively, over the last 16 years.''

One distinct advantage of these cycles, both for the company and for investors, was that Smithfield stock prices also followed a dip-and-rise pattern. With his extra profits, Luter had capitalized on downswings to buy back some 50 percent of the company's shares during the same 16-year period and had increased his individual stake to approximately 20 percent, according to a 1992 *Forbes* article.

To keep Smithfield on the cutting edge, Luter had concentrated on his niche markets, avoided high advertising budgets, and relegated more than half of his production to nonbranded commodity pork sales for the supermarket and food-service industries. Most promising for the future was Luter's quest for the genetically perfect pig: lean, hardy, and easy-to-process. An exclusive contract between Smithfield-Carroll's and National Pig Development Co. (NPD), a family owned British firm, proved to supply the answer. The first generations of NPD's transplanted stock were raised at the North Carolina facility. In July 1992, according to David Ress, ''Mr. Luter ran some tests on a 265-pound hog . . . comparing it with an especially lean American hog culled from the best of Smithfield's current stock. The American pig had an inch of fat on its back. The British pig had less than half that, Mr. Luter said. The raw, or 'green' ham from the American pig yielded 52 percent lean meat after boning and after the fat was trimmed. The British pig's yield was 62 percent.'' Development and marketing of the pigs was expected to continue, particularly through Smithfield's formation of Brown's of Carolina and its centerpiece, a state-of-the-art slaughtering plant located in Bladen County, North Carolina, which opened for production in September 1992. Around this time, the company phased out a dated Baltimore facility, acquired a John Morrell plant in Wilson, North Carolina, and searched for a plant situated to serve the West Coast.

1990s and Beyond: Becoming a Pork-Industry Global Force

The Bladen County plant played a pivotal role in Smithfield Foods' transition from a small, regional packer to the largest

Key Dates:

1936: Smithfield Packing Co. is founded by Joe Luter, Sr.
1962: Joe Luter II dies. Joe III graduates from Wake Forest University and joins Smithfield Foods.
1966: Luter, age 26, becomes president of Smithfield Foods.
1969: Controlling stake of Smithfield Foods is sold to Liberty Equities Corp.; Luter leaves the company.
1975: Luter returns as president/chief operating officer.
1978: The company purchases a financially troubled North Carolina plant.
1981: Smithfield Foods buys their competitor Gwaltney.
1984: The company acquires Patrick Cudahy, Inc. and Esskay (processing only).
1987: Smithfield Foods begins joint hog production with Carroll's Foods.
1991: The company negotiates exclusive U.S. and Mexico rights to National Pig Development Co. (NPD) genetics.
1992: Smithfield Foods buys 82 percent interest in Browns of North Carolina; and opens a new $76 million Bladen County, North Carolina plant.
1995: The company purchases John Morrell & Co.
1998: Smithfield Foods buys North Side Foods (who supplies precooked sausage to McDonalds); and acquires Schneider Corp.
1999: Bladen County plant operates at capacity of 32,000 hogs per day.
1999: The company acquires the following: SFGP (French ham, sausage, hot dog producer); Animex SA (Poland's largest meat processing firm); and Carroll's Foods; in addition company announces intention to buy Murphy Family Farms.
2000: Smithfield Foods announces decision to purchase Farmland Foods' Dubuque, Iowa plant.

pork-packer in the world. By April 1998 operations expanded, changing the primary nature of the facility from a pork-processing plant to the central warehousing/distribution center for Smithfield Packing Co. In 1999, Smithfield received approval to increase processing from 24,000 to more than 30,000 hogs a day. In 2001 the plant killed 32,000 hogs per day, twice the capacity of a typical plant.

By the mid-1990s, pork processing was an industry in flux. Production was becoming more horizontally concentrated and vertically integrated. At this time, the meat-processing industry faced mounting federal regulations, a seesaw marketplace, and food-safety challenges. But at Smithfield, the company saw a smoother road. A trade publication, *National Provisioner,* described Smithfield Foods as the market leader in vertically integrated fresh pork production, with the implementation system necessary to support future growth: long-term production agreements for hogs, and its high-tech North Carolina facility designed to ensure product consistency and quality.

Even in 1998, a year that saw a struggling pork industry, Smithfield was thriving. Planning and strategic initiatives contributed to sales of almost $4 billion in pork products, with profitable product sales and marketing achievements that allowed the company to turn its attention to global expansion. Product development strides included a new line of low-fat Italian sausage and a new precooked sausage line by Smithfield's Wisconsin-based Patrick Cudahy division. But Luter knew that turning America's chicken eaters into pork lovers wouldn't be easy. The company's meat would have to go outside this country. Smithfield Foods entered long-term production agreements with customers in Japan. And the company acquired Canada's Schneider Corp. (Kitchener, Ontario) a pork producer, in February 1999, a year after it first started pursuing the company. In August 1999 Smithfield further pursued its international expansion through a 50 percent owned integrated pork joint venture in Mexico. In September 1998 Smithfield acquired the largest private-label manufacturer of ham, pork shoulder, and bacon products in France. The following year, Smithfield acquired a French meat processor, which doubled the company's processed meats business in that country. Later Smithfield acquired Poland's largest meat-packing firm, Animex SA. Today, environmental and other concerns prohibit Smithfield from expanding in some of the richest hog-producing areas of the United States.

In recent years, Smithfield Foods has faced a minefield of opposition to corporate pig farming. In 1997 Smithfield Foods drew the largest civil penalty ever, assessed for violations of the Clean Water Act, a $12.6 million fine. It was also ordered to pay $3.8 million for about 22,000 pollution violations in Virginia. In September 2000 Smithfield Foods and its North Carolina swine-production firms signed an agreement with the state of North Carolina that included a $15 million research and development commitment to conduct research on environmentally superior swine waste technology to protect the state's water quality. Environmentalists, animal-rights activists, and independent farmers continued to rail against the company in 2001, with lawsuits charging that Smithfield Foods for years intentionally and systematically violated environmental laws including the Clean Water Act. In March 2001 a North Carolina judge dismissed two lawsuits brought against the company and its hog-production subsidiaries in the state.

In this hostile climate, Smithfield needed to diversify its offerings to supermarkets and find new arenas for growth. Between 1998 and 2000, Smithfield purchased or invested in 12 companies, many outside the United States. The acquisitions provided production operations to offset declining meat-processing margins. Because there was more money in raising pigs than slaughtering them, Smithfield bought out its hog-farm partners in 1999 and 2000 as the price of hogs fell to a historic low. Today, huge economies of scale enable Smithfield to raise pigs more cost-effectively than other producers.

Meanwhile, NPD genetics played a role in Smithfield's Lean Generation Pork Products, which Luter believed could emulate Purdue and Tyson's heart-healthy branding of chicken products. By late 2000 Smithfield was one of the few stocks that resisted the market's downswing, thanks to a contract to supply Wal-Mart with prepackaged meats, an agreement Luter predicted would triple Smithfield's sales of fresh-wrapped pork.

In early 2001 Smithfield and Tyson, the nation's largest poultry company, had fought for IBP, the country's largest beef company, which would have made either contender the nation's largest meat producer. Tyson prevailed, but later cut off the merger deal. Smithfield had no immediate plans to resume its pursuit of IBP. Shortly thereafter Smithfield agreed to buy Moyer Packing Co., a smaller beef processor. The acquisition broadened the company's line of prepackaged, branded meat, which doubles the profit margins of commodity meats. Meanwhile, the outbreak of ''mad cow'' and hoof-and-mouth disease in Europe portended well for Smithfield, as analysts speculated that the company might be able to boost exports to Europe, where it has a broad distribution network.

Principal Subsidiaries

Meat Processing: The Smithfield Packing Company, Incorporated; John Morrell & Co.; Gwaltney of Smithfield, Ltd.; Patrick Cudahy Incorporated; North Side Foods Corp. Hog Production: Brown's of Carolina, Inc.; Carroll's Foods, Inc.; Murphy Family Foods, Inc.

Principal Competitors

IBP Inc.; Tyson Foods Inc.; Hormel; ConAgra.

Further Reading

Arrandale, Tom, ''The EPA and the 'Virginia Problem,' '' *Governing Magazine,* October 1997, p. 13.

DiLorenzo, Jim, ''Man with a Mission,'' *National Provisioner,* August 1995, p. 26.

''Esskay, Inc. to Phase Out Production at Baltimore Plant,'' Company Press Release, September 30, 1992.

Forster, Julie, ''Who's Afraid of a Little Mud?,'' *Business Week,* May 21, 2001, p. 112.

Hinden, Stan, ''Interest in Smithfield Stock Sparks a Flurry of Trading,'' *Washington Post,* April 10, 1989.

Jaffe, Thomas, ''Pig Out,'' *Forbes,* December 1, 1986.

Koselka, Rita, ''$ Oink, $ Oink,'' *Forbes,* February 3, 1992 .

Marbery, Steve, ''Smithfield Foods Brainstorms Western Venture,'' *Feedstuffs,* November 16, 1992.

McComas, Maggie, ''Smithfield Foods Inc.,'' *Fortune,* February 16, 1987.

Miller, Dale, ''Straight Talk from Smithfield's Joe Luter,'' *National Hog Farmer,* May 2000.

Norton, Leslie P., ''What's Your Beef?,'' *Barron's, Chicopee,* November 27, 2000, p. 14.

Reier, Sharon, ''High on the Hog,'' *Financial World,* June 28, 1988.

Ress, David, ''Britain's Low-Fat Pigs Expected to Beef up U.S. Pork Market,'' *Journal of Commerce and Commercial,* July 1, 1992.

Simon, Stephanie, ''U.S. Top Hog Processor Accused of Planned Pollution in Lawsuit,'' *Los Angeles Times,* March 1, 2001, p. A5.

Stovall, Robert H., ''Small Stocks with Big Names,'' *Financial World,* May 12, 1992.

''Top 200: Top 10 Snapshot,'' National Provisioner, May 1999, p. 48.

Wal, Gretchen, ''Waterkeeper Lawsuits Target Pork Industry,'' *National Hog Farmer,* May 15, 2001.

Young-Huguenin, Barbara, ''Making Waves,'' *National Provisioner,* December 1994, p.24.

Young-Huguenin, Barbara, ''Solid Foundation,'' *National Provisioner,* December 1994, p.32.

—Jay P. Pederson
—update: Michelle Feder

The Sports Authority, Inc.

3383 North State Road 7
Fort Lauderdale, Florida 33319
U.S.A.
Telephone: (954) 735-1701
Toll-free: (877) 872-3909
Fax: (954) 484-0837
Web site: http://www.sportsauthority.com

Public Company
Incorporated: 1987
Employees: 11,000
Sales: $1,501.6 million (2000)
Stock Exchanges: New York
Ticker Symbol: TSA
NAIC: 45111 Sporting Goods Stores; 45411 Electronic Shopping and Mail-Order Houses

The Sports Authority, Inc. is the world's largest full-line sporting goods retailer. From its 198 stores, located in 32 states, the company sells sporting goods in over 1,200 merchandise categories. Its large format stores, virtually all of which exceed 40,000 square feet, carry more than 700 brand names, including adidas, Asics, Champion, Coleman, K2, Nike, Salomon, Timberland, and Wilson. Over half of the company's annual revenue is generated from the sale of hard lines—equipment for team sports, fitness, hunting, fishing, camping, golf, racquet sports, cycling, water sports, marine, snow sports, and general merchandise. Soft lines—apparel and footwear, its most profitable products—make up the rest. The first comprehensive sporting goods store to top $1 billion in sales, The Sports Authority competes in a $35 billion market that includes traditional and specialty sporting goods retailers, as well as large format sporting goods retailers and mass merchandisers.

Early History

The idea behind the company that would grow to become the nation's largest sporting goods chain in just five years came from Jack Smith, a former CEO of Herman's World of Sports, who opened the first Sports Authority store in Fort Lauderdale, Florida, in 1987. While at Herman's, Smith tried unsuccessfully to bring the same comprehensive megastore concept that had fueled the tremendous growth of Toys "R" Us and Home Depot to the sporting goods industry. With the backing of a group of venture capitalists, he got another chance and set out to build his own sporting goods giant. By 1990, he was running eight megastores, mainly in Florida, and while his company had yet to turn a profit, the then 55-year-old fitness enthusiast was convinced he could make the idea work if he could obtain the capital to fund full-scale expansion.

Joseph Antonini, then chairman of Kmart Corporation, shared Smith's confidence and acquired the sporting goods minichain for $75 million in March of that same year. With the financial backing of the multi-billion-dollar retail giant, Smith now had the resources he needed to implement his plans fully and begin an expansion program that would see The Sports Authority grow to 100 stores four years later. In 1990, the company more than doubled its size to 19 stores. While such rapid growth was accompanied by proportional gains in total revenue, it did not yet translate well onto the balance sheet. At the end of the fiscal year, the company reported a loss of $3.3 million, its fourth consecutive year in the red.

Although the company was unable to realize a profit during these developmental years, it succeeded in building the technological infrastructure needed to support more important long-term growth. At the expense of short-term profits, the experienced sporting goods executive had the foresight to invest heavily in state-of-the-art computer systems that closely monitored inventory. Not only would this give Sports Authority an early technological edge on the competition; it would enable the company to keep its shelves stocked without the use of a distribution facility. The accuracy and availability of information housed in the company's extensive computer system would allow vendors to ship directly to individual stores.

Early 1990s Growth

In 1991, as revenue rose to $240 million, the company enjoyed its first profitable year of operation, reporting an operating

Company Perspectives:

Our mission is simple—create a shopping experience establishing The Sports Authority as the first choice for the sports, leisure and recreational customer. Our strategy to achieve this goal is offer our customers: an extensive selection of quality brand name merchandise; powerfully merchandised megastores that provide ease of shopping; competitive prices that create value; premium customer service and product knowledge; and convenient locations throughout our markets.

income of $3.3 million. With financial support from Kmart, it was also able to again more than double the size of its operations, building 11 new stores and taking over six existing stores. The company's 36 stores now occupied a total of more than 1.5 million square feet. Although the company, at this time, had not yet won over many of the major brand names in the industry, such as Nike, its strong growth suggested that Smith's version of the sporting goods superstore was quickly gaining in popularity. One of the key factors to its success was its ability to combine the best features of the small specialty sporting goods store and the large discount store. While other companies preceded Sports Authority in introducing the public to the idea of a sporting goods megastore, their stores quickly gained a reputation for being warehouse type operations that offered poor service and an unpleasant shopping environment. What Smith contributed to the field were significant improvements on both counts. He made merchandise displays more attractive, investing in high-quality displays that added to the shopping experience, and staffed his stores with enough well-trained employees to give customers the type of service they might receive at a specialty store. In short, he was able to make the "big box" of the superstore workable.

The company's rapid expansion program unfolded at an even faster rate over the next two years. In 1992, sales climbed more than 70 percent while income more than tripled as 20 new stores were opened. The following year, sales increased 50 percent as earnings doubled and 24 new stores entered the fold. Again, Sports Authority followed its simple, time-honored retailing philosophy, described by Smith in *Discount Store News* as "the simple blocking and tackling of retail": keeping shelves stocked, keeping stores clean, and providing good service. Patterned after category killers such as Home Depot and Toys "R" Us, the company did not attempt to beat the competition by undercutting their prices; instead, it tried to win customers over with shelves so densely stocked that virtually anyone would have a difficult time leaving the store empty-handed. The company's receipts at the cash register, in keeping with its policy of "consistent everyday fair pricing," would likely fall somewhere between those of specialty sporting goods retailers and mass merchandisers. And while the company tried to keep its prices comparable to other sporting goods superstores, it did not—unlike many of its competitors—take temporary price reductions to promote product sales. It simply relied on the product quality strength of its ever-increasing stable of brand names.

By the start of 1993, Sports Authority had become less dependent on Kmart and had gained enough financial strength to fund the opening of 10 new stores on its own during the first six months of the year. As intense competition from Wal-Mart threatened Kmart's future ability to support the expansion of its top subsidiaries, Sports Authority's increasing sense of autonomy became an even more important factor. At this time, the company also stepped up its bid to increase its share and presence by opening up multiple stores in major markets. This growth strategy—known as "cannibalizing" because new stores sometimes "eat up" sales from existing stores in an attempt to capture a dominant overall market share—enabled the company to take advantage of economies of scale in advertising and promotion in Florida locations such as Dade and Broward counties, where it had 10 stores by the end of the year. The company also attempted to make a strong entrance in major markets such as Seattle and New York City, where it opened 15 stores.

Initial Public Offering

Just as Sports Authority was fast becoming the largest sporting goods store in the nation, its parent company, Kmart, the second largest retail company in the United States, struggled in the face of increasing competition from Wal-Mart, Target, and other top retailers. In August 1994, following a record $974 million loss the previous year, Kmart made the decision to take its three most successful specialty shops public to fund the renovation of its older stores and the introduction of Super Kmart Centers. Sports Authority, along with OfficeMax and Borders-Walden bookstores, were subsequently approved for initial public offerings with the hope of raising more than $1 billion. Kmart's loss, however, proved to be a boon for Smith and Sports Authority. On November 18, 71 percent of the company was sold to the public for around $270 million. Although Sports Authority had always essentially run its own business, its growth would no longer be hindered by the retail giant.

That same year, Sports Authority opened its 100th store as it recorded another record-breaking performance: sales increased to $838 million, up 38 percent from the previous year, and earnings rose to $16.9 million, a 33 percent jump. While growing at such a rapid rate, the company managed to maintain a strong balance sheet and cash flow. With equity in excess of $250 million, cash and cash equivalents of around $37 million, and—most notably—no long-term debt, the company placed itself in a favorable position to continue its aggressive national expansion program, focusing its growth on the New York metropolitan area, where it opened six stores, and Chicago, where it opened four. In addition to opening 12 stores in existing markets, the company entered several new markets, including Anchorage, Sacramento, and Tucson.

The Sports Authority complemented its efforts toward dominating the domestic sporting goods market by also launching an international program in 1994. Its first movement outside of the United States' borders consisted of a plan to open five new stores in Toronto. Not only did Canada offer the company a market with characteristics and dynamics similar to those in the U.S., but it also featured an easily accessible supply line from existing vendors, most of whom already had Canadian operations. That same year, the company also laid the groundwork for overseas expansion, signing a joint venture agreement with JUSCO Co., Ltd., to operate Sports Authority stores in Japan. The country's third-largest retailer, JUSCO brought to the table

Key Dates:

1987: Founder Jack Smith opens first store in Fort Lauderdale, Florida.
1990: Company is acquired by Kmart Corporation.
1994: Company is spun off from Kmart with an IPO.
1994: One hundredth store is opened.
1995: Company sales top $1 billion.
2001: New CEO Martin Hanaka refinances and refocuses company amid tumultuous times.

a wealth of experience in property management and retail sight selection as well as broad experience in working with other Western-based retailers. With an estimated size of $16 billion, the Japanese sporting goods market presented the opportunity to tap a densely populated market with high disposable income, a strong attraction to branded products, and a commitment to sports and leisure activities.

Perhaps the most visible sign of the company's arrival, though, was the addition of one of the most popular vendors in the industry, Nike. After seven years of refusing to sell to The Sports Authority, the footwear and apparel giant began selling to the fast-growing chain, paving the way for a number of upscale brands to enter the fold. Timberland and Teva quickly followed suit, adding significantly to the company's bid to offer its customers the most comprehensive array of products in the industry.

Breaking the Billion-Dollar Barrier

In 1995, its first full year of operation as a publicly traded company, Sports Authority became the first full-line sporting goods retailer to top $1 billion in sales. The now 136-store chain also proved to its investors that such unprecedented growth did not come without a concomitant boost in earnings, which increased 32 percent. A number of strategic moves contributed to the record-breaking success of the company and provided a foundation for continued growth over the long run.

Although the company had long earned high marks for its extensive product line, its reputation for customer service had not been as strong. In an effort to set itself apart from other large-format sporting goods retailers and other mass merchandisers, Sports Authority launched a company-wide initiative to enhance customer service in each one of its stores. Known as TSA 2000, the new standard tried to address the most common complaint against the company: employees too busy stocking shelves to devote full attention to the needs of customers. TSA 2000 attempted to eliminate this problem by moving receiving and stocking duties, as well as other non-selling functions, to the hours immediately prior to opening or shortly after closing, enabling associates to place a greater emphasis on listening to customers and providing information about products.

In keeping with the year's focus on improving the environment of its stores, the company also invested $4 million in new ''ladder-style'' apparel fixtures designed to display and coordinate merchandise in a more user-friendly manner. Installed to replace conventional gondolas, the in-house designed ladder fixtures enabled stores to combine graphics and coordinate presentations on the same fixture to make a more powerful impression on the customer and save store space at the same time. Another significant merchandising presentation innovation implemented that year was the use of ''statement shops''—designated areas located near the front of the store that feature specialized footwear and related apparel from top manufactures. A New Jersey store, for instance, created a Rugged Apparel shop—complete with a wooden sign with carved letters outlined in green—that featured hiking boots as well as shirts, shorts, and winter flannel apparel from upscale vendors such as Woolrich, Columbia, and Jansport.

As Smith looked forward to the second half of the decade, he predicted that by the year 2000 his company would reach $5 billion in annual sales and expand to 500 stores in the United States alone. His strategy for achieving that goal did not promise to deviate from the ''simple blocking and tackling'' business fundamentals that allowed for its rise to the top of the industry. Setting a market share goal of 35 percent in each of its markets, the company intended to continue its practice of cannibalizing existing store sales to take business away from mass merchandisers and traditional sporting goods retailers. It planned to finance further expansion—at least 30 stores were scheduled to open in 1996—with proceeds from the $160 million sale of the remaining 29 percent of the company.

According to analysts' long-term predictions, the sporting goods industry was expected to continue expanding as baby boomers gained more disposable income and leisure time, and as greater numbers of people took up some form of exercise. With its strong financial base, economies of scale, and technological edge, The Sports Authority expected to lead the competition in taking advantage of these trends.

On The Comeback Trail

The latter half of the 1990s, however, brought tumultuous times to the company. By 1998, when Martin Hanaka replaced the spirited, long-time CEO Jack Smith, the company was in dire need of a turnaround. Hanaka, with formidable experience at retailers Staples and Sears Roebuck & Co., inherited a litany of woes, including weakening sales of athletic shoes and clothing, burgeoning debt from years of over-expansion, and nonproducing stores, all of which had placed the company in distressed territory. For a successful turnaround, stabilizing the company and stopping losses resulting from the over-expansion, and restoring a modest level of profitability were paramount—no small tasks. One of the first steps Hanaka took was to refinance the company, fortifying the capital structure and speeding vendor payments.

The ambitious new store program was scrapped and money-losing stores were closed, including all Canadian locations. By 2000, the company had completely exited the Canadian market and reduced its ownership interest in JUSCO, the joint venture in Japan. Competitors as well struggled against mounting difficulties such as relentless promotional pressure, increasing markdowns, and oversaturation in the sporting goods sector. Industry insiders speculated about potential mergers, and sure enough, merger proposals were announced by both Gart Sports and Venator Group, neither of which succeeded.

The next step for Hanaka's newly assembled management team was to revive the productivity of existing stores. A store-by-store edit of merchandise categories culminated in a new, variable merchandising plan by market, which increased margin rates and sales while reducing advertising costs. To encourage cross-shopping and higher average tickets, a new floor plan was designed to showcase apparel in four specialty quadrants, which created a more appealing ambience than the previous warehouse look and feel. A $30 million investment in new point-of purchase and merchandising technology systems helped reduce inventories and increase sales; a $9.7 million refurbishing plan gave badly needed facelifts to several existing stores.

Sales in fiscal years ending 2000 and 2001 were relatively flat; however, the company continued to narrow its losses. In 2001, the company was scheduled to pay its first bonus in five years. According to CEO Hanaka in *Daily News Record* (March 19, 2001), ''We didn't hit a grand slam homer, but we scored some runs and we returned to a moderate level of profitability.'' There were no plans to open new stores in 2001, but the company was considering modest expansion for 2002 and 2003.

Their sales strategy, signified by the slogan ''Get out and play,'' was designed to inspire consumers to participate or attend any type of sports, leisure, or recreational activity, and make it a meaningful part of their lifestyle. As Hanaka described to *Daily News Record*, ''Our job is not just to sell product. Our job is to have fun and make sure [shoppers] have fun. We want Sports Authority to be their place for fun.'' The company also embarked on a grass-roots effort to promote youth physical fitness. Partnering with the Boys & Girls Clubs of America, it helped educate children on fitness and nutrition, and offered instructional clinics and fitness programs. More than 100,000 children participated in the inaugural year, culminating in championships in Ft. Lauderdale with Kickball Olympics and Basketball Biathlon.

Principal Subsidiaries

Authority International, Inc.; The Sports Authority Florida, Inc.; The Sports Authority Michigan, Inc.; The Sports Authority Puerto Rico, Inc.

Principal Competitors

Gart Sports Company; Venator Group, Inc.; Wal-Mart Stores, Inc.

Further Reading

Book, Esther Wachs, ''Here Comes a Cat Killer,'' *Forbes*, April 22, 1996, pp. 49, 52.

Boyd, Christopher, ''Agassi Vs. Courier,'' *Florida Trend*, October 1993, pp. 60–64.

Butler, Simon, ''Sports Authority Joins Global Sports as Latest Partner in Online Venture,'' *Footwear News*, May 24, 1999, p. 2.

''Chains Square Off to Take Manhattan,'' *Sporting Goods Business*, December 1994, p. 10.

Edelson, Sharon, ''Smith Leaves Sports Authority,'' *WWD*, April 19, 1999, p. 14.

Fickes, Michael, ''Fighting Back,'' *Sporting Goods Business*, January 19, 2001, p. 72.

Gaffney, Andrew, ''Jack Smith,'' *Sporting Goods Business*, June 25, 1995, pp. 62–63.

Halverson, Richard, ''Sports Authority Aims for $5B in Sales, 500 Stores by Year 2000,'' *Discount Store News*, July 17, 1995, pp. 15–16.

''Image, Presentation Key to Merchandising,'' *Discount Store News*, July 17, 1995, pp. 19–20.

Lloyd, Brenda, ''At Sports Authority, The Fix Is In,'' *Daily News Record*, March 19, 2001, p. 2.

Ono, Yumiko, ''Venator Cancels Plans to Acquire Sports Authority,'' *Wall Street Journal*, September 11, 1998, p. B8.

Pratt, Ben, ''Sports Authority Continues Its Slide,'' *Mergers & Acquisitions Report*, November 8, 1999.

Ryan, Thomas J., ''TSA Braces for Deeper Quarter Loss,'' *WWD*, October 7, 1998, p. 2.

Thompson, Kelly, ''The Sports Authority Pares Qtr. Loss,'' *Footwear News*, June 4, 2001, p. 6.

Troy, Mike, ''TSA Turnaround Inches from Endzone,'' *DSN Retailing Today*, April 16, 2001, p. 3.

Young, Vicki M., ''Sports Authority Net Should Exceed Plan,'' *WWD*, January 9, 2001, p. 12.

—Jason Gallman
—update: Suzanne Selvaggi

Stearns, Inc.

1100 Stearns Drive
Sauk Rapids, Minnesota 56379-2522
U.S.A.
Telephone: (320) 252-1642
Toll Free: (800) STEARNS; (800) 783-2767
Fax: (320) 252-4425
Web site: http://www.stearnsinc.com

Wholly Owned Subsidiary of K2 Inc.
Incorporated: 1943 as Stearns Manufacturing Company
Employees: 550
Sales: $65 million (2000 est.)
NAIC: 339113 Life Preservers Manufacturing; 339920 Wet Suits Manufacturing; 326299 All Other Rubber Product Manufacturing; 315299 All Other Cut and Sew Apparel Manufacturing; 315999 Other Apparel Accessories and Other Apparel Manufacturing

Stearns, Inc., a subsidiary of K2 Inc., is a leading manufacturer of moderately priced recreational and industrial water safety and water sports products. Through its six major product lines, Stearns offers a diverse range of items for the outdoors and water sports enthusiast. The company's divisions include: Stearns Water Sports, manufacturing personal flotation devices (PFDs), wetsuits, and swim and dive products; Stearns Outdoors, marketing inflatable kayaks, self-inflating sleeping pads, waterproof bags, and hydration water filters; Mad Dog, offering hunting backpacks, daypacks, and other accessories; Fly Tech, featuring rubberized fishing waders, boots, and related gear; Stearns Industrial Safety, manufacturing cold-water immersion and rescue suits as well as Drywear rainsuits and work vests; and Goldeneye Marine, producing watersport ropes and dock and anchor lines.

The Early Years

In 1927 a Minnesotan named William P. Hilger began a small company which he named the Minnesota Sales Corporation. He had invented an accessory for advertising on the back of a motorcar. Hilger's first product, the Kar-onof-ad, proved unsuccessful, but he persisted and within the year turned to the manufacture of another automotive accessory, the frost shield. In an age when car heaters were primitive at best, the frost shield—an electrically heated and vacuum-sealed barrier between a motor car's windshield and the natural elements—was essential to safety in cold climates. The development of the frost shield and innovations related to it turned the Minnesota Sales Corporation, now renamed Hilco, into one of the fastest growing companies in central Minnesota in the early 1930s.

Throughout the 1930s and into the early 1940s Hilco's frost shields were in demand all over the United States. General Motors contracted Hilco to produce special brands for their vehicles, and other customers from as far away as California and Maine kept the company adding employees to keep up with demand. By 1936 Hilco had produced more than a million frost shields, sometimes turning out as many as several thousand shields a day. Government contracts with Hilco during World War II and for construction vehicles creating the Alaskan Highway were to follow.

Amidst the war, in 1943, Hilco's automotive accessory division was sold to B. Howard ''Pat'' Flanagan and Maurice O'Link. O'Link had been in charge of frost shield operations at Hilco for five years before teaming up with Flanagan to purchase the company. O'Link, a chemical engineer with a degree from the University of Minnesota, served as the company's general manager for many years. Flanagan had entered officers candidate school and was stationed at Fort Snelling in St. Paul and, upon release from his commission following the war, got involved with company operations.

A Shift in Direction

The new company was named Stearns Manufacturing Company, after the central Minnesota county in which it resided, and with the new name and leadership the company took a new direction as well. The improved heating systems in cars and trucks in the 1940s and 1950s greatly affected the sale of frost shields nationwide. With decreasing demand for the company's core product, O'Link turned to the manufacture of plastic products, an area in which, because of his degree in chemical

Company Perspectives:

Stearns is committed to total customer satisfaction through the dedication of all employees to excellence. The pathway to excellence is comprised of our focus on the continuous improvement of products and services while realizing long-term profitability.

Key Dates:

1927: William Hilger develops an automobile accessory and starts Minnesota Sales Corporation; after Hilger's first product fails, he begins producing frost shields for cars and renames his operation Hilco.
1936: Over one million frost shields are sold.
1938: Explosion occurs at the production facility; plant is quickly rebuilt and resumes operation.
1943: Frost shield division is sold to B. Howard ''Pat'' Flanagan and Maurice O'Link, who rename the business Stearns Manufacturing Company.
1950s: Stearns Manufacturing shifts directions from automotive accessories to sporting and camping gear; Stearns begins producing personal flotation devices (PFDs) and various plastic products.
1961: Stearns Manufacturing Company becomes a subsidiary of Plastics Corporation of America; production of plastic boat interiors becomes Stearns's strongest business.
1971: The Federal Boat Safety Act allows for the development of new designs of PFDs.
1973: Stearns develops its most successful product to date, the Type III PFD.
1988: Anthony Industries (later renamed K2 Inc.) purchases Stearns Manufacturing Company for an undisclosed amount of money.
2001: Stearns closes two of its four manufacturing plants.

engineering, he had some expertise. The developing plastics industry was in its genesis and to O'Link and Flanagan, whose frost shield business was quickly becoming an anachronism, manufacturing plastic products was forward-thinking.

Like Hilger, the duo of O'Link and Flanagan allowed local influences to determine their company's product development. While Hilger was strongly motivated by the cold Minnesota climate in his development of the frost shield, O'Link and Flanagan were influenced by the hunting and fishing culture of their central Minnesota surroundings. The two moved the company production into outdoor and recreational gear.

The early products manufactured at Stearns were vinyl gun cases, sleeping bags, and plastic products for camping and hunting. Stearns Manufacturing also took the lead in producing plastic marine products, particularly life jackets, water ski belts, and plastic boat interiors for pontoon boats, another local industry. This shift toward sporting/leisure goods continued to define Stearns for the next half century.

A change in law in the 1960s made a huge impact on the St. Cloud area company. The Federal Boat Safety Act of 1971 allowed manufacturing companies to develop new designs for PFDs as long as they were consistent with U.S. Coast Guard guidelines. This resulted in the manufacture of more Type II PFDs—the bright orange, front-fastening, and cumbersome life jackets with which most people are familiar—but it also allowed for new innovations in the industry.

In 1973 Stearns designed what proved to be its most enduring success—the Type III PFD. The new design met federal regulations but more importantly it was comfortable, which meant that consumers would use it. This particular design was that of a zippered vest that kept the swimmer afloat equally as well as the Type II design but without having the swimmer's neck area so restricted. Stearns Manufacturing's Type III PFD was lauded as a reason for the decline of boating-related fatalities nationwide.

Part of a Conglomerate: 1988

Stearns Manufacturing Company was a leader in producing recreational gear, so it came as little surprise when in October 1988 Anthony Industries, a California company specializing in recreational products, bought it. Anthony Industries began as a swimming pool manufacturer and diversified to include two major business operations: recreational products and industrial products. In adding Stearns Manufacturing, Anthony Industries further diversified its recreational holdings, which already included K2 skis, Hilton active apparel, Shakespeare fishing gear, and its original pool division.

In the early 1990s Anthony Industries sold off its pool division and renamed itself K2 Sports (later, K2 Inc.). This was in large part due to K2 skis, the company's most internationally recognized brand name.

Despite operating under K2's corporate structure, Stearns, Inc., as it was now called, maintained its regional production and identity. All four of Stearns's manufacturing facilities were within a 100-mile radius of the company's headquarters in Sauk Rapids, Minnesota. The Sauk Rapids facility, in addition to the company offices, provided warehousing, manufacturing, and distribution. The close proximity of the manufacturing plants to Stearns's headquarters allowed regular monitoring of all aspects of operations and firm quality control over its product lines.

Throughout the 1990s sales for the company remained strong, in part through the development of new merchandise. Stearns Outdoors experienced great success with its towable rubberized rafts and its inflatable kayaks. The 1990s saw an increase in the use of rubber inner-tube-like rafts for recreational use with boats, snowmobiles, and personal watercraft. Stearns inflatable kayaks proved successful in the outdoor sporting goods market, with sales exceeding expectations. The profit Stearns turned with these products helped to boost the company, making up in part for losses in K2's inline skate and ski sales.

According to company sources, Stearns as it entered the 2000s was distributing the following products: personal flotation devices; wetsuits; inflatable towables; swim and dive products; marine products; self-inflating sleeping pads; waterproof, floatable dry bags; SunShower products; hydration/water filters; hunting packs and accessories; work vests; flotation jackets and coveralls; ice rescue suits; cold water immersion suits; and waders and boots.

Stearns appeared to be a steady company that had developed a significant keystone product with the type III PFD. Its many divisions seemed situated to address the interests of the outdoor sports enthusiast. Most significantly, throughout its history, new product development at Stearns appeared to be closely following and sometimes anticipating market trends while meeting with a good measure of success. The fact that in April 2001 the company closed two of its four manufacturing plants was not necessarily indicative of declines in revenues or earnings. The bulk of Stearns's workforce, housed at its main offices and production site in Sauk Rapids, remained intact, dedicated to further strengthening the Stearns brand name through quality sporting, recreational, and leisure products.

Principal Divisions

Stearns Water Sports; Stearns Outdoors; Mad Dog Gear; Fly Tech; Industrial Safety; Goldeneye Marine.

Principal Competitors

Eastman Outdoors; The North Face, Inc.; Sealine; Sierra Designs, Inc.; Johnson Worldwide; Recreational Equipment, Inc.

Further Reading

"Anthony Industries Announces the Acquisition of Stearns Manufacturing, Inc.," *Business Wire,* October 13, 1988.

Bamett, Chris, "Anthony Industries: Combining R & D with Luck," *California Business,* January 1992, p. 12.

"Branch Is Sold," *St. Cloud Times,* May 18, 1943.

"Firm Triples Size in Three Years, Material Shortage Hits Stearns Manufacturing Company," *St. Cloud Times,* January 26, 1946.

Halena, Sue, "Stearns Inc. Closes Paynesville, Carlton Plants," *St. Cloud Times,* April 1, 2001, p. 1B.

"K2 Can Do," *Forbes,* January 22, 1990, p. 156.

McEvoy, Christopher, "Acquiring Minds," *Sport Goods Business,* August 1995, p. 44.

Mehlman, William, "Anthony Synthesizes Winner from Pools, Skis, Industrials," *Insider's Chronicle,* June 12,1989, p.1.

Paris, Ellen, "A Conglomerate That Works," *Forbes,* November 28,1988, p.52.

"Stearns Associates with PCA," *St. Cloud Times,* September 29, 1961.

Stelling, Linda, "Stearns Manufacturing Helps Make-a-Wish," www.paynesvillearea.com/NewsHeadlinesArticles/archives11/18/98StearnsManufact.

"Windstorm in St. Cloud Brings Damage Reports," *St. Cloud Times,* June, 23, 1950, p. 1.

—Susan B. Culligan

Stone Manufacturing Company

200 Brozzini Ct.
Greenville, South Carolina 29615
U.S.A.

Private Company
Incorporated: 1945
Sales: $400 million (1998 est.)
NAIC: 315221 Men's and Boys' Cut and Sew Underwear and Nightwear Manufacturing

Stone Manufacturing Company once ranked as one of the largest apparel manufacturers in the United States. From late 1997 until mid-1999, the company was known as Umbro International, in recognition of its production of the Umbro brand of soccer clothing, a business the company first became involved in during the early 1980s. After the $145 million sale of the Umbro segment in 1999, the company reverted to its original name and continued to manufacture one of its original mainstays, men's underwear.

Depression-Era Origins

Stone Manufacturing Company was the brainchild of Eugene E. Stone III. Stone was born in Spartanburg, South Carolina, and attended Fishburne Military School in Waynesboro, Virginia. He went on to Georgia Tech University in Atlanta and later graduated with a degree in geology from the University of South Carolina.

In 1929 Stone set out to strike it rich in the oil fields of east Texas. He joined the Seaport Oil Company working out of Houston and developed a close friendship with the man who started the company. At the time, drilling for oil seemed to be an easy route to success. Seaport Oil drilled seven wells and came up with seven oil gushers. However, Seaport Oil was just one of many companies that found oil, and, within a bare six months, the oil market was completely glutted. As a result, the price of a barrel dropped from a high of one dollar to a low of just six cents. Stone's dreams of wealth were shattered, and he returned to Greenville a poorer but wiser man.

Back in Greenville, Stone soon found that conditions were even worse than in Texas. The entire nation was in the grip of the Great Depression, and South Carolina was particularly hard hit. Property values for both residential and commercial real estate had dropped dramatically, and wages were approximately one-third of what they had been before the Wall Street crash of 1929. Small farms in rural South Carolina hd suffered the same fate as farms in the Dust Bowl of the plains states, and many families moved to cities in order to find work at factories or small businesses.

One of the small apparel manufacturing companies in Greenville was also struggling to survive. The firm was forced to reduce the wages of its employees so that it could continue business operations. An embittered worker sabotaged the firm's boiler and left the entire factory and all its personnel working in the cold. When Stone's father, the owner of the building, was asked to repair the boiler, the younger Stone, who had gained some experience fixing boilers in his student days, volunteered to tackle the problem. Stone fixed the boiler, the company resumed its normal operations, and the young man was offered a job at ten cents an hour for 68 hours per week. Stone assumed the job with his usual enthusiasm, and despite the long hours found the time to court and marry Allene Wyman, known affectionately by her friends and family as ''Linky.'' Stone and Linky left on their honeymoon with a guarantee from his boss that they would not only receive the two weeks' pay for his time off, but a new icebox upon their return.

After the honeymoon, however, they discovered that there would be neither a two-week paycheck nor an icebox. Stone immediately resigned, and with the skills he had acquired at the apparel manufacturing company, he opened the Stone Manufacturing Company on July 9, 1933. Stone hired five seamstresses and purchased eight sewing machines that formed the cornerstone of his company for the first few years. Stone himself did all the fabric cutting, as well as all the packaging and shipping. His wife was in charge of designing all clothes.

The first order received by Stone Manufacturing Company was from Sterling Stores of Little Rock, Arkansas, for the production of 25 dozen pink bloomers of knit jersey made from cotton. Although the shipment got lost in transit, Sterling Stores

Key Dates:

1933: Stone Manufacturing begins making swimsuits and underwear.
1948: After years of growth, a second plant opens.
1951: World's largest clothing factory opens.
1981: U.S. rights to Umbro brand are acquired.
1992: Stone buys U.K.-based Umbro Ltd.
1997: Company changes name to Umbro International Inc. and post sales of $600 million; Umbro's bottom line, however, is showing signs of strain.
1998: Umbro International closes its U.S. manufacturing operations in favor of outsourcing.
1999: Stone sells Umbro's world business and returns to underwear manufacturing.

gave Stone another chance and soon developed into one of his most loyal customers. Also during the company's first year of business, Stone made a sales call to G.C. Murphy Company, a retailer with stores throughout Pennsylvania. Before he finished showing the buyer his entire line of clothing, the buyer began filing out an order pad. After the meeting, Stone happily announced that the company had enough orders for the entire year.

During the mid-1930s, the nation was still in the midst of the Great Depression. Stone Manufacturing employees worked in cold, damp conditions since the company was only able to afford one potbellied stove for heat. Yet the firm produced high-quality clothes that people could afford, which was quite an accomplishment during the Depression. By 1935 the company was not merely surviving but making a profit, and Stone decided to buy a furnace for the clothing plant. One of the few apparel manufacturing firms in the country whose sales were always increasing during the 1930s, Stone Manufacturing Company was the envy of the entire industry.

In the late 1930s, due to its rapid growth, the company moved to a larger facility and at the same time expanded its product line. Stone Manufacturing was making dresses, aprons, slips, panties, dustcaps, and sunsuits. The sunsuits sold at Woolworth Department Stores for ten cents. The company held to a high standard of quality: for example, while most bloomers at the time were made with eight or nine stitches to the inch, Stone bloomers were sewn with 15 stitches per inch. As a result, the clothing made by Stone Manufacturing gained the reputation of keeping its shape through continual wear and washing.

By the beginning of World War II, sales at Stone Manufacturing were growing approximately 30 percent per year. The U.S. government contracted the company to make clothes for its soldiers in various theaters of war, and was given a production allotment. This allotment meant that one-quarter of the company's manufacturing facilities had to be set aside for producing clothing for the government. One of the firm's most important products during this time was mattress covers. These covers were so well made that sailors reportedly inflated them and used them as floats to wait for rescue boats when ships sank. By the time the war ended, Stone Manufacturing Company employed over 300 seamstresses.

Postwar Drawers

After the war, Stone Manufacturing planned to take advantage of the demand for clothing necessitated by the return of servicemen to the United States. Stone himself thought that items such as the boxer shorts issued by the government and worn by military personnel during the war, popularly known as ''skivvies,'' would transform the country's buying patterns. Stone purchased a new plant in Columbia, South Carolina, to foster its growth.

During the postwar years, as demand for its products grew, Stone Manufacturing began examining ways to improve the performance of the sewing machine. One of Eugene Stone's own inventions was the ''clipper foot,'' a small attachment located next to the needle of the sewing machine to cut the thread after the seam was completed. This labor-saving device allowed the seamstress to continue sewing without having to stop and reach for a pair of scissors. Stone's invention was so efficient that sewing machine companies soon incorporated the ''clipper foot'' into the manufacture of their machines.

By 1949 Stone Manufacturing Company had grown so rapidly and had become so successful that it was profiled in *Life Magazine* as one of the leading clothing firms in the United States. The company had grown from a mere five employees in 1933 to over 2,000 by the end of the 1940s. Production was so efficient that it had doubled a total of five times in just 13 years. The new plant in Columbia was fast becoming the largest manufacturing facility of men's and boys' underwear in the world. Women's clothing items, a specialty of Stone Manufacturing, were also produced in ever greater quantities to meet the burgeoning demands of a populace entering a national economic boom.

During the 1950s, the company prepared to meet the growth in consumer demand by designing and constructing an entirely new manufacturing facility in Cherrydale, South Carolina. When the plant began operation in 1951, it was heralded as the biggest apparel production facility in the world. At a time when planning, outfitting, and operating a clothing manufacturing plant with 300 sewing machines seemed nearly impossible, the company's new Cherrydale plant included over 1,000 sewing machines.

The company's success continued into the 1960s. Stone Manufacturing broadened its product line to include more children's clothing such as T-shirts, pants, shorts, and underwear. The company's line of women's clothing also continued to expand, and began to gain a greater share of the domestic market. Men's clothing and boys' clothing, the firm's two mainstays, were enjoying their greatest popularity ever. Sales for men's underwear, especially the company's line of boxer shorts, were growing rapidly. Although far from the spotlight of Paris or New York fashions, Stone Manufacturing Company remained abreast of current trends within the fashion industry that affected the styles of clothing for both men and women.

With the advent of the 1970s, Stone Manufacturing Company expanded its line of children's wear and women's clothing. New product lines such as children's sweaters and women's jackets quickly gained the attention of consumers throughout the United States. In the mid-1970s, the physical fitness craze caught on in the United States, and Americans began to exercise on a more regular and vigorous basis. By the end of the decade, it was evident that this movement had become a permanent feature in the daily lives of millions of people. Management at Stone Manufacturing Company recognized the potential of such a new market and began to produce the simplest of exercise clothing—running shorts.

Soon Stone began to produce athletic socks, T-shirts, underwear, jerseys, sweatshirts, sweatpants, basketball shorts, and many other items. Then, in 1981, Stone Manufacturing acquired the rights to manufacture the Umbro brand of soccer clothing in the United States. It dedicated the Cherrydale plant in Greenville to the Umbro line. In 1982, Stone Manufacturing and Umbro Ltd. entered a joint venture to make and sell clothes in the world market outside Great Britain.

Umbro was a well-established brand of soccer apparel whose operations were based in Manchester, England. It had been started by brothers Harold and Wallace Humphreys in 1924. The first professional club to sport Umbro gear was Manchester City, which won the FA Cup final in 1934. Umbro outfitted dozens of winning professional soccer teams after that, including Manchester United, as well as the Scottish, English, Norwegian, and Brazilian national teams.

As Jack Stone, son of founder Gene Stone, later recalled, the company at the time faced a choice on whether to direct its resources into marginal businesses or high-growth ones. It chose the latter, selling its lingerie business in 1984. The younger Stone was appointed CEO in 1982 as the U.S. apparel industry was consolidating in the wake of a recession.

Stone Manufacturing had annual revenues of more than $100 million at the time of its 50th anniversary in 1983. It employed 4,000 workers at a dozen plants in the Carolinas and Georgia, half of them in Greenville County, South Carolina. Gene Stone boasted of never having to lay anyone off in five decades of business. Automation allowed each employee at the Cherrydale facility to control 2.5 machines.

Not O.K. with Elkay in 1985

Stone entered a partnership with apparel company Elkay Industries in November 1985. Headquartered in Wilkes Barre, Pennsylvania, Elkay operated a dozen factories in South Carolina. The combined company would employ over 8,000 workers and would be the third largest manufacturer of children's clothing in the United States. However, although Stone acquired management control, it never formally bought more than 11 percent of Elkay.

Elkay was licensed to make clothes under the Cabbage Patch name, and when the popularity of those dolls faded in 1985, it began to run into financial problems. Consolidation among department stores in the 1980s also lead to increased competition from large overseas manufacturers.

Stone sold Elkay its youthwear division for $7 million in March 1988. The $7 million was to be paid off through six-year leases on four of Stone's facilities. However, Elkay missed a payment in April 1989. The leases were canceled, one of the manufacturing sites was shut down, and Jack Stone was replaced as Elkay CEO by Marvin Crow, formerly president of J.P. Stevens & Co. Stone, however, remained chairman of Elkay until shortly before it filed for Chapter 11 protection in July 1990. Stone Manufacturing stood to lose some $10 million that it was still owed.

Elkay had arranged for new financing through Marine Midland Business Loans Inc. of New York but had been in default several times during the year. To stay in business, Elkay was required to relocate its headquarters to Camden, South Carolina, which had offered a $500,000 incentive loan.

Stone Manufacturing's sales were about $100 million a year at the end of the 1980s. Employment was more than 2,000. Stone closed its chain of S-Mart outlet stores in late 1989, when annual sales were about $75 million. It still made half the boxer shorts produced in the United States and led the soccer clothing market. Sales of Umbro soccer shorts continued to rise.

Internationalized in the 1990s

Fully committed to its premier brand, Stone bought Umbro Ltd. for £2.9 million in September 1992. It had reportedly offered £14.8 million for the U.K. company, but reduced the price since Umbro's financing was coming due and Britain was in a recession.

Umbro had pretax profits of £2.1 million on revenues of £65 million in 1992. Stone Manufacturing's revenues were about $200 million. After acquiring all the U.K. rights to Umbro, Stone cut its squash and rugby offerings and focused the unit on soccer exclusively. Stone soon opened five East Coast outlet stores dedicated to Umbro merchandise.

In 1994, Umbro posted after-tax profits of £4.2 million on U.K. sales of £75 million alone, as soccer made a comeback in Britain. Umbro was supplying more than 60 professional teams. The worldwide soccer equipment industry, including footwear, was estimated to be worth £2.7 billion a year.

Umbro had subsidiaries in Germany, France, Brazil, and the United States. It was also developing markets in Japan and Africa and becoming more dependent on outsourcing manufacturing as its operations became more internationalized. Stone used a high-tech fabric imported from Europe for Umbro's new, radically styled referees' uniforms. The Recovery polyester yarn, made from recycled plastic bottles, was woven in England and finished in Spain. Officials appreciated the superior coolness of the jerseys.

A new gray uniform designed for Manchester United, Britain's largest soccer club, was not as well accepted. Players blamed the uniforms for a losing streak early in the 1996 season and refused to wear them. Fortunately for Umbro, the white replacement shirts were a great success. Umbro was paying £10 million a year to sponsor Manchester United; other makers of soccer clothing also competed vigorously for these rights.

Plans to float Umbro as a public company in late 1996 never came to fruition. Analysts predicted such an offering would be valued between £100 million and £200 million. Stuart Humphreys and Ben Humphreys, son and grandson of Harold Humphreys, threatened to sue Stone Manufacturing, claiming the £2.9 million that Umbro had sold for in 1992 was not a fair price.

Instead of a successful IPO, what followed was Stone Manufacturing's annus terribilis. Company founder Eugene Stone III (Gene) died in June 1997. His son, Jack Stone, already CEO, succeeded him as chairman. The same year, the company had to sue to wrest the Internet domain name Umbro.com from the hands of a Canadian pornographer and the domain name registrar Network Solutions, Inc.

Umbro International had difficulty matching its vigorous competitors in the marketplace. Adidas had been strong in soccer for decades and another multi-sport apparel company, Nike, quickly gained market share in the late 1990s. While Umbro was also expanding aggressively, it overextended itself and defaulted on its debt.

Stone Manufacturing officially changed its name to Umbro International Inc. in late 1997. It posted sales of more than $600 million for the year, in a market spanning 55 countries. The U.S. division lost money in 1997, though the British business remained profitable. As financial pressures mounted, employees were furloughed for eight weeks in August 1997. They were laid off for another two weeks in February 1998.

Leaving the Soccer Field in 1998

By this time, the company was looking for a new CEO. It hired turnaround specialist Larry Ramaekers, who soon closed the Greenville plant entirely and returned manufacturing operations to Manchester, England. Umbro was also planning to sell two plants in Merseyside and Stoke-on-Trent in England as well as its Kaepa volleyball subsidiary.

The Cherrydale plant had been serving as Umbro International's U.S. headquarters and distribution center. Its closing left 220 administrative employees and 342 factory workers jobless. Employment there had been double that a decade earlier and reached 2,200 in the 1950s. The company did not offer a severance package, only a bonus equal to a week's pay to workers who stayed through the final weeks.

By the end of the summer, developers were planning to place a shopping mall on the site, and demolition began in July 1999. Plans were made to relocate a historic residence on the property to nearby Furman University, whose founder originally built the house. The Stone family had remodeled the Cherrydale residence in 1997, intending to use it as a corporate guesthouse. Stone's historic building on Court Street in downtown Greenville was sold to Kent Manufacturing Company, the venerable wool producer.

Two thousand sewing machines were among the equipment auctioned off in September 1998. In the same month, Umbro International licensed Signal Apparel and Riddell Sports Inc. (through its Memphis-based Varsity Spirit subsidiary) to make and market Umbro products in the United States. Signal had found its greatest success marketing sweatshirts and T-shirts to discount department stores, while Riddell was best known for its protective football equipment.

Umbro America, led by longtime Umbro executive Ian McLaren, continued to develop and market Umbro products from Greenville, though production was coordinated by Varsity in Memphis. Riddell/Varsity focused on making clothes for soccer teams; Signal in New York continued to specialize in department store sales.

In April 1999, Umbro Europe Holdings Ltd. and Umbro World were sold for $145 million to a unit of London investment firm Doughty Hanson & Co. Umbro Holdings Ltd. (the new name for the Cheshire-based company) had subsidiaries in the United Kingdom, Germany, France, and Hong Kong and licensing agreements with 52 other countries. After the sale, Umbro International changed its name back to Stone Manufacturing Company. It continued making men's underwear, though its glory days appeared to be over.

Principal Competitors

Courtalds plc; Sara Lee Underwear Co.

Further Reading

Bennett, Jeff, ''Stone Gets Out of Soccer Field,'' *Greenville News,* April 30, 1999, pp. 1D, 2D.

——, ''Stone's Walls Tumbling Down,'' *Greenville News,* July 14, 1999, p. 1D.

——, ''Umbro Denies British Report It Is for Sale,'' *Greenville News,* September 15, 1998, p. 6B.

——, ''Umbro Move Costs 562 Jobs,'' *Greenville News,* March 10, 1998, p.. 1A, 7A.

——, ''Umbro Picks Companies to Handle Soccer Gear,'' *Greenville News,* September 16, 1998, pp. 1D, 2D.

Bennett, Jeff, and Ed O'Donoghue, ''Umbro Workers to Get Week's Pay,'' *Greenville News,* March 11, 1998, pp. 3A-4A.

Curan, Catherine, ''Wall St. Bullish on WR Shirts,'' *Daily News Record,* April 21, 1995, p. 1.

——, ''Men's First Period Financial Results Better Than Women's,'' *Daily News Record,* June 28, 1994, p. 2.

DuPlessis, Jim, ''Stone Manufacturing: Retrenching After Some 'Tough Times','' *Greenville News,* July 30, 1990, pp. 1C, 3C.

Fox, Tally S., ''New Stone Plant Serves As Guinea Pig in Production: Air-Conditioned Factory Expected to Increase Yield Ten Per Cent,'' *Greenville Piedmont,* August 24, 1948.

Gellers, Stan, ''Designers Love Linen,'' *Daily News Record,* July 1, 1993, p. 6.

——, ''Clothing Coming of Age,'' *Daily News Record,* May 22, 1992, p. 93.

Hancox, Clara, ''What Will It Take to Survive into the Next Century,'' *Daily News Record,* June 28, 1993, p. 23.

Harverson, Patrick, ''Family That Sold Umbro Plans Lawsuit,'' *Financial Times,* February 26, 1996, p. 22.

——, ''Grey Day for Umbro As Strip Is Torn Off by Manchester United,'' *Financial Times,* April 16, 1996, p. 20.

Hedges, Stephen J., ''Stone Manufacturing Celebrates Fifty Good Years of Apparel Business,'' *Greenville Piedmont,* August 11, 1983.

Knight, Beverly, ''Umbro America Alive and Kicking,'' *Business Greenville,* September 3, 1999, B19, B27.

Lesley, Wanda, ''Volume Makes Style Key,'' *Greenville News,* July 31, 1977, p. C1.

Rivlin, Richard, ''Umbro United,'' *Sunday Telegraph,* City Section, August 4, 1996, p. 4.

Salfino, Catherine, ''Men's Apparel Execs Cheer Results of 1994 Federal Election,'' *Daily News Record,* November 10, 1994, p. 12.

——, "More Vendors See $ in the SSS Sports," *Daily News Record,* April 24, 1995, p. 6.

Shelton, Ted, "Stone Plant Is Expanding," *Greenville Piedmont,* September 22, 1958.

Stewart, Hank, "'Blood, Sweat, Tears' Make Line of Clothing," *Greenville News,* August 4, 1975.

Stone, Eugene E., III, *Stone Manufacturing Company: The First Half Century of Clothing a Changing World,* New York: Newcomen Society, 1985.

"Stone Manufacturing's Relationship with Elkay Industries Was Troubled," *Greenville News,* July 30, 1990.

"The Story of Stone Manufacturing," *Life Magazine,* August 1949, pp. 39–44.

"Umbro Kicks Off New Season," *Commerce Business Magazine,* December 29, 1997.

Vargo, Julie, "Work Clothes Bring Fashion to the Street," *Daily News Record,* November 18, 1994, p. 3.

Walsh, Peter, "Outside Forces That Influenced Fashion," *Daily News Record,* May 22, 1992, p. 60.

Warren, Elizabeth, "Stone Family Asks County to Relocate Graves for Complex," *Greenville News,* August 31, 1998, pp. 1B, 2B.

Yates, Andrew, "Umbro Sacks US Workforce to Stave Financial Crisis," *The Independent,* March 21, 1998, p. 25.

—Thomas Derdak
—update: Frederick C. Ingram

Swinerton Inc.

580 California Street, Suite 1200
San Francisco, California 94104
U.S.A.
Telephone: (415) 421-2980
Fax: (415) 433-0943
Web Site: http://www.swinerton.com

Private Company
Incorporated: 1888 as Boyd, Sharples & Lindgren
Employees: 1,400
Sales: $1.07 billion (2000 est.)
NAIC: 23332 Commercial and Institutional Building Construction; 23499 All Other Heavy Construction

Swinerton Inc. is the holding company for several firms that handle all aspects of construction including general contracting, project management and consulting, and property management. Some of the most famous buildings in San Francisco—the Opera House, the Public Library, the Pacific Telephone and Telegraph Building, the Ghirardelli Square retail complex—were built by this company whose origins go back to the 1880s and the dreams of a Swedish immigrant who had come to seek his fortune.

Joining the Land Rush in the 1880s

California in the 1880s was a booming place. The gold rush of 1848 had put California on the map, and the construction of new rail lines set up a competition that made it ridiculously inexpensive to come West. The first Santa Fe Railroad train pulled into Los Angeles in the spring of 1887; thanks to the rivalry between the Santa Fe and Southern Pacific rail lines, the rail fare from Chicago to Los Angeles dropped to a dollar.

Not surprisingly, this caused a ''land rush'' not unlike the gold rush of half a century earlier. Among the budding entrepreneurs that traveled to California was Charles Lindgren, a young man who had emigrated from Sweden to Chicago several years earlier. The son of a stonemason, he reasoned that the population boom in California would mean a construction boom, so he moved his young family to Los Angeles. Lindgren met many others like himself in Los Angeles, and he began a business with two men, James Boyd and Frank Sharples. The firm of Boyd, Sharples & Lindgren advertised in the Los Angeles city directory as brick masons and contractors, and initially they met with success.

Unfortunately, the land boom in Southern California had inflated prices so sharply that the market was unable to sustain itself. A collapse of the real estate market in 1889 put many people out of business, including Boyd, Sharples & Lindgren. Lindgren continued to work as a brick mason, always watching out for new challenges. One such challenge came in July, when the city of Bakersfield (north of Santa Barbara) suffered a devastating fire. Bakersfield needed experienced builders, and Lindgren was among those who headed north to help reconstruct the city.

Lindgren proved his skills as a contractor in Bakersfield, where he resettled his family. Over the next decade his business expanded and thrived, and he earned a reputation for work that was both high quality and finished ahead of schedule. Bakersfield and the surrounding communities provided plenty of work for Lindgren, but he was ambitious for greater challenges. At around this time, a new building boom was beginning, this time in San Francisco, and Lindgren was intrigued enough to explore the possibility of expanding his business there. He made his first definitive move in this direction in 1900, when he formed a partnership with a Berkeley engineer named Lewis Hicks.

A New Way of Building in the 20th Century

Hicks brought two attributes to this partnership. First, he was well connected in the San Francisco community, which opened up opportunities for larger projects. Second and more important, he was a pioneer in steel-reinforced concrete construction. Hicks was convinced that steel-reinforced concrete would replace traditional wood and brick, in part because it would be more durable against disasters such as earthquakes and fires. He convinced Lindgren, and the two men introduced the new technique into the Bay Area. Not surprisingly, their efforts were met with resistance, in part because the new technique as more expensive than traditional brick and wood con-

Company Perspectives:

Because we started providing construction services before the invention of the light bulb, the airplane, and the automobile, we've learned to adapt to continuous change over the course of 110 years. But the Swinerton companies haven't simply adapted. We've also set new standards for construction and championed changes in technology that have provided our customers with innovative approaches to their projects, resulting in successful and time-tested buildings and facilities.

struction. Many buildings continued to be constructed this way in San Francisco and its environs.

It took a disaster to change attitudes permanently in San Francisco. The earthquake that hit on April 18, 1906, left much of the city in ruins. Many of the buildings the earthquake left standing were consumed by the fires that engulfed the city for days afterward. Experts examined the buildings that remained standing over the next several months; while some brick and masonry structures had suffered relatively minor damage, it was the steel-reinforced concrete structures that had fared best. Once people realized this, it was clear that there would be no going back to traditional building materials.

One of the buildings damaged in the earthquake was the Fairmount Hotel, which had been scheduled to open in the spring of 1906. The damage resulted from fire, which had burned crates of furnishings in the hotel and gutted the building. A number of the steel columns had buckled and needed to be replaced. This Lindgren Hicks did, under the supervision of a young architect named Julia Morgan (who would later become famous as the architect for San Simeon, the ''Hearst Castle.'')

As the recognized experts on steel-reinforced concrete, Lindgren Hicks grew quickly. However, Lindgren and Hicks ended their partnership in 1908, apparently the result of a business disagreement. Lindgren formed a new company with his brother, Fred, and set about building a still stronger operation by hiring the most talented people he could find. One of these new hires was a young man who had been studying engineering at Stanford until the earthquake convinced him that a career in building would be more challenging. His name was Alfred Bingham Swinerton.

Bringing a New Focus in the early 1900s

Swinerton's talent and abilities were evident almost from the beginning, and he rose quickly up the Lindgren ladder. By 1911 he was a shareholder and a member of Lindgren's board of directors. In 1913, when Charles Lindgren died, the 30-year-old Swinerton was named vice-president. A year later, Swinerton married Jane Hotaling, a member of one of San Francisco's wealthiest and most prominent families. Jane Hotaling Swinerton was as savvy about business as her husband, and she was named to the Lindgren board of directors shortly after the marriage.

The next few years were busy for Lindgren. Among its achievements were the French Pavilion and the Exposition Auditorium for the Pan Pacific International Exposition, the San Francisco Public Library, and the Southern Pacific Building. Lindgren was earning a reputation not just for quality and speed but also safety. The Southern Pacific building—at the time the largest office building west of Chicago—took less than a year to complete, during which time there were no serious injuries to any of the crew.

In April 1917 the U.S. entered World War I, and Lindgren was chosen by the government to build an army training facility, Camp Fremont, in San Mateo. War projects like this were particularly important to companies like Lindgren, since civilian construction all but halted while the U.S. was at war. The wartime contracts helped keep Lindgren busy until construction began to pick up again in the early 1920s.

Lindgren saw its business grow steadily throughout the 1920s; among its projects were the Pacific Telephone and Telegraph building and the Francis Drake Hotel. The combination of more sturdy building materials and the development of high-speed elevators allowed companies to build taller buildings. Alfred Swinerton how headed Lindgren, and in recognition of his hard work and contributions, the board of directors voted in 1923 to change the company's name to Lindgren & Swinerton, Inc.

During the 1920s, architects, engineers, and contractors became increasingly vocal about their belief that builders should be licensed. In part this was because the building boom was attracting so many new contractors that it was difficult to know which ones were most experienced or had the best safety record. Some saw licensing as a means of keeping the best jobs in the hands of only a select few contractors, so the issue was debated throughout the decade. The California legislature finally passed a licensing law in 1929. Lindgren & Swinerton was the 92nd company out of some 28,000 to apply for licenses that first year; the company's license number remains 92 to the present day.

Struggling Through the Depression

Businesses across the board were optimistic about the 1930s. The stock market crash in October 1929 was viewed as a temporary blip in a strong economy, but as it became clear that a severe depression was at hand, industries suffered severe losses. In 1932, three years after the crash, nearly 500 construction contractors had gone bankrupt, with liabilities of more than $42 million. Projects became harder to come by. Moreover, union activity in the construction trade, which had been weak since the end of World War I, was increasing; as unions gained strength, wages went up.

Lindgren & Swinerton had enough backlogged projects that the company was spared some of the pain of the Great Depression, at least in the beginning. However, there came a point during which work seemed to dry up. Lindgren & Swinerton had put in bids for both Boulder Dam and the Golden Gate Bridge but had failed in both attempts. Swinerton and Walberg debated whether it might be better to close the company during the depression, but they decided instead to take a risk and spend additional money to build on their strengths.

By the mid-1930s things seemed to be getting better, but the country was hardly out of the woods. In the late 1930s,

Key Dates:

1888: Charles Lindgren begins contracting business with two partners in Los Angeles.
1889: Lindgren helps rebuild city of Bakersfield; establishes business there.
1900: Lindgren forms partnership with engineer Lewis Hicks.
1908: Lindgren forms partnership with brother, Fred; hires Alfred Swinerton as estimator.
1913: Charles Lindgren dies; Swinerton names vice-president.
1917: U.S. government hires Lindgren Co. to build World War I training camp in San Mateo.
1923: Company renamed Lindgren & Swinerton.
1928: Swinerton hires engineer Richard Walberg.
1939: Lindgren & Swinerton build 263-mile Barco pipeline across Andes Mountains.
1942: Lindgren & Swinerton forms new general partnership called Swinerton & Walberg.
1955: Atomic Energy Commission chooses Swinerton & Walberg to build Rocky Flats plutonium production center near Denver.
1963: Alfred Swinerton dies.
1964: Swinerton & Walberg begins construction of Ghirardelli Square in San Francisco.
1976: Walberg retires.
1982: Swinerton & Walberg launches Interiors division for high-end office space.
1996: Reorganization of company leads to creation of Swinerton Inc. as holding company.
2000: Swinerton reaches $1 billion in revenue.

Lindgren & Swinerton was once again getting large projects, including a 312-mile long pipeline from Bakersfield to Martinez and a 263-mile pipeline running over the Andes Mountains through Colombia and Venezuela. These jobs were lucrative, but Lindgren & Swinerton needed capital. The company's bank was unwilling to grant a loan, but Jane Swinerton came to the rescue, putting up money from her estate. In the end, the projects were successful. The Barco project was particularly grueling, since it exposed workers to conditions they had never before experienced. Mosquitoes carrying malaria and other diseases proliferated, poisonous snakes were also a hazard. Sanitation and refrigeration as these workers knew it were non-existent. Occasionally the workers were even attacked by members of indigenous tribes. Lindgren & Swinerton enlisted the aid of a public health official from San Diego to supervise sanitation efforts at the project site. A water purification plant was built, and electric refrigerators were provided (they had to be floated up the Magdalena River). Workers were also required to remain inside their mosquito netting after sunset.

The War Years

The 1930s closed out with some economic promise, but the specter of World War II hung over U.S. citizens. Even without direct U.S. participation, U.S. supplies were being sent overseas. When the United States officially entered the war in December 1941, production at all levels was turned to the war effort. Lindgren & Swinerton had the reputation, but not the cash flow. The Depression years had left the company strapped despite the projects it had built, and its primary bank, the Anglo-California, was extremely cautious. New projects, such as a joint venture with another contractor to build an Army installation in Panama, held out promise, but cash flow was still a critical problem. By the summer of 1941, relations between Lindgren & Swinerton and Anglo-California were so bad that no one knew what the contractor's fate would be. Once again, help came in the form of Jane Swinerton, who, using money from the Hotaling estate, paid off all loans owed to Anglo-California and vowed that her husband's company would never again do business with that bank. Lindgren & Swinerton entered into a new banking arrangement with the much more helpful American Trust company, and the company was able to devote its energies to its business.

In 1942, partly to shield itself from changes in federal tax law that taxed corporations as high as 50 percent of net earnings, the corporation of Lindgren & Swinerton became a general partnership called Swinerton & Walberg.

Postwar Construction Boom

Wartime construction had peaked around 1943 and then fell off, with the U.S. government putting most of its efforts behind manufacturing. Construction companies struggled, but when the war ended they were in for the most widespread building boom the U.S. had ever witnessed. Construction of post-war factories, housing and highways soared; these paved the way for the construction of schools, hospitals, and shopping centers.

In fact, the U.S. government did not eliminate wartime production controls immediately after the war. Fearing that overly rapid growth could lead to inflation, they opted for a more gradual return to pre-war standards. Far from being detrimental to businesses, it gave them a chance to regroup—and also to plan out their futures.

Swinerton & Walberg was able to take its first breath in nearly a decade. And, with its reputation for superior work and integrity, it was able to land numerous important deals during the post-war years. Among the companies that turned to the Swinerton organization in the 1940s and 1950s were General Motors, Kodak, Safeway, American Can, General Foods, Dow Chemical, Hunt Foods, and Kimberly Clark.

Defense production became a major source of business in the United States as well. Swinerton & Walberg participated in defense construction, including a plutonium production facility in Rocky Flats (outside Denver) commissioned by the Atomic Energy Commission in 1955.

The building frenzy did eventually slow down, and toward the end of the 1950s Swinerton & Walberg began to feel the effects. The company looked to different solutions and decided to divest itself of its pipeline division. It also decided to focus more on real estate development, as well as hotel and resort construction. In the early 1960s the company began building in Hawaii, where demand for hotels was high.

During this time the company began to restructure its business. Previously, it operated more like a series of several different companies, each focusing on a particular specialty. Now it would have a more unified, consolidated corporate structure. This was one of the major changes for the company during this time. In May 1963, another unexpected change took place: company chairman Alfred Swinerton, who had started with Lindgren more than 50 years earlier, died at the age of 79. The transition was smooth; Walberg was named chairman and Swinerton's son William was named president. But to longtime employees it was the end of an era for the company.

Continued Growth: 1960s–80s

Swinerton & Walberg in the 1960s was a strong and healthy company. With such projects as Ghirardelli Square retail complex and additional hotels in Hawaii, Swinerton continued to grow. It also looked for ways to increase its range as a means of fending off dips in the economy. The acquisition of Rothschild & Raffin, specialists in heavy construction projects, helped toward this goal, as did continued expansion into the hotel-resort market.

In 1976, chairman Richard Walberg retired after 48 years with the company, and Milo "Ned" Gates was named president. William Swinerton stayed on as chairman. Another big change that took place within the company's structure was that it became a 100 percent employee-owned company; this involved a stock repurchase plan that bought up some 3,000 shares of stock held by members of the Swinerton and Walberg families who were not otherwise associated with the company. It was believed that employee ownership would give management a stronger stake in the company's long-term performance.

Building recessions in the 1970s turned to construction booms in the 1980s, as an office building boom seemed to sweep the country much as the housing boom had some 30 years earlier. Swinerton & Walberg took advantage of this boom and built many of the premier office buildings in San Francisco and other cities during these years.

The 1980s opened Swinerton up to a problem it had virtually never faced in its history: safety problems. Swinerton had long prided itself on its decades-long outstanding safety record. But a series of accidents made the company rethink its safety programs. A crane accident at a Los Angeles site in 1981 killed two Swinerton employees and injured three others. Immediately the company re-examined all its safety efforts, including education programs and closer supervision of all subcontractors. A 1985 crane accident, also in Los Angeles, killed three workers. Again safety measures were examined carefully, and again the company spared no efforts. However, a 1989 crane accident in San Francisco killed five people and injured 21 others. These accidents ultimately led to a strengthening of crane operation safety regulations.

Entering the Second Century

In 1988, Swinerton & Walberg celebrated the company's centennial in the lobby of the Fairmount Hotel, where more than 80 years earlier Lindgren and Hicks had been feted for rebuilding the fire-damaged edifice. Dave Grubb, who had been rising in the Swinerton ranks for some years, was named president, as William Swinerton stepped down as chairman and Milo Gates replaced him in that role.

The 1990s start off badly for the construction industry, with the collapse of the office construction boom in the late 1980s compounded by the 1991 recession. Swinerton & Walberg had enough work to keep the steady through the early 1990s but realized that planning for a sound future still had to be a top priority.

Throughout the 1990s, the company added a number of companies to its family through mergers and acquisition. These included Tucson-based contractor Conelly Construction (1994), heavy construction company William P. Young (1997), Salt Lake City-based Bud Bailey Construction Co. (1997), and El Monte, CA-based Keller Builders (1999). The company continued its efforts to diversify, getting involved in construction management and consulting, and remained involved in property management. The company reached a milestone in 2000 when for the first time it posted revenues of over $1 billion.

In 1996, the Swinerton group was organized under the umbrella company Swinerton Inc., with Dave Grubb as chairman. In addition to the acquisitions above, Swinerton Inc. also included Swinerton & Walberg, Swinerton Management & Consulting, Westwood Swinerton (based in Oregon), and Swinerton & Walberg Property Services. Swinerton believed that its demonstrated commitment to quality and safety, coupled with its ability to adapt to market changes, will make for a strong and profitable future.

Principal Operating Units

Bud Bailey Construction; Keller Builders; Swinerton Management & Consulting; Swinerton & Walberg; Swinerton & Walberg Property Services; Westwood Swinerton; William P. Young Construction.

Principal Competitors

Bechtel Corporation, Bovis Lend Lease, Hathaway Dinwiddie.

Further Reading

Abrahamson, Eric. *A Builder in the West: The History of the Swinerton Organization,* Redwood City, Calif.: Prologue Group, 1998.

"Accident Revives Question: Is State Lax in Regulating Cranes?," *Los Angeles Times,* January 19, 1990, p. B1.

"California Mark IV," *Economist,* June 4, 1994, p. A23.

"Economic Recovery Taking Hold but Too Late for 1993 Billings," *ENR*, April 4, 1994, p. 35.

Roberts, Steven V., "California Crumbling," *U.S. News & World Report,* September 14, 1992, p. 69.

—George A. Milite

CHAMPAGNE
TAITTINGER
Reims

Taittinger S.A.

9, Place Saint-Nicaise
51100 Reims
France
Telephone: +33 03 26 85 45 35
Fax: +33 03 26 50 14 30
Web site: http://www.taittinger.com

Public Company
Incorporated: 1734 as Forest Fourneaux
Employees: 7,712 (2000)
Sales: EUR 816.05 million (2000)
Stock Exchanges: Paris
Ticker Symbol: TTT
NAIC: 312130 Wineries; 422820 Wine and Distilled Alcoholic Beverage Wholesalers; 721110 Hotels (except Casinos) and Motels; 522210 Credit Card Issuing

Reputedly James Bond's favorite brand of champagne, regularly recognized in such publications as *Wine Spectator*, *Vintage*, *Vogue*, *Wine World*, and *The New York Times*, Taittinger S.A. is one of the most recognized brands of champagne in the world, and its vineyards cover almost 650 acres of prime winemaking country. That's is partly due to market savvy—Taittinger was the first champagne house to engage in commercial advertising, and with the Artist Collection series, the company has clothed fine vintages in the work of some of Europe's most distinguished modern artists—and partly due to the production of award-winning champagne. With Taittinger's diversification, primarily via the Société du Louvre, into hotel ownership and management, fine crystal, perfume, and other industries, the company name has become associated with luxury.

Taittinger S.A. is also, thanks in part to this diversification, one of the 250 largest enterprises in France. With the establishment of its American subsidiary, Domaine Carneros, in 1987, Taittinger has become a truly international concern. Despite this and the fact that the company is publicly traded in France, it remains in many respects an old-fashioned family venture: Claude and Pierre-Emmanuel, respectively the son and grandson of the company's founding father, are senior executives, and other members of the family are in senior management in the Société du Louvre. Under the direction of Claude Taittinger, who took over leadership of the company in 1960, Taittinger's distribution expanded to 120 markets outside of France.

An Ancient History

Although the Taittinger family came into winemaking only in the twentieth century, the company built itself on deep roots. The Taittinger cellars were established in Reims, the heart of champagne country; many other houses, including Piper-Heidsieck, Louis Roederer, and Ruinart, were established there. In the thirteenth century, the land belonged to Saint-Nicaise Abbey. Here the Benedictine order cultivated grapes and manufactured wine, in keeping with the order's emphasis on manual labor. Winemaking was common in the region, and Saint-Nicaise was only one of several abbeys engaged in the occupation. Although the French Revolution ended the abbey's winemaking activities and destroyed the abbey itself, the same land was later acquired by Taittinger and became the site of the company's main cellars and home office.

The company that would later become Taittinger was established in this region in 1734. Jacques Fourneaux founded the third champagne house in the country; by 1931, the firm was known as Forest, Fourneaux, et Cie and was acquired by Pierre-Charles Taittinger. The Taittinger family left the region of Lorraine in 1871 and settled near Paris. Pierre-Charles, who already ran a champagne distribution and export business, was stationed in the Champagne region from which the variety of wine draws its name during World War I. In addition to the company, he also purchased the Château de la Marquetterie and its surrounding vineyards, as well as the palace of the Comtes de Champagne, located in Reims. Despite the fact that the business has acquired such traditional trappings, however, the Taittinger house has been determinedly twentieth century in its outlook.

From the beginning, Pierre-Charles Taittinger set out to create a champagne that was not only distinctive—a prescient example of branding—but that also fit with rising trends in cuisine. A notable gastronome (his son Claude created the

Company Perspectives:

Taittinger is recognized worldwide for producing some of the finest champagnes available. One of the last remaining family-owned and operated champagne houses, Taittinger can rely on 642 acres of its own prime vineyards to assure the consistently outstanding quality that is part of its long tradition.

Pierre Taittinger International Culinary Prize in his honor in 1967) Taittinger predicted a tendency toward lighter, more delicate fare, and crafted a champagne to match. With the assistance of chef Fernand Point, he metamorphosed champagne from a dessert drink to one suitable for any course.

The Next Generation

It was with the accession of Claude Taittinger, son of Pierre-Charles, to the directorship of the company that Taittinger's business and reputation expanded, beginning the firm's rise to become one of the world's best-known champagne producers. Although he had assisted his elder brother François in the management of the company, the death of François in an automobile accident in 1960 put Claude in the driver's seat.

The younger Taittinger had already done much for the family firm, notably creating the Comtes de Champagne Blanc de Blancs, a chardonnay champagne that remains one of the company's flagship wines. It is also, despite what the films may indicate, reputed to be James Bond's favorite vintage, according to Ian Fleming's novel *Casino Royale*. This champagne, in keeping with the distinctive lightness and delicacy that Pierre-Charles Taittinger had already caused to be associated with the family name, did much to enhance the company's reputation. Prior to World War II, the fashion in champagne was for heavy, sweeter taste, so the Blanc de Blancs represented a radical shift.

In the 1950s, however, other expansions were already under way. Taittinger had already taken over the old cellars of the Saint-Nicaise Abbey for the company's own use, but rising production made it necessary to enlarge the cellars. During the construction, Taittinger unearthed perhaps a few dozen empty bottles in the older, potbellied style used by the Benedictines in bottling champagne. Taittinger adopted the design for its Comtes de Champagne line.

While respecting tradition, however, Claude Taittinger was not blind to the commercial possibilities of the twentieth century. In 1963, Taittinger became the first champagne company to advertise its products, taking care to be as distinctive in its advertising as it is with its champagne. Claude continued to take active part in the company's advertisements, designing posters as recently as 1988. (Such posters have lately been sought by collectors, particularly since legislation in France enacted in the early 1990s limits the advertising of alcoholic beverages.)

Claude Taittinger also created the Artist Collection Series, beginning with the 1978 vintage, which premiered in 1983, nominally for the purpose of commemorating the house's 250th anniversary. A sort of limited edition, the Collection Series was defined to consist only of vintage champagnes. Each bottle was swathed in modern artwork courtesy of a well-known twentieth-century artist; this sheath was then laser-sealed to protect the bottle's contents from variations in light and temperature. The 1983 edition was done by Hungarian artist Victor Vasarely; other contributors have included surrealist Andre Masson, abstract artist Toshimitsu Imai, and even Roy Lichtenstein, who according to Claude "considered champagne to be the result of a collaboration between nature and human ingenuity."

Diversification

It was also under Claude Taittinger's leadership that the company diversified from its initial industry of winemaking, which as of the year 2000 comprised only twelve percent of the business. In 1954, Claude's father, Pierre-Charles, acquired a stake in the growing hotel firm Société du Louvre, which had started out in 1855 as a department store next door to the recently constructed Grand Hotel du Louvre. By the 1970s, the Société had largely abandoned its retail activities in favor of concentrating on its luxury hotel business, grouped under the name Concorde. During the 1970s, the Société diversified its business into budget hotels, light industry, the Banque du Louvre, Annick Goutal perfumes and the Baccarat crystal company, but hotels continued to account for approximately two-thirds of the company's business.

The Taittinger family was closely involved with all of these expansions. The Concorde luxury hotel group, founded in 1973, was established by Guy Taittinger, while Anne-Claire Taittinger became the head of the Société's board of directors in 1997 and took over the Baccarat crystal company in the 1990s. To refurbish the crystal company's somewhat dusty image, Anne-Claire set out to redecorate the Château de Baccarat in eastern France. "We made it very simple—but also very French because we are French," she told CNN. The Concorde group included such luxury establishments as the prestigious Hotel de Crillon in Paris, whose Grand Bernstein suite—named for the famous composer—features his piano, has more square footage than many suburban houses, and overlooks the Place de la Concorde. More than that, however, the entire hotel was designed to feature the opulent elegance that is associated with the Taittinger name. As Claude Taittinger put it: "I myself don't have any sensitivity for equipping cars or making television sets, none at all, but I do have a feeling for what is nice, what is beautiful."

However, Taittinger did not neglect the business for which it had primarily become known. In 1974, the company acquired the Bouvet-Ladubay winery, which was founded in the Loire Valley in France in 1851 and had since enjoyed a solid reputation for fine wines.

Taittinger has also expanded its operations into the United States. In 1947, Claude Taittinger visited northern California and, according to company legend, determined one day to settle there. In 1986, the company began a partnership with American importer Kobrand Corporation, which led to the establishment of the Domaine Carneros winery in 1989. As of 2001, Taittinger owned 83.4 percent of the company.

Established in the region that bears its name, intersecting the Sonoma and Napa valleys in northern California, Domaine

Key Dates:

1734: Jacques Fourneaux establishes one of the first champagne houses in France.
1870: The Taittinger family leaves its native province of Lorraine and settles in the vicinity of Paris.
1917: Pierre-Charles Taittinger, a cavalry officer during World War I, visits the Château de la Marquetterie in the Champagne region.
1931: Pierre-Charles Taittinger purchases what is now known as the Forest-Fourneaux Company, as well as the family house of the Counts of Champagne.
1932: Pierre-Charles Taittinger purchases the Château de la Marquetterie that he visited during World War I.
1945: François, Jean, and Claude Taittinger, all sons of Pierre, join the company.
1947: Claude Taittinger visits the United States, particularly northern California.
1950: While enlarging the underground structure of Saint-Nicaise Abbey in Reims, Taittinger discovers several empty bottles with a rounder shape than those used today, dating from when Benedictine monks occupied the land. The shape is used in the production of Comtes de Champagne cuvee.
1954: Pierre Taittinger acquires a stake in Société du Louvre, which owns and operates a group of luxury hotels.
1955: Pierre Taittinger becomes managing director of the Société du Louvre.
1956: Claude Taittinger creates the Comtes de Champagne Blanc de Blancs.
1960: François Taittinger is killed in an automobile accident; his brother Claude takes over leadership of the company.
1963: Tattinger is the first champagne house to advertise its products.
1967: Claude Taittinger establishes the Pierre Taittinger International Culinary Prize in honor of his father.
1978: Claude Taittinger develops the Taittinger Collection, a series of specialty bottles designed by various artists.
1983: Hungarian artist Victor Vasarely creates the first bottle in the Taittinger Collection.
1987: Taittinger founds the Domaine Carneros winery in northern California with the assistance of its United States importer, Kobrand.
1989: Taittinger acquires a 10 percent interest in Euro Disneyland SNC.
1991: Taittinger increases interest in La Distilleries Dalaruan (Scotland), Domaine Carneros (California), Baccarat, Porcelaines Haviland, L'Orfèvre Odiot, Faienceries de Gien, and Parfums Annick Goutal. Taittinger also acquires Société Samazeuilh (Bordeaux) and Maison Garres-Fourche.
1992: Taittinger increases interest in Baccarat.
1993: Taittinger establishes Société Saint-Evremond, a producer of champagne.
1997: Anne-Claire Taittinger becomes CEO of the Société du Louvre.
1998: Société du Louvre decreases interest in the Banque du Louvre, and disposes of all interest in Porcelaines Haviland. Investor Asher Edelman seeks a controlling stake in the Société du Louvre.
1999: Taittinger issues a commemorative millennium edition champagne.
2000: Edelman's attempt to reduce Taittinger's voting rights in Société du Louvre is rejected by Paris courts.

Carneros covered 138 acres of prime wine-growing country. The vineyards produced pinot noir and chardonnay grapes, which are used in champagne production. However, Domaine Carneros sparkling wines did not bear the champagne appellation; Taittinger retained the tradition of only applying the label to wines that are actually produced in the Champagne region of France. Domaine Carneros also produced Pinot Noir red wines.

As with Taittinger's production in France, Domaine Carneros used handpicked grapes from its vineyards, and only juice from the first pressing of the grapes was used to make the wine. The winery itself also reflected the company's origins, with a château consciously modeled on Taittinger's Château de la Marquetterie. Ever since its inception, Domaine Carneros produced well-regarded wines, including the *Le Reve* (''The Dream'') vintage cuvee, an homage to Claude Taittinger's dream of a northern California establishment.

The New Millennium

Through the 1990s and into the new millennium, Taittinger sought both to remain a family-centered organization, and to compete in a modern, increasingly global environment. Although, as Claude Taittinger put it, ''Champagne is a small world. We do not compete. We share quality and tradition,'' the company faced a different kind of competition as the world moved toward a more global economy. In 1998, institutional investor Asher Edelman, who at the time owned an 11 percent stake in the Société du Louvre (Taittinger owned 36.6 percent), attempted to take control of the group and split it into three companies. The resulting conflict highlighted significant differences between American and European methods of doing business; as Jean Peyrelevade, chairman of Crédit Lyonnais, commented in the *Wall Street Journal*, ''In France, a company cannot be reduced to the financial interest of shareholders.'' Or as Jacques-Henri Bourdois, who managed a French organization of family businesses, put it, ''It's a face-off between two completely different worlds.'' While Taittinger always emphasized the familial nature of the business, Edelman claimed that the company was seriously—and deliberately—undervalued, and that if the Société du Louvre were truly a family business, then it should not be publicly traded.

Similarly, another investor, Guy Wyser-Pratte, who at the time owned a 13 percent stake in Taittinger itself, was also determined to focus less on patrimony and more on profit. ''The

Taittingers operate for the benefit of the family,'' Wyser-Pratte observed in the *Wall Street Journal*. ''That's not what modern-day capitalism is all about.'' Anne-Claire Taittinger, who at the time had been at the helm of the Société du Louvre for less than two years, acknowledged that both Taittinger and the Société were family affairs, but denied that this would be bad for either business, or for either company's shareholders. And Claude Taittinger said: ''I don't cheat; I tell that to shareholders. We're a safe investment, a sort of savings bank. There should be room for different sorts of companies on a stock market.'' He also said, in 1998, ''I run the company as a family company. If these people want immediate returns, maybe they should buy computer-company stocks.''

In fact, all of the divisions of the Société du Louvre have traditionally been led by members of the family. This occasionally led to some business decisions that would be a surprise in America, such as the Société's retention of light-industry company Deville, which has generally been a financial loss for the group. However, it became part of the Société when Jean Taittinger married Corinne Deville, and Jean was loath to abandon it. However, when Anne-Claire Taittinger succeeded to the Société's directorship in 1997, she began to increasingly emphasize the group's bottom line. Even so, Claude Taittinger firmly stated the family's point of view to *Wine Spectator* in early 1999: ''I am absolutely convinced that Taittinger and Société du Louvre will remain for many years under the control of the family. Business is very good.''

The conflict escalated, eventually coming before the Paris courts as Edelman attempted to reduce the Taittinger family's voting rights in the Société du Louvre. The court rejected the request, and both Edelman and Wyser-Pratte retreated, selling part of their stakes in their respective investments. However, Anne-Claire Taittinger's disagreement with Edelman had less to do with the importance of profits than with how profits should be made, and even while the battle raged, she took steps to streamline the company. These included unloading a small heating company called Leblanc, which did not quite fit with the company's luxurious image, and diversifying Baccarat's product lines to turn the company profitable.

Looking Forward: 1999 and Beyond

Of course, Taittinger did not merely see in the new millennium by fending off corporate raiders from the United States. In late 1999, the winery released a special, limited-edition millennium vintage, which received good reviews and retailed for $175. That was pricey, but as the demand for champagne increased, it seemed as though higher prices for good quality were justified. Claude Taittinger opined that ''There's been an extraordinary expansion, a fantastic prosperity'' in the champagne business overall. That opinion, ventured in 1989, seemed equally true a decade later.

The company continued to look forward, not only in terms of its business, but also in terms of handing over the reins to the next generation of Taittingers. Claude Taittinger turned 72 in 1999, although he did not seem to slow down. Family luncheons, such as one detailed by Mary Blume in *Food & Wine*, served not only as convivial clan gatherings, but as a chance for younger family members to develop the nose and taste required to recognize and produce fine champagne. At such gatherings it has been Claude's practice to ''try to develop even among the youngest a certain interest in wines.''

At the same time, Taittinger also continued to delve, however tastefully, into commercial branding. This ranged from sponsorship of the Tony Awards—and a gift basket for each nominee—to being named the ''official champagne of the Original Avengers'' when A&E Home Video re-released the TV episodes of the British spy series to coincide with the 1998 theatrical release of the Avengers. The company also worked with Kobrand, its United States partner, to create champagne-tasting events that combined with another luxury pastime: shoe shopping. Name designers, such as Vera Wang, were invited to create new shoes for a New York Taittinger tasting, after which the new designs were distributed to tony retailers around the United States, premiering at similar events in several cities.

Having weathered the storms of corporate economics, solidified both its business and its family base, and introduced a new vintage to celebrate the millennium, Taittinger entered 2001 on a distinct high note.

Principal Subsidiaries

Bouvet-Ladubay; Domaine Carneros (83.4%); Société du Louvre (37.7%).

Principal Competitors

Accor; LVMH; Remy Cointreau.

Further Reading

Bilefsky, Dan, ''Fre're Invests in Luxury Stakes,'' *Financial Times*, January 9, 2001, p. 36.

''Bond Is the Name, Food Is the Game,'' *Financial Times*, November 20, 1999, p. 14.

Blume, Mary, ''Pop Culture,'' *Food & Wine*, September 1999.

Coates, Clive, *An Encyclopedia of the Wines and Domaines of France*, Berkeley/Los Angeles: University of California Press, 2000.

Deutschman, Alan, ''Bubble, Bubble,'' *Fortune*, December 18, 1989, p. 210.

''Effort Dissolved on Cracking Taittinger Control of Group,'' *The New York Times*, September 21, 2000, p. C10.

''Europe: Edelman Checks Out Hotels Group,'' *Financial Times*, August 14, 1998, p. 22.

Faith, Nicholas, *The Story of Champagne*, New York: Facts on File, Inc., 1989.

''Family Fizz,'' *Financial Times*, January 8, 2001, p. 23.

''The Fizz Biz,'' *The Economist*, October 31, 1998, p. 71.

Howard, Theresa, ''Peripatetic 2000 Set for Taittinger's Fancy Shoes,'' *Brandweek*, October 25, 1999, p. 12.

James, Jill, ''Paris: It's a Snip at Pounds 7500 a Night,'' *Financial Times*, September 16, 2000, p. 20.

Kamm, Thomas, ''American Raider Mounts a Challenge to France's Taittinger Family Dynasty,'' *Wall Street Journal*, November 11, 1998, p. A1.

Klensch, Elsa, ''A Marriage of Modern and Classic at Château de Baccarat,'' *CNN.com*, posted March 21, 2000, http://www.cnn.com.

''Looking Ahead to the Next Millennium,'' *The Daily Ardmorette*, November 25, 1999.

MacDonough, Giles, ''Bubbling to the Top of the Pile,'' *Financial Times*, November 23, 1996, p. 10.

Matlack, Carol, ''The Raiders Are Coming! The Raiders Are Coming!,'' Business Week, April 24, 2000, p. 138.

Meitus, Marty, ''All Smiles Over 'Champagne Time,' '' *Rocky Mountain News*, April 4, 2001, p. 4D.

Nigro, Dana, ''Champagne's Taittinger Family Battles Corporate Raider,'' *Wine Spectator*, January 31, 1999, p. 10.

''A Raider Follows a Champagne Dream,'' *The New York Times*, January 23, 2000, p. BU2.

Rafferty, Jean Bond, ''Trés Chic,'' *Town & Country*, November 2000, p. 274.

Reier, Sharon, ''Edelman Returns with a Continental Accent,'' *International Herald Tribune*, April 10, 1999, p. 17.

Robinson, Jancis, ed., *The Oxford Companion to Wine*, Oxford: Oxford University Press, 1994.

Sforza, Nicole, ''A French Toast,'' *Wine Spectator*, October 15, 1998.

Taittinger, Claude, *Champagne par Taittinger*, Relié, 1996.

Taittinger, Claude, *Thibaud le chansonnier, comte de Champagne*, Broché, 1987.

''Taittinger Glams It Up with Millennium Edition Vintage,'' *Brandweek*, December 7, 1998, p. 8.

Tagliabue, John, ''U.S. Investors Lose Court Decision,'' *The New York Times*, July 5, 2000, p. C4.

Tillier, Alan, ''Taittinger Family Fights 'Unmentionable' Raiders,'' *The European*, August 24, 1998, p. 22.

—Genevieve Williams

Tattered Cover Book Store

Denver, Colorado

Tattered Cover Book Store

1628 Sixteenth Street
Denver, Colorado 80202
U.S.A.
Telephone: (303) 322-1965
Toll Free: (800) 833-9327
Fax: (303) 629-1704
Web site: http://www.tatteredcover.com

Private Company
Incorporated: 1980
Employees: 310 (2000)
Sales: $40 million (1998 est.)
NAIC: 451211 Book Stores

Among book lovers everywhere and within the book industry, the Tattered Cover Book Store is a legend. One of the largest independent bookstores in the country, the Tattered Cover carries a diverse selection of books from small literary presses and publishing houses as well as from the major publishing companies. Together the company's two bookstores house over 150,000 book titles and more than a half million books purchased from 9,600 different publishers and distributors. The Tattered Cover also carries more than 1,200 newspapers, periodicals, and magazines, including foreign language magazines. Both of the Tattered Cover Book Stores offer patrons the setting of a home library, with sitting areas for browsing through books. Antique library desks, rich, green carpet, and dark, golden-brown shelves, placed to form nooks and alcoves, create the intimate ambiance of an Old World bookshop. The Tattered Cover Book Stores are centers of intellectual community for Denver, with more than 300 author appearances and book-related events each year. Customer service is a key component to the Tattered Cover's success; the staff is knowledgeable about books and the company has an international reputation for finding little-known and hard-to-find books.

1970s: From Bookshop to Super Store

When Joyce Meskis purchased the three-year-old Tattered Cover Book Store in 1974, the 950-square-foot shop carried 12,000 books and employed one person. Located in the Cherry Creek district southeast of downtown Denver, the Tattered Cover was not Meskis's first venture into bookselling. Employed in bookstores and libraries for many years, Meskis originally opened the Parker Book Shop, in a small town 20 miles southeast of Denver. The planned development community surrounding the bookstore failed to materialize and Meskis closed the store within one year. When the Tattered Cover went on the market, Meskis raised $30,000 to buy the bookstore with money borrowed from relatives and friends.

Meskis transformed the Tattered Cover into a European-style bookshop modeled on a student reading room at Purdue University, where Meskis had majored in English, and on world-renowned bookshops in London. Meskis hoped to foster the love of books by creating the setting of a home library, with comfortable antique chairs and couches placed throughout the store as an invitation to browse. She wanted to provide customers with a broad selection of books, beyond the narrow range of merchandise offered by the chain bookstores, such as B. Dalton and Waldenbooks, which had become the dominant booksellers in the 1970s. Meskis sought to bring people and books together by helping customers find any book, and special orders became a mainstay of the business.

During the first decade under Meskis's ownership, the Tattered Cover expanded eight times. The first expansion of the store began with the dismantling of a bathroom and its walls to provide space for a few bookshelves. When neighbors vacated adjacent retail stores, Meskis leased those spaces until the store reached 6,000 square feet. In 1983 the Tattered Cover opened a second location only one block from the original store. The new locale accommodated over 11,000 square feet of retail space on two floors. With additional chairs, sofas, and reading lamps Meskis preserved the welcoming ambiance of the ''Old Store.'' The company maintained offices and sold bargain books—special reprints and publisher overstock—and supplemental product lines at the original location, while book receiving operations and the core retail operations moved to the new location. With the help of 75 customer volunteers, Tattered Cover's staff of 54 moved 3,000 boxes containing 125,000 books in one weekend.

By 1986 the Tattered Cover outgrew its new space, and Meskis and the Tattered Cover staff began to explore their

> **Company Perspectives:**
>
> *Books are more than a product—the ideas they contain are the past, present, and future of our society. The business of books is more than just a business. Our commitment, as always, is to bring you the best selection and service we possibly can.*

options for improving operations. They decided to consolidate the two stores into one large facility and to update its paper-based methods of record keeping. While the company had grown continuously over the years, the company's paper process for managing operations remained the same. It had become impossible to use index cards to keep account of more than 200 special orders per day and a growing inventory of 200,000 books. To resolve the problem Meskis and the staff decided to implement a computer-based inventory system.

Concurrent with the technological switch to handle the growing inventory, Meskis found a new store only a few blocks from the original store, a 40,000-square-foot space where a department store was in the process of liquidating. The Tattered Cover's new retail space covered three floors plus a 2,000-square-foot basement that the company used for back office functions. Again, the Tattered Cover's loyal customers volunteered to move books; so many people wanted to help that the staff posted a sign-up sheet. Professional movers handled the heavy equipment and furniture, while 130 employees and 120 volunteers moved cartons of books. Despite the problems of moving as the Christmas shopping season commenced, relocating the store, as well as implementing the computer system, had been essential to better serve the company's customers.

Status Grows in the Late 1980s

With more than double the company's previous retail selling space, the Tattered Cover blossomed as one of the premier independent bookstores in the country. Though the new store housed 700 bookshelves, staff also stacked books along the edges of the wide, three-story staircase. The company featured new releases and seasonal titles on display cases on the landings between each floor and on antique tables throughout the store. The company scattered additional overstuffed armchairs and reading lamps amidst the alcoves of bookshelves to accommodate customer browsing. Unusual decorative touches included a church pew in the religion section and, in the psychology section, a couch like one that Sigmund Freud might have had in his office. Meskis had the computers painted brown to blend with the atmosphere of the store. The new store also provided a larger area for author readings and autograph sessions.

The Tattered Cover became a local center of the intellectual community as author appearances and book-oriented events occurred almost daily. A variety of seminars, such as brown bag lunch seminars by business writers, attracted a diverse customer base. The staff developed programs on First Amendment rights and on how to organize a book club reading and discussion group, as well as children's activities and contests. The store published the *Tattered Times* newsletter, featuring articles on authors and new books and an events schedule. As part of a renaissance of independent bookstores in the 1980s, the Tattered Cover became a model for bookstores elsewhere.

While the Tattered Cover had become a landmark among Denver residents, nationwide the bookstore had become a legend. The store had gained the respect of major and minor publishers and attracted national celebrities and politicians. (Both the *New York Times* and the *Christian Science Monitor* featured the bookstore in articles during this time.) While the Tattered Cover became a favorite stop for authors, Denverites took special care to bring out-of-town visitors to the store. In 1989 U.S. Senator Tim Wirth introduced a proclamation into *The Congressional Record*, officially naming the Tattered Cover Book Store as a state treasure.

Despite the relatively small population of Denver, per capita book sales at Tattered Cover ranked 17th in the United States in 1989. Fiction comprised approximately 7 percent of sales and bargain books comprised about 6 percent of sales, unusually large volumes. The staff of 170 employees included 15 buyers of back-listed books and four buyers of new releases. An inventory of nearly 400,000 books covered over 100,000 titles while an additional 75,000 titles were available on the computer database. This access to a large selection of books resulted in 250 to 350 special orders each day. The Tattered Cover required three switchboards and 24 telephone lines to meet the demand for customer service.

Further Growth in the 1990s

Handling over 2,000 transactions on an average business day, the Tattered Cover continued to find new ways to organize operations. In early 1990 the company leased warehouse space near the store for book receiving operations and mail-order services until a permanent facility could be acquired. Meskis began to search for a building to purchase, preferring a historical building which she viewed as compatible with the company philosophy, and found a complex of four buildings in historic Lower Downtown (LoDo) Denver. She and John Hickenloope, owner of the Wynkoop Brewing Company, a LoDo restaurant and microbrewery, purchased the buildings for $2.3 million. Plans for the historic buildings, a total of 225,000 square feet of space, included a Tattered Cover bookstore, other retail stores, and 60 to 80 housing units, with two-thirds of the units to be designated for low to moderate income residents.

With the space to grow, the Tattered Cover reorganized its behind-the-scenes operations. In August 1990 the company moved shipping and receiving operations into a 30,000-square-foot warehouse space in one of the LoDo buildings, followed in September by administrative functions which relocated into a 25,000-square-foot office space. Of the company's 230 employees, about 120 worked at the LoDo facility. Meskis also leased the fourth story of the Cherry Creek building. Certain back office functions were moved from the basement to the fourth floor, clearing the basement for more books.

Meskis opened a second Tattered Cover Book Store in one of the LoDo buildings in October 1994. The $250,000 project involved the restoration of the original oak staircase, hardwood floors, and brick. The LoDo store opened with 5,000 square feet

Key Dates:

1974: Company is acquired by Joyce Meskis.
1975: Company begins first of several expansions.
1983: Tattered Cover relocates to larger retail space.
1986: A second relocation more than doubles retail space.
1989: Company is introduced into *The Congressional Record* as a Colorado state treasure.
1994: New store opens in Lower Downtown Denver.
1995: The company opens the Fourth Story Restaurant.
1997: Tattered Cover launches online sales on website.
2000: Meskis receives first Lifetime Achievement Award from the American Booksellers Association.

of retail space on the first floor while renovation of the upper floors of the building continued. The store carried 30,000 titles and an inventory of more than 45,000 books and also included a coffee bar. Like the Cherry Creek store, the LoDo bookstore featured dark, wood shelves and sitting areas of antique furniture scattered throughout the store. Old, wood library desks served as customer service desks and the computers were given a low-tech facade with brown paint.

Changes at the Cherry Creek store included the opening of a coffee bar in November 1994 and the addition of a restaurant on the fourth floor after the Tattered Cover relocated the fourth floor office functions to the LoDo facility. The Fourth Story Restaurant opened in March 1995 serving Colorado and American cuisine at lunch and dinner; the restaurant also prepared Sunday brunch and afternoon tea.

The upper floors of the Tattered Cover LoDo store opened in October 1996. The additional floors added 30,000 square feet of retail space, including an events center with seating for 250 people. The coffee bar expanded with food items for the downtown lunch crowd; several dark wood magazine racks provided a border around the dining area and its antique tables and chairs. The store carried fewer titles than the Cherry Creek store, providing a more spacious atmosphere. Also, hardwood floors on the first floor and exposed brick throughout the store gave the LoDo bookstore a more urban atmosphere than its Cherry Creek counterpart.

Challenges to Independent Bookstores

While the Tattered Cover expanded, independent booksellers nationwide faced increased competition from chain bookstores and Internet-based commerce. Chain bookstores, such as Barnes & Noble, Borders, and Media Play, received volume discounts from major publishers, enabling them to offer new book releases for up to 50 percent off the regular cover price, both in the stores and on their web sites. Because Denver had an avid reading population above the national average, chain bookstores were attracted to the area. Media Play opened a store in downtown Denver in 1994, less than a mile from the Tattered Cover LoDo store, while Barnes & Noble opened five stores in the Denver metropolitan area between 1991 and 1995. Among those new stores was the fall 1994 opening of a 35,000-square-foot store, including a Starbucks coffee bar, about two miles from Tattered Cover's Cherry Creek location. As a result, Tattered Cover experienced no sales growth during the 1994 Christmas shopping season compared to 1993.

Overall development and growth in population in the Denver area also affected Tattered Cover's bottom line. The 1996 opening of an upscale shopping mall in southeast Denver drew customers away from the Cherry Creek Mall across the street from the Tattered Cover. In 1996 the Tattered Cover froze employee salaries for one year; after terminating the freeze, Meskis asked employees to contribute to their benefits package. In 1998 Barnes & Noble opened its eighth Denver area bookstore in a new downtown shopping center one mile from the Tattered Cover LoDo store.

The Tattered Cover also experienced competition from Amazon.com and other online booksellers who offered books at discount rates from 20 percent to 50 percent off the regular cover price. Even after customers paid for shipping and handling fees, Amazon.com offered new book releases at a lower cost, and more conveniently, than the Tattered Cover and other independent booksellers. In many cases, even a large bookseller like the Tattered Cover could not purchase the books wholesale for less than the retail price offered by Amazon.com and chain bookstores. Special orders also declined at the Tattered Cover with the advent of online commerce. Additionally, because online booksellers were not required to charge a sales tax, they possessed an added competitive edge.

The Tattered Cover took a number of measures to compete with chain bookstores and online booksellers. Though the idea of adding a coffee bar to the Cherry Creek store had been discussed previously, Meskis added the coffee bar and restaurant as a response to competition from the Barnes & Noble bookstore near the Cherry Creek store. With the Fourth Story Restaurant and extended hours at the Cherry Creek store (from a 9:00 p.m. to a 11:00 p.m. closing time) Meskis hoped to draw customers to the bookstore for browsing before or after a drink or a meal. Meskis also moved bargain books to more visible locations in the two bookstores. Sales increased after the Tattered Cover launched its online store by incorporating its database of book titles to the Tattered Cover web site in June 1997. The company had to stop investing in the web site by early 1998, however, as the store could not compete with Amazon.com's superior technology. Funds spent on the web site diverted money from buying books, resulting in fewer books on the shelves, Meskis's priority.

As competition from chain bookstores led to the closure of independent bookstores, independent booksellers banded together. In 1998 the Tattered Cover joined with 25 other plaintiffs in a lawsuit filed by the American Booksellers Association (ABA) against Barnes & Noble, Inc. and Borders Group, Inc. The antitrust suit claimed that these companies had an unfair advantage because they received preferential treatment in negotiating contracts with book vendors. Independent bookstores did not receive the same benefits which included discount rates on wholesale purchases, lenient book return policies, and cooperative advertising and other promotions. Certain special deals were not related to the volume of purchases. This information had come to light during the out-of-court settlement of a similar suit in 1994.

The ABA suit cited the Robinson-Patman Act of 1936. The federal law protected small businesses from discriminatory practices that favored large businesses. Between 1991 and 1996 the market share for book sales at independent booksellers declined 22 percent while the market share for chain stores increased 58 percent; by 1998 market share for independent bookstores declined 40 percent. The plaintiffs in the lawsuit claimed that discriminatory deals had facilitated the growth of chain bookstores by giving them an unfair, competitive advantage over independent bookstores. The suit was scheduled to be brought to trial in 2001.

Independent bookstores also sought to improve their competitive position through other means. In response to online bookselling, Meskis and other independent booksellers emphasized the tactile experience of taking a book off the store shelf and turning its pages, an experience special to book lovers everywhere. In a letter to her customers Meskis expressed her concerns with the idea of community responsibility, basing the quality of a community on the kinds of businesses one found in it and on money spent in the local community where it continued to circulate, rather than go to a company in another city.

A third concern of independent booksellers involved the large degree of control that chain booksellers have had in what books get published and distributed. More than 1,000 bookstores banded together as Book Sense 76, an association of independent bookstores dedicated to making a variety of books available in a democratic, free society, maintaining ''Independent bookstores for independent minds.'' The Tattered Cover set up displays of books by lesser-known authors and from small publishing houses which have been suggested by Book Sense members and their customers.

While Meskis had been recognized for her work by various organizations in the past, in June 2000 the ABA honored her with its first Lifetime Achievement Award at the annual Book Expo America in Chicago. As a founding member of the American Booksellers Foundation for Free Expression, Meskis fought bans on such books as Mark Twain's *The Adventures of Huckleberry Finn* and the *American Heritage Dictionary*. She served in several positions of responsibility with the ABA, including president from 1990 to 1992. Meskis promoted the idea of the bookstore ''superstore'' and provided leadership and support for booksellers to enhance the atmosphere of bookstores.

Principal Competitors

Amazon.com, Inc.; Barnes & Noble, Inc.; Borders Group, Inc.; Media Play.

Further Reading

Accola, John, ''Tattered Cover Takes Aim: Retailer Joins 25 Others in Antitrust Suit, Citing Chapter, Verse on Why Chains Stifle Competition,'' *Rocky Mountain News*, March 19, 1998, p. B1.

Atchison, Sandra, ''Chain-Store Massacre in Bookland?,'' *Business Week*, February 27, 1995, p. 20.

''Book-Wise Denverite Lauded in Her Pursuit of Civil Liberties,'' *Denver Post*, October 22, 1995, p. G2.

Booth, Michael, ''Online Retailers Getting Free Ride,'' *Denver Post*, March 23, 2000, p. B2.

Carlin, Margaret, ''Bookstore's Tale a Moving Story,'' *Rocky Mountain News*, January 25, 1983, p. 37.

Colman, Price, ''Tattered Cover Dipping into Software,'' *Rocky Mountain News*, January 4, 1994.

Conner, Chance, ''Barnes Opens Bookstore Brawl,'' *Denver Post*, September 30, 1993, p. C1.

''Denverite Wins National PEN Award,'' *Denver Post*, April 13, 1995, p. A2.

Fein, Esther B., ''A Book Stop in Colorado,'' *New York Times*, December 23, 1992, p. C15.

Finan, Christopher, ''Joyce Meskis: Pushing Books and Free Speech,'' *Human Rights*, October 1, 2000, pp. 10–13.

Gyure, Michelle, ''Glitz, Glamour & Tattered Covers,'' *Colorado Business Magazine*, April 1991, p. 10.

Jacobs, Andrea, ''The Mother of Denver's Famous Landmark,'' *Intermountain Jewish News*, January 25, 1996, p. 4.

Katz, Alan, ''Tattered Cover's Meskis Stands Up for Hometown Values,'' *Denver Post Magazine*, December 24, 1995, p. 8.

Knox, Don, ''Indie Bookstores Win Battle in War with Chains,'' *Denver Post*, June 3, 1999, p. C1.

Locke, David, ''Buy the Book: At the Tattered Cover, Joyce Meskis Shows How Reading—and Selling—are Fundamental,'' *Sales & Marketing Management*, May 1995, p. 26.

Mason, M. S., ''In Rocky Mountain Book Heaven,'' *Christian Science Monitor*, October 22, 1989, p. 12.

McDowell, Edwin, ''Bookstore Thrives on Independence,'' *New York Times*, July 17, 1989, p. D1.

McPhee, Mike, ''Bookstore Wants Last Word with Cops,'' *Denver Post*, April 12, 2000, p. B1.

Nelton, Sharon, ''A Business That Sweats the Details,'' *Nation's Business*, March 1992, p. 38.

O'Brien, Maureen, ''Huge Expansion Planned for Denver's Tattered Cover,'' *Publishers Weekly*, February 8, 1993, p. 9.

Parker, Penny, ''Bookstore Battle Heats Up,'' *Denver Post*, March 6, 1995, p. C1.

——, ''Tattered Cover Expands Store, Celebrates in LoDo,'' *Denver Post*, October 9, 1996, p. C3.

Raabe, Steve, and Jeffrey Leib, ''Tattered Cover Seeks Downtown Space for Mail-Order Operations,'' *Denver Post*, March 16, 1990, p. C1.

Reed, Carson, ''The Tattered Cover; Swamped by Success, a Denver Bookstore Computerized,'' *Colorado Business Magazine*, February 1990, p. 24.

Schwab, Robert, ''Local Booksellers Join Lawsuit: Barnes & Noble, Borders Accused of Negotiating Unfair Advantage,'' *Denver Post*, March 19, 1998, p. C1.

Wood, Christopher, ''Taking a Page from LoDo History: Tattered Cover Plan is 'Tough' One,'' *Denver Business Journal*, October 18, 1991, p. 3.

—Mary Tradii

TBWA\Chiat\Day

5353 Grosvenor Blvd.
Los Angeles, California 90066-6319
U.S.A.
Telephone: (310) 305-5000
Fax: (310) 305-6000
Web site: http://www.tbwachiat.com

Wholly Owned Subsidiary of Omnicom Group Inc.
Incorporated: 1968 as Chiat/Day Inc. Advertising; 1970 as TBWA International
Employees: 1,200
Gross Billings: $1.8 billion (2000 est.)
NAIC: 54181 Advertising Agencies

The fifteenth largest advertising agency in the United States, TBWA\Chiat\Day is the result of the 1995 merger between Chiat/Day and the North American operations of TBWA Worldwide, an Omnicom Group subsidiary with global billings of $5.7 billion. Daring, controversial, and visionary from its inception, Chiat/Day revolutionized Madison Avenue from its earliest days to its last as an independent agency. When Chiat was acquired by Omnicom Group, the third largest advertising holding company in the world, many thought the smaller agency's irreverence and in-your-face style would be stifled. They were wrong; the latest incarnation of the gonzo ad agency is still outrageously creative and continues to attract major clients and the industry's top awards. Although its Omnicom brethren include top-notch rivals DDBO Worldwide and DDB Needham Worldwide, TBWA\Chiat\Day has revitalized Apple Computer, introduced the public to new Nissan cars, brought fame to the Taco Bell chihuahua, taken PlayStation to the top of the electronic gaming industry, and ushered in a new staple of blue jeans-wearing customers for Levi Strauss & Company. Given its history and penchant for guerilla warfare, few would bet against TBWA\Chiat\Day to remain one of the world's top advertising agencies well into the 21st century.

Merger of Chiat & Day: 1960s–70s

Chiat/Day was established when two competitors combined their talents to take on the bigger agencies in the Los Angeles area. Jay Chiat & Associates, founded in 1962, had billings of $3 million when Guy Day of Faust/Day Advertising, a $5 million agency, proposed a merger. Chiat agreed with Day to pool their creative and financial resources, and by October 1968 Chiat/Day was in operation. Day, after winning a coin toss, became company president.

From the beginning the agency eschewed standard practices and created its own unique brand of advertising. Chiat/Day was among the first to use the English concept of ''account planners,'' liaisons between the agency and targeted consumers who traveled the country conducting individual and group interviews. Account planners not only gauged audience response and understanding of ads, but also served as a crucial link between the client and the buying public. A second Chiat/Day innovation was the requirement that clients actively participate in the creative process by attending an initial brainstorming or strategy session, as well as a subsequent planning session. Chiat/Day turned away business when clients refused this interaction. Third, Chiat/Day believed all staff members should be involved in a campaign via a ''task force'' approach. But Chiat/Day's greatest innovations were the ad campaigns themselves, work that demonstrated the agency's relentless pursuit of quality and its unflagging ambition to create the best ads in the industry.

After the merging agencies combined their existing accounts and dropped any conflicts of interest, Chiat/Day was ready to take the advertising world by storm. In 1969, the agency picked up Western Harness Racing as a client by betting its president they could raise attendance 15 percent with their ads. Another account included a public service ad addressing racism for the Los Angeles County Commission on Human Relations. Chiat/Day's ''My Hero, the Pimp'' ads of 1970 raised large amounts of money for Direction Sports, an organization involved in helping urban youth. In short, Chiat/Day pushed the public's buttons as it grew in both recognition and billings.

Company Perspectives:

Our Product Is: Insight and Ideas. We Value: The people who create, support, nurture, enhance and sell them. We Are Enriched By: Our multinational and multicultural heritage. Our Goal Is: To become indispensable to our clients.

Jay Chiat's now classic maxim "Good enough is not enough" emerged as a defining concept for the company and a testament to his vision of advertising. With a pronounced ability to stir things up, according to Day and others, Chiat traditionally drove his creative teams to the "breaking point," the point where desperation often gave way to sudden inspiration. In 1971, the company hired Lee Clow, a man who came to embody the creative soul of the agency in the years to come. While serving as the architect of many of Chiat/Day's most memorable campaigns, Clow rose through the ranks to become president and executive creative director worldwide. According to Karen Stabiner in *Inventing Desire,* the rare chemistry between Jay Chiat and Lee Clow, perhaps as much as anything, propelled Chiat/Day into the limelight.

Throughout the 1970s, Chiat/Day experimented in style and substance, employing psychedelic colors in its ads for Viviane Woodard Cosmetics, scenic wonders for Rancho California, offbeat ads for KNBC and Motel 6, and a series of breakthrough ads for Honda's new automobiles. In 1975, however, Honda, responsible for half of Chiat/Day's billings and three-quarters of its income, left for another ad agency. This proved the first of many blows to the fledgling agency, as small accounts would become giants thanks to Chiat/Day's ads and then abandon the company for bigger, "full-service" agencies.

The following year, Chiat/Day ran a series of trade ads targeting the food, airline, pet, and motorcycle industries. These ads paid off, and Chiat soon landed clients including Yamaha, Midori, Alaska Airlines, and the Olympia Brewing Company. During this time, Guy Day, wishing to spend more time with his family and pursue his interest in writing, sold his agency holdings and left Chiat/Day in his partner's hands. By the end of the decade, Chiat/Day had opened an office in New York and had purchased an established agency in San Francisco.

Setting the Standard: 1980s

In 1980 the company was named Agency of the Year by *Advertising Age* magazine, which would again bestow that title on Chiat/Day later in the decade. The next year, as Chiat/Day was hitting its stride and becoming one of the fastest growing privately held agencies in the United States, Guy Day rejoined the company to help steer its course. Also during this time, the foundation for what many consider the greatest ad in history was laid. Chiat/Day was steadily garnering attention for Apple Computer, a client of the agency's San Francisco office, through a series of popular ads. Then, in 1983, the agency began work on a TV spot introducing the Macintosh, a computer destined to revolutionize the industry, scheduled to air during the third quarter of the January 1984 Super Bowl.

Using an abandoned print ad, staffers worked around the slogan "Why 1984 won't be like *1984.*" Apple liked the idea, and British film director Ridley Scott was hired for the filming. Yet the disturbingly Orwellian commercial, featuring an athletic-looking young woman (symbolizing Macintosh) hurling a sledgehammer at a Big Brother TV screen (IBM), proved too brash a statement even for Apple's executives. Before air-time on Super Bowl Sunday a reluctant Apple tried to pull the plug, finally insisting Chiat/Day sell the air time. Fortunately, only half of the scheduled time could be sold, and the "1984" ad was run. Chiat/Day held its collective breath and waited for the fallout.

"The commercial changed advertising; the product changed the ad business; the technology changed the world," wrote Bradley Johnson of *Advertising Age* in a January 1994 retrospective. "It turned the Super Bowl from a football game into advertising's Super Event of the year," Johnson contended, "and it ushered in the era of advertising as news." Costing a total of $900,000 to produce and air, "1984" resulted in millions for both Apple and Chiat/Day, as the spot was rebroadcast during evening newscasts and on *Entertainment Tonight.* The "1984" spot not only swept the year's awards, winning the Grand Effie, the Cannes Gold, the Belding Sweepstakes, and the Clio, but it was later dubbed *Advertising Age*'s Commercial of the Decade. "This is what happens," Johnson concluded, "when breakthrough technology is given the benefit of the greatest TV commercial ever made."

In the wake of this success, Chiat/Day secured many new accounts, including Nike, Porsche, and Pizza Hut. The ads Chiat/Day produced for Pizza Hut spawned a lawsuit from competitor Godfather's Pizza. Setting an industry precedent, a California state court enjoined Chiat/Day from sharing confidential information learned while bidding previously for the Godfather account. The court also forbade any agency staffers who worked on the Godfather pitch from working on rival Pizza Hut's account. In November 1984, an appellate court struck down the second part of the ruling, a victory for Chiat/Day and all ad agencies. Yet the remaining injunction seemed a moot point, since agency standards precluded the use of confidential information anyway.

In 1986 and 1987, Chiat/Day continued to prosper, with dynamic media ads for California Coolers, Nike, Teddy Ruxpin, and celebrity spots for Mitsubishi's 35-inch television by Bob Fosse, Jim Henson, John Huston, and Martin Scorsese. But with the highs came more lows, as both Apple and Nike (like Honda before them) departed for other agencies. According to the *Economist:* "No other agency has got so big while maintaining such a fine reputation for cutting-edge work. But nor has any been so sharply criticized for putting self-indulgent 'creativity' ahead of selling products. That has made for a history of stunning ads—and devastating client defections." After six years, Guy Day also left the agency again, this time for good.

Yet 1987's acquisition of the Nissan Motor account heralded a new era for Chiat/Day. Not only did Nissan consolidate its regional marketing with the agency in 1988 (adding another $90 million in billings), but it helped catapult the agency into the big time. With gross billings of $500 million, Chiat/Day was now ranked among the industry's top 25 agencies. To handle the

Key Dates:

1968: Agency is created through merger of Jay Chiat & Associates and Faust/Day.
1970: TBWA International is founded by Bill *T*ragos, Claude *B*onnage, Uli *W*iesendanger, and Paolo *A*joldi.
1980: Chiat/Day is named Agency of the Year by *Advertising Age* magazine.
1984: Chiat's Apple Computer ''1984'' ad debuts during Super Bowl.
1986: Apple Computer boots Steve Jobs and Chiat/Day.
1988: Chiat/Day is again named *Advertising Age*'s Agency of the Year.
1990: Chiat receives Agency of the Decade title from *Advertising Age.*
1994: The agency ushers in the ''virtual'' workspace.
1995: Chiat/Day merges with Omnicom subsidiary TBWA Worldwide; under the new name TBWA\Chiat\Day, the maverick agency retains much of its former autonomy.
1997: Jobs returns to Apple and rehires the agency; ''Think Different'' ads hit TV and billboards.
2000: TBWA\Chiat\Day creates successful ads heralding the Summer Olympic Games in Sydney, Australia.

influx of new business, Chiat hired almost 200 additional staffers and recapitalized to pay off senior executives and other equity holders by borrowing in excess of $50 million in 1988. By the end of 1988 and throughout 1989, the agency had expanded by acquiring a design firm, two public relations operations, a direct-marketing company, and a sales promotion firm. The pinnacle of Chiat's growth during the 1980s came with the purchase of Mojo MDA Group Ltd., Australia's largest advertising agency, with $180 million in billings.

One of Australia's savviest agencies, Mojo was at its peak when the merger came through in 1989. Renaming the conglomerate Chiat/Day/Mojo, Jay Chiat was intent on building the world's premier advertising and communications firm, a full-service provider that could become ''big'' without sacrificing its reputation for innovation. To facilitate the necessary restructuring and eventual management transition, Chiat removed himself from direct involvement with the company and appointed Bob Wolf to take his place. However, amidst internal dissension and severe economic pressures, according to Stabiner in *Business Month,* Chiat returned to the helm the following year.

Bigger Not Always Better: 1990–94

Chiat/Day/Mojo's billings hit $1.2 billion in 1991, with Toshiba, Reebok, American Express, and Microsoft all signing on. Next in line was Nissan's Australian accounts, which Chiat believed would be brought in with ease, given Mojo's reputation and connections. However, Mojo failed to deliver Nissan or other international accounts, and instead began losing clients. Moreover, Shearson Lehman Brothers ($20 million), Chemical Manufacturers Association ($10 million), and AmEx Green Card ($60 million) all deserted Chiat. The industry was rife with speculation about Chiat/Day's debt load, wondering how the agency would handle its rising interest payments. With heavy losses and the recession hitting hard, the agency seemed at a dangerous crossroads, readying itself for massive layoffs or even acquisition.

By November 1992, Chiat/Day had unloaded Mojo to rival Foote, Cone & Belding for an undisclosed sum. ''It was a mix of cultures that wouldn't marry,'' original Mojo founding partner Alan Morris (the ''Mo''of Mojo) told Tony Burrett of *Adweek* magazine. Jay Chiat, on the other hand, was more circumspect, telling the *Wall Street Journal,* ''The initial reason for being in Australia and New Zealand was to service international accounts. But none of that has been fruitful, and it was time to move on.'' Luckily for Chiat/Day, a month before deciding to sell off Mojo, the agency had received some good news: Nissan offered the agency its Infiniti division, worth approximately $90 million in billings. One year later, according to Larry Armstrong of *Business Week,* Chiat had an estimated $850 million in billings, more than 40 percent of which were due to Nissan alone.

Although the early 1990s had been tumultuous, 1993 proved even more so, as the agency celebrated its 25th anniversary and unprecedented losses struck at its core. National Car Rental Systems and *TV Guide* defected, and then the agency was unceremoniously bounced from the $80 million Reebok account, which it had won back after a similar dumping three years earlier. With characteristic aplomb and irreverence, Chiat/Day took out full-page ads in both the *Los Angeles* and *New York Times* that read ''Now we know how Dan felt,'' referring to Dan O'Brien, who had been featured in a $30 million Reebok ad campaign with Dave Johnson, his decathlon rival for the upcoming Olympic Games. Unbelievably, O'Brien failed to qualify for the Olympics. Stunned, Chiat/Day averted disaster with a new campaign heralding athletes in general, still featuring O'Brien.

Yet like O'Brien, who went on to shatter a world record, Chiat/Day rallied, snagging Cherry Coke, the consolidation of NYNEX's media spending (having previously scored with the humorous ''human cartoons'' yellow pages ads), and Starter Rugged Terrain shoes to its client list. The latter's full-page ads ended with a teaser, an apt motto for Chiat/Day: ''You haven't heard the last of us, either.'' Yet throughout the ups and downs and the Mojo debacle, Chiat/Day still had its integrity and us-versus-them mentality. It took comfort in the backhanded compliments of friends and foes alike, such as Christy Marshall's comments in *Business Month* magazine: ''One of the few independents left in an industry dominated by mega-agencies, Los Angeles-based Chiat/Day is the personification of its founder and chief executive officer—a place where success breeds arrogance, where enthusiasm borders on fanaticism and where intensity looks suspiciously like neurosis. It is also a bone in the throat of Madison Avenue, which derides its inventive, often riveting ads as irresponsible and ineffective—and then mimics them.''

Chiat/Day was also unveiling another revolutionary scheme called Project Chrysalis, which propelled the agency away from its current restraints of time and space and into the industry's first ''virtual'' office—a fully portable, organic workplace featuring state-of-the-art technology. In January 1994 the ''virtual office'' concept was officially implemented; traditional desks and cubicles were replaced by electronic calendars and electronic mail, lockers, laptops, beepers, and cellular phones. The excitement, however, was short-lived; the agency Madison Avenue loved to hate soon found itself in a do-or-die situation once again.

Neither a Whimper Nor a Bang: 1995–98

''The key to this agency,'' Jay Chiat had told *Business Month* years earlier, in 1988, ''is the premise that it is very important never to peak, because once you do, you're down the other side of the mountain.'' Had Chiat/Day peaked and begun to slide? By 1995 the agency was deeply in debt; creativity was still king, but he could no longer dress in the manner to which he was accustomed. His raiments lacked luster and his subjects were restless. Furthermore, though the rebels of Chiat/Day wore their independence and the lack of corporate structure as a badge of honor, the agency had followed many predecessors into debt and disillusionment. When TBWA Worldwide (originally founded in 1970 and then bought by Omnicom Group in 1993) showed an acquisitive interest, Chiat/Day became part of one of the industry's largest ''mega-agencies.'' Although its name was now TBWA\Chiat\Day, its commitment to ingenuity remained intact.

There were, however, jobs lost in the transition. Jay Chiat stayed on as a consultant for awhile, and defections became an ongoing occurrence over the next several years. Some players still had not adjusted to the virtual office concept, which completely did away with personal space in favor of impersonal, rotating work stations. Chiat/Day's $20 million Frank Gehry-designed headquarters in Venice Beach, including some $8 million worth of the best and brightest electronic toys, was still a monument to the agency's inimitable style but more a talisman to its past. Yet under the TBWA umbrella, the agency was reborn in 1996 and took on the electronic gaming marketplace, long dominated by Sega and Nintendo. TBWA\Chiat\Day came up with edgy, rowdy ads for PlayStation (owned by the Sony Corporation), appealing to what it called the ''wary and distrustful 17-year-old boy'' in every man.

PlayStation consoles and games rocketed in sales and the agency creatives had scored again, only to almost unwittingly upstage themselves with the popularity of their new ads for Taco Bell. In July 1997 four Taco Bells ads were unveiled, one featuring a talking dog who said ''Yo quiero Taco Bell.'' The charming chihuahua struck a cord with Americans of all ages and Taco Bell experienced a surge in sales. Many new Taco Bell ads featuring the chihuahua and introducing the masses to ''Gorditas'' followed to great success. Another boon was on the way: Steve Jobs returned to Apple Computer and immediately brought his old ad agency on board. TBWA\Chiat\Day and Apple Computer were back with a vengeance with the debut of the ''Think Different'' campaign, featuring a parade of freethinkers and innovative heroes including Muhammad Ali, Amelia Earhart, Albert Einstein, Gandhi, Pablo Picasso, and others. The dynamic duo introduced the world to the PowerBook G3, then the phenomenally successful iMac (in five hip colors), followed by the iBook. The Apple collaboration even earned TBWA\Chiat\Day *Advertising Age's* U.S. Agency of the Year award for 1997.

In 1998 the burgeoning agency moved to new headquarters, a 120,000-square-foot refurbished loft located in Playa del Ray. Designed by Clive Wilkinson Architects for the company's 500 employees, the offices were not ''virtual,'' but still far from conventional, with both public and private meeting areas and a small-town atmosphere referred to as ''Chiatown.'' The agency continued to win new accounts and satisfy old ones. Ads for TBWA's longtime client Absolut Vodka were still inventive visions guaranteed to turn heads and induce thirst; hip commercials for Levi's included one largely addressed to a new demographic, gays and lesbians, and another featured an amorous invisible couple who were embraced by TV audiences. TBWA\Chiat\Day also picked up Kinko's and the online division of Barnes & Noble, Inc. (www.barnesandnoble.com), and won the ''Best of Show'' creative excellence award at the 56th annual Obie Awards, sponsored by the Outdoor Advertising Association of America. Year-end numbers further backed up the agency's fortunes, topping $1.9 billion in billings.

Higher Highs, Lower Lows: 1999 and 2000

Like many years before, 1999 was a rollercoaster ride for TBWA\Chiat\Day. A low point was the loss of New York Life, a client of more than 12 years, followed by an upturn with a new top honor, this time an Effie Award from the American Marketing Association for its Taco Bell ads. Next came a new coveted client, the Summer Olympic Games in Sydney, Australia. Then another downturn arrived when Taco Bell, frustrated by slumping summer sales, dumped the agency. But the proliferation of dot-com companies suggested an entirely new realm of trade for TBWA\Chiat\Day, and these startups accounted for a sizeable chunk of its $600 million in new client revenue. Eager for the challenge of e-commerce advertising as well as a brand new century, TBWA\Chiat\Day ventured into 2000 with the old guard (including Clow, who was chairman and chief creative officer for both TBWA\Chiat\Day and TBWA\Worldwide, and Bob Kuperman, who was president and CEO of TBWA\Chiat\Day North America), and a slew of younger employees poised to make their mark.

Although the agency's notorious successes often appeared to come easily, everyone at Chiat/Day and its later equivalent, TBWA\Chiat\Day, knew there were never any long-term guarantees. Of course, such has always been the nature of highly competitive, big-name advertising, but with TBWA\Chiat\Day both the rewards and the losses seemed magnified. To paraphrase one industry observer: the list of clients this agency had *lost,* let alone *won* over the years was enough to satisfy even the hungriest of its competitors—and equally enough to put most agencies out of business. The secret to the dynamism, staying power, and uniqueness of the company was in part due to the personality and drive of its founder, Jay Chiat; yet long after Chiat left his invention, Lee Clow emerged as the guru who inspired the audacious, edgy, wry advertising for a who's who of international clients. The past, and the future, were effectively commingled.

Principal Competitors

Bates Worldwide, Inc.; Goldberg Moser O'Neill; Hal Riney & Partners; The Interpublic Group of Companies, Inc.; J. Walter Thompson Co. Worldwide; Leo Burnett Company, Inc.; Saatchi

& Saatchi; True North Communications Inc; WPP Group plc; Young & Rubicam Inc.

Further Reading

''Agency Report,'' *Advertising Age,* April 13, 1994, pp. 16, 24.

Alter, Stewart, ''Fallout Lingers from Godfather's-Chiat Suit,'' *Advertising Age,* May 13, 1985, p. 60.

Armstrong, Larry, and Geoffrey Smith, ''It's Reebok Out—and Nissan In,'' *Business Week,* October 4, 1993, p. 38.

''Brand New Day,'' *Economist,* June 19, 1993, pp. 70–71.

Burrett, Tony, ''FCB Has Got Mojo Working Again,'' *Adweek,* May 2, 1994, p. 46.

Cuneo, Alice Z., and Laura Petrecca, ''The Best Agencies; Different Thinking and Business Wins Make TBWA Chiat/Day Agency of the Year,'' *Advertising Age*, March 30, 1998, p. S1.

Farrell, Greg, ''Chiat's End Game,'' *Adweek,* July 12, 1993, pp. 26–34.

Flynn, Gillian, ''An Ad Agency Pitches for the Virtual Office,'' *Workforce*, November 1997, p. 56.

Goldman, Kevin, ''Chiat/Day Pulls Up Down Under, Selling Mojo Shop to Foote Cone,'' *Wall Street Journal,* November 11, 1992, p. B11.

Horton, Cleveland, ''A Day in the 'Virtual' Life of a Chiat/Day Executive,'' *Advertising Age,* March 14, 1994, pp. 19–20.

''How Agencies Fared Around the World,'' *Adweek Special Report,* March 20, 1989, p. N34.

Johnson, Bradley, ''10 Years After '1984,' '' *Advertising Age,* January 10, 1994, pp. 1, 12–14.

Johnson, Bradley, and Laura Petrecca, ''Reunited: Jobs, Clow Aim to Rebuild Apple 'Very Quickly,' '' *Advertising Age*, August 11, 1997, p. 3.

——, ''Dot-Coms Are Set to Spend $2 Billion on Ads This Fall,'' *Advertising Age*, November 1, 1999, p. S3.

Karo, Monica, ''Olympic Effort with Far-Flung Group of Media Directors Pushes TBWA/Chiat/Day Ahead,'' *Advertising Age*, September 13, 1999, p. S4.

Kessler, Stephen, *Chiat/Day: The First Twenty Years,* New York: Rizzoli International Publications, 1990.

Landler, Mark, ''Chiat/Day Is Winning, After Losing, After Winning . . . ,'' *Business Week,* December 2, 1991, p. 120.

Marshall, Christy, ''Smart Guy,'' *Business Month,* April 1988, pp. 32–35.

McCarthy, Michael, ''The Duke of Chiat/Day,'' *Adweek*, May 31, 1999, p. 12.

McGinn, Daniel, ''Chiat's New Day,'' *Newsweek*, August 3, 1998, p. 40.

Petrecca, Laura, and Alice Z. Cuneo, ''TBWA Chiat/Day Extends Win Streak: Kinko's, Barnes & Noble Online Add $75 Million More in Billings,'' *Advertising Age*, July 27, 1998, p. 14.

Rapaport, Richard, ''Jay Chiat Tears Down the Walls,'' *Forbes ASAP,* October 25, 1993, pp. 25–28.

''Reebok Fires Chiat/Day and Hires Burnett,'' *Wall Street Journal,* September 15, 1993, p. B7.

Sharkey, Betsy, ''Chiat/Day Comes of Age,'' *Adweek Special Report,* March 20, 1989, pp. N8–N9, N12.

——, ''Going Virtual,'' *Adweek,* May 16, 1994, pp. 28–35.

Stabiner, Karen, *Inventing Desire,* Simon & Schuster: New York, 1993.

''Three Cs: Clow, Clout, Creativity,'' *Advertising Age*, January 31, 2000, p. S21.

Vagnoni, Anthony, ''New Start: Lee Clow, Geoff Thompson, and John Fawcett Redefine a Complicated Role As They Take on the World,'' *Advertising Age*, June 21, 1999, p. 3.

——, ''Having Ad Bosses Focus on the Work Key to Cult of Clow,''*Advertising Age*, April 27, 1998, p. 22.

Wells, Melanie, ''Behind Scenes, Chiat Talks of HQ Sale,'' *Advertising Age,* April 28, 1993, p. 50.

''Working Without Walls,'' *Advertising Age,* November 22, 1993, p. 8.

Yeoung, Mary, ''If It's in There, It's Outrageous,'' *Marketing & Media Decisions,* August 1989, pp. 26–27.

—Nelson Rhodes and Jay P. Pederson
—update: Nelson Rhodes

Telecom Italia S.p.A.

Via Flaminia 189
I-00196 Rome
Italy
Telephone: (39) 636881
Fax: (39) 6 36883445
Web site: http://www.telecomitalia.it

Public Company
Incorporated: 1994, privatized in 1997
Employees: 119,183
Sales: $23,960.9 million (2000)
Stock Exchanges: NYSE
Ticker Symbol: TI
NAIC: 513322 Cellular and Other Wireless Telecommunications; 513310 Wired Telecommunications Carriers; 334210 Telephone Apparatus Manufacturing; 551112 Offices of Other Holding Companies

Telecom Italia S.p.A. is a leader in fixed-line and wireless telecommunication services in Italy. As a holding company with majority ownership in numerous subsidiaries, it provides domestic and international fixed-line and wireless telecommunication operations as well as Internet, information technology and satellite communication services. Its international operations include fixed-line and wireless communications in Latin America and the Mediterranean region. It is the majority owner of Telecom Italia Mobile (TIM), Italy's leading provider of wireless communications. Telecom Italia is the former government telephone monopoly, which was privatized in 1997 and controlled by Olivetti in 1999 in a hostile takeover. Telecom Italia faces increasing competition in both domestic and international markets.

Origins in Government Monopoly

As telephones were introduced in Italy during the last two decades of the 19th century, private companies and entrepreneurs mainly financed the development of local networks. In 1881, 37 telephone franchises had been granted to private businesses; ten years later, more than 11,000 subscribers were served by 56 telephone franchises. After initial interest, investment and development waned, and at the turn of the century, Italy had one of the lowest telephone densities in Europe—one telephone per 2,243 inhabitants, compared with one per 690 people in France, one per 214 in England, and one per 70 in Sweden.

Early investment and development of the telephone network was largely deterred by an 1892 law requiring telephone installations to be transferred to the state upon termination of the franchise term. State involvement broadened when two of the largest private franchises relinquished their installations in 1907. Eventually, the government acquired the main networks of the most dynamic, economically prosperous regions of the country (mainly in the North), which offered greater potential for development. The government promoted its growing role as an opportunity to modernize the national telephone network and better support demand for new services, but government management fell short of expectations.

With the onset of World War I, there were scant resources to invest in a telephone network. In 1923, the Mussolini government decided to grant new franchises rather than group existing licensees together. This prevented the entire telephone system from being in the hands of one company or a foreign power. It also offered attractive political opportunities to the government—allowing it to create tighter controls, broaden its web of industrial connections, and save itself from possible competition should any one of the franchises become a powerful market force.

During the Depression, demand for telephone service was virtually non-existent and most telephone companies struggled to survive. In 1933, the government established a number of public entities to assist the failing companies, one of which was the Societa Italiana L Esercizio Telecom (STET). STET ultimately fell under control of the Institute for Industrial Reconstruction (IRI), a large public company that dominated the Italian economy. Smaller telephone companies within the larger IRI family often forged alliances and were absorbed into STET, further bolstering government control over the network.

Much of Italy's telephone network survived World War II, but its technology was hopelessly outdated. During post-war

Company Perspectives:

With its new, dynamic culture, Telecom Italia is poised to compete with top telecommunications companies in Italy and worldwide. Telecom Italia is a group on the move—innovative and ready to embrace globalization, technological advance, and all the challenges of the New Economy, dynamic and ready to meet the demands of an ever-changing market, global and present in every part of the communications industry.

financial and structural recovery, Italy gained access to technologies that had been developed in the United States and England in the previous decade and rapidly improved its local and long-distance networks.

In the 1960s, demand for local and long-distance services was strong; expansion of a telecommunications network paralleled the greater development seen throughout Italy in the ''the Miracle Years.'' STET's activities expanded to satellite and data communications. However, the number and complexity of STET's holdings—the telephone companies and franchises that provided the services—resulted in highly fragmented and inefficient service coordination.

By the 1970s, STET had solidified as an expansive monopoly with vast holdings in telephone and telecommunications research, production, parts purchasing, installation, product servicing and network management. Telephone density continued to grow, but an economic recession made technological upgrades and newer services became unaffordable.

The transition from mechanical to electronic equipment gained pace in the 1980s. The STET monopoly maintained support on nationalistic grounds, but telephone services and network development suffered from the effects of bureaucracy, high taxes, and widespread corruption. The difficulties in obtaining fixed-line services ultimately led to great success in the wireless market.

1987–98: Market Privatization

For decades, the European Union Council (EC) had been working on plans to remove continent-wide trade barriers. The EC's Green Paper in 1987 sparked the transformation of the European telecommunications industry. Faced with privatization by January 1, 1998, government-run telephone monopolies prepared for competition in an open market.

STET was originally scheduled for reorganization by 1994, including IRI and its greater holdings. By then, IRI had become Italy's biggest state holding company and the seventh largest conglomerate in the world. The government was slow to implement EC directives and privatization plans were repeatedly delayed, while public offerings were planned in Spain, Portugal, Denmark and the Netherlands.

In August 1994, Telecom Italia S.p.A. was formed by the merger of five state-run companies—SIP (domestic phone operations), Iritel (domestic long-distance services), Italcable (intercontinental long-distance services), Telespazio (satellite communications), and SIRM (maritime communications). Telecom Italia had more than 25 million subscribers and a 96.3 percent market share of residential fixed-line services, making it the sixth largest telecom company in the world. The company's shares were listed on the New York Stock Exchange in July 1995.

Telecom Italia essentially operated as a monopoly. Nowhere was this more evident than in the mobile services market, where the company had been providing wireless services without any competition or a formal license. The company was accused of anti-competitive behavior and withholding wireless licenses from new entrants. Antitrust authorities intervened and succeeded in granting a second GSM (global system for mobile communications) license to Omnitel Pronto Italia. Omnitel was owned by Olivetti and was its first foray into telecommunications. It quickly became Telecom Italia's most formidable competitor in the wireless market.

In July 1995, the company spun off its thriving mobile communications arm to form Telecom Italia Mobile (TIM). With limited competition, it held more than 90 percent of Italy's wireless subscriber market. The next step toward privatization came in 1997, when the company merged with STET (retaining the Telecom Italia name) and the Italian government sold nine percent of its stock to an investor group comprised of Italian insurers and banks.

What followed amounted to the biggest privatization move in modern Italian history. In October 1997, the government sold an additional 34 percent of its Telecom Italia stake for nearly $12 billion, trumpeting the privatization as the largest in Europe and the second largest in the world. Investors worldwide snapped up the shares.

After privatization, the company faced daunting challenges—to address increased competition, an employee headcount bursting at the seams, and a failure to sustain strategic partnerships with AT&T and Cable & Wireless. Telecom Italia also contended with a series of bitter management upheavals with political overtones.

Chairman Guido Rossi resigned only one month after privatization, and the company proceeded without a chairman for two months until it tapped Gian Mario Rossignolo for the role in early 1998. Rossignolo's approach prompted the resignation of the chief executive officer, Tommaso Tommasi di Vignano, and created a thick atmosphere of resentment that played a hand in Rossignolo's downfall only a few months later. When Rossignolo showed union leaders worst-case profit projections to support an argument for labor concessions, the projections were leaked to the press and share prices plunged. In his attempt to allay investor fears, Rossignolo explained that the projections were only used to wring out labor concessions. The board demanded his resignation and for the second time in less than one year, Telecom Italia found itself without a leader.

1999: Takeover Transforms European Corporate Landscape

Franco Bernabe was appointed to the role of chairman. Bernabe had so successfully masterminded the turnaround of ENI, the Italian oil giant, that his story was a Harvard Business

Key Dates:

1933: A state-run holding company of telephone operators and service providers forms, known as STET.
1992: Restructuring of the Italian telecommunications sector gains approval.
1994: The merger of five main telephone and telecommunications providers forms Telecom Italia S.p.A.
1995: The mobile phone unit spins off, creating Telecom Italia Mobile S.p.A. (TIM).
1997: Company merges with STET and opens to investors in privatization, making it the largest telecommunications company in Europe and second largest in the world.
1999: Olivetti acquires a majority interest with a hostile takeover bid.
2000: Major restructuring of international operations is completed, eliminating STET.

School case study. He began to work on an international plan and, in an effort to initiate a strategic partnership, approached Deutsche Telekom in early 1999.

Despite the turmoil since its privatization in 1997, the company had a high cash flow and was virtually debt-free. That, combined with management instability, made it an attractive prospect for a takeover, and Roberto Colaninno, chief executive officer of Olivetti, recognized the opportunity. Colaninno had previously rescued Olivetti, selling its aging computer business and boldly introducing its telecom player, Omnitel Pronto Italia, to the burgeoning wireless market. Omnitel had quickly become a viable competitor in the fixed-line and wireless markets. To raise money and stave off anti-trust controversy in a takeover bid, Olivetti planned to sell its interest in Omnitel and Infostrada to Mannesmann AG (Vodafone).

In February 1999, Olivetti announced its daring takeover bid. As a hostile bid initiated by a company one-fifth the size of Italy's largest telecom provider, it seemed preposterous. A battle for investor support and shareholder allegiance ensued, becoming highly public and contentious. Bernabe's idea of a strategic alliance with Deutsche Telekom escalated into a desperate attempt to secure a white-knight merger partner and fend off Olivetti.

The prospective merger with Deutsche Telekom was poorly received. The German government, which owned 72 percent of Deutsche Telekom, and investors objected to the idea of the main telecommunications provider falling into the hands of a company controlled by a foreign government. Investors also were concerned that a merger might produce a company without the agility to compete in a fast-paced industry.

Olivetti outmaneuvered the opposition, convincing shareholders to support its takeover bid. On May 21, 1999 Olivetti acquired majority ownership—51.02 percent—of Telecom Italia for $65 billion in cash and securities. The takeover was heralded as a transformation of the European corporate landscape. As Europe's largest hostile takeover and the first financed by the Euro dollar, it came at the moment when all of Europe seemed eager to test its flourishing markets. That tiny Olivetti could successfully orchestrate the hostile takeover of the former state-run monopoly was shocking, drawing comparisons to both David and Goliath and the sensational Wall Street battles of the 1980s. European companies immediately recognized their vulnerability, and accepted the concept of a shareholder voice, which had been ignored in favor of the established, inside management. The deal set off a wave of merger activity in the telecom industry and other European markets.

Global Competition in the New Millennium

Roberto Colaninno succeeded as chairman in June 1999. His management was Telecom's fourth since its privatization in 1997. He pledged to restore direction and purpose to the company, and set to work on many of the domestic and international issues that plagued the company and his predecessors. Competition was still limited as a result of the government's failure to cultivate it, but expected to increase significantly, particularly in the wireless sector. The company needed to address widely dispersed holdings and bloated staffing levels, as well as establish an international presence. The takeover had saddled the company and its majority owner, Olivetti, with massive debt. A plan to transfer the company's most valuable asset, Telecom Italia Mobile, to Tecnost, a shell company that Olivetti used to finance the hostile takeover, was met with shareholder disapproval and quickly aborted.

In 2000, a successful restructuring program consolidated all international fixed and integrated (fixed-wireless) network operations under Telecom Italia, and international mobile network operations under Telecom Italia Mobile. Approximately 10,000 jobs were trimmed. The company sold nonessential assets in installations and manufacturing, insurance, property and leasing companies, including Italtel (telecom equipment) and Sirti (installations).

The company adopted an organization model to define its business units—Telecom Italia Wireline Services for fixed-line and data-traffic services, Telecom Italia Mobile (TIM) for mobile communications, Telespazio for satellite communications, Tin.it for Internet service (SEAT-Tin.it), I.T. Telecom for information technology services, and Telecom Italia Lab for research, innovation and development.

Despite cost-cutting measures that saved $2.5 billion, the company's debt levels continued to rise, primarily because of exorbitant costs in high-speed, ''third-generation'' (3G) licensing and infrastructure of mobile telephone systems. In 2000, Telecom Italia spent EUR 3.68 billion on acquisitions of mobile and fixed-line operations throughout South America. It was the first to acquire operating licenses to provide wireless services throughout Brazil.

Its Wireline unit invested $1.56 billion to upgrade the fixed-line network, which accounted for 62 percent of the company's estimated $27.1 billion is sales in 2000. The company had introduced high-speed ADSL (asymmetric digital subscriber line) technology in more than 152 cities in Italy, and planned to reach 600 cities and 80 percent of the population by the end of 2002. Through a partnership with Lucent Technologies, the company began building a 6,900-mile fiber-optic network across Europe. Its Internet service provider joined SEAT Pagine Gialle to form one of Europe's largest Internet firms, Telecom Italia Net.

Telecom Italia generated more than 94 percent of the annual sales and 90 percent of the cash flow at Olivetti. Both companies were suffering from enormous debt—Telecom Italia at EUR 19 billion, and Olivetti at EUR 18.5 billion.

In 2001, Colaninno introduced a complex shareholder proposal wherein Telecom Italia would buy back shares from Olivetti, reducing Olivetti's stakes in the company from 54 percent to 40 percent. Proceeds would enable Olivetti to reduce its debt load and give Telecom Italia greater financial flexibility to better forge strategic alliances. The proposal prompted threats of shareholder lawsuits and speculation that the company was being positioned for a merger in Colaninno's quest to position Olivetti as a diversified holding company with interests in lucrative New Economy technologies.

Italian anti-trust authorities fined the company EUR 59 million for abusing its dominant position in the ADSL broadband market, after 27 telecommunications companies filed complaints. The company contended with controversial board resignations and additional inquiries.

Telecom Italia remained Italy's dominant provider in fixed-line services, holding 89 percent of the total market and claiming approximately 20 million fixed-line subscribers with 27 million connections. Telecom Italia Mobile, its wireless unit, offered GSM and analog services and continued to lead the domestic market with 20 million connections. Infostrada, its main competitor in fixed-line and ISP markets, held 3.5 million and 4.1 million subscribers, respectively; Omnitel, its main wireless competitor, held 15 million subscribers. Although Telecom Italia also boasted 16 million foreign subscribers through its international operations, it did not have a significant wireless presence in other European markets.

Along with its key competitors, the company faced widespread market skepticism and the prospect of merger activity in a global industry shakeout. In addition to maintaining a leading position in fixed-line and wireless service markets, the company had ambitious plans to dominate the Italian information technology sector and augment its international presence in emerging growth businesses, the Internet, broadband services and data transmission. It acquired numerous holdings in South America including Argentina, Brazil, Bolivia, Chile, Peru, and Venezuela, along with Cuba. Its holdings in Europe and the Mediterranean region included France, the United Kingdom, Spain, Austria, the Czech Republic, Netherlands, Turkey, Greece, Israel, and Serbia.

Colaninno summarized his vision for the company in a June 2001 commencement speech at the University of Lecce: ''What has been achieved with Telecom Italia will be remembered as a turning point in Italy's industrial history.''

Principal Subsidiaries

Telecom Italia Wireline Services; Telecom Italia Mobile S.p.A.(60%); Telespazio S.p.A.; STET International Netherlands NV; Sodalia S.p.A.; Finsiel S.p.A.; SEAT Pagine Gialle S.p.A (60%); Telesoft S.p.A. (60%); Entel Chile (54.76%); Digitel (56.5%).

Principal Business Units

Telecom Italia Wireline; Telecom Italia Mobile (TIM); Telespazio; SEAT-Tin.it; I.T. Telecom; Telecom Italia Lab.

Principal Competitors

Omnitel Pronto Italia S.p.A.; Infostrada S.p.A.; France Telecom; Vodafone Group PLC; Deutsche Telekom AG; British Telecommunications plc.

Further Reading

''Along Better Lines,'' *Economist*, October 18, 1997, p. 62.
Arnaboldi, Luca, ''Italy,'' *International Financial Law Review*, August, 1997, pp. 45–47.
Ball, Deborah, ''Olivetti to Shuffle Telecom Italia Shares,'' *Wall Street Journal*, February 6, 2001, p. A15.
—— ''Olivetti's Win May Shape Telecom Industry,'' *Wall Street Journal*, May 24, 1999, p. A22.
Baroncelli, Alessandro, ''Telecom Italia: Merging Five Companies into One,'' *Long Range Planning*, June, 1998, p. 377.
Cazzani, Stefano, ''Fixed Line is Superceded by Cellular,'' *Telecommunications*, October, 1999, pp. 71–74.
Colby, Laura, and Stewart Fleming, ''Telecom Italia Under Siege,'' *Institutional Investor*, May, 1999, pp. 52–61.
Cooper, Ron, ''Deals of the Year: A Firefly Changes the Face of Europe: Tiny Olivetti Nabs a Prize in Italy,'' *Investment Dealer's Digest*, January 13, 1999, p. 23.
Currie, Antony, ''Telecom Italia's Long and Bumpy Ride,'' *Euromoney*, November, 1997, p. 14.
Edmondson, Gail, John Rossant, and David Fairlamb, ''Olivetti: Back to the Bad Old Ways?,'' *Business Week*, October 18, 1999, p. 172.
Edmondson, Gail, Julia Flynn, Karen Lowry Miller, and Patrick Oster, ''A Feeding Frenzy in European Telecom,'' *Business Week*, November 21, 1994, p. 119.
Edmondson, Gail, and Kerry Capell, ''Telecom Italia: Gone Courting: A Debt Reduction Plan Could Raise Its Merger Appeal,'' *Business Week*, February 19, 2001, p. 27.
Jawkes, Stephen, ''Telecom Takeover,'' *Europe*, October, 1999, pp. 31–32.
Lanchner, David, ''The Battle for Telecom Italia, Part II,'' *Institutional Investor*, April 2001, pp. 73–80.
''New Chief Executive for Telecom Italia,'' *European Telecommunications*, November 27, 1998, p. 1.
''Next Job: Make It Work,'' *Business Week*, June 7, 1999, p. 26.
''On Hold,'' *The Economist*, December 31, 1999, pp. S29–S31.
Perrazzelli, Alessandro, ''Italian GSM Second Operator,'' *Telecommunications*, March, 1995, p. 16.
——, ''Italy: Telecoms Deregulation?,'' *Telecommunications*, November, 1994, p. 109.
Platt, Gordon, ''Telecom Italia Issue Oversubscribed,'' *Global Finance*, May, 2001, p. 16.
Racanelli, Vito J., ''European Trader: A Cost-Cutting Way Out of Europe's Telecom Mess,'' *Barron's*, February 19, 2001, p. MW6.
''Raiders at the Gate,'' *Business Week*, March 8, 1999, p. 14.
Tagliabue, John, ''Olivetti Prevails in Hostile Bid for Far Bigger Telecom Italia,'' *New York Times*, May 22, 1999, p. B1.
—— ''Telecom Italia's Chief and Board Resign,'' *New York Times*, May 26, 1999, p. C5.
''Telecom Italia's $2.6BN Broadband Investment,'' *Cable Europe*, May 2, 2001.

''Telecom Italia Acquires License to Provide Services in All Brazil,'' *EFE World News Service*, May 21, 2001.
''Telecom Italia Completes Reorganisation of International Activities,'' *Tech Europe*, January 19, 2001, p. 301.
''Telecom Italia Fined Euro 59 Million for Abuse of Dominant Position,'' *Tech Europe*, May 11, 2001, p. 203.
''Telecom Italia Will Sell Real-Estate Assets to Reduce Debt,'' *Wall Street Journal*, November 24, 2000, p. A10.
Trofimov, Yaroslav, ''Olivetti Splits Off Cellular Operations from Telecom Italia in Big Revamp,'' *Wall Street Journal*, September 29, 1999, p. A19.
''What Next?,'' *The Economist*, October 17, 1998, pp. 70–73.
''Wheeling and Dealing in Europe,'' *Communications Today*, April 19, 1999.
Willan, Philip, ''Telecom Italia to Link Europe with Fiber Network,'' *InfoWorld*, December 4, 2000, p. C48.

—Suzanne Selvaggi

Terra Lycos, Inc.

Calle Nicaragua, 54
Barcelona
Spain
Telephone: 34-91452-3000
Web site: http://www.terralycos.com
400-2 Totten Pond Road
Waltham, Massachusetts 02451
U.S.A.
Telephone: (781) 370-2700
Fax: (781) 370-2600

Public Subsidiary of Telefónica, S.A.
Incorporated: 1995 as Lycos, Inc.
Employees: 3,196
Sales: $40.6 million (1999)
Stock Exchanges: New York Mercado Continuo
Ticker Symbols: TRLY (ADR); TRR
NAIC: 514191 On-Line Information Services

Terra Lycos, Inc. was formed in October 2000 by the merger of Spain's Terra Networks, S.A. and the popular Internet portal and search engine firm Lycos, Inc. Pittsburgh-based Lycos grew from its origin in 1995 as a search engine to become a multi-branded Internet portal operating several different web sites that offered a variety of services. Lycos formed partnerships with numerous content providers for such areas as books, health information, news, and more. After going public in 1996 it acquired a wide range of companies providing content and services. It also expanded internationally by forming joint ventures in Asia, Japan, Latin America, and Europe. The acquisition of Lycos by Terra Networks gave Terra Lycos unprecedented access to more than 50 million telephony and wireless customers throughout the world.

A Leading Internet Search Engine: 1995–97

Lycos, Inc. was created in 1995 when CMG@Ventures, the strategic investment and development arm of CMG Information Services, Inc., purchased the exclusive rights to Lycos Spider Technology from Carnegie Mellon University. Lycos was established as a subsidiary of CMG@Ventures, which later became CMGI Inc., to develop and market the technology. Lycos Spider Technology utilized software ''robots'' to scan the Internet and abstract the home pages that it found. Michael Mauldin, who led the development of the technology at Carnegie Mellon, became Lycos's chief scientist. Carnegie Mellon received $500,000 in cash, a 20 percent stake in the company, and royalties. Later, when a patent was awarded for the spidering technology that Lycos used, it was granted to Carnegie Mellon University but was owned by Lycos. The name Lycos was derived from a Latin word for a special kind of spider that leaves its web to hunt.

At the time Lycos was established as a separate company, it had built a catalog of more than 3.7 million Internet pages and had nearly 3.5 million hits a week. Lycos planned to offer advertising space on its site, to license key components of its search technology, and to develop products based on its technology. One of the first products under development was called Spider in a Box. Lycos planned to ship this shrink-wrapped version of its web crawler in 1996 for use in corporate intranets and wide-area networks (WANs). In early 1996 Lycos offered a free product called a2z, which categorized Lycos's database of 19 million URLs by subject. However, a2z was dropped later in the year, but Lycos would continue to try to create a classified directory of web sites.

In April 1996 Lycos was one of four search engine companies that had their IPOs that year. Yahoo!, the best-known search engine, InfoSeek, and Excite.com, which was produced by Architext, also went public. Following their successful IPOs, other companies announced plans to go public or provide commercial searching products. Digital Equipment Company (DEC), which developed the AltaVista searching technology, planned to develop products for the corporate intranet market.

Lycos launched its licensing program in April 1996 through an agreement with the Scandinavian newspaper the *Swedish Post.* Lycos was the first Internet search engine to license its search and index technology to smaller sites. In another partnership Lycos and book publisher Simon & Schuster formed the Lycos Press as a three-year co-publishing venture. The first title was to be called *Lycos' 250,000 Best World Wide Web Sites.*

Company Perspectives:

Terra Lycos's mission is to become the world's leading online destination. Through a unique platform that combines the benefits of the convergence of Internet services and next-generation communication technologies with the broadest, most comprehensive array of popular products and services, Terra Lycos provides users a compelling network of web brands and gives advertisers access to a vast and diverse audience.

Throughout 1996 Lycos continued to upgrade its search engine. The first upgrade, called CentiSpeed, performed 4,000 queries per second, four times as many as its nearest competitor. It also supported multiple search crawlers and employed a technology that let the spider continue to search while waiting for a slow site to connect. Through an agreement with InfoSpace Inc., Lycos users could access InfoSpace's People Directory, which contained more than 100 million U.S. and Canadian business and public telephone numbers, and AccuMail, a large e-mail directory. Later in 1996 Lycos added the capability to search for individual sound, video, and other multimedia files. Lycos claimed that it was the first search engine to enable users to search for individual multimedia files. Lycos also added a city guide that featured 400 cities, and it established a Club Lycos for users that provided them with discounts with merchants such as Southwest Airlines and Avis car rentals. In addition to adding new features and upgrading its search engine in 1996, Lycos redesigned its graphic interface to look like an Internet portal.

Lycos's first international venture was Lycos Europe, which was formed in May 1997 as a joint venture with German media conglomerate Bertelsmann AG. The venture planned to provide native-language Internet navigation centers in 37 European countries.

In mid-1997 Lycos announced it would introduce two Intranet search engines that combined Lycos search technology with a publishing engine from Inmagic Inc. The Lycos Intranet Spider, priced at $995, performed basic intranet searches and navigation, while DB/Text Index Spider ($7,500) performed database searches.

For its fiscal year ending July 31, Lycos's revenue jumped from $5.3 million in fiscal 1996 to $22.3 million in 1997. Later in the year Lycos surprised analysts when it reported its first profitable quarter ending October 31, 1997. Analysts noted that Lycos had recently signed a three-year agreement with Barnes & Noble, whereby BarnesandNoble.com became the exclusive bookseller for Lycos. Lycos would receive a percentage of book sales generated through its site.

Adding Content Providers, Making Acquisitions, Pursuing Multiple Branding Strategy: 1998

In early 1998 Lycos announced it would acquire Tripod Inc., for $58 million in stock. Tripod provided free web pages to about one million users, with news and commentary tailored to young adults. The acquisition was expected to increase traffic to the Lycos site and was part of Lycos's strategy to build online communities around targeted content. Both Lycos and Tripod were among the top ten most visited sites on the Web, with Lycos recently introducing e-mail and chat capabilities.

Throughout 1998 Lycos continued to add content providers to its site. In March, Preview Travel became the exclusive multi-service provider of travel reservations on Lycos's Travel Web Guide and Travel Network in a deal valued at $4.2 million. CDNow became the exclusive retailer of music-related products on Lycos and Tripod sites, with CDNow paying Lycos $18.5 million over three years to be featured on Lycos's Shopping Network and Entertainment Web Guides as well as on music-related search results pages, banner ads, and links. Other deals were struck with contact management site PlanetAll and career sites The Monster Board and Online Career Center. Lycos also took a minority interest in its e-mail provider, GlobeComm Inc., for about $4 million.

According to one survey, Lycos ranked sixth among popular sites with 15 million unique visitors in March 1998, behind leader Yahoo! with 32 million. Lycos acquired Pittsburgh-based WiseWire, a software firm whose technology Lycos had been licensing since November 1997, for nearly $40 million in stock. WiseWire software was used to create Lycos's search categories as well as to rate sites by Lycos users. Lycos CEO Bob Davis claimed that Lycos's categories were ''incredibly more expansive'' than Yahoo!'s because of the software, and Lycos planned to build a directory of web sites, a project it had started in 1996 with a2z but later abandoned. Ken Lang, who founded WiseWire in 1995 and was a former student of Michael Mauldin at Carnegie Mellon, became Lycos's chief technology officer.

In mid-1998 Lycos entered into a three-year agreement with AT&T Corp. to market each other's services online, under the banner ''Lycos Online Powered by AT&T WorldNet Service.'' Lycos users would begin to see promotions for AT&T services, and AT&T would promote the Lycos site and its roster of services. In addition, a co-branded AT&T Communication Center was launched on the Lycos site.

In July 1998 Lycos introduced its free SafetyNet service, which filtered out objectionable content from web site searches. The company also became the designated content provider for Juno Web, which had 5.5 million subscribers to its free e-mail service. New content on the Lycos site included the science fiction web comic strip ''WhirlGirl.''

Lycos took a big step toward becoming the gateway to the Internet with the $133 million stock purchase of WhoWhere Inc. in August 1998. The acquisition included the popular WhoWhere Internet white pages; MailCity, a free electronic mail system; and Angelfire, a free web page hosting service. MailCity had 9.3 million registered users, and Angelfire had 1.3 million users. Lycos also acquired GuestWorld, a publishing services site, for $4 million in August.

In its September 1, 1998 review of Lycos, *PC Magazine* wrote, ''If you want to make friends on the Internet, no portal offers you more opportunities than Lycos, from its chat and gaming features to its free Tripod Web-page community.'' The review noted that the Lycos community was ''a vast and varied body,'' but it also complained that the site was difficult to

Key Dates:

1995: Lycos, Inc. is founded.
1996: Lycos goes public and raises $46 million in its initial public offering (IPO).
1997: Lycos Europe is formed through a joint venture with German media conglomerate Bertelsmann AG.
1998: Spanish telephone company Telefónica creates Telefónica Interactiva, an Internet company.
1999: Telefónica Interactiva goes public and becomes Terra Networks, S.A.
2000: Terra Networks acquires Lycos, Inc. for $12.5 billion; the two companies combine to form Terra Lycos, Inc.

navigate and could frustrate users. It concluded by ranking Lycos behind America Online, Excite, and Yahoo! in terms of ease of use.

In September 1998 Lycos became one of four search engines to be listed on Microsoft's MSN.com web portal. The four search engines—Lycos, AltaVista, Infoseek, and Snap!—together with a new MSN-branded search engine to be launched later in the year, would be rotated as the default search engine on MSN.com.

Lycos made another major acquisition in October 1998 when it purchased Wired Digital Inc.'s online products, including the popular HotBot search engine, Wired News and HotWired news sites, and other content sites offering shopping, e-mail, chat, and travel services. Wired Digital was the last remaining piece of Wired Ventures Inc., which debuted *Wired* magazine in 1993 and sold it to Condé Nast Publications in 1998.

Lycos's acquisitions were part of the company's new strategy for growth through multiple brands and products. In acquiring a variety of brands and products, Lycos was becoming a ''super site'' that offered a portfolio of products for a variety of users. As one Lycos spokesperson told the *San Jose Mercury News,* ''We are looking more and more like a traditional media company, having multiple brands across the network.'' For fiscal 1998 Lycos reported revenue of $56 million but still posted a loss.

In November Lycos introduced its first national TV advertising campaign, which featured a black Labrador named Lycos under the tagline, ''Lycos, go get it.'' The campaign also included radio spots in 11 major cities and was estimated to cost $25 million. Around this time Lycos added technology from Bidder's Edge that monitored several online auction sites. Lycos also began running services for other web sites, renaming its Lycos Affiliates Program as Lycos Network Services. Lycos was providing services for more than 80 sites, including The New York Times Company, Salon, and iVillage, and planned to expand its co-branding efforts through syndicated distribution of its e-mail, web site building, and other services. At the end of 1998 it was announced that Lycos and the National Football League would create Superbowl.com, the official web site for Super Bowl XXXIII in 1999.

Remaining Independent: 1999

At the beginning of 1999 Lycos was enjoying tremendous growth. According to a Media Metrix report, Lycos attracted 26.3 million visitors monthly and was the fastest-growing web portal. Its audience reach had grown to 46.5 percent of Internet users, only three percentage points behind Yahoo! Inc.

In February 1999 Lycos announced it would be the first major portal site to provide a directory of online songs available for downloading through MP3 technology, which coded music into compact files. Through a joint venture with Norway's Fast Search & Transfer, Lycos's directory would provide links to more than a half a million songs. Following the announcement, Lycos agreed to work with the Recording Industry Association of America (RIAA) to develop procedures for eliminating sites with pirated recordings from its directory.

In early 1999 Lycos was one of the few remaining independent Internet portals. Walt Disney Company owned a significant portion of Infoseek, Netscape was sold to AOL, Snap was 60 percent owned by NBC, and Excite was being absorbed by @Home (At Home Corporation). Compaq Computer planned to spin off AltaVista stock to the public while retaining a majority share. In February 1999 it was announced that cable company USA Networks, which also owned Ticketmaster and Home Shopping Network, would acquire Lycos to create USA/Lycos Interactive Networks Inc. in a deal valued at $22 billion. However, the takeover was opposed by CMGI Inc., Lycos's largest shareholder with a 22 percent interest in the company. One reason for CMGI's opposition was that in the two days following the merger announcement, Lycos's shares lost nearly one-third of their value. Lycos's fate was in limbo, until the deal was declared officially dead in May 1999.

Meanwhile, Lycos's revenue continued to climb. Under a three-year agreement, WebMD would pay Lycos $52.5 million to be its exclusive health information provider. In April 1999 Lycos launched Lycos Clubs, which included a suite of communication tools that let members create virtual clubhouses around shared interests. While Lycos established some clubs based on the known interests of its users, the company expected more clubs to form organically.

According to figures released by Media Metrix Inc., Lycos passed Yahoo! in number of users for the first time. Just under 32 million people, or 51.8 percent of U.S. Internet users, visited Lycos in March 1999, compared to 31.2 million visitors, or 50.8 percent, to Yahoo!. The figure for Lycos included the Tripod and Angelfire web site hosting services, the WhoWhere Internet directory service, the Wired Digital news service, and the Lycos and HotBot Internet search sites, all of which were run as separate entities under the Lycos Network.

In April 1999 Lycos replaced its proprietary directories on Lycos and Hotbot with the Open Directory, a guide to the web that was operated by some 8,000 volunteers. The Open Directory had been acquired by Netscape Communications in December 1998. It became part of Netscape's Mozilla.org group, and Netscape released the source code for free. Lycos's attempt to build its own directory using WiseWire technology had not paid off.

Also in April the Lycos Radio Network was introduced, making Lycos the first portal to incorporate streaming audio and video. The Lycos Radio player browser interface featured an embedded video playback area, an area for banner ads, and navigational links.

In mid-1999 Lycos acquired search engine technology from IntelliSeek, giving it access to more than 7,000 databases from Invisible Web, a previously inaccessible index of information. During the same period Bertelsmann, Lycos's international joint venture partner, invested $12 million for the expansion of Tripod Europe. Launched in October 1998, Tripod was the fastest growing online community in Europe. In addition, Lycos's largest shareholder, CMGI Inc., acquired AltaVista from Compaq for $2.3 billion.

In July 1999 Lycos integrated auctions into its Lycos and Tripod Networks of web sites. Dubbed auctions.lycos.com and auctions.tripod.com, the two services shared listings and started with 7,000 to 8,000 items for auction. Also in July Lycos formed Lycos Ventures, a $70 million venture capital fund whose partners included Microsoft cofounder Paul Allen. For the fiscal year ending July 31, 1999, Lycos reported a net loss of $4.4 million on revenue of $40.6 million.

In August Lycos strengthened its position among music-oriented users by acquiring Internet Music Distribution Inc. for about $38 million in stock. Internet Music's music-playing software, Sonique, allowed users to download music files and play them on their personal computers. Lycos planned to give away Sonique through free downloads, hoping it would boost the popularity of its music-oriented web sites. Later in the year Lycos announced the formation of music.lycos.com, a comprehensive online music destination that offered MP3 search and hosting areas, legal MP3 downloads, 35 radio channels, music news, reviews, chat rooms, message boards, commerce, and an MP3 player download. The site also served independent musicians by offering a hosting service for artists to create their own home page, add songs to the download directory, and provide other information.

Continuing its string of acquisitions, Lycos purchased Quote.com Inc. for about $78 million in stock. Quote.com provided stock quotes and other financial information and had over 600,000 Internet visitors in the most recent month. The company also operated a service that provided real-time stock quotes to the web sites of other financial companies. Lycos planned to build chat rooms, message boards, and other features linked to Quote.com to create a community of users interested in financial information.

Lycos expanded internationally in the final four months of calendar 1999. In September Lycos and Singapore Telecom formed a pan-Asian joint venture, Lycos Asia. In December 1999 Lycos Asia launched a site in Singapore and planned to go online in Malaysia and the Philippines. Other plans called for setting up customized versions of Lycos in ten Asian cities.

In October 1999 Lycos launched 12 country-specific sites for Latin America and two sites for Spanish speakers in the United States. In November Lycos Japan gained a $32 million investment from Kadokawa Shoten Publishing Co. Ltd., a major Japanese media company, which became one of several joint venture partners there. Lycos also launched a Japanese version of Tripod, its community web site subsidiary.

In November 1999 Lycos purchased Gamesville.com, an online game company that had 2.2 million registered users, for $207 million in stock. In preparation for the 1999 holiday shopping season, Lycos announced it would offer a range of new shopping services, including product reviews, comparison shopping, and consumer ratings. The Lycos WebShopper was a new comparison shopping tool, and Lycos added links to epinions.com and other sites that provided consumer and professional product reviews. The company also launched Lycoshop, which featured listings from major retailers as well as the abovementioned services. As a result, Lycos was able to report a 450 percent increase in the number of unique shoppers for the holiday season over the previous year. As of December 1999 Lycos claimed an audience of 29 million users.

Merger with Spain's Terra Networks: 2000

In February 2000 Lycos made investments in two software firms that specialized in building web sites and online communities by taking a minority interest in Trellix Corp. and acquiring Valent Software Corp. for $45 million in stock. Around this time Lycos also formed a joint venture with Bell Canada.

In May 2000 news surfaced that Lycos was holding merger talks with Terra Networks, the Internet unit of Spanish telephone company Telefónica, S.A. Unlike the 1999 announcement of USA Networks' proposed takeover of Lycos, though, this information had the effect of boosting Lycos's stock by about 12 percent. Before the month was over, it was announced that Lycos would be acquired for $12.5 billion by Terra Networks. Wall Street jitters then sent Lycos's stock down more than 20 percent. With support from CMGI, the merger closed in October 2000, and Lycos combined with Terra Networks to create Terra Lycos, Inc.

Terra Networks was originally established in December 1998 as Telefónica Interactiva by Spain's largest telephone company, Telefónica, S.A. In April 1999 Telefónica Interactiva acquired a Spanish portal company and an Internet service provider (ISP) to become the top-ranked portal and ISP in Spain. Later in 1999 the company acquired ISPs and Internet portals in Brazil, Central America, Mexico, Argentina, Chile, and Peru. In November 1999 Telefónica Interactiva went public and changed its name to Terra Networks, S.A.

Bertelsmann, a longtime partner of Lycos, also participated in the formation of Terra Lycos. Bertelsmann agreed to provide content to Terra Lycos and to purchase $325 million of services from Terra Lycos in the first two years. It also committed to purchase up to $675 million of services in years three through five, with Telefónica committing to purchase any portion of those services not bought by Bertelsmann. Bertelsmann was the third largest media company in the world, with operations in 54 countries.

Through its alliances with Bertelsmann and Telefónica, Terra Lycos was in a unique position to benefit from the convergence of media, wireless communications, and interactive content. A joint venture with Telefónica Móviles, S.A., gave Terra Lycos access to 20 million wireless users, for whom

Terra Lycos planned to develop unique content and e-commerce products. Terra Lycos also had access to Telefónica's 35 million telephony subscribers, for whom it planned to offer expanded services.

At the end of 2000 Terra Lycos was providing Internet access to more than five million customers worldwide. The company offered both paid and free subscription services and was the leading ISP in Spain, Chile, Peru, and Guatemala. It was also expanding in Asia through Lycos Asia, its joint venture with Singapore Telecom. In September 2000 Lycos Asia received permission from the Chinese government to operate a web portal from Shanghai. Lycos Indonesia was launched in October 2000, and the launch of Lycos Thailand in December 2000 gave Terra Lycos an international presence in 41 countries.

Lycos also appeared committed to adding new content and services to its web portal. In July 2000 Lycos acquired Matchmaker.com, a Texas-based online dating service, for $44 million. Other new services introduced in selected markets during 2000 included Lycos TV Online and a voice-based information service. The company also continued to strengthen its brand through a $20 million national advertising campaign and high-profile partnerships that included building web sites for the 2000 Olympics in Sydney, Australia.

Principal Subsidiaries

Lycos Europe; Lycos Asia; Lycos Japan; AnimationExpress.com; Angelfire.com; Gamesville.com; HotBot.com; Matchmaker.com; Quote.com; Rumbo.com; Sonique; Tripod.com; Whowhere.com; Wired News.

Principal Competitors

AOL Time Warner, Inc.; Yahoo! Inc.; At Home Corporation; AltaVista Company; Microsoft Corporation.

Further Reading

Albright, Mark, ''Lycos Shares Soar on News of No Deal with USA Networks,'' *Knight-Ridder/Tribune Business News,* May 12, 1999.

Andrews, Whit, ''Deal in Limbo, Lycos Plows Ahead,'' *Internet World,* April 26, 1999, p. 1.

Cheng, Kipp, ''Community Service: Lycos Launches 'Sticky' Clubs,'' *Brandweek,* April 5, 1999, p. 38.

——, ''Going Once, Going Twice: Lycos Launches Auctions,'' *Brandweek,* July 12, 1999, p. 32.

——, ''Lycos Wins Portal Race to Add Streaming Radio,'' *Mediaweek,* April 26, 1999, p. 43.

Creedy, Steve, ''Lycos Expands Internet Search Capabilities,'' *Knight-Ridder/Tribune Business News,* September 18, 1996.

Deck, Stewart, ''Searching for Internet Profits,'' *Computerworld,* June 2, 1997, p. 115.

''Filtering Product,'' *Computerworld,* July 6, 1998, p. 37.

Fitzpatrick, Eileen, ''Web Music Sector Gains Ground: Lycos Targets Artists, Fans,'' *Billboard,* November 20, 1999, p. 1.

Ha, K. Oanh, ''Internet Search Service Lycos to Acquire California Firm's Online Products,'' *Knight-Ridder/Tribune Business News,* October 7, 1998.

Healey, Jon, ''Web Portal Lycos Launches Free 12-Channel TV Online,'' *Knight-Ridder/Tribune Business News,* May 16, 2000.

''Holiday Shoppers at LYCOShop up 450%,'' *Content Factory,* January 5, 2000.

Holland, Bill, ''Lycos Cooperating with RIAA over New MP3 Database,'' *Billboard,* February 13, 1999, p. 111.

Homaday, Bill W., ''Lycos to Purchase Bedford, Texas-Based Online Matchmaker for $44 Million,'' *Knight-Ridder/Tribune Business News,* July 16, 2000.

Howe, Peter J., ''Lycos Debuts New Voice-Based Telephone Web-Surfing Network,'' *Knight-Ridder/Tribune Business News,* October 10, 2000.

——, ''Shares of Web Portal Lycos, Spanish Phone Firm Fall on Worries About Takeover,'' *Knight-Ridder/Tribune Business News,* May 18, 2000.

——, ''Spanish Company to Acquire Web Portal Lycos,'' *Knight-Ridder/Tribune Business News,* May 17, 2000.

Janah, Monua, ''Lycos Move Raises Questions About Open Standards Among Internet Portals,'' *Knight-Ridder/Tribune Business News,* April 20, 1999.

Johnson, Bradley, ''Microsoft Inks $60 Mil Deal with Search Engines,'' *Advertising Age,* September 21, 1998, p. 4.

Kerstetter, Jim, ''Lycos, Verity Expand Searching,'' *PC Week,* June 9, 1997, p. 10.

Kinsella, Bridget, and Diane Patrick-Wexler, ''S&S Sells Gousha, Acquires Mergent, Co-Ventures with Lycos and China,'' *Publishers Weekly,* April 29, 1996, p. 20.

Kirkpatrick, David, ''Why Have Investors Ignored Lycos for So Long?,'' *Fortune,* February 1, 1999, p. 150.

Kong, Deborah, ''Lycos, AltaVista Try to Boost Online Shopping,'' *Knight-Ridder/Tribune Business News,* October 25, 1999.

Kovatch, Karen, ''Lycos Buys WiseWire Corp. in $39.75 Million Stock Deal,'' *Pittsburgh Business Times,* May 1, 1998, p. 1.

——, ''Lycos Patent Could Bring Payoff to Carnegie Mellon,'' *Pittsburgh Business Times,* June 19, 1998, p. 1.

Kuchinskas, Susan, ''Lycos Comes Knocking, Unveils Syndication Plans,'' *Brandweek,* December 14, 1998, p. 46.

Kwon, Regina, ''Building the Network to Back Lycos' Deals,'' *Internet World,* April 20, 1998, p. 28.

Leger, Jill, ''Lycos,'' *PC Magazine,* September 1, 1998, p. 124.

''Lycos, CDNow Form Three-Year Partnership,'' *Internet World,* April 6, 1998, p. 52.

''Lycos Chief Discusses Failed USA Networks Deal,'' *Knight-Ridder/Tribune Business News,* May 12, 1999.

''Lycos, GeoCities Claim Audience Gains,'' *Content Factory,* January 20, 1999.

''Lycos Gets Boost from Bertelsmann,'' *Content Factory,* June 17, 1999.

''Lycos Goes Latin,'' *Content Factory,* October 20, 1999.

''Lycos Japan Raises $32 Million,'' *Content Factory,* November 8, 1999.

''Lycos on Yahoo's Heels with $78M Buy,'' *ISP Business News,* September 13, 1999.

''Lycos, Paul Allen Form Venture Fund,'' *Content Factory,* July 21, 1999.

''Lycos Sets Sights Higher,'' *PC Week,* January 11, 1999, p. 32.

''Lycos Teams with NFL for Bowl Site,'' *Content Factory,* December 31, 1998.

MacArthur, Kate, ''Lycos Leashes Labrador in New $20 Mil Ad Effort,'' *Advertising Age,* October 9, 2000, p. 8.

Machlis, Sharon, ''Lycos Buys Tripod to 'Complete' Itself,'' *Computerworld,* February 9, 1998, p. 12.

Maloney, Janice, ''Yahoo! Still Searching for Profits on the Internet,'' *Fortune,* December 9, 1996, p. 174.

Nadile, Lisa, ''Lycos Leads Search Firms with Value-Added Products,'' *PC Week,* November 13, 1995, p. 83.

——, ''Lycos Upgrade Enhances Support for Web Crawlers,'' *PC Week,* May 27, 1996, p. 10.

——, ''Search Firms Rev up Offerings for the Web,'' *PC Week,* March 11, 1996, p. 46.

Null, Christopher, ''Rules to Get Rich By,'' *PC/Computing,* December 1999, p. 78.

Poole, Jackie, ''Lycos, InMagic Combine Forces to Organize Intranets,'' *InfoWorld,* June 23, 1997, p. 83.

''Portal Combat,'' *Business Week,* January 17, 2000, p. 96.

''Preview Travel, Lycos Team Up,'' *Internet World,* March 30, 1998, p. 42.

Reid, Calvin, ''B&N.com, Lycos Ink Book Web Pact,'' *Publishers Weekly,* August 25, 1997, p. 14.

Roth, Daniel, ''The Revenge of the Search Engine,'' *Forbes,* March 9, 1998, p. 48.

Stahl, Stephanie, et al., ''The Search Is On,'' *InformationWeek,* May 13, 1996, p. 35.

Taylor, Cathy, ''Search for Tomorrow: Three Internet Search Engines Are Set to Start Selling Stock,'' *Mediaweek,* April 1, 1996, p. 31.

Tedesco, Richard, ''Lycos Puts New Spin on 'Net Biz,'' *Broadcasting & Cable,* July 27, 1998, p. 45.

''Tuned into the Web,'' *Byte,* December 1996, p. 40.

''The Urge to Merge,'' *U.S. News & World Report,* February 8, 1999, p. 42.

—David P. Bianco

The 3DO Company

600 Galveston Drive
Redwood City, California 94063
U.S.A.
Telephone: (650) 261-3000
Fax: (650) 261-3120
Web site: http://www.3do.com

Public Company
Incorporated: 1991
Employees: 495
Sales: $122.2 million (2000)
Stock Exchanges: NASDAQ
Ticker Symbol: THDO
NAIC: 42143 Computer and Computer Peripheral Equipment and Software Wholesalers; 511210 Software Publishers; 514191 On-Line Information Services

The 3DO Company develops and publishes CD-based entertainment software for personal computers (PCs) and for advanced game system consoles, such as Nintendo 64 and Game Boy Color for Nintendo of America and PlayStation and PlayStation2 for Sony Computer Entertainment. 3DO's most popular game brands include Army Men; BattleTanx; Heroes of Might and Magic; High Heat Baseball; and Vegas Games. The company also offers the ''Meridian 59'' series for play over the Internet by subscription. 3DO publishes and distributes entertainment software worldwide.

A Love of Video Games Spawns New Technology

Before starting 3DO in 1991, Trip Hawkins had been involved in the design of Apple's Macintosh computer and in the 1982 founding of Electronic Arts, creator of entertainment software for video game consoles. Hawkins' fascination with electronic games originated with ''Pong,'' the first electronic game. He designed his first computer game, ''AccuStat,'' a football game based on the 1974 Super Bowl, as a student of Strategy and Applied Game Theory at Harvard University. As a game designer at Electronic Arts Hawkins became a leader in the new video game industry. Hawkins formed 3DO because he wanted to develop a new technology which would surpass the technical capabilities of existing Nintendo and Sega consoles, as well as bypass the stringent license requirements of those companies. Hawkins planned to license the hardware design specification to electronics manufacturers and to form cooperative links between hardware and software developers.

Originally called SMSG, Inc., 3DO began as a subsidiary of Electronic Arts and became an independent company in 1993 with several prominent investors. While Electronic Arts maintained 24.3 percent ownership in the company, other equity partners included Matsushita Electric Industrial Company, maker of the Panasonic brand of electronic appliances, and Time Warner, each with 17.6 percent ownership; venture capital firm Kleiner Perkers with 14.8 percent; Trip Hawkins with 6.2 percent ownership and AT&T with 6.1 percent. Both Matsushita and AT&T planned to produce and market the game system.

In January 1993, 3DO and Matsushita unveiled a prototype of the company's interactive multimedia system at the Consumer Electronics Show. Hawkins hoped 3DO's technology would set a new standard in gaming technology, with exceptional quality graphics and color, three dimensional sound, and realistic motion. A double speed CD-ROM generated 50 times the processing capacity of similar existing technology, including new products, such as the Philips CD-I and Tandy's VIS. The final product was to be ready for retail introduction in fall 1993, in time for the holiday shopping season.

The product's high price retail price of $699 contained an element of risk. The CD-ROM drives necessary for 32-bit players cost more than cartridges, but the game required a base of users to compete with established video game console manufacturers. Like VCRs and PCs, which initially sold at high prices, Hawkins expected the price of the 3DO console to drop within two years. Hawkins hoped the 3DO system would become a common household appliance as a ''multiplayer'' capable of playing standard audio CDs, Kodak's CD-based electronic photo albums, and, in the future, motion pictures, referred to as Full Motion Video (FMV).

Company Perspectives:

Our mission at 3DO is to get everyone in the world to play video games.

Hawkins promoted hardware manufacturing and software development with low royalty rates. The seven-year hardware license agreement required no royalty payments, though 3DO charged a fee for certification that each console met design standards. Otherwise, Hawkins required only that the 3DO logo appear on the machines. For software licenses 3DO charged a $3 fee for each CD produced, compared to $15 to $20 for Nintendo and Sega. Unlike Sega and Nintendo, the agreement allowed for unlimited title development. 3DO supplied software licensees, over 80 at the time of the January tradeshow, with a development kit with sound effects, music, video clips, and copyrighted photographs from MCA, then a subsidiary of Matsushita, and Time Warner. 3DO authorized Warner Music Group, a subsidiary of Time Warner, to replicate CDs for software licensees.

Despite the fact that 3DO did not have a finished product and had not generated any sales, an initial public offering of 2.9 million shares of stock in March raised $40 million. Research and development had cost $13.2 million since the company's inception in September 1991, while assets accounted for $6.4 million. Delays in the development of 32-bit microprocessor chips for custom animation, graphics, and sound resulted in delays in completion of license agreements. Matsushita signed an agreement shortly after the stock offering and Sanyo signed in July.

In August 3DO and Matsushita announced that the Panasonic FZ-1 REAL (Realistic Entertainment Active Learning) Interactive Multiplayer would be introduced in consumer electronics and video game software stores in October. The retail price of $699 compared to Nintendo and Sega 16-bit games at $99, with dealer margins at approximately 27 percent. The final product included a control pad, and two ports for additional control pads, allowing up to eight players to participate at once. Matsushita packaged the console with a free copy of ''Crash N Burn,'' a game software which maximized the capabilities of the technology.

Marketing for the 3DO console targeted ''early adopters,'' consumers who buy the latest technology regardless of price, with joint promotions with electronics dealers. A mall tour allowed potential customers to experience the system's performance directly. Cities on the tour included Boston; Los Angeles; Washington D.C.; Dallas; Paramus, New Jersey; and Minneapolis, at the Mall of America. Marketing strategies included in-store kiosks, commercials in 1600 movie theaters, local and national print advertising and cable and network television commercials.

Sales of the Panasonic console did not meet expectations during the 1993 holiday shopping season. While 3DO did not release information about how many units sold, industry insider estimates ranged from 22,000 to 50,000 units. 3DO predicted sales of 100,000 units, expecting stronger sales to early adopters. The company attributed the poor sales to the high price tag and the lack of software titles, with only ten available; several new titles were finally released in January. Higher priced personal computers with CD-ROMs proved to be an unexpected competitor due to the multiple uses of computers. Also, Hawkins had expected up to six licensees to have the multiplayer available for sale.

3DO Game Technology Struggles for Market Share

3DO took a variety of measures to promote the game technology as brand loyalty would determine its ability to compete with established game consoles. A software agreement between 3DO and Park Place Productions set a retail price of $8 for each game compared to Sega and Nintendo games at $18 to $28 each. A decrease in manufacturing overhead and component costs allowed Matsushita to reduce the price of the Panasonic 3DO system to $399 retail by February 1994. With new hardware license agreements with Goldstar, Samsung, and Toshiba, Matsushita also wanted to sell at a competitive price. To compensate for the lower price 3DO offered a stock incentive to licensees, paying two shares of 3DO stock for each player sold by September 30.

Panasonic's interactive multiplayer found a ready audience in Japan when Matsushita launched the product in March 1994 at the yen equivalent of $525. By mid-February advanced orders resulted in a backorder of 40,000 units and 150,000 software items. Some dealers sold the consoles at $425 and software at 20 percent off suggested retail price. Matsushita introduced eleven new software titles and planned to launch a total of 60 titles by the end of the year. The success of 3DO in Japan led to several new software license agreements with developers in Japan: Capcom, Konami, Taito, Koei, Bandai, and Tomy. In June Matsushita released the MPEG adapter cartridge for FMV for $249.95 retail; the first movie disc released was the 1991 movie *Total Recall.*

Operating at a loss, 3DO needed to raise funds for working capital to continue its difficult task of building an installed customer base. For 1994 the company reported revenues of $10.3 million and a loss of $51.5 million, including a $21.4 million operating charge for the acquisition of NTG, the developer of the 3DO technology. Sale of stock to original investors included Hawkins's investment of an additional $12.5 million. New investors included Goldstar, Creative Technology, and Sim Wong Hoo, chair of Creative Technology. Inside investment renewed public confidence in the company for a May 1994 public offering of stock at $12.35 per share. The private and public offerings raised $37 million.

Software development presented a number of problems leading 3DO to form Studio 3DO, an in-house software development group. Few titles had been published for exclusive use with 3DO technology, with most titles as port transfers from 16-bit titles. As such, existing game software for 3DO did not make full use of the 32-bit technology's capacities. Many developers were reluctant to expend time on producing 3DO titles given the low consumer response to the product. Also, a best-selling game title did not emerge to compel consumers to want the 3DO multiplayer. Hawkins did not want to compete with software licensees and planned only to create a few new games each year. 3DO also began to publish software for other devel-

Key Dates:

1993: Matsushita introduces Panasonic FZ1 REAL Interactive Multiplayer with 3DO-designed hardware.
1994: 3DO forms in-house game software studio.
1995: Poor sales of game console indicate failure to attain an installed base of users.
1997: 3DO halts hardware development; sells rights to M2 technology to Matsushita.
1998: Company launches Internet multiplayer game, ''Meridian 59.'' 2000: 3DO makes first profit, $205,000.

opera. In a joint project with Creative Technology, 3DO sought to create a 3DO card which would make 3DO entertainment and education CDs compatible with PC CD-ROMs.

To raise consumer awareness of the 3DO technology, the company launched a multi-million marketing campaign. Television and print advertising targeted men aged 18 to 30 years old, incorporating game footage in advertisements on MTV, ESPN, Turner Sports Network, and the 100th episode of the animated comedy *The Simpsons.* Specialty magazines included *Electronic Entertainment* and *Electronic Gaming Monthly*, while general publications included *TV Guide* and *USA Today*. Radio advertisements aired in 50 major markets. Also, Matsushita included a free ''Total Eclipse'' space combat game with units sold before October 31.

In September 3DO announced that it was completing development of the M2 Accelerator which upgraded 3DO hardware to 64-bit capacity. The M2 used IBM's Power PC 602 microprocessor to enhance the speed and quality of graphics. The technology performs a number of software development tasks, such as scale, detail, texture, and surface curves, thus improving the realism of the graphics. 3DO hoped an add-on cartridge would be available by fall 1995 to compete with new 64-bit game consoles from Nintendo, Sega, and Sony.

Sanyo and Goldstar launched their versions of a 3DO game console in fall 1994. Sanyo introduced the 3DO system in Japan under the name TRY for the yen equivalent of $548. Goldstar produced a sleek-looking machine, the GPA 101 M3DO Multiplayer, which the company launched in the United States for $399 through software chains Babbages, Electronics Boutique, and Software Etc., as well as Toys ''R'' Us, Kay-Bee Toys, and FAO Schwarz. Goldstar planned to introduce the system through regional and national mass merchants in 1995 and 1996, respectively. Marketing involved flexible in-store displays and a special software package which included ''Shock Wave,'' a science fiction game, children's ''Putt-Putt,'' and a Photo CD processing coupon from Eastman Kodak, a $150 retail value.

As the 1994 holiday season approached, Hawkins recognized that slow sales determined the future feasibility of the 3DO multiplayer. Because the game makers planned to introduce new game technology in 1995, holiday sales declined dramatically for Nintendo and Sega, as well as 3DO. Sales in Japan, however, were double that of those in the United States, as the Panasonic REAL multiplayer sold well in Matsushita-owned stores. Goldstar sought to improve sales by repackaging its 3DO multiplayer console with ''FIFA International Soccer'' and ''Shockwave.'' It bundled the FMV attachment, called the Digital Video Module (DVM), with a ''Total Recall'' CD for a retail price of $200. The DVM module also enabled full motion video games and Goldstar planned to open a software development studio to create titles for DVM use.

The 3DO hardware began to gain more acceptance in the retail marketplace. Wal-Mart agreed to carry the Panasonic REAL multiplayer in 2,300 stores in spring 1995. Other new distribution included toy stores, mass merchant retailers, and department stores. Available in 2,000 stores at the beginning of 1995, 3DO set a goal to be in 12,000 stores and to have 300 software titles available by the Christmas season. The 3DO technology was available in 10,000 stores by July.

In anticipation of competition from new game technology by Sega, Nintendo, and Sony, Goldstar and Matsushita cut the retail price of their 3DO systems $100 to $299, resulting in a sudden increase in sales. In April 1995 Sega launched a 64-bit technology at $399 with one software title and sold 120,000 copies in the first six months. The following October the Sony PlayStation, at $299 per unit, sold 100,000 machines its first month in the stores. After two years on the market, 3DO had sold 300,000 units in the United States, an indication that 3DO would not attain a critical mass of users to merit continued upgrading of the technology and supplemental equipment and software. Goldstar and Matsushita responded by reducing the price of 3DO multiplayer to $199. The Panasonic REAL console continued to sell well in Japan, with almost a half million units sold.

3DO Makes Transition to Software Development

Taking a dramatic step to reduce losses—$46 million on revenues of $30.4 million in fiscal 1995—3DO signed an $100 million licensing agreement with Matsushita. Under the agreement Matsushita paid a $100 million licensing fee plus royalties to 3DO for its exclusive use of the M2 Acceleration technology. 3DO retained a nonexclusive license to use the technology for personal computing applications, as a tool in software development, and for coin-operated arcade games. Matsushita planned to sublease the technology and to use the technology in DVD players, car navigation hardware, kiosk hardware, interactive television set-top boxes, as well as video games. As a result of the deal, LG Electronics, (formerly Goldstar) decided to discontinue production of the 3DO console.

3DO continued to focus on software and hardware development. In December 1995 3DO acquired the 15-employee Cyclone Studios which produced arcade-style video games, with plans to apply the M2 technology to improve arcade games. In July the company acquired New World Computing for $18 million in stock and the assumption of debt. New World Computing was known for the popular video games series, ''Heroes of Might and Magic'' and ''Wages of War.'' In hardware 3DO launched MPEG Express 1000, a digital encoding and decoding product for television and computer monitors, for license in March 1996. The MPEG Express 1250 provided high-speed data transfer.

By September 1996 3DO decided to discontinue the hardware development and licensing operations, making a definitive switch to game software design. Hawkins gave control of the company to Hugh Martin, president of 3DO. While retaining his position as Chair and CEO, Hawkins became the creative director of Studio 3DO. The company's first games included ''Meridian 59,'' a multiuser, role-playing fantasy game, the first important multiplayer Internet game. While consumers purchased the disc in retail stores, actual play occurred on the Internet by subscription only. For the PC platform 3DO released ''3DO Games: Decathlon,'' ''Captain Quasar,'' and ''Star Fighter.'' The top selling game for PCs, ''Magic,'' sold over 500,000 units, becoming one of the all-time best-selling video games.

3DO settled its business arrangements by selling hardware-related assets. Samsung bought the company's hardware business for $20 million in June 1997. In negotiations with Matsushita, 3DO exchanged future claims to royalties from M2 technology for 3.2 million shares of 3DO stock. 3DO relinquished the right to develop software and peripherals related to M2 technology and Matsushita obtained the right to further develop the M2 technology.

The agreement solidified 3DO's shift to game development, with special interest in the Internet game industry. The company promoted online gaming with reduced rates, to $2.49 per 24-hour day, with maximum charge of $7.47 per week. 3DO eliminated the $14.95 activation fee and reduced the minimum monthly rate to under $5.00. ''M59 Revelation'' debuted in October and ''M59 Renaissance'' launched in early 1998. Aries Online Games and Game Storm distributed 3DO Internet games. 3DO sold its first server license to Computec, a publisher of magazines and a game site owner based in Germany.

The company continued to create games for PCs and began software development for other game platforms. In fiscal 1998 3DO launched three new PC games, ''High Heat Baseball,'' ''Army Men,'' and ''Heroes of Might and Magic IV.'' By fiscal 1999 that number increased to 14 titles, ten for PCs, three for PlayStation, and one for Nintendo. ''BattleTanx,'' released in early 1999, sold 65,000 copies during the first three weeks available. Other best-sellers included the ''Army Men'' series, ''Heroes Might and Magic VII,'' and ''Uprising.'' 3DO also introduced ''M59 Liberation'' for Internet play by subscription in July 1999. The company launched ''Sammy Sosa High Heat Baseball'' after obtaining an endorsement from the record hitting baseball player in January 2000. In fiscal 2000 3DO had increased its rate of new game releases to 31 new titles, 16 for PCS, ten for PlayStation, three for Game Boy Color, and two for Nintendo 64.

By returning to his love of games, Hawkins turned 3DO into a viable company. Fiscal 1999 revenues of $48 million resulted in low losses, relative to the past, at $13 million. With the turnaround in process, 3DO initiated a August public offering of stock and raised $43 million for continuing operations. In December 1999 the company received a patent for ideas related to a new network entertainment system. In anticipation of continued success, 3DO hired several video game industry veterans for crucial executive positions. Operations opened in the United Kingdom to begin distribution throughout Europe. 3DO realized its first profit in fiscal year ending March 31, 2000. With revenues of $122.2 million, 3DO garnered a net income of $205,000. The company expected revenues to continue to grow in the future, but research and development would curtail profits.

Future game releases involved multiple game platforms and leading edge technology. While some titles were being adapted to alternate platforms, new titles included sequels to ''Army Men'' and new game brands included ''Warriors of Might and Magic'' and ''World Destruction League.'' The company expected to produce several games for Sony's PlayStation2, launched in fall 2000. The company also planned to launch a new Internet game, ''Legends of Might and Magic.'' 3DO expected the network capabilities of the Internet as a game platform to be a major factor in software development and company growth.

Principal Subsidiaries

Studio 3DO K.K. (Japan); 3DO Europe Ltd. (United Kingdom).

Principal Competitors

Activision, Inc.; CUC International; Disney Interactive; Electronic Arts Inc.; GT Interactive Software Corp.; LucasArts Entertainment Company; Mattel, Inc.; Microsoft Corp.; Sierra On-Line, Inc.

Further Reading

''3DO Commits to Online,'' *Television Digest*, September 15, 1997, p. 18.

''The 3DO Company Expects 70 Percent Revenue Growth In Fiscal 2001,'' *PR Newswire*, June 8, 2000.

''3DO Dropping Hardware,'' *Television Digest*, September 23, 1996, p. 12.

''3DO Hits Retail Shelves,'' *Television Digest*, October 4, 1993, p. 15.

''3DO Ships 'Groovy Bunch of Games','' *PR Newswire*, August 29, 2000.

''Company and Person to Watch: Trip Hawkins, 3DO,'' *San Francisco Business Times,* December 30, 1994, p. 10A.

''A Done Deal: U.S., Korea OK Samsung Buying 3DO,'' *HFN—The Weekly Newspaper for the Home Furnishings Network,* June 30, 1997, p. 29.

Elmer-Dewitt, Philip, ''Playing for Keeps,'' *Time*, December 19, 1994, p. 58.

Gillen, Marilyn A., ''3DO Previews its 64-Bit Upgrade,'' *Billboard,* May 13, 1995, p. 90.

——, ''Warner Offers Package Deal to 3DO Licensees,'' *Billboard,* October 9, 1993, p. 6.

Goldfisher, Alastair, ''Electronic Arts Spinoff 3DO Finds New Legs in Video Game Software,'' *Business Journal,* August 24, 1998, p. 3.

Landberg, Mike, ''3DO Home Video-Game Maker's Stock See-Saw Amid High Competitive Risks,'' *Knight-Ridder/Tribune Business News,* June 5, 1994.

McConville, James A., ''3DO Aims for Users, Awareness Prior to Arrival of New Machines,'' *HFD—The Weekly Home Furnishings Newspaper*, March 27, 1995, p. 52.

——, ''3DO Takes its Message to the Public,'' *HFD—The Weekly Home Furnishings Newspaper*, May 2, 1994, p. 145.

McConville, James A., ''Interactive Dreaming; 3DO Co. Plots Home Multimedia System That Will Bring Together Elements of Hollywood and Silicon Valley,'' *HFD—The Weekly Home Furnishings Newspaper*, May 31, 1993, p. 54.

''No 3DO from AT&T this year,'' *Television Digest*, June 13, 1994, p. 18.

''Panasonic's Plans for 3DO,'' *Television Digest,* May 17, 1993, p. 16.

''Positioning its Player,'' *Television Digest,* April 25, 1994, p. 11.

Robson, Douglas, ''Trip Hawkins Grabs for Space: Re-Energized 3DO Pushes to Triple Size with New Peninsula Digs,'' *San Francisco Business Times,* May 28, 1999, p. 1.

Veilleux, C. Thomas, ''3DO Forces Pin Hopes on Software,'' *HFN—The Weekly Newspaper for the Home Furnishings Network,* October 16, 1995, p. 89.

——, ''3DO's Deeper in the Game,'' *HFN—The Weekly Newspaper for the Home Furnishings Network,* April 22, 1996, p. 173.

——, ''Fate of LGE 3DO game no great surprise,'' *HFN—The Weekly Newspaper for the Home Furnishings Network,* January 22, 1996, p. 83.

——, ''LG Jumps in 3DO Price Cut Fray,'' *HFN—The Weekly Newspaper for the Home Furnishings Network,* December 11, 1995, p. 56.

——, ''Price Pushes 3DOs: Cuts Jumpstart Sales of Systems,'' *HFN—The Weekly Newspaper for the Home Furnishings Network,* July 31, 1995, p. 45.

—Mary Tradii

TV Guide, Inc.

7140 S. Lewis Ave.
Tulsa, Oklahoma 74136-5422
U.S.A.
Telephone: (918) 488-4000
Toll Free: (800) 477-7388
Fax: (918) 488-4637
Web site: http://www.tvguideinc.com

Wholly Owned Subsidiary of Gemstar-TV Guide International
Incorporated: 1965 as United Video
Employees: 2,700 (2000)
Sales: $1,150.3 million (2000)
Stock Exchanges: NASDAQ
Ticker Symbol: GMST
NAIC: 511120 Periodical Publishers; 513210 Cable Networks; 513220 Cable and Other Program Distribution; 513340 Satellite Telecommunications; 551112 Offices of Other Holding Companies; 541519 Other Computer Related Services

A wholly-owned subsidiary of Gemstar-TV Guide International, TV Guide, Inc. (formerly United Video Satellite Group) oversees a diversified group of companies that provides information and communication services to cable television systems, home satellite dishes, radio networks, data communications networks, and private business and government agencies.

TV Guide, Inc.'s United Video Group is a conglomeration of companies operating satellite delivery services, including SNG (Superstar), which provides programming services to some 60 percent of the direct-to-home satellite dish market. UVTV, the oldest company in the United Video Group, is a domestic and international marketer, distributor, and deliverer of television networks, including WPIX in New York, KTLA in Los Angeles, and CBS, NBC, ABC, PBS, and affiliated stations. TV Guide, Inc.'s 70 percent ownership of SSDS, Inc. adds that company's expertise in designing, building, and maintaining information infrastructure services, such as corporate networks, intranets, and Web sites, with an emphasis on electronic commerce capabilities. SpaceCom Systems is TV Guide, Inc.'s satellite transmission technology and services arm, providing satellite services to paging companies, financial data networks, radio networks, weather information services, and private business networks.

TV Guide, Inc.'s Entertainment Group is perhaps the fastest growing and changing branch of the company. With its merger with Gemstar in 2000, TV Guide became the leading provider of electronic programs guides and pay-per-view promotional services, including TV Guide Interactive (available in 2 million households in 2000, and growing by 5,000 homes per day), TV Guide Channel (reaching 54.5 million U.S. Nielsen households), TV Guide Online, Sneak Prevue, and TV Guide International. TV Guide, Inc.'s Magazine Group, which includes the flagship *TV Guide* magazine, the most widely read weekly publication in the United States (35 million readers and a circulation of 10.8 million), also publishes *The Cable Guide*, TV Guide Ultimate Cable, and *DirecTV TV Guide*, among other publications. Through TV Guide Distribution, TV Guide, Inc. represents 85 major consumer magazines like *Business Week*, *Seventeen*, *Reader's Digest*, and *Soap Opera Digest*.

TV Guide, Inc.'s merger with Gemstar gave Gemstar shareholders 55 percent of the combined company. In 2000, TV Guide, Inc. had sales of $1,150 million, and a one-year employee growth of 18.2 percent (to 2,700), reflecting the company's fast-growth and dominance in the fledgling interactive program guide (IPG) industry.

A Cable Pioneer's Offshoot in the 1960s

The history of TV Guide, Inc. begins with the history of United Video Satellite Group. Founded in 1965 as a division of United Cable Television Corp., United Video could already trace its roots back to the origins of cable television. United Cable was started by Gene Schneider, who had pioneered the industry in 1953 when he helped his brother design and build the country's first cable television system in Casper, Wyoming. In the mid-1960s, Schneider moved to Tulsa, Oklahoma, to start his own cable company, United Cable. Tulsa was wired for cable by 1973, but Schneider had also formed a second division

Company Perspectives:

Generations of television viewers have turned to TV Guide *magazine to learn what's on television, transforming the magazine into a trusted American icon. Now viewers can trust TV Guide, Inc. to guide them into the future of television entertainment and beyond. From print media to the Internet to electronic program guides,* TV Guide *tells viewers what's on across multiple platforms—in print, on the air, online, and on demand.*

of the company—later United Video—to build a larger microwave-based television distribution network. Roy Bliss, a family friend who had known Schneider as a child, joined United Cable in 1969, and took charge of building the United Video division.

United Cable began building its microwave network to bring programming to its own and other small cable systems. As Bliss, who became president of United Video, explained to *Tulsa World,* in many rural locations throughout the U.S., "[Y]ou either had cable or you didn't have television." Cable television found less success in larger cities, where broadcast television was more readily available. The addition of high-profile cable programming, such as the then new movie network HBO, was essential to cable systems—especially those in larger urban areas—for signing up subscribers.

In 1975, HBO began sending its signal via satellite transmission. Other programmers shortly followed suit, including Turner Broadcasting, which began satellite transmission in 1977. This new availability of programming prompted cable television's first boom, but the satellite technology also quickly replaced microwave networks as the primary means of transmission. Bliss saw the technology's potential early as well as the need for a company that could distribute the satellite signals to cable systems. In 1976, Bliss, backed by financing from Lawrence Flinn, bought out the United Video division of United Cable. Flinn, who had previously worked for the Morgan Stanley investment firm, became United Video's chairman and chief executive office and the owner of more than 90 percent of the company. Bliss was named president.

United Video sought to enter the satellite transmission market, but the expenses were too high for the newly independent company. The cable television industry was strictly regulated by the Federal Communications Commission (FCC). However, when deregulation of the cable industry took place in 1977, the cost of building an antenna, as well as its size requirement, dropped. In 1978, the company rented a satellite transponder—the last one available on the only commercial satellite in orbit at the time—at a cost of $100,000 per month. FCC approval came a month after the company's transponder lease began. Another month later, United Video began transmitting WGN and its Chicago Cubs coverage. The company struggled for its first year as a satellite transmission company as cable systems were slow to add satellite reception capacity. By 1979, the company had begun to recoup its investment, building revenues to $2 million per year.

Growth and Change in the 1990s

Led by the popularity of superstation WGN, United Video rapidly expanded its number of cable system customers during the 1980s. The company early on began to add other satellite-based services to complement its transmission capacity. Bliss and Flinn saw a need for more services in order to fuel cable television's future growth. As Bliss told *Tulsa World,* "My vision of cable television has always been more—more services, more entertainment, more technology-driven." United Video formed as a holding company, called United Video Holdings, Inc. and began the in-house development of new services. The first service added by the company brought United Video into providing content, in the form of the on-screen cable program guides. Originally named Trakker, Inc., the unit later became known as the Prevue Network, which proved to be a foreshadow of things to come.

By the mid-1980s, as the launching of more commercial satellites opened up more opportunities, the company expanded into two new areas. Prior to 1986, owners of large-dish (C-band) home satellite dishes could pull in any satellite signal. But HBO began scrambling its signal in 1986, and soon other satellite-based networks followed suit. United Video recognized a new market for its distribution services, and formed Superstar Entertainment, which packaged programming and sold it as subscriptions to home satellite dish owners. Superstar quickly became profitable and proved a strong engine for United Video's revenue growth, despite the fact that the scrambling technology employed at the time was relatively easy for dish owners to defeat. United Video's SpaceCom Systems brought the company into a new area: providing audio and data transmission for radio stations, government agencies, corporations, and others.

By 1990, the company's Cable Video Services Group distributed superstation WGN, which lagged behind only Turner Broadcasting, New York's WPIX, Los Angeles's KTLA, and the Dallas/Ft. Worth station KTVT in subscriber numbers, as well as radio stations, including WFMT of Chicago and KKJZ of Los Angeles. Meanwhile, Prevue Networks had expanded onto 800 cable systems, reaching more than 20 million homes, and soon added a sister channel, Sneak Prevue, which offered an on-screen program guide for pay-per-view programs. Together, United Video's companies reached more than 41 million homes through some 14,000 cable systems. The company's sales had reached $46 million, and United Video showed a strong profit of $4.5 million.

By 1993, the company's revenues had more than doubled, to $114 million. In November of that year, United Video reorganized as United Video Satellite Group. The following month, United Video went public, selling 4.1 million shares and raising $60.4 million in the offering. Flinn remained in control of 90 percent of the company. The company was branching out again, now into the promising arena of interactive services, which offered the home viewer, among other potential services, the ability to search the company's on-screen program guide. The United Video group added another service, Prevue Interactive, in 1993.

Meanwhile, United Video was receiving a big boost on another front. In 1993, satellite transmitters implemented a new scrambling technology that made it more difficult to pirate

Key Dates:

1965: United Video is founded by Gene Schneider as a division of United Cable Television Corp.
1969: Roy Bliss joins United Cable and is placed in charge of building the United Video division.
1976: Bliss, backed by Lawrence Flinn, buys out United Video from United Cable.
1993: United Video reorganizes to become United Video Satellite Group (USVG).
1995: UVSG becomes a subsidiary of Tele-Communications Inc. (TCI).
1996: Bliss leaves the company.
1997: Flinn steps down as chairman and CEO of UVSG.
1998: UVSG acquires TV Guide, and the new company becomes TV Guide, Inc.
1999: Rupert Murdoch and The News Corporation Limited acquires *TV Guide* magazine for $2 billion.
2000: Gemstar acquires TV Guide, making the company a subsidiary of the new Gemstar-TV Guide International.

satellite transmissions. Paying subscriptions quickly tripled, to some 1.9 million homes, and United Video picked up a strong share of the new subscribers, building from 150,000 to 540,000 and surpassing Tele-Communications Inc. (TCI) as the number one provider of C-band satellite transmission services. Superstar's growth helped boost the company's 1994 revenues to $196 million.

In 1994, United Video purchased a 10 percent stake in SSDS, Inc., a Colorado-based systems integrator whose clients included First Data Corp., Sun Microsystems, and the White House. By 1995, United Video had exercised its option to increase its share in SSDS, raising its stake to a controlling 70 percent interest. SSDS, a fast-growing company with $33 million in revenues, offered United Video enhanced technological and, most importantly, software-development capacity. United Video's revenues continued to grow strongly, reaching $263 million with net earnings of more than $23 million in 1995.

United Video was facing pressures from within the cable and satellite industries, not only from the growth of the direct broadcast satellite market—which threatened to make C-band satellite dishes obsolete within a few years—but also from recent startups, particularly TCI, rival to the company's Prevue revenue engine. In June 1995, United Video announced an agreement with TCI that gave the cable giant control of United Video. The transaction, completed in early 1996, formed United Video as a separate, publicly traded subsidiary of TCI. It also involved an exchange of stock, giving shareholders the more marketable TCI stock. Prevue Networks survived, as TCI dropped development of its own on-screen program guide. Later that year, TCI merged its own C-band satellite programming arm, Liberty Media's Netlink, into Superstar, and moved Netlink's operations to Tulsa.

In late 1996, after disagreements with TCI about plans to drop transmission of WGN (which the company ended up keeping), Bliss left the company he had founded. Lawrence Flinn, who still retained 36 percent of United Video's stock, remained chairman and chief executive until he retired in 1997, relinquishing the helm to Gary S. Howard and taking on the title of Chairman Emeritus. In early 1998, TCI increased its ownership of United Video by buying an additional 12.4 million shares of stock held by Flinn. These shake-ups within United Video were just a sign of even bigger changes to come before the dawn of the new millennium.

TV Guide, Inc. Created in 1999

In 1999, United Video Satellite Group saw the opportunity to purchase TV Guide. Founded in 1953 by publishing magnate Walter Annenberg, *TV Guide* magazine had established itself over the years as an icon of American pop culture. A mix of TV listings, reviews, gossip, and industry news, it quickly became the largest circulated weekly digest in the world, reaching more than 19 million readers at its peak in the mid-1970s. But by the 1980s, like many established magazines, *TV Guide* began to flounder. In 1988, Rupert Murdoch's News Corporation Limited acquired *TV Guide* (along with other properties) for an astonishing $3.2 billion. However at that time, readership had already begun to fall. With the dawn of the 1990s, the magazine seemed stuck on autopilot, as younger, hipper magazines grabbed the spotlight, and Internet Web sites began to thrive. By 1999, circulation had dropped to 10 million.

By buying *TV Guide* from News Corp., UVSG brought the magazine into the lucrative interactive high-tech world, and brought UVSG the brand recognition of the country's most-read magazine. With the 1999 merger (for $800 million in cash, and a 44 percent interest in the resulting company), the new combined company was named TV Guide, Inc.

When all the dust had settled by June of 1999, Joe Kiener (former president and COO of News America Publishing Group) was appointed chairman and CEO, and Peter C. Boynlan III (former president and COO of United Video) became president and COO of TV Guide, Inc. Gary Howard, former CEO of United Video, remained as a director of TV Guide, Inc.

Acquisition by Gemstar in 2000

The acquisition of TV Guide Inc. created legal disputes with Gemstar, owner of the VCR Plus product, which was fiercely defending its many patents in the interactive programming guide (IPG) industry. United Video had actually made an unsuccessful bid to purchase Gemstar two years before acquiring TV Guide Inc. Gemstar had been started a decade earlier by Henry Yuen when he created VCR Plus, a product intended to make it simple for customers to program their VCRs. Although Gemstar was a relatively small company, Yuen wielded an amazing amount of power in the IPG industry, holding 90 key patents that made it virtually impossible to build an electronic program guide without crossing legal paths with him. In 2000, *U.S. News and World Report* called Yuen ''the Bill Gates of TV'' and stated that cable executives referred to Gemstar's mastermind as a ''patent terrorist.'' A deadlocked legal battle with Gemstar over patent disputes finally enabled Gemstar to turn the tables and purchase TV Guide, Inc. for $15 billion in 2000.

The merger between Gemstar and TV Guide, Inc. formed Gemstar-TV Guide International and created a behemoth in the communications industry. With the patent wranglings between Gemstar and United Video/TV Guide finally settled with the merger, the two companies combined for a virtual lock on the IPG industry. TV Guide, Inc. retained its dominance in the TV listings industry, now spanning print, online, and broadcasting markets. With the combined properties and a growing international presence, the company's marketers estimated in 2000 that *TV Guide* reached some 79 million viewers in the United States alone, easily the dominant contender in the lucrative battle for the attention of TV viewers everywhere.

Principal Divisions

Entertainment Group; Magazine Group; United Video Group.

Principal Operating Units

TV Guide Interactive; TV Guide Channel; TV Guide Online; Sneak Prevue; TV Guide International; TV Guide Magazine; TV Guide Ultimate Guide; The Cable Guide; See; MMDI; UVTV; SNG [Superstar]; TVG Network; SpaceCom; SSDS and Knowledge Workers; TV Guide Enterprise Solutions; TV Guide Affiliate Sales; Technology Ventures.

Principal Competitors

DirecTV; Gannett; Vertis.

Further Reading

Curtis, Bruce, ''United Video's Growth Tuned to Industry Trends,'' *Tulsa World*, November 2, 1992, p. G1.

Fattah, Hassan, ''Guide-ing Light,'' *Brandweek*, September 11, 2000, p. 64.

Finnerty, Brian, ''On Screen,'' *Investor's Business Daily*, August 1, 1994, p. A6.

Foisie, Geoffrey, ''United Video: Making Money as Middleman,'' *Broadcasting and Cable*, October 18, 1993, p. 36.

Kerschbaumer, Ken, ''Gemstar-TV Guide Merge Gets DOJ OK,'' *Broadcasting and Cable*, July 17, 2000, p. 16.

Norris, Floyd, ''How United Video's Chairman Can Look Like a Loser and Still Win,'' *New York Times*, June 26, 1995, p. D6.

Parets, Robyn Taylor, ''Orbiting,'' *Investor's Business Daily*, July 26, 1995.

Tuttle, Roy, ''Bliss Resigns USVG Posts; Exec Ripped TCI on WGN,'' *Tulsa World*, December 5, 1996, p. E1.

Vogelstein, Fred, ''Meet the Bill Gates of TV,'' *U.S. News and World Report*, August 7, 2000, p. 50.

—M.L. Cohen
—update: Linda M. Gwilym

Vail Resorts, Inc.

P.O. Box 7
Vail, Colorado 81658
U.S.A.
Telephone: (970) 845-2500
Web site: http://www.vailresorts.com
Public Company
Incorporated: 1997
Employees: 12,000 peak season, 7,500 year-round
Operating Revenues: $553.1 million (2000)
NAIC: 71399 Amusement and Recreation; 53139 Real Estate Agents and Managers; 72111 Hotels and Motels; 72211 Eating Places; 72241 Drinking Places

Vail Resorts, Inc. (formerly Vail Associates, Inc.), is the owner of Vail Mountain, the largest and most popular ski area in the United States, and the owner of Vail Resorts Development Company, their real estate and vacation property division. The company headquarters are at the base of the Vail Mountain resort, some 8,200 feet above sea level in the Colorado Rockies. In addition to Vail, the company also owns Breckenridge Ski Resort, Beaver Creek, and Keystone, three nearby ski resorts, as well as land, lodges, restaurants, golf courses, and other property in the Vail Valley. In 1999, Vail Resorts acquired the Grand Teton Lodge Company in Wyoming, its first resort property outside of Colorado.

Before the 1960s: Making of a Mountain

The Vail Valley, also known as Gore Creek Valley, lies in west-central Colorado near the Continental Divide. Cut off at one end by a pass of 10,600 feet, and at the other end by a canyon about the width of a horse, the valley long maintained an obscure presence in Colorado. For generations it was a place where Native American Utes would come to escape the summer heat. After the Civil War, white settlers pushed into the valley, among the first of whom were miners searching for gold and silver, as well as map surveyors, who charted its canyons, cliffs, and other features. The land was settled by a small number of ranchers, but the steep terrain and cold climate eventually drove most of them away, leaving the area to sheepherders, who used the valley as pastureland during the spring and summer.

During World War II, the U.S. Army set up a training center, Camp Hale, in another isolated valley about 23 miles from Vail. There, the army trained ski troopers of the Tenth Mountain Division, who were later sent to fight in the Apennine mountains of northern Italy. Pete Seibert, one of these troopers, was lucky to have made it through the war alive. Hit by small-arms fire and two mortar shells, Seibert was badly wounded, and one of the shells blew off his right kneecap. Doctors told him he would never again be able to ski. However, a few years later, Seibert was working as a ski instructor at Aspen, the famous Colorado resort, and in 1950 he made the U.S. Ski Team, though torn ligaments kept him from competing. During the next few years he studied at a hotel school in Lausanne, Switzerland.

Like many others in Colorado during the 1950s, Seibert dreamed of a way to establish his own resort, though perhaps with a bit more zeal than the others. ''I had first started thinking of running a resort when I was 12 years old,'' Seibert explained in his book about Vail, noting, ''there was nothing I wanted more in my life than to start a ski area.'' In this endeavor, Siebert would have considerable help from Earl Eaton, another Camp Hale veteran. Born not far from the present Vail resort, Eaton had become a uranium prospector. One day, while searching for uranium in Gore Creek Valley, he arrived at the ridge of an unnamed mountain. Looking south his eyes fell upon a vast expanse of treeless slopes, later called the ''back bowls,'' some of the most famous ski terrain in the United States. In March 1957, Eaton took Seibert to the mountain, and they both trudged seven hours through deep snow up to the ridge. When they arrived, Seibert, too, was stunned by the back bowls, as well as by the view of the towering peaks of the Gore Range.

Their first step was buying land. Although unable to purchase the mountain itself, which was owned by the U.S. Forest Service, they were able to purchase a 500-acre ranch at the base for $55,000 in 1957. Funded by six partners (mostly from Denver), Siebert and Eaton bought the land under the guise of a new company, Transmontane Rod and Gun Club, a name they used to keep their plans a secret from the local residents. During this time, they also searched for a name for their new resort. One suggestion was Shining Mountains, the Ute phrase for the

Company Perspectives:

Vail Resorts is the premier mountain resort operator in North America, with five distinctive mountain resorts. The company and our employees are committed to providing excellence for our customers, sensitivity to our surrounding communities and environment, and profitable growth for our shareholders.

western Colorado region. However, "when mountains shine," Seibert pointed out, "it means they're icy." So they settled on Vail, the name of the pass at the eastern end of the valley, named for Charles D. Vail, a former chief engineer of the Colorado Highway Department.

Late 1950s and early 1960s: Beginnings of a Ski Slope

Next, Siebert and Eaton applied for a "Conditional Special Use Permit." However, the U.S. Forest Service turned them down, claiming there were already enough ski resorts in the White River National Forest. Undeterred, the group appealed the decision and, a year later, they received the permit, allowing them to attract 21 new investors, some from as far away as Texas and New York, and to found a new company, Vail Corp., which was used to raise additional funds. In 1960, again through Transmontane Rod and Gun Club, the group purchased an adjacent property, also of 500 acres. Finally, in 1961, after the group brought in 100 limited partners (each putting up $10,000), Vail Associates, Inc. was born.

Vail Associates got the go-ahead from the U.S. Forest Service in December 1961, and the company wasted no time in developing the foundations of the resort. Ski lifts were ordered, bulldozers pushed the snow out of the way to make room for construction, and trails on the mountain were cut. The mountain's front side was ideal for the kind of gentle, tree-lined, slopes appropriate for beginners and intermediates, while the back bowls were the draw for advanced and expert skiers. Some of the trail names emerged from the early ski experiences of the Vail Associates group. The "Forever" trail in the back bowls, for example, was named one spring day when snow conditions were so perfect that a number of people skied down the back of the mountain; without a ski lift, the walk back up the mountain seemed to last forever.

With about $2 million slated for development, the group was able to cut the necessary trails and construct a nearly two-mile gondola (including a building at its base), two double-chair lifts (holding two persons per chair), a beginners surface lift, a lodge at mid-mountain ("Mid-Vail"), a ski patrol shack at the top, and a bridge across Gore Creek. Bob Parker, also from the Tenth Mountain Division and a former editor of *Skiing Magazine*, became the marketing director of Vail Associates, and his contributions included organizing numerous crowd-gathering events. Especially important was an agreement by the U.S. Ski Team to hold an Olympic training camp at Vail, an event that began on December 23, 1961, just eight days after the resort opened.

1960s: Establishing a Ski Resort

Opening day was hardly indicative of the resort's future greatness. With no snow at the base and snow only about ankle deep at the top, the resort sold a small number of $5 lift tickets, only a few of which actually went to skiers. Most of the tickets were purchased by area residents who wanted to experience the novelty of riding the lifts up and down the mountain. Three weeks later, on January 10, 1963, the resort managed to draw just 12 skiers, bringing in a total of $60 from lift tickets.

However, the resort's fortunes soon improved. Its large amount of gentle terrain attracted families, and its more fearsome back bowls became legendary among experienced skiers. Vail, closer to Denver than its soon-to-be archrival Aspen, began to draw tourists. More importantly, however, Vail also benefited from a tremendous increase in the popularity of skiing during the 1960s and 1970s. The 1960 Winter Olympics, held at Squaw Valley, California, encouraged many Americans to try skiing, as did the new Head metal skis, which made the sport easier. Other important developments included safer ski bindings; "stretch" ski pants, which were more fashionable than the traditional bulky skiwear; heavy promotions by airlines, which saw in skiing a new market for their services; and legal changes that made condominium ownership more practical and appealing.

As a result, Vail took off, growing faster than even the most optimistic hopes of its founders. By 1964, the company had developed enough new terrain to triple skier capacity, and trails and lifts continued to spread east and west across the mountain. Its Golden Peak and Lionshead ski areas opened in 1967 and 1969, respectively. For the base area, the company followed its master plan, which called for an Austrian-style village, complete with winding lanes, footbridges, arcades, and a clock tower, while avoiding such distractions as neon lights. Each building in the town offered unique features, while conforming to the general style. In 1966, however, the town of Vail was incorporated and the company was no longer able to control the town's development.

1960s and 1970s: Expansion and Development

During the late 1960s, Vail continued new resort development projects on both sides of the valley. To help pay for the development, costing some $13 million by 1969, the company sold part of its land in the valley as commercial and residential lots. In 1966, it began to offer its stock over the counter, a move that left Seibert as chairperson while effectively reducing his power. In 1971, the company also spent $4.4 million to purchase 2,200 acres of land ten miles down the road, which would later become the site of its Beaver Creek resort. By 1973, Vail Mountain had some 800 acres of skiable terrain, two gondolas, nine chairlifts, and four restaurants (two on the top of the mountain and two at the bottom). Total revenues were about $7 million.

Even more attention was focused on Vail in 1974, when Gerald Ford took over the U.S. presidency from the resigning Richard Nixon. Ford, in addition to being the first "skiing president," frequently took vacations at Vail and owned a three-bedroom condominium in the center of town. His first Vail ski vacation while president took place in December 1974, but for security reasons he rented out the home of Harry W. Bass, a Texas multimillionaire and Vail board member. Some began to dub this rented home the "Western White House."

Key Dates:

1957: Pete Seibert and Earl Eaton, co-founders of Vail Associates, Inc., first climb the future Vail Mountain.
1961: The U.S. Forest Service issues final approvals and permits to begin building Vail Mountain ski area.
1962: Vail Mountain opens for skiing with two chairlifts, one gondola, and a $5 lift ticket.
1972: Vail Associates purchases 2,200 acres of Beaver Creek property.
1980: Beaver Creek ski area officially opens with 4 chairlifts, 28 runs, and 425 skiable acres.
1985: George Gillett purchases Vail Associates as a subsidiary of Gillett Holdings, Inc.
1989: The World Alpine Ski Championships are held at Vail Mountain and Beaver Creek.
1992: Apollo Ski Partners of New York acquires Vail Associates.
1993: Vail Associates buys Arrowhead's undeveloped real estate and mountain properties near Beaver Creek.
1997: Ralcorp Holdings and resort operations, are merged with Vail Associates, creating Vail Resorts, Inc.; Vail Resorts, Inc. undergoes IPO that raises $213 million.
1998: Vail Resorts purchases the Inn at Keystone; the Village at Breckenridge, a collection of hotel, restaurant, and other properties; arson fires in protest of the company's controversial Category III expansion cause more than $12 million in damages.
1999: World Alpine Ski Championships are held at Vail and Beaver Creek; Vail Resorts acquires the Grand Teton Lodge Company in Grand Teton National Park, Wyoming; purchases VailNet and InterNetWorks, two local technology companies.
2000: Category III expansion, now named Blue Sky Basin, is completed. Vail Mountain regains *SKI Magazine*'s title as the #1 ski resort in North America; Vail Resorts acquires a 51 percent stake in Renaissance Resort and Spa in Jackson Hole, Wyoming; the property is renovated and renamed Snake River Lodge and Spa.

Mid-1970s: Tragedy Strikes

Vail's next major source of publicity was the result of a tragic accident. On March 26, 1976, a frayed cable on the Lionshead gondola got caught in one of the lift towers, causing the passing cars to bounce and shake. Two cars then fell off, plummeting 125 feet to the ground, while the rest of the lift came to a halt. Although the ski patrol was able to rescue those trapped in the stalled lift, four people died and eight others were injured. At the time, this was the worst accident at a U.S. ski resort.

The tragedy was bad publicity for Vail and, worse, prompted a wave of lawsuits totaling more than $50 million. Fearing its liability in the accident, the board decided to sell the company, and, in late 1976, Harry Bass was able to gain controlling interest in Vail Associates for $13 million. Soon afterward, Seibert was forced out of the company, reportedly because of a personality clash with Bass. Ironically, Vail Associates eventually settled all the lawsuits out of court for only a fraction of the total claim.

1976–85: New Site Improves Image

During this time, the company's Beaver Creek site was chosen to host the downhill event for the Winter Olympics, scheduled to take place in Colorado in 1976. However, the Olympic offer was turned down by Colorado voters and, instead, the games were held at Innsbruck, Austria. Initially seen as a setback, the loss of the Olympic games gave the company more time to plan Beaver Creek; in fact, the planning alone would take seven years and cost $50 million.

Ultimately, Beaver Creek became not merely a ski resort but an elegant, truly luxurious, all-season resort area, which included facilities for conventions and conferences. Opened on December 14, 1980, Beaver Creek initially offered 450 acres of skiable terrain, boosted to some 1,000 acres by the decade's end. During this period, Vail Associates was also marketing the valley as a summer vacation area, where people could hike, raft, ride the gondola, shop at the more than 200 stores, or golf at one of the four 18-hole courses.

By 1982, Vail Associates had assets of nearly $100 million and revenues of $43.7 million—$31 million from its ski resorts and another $12 million from real estate operations. Vail Mountain was without a doubt one of the country's premier ski resorts, and Beaver Creek, though small, had built a reputation for opulence. All boded well for the company save two developments. First, the popularity of skiing in the United States had declined dramatically, and secondly, sales of the Beaver Creek properties were dismal. By the mid-1980s, real estate prices in the valley had collapsed, causing the near failure of Vail Associates. Problems for the company were further complicated in 1984 by a confrontation between Bass and his children, whose trust, established by Bass, owned enough Vail stock to oust him from the chairmanship.

1985–90: New Owner Invests in Improvements and Expansion

In the summer of 1985, Vail Associates was purchased for $115 million by George Gillett, head of Gillett Holdings Inc., which at the time owned nine television stations, 21 newspapers, two radio stations, and a meatpacking plant. George Gillett had been a customer at Vail since 1963 and was an enthusiastic skier prepared to make large capital investments. However, his appraisal of the resort's recent past was harsh. He noted that Vail was not making money and that it had over six years of condominium inventory in Beaver Creek. Gillett also criticized the company for maintaining an entire department devoted to real estate development when there was no demand. Employee attitudes towards the customers were cited as poor, and the people who owned many of the businesses in town viewed skiers as intruders on their peaceful lifestyle.

Gillett set out to change this environment, emphasizing the simple principle that ''the customer is king.'' One of the first areas he focused on was training. Gillett personally led every employee-training program at the Vail resort, as well as additional training programs for city employees, restaurant workers, bus drivers, and cab companies. He arranged to have television crews follow several families on a Vail vacation—from the moment they made their reservations until they left the resort for home—and then showed a film of these trips to Vail's management. Among the problems they discovered was the lack of a central reservations system; the high incidence of lost baggage at the airport; long lines at ticket windows and lifts; and the lack of children's activities after skiing.

From 1985 to 1989, the company invested $60 million in capital improvements. Part of this sum went to the China Bowl expansion, which opened up an immense new area of advanced terrain on the back side of the mountain, in the process doubling the resort's skiable terrain to 3,787 acres. With the addition of China Bowl, Vail became the country's largest ski resort, surpassing the former leader, Mammoth Mountain in California. By 1989, it had also installed six high-speed quad lifts (with four-person chairs), which, though costing several million dollars each, considerably reduced lift lines. For children, the company opened a kids-only hill, which included Ft. Whippersnapper, an adventure park with mock hunting camps, and an Indian village. Remarkably, by 1989, all the condominiums in Beaver Creek were occupied.

The readers' poll of *SKI Magazine* rated Vail Mountain the top resort in North America three years in a row—1989, 1990, and 1991—and the company also set attendance records, with over 1.5 million ''skier visits'' each year at Vail Mountain and more than 400,000 at Beaver Creek. Capital improvements continued as Vail constructed a public bobsled course in 1990 and installed its tenth high-speed quad in 1992. By 1993, it had 4,020 acres of skiable terrain and a total of 25 lifts. Vail was also the host of the 1989 World Alpine Ski Championships, an event that hadn't been held in the United States since 1950. The event gave Vail extensive international press coverage, which Vail Associates hoped would encourage skiers from other countries to visit the resort.

However, while Vail thrived, its parent, Gillett Holdings, was collapsing under the weight of failed junk bonds (high-risk, high-yielding debt certificates), issued in the 1980s to finance its acquisitions. The holding company filed for bankruptcy on June 25, 1991, and its eventual reorganization transferred the ownership of Vail Associates to Apollo Advisors, L.P. of New York, a company headed by Leon Black, a former Drexel Burnham banker. Nevertheless, George Gillett continued to serve as chairman of Vail Associates.

1990s: Business Booms and Expansion Accelerates Amid Controversy and IPO

Despite the financial complications of its parent company, the day-to-day operations of Vail Associates remained profitable, and the company continued to make ambitious expansion plans. In 1993, Vail sought approval from the U.S. Forest Service to develop a giant, north-facing bowl, which would again almost double the resort's already huge amount of skiable terrain. Further west, the company had purchased Arrowhead, a new, small ski resort next to Beaver Creek, and plans were underway to connect the two resorts with a chair lift. However, the many projects taken on by Vail Associates were also reflected in the price of Vail Mountain's daily lift ticket, which increased from $30 in 1986 to $46 in 1994.

Vail Associates was not alone in its plans for expanding terrain and upgrading facilities, nor in its raising of lift ticket prices. Many other resort owners—noting that Americans were increasingly going to the biggest and best-equipped ski areas—were also investing in expansion projects, while small ski areas, unable to compete, were failing at a rapid rate. Vail Mountain had managed to remain at the top of North American ski resorts, though not without competition. Nearby Aspen, for example, with its four separate ski mountains, continued to benefit from its reputation as a more ''authentic,'' culturally sophisticated town. Moreover, several Utah resorts offered drier snow and steeper terrain. Farther north, Whistler and Blackcomb, contiguous resorts in British Columbia, Canada, both had a much larger vertical drop (the difference in elevation between the base and the summit) and, when viewed as a single ski area, a greater amount of skiable terrain.

In 1996, Vail Associates signed a deal with Ralcorp Holdings, Inc., purchasing nearby Breckenridge and Keystone resorts and establishing Vail Resorts, Inc. Now skiers had access to four ski resorts and the Arapaho Basin. That year, the company also invested $30 million in improvements at Vail, including more ski lifts, a 12-passenger gondola, and a new base lodge that catered to a variety of customers.

The popularity of snowboarding meant Vail had to expand not only in a geographic sense but also in a business sense. Snowboarders were typically a different demographic than the affluent skiers of Vail's majority; the company also recognized the need to establish Vail as not just a place to ski but also a place to vacation. Adventure Ridge, a winter-amusement park, soon opened at the top of the Lionshead gondola. The park included four new restaurants, bars featuring live music, extreme snowboarding movies, and an upscale restaurant, primarily geared toward a younger crowd. By 1997, new CEO Adam Aron had tripled sales of season passes and planned to spend another $74 million in added improvements and expansion efforts.

In February 1997, Vail Resorts became the first North American ski resort to go public. The initial public offering raised $213 million, a welcome contribution to Vail's expansion efforts. Investor Ronald Baron, Ralcorp Holdings, and Apollo Advisors together controlled about 75 percent of the company's stock.

However, continued expansion proved to be challenging. Vail Resort's plans for an 885-acre Category III project in the Vail Mountain back bowls met with opposition from the townspeople and from environmental groups. Locals and animal rights activists protested vehemently in March 1998, objecting to what they viewed as the project's reckless encroachment on the habitats of elk and the Canada lynx. Although lawsuits were filed against the development, the project was ultimately approved by the U.S. Forest Service and by the Eagle County Commission. In October, on the day construction was to commence, fire broke out, damaging four chair lifts and destroying the $5 million Two Elk Lodge and ski patrol headquarters. Damage totaled $12 million. Members of the activist group Earth Liberation Front (ELF) claimed responsibility.

Ironically, the fire invoked local sympathy for Vail and the expansion continued as planned. By 1999 Vail Mountain had repaired the fire damage and, along with Beaver Creek, hosted the 1999 World Alpine Skiing Championships, making them the only North American venues to twice host the event. In 2000, the Category III expansion, now named Blue Sky Basin, was completed and opened for business.

Also in 1999, Vail Resorts finalized acquisition of the Grand Teton Lodge Company in Grand Teton National Park, Wyoming, its first resort property outside of Colorado. In 2000, the company acquired a 51 percent stake in, and assumed management of, the Renaissance Resort and Spa in Jackson Hole, Wyoming, near Grand Teton National Park. The property was renovated and renamed Snake River Lodge and Spa. Also in 2000, Vail Mountain was voted the number one ski resort in North America by readers of *SKI Magazine* for the third time since 1996 and for the tenth time since the poll began in 1987. Vail Resorts' other Colorado ski properties— Breckenridge, Keystone, and Bear Creek—all earned high ratings in the poll.

Into the New Millennium: Technology, Quality Experiences, and Profits

The 2000-2001 season set a new attendance record of 4.9 million skiers at Vail Resorts' four Colorado properties, and the company entered the new millennium employing handheld computers to register ski students, check in rental equipment, and verify ski passes at the lift. Moving forward, their goals are to maintain the ''best resort'' rating, continue improving the resort experiences of a broad base of clientele, sustain strategic expansions and acquisitions, leverage new Internet technologies to provide areas of growth and benefit core business, and increase profits and stock prices for investors.

Principal Subsidiaries

Vail Resorts Development Company.

Principal Operating Units

Vail Mountain; Breckenridge Ski Resort; Keystone; Beaver Creek; Grand Teton Lodge Company.

Principal Competitors

Intrawest Corporation; American Skiing Company; Booth Creek Ski Holdings, Inc.; Aspen Skiing Company.

Further Reading

''Apollo Ski's Vail Unit Agrees to Purchase a Resort in Colorado,'' *Wall Street Journal*, September 1, 1993, p. A5.

''Aspen and Vail Combine Efforts to Lure International Ski Market,'' *Travel Weekly*, June 22, 1992, p. 17.

''Beaver Creek: The Beverly Hills of Resorts,'' *Colorado Business*, February 1981, pp. 83–84.

Blevins, Jason, ''Vail, Colo. Resort Company's Ski Season Gets Big Lift,'' *The Denver Post*, June 7, 2001.

Brizzolara, Kim, ''Riding the Seesaw,'' *Skiing*, October 1991, pp. 26–27.

Charlier, Marj, ''Vail, Miffed at Loss of No. 1 Ranking in Skier Survey, Printed Fake Ballots,'' *Wall Street Journal*, February 22, 1993, p. A5.

Gillett, George, ''George Gillett, Director of Quality Control,'' *Colorado Business Magazine*, November 1989, p. 44.

Glick, Daniel, *Powder Burn: Arson, Money and Mystery on Vail Mountain*. New York: Public Affairs, 2001.

Glick, Daniel, and Sarah Van Boven, ''Fire on the Mountain,'' *Newsweek*, November 2, 1998, pp. 46–47.

Higgins, Kelly Jackson, ''Wireless LAN, Windows CE Devices Hit the Slopes,'' *Computer Reseller News*, October 4, 1999, p. 101.

Jesitus, John, ''Merger Forms Ski-Resort Giant,'' *Hotel and Motel Management*, September 16, 1996, p. 3.

Johnson, William Oscar, ''A Vision Fulfilled: From One Man's Dream, Vail Has Grown into America's Biggest Ski Resort,'' *Sports Illustrated*, January 30, 1989, pp. 70–82.

Marcial, Gene G., ''Good Conditions at Vail,'' *Business Week*, July 28, 1997, p. 73.

Markels, Alex, ''Backfire,'' *Mother Jones*, March 1999, p. 60.

May, Clifford D., ''Sampling New Terrain at Vail,'' *New York Times*, January 15, 1989, Sec. 10, p. 8.

Metz, Robert, ''Market Place: A Skiing Lesson for Wall Street,'' *New York Times*, May 30, 1973, p. 52.

Olson, Eric M., Stanley F. Slater, and Toni Anthony, ''Staying on Top at Vail,'' *Marketing Management*, Fall 1998, pp. 47–53.

Parker, Bob, ''Looking Back on Vail,'' *Skiing*, December 1982, p. 42.

Purdy, Penelope, ''Success Sampler: Three of the Best,'' *Colorado Business*, May 1983, p. 40.

Rebchook, John, ''Vail Resorts to Begin Building in Breckenridge,'' *Denver Rocky Mountain News*, March 23, 2001, p. 2B.

Seibert, Pete, *Vail: Triumph of a Dream*, Publisher's Group West, 2000.

Simonton, June, *Vail: Story of a Colorado Mountain Valley*, Dallas: Taylor Publishing Co., 1987.

Sterba, James P., ''Vail, Colo., Tries to Stay Calm While It Awaits a Special Skier,'' *New York Times*, December 15, 1974, p. 59.

Stern, Richard L., ''Bailing Out Vail,'' *Forbes*, May 27, 1991, p. 16.

Stern, Richard L., ''Downhill Bracer,'' *Forbes*, May 27, 1991, pp. 55–64.

Walter, Claire, ''Vail Parent in Chapter 11,'' *Skiing Trade News*, September 1991, p. 12.

—Thomas Riggs
—update: Kerri DeVault

Veit Companies

14000 Veit Place
Rogers, Minnesota 55374-9583
U.S.A.
Telephone: (763) 428-2242
Fax: (763) 428-8348
Web site: http://www.veitcompanies.com

Private Company
Incorporated: 1928 as Veit & Company, Inc.
Employees: 300
Sales: $50 million (2000 est.)
NAIC: 23594 Wrecking and Demolition Contractors; 23593 Excavation Contractors; 562212 Solid Waste Landfills; 562219 Other Nonhazardous Waste Treatment and Disposal; 562211 Hazardous Waste Treatment and Disposal

Veit Companies is a privately owned corporation specializing in large scale earthwork, demolition, waste disposal, environmental abatement, and sewer reparation projects throughout the upper Midwest. Considered an industry leader in large-scale demolition and removal, Veit has completed contracts for numerous prominent projects, including the dismantling of civic arenas and sports stadiums and the destruction of some 150 Minuteman III missile silos in North Dakota under contract with the Army Corps of Engineers. In addition, subsidiary Veit Disposal Systems boasts one of the largest roll-off container operations in the United States and provides sanitation services and recycling in key metropolitan areas of Minnesota. Veit's other subsidiaries include Veit Container Corporation, Veit Demolition Disposal, Veit Environmental, and Veit Utility.

From Family Farm to Family-Run Company

Few would have thought that in 1928, when Frank Veit began leasing his produce farm trucks to Hennepin County for their road construction projects, that it would mark the beginning of one of the largest excavating and demolition companies in the upper Midwest.

Frank Veit began Veit & Company, Inc. as a sideline to his produce farm. During the Depression of the 1930s the Veit family would supplement their income through lease agreements with Hennepin County, which encompassed Minneapolis and the western half of the Twin Cities metro area, for use of the family's equipment. Like the Veit family farm, Veit's corporate history is very much a family history as well.

In 1928, having purchased one Chevy dump truck specifically for construction work, Frank Veit founded the company. His son Arthur joined the operation in 1931. Arthur made Veit his life's work and began to acquire more equipment throughout the 1930s. These were primarily trucks, but in 1941 Arthur purchased the company's first excavating equipment and used it primarily for small residential and commercial development projects. The projects were local initially but as the company grew so did the area that it served. Construction was at a peak in the following decade and Veit Companies (as it was eventually named), in addition to its new role in excavation, served the region by hauling construction equipment to job sites.

The expansion of the company led to a more permanent shop in Brooklyn Park in 1946, and in keeping with the conservative family ethic, many of the materials used in that construction were recycled from a demolition project with which the company was involved.

Coinciding with the rapid growth of the 1940s Veit made its focus the earthwork contracting needed to build subdivisions and the many municipal streets that now line the northern suburbs of Minneapolis, Minnesota. With the Great Depression of the 1930s well out of the way and the economic expansion that followed World War II, Veit Companies grew steadily. The demand for new housing was spurred by a growing population and an overall sense of economic well-being.

In the mid-1950s Vaughn Veit, Arthur's only son, began to work for the company in the field. From general laborer, he moved up the ranks, experiencing most aspects of the company's operations. It was at this time that the company began to purchase equipment that had not been previously used in the area. The first was a Caterpillar rubber-tired loader that proved more efficient than the track loaders then commonly in use. In

Company Perspectives:

Veit Companies is a third generation progressive company that originated in 1928 and has built its reputation on quality workmanship and services. Our mission is to provide our clientele with the most competitive advantage by delivering quality construction services of unmatched value.

1960 Veit purchased its first low-boy tractor and, in 1969, its first Caterpillar articulated loader, steps that would help position Veit as a company of choice for large excavating and demolition jobs in Minnesota.

In the 1950s and 1960s many of the downtown buildings in the Minneapolis and St. Paul area had begun to fall into disrepair. This was an era when new construction, rather than restoration, appealed to city planners, and Veit was hired to demolish significant numbers of older buildings and warehouses dotting the cityscape.

Seven years after he had begun working in the family company, Vaughn Veit was given a management role, and then promoted to president of the company in 1966. In 1975 Arthur retired from his role as chairman and CEO and Vaughn bought the company. Vaughn's strategy was and continued to be one of expansion.

The growth of the Twin Cities metro area led many businesses to evaluate the placement of their company operation centers and Veit was no exception. In 1958 Veit had moved its shop to the northwest suburb of Osseo, building its first landfill operation there; then, in 1981, the company moved its headquarters further west to Rogers, Minnesota. Strategically located between the Twin Cities metro area and the city of St. Cloud, Veit was thus allowed to play a more significant role in the future of greater Minnesota and surrounding areas.

The 1990s: Rapid Diversification

In 1990 Don Rachel was appointed president of Veit Companies. Vaughn Veit remained as chairman and CEO, leaving many of the day to day operations to Rachel. Under Vaughn Veit and Don Rachel's leadership the company branched out into new areas related to its earthwork and demolition, creating a family of companies under the Veit logo.

In 1990 Vaughn Veit saw an opportunity for expansion and launched Veit Disposal Systems (VDS). VDS began with one truck and 30 container boxes and expanded to more than 45 trucks and 1,500 containers. In 1996 Veit grew its Twin Cities sanitation services with the addition of Disposal Systems, Inc.

In 1998, Veit continued the expansion of VDS with the acquisition of Adams Roll-Off Container in Rochester, Minnesota. The addition of Adams allowed Veit to enlarge its service area into the Rochester/Austin market, where Adams already had a large customer base.

Veit's disposal division grew substantially and was now operating in the St. Paul/Minneapolis, St. Cloud, and Rochester/Austin sales areas. A new start-up operation in the Duluth/Superior area in 1999 began with two trucks and 60 boxes.

The increase in customers led the company to develop two new landfills. To keep up with demand, VDS opened landfills in Big Lake, Minnesota, in 1993, and Austin, Minnesota, in 1998. In addition to its waste disposal, VDS concentrated its efforts in recycling as well. At Veit's Rochester facility, recyclables were sorted and compacted and then temporarily stored at the building. Veit took pride in its recycling record: "70% of construction/demolition debris," was, according to the company, "recycled or reduced with the remainder going to Veit's demolition debris landfill near Austin, Minnesota."

Veit, through its work on a series of demolition projects, gained a regional reputation for demolishing and clearing away antiquated sports stadiums. The Memorial Stadium at the University of Minnesota was the first notable sports facility that Veit tore down and disposed of. Then, in 1995, Veit razed the Metropolitan Stadium in Bloomington, which became home to the internationally known Mall of America. In 1999 the demolition of the St. Paul Civic Center with its River Centre Arena was also tackled by Veit. In the case of the St. Paul Civic Center, Veit was awarded contracts to tear down the Center, and to do the earthwork for the new Excel Energy Center, which would be home to the National Hockey League expansion team the Minnesota Wild.

In 1998 Veit Companies began a $3.9 million earthwork project for the city of Minneapolis. The Minneapolis Water Works needed to expand its water reserves and called upon Veit to excavate a 40-million gallon, 450-foot by 432-foot reservoir on a hilltop site in New Brighton. The hilltop site was at the highest elevation in the Twin Cities metropolitan area, which in case of a water emergency would allow gravity to take the water to the city's customers. The completion of the new water storage facility increased water supplies by 30 percent for well over half a million water works customers.

Larger Projects, Greater Capabilities: Late 1990s–Early 2000s

Although best known for its work with sports arenas, Veit in the late 1990s oversaw a broad spectrum of demolition jobs. On October 6, 1999, Veit began to fulfill a $12.1 million contract for the implosion of 150 Minuteman III missile silos just outside Langdon, North Dakota. This historic three-year project included the permanent destruction of the launch facilities and the standby power facilities connected to the silos. These underground control centers were imploded and the debris was buried and sealed with concrete slabs. Operating under the Strategic Arms Reduction Treaty (START), the Air Force had begun compliance with the treaty in 1994, moving the missiles from the silos near Langdon in 1995.

The completion date of the Minuteman silo demolition was scheduled for the end of 2001, in compliance with the terms of the treaty. As with all of Veit's projects, a good number of salvageable materials were hauled away to be recycled at Veit's demolition disposal site in Austin, Minnesota.

Veit Environmental first appeared under the Veit umbrella of companies in 1999. Due to a growing area of public health

Key Dates:

1927: Frank Veit founds Veit & Company, Inc.
1931: Arthur Veit, Frank's son, joins the company.
1939: Frank Veit dies.
1941: Arthur Veit purchases first excavating equipment.
1955: Vaughn Veit, Arthur's son, begins working at Veit Companies.
1966: Vaughn Veit takes over as president; Arthur remains as chairman and CEO.
1975: Arthur retires; Vaughn Veit purchases the company and becomes chairman and CEO.
1981: Company establishes new headquarters in Rogers, Minnesota.
1990: Company launches Veit Disposal Systems (VDS); Don Rachel is appointed president.
1999: Veit Utility, specializing in sewer construction, storm sewers, and water mains, is formed; Veit Environmental is created to provide asbestos, lead, and mold abatement services.

concern, Veit created its environmental agency to provide abatement services for problem materials such as asbestos, lead, and mold. Many public and private buildings still harbored such hazardous materials and the demand for services appeared to be expanding with what some epidemiologists interpreted as an increased environmental sensitivity in the population. Legislative enactments were leading to mandated removal of hazardous materials in public spaces and Veit predicted a lucrative future in the abatement industry.

Another growing field related to Veit's earthwork business was in the geotechnical arena, specifically in the construction and repair of storm sewers and water mains. Veit acquired Solidification in the fall of 1999. Solidification, a specialty grouting and concrete plumbing company, had been operating in the Minneapolis/St. Paul area for over three decades. Making use of sophisticated developments in the area of robotics, Solidification used video components and robotic technology to repair damaged sewers and pipelines. These aging water systems were leaking and causing contamination to city water supplies and, in the case of sewer systems, contaminated ground water. Veit believed its acquisition of Solidification would capture a large market share of this growing industry.

In 2000 Veit began working on concurrent projects in downtown Minneapolis at the Conservatory, the old Minnegasco building, the Federal Reserve building, and the Old Milwaukee depot. Entering a new century, Veit continued as a well recognized name in the construction and demolition industries. It was well diversified, having adapted to meet new opportunities for growth within its areas of expertise. Veit seemed well placed to be a strong competitor in its region, providing both equipment and services that would meet the challenges of some of the largest jobs the area had to offer. While there were many smaller contractors capable of providing services on a lesser scale, Veit stood out among its peers as a leader in both the range of services it could deliver and the magnitude of the jobs it was able to complete.

Principal Subsidiaries

Veit Disposal Systems; Veit Container Corporation; Veit Environmental; Veit Demolition Disposal; Veit Utility.

Principal Competitors

Carl Bolander & Sons; Zenith Kremer Recycling and Disposal; Watson's Rochester Disposal; Abatement Services; Environmental Control Inc.; Jacobsen Excavating and Trucking Company; Container Service; Quality Disposal; Herbst & Sons Demolition Co. Inc.

Further Reading

Bartemio, Nicholas, "The Wild Arrival; New Arena for The Minnesota Wild Hockey Team," *Demolition,* January/February 1999.

"End of an Era; Minuteman III Missile Silos Go Out with a Bang in North Dakota," *Construction Bulletin Magazine,* November 5,1999.

"Growing from the Ground Up," *Veit Vibes,* Spring 2000.

"Series III, Conquers Downtown Demolition," *Attachment Briefings,* Summer 1998.

"Site Preparation: The Campaign for Rebuild Academy Project Celebrates Actual Start of Construction at Blaine, Minn., Site," *Construction Bulletin Magazine,* January 16, 1998.

Thornley, Stew, "New Reservoir; Construction Actively Kick's into High Gear at the City of Minneapolis' Hilltop Reservoir Site," *Construction Bulletin Magazine,* May 15,1998.

—Susan B. Culligan

Verizon Communications

1095 Avenue of the Americas
New York, New York 10036
U.S.A.
Telephone: (212) 395-2121
Fax: (212) 869-3265
Web site: http://www.verizon.com

Public Company
Incorporated: 2000
Employees: 261,153
Sales: $64.7 billion (2000)
Stock Exchanges: New York
Ticker Symbol: VZ
NAIC: 513310 Wired Telecommunications Carriers; 513322 Cellular and Other Wireless Telecommunications

Verizon Communications was formed in June 2000 with the merger of Bell Atlantic and GTE. Verizon Wireless evolved from the merger of Vodafone Airtouch, Bell Atlantic, and GTE. The company operates in four basic business segments: Domestic Telecom, which consists of their 16 telephone operating subsidiaries and include Internet access; Domestic Wireless; International, including wireless; and Information Services, which provides online and print directories and content.

A Brief History of Bell Atlantic

In January 1982, the U.S. Department of Justice ended a 13-year antitrust suit against the world's largest corporation, the American Telephone and Telegraph Company (AT&T). Pursuant to a consent decree, AT&T maintained its manufacturing and research facilities, as well as its long-distance operations. On January 1, 1984, AT&T divested itself of 22 local operating companies, which were divided among seven regional holding companies (RHCs).

Thus Bell Atlantic was formed from AT&T. The new company served the northern Atlantic states and oversaw seven telephone subsidiaries. AT&T as a competitor proved an immediate and ever-present challenge for Bell Atlantic. In February 1984 the company announced the formation of Bell Atlanticom Systems, a systems and equipment subsidiary to market traditional, cordless, and decorator telephones; wiring components; and home security and healthcare systems. Bell Atlantic Mobile Systems took off early from the starting gate: in March 1984 the company introduced Alex, a cellular telephone service to commence a month later in the Washington, D.C., and Baltimore, Maryland, markets. Bell Atlantic Mobile Systems invested $15.1 million in the fledgling cellular service.

In April 1984 Bell Atlantic went to court over the Federal Communications Commission's (FCC) delay in charging tariffs for customers accessing the local network. Delaying implementation of the access fee not only violated the consent decree, Bell Atlantic charged, but it also caused Bell Atlantic and its sibling RHCs to cover some of AT&T's service costs in the interim. To make matters worse, because Bell Atlantic was the lowest-cost provider of all the RHCs, it was losing the most money. (The FCC system was one of allocation, with access-fee funds collected first, then distributed to RHCs based on the company's cost.) Bell Atlantic planned to succeed in spite of the access fee tangle and subsequently allotted more than half of its construction budget for improvement of the network. Bell Atlantic became the first RHC to employ the use of digital termination systems, a microwave technology for local electronic message distribution. The company experimented with a local area data transport system, and planned to install 50,000 miles of optical fiber within a year.

Carving a Niche: Late 1984

Bell Atlantic made several major acquisitions in its first year of operation, including Telecommunications Specialists, Inc. (TSI), a Houston-based interconnect firm; New Jersey's Tri-Continental Leasing Corporation (Tri-Con), a computer and telecommunications equipment provider; and MAI's Sorbus Inc. division, the second-largest U.S. computer service firm.

With the most aggressive diversification of all the RHCs, Bell Atlantic planned to be a full-service company in the increasingly related merging telecommunications and computer

Company Perspectives:

Driven by our belief in the power of networks, the value of customer connections, and the magic of a unified brand, Verizon is becoming one of the world's leading communications companies. With our unparalleled national scale in landline and wireless networks and a significant global presence, Verizon delivers the benefits of communications—voice, high-speed data, Internet access, and wireless—to millions of customers every day.

sectors. As a struggle for large customers was inevitable, and because the larger customers could potentially set up their own information systems, the company decided to target medium-sized customers. Bell Atlantic offered this customer base everything from information services equipment and data processing to computer maintenance.

Baby Bell Legal Skirmishes in 1985

Of all the unregulated businesses Bell Atlantic was just entering, competition threatened to be even stiffer in the private branch exchange (PBX) market. By early 1985 IBM and Digital Equipment were offering maintenance for their mainframe users, a large portion of Bell Atlantic's recently acquired Sorbus customer base. One yearandahalf after divestiture, Bell Atlantic, along with its sibling RHCs and other companies, realized that convergence of telephone hardware and computer data processing was a huge business. Over the next several years the RHCs repeatedly petitioned the Department of Justice for business waivers to become more competitive in not only the national but international telecommunications market.

By the end of 1985 Bell Atlantic earnings were $1.1 billion on revenues of $9.1 billion. Rated against its competitors, Bell Atlantic was the only RHC close to turning a profit on its unregulated businesses, worth $600 million in revenues. While profits remained strong in Bell Atlantic's local phone service, its Yellow Pages directory publishing division, due to a disagreement, began to compete with Reuben H. Donnelly Corporation, its previous publisher.

In the meantime, the long-distance market moved uncomfortably close to the RHC's local turf. AT&T and other carriers began competing to carry toll calls in local areas. While this would seem to benefit the residential consumer, it did not; outside competitors cutting into RHC profits merely threatened the very profit margin that helped subsidize the cost of local service. Ending its second year in operation, Bell Atlantic's chairman and CEO, Thomas Bolger, described the restrictions on RHCs as "the most significant problem in the telecommunications industry" in *Telephone Engineer & Management's* mid-December 1985 issue and he requested the Justice Department come to a decision before the scheduled January 1, 1987 date. If the purpose of the breakup was to promote maximum competition in the industry, the RHCs reasoned that they, the most likely competitors of industry leaders AT&T and IBM, should not be prohibited from fully competing.

Diversification and More Legal Battles: 1986–88

In July 1987 Bell Atlantic announced a restructuring plan, combining operations of basic telephone service and unregulated businesses. The plan also called for all staff of separate Bell Atlantic telephone companies to report to their respective presidents.

The tables turned rather quickly for Bell Atlantic. In January 1988 the company found itself, along with BellSouth, accused of misconduct in bidding attempts to win government contracts. Senator John Glenn of Ohio led the accusations that the two RHCs had been given confidential price information by a General Services Administration chief. Bell Atlantic disputed the charges entirely, claiming that the senator's report was inaccurate.

A New Era in the Late 1980s

Bell Atlantic implemented another reorganization in 1989 by trimming its management staff less 1,700 employees through voluntary retirement and other incentive plans. During this time, Bell Atlantic invested $2.3 billion in network services to upgrade telephone facilities.

To compete in mobile communications, the company marketed an extremely lightweight cellular telephone; at the same time, Bell Atlantic Paging's customer base grew, with a 16 percent increase. In partnership with GTE, Bell Atlantic Yellow Pages increased its customer base through a new subsidiary, the Chesapeake Directory Sales Company. Bell Atlantic Systems Integration was formed in 1989 to research and explore marketing capabilities in voice and data communications, as well as in artificial intelligence.

Perhaps the biggest opportunity for Bell Atlantic came at year-end 1989, when it stepped up activity in the international arena. Economic changes in the Soviet Union and Eastern Europe opened up entirely new possibilities in global telecommunications. Slowly exploring opportunities abroad since divestiture, Bell Atlantic was, by 1989, assisting in the installation of telephone software systems for the Dutch national telephone company, PTT Telecom, B.V., as well as for the national telephone company in Spain. A Bell Atlantic German subsidiary was awarded a contract to install microcomputers and related equipment at U.S. Army locations in Germany, Belgium, and the United Kingdom. With consultants located in Austria, France, Italy, and Switzerland, Bell Atlantic planned a European headquarters, Bell Atlantic Europe, S.A., to be located in Brussels, Belgium.

In the United States, however, Bell Atlantic kept running into challenges. In April 1990, the company's Chesapeake and Potomac Telephone Company was charged with fraud and barred from seeking federal contracts. Bell Atlantic fought back, citing a double standard in that the U.S. Department of Treasury allowed AT&T to win contracts without necessarily having all the required equipment immediately available, while it had barred the Chesapeake and Potomac Telephone Company from doing so. Undaunted by its squabbles with the government, Bell Atlantic had created the world's largest independent computer maintenance organization by 1990, able to service some 500 brands of computers. With the January 1990 purchase of Control Data Corporation's third-party maintenance business, Bell

Key Dates:

2000: Verizon Communications is formed by the merger of Bell Atlantic and GTE. The company purchases OnePoint Communications Corp., and is renamed Verizon Avenue.

2001: Verizon earns federal approval to offer long distance service in Connecticut and Pennsylvania: Verizon Wireless joins forces with Lucent Technologies. Verizon Avenue offers high-speed Internet access service nationwide.

Atlantic sealed its position as the leader in maintenance of both IBM and Digital Equipment Corporation systems.

In the early and mid-1990s Bell Atlantic's international division thrived. In 1990 alone the corporation made several significant ventures, which included teaming up with the Korean Telecommunications Authority in a variety of research, marketing, and information exchanges; joining U.S. West to modernize Czechoslovak telecommunications; and partnering with Ameritech and two New Zealand companies to acquire the Telecom Corporation of New Zealand.

Distinguishing Itself: 1991–96

In 1992 Bell Atlantic acquired Metro Mobile, the second-largest independent cellular radio telecommunications provider in the United States. This particular transaction gave Bell Atlantic the most extensive cellular phone coverage on the East Coast, while a joint venture with NYNEX and GTE to combine their respective cellular networks into one huge national service made news from coast to coast.

The year of 1995 proved pivotal for Bell Atlantic's future. A long-awaited ruling in the federal courts gave the company a sweet victory; a federal judge finally ruled in favor of the Baby Bells to offer long-distance services. Bell Atlantic wasted little time, becoming the first Baby Bell to jump into the long-distance market by recruiting customers in Florida, Illinois, North and South Carolina, and Texas in early 1996.

Another major development in 1996 was the announcement that Bell Atlantic and NYNEX would merge and become the nation's second-largest telephone company. Though the official announcement came as a surprise to few (rumors had been swirling for months), the deal was at once controversial and ironic—once-struggling Baby Bells were beginning to rival their old parent company. Soon after news of the merger was made public, a new operating unit called Bell Atlantic Internet Solutions debuted, giving customers in Washington, D.C., Philadelphia, and New Jersey a wide range of both business and residential Internet-based products and services.

The New Bell Atlantic: 1997–2000

Bell Atlantic's merger with NYNEX was completed in early 1997. The new company's assets serviced 25 percent of the overall U.S. market in 13 states and accounted for about 140 billion minutes of long-distance traffic; the region not only held one-third of the *Fortune* 500's headquarters, but the U.S. government's nerve center as well. South of the border, Bell Atlantic continued its varied international coups, this time investing another $50 million in its Mexican venture to gain controlling interest in Grupo Iusacell, of which it had previously owned 42 percent.

By early 1998 the new Bell Atlantic had 39.7 million domestic access lines, 5.4 million domestic wireless customers, 6.3 million global wireless customers, and services in 21 countries worldwide. The company was also the world's largest publisher of both print and electronic directories, with over 80 million distributed annually. After a rocky road as Bell Atlantic's local markets were forced open to competitors, the company was taking advantage of new opportunities in the $20 billion long-distance market and the $8 billion video market, and was continuing to expand globally.

A Brief History of GTE

In March 1990, the largest merger in the history of the telecommunications industry united two former U.S. competitors, GTE Corporation and Contel Corporation, under the GTE name. With a market value of $28 billion, the merged company became a telecommunications powerhouse. Designed to take advantage of the two companies' complementary businesses, the merger strengthened GTE's assets in two of its three major areas of operations: telephone service and telecommunications products.

GTE Beginnings

GTE's heritage can be traced to 1918, when three Wisconsin public utility accountants pooled $33,500 to purchase the Richland Center Telephone Company, serving 1,466 telephones in the dairy belt of southern Wisconsin. From the outset, John F. O'Connell, Sigurd L. Odegard, and John A. Pratt worked under the guiding principle that better telephone service could be rendered to small communities if a number of exchanges were operated under one managing body.

The first two decades of operation involved numerous acquisitions and growth. By 1935 the company resurfaced as General Telephone Corporation, operating 12 newly consolidated companies. John Winn, a 26-year veteran of the Bell System, was named president. In 1936 General Telephone created a new subsidiary, General Telephone Directory Company, to publish directories for the parent's entire service area.

In 1940 LaCroix was elected General Telephone's first chairman, and Harold Bozell, a former banker for Associated Telephone Utilities, was named president. Like other businesses, the telephone industry was under government restrictions during World War II, and General Telephone was called upon to increase services at military bases and war-production factories.

Following the war, General Telephone reactivated an acquisitions program that had been dormant for more than a decade and purchased 118,000 telephone lines between 1946 and 1950. In 1950 General Telephone purchased its first telephone equipment manufacturing subsidiary, Leich Electric Company, along with the related Leich Sales Corporation.

In 1959 General Telephone and Sylvania Electric Products merged, and the parent's name was changed to General Telephone & Electronics Corporation (GT&E). The merger gave Sylvania; a leader in such industries as lighting, television and radio, and chemistry and metallurgy; the needed capital to expand. For General Telephone, the merger meant the added benefit of Sylvania's extensive research and development capabilities in the field of electronics. Other acquisitions in the late 1950s included Peninsular Telephone Company in Florida, with 300,000 lines, and Lenkurt Electric Company, Inc., a leading producer of microwave and data transmissions system.

The middle of the century saw more deals and acquisitions for GT&E, as well as some dangerous controversy. In March 1970 GT&E's New York City headquarters was bombed by a radical antiwar group in protest of the company's participation in defense work. In December of that year the GT&E board agreed to move the company's headquarters to Stamford, Connecticut.

After initially proposing to build separate satellite systems, GT&E and its telecommunications rival, American Telephone and Telegraph Company, announced in 1974 joint venture plans for the construction and operation of seven earth-based stations interconnected by two satellites. That same year Sylvania acquired name and distribution rights for Philco television and stereo products. GT&E International expanded its activities during the same period, acquiring television manufacturers in Canada and Israel and a telephone manufacturer in Germany.

In 1976, the company reorganized along five global product lines: communications, lighting, consumer electronics, precision materials, and electrical equipment. GT&E International was phased out during the reorganization, and GTE Products Corporation was formed to encompass both domestic and foreign manufacturing and marketing operations. At the same time, GTE Communications Products was formed to oversee operations of Automatic Electric, Lenkurt, Sylvania, and GTE Information Systems.

Another reorganization followed in 1979. GT&E Products Group was eliminated as an organizational unit and GTE Electrical Products, consisting of lighting, precision materials, and electrical equipment was formed. Vanderslice also revitalized the GT&E Telephone Operating Group in order to develop competitive strategies for anticipated regulatory changes in the telecommunications industry.

GT&E sold its consumer electronics businesses, including the accompanying brand names of Philco and Sylvania in 1980, after watching revenues from television and radio operations decrease precipitously with the success of foreign manufacturers. Following AT&T's 1982 announcement that it would divest 22 telephone operating companies, GT&E made a number of organizational and consolidation moves.

In 1982 the company adopted the name GTE Corporation and formed GTE Mobilnet Incorporated, to handle the company's entrance into the new cellular telephone business. In 1983 GTE sold its electrical equipment, brokerage information services, and cable television equipment businesses.

GTE became the third-largest long-distance telephone company in 1983 through the acquisition of Southern Pacific Communications Company. At the same time, Southern Pacific Satellite Company was acquired, and the two firms were renamed GTE Sprint Communications Corporation and GTE Spacenet Corporation, respectively. Through an agreement with the Department of Justice, GTE conceded to keep Sprint Communications separate from its other telephone companies and limit other GTE telephone subsidiaries in certain markets.

In 1984 GTE formalized its decision to concentrate on three core businesses: telecommunications, lighting, and precision metals. That same year, the company's first satellite was launched, and GTE's cellular telephone service went into operation, and GTE's earnings exceeded $1 billion for the first time.

Beginning in 1986 GTE spun off several operations to form joint ventures. In 1986 GTE Sprint and United Telecommunication's long distance subsidiary, U.S. Telecom, agreed to merge and form US Sprint Communications Company, with each parent retaining a 50 percent interest in the new firm. That same year, GTE transferred its international transmission, overseas central office switching, and business systems operations to a joint venture with Siemens AG of Germany, which took 80 percent ownership of the new firm. The following year, GTE transferred its business systems operations in the United States to a new joint venture, Fujitsu GTE Business Systems, Inc., formed with Fujitsu Limited, which retained 80 percent ownership. In 1987, the company organized its telephone companies around a single national organization headquartered in the Dallas, Texas area.

In 1988, GTE divested its consumer communications products unit as part of a telecommunications strategy to place increasing emphasis on the services sector. The following year GTE sold the majority of its interest in US Sprint to United Telecommunications and its interest in Fujitsu GTE Business Systems to Fujitsu.

In 1989 GTE and AT&T formed the joint venture company AG Communication Systems Corporation, designed to bring advanced digital technology to GTE's switching systems. GTE retained 51 percent control over the joint venture, with AT&T pledging to take complete control of the new firm in 15 years.

With an increasing emphasis on telecommunications, in 1989 GTE launched a program to become the first cellular provider offering nationwide service, and introduced the nation's first rural service area providing cellular service on the Hawaiian island of Kauai. The following year GTE acquired the Providence Journal Company's cellular properties in five southern states for $710 million and became the second-largest cellular-service provider in the United States.

In 1990 GTE reorganized its activities around three business groups: telecommunications products and services, telephone operations, and electrical products. That same year, GTE and Contel Corporation announced merger plans that would strengthen GTE's telecommunications and telephone sectors. Following action or review by more than 20 governmental bodies, in March 1991 the merger of GTE and Contel was approved.

Contel Corporation

GTE Corporation ranked as the world's third-largest publicly owned telecommunications company in 1996. With over

20 million telephone access lines in 40 states, the communications conglomerate was America's leading provider of local telephone services. The $6.6 billion acquisition of Contel Corporation in 1990 nearly doubled GTE's Mobilnet cellular operations, making it the second-largest provider of cellular telephone services in the United States, with over two million customers. GTE's strategy for the mid- to late-1990s focused on technological enhancement of wireline and wireless systems, expansion of data services, global expansion, and diversification into video services.

In 1990 Contel completed the biggest acquisition in its history, a $1.3 billion purchase of McCaw Cellular Communications, Inc.'s controlling interests in 13 cellular markets, added more than six million potential customers and doubled Contel's cellular potential population market (known in the industry as POPs). While important, that move was eclipsed by the merger with GTE announced later that same year. Through that transition, the two former competitors were expected to integrate telephone and mobile-cellular operations and capitalize on business unit similarities in the field of satellitecommunications as well as in communications systems and services targeting government entities.

Over half of Contel's $6.6 billion purchase price, $3.9 billion, was assumed debt. In 1992, in order to reduce that obligation, the company sold its North American Lighting business to a Siemens affiliate for over $1 billion, shaved off local exchange properties in Idaho, Tennessee, Utah, and West Virginia to generate another $1 billion, divested its interest in Sprint in 1992, and sold its GTE Spacenet satellite operations to General Electric in 1994.

The long-heralded telecommunications bill, expected to go into effect in 1996, promised to encourage competition among local phone providers, long-distance services, and cable television companies. Many leading telecoms prepared for the new competitive realities by aligning themselves with entertainment and information providers. GTE, on the other hand, continued to focus on its core operations, seeking to make them as efficient as possible. In 1992 a sweeping reorganization effort was launched that was characterized by *Telephony* magazine as ''easily one of the nation's largest re-engineering processes.''

Among other goals, GTE planned to double revenues and slash costs by $1 billion per year by focusing on five key areas of operation: technological enhancement of wireline and wireless systems, expansion of data services, global expansion, and diversification into video services. GTE hoped to cross-sell its large base of wireline customers on wireless, data and video services by launching Tele-Go, a user-friendly service that combined cordless and cellular phone features. The company bought broadband spectrum cellular licenses in Atlanta, Seattle, Cincinnati and Denver, and formed a joint venture with SBC Communications to enhance its cellular capabilities in Texas. In 1995 the company undertook a 15-state test of videoconferencing services, as well as a video dialtone (VDT) experiment that proposed to offer cable television programming to 900,000 homes by 1997. GTE also formed a video programming and interservices joint venture with Ameritech Corporation, BellSouth Corporation, SBC Communications, and The Walt Disney Company in the fall of 1995. Foreign efforts included affiliations with phone companies in Argentina, Mexico, Germany, Japan, Canada, the Dominican Republic, Venezuela, and China. The early 1990s reorganization included a 37.5 percent workforce reduction, from 177,500 in 1991 to 111,000 by 1994. The fivefold strategy had begun to bear fruit by the mid-1990s. While the communication conglomerate's sales remained rather flat, at about $19.8 billion, from 1992 through 1994, its net income increased by 43.7 percent, from $1.74 billion to a record $2.5 billion during the same period.

By 1996 GTE Corporation ranked as the world's third-largest publicly owned telecommunications company. With over 20 million telephone access lines in 40 states, the communications conglomerate was America's leading provider of local telephone services. The $6.6 billion acquisition of Contel Corporation in 1990 nearly doubled GTE's Mobilnet cellular operations, making it the second-largest provider of cellular telephone services in the United States, with over two million customers.

The Telecommunications Act of 1996

The year 1996 would be as pivotal as 1984 in the telecommunications industry. The Telecommunications Act was designed to meet the needs of communications for the new century. By this time communications had invaded all aspects of life: wireless, television, computer, the Internet, commerce, education, and research. Until then the communications industry had consisted of telephone service. Broadcast, electricity, and computing had their own industries.

The new law eradicated these boundaries. The Telecommunications Act allowed for any company to compete in any industry. Electric companies could provide Internet access if they wanted. Cable bills could be consolidated with phone bills. The heart of the Telecommunications Act was to allow more competition among communications providers. This also meant that different companies could offer different parts of a phone service, and consumers could choose which company they wanted to pay for each part (for ''local'' versus ''long'' distance).

The concept was not new; what was new was the advent of advanced equipment and technology that allowed such industries to meld. The Telecommunications Act not only allowed for companies to interconnect—it required it.

Because of the available technology and the freedom to offer more services, phone companies began massive restructuring and acquisitions. Four of seven Regional Bell operating companies disappeared shortly after the Telecommunications Act was passed; in addition to these, Bell Atlantic joined the buying frenzy by purchasing NYNEX, Vodafone AirTouch, and GTE. This new conglomerate formed Verizon Communications and Verizon Wireless in April 2000.

Verizon Communications Forms

Verizon, whose name is a combination of the Latin word *veritas* and the word ''horizon,'' combined consumer and business services into one massive $58 billion deal. The wireless division got underway first; the Verizon moniker and logos appeared soon after. The re-branding and melding of the two companies was a formidable task; when the merger was first announced in July 1998 Bell Atlantic operated in 13 Mid-Atlantic states and encompassed local telephone service, video, Internet, and wireless divisions. GTE had wireless, Internet, video, local telephone, and long-distance service in 28 (mostly western) states.

By July 2000, the merger had been approved by the FCC and Verizon was on its way to establishing a complete communications business. However, the company faced several problems from the start: an 18-day strike left the company with 280,000 repair requests to handle; plans to sell DSL Internet connection services were delayed; the company was not allowed to offer long distance in 12 of 13 of its home states; and an initial public offering of Verizon Wireless was postponed several times due to lack of investor interest. In addition, profits for the year fell below expectations, and the initial forecast for 2001 was reduced a third.

More trouble came for Verizon at the end of the year when it pulled out of a merger with NorthPoint, a DSL business. The $800 million deal was to commence at the start of 2001 but Verizon discontinued it at the last minute, citing NorthPoint's weakening financial position. Verizon had hoped to expand its out-of-region service and compete with cable companies for Internet service. In December NorthPoint sued Verizon for $1 billion in damages. At the time of this writing the case was scheduled to proceed in a San Francisco court.

Despite these obstacles, the company remained optimistic. The company was especially proud of its 28 million customers, 63 million phone lines, and coverage in 67 of the country's biggest cities. With telecom service regulations lifted, Verizon set out to offer complete packages of services. The wireless side of the company was optimistic as well; Verizon Wireless planned to spend more than $3 billion to upgrade its network. They also struck a deal with Nortel Networks to supply equipment over a two-year period.

Looking Ahead

Verizon's visions for 2001 focused on international expansion. While they already had some links to Toronto, Hong Kong, and Tokyo, the company wanted to expand into major cities in Europe, Asia, and Latin America. They would also offer their Internet services (under the Genuity brand name). New York would be the connecting state while the company waited for approval to add other regions. The company planned a 5-year, $1 billion expansion.

In March 2001, Verizon Wireless joined forces with Lucent Technologies in a $5 billion deal to offer the next generation of high-speed Internet services and wireless technology. With Sprint on their heels, the two companies planned to work on advancements in high-speed mobile Internet services. Verizon Wireless had 27.5 million voice and data customers. The deal would double Verizon's existing voice capacity.

After a little more than a year, Verizon was operating in 40 different countries, had 27.5 million customers, and $65 billion in annual revenue. Further expansion, advanced Internet technologies, and broader service was on the agenda for the immediate future.

Principal Operating Units

Verizon Wireless; Verizon Avenue; Verizon Directories.

Principal Competitors

AT&T; Sprint FON; WorldCom.

Further Reading

"Bad Connection?," *Business Week,* August 28, 2000, p. 56.

Barrett, Paul M., "Legal Beat: Justices Question Congress' Ban on Phone Concerns Offering Cable," *Wall Street Journal,* December 7, 1995, p. B10.

Bernier, Paula, "AT&T, GI Win Round 1 of GTE's Video Rollout," *Telephony,* March 13, 1995, p. 6.

Bradbury, Steven, and Kasler, Kelion, "Verizon Communications: The Merger of Bell Atlantic and GTE," *Coporate Finance,* November 2000, pp. 47–48.

Byrne, Harlan S., "Sleepy No More," *Barron's,* January 16, 1995, p. 15.

Cauley, Leslie, "Bell Atlantic and NYNEX Discuss Merger to Form Second-Biggest Phone Firm," *Wall Street Journal,* December 18, 1995, p. A3.

——, "Bell Atlantic and NYNEX Merger Talks Highlight Roles of Smith and Seidenberg," *Wall Street Journal,* December 19, 1995, p. A3.

——, "Technology & Telecommunications: Baby Bells Square Off Against AT&T on Calling Cards, U.S. West Agreement," *Wall Street Journal,* October 27, 1995, p. B3.

Gold, Howard, "Tom Bolger's OneStopShop," *Forbes,* March 25, 1985.

Gold, Jacqueline S., "GTE: Poor Connection," *Financial World,* October 26, 1993, p. 19.

Greene, Tim, "Those Baby Bells Are Growing up Fast," *Network World Fusion,* November 20, 2000.

Grice, Corey, "Digital Darwinism," *CNET News.com,* posted February 1, 2001, http://www.cnet.com.

——, "Verizon Who?" *CNET News.com,* posted April 3, 2000, http://www.cnet.com.

"GTE's New Twist on Cellular," *Electronics,* April 25, 1994, p. 1.

Heskitt, Ben, "Nortel Nabs $500 Million Deal with Verizon," *CNET News.com,* posted April 12, 2000, http://www.cnet.com.

Jones, Jennifer, "Verizon's Top Lawyer Blasts FCC," *InfoWorld,* August 22, 2000.

King, Carol, "Lucent, Verizon Bet $5 Billion on 3G," *InternetNews,* March 19, 2001.

Klebnikov, Paul, "TechnoSkeptic," *Forbes,* February 26, 1996, p. 42.

Lannon, Larry, "Bell Atlantic's Bolger Demands His Freedom," *Telephony,* July 14, 1986.

Lavin, Douglas, "European Phone Giants Challenge Italy," *Wall Street Journal,* November 16, 1995, p. A14.

"Lucent, Verizon in Major Wireless Deal," *Reuters,* March 19, 2001.

Martin, Michael, "Verizon Expands International Telecom Horizons," *Network World,* February 12, 2001, p. 10.

——, "Verizon Leaves NorthPoint at the Altar," *Network World,* December 4, 2000, p. 98.

Mason, Charles, "RHC Barred Federal Contracts," *Telephony,* April 16, 1990.

——, "Sculpting a New Industry Structure," *Telephony,* April 19, 1993, p. 88.

McCarthy, Thomas E., "The History of GTE: The Evolution of One of America's Great Corporations, Stamford, Conn.," *GTE Corporation,* 1990.

Meeks, Fleming, " 'Fail' Is Not a Four-Letter Word," *Forbes,* April 30, 1990.

Mikolas, Mark, "What Makes Charles Run," *TE&M,* April 1, 1987.

Naik, Gautam, ''Technology & Telecommunications: Bells Venture Likely to Place Cellular Order,'' *Wall Street Journal,* November 10, 1995, p. B2.

Naraine, Ryan, ''Verizon Slams 'Broadband Bill,' '' *Internet.com,* posted May 23, 2001, http://www.internet.com.

Neighly, Patrick, ''Verizon Wireless Announces First Boss,'' *America's Network,* May 15, 2000, p. 8.

Ryan, Vincent, ''Download: Only the Beginning,'' *Telephony,* June 26, 2000.

Stone, Martin, ''NorthPoint's $1B Suit against Verizon Proceeds,'' *The Washington Post,* February 16, 2001.

Tell, Lawrence J., ''Footloose and Fancy Free,'' *Barron's,* November 12, 1984.

''The Foreign Invasion: New Zealand Discovered the Benefits of Letting Global Companies Be a Part of Reform,'' *Wall Street Journal,* October 2, 1995, p. R16.

''Verizon and NorthPoint Merge DSL Businesses,'' *America's Network,* September 2000, pp. 32–33.

''Verizon Faces Lawsuit,'' *Utility Business,* January 2001, p. 12.

''Verizon, Lucent Enter 3-Year, $5B Partnership,'' *Capital Distict Business Review,* March 19, 2001.

Waters, Richard, ''Verizon Plans $1bn Expansion,'' *Financial Times FT.com,* posted February 6, 2001, http://news.ft.com/home/us/.

Weber, Tony, ''Verizon Stumbles out of the Blocks,'' *Telephony,* August 14, 2000, p. 28.

Welti, Patty, ''Dream Job for GTE, IBM,'' *America's Network,* January 1, 1996, p. 18.

Woolley, Scot, ''The New Ma Bell,'' *Forbes,* April 16, 2001, pp. 68–71.

—update: Kerri DeVault

Vinci

1 cours Ferdinand-de-Lesseps
92851 Rueil-Malmaison Cedex,
France
Telephone: (+33) 1-47-16-35-00
Fax: (+33) 1-47-51-91-02
Web site: http://www.groupe-vinci.com

Public Company
Incorporated: 1899 as Giros et Loucheur
Employees: 115,000
Sales: EUR 17.33 billion (2000)
Stock Exchanges: Euronext Paris
Ticker Symbol: DG
NAIC: 541330 Engineering Services; 234120 Bridge and Tunnel Construction; 234110 Highway and Street Construction; 234930 Industrial Nonbuilding Structure Construction; 234990 All Other Heavy Construction

The big got bigger when GTM Group agreed to be absorbed into Vinci in October 2000, making the latter the world's largest construction, public works, and concessions company, with revenues of more than EUR 17 billion. Vinci, formerly known as Société Générale des Entreprises (SGE) and spun off from parent Vivendi (formerly Société Générale des Eaux) in 1999, operates as a holding company for its subsidiaries, structured under four primary business areas. Concessions, generating 8 percent of sales, includes parking subsidiaries Sogeparc and GTM Parc; toll-road operations through Cofiroute; and other operating concessions for various facilities, including the Stade de France in Paris, the Tagus river crossings, and a number of bridges and airports around the world. The Energy and Information division, accounting for 20 percent of total sales, features GTIE, itself a grouping of some 700 local businesses. The company's Roadworks division includes the Eurovia and Jean Lefebvre subsidiaries, which combine to form 30 percent of Vinci's annual sales. Construction represents Vinci's largest single division, with 42 percent of revenues, and combining the activities of subsidiaries Campenon Bernard, Dumez-GTM, Feyssinet, GTM Construction, and Sogea.

Founding a Construction Giant for the 20th Century

Vinci traces its origins to the beginning of the 20th century. In 1899, Alexandre Giros and Louis Loucheur formed Giros et Loucheur, a small construction company dedicated to public works projects. The company quickly became known as Girolou, which served as the company's telephone number. Giros and Loucheur eyed greater growth in the early 1900s, as France prepared to enter a period of modernization. The restructuring of the country's infrastructure, spurred on the growing use of electricity, automobiles, and other new inventions of the late 19th and early 20th century created new demands for large-scale public works projects and for the companies that could build them. In 1908, Giros and Loucheur changed the name of their company to the more imposing Société Générale des Entreprises (SGE) and set out to become one of France's largest construction companies.

SGE participated in a number of France's most important public works projects, ranging from the construction of factories, such as the building of the Comines factory in 1922, to the works for the hydroelectric industry, such as the construction of the Chastang dam on the river Dordogne, completed in 1955. SGE also branched out into other areas related to the construction industry, such as electrical installations and power generation. These diversified activities brought the company under the sway of Compagnie Générale d'Electricité, one of France's largest companies and eagerly seeking to expand its own construction and public works operations since the French government had nationalized the electrical power industry in the late 1940s.

Compagnie Générale d'Electricité began the process of transforming SGE into a holding company for its varied construction, public works, and related projects. In 1970, SGE received control of the engineering, construction, and public works activities of its parent company, while Compagnie Générale d'Electricité took over SGE's electrical business and added it to its CGEE-Alsthom subsidiary. Ten years later, Compagnie Générale d'Electricité once again expanded SGE on a grand scale, merging it with another of its subsidiaries, Sainrapt et Brice. The new company, which took the form of a holding company overseeing the extensive operations of both companies, became known as SGESB.

Company Perspectives:

With a presence in more than one hundred countries, VINCI is the world's leading company in construction and associated services, operating through its 2,500 local business units, for the most part in Europe, where it does more than 90% of its business.

By then, SGE had already added an important new component, that of highway construction and toll road concessions, as France began construction of its Autoroute network. SGE took part in the formation of Cofiroute—later building a majority share—and took over the operations and concessions of the A10 Paris-Poitiers highway and the A11 Paris-Le Mans highway. Cofiroute was to extend its highway operations through the 1970s and 1980s, becoming one of France's top toll road operators.

Constructing a Construction Leader in the 1980s

While many of France's industries were undergoing an ambitious nationalization program under the government led by François Mitterand, the country's major companies were playing a particularly French form of musical chairs, as the companies transferred their shareholding positions among a number of entities, including SGESB. As such, by 1984 SGESB had come under the majority control of a new owner, diversified conglomerate Saint Gobain, which had achieved its majority position through the transfer of the main pieces of its "Enterprise" division. By the mid-1990s, SGE had re-simplified its name and added a number of new company names to its list of holdings, including Saunier Duval, Tunzini, Wanner Isofi, and Sobea.

This last company, a construction and public works specialist, had originally been founded as Etablissements Girault in 1878. In 1918, after coming under control of the Pont-a-Mousson group (itself later merged into Saint Gobain), the company took on the name Eau et Assainissement. The company went on to develop expertise in hydraulics and civil engineering projects as well as major construction projects. After its merger with another water services company, Socoman in 1961, it took on the new name of Socea, before becoming the lead company of the newly merged Saint Gobain-Pont-a-Mousson group's Entreprises et Services in 1970. The addition of rival Balency-Briard, in 1979, gave the company a new name, Sobea.

In 1985, the newly enlarged SGE merged its existing construction and public works subsidiary, SGE-BTP, with its new Sobea assets, creating the new company Sogea, one of the world's top ten construction companies. Three years later, SGE was to find itself under new management—and expanded to a new scale. The acquisition of majority control of SGE by the French industrial and water services group Générale des Eaux (later Vivendi) was accompanied by two immediate steps. The first was the purchase, by Générale des Eaux, of Saint Gobain's insulation and heating and air conditioning subsidiary, G+H Montage, which not only added its expertise, but gave SGE a strong entry into its new subsidiaries German domestic market. The second move by Générale des Eaux was to transfer its own construction and public works subsidiaries, including Viafrance, Campenon Bernard, and Freyssinet, to SGE.

Freyssinet had taken its name from civil engineering genius Eugene Freyssinet. One of 20th-century France's leading bridge and industrial building designers, Freyssinet had also developed a new form of pre-stressed concrete that made possible new types of large scale construction techniques. The Freyssinet company, originally known as the Société Technique pour l'Utilisation de la Précontrainte (Stup), was formed in 1943 in order to exploit an exclusive right to use the prestressed concrete. Stup quickly expanded onto the international scene, and became known worldwide for such construction projects as the Caracas Viaducts in Venezuela, the bridge over Lake Pontchartrain in the United States, a series of bridges over the Marne river, and many others. The loss of the company's prestressed concrete monopoly encouraged Stup—renamed Freyssinet—to diversify its activities in the 1960s and 1970s, in particular into the construction subcontracting category. The company's diversification continued into the 1980s, leading to the construction of nuclear power facilities, the Gladesville bridge in Australia, the Montreal Olympics complex, and more.

When Freyssinet came under control of Générale des Eaux, it found itself in the company of another Générale des Eaux subsidiary, Campenon Bernard (which had joined in the founding of Stup). Campenon had been founded in the 1920s by Edmé Campenon and André Bernard. The company presented diversified interests from its start, with construction projects ranging from railroad and highway construction to industrial facilities. Campenon Bernard was also largely responsible for the building of structures for the famed Maginot Line defense system. The company's diversified interests enabled it to become one of pre-World War II France's largest public works companies. In the postwar period, Campenon Bernard was highly active in helping to reconstruct the damage to France's infrastructure, before turning its attention to international expansion. Apart from construction of many of the world's largest bridges, the company also became a prominent builder of nuclear power facilities, as well as developing expertise in constructing tunnels and viaducts.

World Leader for the 21st Century

Campenon Bernard became a spearhead for SGE's expanded construction and public works holdings. In 1992, SGE transferred its Sogea subsidiary's operations to Campenon Bernard, which then became known as Campenon Bernard SGE. By then, SGE had been undergoing its own international expansion drive in the run-up to the unification of the European Union's economic interests. In 1989, SGE acquired 55 percent of the United Kingdom's Norwest Holst, a position the company was to increase to 100 percent control in 1991, after expanding Norwest Holst in 1990 with the addition of fellow U.K. company Rosser & Russell. SGE also looked across the French border to Germany, where it acquired OBG and VU, the first a construction company, the latter a roadworks company, both based in the former East Germany. SGE continued to acquire companies in that part of Germany, taking over MLTU and OBAG in 1992. SGE's German acquisitions were to continue into the mid-1990s, with the takeovers of Controlmatic and Klee.

Key Dates:

1899: Giros et Loucheur is formed.
1908: Company changes name to Société Générale des Entreprises (SGE).
1966: SGE is acquired by Compagnie Générale de l'Electricité (CGE).
1970: Subsidiary SGE acquires parent CGE's construction and roadworks operations.
1980: SGE, still a subsidiary of CGE, merges with Sainrapt et Brice to form SGESB.
1984: Conglomerate Saint Gobain takes over SGESB.
1988: Industrial and water services giant Générale des Eaux acquires SGESB, which merges with diversified construction subsidiary Campenon Bernard.
1997: SGE (its name shortened once again) transfers waste management, real estate, and water distribution subsidiaries to Générale des Eaux.
2000: Vivendi (Générale des Eaux) exits SGE shareholding; SGE renames itself Vinci; Vinci acquires GTM Group.

Back home in France, SGE was also expanding its holdings, notably with the purchase of highway group Moter, based in the south of France. Through its Campenon Bernard SGE subsidiary, SGE was meanwhile posting a number of construction triumphs, such as the 17-kilometer-long Vasco de Gama bridge in Lisbon, the first nuclear power plant built in China's Daya Bay, and the completion of the Normandy bridge in 1995. That year also marked the award of the contract to conceive and build the Stade de France in Paris, which was completed for the Soccer World Cup in 1998. In 1997, Campenon Bernard SGE took control of the French and European operations of the construction business of CBC, another Générale des Eaux subsidiary, giving SGE a greater balance between its construction and civil engineering operations, while also strengthening its international presence. Nonetheless, nearly 95 percent of SGE's business came from Europe, and some 75 percent of its business was generated among France, Germany, and the United Kingdom.

The transition from SGE to Vinci began in earnest in the late 1990s. In 1997, Générale des Eaux began a reorganization process that was to transform it into Vivendi (and later Vivendi Universal). As part of this process, SGE was refocused on its core construction, public works, concessions, and related services operations, and a number of its assets—including its waste management subsidiaries, water distribution operations, real estate—were transferred to Générale des Eaux. At the same time, Générale des Eaux shifted a number of its holdings under SGE, including its GTIE and Santerne electric works subsidiaries. The transfer increased Générale des Eaux's holding in SGE to more than 85 percent—which Générale des Eaux then reduced to just over 50 percent by the end of that year.

As Générale des Eaux became Vivendi, SGE itself was preparing to be launched as an independent company for the first time since the mid-1960s. In 1998 and 1999, SGE began its own restructuring of its holdings, grouping its subsidiaries under four divisions: Concessions, Equipment (which then became Energy and Information), Road Works, and Construction. SGE accompanied its reorganization with a new commitment to external growth. Beginning in 1998, the company's subsidiaries began to make a series of important acquisitions, including Freyssinet's purchase of Terre Armée Internationale in 1998; three fire protection companies, Calanbau, Mecatiss, and Vraco in 1999; and then Ménard Soltraitement, Teerbau, the German roadworks leader, and lastly, the French parking garage and parking lot leader Sogeparc.

In February 2000, Vivendi—which, after its merger with Universal and acquisition of Seagrams, was in the process of redefining itself as a world-leading communications and entertainment company—substantially reduced its remaining holding in SGE, selling another 32 percent of its shares, reducing its holding to just 17 percent. By the end of that year, Vivendi had all but exited from SGE's capital. The company's newly acquired independent status, as well as its increasing interest in global development, led it to change its name to Vinci in May 2000.

In October 2000, Vinci took on an entirely new scale, when it reached an agreement to acquire another leading French construction and concessions company, GTM Group. That acquisition catapulted Vinci to the top of its industry, making it the world's leading construction group, ahead of fellow French company Bouygues, with more than EUR 17 billion in 2000 revenues.

Principal Divisions

Vinci Concessions; Vinci Roads; Vinci Energy and Information; Vinci Construction.

Principal Competitors

AMEC plc; Autostrade—Concessioni e Costruzioni Autostrade S.p.A; Bechtel Group Inc.; Colas S.A.; Eiffage S.A.; HOCHTIEF A.G.; Louis Berger Group Inc.; Philipp Holzmann Group; Schneider Electric S.A.; WS Atkins Plc.

Further Reading

Le Goff, Delphine, "La Renaissance de la SGE," *Strategies*, June 16, 2000.
"Le nouveau groupe Vinci-GTM va jouer la carte des concessions à l'international," *La Tribune*, July 18, 2000.
"Vinci nouveau numéro un mondial de la construction," *Le Figaro Economie*, July 13, 2000.
"Vinci to Launch Bid for GTM In Euro 1.83 Billion, All-Share Deal," *Wall Street Journal*, July 14, 2000.

—M.L. Cohen

Waters

Waters Corporation

34 Maple Street
Milford, Massachusetts 01757
U.S.A.
Telephone: (508) 478-2000
Fax: (508) 482-3361
Web site: http://www.waters.com

Public Company
Incorporated: 1962 as Waters Associates
Employees: 3,200
Sales: $795.07 million (2000)
Stock Exchanges: New York
Ticker Symbol: WAT
NAIC: 325414 Biological Products (Except Diagnostic Substances) Manufacturing; 334513 Instruments and Related Products Manufacturing for Measuring; 334516 Analytical Laboratory Instrument Manufacturing

Waters Corporation, an analytical instrument manufacturer, holds worldwide leading positions in three complementary analytical technologies: high performance liquid chromatography (HPLC), thermal analysis, and mass spectrometry (MS). The company has the largest HPLC market share in the United States, Europe, and non-Japan Asia, and holds a leading position in Japan. HPLC, the largest product segment of the analytical instrument market, is utilized in a broad range of industries to detect, identify, monitor, and measure the chemical, physical, and biological composition of materials as well as to purify a full range of compounds. Micromass Ltd., a Waters subsidiary, develops, manufactures, and distributes mass spectrometry instruments, which are complementary products that can be integrated and used with other analytical instruments, especially HPLC. Through another subsidiary, TA Instruments Inc., Waters provides thermal analysis and rheology instruments. Waters products are used by pharmaceutical, life science, industrial, university and government scientists in research, development, and quality assurance, as well as in other laboratories. Waters operates 17 facilities in the United States and 71 international facilities. International sales represent nearly 57 percent of company revenue. Since 1995, the company has reported 21 consecutive quarters of double-digit earnings growth and twice effected a two-for-one stock split. Waters is listed in *Standard & Poors Midcap 400 Index.*

1958–73: Into New Lands with New Analytical Tools

James Logan Waters, industry pioneer and entrepreneur, was a descendant of immigrants who settled Salem, Massachusetts, in 1640. Drawn by the desire to till the fertile plains of the Midwest, the Waters clan established themselves in Nebraska in 1865. In 1942 Jim Waters's family returned to Massachusetts when his father became president of Boston and Worcester Bus Lines.

After matriculating in physics at Columbia University, Jim Waters taught math at the university, served as a naval officer, then worked as a project engineer. He designed and built his first analytical instrument in his mother's basement.

In 1958, Waters founded Waters Associates (WA) in order to invent instruments for others. He worked with five employees in the rented basement of the Framingham, Massachusetts, police station, to build one-of-a-kind process-control instruments, including a balloon hydrometer, a nerve gas detector, and a lab refractometer. The company's first major breakthrough occurred in 1961 when John Moore, a chemist at Dow Chemical Company, called for help. Backed by Dow's funds, WA developed a 0.1 milliliter volume flow cell, which enabled Moore to invent an instrument that used gel columns to analyze polymers (naturally occurring or synthetic substances consisting of giant molecules).

In 1963, WA obtained an exclusive license to Dow's patent for Gel Permeation Chromatography (GPC) and introduced WA's first Liquid Chromatography (LC) system, the GPC 100, an instrument larger than a refrigerator and weighing five times as much. Geoffrey Smith, in the May 14, 1979 issue of *Forbes* magazine, explained that LC was "a process for breaking down complex chemical compounds into their individual components for analysis or purification, a process that was first developed by a Russian scientist around 1900."

However, WA was to experience growing pains before profiting from sales of its new product. From 1952 to 1962, gas

Company Perspectives:

Waters Corporation's technologies provide pharmaceutical, life-science, industrial, university, and government scientists with fundamental data on chemical mixtures and materials. Then, by turning these analytical data into useful information, we help scientists understand the complexities of chemistry and of life itself.

chromatography (GC) was the most prevalent analytical technique and WA ''quickly saturated people who had a very immediate obvious need for that product. We were creaming the market—a classic problem for entrepreneurial companies,'' President Zenie later explained to *Forbes'* news writer Smith. Only about 15 percent of one million organic compounds were volatile enough for GC analysis. The remaining 85 percent were non-volatile polymers, carbohydrates, proteins, lipids, amino acids, and other compounds. Waters, however, believed that LC had the potential to make waves in the hitherto untapped 85 percent market.

The economy was softening, but friends lent a helping hand. In 1964 Dow made a $400,000 equity investment in WA. In 1967 WA introduced the ALC 100, a high-pressure LC system (HPLC) which produced ultra-precise separation of the various chemicals in a mixture. This HPLC technique drove ''liquid rapidly through a column packed with fine silica particles,'' McElheny explained in a March 8, 1978 issue of *The New York Times,* adding that HPLC ''separates the chemicals because different compounds travel at different speeds down the column. The chemicals' varying size or electrical properties give each a different affinity for the particles in the column. Under high pressure, chemical separations that used to take hours now are performed in minutes.''

In 1967 Waters appointed Dimitri D'Arbeloff, then president of Millipore Corporation, to WA's board of directors. Millipore was a leader in markets related to membrane technology. In 1970 Millipore made a $600,000 equity investment in WA.

Waters's reputation as an inventor and entrepreneur led Harvard University's Dr. Robert Woodward—recipient of the 1965 Nobel Prize for Chemistry for his work in synthesizing chlorophyll—to call Waters for help. According to *Today's Chemist*, Waters recalled that ''Woodward was trying to synthesize vitamin B12, but the molecule kept rearranging. He wanted us to purify the positional isomers, which were needed to give him the right compound for the final stages of the synthesis.'' Waters brought a LC instrument to Harvard where he worked ten days with Dr. Hamberger, Woodward's chief assistant. They developed a separation, obtained larger columns to scale up the separation, prepped the material, and gave Woodward 200 micrograms of the isolated and purified precursor compound.

Energized by his success, Waters went on an all-out marketing spree for LC sales. Soon, the name Waters Associates became a synonym for liquid chromatography. Unfortunately, though, WA's former emphasis on GPC stalled sales of the new LC technical process; furthermore, the slow economy of the 1970s was wreaking havoc on the company's cash flow. According to the April 1979 issue of *INC.* magazine, Waters was now ''constantly torn between his two most demanding tasks: overseeing production and designing new products.'' He hired Francis H. Zenie as production vice-president. Zenie was an M.I.T. electrical engineer who had left his job as manufacturing manager of Foxboro Company. With Zenie's help, Waters cut the workforce from 175 to 125, stepped up his marketing effort, and reorganized the company. ''We were a $4 million company organized and staffed like a $10 million one,'' Waters explained. Not only had Millipore's 1970 investment in WA upheld the fledgling company's entrepreneurial thrust, but Millipore President Dimitri D'Arbeloff's position on WA's board of directors helped to steer the company back to profitability.

Frank Zenie was promoted to general manager in 1971 and appointed president in 1972. Waters remained chairman of the board and manager of special projects; he opened a WA subsidiary in Japan, did computer and systems programming, and directed a special marketing task force. In 1972 WA introduced its M6000 pump—the industry's first dual-piston reciprocating pump and the firm's first product to win the prestigious *Industrial Research Magazine's* R&D 100 Award.

1973–94: Going Public, Merger, Continuing Recession

During the mid-1970s, company sales grew from $4.7 million in 1972 to $37.7 million in 1977; earnings rose from $346,000 to $4.4 million. Waters gradually ceded more control to his senior managers, thereby removing himself from day-to-day operations. Later, when the *INC.* analyst asked if he regretted losing control of the company, the former chairman, president, and CEO quipped: ''Ambition overcame pride. I wanted that company to succeed more than I wanted to hold on or control of it. The company would have stopped growing it I'd kept my hands in every pie. The entrepreneur makes his biggest contribution simply by picking good people—and then staying out of their way.'' In 1973 WA moved its headquarters from Framingham to Milford, Massachusetts, and made an initial public stock offering on NASDAQ.

Despite a bear market, WA remained a solid competitor even with such industry giants as Hewlett-Packard and DuPont. Zenie attributed the survival to WA's focus on one field, HPCL, and to technical support and software tailored to many specialized customers. For instance, WA designed equipment modules for each of LC's separate stages and in 1977 began to equip the modules with microprocessors. The first of these devices was the Waters Intelligent Sample Processor (WISP), which could ''be loaded with up to 48 separate vials containing different samples and automatically feed each of them into LC analysis,'' wrote McElheny.

The company also developed the first solid-phase extraction (SPE) cartridge and a new integrated high-temperature GPC system, known as the Waters 150C. In 1980 WA's sales outside the United States exceeded those from within the country. That same year, Millipore began to diversify by acquiring WA in a stock transaction valued at $167 million; WA was renamed Waters Chromatography Division (WCD) and merged with Millipore Corporation.

Key Dates:

1958: James L. Waters founds Waters Associates.
1962: Waters Associates is incorporated.
1963: Waters Associates introduces the industry's first liquid chromatography (LC) system.
1964: Dow Chemical invests $400,000 in Waters Associates.
1970: Millipore invests $600,000 in Waters Associates.
1973: Company's stock is issued on NASDAQ and headquarters are moved to Milford, Massachusetts.
1977: Company introduces the first variable-volume autosampler: WISP.
1980: Millipore Corporation acquires Waters Associates, which changes name to Waters Chronology Division (WCD).
1986: WCD launches the first data networking software: ExpertEase.
1995: Having been sold by Millipore, WCD becomes Waters Corporation and is listed on the New York Stock Exchange.
1998: Waters is listed among the top 50 New England publicly held companies.
2000: Waters debuts c.shop.waters.com, an online venue for orders and support.

The new division was highly profitable at the time of the merger, but around 1985 it became clear that the two companies lacked synergy. Millipore's business depended on products made to customer specifications, while WCD focused on developing innovative products to meet special needs—and continued to do so despite the uncertain financial climate of the mid-1980s. WCD launched its first personal computer software—known as ExpertEase—and introduced Millennium 2020 Chromatography Software for networked data management. Other first-of-a-kind products included new chemistries, Microsoft Windows-based software, a system for amino acid analysis, and new detectors.

Meanwhile, sales of chromatography products continued to slow down in both the United States and Europe. By the late 1980s and into the early 1990s, depressed worldwide economic conditions, a stronger U.S. dollar, anemic growth of the analytical instruments market, and concern over healthcare reform in the United States had a negative effect on sales growth. However, although sales from pharmaceutical customers continued to be depressed, sales to generic pharmaceutical companies increased and became a more significant segment of WCD's business, as did requests from the chemical manufacturing industry, which was recovering from cyclical lows. Millipore decided to reorganize its operation, placed many capital spending plans on hold, and in 1993 put WCD up for sale.

1994–99: Independence Regained and a Sharper Focus

In 1994, an investor group led by WCD's management bought WCD for $360 million, forming the independent Waters Corporation. Under the aegis of Douglas A. Berthiaume—Waters chairman, president, and chief executive officer—in 1994 the company began to renew its focus and regain its entrepreneurial spirit with the introduction of Symmetry HPLC columns for the future. Then came the Integrity LC/MS (Liquid Chromatography/Mass Spectrometry) Thermal Beam Electron Ionization (TBEI) system, the industry's first fully integrated benchtop LC/MS system for identifying unknown compounds in chemical mixtures. The Integrity system was user-friendly; for instance, it incorporated ease-of-use features—such as a ''No Tools'' approach to maintenance, automatic tuning and calibration—and helpful ''wizards'' in Millennium software. No longer did a chromatographer have to be an MS expert to obtain MS sample data.

Waters expanded its sales and profitability through the acquisition of closely related businesses and product lines. The company went public on the New York Stock Exchange in November 1995. In May 1996, for $84 million in cash, Waters acquired New Castle, Delaware-based TA Instruments Inc. (TAI), the leading maker of thermal analysis instruments that test how polymer materials (such as plastic and asphalt) react to heat. This acquisition expanded the company's product offerings to include thermal analysis and rheology products.

Then, targeting pharmaceutical scientists in regulated laboratories seeking to conform to the Food and Drug Administration's streamlining of the drug-approval process, Waters introduced its family of Alliance HPLC Systems. These systems had been designed for ''analytical method flexibility, superior sensitivity, and the information-rich detection required for bioanalysis,'' according to the September 1997 issue of *Chemical Business*. Alliance reached the market just as mass spectrometry was gaining importance.

In September 1997 Waters acquired Manchester, England-based Micromass Ltd. for $178 million and established its position as a leader of LC/MS instruments. Micromass was a market leader in the development, manufacture, and distribution of MS instruments, complementary products that could be integrated and used with other analytical instruments, especially HPLC. ''Both Micromass and Waters sold a large portion of their hardware to drug and biotech companies, but Waters' distribution network was five times the size of the Micromass network, enabling it to plug its new MS line into a much larger selling organization,'' according to Loren Fleckenstein in the April 1998 issue of *Investor's Business Daily*.

In early 1998, Waters launched Millennium 32, a 32-bit updated version of Millennium software for Microsoft Windows 95 and NT environments. Indianapolis, Indiana-based drug giant Eli Lilly & Co. contracted with Waters to be its sole provider of LC software. That same year, Waters opened a state-of-the-art consumables manufacturing plant in Wexford, Ireland. Thus, in 1998, Waters celebrated 40 years of innovation in technology and chromatography and entered the ranks of New England's top 50 publicly held corporations. Net sales peaked at $618.81 million in 1998, compared to net sales of $465.47 million in 1997.

In January 1999, Waters was awarded its largest single order to date when Japan's National Police Agency signed an $8-million contract for 50 LC/MS systems for use in forensics.

Waters' Japanese subsidiary, Tokyo-based Nihon Waters K.K., worked with the Agency to educate, train, and support the contingent of scientists assigned to operate the instrumentation.

Demand was strongest for Waters' MS family of products; particularly for time-of-flight mass spectrometry products for protein analysis and high-throughput drug discovery. Waters also established itself as an industry leader in proteomics, with 70 percent of the instrument market. The goal of proteomics was to define the proteins that genes express, their interactions with each other, and their relationships to disease states. Waters partnered with Bio-Rad Laboratories to introduce an integrated proteomics workstation and analysis system, anchored by Waters industry leading Q-TOF mass spectrometer, first introduced in 1996 as a tandem quadruple time-of-flight mass spectrometer. ProteomeWorks was the definitive system for determining the function of proteins *in vivo*, the major analytical challenge of the post-genomic era.

Waters introduced a number of other new products for drug discovery, including the Alliance HT and CapLC Systems, instrument products aimed squarely at scientists seeking new drugs. Alliance HT could process up to 1,500 samples per run; CapLC System could detect trace particles too small to be found by Waters' older products, thereby creating the possibility of new drugs. Waters also launched the XTerra family of chromatographic columns, which used an organic/inorganic hybrid packing that extended HPLC performance limits and set a new standard for HPLC column speed, peak shape, and operating pH range.

In June 1999, Waters entered into an agreement with Mantra Software Corporation to develop and market a NuGenesis Archive software application for Waters Millennium 32 Chromatography. This new technology allowed laboratory professionals to reliably and easily capture, catalog and store raw data and associated methods within moments of their creation, or alteration, thus improving both workflow and compliance practices. In July, Waters introduced the Oasis HLB 96-Well Extraction Plate, for which *R&D Magazine* granted Waters its fifth "R&D 100 Award" for technological innovation. Scientists used Oasis HLB sorbent in a variety of formats for isolating a wide range of organic compounds in aqueous samples—such as drugs and their metabolites in biofluids or agrochemicals in soil, water, and food.

During 1999, Waters Corporation was named to *Standard & Poors Midcap 400 Index* and announced a two-for-one stock split. For fiscal 1999, net sales rose to $704.4 million, an increase of 14 percent over 1998. Net income was $121.88 million, compared to $74.4 million in 1998.

2000 and Beyond: Horizons Unlimited

At the beginning of the new millennium, the major reasons for Waters' continuing growth were its pursuit of improved capabilities and technological breakthroughs. For instance, from 1999 through the first quarter of 2001, the company introduced the Alliance HT and CapLC chromatographs, and the XTerra family of chromatographic columns—as was mentioned above. In July *R&D Magazine*, for the sixth time granted Waters an award for technological innovation. The 2000 R&D 100 Award was for XTerra reversed-phase HPLC columns that extended the limits of HPLC performance.

Furthermore, Waters launched the Q-TOF II and the Quattro Ultima mass spectrometers, the ZQ Mass Detector, and the MassLynx software which handled LC/MS data and controlled the ZQ Detector. The ZQ Mass Detector, created in collaboration by Waters and Micromass, was part of Waters LC/MS system solution, which included hardware, software, columns and chemistries designed to work together for reliability and convenience.

In February Waters launched an inclusive online venue (c.shop.waters.com) from which U.S. scientists could locate, view, price, and place orders for more than 8,000 different Waters HPLC columns, sample preparation and filtration products, and Waters Quality Parts. In September 2000 c.shop became available to scientists and purchasing agents in the United Kingdom, Netherlands, Belgium, Canada, Puerto Rico, and Mexico. In October c.shop became available in Europe and in March 2001 in India, Singapore, Hong Kong, Taiwan, and Australia. C.shop was available 24 hours, seven days a week; it could link scientists to Waters' worldwide-information network to check product availability, order status, delivery timetables, and customer-specific pricing.

Since 1995 Waters had focused aggressively on the HPLC market. However, in February 2000, when *Instrument Business Outlook* interviewed Berthiaume, the president/CEO remarked that "growing genetic sequencing activity" was only the beginning of the biotechnology revolution that would soon follow. Citing forecasts that proteomics "would grow to be a larger size than the DNA sequencing world," Berthiaume explained that "Waters was far and away the leader in the proteomics marketplace . . . and our Q-TOF is far and away the best instrument in that high sensitivity segment of the marketplace. We think our market share for 1999 [was] over 70 percent." He then went on to say that Waters wanted to expand into the whole residual DNA market, but not necessarily through full-scale acquisitions. Waters had already benefitted from joint ventures, such as those with Bio-Rad Laboratories and Mantra Software Corporation.

In June 2000 Waters formed a strategic alliance with Cambridge, Massachusetts-based Variagenics, Inc. to develop and commercialize "SNP" (single nucleotide polymorphisms) analysis capabilities for the emerging field of pharmacogenomics. (Genomics is the study of the collection of genes within an organism.) Micromass also established a partnership with Manchester, England-based Caprion Pharmaceuticals Inc. in order to develop new processes for research in proteomics, which explored the nature and function of all proteins. With the completion of the sequencing of the human genome, the discovery of the proteome stood as the next great challenge in biotechnology. Caprion applied proprietary processes in sub-cellular biology together with large-scale MS to create an unprecedented base of knowledge and understanding of the proteome.

Midway through 2000, Waters Corporation became free of net debt; by the end of the year the company had accumulated $75 million of cash and short-term investments. In August, Waters introduced a new HPLC system designed for laboratories having limited financial and technical resources but needing basic HPLC-derived information. Waters Breeze HPLC System was an all-in-one system consisting of a binary or isocratic pump, automated or manual injector, UV or refractive index detector, and Breeze software.

Fiscal year 2000 combined net sales peaked at $795.07 million, representing a 13 percent increase over 1999. Consistent with the past several years, sales growth was led again by life science customer demand, particularly by requests for MS products. Company sales from operations outside the United States accounted for 57 percent of the company's net sales. Operating income for 2000 was $210.83 million, an increase of 19 percent over the $176.5 million generated in 1999. Net income per basic common share was $1.22 in fiscal 2000, compared to $.99 in 1999. In 2000, Waters announced its second two-for-one stock split.

In May 2001, Waters exhibited its best-selling MS detector: the ZQ. This instrument was a single-quadrupole, atmospheric pressure ionization (API) mass spectrometry detector; it required only about 15 inches of linear bench space and was the centerpiece of Waters two new FractionLynx Systems for autopurification. Optimized for use with Waters 600 Solvent Delivery Module, the ZQ detector also operated with HPLC systems made by other manufacturers. Waters reported that first quarter 2001 sales increased by 17 percent, as measured in local currencies. Earnings per diluted share were $0.28 for the quarter, representing a 27 percent increase over those of first quarter 2000.

From its earliest years, Waters Corporation built on its ability to bring innovative new products to market and established lasting ties in the drug and biotech industries. With the race on to map the human genome in order to link genes to human diseases, scientists could use Waters instruments to generate, organize, and analyze huge amounts of data. As research intensified, the need for Waters' advanced separations, mass spectrometry, and informatic technologies increased; the company leveraged technologies that positioned Waters as an essential element of the future, particularly of life science research.

Principal Subsidiaries

Waters Technologies Corporation; Extrel FTMS, Inc.; Phase Separations, Ltd.; TA Instruments Inc.; Micromass Ltd. (U.K.); Waters Ltd. (U.K.); Nihon Waters K.K. (Japan).

Principal Competitors

Agilent Technologies, Inc.; APBiotech Inc.; Applera Corporation; Beckman Instruments; E.I. du Dupont de Nemours and Company; Hewlett-Packard Co.; Hitachi Ltd.; Millipore Corporation; Perkin-Elmer, Inc.; Shimadzu Corp.; Shiseido Company, Ltd.; Sigma-Aldrich Corporation; Varian Associates.

Further Reading

Biederman, David, "Organized for Effective Exporting," *Traffic World*, August 3, 1998, p. 47.

Elliott, Alan R., "Drug Makers Drive Sales of Analysis Gear," *Investor's Business Daily*, October 20, 1998.

Fleckenstein, Loren, "Souping Up Analysis Skills Via Acquisitions," *Investor's Business Daily*, April 14, 1998.

McElheny, Victor K., "Separating Chemicals in a Mixture," *New York Times*, March 8, 1978.

"One Boss Who Knew How to Let Go," *INC.*, April 1979, p. 47.

"Pioneer Profiles: Jim Waters, Gordon Wilkinson," *Today's Chemist at Work*, October 1990.

Smith, Geoffrey, "Knowing When to Bow Out," *Forbes*, May 14, 1979. pp. 162.

"Waters Alliance HPLC Systems," *Chemical Business*, September 1997, p. 73.

"Waters Rise and How It Plans to Stay on Top," *Instrument Business Outlook*, February 29, 2000.

Young, Alison, "Tech Primes Itself for Role in Genetic Work," *Investor's Business Daily*, August 8, 2000.

—Gloria A. Lemieux

WELLS-GARDNER
ELECTRONICS CORPORATION

Wells-Gardner Electronics Corporation

9500 West 55th Street
McCook, Illinois 60525
U.S.A.
Telephone: (708) 290-2100
Toll Free: (800) 336-6630
Fax: (708) 290-2200
Web site: http://www.wellsgardner.com

Public Company
Incorporated: 1925 as Wells Radio Manufacturing Company
Employees: 205
Sales: $50.6 million (2000)
Stock Exchanges: American
Ticker Symbol: WGA
NAIC: 334119 Other Computer Peripheral Equipment Manufacturing; 334419 Other Electronic Component Manufacturing

Wells-Gardner Electronics Corporation designs, manufacturers, and distributes color video monitors, liquid crystal and plasma displays, coin doors and mechanisms, and related supplies. While the company's primary market is the gaming industry, Wells-Gardner products are also used for coin-operated video games, leisure and fitness machines, automotive analysis systems, and medical displays. Most of the company's inventory is manufactured through a joint venture in Malaysia. A subsidiary, American Gaming & Electronics, provides parts and service to the gaming industry in North America and refurbishes used gaming machines for international markets.

Early History in Radio and Television Manufacturing

Albert S. Wells and Frank Dillbauer formed the Wells Radio Manufacturing Company in Chicago in 1925. The company produced radios for private label brands, including Montgomery Ward and Gambles, as well as under its own name. George Gardner, whom Wells knew from employment with a Milwaukee business which sold batteries and power generators, joined the company in 1926, and the company took the name Wells-Gardner & Company to reflect the new ownership. Wells-Gardner did well through the end of the prosperous 1920s and survived the Great Depression.

In 1936, Wells-Gardner began production of what would become two of its most memorable radios: the Airline model 62-197 and the distinct ''movie dial'' radio for Montgomery Ward. The movie dial sets were distinguished by their chrome chassis and black crackle finishes. The top-of-the-line model contained 13 tubes and electric tuning, generating a 20-watt output over two 12-inch speakers. The Airline model 62-197 radio channeled 30 watts of power through two 12-inch speakers; its chrome and black exterior was enhanced by modern chrome-plated speakers. Moreover, its three shortwave bands proved optimal for tracking overseas news during World War II. A prototype of this Airline model was highlighted at the ''Century of Progress'' World's Fair held in Chicago in 1933–34. Wells-Gardner stamped its radios ''W.G. 24.''

During World War II, Wells-Gardner produced radio-related equipment, including receivers and transmitters. The company often produced these items far below the budget allowed by wartime contracts, receiving many commendations for the effort, including the Army-Navy ''E'' award in 1944. That year revenues peaked at $21.5 million with net income reaching $450,000; the following year, the last year of the war, revenues declined rapidly to $8.9 million.

The company returned to production of civilian goods as a public company traded on the American Stock Exchange in 1945. In addition to manufacturing radios, Wells-Gardner began to manufacture television sets for Montgomery Ward, Gambles, Western Auto (for auto analysis systems), J.C. Penney, White's (in Texas), and W.T. Grant. During this postwar era, Wells-Gardner manufactured an estimated 3 percent of all televisions in the United States. The company also began manufacturing high fidelity stereo systems, electric organs, and various consumer electronics. The company's factory had expanded from 140,600 square feet in the 1940s to 270,000 square feet. Wells-Gardner owned the building, machinery, and equipment.

Production peaked with the popularity of color television in 1966. Sales rose from $25 million in 1960 to $46.3 million in 1966, with net income of $1.9 million. Unfilled orders at the end

Key Dates:

1925: Wells Radio Manufacturing Company is founded.
1936: Company begins manufacturing "movie dial" radios for Montgomery Ward.
1945: Company goes public.
1960: Name is changed to Wells Gardner & Company.
1966: Production of color television sets peaks.
1974: Lower-priced, better quality Japanese products cuts market share; company produces its last radio.
1978: Wells-Gardner begins manufacturing video game monitors.
1980: Production of video monitors exceeds production of televisions.
1991: Company produces its last television.
2000: A joint venture, WEA, based in Malaysia, is established for overseas manufacturing.
2001: Company obtains three-year, $35 million contract for gaming monitors.

of the year valued at $20.1 million. In 1967 Wells-Gardner acquired Rocket Manufacturing, a woodworking company which produced television and radio cabinets at two plants in Illinois and Indiana, adding 200,000 square feet of production capacity.

A Shift in Manufacturing Emphasis in 1970s

In the late 1960s and early 1970s, American electronic manufacturing entered a period of decline as good quality, lower priced Japanese products overtook the market. In 1974 Wells-Gardner lost $1 million on sales of $33 million, as Montgomery Ward switched to overseas production of its private label televisions. The company did generate some business as a final quality control inspector for foreign-built sets, but this did not compensate for the loss of manufacturing business. Wells-Gardner produced the last of several of its products at this time: its last electronic organ in 1969, its last black and white television in 1971; its last radio in 1974; and its last console stereo and portable color television in 1975. Wells-Gardner verged on bankruptcy in 1977, with a $3 million net loss on $8.2 million in sales. A 44 percent decline in revenue from 1976 resulted from market saturation of 19'' color televisions as well as market resistance to 25-inch sets after a problem with a competent part in 1976.

The company survived on short-term loans and two new manufacturing opportunities. The first involved a contract to assemble 19-inch and 25-inch television receivers for Teknika Electronics Corporation, using parts engineered and manufactured overseas by its parent company, The General Corporation of Japan. The second opportunity was presented when Bally Manufacturing asked the company to make video monitors for arcade games. Albert Wells was reportedly so intent on the opportunity that he ordered the doors locked, refusing to let his managers and engineers go home until they had determined how to fill the purchase order.

Using subassembly parts from Teknika, the engineers made a few changes to the basic television receiver to create a video game monitor. As a result, game monitors contributed to total revenues of $14 million in 1978, though the company still suffered a loss of $1 million. This was the fifth consecutive year in which Wells-Gardner had reported a loss, but the change in manufacturing proved positive in the short term. Seeking to develop more products for the video monitor market, the company doubled its engineering staff to 64.

Wells-Gardner was almost alone in the game monitor market when PacMan, Centipede, Space Invaders, and other coin-operated video games became popular. In fact, it was the only company to produce monitors for PacMan. Sales skyrocketed with the introduction of a color game monitor in 1979. In 1980 the game monitors became the major product of the company, exceeding television sales by 230 percent. Revenues and net income peaked at $79.5 million and $7.7 million, respectively, in 1981; video game monitors comprised 89.2 percent of sales, at $68.6 million. Other new products included a monochromatic graphic display game monitor, 13-inch and 19-inch color game monitors, and data display monitors for computers. During this time, the company sold the Rocket woodworking plant in Indiana and began to manufacture cabinets for video games at the plant in Chicago. Also, in 1980 Teknika introduced three new models of portable color televisions in 1980, increasing production 60 percent in 1981.

As quickly as revenues rose, revenues fell due to a decline in demand from coin-operated game manufacturers. Consolidation and bankruptcies in the game manufacturing industry lowered demand, as did market saturation of existing games and lack of new, replacement games due to economic recession. While Wells-Gardner maintained a dominant position in the market, foreign competition necessitated lower price points. Video monitors comprised $22.8 million of total sales of $28.1 million in 1983, with a profit of only $115,000. An increase in color television sales and data display monitors offset the decline in revenues. Sales of Teknika sets rose 73 percent, while computer monitors rose 678 percent, with several new customers such as NBI, Teletype, and Mohawk Data Sciences. With two new products, a 13-inch color raster used in video slot machines and video card games and a 19-inch XY color monitors for three-dimensional effects, Wells-Gardner was ready for a revival in demand for game monitors.

Fluctuating Fortunes in the 1980s

The company's financial situation continued to fluctuate through the rest of the 1980s and into the 1990s. Revenues declined 58 percent in 1984, to $17.8 million, and in 1985 an important contract for video lottery machines was canceled. Demand for video game monitors rebounded in 1986 and 1987, but in 1988 a contract to produce Teknika televisions for Fujitsu expired and was not renewed. In 1989 a major client discontinued products which used Wells-Gardner's video display monitors.

Wells-Gardner experienced a brief and final upswing in its television manufacturing in 1990, when D&H Distributing sought to revive the Majestic brand of televisions, popular in the 1930s to 1950s, for two-step marketing by a new affiliate company, Majestic Industries, Inc. A three-year contract with Wells-Gardner involved a line of 11 television sets, with 20- to 27-inch screens, including five console sets. Sales were estimated at $35 million with first year sales at $10 million, with production utilizing 50 percent of Wells-Gardner's excess factory capacity. However, a slow consumer market resulted in disappointing retail sales. Majestic Industries discontinued the line of television sets in February 1991, and this marked the last time Wells-Gardner produced a television.

Soon thereafter, the company instituted a restructuring plan which involved a voluntary early retirement plan for some of its workforce and a write-off of inventory and equipment, valued at $1 million. Wells-Gardner also discontinued its distribution of switching power supplies and touch screen panel lines. The company had acquired the business with Energetic Systems, Inc. in 1987 and sold it in 1990.

Unexpectedly, sales of video monitors increased in 1990, with demand rising for larger screens to be used on coin-operated video games and other amusement applications. The strength of Wells-Gardner at the time was its ability to partially customize monitors to client needs, thus enabling it to provide supplies for nine of the ten most popular video arcade games. Revenues climbed to $45.1 million. In 1992 a sudden demand for monitors for video lottery terminals resulted in a 150 percent increase in revenues. James Industries acted as representative for Wells-Gardner in international markets, finding new business for coin-operated video games in Europe, Mexico, and Central America, with notable success in Britain and Mexico. The company also expanded into new areas of business, manufacturing monitors for automotive test and diagnostic equipment, such as emissions testing, and leisure equipment, such as Liferower exercise equipment and scoring monitors in bowling alleys.

New Leadership in the 1990s

When Anthony Spier, a board member since 1990, became CEO and chairman at Wells-Gardner in 1994, he confronted a number of persistent problems: erratic revenues; oscillation between profit and loss; competitive pricing from off-shore manufacturers of video monitors; low inventory turnover; rapid obsolescence; and a lack of shareholder benefits.

Revenues were in decline when Spier took the helm at Wells-Gardner, as the video game market slowed. The popularity of ''Mortal Kombat'' arcade game invigorated sales of game monitors in 1992, but market saturation and lack of exciting new games resulted in lower revenues in 1993 and 1994. This decline was offset by orders for video lottery monitors from Loto-Quebec in 1994; Wells-Gardner obtained 100 percent of the Loto-Quebec order from three terminal manufacturing customers. The company benefited from being the only manufacturer of a state-of-the-art touch screen monitor, introduced in 1994.

Reduction of overhead was a major factor in cultivating financial stability, enabling the company to profit, even in periods of slack demand. Since late 1992, the company had reduced overhead by 25 percent, to an annual break-even point of $33 million. Spier sought to reduce that figure to $30 million, and toward that end he streamlined the product line from 75 models to 25 models, minimizing losses related to obsolescence and slow inventory turnover. Moreover, the company implemented use of standardized, interchangeable components in new products, while maintaining development of advanced technology within those standards. Standard VGA and SVGA high-resolution color monitors were upgraded with the intent of serving 75 percent of demand. Overseas production also reduced costs for a competitive price advantage. Standardization reconciled the difficulty of forecasting demand for the unpredictable video game market and the need for 12 to 16 weeks lead time to order components and assemblies. Also, the company attained ISO 9001 quality certification for manufacturing of color monitors, becoming the first in its industry to do so.

Wells-Gardner possessed several strengths from which to renew itself, such as freedom from long-term debt and a reputation in the industry for responsiveness to client needs. Wells-Gardner was the dominant supplier for video lottery monitors and coin-operated video game monitors, supplying five of the six leading manufacturers of lottery terminals and nine of the ten major producers of game manufacturers. The company was also the leading supplier of monitors for automotive diagnostics, as well as the number-two supplier of bowling score monitors to such bowling equipment manufacturers as AMF and Brunswick.

The company used its strengths to expand into new markets. While sales of coin-operated video monitors and video lottery monitors declined 52 percent in 1995, the company entered new markets and grew within other markets. Sales of products for casino gaming and the bartop market more than tripled, and sales to leisure and fitness companies grew 42 percent on the release of a new 27-inch VGA monitor. Video-wall displays and presentation and transportation applications provided new markets for Wells-Gardner products, while a new service group for refurbishing monitors also performed well. Although the automotive diagnostics market was in decline (as that industry consolidated and switched to personal computers), productivity improved with lower overhead on fixed costs, while quality improved with a reject rate below 9 percent, compared to 20 percent in April 1994.

By 1997, Wells-Gardner's transition to stability was secure. The company recorded a modest profit for the second year in a row, with sales at $42.9 million and net income of $775,000. Offshore manufacturing improved profit margins, and the 32 products launched since January 1995 accounted for 94 percent of revenues. In 1997 Wells-Gardner introduced 12 voltage-free products for use worldwide, including the WG2 line of high value monitors. Over the next few years Wells-Gardner received a steady stream of revenues and contracts for new business in medical, gaming, amusement, and video wall markets.

Into the 21st Century

At the end of the 1990s Wells-Gardner pursued a strategy of growth through acquisition and diversification in services related to the gaming industry. The company decide to serve four segments: monitor manufacturing; distribution of parts produced by Wells-Gardner and other companies; installation and service of new gaming equipment; and refurbishment of used equipment for international clients. The June 1998 acquisition of the coin door business of Coin Controls, Inc., for $3.2 million, included rights to worldwide distribution and manufacturing of coin doors and coin mechanical products. In February 1999 the company began to distribute JCM and Mars dollar bill validators with the coin door products often placed side-by-side. A January 2000 agreement with Pacific Electronics Corporation involved distribution of power supplies, line filters and motors, and other items.

New products at this time involved flat panel displays and digitally controlled multiscan products for the gaming industry. The flat panel monitors—in 12-, 14-, 15-, and 18-inch models—used plasma and liquid crystal display technology. The lightweight monitors needed less space and used less power as they provided high contrast ratios. The technology adjusted to touch screen applications for gaming, industrial, bartop, and digital information display markets. Wells-Gardner's marketing emphasized digital technology for ease of installation and long-term usage. While Wells-Gardner held a second place in the gaming market, as the leader in digital technology, estimated at 18 months development time, Spier believed the company could attain the dominant market position in 2002. Production of new monitors continued overseas as Wells-Gardner formed Wells Eastern Asia Displays (WEA). a joint venture with Eastern Asia Technology, Ltd., of Singapore.

In January 2000 Wells-Gardner acquired American Gaming and Electronics, Inc. (AG&E), the largest independent distributor of gaming parts and service in North American, serving 500 casinos. AG&E also remanufactured used gaming equipment and sold new gaming machines in New Jersey and Connecticut. With offices in Las Vegas, New Jersey, and Florida, under Wells-Gardner AG&E opened offices in Palm Springs, California, to take advantage of legalized gambling on Indian reservations, as well as in Chicago and Reno. AG&E obtained a distribution and service agreement to provide computer touch screen display products to Micro Touch Systems, Inc. and Money Controls. A contract with a major manufacture gave AG&E the first right of refusal on used gaming equipment for refurbishment.

International business expanded with the opening of a sales, service, and distribution network in the summer of 2000. The company appointed Eurocoin in the Netherlands and S&M in Germany to sell Wells-Gardner products abroad.

Sales in 2000 reached $50.6 million with net earnings of $851,000. While net earnings were not stable, with a net loss in 1999, Wells-Gardner paid a dividend for the third year in a row. Based on revenues from 1995 to 1999, the company was named one of the 50 fastest growing companies in the Chicago area. Also in 2000, the company sold its factory and headquarters in Chicago, relocating to the nearby suburb of McCook in June 2001. Spier hoped to attract a stronger workforce at a more desirable location on the northwest side of Chicago. Wells-Gardner looked poised for a stable future as, in April 2001, the company obtained a three-year contract for gaming monitors, valued at $35–$45 million, intended for worldwide distribution.

Principal Subsidiaries

American Gaming & Electronics; Wells Eastern Asia Displays (M) SDN BHD (Malaysia; 50%).

Principal Competitors

Alliance Gaming Corporation; Sharp Corporation; ViewSonic Corporation; Display Technologies, Inc.

Further Reading

''American Gaming & Electronics Reaches Agreement to Distribute & Service MicroTouch and Money Controls Products,'' *PR Newswire*, May 16, 2000.

''Canceled Lottery Machines Add to W-Gardner's Woes,'' *Crain's Chicago Business*, April 29, 1985, p. 24.

''Catching the Action in Video,'' *Business Week*, July 20, 1992, p. 81.

''Early Names Back in TV—Majestic, Wells-Gardner,'' *Television Digest*, February 5, 1990, p. 10.

Gross, Lisa, ''The Party's Over,'' *Forbes*, December 20, 1982, p. 95.

''Majestic Brand Dropped,'' *Television Digest*, March 18, 1991, p. 15.

''Video Game Rebound Helps Wells-Gardner,'' *Crain's Chicago Business*, May 4, 1987, p. 54.

''Wells-Gardner Announces Acquisition of American Gaming & Electronics, Inc. of Las Vegas, New Jersey, and Florida,'' *PR Newswire*, January 13, 2000.

''Wells-Gardner Announces Business by E-Commerce,'' *PR Newswire*, August 16, 1999.

''Wells-Gardner Announces Distribution Agreement with Pacific Electronics,'' *PR Newswire*, January 6, 2000.

''Wells-Gardner Announces $2 Million Intranet Order,'' *PR Newswire*, March 9, 1998.

''Wells-Gardner Hits Europe,'' *AB Europe*, May 2000, p. 23.

—Mary Tradii

White Wave

1990 N. 57th Ct.
Boulder, Colorado 80301
Telephone: (303) 443-3470
Fax: (303) 443-3952
Web sites: www.whitewave.com; www.silkissoy.com

Private Company
Incorporated: 1977
Employees: 100+
Sales: $85 million (2001)
NAIC: 311999 All Other Miscellaneous Food Manufacturing

White Wave has made a name for itself recently due to the success of its most popular product, the soy milk known as Silk. The soy foods company produces more than 40 products sold at 24,000 stores, including Silk, Silk yogurt, Silk creamers, tempeh, and tofu. Started by CEO Steve Demos in 1977, the company has grown to include more than 100 employees, seven production facilities, and $85 million in revenue. Silk was rated best-tasting soy milk by the American Taste Institute in June 1999. Today, White Wave commands more than 30 percent of the market share for tofu and has been the fastest-growing soy milk maker at the close of the twentieth century.

White Wave Begins With a Passion for Soy

Born in 1949, Steve Demos is a self-proclaimed hippie. In 1977, he had just returned from spending three years traveling through India and other parts of East Asia. He was in the middle of an eight-week meditation retreat in California, when he decided to start a tofu company for vegetarians and others who didn't want to consume dairy products. Demos believed in the benefits of soy and was determined to make a quality tofu. He knew he wanted to be an entrepreneur; his penchant for healthy food and enthusiasm for soy foods led him to start White Wave in 1977 with $500 in startup capital. There was no IPO.

Demos made his tofu by hand in a bucket and delivered it to health-food stores in a red wagon. In the beginning, his company struggled, and the market for tofu didn't grow substantially from one year to the next. ''When I used to tell banks, 'I make tofu,' they would apologize,'' said Demos.

Until recently, soy was regarded as ''hippie food.'' It suffered from a health-food reputation that mainstream markets wouldn't touch. The general public wasn't yet aware of the health benefits of soy, and the quality of available tofu unfortunately lived up to its stereotype: bland, tasteless, and hard to work with. ''Tofu is such a foreign product,'' said Demos, ''Consumers [in the United States] don't know what to do with it. A block of white stuff floating in a salt water is not American.''

By the mid-1990s however, there was a growing trend toward healthy eating, and Demos was quick to pick up on the slowly increasing popularity of soy milk. In 1996, Demos led the mainstreaming of soy milk with a move hailed as ingenious by food marketers: he began offering soy milk in milk-like cartons, and sold it in the refrigerated dairy case, right next to the cow's milk.

Before Demos' innovation, soy milk was found almost exclusively in health food stores or in health food sections at supermarkets. While there had been many varieties of non-dairy milks available (such as chocolate, vanilla, rice, and oat milks), all were packaged the same in brick-like aseptic cartons and set off from ''regular'' food on a warm shelf next to organic snack foods and fat-free salad dressings. White Wave was banking on the idea that it made sense to package soy milk like cow's milk. White Wave's goal was to bring soy milk to the mainstream table, and by presenting it next to the other milks, it would be easy for consumers to choose the Silk brand instead of their usual milk.

The move was a success from the start. Silk sales doubled every year since it debuted. In 1999, the Silk line accounted for about half of White Wave's sales and was the fastest-growing non-dairy beverage in the industry, according to Spence Information Services.

Soy Makes a Big Entrance to Mainstream Cuisines

Demos' desire to incorporate more soy into the diets of mainstream consumers came at a time when a major shift in food

> **Company Perspectives:**
>
> *"Our interest is in promoting the use of foods we consider the world better off with, rather than without."*
>
> *This quote from our president, Steve Demos, really sums up the philosophy of White Wave. As a company, we seek to creatively integrate healthy, natural, vegetarian foods into the American diet. That's it. We're not out to take over the world. We just want you to enjoy more soy. So relax.*

labeling occurred. Thanks to a change in the rules regarding food benefit claims, the soy market was about to really take off.

In 1998 the Food & Drug Administration made a landmark announcement that would provide the catalyst for increased soy consumption. Makers of soy products were allowed for the first time to promote soy as beneficial for one's diet; they could state on product labels that soy can reduce heart disease. According to the FDA, those foods that contained soy may lower heart disease risk by reducing blood levels of total cholesterol and LDL (''bad'') cholesterol. Their studies concluded that 25 grams of soy a day could beneficially affect cholesterol levels. To be able to claim the soy product as cholesterol-reducing, the food had to contain at least 6.25 grams of soy. That requirement was no problem for White Wave because most its tofu and soy milk comfortably exceeded that number.

This ability to point out health benefits was pivotal to the success of soy products in the United States. The country was paying attention to heart-healthy and diet-improving foods. More Americans were considering themselves vegetarians or at least following a vegetarian diet part of the time. An Archer Daniels Midland survey found meatless entrees on the menus at 97 percent of colleges and universities. Sales of vegetarian foods had increased 37 percent over the past 5 years, according to *American Demographics*. Now that White Wave could promote its Silk as healthy, it could reach an even greater audience and increase awareness of soy consumption in general. And it did.

Their success was enough to make Dean Foods, Inc. take notice. Dean Foods was the maker of Dean Dip and Marie's Dressing, among other well-known foods. In August of 1999 they bought a minority share of White Wave. While White Wave didn't need an investor because of financial trouble, the company wanted some help in packaging and product distribution. The deal gave Dean Foods a 36 percent interest in White Wave with an option to buy the remaining shares in September 2002.

Get Your Soy with Silk

With the distribution and packaging problems solved, White Wave was ready to market its Silk soy milk to the mainstream public. The company had been focusing its advertising on health-food publications up to this point with relative success; with the popularity of soy milk soaring, it was time to aggressively introduce Silk to the rest of the world. Demo's goal was to expand distribution to 10,000 stores by 2000 and to further ''integrate natural soy products into the average American's diet.''

They hired Carmichael Lynch Spong of Chicago to run their new ad campaign. Carmichael Lynch Spong decided to promote Silk as ''fun and approachable,'' in an attempt to shed the health-food image of soy milk. The goal was to make Silk a ''contemporary'' beverage for the public.

With a budget of more than $10 million, the company set to work creating ads that suggested ways to incorporate soy milk into one's diet and targeted women aged 32–55. One ad featured chocolate cereal, intentionally choosing not to use a healthy cereal in order to create more of the ''fun'' image. Their tagline was ''Get your soy with Silk.'' The company placed ads in major magazines such as *People*, *The Oprah Magazine*, and *Real Simple*.

The ads worked; sales were up more than six times from the previous year in the first week the ads were rolled out. Radio ads in select cities soon followed. White Wave soon established itself as the fastest-growing soy foods manufacturer. In 2000 the company generated revenues of $80 million, compared to $8 million only 5 years before.

White Wave Files Complaint Against Dean Foods

A wrinkle in the Dean Foods-White Wave relationship occurred in June 2001 when White Wave filed suit against Dean Foods and Suiza Corp. over the two companies' proposed $15 billion merger. The complaint, filed in the U.S. District Court in Denver, alleged the merger would cause a contract violation and irreparable harm to White Wave. Suiza, based in Dallas, made Sun Soy, a direct competitor to Silk. White Wave wanted to prevent complete control of its operations by Suiza.

According to a prior agreement, Dean Foods was prohibited from transferring their shares or interest to any company without giving White Wave the option to buy them first. White Wave also claims Suiza improperly induced the violation. The proposed merger between Suiza and Dean would transfer the 36 percent of White Wave stock owned by Dean to Suiza.

White Wave sought to stop any process that involved it shares. If Suiza gained them, they could control White Wave's rights, elect members to the board, and have access to proprietary information. Demos said in a June 14 press release, ''Our agreements with Dean Dip were specifically designed to prevent a direct competitor or ours, such as Suiza, from obtaining the control over our business that they will obtain in this merger. While we are not trying to disrupt the Suiza/Dean Foods merger, we will pursue all remedies necessary to make certain that our contractual rights and our shareholders' interests are protected.''

Suiza vowed to fight the action, claiming the contract was interpreted incorrectly. In May 2001, the Justice department had issued a second request for information about the merger.

New Products and Expansion

White Wave's business wasn't limited to just soy milk. By 2000 the company was also offering yogurt, tofu, tempeh, flavored baked tofus, and creamers. Besides the vanilla, plain, and chocolate varieties of Silk, two new flavors were added: mocha and chai. Since consumer response to the holiday offering of Silk Nog the year before was so positive, White Wave felt even

Key Dates:

1977: Steve Demos founds White Wave as a tofu manufacturer.
1996: Silk brand of soy milk is introduced and marketed in the dairy case.
1999: Dean Foods buys minority share of White Wave.
2000: Silk yogurt and new flavors of Silk introduced; sales reach more than $80 million.
2001: White Wave files complaint against Dean Foods and Suiza proposed merger.

more flavors of Silk would be welcome. In fact, their chocolate Silk had beaten Hershey's chocolate milk (dairy milk) in a Good Housekeeping taste test earlier that year, an achievement especially welcome since in July it had to recall its Chocolate Silk because a batch may have contained dairy milk residue, to which some people are allergic.

At the end of the year White Wave introduced yet another product: Silk soy yogurt. White Wave yogurt had been on the market since 1994, but the company thought a whole new product was in order. They reformulated the taste, improved the packaging, and added 11 new flavors. In addition, each six-ounce cup contained half the daily allowance of calcium. The new formula won White Wave a Gold Medal Award of Excellence from the American Tasting Institute.

In the tofu side of business, new flavors of baked tofu were taking off as well; some examples included lemon pepper, tangy barbeque, oriental, Thai, and Mexican. White Wave also offered five varieties of tempeh, and four kinds of regular tofu as well.

Not only did the company expand its product line, but two new production facilities were in the works as well; one in New Jersey and the other in Utah, bringing production to seven different factories in the U.S.

Keeping the public aware and buying soy foods continued to be White Wave's goal into the later half of 2001. Their web site not only included a bevy of information about soy consumption and benefits, but offered ways to cook tofu, incorporate it into a diet, and where to buy it. It even included a meal planner with suggestions and a shopping list function. The company liked to refer to itself as a ''23-year startup,'' and this self-identification continued to be the driving force behind its philosophy for success.

Principal Competitors

Hain Celestial; Suiza Foods; Tofutti Brands

Further Reading

Baar, Aaron, ''Need Milk? Got Soy, Say CL Ads,'' *Adweek*, May 15, 2000, p8.

Chen, I-Chun, ''White Wave Sues Over Suiza-Dean Foods Merger,'' *The Denver Business Journal*, June 15, 2001.

Chura, Hillary, ''Soy Milk Goes Mainstream with Ads,'' *Advertising Age*, May 8, 2000.

Kelly, Barbara J. ''White Wave's Silk Soy Milk Gains Foothold in Dairy Case,'' *Boulder County Business Report*, 2000.

Lavelle, Terri, ''Oh Soy!,'' ebody.com, posted July 31, 2001, http://www.ebody.com.

Robertson, Robin, ''Got Soy, Almond, Rice Milk?'' *Vegetarian Times*, February 2000.

''Personality Profile: Steven Demos,'' *Beverage Industry*, July 2000, p. 78.

Stewart, Kim, ''Dean Foods Buys Minority Share In White Wave,'' *Natural Foods Merchandiser*, October 1999.

Sweeney, Patrick, ''Riding a White Wave of Success in Boulder,'' *The Denver Business Journal*, October 13, 2000.

''White Wave Announces Two New Soymilk Flavors,'' *The SoyFanClub*, accessed October 1, 2001, http://www.thesoyfanclub.com.

''White Wave Files Suit Against Suiza, Dean-Foods,'' *Forbes.com*, posted June 14, 2001, http://www.forbes.com.

''White Wave Sues Dean Foods Over Merger,'' *Chicago Sun-Times*, June 14, 2001.

—Kerri DeVault

WIPRO
Applying Thought

Wipro Limited

Doddakannelli, Sarjapur Road
Bangalore, Karnataka 560 035
India
Telephone: +91-80-8440315
Fax: +91-80-8440256
Web site: http://www.wiproindia.com; http://www.wipro.com

Public Company
Incorporated: 1945
Employees: 12,000
Sales: $662 million (2001 est.)
Stock Exchanges: Ahmedabad Bangalore Cochin Mumbai New York
Ticker Symbol: WIT
NAIC: 334111 Electronic Computer Manufacturing; 334113 Computer Terminal Manufacturing; 511210 Software Publishers; 514191 On-Line Information Services; 334220 Radio and Television Broadcasting and Wireless Communications Equipment Manufacturing; 311223 Other Oilseed Processing; 333298 All Other Industrial Machinery Manufacturing; 335110 Electric Lamp Bulb and Part Manufacturing; 325620 Toilet Preparation Manufacturing;

The third-largest company in India, Bangalore-based Wipro Limited is an ever-growing and ever-diversifying global company that manufactures and sells products and services ranging from cooking oil and soaps to healthcare instruments and information technology (IT) consulting. Although Wipro's chairman and managing director Azim Hasham Premji is committed to the company's diversified business model, its future clearly lies in its continued successes in software and IT services, which make up nearly half of the company's sales and has consistently outpaced the growth of Wipro's other businesses. Wipro's world-class technologies division provides a range of high-tech services such as global IT consulting, e-business integration, and legacy systems maintenance to clients such as Cisco Systems, Thomas Cooke, and NEC. Wipro's IT efforts are so reliable that in 1998 the company became the first in the world to have been awarded the Software Engineering Institute's (SEI) coveted Level 5 Certification for quality. After an impressive debut on the New York Stock Exchange in 2000, Premji, who owns 75 percent of Wipro, became one of the top billionaires in the world.

Humble Beginnings: Mid-1940s to Early1970s

Western India Vegetable Products Ltd. (Wipro Limited) was founded in 1945 by M.H. Premji. The company sold vanaspati solidified sunflower oil to retailers, who sold it in bulk, scooping 50 and 100 grams for customers who brought along their own containers. In 1947 the same year that India gained independence from British rule, 32-year-old Premji laid the foundations of a vegetable oil mill at Amalner in Maharashtra. When Pakistan's prime minister offered him a position as finance minister, Premji turned it down, citing his loyalty to India and his fledgling cooking oil business. Little did either man know that later, in the new millennium, Wipro's value would dwarf Pakistan's gross domestic product. Wipro went public in 1947 for roughly $30,000.

Premji continued his political career along with his business in India. He became the first Indian chairman of Bombay Electricity Board and a board member of the Reserve Bank of India, the State Bank of India and the Life Insurance Corporation of India. But Premji's untimely demise occurred in 1966, due to a heart attack. Soon after, his 21-year-old son Azim left his unfinished studies in engineering at Stanford University in the United States and returned home to India to take over the business. What used to be a sleepy business run by various members of the family now became a highly professional one, leaving Azim Premji as the only one in the family working at Wipro—a characteristic that still would hold true decades later.

Premji planned to professionalize, diversify and expand his father's business, which was already valued at about $3 million. He immediately recruited top-notch managers from the renowned Indian Institute of Management (IIM), where top graduates are also courted by blue-chip firms in the West. ''We were

Company Perspectives:

Wipro is an integrated corporation that offers a diverse range of products, solutions and services in systems, software, consumer care, healthcare, lighting and infrastructure technology. We are driven by our passion for quality and our commitment to customers. This drive has catapulted us among the ten most admired companies in India. Through constant innovation and a people-first attitude, we strive to assume leadership positions in all our businesses in the new millennium.

the pioneers in packaging for the mass market,'' explains Premji. ''We went from bulk packs of vanaspati to [single-use] consumer packs.'' The packaging innovation took off, and the marketing and distribution network expanded into rural areas. At this point, the company had no plans to go global. By 1971 business nearly doubled from when Azim Premji took over.

Going High-Tech: Mid-1970s to Late1980s

The company's first departure from its main cooking oil business came about in 1975. Drawing Azim Premji's his engineering background, and at the suggestion of one of the new IIM recruits, M. Seethapathy Rao, Premji launched Wipro Fluid Power, an operation that manufactured hydraulic and pneumatic cylinders. And under the direction of P.S. Pai, Wipro's consumer care division expanded beyond oil in 1979, establishing operations in soaps, toiletries, and baby care products. Along with major expansions in distribution, Wipro's consumer care division gained so much financial strength for the company that the company was able to further diversify into IT and healthcare instruments.

Wipro would diversify into computers almost as soon as India's computer industry began to develop in the mid-1970s. At the time, the Indian government was the largest purchaser of computers sold in India, and was standardized on the Unix-based platform, which helped Indian companies build a solid reputation in Unix-based software development. The growing IT industry in India attracted multinationals such as IBM, Motorola, and Texas Instruments, who took advantage of India's wealth of low-cost engineering labor. But in 1977 the Indian government decided to throw out U.S. computer giant IBM over a dispute about investment and intellectual property, creating what Premji saw as a golden business opportunity. He quickly set up an electronics unit. But instead of luring ex-IBM employees into his business, Premji hired managers from a truck maker and a refrigeration company.

In 1980 Wipro launched information technology services for the domestic market, setting up in Bangalore a crack-team of R&D and marketing managers, headed by Ashok Narasimhan. Their professionalism, innovation and insistence on quality were to make Wipro the No. 1 listed information technology company in the country within the next 15 years. By 1984 the company diversified into software, which it would discontinue by 1990, but it led to Wipro's foray into its growth business, software services. Wipro began manufacturing PCs and workstations in 1985, quickly building brand recognition and securing the enviable position of commanding a premium price over the competitions' cheap clones. Wipro assembled and redistributed hardware for U.S. companies like Nortel, Sun Microsystems, and Cisco Systems.

India's $80-million market in medical equipment attracted General Electric Co. (GE), which in 1989 chose Wipro for a joint venture to develop and distribute ultrasound devices and other medical instruments, especially throughout India and South Asia. In addition to creating a new business segment for Wipro, the joint venture instantly secured Wipro's reputation as a software integrator and led to scores of R&D contracts with major companies, including Cisco Systems, Hitachi, and Alcatel. Wipro GE came to be the largest exporter of medical systems.

Rapid Growth and Expansion in the 1990s

India's software industry continued to take off throughout the nineties, at a compounded annual rate of nearly 60 percent for most of the decade. India quickly became the third-largest supplier of IT labor, and its communications infrastructure rapidly improved. Part of this growth was driven by a growing number of U.S. corporations that began to tap into the cheap IT labor market in India, often for 40 percent to 60 percent less than the cost of U.S. labor. As a result, Wipro typically contracted out teams of engineers to work at U.S.-based companies. As successful as this model was, it could not be counted on to last, due to mounting competition and Wipro's growing need to offer more sophisticated technology solutions.

Wipro began to shift its IT business away from costly on-site development projects in the United States, to more profitable offshore development closer to home. To help keep its competitive edge, the company replicated the development labs of some of its major clients, including AT&T, IBM, and Intel Corporation. And while Wipro continued to offer a range of programming services, including hardware design, networking, and communications and operating system support—it continued to diversify into other lines of business. In 1992 the company established a new lighting business, offering a range of lighting solutions for domestic, commercial, industrial, and pharmaceutical lab environments. Wipro discarded its PC brand in 1995 when it formed a joint venture with Acer, a Taiwan-based computer and peripherals manufacturer and distributor.

By 1998, Bangalore became one of the many IT centers in India, with about 250 high-tech firms, plus about 100 just outside the city's limits. And Wipro became the center of this Indian ''Silicon Valley,'' as India's second-biggest software exporter. Both software and hardware businesses generated 57 percent of the company's sales, and 75 percent of its profits, with software employees numbering over 5,600 of the company's 9,000 total. Still, Premji saw continued value in keeping Wipro's non-IT businesses, which he was always quick to point out were the best in their niche markets. The company invested about 25 percent of its advertising budget into branding for its consumer care and lighting division. The Santoor brand, for example, grew by 20 percent in 1997. Wipro's power cylinder business grew at a similar rate as its hardware business, and kept the company well poised to benefit from any boom in future infrastructure expenditures. In 1998 Wipro started exporting

Key Dates:

1945: Wipro Limited is incorporated.
1947: An oil mill and hydrogenated cooking medium plant is built; Wipro goes public in India, for roughly $30,000.
1966: Founder M.H. Hasham Premji dies.
1968: Founder's son, Azim Hasham Premji assumes leadership of company.
1975: Wipro begins to manufacture hydraulic and pneumatic cylinders.
1980: Wipro employs information technology services.
1985: Wipro begins to manufacture toilet soaps, PCs, and dot-matrix printers.
1989: General Electric and Wipro create a joint venture for medical systems.
1990: Product software business is discontinued; software services begin.
1992: Lighting business is established.
1999: Wipro's software business receives prestigious SEI Level 5 Certification; company restructures to address the Internet market.
2000: Wipro debuts on the New York Stock Exchange.

hydraulic cylinders throughout Southeast Asia. Also, a lot of synergies existed between the medical systems and IT businesses within Wipro. Wipro GE emerged as the largest healthcare systems company in South Asia in 1998, and in that same year, became the top exporter of such systems in India.

Wipro proved to be a nimble and formidable competitor throughout the nineties. From 1991 to 1997, for example, Wipro went through six corporate restructurings, keeping the company ready to adapt to the constantly changing technological landscape. By September of 2000 Wipro's technologies division completed what may have been the most significant restructuring effort, re-engineering the division's operations toward four major market sectors: content housing platforms (computers and Web servers), content transportation (networking media), content access devices (mobile phones, PCs, etc.), and service providers. And even its Six Sigma quality initiative, which aimed to reduce the defect rate to virtually nothing, already led to an eightfold gain over the investments in its first 20 months, which began in 1997. Wipro projected that it would apply the Six Sigma concept, allowing a maximum of 3.4 mistakes for every one million opportunities for error, to every key process by 2002.

Going Global in the 21st Century

Wipro seemed to have survived the effects of the U.S. economic slowdown of 2000, with massive layoffs and profit warnings, and raced ahead in 2001 amid its own soaring growth rates and a huge expansion in its operating margins. Given that 60 percent of India's IT-related services and software exports were tied to the U.S., Wipro's unscathed emergence was remarkable. By the end of March 2001, the company's net income hit a record $138 million (up 106 percent from the previous year), and operating margins grew from 18 to 24 percent that same year. While revenues from U.S. clients declined to 64 percent from 70 percent, revenues from Europe climbed from 24 percent to 29 percent, and revenues from Japan did the same from 5 to 6 percent. With a fleet of 150 Japanese-speaking engineers, and some 800 engineers dedicated to Japanese customers including Fujitsu, NEC, Daiwa, Sony, Toshiba, and NTT DoCoMo, Wipro's Japanese business promised to grow along with other continued investments in a diversified customer base. Wipro decided to set up an Asia-Pacific regional base in Singapore in 2001. By this time, Wipro had a total of 209 active clients, the top five of whom were: fiber-optic network equipment major Nortel Networks; British gas transport firm Transco; U.S. conglomerate GE; telecom equipment manufacturer Lucent Technologies; and French telecom equipment maker Alcatel.

Along with diversifying its customer base, Wipro set out to expand and deepen its IT service offerings and become a global tech powerhouse that directly competes with giants such as IBM Global Consulting, Accenture, and Electronic Data Service. Even though Wipro came out of 2000 quite well, India's IT industry quickly became flanked with growing competition from countries such as Ireland, China, Vietnam, and the Philippines. And even though 60 percent of Indian software exports were absorbed by businesses in the U.S. in 1999, that accounted for only 2 percent of the global total.

Wipro decided to go beyond the unglamorous back-office code-writing on contract, and pursue even more high-profile, high-paying projects that involved e-business development, new software products, and end-to-end business/system consulting. Instead of doing small portions of large IT software solutions, Wipro would set out to develop comprehensive, end-to-end solutions, which included both software services and hardware, and often involved outsourcing the simpler code work to other countries. For example, in August of 2000, Wipro launched a ''Portal-in-a-Box,'' which was a fixed-price, end-to-end solution to help businesses create a sales presence on the Web. Wipro's new ''upstream'' strategy would not only help stave off the growing competition, but also enable Wipro to continue its growth, and keep its staff immune from the temptation to go West and start up their own software companies. Wipro also continued to aggressively refocus on offshore projects and expand its efforts in the domestic market.

Wipro has come a long way from its simple sunflower oil business. At the start of the new millennium, Wipro continued to prove itself a pioneer in three main businesses—consumer care and lighting, healthcare technology services, and information technology—altogether encompassing a broad range of high-quality products and services. With its solid reputation in these businesses, deep ties with major world companies, and newly opened offices including the United Kingdom, Germany, Paris, Singapore, the Middle East, and the United States, Wipro promised to quickly become a true multinational corporation.

Principal Subsidiaries

Wipro Inc. (United States); Enthink Inc. (United States); Wipro Japan KK (Japan); Wipro Welfare Limited; Wipro Prosper Limited; Wipro Trademarks Holding Limited.

Principal Divisions

Information Technology; Consumer Care & Lighting; Healthcare Technology Services.

Principal Competitors

Accenture; Booz-Allen; Cambridge Technology; Cognizant Technology Solutions; Compaq; Computer Sciences; Deloitte Touche Tohmatsu; EDS; Ernst & Young; GE; Getronics; Hewlett-Packard; Hindustan Lever; IBM; Infosys Technologies; Johnson & Johnson; McKinsey & Company; KPMG; Perot Systems; Philips Electronics; PricewaterhouseCoopers; Procter & Gamble; Sapient; Satyam; Siemens; Silverline Technologies; Tata Enterprises; Unilever; Zenith.

Further Reading

Beltran, Eamon, ''Wipro Launches Operations in Germany,'' *Business Wire,* posted May 17, 2001, http://www.businesswire.com.

Chakravarty, Subrata N., ''What's Cooking at Wipro?,'' *Forbes,* December 14, 1998, pp. 74–65.

Chanda, Nayan, ''How Precarious Is India's Perch?,'' *Far Eastern Economic Review,* April 12, 2001.

Dhume, Sadanand, ''Who's That Man?,'' *Far Eastern Economic Review,* August 19, 1999, pp. 48–49.

Einhorn, Bruce, Manjeet Kripalani, and Pete Engardio, ''India 3.0,'' *Business Week,* February 26, 2001, pp. 44–46.

Engardio, Pete, ''An Ultrasound Foothold in Asia,'' *Business Week,* November 8, 1993, p. 68.

Erwin, Jane, and P. C. Douglas, ''It's Not Difficult to Change Company Culture,'' *Supervision,* November 2000.

Fai, Tang Weng, ''A Look at Three Indian Examples,'' *The Business Times (Singapore),* March 19, 2001, p. SS2.

Field, Tom, ''For a Few Rupees More,'' *CIO,* December 1, 2000, pp. 168–78.

''From Fringes to Dominance,'' *DataQuest (India),* July 15, 1997.

Glatzer, Hal, ''Software Intrigues India,'' *Software Magazine,* January, 1989.

Guha, Krishna, ''Software Successes Gives Wipro Hard-Core Problem: Diversified Indian Group Must Decide What to Do with Its Other Activities,'' *Financial Times (London),* January 7, 1999, p.32.

James, David, ''India Starts Up,'' *Upside,* April 2000.

Lincoln, Kaye, ''Coming Crisis,'' *Far Eastern Economic Review,* July 10, 1997, pp. 66–68.

Mazumdar, Sudip, ''Bangalore, India,'' *Newsweek,* November 9, 1998, p. 52.

Merchant, Khozem, ''Defining the Indian Software Brand in a Competitive World: Global Strategies,'' *The Financial Times (London),* February 21, 2001, p. 14.

——, ''Survey: IT Indian Sub-Continent,'' *Financial Times (London),* July 4, 2000, p. 3.

Paradkar, Bageshree, ''Second-Richest Man, After You-Know-Who,'' *The Toronto Star,* August 6, 2000.

Popham, Peter, ''He Drives an Escort and Hates Luxury. Meet Mr. Premji, The World's Third Richest Man,'' *The Independent (London),* February 22, 2000, p. 3.

''Profit Soars at Indian Software Tiger Wipro,'' *Reuters,* January 19, 2001.

''Richest Man in India Is Mr. Integrity,'' *The Straits Times,* March 5, 2000, p. 16.

''Stop the Underselling: Azim Premji,'' *The Hindu Online,* posted December 28, 2000, http://www.hinduonnet.com.

Taylor, Paul, ''Survey: South Asian Software,'' *Financial Times (London),* July 1, 1998, p. 1.

——, ''Survey of India,'' *Financial Times (London),* November 17, 1995, p. 7.

Vasuki, S.N., ''Not Easy for India's Big Guns,'' *Business Times (Singapore),* September 27, 1993, p. 2.

Vijayan, Jaikumar, ''Look out, Here Comes India,'' *Computerworld,* February 26, 1996, p. 100.

''Wipro Bucks Trend, Races Ahead,'' *Computers Today,* May 31, 2001, p. 9.

''Wipro Infotech's E-Com Services,'' *The Hindu Online,* posted August 30, 2000, http://www.hinduonnet.com.

''Wipro Launches B2B Portal for IT Industry,'' *The Hindu Online,* posted September 20, 2000, http://www.hinduonnet.com.

''Wipro Rides High on Software Boom,'' *The Hindu,* June 1, 1998.

''Wipro to Focus on Offsite Projects,'' *The Hindu Online,* posted April 25, 2001, http://www.hinduonnet.com.

—Heidi Wrightsman

WMC, Limited

Level 16, IBM Centre
60 City Road
Southbank, Victoria 3006
Australia
Telephone: +61 03 9685 6000
Fax: +61 03 9686 3569
Web site: http://www.wmc.com.au

Public Company
Incorporated: 1933
Employees: 3,483 (2000)
Sales: A$3,403.8 million (2000)
Stock Exchanges: Australia, New York
Ticker Symbol: WMC
NAIC: 212221 Gold Mining Ore; 212399 All Other Nonmetallic Mineral Mining; 211111 Crude Petroleum and Natural Gas Extraction; 212231 Lead Ore and Zinc Ore Mining; 325312 Phosphatic Fertilizer Manufacturing; 551112 Offices of Other Holding Companies

WMC, Limited is the Australian holding company for a diversified group of mining enterprises operating throughout the world. It is the world's third-ranked nickel producer and one of Australia's leading gold producers. It owns 40 percent of Alcoa World Alumina and Chemicals, the world's largest producer of bauxite, alumina, and alumina-based chemicals. It produces substantial amounts of copper, uranium, and talc. The company's headquarters and the majority of its operations are in Australia, but its subsidiaries undertake mining activities in at least 20 nations on every continent except Antarctica.

1930–45: Founded on Gold

As a very young man, William Sydney Robinson was a partner with his older brother in a stock brokerage firm that helped finance the Australian gold rush of the late 19th and early 20th century. The Robinsons moved to London, established a business there, and continued their involvement in financing the global mining industry. Even when most mines closed as countries mobilized to fight World War I, the younger Robinson maintained a particular interest in the Australian mining business.

After the War, Robinson returned to Australia frequently. On those trips, he observed the continued devastation of the industry that resulted from maintaining the gold standard at prewar prices in the face of substantial postwar inflation. He also observed Australia's inability to export its agricultural or mineral products to other nations because the Australian dollar was overvalued in terms of other currencies. These observations led him to believe that Australia would soon devalue its dollar to make its products less expensive on the world market. Devaluation would also raise the price of gold in Australian dollars. Robinson began to set in motion arrangements that would allow him to exploit this opportunity when it came.

In 1930, Robinson incorporated Gold Mines of Australia (GMA) in London to raise money to buy options on mining properties throughout Australia. The shareholders of this enterprise included New Consolidated Gold Fields, Ltd., of South Africa, with a 60 percent share of the company; Zinc Corporation, Ltd, of which Robinson was Managing Director; Imperial Smelting Corporation, Ltd., and some private parties. In 1931, the Australian dollar was devalued from A$1 per British pound to A$1.25 per pound. This increased the price of gold by 25 percent and again made mining profitable for at least a few years.

GMA began to accumulate and prospect promising properties, and, in a few cases, produce and sell gold. By 1933, the company had purchased several existing mines in Eastern Australia, and it was about to acquire the rights to explore and prospect in areas near existing mines in Western Australia. The greater risk attending the Western Australian activities made it advisable to form a new company to manage them. The Western Mining Corporation, Limited (WMC) was incorporated in 1933 for that purpose.

A further reorganization of the companies occurred in 1935. The original organizers of GMA had been the primary sources of finance until then, but by 1935 sufficient property had been accumulated that required new sources of finance to support large-scale exploration and development. The Gold Exploration and Finance Company of Australia, Limited (GEFCA) was

Company Perspectives:

WMC is an Australian-based minerals company determined to be "best"—symbolising our commitment to strive for optimal bottom-line, environment, safety and team performance. Our aim is to create shareholder value by finding, acquiring, developing, and operating high-quality mineral resource projects around the world. We will maintain a diversified portfolio of commodities and exercise prudent financial management.

therefore incorporated in London. This new company, with substantial financial participation of additional South African mining interests, was to serve as the new financing vehicle. It bought out both GMA and WMC and made them Australian operating subsidiaries.

The 1930s and prewar 1940s saw Robinson's companies complete substantial exploration, acquisition, and development of mining properties throughout Australia. Some of these mines were brought into production. Nevertheless, the companies struggled to survive because financing was difficult to secure during the Great Depression. In 1935, gold prices again fell; making it even more of a problem to secure needed financing. By the time most operations were mothballed for the duration of Australia's mobilization for World War II, the companies operated ten producing mines, but those mines had not yet generated significant profits.

1945–49: The Struggle to Survive

The years immediately after the the Second World War were challenging for Australian gold miners. The Bretton Woods agreements of 1944 had fixed the price of gold in terms of the US dollar and tied the exchange rates of other currencies to the dollar. The price of gold would not change, therefore, unless a nation devalued its currency in relation to the dollar. But when a nation did that, anything it imported would immediately become more expensive. This was a particular problem for the Australian mining industry because it had to import most of its heavy operating equipment.

Two additional difficulties affected the Australian mining industry: The nation experienced significant inflation, which increased the cost of labor and of what equipment could be procured domestically. And much of Europe had been destroyed by the War, so international commerce, on which the extractive resource industries of the nation depended, did not immediately recover.

Facing these difficulties, GEFCA and its subsidiaries, GMA and WMC, reopened the mines that were closed during the War, opened a few new ones, and continued their exploration activities. The companies, however, found it difficult to raise additional capital to support these efforts. The South African mines that were GEFCA's primary investors found better uses for their money in South Africa, and its other London-based sources of capital were likewise uninterested in Australian gold. Consequently, the London shareholders of GEFCA were receptive to a takeover offer from WMC. In 1949, WMC purchased GEFCA, including its 62 percent interest in GMA. From that time, WMC was a company headquartered in Australia and controlled by Australians.

1949–79: Diversification

WMC's establishment as an Australian company brought with it a slight improvement in its ability to obtain financing. Australian law did not tax dividends paid by gold mining companies. Wealthy Australians, who would not otherwise do so often invested in such companies as a means of reducing their tax obligations. This additional source of investment was not, however, sufficient to meet WMC's needs. Indeed, it had a major disadvantage: it required the company to pay out a substantial portion of its cash profits in dividends each year, leaving relatively little cash surplus to be reinvested in exploration and development activities.

By the early 1950s, WMC's board concluded that the company would probably not survive if it continued to mine only gold. In 1953, Sir Lindesay Clark, the company's third chairman, announced a significant revision of the company's business strategy. WMC would continue to produce gold, but it would expand its exploration efforts to seek and exploit base metal deposits. Such diversification would enable the company to produce and sell products whose prices were set by the market rather than established by international economic agreements and institutions. Base metals might also experience price cycles different from each other and from gold, thus smoothing the boom and bust gold cycles.

During the next six years, the company explored and prospected uranium, copper, iron ore, talc, bauxite, and nickel prospects. The uranium and copper properties could not be developed economically. Policies of the government of Western Australia and of the national government prevented the development of iron ore properties for export to the emerging market of Japan.

One of the first positive results of the diversification strategy was the acquisition of 50 percent of a high-grade talc mine in Western Australia in 1960. The mine was small, but very profitable. More significant was WMC's entry into the production of bauxite and its product, alumina.

During the decade of the 1950s, Japan had emerged as a resource-poor manufacturing nation. Resource-rich Australia was geographically positioned as an ideal supplier of metal products to that increasingly important market. One of the resources the nation had in abundance was bauxite, previously not exploited because known deposits were not considered economical to mine.

Acting on a newly established diversification strategy, Sir Lindesay Clark ordered a reevaluation of bauxite deposits in Western Australia in 1953. These deposits had been identified previously but had been dismissed as uneconomical. Sir Lindesay, as he stated in his memoirs, believed that times had changed. Preliminary results were sufficiently promising that WMC formed Western Aluminum, NL (WANL) with two other Australian mining companies and a bank as partners.

WANL initiated intensive exploration and development of the Western Australia bauxite deposits, laboratory testing to establish the quality of the bauxite found, and negotiations with major industrial companies in Japan. It rapidly emerged as an

Key Dates:

1933: Western Mining Corporation, Ltd., is incorporated by the directors of Gold Mines of Australia.
1935: WMC becomes a subsidiary of The Gold Exploration and Finance Company of Australia, Ltd.
1949: WMC takes over GEFCA and becomes a company based in Australia and owned by Australians.
1953: WMC diversifies beyond gold.
1960: WMC acquires 50% of a talc mine.
1961: ALCOA and WMC form joint venture Alcoa of Australia.
1967: WMC exports its first nickel concentrates.
1970: WMC exports its first refined nickel products.
1979: Western Mining Corporation Holdings, Ltd., incorporated as the holding company for all WMC holdings.
1988: Production of copper and uranium begins at Olympic Dam.
2000: Queensland Fertilizer Plant begins operation.

industrial power and market for Australian resources. The company also negotiated with the Western Australia government that wanted to export finished alumina products rather than unprocessed bauxite.

This required the construction of a smelter, a fabricating plant, and a power plant to supply them with the massive amounts of electricity required for processing bauxite. The power plant, in turn, required massive amounts of coal to fuel it. By 1959, the planning and legal arrangements for the creation of these prerequisites of an integrated aluminum industry were in place. But it was evident that WANL lacked the financial resources necessary to build and operate the necessary facilities. Sir Lindesay, therefore, began the search for a major aluminum producer that could contribute the financial support and the expertise required to create the facilities needed.

Sir Lindesay felt some urgency in completing these negotiations. Bauxite was in plentiful supply at the time, and it was expected that large deposits in West Africa would soon add to that supply. The Australians wanted to create a partnership and begin production before potential partners lost interest in the Australian resource and focused instead on Africa. Moreover, WMC itself was in danger of being taken over. Its capital was relatively small, and its 78 percent interest in WANL and its assets was quite attractive. A partnership with a financially strong business would make a hostile takeover more difficult.

In 1960, WMC initiated negotiations with the Aluminum Company of America (ALCOA). That company was interested in establishing a market for aluminum in Japan, and Australia seemed an ideal location from which to undertake this. ALCOA made two requests of WMC/WANL. They wanted a confirmed Japanese market for the Australian alumina products, and they wanted 100 million tons of the bauxite reserves to be made available for ALCOA's exclusive use. These conditions were easily met. Mitsubishi of Japan had already negotiated a first order for 150,000 tons of alumina with WANL. The company also guaranteed the necessary bauxite to ALCOA.

In 1961, ALCOA and WANL incorporated Alcoa of Australia, Ltd. (ALCOA-Aus), with the Australian partners holding a 49 percent interest. During the next three years, ALCOA-Aus built a refinery, a smelter, a fabricating plant, and a power plant. The first shipment of alumina was sent to Japan in 1964. In 1968, the first shipment of bauxite went to ALCOA refineries.

In 1979, WMC acquired most of BH South, Ltd. It sold most of its holdings, but retained a 13 percent interest in ALCOA-Aus, thus bringing WMC's interest in the venture to 40 percent. WMC merged all of its alumina assets with ALCOA's global alumina and alumina chemicals business in 1995 to form Alcoa World Alumina and Chemicals (AWAC), the world's largest alumina producer. This enterprise, of which WMC is a 40 percent partner, supplies 27 percent of the world's alumina consumption.

WMC first located nickel in 1954, but it was ten years later when the company performed sufficient geologic evaluation to determine that the deposit was worth exploration. In 1965, the company applied to the Western Australia government for exploration rights covering 527 square miles surrounding the first nickel find and the rights to take up mineral leases in the area as necessary for mining. Serious exploration was then begun, and two major ore deposits were identified early in 1966.

In this case, too, world supply of the metal influenced decision making about how rapidly to attempt to bring the deposits to production, and how much risk would attend the project. Nickel was in worldwide shortage, and INCO of Canada controlled most of the available supply. A decision to begin rapidly building a mine was risky because full evaluation of the prospect was not complete, and unexpected complications might develop as the mine was constructed. But a decision to wait until exploration advanced further could mean that WMC nickel would come to market at a time when supply had increased.

Work on the first nickel mine was therefore initiated in late 1966. This entailed not only sinking mine shafts and making the ore accessible to the miners. It also required building a mill, a concentrator, power plants, and offices to support the mine. Construction of a town and its attendant infrastructure was also necessary to house the workers. The first nickel concentrates were shipped to Japan and Canada in 1967. In 1968, construction of a nickel refinery began. It was completed in 1970, and the WMC's first refined nickel products were exported in June of that year. This was the beginning of WMC's extremely profitable integrated nickel operations.

To finance these undertakings, WMC floated two secondary stock issues. In 1966, such an offering raised A$7.5 million, of which A$5 million was used in the construction of the mine and its attendant infrastructure. A 1968 offering raised another A$46 million, of which at least A$45 million was spent on construction of the refinery; on needed railway links among the mine, the concentrator and the refinery, and on further improvements to the associated town.

1979–Present: Reorganization, Further Diversification, and Consolidation

By 1979, WMC had sufficiently diverse operations that its fourth Chairman, Sir Arvi Parbo, restructured the company. In 1964, WMC had bought the portion of GMA it did not already own. But since WMC's buyout of GEFCA in 1949, many projects and even individual mines had been operated as separate subsidiaries of the parent company. The restructuring created Western Mining Corporation Holdings, Ltd., and made it the holding company for all WMC properties and operations.

Sir Arvi's chairmanship also saw the culmination of the process of diversification initiated in 1953. The first minerals the company sought after that date had been copper and uranium. The company had located copper deposits, but for the most part, these were small or not suitable for exploitation. Only in 1972 did the company find a promising uranium deposit near Yeelirrie, Western Australia. Until 1975, governmental opposition to uranium production inhibited work on the project. At the end of that year, however, exploration recommenced and work toward an environmental impact statement began. In 1977, the Western Australia and federal governments approved further development of the project.

In 1978, WMC formed a joint venture to develop the project. WMC held a 75 percent interest; Esso Exploration and Production Company of Australia, Inc., held 15 percent, and Urangesellschaft mbH and Co. held 10 percent. A research plant was completed in 1979, and trial mining began. The conceptual work prerequisite to full development of the site was complete, and negotiations with potential customers were underway when the federal government again adopted restrictive policies toward uranium mining. Permission to develop the site was withdrawn. Work stopped in 1983.

Yeelirrie was not WMC's only venture into uranium mining. Its experience at Olympic Dam near Roxby Downs in South Australia has been a success. The company began a search for copper in 1972. By 1975, it had located a rich deposit of copper and uranium under 350 meters of barren rock at the Olympic Dam site. By 1979, WMC had determined that the site contained enormous quantities of both metals. They found a joint venture partner in BP of Australia, which took a 49 percent interest in the project, leaving majority ownership and management responsibility with WMC. After substantial development of the site, production of both uranium and copper began in 1988. In 2000, Olympic Dam produced 4,500 tons of uranium oxide and 200,400 tons of refined copper.

The most recent addition to WMC's product mix was phosphate fertilizer. As previously mentioned, WMC took over BH South, Ltd., in 1979. At that time, it retained not only its interest in ALCOA-Aus, but also its wholly owned subsidiary, Queensland Phosphate, Ltd. This property was composed of rich phosphate deposits, but was not then in production. WMC resumed small-scale production in 1981, but stopped production in 1983 because it could not get an adequate price for its product. Continued exploration of the property revealed that the site contained a phosphate resource totaling about 107 million tons. But the exploitation of the resource would require a construction project totaling hundreds of millions of Australian dollars. Moreover, the site lacked a needed supply of natural gas.

WMC put the project on hold, but continued to arrange for eventual production. In 1988, it had acquired Hi Fert, Ltd., a major Australian blender and distributor of high analysis fertilizers. In 1996, the company changed names from Queensland Phosphate, Ltd, to WMC Fertilizers, Ltd, and announced the decision to develop a A$700 million fertilizer project at the site. Australia imported all the fertilizer used in its agricultural activities. WMC expected to be able to supply the internal market, and to export a substantial quantity of phosphate fertilizer as well.

In 1998, WMC Fertilizers contracted with Cargill, Inc., to export up to half a million tons of fertilizer per year for five years. By 2000, the Queensland Fertilizer Plant was fully commissioned, and was expected to produce at a full capacity of one million tons per year by 2002.

The beginning of the twenty-first century brought signs that WMC was consolidating. In 2000, it announced the intended sale of its talc operations. The first months of 2001 saw speculation in *The Financial Times* of London that the company planned to sell its gold operations. Later reports from the Dow Jones Newswire said that WMC was looking for a means to enhance the value of those operations, but they did not deny that a sale would be one way of achieving this.

Principal Subsidiaries

Westminster International Holdings Pty, Ltd.; Alcoa Worldwide Alumina and Chemicals; WMC Fertilizers Pty, Ltd.; WMC Finance, Ltd.; WMC Finance USA, Ltd.; Wmc Pty, Ltd.; Wmc Resources, Ltd.

Principal Competitors

Alcan; Alcoa; Anglo American; Barrick Gold; BHP; Billiton; Cameco; Carso; COGEMA; Cominco; Freeport-McMoRan Copper and Gold; Gold Fields Limited; Homestake Mining; Inco Limited; Kaiser Aluminum; Newmont Mining; Noranda; Norlisk Nickel; Phelps Dodge; Placer Dome; Rio Algom; Rio Tinto Limited; Rio Tinto plc; UM.

Further Reading

''Australia's WMC: Eight Cos Help with Review of Gold Ops,'' *Wall Street Journal.com*, posted May 15, 2001, http://wsj.com.

Blainey, Geoffrey, *White Gold: The Story of Alcoa in Australia*, St. Leonards, NSW: Allen & Unwin, 1997.

Brodie-Hill, L.C., *Brodie: Memoirs of Sir Lawrence Brodie-Hall*, Perth: Access Press, 1994.

Campbell, J.D., *Hidden Gold: The Central Norseman Story*, Melbourne: Australian Institute of Mines and Minerals, 1990.

Caroll, B., *Built on Silver: A History of Broken Hill South*, Melbourne: Hill of Content, 1986.

Clark, G. Lindesay, *Built on Gold: Recollections of Western Mining*, Melbourne: Hill of Content, 1983.

Gresham, J.J., *Kambalda: History of a Mining Town*, Melbourne: Western Mining Corporation, 1991.

Marsh, Virginia, ''WMC Puts Bold Business Up for Sale,'' *Financial Times.com*, posted May 16, 2001, http://www.news.ft.com.

Reid, D., *They Searched: A History of Exploration Within WMC, Part I—The First Twenty Years,* Adelaide: Western Mining Corporation, 1981.

Reid, D., *They Searched: A History of Mining Within WMC, Part II—The Years of Growth*, Adelaide: WMC Resources, Ltd, 1998.

—Anne L. Potter

WORKING ASSETS®

Working Assets Funding Service

101 Market Street, Suite 700
San Francisco, CA 94105
U.S.A.
Telephone: (415) 788-0777
Toll Free: (800) 788-8588
Fax: (415) 788-7572
Web site: http://www.workingassets.com;
http://www.workingforchange.com

Private Company
Incorporated: 1985
Employees: 100
Sales: $140 million (2000 est.)
NAIC: 522210 Credit Card Issuing; 513322 Cellular and Other Wireless Communications; 514191 On-Line Information Services

Working Assets Funding Service is a long-distance, Internet, and credit card company that donates a portion of its revenues to politically active and philanthropic nonprofit groups. The company's phone service donates one percent of customers' phone charges to organizations such as Amnesty International, Oxfam America, and Planned Parenthood, and ten cents is donated every time a customer makes a transaction using the Working Assets credit card. In 2001, the company reported it had donated approximately $25 million dollars since its inception in 1985.

Working Assets provides customers with free phone calls and company-generated letters to Congress, the White House, and business leaders on matters of national debate. Says Laura Scher, the CEO of Working Assets, ''We provide a way for people to become effective activists and philanthropists through their everyday activities, at little or no cost to them. . . . We're all about building a world that is just, humane, and environmentally sustainable.''

Although Working Assets measures its success in terms of dollars donated rather than money earned (Sher points to 2000 as the company's most successful year because Working Assets donated $5 million and generated 900,000 letters and calls), the privately held company has succeeded according to more traditional business criteria, as well. Working Assets' revenues for 2000 totaled $140 million, and the company has appeared five times on *Inc* magazine's list of the 500 fastest-growing enterprises in the United States.

Beginning in Social Consciousness

Working Assets sprouted roots in 1983 as a socially conscious investment house. The firm, called the Working Assets Money Market Fund, was founded by a group of eight partners headed by environmental activist Peter Barnes. The fund targeted investors looking for a way to invest money in a way that was socially and environmentally responsible. As Barnes told *The Progressive* in 1983, ''We're offering a choice that hasn't been there before. What's important for an investor to understand is that other criteria can be applied to investment than maximizing the bottom line.''

The Working Assets fund avoided interest in companies that engaged in unfair labor practices, violated environmental standards, invested in nuclear power, or conducted business in South Africa, which at that time followed the government-sanctioned policies of racial segregation (apartheid was abolished in the early 1990s).

Instead, the fund focused on such investments as alternative energy sources, certificates of deposit in financial institutions that funded farmers, and government loan programs for students, small businesses, and housing development. Despite industry skepticism and the difficulties inherent in ensuring the integrity of all their investments (for example, avoiding South African interests was particularly difficult, as South African stocks made up more than half of the market capitalization of the S&P 500), the fund had attracted $63 million by 1985. That year, Barnes became interested in playing a more active role in the causes Working Assets believed in. Realizing that many similarly-minded people didn't have $1,000 to open a money market account, he decided that offering services and products linked to charitable giving would be a more efficient and popular way to support these causes. The subsidiary Working Assets Funding Service was founded, and Barnes hired Laura Scher,

Company Perspectives:

Working Assets is a long distance, credit card, and online services company that was created to build a world that is more just, humane, and environmentally sustainable. The company was established in 1985 to help busy people make a difference in the world through progressive philanthropy and political activism.

Working Assets donates a portion of its revenue to nonprofit groups working for peace, human rights, equality, education, and the environment. The company also serves as a strong political force, dedicated to giving its customers the opportunity to speak out on critical public issues.

who had just graduated from the Harvard Business School, to head the venture.

From Conscience to Contributions

''For three months, I was the only employee,'' Scher said in 2000, remembering the early days of Working Assets Funding Service. ''I had to do everything from customer service to marketing to bookkeeping.'' Her primary responsibility was to develop the products that would carry out the new company's goal of promoting social responsibility. The first product was the Working Assets Visa Card, loosely modeled on a summer-long project conducted by American Express to fund the renovation of the Statue of Liberty. Working Assets donated five cents for every transaction made using the Visa card (this would later be raised to ten cents)—without cost to the customer and while maintaining a relatively low interest rate. While such ''affinity cards''—cards that offer perks such as frequent flier miles—later became widely popular, in 1985 they were virtually unheard of.

Finding a bank willing to support such a card—and keep annual rates lower than the 20 percent typically charged at that time—was a major challenge. A Massachusetts bank launched the card with a 17.5 percent interest rate. By the end of the first summer, Working Assets had 10,000 customers—the number the bank had projected would be signed up by the end of the third year. The bank told Working Assets to stop signing up customers, forcing the company to find other banks to issue the card. In its first year, Working Assets donated $32,000 in proceeds from the card to 16 charities.

During the early years, Working Assets established the policy that would distinguish its donations from other corporate gifts and that would remain in effect throughout the life of the company: The donations would be made from revenues, not the bottom line. In other words, the company would donate regardless of whether it earned a profit. ''Making money is not the company's goal,'' said Scher in 1985.

Despite this unorthodox business plan, the company thrived. By 1987, revenues—and donations—had tripled. That year, 55,000 cardholders generated $109,000, which was distributed among 32 organizations, and a Working Assets MasterCard soon followed. In 1988, Working Assets began allowing its cardholders to cast ballots to determine the percentage of donations allocated to these organizations. Also in 1988, the company offered a Working Assets Women's Card, which made donations only to organizations that helped women and children.

With Working Assets Funding Service growing rapidly, the money market fund, which by then had $100 million under management, was spun off into its own entity in 1988. It would later become Citizens Fund, one of the largest socially responsible funds, with $765 million in assets by 1999.

Dialing for Donations

Newly autonomous and inspired by the success of its credit cards, Working Assets set about in 1988 to develop its next socially responsible product—long-distance phone service. Working Assets began the venture as a sales-agent for U.S. Sprint, using the same donation model it had used for its credit cards. Working Assets marketed donation-linked service wherein one percent of customers' phone bills was donated—without cost to the customer—and Sprint provided the phone service. In 1989, 32 groups benefited from revenues generated by the long-distance service, and by 1991, Working Assets had attracted more than 50,000 customers.

That year, the company changed its method of providing long-distance service. As a sales-agent, Working Assets received a small marketing fee, which was roughly equal to its one percent donation and not enough to keep the operation afloat. Further, working with such a large carrier didn't allow Working Assets control over its billing or the ability to customize its service to fit the needs of its subscribers. Working Assets became a reseller, buying discounted long-distance time in bulk from the major long-distance carriers and selling it to its customers at a competitive price (Working Assets rates would consistently stay about a penny cheaper than larger carriers). Operating as a reseller proved enormously successful for Working Assets. Revenues jumped from $2 million to $15 million in 1992, $1 million of which was donated. In 1993, revenues rose to $35 million, long-distance subscriber rates climbed to 130,000, and, as of the third quarter of that year, the company turned a profit for the first time. Working Assets also added business long-distance service in 1993.

Freed from its ties to Sprint, Working Assets was able to control its billing, and in 1991 it introduced the phone bill that Laura Scher called the company's greatest innovation. ''No one else thinks of the bill as a product,'' she told the *New York Times* in 1993, ''This is the crux of our whole operation and this is where we have fun.'' Each Working Assets bill was printed with soy-based ink on 100 percent post-consumer recycled paper. The company felt compelled to plant trees to replace those felled to make the paper originally, and between 1991 and 2000 donated $400,000 to tree-planting groups all over the world.

Working Assets customers were given the option to ''round up'' their bills (for example, paying $37 on a $36.14 bill). The rounded-up funds, which averaged $50,000 a month in 1993, were added to the one percent of revenues set aside for charitable donations. At the end of the year, customers were issued a ballot and could vote on the organizations they wished to receive the money.

Key Dates:

1983: The Working Assets Money Market fund is established.
1985: The Working Assets Funding Service is incorporated; Laura Scher becomes CEO; the company offers its first credit card.
1988: The mutual fund business spins off; the company offers phone services.
1991: Working Assets Long Distance is established.
1993: The company becomes profitable for the first time.
1997: The company offers Internet access services.
1999: The company launches three ''e-philanthropy'' Web sites.
2000: The company offers wireless services.

Working Assets wanted its bill to serve as a lobbying tool as well as a fund-raising tool, and with the creation of the Citizen Acton program, it provided customers with easy ways to speak out on issues important to the company. Each bill highlighted two current issues, listed contact information, and encouraged customers—through free and discounted calls, and later company-generated letters—to contact the people making decisions about those issues. Later, the bill evolved to include a ''recommended reading'' list of books in line with the company's political philosophies. Customers could order the books directly on the bill at a ten percent discount, with one percent of the price going into the donations pool.

By 1997, Working Assets' donations had grown to $2.5 million, and *E* magazine called the company the ''granddaddy'' of the burgeoning movement of socially and environmentally progressive long-distance companies. The bulk of the company's revenues and donations came from the long-distance service, which had 250,000 subscribers. New subscribers were given a coupon for a free pint of Ben and Jerry's ice cream each month for the first year of service.

Citizen Action Victories

Working Assets was generating between 30,000 and 50,000 calls and letters each month from the Citizen Action alerts included their bills, and the lobbying efforts were beginning to bear fruit. In a 1997 interview with the environmental organization SEE Green, Scher reported that Working Assets had asked subscribers to lobby Mercedes Benz to pay reparations to Holocaust survivors who had been slave laborers for the company during World War II. The campaign generated more than 30,000 letters and calls, and within months, Mercedes Benz had contributed to a $2 billion reparations fund, along with several other German companies.

Working Assets-generated letters and calls also accounted for about 44,000 of the 200,000 received by the USDA that led the agency to apply strict labeling standards for organic foods. The Capital Research Center, a group that studies nonprofit organizations, reported that 24 percent of the 26 Citizens Actions headed by Working Assets in 1999 resulted in success, including a campaign to back a bill to encourage wind energy production through a tax credit. In its press kit, Working Assets counts ''renewing the Violence Against Women Act, protecting the Tongass Rainforest in Alaska, and convincing Congress to invest $12 billion in conservation initiatives'' among its 2000 Citizens Action victories. ''We don't win all the time, but we win enough to make a significant impact,'' Scher told SEE Green.

Working Assets in the Internet Age

Working Assets continued in its quest to add products and services, and in 1997, it introduced Internet access. The service was provided in partnership with the nationwide Internet service provider Earthlink Network, Inc. Earthlink provided the service and customers were billed via their Working Assets bill. Working Assets' donation model was applied to the new venture: the company contributed one percent of the $19.95 monthly service fees to nonprofit groups selected by members.

In 1999, the company launched a trio of ''e-philanthropy'' Web sites that promoted the company's commitment to social change. Giveforchange.com allowed visitors to make online donations directly, giving them access to hundreds of nonprofit groups in one location. Volunteerforchange.com helped individuals nationwide find volunteer opportunities at more than 20,000 nonprofits and public sector organizations. Shopforchange.com provided a portal to 60 popular online merchants such as Amazon.com, Land's End, and the Sharper Image. A percentage of the price of every item purchased was donated to nonprofit organizations. The site also maintained lists of progressive merchants, tips on socially responsible shopping, and a Citizens Action program similar to the one connected with the Working Assets long distance service. In the first five months of its existence, shopforchange.com registered 100,000 customers.

Challenges Ahead

The turn of the century was challenging for Working Assets. An attempt to enter the local phone service market in 1999 failed after the company experienced difficulty working with Pacific Bell. Working Assets also attempted to enter the broadcasting arena by starting an AM radio station, KWAB 1490 in Boulder, Colorado, that broadcast simultaneously on the Internet. While the station won awards for its coverage, it was unsustainable as either a traditional broadcast business or as an Internet broadcaster. Working Assets sold the station to Colorado Public Radio in May of 2001.

Working Assets' growth also slowed somewhat at the end of the decade. Revenues between 1998 and 1999 grew by $10 million, a small increase compared to the exponential leaps made in the early 1990s. In response, Working Assets looked for a way to expand its service line. ''To continue growing at the pace that Working Assets is growing at, we need to offer new products,'' Scher told the *San Francisco Business Times* in 2000.

Working Assets became one of the first wireless resellers in the country when it began offering digital wireless phone service in 2000. Initially, the service was available only in Seattle and San Francisco, but it soon expanded into 20 major metropolitan areas. As with its other services, Working Assets donates one percent of its wireless revenues. Working Assets also began exploring the possibility of providing electricity to customers in parts of the country. However, in 2001, Working Assets' primary future business goals underscored the emphasis it had always placed on philanthropy over profits: to donate $10 million dollars a year and to generate two million political calls and letters a year. "We're highly motivated to growing our business," Scher told SEE Green, "We need to be bigger."

Principal Competitors

AT&T; Sprint FON; WorldCom.

Further Reading

Anderson, Mae, "Working Their Assets," *ADWEEK Eastern Edition*, May 7, 2001, p. 5.

Baldwin, William, "Morality Plays," *Forbes*, July 29, 1985, pp. 42–43.

Boudreau, John, "Goodall Eyes Valley Philanthropists,"San Jose Mercury News, February 9, 2001.

"Charity Begins at the Home Page," *Promo*, February, 2000.

Cockburn, Alexander, "Beat the Devil: The Conscience Industry," *The Nation*, November 9, 1998.

"Dialing Dollars for the Environment," *Environment*, January-February 1990, p. 24.

Elliott, Stuart, "Working Assets Funding Service," *The New York Times*, August 16, 1991, p. C4.

Fefer, Mark D., "20 Companies on a roll: Working Assets," *Fortune*, Autumn 1993/Winter 1994, p. 28.

Fernandes, Lorna, "Working Assets Hangs up Service," *San Francisco Business Times*, January 29, 1999, pp. 1–2.

Fraser, Jill Andresky, "Changing of the Card," *Inc.*, 1997, Vol. 19, Issue 15, p. 84.

Frons, Marc, "Laura Scher: Doing Good Business Helps Good Causes," *Business Week*, October 26, 1987, p. 76.

Garfield, Charles A., "Do Profits & Social Responsibility Mix?," *Executive Excellence*, March 1992, p. 5.

Gibeau, Dawn, "Want Peace, Rights and a Safe Environment? Charge It," *National Catholic Reporter*, December 20, 1991, pp. 6–7.

Ginsberg, Steve, "Working Assets Make Energy Call," *San Francisco Business Times*, June 12, 1998, p.5.

Glickman, Marshall, "Dialing for Dolphins: Activist Phone Companies Give to the Cause and Reduce Rates, Too," *E*, March-April, 1997, pp. 44–47.

Goerne, Carrie, "Reach Out and Change the World: Long-Distance Service Helps Users Make a Difference the Easy Way," *Marketing News*, March 16, 1992, p. 10.

Gonzales, Monica, "The Women's Card," *American Demographics*, January, 1988, p. 23.

Gould, Carole, "A Social Responsibility Shake-Up," *The New York Times*, June 12, 1994, p. F14.

—— "Socially Attuned and Indexed, Too," *The New York Times*, June 18, 1995, p. F7.

"Greens Tell Working Assets It's Not Being Green Enough," *The Electricity Journal*, August/September, 1997, pp. 3–4.

Gross, Jane, "She Took One Look at the Age of Greed and Made a Quick Left," *The New York Times*, November 7, 1993, p. F8.

Gupta, Udayan, "Four Companies Hope to Turn Customers into Activists," *The Wall Street Journal*, January 21, 1993, p. B2.

—— "Working Assets Seeks Wall Street Ties'," *The Wall Street Journal*, September 29, 1992, p. B1.

Hammer, Marion P., "Working Assets: The Long Distance Phone Service You Need to Hang-up on," *American Rifleman*, January 1997, p. 12.

Hansen, Larry, "Doing Well with Do-Good Funds," *Fact*, June, 1984, pp. 58–59.

Horowitz, Jed, "Selling Social Responsibility," *On Wall Street*, January 1, 1999, p. 1.

"Invasion of the MBA Liberals," *Business Week*, October 19, 1992, p. 33.

Jacobs, Kathleen, "Laura Scher," *Working Woman*, June, 2000, p. 79.

Jordan, Patrick, "Plastic or Principle? To Choose or Not to Choose," *Commonweal*, October 9, 1992, pp. 5–6.

Kallen, Barbara, "Cleaner Than Thou," *Forbes*, November 21, 1983, pp. 334–335.

Krizmanic, Judy, "Peter Barnes' Cents of Responsibility," *Vegetarian Times*, July 1990, pp. 62–68.

Levine, Daniel S., "Working Assets Goes Wireless with New Offering," *San Francisco Business Times*, September 29, 2000, p. 8.

"Making Money While Making a Difference," *Working Woman*, February, 1992, pp. 31–32.

Miller, Annetta, "Reach Out and Prod Someone," *Newsweek*, October 14, 1991, p. 50.

Miller, Samantha, "Profit Sharing: Working Assets CEO Laura Scher Turns Bills into Bonanzas for Causes Her Customers Believe in," *People Weekly*, Sept 4, 2000 v54 i10 pp. 151–153.

Moskowitz, Milton, "Social Investment Funds: Fortune or Folly?," *Business and Society Review*, Spring, 1984, pp. 10–14.

Ojala, Marydee, "Finding Socially Responsible Companies," *Database Magazine*, October 20, 1994.

Patron, Eugene J., "Using Money to Make Change," *The Advocate*, December 17, 1991, pp. 70–71.

Peregrin, Tony C., "Win-Win Situation," *Telephony*, May 3, 1999, p. 50.

Philip, Christine, "Mutual Funds Drop South African Divestment Rules," *Pensions & Investments*, February 21, 1994, p. 7.

"Prizes, Prizes, and Prizes for Good Companies," *Business and Society Review*, 1996, p. 71.

Robinson, Susan, "Socially Responsible Mutual Funds, 'Progressives' Put Their Money Where Their Hearts Are," *San Francisco Business Journal*, July 29, 1985 pp. 9–11.

Rothman, Matt, "A Bull Market for Radicals," *The Progressive*, December, 1993, pp. 16–17.

Rowe, Jonathan, "A Choice Worth Making," *The Christian Science Monitor*, November 14, 1991, p. 13.

Scher, Laura and Nancy Nachman-Hunt, "When Does a CEO Decide to Become One?," *Natural Business LOHAS Journal*, May/June, 2000, p. 64.

Stovall, Robert H., "When Do-Gooders Do Good," *Financial World*, September 1, 1992, p. 68.

Wallen, Esther, "Phone Service Gives Customers Chance to Be Social, Political Activists," *Knight-Ridder/Tribune News Service*, July 13, 1993.

Woolard, Andrea L., "Funds with Social Themes: Investing Principal in your Principles," *The Christian Science Monitor*, August 14, 1986, p. 19.

"Working Assets Affinity Cards Gather Support," *San Francisco Business Times*, February 8, 1988, p. 10.

"Working Assets Makes Donations, Promotes Charitable Giving," *Fund Raising Management*, February, 2000, p. 12.

—Lisa Whipple

INDEX TO COMPANIES

Index to Companies

Listings in this index are arranged in alphabetical order under the company name. Company names beginning with a letter or proper name such as Eli Lilly & Co. will be found under the first letter of the company name. Definite articles (The, Le, La) are ignored for alphabetical purposes as are forms of incorporation that precede the company name (AB, NV). Company names printed in bold type have full, historical essays on the page numbers appearing in bold. Updates to entries that appeared in earlier volumes are signified by the notation **(upd.)**. Company names in light type are references within an essay to that company, not full historical essays. This index is cumulative with volume numbers printed in bold type.

A & A Die Casting Company, **25** 312
A and A Limousine Renting, Inc., **26** 62
A & C Black Ltd., **7** 165
A&E Plastics, **12** 377
A&E Television Networks, IV 627; **19** 204; **32 3–7**
A. & J. McKenna, **13** 295
A&K Petroleum Company. *See* Kerr-McGee Corporation.
A & M Instrument Co., **9** 323
A&M Records, **23** 389
A&N Foods Co., **II** 553
A&P. *See* Great Atlantic & Pacific Tea Company, Inc.
A&P Water and Sewer Supplies, Inc., **6** 487
A. and T. McKenna Brass and Copper Works, **13** 295
A & W Brands, Inc., II 595; **25 3–5**
A-1 Supply. *See* International Game Technology.
A.A. Housman & Co., **II** 424; **13** 340
A.A. Mathews. *See* CRSS Inc.
A. Ahlström Oy, **IV** 276–77
A.B. Chance Industries Co., Inc., **II** 20; **31** 259
A.B.Dick Company, II 25; **28 6–8**
A.B. Hemmings, Ltd., **13** 51
A.B. Leasing Corp., **13** 111–12
A-B Nippondenso, **III** 593
A-BEC Mobility, **11** 487
A.C. Delco, **26** 347, 349
A.C. Moore Arts & Crafts, Inc., 30 3–5
A.C. Nielsen Company, IV 605; **13 3–5**. *See also* ACNielsen Corporation.
A.C. Wickman, **13** 296
A.D. International (Australia) Pty. Ltd., **10** 272
A. Dager & Co., **I** 404
A. Dunkelsbuhler & Co., **IV** 20–21, 65; **7** 122
A/E/C/ Systems International, **27** 362
A.E. Fitkin & Company, **6** 592–93
A.E. Gutman, **16** 486
A.E. LePage, **II** 457
A.E. Lottes, **29** 86
A.G. Becker, **II** 259–60; **11** 318; **20** 260
A.G. Edwards, Inc., 8 3–5; **19** 502; **32 17–21 (upd.)**
A.G. Industries, Inc., **7** 24
A.G. Morris, **12** 427
A.G. Spalding & Bros., Inc., **I** 428–29; **24** 402–03
A.G. Stanley Ltd., **V** 17, 19; **24** 75
A. Gettelman, Co., **I** 269
A. Goertz and Co., **IV** 91
A.H. Belo Corporation, IV 605; **10 3–5**; **28** 367, 369; **30 13–17 (upd.)**
A.H. Robins Co., **10** 70; **12** 188; **16** 438
A. Hirsh & Son, **30** 408
A.I. Credit Corp., **III** 196
A.J. Caley and Son. Ltd., **II** 569
A.J. Oster Co., **III** 681
A. Johnson & Co. *See* Axel Johnson Group.
A.L. Laboratories Inc., **12** 3
A.L. Pharma Inc., 12 3–5. *See also* Alpharma Inc.
A.L. Van Houtte Inc. *See* Van Houtte Inc.
A. Lambert International Inc., **16** 80
A.M. Castle & Co., 25 6–8
A.M. Collins Manufacturing Co., **IV** 286
A.O. Smith Corporation, 7 139; **22** 181, **11 3–6**; **24** 499; **40 3–8 (upd.)**
A-1 Steak Sauce Co., **I** 259
A-1 Supply, **10** 375
A.P. Green Refractories, **22** 285
A.R. Pechiney, **IV** 173
A. Roger Perretti, **II** 484
A.S. Abell Co., **IV** 678
A.S. Aloe, **III** 443
A.S. Cameron Steam Pump Works, **III** 525
A/S Titan, **III** 418
A.S. Watson & Company, **18** 254
A.S. Yakovlev Design Bureau, 15 3–6
A. Schilling & Company. *See* McCormick & Company, Incorporated.
A. Schulman, Inc., 8 6–8
A. Sulka & Co., **29** 457
A.T. Cross Company, 17 3–5
A.T. Massey Coal Company, **34** 164
A-T-O Inc. *See* Figgie International, Inc.
A.V. Roe & Co., **I** 50, 81; **III** 508; **24** 85
A.W. Bain Holdings, **III** 523
A.W. Shaw Co., **IV** 635
A.W. Sijthoff, **14** 555
A-Z International Companies, **III** 569; **20** 361
AA Development Corp., **I** 91
AA Distributors, **22** 14
AA Energy Corp., **I** 91
AAA Development Corp., **17** 238
Aardman Animations, **43** 143
Aachener und Münchener Feuer-Versicherungs-Gesellschaft, **III** 376
Aachener und Münchener Gruppe, **III** 349–50
Aachener Union, **II** 385
AAE Ahaus Alstatter Eisenbahn Holding AG, **25** 171
AAF-McQuay Incorporated, 26 3–5
AAI Corporation, **37** 399
Aalborg, **6** 367
Aansworth Shirt Makers, **8** 406
AAON, Inc., 22 3–6
AAR Corp., III 687; **IV** 60; **28 3–5**
Aargauische Portlandcement-Fabrik Holderbank-Wildegg, **III** 701
Aaron Brothers, Inc., **17** 320, 322
Aaron Rents, Inc., 14 3–5; **33** 368; **35 3–6 (upd.)**
AARP, 27 3–5
Aasche Transportation, **27** 404
Aastrom Biosciences, Inc., **13** 161
AAV Cos., **13** 48; **41** 22
Aavant Health Management Group, Inc., **11** 394
Aavid Thermal Technologies, Inc., 29 3–6
AB Capital & Investment Corporation, **23** 381
AB Ingredients Limited, **41** 32
AB-PT. *See* American Broadcasting-Paramount Theatres, Inc.
ABA. *See* Aktiebolaget Aerotransport.

Abacus Fund, Inc., **II** 445; **22** 405
ABACUS International Holdings Ltd., **26** 429
Abana Pharmaceuticals, **24** 257
Abar Staffing, **25** 434
ABB Asea Brown Boveri Ltd., II 1–4, 13; **III** 427, 466, 631–32; **IV** 66, 109, 204, 300; **15** 483; **22 7–12 (upd.)**, 64, 288; **28** 39; **34** 132
ABB Hafo AB. *See* Mitel Corp.
ABB RDM Service, **41** 326
Abba Seafood AB, **18** 396
Abbatoir St.-Valerien Inc., **II** 652
Abbey Business Consultants, **14** 36
Abbey Home Entertainment, **23** 391
Abbey Life Group PLC, **II** 309
Abbey Medical, Inc., **11** 486; **13** 366–67
Abbey National plc, 10 6–8; **39 3–6 (upd.)**
Abbey Rents, **II** 572
Abbey Road Building Society, **10** 6–7
Abbott Laboratories, I 619–21, 686, 690, 705; **II** 539; **10** 70, 78, 126; **11 7–9 (upd.)**, 91, 494; **12** 4; **14** 98, 389; **22** 75; **25** 55; **36** 38–39; **40 9–13 (upd.)**
Abbott, Proctor & Paine, **II** 445; **22** 405
ABC Appliance, Inc., 10 9–11
ABC Carpet & Home Co. Inc., 26 6–8
ABC, Inc., **I** 463–64; **II** 89, 129–33, 151, 156, 170, 173; **III** 188, 214, 251–52; **6** 157–59, 164; **11** 197–98; **17** 150; XVIII 65; **19** 201; **21** 25; **24** 516–17; **32** 3. *See also* Capital Cities/ABC Inc.
ABC Markets, **17** 558
ABC Rail Products Corporation, 18 3–5
ABC Records, **II** 144
ABC Supply Co., Inc., 22 13–16
ABC Treadco, **19** 455
ABD Securities Corp., **II** 239, 283
ABECOR. *See* Associated Banks of Europe Corp.
Abell-Howe Construction Inc., **42** 434
Abercom Holdings, **IV** 92
Abercrombie & Fitch Co., V 116; **15 7–9**; **17** 369; **25** 90; **35 7–10 (upd.)**
Aberthaw Cement, **III** 671
Abex Aerospace, **III** 512
Abex Corp., **I** 456; **10** 553; **18** 3
Abex Friction Products, **III** 512
ABF. *See* Associated British Foods PLC.
ABF Freight System, Inc., **16** 39–41
ABI. *See* American Furniture Company, Inc.
Abigail Adams National Bancorp, Inc., 23 3–5
Abington Shoe Company. *See* The Timberland Company.
Abitec Corporation, **41** 32–33
Abitibi-Consolidated, Inc., 25 9–13 (upd.); **26** 445
Abitibi-Price Inc., IV 245–47, 721; **9** 391
Abko Realty Inc., **IV** 449
ABM Industries Incorporated, 25 14–16 (upd.)
ABN. *See* Algemene Bank Nederland N.V.
ABN AMRO Rothschild, **39** 295
Above The Belt, Inc., **16** 37
ABR Foods, **II** 466
Abraham & Straus, **V** 168; **8** 443; **9** 209; **31** 192
Abraham Schaaffhausenscher Bankverein, **IV** 104
Abrams Industries Inc., 23 6–8
Abri Bank Bern, **II** 378
Absolut Company, **31** 458, 460
Abu Dhabi National Oil Company, IV 363–64, 476
Abu Qir Fertilizer and Chemical Industries Co., **IV** 413
AC Design Inc., **22** 196
AC Humko Corporation, **41** 32–33
ACA Corporation, **25** 368
Academic Press, **IV** 622–23
Academy Sports & Outdoors, 27 6–8
Acadia Entities, **24** 456
Acadia Investors, **23** 99
Acadia Partners, **21** 92
Acadian Ambulance & Air Med Services, Inc., 39 7–10
Access Dynamics Inc., **17** 255
Access Graphics Technology Inc., **13** 128
Access Technology, **6** 225
Accessory Network Group, Inc., **8** 219
Accident and Casualty Insurance Co., **III** 230–31
Acclaim Entertainment Inc., 13 115; **24 3–8**, 538
ACCO World Corporation, 7 3–5; **12** 264
Accolade Inc., **35** 227
Accor SA, 10 12–14; **13** 364; **27 9–12 (upd.)**
Accord Energy, **18** 367
Accountants on Call, **6** 10
Accounting and Tabulating Corporation of Great Britain, **6** 240
Acctex Information Systems, **17** 468
Accuralite Company, **10** 492
Accurate Forming Co., **III** 643
AccuRead Limited, **42** 165, 167
Accuride Corp., **IV** 179
Accuscan, Inc., **14** 380
ACE Cash Express, Inc., 33 3–6
Ace Comb Company, **12** 216
Ace Electric Co., **I** 156
Ace Hardware Corporation, 12 6–8; **35 11–14 (upd.)**
Ace Medical Company, **30** 164
Ace Novelty Company, **26** 374
Ace Refrigeration Ltd., **I** 315; **25** 81
Acer Inc., 6 244; **10** 257; **16 3–6**
Acer Sertek, **24** 31
Aceralia, **42** 414
Aceros Fortuna S.A. de C.V., **13** 141
Aceto Corp., 38 3–5
ACF Industries, **30** 282
Acheson Graphite Corp, **I** 399; **9** 517
ACI Holdings Inc., **I** 91; **28** 24
ACI Ltd., **29** 478
Aciéries de Ploërmel, **16** 514
Aciéries et Minières de la Sambre, **IV** 52
Aciéries Réunies de Burbach-Eich-Dudelange S.A. *See* ARBED S.A.
Acker Drill Company, **26** 70
Ackerley Communications, Inc., 9 3–5
Acklin Stamping Company, **8** 515
ACLC. *See* Allegheny County Light Company.
ACLI Government Securities Inc., **II** 422
ACM. *See* Advanced Custom Molders, Inc.
Acme Boot, **I** 440–41
Acme Brick Company, **19** 231–32
Acme Can Co., **I** 601; **13** 188
Acme Carton Co., **IV** 333
Acme-Cleveland Corp., I 531; **13 6–8**
Acme Corrugated Cases, **IV** 258
Acme Cotton Products, **13** 366
Acme-Delta Company, **11** 411
Acme Fast Freight Inc., **27** 473
Acme Market. *See* American Stores Company.
Acme Newspictures, **25** 507
Acme Quality Paint Co., **III** 744
Acme Quilting Co., Inc., **19** 304
Acme Road Machinery, **21** 502
Acme Screw Products, **14** 181
ACMI, **21** 118–19
ACNielsen Corporation, 38 6–9 (upd.)
Acordis, **41** 10
Acorn Computer, **III** 145
Acorn Financial Corp., **15** 328
Acoustics Development Corporation, **6** 313
Acova S.A., **26** 4
Acquired Systems Enhancement Corporation, **24** 31
ACR. *See* American Capital and Research Corp.
AcroMed Corporation, **30** 164
Act III Theatres, **25** 453
Actava Group, **14** 332
Action, **6** 393
Action Furniture by Lane, **17** 183
Action Labs Inc., **37** 285
Action Performance Companies, Inc., 27 13–15; **32** 344; **37** 319
Action Temporary Services, **29** 273
Activenture Corporation, **16** 253; **43** 209
Activision, Inc., 24 3; **32 8–11**
Acton Bolt Ltd., **IV** 658
Acumos, **11** 57
Acuson Corporation, 10 15–17; **36 3–6 (upd.)**
ACX Technologies, **13** 11; **36** 15
Acxiom Corporation, 35 15–18
Ad Astra Aero, **I** 121
AD-AM Gas Company, **11** 28
Adage Systems International, Inc., **19** 438
Adam, Meldrum & Anderson Company (AM&A), **16** 61–62
Adam Opel AG, 7 6–8; **11** 549; **18** 125; **21 3–7 (upd.)**
Adams Childrenswear, **V** 177
Adams Express Co., **II** 380–81, 395–96; **10** 59–60; **12** 533
Adams Golf, Inc., 37 3–5
Adams Industries, **19** 414
Adams/Cates Company, **21** 257
Adanac General Insurance Company, **13** 63
Adaptec, Inc., 11 56; **31 3–6**
Adaptive Data Systems, **25** 531
Adar Associates, Inc. *See* Scientific-Atlanta, Inc.
ADC of Greater Kansas City, Inc., **22** 443
ADC Telecommunications, Inc., 10 18–21; **30 6–9 (upd.)**
Adco Products, **I** 374
Addison Corporation, **31** 399
Addison Structural Services, Inc., **26** 433
Addison Wesley, **IV** 659
Addressograph-Multigraph, **11** 494
Adecco S.A., 26 240; **35** 441–42; **36 7–11 (upd.)**
Adelphi Pharmaceutical Manufacturing Co., **I** 496
Adelphia Communications Corp., 17 6–8
Ademco. *See* Alarm Device Manufacturing Company.
ADESA Corporation, **34** 286
Adesso-Madden, Inc., **37** 372
Adger Assuranceselskab, **III** 310
Adhere Paper Co., **IV** 252; **17** 29

ADI Group Limited. *See* AHL Services, Inc.
Adia S.A., 6 9–11; **9** 327. *See also* Adecco S.A.
Adiainvest S.A., **6** 9, 11
adidas AG, 8 392–93; **13** 513; **14 6–9**; **17** 244; **22** 202; **23** 472, 474; **25** 205, 207; **36** 344, 346
adidas-Salomon AG, 33 7–11 (upd.)
Adirondack Industries, **24** 403
Adjusters Auto Rental Inc. **16** 380
Adler, **23** 219
Adler and Shaykin, **III** 56; **11** 556–57
Adler Line. *See* Transatlantische Dampfschiffahrts Gesellschaft.
Adley Express, **14** 567
ADM. *See* Archer-Daniels-Midland Co.
Administracion Corporativa y Mercantil, S.A. de C.V., **37** 178
Admiral Co., **II** 86; **III** 573
Admiral Cruise Lines, **6** 368; **27** 91
Adnan Dabbagh, **6** 115
ADNOC. *See* Abu Dhabi National Oil Company.
Adobe Systems Incorporated, 10 22–24; **15** 149; **20** 46, 237; **33 12–16 (upd.)**; **43** 151
Adolph Coors Company, I 236–38, 255, 273; **13 9–11 (upd.)**; **18** 72; **26** 303, 306; **34** 37; **36 12–16 (upd.)**
Adolphe Lafont, **17** 210
Adonis Radio Corp., **9** 320
Adorence, **16** 482
ADP, Inc., **18** 297
Adria Produtos Alimenticos, Ltd., **12** 411
Adria Steamship Company, **6** 425
Adrian Hope and Company, **14** 46
Adriatico Banco d'Assicurazione, **III** 206, 345–46
Adrienne Vittadini, **15** 291
ADS. *See* Aerospace Display Systems.
Adsega, **II** 677
Adstaff Associates, Ltd., **26** 240
ADT Ltd., **26** 410; **28** 486
ADT Security Systems, Inc., 12 9–11
Adtel, Inc., **10** 358
Adtran Inc., 22 17–20
Adtranz **34** 128, 132–33, 136; **42** 45. *See also* ABB ASEA Brown Boveri Ltd.
Advacel, **18** 20; **43** 17
Advance Chemical Company, **25** 15
Advance Foundry, **14** 42
Advance Publications Inc., **IV 581–84**; **13** 178, 180, 429; **19 3–7 (upd.)**; **31** 376, 378
Advance-Rumely Thresher Co., **13** 16
Advance Transformer Co., **13** 397
Advance/Newhouse Communications, **42** 114
Advanced Casino Systems Corporation, **21** 277
Advanced Communications Engineering. *See* Scientific-Atlanta, Inc.
Advanced Communications Inc. *See* Metrocall, Inc.
Advanced Custom Molders, Inc., **17** 533
Advanced Data Management Group S.A., **23** 212
Advanced Entertainment Group, **10** 286
Advanced Fiberoptic Technologies, **30** 267
Advanced Gravis, **28** 244
Advanced Logic Research, Inc., **27** 169
Advanced Marine Enterprises, Inc., **18** 370
Advanced Marketing Services, Inc., 24 354; **34 3–6**
Advanced Medical Technologies, **III** 512
Advanced Metal Technologies Inc., **17** 234
Advanced Metallurgy, Inc., **29** 460
Advanced Micro Devices, Inc., 6 215–17; **9** 115; **10** 367; **11** 308; **16** 316; **18** 18–19, 382; **19** 312; **20** 175; **30 10–12 (upd.)**; **32** 498; **43** 15–16;
Advanced MobilComm, **10** 432
Advanced Structures, Inc., **18** 163
Advanced System Applications, **11** 395
Advanced Technology Laboratories, Inc., 9 6–8
Advanced Telecommunications Corporation, **8** 311
Advanced Tissue Sciences Inc., **41** 377
Advanced Web Technologies, **22** 357
Advanstar Communications, **27** 361
Advanta Corporation, 8 9–11; **11** 123; **38 10–14 (upd.)**
Advanta Partners, LP, **42** 322
Advantage Company, **8** 311; **27** 306
The Advantage Group, Inc., **25** 185–86
Advantage Health Plans, Inc., **11** 379
Advantage Health Systems, Inc., **25** 383
Advantage Insurers, Inc., **25** 185, 187
Advantage Publishers Group, **34** 5
Advantest Corporation, **39** 350, 353
Advantica Restaurant Group, Inc., 27 16–19 (upd.); **29** 150
Advent Corporation, **22** 97
Advertising Unlimited, Inc., **10** 461
Advo, Inc., 6 12–14
AEA. *See* United Kingdom Atomic Energy Authority.
AEA Investors Inc., **II** 628; **13** 97; **22** 169, 171; **28** 380; **30** 328
AEG A.G., I 151, 193, **409–11**; **II** 12, 119, 279; **III** 466, 479; **IV** 167; **6** 489; IX 11; **14** 169; **15** 142; **22** 28; **23** 495; **34** 131–32
Aegis Group plc, 6 15–16
Aegis Insurance Co., **III** 273
AEGON N.V., III 177–79, 201, 273; **33** 418–20. *See also* Transamerica–An AEGON Company
AEI Music Network Inc., 35 19–21
AEL Ventures Ltd., **9** 512
Aeneas Venture Corp., **26** 502
AEON Group, **V** 96–99; **11** 498–99; **31** 430–31; **37** 227
AEP. *See* American Electric Power Company.
AEP Industries, Inc., 36 17–19
AEP-Span, **8** 546
Aer Lingus Group plc, 6 59; **12** 367–68; **34 7–10**; **35** 382–84; **36** 230–31
Aera Energy LLC, **41** 359
Aérazur, **36** 529
Aerial Communications Inc., **31** 452
Aeritalia, **I** 51, 74–75, 467; **24** 86
Aero-Coupling Corp., **III** 641
Aero Engines, **9** 418
Aero International (Regional) SAS, **24** 88
Aero International Inc., **14** 43
Aero Mayflower Transit Company. *See* Mayflower Group Inc.
Aero O/Y, **6** 87–88
Aero-Portuguesa, **6** 125
Aeroflot—Russian International Airlines, 29 7–10 (upd.)
Aeroflot Soviet Airlines, I 105, 110, 118; **6 57–59**; **14** 73; **27** 475
Aerojet, **8** 206, 208
Aerojet-General Corp., **9** 266
Aerolíneas Argentinas S.A., I 107; **6** 97; **33 17–19**; **36** 281
Aeroméxico, **20** 168
Aeronautics Leasing, Inc., **39** 33
Aéroports de Paris, 33 20–22
Aeroquip Corporation, III 640–42; **V** 255; **16 7–9**; **19** 508
Aerospace Avionics, **III** 509
Aerospace Display Systems, **36** 158
Aerospace International Services, **41** 38
The Aérospatiale Group, I 41–42, 46, 50, 74, 94; **7 9–12**; **12** 190–91; **14** 72; **21 8–11 (upd.)**; **24** 84–86, 88–89; **26** 179
Aerostar, **33** 359–61
The AES Corporation, 10 25–27; **13 12–15 (upd.)**; **24** 359
Aetna, Inc., 20 59; **21 12–16 (upd.)**, 95; **22** 139, 142–43; **30** 364
Aetna Life and Casualty Company, II 170–71, 319; **III** 78, **180–82**, 209, 223, 226, 236, 254, 296, 298, 305, 313, 329, 389; **IV** 123, 703; **10** 75–76; **12** 367; **15** 26; **17** 324; **23** 135; **40** 199
Aetna National Bank, **13** 466
Aetna Oil Co., **IV** 373
AFC Enterprises, Inc., 32 12–16 (upd.); **36** 517, 520
AFCO Industries, Inc., **III** 241; **IV** 341
Afcol, **I** 289; **24** 449–50
AFE Ltd., **IV** 241
Affiliated Enterprises Inc., **I** 114
Affiliated Hospital Products Inc., **37** 400
Affiliated Music Publishing, **22** 193
Affiliated Paper Companies, Inc., **31** 359, 361
Affiliated Products Inc., **I** 622
Affiliated Publications, Inc., 6 323; **7 13–16**; **19** 285
Affordable Inns, **13** 364
AFG Industries Inc., **I** 483; **9** 248
AFIA, **22** 143
Afianzadora Insurgentes Serfin, **19** 190
AFL. *See* American Football League.
AFLAC Incorporated, 10 28–30 (upd.); **38 15–19 (upd.)**
AFP. *See* Australian Forest Products.
AFRA Enterprises Inc., **26** 102
African and European Investment, **IV** 96
African Coasters, **IV** 91
African Explosive and Chemical Industries, **IV** 22
AFT. *See* Advanced Fiberoptic Technologies.
AFW Fabric Corp., **16** 124
AG&E. *See* American Electric Power Company.
Ag-Chem Equipment Company, Inc., 17 9–11
AG Communication Systems Corporation, **15** 194; **43** 446
AGA, **I** 358
Agan Chemical Manufacturers Ltd., **25** 266–67
Agar Manufacturing Company, **8** 2
Agatha Christie Ltd., **31** 63 67
AGCO Corp., 13 16–18
Agefi, **34** 13
AGEL&P. *See* Albuquerque Gas, Electric Light and Power Company.
Agence France-Presse, IV 670; **34 11–14**
Agency, **6** 393
Agency Rent-A-Car, **16** 379

AGF, **III** 185; **27** 515
AGFA, **I** 310–11
Agfa-Ansco Corporation, **I** 337–38; **22** 225–27
Agfa-Gevaert, **III** 487; **18** 50, 184–86; **26** 540–41
Aggregate Industries plc, **36 20–22**
Agiba Petroleum, **IV** 414
Agilent Technologies Inc., **38 20–23**
Agip SpA, **IV** 419–21, 454, 466, 472–74, 498; **12** 153
Agiv AG, **39** 40–41
AGLP, **IV** 618
AGO, **III** 177, 179, 273, 310
Agor Manufacturing Co., **IV** 286
Agouron Pharmaceuticals, Inc., **38** 365
AGRAN, **IV** 505
AGRANA, **27** 436, 439
AgriBank FCB, **8** 489
Agribrands International, Inc., **40** 89
Agrico Chemical Company, **IV** 82, 84, 576; **7** 188; **31** 470
Agricole de Roquefort et Maria Grimal, **23** 219
Agricultural Insurance Co., **III** 191
Agricultural Minerals and Chemicals Inc., **IV** 84; **13** 504
Agrifan, **II** 355
Agrifull, **22** 380
Agrigenetics, Inc., **I** 361. *See also* Mycogen Corporation.
Agrippina Versicherungs AG, **III** 403, 412
Agrobios S.A., **23** 172
Agroferm Hungarian Japanese Fermentation Industry, **III** 43
Agromán S.A., **40** 218
AGTL. *See* Alberta Gas Trunk Line Company, Ltd.
Agua de la Falda S.A., **38** 231
Agua Pura Water Company, **24** 467
Aguila (Mexican Eagle) Oil Co. Ltd., **IV** 657
Agway, Inc., **7 17–18**; **21 17–19 (upd.)**; **36** 440
AHL Services, Inc., **26** 149; **27 20–23**
Ahmanson. *See* H.F. Ahmanson & Company.
AHMSA. *See* Altos Hornos de México, S.A. de C.V.
Ahold. *See* Koninklijke Ahold NV.
AHP. *See* American Home Products Corporation.
AHS. *See* American Hospital Supply Corporation.
AHSC Holdings Corp., **III** 9–10
Ahtna AGA Security, Inc., **14** 541
AI Automotive, **24** 204
AIC. *See* Allied Import Company.
AICA, **16** 421; **43** 308
Aichi Bank, **II** 373
Aichi Kogyo Co., **III** 415
Aichi Steel Works, **III** 637
Aid Auto, **18** 144
Aida Corporation, **11** 504
AIG. *See* American International Group, Inc.
AIGlobal, **III** 197
Aiken Stores, Inc., **14** 92
Aikenhead's Home Improvement Warehouse, **18** 240; **26** 306
Aikoku Sekiyu, **IV** 554
AIM Create Co., Ltd., **V** 127
Ainsworth National, **14** 528
Air & Water Technologies Corporation, **6 441–42**. *See also* Aqua Alliance Inc.
Air BP, **7** 141
Air Brasil, **6** 134; **29** 496
Air Canada, **6 60–62**; **23 9–12 (upd.)**; **29** 302; **36** 230
Air Compak, **12** 182
Air de Cologne, **27** 474
Air Express International Corporation, **13 19–20**; **40** 138
Air France, **I** 93–94, 104, 110, 120; **II** 163; **6** 69, 373; **8** 313; **12** 190; **24** 86; **27** 26; **33** 21, 50, 377. *See also* Groupe Air France *and* Societe Air France.
Air-India Limited, **6 63–64**; **27 24–26 (upd.)**; **41** 336–37
Air Inter. *See* Groupe Air France.
Air La Carte Inc., **13** 48
Air Lanka Catering Services Ltd., **6** 123–24; **27** 464
Air Liberté, **6** 208
Air London International, **36** 190
Air Micronesia, **I** 97; **21** 142
Air Midwest, Inc., **11** 299
Air New Zealand Limited, **14 10–12**; **24** 399–400; **27** 475; **38 24–27 (upd.)**
Air Nippon Co., Ltd., **6** 70
Air Pacific, **24** 396, 400
Air Products and Chemicals, Inc., **I 297–99**, 315, 358, 674; **10 31–33 (upd.)**; **11** 403; **14** 125
Air Russia, **24** 400
Air Southwest Co. *See* Southwest Airlines Co.
Air Spec, Inc., **III** 643
Airborne Accessories, **II** 81
Airborne Freight Corporation, **6 345–47** 345; **13** 19; **14** 517; **18** 177; **34 15–18 (upd.)**
Airbus Industrie, **6** 74; **7** 9–11, 504; **9** 418; **10** 164; **13** 356; **21** 8; **24** 84–89; **34** 128, 135. *See also* G.I.E. Airbus Industrie.
AirCal, **I** 91
Airco, **25** 81–82; **26** 94
Aircraft Marine Products, **II** 7; **14** 26
Aircraft Modular Products, **30** 73
Aircraft Services International, **I** 449
Aircraft Transport & Travel Ltd., **I** 92
Aircraft Turbine Center, Inc., **28** 3
Airex Corporation, **16** 337
Airguard Industries, Inc., **17** 104, 106
Airlease International, **II** 422
Airline Interiors Inc., **41** 368–69
Airlines of Britain Holdings, **34** 398; **38** 105–06
Airlink, **24** 396
Airmark Plastics Corp., **18** 497–98
Airmec-AEI Ltd., **II** 81
Airpax Electronics, Inc., **13** 398
Airport Ground Service Co., **I** 104, 106
Airshop Ltd., **25** 246
Airstream. *See* Thor Industries, Inc.
Airtel, **IV** 640
AirTouch Communications, **11 10–12**. *See also* Vodafone Group PLC.
Airtours Plc, **II** 164; **27 27–29**, 90, 92
AirTran Holdings, Inc., **22 21–23**; **28** 266; **33** 302; **34** 32
AirWair Ltd., **23** 399, 401–02
AirWays Corporation. *See* AirTran Holdings, Inc.
Airways Housing Trust Ltd., **I** 95
Airwick Industries, **II** 567
Aisin Seiki Co., Ltd., **III 415–16**; **14** 64
Aitken, Inc., **26** 433
AITS. *See* American International Travel Service.
Aiuruoca, **25** 85
Aiwa Co., Ltd., **28** 360; **30 18–20**
Ajax, **6** 349
Ajax Iron Works, **II** 16
Ajinomoto Co., Inc., **II 463–64**, 475; **III** 705; **28 9–11 (upd.)**
Ajman Cement, **III** 760
AJS Auto Parts Inc., **15** 246
AK Steel Holding Corporation, **19 8–9**; **41 3–6 (upd.)**
Akane Securities Co. Ltd., **II** 443
Akashic Memories, **11** 234
Akemi, **17** 310; **24** 160
Aker RGI, **32** 99
AKH Co. Inc., **20** 63
Akin, Gump, Strauss, Hauer & Feld, L.L.P., **18** 366; **33 23–25**
AKO Bank, **II** 378
Akorn, Inc., **32 22–24**
Akro-Mills Inc., **19** 277–78
Akron Brass Manufacturing Co., **9** 419
Akron Corp., **IV** 290
Akroyd & Smithers, **14** 419
Akseli Gallen-Kallela, **IV** 314
Aktiebolaget Aerotransport, **I** 119
Aktiebolaget Electrolux, **22 24–28 (upd.)**
Aktiebolaget SKF, **III 622–25**; **IV** 203; **38 28–33 (upd.)**
Aktiengesellschaft für Berg- und Hüttenbetriebe, **IV** 201
Aktiengesellschaft für Maschinenpapier-Zellstoff-Fabrikation, **IV** 323
Aktiv Placering A.B., **II** 352
Akzo Nobel N.V., **I** 674; **II** 572; **III** 44; **13 21–23**, 545; **14** 27; **15** 436; **16** 69, 462; **21** 466; **41 7–10 (upd.)**
Al Copeland Enterprises, Inc., **7** 26–28; **32** 13–15
Alaadin Middle East-Ersan, **IV** 564
Alabama Bancorp., **17** 152
Alabama Gas Corporation, **21** 207–08
Alabama Power Company, **38** 445, 447–48
Alabama Shipyards Inc., **21** 39–40
Alabaster Co., **III** 762
Aladdin Industries, **16** 487
Aladdin Mills Inc., **19** 276
Aladdin's Castle, **III** 430, 431
Alagasco, **21** 207–08
Alais et Camargue, **IV** 173
Alamac Knit Fabrics, Inc., **16** 533–34; **21** 192
Alamito Company, **6** 590
Alamo Engine Company, **8** 514
Alamo Group Inc., **32 25–28**
Alamo Rent A Car, Inc., **6 348–50**; **24 9–12 (upd.)**; **25** 93; **26** 409
Alania, **24** 88
ALANTEC Corporation, **25** 162
Alarm Device Manufacturing Company, **9** 413–15
Alaron Inc., **16** 357
Alascom, **6** 325–28; **26** 358
Alaska Air Group, Inc., **6 65–67**; **11** 50; **29 11–14 (upd.)**
Alaska Co., **III** 439
Alaska Commercial Company, **12** 363
Alaska Hydro-Train, **6** 382; **9** 510
Alaska Junk Co., **19** 380
Alaska Natural Gas Transportation System, **V** 673, 683

Alaska Pulp Co., **IV** 284, 297, 321
Alaska Steel Co., **19** 381
Alatas Mammoet, **26** 279
Alba Foods, **III** 619–20; **27** 197; **43** 218
Alba-Waldensian, Inc., **30 21–23**
Albany and Susquehanna Railroad, **II** 329
Albany Assurance Co., Ltd., **III** 293
Albany Cheese, **23** 219
Albany Felt Company. *See* Albany International Corp.
Albany International Corp., **8 12–14**
Albemarle Paper Co., **I** 334–35; **10** 289
Albers Brothers Milling Co., **II** 487
Albert E. Reed & Co. Ltd. *See* Reed International PLC.
The Albert Fisher Group plc, **41 11–13**
Albert Heijn NV, **II** 641–42; **38** 200, 202
Albert Nipon, Inc., **8** 323
Albert Willcox & Co., **14** 278
Alberta Distillers, **I** 377
Alberta Energy Company Ltd., **16 10–12**; **43 3–6 (upd.)**
Alberta Gas Trunk Line Company, Ltd., **V** 673–74
Alberta Sulphate Ltd., **IV** 165
Alberto-Culver Company, **II** 641–42; **8 15–17**; **36 23–27 (upd.)**
Albertson's Inc., **II 601–03**, 604–05, 637; **7 19–22 (upd.)**; **8** 474; **15** 178, 480; **16** 249; **18** 8; **22** 38; **27** 247, 290, 292; **30 24–28 (upd.)**; **33** 306; **40** 366
Albi Enterprises, **III** 24
Albion Industries, Inc., **16** 357
Albion Reid Proprietary, **III** 673
Albright & Friel, **I** 313; **10** 154
Albright & Wilson Ltd., **I** 527; **IV** 165; **12** 351; **16** 461; **38** 378, 380
Albuquerque Gas & Electric Company. *See* Public Service Company of New Mexico.
Albuquerque Gas, Electric Light and Power Company, **6** 561–62
Albury Brickworks, **III** 673
Alcan Aluminium Limited, **II** 415; **IV 9–13**, 14, 59, 154–55; **9** 512; **14** 35; **31 7–12 (upd.)**
Alcantara and Sores, **II** 582
Alcatel Alsthom Compagnie Générale d'Electricité, **II** 13, 69, 117; **6** 304; **7** 9; **9 9–11**, 32; **11** 59, 198; **15** 125; **17** 353; **18** 155; **19** 164, 166; **21** 233
Alcatel S.A., **36 28–31 (upd.)**; **42** 375–76
Alchem Capital Corp., **8** 141, 143
Alchem Plastics, **19** 414
Alco Capital Group, Inc., **27** 288
Alco Health Services Corporation, **III 9–10**. *See also* AmeriSource Health Corporation.
Alco Hydro-Aeroplane, **I** 64
Alco Office Products Inc., **24** 362
Alco Standard Corporation, **I 412–13**; **III** 9; **9** 261; **16** 473–74
ALCO Trade Show Services, **26** 102
Alcoa. *See* Aluminum Company of America.
Alcon Laboratories, **II** 547; **7** 382; **10** 46, 48; **30** 30–31
Alcudia, **IV** 528
Alden Merrell Corporation, **23** 169
Aldermac Mines Ltd., **IV** 164
Aldi Group, **11** 240; **13 24–26**; **17** 125
Aldine Press, **10** 34
Aldiscon, **37** 232
Aldrich Chemical Co., **I** 690
Aldus Corporation, **10 34–36**
Aldwarke Main & Car House Collieries, **I** 573
Alenia, **7** 9, 11
Alert Centre Inc., **32** 373
Alert Management Systems Inc., **12** 380
Alessio Tubi, **IV** 228
Alestra, **19** 12
Alex & Ivy, **10** 166–68
Alex Lee Inc., **18 6–9**
Alexander & Alexander Services Inc., **III** 280; **10 37–39**; **13** 476; **22** 318
Alexander & Baldwin, Inc., **I** 417; **10 40–42**; **24** 32; **29** 307; **40 14–19 (upd.)**
Alexander and Lord, **13** 482
Alexander Grant & Co., **I** 481, 656
Alexander Hamilton Life Insurance Co., **II** 420; **29** 256
Alexander Howden Group, **III** 280; **10** 38–39; **22** 318
Alexander Martin Co., **I** 374
Alexander-Schroder Lumber Company, **18** 514
Alexander Smith, Inc., **19** 275
Alexander's Inc., **10** 282; **12** 221; **26** 111
Alexis Lichine, **III** 43
Alfa-Laval AB, **III 417–21**; **IV** 203; **8** 376
Alfa Romeo, **I** 163, 167; **11** 102, 104, 139, 205; **13 27–29**, 218–19; **36 32–35 (upd.)**, 196–97
Alfa, S.A. de C.V., **II** 262; **11** 386; **19 10–12**; **37** 176
Alfa Trading Company, **23** 358
Alfalfa's Markets, **19** 500–02
Alfinal, **III** 420
Alfred A. Knopf, Inc., **13** 428, 429; **31** 376–79
Alfred Bullows & Sons, Ltd., **21** 64
Alfred Dunhill Limited, **19** 369; **27** 487–89
Alfred Hickman Ltd., **III** 751
Alfred Marks Bureau, Ltd., **6** 9–10
Alfred Nobel & Co., **III** 693
Alfred Teves, **I** 193
Alfried Krupp von Bohlen und Halbach Foundation, **IV** 89
ALG. *See* Arkla, Inc.
Alga, **24** 83
Algemeen Burgerlijk Pensioenfonds, **26** 421
Algemeene Bankvereeniging en Volksbank van Leuven, **II** 304
Algemeene Friesche, **III** 177–79
N.V. Algemeene Maatschappij tot Exploitatie van Verzekeringsmaatschappijen, **III** 199
Algemeene Maatschappij van Levensverzekering en Lijfrente, **III** 178
Algemeene Maatschappij voor Nijverheidskrediet, **II** 304–05
Algemeene Nederlandsche Maatschappij ter begunstiging van de Volksvlijt, **II** 294
Algemene Bank Nederland N.V., **II 183–84**, 185, 239, 527; **III** 200
Algo Group Inc., **24 13–15**
Algoma Steel Corp., **IV** 74; **8** 544–45; **24** 143
Algonquin Energy, Inc., **6** 487
Algonquin Gas Transmission Company, **6** 486; **14** 124–26
ALI. *See* Aeronautics Leasing, Inc.
Alidata, **6** 69
Aligro Inc., **II** 664
Alimenta (USA), Inc., **17** 207
Alimentana S.A., **II** 547
Alimondo, **17** 505
Alitalia–Linee Aeree Italiana, S.p.A., **I** 110, 466–67; **6** 96, **68–69**; **24** 311; **29 15–17 (upd.)**
Alken, **II** 474
Oy Alkoholiliike Ab, **IV** 469
Alkor-Oerlikon Plastic GmbH, **7** 141
All American Airways. *See* USAir Group, Inc.
All American Communications Inc., **20 3–7**; **25** 138
All American Gourmet Co., **12** 178, 199
All American Sports Co., **22** 458–59
All British Escarpment Company LTD, **25** 430
All-Clad Metalcrafters Inc., **34** 493, 496–97
All Nippon Airways Co., Ltd., **I** 106, 493; **6 70–71** 118, 427; **16** 168; **24** 326; **33** 50–51; **38 34–37 (upd.)**
All Seasons Vehicles, Inc. *See* ASV, Inc.
All Woods, Inc., **18** 514
Allami Biztosito, **III** 209; **15** 30
Allcom, **16** 392
Allders plc, **37 6–8**
Alleanza & Unione Mediterranea, **III** 208
Alleanza-Securitas-Esperia, **III** 208
Alleghany Corporation, **II** 398; **IV** 180–81; **10 43–45**; **19** 319; **22** 494
Allegheny Airlines. *See* USAir Group, Inc. *and* US Airways Group, Inc.
Allegheny Beverage Corp., **7** 472–73
Allegheny County Light Company, **6** 483–84
Allegheny Energy, Inc., **38 38–41 (upd.)**
Allegheny International, Inc., **III** 732; **8** 545; **9** 484; **22** 3, 436
Allegheny Ludlum Corporation, **I** 307; **II** 402; **8 18–20**; **9** 484; **21** 489
Allegheny Power System, Inc., **V 543–45**
Allegheny Steel and Iron Company, **9** 484
Allegiance Life Insurance Company, **22** 268
Allegis, Inc. *See* United Airlines.
Allegmeine Transpotmittel Aktiengesellschaft, **6** 394; **25** 169
Allegretti & Co., **22** 26
Allen & Co., **I** 512, 701; **II** 136; **12** 496; **13** 366; **25** 270
Allen & Ginter, **12** 108
Allen & Hanbury's, **I** 640
Allen-Bradley Co., **I** 80; **II** 110; **III** 593; **11** 429–30; **17** 478; **22** 373; **23** 211
Allen-Liversidge Ltd., **I** 315; **25** 80
Allen Organ Company, **33 26–29**
Allen Tank Ltd., **21** 499
Allen's Convenience Stores, Inc., **17** 170
Allergan, Inc., **10 46–49**; **23** 196; **30 29–33 (upd.)**
Allforms Packaging Corp., **13** 442
Allgemeine Deutsche Creditanstalt, **II** 211, 238, 383; **12** 536
Allgemeine Eisenbahn-Versicherungs-Gesellschaft, **III** 399
Allgemeine Elektricitäts-Gesellschaft. *See* AEG A.G.
Allgemeine Handelsgesellschaft der Verbraucher AG. *See* AVA AG.
Allgemeine Rentenstalt Lebens- und Rentenversicherung, **II** 258
Allgemeine Schweizerische Uhrenindustrie, **26** 480

Allgemeine Versicherungs-Gesellschaft Helvetia, **III** 375
Alliance Agro-Alimentaires S.A., **II** 577
Alliance Amusement Company, **10** 319
Alliance Assurance Co., **III** 369–73
Alliance Atlantis Communications Inc., **35** 69; **39 11–14**
Alliance Brothers, **V** 356
Alliance Capital Management Corp., **22** 189
Alliance Entertainment Corp., **17 12–14**; **35** 430
Alliance Gaming Corp., **15** 539; **24** 36
Alliance Insurance Co., **III** 224
Alliance Manufacturing Co., **13** 397
Alliance Marine, **III** 373
Alliance Mortgage Co., **I** 610
Alliance Packaging, **13** 443
Alliance Paper Group, **IV** 316
Alliance Tire and Rubber Co., **II** 47; **25** 267
AllianceWare, Inc., **16** 321
Alliant Energy Corp., **39** 261
Alliant Techsystems Inc., **8 21–23**; **30 34–37 (upd.)**
Allianz AG Holding, **I** 411, 426; **II** 239, 257, 279–80; **III 183–86**, 200, 250, 252, 299–301, 347–48, 373, 377, 393; **IV** 222; **14** 169–70; **15 10–14 (upd.)**
Allibert, **III** 614
Allied Bakeries Ltd., **II** 465–66; **13** 52–53
Allied Breweries Ltd., **I** 215; **III** 105; **IV** 712
Allied Chemical, **I** 310, 332, 351–52; **8** 526; **9** 521–22; **13** 76; **22** 5. *See also* General Chemical Corp.
Allied Chemical & Dye Corp., **I** 414; **7** 262; **9** 154; **22** 29
Allied Color Industries, **8** 347
Allied Communications Group, **18** 77; **22** 297
Allied Construction Products, **17** 384
Allied Container Corp., **IV** 345
Allied Corporation, **I** 68, 141, 143, 414, 534; **III** 118, 511; **6** 599; **7** 356; **9** 134; **11** 435; **24** 164; **25** 224; **31** 135. *See also* AlliedSignal Inc.
Allied Crude Vegetable Oil Refining Co., **II** 398; **10** 62
Allied Distributing Co., **12** 106
Allied Domecq PLC, **24** 220; **29 18–20**, 85
Allied Dunbar, **I** 427
Allied Engineering Co., **8** 177
Allied Fibers, **19** 275
Allied Food Markets, **II** 662
Allied Gas Company, **6** 529
Allied Grape Growers, **I** 261
Allied Health and Scientific Products Company, **8** 215
Allied Healthcare Products, Inc., **24 16–19**
Allied Holdings, Inc., **24** 411
Allied Import Company, **V** 96
Allied Irish Banks, plc, **16 13–15**; **43 7–10 (upd.)**
Allied Leisure, **40** 296–98
Allied-Lyons plc, **I 215–16**, 258, 264, 438; **IV** 721; **9** 100, 391; **10** 170; **13** 258; **21** 228, 323; **29** 18, 84
Allied Maintenance Corp., **I** 514
Allied Mills, Inc., **10** 249; **13** 186; **43** 121
Allied Oil Co., **IV** 373
Allied Overseas Trading Ltd., **I** 216
Allied Plywood Corporation, **12** 397
Allied Polymer Group, **I** 429
Allied Products Corporation, **21 20–22**
Allied Radio, **19** 310
Allied Safety, Inc., **V** 215
Allied Shoe Corp., **22** 213
Allied-Signal Corp., **I** 85, 141, 143, **414–16**; **III** 511–12; **V** 605; **6** 599–600; **9** 519; **11** 435, 444; **13** 227; **16** 436; **17** 20; **21** 200, 396–97; **40** 35; **43** 320
Allied Signal Engines, **9 12–15**
Allied Steel and Conveyors, **18** 493
Allied Steel and Wire Ltd., **III** 495
Allied Stores Corporation, **II** 350, 611–12; **V** 25–28; **9** 211; **10** 282; **13** 43; **15** 94, 274; **16** 60; **22** 110; **23** 59–60; **25** 249; **31** 192; **37**
Allied Structural Steel Company, **10** 44
Allied Supermarkets, Inc., **7** 570; **28** 511
Allied Suppliers, **II** 609
Allied Telephone Company. *See* Alltel Corporation.
Allied Tin Box Makers Ltd., **I** 604
Allied Towers Merchants Ltd., **II** 649
Allied Van Lines Inc., **6** 412, 414; **14** 37
Allied Vintners, **I** 215
AlliedSignal Inc., **22 29–32 (upd.)**; **29** 408; **31** 154; **37** 158
Allis Chalmers Corporation, **I** 163; **II** 98, 121; **III** 543–44; **9** 17; **11** 104; **12** 545; **13** 16–17, 563; **14** 446; **21** 502–03; **22** 380
Allis-Gleaner Corp. *See* AGCO Corp.
Allison Engine Company, **21** 436
Allison Engineering Company. *See* Rolls-Royce Allison.
Allison Gas Turbine Division, **9 16–19**, 417; **10** 537; **11** 473
Allmanna Svenska Elektriska Aktiebolaget. *See* ABB ASEA Brown Boveri Ltd.
Allmänna Telefonaktiebolaget L.M. Ericsson, **V** 334
Allnatt London & Guildhall Properties, **IV** 724
Allnet, **10** 19
Allo Pro, **III** 633
Allor Leasing Corp., **9** 323
Allou Health & Beauty Care, Inc., **28 12–14**
Alloy & Stainless, Inc., **IV** 228
Alloys Unlimited, **II** 82
Allserve Inc., **25** 367
Allsport plc., **31** 216, 218
The Allstate Corporation, **I** 23; **III** 231–32, 259, 294; **V** 180, 182; **6** 12; **10 50–52**; **13** 539; **18** 475; **21** 96–97; **22** 495; **23** 286–87; **25** 155; **27 30–33 (upd.)**; **29** 397
Alltel Corporation, **6 299–301**; **16** 318; **20** 440
Alltrans Group, **27** 472
Alltrista Corporation, **30 38–41**
Allwaste, Inc., **18 10–13**
Almac Electronics Corporation, **10** 113
Almac's Inc., **17** 558–59
Almacenes de Baja y Media, **39** 201, 204
Almaden Vineyards, **I** 377–78; **13** 134; **34** 89
Almanij. *See* Algemeene Maatschappij voor Nijverheidskrediet.
Almay, Inc., **III** 54
Almeida Banking House. *See* Banco Bradesco S.A.
Almours Security Co., **IV** 311; **19** 266
Almys, **24** 461
Aloe Vera of America, **17** 187
Aloha Airlines, Incorporated, **I** 97; **9** 271–72; **21** 142; **22** 251; **24 20–22**
Alp Sport Sandals, **22** 173
Alpen-Elektrowerke Aktiengesellschaft, **IV** 230
Alpex Computer Corp., **III** 157
Alpex, S.A. de C.V., **19** 12
Alpha Beta Co., **II** 605, 625, 653; **17** 559
Alpha Engineering Group, Inc., **16** 259–60
Alpha Healthcare Ltd., **25** 455
Alpha Processor Inc., **41** 349
Alpha Technical Systems, **19** 279
Alphaform, **40** 214–15
Alphanumeric Publication Systems, Inc., **26** 518
Alpharma Inc., **35 22–26 (upd.)**
Alphonse Allard Inc., **II** 652
Alpina Versicherungs-Aktiengesellschaft, **III** 412
Alpine, **IV** 234
Alpine Electronics, Inc., **II** 5; **13 30–31**
Alpine Lace Brands, Inc., **18 14–16**
Alpine Securities Corporation, **22** 5
Alpre, **19** 192
Alps Electric Co., Ltd., **II 5–6**; **13** 30
Alric Packing, **II** 466
Alsen-Breitenbury, **III** 702
ALSO Holding AG, **29** 419, 422
Alsons Corp., **III** 571; **20** 362
Alsthom, **II** 12
Alsthom-Atlantique, **9** 9
Alta Dena, **25** 83, 85
Alta Electric Company, **25** 15
Alta Gold Co., **IV** 76
ALTA Health Strategies, Inc., **11** 113
Alta Holidays Ltd., **I** 95
Altamil Corp., **IV** 137
Altana AG, **23** 498
AltaVista Company, **43 11–13**
Alte Leipziger, **III** 242
Altec Electronics, **I** 489–90
ALTEC International, **21** 107–09
Altenburg & Gooding, **22** 428
Altera Corporation, **18 17–20**; **43 14–18 (upd.)**
Alternate Postal Delivery, **6** 14
Alternative Living Services. *See* Alterra Healthcare Corporation.
Alternative Youth Services, Inc., **29** 399–400
Alterra Healthcare Corporation, **42 3–5**
Altex, **19** 192–93
Althoff KG, **V** 101
Althouse Chemical Company, **9** 153
Althus Corp, **I** 361
Altman Weil Pensa, **29** 237
Alton & Eastern Railroad Company, **6** 504
Alton Box Board Co., **IV** 295; **19** 225
Altos Computer Systems, **6** 279; **10** 362
Altos Hornos de México, S.A. de C.V., **13** 144; **19** 220; **39** 188; **42 6–8**
Altron Incorporated, **20 8–10**
Altura Energy Ltd., **41** 359
Aluar. *See* Aluminios Argentinos.
Aluma Systems Corp., **9** 512; **22** 14
Alumax Inc., **I** 508; **III** 758; **IV** 18–19; **8** 505–06; **22** 286
Alumina Partners of Jamaica, **IV** 123
Aluminate Sales Corp, **I** 373
Aluminio de Galicia, **IV** 174
Aluminios Argentinos, **26** 433
Aluminium Co. of London, **IV** 69

L'Aluminium Francais, **IV** 173
Aluminium Ltd., **IV** 9–11, 14, 153
Aluminium-Oxid Stade GmbH, **IV** 231
Aluminium Plant and Vessel Co., **III** 419
Aluminum Can Co., **I** 607
Aluminum Company of America, **I** 373, 599; **II** 315, 402, 422; **III** 490–91, 613; **IV** 9–12, **14–16**, 56, 59, 121–22, 131, 173, 703; **6** 39; **12** 346; **19** 240, 292; **20 11–14 (upd.)**; **22** 455; **42** 438
Aluminum Company of Canada Ltd., **II** 345; **IV** 10–12, 154
Aluminum Cooking Utensil Co., **IV** 14
Aluminum Forge Co., **IV** 137
Aluminum Norf GmbH, **IV** 231
Aluminum of Korea, **III** 516
Aluminum Rolling Mills, **17** 280
Aluminum Sales Corporation, **12** 346
Aluminum Seating Corp., **I** 201
Alun Cathcart, **6** 357
Alup-Kompressoren Pressorun, **III** 570; **20** 361
Alupak, A.G., **12** 377
Alusaf, **IV** 92
Alusuisse Lonza Group Ltd., **IV** 12; **31** 11
Alva Jams Pty., **I** 437
Alvic Group, **20** 363
Alyeska Pipeline Service Co., **IV** 522, 571; **14** 542; **24** 521; **40** 356
Alyeska Seafoods Co., **II** 578
ALZA Corporation, **10 53–55**; **36 36–39 (upd.)**; **40** 11; **41** 200–01
Alzwerke GmbH, **IV** 230
AM Acquisition Inc., **8** 559–60
AM Cosmetics, Inc., **31** 89
Am-Par Records, **II** 129
Am-Safe, Inc., **16** 357
AM-TEX Corp., Inc., **12** 443
Amagasaki Co., **I** 492; **24** 325
Amagasaki Spinners Ltd., **V** 387
Amagasaki Steel Co., Ltd., **IV** 130
Amalgamaize Co., **14** 18
Amalgamated Chemicals, Ltd., **IV** 401
Amalgamated Dental International, **10** 271–72
Amalgamated Distilled Products, **II** 609
Amalgamated Press, **IV** 666; **7** 244, 342; **17** 397
Amalgamated Roadstone Corp., **III** 752; **28** 449
Amalgamated Sugar Co., **14** 18; **19** 467–68
Amalgamated Weatherware, **IV** 696
Amana Refrigeration Company, **II** 86; **11** 413; **18** 226; **38** 374; **42** 159
Amaray International Corporation, **12** 264
Amarillo Gas Company. *See* Atmos Energy Corporation.
Amarillo Railcar Services, **6** 580
Amarin Plastics, **IV** 290
Amax Gold, **36** 316
AMAX Inc., **I** 508; **III** 687; **IV 17–19**, 46, 139, 171, 239, 387; **6** 148; **12** 244; **22** 106, 286
Amazon.com, Inc., **25 17–19**
Amazôna Mineracao SA, **IV** 56
Ambac Industries, **I** 85
AmBase Corp., **III** 264
Amber's Stores, Inc., **17** 360
Amblin Entertainment, **21 23–27**; **33** 431
Ambrose Shardlow, **III** 494
AMC Entertainment Inc., **12 12–14**; **14** 87; **21** 362; **23** 126; **35 27–29 (upd.)**
AMCA International Corporation, **7** 513; **8** 545; **10** 329; **23** 299
AMCC. *See* Applied Micro Circuits Corporation.
Amcell. *See* American Cellular Network.
Amchem Products Inc., **I** 666
AMCO, Inc., **13** 159
Amcor Limited, **IV 248–50**; **19 13–16 (upd.)**
Amcraft Building Products Co., Inc., **22** 15
AMD. *See* Advanced Micro Devices, Inc.
Amdahl Corporation, **III 109–11**, 140; **6** 272; **12** 238; **13** 202; **14 13–16 (upd.)**; **16** 194, 225–26; **22** 293; **25** 87; **40 20–25 (upd.)**; **42** 147. *See also* Fujitsu Limited.
AME Finanziaria, **IV** 587; **19** 19
AMEC plc, **I** 568; **36** 322
Amedco, **6** 295
Amer Group plc, **24** 530; **41 14–16**
Amer Sport, **22** 202
Amerada Hess Corporation, **IV 365–67**, 400, 454, 522, 571, 658; **11** 353; **21 28–31 (upd.)**; **24** 521
Amerco, **6 351–52**
Ameri-Kart Corp., **19** 277, 279
America Japan Sheet Glass Co., **III** 714
America Latina Companhia de Seguros, **III** 289
America Online, Inc., **10 56–58**, 237; **13** 147; **15** 54, 265, 321; **18** 24; **19** 41; **22** 52, 519, 522; **26 16–20 (upd.)**; **27** 20, 106, 301, 430, 517–18; **29** 143, 227; **32** 163; **33** 254; **34** 361; **35** 304, 306; **38** 269–71. *See also* CompuServe Interactive Services, Inc.
America Publishing Company, **18** 213
America Today, **13** 545
America Unplugged, **18** 77
America West Airlines, **6 72–74**, 121
America West Express, **32** 334
America West Holdings Corporation, **34 22–26 (upd.)**
America's Favorite Chicken Company, Inc., **7 26–28**. *See also* AFC Enterprises, Inc.
American & Efird, Inc., **12** 501; **23** 260
American Agricultural Chemical Co., **IV** 401
American Air Conditioning, **25** 15
American Air Filter, **26** 3–4
American Airlines, **I** 30–31, 48, 71, **89–91**, 97, 106, 115, 118, 124–26, 130, 132, 512, 530; **III** 102; **6** 60, 81, **75–77 (upd.)**, 121, 129–31; **9** 271–72; **10** 163; **11** 279; **12** 190, 192, 379, 381, 487, **13** 173; **14** 73; **16** 146; **18** 73; **21** 141, 143; **24** 21, 399–400; **25** 90–91, 403, 421–22; **26** 427–28, 441; **31** 103, 306; **33** 270, 302; **34** 118; **38** 105. *See also* AMR Corporation.
American Alliance Co., **III** 191
American Allsafe Co., **8** 386
American Amusements, Inc., **III** 430
American Appliance Co., **II** 85; **11** 411
American Arithmometer Company. *See* Burroughs Corporation.
American Asiatic Underwriters, **III** 195
American Association of Retired Persons, **9** 348. *See also* AARP.
American Automar Inc., **12** 29
American Automated, **11** 111
American Automobile Insurance Co., **III** 251
American Aviation and General Insurance Co., **III** 230
American Aviation Manufacturing Corp., **15** 246
American Avitron Inc, **I** 481
American Bakeries Company, **12** 275–76
American Bancorp, **11** 295
American Bancshares, Inc., **11** 457
American Bank, **9** 474–75
American Bank Note, **IV** 599
American Bank of Vicksburg, **14** 41
American Bankcorp, Inc., **8** 188
American Banker/Bond Buyer, **8** 526
American Banknote Corporation, **30 42–45**
American Bar Association, **35 30–33**
American Barge and Towing Company, **11** 194
American Beauty Cover Company, **12** 472
American Beef Packers, Inc., **16** 473
American Beet Sugar Company, **11** 13–14
American Bell Telephone Company, **V** 259; **14** 336
American Beryllium Co., Inc., **9** 323
American Beverage Corp., **II** 528
American Biltrite Inc., **16 16–18**; **18** 116, 118; **43 19–22 (upd.)**
American Biodyne Inc., **9** 348
American Biomedical Corporation, **11** 333
American Biscuit Co., **II** 542
American Box Board Company, **12** 376
American Box Co., **IV** 137
American Brake Shoe and Foundry Company, **I** 456. *See also* ABC Rail Products Corporation.
American Brands, Inc., **II** 468, 477; **IV** 251; **V 395–97**, 398–99, 405; **7** 3–4; **9** 408; **12** 87, 344; **14** 95, 271–72; **16** 108, 110, 242; **19** 168–69; **38** 169. *See also* Fortune Brands, Inc.
American Bridge Co., **II** 330; **IV** 572; **7** 549
American Broadcasting Co., **25** 418. *See also* ABC, Inc. *and* Capital Cities/ABC Inc.
American Builders & Contractors Supply Co. *See* ABC Supply Co., Inc.
American Builders, Inc., **8** 436
American Building Maintenance Industries, Inc., **6 17–19**. *See also* ABM Industries Incorporated.
American Bus Lines Inc., **24** 118
American Business Information, Inc., **18 21–25**
American Business Interiors. *See* American Furniture Company, Inc.
American Business Products, Inc., **20 15–17**
American Cable Systems, Inc. *See* Comcast Corporation.
American Cablesystems, **7** 99
American Cafe, **I** 547
American Can Co., **IV** 36, 290; **8** 476; **10** 130; **11** 29, 197; **12** 408; **13** 255; **15** 127–28; **17** 106; **22** 210; **23** 98. *See also* Primerica Corp.
The American Cancer Society, **24 23–25**
American Capital and Research Corp., **28** 201
American Car & Foundry Inc., **21** 503
American Carbide Corporation, **7** 584
American Cash Register Co., **III** 150; **6** 264
American Casualty Co., **III** 230–31, 404

American Casualty Co. of Dallas, **III** 203
American Cellular Network, **7** 91; **24** 122
American Cellulose and Chemical Manufacturing Co., **I** 317
American Cement Co. *See* Giant Cement Holding, Inc.
American Central Insurance Co., **III** 241
American Cereal Co., **II** 558; **12** 409
American Chicle Co., **I** 711; **21** 54; **38** 363–64
American Chocolate & Citrus Co., **IV** 409
American Chrome, **III** 699
American Classic Voyages Company, **22** 340, **27 34–37**
American Clay Forming Company, **8** 178
American Clip Company, **7** 3
American Coin Merchandising, Inc., **28 15–17**
American Colloid Co., **13 32–35**
American Commercial Bank, **II** 336
American Commercial Lines Inc., **22** 164, 166–67
American Commonwealths Power Corporation, **6** 579
American Community Grocers, **II** 670
American Computer Systems. *See* American Software Inc.
American Construction Lending Services, Inc., **39** 380, 382
American Continental Insurance Co., **III** 191–92
American Cotton Cooperative Association, **17** 207; **33** 85
American Cotton Oil Co., **II** 497
American Council on Education, **12** 141
American Courier Express, Inc., **24** 126
American Crayon Company, **12** 115
American Credit Corporation, **II** 236; **20** 59
American Crystal Sugar Company, **7** 377; **11 13–15**; **32 29–33 (upd.)**
American Cyanamid, **I 300–02**, 619; **III** 22; **IV** 345, 552; **8 24–26 (upd.)**; **10** 269; **11** 494; **13** 231–32; **14** 254, 256; **16** 68; **22** 147; **27** 115–16
American Dairy Queen Corporation, **10** 373
American Data Technology, Inc., **11** 111
American Digital Communications, Inc., **33** 329
American Distilling Co., **I** 226; **10** 180–81
American District Telegraph Co., **III** 644; **12** 9
American Diversified Foods, Inc., **14** 351
American Drew, Inc., **12** 301
American Drug Company, **13** 367
American Eagle Airlines, Inc., **28** 22
American Eagle Fire Insurance Co., **III** 240–41
American Eagle Outfitters, Inc., **14** 427; **24 26–28**; **25** 121
American Education Press, **10** 479
American Electric Company, **II** 27; **12** 193; **22** 10
American Electric Power Company, **II** 3; **IV** 181; **V 546–49**; **6** 449, 524; **11** 516
American Empire Insurance Co., **III** 191
American Emulsions Co., **8** 455
American Encaustic Tiling Co., **22** 170
American Energy Management Inc., **39** 261
American Envelope Co., **III** 40; **16** 303; **28** 251; **43** 257
American Equipment Co., **I** 571
American Export Steamship Lines, **I** 89
American Express Company, **I** 26–27, 480, 614; **II** 108, 176, 309, 380–82, **395–99**, 450–52, 544; **III** 251–52, 319, 340, 389; **IV** 637, 721; **6** 206–07, 409; **8** 118; **9** 335, 343, 391, 468–69, 538; **10** 44–45, **59–64 (upd.)**; **11** 41, 416–17, 532; **12** 533; **14** 106; **15** 50; **18** 60, 112, 516, 543; **21** 97, 127; **23** 229; **26** 516; **33** 394–96; **38 42–48 (upd.)**
American Factors, Ltd. *See* Amfac/JMB Hawaii L.L.C.
American Family Corporation, **III 187–89**. *See also* AFLAC Inc.
American Family Life Insurance Company, **33** 407
American Family Publishers, **23** 393–94
American Feldmühle Corp., **II** 51; **21** 330
American Filtrona Corp., **IV** 260–61
American Finance Systems, **II** 349
American Financial Corporation, **II** 596; **III 190–92**, 221; **8** 537; **9** 452; **18** 549
American Fine Wire, Inc., **33** 248
American First National Supermarkets, **16** 313
American Fitness Centers, **25** 40
American Flange, **30** 397
American Flavor & Fragrance Company, **9** 154
American Flyer Trains, **16** 336–37
American Food Management, **6** 45
American Foods Group, **43 23–27**
American Football League, **29** 346
American Fore Group, **III** 241–42
American Foreign Insurance Association, **III** 223, 226. *See also* AFIA.
American Forest Products Co., **IV** 282; **9** 260
American Freightways Corporation, **42** 141
American Fructose Corp., **14** 18–19
American Fur Company, **25** 220
American Furniture Company, Inc., **12** 300; **21 32–34**
American Gage Co., **I** 472
American Gaming and Electronics, Inc., **43** 461
American Gas & Electric. *See* American Electric Power Company.
American Gasoline Co., **IV** 540
American General Capital Corp., **I** 614
American General Corporation, **III 193–94**; **10 65–67 (upd.)**; **11** 16
American General Finance Corp., **11 16–17**
American General Life Insurance Company, **6** 294
American Graphics, **23** 100
American Greetings Corporation, **7 23–25**; **12** 207–08; **15** 507; **16** 256; **21** 426–28; **22 33–36 (upd.)**
American Grinder and Manufacturing Company, **9** 26
American Hardware & Supply Company. *See* TruServ Corporation.
American Harvester, **II** 262
American Hawaii Cruises, **27** 34
American Health & Life Insurance Company, **27** 47
American Heritage Savings, **II** 420
American Hoechst Corporation. *See* Hoechst Celanese Corporation.
American Hoist & Derrick Co., **8** 544
American Home Assurance Co., **III** 196–97
American Home Assurance Co. of New York, **III** 203
American Home Products, **I** 527, **622–24**, 631, 676–77, 696, 700; **III** 18, 36, 444; **8** 282–83; **10 68–70 (upd.)**, 528; **11** 35; **15** 64–65; **16** 191, 438; **21** 466; **24** 288; **25** 477; **36** 87; **38** 365
American Home Publishing Co., Inc., **14** 460
American Home Shield, **6** 46; **23** 428, 430
American Home Video, **9** 186
American Homestar Corporation, **18 26–29**; **41 17–20 (upd.)**
American Homeware Inc., **15** 501
American Honda Motor Co., **I** 174; **10** 352
American Hospital Association, **10** 159
American Hospital Supply Co., **I** 627, 629; **III** 80; **10** 141–43; **11** 459, 486; **19** 103; **21** 118; **30** 496
American Hydron, **13** 366; **25** 55
American I.G. Chemical Corporation. *See* GAF Corporation.
American Impacts Corporation, **8** 464
American Improved Cements. *See* Giant Cement Holding, Inc.
American Independent Oil Co., **IV** 522, 537. *See also* Aminoil, Inc.
American Industrial Manufacturing Co., **I** 481
American Information Services, Inc., **11** 111
American Institutional Products, Inc., **18** 246
American Instrument Co., **I** 628; **13** 233
American Insurance Agency, **III** 191, 352
American Insurance Co., **III** 251
American International Airways, Inc., **17** 318; **22** 311
American International Group, Inc., **II** 422; **III 195–98**, 200; **6** 349; **10** 39; **11** 532–33; **15 15–19 (upd.)**; **18** 159
American International Travel Service, **6** 367; **27** 90
American Iron and Steel Manufacturing Co., **IV** 35; **7** 48
American Isuzu Motors, Inc. *See* Isuzu Motors, Ltd.
American Italian Pasta Company, **27 38–40**
American Janitor Service, **25** 15
American Jet Industries, **7** 205
American Ka-Ro, **8** 476
American Knitting Mills of Miami, Inc., **22** 213
American La-France, **10** 296
American Laboratories, **III** 73
American Land Cruiser Company. *See* Cruise America Inc.
American Lawyer Media Holdings, Inc., **32 34–37**
American Learning Corporation, **7** 168
American Life Insurance Co., **III** 195–96
American Light and Traction. *See* MCN Corporation.
American Lightwave Systems, Inc., **10** 19
American Limestone Co., **IV** 33
American Limousine Corp., **26** 62
American Linseed Co, **II** 497
American Locker Group Incorporated, **34 19–21**
American Machine and Foundry Co., **II** 7; **III** 443; **7** 211–13; **11** 397; **25** 197
American Machine and Metals, **9** 23
American Machinist Press, **IV** 634

American Magnesium Products Co., **I** 404
American Maize-Products Co., 14 17–20; 23 464
American Management Systems, Inc., 11 18–20
American Manufacturers Mutual Insurance Co., **III** 269, 271; **15** 257
American-Marietta Corp., **I** 68, 405
American Materials & Technologies Corporation, **27** 117
American Media, Inc., 27 41–44
American Medical Association, 39 15–18
American Medical International, Inc., III 73–75, 79; **14** 232
American Medical Optics, **25** 55
American Medical Response, Inc., 39 19–22
American Medical Services, **II** 679–80; **14** 209
American Medicorp, Inc., **III** 81; **6** 191; **14** 432; **24** 230
American Melamine, **27** 317
American Merchandising Associates Inc., **14** 411
American Merchants Union Express Co., **II** 396
American Metal Climax, Inc. *See* AMAX.
American Metal Co. Ltd. *See* AMAX.
American Metal Products Company. *See* Lear Seating Corporation.
American Metal Products Corp., **I** 481
American Metals and Alloys, Inc., **19** 432
American Metals Corp., **III** 569; **20** 361
American Micro Devices, Inc., **16** 549
American Microsystems, **I** 193
American Milk Products Corp., **II** 487
The American Mineral Spirits Company, **8** 99–100
American Motorists Insurance Co., **III** 269, 271; **15** 257
American Motors Corp., I 135–37, 145, 152, 190; **II** 60, 313; **III** 543; **6** 27, 50; **8** 373; **10** 262, 264; **18** 493; **26** 403
American Movie Classics Co., **II** 161
American Multi-Cinema. *See* AMC Entertainment Inc.
American National Bank, **13** 221–22
American National Bank and Trust Co., **II** 286
American National Can Co., **III** 536; **IV** 173, 175; **26** 230
American National Corp., **II** 286
American National Fire Insurance Co., **III** 191
American National General Agencies Inc., **III** 221; **14** 109; **37** 85
American National Insurance Company, 8 27–29; 27 45–48 (upd.); 39 158
American Natural Resources Co., **I** 678; **IV** 395; **13** 416
American Natural Snacks Inc., **29** 480
American Newspaper Publishers Association, **6** 13
American of Philadelphia, **III** 234
American Oil Co., **IV** 369–70; **7** 101; **14** 22
American Olean Tile Company, **III** 424; **22** 48, 170
American Optical Co., **I** 711–12; **III** 607; **7** 436; **38** 363–64
American Overseas Airlines, **12** 380
American Overseas Holdings, **III** 350
American Pad & Paper Company, 20 18–21
American Paging, **9** 494–96
American-Palestine Trading Corp., **II** 205–06
American Paper Box Company, **12** 376
American Patriot Insurance, **22** 15
American Payment Systems, Inc., **21** 514
American Petrofina, Inc., **IV** 498; **7** 179–80; **19** 11
American Pfauter, **24** 186
American Phone Centers, Inc., **21** 135
American Photographic Group, **III** 475; **7** 161
American Physicians Service Group, Inc., **6** 45; **23** 430
American Platinum Works, **IV** 78
American Postage Meter Co., **III** 156
American Potash and Chemical Corporation, **IV** 95, 446; **22** 302
American Power & Light Co., **6** 545, 596–97; **12** 542
American Power Conversion Corporation, 24 29–31
American Premier Underwriters, Inc., 10 71–74
American Prepaid Professional Services, Inc. *See* CompDent Corporation.
American President Companies Ltd., III 512; **6 353–55**
American Printing House for the Blind, 26 13–15
American Protective Mutual Insurance Co. Against Burglary, **III** 230
American Public Automotive Group, **37** 115
American Publishing Co., **IV** 597; **24** 222
American Pure Oil Co., **IV** 497
American Radiator & Standard Sanitary Corp., **III** 663–64
American Railway Express Co., **II** 382, 397; **10** 61
American Railway Publishing Co., **IV** 634
American Re Corporation, III 182; **10 75–77; 35 34–37 (upd.)**
American Record Corp., **II** 132
American Recreation Company Holdings, Inc., **16** 53
American Red Cross, 40 26–29
American Ref-Fuel, **V** 751
American Refrigeration Products S.A, **7** 429
American Republic Assurance Co., **III** 332
American Research and Development Corp., **II** 85; **III** 132; **6** 233; **19** 103
American Residential Mortgage Corporation, 8 30–31
American Residential Services, **33** 141
American Resorts Group, **III** 103
American Retirement Corporation, 42 9–12; 43 46
American Rice, Inc., 17 161–62; **33 30–33**
American River Transportation Co., **I** 421; **11** 23
American Robot Corp., **III** 461
American Rolling Mill Co., **IV** 28; **8** 176–77
American Royalty Trust Co., **IV** 84; **7** 188
American Rug Craftsmen, **19** 275
American RX Pharmacy, **III** 73
American Safety Equipment Corp., **IV** 136
American Safety Razor Company, III 27–29; **20 22–24**
American Saint-Gobain, **16** 121
American Sales Book Co., Ltd., **IV** 644
American Salt Co., **12** 199
American Satellite Co., **6** 279; **15** 195
American Savings & Loan, **10** 117
American Savings Bank, **9** 276; **17** 528, 531
American Sealants Company. *See* Loctite Corporation.
American Seating Co., **I** 447; **21** 33
American Seaway Foods, Inc, **9** 451
American Service Corporation, **19** 223
American Sheet Steel Co., **IV** 572; **7** 549
American Shipbuilding, **18** 318
American Skiing Company, 28 18–21; 31 67, 229
American Sky Broadcasting, **27** 305; **35** 156
American Smelting and Refining Co., **IV** 31–33. *See also* ASARCO.
The American Society of Composers, Authors and Publishers (ASCAP), 29 21–24
American Software Inc., 22 214; **25 20–22**
American-South African Investment Co. Ltd., **IV** 79
American Southern Insurance Co., **17** 196
American Standard Companies Inc., 30 46–50 (upd.)
American Standard Inc., III 437, **663–65; 19** 455; **22** 4, 6; **28** 486; **40** 452
American States Insurance Co., **III** 276
American Steamship Company, **6** 394–95; **25** 168, 170
American Steel & Wire Co., **I** 355; **IV** 572; **7** 549; **13** 97–98; **40** 70, 72
American Steel Foundries, **7** 29–30
American Stock Exchange, **10** 416–17
American Stores Company, II 604–06; 12 63, 333; **13** 395; **17** 559; **18** 89; **22 37–40 (upd.); 25** 297; **27** 290–92; **30** 24, 26–27
American Sugar Refining Company. *See* Domino Sugar Corporation.
American Sumatra Tobacco Corp., **15** 138
American Superconductor Corporation, **41** 141
American Surety Co., **26** 486
American Systems Technologies, Inc., **18** 5
American Teaching Aids Inc., **19** 405
American Technical Services Company. *See* American Building Maintenance Industries, Inc. *and* ABM Industries Incorporated.
American Telephone and Telegraph Company. *See* AT&T.
American Television and Communications Corp., **I** 534–35; **II** 161; **IV** 596, 675; **7** 528–30; **18** 65
American Textile Co., **III** 571; **20** 362
American Thermos Bottle Company. *See* Thermos Company.
American Tile Supply Company, **19** 233
American Tin Plate Co., **IV** 572; **7** 549
American Tissue Company, **29** 136
American Title Insurance, **III** 242
American Tobacco Co., **I** 12–14, 28, 37, 425; **V** 395–97, 399, 408–09, 417–18, 600; **14** 77, 79; **15** 137–38; **16** 242; **18** 416; **27** 128–29; **33** 82; **43** 126. *See also* American Brands Inc., B.A.T. Industries PLC., *and* Fortune Brands, Inc.
American Tool & Machinery, **III** 420
American Tool Company, **13** 563

American Totalisator Corporation, **10** 319–20
American Tourister, Inc., **10** 350; **13** 451, 453; **16** **19–21**. *See also* Samsonite Corporation.
American Tower Corporation, **33** **34–38**
American Tractor Corporation, **10** 379
American Trading and Production Corporation, **7** 101
American Trans Air, **34** 31
American Transport Lines, **6** 384
American Trust and Savings Bank, **II** 261
American Trust Co., **II** 336, 382; **12** 535
American Twist Drill Co., **23** 82
American Ultramar Ltd., **IV** 567
American VIP Limousine, Inc., **26** 62
American Viscose Corp. *See* Avisco.
American Water Works Company, Inc., **V** 543–44; **6** **443–45**; **26** 451; **38** **49–52** **(upd.)**
American Window Glass, **16** 120
American Wood Reduction Company, **14** 174
American Woodmark Corporation, **31** **13–16**
American Woolen, **I** 529
American Yard Products, **22** 26, 28
American Yearbook Company, **7** 255; **25** 252
American-Strevell Inc., **II** 625
Americana Entertainment Group, Inc., **19** 435
Americana Foods, Inc., **17** 474–75
Americana Healthcare Corp., **15** 522
Americana Hotel, **12** 316
AmeriFirst Bank, **11** 258
Amerifirst Federal Savings, **10** 340
AmeriGas Partners, L.P., **12** 498
AmeriGas Propane, Inc., **12** 500
Amerihost Properties, Inc., **30** **51–53**
AmeriKing Corp., **36** 309
Amerimark Inc., **II** 682
Amerin Corporation. *See* Radian Group Inc.
AmeriServe Food Distribution. *See* Holberg Industries, Inc.
AmeriSource Health Corporation, **37** **9–11** **(upd.)**
Ameristar Casinos, Inc., **33** **39–42**
Amerisystems, **8** 328
Ameritech Corporation, **V** **265–68**; **6** 248; **7** 118; **10** 431; **11** 382; **12** 137; **14** 252–53, 257, 259–61, 364; **15** 197; **18** **30–34** **(upd.)**; **25** 499; **41** 288–90; **43** 447
Ameritech Illinois. *See* Illinois Bell Telephone Company.
Ameritrade Holding Corporation, **34** **27–30**
Ameritrust Corporation, **9** 476
Ameriwood Industries International Corp., **17** **15–17**
Amerock Corp., **13** 41
Amerotron, **I** 529
Amersil Co., **IV** 78
Ames Department Stores, Inc., **V** 197–98; **9** **20–22**; **10** 497; **15** 88; **19** 449; **30** **54–57** **(upd.)**
Ametek Inc., **9** **23–25**; **12** 88; **38** 169
N.V. Amev, **III** **199–202**
Amey Roadstone Corp., **III** 503; **7** 209
AMF Bowling, Inc., **19** 312; **23** 450; **40** **30–33**
Amfac Inc., **I** **417–18**, 566; **IV** 703; **10** 42; **23** 320
Amfac/JMB Hawaii L.L.C., **24** **32–35** **(upd.)**
Amfas, **III** 310
AMFM Inc., **35** 221, 245, 248; **37** 104; bf]XLI 384
Amgen, Inc., **I** 266; **8** 216–17; **10** **78–81**; **13** 240; **14** 255; **21** 320; **30** **58–61** **(upd.)**; **38** 204
Amherst Coal Co., **IV** 410; **7** 309
AMI. *See* Advanced Metallurgy, Inc.
Amiga Corporation, **7** 96
Aminoil, Inc., **IV** 523. *See also* American Independent Oil Co.
AMISA, **IV** 136
Amisys Managed Care Information Systems, **16** 94
Amitron S.A., **10** 113
Amity Leather Products Company. *See* AR Accessories Group, Inc.
AMK Corporation, **II** 595; **7** 85; **21** 111
Amkor, **23** 17
AMLI Realty Company, **33** 418, 420
Amling Co., **25** 89
Ammirati Puris Lintas, **14** 316; **22** 294
Ammo-Phos, **I** 300; **8** 24
L'Ammoniac Sarro-Lorrain S.a.r.l., **IV** 197
Amoco Corporation, **I** 516, 202; **II** 376; **III** 611; **IV** **368–71**, 412, 424–25, 453, 525; **7** 107, 443; **10** 83–84; **11** 441; **12** 18; **14** **21–25** **(upd.)**, 494; **18** 365; **19** 297; **26** 369
Amoseas, **IV** 453–54
Amoskeag Company, **6** 356; **8** **32–33**; **9** 213–14, 217; **22** 54; **31** 199
Amot Controls Corporation, **15** 404
AMP, Inc., **II** **7–8**; **11** 319; **13** 344; **14** **26–28** **(upd.)**; **17** 274; **22** 542; **28** 486; **36** 158
Ampad Holding Corporation. *See* American Pad & Paper Company.
AMPAL. *See* American-Palestine Trading Corp.
AMPCO Auto Parks, Inc. *See* American Building Maintenance Industries, Inc. *and* ABM Industries Incorporated.
AMPEP, **III** 625
Ampex Corporation, **III** 549; **6** 272; **17** **18–20**
Amphenol Corporation, **40** **34–37**
Ampol Petroleum Ltd., **III** 729; **27** 473
Ampro, **25** 504–05
AMR. *See* American Medical Response, Inc.
AMR Combs Inc., **36** 190
AMR Corporation, **I** 90–91; **6** 76; **8** 315; **22** 252; **26** 427–28; **28** **22–26** **(upd.)**; **29** 409; **33** 19; **34** 119
AMR Information Services, **9** 95
Amram's Distributing Limited, **12** 425
AMRE, **III** 211
AMREP Corporation, **I** 563; **21** **35–37**; **24** 78
Amro. *See* Amsterdam-Rotterdam Bank N.V.
Amrop International Australasia, **34** 249
AMS. *See* Advanced Marketing Services, Inc.
AMS Trading Co., **III** 112
Amsco International, **29** 450
AmSouth Bancorporation, **12** **15–17**
Amstar Corp., **14** 18
Amstar Sugar Corporation, **II** 582; **7** 466–67; **26** 122
Amsted Industries Incorporated, **7** **29–31**
Amstel Brewery, **I** 257; **34** 201
Amsterdam-Rotterdam Bank N.V., **II** 184, **185–86**, 279, 295, 319; **III** 200; **14** 169; **17** 324
Amstrad plc, **III** **112–14**
AMT. *See* American Materials & Technologies Corporation.
Amtech. *See* American Building Maintenance Industries, Inc. *and* ABM Industries Incorporated.
Amtech Systems Corporation, **11** 65; **27** 405
Amtel, Inc., **8** 545; **10** 136
Amtliches Bayerisches Reisebüro, **II** 163
Amtorg, **13** 365
Amtrak, **II** 2; **10** 73; **19** 141; **26** 440. *See also* National Railroad Passenger Corporation.
Amtran, Inc., **34** **31–33**
AmTrans. *See* American Transport Lines.
Amvent Inc., **25** 120
Amway Corporation, **III** **11–14**; **13** **36–39** **(upd.)**; **17** 186; **18** 67, 164; **20** 435; **23** 509; **29** 493; **30** **62–66** **(upd.)**; **31** 327
Amylum, **II** 582
ANA. *See* All Nippon Airways Co., Ltd.
Anacomp, Inc., **11** 19
Anaconda Aluminum, **11** 38
Anaconda Co., **III** 644; **IV** 33, 376; **7** 261–63
Anaconda-Jurden Associates, **8** 415
Anadarko Petroleum Corporation, **10** **82–84**
Anadex, Inc., **18** 435–36
Anaheim Imaging, **19** 336
Analog Devices, Inc., **10** **85–87**; **18** 20; **19** 67; **38** 54; **43** 17, 311
Analogic Corporation, **23** **13–16**
Analysts International Corporation, **36** **40–42**
Analytic Sciences Corporation, **10** **88–90**; **13** 417
Analytical Surveys, Inc., **33** **43–45**
Anam Group, **21** 239; **23** **17–19**
Anamax Mining Co., **IV** 33
AnAmo Co., **IV** 458
Anarad, Inc., **18** 515
Anaren Microwave, Inc., **33** **46–48**
ANB Bank, **I** 55
Anchor Bancorp, Inc., **10** **91–93**
Anchor Brake Shoe, **18** 5
Anchor Cable, **III** 433
Anchor Corporation, **12** 525
Anchor Gaming, **24** **36–39**; **41** 216
Anchor Hocking Glassware, **I** 609–10; **13** **40–42**; **14** 483; **26** 353
Anchor Motor Freight, Inc., **12** 309–10
Anchor National Financial Services, Inc., **11** 482
Anchor National Life Insurance Company, **11** 482
Anchor Oil and Gas Co., **IV** 521
Anchor Records, **II** 130
Ancienne Mutuelle, **III** 210
Anders Wilhelmsen & Co., **22** 471
Andersen Consulting, **38** 430
Andersen Corporation, **9** 344; **10** **94–95**; **11** 305; **22** 346; **39** 324
Andersen Worldwide, **29** **25–28** **(upd.)**
Anderson & Kerr Drilling Co., **IV** 445

Anderson and Campbell, **II** 479
Anderson Box Co., **IV** 342; **8** 267
Anderson Clayton & Co., **II** 560; **12** 411
Anderson, Greenwood & Co., **11** 225–26
Anderson Testing Company, Inc., **6** 441
The Andersons, Inc., **31 17–21**
Anderton, **III** 624
Andes Candies, **II** 520–21
Andian National Corp. Ltd., **IV** 415–16
André Courrèges, **III** 47; **8** 342–43
Andreas Christ, **26** 243
Andreas Stihl, **16 22–24**
Andrew Corporation, **10 96–98**; **32 38–41 (upd.)**
Andrew Jergens Co., **III** 38; **25** 56
Andrew Weir & Co., **III** 273
Andrews, Clark & Company, **IV** 426; **7** 169
Andrews Group, Inc., **10** 402
Andrews McMeel Universal, **40 38–41**
Andrews Office Supply and Equipment Co., **25** 500
Andritz AG, **27** 269
Anfor, **IV** 249–50
Angele Ghigi, **II** 475
Angelica Corporation, **15 20–22**; **43 28–31 (upd.)**
Angelo's Supermarkets, Inc., **II** 674
ANGI Ltd., **11** 28
Angle Steel, **25** 261
Anglian Water Plc, **38** 51
Anglo-American Chewing Gum Ltd., **II** 569
Anglo-American Clays Corp., **III** 691; **IV** 346
Anglo American Corporation of South Africa Limited, **I** 289, 423; **IV 20–23**, 56–57, 64–68, 79–80, 90, 92, 94–96, 118–20, 191, 239–40; **7** 121–23, 125; **16 25–30 (upd.)**, 292; **21** 211, 354; **22** 233; **28** 88, 93
Anglo-American Oil Company Limited, **IV** 427; **7** 170
Anglo American Paper Co., **IV** 286
Anglo-American Telegraph Company Ltd., **IV** 668; **25** 98
Anglo-Belge, **II** 474
Anglo-Canadian, **III** 704
Anglo-Canadian Mining & Refining, **IV** 110
Anglo-Canadian Telephone Company of Montreal. *See* British Columbia Telephone Company.
Anglo-Celtic Watch Company, **25** 430
Anglo Company, Ltd., **9** 363
Anglo-Dutch Unilever group, **9** 317
Anglo-Egyptian D.C.O., **II** 236
Anglo-Egyptian Oilfields, **IV** 412, 414
Anglo-Elementar-Versicherungs-AG, **III** 185
Anglo Energy, Ltd., **9** 364
Anglo-Huronian Ltd., **IV** 164
Anglo-Iranian Oil Co., **IV** 379, 419, 435, 450, 466, 559; **7** 57, 141; **21** 81
Anglo-Lautaro Nitrate Corporation, **9** 363
Anglo Mexican Petroleum Co. Ltd., **IV** 657
Anglo-Palestine Co., **II** 204
Anglo-Persian Oil Co., **IV** 363, 378–79, 381, 429, 450, 466, 515, 524, 531, 557–59; **7** 56–57, 140; **21** 80–81
Anglo-Swiss Condensed Milk Co., **II** 545
Anglo-Thai Corp., **III** 523
Anglo-Transvaal Consolidated, **IV** 534
Anglovaal Industries Ltd., **20** 263
Angus Hill Holdings, **IV** 249
Anheuser-Busch Companies, Inc., **34 34–37 (upd.)**; **36** 12–15, 163
Anheuser-Busch Company, Inc., **I** 32, **217–19**, 236–37, 254–55, 258, 265, 269–70, 290–91, 598; **IV** 624; **6** 20–21, 48; **9** 100; **10 99–101 (upd.)**, 130; **11** 421; **12** 337–38; **13** 5, 10, 258, 366; **15** 429; **17** 256; **18** 65, 70, 72–73, 499, 501; **19** 221, 223; **21** 229, 319–20; **22** 421; **23** 403; **25** 281–82, 368; **26** 432; **29** 84–85; **29** 218; **31** 381, 383
ANIC Gela, **IV** 421
Anikem, **I** 374
Anitec Image Technology Corp., **IV** 287; **15** 229
Annabelle's, **II** 480–81; **26** 57
Anne Klein & Co., **15** 145–46; **24** 299; **40** 277–78
Anneplas, **25** 464
AnnTaylor Stores Corporation, **V** 26–27; **13 43–45**; **15** 9; **25** 120–22; **37 12–15 (upd.)**
Annuaries Marcotte Ltd., **10** 461
Anocout Engineering Co., **23** 82
Anonima Infortunia, **III** 208
ANR Pipeline Co., **17 21–23**; **31** 119
Ansa Software, **9** 81
Ansaldo, **II** 191
Ansbacher-Siegle Corp., **13** 460
Anschütz & Co. GmbH, **III** 446
The Anschutz Corporation, **12 18–20**; **36 43–47 (upd.)**; **37** 312
Anschütz-Kaempfe, **III** 446
Ansell, **I** 215
Ansell Rubber Company, **10** 445
Anselmo L. Morvillo S.A., **19** 336
Ansett Airlines, **6** 73; **14** 11; **27** 475
Ansett Australia, **24** 398, 400; **26** 113
Ansett Transport Industries Limited, **V** 523–25; **27** 473
Ansonia Brass and Battery Co., **IV** 176–77
Ansonia Manufacturing Co., **IV** 176
Ant Nachrichtentechnik GmbH., **I** 411
Anta Corporation, **6** 188; **25** 308
Antalis, **34** 38, 40
Antar group, **IV** 544, 546
Antares Alliance Group, **14** 15
Antares Electronics, Inc., **10** 257
Ante Corp., **22** 222
Antenna Company, **32** 40
ANTEX. *See* American National Life Insurance Company of Texas.
Anthem Electronics, Inc., **13 46–47**; **17** 276
Anthem P&C Holdings, **15** 257
Anthes Imperial Ltd., **I** 274; **26** 304
Anthes Industries Inc., **9** 512
Anthony Industries Inc. *See* K2 Inc.
Anthony Stumpf Publishing Company, **10** 460
Anthropologie, **14** 524–25
Antillaase Bank-Unie N.V., **II** 184
Antinori. *See* Marchesi Antinori SRL.
The Antioch Company, **40 42–45**
Antique Street Lamps, **19** 212
ANTK Tupolev. *See* Aviacionny Nauchno-Tehnicheskii Komplex im. A.N. Tupoleva.
Antoine Saladin, **III** 675
Antwerp Co., **IV** 497
ANZ. *See* Australia and New Zealand Banking Group Ltd.
ANZ Securities, **24** 400
Anzon Ltd., **III** 681
AOE Plastic GmbH, **7** 141
Aoki Corporation, **9** 547, 549; **29** 508
AOL. *See* America Online, Inc.
Aon Corporation, **III 203–05**; **22** 495
AP. *See* The Associated Press.
AP Bank, Ltd., **13** 439
AP Support Services, **25** 13
AP&L. *See* American Power & Light Co.
AP-Dow Jones/Telerate Company, **10** 277
APAC, Inc., **IV** 374
Apache Corporation, **10 102–04**; **11** 28; **18** 366; **32 42–46 (upd.)**
Apache Energy Ltd., **25** 471
APACHE Medical Systems, Inc., **16** 94
Apartment Furniture Rental, **26** 102
APCOA/Standard Parking. *See* Holberg Industries, Inc.
Apex, **17** 363
Apex Financial Corp., **8** 10
Apex Oil, **37** 310–11
Apex One Inc., **31** 137
Apex Smelting Co., **IV** 18
APH. *See* American Printing House for the Blind.
Apita, **V** 210
APL. *See* American President Companies Ltd.
APL Corporation, **9** 346
APL Ltd., **41** 399
Aplex Industries, Inc., **26** 363
Apline Guild, **12** 173
Aplix, **19** 477
APM Ltd., **IV** 248–49
Apogee Enterprises, Inc., **8 34–36**; **22** 347
Apollo Advisors L.P., **16** 37; **26** 500, 502; **43** 438
Apollo Apparel Partners, L.P., **12** 431
Apollo Computer, **III** 143; **6** 238; **9** 471; **11** 284
Apollo Group, Inc., **24 40–42**
Apollo Heating & Air Conditioning Inc., **15** 411
Apollo Investment Fund Ltd., **31** 211; **39** 174
Apollo Ski Partners LP of New York, **11** 543, 545
Apollo Technologies, **I** 332
Apotekarnes Droghandel A.B., **I** 664–65
Apothekernes Laboratorium A.S., **12** 3–5
Appalachian Computer Services, **11** 112
Appalachian Travel Services, Inc., **25** 185, 187
Applause Inc., **17** 461; **24 43–46**
Apple Computer, Inc., **II** 6, 62, 103, 107, 124; **III** 114, **115–16**, 121, 125, 149, 172; **6 218–20 (upd.)**, 222, 225, 231, 244, 248, 254–58, 260, 289; **8** 138; **9** 166, 170–71, 368, 464; **10** 22–23, 34, 57, 233, 235, 404, 458–59, 518–19; **11** 45, 50, 57, 62, 490; **12** 139, 183, 335, 449, 455, 470; **13** 90, 388, 482; **16** 195, 367–68, 372, 417–18; **18** 93, 511, 521; **20** 31; **21** 391; **23** 209; **24** 370; **25** 299–300, 348, 530–31; **28** 244–45; **33** 12–14; **34** 512; **36 48–51 (upd.)**, 168; **38** 69
Apple Container Corp., **III** 536; **26** 230
Apple Orthodontix, Inc., **35** 325
Apple South, Inc., **21** 362; **35** 39. *See also* Avado Brands, Inc.

Applebee's International Inc., **14 29–31**; **19** 258; **20** 159; **21** 362; **31** 40; **35 38–41 (upd.)**
Appleton & Cox, **III** 242
Appleton Papers, **I** 426
Appleton Wire Works Corp., **8** 13
Appliance Buyers Credit Corp., **III** 653
Appliance Recycling Centers of America, Inc., **42 13–16**
Applica Incorporated, **43 32–36 (upd.)**
Les Applications du Roulement, **III** 623
Applied Beverage Systems Ltd., **21** 339
Applied Bioscience International, Inc., **10 105–07**
Applied Color Systems, **III** 424
Applied Communications, Inc., **6** 280; **11** 151; **25** 496; **29** 477–79
Applied Data Research, Inc., **6** 225; **18** 31–32
Applied Digital Data Systems Inc., **II** 83; **9** 514
Applied Engineering Services, Inc. *See* The AES Corporation.
Applied Films Laboratory Inc., **12** 121; **35** 148
Applied Industrial Materials Corporation, **22** 544, 547
Applied Komatsu Technology, Inc., **10** 109
Applied Laser Systems, **31** 124
Applied Learning International, **IV** 680
Applied Materials, Inc., **10 108–09**; **18** 382–84
Applied Micro Circuits Corporation, **38 53–55**
Applied Network Technology, Inc., **25** 162
Applied Power Inc., **9 26–28**; **32 47–51 (upd.)**
Applied Programming Technologies, Inc., **12** 61
Applied Solar Energy, **8** 26
Applied Technology Corp., **11** 87
Applied Thermal Technologies, Inc., **29** 5
Approvisionnement Atlantique, **II** 652
Appryl, **I** 303
Apria Healthcare Inc., **43** 266
Aprilia SpA, **17 24–26**
APS. *See* Arizona Public Service Company.
APS Healthcare, **17** 166, 168
Apura GmbH, **IV** 325
APUTCO, **6** 383
Aqua Alliance Inc., **32 52–54 (upd.)**
Aqua-Chem, Inc., **I** 234; **10** 227
Aqua Glass, **III** 570; **20** 362
Aqua Pure Water Co., **III** 21
Aquafin N.V., **12** 443; **38** 427
Aquarium Supply Co., **12** 230
Aquarius Group, **6** 207
Aquila, **IV** 486
Aquila Energy Corp., **6** 593
Aquitaine. *See* Société Nationale des Petroles d'Aquitaine.
AR Accessories Group, Inc., **23 20–22**
AR-TIK Systems, Inc., **10** 372
ARA Services, **II 607–08**; **21** 507; **25** 181
Arab Contractors, **III** 753
Arab Japanese Insurance Co., **III** 296
Arab Petroleum Pipeline Co., **IV** 412
Arabian American Oil Co., **I** 570; **IV** 386, 429, 464–65, 512, 536–39, 552, 553, 559; **7** 172, 352; **14** 492–93; **41** 392. *See also* Saudi Arabian Oil Co.
Arabian Gulf Oil Co., **IV** 454
Arabian Investment Banking Corp., **15** 94; **26** 53
Arabian Oil Co., **IV** 451
Aral, **IV** 487
ARAMARK Corporation, **13 48–50**; **16** 228; **21** 114–15; **35** 415; **41 21–24**
Aramco. *See* Arabian American Oil Co. *and* Saudi Arabian Oil Company.
Aramis Inc., **30** 191
Arandell Corporation, **37 16–18**
Arapuã. *See* Lojas Arapuã S.A.
Aratex Inc., **13** 49
Aratsu Sekiyu, **IV** 554
ARBED S.A., **IV 24–27**, 53; **22 41–45 (upd.)**; **26** 83; **42** 414
Arbeitsgemeinschaft der öffentlich-rechtlichen Rundfunkanstalten der Bundesrepublick. *See* ARD.
The Arbitron Company, **III** 128, **10** 255, 359; **13** 5; **38 56–61**
Arbor Acres, **13** 103
Arbor Drugs Inc., **12 21–23**
Arbor International, **18** 542
Arbor Living Centers Inc., **6** 478
Arbuthnot & Co., **III** 522
Arby's Inc., **II** 614; **8** 536–37; **14 32–34**, 351
ARC. *See* American Rug Craftsmen.
ARC International Corporation, **27** 57
ARC Ltd., **III** 501
ARC Materials Corp., **III** 688
ARC Propulsion, **13** 462
ARCA. *See* Appliance Recycling Centers of America, Inc.
Arcadia Company, **14** 138
Arcadia Group plc, **28 27–30 (upd.)**, 95–96
Arcadia Partners, **17** 321
Arcadian Corporation, **18** 433; **27** 317–18
Arcadian Marine Service, Inc., **6** 530
Arcadis NV, **26 21–24**
Arcata Corporation, **12** 413
Arcata National Corp., **9** 305
Arcelik, **I** 478
Arch Mineral Corporation, **IV** 374; **7 32–34**
Arch Petroleum Inc., **39** 331
Arch Wireless, Inc., **39 23–26**; **41** 265, 267
Archbold Container Co., **35** 390
Archbold Ladder Co., **12** 433
Archer-Daniels-Midland Co., **I 419–21**; **IV** 373; **7** 432–33, 241 **8** 53; **11 21–23 (upd.)**; **17** 207; **22** 85, 426; **23** 384; **25** 241; **31** 234; **32 55–59 (upd.)**
Archer Drug, **III** 10
Archer Management Services Inc., **24** 360
Archers Gilles & Co., **II** 187
Archibald Candy Corporation, **36** 309
Archway Cookies, Inc., **29 29–31**
ARCO. *See* Atlantic Richfield Company.
ARCO Chemical Company, **IV** 376–77, 456–57; **10 110–11**
ARCO Comfort Products Co., **26** 4
Arco Electronics, **9** 323
Arco Pharmaceuticals, Inc., **31** 346
Arco Societa Per L'Industria Elettrotecnica, **II** 82
Arcon Corporation, **26** 287
Arctco, Inc., **12** 400–01; **16 31–34**; **35** 349, 351
Arctic, **III** 479
Arctic Alaska Fisheries Corporation, **14** 515
Arctic Cat Inc., **40 46–50 (upd.)**
Arctic Enterprises, **34** 44
Arctic Slope Regional Corporation, **38 62–65**
ARD, **41 25–29**
Ardal og Sunndal Verk AS, **10** 439
Arden Group, Inc., **29 32–35**
Ardent Computer Corp., **III** 553
Ardent Risk Services, Inc. *See* General Re Corporation.
Areal Technologies, **III** 715
Argbeit-Gemeinschaft Lurgi und Ruhrchemie, **IV** 534
Argentine National Bank, **14** 46
Argo Communications Corporation, **6** 300
Argon Medical, **12** 327
Argonaut, **I** 523–24; **10** 520–22
Argos, **I** 426; **22** 72
Argos Soditic, **43** 147, 149
Argosy Gaming Company, **21 38–41**
Argosy Group LP, **27** 197
Argus Chemical Co., **I** 405
Argus Corp., **IV** 22, 272, 611
Argus Energy, **7** 538
Argus Motor Company, **16** 7
Argyle Television Inc., **19** 204
Argyll Group PLC, **I** 241; **II 609–10**, 656; **12** 152–53; **24** 418
Aria Communications, Inc. *See* Ascend Communications, Inc.
Ariba Inc., **38** 432
Ariel Capital Management, **28** 421
Aries Technology, **25** 305
Aris Industries, Inc., **15** 275; **16 35–38**
Aristech Chemical Corp., **12** 342
Arizona Airways, **22** 219
Arizona Copper Co., **IV** 177
Arizona Edison Co., **6** 545
Arizona Growth Capital, Inc., **18** 513
AriZona Iced Tea. *See* Ferolito, Vultaggio & Sons.
Arizona One, **24** 455
Arizona Public Service Company, **6** 545–47; **19** 376, 412; **26** 359; **28** 425–26
Arizona Refrigeration Supplies, **14** 297–98
Arjo Wiggins Appleton p.l.c., **13** 458; **27** 513; **34 38–40**
Ark Restaurants Corp., **20 25–27**
Ark Securities Co., **II** 233
Arkady Co., Ltd., **I** 421; **11** 23
Arkansas Best Corporation, **16 39–41**; **19** 455; **42** 410
Arkansas Breeders, **II** 585
Arkansas Chemicals Inc., **I** 341
Arkansas Louisiana Gas Company. *See* Arkla, Inc.
Arkansas Power & Light, **V** 618
Arkay Computer, **6** 224
ARKE, **II** 164
Arkia, **23** 184, 186–87
Arkla, Inc., **V 550–51**; **11** 441
Arlesey Lime and Portland Cement Co., **III** 669
Arlington Corporation, **6** 295
Arlington Motor Holdings, **II** 587
Arlington Securities plc, **24** 84, 87–89
Arlon, Inc., **28** 42, 45
Armaturindistri, **III** 569
Armco Inc., **III** 259, 721; **IV 28–30**, 125, 171; **10** 448; **11** 5, 255; **12** 353; **19** 8; **26** 407; **30** 282–83; **41** 3, 5
Armin Corp., **III** 645
Armin Poly Film Corp., **III** 645

Armitage Shanks, **III** 671
Armor All Products Corp., **12** 333; **15** 507; **16 42–44**; **22** 148; **26** 349
Armor Elevator, **11** 5
Armor Holdings, Inc., **27 49–51**
Armour. *See* Tommy Armour Golf Co.
Armour & Company, **8** 144; **12** 198; **13** 21, 506; **23** 173
Armour-Dial, **I** 14; **8** 144; **23** 173–74
Armour Food Co., **I** 449–50, 452; **II** 494, 518; **12** 81, 370; **13** 270; **42** 92
Armour Pharmaceutical Co., **III** 56
Armstrong Advertising Co., **I** 36
Armstrong Air Conditioning Inc. *See* Lennox International Inc.
Armstrong Autoparts, **III** 495
Armstrong Communications, **IV** 640
Armstrong Cork Co., **18** 118
Armstrong Nurseries, **I** 272
Armstrong Rees Ederer Inc., **IV** 290
Armstrong-Siddeley Co., **III** 508
Armstrong Tire Co., **15** 355
Armstrong, Whitworth & Co. Ltd., **I** 50; **III** 508; **IV** 257; **24** 85
Armstrong World Industries, Inc., **III 422–24**; **9** 466; **12** 474–75; **22 46–50 (upd.)**, 170–71; **26** 507
Armtek, **7** 297
Army and Air Force Exchange Service, **39 27–29**
Army Cooperative Fire Insurance Company, **10** 541
Army Ordnance, **19** 430
Army Signal Corps Laboratories, **10** 96
Arndale, **IV** 696
Arno Press, **IV** 648; **19** 285
Arnold & Porter, **35 42–44**
Arnold Communications, **25** 381
Arnold Electric Company, **17** 213
Arnold Foods Co., **II** 498
Arnold Industries Inc., **35** 297
Arnold, Schwinn & Company. *See* Schwinn Cycle and Fitness L.P.
Arnold Thomas Co., **9** 411
Arnoldo Mondadori Editore S.p.A., **IV 585–88**, 675; **19 17–21 (upd.)**
Arnotts Ltd., **II** 481; **26** 57–59
Aro Corp., **III** 527; **14** 477, 508; **15** 225
Aromat Corporation, **III** 710; **7** 303
Aromatic Industries, **18** 69
Arpet Petroleum, **III** 740; **IV** 550
Arpic, **III** 426
Arrosto Coffee Company, **25** 263
Arrow Electronics, Inc., **10 112–14**; **13** 47; **19** 310–11, 313; **29** 414; **30** 175
Arrow Food Distributor, **II** 675
Arrow Furniture Co., **21** 32
Arrow Oil Co., **IV** 401
Arrow Oil Tools, **III** 570; **20** 360
Arrow Pump Co., **I** 185
Arrow Shirt Co., **24** 384
Arrow Specialty Company, **III** 570; **20** 360
Arrowhead Mills Inc., **27** 197–98; **43** 218–19
Arrowsmith & Silver, **I** 428
Arsam Investment Co., **26** 261
A.B. Arsenalen, **II** 352
Arsynco, Inc., **38** 4
The Art Institute of Chicago, **29 36–38**
Art Van Furniture, Inc., **28 31–33**
Artal Luxembourg SA, **33** 446, 449
Artal NV, **40** 51
Artec, **III** 420; **12** 297
Artech Digital Entertainments, Inc., **15** 133
Artek Systems Corporation, **13** 194
Artémis Group, **27** 513
Artesian Manufacturing and Bottling Company, **9** 177
Artex Enterprises, **7** 256; **25** 167, 253
Arthur Andersen & Company, Société Coopérative, **III** 143; **6** 244; **10 115–17**, 174; **16** 92; **25** 358; **29** 392. *See also* Andersen Worldwide.
Arthur D. Little, Inc., **35 45–48**
Arthur H. Fulton, Inc., **42** 363
Arthur Murray International, Inc., **32 60–62**
Arthur Ovens Motor Freight Co., **6** 371
Arthur Rank Organisation, **25** 328
Arthur Tappan & Co., **IV** 604
Arthur Young & Company, **IV** 119; **10** 386; **19** 311; **33** 235. *See also* Ernst & Young.
Artisan Entertainment Inc., **32 63–66 (upd.)**
Artisan Life Insurance Cooperative, **24** 104
Artisoft, Inc., **18** 143
Artistic Direct, Inc., **37** 108
Artists & Writers Press, Inc., **13** 560
Artists Management Group, **38** 164
ArtMold Products Corporation, **26** 342
Artra Group Inc., **40** 119–20
Arts and Entertainment Network. *See* A&E Television Networks.
Arvey Corp., **IV** 287
Arvida Corp., **IV** 703
Arvin Industries, Inc., **8 37–40**
ASAB, **III** 480
Asahi Breweries, Ltd., **I 220–21**, 282, 520; **13** 454; **20 28–30 (upd.)**; **21** 230, 319–20; **26** 456; **36** 404–05
Asahi Chemical Industry Co., **I** 221; **III** 760; **IV** 326
Asahi Corporation, **16** 84; **40** 93
Asahi Glass Company, Limited, **I** 363; **III 666–68**; **11** 234–35
Asahi Kasei Industry Co. Ltd., **IV** 476
Asahi Komag Co., Ltd., **11** 234
Asahi Kyoei Co., **I** 221
Asahi Manufacturing, **III** 592
Asahi Medix Co., Ltd., **36** 420
Asahi Milk Products, **II** 538
Asahi National Broadcasting Company, Ltd., **9 29–31**
Asahi Oil, **IV** 542
Asahi Real Estate Facilities Co., Ltd., **6** 427
Asahi Seiko, **III** 595
Asahi Shimbun, **9** 29–30
Asahi Trust & Banking, **II** 323
Asano Group, **III** 718
Asanté Technologies, Inc., **20 31–33**
ASARCO Incorporated, **I** 142; **IV 31–34**; **40** 220–22, 411
ASB Agency, Inc., **10** 92
Asbury Associates Inc., **22** 354–55
Asbury Group, **26** 501
ASCAP. *See* The American Society of Composers, Authors and Publishers.
Ascend Communications, Inc., **24 47–51**; **34** 258
Aschaffenburger Zellstoffwerke AG, **IV** 323–24
ASCO Healthcare, Inc., **18** 195–97
Asco Products, Inc., **22** 413
Ascom AG, **9 32–34**; **15** 125
Ascometal, **IV** 227
Ascotts, **19** 122
ASD, **IV** 228
ASDA Group plc, **II 611–12**, 513, 629; **11** 240; **28 34–36 (upd.)**
ASEA AB. *See* ABB ASEA Brown Boveri Ltd.
Asean Bintulu Fertilizer, **IV** 518
Asepak Corp., **16** 339
A.B. Asesores Bursatiles, **III** 197–98; **15** 18
ASF. *See* American Steel Foundries.
Asgrow Florida Company, **13** 503
Asgrow Seed Co., **29** 435; **41** 306
Ash Company, **10** 271
Ash Resources Ltd., **31** 398–99
Ashanti Goldfields Company Limited, **43 37–40**
Ashbourne PLC, **25** 455
Ashitaka Rinsan Kogyo, **IV** 269
Ashland Inc., **19 22–25**; **27** 316, 318
Ashland Iron and Mining Co., **IV** 28
Ashland Oil, Inc., **I** 420; **IV** 71, 198, 366, **372–74**, 472, 658; **7** 32–33; **8** 99; **9** 108; **11** 22; **18** 279
Ashley Furniture Industries, Inc., **35 49–51**
Ashtead Group plc, **34 41–43**
Ashton Joint Venture, **IV** 60, 67
Ashton Mining, **IV** 60
Ashton-Tate Corporation, **9** 81–82; **10** 504–05
Ashworth, Inc., **26 25–28**
Asia Life Insurance Co., **III** 195–96
Asia Oil Co., Ltd., **IV** 404, 476
Asia Pulp & Paper, **38** 227
Asia Television, **IV** 718; **38** 320
Asia Terminals Ltd., **IV** 718; **38** 319
AsiaInfo Holdings, Inc., **43 41–44**
Asian Football Confederation, **27** 150
Asiana, **24** 400
Asiatic Petroleum Co., **IV** 434, 530
ASICS Corp., **24** 404
Asil çelik, **I** 479
ASK Group, Inc., **9 35–37**; **25** 34
Ask Mr. Foster Agency, **22** 127; **26** 308
Asland SA, **III** 705, 740
Aso Cement, **III** 705
Aspect Telecommunications Corporation, **16** 392–93; **22 51–53**
Aspen Imaging International, Inc., **17** 384
Aspen Mountain Gas Co., **6** 568
Aspen Skiing Company, **II** 170; **15 23–26**, 234; **43** 438
Aspen Systems, **14** 555
Asplundh Tree Expert Co., **20 34–36**
Assam Co. Ltd., **III** 522–23
Assam Oil Co., **IV** 441, 483–84
Asset Management Company, **25** 86
Asset Marketing Inc. *See* Commercial Financial Services, Inc.
L'Assicuratrice Italiana, **III** 346–47
Assicurazioni Generali SpA, **II** 192; **III 206–09**, 211, 296, 298; **14** 85; **15 27–31 (upd.)**
Assisted Living Concepts, Inc., **43 45–47**
Associate Venture Investors, **16** 418
Associated Anglo-Atlantic Corp., **III** 670
Associated Aviation Underwriters, **III** 220
Associated Banks of Europe Corp., **II** 184, 239
Associated Biscuit Co., **II** 631
Associated Book Publishers, **8** 527
Associated Bowater Industries, **IV** 258
Associated Brewing Co., **I** 254

Associated British Foods plc, II 465–66, 565, 609; **11** 526; **13 51–53 (upd.)**; **24** 475; **41 30–33 (upd.)**
Associated British Maltsters, **II** 500
Associated British Picture Corporation, **I** 531; **II** 157; **22** 193
Associated Bulk Carriers Ltd., **38** 345
Associated City Investment Trust, **IV** 696
Associated Communications Companies, **7** 78; **23** 479
Associated Container Transportation, **23** 161
Associated Cooperative Investment Trust Ltd., **IV** 696
Associated Dairies Ltd., **II** 611
Associated Dry Goods Corp., **V** 134; **12** 54–55; **24** 298
Associated Electrical Industries, Ltd., **II** 25; **III** 502
Associated Employers General Agency, **III** 248
Associated Estates Realty Corporation, 25 23–25
Associated Fire Marine Insurance Co., **26** 486
Associated Food Holdings Ltd., **II** 628
Associated Fresh Foods, **II** 611–12
Associated Fuel Pump Systems Corp., **III** 593
Associated Gas & Electric Company, **V** 621, 629–30; **6** 534; **14** 124
Associated Gas Services, Inc., **11** 28
Associated Grocers, Incorporated, 9 38–40; **19** 301; **31 22–26 (upd.)**
Associated Grocers of Arizona, **II** 625
Associated Grocers of Colorado, **II** 670
The Associated Group, **10** 45
Associated Hospital Service of New York, **III** 245–46
Associated Iliffe Press, **IV** 666; **17** 397
Associated Indemnity Co., **III** 251
Associated Inns and Restaurants Company of America, **14** 106; **25** 309; **26** 459
Associated Insurance Cos., **III** 194
Associated International Insurance Co. *See* Gryphon Holdings, Inc.
Associated Lead Manufacturers Ltd., **III** 679, 680–81
Associated London Properties, **IV** 705
Associated Madison Insurance, **I** 614
Associated Merchandisers, Inc., **27** 246
Associated Merchandising Corp., **16** 215
Associated Milk Producers, Inc., 11 24–26
Associated National Insurance of Australia, **III** 309
Associated Natural Gas Corporation, 11 27–28
Associated Newspapers Holdings P.L.C., **IV** 686; **19** 118, 120; **37** 121
Associated Octel Company Limited, **10** 290
Associated Oil Co., **IV** 460
Associated Pipeline Contractors, **III** 559
Associated Piping & Engineering Corp., **III** 535
Associated Portland Cement Manufacturers (1900) Ltd., **III** 669–71
The Associated Press, IV 629, 669–70; **7** 158; **10** 277; **13 54–56**; **25** 506; **31 27–30 (upd.)**; **34** 11
Associated Publishing Company, **19** 201
Associated Pulp & Paper Mills, **IV** 328
Associated Sales Agency, **16** 389
Associated Spring Co., **III** 581; **13** 73
Associated Stationers, **14** 521, 523
Associated Television, **7** 78
Associated Timber Exporters of British Columbia Ltd., **IV** 307
Associated TV, **IV** 666; **17** 397
Associates First Capital Corporation, **22** 207
Associates Investment Co., **I** 452
Association des Centres Distributeurs E. Leclerc, 37 19–21
Assubel, **III** 273
Assurances du Groupe de Paris, **III** 211
Assurances Générales de France, **III** 351; **27** 513; **42** 151
AST Holding Corp., **III** 663, 665
AST Research, Inc., 9 41–43; **10** 459, 518–19; **12** 470; **18** 260
Asta Pharma AG, **IV** 71
Asta Werke AG, **IV** 71
Astech, **18** 370
Asteroid, **IV** 97
Astley & Pearce, **10** 277
Aston Brooke Software, **14** 392
Aston Villa plc, 41 34–36
Astor Holdings Inc., **22** 32
Astor Trust Co., **II** 229
Astra AB, I 625–26, 635, 651; **11** 290; **20 37–40 (upd.)**; **34** 282, 284
Astra Resources, **12** 543
Astrolac, **IV** 498
Astronics Corporation, 35 52–54
Astrotech Space Operations, L.P., **11** 429; **37** 365
Astrum International Corp., **12** 88; **13** 453; **16** 20–21; **43** 355
ASV, Inc., 34 44–47
ASW. *See* American Steel & Wire Corp.
Asylum Life Assurance Co., **III** 371
Asylum Records, **23** 33; **26** 150
Asymetrix, **6** 259
AT&E Corp., **17** 430
AT&T Bell Laboratories, Inc., 13 57–59; **22** 17
AT&T Corp., I 462; **II** 13, 54, 61, 66, 80, 88, 120, 125, 252, 403, 430–31, 448; **III** 99, 110–11, 130, 145, 149, 160, 162, 167, 246, 282; **IV** 95, 287; **V 259–64**, 265–68, 269, 272–75, 302–04, 308–12, 318–19, 326–30, 334–36, 339, 341–342, 344–346; **6** 267, 299, 306–07, 326–27, 338–40; **7** 88, 118–19, 146, 288–89, 333; **8** 310–11; **9** 32, 43, 106–07, 138, 320, 321, 344, 478–80, 495, 514; **10** 19, 58, 87, 97, 175, 202–03, 277–78, 286, 431, 433, 455–57; **11** 10, 59, 91, 183, 185, 196, 198, 302, 395, 500–01; **12** 9, 135–36, 162, 544; **13** 212–13, 326, 402, 448; **14** 15, 95, 251–53, 257–61, 318, 336–37, 345, 347, 354, 363–64; **15** 125–26, 228, 455; **16** 223, 318, 368, 467; **18** 30, 32, 74, 76, 111–12, 155, 164–65, 368, 516–18, 569–70; **19** 12, 41; **20** 34, 313; **21** 70, 200–01, 514; **22** 51; **23** 135; **25** 100, 256, 301, 495–99; **26** 187, 225, 431, 520; **27** 363; **28** 242; **29** 59, **39–45 (upd.)**; **30** 99, 339; **33** 34–35, 37, 91, 93–94; **34** 257–59; **38** 269–70, 416; **42** 224; **43** 50, 222, 443
AT&T Istel Ltd., 14 35–36
At Home Corporation, 43 48–51
Ataka & Co., **I** 433; **II** 361
Atari Corporation, II 176; **III** 587; **IV** 676; **6** 244; **7** 395–96; **9 44–47**; **10** 284, 482, 485; **13** 472; **23 23–26 (upd.)**; **28** 319; **32** 8
ATAS International, **26** 527, 530
ATC, **III** 760; **13** 280
Atchison Casting Corporation, 24 144; **39 30–32**
Atchison, Topeka and Santa Fe Railroad, **V** 507–08; **12** 19–20; **27** 86
ATCO Ltd., **13** 132
ATD Group, **10** 113
ATE Investment, **6** 449
Atelier de Construction Electrique de Delle, **9** 9
ATEQ Corp., **III** 533
Atex, Inc., **III** 476; **7** 162; **10** 34; **36** 172, 174
ATH AG, **IV** 221
Atha Tool Co., **III** 627
Athalon Products, Ltd., **10** 181; **12** 313
Athena Assurances, **27** 513, 515
Athenia Steel Co., **13** 369
Athens National Bank, **III** 190
Athens Piraeus Electricity Co., **IV** 658
Athern, **16** 337
Athlete's Foot, **29** 186
Athletic Attic, **19** 230
Athletic Shoe Company, **17** 243
Athletic Textile Company, Inc., **13** 532
Athletic X-Press, **14** 293
Athol Machine Co., **13** 301
ATI, **IV** 651; **7** 390
Atlalait, **19** 50
Atlanta Gas Light Company, 6 446–48; **23 27–30 (upd.)**
Atlanta-LaSalle Corporation, **43** 54
Atlanta National Bank, **16** 521
Atlanta National League Baseball Club, Inc., 43 52–55
Atlanta Paper Co., **IV** 311; **19** 267
Atlantic & Pacific Tea Company (A&P). *See* Great Atlantic & Pacific Tea Company, Inc.
Atlantic Acceptance Corporation, **7** 95
Atlantic Aircraft Corp., **I** 34; **17** 197
Atlantic American Corp., **23** 413
Atlantic Auto Finance Corp. *See* United Auto Group, Inc.
Atlantic Cellular, **43** 341
Atlantic Cement Co., **III** 671
Atlantic Coast Carton Company, **19** 77
Atlantic Coast Line Railroad Company. *See* CSX Corporation.
Atlantic Computers, **14** 35
Atlantic Container Lines Ltd., **23** 161
Atlantic Energy, Inc., 6 449–50
The Atlantic Group, 23 31–33
Atlantic Gulf and Caribbean Airways, **I** 115
Atlantic Import, **I** 285
Atlantic Mills, **27** 188
Atlantic Mutual, **41** 65
Atlantic Precision Instrument Company, **13** 234
Atlantic Precision Works, **9** 72
Atlantic Records, **II** 176; **18** 458; **26** 150
Atlantic Refining Co., **III** 497; **III** 498; **IV** 375–76, 456, 504, 566, 570; **24** 520–21
Atlantic Research Corp., **13** 462
Atlantic Richfield Company, I 452; **II** 90, 425; **III** 740; **IV 375–77**, 379, 435, 454, 456–57, 467, 494, 522, 536, 571; **7** 57, 108, 537–38, 558–59; **8** 184, 416; **10**

110; **13** 13, 341; **19** 175; **24** 521, 524; **26** 4, 372; **31 31–34 (upd.)**; **40** 358
Atlantic Sea Products, **13** 103
The Atlantic Seaboard Dispatch. *See* GATX.
Atlantic Securities Ltd., **II** 223; **III** 98
Atlantic Southeast, **26** 439
Atlantic Southern Properties, Inc., **6** 449–50
Atlantic Surety Co., **III** 396
Atlantic Transport Company, **19** 198
Atlantic-Union Oil, **IV** 570; **24** 520
Atlantic Wholesalers, **II** 631
Atlantis Group, Inc., **17** 16; **19** 50, 390
Atlantis Ltd., **II** 566
Atlantis Resort and Casino. *See* Sun International Hotels Limited.
Atlas Air, Inc., 39 33–35
Atlas America, Inc., **42** 311
Atlas Assurance Co., **III** 370
Atlas Cement Company, **31** 252
Atlas Chemical Industries, **I** 353
Atlas Copco AB, **III 425–27**, 480; **IV** 203; **28 37–41 (upd.)**
Atlas Corp., **I** 58, 512; **10** 316
Atlas Eléctrica S.A., **22** 27
Atlas Hotels, Inc., **V** 164
Atlas Petroleum Ltd., **IV** 449
Atlas Plastics, **19** 414
Atlas Powder Company, **I** 343–44; **22** 260
Atlas Shipping, **I** 285
Atlas Steel Works, **I** 572
Atlas Steels, **IV** 191
Atlas Supply Co., **IV** 369
Atlas Tag & Label, **9** 72
Atlas Van Lines, Inc., 14 37–39
Atlas Ventures, **25** 96
Atlas-Werke AG, **IV** 88
Atlas Works, **I** 531
Atlatec SA de CV, **39** 192
Atle Byrnestad, **6** 368; **27** 92
Atmel Corporation, **17 32–34**; **19** 313
Atmos Energy Corporation, 43 56–58
Atmos Lebensmitteltechnik, **III** 420
Atmospherix Ltd. *See* Blyth Industries, Inc.
ATO Chimie, **I** 303; **IV** 560
Atochem S.A., **I 303–04**, 676; **IV** 525, 547; **7** 484–85
AtoHaas Americas, **26** 425
Atom-Energi, **II** 2; **22** 9
Atomic Austria GmbH, **41** 14–16
ATR, **7** 9, 11
ATS. *See* Magasins Armand Thiéry et Sigrand.
ATT Microelectrica España, **V** 339
Attachmate Corp., **11** 520
Atvidabergs Industrier, **25** 463
Atwater McMillian. *See* St. Paul Companies, Inc.
Atwood Resources Inc., **17** 372
ATX Technologies, Inc., **32** 374
ATx Telecom Systems Inc., **31** 124
Au Bon Marché, **26** 160
Au Bon Pain Co., Inc., 18 35–38
Au Printemps S.A., **V 9–11**; **17** 124; **41** 114. *See also* Pinault-Printemps-Redoute S.A.
Aubrey G. Lanston Co., **II** 301
Auchan, **10** 205; **23** 230; **27** 94; **37 22–24**; **39** 183–85
AUDI AG, **I** 202; **IV** 570; **34** 55
Audio Accessories, Inc., **37** 301
Audio Development Company, **10** 18
Audio International Inc., **36** 159
Audio King Corporation, **24 52–54**
Audio/Video Affiliates, Inc., **10** 468–69
Audiotronic Holdings, **III** 112
Audiovox Corporation, **34 48–50**
Audits & Surveys Worldwide Inc., **28** 501, 504
Aufina Bank, **II** 378
Aug. Stenman A.B., **III** 493
Aughton Group, **II** 466
Augsburger Aktienbank, **III** 377
Auguri Mondadori S.p.A., **IV** 586
August Max Woman, **V** 207–08
August Schell's Brewing Co., **22** 421
August Thyssen-Hütte AG, **IV** 221–22
Auguste Metz et Cie, **IV** 24
Ault Incorporated, **34 51–54**
Aunor Gold Mines, Ltd., **IV** 164
Aunt Fanny's Bakery, **7** 429
Auntie Anne's, Inc., 35 55–57
Aura Books plc, **34** 5
Aurora Dairy Corporation, **37** 195, 198
Aurora Foods Inc., **26** 384; **32 67–69**
Aurora Products, **II** 543
Aurora Systems, Inc., **21** 135
Aurrera S.A., **35** 459
Aurum Corp., **38** 431
Ausilio Generale di Sicurezza, **III** 206
Ausimont N.V., **8** 271
Ausplay, **13** 319
AUSSAT Ltd., **6** 341
Aussedat-Rey, **IV** 288; **23** 366, 368
The Austin Company, **8 41–44**
Austin Industries, **25** 402
Austin-Morris, **III** 494
Austin Motor Company, **I** 183; **III** 554; **7** 458
Austin Nichols, **I** 248, 261, 280–81
Austin Quality Foods, **36** 313
Austin Rover, **14** 321
Austral Waste Products, **IV** 248
Australasian Paper and Pulp Co. Ltd., **IV** 248
Australasian Sugar Co., **III** 686
Australasian United Steam Navigation Co., **III** 522
Australia and New Zealand Banking Group Ltd., **II 187–90**
Australia Gilt Co. Group, **II** 422
Australia National Bank, Limited, **10** 170
Australian Airlines, **6** 91, 112; **24** 399–400; **27** 475
Australian and Kandos Cement (Holdings) Ltd., **III** 687, 728; **28** 83
Australian and Overseas Telecommunications Corporation, **6** 341–42
Australian Associated Press, **IV** 669
Australian Automotive Air, Pty. Ltd., **III** 593
Australian Blue Asbestos, **III** 687
Australian Consolidated Investments, Limited, **10** 170
Australian Consolidated Press, **27** 42
Australian Forest Products, **I** 438–39
Australian Guarantee Corp. Ltd., **II** 389–90
Australian Gypsum Industries, **III** 673
Australian Iron & Steel Company, **IV** 45; **22** 105
Australian Metal Co., **IV** 139
Australian Mutual Provident Society, **IV** 61, 697
Australian Paper Co., **IV** 248
Australian Petroleum Pty. Ltd., **25** 471
Australian Tankerships Pty. Ltd., **25** 471
Australian Telecommunications Corporation, **6** 342
Australian United Corp., **II** 389
Australian Window Glass, **III** 726
Austrian Airlines AG (Österreichische Luftverkehrs AG), **27** 26; **33 49–52**; **34** 398
Austrian Industries, **IV** 485, 486
Austrian National Bank, **IV** 230
Austro-Americana, **6** 425
Austro-Daimler, **I** 138, 206; **11** 31
Authentic Fitness Corp., **16** 511; **20 41–43**
Auto Avio Costruzione, **13** 219
Auto Coil Springs, **III** 581
Auto-Flo Corp., **III** 569; **20** 360
Auto Ordnance Corporation, **19** 430–31
Auto Parts Wholesale, **26** 348
Auto Shack. *See* AutoZone, Inc.
Auto Strop Safety Razor Co., **III** 27–28
Auto-Trol Technology, **14** 15
Auto Union, **I** 150
Auto Value Associates, Inc., **25 26–28**
Autodesk, Inc., **10 118–20**
Autogrill, **24** 195
Autolite, **I** 29, 142; **III** 555
Autoliv AB, **41** 369
Autologic Information International, Inc., **20 44–46**; **26** 518–20
Automat, **II** 614
Automated Building Components, **III** 735
Automated Communications, Inc., **8** 311
Automated Design Systems, **25** 348
Automated Loss Prevention Systems, **11** 445
Automated Security (Holdings) PLC, **11** 444
Automated Wagering Systems, **III** 128
Automatic Coil Corp., **33** 359, 361
Automatic Data Processing, Inc., **III 117–19**; **9 48–51 (upd.)**, 125, 173; **21** 69
Automatic Fire Alarm Co., **III** 644
Automatic Manufacturing Corporation, **10** 319
Automatic Payrolls, Inc., **III** 117
Automatic Retailers of America, Inc., **II** 607; **13** 48
Automatic Sprinkler Corp. of America. *See* Figgie International, Inc.
Automatic Telephone & Electric, **II** 81
Automatic Toll Systems, **19** 111
Automatic Vaudeville Arcades Co., **II** 154
Automatic Voting Machine Corporation. *See* American Locker Group Incorporated.
Automobile Insurance Co., **III** 181–82
Automobiles Citroen, **I** 162, 188; **III** 676; **IV** 722; **V** 237; **7 35–38**; **11** 103; **16** 121, 420
Automobili Lamborghini Holding S.p.A., 34 55–58 (upd.)
Automobili Lamborghini S.p.A., **13 60–62**, 219
Automotive Components Group Worldwide, **10** 325
Automotive Diagnostics, **10** 492
Automotive Group. *See* Lear Seating Corporation.
Automotive Industries Holding Inc., **16** 323
AutoNation USA, **41** 239. *See also* Republic Industries, Inc.
Autonet, **6** 435
Autophon AG, **9** 32

Autotote Corporation, 20 47–49
AutoTrol Technology, **III** 111
AUTOWORKS Holdings, Inc., **24** 205
AutoZone, Inc., 9 52–54; 26 348; **31 35–38 (upd.); 36** 364
AVA AG (Allgemeine Handelsgesellschaft der Verbraucher AG), 33 53–56
Avado Brands, Inc., 31 39–42
Avalon Publishing Group. *See* Publishers Group, Inc.
Avana Group, **II** 565
Avantel, **27** 304
Avaya Inc., **41** 287, 289–90
Avco. *See* Aviation Corp. of the Americas.
Avco Corp., **34** 433
Avco Financial Services Inc., 13 63–65
Avco National Bank, **II** 420
Avdel, **34** 433
Avecor Cardiovascular Inc., **8** 347; **22** 360
Aveda Corporation, 24 55–57
Avedis Zildjian Co., 38 66–68
Avendt Group, Inc., **IV** 137
Avenir, **III** 393
Avenor Inc., **25** 13
Aventis, **34** 280, 283–84; **38** 378, 380
Avery Dennison Corporation, IV 251–54; 15 229, 401; **17 27–31 (upd.),** 445
Avesta Steel Works Co., **I** 553–54
Avex Electronics Inc., **40** 68
Avfuel, **11** 538
Avgain Marine A/S, **7** 40; **41** 42
Avia Group International, Inc., **V** 376–77; **26** 397–99
Aviacion y Comercio, **6** 95–96
Aviacionny Nauchno-Tehnicheskii Komplex im. A.N. Tupoleva, 24 58–60
AVIACO. *See* Aviacion y Comercio.
Avianca Aerovías Nacionales de Colombia SA, 36 52–55
Aviation Corp. of the Americas, **I** 48, 78, 89, 115, 530; **III** 66; **6** 75; **9** 497–99; **10** 163; **11** 261, 427; **12** 379, 383; **13** 64
Aviation Inventory Management Co., **28** 5
Aviation Power Supply, **II** 16
Aviation Sales Company, 41 37–39
Aviation Services West, Inc. *See* Scenic Airlines, Inc.
Avid Technology Inc., 38 69–73
Avion Coach Corporation, **I** 76; **III** 484; **11** 363; **22** 206
Avions Marcel Dassault-Breguet Aviation, I 44–46; 7 11; **7** 205; **8** 314. *See also* Groupe Dassault Aviation SA.
Avis, Inc., I 30, 446, 463; **II** 468; **III** 502; **IV** 370; **6** 348–49, **356–58**, 392–93; **8** 33; **9** 284; **10** 419; **11** 198; **16** 379–80; **22** 524
Avis Rent A Car, Inc., 22 54–57 (upd.); 24 9; **25** 93, 143, 420–22
Avisco, **I** 317, 365, 442–43; **V** 359; **17** 117
Avisun Corp., **IV** 371
Avnet Electronics Supply Co., **19** 311, 313
Avnet Inc., 9 55–57; 10 112–13; **13** 47
Avon Products, Inc., III 13, **15–16**, 62; **8** 329; **9** 331; **11** 282, 366; **12** 314, 435; **13** 38; **14** 501–02; **17** 186; **19 26–29 (upd.),** 253; **21** 49, 51; **25** 292; 456; **27** 429; **30** 64, 308–09
Avon Publications, Inc., **IV** 627; **19** 201, 204
Avon Rubber plc, **23** 146
Avoncraft Construction Co., **I** 512
Avondale Industries, Inc., I 512–14; **7 39–41; 41 40–43 (upd.)**
Avondale Mills, Inc., **8** 558–60; **9** 466
Avondown Properties Ltd., **IV** 711
Avro. *See* A.V. Roe & Company.
AVS, **III** 200
Avstar, **38** 72
Avtech Corp., **36** 159
Avtex Fibers Inc., **I** 443; **11** 134
AVX Corporation, **21** 329, 331
AWA. *See* America West Holdings Corporation.
AWA Defence Industries (AWADI). *See* British Aerospace Defence Industries.
Award Foods, **II** 528
Awesome Transportation, Inc., **22** 549
AXA Colonia Konzern AG, III 209, **210–12; 15** 30, **21** 147. **27 52–55**
Axe-Houghton Associates Inc., **41** 208
Axel Johnson Group, I 553–55
Axel Springer Verlag AG, IV 589–91; 20 50–53 (upd.); 23 86; **35** 452
Axelrod Foods, **II** 528
Axon Systems Inc., **7** 336
Ayco Corp., **II** 398; **10** 62
Aydin Corp., 19 30–32
Ayerst, **I** 623
Ayr-Way Stores, **27** 452
AYS. *See* Alternative Youth Services, Inc.
Ayshire Collieries, **IV** 18
Azcon Corporation, 23 34–36
Azerty, **25** 13
Azienda Generale Italiana Petroli. *See* Agip SpA.
Azienda Nazionale Idrogenazione Combustibili, **IV** 419–22
AZL Resources, **7** 538
Aznar International, **14** 225
Azon Limited, **22** 282
AZP Group Inc., **6** 546
Aztar Corporation, 13 66–68
Azteca, **18** 211, 213
Azuma Leather Co. Ltd., **V** 380
Azuma Shiki Manufacturing, **IV** 326
Azusa Valley Savings Bank, **II** 382

B&G Foods, Inc., 40 51–54
B & K Steel Fabrications, Inc., **26** 432
B&M Baked Beans, **40** 53
B & O. *See* Baltimore and Ohio Railroad.
B&Q plc, **V** 106, 108; **24** 266, 269–70
B&S. *See* Binney & Smith Inc.
B&W Diesel, **III** 513
B.A.T. Industries PLC, 14 77; **16** 242; **22 70–73 (upd.); 25** 154–56; **29** 196. *See also* Brown & Williamson Tobacco Corporation
B. B. & R. Knight Brothers, **8** 200; **25** 164
B.B. Foods, **13** 244
B-Bar-B Corp., **16** 340
B.C. Rail Telecommunications, **6** 311
B.C. Sugar, **II** 664
B.C. Ziegler and Co. *See* The Ziegler Companies, Inc.
B. Dalton Bookseller Inc., 10 136; **13** 545; **16** 160; **18** 136; **25 29–31; 30** 68
B-E Holdings, **17** 60
B/E Aerospace, Inc., 30 72–74
B.F. Ehlers, **I** 417; **24** 32
B.F. Goodrich Co. *See* The BFGoodrich Company.
B.F. Walker, Inc., **11** 354
B.I.C. America, **17** 15, 17
B.J.'s Wholesale, **12** 335
The B. Manischewitz Company, LLC, 31 43–46
B. Perini & Sons, Inc., **8** 418
B.R. Simmons, **III** 527
B.S. Bull & Company. *See* Supervalu Inc.
B. Stroh Brewing Co., **I** 290
B.T.I. Chemicals Ltd., **I** 313; **10** 154
B Ticino, **21** 350
B.V. Tabak Export & Import Compagnie, **12** 109
BA. *See* British Airways.
BAA plc, 10 121–23; 29 509, 511; **33 57–61 (upd.); 37** 8
Bålforsens Kraft AB, **28** 444
Baan Company, 25 32–34; 26 496, 498
Babbage's, Inc., 10 124–25
Babcock & Wilcox Co., **III** 465–66, 516, 559–60, **V** 621, **23** 199, **37** 242–45
Baby Furniture and Toy Supermarket, **V** 203
Baby Superstore, Inc., 15 32–34
Babybird Co., Ltd., **V** 150
BabyCenter.com, **37** 130
Babyliss, S.A., **17** 110
BAC. *See* Barclays American Corp. *and* British Aircraft Corporation.
Bacardi Limited, 18 39–42
Baccarat, 23 241; **24 61–63; 27** 421, 423
Bache & Company, **III** 340; **8** 349
Bachman Foods, **15** 139
Bachman Holdings, Inc., **14** 165; **34** 144–45
Bachman's Inc., 22 58–60; 24 513
Bachoco. *See* Industrias Bacholo, S.A. de C.V.
Bachrach Advertising, **6** 40
Back Bay Restaurant Group, Inc., 20 54–56
Backer & Spielvogel, **I** 33; **12** 168; **14** 48–49; **22** 296
Backer Spielvogel Bates Worldwide **42** 329. *See also* Bates Worldwide, Inc.
Backroom Systems Group, **II** 317
Bacon & Matheson Drop Forge Co., **I** 185
Bacova Guild, Ltd., **17** 76
Bad Boy Entertainment, **31** 269
Baddour, Inc. *See* Fred's, Inc.
Badger Co., **II** 86
Badger Illuminating Company, **6** 601
Badger Meter, Inc., 22 61–65
Badger Paint and Hardware Stores, **II** 419
Badger Paper Mills, Inc., 15 35–37
Badin-Defforey, **27** 93
Badische Analin & Soda Fabrik A.G., **I** 305
BAe. *See* British Aerospace plc.
BAE Systems, **41** 412
BAFS. *See* Bangkok Aviation Fuel Services Ltd.
Bahia de San Francisco Television, **IV** 621
Bailey, Banks & Biddle, **16** 559
Bailey Controls, **III** 560
Bain & Co., **III** 429; **9** 343; **21** 143
Bain Capital, Inc., **14** 244–45; **16** 466; **20** 18; **24** 456, 482; **25** 254; **26** 184; **38** 107–09
Baird, **7** 235, 237
Bairnco Corporation, 28 42–45
Bajaj Auto Limited, 39 36–38
BÅKAB. *See* Bålforsens Kraft AB.
Bakelite Corp., **I** 399; **9** 517; **13** 231
Baker and Botts, L.L.P., 28 46–49
Baker & Co., **IV** 78

Baker & Crane, **II** 318; **17** 323
Baker & Hostetler LLP, 40 55–58
Baker & McKenzie, 10 126–28; 42 17–20 (upd.)
Baker & Taylor Corporation, I 548; **16 45–47; 43 59–62 (upd.)**
Baker Casing Shoe Co., **III** 429
Baker Cummins Pharmaceuticals Inc., **11** 208
Baker Extract Co., **27** 299
Baker Hughes Incorporated, III 428–29; 11 513; **22 66–69 (upd.); 25** 74
Baker Industries, Inc., **III** 440; **8** 476; **13** 124
Baker International Corp., **III** 428–29
Baker Oil Tools. *See* Baker Hughes Incorporated.
Baker-Raulang Co., **13** 385
Bakers Best Snack Food Corporation, **24** 241
Bakers Square. *See* VICORP Restaurants, Inc.
Bakersfield Savings and Loan, **10** 339
Bakery Products Inc., **IV** 410
Balair Ltd., **I** 122
Balance Bar Company, 32 70–72
Balchem Corporation, 42 21–23
Balco, Inc., **7** 479–80; **27** 415
Balcor Co., **II** 398; **IV** 703
Balcor, Inc., **10** 62
Baldor Electric Company, 21 42–44
Baldwin-Ehret-Hill Inc., **28** 42
Baldwin Filters, Inc., **17** 104
Baldwin Hardware Manufacturing Co., **III** 570; **20** 361
Baldwin-Montrose Chemical Co., Inc., **31** 110
Baldwin Piano & Organ Company, 16 201; **18 43–46**
Baldwin Rubber Industries, **13** 79
Baldwin Technology Company, Inc., 25 35–39
Baldwin-United Corp., **III** 254, 293
Baldwins Ltd., **III** 494
Bålforsens Kraft AB, **IV** 339–40; **28** 444
Balfour Beatty Construction Ltd., III 433–34; **36 56–60 (upd.)**
Balfour Company, L.G., **19** 451–52
Balikpapan Forest Industries, **I** 504
Ball & Young Adhesives, **9** 92
Ball-Bartoe Aircraft Corp., **I** 598; **10** 130
Ball Corporation, I 597–98; 10 129–31 (upd.); 13 254, 256; **15** 129; **16** 123; **30** 38
The Ball Ground Reps, Inc., **26** 257
Ball Industries, Inc., **26** 539
Ball Stalker Inc., **14** 4
Ballantine & Sons Ltd., **I** 263
Ballantine Beer, **6** 27
Ballantine Books, **13** 429; **31** 376–77, 379
Ballantyne of Omaha, Inc., 27 56–58
Ballard & Ballard Co., **II** 555
Ballard Medical Products, 21 45–48
Ballast Nedam Group, **24** 87–88
Balli Group plc, **26** 527, 530
Bally Entertainment Corp., **19** 205, 207
Bally Gaming International, **15** 539
Bally Manufacturing Corporation, III 430–32; 6 210; **10** 375, 482; **12** 107; **15** 538–39; **17** 316–17, 443; **41** 214–15
Bally Total Fitness Holding Corp., 25 40–42
Bâloise-Holding, 40 59–62
Baltek Corporation, 34 59–61
AB Baltic, **III** 418–19
Baltic Cable, **15** 521
Baltica, **27** 54
Baltimar Overseas Limited, **25** 469
Baltimore & Ohio Railroad, **I** 584; **II** 329. *See also* CSX Corporation.
Baltimore Aircoil Company, **7** 30–31
Baltimore Gas and Electric Company, V 552–54; 11 388; **25 43–46 (upd.)**
Baltimore Paper Box Company, **8** 102
Baltimore Technologies Plc, 42 24–26
Baltino Foods, **13** 383
Balzaretti-Modigliani, **III** 676; **16** 121
Bamberger's of New Jersey, **V** 169; **8** 443
Banamex, **22** 285; **23** 170; **34** 81. *See also* Banco Nacional de Mexico.
Banana Boat Holding Corp., **15** 359
Banana Brothers, **31** 229
Banana Importers of Ireland, **38** 197
Banana Republic Inc., V 61–62; **18** 193–94; **25 47–49; 31** 51–52
Banc One Corporation, 9 475; **10** 132–34; **11** 181. *See also* Bank One Corporation.
Banca Brasiliana Italo-Belga, **II** 270
Banca Coloniale di Credito, **II** 271
Banca Commerciale Italiana SpA, I 368, 465, 467; **II 191–93**, 242, 271, 278, 295, 319; **III** 207–08, 347; **17** 324
BancA Corp., **11** 305
Banca d'America e d'Italia, **II** 280
Banca Dalmata di Sconto, **II** 271
Banca de Gottardo, **II** 361
Banca di Genova, **II** 270
Banca Internazionale Lombarda, **II** 192
Banca Italiana di Sconto, **II** 191
Banca Italo-Cinese, **II** 270
Banca Italo-Viennese, **II** 270
Banca Jacquet e Hijos, **II** 196
Banca Luis Roy Sobrino, **II** 196
Banca Nazionale de Lavoro, **II** 239
Banca Nazionale dell'Agricoltura, **II** 272
Banca Nazionale di Credito, **II** 271
Banca Serfin. *See* Grupo Financiero Serfin, S.A.
Banca Unione di Credito, **II** 270
Bancard Systems, **24** 395
BancFinancial Services Corporation, **25** 187
BancItaly Corp., **II** 226–27, 288, 536; **13** 528
BancMortgage Financial Corp., **25** 185, 187
Banco Aleman-Panameno, **II** 521
Banco Aliança S.A., **19** 34
Banco Azteca, **19** 189
Banco Bilbao Vizcaya, S.A., II 194–96
Banco Bradesco S.A., 13 69–71; 19 33
Banco Capitalizador de Monterrey, **19** 189
Banco Central, II 197–98. *See also* Banco Santander Central Hispano S.A.
Banco Central de Crédito. *See* Banco Itaú.
Banco Chemical (Portugal) S.A. *See* Chemical Banking Corp.
Banco Comercial, **19** 188
Banco Comercial de Puerto Rico, **41** 311
Banco Credito y Ahorro Ponceno, **41** 312
Banco da América, **19** 34
Banco de Londres, Mexico y Sudamerica. *See* Grupo Financiero Serfin, S.A.
Banco de Madrid, **40** 147
Banco de Mexico, **19** 189
Banco de Ponce, **41** 313
Banco del Norte, **19** 189
Banco di Roma, **I** 465, 467; **II** 191, 257, 271
Banco di Santo Spirito, **I** 467
Banco do Brasil S.A., II 199–200
Banco Español de Credito, **II** 195, 198; **IV** 160
Banco Espírito Santo e Comercial de Lisboa S.A., 15 38–40
Banco Federal de Crédito. *See* Banco Itaú.
Banco Frances y Brasiliero, **19** 34
Banco Industrial de Bilbao, **II** 195
Banco Industrial de Monterrey, **19** 189
Banco Italo-Belga, **II** 270, 271
Banco Italo-Egiziano, **II** 271
Banco Itaú S.A., 19 33–35
Banco Nacional de Cuba, **II** 345
Banco Nacional de Mexico, **9** 333; **19** 188, 193
Banco Pinto de Mahalhãhes, **19** 34
Banco Popolar, **III** 348; **6** 97. *See also* Popular, Inc.
Banco Português do Brasil S.A., **19** 34
Banco Santander Central Hispano S.A., 36 61–64 (upd.); 42 349
Banco Serfin, **34** 82
Banco Sul Americano S.A., **19** 34
Banco Trento & Bolanzo, **II** 240
Banco União Comercial, **19** 34
Banco Vascongado, **II** 196
BancOhio National Bank in Columbus, **9** 475
Bancomer, **19** 12
Bancorp Leasing, Inc., **14** 529
BancorpSouth, Inc., **14** 40–41
Bancroft Racket Co., **III** 24
BancSystems Association Inc., **9** 475, 476
Bandag, Inc., 19 36–38, 454–56
Bandai America Inc., **23** 388; **25** 488
Bandai Co., Ltd., **38** 415
Banesto. *See* Banco Español de Credito.
Banexi, **II** 233
Banfi Products Corp., 36 65–67
Bang & Olufsen Holding A/S, 37 25–28
Bangkok Airport Hotel, **6** 123–24
Bangkok Aviation Fuel Services Ltd., **6** 123–24
Bangladesh Krishi Bank, **31** 220
Bangor and Aroostook Railroad Company, **8** 33
Bangor Mills, **13** 169
Bangor Punta Alegre Sugar Corp., **30** 425
Bangor Punta Corp., **I** 452, 482; **II** 403
Banister Continental Corp. *See* BFC Construction Corporation.
Bank Austria AG, 23 37–39
Bank Brussels Lambert, II 201–03, 295, 407
Bank Bumiputra, **IV** 519
Bank Central Asia, **18** 181
Bank CIC-Union Européenne A.G., **II** 272
Bank du Louvre, **27** 423
Bank Européene de Creditä Moyen Terme, **II** 319; **17** 324
Bank for International Settlements, **II** 368
Bank für Elektrische Unternehmungen. *See* Elektrowatt AG.
Bank für Gemeinwirtschaft, **II** 239
Bank Hapoalim B.M., II 204–06; 25 266, 268
Bank Hofmann, **21** 146–47
Bank Leu, **I** 252; **21** 146–47
Bank Leumi Le-Israel, **25** 268
Bank of Adelaide, **II** 189

Bank of America, **I** 536–37; **II** 226–28, 252–55, 280, 288–89, 347, 382; **III** 218; **6** 385; **8** 94–95; **9** 50, 123–24, 333, 536; **12** 106, 466; **13** 69; **14** 170; **18** 516; **22** 542; **25** 432; **26** 486. *See also* BankAmerica Corporation.
Bank of America National Trust and Savings Assoc. (NT & SA), **I** 536; **II** 227, 288; **13** 528. *See also* BankAmerica Corporation.
Bank of Antwerp, **IV** 497
Bank of Asheville, **II** 336
Bank of Australasia, **II** 187–89
The Bank of Bishop and Co., Ltd., **11** 114
Bank of Boston Corporation, II 207–09; **7** 114; **12** 31; **13** 467; **14** 90
Bank of Brandywine Valley, **25** 542
Bank of Britain, **14** 46–47
Bank of British Columbia, **II** 244, 298
Bank of British Honduras, **II** 344
Bank of British North America, **II** 220
Bank of California, **II** 322, 490. *See also* Union Bank of California.
Bank of Canada, **II** 210, 376
Bank of Central and South America, **II** 344
Bank of Chicago, **III** 270
Bank of China, **II** 298
Bank of Chosen, **II** 338
Bank of Commerce, **II** 331
Bank of Delaware, **25** 542
Bank of England, **II** 217, 235–36, 306–07, 318–19, 333–34, 357, 421–22, 427–28; **III** 234, 280; **IV** 119, 366, 382, 705, 711; **10** 8, 336; **14** 45–46; **17** 324–25
Bank of Finland, **III** 648
Bank of France, **II** 232, 264–65, 354; **III** 391
Bank of Hamilton, **II** 244
Bank of Hindustan, **IV** 699
Bank of Ireland, **16** 13–14; **19** 198
Bank of Israel, **II** 206
Bank of Italy, **I** 536; **II** 192, 226, 271–72, 288; **III** 209, 347; **8** 45
The Bank of Jacksonville, **9** 58
Bank of Japan, **I** 519; **II** 291, 325
Bank of Kobe, **II** 371
Bank of Lee County, **14** 40
Bank of Liverpool, **II** 236
Bank of London and South America, **II** 308
Bank of Manhattan Co., **II** 247–48
Bank of Mexico Ltd., **19** 188
The Bank of Milwaukee, **14** 529
Bank of Mississippi, Inc., 14 40–41
Bank of Montreal, II 210–12, 231, 375; **26** 304
Bank of Nettleton, **14** 40
Bank of New Brunswick, **II** 221
Bank of New England Corporation, II 213–15; **9** 229
Bank of New Orleans, **11** 106
Bank of New Queensland, **II** 188
Bank of New South Wales, **II** 188–89, 388–90
Bank of New York Company, Inc., II 192, **216–19**, 247; **34** 82
Bank of North Mississippi, **14** 41
Bank of Nova Scotia, II 220–23, 345; **IV** 644
Bank of Oklahoma, **22** 4
Bank of Ontario, **II** 210
Bank of Osaka, **II** 360
Bank of Ottawa, **II** 221
Bank of Pasadena, **II** 382
Bank of Queensland, **II** 188
The Bank of Scotland. *See* The Governor and Company of the Bank of Scotland.
Bank of Sherman, **14** 40
Bank of Spain, **II** 194, 197
Bank of the Ohio Valley, **13** 221
Bank of the People, **II** 210
Bank of the United States, **II** 207, 216, 247
Bank of the West, **II** 233
Bank of Tokyo, Ltd., II 224–25, 276, 301, 341, 358; **IV** 151; **12** 138; **16** 496, 498; **24** 358
Bank of Tokyo-Mitsubishi Ltd., 15 41–43 (upd.), 431; **26** 454, 457; **38** 387
Bank of Toronto, **II** 375–76
Bank of Tupelo, **14** 40
Bank of Upper Canada, **II** 210
Bank of Wales, **10** 336, 338
Bank of Western Australia, **II** 187
Bank of Winterthur, **II** 378
Bank One Corporation, 36 68–75 (upd.)
Bank Powszechny Depozytowy, **IV** 119
Bank-R Systems Inc., **18** 517
Bank voor Handel en Nijverheid, **II** 304
BankAmerica Corporation, II 226–28, 436; **8 45–48 (upd.)**, 295, 469, 471; **13** 69; **17** 546; **18** 518; **25** 187; **26** 65. *See also* Bank of America *and* Bank of America National Trust and Savings Assoc.
BankBoston. *See* FleetBoston Financial Corporation.
BankCard America, Inc., **24** 394
Bankers and Shippers Insurance Co., **III** 389
Bankers Co., **II** 230
Bankers Corporation, **14** 473
Bankers Investment, **II** 349
Bankers Life and Casualty Co., **10** 247; **16** 207; **33** 110
Bankers Life Co., **III** 328–30
Bankers National Bank, **II** 261
Bankers National Life Insurance Co., **II** 182; **10** 246
Bankers Trust Co., **38** 411
Bankers Trust New York Corporation, I 601; **II** 211, **229–31**, 330, 339; **III** 84–86; **10** 425; **11** 416; **12** 165, 209; **13** 188, 466; **17** 559; **19** 34; **22** 102; **25** 268; 317
Bankhaus IG Herstatt, **II** 242
BankVermont Corp., **II** 208
BankWatch, **37** 143, 145
Banner Aerospace, Inc., 14 42–44; **37 29–32 (upd.)**
Banner International, **13** 20
Banner Life Insurance Company, **III** 273; **24** 284
BanPonce Corporation, **41** 312
Banque Belge et Internationale en Egypte, **II** 295
Banque Belge pour l'Etranger, **II** 294
Banque Belgo-Zairoise, **II** 294
Banque Bruxelles Lambert. *See* Bank Brussels Lambert.
Banque Commerciale du Maroc, **II** 272
Banque Commerciale-Basle, **II** 270
Banque d'Anvers/Bank van Antwerpen, **II** 294–95
Banque de Bruxelles, **II** 201–02, 239
Banque de Credit et de Depot des Pays Bas, **II** 259
Banque de France, **14** 45–46
Banque de l'Indochine et de Suez, **II** 259
Banque de l'Union Européenne, **II** 94
Banque de l'Union Parisienne, **II** 270; **IV** 497, 557
Banque de la Construction et les Travaux Public, **II** 319; **17** 324
Banque de la Société Générale de Belgique, **II** 294–95
Banque de Louvain, **II** 202
Banque de Paris et des Pays-Bas, **II** 136, 259; **10** 346; **19** 188–89; **33** 179
Banque de Reports et de Depots, **II** 201
Banque du Congo Belge, **II** 294
Banque Européenne pour l'Amerique Latine, **II** 294
Banque Française et Espagnol en Paris, **II** 196
Banque Francaise pour le Commerce et l'Industrie, **II** 232, 270
Banque Génerale des Pays Roumains, **II** 270
Banque Générale du Luxembourg, **II** 294
Banque Indosuez, **II** 429
Banque Internationale de Bruxelles, **II** 201–02
Banque Internationale de Luxembourg, **II** 239; **42** 111
Banque Italo-Belge, **II** 294
Banque Italo-Francaise de Credit, **II** 271
Banque Lambert, **II** 201–02
Banque Nationale de Paris S.A., II 232–34, 239; **III** 201, 392–94; **9** 148; **13** 203; **15** 309; **19** 51; **33** 119. *See also* BNP Paribas Group.
Banque Nationale Pour le Commerce et l'Industrie, **II** 232–33
Banque Nordique du Commerce, **II** 366
Banque Orea, **II** 378
Banque Paribas, **II** 192, 260; **IV** 295; **19** 225. *See* BNP Paribas Group.
Banque Rothschild, **IV** 107
Banque Sino-Belge, **II** 294
Banque Stern, **II** 369
La Banque Suisse et Française. *See* Crédit Commercial de France.
Banque Transatlantique, **II** 271
Banque Worms, **III** 393; **27** 514
Banquet Foods Corp., **II** 90, 494; **12** 81; **42** 91
Banta Corporation, 12 24–26; **19** 333; **32 73–77 (upd.)**
Bantam Ball Bearing Company, **13** 522
Bantam Books, Inc., **III** 190–91
Bantam Doubleday Dell Publishing Group, **IV** 594; **13** 429; **15** 51; **27** 222; **31** 375–76, 378
Banyan Systems Inc., 25 50–52
Banyu Pharmaceutical Co., **I** 651; **11** 290; **34** 283
Baoshan Iron and Steel, **19** 220
BAP of New York, Inc., **15** 246
BAPCO, **III** 745
Bar Technologies, Inc., **26** 408
Barat. *See* Barclays PLC.
Barber Dental Supply Inc., **19** 291
Barber-Greene, **21** 502
Barberet & Blanc, **I** 677
Barcel, **19** 192
Barclay Furniture Co., **12** 300
Barclay Group, **I** 335; **10** 290
Barclay White Inc., **38** 436
Barclays Business Credit, **13** 468
Barclays PLC, I 604–05; **II** 202, 204, **235–37**, 239, 244, 308, 319, 333, 383, 422, 429; **III** 516; **IV** 23, 722; **7**

332–33; **8** 118; **11** 29–30; **17** 324–25; **20 57–60 (upd.)**; **25** 101; **28** 167
BarclaysAmerican Mortgage Corporation, **11 29–30**
Barco Manufacturing Co., **16** 8; **26** 541
Barcolo Manufacturing, **15** 103; **26** 100
Barden Cablevision, **IV** 640; **26** 273
Bardon Group. *See* Aggregate Industries plc.
Bareco Products, **15** 352
Barefoot Inc., **23** 428, 431
Bari Shoes, Inc., **22** 213
Barilla G. e R. Fratelli S.p.A., **17 35–37**
Baring Brothers & Co., Ltd., **39** 5
Barings PLC, **III** 699; **14 45–47**
Barker & Dobson, **II** 629
Barker and Company, Ltd., **13** 286
Barlow Rand Ltd., **I** 288–89, **422–24**; **IV** 22, 96
Barlow Specialty Advertising, Inc., **26** 341
Barmag AG, **39 39–42**
Barmer Bankverein, **II** 238, 241
Barnato Brothers, **IV** 21, 65; **7** 122
Barneda Carton SA, **41** 326
Barnes & Noble, Inc., **10 135–37**; **12** 172; **13** 494, 545; **14** 61–62; **15** 62; **16** 160; **17** 524; **23** 370; **25** 17, 29–30; **30 67–71 (upd.)**; **41** 61; **43** 78, 408
Barnes Group, **III** 581
Barnes-Hind, **III** 56, 727
Barnett Banks, Inc., **9 58–60**
Barnett Brass & Copper Inc., **9** 543
Barnett Inc., **28 50–52**
Barnetts, Hoares, Hanbury and Lloyds, **II** 306
Barney's, Inc., **28 53–55**; **36** 290, 292
Barnstead/Thermolyne Corporation, **14** 479–80
Baroid, **19** 467–68
Baron Philippe de Rothschild S.A., **39 43–46**
Barr & Stroud Ltd., **III** 727
Barr Laboratories, Inc., **26 29–31**
Barranquilla Investments, **II** 138; **24** 193
Barratt Developments plc, **I 556–57**
Barret Fitch North, **II** 445; **22** 405
Barrett Burston, **I** 437
Barrett Business Services, Inc., **16 48–50**
The Barrett Co., **I** 414–15; **18** 116; **22** 29
Barricini Foods Inc., **27** 197
Barrick Gold Corporation, **34 62–65**; **38** 232
Barris Industries, Inc., **23** 225
Barry & Co., **III** 522
Barry Callebaut AG, **29 46–48**
Barry Wright Corporation, **9** 27; **32** 49
Barry's Jewelers. *See* Samuels Jewelers Incorporated.
Barsab Investment Trust. *See* South African Breweries Ltd.
Barsotti's, Inc., **6** 146
Bart Starr, **12** 284
Barth Smelting Corp., **I** 513
Bartlett & Co., **33** 261
Barton & Ludwig, Inc., **21** 96
Barton Beers, Ltd., **29** 219
Barton Brands, **I** 227; **II** 609; **10** 181
Barton, Duer & Koch, **IV** 282; **9** 261
Barton Incorporated, **13** 134; **24** 140; **34** 89
Bartow Food Company, **25** 332
Barwig Medizinische Systeme. *See* OEC Medical Systems, Inc.
Basel AG, **39** 304
BASF Aktiengesellschaft, **I** 275, **305–08**, 309, 319, 346–47, 632, 638; **II** 554; **IV** 70–71; **13** 75; **14** 308; **16** 462; **18 47–51 (upd.)**, 186, 234; **21** 544; **24** 75; **26** 305, 368; **27** 22; **28** 194; **41** 45
Bashas' Inc., **33 62–64**
Basic American Retirement Communities, **III** 103
Basic Resources, Inc., **V** 725
Basics, **14** 295
BASIS Information Technologies, Inc., **11** 112–13, 132
Baskin-Robbins Ice Cream Co., **I** 215; **7** 128, 372; **17** 474–75; **25** 366; **29** 18
Basle A.G., **I** 632–33, 671–72; **8** 108–09
Basle Air Transport, **I** 121
Basler Bankverein, **II** 368
Bass & Co., **I** 142
Bass Brewers Ltd., **15** 441; **29** 85
Bass Brothers Enterprises Inc., **28** 107; **36** 472
Bass Charington, **29** 84
Bass PLC, **I 222–24**; **III** 94–95; **9** 99, 425–26; **15 44–47 (upd.)**; **16** 263; **23** 482; **24** 194; **33** 127; **35** 396; **38 74–78 (upd.)**; **43** 226
Bass Pro Shops, Inc., **42 27–30**
Bassett Boat Company, **30** 303
Bassett Foods, **II** 478
Bassett Furniture Industries, Inc., **18 52–55**; **19** 275
Bassett-Walker Inc., **V** 390–91; **17** 512
Bassins Food Chain, **II** 649
BAT. *See* British-American Tobacco Co., Ltd.
BAT Industries plc, **I 425–27**, 605; **II** 628; **III** 66, 185, 522; **9** 312; **23** 427; **30** 273
Bataafsche Petroleum Maatschappij, **V** 658
Batavia Wine Company, **13** 134
Batchelors Ltd., **I** 315; **25** 81
Bateaux Parisiens, **29** 442
Bateman Eichler Hill Richards, **III** 270
Bates, **16** 545
Bates & Robins, **II** 318; **17** 323
Bates Chemical Company, **9** 154
Bates Manufacturing Company, **10** 314
Bates Worldwide, Inc., **14 48–51**; **26** 500; **33 65–69 (upd.)**
Batesville Casket Company, **10** 349–50
Bath & Body Works, **11** 41; **24** 237
Bath Industries Inc., **18** 117–18
Bath Iron Works Corporation, **12 27–29**; **36 76–79 (upd.)**
Bathurst Bank, **II** 187
Baton Rouge Gas Light Company. *See* Gulf States Utilities Company.
Battelle Laboratories, **25** 260
Battelle Memorial Institute, Inc., **6** 288; **10 138–40**
Batten Barton Durstine & Osborn, **I** 25, 28–31, 33; **16** 70; **41** 88
Battle Creek Food Company, **14** 557–58
Battle Creek Toasted Corn Flake Co., **II** 523; **13** 291
Battle Mountain Gold Company, **IV** 490; **23 40–42**
Battlefield Equipment Rentals, **21** 499, 501
BATUS Inc., **9** 312; **18** 136; **30** 273
Bauborg, **I** 560–61
Baudhuin-Anderson Company, **8** 553
Bauer Audio Visual, Inc., **24** 96
Bauer Nike Hockey Inc., **36** 347
Bauer Publishing Group, **7 42–43**; **20** 53
Baume & Mercier, **27** 487, 489
Bausch & Lomb Inc., **III** 446; **7 44–47**; **10** 46–47; **13** 365–66; **25** 22, **53–57 (upd.)**, 183; **30** 30; **42** 66
Bavaria SA, **36** 52
Bavarian Brewing Limited, **25** 280
Bavarian Railway, **II** 241
Bavarian Specialty Foods, **13** 383
Baxter Estates, **II** 649
Baxter Healthcare, **36** 497–98
Baxter International Inc., **I 627–29**; **9** 346; **10 141–43 (upd.)**, 198–99; **11** 459–60; **12** 325; **18** 469; **22** 361; **25** 82; **26** 433; **36** 92
Baxter Travenol, **21** 119; **24** 75
The Bay, **16** 216
Bay Area Review Course, Inc., **IV** 623
Bay Cities Transportation Company, **6** 382
Bay City, **21** 502
Bay City Cash Way Company, **V** 222; **25** 534
Bay Colony Life Insurance Co., **III** 254
Bay Harbour Management L.C., **28** 55
Bay Networks, Inc., **20** 33, 69; **26** 276; **36** 352
Bay Petroleum, **I** 526
Bay Ridge Savings Bank, **10** 91
Bay Shipbuilding Corporation, **18** 320
Bay State Gas Company, **38 79–82**
Bay State Glass Co., **III** 683
Bay State Iron Manufacturing Co., **13** 16
Bay State Tap and Die Company, **13** 7
Bay West Paper Corporation. *See* Mosinee Paper Corporation.
BayBanks, Inc., **12 30–32**
Bayer A.G., **I** 305–06, **309–11**, 319, 346–47, 350; **II** 279; **12** 364; **13 75–77 (upd.)**; **14** 169; **16** 439; **18** 47, 49, 51, 234; **21** 544; **22** 225; **41 44–48 (upd.)**
Bayer S.p.A., **8** 179
Bayerische Aluminium AG, **IV** 230
Bayerische Hypotheken- und Wechsel-Bank AG, **II 238–40**, 241–42; **IV** 323
Bayerische Kraftwerke AG, **IV** 229–30
Bayerische Landesbank, **II** 257–58, 280; **14** 170
Bayerische Motoren Werke A.G., **I** 73, 75, **138–40**, 198; **II** 5; **III** 543, 556, 591; **11 31–33 (upd.)**; **13** 30; **17** 25; **21** 441; **27** 20, 203; **38 83–87 (upd.)**
Bayerische Rückversicherung AG, **III** 377
Bayerische Rumpler Werke, **I** 73
Bayerische Stickstoff-Werke AG, **IV** 229–30
Bayerische Vereinsbank A.G., **II** 239–40, **241–43**; **III** 401
Bayerische Versicherungsbank, **II** 238; **III** 377
Bayerische Wagnisbeteiligung GmbH, **27** 192
Bayerische Wasserkraftwerke Aktiengesellschaft, **IV** 231
Bayerische Zellstoff, **IV** 325
Bayernwerk AG, **IV** 231–32, 323; **V 555–58**, 698–700; **23 43–47 (upd.)**; **39** 57
Bayliner Marine Corporation, **22** 116
Bayou Boeuf Fabricators, **III** 559
Bayou Steel Corporation, **IV** 234; **31 47–49**
Bayside National Bank, **II** 230
Baystate Corporation, **12** 30
Baytree Investors Inc., **15** 87
Bayview, **III** 673

Bazaar & Novelty. *See* Stuart Entertainment Inc.
Bazar de l'Hotel de Ville, **19** 308
BBA. *See* Bush Boake Allen Inc.
BBAG Osterreichische Brau-Beteiligungs-AG, 38 88–90
BBC. *See* British Broadcasting Corp.
BBC Brown, Boveri Ltd. *See* ABB ASEA Brown Boveri Ltd.
BBDO. *See* Batten Barton Durstine & Osborn.
BBDO Worldwide Network, **22** 394
BBME. *See* British Bank of the Middle East.
BBN Corp., 19 39–42
BBO & Co., **14** 433
BC Development, **16** 481
BC TEL. *See* British Columbia Telephone Company.
BCal. *See* British Caledonian Airways.
BCC, **24** 266, 270
BCE, Inc., **V 269–71**; **6** 307; **7** 333; **12** 413; **18** 32; **36** 351
BCI. *See* Banca Commerciale Italiana SpA.
Bcom3 Group, Inc., **40** 142
BCOP. *See* Boise Cascade Office Products.
BCP Corporation, **16** 228–29
BCPA. *See* British Commonwealth Pacific Airways.
BDB. *See* British Digital Broadcasting plc.
BDB Corp., **10** 136
BDDP. *See* Wells Rich Greene BDDP.
BEA Systems, Inc., 36 80–83
Beach Patrol Inc., **29** 181
BeachviLime Ltd., **IV** 74; **24** 143, 144
Beacon Communications Group, **23** 135
Beacon Manufacturing Company, **I** 377; **19** 304–05
Beacon Oil, **IV** 566
Beacon Participations, **III** 98
Beacon Publishing Co., **IV** 629
Beall-Ladymon, Inc., **24** 458
Bealls, **24** 456
Beamach Group Ltd., **17** 182–83
Beaman Corporation, **16** 96; **25** 390
Bean Fiberglass Inc., **15** 247
Bear Automotive Service Equipment Company, **10** 494
Bear Creek Corporation, **12** 444–45; **38 91–94**; **39** 361
Bear Stearns Companies, Inc., **II 400–01**, 450; **10 144–45 (upd.)**, 382; **20** 313; **24** 272
Beard & Stone Electric Co., **I** 451
Bearings, Inc., **I** 158–59; **13 78–80**
Beasley Industries, Inc., **19** 125–26
Beatrice Company, **I** 353; 440–41; **II 467–69**, 475; **III** 118, 437; **6** 357; **9** 318; **12** 82, 87, 93; **13** 162–63, 452; **14** 149–50; **15** 213–14, 358; **16** 160, 396; **19** 290; **24** 273; **26** 476, 494; **28** 475; **42** 92. *See also* TLC Beatrice International Holdings, Inc.
Beatrice Foods, **21** 322–24, 507, 545; **25** 277–78; **38** 169; **43** 355
Beauharnois Power Company, **6** 502
Beaulieu of America, **19** 276
Beaulieu Winery, **I** 260
Beaumont-Bennett Group, **6** 27
Beauté Prestige International S.A. *See* Shiseido Company Limited.
BeautiControl Cosmetics, Inc., 21 49–52
Beauty Biz Inc., **18** 230
Beaver Lumber Company Limited, **I** 274; **26** 303, 305–06
Beazer Homes USA, Inc., 17 38–41
Beazer Plc., **7** 209
bebe stores, inc., 31 50–52
BEC Group Inc., **22** 35
Bechtel Group, Inc., **I 558–59**, 563; **III** 248; **IV** 171, 576; **6** 148–49, 556; **13** 13; **24 64–67 (upd.)**; **25** 402; **26** 220
Beck & Gregg Hardware Co., **9** 253
Beck's North America, Inc. *See* Brauerei Beck & Co.
Becker Drill, Inc., **19** 247
Becker Group of Germany, **26** 231
Becker Paribas Futures, **II** 445; **22** 406
Becker Warburg Paribas, **II** 259
Beckett Papers, 23 48–50
Beckley-Cardy Co., **IV** 623–24
Beckman Coulter, Inc., 22 74–77
Beckman Instruments, Inc., **I** 694; **14 52–54**; **16** 94
Becton, Dickinson & Company, **I 630–31**; **11 34–36 (upd.)**; **36 84–89 (upd.)**; **42** 182–83
Bed Bath & Beyond Inc., **13 81–83**; **14** 61; **18** 239; **24** 292; **33** 384; **41 49–52 (upd.)**
Bedcovers, Inc., **19** 304
Beddor Companies, **12** 25
Bedford Chemical, **8** 177
Bedford-Stuyvesant Restoration Corp., **II** 673
Bee Chemicals, **I** 372
Bee Discount, **26** 476
Bee Gee Shoe Corporation, **10** 281
Bee Gee Shrimp, **I** 473
Beech Aircraft Corporation, **II** 87; **8 49–52**, 313; **11** 411, 413; **27** 98; **38** 375
Beech Holdings Corp., **9** 94
Beech-Nut Nutrition Corporation, **I** 695; **II** 489; **21 53–56**
Beecham Group PLC, **I** 626, 640, 668; **II** 331, 543; **III** 18, 65–66; **9** 264; **14** 53; **16** 438
Beechwood Insurance Agency, Inc., **14** 472
Beeck-Feinkost GmbH, **26** 59
Beerman Stores, Inc., **10** 281
Beers Construction Company, **38** 437
Beghin Say S.A., **II** 540
Behr-Manning Company, **8** 396
Behringwerke AG, **14** 255
Beiersdorf AG, **29 49–53**; **41** 374–77
Beijerinvest Group, **I** 210
Beijing Contact Lens Ltd., **25** 56
Beijing Dentsu, **16** 168
Beijing Liyuan Co., **22** 487
Beijing Machinery and Equipment Corp., **II** 442
Beijing Yanshan Petrochemical Company, **22** 263
Beirao, Pinto, Silva and Co. *See* Banco Espírito Santo e Comercial de Lisboa S.A.
Bejam Group PLC, **II** 678; **33** 206–07
Beker Industries, **IV** 84
Bekins Company, **15 48–50**; **26** 197
Bel. *See* Fromageries Bel.
Bel Air Markets, **14** 397
Belairbus, **I** 42; **12** 191
Belcher New England, Inc., **IV** 394
Belcher Oil Co., **IV** 394
Belco Oil & Gas Corp., **23** 219; **40 63–65**
Belden Inc., **II** 16; **19 43–45**
Beldis, **23** 219
Beldoch Industries Corp., **17** 137–38
Belfast Banking Co., **II** 318; **17** 323
Belgacom, 6 302–04
Belgian De Vaderlandsche, **III** 309
Belgian Rapid Access to Information Network Services, **6** 304
Belgian Société Internationale Forestière et Minière, **IV** 65
Belglas, **16** 420; **43** 307
Belgo Group plc, **31** 41
Belgochim, **IV** 499
Belize Sugar Industries, **II** 582
Belk Stores Services, Inc., **V 12–13**; **19 46–48 (upd.)**
Bell (Quarry and Concrete), **III** 674
Bell Aerospace, **I** 530; **24** 442; **34** 432–33
Bell Aircraft Company, **I** 529; **11** 267; **13** 267; **34** 431
Bell and Howell Company, **I** 463, **IV** 642; **9** 33, **61–64**; **11** 197; **14** 569; **15** 71; **29 54–58 (upd.)**, 159
Bell Atlantic Corporation, **V 272–74**; **9** 171; **10** 232, 456; **11** 59, 87, 274; **12** 137; **13** 399; **18** 33; **25 58–62 (upd.)**, 91, 497; **27** 22, 365. *See also* Verizon Communications.
Bell Canada Enterprises Inc. *See* BCE, Inc.
Bell Canada International, Inc., **V** 269, 308–09; **6 305–08**; **12** 413; **21** 308; **25** 102
Bell Communications Research, **13** 58; **25** 496
Bell Fibre Products, **12** 377
Bell Helmets Inc., **22** 458
Bell Industries, **13** 47; **18** 498; **19** 311
Bell Laboratories, **II** 33, 60–61, 101, 112; **V** 259–64; **8** 157; **9** 171; **10** 108; **11** 327, 500–01; **12** 61; **14** 52, 281–82; **23** 181; **29** 41, 44; **34** 257–58. *See also* AT&T Bell Labroatories, Inc.
Bell Mountain Partnership, Ltd., **15** 26
Bell-Northern Research, Ltd., **V** 269–71; **15** 131
Bell Pharmacal Labs, **12** 387
Bell Resources, **I** 437–38; **III** 729; **10** 170; **27** 473
Bell Sports Corporation, 16 51–53
Bell System, **II** 72, 230; **6** 338–40; **7** 99, 333; **11** 500; **16** 392–93
Bell Telephone Company, **I** 409; **6** 332, 334
Bell Telephone Company of Pennsylvania, **I** 585
Bell Telephone Manufacturing, **II** 13
Bell's Asbestos and Engineering, **I** 428
Bellcore. *See* Bell Communications Research.
Belle Alkali Co., **IV** 409; **7** 308
Belledune Fertilizer Ltd., **IV** 165
Bellefonte Insurance Co., **IV** 29
Bellemead Development Corp., **III** 220; **14** 108; **37** 84
Bellofram Corp., **14** 43
BellSouth Corporation, **V 276–78**; **9** 171, 321; **10** 431, 501; **15** 197; **18** 23, 74, 76; **19** 254–55; **22** 19; **27** 20; **29 59–62 (upd.)**; **43** 447
Belmin Systems, **14** 36
Belmont Electronics, **II** 85–86; **11** 412
Belmont Plaza, **12** 316
Belmont Savings and Loan, **10** 339
Belmont Springs Water Company, Inc., **I** 234; **10** 227

Belo Corporation. *See* A.H. Belo Corporation
Beloit Corporation, **8** 243; **14 55–57**; **34** 358; **38** 224, 226–28
Beloit Tool Company. *See* Regal-Beloit Corporation.
Beloit Woodlands, **10** 380
Belridge Oil Co., **IV** 541
Belzer Group, **IV** 198–99
Bemis Company, Inc., **8 53–55**; **26** 43
Bemrose group, **IV** 650
Ben & Jerry's Homemade, Inc., **10 146–48**; **35 58–62**
Ben Franklin Retail Stores, Inc. *See* FoxMeyer Health Corporation.
Ben Franklin Savings & Trust, **10** 117
Ben Hill Griffin, **III** 53
Ben Johnson & Co. Ltd., **IV** 661
Ben Line, **6** 398
Ben Myerson Candy Co., Inc., **26** 468
Ben Venue Laboratories Inc., **16** 439; **39** 73
Benchmark Electronics, Inc., **40 66–69**
Benckiser Group, **37** 269
Benckiser N.V. *See* Reckitt Benckiser plc.
Bendicks, **I** 592
Bendix Corporation, **I** 68, **141–43**, 154, 166, 192, 416; **II** 33; **III** 166, 555; **7** 356; **8** 545; **9** 16–17; **10** 260, 279; **11** 138; **13** 356–57; **15** 284; **17** 564; **21** 416; **22** 31
Beneficial Corporation, **II** 236; **8 56–58**, 117; **10** 490
Beneficial Finance Company, **27** 428–29
Beneficial National Bank USA, **II** 286
Beneficial Standard Life, **10** 247
Benefit Consultants, Inc., **16** 145
Benelli Arms S.p.A., **39** 151
Benesse Corporation, **13** 91, 93; **39** 49
Benetton Group S.p.A., **8** 171; **10 149–52**; **15** 369; **18** 193; **25** 56
Bengal Iron and Steel Co., **IV** 205–06
Benihana, Inc., **18 56–59**
Benjamin Allen & Co., **IV** 660
Benjamin Moore and Co., **13 84–87**; **38 95–99 (upd.)**
Benlox Holdings PLC, **16** 465
Benn Bros. plc, **IV** 687
Bennett Biscuit Co., **II** 543
Bennett Industries, Inc., **17** 371–73
Bennett's Smokehouse and Saloon, **19** 122; **29** 201
Bennigan's, **II** 556–57; **7** 336; **12** 373; **13** 408; **19** 286; **25** 181
Bensdorp, **29** 47
Benson & Hedges, Ltd., **V** 398–99; **15** 137; **19** 171
Benson Wholesale Co., **II** 624
Bentalls, **37** 6, 8
Bentley Laboratories, **22** 360
Bentley Mills, Inc., **8** 272
Bentley Motor Ltd., **I** 194; **21** 435
Bentley Systems, **6** 247
Benton & Bowles, **I** 33; **6** 20, 22
Benton International, Inc., **29** 376
Benwood Iron Works, **17** 355
Benxi Iron and Steel Corp., **IV** 167
Benzina, **IV** 487
Benzinol, **IV** 487
N.V. Benzit. *See* N.V. Gemeenschappelijk Benzit van Aandeelen Philips Gloeilampenfabriken.
Berec Group, **III** 502; **7** 208
Beresford International plc, **24** 335; **27** 159
Beretta. *See* Fabbrica D' Armi Pietro Beretta S.p.A.
Berg Manufacturing Sales Co., **I** 156
Berg- und Metallbank, **IV** 139–40
Bergdorf Goodman, **I** 246; **V** 30–31; **25** 177
Bergedorfer Eisenwerk, **III** 417–20
Bergen Bank, **II** 352
Bergen Brunswig Corporation, **I** 413; **V 14–16**, 152; **13 88–90 (upd.)**; **18** 97
Berger Associates, Inc., **26** 233
Berger, Jenson and Nicholson, **I** 347; **18** 236
Berger Manufacturing Company, **26** 405
Bergische-Markische Bank, **II** 278
Berglen, **III** 570; **20** 362
Bergmann & Co., **II** 27
Bergstrom Paper Company, **8** 413
Bergswerksgesellschaft Hibernia, **I** 349; **IV** 194
Bergvik & Ala, **IV** 336, 338–39
Beringer Wine Estates Holdings, Inc., **22 78–81**; **36** 472
Berisford International plc, **19** 492, 494
Berjaya Group, **22** 464–65
Berkeley Computers, **III** 109; **14** 13
Berkey Photo Inc., **I** 447; **III** 475; **36** 171
Berkley Dean & Co., **15** 525
Berkline Corp., **17** 183; **20** 363; **39** 267
Berkshire Hathaway Inc., **III 213–15**; **18 60–63 (upd.)**; **29** 191; **30** 411; **36** 191; **38** 98; **40** 196, 199, 398; **39** 232, 235; **42 31–36 (upd.)**
Berkshire International, **V** 390–91; **17** 512
Berkshire Partners, **10** 393
Berleca Ltd., **9** 395; **42** 269
Berlex Laboratories, **I** 682; **10** 214
Berli Jucker, **18** 180–82
Berlin Exchange, **I** 409
Berlin Göring-Werke, **IV** 233
BerlinDat Gesellschaft für Informationsverarbeitung und Systemtechnik GmbH, **39** 57
Berliner Bank, **II** 256
Berliner Bankverein, **II** 278
Berliner Handels- und Frankfurter Bank, **II** 242
Berliner Union, **I** 409
Berlinische Bodengesellschaft, **I** 560
Berlitz International, Inc., **IV** 643; **7** 286, 312; **13 91–93**; **39 47–50 (upd.)**
Berman Brothers Fur Co., **21** 525
Berman Buckskin, **21** 525
Bernard C. Harris Publishing Company, Inc., **39 51–53**
Bernard Chaus, Inc., **27 59–61**
Bernardin Ltd., **30** 39
Bernheim-Meyer: A l'Innovation. *See* GIB Group.
Berni Inns, **I** 247
Bernie Schulman's, **12** 132
Bernstein Macauley, Inc., **II** 450
Berrios Enterprises, **14** 236
Berry Bearing Company, **9** 254
Berry Industries, **III** 628
Berry Plastics Corporation, **21 57–59**
Bert L. Smokler & Company, **11** 257
Bertea Corp., **III** 603
Bertelsmann A.G., **IV 592–94**, 614–15; **10** 196; **15 51–54 (upd.)**; **17** 399; **19** 285; **22** 194; **26** 19, 43; **30** 67, 70; **31** 375, 378; **43 63–67 (upd.)**, 422
Bertolini's Authentic Trattorias, **30** 329
Bertram & Graf Gmbh, **28** 45
Bertron Griscom & Company, **V** 641
Bertucci's Inc., **16 54–56**, 447
Berwick Industries, Inc., **35** 130–31
Berwind Corp., **14** 18
Beryl Corp., **26** 149
Beryllium Resources, **14** 80
Berzelius Metallhütten Gesellschaft, **IV** 141
Berzelius Umwelt-Service, **III** 625; **IV** 141
Besi, **26** 498
Besnier SA, **19 49–51**; **23** 217, 219; **24** 444–45; **25** 83, 85
Bess Mfg., **8** 510
Bessemer Capital Partners L.P., **15** 505
Bessemer Gas Engine Co., **II** 15; **20** 163
Bessemer Limestone & Cement Co., **IV** 409; **31** 454
Bessemer Steamship, **IV** 572; **7** 549
Besser Vibrapac, **III** 673
Best Apparel, **V** 156
Best Buy Co., Inc., **9 65–66**; **10** 305; **17** 489; **18** 532–33; **19** 362; **23 51–53 (upd.)**; **24** 52, 502; **29** 120, 123; **30** 464, 466; **38** 315
best energy GmbH, **39** 54, 57
Best Fabric Outlets, **16** 198
Best Holding Corporation. *See* Arkansas Best Corporation.
Best Manufacturing, **15** 490
Best Power, **24** 29
Best Products Inc., **19** 396–97
Best Read Guides Franchise Corp., **36** 341
Best Western, **14** 106; **25** 308
Bestfoods, **II** 496–97; **22 82–86 (upd.)**
Bestline Products, **17** 227
Bestop Inc., **16** 184
Bestwall Gypsum Co., **IV** 281; **9** 259
Bestway Distribution Services, Inc., **24** 126
Bestway Transportation, **14** 505
Beswick, **II** 17
BET Holdings, Inc., **18 64–66**; **22** 224; **25** 213; **34** 43
Beta West Properties, **25** 496–97
Bethesda Research Laboratories, Inc., **I** 321; **17** 287, 289
Bethlehem Steel Corporation, **IV 35–37**, 228, 572–73; **6** 540; **7 48–51 (upd.)**, 447, 549–50; **11** 65; **12** 354; **13** 97, 157; **18** 378; **22** 285; **23** 305; **25** 45; **26** 405; **27 62–66 (upd.)**
Beton Union, **III** 738
Better Brands Ltd., **32** 518–19
Better Communications, **IV** 597
Betz Laboratories, Inc., **I** 312–13; **10 153–55 (upd.)**; **15** 536
Bevan and Wedd Durlacher Morduant & Co., **II** 237
Beveridge-Marvellum Company, **8** 483
Beverly Enterprises, Inc., **III 76–77**, 80; **14** 242; **16 57–59 (upd.)**; **25** 309
Beverly Hills Savings, **II** 420
Beverly Pest Control, **25** 15
Bevis Custom Furniture, Inc., **12** 263
Bevrachtingskantoor, **26** 280
Bewag AG, **38** 449; **39 54–57**
Bezeq, **25** 266
BFC Construction Corporation, **25 63–65**
The BFGoodrich Company, **I** 28, 428, 440; **II** 414; **III** 118, 443; **V 231–33**; **8** 80–81, 290; **9** 12, 96, 133; **10** 438; **11** 158; **19 52–55 (upd.)**; **20** 260, 262; **21** 260; **22** 114; **23** 170; **25** 70; **30** 158; **31** 135

BFI. *See* Browning-Ferris Industries, Inc.
BFP Holdings Corp. *See* Big Flower Press Holdings, Inc.
BG Freight Line Holding B.V., **30** 318
BG plc, **29** 104
BG&E. *See* Baltimore Gas and Electric Company.
BGC Finance, **II** 420
BGJ Enterprises, Inc. *See* Brown Printing Company.
BH Acquisition Corporation, **22** 439
Bharat Coking Coal Ltd., **IV** 48–49
Bharat Petroleum Ltd., **IV** 441
Bharti Telecom, **16** 84
BHC Communications, Inc., 9 119; **26 32–34; 31** 109
BHP. *See* Broken Hill Proprietary Company Ltd.
BHP Steel of Australia, **18** 380
Bhs plc, 16 466; **17 42–44**, 334–35
BHV. *See* Bazar de l'Hotel de Ville.
Bi-Lo Inc., **II** 641; **V** 35; **16** 313
Biacore International AB, **25** 377
Bianchi, **13** 27
Bibb Co., **31** 199
BIC Corporation, III 29; **8 59–61; 20** 23; **23 54–57 (upd.)**
BICC PLC, III 433–34; 11 520. *See also* Balfour Beatty plc.
BICE Med Grille, **16** 447
Bicoastal Corporation, II 9–11
Bidermann Industries, **22** 122; **41** 129
Biederman & Company, **14** 160
Biedermann Motech, **37** 112
Bieffe, **16** 52
Bienfaisance, **III** 391
Bierbrauerei Wilhelm Remmer, **9** 86
Biesemeyer Manufacturing Corporation, **26** 363
Biffa Waste Services Ltd. *See* Severn Trent PLC.
Big B, Inc., 17 45–47
Big Bear Stores Co., 13 94–96
Big Boy, **III** 102–03
Big D Construction Corporation, **42** 432
Big 5 Sporting Goods, **12** 477
Big Flower Press Holdings, Inc., 21 60–62; 32 465–66
Big Foot Cattle Co., **14** 537
Big Horn Mining Co., **8** 423
Big M, **8** 409–10
Big O Tires, Inc., 20 61–63
Big Rivers Electric Corporation, 11 37–39
Big Sky Western Bank, **35** 197, 199
Big Three Industries, **I** 358
Big V Supermarkets, Inc., 25 66–68
Big Y Foods, Inc., **23** 169
Bigelow-Sanford, Inc., **31** 199
BII. *See* Banana Importers of Ireland.
Bike Athletics, **23** 449
BIL. *See* Brierley Investments.
Bilbao Insurance Group, **III** 200
Bilfinger & Berger Bau A.G., I 560–61
Bill & Melinda Gates Foundation, 41 53–55, 119
Bill Blass Ltd., 32 78–80
Bill France Racing, **19** 222
Billboard Publications, Inc., **7** 15
Billerud, **IV** 336
Billing Concepts Corp., 26 35–38
Billiton International, **IV** 56, 532; **22** 237
Bill's Casino, **9** 426
Bilsom, **40** 96–97
Bilt-Rite Chase-Pitkin, Inc., **41** 416
Biltwell Company, **8** 249
Bimar Foods Inc., **19** 192
Bimbo Bakeries USA, **29** 341
Bimbo, S.A., **36** 162, 164
Binder Hamlyn, **IV** 685
Binderline Development, Inc., **22** 175
Bindley Western Industries, Inc., 9 67–69
Bing Crosby Productions, **IV** 595
Bingham Dana LLP, 43 68–71
Binghamton Container Company, **8** 102
Bingo King. *See* Stuart Entertainment Inc.
Binks Sames Corporation, 21 63–66
Binney & Smith Inc., II 525; **IV** 621; **13** 293; **25 69–72**
Binnie & Partners, **22** 89
Binny & Co. Ltd., **III** 522
Binter Canarias, **6** 97
Bio-Clinic, **11** 486–87
Bio-Dynamics, Inc., **10** 105, 107; **37** 111
Bio Foods Inc. *See* Balance Bar Company.
Bio Synthetics, Inc., **21** 386
Bio-Toxicological Research Laboratories, **IV** 409
Biodevelopment Laboratories, Inc., **35** 47
Biofermin Pharmaceutical, **I** 704
Biogen Inc., I 638, 685; **8** 210; **14 58–60; 36 90–93 (upd.)**
Bioindustrias, **19** 475
Biokyowa, **III** 43
Biological Research, **III** 443
Biological Technology Corp., **IV** 252; **17** 29
Biomedical Reference Laboratories of North Carolina, **11** 424
Biomega Corp., **18** 422
Biomet, Inc., 10 156–58
Bionaire, Inc., **19** 360
BioSensor A.B., **I** 665
Biotechnica International, **I** 286
Bioteknik-Gruppen, **I** 665
Bioter-Biona, S.A., **II** 493
Bioter S.A., **III** 420
Biotherm, **III** 47
Bird & Sons, **22** 14
Bird Corporation, 19 56–58
Birdair, Inc., **35** 99–100
Birds Eye, **32** 474
Birdsall, Inc., **6** 529, 531
Bireley's, **22** 515
Birfield Ltd., **III** 494
Birkbeck, **10** 6
Birkenstock Footprint Sandals, Inc., 12 33–35; 42 37–40 (upd.)
Birmingham & Midland Bank. *See* Midland Bank plc.
Birmingham Joint Stock Bank, **II** 307
Birmingham Screw Co., **III** 493
Birmingham Slag Company, **7** 572–73, 575
Birmingham Steel Corporation, 13 97–98; 18 379–80; **19** 380; **40 70–73 (upd.)**
Birra Moretti, **25** 281–82
Birtman Electric Co., **III** 653; **12** 548
Biscayne Bank. *See* Banco Espírito Santo e Comercial de Lisboa S.A.
Biscayne Federal Savings and Loan Association, **11** 481
Biscuiterie Nantaise, **II** 502; **10** 323
Biscuits Belin, **II** 543
Biscuits Delacre, **II** 480; **26** 56
Biscuits Gondolo, **II** 543
Bishop & Babcock Manufacturing Co., **II** 41
Bishop & Co. Savings Bank, **11** 114
Bishop National Bank of Hawaii, **11** 114
Bishopsgate Insurance, **III** 200
BISSELL, Inc., 9 70–72; 30 75–78 (upd.)
Bit Software, Inc., **12** 62
Bits & Pieces, **26** 439
Bitumax Proprietary, **III** 672
Bitumen & Oil Refineries (Australia) Ltd., **III** 672–73
BIW. *See* Bath Iron Works.
BIZ Enterprises, **23** 390
BizBuyer.com, **39** 25
Bizmark, **13** 176
BizMart, **6** 244–45; **8** 404–05
BJ Services Company, 15 534, 536; **25 73–75**
BJ's Wholesale Club, **12** 221; **13** 547–49; **33** 198
BJK&E. *See* Bozell Worldwide Inc.
Björknäs Nya Sågverks, **IV** 338
BK Tag, **28** 157
BKW, **IV** 229
BL Ltd., **I** 175; **10** 354
BL Systems. *See* AT&T Istel Ltd.
The Black & Decker Corporation, I 667; **III 435–37**, 628, 665; **8** 332, 349; **15** 417–18; **16** 384; **17** 215; **20 64–68 (upd.)**; **22** 334; **43** 101, 289
Black & Veatch LLP, 22 87–90
Black Arrow Leasing, **II** 138; **24** 193
Black Box Corporation, 20 69–71
Black Clawson Company, **24** 478
Black Entertainment Television. *See* BET Holdings, Inc.
Black Flag Co., **I** 622
Black Hawk Broadcasting Group, **III** 188; **10** 29; **38** 17
Black Hills Corporation, 20 72–74
Black Pearl Software, Inc., **39** 396
Black Spread Eagle, **II** 235
Blackburn Group, **III** 508; **24** 85
Blackhawk, **9** 26
Blackhorse Agencies, **II** 309
Blackmer Pump Co., **III** 468
Blacks Leisure Group plc, 39 58–60
Blackstone Capital Partners L.P., **V** 223; **6** 378; **17** 366
The Blackstone Group, **II** 434, 444; **IV** 718; **11** 177, 179; **13** 170; **17** 238, 443; **22** 404, 416; **26** 408; **37** 309, 311
Blackstone Hotel Acquisition Co., **24** 195
Blaine Construction Company, **8** 546
Blair and Co., **II** 227
Blair Corporation, 25 76–78; 31 53–55
Blair Paving, **III** 674
Blair Radio, **6** 33
Blakiston Co., **IV** 636
Blane Products, **I** 403
Blanes, S.A. de C.V., **34** 197
Blatz Breweries, **I** 254
Blaupunkt-Werke, **I** 192–93
BLC Insurance Co., **III** 330
BLD Europe, **16** 168
Bleichröder, **II** 191
Blendax, **III** 53; **8** 434; **26** 384
Blessings Corp., 14 550; **19 59–61**
Blimpie International, Inc., 15 55–57; 17 501; **32** 444
Bliss Manufacturing Co., **17** 234–35
Blitz-Weinhart Brewing, **18** 71–72
Bloch & Guggenheimer, Inc., **40** 51–52
Blochman Lawrence Goldfree, **I** 697

Block Drug Company, Inc., **6** 26; **8 62–64**; **27 67–70 (upd.)**
Block Financial Corporation, **17** 265; **29** 227
Block Management, **29** 226
Block Medical, Inc., **10** 351
Blockbuster Entertainment Corporation, **II** 161; **IV** 597; **9 73–75**, 361; **11** 556–58; **12** 43, 515; **13** 494; **18** 64, 66; **19** 417; **22** 161–62; **23** 88, 503; **25** 208–10, 222; **26** 409; **28** 296; **29** 504
Blockbuster Inc., **31 56–60 (upd.)**, 339–40
Blockson Chemical, **I** 380; **13** 379
Bloedel, Stewart & Welch, **IV** 306–07
Blohm & Voss, **I** 74
Bloomberg L.P., **18** 24; **21 67–71**
Bloomingdale's Inc., **I** 90; **III** 63; **IV** 651, 703; **9** 209, 393; **10** 487; **12 36–38**, 307, 403–04; **16** 328; **23** 210; **25** 257; **31** 190
Blount International, Inc., **I** 563; **12 39–41**; **24** 78; **26** 117, 119, 363
BLT Ventures, **25** 270
Blue Arrow PLC, **II** 334–35; **9** 327; **30** 300
Blue Bell Creameries L.P., **30 79–81**
Blue Bell, Inc., **V** 390–91; **12** 205; **17** 512
Blue Bird Corporation, **35 63–66**
Blue Bunny Ice Cream. *See* Wells' Dairy, Inc.
Blue Byte, **41** 409
Blue Chip Stamps, **III** 213–14; **30** 412
Blue Circle Industries PLC, **III 669–71**, 702
Blue Cross and Blue Shield Association, **10 159–61**; **14** 84
Blue Cross and Blue Shield Mutual of Northern Ohio, **12** 176
Blue Cross and Blue Shield of Colorado, **11** 175
Blue Cross and Blue Shield of Greater New York, **III** 245, 246
Blue Cross and Blue Shield of Ohio, **15** 114
Blue Cross Blue Shield of Michigan, **12** 22
Blue Cross of California, **25** 525
Blue Cross of Northeastern New York, **III** 245–46
Blue Diamond Growers, **28 56–58**
Blue Dot Services, **37** 280, 283
Blue Funnel Line, **I** 521; **6** 415–17
Blue Line Distributing, **7** 278–79
Blue Metal Industries, **III** 687; **28** 82
Blue Mountain Arts, Inc., **IV** 621; **29 63–66**
Blue Ribbon Beef Pack, Inc., **II** 515–16
Blue Ribbon Sports. *See* Nike, Inc.
Blue Ridge Grocery Co., **II** 625
Blue Ridge Lumber Ltd., **16** 11
Blue Shield of California, **25** 527
Blue Square Israel Ltd., **41 56–58**
Blue Tee Corporation, **23** 34, 36
Blue Water Food Service, **13** 244
Bluebird Inc., **10** 443
Bluffton Grocery Co., **II** 668
Blumberg Communications Inc., **24** 96
Blunt Ellis & Loewi, **III** 270
Blyth and Co., **I** 537; **13** 448, 529
Blyth Eastman Dillon & Company, **II** 445; **22** 405–06
Blyth Industries, Inc., **18 67–69**
Blyth Merrill Lynch, **II** 448
Blythe Colours BV, **IV** 119
BMC Industries, Inc., **6** 275; **17 48–51**
BMC Software Inc., **14** 391
BMG/Music, **IV** 594; **15** 51; **37** 192–93
BMI. *See* Broadcast Music Inc.
BMI Ltd., **III** 673
BMI Systems Inc., **12** 174
BMO Corp., **III** 209
BMW. *See* Bayerische Motoren Werke.
BNA. *See* Banca Nazionale dell'Agricoltura *or* Bureau of National Affairs, Inc.
BNCI. *See* Banque Nationale Pour le Commerce et l'Industrie.
BNE. *See* Bank of New England Corp.
BNG, Inc., **19** 487
BNP Paribas Group, **36 94–97 (upd.)**; **42** 349
BNS Acquisitions, **26** 247
Boa Shoe Company, **42** 325
BOAC. *See* British Overseas Airways Corp.
Boardwalk Regency, **6** 201
Boart and Hard Metals, **IV** 22
Boart Longyear Company, **26 39–42**, 69
Boase Massimi Pollitt, **6** 48
Boatmen's Bancshares Inc., **15 58–60**
BoatsDirect.com, **37** 398
Bob Evans Farms, Inc., **9 76–79**; **10** 259; **35** 83–84
Bobbie Brooks Inc., **17** 384
Bobbs-Merrill, **11** 198
Bobingen A.G., **I** 347
Bobro Products. *See* BWP Distributors.
BOC Group plc, **I 314–16**, 358; **11** 402; **12** 500; **25 79–82 (upd.)**
Boca Resorts, Inc., **37 33–36**
BOCAP Corp., **37** 372
Bochumer Verein für Gusstahlfabrikation, **IV** 88
Bock Bearing Co., **8** 530
Bodcaw Co., **IV** 287; **15** 228
Boddington, **21** 247
Bodegas, **8** 556
Bodeker Drug Company, **16** 399
The Body Shop International PLC, **11 40–42**
Boehringer Ingelheim GmbH. *See* C.H. Boehringer Sohn.
Boehringer Mannheim Companies, **37** 111–12
The Boeing Company, **I** 41–43, **47–49**, 50, 55–56, 58, 61, 67–68, 70–72, 74, 77, 82, 84–85, 90, 92–93, 96–97, 100, 102, 104–05, 108, 111–13, 116, 121–22, 126, 128, 130, 195, 489–90, 511, 530; **II** 7, 32–33, 62, 442; **III** 512, 539; **IV** 171, 576; **6** 68, 96, 130, 327; **7** 11, 456, 504; **8** 81, 313, 315; **9** 12, 18, 128, 194, 206, 232, 396, 416–17, 458–60, 498; **10 162–65 (upd.)**, 262, 316, 369, 536; **11** 164, 267, 277–79, 363, 427; **12** 180, 190–91, 380; **13** 356–58; **21** 140, 143, 436; **24** 21, 84, 85–86, 88–89, 442; **25** 34, 224, 430–31; **26** 117; **28** 195, 225; **32 81–87 (upd.)**; **36** 122, 190; **38** 372
Boeke & Huidekooper, **III** 417
Boerenbond, **II** 304
Boettcher & Co., **III** 271
Bofors Nobel Inc., **9** 380–81; **13** 22
Bogen Company, **15** 213
Bohemia, Inc., **13 99–101**; **31** 467
Bohm-Allen Jewelry, **12** 112
Böhme-Fettchemie, Chenmitz, **III** 32
Bohn Aluminum & Brass, **10** 439
Boise Cascade Corporation, **I** 142; **III** 499, 648, 664; **IV 255–56**, 333; **6** 577; **7** 356; **8 65–67 (upd.)**, 477; **15** 229; **16** 510; **19** 269, 445–46; **22** 154; **31** 13; **32 88–92 (upd.)**; **36** 509; **37** 140
Bokaro Steel Ltd., **IV** 206
Bolands Ltd., **II** 649
Bolar Pharmaceutical Co., **16** 529
Boley G.m.b.H., **21** 123
Boliden Mining, **II** 366
Bolinder-Munktell, **I** 209; **II** 366
Bolitho Bank, **II** 235
Bölkow GmbH, **I** 74
Bolles & Houghton, **10** 355
The Bolsa Chica Company, **8** 300
Bolt, Beranek & Newman Inc., **26** 520
Bolt Security, **32** 373
BOMAG, **8** 544, 546
Bombadier Defence Services UK, **41** 412
Bombardier Aerospace Group, **36** 190–91
Bombardier, Inc., **12** 400–01; **16** 78; **25** 423; **27** 281, 284; **34** 118–19; **35** 350–51; **42 41–46 (upd.)**
The Bombay Company, Inc., **III** 581; **10 166–68**; **27** 429
Bon Appetit, **II** 656
Bon Dente International Inc., **39** 320
The Bon Marché, Inc., **V** 25; **9** 209; **19** 88, 306, 309; **23 58–60**; **26** 158, 160
Bon Secours Health System, Inc., **24 68–71**
The Bon-Ton Stores, Inc., **16 60–62**
Bonanza, **7** 336; **10** 331; **15** 361–63
Bonanza Steakhouse, **17** 320
Bonaventura, **IV** 611
Bonaventure Liquor Store Co., **I** 284
Bond Brewing International, **23** 405
Bond Corporation Holdings Limited, **I** 253, 255; **10 169–71**
Bondex International, **8** 456
Bonduel Pickling Co. Inc., **25** 517
Bongrain SA, **19** 50; **23** 217, 219; **25 83–85**
Boni & Liveright, **13** 428
Bonifiche Siele, **II** 272
Bonimart, **II** 649
Bonneville International Corporation, **29 67–70**; **30** 15
Bontrager Bicycles, **16** 495
Bonwit Teller, **13** 43; **17** 43
Book-Mart Press, Inc., **41** 111
Book-of-the-Month Club, Inc., **IV** 661, 675; **7** 529; **13 105–07**
Booker plc, **13 102–04**; **31 61–64 (upd.)**
Booker Tate, **13** 102
Booklink Technologies, **26** 19
Bookmasters, **10** 136
Books-A-Million, Inc., **14 61–62**; **16** 161; **41 59–62 (upd.)**
Bookstop, **10** 136
Boole & Babbage, Inc., **25 86–88**
Booth Bay, Ltd., **16** 37
Booth Creek Ski Holdings, Inc., **31 65–67**
Booth Fisheries, **II** 571
Booth, Inc., **II** 420
Booth-Kelly Lumber Co., **IV** 281; **9** 259
Booth Leasing, **I** 449
Bootprint Entertainment, **31** 240
The Boots Company PLC, **I** 640, 668, 708; **II** 650; **V 17–19**; **8** 548; **19** 122; **24 72–76 (upd.)**
Boots Pharmaceuticals, **18** 51
Booz Allen & Hamilton Inc., **10 172–75**

Boral Limited, III 672–74; 43 72–76 (upd.)
Borax Holdings, **IV** 191
Bordas, **IV** 615
Borden Cabinet Corporation, **12** 296
Borden, Inc., II 470–73, 486, 498, 538, 545; **IV** 569; **7** 127, 129, 380; **11** 173; **15** 490; **16** 43; **17** 56; **22** 84, **91–96 (upd.)**; **24** 273, 288, 520; **27** 38, 40, 316, 318
Border Fine Arts, **11** 95
Border Television, **41** 352
Borders Group, Inc., 9 361; **10** 137; **15 61–62**; **17** 522; **18** 286; **25** 17; **30** 69; **43 77–79 (upd.)**, 408
Borders, Perrin and Norrander, **23** 480
Borealis A/S, **30** 205
Borg Instruments, **23** 494
Borg-Warner Automotive, Inc., 14 63–66; **23** 171; **32 93–97 (upd.)**
Borg-Warner Corporation, I 193, 339, 393; **III** 428, **438–41**; **14** 63, 357; **22** 228; **25** 74, 253
Borg-Warner Security Corporation, **13** 123–25; **14** 63, 65, 541; **41** 79
Borland International, Inc., 6 255–56; **9 80–82**; **10** 237, 509, 519, 558; **15** 492; **25** 300–01, 349; **38** 417
Borman's, Inc., **II** 638; **16** 249
Borneo Airways. *See* Malaysian Airlines System BHD.
Borneo Co., **III** 523
Borregaard Osterreich AG, **18** 395
Borror Corporation. *See* Dominion Homes, Inc.
Borsheim's, **III** 215; **18** 60
Borun Bros., **12** 477
Bosanquet, Salt and Co., **II** 306
Bosch. *See* Robert Bosch GmbH.
Boschert, **III** 434
Boscov's Department Store, Inc., 31 68–70
Bose Corporation, 13 108–10; **36 98–101 (upd.)**
Bosendorfer, L., Klavierfabrik, A.G., **12** 297
Bosert Industrial Supply, Inc., **V** 215
Boso Condensed Milk, **II** 538
Bostich, **III** 628
Boston Acoustics, Inc., 22 97–99
Boston and Maine Corporation, **16** 350
Boston Beer Company, 18 70–73; **22** 422; **31** 383
Boston Brewing Company, **18** 502
Boston Casualty Co., **III** 203
Boston Celtics Limited Partnership, 14 67–69
Boston Chicken, Inc., 12 42–44; **23** 266; **29** 170, 172
Boston Co., **II** 451–52
Boston Consulting Group, **I** 532; **9** 343; **18** 70; **22** 193
Boston Corp., **25** 66
Boston Distributors, **9** 453
Boston Edison Company, 12 45–47
Boston Educational Research, **27** 373
Boston Fruit Co., **II** 595
Boston Garden Arena Corporation, **14** 67
Boston Gas Company, **6** 486–88
Boston Globe, **7** 13–16
Boston Herald, **7** 15
Boston Industries Corp., **III** 735
Boston Marine Insurance Co., **III** 242
Boston National Bank, **13** 465
Boston News Bureau, **IV** 601
Boston Overseas Financial Corp., **II** 208
Boston Popcorn Co., **27** 197–98; **43** 218
Boston Professional Hockey Association Inc., 39 61–63
Boston Properties, Inc., 22 100–02
Boston Scientific Corporation, 37 37–40
Boston Technology, **43** 117
Boston Ventures Limited Partnership, **17** 444; **27** 41, 393
Boston Whaler, Inc., **V** 376–77; **10** 215–16; **26** 398
Bostrom Seating, Inc., **23** 306
BOTAS, **IV** 563
Botsford Ketchum, Inc., **6** 40
Botswana General Insurance Company, **22** 495
Botto, Rossner, Horne & Messinger, **6** 40
Bottu, **II** 475
BOTWEB, Inc., **39** 95
Bougainville Copper Pty., **IV** 60–61
Boulanger, **37** 22
Boulder Creek Steaks & Saloon, **16** 447
Boulder Natural Gas Company, **19** 411
Boulet Dru DuPuy Petit Group. *See* Wells Rich Greene BDDP.
Boulevard Bancorp, **12** 165
Boulton & Paul Ltd., **31** 398–400
Boundary Gas, **6** 457
Boundary Healthcare, **12** 327
Bouquet, **V** 114
Bourdon, **19** 49
Bourjois, **12** 57
Boussois Souchon Neuvesel, **II** 474; **III** 677; **16** 121–22
Bouygues S.A., I 562–64; **13** 206; **23** 475–76; **24 77–80 (upd.)**; **31** 126, 128
Bouzan Mines Ltd., **IV** 164
Bovaird Seyfang Manufacturing Co., **III** 471
Bovis Construction, **38** 344–45
Bovis Ltd., **I** 588
Bow Bangles, **17** 101, 103
Bowater PLC, III 501–02; **IV 257–59**; **7** 208; **8** 483–84; **25** 13; **30** 229
Bower Roller Bearing Company. *See* Federal-Mogul Corporation.
Bowery and East River National Bank, **II** 226
Bowery Savings Bank, **II** 182; **9** 173
Bowes Co., **II** 631
Bowman Gum, Inc., **13** 520
Bowmar Instruments, **II** 113; **11** 506
Bowne & Co., Inc., 18 331–32; **23 61–64**
Bowthorpe plc, 33 70–72
Box Innards Inc., **13** 442
Box Office Attraction Co., **II** 169
BoxCrow Cement Company, **8** 259
The Boy Scouts of America, 34 66–69
Boyd Bros. Transportation Inc., 39 64–66
Boyd Gaming Corporation, 43 80–82
The Boyds Collection, Ltd., 29 71–73
Boyer Brothers, Inc., **14** 17–18
Boyer's International, Inc., **20** 83
Boykin Enterprises, **IV** 136
Boyles Bros. Drilling Company. *See* Christensen Boyles Corporation.
Boys Market, **17** 558–59
Boz, **IV** 697–98
Bozel Électrométallurgie, **IV** 174
Bozell, Jacobs, Kenyon, and Eckhardt Inc. *See* True North Communications Inc.
Bozell Worldwide Inc., 25 89–91
Bozkurt, **27** 188
Bozzuto's, Inc., 13 111–12
BP. *See* British Petroleum Company PLC.
BP Amoco plc, **31** 31, 34; **40** 358
BPB, **III** 736
BPD, **13** 356
BPI Communications, Inc., **7** 15; **19** 285; **27** 500
BR. *See* British Rail.
Braas, **III** 734, 736
Brabant, **III** 199, 201
Brabazon, **III** 555
Brach and Brock Confections, Inc., 15 63–65; **29** 47
Brad Foote Gear Works, **18** 453
Bradbury Agnew and Co., **IV** 686
Braden Manufacturing, **23** 299–301
Bradford District Bank, **II** 333
Bradford Exchange Ltd. Inc., **21** 269
Bradford Insulation Group, **III** 687
Bradford Pennine, **III** 373
Bradlees Discount Department Store Company, II 666–67; **12 48–50**; **24** 461
Bradley Lumber Company, **8** 430
Bradley Producing Corp., **IV** 459
Bradstreet Co., **IV** 604–05; **19** 133
Braegen Corp., **13** 127
Bragussa, **IV** 71
BRAINS. *See* Belgian Rapid Access to Information Network Services.
Bramalea Ltd., 9 83–85; **10** 530–31
Brambles Industries Limited, III 494–95; **24** 400; **42 47–50**
Bramco, **III** 600
Bramwell Gates, **II** 586
Bran & Lübbe, **III** 420
Brand Companies, Inc., **9** 110; **11** 436
Branded Restaurant Group, Inc., **12** 372
Brandeis & Sons, **19** 511
Brandenburgische Motorenwerke, **I** 138
Brandywine Asset Management, Inc., **33** 261
Brandywine Insurance Agency, Inc., **25** 540
Brandywine Iron Works and Nail Factory, **14** 323
Brandywine Valley Railroad Co., **14** 324
Braniff Airlines, **I** 97, 489, 548; **II** 445; **6** 50, 119–20; **16** 274; **17** 504; **21** 142; **22** 406; **36** 231
Branigar Organization, Inc., **IV** 345
Brascade Resources, **IV** 308
Brascan Ltd., **II** 456; **IV** 165, 330; **25** 281
Braspetro, **IV** 454, 501–02
Brass Craft Manufacturing Co., **III** 570; **20** 361
Brass Eagle Inc., 34 70–72
Brasseries Kronenbourg, **II** 474–75
Braswell Motor Freight, **14** 567
Braud & Faucheux. *See* Manitou BF S.A.
Brauerei Beck & Co., 9 86–87; **33 73–76 (upd.)**
Braun, **III** 29; **17** 214–15; **26** 335
Braunkohlenwerk Golpa-Jessnitz AG, **IV** 230
Brauns Fashions Corporation. *See* Christopher & Banks Corporation.
Brazilian Central Bank, **IV** 56
Brazos Gas Compressing, **7** 345
Brazos Sportswear, Inc., 23 65–67
Breakstone Bros., Inc., **II** 533
Breakthrough Software, **10** 507
Breckenridge-Remy, **18** 216

Breco Holding Company, **17** 558, 561
Bredel Exploitatie B.V., **8** 546
Bredell Paint Co., **III** 745
Bredero's Bouwbedrijf of Utrecht, **IV** 707–08, 724
BREED Technologies, Inc., **22** 31
Breedband NV, **IV** 133
Brega Petroleum Marketing Co., **IV** 453, 455
Breguet Aviation, **I** 44; **24** 86
Breitenburger Cementfabrik, **III** 701
Bremner Biscuit Co., **II** 562; **13** 426
Brenco Inc., **16** 514
Brenda Mines Ltd., **7** 399
Brennan College Services, **12** 173
Brenntag AG, 8 68–69, 496; **23 68–70 (upd.)**, **23** 453–54
Bresler's Industries, Inc., **35** 121
Breslube Enterprises, **8** 464
Bresser Optik, **41** 264
Brewster Lines, **6** 410
Breyers Ice Cream Co. *See* Good Humor-Breyers.
BRI Bar Review Institute, Inc., **IV** 623; **12** 224
BRI International, **21** 425
Brian Mills, **V** 118
Briarpatch, Inc., **12** 109
Brickwood Breweries, **I** 294
Bricorama, **23** 231
Bricotruc, **37** 259
Bridas S.A., **24** 522
Bridel, **19** 49–50; **25** 85
Bridge Communications Inc., **34** 442–43
Bridge Oil Ltd., **I** 438
Bridge Technology, Inc., **10** 395
Bridgeman Creameries, **II** 536
Bridgeport Brass, **I** 377
Bridgeport Machines, Inc., 17 52–54
Bridgestone Corporation, V 234–35; 15 355; **20** 262; **21 72–75 (upd.)**
Bridgestone Liquefied Gas, **IV** 364
Bridgestone/Firestone, **19** 454, 456
Bridgeway Plan for Health, **6** 186
Bridgford Company, **13** 382
Bridgford Foods Corporation, 27 71–73
Brier Hill, **IV** 114
Brierly Investment Limited, **19** 156; **24** 399
Briggs & Stratton Corporation, III 597; **8 70–73; 27 74–78 (upd.)**
Briggs and Lundy Lumber Cos., **14** 18
Brigham's Inc., **15** 71
Bright Horizons Family Solutions, Inc., 31 71–73
Bright of America Inc., **12** 426
Bright Star Technologies, **13** 92; **15** 455; **41** 362
Brighter Vision Learning Adventures, **29** 470, 472
Brighton & Hove Bus and Coach Company, **28** 155–56
Brighton Federal Savings and Loan Assoc., **II** 420
Brightpoint, Inc., 18 74–77
Brightwork Development Inc., **25** 348
Briker, **23** 231
Brillion Iron Works Inc., **23** 306
Brimsdown Lead Co., **III** 680
Brin's Oxygen Company Limited. *See* BOC Group plc.
Brinco Ltd., **II** 211
Brink's, Inc., **IV** 180–82; **19** 319
Brinker International, Inc., 10 176–78; 18 438; **38 100–03 (upd.)**
Brinson Partners Inc., **41** 198
BRIntec, **III** 434
Brinton Carpets, **III** 423
BRIO AB, 24 81–83
Brio Technology, **25** 97
Briones Alonso y Martin, **42** 19
Brisbane Gas Co., **III** 673
Brisco Engineering, **41** 412
Bristol Aeroplane, **I** 50, 197; **10** 261; **24** 85
Bristol-BTR, **I** 429
Bristol-Erickson, **13** 297
Bristol Gaming Corporation, **21** 298
Bristol Hotel Company, 23 71–73; 38 77
Bristol-Myers Squibb Company, I 26, 30, 37, 301, 696, 700, 703; **III 17–19**, 36, 67; **IV** 272; **6** 27; **7** 255; **8** 210, 282–83; **9 88–91 (upd.)**; **10** 70; **11** 289; **12** 126–27; **16** 438; **21** 546; **25** 91, 253, 365; **32** 213; **34** 280, 282, 284; **37 41–45 (upd.)**
Bristol PLC, **IV** 83
Bristol-Siddeley, Ltd., **I** 50; **24** 85
Britannia Airways, **8** 525–26
Britannia Security Group PLC, **12** 10
Britannia Soft Drinks Limited, **38** 77
Britannica Software, **7** 168
Britannica.com, **39** 140, 144
Britches of Georgetowne, **10** 215–16
BRITE. *See* Granada Group PLC.
Brite Voice Systems, Inc., 20 75–78
BriteSmile, Inc., **35** 325
British & Commonwealth Shipping Company, **10** 277
British Aerospace plc, I 42, 46, **50–53**, 55, 74, 83, 132, 532; **III** 458, 507; **V** 339; **7** 9, 11, 458–59; **8** 315; **9** 499; **11** 413; **12** 191; **14** 36; **18** 125; **21** 8, 443; **24 84–90 (upd.)**; **27** 474
British Airways plc, I 34, 83, **92–95**, 109; **IV** 658; **6** 60, 78–79, 118, 132; **14 70–74 (upd.)**; **18** 80; **22** 52; **24** 86, 311, 396, 399–400; **26** 115; **27** 20–21, 466; **28** 25, 508; **31** 103; **33** 270; **34** 398; **37** 232; **38** 104–05; **39** 137–38; **43 83–88 (upd.)**
British Aluminium, Ltd., **II** 422; **IV** 15
British American Cosmetics, **I** 427
British American Financial Services, **42** 450
British American Insurance Co., **III** 350
British American Nickel, **IV** 110
British-American Tobacco Co., Ltd., **V** 396, 401–02, 417; **9** 312; **29** 194–95; **34** 39
British and Dominion Film Corp., **II** 157
British and Foreign Marine, **III** 350
British and Foreign Steam Navigation Company, **23** 160
British and French Bank, **II** 232–33
British and North American Royal Mail Steam Packet Company. *See* Cunard Line Ltd.
British Bank of North America, **II** 210
British Bank of the Middle East, **II** 298
British-Borneo Oil & Gas PLC, 34 73–75
British Borneo Timber Co., **III** 699
British Broadcasting Corporation Ltd., III 163; **IV** 651; **7 52–55; 21 76–79 (upd.)**; **24** 192; **39** 198; **42** 114, 116
British Caledonian Airways, **I** 94–95; **6** 79
British Can Co., **I** 604
British Car Auctions, **14** 321
British Celanese Ltd., **I** 317
British Cellulose and Chemical Manufacturing Co., **I** 317
British Chrome, **III** 699
British Coal Corporation, IV 38–40
British Columbia Forest Products Ltd., **IV** 279; **19** 155
British Columbia Packers, **II** 631–32
British Columbia Resources Investment Corp., **IV** 308
British Columbia Telephone Company, IV 308; **6 309–11**
British Commonwealth Insurance, **III** 273
British Commonwealth Pacific Airways, **6** 110; **24** 398
British Continental Airlines, **I** 92
British Credit Trust, **10** 443
British Data Management, Ltd., **33** 212, 214
British Digital Broadcasting plc, **24** 192, 194
British Dyestuffs Corp., **I** 351
British Dynamite Co., **I** 351
British Energy Group, **19** 391
British Engine, **III** 350
British European Airways, **I** 93, 466
British Executive and General Aviation, **I** 50; **24** 85
British Fuels, **III** 735
British Gas plc, II 260; **V 559–63; 6** 478–79; **11** 97; **18** 365–67; **38** 408. *See also* Centrica plc.
British Gauge and Instrument Company, **13** 234
British General, **III** 234
British General Post Office, **25** 99–100
British Goodrich Tyre Co., **I** 428
British Home Stores PLC. *See* Storehouse PLC.
British Hovercraft Corp., **I** 120
British Independent Television Enterprises Ltd. *See* Granada Group PLC.
British India and Queensland Agency Co. Ltd., **III** 522
British India Steam Navigation Co., **III** 521–22
British Industrial Solvents Ltd., **IV** 70
British Industry, **III** 335
British Insulated and Helsby Cables Ltd., **III** 433–34
British Interactive Broadcasting Ltd., **20** 79
British Isles Transport Co. Ltd., **II** 564
British Land Company, **10** 6
British Leyland Motor Corporation, **I** 175, 186; **III** 516, 523; **13** 286–87; **14** 35–36
British Linen Bank, **10** 336
British Marine Air Navigation, **I** 92
British Metal Corp., **IV** 140, 164
British Midland plc, 34 398; **38 104–06**
British Motor Corporation, **III** 555; **7** 459; **13** 286
British Motor Holdings, **7** 459
British National Films Ltd., **II** 157
British National Oil Corp., **IV** 40
British Newfoundland Corporation, **6** 502
British Nuclear Fuels PLC, I 573; **6 451–54; 13** 458
British Nylon Spinners (BNS), **17** 118
British Overseas Airways Corp., **I** 51, 93, 120–21; **III** 522; **6** 78–79, 100, 110, 112, 117; **14** 71; **24** 86, 397
British Oxygen Co. *See* BOC Group.
The British Petroleum Company plc, I 241, 303; **II** 449, 563; **IV** 61, 280,

363–64, **378–80**, 381–82, 412–13, 450–54, 456, 466, 472, 486, 497–99, 505, 515, 524–25, 531–32, 557; **6** 304; **7 56–59 (upd.)**, 140–41, 332–33, 516, 559; **9** 490, 519; **11** 538; **13** 449; **14** 317; **16** 394, 461–62; **19** 155, 391; **21 80–84 (upd.)**, 352; **25** 101; **26** 366, 369; **30** 86, 88
British Plasterboard, **III** 734
British Portland Cement Manufacturers, **III** 669–70
British Printing and Communications Corp., **IV** 623–24, 642; **7** 312; **12** 224
British Prudential Assurance Co., **III** 335
British Rail, **III** 509; **V** 421–24; **10** 122; **27** 474
British Railways, **6** 413
British Railways Board, **V 421–24**
British Road Services, **6** 413
British Royal Insurance Co., Ltd., **III** 242
British Satellite Broadcasting, **10** 170
British Shoe Corporation, **V** 178
British Sky Broadcasting Group Plc, **20 79–81**; **24** 192, 194
British South Africa Co., **IV** 23, 94
British South American Airways, **I** 93
British South American Corporation, **6** 95
British Steel Brickworks, **III** 501; **7** 207
British Steel plc, **III** 494–95; **IV** 40, **41–43**, 128; **17** 481; **19 62–65 (upd.)**, 391; **24** 302
British Sugar plc, **II** 514, 581–82; **13** 53; **41** 30, 32–33
British Tabulating Machine Company, **6** 240
British Telecommunications plc, **I** 83, 330; **II** 82; **V 279–82**; **6** 323; **7** 332–33; **8** 153; **9** 32; **11** 59, 185, 547; **15 66–70 (upd.)**, 131; **16** 468; **18** 155, 345; **20** 81; **21** 233; **24** 370; **25** 101–02, 301; **27** 304; **29** 44
British Thermoplastics and Rubber. *See* BTR plc.
British Timken Ltd., **8** 530
British Trimmings Ltd., **29** 133
British Twin Disc Ltd., **21** 504
British Tyre and Rubber Co., **I** 428
British United Airways, **I** 94
British Vita plc, **9 92–93**; **19** 413–15; **33 77–79 (upd.)**
British World Airlines Ltd., **18 78–80**
British Zaire Diamond Distributors Ltd., **IV** 67
Britoil, **IV** 380; **21** 82
Britt Airways, **I** 118
Britt Lumber Co., Inc., **8** 348
Brittains Bricks, **III** 673
Brittania Sportswear, **16** 509
Britvic Soft Drinks Limited, **38** 74, 77
BritWill Healthcare Corp., **25** 504
BRK Brands, Inc., **28** 134
BRK Electronics, **9** 414
Bro-Well, **17** 56
Broad, Inc., **11** 482
Broad River Power Company, **6** 575
Broadband Networks Inc., **36** 352
Broadcast Music Inc., **23 74–77**; **29** 22–23
Broadcast Technology Systems, Inc., **13** 398
Broadcaster Press, **36** 341
Broadcom Corporation, **34 76–79**; **36** 123
Broadcom Eireann Research, **7** 510
Broadcort Capital Corp., **13** 342
The Broadmoor Hotel, **30 82–85**
BroadPark, **II** 415
BroadVision Inc., **18** 543; **38** 432
Broadway & Seymour Inc., **17** 264; **18** 112
Broadway-Hale Stores, Inc., **12** 356
Broadway Stores, Inc., **31** 193
Brobeck, Phleger & Harrison, LLP, **31 74–76**
Brock Candy Company. *See* Brach and Brock Confections, Inc.
Brock Hotel Corp., **13** 472–73; **31** 94
Brock Residence Inn, **9** 426
Brockway Glass Co., **I** 524; **15** 128
Brockway Standard Holdings Corporation. *See* BWAY Corporation.
Broder Bros. Co., **38 107–09**
Broderbund Software, Inc., **10** 285; **13 113–16**; **25** 118; **29 74–78 (upd.)**
Broederlijke Liefdebeurs, **III** 177
Broken Hill Proprietary Company Ltd., **I** 437–39; **II** 30; **III** 494; **IV 44–47**, 58, 61, 171, 484; **10** 170; **21** 227; **22 103–08 (upd.)**; **26** 248
The Bronfman Group, **6** 161, 163; **23** 124–25
Bronson Laboratories, Inc., **34** 460
Bronson Pharmaceuticals, **24** 257
Brooke Bond, **32** 475
Brooke Group Ltd., **15 71–73**. *See also* Vector Group Ltd.
Brooke Partners L.P., **11** 275
Brookfield Athletic Shoe Company, **17** 244
Brookfield International Inc., **35** 388
Brooklyn Flint Glass Co., **III** 683
Brooklyn Trust Co., **II** 312
Brooklyn Union Gas, **6 455–57**; **27** 264–66
Brooks Brothers Inc., **V** 26–27; **13** 43; **22 109–12**; **24** 313, 316
Brooks Fashion, **29** 164
Brooks Fiber Communications, **41** 289–90
Brooks Fiber Properties, Inc., **27** 301, 307
Brooks, Harvey & Company, Inc., **II** 431; **16** 376
Brooks-Scanlon Lumber Co., **IV** 306
Brooks Shoe Manufacturing Co., **16** 546
Brooks, Shoobridge and Co., **III** 669
Brooks Sports Inc., **32 98–101**
Brookshire Grocery Company, **16 63–66**
Brookstone, Inc., **II** 560; **12** 411; **18 81–83**
Brookville Telephone Company, **6** 300
Brookwood Health Services, **III** 73
Brother Industries, Ltd., **13** 478; **14 75–76**
Brother International, **23** 212
Brothers Foods, **18** 7
Brothers Gourmet Coffees, Inc., **20 82–85**
Brotherton Chemicals, **29** 113
Broughton Foods Co., **17 55–57**
Brown & Bigelow, **27** 193
Brown & Brown, Inc., **41 63–66**
Brown & Dureau Ltd., **IV** 248–49; **19** 14
Brown & Haley, **23 78–80**
Brown & Root, Inc., **III** 498–99, 559; **13 117–19**; **25** 190–91; **37** 244; **38** 481
Brown & Sharpe Manufacturing Co., **23 81–84**
Brown and Williamson Tobacco Corporation, **I** 426; **14 77–79**; **15** 72; **22** 72–73; **33 80–83 (upd.)**
Brown Bibby & Gregory, **I** 605
Brown Boveri. *See* BBC Brown Boveri.
Brown Co., **I** 452; **IV** 289
Brown Corp., **IV** 286
Brown Drug, **III** 9
Brown-Forman Corporation, **I 225–27**; **III** 286; **10 179–82 (upd.)**; **12** 313; **18** 69; **38 110–14 (upd.)**
Brown Foundation, **III** 498
Brown Group, Inc., **V 351–53**; **9** 192; **10** 282; **16** 198; **20 86–89 (upd.)**
Brown Instrument Co., **II** 41
Brown Jordan Co., **12** 301
Brown Oil Tools, **III** 428
Brown Paper Mill Co., **I** 380; **13** 379
Brown Printing Company, **26 43–45**
Brown-Service Insurance Company, **9** 507
Brown Shipbuilding Company. *See* Brown & Root, Inc.
Brown-Shipley Ltd., **II** 425; **13** 341
Brown Shoe Co., **V** 351–52; **14** 294
Browne & Nolan Ltd., **IV** 294; **19** 225
Browning-Ferris Industries, Inc., **V 749–53**; **8** 562; **10** 33; **17** 552; **18** 10; **20 90–93 (upd.)**; **23** 491; **33** 382
Browning Manufacturing, **II** 19
Browning Telephone Corp., **14** 258
Broyhill Furniture Industries, Inc., **III** 528, 530; **10 183–85**; **12** 308; **39** 170, 173–74
BRS Ltd., **6** 412–13
Bruce Foods Corporation, **39 67–69**
Bruce's Furniture Stores, **14** 235
Bruckmann, Rosser, Sherill & Co., **27** 247; **40** 51
Bruegger's Bagel Bakery, **29** 171
Brufina, **II** 201–02
Brugman, **27** 502
Brummer Seal Company, **14** 64
Brunner Mond and Co., **I** 351
Bruno's Inc., **7 60–62**; **13** 404, 406; **23** 261; **26 46–48 (upd.)**
Brunswick Corporation, **III 442–44**, 599; **9** 67, 119; **10** 262; **17** 453; **21** 291; **22 113–17 (upd.)**, 118; **30** 303; **40** 30
Brunswick Pulp & Paper Co., **IV** 282, 311, 329; **9** 260; **19** 266
The Brush Electric Light Company, **11** 387; **25** 44
Brush Electrical Machines, **III** 507–09
Brush Moore Newspaper, Inc., **8** 527
Brush Wellman Inc., **14 80–82**
Bryan Bros. Packing, **II** 572
Bryant Heater Co., **III** 471
Bryce & Co., **I** 547
Bryce Brothers, **12** 313
Bryce Grace & Co., **I** 547
Brylane Inc., **29** 106–07
Brymbo Steel Works, **III** 494
Bryn Mawr Stereo & Video, **30** 465
Brynwood Partners, **13** 19
BSA. *See* The Boy Scouts of America.
BSB, **IV** 653; **7** 392
BSC. *See* Birmingham Steel Corporation.
BSC (Industry) Ltd., **IV** 42
BSkyB, **IV** 653; **7** 392; **29** 369, 371; **34** 85
BSN Groupe S.A., **II 474–75**, 544; **22** 458; **23** 448. *See also* Groupe Danone
BSN Medical, **41** 374, 377
BSR, **II** 82
BT. *See* British Telecommunications, plc.
BTI Services, **9** 59
BTM. *See* British Tabulating Machine Company.
BTR Dunlop Holdings, Inc., **21** 432

BTR plc, **I 428–30**; **III** 185, 727; **8** 397; **24** 88
BTR Siebe plc, **27 79–81**
Buca, Inc., **38 115–17**
Buchanan, **I** 239–40
Buchanan Electric Steel Company, **8** 114
Buck Consultants Inc., **32** 459
Buckaroo International. *See* Bugle Boy Industries, Inc.
Buckeye Business Products Inc., **17** 384
Buckeye Technologies, Inc., **42 51–54**
Buckeye Tractor Ditcher, **21** 502
Buckeye Union Casualty Co., **III** 242
Buckhorn, Inc., **19** 277–78
Buckingham Corp., **I** 440, 468
The Buckle, Inc., **18 84–86**
Buckler Broadcast Group, **IV** 597
Buckley/DeCerchio New York, **25** 180
Bucyrus Blades, Inc., **14** 81
Bucyrus-Erie Company, **7** 513
Bucyrus International, Inc., **17 58–61**
Bud Bailey Construction, **43** 400
Budapest Bank, **16** 14
The Budd Company, **III** 568; **IV** 222; **8 74–76**; **20** 359
Buderus AG, **III** 692, 694–95; **37 46–49**
Budget Group, Inc., **25 92–94**
Budget Rent a Car Corporation, **I** 537; **6** 348–49, 393; **9 94–95**; **13** 529; **22** 524; **24** 12, 409; **25** 143; **39** 370; **41** 402
Budgetel Inn. *See* Marcus Corporation.
Budweiser, **18** 70
Budweiser Japan Co., **21** 320
Buena Vista Distribution, **II** 172; **6** 174; **30** 487
Bufete Industrial, S.A. de C.V., **34 80–82**
Buffalo Forge Company, **7** 70–71
Buffalo Insurance Co., **III** 208
Buffalo Mining Co., **IV** 181
Buffalo News, **18** 60
Buffalo Paperboard, **19** 78
Buffalo-Springfield, **21** 502
Buffets, Inc., **10 186–87**; **22** 465; **32 102–04 (upd.)**
Buffett Partnership, Ltd., **III** 213
Bugaboo Creek Steak House Inc., **19** 342
Bugatti Industries, **14** 321
Bugle Boy Industries, Inc., **18 87–88**
Buhrmann NV, **41 67–69**
Buick Motor Co., **I** 171; **III** 438; **8** 74; **10** 325
Builders Emporium, **13** 169; **25** 535
Builders Square, **V** 112; **9** 400; **12** 345, 385; **14** 61; **16** 210; **31** 20; **35** 11, 13
Building One Services Corporation. *See* Encompass Services Corporation.
Building Products of Canada Limited, **25** 232
Buitoni SpA, **II** 548; **17** 36
Bulgari S.p.A., **20 94–97**
Bulgarian Oil Co., **IV** 454
Bulgheroni SpA, **27** 105
Bulkships, **27** 473
Bull. *See* Compagnie des Machines Bull S.A.
Bull-GE, **III** 123
Bull HN Information Systems, **III** 122–23
Bull Motors, **11** 5
Bull Run Corp., **24** 404
Bull S.A., **III** 122–23; **43 89–91 (upd.)**
Bull Tractor Company, **7** 534; **16** 178; **26** 492
Bull-Zenith, **25** 531
Bulldog Computer Products, **10** 519
Bullock's, **III** 63; **31** 191
Bulolo Gold Dredging, **IV** 95
Bulova Corporation, **I** 488; **II** 101; **III** 454–55; **12** 316–17, 453; **13 120–22**; **14** 501; **21** 121–22; **36** 325; **41 70–73 (upd.)**
Bumble Bee Seafoods, Inc., **II** 491, 508, 557; **24** 114
Bumkor-Ramo Corp., **I** 539
Bunawerke Hüls GmbH., **I** 350
Bundy Corporation, **17 62–65**, 480
Bunker Ramo Info Systems, **III** 118
Bunte Candy, **12** 427
Bunzl plc, **IV 260–62**; **12** 264; **31 77–80 (upd.)**
Buquet, **19** 49
Burbank Aircraft Supply, Inc., **14** 42–43; **37** 29, 31
Burberry Ltd., **41 74–76 (upd.)**
Burberrys Ltd., **V** 68; **10** 122; **17 66–68**; **19** 181
Burda Holding GmbH. & Co., **20** 53; **23 85–89**
Burdines, **9** 209; **31** 192
Bureau de Recherches de Pétrole, **IV** 544–46, 559–60; **7** 481–83; **21** 203–04
The Bureau of National Affairs, Inc., **23 90–93**
Burelle S.A., **23 94–96**
Burger and Aschenbrenner, **16** 486
Burger Boy Food-A-Rama, **8** 564
Burger Chef, **II** 532
Burger King Corporation, **I** 21, 278; **II** 556–57, **613–15**, 647; **7** 316; **8** 564; **9** 178; **10** 122; **12** 43, 553; **13** 408–09; **14** 25, 32, 212, 214, 452; **16** 95–97, 396; **17 69–72 (upd.)**, 501; **18** 437; **21** 25, 362; **23** 505; **24** 140–41; **25** 228; **26** 284; **33** 240–41; **36** 517, 519
Burgess, Anderson & Tate Inc., **25** 500
Bürhle, **17** 36
Burhmann-Tetterode, **22** 154
Burke Scaffolding Co., **9** 512
BURLE Industries Inc., **11** 444
Burlesdon Brick Co., **III** 734
Burlington Coat Factory Warehouse Corporation, **10 188–89**
Burlington Homes of New England, **14** 138
Burlington Industries, Inc., **V** 118, **354–55**; **8** 234; **9** 231; **12** 501; **17 73–76 (upd.)**, 304–05; **19** 275
Burlington Mills Corporation, **12** 117–18
Burlington Motor Holdings, **30** 114
Burlington Northern, Inc., **IV** 182; **V 425–28**; **10** 190–91; **11** 315; **12** 145, 278
Burlington Northern Santa Fe Corporation, **27 82–89 (upd.)**; **28** 495
Burlington Resources Inc., **10 190–92**; **11** 135; **12** 144
Burmah Castrol PLC, **IV** 378, **381–84**, 440–41, 483–84, 531; **7** 56; **15** 246; **21** 80; **30 86–91 (upd.)**
Burmeister & Wain, **III** 417–18
Burn & Co., **IV** 205
Burn Standard Co. Ltd., **IV** 484
Burnards, **II** 677
Burndy, **19** 166
Burnham and Co., **II** 407–08; **6** 599; **8** 388
Burns & Ricker, Inc., **40** 51, 53
Burns & Wilcox Ltd., **6** 290
Burns-Alton Corp., **21** 154–55
Burns Companies, **III** 569; **20** 360
Burns Fry Ltd., **II** 349
Burns International Security Services, **III** 440; **13 123–25**; **42** 338. *See also* Securitas AB.
Burns International Services Corporation, **41 77–80 (upd.)**
Burns Philp & Company Limited, **21** 496–98
Burnup & Sims, Inc., **19** 254; **26** 324
Burpee & Co. *See* W. Atlee Burpee & Co.
Burr & Co., **II** 424; **13** 340
Burr-Brown Corporation, **19 66–68**
Burrill & Housman, **II** 424; **13** 340
Burris Industries, **14** 303
Burroughs Corp., **I** 142, 478; **III** 132, 148–49, 152, 165–66; **6** 233, 266, 281–83; **18** 386, 542. *See also* Unisys Corporation.
Burroughs Mfg. Co., **16** 321
Burroughs Wellcome & Co., **I** 713; **8** 216
Burrows, Marsh & McLennan, **III** 282
Burrups Ltd., **18** 331, 333
Burry, **II** 560; **12** 410
Bursley & Co., **II** 668
Burt Claster Enterprises, **III** 505
Burthy China Clays, **III** 690
Burton-Furber Co., **IV** 180
Burton Group plc, **V 20–22**. *See also* Arcadia Group plc.
Burton J. Vincent, Chesley & Co., **III** 271
Burton, Parsons and Co. Inc., **II** 547
Burton Retail, **V** 21
Burton Rubber Processing, **8** 347
Burton Snowboards Inc., **22 118–20**, 460
Burtons Gold Medal Biscuits Limited, **II** 466; **13** 53
Burwell Brick, **14** 248
Bury Group, **II** 581
Busch Entertainment Corporation, **34** 36
Bush Boake Allen Inc., **IV** 346; **30 92–94**; **38** 247
Bush Hog, **21** 20–22
Bush Industries, Inc., **20 98–100**
Bush Terminal Company, **15** 138
Business Communications Group, Inc. *See* Caribiner International, Inc.
Business Depot, Limited, **10** 498
Business Expansion Capital Corp., **12** 42
Business Express Airlines, Inc., **28** 22
Business Information Technology, Inc., **18** 112
Business Men's Assurance Company of America, **III** 209; **13** 476; **14 83–85**; **15** 30
Business Objects S.A., **25 95–97**
Business Resources Corp., **23** 489, 491
Business Science Computing, **14** 36
Business Software Association, **10** 35
Business Software Technology, **10** 394
Business Wire, **25** 240
Businessland Inc., **III** 153; **6** 267; **10** 235; **13** 175–76, 277, 482
Busse Broadcasting Corporation, **7** 200; **24** 199
Büssing Automobilwerke AG, **IV** 201
Buster Brown, **V** 351–52
BUT S.A., **24** 266, 270
Butano, **IV** 528
Butler Bros., **21** 96
Butler Cox PLC, **6** 229
Butler Group, Inc., **30** 310–11
Butler Manufacturing Co., **12 51–53**; **43** 130
Butler Shoes, **16** 560
Butterfield & Butterfield, **32** 162

Butterfield & Swire. *See* Swire Pacific Ltd.
Butterfield, Wasson & Co., **II** 380, 395; **10** 59; **12** 533
Butterick Co., Inc., 23 97–99
Butterley Company, **III** 501; **7** 207
Butterworth & Co. (Publishers) Ltd., **IV** 641; **7** 311; **17** 398
Buttrey Food & Drug Stores Co., 18 89–91
Butz Thermo-Electric Regulator Co., **II** 40; **12** 246
Buxton, **III** 28; **23** 21
Buzzard Electrical & Plumbing Supply, **9** 399; **16** 186
BVA Investment Corp., **11** 446–47
BVD, **25** 166
BWAY Corporation, 24 91–93
BWP Distributors, **29** 86, 88
Byerly's, Inc. *See* Lund Food Holdings, Inc.
Byers Machines, **21** 502
Byrnes Long Island Motor Cargo, Inc., **6** 370
Byron Jackson, **III** 428, 439. *See also* BJ Services Company.
Byron Weston Company, **26** 105
Bytrex, Inc., **III** 643

C&A, 40 74–77 (upd.)
C&A Brenninkmeyer KG, V 23–24
C&E Software, **10** 507
C.&E. Cooper Co., **II** 14
C & G Systems, **19** 442
C.&G. Cooper Company, **II** 14; **20** 162
C & H Distributors, Inc., **27** 177
C & O. *See* Chesapeake and Ohio Railway.
C&R Clothiers, **17** 313
C&S Bank, **10** 425–26
C&S/Sovran Corporation, **10** 425–27; **18** 518; **26** 453
C-COR.net Corp., 38 118–21
C-Cube Microsystems, Inc., 37 50–54; 43 221–22
C.A. Delaney Capital Management Ltd., **32** 437
C.A. Pillsbury and Co., **II** 555
C.A. Reed Co., **IV** 353; **19** 498
C.A.S. Sports Agency Inc., **22** 460, 462
C.A. Swanson & Sons. *See* Vlasic Foods International Inc.
C. Bechstein, **III** 657
C. Brewer, **I** 417; **24** 32
C.D. Haupt, **IV** 296; **19** 226
C.D. Kenny Co., **II** 571
C.D. Magirus AG, **III** 541
C.E. Chappell & Sons, Inc., **16** 61–62
C.E.T. *See* Club Européen du Tourisme.
C.F. Burns and Son, Inc., **21** 154
C.F. Hathaway Company, **12** 522
C.F. Martin & Co., Inc., 42 55–58
C.F. Mueller Co., **I** 497–98; **12** 332
C.F. Orvis Company. *See* The Orvis Company, Inc.
C. Francis, Son and Co., **III** 669
C.G. Conn, **7** 286
C.H. Boehringer Sohn, 39 70–73
C.H. Dexter & Co., **I** 320
C.H. Heist Corporation, 24 111–13
C.H. Knorr Company, **II** 497; **22** 83
C.H. Masland & Sons. *See* Masland Corporation.
C.H. Musselman Co., **7** 429
C.H. Robinson, Inc., 8 379–80; **11 43–44; 23** 357
C.H. Robinson Worldwide, Inc., 40 78–81 (upd.)
C-I-L, Inc., **III** 745; **13** 470
C. Itoh & Co., I 431–33, 492, 510; **II** 273, 292, 361, 442, 679; **IV** 269, 326, 516, 543; **7** 529; **10** 500; **17** 124; **24** 324–25; **26** 456. *See also* ITOCHU Corporation.
C.J. Devine, **II** 425
C.J. Lawrence, Morgan Grenfell Inc., **II** 429
C.J. Smith and Sons, **11** 3
C.L. Bencard, **III** 66
C. Lee Cook Co., **III** 467
C.M. Aikman & Co., **13** 168
C.M. Armstrong, Inc., **14** 17
C.M. Barnes Company, **10** 135
C.M. Page, **14** 112
C.O. Lovette Company, **6** 370
C.O.M.B. Company, **18** 131–33
C/P Utility Services Company, **14** 138
C.P.U., Inc., **18** 111–12
C.R. Anthony Company, **24** 458
C.R. Bard Inc., IV 287; **9 96–98; 22** 360–61
C.R. Eggs, Inc., **25** 332
C. Reichenbach'sche Maschinenfabrik, **III** 561
C. Rowbotham & Sons, **III** 740
C.S. Rolls & Co., **I** 194
C.T. Bowring, **III** 280, 283; **22** 318
C-Tec Corp. *See* Commonwealth Telephone Enterprises, Inc.
C.V. Buchan & Co., **I** 567
C.V. Gebroeders Pel, **7** 429
C.V. Mosby Co., **IV** 677–78
C.W. Acquisitions, **27** 288
C.W. Costello & Associates Inc., **31** 131
C.W. Holt & Co., **III** 450
C.W. Zumbiel Company, **11** 422
C. Wuppesahl & Co. Assekuranzmakler, **25** 538
CAA. *See* Creative Artists Agency LLC.
Cabela's Inc., 26 49–51
Cable & Wireless HKT, 30 95–98 (upd.). *See also* Hong Kong Telecomminications Ltd.
Cable and Wireless plc, IV 695; **V 283–86; 7** 332–33; **11** 547; **15** 69, 521; **17** 419; **18** 253; **25 98–102 (upd.); 26** 332; **27** 307
Cable Communications Operations, Inc., **6** 313
Cable London, **25** 497
Cable Management Advertising Control System, **25** 497
Cable News Network, **II** 166–68; **6** 171–73; **9** 30; **12** 546
Cablec Corp., **III** 433–34
Cableform, **I** 592
Cabletron Systems, Inc., 10 193–94; 10 511; **20** 8; **24** 183; **26** 276
Cablevision Electronic Instruments, Inc., 32 105–07
Cablevision Systems Corporation, 7 63–65; 18 211; **30 99–103 (upd.)**106. *See also* Cablevision Electronic Instruments, Inc.
Cabot, Cabot & Forbes, **22** 100
Cabot Corporation, 8 77–79; 29 79–82 (upd.)
Cabot Medical Corporation, **21** 117, 119
Cabot-Morgan Real Estate Co., **16** 159
Cabot Noble Inc., **18** 503, 507
Cabrera Vulcan Shoe Corp., **22** 213
Cache Incorporated, 30 104–06
CACI International Inc., 21 85–87
Cacique, **24** 237
Cadadia, **II** 641–42
Cadbury Schweppes PLC, I 25–26, 220, 288; **II 476–78**, 510, 512, 592; **III** 554; **6** 51–52; **9** 178; **15** 221; **22** 513; **25** 3, 5; **39** 383, 385
CADCAM Technology Inc., **22** 196
Caddell Construction Company, **12** 41
Cademartori, **23** 219
Cadence Design Systems, Inc., 6 247; **10** 118; **11 45–48**, 285, 490–91; **24** 235; **35** 346; **38** 188
Cadence Industries Corporation, **10** 401–02
Cadet Uniform Services Ltd., **21** 116
Cadillac Automobile Co., **I** 171; **10** 325
Cadillac Fairview Corp., **IV** 703
Cadillac Plastic, **8** 347
Cadisys Corporation, **10** 119
Cadmus Communications Corporation, 16 531; **23 100–03**
Cadoricin, **III** 47
CAE Systems Inc., **8** 519
Caere Corporation, 20 101–03
Caesar-Wollheim-Gruppe, **IV** 197
Caesars World, Inc., 6 199–202; 17 318
Caf'Casino, **12** 152
Café Grand Mère, **II** 520
Caffarel, **27** 105
CAFO, **III** 241
Cagiva Group, **17** 24; **30** 172; **39** 37
Cagle's, Inc., 20 104–07
Cahners Business Information, 43 92–95
Cahners Publishing, **IV** 667; **12** 561; **17** 398; **22** 442
CAI Corp., **12** 79
Cailler, **II** 546
Cain Chemical, **IV** 481
Cains Marcelle Potato Chips Inc., **15** 139
Caisse Commericale de Bruxelles, **II** 270
Caisse de dépôt et placement du Quebec, **II** 664
Caisse des Dépôts, **6** 206
Caisse National de Crédit Agricole, **II** 264–66
Caisse Nationale de Crédit Agricole, **15** 38–39
Caithness Glass Limited, **38** 402
Caja General de Depositos, **II** 194
Cajun Bayou Distributors and Management, Inc., **19** 301
Cajun Electric Power Cooperative, Inc., **21** 470
CAK Universal Credit Corp., **32** 80
CAL. *See* China Airlines.
Cal Circuit Abco Inc., **13** 387
CAL Corporation, **21** 199, 201
Cal-Dive International Inc., **25** 104–05
Cal-Van Tools. *See* Chemi-Trol Chemical Co.
Cal/Ink, **13** 228
Cala, **17** 558
Calais Railroad Company, **16** 348
Calcined Coke Corp., **IV** 402
Calcitherm Group, **24** 144
Calco, **I** 300–01
CalComp Inc., 13 126–29
Calcot Ltd., 33 84–87
Calculating-Tabulating-Recording Company. *See* International Business Machines Corporation.

Calcutta & Burmah Steam Navigation Co., **III** 521
Caldbeck Macgregor & Co., **III** 523
Calder Race Course, Inc., **29** 118
Caldera Systems Inc., **38** 416, 420
Caldor Inc., 12 54–56, 508; **30** 57
Caledonian Airways. *See* British Caledonian Airways.
Caledonian Bank, **10** 337
Caledonian Paper plc, **IV** 302
Calédonickel, **IV** 107
Calgary Power Company. *See* TransAlta Utilities Corporation.
Calgene, Inc., **29** 330; **41** 155
Calgon Corporation, **6** 27; **16** 387; **34** 281
Calgon Vestal Laboratories, **37** 44
Calgon Water Management, **15** 154; **40** 176
Cali Realty. *See* Mack-Cali Realty Corporation.
California Arabian Standard Oil Co., **IV** 536, 552
California Automated Design, Inc., **11** 284
California Bank, **II** 289
California Charter Inc., **24** 118
California Cheese, **24** 444
California Computer Products, Inc. *See* CalComp Inc.
California Cooler Inc., **I** 227, 244; **10** 181
California Dental Supply Co., **19** 289
California Design Studio, **31** 52
California Federal Bank, **22** 275
California First, **II** 358
California Fruit Growers Exchange. *See* Sunkist Growers, Inc.
California Ink Company, **13** 227
California Institute of Technology, **9** 367
California Insurance Co., **III** 234
California Oilfields, Ltd., **IV** 531, 540
California Pacific, **22** 172
California Perfume Co., **III** 15
California Petroleum Co., **IV** 551–52
California Pizza Kitchen Inc., 15 74–76
California Plant Protection, **9** 408
California Portland Cement Co., **III** 718; **19** 69
California Pro Sports Inc., **24** 404
California Slim, **27** 197
California Steel Industries, **IV** 125
California Telephone and Light, **II** 490
California Test Bureau, **IV** 636
California Texas Oil Co., **III** 672
California Tile, **III** 673
California-Western States Life Insurance Co., **III** 193–94
California Woodfiber Corp., **IV** 266
Caligen, **9** 92
Caligor. *See* Henry Schein Medical.
Call-Chronicle Newspapers, Inc., **IV** 678
Callaghan & Company, **8** 526
Callard and Bowser, **II** 594
Callaway Golf Company, 15 77–79; **16** 109; **19** 430, 432; **23** 267, 474; **37** 4
Callaway Wines, **I** 264
Callebaut, **II** 520–21
Callender's Cable and Construction Co. Ltd., **III** 433–34
Calloway's Nursery Inc., **12** 200
Calma, **II** 30; **12** 196
Calmar Co., **12** 127
CalMat Co., III 718; **19 69–72**
Calmic Ltd., **I** 715
Calor Group, **IV** 383
Caloric Corp., **II** 86
Calpine Corporation, 36 102–04
Calsil Ltd., **III** 674
Caltex Petroleum Corporation, II 53; **III** 672; **IV** 397, 434, 440–41, 479, 484, 492, 519, 527, 536, 545–46, 552, 560, 562, 718; **7** 483; **19 73–75**; **21** 204; **25** 471; **38** 320; **41** 392–93
Calumatic Group, **25** 82
Calumet & Arizona Mining Co., **IV** 177
Calumet Electric Company, **6** 532
Calvert & Co., **I** 293
Calvert Insurance Co. *See* Gryphon Holdings, Inc.
Calvin Bullock Ltd., **I** 472
Calvin Klein, Inc., 9 203; **22 121–24**; **25** 258; **27** 329; **32** 476
Calyx & Corolla Inc., **37** 162–63
Camargo Foods, **12** 531
Camas. *See* Aggregate Industries plc.
CamBar. *See* Cameron & Barkley Company.
Camber Corporation, **25** 405
Cambex, **12** 147–48
Cambrex Corporation, 16 67–69
Cambria Steel Company, **IV** 35; **7** 48
Cambrian Wagon Works Ltd., **31** 369
Cambridge Applied Nutrition Toxicology and Biosciences Ltd., **10** 105
Cambridge Biotech Corp., **13** 241
Cambridge Electric Co., **14** 124, 126
Cambridge Gas Co., **14** 124
The Cambridge Instrument Company, **35** 272
Cambridge Interactive Systems Ltd., **10** 241
Cambridge SoundWorks, Inc., **36** 101
Cambridge Steam Corp., **14** 124
Cambridge Technology Partners, Inc., 36 105–08
Camco Inc., **IV** 658
Camden Wire Co., Inc., **7** 408; **31** 354–55
CAMECO, **IV** 436
Camelot Barthropp Ltd., **26** 62
Camelot Group plc, **34** 140
Camelot Music, Inc., 26 52–54
Cameron & Barkley Company, 13 79; **28 59–61**
Cameron Ashley Inc., **19** 57
Cameron-Brown Company, **10** 298
Cameron Iron Works, **II** 17
Cameron Oil Co., **IV** 365
CAMI Automotive, **III** 581
Camintonn, **9** 41–42
Camp Manufacturing Co., **IV** 345; **8** 102
Campbell Box & Tag Co., **IV** 333
Campbell Cereal Company. *See* Malt-O-Meal Company.
Campbell, Cowperthwait & Co., **17** 498
Campbell-Ewald Co., **I** 16–17
Campbell Hausfeld. *See* Scott Fetzer Company.
Campbell Industries, Inc., **11** 534
Campbell-Mithun-Esty, Inc., 13 516; **16 70–72**
Campbell Soup Company, I 21, 26, 31, 599, 601; **II 479–81**, 508, 684; **7 66–69 (upd.)**, 340; **10** 382; **11** 172; **18** 58; **25** 516; **26 55–59 (upd.)**; **33** 32; **43** 121
Campbell Taggart, Inc., **I** 219; **19** 135–36, 191; **34** 36
Campeau Corporation, IV 721; **V 25–28**; **9** 209, 211, 391; **12** 36–37; **13** 43; **15** 94; **17** 560; **22** 110; **23** 60; **31** 192; **37** 13
Campo Electronics, Appliances & Computers, Inc., 16 73–75
Campo Lindo, **25** 85
Campofrio Alimentacion, S.A., **18** 247
CAMPSA. *See* Compañia Arrendataria del Monopolio de Petróleos Sociedad Anónima.
Campus Services, Inc., **12** 173
Canada & Dominion Sugar Co., **II** 581
Canada Cable & Wire Company, **9** 11
Canada Cement, **III** 704–05
Canada Cup, **IV** 290
Canada Development Corp., **IV** 252; **17** 29
Canada Dry, **I** 281
Canada, Limited, **24** 143
Canada Packers Inc., II 482–85; **41** 249
Canada Safeway Ltd., **II** 650, 654
Canada Surety Co., **26** 486
Canada Trust. *See* CT Financial Services Inc.
Canada Tungsten Mining Corp., Ltd., **IV** 18
Canada Wire & Cable Company, Ltd., **IV** 164–65; **7** 397–99
Canadair, Inc., I 58; **7** 205; **13** 358; **16 76–78**
Canadian Ad-Check Services Inc., **26** 270
Canadian Airlines International Ltd., **6** 61–62, 101; **12** 192; **23** 10; **24** 400
Canadian Bank of Commerce, **II** 244–45
Canadian British Aluminum, **IV** 11
The Canadian Broadcasting Corporation (CBC), 37 55–58
Canadian Cellucotton Products Ltd., **III** 40; **16** 302; **43** 256
Canadian Copper, **IV** 110
Canadian Copper Refiners, Ltd., **IV** 164
Canadian Dominion Steel and Coal Corp., **III** 508
Canadian Eastern Finance, **IV** 693
Canadian Fina Oil, **IV** 498
Canadian Football League, **12** 457
Canadian Forest Products, **IV** 270. *See also* Canfor Corporation.
Canadian Fuel Marketers, **IV** 566
Canadian General Electric Co., **8** 544–45
Canadian Government Merchant Marine, **6** 360–61
Canadian Gridoil Ltd., **IV** 373
Canadian Imperial Bank of Commerce, II 244–46; **IV** 693; **7** 26–28; **10** 8; **32** 12, 14
Canadian Industrial Alcohol Company Limited, **14** 141
Canadian International Paper Co., **IV** 286–87; **15** 228
Canadian Keyes Fibre Company, Limited of Nova Scotia, **9** 305
Canadian National Railway System, I 284; **6 359–62**; **12** 278–79; **22** 444; **23** 10
Canadian Odeon Theatres, **6** 161; **23** 123
Canadian Overseas Telecommunications Corporation, **25** 100
Canadian Pacific Enterprises, **III** 611
Canadian Pacific Limited, V 429–31; **8** 544–46
Canadian Pacific Railway, **I** 573; **II** 210, 220, 344; **III** 260; **IV** 272, 308, 437; **6** 359–60; **25** 230
Canadian Packing Co. Ltd., **II** 482
Canadian Petrofina, **IV** 498
Canadian Radio-Television and Telecommunications Commission, **6** 309

Canadian Steel Foundries, Ltd., **39** 31
Canadian Telephones and Supplies, **6** 310
Canadian Tire Corporation, Limited, **25** 144
Canadian Transport Co., **IV** 308
Canadian Utilities Limited, 13 130–32
Canadian Vickers, **16** 76
Canal Bank, **11** 105
Canal Electric Co., **14** 125–26
Canal Plus, III 48; **7** 392; **10 195–97**, 345, 347; **23** 476; **29** 369, 371; **31** 330; **33** 181; **34 83–86 (upd.)**
CanalSatellite, **29** 369, 371
CanAmera Foods, **7** 82
Canandaigua Brands, Inc., 34 87–91 (upd.)
Canandaigua Wine Company, Inc., 13 133–35
Cananwill, **III** 344
Canary Wharf Group Plc, 30 107–09
Candie's, Inc., 31 81–84
Candle Corporation of America. *See* Blyth Industries, Inc.
Candlewood Hotel Company, Inc., 41 81–83
Candy SpA, **22** 350
Canfor Corporation, IV 321; **17** 540; **42 59–61**
Cannell Communications, **25** 418
Cannon Assurance Ltd., **III** 276
Cannon Mills, Co., **9** 214–16
Cannondale Corporation, 16 494; **21 88–90**; **26** 183, 412
Canon Inc., I 494; **II** 103, 292; **III 120–21**, 143, 172, 575, 583–84; **6** 238, 289; **9** 251; **10** 23; **13** 482; **15** 150; **18 92–95 (upd.)**, 186, 341–42, 383, 386–87; **24** 324; **26** 213; **33** 13; **43** 152, 283–84
Canpet Exploration Ltd., **IV** 566
Canpotex Ltd., **18** 432
Canrad-Hanovia, **27** 57
Cans Inc., **I** 607
Canstar Sports Inc., 15 396–97; **16 79–81**
Canteen Corp., **I** 127; **II** 679–80; **12** 489; **13** 321
Cantel Corp., **11** 184; **18** 32; **20** 76; **30** 388
Canterbury Park Holding Corporation, 42 62–65
Canton Chemical, **I** 323; **8** 147
Canton Railway Corp., **IV** 718; **38** 320
Cantor Fitzgerald Securities Corporation, **10** 276–78
CanWest Global Communications Corporation, 35 67–70; **39** 13
Canyon Cafes, **31** 41
Cap Gemini Ernst & Young, 37 59–61
Cap Rock Electric Cooperative, **6** 580
Capacity of Texas, Inc., **33** 105–06
CAPCO. *See* Central Area Power Coordination Group *or* Custom Academic Publishing Company.
Capco Energy, Inc., **33** 296
Capcom Co., **7** 396
Cape and Vineyard Electric Co., **14** 124–25
Cape Cod-Cricket Lane, Inc., **8** 289
Cape Cod Potato Chip Company, Inc., **41** 233
Cape Horn Methanol, **III** 512
Cape May Light and Power Company, **6** 449
Cape PLC, **22** 49
Cape Wine and Distillers, **I** 289
Capehart-Farnsworth, **I** 463; **11** 197
Capex, **6** 224
AB Capital & Investment Corporation, **6** 108; **23** 381
Capital Advisors, Inc., **22** 4
Capital Airlines, **I** 128; **III** 102; **6** 128
Capital and Counties Bank, **II** 307; **IV** 91
Capital Bank N.A., **16** 162
Capital Cities/ABC Inc., II 129–31; **III** 214; **IV** 608–09, 613, 652; **11** 331; **15** 464; **18** 60, 62–63, 329; **30** 490; **42** 31, 33–34. *See also* ABC, Inc.
Capital Concrete Pipe Company, **14** 250
Capital Controls Co., Inc. *See* Severn Trent PLC.
Capital Distributing Co., **21** 37
Capital Financial Services, **III** 242
Capital-Gazette Communications, Inc., **12** 302
Capital Grille, **19** 342
Capital Group, **26** 187
Capital Holding Corporation, III 216–19
Capital Life Insurance Company, **11** 482–83
Capital Management Services. *See* CB Commercial Real Estate Services Group, Inc.
Capital One, **18** 535
Capital Radio plc, 35 71–73; **39** 199
Capital Trust Corp., **17** 498
Capitol-EMI, **I** 531–32; **11** 557
Capitol Film + TV International, **IV** 591
Capitol Films, **25** 270
Capitol Pack, Inc., **13** 350
Capitol Printing Ink Company, **13** 227–28
Capitol Publishing, **13** 560
Capitol Radio Engineering Institute, **IV** 636
Capitol Records, **22** 192–93
Capper Pass, **IV** 191
Capseals, Ltd., **8** 476
CapStar Hotel Company, 21 91–93
Capsugel, **I** 712
Car-lac Electronic Industrial Sales Inc., **9** 420
Car-X, **10** 415
Caracas Petroleum Sociedad Anónima, **IV** 565–66
Caradon plc, 18 561; **20 108–12 (upd.)**
Carando Foods, **7** 174–75
Carat Group, **6** 15–16
Caratti Sports, Ltd., **26** 184
Caraustar Industries, Inc., 19 76–78
Caravali, **13** 493–94
Caravelle Foods, **21** 500
The Carbide/Graphite Group, Inc., 40 82–84
Carbide Router Co., **III** 436
Carbis China Clay & Brick Co., **III** 690
Carbocol, **IV** 417
Carboline Co., **8** 455
CarboMedics, **11** 458–60
Carbon Research Laboratories, **9** 517
Carbone Lorraine S.A., 33 88–90
La Carbonique, **23** 217, 219
Carborundum Company, III 610; **15 80–82**
Cardàpio, **29** 444
Cardboard Containers, **IV** 249
Cardem Insurance Co., **III** 767; **22** 546
Cardiac Pacemakers, Inc., **I** 646; **11** 90; **11** 458; **22** 361
Cardinal Distributors Ltd., **II** 663
Cardinal Freight Carriers, Inc., **42** 365
Cardinal Health, Inc., 18 96–98
Cardiotronics Systems, Inc., **21** 47
Cardon-Phonocraft Company, **18** 492
Care Advantage, Inc., **25** 383
Care Group, **22** 276
CareerCom Corp., **25** 253
CareerStaff Unlimited Inc., **25** 455
Caremark International Inc., 10 143, **198–200**; **33** 185
Carenes, SA, **12** 377
CarePlus, **6** 42
CareUnit, Inc., **15** 123
CareWise, Inc., **36** 365, 367–68
Carey Canada Inc., **III** 766; **22** 546
Carey International, Inc., 26 60–63
Carey-McFall Corp., **V** 379; **19** 421
Carey Straw Mill, **12** 376
S.A. CARFUEL, **12** 152
Cargill, Incorporated, II 494, 517, **616–18**; **11** 92; **13 136–38 (upd.)**, 186, 351; **18** 378, 380; **21** 290, 500; **22** 85, 426; **25** 332; **31** 17, 20; **40 85–90 (upd.)**; **41** 306
Cargill Trust Co., **13** 467
Cargo Express, **16** 198
Cargo Furniture, **31** 436
CARGOSUR, **6** 96
Carhartt, Inc., 30 110–12
Cariani Sausage Co., **II** 518
Caribair, **I** 102
Caribbean Chemicals S.A., **I** 512
Caribe Co., **II** 493
Caribe Shoe Corp., **III** 529
Caribiner International, Inc., 24 94–97
Cariboo Pulp & Paper Co., **IV** 269
Caribou Coffee Company, Inc., 28 62–65
Carintusa Inc., **8** 271
CARIPLO, **III** 347
Carisam International Corp., **29** 511
Carita S.A., **III** 63; **22** 487
Caritas Foundation, **22** 411, 413
Carl Byoir & Associates, **I** 14
Carl Karcher Enterprises, Inc., **19** 435
Carl Marks & Co., **11** 260–61
Carl-Zeiss-Stiftung, III 445–47, 583; **33** 218; **34 92–97 (upd.)**
Carl's Superstores, **9** 452
Carlan, **III** 614
Carless Lubricants, **IV** 451
Carleton Financial Computations Inc., **II** 317
Carlin Gold Mining Company, **7** 386–87
Carling O'Keefe Ltd., **I** 218, 229, 254, 269, 438–39; **7** 183; **12** 337; **26** 305
Carlingford, **II** 298
Carlisle Companies Incorporated, 8 80–82
Carlisle Memory Products, **14** 535
Carlo Erba S.p.A., **I** 635
Carlon, **13** 304–06
Carlova, Inc., **21** 54
Carlsberg A/S, I 247; **9 99–101**; **29 83–85 (upd.)**
Carlson Companies, Inc., 6 363–66; **22 125–29 (upd.)**; **26** 147, 439–40; **27** 9, 11; **29** 200; **38** 387
Carlton and United Breweries Ltd., I 228–29, 437–39; **7** 182–83
Carlton Cards, **39** 87
Carlton Communications plc, 15 83–85; **23** 111, 113; **24** 194
Carlton Investments L.P., **22** 514

The Carlyle Group, **11** 364; **14** 43; **16** 47; **21** 97; **30** 472; **43** 60
CarMax, **26** 410; **29** 120, 123
Carmeda AB, **10** 439
Carmichael Lynch Inc., 28 66–68
Carmike Cinemas, Inc., 14 86–88; 21 362; **37 62–65 (upd.)**
Carmine's Prime Meats, Inc., **35** 84
Carnation Company, I 269; **II 486–89**, 518, 548; **7** 339, 383, 429; **10** 382; **12** 337; **28** 311
Carnaud Basse-Indre, **IV** 228
Carnaud Metalbox, **13** 190; **20** 111; **32** 125–26
Carnegie Brothers & Co., Ltd., **9** 407
Carnegie Corporation of New York, 35 74–77
Carnegie Foundation for the Advancement of Teaching, **12** 141
Carnegie Group, **41** 371–72
Carnegie Steel Co., **II** 330; **IV** 572; **7** 549; **35** 74
Carnival Corporation, 27 90–92 (upd.); **36** 194
Carnival Cruise Lines, Inc., 6 367–68; **21** 106; **22** 444–46, 470; **27** 27
Caro Produce and Institutional Foods, **31** 359–61
Carol-Braugh-Robinson Co., **II** 624
Carol Moberg, Inc., **6** 40
Carol's Shoe Corp., **22** 213
Carolco Pictures Inc., **III** 48; **10** 196
Carolina Biological Supply, **11** 424
Carolina Coach Co., **13** 397–98
Carolina Coin Caterers Corporation, **10** 222
Carolina Energies, Inc., **6** 576
Carolina First Corporation, 31 85–87
Carolina First National, **II** 336
Carolina Freight Corporation, 6 369–72
Carolina Paper Board Corporation. *See* Caraustar Industries, Inc.
Carolina Power & Light Company, V 564–66; 23 104–07 (upd.)
Carolina Telephone and Telegraph Company, 10 201–03
Carolinas Capital Funds Group, **29** 132
Carolinas-Virginia Nuclear Power Association, **27** 130
Carpenter Investment and Development Corporation, **31** 279
Carpenter Paper Co., **IV** 282; **9** 261
Carpenter Technology Corporation, 13 139–41
CarpetMAX, **25** 320
Carpets International Plc., **8** 270–71
CARQUEST Corporation, 26 348; **29 86–89**
Carr Fowler, **III** 673
Carr-Gottstein Foods Co., 17 77–80
Carr-Lowrey Glass Co., **13** 40
Carr-Union Line, **6** 397
Carr's of Carlisle, **I** 604; **II** 594
Carrabba's Italian Grill, **12** 373–75
Carre Orban International, **34** 248
Carrefour SA, II 628; **8** 404–05; **10 204–06**; **12** 153; **19** 98, 309; **21** 225; **23** 230–32; 246–47, 364; **24** 475; **27** 207, **93–96 (upd.)**; **34** 198; **37** 21, 23
Carreras, Limited, **V** 411–12; **19** 367–69
Carriage Services, Inc., 37 66–68
Carrier Corporation, I 85; **III** 329; **7 70–73**; **13** 507; **22** 6; **26** 4; **29** 216
Carrington Laboratories, **33** 282
Carroll County Electric Company, **6** 511
Carroll Reed Ski Shops, Inc., **10** 215
Carroll's Foods, **7** 477; **22** 368; **43** 382
Carrows, **27** 16, 19
Carry Machine Supply, Inc., **18** 513
The Carsey-Werner Company, L.L.C., 37 69–72
Carso Global Telecom S.A. de C.V., **34** 362
Carson, Inc., 31 88–90
Carson Pirie Scott & Company, II 669; **9** 142; **15 86–88**; **19** 324, 511–12; **41** 343–44
Carson Water Company, **19** 411
CART. *See* Championship Auto Racing Teams, Inc.
Carte Blanche, **9** 335
CarTemps USA. *See* Republic Industries, Inc.
Carter & Co., **IV** 644
Carter Automotive Co., **I** 159
Carter, Berlind, Potoma & Weill, **II** 450
Carter Hawley Hale Stores, I 246; **V 29–32**; **8** 160; **12** 356; **15** 88; **16** 466; **17** 43, 523; **18** 488; **25** 177
Carter Holt Harvey Ltd., **IV** 280; **15** 229; **19** 155
Carter Oil Company, **IV** 171; **11** 353
Carter-Wallace, Inc., 6 27; **8 83–86**; **38 122–26 (upd.)**
Carteret Savings Bank, **III** 263–64; **10** 340
Carterphone, **22** 17
Cartier, **27** 329, 487–89
Cartier Monde, IV 93; **V** 411, 413; **29 90–92**
Cartier Refined Sugars Ltd., **II** 662–63
Cartiera F.A. Marsoni, **IV** 587
Cartiere Ascoli Piceno, **IV** 586
Cartiers Superfoods, **II** 678
Cartillon Importers, Ltd., **6** 48
Carton Titan S.A. de C.V., **37** 176–77
Cartotech, Inc., **33** 44
Carvel Corporation, 35 78–81
Carver Pump Co., **19** 36
Carworth Inc., **I** 630; **11** 34
Cary-Davis Tug and Barge Company. *See* Puget Sound Tug and Barge Company.
CASA. *See* Construcciones Aeronautics S.A.
Casa Bancária Almeida e Companhia. *See* Banco Bradesco S.A.
Casa Bonita, **II** 587
Casa Cuervo, S.A. de C.V., 31 91–93
Casa Ley, S.A. de C.V., **24** 416
Casa Saba. *See* Grupo Casa Saba, S.A. de C.V.
Casablanca Records, **23** 390
Casarotto Security, **24** 510
Cascade Communications Corp., **16** 468; **20** 8; **24** 50
Cascade Fertilizers Ltd., **25** 232
Cascade Fiber, **13** 99
Cascade Lumber Co., **IV** 255; **8** 65
Cascade Natural Gas Corporation, 6 568; **9 102–04**
Cascade Steel Rolling Mills, Inc., **19** 380–81
CasChem, Inc. *See* Cambrex Corporation.
Casco Northern Bank, 14 89–91
Case Corporation. *See* CNH Global N.V.
Case Manufacturing Corp., **I** 512
Case, Pomeroy & Co., Inc., **IV** 76
Case Technologies, Inc., **11** 504
Casein Co. of America, **II** 471
Casey's General Stores, Inc., 19 79–81
Cash America International, Inc., 20 113–15; **33** 4
Cash Wise Foods and Liquor, **30** 133
Casino, **10** 205; **23** 231; **26** 160; **27** 93–94
Casino. *See* Etablissements Economiques de Casino Guichard, Perrachon et Cie, S.C.A.
Casino America, Inc. *See* Isle of Capri Casinos, Inc., **41** 218
Casino Frozen Foods, Inc., **16** 453
Casino Guichard S.A., **37** 23
Casino S.A., **22** 515
Casino USA, **16** 452
Casinos International Inc., **21** 300
CASIO Computer Co., Ltd., III 448–49, 455; **IV** 599; **10** 57; **16 82–84 (upd.)**; **21** 123; **26** 18; **40 91–95 (upd.)**
Cassa Generale Ungherese di Risparmio, **III** 207
Cassady Broiler Co., **II** 585
Cassandra Group, **42** 272
Cassatt, **II** 424
Cassco Ice & Cold Storage, Inc., **21** 534–35
CAST Inc., **18** 20; **43** 17
Cast-Matic Corporation, **16** 475
Castex, **13** 501
Castings, Inc., **29** 98
Castle & Cooke, Inc., I 417; **II 490–92**; **9** 175–76; **10** 40; **20 116–19 (upd.)**; **24** 32, 115. *See also* Dole Food Company, Inc.
Castle Brewery, **I** 287
Castle Cement, **31** 400
Castle Communications plc, **17** 13
Castle Harlan Investment Partners III, **36** 468, 471
Castle Rock Pictures, **23** 392
Castle Rubber Co., **17** 371
Castle Tretheway Mines Ltd., **IV** 164
Castlemaine Tooheys, **10** 169–70
Castorama S.A., **37** 258–60. *See also* Groupe Castorama-Dubois Investissements.
Castro Convertibles. *See* Krause's Furniture, Inc.
Castrol Ltd., **IV** 382–83
Castrorama, **10** 205; **27** 95
Casual Corner Group, Inc., V 207–08; **25** 121; **43 96–98**
Catalina Lighting, Inc., 43 99–102 (upd.)
Catalina Marketing Corporation, 18 99–102
Catalogue Marketing, Inc., **17** 232
Catalyst Telecom, **29** 414–15
Catamaran Cruisers, **29** 442
Catamount Petroleum Corp., **17** 121
Cataract, Inc., **34** 373
CATCO. *See* Crowley All Terrain Corporation.
Catellus Development Corporation, 24 98–101; **27** 88
Caterair International Corporation, **16** 396
Caterpillar Inc., I 147, 181, 186, 422; **III 450–53**, 458, 463, 545–46; **9** 310; **10** 274, 377, 381, 429; **11** 473; **12** 90; **13** 513; **15 89–93 (upd.)**, 225; **16** 180, 309–10; **18** 125; **19** 293; **21** 173, 499–501, 503; **22** 542; **34** 44, 46–47
Cathay Insurance Co., **III** 221; **14** 109
Cathay Pacific Airways Limited, I 522; **II** 298; **6** 71, **78–80**; **16** 480–81; **18** 114–15; **34 98–102 (upd.)**

Catherines Stores Corporation, 15 94–97; 38 129
Cathodic Protection Services Co., **14** 325
Catholic Order of Foresters, 24 102–05
Cato Corporation, 14 92–94
Cato Oil and Grease Company, **IV** 446; **22** 302
Catteau S.A., **24** 475
Cattleman's, Inc., 20 120–22
Cattybrook Brick Company, **14** 249
CATV, **10** 319
Caudill Rowlett Scott. *See* CRSS Inc.
Caudle Engraving, **12** 471
CAV, **III** 554–55
Cavallo Pipeline Company, **11** 441
Cavedon Chemical Co., **I** 341
Cavendish International Holdings, **IV** 695
Cavendish Land, **III** 273
Cavenham Ltd., **7** 202–03; **28** 163
Caves Altovisto, **22** 344
Caves de Roquefort, **19** 51; **24** 445
Cawoods Holdings, **III** 735
Caxton Holdings, **IV** 641
CB Commercial Real Estate Services Group, Inc., 21 94–98
CB&I, **7** 76–77
CB&Q. *See* Chicago, Burlington and Quincy Railroad Company.
CB&T. *See* Synovus Financial Corp.
CBC Film Sales Co., **II** 135
CBE Technologies Inc., **39** 346
CBI Industries, Inc., 7 74–77; 22 228
CBM Realty Corp., **III** 643
CBN Cable Network, **13** 279–81
CBN Satellite Services, **13** 279
CBOT. *See* Chicago Board of Trade.
CBR-HCI Construction Materials Corp., **31** 253
CBRL Group, Inc., 35 82–85 (upd.)
CBS Corporation, 28 69–73 (upd.); 30 269, 272
CBS Inc., I 29, 488; **II** 61, 89, 102–03, 129–31, **132–34**, 136, 152, 166–67; **III** 55, 188; **IV** 605, 623, 652, 675, 703; **6 157–60 (upd.); 11** 327; **12** 75, 561; **16** 201–02; **17** 150, 182; **19** 210, 426, 428; **21** 24; **24** 516–17; **25** 330, 418; **26** 102; **36** 326; **43** 170–71
CBS Musical Instruments, **16** 201–02; **43** 170–71
CBS Radio Network, **37** 192
CBS Records, **II** 103, 134, 177; **6** 159; **22** 194; **23** 33; **28** 419; **40** 406
CBSI. *See* Complete Business Solutions, Inc.
CBT Corp., **II** 213–14
CBW Inc., **42** 129
CBWL-Hayden Stone, **II** 450
CC Soft Drinks Ltd., **I** 248
cc:Mail, Inc., **25** 300
CCA. *See* Container Corporation of America *and* Corrections Corporation of America.
CCAir Inc., **11** 300
CCB Financial Corp., **33** 293
CCC Franchising Corporation. *See* Primedex Health Systems, Inc.
CCG. *See* The Clark Construction Group, Inc.
CCH Computax, **7** 93–94
CCH Inc., 7 93; **14 95–97; 33** 461
CCI Asia-Pacific Ltd., **27** 362
CCI Electronique, **10** 113
CCL Industries, Ltd., **15** 129
CCM Inc. *See* The Hockey Company.
CCM Sport Maska, Inc., **15** 396
CCP Insurance, Inc., **10** 248
CCR, Inc. *See* Rica Foods, Inc.
CCS Automation Systems Inc., **I** 124
CCT. *See* Crowley Caribbean Transport.
CD Titles, Inc., **22** 409
CDC. *See* Canada Development Corporation *or* Control Data Corporation.
CdF-Chimie, **I** 303; **IV** 174, 198, 525
CDG Books Canada Inc., **27** 224
CDI. *See* Centre de Dechets Industriels Group.
CDI Corporation, 6 139–41
CDMS. *See* Credit and Data Marketing Services.
CDR. *See* Consortium de Realisation.
CDR International, **13** 228
CDS Holding Corp., **22** 475
CDW Computer Centers, Inc., 16 85–87
CDX Audio Development, Inc., **18** 208
CE-Minerals, **IV** 109
CEAG AG, **23** 498
Ceat Ltd., **III** 434; **20** 263
CEC Entertainment, Inc., 31 94–98 (upd.)
Ceco Doors, **8** 544–46
Ceco Industries, Inc. *See* Robertson-Ceco Corporation.
CECOS International, Inc., **V** 750
Cedar Engineering, **III** 126
Cedar Fair, L.P., 22 130–32
Cedarapids, Inc., **11** 413; **38** 374, 376; **40** 432
Cedec S.A., **14** 43
Cederroth International AB, **8** 17; **36** 25–26
CEDIS, **12** 153
Cedric Chivers, **35** 243–44
Cegedur, **IV** 174
Cegetel SA, **38** 300
CEIR, **10** 255
Celadon Group Inc., 30 113–16
Celanese Corp., I 317–19, 347; **19** 192. *See also* Hoechst Celanese Corporation.
Celebrity Entertainment, Inc., **27** 43
Celebrity, Inc., 22 133–35, 472
Celeron Corporation, **20** 258, 262–63
Celestial Farms, **13** 383
Celestial Seasonings, Inc., II 534; **16 88–91**. *See also* The Hain Celestial Group, Inc.
Celestron International, **41** 262–63
Celfor Tool Company. *See* Clark Equipment Company.
Celite Corporation, **III** 706; **7** 291; **10** 43, 45
Cella Italian Wines, **10** 181
CellAccess Technology, Inc., **25** 162
Cellnet Data Systems, **11** 547; **22** 65
Cellonit-Gesellschaft Dreyfus & Cie., **I** 317
Cellstar Corporation, **18** 74
Cellu-Products Co., **14** 430
Cellular America, **6** 300
Cellular One, **9** 321
Cellular 2000. *See* Rural Cellular Corporation.
CellularOne. *See* Rural Cellular Corporation.
CellularVision, **13** 399
Cellulosa d'Italia, **IV** 272
Cellulose & Chemical Manufacturing Co., **I** 317
Cellulose & Specialties, **8** 434
Cellulose du Pin, **III** 677, 704; **16** 121–22; **19** 226–27
Celotex Corporation, **III** 766–67; **22** 545
Celsius Energy Company, **6** 569
Celtex **I** 388–89. *See also* Pricel.
Cementia, **III** 705
Cementos Portland Moctezuma, **21** 261
Cementownia Chelm, **31** 398, 400
Cemex SA de CV, 20 123–26
Cemij, **IV** 132
Cemp Investments Ltd., **16** 79–80
Cemsto, **13** 545
CenCall Communications, **10** 433
Cenco, Inc., **6** 188; **10** 262–63; **25** 308; **35** 135
Cencor, **25** 432
Cendant Corporation, **41** 363
Cenex Cooperative, **21** 342
Cenex Inc., **II** 536; **19** 160
Cengas, **6** 313
Centaur Communications, **43** 204, 206
Centel Corporation, 6 312–15, 593; **9** 106, 480; **10** 203; **14** 258; **16** 318; **17** 7
Centennial Communications Corporation, 39 74–76
Center Rental & Sales Inc., **28** 387
Centerior Energy Corporation, V 567–68
Centerra Corporation, **24** 79
Centertel, **18** 33
Centex Corporation, 8 87–89, 461; **11** 302; **23** 327; **29 93–96 (upd.)**
Centocor Inc., 14 98–100; 36 306
CentraBank, **II** 337; **10** 426
Central Alloy Steel Corporation. *See* Republic Engineered Steels, Inc.
Central and South West Corporation, V 569–70; 21 197–98
Central Area Power Coordination Group, **V** 677
Central Arizona Light & Power Company, **6** 545
Central Asia Gas Pipeline Ltd, **24** 522
Central Bancorp of Cincinnati, **II** 342
Central Bank for Railway Securities, **II** 281
Central Bank of Italy, **II** 403
Central Bank of London, **II** 318; **17** 323
Central Bank of Oman, **IV** 516
Central Bank of Scotland, **10** 337
Central Coalfields Ltd., **IV** 48–49
Central Computer Systems Inc., **11** 65
Central Covenants, **II** 222
Central Detallista, S.A. de C.V., **12** 154; **16** 453
Central Electric & Gas Company. *See* Centel Corporation.
Central Electric and Telephone Company, Inc. *See* Centel Corporation.
Central Elevator Co., **19** 111
Central Fiber Products Company, **12** 376
Central Finance Corporation of Canada, **II** 418; **21** 282
Central Florida Press, **23** 101
Central Foam Corp., **I** 481, 563; **16** 322
Central Garden & Pet Company, 23 108–10
Central Hankyu Ltd., **V** 71
Central Hardware, **III** 530
Central Hudson Gas And Electricity Corporation, 6 458–60
Central Illinois Public Service Company. *See* CIPSCO Inc.

Central Independent Television, 7 78–80; **15** 84; **23 111–14 (upd.)**
Central India Spinning, Weaving and Manufacturing Co., **IV** 217
Central Indiana Power Company, **6** 556
Central Investment Corp., **12** 184
Central Japan Heavy Industries, **III** 578–79; **7** 348
Central Japan Railway Company, 43 103–06
Central Maine Power, 6 461–64; **14** 126
Central Maloney Transformer, **I** 434
Central Mining and Investment Corp., **IV** 23, 79, 95–96, 524, 565
Central National Bank, **9** 475
Central National Bank & Trust Co., **13** 467
Central National Life Insurance Co., **III** 463; **21** 174
Central Nebraska Packing, **10** 250
Central Newspapers, Inc., 10 207–09
Central Pacific Railroad, **II** 381; **13** 372
Central Park Bank of Buffalo, **11** 108
Central Parking Corporation, 18 103–05
Central Penn National Corp., **11** 295
Central Planning & Design Institute, **IV** 48
Central Point Software, **10** 509
Central Public Service Corporation, **6** 447; **23** 28
Central Public Utility Corp., **13** 397
Central Research Laboratories, **22** 194
Central Savings and Loan, **10** 339
Central Solvents & Chemicals Company, **8** 100
Central Songs, **22** 193
Central Soya Company, Inc., 7 81–83; **31** 20; **36** 185, 187
Central Sprinkler Corporation, 29 97–99
Central States Indemnity, **18** 62
Central Supply Company. *See* Granite Rock Company.
Central Telephone & Utilities Corporation. *See* Centel Corporation.
Central Terminal Company, **6** 504
Central Textile, **16** 36
Central Transformer, **I** 434
Central Trust Co., **II** 313; **11** 110
Central Union Telephone Company, **14** 251, 257
Central Union Trust Co. of New York, **II** 313
Central West Public Service Company. *See* Centel Corporation.
Centralab Inc., **13** 398
Centrale Verzorgingsdienst Cotrans N.V., **12** 443
Centran Corp., **9** 475
Centre de Dechets Industriels Group, **IV** 296; **19** 226
Centre Lait, **II** 577
Centre Partners Management LLC, **18** 355; **24** 482
Centrica plc, 29 100–05 (upd.)
Centron DPL Company, Inc., **25** 171
Centronics Corp., **16** 192
Centros Commerciales Pryca, **23** 246, 248
Centrum Communications Inc., **11** 520
CenTrust Federal Savings, **10** 340
Centura Software, **10** 244
Centurion Brick, **14** 250
Century Bakery. *See* Dawn Food Products, Inc.
Century Bank, **II** 312
Century Brewing Company. *See* Rainier Brewing Company.
Century Cellular Network, Inc., **18** 74
Century Communications Corp., 10 210–12
Century Data Systems, Inc., **13** 127
Century Electric Company, **13** 273
Century Finance, **25** 432
Century Hutchinson, Ltd., **13** 429
Century Manufacturing Company, **26** 363
Century Papers, Inc., **16** 387
Century Savings Assoc. of Kansas, **II** 420
Century Supply Corporation, **39** 346
Century Telephone Enterprises, Inc., 9 105–07
Century Theatres, Inc., 31 99–101
Century Tool Co., **III** 569; **20** 360
Century 21 Real Estate, **I** 127; **II** 679; **III** 293; **11** 292; **12** 489; **21** 97; **25** 444
CEPA. *See* Consolidated Electric Power Asia.
CEPAM, **21** 438
CEPCO. *See* Chugoku Electric Power Company Inc.
CEPSA. *See* Compañia Española de Petroleos S.A.
Cera Trading Co., **III** 756
Ceramesh, **11** 361
Ceramic Art Company, **12** 312
Ceramic Supply Company, **8** 177
Cerberus Limited, **6** 490
Cereal and Fruit Products, **32** 519
Cereal Industries, **II** 466
Cereal Packaging, Ltd., **13** 294
Cereal Partners Worldwide, **10** 324; **13** 294; **36** 234, 237
Cerebos, **II** 565
Cereol, **36** 185
Cerestar, **36** 185, 187
Ceresucre, **36** 185
Cerex, **IV** 290
Ceridian Corporation, **10** 257; **38** 58
Cermalloy, **IV** 100
Cerner Corporation, 16 92–94
Cerro Corp., **IV** 11, 136
Cerro de Pasco Corp., **IV** 33; **40** 411
Cerro Metal Products Company, **16** 357
CertainTeed Corporation, III 621, 677–78, 762; **16** 8, 121–22; **19** 58; **35 86–89**
Certanium Alloys and Research Co., **9** 419
Certified Grocers of Florida, Inc., **15** 139
Certified Laboratories, **8** 385
Certified TV and Appliance Company, **9** 120
Certus International Corp., **10** 509
Cerus, **23** 492
Cerveceria Cuahtémoc Moctezuma, **25** 281
Cerveceria Cuauhtemoc, **19** 10
Cerveceria Moctezuma, **23** 170
Cerveceria Polar, I 230–31
Cessna Aircraft Company, III 512; **8** 49–51, **90–93**, 313–14; **26** 117; **27 97–101 (upd.)**; **34** 431, 433; **36** 190
CET. *See* Compagnie Européenne de Télésecurité.
Cetelem S.A., 21 99–102
Cetus Corp., **I** 637; **III** 53; **7** 427; **10** 78, 214; **41** 201
CF AirFreight, **6** 390; **25** 149
CF Braun, **13** 119
CF Holding Corporation, **12** 71
CF Industries, **IV** 576
CF&I Steel Corporation, **8** 135
CFC Investment Company, **16** 104
CFM. *See* Compagnie Française du Méthane.
CFP. *See* Compagnie Française des Pétroles.
CFS Continental, Inc., **II** 675; **26** 504
CG&E. *See* Cincinnati Gas & Electric Company.
CGCT, **I** 563
CGE. *See* Alcatel Alsthom.
CGM. *See* Compagnie Générale Maritime.
CGR-MeV, **III** 635
Chace Precision Metals, Inc., **29** 460–61
Chaco Energy Corporation, **V** 724–25
Chadbourne & Parke, 36 109–12
Chadwick's of Boston, Ltd., V 197–98; **27** 348; **29 106–08**
Chalet Suisse International, Inc., **13** 362
Chalk's International Airlines, **12** 420
Challenge Corp. Ltd. *See* Fletcher Challenge Ltd.
Challenger Airlines, **22** 219
Challenger Minerals Inc., **9** 267
The Chalone Wine Group, Ltd., 36 113–16
Chamberlain Group, Ltd., **23** 82
Chambers Corporation, **8** 298; **17** 548–49
Chambosse Brokerage Co., **29** 33
Champ Industries, Inc., **22** 15
Champalimaud, **36** 63
Champion Engineering Co., **III** 582
Champion Enterprises, Inc., 17 81–84; **22** 207
Champion Forge Co., **41** 366
Champion, Inc., **8** 459; **12** 457
Champion Industries, Inc., 28 74–76
Champion International Corporation, III 215; **IV 263–65**, 334; **12** 130; **15** 229; **18** 62; **20 127–30 (upd.)**; **22** 352; **26** 444
Champion Modular Restaurant Company, Inc. *See* Checkers Drive-Up Restaurants Inc.
Champion Products Inc., **27** 194
Champion Spark Plug Co., **II** 17; **III** 593
Champion Valley Farms, **II** 480; **26** 56
Championship Auto Racing Teams, Inc., 37 73–75
Champlin Petroleum Company, **10** 83
Champps Americana, **27** 480–82
Champs Sports, **14** 293, 295. *See also* Venator Group Inc.
Chance Bros., **III** 724–27
Chance Vought Aircraft Co., **I** 67–68, 84–85, 489–91
Chancellor Media Corporation, 24 106–10; **35** 247
Chancery Law Publishing Ltd., **17** 272
Chanco Medical Industries, **III** 73
Chandeleur Homes, Inc., **17** 83
The Chandris Group, **11** 377
Chanel, 12 57–59; **23** 241
Channel Master Corporation, **II** 91; **15** 134
Channel One Communications Corp., **22** 442
Channel Tunnel Group, **13** 206
Chansam Investments, **23** 388
Chantex Inc., **18** 519
Chantiers de l'Atlantique, **9** 9
Chaparral Steel Co., 8 522–24; **13 142–44**; **18** 379; **19** 380
Chapman Printing Company. *See* Champion Industries, Inc.

Chapman Valve Manufacturing Company, **8** 135
Chappel Music, **23** 389
Charan Industries Inc., **18** 519
Charan Toy Co., Inc., **18** 519
Chargeurs International, **6 373–75**, 379; **20** 79; **21 103–06 (upd.)**; **29** 369, 371
Charise Charles Ltd., **9** 68
Charisma Communications, **6** 323
Charles A. Eaton Co., **III** 24
Charles B. Perkins Co., **II** 667; **24** 461
Charles Barker, plc, **25** 91
Charles D. Burnes Co., Inc. *See* The Holson Burnes Group, Inc.
Charles Hobson, **6** 27
Charles Huston & Sons, **14** 323
Charles Luckman Assoc., **I** 513
Charles M. Schulz Creative Associates, **39** 95
Charles of the Ritz Group Ltd., **I** 695–97; **III** 56; **23** 237
Charles Pfizer Co., **I** 96
Charles Phillips & Co. Ltd., **II** 677
Charles R. McCormick Lumber Company, **12** 407
Charles River Laboratories International, Inc., **25** 55; **42 66–69**
The Charles Schwab Corporation, **II** 228; **8 94–96**; **18** 552; **22** 52; **26 64–67 (upd.)**; **34** 407; **38** 430
Charles Scribner's Sons, **7** 166
The Charles Stark Draper Laboratory, Inc., **35 90–92**
Charleston Consolidated Railway, Gas and Electric Company, **6** 574
Charlestown Foundry, **III** 690
Charley Brothers, **II** 669
Charley's Eating & Drinking Saloon, **20** 54
Charlie Browns, **24** 269–70
Charlotte Russe Holding, Inc., **35 93–96**
Charmin Paper Co., **III** 52; **IV** 329; **8** 433; **26** 383
Charming Shoppes, Inc., **8 97–98**; **38 127–29**; **39** 287, 289
Charrington & Co., **I** 223
Charrington United Breweries, **38** 76
Chart House Enterprises, Inc., **II** 556, 613–14; **17** 70, 71, **85–88**
Chart Industries, Inc., **21 107–09**
Charter Bank, **II** 348
Charter Club, **9** 315
Charter Communications, Inc., **33 91–94**
Charter Consolidated, **IV** 23, 119–20; **16** 293
Charter Corp., **III** 254; **14** 460
Charter Golf, Inc. *See* Ashworth, Inc.
Charter Medical Corporation, **31** 356
Charter National Life Insurance Company, **11** 261
Charter Oil Co., **II** 620; **12** 240
Charter Security Life Insurance Cos., **III** 293
Chartered Bank, **II** 357
Chartered Co. of British New Guinea, **III** 698
Chartered Mercantile Bank of India, London and China, **II** 298
Charterhouse Japhet, **24** 269
Charterhouse Petroleum, **IV** 499
Chartwell Associates, **III** 16; **9** 331
Chartwell Land plc, **V 106**; **24** 266, 269
Chas. A. Stevens & Co., **IV** 660
Chas. H. Tompkins Co., **16** 285–86
Chase & Sanborn, **II** 544
Chase Corp., **II** 402
Chase Drier & Chemical Co., **8** 177
Chase, Harris, Forbes, **II** 402
The Chase Manhattan Corporation, **I** 123, 334, 451; **II** 202, 227, **247–49**, 256–57, 262, 286, 317, 385, 397, 402; **III** 104, 248; **IV** 33; **6** 52; **9** 124; **10** 61; **13 145–48 (upd.)**, 476; **14** 48, 103; **15** 38–39; **16** 460; **17** 498; **23** 482; **36** 358. *See* J.P. Morgan Chase & Co.
Chase National Bank, **25** 114
Chastain-Roberts Company, **II** 669; **18** 504
Chaston Medical & Surgical Products, **13** 366
Chateau Cheese Co. Ltd., **II** 471
Chateau Communities, Inc., **37 76–79**
Chateau Grower Winery Co., **II** 575
Chateau St. Jean, **22** 80
Chateau Souverain, **22** 80
Chateau Ste. Michelle Winery, **42** 245, 247
Chateaux St. Jacques, **24** 307
Chatfield & Woods Co., **IV** 311; **19** 267
Chatfield Paper Co., **IV** 282; **9** 261
Chatham and Phenix National Bank of New York, **II** 312
Chatham Bank, **II** 312
Chatham Technologies Inc., **38** 189
Chatillon. *See* John Chatillon & Sons Inc.
Chattanooga Gas Company, Inc., **6** 577
Chattanooga Gas Light Company, **6** 448; **23** 30
Chattanooga Medicine Company. *See* Chattem, Inc.
Chattem, Inc., **17 89–92**
Chatto, Virago, Bodley Head & Jonathan Cape, Ltd., **13** 429; **31** 376
Chautauqua Airlines, Inc., **38 130–32**
Chaux et Ciments de Lafarge et du Teil, **III** 703–04
Chaux et Ciments du Maroc, **III** 703
Check Express, **33** 4–5
Check Point Software Technologies Ltd., **20** 238
Checker Auto Parts. *See* CSK Auto Corporation.
Checker Holding, **10** 370
Checker Motors Corp., **10** 369
Checkers Drive-Up Restaurants Inc., **14** 452; **16 95–98**
CheckFree Corporation, **22** 522
Checkpoint Systems, Inc., **39 77–80**
The Cheesecake Factory Inc., **17 93–96**
Chef-Boy-Ar-Dee Quality Foods Inc., **I** 622
Chef Boyardee, **10** 70
Chef Francisco, **13** 383
Chef Pierre, **II** 572
Chef's Orchard Airline Caterers Inc., **I** 513
Cheil Sugar Co., **I** 515
Cheil Wool Textile Co., **I** 515
Chelan Power Company, **6** 596
Chelsea GCA Realty, Inc., **27** 401
Chelsea Milling Company, **29 109–11**
Chem-Nuclear Systems, Inc., **9** 109–10
Chemap, **III** 420
Chemcentral Corporation, **8 99–101**
Chemcut, **I** 682
Chemdal Corp., **13** 34
Chemed Corporation, **13 149–50**; **15** 409–11; **16** 386–87
Chemetron Process Equipment, Inc., **8** 545
Chemex Pharmaceuticals, Inc., **8** 63; **27** 69
Chemfab Corporation, **35 97–101**
ChemFirst, Inc., **27** 316
Chemgas Holding BV, **41** 340
Chemgrout, **26** 42
Chemi-Trol Chemical Co., **16 99–101**
Chemical Banking Corporation, **II** 234, **250–52**, 254; **9** 124, 361; **12** 15, 31; **13** 49, 147, 411; **14 101–04 (upd.)**; **15** 39; **21** 138; **26** 453; **38** 253
Chemical Coatings Co., **I** 321
Chemical Process Co., **IV** 409; **7** 308
Chemical Products Company, **13** 295
Chemical Specialties Inc., **I** 512
Chemical Waste Management, Inc., **V** 753; **9 108–10**; **11** 435–36
Chemie Linz, **16** 439
Chemins de fer de Paris à Lyon et à la Méditerranée, **6** 424
Chemins de fer du Midi, **6** 425
Chemins de Fer Fédéraux, **V** 519
Chemisch-Pharmazeutische AG, **IV** 70
Chemische Fabrik auf Actien, **I** 681
Chemische Fabrik Friesheim Elektron AG, **IV** 229
Chemische Fabrik vormals Sandoz, **I** 671
Chemische Fabrik Wesseling AG, **IV** 70–71
Chemische Werke Hüls GmbH. *See* Hüls A.G.
Chemise Lacoste, **9** 157
ChemLawn, **13** 199; **23** 428, 431; **34** 153
Chemmar Associates, Inc., **8** 271
Chemonics Industries–Fire-Trol, **17** 161–62
Chemonics International–Consulting, **17** 161–62
Chempump, **8** 135
Chemurgic Corporation, **6** 148
Chemway Corp., **III** 423
Cheney Bigelow Wire Works, **13** 370
CHEP Pty Ltd., **42** 50
Cheplin Laboratories, **III** 17
Cherokee Inc., **18 106–09**
Cherokee Insurance Co., **I** 153; **10** 265
Cherry-Burrell Process Equipment, **8** 544–45
Cherry Company Ltd., **I** 266; **21** 319
Cherry Hill Cheese, **7** 429
Cherry-Levis Co., **26** 172
Chesapeake and Ohio Railroad, **II** 329; **V** 438–40; **10** 43; **13** 372. *See also* CSX Corporation.
Chesapeake Corporation, **8 102–04**; **10** 540; **25** 44; **30 117–20 (upd.)**
Chesapeake Microwave Technologies, Inc., **32** 41
Chesebrough-Pond's USA, Inc., **II** 590; **7** 544; **8 105–07**; **9** 319; **17** 224–25; **22** 123; **32** 475
Cheshire Wholefoods, **II** 528
Chester Engineers, **10** 412
Chester G. Luby, **I** 183
Chester Oil Co., **IV** 368
Cheung Kong (Holdings) Limited, **I** 470; **IV 693–95**; **18** 252; **20 131–34 (upd.)**; **23** 278, 280. *See also* Hutchison Whampoa Ltd.
Chevrolet, **V** 494; **9** 17; **19** 221, 223; **21** 153; **26** 500
Chevron Corporation, **II** 143; **IV** 367, **385–87**, 452, 464, 466, 479, 484, 490, 523, 531, 536, 539, 563, 721; **9** 391; **10** 119; **12** 20; **17** 121–22; **18** 365, 367; **19** 73, 75, **82–85 (upd.)**; **25** 444; **29** 385; **40** 354, 357–58; **41** 391, 394–95
Chevron U.K. Ltd., **15** 352

Chevy Chase Savings Bank, **13** 439
Chevy's, Inc., **33** 140
Chevy's Mexican Restaurants, **27** 226
ChexSystems, **22** 181
Cheyenne Software, Inc., **12 60–62**; **25** 348–49
CHF. *See* Chase, Harris, Forbes.
Chi-Chi's Inc., **13 151–53**; **14** 195; **25** 181
Chiat/Day Inc. Advertising, **9** 438; **11 49–52**. *See also* TBWA/Chiat/Day.
Chiba Riverment and Cement, **III** 760
Chibu Electric Power Company, Incorporated, **V 571–73**
Chic by H.I.S, Inc., **20 135–37**
Chicago & Calumet Terminal Railroad, **IV** 368
Chicago and Alton Railroad, **I** 456
Chicago and North Western Holdings Corporation, **I** 440; **6 376–78**
Chicago and Southern Airlines Inc., **I** 100; **6** 81
Chicago Bears Football Club, Inc., **IV** 703 **33 95–97**
Chicago Board of Trade, **41 84–87**
Chicago Bridge & Iron Company, **7** 74–77
Chicago Burlington and Quincy Railroad, **III** 282; **V** 425–28
Chicago Chemical Co., **I** 373; **12** 346
Chicago Corp., **I** 526
Chicago Cubs, **IV** 682–83
Chicago Cutlery, **16** 234
Chicago Directory Co., **IV** 660–61
Chicago Edison, **IV** 169
Chicago Flexible Shaft Company, **9** 484
Chicago Heater Company, Inc., **8** 135
Chicago Magnet Wire Corp., **13** 397
Chicago Medical Equipment Co., **31** 255
Chicago Motor Club, **10** 126
Chicago Musical Instrument Company, **16** 238
Chicago Pacific Corp., **I** 530; **III** 573; **12** 251; **22** 349; **23** 244; **34** 432
Chicago Pneumatic Tool Co., **III** 427, 452; **7** 480; **21** 502; **26** 41; **28** 40
Chicago Radio Laboratory, **II** 123
Chicago Rawhide Manufacturing Company, **8** 462–63
Chicago Rock Island and Peoria Railway Co., **I** 558
Chicago Rollerskate, **15** 395
Chicago Screw Co., **12** 344
Chicago Shipbuilding Company, **18** 318
Chicago Steel Works, **IV** 113
Chicago Sun-Times Distribution Systems, **6** 14
Chicago Times, **11** 251
Chicago Title and Trust Co., **III** 276; **10** 43–45
Chicago Tribune. *See* Tribune Company.
Chick-fil-A Inc., **23 115–18**
Chicken of the Sea International, **24 114–16 (upd.)**
Chicopee Manufacturing Corp., **III** 35
Chief Auto Parts, **II** 661; **32** 416
Chieftain Development Company, Ltd., **16** 11
Chiers-Chatillon-Neuves Maisons, **IV** 227
Chilcott Laboratories Inc., **I** 710–11
Child World Inc., **13** 166; **18** 524
Childers Products Co., **21** 108
Children's Book-of-the-Month Club, **13** 105
Children's Comprehensive Services, Inc., **42 70–72**
The Children's Place Retail Stores, Inc., **37 80–82**
Children's Record Guild, **13** 105
Children's Television Workshop, **12** 495; **13** 560; **35** 75
Children's World Learning Centers, **II** 608; **V** 17, 19; **13** 48; **24** 75
Childtime Learning Centers, Inc., **34 103–06**
Chiles Offshore Corporation, **9 111–13**
Chili's Grill & Bar, **10** 331; **12** 373–74; **19** 258; **20** 159
Chillicothe Co., **IV** 310; **19** 266
Chilton Corp., **III** 440; **25** 239; **27** 361
Chilton Publications. *See* Cahners Business Information.
Chiminter, **III** 48
Chimio, **I** 669–70; **8** 451–52
China Airlines, **6** 71; **34 107–10**; **39** 33–34
China Borneo Co., **III** 698
China Canada Investment and Development Co., **II** 457
China Coast, **10** 322, 324; **16** 156, 158
China Communications System Company, Inc. (Chinacom), **18** 34
China Development Corporation, **16** 4
China Eastern Airlines Co. Ltd., **31 102–04**
China Electric, **II** 67
China Foreign Transportation Corporation, **6** 386
China Industries Co., **II** 325
China International Capital Corp., **16** 377
China International Trade and Investment Corporation, **II** 442; **IV** 695; **6** 80; **18** 113, 253; **19** 156; **25** 101; **34** 100. *See also* CITIC Pacific Ltd.
China Light & Power, **6** 499; **23** 278–80
China Mutual Steam Navigation Company Ltd., **6** 416
China National Automotive Industry Import and Export Corp., **III** 581
China National Aviation Corp., **I** 96; **18** 115; **21** 140
China National Cereals, Oils & Foodstuffs Import and Export Corporation, **24** 359
China National Chemicals Import and Export Corp., **IV** 395; **31** 120
China National Heavy Duty Truck Corporation, **21** 274
China National Machinery Import and Export Corporation, **8** 279
China National Petroleum Corp. (SINOPEC), **18** 483
China Navigation Co., **I** 521; **16** 479–80
China Orient Leasing Co., **II** 442
China Resources (Shenyang) Snowflake Brewery Co., **21** 320
China Southern Airlines Company Ltd., **31** 102; **33 98–100**
China Zhouyang Fishery Co. Ltd., **II** 578
Chinese Electronics Import and Export Corp., **I** 535
Chinese Metallurgical Import and Export Corp., **IV** 61
Chinese Petroleum Corporation, **IV 388–90**, 493, 519; **31 105–108 (upd.)**
Chinese Steel Corp., **IV** 184
The Chinet Company, **30** 397
Chino Mines Co., **IV** 179
Chinon Industries, **III** 477; **7** 163
Chipcom, **16** 392
Chippewa Shoe, **19** 232
CHIPS and Technologies, Inc., **6** 217; **9 114–17**
Chiquita Brands International, Inc., **II** 595–96; **III** 28; **7 84–86**; **21 110–13 (upd.)**; **38** 197
ChiRex, **38** 380
Chiro Tool Manufacturing Corp., **III** 629
Chiron Corporation, **7** 427; **10 213–14**; **36 117–20 (upd.)**
Chisholm-Mingo Group, Inc., **41 88–90**
Chisso Chemical, **II** 301
Chiswick Products, **II** 566
Chita Oil Co., **IV** 476
Chitaka Foods International, **24** 365
Chivers, **II** 477
Chiyoda Bank, **I** 503; **II** 321
Chiyoda Chemical, **I** 433
Chiyoda Fire and Marine, **III** 404
Chiyoda Kogaku Seiko Kabushiki Kaisha, **III** 574–75; **43** 282
Chiyoda Konpo Kogyo Co. Ltd., **V** 536
Chiyoda Mutual, **II** 374
Chloé Chimie, **I** 303
Chloride S.A., **I** 423
Choay, **I** 676–77
Chock Full o'Nuts Corp., **17 97–100**; **20** 83
Chocoladefabriken Lindt & Sprüngli AG, **27 102–05**; **30** 220
Chocolat Ibled S.A., **II** 569
Chocolat-Menier S.A., **II** 569
Chocolat Poulait, **II** 478
Chogoku Kogyo, **II** 325
Choice Hotels International Inc., **6** 187, 189; **14 105–07**; **25** 309–10; **26** 460
ChoiceCare Corporation, **24** 231
ChoicePoint Services, Inc., **31** 358
Chorlton Metal Co., **I** 531
Chorus Line Corporation, **25** 247; **30 121–23**
Chosen Sekiyu, **IV** 554
Chotin Transportation Co., **6** 487
Chouinard Equipment. *See* Lost Arrow Inc.
Chow Tai Fook Jewellery Co., **IV** 717
Chris-Craft Industries, Inc., **II** 176, 403; **III** 599–600; **9 118–19**; **26** 32; **31 109–112 (upd.)**
Christal Radio, **6** 33
Christensen Boyles Corporation, **19** 247; **26 68–71**
Christensen Company, **8** 397
Christiaensen, **26** 160
Christian Bourgois, **IV** 614–15
Christian Broadcasting Network, **13** 279
Christian Dalloz SA, **40 96–98**
Christian Dior S.A., **I** 272; **19 86–88**; **23** 237, 242
Christiana Bank og Kredietklasse, **40** 336
Christie, Mitchell & Mitchell, **7** 344
Christie's International plc, **15 98–101**; **39 81–85 (upd.)**
Christofle SA, **40 99–102**
Christopher & Banks Corporation, **42 73–75**
Christopher Charters, Inc. *See* Kitty Hawk, Inc.
Chromalloy American Corp., **13** 461
Chromalloy Gas Turbine Corp., **13** 462
Chromatic Color, **13** 227–28
Chromcraft Revington, Inc., **15 102–05**; **26** 100

The Chronicle Publishing Company, Inc., **23 119–22**
Chronimed Inc., **26 72–75**
Chronoservice, **27** 475
Chrysalis Group plc, **22** 194; **40 103–06**
Chrysler Corporation, **I** 10, 17, 28, 38, 59, 79, 136, **144–45**, 152, 162–63, 172, 178, 182, 188, 190, 207, 420, 504, 516, 525, 540; **II** 5, 313, 403, 448; **III** 439, 517, 544, 568, 591, 607, 637–38; **IV** 22, 449, 676, 703; **7** 205, 233, 461; **8** 74–75, 315, 505–07; **9** 118, 349–51, 472; **10** 174, 198, 264–65, 290, 317, 353, 430; **11 53–55 (upd.)**, 103–04, 429; **13** 28–29, 61, 448, 501, 555; **14** 321, 367, 457; **16** 184, 322, 484; **17** 184; **18** 173–74, 308, 493; **20** 359–60; **22** 52, 55, 175, 330; **23** 352–54; **25** 89–91, 93, 142–44, 329; **26** 403, 501; **31** 130; **36** 34, 242; **38** 480–81; **43** 163–64. *See also* DaimlerChrysler AG
CH2M Hill Ltd., **22 136–38**
Chu Ito & Co., **IV** 476
Chubb Corporation, **II** 84; **III** 190, **220–22**, 368; **11** 481; **14 108–10 (upd.)**; **29** 256; **37 83–87 (upd.)**
Chubu Electric Power Co., **IV** 492
Chuck E. Cheese, **13** 472–74; **31** 94
Chugai Pharmaceutical Company, **8** 215–16; **10** 79
Chugai Shogyo Shimposha, **IV** 654–55
Chugoku Electric Power Company Inc., **V 574–76**
Chunghwa Picture Tubes, **23** 469
Chuo Trust & Banking Co. *See* Yasuda Trust and Banking Company, Limited.
Chupa Chups S.A., **38 133–35**
Church & Dwight Co., Inc., **29 112–15**
Church and Tower Group, **19** 254
Church, Goodman, and Donnelley, **IV** 660
Church's Fried Chicken, Inc., **I** 260; **7** 26–28; **15** 345; **23** 468; **32** 13–14
Churchill Downs Incorporated, **29 116–19**
Churchill Insurance Co. Ltd., **III** 404
Churny Co. Inc., **II** 534
Cianbro Corporation, **14 111–13**
Cianchette Brothers, Inc. *See* Cianbro Corporation.
Ciba-Geigy Ltd., **I** 625, **632–34**, 671, 690, 701; **III** 55; **IV** 288; **8** 63, **108–11 (upd.)**, 376–77; **9** 153, 441; **10** 53–54, 213; **15** 229; **18** 51; **21** 386; **23** 195–96; **25** 55; **27** 69; **28** 193, 195; **30** 327; **36** 36, 119. *See also* Novartis AG.
CIBC. *See* Canadian Imperial Bank of Commerce.
CIBC Wood Gundy Securities Corp., **24** 482
Ciber, Inc., **18 110–12**
Ciby 2000, **24** 79
CICI, **11** 184
CIDLA, **IV** 504–06
Cie Continental d'Importation, **10** 249
Cie des Lampes, **9** 9
Cie Générale d'Electro-Ceramique, **9** 9
Cie. Generale des Eaux S.A., **24** 327
Cifra, S.A. de C.V., **8** 556; **12 63–65**; **26** 524; **34** 197–98; **35** 320. *See also* Wal-Mart de Mexico, S.A. de C.V.
Cigarrera La Moderna, **21** 260; **22** 73
Cigarros la Tabacelera Mexicana (Cigatam), **21** 259
CIGNA Corporation, **III** 197, **223–27**, 389; **10** 30; **11** 243; **22 139–44 (upd.)**, 269; **38** 18
CIGWELD, **19** 442
Cii-HB, **III** 123, 678; **16** 122
Cilag-Chemie, **III** 35–36; **8** 282
Cilbarco, **II** 25
Cilva Holdings PLC, **6** 358
Cima, **14** 224–25
Cimaron Communications Corp., **38** 54
Cimarron Utilities Company, **6** 580
CIMCO Ltd., **21** 499–501
Cimenteries CBR S.A., **23** 325, 327
Ciments d'Obourg, **III** 701
Ciments de Chalkis Portland Artificiels, **III** 701
Ciments de Champagnole, **III** 702
Ciments de l'Adour, **III** 702
Ciments Français, **40 107–10**
Ciments Lafarge France, **III** 704
Ciments Lafarge Quebec, **III** 704
Cimos, **7** 37
Cinar Corporation, **40 111–14**
Cincinnati Bell, Inc., **6 316–18**; **29** 250, 252
Cincinnati Chemical Works, **I** 633
Cincinnati Electronics Corp., **II** 25
Cincinnati Financial Corporation, **16 102–04**
Cincinnati Gas & Electric Company, **6 465–68**, 481–82
Cincinnati Milacron Inc., **12 66–69**
Cincom Systems Inc., **15 106–08**
Cine-Groupe, **35** 279
Cineamerica, **IV** 676
Cinecentrum, **IV** 591
Cinema International Corp., **II** 149
Cinemark, **21** 362; **23** 125
Cinemax, **IV** 675; **7** 222–24, 528–29; **23** 276
Cineplex Odeon Corporation, **II** 145, **6 161–63**; **14** 87; **23 123–26 (upd.)**; **33** 432
Cinnabon Inc., **13** 435–37; **23 127–29**; **32** 12, 15
Cinquième Saison, **38** 200, 202
Cinram International, Inc., **43 107–10**
Cintas Corporation, **16** 228; **21 114–16**, 507; **30** 455
Cintel, **II** 158
Cintra. *See* Concesiones de Infraestructuras de Transportes, S.A. *or* Corporacion Internacional de Aviacion, S.A. de C.V.
Cipal-Parc Astérix, **27** 10
Ciprial S.A., **27** 260
CIPSCO Inc., **6 469–72**, 505–06
Circa Pharmaceuticals, **16** 529
Circle A Ginger Ale Company, **9** 177
Circle International, Inc., **17** 216
The Circle K Company, **II 619–20**; **V** 210; **7** 113–14, 372, 374; **20 138–40 (upd.)**; **25** 125; **26** 447
Circle Plastics, **9** 323
Circon Corporation, **21 117–20**
Circuit City Stores, Inc., **9** 65–66, **120–22**; **10** 235, 305–06, 334–35, 468–69; **12** 335; **14** 61; **15** 215; **16** 73, 75; **17** 489; **18** 533; **19** 362; **23** 51–53, 363; **24** 52, 502; **26** 410; **29 120–24 (upd.)**; **30** 464–65
Circus Circus Enterprises, Inc., **6** 201, **203–05**; **19** 377, 379
Circus Knie, **29** 126
Circus World, **16** 389–90
Cirque du Soleil Inc., **29 125–28**
Cirrus Logic, Incorporated, **9** 334; **11 56–57**; **25** 117
Cisco Systems, Inc., **11 58–60**, 520; **13** 482; **16** 468; **19** 310; **20** 8, 33, 69, 237; **25** 499; **26** 276–77; **34 111–15 (upd.)**, 441, 444; **36** 300; **38** 430; **43** 251
Cise, **24** 79
CIT Alcatel, **9** 9–10
CIT Financial Corp., **II** 90, 313; **8** 117; **12** 207
CIT Group/Business Credit, Inc., **13** 446
CIT Group/Commercial Services, **13** 536
Citadel Communications Corporation, **35 102–05**
Citadel General, **III** 404
Citadel, Inc., **27** 46
CitFed Bancorp, Inc., **16 105–07**
CITGO Petroleum Corporation, **II** 660–61; **IV 391–93**, 508; **7** 491; **31 113–117 (upd.)**; **32** 414, 416–17
Citibanc Group, Inc., **11** 456
Citibank, **II** 227, 230, 248, 250–51, 253–55, 331, 350, 358, 415; **III** 243, 340; **6** 51; **9** 124; **10** 150; **11** 418; **13** 146; **14** 101; **23** 3–4, 482; **25** 180, 542. *See also* Citigroup Inc
Citibank of Mexico, **34** 82
CITIC Pacific Ltd., **16** 481; **18 113–15**; **20** 134. *See also* China International Trade and Investment Corporation.
Citicasters Inc., **23** 293–94
Citicorp, **II** 214, **253–55**, 268, 275, 319, 331, 361, 398, 411, 445; **III** 10, 220, 397; **7** 212–13; **8** 196; **9 123–26 (upd.)**, 441; **10** 463, 469; **11** 140; **12** 30, 310, 334; **13** 535; **14** 103, 108, 235; **15** 94, 146, 281; **17** 324, 559; **21** 69, 145; **22** 169, 406; **25** 198, 542
Cities Service Company, **IV** 376, 391–92, 481, 575; **12** 542; **22** 172
Citifor, **19** 156
Citigroup Inc., **30 124–28 (upd.)**; **42** 332
Citinet. *See* Hongkong Telecommunications Ltd.
Citivision PLC, **9** 75
Citizen Watch Co., Ltd., **III 454–56**, 549; **13** 121–22; **21 121–24 (upd.)**; **23** 212; **41** 71–82
Citizen's Electric Light & Power Company, **V** 641
Citizen's Federal Savings Bank, **10** 93
Citizen's Fidelity Corp., **II** 342
Citizen's Industrial Bank, **14** 529
Citizens and Southern Bank, **II** 337; **10** 426
Citizens Bank, **11** 105
Citizens Bank of Hamilton, **9** 475
Citizens Bank of Savannah, **10** 426
Citizens Building & Loan Association, **14** 191
Citizens Federal Savings and Loan Association, **9** 476
Citizens Financial Group, Inc., **12** 422; **42 76–80**
Citizens Gas Co., **6** 529
Citizens Gas Fuel Company. *See* MCN Corporation.
Citizens Gas Light Co., **6** 455
Citizens Gas Supply Corporation, **6** 527
Citizens Mutual Savings Bank, **17** 529–30
Citizens National Bank, **II** 251; **13** 466; **25** 114; **41** 312
Citizens National Gas Company, **6** 527

Citizens Saving and Trust Company, **17** 356
Citizens Savings & Loan Association, **9** 173
Citizens Savings and Loan Society. *See* Citizens Mutual Savings Bank.
Citizens State Bank, **41** 178, 180
Citizens Telephone Company, **14** 257–58
Citizens Trust Co., **II** 312
Citizens Utilities Company, **7 87–89**; **37** 124–27
Citizens' Savings and Loan, **10** 339
Citroën. *See* Automobiles Citroen *and* PSA Peugeot Citroen S.A.
City and St. James, **III** 501
City and Suburban Telegraph Association and Telephonic Exchange, **6** 316–17
City and Village Automobile Insurance Co., **III** 363
City Auto Stamping Co., **I** 201
City Bank Farmers' Trust Co., **II** 254; **9** 124
City Bank of New York, **II** 250, 253
City Brewery, **I** 253
City Capital Associates, **31** 211
City Centre Properties Ltd., **IV** 705–06
City Finance Company, **10** 340; **11** 261
City Ice Delivery, Ltd., **II** 660
City Investing Co., **III** 263; **IV** 721; **9** 391; **13** 363
City Light and Traction Company, **6** 593
City Light and Water Company, **6** 579
City Market Inc., **12** 112
City Mutual Life Assurance Society, **III** 672–73
City National Bank of Baton Rouge, **11** 107
City National Leasing, **II** 457
City of London Real Property Co. Ltd., **IV** 706
City of Seattle Water Department, **12** 443
The City Post Publishing Corp., **12** 359
City Products Corp., **II** 419
City Public Service, **6 473–75**
City Savings, **10** 340
City Stores Company, **16** 207
Cityhome Corp., **III** 263
Civic Drugs, **12** 21
Civic Parking LLC, **18** 105
Civil & Civic Pty. Ltd., **IV** 707–08; **17** 286
Civil Aviation Administration of China, **31** 102; **33** 98
Civil Service Employees Insurance Co., **III** 214
CJ Banks. *See* Christopher & Banks Corporation.
CKE Restaurants, Inc., **19 89–93**, 433, 435; **25** 389; **27** 19; **29** 203; **37** 349–51
CKS Group Inc. *See* marchFIRST, Inc.
CKS Inc., **23** 479
Clabir Corp., **12** 199
Claeys, **22** 379–80
Claire's Stores, Inc., **17 101–03**; **18** 411
Clairol, **III** 17–18; **17** 110
Clairton Steel Co., **IV** 572; **7** 550
Clal Electronic Industries Ltd., **24** 429
Clal Group, **18** 154
CLAM Petroleum, **7** 282
Clancy Paul Inc., **13** 276
Clapp-Eastham Company. *See* GenRad, Inc.
Clara Candy, **15** 65
Clarcor Inc., **17 104–07**
Claremont Technology Group Inc., **31** 131
Clares Equipment Co., **I** 252
Clariden Bank, **21** 146–47
Claridge Group, **25** 266, 268
Clarify Corp., **38** 431
Clarion Hotels and Resorts, **25** 309
Clark & Co., **IV** 301
Clark & McKenney Hardware Co. *See* Clarcor Inc.
Clark & Rockefeller, **IV** 426
Clark Bros. Co., **III** 471
The Clark Construction Group, Inc., **8 112–13**
Clark, Dietz & Associates-Engineers. *See* CRSS Inc.
Clark Equipment Company, **I** 153; **7** 513–14; **8 114–16**; **10** 265; **13** 500; **15** 226
Clark Estates Inc., **8** 13
Clark Filter, Inc., **17** 104
Clark Materials Handling Company, **7** 514
Clark Motor Co., **I** 158; **10** 292
Clark Retail Enterprises Inc., **37** 311
Clark-Schwebel, Inc., **28** 195
Clarkins, Inc., **16** 35–36
Clarkson International Tools, **I** 531
CLASSA. *See* Compañia de Líneas Aéreas Subvencionadas S.A.
Classic FM plc, **39** 198–200
Claudel Roustand Galac, **19** 50
Claussen Pickle Co., **12** 371
Clayco Construction Company, **41** 225–26
Clayton & Dubilier, **III** 25
Clayton Brown Holding Company, **15** 232
Clayton Dubilier & Rice Inc., **25** 501; **29** 408; **40** 370
Clayton Homes Incorporated, **13 154–55**; **37** 77
Clayton-Marcus Co., **12** 300
Clayton/National Courier Systems, Inc., **24** 126
CLE. *See* Compagnie Laitière Européenne.
Clean Window Remodelings Co., **III** 757
Cleanaway Ltd., **III** 495
Cleancoal Terminal, **7** 582, 584
Clear Channel Communications, Inc., **23 130–32**, 294; **25** 418; **27** 278; **33** 322, 324; **35** 219–21, 233; **36** 422, 424; **37** 104–05
Clear Shield Inc., **17** 157, 159
Clearing Inc., **III** 514
Clearwater Tissue Mills, Inc., **8** 430
Cleary, Gottlieb, Steen & Hamilton, **35 106–09**
Cleco Corporation, **37 88–91**
Clef, **IV** 125
Clemente Capital Inc., **25** 542
Clements Energy, Inc., **7** 376
Cleo Inc., **12** 207–09; **35** 131
Le Clerc, **21** 225–26
Cletrac Corp., **IV** 366
Cleve-Co Jig Boring Co., **23** 82
Cleveland and Western Coal Company, **7** 369
Cleveland-Cliffs Inc., **13 156–58**; **17** 355
Cleveland Cotton Products Co., **37** 393
Cleveland Electric Illuminating Company. *See* Centerior Energy Theodor.
Cleveland Fabric Centers, Inc. *See* Fabri-Centers of America Inc.
Cleveland Grinding Machine Co., **23** 82
Cleveland Indians Baseball Company, Inc., **37 92–94**
Cleveland Iron Mining Company. *See* Cleveland-Cliffs Inc.
Cleveland Oil Co., **I** 341
Cleveland Paper Co., **IV** 311; **19** 267
Cleveland Pneumatic Co., **I** 457; **III** 512
Cleveland Precision Instruments, Inc., **23** 82
Cleveland Twist Drill Company. *See* Acme-Cleveland Corp.
Clevepak Corporation, **8** 229; **13** 442
Clevite Corporation, **14** 207
CLF Research, **16** 202; **43** 170
Click Messenger Service, Inc., **24** 126
Clifford & Wills, **12** 280–81
Clifford Chance LLP, **38 136–39**
Cliffs Corporation, **13** 157; **27** 224
Climax Molybdenum Co., **IV** 17–19
Clinchfield Coal Corp., **IV** 180–81; **19** 320
Clinical Assays, **I** 628
Clinical Partners, Inc., **26** 74
Clinical Pathology Facility, Inc., **26** 391
Clinical Science Research Ltd., **10** 106
Clinique Laboratories, Inc., **30** 191
Clinton Cards plc, **39 86–88**
Clinton Pharmaceutical Co., **III** 17; **37** 41
Clipper Group, **12** 439
Clipper, Inc., **IV** 597
Clipper Manufacturing Company, **7** 3
Clipper Scafoods, **II** 587
La Cloche d'Or, **25** 85
Clopay Corp., **34** 195
The Clorox Company, **III 20–22**, 52; **8** 433; **22 145–48 (upd.)**, 436; **26** 383
Close Brothers Group plc, **39 89–92**
The Clothestime, Inc., **20 141–44**
Clouterie et Tréfilerie des Flandres, **IV** 25–26
Clover Leaf Creamery, **II** 528
Clover Milk Products Co., **II** 575
Clovis Water Co., **6** 580
CLSI Inc., **15** 372; **43** 182
Club Aurrera, **8** 556
Club Corporation of America, **26** 27
Club de Hockey Canadien Inc., **26** 305
Club Européen du Tourisme, **6** 207
Club Méditerranée S.A., **I** 286; **6 206–08**; **21 125–28 (upd.)**; **27** 10
ClubCorp, Inc., **33 101–04**
Clubhôtel, **6** 207
Cluett Corporation, **22** 133
Cluett, Peabody & Co., Inc., **II** 414; **8** 567–68
Clyde Iron Works, **8** 545
Clydebank Engineering & Shipbuilding Co., **I** 573
Clydesdale Group, **19** 390
Clyne Maxon Agency, **I** 29
CM&M Equilease, **7** 344
CM&P. *See* Cresap, McCormick and Paget.
CM Industries, **I** 676
CMAC Investment Corporation. *See* Radian Group Inc.
CMB Acier, **IV** 228
CMB Packaging, **8** 477
CMC. *See* Commercial Metals Company.
CME. *See* Campbell-Mithun-Esty, Inc.
CMGI, Inc., **43** 11, 13, 420, 422
CMI International, Inc., **27** 202, 204
CML Group, Inc., **10 215–18**; **22** 382, 536; **38** 238
CMP Media Inc., **26 76–80**; **28** 504
CMP Properties Inc., **15** 122
CMS Energy Corporation, **IV** 23; **V 577–79**; **8** 466; **14 114–16 (upd.)**

CMS Healthcare, **29** 412
CMT Enterprises, Inc., **22** 249
CN. *See* Canadian National Railway System.
CNA Financial Corporation, **I** 488; **III 228–32**, 339; **12** 317; **36** 325, 327; **38 140–46 (upd.)**
CNA Health Plans, **III** 84
CNB Bancshares Inc., **31** 207
CNBC, Inc., **28** 298
CNC Holding Corp., **13** 166
CNCA. *See* Caisse National de Crédit Agricole.
CNEP. *See* Comptoir National d'Escompte de Paris.
CNF Transportation. *See* Consolidated Freightways Corporation.
CNG. *See* Consolidated Natural Gas Company.
CNH Global N.V., **38 147–56 (upd.)**
CNN. *See* Cable News Network.
CNP. *See* Compagnie Nationale à Portefeuille.
CNS, Inc., **20 145–47**
Co-Axial Systems Engineering Co., **IV** 677
Co-Counsel, Inc., **29** 364
Co. Luxemburgeoise de Banque S.A., **II** 282
Co. of London Insurers, **III** 369
Co-Op Blue Square Consumer Cooperative Society, **41** 56–58
Co-Steel International Ltd., **8** 523–24; **13** 142–43; **24** 144
Coach and Car Equipment Corp., **41** 369
Coach Leatherware, **10 219–21**; **12** 559
Coach Specialties Co. *See* Fleetwood Enterprises, Inc.
Coach USA, Inc., **24 117–19**; **30** 431, 433
Coachmen Industries Inc., **21** 153; **39** 393
Coal India Limited, **IV 48–50**
Coalport, **12** 528
Coast American Corporation, **13** 216
Coast Consolidators, Inc., **14** 505
Coast to Coast Hardware. *See* TruServ Corporation.
Coast-to-Coast Stores, **II** 419; **12** 8
Coastal Coca-Cola Bottling Co., **10** 223
Coastal Container Line Inc., **30** 318
Coastal Corporation, **IV** 366, **394–95**; **7** 553–54; **31 118–121 (upd.)**
Coastal Lumber, S.A., **18** 514
Coastal States Corporation, **11** 481
Coastal States Life Insurance Company, **11** 482
Coastal Valley Canning Co., **I** 260
CoastAmerica Corp., **13** 176
Coates/Lorilleux, **14** 308
Coating Products, Inc., **III** 643
Coats Viyella Plc, **V 356–58**
CoBank. *See* National Bank for Cooperatives.
Cobb & Branham, **14** 257
Cobb, Inc., **II** 585; **14** 515
COBE Laboratories, Inc., **13 159–61**; **22** 360
Cobham plc, **30 129–32**
Coborn's, Inc., **30 133–35**
Cobra Electronics Corporation, **14 117–19**
Cobra Golf Inc., **16 108–10**; **23** 474
Cobra Ventilation Products, **22** 229
Coburn Optical Industries, **III** 56
Coburn Vision Care, **III** 727
Coca-Cola Bottling Co. Consolidated, **II** 170, 468; **10 222–24**; **15** 299
Coca-Cola Bottling Company of Northern New England, Inc., **21** 319
The Coca-Cola Company, **I** 17, **232–35**, 244, 248, 278–79, 286, 289, 440, 457; **II** 103, 136–37, 477–78; **III** 215; **IV** 297; **6** 20–21, 30; **7** 155, 383, 466; **8** 399; **9** 86, 177; **10** 130, 222–23, **225–28 (upd.)**; **11** 421, 450–51; **12** 74; **13** 284; **14** 18, 453; **15** 428; **16** 480–81; **17** 207; **18** 60, 62–63, 68, 467–68; **19** 391; **21** 337–39, 401; **23** 418–20; **24** 516; **25** 183; **27** 21, 150; **28** 271, 473; **29** 85; **31** 243; **32** 59, **111–16 (upd.)**; **40** 350–52; **42** 31, 34–35
Coca-Cola Enterprises, Inc., **10** 223; **13 162–64**; **23** 455–57; **32** 115
Cochrane Corporation, **8** 135
Cochrane Foil Co., **15** 128
Cockburn & Campbell Ltd., **38** 501
Cockburn-Adelaide Cement, **31** 398, 400
Cockerill Sambre Group, **IV** 26–27, **51–53**; **22** 44; **26 81–84 (upd.)**; **42** 416
Coco's, **I** 547; **27** 16, 19
Code Hennessey & Simmons Limited, **39** 358
Codec, **19** 328
Codelco. *See* Corporacion Nacional del Cobre de Chile.
Codex Corp., **II** 61
Codville Distributors Ltd., **II** 649
Coeur d'Alene Mines Corporation, **20 148–51**
Coffee People, Inc., **40** 152–54
Cofica, **21** 99
COFINA, **III** 347
COFIRED, **IV** 108
Cofitel SA, **25** 466
Coflexip S.A., **25 103–05**
Cofroma, **23** 219
Cogéma, **IV** 108
COGEMA Canada, **IV** 436
Cogeneracion Prat SA, **41** 325, 327
Cogeneration Development Corp., **42** 387–88
Cogent Data Technologies, Inc., **31** 5
Cogentrix Energy, Inc., **10 229–31**
Cogetex, **14** 225
Cogifer, S.A., **18** 4; **31** 156, 158
Cognex Corp., **22** 373
CogniSeis Development, Inc., **18** 513, 515
Cognitive Solutions, Inc., **18** 140
Cognos Corp., **11** 78; **25** 97
Cohasset Savings Bank, **13** 468
Coherent, Inc., **31 122–25**
Cohn-Hall-Marx Co. *See* United Merchants & Manufacturers, Inc.
Cohoes Bancorp Inc., **41** 212
Cohu, Inc., **32 117–19**
Coils Plus, Inc., **22** 4
Coinamatic Laundry Equipment, **II** 650
Coinmach Laundry Corporation, **20 152–54**
Coktel Vision, **15** 455
Colas S.A., **31 126–29**
Colbert Television Sales, **9** 306
Colchester Car Auctions, **II** 587
Cold Spring Granite Company, **16 111–14**
Coldwater Creek Inc., **21 129–31**
Coldwell Banker, **IV** 715, 727; **V** 180, 182; **11** 292; **12** 97; **18** 475, 478; **27** 32. *See also* CB Commercial Real Estate Services Group, Inc.
Cole & Weber Inc., **I** 27
Cole Haan Holdings Incorporated, **36** 346
Cole National Corporation, **13 165–67**, 391
Cole Sewell Corporation, **39** 322, 324
Cole's Craft Showcase, **13** 166
Coleco Industries, Inc., **III** 506; **18** 520; **21** 375; **43** 229, 232
Coleman & Co., **II** 230
The Coleman Company, Inc., **III** 485; **9 127–29**; **22** 207; **26** 119; **28** 135, 247; **30 136–39 (upd.)**
Coleman Outdoor Products Inc., **21** 293
Colemans Ltd., **11** 241
Coles Book Stores Ltd., **7** 486, 488–89
Coles Express Inc., **15 109–11**
Coles Myer Ltd., **V 33–35**; **18** 286; **20 155–58 (upd.)**
Colex Data, **14** 556
Colgate-Palmolive Company, **I** 260; **II** 672; **III 23–26**; **IV** 285; **9** 291; **11** 219, 317; **14 120–23 (upd.)**, 279; **17** 106; **25** 365; **27** 212–13, 390; **35 110–15 (upd.)**
Colgens, **22** 193
Collabra Software Inc., **15** 322
College Construction Loan Insurance Assoc., **II** 455; **25** 427
College Entrance Examination Board, **12** 141
College Survival, Inc., **10** 357
Collegiate Arlington Sports Inc., **II** 652
Collett Dickinson Pearce International Group, **I** 33; **16** 168
Collins & Aikman Corporation, **I** 483; **13 168–70**; **25** 535; **41 91–95 (upd.)**
Collins Industries, Inc., **33 105–07**
Collins Radio Co., **III** 136; **11** 429
Collins Stewart, **41** 371–72
Colo-Macco. *See* CRSS Inc.
Cologne Re. *See* General Re Corporation *or* Kölnische Rückversicherungs-Gesellschaft AG.
Cologne Reinsurance Co., **III** 273, 299
Colombia Graphophone Company, **22** 192
Colombo, **25** 84
Colonia, **III** 273, 394
Colonia Versicherung Aktiengesellschaft. *See* AXA Colonia Konzern AG.
Colonial & General, **III** 359–60
Colonial Air Transport, **I** 89, 115; **12** 379
Colonial Airlines, **I** 102
Colonial Bancorp, **II** 208
Colonial Bank, **II** 236
Colonial Candle of Cape Cod, **18** 69
Colonial Container, **8** 359
Colonial Food Stores, **7** 373
Colonial Healthcare Supply Co., **13** 90
Colonial Insurance Co., **IV** 575–76
Colonial Life Assurance Co., **III** 359
Colonial Life Insurance Co. of America, **III** 220–21; **14** 108–09
Colonial Life Insurance Company, **11** 481
Colonial National Bank, **8** 9; **38** 10–12
Colonial National Leasing, Inc., **8** 9
Colonial Packaging Corporation, **12** 150
Colonial Penn Group Insurance Co., **11** 262; **27** 4
Colonial Penn Life Insurance Co., **V** 624
Colonial Rubber Works, **8** 347
Colonial Stores, **II** 397
Colonial Sugar Refining Co. Ltd. *See* CSR Limited.

Colony Capital, Inc., **27** 201
Colony Communications, **7** 99
Colony Gift Corporation, Ltd., **18** 67, 69
Color-Box, Inc., **8** 103
Color Corporation of America, **8** 553
Color Me Mine, **25** 263
Color Tile, **31** 435
Colorado Belle Casino, **6** 204
Colorado Cooler Co., **I** 292
Colorado Electric Company. *See* Public Service Company of Colorado.
Colorado Fuel & Iron (CF&I), **14** 369
Colorado Gaming & Entertainment Co., **21** 335
Colorado Gathering & Processing Corporation, **11** 27
Colorado Interstate Gas Co., **IV** 394
Colorado National Bank, **12** 165
Colorado Technical University, Inc., **41** 419
Colorcraft, **I** 447
Colorfoto Inc., **I** 447
Colortree. *See* National Envelope Corporation.
Colossal Pictures, **10** 286
Colson Co., **III** 96; **IV** 135–36
Colt, **19** 430–31
Colt Industries Inc., I 434–36, 482, 524; **III** 435
Colt Pistol Factory, **9** 416
COLT Telecom Group plc, 41 96–99
Colt's Manufacturing Company, Inc., 12 70–72
Coltec Industries Inc., **30** 158; **32** 96
Columbia Brewery, **25** 281
Columbia Broadcasting System. *See* CBS Corporation.
Columbia Chemical Co. *See* PPG Industries, Inc.
Columbia Electric Street Railway, Light and Power Company, **6** 575
Columbia Forest Products, **IV** 358
Columbia Gas & Electric Company, **6** 466. *See also* Columbia Gas System, Inc.
Columbia Gas Light Company, **6** 574
Columbia Gas of New York, Inc., **6** 536
The Columbia Gas System, Inc., V 580–82; 16 115–18 (upd.)
Columbia Gas Transmission Corporation, **6** 467
Columbia General Life Insurance Company of Indiana, **11** 378
Columbia Hat Company, **19** 94
Columbia House, **IV** 676
Columbia Insurance Co., **III** 214
Columbia News Service, **II** 132
Columbia Paper Co., **IV** 311; **19** 266
Columbia Pictures Entertainment, Inc., II 103, 134, **135–37**, 170, 234, 619; **IV** 675; **10** 227; **12** 73, 455; **21** 360; **22** 193; **25** 139; **28** 71. *See also* Columbia TriStar Motion Pictures Companies.
Columbia Railroad, Gas and Electric Company, **6** 575
Columbia Records, **II** 132; **16** 201; **26** 150
Columbia Records Distribution Corp., **43** 170
Columbia River Packers, **II** 491
Columbia Savings & Loan, **II** 144
Columbia Sportswear Company, 19 94–96; 41 100–03 (upd.)
Columbia Steamship Company, **17** 356
Columbia Steel Co., **IV** 28, 573; **7** 550
Columbia Transportation Co., **17** 357
Columbia TriStar Motion Pictures Companies, 12 73–76 (upd.); **28** 71
Columbia TriStar Television Distribution, **17** 149
Columbia/HCA Healthcare Corporation, 13 90; **15 112–14**; **22** 409–10; **27** 356
Columbian Carbon Company, **25** 70–71
Columbian Chemicals Co., **IV** 179; **28** 352, 356
Columbian Peanut Co., **I** 421; **11** 23
Columbus & Southern Ohio Electric Company (CSO), **6** 467, 481–82
Columbus Bank & Trust. *See* Synovus Financial Corp.
Columbus McKinnon Corporation, 37 95–98
Columbus-Milpar, **I** 544
Columbus Realty Trust, **26** 378
Columbus Savings and Loan Society, **I** 536; **13** 528
Colwell Systems, **19** 291; **22** 181
Com Dev, Inc., **32** 435
Com Ed. *See* Commonwealth Edison.
Com-Link 21, Inc., **8** 310
Comair Holdings Inc., 13 171–73; **31** 420; **34 116–20 (upd.)**
Comalco Fabricators (Hong Kong) Ltd., **III** 758
Comalco Ltd., **IV** 59–61, 122, 191
Comark, **24** 316; **25** 417–18
Comat Services Pte. Ltd., **10** 514
Comau, **I** 163
Combibloc Inc., **16** 339
Combined American Insurance Co. of Dallas, **III** 203
Combined Casualty Co. of Philadelphia, **III** 203
Combined Communications Corp., **II** 619; **IV** 612; **7** 191
Combined Insurance Co. of America, **III** 203–04
Combined International Corp., **III** 203–04
Combined Mutual Casualty Co. of Chicago, **III** 203
Combined Properties, Inc., **16** 160
Combined Registry Co., **III** 203
Combustion Engineering Group, **22** 11; **25** 534
Combustiveis Industriais e Domésticos. *See* CIDLA.
Comcast Corporation, 7 90–92; **9** 428; **10** 432–33; **17** 148; **22** 162; **24 120–24 (upd.)**; **27** 342, 344
ComCore Semiconductor, Inc., **26** 330
Comdata, **19** 160
Comdial Corporation, 21 132–35
Comdisco, Inc., 9 130–32; **11** 47, 86, 484, 490
Comdor Flugdienst GmbH., **I** 111
Comer Motor Express, **6** 370
Comerci. *See* Controladora Comercial Mexicana, S.A. de C.V.
Comercial Mexicana, S.A. *See* Controladora Comercial Mexicana, S.A. de C.V.
Comerco, **III** 21; **22** 147
Comerica Incorporated, 40 115–17
Comet, **II** 139; **V** 106–09; **24** 194, 266, 269–70
Comet American Marketing, **33** 31
Comet Rice, Inc., **33** 31
Cometra Oil, **IV** 576
ComFed Bancorp, **11** 29
COMFORCE Corporation, 40 118–20
Comfort Inns, **21** 362
Comforto GmbH, **8** 252; **39** 206
Cominco Ltd., 37 99–102 55
Comision Federal de Electricidad de Mexico (CFE), **21** 196–97
Comitato Interministrale per la Ricostruzione, **I** 465
Comm-Quip, **6** 313
CommAir. *See* American Building Maintenance Industries, Inc.
Commander Foods, **8** 409
Commander-Larabee Co., **I** 419; **25** 242
Commemorative Brands Inc., **19** 453
Commentry, **III** 676; **16** 120
Commerce and Industry Insurance Co., **III** 196, 203
Commerce Clearing House, Inc., 7 93–94. *See also* CCH Inc.
Commerce Group, **III** 393
Commerce.TV, **42** 323
Commerce Union, **10** 426
Commercial & General Life Assurance Co., **III** 371
Commercial Air Conditioning of Northern California, **25** 15
Commercial Air Lines, Inc., **23** 380
Commercial Alliance Corp. of New York, **II** 289
Commercial Aseguradora Suizo Americana, S.A., **III** 243
Commercial Assurance, **III** 359
Commercial Bank of Australia Ltd., **II** 189, 319, 388–89; **17** 324
Commercial Bank of London, **II** 334
Commercial Bank of Tasmania, **II** 188
Commercial Banking Co. of Sydney, **II** 187–89
Commercial Bureau (Australia) Pty., **I** 438
Commercial Chemical Company, **16** 99
Commercial Credit Company, III 127–28; 8 117–19; **10** 255–56; **15** 464
Commercial Exchange Bank, **II** 254; **9** 124
Commercial Federal Corporation, 12 77–79
Commercial Filters Corp., **I** 512
Commercial Financial Services, Inc., 26 85–89
Commercial Insurance Co. of Newark, **III** 242
Commercial Life, **III** 243
Commercial Life Assurance Co. of Canada, **III** 309
Commercial Metals Company, 15 115–17; 42 81–84 (upd.)
Commercial Motor Freight, Inc., **14** 42
Commercial National Bank, **II** 261; **10** 425
Commercial National Bank & Trust Co., **II** 230
Commercial National Bank of Charlotte, **II** 336
Commercial Realty Services Group, **21** 257
Commercial Ship Repair Co., **I** 185
Commercial Union plc, II 272, 308; **III** 185, **233–35**, 350, 373; **IV** 711
Commerzbank A.G., II 239, 242, **256–58**, 280, 282, 385; **IV** 222; **9** 283; **14** 170
Commerzfilm, **IV** 591
CommLink Corp., **17** 264
Commodity Credit Corp., **11** 24
Commodore Corporation, **8** 229
Commodore International, Ltd., II 6; **III** 112; **6** 243–44; **7 95–97**, 532; **9** 46; **10** 56, 284; **23** 25; **26** 16

Commonwealth & Southern Corporation, **V** 676
Commonwealth Aluminium Corp., Ltd. *See* Comalco Ltd.
Commonwealth Bank, **II** 188, 389
Commonwealth Board Mills, **IV** 248
Commonwealth Edison, **II** 28, 425; **III** 653; **IV** 169; **V 583–85**; **6** 505, 529, 531; **12** 548; **13** 341; **15** 422
Commonwealth Energy System, **14 124–26**
Commonwealth Hospitality Ltd., **III** 95
Commonwealth Industrial Gases, **25** 82
Commonwealth Industries, **III** 569; **11** 536; **20** 360
Commonwealth Insurance Co., **III** 264
Commonwealth Land Title Insurance Co., **III** 343
Commonwealth Life and Accident Insurance Company, **27** 46–47
Commonwealth Life Insurance Co., **III** 216–19
Commonwealth Limousine Services, Ltd., **26** 62
Commonwealth Mortgage Assurance Co., **III** 344
Commonwealth National Financial Corp., **II** 316
Commonwealth Oil Refining Company, **II** 402; **7** 517
Commonwealth Power Railway and Light Company, **14** 134
Commonwealth Southern Corporation, **14** 134
Commonwealth Telephone Enterprises, Inc., **25 106–08**
Commtron, Inc., **V** 14, 16; **11** 195; **13** 90
Communication Services Ltd. *See* Hongkong Telecommunications Ltd.
Communications and Systems Specialists, **18** 370
Communications Consultants, Inc., **16** 393
Communications Corp. of America, **25** 418
Communications Data Services, Inc., **IV** 627; **19** 204
Communications Industries Inc., **25** 496
Communications Network Consultants, **29** 400
Communications Properties, Inc., **IV** 677
Communications Solutions Inc., **11** 520
Communications Technology Corp. (CTC), **13** 7–8
Communicorp, **III** 188; **10** 29; **38** 17
Community Direct, Inc., **7** 16
Community HealthCare Services, **6** 182
Community Hospital of San Gabriel, **6** 149
Community Medical Care, Inc., **III** 245
Community National Bank, **9** 474
Community Power & Light Company, **6** 579–80
Community Psychiatric Centers, **15 118–20**
Community Public Service Company, **6** 514
Community Savings and Loan, **II** 317
Comnet Corporation, **9** 347
Comp-U-Card of America, Inc. *See* CUC International Inc.
Compac Corp., **11** 535
Compactom, **I** 588
Compagnia di Assicurazioni, **III** 345
Compagnia di Genova, **III** 347
Compagnia di Participazioni Assicurative ed Industriali S.p.A., **24** 341
Compagnie Auxilaire de Navigation, **IV** 558
Compagnie Bancaire, **II** 259; **21** 99–100
Compagnie Belge pour l'industrie, **II** 202
Compagnie Continentale, **I** 409–10
Compagnie d'Assurances Générales, **III** 391
Compagnie d'assurances Mutuelles contre l'incendie dans les départements de la Seine Inférieure et de l'Eure, **III** 210
Compagnie d'Investissements de Paris, **II** 233
Compagnie de Compteurs, **III** 617; **17** 418
Compagnie de Five-Lille, **IV** 469
Compagnie de Mokta, **IV** 107–08
Compagnie de Navigation Mixte, **III** 185
Compagnie de Reassurance Nord-Atlantique, **III** 276
Compagnie de Recherche et d'Exploitation du Pétrole du Sahara, **IV** 545; **21** 203
Compagnie de Saint-Gobain S.A., **II** 117, 474–75; **III 675–78**, 704; **8** 395, 397; **15** 80; **16 119–23 (upd.)**; **19** 58, 226; **21** 222; **26** 446; **33** 338, 340; **35** 86, 88
Compagnie de Transport Aerien, **I** 122
Compagnie des Cristalleries de Baccarat. *See* Baccarat.
Compagnie des Machines Bull S.A., **II** 40, 42, 70, 125; **III 122–23**, 154; **IV** 600; **12** 139; **13** 574; **25** 33. *See also* Bull S.A. *and* Groupe Bull.
Compagnie des Messageries Maritimes, **6** 379
Compagnie des Produits Chimiques et Électrométallurgiques d'Alais, Froges et Camargue, **IV** 173–74
Compagnie du Midi, **III** 209, 211
Compagnie du Nord, **IV** 108
Compagnie Européenne de Publication, **IV** 614–15
Compagnie Européenne de Télésecurité, **32** 374
Compagnie Financier Richemont AG, **19** 367, 369–70
Compagnie Financiere Alcatel, **9** 10
Compagnie Financière Belge des Pétroles. *See* PetroFina S.A.
Compagnie Financière de Paribas, **II** 192, **259–60**; **III** 185; **21** 99; **27** 138; **33** 339. *See also* BNP Paribas Group.
Compagnie Financière de Richemont AG, **29** 90
Compagnie Financière de Suez. *See* Suez Lyonnaise des Eaux.
Compagnie Financiere du Groupe Victoire, **27** 54
Compagnie Financière Richemont AG, **27** 487; **29** 91–92
Compagnie Française Chaufour Investissement, **27** 100
Compagnie Française de Distribution en Afrique, **IV** 559
Compagnie Française de Manutention, **27** 295
Compagnie Française de Raffinage, **IV** 558–60
Compagnie Française des Lubricants, **I** 341
Compagnie Française des Minerais d'Uranium, **IV** 108
Compagnie Française des Mines de Diamants du Cap, **IV** 64; **7** 121
Compagnie Française des Pétroles. *See* TOTAL S.A.
Compagnie Française des Produits d'Orangina, **I** 281
Compagnie Française du Méthane, **V** 626
Compagnie Française Thomson-Houston, **I** 357; **II** 116. *See also* Thales S.A.
Compagnie Fromagère de la Vallée de l'Ance, **25** 84
Compagnie Générale d'Électricité, **I** 193; **II 12–13**, 25; **IV** 174, 615; **9** 9–10
Compagnie Generale de Cartons Ondules, **IV** 296; **19** 226
Compagnie Generale de Radiologie, **II** 117
Compagnie Generale de Telegraphie Sans Fils, **II** 116
Compagnie Générale des Eaux, **V** 632–33; **6** 441. *See also* Vivendi SA.
Compagnie Générale des Établissements Michelin, **V 236–39**; **19** 508; **42 85–89 (upd.)**
Compagnie Générale Maritime et Financière, **6 379–81**
Compagnie Industriali Riunite S.p.A., **IV** 587–88
Compagnie Industrielle de Matérials de Manutention, **27** 296
Compagnie Industrielle des Fillers. *See* L'Entreprise Jean Lefebvre.
Compagnie Internationale de l'Informatique, **III** 123
Compagnie Internationale Express, **25** 120
Compagnie Internationale Pirelli S.A., **V** 249
Compagnie Laitière Européenne, **25** 83, 85
Compagnie Luxembourgeoise de Télédiffusion, **15** 54
Compagnie Nationale à Portefeuille, **29** 48
Compagnie Nationale de Navigation, **27** 515
Compagnie Navale Des Pétroles, **IV** 558
Compagnie Parisienne de Garantie, **III** 211
Compagnie Pneumatique Commerciale, **III** 426
Compagnie Tunisienne de Ressorts a Lames, **III** 581
Companhia Brasileira de Aluminio, **IV** 55
Companhia Brasileira de Mineracão e Siderugica, **IV** 54
Companhia de Celulose do Caima, **14** 250
Companhia de Diamantes de Angola, **IV** 21
Companhia de Minerales y Metales, **IV** 139
Companhia de Pesquisas Mineras de Angola, **IV** 65; **7** 122
Companhia de Seguros Argos Fluminense, **III** 221
Companhia de Seguros Tranquilidade Vida, S.A. *See* Banco Espírito Santo e Comercial de Lisboa S.A.
Companhia Siderúrgica de Tubarao, **IV** 125
Companhia Siderúrgica Mannesmann S.A., **III** 565–66
Companhia Siderúrgica Nacional, **II** 199; **43** 112
Companhia Uniao Fabril, **IV** 505
Companhia Vale do Rio Doce, **IV 54–57**; **43 111–14 (upd.)**
Compañia Arrendataria del Monopolio de Petróleos Sociedad Anónima, **IV** 396–97, 527–29
Compañia de Investigacion y Exploitaciones Petrolifera, **IV** 397

Compañia de Líneas Aéreas Subvencionadas S.A., **6** 95
Compañia Española de Petroleos S.A., IV 396–98, 527
Compania Fresnillo, **22** 286
Compania General de Aceptaciones. *See* Financiera Aceptaciones.
Compania Hulera Euzkadi, **21** 260; **23** 170
Compañia Mexicana de Transportación Aérea, **20** 167
Compania Minera de Penoles. *See* Industrias Penoles, S.A. de C.V.
Compañia Minera La India, **IV** 164
Compania Minera Las Torres, **22** 286
Compañia Nacional Minera Petrólia del Táchira, **IV** 507
Compania Siderurgica Huachipato, **24** 209
Compañía Telefónica Nacional de España S.A., **V** 337
Compaq Computer Corporation, II 45; **III** 114, **124–25; 6** 217, **221–23 (upd.)**, 230–31, 235, 243–44; **9** 42–43, 166, 170–71, 472; **10** 87, 232–33, 366, 459, 518–19; **12** 61, 183, 335, 470; **13** 388, 483; **16** 4, 196, 367–68; **17** 274; **21** 123, 391; **22** 288; **25** 184, 239, 498, 531; **26 90–93 (upd.)**; **27** 365; **28** 191; **29** 439; **30** 12; **36** 384; **43** 13
Compart, **24** 341
Compass Airlines, **27** 475
Compass Design Automation, **16** 520
Compass Group PLC, 6 193; **24** 194; **27** 482; **34 121–24**
CompDent Corporation, 22 149–51
Compeda, Ltd., **10** 240
Competence ApS, **26** 240
Competition Tire East/West, **V** 494; **19** 292
Competrol Ltd., **22** 189
Compex, **II** 233
CompHealth Inc., 25 109–12
Complete Business Solutions, Inc., 31 130–33
Completion Bond Co., **26** 487
Components Agents Ltd., **10** 113
Composite Craft Inc., **I** 387
Composite Research & Management Co., **17** 528, 530
Comprehensive Care Corporation, 15 121–23
Comprehensive Resources Corp., **IV** 83
Compressed Industrial Gases, **I** 297
Compression Labs Inc., **10** 456; **16** 392, 394; **27** 365
Compressor Controls Corporation, **15** 404
Comptoir d'Escompte de Mulhouse, **II** 232
Comptoir des Textiles Artificielles, **I** 122, 388–89
Comptoir Général de la Photographie. *See* Gaumont SA.
Comptoir Métallurgique Luxembourgeois, **IV** 25
Comptoir National d'Escompte de Paris, **II** 232–33, 270
Comptoirs Modernes S.A., 19 97–99
Compton Communications, **I** 33
Compton Foods, **II** 675
Compton's MultiMedia Publishing Group, Inc., **7** 165
Compton's New Media, Inc., **7** 168
Compu-Notes, Inc., **22** 413
CompuAdd Computer Corporation, 11 61–63
CompuChem Corporation, **11** 425
CompuCom Systems, Inc., 10 232–34, 474; **13** 176
Compugraphic, **III** 168; **6** 284
Compumech Technologies, **19** 312
Compumotor, **III** 603
CompuPharm, Inc., **14** 210
CompUSA, Inc., 10 235–36; 35 116–18 (upd.)
CompuServe Incorporated, 9 268–70; **10 237–39; 12** 562; **13** 147; **15** 265; **16** 467, 508; **26** 16; **29** 224, 226–27; **34** 361. *See also* America Online, Inc.
CompuServe Interactive Services, Inc., 27 106, **106–08 (upd.)**, 301, 307. *See also* America Online, Inc.
Computax, **6** 227–28
Computer Associates International, Inc., 6 224–26; 10 394; **12** 62; **14** 392; **27** 492
Computer City, **12** 470; **36** 387
The Computer Company, **11** 112
Computer Consoles Inc., **III** 164
Computer Data Systems, Inc., 14 127–29
The Computer Department, Ltd., **10** 89
Computer Depot, **6** 243
Computer Discount Corporation. *See* Comdisco, Inc.
Computer Dynamics, Inc., **6** 10
Computer Engineering Associates, **25** 303
Computer Factory, Inc., **13** 176
Computer Learning Centers, Inc., 26 94–96
Computer Network, **20** 237
Computer Peripheral Manufacturers Association, **13** 127
Computer Plaza K.K., **IV** 542–43
Computer Power, **6** 301
Computer Renaissance, Inc., **18** 207–8
Computer Research Corp., **III** 151; **6** 265
Computer Resources Management, Inc., **26** 36
Computer Sciences Corporation, 6 25, **227–29; 13** 462; **15** 474; **18** 370
Computer Shoppe, **V** 191–92
Computer Systems and Applications, **12** 442
Computer Systems Division (CDS), **13** 201
Computer Terminal Corporation, **11** 67–68
ComputerCity, **10** 235
ComputerCraft, **27** 163
Computerized Lodging Systems, Inc., **11** 275
ComputerLand Corp., 6 243; **9** 116; **10** 233, 563; **12** 335; **13 174–76**, 277; **33** 341–42
Computervision Corporation, 6 246–47; **7** 498; **10 240–42; 11** 275; **13** 201; **24** 234
Computing Scale Company of America. *See* International Business Machines Corporation.
Computing-Tabulating-Recording Co., **III** 147
Compuware Corporation, 10 243–45; 30 140–43 (upd.); **38** 482
CompX International, Inc., **19** 466, 468
Comsat Corporation, II 425; **12** 19; **13** 341; **23 133–36; 28** 241; **29** 42
Comshare Inc., 23 137–39
Comstock Canada, **9** 301
Comtel Electronics, Inc., **22** 409
Comunicaciones Avanzados, S.A. de C.V., **39** 195
Comverse Technology, Inc., 15 124–26; 43 115–18 (upd.)
Comviq GSM AB, **26** 331–33
Con Ed. *See* Consolidated Edison of New York, Inc.
Con-Ferro Paint and Varnish Company, **8** 553
ConAgra, Inc., II 493–95, 517, 585; **7** 432, 525; **8** 53, 499–500; **12 80–82 (upd.)**; **13** 138, 294, 350, 352; **14** 515; **17** 56, 240–41; **18** 247, 290; **21** 290; **23** 320; **25** 243, 278; **26** 172, 174; **36** 416; **42 90–94 (upd.)**
Conahay & Lyon, **6** 27
Conair Corp., 16 539; **17 108–10; 24** 131; **25** 56
Concept, Inc., **23** 154
Concepts Direct, Inc., 39 93–96
Concepts in Community Living, Inc., **43** 46
Concert Communications Company, **15** 69; **27** 304–05
Concesiones de Infraestructuras de Transportes, S.A., **40** 217
Concession Air, **16** 446
Concord Camera Corporation, 41 104–07
Concord Fabrics, Inc., 16 124–26
Concord International, **II** 298
Concord Watch Company, S.A., **28** 291
Concorde Hotels, **27** 421
Concordia, **IV** 497
Concrete Industries (Monier) Ltd., **III** 735
Concurrent Logic, **17** 34
The Condé Nast Publications Inc., IV 583–84; **13 177–81; 19** 5; **23** 98
Condor Systems Inc., **15** 530
Cone Communications, **25** 258
Cone Mills Corporation, 8 120–22
Conelectron, **13** 398
Conestoga National Bank, **II** 316
Conexant Systems, Inc., 36 121–25; 43 328
Confectionaire, **25** 283
Confederacion Norte-Centromericana y del Caribe de Futbol, **27** 150
Confederacion Sudamericana de Futbol, **27** 150
Confederation Africaine de Football, **27** 150
Confederation Freezers, **21** 501
Confederation of Engineering Industry, **IV** 484
Confidata Corporation, **11** 111
Confindustria, **I** 162
Confiserie-Group Hofbauer, **27** 105
Congas Engineering Canada Ltd., **6** 478
Congoleum Corp., 12 28; **16** 18; **18 116–19; 36** 77–78; **43** 19, 21
Congress Financial Corp., **13** 305–06; **19** 108; **27** 276
Congressional Information Services, **IV** 610
Conic, **9** 324
Conifer Group, **II** 214
Conill Corp., **II** 261
Coniston Partners, **I** 130; **II** 680; **III** 29; **6** 130; **10** 302
CONNA Corp., **7** 113; **25** 125
Connect Group Corporation, **28** 242
Connecticut Bank and Trust Co., **II** 213–14
Connecticut General Corporation. *See* CIGNA Corporation.

Connecticut Health Enterprises Network, **22** 425
Connecticut Light and Power Co., **13 182–84**; **21** 514
Connecticut Mutual Life Insurance Company, **III** 225, **236–38**, 254, 285
Connecticut National Bank, **13** 467
Connecticut River Banking Company, **13** 467
Connecticut Telephone Company. *See* Southern New England Telecommunications Corporation.
Connecticut Trust and Safe Deposit Co., **II** 213
Connecticut Yankee Atomic Power Company, **21** 513
Connecting Point of America, **6** 244
The Connection Group, Inc., **26** 257
Connectix Corporation, **28** 245
The Connell Company, **29 129–31**
Conner Corp., **15** 327
Conner Peripherals, Inc., **6 230–32**; **10** 403, 459, 463–64, 519; **11** 56, 234; **18** 260
Connie Lee. *See* College Construction Loan Insurance Assoc.
Connoisseur Communications, **37** 104
Connolly Data Systems, **11** 66
Connolly Tool and Machine Company, **21** 215
Connors Brothers, **II** 631–32
Connors Steel Co., **15** 116
Conoco Inc., **I** 286, 329, 346, 402–04; **II** 376; **IV** 365, 382, 389, **399–402**, 413, 429, 454, 476; **6** 539; **7** 346, 559; **8** 152, 154, 556; **11** 97, 400; **16 127–32 (upd.)**; **18** 366; **21** 29; **26** 125, 127
Conorada Petroleum Corp., **IV** 365, 400
Conover Furniture Company, **10** 183
ConQuest Telecommunication Services Inc., **16** 319
Conquistador Films, **25** 270
Conrad International Hotels, **III** 91–93
Conrail Inc., **22** 167, 376. *See also* Consolidated Rail Corporation.
Conran Associates, **17** 43
Conrock Co., **19** 70
Conseco Inc., **10 246–48**; **15** 257; **33 108–12 (upd.)**
Consgold. *See* Consolidated Gold Fields of South Africa Ltd. *and* Consolidated Gold Fields PLC.
Conshu Holdings, **24** 450
Conso International Corporation, **29 132–34**
Consolidated Aircraft Corporation, **9** 16, 497
Consolidated Aluminum Corp., **IV** 178
Consolidated Asset Management Company, Inc., **25** 204
Consolidated-Bathurst Inc., **IV** 246–47, 334; **25** 11; **26** 445
Consolidated Brands Inc., **14** 18
Consolidated Cable Utilities, **6** 313
Consolidated Cement Corp., **III** 704
Consolidated Cigar Holdings, Inc., **I** 452–53; **15** 137–38; **27** 139–40; **28** 247
Consolidated Coal Co., **IV** 82, 170–71
Consolidated Coin Caterers Corporation, **10** 222
Consolidated Controls, **I** 155
Consolidated Converting Co., **19** 109
Consolidated Copper Corp., **13** 503
Consolidated Delivery & Logistics, Inc., **24 125–28**
Consolidated Denison Mines Ltd., **8** 418
Consolidated Diamond Mines of South-West Africa Ltd., **IV** 21, 65–67; **7** 122–25; **16** 26
Consolidated Distillers Ltd., **I** 263
Consolidated Edison Company of New York, Inc., **I** 28; **V 586–89**; **6** 456; **35** 479
Consolidated Electric & Gas, **6** 447; **23** 28
Consolidated Electric Power Asia, **38** 448
Consolidated Electric Supply Inc., **15** 385
Consolidated Electronics Industries Corp. (Conelco), **13** 397–98
Consolidated Foods Corp., **II** 571–73, 584; **III** 480; **12** 159, 494; **22** 27; **29** 132
Consolidated Freightways Corporation, **V 432–34**; **6** 280, 388; **12** 278, 309; **13** 19; **14** 567; **21 136–39 (upd.)**; **25** 148–50
Consolidated Gas Company. *See* Baltimore Gas and Electric Company.
Consolidated Gold Fields of South Africa Ltd., **IV** 94, 96, 118, 565, 566
Consolidated Gold Fields PLC, **II** 422; **III** 501, 503; **IV** 23, 67, 94, 97, 171; **7** 125, 209, 387
Consolidated Grocers Corp., **II** 571
Consolidated Insurances of Australia, **III** 347
Consolidated Marketing, Inc., **IV** 282; **9** 261
Consolidated Mines Selection Co., **IV** 20, 23
Consolidated Mining and Smelting Co., **IV** 75
Consolidated National Life Insurance Co., **10** 246
Consolidated Natural Gas Company, **V 590–91**; **19 100–02 (upd.)**
Consolidated Oatmeal Co., **II** 558
Consolidated Papers, Inc., **8 123–25**; **36 126–30 (upd.)**
Consolidated Plantations Berhad, **36** 434–35
Consolidated Power & Light Company, **6** 580
Consolidated Power & Telephone Company, **11** 342
Consolidated Press Holdings, **8** 551; **37** 408–09
Consolidated Products, Inc., **14 130–32**, 352
Consolidated Rail Corporation, **II** 449; **V 435–37**, 485; **10** 44; **12** 278; **13** 449; **14** 324; **29** 360; **35** 291. *See also* Conrail Inc.
Consolidated Rand-Transvaal Mining Group, **IV** 90; **22** 233
Consolidated Rock Products Co., **19** 69
Consolidated Specialty Restaurants, Inc., **14** 131–32
Consolidated Steel, **I** 558; **IV** 570; **24** 520
Consolidated Stores Corp., **13** 543; **29** 311; **35** 254
Consolidated Temperature Controlling Co., **II** 40; **12** 246
Consolidated Theaters, Inc., **14** 87
Consolidated Tire Company, **20** 258
Consolidated Trust Inc., **22** 540
Consolidated Tyre Services Ltd., **IV** 241
Consolidated Vultee, **II** 7, 32
Consolidated Zinc Corp., **IV** 58–59, 122, 189, 191
Consolidation Coal Co., **IV** 401; **8** 154, 346–47
Consorcio G Grupo Dina, S.A. de C.V., **36 131–33**
Consortium, **34** 373
Consortium de Realisation, **25** 329
Consortium De Realization SAS, **23** 392
Consoweld Corporation, **8** 124
Constar International Inc., **8** 562; **13** 190; **32** 125
Constellation, **III** 335
Constellation Energy Corporation, **24** 29
Constellation Enterprises Inc., **25** 46
Constellation Insurance Co., **III** 191–92
Constinsouza, **25** 174
Construcciones Aeronauticas S.A., **I** 41–42; **7** 9; **12** 190; **24** 88
Construcciones y Contratas, **II** 198
Construction DJL Inc., **23** 332–33
Construtora Moderna SARL, **IV** 505
Consul Restaurant Corp., **13** 152
Consumer Access Limited, **24** 95
Consumer Products Company, **30** 39
Consumer Value Stores, **V** 136–37; **9** 67; **18** 199; **24** 290
Consumer's Gas Co., **I** 264
Consumers Cooperative Association, **7** 174
Consumers Distributing Co. Ltd., **II** 649, 652–53
Consumers Electric Light and Power, **6** 582
The Consumers Gas Company Ltd., **6 476–79**; **43** 154. *See also* Enbridge Inc.
Consumers Mutual Gas Light Company. *See* Baltimore Gas and Electric Company.
Consumers Power Co., **V** 577–79, 593–94; **14** 114–15, **133–36**
Consumers Public Power District, **29** 352
Consumers Union, **26 97–99**
Consumers Water Company, **14 137–39**; **39** 329
Contact Software International Inc., **10** 509
Contadina, **II** 488–89
Container Corporation of America, **IV** 295, 465; **V** 147; **7** 353; **8** 476; **19** 225; **26** 446
The Container Store, **36 134–36**
Container Transport International, **III** 344
Containers Packaging, **IV** 249
Contaminant Recovery Systems, Inc., **18** 162
Conte S.A., **12** 262
Contech, **10** 493
Contel Corporation, **II** 117; **V** 294–98; **6** 323; **13** 212; **14** 259; **15** 192; **43** 447
Contempo Associates, **14** 105; **25** 307
Contempo Casuals, Inc. *See* The Wet Seal, Inc.
Contemporary Books, **22** 522
Content Technologies Inc., **42** 24–25
Contex Graphics Systems Inc., **24** 428
Contherm Corp., **III** 420
Conti-Carriers & Terminals Inc., **22** 167
ContiCommodity Services, Inc., **10** 250–51
ContiGroup Companies, Inc., **43 119–22 (upd.)**
Continental AG, **9** 248; **15** 355
Continental Airlines, Inc., **I 96–98**, 103, 118, 123–24, 129–30; **6** 52, 61, 105, 120–21, 129–30; **12** 381; **20** 84, 262; **21**

140–43 (upd.); **22** 80, 220; **25** 420, 423; **26** 439–40; **34** 398
Continental Aktiengesellschaft, **V 240–43**, 250–51, 256; **8** 212–14; **19** 508
Continental American Life Insurance Company, **7** 102
Continental Assurance Co., **III** 228–30
Continental Baking Co., **I** 463–64; **II** 562–63; **7** 320–21; **11** 198; **12** 276; **13** 427; **19** 192; **27** 309–10; **38** 252
Continental Bancor, **II** 248
Continental Bank and Trust Co., **II** 251; **14** 102
Continental Bank Corporation, **I** 526; **II 261–63**, 285, 289, 348; **IV** 702
Continental Bio-Clinical Laboratories, **26** 391
Continental Blacks Inc., **I** 403
Continental Cablevision, Inc., **7 98–100**; **17** 148; **19** 201
Continental Can Co., Inc., **I** 597; **II** 34, 414; **III** 471; **10** 130; **13** 255; **15 127–30**; **24** 428; **26** 117, 449; **32** 125
Continental-Caoutchouc und Gutta-Percha Compagnie, **V** 240
Continental Carbon Co., **I** 403–05; **II** 53; **IV** 401; **36** 146–48
Continental Care Group, **10** 252–53
Continental Casualty Co., **III** 196, 228–32; **16** 204
Continental Cities Corp., **III** 344
Continental Corporation, **III** 230, **239–44**, 273; **10** 561; **12** 318; **15** 30; **38** 142
Continental Cos., **III** 248
Continental Divide Insurance Co., **III** 214
Continental Electronics Corporation, **18** 513–14
Continental Emsco, **I** 490–91; **24** 305
Continental Equipment Company, **13** 225
Continental Express, **11** 299
Continental Fiber Drum, **8** 476
Continental Gas & Electric Corporation, **6** 511
Continental General Tire Corp., **23 140–42**
Continental Grain Company, **10 249–51**; **13 185–87 (upd.)**; **30** 353, 355; **40** 87. *See also* ContiGroup Companies, Inc.
Continental Group Co., **I 599–600**, 601–02, 604–05, 607–09, 612–13, 615; **IV** 334; **8** 175, 424; **17** 106
Continental Gummi-Werke Aktiengesellschaft, **V** 241; **9** 248
Continental Hair Products, Inc. *See* Conair Corp.
Continental Health Affiliates, **17** 307
Continental Homes, **26** 291
Continental Illinois Corp. *See* Continental Bank Corporation.
Continental Illinois Venture Co., **IV** 702
Continental Insurance Co., **III** 239–42, 372–73, 386
Continental Insurance Cos. of New York, **III** 230
Continental Investment Corporation, **9** 507; **12** 463; **22** 541; **33** 407
Continental Life Insurance Co., **III** 225
Continental Medical Systems, Inc., **10 252–54**; **11** 282; **14** 233; **25** 111; **33** 185
Continental Milling Company, **10** 250
Continental Motors Corp., **I** 199, 524–25; **10** 521–22
Continental Mutual Savings Bank, **17** 529
Continental National American Group, **III** 230, 404
Continental National Bank, **II** 261; **11** 119
Continental-National Group, **III** 230
Continental Oil Co., **IV** 39, 365, 382, 399–401, 476, 517, 575–76
Continental Packaging Inc., **13** 255
Continental Plastic Containers, Inc., **25** 512
Continental Radio, **IV** 607
Continental Reinsurance, **11** 533
Continental Research Corporation, **22** 541
Continental Restaurant Systems, **12** 510
Continental Risk Services, **III** 243
Continental Savouries, **II** 500
Continental Scale Works, **14** 229–30
Continental Securities Corporation, **II** 444; **22** 404
Continental Telephone Company, **V** 296–97; **9** 494–95; **11** 500; **15** 195
Continental Wood Preservers, Inc., **12** 397
Continentale Allgemeine, **III** 347
ContinueCare Corporation, **25** 41
Contran Corporation, **19** 467
Contrans Acquisitions, Inc., **14** 38
Contred Ltd., **20** 263
Control Data Corporation, **17** 49; **19** 110, 513–15; **25** 496; **30** 338; **38** 58
Control Data Systems, Inc., **III** 118, **126–28**, 129, 131, 149, 152, 165; **6** 228, 252, 266; **8** 117–18, 467; **10 255–57**, 359, 458–59; **11** 469; **16** 137
Controladora Comercial Mexicana, S.A. de C.V., **36 137–39**
Controladora PROSA, **18** 516, 518
Controlled Materials and Equipment Transportation, **29** 354
Controlonics Corporation, **13** 195
Controls Company of America, **9** 67
Controlware GmbH, **22** 53
Convair, **I** 82, 121, 123, 126, 131; **II** 33; **9** 18, 498; **13** 357
Convenient Food Mart Inc., **7** 114; **25** 125
Convergent Technologies, **III** 166; **6** 283; **11** 519
Converse Inc., **III** 528–29; **V** 376; **9 133–36**, 234; **12** 308; **31 134–138 (upd.)**, 211; **39** 170, 172–74
Conway Computer Group, **18** 370
Conwest Exploration Company Ltd., **16** 10, 12; **43** 3
Conycon. *See* Construcciones y Contratas.
Conzinc Riotinto of Australia. *See* CRA Limited.
Cook Bates Inc., **40** 347–48
Cook Data Services, Inc., **9** 73
Cook Industrial Coatings, **I** 307
Cook Standard Tool Co., **13** 369
Cook United, **V** 172
Cooke Engineering Company, **13** 194
The Cooker Restaurant Corporation, **20 159–61**
Cooking and Crafts Club, **13** 106
Cookson Group plc, **III 679–82**; **16** 290
CoolBrands International Inc., **35 119–22**
Coolerator, **I** 463
Coolidge Mutual Savings Bank, **17** 529
Cooper Cameron Corporation, **20 162–66 (upd.)**
Cooper Canada Ltd., **16** 80
The Cooper Companies, Inc., **39 97–100**
Cooper Industries, Inc., **II 14–17**; **14** 564; **19** 43, 45, 140; **30** 266
Cooper Laboratories, **I** 667, 682
Cooper LaserSonics Inc., **IV** 100
Cooper McDougall & Robertson Ltd., **I** 715
Cooper Tire & Rubber Company, **8 126–28**; **23 143–46 (upd.)**
Cooper-Weymouth, **10** 412
Cooper's, Inc., **12** 283
Cooperative Grange League Federation Exchange, **7** 17
Coopers & Lybrand, **9 137–38**; **12** 391; **25** 383. *See also* PricewaterhouseCoopers.
CooperVision, **7** 46; **25** 55
Coordinated Caribbean Transport. *See* Crowley Caribbean Transport.
Coors Company. *See* Adolph Coors Company.
Coorsh and Bittner, **7** 430
Coos Bay Lumber Co., **IV** 281; **9** 259
Coosa River Newsprint Co., **III** 40; **16** 303; **43** 257
Coote & Jurgenson, **14** 64
Cooymans, **I** 281
Copart Inc., **23 147–49**, 285, 287
Copeland Corp., **II** 20
Copeman Ridley, **13** 103
Copland Brewing Co., **I** 268; **25** 280
Copley Pharmaceuticals Inc., **13** 264
The Copley Press, Inc., **23 150–52**
Copley Real Estate Advisors, **III** 313
Copolymer Corporation, **9** 242
Copper Queen Consolidated Mining Co., **IV** 176–77
Copper Range Company, **IV** 76; **7** 281–82
Copperweld Steel Co., **IV** 108–09, 237
The Copps Corporation, **32 120–22**
Copycat Ltd., **8** 383
Cora Verlag, **IV** 590
Coral Drilling, **I** 570
Coral Energy, **41** 359
Coral Leisure Group, **I** 248
Coral Petroleum, **IV** 395
Corange, Ltd., **37** 111–13
Corbett Canyon. *See* The Wine Group, Inc.
Corbett Enterprises Inc., **13** 270
Corbis Corporation, **31 139–42**
Corby Distilleries Limited, **14 140–42**
Corco. *See* Commonwealth Oil Refining Company.
Corco, Inc. *See* Liqui-Box Corporation.
Corcoran & Riggs. *See* Riggs National Corporation.
Cordiant plc. *See* Saatchi & Saatchi plc.
Cordis Corp., **19 103–05**; **36** 306
Cordon & Gotch, **IV** 619
Cordon Bleu, **II** 609
Cordovan Corp., **IV** 608
Core Laboratories Inc., **I** 486; **11** 265
Corel Corporation, **15 131–33**; **33 113–16 (upd.)**
CoreStates Financial Corp, **17 111–15**
CoreTek, Inc., **36** 353
Corfuerte S.A. de C.V., **23** 171
Corimon, **12** 218
Corinthian Broadcast Corporation, **IV** 605; **10** 4
Corinthian Colleges, Inc., **39 101–04**
Corio Inc., **38** 188, 432
Cormetech, **III** 685
Corn Exchange Bank, **II** 316
Corn Exchange Bank Trust Co., **II** 251; **14** 102
Corn Exchange National Bank, **II** 261
Corn Products Company. *See* Bestfoods.

Corn Sweetners Inc., **I** 421; **11** 23
Cornelia Insurance Agency. *See* Advantage Insurers, Inc.
Cornell Corrections, **28** 255
Cornerstone Direct Marketing, **8** 385–86
Cornerstone Propane Partners, L.P., **37** 280, 283
Cornerstone Title Company, **8** 461
Cornhill Insurance Co., **I** 429; **III** 185, 385
Cornhusker Casualty Co., **III** 213
Corning Asahi Video Products Co., **III** 667
Corning Clinical Laboratories, **26** 390–92
Corning Consumer Products Company, **27** 288
Corning Incorporated, **I** 609; **III** 434, 667, **683–85**, 720–21; **8** 468; **11** 334; **13** 398; **22** 454; **25** 254; **30** 151–52
Coro International A.V.V., **39** 346
Coronado Corp., **II** 112
Coronet Industries, Inc., **II** 90; **14** 436
Corporacion Durango, S.A. de C.V., **37** 178
Corporacion Estatal Petrolera Ecuatoriana, **IV** 510–11
Corporación Internacional de Aviación, S.A. de C.V. (Cintra), **20 167–69**
Corporación Moctezuma, **21** 261
Corporacion Nacional del Cobre de Chile, **38** 231; **40 121–23**
Corporacion Siderurgica Integral, **22** 44
Corporación Venezolana de Petroleo, **IV** 507
Corporate Childcare Development, Inc. *See* Bright Horizons Family Solutions, Inc.
Corporate Express, Inc., **22 152–55**, 531; **41** 67–69
Corporate Microsystems, Inc., **10** 395
Corporate Partners, **12** 391
Corporate Software Inc., **9 139–41**
CorporateFamily Solutions. *See* Bright Horizons Family Solutions, Inc.
Corporation for Public Broadcasting, **14 143–45**
Corporation of Lloyd's, **III** 278–79
Corporation Trust Co. *See* CCH Inc.
Corpoven, **IV** 508
Corrado Passera, **IV** 588
Corral Midwest, Inc., **10** 333
Correctional Services Corporation, **30 144–46**
Corrections Corporation of America, **23 153–55**; **28** 255
Corrigan-McKinney Steel Company, **13** 157
Corrigan's, **16** 559
Corroon & Black. *See* Willis Corroon Group Plc.
Corrpro Companies, Inc., **20 170–73**
Corrugated Paper, **IV** 249
CORT Business Services Corporation, **26 100–02**
El Corte Inglés Group, **26 128–31 (upd.)**
Cortec Corporation, **14** 430
Corvallis Lumber Co., **IV** 358
Cory Bros & Co. Ltd., **31** 367, 369
Cory Components, **36** 158
Cory Corp., **II** 511
Cory Food Services, Inc., **II** 608
Cory Orchard and Turf. *See* Chemi-Trol Chemical Co.
Cosco Pacific, **20** 313
Cosden Petroleum Corp., **IV** 498; **26** 367
Cosgrove & Co., **III** 283
Cosmair Inc., **III** 47–48; **8 129–32**, 342–44; **12** 404; **31** 418
Cosmar Corp., **37** 269–71
The Cosmetic Center, Inc., **22 156–58**
Cosmetic Technology International, Inc., **22** 409
Cosmo Oil Co., Ltd., **IV 403–04**
Cosmopolitan Productions, **IV** 626; **19** 203
Cosorzio Interprovinciale Vini, **10** 181
Cost Plus, Inc., **12** 393; **27 109–11**; **34** 337, 340
Costa Apple Products, **II** 480; **26** 57
Costa Cruise Lines, **27** 29, 90, 92
Costa e Ribeiro Ltd., **IV** 504
Costa Rica International, Inc., **41** 329
Costain Civil Engineering Ltd., **III** 495; **13** 206
Costain Homes, **31** 386
Costco Wholesale Corporation, **V** 36, **10** 206; **11** 240; **14** 393–95; **15** 470; **25** 235; **27** 95; **43 123–25 (upd.)**
Costruzioni Meccaniche Nazionalia, **13** 218
Côte d'Or, **II** 521
Cott Beverage Corporation, **9** 291
Cottees General Foods, **II** 477
Cotter & Company, **V 37–38**; **12** 8. *See also* TruServ Corporation.
Cotter Corporation, **29** 488
Cotton Producers Association. *See* Gold Kist Inc.
Coty, Inc., **36 140–42**; **37** 270
Coudert Brothers, **30 147–50**
Coulter Corporation. *See* Beckman Coulter, Inc.
Counselor Co., **14** 230
Country Fresh, Inc., **26** 449
Country Kitchen Foods, **III** 21
Country Kitchen International, **22** 127
Country Music Television, **11** 153
Country Poultry, Inc., **II** 494
Country Seat Stores, Inc., **15** 87
Country Store of Concord, Inc., **10** 216
Countrywide Credit Industries, Inc., **16 133–36**
County Bank, **II** 333
County Catering Co., **13** 103
County Data Corporation, **18** 24
County Fire Insurance Co., **III** 191
County Market, **II** 670
County NatWest, **II** 334–35
County Perfumery, **III** 65
County Seat Stores Inc., **II** 669; **9 142–43**
County Trust Co., **II** 230
Cour des Comptes, **II** 233
Courage Brewing Group., **I** 229, 438–39; **III** 503
Courcoux-Bouvet, **II** 260
Courier Corporation, **41 108–12**
Courir S.A., **39** 183–85
Courrèges Parfums, **III** 48; **8** 343
The Courseware Developers, **11** 19
Court Courier Systems, Inc., **24** 126
Court House Square, **10** 44
Courtaulds plc, **I** 321; **IV** 261, 670; **V** 356–57, **359–61**; **12** 103; **17 116–19 (upd.)**; **33** 134; **41** 9
Courtney Wines International, **II** 477
Courtot Investments, **II** 222
Courtyard by Marriott, **9** 427
Cousins Mortgage and Equity Investments, **12** 393
Coutts & Co., **II** 333–34
Couvrette & Provost Ltd., **II** 651
Covance Inc., **30 151–53**
Covantage, **11** 379
Covenant Life Insurance, **III** 314
Coventry Climax Engines, Ltd., **13** 286
Coventry Co., **III** 213
Coventry Corporation, **17** 166, 168
Coventry Machinists Company, **7** 458
Coventry Ordnance Works, **I** 573
Coventry Union Banking Co., **II** 318; **17** 323
Covidea, **II** 252
Coville Inc., **16** 353
Covington & Burling, **40 124–27**
Cow & Gate Ltd., **II** 586–87
Cowham Engineering, **III** 704
Cowles Media Company, **IV** 613, 648; **7** 191; **19** 285; **23 156–58**; 344
Cox & Co., **II** 236, 307–08
Cox Cable Communications, Inc., **42** 114
Cox Enterprises, Inc., **IV** 246, **595–97**; **6** 32; **7** 327; **9** 74; **17** 148; **22 159–63 (upd.)**; **24** 120; **30** 217; **38** 307–08
Cox Medical Enterprises, Inc., **21** 47
Cox Newsprint, Inc., **25** 11
Cox Pharmaceuticals, **35** 25
Cox Woodlands Company, **25** 11
Coz Chemical Co., **21** 20, 22
CP. *See* Canadian Pacific Limited.
CP Air, **6** 60–61
CP National, **6** 300; **19** 412
CP/AAON. *See* AAON, Inc.
CP8, **43** 89
CPC International Inc., **II** 463, **496–98**; **27** 40. *See also* Bestfoods.
CPI Corp., **38 157–60**
CPL. *See* Carolina Power & Light Company.
CRA Limited, **IV 58–61**, 67, 192; **7** 124. *See also* Rio Tinto plc.
Crabtree Electricals, **III** 503; **7** 210
Cracker Barrel Old Country Store, Inc., **10 258–59**. *See also* CBRL Group, Inc.
Craft House Corp., **8** 456
Craftique, Inc., **33** 350–51
Craig Bit Company, **13** 297
Crain Communications, Inc., **12 83–86**; **35 123–27 (upd.)**
Cramer, Berkowitz & Co., **34 125–27**
Cramer Electronics, **10** 112
Cranberry Canners, Inc. *See* Ocean Spray Cranberries, Inc.
Crane & Co., Inc., **26 103–06**; **30** 42
Crane Co., **8 133–36**, 179; **24** 332; **30 154–58 (upd.)**
Crane Packing Company, **19** 311
Crane Supply Company, **8** 135
Cranston Mills, **13** 168
Cranswick plc, **40 128–30**
Crate and Barrel, **9 144–46**; **27** 429; **36** 135. *See also* Euromarket Designs Inc.
Cravath, Swaine & Moore, **27** 325; **43 126–28**
Craven Tasker Ltd., **I** 573–74
Crawford and Watson, **IV** 278
Crawford Gosho Co., Ltd., **IV** 442
Crawford Group, Inc., **17** 372
Crawford Supply Company, **6** 392
Cray Research, Inc., **III** 126, 128, **129–31**; **10** 256; **16 137–40 (upd.)**; **21** 391; **22** 428; **29** 440
Crayfish Company, Ltd., **36** 153
Crazy Eddie Inc., **23** 373
CRD Total France, **IV** 560
Cream City Railway Company, **6** 601

Cream of Wheat Corp., **II** 543; **22** 427
Creamola Food Products, **II** 569
Creasy Co., **II** 682
Creative Artists Agency LLC, **10** 228; **22** 297; **23** 512, 514; **32** 115; **38 161–64**
Creative Artists Associates, **43** 235
Creative BioMolecules, Inc., **29** 454
Creative Business Concepts, Inc., **39** 346
Creative Concepts in Advertising, **27** 194
Creative Displays, Inc., **27** 279
Creative Engineering Inc., **13** 472
Creative Food 'N Fun Co., **14** 29
Creative Forming, Inc., **8** 562
Creative Homes, Inc., **IV** 341
Creative Integration and Design Inc., **20** 146
Creative Memories, **40** 44
Creative Technologies Corp., **15** 401
Credit & Risk Management Associates, Inc., **18** 170
Credit Acceptance Corporation, **18 120–22**
Crédit Agricole, **II 264–66**, 355; **19** 51
Credit and Data Marketing Services, **V** 118
Credit Clearing House, **IV** 605
Crédit Commercial de France, **25** 173
Crédit Communal de Belgique, **42** 111
Credit du Nord, **II** 260
Crédit Foncier, **II** 264
Crédit Général de Belgique, **II** 304
Credit Immobilier, **7** 538
Crédit Liégiois, **II** 270
Crédit Local de France, **42** 111
Crédit Lyonnais, **II** 242, 257, 354; **6** 396; **7** 12; **9 147–49**; **19** 34, 51, 166; **21** 226; **25** 170, 329; **33 117–21 (upd.)**
Credit Mobilier, **II** 294
Crédit National S.A., **9 150–52**
Credit Service Exchange, **6** 24
Credit Suisse First Boston. *See* Financière Crédit Suisse-First Boston.
Crédit Suisse Group, **II 267–69**, 369–70, 378–79, 402–04; **21 144–47 (upd.)**. *See also* Schweizerische Kreditanstalt.
Creditanstalt-Bankverein, **II** 242, 295
CrediThrift Financial, **11** 16
Credithrift Financial of Indiana, **III** 194
Credito de la Union Minera, **II** 194
Credito Italiano, **I** 368, 465, 567; **II** 191, **270–72**; **III** 347
Credito Minero y Mercantil, S.A., **22** 285
Credito Provincial Hipotecario, **19** 189
Creditrust Corp., **42** 259
Cree Research, Inc., **13** 399
Crellin Holding, Inc., **8** 477
Crellin Plastics, **8** 13
Crenlo Corp., **16** 180
Creole Petroleum Corporation, **IV** 428; **7** 171
Cresap, McCormick and Paget, **32** 458
Crescendo Productions, **6** 27
Crescent Box & Printing Co., **13** 442
Crescent Chemical, **I** 374
Crescent Niagara Corp., **II** 16
Crescent Real Estate Equities Company, **25** 454
Crescent Software Inc., **15** 373
Crescent Vert Company, Ltd., **II** 51; **21** 330
Crescent Washing Machine Company, **8** 298
Crescott, Inc., **15** 501
Cressbrook Dairy Co., **II** 546
Cressey Dockham & Co., **II** 682
Crest Fruit Co., **17** 458
Crest Ridge Homes, Inc., **17** 83
Crest Service Company, **9** 364
Crestbrook Forest Industries Ltd., **IV** 285
Crestmont Financial Corporation, **14** 472
Creusot-Loire, **II** 93–94; **19** 166
Crevettes du Cameroun, **13** 244
CRH plc, **37** 203, 206
Crimson Associates L.P., **26** 48
Crist Partners, **34** 249
Criterion Casualty Company, **10** 312
Criterion Life Insurance Company, **10** 311
Critikon, Inc., **III** 36
Crocker National Bank, **II** 226, 317, 319, 383; **13** 535; **17** 324–25
Crocker National Corporation, **12** 536
Crockett Container Corporation, **8** 268
Croda International Ltd., **IV** 383
Croitex S.A., **26** 374
Crompton & Knowles Corp., **I** 633; **9 153–55**
Crompton Corporation, **36 143–50 (upd.)**
Crop Production Services, Inc., **IV** 576
Crosby Enterprises, **17** 19
Croscill Home Fashions, **8** 510
Croscill, Inc., **42 95–97**
Crosfield, Lampard & Co., **III** 696
Cross & Trecker Corporation, **10** 330
Cross-Continent Auto Retailers, **26** 501
Cross Country Group, **25** 358
Cross Creek Apparel, Inc., **30** 400
Cross Pointe Paper Corporation, **26** 363
Cross/Tessitore & Associates, **16** 259
Crossair, **I** 121
Crosse and Blackwell, **II** 547
Crossett Lumber Co., **IV** 281; **9** 259
Crossland Capital Corp., **III** 293
Crossley Motors, Ltd., **13** 285
Crothall, **6** 44
Crothers Properties, Ltd., **21** 500
Crouse-Hinds Co., **II** 16; **19** 45
Crow Catchpole, **III** 752; **28** 448
Crowell-Collier Publishing Company, **IV** 310; **7** 286
Crowell Publishing Company, **19** 266
Crowley Foods, Inc., **II** 528
Crowley Maritime Corporation, **6 382–84**; **9** 510–11; **28 77–80 (upd.)**
Crowley, Milner & Company, **19 106–08**
Crown Advertising Agency. *See* King Kullen Grocery Co., Inc.
Crown Aluminum, **I** 544
Crown America Corp., **13** 393
Crown Books Corporation, **14** 61; **16** 159–61; **21 148–50**; **41** 61
Crown Can Co., **I** 601
Crown Center Redevelopment Corp., **IV** 621
Crown Central Petroleum Corporation, **7 101–03**
Crown, Cork & Seal Company, Inc., **I 601–03**; **13 188–90 (upd.)**; **15** 129; **17** 106; **24** 264; **30** 475; **32 123–27 (upd.)**
Crown Courier Systems, Inc., **24** 126
Crown Crafts, Inc., **16 141–43**
Crown Drugs, **II** 673
Crown Equipment Corporation, **15 134–36**
Crown Forest Industries, **IV** 279; **19** 155
Crown Life Insurance Company, **III** 261; **6** 181–82
Crown Oil and Refining Company, **7** 101
Crown Packaging, **19** 155
Crown Pet Foods Ltd., **39** 356
Crown Publishing Group, **IV** 584; **13** 429; **31** 376, 379
Crown Radio, **17** 123–24; **41** 114
Crown Technical Systems, Inc., **37** 215
Crown Vantage Inc., **29 135–37**
Crown Zellerbach Corporation, **IV** 290, 345; **8** 261; **22** 210; **24** 247
Crownx Inc., **6** 181–82
Crowson and Son Ltd., **23** 219
CRSS Inc., **6 142–44**; **23** 491
CRTC. *See* Canadian Radio-Television and Telecommunications Commission.
Crucible Steel, **I** 434–35
Crude Oil Pipe Line Co., **IV** 400
Cruden Investments Pty Ltd., **IV** 651; **7** 390
Cruise America Inc., **21 151–53**
Cruise Associates, **22** 471
Crum & Forster Holdings, Inc., **II** 448; **III** 172; **6** 290; **13** 448; **26** 546
Crump E & S, **6** 290
Crump Inc., **I** 584
Crush International, **II** 478; **III** 53
Crushed Stone Sales Ltd., **IV** 241
Cruzan Rum Distillery, Ltd., **27** 478
Cruzcampo, **18** 501
Cruzeiro do Sul Airlines, **6** 133
Cryenco Sciences Inc., **21** 109
Cryomedics Inc., **I** 667
Crystal Brands, Inc., **9 156–58**; **12** 431
Crystal Market, **41** 174
Crystal Oil Co., **IV** 180, 548
CS Crable Sportswear Inc., **23** 66
CS First Boston Inc., **II** 269, **402–04**; **III** 289; **12** 209; **21** 146. *See also* Credit Suisse Group.
CS Holding. *See* Credit Suisse Group.
CS Life, **21** 146–47
CSA. *See* China Southern Airlines Company Ltd.
CSA Press, **IV** 661
CSC. *See* Computer Sciences Corporation.
CSC Holdings, Inc., **32** 105
CSC Industries, Inc., **IV** 63
CSE Corp., **III** 214
CSFB. *See* Financière Crédit Suisse-First Boston *and* Credit Suisse Group.
CSK, **10** 482
CSK Auto Corporation, **38 165–67**
CSO. *See* Columbus & Southern Ohio Electric Company.
CSR Limited, **III 686–88**, 728, 735–36; **IV** 46; **22** 106; **28 81–84 (upd.)**
CSS Industries, Inc., **35 128–31**
CST Office Products, **15** 36; **42** 416
CSX Corporation, **V 438–40**, 485; **6** 340; **9** 59; **13** 462; **22 164–68 (upd.)**; **29** 360–61
CSY Agri-Processing, **7** 81–82
CT Financial Services Inc., **V** 401–02
CT&T. *See* Carolina Telephone and Telegraph Company.
CTA. *See* Comptoir des Textiles Artificielles.
CTB International Corporation, **43 129–31 (upd.)**
CTG, Inc., **11 64–66**
CTI. *See* Cosmetic Technology International, Inc.
CTNE, **I** 462
CTR. *See* International Business Machines Corporation.
CTS Corporation, **19** 104; **39 105–08**

CTV Network, **35** 69
CTX Mortgage Company, **8** 88
Cub Foods, **II** 669–70; **14** 411; **17** 302; **18** 505; **22** 327
Cuban-American Manganese Corp., **IV** 81; **7** 186
Cuban American Nickel Co., **IV** 82; **7** 186
Cuban American Oil Company, **8** 348
Cuban Telephone Co., **I** 462–63
Cubic Corporation, 19 109–11
Cubitts Nigeria, **III** 753
CUC International Inc., 16 144–46
Cuckler Steel Span Co., **I** 481
Cudahy Corp., **12** 199
Cuisinart Corporation, **17** 110; **24 129–32**
Culbro Corporation, **14** 19; **15 137–39**
Culinary Foods, Inc., **14** 516
Cullen/Frost Bankers, Inc., 25 113–16
Culligan International Company, **I** 373; **II** 468; **12 87–88**, 346; **16** 20
Culligan Water Technologies, Inc., 38 168–70 (upd.)
Cullinet Software Corporation, **6** 225; **14** 390; **15** 108
Cullman Bros. *See* Culbro Corporation.
Cullum Companies, **II** 670
Culp, Inc., 29 138–40
Culter Industries, Inc., **22** 353
Cumberland Farms, Inc., 17 120–22; **26** 450
Cumberland Federal Bancorporation, **13** 223; **31** 206
Cumberland Newspapers, **IV** 650; **7** 389
Cumberland Packing Corporation, 26 107–09
Cumberland Paper Board Mills Ltd., **IV** 248
Cumberland Pipeline Co., **IV** 372
Cumberland Property Investment Trust Ltd., **IV** 711
Cummins Cogeneration Co. *See* Cogeneration Development Corp.
Cummins Engine Co., Inc., I 146–48, 186; **III** 545; **IV** 252; **10** 273–74; **12 89–92 (upd.)**; **16** 297; **17** 29; **19** 293; **21** 503; **26** 256; **40 131–35 (upd.)**; **42** 387
Cumo Sports, **16** 109
Cumulus Media Inc., 37 103–05
CUNA Mutual Insurance Group, **11** 495
Cunard Line Ltd., **I** 573; **23 159–62**; **27** 90, 92; **36** 323; **38** 341, 344
Cuno Kourten, **13** 353
Cupples Products Co., **IV** 15
Current, Inc., 37 106–09
Currys Group PLC, **V** 49; **19** 123
Cursenir, **I** 280
Curtice-Burns Foods, Inc., **7** 17–18, **104–06**; **21** 18, **154–57 (upd.)**
Curtin & Pease/Peneco, **27** 361
Curtis Circulation Co., **IV** 619
Curtis Homes, **22** 127
Curtis Industries, **13** 165
Curtis 1000 Inc. *See* American Business Products, Inc.
Curtis Squire Inc., **18** 455
Curtiss Candy Co., **II** 544
Curtiss-Wright Corporation, **I** 524; **III** 464; **7** 263; **8** 49; **9** 14, 244, 341, 417; **10 260–63**; **11** 427; **21** 174; **23** 340; **35 132–37 (upd.)**
Curver Group, **III** 614
Curver-Rubbermaid, **III** 615
Cushman Motor Works, **III** 598
Custom Academic Publishing Company, **12** 174
Custom Chrome, Inc., 16 147–49
Custom Electronics, Inc., **9** 120
Custom Expressions, Inc., **7** 24; **22** 35
Custom Hoists, Inc., **17** 458
Custom Metal Products, Inc., **III** 643
Custom Organics, **8** 464
Custom Primers, **17** 288
Custom Products Inc., **III** 643
Custom Publishing Group, **27** 361
Custom Technologies Corp., **19** 152
Custom Thermoform, **24** 512
Custom Tool and Manufacturing Company, **41** 366
Custom Transportation Services, Inc., **26** 62
Custom Woodwork & Plastics Inc., **36** 159
Customized Transportation Inc., **22** 164, 167
AB Custos, **25** 464
Cutler-Hammer Inc., **I** 155; **III** 644–45
Cutter & Buck Inc., 27 112–14
Cutter Laboratories, **I** 310
Cutter Precision Metals, Inc., **25** 7
CVE Corporation, Inc., **24** 395
CVG Aviation, **34** 118
CVI Incorporated, **21** 108
CVL Inc., **II** 457
CVN Companies, **9** 218
CVS. *See* Consumer Value Stores.
CVS Corporation, **32** 166, 170; **34** 285
CWM. *See* Chemical Waste Management, Inc.
CWP. *See* Custom Woodwork & Plastics Inc.
CWT Farms International Inc., **13** 103
CXT Inc., **33** 257
Cyber Communications Inc., **16** 168
CyberCash Inc., **18** 541, 543
Cybermedia, Inc., 25 117–19, 349
Cybernet Electronics Corp., **II** 51; **21** 330
Cybernex, **10** 463
CyberSource Corp., **26** 441
CYBERTEK Corporation, **11** 395
CyberTel, **IV** 596–97
CyberTrust Solutions Inc., **42** 24–25
Cycle & Carriage Ltd., **20** 313
Cycle Video Inc., **7** 590
Cyclo Chemical Corp., **I** 627
Cyclo Getriebebau Lorenz Braren GmbH, **III** 634
Cyclone Co. of Australia, **III** 673
Cyclops Corporation, **10** 45; **13** 157
Cydsa. *See* Grupo Cydsa, S.A. de C.V.
Cygna Energy Services, **13** 367
Cygne Designs, Inc., 25 120–23; **37** 14
Cymbal Co., Ltd., **V** 150
Cynosure Inc., **11** 88
Cyphernetics Corp., **III** 118
Cypress Amax Minerals Co., **13** 158; **22** 285–86
Cypress Insurance Co., **III** 214
Cypress Semiconductor Corporation, **6** 216; **18** 17, 383; **20 174–76**; **43** 14
Cyprus Amax Coal Company, **35** 367
Cyprus Amax Minerals Company, 21 158–61
Cyprus Minerals Company, 7 107–09
Cyrix Corp., **10** 367; **26** 329
Cyrk Inc., 19 112–14; **21** 516; **33** 416
Cytec Industries Inc., 27 115–17
Czarnikow-Rionda Company, Inc., 32 128–30
D&D Enterprises, Inc., **24** 96
D&F Industries, Inc., **17** 227; **41** 204
D&K Wholesale Drug, Inc., 14 146–48
D&N Systems, Inc., **10** 505
D&O Inc., **17** 363
D & P Studios, **II** 157
D&W Computer Stores, **13** 176
D & W Food Stores, Inc., **8** 482; **27** 314
D.B. Kaplan's, **26** 263
D.B. Marron & Company, **II** 445; **22** 406
D.C. Heath & Co., **II** 86; **11** 413; **36** 273; **38** 374
D.C. National Bancorp, **10** 426
D. Connelly Boiler Company, **6** 145
D. de Ricci-G. Selnet et Associes, **28** 141
d.e.m.o., **28** 345
D.E. Makepeace Co., **IV** 78
D.E. Shaw & Co., **25** 17; **38** 269
D.E. Winebrenner Co., **7** 429
D.G. Calhoun, **12** 112
D.G. Yuengling & Son, Inc., 38 171–73
D. Hald & Co., **III** 417
D.I. Manufacturing Inc., **37** 351
D.K. Gold, **17** 138
D.L. Rogers Group, **37** 363
D.L. Saslow Co., **19** 290
D.M. Nacional, **23** 170
D.M. Osborne Co., **III** 650
D.R. Horton Inc., **25** 217; **26** 291
D.W. Mikesell Co. *See* Mike-Sell's Inc.
Da Gama Textiles Company, **24** 450
Dabney, Morgan & Co., **II** 329
Dade Reagents Inc., **19** 103
Dade Wholesale Products, **6** 199
DADG. *See* Deutsch-Australische Dampfschiffs-Gesellschaft.
Dae Won Kang Up Co., **III** 581
Daejin Shipping Company, **6** 98; **27** 271
Daesung Heavy Industries, **I** 516
Daewoo Group, **I** 516; **II** 53; **III 457–59**, 749; **12** 211; **18 123–27 (upd.)**; **30** 185
DAF, **I** 186; **III** 543; **7** 566–67
Daffy's Inc., 26 110–12
NV Dagblad De Telegraaf. *See* N.V. Holdingmaatschappij De Telegraaf.
Dage-Bell, **II** 86
Dagincourt. *See* Compagnie de Saint-Gobain S.A.
D'Agostino Supermarkets Inc., 19 115–17
Dagsbladunie, **IV** 611
DAH. *See* DeCrane Aircraft Holdings Inc.
Dahl Manufacturing, Inc., **17** 106
Dahlberg, Inc., **18** 207–08
Dahlgren, **I** 677
Dahlonega Equipment and Supply Company, **12** 377
Dai-Ichi. *See also listings under* Daiichi.
Dai-Ichi Bank, **I** 507, 511; **IV** 148
Dai-Ichi Kangyo Bank Ltd., II 273–75, 325–26, 360–61, 374; **III** 188
Dai-Ichi Mokko Co., **III** 758
Dai-Ichi Mutual Life Insurance Co., **II** 118; **III** 277, 401; **25** 289; **26** 511; **38** 18
Dai Nippon. *See also listings under* Dainippon.
Dai Nippon Brewery Co., **I** 220, 282; **21** 319
Dai Nippon Ink and Chemicals, **I** 303
Dai Nippon Mujin, **II** 371

Dai Nippon Printing Co., Ltd., IV 598–600, 631, 679–80
Dai Nippon X-ray Inc., **II** 75
Dai Nippon Yuben Kai, **IV** 631–32
Daido Boeki, **24** 325
Daido Spring Co., **III** 580
Daido Steel Co., Ltd., IV 62–63
Daido Trading, **I** 432, 492; **24** 324
The Daiei, Inc., V 11, **39–40**; **17 123–25 (upd.)**; **18** 186, 285; **19** 308; **36** 418–19; **41 113–16 (upd.)**
Daig Corporation, **43** 349–50
Daignault Rolland, **24** 404
Daihatsu Motor Company, Ltd., 7 110–12; **21 162–64 (upd.)**; **38** 415
Daiichi. *See also listings under* Dai-Ichi.
Daiichi Atomic Power Industry Group, **II** 22
Daiichi Bussan Kaisha Ltd., **I** 505, 507
Daiichi Fire, **III** 405
Daijugo Bank, **I** 507
Daiken Company. *See* Marubeni Corporation.
Daikin Industries, Ltd., III 460–61
Daikyo Oil Co., Ltd., **IV** 403–04, 476
Dailey & Associates, **I** 16
Daily Chronicle Investment Group, **IV** 685
Daily Mail and General Trust plc, 19 118–20; **39** 198–99
Daily Mirror, **IV** 665–66; **17** 397
Daily Press Inc., **IV** 684; **22** 522
The Daimaru, Inc., V 41–42, 130; **42 98–100 (upd.)**
Daimler Airway, **I** 92
Daimler-Benz Aerospace AG, 16 150–52; **24** 84
Daimler-Benz AG, I 27, 138, **149–51**, 186–87, 192, 194, 198, 411, 549; **II** 257, 279–80, 283; **III** 495, 523, 562, 563, 695, 750; **7** 219; **10** 261, 274; **11** 31; **12** 192, 342; **13** 30, 286, 414; **14** 169; **15 140–44 (upd.)**; **20** 312–13; **22** 11; **26** 481, 498
DaimlerChrysler AG, 34 128–37 (upd.), 306
Dain Bosworth Inc., **15** 231–33, 486
Dain Rauscher Corporation, 35 138–41 (upd.)
Daina Seikosha, **III** 620
Daini-Denden Incorporated, **12** 136–37
Daini-Denden Kikaku Company, Ltd., **II** 51. *See also* DDI Corporation.
Dainippon. *See also listings under* Dai-Nippon.
Dainippon Celluloid Company, **I** 509; **III** 486; **18** 183
Dainippon Ink & Chemicals, Inc., **IV** 397; **10** 466–67; **13** 308, 461; **17** 363; **28** 194
Dainippon Shurui, **III** 42
Dainippon Spinning Company, **V** 387
Daio Paper Corporation, IV 266–67, 269
Dairy Crest Group plc, 32 131–33
Dairy Farm Ice and Cold Storage Co., **IV** 700
Dairy Farm Management Services Ltd., **I** 471; **20** 312
Dairy Fresh, Inc., **26** 449
Dairy Maid Products Cooperative, **II** 536
Dairy Mart Convenience Stores, Inc., 7 113–15; **17** 501; **25 124–27 (upd.)**
Dairy Queen. *See* International Dairy Queen, Inc.
Dairy Queen National Development Company, **10** 372
Dairy Supply Co., **II** 586; **III** 418, 420
Dairyland Food Laboratories, **I** 677
Dairymen, Inc., **11** 24
Daishowa Paper Manufacturing Co., Ltd. II 361; **IV 268–70**, 326, 667; **17** 398
Daisy Manufacturing Company, Inc., **34** 72
Daisy Systems Corp., **11** 46, 284–85, 489
Daisy/Cadnetix Inc., **6** 248; **24** 235
Daisytek International Corporation, 18 128–30
Daiwa Bank, Ltd., II 276–77, 347, 438; **26** 457; **39 109–11 (upd.)**
Daiwa Securities Company, Limited, II 276, 300, **405–06**, 434; **9** 377
Daka, Inc. *See* Unique Casual Restaurants, Inc.
Dakin Inc., **24** 44; **33** 415
Dakota Power Company, **6** 580; **20** 73
Dakotah Mills, **8** 558–59; **16** 353
Daksoft, Inc., **20** 74
Daktronics, Inc., 32 134–37
Dal-Tile International Inc., 22 46, 49, **169–71**
Dalberg Co., **II** 61
Dale Carnegie Training, Inc., 28 85–87
Dale Electronics, **21** 519
Daleville & Middletown Telephone Company, **14** 258
Dalfort Corp., **15** 281
Dalgety PLC, II 499–500; **III** 21; **12** 411; **22** 147; **27** 258, 260. *See also* PIC International Group PLC
Dalian, **14** 556
Dalian Cement Factory, **III** 718
Dalian International Nordic Tire Co., **20** 263
D'Allaird's, **24** 315–16
Dallas Airmotive, **II** 16
Dallas Ceramic Co. *See* Dal-Tile International Inc.
Dallas Cowboys Football Club, Ltd., 33 122–25
Dallas-Fort Worth Suburban Newspapers, Inc., **10** 3
Dallas Lumber and Supply Co., **IV** 358
Dallas Power & Light Company, **V** 724
Dallas Semiconductor Corporation, 13 191–93; **31 143–46 (upd.)**
Dallas Southland Ice Co., **II** 660
Daltex General Agency, Inc., **25** 115
Damar, **IV** 610
Damark International, Inc., 18 131–34
Damart, **25** 523
Dameron-Pierson Co., **25** 500
Dames & Moore, Inc., 25 128–31
Dammann Asphalt, **III** 673
Damodar Valley Corp., **IV** 49
Damon, **21** 153
Damon Clinical Laboratories Inc., **26** 392
Damon Corporation, **11** 334
Dan River Inc., 35 142–46
Dan's Supreme, **24** 528
Dana Alexander Inc., **27** 197; **43** 218
Dana Corporation, I 152–53; **10 264–66 (upd.)**; **23** 170–71
Dana Design Ltd., **16** 297
Danaher Corporation, 7 116–17
Danair A/S, **I** 120
Danapak Holding Ltd., **11** 422
Danat-Bank, **I** 138
Danbury Mint, **34** 370
Danbury Phamacal Inc., **31** 254
Dancer Fitzgerald Sample, **I** 33; **23** 505
Daniel Industries, Inc., 16 153–55
Daniel International Corp., **I** 570–71; **8** 192
Daniel James Insurance Group, **41** 64
Daniel P. Creed Co., Inc., **8** 386
Daniel's Jewelers, **16** 559
Danieli & C. Officine Meccaniche, **13** 98
Daniels Linseed Co., **I** 419
Daniels Packaging, **12** 25
Daniels Pharmaceuticals, Inc., **24** 257
Danish Aalborg, **27** 91
Danish Almindelinge Brand-Assurance-Compagni, **III** 299
Danley Machine Corp., **I** 514
Danner Shoe Manufacturing Co., **18** 300
Dannon Co., Inc., II 468, 474–75; **14 149–51**
Danone Group, **25** 85; **35** 394, 397
Danray, **12** 135
Dansk Bioprotein, **IV** 406–07
Dansk International Designs Ltd., **10** 179, 181; **12** 313
Dansk Metal and Armaturindistri, **III** 569; **20** 361
Dansk Rejsebureau, **I** 120
Danskin, Inc., 12 93–95; **15** 358
Danville Resources, Inc., **13** 502
Danzas Group, V 441–43; **40 136–39 (upd.)**
DAP, Inc., **III** 66; **12** 7; **18** 549
DAP Products Inc., **36** 396
Dara Michelle, **17** 101–03
D'Arcy Masius Benton & Bowles, Inc., I 233–34; **6 20–22**; **10** 226–27; **26** 187; **28** 137; **32 138–43 (upd.)**
Darden Restaurants, Inc., 16 156–58; **36** 238
Darigold, Inc., 9 159–61
Darling and Hodgson, **IV** 91
Darling, Brown & Sharpe. *See* Brown & Sharpe Manufacturing Co.
Darmstadter, **II** 282
Darracq, **7** 6
Darrell J. Sekin Transport Co., **17** 218
Dart & Kraft Financial Corp., **II** 534; **III** 610–11; **7** 276; **12** 310; **14** 547
Dart Group Corporation, II 645, 656, 667, 674; **12** 49; **15** 270; **16 159–62**; **21** 148; **23** 370; **24** 418; **27** 158; **32** 168
Dart Industries, **II** 533–34; **III** 610; **9** 179–80. *See also* Premark International Inc.
Dart Transit Co., **13** 550
Dart Truck Co., **I** 185
Dartex, **18** 434
Darty S.A., 27 118–20
Darvel Realty Trust, **14** 126
Darya-Varia Laboratoria, **18** 182
DASA. *See* Daimler-Benz Aerospace AG *or* Deutsche Aerospace Airbus.
Dashwood Industries, **19** 446
Dassault Aviation SA, **21** 11
Dassault-Breguet. *See* Avions Marcel Dassault-Breguet Aviation.
Dassault Systèmes S.A., 25 132–34; **26** 179. *See also* Groupe Dassault Aviation SA.
Dassler, **14** 6
Dastek Inc., **10** 464; **11** 234–35
DAT GmbH, **10** 514
Dat Jidosha Seizo Co., **I** 183
Data Acquisition Systems, Inc., **16** 300
Data Architects, **14** 318
Data Base Management Inc., **11** 19

Data-Beam Corp., **25** 301
Data Broadcasting Corporation, 31 147–50
Data Business Forms, **IV** 640
Data Card Corp., **IV** 680
Data Corp., **IV** 311; **19** 267
Data Documents, **III** 157
Data Force Inc., **11** 65
Data General Corporation, II 208; **III** 124, 133; **6** 221, 234; **8 137–40**; **9** 297; **10** 499; **12** 162; **13** 201; **16** 418; **20** 8
Data One Corporation, **11** 111
Data Preparation, Inc., **11** 112
Data Printer, Inc., **18** 435
Data Resources, Inc., **IV** 637
Data Specialties Inc. *See* Zebra Technologies Corporation.
Data Structures Inc., **11** 65
Data Systems Technology, **11** 57; **38** 375
Data Technology Corp., **18** 510
Data 3 Systems, **9** 36
Datac plc, **18** 140
Datachecker Systems, **II** 64–65; **III** 164; **11** 150
Datacraft Corp., **II** 38
DataFocus, Inc., **18** 112
Datamatic Corp., **II** 41, 86; **12** 247
Datapoint Corporation, 11 67–70
Datapro Research Corp., **IV** 637
Dataquest Inc., **10** 558; **21** 235, 237; **22** 51; **25** 347
Datas Incorporated, **I** 99; **6** 81
Datascope Corporation, 39 112–14
Dataset Communications Inc., **23** 100
Datastream International Ltd., **IV** 605; **10** 89; **13** 417
DataTimes Corporation, **29** 58
Datavision Inc., **11** 444
Datec, **22** 17
Datek Online Holdings Corp., 32 144–46
Datext, **IV** 596–97
Datran, **11** 468
Datsun. *See* Nissan Motor Company, Ltd.
Datteln, **IV** 141
Datura Corp., **14** 391
Dauphin Deposit Corporation, 14 152–54
Dauphin Distribution Services. *See* Exel Logistics Ltd.
Daut + Rietz and Connectors Pontarlier, **19** 166
Dave & Buster's, Inc., 33 126–29
Davenport & Walter, **III** 765
Davenport Mammoet Heavy Transport Inc., **26** 280
The Davey Tree Expert Company, 11 71–73
The David and Lucile Packard Foundation, 41 117–19
David B. Smith & Company, **13** 243
David Berg & Co., **14** 537
David Brown & Son. *See* Brown & Sharpe Manufacturing Co.
David Brown, Ltd., **10** 380
David Clark, **30** 357
David Crystal, Inc., **II** 502; **9** 156; **10** 323
David Hafler Company, **43** 323
The David J. Joseph Company, 14 155–56; **19** 380
David Sandeman Group, **I** 592
David Sassoon & Co., **II** 296
David Williams and Partners, **6** 40
David's Bridal, Inc., 33 130–32
David's Supermarkets, **17** 180
Davidson & Associates, **16** 146
Davidson & Leigh, **21** 94
Davidson Automatic Merchandising Co. Inc., **II** 607
Davidson Brothers Co., **19** 510
Davies, William Ltd., **II** 482
Davis & Geck, **I** 301; **27** 115
Davis & Henderson Ltd., **IV** 640
Davis Coal & Coke Co., **IV** 180
Davis Estates, **I** 592
Davis Manufacturing Company, **10** 380
Davis Polk & Wardwell, 36 151–54
Davis-Standard Company, **9** 154; **36** 144
Davis Vision, Inc., **27** 209
Davis Wholesale Company, **9** 20
Davison Chemical Corp., **IV** 190
Davlyn Industries, Inc., **22** 487
Davox Corporation, **18** 31
Davy Bamag GmbH, **IV** 142
Davy McKee AG, **IV** 142
DAW Technologies, Inc., 25 135–37
Dawe's Laboratories, Inc., **12** 3
Dawn Food Products, Inc., 17 126–28
Dawnay Day, **III** 501
Dawson Holdings PLC, 43 132–34
Dawson Mills, **II** 536
Day & Zimmermann Inc., 6 579; **9 162–64**; **31 151–155 (upd.)**
Day Brite Lighting, **II** 19
Day-Glo Color Corp., **8** 456
Day International, **8** 347
Day-Lee Meats, **II** 550
Day-N-Nite, **II** 620
Day Runner, Inc., 14 157–58; **41 120–23 (upd.)**
Daybridge Learning Centers, **13** 49, 299
Dayco Products, **7** 297
Days Inns of America, Inc., **III** 344; **11** 178; **13** 362, 364; **21** 362
Daystar International Inc., **11** 44
Daystrom, **III** 617; **17** 418
Daytex, Inc., **II** 669; **18** 505
Dayton Engineering Laboratories, **I** 171; **9** 416; **10** 325
Dayton Flexible Products Co., **I** 627
Dayton Hudson Corporation, V 43–44; **8** 35; **9** 360; **10** 136, 391–93, 409–10, 515–16; **13** 330; **14** 376; **16** 176, 559; **18** 108, **135–37 (upd.)**; **22** 59
Dayton Power & Light Company, **6** 467, 480–82
Dayton Walther Corp., **III** 650, 652
Daytron Mortgage Systems, **11** 485
Dazey Corp., **16** 384; **43** 289
DB. *See* Deutsche Bundesbahn.
DB Reise & Touristik AG, **37** 250
DBA Holdings, Inc., **18** 24
DBMS Inc., **14** 390
DC Comics Inc., 25 138–41
DCA Advertising, **16** 168
DCA Food Industries, **II** 554; **27** 258–60, 299
DCL BioMedical, Inc., **11** 333
DCMS Holdings Inc., **7** 114; **25** 125
DDB Needham Worldwide, 14 159–61; **22** 394
DDI Corporation, 7 118–20; **13** 482; **21** 330–31
De Beers Consolidated Mines Limited / De Beers Centenary AG, I 107; **IV** 20–21, 23, 60, **64–68**, 79, 94; **7 121–26 (upd.)**; **16** 25–26, 29; **21** 345–46; **28 88–94 (upd.)**
De Bono Industries, **24** 443
De Dietrich & Cie., 31 156–59
De Grenswisselkantoren NV, **III** 201
De Groote Bossche, **III** 200
de Havilland Aircraft Co., **I** 82, 92–93, 104, 195; **III** 507–08; **7** 11. *See also* Bombardier Inc.
de Havilland Holdings, Ltd., **24** 85–86
De La Rue plc, 10 267–69; **34 138–43 (upd.)**
De Laurentiis Entertainment Group, **III** 84; **25** 317
De Laval Turbine Company, **III** 418–20; **7** 236–37
De Leuw, Cather & Company, **8** 416
De Nederlandse Bank, **IV** 132
De-sta-Co., **III** 468
De Ster 1905 NV, **III** 200
De Tomaso Industries, **11** 104
De Trey Gesellchaft, **10** 271
De Vito/Verdi, **26** 111
De Walt, **III** 436
de Wendel, **IV** 226–27
DEA Group, **23** 83
Dealer Equipment and Services, **10** 492
Dean & Barry Co., **8** 455
Dean & DeLuca, Inc., 36 155–57
Dean-Dempsy Corp., **IV** 334
Dean Foods Company, 7 127–29; **17** 56; **21** 157, **165–68 (upd.)**; **26** 447; **29** 434
Dean Witter, Discover & Co., II 445; **IV** 186; **V** 180, 182; **7** 213; **12 96–98**; **18** 475; **21** 97; **22** 405–07. *See also* Morgan Stanley Dean Witter & Company.
Dearborn Publishing Group, **42** 211
Death Row Records, 27 121–23
Deb Shops, Inc., 16 163–65
DeBartolo Realty Corp., **27** 401
Debenhams Plc, V 20–22; **28** 29–30, **95–97**; **39** 88
Debevoise & Plimpton, 39 115–17
Debis, **26** 498
DeBoles Nutritional Foods Inc., **27** 197–98; **43** 218–19
Debron Investments Plc., **8** 271
DEC. *See* Digital Equipment Corp.
Decafin SpA, **26** 278, 280
Decathlon S.A., **39** 183–84
Decca Record Company Ltd., **II** 81, 83, 144; **23** 389
Dechert, 43 135–38
Decision Base Resources, **6** 14
Decision Systems Israel Ltd. (DSI), **21** 239
DecisionQuest, Inc., **25** 130
Decker, Howell & Co., **26** 451
Deckers Outdoor Corporation, 22 172–74
Deco Industries, Inc., **18** 5
Deco Purchasing Company, **39** 211
Decoflex Ltd., **IV** 645
Decolletage S.A. St.-Maurice, **14** 27
Decora Industries, Inc., 31 160–62
DeCrane Aircraft Holdings Inc., 36 158–60
Dee and Cee Toy Co., **25** 312
Dee Corporation plc, **I** 549; **II** 628–29, 642; **24** 269
Deeks McBride, **III** 704
Deep Oil Technology, **I** 570
Deep Rock Oil Company. *See* Kerr-McGee Corporation.
Deep Rock Water Co., **III** 21
DeepFlex Production Partners, L.P., **21** 171
Deepsea Ventures, Inc., **IV** 152; **24** 358

DeepTech International Inc., 21 169–71
Deepwater Light and Power Company, **6** 449
Deer Park Spring Water Co., **III** 21
Deere & Company, **I** 181, 527; **III 462–64**, 651; **10** 377–78, 380, 429; **11** 472; **13** 16–17, 267; **16** 179; **17** 533; **21 172–76 (upd.)**; **22** 542; **26** 492; **42 101–06 (upd.)**
Deering Harvesting Machinery Company. *See* Navistar.
Deering Milliken & Co. *See* Milliken & Co.
Def Jam Records, Inc., **23** 389, 391; **31** 269; **33** 373–75
Defense Plant Corp., **IV** 10, 408
Defense Technology Corporation of America, **27** 50
Defiance, Inc., 22 175–78
Deflecta-Shield Corporation, **40** 299–300
Deft Software, Inc., **10** 505
DEG. *See* Deutsche Edison Gesellschaft.
Degussa Group, **I** 303; **IV 69–72**, 118
Degussa-Hüls AG, **32 147–53 (upd.)**; **34** 209
Deinhard, **I** 281
DeKalb AgResearch Inc., **9** 411; **41** 304–06
Dekalb Energy Company, **18** 366
DeKalb Farmers Market, **23** 263–64
DeKalb Genetics Corporation, **17 129–31**; **29** 330
DeKalb Office Supply, **25** 500
Del Laboratories, Inc., **28 98–100**
Del Mar Avionics, **26** 491
Del Monte Corporation, **II** 595; **7 130–32**; **12** 439; **14** 287; **25** 234
Del Monte Foods Company, **23 163–66 (upd.)**; **36** 472; **38** 198
Del-Rey Petroleum, **I** 526
Del Webb Corporation, **14 162–64**; **17** 186–87; **19** 377–78; **26** 291
Delafield, Harvey, Tabrell, Inc., **17** 498
Delafield Industries, **12** 418
Delagrange, **I** 635
Delaware and Hudson Railway Company, **16** 350
Delaware Charter Guarantee & Trust Co., **III** 330
Delaware Guarantee and Trust Co. *See* Wilmington Trust Company.
Delaware Lackawanna & Western, **I** 584
Delaware Management Holdings, **III** 386
Delaware North Companies Incorporated, **7 133–36**
Delbard, **I** 272
Delchamps, Inc., **II** 638; **27** 247
Delco Electronics, **II** 32–35; **III** 151; **6** 265; **25** 223–24
Delhaize Freres & Cie, **II** 626; **15** 176
Delhaize Frères-Le-Lion, **27** 94
Delhi Gas Pipeline Corporation, **7** 551
Delhi International Oil Corp., **III** 687; **28** 83
Deli Universal, **13** 545
dELiA*s Inc., **29 141–44**
Delicious Foods, **13** 383
Delimaatschappij, **13** 545
Dell Computer Corporation, **9 165–66**; **10** 309, 459; **11** 62; **16** 5, 196; **24** 31; **25** 254; **27** 168; **31 163–166 (upd.)**
Dell Distributing, **25** 483
Dell Publishing Co., **13** 560
Dellwood Elevator Co., **I** 419
Delmar Chemicals Ltd., **II** 484
Delmar Paper Box Co., **IV** 333
Delmarva Properties, Inc., **8** 103; **30** 118
Delmonico Foods Inc., **II** 511
Delmonico International, **II** 101
Deloitte & Touche, **9 167–69**, 423; **24** 29
Deloitte Touche Tohmatsu International, **29 145–48 (upd.)**
DeLong Engineering Co., **III** 558
DeLorean Motor Co., **10** 117; **14** 321
Delphax, **IV** 252; **17** 29
Delphi, **22** 52; **25** 223
Delphi Automotive Systems, **36** 243; **37** 429
Delprat, **IV** 58
Delta and Pine Land Company, **21** 386; **33 133–37**
Delta Acceptance Corporation Limited, **13** 63
Delta Air Lines, Inc., **I** 29, 91, 97, **99–100**, 102, 106, 120, 132; **6** 61, **81–83 (upd.)**, 117, 131–32, 383; **12** 149, 381; **13** 171–72; **14** 73; **21** 141, 143; **22** 22; **25** 420, 422–23; **26** 439; **27** 20, 409; **33** 50–51, 377; **34** 116–17, 119; **39 118–21 (upd.)**
Delta Biologicals S.r.l., **11** 208
Delta Biotechnology Ltd., **25** 82
Delta Campground Management Corp., **33** 399
Delta Communications, **IV** 610
Delta Education, **29** 470, 472
Delta Faucet Co., **III** 568–69; **39** 263
Delta International Machinery Corp., **26** 361–63
Delta Lloyd, **III** 235
Delta Manufacturing, **II** 85
Delta Motors, **III** 580
Delta Pride Catfish Inc., **18** 247
Delta Queen Steamboat Company, **27** 34–35
Delta Resources Inc., **26** 519
Delta Savings Assoc. of Texas, **IV** 343
Delta Steamship Lines, **9** 425–26
Delta V Technologies, Inc., **33** 348
Delta Woodside Industries, Inc., **8 141–43**; **17** 329; **30 159–61 (upd.)**; **42** 118
Deltak Corp., **23** 300
Deltic Timber Corporation, **32** 339, 341
Deluxe Corporation, **7 137–39**; **19** 291; **22 179–82 (upd.)**; **37** 107–08
Deluxe Data, **18** 518
DeLuxe Laboratories, **IV** 652
Deluxe Upholstering Ltd., **14** 303
Delvag Luftürsicherungs A.G., **I** 111
Demag AG, **II** 22; **III** 566; **IV** 206
Demerara Company, **13** 102
Deminex, **IV** 413, 424
Deming Company, **8** 135
Demka, **IV** 132–33
Demko, **30** 469
DeMoulas / Market Basket Inc., **23 167–69**
Dempsey & Siders Agency, **III** 190
Den Fujita, **9** 74
Den Norske Bank, **22** 275
Den norske Creditbank, **II** 366
Den Norske Stats Oljeselskap AS, **IV 405–07**, 486
Den-Tal-Ez, **I** 702
Denain-Nord-Est-Longwy, **IV** 227
DenAmerica Corporation, **29 149–51**
Denault Ltd., **II** 651
Denison Corp., **III** 628
Denison Mines, Ltd., **12** 198
Denker & Goodwin, **17** 498
Denki Seikosho, **IV** 62
Denney-Reyburn, **8** 360
Dennison Manufacturing Company. *See* Avery Dennison Corporation.
Denny's Restaurants Inc., **II** 680; **III** 103; **V** 88–89; **12** 511; **13** 526; **27** 16–18
Denshi Media Services, **IV** 680
Dent & Co., **II** 296
Dental Capital Corp., **19** 290
Dental Research, **25** 56
DentiCare, Inc., **22** 149
Dentons Green Brewery, **21** 246
Dentsply International Inc., **10 270–72**
Dentsu Inc., **I 9–11**, 36, 38; **6** 29; **9** 30; **13** 204; **16 166–69 (upd.)**; **25** 91; **40 140–44 (upd.)**
Denver & Rio Grande Railroad, **12** 18–19
Denver Chemical Company, **8** 84; **38** 124
Denver Gas & Electric Company. *See* Public Service Company of Colorado.
DEP Corporation, **20 177–80**; **34** 209
Department 56, Inc., **14 165–67**; **22** 59; **34 144–47 (upd.)**
Department Stores International, **I** 426; **22** 72
Deposit Guaranty Corporation, **17 132–35**
Deposito and Administratie Bank, **II** 185
Depositors National Bank of Durham, **II** 336
DePree Company, **17** 90–91
DePuy, Inc., **10** 156–57; **30 162–65**; **36** 306; **37 110–13 (upd.)**
Der Anker, **III** 177
Derby Commercial Bank, **II** 318; **17** 323
Derby Outdoor, **27** 280
Derbyshire Stone and William Briggs, **III** 752
Deritend Computers, **14** 36
Dermablend, Inc., **31** 89
Deruluft, **6** 57
Derwent Publications, **8** 526
Des Moines Electric Light Company, **6** 504
DESA Industries, **8** 545
Desc, S.A. de C.V., **23 170–72**
Deseret Management Corporation, **29** 67
Deseret National Bank, **11** 118
Deseret Pharmaceutical Company, **21** 45
Desert Partners, **III** 763
Design-Center Southwest, **19** 411
Design Craft Ltd., **IV** 640
Design Trend, Inc., **37** 394
Designcraft Inc. *See* Sloan's Supermarkets Inc.
Designer Holdings Ltd., **20 181–84**; **22** 123
Desmarais Frères, **IV** 557, 559
DeSoto, Inc., **8** 553; **13** 471
Desoutter Brothers plc, **III** 427; **28** 40
Destec Energy, Inc., **12 99–101**
Det Danske/Norske Luftartselskab, **I** 119
Detroit Aircraft Corp., **I** 64; **11** 266
Detroit Automobile Co., **I** 164
Detroit Ball Bearing Co., **13** 78
Detroit Chemical Coatings, **8** 553
Detroit City Gas Company. *See* MCN Corporation.
Detroit Copper Co., **IV** 176–77
Detroit Diesel Corporation, **V** 494–95; **9** 18; **10 273–75**; **11** 471; **12** 90–91; **18** 308; **19** 292–94; **21** 503

The Detroit Edison Company, I 164; V **592–95**; 7 377–78; 11 136; 14 135; 18 320. *See also* DTE Energy Co.
Detroit Fire & Marine Insurance Co., III 191
Detroit Gear and Machine Co., III 439
Detroit-Graphite Company, 8 553
The Detroit Pistons Basketball Company, **41 124–27**
Detroit Radiator Co., III 663
Detroit Red Wings, 7 278–79; 24 293; 37 207
Detroit Steel Products Co., Inc., IV 136; 13 157; 16 357
Detroit Stoker Company, 37 399–401
Detroit Tigers, 24 293; 37 207
Detroit Toledo & Ironton Railroad, I 165
Detroit Vapor Stove Co., III 439
Detrola, II 60
Dettmers Industries Inc., 36 159–60
Deutsch-Australische Dampfschiffs-Gesellschaft, 6 398
Deutsch Erdol A.G., IV 552
Deutsch, Inc., **42 107–10**
Deutsch-Luxembergische Bergwerks und Hütten AG, I 542; IV 105
Deutsch-Österreichische Mannesmannröhren-Werke Aktiengesellschaft, III 564–65
Deutsch Shea & Evans Inc., I 15
Deutsch-Skandinavische Bank, II 352
Deutsche Aerospace Airbus, I 41–42; 7 9, 11; 12 190–91; 21 8
Deutsche Allgemeine Versicherungs-Aktiengesellschaft, III 412
Deutsche Anlagen Leasing GmbH, II 386
Deutsche-Asiatische Bank, II 238, 256
Deutsche BA, 14 73; 24 400; 26 115
Deutsche Babcock AG, II 386; III **465–66**
Deutsche Bahn AG, 37 250, 253
Deutsche Bank AG, I 151, 409, 549; II 98, 191, 239, 241–42, 256–58, **278–80**, 281–82, 295, 319, 385, 427, 429; III 154–55, 692, 695; IV 91, 141, 229, 232, 378, 557; V 241–42; **14 168–71 (upd.)**; 15 13; 16 364–65; 17 324; 21 147, 34 29; **40 145–51 (upd.)**
Deutsche Börse, 37 131–32
Deutsche BP Aktiengesellschaft, 7 **140–43**
Deutsche Bundepost Telekom, V **287–90**; 18 155
Deutsche Bundesbahn, V **444–47**; 6 424–26
Deutsche Edelstahlwerke AG, IV 222
Deutsche Edison Gesellschaft, I 409–10
Deutsche Erdol Aktiengesellschaft, 7 140
Deutsche Gold-und Silber-Scheideanstalt vormals Roessler, IV 69, 118, 139
Deutsche Grammophon Gesellschaft, 23 389
Deutsche Hydrierwerke, III 32
Deutsche Industriewerke AG, IV 230
Deutsche Kreditbank, 14 170
Deutsche Länderbank, II 379
Deutsche Lufthansa Aktiengesellschaft, I 94, **110–11**, 120; 6 59–60, 69, 95–96, 386; 12 191; 25 159; **26 113–16 (upd.)**; 27 465; 33 49; 36 426
Deutsche Marathon Petroleum, IV 487
Deutsche Mineralöl-Explorationsgesellschaft mbH, IV 197
Deutsche-Nalco-Chemie GmbH., I 373
Deutsche Nippon Seiko, III 589
Deutsche Petroleum-Verkaufsgesellschaft mbH, 7 140
Deutsche Post AG, **29 152–58**; 40 138
Deutsche Reichsbahn. *See* Deutsche Bundesbahn.
Deutsche Schiff-und Maschinenbau Aktiengesellschaft ''Deschimag,'' IV 87
Deutsche Shell, 7 140
Deutsche Spezialglas AG, III 446
Deutsche Strassen und Lokalbahn A.G., I 410
Deutsche Telekom, 18 155; 25 102; 38 296
Deutsche Texaco, V 709
Deutsche Union, III 693–94
Deutsche Union-Bank, II 278
Deutsche Wagnisfinanzierung, II 258
Deutsche Werke AG, IV 230
Deutscher Aero Lloyd, I 110
Deutscher Automobil Schutz Allgemeine Rechtsschutz-Versicherung AG, III 400
Deutscher Kommunal-Verlag Dr. Naujoks & Behrendt, 14 556
Deutscher Ring, 40 61
Deutsches Reisebüro DeR, II 163
Deutz AG, III 541; **39 122–26**
Deutz-Allis, III 544. *See also* AGCO Corp.
Deutz Farm Equipment, 13 17
Devcon Corporation, III 519; 22 282
Deveaux S.A., **41 128–30**
Developer's Mortgage Corp., 16 347
Development Finance Corp., II 189
Devenish, 21 247
DeVilbiss Company, 8 230
DeVilbiss Health Care, Inc., 11 488
Deville, 27 421
Devoe & Raynolds Co., 12 217
Devoke Company, 18 362
Devon Energy Corporation, 22 304
DeVry Incorporated, 9 63; 29 56, **159–61**
Dewars Brothers, I 239–40
Dewey & Almy Chemical Co., I 548
Dexer Corporation, 41 10
Dexia Group, **42 111–13**
The Dexter Corporation, I **320–22**; 12 **102–04 (upd.)**; 17 287
Dexter Shoe, 18 60, 63
DFS Dorland Worldwide, I 35
DFS Group Ltd., 33 276
DFW Printing Company, 10 3
DG Bank, 33 358
DG&E. *See* Denver Gas & Electric Company.
DH Compounding, 8 347
DH Technology, Inc., **18 138–40**
Dharma Juice, 31 350
DHI Corp., II 680
DHJ Industries, Inc., 12 118
DHL Worldwide Express, 6 **385–87**; 18 177, 316; **24 133–36 (upd.)**; 26 441; 27 471, 475; 29 152
Di Giorgio Corp., II 602; **12 105–07**; 24 528–29
Di-Rite Company, 11 534
Dia Prosim, S.A., IV 409
Diageo plc, **24 137–41 (upd.)**; 25 411; 29 19; 31 92; 34 89; 36 404; 42 223
Diagnostic Health Corporation, 14 233
Diagnostic Imaging Services, Inc., 25 384
Diagnostics Pasteur, I 677
Dial-A-Mattress Inc., 32 427
The Dial Corporation, **8 144–46**; **23 173–75 (upd.)**; 29 114; 32 230; 34 209
Dial Home Shopping Ltd., 28 30
Dial-Net Inc., 27 306
Dialight Corp., 13 397–98
Dialog Information Services, Inc., IV 630
Dialogic Corporation, **18 141–43**
Diamandis Communications Inc., IV 619, 678
Diamang, IV 65, 67
Diamedix, 11 207
Diamond Animal Health, Inc., 39 216
Diamond Communications, 10 288
Diamond Corporation Ltd., IV 21, 66–67; 7 123
Diamond Crystal Brands, Inc., 32 274, 277
Diamond Electronics, 24 510
Diamond Fields Resources Inc., 27 457
Diamond Head Resources, Inc. *See* AAON, Inc.
Diamond International Corp., IV 290, 295; 13 254–55; 19 225; 26 446
Diamond M Offshore Inc., 12 318
Diamond Match Company, 14 163
Diamond Offshore Drilling, Inc., 36 325; 43 202
Diamond Oil Co., IV 548
Diamond Park Fine Jewelers, 16 559
Diamond Rug & Carpet Mills, 19 276
Diamond Savings & Loan, II 420
Diamond Shamrock Corporation, IV **408–11**, 481; 7 34, 308–099, 345; 13 118; 19 177. *See also* Ultramar Diamond Shamrock Corporation.
Diamond-Star Motors Corporation, 9 349–51
Diamond Trading Company, IV 66–67; 7 123
Diamond Walnut Growers, 7 496–97
Dianatel, 18 143
Diasonics Ultrasound, Inc., 27 355
Dibrell Brothers, Incorporated, 12 **108–10**; 13 492
dick clark productions, inc., **16 170–73**
Dick Simon Trucking, Inc. *See* Simon Transporation Services Inc.
Dickerman, 8 366
Dickson Forest Products, Inc., 15 305
Dickstein Partners, L.P., 13 261
Dictaphone Corp., III 157
Didier Lamarthe, 17 210
Didier Werke AG, IV 232
Diebold, Incorporated, 7 **144–46**; 22 **183–87 (upd.)**
Diedrich Coffee, Inc., **40 152–54**
Diehl Manufacturing Co., II 9
Diemakers Inc., IV 443
Diesel Nacional, S.A. *See* Consorcio G Grupo Dina, S.A. de C.V.
Diesel SpA, **40 155–57**
Diesel United Co., III 533
AB Diesels Motorer, III 425–26
Diet Center, 10 383
Dieter Hein Co., 14 537
Dieterich Standard Corp., III 468
Dietrich & Cie. *See* De Dietrich & Cie.
Dietrich Corp., II 512; 15 221
Dietrich's Bakeries, II 631
DiFeo Automotive Group, 26 500–01
DiFranza Williamson, 6 40
DIG Acquisition Corp., 12 107
Digi International Inc., 9 **170–72**; 20 237
Digicom, 22 17
Digidesign Inc., 38 70, 72
DiGiorgio Corporation, 25 421
Digital Audio Disk Corp., II 103
Digital City, Inc., 22 522

Digital Data Systems Company, **11** 408
Digital Devices, Inc., **III** 643
Digital Directory Assistance, **18** 24
Digital Entertainment Network, **42** 272
Digital Equipment Corporation, **II** 8, 62, 108; **III** 118, 128, **132–35**, 142, 149, 166; **6** 225, **233–36 (upd.)**, 237–38, 242, 246–47, 279, 287; **8** 137–39, 519; **9** 35, 43, 57, 166, 170–71, 514; **10** 22–23, 34, 86, 242, 361, 463, 477; **11** 46, 86–88, 274, 491, 518–19; **12** 147, 162, 470; **13** 127, 202, 482; **14** 318; **15** 108; **16** 394, 418; **18** 143, 345; **19** 310; **21** 123; **25** 499; **26** 90, 93; **34** 441–43; **36** 81, 287; **43** 13
Digital Marketing, Inc., **22** 357
Digital Research in Electronic Acoustics and Music S.A., **17** 34
Digitech, **19** 414
Dii Group Inc., **38** 188–89
Diligent Engine Co., **III** 342
Dill & Collins, **IV** 311; **19** 266
Dill Enterprises, Inc., **14** 18
Dillard Department Stores, Inc., **V 45–47**; **10** 488; **11** 349; **12** 64; **13** 544–45; **16 174–77 (upd.)**, 559; **19** 48, 324; **27** 61
Dillard Paper Company, **11 74–76**
Dillingham Corp., **I 565–66**
Dillingham Holdings Inc., **9** 511
Dillon Companies Inc., **II** 645; **12 111–13**; **15** 267; **22** 194
Dillon Paper, **IV** 288
Dillon, Read, and Co., Inc., **I** 144, 559; **III** 151, 389; **6** 265; **11** 53; **20** 259; **24** 66
Dime Banking and Loan Association of Rochester, **10** 91
Dime Savings Bank of New York, F.S.B., **9 173–74**
Dimeling, Schrieber & Park, **11** 63
Dimensions in Sport, Ltd., **37** 5
Dimeric Development Corporation, **14** 392
DIMON Inc., **12** 110; **27 124–27**
Dina. *See* Consorcio G Grupo Dina, S.A. de C.V.
Dinamica, S.A., **19** 12
Dine S.A., **23** 170–72
Diners Club, **II** 397; **6** 62; **9** 335; **10** 61
Dinner Bell Foods, Inc., **11** 93
de Dion, **III** 523
Dirección General de Correos y Telecomunicaciónes, **V** 337
Dirección Nacional de los Yacimientos Petrolíferos Fiscales, **IV** 577–78
Direct Container Lines, **14** 505
Direct Friends, **25** 91
Direct Line, **12** 422
Direct Mail Services Pty. Ltd., **10** 461
Direct Marketing Technology Inc., **19** 184
Direct Spanish Telegraph Co., **I** 428
Direct Transit, Inc., **42** 364
Direction Générale des Télécommunications, **V** 471
DirectLine Insurance, **22** 52
Directorate General of Telecommunications, **7 147–49**
DIRECTV, Inc., **21** 70; **35** 156, 158–59; **38 174–77**
Dirr's Gold Seal Meats, **6** 199
Disc Go Round, **18** 207, 209
Disc Manufacturing, Inc., **15** 378
Disclosure, Inc., **18** 24
Disco SA, **V** 11; **19** 308–09
Disconto-Gesellschaft, **II** 238, 279
Discount Auto Parts, Inc., **18 144–46**; **26** 348
Discount Bank, **II** 205
Discount Corporation, **12** 565
Discount Drug Mart, Inc., **14 172–73**
Discount Investment Corporation Ltd., **24** 429
Discount Labels, Inc., **20** 15
Discount Tire Co., **19** 294; **20** 263
Discover, **9** 335; **12** 97
Discovery Communications, Inc., **42 114–17**
Discovery Toys, Inc., **19** 28
Discovery Zone, **31** 97
DiscoVision Associates, **III** 605
Discreet Logic Inc., **20 185–87**
Disctronics, Ltd., **15** 380
Disney Channel, **6** 174–75; **13** 280
Disney Co. *See* The Walt Disney Company.
Disney Studios, **II** 408; **6** 174, 176; **43** 229–30, 233
Disneyland, **6** 175
Disneyland Paris. *See* Euro Disneyland SCA.
Dispatch Communications, **10** 432
Display Components Inc., **II** 110; **17** 479
Displayco Midwest Inc., **8** 103
Disposable Hospital Products, **I** 627
Distillers and Cattle Feeders Trust, **I** 376
Distillers Co. plc, **I 239–41**, 252, 263, 284–85; **II** 429, 609–10; **IV** 70; **43** 214
Distillers Securities, **I** 376
Distinctive Printing and Packaging Co., **8** 103
Distinctive Software Inc., **10** 285
Distribuidora Bega, S.A. de C.V., **31** 92
Distribution Centers Incorporated. *See* Exel Logistics Ltd.
Distribution Services, Inc., **10** 287
Distribution Solutions International, Inc., **24** 126
District Bank, **II** 333
District Cablevision, **II** 160
District News Co., **II** 607
Distrigas, **IV** 425
DITAS, **IV** 563
Ditzler Color Co., **III** 732
DIVAL, **III** 347
Divani & Divani. *See* Industrie Natuzzi S.p.A.
Divco-Wayne Corp., **17** 82
DIVE!, **26** 264
Diversey Corp., **I** 275, 333; **13** 150, 199; **26** 305–06; **32** 476
Diversified Agency Services, **I** 32
Diversified Foods Inc., **25** 179
Diversified Retailing Co., **III** 214
Diversified Services, **9** 95
Diversifoods Inc., **II** 556; **13** 408
Diversity Consultants Inc., **32** 459
DiviCom, **43** 221–22
Dixie Airline, **25** 420
Dixie Bearings, Inc., **13** 78
Dixie Carriers, Inc., **18** 277
Dixie Container Corporation, **12** 377
Dixie Crystals Brands, Inc., **32** 277
The Dixie Group, Inc., **20 188–90**
Dixie Hi-Fi, **9** 120–21
Dixie Home Stores, **II** 683
Dixie-Narco Inc., **III** 573; **22** 349
Dixie Paper, **I** 612–14
Dixie Power & Light Company, **6** 514
Dixie Yarns, Inc., **9** 466; **19** 305
Dixieland Food Stores, **II** 624
Dixon Industries, Inc., **26 117–19**
Dixon Ticonderoga Company, **12 114–16**
Dixons Group plc, **II** 139; **V 48–50**; **9** 65; **10** 45, 306; **19 121–24 (upd.)**; **23** 52; **24** 194, 269–70
DIY Home Warehouse, **16** 210
DJ Moldings Corp., **18** 276
Djedi Holding SA, **23** 242
DKB. *See* Dai-Ichi Kangyo Bank Ltd.
DLC. *See* Duquesne Light Company.
DLJ. *See* Donaldson, Lufkin & Jenrette.
DLJ Merchant Banking Partners II, **21** 188; **36** 158–59
DM Associates Limited Partnership, **25** 127
DMA, **18** 510
DMB&B. *See* D'Arcy Masius Benton & Bowles.
DMGT. *See* Daily Mail and General Trust.
DMP Mineralöl Petrochemie GmbH, **IV** 487
DNATA, **39** 137, 139
DNAX Research Institute, **I** 685; **14** 424
DNEL-Usinor, **IV** 227
DNN Galvanizing Limited Partnership, **24** 144
DNP DENMARK A/S, **IV** 600
Do It All, **24** 75
Do it Best Corporation, **30 166–70**
Dobbs House, **21** 54
Dobbs Houses Inc., **I** 696–97; **15** 87
Dobrolet, **6** 57
Dobson Park Industries, **38** 227
Docks de France, **37** 23; **39** 183–84
Doctors' Hospital, **6** 191
Documentation Resources, **11** 65
DOD Electronics Corp., **15** 215
Dodd, Mead & Co., **14** 498
Dodge & Day. *See* Day & Zimmermann, Inc.
Dodge Corp., **I** 144; **8** 74; **11** 53
The Dodge Group, **11** 78
Dodge Manufacturing Company, **9** 440
Dodge Motor Company, **20** 259
Doduco Corporation, **29** 460–61
Dodwell & Co., **III** 523
Doe Run Company, **12** 244
Doeflex PLC, **33** 79
Dofasco Inc., **IV 73–74**; **24 142–44 (upd.)**
Doherty Clifford Steers & Sherfield Inc., **I** 31
Doherty, Mann & Olshan. *See* Wells Rich Greene BDDP.
Dolby Laboratories Inc., **20 191–93**
Dole Food Company, Inc., **I** 565; **II** 491–92; **9 175–76**; **20** 116; **31 167–170 (upd.)**
Dolland & Aitchison Group, **V** 399
Dollar Bills, Inc. *See* Dollar Tree Stores, Inc.
Dollar General, **26** 533
Dollar Rent A Car, **6** 349; **24** 10
Dollar Steamship Lines, **6** 353
Dollar Thrifty Automotive Group, Inc., **25** 92, **142–45**
Dollar Tree Stores, Inc., **16** 161; **23 176–78**
Dollfus Mieg & Cie. *See* Groupe DMC.
Dolphin Book Club, **13** 106
Dom Perignon, **25** 258
Domain Technology, **6** 231
Domaine Carneros, **43** 401

Domaine Chandon, **I** 272
Domaines Barons de Rothschild, **36** 113, 115
Dombrico, Inc., **8** 545
Domco Industries, **19** 407
Dome Laboratories, **I** 654
Dome Petroleum, Ltd., **II** 222, 245, 262, 376; **IV** 371, 401, 494; **12** 364
Domestic Electric Co., **III** 435
Domestic Operating Co., **III** 36
Dominick International Corp., **12** 131
Dominick's Finer Foods, **9** 451; **13** 25, 516; **17** 558, 560–61
Dominion Bank, **II** 375–76
Dominion Bridge Company, Limited, **8** 544
Dominion Cellular, **6** 322
Dominion Dairies, **7** 429
Dominion Engineering Works Ltd., **8** 544
Dominion Far East Line, **I** 469; **20** 311
Dominion Foils Ltd., **17** 280
Dominion Foundries and Steel, Ltd., **IV** 73–74
Dominion Hoist & Shovel Co., **8** 544
Dominion Homes, Inc., 19 125–27
Dominion Industries Ltd., **15** 229
Dominion Life Assurance Co., **III** 276
Dominion Mushroom Co., **II** 649–50
Dominion Ornamental, **III** 641
Dominion Paper Box Co. Ltd., **IV** 645
Dominion Resources, Inc., **V** 591, **596–99**
Dominion Securities, **II** 345; **21** 447
Dominion Steel Castings Company, Ltd. *See* Dofasco Inc.
Dominion Stores Ltd., **II** 650, 652
Dominion Tar & Chemical Co. Ltd., **IV** 271–72
Dominion Terminal Associates, **IV** 171; **7** 582, 584
Dominion Textile Inc., **V** 355; **8** 559–60; **12 117–19**
Domino Sugar Corporation, **26 120–22**; **42** 370
Domino Supermarkets, **24** 528
Domino's Pizza, Inc., **7 150–53**; **9** 74; **12** 123; **15** 344, 346; **16** 447; **21 177–81 (upd.)**; **22** 353; **24** 295; **25** 179–80, 227–28; **26** 177; **33** 388; **37** 208
Domtar Inc., **IV 271–73**, 308
Don Baxter Intravenous Products Co., **I** 627
Don Massey Cadillac, Inc., **37 114–16**
Don's Foods, Inc., **26** 164
Donac Company, **V** 681
Donald L. Bren Co., **IV** 287
Donaldson Co. Inc., **16 178–81**
Donaldson, Lufkin & Jenrette, Inc., **II** 422, 451; **III** 247–48; **9** 115, 142, 360–61; **18** 68; **22 188–91**; **26** 348; **35** 247; **41** 197
Donaldson's Department Stores, **15** 274
Doncaster Newspapers Ltd., **IV** 686
Dong-A Motor, **III** 749
Dong-Myung Industrial Co. Ltd., **II** 540
Dongbang Life Insurance Co., **I** 515
Dongguan Shilong Kyocera Optics Co., Ltd., **21** 331
Dongil Frozen Foods Co., **II** 553
Dongsu Industrial Company, **III** 516; **7** 232
Donn, Inc., **18** 162
Donna Karan Company, **15 145–47**; **24** 299; **25** 294, 523
Donnelley, Gassette & Loyd, **IV** 660
Donnellon McCarthy Inc., **12** 184
Donnelly Corporation, **12 120–22**; **35 147–50 (upd.)**
Donnkenny, Inc., **17 136–38**
Donohue Inc., **12** 412
Donohue Meehan Publishing Co., **27** 362
Donruss Leaf Inc., **19** 386
Donzi Marine Corp., **III** 600
Dooner Laboratories, **I** 667
Door-to-Door, **6** 14
Dorado Beach Development Inc., **I** 103
Dordrecht, **III** 177–78
Dorenbecher Properties, **19** 381
Doric Corp., **19** 290
Dorling Kindersley Holdings plc, **20 194–96**
Dorman Long & Co. Ltd., **IV** 658
Dorman's, Inc., **27** 291
Dorney Park, **22** 130
Dornier, **I** 46, 74, 151; **15** 142; **34** 131
Dorothy Hamill International, **13** 279, 281
Dorothy Perkins, **V** 21
Dorr-Oliver Inc., **35** 134–35
Dortmunder Union, **II** 240; **IV** 103, 105
Doskocil Companies, Inc., **12 123–25**. *See also* Foodbrands America, Inc.
Doty Agency, Inc., **41** 178, 180
Double A Products Co., **23** 82–83
Doubleday Book Shops, Inc., **10** 136; **25** 31; **30** 68
Doubleday-Dell, **IV** 594, 636
Doubletree Corporation, **21 182–85**; **41** 81–82
Douglas & Lomason Company, **16 182–85**
Douglas Aircraft Co., **I** 48, 70, 76, 96, 104, 195; **II** 32, 425; **III** 601; **9** 12, 18, 206; **10** 163; **13** 48, 341; **16** 77; **21** 141; **24** 375
Douglas-Dahlin Co., **I** 158–59
Douglas Dynamics L.L.C., **41** 3
Douglas Oil Co., **IV** 401
Doulton Glass Industries Ltd., **IV** 659
Douwe Egberts, **II** 572
Dove International, **7** 299–300
Dover Corporation, **III 467–69**; **28 101–05 (upd.)**
Dover Downs Entertainment, Inc., **43 139–41**
Dover Publications Inc., **34 148–50**; **41** 111
Dovrat Shrem, **15** 470
Dow Chemical Co., **I 323–25**, 334, 341–42, 360, 370–71, 708; **II** 440, 457; **III** 617, 760; **IV** 83, 417; **8 147–50 (upd.)**, 153, 261–62, 548; **9** 328–29, 500–1; **10** 289; **11** 271; **12** 99–100, 254, 364; **14** 114, 217; **16** 99; **17** 418; **18** 279; **21** 387; **28** 411; **38** 187
Dow Corning, **II** 54; **III** 683, 685
Dow Jones & Company, Inc., **IV 601–03**, 654, 656, 670, 678; **7** 99; **10** 276–78, 407; **13** 55; **15** 335–36; **19 128–31 (upd.)**, 204; **21** 68–70; **23** 157
Dow Jones Telerate, Inc., **10 276–78**
DOW Stereo/Video Inc., **30** 466
Dowdings Ltd., **IV** 349
DowElanco, **21** 385, 387
Dowell Australia Ltd., **III** 674
Dowell Schlumberger. *See* Schlumberger Limited.
Dowidat GmbH, **IV** 197
Dowlais Iron Co., **III** 493
Down River International, Inc., **15** 188
Downe Communications, Inc., **14** 460
Downingtown Paper Company, **8** 476
Downyflake Foods, **7** 429
Dowty Aerospace, **17** 480
Doyle Dane Bernbach, **I** 9, 20, 28, 30–31, 33, 37, 206; **11** 549; **14** 159; **22** 396
DP&L. *See* Dayton Power & Light Company.
DPCE, **II** 139; **24** 194
DPF, Inc., **12** 275; **38** 250–51
DPL Inc., **6 480–82**
DQE, **6 483–85**; **38** 40
DR Holdings, Inc., **10** 242
Dr Pepper/Seven Up, Inc., **32 154–57 (upd.)**
Dr. Gerhard Mann Pharma, **25** 56
Dr. Ing he F. Porsche GmbH, **13** 413–14
Dr. Karl Thomae GmbH, **39** 72–73
Dr. Martens, **23** 399, 401
Dr. Miles' Medical Co., **I** 653
Dr Pepper/7Up Companies, Inc., **I** 245; **II** 477; **9 177–78**
Dr. Richter & Co., **IV** 70
Dr. Solomon's Software Ltd., **25** 349
Dr. Tigges-Fahrten, **II** 163–64
Drackett Professional Products, **III** 17; **12 126–28**
DraftDirect Worldwide, **22** 297
Draftline Engineering Co., **22** 175
Dragados y Construcciones S.A., **II** 198
Dragon, **III** 391
Dragon International, **18** 87
Dragonair, **16** 481; **18** 114. *See also* Hong Kong Dragon Airlines.
The Drake, **12** 316
Drake Bakeries, **II** 562
Drake Beam Morin, Inc., **IV** 623
Drake Steel Supply Co., **19** 343
Drallos Potato Company, **25** 332
Draper & Kramer, **IV** 724
Draper Corporation, **14** 219; **15** 384
Drathen Co., **I** 220
Dravo Corp., **6** 143
Draw-Tite, Inc., **11** 535
Drayton Corp., **II** 319; **17** 324
DreamWorks SKG, **17** 72; **21** 23, 26; **26** 150, 188; **43 142–46**
The Drees Company, Inc., **41 131–33**
Dreher Breweries, **24** 450
Dresdner Bank A.G., **I** 411; **II** 191, 238–39, 241–42, 256–57, 279–80, **281–83**, 385; **III** 201, 289, 401; **IV** 141; **14** 169–70; **15** 13
Dresdner Feuer-Versicherungs-Gesellschaft, **III** 376
Dresdner RCM Global Investors, **33** 128
The Dress Barn, Inc., **24 145–46**
Dresser Industries, Inc., **I** 486; **III** 429, **470–73**; 499, 527, 545–46; **12** 539; **14** 325; **15** 225–26, 468; **16** 310; **18** 219; **24** 208; **25** 188, 191
Dresser Power, **6** 555
Drew Graphics, Inc., **13** 227–28
Drew Industries Inc., **28 106–08**
Drewry Photocolor, **I** 447
Drexel Burnham Lambert Incorporated, **II** 167, 329–30, **407–09**, 482; **III** 10, 253, 254–55, 531, 721; **IV** 334; **6** 210–11; **7** 305; **8** 327, 349, 388–90, 568; **9** 346; **12** 229; **13** 169, 299, 449; **14** 43; **15** 71, 281, 464; **16** 535, 561; **20** 415; **22** 55, 189; **24** 273; **25** 313; **33** 253. *See also* New Street Capital Inc.

Drexel Heritage Furnishings Inc., **III** 571; **11** 534; **12 129–31**; **20** 362; **39** 266
Dreyer's Grand Ice Cream, Inc., **10** 147–48; **17 139–41**; **30** 81; **35** 59–61
Dreyfus Interstate Development Corp., **11** 257
DRI. *See* Dominion Resources, Inc.
Dribeck Importers Inc., **9** 87
Drip In Irrigation, **26** 494
Drogueros S.A., **39** 188
Drott Manufacturing Company, **10** 379
Drouot Group, **III** 211
DRS Investment Group, **27** 370
Drug City, **II** 649
Drug Emporium, Inc., **12 132–34**, 477
Drug House, **III** 9
Drug, Inc., **III** 17; **37** 42
Drummond Lighterage. *See* Puget Sound Tug and Barge Company.
Drummonds' Bank, **12** 422
Druout, **I** 563; **24** 78
Dry Milks Inc., **I** 248
DryClean U.S.A., **14** 25
Dryden and Co., **III** 340
Drypers Corporation, **18 147–49**
Drysdale Government Securities, **10** 117
DSC Communications Corporation, **9** 170; **12 135–37**
DSL Group Ltd., **27** 49
DSM Melamine America, **27** 316–18
DSM N.V., **I 326–27**; **III** 614; **15** 229
DST Systems Inc., **6** 400–02; **26** 233
DTAG. *See* Dollar Thrifty Automotive Group, Inc.
DTE Energy Company, **20 197–201 (upd.)**
Du Bouzet, **II** 233
Du Mont Company, **8** 517
Du Pareil au Même, **43 147–49**
Du Pont. *See* E.I. du Pont de Nemours & Co.
Du Pont Fabricators, **III** 559
Du Pont Glore Forgan, Inc., **III** 137
Du Pont Photomask, **IV** 600
Duane Reade Holding Corp., **21 186–88**
Dublin and London Steam Packet Company, **V** 490
DuBois Chemicals Division, **13** 149–50; **22** 188; **26** 306
Ducatel-Duval, **II** 369
Ducati Motor Holding S.p.A., **17** 24; **30 171–73**; **36** 472
Duck Head Apparel Company, Inc., **8** 141–43; **30** 159; **42 118–21**
Ducks Unlimited, **28** 306
Duckwall-ALCO Stores, Inc., **24 147–49**
Duco Ltd., **25** 104–05
Ducommun Incorporated, **30 174–76**
Ducon Group, **II** 81
Ducros, **36** 185, 187–88
Dudley Stationery Ltd., **25** 501
Duff & Phelps Credit Rating, **37** 143, 145
Duff Bros., **III** 9–10
Duffy Meats, **27** 259
Duffy-Mott, **II** 477
Duke Energy Corporation, **27 128–31 (upd.)**; **40** 354, 358
Duke Energy Field Services, Inc., **24** 379; **40** 354, 358
Duke Power Company, **V 600–02**
Dumes SA, **13** 206
Dumez, **V** 655–57
Dumont Broadcasting Corporation, **7** 335
The Dun & Bradstreet Corporation, **I** 540; **IV 604–05**, 643, 661; **8** 526; **9** 505; **10** 4, 358; **13** 3–4; **19 132–34 (upd.)**; **38** 6
Dun & Bradstreet Software Services Inc., **11 77–79**; **43** 183
Dunbar-Stark Drillings, Inc., **19** 247
Duncan Foods Corp., **I** 234; **10** 227
Duncan, Sherman & Co., **II** 329
Duncanson & Holt, Inc., **13** 539
Dundee Acquisition Corp., **19** 421
Dundee Bancorp, **36** 314
Dundee Cement Co., **III** 702; **8** 258–59
Dunfey Brothers Capital Group, **12** 368
Dunfey Hotels Corporation, **12** 367
Dunhams Stores Corporation, **V** 111
Dunhill Holdings, **IV** 93; **V** 411
Dunkin' Donuts, **II** 619; **21** 323; **29** 18–19
Dunlop Coflexip Umbilicals Ltd. *See* Duco Ltd.
Dunlop Holdings, **I** 429; **III** 697; **V** 250, 252–53
Dunlop Ltd., **25** 104
Dunn Bennett, **38** 401
Dunn Bros., **28** 63
Dunn Manufacturing Company, **25** 74
Dunn Paper Co., **IV** 290
Dunning Industries, **12** 109
Dunoyer. *See* Compagnie de Saint-Gobain S.A.
Dunwoodie Manufacturing Co., **17** 136
Duo-Bed Corp., **14** 435
Dupey Enterprises, Inc., **17** 320
Dupil-Color, Inc., **III** 745
Duplainville Transport, **19** 333–34
Duplex Products, Inc., **17 142–44**, 445
Dupol, **III** 614
Dupont. *See* E.I. du Pont de Nemours & Company.
Dupont Chamber Works, **6** 449
Duquesne Light Company, **6** 483–84
Duquesne Systems, **10** 394
Dura Convertible Systems, **13** 170
Dura Corp., **I** 476
Dura-Vent, **III** 468
Duracell International Inc., **9 179–81**; **12** 559; **13** 433; **17** 31; **24** 274; **39** 336, 339
Durametallic, **17** 147; **21 189–91**
Durand & Huguenin, **I** 672
Durango-Mapimi Mining Co., **22** 284
Duray, Inc., **12** 215
Durban Breweries and Distillers, **I** 287
D'Urban, Inc., **41** 169
Durham Chemicals Distributors Ltd., **III** 699
Durham Raw Materials Ltd., **III** 699
Duriron Company Inc., **17 145–47**; **21** 189, 191
Durkee Famous Foods, **II** 567; **7** 314; **8** 222; **17** 106; **27** 297
Durr-Fillauer Medical Inc., **13** 90; **18** 97
Dutch Boy, **II** 649; **III** 745; **10** 434–35
Dutch Crude Oil Company. *See* Nederlandse Aardolie Maatschappij.
Dutch East Indies Post, Telegraph and Telephone Service, **II** 67
Dutch Nuts Chocoladefabriek B.V., **II** 569
Dutch Pantry, **II** 497
Dutch State Mines. *See* DSM N.V.
Dutchland Farms, **25** 124
Dutton Brewery, **I** 294
Duttons Ltd., **24** 267
Duty Free International, Inc., **11 80–82**. *See also* World Duty Free Americas, Inc.
Duval Corp., **IV** 489–90; **7** 280; **25** 461
DWG Corporation. *See* Triarc Companies, Inc.
Dyckerhoff AG, **35 151–54**
Dyersburg Corporation, **21 192–95**
Dyke and Dryden, Ltd., **31** 417
Dylex Limited, **29 162–65**
Dymed Corporation. *See* Palomar Medical Technologies, Inc.
Dynaco Corporation, **III** 643; **22** 409
DynaMark, Inc., **18** 168, 170, 516, 518
Dynamatic Corp., **I** 154
Dynamem Corporation, **22** 409
Dynamic Capital Corp., **16** 80
Dynamic Controls, **11** 202
Dynamic Microprocessor Associated Inc., **10** 508
Dynamics Corporation of America, **39** 106
Dynamit Nobel AG, **III** 692–95; **16** 364; **18** 559
Dynamix, **15** 455
Dynapar, **7** 116–17
Dynaplast, **40** 214–15
Dynascan AK, **14** 118
Dynasty Footwear, Ltd., **18** 88
Dynatech Corporation, **13 194–96**
Dynatron/Bondo Corporation, **8** 456
Dynell Electronics, **I** 85
Dyno Industrier AS, **13** 555
Dyonics Inc., **I** 667
DYR, **I** 38; **16** 167
Dystrybucja, **41** 340

E. & B. Carpet Mills, **III** 423
E&B Company, **9** 72
E&B Marine, Inc., **17** 542–43
E & H Utility Sales Inc., **6** 487
E. & J. Gallo Winery, **I** 27, **242–44**, 260; **7 154–56 (upd.)**; **15** 391; **28 109–11 (upd.)**, 223
E&M Laboratories, **18** 514
E & S Retail Ltd. *See* Powerhouse.
E! Entertainment Television Inc., **17 148–50**; **24** 120, 123
E-Stamp Corporation, **34** 474
E-Systems, Inc., **I** 490; **9 182–85**
E*Trade Group, Inc., **20 206–08**; **38** 439
E-II Holdings Inc., **II** 468; **9** 449; **12** 87; **43** 355. *See also* Astrum International Corp.
E-Z Haul, **24** 409
E-Z Serve Corporation, **15** 270; **17 169–71**
E.A. Miller, Inc., **II** 494
E.A. Pierce & Co., **II** 424; **13** 340
E.A. Stearns & Co., **III** 627
E.B. Badger Co., **11** 413
E.B. Eddy Forest Products, **II** 631
E.C. Snodgrass Company, **14** 112
E.C. Steed, **13** 103
E. de Trey & Sons, **10** 270–71
E.F. Hutton Group, **I** 402; **II** 399, 450–51; **8** 139; **9** 469; **10** 63
E.F. Hutton LBO, **24** 148
E. Gluck Trading Co., **III** 645
E.H. Bindley & Company, **9** 67
E.I. du Pont de Nemours & Company, **I** 21, 28, 305, 317–19, 323, **328–30**, 334, 337–38, 343–44, 346–48, 351–53, 365, 377, 379, 383, 402–03, 545, 548, 675; **III** 21; **IV** 69, 78, 263, 371, 399,

401–02, 409, 481, 599; **V** 360; **7** 546; **8** **151–54 (upd.)**, 485; **9** 154, 216, 352, 466; **10** 289; **11** 432; **12** 68, 365, 416–17; **13** 21, 124; **16** 127, 130, 201, 439, 461–62; **19** 11, 223; **21** 544; **22** 147, 260, 405; **24** 111, 388; **25** 152, 540; **26** **123–27 (upd.)**; **34** 80, 283–84; **37** 111; **40** 370
E.J. Brach & Sons, **II** 521. *See also* Brach and Brock Confections, Inc.
E.J. Longyear Company. *See* Boart Longyear Company.
E. Katz Special Advertising Agency. *See* Katz Communications, Inc.
E.L. Phillips and Company, **V** 652–53
E.M. Warburg Pincus & Co., **7** 305; **13** 176; **16** 319; **25** 313; **29** 262
E. Missel GmbH, **20** 363
E.N.V. Engineering, **I** 154
E.R. Squibb, **I** 695; **21** 54–55
E. Rabinowe & Co., Inc., **13** 367
E.S. Friedman & Co., **II** 241
E.S. International Holding S.A. *See* Banco Espírito Santo e Comercial de Lisboa S.A.
E.W. Bliss, **I** 452
E.W. Oakes & Co. Ltd., **IV** 118
The E.W. Scripps Company, **IV** **606–09**; **7** **157–59 (upd.)**; **24** 122; **25** 507; **28** **122–26 (upd.)**
E.W.T. Mayer Ltd., **III** 681
EADS. *See* European Aeronautic Defence and Space Company.
Eagle Airways Ltd., **23** 161
Eagle Credit Corp., **10** 248
Eagle Distributing Co., **37** 351
Eagle Family Foods, Inc., **22** 95
Eagle Floor Care, Inc., **13** 501; **33** 392
Eagle Gaming, L.P., **16** 263; **43** 226
Eagle Hardware & Garden, Inc., **9** 399; **16** **186–89**; **17** 539–40
Eagle Industries Inc., **8** 230; **22** 282; **25** 536
Eagle-Lion Films, **II** 147; **25** 328
Eagle Managed Care Corp., **19** 354, 357
Eagle Oil Transport Co. Ltd., **IV** 657
Eagle-Picher Industries, Inc., **8** **155–58**; **23** **179–83 (upd.)**
Eagle Plastics, **19** 414
Eagle Printing Co. Ltd., **IV** 295; **19** 225
Eagle Sentry Inc., **32** 373
Eagle Snacks Inc., **I** 219; **34** 36–37
Eagle Square Manufacturing Co., **III** 627
Eagle Star Insurance Co., **I** 426–27; **III** 185, 200
Eagle Supermarket, **II** 571
Eagle Thrifty Drug, **14** 397
Eagle Travel Ltd., **IV** 241
Earl Scheib, Inc., **32** **158–61**
Early American Insurance Co., **22** 230
Early Learning Centre, **39** 240, 242
Earth Resources Company, **IV** 459; **17** 320
Earth Wise, Inc., **16** 90
Earth's Best, Inc., **21** 56; **36** 256
The Earthgrains Company, **36** **161–65**
EarthLink, Inc., **33** 92; **36** **166–68**; **38** 269
EAS. *See* Executive Aircraft Services.
Easco Hand Tools, Inc., **7** 117
Eason Oil Company, **6** 578; **11** 198
East African External Communications Limited, **25** 100
East Chicago Iron and Forge Co., **IV** 113
East Hartford Trust Co., **13** 467
East India Co., **I** 468; **III** 521, 696; **IV** 48; **20** 309
East Japan Heavy Industries, **III** 578–79; **7** 348
East Japan Railway Company, **V** **448–50**
East Midlands Electricity, **V** 605
The East New York Savings Bank, **11** 108–09
East of Scotland, **III** 359
East Texas Pulp and Paper Co., **IV** 342, 674; **7** 528
East-West Airlines, **27** 475
East-West Federal Bank, **16** 484
East West Motor Express, Inc., **39** 377
Easter Enterprises, **8** 380; **23** 358
Easterday Supply Company, **25** 15
Eastern Air Group Co., **31** 102
Eastern Airlines, **I** 41, 66, 78, 90, 98–99, **101–03**, 116, 118, 123–25; **III** 102; **6** 73, 81–82, 104–05; **8** 416; **9** 17–18, 80; **11** 268, 427; **12** 191, 487; **21** 142, 143; **23** 483; **26** 339, 439; **39** 120
Eastern Associated Coal Corp., **6** 487
Eastern Australia Airlines, **24** 396
Eastern Aviation Group, **23** 408
Eastern Bank, **II** 357
Eastern Carolina Bottling Company, **10** 223
Eastern Coal Corp., **IV** 181
Eastern Coalfields Ltd., **IV** 48–49
Eastern Corp., **IV** 703
Eastern Electricity, **13** 485
Eastern Enterprises, **IV** 171; **6** **486–88**
Eastern Gas and Fuel Associates, **I** 354; **IV** 171
Eastern Indiana Gas Corporation, **6** 466
Eastern Kansas Utilities, **6** 511
Eastern Machine Screw Products Co., **13** 7
Eastern Market Beef Processing Corp., **20** 120
Eastern Operating Co., **III** 23
Eastern Pine Sales Corporation, **13** 249
Eastern Software Distributors, Inc., **16** 125
Eastern States Farmers Exchange, **7** 17
Eastern Telegraph Company, **V** 283–84; **25** 99–100
Eastern Texas Electric. *See* Gulf States Utilities Company.
Eastern Tool Co., **IV** 249
Eastern Torpedo Company, **25** 74
Eastern Wisconsin Power, **6** 604
Eastern Wisconsin Railway and Light Company, **6** 601
Eastex Pulp and Paper Co., **IV** 341–42
Eastman Chemical Company, **14** **174–75**; **25** 22; **38** **178–81 (upd.)**
Eastman Christensen Company, **22** 68
Eastman Kodak Company, **I** 19, 30, 90, 323, 337–38, 690; **II** 103; **III** 171–72, **474–77**, 486–88, 547–48, 550, 584, 607–09; **IV** 260–61; **6** 288–89; **7** **160–64 (upd.)**, 436–38; **8** 376–77; **9** 62, 231; **10** 24; **12** 342; **14** 174–75, 534; **16** 168, 449; **18** 184–86, 342, 510; **25** 153; **29** 370; **36** **169–76 (upd.)**; **38** 178–79; **41** 104, 106; **43** 284
Eastman Radio, **6** 33
Eastmaque Gold Mines, Ltd., **7** 356
Eastover Mining, **27** 130
Eastpak, Inc., **30** 138
Eastwynn Theatres, Inc., **37** 63
easyJet Airline Company Limited, **39** **127–29**
Eatco, Inc., **15** 246
Eateries, Inc., **33** **138–40**
Eaton Axle Co., **I** 154
Eaton, Cole & Burnham Company, **8** 134
Eaton Corporation, **I** **154–55**, 186; **III** 645; **10** **279–80 (upd.)**; **12** 547; **27** 100
Eaton Vance Corporation, **18** **150–53**
Eavey Co., **II** 668
Ebamsa, **II** 474
EBASCO. *See* Electric Bond and Share Company.
Ebasco Services, **III** 499; **V** 612; **IV** 255–56
eBay Inc., **32** **162–65**
EBC Amro Ltd., **II** 186
Eberhard Faber, **12** 115
Eberhard Foods, **8** 482
EBIC. *See* European Banks' International Co.
Ebiex S.A., **25** 312
EBS. *See* Electric Bond & Share Company *or* Electronic Bookshelf.
EBSCO Industries, Inc., **17** **151–53**; **40** **158–61 (upd.)**
EC Comics, **25** 139
EC Erdolchemie GmbH, **7** 141
ECC. *See* Educational Credit Corporation.
ECC Group plc, **III** **689–91**. *See also* English China Clays plc.
ECC International Corp., **42** **122–24**
Ecce, **41** 129
ECCO. *See* Adecco S.A.
Echigoya Saburobei Shoten, **IV** 292
Echlin Inc., **I** **156–57**; **11** **83–85 (upd.)**; **15** 310
Echo Bay Mines Ltd., **IV** **75–77**; **23** 40; **38** **182–85 (upd.)**
Les Echos, **IV** 659
EchoStar Communications Corporation, **35** **155–59**
EchoStar Satellite Corp., **39** 400
ECI Telecom Ltd., **18** **154–56**
Eckerd Corporation, **9** **186–87**; **18** 272; **24** 263; **43** 247. *See also* J.C. Penney Company, Inc.
Eckert-Mauchly Corp., **III** 166
Ecko-Ensign Design, **I** 531
Ecko Products, **I** 527
ECL, **16** 238
Eclipse Candles, Ltd., **18** 67, 69
Eclipse Machine Co., **I** 141
Eclipse Telecommunications, Inc., **29** 252
Eco Hotels, **14** 107
Ecolab Inc., **I** **331–33**; **13** **197–200 (upd.)**; **26** 306; **34** **151–56 (upd.)**, 205, 208
Ecology and Environment, Inc., **39** **130–33**
Econo Lodges of America, **25** 309
Econo-Travel Corporation, **13** 362
Economist Group, **15** 265
Economy Book Store, **10** 135
Economy Fire & Casualty, **22** 495
Economy Grocery Stores Company. *See* The Stop & Shop Companies, Inc.
Ecopetrol. *See* Empresa Colombiana de Petróleos.
EcoSystems Software, Inc., **10** 245; **30** 142
EcoWater Systems, Inc., **16** 357
ECS S.A, **12** **138–40**
Ecton, Inc., **36** 5
Ecusta Corporation, **8** 414
ed bazinet international, inc., **34** 144–45
Edah, **13** 544–45

Eddie Bauer, Inc., **II** 503; **V** 160; **9 188–90**; **9** 316; **10** 324, 489, 491; **11** 498; **15** 339; **25** 48; **27** 427, 429–30; **29** 278; **36 177–81 (upd.)**
Eddy Bakeries, Inc., **12** 198
Eddy Paper Co., **II** 631
Edeka Zentrale AG, **II 621–23**; **33** 56
Edelbrock Corporation, **37 117–19**
Edelhoff AG & Co., **39** 415
Edelstahlwerke Buderus AG, **III** 695
Edenhall Group, **III** 673
Edenton Cotton Mills, **12** 503
EDF. *See* Electricité de France.
Edgars, **I** 289
Edgcomb Metals, **IV** 575–76; **31** 470–71
Edge Research, **25** 301
Edgell Communications Inc., **IV** 624
Edgewater Hotel and Casino, **6** 204–05
EDI, **26** 441
Edina Realty Inc., **13** 348
Edison Brothers Stores, Inc., **9 191–93**; **17** 369, 409; **33** 126–28
Edison Electric Appliance Co., **II** 28; **12** 194
Edison Electric Co., **I** 368; **II** 330; **III** 433; **6** 572
Edison Electric Illuminating Co., **II** 402; **6** 595, 601; **14** 124
Edison Electric Illuminating Company of Boston, **12** 45
Edison Electric Light & Power, **6** 510
Edison Electric Light Co., **II** 27; **6** 565, 595; **11** 387; **12** 193
Edison General Electric Co., **II** 27, 120, 278; **12** 193; **14** 168; **26** 451
Edison Machine Works, **II** 27
Edison Phonograph, **III** 443
Edison Schools Inc., **37 120–23**
Editions Albert Premier, **IV** 614
Editions Bernard Grasset, **IV** 618
Editions Dalloz, **IV** 615
Editions Jean-Baptiste Baillière, **25** 285
Editions Nathan, **IV** 615
Editions Ramsay, **25** 174
Editorial Centro de Estudios Ramón Areces, S.A., **V** 52; **26** 130
Editorial Televisa, **18** 211, 213; **23** 417
Editoriale L'Espresso, **IV** 586–87
Editoriale Le Gazzette, **IV** 587
EdK. *See* Edeka Zentrale A.G.
Edmark Corporation, **14 176–78**; **41 134–37 (upd.)**
Edmonton City Bakery, **II** 631
Edogawa Oil Co., **IV** 403
EdoWater Systems, Inc., **IV** 137
Edper Equities, **II** 456
EDS. *See* Electronic Data Systems Corporation.
Education Association Mutual Assurance Company. *See* Horace Mann Educators Corporation.
The Education Finance Group, **33** 418, 420
Education Funds, Inc., **II** 419
Education Management Corporation, **35 160–63**
Education Systems Corporation, **7** 256; **25** 253
Educational & Recreational Services, Inc., **II** 607
Educational Computer International, Inc. *See* ECC International Corp.
Educational Credit Corporation, **8** 10; **38** 12
Educational Loan Administration Group, Inc., **33** 420
Educational Publishing Corporation, **22** 519, 522
Educational Supply Company, **7** 255; **25** 252
Educational Testing Service, **12 141–43**; **42** 209–10, 290
Educorp, Inc., **39** 103
EduQuest, **6** 245
EduServ Technologies, Inc., **33** 420
Edusoft Ltd., **40** 113
Edw. C. Levy Co., **42 125–27**
Edward Ford Plate Glass Co., **III** 640–41, 731
Edward J. DeBartolo Corporation, **V** 116; **8 159–62**
Edward Jones, **30 177–79**
Edward Lloyd Ltd., **IV** 258
Edward P. Allis Company, **13** 16
Edward Smith & Company, **8** 553
Edwards & Jones, **11** 360
Edwards Dunlop & Co. Ltd., **IV** 249
Edwards Food Warehouse, **II** 642
Edwards George and Co., **III** 283
Edwards Industries, **IV** 256
Edwards Theatres Circuit, Inc., **31 171–73**
Edwardstone Partners, **14** 377
EEC Environmental, Inc., **16** 259
Eerste Nederlandsche, **III** 177–79
Eff Laboratories, **I** 622
Effectenbank, **II** 268; **21** 145
EFM Media Management, **23** 294
Efnadruck GmbH, **IV** 325
Efrat Future Technology Ltd. *See* Comverse Technology, Inc.
EFTEC, **32** 257
EG&G Incorporated, **8 163–65**; **18** 219; **22** 410; **29 166–69 (upd.)**
EGAM, **IV** 422
Egerton Hubbard & Co., **IV** 274
Egghead Inc., **9 194–95**; **10** 284
Egghead.com, Inc., **31 174–177 (upd.)**
EGPC. *See* Egyptian General Petroleum Corporation.
EGUZKIA-NHK, **III** 581
EgyptAir, **I** 107; **6 84–86**; **27 132–35 (upd.)**
Egyptian General Petroleum Corporation, **IV 412–14**; **32** 45
EHAPE Einheitspreis Handels Gesellschaft mbH. *See* Kaufhalle AG.
Eidgenössische Bank, **II** 378
Eidgenössische Versicherungs- Aktien-Gesellschaft, **III** 403
Eiffage, **27 136–38**
Eiffel Construction Metallique, **27** 138
800-JR Cigar, Inc., **27 139–41**
84 Lumber Company, **9 196–97**; **39 134–36 (upd.)**
Eildon Electronics Ltd., **15** 385
EIMCO, **I** 512
Einstein/Noah Bagel Corporation, **29 170–73**
eircom plc, **31 178–181 (upd.)**
EIS Automotive Corp., **III** 603
Eisai Company, **13** 77
Eisen-und Stahlwerk Haspe AG, **IV** 126
Eisen-und Stahlwerk Hoesch, **IV** 103
Eisenhower Mining Co., **IV** 33
EKA AB, **I** 330; **8** 153
Eka Nobel AB, **9** 380
Ekco Group, Inc., **12** 377; **16 190–93**
El Al Israel Airlines Ltd., **I** 30; **23 184–87**
El Camino Resources International, Inc., **11 86–88**
El Chico Restaurants, Inc., **19 135–38**; **36** 162–63
El Corte Inglés, S.A., **V 51–53**; **26 128–31 (upd.)**
El Dorado Investment Company, **6** 546–47
El-Mel-Parts Ltd., **21** 499
El Paso & Southwestern Railroad, **IV** 177
El Paso Electric Company, **21 196–98**
El Paso Healthcare System, Ltd., **15** 112; **35** 215
El Paso Natural Gas Company, **10** 190; **11** 28; **12 144–46**; **19** 411; **27** 86
El Pollo Loco, **II** 680; **27** 16–18
El Taco, **7** 505
ELAN, **IV** 486
Elan Corp. plc, **10** 54
Elan Ski Company, **22** 483
Elano Corporation, **14 179–81**
Elastic Reality Inc., **38** 70
Elcat Company, **17** 91
Elco Corporation, **21** 329, 331
Elco Industries Inc., **22** 282
Elco Motor Yacht, **I** 57
Elda Trading Co., **II** 48; **25** 267
Elder-Beerman Stores Corporation, **10 281–83**; **19** 362
Elder Dempster Line, **6** 416–17
Elder Smith Goldsbrough Mort Ltd., **21** 227
Elder's Insurance Co., **III** 370
Elders IXL Ltd., **I** 216, 228–29, 264, **437–39**, 592–93; **7** 182–83; **21** 227; **26** 305; **28** 201
Elders Keep, **13** 440
Eldorado Gold Corporation, **22** 237
ele Corporation, **23** 251
Electra Corp., **III** 569; **20** 361–62
Electra/Midland Corp., **13** 398
Electralab Electronics Corp., **III** 643
Electric Boat Co., **I** 57–59, 527; **II** 7; **10** 315
Electric Bond & Share Company, **V** 564–65; **6** 596
Electric Clearinghouse, Inc., **18** 365, 367
Electric Energy, Inc., **6** 470, 505
Electric Fuels Corp., **V** 621; **23** 200
Electric Heat Regulator Co., **II** 40; **12** 246
Electric Iron and Steel, **IV** 162
Electric Light and Power Company, **6** 483
Electric Light Company of Atlantic City. *See* Atlantic Energy, Inc.
Electric Lightwave, Inc., **37 124–27**
Electric Storage Battery Co., **39** 338
Electric Thermostat Co., **II** 40; **12** 246
Electric Transit, Inc., **37** 399–400
Electrical Lamp Service Co. *See* EMI Group plc.
Electricité de France, **I** 303; **V 603–05**, 626–28; **41 138–41 (upd.)**
Electro-Alkaline Company. *See* The Clorox Company.
Electro-Chemische Fabrik Natrium GmbH, **IV** 69–70
Electro Dynamics Corp., **I** 57, 484; **11** 263
Electro-Flo, Inc., **9** 27
Electro-Mechanical Research, **III** 617; **17** 417
Electro Metallurgical Co., **I** 400; **9** 517; **11** 402

Electro-Motive Engineering Company, **10** 273
Electro-Nite International N.V., **IV** 100
Electro-Optical Systems, **III** 172; **6** 289
Electro Refractories and Abrasives Company, **8** 178
Electro String Instrument Corporation, **16** 201; **43** 169
Electrobel, **II** 202
ElectroData Corp., **III** 165; **6** 281
Electrolux Group, **II** 69, 572; **III** 420, **478–81**; **IV** 338; **6** 69; **11** 439; **12** 158–59, 250; **13** 562, 564; **17** 353; **21** 383. *See also* Aktiebolaget Electrolux.
Electromagnetic Sciences Inc., **21 199–201**
Electromedics, **11** 460
Electronic Arts Inc., **10 284–86**; **13** 115; **29** 76; **35** 227
Electronic Banking Systems, **9** 173
Electronic Book Technologies, Inc., **26** 216 **29** 427
Electronic Data Systems Corporation, **I** 172; **II** 65; **III 136–38**, 326; **6** 226; **9** 36; **10** 325, 327; **11** 62, 123, 131; **13** 482; **14** 15, 318; **22** 266; **27** 380; **28 112–16 (upd.)**; **241**; **XXIX** 375; **36** 242. *See also* Perot Systems Corporation.
Electronic Engineering Co., **16** 393
Electronic Hair Styling, Inc., **41** 228
Electronic Rentals Group PLC, **II** 139; **24** 194
Electronic Tool Company, **16** 100
Electronics Corp. of Israel Ltd. *See* ECI Telecom Ltd.
Electronics for Imaging, Inc., **15 148–50**; **43 150–53 (upd.)**
Electrorail, **II** 93; **18** 472
Electrowatt Ltd., **21** 146–47
Electrowerke AG, **IV** 230
Elekom, **31** 176
Elektra. *See* Grupo Elektra, S.A. de C.V.
Elektra Records, **III** 480; **23** 33
Elektriska Aktiebolaget. *See* ABB Asea Brown Boveri Ltd.
Elektrizitäts-Gesellschaft Laufenburg, **6** 490
Elektrizitätswerk Wesertal GmbH, **30** 206
Elektrizitätswerk Westfalen AG, **V** 744
ElektroHelios, **III** 479; **22** 26
Elektromekaniska AB, **III** 478
Elektromekano, **II** 1
Elektrowatt AG, **6 489–91**
Eleme Petrochemicals Co., **IV** 473
Elementis plc, **40 162–68 (upd.)**
Eletson Corp., **13** 374
Elettra Broadcasting Corporation, **14** 509
Elettrofinanziaria Spa, **9** 152
Eleventh National Bank, **II** 373
Elf Aquitaine SA, **21 202–06 (upd.)**; **23** 236, 238; **24** 494; **25** 104; **26** 369, 425. *See also* Société Nationale Elf Aquitaine.
Elfa International, **36** 134–35
Elgin Blenders, Inc., **7** 128
Elgin Exploration, Inc., **19** 247; **26** 70
Eli Lilly & Co., **I** 637, **645–47**, 666, 679, 687, 701; **III** 18–19, 60–61; **8** 168, 209; **9** 89–90; **10** 535; **11** 9, **89–91 (upd.)**, 458, 460; **12** 187, 278, 333; **14** 99–100, 259; **17** 437; **18** 420, 422; **19** 105; **21** 387; **26** 31; **32** 212
Eli Witt Company, **15** 137, 139; **43** 205
Elias Brothers Restaurants, **III** 103
Elit Circuits Inc., **I** 330; **8** 153
Elite Microelectronics, **9** 116
Elite Sewing Machine Manufacturing Co., **III** 415
Elizabeth Arden, Inc., **I** 646, **III** 48; **8 166–68**, 344; **9** 201–02, 428, 449; **11** 90; **12** 314; **30** 188; **32** 476; **40 169–72 (upd.)**
Eljer Industries, Inc., **II** 420; **24 150–52**
Elk River Resources, Inc., **IV** 550
Elka, **III** 54
Elke Corporation, **10** 514
Elko-Lamoille Power Company, **11** 343
Ellenville Electric Company, **6** 459
Ellerbe Becket, **41 142–45**
Ellesse International S.p.A., **V** 376; **26** 397–98
Ellett Brothers, Inc., **17 154–56**
Ellington Recycling Center, **12** 377
Elliott Automation, **II** 25; **6** 241; **13** 225
Elliott Bay Design Group, **22** 276
Elliott Paint and Varnish, **8** 553
Ellis & Everard, **41** 341
Ellis Adding-Typewriter Co., **III** 151; **6** 265
Ellis Banks, **II** 336
Ellis, Chafflin & Co. *See* Mead Corporation.
Ellis-Don Ltd., **38** 481
Ellis Paperboard Products Inc., **13** 442
Ellis Park Race Course, **29** 118
Ellisco Co., **35** 130
Ellos A.B., **II** 640
ELMA Electronic, **III** 632
Elmendorf Board, **IV** 343
Elmer's Products, Inc. *See* Borden, Inc.
Elmer's Restaurants, Inc., **42 128–30**
Elphinstone, **21** 501
Elrick & Lavidge, **6** 24
Elrick Industries, Inc., **19** 278
Elscint Ltd., **20 202–05**
Elsevier NV, **IV 610–11**, 643, 659; **7** 244; **14** 555–56; **17** 396, 399. *See also* Reed Elsevier.
Elsi, **II** 86
Elsinore L.P., **36** 158
ELTO Outboard Motor Co., **III** 597
Eltra Corporation, **I** 416, 524; **22** 31; **31** 135
Elwerath, **IV** 485
ELYO, **42** 387–88
Elyria Telephone Company, **6** 299
Email Ltd., **III** 672–73
EMAP plc, **35** 71–72, **164–66**, 242–44
Emballage, **III** 704
Embankment Trust Ltd., **IV** 659
Embassy Book Co., Ltd., **IV** 635
Embassy Hotel Group, **I** 216; **9** 426
Embassy Suites, **9** 425; **24** 253
Embedded Support Tools Corporation, **37** 419, 421
Embers America Restaurants, **30 180–82**
Embraer. *See* Empresa Brasileira de Aeronáutica S.A.
Embry-Riddle, **I** 89
EMC Corporation, **12 147–49**; **20** 8
EMC Technology Services, Inc., **30** 469
Emco, **III** 569; **20** 361
EMD Technologies, **27** 21; **40** 67
Emerald Coast Water Co., **III** 21
Emerald Technology, Inc., **10** 97
Emerson-Brantingham Company, **10** 378
Emerson Drug, **I** 711
Emerson Electric Co., **II 18–21**, 92; **III** 625; **8** 298; **12** 248; **13** 225; **14** 357; **15** 405–06; **21** 43; **22** 64; **25** 530; **36** 400
Emerson Foote, Inc., **25** 90
Emerson Radio Corp., **30 183–86**
Emery Air Freight Corporation, **6** 345–46, 386, **388–91**; **18** 177. *See also* Emery Worldwide Airlines, Inc.
Emery Group, **I** 377; **III** 33
Emery Worldwide Airlines, Inc., **21** 139; **25 146–50 (upd.)**
Emeryville Chemical Co., **IV** 408
Emge Packing Co., Inc., **11 92–93**
Emhart Corp., **III** 437; **8** 332; **20** 67
EMI Group plc, **I** 531; **6** 240; **22 192–95 (upd.)**; **24** 485; **26** 188, 314. *See also* Thorne EMI plc.
The Emirates Group, **24** 400; **39 137–39**
Empain, **18** 472; **19** 165
Empain-Schneider, **II** 93
Empaques de Carton Titan, **19** 10–11
Empex Hose, **19** 37
Empi, Inc., **27 132–35**
Empire Blue Cross and Blue Shield, **III 245–46**; **6** 195
Empire Brewery, **I** 253
Empire Co., **II** 653
Empire Cos., **IV** 391
Empire District Electric, **IV** 391
Empire Family Restaurants Inc., **15** 362
Empire Gas & Fuel, **IV** 391
Empire Hanna Coal Co., Ltd., **8** 346
Empire Inc., **II** 682
Empire Life and Accident Insurance Co., **III** 217
Empire National Bank, **II** 218
Empire of America, **11** 110
Empire Pencil, **III** 505; **43** 230
Empire Savings, Building & Loan Association, **8** 424
Empire State Group, **IV** 612
Empire State Petroleum, **IV** 374
Empire State Pickling Company, **21** 155
Empire Steel Castings, Inc., **39** 31–32
Empire Stores, **19** 309
Empire Trust Co., **II** 218
Employee Solutions, Inc., **18 157–60**
employeesavings.com, **39** 25
Employers' Liability Assurance, **III** 235
Employer's Overload, **25** 432
Employers Reinsurance Corp., **II** 31; **12** 197
Empresa Brasileira de Aeronáutica S.A. (Embraer), **36 182–84**
Empresa Colombiana de Petróleos, **IV 415–18**
Empresa de Obras y Montajes Ovalle Moore, S.A., **34** 81
Empresa Nacional de Electridad, **I** 459
Empresa Nacional del Petroleo, **IV** 528
Empresa Nacional Electrica de Cordoba, **V** 607
Empresa Nacional Hidro-Electrica del Ribagorzana, **I** 459; **V** 607
Empresa Nacional Hulleras del Norte, **I** 460
Empresas Emel S.A., **41** 316
Empresas Frisco, **21** 259
Empresas ICA, **34** 82
Empresas ICA Sociedad Controladora, S.A. de C.V., **41 146–49**
Empresas La Moderna, **21** 413; **29** 435
Empresas Tolteca, **20** 123
Emprise Corporation, **7** 134–35

EMS-Chemie Holding AG, **III** 760; **32** 257
EMS Technologies, Inc., **21** 199, 201; **22** 173
Enagas, **IV** 528
Enbridge Inc., 43 154–58
ENCAD, Incorporated, 25 151–53
ENCASO, **IV** 528
ENCI, **IV** 132
Encompass Services Corporation, 33 141–44
Encore Computer Corporation, 13 201–02
Encore Distributors Inc., **17** 12–13
Encryption Technology Corporation, **23** 102
Encyclopedia Britannica, Inc., 7 165–68; 12 435, 554–55; **16** 252; **39 140–44 (upd.)**; **43** 208
Endata, Inc., **11** 112
ENDESA Group, V 606–08
Endevco Inc., **11** 28
Endiama, **IV** 67
Endicott Trust Company, **11** 110
Endo Vascular Technologies, Inc., **11** 460
Endovations, Inc., **21** 47
ENECO. *See* Empresa Nacional Electrica de Cordoba.
ENEL. *See* Ente Nazionale per l'Energia Elettrica.
Enerchange LLC, **18** 366
Enercon, Inc., **6** 25
Energas Company, **43** 56–57
Energen Corporation, 6 583; **21 207–09**
Energie-Verwaltungs-Gesellschaft, **V** 746
Energieversorgung Ostbayern AG, **23** 47
Energizer Holdings, Inc., 9 180; **32 171–74; 39** 336, 339
Energy & Minerals, Inc., **42** 354
Energy Absorption Systems, Inc., **15** 378
Energy Biosystems Corp., **15** 352
Energy Coatings Co., **14** 325
Energy Corp. of Louisiana, **V** 619
Energy Film Library, **31** 216, 218
Energy Foundation, **34** 386
The Energy Group, **26** 359
Energy Increments Inc., **19** 411
Energy National, Inc., **27** 485
Energy Resources, **27** 216
Energy Steel Corporation, **19** 472
Energy Systems Group, Inc., **13** 489
Energy Transportation Systems, Inc., **27** 88
Energyline Systems, **26** 5
EnergyOne, **19** 487
Enerplus Resources, **21** 500
Enesco Corporation, 11 94–96; 15 475, 477–78
Engelhard Corporation, II 54; **IV** 23, **78–80; 16** 28; **21 210–14 (upd.)**
Engen, **IV** 93; **22** 236
Engineered Polymers Co., **I** 202
Engineering Co. of Nigeria, **IV** 473
Engineering Company, **9** 16
Engineering for the Petroleum and Process Industries, **IV** 414
Engineering Plastics, Ltd., **8** 377
Engineering Research Associates, **III** 126, 129
Engineers & Fabricators, Inc., **18** 513
England Corsair Furniture, **14** 302
Englander Co., **I** 400
Engles Management Corp., **26** 448
English China Clays Ltd., III 689–91; **15 151–54 (upd.)**; **36** 20; **40 173–77 (upd.)**
English Condensed Milk Co., **II** 545
English Electric Co., **I** 50; **II** 25, 81; **6** 241; **24** 85
English Mercantile & General Insurance Co., **III** 376
English Property Corp., **IV** 712
English, Scottish and Australian Bank Ltd., **II** 187–89
Engraph, Inc., 12 150–51
Enhanced Services Billing, Inc. *See* Billing Concepts Corp.
ENHER. *See* Empresa Nacional Hidro-Electrica del Ribagorzana.
ENI. *See* Ente Nazionale Idrocarburi.
ENI S.p.A., **34** 75
ENIEPSA, **IV** 528
Enimont, **IV** 422, 525
Ennia, **III** 177, 179, 310
Ennis Business Forms, Inc., 21 215–17
Eno Proprietaries, **III** 65
Enocell Oy, **IV** 277
The Enoch F. Bills Co., **25** 365
Enogex, Inc., **6** 539–40
Enova Corporation. *See* Sempra Energy.
ENPAC Corporation, **18** 162
Enpetrol, **IV** 528
Enquirer/Star Group, Inc., 10 287–88; 12 358. *See also* American Media, Inc.
Enrich International, Inc., 33 145–48; 37 340, 342
Enron Corporation, III 197; **V** 609–10; **6** 457, 593; **18** 365; **19 139–41**, 162, 487; **27** 266; **34** 82
Enseco, **III** 684
Enserch Corp., V 611–13
Ensidesa, **I** 460
Ensign Oil Company, **9** 490
Enskilda S.A., **II** 352–53
Enso-Gutzeit Oy, IV 274–77; 17 539. *See also* Stora Enso Oyj
ENSTAR Corporation, **IV** 567; **11** 441
Enstar Group Inc., **13** 299
Ensys Environmental Products, Inc., **10** 107
ENTASA, **IV** 528
Ente Gestione Aziende Minerarie, **I** 466
Ente Nazionale di Energia Elettrica, **I** 466
Ente Nazionale Idrocarburi, I 369; **IV** 412, **419–22**, 424, 453, 466, 470, 486, 546; **V** 614–17
Ente Nazionale per l'Energia Elettrica, V 614–17
Entenmann's Bakery, **I** 246, 712; **10** 551; **35** 415; **38** 364
Entergy Corp., V 618–20; 6 496–97
Enterprise Development Company, **15** 413
Enterprise Electronics Corporation, **18** 513–15
Enterprise Federal Savings & Loan, **21** 524
Enterprise Integration Technologies, **18** 541
Enterprise Leasing, 6 392–93
Enterprise Metals Pty. Ltd., **IV** 61
Enterprise Oil plc, 11 97–99
Enterprise Rent-A-Car, Inc., **16** 380; **33** 192
Enterra Corp., **25** 546
Entertainment Publications, **16** 146
Entertainment UK, **24** 266, 269
Entertainment Zone, Inc., **15** 212
Entex Information Services, **24** 29
Entity Software, **11** 469
Entrada Industries Incorporated, **6** 568–69; **26** 387
Entravision Communications Corporation, 41 150–52
Entré Computer Centers, **6** 243–44; **13** 175
Entremont, **I** 676
Entreprise de Recherches et d'Activités Pétrolières, **IV** 453, 467, 544, 560; **7** 481, 483–84
Entreprise Nationale Sonatrach, IV 423–25; V 626, 692; **10** 83–84; **12** 145
Entrex, Inc., **III** 154
Entrust Financial Corp., **16** 347
Envergure, **27** 421
Envirex, **11** 361
Envirodrill Services, Inc., **19** 247
Envirodyne Industries, Inc., 17 157–60
EnviroLease, Inc., **25** 171
ENVIRON International Corporation, **10** 106
Environmental Defense Fund, **9** 305
Environmental Industries, Inc., 31 182–85
Environmental Planning & Research. *See* CRSS Inc.
Environmental Research and Technology, Inc., **23** 135
Environmental Systems Corporation, **9** 109
Environmental Testing and Certification Corporation, **10** 106–07
Environmentals Incorporated. *See* Angelica Corporation.
Enviroscicnces Pty. Ltd., **16** 260
Envision Corporation, **24** 96
Enwright Environmental Consulting Laboratories, **9** 110
Enzafruit Worldwide, **38** 202
Enzo Biochem, Inc., 41 153–55
Enzyme Bio-Systems, Ltd., **21** 386
Enzyme Technologies Corp., **I** 342; **14** 217
Eon Productions, **II** 147; **25** 328
Eon Systems, **III** 143; **6** 238; **38** 409
l'Epargne, **12** 152
EPE Technologies, **18** 473
EPI Group Limited, **26** 137
Les Epiceries Presto Limitée, **II** 651
Epiphone, **16** 238–39
Epoch Systems Inc., **9** 140; **12** 149
ePOWER International, **33** 3, 6
Eppler, Guerin & Turner, Inc., **III** 330
Eppley, **III** 99
Epsilon Trading Corporation, **6** 81
Epson, **18** 386–87, 435
Equator Bank, **II** 298
EQUICOR-Equitable HCA Corp., **III** 80, 226
Equicor Group Ltd., **29** 343
Equifax, Inc., 6 23–25; 25 182, 358; **28 117–21 (upd.)**
Equilink Licensing Group, **22** 458
Equilon Enterprises LLC, **41** 359, 395
EquiStar Hotel Investors L.P. *See* CapStar Hotel Co.
Equitable Bancorporation, **12** 329
Equitable Equipment Company, **7** 540
Equitable Life Assurance Society of the United States, II 330; **III** 80, 229, 237, **247–49**, 274, 289, 291, 305–06, 316, 329, 359; **IV** 171, 576, 711; **6** 23; **13** 539; **19** 324, 511; **22** 188–90; **23** 370, 482; **27** 46
Equitable Resources, Inc., 6 492–94
Equitable Trust Co., **II** 247, 397; **10** 61
Equitas, **22** 315
Equitec Financial Group, **11** 483
Equitex Inc., **16** 431
Equity & Law, **III** 211
Equity Corp. Tasman, **III** 735

Equity Corporation, **6** 599; **37** 67–68
Equity Group Investment, Inc., **22** 339
Equity Marketing, Inc., **26 136–38**
Equity Title Services Company, **13** 348
Equivalent Company, **12** 421
Equus Capital Corp., **23** 65
Equus II Inc., **18** 11
Eramet, **IV** 108
ERAP. *See* Entreprise de Recherches et d'Activités Pétrolières.
Erasco Group, **II** 556; **26** 58
EraSoft Technologies, **27** 492
Ercea, **41** 128–29
ERCO Systems Group, **16** 461–63
ERDA Inc., **36** 160
Erdal, **II** 572
Erdölsproduktions-Gesellschaft AG, **IV** 485
Erftwerk AG, **IV** 229
Ericson Yachts, **10** 215
Ericssan, AB, **11** 501
Ericsson, **9** 32–33; **11** 196; **17** 33, 353; **18** 74. *See also* L.M. Ericsson.
Eridania Béghin-Say S.A., **14** 17, 19; **36 185–88**
Erie and Pennyslvania, **I** 584
Erie County Bank, **9** 474
Erie Indemnity Company, **35 167–69**
Erie Railroad, **I** 584; **II** 329; **IV** 180
Erie Scientific Company, **14** 479–80
Eritsusha, **IV** 326
erizon, **36** 264
ERKA. *See* Reichs Kredit-Gesellschaft mbH.
ERLY Industries Inc., **17 161–62**; **33** 30–31
Ernest Oppenheimer and Sons, **IV** 21, 79
Ernst & Young, **I** 412; **9 198–200**, 309, 311; **10** 115; **25** 358; **29 174–77 (upd.)**, 236, 392
Ernst, Homans, Ware & Keelips, **37** 224
Erol's, **9** 74; **11** 556
ERPI, **7** 167
Ersco Corporation, **17** 310; **24** 160
Erste Allgemeine, **III** 207–08
The Ertl Company, **37** 318
Erving Distributor Products Co., **IV** 282; **9** 260
Erving Healthcare, **13** 150
Erwin Wasey & Co., **I** 17, 22
Erzbergbau Salzgitter AG, **IV** 201
ES&A. *See* English, Scottish and Australian Bank Ltd.
Esanda, **II** 189
Esaote Biomedica, **29** 298
ESB Inc., **IV** 112; **18** 488
Esbjerg Thermoplast, **9** 92
Escada AG, **14** 467
Escalade, Incorporated, **19 142–44**
Escambia Chemicals, **I** 298
Escan, **22** 354
Escanaba Paper Co., **IV** 311; **19** 266
Escaut et Meuse, **IV** 227
Escher Wyss, **III** 539, 632
Eschweiler Bergwerks-Verein AG, **IV** 25–26, 193
ESCO Electronics Corporation, **17** 246, 248; **24** 425
Esco Trading, **10** 482
Escoffier Ltd., **I** 259
Escotel Mobile Communications, **18** 180
Esdon de Castro, **8** 137
ESE Sports Co. Ltd., **V** 376; **26** 397
ESGM. *See* Elder Smith Goldsbrough Mort.
ESI Energy, Inc., **V** 623–24
Eskay Screw Corporation, **11** 536
Eskilstuna Separator, **III** 419
Eskimo Pie Corporation, **21 218–20**; **35** 119, 121
Esmark, Inc., **I** 441; **II** 448, 468–69; **6** 357; **12** 93; **13** 448; **15** 357; **19** 290; **22** 55, 513
Esperance-Longdoz, **IV** 51–52
Espírito Santo. *See* Banco Espírito Santo e Comercial de Lisboa S.A.
ESPN Inc., **II** 131; **IV** 627; **19** 201, 204; **24** 516
Esporta plc, **35 170–72**
Esprit de Corp., **8 169–72**; **29 178–82 (upd.)**
La Espuela Oil Company, Ltd., **IV** 81–82; **7** 186
Esquire Education Group, **12** 173
Esquire Inc., **I** 453; **IV** 672; **13** 178; **19** 405
ESS Technology, Inc., **22 196–98**
Essanelle Salon Co., **18** 455
Essantee Theatres, Inc., **14** 86
Essef Corporation, **18 161–63**
Esselte Pendaflex Corporation, **11 100–01**
Essence Communications, Inc., **24 153–55**
Essener Reisebüro, **II** 164
Essex International Ltd., **19** 452
Essex Outfitters Inc., **9** 394; **42** 268–69
Essilor International, **18** 392; **21 221–23**; **40** 96–98
Esso Petroleum, **I** 52; **II** 628; **III** 673; **IV** 46, 276, 397, 421, 423, 432–33, 439, 441, 454, 470, 484, 486, 517–19, 531, 555, 563; **7** 140, 171; **11** 97; **13** 558; **22** 106; **24** 86; **25** 229, 231–32. *See also* Imperial Oil Limited *and* Standard Oil Company of New Jersey.
Essroc Corporation, **40** 108
Estat Telecom Group plc, **31** 180
Estech, Inc., **19** 290
Estee Corp., **27** 197; **43** 218
The Estée Lauder Companies Inc., **30 187–91 (upd.)**
Estée Lauder Inc., **I** 696; **III** 56; **8** 131; **9 201–04**; **11** 41; **24** 55
Estel N.V., **IV** 105, 133
Esterline Technologies Corp., **15 155–57**
Eston Chemical, **6** 148
Estronicks, Inc., **19** 290
ETA Systems, Inc., **10** 256–57
Etablissement Mesnel, **I** 202
Etablissement Poulenc-Frères, **I** 388
Etablissements Badin-Defforey, **19** 98
Etablissements Braud. *See* Manitou BF S.A.
Etablissements Economiques du Casino Guichard, Perrachon et ie, S.C.A., **12 152–54**; **16** 452
Etablissements Pierre Lemonnier S.A., **II** 532
Etablissements Robert Ouvrie S.A., **22** 436
Etam, **35** 308
Eteq Microsystems, **9** 116
Ethan Allen Interiors, Inc., **III** 530–31; **10** 184; **12** 307; **12 155–57**; **39 145–48 (upd.)**, **39** 173–74
Ethical Personal Care Products, Ltd., **17** 108
Ethicon, Inc., **III** 35; **8** 281; **10** 213; **23 188–90**
Ethyl Corp., **I 334–36**, 342; **IV** 289; **10 289–91 (upd.)**; **14** 217
Etienne Aigner, **14** 224
Etimex Kunstoffwerke GmbH, **7** 141
Etkin Skanska, **38** 437
L'Etoile, **II** 139
Etos, **II** 641
EToys, Inc., **37 128–30**
ETPM Entrêpose, **IV** 468
ETS. *See* Educational Testing Service.
Euclid, **I** 147; **12** 90
Euclid Chemical Co., **8** 455–56
Euclid Crane & Hoist Co., **13** 385
Euralux, **III** 209
Eurasbank, **II** 279–80; **14** 169
The Eureka Company, **III** 478, 480; **12 158–60**; **15** 416; **22** 26. *See also* White Consolidated Industries Inc.
Eureka Insurance Co., **III** 343
Eureka Specialty Printing, **IV** 253; **17** 30
Eureka Technology, **18** 20; **43** 17
Eureka Tent & Awning Co., **III** 59
Eureka X-Ray Tube, Inc., **10** 272
Eurex, **41** 84, 87
Euris, **22** 365
Euro Disneyland SCA, **6** 174, 176; **20 209–12**
Euro-Pacific Finance, **II** 389
Euro RSCG Worldwide S.A., **10** 345, 347; **13 203–05**; **16** 168; **33** 181
Eurobel, **II** 139; **III** 200; **24** 193
Eurobrokers Investment Corp., **II** 457
Eurocan Pulp & Paper Co. Ltd., **III** 648; **IV** 276, 300
Eurocard France, **II** 265
Eurocom S.A. *See* Euro RSCG Worldwide S.A.
Eurocopter SA, **7** 9, 11; **21** 8
EuroDollar Rent A Car. *See* Republic Industries, Inc.
Eurofighter Jagdflugzeug GmbH, **24** 84
Eurofilter Airfilters Ltd., **17** 106
Eurogroup, **V** 65
Euroimpex, **18** 163
Euromarché SA, **10** 205; **19** 308–09; **23** 231; **27** 94–95
Euromarket Designs Inc., **9** 144; **31 186–189 (upd.)**; **34** 324, 327
Euromissile Dynamics Group, **7** 9; **24** 84
Euromoney Publications, **19** 118, 120
Euronda, **IV** 296; **19** 226
Euronext Paris S.A., **37 131–33**
Euronova S.R.L., **15** 340
Europa Discount Sud-Ouest, **23** 248
Europa Metalli, **IV** 174
Europaischen Tanklager- und Transport AG, **7** 141
Europate, S.A., **36** 162–63
Europcar Chauffeur Drive U.K. International, **26** 62
Europcar International Corporation, Limited, **25** 142, 144, **27** 9, 11
Europcar Interrent, **10** 419
Europe Computer Systems. *See* ECS S.A.
Europe Craft Imports, Inc., **16** 37
European Aeronautic Defence and Space Company, **34** 128, 135
European-American Bank & Trust Company, **14** 169
European-American Banking Corp., **II** 279, 295
European and African Investments Ltd., **IV** 21
European Banking Co., **II** 186

European Banks' International Co., **II** 184–86, 295
European Coal and Steel, **II** 402
European Gas Turbines, **13** 356
European Investment Bank, **6** 97
European Periodicals, Publicity and Advertising Corp., **IV** 641; **7** 311
European Petroleum Co., **IV** 562
European Retail Alliance (ERA), **12** 152–53
European Silicon Structures, **17** 34
European Software Company, **25** 87
Europeia, **III** 403
Europemballage, **I** 600
Europene du Zirconium (Cezus), **21** 491
Europensiones, **III** 348
Europoligrafico SpA, **41** 326
Eurosar S.A., **25** 455
Eurotec, **IV** 128
Eurotech BV, **25** 101
Eurotechnique, **III** 678; **16** 122
Eurotunnel Group, 37 134–38 (upd.)
Eurotunnel PLC, 13 206–08
Eurovida, **III** 348
Euthenics Systems Corp., **14** 334
EVA Airways Corporation, **13** 211
Evaluation Associates, Inc., **III** 306
Evan Picone, **III** 55
Evans, **V** 21
Evans & Sutherland Computer Corporation, 19 145–49
Evans-Aristocrat Industries, **III** 570; **20** 361
Evans, Inc., 30 192–94
Evans Products Co., **13** 249–50, 550
Evans Rents, **26** 101
Evansville Veneer and Lumber Co., **12** 296
Eve of Roma, **III** 28
Evelyn Haddon, **IV** 91
Evelyn Wood, Inc., **7** 165, 168
Evence Coppée, **III** 704–05
Evenflo Companies, Inc., **19** 144
Evening News Association, **IV** 612; **7** 191
Ever Ready Label Corp., **IV** 253; **17** 30
Ever Ready Ltd., **7** 209; **9** 179–80; **30** 231
Everan Capital Corp., **15** 257
Everest & Jennings, **11** 200
Everett Pulp & Paper Company, **17** 440
Everex Systems, Inc., 12 162; **16 194–96**
Everfresh Beverages Inc., **26** 326
Evergenius, **13** 210
Evergreen Healthcare, Inc., **14** 210
Evergreen Marine Corporation Taiwan Ltd., 13 209–11
Evergreen Media Corporation, **24** 106
Evergreen Resources, Inc., **11** 28
Everlaurel, **13** 210
Everready Battery Co., **13** 433; **39** 338
Eversharp, **III** 28
Everyday Learning Corporation, **22** 519, 522
Everything for the Office, **22** 154
Everything Yogurt, **25** 180
Everything's A Dollar Inc. (EAD), **13** 541–43
EVI, Inc., **39** 416
Evian, **6** 47, 49
Evinrude-ELTO, **III** 597
Evinrude Motor Co., **III** 597–99
Evinrude Outboard Motor Company, **27** 75
Ewell Industries, **III** 739
Ewo Breweries, **I** 469; **20** 311
Ex-Cell-O Corp., **IV** 297
Ex-Lax Inc., **15** 138–39
Exabyte Corporation, 12 161–63; **26** 256; **40 178–81 (upd.)**
Exacta, **III** 122
Exar Corp., 14 182–84
Exatec A/S, **10** 113
Exbud, **38** 437
Excaliber, **6** 205
EXCEL Communications Inc., 18 164–67
Excel Corporation, **11** 92–93; **13** 138, 351
Excel Mining Systems, Inc., **13** 98
Excelsior Life Insurance Co., **III** 182; **21** 14
Excelsior Printing Company, **26** 105
Excerpta Medica International, **IV** 610
Exchange & Discount Bank, **II** 318; **17** 323
Exchange Bank of Yarmouth, **II** 210
Exchange Oil & Gas Corp., **IV** 282; **9** 260
Excite, Inc., **22** 519; **27** 517. *See also* At Home Corporation.
Exco International, **10** 277
Execu-Fit Health Programs, **11** 379
Executive Aircraft Services, **27** 21
Executive Airlines, Inc., **28** 22
Executive Fund Life Insurance Company, **27** 47
Executive Gallery, Inc., **12** 264
Executive Income Life Insurance Co., **10** 246
Executive Jet, Inc., 36 189–91; **42** 35
Executive Life Insurance Co., **III** 253–55; **11** 483
Executive Risk Inc., **37** 86
Executive Systems, Inc., **11** 18
Executone Information Systems, Inc., 13 212–14; **15** 195
ExecuTrain. *See* International Data Group, Inc.
Executrans, Inc., **21** 96
Exel Logistics Ltd., **6** 412, 414
Exel Ltd., **13** 150
Exeter & Hampton Electric Company, **37** 406
Exeter Oil Co., **IV** 550
Exide Electronics Group, Inc., 9 10; **20 213–15**; **24** 29
Exmark Manufacturing Company, Inc., **26** 494
Exors. of James Mills, **III** 493
Exp@nets, **37** 280, 283
Expeditors International of Washington Inc., 17 163–65
Expercom, **6** 303
Experian Inc., **28** 120
Experience, **III** 359
Exploitasi Tambang Minyak Sumatra Utara, **IV** 492
Explorer Motor Home Corp., **16** 296
Explosive Fabricators Corp., **III** 643
Export & Domestic Can Co., **15** 127
Export-Import Bank, **IV** 33, 184
Express Airlines, Inc., **28** 266
Express Baggage Reclaim Services Limited, **27** 21
Express Foods Inc, **I** 247–48
Express Newspapers plc, **IV** 687; **28** 503
Express Rent-a-Tire, Ltd., **20** 113
Express Scripts Incorporated, 17 166–68
Expression Homes, **22** 205, 207
Extel Corp., **II** 142; **III** 269–70
Extel Financial Ltd., **IV** 687
Extended Stay America, Inc., 41 156–58
Extendicare Health Services, Inc., III 81; **6 181–83**
Extracorporeal Medical Specialties, **III** 36
Extron International Inc., **16** 538; **43** 33
Exx Inc., **40** 334
Exxon Corporation, I 16–17, 360, 364; **II** 16, 62, 431, 451; **IV** 171, 363, 365, 403, 406, **426–30**, 431–33, 437–38, 454, 466, 506, 508, 512, 515, 522, 537–39, 554; **V** 605; **7 169–73 (upd.)**, 230, 538, 559; **9** 440–41; **11** 353; **14** 24–25, 291, 494; **12** 348; **16** 489, 548; **20** 262; **23** 317; **25** 229–30; **26** 102, 369; **27** 217; **32 175–82 (upd.)**
Exxon Mobil Corporation, **40** 358
Eye Masters Ltd., **23** 329
Eyeful Home Co., **III** 758
Eyelab, **II** 560; **12** 411
EZ Paintr Corporation, **9** 374
EZCORP Inc., 43 159–61
EZPor Corporation, **12** 377

F. & F. Koenigkramer Company, **10** 272
F&G International Insurance, **III** 397
F. & J. Heinz, **II** 507
F & J Meat Packers, Inc., **22** 548–49
F & M Distributors, **12** 132
F. & M. Schaefer Brewing Corporation, **I** 253, 291, **III** 137; **18** 500
F & M Scientific Corp., **III** 142; **6** 237
F & R Builders, Inc., **11** 257
F.A. Computer Technologies, Inc., **12** 60
F.A. Ensign Company, **6** 38
F.A.I. Insurances, **III** 729
F.A.O. Schwarz, **I** 548
F. Atkins & Co., **I** 604
F.B. McFarren, Ltd., **21** 499–500
F.E. Compton Company, **7** 167
F. Egger Co., **22** 49
F.F. Dalley Co., **II** 497
F.F. Publishing and Broadsystem Ltd., **IV** 652; **7** 392
F.H. Tomkins Buckle Company Ltd., **11** 525
F. Hoffmann-La Roche & Co. A.G., I 637, 640, **642–44**, 657, 685, 693, 710; **7** 427; **9** 264; **10** 80, 549; **11** 424–25; **14** 406; **32** 211–12
F.J. Walker Ltd., **I** 438
F.K.I. Babcock, **III** 466
F. Kanematsu & Co., Ltd. *See* Kanematsu Corporation.
F.L. Industries Inc., **I** 481, 483
F.L. Moseley Co., **III** 142; **6** 237
F.N. Burt Co., **IV** 644
F. Perkins, **III** 651–52
F.S. Smithers, **II** 445; **22** 405
F.W. Dodge Corp., **IV** 636–37
F.W. Means & Company, **11** 337
F.W. Sickles Company, **10** 319
F.W. Williams Holdings, **III** 728
F.W. Woolworth & Co. Ltd. *See* Kingfisher plc.
F.W. Woolworth Co. *See* Woolworth Corporation.
F.X. Matt Brewing Co., **18** 72
Fab-Asia, Inc., **22** 354–55
Fab Industries, Inc., 27 142–44
Fab 9, **26** 431
Fabbrica D' Armi Pietro Beretta S.p.A., 39 149–51
Fabco Automotive Corp., **23** 306; **27** 203
Fabergé, Inc., **II** 590; **III** 48; **8** 168, 344; **11** 90; **32** 475

Fabri-Centers of America Inc., 15 329; **16 197–99; 18** 223; **43** 291
Fabrica de Cemento El Melan, **III** 671
Facchin Foods Co., **I** 457
Facit, **III** 480; **22** 26
Facom S.A., 32 183–85; 37 143, 145
Facts on File, Inc., **14** 96–97; **22** 443
Fafnir Bearing Company, **13** 523
FAG Kugelfischer, **11** 84
Fagersta, **II** 366; **IV** 203
Fahr AG, **III** 543
Fahrzeugwerke Eisenach, **I** 138
FAI, **III** 545–46
Failsafe, **14** 35
Fair, Isaac and Company, 18 168–71, 516, 518
Fairbanks Morse Co., **I** 158, 434–35; **10** 292; **12** 71
Fairchild Aircraft, Inc., 9 205–08, 460; **11** 278
Fairchild Camera and Instrument Corp., **II** 50, 63; **III** 110, 141, 455, 618; **6** 261–62; **7** 531; **10** 108; **11** 503; **13** 323–24; **14** 14; **17** 418; **21** 122, 330; **26** 327
Fairchild Communications Service, **8** 328
The Fairchild Corporation, **37** 30
Fairchild Industries, **I** 71, 198; **11** 438; **14** 43; **15** 195; **34** 117
Fairchild Semiconductor Corporation, **II** 44–45, 63–65; **III** 115; **6** 215, 247; **10** 365–66; **16** 332; **24** 235; **41** 201
Fairclough Construction Group plc, I 567–68
Fairey Industries Ltd., **IV** 659
Fairfax, **IV** 650
Fairfield Communities, Inc., 36 192–95
The Fairfield Group, **33** 259–60
Fairfield Manufacturing Co., **14** 43
Fairfield Publishing, **13** 165
Fairmont Foods Co., **7** 430; **15** 139
Fairmont Insurance Co., **26** 487
Fairmount Glass Company, **8** 267
Fairport Machine Shop, Inc., **17** 357
Fairway Marketing Group, Inc., **24** 394
Fairway Outdoor Advertising, Inc., **36** 340, 342
Faiveley S.A., 39 152–54
Falcon Oil Co., **IV** 396
Falcon Products, Inc., 33 149–51
Falcon Seaboard Inc., **II** 86; **IV** 410; **7** 309
Falconbridge, Ltd., **IV** 165–66
Falconbridge Nickel Mines Ltd., **IV** 111
Falconet Corp., **I** 45
Falley's, Inc., **17** 558, 560–61
Fallon McElligott Inc., 22 199–201
Falls Financial Inc., **13** 223; **31** 206
Falls National Bank of Niagara Falls, **11** 108
Falls Rubber Company, **8** 126
FAME Plastics, Inc., **18** 162
Family Bookstores, **24** 548
Family Channel. *See* International Family Entertainment Inc.
Family Dollar Stores, Inc., 13 215–17
Family Golf Centers, Inc., 29 183–85
Family Health Program, **6** 184
Family Life Insurance Co., **II** 425; **13** 341
Family Mart Group, **V** 188; **36** 418, 420
Family Restaurants, Inc., **14** 194
Family Steak Houses of Florida, Inc., **15** 420
Famosa Bakery, **II** 543
Famous Amos Chocolate Chip Cookie Corporation, **27** 332
Famous Atlantic Fish Company, **20** 5
Famous Dave's of America, Inc., 40 182–84 4
Famous Players-Lasky Corp., **I** 451; **II** 154; **6** 161–62; **23** 123
Famous Restaurants Inc., **33** 139–40
FAN, **13** 370
Fancom Holding B.V., **43** 130
Fannie Mae. *See* Federal National Mortgage Association.
Fannie May Candy Shops Inc., **36** 309
Fansteel Inc., 19 150–52
Fantastic Sam's, **26** 476
Fantle's Drug Stores, **16** 160
Fantus Co., **IV** 605
Fanuc Ltd., III 482–83; 17 172–74 (upd.)
Fanzz, **29** 282
Faprena, **25** 85
Far East Airlines, **6** 70
Far East Machinery Co., **III** 581
Far Eastern Air Transport, Inc., **23** 380
Far West Restaurants, **I** 547
Faraday National Corporation, **10** 269
Farah Incorporated, 24 156–58
Farben. *See* I.G. Farbenindustrie AG.
Farbenfabriken Bayer A.G., **I** 309
Farberware, Inc., **27** 287–88
Farbwerke Hoechst A.G., **I** 346–47; **IV** 486; **13** 262
Farine Lactée Henri Nestlé, **II** 545
Farinon Corp., **II** 38
Farley Candy Co., **15** 190
Farley Industries, **25** 166
Farley Northwest Industries Inc., I 440–41
Farm Credit Bank of St. Louis, **8** 489
Farm Credit Bank of St. Paul, **8** 489–90
Farm Electric Services Ltd., **6** 586
Farm Family Holdings, Inc., 39 155–58
Farm Fresh Foods, **25** 332
Farm Journal Corporation, 42 131–34
Farm Power Laboratory, **6** 565
Farmer Jack, **16** 247
Farmers and Mechanics Bank of Georgetown, **13** 439
Farmers and Merchants Bank, **II** 349
Farmers Bank of Delaware, **II** 315–16
Farmers Insurance Group of Companies, 23 286; **25 154–56; 29** 397
Farmers' Loan and Trust Co., **II** 254; **9** 124
Farmers National Bank & Trust Co., **9** 474
Farmers Regional Cooperative, **II** 536
Farmland Foods, Inc., IV 474; **7** 17, **7 174–75**
Farmland Industries, Inc., **39** 282
Farnam Cheshire Lime Co., **III** 763
Farrar, Straus and Giroux Inc., 15 158–60; 35 451
FASC. *See* First Analysis Securities Corporation.
Fasco Consumer Products, **19** 360
Fasco Industries, **III** 509; **13** 369
Faserwerke Hüls GmbH., **I** 350
Fashion Bar, Inc., **24** 457
Fashion Bug, **8** 97
Fashion Co., **II** 503; **10** 324
Fasquelle, **IV** 618
Fasson. *See* Avery Dennison Corporation.
Fast Air, **31** 305
Fast Fare, **7** 102
Fastenal Company, 14 185–87; 42 135–38 (upd.)
Fata European Group, **IV** 187; **19** 348
Fateco Förlag, **14** 556
FATS, Inc., **27** 156, 158
Fatum, **III** 308
Faugere et Jutheau, **III** 283
Faulkner, Dawkins & Sullivan, **II** 450
Fauquet, **25** 85
Favorite Plastics, **19** 414
Fawcett Books, **13** 429
Fay's Inc., 17 175–77
Fayette Tubular Products, **7** 116–17
Fayva, **13** 359–61
Fazoli's Systems, Inc., 13 321; **27 145–47**
FB&T Corporation, **14** 154
FBC. *See* First Boston Corp.
FBO. *See* Film Booking Office of America.
FC Holdings, Inc., **26** 363
FCBC, **IV** 174
FCC. *See* Federal Communications Commission.
FCC National Bank, **II** 286
FCI. *See* Framatome SA.
FDIC. *See* Federal Deposit Insurance Corp.
Fearn International, **II** 525; **13** 293
Feather Fine, **27** 361
Featherlite Inc., 28 127–29
Feature Enterprises Inc., **19** 452
Fechheimer Bros. Co., **III** 215; **18** 60, 62
Fedders Corporation, 18 172–75; 43 162–67 (upd.)
Federal Barge Lines, **6** 487
Federal Bearing and Bushing, **I** 158–59
Federal Bicycle Corporation of America, **11** 3
Federal Cartridge, **26** 363
Federal Coca-Cola Bottling Co., **10** 222
Federal Communications Commission, **6** 164–65; **9** 321
Federal Deposit Insurance Corp., **II** 261–62, 285, 337; **12** 30, 79
Federal Electric, **I** 463; **III** 653
Federal Express Corporation, II 620; **V 451–53; 6** 345–46, 385–86, 389; **12** 180, 192; **13** 19; **14** 517; **17** 504–05; **18** 315–17, 368, 370; **24** 22, 133; **25** 148; **26** 441; **27** 20, 22, 471, 475; **34** 15, 17; **39** 33, 35; **41** 245–47. *See also* FedEx Corporation.
Federal Home Life Insurance Co., **III** 263; **IV** 623
Federal Home Loan Bank, **II** 182
Federal Home Loan Mortgage Corp., **18** 168; **25** 427
Federal Insurance Co., **III** 220–21; **14** 108–109; **37** 83–85
Federal Lead Co., **IV** 32
Federal Light and Traction Company, **6** 561–62
Federal Mining and Smelting Co., **IV** 32
Federal-Mogul Corporation, I 158–60; III 596; **10 292–94 (upd.); 26 139–43 (upd.)**
Federal National Mortgage Association, II 410–11; 18 168; **25** 427
Federal Pacific Electric, **II** 121; **9** 440
Federal Packaging and Partition Co., **8** 476
Federal Packaging Corp., **19** 78
Federal Paper Board Company, Inc., I 524; **8 173–75; 15** 229
Federal Paper Mills, **IV** 248
Federal Power, **18** 473

Federal Prison Industries, Inc., 34 157–60
Federal Reserve Bank of New York, **21** 68
Federal Savings and Loan Insurance Corp., **16** 346
Federal Signal Corp., 10 295–97
Federal Steel Co., **II** 330; **IV** 572; **7** 549
Federal Trade Commission, **6** 260; **9** 370
Federal Yeast Corp., **IV** 410
Federale Mynbou, **IV** 90–93
Federated Department Stores Inc., IV 703; **V** 25–28; **9 209–12**; **10** 282; **11** 349; **12** 37, 523; **13** 43, 260; **15** 88; **16** 61, 206; **17** 560; **18** 523; **22** 406; **23** 60; **27** 346–48; **30** 379; **31 190–194 (upd.)**; **35** 368; **36** 201, 204; **37** 13
Federated Development Company, **8** 349
Federated Metals Corp., **IV** 32
Federated Publications, **IV** 612; **7** 191
Federated Timbers, **I** 422
Fédération Internationale de Football Association, 27 148–51
Federation Nationale d'Achats des Cadres. *See* FNAC.
FedEx Corporation, 18 128, **176–79 (upd.)**, 535; **33** 20, 22; **34** 474; **42 139–44 (upd.)**
Fedmart, **V** 162
FEE Technology, **29** 461–62
Feed-Rite Controls, Inc., **16** 270
Feffer & Simons, **16** 46
Feikes & Sohn KG, **IV** 325
Feinblech-Contiglühe, **IV** 103
Felco. *See* Farmers Regional Cooperative.
Feld Entertainment, Inc., 32 186–89 (upd.)
Feldmühle Nobel AG, II 50–51; **III 692–95**; **IV** 142, 325, 337; **21** 330; **36** 449
Felixstowe Ltd., **18** 254
Fellowes Manufacturing Company, 28 130–32
Felten & Guilleaume, **IV** 25
Femsa, **19** 473. *See also* Formento Económico Mexicano, S.A. de C.V.
Femtech, **8** 513
Fendall Company, **40** 96, 98
Fendel Schiffahrts-Aktiengesellschaft, **6** 426
Fender Musical Instruments Company, 16 200–02; **43 168–72 (upd.)**
Fenestra Inc., **IV** 136
Fenicia Group, **22** 320
Fenn, Wright & Manson, **25** 121–22
Fenner & Beane, **II** 424
Fenton Hill American Limited, **29** 510
Fenwal Laboratories, **I** 627; **10** 141
Fenwick & West LLP, 34 161–63, 512
Ferembal S.A., **25** 512
Ferfin, **24** 341
Fergus Brush Electric Company, **18** 402
Ferguson Machine Co., **8** 135
Ferguson Manufacturing Company, **25** 164
Ferguson Radio Corp., **I** 531–32
Ferienreise GmbH., **II** 164
Fermec Manufacturing Limited, **40** 432
Fermentaciones Mexicanas, **III** 43
Fernando Roqué, **6** 404; **26** 243
Ferngas, **IV** 486
Ferolito, Vultaggio & Sons, 27 152–55
Ferranti Business Communications, **20** 75
Ferranti Ltd., **II** 81; **6** 240
Ferrari S.p.A., I 162; **11** 103; **13 218–20**; **36 196–200 (upd.)**
Ferrellgas Partners, L.P., 35 173–75
Ferrier Hodgson, **10** 170
Ferro Corporation, III 536; **8 176–79**; **9** 10; **26** 230
Ferro Engineering Co., **17** 357
Ferrovial. *See* Grupo Ferrovail
Ferroxcube Corp. of America, **13** 397
Ferrum Inc., **24** 144
Ferruzzi Agricola Finanziario, **I** 369; **7** 81–83
Ferruzzi Finanziaria S.p.A., **24** 341; **36** 186
Fesca, **III** 417–18
Fetzer Vineyards, **10** 182
FFI Fragrances. *See* Elizabeth Arden, Inc.
FHP International Corporation, 6 184–86; **17** 166, 168
Fianzas Monterrey, **19** 189
Fiat S.p.A., I 154, 157, **161–63**, 459–60, 466, 479; **II** 280; **III** 206, 543, 591; **IV** 420; **9** 10; **11 102–04 (upd.)**, 139; **13** 17, 27–29, 218–20; **16** 322; **17** 24; **22** 379–81; **36** 32–34, 196–97, 199, 240, 243
Fibamex, **17** 106
Fiber Chemical Corporation, **7** 308
Fiberglas Canada, **III** 722
Fiberite, Inc., **27** 117; **28** 195
FiberMark, Inc., 37 139–42
Fibermux Corporation, **10** 19; **30** 7
Fibic Corp., **18** 118
Fibre Containers, **IV** 249
Fibreboard Corporation, IV 304; **12** 318; **14** 110; **16 203–05**
FibreChem, Inc., **8** 347
Fibro Tambor, S.A. de C.V., **8** 476
Fichtel & Sachs AG, **III** 566; **14** 328; **38** 299
Fidata Corp., **II** 317
Fidelco Capital Group, **10** 420
Fidelio Software GmbH, **18** 335, 337
Fidelity and Casualty Co. of New York, **III** 242
Fidelity and Guaranty Life Insurance Co., **III** 396–97
Fidelity Exploration & Production Company, **42** 249, 253
Fidelity Federal Savings and Loan, **II** 420
Fidelity Fire Insurance Co., **III** 240
Fidelity Insurance of Canada, **III** 396–97
Fidelity Investments Inc., II 412–13; **III** 588; **8** 194; **9** 239; **14 188–90 (upd.)**; **18** 552; **19** 113; **21** 147; **22** 52. *See also* FMR Corp.
Fidelity Leasing Corporation, **42** 312–13
Fidelity Life Association, **III** 269
Fidelity Mutual Insurance Co., **III** 231
Fidelity National Life Insurance Co., **III** 191
Fidelity National Title, **19** 92
Fidelity Oil Group, **7** 324
Fidelity-Phenix Fire Insurance Co., **III** 240–42
Fidelity Title and Trust Co., **II** 315
Fidelity Trust Co., **II** 230; **33** 293
Fidelity Union Life Insurance Co., **III** 185
Fidenas Investment Ltd., **30** 185
Fides Holding, **21** 146
Field Corporation, **18** 355
Field Enterprises Educational Corporation, **16** 252; **26** 15; **43** 208
Field Enterprises, Inc., **IV** 672; **12** 554; **19** 404
Field Group plc, **30** 120
Field Limited Partnership, **22** 441
Field Oy, **10** 113
Fieldale Farms Corporation, 23 191–93; **25** 185–86
Fieldco Guide Dog Foundation, **42** 207
Fieldcrest Cannon, Inc., 8 32–33; **9 213–17**; **16** 535; **19** 276, 305; **31 195–200 (upd.)**; **41** 299–301
Fieldstone Cabinetry, **III** 571; **20** 362
Fielmann AG, 31 201–03
Fiesta Restaurants Inc., **33** 139–40
FIFA. *See* Fédération Internationale de Football Association.
Fifa International, **39** 58
Fifteen Oil, **I** 526
Fifth Generation Systems Inc., **10** 509
Fifth Third Bancorp, II 291; **9** 475; **11** 466; **13 221–23**; **31 204–208 (upd.)**
50-Off Stores, **23** 177. *See also* LOT$OFF Corporation.
Figgie International Inc., 7 176–78; **24** 403–04
Figi's Inc., **9** 218, 220
FII Limited, **38** 197
Fil-Mag Group, **29** 461
Fila Holding S.p.A., 20 216–18; **39** 60
Filene's, **V** 132, 134
Filene's Basement. *See* Value City Department Stores, Inc.
Filergie S.A., **15** 355
Filipacchi Medias S.A. *See* Hachette Filipacchi Medias S.A.
Filiz Lastex, S.A., **15** 386
Filles S.A. de C.V., **7** 115; **25** 126
Film Booking Office of America, **II** 88
Films for the Humanities, Inc., **22** 441
Filofax Inc., **41** 120, 123
Filter Queen-Canada, **17** 234
Filterfresh Corporation, **39** 409
Filtertek, Inc., **24** 425
Filtrol Corp., **IV** 123
Filtrona International Ltd., **31** 77
Filtros Baldwin de Mexico, **17** 106
Filtros Continental, **17** 106
Fimalac S.A., 37 143–45
Fimaser, **21** 101
Fimestic, **21** 101
Fin. Comit SpA, **II** 192
FINA, Inc., 7 179–81; **26** 368
Finalrealm Limited, **42** 404
Financial Computer Services, Inc., **11** 111
Financial Corp. of Indonesia, **II** 257
Financial Data Services, Inc., **11** 111
Financial Investment Corp. of Asia, **III** 197
Financial Network Marketing Company, **11** 482
Financial News Ltd., **IV** 658
Financial News Network, Inc., **25** 507; **31** 147
Financial Security Assurance Inc., **III** 765; **25** 497
Financial Services Corp., **III** 306–07
Financial Services Corporation of Michigan, **11** 163
Financial Systems, Inc., **11** 111
Financial Technologies International, **17** 497
Financiera Aceptaciones, **19** 189
Financière Crédit Suisse-First Boston, **II** 268, 402–04
Financiere de Suez, **II** 295
Financière Saint Dominique, **9** 151–52
FinansSkandic A.B., **II** 352–53

Finast. *See* First National Supermarkets, Inc.
Fincantieri, **I** 466–67
Find-A-Home Service, Inc., **21** 96
Findomestic, **21** 101
Findus, **II** 547; **25** 85
Fine Art Developments Ltd., **15** 340
Fine Fare, **II** 465, 609, 628–29
Fine Fragrances, **22** 213
Finelettrica, **I** 465–66
Finesco, LLC, **37** 200–01
Finevest Services Inc., **15** 526
Fingerhut Companies, Inc., **I** 613; **V** 148; **9 218–20**; **15** 401; **18** 133; **31** 190; **34** 232; **36 201–05 (upd.)**; **37** 130
Fininvest Group, **IV** 587–88
The Finish Line, Inc., **29 186–88**
FinishMaster, Inc., **17** 310–11; **24 159–61**
Finland Wood Co., **IV** 275
Finlay Enterprises, Inc., **16 206–08**
Finlay Forest Industries, **IV** 297
Finmare, **I** 465, 467
Finmeccanica S.p.A., **II** 86; **13** 28; **23** 83; **36** 34
Finnair Oy, **I** 120; **6 87–89**; **25 157–60 (upd.)**; **33** 50; **34** 398
Finnforest Oy, **IV** 316
Finnigan Corporation, **11** 513
Finnish Cable Works, **II** 69; **17** 352
Finnish Fiberboard Ltd., **IV** 302
Oy Finnish Peroxides Ab, **IV** 300
Finnish Rubber Works, **II** 69; **17** 352
Oy Finnlines Ltd., **IV** 276
Finsa, **II** 196
FinSer Capital Corporation, **17** 262
Finservizi SpA, **II** 192
Finsider, **I** 465–66; **IV** 125
Firan Motor Coach, Inc., **17** 83
Fire Association of Philadelphia, **III** 342–43
Firearms Training Systems, Inc., **27 156–58**
Fireman's Fund Insurance Company, **I** 418; **II** 398, 457; **III** 214, **250–52**, 263; **10** 62
Firemen's Insurance Co. of Newark, **III** 241–42
Firestone Tire and Rubber Co., **III** 440, 697; **V** 234–35; **8** 80; **9** 247; **15** 355; **17** 182; **18** 320; **20** 259–62; **21** 73–74
Firma Hamburger Kaffee-Import- Geschäft Emil Tengelmann. *See* Tengelmann Group.
The First, **10** 340
First Acadiana National Bank, **11** 107
First Albany Companies Inc., **37 146–48**
First Alert, Inc., **28 133–35**
First American Bank Corporation, **8** 188; **41** 178
First American Media, Inc., **24** 199
First American National Bank, **19** 378
First American National Bank-Eastern, **11** 111
First Analysis Securities Corporation, **22** 5
First and Merchants, **10** 426
First Atlanta Corporation, **16** 523
First Atlantic Capital, Ltd., **28** 340, 342
First Bancard, Inc., **11** 106
First BanCorporation, **13** 467
First Bank and Trust of Mechanicsburg, **II** 342
First Bank of Savannah, **16** 522
First Bank of the United States, **II** 213, 253
First Bank System Inc., **11** 130; **12 164–66**; **13** 347–48; **24** 393. *See also* U.S. Bancorp
First Boston Corp., **II** 208, 257, 267–69, 402–04, 406–07, 426, 434, 441; **9** 378, 386; **12** 439; **13** 152, 342; **21** 145–46. *See also* CSFB.
First Brands Corporation, **8 180–82**; **16** 44
First Capital Financial, **8** 229
First Carolina Investors Inc., **17** 357
First Chicago Corporation, **II 284–87**. *See also* Bank One Corporation.
First Chicago Venture Capital, **24** 516
First Choice Holidays PLC, **40 185–87**, 284–85
First Cincinnati, Inc., **41** 133
First City Bank of Rosemead, **II** 348
First Colony Farms, **II** 584
First Colony Life Insurance, **I** 334–35; **10** 290
First Commerce Bancshares, Inc., **15 161–63**
First Commerce Corporation, **11 105–07**
First Commercial Savings and Loan, **10** 340
First Consumers National Bank, **10** 491; **27** 429
First Dallas, Ltd., **II** 415
First Data Corporation, **10** 63; **18** 516–18, 537; **24** 393 **30 195–98 (upd.)**
First Data Management Company of Oklahoma City, **11** 112
First Delaware Life Insurance Co., **III** 254
First Deposit Corp., **III** 218–19
First Empire State Corporation, **11 108–10**
First Engine and Boiler Insurance Co. Ltd., **III** 406
First Executive Corporation, **III 253–55**
First Federal Savings & Loan Assoc., **IV** 343; **9** 173
First Federal Savings and Loan Association of Crisp County, **10** 92
First Federal Savings and Loan Association of Hamburg, **10** 91
First Federal Savings and Loan Association of Fort Myers, **9** 476
First Federal Savings and Loan Association of Kalamazoo, **9** 482
First Federal Savings Bank of Brunswick, **10** 92
First Fidelity Bank, N.A., New Jersey, **9 221–23**
First Fidelity Bank of Rockville, **13** 440
First Financial Insurance, **41** 178
First Financial Management Corporation, **11 111–13**; **18** 542; **25** 183; **30** 195
First Florida Banks, **9** 59
First Hawaiian, Inc., **11 114–16**
First Health, **III** 373
FIRST HEALTH Strategies, **11** 113
First Healthcare, **14** 242
First Heights, fsa, **8** 437
First Hospital Corp., **15** 122
First Industrial Corp., **II** 41
First Insurance Agency, Inc., **17** 527
First Insurance Co. of Hawaii, **III** 191, 242
First International Trust, **IV** 91
First Interstate Bancorp, **II** 228, **288–90**; **8** 295; **9** 334; **17** 546
First Investment Advisors, **11** 106
First Investors Management Corp., **11** 106
First Jersey National Bank, **II** 334
First Leisure Corporation plc. *See* Esporta plc.
First Liberty Financial Corporation, **11** 457
First Line Insurance Services, Inc., **8** 436
First Madison Bank, **14** 192
First Maryland Bancorp, **16** 14
First Mid America, **II** 445; **22** 406
First Mississippi Corporation, **8 183–86**. *See also* ChemFirst, Inc.
First Mississippi National, **14** 41
First National Bank, **10** 298; **13** 467
First National Bank (Revere), **II** 208
First National Bank and Trust Company, **22** 4
First National Bank and Trust Company of Kalamazoo, **8** 187–88
First National Bank and Trust of Oklahoma City, **II** 289
First National Bank in Albuquerque, **11** 119
First National Bank of Akron, **9** 475
First National Bank of Allentown, **11** 296
First National Bank of Atlanta, **16** 522
First National Bank of Azusa, **II** 382
First National Bank of Boston, **II** 207–08, 402; **12** 310; **13** 446
First National Bank of Carrollton, **9** 475
First National Bank of Chicago, **II** 242, 257, 284–87; **III** 96–97; **IV** 135–36
First National Bank of Commerce, **11** 106
First National Bank of Harrington, Delaware. *See* J.C. Penny National Bank.
First National Bank of Hartford, **13** 466
First National Bank of Hawaii, **11** 114
First National Bank of Highland, **11** 109
First National Bank of Houma, **21** 522
The First National Bank of Lafayette, **11** 107
The First National Bank of Lake Charles, **11** 107
First National Bank of Lake City, **II** 336; **10** 425
First National Bank of Mexico, New York, **II** 231
First National Bank of Minneapolis, **22** 426–27
First National Bank of New York, **II** 254, 330
First National Bank of Raleigh, **II** 336
First National Bank of Salt Lake, **11** 118
First National Bank of Seattle, **8** 469–70
First National Bank of York, **II** 317
First National Bankshares, Inc., **21** 524
First National Boston Corp., **II** 208
First National Casualty Co., **III** 203
First National City Bank, **9** 124; **16** 13
First National City Bank of New York, **II** 254; **9** 124
First National City Corp., **III** 220–21
First National Holding Corporation, **16** 522
First National Insurance Co., **III** 352
First National Life Insurance Co., **III** 218
First National Supermarkets, Inc., **II** 641–42; **9** 452
First Nationwide Bank, **8** 30; **14 191–93**
First Nationwide Financial Corp., **I** 167; **11** 139
First Nationwide Holdings Inc., **28** 246
First New England Bankshares Corp., **13** 467

First Nitrogen, Inc., **8** 184
First of America Bank Corporation, 8 187–89
First of America Bank-Monroe, **9** 476
First of Boston, **II** 402–03
First Omni Bank NA, **16** 14; **18** 518; **43** 8
First Pacific Company Limited, 18 180–82
First Penn-Pacific Life Insurance Co., **III** 276
First Physician Care, Inc., **36** 367
First Pick Stores, **12** 458
First Railroad and Banking Company, **11** 111
First Republic Bank of Texas, **II** 336
First Republic Corp., **III** 383; **14** 483
First RepublicBank Corporation, **II** 337; **10** 425–26
First Savings and Loan, **10** 339
First Seattle Dexter Horton National Bank, **8** 470
First Security Bank of Missoula, **35** 197–99
First Security Corporation, 11 117–19; 38 491
First Signature Bank and Trust Co., **III** 268
First Sport Ltd., **39** 60
1st State Bank & Trust, **9** 474
First State Bank Southwest Indiana, **41** 178–79
First SunAmerican Life Insurance Company, **11** 482
First Team Sports, Inc., 15 396–97; **22 202–04**
First Tennessee National Corporation, 11 120–21
First Texas Pharmaceuticals, **I** 678
First Trust and Savings Bank, **II** 284
First Trust Bank, **16** 14
First Union Corporation, 10 298–300; 24 482; **37** 148
First Union Trust and Savings Bank, **II** 284–85; **11** 126; **22** 52
First United Financial Services Inc., **II** 286
First USA, Inc., 11 122–24
First USA Paymentech, **24** 393
First Virginia Banks, Inc., 11 125–26
First Westchester National Bank of New Rochelle, **II** 236
First Western Bank and Trust Co., **II** 289
First Women's Bank of New York, **23** 3
First Worth Corporation, **19** 232
Firstamerica Bancorporation, **II** 288–89
Firstar Corporation, 11 127–29; 33 152–55 (upd.)
FirstBancorp., **13** 467
FirstGroup plc, **38** 321
FirstMiss, Inc., **8** 185
FirstPage USA Inc., **41** 265
Firth Carpet, **19** 275
Fischbach & Moore, **III** 535
Fischbach Corp., **III** 198; **8** 536–37
FISCOT, **10** 337
Fiserv Inc., 11 130–32; 33 156–60 (upd.)
Fisher & Company, **9** 16
Fisher Body Company, **I** 171; **10** 325
Fisher Broadcasting Co., **15** 164
Fisher-Camuto Corp., **14** 441
Fisher Companies, Inc., 15 164–66
Fisher Controls International, Inc., 13 224–26; 15 405, 407; **29** 330
Fisher Foods, Inc., **II** 602; **9** 451, 452; **13** 237; **41** 11, 13
Fisher Marine, **III** 444; **22** 116
Fisher Nut, **14** 275
Fisher-Price Inc., II 559–60; **12 167–69,** 410–11; **13** 317; **25** 314, 380; **32 190–94 (upd.); 34** 365
Fisher Scientific International Inc., III 511–12; **24 162–66; 25** 260
Fishers Agricultural Holdings, **II** 466
Fishers Nutrition, **II** 466
Fishers Seed and Grain, **II** 466
Fishery Department of Tamura Kisen Co., **II** 552
Fisk Telephone Systems, **6** 313
Fiskars Corporation, 33 161–64
Fisons plc, 9 224–27; 23 194–97 (upd.)
Fitch IBCA Inc., **37** 143, 145
Fitch Lovell PLC, **13** 103
Fitchburg Daily News Co., **IV** 581
Fitchburg Gas and Electric Light, **37** 406
Fitchell and Sachs, **III** 495
Fitel, **III** 491
Fitzsimmons Stores Inc., **16** 452
Fitzwilton Public Limited Company, **12** 529; **34** 496
Five Bros. Inc., **19** 456
Five Star Entertainment Inc., **28** 241
FKM Advertising, **27** 280
FL Industries Holdings, Inc., **11** 516
Flachglass A.G., **II** 474
Flagship Resources, **22** 495
Flagstar Companies, Inc., 10 301–03; 29 150. *See also* Advantica Restaurant Group, Inc.
Flair Corporation, **18** 467
Flair Fold, **25** 11
Flanagan McAdam Resources Inc., **IV** 76
Flapdoodles, **15** 291
Flashes Publishers, Inc., **36** 341
Flatbush Gas Co., **6** 455–56
Flatiron Mandolin Company, **16** 239
Flatow, Moore, Bryan, and Fairburn, **21** 33
Flavors Holdings Inc., **38** 294
Fleck Controls, Inc., **26** 361, 363
Fleer Corporation, 10 402; **13** 519; **15 167–69; 19** 386; **34** 447; **37** 295
Fleet Call, Inc., **10** 431–32
Fleet Financial Group, Inc., IV 687; **9 228–30; 12** 31; **13** 468; **18** 535; **38** 13, 393
Fleet Holdings, **28** 503
FleetBoston Financial Corporation, 36 206–14 (upd.)
Fleetway, **7** 244
Fleetwood Enterprises, Inc., III 484–85; 13 155; **17** 83; **21** 153; **22 205–08 (upd.); 33** 399
Fleischmann Co., **II** 544; **7** 367
Fleischmann Malting Co., **I** 420–21; **11** 22
Fleming Chinese Restaurants Inc., **37** 297
Fleming Companies, Inc., II 624–25, 671; **7** 450; **12** 107, 125; **13** 335–37; **17 178–81 (upd.); 18** 506–07; **23** 407; **24** 529; **26** 449; **28** 152, 154; **31** 25; **34** 198
Fleming Foodservice, **26** 504
Fleming Machine Co., **III** 435
Fleming-Wilson Co., **II** 624
Fletcher Challenge Ltd., III 687; **IV** 250, **278–80; 19 153–57 (upd.); 25** 12
Fleury Michon S.A., 39 159–61
Fleuve Noir, **IV** 614
Flex Elektrowerkzeuge GmbH, **26** 363
Flex Interim, **16** 421; **43** 308
Flex-O-Lite, **14** 325
Flexi-Van Corporations, **II** 492; **20** 118
Flexible Packaging, **I** 605
Flexsteel Industries Inc., 15 170–72; 41 159–62 (upd.)
Flextronics International Ltd., 12 451; **38 186–89**
Flexys, **16** 462
FLGI Holding Company, **10** 321
Flick Industrial Group, **II** 280, 283; **III** 692–95
Flight One Logistics, Inc., **22** 311
Flight Refuelling Limited. *See* Cobham plc.
Flight Transportation Co., **II** 408
FlightSafety International, Inc., 9 231–33; 29 189–92 (upd.)
Flint and Walling Water Systems, **III** 570; **20** 362
Flint Eaton & Co., **I** 627
Flint Ink Corporation, 13 227–29; 41 163–66 (upd.)
Flip Chip Technologies, LLC, **33** 248
Florafax International, Inc., **37** 162
Floral City Furniture Company, **14** 302–03
Flori Roberts, Inc., **11** 208
Florida Crystals Inc., 35 176–78
Florida Cypress Gardens, Inc., **IV** 623
Florida Distillers Company, **27** 479
Florida East Coast Railway Company, **8** 486–87; **12** 278
Florida Frozen Foods, **13** 244
Florida Gas Co., **15** 129
Florida Gas Transmission Company, **6** 578
Florida National Banks of Florida, Inc., **II** 252
Florida Panthers Hockey Club, Ltd., **37** 33, 35
Florida Presbyterian College, **9** 187
Florida Progress Corp., V 621–22; 23 198–200 (upd.)
Florida Rock Industries Inc., **23** 326
Florida Steel Corp., **14** 156
Florida Telephone Company, **6** 323
FloridaGulf Airlines, **11** 300
Florimex Verwaltungsgesellschaft mbH, **12** 109
Florists' Transworld Delivery, Inc., 28 136–38
Florsheim Shoe Group Inc., III 528–29; **9** 135, **234–36; 12** 308; **16** 546; **31 209–212 (upd.); 39** 170, 172, 174
Flow Laboratories, **14** 98
Flow Measurement, **26** 293
Flower Gate Inc., **I** 266; **21** 320
Flower Time, Inc., **12** 179, 200
Flowers Industries, Inc., 12 170–71; 35 179–82 (upd.). *See also* Keebler Foods Company.
Flowserve Corporation, 33 165–68
Floyd West & Co., **6** 290
Fluent, Inc., **29** 4–6
Fluf N'Stuf, Inc., **12** 425
Fluke Corporation, 15 173–75
Flunch, **37** 22
Fluor Corporation, I 569–71, 586; **III** 248; **IV** 171, 533, 535, 576; **6** 148–49; **8 190–93 (upd.); 12** 244; **26** 220, 433; **34 164–69 (upd.)**
Fluor Daniel Inc., **41** 148
The Fluorocarbon Company. *See* Furon Company.
Flushing Federal Savings & Loan Association, **16** 346
Flushing National Bank, **II** 230
Flying J Inc., 19 158–60

Flying Tiger Line, **V** 452; **6** 388; **25** 146; **39** 33
Flymo, **III** 478, 480; **22** 26
FMC Corp., **I 442–44**, 679; **II** 513; **11 133–35 (upd.)**; **14** 457; **22** 415; **30** 471
FMR Corp., **II** 412; **8 194–96**; **14** 188; **22** 413; **30** 331; **32 195–200 (upd.)**
FMXI, Inc. *See* Foamex International Inc.
FN Life Insurance Co., **III** 192
FN Manufacturing Co., **12** 71
FNAC, **21 224–26**; **26** 160
FNC Comercio, **III** 221
FNCB. *See* First National City Bank of New York.
FNMA. *See* Federal National Mortgage Association.
FNN. *See* Financial News Network.
Foamex International Inc., **17 182–85**; **26** 500
Focal Surgery, Inc., **27** 355
Focke-Wulf, **III** 641; **16** 7
Fodens Ltd., **I** 186
Fodor's Travel Guides, **13** 429
Fogdog Inc., **36** 347
Fokker. *See* N.V. Koninklijke Nederlandse Vliegtuigenfabriek Fokker.
Fokker Aircraft Corporation of America, **9** 16
Fokker-VFW, **I** 41–42; **12** 191
Foley & Lardner, **28 139–42**
Folgers, **III** 52
Folland Aircraft, **I** 50; **III** 508; **24** 85
Follett Corporation, **12 172–74**; **16** 47; **39 162–65 (upd.)**; **43** 61
Follis DeVito Verdi. *See* De Vito/Verdi.
Fomento de Valores, S.A. de C.V., **23** 170
Fomento Economico Mexicano, S.A. de C.V. *See* Femsa.
Fonda Group, **36** 462
Fondiaria Group, **III** 351
Fonditalia Management, **III** 347
Font & Vaamonde, **6** 27
Font Vella, **II** 474
FONTAC, **II** 73
Fontana Asphalt, **III** 674
Food City, **II** 649–50
Food Fair, **19** 480
Food 4 Less Supermarkets, Inc., **II** 624; **17** 558–61
Food Giant, **II** 670
Food Ingredients Technologies, **25** 367
Food Investments Ltd., **II** 465
Food King, **20** 306
Food Lion, Inc., **II 626–27**; **7** 450; **15 176–78 (upd.)**, 270; **18** 8; **21** 508; **33** 306
Food Machinery Corp. *See* FMC Corp.
Food Marketing Corp., **II** 668; **18** 504
Food Town Inc., **II** 626–27
Food World, **26** 46; **31** 372
Foodarama Supermarkets, Inc., **28 143–45**
FoodBrands America, Inc., **21** 290; **22** 510; **23 201–04**. *See also* Doskocil Companies, Inc.
FoodLand Distributors, **II** 625, 645, 682
Foodmaker, Inc., **II** 562; **13** 152, 426; **14 194–96**
Foodstuffs, **9** 144
Foodtown, **II** 626; **V** 35; **15** 177; **24** 528
FoodUSA.com, **43** 24
Foodways National, Inc., **12** 531; **13** 383
Foot Locker, **V** 226; **14** 293–95. *See also* Venator Group Inc.
Footaction. *See* Footstar, Incorporated.
Foote Cone & Belding Communications Inc., **I 12–15**, 28, 34; **11** 51; **13** 517; **22** 395; **25** 90–91. *See also* True North Communications Inc.
Foote Mineral Company, **7** 386–87
Footquarters, **14** 293, 295
Footstar, Incorporated, **24 167–69**
Forages et Exploitations Pétrolières. *See* Forex.
Forbes Inc., **30 199–201**
The Ford Foundation, **34 170–72**
Ford Motor Company, **I** 10, 14, 20–21, 136, 142, 145, 152, 154–55, 162–63, **164–68**, 172, 183, 186, 201, 203–04, 280, 297, 337, 354, 423, 478, 484, 540, 693; **II** 7–8, 33, 60, 86, 143, 415; **III** 58, 259, 283, 439, 452, 495, 515, 555, 568, 591, 603, 637–38, 651, 725; **IV** 22, 187, 597, 722; **6** 27, 51; **7** 377, 461, 520–21; **8** 70, 74–75, 117, 372–73, 375, 505–06; **9** 94, 118, 126, 190, 283–84, 325, 341–43; **10** 32, 241, 260, 264–65, 279–80, 290, 353, 407, 430, 460, 465; **11** 53–54, 103–04, **136–40 (upd.)**, 263, 326, 339, 350, 528–29; **12** 68, 91, 294, 311; **13** 28, 219, 285, 287, 345, 555; **14** 191–92; **15** 91, 171, 513, 515; **16** 321–22; **17** 183, 303–04; **18** 112, 308, 319; **19** 11, 125, 221, 223, 482, 484; **20** 359; **21** 153, 200, 503; **22** 175, 380–81; **23** 143, 339–41, 434; **24** 12; **25** 90, 93, 142–43, 224, 226, 358; **26** 176, 452, 501; **27** 20, 202; **29** 265; **34** 133–34, 136, 303, 305; **36** 34, 180, 198, **215–21 (upd.)**, 242–43; **38** 86, 458–59; **40** 134; **41** 280–81
Ford Motor Company, S.A. de C.V., **20 219–21**
Ford New Holland, Inc. *See* New Holland N.V.
Ford Transport Co., **I** 112; **6** 103
Fordyce Lumber Co., **IV** 281; **9** 259
FORE Systems, Inc., **25 161–63**; **33** 289
Forefront Communications, **22** 194
Foreman State Banks, **II** 285
Foremost Dairy of California, **I** 496–97
Foremost-McKesson Inc., **I** 496–97, **III** 10; **11** 211; **12** 332
Foremost Warehouse Corp., **14** 372
Forenza, **V** 116
Forest City Auto Parts, **23** 491
Forest City Enterprises, Inc., **16 209–11**
Forest City Ratner Companies, **17** 318
Forest E. Olson, Inc., **21** 96
Forest Laboratories, Inc., **11 141–43**
Forest Oil Corporation, **19 161–63**
Forest Products, **III** 645
Forestry Corporation of New Zealand, **19** 156
Företagsfinans, **25** 464
Forethought Group, Inc., **10** 350
Forever Living Products International Inc., **17 186–88**
Forex Chemical Corp., **I** 341; **14** 216; **17** 418
Forex-Neptune, **III** 617
Forge Books. *See* Tom Doherty Associates Inc.
Forges d'Eich–Le Gallais, Metz et Cie, **IV** 24; **22** 42
Forges de la Providence, **IV** 52
Formento Económico Mexicano, S.A. de C.V., **25** 279, 281
Formica Corporation, **10** 269; **13 230–32**
Forming Technology Co., **III** 569; **20** 361
Formonix, **20** 101
Formosa Plastics Corporation, **11** 159; **14 197–99**; **16** 194, 196
Formosa Plastics Group, **31** 108
Formosa Springs, **I** 269; **12** 337
Formularios y Procedimientos Moore, **IV** 645
Formule 1, **13** 364; **27** 10
Forney Fiber Company, **8** 475
Forsakrings A.B. Volvia, **I** 20
Forstmann Little & Co., **I** 446, 483; **II** 478, 544; **III** 56; **7** 206; **10** 321; **12** 344, 562; **14** 166; **16** 322; **19** 372–73, 432; **22** 32, 60; **30** 426; **34** 145, 448; **36** 523; **38 190–92**
Fort Associates, **I** 418
Fort Bend Utilities Company, **12** 269
Fort Dummer Mills, **III** 213
Fort Garry Brewery, **26** 304
Fort Howard Corporation, **8 197–99**; **15** 305; **22** 209. *See also* Fort James Corporation.
Fort James Corporation, **22 209–12 (upd.)**; **29** 136
Fort Mill Manufacturing Co., **V** 378
Fort William Power Co., **IV** 246; **25** 10
Forte Plc, **15** 46; **16** 446; **24** 195; **29** 443
Forte's Holdings Ltd., **III** 104–05
Fortis, Inc., **15 179–82**
Fortum Corporation, **30 202–07 (upd.)**
Fortun Foods, **26** 59
Fortuna Coffee Co., **I** 451
Fortune Brands, Inc., **19** 168; **29 193–97 (upd.)**
Fortune Enterprises, **12** 60
Fortunoff Fine Jewelry and Silverware Inc., **26 144–46**
Forum Cafeterias, **19** 299–300
Forum Hotels, **I** 248
Foseco plc, **IV** 383
Fosgate Electronics, **43** 322
Foss Maritime Co., **9** 509, 511
Fossil, Inc., **17 189–91**
Foster & Kleiser, **7** 335; **14** 331
Foster & Marshall, **II** 398; **10** 62
Foster and Braithwaite, **III** 697
Foster Forbes, **16** 123
Foster Grant, **I** 670; **II** 595–96; **12** 214
Foster Management Co., **11** 366–67
Foster Medical Corp., **III** 16; **11** 282
Foster Poultry Farms, **32 201–04**
Foster-Probyn Ltd., **38** 501
Foster Sand & Gravel, **14** 112
Foster Wheeler Corporation, **I** 82; **6 145–47**; **23 205–08 (upd.)**; **25** 82
Foster's Brewing Group Ltd., **7 182–84**; **21 227–30 (upd.)**; **26** 303, 305–06; **36** 15
Fotomat Corp., **III** 549
Fougerolle, **27** 136, 138
Foundation Computer Systems, Inc., **13** 201
Foundation Fieldbus, **22** 373
Foundation Health Corporation, **11** 174; **12 175–77**
Founders Equity Inc., **14** 235
Founders of American Investment Corp., **15** 247
Fountain Powerboats Industries, Inc., **28 146–48**
Four Media Co., **33** 403
Four-Phase Systems, Inc., **II** 61; **11** 327

Four Seasons Hotels Inc., **II** 531; **9** 237–38; **29 198–200 (upd.)**
Four Seasons Nursing Centers, Inc., **6** 188; **25** 308
Four Winds, **21** 153
Four Winns, **III** 600
Fournier Furniture, Inc., **12** 301
4P, **30** 396–98
Fourth Financial Corporation, **11 144–46**; **15** 60
Foussard Associates, **I** 333
Fowler Road Construction Proprietary, **III** 672
Fowler, Roenau & Geary, LLC, **37** 224
Fowler-Waring Cables Co., **III** 162
Fox & Jacobs, **8** 87
Fox Broadcasting Co., **II** 156; **IV** 608, 652; **7** 391–92; **9** 428; **21** 25, 360; **24** 517; **25** 174, 417–18
Fox Children's Network, **21** 26
Fox Entertainment Group, Inc., **43 173–76**
Fox Family Worldwide, Inc., **24 170–72**
Fox Film Corp., **II** 146–47, 154–55, 169; **25** 327–28
Fox, Fowler & Co., **II** 307
Fox Glacier Mints Ltd., **II** 569
Fox Grocery Co., **II** 682
Fox, Inc., **12** 359; **25** 490
Fox Network, **29** 426
Fox Paper Company, **8** 102
Fox Photo, **III** 475; **7** 161
Fox-Vliet Drug Company, **16** 212
Foxboro Company, **13 233–35**; **27** 81
FoxMeyer Health Corporation, **V** 152–53; **8** 55; **16 212–14**
Foxmoor, **29** 163
Foxx Hy-Reach, **28** 387
FP&L. *See* Florida Power & Light Co.
FPK LLC, **26** 343
FPL Group, Inc., **V 623–25**
FR Corp., **18** 340; **43** 282
Fragrance Express Inc., **37** 271
Fram Corp., **I** 142, 567
Framatome SA, **9** 10; **19 164–67**
Framingham Electric Company, **12** 45
Franc-Or Resources, **38** 231–32
France Cables et Radio, **6** 303
France 5, **6** 374; **21** 105
France-Loisirs, **IV** 615–16, 619
France Quick, **12** 152; **26** 160–61; **27** 10
France Telecom Group, **V 291–93**, 471; **9** 32; **14** 489; **18** 33; **21 231–34 (upd.)**; **25** 96, 102; **34** 13
Franchise Associates, Inc., **17** 238
Franchise Business Systems, Inc., **18** 207
Franchise Finance Corp. of America, **19** 159; **37** 351
Francis H. Leggett & Co., **24** 527
Franciscan Vineyards, Inc., **34** 89
Franco-Américaine de Constructions Atomiques, **19** 165
Franco-American Food Co., **I** 428; **II** 479
Frank & Hirsch, **III** 608
Frank & Schulte GmbH, **8** 496
Frank Dry Goods Company, **9** 121
Frank H. Nott Inc., **14** 156
Frank J. Rooney, Inc., **8** 87
Frank J. Zamboni & Co., Inc., **34 173–76**
Frank Schaffer Publications, **19** 405; **29** 470, 472
Frank W. Horner, Ltd., **38** 123
Frank's Nursery & Crafts, Inc., **12 178–79**, 198–200
Frankel & Co., **39 166–69**
Fränkel & Selz, **II** 239
Frankenberry, Laughlin & Constable, **9** 393
Frankford-Quaker Grocery Co., **II** 625
Frankfort Oil Co., **I** 285
Frankfurter Allgemeine Versicherungs-AG, **III** 184
Franklin Assurances, **III** 211
Franklin Baker's Coconut, **II** 531
Franklin Brass Manufacturing Company, **20** 363
Franklin Container Corp., **IV** 312; **19** 267
Franklin Corp., **14** 130; **41** 388
Franklin Covey Company, **37 149–52 (upd.)**
Franklin Electric Company, Inc., **43 177–80**
Franklin Electronic Publishers, Inc., **23 209–13**
Franklin Life Insurance Co., **III** 242–43; **V** 397; **29** 195
Franklin Mint, **IV** 676; **9** 428; **37** 337–38
Franklin National Bank, **9** 536
Franklin Plastics, **19** 414
Franklin Quest Co., **11 147–49**; **41** 121. *See also* Franklin Covey Company.
Franklin Rayon Yarn Dyeing Corp., **I** 529
Franklin Research & Development, **11** 41
Franklin Resources, Inc., **9 239–40**
Franklin Sports, Inc., **17** 243
Franklin Steamship Corp., **8** 346
Franks Chemical Products Inc., **I** 405
Frans Maas Beheer BV, **14** 568
Franz and Frieder Burda, **IV** 661
Franz Foods, Inc., **II** 584
Franz Ströher AG, **III** 68–69
Franzia. *See* The Wine Group, Inc.
Fraser & Chalmers, **13** 16
Fraser Cos. Ltd., **IV** 165
Fratelli Manzoli, **IV** 585
Fratelli Treves, **IV** 585
Fraternal Assurance Society of America, **III** 274
Fray Data International, **14** 319
Fre Kote Inc., **I** 321
Frears, **II** 543
Fred Campbell Auto Supply, **26** 347
Fred Harvey Hotels, **I** 417
Fred Meyer, Inc., **II** 669; **V 54–56**; **18** 505; **20 222–25 (upd.)**; **35** 370
Fred S. James and Co., **III** 280; **I** 537; **22** 318
Fred Sammons Co., **9** 72
Fred Sammons Company of Chicago, **30** 77
Fred Sands Realtors, **IV** 727
Fred Schmid Appliance & T.V. Co., Inc., **10** 305; **18** 532
The Fred W. Albrecht Grocery Co., **13 236–38**
Fred's, Inc., **23 214–16**
Freddie Mac. *See* Federal Home Loan Mortgage Corporation.
Fredelle, **14** 295
Frederick & Nelson, **17** 462
Frederick Atkins Inc., **16 215–17**
Frederick Bayer & Company, **22** 225
Frederick Gas Company, **19** 487
Frederick Manufacturing Corporation, **26** 119
Frederick Miller Brewing Co., **I** 269
Frederick's of Hollywood Inc., **16 218–20**; **25** 521
Free-lance Uitzendburo, **26** 240
Freeborn Farms, **13** 244
Freedom Communications, Inc., **36 222–25**
Freedom Group Inc., **42** 10–11
Freedom Technology, **11** 486
Freedom-Valvoline Oil Co., **IV** 373; **19** 23
Freeman, Spogli & Co., **17** 366; **18** 90; **32** 12, 15; **35** 276; **36** 358–59
Freemans, **V** 177
FreeMark Communications, **38** 269
Freeport-McMoran Inc., **IV 81–84**; **7 185–89 (upd.)**; **16** 29; **23** 40
Freeport Power, **38** 448
Freezer House, **II** 398; **10** 62
Freezer Queen Foods, Inc., **21** 509
Freezer Shirt Corporation, **8** 406
Freiberger Papierfabrik, **IV** 323
Freight Car Services, Inc., **23** 306
Freight Outlet, **17** 297
Freightliner, **I** 150; **6** 413
FreightMaster, **III** 498
Frejlack Ice Cream Co., **II** 646; **7** 317
Fremlin Breweries, **I** 294
Fremont Butter and Egg Co., **II** 467
Fremont Canning Company, **7** 196
Fremont Group, **21** 97
Fremont Investors, **30** 268
Fremont Partners, **24** 265
Fremont Savings Bank, **9** 474–75
French and Richards & Co., **I** 692
French Bank of California, **II** 233
French Connection Group plc, **41 167–69**
French Fragrances, Inc., **22 213–15**; **40** 170. *See also* Elizabeth Arden, Inc.
French Kier, **I** 568
French Petrofina, **IV** 497
French Quarter Coffee Co., **27** 480–81
Frequency Sources Inc., **9** 324
Fresenius Ag, **22** 360
Fresh America Corporation, **20 226–28**
Fresh Choice, Inc., **20 229–32**
Fresh Fields, **19** 501
Fresh Foods, Inc., **25** 391; **29 201–03**
Fresh Start Bakeries, **26** 58
Freshbake Foods Group PLC, **II** 481; **7** 68; **25** 518; **26** 57
Fretter, Inc., **9** 65; **10** 9–10, **304–06**, 502; **19** 124; **23** 52
Freudenberg & Co., **41 170–73**
Frialco, **IV** 165
Frictiontech Inc., **11** 84
Friday's Front Row Sports Grill, **22** 128
Friden, Inc., **II** 10; **30** 418
Fridy-Gauker & Fridy, **I** 313; **10** 154
Fried, Frank, Harris, Shriver & Jacobson, **35 183–86**
Fried. Krupp AG Hoesch- Krupp. *See* Thyssen Krupp AG.
Fried. Krupp GmbH, **II** 257; **IV** 60, **85–89**, 104, 128, 203, 206, 222, 234
Friedman's Inc., **29 204–06**
Friedrich Flick Industrial Corp., **I** 548; **III** 692
Friedrich Roessler Söhne, **IV** 69
Friedrichshütte, **III** 694
Friendly Hotels PLC, **14** 107
Friendly Ice Cream Corp., **II** 511–12; **15** 221; **30 208–10**
Friesch-Groningsche Hypotheekbank, **III** 179

Frigidaire Home Products, **III** 572; **13** 564; **19** 361; **22** 28, **216–18**, 349
Frigo, **II** 587
Friguia, **IV** 165
Frisby P.M.C. Incorporated, **16** 475
Frisch's Restaurants, Inc., **35 187–89**
Frisdranken Industries Winters B.V., **22** 515
Frisia Group, **IV** 197–98
Frito-Lay Company, **I** 219, 278–79; **III** 136; **22** 95; **32 205–10**; **38** 347
Fritz Companies, Inc., **12 180–82**
Fritz Thyssen Stiftung, **IV** 222
Fritz W. Glitsch and Sons, Inc. *See* Glitsch International, Inc.
Fritzsche Dodge and Ollcott, **I** 307
Froebel-Kan, **IV** 679
Frolic, **16** 545
Fromagerie d'Illoud. *See* Bongrain SA.
La Fromagerie du Velay, **25** 85
Fromagerie Paul Renard, **25** 85
Fromageries Bel, **II** 518; **6** 47; **19** 51; **23 217–19**; **25 83–84**
Fromageries des Chaumes, **25** 84
Fromarsac, **25** 84
Frome Broken Hill Co., **IV** 59
Fromm & Sichel, **I** 285
Frontec, **13** 132
Frontenac Co., **24** 45
Frontier Airlines, Inc., **I** 97–98, 103, 118, 124, 129–30; **6** 129; **11** 298; **21** 141–42; **22 219–21**; **25** 421; **26** 439–40; **39** 33
Frontier Communications, **32** 216, 218
Frontier Corp., **16 221–23**; **18** 164
Frontier Electronics, **19** 311
Frontier Expeditors, Inc., **12** 363
Frontier Oil Co., **IV** 373
Frontier Pacific Insurance Company, **21** 263
Frosch Touristik, **27** 29
Frost National Bank. *See* Cullen/Frost Bankers, Inc.
Frozen Food Express Industries, Inc., **20 233–35**; **27** 404
Fru-Con Corp., **I** 561
Fruehauf Corp., **I 169–70**, 480; **II** 425; **III** 652; **7** 259–60, 513–14; **13** 341; **27** 202–03, 251; **40** 432
Fruit of the Loom, Inc., **8 200–02**; **16** 535; **25 164–67 (upd.)**
Fry's Diecastings, **III** 681
Fry's Food Stores, **12** 112
Fry's Metal Foundries, **III** 681
Frye Copy Systems, **6** 599
Frymaster Corporation, **27 159–62**
FSA Corporation, **25** 349
FSI International, Inc., **17 192–94**. *See also* FlightSafety International, Inc.
FSP. *See* Frank Schaffer Publications.
FTD, **26** 344. *See also* Florists Transworld Delivery, Inc.
F3 Software Corp., **15** 474
FTP Software, Inc., **20 236–38**
Fubu, **29 207–09**
Fuddruckers, **27** 480–82
Fuel Pipeline Transportation Ltd., **6** 123–24; **27** 464
Fuel Resources Development Co., **6** 558–59
Fuel Resources Inc., **6** 457
FuelMaker Corporation, **6** 569
Fuji, **18** 94, 342, 511
Fuji Bank, Ltd., **I** 494; **II 291–93**, 360–61, 391, 422, 459, 554; **III** 405, 408–09; **17** 556–57; **24** 324; **26** 455
Fuji Electric Co., Ltd., **II 22–23**, 98, 103; **III** 139; **13** 356; **18** 511; **22** 373; **42** 145
Fuji Gen-Gakki, **16** 202; **43** 171
Fuji Heavy Industries, **I** 207; **III** 581; **9** 294; **12** 400; **13** 499–501; **23** 290; **36** 240, 243
Fuji Iron & Steel Co., Ltd., **I** 493; **II** 300; **IV** 130, 157, 212; **17** 349–50; **24** 325
Fuji Kaolin Co., **III** 691
Fuji Paper, **IV** 320
Fuji Photo Film Co., Ltd., **III** 172, 476, **486–89**, 549–50; **6** 289; **7** 162; **18** 94, **183–87 (upd.)**, 341–42; **36** 172, 174; **43** 284
Fuji Seito, **I** 511
Fuji Television, **7** 249; **9** 29
Fuji Xerox. *See* Xerox Corporation.
Fuji Yoshiten Co., **IV** 292
Fujian Hualong Carburetor, **13** 555
Fujikoshi Kozai, **III** 595
Fujimoto Bill Broker & Securities Co., **II** 405
Fujisawa Pharmaceutical Co., **I 635–36**; **III** 47; **8** 343
Fujita Airways, **6** 70
Fujitsu-ICL Systems Inc., **11 150–51**
Fujitsu Limited, **I** 455, 541; **II** 22–23, 56, 68, 73, 274; **III** 109–11, 130, **139–41**, 164, 482; **V** 339; **6** 217, 240–42; **10** 238; **11** 308, 542; **13** 482; **14** 13–15, 512; **16** 139, **224–27 (upd.)**; **17** 172; **21** 390; **27** 107; **40** 20; **145–50 (upd.)**; **43** 285
Fujitsu Takamisawa, **28** 131
Fujiyi Confectionery Co., **II** 569
Fukuin Electric Works, Ltd., **III** 604
Fukuin Shokai Denki Seisakusho, **III** 604
Fukuju Fire, **III** 384
Fukuoka Paper Co., Ltd., **IV** 285
Fukutake Publishing Co., Ltd., **13** 91, 93
Ful-O-Pep, **10** 250
Fulbright Jaworski & Reavis McGrath, **22** 4
Fulcrum Communications, **10** 19
The Fulfillment Corporation of America, **21** 37
Fulham Brothers, **13** 244
Fullbright & Jaworski, **28** 48
Fuller Brush Co., **II** 572; **15** 475–76, 78
Fuller Co., **6** 395–96; **25** 169–70
Fuller Manufacturing Company **I** 154. *See also* H.B. Fuller Company.
Fuller Smith & Turner P.L.C., **38 193–95**
Fulton Bank, **14** 40
Fulton Co., **III** 569; **20** 361
Fulton Insurance Co., **III** 463; **21** 173
Fulton Manufacturing Co., **11** 535
Fulton Municipal Gas Company, **6** 455
Fulton Performance Products, Inc., **11** 535
Funai-Amstrad, **III** 113
Funco, Inc., **20 239–41**
Fund American Cos., **III** 251–52
Fundimensions, **16** 337
Funk & Wagnalls, **IV** 605; **22** 441
Funk Software Inc., **6** 255; **25** 299
Funnel Cake Factory, **24** 241
Fuqua Enterprises, Inc., **17 195–98**
Fuqua Industries Inc., **I 445–47**, 452; **8** 545; **12** 251; **14** 86; **37** 62
Furalco, **IV** 15
Furnishings International Inc., **20** 359, 363; **39** 267
Furniture Brands International, Inc., **31** 246, 248; **39 170–75 (upd.)**
The Furniture Center, Inc., **14** 236
Furon Company, **28 149–51**
Furr's Supermarkets, Inc., **II** 601; **28 152–54**
Furst Group, **17** 106
Furukawa Electric Co., Ltd., **II** 22; **III** 139, **490–92**; **IV** 15, 26, 153; **15** 514; **22** 44
Fusi Denki, **II** 98
Fuso Marine Insurance Co., **III** 367
Fuso Metal Industries, **IV** 212
Futagi Co., Ltd., **V** 96
Futronix Corporation, **17** 276
Future Diagnostics, Inc., **25** 384
Future Graphics, **18** 387
Future Now, Inc., **6** 245; **12 183–85**
Futurestep, Inc., **34** 247, 249
Fuyo Group, **II** 274, 291–93, 391–92, 554
FWD Corporation, **7** 513
Fyffes Plc, **38 196–99**, 201

G&G Shops, Inc., **8** 425–26
G & H Products, **III** 419
G&K Services, Inc., **16 228–30**; **21** 115
G&L Albu, **IV** 90
G&L Inc., **16** 202; **43** 170
G&R Pasta Co., Inc., **II** 512
G. and T. Earle, **III** 669, 670
G.A. Serlachius Oy, **IV** 314–15
G.B. Lewis Company, **8** 359
G. Bruss GmbH and Co. KG, **26** 141
G.C.E. International Inc., **III** 96–97
G.C. Murphy Company, **9** 21
G.C. Smith, **I** 423
G.D. Searle & Co., **I** 365–66, **686–89**; **III** 47, 53; **8** 343, 398, 434; **9** 356–57; **10** 54; **12 186–89 (upd.)**; **16** 527; **26** 108, 383; **29** 331; **29** 331; **34 177–82 (upd.)**
G. Felsenthal & Sons, **17** 106
G.H. Bass & Co., **15** 406; **24** 383
G.H. Besselaar Associates, **30** 151
G.H. Rinck NV, **V** 49; **19** 122–23
G.H. Wetterau & Sons Grocery Co., **II** 681
G. Heileman Brewing Co., **I 253–55**, 270; **10** 169–70; **12** 338; **18** 501; **23** 403, 405
G.I.E. Airbus Industrie, **I**
G.I. Joe's, Inc., **30 221–23 41–43**, 49–52, 55–56, 70, 72, 74–76, 107, 111, 116, 121; **9** 458, 460; **11** 279, 363; **12 190–92 (upd.)**
G-III Apparel Group, Ltd., **22 222–24**
G.J. Coles & Coy. Ltd., **20** 155
G.L. Kelty & Co., **13** 168
G.L. Rexroth GmbH, **III** 566; **38** 298, 300
G.M. Pfaff AG, **30** 419–20
G.P. Group, **12** 358
G.P. Putnam's Sons, **II** 144
G.R. Foods, Inc. *See* Ground Round, Inc.
G.R. Herberger's Department Stores, **19** 324–25; **41** 343–44
G.R. Kinney Corporation, **V** 226, 352; **14** 293; **20** 88
G. Riedel Kälte- und Klimatechnik, **III** 420
G.S. Blodgett Corporation, **15 183–85**; **22** 350
G.S. Capital Partners II L.P. *See* Goldman, Sachs & Company.
G. Washington Coffee Refining Co., **I** 622

Gabelli Asset Management Inc., **13** 561; **30 211–14**. *See also* Lynch Corporation.
Gable House Properties, **II** 141
Gabriel Industries, **II** 532
GAC. *See* The Goodyear Tire & Rubber Company.
GAC Corp., **II** 182; **III** 592
GAC Holdings L.P., **7** 204; **28** 164
Gadzooks, Inc., **18 188–90**; **33** 203
GAF, **I 337–40**, 524–25, 549; **II** 378; **III** 440; **8** 180; **9** 518; **18** 215; **22** 14, **225–29 (upd.)**; **25** 464
Gage Marketing Group, **26 147–49**; **27** 21
Gagliardi Brothers, **13** 383
Gaiam, Inc., **41 174–77**
Gail Borden, Jr., and Company. *See* Borden, Inc.
Gain Technology, Inc., **10** 505
Gaines Dog Food Co., **II** 531
Gaines Furniture Manufacturing, Inc., **43** 315
Gainsborough Craftsmen Ltd., **II** 569
Gainsco, Inc., **22 230–32**
Gair Paper Co., **I** 599
Galas Harland, S.A., **17** 266, 268
Galavision, Inc., **24** 515–17
Galaxy Carpet Mills Inc., **19** 276
Galaxy Energies Inc., **11** 28
Galbreath Escott, **16** 474
The Gale Group, Inc., **34** 437
Gale Research Inc., **8** 526; **23** 440
Galen Health Care, **15** 112; **35** 215–16
Galen Laboratories, **13** 160
Galerías Preciados, **26** 130
Galeries Lafayette S.A., **V 57–59**; **23 220–23 (upd.)**
Galesburg Coulter Disc Co., **III** 439–40
Galey & Lord, Inc., **20 242–45**
Gallaher Limited, **IV** 260; **V 398–400**; **19 168–71 (upd.)**; **29** 195
Gallatin Bank, **II** 312
Gallatin Steel Company, **18** 380; **24** 144
Galletas, **II** 543
Gallimard, **IV** 618
Gallo Winery. *See* E. & J. Gallo Winery.
Gallop Johnson & Neuman, L.C., **26** 348
The Gallup Organization, **37 153–56**; **41** 196–97
Galoob Toys. *See* Lewis Galoob Toys Inc.
Galor, **I** 676
GALP, **IV** 505
Galvanizing Co., **IV** 159
Galveston *Daily News*, **10** 3
Galvin Manufacturing Corp., **II** 60; **11** 326
GALVSTAR, L.P., **26** 530
Gamble-Skogmo Inc., **13** 169; **25** 535
The Gambrinus Company, **29** 219; **40 188–90**
Gambro Engstrom AB, **13** 159–61, 327–28
Gamebusters, **41** 409
Gamesa, **II** 544; **19** 192
GameTime, Inc., **19** 387; **27** 370–71
GAMI. *See* Great American Management and Investment, Inc.
Gamlestaden, **9** 381–82
Gamlestadens Fabriker, **III** 622
Gamma Capital Corp., **24** 3
Gammalink, **18** 143
Gander Mountain, Inc., **20 246–48**
Gang-Nail Systems, **III** 735
Gannett Co., Inc., **III** 159; **IV 612–13**, 629–30; **7 190–92 (upd.)**; **9** 3; **18** 63; **23** 157–58, 293; **24** 224; **25** 371; **30 215–17 (upd.)**; **32** 354–55; **41** 197–98
Gannett Supply, **17** 282
Gantos, Inc., **17 199–201**
The Gap, Inc., **V 60–62**; **9** 142, 360; **11** 499; **18 191–94 (upd.)**; **24** 27; **25** 47–48; **31** 51–52
GAR Holdings, **19** 78
Garamond Press, **23** 100
Garan, Inc., **16 231–33**
Garantie Mutuelle des Fonctionnaires, **21** 225
Garden Botanika, **11** 41
Garden City Newspapers Inc., **38** 308
Garden Escape, **26** 441
Garden Fresh Restaurant Corporation, **31 213–15**
Garden of Eatin' Inc., **27** 198; **43** 218–19
Garden Ridge Corporation, **27 163–65**
Garden State BancShares, Inc., **14** 472
Garden State Life Insurance Company, **10** 312; **27** 47–48
Garden State Paper, **38** 307–08
Gardenburger, Inc., **33 169–71**
Gardener's Eden, **17** 548–49
Gardenia, **II** 587
Gardner & Harvey Container Corporation, **8** 267
Gardner Advertising. *See* Wells Rich Green BDDP.
Gardner Cryogenics, **13** 140
Gardner-Denver Co., **II** 16
Gardner Merchant Ltd., **III** 104; **11** 325; **29** 442–44
Gardner Rubber Co. *See* Tillotson Corp.
Garelick Farms, Inc., **26** 449
Garfield Weston, **13** 51
Garfinckel, Brooks Brothers, Miller & Rhodes, Inc., **15** 94; **22** 110
Garfinckels, **37** 12
Garland-Compton, **42** 328
Garlock, **I** 435
Garnier, **III** 47
A.B. Garnisonen, **II** 352
Garrard Engineering, **II** 82
Garrett, **9** 18; **11** 472
Garrett & Company, **27** 326
Garrett AiResearch, **9** 18
Garrett-Buchanan, **I** 412
Garrett Poultry Co., **II** 584; **14** 514
Garrick Investment Holdings Ltd., **16** 293
Garrido y Compania, Inc., **26** 448
Gart Sports Company, **24 173–75**
Gartner Group, Inc., **21 235–37**; **25** 22
Gartrell White, **II** 465
Garuda Indonesia, **I** 107; **6 90–91**
Gary Fisher Mountain Bike Company, **16** 494
Gary Industries, **7** 4
Gary-Wheaton Corp., **II** 286
Gary-Williams Energy Corporation, **19** 177
Gas Authority of India Ltd., **IV** 484
Gas Corp. of Queensland, **III** 673
Gas Energy Inc., **6** 457
Gas Group, **III** 673
Gas Light and Coke Company. *See* British Gas plc.
Gas Light Company. *See* Baltimore Gas and Electric Company.
Gas Machinery Co., **I** 412
Gas Service Company, **6** 593; **12** 542
Gas Supply Co., **III** 672
Gas Tech, Inc., **11** 513
Gas Utilities Company, **6** 471
Gaston Paper Stock Co., Inc., **8** 476
Gasunie. *See* N.V. Nederlandse Gasunie.
GATC. *See* General American Tank Car Company.
Gate City Company, **6** 446
The Gates Corporation, **9 241–43**
Gates Distribution Company, **12** 60
Gates Radio Co., **II** 37
Gates Rubber, **26** 349
Gates/FA Distributing Inc., **29** 413–14
Gateway Books, **14** 61
Gateway Corporation Ltd., **II** 612, **628–30**, 638, 642; **10** 442; **16** 249; **25** 119
Gateway Foodmarkets Ltd., **II** 628; **13** 26
Gateway, Inc., **27 166–69 (upd.)**
Gateway International Motorsports Corporation, Inc., **43** 139–40
Gateway State Bank, **39** 381–82
Gateway 2000, Inc., **10 307–09**; **11** 240; **22** 99; **24** 31; **25** 531
Gatliff Coal Co., **6** 583
Gattini, **40** 215
Gatwick Handling, **28** 157
GATX, **6 394–96**; **25 168–71 (upd.)**
Gaultier. *See* Groupe Jean-Paul Gaultier.
Gaumont SA, **II** 157–58; **25 172–75**; **29** 369–71
Gauntlet Developments, **IV** 724
Gavilan Computer Corp., **III** 124; **6** 221
Gaya Motor, P.T. **23** 290
Gaylord Container Corporation, **8 203–05**; **24** 92
Gaylord Entertainment Company, **11 152–54**; **36 226–29 (upd.)**; **38** 456
Gaymer Group, **25** 82
Gaz de France, **IV** 425; **V 626–28**; **38** 407; **40 191–95 (upd.)**
Gazelle Graphics Systems, **28** 244
Gazprom, **18** 50; **30** 205. *See also* OAO Gazprom.
GB Foods Inc., **19** 92
GB-Inno-BM, **II** 658; **V** 63
GB Papers, **IV** 290
GB s.a. *See* GIB Group.
GB Stores, Inc., **14** 427
GBL, **IV** 499
GC Companies, Inc., **25 176–78**
GCFC. *See* General Cinema Finance Co.
GD Express Worldwide, **27** 472, 475; **30** 463
GDE Systems, Inc., **17** 492
GDF. *See* Gaz de France.
GDS, **29** 412
GE. *See* General Electric Company.
GE Aircraft Engines, **9 244–46**
GE Capital Aviation Services, **36 230–33**
GE Capital Corporation, **29** 428, 430
GE Capital Services, **27** 276
GE SeaCo SRL, **29** 428, 431
GEA AG, **27 170–74**
GEAC Computer Corporation Ltd., **43 181–85**
Geant Casino, **12** 152
Gearhart Industries Inc., **III** 499; **15** 467
Gearmatic, **I** 185
Gebrüder Kiessel GmbH, **IV** 197
Gebrüder Sulzer Aktiengesellschaft. *See* Sulzer Brothers Limited.
Gebrüder Volkart, **III** 402
Gebrueder Ahle GmbH, **III** 581
GEC. *See* General Electric Company.
GECAS. *See* GE Capital Aviation Services.
Gecina SA, **42 151–53**

GECO, **III** 618; **17** 419
Geco Mines Ltd., **IV** 165; **7** 398
Geer Drug, **III** 9–10
Geest Plc, **38** 198, **200–02**
Geffen Records Inc., **21** 26; **23** 33; **26 150–52**; **43** 143
GEGC, **III** 434
GEHE AG, **27 175–78**
Gehl Company, **19 172–74**
GEICO Corporation, **III** 214, 248, 252, 273, 448; **10 310–12**; **18** 60, 61, 63; **40 196–99 (upd.)**; **42** 31–34
Gelatin Products Co., **I** 678
Gelco Express, **18** 177
Gelco Truck Services, **19** 293
Gellatly, Hankey and Sewell, **III** 521
Gelsenberg AG, **IV** 454; **7** 141
Gelsenkirchener Bergwerks AG, **I** 542; **IV** 194
Gelson's, **29** 32
Gem State Utilities, **6** 325, 328
GEMA Gesellschaft für Maschinen- und Apparatebau mbH, **IV** 198
Gemco, **17** 366
Gemcolite Company, **8** 178
N.V. Gemeenschappelijk Benzit van Aandeelen Philips Gloeilampenfabriken, **II** 79; **13** 396
Gemeinhardt Co., **16** 201; **43** 170
Gemey, **III** 47
Gemina, **I** 369
Gemini Computer Systems, **III** 109; **14** 13; **37** 59–60
Gemini Group Limited Partnership, **23** 10
Gemini Industries, **17** 215
GemPlus, **18** 543
Gemstar-TV Guide International, **43** 431
Genbel Investments Ltd., **IV** 92
GenCare Health Systems, **17** 166–67
Gencor Ltd., **I** 423; **IV 90–93**, 95; **22 233–37 (upd.)**
GenCorp Inc., **8** 206–08; **9 247–49**; **13** 381
Gendex Corp., **10** 270, 272
Gene Reid Drilling, **IV** 480
Gene Upton Co., **13** 166
Genender International Incorporated, **31** 52
Genentech Inc., **I** 628, **637–38**; **III** 43; **8 209–11 (upd.)**, 216–17; **10** 78, 80, 142, 199; **17** 289; **29** 386; **30** 164; **32 211–15 (upd.)**; **37** 112; **38** 204, 206; **41** 153, 155
General Accident plc, **III 256–57**, 350
General America Corp., **III** 352–53
General American Oil Co., **IV** 523
General American Tank Car Company. *See* GATX Corporation.
General Aniline and Film Corporation. *See* GAF Corporation.
General Aquatics, Inc., **16** 297
General Artificial Silk Co., **IV** 310; **19** 265
General Atlantic Partners, **25** 34; **26** 94
General Automotive Parts Corp., **I** 62; **9** 254
General Aviation Corp., **I** 54; **9** 16
General Battery Corp., **I** 440–41
General Binding Corporation, **10 313–14**
General Box Corp., **IV** 342
General Brewing Corp, **I** 269
General Bussan Kaisha, Ltd., **IV** 431–32, 555
General Cable Corporation, **IV** 32; **7** 288; **8** 367; **18** 549; **40 200–03**
General Casualty Co., **III** 258, 343, 352, 404
The General Chemical Group Inc., **I** 414; **22** 29, 115, 193, 349, 541; **29** 114; **37 157–60**
General Chocolate, **II** 521
General Cigar Company, **43** 204–05. *See also* Culbro Corporation.
General Cigar Holdings, Inc., **27** 139–40
General Cinema Corporation, **I 245–46**; **II** 478; **IV** 624; **12** 12–13, 226, 356; **14** 87; **19** 362; **26** 468; **27** 481
General Cinema Finance Co., **II** 157–58
General Cinema Theaters. *See* GC Companies, Inc.
General Co. for Life Insurance and Superannuation, **III** 309
General Corporation, **9** 173
General Credit Ltd., **II** 389
General Crude Oil Co., **II** 403; **IV** 287; **15** 228
General DataComm Industries, Inc., **14 200–02**
General Diaper Corporation, **14** 550
General Dynamics Corporation, **I** 55, **57–60**, 62, 71, 74, 77, 482, 525, 527, 597; **6** 79, 229; **7** 520; **8** 51, 92, 315, 338; **9** 206, 323, 417–18, 498; **10 315–18 (upd.)**, 522, 527; **11** 67, 165, 269, 278, 364; **13** 374; **16** 77–78; **18** 62, 554; **27** 100; **30** 471; **36** 76, 78–79; **40 204–10 (upd.)**
General Electric Capital Corp., **15** 257, 282; **19** 190
General Electric Company, **I** 41, 52, 82–85, 195, 321, 454, 478, 532, 534, 537; **II** 2, 16, 19, 22, 24, **27–31**, 38–39, 41, 56, 58–59, 66, 82, 86, 88–90, 98–99, 116–17, 119–21, 143, 151–52, 330, 349, 431, 604; **III** 16, 110, 122–23, 132, 149, 152, 154, 170–71, 340, 437, 440, 443, 475, 483, 502, 526, 572–73, 614, 655; **IV** 66, 203, 287, 596, 675; **V** 564; **6** 13, 27, 32, 164–66, 240, 261, 266, 288, 452, 517; **7** 123, 125, 161, 456, 520, 532; **8** 157, 262, 332, 377; **9** 14–18, 27, 128, 162, 244, 246, 352–53, 417–18, 439, 514; **10** 16, 241, 536–37; **11** 46, 313, 318, 422, 472, 490; **12** 68, 190, **193–97 (upd.)**, 237, 247, 250, 252, 484, 544–45, 550; **13** 30, 124, 326, 396, 398, 501, 529, 554, 563–64; **15** 196, 228, 285, 380, 403, 467; **17** 149, 173, 272; **18** 228, 369; **19** 110, 164–66, 210, 335; **20** 8, 152; **22** 37, 218, 406; **23** 104–05, 181; **26** 371; **28** 4–5, 8, 298; **30** 490; **31** 123; **34 183–90 (upd.)**; **41** 366; **43** 447, 466
General Electric Company, PLC, **I** 411, 423; **II** 3, 12, **24–26**, 31, 58, 72, 80–83; **III** 509; **9** 9–10; **13** 356; **20** 290; **24** 87; **42** 373, 377. *See also* Marconi plc.
General Electric Credit Corporation, **19** 293; **20** 42
General Electric Railcar Wheel and Parts Services Corporation, **18** 4
General Electric Venture Capital Corporation, **9** 140; **10** 108
General Electronics Co., **III** 160
General Elevator Corporation, **25** 15
General Europea S.A., **V** 607
General Export Iron and Metals Company, **15** 116
General Felt Industries Inc., **I** 202; **14** 300; **17** 182–83
General Film Distributors Ltd., **II** 157
General Finance Corp., **II** 419; **III** 194, 232; **11** 16
General Finance Service Corp., **11** 447
General Fire and Casualty, **I** 449
General Fire Extinguisher Co. *See* Grinnell Corp.
General Foods Corp., **I** 26, 36, 608, 712; **II** 414, 463, 477, 497, 502, 525, 530–34, 557, 569; **III** 66; **V** 407; **7** 272–74; **10** 323, 551; **12** 167, 372; **13** 293; **18** 416, 419; **25** 517; **26** 251; **36** 236
General Foods, Ltd., **7** 577
General Furniture Leasing. *See* CORT Business Services Corporation.
General Gas Co., **IV** 432
General Glass Corporation, **13** 40
General Growth Properties, **III** 248
General Health Services, **III** 79
General Host Corporation, **7** 372; **12** 178–79, **198–200**, 275; **15** 362; **17** 230–31
General Housewares Corporation, **16 234–36**; **18** 69
General Instrument Corporation, **II** 5, 112, 160; **10 319–21**; **17** 33; **34** 298
General Insurance Co. of America, **III** 352–53
General Jones Processed Food, **I** 438
General Learning Corp., **IV** 675; **7** 528
General Leisure, **16** 33
General Life Insurance Co. of America, **III** 353
General Medical Corp., **18** 469
General Merchandise Company, **V** 91
General Merchandise Services, Inc., **15** 480
General Milk Co., **II** 487; **7** 429
General Milk Products of Canada Ltd., **II** 586
General Mills, Inc., **II** 493, **501–03**, 525, 556, 576, 684; **III** 505; **7** 547; **8** 53–54; **9** 156, 189–90, 291; **10** 177, **322–24 (upd.)**; **11** 15, 497–98; **12** 80, 167–68, 275; **13** 244, 293–94, 408, 516; **15** 189; **16** 71, 156–58, 337; **18** 225, 523; **22** 337–38; **25** 90, 241, 243, 253; **30** 286; **31** 429–31; **33** 359; **36** 179–80, **234–39 (upd.)**
General Mining and Finance Corporation. *See* Gencor Ltd.
General Mortgage and Credit Corp., **II** 256
General Motors Acceptance Corporation, **21** 146; **22** 55
General Motors Corporation, **I** 10, 14, 16–17, 54, 58, 78–80, 85, 101–02, 125, 136, 141, 144–45, 147, 154–55, 162–63, 165–67, **171–73**, 181, 183, 186–87, 203, 205–06, 280, 328–29, 334–35, 360, 448, 464, 481–82, 529, 540; **II** 2, 5, 15, 32–35, 268, 431, 608; **III** 55, 136–38, 292, 442, 458, 482–83, 536, 555, 563, 581, 590–91, 637–38, 640–42, 760; **6** 140, 256, 336, 356, 358; **7** 6–8, 427, 461–64, 513, 565, 567, 599; **8** 151–52, 505–07; **9** 16–18, 36, 283, 293–95, 341, 343, 344, 439, 487–89; **10** 198, 232, 262, 264, 273–74, 279–80, 288–89, **325–27 (upd.)**, 419–20, 429, 460, 537; **11** 5, 29, 53, 103–04, 137–39, 339, 350, 427–29, 437–39, 471–72, 528, 530; **12** 90, 160, 309, 311, 487; **13** 109, 124, 179, 344–45, 357; **16** 321–22,

436, 484; **17** 173, 184, 304; **18** 125–26, 168, 308; **19** 293–94, 482, 484; **21** 3, 6, 444; **22** 13, 169, 175, 216; **23** 267–69, 288–91, 340, 459–61; **25** 142–43, 149, 223–24, 300; **29** 375, 407–08; **34** 133–35, 303; **36** 32, **240–44 (upd.)**, 298; **38** 86, 458, 461; **43** 319
General Nucleonics Corp., **III** 643
General Nutrition Companies, Inc., **11 155–57**; **24** 480; **29 210–14 (upd.)**; **31** 347; **37** 340, 342
General Office Products Co., **25** 500
General Packing Service, Inc., **19** 78
General Parts Inc., **29** 86
General Petroleum and Mineral Organization of Saudi Arabia, **IV** 537–39
General Petroleum Corp., **IV** 412, 431, 464; **7** 352
General Physics Corporation, **13** 367
General Portland Cement Co., **III** 704–05; **17** 497
General Portland Inc., **28** 229
General Precision Equipment Corp., **II** 10; **30** 418
General Printing and Paper, **II** 624–25
General Printing Ink Corp. *See* Scqua Corp.
General Property Trust, **IV** 708
General Public Utilities Corporation, **V 629–31**; **6** 484, 534, 579–80; **11** 388; **20** 73
General Radio Company. *See* GenRad, Inc.
General Railway Signal Company. *See* General Signal Corporation.
General Re Corporation, **III 258–59**, 276; **24 176–78 (upd.)**; **42** 31, 35
General Rent A Car, **6** 349; **25** 142–43
General Research Corp., **14** 98
General Seafoods Corp., **II** 531
General Sekiyu K.K., **IV 431–33**, 555; **16** 490
General Signal Corporation, **III** 645; **9 250–52**; **11** 232
General Spring Products, **16** 321
General Steel Industries Inc., **14** 324
General Supermarkets, **II** 673
General Telephone and Electronics Corp., **II** 47; **V** 295, 345–46; **13** 398; **19** 40; **25** 267
General Telephone Corporation, **V** 294–95; **9** 478, 494
General Time Corporation, **16** 483
General Tire, Inc., **8** 206–08, **212–14**; **9** 247–48; **20** 260, 262; **22** 219
General Transistor Corporation, **10** 319
General Utilities Company, **6** 555
General Waterworks Corporation, **40** 449
Generale Bank, **II 294–95**
Genérale Biscuit S.A., **II** 475
Générale de Banque, **36** 458
Générale de Mécanique Aéronautique, **I** 46
Générale des Eaux Group, **V 632–34**; **21** 226
Generale du Jouet, **16** 428
Générale Occidentale, **II** 475; **IV** 614–15
Générale Restauration S.A., **34** 123
Generali. *See* Assicurazioni Generali.
Génération Y2K, **35** 204, 207
GenerComit Gestione SpA, **II** 192
Genesco Inc., **14** 501; **17 202–06**; **27** 59
Genesee & Wyoming Inc., **27 179–81**
Genesee Brewing Co., **18** 72
Genesee Iron Works. *See* Wickes Inc.
Genesis, **II** 176–77
Genesis Health Ventures, Inc., **18 195–97**; **25** 310
Genetic Anomalies, Inc., **39** 395
Genetic Systems Corp., **I** 654; **III** 18; **37** 43
Genetics Institute, Inc., **8 215–18**; **10** 70, 78–80
Geneva Metal Wheel Company, **20** 261
Geneva Pharmaceuticals, Inc., **8** 549; **22** 37, 40
Geneva Rubber Co., **17** 373
Geneva Steel, **7 193–95**
Genex Corp., **I** 355–56; **26** 246
GENIX, **V** 152
Genix Group. *See* MCN Corporation.
Genossenschaftsbank Edeka, **II** 621–22
Genosys Biotechnologies, Inc., **36** 431
Genovese Drug Stores, Inc., **18 198–200**; **21** 187; **32** 170; **43** 249
Genpack Corporation, **21** 58
GenRad, Inc., **24 179–83**
GenSet, **19** 442
Genstar, **22** 14; **23** 327
Genstar Gypsum Products Co., **IV** 273
Genstar Stone Products Co., **III** 735; **15** 154; **40** 176
GenTek Inc., **37** 157; **41** 236
Gentex Corporation, **26 153–57**; **35** 148–49
Gentex Optics, **17** 50; **18** 392
GenTrac, **24** 257
Gentry Associates, Inc., **14** 378
Gentry International, **I** 497
Genty-Cathiard, **39** 183–84
Genuardi's Family Markets, Inc., **35 190–92**
Genuin Golf & Dress of America, Inc., **32** 447
Genuine Parts Company, **9 253–55**
Genung's, **II** 673
Genus, **18** 382–83
Genzyme Corporation, **13 239–42**; **38 203–07 (upd.)**
Genzyme Transgenics Corp., **37** 44
Geo Space Corporation, **18** 513
GEO Specialty Chemicals, Inc., **27** 117
Geo. W. Wheelwright Co., **IV** 311; **19** 266
Geodynamics Oil & Gas Inc., **IV** 83
Geographics, Inc., **25** 183
Geomarine Systems, **11** 202
The Geon Company, **11 158–61**
Geon Industries, Inc. *See* Johnston Industries, Inc.
Geophysical Service, Inc., **II** 112; **III** 499–500; **IV** 365
GeoQuest Systems Inc., **17** 419
Georesources, Inc., **19** 247
Georg Fischer Foundries Group, **38** 214
George A. Hormel and Company, **II 504–06**; **7** 547; **12** 123–24; **18** 244. *See also* Hormel Foods Corporation.
George A. Touche & Co., **9** 167
George Batten Co., **I** 28
George Booker & Co., **13** 102
George Buckton & Sons Limited, **40** 129
George Fischer, Ltd., **III** 638
George H. Dentler & Sons, **7** 429
The George Hyman Construction Company, **8** 112–13; **25** 403
George J. Ball, Inc., **27** 507
George K. Baum & Company, **25** 433
George K. Smith & Co., **I** 692
George Kent, **II** 3; **22** 10
George Newnes Company, **IV** 641; **7** 244
George Peabody & Co., **II** 329, 427
George R. Newell Company. *See* Supervalu Inc.
George R. Rich Manufacturing Company. *See* Clark Equipment Company.
George Smith Financial Corporation, **21** 257
George W. Neare & Co., **III** 224
George Weston Limited, **II 631–32**; **36 245–48 (upd.)**; **41** 30, 33
George Wimpey PLC, **12 201–03**; **28** 450
Georges Renault SA, **III** 427; **28** 40
Georgetown Group, Inc., **26** 187
Georgetown Steel Corp., **IV** 228
Georgia Carpet Outlets, **25** 320
Georgia Cotton Producers Association. *See* Gold Kist Inc.
Georgia Credit Exchange, **6** 24
Georgia Federal Bank, **I** 447; **11** 112–13; **30** 196
Georgia Gulf Corporation, **IV** 282; **9 256–58**, 260
Georgia Hardwood Lumber Co., **IV** 281; **9** 259
Georgia International Life Insurance Co., **III** 218
Georgia Kraft Co., **IV** 312, 342–43; **8** 267–68; **19** 268
Georgia Natural Gas Corporation, **6** 447–48
Georgia-Pacific Corporation, **IV 281–83**, 288, 304, 345, 358; **9** 256–58, **259–62 (upd.)**; **12** 19, 377; **15** 229; **22** 415, 489; **31** 314
Georgia Power & Light Co., **V** 621; **6** 447, 537; **23** 28; **27** 20
Georgia Power Company, **38** 446–48
Georgia Railway and Electric Company, **6** 446–47; **23** 28
Georgie Pie, **V** 35
GeoScience Corporation, **18** 515
Geosource Inc., **III** 182; **21** 14; **22** 189
Geotec Boyles Brothers, S.A., **19** 247
Geotek Communications Inc., **21 238–40**
GeoTel Communications Corp., **34** 114
Geothermal Resources International, **11** 271
GeoVideo Networks, **34** 259
Geoworks Corporation, **25** 509
Geraghty & Miller Inc., **26** 23
Gerald Stevens, Inc., **37 161–63**
Gérard, **25** 84
Gerber Products Company, **II** 481; **III** 19; **7 196–98**, 547; **9** 90; **11** 173; **21** 53–55, **241–44 (upd)**; **25** 366; **34** 103; **36** 256
Gerber Scientific, Inc., **12 204–06**
Gerbes Super Markets, Inc., **12** 112
Gerbo Telecommunicacoes e Servicos Ltda., **32** 40
Geren Associates. *See* CRSS Inc.
Geriatrics Inc., **13** 49
Gerling of Cologne, **III** 695
Germaine Monteil Cosmetiques Corp., **I** 426; **III** 56
German American Bancorp, **41 178–80**
German-American Car Company. *See* GATX.
German-American Securities, **II** 283
German Cargo Service GmbH., **I** 111
German Mills American Oatmeal Factory, **II** 558; **12** 409
Germania Refining Co., **IV** 488–89

Germplasm Resource Management, **III** 740
Gerresheimer Glas AG, **II** 386; **IV** 232; **43 186–89**
Gerrity Oil & Gas Corporation, **11** 28; **24** 379–80
Gervais Danone, **II** 474
GESA. *See* General Europea S.A.
Gesbancaya, **II** 196
Gesellschaft für Chemische Industrie im Basel, **I** 632
Gesellschaft für den Bau von Untergrundbahnen, **I** 410
Gesellschaft für Linde's Eisenmachinen, **I** 581
Gesellschaft für Markt- und Kühlhallen, **I** 581
Gesparal, **III** 47; **8** 342
Gestettner, **II** 159
Gestione Pubblicitaria Editoriale, **IV** 586
GET Manufacturing Inc., **36** 300
Getronics NV, **39 176–78**
Getty Images, Inc., **31 216–18**
Getty Oil Co., **II** 448; **IV** 367, 423, 429, 461, 479, 488, 490, 551, 553; **6** 457; **8** 526; **11** 27; **13** 448; **17** 501; **18** 488; **27** 216; **41** 391, 394–95
Getz Corp., **IV** 137
Geyser Peak Winery, **I** 291
Geysers Geothermal Co., **IV** 84, 523; **7** 188
GFS. *See* Gordon Food Service Inc.
GFS Realty Inc., **II** 633
GHH, **II** 257
GHI, **28** 155, 157
Ghirardelli Chocolate Company, **24** 480; **27** 105; **30 218–20**
GI Communications, **10** 321
GI Export Corp. *See* Johnston Industries, Inc.
GIAG, **16** 122
Gianni Versace SpA, **22 238–40**
Giant Bicycle Inc., **19** 384
Giant Cement Holding, Inc., **23 224–26**
Giant Eagle, Inc., **12** 390–91; **13** 237
Giant Food Inc., **II 633–35**, 656; **13** 282, 284; **15** 532; **16** 313; **22 241–44 (upd.)**; **24** 462
Giant Industries, Inc., **19 175–77**
Giant Resources, **III** 729
Giant Stores, Inc., **7** 113; **25** 124
Giant TC, Inc. *See* Campo Electronics, Appliances & Computers, Inc.
Giant Tire & Rubber Company, **8** 126
Giant Video Corporation, **29** 503
Giant Wholesale, **II** 625
GIB Group, **V 63–66**; **22** 478; **23** 231; **26 158–62 (upd.)**
Gibbons, Green, van Amerongen Ltd., **II** 605; **9** 94; **12** 28; **19** 360
Gibbs Automatic Molding Co., **III** 569; **20** 360
Gibbs Construction, **25** 404
GIBCO Corp., **I** 321; **17** 287, 289
Gibraltar Casualty Co., **III** 340
Gibraltar Financial Corp., **III** 270–71
Gibraltar Steel Corporation, **37 164–67**
Gibson, Dunn & Crutcher LLP, **36 249–52**; **37** 292
Gibson Greetings, Inc., **7** 24; **12 207–10**; **16** 256; **21** 426–28; **22** 34–35
Gibson Guitar Corp., **16 237–40**
Gibson McDonald Furniture Co., **14** 236
GIC. *See* The Goodyear Tire & Rubber Company.
Giddings & Lewis, Inc., **8** 545–46; **10 328–30**; **23** 299; **28** 455
Giftmaster Inc., **26** 439–40
Gil-Wel Manufacturing Company, **17** 440
Gilbane, Inc., **34 191–93**
Gilbert & John Greenall Limited, **21** 246
Gilbert-Ash Ltd., **I** 588
Gilbert Lane Personnel, Inc., **9** 326
Gilde-Verlag, **IV** 590
Gilde-Versicherung AG, **III** 400
Gildon Metal Enterprises, **7** 96
Gilkey Bros. *See* Puget Sound Tug and Barge Company.
Gill and Duffus, **II** 500
Gill Industries, **II** 161
Gill Interprovincial Lines, **27** 473
Gillett Holdings, Inc., **7 199–201**; **11** 543, 545; **43** 437–38
The Gillette Company, **III 27–30**, 114, 215; **IV** 722; **8** 59–60; **9** 381, 413; **17** 104–05; **18** 60, 62, 215, 228; **20 249–53 (upd.)**; **23** 54–57; **26** 334; **28** 247; **39** 336
Gilliam Furniture Inc., **12** 475
Gilliam Manufacturing Co., **8** 530
Gilman & Co., **III** 523
Gilman Fanfold Corp., Ltd., **IV** 644
Gilman Paper Co., **37** 178
Gilmore Brother's, **I** 707
Gilmore Steel Corporation. *See* Oregon Steel Mills, Inc.
Gilroy Foods, **27** 299
Giltspur, **II** 587
Gimbel Brothers, Inc. *See* Saks Holdings, Inc.
Gimbel's Department Store, **I** 426–27; **8** 59; **22** 72
Gindick Productions, **6** 28
Ginn & Co., **IV** 672; **19** 405
Ginnie Mae. *See* Government National Mortgage Association.
Gino's, **III** 103
Gino's East, **21** 362
Ginsber Beer Group, **15** 47; **38** 77
Giorgio Beverly Hills, Inc., **26** 384
Giorgio, Inc., **III** 16; **19** 28
Girard Bank, **II** 315–16
Girbaud, **17** 513; **31** 261
Girl Scouts of the USA, **35 193–96**
Girling, **III** 556
Giro Sport Designs, **16** 53
Girod, **19** 50
Girsa S.A., **23** 170
Girvin, Inc., **16** 297
Gist-Brocades Co., **III** 53; **26** 384
The Gitano Group, Inc., **8 219–21**; **20** 136 **25** 167; **37** 81
Givaudan SA, **43 190–93**
GJM International Ltd., **25** 121–22
GK Technologies Incorporated, **10** 547
GKH Partners, **29** 295
GKN plc, **III 493–96**, 554, 556; **38 208–13 (upd.)**; **42** 47
Glaceries de Saint-Roch, **III** 677; **16** 121
Glaces de Boussois, **II** 474–75
Glacier Bancorp, Inc., **35 197–200**
Glacier Park Co., **10** 191
Gladieux Corp., **III** 103
Glamar Group plc, **14** 224
Glamor Shops, Inc., **14** 93
Glanbia Group, **38** 196, 198
Glasrock Home Health Care, **I** 316; **25** 81
Glass Containers Corp., **I** 609–10
Glass Fibres Ltd., **III** 726
Glasstite, Inc., **33** 360–61
GlasTec, **II** 420
Glatfelter Wood Pulp Company, **8** 413
Glaverbel, **III** 667
Glaxo Holdings plc, **I 639–41**, 643, 668, 675, 693; **III** 66; **6** 346; **9 263–65 (upd.)**; **10** 551; **11** 173; **20** 39; **26** 31; **34** 284; **38** 365
Gleason Corporation, **24 184–87**
Glen & Co, **I** 453
Glen Alden Corp., **15** 247
Glen Cove Mutual Insurance Co., **III** 269
Glen-Gery Corporation, **14** 249
Glen Iris Bricks, **III** 673
Glen Line, **6** 416
Glencairn Ltd., **25** 418
Glendale Federal Savings, **IV** 29
The Glenlyte Group, **29** 469
Glenlyte Thomas Group LLC, **29** 466
Glenn Advertising Agency, **25** 90
Glenn Pleass Holdings Pty. Ltd., **21** 339
Glens Falls Insurance Co., **III** 242
GLF-Eastern States Association, **7** 17
The Glidden Company, **I** 353; **8 222–24**; **21** 545
Glimcher Co., **26** 262
Glitsch International, Inc., **6** 146; **23** 206, 208
Global Access, **31** 469
Global Apparel Sourcing Ltd., **22** 223
Global Crossing Ltd., **32 216–19**
Global Energy Group, **II** 345
Global Engineering Company, **9** 266
Global Health Care Partners, **42** 68
Global Industries, Ltd., **37 168–72**
Global Information Solutions, **34** 257
Global Interactive Communications Corporation, **28** 242
Global Marine Inc., **9 266–67**; **11** 87
Global Natural Resources, **II** 401; **10** 145
Global Telesystems Ltd. *See* Global Crossing Ltd.
Global Transport Organization, **6** 383
GlobalCom Telecommunications, Inc., **24** 122
GlobaLex, **28** 141
Globe & Rutgers Insurance Co., **III** 195–96
Globe Business Furniture, **39** 207
Globe Co. **I** 201
Globe Electric Co., **III** 536
Globe Feather & Down, **19** 304
Globe Files Co., **I** 201
Globe Grain and Milling Co., **II** 555
Globe Industries, **I** 540
Globe Insurance Co., **III** 350
Globe Life Insurance Co., **III** 187; **10** 28; **38** 15
Globe National Bank, **II** 261
Globe Newspaper Co., **7** 15
Globe Pequot Press, **36** 339, 341
Globe Petroleum Ltd., **IV** 401
Globe Steel Abrasive Co., **17** 371
Globe Telegraph and Trust Company, **25** 99
Globe-Union, **III** 536; **26** 229
Globe-Wernicke Co., **I** 201
Globelle Corp., **43** 368
Globetrotter Communications, **7** 199
Globo, **18** 211
Glock Ges.m.b.H., **42 154–56**
Gloria Jean's Gourmet Coffees, **20** 83
La Gloria Oil and Gas Company, **7** 102
Gloria Separator GmbH Berlin, **III** 418

Glosser Brothers, **13** 394
Gloster Aircraft, **I** 50; **III** 508; **24** 85
Gloucester Cold Storage and Warehouse Company, **13** 243
Glovatorium, **III** 152; **6** 266; **30** 339
Glycomed Inc., **13** 241
Glyn, Mills and Co., **II** 308; **12** 422
GM. *See* General Motors Corp.
GM Hughes Electronics Corporation, II 32–36; **10** 325. *See also* Hughes Electronics Corporation.
GMARA, **II** 608
GMFanuc Robotics, **III** 482–83
GMR Properties, **21** 257
GNB International Battery Group, **10** 445
GND Holdings Corp., **7** 204; **28** 164
GNMA. *See* Government National Mortgage Association.
The Go-Ahead Group Plc, 28 155–57
Go Fly Ltd., **39** 128
Go-Gro Industries, Ltd., **43** 99
Go Sport. *See* Groupe Go Sport S.A.
Go-Video, Inc. *See* Sensory Science Corporation.
Goal Systems International Inc., **10** 394
Godfather's Pizza Incorporated, II 556–57; **11** 50; **12** 123; **14** 351; **17** 86; **25 179–81**
Godfrey Co., **II** 625
Godfrey L. Cabot, Inc., **8** 77
Godiva Chocolatier, **II** 480; **26** 56
Godo Shusei, **III** 42
Godsell, **10** 277
Godtfred Kristiansen, **13** 310–11
Goebel & Wetterau Grocery Co., **II** 681
Goelitz Confectionary. *See* Herman Goelitz, Inc.
Goering Werke, **II** 282
Göhner AG, **6** 491
Gokey Company, **10** 216; **28** 339
Gold Bond Stamp Company, **6** 363–64; **22** 125
Gold Crust Bakeries, **II** 465
Gold Dust Corp., **II** 497
Gold Exploration and Mining Co. Limited Partnership, **13** 503
Gold Fields of South Africa Ltd., I 423; **IV** 91, **94–97**
Gold Kist Inc., **7** 432; **17 207–09**; **26 166–68**
Gold Lance Inc., **19** 451–52
Gold Lion, **20** 263
Gold Seal, **II** 567
Gold Star Foods Co., **IV** 410
Gold's Gym Enterprises, **25** 450
Goldblatt Bros., **IV** 135
Goldblatt's Department Stores, **15** 240–42
Golden, **III** 47
Golden Bear International, **33** 103; **42** 433
Golden Belt Manufacturing Co., 16 241–43
Golden Books Family Entertainment, Inc., 28 158–61
Golden Circle Financial Services, **15** 328
Golden Corral Corporation, 10 331–33
Golden Eagle Exploration, **IV** 566–67
Golden Enterprises, Inc., 26 163–65
Golden Gate Airlines, **25** 421
Golden Grain Macaroni Co., **II** 560; **12** 411; **30** 219; **34** 366
Golden Hope Rubber Estate, **III** 697, 699
Golden Nugget, Inc. *See* Mirage Resorts, Incorporated.
Golden Partners, **10** 333
Golden Peanut Company, **17** 207
Golden Poultry Company, **26** 168
Golden Press, Inc., **13** 559–61
Golden Sea Produce, **10** 439
Golden Skillet, **10** 373
Golden State Bank, **II** 348
Golden State Foods Corporation, 32 220–22
Golden State Newsprint Co. Inc., **IV** 296; **19** 226; **23** 225
Golden State Sanwa Bank, **II** 348
Golden State Vintners, Inc., 33 172–74
Golden Tulip International, **I** 109
Golden West Homes, **15** 328
Golden West Publishing Corp., **38** 307–08
Golden Wonder, **II** 500; **III** 503
Golden Youth, **17** 227
Goldenberg Group, Inc., **12** 396
Goldenlay Eggs, **II** 500
Goldfield Corp., **12** 198
Goldfine's Inc., **16** 36
Goldkuhl & Broström, **III** 419
Goldline Laboratories Inc., **11** 208
Goldman, Sachs & Co., II 11, 268, 326, 361, **414–16**, 432, 434, 448; **III** 80, 531; **IV** 611; **9** 378, 441; **10** 423; **12** 405; **13** 95, 448, 554; **15** 397; **16** 195; **20 254–57 (upd.)**, 258; **21** 146; **22** 427–28; **26** 456; **27** 317; **29** 508; **36** 190–91; **38** 289, 291
Goldome Savings Bank, **11** 110; **17** 488
Goldsbrough Mort & Co., **I** 437
Goldsmith's, **9** 209
Goldstar Co., Ltd., II 5, 53–54; **III** 517; **7** 233; **12 211–13**; **13** 213; **30** 184; **43** 428
Goldwell, **III** 38
Goldwyn Films. *See* Metro-Goldwyn-Mayer Inc.
Goleta National Bank, **33** 5
Golf Day, **22** 517
The Golub Corporation, 26 169–71
Gomoljak, **14** 250
Gonnella Baking Company, 40 211–13
Good Foods, Inc., **II** 497
The Good Guys!, Inc., 10 334–35; **30 224–27 (upd.)**
The Good Humor-Breyers Ice Cream Company, II 533; **14 203–05**; **15** 222; **17** 140–41; **32** 474, 476
Good Natural Café, **27** 481
Good Times, Inc., **8** 303
Good Vibrations, Inc., **28** 345
Good Weather International Inc., **III** 221; **14** 109
Goodbody & Company, **II** 425; **13** 341; **22** 428
Goodbody James Capel, **16** 14
Goodby, Berlin & Silverstein, **10** 484
Goodebodies, **11** 41
Gooderham and Worts, **I** 216, 263–64
Goodlass, Wall & Co., **III** 680–81
Goodman Bros. Mfg. Co., **14** 436
Goodman Fielder, Wattie's, Ltd., **II** 565; **7** 577
Goodman Holding Company, 42 157–60
GoodMark Foods, Inc., 26 172–74
Goodrich Oil Co., **IV** 365
Goodrich, Tew and Company, **V** 231
Goodrich Tire Company, **V** 240–41; **6** 27
Goodson Newspaper Group, **29** 262
GoodTimes Entertainment, **31** 238
Goodwill Industries International, Inc., 15 511; **16 244–46**
Goodwin & Co., **12** 108
Goodwin, Dannenbaum, Littman & Wingfield, **16** 72
Goody Products, Inc., 12 214–16
Goody's Family Clothing, Inc., 20 265–67
The Goodyear Tire & Rubber Company, I 21; **II** 304; **III** 452; **V 244–48**; **8** 81, 291–92, 339; **9** 324; **10** 445; **15** 91; **16** 474; **19** 221, 223, 455; **20 259–64 (upd.)**; **21** 72–74
Gordon A. Freisen, International, **III** 73
Gordon B. Miller & Co., **7** 256; **25** 254
Gordon Capital Corp., **II** 245
Gordon Food Service Inc., 8 225–27; **39 179–82 (upd.)**
Gordon Investment Corp., **II** 245
Gordon Jewelry Corporation, **16** 559, 561; **40** 472
Gordon Manufacturing Co., **11** 256
Gordon Publications, **IV** 610
Gordon S. Black Corporation, **41** 197–98
Gordon-Van Cheese Company, **8** 225
Gordy Company, **26** 314
Gore Newspapers Company, **IV** 683; **22** 521
Gorges Foodservice, Inc., **14** 516
Gorham Silver, **12** 313
Gorilla Sports Club, **25** 42
Gorman Eckert & Co., **27** 299
The Gorman-Rupp Company, 18 201–03
Gormully & Jeffrey, **IV** 660
Gorton's, II 502; **10** 323; **13 243–44**
The Gosho Co. *See* Kanematsu Corporation.
Goss Holdings, Inc., 43 194–97
Gotaas-Larsen Shipping Corp., **6** 368; **27** 91
Götabanken, **II** 303, 353
Göteborgs Handelsbank, **II** 351
Göteborgs Handelskompani, **III** 425
Gothenburg Light & Power Company, **6** 580
Gothenburg Tramways Co., **II** 1
Gott Corp., **III** 614; **21** 293
Gottleib Group, **38** 437
Gottschalks, Inc., 18 204–06; **26** 130
Goulard and Olena, **I** 412
Gould Electronics, Inc., III 745; **11** 45; **13** 127, 201; **14 206–08**; **21** 43
Goulding Industries Ltd., **IV** 295; **19** 225
Goulds Pumps Inc., 24 188–91
Gourmet Award Foods, **29** 480–81
Gourmet Foods, **II** 528
Government Bond Department, **9** 369
Government Employees Insurance Company. *See* GEICO Corporation.
Government National Mortgage Assoc., **II** 410
Governor and Company of Adventurers of England. *See* Hudson's Bay Company.
The Governor and Company of the Bank of Scotland, II 422; **III** 360; **V** 166; **10 336–38**
Goya Foods Inc., 22 245–47; **24** 516
GP Group Acquisition Limited Partnership, **10** 288; **27** 41–42
GPE. *See* General Precision Equipment Corporation.
GPI. *See* General Parts Inc.
GPM Gas Corporation, **40** 357–58
GPS Pool Supply, **29** 34
GPT, **15** 125

GPU. *See* General Public Utilities Corporation.
GPU, Inc., 27 182–85 (upd.)
Graber Industries, Inc., **V** 379; **19** 421
Grace. *See* W.R. Grace & Co.
Grace Drilling Company, **9** 365
Grace-Sierra Horticultural Products Co., **22** 475
Graco Inc., 19 178–80
Gradco Systems, Inc., **6** 290
Gradiaz, Annis & Co., **15** 138
Gradmann & Holler, **III** 283
Graef & Schmidt, **III** 54
Graf, **23** 219
Graf Bertel Dominique/New York, **6** 48
Graficas e Instrumentos S.A., **13** 234
Graftek Press, Inc., **26** 44
Graham Brothers, **27** 267, 269
Graham Container Corp., **8** 477
Graham Page, **III** 568; **20** 359
Grahams Builders Merchants, **I** 429
Gralla, **IV** 687
Grameen Bank, 31 219–22
Gramercy Pictures, **23** 391
Gramophone Company, **22** 192
Grampian Electricity Supply Company, **13** 457
Gran Central Corporation, **8** 487
Granada Group PLC, II 70, **138–40**; **17** 353; **24 192–95 (upd.)**, 269; **25** 270; **32** 404
Granada Royale Hometels, **9** 426
Granaria Holdings B.V., **23** 183
GranCare, Inc., 14 209–11; **25** 310
Grand Bazaar Innovations Bon Marché, **13** 284; **26** 159–60
Grand Casinos, Inc., 20 268–70; **21** 526; **25** 386
Grand Department Store, **19** 510
Grand Hotel Krasnapolsky N.V., 23 227–29
Grand Magasin de Nouveautés Fournier d'Annecy, **27** 93
Grand Metropolitan plc, I 247–49, 259, 261; **II** 555–57, 565, 608, 613–15; **9** 99; **13** 391, 407, 409; **14 212–15 (upd.)**; **15** 72; **17** 69, 71; **20** 452; **21** 401; **26** 58; **33** 276; **34** 121; **35** 438; **42** 223; **43** 215. *See also* Diageo plc.
Grand Ole Opry. *See* Gaylord Entertainment Company.
Grand Prix Association of Long Beach, Inc., **43** 139–40
Grand Rapids Carpet Sweeper Company, **9** 70
Grand Rapids Gas Light Company. *See* MCN Corporation.
Grand Rapids Wholesale Grocery Company, **8** 481
Grand Trunk Corp., **6** 359–61
Grand Union Company, II 637, 662; **7 202–04**; **8** 410; **13** 394; **16** 249; **28 162–65 (upd.)**
Grand Valley Gas Company, **11** 28
Grand-Perret, **39** 152–53
Grandes Superficies S.A., **23** 247
Grandmet USA, **I** 248
Les Grands Magasins Au Bon Marché, **26** 159–60
Grands Magasins L. Tietz, **V** 103
GrandVision S.A., 43 198–200
Grandy's, **15** 345
Granger Associates, **12** 136
Gränges, **III** 480; **22** 27
Granite Broadcasting Corporation, 42 161–64
Granite City Steel Company, **12** 353
Granite Furniture Co., **14** 235
Granite Rock Company, 26 175–78
Granite State Bankshares, Inc., 37 173–75
Grant Oil Tool Co., **III** 569; **20** 361
Grant Street National Bank, **II** 317
Grantham, Mayo, Van Otterloo & Co. LLC, **24** 407
Grantree Corp., **14** 4; **33** 398
Graphic Controls Corp., **IV** 678
Graphic Industries Inc., 25 182–84; **36** 508
Graphic Research, Inc., **13** 344–45
Graphic Services, **III** 166; **6** 282
Graphics Systems Software, **III** 169; **6** 285; **8** 519
Graphite Oil Product Co., **I** 360
Graphix Zone, **31** 238
Grass Valley Group, **8** 518, 520
Grasselli Chemical Company, **22** 225
Grasselli Dyestuffs Corp., **I** 337
Grasset, **IV** 617–18
Grasso Production Management Inc., **37** 289
Grattan Plc, **V** 160; **29** 356
The Graver Company, **16** 357
Gray Communications Systems, Inc., 24 196–200
Gray Dawes & Co., **III** 522–23
Gray Drug Stores, **III** 745
Gray Dunn and Co., **II** 569
Gray Line, **24** 118
Gray, Siefert & Co., Inc., **10** 44; **33** 259–60
Grayarc, **III** 157
Grayrock Capital, **I** 275
Grays Harbor Mutual Savings Bank, **17** 530
Greaseater, Ltd., **8** 463–64
Great Alaska Tobacco Co., **17** 80
Great American Bagel and Coffee Co., **27** 482
Great American Broadcasting Inc., **18** 65–66; **22** 131; **23** 257–58
Great American Cookie Company. *See* Mrs. Fields' Original Cookies, Inc.
Great American Entertainment Company, **13** 279
Great American First Savings Bank of San Diego, **II** 420
Great American Life Insurance Co., **III** 190–92
Great American Lines Inc., **12** 29
Great American Management and Investment, Inc., 8 228–31
Great American Reserve Insurance Co., **IV** 343; **10** 247
Great American Restaurants, **13** 321
The Great Atlantic & Pacific Tea Company, Inc., II 636–38, 629, 655–56, 666; **13** 25, 127, 237; **15** 259; **16** 63–64, **247–50 (upd.)**; **17** 106; **18** 6; **19** 479–80; **24** 417; **26** 463; **33** 434
Great Bagel and Coffee Co., **27** 480–81
Great Beam Co., **III** 690
Great Eastern Railway, **6** 424
Great 5¢ Store, **V** 224
Great Halviggan, **III** 690
Great Lakes Bancorp, 8 232–33
Great Lakes Bankgroup, **II** 457
Great Lakes Carbon Corporation, **12** 99
Great Lakes Chemical Corp., I 341–42; **8** 262; **14 216–18 (upd.)**
Great Lakes Corp., **IV** 136
Great Lakes Energy Corp., **39** 261
Great Lakes Pipe Line Co., **IV** 400, 575; **31** 470
Great Lakes Steel Corp., **IV** 236; **8** 346; **12** 352; **26** 528
Great Lakes Window, Inc., **12** 397
Great Land Seafoods, Inc., **II** 553
Great Northern, **III** 282
Great Northern Import Co., **I** 292
Great Northern Nekoosa Corp., **IV** 282–83, 300; **9** 260–61
Great Northern Railway Company, **6** 596
Great Plains Software Inc., **38** 432
Great Plains Transportation, **18** 226
Great Shoshone & Twin Falls Water Power Company, **12** 265
The Great Universal Stores plc, V 67–69; **15** 83; **17** 66, 68; **19 181–84 (upd.)**; **41** 74, 76
Great-West Lifeco Inc., III 260–61; **21** 447. *See also* Power Corporation of Canada.
The Great Western Auction House & Clothing Store, **19** 261
Great Western Billiard Manufactory, **III** 442
Great Western Financial Corporation, 10 339–41
Great Western Foam Co., **17** 182
Great Western Railway, **III** 272
Great World Foods, Inc., **17** 93
Greatamerica Corp., **I** 489; **10** 419; **24** 303
Greater All American Markets, **II** 601; **7** 19
Greater New York Film Rental Co., **II** 169
Greater Washington Investments, Inc., **15** 248
Greb Industries Ltd., **16** 79, 545
Grebner GmbH, **26** 21
Grede Foundries, Inc., 38 214–17
Greeley Beef Plant, **13** 350
Greeley Gas Company, **43** 56–57
Green Acquisition Co., **18** 107
Green Bay Food Company, **7** 127
The Green Bay Packers, Inc., 32 223–26
Green Capital Investors L.P., **23** 413–14
Green Cross K.K., **I** 665
Green Giant, **II** 556; **13** 408; **14** 212, 214; **24** 140–41
Green Island Cement (Holdings) Ltd. Group, **IV** 694–95
Green Line Investor Services, **18** 553
Green Mountain Coffee, Inc., 31 227–30
Green Power & Light Company. *See* UtiliCorp United Inc.
Green River Electric Corporation, **11** 37
Green Thumb, **II** 562
Green Tree Financial Corporation, 11 162–63. *See also* Conseco, Inc.
The Greenalls Group PLC, 21 245–47
The Greenbrier Companies, 19 185–87
Greene King plc, 31 223–26
Greenfield Healthy Foods, **26** 58
Greenfield Industries Inc., **13** 8
Greenham Construction Materials, **38** 451–52
Greenleaf Corp., **IV** 203
Greenman Brothers Inc. *See* Noodle Kidoodle.
GreenPoint Financial Corp., 28 166–68

Greensboro Life Insurance Company, **11** 213
Greenville Insulating Board Corp., **III** 763
Greenville Tube Corporation, **21** 108
Greenwell Montagu Gilt-Edged, **II** 319; **17** 325
Greenwich Associates, **19** 117
Greenwich Capital Markets, **II** 311
Greenwood Mills, Inc., 14 219–21
Greenwood Publishing Group, **IV** 610
Greenwood Trust Company, **18** 478
Gregg Publishing Co., **IV** 636
Greif Bros. Corporation, 15 186–88
Grenfell and Colegrave Ltd., **II** 245
Gresham Insurance Company Limited, **24** 285
Gresham Life Assurance, **III** 200, 272–73
GretagMacbeth Holdings AG, **18** 291
Gretel's Pretzels, **35** 56
Grey Advertising, Inc., I 175, 623; **6 26–28; 10** 69; **14** 150; **22** 396; **25** 166, 381
Grey United Stores, **II** 666
Grey Wolf, Inc., 43 201–03
Greyhound Corp., I 448–50; II 445; **6** 27; **8** 144–45; **10** 72; **12** 199; **16** 349; **22** 406, 427; **23** 173–74; **27** 480; **42** 394
Greyhound Lines, Inc., 32 227–31 (upd.)
Greyhound Temporary Services, **25** 432
Greylock Mills, **III** 213
GRiD Systems Corp., **II** 107
Griesheim Elektron, **IV** 140
Grieveson, Grant and Co., **II** 422–23
Griffin and Sons, **II** 543
Griffin Bacal, **25** 381
Griffin Land & Nurseries, Inc., 43 204–06
Griffin Pipe Products Co., **7** 30–31
Griffin Wheel Company, **7** 29–30
Griffon Corporation, 34 194–96
Griffon Cutlery Corp., **13** 166
Grigg, Elliot & Co., **14** 555
Grimes Aerospace, **22** 32
Grindlays Bank, **II** 189
Gringoir/Broussard, **II** 556
Grinnell Corp., III 643–45; **11** 198; **13 245–47**
Grip Printing & Publishing Co., **IV** 644
Grisewood & Dempsey, **IV** 616
Grist Mill Company, 15 189–91; 22 338
Gristede Brothers, **23** 407; **24** 528–29
Gristede's Sloan's, Inc., 31 231–33
GRM Industries Inc., **15** 247–48
Grocer Publishing Co., **IV** 638
Grocery Store Products Co., **III** 21
Grocery Warehouse, **II** 602
Groen Manufacturing, **III** 468
Grogan-Cochran Land Company, **7** 345
Grolier Inc., IV 619; **16 251–54; 43 207–11 (upd.)**
Grolier Interactive, **41** 409
Groot-Noordhollandsche, **III** 177–79
Groovy Beverages, **II** 477
Gross Brothers Laundry. *See* G&K Services, Inc.
Gross Townsend Frank Hoffman, **6** 28
Grosset & Dunlap, Inc., **II** 144; **III** 190–91
Grosskraftwerk Franken AG, **23** 47
Grossman's Inc., 13 248–50
Grossmith Agricultural Industries, **II** 500
Grosvenor Marketing Co., **II** 465
Groton Victory Yard, **I** 661
Ground Round, Inc., 21 248–51
Ground Services Inc., **13** 49
Group Arnault, **32** 146
Group 4 Falck A/S, 42 165–68, 338
Group Health Cooperative, 41 181–84
Group Hospitalization and Medical Services, **10** 161
Group Lotus, **13** 357
Group Maintenance America Corp. *See* Encompass Services Corporation.
Group Schneider S.A., **20** 214
Groupe AB, **19** 204
Groupe AG, **III** 201–02
Groupe Air France, 6 92–94. *See also* Air France *and* Societe Air France.
Groupe Ancienne Mutuelle, **III** 210–11
Groupe André, 17 210–12
Groupe Axime, **37** 232
Groupe Barthelmey, **III** 373
Groupe Bisset, **24** 510
Groupe Bollore, **37** 21
Groupe Bruxelles Lambert, **26** 368
Groupe Bull, **10** 563–64; **12** 246; **21** 391; **34** 517. *See also* Compagnie des Machines Bull.
Groupe Casino. *See* Etablissements Economiques de Casino Guichard, Perrachon et Cie, S.C.A.
Groupe Castorama-Dubois Investissements, 23 230–32
Groupe Danone, 14 150; **32 232–36 (upd.)**
Le Groupe Darty, **24** 266, 270
Groupe Dassault Aviation SA, 26 179–82 (upd.); 42 373, 376
Groupe de la Cité, IV 614–16, 617
Groupe de la Financière d'Angers, **IV** 108
Groupe DMC (Dollfus Mieg & Cie), 27 186–88
Groupe Go Sport S.A., 39 183–85
Groupe Guillin SA, 40 214–16
Groupe Jean Didier, **12** 413
Groupe Jean-Paul Gaultier, **34** 214
Groupe Lagardère S.A., **15** 293; **21** 265, 267
Groupe Lapeyre S.A., 33 175–77
Groupe Legris Industries, 23 233–35
Groupe Les Echos, 25 283–85
Groupe Pechiney, **33** 89
Groupe Pinault-Printemps-Redoute, **19** 306, 309; **21** 224, 226
Groupe Poron, **35** 206
Groupe Promodès S.A., 19 326–28
Groupe Rallye, **39** 183–85
Groupe Rothschild, **22** 365
Groupe Rougier SA, 21 438–40
Groupe Roussin, **34** 13
Groupe Salvat, **IV** 619
Groupe SEB, 35 201–03
Groupe Sidel S.A., 21 252–55
Groupe Victoire, **III** 394
Groupe Vidéotron Ltée., 20 271–73
Groupe Yves Saint Laurent, 23 236–39
Groupe Zannier S.A., 35 204–07
Groupement des Exploitants Pétroliers, **IV** 545
Groupement des Mousquetaires. *See* ITM Entreprises SA.
Groupement Français pour l'Investissement Immobilier, **42** 153
Groupement Laitier du Perche, **19** 50
Groupement pour le Financement de la Construction. *See* Gecina SA.
GroupMAC. *See* Encompass Services Corporation.
Groux Beverage Corporation, **11** 451
Grove Manufacturing Co., **I** 476–77; **9** 393
Grow Biz International, Inc., 18 207–10
Grow Group Inc., 12 217–19, 387–88
Growing Healthy Inc., **27** 197; **43** 218
Growmark, **I** 421; **11** 23
Growth International, Inc., **17** 371
Grubb & Ellis Company, 21 256–58
Gruene Apotheke, **I** 681
Gruma, S.A. de C.V., 19 192; **31 234–36**
Grumman Corp., I 58–59, **61–63,** 67–68, 78, 84, 490, 511; **7** 205; **8** 51; **9** 17, 206–07, 417, 460; **10** 316–17, 536; **11 164–67 (upd.),** 363–65, 428; **15** 285; **28** 169
Grün & Bilfinger A.G., **I** 560–61
Grundig AG, I 411; **II** 80, 117; **13** 402–03; **15** 514; **27 189–92**
Grundig Data Scanner GmbH, **12** 162
Grunenthal, **I** 240
Gruner + Jahr AG & Co., **IV** 590, 593; **7** 245; **15** 51; **20** 53; **22** 442; **23** 85
Gruntal & Co., L.L.C., III 263; **20 274–76**
Gruntal Financial Corp., **III** 264
Grupo Acerero del Norte,
Grupo Acerero del Norte, S.A. de C.V., **22** 286; **42** 6
Grupo Bimbo, S.A. de C.V., **31** 236
Grupo Bufete. *See* Bufete Industrial, S.A. de C.V.
Grupo Cabal S.A., **23** 166
Grupo Campi, S.A. de C.V., **39** 230
Grupo Carso, S.A. de C.V., 14 489; **21 259–61**
Grupo Casa Saba, S.A. de C.V., 39 186–89
Grupo Corvi S.A. de C.V., **7** 115; **25** 126
Grupo Cruzcampo S.A., **34** 202
Grupo Cuervo, S.A. de C.V., **31** 91–92
Grupo Cydsa, S.A. de C.V., 39 190–93
Grupo de Ingenieria Ecologica, **16** 260
Grupo Dina. *See* Consorcio G Grupo Dina, S.A. de C.V.
Grupo DST, **41** 405–06
Grupo Elektra, S.A. de C.V., 39 194–97
Grupo Ferrovial, S.A., 40 217–19
Grupo Financiero Banamex-Accival, **27** 304
Grupo Financiero Inbursa, **21** 259
Grupo Financiero Inverlat, S.A., **39** 188
Grupo Financiero Serfin, S.A., 19 188–90, 474; **36** 63
Grupo Gigante, S.A. de C.V., 34 197–99
Grupo Hecali, S.A., **39** 196
Grupo Herdez, S.A. de C.V., 35 208–10
Grupo Hermes, **24** 359
Grupo Industrial Alfa, S.A. *See* Alfa, S.A. de C.V.
Grupo Industrial Atenquique, S.A. de C.V., **37** 176
Grupo Industrial Bimbo, 19 191–93; 29 338
Grupo Industrial Durango, S.A. de C.V., 37 176–78
Grupo Industrial Maseca S.A. de C.V. (Gimsa). *See* Gruma, S.A. de C.V.
Grupo Irsa, **23** 171
Grupo Mexico, S.A. de C.V., 40 220–23, 413
Grupo Modelo, S.A. de C.V., 29 218–20
Grupo Nacional Provincial, **22** 285
Grupo Pipsamex S.A., **37** 178
Grupo Protexa, **16** 210

Grupo Pulsar. *See* Pulsar Internacional S.A.
Grupo Quan, **19** 192–93
Grupo Salinas, **39** 196
Grupo Sanborns S.A. de C.V., **35** 118
Grupo TACA, **38 218–20**
Grupo Televisa, S.A., **9** 429; **18 211–14**; **19** 10; **24** 515–17; **39** 188, 398
Grupo Tribasa, **34** 82
Grupo Tudor, **IV** 471
Grupo Xtra, **39** 186, 188
Grupo Zeta, **IV** 652–53; **7** 392
Gruppo Coin S.p.A., **41 185–87**
Gruppo GFT, **22** 123
Gruppo IRI, **V** 325–27
Gryphon Development, **24** 237
Gryphon Holdings, Inc., **21 262–64**
GSG&T, **6** 495
GSG Holdings Ltd., **39** 87
GSI. *See* Geophysical Service, Inc.
GSI Acquisition Co. L.P., **17** 488
GSR, Inc., **17** 338
GSU. *See* Gulf States Utilities Company.
GT Bicycles, **26 183–85**, 412
GT Interactive Software, **19** 405; **31 237–41**. *See also* Infogrames Entertainment S.A.
GTE Corporation, **II** 38, 47, 80; **III** 475; **V 294–98**; **9** 49, 171, 478–80; **10** 19, 97, 431; **11** 500; **14** 259, 433; **15 192–97 (upd.)**; **18** 74, 111, 543; **22** 19; **25** 20–21, 91; **26** 520; **27** 302, 305. *See also* British Columbia Telephone Company *and* Verizon Communications.
GTE Northwest Inc., **37** 124–26
GTECH Holdings, Inc., **27** 381
GTI Corporation, **29** 461–62
GTM-Entrepose, **23** 332
GTM Group, **43** 450, 452
GTO. *See* Global Transport Organization.
GTS Duratek, Inc., **13** 367–68
Guangzhou M. C. Packaging, **10** 130
Guaranty Bank & Trust Company, **13** 440
Guaranty Federal Bank, F.S.B., **31** 441
Guaranty Federal Savings & Loan Assoc., **IV** 343
Guaranty Properties Ltd., **11** 258
Guaranty Savings and Loan, **10** 339
Guaranty Trust Co., **II** 329–32, 428; **IV** 20; **16** 25; **22** 110; **36** 152
Guardian, **III** 721
Guardian Bank, **13** 468
Guardian Federal Savings and Loan Association, **10** 91
Guardian Mortgage Company, **8** 460
Guardian National Bank, **I** 165; **11** 137
Guardian Refrigerator Company. *See* Frigidaire Home Products.
Guardian Royal Exchange Plc, **III** 350; **11 168–70**; **33** 319
Gubor Schokoladen, **15** 221
Guccio Gucci, S.p.A., **12** 281; **15 198–200**; **27** 329
GUD Holdings, Ltd., **17** 106
Guelph Dolime, **IV** 74
Guerdon Homes, Inc., **41** 19
Guerlain, **23 240–42**; **33** 272
Guernsey Banking Co., **II** 333
Guess, Inc., **15 201–03**; **17** 466; **23** 309; **24** 157; **27** 329
Guest, Keen and Nettlefolds plc. *See* GKN plc.
Guest Supply, Inc., **18 215–17**
Gueyraud et Fils Cadet, **III** 703
Guidant Corp., **30** 316; **37** 39; **43** 351
Guideoutdoors.com Inc., **36** 446
Guilbert S.A., **42 169–71**
Guild Press, Inc., **13** 559
Guild Wineries, **13** 134; **34** 89
Guilford Industries, **8** 270–72
Guilford Mills Inc., **8 234–36**; **40 224–27 (upd.)**
Guilford of Maine, Inc., **29** 246
Guilford Transportation Industries, Inc., **16** 348, 350
Guillemot Corporation, **41 188–91**, 407, 409
Guillin. *See* Groupe Guillin SA
Guinness Mahon, **36** 231
Guinness Overseas Ltd., **25** 281
Guinness Peat Aviation, **10** 277; **36** 426
Guinness plc, **I** 239, 241, **250–52**, 268, 272, 282; **II** 428–29, 610; **9** 100, 449; **10** 399; **13** 454; **18** 62, 501; **29** 84; **33** 276; **36** 405–06. *See also* Diageo plc.
Guinness/UDV, **43 212–16 (upd.)**
Guitar Center, Inc., **29 221–23**
Gujarat State Fertilizer Co., **III** 513
Gulco Industries, Inc., **11** 194
Güldner Aschaffenburg, **I** 582
Gulf + Western Inc., **I** 418, **451–53**, 540; **II** 147, 154–56, 177; **III** 642, 745; **IV** 289, 672; **7** 64; **10** 482; **13** 121, 169, 470; **22** 210; **24** 33; **25** 328, 535; **33** 3; **41** 71
Gulf + Western Industries, **22** 122. *See also* Paramount Communications.
Gulf Air, **6** 63; **27** 25; **39** 137–38
Gulf Canada Ltd., **I** 216, 262, 264; **IV** 495, 721; **6** 478; **9** 391; **13** 557–58
Gulf Caribbean Marine Lines, **6** 383
Gulf Coast Sportswear Inc., **23** 65
Gulf Energy Development, **22** 107
Gulf Engineering Co. Ltd., **IV** 131
Gulf Exploration Co., **IV** 454
Gulf Marine & Maintenance Offshore Service Company, **22** 276
Gulf Mobile and Northern Railroad, **I** 456
Gulf Mobile and Ohio Railroad, **I** 456; **11** 187
Gulf of Suez Petroleum Co., **IV** 412–14
Gulf Oil Chemical Co., **13** 502
Gulf Oil Corp., **I** 37, 584; **II** 315, 402, 408, 448; **III** 225, 231, 259, 497; **IV** 198, 287, 385–87, 392, 421, 450–51, 466, 470, 472–73, 476, 484, 508, 510, 512, 531, 538, 565, 570, 576; **17** 121–22; **21** 494; **24** 521; **25** 444; **33** 253
Gulf Plains Corp., **III** 471
Gulf Power Company, **38** 446, 448
Gulf Public Service Company, Inc, **6** 580; **37** 89
Gulf Resources & Chemical Corp., **15** 464
Gulf States Paper, **IV** 345
Gulf States Steel, **I** 491
Gulf States Utilities Company, **6 495–97**; **12** 99
Gulf United Corp., **III** 194
Gulfstream Aerospace Corporation, **7 205–06**; **13** 358; **24** 465; **28 169–72 (upd.)**; **36** 190–91
Gulfstream Banks, **II** 336
Gulfwind Marine USA, **30** 303
Gulistan Holdings Inc., **28** 219
Gulton Industries Inc., **7** 297; **19** 31
Gummi Werke, **I** 208
Gump's, **7** 286
Gunder & Associates, **12** 553
Gunderson, Inc. *See* The Greenbrier Companies.
Gunfred Group, **I** 387
Gunite Corporation, **23** 306
The Gunlocke Company, **12** 299; **13** 269; **23 243–45**
Gunnite, **27** 203
Gunns Ltd., **II** 482
Gunpowder Trust, **I** 379; **13** 379
Gunter Wulff Automaten, **III** 430
Gunther, S.A., **8** 477
Gupta, **15** 492
Gurneys, Birkbeck, Barclay & Buxton, **II** 235
Gusswerk Paul Saalmann & Sohne, **I** 582
Gustav Schickendanz KG, **V** 165
Gustavus A. Pfeiffer & Co., **I** 710
Gustin-Bacon Group, **16** 8
Gutehoffnungshütte Aktienverein AG, **III** 561, 563; **IV** 104, 201
Guthrie Balfour, **II** 499–500
Guthy-Renker Corporation, **32 237–40**
Gutta Percha Co., **I** 428
Gutteridge, Haskins & Davey, **22** 138
Gutzeit. *See* W. Gutzeit & Co.
Guy Carpenter & Co., **III** 282
Guy Motors, **13** 286
Guy Pease Associates, **34** 248
Guy Salmon Service, Ltd., **6** 349
Guyenne et Gascogne, **23 246–48**
Guyomarc'h, **39** 356
GW Utilities Ltd., **I** 264; **6** 478
Gwathmey Siegel & Associates Architects LLC, **II** 424; **13** 340; **26 186–88**
GWC. *See* General Waterworks Corporation.
GWR Group plc, **39 198–200**
Gymboree Corporation, **15 204–06**
Gynecare Inc., **23** 190
Gynetics, Inc., **26** 31
Gypsum, Lime, & Alabastine Canada Ltd., **IV** 271

H&D. *See* Hinde & Dauch Paper Company.
H&H Craft & Floral, **17** 322
H & H Plastics Co., **25** 312
H & R Block, Incorporated, **9 268–70**; **25** 434; **27** 106, 307; **29 224–28 (upd.)**
H.A. Job, **II** 587
H.B. Claflin Company, **V** 139
H.B. Fenn and Company Ltd., **25** 485
H.B. Fuller Company, **8 237–40**; **32 254–58 (upd.)**
H.B. Nickerson & Sons Ltd., **14** 339
H.B. Reese Candy Co., **II** 511
H.B. Tuttle and Company, **17** 355
H.B. Viney Company, Inc., **11** 211
H. Berlind Inc., **16** 388
H.C. Christians Co., **II** 536
H.C. Frick Coke Co., **IV** 573; **7** 550
H.C. Petersen & Co., **III** 417
H.C. Prange Co., **19** 511–12
H Curry & Sons. *See* Currys Group PLC.
H.D. Lee Company, Inc. *See* Lee Apparel Company, Inc.
H.D. Pochin & Co., **III** 690
H. Douglas Barclay, **8** 296
H.E. Butt Grocery Company, **13 251–53**; **32 259–62 (upd.)**; **33** 307
H.E. Moss and Company Tankers Ltd., **23** 161

H.F. Ahmanson & Company, **II 181–82**; **10 342–44 (upd.)**; **28** 167
H. Fairweather and Co., **I** 592
H.G. Anderson Equipment Corporation, **6** 441
H.H. Brown Shoe Company, **18** 60, **18** 62
H.H. Cutler Company, **17** 513
H.H. Robertson, Inc., **19** 366
H.H. West Co., **25** 501
H. Hackfeld & Co., **I** 417
H. Hamilton Pty, Ltd., **III** 420
H.I.G. Capital L.L.C., **30** 235
H.I. Rowntree and Co., **II** 568
H.J. Green, **II** 556
H.J. Heinz Company, **I** 30–31, 605, 612; **II** 414, 480, 450, **507–09**, 547; **III** 21; **7** 382, 448, 576, 578; **8** 499; **10** 151; **11 171–73 (upd.)**; **12** 411, 529, 531–32; **13** 383; **21** 55, 500–01; **22** 147; **25** 517; **27** 197–98; **33** 446–49; **36 253–57 (upd.)**; **43** 217–18
H.J. Justin & Sons. *See* Justin Industries, Inc.
H.K. Ferguson Company, **7** 355
H.K. Porter Company, Inc., **19** 152
H.L. Green Company, Inc., **9** 448
H.L. Judd Co., **III** 628
H.L. Yoh Company. *See* Day & Zimmerman, Inc.
H. Lewis and Sons, **14** 294
H.M. Byllesby & Company, Inc., **6** 539
H.M. Goush Co., **IV** 677–78
H.M. Spalding Electric Light Plant, **6** 592
H. Miller & Sons, Inc., **11** 258
H N Norton Co., **11** 208
H.O. Houghton & Company, **10** 355
H-P. *See* Hewlett-Packard Co.
H.P. Foods, **II** 475
H.P. Hood, **7** 17–18
H.P. Smith Paper Co., **IV** 290
H.R. MacMillan Export Co., **IV** 306–08
H. Reeve Angel & Co., **IV** 300
H. Salt Fish and Chips, **13** 320
H.T. Cherry Company, **12** 376
H.V. McKay Proprietary, **III** 651
H.W. Heidmann, **I** 542
H.W. Johns Manufacturing Co., **III** 663, 706–08; **7** 291
H.W. Madison Co., **11** 211
H.W.S. Solutions, **21** 37
H.W. Wilson Company, **17** 152; **23** 440
H. Williams and Co., Ltd., **II** 678
Ha-Lo Industries, Inc., **27 193–95**
Häagen-Dazs, **II** 556–57, 631; **10** 147; **14** 212, 214; **19** 116; **24** 140, 141
Haake-Beck Brauerei AG, **9** 86
Haas, Baruch & Co. *See* Smart & Final, Inc.
Haas Corp., **I** 481
Haas Publishing Companies, Inc., **22** 442
Haas Wheat & Partners, **15** 357
Habersham Bancorp, **25 185–87**
Habirshaw Cable and Wire Corp., **IV** 177
Habitat for Humanity International, **36 258–61**
Habitat/Mothercare PLC. *See* Storehouse PLC.
Hach Co., **14** 309; **18 218–21**
Hachette Filipacchi Medias S.A., **21 265–67**; **33** 310
Hachette S.A., **IV** 614–15, **617–19**, 675; **10** 288; **11** 293; **12** 359; **16** 253–54; **17** 399; **21** 266; **22** 441–42; **23** 476; **43** 210. *See also* Matra-Hachette S.A.
Hachmeister, Inc., **II** 508; **11** 172
Hacker-Pschorr Brau, **II** 242; **35** 331
Hadco Corporation, **24 201–03**
Hadleigh-Crowther, **I** 715
Haemocell, **11** 476
Haemonetics Corporation, **20 277–79**
Hafez Insurance Co., **III** 242
Hagemeyer N.V., **18** 180–82; **39 201–04**
Haggar Corporation, **19 194–96**; **24** 158
Haggen Inc., **38 221–23**
Haggie, **IV** 91
Hahn Automotive Warehouse, Inc., **24 204–06**
Hahn Department Stores. *See* Allied Stores Corp.
Hahn, Inc., **17** 9
Haile Mines, Inc., **12** 253
The Hain Celestial Group, Inc., **43 217–20 (upd.)**
Hain Food Group, Inc., **I** 514; **27 196–98**; **36** 256
Hainaut-Sambre, **IV** 52
A.B. Hakon Swenson, **II** 639
Hakuhodo, Inc., **6 29–31**, 48–49; **16** 167; **42 172–75 (upd.)**
Hakunetsusha & Company, **12** 483
HAL Inc., **6** 104; **9 271–73**. *See also* Hawaiian Airlines, Inc.
Halcon International, **IV** 456
Hale and Dorr, **31** 75
Haleko Hanseatisches Lebensmittel Kontor GmbH, **29** 500
Halewood, **21** 246
Half Price Books, Records, Magazines Inc., **37 179–82**
Halfords Ltd., **IV** 17, 19, 382–83; **24** 75
Halifax Banking Co., **II** 220
Halifax Timber, **I** 335
Hall & Levine Agency, **I** 14
Hall and Co., **III** 737
Hall and Ham River, **III** 739
Hall Bros. Co., **IV** 620–21; **7** 23
Hall Containers, **III** 739
Hall-Mark Electronics, **23** 490
Hallamore Manufacturing Co., **I** 481
La Halle aux Chaussures, **17** 210
Haller, Raymond & Brown, Inc., **II** 10
Halliburton Company, **II** 112; **III** 473, **497–500**, 617; **11** 505; **13** 118–19; **17** 417; **25 188–92 (upd.)**
Hallivet China Clay Co., **III** 690
Hallmark Cards, Inc., **IV 620–21**; **7** 23–25; **12** 207, 209; **16 255–57 (upd.)**, 427; **18** 67, 69, 213; **21** 426–28; **22** 33, 36; **24** 44, 516–17; **25** 69, 71, 368; **28** 160; **29** 64; **39** 87; **40 228–32 (upd.)**
Hallmark Chemical Corp., **8** 386
Hallmark Investment Corp., **21** 92
Halo Lighting, **30** 266
Haloid Company. *See* Xerox Corporation.
Halsam Company, **25** 380
Halsey, Stuart & Co., **II** 431; **III** 276
Halstead Industries, **26** 4
Halter Marine, **22** 276
Hamada Printing Press, **IV** 326
Hamashbir Lata'asiya, **II** 47; **25** 267
Hambrecht & Quist Group, **10** 463, 504; **26** 66; **27** 447; **31** 349
Hambro American Bank & Trust Co., **11** 109
Hambro Countrywide Security, **32** 374
Hambro Life Assurance Ltd., **I** 426; **III** 339
Hambros Bank, **II** 422; **16** 14; **27** 474; **43** 7
Hamburg-Amerikanische-Packetfahrt-Actien-Gesellschaft, **6** 397–98
Hamburg Banco, **II** 351
Hamburg-Amerika, **I** 542
Hamburger Flugzeubau GmbH., **I** 74
Hamelin Group, Inc., **19** 415
Hamer Hammer Service, Inc., **11** 523
Hamersley Holdings, **IV** 59–61
Hamil Textiles Ltd. *See* Algo Group Inc.
Hamilton Aero Manufacturing, **I** 47, 84; **10** 162
Hamilton Beach/Proctor-Silex Inc., **7** 369–70; **16** 384; **17 213–15**; **24** 435; **43** 289
Hamilton Blast Furnace Co., **IV** 208
Hamilton Brown Shoe Co., **III** 528
Hamilton Group Limited, **15** 478
Hamilton Industries, Inc., **25** 261
Hamilton Malleable Iron Co., **IV** 73; **24** 142
Hamilton National Bank, **13** 465
Hamilton Oil Corp., **IV** 47; **22** 107
Hamilton Standard, **9** 417
Hamilton Steel and Iron Co., **IV** 208
Hamilton/Hall-Mark, **19** 313
Hamish Hamilton, **IV** 659; **8** 526
Hammacher Schlemmer & Company, **21 268–70**; **26** 439–40
Hammamatsu Commerce Bank, **II** 291
Hammarplast, **13** 493
Hammarsforsens Kraft, **IV** 339
Hammerich & Lesser, **IV** 589
Hammermill Paper Co., **IV** 287; **15** 229; **23** 48–49
Hammers Plastic Recycling, **6** 441
Hammerson plc, **40 233–35**
Hammerson Property Investment and Development Corporation PLC, **IV 696–98**; **26** 420
Hammery Furniture Company, **14** 302–03
Hammes Co., **38** 482
Hamming-Whitman Publishing Co., **13** 559
Hammond Corp., **IV** 136
Hammond Lumber Co., **IV** 281; **9** 259
Hammond's, **II** 556
Hammonton Electric Light Company, **6** 449
Hamomag AG, **III** 546
Hampton Industries, Inc., **20 280–82**
Hampton Inns, **9** 425–26
Hampton Roads Food, Inc., **25** 389
Hamworthy Engineering Ltd., **31** 367, 369
Han Kook Fertilizer Co., **I** 516
Hanbury, Taylor, Lloyd and Bowman, **II** 306
Hancock Fabrics, Inc., **16** 197–99; **18 222–24**
Hancock Holding Company, **15 207–09**
Hancock Jaffe Laboratories, **11** 460
Hancock Park Associates. *See* Leslie's Poolmart, Inc.
Hancock Textile Co., Inc., **27** 291
Hand in Hand, **III** 234
Handelsbank of Basel, **III** 375
Handelsfinanz Bank of Geneva, **II** 319; **17** 324
Handelsmaatschappij Montan N.V., **IV** 127
Handelsunion AG, **IV** 222
Handleman Company, **15 210–12**
Handley Page Transport Ltd., **I** 50, 92–93; **24** 85
Handy & Harman, **23 249–52**

Handy Andy Home Improvement Centers, Inc., **16** 210; **26** 160–61
Handy Dan, **V** 75
Hanes Corp., **II** 572–73; **8** 202, 288; **15** 436; **25** 166
Hanes Holding Company, **11** 256
Hang Chong, **18** 114
Hang Seng Bank, **II** 298; **IV** 717
Hanger Orthopedic Group, Inc., 41 192–95
Haniel & Cie. GmbH, **27** 175
Hanil Development Company, **6** 98
Hanjin Group, **6** 98; **27** 271–72
Hankook Tyre Manufacturing Company, **V** 255–56; **19** 508
Hankuk Glass Industry Co., **III** 715
Hankyu Corporation, V 454–56; 23 253–56 (upd.)
Hankyu Department Stores, Inc., V 70–71
Hanley Brick, **14** 250
Hanmi Citizen Precision Industry, **III** 455
Hanna-Barbera Cartoons Inc., 7 306; **18** 65; **23 257–59**, 387; **25** 313; **33** 432
Hanna Iron Ore Co., **IV** 236; **26** 528
Hanna Mining Co., **8** 346–47
Hanna Ore Mining Company, **12** 352
Hannaford Bros. Co., 12 220–22
Hannen Brauerei GmbH, **9** 100
Hannifin Corp., **III** 602
Hannoversche Bank, **II** 278
Hanover Bank, **II** 312–13
Hanover Direct, Inc., 36 262–65
Hanover Foods Corporation, 35 211–14
Hanover House, Inc., **24** 154
Hanovia Co., **IV** 78
Hanrstoffe-und Düngemittelwerk Saar-Lothringen GmbH, **IV** 197
Hans Grohe, **III** 570; **20** 362
Hansa Linie, **26** 279–80
Hanseco Reinsurance Co., **III** 343
Hansen Natural Corporation, 31 242–45
Hanson PLC, I 438, 475, 477; **III 501–03**, 506; **IV** 23, 94, 97, 169, 171, 173, 290; **7 207–10 (upd.)**; **13** 478–79; **17** 39–40, 325; **23** 296–97; **27** 287–88; **30 228–32 (upd.)**, 441; **37** 6–7, 205; **39** 345
Hansvedt Industries Inc., **25** 195
Hapag-Lloyd Ag, 6 397–99; 42 283
Happy Air Exchangers Ltd., **21** 499
Happy Eater Ltd., **III** 106
Happy Kids Inc., 30 233–35
Haralambos Beverage Corporation, **11** 451
Harald Quant Group, **III** 377
Harbert Corporation, 13 98; **14 222–23**
Harbison-Walker Refractories Company, III 472; **24 207–09**
Harbor Group, **41** 262–63
Harbor Tug and Barge Co., **6** 382
Harborlite Corporation, **10** 45
Harbour Group, **24** 16
Harco, Inc., **37** 31
Harcourt Brace and Co., IV 622; **12 223–26**
Harcourt Brace Jovanovich, Inc., II 133–34; **III** 118; **IV 622–24**, 642, 672; **7** 312; **12** 224; **13** 106; **14** 177; **19** 404; **25** 177
Harcourt General, Inc., 12 226; **20 283–87 (upd.)**; **25** 178
Harcros Chemical Group, **III** 699
Harcros Investment Trust Ltd., **III** 698–99
Hard Rock Cafe International, Inc., 12 227–29; **25** 387; **27** 201; **32 241–45 (upd.)**; **37** 191; **41** 308
Hardee's Food Systems Inc., **II** 679; **7** 430; **8** 564; **9** 178; **15** 345; **16** 95; **19** 93; **23** 505; **27** 16–18
Hardin Stockton, **21** 96
Harding Lawson Associates Group, Inc., 16 258–60
Hardinge Inc., 25 193–95
Hardison & Stewart Oil, **IV** 569; **24** 519
Hardman Inc., **III** 699
Hardware Wholesalers Inc., **12** 8. *See also* Do it Best Corporation.
Hardwick Stove Company, **III** 573; **22** 349
Hardy Oil & Gas, **34** 75
Hardy Spicer, **III** 595
Harima Shipbuilding & Engineering Co., Ltd., **I** 511, 534; **III** 513, 533; **12** 484
Harima Zosenjo, Ltd., **IV** 129
Harken Energy Corporation, **17** 169–70
Harland and Wolff Holdings plc, 19 197–200
Harlem Globetrotters, **7** 199, 335
Harlequin Enterprises Ltd., **IV** 587, 590, 617, 619, 672; **19** 405; **29** 470–71, 473
Harley-Davidson, Inc., III 658; **7 211–14**; **13** 513; **16** 147–49; **21** 153; **23** 299–301; **25** 22, **196–200 (upd.)**; **40** 31
Harleysville Group Inc., 37 183–86
Harlow Metal Co. Ltd., **IV** 119
Harman International Industries Inc., 15 213–15; **36** 101
Harmon Industries, Inc., 25 201–04
Harmon Publishing Company, **12** 231
Harmonic Inc., 43 221–23
Harmsworth Brothers, **17** 396
Harmsworth Publishing, **19** 118, 120
Harnischfeger Industries, Inc., I 186; **8 241–44**; **14** 56; **26** 355; **38 224–28 (upd.)**
Harold A. Wilson & Co., **I** 405
Harold's Stores, Inc., 22 248–50
Harp Lager Ltd., **15** 442; **35** 395, 397
Harper Group Inc., 12 180; **13** 20; **17 216–19**
Harper House, Inc. *See* Day Runner, Inc.
Harper Robinson and Company, **17** 163
HarperCollins Publishers, IV 652; **7** 389, 391; **14** 555–56; **15 216–18**; **23** 156, 210; **24** 546
Harpers, Inc., **12** 298
Harpo Entertainment Group, 28 173–75; **30** 270
Harrah's Entertainment, Inc., 9 425–27; **16 261–63**; **27** 200; **43 224–28 (upd.)**
Harrell International, **III** 21; **22** 146
Harriman Co., **IV** 310; **19** 266
Harriman, Ripley and Co., **II** 407
Harris Abattoir Co., **II** 482
Harris Adacom Corporation B.V., **21** 239
Harris Bankcorp, **II** 211
Harris Corporation, II 37–39; **11** 46, 286, 490; **20 288–92 (upd.)**; **27** 364
Harris Daishowa (Australia) Pty., Ltd., **IV** 268
Harris-Emery Co., **19** 510
Harris Financial, Inc., **11** 482
Harris Interactive Inc., 41 196–99
Harris Laboratories, **II** 483; **14** 549
Harris Manufacturing Company, **25** 464
Harris Microwave Semiconductors, **14** 417
Harris Oil Company, **17** 170
Harris Pharmaceuticals Ltd., **11** 208
Harris Publications, **13** 179
Harris Publishing. *See* Bernard C. Harris Publishing Company, Inc.
Harris Queensway, **24** 269
Harris Teeter Inc., 23 260–62
Harris Transducer Corporation, **10** 319
Harrisburg National Bank and Trust Co., **II** 315–16
Harrison & Sons (Hanley) Ltd., **III** 681
Harrisons & Crosfield plc, III 696–700. *See also* Elementis plc.
Harrods, **21** 353
Harrow Stores Ltd., **II** 677
Harry and David. *See* Bear Creek Corporation.
Harry F. Allsman Co., **III** 558
Harry Ferguson Co., **III** 651
Harry N. Abrams, Inc., **IV** 677; **17** 486
Harry's Farmers Market Inc., 23 263–66
Harry's Premium Snacks, **27** 197; **43** 218
Harsah Ceramics, **25** 267
Harsco Corporation, 8 245–47; **11** 135; **30** 471
Harshaw Chemical Company, **9** 154; **17** 363
Harshaw/Filtrol Partnership, **IV** 80
Hart Glass Manufacturing, **III** 423
Hart Press, **12** 25
Hart Schaffner & Marx. *See* Hartmarx Corporation.
Hart Son and Co., **I** 592
Harte & Co., **IV** 409; **7** 308
Harte-Hanks Communications, Inc., 17 220–22
Harter Bank & Trust, **9** 474–75
Hartford Container Company, **8** 359
Hartford Electric Light Co., **13** 183
Hartford Financial Services Group, **41** 64
Hartford Fire Insurance, **11** 198
Hartford Insurance Group, **I** 463–64; **22** 428
Hartford Machine Screw Co., **12** 344
Hartford National Bank and Trust Co., **13** 396
Hartford National Corporation, **13** 464, 466–67
Hartford Trust Co., **II** 213
Hartley's, **II** 477
Hartmann & Braun, **III** 566; **38** 299
Hartmann Fibre, **12** 377
Hartmann Luggage, **12** 313
Hartmarx Corporation, 8 248–50; **25** 258; **32 246–50 (upd.)**
The Hartstone Group plc, 14 224–26
The Hartz Mountain Corporation, 12 230–32
Harvard Private Capital Group Inc., **26** 500, 502
Harvard Sports, Inc., **19** 144
Harvard Table Tennis, Inc., **19** 143–44
Harvard Ventures, **25** 358
Harvest Day, **27** 291
Harvest International, **III** 201
Harvest Partners, Inc., **40** 300
Harvestore, **11** 5
Harvey Aluminum Inc., **I** 68; **22** 188
Harvey Benjamin Fuller, **8** 237–38
Harvey Group, **19** 312
Harvey Hotel Corporation, **23** 71, 73
Harvey Lumber and Supply Co., **III** 559
Harveys Casino Resorts, 27 199–201
Harwood Homes, **31** 386
Harza Engineering Company, 14 227–28

Hasbro, Inc., **III 504–06**; **IV** 676; **7** 305, 529; **12** 168–69, 495; **13** 561; **16 264–68 (upd.)**; **17** 243; **18** 520–21; **21** 375; **25** 313, 380–81, 487–89; **28** 159; **34** 369; **43 229–34 (upd.)**
Haslemere Estates, **26** 420
Hasler Holding AG, **9** 32
Hassenfeld Brothers Inc., **III** 504
Hasten Bancorp, **11** 371
Hastings Entertainment, Inc., **29 229–31**
Hastings Filters, Inc., **17** 104
Hastings Manufacturing Company, **17** 106
Hatch Grinding, **29** 86, 88
Hatersley & Davidson, **16** 80
Hatfield Jewelers, **30** 408
Hathaway Manfacturing Co., **III** 213
Hathaway Shirt Co., **I** 25–26
Hattori Seiko Co., Ltd. *See* Seiko Corporation.
Hausted, Inc., **29** 451
Havas, SA, **IV** 616; **10** 195–96, **345–48**; **13** 203–04; **33 178–82 (upd.)**; **34** 83. *See also* Vivendi Universal Publishing
Haven Automation International, **III** 420
Haverty Furniture Companies, Inc., **31 246–49**
Havertys, **39** 174
Haviland Candy Co., **15** 325
Hawaii National Bank, **11** 114
Hawaiian Airlines Inc., **9** 271–73; **22 251–53 (upd.)**; **24** 20–22; **26** 339. *See also* HAL Inc.
Hawaiian Dredging & Construction Co., **I** 565–66
Hawaiian Electric Industries, Inc., **9 274–77**
Hawaiian Fertilizer Co., **II** 490
Hawaiian Pineapple Co., **II** 491
Hawaiian Tug & Barge, **9** 276
Hawaiian Tuna Packers, **II** 491
Hawker Siddeley Group Public Limited Company, **I** 41–42, 50, 71, 470; **III 507–10**; **8** 51; **12** 190; **20** 311; **24** 85–86
Hawkeye Cablevision, **II** 161
Hawkins Chemical, Inc., **16 269–72**
Hawley & Hazel Chemical Co., **III** 25
Hawley Group Limited, **12** 10
Hawley Products, **16** 20
Haworth Inc., **8 251–52**; **27** 434; **39 205–08 (upd.)**
Hawthorn Company, **8** 287
Hawthorn-Mellody, **I** 446; **11** 25
Hawthorne Appliance and Electronics, **10** 9–11
Haxton Foods Inc., **21** 155
Hay Group, **I** 33; **42** 329–30
Hayakawa Electrical Industries, **II** 95–96
Hayakawa Metal Industrial Laboratory, **II** 95; **12** 447
Hayaku Zenjiro, **III** 408
Hayama Oil, **IV** 542
Hayashi Kane Shoten, **II** 578
Hayashikane Shoten K.K., **II** 578
Hayden Clinton National Bank, **11** 180
Hayden Publications, **27** 499
Hayden Stone, **II** 450; **9** 468
Hayes Conyngham & Robinson, **24** 75
Hayes Corporation, **24 210–14**
Hayes Industries Inc., **16** 7
Hayes Lemmerz International, Inc., **27 202–04**
Hayes Microcomputer Products, **9** 515
Hayes Wheel Company, **7** 258
Hayne, Miller & Swearingen, Inc., **22** 202
Hays Petroleum Services, **IV** 451
Hays Plc, **27 205–07**
Hazard, **I** 328
HAZCO International, Inc., **9** 110
Hazel-Atlas Glass Co., **I** 599; **15** 128
Hazel Bishop, **III** 55
Hazelden Foundation, **28 176–79**
Hazell Sun Ltd., **IV** 642; **7** 312
Hazeltine, Inc., **II** 20
Hazlenut Growers of Oregon, **7** 496–97
Hazleton Laboratories Corp., **30** 151
Hazlewood Foods plc, **32 251–53**
Hazzard and Associates, **34** 248
HBO. *See* Home Box Office Inc.
HCA - The Healthcare Company, **35 215–18 (upd.)**
HCI Holdings, **I** 264
HCL America, **10** 505
HCL Sybase, **10** 505
HCR Manor Care, **25** 306, 310
HCS Technology, **26** 496–97
HDM Worldwide Direct, **13** 204; **16** 168
HDR Inc., **I** 563
HDS. *See* Heartland Express, Inc.
Head Sportswear International, **15** 368; **16** 296–97; **43** 374
Headrick Outdoor, **27** 280
Heads and Threads, **10** 43
Headway Corporate Resources, Inc., **40 236–38**
Heal's, **13** 307
Heald Machine Co., **12** 67
Healey & Baker, **IV** 705
Healing Arts Publishing, Inc., **41** 177
Health & Tennis Corp., **III** 431; **25** 40
Health and Diet Group, **29** 212
Health Care & Retirement Corporation, **III** 79; **22 254–56**; **25** 306, 310
Health Care International, **13** 328
Health Maintenance Organization of Pennsylvania. *See* U.S. Healthcare, Inc.
Health Maintenance Organizations, **I** 545
Health Management Center West, **17** 559
Health-Mor Inc. *See* HMI Industries.
Health O Meter Products Inc., **14 229–31**; **15** 307
Health Plan of America, **11** 379
Health Plan of Virginia, **III** 389
Health Products Inc., **I** 387
Health Risk Management, Inc., **24 215–17**
Health Services, Inc., **10** 160
Health Systems International, Inc., **11 174–76**; **25** 527
Health Way, Inc., **II** 538
HealthAmerica Corp., **III** 84
Healthcare, L.L.C., **29** 412
HealthCare USA, **III** 84, 86
HealthCo International, Inc., **19** 290
Healthdyne, Inc., **17** 306–09; **25** 82
Healthmagic, Inc., **29** 412
HealthRider Corporation, **38** 238
Healthshares L.L.C, **18** 370
Healthsource Inc., **22** 143
HealthSouth Corporation, **33 183–86 (upd.)**
HealthSouth Rehabilitation Corporation, **14 232–34**; **25** 111
Healthtex, Inc., **17 223–25**, 513
HealthTrust, **III** 80; **15** 112; **35** 215, 217
Healthy Choice, **12** 531
The Hearst Corporation, **IV** 582, 596, 608, **625–27**; **12** 358–59; **19 201–204 (upd.)**; **21** 404; **22** 161; **32** 3
Hearthstone Insurance Co. of Massachusetts, **III** 203
Heartland Building Products, **II** 582
Heartland Components, **III** 519; **22** 282
Heartland Express, Inc., **13** 550–51; **18 225–27**
Heartland Homes, Inc., **41** 19
Heartland Industrial Partners L.P., **41** 94
Heartland Securities Corp., **32** 145
Heartstream Inc., **18** 423
Heat Transfer Pty. Ltd., **III** 420
Heatcraft Inc., **8** 320–22
Heath Co., **II** 124; **13** 573; **34** 516
Heath Steele Mines Ltd., **IV** 18
Heatilator Inc., **13** 269
Heavy Duty Parts, Inc., **19** 37
Hebrew National Kosher Foods, **III** 24
Hechinger Company, **12 233–36**; **28** 51
Hecker-H-O Co., **II** 497
Heckett Technology Services Inc., **8** 246–47
Heckler & Koch GmbH, **24** 88
Hecla Mining Company, **17** 363; **20** 149, **293–96**
Heco Envelope Co., **IV** 282; **9** 261
Heekin Can Inc., **10** 130; **13 254–56**
HEFCO, **17** 106
Hefei Rongshida Group Corporation, **22** 350
HEI Investment Corp., **9** 276
HEICO Corporation, **15** 380; **30 236–38**
Heidelberger Druckmaschinen AG, **III** 701; **33** 346; **40 239–41**
Heidelberger Zement AG, **23** 325–26; **31 250–53**
Heidelburger Drueck, **III** 301
Heidemij. *See* Arcadis NV.
Heidi Bakery, **II** 633
Heidrick & Struggles International, Inc., **14** 464; **28 180–82**
Heights of Texas, fsb, **8** 437
Heil Company, **28** 103
Heil-Quaker Corp., **III** 654
Heileman Brewing Co. *See* G. Heileman Brewing Co.
Heilig-Meyers Company, **14 235–37**; **23** 412, 414; **40 242–46 (upd.)**
Heim-Plan Unternehmensgruppe, **25** 455
Heimstatt Bauspar AG, **III** 401
Heineken N.V., **I** 219, **256–58**, 266, 288; **II** 642; **13 257–59 (upd.)**; **14** 35; **17** 256; **18** 72; **21** 319; **25** 21–22; **26** 305; **34 200–04 (upd.)**
Heinkel Co., **I** 74
Heinrich Bauer North America, **7** 42–43
Heinrich Bauer Verlag, **23** 85–86
Heinrich Koppers GmbH, **IV** 89
Heinrich Lanz, **III** 463; **21** 173
Heinz Co. *See* H.J. Heinz Company.
Heinz Deichert KG, **11** 95
Heinz Italia S.p.A., **15** 221
Heisers Inc., **I** 185
Heisey Glasswork Company, **19** 210
Heiwa Sogo Bank, **II** 326, 361
Heizer Corp., **III** 109–11; **14** 13–15
HEL&P. *See* Houston Electric Light & Power Company.
Helados La Menorquina S.A., **22** 515
Helemano Co., **II** 491
Helen of Troy Corporation, **18 228–30**
Helen's Arts & Crafts, **17** 321

Helena Rubenstein, Inc., **III** 24, 48; **8** 343–44; **9** 201–02; **14** 121; **30** 188; **35** 111
Helene Curtis Industries, Inc., **I** 403; **8** **253–54**; **18** 217; **22** 487; **28** **183–85 (upd.)**; **32** 476
Heliotrope Studios, Inc., **39** 396
Helix Biocore, **11** 458
Hellefors Jernverk, **III** 623
Heller, Ehrman, White & McAuliffe, **41** **200–02**
Heller Financial, Inc., **7** 213; **16** 37; **25** 198
Hellman, Haas & Co. *See* Smart & Final, Inc.
Hellschreiber, **IV** 669
Helly Hansen ASA, **18** 396; **25** **205–07**
Helme Products, Inc., **15** 139
Helmerich & Payne, Inc., **18** **231–33**
Helmsley Enterprises, Inc., **9** **278–80**; **39** **209–12 (upd.)**
Helmut Delhey, **6** 428
Helmuth Hardekopf Bunker GmbH, **7** 141
Help-U-Sell, Inc., **III** 304
Helvetia General, **III** 376
Helvetia Milk Condensing Co., **II** 486; **7** 428
Helvetia Schweizerische Feuerversicherungs-Gesellschaft St. Gallen, **III** 375
Hely Group, **IV** 294; **19** 225
Helzberg Diamonds, **18** 60, 63; **40** **247–49**
Hemelinger Aktienbrauerei, **9** 86
Hemex, **11** 458
Hemlo Gold Mines Inc., **9** **281–82**; **23** 40, 42
Hemma, **IV** 616
A.B. Hemmings, Ltd., **II** 465
Henderson Brothers Holdings, Inc., **37** 225
Henderson-Union Electric Cooperative, **11** 37
Henderson's Industries, **III** 581
Henijean & Cie, **III** 283
Henkel KGaA, **III** 21, **31–34**, 45; **IV** 70; **9** 382; **13** 197, 199; **22** 145, 257; **30** 291; **34** 153, **205–10 (upd.)**
Henkel Manco Inc., **22** **257–59**
Henley Drilling Company, **9** 364
The Henley Group, Inc., **I** 416; **III** **511–12**; **6** 599–600; **9** 298; **11** 435; **12** 325; **17** 20; **37** 158
Henlys Group plc, **35** 63, 65
Hennes & Mauritz AB, **29** **232–34**
Hennessy Company, **19** 272
Henney Motor Company, **12** 159
Henredon Furniture Industries, **III** 571; **11** 534; **20** 362; **39** 266
Henri Bendel Inc., **17** 203–04
Henry Broderick, Inc., **21** 96
Henry Denny & Sons, **27** 259
Henry Grant & Co., **I** 604
Henry Holt & Co., **IV** 622–23; **13** 105; **27** 223; **35** 451
Henry I. Siegel Co., **20** 136
Henry J. Kaiser Company, Ltd., **28** 200
Henry J. Tully Corporation, **13** 531
The Henry Jones Co-op Ltd., **7** 577
Henry Jones Foods, **I** 437–38, 592; **7** 182; **11** 212
Henry L. Doherty & Company, **IV** 391; **12** 542
Henry Lee Company, **16** 451, 453
Henry, Leonard & Thomas Inc., **9** 533
Henry Meadows, Ltd., **13** 286
Henry Modell & Company Inc., **32** **263–65**
Henry Pratt Company, **7** 30–31
Henry S. King & Co., **II** 307
Henry S. Miller Companies, **21** 257
Henry Schein, Inc., **29** 298; **31** **254–56**
Henry Tate & Sons, **II** 580
Henry Telfer, **II** 513
Henry Waugh Ltd., **I** 469; **20** 311
Henry Willis & Co. *See* Willis Corroon Group Plc.
Henthy Realty Co., **III** 190
HEPCO. *See* Hokkaido Electric Power Company Inc.
Her Majesty's Stationery Office, **7** **215–18**
Heraeus Holding GmbH, **IV** **98–100**, 118
Herald and Weekly Times, **IV** 650, 652; **7** 389, 391
Herald Publishing Company, **12** 150
Heralds of Liberty, **9** 506
Herbalife International, Inc., **17** **226–29**; **18** 164; **41** **203–06 (upd.)**
Herbert Clough Inc., **24** 176
Herbert W. Davis & Co., **III** 344
Herby's Foods, **36** 163
Herco Technology, **IV** 680
Hercofina, **IV** 499
Hercules Filter, **III** 419
Hercules Inc., **I** **343–45**, 347; **III** 241; **19** 11; **22** **260–63 (upd.)**; **28** 195; **30** 36
Hercules Nut Corp., **II** 593
Hercules Offshore Drilling, **28** 347–48
Hereford Paper and Allied Products Ltd., **14** 430
Herff Jones, **II** 488; **25** 254
Heritage Bankcorp, **9** 482
Heritage Communications, **II** 160–61
Heritage Federal Savings and Loan Association of Huntington, **10** 92
Heritage House of America Inc., **III** 81
Heritage Life Assurance, **III** 248
Heritage Media Group, **25** 418
Heritage National Health Plan, **III** 464
Heritage Springfield $$Heritage Springfield, **14** 245
Herley Industries, Inc., **33** **187–89**
Herman Goelitz, Inc., **28** **186–88**
Herman Miller, Inc., **8** 251–52, **255–57**; **39** 205–07
Herman's World of Sports, **I** 548; **II** 628–29; **15** 470; **16** 457; **43** 385
Hermann Pfauter Group, **24** 186
Hermannshütte, **IV** 103, 105
Hermès International S.A., **34** **211–14 (upd.)**
Hermes Kreditversicherungsbank, **III** 300
Hermès S.A., **14** **238–40**
Herrburger Brooks P.L.C., **12** 297
Herrick, Waddell & Reed. *See* Waddell & Reed, Inc.
Herring-Hall-Marvin Safe Co. of Hamilton, Ohio, **7** 145
Hersey Products, Inc., **III** 645
Hershey Bank, **II** 342
Hershey Foods Corporation, **I** 26–27; **II** 478, 508, **510–12**, 569; **7** 300; **11** 15; **12** 480–81; **15** 63–64, **219–22 (upd.)**, 323; **27** 38–40; **30** 208–09
Hertel AG, **13** 297
Hertford Industrial Estates, **IV** 724
Hertie Waren- und Kaufhaus GmbH, **V** **72–74**; **19** 234, 237
Herts & Beds Petroleum Co., **IV** 566
Herts Pharmaceuticals, **17** 450; **41** 375–76
The Hertz Corporation, **I** 130; **II** 90; **6** 52, 129, 348–50, 356–57, 392–93; **V** 494; **9** **283–85**; **10** 419; **11** 494; **16** 379; **21** 151; **22** 54, 56, 524; **24** 9, 409; **25** 143; **33** **190–93 (upd.)**; **36** 215
Hertz-Penske Leasing. *See* Penske Corporation.
Hervillier, **27** 188
Heska Corporation, **39** **213–16**
Hespeler Hockey Inc., **22** 204
Hess Department Stores Inc., **16** 61–62; **19** 323–24; **41** 343
Hess Oil & Chemical Corp., **IV** 366
Hessische Berg- und Hüttenwerke AG, **III** 695
Hessische Landesbank, **II** 385–86
Hessische Ludwigs-Eisenbahn-Gesellschaft, **6** 424
Hesston Corporation, **13** 17; **22** 380
Hetteen Hoist & Derrick. *See* Polaris Industries Inc.
Heublein Inc., **I** 226, 246, 249, **259–61**, 281; **7** 266–67; **10** 180; **14** 214; **21** 314–15; **24** 140; **25** 177; **31** 92; **34** 89
Heuer. *See* TAG Heuer International SA.
Heuga Holdings B.V., **8** 271
Hewitt & Tuttle, **IV** 426; **17** 355–56
Hewitt Motor Company, **I** 177; **22** 329
Hewlett-Packard Company, **II** 62; **III** 116, **142–43**; **6** 219–20, 225, **237–39 (upd.)**, 244, 248, 278–79, 304; **8** 139, 467; **9** 7, 35–36, 57, 115, 471; **10** 15, 34, 86, 232, 257, 363, 404, 459, 464, 499, 501; **11** 46, 234, 274, 284, 382, 491, 518; **12** 61, 147, 162, 183, 470; **13** 128, 326, 501; **14** 354; **15** 125; **16** 5, 139–40, 299, 301, 367, 394, 550; **18** 386–87, 434, 436, 571; **19** 515; **20** 8; **25** 96, 118, 151–53, 499, 531; **26** 177, 520; **27** 221; **28** **189–92 (upd.)**; **33** 15; **36** 3, 81–82, 299–300; **38** 20, 187, 417–19; **41** 117, 288; **43** 294
Hexalon, **26** 420
Hexatec Polymers, **III** 742
Hexcel Corporation, **11** 475; **27** 50; **28** **193–95**
Heyden Newport Chemical Corp., **I** 526
Heyer-Schulte, **26** 286
Heytesbury Party Ltd., **34** 422
HFC. *See* Household Finance Corporation.
HFS Inc., **21** 97; **22** 54, 56
HG Hawker Engineering Co. Ltd., **III** 508
HGCC. *See* Hysol Grafil Composite Components Co.
HH Finch Ltd., **38** 501
HI. *See* Houston Industries Incorporated.
Hi-Bred Corn Company, **9** 410
Hi-Lo Automotive, Inc., **26** 348–49
Hi-Mirror Co., **III** 715
Hi Tech Consignments, **18** 208
Hi-Tek Polymers, Inc., **8** 554
Hibbett Sporting Goods, Inc., **26** **189–91**
Hibbing Transportation, **I** 448
Hibernia & Shamrock-Bergwerksgesellschaft zu Berlin, **I** 542–43
Hibernia Bank, **18** 181
Hibernia Corporation, **37** **187–90**
Hibernian Banking Assoc., **II** 261
Hickman Coward & Wattles, **24** 444
Hickory Farms, Inc., **12** 178, 199; **17** **230–32**
Hickorycraft, **III** 571; **20** 362

Hicks & Greist, **6** 40
Hicks & Haas, **II** 478
Hicks, Muse, Tate & Furst, Inc., **24** 106; **30** 220; **36** 423
Hicksgas Gifford, Inc., **6** 529
Hidden Creek Industries, Inc., **16** 397; **24** 498
HiFi Buys, **30** 465
Higginson et Hanckar, **IV** 107
Higgs & Young Inc., **I** 412
High Point Chemical Corp., **III** 38
High Retail System Co., Ltd., **V** 195
Highgate Hotels, Inc., **21** 93
Highland Container Co., **IV** 345
Highland Superstores, **9** 65–66; **10** 9–10, 304–05, 468; **23** 51–52
Highland Telephone Company, **6** 334
Highlander Publications, **38** 307–08
Highlands Insurance Co., **III** 498
Highmark Inc., **I** 109; **27 208–11**
Highveld Steel and Vanadium Corp., **IV** 22
Higo Bank, **II** 291
Hilbun Poultry, **10** 250
Hilco Technologies, **III** 143; **6** 238
Hildebrandt International, **29 235–38**
Hilex Poly Co., Inc., **8** 477
Hill & Knowlton Inc. *See* WPP Group PLC.
Hill Publishing Co., **IV** 634
Hill-Rom Company, **10** 349–50
Hill Stores, **II** 683
Hill's Pet Nutrition, Inc., **14** 123; **26** 207; **27 212–14**, 390. *See also* Colgate-Palmolive Company.
Hillard Oil and Gas Company, Inc., **11** 523
Hillards, PLC, **II** 678
Hillenbrand Industries, Inc., **6** 295; **10 349–51**; **16** 20
Hiller Aircraft Company, **9** 205
Hiller Group, **14** 286
Hillerich & Bradsby Co., **24** 403
The Hillhaven Corporation, **III** 76, 87–88; **6** 188; **14 241–43**; **16** 57, 515, 517; **25** 307, 456
Hillin Oil, **IV** 658
Hillman, **I** 183
Hills & Dales Railway Co. *See* Dayton Power & Light Company.
Hills Brothers Inc., **II** 548; **7** 383; **28** 311
Hills Pet Products, **III** 25
Hills Stores Company, **11** 228; **13 260–61**; **21** 459; **30** 57
Hillsborough Holdings Corporation. *See* Walter Industries, Inc.
Hillsdale Machine & Tool Company, **8** 514
Hillsdown Holdings, PLC, **II 513–14**; **24 218–21 (upd.)**; **28** 490; **41** 252
Hillshire Farm, **II** 572
Hillside Industries Inc., **18** 118
Hilo Electric Light Company, **9** 276
Hilton, Anderson and Co., **III** 669
Hilton Athletic Apparel, **16** 296–97
Hilton Gravel, **III** 670
Hilton Hotels Corporation, **II** 208; **III 91–93**, 98–99, 102; **IV** 703; **6** 201, 210; **9** 95, 426; **19 205–08 (upd.)**; **21** 91, 93, 182, 333, 363; **23** 482; **27** 10
Hilton International Co., **6** 385; **12** 489
Himley Brick, **14** 248
Himolene, Inc., **8** 181
Hinde & Dauch Ltd., **IV** 272
Hinde & Dauch Paper Company, **19** 496
Hindell's Dairy Farmers Ltd., **II** 611–12
Hinds, Hayden & Eldredge, **10** 135
Hindustan Petroleum Corp. Ltd., **IV** 441
Hindustan Shipyard, **IV** 484
Hindustan Steel Ltd., **IV** 205–07
Hino Motors, Ltd., **7 219–21**; **21** 163, **271–74 (upd.)**; **23** 288
Hinode Life Insurance Co., Ltd., **II** 360; **III** 365
Hinomaru Truck Co., **6** 428
HIP Health Plan, **22** 425
Hip Hing Construction Company Limited, **IV** 717; **38** 319
Hipercor, S.A., **V** 52; **26** 129
Hiram Walker Resources Ltd., **I** 216, **262–64**; **IV** 721; **6** 478; **9** 391; **18** 41
Hiram Walker-Consumers' Home Ltd. *See* Consumers' Gas Company Ltd.
Hiram Walker-Gooderham & Worts Ltd., **29** 18
Hire-Purchase Company of Ireland, **16** 13; **43** 7
Hiroshima Yakult Co., **25** 449
The Hirsh Company, **17** 279
Hirth-Krause Company. *See* Wolverine World Wide Inc.
Hirz, **25** 85
Hispanic Broadcasting Corporation, **35 219–22**; **41** 383, 385
Hispanica de Petroleos, **IV** 424, 527, 546
Hispano Aviacion, **I** 74
HISPANOBRAS, **IV** 55
Hispanoil. *See* Hispanica de Petroleos.
Hispeed Tools, **I** 573
Hisshin-DCA foods, **II** 554
History Book Club, **13** 105–06
HIT Entertainment PLC, **40 250–52**
Hit or Miss, **V** 197–98
Hitachi, Ltd., **I 454–55**, 494, 534; **II** 5, 30, 59, 64–65, 68, 70, 73, 75, 114, 273–74, 292–91; **III** 130, 140, 143, 464, 482; **IV** 101; **6** 238, 262; **7** 425; **9** 297; **11** 45, 308, 507; **12 237–39 (upd.)**, 484; **14** 201; **16** 139; **17** 353, 556; **18** 383; **19** 11; **21** 174–75, 390; **23** 53; **24** 324; **40 253–57 (upd.)**
Hitachi Metals, Ltd., **IV 101–02**
Hitachi Zosen Corporation, **III 513–14**; **8** 449
Hitchiner Manufacturing Co., Inc., **23 267–70**
Hitco, **III** 721–22
Hjalmar Blomqvist A.B., **II** 639
HL&P. *See* Houston Lighting and Power Company.
HLH Products, **7** 229
HMI Industries, Inc., **17 233–35**
HMO-PA. *See* U.S. Healthcare, Inc.
HMT Technology Corp., **IV** 102
HMV, **I** 531
Hoan Products Ltd. *See* Lifetime Hoan Corporation.
Hoare Govett Ltd., **II** 349
HOB Entertainment, Inc., **37 191–94**
Hobart Corporation, **II** 534; **III** 610–11, 654; **7** 276; **12** 549; **22** 282, 353
Hobart Manufacturing Company, **8** 298
Hobbes Manufacturing, **I** 169–70
Hobby Lobby Stores Inc., **17** 360
Hobson, Bates & Partners, Ltd., **14** 48
Hochschild, Kohn Department Stores, **II** 673
Hochtief AG, **14** 298; **17** 376; **24** 88; **33 194–97**
The Hockey Company, **34 215–18**
Hocking Glass Company, **13** 40
Hoden Oil, **IV** 478
Hodenpyl-Walbridge & Company, **14** 134
Hodgart Consulting. *See* Hildebrandt International.
Hodgkin, Barnett, Pease, Spence & Co., **II** 307
Hoechst AG, **I** 305–06, 309, 317, **346–48**, 605, 632, 669–70; **IV** 451; **8** 262, 451–53; **13** 75, 262–64; **18** 47, 49, 51, **234–37 (upd.)**, 401; **21** 544; **22** 32; **25** 376; **34** 284; **35** 455–57; **38** 380
Hoechst Celanese Corporation, **8** 562; **11** 436; **12** 118; **13** 118, **262–65**; **22** 278; **24** 151; **26** 108
Hoeganaes Corporation, **8** 274–75
Hoenig Group Inc., **41 207–09**
Hoerner Waldorf Corp., **IV** 264; **20** 129
Hoesch AG, **IV 103–06**, 128, 133, 195, 228, 232, 323
Hofbräubierzentrale GmbH Saarbrücken, **41** 222
Hoffman Enclosures Inc., **26** 361, 363
Hoffmann-La Roche & Co. *See* F. Hoffmann- La Roche & Co.
Hoffritz, **27** 288
Hofmann Herbold & Partner, **34** 249
Högbo Stål & Jernwerks, **IV** 202
Högforsin Tehdas Osakeyhtiö, **IV** 300
Hojalata y Laminas S.A., **19** 10
Hojgaard & Schultz, **38** 436
Hokkaido Butter Co., **II** 575
Hokkaido Colonial Bank, **II** 310
Hokkaido Dairy Cooperative, **II** 574
Hokkaido Dairy Farm Assoc., **II** 538
Hokkaido Electric Power Company Inc., **V 635–37**
Hokkaido Forwarding, **6** 428
Hokkaido Rakuno Kosha Co., **II** 574
Hokkaido Takushoku Bank, **II** 300
Hokoku Cement, **III** 713
Hokoku Fire, **III** 384
Hokuetsu Paper Manufacturing, **IV** 327
Hokuriku Electric Power Company, **V 638–40**
Hokusin Kai, **IV** 475
Hokuyo Sangyo Co., Ltd., **IV** 285
Holberg Industries, Inc., **36 266–69**
Holbrook Grocery Co., **II** 682
Holco BV, **41** 12
Holcroft & Company, **7** 521
Hold Everything, **17** 548–50
Holden Group, **II** 457
Holderbank Financière Glaris Ltd., **III 701–02**; **8** 258–59, 456; **39** 217. *See also* Holnam Inc
N.V. Holdingmaatschappij De Telegraaf, **23 271–73**
Holec Control Systems, **26** 496
Holes-Webway Company, **40** 44
Holga, Inc., **13** 269
Holgate Toys, **25** 379–80
Holiday Corp., **16** 263; **22** 418; **38** 76; **43** 226
Holiday Inns, Inc., **I** 224; **III 94–95**, 99–100; **6** 383; **9** 425–26; **10** 12; **11** 178, 242; **13** 362; **14** 106; **15** 44, 46; **16** 262; **18** 216; **21** 361–62; **23** 71; **24** 253; **25** 386; **27** 21. *See also* The Promus Cos., Inc.
Holiday Magic, Inc., **17** 227
Holiday Mart, **17** 124; **41** 114–15
Holiday Rambler Corporation, **7** 213; **25** 198

Holiday RV Superstores, Incorporated, 26 192–95
Holland & Barrett, **13** 103; **31** 346, 348
Holland America Line, **6** 367–68; **26** 279; **27** 90–91
Holland Casino, **23** 229
Holland Electro B.V., **17** 234
Holland Hannen and Cubitts, **III** 753
Holland House, **I** 377–78
Holland Motor Express, **14** 505
Holland Studio Craft, **38** 402
Holland van 1859, **III** 200
Hollandsche Bank-Unie, **II** 184–85
Hollandse Signaalapparaten, **13** 402
Holley Carburetor, **I** 434
Hollinger International Inc., 24 222–25; 32 358
Hollingsead International, Inc., **36** 158–60
Hollingsworth & Whitney Co., **IV** 329
Hollostone, **III** 673
Holly Corporation, 12 240–42
Holly Farms Corp., **II** 585; **7** 422–24; **14** 515; **23** 376–77
Holly Sugar Company. *See* Imperial Holly Corporation.
Hollywood Casino Corporation, 21 275–77
Hollywood Entertainment Corporation, 25 208–10; 29 504; **31** 339
Hollywood Park, Inc., 20 297–300
Hollywood Park Race Track, **29** 118
Hollywood Pictures, **II** 174; **30** 487
Hollywood Records, **6** 176
Holme Roberts & Owen LLP, 28 196–99
Holmen Hygiene, **IV** 315
Holmen S.A., **IV** 325
Holmens Bruk, **IV** 317–18
Holmes Electric Protective Co., **III** 644
Holmes International. *See* Miller Industries, Inc.
Holmsund & Kramfors, **IV** 338
Holnam Inc., III 702; **8 258–60; 39 217–20 (upd.)**
Holophane Corporation, 19 209–12
Holson Burnes Group, Inc., 14 244–45
Holsten Brauerei AG, **35** 256, 258
Holt Manufacturing Co., **III** 450–51
Holt, Rinehart and Winston, Inc., **IV** 623–24; **12** 224
Holt's Cigar Holdings, Inc., 42 176–78
Holthouse Furniture Corp., **14** 236
Holtzbrinck. *See* Verlagsgruppe Georg von Holtzbrinck.
Holvick Corp., **11** 65
Holvis AG, **15** 229
Holyman Sally Ltd., **29** 431
Holyoke Food Mart Inc., **19** 480
Holzer and Co., **III** 569; **20** 361
Holzverkohlungs-Industrie AG, **IV** 70
Homart Development, **V** 182
Home & Automobile Insurance Co., **III** 214
Home and Community Care, Inc., **43** 46
Home Box Office Inc., II 134, 136, 166–67, 176–77; **IV** 675; **7 222–24,** 528–29; **10** 196; **12** 75; **18** 65; **23 274–77 (upd.)**, 500; **25** 498; **28** 71
Home Builders Supply, Inc. *See* Scotty's, Inc.
Home Centers of America, Inc., **18** 286
Home Charm Group PLC, **II** 141
Home Choice Holdings, Inc., **33** 366–67
The Home Depot, Inc., V 75–76; 9 400; **10** 235; **11** 384–86; **12** 7, 235, 345, 385; **13** 250, 548; **16** 187–88, 457; **17** 366; **18 238–40 (upd.); 19** 248, 250; **21** 356, 358; **22** 477; **23** 232; **26** 306; **27** 416, 481; **31** 20; **35** 11–13; **39** 134; **43** 385
Home Entertainment of Texas, Inc., **30** 466
Home Furnace Co., **I** 481
Home Insurance Company, I 440; **III 262–64**
Home Interiors, **15** 475, 477
Home Nutritional Services, **17** 308
Home Office Reference Laboratory, Inc., **22** 266
Home Oil Company Ltd., **I** 264; **6** 477–78
Home Products Corp., **18** 492
Home Properties Co., Inc., **21** 95
Home Properties of New York, Inc., 42 179–81
Home Quarters Warehouse, Inc., **12** 233, 235
Home Savings of America, **II** 181–82; **10** 342–43; **16** 346; **28** 167
The Home School, Inc., **41** 111
Home Shopping Network, Inc., V 77–78; 9 428; **18** 76; **24** 517; **25 211–15 (upd.); 26** 441; **33** 322
Home Telephone and Telegraph Company, **10** 201
Home Telephone Company. *See* Rochester Telephone Corporation.
Home Vision Entertainment Inc., **31** 339–40
HomeBase, Inc., II 658; **13** 547–48; **33 198–201 (upd.)**
HomeClub Inc., **13** 547–48; **16** 187; **17** 366. *See also* HomeBase, Inc.
Homécourt, **IV** 226
HomeFed Bank, **10** 340
Homegrocer.com Inc., **38** 223
Homelite, **21** 175
Homemade Ice Cream Company, **10** 371
Homemakers Furniture. *See* John M. Smyth Co.
HomeMax, Inc., **41** 20
Homer McKee Advertising, **I** 22
Homes By Oakwood, Inc., **15** 328
Homestake Mining Company, IV 18, 76; **12 243–45; 20** 72; **27** 456; **38 229–32 (upd.)**
HomeTown Buffet, Inc., **19** 435; **22** 465. *See also* Buffets, Inc
Hometté Corporation, **30** 423
Homewood Stores Co., **IV** 573; **7** 550
Homewood Suites, **9** 425–26
Hominal Developments Inc., **9** 512
Hon Industries Inc., 13 266–69; 23 243–45
Honam Oil Refinery, **II** 53
Honcho Real Estate, **IV** 225; **24** 489
Honda Giken Kogyo Kabushiki Kaisha. *See* Honda Motor Company Limited.
Honda Motor Company Limited, I 9–10, 32, **174–76,** 184, 193; **II** 5; **III** 495, 517, 536, 603, 657–58, 667; **IV** 443; **7** 212–13, 459; **8** 71–72; **9** 294, 340–42; **10 352–54 (upd.); 11** 33, 49–50, 352; **12** 122, 401; **13** 30; **16** 167; **17** 25; **21** 153; **23** 289–90, 338, 340; **25** 197–99; **27** 76; **29 239–42 (upd.); 34** 305–06; **36** 243
Hondo Oil & Gas Co., **IV** 375–76
Honeywell Inc., I 63; **II** 30, **40–43,** 54, 68; **III** 122–23, 149, 152, 165, 535, 548–49, 732; **6** 266, 281, 283, 314; **8** 21; **9** 171, 324; **11** 198, 265; **12 246–49 (upd.); 13** 234, 499; **17** 33; **18** 341; **22** 373, 436; **23** 471; **29** 464; **30** 34; **33** 334, 337; **43** 284
Hong Kong Aircraft Engineering Co., **I** 522; **6** 79; **16** 480
Hong Kong Airways, **6** 78–79; **16** 480
Hong Kong and Kowloon Wharf and Godown Co., **I** 470; **IV** 699
Hong Kong Dragon Airlines, **18** 114
Hong Kong Industrial Co., Ltd., **25** 312
Hong Kong Island Line Co., **IV** 718
Hong Kong Mass Transit Railway Corp., **19** 111
Hong Kong Resort Co., **IV** 718; **38** 320
Hong Kong Telecommunications Ltd., IV 700; **V** 285–86; **6 319–21; 18** 114; **25** 101–02. *See also* Cable & Wireless HKT.
Hong Leong Corp., **III** 718
Hong Leong Group Malaysia, **26** 3, 5
Hongkong & Kowloon Wharf & Godown Company, **20** 312
Hongkong and Shanghai Banking Corporation Limited, II 257, **296–99,** 320, 358; **III** 289; **17** 325; **18** 253; **25** 12. *See also* HSBC Holdings plc.
Hongkong Electric Company Ltd., 6 498–500; 20 134
Hongkong Electric Holdings Ltd., 23 278–81 (upd.)
Hongkong Land Holdings Ltd., I 470–71; **IV 699–701; 6** 498–99; **20** 312–13; **23** 280
Honig-Copper & Harrington, **I** 14
Honjo Copper Smeltery, **III** 490
Honolua Plantation Land Company, Inc., **29** 308
Honolulu Oil, **II** 491
Honolulu Sugar Refining Co., **II** 490
Honshu Paper Co., Ltd., IV 268, **284–85,** 292, 297, 321, 326
Hood Rubber Company, **15** 488–89
Hood Sailmakers, Inc., **10** 215
Hoogovens. *See* Koninklijke Nederlandsche Hoogovens en Staalfabricken NV.
Hooiberg, **I** 256
Hook's Drug Stores, **9** 67
Hooker Chemical, **IV** 481
Hooker Corp., **19** 324
Hooker Furniture Corp. *See* Bassett Furniture Industries, Inc.
Hooker Petroleum, **IV** 264
Hooper Holmes, Inc., 22 264–67
Hoosier Park L.P., **29** 118
Hooters of America, Inc., 18 241–43
Hoover Ball and Bearing Co., **III** 589
The Hoover Company, II 7; **III** 478; **12** 158, **250–52; 15** 416, 418; **21** 383; **30** 75, 78; **40 258–62 (upd.)**
Hoover Group Inc., **18** 11
Hoover Industrial, **III** 536; **26** 230
Hoover-NSK Bearings, **III** 589
Hoover Treated Wood Products, Inc., **12** 396
Hopkinton LNG Corp., **14** 126
Hopper Soliday and Co. Inc., **14** 154
Hops Restaurant Bar and Brewery, **31** 41
Hopwood & Company, **22** 427
Horace Mann Educators Corporation, 22 268–70
Horizon Air Industries, Inc. *See* Alaska Air Group, Inc.
Horizon Bancorp, **II** 252; **14** 103
Horizon Corporation, **8** 348

Horizon Group Inc., **27** 221
Horizon Healthcare Corporation, **25** 456
Horizon Holidays, **14** 36
Horizon Industries, **19** 275
Horizon Organic Holding Corporation, 37 195–99
Horizon Travel Group, **8** 527
Horizon/CMS Healthcare Corp., **25** 111, 457; **33** 185
Horizons Laitiers, **25** 85
Hormel Foods Corporation, 18 244–47 (upd.)
Horn & Hardart, **II** 614
Horn Silver Mines Co., **IV** 83; **7** 187
Horn Venture Partners, **22** 464
Hornblower & Co., **II** 450
Hornbrook, Inc., **14** 112
Horne's, **I** 449; **16** 62
Hornsberg Land Co., **I** 553
Horsham Corp. *See* TrizecHahn.
Horst Breuer GmbH, **20** 363
Horst Salons Inc., **24** 56
Horten, **II** 622
Horton Homes, Inc., 25 216–18
Hospital Corporation of America, II 331; **III 78–80**; **15** 112; **23** 153; **27** 237. *See also* HCA - The Healthcare Company.
Hospital Cost Consultants, **11** 113
Hospital Products, Inc., **10** 534
Hospital Service Association of Pittsburgh, **III** 325
Hospital Specialty Co., **37** 392
Hospitality Franchise Systems, Inc., 11 177–79; **14** 106; **17** 236
Hospitality Worldwide Services, Inc., 26 196–98
Hosposable Products, Inc. *See* Wyant Corporation.
Host Communications Inc., **24** 404
Host Marriott Corporation, **21** 366
Host Marriott Services Corp., **III** 103; **16** 446; **17** 95
Hot 'n Now, **16** 96–97
Hot Dog Construction Co., **12** 372
Hot Sam Co., **12** 179, 199. *See also* Mrs. Fields' Original Cookies, Inc.
Hot Shoppes Inc., **III** 102
Hot Topic, Inc., 33 202–04
Hotchkiss-Brandt, **II** 116; **42** 378
Hoteiya, **V** 209–10
Hotel Corporation of America, **16** 337
Hotel Corporation of India, **27** 26
Hotel Properties Ltd., **30** 107
Hotel Scandinavia K/S, **I** 120
HotRail Inc., **36** 124
Houbigant, **37** 270
Houdry Chemicals, **I** 298
Houghton Mifflin Company, 10 355–57; **26** 215; **36 270–74 (upd.)**
Houlihan's Restaurant Group, **25** 546
Housatonic Power Co., **13** 182
House and Land Syndicate, **IV** 710
House of Blues, **32** 241, 244
House of Fabrics, Inc., 16 197–98; **18** 223; **21 278–80**
House of Fraser Plc., **21** 353; **37** 6, 8
House of Miniatures, **12** 264
House of Windsor, Inc., **9** 533
Household International, Inc., I 31; **II 417–20**, 605; **7** 569–70; **8** 117; **10** 419; **16** 487–88; **21 281–86 (upd.)**; **22** 38, 542; **24** 152
Household Products Inc., **I** 622; **10** 68
Household Rental Systems, **17** 234
Housing Development Finance Corporation, **20** 313
Housmex Inc., **23** 171
Houston, Effler & Partners Inc., **9** 135
Houston General Insurance, **III** 248
Houston Industries Incorporated, V 641–44; **7** 376
Houston International Teleport, Inc., **11** 184
Houston Natural Gas Corp., **IV** 395; **V** 610
Houston Oil & Minerals Corp., **11** 440–41
Houston Oil Co., **IV** 342, 674
Hoveringham Group, **III** 753; **28** 450
Hoving Corp., **14** 501
Hovis-McDougall Co., **II** 565
Hovnanian Enterprises, Inc., 29 243–45
Howaldtswerke-Deutsche Werft AG, **IV** 201
Howard B. Stark Candy Co., **15** 325
Howard Flint Ink Company, **13** 227
Howard H. Sweet & Son, Inc., **14** 502
Howard Hughes Medical Institute, II 33, 35; **39 221–24**
Howard Hughes Properties, Ltd., **17** 317
Howard Humphreys, **13** 119
Howard Johnson International, Inc., III 94, 102–03; **6** 27; **7** 266; **11** 177–78; **15** 36; **16** 156; **17 236–39**; **25** 309
Howard Printing Co., **III** 188; **10** 29
Howard Research and Development Corporation, **15** 412, 414
Howard, Smith & Levin, **40** 126
Howard Smith Paper Mills Ltd., **IV** 271–72
Howden. *See* Alexander Howden Group.
Howdy Company, **9** 177
Howe & Fant, Inc., **23** 82
Howe and Brainbridge Inc., **I** 321
Howe Sound Co., **12** 253
Howe Sound Inc., **IV** 174
Howe Sound Pulp and Paper Ltd., **IV** 321
Howmedica, **29** 455
Howmet Corporation, 12 IV 174; **253–55**; **22** 506
Hoya Corp., **III** 715
Hoyt Archery Company, **10** 216
HQ Office International, **8** 405; **23** 364
HRB Business Services, **29** 227
Hrubitz Oil Company, **12** 244
HSBC Holdings plc, 12 256–58; **17** 323, 325–26; **26 199–204 (upd.)**
HSN Inc., **25** 411
HTH, **12** 464
HTM Goedkoop, **26** 278–79
H2O Plus, **11** 41
Hua Bei Oxygen, **25** 82
Huaneng Raw Material Corp., **III** 718
Hub Group, Inc., 26 533; **38 233–35**
Hub Services, Inc., **18** 366
Hubbard Air Transport, **10** 162
Hubbard, Baker & Rice, **10** 126
Hubbard Broadcasting Inc., 24 226–28
Hubbard Construction Co., **23** 332
Hubbard, Westervelt & Motteley, **II** 425; **13** 341
Hubbell Incorporated, 9 286–87; **31 257–259 (upd.)**
Hubinger Co., **II** 508; **11** 172; **36** 254
Huck Manufacturing Company, **22** 506
Huddart Parker, **III** 672
Hudepohl-Schoenling Brewing Co., **18** 72
Hudnut, **I** 710
Hudson Automobile Company, **18** 492
The Hudson Bay Mining and Smelting Company, Limited, 12 259–61; **13** 502–03; **16** 29
Hudson Engineering Corp., **III** 559
Hudson Foods Inc., 13 270–72
Hudson Housewares Corp., **16** 389
Hudson Motor Car Co., **I** 135, 158; **III** 568; **10** 292; **20** 359
Hudson Packaging & Paper Co., **IV** 257
Hudson Pharmaceutical Corp., **31** 347
Hudson River Bancorp, Inc., 41 210–13
Hudson River Railroad, **II** 396
Hudson River Rubber Company, **V** 231
Hudson Scott & Sons, **I** 604
Hudson Software, **13** 481
Hudson Underground Telephone Company, **6** 299
Hudson's. *See* Dayton Hudson Corporation.
Hudson's Bay Company, I 284; **IV** 400–01, 437; **V 79–81**; **6** 359; **8** 525; **12** 361; **25 219–22 (upd.)**, 230
Hue International, **8** 324
Hueppe Duscha, **III** 571; **20** 362
Huff Daland Dusters, **I** 99; **6** 81
Huffco, **IV** 492
Huffman Manufacturing Company, **7** 225–26
Huffy Bicycles Co., **19** 383
Huffy Corporation, 7 225–27; **26** 184, 412; **30 239–42 (upd.)**
Hugerot, **19** 50
Hugh O'Neill Auto Co., **12** 309
Hughes Air West, **25** 421
Hughes Aircraft Corporation, **I** 172, 484, 539; **III** 428, 539; **7** 426–27; **9** 409; **10** 327; **11** 263, 540; **13** 356, 398; **15** 528, 530; **21** 201; **23** 134; **24** 442; **25** 86, 223; **30** 175. *See also* GM Hughes Electronics Corporation.
Hughes Communications, Inc., **13** 398; **18** 211
Hughes Corp., **18** 535
Hughes Electric Heating Co., **II** 28; **12** 194
Hughes Electronics Corporation, 25 223–25; **36** 240, 243; **38** 175, 375
Hughes Helicopter, **26** 431
Hughes Markets, Inc., 22 271–73
Hughes Network Systems Inc., **21** 239
Hughes Properties, Inc., **17** 317
Hughes Space and Communications Company, **33** 47–48
Hughes Supply, Inc., 14 246–47; **39** 360
Hughes Television Network, **11** 184
Hughes Tool Co., **I** 126; **II** 32; **12** 488; **15** 467; **25** 74; **35** 425. *See also* Baker Hughes Incorporated.
Hugo Neu Corporation, **19** 381–82
Hugo Stinnes GmbH, **I** 542; **8** 69, 494–95
Huguenot Fenal, **IV** 108
Huhtamaki, **30** 396, 398
Hüls A.G., I 349–50; **25** 82. *See also* Degussa-Hüls AG.
Hulton, **17** 397
Hulton Getty, **31** 216–17
Humana Inc., III 79, **81–83**; **6** 28, 191–92, 279; **15** 113; **24 229–32 (upd.)**; **35** 215–16
Humanetics Corporation, **29** 213
Humanities Software, **39** 341
Humason Manufacturing Co., **III** 628
Humber, **I** 197
Humberside Sea & Land Services, **31** 367

Humble Oil & Refining Company, **III** 497; **IV** 373, 428; **7** 171; **13** 118; **14** 291. *See also* Exxon.
Humboldt-Deutz-Motoren AG, **III** 541–42, 543; **IV** 126
Hummel, **II** 163–64
Hummer, Winblad Venture Partners, **36** 157
Hummingbird, **18** 313
Humongous Entertainment, Inc., **31** 238–40
Humphrey Instruments, **I** 693
Humphrey's Estate and Finance, **IV** 700
Humphreys & Glasgow Ltd., **V** 612
Hunco Ltd., **IV** 640; **26** 273
Hungária Biztositó, **III** 185
Hungarian-Soviet Civil Air Transport Joint Stock Company. *See* Malæv Plc.
Hungarotex, **V** 166
Hungry Howie's Pizza and Subs, Inc., 25 226–28
Hunt Consolidated, Inc., 27 215–18 (upd.)
Hunt Lumber Co., **IV** 358
Hunt Manufacturing Company, 12 262–64
Hunt Oil Company, IV 367, 453–54; **7 228–30**, 378. *See also* Hunt Consolidated, Inc.
Hunt-Wesson, Inc., 17 240–42; **25** 278
Hunter-Douglas, **8** 235
Hunter Engineering Co., **IV** 18
Hunter Fan Company, 13 273–75
Hunter-Hayes Elevator Co., **III** 467
Hunters' Foods, **II** 500
Hunting Aircraft, **I** 50; **24** 85
Huntingdon Life Sciences Group plc, 42 182–85
Huntington Bancshares Inc., 11 180–82
Huntley and Palmer Foods, **II** 544
Huntley Boorne & Stevens, **I** 604
Hunton & Williams, 35 223–26
Huntsman Chemical Corporation, 8 261–63; **9** 305
Hupp Motor Car Company, **III** 601; **8** 74; **10** 261
Hurd & Houghton, **10** 355
Hurlburt Paper Co., **IV** 311; **19** 267
Huron Steel Company, Inc., **16** 357
Huse Food Group, **14** 352
Husky Oil Ltd., **IV** 454, 695; **V** 673–75; **18** 253–54; **19** 159
Husqvarna Forest & Garden Company, **III** 480; **13** 564; **22** 26–27
Hussmann Corporation, **I** 457–58; **7** 429–30; **10** 554; **13** 268; **22** 353–54
Hutcheson & Grundy, **29** 286
Hutchinson-Mapa, **IV** 560
Hutchinson Technology Incorporated, 18 248–51
Hutchinson Wholesale Grocery Co., **II** 624
Hutchison, **I** 470
Hutchison Microtel, **11** 548
Hutchison Whampoa Ltd., IV 694–95; **18** 114, **252–55**; **20** 131, 312–13; **25** 101
Huth Manufacturing Corporation, **10** 414
Hüttenwerk Oberhausen AG, **IV** 222
Hüttenwerk Salzgitter AG, **IV** 201
Huttig Building Products, **31** 398, 400
Huttig Sash & Door Company, **8** 135
Hutton, E.F. *See* E.F. Hutton.
Huyck Corp., **I** 429
Hvide Marine Incorporated, 22 274–76
HWI. *See* Hardware Wholesalers, Inc.
Hy-Form Products, Inc., **22** 175
Hy-Vee, Inc., 36 275–78; **42** 432
Hyatt Corporation, II 442; **III** 92, **96–97**; **9** 426; **16 273–75 (upd.)**; **22** 101; **23** 482
Hyatt Legal Services, **20** 435; **29** 226
Hyatt Medical Enterprises, **III** 73
Hyatt Roller Bearing Co., **I** 171–72; **9** 17; **10** 326
Hybridtech, **III** 18
Hyde Athletic Industries, Inc., 17 243–45. *See* Saucony Inc.
Hyde Company, A.L., **7** 116–17
Hyder plc, 34 219–21
Hydra Computer Systems, Inc., **13** 201
Hydrac GmbH, **38** 300
Hydraulic Brake Co., **I** 141
Hydro Aire Incorporated, **8** 135
Hydro Carbide Corp., **19** 152
Hydro-Carbon Light Company, **9** 127
Hydro Electric, **19** 389–90
Hydro-Electric Power Commission of Ontario, **6** 541; **9** 461
Hydro Med Sciences, **13** 367
Hydro-Quebéc, 6 501–03; **32 266–69 (upd.)**
Hydrocarbon Services of Nigeria Co., **IV** 473
Hydroponic Chemical Co., **III** 28
Hydrox Corp., **II** 533
Hyer Boot, **19** 232
Hygeia Sciences, Inc., **8** 85, 512
Hygienic Ice Co., **IV** 722
Hygrade Containers Ltd., **IV** 286
Hygrade Foods, **III** 502; **7** 208; **14** 536
Hyland Laboratories, **I** 627
Hylsa. *See* Hojalata y Laminas S.A.
Hylsamex, S.A. de C.V., 39 225–27
Hyosung Group, **III** 749
Hyper Shoppes, Inc., **II** 670; **18** 507
Hypercom Corporation, 27 219–21
Hyperion Press, **6** 176
Hyperion Software Corporation, 22 277–79
Hypermart USA, **8** 555–56
Hyplains Beef, **7** 175
Hypo-Bank. *See* Bayerische Hypotheken- und Wechsel-Bank AG.
Hypobaruk, **III** 348
Hyponex Corp., **22** 475
Hypro Engineering Inc., **I** 481
Hysol Corp., **I** 321; **12** 103
Hyster Company, 17 246–48; **33** 364
Hyster-Yale Materials Handling, Inc., **I** 424; **7** 369–71
Hystron Fibers Inc., **I** 347
Hyundai Group, I 207, 516; **II** 53–54, 122; **III** 457–59, **515–17**; **7 231–34 (upd.)**; **9** 350; **10** 404; **12** 211, 546; **13** 280, 293–94; **18** 124; **23** 353; **25** 469; **29** 264, 266

I Can't Believe It's Yogurt, Inc., **17** 474; **35** 121
I. Appel, **30** 23
I.B. Kleinert Rubber Company, **37** 399
I.C.H. Corp., **I** 528
I.C. Isaacs & Company, 31 260–62
I.C. Johnson and Co., **III** 669
I.D. Systems, Inc., **11** 444
I-DIKA Milan SRL, **12** 182
I. Feldman Co., **31** 359
I.G. Farbenindustrie AG, **I** 305–06, 309–11, 337, 346–53, 619, 632–33, 698–99; **II** 257; **III** 677, 694; **IV** 111, 485; **8** 108–09; **11** 7; **13** 75–76, 262; **16** 121; **18** 47; **21** 544; **22** 225–26; **26** 452. *See also* BASF A.G. *and* Bayer A.G. *and* Hoechst A.G.
I.J. Stokes Corp., **I** 383
I.M. Pei & Associates, **I** 580; **III** 267; **41** 143
I.M. Singer and Co., **II** 9
I. Magnin Inc., **8** 444; **15** 86; **24** 422; **30** 383; **31** 191, 193
I.N. Kote, **IV** 116; **19** 219
I.N. Tek, **IV** 116; **19** 219
I.R. Maxwell & Co. Ltd., **IV** 641; **7** 311
I-T-E Circuit Breaker, **II** 121
I-X Corp., **22** 416
IAM/Environmental, **18** 11
Iams Company, 26 205–07; **27** 213
IBANCO, **26** 515
IBC Holdings Corporation, **12** 276
IBCA. *See* International Banking and Credit Analysis.
Iberdrola, **V** 608
Iberia Líneas Aéreas De España S.A., I 110; **6 95–97**; **33** 18; **36 279–83 (upd.)**
IBERIABANK Corporation, 37 200–02
Ibero-Amerika Bank, **II** 521
Iberswiss Catering, **6** 96
Ibex Engineering Co., **III** 420
IBH Holding AG, **7** 513
IBJ. *See* The Industrial Bank of Japan Ltd.
IBM. *See* International Business Machines Corporation.
IBP, Inc., II 515–17; **7** 525; **21 287–90 (upd.)**; **23** 201
IBS Conversions Inc., **27** 492
Ibstock Brick Ltd., 37 203–06 (upd.)
Ibstock plc, III 735; **14 248–50**
IC Industries Inc., I 456–58; **III** 512; **7** 430; **10** 414, 553; **18** 3; **22** 197; **43** 217. *See also* Whitman Corporation.
ICA AB, II 639–40
ICA Fluor Daniel, S. de R.L. de C.V., **41** 148
ICA Mortgage Corporation, **8** 30
ICA Technologies, Ltd., **III** 533
Icahn Capital Corp., **35** 143
Icarus Consulting AG, **29** 376
ICE, **I** 333
ICEE-USA, **24** 240
Iceland Group plc, 33 205–07
ICF Kaiser International, Inc., 28 200–04
ICH Corporation, **19** 468
Ichikoh Industries Ltd., **26** 154
ICI. *See* Imperial Chemical Industries plc.
ICI Canada, **22** 436
ICL plc, II 65, 81; **III** 141, 164; **6 240–42**; **11** 150; **16** 226
ICM Mortgage Corporation, **8** 436
ICOA Life Insurance, **III** 253
Icon Health & Fitness, Inc., 38 236–39
Icon International, **24** 445
iConcepts, Inc., **39** 95
Icot Corp., **18** 543
ICS. *See* International Care Services.
ICS, **26** 119
ICX, **IV** 136
ID, Inc., **9** 193
id Software, **31** 237–38; **32** 9
Idaho Frozen Foods, **II** 572–73
Idaho Power Company, 12 265–67

IDB Communications Group, Inc., **11 183–85**; **20** 48; **27** 301, 307
IDC, **25** 101
Ide Megumi, **III** 549
Ideal Basic Industries, **III** 701–02; **8** 258–59; **12** 18
Ideal Corp., **III** 602; **23** 335
Ideal Loisirs Group, **23** 388
IDEC Pharmaceuticals Corporation, **32** 214
Idemitso Petrochemicals, **8** 153
Idemitsu Kosan K.K., **II** 361; **IV 434–36**, 476, 519
Identification Business, Inc., **18** 140
IDEXX Laboratories, Inc., **23 282–84**
IDG Books Worldwide, Inc., **27 222–24**. *See also* International Data Group, Inc.
IDG Communications, Inc, **7** 238
IDG World Expo Corporation, **7** 239
IDI, **22** 365
IDI Temps, **34** 372
IDO. *See* Nippon Idou Tsushin.
IDS Ltd., **22** 76
IDT Corporation, **34 222–24**
IEC Electronics Corp., **42 186–88**
IEL. *See* Industrial Equity Ltd.
IFC Disposables, Inc., **30** 496–98
IFF. *See* International Flavors & Fragrances Inc.
IFI, **I** 161–62; **III** 347
Ifil, **27** 515
IFM, **25** 85
IFS Industries, **6** 294
IG. *See* Integrated Genetics.
IG Farben. *See* I.G. Farbenindustrie AG.
IG Holdings, **27** 430
IGA, **II** 624, 649, 668, 681–82; **7** 451; **15** 479; **18** 6, 9; **25** 234
Iggesund Bruk, **IV** 317–18
Igloo Products Corp., **21 291–93**; **22** 116
IGT-International, **10** 375–76
IGT-North America, **10** 375
IHI. *See* Ishikawajima Harima Heavy Industries.
IHI Granitech Corp., **III** 533
IHOP Corporation, **17 249–51**; **19** 435, 455
Iida & Co., **I** 493; **24** 325
IinteCom, **III** 169
IIS, **26** 441
IISCO-Ujjain Pipe and Foundry Co. Ltd., **IV** 206
IK Coach, Ltd., **23** 290
IKEA Group, **V 82–84**
IKEA International A/S, **26** 161, **208–11 (upd.)**
Il Fornaio (America) Corporation, **27 225–28**
Il Giornale, **13** 493
Ilaco, **26** 22
ILFC. *See* International Lease Finance Corporation.
Ilitch Holdings Inc., **37 207–210**
Illco Toy Co. USA, **12** 496
Illinois Bell Telephone Company, **IV** 660; **14 251–53**; **18** 30
Illinois Central Corporation, **I** 456, 584; **8** 410; **10** 553; **11 186–89**
Illinois Glass Co., **I** 609
Illinois Merchants Trust Co., **II** 261
Illinois National Bank & Trust Co., **III** 213–14
Illinois Power Company, **6** 470, **504–07**
Illinois Steel Co., **IV** 572; **7** 549; **8** 114
Illinois Terminal Company, **6** 504
Illinois Tool Works Inc., **III 518–20**; **22 280–83 (upd.)**
Illinois Traction Company, **6** 504
Illinois Trust and Savings Bank, **II** 261
Illinova Energy Partners, **27** 247
Ilmor Engineering of Great Britain, **V** 494
Ilse-Bergbau AG, **IV** 229–30
Ilselder Hütte, **IV** 201
Ilwaco Telephone and Telegraph Company. *See* Pacific Telecom, Inc.
Ilyushin, **24** 60
IMA Bancard, Inc., **24** 395
IMA Holdings Corp., **III** 73–74
Imabari, **25** 469
Image Business Systems Corp., **11** 66
Image Industries, Inc., **25** 320–21
Image Technologies Corporation, **12** 264
Imageline Inc., **25** 348
Imagine Entertainment, **43** 144
ImagiNet, **41** 97
Imaging Technologies, **25** 183
Imaje, S.A., **28** 104
IMall Inc., **26** 441
Imasa Group, **IV** 34
Imasco Limited, **I** 514; **II** 605; **V 401–02**
Imation Corporation, **20 301–04**; **33** 348. *See also* Minnesota Mining & Manufacturing Company.
Imatran Voima Oy, **IV** 469. *See also* Fortum Corporation
Imax Corporation, **21** 362; **28 205–08**
IMC. *See* Intertec Marine Corporation.
IMC Drilling Mud, **III** 499
IMC Fertilizer Group, Inc., **8 264–66**
Imcera Group, Inc., **8** 264, 266
IMCO Recycling, Incorporated, **32 270–73**
IMED Corp., **I** 712; **III** 511–12; **10** 551; **38** 364
Imerys S.A., **40** 176, **263–66 (upd.)**
Imetal S.A., **IV 107–09**
IMG. *See* International Management Group.
IMI plc, **III** 593; **9 288–89**; **29** 364
Imigest Fondo Imicapital, **III** 347
Imlo, **26** 22
Immersion Corporation, **28** 245
Immobilier Batibail, **42** 152
Immunex Corporation, **8** 26; **14 254–56**
Immuno Serums, Inc., **V** 174–75
Immuno Therapeutics, Inc., **25** 382
Imo Industries Inc., **7 235–37**; **27 229–32 (upd.)**
IMO Ltd., **III** 539
Impala Platinum Holdings, **IV** 91–93
Impark Limited, **42** 433
Imperial Airways. *See* British Overseas Airways Corporation.
Imperial and International Communications Limited, **25** 100
Imperial Bank of Canada, **II** 244–45
Imperial Bank of Persia, **II** 298
Imperial British East Africa Co., **III** 522
Imperial Business Forms, **9** 72
Imperial Chemical Industries plc, **I** 303, **351–53**, 374, 605, 633; **II** 448, 565; **III** 522, 667, 677, 680, 745; **IV** 38, 110, 698; **7** 209; **8** 179, 222, 224; **9** 154, 288; **10** 436; **11** 97, 361; **12** 347; **13** 448, 470; **16** 121; **17** 118; **18** 50; **21** 544
Imperial Feather Company, **19** 304
Imperial Fire Co., **III** 373
Imperial Goonbarrow, **III** 690
Imperial Group Ltd., **II** 513; **III** 503; **7** 209; **17** 238
Imperial Holly Corporation, **12 268–70**. *See also* Imperial Sugar Company.
Imperial Japanese Government Steel Works, **17** 349–50
Imperial Life Co., **III** 288, 373
Imperial Marine Insurance Co., **III** 384, 405–06
Imperial Metal Industries Ltd. *See* IMI plc.
Imperial Oil Limited, **IV** 428, **437–39**, 494; **25 229–33 (upd.)**; **32** 179–80
Imperial Outdoor, **27** 280
Imperial Packing Co. *See* Beech-Nut Nutrition Corp.
Imperial Paper, **13** 169
Imperial Pneumatic Tool Co., **III** 525
Imperial Premium Finance, **III** 264
Imperial Savings Association, **8** 30–31
Imperial Smelting Corp., **IV** 58
Imperial Sports, **19** 230
Imperial Sugar Company, **32 274–78 (upd.)**
Imperial Tobacco Company, **I** 425–26, 605; **IV** 260; **V** 401. *See also* B.A.T. Industries PLC.
Imported Auto Parts, Inc., **15** 246
Impressions Software, **15** 455
Imprimis, **8** 467
Impulse, **9** 122
Impulse Designs, **31** 435–36
Imreg, **10** 473–74
IMRS. *See* Hyperion Software Corporation.
IMS International, Inc., **10** 105
In Focus Systems, Inc., **22 287–90**
In Home Health, Inc., **25** 306, 309–10
In-N-Out Burger, **19 213–15**
In-Sink-Erator, **II** 19
INA Corporation, **II** 403; **III** 79, 208, 223–25, 226; **11** 481; **22** 269. *See also* CIGNA Corporation.
INA-Naftaplin, **IV** 454
INA Wälzlager Schaeffler, **III** 595
Inabata & Co., **I** 398
InaCom Corporation, **13** 176, **276–78**; **19** 471
Incasso Bank, **II** 185
Incentive Group, **27** 269
Inchcape PLC, **II** 233; **III 521–24**; **16 276–80 (upd.)**
Incheon Iron & Steel Co., **III** 516
Inchon Heavy Industrial Corp., **IV** 183
INCO-Banco Indústria e Comércio de Santa Catarina, **13** 70
Inco Limited, **IV** 75, 78, **110–12**; **39** 338
Incola, S.A., **II** 471; **22** 93
Incon Research Inc., **41** 198
InControl Inc., **11** 460
Incredible Universe, **12** 470; **17** 489; **36** 387
Ind Coope, **I** 215
Indemnité, **III** 391
Indemnity Insurance Company. *See* CIGNA Corporation.
Indentimat Corp., **14** 542
Independent Breweries Company, **9** 178
Independent Delivery Services, Inc., **37** 409
Independent Exhibitions Ltd., **27** 362
Independent Grocers Alliance. *See* IGA.
Independent Lock Co., **13** 166
Independent Metal Products Co., **I** 169
Independent Oil & Gas Co., **IV** 521
Independent Petrochemical, **14** 461

Independent Power Generators, **V** 605
Independent Stave Company, **28** 223
Independent Torpedo Company, **25** 73
Independent Warehouses, Inc., **IV** 180
India Exotics, Inc., **22** 133
India General Steam Navigation and Railway Co., **III** 522
India Life Assurance Co., **III** 359
India Rubber, Gutta Percha & Telegraph Works Co., **I** 428
Indian, **7** 211; **25** 196
Indian Airlines Corporation. *See* Air-India.
Indian Archery and Toy Corp., **19** 142–43
Indian Iron & Steel Co. Ltd., **IV** 49, 205–07
Indian Oil Corporation Ltd., **IV 440–41**, 483
Indian Point Farm Supply, Inc., **IV** 458–59
Indiana Bearings, Inc., **13** 78
Indiana Bell Telephone Company, Incorporated, **14 257–61**; **18** 30
Indiana Board and Filler Company, **12** 376
Indiana Electric Corporation, **6** 555
Indiana Energy, Inc., **27 233–36**
Indiana Gaming Company, **21** 40
Indiana Gas & Water Company, **6** 556
Indiana Group, **I** 378
Indiana Oil Purchasing Co., **IV** 370
Indiana Parts and Warehouse, **29** 86, 88
Indiana Power Company, **6** 555
Indiana Refining Co., **IV** 552
Indiana Tube Co., **23** 250
Indianapolis Air Pump Company, **8** 37
Indianapolis Brush Electric Light & Power Company, **6** 508
Indianapolis Cablevision, **6** 508–09
Indianapolis Light and Power Company, **6** 508
Indianapolis Motor Speedway Company, **9** 16
Indianapolis Power & Light Company, **6** 508–09
Indianapolis Pump and Tube Company, **8** 37
Indianhead Truck Lines, **6** 371
Indigo NV, **26 212–14**, 540–41
Indo-Asahi Glass Co., Ltd., **III** 667
Indo-China Steam Navigation Co., **I** 469; **20** 311
Indola Cosmetics B.V., **8** 16
Indonesia Petroleum Co., **IV** 516
Indresco, Inc., **22** 285
Induba, S.A. de C.V., **39** 230
Induban, **II** 196
Indura SA Industria Y Commercio, **25** 82
Industri Kapital, **27** 269
Industria Gelati Sammontana, **II** 575
Industria Metalgrafica, **I** 231
Industria Raffinazione Oli Minerali, **IV** 419
Industrial & Trade Shows of Canada, **IV** 639
Industrial Acceptance Bank, **I** 337
Industrial Air Products, **19** 380–81
Industrial Air Tool, **28** 387
Industrial Bancorp, **9** 229
Industrial Bank of Japan, Ltd., **II 300–01**, 310–11, 338, 369, 433, 459; **17** 121
Industrial Bank of Scotland, **10** 337
Industrial Bio-Test Laboratories, **I** 374, 702
Industrial Cartonera, **IV** 295; **19** 226
Industrial Chemical and Equipment, **16** 271
Industrial Circuits, **IV** 680
Industrial Computer Corp., **11** 78
Industrial Development Corp., **IV** 22, 92, 534
Industrial Development Corp. of Zambia Ltd., **IV** 239–41
Industrial Engineering, **III** 598
Industrial Engineering Associates, Inc., **II** 112
Industrial Equity Ltd., **I** 438; **17** 357
Industrial Fuel Supply Co., **I** 569
Industrial Gas Equipment Co., **I** 297
Industrial Gases Lagos, **25** 82
Industrial Instrument Company. *See* Foxboro Company.
Industrial Light & Magic, **12** 322
Industrial Mutual Insurance, **III** 264
Industrial National Bank, **9** 229
Industrial Powder Coatings, Inc., **16** 475
Industrial Publishing Company, **9** 413; **27** 361
Industrial Reorganization Corp., **III** 502, 556
Industrial Resources, **6** 144
Industrial Shows of America, **27** 362
Industrial Tectonics Corp., **18** 276
Industrial Trade & Consumer Shows Inc., **IV** 639; **26** 272
Industrial Trust Co. of Wilmington, **25** 540
Industrial Trust Company, **9** 228
Industrial Vehicles Corp. B.V., **III** 543–44
Industrias Bachoco, S.A. de C.V., **39 228–31**
Industrias Nacobre, **21** 259
Industrias Negromex, **23** 170
Industrias Penoles, S.A. de C.V., **22 284–86**
Industrias Resistol S.A., **23** 170–71
Industrias y Confecciones, S.A. **V** 51; **26** 129
Industrie-Aktiengesellschaft, **IV** 201
Industrie Natuzzi S.p.A., **18 256–58**
Industrie Regionale du Bâtiment, **IV** 108
Industriegas GmbH., **I** 581
Les Industries Ling, **13** 443
Industriförvaltnings AB Kinnevik, **26** 331–33; **36** 335
Industrionics Control, Inc., **III** 643
AB Industrivärden, **II** 366; **32** 397
Induyco. *See* Industrias y Confecciones, S.A.
Indy Lighting, **30** 266
Indy Racing League, **37** 74
Inelco Peripheriques, **10** 459
Inespo, **16** 322
Inexco Oil Co., **7** 282
Infinity Broadcasting Corporation, **11 190–92**; **22** 97; **23** 510; **28** 72; **35** 232
Infinity Partners, **36** 160
INFLEX, S.A., **8** 247
Inflight Sales Group Limited, **11** 82; **29** 511
InfoAsia, **28** 241
Infobase Services, **6** 14
Infocom, **32** 8
Infogrames Entertainment S.A., **35 227–30**; **41** 407
Infonet Services Corporation, **6** 303; **27** 304
Infoplan, **14** 36
Informatics General Corporation, **III** 248; **11** 468; **25** 86
Informatics Legal Systems, **III** 169; **6** 285
Information Access Company, **12** 560–62; **17 252–55**; **34** 438. *See also* The Thomson Corporation.
Information and Communication Group, **14** 555
Information Associates Inc., **11** 78
Information Builders, Inc., **14** 16; **22 291–93**
Information Consulting Group, **9** 345
Information, Dissemination and Retrieval Inc., **IV** 670
Information International. *See* Autologic Information International, Inc.
Information Management Reporting Services. *See* Hyperion Software Corporation.
Information Management Science Associates, Inc., **13** 174
Information Please LLC, **26** 216
Information Resources, Inc., **10 358–60**; **13** 4; **25** 366
Information Unlimited Software, **6** 224
Informix Corporation, **10 361–64**, 505; **30 243–46 (upd.)**
Infoseek Corporation, **27** 517; **30** 490
InfoSoft International, Inc. *See* Inso Corporation.
Infostrada S.p.A., **38** 300
Infosys Technologies Ltd., **38 240–43**
Infotech Enterprises, Ltd., **33** 45
Infotechnology Inc., **25** 507–08
Infrasud, **I** 466
Infun, S.A., **23** 269
ING, B.V., **14** 45, 47
Ing. C. Olivetti & C., S.p.A., **III** 122, **144–46**, 549, 678; **10** 499; **16** 122; **25** 33. *See also* Olivetti S.p.A
Ingalls Quinn and Johnson, **9** 135
Ingalls Shipbuilding, Inc., **I** 485; **11** 264–65; **12** 28, **271–73**; **36** 78–79; **41** 42
Ingear, **10** 216
Ingersoll-Rand Company, **III** 473, **525–27**; **10** 262; **13** 27, 523; **15** 187, **223–26 (upd.)**; **22** 542; **33** 168; **34** 46
Ingka Holding B.V. *See* IKEA International A/S.
Ingleby Enterprises Inc. *See* Caribiner International, Inc.
Inglenook Vineyards, **13** 134; **34** 89
Ingles Markets, Inc., **20 305–08**
Inglis Ltd., **III** 654; **12** 549
Ingram Book Group, **30** 70
Ingram Corp. Ltd., **III** 559; **IV** 249
Ingram Industries, Inc., **10** 518–19; **11 193–95**; **13** 90, 482
Ingram Micro Corporation, **24** 29
AB Ingredients, **II** 466
Ingredients Technology Corp., **9** 154
Ingres Corporation, **9** 36–37; **25** 87
Ingwerson and Co., **II** 356
INH. *See* Instituto Nacional de Hidrocarboros.
Inha Works Ltd., **33** 164
Inhalation Therapy Services, **III** 73
INI. *See* Instituto Nacional de Industria.
Inktomi Corporation, **41** 98
Inland Container Corporation, **IV** 311, 341–42, 675; **7** 528; **8 267–69**; **19** 267
Inland Motors Corporation, **18** 291
Inland Paperboard and Packaging, Inc., **31** 438
Inland Pollution Control, **9** 110
Inland Specialty Chemical Corp., **I** 342; **14** 217
Inland Steel Industries, Inc., **II** 403; **IV 113–16**, 158, 703; **7** 447; **13** 157; **15**

249–50; **17** 351; **19** 9, **216–20 (upd.)**, 311, 381; **23** 35; **30** 254; **40** 269, 381; **41** 4
Inland Valley, **23** 321
Inmac, Inc., **16** 373
Inmos Ltd., **I** 532; **11** 307; **29** 323
InnCOGEN Limited, **35** 480
InnerCity Foods Joint Venture Company, **16** 97
Inno-BM, **26** 158, 161
Inno-France. *See* Societe des Grandes Entreprises de Distribution, Inno-France.
Innova International Corporation, **26** 333
Innovacom, **25** 96
Innovation, **26** 158
Innovative Marketing Systems. *See* Bloomberg L.P.
Innovative Pork Concepts, **7** 82
Innovative Products & Peripherals Corporation, **14** 379
Innovative Software Inc., **10** 362
Innovative Sports Systems, Inc., **15** 396
Innovative Valve Technologies Inc., **33** 167
Innovex Ltd., **21** 425
Inns and Co., **III** 734
Innwerk AG, **IV** 229
Inoue Electric Manufacturing Co., **II** 75–76
Inpaco, **16** 340
Inpacsa, **19** 226
Inprise/Borland Corporation, **33** 115
Input/Output, Inc., **11** 538
INS. *See* International News Service.
Insalaco Markets Inc., **13** 394
INSCO, **III** 242
Inserra Supermarkets, **25 234–36**
Insight Enterprises, Inc., **18 259–61**
Insilco Corporation, **I** 473; **12** 472; **16 281–83**; **23** 212; **36** 469–70
Insley Manufacturing Co., **8** 545
Inso Corporation, **26 215–19**; **36** 273
Inspiration Resources Corporation, **12** 260; **13** 502–03
Inspirations PLC, **22** 129
Insta-Care Holdings Inc., **16** 59
Insta-Care Pharmacy Services, **9** 186
Instant Auto Insurance, **33** 3, 5
Instant Interiors Corporation, **26** 102
Instant Milk Co., **II** 488
Instapak Corporation, **14** 429
Instinet Corporation, **34 225–27**
Institut de Sérothérapie Hémopoiétique, **I** 669
Institut für Gemeinwohl, **IV** 139
Institut Merieux, **I** 389
Institut Ronchese, **I** 676
Institute de Development Industriel, **19** 87
Institute for Professional Development, **24** 40
Institute for Scientific Information, **8** 525, 528
Institution Food House. *See* Alex Lee Inc.
Institutional Financing Services, **23** 491
Instituto Nacional de Hidrocarboros, **IV** 528
Instituto Nacional de Industria, **I 459–61**; **V** 606–07; **6** 95–96
Instituto per la Ricostruzione Industriale, **V** 614
Instone Airline, **I** 92
Instromet International, **22** 65
Instrument Systems Corp. *See* Griffon Corporation.
Instrumentarium Corp., **13** 328; **25** 82
Instrumentation Laboratory Inc., **III** 511–12; **22** 75
Instrumentation Scientifique de Laboratoire, S.A., **15** 404
Insulite Co. of Finland, **IV** 275
Insurance Auto Auctions, Inc., **23** 148, **285–87**
Insurance Co. against Fire Damage, **III** 308
Insurance Co. of Scotland, **III** 358
Insurance Co. of the State of Pennsylvania, **III** 196
Insurance Company of North America. *See* CIGNA Corporation.
Insurance Corp. of Ireland (Life), **III** 335
Insurance Partners L.P., **15** 257
InSync Communications, **42** 425
Intabex Holdings Worldwide, S.A., **27** 126
Intalco Aluminum Corp., **12** 254
Intamin, **17** 443
Intarsia Corp., **38** 187
INTEC, **6** 428
InteCom Inc., **6** 285
Integon Corp., **IV** 374
Integra-A Hotel and Restaurant Company, **13** 473
Integral Corporation, **14** 381; **23** 446; **33** 331
Integrated Business Information Services, **13** 5
Integrated Computer Systems. *See* Learning Tree International Inc.
Integrated Data Services Co., **IV** 473
Integrated Genetics, **I** 638; **8** 210; **13** 239; **38** 204, 206
Integrated Health Services, Inc., **11** 282
Integrated Medical Systems Inc., **12** 333
Integrated Resources, Inc., **11** 483; **16** 54; **19** 393
Integrated Silicon Solutions, Inc., **18** 20; **43** 17
Integrated Software Systems Corporation, **6** 224; **11** 469
Integrated Systems Operations. *See* Xerox Corporation.
Integrated Systems Solutions Corp., **9** 284; **11** 395; **17** 264
Integrated Technology, Inc., **6** 279
Integrated Telecom Technologies, **14** 417
Integrity Life Insurance, **III** 249
Intel Corporation, **II 44–46**, 62, 64; **III** 115, 125, 455; **6** 215–17, 222, 231, 233, 235, 257; **9** 42–43, 57, 114–15, 165–66; **10 365–67 (upd.)**, 477; **11** 62, 308, 328, 490, 503, 518, 520; **12** 61, 449; **13** 47; **16** 139–40, 146, 394; **17** 32–33; **18** 18, 260; **19** 310, 312; **20** 69, 175; **21** 36, 122; **22** 542; **24** 233, 236, 371; **25** 418, 498; **26** 91, 432; **27** 365–66; **30** 10; **34** 441; **36** 123, **284–88 (upd.)**; **38** 71, 416; **41** 408; **43** 14–16
Intelcom Support Services, Inc., **14** 334
Intelicom Solutions Corp., **6** 229
IntelliCorp, **9** 310; **31** 298
Intelligent Electronics, Inc., **6 243–45**; **12** 184; **13** 176, 277
Intelligent Software Ltd., **26** 275
Intelligraphics Inc., **33** 44
Intellimetrics Instrument Corporation, **16** 93
Inter American Aviation, Inc. *See* SkyWest, Inc.
Inter-American Development Bank, **IV** 55
Inter-American Satellite Television Network, **7** 391
Inter-City Gas Ltd., **III** 654; **19** 159
Inter-City Western Bakeries Ltd., **II** 631
Inter-City Wholesale Electric Inc., **15** 385
Inter-Comm Telephone, Inc., **8** 310
Inter-Continental Hotels and Resorts, **38** 77
Inter IKEA Systems B.V., **V** 82
Inter-Island Airways, Ltd., **22** 251; **24** 20
Inter-Island Steam Navigation Co. *See* Hawaiian Airlines.
Inter Island Telephone, **6** 326, 328
Inter-Mountain Telephone Co., **V** 344
Inter-Ocean Corporation, **16** 103
Inter Parfums Inc., **35 235–38**
Inter-Regional Financial Group, Inc., **15 231–33**. *See also* Dain Rauscher Corporation.
Inter State Telephone, **6** 338
Inter Techniek, **16** 421
Interactive Computer Design, Inc., **23** 489, 491
Interactive Systems, **7** 500
Interamericana de Talleras SA de CV, **10** 415
Interbake Foods, **II** 631
InterBold, **7** 146; **11** 151
Interbrás, **IV** 503
Interbrew S.A., **16** 397; **17 256–58**; **25** 279, 282; **26** 306; **34** 202; **38** 74, 78
Interchemical Corp., **13** 460
Intercity Food Services, Inc., **II** 663
Interco Incorporated, **III 528–31**; **9** 133, 135, 192, 234–35; **10** 184; **12** 156, 306–08; **22** 49; **29** 294; **31** 136–37, 210; **39** 146. *See also* Furniture Brands International, Inc.
Intercolonial, **6** 360
Intercomi, **II** 233
Intercontessa AG, **35** 401; **36** 294
Intercontinental Apparel, **8** 249
Intercontinental Breweries, **I** 289
Intercontinental Electronics Corp. *See* IEC Electronics Corp.
Intercontinental Hotels, **I** 248–49
Intercontinental Mortgage Company, **8** 436
Intercontinental Rubber Co., **II** 112
Intercontinentale, **III** 404
Intercord, **22** 194
Intercostal Steel Corp., **13** 97
Interdesign, **16** 421
Interealty Corp., **43** 184
Interedi-Cosmopolitan, **III** 47
Interep National Radio Sales Inc., **35 231–34**
Interessen Gemeinschaft Farbenwerke. *See* I.G. Farbenindustrie AG.
Interface Group, **13** 483
Interface, Inc., **8 270–72**; **18** 112; **29 246–49 (upd.)**
Interferon Sciences, Inc., **13** 366–67
Interfinancial, **III** 200
InterFirst Bankcorp, Inc., **9** 482
Interfood Ltd., **II** 520–21, 540
Interglas S.A., **22** 515
Intergram, Inc., **27** 21
Intergraph Corporation, **6 246–49**; **10** 257; **24 233–36 (upd.)**
Interhandel, **I** 337–38; **II** 378; **22** 226
INTERIM Services, Inc., **9** 268, 270; **25** 434; **29** 224, 227
Interinvest S.A., **33** 19
Interlabor, **16** 420–21
Interlabor Interim, **43** 308

The Interlake Corporation, **8 273–75**; **38** 210
Interlake Steamship Company, **15** 302
Intermaco S.R.L., **43** 368
Intermagnetics General Corp., **9** 10
Intermarché, **35** 398, 401. *See also* ITM Entreprises SA.
Intermark, Inc., **12** 394; **34** 338–39
Intermec Corporation, **29** 414
Intermed, **I** 429
Intermedia, **25** 499
Intermedics, **III** 633; **11** 458–59; **12** 325–26; **40** 66–67
Intermedics Intraocular Inc., **I** 665
Intermet Corporation, **32 279–82**
Intermoda, **V** 166
Intermountain Broadcasting and Television Corp., **IV** 674
Intermountain Health Care, Inc., **27 237–40**
ITM International, **IV** 239
International Aero Engines, **9** 418
International Agricultural Corporation, **8** 264–65
International Air Service Co., **24** 21
International Assurance Co., **III** 195
International Bank, **II** 261
International Bank of Japan, **17** 122
International Bank of Moscow, **II** 242
International Banking and Credit Analysis (IBCA), **37** 144
International Banking Corp., **II** 253; **9** 123
International Banking Technologies, Inc., **11** 113
International Basic Economy Corporation, **13** 103
International Beauty Supply, Ltd. *See* L.L. Knickerbocker Co., Inc.
International Brewing Holdings Pty., **21** 229
International Brotherhood of Teamsters, **37 211–14**
International Business Directories, Inc., **26** 484
International Business Machines Corporation, **I** 26, 455, 523, 534, 541; **II** 6, 8, 10, 42, 44–45, 56, 62, 68, 70, 73, 86, 99, 107, 113, 134, 159, 211, 274, 326, 379, 397, 432, 440; **III** 9, 109–11, 113–18, 121–28, 130, 132–34, 136, 139–43, 145, **147–49**, 151–52, 154–55, 157, 165–72, 200, 246, 313, 319, 326, 458, 475, 549, 618, 685; **IV** 443, 711; **6** 51, 218–25, 233–35, 237, 240–42, 244–48, **250–53 (upd.)**, 254–60, 262, 265, 269–71, 275–77, 279, 281–89, 320, 324, 346, 390, 428; **7** 145–46, 161; **8** 138–39, 466–67; **9** 36, 41–42, 48, 50, 114–15, 131, 139, 165–66, 170–71, 184, 194, 284, 296–97, 310, 327, 463–64; **10** 19, 22–24, 58, 119, 125, 161, 194, 232, 237, 243–44, 255–56, 309, 361–62, 366–67, 394, 456, 463, 474, 500–01, 505, 510, 512–13, 518–19, 542; **11** 19, 45, 50, 59, 61–62, 64–65, 68, 86–88, 150, 273–74, 285, 364, 395, 469, 485, 491, 494, 506, 519; **12** 61, 138–39, 147–49, 161–62, 183, 204, 238, 278, 335, 442, 450, 469–70, 484; **13** 47, 127, 174, 214, 326, 345, 387–88, 403, 482; **14** 13–15, 106, 268–69, 318, 354, 391, 401, 432–33, 446, 533; **15** 106, 440, 454–55, 491–92; **16** 4, 94, 140, 224–26, 301, 367–68, 372; **17** 353, 418, 532–34; **18** 94, 110, 112, 162, 250, 292, 305–07, 344, 434–36; **19** 41, 110, 310, 312, 437; **20** 237, 313; **21** 86, 391; **23** 135, 138, 209, 470; **24** 234; **25** 20–21, 34, 86–87, 96, 133–34, 149, 298–301, 356, 358, 530–32; **26** 90, 187, 275–76, 427, 429, 441, 540, 542; **28** 112, 189; **29** 375, 414; **30 247–51 (upd.)**, 140, 300, 337–38; **34** 442–43; **36** 81–82, 171, 480–81; **38** 54–55, 250, 417; **43** 126–27
International Care Services, **6** 182
International Cellucotton Products Co., **III** 40; **16** 302–03; **43** 256–57
International Cementers Inc., **25** 74
International Commercial Bank, **II** 257
International Communication Materials, Inc., **18** 387
International Computers. *See* ICL plc.
International Controls Corporation, **10 368–70**
International Corona Corporation, **12** 244
International Creative Management, Inc., **38** 161; **43 235–37**
International Credit Card Business Assoc., **II** 436
International Dairy Queen, Inc., **7** 266; **10 371–74**; **39 232–36 (upd.)**
International Data Group, Inc., **7 238–40**; **12** 561; **25 237–40 (upd.)**; **27** 222
International Development Bank, **IV** 417
International Digital Communications, Inc., **6** 327
International Distillers & Vintners Ltd., **31** 92
International Egyptian Oil Co., **IV** 412
International Engineering Company, Inc., **7** 355
International Epicure, **12** 280
International Equities Corp., **III** 98
International Factoring Corp., **II** 436
International Factors, Limited, **II** 208
International Family Entertainment Inc., **13 279–81**
International Finance Corp., **19** 192
International Flavors & Fragrances Inc., **9 290–92**; **38 244–48 (upd.)**
International Foods, **II** 468
International Fuel Cells Inc., **39** 394
International Game Technology, **10 375–76**; **24** 37 **25** 313; **41 214–16 (upd.)**
International Graphics Corp., **IV** 645
International Group, **13** 277
International Harvester Co., **III** 473, 650, 651; **10** 264, 280, 378, 380, 528; **13** 16; **17** 158; **22** 380. *See also* Navistar International Corporation.
International Healthcare, **III** 197
International Home Foods, Inc., **42** 94
International House of Pancakes. *See* IHOP Corporation.
International Hydron, **10** 47; **13** 367
International Imaging Limited, **29** 58
International Income Property, **IV** 708
International Industries, **17** 249
International Learning Systems Corp. Ltd., **IV** 641–42; **7** 311
International Lease Finance Corp., **III** 198; **6** 67; **36** 231
International Light Metals Corp., **IV** 163
International MacGregor, **27** 269
International Management Group, **18 262–65**
International Marine Oil Co., **IV** 363
International Marine Services, **22** 276
International Match, **12** 463
International Mercantile Marine Co., **II** 330
International Milling. *See* International Multifoods Corporation.
International Mineral & Chemical, Inc., **8** 265–66
International Minerals and Chemical Corporation, **19** 253
International Multifoods Corporation, **II** 493; **7 241–43**; **12** 80, 125; **14** 515; **21** 289; **23** 203; **25 241–44 (upd.)**; **28** 238
International Music Co., **16** 202; **43** 171
International News Service, **IV** 626–27; **19** 203; **25** 507
International Nickel Co. of Canada, Ltd., **III** 677; **IV** 78, 110–12
International Nickel Corporation, **16** 122; **18** 488
International Nutrition Laboratories, **14** 558
International Organization of Consumers Unions, **26** 98
International Pacific Corp., **II** 389
International Paper Company, **I** 27; **II** 208, 403; **III** 693, 764; **IV** 16, 245, **286–88**, 289, 326; **8** 267; **11** 76, 311; **15 227–30 (upd.)**; **16** 349; **17** 446; **23** 48–49, 366, 368; **25** 9; **26** 444; **30** 92, 94; **32** 91, 346
International Parts Corporation, **10** 414
International Periodical Distributors, **34** 5
International Permalite, **22** 229
International Petroleum Co., Ltd., **IV** 415–16, 438, 478; **25** 230
International Petroleum Corp., **IV** 454, 484
International Playtex, Inc., **12** 93
International Proteins Corporation, **21** 248
International Publishing Corp., **IV** 641, 666–67; **7** 343; **17** 397; **23** 350
International Raw Materials, Ltd., **31** 20
International Rectifier Corporation, **31 263–66**
International Roofing Company, **22** 13–14
International Sealants Corporation, **8** 333
International Shipholding Corporation, Inc., **27 241–44**
International Shoe Co., **III** 528–30
International Silver Company, **I** 30; **12** 472; **14** 482–83
International Specialty Products, Inc., **22** 225, 228–29
International Speedway Corporation, **19 221–23**; **32** 439
International Standard Electric, **II** 66–68
International Stores, **I** 427
International Supply Consortium, **13** 79
International Talent Group, **25** 281
International Talent Management, Inc. *See* Motown Records Company L.P.
International Telcell Group, **7** 336
International Telephone & Telegraph Corporation, **I** 434, 446, **462–64**, 544; **II** 13, 66, 68, 86, 130, 331; **III** 98–99, 162–64, 166, 644–45, 684; **V** 334–35, 337–38; **6** 356; **8** 157; **9** 10–11, 324; **10** 19, 44, 301; **11 196–99 (upd.)**, 337, 516; **12** 18; **13** 246; **14** 332, 488; **19** 131, 205, 208; **22** 55; **25** 100, 432
International Television Corporation Entertainment Group, **23** 391

International Thomson Organisation Ltd. *See* The Thomson Corporation.
International Thomson Organization Ltd., **23** 92
International Time Recording Company. *See* International Business Machines Corporation.
International Total Services, Inc., 37 215–18
International Trust and Investment Corp., **II** 577
International Trust Co., **II** 207
International Utilities Corp., **IV** 75–76; **6** 444
International Western Electric Co., **I** 462; **II** 66; **III** 162; **11** 196
International Wind Systems, **6** 581
International Wine & Spirits Ltd., **9** 533
International Wire Works Corp., **8** 13
International Wireless Inc., **21** 261
Internationale Industriële Beleggung Maatschappij Amsterdam BV, **IV** 128
Internationale Nederlanden Group, **24** 88
Internet Shopping Network, **26** 441
InterNorth, Inc., **II** 16; **V** 610
Interocean Management Corp., **9** 509–11
Interpac Belgium, **6** 303
Interprovincial Pipe Line Ltd., **I** 264; **IV** 439; **25** 231. *See also* Enbridge Inc.
The Interpublic Group of Companies, Inc., I 16–18, 31, 36; **6** 53; **14** 315; **16** 70, 72, 167; **20** 5; **22 294–97 (upd.)**; **23** 478; **28** 66–67; **32** 142; **42** 107
Interra Financial. *See* Dain Rauscher Corporation.
InterRedec, Inc., **17** 196
Interscience, **17** 271
Interscope Communications, Inc., **23** 389, 391; **27** 121
Interscope Music Group, 31 267–69
Intersec, Inc., **27** 21
Intersil Inc., **II** 30; **12** 196; **16** 358
Interstate & Ocean Transport, **6** 577
Interstate Bag, **I** 335
Interstate Bakeries Corporation, **7** 320; **12 274–76**; **27** 310; **38 249–52 (upd.)**
Interstate Brick Company, **6** 568–69
Interstate Electric Manufacturing Company. *See* McGraw Electric Company.
Interstate Finance Corp., **11** 16
Interstate Financial Corporation, **9** 475
Interstate Iron and Steel Company. *See* Republic Engineered Steels, Inc.
Interstate Logos, Inc., **27** 278
Interstate Paint Distributors, Inc., **13** 367
Interstate Power Company, **6** 555, 605; **18** 404
Interstate Public Service Company, **6** 555
Interstate Stores Inc., **V** 203; **15** 469; **18** 522
Interstate Supply Company. *See* McGraw Electric Company.
Interstate United Corporation, **II** 679; **III** 502; **13** 435
Intertec Design, Inc., **34** 371–72
Intertec Publishing Corp., **22** 441
Intertechnique SA, **36** 530
Interturbine Holland, **19** 150
Intertype Corp., **II** 37
Interunfall, **III** 346
Intervideo TV Productions-A.B., **II** 640
Intervision Express, **24** 510
Interweb, **IV** 661
InterWest Partners, **16** 418
Intimate Brands, Inc., 24 237–39' **29** 357
InTouch Systems, Inc., **43** 118
Intrac Handelsgesellschaft mbH, **7** 142
Intradal, **II** 572
Intraph South Africa Ltd., **6** 247
IntraWest Bank, **II** 289
The Intrawest Corporation, **15 234–36**; **31** 67; **43** 438
Intrepid Corporation, **16** 493
IntroGene B.V., **13** 241
Intuit Inc., **13** 147; **14 262–64**; **23** 457; **33 208–11 (upd.)**
Invacare Corporation, **11 200–02**, 486
Invenex Laboratories, **17** 287
Invento Products Corporation, **21** 269
Invep S.p.A., **10** 150
Inveresk Paper Co., **III** 693; **IV** 685
Invergordon Distillers, **III** 509
Inversale, **9** 92
INVESCO MIM Management Limited, **21** 397
Invesgen S.A., **26** 129
InvestCorp International, **15** 200; **24** 195, 420; **25** 205, 207
Investcorp S.A. *See* Arabian Investment Banking Corp.
Investimentos Itaú S.A., **19** 33
Investors Bank and Trust Company, **18** 152
Investors Diversified Services, Inc., **II** 398; **6** 199; **8** 348–49; **10** 43–45, 59, 62; **21** 305; **25** 248; **38** 42
Investors Group, **III** 261. *See also* Power Corporation of Canada.
Investors Management Corp., **10** 331
Investors Overseas Services, **10** 368–69
Investrónica S.A., **26** 129
Invista Capital Management, **III** 330
The Invus Group, Ltd., **33** 449
Iolab Corp., **III** 36
Iomega Corporation, **18** 509–10; **21 294–97**
IONA Technologies plc, 43 238–41
Ionpure Technologies Corporation, **6** 486–88
Iowa Beef Packers, **21** 287
Iowa Beef Processors, **II** 516–17; **IV** 481–82; **13** 351
Iowa Manufacturing, **II** 86
Iowa Mold Tooling Co., Inc., **16** 475
Iowa Public Service Company, **6** 524–25
IP Gas Supply Company, **6** 506
IP Services, Inc., **IV** 597
IP Timberlands Ltd., **IV** 288
IP&L. *See* Illinois Power & Light Corporation.
Ipalco Enterprises, Inc., 6 508–09
IPC. *See* International Publishing Corp.
IPC Communications, Inc., **15** 196
IPC Magazines Limited, **IV** 650; **7 244–47**
IPD. *See* International Periodical Distributors.
IPEC Holdings Ltd., **27** 474–75
Ipko-Amcor, **14** 225
IPL Energy Inc. *See* Enbridge Inc.
IPS Praha a.s., **38** 437
IPS Publishing, **39** 341–42
IPSOA Editore, **14** 555
IPSOS, S.A., **24** 355
IQUE, Inc., **21** 194
Iran Air, **6** 101
Iran Pan American Oil Co., **IV** 466
Iranian Oil Exploration and Producing Co., **IV** 466–67
Iraq Petroleum Co., **IV** 363, 386, 429, 450, 464, 558–60
Irby-Gilliland Company, **9** 127
Irdeto, **31** 330
IRI. *See* Instituto per la Ricostruzione Industriale.
Irideon, Inc., **35** 435
Iris Associates, Inc., **25** 299, 301
IRIS Holding Co., **III** 347
Irish Air. *See* Aer Lingus Group plc.
Irish Life Assurance Company, **16** 14; **43** 7
Irish Paper Sacks Ltd., **IV** 295; **19** 225
Irish Sugar Co., **II** 508
Iron and Steel Corp., **IV** 22, 41, 92, 533–34
Iron and Steel Press Company, **27** 360
Iron Cliffs Mining Company, **13** 156
Iron Mountain Forge, **13** 319
Iron Mountain, Inc., 33 212–14
Iron Ore Company of Canada, **8** 347
Iroquois Gas Corporation, **6** 526
Irvin Feld & Kenneth Feld Productions, Inc., 15 237–39. *See also* Feld Entertainment, Inc.
Irving Bank Corp., **II** 192
Irving Tanning Company, **17** 195
Irving Trust Coompany, **II** 257; **22** 55
Irvington Smelting, **IV** 78
Irwin Lehrhoff Associates, **11** 366
Irwin Toy Limited, **14 265–67**
Isabela Shoe Corporation, **13** 360
Isagro S.p.A., **26** 425
Iscor. *See* Iron and Steel Corporation.
Isetan Company Limited, **V 85–87**; **36 289–93 (upd.)**
Iseya Tanji Drapery, **V** 85
Ishikawajima-Harima Heavy Industries Co., Ltd., **I** 508, 511, 534; **II** 274; **III 532–33**; **9** 293; **12** 484; **41** 41
Ishizaki Honten, **III** 715
Isis Distributed Systems, Inc., **10** 501
Island Air, **24** 22
Island Equipment Co., **19** 381
Island Holiday, **I** 417
Island Pictures Corp., **23** 389
Island Records, **23** 389
Islands Restaurants, **17** 85–87
Isle of Capri Casinos, Inc., **33** 41; **41 217–19**
Isolite Insulating Products Co., **III** 714
Isosceles PLC, **II** 628–29; **24** 270
Isotec Communications Incorporated, **13** 213
Isover, **III** 676; **16** 121
Ispat Inland Inc., **40 267–72 (upd.)**, 381
Ispat International N.V., **30 252–54**
ISS International Service System, Inc., **8** 271
ISS Securitas, **42** 165, 167
Istanbul Fertilizer Industry, **IV** 563
Istante Vesa s.r.l., **22** 239
Istituto per la Ricostruzione Industriale S.p.A., **I** 207, 459, **465–67**; **II** 191–92, 270–71; **IV** 419; **11 203–06**; **13** 28, 218
Isuzu Motors, Ltd., **II** 274; **III** 581, 593; **7** 8, 219; **9 293–95**; **10** 354; **23 288–91 (upd.)**; **36** 240, 243
Isuzu Motors of Japan, **21** 6
IT Group, **28** 203
IT International, **V** 255
Itabira Iron Ore Co. Ltd., **IV** 54; **43** 111
ITABRASCO, **IV** 55
Italcarta, **IV** 339
Italcementi, **IV** 420

Italcimenti Group, **40** 107–08
Italianni's, **22** 128
Italiatour, **6** 69
Italmobiliare, **III** 347
Italstate. *See* Societa per la Infrastrutture e l'Assetto del Territoria.
Italtel, **V** 326–27
Italware, **27** 94
Itaú. *See* Banco Itaú S.A.
Itaú Winterthur Seguradura S.A., **III** 404
Itaúsa. *See* Investimentos Itaú S.A.
Itek Corp., **I** 486; **11** 265
Itel Corporation, **II** 64; **III** 512; **6** 262, 354; **9** 49, **296–99**; **15** 107; **22** 339; **26** 328, 519
Items International Airwalk Inc., **17 259–61**
Ithaca Gas & Electric. *See* New York State Electric and Gas.
ITI Education Corporation, **29** 472
ITM Entreprises SA, **36 294–97**
Ito Carnation Co., **II** 518
Ito Food Processing Co., **II** 518
Ito Gofuku Co. Ltd., **V** 129
Ito Meat Processing Co., **II** 518
Ito Processed Food Co., **II** 518
Ito-Yokado Co., Ltd., **II** 661; **V 88–89**; **32** 414, 416–17; **42 189–92 (upd.)**
Itochu and Renown, Inc., **12** 281
ITOCHU Corporation, **19** 9; **32 283–87 (upd.)**; **34** 231; **42** 342
Itochu Housing, **38** 415
Itochu of Japan, **14** 550
Itoh. *See* C. Itoh & Co.
Itoham Foods Inc., **II 518–19**
Itokin, **III** 48
Itoman & Co., **26** 456
ITT, **21** 200; **24** 188, 405; **30** 101. *See also* International Telephone and Telegraph Corporation.
ITT Aerospace, **33** 48
ITT Educational Services, Inc., **33 215–17**
ITT Sheraton Corporation, **III 98–101**; **23** 484
ITT World Directories, **27** 498, 500
iTurf Inc., **29** 142–43
ITW. *See* Illinois Tool Works Inc.
ITW Devcon, **12** 7
IU International, **23** 40
IURA Edition, **14** 556
IV Therapy Associates, **16** 440
IVAC Corp., **I** 646; **11** 90
IVACO Industries Inc., **11** 207
Ivanhoe, Inc., **II** 662, 664
IVAX Corporation, **11 207–09**; **41** 420–21
Iveco, **I** 148; **12** 91
Ives Trains, **16** 336
Ivy Mortgage Corp., **39** 380, 382
Iwai & Co., **I** 492, 509–10; **IV** 151; **24** 325, 358
Iwata Air Compressor, **III** 427
Iwerks Entertainment, Inc., **33** 127; **34 228–30**
IXC Communications, Inc., **29 250–52**; **37** 127
IXI Ltd., **38** 418–19
IYG Holding Company of Japan, **7** 492; **32** 414, 417
The IZOD Gant Corporation, **24** 385
Izod Lacoste, **II** 502–03; **9** 156–57; **10** 324
Izumi Fudosan, **IV** 726
Izumiya, **V** 477; **36** 418
J&E Davy, **16** 14
J&G Meakin, **12** 529
J&J Colman, **II** 566
J&J Corrugated Box Corp., **IV** 282; **9** 261
J & J Snack Foods Corporation, **24 240–42**
J&L Industrial Supply, **13** 297
J&L Steel. *See* Jones & Laughlin Steel Corp.
J&R Electronics Inc., **26 224–26**
J. & W. Seligman and Co., **17** 498
J.A. Baldwin Manufacturing Company, **17** 106
J.A. Jones, Inc., **16 284–86**; **17** 377
J. Aron & Co., **II** 415
J.B. Hudson & Son, **18** 136
J.B. Hunt Transport Services Inc., **12 277–79**; **15** 440; **26** 533
J.B. Lippincott & Company, **IV** 652; **14** 554–56; **33** 460
J.B. McLean Publishing Co., Ltd., **IV** 638
J.B. Williams Company, **III** 66; **8** 63
J.B. Wolters Publishing Company, **14** 554
J. Baker, Inc., **13** 361; **31 270–73**
J. Beres & Son, **24** 444–45
J Bibby & Sons, **I** 424
J Bibby Agriculture Limited, **13** 53
J. Bulova Company. *See* Bulova Corporation.
J. Byrons, **9** 186
J.C. Baxter Co., **15** 501
J.C. Hillary's, **20** 54
J.C. Penney Company, Inc., **I** 516; **V 90–92**; **6** 336; **8** 288, 555; **9** 156, 210, 213, 219, 346–94; **10** 409, 490; **11** 349; **12** 111, 431, 522; **14** 62; **16** 37, 327–28; **17** 124, 175, 177, 366, 460; **18** 108, 136, 168, 200, **269–73 (upd.)**, 373, 478; **19** 300; **21** 24, 527; **25** 91, 254, 368; **26** 161; **27** 346, 429; **31** 260–61; **32** 166, 168–70; **39** 270; **41** 114–15; **43 245–50 (upd.)**
J. Crew Group Inc., **12 280–82**; **25** 48; **34 231–34 (upd.)**; **36** 472
J.D. Bassett Manufacturing Co. *See* Bassett Furniture Industries, Inc.
J.D. Edwards & Company, **14 268–70**; **38** 431
J.D. Power and Associates, **9** 166; **32 297–301**
J.E. Baxter Co., **I** 429
J.E. Nolan, **11** 486
J.E. Sirrine. *See* CRSS Inc.
J.E. Smith Box & Printing Co., **13** 441
J. Edward Connelly Associates, Inc., **22** 438
J. Evershed & Son, **13** 103
J.F. Corporation, **V** 87
J.F. Lauman and Co., **II** 681
J. Fielding & Co., **IV** 249
J.G. McMullen Dredging Co., **III** 558
J. Gadsden Paper Products, **IV** 249
J. George Leyner Engineering Works Co., **III** 525–26
J.H. Heafner Co., **20** 263
J.H. Stone & Sons, **IV** 332
J.H. Whitney & Company, **9** 250; **32** 100
J. Homestock. *See* R.H. Macy & Co.
J.I. Case Company, **I** 148, 527; **III** 651; **10 377–81**; **13** 17; **22** 380. *See also* CNH Global N.V.
The J. Jill Group, Inc., **35 239–41**
J.K. Armsby Co., **7** 130–31
J.K. Starley and Company Ltd, **7** 458
J.L. Clark, Inc. *See* Clarcor Inc.
J.L. Hudson Company. *See* Dayton Hudson Corporation.
J.L. Kraft & Bros. Co., **II** 532
J.L. Shiely Co., **III** 691
J.L. Wright Company, **25** 379
J. Levin & Co., Inc., **13** 367
J. Lyons & Co., **I** 215
J.M. Brunswick & Brothers, **III** 442
J.M. Douglas & Company Limited, **14** 141
J.M. Horton Ice Cream Co., **II** 471
J.M. Huber Corporation, **40** 68
J.M. Jones Co., **II** 668; **18** 504
J.M. Kohler Sons Company, **7** 269
The J.M. Smucker Company, **11 210–12**
J.M. Tull Metals Co., Inc., **IV** 116; **15** 250; **19** 219
J.M. Voith AG, **33 222–25**
J. Mandelbaum & Sons, **19** 510
J-Mar Associates, **31** 435–36
J-Mass, **IV** 289
J. Muirhead Ltd., **I** 315; **25** 81
J.P. Heilwell Industries, **II** 420
J.P. Morgan & Co. Incorporated, **II** 281, **329–32**, 407, 419, 427–28, 430–31, 441; **III** 237, 245, 380; **IV** 20, 180, 400; **9** 386; **11** 421; **12** 165; **13** 13; **16** 25, 375; **19** 190; **26** 66, 500; **30 261–65 (upd.)**; **33** 464; **35** 74; **36** 151–53
J.P. Morgan Chase & Co., **38 253–59 (upd.)**
J.P. Stevens Inc., **8** 234; **12** 404; **16** 533–35; **17** 75; **19** 420; **27** 468–69; **28** 218
J.P. Wood, **II** 587
J.R. Brown & Sharpe. *See* Brown & Sharpe Manufacturing Co.
J.R. Geigy S.A., **I** 632–33, 635, 671; **8** 108–10; **39** 72
J.R. Parkington Co., **I** 280
J.R. Simplot Company, **16 287–89**; **21** 508; **26** 309
J.R. Wyllie & Sons, **I** 437
J. Ray McDermott & Co., **III** 558–59
J.S. Fry & Sons, **II** 476
J.S. Morgan & Co., **II** 329, 427
J Sainsbury plc, **II 657–59**, 677–78; **10** 442; **11** 239, 241; **13 282–84 (upd.)**; **17** 42; **21** 335; **22** 241; **32** 253; **38 260–65 (upd.)**
J. Sanders & Sons, **IV** 711
J. Sears & Company, **V** 177
J. Spiegel and Company. *See* Spiegel, Inc.
J.T. Wing and Co., **I** 158
J.U. Dickson Sawmill Inc. *See* Dickson Forest Products, Inc.
J.W. Bateson, **8** 87
J.W. Buderus and Sons, **III** 694
J.W. Charles Financial Services Inc., **25** 542
J.W. Childs Equity Partners LP, **40** 274
J.W. Foster and Sons, Inc. *See* Reebok International Ltd.
J.W. Higman & Co., **III** 690
J.W. Spear, **25** 314
J.W. Wassall Ltd. *See* Wassall PLC.
J. Walter Thompson Co., **I** 9, 17, 25, 37, 251, 354, 623; **10** 69; **11** 51; **12** 168; **16** 167
J. Weingarten Inc., **7** 203; **28** 163
J. Wiss & Sons Co., **II** 16
J.Z. Sales Corp., **16** 36

J. Zinmeister Co., **II** 682
Jabil Circuit, Inc., 36 298–301
Jacintoport Corporation, **7** 281
Jack Daniel Distillery, **10** 180
Jack Daniel's. *See* Brown-Forman Corporation.
Jack Eckerd Corp., **16** 160; **19** 467
Jack Frain Enterprises, **16** 471
Jack Henry and Associates, Inc., 17 262–65
Jack Houston Exploration Company, **7** 345
Jack in the Box, Inc. *See* Foodmaster, Inc.
Jack Schwartz Shoes, Inc., 18 266–68
Jackpot Enterprises Inc., 21 298–300; 24 36
Jackson & Curtis, **II** 444; **22** 405
Jackson & Perkins. *See* Bear Creek Corporation.
Jackson Box Co., **IV** 311; **19** 267
Jackson Cushion Spring Co., **13** 397
Jackson Ice Cream Co., **12** 112
Jackson Marine Corp., **III** 499
Jackson Mercantile Co. *See* Jitney-Jungle Stores of America, Inc.
Jackson National Life Insurance Company, III 335–36; **8 276–77**
Jackson Purchase Electric Cooperative Corporation, **11** 37
Jacksonville Shipyards, **I** 170
Jaco Electronics, Inc., 19 311; **30 255–57**
Jacob Holm & Sons A/S, **22** 263
Jacob Leinenkugel Brewing Company, 12 338; **28 209–11**
Jacobs Brake Manufacturing Company, **7** 116–17
Jacobs Engineering Group Inc., 6 148–50; 26 220–23 (upd.)
Jacobs Suchard (AG), II 520–22, 540, 569; **15** 64; **29** 46–47. *See also* Kraft Jacobs Suchard AG.
Jacobson Stores Inc., 21 301–03
Jacoby & Meyers, **20** 435
Jacor Communications, Inc., 6 33; **23 292–95; 24** 108; **27** 339; **35** 220
Jacques Borel International, **II** 641; **10** 12
Jacques Fath Perfumes, **III** 47
Jacuzzi Inc., 7 207, 209; **23 296–98**
Jade Accessories, **14** 224
Jade KK, **25** 349
Jadepoint, **18** 79–80
JAF Pampryl, **I** 281
Jafra Cosmetics, **15** 475, 477
Jagenberg AG, **9** 445–46; **14** 57
Jaguar Cars, Ltd., III 439, 495; **11** 140; **13** 28, 219, **285–87**, 414; **36** 198, 217. *See also* Ford Motor Company.
JAI Parabolic Spring Ltd., **III** 582
JAIX Leasing Company, **23** 306
Ab Jakobstads Cellulosa-Pietarsaaren Selluloosa Oy, **IV** 302
JAL. *See* Japan Air Lines.
Jalate Inc., 25 245–47
Jaluzot & Cie. *See* Pinault-Printemps-Redoute S.A.
Jamaica Gas Light Co., **6** 455
Jamaica Plain Trust Co., **II** 207
Jamaica Water Supply Company. *See* JWP Inc.
JAMCO, **III** 589
James A. Ryder Transportation (Jartran), **V** 505
James Bay Development Corporation, **6** 502
James Beam Distilling Co., **I** 226; **10** 180
James Beattie plc, 43 242–44
James Burn/American, Inc., **17** 458
James C. Heintz Company, **19** 278
James Ericson, **III** 324
James Felt Realty, Inc., **21** 257
James Fison and Sons. *See* Fisons plc.
James Fleming, **II** 500
James G. Fast Company. *See* Angelica Corporation.
James Gulliver Associates, **II** 609
James Hardie Industries Limited, **IV** 249; **26** 494
James Hartley & Son, **III** 724
James Heekin and Company, **13** 254
James Lyne Hancock Ltd., **I** 428
James Magee & Sons Ltd., **IV** 294; **19** 224
James McNaughton Ltd., **IV** 325
James O. Welch Co., **II** 543
James Publishing Group, **17** 272
James R. Osgood & Company, **10** 356
James River Corporation of Virginia, IV 289–91; 8 483; **22** 209; **29** 136. *See also* Fort James Corporation.
James Stedman Ltd., **II** 569
James Talcott, Inc., **11** 260–61
James Thompson, **IV** 22
James Wellbeloved, **39** 354, 356
James Wholesale Company, **18** 7
James Wrigley & Sons, **IV** 257
Jamestown Publishers, **22** 522
Jamesway Corporation, **IV** 136; **13** 261; **23** 177
Jamie Scott, Inc., **27** 348
Jamieson & Co., **22** 428
Jamna Auto Industries Pvt. Ltd., **III** 581
Jämsänkoski Oy, **IV** 347
Jan Bell Marketing Inc., **24** 335. *See also* Mayor's Jewelers, Inc.
Janata Bank, **31** 219
Jane Jones Enterprises, **16** 422; **43** 309
Jane's Information Group, **8** 525
Janesville Electric, **6** 604
Janet Frazer, **V** 118
Janin, S.A., **36** 163
Janna Systems Inc., **38** 433
Janson Publications, **22** 522
Janssen-Kyowa, **III** 43
N.V. Janssen M&L, **17** 147
Janssen Pharmaceutica, **III** 36; **8** 282
JANT Pty. Ltd., **IV** 285
Jantzen Inc., **V** 391; **17** 513
Janus Capital Corporation, **6** 401–02; **26** 233
Japan Acoustics, **II** 118
Japan Advertising Ltd., **16** 166
Japan Air Filter Co., Ltd., **III** 634
Japan Airlines Company, Ltd., I 104–06; 6 70–71, 118, 123, 386, 427; **24** 399–400; **27** 464; **32 288–92 (upd.)**
Japan Brewery. *See* Kirin Brewery Company, Limited.
Japan Broadcasting Corporation, I 586; **II** 66, 101, 118; **7 248–50; 9** 31
Japan-California Bank, **II** 274
Japan Commerce Bank, **II** 291
Japan Copper Manufacturing Co., **II** 104; **IV** 211
Japan Cotton Co., **IV** 150; **24** 357
Japan Creative Tours Co., **I** 106
Japan Credit Bureau, **II** 348
Japan Dairy Products, **II** 538
Japan Day & Night Bank, **II** 292
Japan Development Bank, **II** 300, 403
Japan Dyestuff Manufacturing Co., **I** 397
Japan Elanco Company, Ltd., **17** 437
Japan Electricity Generation and Transmission Company (JEGTCO), **V** 574
Japan Energy Corporation, **13** 202; **14** 206, 208
Japan Food Corporation, **14** 288
Japan International Bank, **II** 292
Japan International Liquor, **I** 220
Japan Iron & Steel Co., Ltd., **IV** 157; **17** 349–50
Japan Leasing Corporation, 8 278–80; 11 87
Japan Medico, **25** 431
Japan National Oil Corp., **IV** 516
Japan National Railway, **V** 448–50; **6** 70
Japan Oil Development Co., **IV** 364
Japan Petroleum Development Corp., **IV** 461
Japan Petroleum Exploration Co., **IV** 516
Japan Pulp and Paper Company Limited, IV 292–93, 680
Japan Reconstruction Finance Bank, **II** 300
Japan Special Steel Co., Ltd., **IV** 63
Japan Steel Manufacturing Co., **IV** 211
Japan Steel Works, **I** 508
Japan Telecom, **7** 118; **13** 482
Japan Telegraphic Communication Company (Nihon Denpo-Tsushin Sha), **16** 166
Japan Tobacco Incorporated, V 403–04; 30 387
Japan Trust Bank, **II** 292
Japan Try Co., **III** 758
Japan Vilene Company Ltd., **41** 170–72
Japanese and Asian Development Bank, **IV** 518
Japanese Electronic Computer Co., **III** 140
Japanese Enterprise Co., **IV** 728
Japanese National Railway, **I** 579; **III** 491; **43** 103
Japanese Victor Co., **II** 118
Japex Oman Co., **IV** 516
Japonica Partners, **9** 485
Jara Enterprises, Inc., **31** 276
Jarcho Brothers Inc., **I** 513
Jardinay Manufacturing Corp., **24** 335
Jardine Matheson Holdings Limited, I 468–71, 521–22, 577, 592; **II** 296; **IV** 189, 699–700; **16** 479–80; **18** 114; **20 309–14 (upd.)**
Jartran Inc., **V** 505; **24** 410
Järvenpään Kotelo Oy, **IV** 315
Jarvis plc, 39 237–39
Jas, Hennessy & Co., **I** 272
Jas. I. Miller Co., **13** 491
JASCO Products, **III** 581
Jason Incorporated, 23 299–301
Jasper Corporation, **III** 767; **22** 546. *See also* Kimball International, Inc.
JAT, **27** 475
Jato, **II** 652
Jauch & Hübener, **14** 279
Java-China-Japan Line, **6** 403–04; **26** 242
Java Software, **30** 453
Javelin Software Corporation, **10** 359
Javex Co., **IV** 272
Jax, **9** 452
Jay Cooke and Co., **III** 237; **9** 370
Jay Jacobs, Inc., 15 243–45
Jay-Ro Services, **III** 419
Jay's Washateria, Inc., **7** 372
Jayco Inc., 13 288–90
Jaywoth Industries, **III** 673

JB Oxford Holdings, Inc., 32 293–96
JBA Holdings PLC, **43** 184
JBL, **22** 97
JCB, **14** 321
JCJL. *See* Java-China-Japan Line.
JD Wetherspoon plc, 30 258–60
JDS Uniphase Corporation, 34 235–37
Jean-Jacques, **19** 50
Jean Lassale, **III** 619–20; **17** 430
Jean Lincet, **19** 50
Jean Nate, **I** 695
Jean Pagées et Fils, **III** 420
Jean-Philippe Fragrances, Inc. *See* Inter Parfums, Inc.
Jean Prouvost, **IV** 618
Jeanmarie Creations, Inc., **18** 67, 69
Jeanne Piaubert, **III** 47
Jefferies Group, Inc., 25 248–51
Jefferson Bancorp, Inc., **37** 201
Jefferson Chemical Co., **IV** 552
Jefferson Fire Insurance Co., **III** 239
Jefferson National Life Group, **10** 247
Jefferson-Pilot Corporation, 11 213–15; 29 253–56 (upd.)
Jefferson Smurfit Group plc, IV 294–96; 16 122; **19 224–27 (upd.)**. *See also* Smurfit-Stone Container Corporation.
Jefferson Standard Life Insurance, **11** 213–14
Jefferson Ward, **12** 48–49
Jefferson Warrior Railroad Company, **III** 767; **22** 546
Jeffery Sons & Co. Ltd., **IV** 711
Jeffrey Galion, **III** 472
JEGTCO. *See* Japan Electricity Generation and Transmission Company (JEGTCO).
JELD-WEN, Inc., **33** 409
Jell-O Co., **II** 531
Jem Development, **17** 233
Jenaer Glaswerk Schott & Genossen, **III** 445, 447
Jenn-Air Corporation, **III** 573; **22** 349
Jennie-O Foods, **II** 506
Jennifer Convertibles, Inc., 31 274–76
Jenny Craig, Inc., 10 382–84; **12** 531; **29 257–60 (upd.)**
Jeno's, **13** 516; **26** 436
Jenoptik AG, 33 218–21
Jensen Salsbery, **I** 715
Jenson, Woodward & Lozier, Inc., **21** 96
JEORA Co., **IV** 564
Jeppesen Sanderson, Inc., **IV** 677; **17** 486
Jepson Corporation, **8** 230
Jeri-Jo Knitwear, Inc., **27** 346, 348
Jerome Increase Case Machinery Company. *See* J.I. Case Company.
Jerrico Inc., **27** 145
Jerrold Corporation, **10** 319–20
Jerry Bassin Inc., **17** 12–14
Jerry's Famous Deli Inc., 24 243–45
Jerry's Restaurants, **13** 320
Jersey Central Power & Light Company, **27** 182
Jersey Paper, **IV** 261
Jersey Standard. *See* Standard Oil Co. of New Jersey.
Jervis B. Webb Company, 24 246–49
Jesse Jones Sausage Co. *See* GoodMark Foods, Inc.
Jesse L. Lasky Feature Play Co., **II** 154
Jessup & Moore Paper Co., **IV** 351; **19** 495
Jet America Airlines, **I** 100; **6** 67, 82
Jet Capital Corp., **I** 123
Jet Petroleum, Ltd., **IV** 401
Jet Research Center, **III** 498
Jet Set Corporation, **18** 513
Jetro Cash & Carry Enterprises Inc., 38 266–68
Jetway Systems, **III** 512
Jeumont-Industrie, **II** 93
Jeumont-Schneider Industries, **II** 93–94; **9** 10; **18** 473
Jewel Companies, Inc., **II** 605; **6** 531; **12** 63; **18** 89; **22** 38; **26** 476; **27** 291
Jewel Food Stores, **7** 127–28; **13** 25
Jewell Ridge Coal Corp., **IV** 181
JFD-Encino, **24** 243
JG Industries, Inc., 15 240–42
Jheri Redding Products, Inc., **17** 108
JHT, Inc., **39** 377
Jiamusi Combine Harvester Factory, **21** 175
JIB Group plc, **20** 313
Jiffee Chemical Corporation, **III** 21; **22** 146
Jiffy Auto Rental, **16** 380
Jiffy Convenience Stores, **II** 627
Jiffy Lube International, Inc., **IV** 490; **21** 541; **24** 339; **25** 443–45
Jiffy Mixes, **29** 109–10
Jiffy Packaging, **14** 430
Jiji, **16** 166
Jillian's Entertainment Holdings, Inc., 40 273–75
Jim Beam Brands Co., 14 271–73; 29 196
Jim Cole Enterprises, Inc., **19** 247
The Jim Henson Company, 23 302–04
The Jim Pattison Group, 37 219–22
Jim Walter Corporation. *See* Walter Industries, Inc.
Jim Walter Papers, **IV** 282; **9** 261
Jimmy Carter Work Project. *See* Habitat for Humanity International.
Jitney-Jungle Stores of America, Inc., 27 245–48
Jitsugyo no Nihon-sha, **IV** 631
Jitsuyo Jidosha Seizo Co., **I** 183
JJB Sports plc, 32 302–04
JLA Credit, **8** 279
JMB Internacionale S.A., **25** 121
JMB Realty Corporation, IV 702–03. *See also* Amfac/JMB Hawaii L.L.C.
Jno. H. Swisher & Son. *See* Swisher International Group Inc.
JNR. *See* Japan National Railway.
Jo-Ann Fabrics and Crafts, **16** 197
Jo-Gal Shoe Company, Inc., **13** 360
Joanna Cotton Mills, **14** 220
Joannes Brothers, **II** 668
Jobete Music. *See* Motown Records Company L.P.
JobWorks Agency, Inc., **16** 50
Jockey International, Inc., 12 283–85; 34 238–42 (upd.)
Joe Alexander Press, **12** 472; **36** 469
Joe B. Hughes, **III** 498
Joe's American Bar & Grill, **20** 54
Joe's Crab Shack, **15** 279
Joh. A. Benckiser GmbH, **36** 140
Joh. Parviaisen Tehtaat Oy, **IV** 276
Johann Jakob Rieter & Co., **III** 402
Johannesburg Consolidated Investment Co. Ltd., **IV** 21–22, 118; **16** 293
John A. Frye Shoe Company, **V** 376; **8** 16; **26** 397–98; **36** 24
John A. Pratt and Associates, **22** 181
John Alden Life Insurance, **10** 340
John B. Sanfilippo & Son, Inc., 14 274–76
John Bean Spray Pump Co., **I** 442
John Blair & Company, **6** 13
John Brown plc, I 572–74
John Bull, **II** 550
John Carr Group, **31** 398–400
John Chatillon & Sons Inc., **29** 460
John Crane International, **17** 480
John Crosland Company, **8** 88
The John D. and Catherine T. MacArthur Foundation, 34 243–46
John de Kuyper and Son, **I** 377
John Deere. *See* Deere & Company.
John F. Jelke Company, **9** 318
John F. Murray Co., **I** 623; **10** 69
John Fairfax Holdings Limited, 7 251–54
John Gardner Catering, **III** 104
John Govett & Co., **II** 349
John Gund Brewing Co., **I** 253
John H. Harland Company, 17 266–69
John H.R. Molson & Bros. *See* The Molson Companies Limited.
John Hancock Financial Services, Inc., 42 193–98 (upd.)
John Hancock Mutual Life Insurance Company, III 265–68, 291, 313, 332, 400; **IV** 283; **13** 530; **25** 528
John Hill and Son, **II** 569
John Holroyd & Co. of Great Britain, **7** 236
John L. Wortham & Son Agency, **III** 193
John Labatt Ltd., **I** 267; **II** 582; **8** 399; **16** 397; **17** 256–57. *See also* Labatt Brewing Company Limited.
John Laing plc, I 575–76, 588
John Lewis Partnership plc, V 93–95; 13 307; **42 199–203 (upd.)**
John Lucas Co., **III** 745
John Lysaght, **III** 493–95
John M. Hart Company, **9** 304
John M. Smyth Co., **15** 282
John Macfarlane and Sons, **II** 593
John Mackintosh and Sons, **II** 568–69
John McConnell & Co., **13** 102
John McLean and Sons Ltd., **III** 753
John Menzies plc, 39 240–43
John Morrell and Co., **II** 595–96; **21** 111
John Nicholls & Co., **III** 690
The John Nuveen Company, III 356; **21 304–06**; **22** 492, 494–95
John Oster Manufacturing Company. *See* Sunbeam-Oster.
John Paul Mitchell Systems, 24 250–52
John Pew & Company, **13** 243
John Q. Hammons Hotels, Inc., 24 253–55
John R. Figg, Inc., **II** 681
John Rogers Co., **9** 253
John Sands, **22** 35
John Schroeder Lumber Company, **25** 379
John Sexton & Co., **26** 503
John Strange Paper Company, **8** 358
John Swire & Sons Ltd. *See* Swire Pacific Ltd.
John Walker & Sons, **I** 239–40
John Wanamaker, **22** 110
John Wiley & Sons, Inc., 17 270–72
John Williams, **III** 691
John Wyeth & Bro., **I** 713
John Yokley Company, **11** 194
John Zink Company, **22** 3–4; **25** 403

Johnny Rockets Group, Inc., 31 277–81
Johns Manville Corporation, **III** 708; **7** 293; **11** 420; **19** 211–12
Johns Perry, **III** 673
Johnsen, Jorgensen and Wettre, **14** 249
Johnson. *See* Axel Johnson Group.
Johnson & Higgins, 14 277–80
Johnson and Howe Furniture Corporation, **33** 151
Johnson & Johnson, III 18, **35–37**; **IV** 285, 722; **7** 45–46; **8 281–83 (upd.)**, 399, 511–12; **9** 89–90; **10** 47, 69, 78, 80, 534–35; **15** 357–58, 360; **16** 168, 440; **17** 104–05, 340, 342–43, 533; **19** 103, 105; **25** 55–56; **34** 280, 283–84; **36 302–07 (upd.)**; **37** 110–11, 113; **41** 154–55
Johnson and Patan, **III** 671
Johnson and Sons Smelting Works Ltd., **IV** 119
Johnson Brothers, **12** 528
Johnson, Carruthers & Rand Shoe Co., **III** 528
Johnson Controls, Inc., III 534–37; **13** 398; **16** 184, 322; **26 227–32 (upd.)**
Johnson Diversified, Inc., **III** 59
Johnson Engineering Corporation, **37** 365
Johnson Matthey PLC, II 390; **IV** 23, **117–20**; **16** 28, **290–94 (upd.)**, 439
Johnson Motor Co., **III** 597–99
Johnson Products Co., Inc., **11** 208; **31** 89
Johnson Publishing Company, Inc., 27 361; **28 212–14**
Johnson Systems, **6** 224
Johnson Wax. *See* S.C. Johnson & Son, Inc.
Johnson Worldwide Associates, Inc., 24 530; **28 215–17**, 412
Johnston Coca-Cola Bottling Company of Chattanooga, **13** 163–64
Johnston Evans & Co., **IV** 704
Johnston Foil Co., **IV** 18
Johnston Harvester Co., **III** 650
Johnston Industries, Inc., 15 246–48
Johnston Press plc, 35 242–44
Johnstown America Industries, Inc., 23 305–07
Johnstown Sanitary Dairy, **13** 393
Jointless Rim Ltd., **I** 428
Jokisch, **II** 556
Jonathan Backhouse & Co., **II** 235
Jonathan Logan Inc., **13** 536
Jonell Shoe Manufacturing Corporation, **13** 360
Jones & Babson, Inc., **14** 85
Jones & Johnson, **14** 277
Jones & Laughlin Steel Corp., **I** 463, 489–91; **IV** 228; **11** 197
Jones Apparel Group, Inc., 11 216–18; **27** 60; **30** 310–11; **39 244–47 (upd.)**, 301, 303
Jones Brothers Tea Co., **7** 202
Jones, Day, Reavis & Pogue, 33 226–29
Jones Environmental, **11** 361
Jones Financial Companies, L.P. *See* Edward Jones.
Jones Intercable, Inc., 14 260; **17** 7; **21 307–09**; **24** 123; **25** 212
Jones Janitor Service, **25** 15
Jones Medical Industries, Inc., 24 256–58; **34** 460
Jones Motor Co., **10** 44
Jones-Rodolfo Corp. *See* Cutter & Buck, Inc.
Jonker Fris, **II** 571
Jonkoping & Vulcan, **12** 462
Jordache Enterprises, Inc., 15 201–02; **23 308–10**
The Jordan Co., **11** 261; **16** 149
Jordan Industries, Inc., 36 308–10
Jordan Marsh, **III** 608; **V** 26; **9** 209
Jordan Valley Electric Cooperative, **12** 265
Jos. A. Bank Clothiers, Inc., II 560; **12** 411; **31 282–85**
Josef Meys, **III** 418
Joseph Bellamy and Sons Ltd., **II** 569
Joseph Campbell Company. *See* Campbell Soup Company.
Joseph Crosfield, **III** 31
Joseph E. Seagram & Sons Inc., **I** 266, 285; **21** 319
Joseph Garneau Co., **I** 226; **10** 180
Joseph Leavitt Corporation, **9** 20
Joseph Littlejohn & Levy, **27** 204
Joseph Lucas & Son, **III** 554–56
Joseph Lumber Company, **25** 379
Joseph Magnin, **I** 417–18; **17** 124; **41** 114
Joseph Malecki Corp., **24** 444–45
Joseph Nathan & Co., **I** 629–40
Joseph Rank Limited, **II** 564
Joseph Schlitz Brewing Company, **25** 281
Joseph T. Ryerson & Son, Inc., IV 114; **15 249–51**; **19** 217, 381. *See also* Ryerson Tull, Inc.
Josephson International, **27** 392; **43** 235
Joshin Denki, **13** 481
Joshu Railway Company, **6** 431
Joshua's Christian Bookstores, **31** 435–36
Josiah Wedgwood and Sons Limited. *See* Waterford Wedgewood plc..
Jostens, Inc., 7 255–57; **25 252–55 (upd.)**; **36** 470
Journal Register Company, 29 261–63
Journey's End Corporation, **14** 107
Jovan, **III** 66
Jove Publications, Inc., **II** 144; **IV** 623; **12** 224
Jovi, **II** 652
Joy Manufacturing, **III** 526
Joy Planning Co., **III** 533
Joy Technologies Inc., **II** 17; **26** 70; **38** 227
Joyce International, Inc., **16** 68
JP Foodservice Inc., **24** 445
JP Household Supply Co. Ltd., **IV** 293
JP Information Center Co., Ltd., **IV** 293
JP Planning Co. Ltd., **IV** 293
JPC Co., **IV** 155
JPF Holdings, Inc. *See* U.S. Foodservice.
JPS Automotive L.P., **17** 182–84
JPS Textile Group, Inc., 28 218–20
JPT Publishing, **8** 528
JR Central, **43** 103
JR Tokai, **43** 103
JT Aquisitions, **II** 661
JTL Corporation, **13** 162–63
JTN Acquisition Corp., **19** 233
JTS Corporation, **23** 23, 26
Jude Hanbury, **I** 294
Judel Glassware Co., Inc., **14** 502
Judson Dunaway Corp., **12** 127
Judson Steel Corp., **13** 97
Jugend & Volk, **14** 556
Jugo Bank, **II** 325
Juice Bowl Products, **II** 480–81; **26** 57
Juice Works, **26** 57
Jujamycn, **24** 439
Jujo Paper Co., Ltd., IV 268, 284–85, 292–93, **297–98**, 321, 326, 328, 356
JuJu Media, Inc., **41** 385
Julius Berger-Bauboag A.G., **I** 560–61
Julius Garfinckel & Co., Inc., **22** 110
Jumping-Jacks Shoes, Inc., **17** 390
Jung-Pumpen, **III** 570; **20** 361
Junghans Uhren, **10** 152
Juniper Networks, Inc., 43 251–55
Junkers Luftverkehr, **I** 110, 197; **6** 87–88
Juno Lighting, Inc., 30 266–68
Juno Online Services, Inc., 38 269–72; **39** 25–26
Juovo Pignone, **13** 356
Jupiter National, **15** 247–48; **19** 166
Jurgens, **II** 588–89
Jurgensen's, **17** 558
Jurgovan & Blair, **III** 197
Juristförlaget, **14** 556
Jusco Car Life Company, **23** 290
JUSCO Co., Ltd., V 96–99; **11** 498; **36** 419; **43** 386
Jusco Group, **31** 430
Just Born, Inc., 32 305–07
Just For Feet, Inc., 19 228–30
Just Squeezed, **31** 350
Just Toys, Inc., **29** 476
Justin Industries, Inc., 19 231–33
JVC. *See* Victor Company of Japan, Ltd.
JW Aluminum Company, **22** 544
JW Bernard & Zn., **39** 203
JWP Inc., 9 300–02; **13** 176
JWT Group Inc., I 9, **19–21**, 23; **6** 53. *See also* WPP Group plc.
Jylhävaara, **IV** 348
JZC. *See* John Zink Company.

K&B Inc., 12 286–88; **17** 244
K&F Manufacturing. *See* Fender Musical Instruments.
K & G Men's Center, Inc., 21 310–12
K&K Insurance Group, **26** 487
K&K Toys, Inc., **23** 176
K&L, **6** 48
K&M Associates L.P., **16** 18; **43** 19
K & R Warehouse Corporation, **9** 20
K-C Aviation, **III** 41; **16** 304; **43** 258
K-Graphics Inc., **16** 306; **43** 261
K-Group, **27** 261
K-H Corporation, **7** 260
K-Swiss, Inc., 33 243–45
K-tel International, Inc., 21 325–28
K-III Holdings. *See* Primedia Inc.
K.C.C. Holding Co., **III** 192
K.F. Kline Co., **7** 145; **22** 184
K.H. Wheel Company, **27** 202
K. Hattori & Co., Ltd., **III** 454–55, 619–20. *See also* Seiko Corporation.
k.k. Staatsbahnen, **6** 419
K Line. *See* Kawasaki Kisen Kaisha, Ltd.
K.O. Lester Co., **31** 359, 361
K.W. Muth Company, **17** 305
KA Teletech, **27** 365
Ka Wah AMEV Insurance, **III** 200–01
Kabelvision AB, **26** 331–33
Kable News Company. *See* AMREP Corporation.
Kable Printing Co., **13** 559
Kaduna Refining and Petrochemicals Co., **IV** 473
Kaepa, **16** 546
Kaestner & Hecht Co., **II** 120
Kafte Inc., **28** 63
Kaga Forwarding Co., **6** 428

Kagami Crystal Works, **III** 714
Kagle Home Health Care, **11** 282
Kagoshima Central Research Laboratory, **21** 330
Kahan and Lessin, **II** 624–25
Kahn's Meats, **II** 572
Kai Tak Land Investment Co., **IV** 717
Kaiser + Kraft GmbH, **27** 175
Kaiser Aluminum & Chemical Corporation, **IV** 11–12, 15, 59–60, **121–23**, 191; **6** 148; **12** 377; **8** 348, 350; **22** 455. *See also* ICF Kaiser International, Inc.
Kaiser Cement, **III** 501, 760; **IV** 272
Kaiser Company, **6** 184
Kaiser Engineering, **IV** 218
Kaiser Industries, **III** 760
Kaiser Packaging, **12** 377
Kaiser Permanente Corp., **6** 279, **12** 175; **24** 231; **25** 434, 527; **41** 183
Kaiser Steel, **IV** 59
Kaiser's Kaffee Geschäft AG, **27** 461
Kaizosha, **IV** 632
Kajaani Oy, **II** 302; **IV** 350
Kajima Corp., **I 577–78**
Kal Kan Foods, Inc., **22 298–300**
Kalamazoo Paper Co., **IV** 281; **9** 259
Kalbfleish, **I** 300
Kaldveer & Associates, **14** 228
Kalitta Group, **22** 311
Kalua Koi Corporation, **7** 281
Kalumburu Joint Venture, **IV** 67
Kamaishi, **IV** 157; **17** 349
Kaman Corporation, **12 289–92**; **16** 202; **42 204–08 (upd.)**; **43** 171
Kamewa Group, **27** 494, 496
Kaminski/Engles Capital Corp. *See* Suiza Foods Corporation.
Kamioka Mining & Smelting Co., Ltd., **IV** 145, 148
Kammer Valves, A.G., **17** 147
Kampgrounds of America, Inc., **33 230–33**
Kanagawa Bank, **II** 291
Kanda Shokai, **16** 202; **43** 171
Kanders Florida Holdings, Inc., **27** 50
Kane Financial Corp., **III** 231
Kane Foods, **III** 43
Kane Freight Lines, **6** 370
Kane-Miller Corp., **12** 106
Kanebo Spinning Inc., **IV** 442
Kanegafuchi Shoji, **IV** 225
Kanematsu Corporation, **IV 442–44**; **24 259–62 (upd.)**
Kangaroo. *See* Seino Transportation Company, Ltd.
Kangol Ltd., **IV** 136
Kangyo Bank, **II** 300, 310, 361
Kanhym, **IV** 91–92
Kanoldt, **24** 75
Kansai Electric Power Co., Inc., **IV** 492; **V 645–48**
Kansai Seiyu Ltd., **V** 188
Kansai Sogo Bank, **II** 361
Kansallis-Osake-Pankki, **II** 242, **302–03**, 366; **IV** 349
Kansas City Power & Light Company, **6 510–12**, 592; **12** 541–42
Kansas City Securities Corporation, **22** 541
Kansas City Southern Industries, Inc., **6 400–02**; **26 233–36 (upd.)**; **29** 333
Kansas City White Goods Company. *See* Angelica Corporation.
Kansas Fire & Casualty Co., **III** 214
Kansas Power Company, **6** 312
Kansas Public Service Company, **12** 541
Kansas Utilities Company, **6** 580
Kanto Steel Co., Ltd., **IV** 63
Kanzaki Paper Manufacturing Co., **IV** 285, 293
Kao Corporation, **III 38–39**, 48; **16** 168; **20 315–17 (upd.)**
Kaohsiung Refinery, **IV** 388
Kaolin Australia Pty Ltd., **III** 691
Kapalua Land Company, Ltd., **29** 307–08
Kaplan Educational Centers, **12** 143
Kaplan, Inc., **42 209–12**, 290
Kapy, **II** 139; **24** 194
Karafuto Industry, **IV** 320
Karan Co. *See* Donna Karan Company.
Karastan Bigelow, **19** 276
Karg'sche Familienstiftung, **V** 73
Karlsberg Brauerei GmbH & Co KG, **41 220–23**
Karmelkorn Shoppes, Inc., **10** 371, 373; **39** 232, 235
Karstadt Aktiengesellschaft, **V 100–02**; **19 234–37 (upd.)**
Kasado Dockyard, **III** 760
Kasai Securities, **II** 434
Kasco Corporation, **28** 42, 45
Kaset Rojananil, **6** 123
Kash n' Karry Food Stores, Inc., **20 318–20**
Kasmarov, **9** 18
Kaspare Cohn Commercial & Savings Bank. *See* Union Bank of California.
Kasper A.S.L., Ltd., **40 276–79**
Kast Metals, **III** 452; **15** 92
Kasuga Radio Company. *See* Kenwood Corporation.
Kat-Em International Inc., **16** 125
Katalco, **I** 374
Kataoka Electric Co., **II** 5
Katelise Group, **III** 739–40
Katharine Gibbs Schools Inc., **22** 442
Kathleen Investment (Australia) Ltd., **III** 729
Kathy's Ranch Markets, **19** 500–01
Katies, **V** 35
Kativo Chemical Industries Ltd., **8** 239; **32** 256
Katy Industries Inc., **I 472–74**; **14** 483–84; **16** 282
Katz Communications, Inc., **6 32–34**
Katz Drug, **II** 604
Katz Media Group, Inc., **35** 232, **245–48**
Kauffman-Lattimer, **III** 9–10
Kaufhalle AG, **V** 104; **23** 311; **41** 186–87
Kaufhof Holding AG, **II** 257; **V 103–05**
Kaufhof Warenhaus AG, **23 311–14 (upd.)**
Kaufman and Broad Home Corporation, **8 284–86**; **11** 481–83
Kaufmann Department Stores, Inc., **V** 132–33; **6** 243; **19** 262
Kaufring AG, **35 249–52**
Kaukaan Tehdas Osakeyhtiö, **IV** 301
Oy Kaukas Ab, **IV** 300–02; **19** 462
Kaukauna Cheese Inc., **23** 217, 219
Kauppaosakeyhtiö Kymmene Aktiebolag, **IV** 299
Kauppiaitten Oy, **8** 293
Kautex-Bayern GmbH, **IV** 128
Kautex-Ostfriedland GmbH, **IV** 128
Kautex Werke Reinold Hagen AG, **IV** 128
Kawachi Bank, **II** 361; **26** 455
Kawamata, **11** 350
Kawasaki Denki Seizo, **II** 22
Kawasaki Heavy Industries, Ltd., **I** 75; **II** 273–74; **III** 482, 513, 516, **538–40**, 756; **IV** 124; **7** 232; **8** 72; **23** 290
Kawasaki Kisen Kaisha, Ltd., **V 457–60**
Kawasaki Steel Corporation, **I** 432; **II** 274; **III** 539, 760; **IV** 30, **124–25**, 154, 212–13; **13** 324; **19** 8
Kawashimaya Shoten Inc. Ltd., **II** 433
Kawecki Berylco Industries, **8** 78
Kawneer GmbH., **IV** 18
Kawsmouth Electric Light Company. *See* Kansas City Power & Light Company.
Kay-Bee Toy Stores, **V** 137; **15 252–53**; **16** 389–90. *See also* KB Toys.
Kay County Gas Co., **IV** 399
Kay Home Products, **17** 372
Kay's Drive-In Food Service, **II** 619
Kaydon Corporation, **18 274–76**
Kayex, **9** 251
Kaynar Manufacturing Company, **8** 366
Kayser Aluminum & Chemicals, **8** 229
Kayser Roth Corp., **8** 288; **22** 122
Kaysersberg, S.A., **IV** 290
KB Toys, **35 253–55 (upd.)**
KBLCOM Incorporated, **V** 644
KC. *See* Kenneth Cole Productions, Inc.
KC Holdings, Inc., **11** 229–30
KCI Konecranes International, **27** 269
KCPL. *See* Kansas City Power & Light Company.
KCS Industries, **12** 25–26
KCSI. *See* Kansas City Southern Industries, Inc.
KCSR. *See* Kansas City Southern Railway.
KD Acquisition Corporation, **34** 103–04
KD Manitou, Inc. *See* Manitou BF S.A.
KDT Industries, Inc., **9** 20
Keane Inc., **38** 431
The Keds Corp., **37** 377, 379
Keebler Foods Company, **II** 594; **35** 181; **36 311–13**
Keefe Manufacturing Courtesy Coffee Company, **6** 392
Keegan Management Co., **27** 274
Keen, Robinson and Co., **II** 566
Keene Packaging Co., **28** 43
KEG Productions Ltd., **IV** 640; **26** 272
Keihan JUSCO, **V** 96
Keil Chemical Company, **8** 178
Keio Teito Electric Railway Company, **V 461–62**
Keisei Electric Railway, **II** 301
Keith-Albee-Orpheum, **II** 88
Keith Prowse Music Publishing, **22** 193
Keithley Instruments Inc., **16 299–301**
Kelco, **34** 281
Keller Builders, **43** 400
Keller-Dorian Graveurs, S.A., **17** 458
Kelley & Partners, Ltd., **14** 130
Kelley Drye & Warren LLP, **40 280–83**
Kellock, **10** 336
Kellogg Company, **I** 22–23; **II** 463, 502–03, **523–26**, 530, 560; **10** 323–24; **12** 411; **13** 3, **291–94 (upd.)**; **15** 189; **18** 65, 225–26; **22** 336, 338; **25** 90; **27** 39; **29** 30, 110; **36** 236–38
Kellogg Foundation, **41** 118
Kellwood Company, **V** 181–82; **8 287–89**
Kelly & Associates, **III** 306
Kelly & Cohen, **10** 468
Kelly, Douglas and Co., **II** 631
Kelly Nason, Inc., **13** 203

Kelly Services, Inc., **6 35–37**, 140; **9** 326; **16** 48; **25** 356, 432; **26 237–40 (upd.)**; **40** 236, 238
The Kelly-Springfield Tire Company, **8 290–92**; **20** 260, 263
Kelsey-Hayes Group of Companies, **I** 170; **III** 650, 652; **7 258–60**; **27 249–52 (upd.)**
Kelso & Co., **III** 663, 665; **12** 436; **19** 455; **21** 490; **30** 48–49; **33** 92
Kelty Pack, Inc., **10** 215
Kelvinator Inc., **17** 487
KemaNobel, **9** 380–81; **13** 22
Kemet Corp., **14 281–83**
Kemi Oy, **IV** 316
Kemira, Inc., **III** 760; **6** 152
Kemp's Biscuits Limited, **II** 594
Kemper Corporation, **III 269–71**, 339; **15 254–58 (upd.)**; **22** 495; **33** 111; **42** 451
Kemper Financial Services, **26** 234
Kemper Motorenfabrik, **I** 197
Kemper Snowboards, **22** 460
Kemperco Inc., **III** 269–70
Kempinski Group, **II** 258
Kemps Biscuits, **II** 594
Ken-L-Ration, **II** 559
Kendall International, Inc., **I** 529; **III** 24–25; **IV** 288; **11 219–21**; **14** 121; **15** 229; **28** 486
Kendall-Jackson Winery, Ltd., **28** 111, **221–23**
Kenetech Corporation, **11 222–24**
Kennametal, Inc., **IV** 203; **13 295–97**
Kennecott Corporation, **III** 248; **IV** 33–34, 79, 170–71, 179, 192, 288, 576; **7 261–64**; **10** 262, 448; **12** 244; **27 253–57 (upd.)**; **35** 135; **38** 231
Kennedy Automatic Products Co., **16** 8
Kenner, **II** 502; **10** 323; **12** 168
Kenner Parker Toys, Inc., **II** 503; **9** 156; **10** 324; **14** 266; **16** 337; **25** 488–89
Kenneth Cole Productions, Inc., **22** 223; **25 256–58**
Kenneth O. Lester, Inc., **21** 508
Kenny Rogers' Roasters, **22** 464; **29** 342, 344
Kenroy International, Inc., **13** 274
Kent Drugs Ltd., **II** 640, 650
Kent Electronics Corporation, **17 273–76**
Kent Fire, **III** 350
Kent-Moore Corp., **I** 200; **10** 492–93
Kentland-Elkhorn Coal Corp., **IV** 181
Kentrox Industries, **30** 7
Kentucky Bonded Funeral Co., **III** 217
Kentucky Electric Steel, Inc., **31 286–88**
Kentucky Fried Chicken, **I** 260–61; **II** 533; **III** 78, 104, 106; **6** 200; **7** 26–28, 433; **8** 563; **12** 42; **13** 336; **16** 97; **18** 8, 538; **19** 92; **21** 361; **22** 464; **23** 384, 504. *See also* KFC Corporation.
Kentucky Institution for the Education of the Blind. *See* American Printing House for the Blind.
Kentucky Utilities Company, **6 513–15**; **11** 37, 236–38
Kenway, **I** 155
Kenwood Corporation, **I** 532; **19** 360; **23** 53; **31 289–91**
Kenwood Silver Company, Inc., **31** 352
Kenworth Motor Truck Corp., **I** 185–86; **26** 354
Kenyon & Eckhardt Advertising Agency, **25** 89–91
Kenyon Corp., **18** 276
Kenyon Sons and Craven Ltd., **II** 593–94
Kenzo, **25** 122
Keo Cutters, Inc., **III** 569; **20** 360
KEPCO. *See* Kyushu Electric Power Company Inc.
Kerlick, Switzer & Johnson, **6** 48
Kerlyn Oil Co., **IV** 445–46
Kern County Land Co., **I** 527; **10** 379, 527
Kernite SA, **8** 386
Kernkraftwerke Lippe-Ems, **V** 747
Kernridge Oil Co., **IV** 541
Kerr-Addison Mines Ltd., **IV** 165
Kerr Concrete Pipe Company, **14** 250
Kerr Corporation, **14** 481
Kerr Drug Stores, **32** 170
Kerr Group Inc., **III** 423; **10** 130; **22** 48; **24 263–65**; **30** 39
Kerr-McGee Corporation, **IV 445–47**; **13** 118; **22 301–04 (upd.)**
Kerry Group plc, **27 258–60**
Kerry Properties Limited, **22 305–08**; **24** 388
Keski-Suomen Tukkukauppa Oy, **8** 293
Kesko Ltd (Kesko Oy), **8 293–94**; **27 261–63 (upd.)**
Ketchikan International Sales Co., **IV** 304
Ketchikan Paper Company, **31** 316
Ketchikan Pulp Co., **IV** 304
Ketchum Communications Inc., **6 38–40**
Ketner and Milner Stores, **II** 683
Kettle Chip Company, **26** 58
Kettle Restaurants, Inc., **29** 149
Keumkang Co., **III** 515; **7** 231
Kewanee Public Service Company, **6** 505
Kewaunee Scientific Corporation, **25 259–62**
Key Computer Laboratories, Inc., **14** 15
Key Industries, Inc., **26** 342
Key Markets, **II** 628
Key Pharmaceuticals, Inc., **11** 207; **41** 419
Key Tronic Corporation, **14 284–86**
KeyCorp, **8 295–97**; **11** 110; **14** 90
Keyes Fibre Company, **9 303–05**
Keypage. *See* Rural Cellular Corporation.
KeySpan Energy Co., **27 264–66**
Keystone Aircraft, **I** 61; **11** 164
Keystone Consolidated Industries, Inc., **19** 467
Keystone Custodian Fund, **IV** 458
Keystone Foods Corporation, **10** 443
Keystone Franklin, Inc., **III** 570; **9** 543; **20** 362
Keystone Frozen Foods, **17** 536
Keystone Gas Co., **IV** 548
Keystone Health Plan West, Inc., **27** 211
Keystone Insurance and Investment Co., **12** 564
Keystone International, Inc., **11 225–27**; **28** 486
Keystone Life Insurance Co., **III** 389; **33** 419
Keystone Paint and Varnish, **8** 553
Keystone Pipe and Supply Co., **IV** 136
Keystone Portland Cement Co., **23** 225
Keystone Savings and Loan, **II** 420
Keystone Tube Inc., **25** 8
Keytronics, **18** 541
KFC Corporation, **7 265–68**; **10** 450; **21 313–17 (upd.)**; **23** 115, 117, 153; **32** 12–14
KFF Management, **37** 350
Khalda Petroleum Co., **IV** 413
KHBB, **16** 72
KHD AG. *See* Klöckner-Humboldt-Deutz AG.
KHD Konzern, **III 541–44**
KHL. *See* Koninklijke Hollandsche Lloyd.
Kia Motors Corporation, **I** 167; **12 293–95**; **29 264–67 (upd.)**
Kiabi, **37** 22–23
Kickers Worldwide, **35** 204, 207
Kidd, Kamm & Co., **21** 482
Kidde Inc., **I 475–76**; **III** 503; **7** 209; **23** 297; **39** 344–46
Kidder, Peabody & Co., **II** 31, 207, 430; **IV** 84; **7** 310; **12** 197; **13** 465–67, 534; **16** 322; **22** 406
Kidder Press Co., **IV** 644
Kiddie Products, Inc., **24** 413
Kids "R" Us, **V** 203–05; **9** 394; **37** 81
Kids Foot Locker, **14** 293, 295
Kidston Mines, **I** 438
Kiekhaefer Corporation, **III** 443; **22** 115
Kien, **13** 545
Kienzle Apparate GmbH, **III** 566; **38** 299
Kierulff Electronics, **10** 113
Kieser Verlag, **14** 555
Kiewit Diversified Group Inc., **11** 301
Kiewit-Murdock Investment Corp., **15** 129
Kijkshop/Best-Sellers, **13** 545
Kikkoman Corporation, **I** 9; **14 287–89**
Kilburn & Co., **III** 522
Kilgo Motor Express, **6** 370
Kilgore Ceramics, **III** 671
Kilgore Federal Savings and Loan Assoc., **IV** 343
Killington, Ltd., **28** 21
Kilpatrick's Department Store, **19** 511
Kilsby Tubesupply, **I** 570
Kimball International, Inc., **12 296–98**
Kimbell Inc., **II** 684
Kimberley Central Mining Co., **IV** 64; **7** 121
Kimberly-Clark Corporation, **I** 14, 413; **III** 36, **40–41**; **IV** 249, 254, 297–98, 329, 648, 665; **8** 282; **15** 357; **16 302–05 (upd.)**; **17** 30, 397; **18** 147–49; **19** 14, 284, 478; **22** 209; **43 256–60 (upd.)**
Kimco Realty Corporation, **11 228–30**
Kimowelt Medien, **39** 13
Kincaid Furniture Company, **14** 302–03
Kindai Golf Company, **32** 447
Kinden Corporation, **7** 303
KinderCare Learning Centers, Inc., **13 298–300**; **34** 105; **35** 408
Kinear Moodie, **III** 753
Kineret Acquisition Corp. *See* The Hain Celestial Group, Inc.
Kinetic Concepts, Inc., **20 321–23**
King & Spalding, **23 315–18**
The King Arthur Flour Company, **31 292–95**
King Bearing, Inc., **13** 79
King Cullen, **II** 644
King Features Syndicate, **IV** 626; **19** 201, 203–04
King Folding Box Co., **13** 441
King Fook Gold and Jewellery Co., **IV** 717
King Hickory, **17** 183
King Kullen Grocery Co., Inc., **15 259–61**; **19** 481; **24** 528
King Ranch, Inc., **14 290–92**
King-Seeley, **II** 419; **16** 487
King Soopers Inc., **12** 112–13
King World Productions, Inc., **9 306–08**; **28** 174; **30 269–72 (upd.)**

King's Lynn Glass, **12** 528
Kingbird Media Group LLC, **26** 80
Kingfisher plc, **V 106–09**; **10** 498; **19** 123; **24 266–71 (upd.)**; **27** 118, 120; **28** 34, 36
Kings, **24** 528
Kings County Lighting Company, **6** 456
Kings County Research Laboratories, **11** 424
Kings Mills, Inc., **13** 532
Kings Super Markets, **24** 313, 316
Kingsford Corporation, **III** 21; **22** 146
Kingsin Line, **6** 397
Kingsport Pulp Corp., **IV** 310; **19** 266
Kingston Technology Corporation, **20 324–26**; **38** 441
Kinki Nippon Railway Company Ltd., **V 463–65**
Kinko's Inc., **12** 174; **16 306–08**; **18** 363–64; **43 261–64 (upd.)**
Kinnevik. *See* Industriförvaltnings AB Kinnevik.
Kinney Corporation, **23** 32; **24** 373
Kinney National Service Inc., **II** 176; **IV** 672; **19** 404; **25** 140
Kinney Services, **6** 293
Kinney Shoe Corp., **V** 226; **11** 349; **14 293–95**
Kinney Tobacco Co., **12** 108
Kinoshita Sansho Steel Co., **I** 508
Kinpo Electronic, **23** 212
Kinross Gold Corporation, **36 314–16**
Kinson Resources Inc., **27** 38
Kintec Corp., **10** 97
Kirby. *See* Scott Fetzer Company.
Kirby Corporation, **18 277–79**; **22** 275
Kirby Forest Industries, **IV** 305
Kirch Gruppe, **10** 196; **35** 452
Kirchner, Moore, and Co., **II** 408
Kirin Brewery Company, Limited, **I** 220, 258, **265–66**, 282; **10** 78, 80; **13** 258, 454; **20** 28; **21 318–21 (upd.)**; **36** 404–05
Kirk Stieff Company, **10** 181; **12** 313
Kirkland Messina, Inc., **19** 392, 394
Kirkstall Forge Engineering, **III** 494
Kirsch Co., **II** 16
Kirschner Manufacturing Co., **16** 296
Kishimoto & Co., **I** 432, 492; **24** 325
Kishimoto Shoten Co., Ltd., **IV** 168
Kistler, Lesh & Co., **III** 528
Kit Manufacturing Co., **18 280–82**
Kita Consolidated, Ltd., **16** 142
Kita Karafunto Oil Co., **IV** 475
Kita Nippon Paper Co., **IV** 321
Kitagawa & Co. Ltd., **IV** 442
Kitchell Corporation, **14 296–98**
KitchenAid, **III** 611, 653–54; **8 298–99**
Kitchenbell, **III** 43
Kitchens of Sara Lee, **II** 571–73
Kittery Electric Light Co., **14** 124
Kittinger, **10** 324
Kitty Hawk, Inc., **22 309–11**
Kiwi International Airlines Inc., **20 327–29**
Kiwi Packaging, **IV** 250
Kiwi Polish Co., **15** 507
KJJ. *See* Klaus J. Jacobs Holdings.
Kjøbenhavns Bandelsbank, **II** 366
KJPCL. *See* Royal Interocean Lines.
KKK Shipping, **II** 274
KKR. *See* Kohlberg Kravis Roberts & Co.
KLA Instruments Corporation, **11 231–33**; **20** 8
Klaus J. Jacobs Holdings, **29** 46–47
KLC/New City Televentures, **25** 269
Klein Bicycles, **16** 495
Klein Sleep Products Inc., **32** 426
Kleiner, Perkins, Caufield & Byers, **I** 637; **6** 278; **10** 15, 504; **14** 263; **16** 418; **27** 447
Kleinwort Benson Group PLC, **II** 379, **421–23**; **IV** 191; **22** 55
Kline Manufacturing, **II** 16
KLLM Transport Services, **27** 404
KLM Royal Dutch Airlines, **26** 33924 311, 396–97; **27** 474; **29** 15, 17; **33** 49, 51; **34** 397. *See also* Koninklijke Luftvaart Maatschappij N.V.
Klöckner-Humboldt-Deutz AG, **I** 542; **III** 541–44; **IV** 126–27; **13** 16–17
Klöckner-Werke AG, **IV** 43, 60, **126–28**, 201, **19** 64; **39** 125
Klondike, **14** 205
Klopman International, **12** 118
Kloth-Senking, **IV** 201
Klüber Lubrication München KG, **41** 170
Kluwer Publishers, **IV** 611; **14** 555
Klynveld Main Goerdeler, **10** 387
Klynveld Peat Marwick Goerdeler. *See* KPMG Worldwide.
KM&G. *See* Ketchum Communications Inc.
Kmart Canada Co., **25** 222
Kmart Corporation, **I** 516; **V** 35, **110–12**; **6** 13; **7** 61, 444; **9** 361, 400, 482; **10** 137, 410, 490, 497, 515–16; **12** 48, 54–55, 430, 477–78, 507–08; **13** 42, 260–61, 274, 317–18, 444, 446; **14** 192, 394; **15** 61–62, 210–11, 330–31, 470; **16** 35–37, 61, 187, 210, 447, 457; **17** 297, 460–61, 523–24; **18** 137, **283–87 (upd.)**, 477; **19** 511; **20** 155–56; **21** 73; **22** 258, 328; **23** 210, 329; **24** 322–23; **25** 121; **26** 348, 524; **27** 313, 429, 451, 481; **32** 169; **43** 77–78, 293, 385
Kmart Mexico, **36** 139
KMC Enterprises, Inc., **27** 274
KMP Holdings, **I** 531
KN. *See* Kühne & Nagel Group.
Kna-Shoe Manufacturing Company, **14** 302
Knape & Vogt Manufacturing Company, **17 277–79**
Knapp & Tubbs, **III** 423
Knapp Communications Corporation, **II** 656; **13** 180; **24** 418
Knapp-Monarch, **12** 251
Knauf, **III** 721, 736
KNI Retail A/S, **12** 363
Knickerbocker Toy Co., **III** 505
Knickerbocker Trust Company, **13** 465
Knife River Coal Mining Company, **7** 322–25
Knife River Corporation, **42** 249, 253
Knight Paper Co., **III** 766; **22** 545
Knight-Ridder, Inc., **III** 190; **IV** 597, 613, **628–30**, 670; **6** 323; **7** 191, 327; **10** 407; **15 262–66 (upd.)**; **18** 323; **30** 216; **38** 307
Knightsbridge Partners, **26** 476
KNILM, **24** 397
Knoff-Bremse, **I** 138
Knogo Corp., **11** 444; **39** 78
Knoll Group Inc., **I** 202; **14 299–301**
Knoll Pharmaceutical, **I** 682
Knomark, **III** 55
Knorr-Bremse, **11** 31
Knorr Co. *See* C.H. Knorr Co.
Knorr Foods Co., Ltd., **28** 10
Knott, **III** 98
Knott's Berry Farm, **18 288–90**; **22** 130
Knowledge Systems Concepts, **11** 469
KnowledgeWare Inc., **9 309–11**; **27** 491; **31 296–298 (upd.)**
Knox County Insurance, **41** 178
Knox Reeves Advertising Agency, **25** 90
Knoxville Glove Co., **34** 159
Knoxville Paper Box Co., Inc., **13** 442
KNP BT. *See* Buhrmann NV.
KNSM. *See* Koninklijke Nederlandsche Stoomboot Maatschappij.
Knudsen & Sons, Inc., **11** 211
Knudsen Foods, **27** 330
Knutange, **IV** 226
Knutson Construction, **25** 331
KOA. *See* Kampgrounds of America, Inc.
Kobacker Co., **18** 414–15
Kobayashi Tomijiro Shoten, **III** 44
Kobe Shipbuilding & Engine Works, **II** 57
Kobe Steel, Ltd., **I** 511; **II** 274; **IV** 16, **129–31**, 212–13; **8** 242; **11** 234–35; **13** 297; **19 238–41 (upd.)**; **38** 225–26
Kobelco America Inc., **19** 241
Kobelco Middle East, **IV** 131
Kobold. *See* Vorwerk & Co.
Kobrand Corporation, **24** 308; **43** 402
Koç Holdings A.S., **I** 167, **478–80**; **11** 139; **27** 188
Koch Enterprises, Inc., **29 215–17**
Koch Industries, Inc., **IV 448–49**; **20 330–32 (upd.)**; **21** 108; **22** 3
Koch-Light Laboratories, **13** 239; **38** 203–04
Kockos Brothers, Inc., **II** 624
Kodak. *See* Eastman Kodak Company.
Kodansha Ltd., **IV 631–33**; **38 273–76 (upd.)**
Ködel & Böhn GmbH, **III** 543
Koehring Company, **8** 545; **23** 299
Koehring Cranes & Excavators, **7** 513
Koei Real Estate Ltd., **V** 195
Koenig Plastics Co., **19** 414
Kohl's Corporation, **9 312–13**; **22** 72; **30 273–75 (upd.)**
Kohl's Food Stores, Inc., **I** 426–27; **16** 247, 249
Kohlberg Kravis Roberts & Co., **I** 566, 609–11; **II** 370, 452, 468, 544, 645, 654, 656, 667; **III** 263, 765–67; **IV** 642–43; **V** 55–56, 408, 410, 415; **6** 357; **7** 130, 132, 200; **9** 53, 180, 230, 469, 522; **10** 75–77, 302; **12** 559; **13** 163, 166, 363, 453; **14** 42; **15** 270; **17** 471; **18** 3; **19** 493; **22** 55, 91, 441, 513, 544; **23** 163; **24** 92, **272–74**, 416, 418; **25** 11, 278; **26** 46, 48, 352; **27** 11; **28** 389, 475; **30** 386; **32** 408; **33** 255; **35** 35; **38** 190; **40** 34, 36, 366; **43** 355
Kohler Bros., **IV** 91
Kohler Company, **7 269–71**; **10** 119; **24** 150; **32 308–12 (upd.)**
Kohler Mix Specialties, Inc., **25** 333
Kohner Brothers, **II** 531
Koholyt AG, **III** 693
Koike Shoten, **II** 458
Kojiro Matsukata, **V** 457–58
Kokkola Chemicals Oy, **17** 362–63
Kokomo Gas and Fuel Company, **6** 533
Kokuei Paper Co., Ltd., **IV** 327
Kokura Sekiyu Co. Ltd., **IV** 554
Kokura Steel Manufacturing Co., Ltd., **IV** 212

Kokusai Kisen, **V** 457–58
Kokusaku Kiko Co., Ltd., **IV** 327
Kokusaku Pulp Co., **IV** 327
Kolb-Lena, **25** 85
Kolbenschmidt, **IV** 141
Kolker Chemical Works, Inc., **IV** 409; **7** 308
The Koll Company, **8 300–02**; **21** 97; **25** 449
Kollmorgen Corporation, **18 291–94**
Kölnische Rückversicherungs- Gesellschaft AG, **24** 178
Komag, Inc., **11 234–35**
Komatsu Ltd., **III** 453, 473, **545–46**; **15** 92; **16 309–11 (upd.)**
Kommanditgesellschaft S. Elkan & Co., **IV** 140
Kommunale Energie-Beteiligungsgesellschaft, **V** 746
Kompro Computer Leasing, **II** 457
Konan Camera Institute, **III** 487
Kone Corporation, **27 267–70**
Kongl. Elektriska Telegraf-Verket, **V** 331
Kongo Bearing Co., **III** 595
Konica Corporation, **III 547–50**; **30 276–81 (upd.)**; **43** 284
König Brauerei GmbH & Co. KG, **35 256–58 (upd.)**
Koninklijke Ahold N.V., **II 641–42**; **12** 152–53; **16 312–14 (upd.)**
Koninklijke Bols Wessanen, N.V., **29** 480–81
Koninklijke Distilleerderijen der Erven Lucas Böls, **I** 226
Koninklijke Hoogovens NV, **26** 527, 530
Koninklijke Java-China Paketvaart Lijnen. *See* Royal Interocean Lines.
NV Koninklijke KNP BT. *See* Buhrmann NV.
Koninklijke KPN N.V. *See* Royal KPN N.V.
Koninklijke Luchtvaart Maatschappij N.V., **I** 55, **107–09**, 119, 121; **6** 95, 105, 109–10; **14** 73; **28 224–27 (upd.)**
Koninklijke Nederlandsche Hoogovens en Staalfabrieken NV, **IV** 105, 123, **132–34**
Koninklijke Nederlandsche Maatschappig Tot Exploitatie van Petroleumbronnen in Nederlandsch-indie, **IV** 530
Koninklijke Nederlandsche Petroleum Maatschappij, **IV** 491
Koninklijke Nederlandsche Stoomboot Maatschappij, **26** 241
N.V. Koninklijke Nederlandse Vliegtuigenfabriek Fokker, **I** 46, **54–56**, 75, 82, 107, 115, 121–22; **28 327–30 (upd.)**
Koninklijke Nedlloyd Groep N.V., **6 403–05**
Koninklijke Nedlloyd N.V., **26 241–44 (upd.)**
Koninklijke Numico N.V. *See* Royal Numico N.V.
Koninklijke Paketvaart Maatschappij, **26** 242
Koninklijke PTT Nederland NV, **V 299–301**; **27** 471–72, 475. *See also* Royal KPN NV.
Koninklijke Van Ommeren, **22** 275
Koninklijke Wessanen N.V., **II 527–29**
Koninklijke West-Indische Maildienst, **26** 242
Koniphoto Corp., **III** 548
Konishi Honten, **III** 547
Konishi Pharmaceutical, **I** 704
Konishiroku Honten Co., Ltd., **III** 487, 547–49
Konoike Bank, **II** 347
Konrad Hornschuch AG, **31** 161–62
Koo Koo Roo, Inc., **25 263–65**
Koop Nautic Holland, **41** 412
Koopman & Co., **III** 419
Koor Industries Ltd., **II 47–49**; **22** 501; **25 266–68 (upd.)**
Koors Perry & Associates, Inc., **24** 95
Koortrade, **II** 48
Kop-Coat, Inc., **8** 456
Kopin Corp., **13** 399
Köpings Mekaniska Verkstad, **26** 10
Koppel Steel, **26** 407
Koppens Machinenfabriek, **III** 420
Kopper United, **I** 354
Koppers Inc., **I** 199, **354–56**; **III** 645, 735; **6** 486; **17** 38–39
Koppers Industries, Inc., **26 245–48 (upd.)**
Koracorp Industries Inc., **16** 327
Korbel, **I** 226
Korea Automotive Fuel Systems Ltd., **13** 555
Korea Automotive Motor Corp., **16** 436; **43** 319
Korea Development Leasing Corp., **II** 442
Korea Steel Co., **III** 459
Korea Telecommunications Co, **I** 516
Korean Air Lines Co. Ltd., **II** 442; **6 98–99**; **24** 443; **27 271–73 (upd.)**
Korean Development Bank, **III** 459
Korean Tungsten Mining Co., **IV** 183
Kori Kollo Corp., **23** 41
Korn/Ferry International, **34 247–49**
Koro Corp., **19** 414
Korrekt Gebäudereinigung, **16** 420; **43** 307
KorrVu, **14** 430
Kortbetalning Servo A.B., **II** 353
Kortgruppen Eurocard-Köpkort A.B., **II** 353
Korvettes, E.J., **14** 426
Koryeo Industrial Development Co., **III** 516; **7** 232
Koryo Fire and Marine Insurance Co., **III** 747
Koss Corporation, **38 277–79**
Kosset Carpets, Ltd., **9** 467
Kotobukiya Co., Ltd., **V 113–14**
Kowa Metal Manufacturing Co., **III** 758
Koyo Seiko, **III** 595–96, 623–24
KPM. *See* Koninklijke Paketvaart Maatschappij.
KPMG International, **29** 176; **33 234–38 (upd.)**
KPMG Worldwide, **7** 266; **10** 115, **385–87**
KPN. *See* Koninklijke PTT Nederland N.V.
KPR Holdings Inc., **23** 203
Kraft Foods, Inc., **II** 129, **530–34**, 556; **V** 407; **III** 610; **7 272–77 (upd.)**, 339, 433, 547; **8** 399, 499; **9** 180, 290, 318; **11** 15; **12** 372, 532; **13** 408, 515, 517; **14** 204; **16** 88, 90; **17** 56; **18** 67, 246, 416, 419; **19** 51; **22** 82, 85; **23** 219, 384; **25** 366, 517; **26** 249, 251; **28** 479
Kraft Foodservice, **26** 504; **31** 359–60
Kraft Jacobs Suchard AG, **26 249–52 (upd.)**
Kraft-Versicherungs-AG, **III** 183
Kraftco Corporation, **II** 533; **14** 204
KraftMaid Cabinetry, Inc., **20** 363; **39** 267
Kraftwerk Union, **I** 411; **III** 466
Kragen Auto Supply Co., **27** 291. *See also* CSK Auto Corporation.
Kramer, **III** 48
Krämer & Grebe, **III** 420
Kramer Guitar, **29** 222
Kramer Machine and Engineering Company, **26** 117
Krames Communications Co., **22** 441, 443
Kransco, **25** 314
Krasnapolsky Restaurant and Wintergarden Company Ltd., **23** 228
Kraus-Anderson, Incorporated, **36 317–20**
Krause Publications, Inc., **35 259–61**
Krause's Furniture, Inc., **27 274–77**
Krauss-Maffei AG, **I** 75; **II** 242; **III** 566, 695; **14** 328; **38** 299
Kravco, **III** 248
Kredietbank N.V., **II** 295, **304–05**
Kreditanstalt für Wiederaufbau, **IV** 231–32; **29 268–72**
Kreft, **III** 480; **22** 26
Kreher Steel Co., **25** 8
Krelitz Industries, Inc., **14** 147
Krema Hollywood Chewing Gum Co. S.A., **II** 532
Kremers-Urban, **I** 667
Kresge Foundation, **V** 110
Kreuger & Toll, **IV** 338; **12** 462–63
Kreymborg, **13** 544–45
Kriegschemikalien AG, **IV** 229
Kriegsmetall AG, **IV** 229
Kriegswollbedarfs AG, **IV** 229
Krislex Knits, Inc., **8** 235
Krispy Kitchens, Inc., **II** 584
Krispy Kreme Doughnut Corporation, **21 322–24**
Kroeze, **25** 82
The Kroger Company, **II** 605, 632, **643–45**, 682; **III** 218; **6** 364; **7** 61; **12** 111–13; **13** 25, 237, 395; **15** 259, **267–70 (upd.)**, 449; **16** 63–64; **18** 6; **21** 323, 508; **22** 37, 126; **24** 416; **25** 234; **28** 512; **30** 24, 27; **40** 366
Krohn-Fechheimer Shoe Company, **V** 207
Krone AG, **33** 220
Krones A.G., **I** 266; **21** 319
Kronos, Inc., **18 295–97**; **19** 468
Krovtex, **8** 80
Kroy Tanning Company, **17** 195
Krueger Insurance Company, **21** 257
Kruger Inc., **17 280–82**
Krumbhaar Chemical Inc., **14** 308
Krupp, **17** 214; **22** 364. *See also* Fried. Krupp GmbH *and* Thyssen Krupp AG.
Krupp Widia GmbH, **12** 66
Kruse International, **32** 162
The Krystal Company, **33 239–42**
KSSU Group, **I** 107–08, 120–21
KT Contract Services, **24** 118
KTR. *See* Keio Teito Electric Railway Company.
K2 Inc., **16 295–98**; **22** 481, 483; **23** 474; **43** 389
KU Energy Corporation, **6** 513, 515; **11 236–38**
Kubota Corporation, **I** 494; **III 551–53**; **10** 404; **12** 91, 161; **21** 385–86; **24** 324; **39** 37; **40** 134
Kubota, Gonshiro. *See* Gonshiro Oode.
Kuhara Mining Co., **IV** 475
Kuhlman Corporation, **20 333–35**

Kuhlmann, **III** 677; **IV** 174; **16** 121
Kühn + Bayer, **24** 165
Kuhn Loeb, **II** 402–03
Kühne & Nagel International AG, **V 466–69**
Kuitu Oy, **IV** 348
KUK, **III** 577, 712
Kukje Group, **III** 458
Kulicke and Soffa Industries, Inc., **33 246–48**
Kulka Smith Inc., **13** 398
Kulmobelwerk G.H. Walb and Co., **I** 581
Kum-Kleen Products, **IV** 252; **17** 29
Kumagai Gumi Co., **I 579–80**
Kumsung Companies, **III** 747–48
Kunkel Industries, **19** 143
Kunst und Technik Verlag, **IV** 590
Kuo International Ltd., **I** 566
Kuok Group, **28** 84
Kuoni Travel Holding Ltd., **40 284–86**
The Kuppenheimer Company, **8** 248–50; **32** 247
Kureha Chemical Industry, **I** 675
Kureha Spinning, **24** 325
Kureha Textiles, **I** 432, 492
Kurosawa Construction Co., Ltd., **IV** 155
Kurose, **III** 420
Kurt Möller Verlag, **7** 42
Kurushima Dockyard, **II** 339
The Kushner-Locke Company, **25 269–71**
Kuusankoski Aktiebolag, **IV** 299
Kuwait Airways, **27** 135
Kuwait Investment Office, **II** 198; **IV** 380, 452; **27** 206
Kuwait Petroleum Corporation, **IV** 364, **450–52**, 567; **18** 234; **38** 424
Kvaerner ASA, **20** 313; **31** 367, 370; **36 321–23**
KW, Inc. *See* Coca-Cola Bottling Company of Northern New England, Inc.
Kwaishinsha Motor Car Works, **I** 183
Kwik Save Group plc, **11 239–41**; **13** 26
Kwik Shop, Inc., **12** 112
Kwikasair Ltd., **27** 473
KWIM. *See* Koninklijke West-Indische Maildienst.
KWV, **I** 289
Kygnus Sekiyu K.K., **IV** 555
Kymi Paper Mills Ltd., **IV** 302
Kymmene Corporation, **IV** 276–77, **299–303**, 337. *See also* UPM-Kymmene Corporation.
Kyocera Corporation, **II 50–52**; **III** 693; **7** 118; **21 329–32 (upd.)**
Kyodo, **16** 166
Kyodo Dieworks Thailand Co., **III** 758
Kyodo Gyogyo Kaisha, Limited, **II** 552
Kyodo Kako, **IV** 680
Kyodo Kokusan K.K., **21** 271
Kyodo Oil Co. Ltd., **IV** 476
Kyodo Securities Co., Ltd., **II** 433
Kyodo Unyu Kaisha, **I** 502–03, 506; **IV** 713; **V** 481
Kyoei Mutual Fire and Marine Insurance Co., **III** 273
Kyoritsu Pharmaceutical Industry Co., **I** 667
Kyosai Trust Co. *See* Yasuda Trust and Banking Company, Limited.
Kyoto Bank, **II** 291
Kyoto Ceramic Co., Ltd. *See* Kyocera Corporation.
Kyoto Ouchi Bank, **II** 292
Kyowa Hakko Kogyo Co., Ltd., **III 42–43**
Kyusha Refining Co., **IV** 403
Kyushu Electric Power Company Inc., **IV** 492; **V 649–51**; **17** 349
Kyushu Oil Refinery Co. Ltd., **IV** 434
Kywan Petroleum Ltd., **13** 556
KYZ International, **9** 427
KZO, **13** 21

L & G, **27** 291
L. & H. Sales Co., **16** 389
L&W Supply Corp., **III** 764
L.A. Darling Co., **IV** 135–36; **16** 357
L.A. Gear, Inc., **8 303–06**; **11** 349; **31** 413; **32 313–17 (upd.)**
L.A. Mex. *See* Checkers Drive-Up Restaurants Inc.
L.A. T Sportswear, Inc., **26 257–59**
L.B. DeLong, **III** 558
L.B. Foster Company, **33 255–58**
L. Bamberger & Co., **V** 169; **8** 443
L. Bosendorfer Klavierfabrik, A.G., **12** 297
L.C. Bassford, **III** 653
L.D. Canocéan, **25** 104
The L.D. Caulk Company, **10** 271
L. Fish, **14** 236
L.G. Balfour Company, **12** 472; **19** 451–52; **36** 469
L. Greif & Bro. Inc., **17** 203–05
L. Grossman and Sons. *See* Grossman's Inc.
L.H. Parke Co., **II** 571
L.J. Knowles & Bros., **9** 153
L.J. Melody & Co., **21** 97
L.K. Liggett Company, **24** 74
L. Kellenberger & Co. AG, **25** 194
L.L. Bean, Inc., **9** 190, 316; **10 388–90**; **12** 280; **19** 333; **21** 131; **22** 173; **25** 48, 206; **29** 278; **36** 180, 420; **38 280–83 (upd.)**
The L.L. Knickerbocker Co., Inc., **25 272–75**
L. Luria & Son, Inc., **19 242–44**
L.M. Electronics, **I** 489
L.M. Ericsson, **I** 462; **II** 1, 70, 81–82, 365; **III** 479–80; **11** 46, 439; **14** 488
L-N Glass Co., **III** 715
L-N Safety Glass, **III** 715
L-O-F Glass Co. *See* Libbey-Owens-Ford Glass Co.
L. Prang & Co., **12** 207
L.S. DuBois Son and Co., **III** 10
L.S. Starrett Co., **13 301–03**
L. Straus and Sons, **V** 168
L.W. Hammerson & Co., **IV** 696
L.W. Pierce Co., Inc. *See* Pierce Leahy Corporation.
L.W. Singer, **13** 429
La Banque Suisse et Française. *See* Crédit Commercial de France.
La Barge Mirrors, **III** 571; **20** 362
La Cerus, **IV** 615
La Choy Food Products Inc., **II** 467–68; **17** 241; **25 276–78**
La Cinq, **IV** 619
La Cloche d'Or, **25** 85
La Concorde, **III** 208
La Crosse Telephone Corporation, **9** 106
La Cruz del Campo S.A., **9** 100
La Favorita Bakery, **II** 543
La Fromagerie du Velay, **25** 85
La Grange Foundry, Inc., **39** 31
La Halle aux Chaussures, **17** 210
La India Co., **II** 532
La Madeleine French Bakery & Café, **33 249–51**
La Oroya, **22** 286
La Petite Academy, **13** 299
La Poste, **V 270–72**
The La Quinta Companies, **42 213–16 (upd.)**
La Quinta Inns, Inc., **11 242–44**; **21** 362
La Redoute S.A., **19** 306, 309
La Rinascente, **12** 153
La-Ru Truck Rental Company, Inc., **16** 386
La Ruche Meridionale, **12** 153
La Societe Anonyme Francaise Holophane, **19** 211
La Vie Claire, **13** 103
La-Z-Boy Chair Company, **14 302–04**; **31** 248
Laakirchen, **IV** 339–40; **28** 445
LAB. *See* Lloyd Aereo de Bolivia.
The Lab, Inc., **37** 263
LaB Investing Co. L.L.C, **37** 224
LaBakelite S.A., **I** 387
LaBarge Inc., **41 224–26**
Labatt Brewing Company Limited, **I 267–68**; **18** 72; **25 279–82 (upd.)**; **26** 303, 306
Labaz, **I** 676; **IV** 546
Labelcraft, Inc., **8** 360
LaBelle Iron Works, **7** 586
Labor für Impulstechnik, **III** 154
Labor Ready, Inc., **29 273–75**
Laboratoire Michel Robilliard, **IV** 546
Laboratoire Roger Bellon, **I** 389
Laboratoires d'Anglas, **III** 47
Laboratoires de Biologie Végétale Yves Rocher, **35 262–65**
Laboratoires Goupil, **III** 48
Laboratoires Roche Posay, **III** 48
Laboratoires Ruby d'Anglas, **III** 48
Laboratorios Grossman, **III** 55
Laboratorios Liade S.A., **24** 75
Laboratory Corporation of America Holdings, **42 217–20 (upd.)**
Laboratory for Electronics, **III** 168; **6** 284
LaBour Pump, **I** 473
LaBow, Haynes Co., **III** 270
LaBranche & Co. Inc., **37 223–25**
Lachine Rapids Hydraulic and Land Company, **6** 501
Lackawanna Steel & Ordnance Co., **IV** 35, 114; **7** 48
Laclede Steel Company, **15 271–73**
Lacombe Electric. *See* Public Service Company of Colorado.
Lacquer Products Co., **I** 321
LaCrosse Footwear, Inc., **18 298–301**
Lacto Ibérica, **23** 219
Lactos, **25** 85
Lacy Diversified Industries, Ltd., **24** 159–61
Ladbroke Group PLC, **II** 139, **141–42**; **19** 208; **21 333–36 (upd.)**; **24** 194; **42** 64
Ladd and Tilton, **14** 527–28
LADD Furniture, Inc., **12 299–301**; **23** 244
Ladd Petroleum Corp., **II** 30
LADECO, **6** 97; **31** 304; **36** 281
Ladenburg, Thalmann & Co. Inc., **17** 346
Ladenso, **IV** 277
Ladish Co., Inc., **30 282–84**
Lady Foot Locker, **V** 226; **14** 293, 295
Lady Lee, **27** 291

Laerdal Medical, **18** 423
Lafarge Coppée S.A., III 702, **703–05,** 736; **8** 258; **10** 422–23; **23** 333
Lafarge Corporation, 24 332; **28 228–31**
Lafayette Manufacturing Co., **12** 296
Lafayette Radio Electronics Corporation, **9** 121–22
Laflin & Rand Powder Co., **I** 328; **III** 525
Lafuma S.A., 39 248–50
LAG&E. *See* Los Angeles Gas and Electric Company.
LaGard Inc., **20** 363
Lagardère Groupe SCA, **16** 254; **24** 84, 88; **34** 83
Lagoven, **IV** 508
Laidlaw Inc., **39** 19, 21
Laidlaw Transportation, Inc., **6** 410; **32** 227, 231
Laing, **IV** 696
Laing's Properties Ltd., **I** 575
L'Air Liquide, I 303, **357–59; 11** 402
Laitaatsillan Konepaja, **IV** 275
Laiterie Centrale Krompholtz, **25** 84
Laiterie de la Vallée du Dropt, **25** 84
Laiterie Ekabe, **19** 50
SA Laiterie Walhorn Molkerel, **19** 50
Laiteries Prairies de l'Orne, **19** 50
Lake Arrowhead Development Co., **IV** 255
Lake Central Airlines, **I** 131; **6** 131
Lake Erie Screw Corp., **11** 534, 536
Lake Odessa Machine Products, **18** 494
Lake Superior Consolidated Mines Company, **IV** 572; **7** 549; **17** 355–56
Lake Superior Paper Industries, **26** 363
Lakehead Pipe Line Partners, L.P., **43** 155
Lakeland Fire and Casualty Co., **III** 213
Läkemedels-Industri Föreningen, **I** 664
Laker Airways, **I** 94; **6** 79; **24** 399
Lakeside Laboratories, **III** 24
The Lakeside Publishing and Printing Co., **IV** 660
Lakestone Systems, Inc., **11** 469
Lam Research Corporation, IV 213; **11 245–47; 18** 383; **31 299–302 (upd.)**
Lamar Advertising Company, 27 278–80
The Lamaur Corporation, 41 227–29
Lamb Technicon Corp., **I** 486
Lamb Weston, Inc., I 417; **23 319–21; 24** 33–34
Lambda Electronics Inc., **32** 411
Lambert Brothers, Inc., **7** 573
Lambert Brussels Financial Corporation, **II** 407; **11** 532
Lambert Frères, **33** 339
Lambert Kay Company, **8** 84
Lambert Pharmacal Co., **I** 710–11; **III** 28
Lambert Rivière, **41** 340
Lamborghini. *See* Automobili Lamborghini S.p.A.
Lamkin Brothers, Inc., **8** 386
Lamons Metal Gasket Co., **III** 570; **11** 535; **20** 361
Lamontagne Ltd., **II** 651
Lamonts Apparel, Inc., 15 274–76
Lampadaires Feralux, Inc., **19** 472
Lamson & Sessions Co., 13 304–06
Lamson Bros., **II** 451
Lamson Corporation, **7** 145
Lamson Industries Ltd., **IV** 645
Lamson Store Service Co., **IV** 644
Lan Chile S.A., 31 303–06; 33
Lanca, **14** 224
Lancashire, **III** 350
Lancaster Caramel Co., **II** 510
Lancaster Colony Corporation, 8 307–09
Lancaster Cork Works, **III** 422
Lancaster Financial Ltd., **14** 472
Lancaster National Bank, **9** 475
Lancaster Press, **23** 102
Lance, Inc., 14 305–07; 41 230–33 (upd.)
Lancel, **27** 487, 489
Lancer Corporation, 21 337–39
Lanchester Motor Company, Ltd., **13** 286
Lancia, **I** 162; **11** 102
Lancôme, **III** 46–48; **8** 342
Land O'Lakes, Inc., II 535–37; 7 339; **13** 351; **21 340–43 (upd.)**
Land-O-Sun Dairies, L.L.C., **26** 449
Land Securities PLC, IV 704–06
Land-Wheelwright Laboratories, **III** 607; **7** 436
Lander Alarm Co., **III** 740
Lander Company, **21** 54
Länderbank, **II** 282
Landesbank für Westfalen Girozentrale, Münster, **II** 385
Landis International, Inc., **10** 105–06
Landmark Banks, **10** 426
Landmark Communications, Inc., 12 302–05; 22 442
Landmark Financial Services Inc., **11** 447
Landmark Target Media, **IV** 597
Landmark Union Trust, **18** 517
Landoll, Inc., **22** 522
Landor Associates, **I** 94
Landry's Seafood Restaurants, Inc., 15 277–79
Lands' End, Inc., 9 314–16; 12 280; **16** 37; **19** 333; **26** 439; **27** 374, 429; **29 276–79 (upd.)**
Landstar, **26** 533
Lane Bryant, **V** 115–16
The Lane Co., Inc., III 528, 530; **12 306–08; 39** 170, 173–74
Lane Drug Company, **12** 132
Lane, Piper, and Jaffray, Inc. *See* Piper Jaffray Companies.
Lane Processing Inc., **II** 585
Lane Publishing Co., **IV** 676; **7** 529
Lane Rossi, **IV** 421
Laneco, Inc., **II** 682
Lang Exploratory Drilling, **26** 42
Langdon Rieder Corp., **21** 97
Lange International S.A., **15** 462; **43** 375–76
Lange, Maxwell & Springer, **IV** 641; **7** 311
Langford Labs, **8** 25
Lanier Business Products, Inc., **II** 39; **8** 407; **20** 290
Lanman Companies, Inc., **23** 101
Lannet Data Communications Ltd., **18** 345–46; **26** 275–77
Lano Corp., **I** 446
Lansi-Suomen Osake-Pankki, **II** 303
Lanson Pere et Fils, **II** 475
Lantic Industries, Inc., **II** 664
Lanvin, **I** 696; **III** 48; **8** 343
LAPE. *See* Líneas Aéreas Postales Españolas.
Lapeyre S.A. *See* Groupe Lapeyre S.A.
LaPine Technology, **II** 51; **21** 331
Laporte Industries Ltd., **I** 303; **IV** 300
Lapp, **8** 229
Lara, **19** 192
Larami Corp., **14** 486
Lareco, **26** 22
Largardère Groupe, **43** 210
Largo Entertainment, **25** 329
Laroche Navarron, **I** 703
Larousse Group, **IV** 614–15
Larrowe Milling Co., **II** 501; **10** 322
Larry Flynt Publishing Inc., 31 307–10
Larry H. Miller Group, 29 280–83
Larry's Food Products, **36** 163
Larsen & Toubro, **IV** 484
Larsen Company, **7** 128
Larson Lumber Co., **IV** 306
Larwin Group, **III** 231
Las Vegas Gas Company, **19** 411
LaSalle Machine Tool, Inc., **13** 7–8
LaSalle National Bank, **II** 184
LaSalle Steel Corporation, **28** 314
LaSalles & Koch Co., **8** 443
Lasco Shipping Co., **19** 380
Laser Tech Color, **21** 60
Lasercharge Pty Ltd, **18** 130
LaserSoft, **24** 349
Oy Läskelä Ab, **IV** 300
Lasky's, **II** 141; **24** 269
Lasmo, **IV** 455, 499
Lason, Inc., 31 311–13
Latham & Watkins, 33 252–54; 37 292
Latin Communications Group Inc., **41** 151
Latitude Communications, **22** 52
Latrobe Brewing Co., **25** 281
Latrobe Steel Company, **8** 529–31
Lattice Semiconductor Corp., 16 315–17; 43 17
Lauder Chemical, **17** 363
Laura Ashley Holdings plc, 13 307–09; 37 226–29 (upd.)
Laura Scudder's, **7** 429
Laurel Glen, **34** 3, 5
Laurent-Perrier SA, 42 221–23
Laurentien Hotel Co., **III** 99
Lauson Engine Company, **8** 515
LaVista Equipment Supply Co., **14** 545
Lavold, **16** 421; **43** 308
Law Life Assurance Society, **III** 372
Lawn Boy Inc., **7** 535–36; **8** 72; **26** 494
Lawrence Manufacturing Co., **III** 526
Lawrence Warehouse Co., **II** 397–98; **10** 62
Lawrenceburg Gas Company, **6** 466
The Lawson Co., **7** 113; **25** 125
Lawson Inc., **41** 113, 115
Lawson Milk, **II** 572
Lawson Software, 38 284–88
Lawter International Inc., 14 308–10; 18 220
Lawyers Cooperative, **8** 527–28
Lawyers Trust Co., **II** 230
Layer Five, **43** 252
Layne & Bowler Pump, **11** 5
Layne Christensen Company, 19 245–47; 26 71
Layton Homes Corporation, **30** 423
Lazard Freres & Co., **II** 268, 402, 422; **IV** 23, 79, 658–59; **6** 356; **7** 287, 446; **10** 399; **12** 165, 391, 547, 562; **21** 145
Lazard LLC, 38 289–92
Lazare Kaplan International Inc., 21 344–47
LBO Holdings, **15** 459
LBS Communications, **6** 28
LCI International, Inc., 16 318–20
LCP Hotels. *See* CapStar Hotel Co.
LDDS-Metro Communications, Inc., 8 310–12
LDDS WorldCom, Inc., **16** 467–68
LDI. *See* Lacy Diversified Industries, Ltd.

LDS Health Services Corporation, **27** 237
LDX NET, Inc., **IV** 576
Le Bon Marché. *See* Bon Marché.
Le Brun and Sons, **III** 291
Le Buffet System-Gastronomie, **V** 74
Le Chameau, **39** 250
Le Clerc, **21** 225–26
Le Courviour S.A., **10** 351
Le Monde S.A., 33 308–10
Le Rocher, Compagnie de Reassurance, **III** 340
Lea & Perrins, **II** 475
Lea County Gas Co., **6** 580
Lea Lumber & Plywood Co., **12** 300
Lea Manufacturing, **23** 299
Leach McMicking, **13** 274
Lead Industries Group Ltd., **III** 681; **IV** 108
Leadership Housing Inc., **IV** 136
Leaf River Forest Products Inc., **IV** 282, 300; **9** 261
Leahy & Co. *See* Pierce Leahy Corporation.
Leamington Priors & Warwickshire Banking Co., **II** 318; **17** 323
Lean Cuisine, **12** 531
Lear Corporation, **17** 303, 305
Lear Inc., **II** 61; **8** 49, 51
Lear Romec Corp., **8** 135
Lear Seating Corporation, 16 321–23
Lear Siegler Holdings Corporation, **25** 431
Lear Siegler Inc., I 481–83; III 581; **8** 313; **13** 169, 358, 398; **19** 371–72; **30** 426
Learjet Inc., 8 313–16; **9** 242; **27 281–85 (upd.)**
The Learning Company Inc., 24 275–78, 480; **29** 74, 77; **41** 409
Learning Tree International Inc., 24 279–82
LeaRonal, Inc., 23 322–24
Leasco Data Processing Equipment Corp., **III** 342–44; **IV** 641–42; **7** 311
Lease International SA, **6** 358
Leaseway Personnel Corp., **18** 159
Leaseway Transportation Corp., V 494; **12 309–11**; **19** 293
Leatherback Industries, **22** 229
LeBoeuf, Lamb, Greene & MacRae, L.L.P., 29 284–86
Lebr Associates Inc., **25** 246
Lech Brewery, **24** 450
Lechmere Inc., 10 391–93
Lechters, Inc., 11 248–50; **39 251–54 (upd.)**
Leclerc. *See* Association des Centres Distributeurs E. Leclerc.
LeCroy Corporation, 41 234–37
Lectorum Publications, **29** 426
Lederle Laboratories, **I** 300–02, 657, 684; **8** 24–25; **14** 254, 256, 423; **27** 115
Lederle Standard Products, **26** 29
Lee Ackerman Investment Company, **18** 513
Lee Apparel Company, Inc., 8 317–19; **17** 512, 514
Lee Brands, **II** 500
Lee Company, **V** 390–92
Lee Enterprises, Incorporated, 11 251–53
Lee Hecht Harrison, **6** 10
Lee International, **24** 373
Lee National Corporation, **26** 234
Lee Optical, **13** 390
Lee Rubber and Tire Corp., **16** 8
Lee Telephone Company, **6** 313
Lee Way Holding Co., **14** 42
Lee Way Motor Freight, **I** 278
Leeann Chin, Inc., 30 285–88
Leeds & County Bank, **II** 318; **17** 323
Leeds & Northrup Co., **III** 644–45; **28** 484
Lees Carpets, **17** 76
Leewards Creative Crafts Inc., **17** 322
Lefeldt, **III** 417, 418
Lefrak Organization Inc., 8 357; **26 260–62**
Legacy Homes Ltd., **26** 290
Legal & General Group plc, III 272–73; **IV** 705, 712; **24 283–85 (upd.)**; **30** 494; **33** 319
Legal Technologies, Inc., **15** 378
Legault and Masse, **II** 664
Legent Corporation, 10 394–96; **14** 392
Legetojsfabrikken LEGO Billund A/S. *See* Lego A/S.
Legg Mason, Inc., 11 493; **33 259–62**
Leggett & Platt, Incorporated, 9 93; **11 254–56**
Leggett Stores Inc., **19** 48
Lego A/S, 12 495; **13 310–13**; **40 287–91 (upd.)**
Legrand SA, 21 348–50
Lehigh Acquisition Corp., **34** 286
Lehigh Portland Cement Company, 23 325–27; **31** 252
Lehigh Railroad, **III** 258
Lehman Brothers, **I** 78, 125, 484; **II** 192, 259, 398, 448, 450–51; **6** 199; **10** 62–63; **11** 263–64; **13** 448; **14** 145; **22** 445; **25** 301; **38** 411
Lehman Merchant Bank Partners, **19** 324
Lehmer Company. *See* Centel Corporation.
Lehn & Fink, **I** 699
Lehnkering AG, **IV** 140
Lehrman Bros., **III** 419
Lehser Communications, Inc., **15** 265
Leica Camera AG, 35 266–69
Leica Microsystems Holdings GmbH, 35 270–73
Leigh-Mardon Security Group, **30** 44
Leighton Holdings Ltd., **19** 402
Leinenkugel Brewing Company. *See* Jacob Leinenkugel Brewing Company.
Leiner Health Products Inc., 34 250–52
The Leisure Company, **34** 22
Leisure Lodges, **III** 76
Leisure System Inc., **12** 359
Leitz, **III** 583–84
LeMaster Litho Supply, **13** 228
Lemmerz Holding GmbH, **27** 202, 204
Lempereur, **13** 297
Lena Goldfields Ltd., **IV** 94
Lenc-Smith, **III** 430
Lend Lease Corporation Limited, IV 707–09; **17 283–86 (upd.)**
Lender's Bagel, **32** 69
Lending Textiles, **29** 132
Lenel Systems International Inc., **24** 510
Lennar Corporation, 11 257–59
Lennon's, **II** 628
Lennox Industries, Inc., **22** 6
Lennox International Inc., 8 320–22; **28 232–36 (upd.)**
Lenoir Furniture Corporation, **10** 183
Lenox, Inc., I 227; **10** 179, 181; **12 312–13**; **18** 69; **38** 113
Lens, Inc., **30** 267–68
LensCrafters Inc., V 207–08; **13** 391; **17** 294; **23 328–30**; **43** 199
Lentheric, **I** 426
L'Entreprise Jean Lefebvre, 23 331–33
Leo Burnett Company, Inc., I 22–24, 25, 31, 37; **11** 51, 212; **12** 439; **20 336–39 (upd.)**
The Leo Group, **32** 140; **40** 140
Léon Gaumont et Cie. *See* Gaumont SA.
Leonard Bernstein Music Publishing Company, **23** 391
Leonard Development Group, **10** 508
Leonard Express, Inc., **6** 371
Leonard Green & Partners LP, **12** 477–78; **24** 173
Leonard Machinery Corp., **16** 124
Leonard Parker Company, **26** 196
Leonard Silver, **14** 482
Leonardo Editore, **IV** 587
Leonberger Bausparkasse, **II** 258
Lepco Co., **III** 596
Leprino Foods Company, 28 237–39
Lern, Inc., **II** 420
Lerner Plastics, **9** 323
Lerner Stores, **V** 116
Leroy-Merlin, **23** 230; **37** 24
Les Chantiers de l'Atlantique, **II** 13
Les Echos. *See* Groupe Les Echos.
Les Grands Magasins Au Bon Marché: Etablissements Vaxelaire-Claes, **26** 159–60
Les Industries Ling, **13** 443
Les Papeteries du Limousin, **19** 227
L'Escaut, **III** 335
Lesco Inc., 19 248–50
The Leslie Fay Companies, Inc., 8 323–25
The Leslie Fay Company, Inc., 39 255–58 (upd.); **40** 276–77
Leslie Paper, **IV** 288
Leslie's Poolmart, Inc., 18 302–04
Lesser-Goldman, **II** 18
Lester B. Knight & Associates, **II** 19
Lester Ink and Coatings Company, **13** 228
Lestrem Group, **IV** 296; **19** 226
Let op Uw Einde, **III** 199
Lettuce Entertain You Enterprises, **38** 103
Leucadia National Corporation, 6 396; **11** ; **25** 170 **260–62**
Leuna-Werke AG, **7** 142
Level Five Research, Inc., **22** 292
N.V. Levensverzekering Maatschappji Utrecht, **III** 199–200
Lever Brothers Company, I 17, 21, 26, 30, 333; **II** 497, 588–89; **III** 31; **7** 542–43, 545; **9** 291, **317–19**; **13** 199; **14** 314. *See also* Unilever.
Levi Strauss & Co., I 15; **II** 634, 669; **V** 60–61, **362–65**; **9** 142; **12** 430; **16 324–28 (upd.)**, 509, 511; **17** 512; **18** 191–92; **19** 196; **23** 422; **24** 158; **25** 47
Leviathan Gas Pipeline Company, **21** 171
Levine, Huntley, Vick & Beaver, **6** 28
Levitt & Sons, **IV** 728
Levitt Corp., **21** 471
Levitt Homes, **I** 464; **11** 198
Levitt Industries, **17** 331
Levitt Investment Company, **26** 102
Levitz Furniture Inc., 15 280–82; **23** 412, 414
Levtex Hotel Ventures, **21** 363
Levy Bakery Goods, **I** 30
Levy Restaurants L.P., 26 263–65
Lew Liberbaum & Co., **27** 197

The Lewin Group, Inc., **21** 425
Lewis and Marks, **IV** 21–22, 96; **16** 27
Lewis Batting Company, **11** 219
Lewis Construction, **IV** 22
Lewis Galoob Toys Inc., 16 329–31
Lewis Grocer Co., **II** 669; **18** 504
Lewis-Howe Co., **III** 56
Lewis Refrigeration Company, **21** 500
Lewis's, **V** 178
Lewis's Bank, **II** 308
Lex Electronics, **10** 113
Lex Service plc, **19** 312
Lexecon, Inc., **26** 187
Lexington Broadcast Services, **6** 27
Lexington Furniture Industries, **III** 571; **20** 362
Lexington Ice Company, **6** 514
Lexington Insurance Co., **III** 197
Lexington Utilities Company, **6** 514; **11** 237
LEXIS-NEXIS Group, 17 399; **18** 542; **21** 70; **31** 388, 393; **33 263–67**
Lexitron, **II** 87
Lexmark International, Inc., 9 116; **10** 519; **18 305–07; 30** 250
Leybold AG, **IV** 71
Leyland and Birmingham Rubber Co., **I** 429
Leyland Motor Corporation, **7** 459
LFC Financial, **10** 339
LFC Holdings Corp. *See* Levitz Furniture Inc.
LFE Corp., **7** 297
LG Chemical Ltd., **26** 425
LG Electronics Inc., **13** 572, 575; **43** 428
LG Group, **18** 124; **34** 514, 517–18
LG&E Energy Corp., 6 516–18; 18 366–67
Lhomme S.A., **8** 477
Liaison Agency, **31** 216–17
Liaoyang Automotive Spring Factory, **III** 581
Libbey-Owens-Ford Company, **I** 609; **III** 640–42, 707, 714–15, 725–26, 731; **IV** 421; **7** 292; **16** 7–9; **22** 434; **23** 83; **26** 353; **31** 355
Libby, **II** 547; **7** 382
Libby McNeil & Libby Inc., **II** 489
Libeltex, **9** 92
Liber, **14** 556
Liberty Bank of Buffalo, **9** 229
Liberty Brokerage Investment Company, **10** 278
Liberty Can and Sign Company, **17** 105–06
The Liberty Corporation, 22 312–14
Liberty Gauge Company, **17** 213
Liberty Hardware Manufacturing Corporation, **20** 363
Liberty House, **I** 417–18
Liberty Life, **IV** 91, 97
Liberty Livewire Corporation, 42 224–27
Liberty Media Corporation, **18** 66; **19** 282; **25** 214; **34** 224; **42** 114, 224. *See also* Liberty Livewire Corporation.
Liberty Mexicana, **III** 415
Liberty Mutual Insurance Group, **I** 28; **11** 379
Liberty Mutual Savings Bank, **17** 530
Liberty National Bank, **II** 229
Liberty National Insurance Holding Company. *See* Torchmark Corporation.
Liberty National Life Insurance Co., **III** 217; **9** 506–07
Liberty Natural Gas Co., **11** 441
Liberty Software, Inc., **17** 264
Liberty's, **13** 307
Libra Bank Ltd., **II** 271
Librairie de Jacques-Francois Brétif, **IV** 617
Librairie Fayard, **IV** 618
Librairie Générale Francaise, **IV** 618
Librairie Larousse, **IV** 614–16
Librairie Louis Hachette, **IV** 617–18
Librairie Nathan, **IV** 614, 616
Librairie Victor Lecou, **IV** 617
Libyan Arab Airline, **6** 85
Libyan Arab Foreign Bank, **IV** 454
Libyan National Oil Corporation, IV 453–55
Libyan-Turkish Engineering and Consultancy Corp., **IV** 563
Lidköpings Mekaniska Verkstad AB, **III** 623
Lieberman Enterprises, **24** 349
Liebert Corp., **II** 20
Life and Casualty Insurance Co. of Tennessee, **III** 193
Life Assoc. of Scotland, **III** 310
Life Fitness Inc., **III** 431
Life Insurance Co. of Georgia, **III** 310
Life Insurance Co. of Scotland, **III** 358
Life Insurance Co. of Virginia, **III** 204
Life Insurance Securities, Ltd., **III** 288
Life Investors International Ltd., **III** 179; **12** 199
Life of Eire, **III** 273
Life Partners Group, Inc., **33** 111
Life Retail Stores. *See* Angelica Corporation.
Life Savers Corp., **II** 129, 544; **7** 367; **21** 54
Life Science Research, Inc., **10** 105–07
Life Technologies, Inc., I 321; **12** 103; **17 287–89**
Life Uniform Shops. *See* Angelica Corporation.
Lifecycle, Inc., **III** 431; **25** 40
Lifeline Systems, Inc., **32** 374
LifeLink, **11** 378
Lifemark Corp., **III** 74; **14** 232; **33** 183
LIFETIME, **IV** 627; **19** 204
Lifetime Corp., **29** 363–64
Lifetime Foam Products, Inc., **12** 439
Lifetime Hoan Corporation, 27 286–89
Lift Parts Manufacturing, **I** 157
Ligand Pharmaceutical, **10** 48
Liggett & Meyers, **V** 396, 405, 417–18; **18** 416; **29** 195
Liggett Group Inc., **I** 248; **7** 105; **14** 213; **15** 71; **16** 242; **37** 295. *See also* Vector Group Inc.
Light & Power Company, **12** 265
Light Corrugated Box Co., **IV** 332
Light Savers U.S.A., Inc. *See* Hospitality Worldwide Services, Inc.
Light-Servicos de Eletricidade S.A., **II** 456
Lightel Inc., **6** 311
Lighthouse, Ltd., **24** 95
Lighting Corp. of America, **I** 476
LIGHTNET, **IV** 576
Lightwell Co., **III** 634
Lignum Oil Co., **IV** 658
Lil' Champ Food Stores, Inc., **36** 359
LILCO. *See* Long Island Lighting Company.
Lilia Limited, **17** 449
Lille Bonnières et Colombes, **37** 143–44
Lillian Vernon Corporation, 12 314–15; 35 274–77 (upd.)
Lillie Rubin, **30** 104–06
Lilliput Group plc, **11** 95; **15** 478
Lilly & Co. *See* Eli Lilly & Co.
Lilly Industries, **22** 437
Lillybrook Coal Co., **IV** 180
Lillywhites Ltd., **III** 105
Lily Tulip Co., **I** 609, 611; **8** 198
Limburger Fabrik und Hüttenverein, **IV** 103
Limhamns Golvindustri AB. *See* Tarkett Sommer AG.
The Limited, Inc., V 115–16; 9 142; **12** 280, 356; **15** 7, 9; **16** 219; **18** 193, 215, 217, 410; **20 340–43 (upd.); 24** 237; **25** 120–21, 123; **28** 344
Limmer and Trinidad Ltd., **III** 752
LIN Broadcasting Corp., II 331; **6** 323; **9 320–22; 11** 330
Lin Data Corp., **11** 234
Linamar Corporation, 18 308–10
Lincare Holdings Inc., 43 265–67
Lincoln American Life Insurance Co., **10** 246
Lincoln Automotive, **26** 363
Lincoln Benefit Life Company, **10** 51
Lincoln Electric Co., II 19; **13 314–16**
Lincoln Electric Motor Works, **9** 439
Lincoln Federal Savings, **16** 106
Lincoln First Bank, **II** 248
Lincoln Income Life Insurance Co., **10** 246
Lincoln Liberty Life Insurance Co., **III** 254
Lincoln Marketing, Inc., **18** 518
Lincoln Motor Co., **I** 165
Lincoln National Corporation, III 274–77; 6 195; **10** 44; **22** 144; **25 286–90 (upd.)**
Lincoln Property Company, 8 326–28
Lincoln Savings, **10** 340
Lincoln Savings & Loan, **9** 199
Lincoln Snacks Company, 24 286–88
Lincoln Telephone & Telegraph Company, 14 311–13
LinCom Corp., **8** 327
Lindal Cedar Homes, Inc., 29 287–89
Linde A.G., I 297–98, 315, **581–83; 9** 16, 516; **10** 31–32; **11** 402–03; **25** 81
Lindemann's, **I** 220
Lindex, **II** 640
Lindsay Manufacturing Co., 20 344–46
Lindsay Parkinson & Co., **I** 567
Lindt & Sprüngli. *See* Chocoladefabriken Lindt & Sprüngli AG.
Lindustries, **III** 502; **7** 208
Linear Corp., **III** 643
Linear Technology, Inc., 16 332–34
Líneas Aéreas Postales Españolas, **6** 95
Linens 'n Things, Inc., 13 81–82; **24 289–92; 33** 384; **41** 50
Linfood Cash & Carry, **13** 103
Linfood Holdings Ltd., **II** 628–29
Ling Products, **12** 25
Ling-Temco-Vought. *See* LTV Corporation.
Lingerie Time, **20** 143
Linguaphone Group, **43** 204, 206
Linjeflyg, **I** 120
Link-Belt Corp., **I** 443; **IV** 660
Link House Publications PLC, **IV** 687
Link Motor Supply Company, **26** 347
Linmark Westman International Limited, **25** 221–22

Linroz Manufacturing Company L.P., **25** 245
Lintas: Worldwide, **I** 18; **6** 30; **14 314–16**
Lintott Engineering, Ltd., **10** 108
Linz, **16** 559
Lion Corporation, **III 44–45**
Lion Manufacturing, **III** 430; **25** 40
Lion Match Company, **24** 450
Lion Oil, **I** 365
Lion's Head Brewery. *See* The Stroh Brewery Company.
Lionel L.L.C., **12** 494; **16 335–38**; **18** 524
Lionex Corporation, **13** 46
Lions Gate Entertainment Corporation, **35 278–81**
Liontech, **16** 337–38
Lippincott & Margulies, **III** 283
Lippincott Raven Publishers, **14** 556
Lipschutz Bros., Inc., **29** 511
Lipson Alport Glass & Associates, **27** 195
Lipton. *See* Thomas J. Lipton Company.
Liqui-Box Corporation, **16 339–41**
Liquid Ag Systems Inc., **26** 494
Liquid Carbonic, **7** 74, 77
Liquor Barn, **II** 656
Liquorland, **V** 35
Liquorsave, **II** 609–10
LIRCA, **III** 48
Liris, **23** 212
Lisbon Coal and Oil Fuel Co., **IV** 504
Liscaya, **II** 196
Listening Library Inc., **31** 379
Lister, **21** 503
Litco Bancorp., **II** 192
LiTel Communications, Inc., **16** 318
Lithia Motors, Inc., **41 238–40**
Litho-Krome Corp., **IV** 621
LitleNet, **26** 441
Litronix, **III** 455; **21** 122
Littelfuse, Inc., **26 266–69**
Little, Brown & Company, **IV** 675; **7** 528; **10** 355; **36** 270
Little Caesar Enterprises, Inc., **24 293–96 (upd.)**; **27** 481. *See also* Ilitch Holdings Inc.
Little Caesar International, Inc., **7 278–79**; **7** 278–79; **15** 344, 346; **16** 447; **25** 179, 227–28
Little Chef Ltd., **III** 105–06
Little General, **II** 620; **12** 179, 200
Little Giant Pump Company, **8** 515
Little League Baseball, Incorporated, **23** 450
Little Leather Library, **13** 105
Little, Royal, **I** 529–30; **8** 545; **13** 63
Little Switzerland, **19** 451
Little Tikes Co., **III** 614; **12** 169; **13 317–19**
Littlewoods Financial Services, **30** 494
Littlewoods Organisation PLC, **V 117–19**; **24** 316
Littlewoods plc, **42 228–32 (upd.)**
Litton Industries Inc., **I** 85, 452, 476, **484–86**, 523–24; **II** 33; **III** 293, 473, 732; **IV** 253; **6** 599; **10** 520–21, 537; **11 263–65 (upd.)**, 435; **12** 248, 271–72, 538–40; **15** 287; **17** 30; **19** 31, 110, 290; **21** 86; **22** 436. *See also* Avondale Industries.
Litwin Engineers & Constructors, **8** 546
Livanos, **III** 516
LIVE Entertainment Inc., **18** 64, 66; **20 347–49**; **24** 349
Liverpool and London and Globe Insurance Co., **III** 234, 350
Liverpool and London Fire and Life Insurance Co., **III** 349
Liverpool Fire and Life Insurance Co., **III** 350
Liverpool Mexico S.A., **16** 216
Livia, **I** 154; **10** 279
Living Arts, Inc., **41** 174
Living Centers of America, **13** 49
Living Videotext, **10** 508
Livingston Communications, **6** 313
Livingston, Fargo and Co., **II** 380, 395; **10** 59
LivingWell Inc., **12** 326
Liz Claiborne, Inc., **8 329–31**; **16** 37, 61; **25** 258, **291–94 (upd.)**
LKB-Produkter AB, **I** 665
Lloyd A. Fry Roofing, **III** 721
Lloyd Adriatico S.p.A., **III** 377
Lloyd Aereo de Bolivia, **6** 97
Lloyd Creative Staffing, **27** 21
Lloyd George Management, **18** 152
Lloyd Instruments, Ltd., **29** 460–61
Lloyd Italico, **III** 351
Lloyd Thompson Group plc, **20** 313
Lloyd-Truax Ltd., **21** 499
Lloyd's Electronics, **14** 118
Lloyd's of London, **III** 234, **278–81**; **9** 297; **10** 38; **11** 533; **22 315–19 (upd.)**
Lloyds Bank PLC, **II 306–09** 319, 334, 358; **17** 324–25
Lloyds Chemists plc, **27** 177
Lloyds Life Assurance, **III** 351
Lloyds TSB, **39** 6
LM Ericsson. *See* Telefonaktiebolaget LM Ericsson.
LMC Metals, **19** 380
LME. *See* Telefonaktiebolaget LM Ericsson.
LNG Co., **IV** 473–74
LNM Group, **30** 252
Lo-Cost, **II** 609
Lo-Vaca Gathering Co., **IV** 394; **7** 553
Loadometer Co., **III** 435
Lobitos Oilfields Ltd., **IV** 381–82
Loblaw Companies Limited, **II** 631–32; **19** 116; **43 268–72**. *See also* George Weston Limited.
Local Data, Inc., **10** 97
Locations, Inc., **IV** 727
Locke, Lancaster and W.W.&R. Johnson & Sons, **III** 680
Lockhart Catering, **III** 104
Lockhart Corporation, **12** 564
Lockheed Corporation, **I** 13, 41, 48, 50, 52, 54, 61, 63, **64–66**, 67–68, 71–72, 74, 76–77, 82, 84, 90, 92–94, 100, 102, 107, 110, 113, 121, 126, 195, 493–94, 529; **II** 19, 32–33; **III** 84, 539, 601; **IV** 15; **6** 71; **9** 12, 17–18, 272, 417, 458–60, 501; **10** 163, 262–63, 317, 536; **11** 164, 166, **266–69 (upd.)**, 278–79, 363–65; **12** 190; **13** 126, 128; **17** 306; **21** 140; **22** 506; **24** 84–85, 87, 311, 326, 375, 397; **25** 303, 316, 347; **34** 371
Lockheed Martin Corporation, **15 283–86 (upd.)**; **21** 86; **24** 88; **29** 409; **32** 437; **33** 47–48; **38** 372, 376
Lockwood Banc Group, Inc., **11** 306
Lockwood Greene Engineers, Inc., **17** 377
Lockwood National Bank, **25** 114
Lockwood Technology, Inc., **19** 179
Lockwoods Foods Ltd., **II** 513
Loctite Corporation, **8 332–34**; **30 289–91 (upd.)**; **34** 209
Lodding Engineering, **7** 521
Lodestar Group, **10** 19
Lodge-Cottrell, **III** 472
Lodge Plus, Ltd., **25** 430
LodgeNet Entertainment Corporation, **26** 441; **28 240–42**
Lodging Group, **12** 297
Loeb Rhoades, Hornblower & Co., **II** 450–51; **9** 469
Loehmann's Inc., **24 297–99**
Loening Aeronautical, **I** 61; **11** 164
Loew's Consolidated Enterprises, **II** 154
Loew's, Inc., **31** 99
The Loewen Group, Inc., **16 342–44**; **37** 67–68; **40 292–95 (upd.)**
Loewenstein Furniture Group, Inc., **21** 531–33
Loewi Financial Cos., **III** 270
Loews Cineplex Entertainment Corp., **37** 64
Loews Corporation, **I** 245, **487–88**; **II** 134, 148–49, 169; **III** 228, 231; **12 316–18 (upd.)**, 418; **13** 120–21; **19** 362; **22** 73; **25** 177, 326–28; **36 324–28 (upd.)**; **38** 142; **41** 70, 72
LOF Plastics, Inc. *See* Libbey-Owens-Ford.
Loffland Brothers Company, **9** 364
Loft Inc., **I** 276; **10** 451
Logan's Roadhouse, Inc., **19** 287–88; **22** 464; **29 290–92**; **35** 84
Logged Off Land Co., **IV** 355–56
Logic Modeling, **11** 491
Logica plc, **14 317–19**; **37 230–33 (upd.)**
Logicon Inc., **20 350–52**
Logility, **25** 20, 22
Logistics, **III** 431
Logistics Data Systems, **13** 4
Logistics Industries Corporation, **39** 77
Logistics Management Systems, Inc., **8** 33
Logitech International SA, **9** 116; **28 243–45**
Logo Athletic, Inc., **35** 363
Logo 7, Inc., **13** 533
Logon, Inc., **14** 377
Lojas Arapuã S.A., **22 320–22**
Loma Linda Foods, **14** 557–58
Lomak Petroleum, Inc., **24** 380
Lomas & Nettleton Financial Corporation, **III** 249; **11** 122
Lombard North Central, **II** 442
Lombard Orient Leasing Ltd., **II** 442
London and County Bank, **II** 334
London and Hanseatic Bank, **II** 256
London & Hull, **III** 211
London and Lancashire Insurance Co., **III** 350
London & Leeds Development Corp., **II** 141
London & Midland Bank. *See* Midland Bank plc.
London & Rhodesia Mining & Land Company. *See* Lonrho Plc.
London and Scottish Marine Oil, **11** 98
London & Western Trust, **39** 90
London and Westminster Bank, **II** 333–34
London Asiastic, **III** 699
London Assurance Corp., **III** 278, 369–71, 373
London Brick Co., **III** 502; **7** 208; **14** 249
London Brokers Ltd., **6** 290
London Buses Limited, **6** 406
London Cargo Group, **25** 82

London Central, **28** 155–56
London Chartered Bank of Australia, **II** 188
London Clermont Club, **III** 431
London County and Westminster Bank, **II** 334
London County Freehold & Leasehold Properties, **IV** 711
London East India Company, **12** 421
London, Edinburgh and Dublin Insurance Co., **III** 350
London Electricity, **12** 443; **41** 141
London Film Productions Ltd., **II** 157; **14** 399
London Fog Industries, Inc., **16** 61; **29 293–96**
London General Omnibus Company, **6** 406
London Guarantee and Accident Co., **III** 372
London Insurance Group, **III** 373; **36** 372
London Joint-Stock Bank, **II** 318, 388; **17** 324
London Life Assoc., **IV** 711
London Life Insurance Co., **II** 456–57
London Precision Machine & Tool, Ltd., **39** 32
London, Provincial and South Western Bank, **II** 235
London Records, **23** 390
London Regional Transport, **6 406–08**
London South Partnership, **25** 497
London Stock Exchange Limited, **34 253–56**; **37** 131–33
London Transport, **19** 111
London Weekend Television, **IV** 650–51; **7** 389
Londontown Manufacturing Company. *See* London Fog Industries, Inc.
Lone Star and Crescent Oil Co., **IV** 548
Lone Star Brewing Co., **I** 255
Lone Star Gas Corp., **V** 609, 611
Lone Star Industries, **III** 718, 729, 753; **IV** 304; **23** 326; **28** 450; **35** 154
Lone Star Steakhouse, **21** 250
Lone Star Steel, **I** 440–41
Lone Star Technologies, Inc., **22** 3
Long-Airdox Co., **IV** 136
Long Distance Discount Services, Inc., **8** 310; **27** 305
Long Distance/USA, **9** 479
Long Island Airways, **I** 115; **12** 379
Long Island Bancorp, Inc., **16 345–47**
Long Island Cable Communication Development Company, **7** 63
Long Island Daily Press Publishing Co., **IV** 582–83
Long Island Lighting Company, **V 652–54**; **6** 456; **27** 264
Long Island Power Authority, **27** 265
Long Island Rail Road, **35** 290
Long Island Trust Co., **II** 192, 218
Long John Silver's Restaurants Inc., **13 320–22**
Long Lac Mineral Exploration, **9** 282
Long Life Fish Food Products, **12** 230
Long Manufacturing Co., **III** 439; **14** 63
Long-Term Credit Bank of Japan, Ltd., **II** 301, **310–11**, 338, 369
Long Valley Power Cooperative, **12** 265
The Longaberger Company, **12 319–21**
Longchamps, Inc., **38** 385; **41** 388
LongHorn Steaks Inc., **19** 341
Longines-Wittenauer Watch Co., **II** 121
Longman Group Ltd., **IV** 611, 658
Longmat Foods, **II** 494
Longs Drug Stores Corporation, **V 120**; **25 295–97 (upd.)**
Longview Fibre Company, **8 335–37**; **37 234–37 (upd.)**
Longwy, **IV** 227
Lonrho Plc, **IV** 651–52; **10** 170; **21 351–55**; **43** 38
Lonsdale Investment Trust, **II** 421
Lonvest Corp., **II** 456–57
Loomis Fargo Group, **42** 338
Loomis, Sayles & Co., **III** 313
Loose Leaf Metals Co., Inc., **10** 314
Lor-Al, Inc., **17** 10
Loral Corporation, **II** 38; **7** 9; **8 338–40**; **9 323–25**; **13** 356; **15** 283, 285; **20** 262
Lord & Taylor, **13** 44; **14** 376; **15** 86; **18** 137, 372; **21** 302
Lord & Thomas, **I** 12–14; **IV** 660
Lord Baltimore Press, Inc., **IV** 286
L'Oréal, **II** 547; **III 46–49**, 62; **7** 382–83; **8** 129–31; **341–44 (upd.)**; **11** 41; **23** 238, 242; **31** 418
Lorenz, **I** 463
Lorillard Industries, **I** 488; **V** 396, 407, 417; **12** 317; **18** 416; **22** 73; **29** 195; **36** 324, 327
Lorimar Telepictures, **II** 149, 177; **25** 90–91, 329
Loronix Inc., **24** 509
Lorraine-Escaut, **IV** 227
Lorvic Corp., **I** 679
Los Angeles Can Co., **I** 599
Los Angeles Drug Co., **12** 106
Los Angeles Gas and Electric Company, **V** 682; **25** 413
Los Angeles Steamship Co., **II** 490
Los Lagos Corp., **12** 175
Los Nietos Co., **IV** 570; **24** 520
Loss Prevention Inc., **24** 509
Lost Arrow Inc., **22 323–25**
LOT Polish Airlines (Polskie Linie Lotnicze S.A.), **33 268–71**
Lothringer Bergwerks- und Hüttenverein Aumetz-Friede AG, **IV** 126
LOT$OFF Corporation, **24 300–01**
Lotus Cars Ltd., **14 320–22**
Lotus Development Corporation, **IV** 597; **6** 224–25, 227, **254–56**, 258–60, 270–71, 273; **9** 81, 140; **10** 24, 505; **12** 335; **16** 392, 394; **20** 238; **21** 86; **22** 161; **25 298–302 (upd.)**; **30** 251; **38** 417
Lotus Publishing Corporation, **7** 239; **25** 239
Lotus Radio, **I** 531
Louart Corporation, **29** 33–34
Loucks, Hoffman & Company, **8** 412
Loughead Aircraft Manufacturing Co., **I** 64
Louis Allis, **15** 288
Louis B. Mayer Productions, **II** 148; **25** 326–27
Louis C. Edwards, **II** 609
Louis Dreyfus Energy Corp., **28** 471
Louis Harris & Associates, Inc., **22** 188
Louis Kemp Seafood Company, **14** 515
Louis Marx Toys, **II** 559; **12** 410
Louis Rich, Inc., **II** 532; **12** 372
Louis Vuitton, **I** 272; **III** 48; **8** 343; **10 397–99**. *See also* LVMH Moët Hennessy Louis Vuitton SA.
Louisiana & Southern Life Insurance Co., **14** 460
Louisiana Bank & Trust, **11** 106
Louisiana Corporation, **19** 301
Louisiana Energy Services, **27** 130
The Louisiana Land and Exploration Company, **IV** 76, 365, 367; **7 280–83**
Louisiana-Pacific Corporation, **IV** 282, **304–05**; **9** 260; **16** 203; **22** 491; **31 314–317 (upd.)**; **32** 91
Louisville Cement Co., **IV** 409
Louisville Gas and Electric Company. *See* LG&E Energy Corporation.
Louisville Home Telephone Company, **14** 258
Loup River Public Power District, **29** 352
Louthan Manufacturing Company, **8** 178
LoVaca Gathering Company. *See* The Coastal Corporation.
Lovelace Truck Service, Inc., **14** 42
Loveman's, Inc., **19** 323
Lovering China Clays, **III** 690
Lowe Bros. Co., **III** 745
Lowe Group, **22** 294
Lowe's Companies, Inc., **V 122–23**; **11** 384; **12** 234, 345; **18** 239; **21** 324, **356–58 (upd.)**; **27** 416
Lowell Bearing Co., **IV** 136
Lowell Shoe, Inc., **13** 360
Löwenbräu, **I** 220, 257; **II** 240
Lowes Food Stores. *See* Alex Lee Inc.
Lowney/Moirs, **II** 512
Lowrance Electronics, Inc., **18 311–14**
Lowrey's Meat Specialties, Inc., **21** 156
Loyalty Group, **III** 241–43
LPL Investment Group, **40** 35–36
LRL International, **II** 477
LSI. *See* Lear Siegler Inc.
LSI Logic Corporation, **13 323–25**; **18** 382
LTA Ltd., **IV** 22
LTU Group Holding GmbH, **37 238–41**
The LTV Corporation, **I** 62–63, **489–91**; **7** 107–08; **8** 157, 315; **10** 419; **11** 166, 364; **12** 124; **17** 357; **18** 110, 378; **19** 466; **24 302–06 (upd.)**; **26** 406
Luberef, **IV** 538
The Lubrizol Corporation, **30 292–95 (upd.)**
Lubrizol Enterprises, Inc., **I 360–62**; **21** 385–87
Luby's Cafeteria's, Inc., **17 290–93**; **19** 301
Luby's, Inc., **42 233–38 (upd.)**
Lucas Bols, **II** 642
Lucas Digital Ltd., **12** 322
Lucas Girling, **I** 157
Lucas Industries Plc, **III** 509, **554–57**; **27** 251
Lucas Ingredients, **27** 258
Lucas-Milhaupt, Inc., **23** 250
LucasArts Entertainment Company, **32** 9
Lucasfilm Ltd., **9** 368, 472; **12 322–24**; **22** 459; **34** 350; **38** 70
LucasVarity plc, **27** 249, 251
Lucchini, **IV** 228
Lucent Technologies Inc., **18** 154, 180; **20** 8; **22** 19; **26** 275, 277; **29** 44, 414; **34 257–60**; **36** 122, 124; **41** 289–90
Lucky Brand Dungarees, **18** 85
Lucky-Goldstar, **II 53–54**; **III** 457; **13** 574. *See also* Goldstar Co., Ltd.
Lucky Lager Brewing Co, **I** 268; **25** 280
Lucky Stores Inc., **II** 605, 653; **6** 355; **8** 474; **12** 48; **17** 369, 559; **22** 39; **27 290–93**
Lucky Strike, **II** 143
Ludi Wap S.A., **41** 409

Ludlow Corp., **III** 645
Ludovico, **25** 85
Lufkin Rule Co., **II** 16
Luftag, **I** 110
Lufthansa. *See* Deutsche Lufthansa Aktiengesellschaft.
The Luggage Company, **14** 224
Lukens Inc., **14 323–25**; **27** 65
Lukey Mufflers, **IV** 249
LUKOIL. *See* OAO LUKOIL.
Lum's, **6** 199–200
Lumac B.V., **I** 387
Lumbermen's Investment Corp., **IV** 341
Lumbermens Mutual Casualty Co., **III** 269–71; **15** 257
Lumex, Inc., **17** 197
La Lumière Economique, **II** 79
Luminar Plc, **40 296–98**
Lummus Crest, **IV** 169; **26** 496
Lumonics Inc., **III** 635
Lunar Corporation, **29 297–99**
Luncheon Voucher, **27** 10
Lund Food Holdings, Inc., **22 326–28**
Lund International Holdings, Inc., **40 299–301**
Lundstrom Jewelers, **24** 319
Lunenburg Sea Products Limited, **14** 339
Lunevale Products Ltd., **I** 341
L'Unite Hermetique S.A., **8** 515
Lunn Poly, **8** 525–26
Luotto-Pankki Oy, **II** 303
Lurgei, **6** 599
LURGI. *See* Metallurgische Gesellschaft Aktiengesellschaft.
Luria Bros. and Co., **I** 512–13; **6** 151
Lutèce, **20** 26
Luther's Bar-B-Q, **II** 556
Lutheran Brotherhood, **31 318–21**
Lux, **III** 478
Lux Mercantile Co., **II** 624
Luxor, **II** 69; **6** 205; **17** 353
Luxottica SpA, **17 294–96**; **23** 328; **43** 96. *See also* Casual Corner Group, Inc.
Luxury Linens, **13** 81–82
LVMH Moët Hennessy Louis Vuitton SA, **I** 272; **19** 86; **24** 137, 140; **33 272–77 (upd.)**
LVO Cable Inc., **IV** 596
LXE Inc., **21** 199–201
Lycos, **27** 517; **37** 384. *See also* Terra Lycos, Inc.
Lydex, **I** 527
Lykes Corp., **I** 490–91; **24** 303
Lynch Corporation, **43 273–76**
Lynde Company, **16** 269–71
Lynx Express Delivery, **6** 412, 414
Lyon & Healy, **IV** 660
Lyon's Technological Products Ltd., **III** 745
Lyondell Petrochemical Company, **IV** 377, **456–57**; **10** 110
Lyonnaise Communications, **10** 196; **25** 497
Lyonnaise des Eaux-Dumez, **I** 576; **V 655–57**; **23** 332. *See also* Suez Lyonnaise des Eaux.
Lyons. *See* J. Lyons & Co. Ltd.
LyphoMed Inc., **IV** 333; **17** 287
Oy Lypsyniemen Konepaja, **IV** 275–76
Lysaght, **24** 143
Lysaght's Canada, Ltd., **IV** 73
Lystads, **I** 333
Lytag Ltd., **31** 398–99
M & C Saatchi, **42** 330
M&F Worldwide Corp., **38 293–95**
M and G Fund Management, **III** 699
M&J Diesel Locomotive Filter Co., **17** 106
M&M Limited, **7** 299
M and M Manufacturing Company, **23** 143
M&M/Mars, **14** 48; **15** 63–64; **21** 219
M & S Computing. *See* Intergraph Corporation.
M&T Capital Corporation, **11** 109
M/A Com Inc., **6** 336; **14** 26–27
M.A. Hanna Company, **8 345–47**; **12** 352
M.A.N., **III** 561–63; **IV** 86
M.B. McGerry, **21** 94
M-Cell Ltd., **31** 329
M.D.C., **11** 258
M.E.P.C. Ltd., **IV** 711
M.F. Patterson Dental Supply Co. *See* Patterson Dental Co.
M.G. Waldbaum Company, **25** 332–33
M. Guggenheim's Sons, **IV** 31
M.H. McLean Wholesaler Grocery Company, **8** 380
M. Hensoldt & Söhne Wetzlar Optische Werke AG, **III** 446
M-I Drilling Fluids Co., **III** 473; **15** 468
M.I. Schottenstein Homes Inc., **19** 125–26
M.J. Brock Corporation, **8** 460
M.J. Designs, Inc., **17** 360
M.L.C. Partners Limited Partnership, **22** 459
M. Loeb Ltd., **II** 652
M. Lowenstein Corp., **V** 379
M.M. Warburg. *See* SBC Warburg.
M.P. Burke PLC, **13** 485–86
M.P. Pumps, Inc., **8** 515
M. Polaner Inc., **10** 70; **40** 51–52
M-R Group plc, **31** 312–13
M.S. Carriers, Inc., **42** 363, 365
M. Samuel & Co., **II** 208
M. Sobol, Inc., **28** 12
M Stores Inc., **II** 664
M.T.G.I. Textile Manufacturers Group, **25** 121
M.W. Carr, **14** 245
M.W. Kellogg Co., **III** 470; **IV** 408, 534; **34** 81
M-Web Holdings Ltd., **31** 329–30
Ma. Ma-Macaroni Co., **II** 554
Maakauppiaitten Oy, **8** 293–94
Maakuntain Keskus-Pankki, **II** 303
MaasGlas, **III** 667
Maatschappij tot Exploitatie van de Onderneming Krasnapolsky. *See* Grand Hotel Krasnapolsky N.V.
Maatschappij tot Exploitatie van Steenfabrieken Udenhout, voorheen Weyers, **14** 249
MABAG Maschinen- und Apparatebau GmbH, **IV** 198
Mabley & Carew, **10** 282
Mac Frugal's Bargains - Closeouts Inc., **17 297–99**
Mac Publications LLC, **25** 240
Mac Tools, **III** 628
MacAndrews & Forbes Holdings Inc., **II** 679; **III** 56; **9** 129; **11** 334; **28 246–49**; **30** 138; **38** 293–94
MacArthur Foundation. *See* The John D. and Catherine T. MacArthur Foundation.
Macau Telephone, **18** 114
Maccabees Life Insurance Co., **III** 350
MacCall Management, **19** 158
MacDermid Incorporated, **32 318–21**
MacDonald Companies, **15** 87
MacDonald Dettwiler and Associates, **32** 436
MacDonald, Halsted, and Laybourne, **10** 127
Macdonald Hamilton & Co., **III** 522–23
Macey Furniture Co., **7** 493
Macfarlane Lang & Co., **II** 592–93
Macfield Inc., **12** 502
MacFrugal's Bargains Close-Outs Inc., **29** 312
MacGregor Sporting Goods Inc., **III** 443; **22** 115, 458; **23** 449
Mach Performance, Inc., **28** 147
Machine Vision International Inc., **10** 232
Macintosh. *See* Apple Computer, Inc.
Mack-Cali Realty Corporation, **42 239–41**
Mack Trucks, Inc., **I** 147, **177–79**; **9** 416; **12** 90; **22 329–32 (upd.)**
Mack-Wayne Plastics, **42** 439
MacKay-Shields Financial Corp., **III** 316
MacKenzie & Co., **II** 361
Mackenzie Hill, **IV** 724
Mackenzie Mann & Co. Limited, **6** 360
Mackey Airways, **I** 102
Mackie Designs Inc., **30** 406; **33 278–81**
Mackinnon Mackenzie & Co., **III** 521–22
Maclaren Power and Paper Co., **IV** 165
Maclean Hunter Limited, **III** 65; **IV 638–40**, **22** 442; **23** 98
Maclean Hunter Publishing Limited, **26 270–74 (upd.)**; **30** 388
Maclin Co., **12** 127
The MacManus Group, **32** 140; **40** 140
MacMark Corp., **22** 459
MacMarr Stores, **II** 654
Macmillan & Co. Ltd., **35** 452
MacMillan Bloedel Limited, **IV** 165, 272, **306–09**, 721; **9** 391; **19** 444, 446; **25** 12; **26** 445
Macmillan, Inc., **IV** 637, 641–43; **7 284–86**, 311–12, 343; **9** 63; **12** 226; **13** 91, 93; **17** 399; **18** 329; **22** 441–42; **23** 350, 503; **25** 484; **27** 222–23
Macnaughton Blair, **III** 671
The MacNeal-Schwendler Corporation, **25 303–05**
Macneill & Co., **III** 522
Macon Gas Company, **6** 447; **23** 28
Macon Kraft Co., **IV** 311; **11** 421; **19** 267
Maconochie Bros., **II** 569
Macrodata, **18** 87
Macwhyte Company, **27** 415
Macy's. *See* R.H. Macy & Co., Inc.
Macy's California, **21** 129
Mad Dog Athletics, **19** 385
Maddingley Brown Coal Pty Ltd., **IV** 249
Maddux Air Lines, **I** 125; **12** 487
Madge Networks N.V., **18** 346; **26 275–77**
Madison & Sullivan, Inc., **10** 215
Madison Financial Corp., **16** 145
Madison Foods, **14** 557
Madison Furniture Industries, **14** 436
Madison Gas and Electric Company, **6** 605–06; **39 259–62**
Madison Resources, Inc., **13** 502
Madison Square Garden, **I** 452
MAEFORT Hungarian Air Transport Joint Stock Company, **24** 310
Maersk Lines, **22** 167
Maes Group Breweries, **II** 475
Maeva Group, **6** 206

Mafco Holdings, Inc., **28** 248; **38** 293–95
Magasins Armand Thiéry et Sigrand, **V** 11; **19** 308
Magazine and Book Services, **13** 48
Magazins Réal Stores, **II** 651
Magcobar, **III** 472
MagCorp, **28** 198
Magdeburg Insurance Group, **III** 377
Magdeburger Versicherungsgruppe, **III** 377
Magee Company, **31** 435–36
Magellan Corporation, **22** 403
Magic Chef Co., **III** 573; **8** 298; **22** 349
Magic City Food Products Company. *See* Golden Enterprises, Inc.
Magic Marker, **29** 372
Magic Pan, **II** 559–60; **12** 410
Magic Pantry Foods, **10** 382
Magicsilk, Inc., **22** 133
MagicSoft Inc., **10** 557
Magirus, **IV** 126
Maglificio di Ponzano Veneto dei Fratelli Benetton. *See* Benetton.
Magma Copper Company, **7 287–90**, 385–87; **22** 107
Magma Power Company, **11 270–72**
Magna Computer Corporation, **12** 149; **13** 97
Magna Distribuidora Ltda., **43** 368
Magnaflux, **III** 519; **22** 282
Magnavox Co., **13** 398; **19** 393
Magne Corp., **IV** 160
Magnesium Metal Co., **IV** 118
Magnet Cove Barium Corp., **III** 472
MagneTek, Inc., **15 287–89**; **41 241–44(upd.)**
Magnetic Controls Company, **10** 18
Magnetic Peripherals Inc., **19** 513–14
Magnivision, **22** 35
Magnolia Petroleum Co., **III** 497; **IV** 82, 464
Magnus Co., **I** 331; **13** 197
La Magona d'Italia, **IV** 228
Magor Railcar Co., **I** 170
MAGroup Inc., **11** 123
Magyar Viscosa, **37** 428
Mahalo Air, **22** 252; **24** 22
Maharam Fabric, **8** 455
Mahir, **I** 37
Mahou, **II** 474
Mai Nap Rt, **IV** 652; **7** 392
MAI PLC, **28** 504
MAI Systems Corporation, **10** 242; **11 273–76**; **26** 497, 499
Maidenform Worldwide Inc., **20 352–55**
Mail Boxes Etc., **18 315–17**; **25** 500; **41 245–48 (upd.)**. *See also* U.S. Office Products Company.
Mail.com Inc., **38** 271
Mail-Well, Inc., **25** 184; **28 250–52**
Mailson Ferreira da Nobrega, **II** 200
Mailtek, Inc., **18** 518
MAIN. *See* Mid-American Interpool Network.
Main Event Management Corp., **III** 194
Main Plaza Corporation, **25** 115
Main Street Advertising USA, **IV** 597
Maine Central Railroad Company, **16 348–50**
Mainline Industrial Distributors, Inc., **13** 79
Mainline Travel, **I** 114
Maison Blanche Department Stores Group, **35** 129
Maison Bouygues, **I** 563
Maison de Schreiber and Aronson, **25** 283
Maison de Valérie, **19** 309
Maison Louis Jadot, **24 307–09**
Maizuru Heavy Industries, **III** 514
Majestic Contractors Ltd., **8** 419–20
Majestic Industries, Inc., **43** 459
Majestic Wine Warehouses Ltd., **II** 656
Major League Baseball, **12** 457
Major Video Concepts, **6** 410
Major Video, Inc., **9** 74
MaK Maschinenbau GmbH, **IV** 88
Mak van Waay, **11** 453
Makepeace Preserving Co., **25** 365
Makhteshim Chemical Works Ltd., **II** 47; **25** 266–67
Makita Corporation, **III** 436; **20** 66; **22 333–35**
Makiyama, **I** 363
Makovsky & Company, **12** 394
Makro Inc., **18** 286
Malama Pacific Corporation, **9** 276
Malapai Resources, **6** 546
Malayan Breweries, **I** 256
Malayan Motor and General Underwriters, **III** 201
Malaysia LNG, **IV** 518–19
Malaysian Airlines System Berhad, **6** 71, **100–02**, 117, 415; **29 300–03 (upd.)**
Malaysian International Shipping Co., **IV** 518
Malaysian Sheet Glass, **III** 715
Malbak Ltd., **IV** 92–93
Malcolm Pirnie, Inc., **42 242–44**
Malcolm's Diary & Time-Table, **III** 256
Malcus Industri, **III** 624
Malden Mills Industries, Inc., **16 351–53**
Malév Plc, **24 310–12**; **27** 474; **29** 17
Malheur Cooperative Electric Association, **12** 265
Malibu, **25** 141
Mall.com, **38** 271
Mallard Bay Drilling, Inc., **28** 347–48
Malleable Iron Works, **II** 34
Mallinckrodt Group Inc., **III** 16; **IV** 146; **8** 85; **19** 28, **251–53**
Malmö Flygindustri, **I** 198
Malmö Woodworking Factory. *See* Tarkett Sommer AG.
Malmsten & Bergvalls, **I** 664
Malone & Hyde, Inc., **II** 625, 670–71; **9** 52–53; **14** 147; **18** 506
Malrite Communications Group, **IV** 596
Malt-A-Milk Co., **II** 487
Malt-O-Meal Company, **15** 189; **22 336–38**
Mameco International, **8** 455
Mammoet Transport B.V., **26** 241, **278–80**
Man Aktiengesellschaft, **III** 301, **561–63**
MAN Gutehoffnungshütte AG, **15** 226
Management and Training Corporation, **28 253–56**
Management Decision Systems, Inc., **10** 358
Management Engineering and Development Co., **IV** 310; **19** 266
Management Recruiters International, **6** 140
Management Science America, Inc., **11** 77; **25** 20
Manbré and Garton, **II** 582
Manchester and Liverpool District Banking Co., **II** 307, 333
Manchester Board and Paper Co., **19** 77
Manchester Commercial Buildings Co., **IV** 711
Manchester United Football Club plc, **30 296–98**
Manco, Inc., **13** 166. *See also* Henkel Manco Inc.
Mancuso & Co., **22** 116
Mandabach & Simms, **6** 40
Mandalay Pictures, **35** 278–80
Mandalay Resort Group, **32 322–26 (upd.)**
Mandarin, Inc., **33** 128
Mandarin Oriental Hotel Group International Ltd., **I** 471; **IV** 700; **20** 312
Mandel Bros., **IV** 660
Manetta Mills, Inc., **19** 304
Manhattan Card Co., **18** 114
Manhattan Co., **II** 217, 247
Manhattan Construction Company. *See* Rooney Brothers Co.
Manhattan Electrical Supply Co., **9** 517
Manhattan Fund, **I** 614
Manhattan International Limousine Network Ltd., **26** 62
Manhattan Trust Co., **II** 229
Manheim Auctions, Inc. *See* Cox Enterprises, Inc.
Manifatture Cotoniere Meridionali, **I** 466
Manischewitz Company. *See* B. Manischewitz Company.
Manistique Papers Inc., **17** 282
Manistique Pulp and Paper Co., **IV** 311; **19** 266
Manitoba Bridge and Engineering Works Ltd., **8** 544
Manitoba Paper Co., **IV** 245–46; **25** 10
Manitoba Rolling Mill Ltd., **8** 544
Manitou BF S.A., **27 294–96**
Manitowoc Company, Inc., **18 318–21**
Mann Egerton & Co., **III** 523
Mann Theatres Chain, **I** 245; **25** 177
Mann's Wine Company, Ltd., **14** 288
Mannatech Inc., **33 282–85**
Manne Tossbergs Eftr., **II** 639
Mannesmann AG, **I** 411; **III 564–67**; **IV** 222, 469; **14 326–29 (upd.)**; **34** 319; **38 296–301 (upd.)**. *See also* Vodafone Group PLC.
Mannheimer Bank, **IV** 558
Manning, Selvage & Lee, **6** 22
Mannstaedt, **IV** 128
Manor Care, Inc., **6 187–90**; **14** 105–07; **15** 522; **25 306–10 (upd.)**
Manor Healthcare Corporation, **26** 459
Manorfield Investments, **II** 158
Manos Enterprises, **14** 87
Manpower, Inc., **6** 10, 140; **9 326–27**; **16** 48; **25** 432; **30 299–302 (upd.)**; **40** 236, 238
Mantrec S.A., **27** 296
Mantua Metal Products. *See* Tyco Toys, Inc.
Manufactured Home Communities, Inc., **22 339–41**
Manufacturers & Merchants Indemnity Co., **III** 191
Manufacturers and Traders Trust Company, **11** 108–09
Manufacturers Casualty Insurance Co., **26** 486
Manufacturers Fire Insurance Co., **26** 486
Manufacturers Hanover Corporation, **II** 230, 254, **312–14**, 403; **III** 194; **9** 124;

11 16, 54, 415; **13** 536; **14** 103; **16** 207; **17** 559; **22** 406; **26** 453; **38** 253
Manufacturers National Bank of Brooklyn, **II** 312
Manufacturers National Bank of Detroit, **I** 165; **11** 137; **40** 116
Manufacturers Railway, **I** 219; **34** 36
Manufacturing Management Inc., **19** 381
Manus Nu-Pulse, **III** 420
Manville Corporation, **III 706–09**, 721; **7 291–95 (upd.)**; **10** 43, 45; **11** 420–22
Manweb plc, **19** 389–90
MAPCO Inc., **IV 458–59**; **26** 234; **31** 469, 471
Mapelli Brothers Food Distribution Co., **13** 350
Maple Grove Farms of Vermont, Inc., **40** 51–52
Maple Leaf Foods Inc., **41 249–53**
Maple Leaf Mills, **II** 513–14; **41** 252
MAPP. *See* Mid-Continent Area Power Planner.
Mapra Industria e Comercio Ltda., **32** 40
Mar-O-Bar Company, **7** 299
A.B. Marabou, **II** 511
Marantha! Music, **14** 499
Marantz Co., **14** 118
Marathon Insurance Co., **26** 486
Marathon Oil Co., **IV** 365, 454, 487, 572, 574; **7** 549, 551; **13** 458
Marathon Paper Products, **I** 612, 614
Marauder Company, **26** 433
Maraven, **IV** 508
Marblehead Communications, Inc., **23** 101
Marbodal, **12** 464
Marboro Books, Inc., **10** 136
Marbro Lamp Co., **III** 571; **20** 362
Marc's Big Boy. *See* The Marcus Corporation.
Marcade Group. *See* Aris Industries, Inc.
Marceau Investments, **II** 356
March-Davis Bicycle Company, **19** 383
March of Dimes, **31 322–25**
Marchand, **13** 27
Marchesi Antinori SRL, **42 245–48**
marchFIRST, Inc., **34 261–64**
Marchland Holdings Ltd., **II** 649
Marchon Eyewear, **22** 123
Marciano Investments, Inc., **24** 157
Marcillat, **19** 49
Marcon Coating, Inc., **22** 347
Marconi plc, **33 286–90 (upd.)**
Marconi Wireless Telegraph Co. of America, **II** 25, 88
Marconiphone, **I** 531
The Marcus Corporation, **21 359–63**
Marcus Samuel & Co., **IV** 530
Marcy Fitness Products, Inc., **19** 142, 144
Mardon Packaging International, **I** 426–27
Mardorf, Peach and Co., **II** 466
Maremont Corporation, **8** 39–40
Margarete Steiff GmbH, **23 334–37**
Margarine Unie N.V. *See* Unilever PLC (Unilever N.V.).
Marge Carson, Inc., **III** 571; **20** 362
Margo's La Mode, **10** 281–82
Marico Acquisition Corporation, **8** 448, 450
Marie Brizard & Roger International S.A., **22 342–44**
Marie Callender's Restaurant & Bakery, Inc., **13** 66; **28 257–59**
Marie-Claire Album, **III** 47
Marigold Foods Inc., **II** 528
Marinduque Mining & Industrial Corp., **IV** 146
Marine Bank and Trust Co., **11** 105
Marine Bank of Erie, **II** 342
Marine Computer Systems, **6** 242
Marine Diamond Corp., **IV** 66; **7** 123
Marine-Firminy, **IV** 227
Marine Group, **III** 444; **22** 116
Marine Harvest International, **13** 103
Marine Midland Corp., **I** 548; **II** 298; **9** 475–76; **11** 108; **17** 325
Marine Office of America, **III** 220, 241–42
Marine United Inc., **42** 361
Marinela, **19** 192–93
Marineland Amusements Corp., **IV** 623
MarineMax, Inc., **30 303–05**; **37** 396
Marion Brick, **14** 249
Marion Foods, Inc., **17** 434
Marion Freight Lines, **6** 370
Marion Laboratories Inc., **I 648–49**; **8** 149; **9** 328–29; **16** 438
Marion Manufacturing, **9** 72
Marion Merrell Dow, Inc., **9 328–29 (upd.)**
Marionet Corp., **IV** 680–81
Marisa Christina, Inc., **15 290–92**; **25** 245
Maritime Electric Company, Limited, **15** 182
Maritz Inc., **38 302–05**
Mark Controls Corporation, **30** 157
Mark Cross, Inc., **17** 4–5
Mark Goldston, **8** 305
Mark Hopkins, **12** 316
Mark IV Industries, Inc., **7 296–98**; **21** 418; **28 260–64 (upd.)**
Mark Travel Corporation, **30** 448
Mark Trouser, Inc., **17** 338
Markborough Properties, **II** 222; **V** 81; **8** 525; **25** 221
Market Growth Resources, **23** 480
Market Horizons, **6** 27
Market National Bank, **13** 465
Marketime, **V** 55
Marketing Data Systems, Inc., **18** 24
Marketing Equities International, **26** 136
Marketing Information Services, **6** 24
MarketSpan Corp. *See* KeySpan Energy Co.
Markham & Co., **I** 573–74
Marks and Spencer p.l.c., **I** 588; **II** 513, 678; **V 124–26**; **10** 442; **17** 42, 124; **22** 109, 111; **24** 268, 270; **313–17 (upd.)**, 474; **28** 96; **35** 308, 310; **41** 114; **42** 231
Marks-Baer Inc., **11** 64
Marks Brothers Jewelers, Inc., **24 318–20**
Marland Refining Co., **IV** 399–400
Marlene Industries Corp., **16** 36–37
MarLennan Corp., **III** 283
Marley Co., **19** 360
Marley Holdings, L.P., **19** 246
Marley Tile, **III** 735
Marlin-Rockwell Corp., **I** 539; **14** 510
Marlow Foods, **II** 565
Marman Products Company, **16** 8
The Marmon Group, **III** 97; **IV 135–38**; **16 354–57 (upd.)**
Marmon-Perry Light Company, **6** 508
Marolf Dakota Farms, Inc., **18** 14–15
Marotte, **21** 438
Marquam Commercial Brokerage Company, **21** 257
Marquardt Aircraft, **I** 380; **13** 379
Marquette Electronics, Inc., **13 326–28**
Marquette Paper Corporation, **III** 766; **22** 545
Marquis Who's Who, **17** 398
Marriage Mailers, **6** 12
Marriner Group, **13** 175
Marriot Inc., **29** 442
Marriot Management Services, **29** 444
Marriott Corporation, **II** 173, 608; **III** 92, 94, 99–100, **102–03**, 248; **7** 474–75; **9** 95, 426; **15** 87; **17** 238; **18** 216; **19** 433–34; **21** 91, 364; **22** 131; **23** 436–38; **27** 334; **38** 386; **41** 82
Marriott International, Inc., **21** 182, **364–67 (upd.)**; **29** 403, 406; **41** 156–58
Mars, Incorporated, **II** 510–11; **III** 114; **7 299–301**; **22** 298, 528; **40 302–05 (upd.)**
Marschke Manufacturing Co., **III** 435
Marsene Corp., **III** 440
Marsh & McLennan Companies, Inc., **III** 280, **282–84**; **10** 39; **14** 279; **22** 318
Marsh Supermarkets, Inc., **17 300–02**
Marshalk Company, **I** 16; **22** 294
Marshall Die Casting, **13** 225
Marshall Field & Co., **I** 13, 426; **III** 329; **IV** 660; **V** 43–44; **8** 33; **9** 213; **12** 283; **15** 86; **18** 136–37, 488; **22** 72
Marshall Industries, **19** 311
Marshalls Incorporated, **13 329–31**; **14** 62
Marsin Medical Supply Co., **III** 9
Marstellar, **13** 204
The Mart, **9** 120
Marten Transport, **27** 404
Martha, **IV** 486
Martha Lane Adams, **27** 428
Martha Stewart Living Omnimedia, L.L.C., **24 321–23**
Martin & Pagenstecher GMBH, **24** 208
Martin Bros. Tobacco Co., **14** 19
Martin-Brower Corp., **II** 500; **III** 21; **17** 475
Martin Collet, **19** 50
Martin Dennis Co., **IV** 409
Martin Electric Co., **III** 98
Martin Guitar Company. *See* C.F. Martin & Co., Inc.
Martin Marietta Corporation, **I** 47, **67–69**, 71, 102, 112, 142–43, 184, 416; **II** 32, 67; **III** 671; **IV** 60, 163; **7** 356, 520; **8** 315; **9** 310; **10** 162, 199, 484; **11** 166, 277–78, 364; **12** 127, 290; **13** 327, 356; **15** 283; **17** 564; **18** 369; **19** 70; **22** 400; **28** 288. *See also* Lockheed Martin Corporation.
Martin Mathys, **8** 456
Martin Rooks & Co., **I** 95
Martin-Senour Co., **III** 744
Martin Sorrell, **6** 54
Martin Theaters, **14** 86
Martin-Yale Industries, Inc., **19** 142–44
Martin Zippel Co., **16** 389
Martin's, **12** 221
Martindale-Hubbell, **17** 398
Martineau and Bland, **I** 293
Martini & Rossi, **18** 41
Martins Bank, **II** 236, 308
Martinus Nijhoff, **14** 555; **25** 85
Marubeni Corporation, **24 324–27 (upd.)**
Marubeni K.K., **I** 432, **492–95**, 510; **II** 292, 391; **III** 760; **IV** 266, 525; **12** 147; **17** 556
Maruei & Co., **IV** 151; **24** 358

Maruetsu, **17** 124; **41** 114
Marufuku Co., Ltd., **III** 586; **7** 394
Marui Co. Ltd., **V 127**
Marukuni Kogyo Co., Ltd., **IV** 327
Marutaka Kinitsu Store Ltd., **V** 194
Maruzen Co., Limited, **II** 348; **IV** 403–04, 476, 554; **18 322–24**
Marvel Entertainment Group, Inc., **10 400–02**; **18** 426, 520–21; **21** 404; **25** 141; **34** 449
Marvel Metal Products, **III** 570; **20** 361
Marvel-Schebler Carburetor Corp., **III** 438; **14** 63–64
Marvin & Leonard Advertising, **13** 511–12
Marvin H. Sugarman Productions Inc., **20** 48
Marvin Lumber & Cedar Company, **10** 95; **22 345–47**
Marwick, Mitchell & Company, **10** 385
Marwitz & Hauser, **III** 446
Marx, **12** 494
Mary Ann Co. Ltd., **V** 89
Mary Ann Restivo, Inc., **8** 323
Mary Ellen's, Inc., **11** 211
Mary Kathleen Uranium, **IV** 59–60
Mary Kay Corporation, **III** 16; **9 330–32**; **12** 435; **15** 475, 477; **18** 67, 164; **21** 49, 51; **30 306–09 (upd.)**
Maryland Casualty Co., **III** 193, 412
Maryland Cup Company, **8** 197
Maryland Distillers, **I** 285
Maryland Medical Laboratory Inc., **26** 391
Maryland National Corp., **11** 287
Maryland National Mortgage Corporation, **11** 121
Maryland Shipbuilding and Drydock Co., **I** 170
Maryland Steel Co., **IV** 35; **7** 48
Marzotto S.p.A., **20 356–58**
Masayoshi Son, **13** 481–82
Mascan Corp., **IV** 697
Maschinenbauanstalt Humboldt AG, **III** 541
Maschinenfabrik Augsburg-Nürnberg. *See* M.A.N.
Maschinenfabrik Deutschland, **IV** 103
Maschinenfabrik für den Bergbau von Sievers & Co., **III** 541
Maschinenfabrik Gebr. Meer, **III** 565
Maschinenfabrik Sürth, **I** 581
Masco Corporation, **III 568–71**; **11** 385, 534–35; **12** 129, 131, 344; **13** 338; **18** 68; **20 359–63 (upd.)**; **39 263–68 (upd.)**
Masco Optical, **13** 165
Mascon Toy Co., **III** 569; **20** 360
MASCOR, **14** 13
Mase Westpac Limited, **11** 418
Maserati. *See* Officine Alfieri Maserati S.p.A.
Mashantucket Pequot Gaming Enterprise Inc., **35 282–85**
Masinfabriks A.B. Scania, **I** 197
MASkargo Ltd., **6** 101
Masland Corporation, **17 303–05**; **19** 408
Mason & Hamlin, **III** 656
Mason Best Co., **IV** 343
Masonite Corp., **III** 764
Masonite Holdings, **III** 687
Mass Rapid Transit Corp., **19** 111
Massachusetts Bank, **II** 207
Massachusetts Capital Resources Corp., **III** 314
Massachusetts Mutual Life Insurance Company, **III** 110, **285–87**, 305; **14** 14; **25** 528
Massachusetts Technology Development Corporation, **18** 570
Massachusetts's General Electric Company, **32** 267
Massey Burch Investment Grou Master Boot Polish Co., **II** 566
Master Builders, **I** 673
Master Electric Company, **15** 134
Master Glass & Color, **24** 159–60
Master Pneumatic Tool Co., **III** 436
Master Processing, **19** 37
Master Products, **14** 162
Master Shield Inc., **7** 116
Master Tank and Welding Company, **7** 541
MasterBrand Industries Inc., **12** 344–45
MasterCard International, Inc., **9 333–35**; **18** 337, 543; **25** 41; **26** 515; **41** 201
Mastercraft Homes, Inc., **11** 257
Mastercraft Industries Corp., **III** 654
Mastex Industries, **29** 132
Maszovlet. *See* Malév Plc.
Matador Records, **22** 194
Matairco, **9** 27
Matane Pulp & Paper Company, **17** 281
Matchbox Toys Ltd., **12** 168
MatchLogic, Inc., **41** 198
Matco Tools, **7** 116
Material Management and Services Inc., **28** 61
Materials Services Corp., **I** 58
Mathematica, Inc., **22** 291
Mather & Crother Advertising Agency, **I** 25
Mather Co., **I** 159
Mather Metals, **III** 582
Matheson & Co., **IV** 189
Mathews Conveyor Co., **14** 43
Mathieson Chemical Corp., **I** 379–80, 695; **13** 379
Matra, **II** 38, 70; **IV** 617–19; **13** 356; **17** 354; **24** 88
Matra Aerospace Inc., **22** 402
Matra-Hachette S.A., **15 293–97 (upd.)**; **21** 267
Matria Healthcare, Inc., **17 306–09**
Matrix Science Corp., **II** 8; **14** 27
Matson Navigation Company, Inc., **II** 490–91; **10** 40; **41** 399
Matsumoto Medical Instruments, Inc., **11** 476; **29** 455
Matsushita Electric Industrial Co., Ltd., **II** 5, **55–56**, 58, 61, 91–92, 102, 117–19, 361, 455; **III** 476, 710; **6** 36; **7** 163, 302; **10** 286, 389, 403, 432; **11** 487; **12** 448; **13** 398; **18** 18; **20** 81; **26** 511; **33** 432; **36** 399–400, 420
Matsushita Electric Works, Ltd., **III 710–11**; **7 302–03 (upd.)**; **12** 454; **16** 167; **27** 342
Matsushita Kotobuki Electronics Industries, Ltd., **10** 458–59
Matsuura Trading Co., Ltd., **IV** 327
Matsuzakaya Company, **V 129–31**
Mattatuck Bank & Trust Co., **13** 467
Mattel, Inc., **II** 136; **III** 506; **7 304–07**; **12** 74, 168–69, 495; **13** 560–61; **15** 238; **16** 264, 428; **17** 243; **18** 520–21; **25 311–15 (upd.)**, 381, 488; **27** 20, 373, 375; **28** 159; **29** 74, 78; **32** 187; **34** 369–70; **43** 229, 232–33
Matthes & Weber, **III** 32
Matthew Bender & Company, Inc., **IV** 677; **7** 94; **14** 97; **17** 486
Matthews International Corporation, **29 304–06**
Matthews Paint Co., **22** 437
Maud Foster Mill, **II** 566
Maui Electric Company, **9** 276
Maui Land & Pineapple Company, Inc., **29 307–09**
Mauna Kea Properties, **6** 129
Maurice H. Needham Co., **I** 31
Maus Frères, **19** 307
Maus-Nordmann, **V** 10; **19** 308
Max & Erma's Restaurants Inc., **19 258–60**
Max Factor & Co., **III** 54, 56; **6** 51; **12** 314
Max-Grundig-Stiftung, **27** 190–91
Max Klein, Inc., **II** 572
Max Media Properties LLC, **25** 419
Max Television Co., **25** 418
Maxcell Telecom Plus, **6** 323
Maxco Inc., **17 310–11**; **24** 159, 160
Maxell Corp., **I** 500; **14** 534
Maxi-Papier-Markt, **10** 498; **24** 270
Maxi Vac, Inc., **9** 72
Maxicare Health Plans, Inc., **III 84–86**; **25 316–19 (upd.)**
Maxie's of America, **25** 389
The Maxim Group, **25** 88, **320–22**
Maxim Integrated Products, Inc., **16 358–60**
MAXIMUS, Inc., **43 277–80**
Maxis Software, **13** 115
Maxoptix Corporation, **10** 404
Maxpro Sports Inc., **22** 458
Maxpro Systems, **24** 509–10
Maxtor Corporation, **6** 230; **10 403–05**, 459, 463–64
Maxus Energy Corporation, **IV** 410; **7 308–10**; **10** 191; **31** 456
Maxwell Communication Corporation plc, **IV** 605, 611, **641–43**; **7** 286, **311–13 (upd.)**, 343; **10** 288; **13** 91–93; **23** 350; **39** 49
Maxwell Morton Corp, **I** 144, 414
Maxwell Shoe Company, Inc., **30 310–12**
Maxwell Travel Inc., **33** 396
MAXXAM Inc., **IV** 121, 123; **8 348–50**
Maxxim Medical Inc., **12 325–27**
May and Baker, **I** 388
May & Speh Inc., **35** 17
The May Department Stores Company, **I** 540; **II** 414; **V 132–35**; **8** 288; **11** 349; **12** 55, 507–08; **13** 42, 361; **15** 275; **16** 62, 160, 206–07; **18** 414–15; **19 261–64 (upd.)**; **23** 345; **27** 61, 291, 346, 348; **33** 471, 473
Maybelline, **I** 684
Mayer & Schweitzer, **26** 66
Mayfair Foods, **I** 438; **16** 314
Mayfield Dairy Farms, Inc., **7** 128
Mayflower Group Inc., **6 409–11**; **15** 50
Mayne Nickless Ltd., **IV** 248
Mayo Foundation, **9 336–39**; **13** 326; **34 265–69 (upd.)**
Mayor's Jewelers, Inc., **41 254–57**
Maytag Corporation, **III 572–73**; **12** 252, 300; **21** 141; **22** 218, **348–51 (upd.)**; **23** 244; **42** 159; **43** 166
Mayville Metal Products Co., **I** 513

Mazda Motor Corporation, **I** 520; **II** 4, 361; **III** 603; **9 340–42**; **11** 86; **13** 414; **16** 322; **23 338–41 (upd.)**; **36** 215
Mazel Stores, Inc., **29 310–12**
MB Group, **20** 108
MBB. *See* Messerschmitt-Bölkow-Blohm.
MBC. *See* Middle East Broadcasting Centre, Ltd.
MBC Holding Company, **40 306–09**
MBE. *See* Mail Boxes Etc.
MBNA Corporation, **11** 123; **12 328–30**; **33 291–94 (upd.)**
MBPXL Corp., **II** 494
MC Distribution Services, Inc., **35** 298
MCA Inc., **II 143–45**; **6** 162–63; **10** 286; **11** 557; **17** 317; **21** 23, 25–26; **22** 131, 194; **23** 125; **25** 411; **26** 151, 314; **33** 431
McAfee Associates. *See* Network Associates, Inc.
The McAlpin Company, **19** 272
McAndrew & Forbes Holdings Inc., **23** 407; **26** 119
McArthur Glen Realty, **10** 122; **33** 59
MCC. *See* Morris Communications Corporation.
McCaffrey & McCall, **I** 33; **11** 496
McCain Feeds Ltd., **II** 484
McCain Foods, **41** 252
McCall Pattern Company, **22** 512; **23** 99
McCall Printing Co., **14** 460
McCall's Corp., **23** 393
McCann-Erickson Worldwide, **I** 10, 14, 16–17, 234; **6** 30; **10** 227; **14** 315; **16** 167; **18** 68; **22** 294; **32** 114
McCann-Erickson Hakuhodo, Ltd., **42** 174
McCarthy Milling, **II** 631; **27** 245–47
McCaughan Dyson and Co., **II** 189
McCaw Cellular Communications, Inc., **II** 331; **6** 274, **322–24**; **7** 15; **9** 320–21; **10** 433; **15** 125, 196; **27** 341, 343–44; **29** 44, 61; **36** 514–15; **43** 447
McClanahan Oil Co., **I** 341; **14** 216
McClatchy Newspapers, Inc., **23** 156, 158, **342–44**
McCleary, Wallin and Crouse, **19** 274
McClintic-Marshall, **IV** 36; **7** 49
The McCloskey Corporation, **8** 553
The McClure Syndicate, **25** 138
McColl-Frontenac Petroleum Inc., **IV** 439; **25** 232
McComb Manufacturing Co., **8** 287
McCormack & Dodge, **IV** 605; **11** 77
McCormick & Company, Incorporated, **7 314–16**; **17** 104, 106; **21** 497; **27 297–300 (upd.)**; **36** 185, 188
McCormick & Schmick's, **31** 41
McCormick Harvesting Machine Co., **I** 180; **II** 330
McCown De Leeuw & Co., **16** 510
McCracken Brooks, **23** 479; **25** 91
McCrory Stores, **II** 424; **9** 447–48; **13** 340
McCulloch Corp., **III** 436; **8** 348–49
McCullough Environmental Services, **12** 443
McDermott International, Inc., **III 558–60**; **37 242–46 (upd.)**
McDonald Glass Grocery Co. Inc., **II** 669
McDonald's Company (Japan) Ltd., **V** 205
McDonald's Corporation, **I** 23, 31, 129; **II** 500, 613–15 **646–48**; **III** 63, 94, 103; **6** 13; **7** 128, 266–67, 316, **317–19 (upd.)**, 435, 505–06; **8** 261–62, 564; **9** 74, 178, 290, 292, 305; **10** 122; **11** 82, 308; **12** 43, 180, 553; **13** 494; **14** 25, 32, 106, 195, 452–53; **16** 95–97, 289; **17** 69–71; **19** 85, 192, 214; **21** 25, 315, 362; **23** 505; **25** 179, 309, 387; **26 281–85 (upd.)**; **31** 278; **32** 442–44; **33** 240; **36** 517, 519–20; **39** 166, 168
McDonnell Douglas Corporation, **I** 41–43, 45, 48, 50–52, 54–56, 58–59, 61–62, 67–68, **70–72**, 76–77, 82, 84–85, 90, 105, 108, 111, 121–22, 321, 364, 490, 511; **II** 442; **III** 512, 654; **6** 68; **7** 456, 504; **8** 49–51, 315; **9** 18, 183, 206, 231, 271–72, 418, 458, 460; **10** 163–64, 317, 536; **11** 164–65, 267, **277–80 (upd.)**, 285, 363–65; **12** 190–91, 549; **13** 356; **15** 283; **16** 78, 94; **18** 368; **24** 84–85, 87; **28** 225; **32** 81, 83, 85
McDonough Co., **II** 16; **III** 502
McDougal, Littell & Company, **10** 357
McDowell Energy Center, **6** 543
McDowell Furniture Company, **10** 183
McDuff, **10** 305
McElligott Wright Morrison and White, **12** 511
McFadden Holdings L.P., **27** 41
McFadden Industries, **III** 21
McFadden Publishing, **6** 13
McGaughy, Marsha 584, **634–37**, 643, 656, 674; **10** 62; **12** 359; **13** 417; **18 325–30 (upd.)**; **26** 79; **27** 360
McGaw Inc., **11** 208
McGill Manufacturing, **III** 625
McGraw-Edison Co., **II** 17, 87
McGraw Electric Company. *See* Centel Corporation.
The McGraw-Hill Companies, Inc., **II** 398; **IV** 584, **634–37**, 643, 656, 674; **10** 62; **12** 359; **13** 417; **18 325–30 (upd.)**; **26** 79; **27** 360
McGregor Corporation, **6** 415; **26** 102
McGrew Color Graphics, **7** 430
MCI. *See* Manitou Costruzioni Industriali SRL. *or* Melamine Chemicals, Inc.
MCI Communications Corporation, **II** 408; **III** 13, 149, 684; **V 302–04**; **6** 51–52, 300, 322; **7** 118–19; **8** 310; **9** 171, 478–80; **10** 19, 80, 89, 97, 433, 500; **11** 59, 183, 185, 302, 409, 500; **12** 135–37; **13** 38; **14** 252–53, 260, 364; **15** 222; **16** 318; **18** 32, 112, 164–66, 569–70; **19** 255; **25** 358; **26** 102, 441; **27** 430; **29** 42
MCI WorldCom, Inc., **27 301–08 (upd.)**
McIlhenny Company, **20 364–67**
McIlwraith McEachern Limited, **27** 474
McJunkin Corp., **13** 79; **28** 61
McKechnie plc, **34 270–72**
McKee Foods Corporation, **7 320–21**; **27 309–11 (upd.)**
McKenna Metals Company, **13** 295–96
McKesson Corporation, **I** 413, **496–98**, 713; **II** 652; **III** 10; **6** 279; **8** 464; **9** 532; **11** 91; **12 331–33 (upd.)**; **16** 43; **18** 97; **37** 10; **41** 340
McKesson General Medical, **29** 299
McKinsey & Company, Inc., **I** 108, 144, 437, 497; **III** 47, 85, 670; **9 343–45**; **10** 175; **13** 138; **18** 68; **25** 34, 317; **26** 161
McLain Grocery, **II** 625
McLane America, Inc., **29** 481
McLane Company, Inc., **V** 217; **8** 556; **13 332–34**; **36** 269
McLaren Consolidated Cone Corp., **II** 543; **7** 366
McLaughlin Motor Company of Canada, **I** 171; **10** 325
McLean Clinic, **11** 379
McLeodUSA Incorporated, **32 327–30**; **38** 192
McLouth Steel Products, **13** 158
MCM Electronics, **9** 420
McMahan's Furniture Co., **14** 236
McMan Oil and Gas Co., **IV** 369
McManus, John & Adams, Inc., **6** 21
McMoCo, **IV** 82–83; **7** 187
McMoRan, **IV** 81–83; **V** 739; **7** 185, 187
McMullen & Yee Publishing, **22** 442
McMurtry Manufacturing, **8** 553
MCN Corporation, **6 519–22**; **13** 416; **17** 21–23
McNeil Corporation, **26** 363
McNeil Laboratories, **III** 35–36; **8** 282–83
McNellan Resources Inc., **IV** 76
MCO Holdings Inc., **8** 348–49
MCorp, **10** 134; **11** 122
McPaper AG, **29** 152
McQuay International. *See* AAF-McQuay Incorporated.
McRae's, Inc., **19** 324–25; **41** 343–44
MCS, Inc., **10** 412
MCSi, Inc., **41 258–60**
MCT Dairies, Inc., **18** 14–16
McTeigue & Co., **14** 502
McVitie & Price, **II** 592–93
McWhorter Inc., **8** 553; **27** 280
MD Distribution Inc., **15** 139
MD Pharmaceuticals, **III** 10
MDC. *See* Mead Data Central, Inc.
MDI Co., Ltd., **IV** 327
MDS/Bankmark, **10** 247
MDU Resources Group, Inc., **7 322–25**; **42 249–53 (upd.)**
The Mead Corporation, **IV 310–13**, 327, 329, 342–43; **8** 267; **9** 261; **10** 406; **11** 421–22; **17** 399; **19 265–69 (upd.)**; **20** 18; **33** 263, 265
Mead Cycle Co., **IV** 660
Mead Data Central, Inc., **IV** 312; **7** 581; **10 406–08**; **19** 268. *See also* LEXIS-NEXIS Group.
Mead John & Co., **19** 103
Mead Johnson, **III** 17
Mead Packaging, **12** 151
Meade County Rural Electric Cooperative Corporation, **11** 37
Meade Instruments Corporation, **41 261–64**
Meadow Gold Dairies, Inc., **II** 473
Meadowcraft, Inc., **29 313–15**
Means Services, Inc., **II** 607
Mears & Phillips, **II** 237
Measurex Corporation, **8** 243; **14** 56; **38** 227
Mebetoys, **25** 312
MEC - Hawaii, UK & USA, **IV** 714
MECA Software, Inc., **18** 363
Mecair, S.p.A., **17** 147
Mecca Leisure PLC, **I** 248; **12** 229; **32** 243
Mechanics Exchange Savings Bank, **9** 173
Mechanics Machine Co., **III** 438; **14** 63
Mecklermedia Corporation, **24 328–30**; **26** 441; **27** 360, 362
Medal Distributing Co., **9** 542
Medallion Pictures Corp., **9** 320
Medar, Inc., **17** 310–11

Medco Containment Services Inc., 9 346–48; 11 291; 12 333
Medcom Inc., I 628
Medeco Security Locks, Inc., 10 350
Medfield Corp., III 87
Medford, Inc., 19 467–68
Medi Mart Drug Store Company. *See* The Stop & Shop Companies, Inc.
Media Arts Group, Inc., 42 254–57
Media Exchange International, 25 509
Media General, Inc., III 214; **7 326–28**; 18 61; 23 225; **38 306–09 (upd.)**
Media Groep West B.V., 23 271
Media News Corporation, 25 507
Media Play. *See* Musicland Stores Corporation.
MediaBay, 41 61
Mediacom Inc., 25 373
Mediamark Research, 28 501, 504
Mediamatics, Inc., 26 329
MediaOne Group Inc. *See* U S West, Inc.
MEDIC Computer Systems, 16 94
Medical Care America, Inc., 15 112, 114; 35 215–17
Medical Development Corp. *See* Cordis Corp.
Medical Development Services, Inc., 25 307
Medical Economics Data, 23 211
Medical Expense Fund, III 245
Medical Indemnity of America, 10 160
Medical Innovations Corporation, 21 46
Medical Marketing Group Inc., 9 348
Medical Service Assoc. of Pennsylvania, III 325–26
Medical Tribune Group, IV 591; 20 53
Medicare-Glaser, 17 167
Medicine Bow Coal Company, 7 33–34
Medicine Shoppe International. *See* Cardinal Health, Inc.
Medicor, Inc., 36 496
Medicus Intercon International, 6 22
Medifinancial Solutions, Inc., 18 370
MedImmune, Inc., 35 286–89
Medinol Ltd., 37 39
Mediobanca Banca di Credito Finanziario SpA, II 191, 271; III 208–09; 11 205
The Mediplex Group, Inc., III 16; 11 282
Medis Health and Pharmaceuticals Services Inc., II 653
Medite Corporation, 19 467–68
Meditrust, 11 281–83
Medlabs Inc., III 73
MedPartners, 36 367
Medtech, Ltd., 13 60–62
Medtronic, Inc., 8 351–54; 11 459; 18 421; 19 103; 22 359–61; 26 132; **30 313–17 (upd.)**; 37 39; 43 349
Medusa Corporation, 8 135; **24 331–33**; 30 156
Mees & Hope, II 184
The MEGA Life and Health Insurance Co., 33 418–20
MEGA Natural Gas Company, 11 28
MegaBingo, Inc., 41 273, 275
Megafoods Stores Inc., 13 335–37; 17 560
Megasource, Inc., 16 94
Meggitt PLC, 34 273–76
MEI Diversified Inc., 18 455
Mei Foo Investments Ltd., IV 718; 38 319
Meier & Frank Co., 23 345–47
Meijer Incorporated, 7 329–31; 15 449; 17 302; **27 312–15 (upd.)**
Meiji Commerce Bank, II 291
Meiji Fire Insurance Co., III 384–85
Meiji Milk Products Company, Limited, II 538–39
Meiji Mutual Life Insurance Company, II 323; **III 288–89**
Meiji Seika Kaisha, Ltd., I 676; **II 540–41**
Meikosha Co., II 72
Meinecke Muffler Company, III 495; 10 415
Meineke Discount Muffler Shops, 38 208
Meis of Illiana, 10 282
Meisei Electric, III 742
Meisel. *See* Samuel Meisel & Co.
Meisenzahl Auto Parts, Inc., 24 205
Meissner, Ackermann & Co., IV 463; 7 351
Meister, Lucious and Company, 13 262
Meiwa Manufacturing Co., III 758
N.V. Mekog, IV 531
Mel Farr Automotive Group, 20 368–70
Mel Klein and Partners, III 74
Melaleuca Inc., 31 326–28
Melamine Chemicals, Inc., 27 316–18
Melbourne Engineering Co., 23 83
Melbur China Clay Co., III 690
Melco, II 58
Meldisco. *See* Footstar, Incorporated.
Melkunie-Holland, II 575
Mellbank Security Co., II 316
Mello Smello. *See* The Miner Group International.
Mellon Bank Corporation, I 67–68, 584; **II 315–17**, 342, 402; III 275; 9 470; 13 410–11; 18 112
Mellon Financial Corporation, 42 76
Mellon Indemnity Corp., III 258–59; 24 177
Mellon-Stuart Co., I 584–85; 14 334
Melmarkets, 24 462
Mélotte, III 418
Meloy Laboratories, Inc., 11 333
Melroe Company, 8 115–16; 34 46
Melville Corporation, V 136–38; 9 192; 13 82, 329–30; 14 426; 15 252–53;, 16 390; 19 449; 21 526; 23 176; 24 167, 290; 35 253
Melvin Simon and Associates, Inc., 8 355–57; 26 262
Melwire Group, III 673
MEM, 37 270–71
Memco, 12 48
Memorex Corp., III 110, 166; 6 282–83
Memphis International Motorsports Corporation Inc., 43 139–40
The Men's Wearhouse, Inc., 17 312–15; 21 311
Menasco Manufacturing Co., I 435; III 415
Menasha Corporation, 8 358–61
Menck, 8 544
Mendelssohn & Co., II 241
Meneven, IV 508
Menka Gesellschaft, IV 150; 24 357
The Mennen Company, I 19; 6 26; 14 122; 18 69; 35 113
Mental Health Programs Inc., 15 122
The Mentholatum Company Inc., IV 722; **32 331–33**
Mentor Corporation, 26 286–88
Mentor Graphics Corporation, III 143; 8 519; 11 46–47, **284–86**, 490; 13 128
MEPC plc, IV 710–12
Mepco/Electra Inc., 13 398
MeraBank, 6 546
MERBCO, Inc., 33 456
Mercantile Agency, IV 604
Mercantile and General Reinsurance Co., III 335, 377
Mercantile Bancorporation Inc., 33 155
Mercantile Bank, II 298
Mercantile Bankshares Corp., 11 287–88
Mercantile Credit Co., 16 13
Mercantile Estate and Property Corp. Ltd., IV 710
Mercantile Fire Insurance, III 234
Mercantile Mutual, III 310
Mercantile Property Corp. Ltd., IV 710
Mercantile Security Life, III 136
Mercantile Stores Company, Inc., V 139; **19 270–73 (upd.)**
Mercantile Trust Co., II 229, 247
Mercator & Noordstar N.V., 40 61
Mercedes Benz. *See* Daimler-Benz A.G.
Mercedes Benz of North America, 22 52
Merchant Bank Services, 18 516, 518
Merchant Co., III 104
Merchant Distributors, Inc., 20 306
Merchants & Farmers Bank of Ecru, 14 40
Merchants Bank, II 213
Merchants Bank & Trust Co., 21 524
Merchants Bank of Canada, II 210
Merchants Bank of Halifax, II 344
Merchants Dispatch, II 395–96; 10 60
Merchants Distributors Inc. *See* Alex Lee Inc.
Merchants Fire Assurance Corp., III 396–97
Merchants Home Delivery Service, 6 414
Merchants Indemnity Corp., III 396–97
Merchants Life Insurance Co., III 275
Merchants National Bank, 9 228; 14 528; 17 135
Merchants National Bank of Boston, II 213
Merchants Union Express Co., II 396; 10 60
Merchants' Assoc., II 261
Merchants' Loan and Trust, II 261; III 518
Merchants' Savings, Loan and Trust Co., II 261
Mercier, I 272
Merck & Co., Inc., I 640, 646, **650–52**, 683–84, 708; II 414; III 42, 60, 66, 299; 8 154, 548; 10 213; 11 9, 90, **289–91 (upd.)**; 12 325, 333; 14 58, 422; 15 154; 16 440; 20 39, 59; 26 126; **34 280–85 (upd.)**; 36 91, 93, 305; 38 380
Mercury Air Group, Inc., 20 371–73
Mercury Asset Management (MAM), 14 420; 40 313
Mercury Communications, Ltd., V 280–82; **7 332–34**; 10 456; 11 547–48; 25 101–02; 27 365
Mercury General Corporation, 25 323–25
Mercury, Inc., 8 311
Mercury Mail, Inc., 22 519, 522
Mercury Records, 13 397; 23 389, 391
Mercury Telecommunications Limited, 15 67, 69
Meredith and Drew, II 593
Meredith Corporation, IV 661–62; **11 292–94**; 17 394; 18 239; 23 393; **29 316–19 (upd.)**
Merfin International, 42 53
Merial, 34 284
Merico, Inc., 36 161–64

Meridian Bancorp, Inc., **11 295–97**; **17** 111, 114
Meridian Emerging Markets Ltd., **25** 509
Meridian Healthcare, **18** 197
Meridian Insurance Co., **III** 332
Meridian Investment and Development Corp., **22** 189
Meridian Oil Inc., **10** 190–91
Meridian Publishing, Inc., **28** 254
Merillat Industries Inc., **III** 570; **13 338–39**; **20** 362; **39** 266, 268
Merisel, Inc., **10** 518–19; **12 334–36**; **13** 174, 176, 482
Merit Distribution Services, **13** 333
Merit Medical Systems, Inc., **29 320–22**; **36** 497
Merit Tank Testing, Inc., **IV** 411
Merita/Cotton's Bakeries, **38** 251
Meritage Corporation, **26 289–92**
MeritaNordbanken, **40** 336
Meritor Automotive Inc., **43** 328
Merivienti Oy, **IV** 276
Merix Corporation, **36 329–31**
Merkur Direktwerbegesellschaft, **29** 152
Merla Manufacturing, **I** 524
Merlin Gérin, **II** 93–94; **18** 473; **19** 165
Merpati Nusantara Airlines, **6** 90–91
Merrell, **22** 173
Merrell Dow, **16** 438
Merrell Drug, **I** 325
Merrell-Soule Co., **II** 471
Merriam and Morgan Paraffine Co., **IV** 548
Merriam-Webster, Inc., **7** 165, 167; **23** 209–10; **39** 140, 143
Merrill Corporation, **18 331–34**
Merrill Gas Company, **9** 554
Merrill Lynch & Co., Inc., **I** 26, 339, 681, 683, 697; **II** 149, 257, 260, 268, 403, 407–08, 412, **424–26**, 441, 445, 449, 451, 456, 654–55, 680; **III** 119, 253, 340, 440; **6** 244; **7** 130; **8** 94; **9** 125, 187, 239, 301, 386; **11** 29, 122, 348, 557; **13** 44, 125, **340–43 (upd.)**, 448–49, 512; **14** 65; **15** 463; **16** 195; **17** 137; **21** 68–70, 145; **22** 404–06, 542; **23** 370; **25** 89–90, 329; **29** 295; **32** 14, 168; **40 310–15 (upd.)**
Merrill, Pickard, Anderson & Eyre IV, **11** 490
Merrill Publishing, **IV** 643; **7** 312; **9** 63; **29** 57
Merrimack Services Corp., **37** 303
Merry-Go-Round Enterprises, Inc., **8 362–64**; **24** 27
Merry Group, **III** 673
Merry Maids, **6** 46; **23** 428, 430
Merryhill Schools, Inc., **37** 279
The Mersey Docks and Harbour Company, **30 318–20**
Mersey Paper Co., **IV** 258
Mersey White Lead Co., **III** 680
Merv Griffin Enterprises, **II** 137; **12** 75; **22** 431
Mervyn's, **V** 43–44; **10 409–10**; **13** 526; **18** 136–37; **27** 452
Mervyn's California, **39 269–71 (upd.)**
Mesa Air Group, Inc., **32 334–37 (upd.)**
Mesa Airlines, Inc., **11 298–300**
Mesa LP, **IV** 410, 523; **11** 441; **40** 357
Mesa Petroleum, **IV** 392, 571; **24** 521, 522; **27** 217
Mesaba Holdings, Inc., **I** 448; **22** 21; **28 265–67**
Messageries du Livre, **IV** 614
Messerschmitt-Bölkow-Blohm GmbH., **I** 41–42, 46, 51–52, 55, **73–75**, 111; **II** 242; **III** 539; **11** 267; **24** 86
Messner, Vetere, Berger, Carey, Schmetterer, **13** 204
Mesta Machine Co., **22** 415
Mestek, Inc., **10 411–13**
Met Food Corp. *See* White Rose Food Corp.
Met-Mex Penoles. *See* Industrias Penoles, S.A. de C.V.
META Group, Inc., **37** 147
Metabio-Joullie, **III** 47
Metaframe Corp., **25** 312
Metal Box plc, **I 604–06**; **20** 108
Metal-Cal. *See* Avery Dennison Corporation.
Metal Casting Technology, Inc., **23** 267, 269
Metal Closures, **I** 615
Metal Industries, **I** 531–32
Metal Manufactures, **III** 433–34
Metal Office Furniture Company, **7** 493
Metales y Contactos, **29** 461–62
Metaleurop S.A., **IV** 108–09; **21 368–71**
MetalExchange, **26** 530
Metall Mining Corp., **IV** 141; **27** 456
Metallgesellschaft AG, **IV** 17, **139–42**, 229; **16 361–66 (upd.)**
MetalOptics Inc., **19** 212
MetalPro, Inc., **IV** 168
Metals and Controls Corp., **II** 113
Metals Exploration, **IV** 82
Metalurgica Mexicana Penoles, S.A. *See* Industrias Penoles, S.A. de C.V.
Metaphase Technology, Inc., **10** 257
Metcalf & Eddy Companies, Inc., **6** 143, 441; **32** 52
Meteor Film Productions, **23** 391
Meteor Industries Inc., **33 295–97**
Methane Development Corporation, **6** 457
Methanex Corporation, **12** 365; **19** 155–56; **40 316–19**
Methode Electronics, Inc., **13 344–46**
Metinox Steel Ltd., **IV** 203
MetLife General Insurance Agency, **III** 293
MetLife HealthCare, **36** 366
MetMor Financial, Inc., **III** 293
Meto AG, **39** 79
MetPath, Inc., **III** 684; **26** 390
Metra Steel, **19** 381
Metrastock Ltd., **34** 5
Metric Constructors, Inc., **16** 286
Metric Systems, Inc., **18** 513
Metris Companies, **25** 41
Metro AG, **23** 311
Metro Distributors Inc., **14** 545
Metro Drug Corporation, **II** 649–50; **18** 181
Metro Glass, **II** 533
Metro-Goldwyn-Mayer Inc., **25** 173, 253, **326–30 (upd.)**; **33**
Metro Holding AG, **38** 266
Metro Information Services, Inc., **36 332–34**
Metro International SA, **36** 335
Metro-Mark Integrated Systems Inc., **11** 469
Metro-North Commuter Railroad Company, **35** 292
Metro Pacific, **18** 180, 182
Metro-Richelieu Inc., **II** 653
Metro Southwest Construction. *See* CRSS Inc.
Metro Vermögensverwaltung GmbH & Co. of Dusseldorf, **V** 104
Metro-Verwegensverwaltung, **II** 257
Metrocall, Inc., **18** 77; **39** 25; **41 265–68**
Metrol Security Services, Inc., **32** 373
Metroland Printing, Publishing and Distributing Ltd., **29** 471
Metromail Corp., **IV** 661; **18** 170; **38** 370
Metromedia Companies, **II** 171; **6** 33, 168–69; **7** 91, **335–37**; **14 298–300**
Metropolitan Accident Co., **III** 228
Metropolitan Bank, **II** 221, 318; **III** 239; **IV** 644; **17** 323
Metropolitan Baseball Club Inc., **39 272–75**
Metropolitan Broadcasting Corporation, **7** 335
Metropolitan Clothing Co., **19** 362
Metropolitan Distributors, **9** 283
Metropolitan District Railway Company, **6** 406
Metropolitan Edison Company, **27** 182
Metropolitan Estate and Property Corp. Ltd., **IV** 710–11
Metropolitan Financial Corporation, **12** 165; **13 347–49**
Metropolitan Furniture Leasing, **14** 4
Metropolitan Gas Light Co., **6** 455
Metropolitan Housing Corp. Ltd., **IV** 710
Metropolitan Life Insurance Company, **II** 679; **III** 265–66, 272, **290–94**, 313, 329, 337, 339–40, 706; **IV** 283; **6** 256; **8** 326–27; **11** 482; **22** 266; **25** 300; **42** 194
Metropolitan National Bank, **II** 284
Metropolitan Opera Association, Inc., **40 320–23**
Metropolitan Petroleum Corp., **IV** 180–81; **19** 319
Metropolitan Railway, **6** 407
Metropolitan Railways Surplus Lands Co., **IV** 711
Metropolitan Reference Laboratories Inc., **26** 391
Metropolitan Tobacco Co., **15** 138
Metropolitan Transportation Authority, **35 290–92**
Metropolitan Vickers, **III** 670
METSA, Inc., **15** 363
Metsä-Serla Oy, **IV 314–16**, 318, 350
Metso Corporation, **30 321–25 (upd.)**
Mettler-Toledo International Inc., **30 326–28**
Mettler United States Inc., **9** 441
Metwest, **26** 391
Metz Baking Company, **36** 164
Metzdorf Advertising Agency, **30** 80
Metzeler Kautschuk, **15** 354
Mexican Eagle Oil Co., **IV** 365, 531
Mexican Metal Co. *See* Industrias Penoles, S.A. de C.V.
Mexican Original Products, Inc., **II** 585; **14** 515
Mexican Restaurants, Inc., **41 269–71**
Mexofina, S.A. de C.V., **IV** 401
Meyer and Charlton, **IV** 90
Meyer Brothers Drug Company, **16** 212
Meyer Corporation, **27** 288
Meyerland Company, **19** 366
Meyers and Co., **III** 9
Meyers & Muldoon, **6** 40
Meyers Motor Supply, **26** 347

Meyers Parking, **18** 104
Meyr Melnhof Karton AG, **41** 325–27
Meyrin, **I** 122
MFI, **II** 612
MFS Communications Company, Inc., 11 301–03; **14** 253; **27** 301, 307
MG&E. *See* Madison Gas & Electric.
MG Holdings. *See* Mayflower Group Inc.
MG Ltd., **IV** 141
MGD Graphics Systems. *See* Goss Holdings, Inc.
MGM. *See* McKesson General Medical.
MGM Grand Inc., III 431; **6** 210; **17 316–19**; **18** 336–37
MGM Mirage. *See* Mirage Resorts, Incorporated.
MGM/UA Communications Company, I 286, 487; **II** 103, 135, **146–50**, 155, 161, 167, 169, 174–75, 408; **IV** 676; **6** 172–73; **12** 73, 316, 323, 455; **15** 84; **17** 316. *See also* Metro-Goldwyn-Mayer Inc.
MH Alshaya Group, **28** 96
mh Bausparkasse AG, **III** 377
MH Media Monitoring Limited, **26** 270
MHI Group, Inc., **13** 356; **16** 344
MHS Holding Corp., **26** 101
MHT. *See* Manufacturers Hanover Trust Co.
MI. *See* Masco Corporation.
Miami Computer Supply Corporation. *See* MCSi, Inc.
Miami Power Corporation, **6** 466
Miami Subs Corp., **29** 342, 344
Micamold Electronics Manufacturing Corporation, **10** 319
Mich-Wis. *See* Michigan Wisconsin Pipe Line.
Michael Anthony Jewelers, Inc., 24 334–36
Michael Baker Corp., 14 333–35
MICHAEL Business Systems Plc, **10** 257
Michael Foods, Inc., 25 331–34; **39** 319–321
Michael Joseph, **IV** 659
Michael Reese Health Plan Inc., **III** 82
Michael's Fair-Mart Food Stores, Inc., **19** 479
Michaels Stores, Inc., 17 320–22, 360; **25** 368
MichCon. *See* MCN Corporation.
Michelin, **III** 697; **7** 36–37; **8** 74; **11** 158, 473; **20** 261–62; **21** 72, 74; **28** 372. *See also* Compagnie Générale des Établissements Michelin.
Michelin et Compagnie, **V** 236
Michiana Merchandising, **III** 10
Michie Co., **IV** 312; **19** 268; **33** 264–65
Michigan Automotive Compressor, Inc., **III** 593, 638–39
Michigan Automotive Research Corporation, **23** 183
Michigan Bell Telephone Co., 14 336–38; **18** 30
Michigan Carpet Sweeper Company, **9** 70
Michigan Consolidated Gas Company. *See* MCN Corporation.
Michigan Fruit Canners, **II** 571
Michigan General, **II** 408
Michigan International Speedway, **V** 494
Michigan Livestock Exchange, **36** 442
Michigan Motor Freight Lines, **14** 567
Michigan National Corporation, 11 304–06; **18** 517
Michigan Oil Company, **18** 494
Michigan Packaging Company, **15** 188
Michigan Plating and Stamping Co., **I** 451
Michigan Radiator & Iron Co., **III** 663
Michigan Shoe Makers. *See* Wolverine World Wide Inc.
Michigan Spring Company, **17** 106
Michigan State Life Insurance Co., **III** 274
Michigan Steel Corporation, **12** 352
Michigan Tag Company, **9** 72
Michigan Wisconsin Pipe Line, **39** 260
Mick's Inc., **30** 329
Mickey Shorr Mobile Electronics, **10** 9–11
Micro-Circuit, Inc., **III** 645
Micro D, Inc., **11** 194
Micro Decisionware, Inc., **10** 506
Micro Focus Inc., **27** 491
Micro Magic, Inc., **43** 254
Micro Peripherals, Inc., **18** 138
Micro-Power Corp., **III** 643
Micro Power Systems Inc., **14** 183
Micro Switch, **14** 284
Micro/Vest, **13** 175
Micro Warehouse, Inc., 16 371–73
MicroAge, Inc., 16 367–70; **29** 414
Microamerica, **12** 334
Microban Products Company, **27** 288
MicroBilt Corporation, **11** 112
Microcom, Inc., **26** 93
MicroComputer Accessories, **III** 614
Microcomputer Asset Management Services, **9** 168
Microcomputer Systems, **22** 389
Microdot Inc., I 440; **8 365–68**, 545
Microfal, **I** 341
Microform International Marketing Corp., **IV** 642; **7** 312
Microfral, **14** 216
Micromass Ltd., **43** 455
Micromedex, **19** 268
Micron Technology, Inc., III 113; **11 307–09**; **29 323–26 (upd.)**
Micropolis Corp., **10** 403, 458, 463
MicroPro International Corp., **10** 556. *See also* The Learning Company Inc.
Microprocessor Systems, **13** 235
Microprose Inc., **24** 538
Micros Systems, Inc., 18 335–38
Microseal Corp., **I** 341
Microsensor Systems Inc., **43** 366
Microsoft Corporation, III 116; **6** 219–20, 224, 227, 231, 235, 254–56, **257–60**, 269–71; **9** 81, 140, 171, 195, 472; **10** 22, 34, 57, 87, 119, 237–38, 362–63, 408, 477, 484, 504, 557–58; **11** 59, 77–78, 306, 519–20; **12** 180, 335; **13** 115, 128, 147, 482, 509; **14** 262–64, 318; **15** 132–33, 321, 371, 483, 492, 511; **16** 4, 94, 367, 392, 394, 444; **18** 24, 64, 66, 306–7, 345, 349, 367, 541, 543; **19** 310; **20** 237; **21** 86; **24** 120, 233, 236, 371; **25** 21, 32, 34, 96, 117, 119, 184, 298–301, 498–99, 509; **26** 17, 294–95, 441, 520; **27 319–23 (upd.)**, 448, 517; **28** 245, 301; **29** 65, 439; **30** 391, 450; **33** 115–16, 210; **34** 443, 445, 513; **36** 384; **37** 383; **38** 71, 416; **41** 53–54; **42** 424; **43** 240
Microsoft Network, **38** 270–71
Microtek, Inc., **22** 413
Microtel Limited, **6** 309–10
Microware Surgical Instruments Corp., **IV** 137
Microwave Communications, Inc., **V** 302; **27** 302
Mid-America Capital Resources, Inc., **6** 508
Mid-America Dairymen, Inc., II 536; **7 338–40**; **11** 24; **21** 342; **22** 95; **26** 448
Mid-America Industries, **III** 495
Mid-America Interpool Network, **6** 506, 602
Mid-America Packaging, Inc., **8** 203
Mid-America Tag & Label, **8** 360
Mid Bus Inc., **33** 107
Mid-Central Fish and Frozen Foods Inc., **II** 675
Mid-Continent Area Power Planner, **V** 672
Mid-Continent Computer Services, **11** 111
Mid-Continent Life Insurance Co., **23** 200
Mid-Continent Telephone Corporation. *See* Alltel Corporation.
Mid-Georgia Gas Company, **6** 448
Mid-Illinois Gas Co., **6** 529
Mid-Pacific Airlines, **9** 271; **24** 21–22
Mid-Packaging Group Inc., **19** 78
Mid-South Towing, **6** 583
Mid-States Development, Inc., **18** 405
Mid-Texas Communications Systems, **6** 313
Mid-Valley Dairy, **14** 397
Mid-West Drive-In Theatres Inc., **I** 245
Mid-West Paper Ltd., **IV** 286
MidAmerican Communications Corporation, **8** 311
Midas International Corporation, I 457–58; **10 414–15**, 554; **24** 337
MIDCO, **III** 340
MidCon, **IV** 481; **25** 363
Middle East Broadcasting Centre, Ltd., **25** 506, 508
Middle East Tube Co. Ltd., **25** 266
Middle South Utilities, **V** 618–19
Middle West Corporation, **6** 469–70
Middle West Utilities Company, **V** 583–84; **6** 555–56, 604–05; **14** 227; **21** 468–69
Middle Wisconsin Power, **6** 604
Middleburg Steel and Alloys Group, **I** 423
The Middleby Corporation, 22 352–55
Middlesex Bank, **II** 334
Middleton Packaging, **12** 377
Middleton's Starch Works, **II** 566
Middletown Manufacturing Co., Inc., **16** 321
Middletown National Bank, **13** 467
Midhurst Corp., **IV** 658
Midial, **II** 478
Midland Bank plc, II 208, 236, 279, 295, 298, **318–20**, 334, 383; **9** 505; **12** 257; **14** 169; **17 323–26 (upd.)**; **19** 198; **26** 202; **33** 395
Midland Brick, **14** 250
Midland Cooperative, **II** 536
Midland Counties Dairies, **II** 587
Midland Electric Coal Co., **IV** 170
Midland Enterprises Inc., **6** 486–88
Midland Gravel Co., **III** 670
Midland Independent Newspaper plc, **23** 351
Midland Industrial Finishes Co., **I** 321
Midland Insurance, **I** 473
Midland International, **8** 56–57
Midland Investment Co., **II** 7
Midland Linseed Products Co., **I** 419
Midland National Bank, **11** 130
Midland Railway Co., **II** 306

Midland-Ross Corporation, **14** 369
Midland Southwest Corp., **8** 347
Midland Steel Products Co., **13** 305–06
Midland United, **6** 556; **25** 89
Midland Utilities Company, **6** 532
Midlands Electricity, **13** 485
Midlands Energy Co., **IV** 83; **7** 188
Midlantic Corp., **13** 411
Midlantic Hotels Ltd., **41** 83
Midrange Performance Group, **12** 149
Midrex Corp., **IV** 130
Midvale Steel and Ordnance Co., **IV** 35, 114; **7** 48
Midway Airlines Corporation, **6** 105, 120–21; **33 301–03**
Midway Games, Inc., **25 335–38**
Midway Manufacturing Company, **III** 430; **15** 539
Midwest Agri-Commodities Company, **11** 15; **32** 29
Midwest Air Charter, **6** 345
Midwest Biscuit Company, **14** 306
Midwest Com of Indiana, Inc., **11** 112
Midwest Dairy Products, **II** 661
Midwest Express Holdings, Inc., **35 293–95**; **43** 258
Midwest Federal Savings & Loan Association, **11** 162–63
Midwest Financial Group, Inc., **8** 188
Midwest Foundry Co., **IV** 137
Midwest Manufacturing Co., **12** 296
Midwest Realty Exchange, Inc., **21** 257
Midwest Refining Co., **IV** 368
Midwest Resources Inc., **6 523–25**
Midwest Staffing Systems, **27** 21
Midwest Steel Corporation, **13** 157
Midwest Synthetics, **8** 553
Midwinter, **12** 529
Miele & Cie., **III** 418
MIG Realty Advisors, Inc., **25** 23, 25
Miguel Galas S.A., **17** 268
MIH Limited, **31 329–32**
Mikasa, Inc., **28 268–70**
Mike-Sell's Inc., **15 298–300**
Mikemitch Realty Corp., **16** 36
Mikko, **II** 70
Mikko Kaloinen Oy, **IV** 349
Mikohn Gaming Corporation, **39 276–79**
Mikon, Ltd., **13** 345
Milac, **27** 259
Milani Foods, **II** 556; **36** 24
Milbank Insurance Co., **III** 350
Milbank, Tweed, Hadley & McCloy, **27 324–27**
Milbank, Tweed, Hope & Webb, **II** 471
Milcor Steel Co., **IV** 114
Miles Druce & Co., **III** 494
Miles Inc., **22** 148
Miles Kimball Co., **9** 393
Miles Laboratories, **I** 310, **653–55**, 674, 678; **6** 50; **13** 76; **14** 558
Miles Redfern, **I** 429
Milgo Electronic Corp., **II** 83; **11** 408
Milgram Food Stores Inc., **II** 682
Milgray Electronics, **19** 311
Milk Producers, Inc., **11** 24
Milk Specialties Co., **12** 199
Mill-Power Supply Company, **27** 129–30
Millbrook Press Inc., **IV** 616
Millennium Chemicals Inc., **30** 231
Miller Brewing Company, **I** 218–19, 236–37, 254–55, 257–58, **269–70**, 283, 290–91, 548; **10** 100; **11** 421; **12 337–39 (upd.)**, 372; **13** 10, 258; **15** 429; **17** 256; **18** 70, 72, 418, 499, 501; **21** 230; **22** 199, 422; **26** 303, 306; **27** 374; **28** 209–10; **34** 36–37; **36** 12–15
Miller Chemical & Fertilizer Corp., **I** 412
Miller Companies, **17** 182
Miller Container Corporation, **8** 102
Miller Freeman, Inc., **IV** 687; **27** 362; **28** 501, 504
Miller Group Ltd., **22** 282
Miller Industries, Inc., **26 293–95**
Miller, Mason and Dickenson, **III** 204–05
Miller, Tabak, Hirsch & Co., **13** 394; **28** 164
Millet, **39** 250
Millet's Leisure, **V** 177–78
Millicom, **11** 547; **18** 254
Milliken & Co., **V 366–68**; **8** 270–71; **17 327–30 (upd.)**; **29** 246
Milliken, Tomlinson Co., **II** 682
Millipore Corporation, **9** 396; **23** 284; **25 339–43**; **43** 454
Mills Clothing, Inc. *See* The Buckle, Inc.
Millstone Point Company, **V** 668–69
Millville Electric Light Company, **6** 449
Millway Foods, **25** 85
Milne Fruit Products, Inc., **25** 366
Milner, **III** 98
Milsco Manufacturing Co., **23** 299, 300
Milton Bradley Company, **III** 504–06; **16** 267; **17** 105; **21 372–75**; **25** 380; **43** 229, 232
Milton Light & Power Company, **12** 45
Milton Roy Co., **8** 135
Milupa S.A., **37** 341
Milwaukee Brewers Baseball Club, **37 247–49**
Milwaukee Cheese Co. Inc., **25** 517
Milwaukee Electric Manufacturing Co., **III** 534
Milwaukee Electric Railway and Light Company, **6** 601–02, 604–05
Milwaukee Electric Tool, **28** 40
Milwaukee Insurance Co., **III** 242
Milwaukee Mutual Fire Insurance Co., **III** 321
Minatome, **IV** 560
Mindport, **31** 329
Mindset Corp., **42** 424–25
Mindspring Enterprises, Inc., **36** 168
Mine Safety Appliances Company, **31 333–35**
Minemet Recherche, **IV** 108
The Miner Group International, **22 356–58**
Mineral Point Public Service Company, **6** 604
Minerales y Metales, S.A. *See* Industrias Penoles, S.A. de C.V.
Minerals & Chemicals Philipp, **IV** 79–80
Minerals & Metals Trading Corporation of India Ltd., **IV 143–44**
Minerals and Resources Corporation Limited, **IV** 23; **13** 502. *See also* Minorco.
Minerals Technologies Inc., **11 310–12**
Minerec Corporation, **9** 363
Minerva, **III** 359
Minerve, **6** 208
Mines et Usines du Nord et de l'Est, **IV** 226
Minet Group, **III** 357; **22** 494–95
Mini Stop, **V** 97
Mining and Technical Services, **IV** 67
Mining Corp. of Canada Ltd., **IV** 164
Mining Development Corp., **IV** 239–40
Mining Trust Ltd., **IV** 32
MiniScribe, Inc., **6** 230; **10** 404
Minister of Finance Inc., **IV** 519
Minitel, **21** 233
Minivator Ltd., **11** 486
Minneapolis General Electric of Minnesota, **V** 670
Minneapolis Heat Regulator Co., **II** 40–41; **12** 246
Minneapolis-Honeywell Regulator Co., **II** 40–41, 86; **8** 21; **12** 247; **22** 427
Minneapolis Millers Association, **10** 322
Minneapolis Steel and Machinery Company, **21** 502
Minnesota Brewing Company. *See* MBC Holding Company.
Minnesota Cooperative Creamery Association, Inc., **II** 535; **21** 340
Minnesota Linseed Oil Co., **8** 552
Minnesota Mining & Manufacturing Company, **I** 28, 387, **499–501**; **II** 39; **III** 476, 487, 549; **IV** 251, 253–54; **6** 231; **7** 162; **8** 35, **369–71 (upd.)**; **11** 494; **13** 326; **17** 29–30; **22** 427; **25** 96, 372; **26 296–99 (upd.)**
Minnesota Paints, **8** 552–53
Minnesota Power & Light Company, **11 313–16**
Minnesota Power, Inc., **34 286–91 (upd.)**
Minnesota Sugar Company, **11** 13
Minnesota Valley Canning Co., **I** 22
Minnetonka Corp., **II** 590; **III** 25; **22** 122–23
Minntech Corporation, **22 359–61**
Minn-Dak Farmers Cooperative, **32** 29
Minolta Camera Co., Ltd., **III 574–76**, 583–84
Minolta Co., Ltd., **18** 93, 186, **339–42 (upd.)**; **43 281–85 (upd.)**
Minorco, **III** 503; **IV** 67–68, 84, 97; **16** 28, 293
Minstar Inc., **11** 397; **15** 49
Minton China, **38** 401
The Minute Maid Company, **I** 234; **10** 227; **28 271–74**, 473; **32** 116
Minute Tapioca, **II** 531
Minyard Food Stores, Inc., **33 304–07**
Mippon Paper, **21** 546
MIPS Computer Systems, **II** 45; **11** 491
Miracle Food Mart, **16** 247, 249–50
Miracle-Gro Products, Inc., **22** 474
Miraflores Designs Inc., **18** 216
Mirage Resorts, Incorporated, **6 209–12**; **15** 238; **28 275–79 (upd.)**; **29** 127; **43** 82
Miramar Hotel & Investment Co., **IV** 717; **38** 318
Mirant, **39** 54, 57
Mircali Asset Management, **III** 340
Mircor Inc., **12** 413
Mirrlees Blackstone, **III** 509
Mirror Group Newspapers plc, **IV** 641; **7** 244, 312, **341–43**; **23 348–51 (upd.)**
Mirror Printing and Binding House, **IV** 677
Misceramic Tile, Inc., **14** 42
Misr Airwork. *See* AirEgypt.
Misr Bank of Cairo, **27** 132
Misrair. *See* AirEgypt.
Miss Erika, Inc., **27** 346, 348
Miss Selfridge, **V** 177–78
Misset Publishers, **IV** 611
Mission Energy Company, **V** 715
Mission First Financial, **V** 715

Mission Group, **V** 715, 717
Mission Insurance Co., **III** 192
Mission Jewelers, **30** 408
Mississippi Chemical Corporation, **8** 183; **IV** 367; **27** 316; **39 280–83**
Mississippi Drug, **III** 10
Mississippi Gas Company, **6** 577
Mississippi Power & Light, **V** 619
Mississippi Power Company, **38** 446–47
Mississippi River Corporation, **10** 44
Mississippi River Recycling, **31** 47, 49
Missoula Bancshares, Inc., **35** 198–99
Missouri Book Co., **10** 136
Missouri Fur Company, **25** 220
Missouri Gaming Company, **21** 39
Missouri Gas & Electric Service Company, **6** 593
Missouri-Kansas-Texas Railroad, **I** 472; **IV** 458
Missouri Pacific Railroad, **10** 43–44
Missouri Public Service Company. *See* UtiliCorp United Inc.
Missouri Utilities Company, **6** 580
Mist Assist, Inc. *See* Ballard Medical Products.
Mistik Beverages, **18** 71
Mistral Plastics Pty Ltd., **IV** 295; **19** 225
Mitchel & King Skates Ltd., **17** 244
Mitchell Construction, **III** 753
Mitchell Energy and Development Corporation, **7 344–46**
Mitchell Home Savings and Loan, **13** 347
Mitchell Hutchins, Inc., **II** 445; **22** 405–06
Mitchell International, **8** 526
Mitchells & Butler, **I** 223
Mitchum Co., **III** 55
Mitchum, Jones & Templeton, **II** 445; **22** 405
MiTek Industries Inc., **IV** 259
MiTek Wood Products, **IV** 305
Mitel Corporation, **15** 131–32; **18 343–46**
MitNer Group, **7** 377
MITRE Corporation, **26 300–02**
Mitre Sport U.K., **17** 204–05
MITROPA AG, **37 250–53**
Mitsubishi Aircraft Co., **III** 578; **7** 348; **9** 349; **11** 164
Mitsubishi Bank, Ltd., **II** 57, 273–74, 276, **321–22**, 323, 392, 459; **III** 289, 577–78; **7** 348; **15** 41; **16** 496, 498. *See also* Bank of Tokyo-Mitsubishi Ltd.
Mitsubishi Chemical Industries Ltd., **I** 319, **363–64**, 398; **II** 57; **III** 666, 760; **11** 207
Mitsubishi Corporation, **I** 261, 431–32, 492, **502–04**, 505–06, 510, 515, 519–20; **II** 57, 59, 101, 118, 224, 292, 321–25, 374; **III** 577–78; **IV** 285, 518, 713; **6** 499; **7** 82, 233, 590; **9** 294; **12 340–43 (upd.)**; **17** 349, 556; **24** 325, 359; **27** 511
Mitsubishi Electric Corporation, **II** 53, **57–59**, 68, 73, 94, 122; **III** 577, 586; **7** 347, 394; **18** 18; **23** 52–53; **43** 15
Mitsubishi Estate Company, Limited, **IV 713–14**
Mitsubishi Foods, **24** 114
Mitsubishi Group, **V** 481–82; **7** 377; **21** 390
Mitsubishi Heavy Industries, Ltd., **II** 57, 75, 323, 440; **III** 452–53, 487, 532, 538, **577–79**, 685, 713; **IV** 184, 713; **7 347–50 (upd.)**; **8** 51; **9** 349–50; **10** 33; **13** 507; **15** 92; **24** 359; **40 324–28 (upd.)**
Mitsubishi International Corp., **16** 462
Mitsubishi Kasei Corp., **III** 47–48, 477; **8** 343; **14** 535
Mitsubishi Kasei Industry Co. Ltd., **IV** 476
Mitsubishi Marine, **III** 385
Mitsubishi Materials Corporation, **III 712–13**; **IV** 554; **38** 463
Mitsubishi Motors Corporation, **III** 516–17, 578–79; **6** 28; **7** 219, 348–49; **8** 72, 374; **9 349–51**; **23 352–55 (upd.)**; **34** 128, 136; **40** 326
Mitsubishi Oil Co., Ltd., **IV 460–62**, 479, 492
Mitsubishi Paper Co., **III** 547
Mitsubishi Rayon Co. Ltd., **I** 330; **V 369–71**; **8** 153
Mitsubishi Sha Holdings, **IV** 554
Mitsubishi Shipbuilding Co. Ltd., **II** 57; **III** 513, 577–78; **7** 348; **9** 349
Mitsubishi Shokai, **III** 577; **IV** 713; **7** 347
Mitsubishi Trading Co., **IV** 460
Mitsubishi Trust & Banking Corporation, **II 323–24**; **III** 289
Mitsui & Co., Ltd., **I** 282; **IV** 18, 224, 432, 654–55; **V** 142; **6** 346; **7** 303; **13** 356; **24** 325, 488–89; **27** 337; **28 280–85 (upd.)**
Mitsui Bank, Ltd., **II** 273–74, 291, **325–27**, 328, 372; **III** 295–97; **IV** 147, 320; **V** 142; **17** 556
Mitsui Bussan K.K., **I** 363, 431–32, 469, 492, 502–04, **505–08**, 510, 515, 519, 533; **II** 57, 66, 101, 224, 292, 323, 325–28, 392; **III** 295–96, 717–18; **IV** 147, 431; **9** 352–53. *See also* Mitsui & Co., Ltd.
Mitsui Gomei Kaisha, **IV** 715
Mitsui Group, **9** 352; **16** 84; **20** 310; **21** 72
Mitsui House Code, **V** 142
Mitsui Light Metal Processing Co., **III** 758
Mitsui Marine and Fire Insurance Company, Limited, **III** 209, **295–96**, 297
Mitsui Mining & Smelting Co., Ltd., **IV 145–46**, 147–48
Mitsui Mining Company, Limited, **IV** 145, **147–49**
Mitsui Mutual Life Insurance Company, **III 297–98**; **39 284–86 (upd.)**
Mitsui-no-Mori Co., Ltd., **IV** 716
Mitsui O.S.K. Lines, Ltd., **I** 520; **IV** 383; **V 473–76**; **6** 398; **26** 278–80
Mitsui Petrochemical Industries, Ltd., **I** 390, 516; **9 352–54**
Mitsui Real Estate Development Co., Ltd., **IV 715–16**
Mitsui Shipbuilding and Engineering Co., **III** 295, 513
Mitsui Toatsu, **9** 353–54
Mitsui Trading, **III** 636
Mitsui Trust & Banking Company, Ltd., **II 328**; **III** 297
Mitsukoshi Ltd., **I** 508; **V 142–44**; **14** 502; **41** 114
Mitsuya Foods Co., **I** 221
Mitteldeutsche Creditbank, **II** 256
Mitteldeutsche Energieversorgung AG, **V** 747
Mitteldeutsche Privatbank, **II** 256
Mitteldeutsche Stickstoff-Werke Ag, **IV** 229–30
Mitteldeutsches Kraftwerk, **IV** 229
Mity Enterprises, Inc., **38 310–12**
Mixconcrete (Holdings), **III** 729
Miyoshi Electrical Manufacturing Co., **II** 6
Mizuno Corporation, **25 344–46**
Mizushima Ethylene Co. Ltd., **IV** 476
MJB Coffee Co., **I** 28
MK-Ferguson Company, **7** 356
MLC Ltd., **IV** 709
MLH&P. *See* Montreal Light, Heat & Power Company.
MLT Vacations Inc., **30** 446
MMAR Group Inc., **19** 131
MMC Networks Inc., **38** 53, 55
MML Investors Services, **III** 286
MMS America Corp., **26** 317
MNC Financial. *See* MBNA Corporation.
MNC Financial Corp., **11** 447
MND Drilling, **7** 345
MNet, **11** 122
Mo och Domsjö AB, **IV** 315, **317–19**, 340
Moa Bay Mining Co., **IV** 82; **7** 186
Mobay, **I** 310–11; **13** 76
Mobil Corporation, **I** 30, 34, 403, 478; **II** 379; **IV** 93, 295, 363, 386, 401, 403, 406, 423, 428, 454, **463–65**, 466, 472–74, 486, 492, 504–05, 515, 517, 522, 531, 538–39, 545, 554–55, 564, 570–71; **V** 147–48; **6** 530; **7** 171, **351–54 (upd.)**; **8** 552–53; **9** 546; **10** 440; **12** 348; **16** 489; **17** 363, 415; **19** 140, 225, 297; **21 376–80 (upd.)**; **24** 496, 521; **25** 232, 445; **26** 369; **32** 175, 179, 181
Mobil Oil Australia, **24** 399
Mobile America Housing Corporation. *See* American Homestar Corporation.
Mobile and Ohio Railroad, **I** 456
Mobile Corporation, **25** 232
Mobile Mini, Inc., **21** 476
Mobile Telecommunications Technologies Corp., **V** 277–78; **6** 323; **16** 74; **18 347–49**
Mobilefone, Inc., **25** 108
MobileMedia Corp., **39** 23, 24
MobileStar Network Corp., **26** 429
Mobira, **II** 69; **17** 353
Mobley Chemical, **I** 342
Mobu Company, **6** 431
Mobujidosha Bus Company, **6** 431
MOÇACOR, **IV** 505
Mocatta and Goldsmid Ltd., **II** 357
Mochida Pharaceutical Co. Ltd., **II** 553
Moctezuma Copper Co., **IV** 176–77
Modar, **17** 279
Modell's Shoppers World, **16** 35–36
Modell's Sporting Goods. *See* Henry Modell & Company Inc.
Modem Media, **23** 479
Modern Equipment Co., **I** 412
Modern Furniture Rentals Inc., **14** 4; **27** 163
Modern Handling Methods Ltd., **21** 499
Modern Maid Food Products, **II** 500
Modern Merchandising Inc., **19** 396
Modern Patterns and Plastics, **III** 641
Modern Times Group AB, **36 335–38**
Modernistic Industries Inc., **7** 589
Modine Manufacturing Company, **8 372–75**
MoDo. *See* Mo och Domsjö AB.
MoDo Paper AB, **28** 446
Moen Incorporated, **12 344–45**

Moët-Hennessy, **I 271–72**; **10** 397–98; **23** 238, 240, 242. *See also* LVMH Moët Hennessy Louis Vuitton SA.
Mogen David. *See* The Wine Group, Inc.
Mogul Corp., **I** 321; **17** 287
The Mogul Metal Company. *See* Federal-Mogul Corporation.
Mohasco Corporation, **15** 102; **26** 100–01
Mohawk & Hudson Railroad, **9** 369
Mohawk Airlines, **I** 131; **6** 131
Mohawk Carpet Corp., **26** 101
Mohawk Industries, Inc., **19 274–76**; **31** 199
Mohawk Rubber Co. Ltd., **V** 256; **7** 116; **19** 508
Mohegan Tribal Gaming Authority, **37 254–57**
Mohr-Value Stores, **8** 555
Moilliet and Sons, **II** 306
Mojave Foods Corporation, **27** 299
Mojo MDA Group Ltd., **11** 50–51; **43** 412
Mokta. *See* Compagnie de Mokta.
MOL. *See* Mitsui O.S.K. Lines, Ltd.
Molecular Biosystems, **III** 61
Molex Incorporated, **II** 8; **11 317–19**; **14** 27
Moline National Bank, **III** 463; **21** 173
Molinera de México S.A. de C.V., **31** 236
Molinos de Puerto Rico, **II** 493
Molinos Nacionales C.A., **7** 242–43; **25** 241
Molins Co., **IV** 326
Molkerie-Zentrak Sud GmbH, **II** 575
Moll Plasticrafters, L.P., **17** 534
Molloy Manufacturing Co., **III** 569; **20** 360
Mölnlycke AB, **IV** 338–39; **28** 443–45; **36** 26
The Molson Companies Limited, **I 273–75**, 333; **II** 210; **7** 183–84; **12** 338; **13** 150, 199; **21** 320; **23** 404; **25** 279; **26 303–07 (upd.)**; **36** 15
Molycorp, **IV** 571; **24** 521
Mon-Dak Chemical Inc., **16** 270
Mon-Valley Transportation Company, **11** 194
MONACA. *See* Molinos Nacionales C.A.
Monaco Coach Corporation, **31 336–38**
Monadnock Paper Mills, Inc., **21 381–84**
Monarch Air Lines, **22** 219
Monarch Development Corporation, **38** 451–52
Monarch Food Ltd., **II** 571
Monarch Foods, **26** 503
Monarch Marking Systems, **III** 157
MonArk Boat, **III** 444; **22** 116
Mond Nickel Co., **IV** 110–11
Mondadori. *See* Arnoldo Monadori Editore S.p.A.
Mondex International, **18** 543
Mondi Foods BV, **41** 12
Mondi Paper Co., **IV** 22
Monet Jewelry, **II** 502–03; **9** 156–57; **10** 323–24
Money Access Service Corp., **11** 467
Monfort, Inc., **13 350–52**
Monheim Group, **II** 521
Monier Roof Tile, **III** 687, 735
Monis Wineries, **I** 288
Monitor Dynamics Inc., **24** 510
Monitor Group Inc., **33** 257
Monk-Austin Inc., **12** 110
Monmouth Pharmaceuticals Ltd., **16** 439
Monochem, **II** 472; **22** 93
Monogram Aerospace Fasteners, Inc., **11** 536
Monogram Models, **25** 312
Monogramme Confections, **6** 392
Monolithic Memories Inc., **6** 216; **16** 316–17, 549
Monon Corp., **13** 550
Monon Railroad, **I** 472
Monongahela Power, **38** 40
Monoprix, **V** 57–59
Monro Muffler Brake, Inc., **24 337–40**
Monroe Auto Equipment, **I** 527
Monroe Calculating Machine Co., **I** 476, 484
Monroe Cheese Co., **II** 471
Monroe Savings Bank, **11** 109
Monrovia Aviation Corp., **I** 544
Monsanto Company, **I** 310, 363, **365–67**, 402, 631, 666, 686, 688; **III** 741; **IV** 290, 367, 379, 401; **8** 398; **9** 318, **355–57 (upd.)**, 466; **12** 186; **13** 76, 225; **16** 460–62; **17** 131; **18** 112; **22** 107; **23** 170–71; **26** 108; **29 327–31 (upd.)**; **33** 135; **34** 179; **41** 306
Monsavon, **III** 46–47
Monsoon plc, **39 287–89**
Mont Blanc, **17** 5; **27** 487, 489
Montabert S.A., **15** 226
Montan TNT Pty Ltd., **27** 473
Montan Transport GmbH, **IV** 140
Montana-Dakota Utilities Co., **7** 322–23; **37** 281–82; **42** 249–50, 252
Montana Enterprises Inc., **I** 114
Montana Power Company, **6** 566; **7** 322; **11 320–22**; **37** 280, 283
Montana Refining Company, **12** 240–41
Montana Resources, Inc., **IV** 34
Montaup Electric Co., **14** 125
MontBell America, Inc., **29** 279
Montecatini, **I** 368; **IV** 421, 470, 486
Montedison S.p.A., **I 368–69**; **IV** 413, 421–22, 454, 499; **14** 17; **22** 262; **24 341–44 (upd.)**; **26** 367; **36** 185–86, 188
Montefibre, **I** 369
Montefina, **IV** 499; **26** 367
Montell N.V., **24** 343
Monterey Homes Corporation. *See* Meritage Corporation.
Monterey Mfg. Co., **12** 439
Monterey's Acquisition Corp., **41** 270
Monterey's Tex-Mex Cafes, **13** 473
Monterrey, Compania de Seguros sobre la Vida. *See* Seguros Monterrey.
Monterrey Group, **19** 10–11, 189
Montfort of Colorado, Inc., **II** 494
Montgomery Elevator Company, **27** 269
Montgomery Ward & Co., Incorporated, **III** 762; **IV** 465; **V 145–48**; **7** 353; **8** 509; **9** 210; **10** 10, 116, 172, 305, 391, 393, 490–91; **12** 48, 309, 315, 335, 430; **13** 165; **15** 330, 470; **17** 460; **18** 477; **20** 263, **374–79 (upd.)**, 433; **22** 535; **25** 144; **27** 428–30; **43** 292
Montiel Corporation, **17** 321
Montinex, **24** 270
Montreal Bank, **II** 210
Montreal Engineering Company, **6** 585
Montreal Light, Heat & Power Consolidated, **6** 501–02
Montreal Mining Co., **17** 357
Montres Rolex S.A., **8** 477; **13 353–55**; **19** 452; **34 292–95 (upd.)**
Montrose Capital, **36** 358
Montrose Chemical Company, **9** 118, 119
Montrose Chrome, **IV** 92
Monument Property Trust Ltd., **IV** 710
Monumental Corp., **III** 179
MONYCo., **III** 306
Moody's Investment Service, **IV** 605; **16** 506; **19** 133; **22** 189
Moog Inc., **13 356–58**
Moon-Hopkins Billing Machine, **III** 165
Mooney Chemicals, Inc. *See* OM Group, Inc.
Moonlight Mushrooms, Inc. *See* Sylvan, Inc.
Moonstone Mountaineering, Inc., **29** 181
Moore and McCormack Co. Inc., **19** 40
Moore Corporation Limited, **IV 644–46**, 679; **15** 473; **16** 450; **36** 508
Moore Gardner & Associates, **22** 88
The Moore Group Ltd., **20** 363
Moore-Handley, Inc., **IV** 345–46; **39 290–92**
Moore McCormack Resources Inc., **14** 455
Moore Medical Corp., **17 331–33**
Moorhouse, **II** 477
Moran Group Inc., **II** 682
Moran Health Care Group Ltd., **25** 455
MoRan Oil & Gas Co., **IV** 82–83
Moran Towing Corporation, Inc., **15 301–03**
Morana, Inc., **9** 290
Moreland and Watson, **IV** 208
Moretti-Harrah Marble Co., **III** 691
Morgan & Banks Limited, **30** 460
Morgan & Cie International S.A., **II** 431
Morgan Construction Company, **8** 448
Morgan Edwards, **II** 609
Morgan Engineering Co., **8** 545
Morgan Grampian Group, **IV** 687
Morgan Grenfell Group PLC, **II** 280, 329, **427–29**; **IV** 21, 712
Morgan Guaranty International Banking Corp., **II** 331; **9** 124
Morgan Guaranty Trust Co. of New York, **I** 26; **II** 208, 254, 262, 329–32, 339, 428, 431, 448; **III** 80; **10** 150
Morgan Guaranty Trust Company, **11** 421; **13** 49, 448; **14** 297; **25** 541; **30** 261
Morgan, Harjes & Co., **II** 329
Morgan, J.P. & Co. Inc. *See* J.P. Morgan & Co. Incorporated.
Morgan, Lewis & Bockius LLP, **29 332–34**
Morgan, Lewis, Githens & Ahn, Inc., **6** 410
Morgan Mitsubishi Development, **IV** 714
Morgan Schiff & Co., **29** 205
Morgan Stanley Dean Witter & Company, **33 311–14 (upd.)**; **38** 289, 291, 411
Morgan Stanley Group, Inc., **I** 34; **II** 211, 330, 403, 406–08, 422, 428, **430–32**, 441; **IV** 295, 447, 714; **9** 386; **11** 258; **12** 529; **16 374–78 (upd.)**; **18** 448–49; **20** 60, 363; **22** 404, 407; **25** 542; **30** 353–55; **34** 496; **36** 153
Morgan Yacht Corp., **II** 468
Morgan's Brewery, **I** 287
Mori Bank, **II** 291
Moria Informatique, **6** 229
Morino Associates, **10** 394
Morita & Co., **II** 103
Mormac Marine Group, **15** 302
Morning Star Technologies Inc., **24** 49
Morning Sun, Inc., **23** 66
Morris Air, **24** 455

Morris Communications Corporation, 36 339–42
Morris Motors, **III** 256; **7** 459
Morris Travel Services L.L.C., 26 308–11
Morrison Industries Ltd., **IV** 278; **19** 153
Morrison Knudsen Corporation, IV 55; **7 355–58; 11** 401, 553; **28 286–90 (upd.); 33** 442. *See also* The Washington Companies.
Morrison Machine Products Inc., **25** 193
Morrison Restaurants Inc., 11 323–25; 18 464
Morse Chain Co., **III** 439; **14** 63
Morse Equalizing Spring Company, **14** 63
Morse Industrial, **14** 64
Morse Shoe Inc., 13 359–61
Morss and White, **III** 643
Morstan Development Co., Inc., **II** 432
Mortgage & Trust Co., **II** 251
Mortgage Associates, **9** 229
Mortgage Insurance Co. of Canada, **II** 222
Mortgage Resources, Inc., **10** 91
Morton Foods, Inc., **II** 502; **10** 323; **27** 258
Morton International Inc., 9 358–59 (upd.), 500–01; **16** 436; **22** 505–06; **43** 319
Morton Thiokol Inc., I 325, **370–72; 19** 508; **28** 253–54. *See also* Thiokol Corporation.
Morton's Restaurant Group, Inc., 28 401; **30 329–31**
Mos Magnetics, **18** 140
MOS Technology, **7** 95
Mosby-Year Book, Inc., **IV** 678; **17** 486
Moseley, Hallgarten, Estabrook, and Weeden, **III** 389
Mosher Steel Company, **7** 540
Mosinee Paper Corporation, 15 304–06
Moskatel's, Inc., **17** 321
Mosler Safe Co., **III** 664–65; **7** 144, 146; **22** 184
Moss-Rouse Company, **15** 412
Mossgas, **IV** 93
Mossimo, Inc., 27 328–30
Mostek Corp., **I** 85; **II** 64; **11** 307–08; **13** 191; **20** 175; **29** 323
Mostjet Ltd. *See* British World Airlines Ltd.
Móstoles Industrial S.A., **26** 129
Mostra Importaciones S.A., **34** 38, 40
Motel 6 Corporation, 10 13; **13 362–64.** *See also* Accor SA
Mother Karen's, **10** 216
Mother's Oats, **II** 558–59; **12** 409
Mothercare Stores, Inc., **16** 466
Mothercare UK Ltd., 17 42–43, **334–36**
Mothers Work, Inc., 18 350–52
Motif Inc., **22** 288
Motion Designs, **11** 486
Motion Factory, Inc., **38** 72
Motion Picture Association of America, **37** 353–54
Motion Picture Corporation of America, **25** 326, 329
Motiva Enterprises LLC, **41** 359, 395
MotivePower. *See* Wabtec Corporation.
The Motley Fool, Inc., 40 329–31
Moto-Truc Co., **13** 385
Motor Cargo Industries, Inc., 35 296–99
Motor Coaches Industries International Inc., **36** 132
Motor Haulage Co., **IV** 181
Motor Parts Industries, Inc., **9** 363
Motor Transit Corp., **I** 448; **10** 72
Motor Wheel Corporation, **20** 261; **27** 202–04
Motoren-und-Turbinen-Union, **I** 151; **III** 563; **9** 418; **15** 142; **34** 128, 131, 133
Motoren-Werke Mannheim AG, **III** 544
Motorenfabrik Deutz AG, **III** 541
Motorenfabrik Oberursel, **III** 541
Motornetic Corp., **III** 590
Motorola, Inc., I 534; **II** 5, 34, 44–45, 56, **60–62,** 64; **III** 455; **6** 238; **7** 119, 494, 533; **8** 139; **9** 515; **10** 87, 365, 367, 431–33; **11** 45, 308, **326–29 (upd.),** 381–82; **12** 136–37, 162; **13** 30, 356, 501; **17** 33, 193; **18** 18, 74, 76, 260, 382; **19** 391; **20** 8, 439; **21** 123; **22** 17, 19, 288, 542; **26** 431–32; **27** 20, 341–42, 344; **33** 47–48; **34 296–302 (upd.); 38** 188; **43** 15
Motown Records Company L.P., II 145; **22** 194; **23** 389, 391; **26 312–14**
Moulinex S.A., 22 362–65
Mound Metalcraft. *See* Tonka Corporation.
Mount. *See also* Mt.
Mount Hood Credit Life Insurance Agency, **14** 529
Mount Isa Mines, **IV** 61
Mount Vernon Group, **8** 14
Mountain Fuel Supply Company. *See* Questar Corporation.
Mountain Fuel Supply Company, **6** 568–69
Mountain Pass Canning Co., **7** 429
Mountain Safety Research, **18** 445–46
Mountain State Telephone Company, **6** 300
Mountain States Mortgage Centers, Inc., 29 335–37
Mountain States Power Company. *See* PacifiCorp.
Mountain States Telephone & Telegraph Co., **V** 341; **25** 495
Mountain States Wholesale, **II** 602; **30** 25
Mountain West Bank, **35** 197
Mountleigh PLC, **16** 465
Mounts Wire Industries, **III** 673
Mountsorrel Granite Co., **III** 734
Movado Group, Inc., 28 291–94
Movado-Zenith-Mondia Holding, **II** 124
Movie Gallery, Inc., 31 339–41
Movie Star Inc., 17 337–39
Movies To Go, Inc., **9** 74; **31** 57
Movil@ccess, S.A. de C.V., **39** 25, 194
Moving Co. Ltd., **V** 127
The Moving Picture Company, **15** 83
The Mowry Co., **23** 102
MPB Corporation, **8** 529, 531
MPM, **III** 735
MP3.com, **43** 109
Mr. Bricolage S.A., 37 258–60
Mr. Coffee, Inc., 14 229–31; **15 307–09; 17** 215; **27** 275; **39** 406
Mr. D's Food Centers, **12** 112
Mr. Donut, **21** 323
Mr. Gasket Inc., 11 84; **15 310–12**
Mr. Gatti's, **15** 345
Mr. Goodbuys, **13** 545
Mr. How, **V** 191–92
Mr. M Food Stores, **7** 373
Mr. Maintenance, **25** 15
Mr. Payroll Corp., **20** 113
MRC Bearings, **III** 624
MRN Radio Network, **19** 223
Mrs. Baird's Bakeries, 29 338–41
Mrs. Fields' Original Cookies, Inc., 27 331–35
Mrs. Paul's Kitchens, **II** 480; **26** 57–58
Mrs. Smith's Frozen Foods, **II** 525; **13** 293–94; **35** 181
MS-Relais GmbH, **III** 710; **7** 302–03
MSAS Cargo International, **6** 415, 417
MSE Corporation, **33** 44
MSI Data Corp., **10** 523; **15** 482
M6. *See* Métropole Télévision.
MSL Industries, **10** 44
MSNBC, **28** 301
MSR. *See* Mountain Safety Research.
MSU. *See* Middle South Utilities.
Mt. *See also* Mount.
Mt. Beacon Insurance Co., **26** 486
Mt. Carmel Public Utility Company, **6** 506
Mt. Goldsworthy Mining Associates, **IV** 47
Mt. Lyell Investments, **III** 672–73
Mt. Summit Rural Telephone Company, **14** 258
Mt. Vernon Iron Works, **II** 14
MTC. *See* Management and Training Corporation.
MTC Pharmaceuticals, **II** 483
MTel. *See* Mobile Telecommunications Technologies Corp.
MTG. *See* Modern Times Group AB.
MTM Entertainment Inc., **13** 279, 281
MTS Inc., 37 261–64
MTV, **31** 239
MTV Asia, **23** 390
MTVi Group, **37** 194
Mueller Co., **III** 645; **28** 485
Mueller Furniture Company, **8** 252; **39** 206
Mueller Industries, Inc., 7 359–61
Mujirushi Ryohin, **V** 188
Mukluk Freight Lines, **6** 383
Mule Battery Manufacturing Co., **III** 643
Mule-Hide Products Co., **22** 15
Mülheimer Bergwerksvereins, **I** 542
Mullen Advertising, **13** 513
Mullens & Co., **14** 419
Multex Systems, **21** 70
Multi Restaurants, **II** 664
Multibank Inc., **11** 281
Multicom Publishing Inc., **11** 294
Multilink, Inc., **27** 364–65
MultiMed, **11** 379
Multimedia Games, Inc., 41 272–76
Multimedia, Inc., IV 591; **11 330–32; 30** 217
Multimedia Security Services, Inc., **32** 374
Multiple Access Systems Corp., **III** 109
Multiple Properties, **I** 588
MultiScope Inc., **10** 508
Multitech International. *See* Acer Inc.
Multiview Cable, **24** 121
Münchener Rückversicherungs-Gesellschaft. *See* Munich Re.
Munford, Inc., **17** 499
Mungana Mines, **I** 438
Munich Re, II 239; **III** 183–84, 202, **299–301,** 400–01, 747; **35** 34, 37
Municipal Assistance Corp., **II** 448
Munising Paper Co., **III** 40; **13** 156; **16** 303; **43** 257
Munising Woodenware Company, **13** 156
Munksjö, **19** 227
Munksund, **IV** 338
Munsingwear, Inc., **22** 427; **25** 90; **27** 443, 445; **41** 291. *See also* PremiumWear, Inc.
Munson Transportation Inc., **18** 227

Munster and Leinster Bank Ltd., **16** 13
Mura Corporation, **23** 209
Murata, **37** 347
Murdock Madaus Schwabe, 26 315–19, 470
Murfin Inc., **8** 360
Murmic, Inc., **9** 120
Murphey Favre, Inc., **17** 528, 530
Murphy Family Farms Inc., 7 477; **21** 503; **22 366–68**
Murphy Oil Corporation, 7 362–64; 32 338–41 (upd.)
Murphy-Phoenix Company, **14** 122
Murray Bay Paper Co., **IV** 246; **25** 10
Murray Corp. of America, **III** 443
Murray Goulburn Snow, **II** 575
Murray Inc., **19** 383
Murrayfield, **IV** 696
Murtaugh Light & Power Company, **12** 265
Musashino Railway Company, **V** 510
Muscatine Journal, **11** 251
Muscocho Explorations Ltd., **IV** 76
Muse Air Corporation, **6** 120; **24** 454
Muse, Cordero, Chen, **41** 89
Music and Video Club, **24** 266, 270
Music-Appreciation Records, **13** 105
Music Corporation of America. *See* MCA Inc.
Music Go Round, **18** 207–09
Music Man, Inc., **16** 202; **43** 170
Music Plus, **9** 75
Musical America Publishing, Inc., **22** 441
Musician's Friend, **29** 221, 223
Musicland Stores Corporation, 9 360–62; 11 558; **19** 417; **37** 263; **38 313–17 (upd.)**
Musitek, **16** 202; **43** 170
Muskegon Gas Company. *See* MCN Corporation.
Musotte & Girard, **I** 553
Mutoh Industries, Ltd., **6** 247; **24** 234
Mutual Benefit Life Insurance Company, III 243, **302–04**
Mutual Broadcasting System, **23** 509
Mutual Gaslight Company. *See* MCN Corporation.
Mutual Life Insurance Co. of the State of Wisconsin, **III** 321
Mutual Life Insurance Company of New York, II 331; **III** 247, 290, **305–07,** 316, 321, 380
Mutual Marine Office Inc., **41** 284
Mutual Medical Aid and Accident Insurance Co., **III** 331
Mutual of Omaha, **III** 365; **25** 89–90; **27** 47
Mutual Oil Co., **IV** 399
Mutual Papers Co., **14** 522
Mutual Safety Insurance Co., **III** 305
Mutual Savings & Loan Association, **III** 215; **18** 60
Mutualité Générale, **III** 210
Mutuelle d'Orléans, **III** 210
Mutuelle de l'Quest, **III** 211
Mutuelle Vie, **III** 210
Mutuelles Unies, **III** 211
Muzak, Inc., 7 90–91; **18 353–56; 35** 19–20
Muzzy-Lyon Company. *See* Federal-Mogul Corporation.
MVC. *See* Music and Video Club.
Mwinilunga Canneries Ltd., **IV** 241
MXL Industries, **13** 367
MY Holdings, **IV** 92
Myanmar Oil and Gas Enterprise, **IV** 519
MYCAL Group, **V** 154
Myco-Sci, Inc. *See* Sylvan, Inc.
Mycogen Corporation, 21 385–87
Mycrom, **14** 36
Myer Emporium Ltd., **20** 156
Myers Industries, Inc., 19 277–79
Mygind International, **8** 477
Mylan Laboratories Inc., I 656–57; 20 380–82 (upd.)
Myllykoski Träsliperi AB, **IV** 347–48
Myokenya, **III** 757
Myrna Knitwear, Inc., **16** 231
Myson Group PLC, **III** 671
Mysore State Iron Works, **IV** 205

N.A. Otto & Cie., **III** 541
N.A. Woodworth, **III** 519; **22** 282
N. Boynton & Co., **16** 534
N.C. Cameron & Sons, Ltd., **11** 95
N.C. Monroe Construction Company, **14** 112
N.E.M., **23** 228
N.H. Geotech. *See* New Holland N.V.
N.K. Fairbank Co., **II** 497
N.L. Industries, **19** 212
N M Electronics, **II** 44
N M Rothschild & Sons Limited, IV 64, 712; **24** 267; **39 293–95**
N.M.U. Transport Ltd., **II** 569
N.R.F. Gallimard, **IV** 618
N. Shure Company, **15** 477
N.V. *see under first word of company name*
N.W. Ayer & Son, **I** 36; **II** 542
N.W. Ayer and Partners, **32** 140
N.Y.P. Holdings Inc., **12** 360
Na Pali, S.A. *See* Quiksilver, Inc.
Naamloze Vennootschap tot Exploitatie van het Café Krasnapolsky. *See* Grand Hotel Krasnapolsky N.V.
Nabisco, **24** 358
Nabisco Brands, Inc., II 475, 512, **542–44; 7** 128, 365–67; **12** 167; **25** 366. *See also* RJR Nabisco.
Nabisco Foods Group, 7 365–68 (upd.); 9 318; **14** 48
Nabisco Holdings Corporation, **25** 181; **42** 408
Nabisco Ltd., **24** 288
Nabors Industries, Inc., 9 363–65
NACCO Industries, Inc., 7 369–71; 17 213–15, 246, 248
Nacional de Drogas, S.A. de C.V., **39** 188
Nacional Financiera, **IV** 513
NACO Finance Corp., **33** 398
Nadler Sportswear. *See* Donnkenny, Inc.
Naegele Outdoor Advertising Inc., **36** 340
NAFI Corp. *See* Chris-Craft Industries, Inc.
Nagano Seiyu Ltd., **V** 188
Nagasaki Shipyard, **I** 502
Nagasakiya Co., Ltd., V 149–51
Nagasco, Inc., **18** 366
Nagase & Company, Ltd., 8 376–78
Nagase-Alfa, **III** 420
Nagel Meat Markets and Packing House, **II** 643
Nagoya Bank, **II** 373
Nagoya Electric Light Co., **IV** 62
NAI. *See* Network Associates, Inc.
Naigai Tsushin Hakuhodo, **6** 29
Naikoku Tsu-un Kabushiki Kaisha, **V** 477
Naiman Co., **25** 449
Nairn Linoleum Co., **18** 116
Nakai Shoten Ltd., **IV** 292
Nakano Vinegar Co. Ltd., **26** 58
Nalco Chemical Corporation, I 373–75; 12 346–48 (upd.)
Nalfloc, **I** 374
Nalge Co., **14** 479–80
NAM. *See* Nederlandse Aardolie Maatschappij.
Namco, **III** 431
Namibia Breweries Ltd., **33** 75
Namkwang Engineering & Construction Co. Ltd., **III** 749
NAMM. *See* North American Medical Management Company, Inc.
Nampack, **I** 423
Nan Ya Plastics Corp., **14** 197–98
NANA Regional Corporation, **7** 558
Nanfang South China Motor Corp., **34** 132
Nankai Kogyo, **IV** 225; **24** 489
Nansei Sekiyu, **IV** 432
Nantucket Allserve, Inc., 22 369–71
Nantucket Corporation, **6** 226
Nantucket Mills, **12** 285; **34** 240
Nanyo Bussan, **I** 493; **24** 326
NAPA. *See* National Automotive Parts Association.
NAPC. *See* North American Philips Corp.
Napier, **I** 194
NAPP Systems, Inc., **11** 253
Narmco Industries, **I** 544
NAS. *See* National Audubon Society.
NASA. *See* National Aeronautics and Space Administration.
NASCAR. *See* National Association for Stock Car Auto Racing.
NASDAQ, **37** 132
Nash DeCamp Company, **23** 356–57
Nash Finch Company, 8 379–81; 11 43; **23 356–58 (upd.); 40** 80
Nash-Kelvinator Corp., **I** 135; **12** 158
Nash Motors Co., **I** 135; **8** 75
Nashaming Valley Information Processing, **III** 204
Nashua Corporation, 8 382–84
The Nashville Network, **11** 153
Nashville Speedway USA, Inc., **43** 139–41
Nassau Gas Light Co., **6** 455
Nassco Holdings Inc., **36** 79
NASTECH, **III** 590
Nasu Aluminium Manufacturing Co., **IV** 153
Nat Robbins, **37** 269–70
Natal Brewery Syndicate, **I** 287
Natco Corp., **I** 445
NaTec Ltd. *See* CRSS Inc.
Nathan's Famous, Inc., 29 342–44
National, **10** 419
National Acme Company. *See* Acme-Cleveland Corp.
National Advanced Systems, **II** 64–65
National Advertising Company, **27** 280
National Aeronautics and Space Administration, **II** 139; **6** 227–29, 327; **11** 201, 408; **12** 489; **37** 364–65
National Air Transport Co., **I** 128; **6** 128; **9** 416; **11** 427
National Airlines, **I** 97, 116; **6** 388; **21** 141; **25** 146
National Allied Publications. *See* DC Comics Inc.
National Aluminate Corp., **I** 373; **12** 346
National Aluminum Company, **11** 38
National American Corporation, **33** 399

National American Life Insurance Co. of California, **II** 181
National American Title Insurance Co., **II** 181
National Amusements Inc., 28 295–97
National Aniline & Chemical Coompany, **I** 414; **22** 29
National Association for Stock Car Auto Racing, 32 342–44
National Association of Securities Dealers, Inc., 10 416–18
National Audubon Society, 26 320–23
National Australia Bank, **III** 673
National Auto Credit, Inc., 16 379–81
National Automobile and Casualty Insurance Co., **III** 270
National Automotive Fibers, Inc. *See* Chris- Craft Industries, Inc.
National Automotive Parts Association, **26** 348
National Aviation, **I** 117
National Baby Shop, **V** 203
National Bancard Corporation, **11** 111–13
National Bancorp of Arizona, **12** 565
National Bank, **II** 312
National Bank for Cooperatives, **8** 489–90
National Bank für Deutschland, **II** 270
National Bank of Belgium, **II** 294
National Bank of Commerce, **II** 331; **9** 536; **11** 105–06; **13** 467
National Bank of Commerce Trust & Savings Association, **15** 161
National Bank of Detroit, **I** 165. *See also* NBD Bancorp, Inc.
National Bank of Egypt, **II** 355
National Bank of Greece, 41 277–79
The National Bank of Jacksonville, **9** 58
National Bank of New Zealand, **II** 308; **19** 155
National Bank of North America, **II** 334
National Bank of South Africa Ltd., **II** 236
National Bank of the City of New York, **II** 312
National Bank of Turkey, **IV** 557
National Bank of Washington, **13** 440
National BankAmericard Inc. *See* Visa International.
National Bankers Express Co., **II** 396; **10** 60
National Basketball Association, **12** 457
National Bell Telephone Company, **V** 259
National-Ben Franklin Insurance Co., **III** 242
National Benefit and Casualty Co., **III** 228
National Benefit Co., **III** 228
National Beverage Corp., 26 324–26
National Binding Company, **8** 382
National Biscuit Co., **IV** 152; **22** 336. *See also* Nabisco.
National Bridge Company of Canada, Ltd., **8** 544
National Broach & Machine Co., **I** 481–82
National Broadcasting Company, Inc., II 30, 88–90, 129–33, **151–53**, 170, 173, 487, 543; **III** 188, 329; **IV** 596, 608, 652; **6** 157–59, **164–66 (upd.)**; **10** 173; **17** 149–50; **19** 201, 210; **21** 24; **23** 120; **28** 69, **298–301 (upd.)**; **30** 99; **32** 3; **33** 324; **34** 186; **42** 161, 163. *See also* General Electric Company.
National Building Society, **10** 6–7
National Cable & Manufacturing Co., **13** 369
National Cable Television Association, **18** 64
National Can Corp., I 601–02, **607–08**; **IV** 154; **13** 255
National Car Rental System, Inc., I 489; **II** 419–20, 445; **6** 348–49; **10** 373, **419–20**; **21** 284; **22** 406, 524; **24** 9; **25** 93, 143. *See also* Republic Industries, Inc.
National Carbon Co., Inc., **I** 400; **9** 516; **11** 402
National Carriers, **6** 413–14
National Cash Register Company. *See* NCR Corporation.
National Cement Co., **35** 419
National Cheerleaders Association, **15** 516–18
National Chemsearch Corp. *See* NCH Corporation.
National Child Care Centers, Inc., **II** 607
National City Bank, **9** 475
National City Bank of New York, **I** 337, 462; **II** 253–54; **III** 380; **IV** 81
National City Co., **II** 254; **9** 124
National City Corp., 9 475; **15 313–16**
National Cleaning Contractors, **II** 176
National Coal Board, **IV** 38–40
National Coal Development Corp., **IV** 48
National Comics Publications. *See* DC Comics Inc.
National Commercial Bank, **11** 108; **12** 422; **13** 476
National Components Industries, Inc., **13** 398
National Container Corp., **I** 609
National Convenience Stores Incorporated, 7 372–75; **20** 140
National Cranberry Association. *See* Ocean Spray Cranberries, Inc.
National Credit Office, **IV** 604
National CSS, **IV** 605
National Dairy Products Corp., **II** 533; **7** 275; **14** 204
National Data Corporation, **24** 393
National Demographics & Lifestyles Inc., **10** 461
National Development Bank, **IV** 56
National Discount Brokers Group, Inc., 28 302–04
National Disinfectant Company. *See* NCH Corporation.
National Distillers and Chemical Corporation, I 226, **376–78**; **IV** 11; **8** 439–41; **9** 231; **10** 181; **30** 441
National Drive-In Grocery Corporation, **7** 372
National Drug Ltd., **II** 652
National Economic Research Associates, **III** 283
National Education Association, **9** 367
National Educational Corporation, **26** 95
National Electric Company, **11** 388
National Electric Instruments Co., **IV** 78
National Electric Products Corp., **IV** 177
National Employers Life Assurance Co. Ltd., **13** 539
National Enquirer, **10** 287–88
National Envelope Corporation, 32 345–47
National Executive Service. *See* Carey International, Inc.
National Express Laboratories, Inc., **10** 107
National Family Opinion. *See* NFO Worldwide, Inc.
National Fidelity Life Insurance Co., **10** 246
National Fidelity Life Insurance Co. of Kansas, **III** 194; **IV** 343
National Finance Corp., **IV** 22–23
National Fire & Marine Insurance Co., **III** 213–14; **42** 32
National Fire Insurance Co., **III** 229–30
National Football League, 12 457; **29 345–47**; **37** 294
National Freight Corporation, **6** 412–13
National Fuel Gas Company, 6 526–28
National Gateway Telecom, **6** 326–27
National General Corp., **III** 190–91
National Geographic Society, 9 366–68; **30 332–35 (upd.)**; **42** 115, 117
National Grape Co-operative Association, Inc., 20 383–85
National Greyhound Racing Club, **II** 142
National Grid Company, **11** 399–400; **12** 349; **13** 484
National Grocers of Ontario, **II** 631
National Guardian Corp., **18** 33
National Gypsum Company, 8 43; **10 421–24**; **13** 169; **22** 48, 170; **25** 535
National Health Enterprises, **III** 87
National Health Laboratories Incorporated, 11 333–35. *See also* Laboratory Corporation of America Holdings.
National Hockey League, 35 300–03
National Hotel Co., **III** 91
National Housing Systems, Inc., **18** 27
National Hydrocarbon Corp., **IV** 543
National ICEE Corporation, **24** 242
National Import and Export Corp. Ltd., **IV** 240
National Indemnity Co., **III** 213–14; **42** 32–33
National India Rubber Company, **9** 228
National Industries, **I** 446
National Inking Appliance Company, **14** 52
National Instruments Corporation, 22 372–74
National Integrity Life Insurance, **III** 249
National Intergroup, Inc., IV 237, 574; **V 152–53**; **12** 354; **16** 212; **26** 529. *See also* FoxMeyer Health Corporation.
National Iranian Oil Company, III 748; **IV** 370, 374, **466–68**, 484, 512, 535
National Key Company. *See* Cole National Corporation.
National Kinney Corp., **IV** 720; **9** 391
National Law Publishing Company, Inc., **32** 35
National Lead Co., **III** 681; **IV** 32; **21** 489
National Liability and Fire Insurance Co., **III** 214
National Liberty Corp., **III** 218–19
National Life and Accident Insurance Co., **III** 194
National Life Insurance Co., **III** 290
National Life Insurance Co. of Canada, **III** 243
National Living Centers, **13** 49
National Loss Control Service Corp., **III** 269
National Magazine Company Limited, **19** 201
National Manufacturing Co., **III** 150; **6** 264; **13** 6
National Marine Service, **6** 530
National Market System, **9** 369
National Media Corporation, 27 336–40

National Medical Care, **22** 360
National Medical Enterprises, Inc., III 79, **87–88**; **6** 188; **10** 252; **14** 233; **25** 307–08; **33** 185
National Minerals Development Corp., **IV** 143–44
National Mobility Corp., **30** 436
National Mortgage Agency of New Zealand Ltd., **IV** 278; **19** 153
National Mortgage Assoc. of Washington, **II** 410
The National Motor Bearing Company. *See* Federal-Mogul Corporation.
The National Motor Club of America, Inc., **33** 418
National Mutual Life Assurance of Australasia, **III** 249
National Office Furniture, **12** 297
National Oil Corp. *See* Libyan National Oil Corporation.
National Oil Distribution Co., **IV** 524
National Old Line Insurance Co., **III** 179
National Packaging, **IV** 333
National Paper Co., **8** 476
National Parks Transportation Company, **25** 420–22
National Patent Development Corporation, **7** 45; **13 365–68**; **25** 54
National Periodical Publications. *See* DC Comics Inc.
National Permanent Mutual Benefit Building Society, **10** 6
National Petrochemical Co., **IV** 467
National Petroleum Publishing Co., **IV** 636
National Pharmacies, **9** 346
National Picture & Frame Company, **24 345–47**
National Postal Meter Company, **14** 52
National Potash Co., **IV** 82; **7** 186
National Power PLC, **11** 399–400; **12 349–51**; **13** 458, 484
National Presto Industries, Inc., **16 382–85**; **43 286–90 (upd.)**
National Processing, Inc., **24** 394
National Propane Corporation, **8** 535–37
National Provident Institution for Mutual Life Assurance, **IV** 711
National Provincial Bank, **II** 319–20, 333–34; **IV** 722; **17** 324
National Public Radio, **19 280–82**
National Publishing Company, **41** 110
National Quotation Bureau, Inc., **14** 96–97
National R.V. Holdings, Inc., **32 348–51**
National Railroad Passenger Corporation, **22 375–78**
National Railways of Mexico, **IV** 512
National Record Mart, Inc., **29 348–50**
National Register Publishing Co., **17** 399; **23** 442
National Regulator Co., **II** 41
National Reinsurance Corporation. *See* General Re Corporation.
National Rent-A-Car, **6** 392–93
National Research Corporation, **8** 397
National Restaurants Management, Inc., **38** 385–87
National Revenue Corporation, **22** 181
National Rifle Association of America, **37 265–68**
National Rubber Machinery Corporation, **8** 298
National Sanitary Supply Co., **13** 149–50; **16 386–87**
National Satellite Paging, **18** 348
National School Studios, **7** 255; **25** 252
National Science Foundation, **9** 266
National Sea Products Ltd., **14 339–41**
National Seal, **I** 158
National Semiconductor Corporation, **II 63–65**; **III** 455, 618, 678; **6** 215, **261–63**; **9** 297; **11** 45–46, 308, 463; **16** 122, 332; **17** 418; **18** 18; **19** 312; **21** 123; **26 327–30 (upd.)**; **43** 15
National Service Industries, Inc., **11 336–38**
National Shoe Products Corp., **16** 17
National Slicing Machine Company, **19** 359
National-Southwire Aluminum Company, **11** 38; **12** 353
National Stamping & Electric Works, **12** 159
National Standard Co., **IV** 137; **13 369–71**
National Star Brick & Tile Co., **III** 501; **7** 207
National Starch and Chemical Corp., **IV** 253; **17** 30; **32** 256–57
National Starch Manufacturing Co., **II** 496
National Steel and Shipbuilding Company, **7** 356
National Steel Car Corp., **IV** 73; **24** 143–44
National Steel Corporation, **I** 491; **IV** 74, 163, 236–37, 572; **V** 152–53; **7** 549; **8** 346, 479–80; **11** 315; **12 352–54**; **14** 191; **16** 212; **23** 445; **24** 144; **26** 527–29; **28** 325. *See also* FoxMeyer Health Corporation.
National Student Marketing Corporation, **10** 385–86
National Supply Co., **IV** 29
National Surety Co. of New York, **III** 395
National System Company, **9** 41; **11** 469
National Tanker Fleet, **IV** 502
National Tea, **II** 631–32
National Technical Laboratories, **14** 52
National TechTeam, Inc., **41 280–83**
National Telecommunications of Austin, **8** 311
National Telephone and Telegraph Corporation. *See* British Columbia Telephone Company.
National Telephone Co., **III** 162; **7** 332, 508
National Theatres, Inc., **III** 190
National Trading Manufacturing, Inc., **22** 213
National Transcontinental, **6** 360
National Travelers' Insurance Co., **III** 290
National Trust Life Insurance Co., **III** 218
National Tube Co., **II** 330; **IV** 572; **7** 549
National Union Electric Corporation, **12** 159
National Union Fire Insurance Co. of Pittsburgh, Pa., **III** 195–97
National Union Life and Limb Insurance Co., **III** 290
National Utilities & Industries Corporation, **9** 363
National Westminster Bank PLC, **II** 237, **333–35**; **IV** 642; **13** 206
Nationalbank, **I** 409
Nationale Bank Vereeniging, **II** 185
Nationale-Nederlanden N.V., **III** 179, 200–01, **308–11**; **IV** 697
Nationar, **9** 174
NationsBank Corporation, **6** 357; **10 425–27**; **11** 126; **13** 147; **18** 516, 518; **23** 455; **25** 91, 186; **26** 348, 453
NationsRent, **28** 388
Nationwide Cellular Service, Inc., **27** 305
Nationwide Credit, **11** 112
Nationwide Group, **25** 155
Nationwide Income Tax Service, **9** 326
Nationwide Logistics Corp., **14** 504
Nationwide Mutual Insurance Co., **26** 488
NATIOVIE, **II** 234
Native Plants, **III** 43
NATM Buying Corporation, **10** 9, 468
Natomas Co., **IV** 410; **6** 353–54; **7** 309; **11** 271
Natref, **IV** 535
Natronag, **IV** 325
Natronzellstoff-und Papierfabriken AG, **IV** 324
NatTeknik, **26** 333
Natudryl Manufacturing Company, **10** 271
Natural Gas Clearinghouse, **11** 355. *See also* NGC Corporation.
Natural Gas Corp., **19** 155
Natural Gas Pipeline Company, **6** 530, 543; **7** 344–45
Natural Gas Service of Arizona, **19** 411
Natural Wonders Inc., **14 342–44**
NaturaLife International, **26** 470
The Nature Company, **10** 215–16; **14** 343; **26** 439; **27** 429; **28** 306
The Nature Conservancy, **26** 323; **28 305–07**, 422
Nature's Sunshine Products, Inc., **15 317–19**; **26** 470; **27** 353; **33** 145
Nature's Way Products Inc., **26** 315
Natuzzi Group. *See* Industrie Natuzzi S.p.A.
NatWest Bancorp, **38** 393
NatWest Bank, **22** 52. *See also* National Westminster Bank PLC.
Naugles, **7** 506
Nautica Enterprises, Inc., **16** 61; **18 357–60**; **25** 258; **27** 60
Nautilus International, Inc., **III** 315–16; **13** 532; **25** 40; **30** 161
Nautor Ab, **IV** 302
Navaho Freight Line, **16** 41
Navajo Refining Company, **12** 240
Navajo Shippers, Inc., **42** 364
Navale, **III** 209
Navan Resources, **38** 231
Navarre Corporation, **22** 536; **24 348–51**
Naviera Vizcaina, **IV** 528
Navigation Mixte, **III** 348
Navire Cargo Gear, **27** 269
Navistar International Corporation, **I** 152, 155, **180–82**, 186, 525, 527; **II** 330; **10** 280, **428–30 (upd.)**; **17** 327; **33** 254. *See also* International Harvester Co.
Navy Exchange Service Command, **31 342–45**
Navy Federal Credit Union, **33 315–17**
Naxon Utilities Corp., **19** 359
Naylor, Hutchinson, Vickers & Company. *See* Vickers PLC.
NBC **24** 516–17. *See also* National Broadcasting Company, Inc.
NBC Bankshares, Inc., **21** 524
NBC/Computer Services Corporation, **15** 163
NBD Bancorp, Inc., **9** 476; **11 339–41**, 466. *See also* Bank One Corporation.
NBTY, Inc., **31 346–48**

NCA Corporation, **9** 36, 57, 171
NCB. *See* National City Bank of New York.
NCB Brickworks, **III** 501; **7** 207
NCC L.P., **15** 139
NCH Corporation, 8 385–87
Nchanga Consolidated Copper Mines, **IV** 239–40
nChip, **38** 187–88
NCNB Corporation, II 336–37; **12** 519; **26** 453
NCO Group, Inc., 42 258–60
NCR Corporation, I 540–41; **III** 147–52, **150–53**, 157, 165–66; **IV** 298; **V** 263; **6** 250, **264–68 (upd.)**, 281–82; **9** 416; **11** 62, 151, 542; **12** 162, 148, 246, 484; **16** 65; **29** 44; **30 336–41 (upd.)**; **36** 81
NCS. *See* Norstan, Inc.
NCTI (Noise Cancellation Technologies Inc.), **19** 483–84
nCube Corp., **14** 15; **22** 293
ND Marston, **III** 593
NDB. *See* National Discount Brokers Group, Inc.
NDL. *See* Norddeutscher Lloyd.
NEA. *See* Newspaper Enterprise Association.
NEAC Inc., **I** 201–02
Nearly Me, **25** 313
Neatherlin Homes Inc., **22** 547
Nebraska Bell Company, **14** 311
Nebraska Cellular Telephone Company, **14** 312
Nebraska Consolidated Mills Company, **II** 493; **III** 52; **8** 433; **26** 383
Nebraska Furniture Mart, **III** 214–15; **18** 60–61, 63
Nebraska Light & Power Company, **6** 580
Nebraska Power Company, **25** 89
Nebraska Public Power District, 29 351–54
NEBS. *See* New England Business Services, Inc.
NEC Corporation, I 455, 520; **II** 40, 42, 45, 56–57, **66–68**, 73, 82, 91, 104, 361; **III** 122–23, 130, 140, 715; **6** 101, 231, 244, 287; **9** 42, 115; **10** 257, 366, 463, 500; **11** 46, 308, 490; **13** 482; **16** 139; **18** 382–83; **19** 391; **21 388–91 (upd.)**; **25** 82, 531; **36** 286, 299–300
Neches Butane Products Co., **IV** 552
Neckermann Versand AG, **V** 100–02
Nedbank, **IV** 23
Nederland Line. *See* Stoomvaart Maatschappij Nederland.
Nederlander Organization, **24** 439
Nederlands Talen Institut, **13** 544
Nederlandsche Electriciteits Maatschappij. *See* N.E.M.
Nederlandsche Handel Maatschappij, **26** 242
Nederlandsche Heide Maatschappij, **III** 199
Nederlandsche Heidenmaatschappij. *See* Arcadis NV.
Nederlandsche Kunstzijdebariek, **13** 21
Nederlandsche Nieuw Guinea Petroleum Maatschappij, **IV** 491
Nederlandsche Stoomvart Maatschappij Oceaan, **6** 416
Nederlandse Cement Industrie, **III** 701
Nederlandse Credietbank N.V., **II** 248
Nederlandse Dagbladunie NV, **IV** 610
N.V. Nederlandse Gasunie, I 326; **V** 627, **658–61**; **38** 407
Nederlandse Handel Maatschappij, **II** 183, 527; **IV** 132–33
Nederlandse Vliegtuigenfabriek, **I** 54
Nedlloyd Group. *See* Koninklijke Nedlloyd N.V.
Nedsual, **IV** 23; **16** 28
Neeco, Inc., **9** 301
Needham Harper Worldwide, **I** 23, 28, 30–33; **13** 203; **14** 159
Needlecraft, **II** 560; **12** 410
Needleworks, Inc., **23** 66
Neenah Paper Co., **III** 40; **16** 303; **43** 257
Neenah Printing, **8** 360
NEES. *See* New England Electric System.
Neff Corp., 32 352–53
Negromex, **23** 171–72
Neighborhood Restaurants of America, **18** 241
Neilson/Cadbury, **II** 631
Neiman Bearings Co., **13** 78
Neiman-Marcus Co., I 246; **II** 478; **V** 10, 31; **12 355–57**; **15** 50, 86, 291; **17** 43; **21** 302; **25** 177–78; **27** 429
Neisler Laboratories, **I** 400
Neisner Brothers, Inc., **9** 20
Nekoosa Edwards Paper Co., **IV** 282; **9** 261
NEL Equity Services Co., **III** 314
Nelio Chemicals, Inc., **IV** 345
Nelson Bros., **14** 236
Nelson Publications, **22** 442
Nemuro Bank, **II** 291
Nenuco, **II** 567
Neo Products Co., **37** 401
Neodata, **11** 293
Neos, **21** 438
Neoterics Inc., **11** 65
Neozyme I Corp., **13** 240
Nepera, Inc., **I** 682; **16** 69
Neptun Maritime Oyj, **29** 431
Neptune, **22** 63
NER Auction Group, **23** 148
NERCO, Inc., V 689, **7 376–79**
Nesbitt Thomson, **II** 211
Nesco Inc., **28** 6, 8
Nescott, Inc., **16** 36
Nesher Israel Cement Enterprises Ltd., **II** 47; **25** 266
Nespak SpA, **40** 214–15
Neste Oy, IV 435, **469–71**, 519. *See also* Fortum Corporation
Nestlé S.A., I 15, 17, 251–52, 369, 605; **II** 379, 456, 478, 486–89, 521, **545–49**, 568–70; **III** 47–48; **6** 16; **7 380–84 (upd.)**; **8** 131, 342–44, 498–500; **10** 47, 324; **11** 15, 205; **12** 480–81; **13** 294; **14** 214; **15** 63; **16** 168; **19** 50–51; **21** 55–56, 219; **22** 78, 80; **23** 219; **24** 388; **25** 21, 85, 366; **28 308–13 (upd.)**; **32** 115, 234; **36** 234, 237
NetCom Systems AB, 26 331–33
Netherland Bank for Russian Trade, **II** 183
Netherlands Fire Insurance Co. of Tiel, **III** 308, 310
Netherlands India Steam Navigation Co., **III** 521
Netherlands Insurance Co., **III** 179, 308–10
Netherlands Trading Co. *See* Nederlandse Handel Maatschappij.
NetHold B.V., **31** 330
NetLabs, **25** 117
NetMarket Company, **16** 146
NetPlane Systems, **36** 124
Netron, **II** 390
Netscape Communications Corporation, 15 320–22; **35 304–07 (upd.)**
NetStar Communications Inc., **24** 49; **35** 69
NetStar Inc.,
Nettai Sangyo, **I** 507
Nettingsdorfer, **19** 227
Nettle Creek Corporation, **19** 304
Nettlefolds Ltd., **III** 493
Netto, **11** 240
Net2Phone Inc., **34** 224
NetWest Securities, **25** 450
Network Associates, Inc., 25 119, **347–49**
Network Communications Associates, Inc., **11** 409
Network Ten, **35** 68–69
NetZero Inc., **38** 271
Neue Frankfurter Allgemeine Versicherungs-AG, **III** 184
Neue Holding AG, **III** 377
Neuenberger Versicherungs-Gruppe, **III** 404
Neuralgyline Co., **I** 698
Neuro Navigational Corporation, **21** 47
Neutrogena Corporation, 17 340–44; **36** 305
Nevada Bell Telephone Company, V 318–20; **14 345–47**
Nevada Community Bank, **11** 119
Nevada National Bank, **II** 381; **12** 534
Nevada Natural Gas Pipe Line Co., **19** 411
Nevada Power Company, 11 342–44; **12** 265
Nevada Savings and Loan Association, **19** 412
Nevada Southern Gas Company, **19** 411
Neversink Dyeing Company, **9** 153
Nevex Software Technologies, **42** 24, 26
New Access Communications, **43** 252
New America Publishing Inc., **10** 288
New Asahi Co., **I** 221
New Balance Athletic Shoe, Inc., 17 245; **25 350–52**; **35** 388
New Bedford Gas & Edison Light Co., **14** 124–25
New Broken Hill Consolidated, **IV** 58–61
New Century Network, **13** 180; **19** 204, 285
New City Releasing, Inc., **25** 269
New Consolidated Canadian Exploration Co., **IV** 96
New Consolidated Gold Fields, **IV** 21, 95–96
New CORT Holdings Corporation. *See* CORT Business Services Corporation.
New Daido Steel Co., Ltd., **IV** 62–63
New Dana Perfumes Company, 37 269–71
New Departure, **9** 17
New Departure Hyatt, **III** 590
New England Audio Company, Inc. *See* Tweeter Home Entertainment Group, Inc.
New England Business Services, Inc., 18 361–64
New England Confectionery Co., 15 323–25
New England CRInc, **8** 562
New England Electric System, V 662–64
New England Gas & Electric Association, **14** 124–25
New England Glass Co., **III** 640
New England Life Insurance Co., **III** 261

New England Merchants National Bank, **II** 213–14; **III** 313
New England Mutual Life Insurance Co., III 312–14
New England National Bank of Boston, **II** 213
New England Network, Inc., **12** 31
New England Nuclear Corporation, **I** 329; **8** 152
New England Power Association, **V** 662
New England Trust Co., **II** 213
New Fire Office, **III** 371
New Found Industries, Inc., **9** 465
New Galveston Company, Inc., **25** 116
New Guinea Goldfields, **IV** 95
New Halwyn China Clays, **III** 690
New Hampshire Gas & Electric Co., **14** 124
New Hampshire Insurance Co., **III** 196–97
New Hampshire Oak, **III** 512
New Hampton, Inc., **27** 429
New Haven District Telephone Company. *See* Southern New England Telecommunications Corporation.
New Haven Electric Co., **21** 512
New Hokkai Hotel Co., Ltd., **IV** 327
New Holland N.V., 22 379–81. *See also* CNH Global N.V.
New Horizon Manufactured Homes, Ltd., **17** 83
New Hotel Showboat, Inc. *See* Showboat, Inc.
New Ireland, **III** 393
New Jersey Bell, **9** 321
New Jersey Hot Water Heating Company, **6** 449
New Jersey Shale, **14** 250
New Jersey Tobacco Co., **15** 138
New Jersey Zinc, **I** 451
New London City National Bank, **13** 467
New London Ship & Engine, **I** 57
New Look Group plc, 35 308–10
New Mather Metals, **III** 582
New Mitsui Bussan, **I** 507; **III** 296
New Nippon Electric Co., **II** 67
New Orleans Canal and Banking Company, **11** 105
New Orleans Refining Co., **IV** 540
New Plan Realty Trust, 11 345–47
New Process Company, **25** 76–77
New Process Cork Company Inc., **I** 601; **13** 188
New South Wales Health System, **16** 94
New Street Capital Inc., 8 388–90 (upd.). *See also* Drexel Burnham Lambert Incorporated.
New Sulzer Diesel, **III** 633
New Toyo Group, **19** 227
New Trading Company. *See* SBC Warburg.
New United Motor Manufacturing Inc., **I** 205; **38** 461
New UPI Inc., **25** 507
New Valley Corporation, 17 345–47
New Vanden Borre, **24** 266–70
New World Coffee-Manhattan Bagel, Inc., **32** 15
New World Communications Group, **22** 442; **28** 248
New World Development Company Limited, IV 717–19; **8** 500; **38 318–22 (upd.)**
New World Entertainment, **17** 149
New World Hotel (Holdings) Ltd., **IV** 717; **13** 66
New York Air, **I** 90, 103, 118, 129; **6** 129
New York Airways, **I** 123–24
New York and Richmond Gas Company, **6** 456
New York and Suburban Savings and Loan Association, **10** 91
New York Biscuit Co., **II** 542
New York Capital Bank, **41** 312
New York Central Railroad Company, **II** 329, 369; **IV** 181; **9** 228; **10** 43–44, 71–73; **17** 496
New York Chemical Manufacturing Co., **II** 250
New York City Transit Authority, **8** 75
New York Condensed Milk Co., **II** 470
New York Daily News, 32 357–60
New York Electric Corporation. *See* New York State Electric and Gas.
New York Envelope Co., **32** 346
New York Evening Enquirer, **10** 287
New York Fabrics and Crafts, **16** 197
New York Gas Light Company. *See* Consolidated Edison Company of New York.
New York Glucose Co., **II** 496
New York Guaranty and Indemnity Co., **II** 331
New York Harlem Railroad Co., **II** 250
New York Improved Patents Corp., **I** 601; **13** 188
New York, Lake Erie & Western Railroad, **II** 395; **10** 59
New York Life Insurance Company, II 217–18, 330; **III** 291, 305, **315–17**, 332; **10** 382
New York Magazine Co., **IV** 651; **7** 390; **12** 359
New York Manufacturing Co., **II** 312
New York Marine and Gotham Insurance, **41** 284
New York Marine Underwriters, **III** 220
New York Quinine and Chemical Works, **I** 496
New York Quotation Company, **9** 370
New York Restaurant Group, Inc., 32 361–63
New York, Rio and Buenos Aires Airlines, **I** 115
New York State Board of Tourism, **6** 51
New York State Electric and Gas Corporation, 6 534–36
New York Stock Exchange, Inc., 9 369–72; **10** 416–17; **34** 254; **39 296–300 (upd.)**
New York Telephone Co., **9** 321
The New York Times Company, III 40; **IV 647–49**; **6** 13; **15** 54; **16** 302; **19 283–85 (upd.)**; **23** 158; **32** 508; **43** 256
New York Trust Co., **I** 378; **II** 251
New York, West Shore and Buffalo Railroad, **II** 329
New York Zoological Society. *See* Wildlife Conservation Society.
New York's Bankers Trust Co., **12** 107
New York-Newport Air Service Co., **I** 61
New Zealand Aluminum Smelters, **IV** 59
New Zealand Co., **II** 187
New Zealand Countrywide Banking Corporation, **10** 336
New Zealand Forest Products, **IV** 249–50
New Zealand Press Assoc., **IV** 669
New Zealand Sugar Co., **III** 686
New Zealand Wire Ltd., **IV** 279; **19** 154
Newark Electronics Co., **9** 420
Newco Waste Systems, **V** 750
Newcor, Inc., 40 332–35
Newcrest Mining Ltd., **IV** 47; **22** 107
Newell and Harrison Company. *See* Supervalu Inc.
Newell Co., 9 373–76; **12** 216; **13** 40–41; **22** 35; **25** 22
Newey and Eyre, **I** 429
Newfoundland Brewery, **26** 304
Newfoundland Energy, Ltd., **17** 121
Newfoundland Light & Power Co. *See* Fortis, Inc.
Newfoundland Processing Ltd. *See* Newfoundland Energy, Ltd.
Newgateway PLC, **II** 629
Newhall Land and Farming Company, 14 348–50
Newhouse Broadcasting, **6** 33
Newman's Own, Inc., 37 272–75
Newmark & Lewis Inc., **23** 373
Newmont Mining Corporation, III 248; **IV** 17, 20, 33, 171, 576; **7** 287–89, **385–88**; **12** 244; **16** 25; **23** 40; **38** 231–32; **40** 411–12
Newnes, **17** 397
Newport News Shipbuilding and Dry Dock Co., I 58, 527; **13 372–75**; **27** 36
Newport News Shipbuilding Inc., 38 323–27 (upd.); **41** 42
News & Observer Publishing Company, **23** 343
News America Publishing Inc., 12 358–60; **27** 42; **37** 408
News and Westminster Ltd., **IV** 685
News Communications & Media Plc, **35** 242
News Corporation Limited, II 169; **IV 650–53**; **7 389–93 (upd.)**; **8** 551; **9** 429; **12** 358–60; **17** 398; **18** 211, 213, 254; **22** 194, 441; **23** 121; **24** 224; **25** 490; **26** 32; **27** 305, 473; **32** 239; **35** 157–58; **37** 408; **43** 174, 433
News International Corp., **20** 79
Newsfoto Publishing Company, **12** 472; **36** 469
Newspaper Co-op Couponing, **8** 551
Newspaper Enterprise Association, **7** 157–58
Newspaper Proprietors' Assoc., **IV** 669
Newspaper Supply Co., **IV** 607
Newsquest plc, 32 354–56
Newsweek, Inc., **IV** 688
Newth-Morris Box Co. *See* Rock-Tenn Company.
Newtherm Oil Burners, Ltd., **13** 286
Newton Yarn Mills, **19** 305
Newtown Gas Co., **6** 455
Nexar Technologies, Inc., **22** 409
NEXCOM. *See* Navy Exchange Service Command.
NeXT Incorporated, **III** 116, 121; **6** 219; **18** 93; **34** 348; **36** 49
Next plc, 6 25; **29 355–57**
Nextel Communications, Inc., 10 431–33; **21** 239; **26** 389; **27 341–45 (upd.)**
NEXTLINK Communications, Inc., **38** 192
Neyveli Lignite Corp. Ltd., **IV** 49
NFC plc, 6 412–14; **14** 547
NFL Properties, Inc., **22** 223
NFO Worldwide, Inc., 24 352–55
NGC Corporation, 18 365–67
NGI International Precious Metals, Ltd., **24** 335
NHK. *See* Japan Broadcasting Corporation.

NHK Spring Co., Ltd., III 580–82
NI Industries, **20** 362
Niagara Corporation, 28 314–16
Niagara Fire Insurance Co., **III** 241–42
Niagara First Savings and Loan Association, **10** 91
Niagara Insurance Co. (Bermuda) Ltd., **III** 242
Niagara Mohawk Power Corporation, V 665–67; **6** 535; **25** 130
Niagara of Wisconsin, **26** 362–63
Niagara Silver Co., **IV** 644
Niagara Sprayer and Chemical Co., **I** 442
NIBRASCO, **IV** 55
Nicaro Nickel Co., **IV** 82, 111; **7** 186
Nice Day, Inc., **II** 539
Nice Systems, **11** 520
NiceCom Ltd., **11** 520
Nichi-Doku Shashinki Shoten, **III** 574; **43** 281
Nichia Steel, **IV** 159
Nichibo, **V** 387
Nichii Co., Ltd., V 154–55; **15** 470; **36** 418
Nichimen Corporation, II 442; **IV 150–52**, 154; **10** 439; **24 356–59 (upd.)**
Nichimo Sekiyu Co. Ltd., **IV** 555; **16** 490
Nicholas Kiwi Ltd., **II** 572; **15** 436
Nicholas Turkey Breeding Farms, **13** 103
Nicholas Ungar, **V** 156
Nichols & Company, **8** 561
Nichols Copper Co., **IV** 164, 177
Nichols-Homeshield, **22** 14
Nichols Research Corporation, 18 368–70
Nicholson File Co., **II** 16
Nicholson Graham & Jones, **28** 141
Le Nickel. *See* Société Le Nickel.
Nickelodeon, **25** 381
Nicolai Pavdinsky Co., **IV** 118
Nicolet Instrument Company, **11** 513
NICOR Inc., 6 529–31
Niederbayerische Celluloswerke, **IV** 324
Niederrheinische Hütte AG, **IV** 222
Niehler Maschinenfabrick, **III** 602
Nielsen, **10** 358
Nielsen & Petersen, **III** 417
Nielsen Marketing Research. *See* A.C. Nielsen Company.
Niemann Chemie, **8** 464
Niese & Coast Products Co., **II** 681
Niesmann & Bischoff, **22** 207
Nieuw Rotterdam, **27** 54
Nieuwe Eerste Nederlandsche, **III** 177–79
Nieuwe HAV-Bank of Schiedam, **III** 200
Nigeria Airways, **I** 107
Nigerian National Petroleum Corporation, IV 472–74
Nigerian Shipping Operations, **27** 473
Nihol Repol Corp., **III** 757
Nihon Denko, **II** 118
Nihon Keizai Shimbun, Inc., IV 654–56
Nihon Kensetsu Sangyo Ltd., **I** 520
Nihon Kohden Corporation, **13** 328
Nihon Lumber Land Co., **III** 758
Nihon Sangyo Co., **I** 183; **II** 118
Nihon Sugar, **I** 511
Nihon Synopsis, **11** 491
Nihon Teppan, **IV** 159
Nihon Timken K.K., **8** 530
Nihon Waters K.K., **43** 456
Nihon Yusen Kaisha, **I** 503, 506; **III** 577, 712
Nihron Yupro Corp., **III** 756
NII. *See* National Intergroup, Inc.
Niitsu Oil, **IV** 542
NIKE, Inc., V 372–74, 376; **8** 303–04, **391–94 (upd.)**; **9** 134–35, 437; **10** 525; **11** 50, 349; **13** 513; **14** 8; **15** 397; **16** 79, 81; **17** 244–45, 260–61; **18** 264, 266–67, 392; **22** 173; **25** 352; **27** 20; **29** 187–88; **31** 413–14; **36 343–48 (upd.)**
Nikka Oil Co., **IV** 150; **24** 357
Nikka Whisky Distilling Co., **I** 220
Nikkei. *See also* Nihon Keizai Shimbun, Inc.
Nikkei Aluminium Co., **IV** 153–55
Nikkei Shimbun Toei, **9** 29
Nikken Global Inc., 32 364–67
Nikken Stainless Fittings Co., Ltd., **IV** 160
Nikko Copper Electrolyzing Refinery, **III** 490
Nikko International Hotels, **I** 106
Nikko Kido Company, **6** 431
Nikko Petrochemical Co. Ltd., **IV** 476
The Nikko Securities Company Limited, II 300, 323, 383, **433–35**; **9 377–79 (upd.)**; **12** 536
Nikko Trading Co., **I** 106
Nikolaiev, **19** 49, 51
Nikon Corporation, III 120–21, 575, **583–85**; **9** 251; **12** 340; **18** 93, 186, 340, 342; **43** 282
Nile Faucet Corp., **III** 569; **20** 360
Nillmij, **III** 177–79
Nilpeter, **26** 540, 542
Nimas Corp., **III** 570; **20** 362
Nimbus CD International, Inc., 20 386–90
9 Telecom, **24** 79
Nine West Group Inc., 11 348–49; **14** 441; **23** 330; **39** 247, **301–03 (upd.)**
Nineteen Hundred Washer Co., **III** 653; **12** 548
99¢ Only Stores, 25 353–55
Nintendo Co., Ltd., III 586–88; **7 394–96 (upd.)**; **10** 124–25, 284–86, 483–84; **13** 403; **15** 539; **16** 168, 331; **18** 520; **23** 26; **28 317–21 (upd.)**; **31** 237; **38** 415
Nintendo of America, **24** 4
NIOC. *See* National Iranian Oil Company.
Nippon ARC Co., **III** 715
Nippon Breweries Ltd. *See* Sapporo Breweries Ltd.
Nippon Broilers Co., **II** 550
Nippon Cable Company, **15** 235
Nippon Cargo Airlines, **6** 71
Nippon Chemical Industries, **I** 363
Nippon Credit Bank, II 310, **338–39**; **38** 439
Nippon Educational Television (NET). *See* Asahi National Broadcasting Company, Ltd.
Nippon Electric Company, Limited. *See* NEC Corporation.
Nippon Express Co., Ltd., II 273; **V 477–80**
Nippon-Fisher, **13** 225
Nippon Fruehauf Co., **IV** 154
Nippon Fukokin Kinyu Koku, **II** 300
Nippon Funtai Kogyo Co., **III** 714
Nippon Gakki Co., Ltd., **III** 656–58; **16** 554, 557
Nippon Ginko, **III** 408
Nippon Gyomo Sengu Co. Ltd., **IV** 555
Nippon Hatsujo Kabushikikaisha. *See* NHK Spring Co., Ltd.
Nippon Helicopter & Aeroplane Transport Co., Ltd., **6** 70
Nippon Hoso Kyokai. *See* Japan Broadcasting Corporation.
Nippon Idou Tsushin, **7** 119–20
Nippon International Container Services, **8** 278
Nippon Interrent, **10** 419–20
Nippon K.K. *See* Nippon Kokan K.K.
Nippon Kairiku Insurance Co., **III** 384
Nippon Kakoh Seishi, **IV** 293
Nippon Kogaku K.K., **III** 583–84
Nippon Kogyo Co. Ltd. *See* Nippon Mining Co. Ltd.
Nippon Kokan K.K., **IV** 161–63, 184, 212; **8** 449; **12** 354
Nippon Life Insurance Company, II 374, 451; **III** 273, 288, **318–20**; **IV** 727; **9** 469
Nippon Light Metal Company, Ltd., IV 153–55
Nippon Machinery Trading, **I** 507
Nippon Meat Packers, Inc., II 550–51
Nippon Menka Kaisha. *See* Nichimen Corporation.
Nippon Merck-Banyu, **I** 651; **11** 290
Nippon Mining Co., Ltd., III 759; **IV 475–77**; **14** 207
Nippon Motorola Manufacturing Co., **II** 62
Nippon New Zealand Trading Co. Ltd., **IV** 327
Nippon Oil Company, Limited, IV 434, 475–76, **478–79**, 554; **19** 74
Nippon Onkyo, **II** 118
Nippon Paint Co., Ltd, **11** 252
Nippon Pelnox Corp., **III** 715
Nippon Phonogram, **23** 390
Nippon Polaroid Kabushiki Kaisha, **III** 608; **7** 437; **18** 570
Nippon Pulp Industries, **IV** 321
Nippon Rayon, **V** 387
Nippon Sangyo Co., Ltd., **IV** 475
Nippon Sanso Corp., **I** 359; **16** 486, 488
Nippon Seiko K.K., III 589–90, 595
Nippon Sekiyu Co. *See* Nippon Oil Company, Limited.
Nippon Sheet Glass Company, Limited, III 714–16
Nippon Shinpan Company, Ltd., II 436–37, 442; **8** 118
Nippon Silica Kogyo Co., **III** 715
Nippon Soda, **II** 301
Nippon Soken, **III** 592
Nippon Steel Chemical Co., **10** 439
Nippon Steel Corporation, I 466, 493–94, 509; **II** 300, 391; **IV** 116, 130, **156–58**, 184, 212, 228, 298; **6** 274; **14** 369; **17 348–51 (upd.)**, 556; **19** 219; **24** 324–25, 370
Nippon Suisan Kaisha, Limited, II 552–53
Nippon Tar, **I** 363
Nippon Telegraph and Telephone Corporation, II 51, 62; **III** 139–40; **V 305–07**; **7** 118–20; **10** 119; **13** 482; **16** 224; **21** 330; **25** 301; **27** 327, 365
Nippon Television, **7** 249; **9** 29
Nippon Tire Co., Ltd. *See* Bridgestone Corporation.
Nippon Trust Bank Ltd., **II** 405; **15** 42
Nippon Typewriter, **II** 459
Nippon Victor (Europe) GmbH, **II** 119
Nippon Wiper Blade Co., Ltd., **III** 592

Nippon Yusen Kabushiki Kaisha, **IV** 713; **V 481–83**; **6** 398
Nippon Yusoki Company, Ltd., **13** 501
Nippondenso Co., Ltd., **III 591–94**, 637–38
NIPSCO Industries, Inc., **6 532–33**
Nishi Taiyo Gyogyo Tosei K.K., **II** 578
Nishikawaya Co., Ltd., **V** 209
Nishimbo Industries Inc., **IV** 442
Nishizono Ironworks, **III** 595
NiSource, Inc., **38** 81
Nissan Construction, **V** 154
Nissan Motor Acceptance Corporation, **22** 207
Nissan Motor Co., Ltd., **I** 9–10, **183–84**, 207, 494; **II** 118, 292–93, 391; **III** 485, 517, 536, 579, 591, 742, 750; **IV** 63; **7** 111, 120, 219; **9** 243, 340–42; **10** 353; **11** 50–51, **350–52 (upd.)**; **16** 167; **17** 556; **23** 338–40, 289; **24** 324; **27** 203; **34** 133, **303–07 (upd.)**
Nissan Trading Company, Ltd., **13** 533
Nisshin Chemical Industries, **I** 397
Nisshin Chemicals Co., **II** 554
Nisshin Flour Milling Company, Ltd., **II 554**
Nisshin Pharaceutical Co., **II** 554
Nisshin Steel Co., Ltd., **I** 432; **IV** 130, **159–60**; **7** 588
Nissho Iwai K.K., **I** 432, **509–11**; **IV** 160, 383; **V** 373; **6** 386; **8** 75, 392; **15** 373; **25** 449; **27** 107; **36** 345
Nissho Kosan Co., **III** 715
Nissui. *See* Nippon Suisan Kaisha.
Nitratos de Portugal, **IV** 505
Nitroglycerin AB, **13** 22
Nitroglycerin Ltd., **9** 380
Nittetsu Curtainwall Corp., **III** 758
Nittetsu Sash Sales Corp., **III** 758
Nitto Warehousing Co., **I** 507
Nittoku Metal Industries, Ltd., **III** 635
Nittsu. *See* Nippon Express Co., Ltd.
Niugini Mining Ltd., **23** 42
Nixdorf Computer AG, **I** 193; **II** 279; **III** 109, **154–55**; **12** 162; **14** 13, 169; **26** 497
Nixdorf-Krein Industries Inc. *See* Laclede Steel Company.
NKK Corporation, **IV** 74, **161–63**, 212–13; **V** 152; **24** 144; **28 322–26 (upd.)**
NL Industries, Inc., **III** 681; **10 434–36**; **19** 466–68
NLM City-Hopper, **I** 109
NLM Dutch Airlines, **I** 108
NLT Corp., **II** 122; **III** 194; **10** 66; **12** 546
NM Acquisition Corp., **27** 346
NMC Laboratories Inc., **12** 4
NMH Stahlwerke GmbH, **IV** 128
NMT. *See* Nordic Mobile Telephone.
No-Leak-O Piston Ring Company, **10** 492
No-Sag Spring Co., **16** 321
Noah's New York Bagels, **13** 494. *See also* Einstein/Noah Bagel Corporation.
Nobel-Bozel, **I** 669
Nobel Drilling Corporation, **26** 243
Nobel-Hoechst Chimie, **I** 669
Nobel Industries AB, **I** 351; **9 380–82**; **16** 69. *See also* Akzo Nobel N.V.
Nobel Learning Communities, Inc., **37 276–79**
Noble Affiliates, Inc., **11 353–55**; **18** 366
Noble Broadcast Group, Inc., **23** 293
Noble Roman's Inc., **14 351–53**
Nobles Industries, **13** 501
Noblesville Telephone Company, **14** 258
Noblitt-Sparks Industries, Inc., **8** 37–38
Nobody Beats the Wiz. *See* Cablevision Electronic Instruments, Inc.
Nocona Belt Company, **31** 435–36
Nocona Boot Co. *See* Justin Industries, Inc.
Noel Group, Inc., **24** 286–88
Noell, **IV** 201
NOK Corporation, **41** 170–72
Nokia Corporation, **II 69–71**; **IV** 296; **6** 242; **15** 125; **17** 33, **352–54 (upd.)**; **18** 74, 76; **19** 226; **20** 439; **38 328–31 (upd.)**
Noland Company, **35 311–14**
Nolte Mastenfabriek B.V., **19** 472
Noma Industries, **11** 526
Nomai Inc., **18** 510
Nomura Bank of Japan, **34** 221
Nomura Securities Company, Limited, **II** 276, 326, 434, **438–41**; **9** 377, **383–86 (upd.)**; **39** 109
Nomura Toys Ltd., **16** 267; **43** 232
Non-Fiction Book Club, **13** 105
Non-Stop Fashions, Inc., **8** 323
Nonpareil Refining Co., **IV** 488
Noodle Kidoodle, **16 388–91**
Noordwinning Group, **IV** 134
NOP Research Group, **28** 501, 504
Nopco Chemical Co., **IV** 409; **7** 308
Nopri, **V** 63–65
Nor-Am Agricultural Products, **I** 682
Nor-Cal Engineering Co. GmbH, **18** 162
Nora Industrier A/S, **18** 395
NORAND, **9** 411
Noranda Inc., **IV 164–66**; **7 397–99 (upd.)**; **9** 282; **26** 363
Norandex, **16** 204
Norbro Corporation. *See* Stuart Entertainment Inc.
Norcast Manufacturing Ltd., **IV** 165
Norcen Energy Resources, Ltd., **8** 347
Norcliff Thayer, **III** 66
Norco Plastics, **8** 553
Norcon, Inc., **7** 558–59
Norcore Plastics, Inc., **33** 361
Nord-Aviation, **I** 45, 74, 82, 195; **7** 10
Nordarmatur, **I** 198
Nordbanken, **9** 382
Norddeutsche Affinerie, **IV** 141
Norddeutsche Bank A.G., **II** 279
Norddeutscher-Lloyd, **I** 542; **6** 397–98
Nordea AB, **40 336–39**
Nordfinanzbank, **II** 366
Nordic Baltic Holding. *See* Nordea AB.
Nordic Bank Ltd., **II** 366
Nordic Joint Stock Bank, **II** 302
Nordic Mobile Telephone, **II** 70
Nordica, **10** 151; **15** 396–97
NordicTrack, **10** 215–17; **22 382–84**; **38** 238. *See also* Icon Health & Fitness, Inc.
Nordland Papier GmbH, **IV** 300, 302
Nordson Corporation, **11 356–58**
Nordstahl AG, **IV** 201
Nordstjernan, **I** 553–54
Nordstrom, Inc., **V 156–58**; **11** 349; **13** 494; **14** 376; **17** 313; **18 371–74 (upd.)**; **21** 302; **22** 173
Nordwestdeutsche Kraftwerke AG, **III** 466; **V** 698–700
Norelco, **17** 110
Norelco Consumer Products Co., **12** 439; **26 334–36**
Norelec, **27** 138
Norex Laboratories, **I** 699
Norex Leasing, Inc., **16** 397
Norfolk Carolina Telephone Company, **10** 202
Norfolk Southern Corporation, **V 484–86**; **6** 436, 487; **12** 278; **22** 167; **29 358–61 (upd.)**
Norfolk Steel, **13** 97
Norge Co., **III** 439–40; **18** 173–74; **43** 163–64
Noric Corporation, **39** 332
Norinchukin Bank, **II 340–41**
NORIS Bank GmbH, **V** 166
Norlin, **16** 238–39
Norma Cie., **III** 622
Norman BV, **9** 93; **33** 78
Norman J. Hurll Group, **III** 673
Normandy Mining Ltd., **23** 42
Normark Corporation. *See* Rapala-Normark Group, Ltd.
Normond/CMS, **7** 117
Norrell Corporation, **I** 696; **6** 46; **23** 431; **25 356–59**
Norris Cylinder Company, **11** 535
Norris Grain Co., **14** 537
Norsk Hydro ASA, **10 437–40**; **35 315–19 (upd.)**; **36** 322
Norstan, Inc., **16 392–94**
Norstar Bancorp, **9** 229
Nortek, Inc., **I** 482; **14** 482; **22** 4; **26** 101; **34 308–12**; **37** 331
Nortel Networks Corporation, **36 349–54 (upd.)**
Nortex International, **7** 96; **19** 338
North & South Wales Bank, **II** 318; **17** 323
North Advertising, Inc., **6** 27
North African Petroleum Ltd., **IV** 455
North American Aviation, **I** 48, 71, 78, 81, 101; **7** 520; **9** 16; **10** 163; **11** 278, 427
North American Bancorp, **II** 192
North American Carbon, **19** 499
North American Cellular Network, **9** 322
North American Coal Corporation, **7** 369–71
North American Company, **6** 443, 552–53, 601–02
North American Dräger, **13** 328
North American Energy Conservation, Inc., **35** 480
North American Insurance Co., **II** 181
North American InTeleCom, Inc., **IV** 411
North American Life and Casualty Co., **III** 185, 306
North American Light & Power Company, **V** 609; **6** 504–05; **12** 541
North American Managers, Inc., **III** 196
North American Medical Management Company, Inc., **36** 366
North American Mogul Products Co. *See* Mogul Corp.
North American Philips Corporation, **II** 79–80; **19** 393; **21** 520
North American Printed Circuit Corp., **III** 643
North American Printing Ink Company, **13** 228
North American Reinsurance Corp., **III** 377
North American Rockwell Corp., **10** 173
North American Systems, **14** 230
North American Training Corporation. *See* Rollerblade, Inc.
North American Van Lines, **I** 278; **14** 37

North American Watch Company. *See* Movado Group, Inc.
North Atlantic Energy Corporation, **21** 411
North Atlantic Packing, **13** 243
North British Insurance Co., **III** 234–35
North British Rubber Company, **20** 258
North Broken Hill Peko, **IV** 61
North Carolina Motor Speedway, Inc., **19** 294
North Carolina National Bank Corporation, **II** 336; **10** 425–27; **18** 518
North Carolina Natural Gas Corporation, **6** 578
North Carolina Shipbuilding Co., **13** 373
North Central Airlines, **I** 132
North Central Finance, **II** 333
North Central Financial Corp., **9** 475
North Central Utilities, Inc., **18** 405
North Cornwall China Clay Co., **III** 690
North Eastern Bricks, **14** 249
North Eastern Coalfields Ltd., **IV** 48
The North Face, Inc., 8 169; **18 375–77; 25** 206; **41** 103
North Goonbarrow, **III** 690
North Holland Publishing Co., **IV** 610
North New York Savings Bank, **10** 91
North of Scotland Bank, **II** 318; **17** 324
North of Scotland Hydro-Electric Board, **19** 389
North Pacific Paper Corp., **IV** 298
North Pacific Railroad, **II** 330
North Sea Ferries, **26** 241, 243
North Sea Oil and Gas, **10** 337
North Sea Sun Oil Co. Ltd., **IV** 550
North Shore Gas Company, **6** 543–44
North Shore Land Co., **17** 357
North Shore Medical Centre Pty, Ltd., **IV** 708
North Star Egg Case Company, **12** 376
North Star Marketing Cooperative, **7** 338
North Star Mill, **12** 376
North Star Steel Company, 13 138; **18 378–81; 19** 380; **40** 87
North Star Universal, Inc., **25** 331, 333
North Supply, **27** 364
The North West Company, Inc., 12 361–63; 25 219–20
North-West Telecommunications, **6** 327
North West Water Group plc, 11 359–62
Northamptonshire Union Bank, **II** 333
Northbrook Corporation, **24** 32
Northbrook Holdings, Inc., **22** 495
Northcliffe Newspapers, **IV** 685; **19** 118
Northeast Airlines Inc., **I** 99–100; **6** 81
Northeast Federal Corp., **13** 468
Northeast Petroleum Industries, Inc., **11** 194; **14** 461
Northeast Savings Bank, **12** 31; **13** 467–68
Northeast Utilities, V 668–69; 13 182–84; **21** 408, 411
Northeastern Bancorp of Scranton, **II** 342
Northeastern New York Medical Service, Inc., **III** 246
Northern Aluminum Co. Ltd., **IV** 9–10
Northern and Employers Assurance, **III** 235
Northern Arizona Light & Power Co., **6** 545
Northern Border Pipeline Co., **V** 609–10
Northern California Savings, **10** 340
Northern Crown Bank, **II** 344
Northern Dairies, **10** 441
Northern Development Co., **IV** 282
Northern Drug Company, **14** 147
Northern Electric Company. *See* Northern Telecom Limited.
Northern Energy Resources Company. *See* NERCO, Inc.
Northern Engineering Industries Plc, **21** 436
Northern Fibre Products Co., **I** 202
Northern Foods PLC, I 248; **II** 587; **10 441–43**
Northern Illinois Gas Co., **6** 529–31
Northern Indiana Power Company, **6** 556
Northern Indiana Public Service Company, **6** 532–33
Northern Infrastructure Maintenance Company, **39** 238
Northern Joint Stock Bank, **II** 303
Northern Leisure, **40** 296–98
Northern Light Electric Company, **18** 402–03
Northern National Bank, **14** 90
Northern Natural Gas Co., **V** 609–10
Northern Pacific Corp., **15** 274
Northern Pacific Railroad, **II** 278, 329; **III** 228, 282; **14** 168; **26** 451
Northern Paper, **I** 614
Northern Pipeline Construction Co., **19** 410, 412
Northern Rock plc, 33 318–21
Northern Star Co., **25** 332
Northern States Life Insurance Co., **III** 275
Northern States Power Company, V 670–72; 18 404; **20 391–95 (upd.)**
Northern Stores, Inc., **12** 362
Northern Sugar Company, **11** 13
Northern Telecom Limited, II 70; **III** 143, 164; **V** 271; **V 308–10; 6** 242, 307, 310; **9** 479; **10** 19, 432; **11** 69; **12** 162; **14** 259; **16** 392, 468; **17** 353; **18** 111; **20** 439; **22** 51; **25** 34; **27** 342. *See also* Nortel Networks Corporation.
Northern Trust Company, III 518; **9 387–89; 22** 280
Northfield Metal Products, **11** 256
Northgate Computer Corp., **16** 196
Northland. *See* Scott Fetzer Company.
Northland Cranberries, Inc., 38 332–34
Northland Publishing, **19** 231
NorthPrint International, **22** 356
Northrop Corporation, I 47, 49, 55, 59, **76–77**, 80, 84, 197, 525; **III** 84; **9** 416, 418; **10** 162; **11** 164, 166, 266, 269, **363–65 (upd.); 25** 316
Northrop Grumman, **41** 43
Northrup King Co., **I** 672
NorthStar Computers, **10** 313
Northwest Airlines Inc., I 42, 64, 91, 97, 100, 104, **112–14**, 125, 127; **6** 66, 74, 82 **103–05 (upd.)**, 123; **9** 273; **11** 266, 315; **12** 191, 487; **21** 141, 143; **22** 252; **26 337–40 (upd.)**, 441; **27** 20; **28** 226, 265–66; **30** 447; **31** 419–20; **33** 50–51, 302. *See also* Mesaba Holdings, Inc.
Northwest Benefit Assoc., **III** 228
Northwest Engineering, **21** 502
Northwest Engineering Co. *See* Terex Corporation.
Northwest Express. *See* Bear Creek Corporation.
Northwest Industries, **I** 342; **II** 468 **8** 367; **25** 165–66. *See also* Chicago and North Western Holdings Corporation.
Northwest Instruments, **8** 519
Northwest Linen Co., **16** 228
Northwest Outdoor, **27** 280
Northwest Paper Company, **8** 430
Northwest Steel Rolling Mills Inc., **13** 97
Northwest Telecommunications Inc., **6** 598
Northwestern Bell Telephone Co., **V** 341; **25** 495
Northwestern Benevolent Society, **III** 228
NorthWestern Corporation, 37 280–83
Northwestern Engraving, **12** 25
Northwestern Expanded Metal Co., **III** 763
Northwestern Financial Corporation, **11** 29
Northwestern Industries, **III** 263
Northwestern Manufacturing Company, **8** 133
Northwestern Mutual Life Insurance Company, III 321–24, 352; **IV** 333
Northwestern National Bank, **16** 71
Northwestern National Insurance Co., **IV** 29
Northwestern National Life Insurance Co., **14** 233
Northwestern Public Service Company, **6** 524
Northwestern States Portland Cement Co., **III** 702
Northwestern Telephone Systems, **6** 325, 328
Norton Company, III 678; **8 395–97; 16** 122; **22** 68; **26** 70
Norton Healthcare Ltd., **11** 208
Norton McNaughton, Inc., 25 245; **27 346–49**
Norton Opax PLC, **IV** 259; **34** 140
Norton Professional Books. *See* W.W. Norton & Company, Inc.
Norton Simon Industries, **I** 446; **IV** 672; **6** 356; **19** 404; **22** 513
Norwales Development Ltd., **11** 239
Norwalk Truck Lines, **14** 567
NORWEB plc, **13** 458; **24** 270
Norwegian Assurance, **III** 258
Norwegian Caribbean Line, **27** 90
Norwegian Globe, **III** 258
Norwegian Petroleum Consultants, **III** 499
Norweld Holding A.A., **13** 316
Norwest Bank, **19** 412
Norwest Corp., **16** 135
Norwest Mortgage Inc., **11** 29
Norwest Publishing, **IV** 661
Norwich-Eaton Pharmaceuticals, **III** 53; **8** 434; **26** 383
Norwich Pharmaceuticals, **I** 370–71; **9** 358
Norwich Union Fire Insurance Society, Ltd., **III** 242, 273, 404; **IV** 705
Norwich Winterthur Group, **III** 404
Norwood Company, **13** 168
Norwood Promotional Products, Inc., 26 341–43
Nostell Brick & Tile, **14** 249
Notre Capital Ventures II, L.P., **24** 117
Nottingham Manufacturing Co., **V** 357
Nouvelle Compagnie Havraise Pénninsulaire, **27** 514
Nouvelles Galeries Réunies, **10** 205; **19** 308; **27** 95
Nouvelles Messageries de la Presse Parisienne, **IV** 618
Nova Corporation, **18** 365–67; **24** 395
Nova Corporation of Alberta, V 673–75; 12 364–66
Nova Information Systems, **24** 393
Nova Pharmaceuticals, **14** 46
Nova Scotia Steel Company, **19** 186
NovaCare, Inc., 11 366–68; 14 233; **33** 185; **41** 194

Novacor Chemicals Ltd., **12 364–66**
Novagas Clearinghouse Ltd., **18** 367
Novalta Resources Inc., **11** 441
Novamax Technologies Inc., **34** 209
Novanet Semiconductor, **36** 124
Novartis AG, **18** 51; **34** 284; **39 304–10 (upd.)**
Novell, Inc., **6** 255–56, 260, **269–71**; **9** 170–71; **10** 232, 363, 473–74, 558, 565; **11** 59, 519–20; **12** 335; **13** 482; **15** 131, 133, 373, 492; **16** 392, 394; **20** 237; **21** 133–34; **23 359–62 (upd.)**; **25** 50–51, 117, 300, 499; **33** 113, 115; **34** 442–43; **36** 80; **38** 418–19
Novello and Co., **II** 139; **24** 193
Novellus Systems, Inc., **18 382–85**
Novo Industri A/S, **I 658–60**, 697
Novotel. *See* Accor SA.
NOVUM. *See* Industrie Natuzzi S.p.A.
NOVUS Financial Corporation, **33** 314
Nowell Wholesale Grocery Co., **II** 681
Nowsco Well Services Ltd., **25** 73
Nox Ltd., **I** 588
Noxell Corporation, **III** 53; **8** 434; **26** 384
NPC International, Inc., **40 340–42**
NPD Group, **13** 4
NPD Trading (USA), Inc., **13** 367
NPS Waste Technologies, **13** 366
NRG Energy, Inc., **11** 401
NS. *See* Norfolk Southern Corporation.
NS Group, **31** 287
NS Petites Inc., **8** 323
NSG Information System Co., **III** 715
NSK. *See* Nippon Seiko K.K.
NSK Ltd., **42** 384
NSK-Warner, **14** 64
NSMO. *See* Nederlandsche Stoomvart Maatschappij Oceaan.
NSN Network Services, **23** 292, 294
NSP. *See* Northern States Power Company.
NSU Werke, **10** 261
NTC Publishing Group, **22** 519, 522
NTCL. *See* Northern Telecom Limited.
NTN Corporation, **III 595–96**, 623; **28** 241
NTRON, **11** 486
NTT. *See* Nippon Telegraph and Telephone Corp.
NTTPC. *See* Nippon Telegraph and Telephone Public Corporation.
NU. *See* Northeast Utilities.
Nu-Era Gear, **14** 64
Nu-kote Holding, Inc., **18**
Nu Skin Enterprises, Inc., **27 350–53**; **31** 327 **386–89**
Nuclear Electric, **6** 453; **11** 399–401; **12** 349; **13** 484
Nuclear Power International, **19** 166
Nucoa Butter Co., **II** 497
Nucor Corporation, **7 400–02**; **13** 143, 423; **14** 156; **18** 378–80; **19** 380; **21 392–95 (upd.)**; **26** 407
Nucorp Energy, **II** 262, 620
NUG Optimus Lebensmittel-Einzelhandelgesellschaft mbH, **V** 74
Nugget Polish Co. Ltd., **II** 566
NUMAR Corporation, **25** 192
Numerax, Inc., **IV** 637
NUMMI. *See* New United Motor Manufacturing, Inc.
Nuovo Pignone, **IV** 420–22
NUR Touristic GmbH, **V** 100–02
Nurad, **III** 468
Nurotoco Inc. *See* Roto-Rooter Service Company.
Nursefinders, **6** 10
Nutmeg Industries, Inc., **17** 513
Nutraceutical International Corporation, **37 284–86**
NutraSweet Company, **II** 463, 582; **8 398–400**; **26** 108; **29** 331
Nutrena, **II** 617; **13** 137
Nutri-Foods International, **18** 467–68
Nutri/System Inc., **29** 258
Nutrilite Co., **III** 11–12
NutriSystem, **10** 383; **12** 531
Nutrition for Life International Inc., **22 385–88**
Nuveen. *See* John Nuveen Company.
NV Dagblad De Telegraaf. *See* N.V. Holdingmaatschappij De Telegraaf.
NVR L.P., **8 401–03**
NWA, Inc. *See* Northwest Airlines Corporation.
NWK. *See* Nordwestdeutsche Kraftwerke AG.
NWL Control Systems, **III** 512
NWS BANK plc, **10** 336–37
Nya AB Atlas, **III** 425–26
Nydqvist & Holm, **III** 426
Nyhamms Cellulosa, **IV** 338
NYK. *See* Nihon Yusen Kaisha, Nippon Yusen Kabushiki Kaisha *and* Nippon Yusen Kaisha.
Nyland Mattor, **25** 464
Nylex Corp., **I** 429
NYLife Care Health Plans, Inc., **17** 166
Nylon de Mexico, S.A., **19** 10, 12
NYMAGIC, Inc., **41 284–86**
Nyman & Schultz Affarsresbyraer A.B., **I** 120
Nymofil, Ltd., **16** 297
NYNEX Corporation, **V 311–13**; **6** 340; **11** 19, 87; **13** 176; **25** 61–62, 102; **26** 520; **43** 445
NYRG. *See* New York Restaurant Group, Inc.
Nyrop, **I** 113
Nysco Laboratories, **III** 55
NYSEG. *See* New York State Electric and Gas Corporation.
NZI Corp., **III** 257

O&K Rolltreppen, **27** 269
O&Y. *See* Olympia & York Developments Ltd.
O.B. McClintock Co., **7** 144–45
O.G. Wilson, **16** 560
O. Kraft & Sons, **12** 363
O.N.E. Color Communications L.L.C., **29** 306
O-Pee-Chee, **34** 447–48
O.S. Designs Inc., **15** 396
O.Y.L. Industries Berhad, **26** 3, 5
Oahu Railway & Land Co., **I** 565–66
Oak Creek Homes Inc., **41** 18
Oak Farms Dairies, **II** 660
Oak Hill Investment Partners, **11** 490
Oak Hill Sportswear Corp., **17** 137–38
Oak Industries Inc., **III** 512; **21 396–98**
Oak Technology, Inc., **22 389–93**
Oakley, Inc., **18 390–93**
OakStone Financial Corporation, **11** 448
Oaktree Capital Management, **30** 185
OakTree Health Plan Inc., **16** 404
Oakville, **7** 518
Oakwood Homes Corporation, **13** 155; **15 326–28**
OAO Gazprom, **42 261–65**
OAO LUKOIL, **40 343–46**
OASIS, **IV** 454
Oasis Group P.L.C., **10** 506
OASYS, Inc., **18** 112
ÖBB. *See* Österreichische Bundesbahnen GmbH.
Obbola Linerboard, **IV** 339
Oberheim Corporation, **16** 239
Oberland, **16** 122
Oberrheinische Bank, **II** 278
Oberschlesische Stickstoff-Werge AG, **IV** 229
Oberusel AG, **III** 541
Obi, **23** 231
Object Design, Inc., **15** 372
O'Boy Inc. *See* Happy Kids Inc.
O'Brien Kreitzberg, Inc., **25** 130
Obunsha, **9** 29
Occidental Bank, **16** 497
Occidental Chemical Corp., **19** 414
Occidental Insurance Co., **III** 251
Occidental Life Insurance Company, **I** 536–37; **13** 529; **26** 486–87; **41** 401
Occidental Overseas Ltd., **11** 97
Occidental Petroleum Corporation, **I** 527; **II** 432, 516; **IV** 264, 312, 392, 410, 417, 453–54, 467, **480–82**, 486, 515–16; **7** 376; **8** 526; **12** 100; **19** 268; **25 360–63 (upd.)**; **29** 113; **31** 115, 456; **37** 309, 311
Occidental Petroleum Great Britain Inc., **21** 206
Océ N.V., **24 360–63**
Ocean, **III** 234
Ocean Combustion Services, **9** 109
Ocean Drilling and Exploration Company. *See* ODECO.
Ocean Group plc, **6 415–17**
Ocean Reef Management, **19** 242, 244
Ocean Salvage and Towage Co., **I** 592
Ocean Scientific, Inc., **15** 380
Ocean Specialty Tankers Corporation, **22** 275
Ocean Spray Cranberries, Inc., **7 403–05**; **10** 525; **19** 278; **25 364–67 (upd.)**; **38** 334
Ocean Steam Ship Company. *See* Malaysian Airlines System BHD.
Ocean Systems Inc., **I** 400
Ocean Transport & Trading Ltd., **6** 417
Oceania Football Confederation, **27** 150
Oceanic Contractors, **III** 559
Oceanic Properties, **II** 491–92
Oceanic Steam Navigation Company, **19** 197; **23** 160
Oceans of Fun, **22** 130
Ocelet Industries Ltd., **25** 232
O'Charley's Inc., **19 286–88**
OCL. *See* Overseas Containers Ltd.
Ocoma Foods, **II** 584
Octek, **13** 235
Octel Communications Corp., **III** 143; **14** 217, **354–56**; **16** 394
Octel Messaging, **41 287–90 (upd.)**
Octopus Publishing, **IV** 667; **17** 398
Oculinum, Inc., **10** 48
Odakyu Electric Railway Company Limited, **V 487–89**
Odam's and Plaistow Wharves, **II** 580–81
Odd Job Trading Corp., **29** 311–12
Odd Lot Trading Company, **V** 172–73

Odda Smelteverk A/S, **25** 82
Odeco Drilling, Inc., **7** 362–64; **11** 522; **12** 318; **32** 338, 340
Odegard Outdoor Advertising, L.L.C., **27** 280
Odeon Theatres Ltd., **II** 157–59
Odetics Inc., 14 357–59
Odhams Press Ltd., **IV** 259, 666–67; **7** 244, 342; **17** 397–98
ODM, **26** 490
ODME. *See* Toolex International N.V.
O'Donnell-Usen Fisheries, **II** 494
Odwalla, Inc., 31 349–51
Odyssey Holdings, Inc., **18** 376
Odyssey Partners Group, **II** 679; **V** 135; **12** 55; **13** 94; **17** 137; **28** 218
Odyssey Press, **13** 560
OEC Medical Systems, Inc., 27 354–56
Oelwerken Julias Schindler GmbH, **7** 141
OEN Connectors, **19** 166
Oertel Brewing Co., **I** 226; **10** 180
Oësterreichischer Phönix in Wien, **III** 376
Oetker Group, **I** 219
Off the Rax, **II** 667; **24** 461
Off Wall Street Consulting Group, **42** 313
Office Depot Incorporated, 8 404–05; 10 235, 497; **12** 335; **13** 268; **15** 331; **18** 24, 388; **22** 154, 412–13; **23 363–65 (upd.)**; **27** 95; **34** 198; **43** 293
Office Mart Holdings Corporation, **10** 498
Office National du Crédit Agricole, **II** 264
Office Systems Inc., **15** 407
The Office Works, Inc., **13** 277; **25** 500
OfficeMax Inc., 8 404; **15 329–31; 18** 286, 388; **20** 103; **22** 154; **23** 364–65; **43 291–95 (upd.)**
Official Airline Guides, Inc., **IV** 605, 643; **7** 312, 343; **17** 399
Officine Alfieri Maserati S.p.A., 11 104; **13** 28, **376–78**
Offset Gerhard Kaiser GmbH, **IV** 325
The Offshore Company, **III** 558; **6** 577; **37** 243
Offshore Food Services Inc., **I** 514
Offshore Logistics, Inc., 37 287–89
Offshore Transportation Corporation, **11** 523
Ogden Corporation, I 512–14, 701; **6 151–53**, 600; **7** 39; **25** 16; **27** 21, 196; **41** 40–41; **43** 217
Ogden Food Products, **7** 430
Ogden Gas Co., **6** 568
Ogden Ground Services, **39** 240, 242
Ogilvie Flour Mills Co., **I** 268; **IV** 245; **25** 9, 281
Ogilvy & Mather, **22** 200
Ogilvy Group Inc., I 20, **25–27**, 31, 37, 244; **6** 53; **9** 180. *See also* WPP Group.
Oglebay Norton Company, 17 355–58
Oglethorpe Power Corporation, 6 537–38
O'Gorman and Cozens-Hardy, **III** 725
Ogura Oil, **IV** 479
Oh la la!, **14** 107
Ohbayashi Corporation, I 586–87
The Ohio Art Company, 14 360–62
Ohio Ball Bearing. *See* Bearings Inc.
Ohio Barge Lines, Inc., **11** 194
Ohio Bell Telephone Company, 14 363–65; 18 30
Ohio Boxboard Company, **12** 376
Ohio Brass Co., **II** 2
Ohio Casualty Corp., III 190; **11 369–70**
Ohio Crankshaft Co. *See* Park-Ohio Industries Inc.
Ohio Edison Company, V 676–78
Ohio Electric Railway Co., **III** 388
Ohio Mattress Co., **12** 438–39
Ohio Oil Co., **IV** 365, 400, 574; **6** 568; **7** 551
Ohio Pizza Enterprises, Inc., **7** 152
Ohio Power Shovel, **21** 502
Ohio Pure Foods Group, **II** 528
Ohio River Company, **6** 487
Ohio-Sealy Mattress Mfg. Co., **12** 438–39
Ohio Valley Electric Corporation, **6** 517
Ohio Ware Basket Company, **12** 319
Ohlmeyer Communications, **I** 275; **26** 305
Ohlsson's Cape Breweries, **I** 287–88; **24** 449
OHM Corp., **17** 553
Ohmeda. *See* BOC Group plc.
Ohmite Manufacturing Co., **13** 397
Ohrbach's Department Store, **I** 30
Ohta Keibin Railway Company, **6** 430
ÖIAG, **IV** 234
Oil Acquisition Corp., **I** 611
Oil and Natural Gas Commission, IV 440–41, **483–84**
Oil and Solvent Process Company, **9** 109
Oil City Oil and Grease Co., **IV** 489
Oil Co. of Australia, **III** 673
Oil Distribution Public Corp., **IV** 434
Oil-Dri Corporation of America, 20 396–99
Oil Drilling, Incorporated, **7** 344
Oil Dynamics Inc., **43** 178
Oil Equipment Manufacturing Company, **16** 8
Oil India Ltd., **IV** 440, 483–84
Oil Shale Corp., **IV** 522; **7** 537
Oilfield Industrial Lines Inc., **I** 477
Oilfield Service Corp. of America, **I** 342
Oita Co., **III** 718
Oji Paper Co., Ltd., I 506, 508; **II** 326; **IV** 268, 284–85, 292–93, 297–98, **320–22**, 326–27
OK Bazaars, **I** 289; **24** 450
OK Turbines, Inc., **22** 311
Okadaya Co. Ltd., **V** 96
O'Keefe Marketing, **23** 102
Oki Electric Industry Company, Limited, II 68, **72–74**; **15** 125; **21** 390
Okidata, **9** 57; **18** 435
Okinoyama Coal Mine, **III** 759
Oklahoma Airmotive, **8** 349
Oklahoma Entertainment, Inc., **9** 74
Oklahoma Gas and Electric Company, 6 539–40; 7 409–11
Oklahoma Oil Co., **I** 31
Oklahoma Publishing Company, **11** 152–53; **30** 84
Okonite, **I** 489
Okura & Co., Ltd., I 282; **IV 167–68**
Oland & Sons Limited, **25** 281
Olathe Manufacturing, **26** 494
OLC. *See* Orient Leasing Co., Ltd.
Olcott & McKesson, **I** 496
Old America Stores, Inc., 17 359–61
Old Colony Envelope Co., **32** 345–46
Old Colony Trust Co., **II** 207; **12** 30
Old Country Buffet Restaurant Co. (OCB). *See* Buffets, Inc.
Old Dominion Power Company, **6** 513, 515
Old El Paso, **I** 457; **14** 212; **24** 140–41
Old Harbor Candles, **18** 68
Old Kent Financial Corp., 11 371–72
Old Line Life Insurance Co., **III** 275
Old Mutual, **IV** 23, 535
Old National Bancorp, 14 529; **15 332–34**
Old Navy Clothing Company, **18** 193
Old Quaker Paint Company, **13** 471
Old Republic International Corp., 11 373–75
Old Spaghetti Factory International Inc., 24 364–66
Old Stone Trust Company, **13** 468
Oldach Window Corp., **19** 446
Oldham Estate, **IV** 712
Oldover Corp., **23** 225
Olds Motor Vehicle Co., **I** 171; **10** 325
Olds Oil Corp., **I** 341
Ole's Innovative Sports. *See* Rollerblade, Inc.
Olean Tile Co., **22** 170
Oleochim, **IV** 498–99
OLEX. *See* Deutsche BP Aktiengesellschaft.
Olex Cables Ltd., **10** 445
Olin Corporation, I 318, 330, **379–81**, 434, 695; **III** 667; **IV** 482; **8** 23, 153; **11** 420; **13 379–81 (upd.)**; **16** 68, 297; **32** 319
Olinkraft, Inc., **II** 432; **III** 708–09; **11** 420; **16** 376
Olins Rent-a-Car, **6** 348
Olinvest, **IV** 454
Olive Garden Italian Restaurants, **10** 322, 324; **16** 156–58; **19** 258; **35** 83
Oliver Rubber Company, **19** 454, 456
Olivetti S.p.A., 34 316–20 (upd.); **38** 300
Olivine Industries, Inc., **II** 508; **11** 172; **36** 255
Olmstead Products Co., **23** 82
Olofsson, **I** 573
Olohana Corp., **I** 129; **6** 129
Olsen Dredging Co., **III** 558
Olson & Wright, **I** 120; **34** 398
Olsonite Corp., **I** 201
Olsten Corporation, 6 41–43; 9 327; **29 362–65 (upd.)**. *See also* Adecco S.A.
Olveh, **III** 177–79
Olympia & York Developments Ltd., IV 245, 247, 712, **720–21**; **6** 478; **8** 327; **9 390–92 (upd.)**; **25** 11–12; **30** 108
Olympia Arenas, Inc., **7** 278–79; **24** 294
Olympia Brewing, **I** 260; **11** 50
Olympia Entertainment, **37** 207
Olympia Floor & Tile Co., **IV** 720
Olympiaki, **III** 401
Olympic Airways, **II** 442
Olympic Courier Systems, Inc., **24** 126
Olympic Fastening Systems, **III** 722
Olympic Insurance Co., **26** 486
Olympic Packaging, **13** 443
Olympus Communications L.P., **17** 7
Olympus Optical Company, Ltd., **15** 483
Olympus Sport, **V** 177–78
Olympus Symbol, Inc., **15** 483
OM Group, Inc., 17 362–64
Omaha Cold Store Co., **II** 571
Omaha Public Power District, **29** 353
Oman Oil Refinery Co., **IV** 516
Omega Gas Company, **8** 349
Omega Gold Mines, **IV** 164
Omega Protein Corporation, **25** 546
O'Melveny & Myers, 37 290–93
Omex Corporation, **6** 272

OMI Corporation, **IV** 34; **9** 111–12; **22** 275
Omlon, **II** 75
Ommium Française de Pétroles, **IV** 559
Omnes, **17** 419
Omni Construction Company, Inc., **8** 112–13
Omni Hearing Aid Systems, **I** 667
Omni Hotels Corp., 12 367–69
Omni-Pac, **12** 377
Omni Products International, **II** 420
Omnibus Corporation, **9** 283
Omnicare, Inc., **13** 150
Omnicom Group Inc., I 28–32, 33, 36; **14** 160; **22 394–99 (upd.)**; **23** 478; **43** 410. *See also* TBWA Worldwide.
Omnipoint Communications Inc., **18** 77
OmniSource Corporation, 14 366–67
Omnitel Pronto Italia SpA, **38** 300
Omron Corporation, 28 331–35 (upd.)
Omron Tateisi Electronics Company, II 75–77; **III** 549
ÖMV Aktiengesellschaft, IV 234, 454, **485–87**
On Assignment, Inc., 20 400–02
On Command Video Corp., **23** 135
On Cue, **9** 360
On-Line Software International Inc., **6** 225
On-Line Systems. *See* Sierra On-Line Inc.
Onan Corporation, **8** 72
Onbancorp Inc., **11** 110
Once Upon A Child, Inc., **18** 207–8
Oncogen, **III** 18
Ondal GmbH, **III** 69
Ondulato Imolese, **IV** 296; **19** 226
1-800-FLOWERS, Inc., 26 344–46; **28** 137
One For All, **39** 405
One Hundred Thirtieth National Bank, **II** 291
One Hundredth Bank, **II** 321
One Price Clothing Stores, Inc., 20 403–05
O'Neal, Jones & Feldman Inc., **11** 142
Oneida Bank & Trust Company, **9** 229
Oneida County Creameries Co., **7** 202
Oneida Gas Company, **9** 554
Oneida Ltd., 7 406–08; **31 352–355 (upd.)**
ONEOK Inc., 7 409–12
Onex Corporation, 16 395–97; **22** 513; **24** 498; **25** 282
OneZero Media, Inc., **31** 240
Onitsuka Tiger Co., **V** 372; **8** 391; **36** 343–44
Online Distributed Processing Corporation, **6** 201
Online Financial Communication Systems, **11** 112
Only One Dollar, Inc. *See* Dollar Tree Stores, Inc.
Onoda Cement Co., Ltd., I 508; **III 717–19**
Onomichi, **25** 469
Onsale Inc., **31** 177
Onstead Foods, **21** 501
OnTarget Inc., **38** 432
Ontario Hydro Services Company, 6 541–42; **9** 461; **32 368–71 (upd.)**
Ontel Corporation, **6** 201
OnTrak Systems Inc., **31** 301
Oode Casting Iron Works, **III** 551
O'okiep Copper Company, Ltd., **7** 385–86
Opel. *See* Adam Opel AG.
Open Board of Brokers, **9** 369
Open Cellular Systems, Inc., **41** 225–26
Open Market, Inc., **22** 522
OpenTV, Inc., **31** 330–31
Operadora de Bolsa Serfin. *See* Grupo Financiero Serfin, S.A.
Operon Technologies Inc., **39** 335
Opinion Research Corp., **35** 47
Opp and Micolas Mills, **15** 247–48
Oppenheimer. *See* Ernest Oppenheimer and Sons.
Oppenheimer & Co., **17** 137; **21** 235; **22** 405; **25** 450
Opryland USA, **11** 152–53; **25** 403; **36** 229
Optel Corp., **17** 331
OPTi Computer, **9** 116
Opti-Ray, Inc., **12** 215
Optical Radiation Corporation, **27** 57
Optilink Corporation, **12** 137
Optima Pharmacy Services, **17** 177
Optimum Financial Services Ltd., **II** 457
Opto-Electronics Corp., **15** 483
Optronics, Inc., **6** 247; **24** 234
Optus Communications, **25** 102
Optus Vision, **17** 150
Opus Group, 34 321–23
OPW, **III** 467–68
Oracle Corporation, 24 367–71 (upd.); **25** 34, 96–97, 499
Oracle Systems Corporation, 6 272–74; **10** 361, 363, 505; **11** 78; **13** 483; **14** 16; **15** 492; **18** 541, 543; **19** 310; **21** 86; **22** 154, 293
Orange Julius of America, **10** 371, 373; **39** 232, 235
Orange Line Bus Company, **6** 604
Orange PLC, **24** 89; **38** 300
Orb Books. *See* Tom Doherty Associates Inc.
Orbis Entertainment Co., **20** 6
Orbis Graphic Arts. *See* Anaheim Imaging.
Orbital Engine Corporation Ltd., **17** 24
Orbital Sciences Corporation, 22 400–03
Orchard Supply Hardware Stores Corporation, 17 365–67; **25** 535
Orcofi, **III** 48
OrderTrust LLP, **26** 440
Ore and Chemical Corp., **IV** 140
Ore-Ida Foods Incorporated, II 508; **11** 172; **12** 531; **13 382–83**; **36** 254, 256
Orebehoved Fanerfabrik, **25** 464
Oregon Ale and Beer Company, **18** 72
Oregon Craft & Floral Supply, **17** 322
Oregon Cutting Systems, **26** 119
Oregon Metallurgical Corporation, 20 406–08
Oregon Pacific and Eastern Railway, **13** 100
Oregon Steel Mills, Inc., 14 368–70; **19** 380
O'Reilly Automotive, Inc., 26 347–49
Orford Copper Co., **IV** 110
Organización Soriana, S.A. de C.V., 35 320–22
Organon, **I** 665
Oriel Foods, **II** 609
Orient, **21** 122
Orient Express Hotels Inc., **29** 429–30
Orient Glass, **III** 715
Orient Leasing. *See* Orix Corporation.
Orient Overseas, **18** 254
Oriental Brewery Co., Ltd., **21** 320
Oriental Cotton Trading. *See* Tomen Corporation.
Oriental Land Co., Ltd., **IV** 715
Oriental Precision Company, **13** 213
Oriental Trading Corp., **22** 213
Oriental Yeast Co., **17** 288
Origin Energy Limited, **43** 75. *See also* Boral Limited.
Origin Systems Inc., **10** 285
Origin Technology, **14** 183
Original Arizona Jean Company. *See* J.C. Penney Company, Inc.
Original Cookie Co., **13** 166. *See also* Mrs. Fields' Original Cookies, Inc.
Original Musical Instrument Company (O.M.I.), **16** 239
Original Wassertragers Hummel, **II** 163
Origins Natural Resources Inc., **30** 190
Orinoco Oilfields, Ltd., **IV** 565
Orion, **III** 310
Orion Bank Ltd., **II** 271, 345, 385
Orion Healthcare Ltd., **11** 168
Orion Personal Insurances Ltd., **11** 168
Orion Pictures Corporation, II 147; **6 167–70**; **7** 336; **14** 330, 332; **25** 326, 328–29; **31** 100
Orit Corp., **8** 219–20
Orix Corporation, II 442–43, 259, 348
Orkem, **IV** 547, 560; **21** 205
Orkin Pest Control, **11** 431–32, 434
Orkla A/S, 18 394–98; **25** 205–07; **36** 266
Orm Bergold Chemie, **8** 464
Ormco Corporation, **14** 481
ÖROP, **IV** 485–86
Orowheat Baking Company, **10** 250
La Oroya, **22** 286
ORSCO, Inc., **26** 363
Ortho Diagnostic Systems, Inc., **10** 213; **22** 75
Ortho Pharmaceutical Corporation, **III** 35; **8** 281; **10** 79–80; **30** 59–60
Orthodontic Centers of America, Inc., 35 323–26
Orthopedic Services, Inc., **11** 366
Orval Kent Food Company, Inc., **7** 430
Orville Redenbacher/Swiss Miss Foods Co., **17** 241
The Orvis Company, Inc., 28 336–39
Oryx Energy Company, IV 550; **7 413–15**
Osaka Aluminium Co., **IV** 153
Osaka Beer Brewing Co., **I** 220, 282; **20** 28
Osaka Electric Tramway, **V** 463
Osaka Gas Co., Ltd., V 679–81
Osaka General Bussan, **IV** 431
Osaka Iron Works, **III** 513
Osaka Marine and Fire Insurance Co., **III** 367
Osaka Nomura Bank, **II** 276, 438–39
Osaka North Harbor Co. Ltd., **I** 518
Osaka Shinyo Kumiai, **15** 495
Osaka Shosen Kaisha, **I** 503; **V** 473–74, 481–82
Osaka Spinning Company, **V** 387
Osaka Sumitomo Marine and Fire Insurance Co., Ltd., **III** 367
Osaka Textile Co., **I** 506
Osakeyhtiö Gustaf Cederberg & Co., **IV** 301
Osakeyhtiö T. & J. Salvesen, **IV** 301
Osborne Books, **IV** 637

Oscar Mayer Foods Corp., **II** 532; **7** 274, 276; **12** 123, **370–72**
Osco Drug, **II** 604–05
OSF Japan Ltd., **24** 365
Oshawa Group Limited, **II 649–50**
OshKosh B'Gosh, Inc., **9 393–95**; **42 266–70 (upd.)**
Oshkosh Electric Power, **9** 553
Oshkosh Gas Light Company, **9** 553
Oshkosh Truck Corporation, **7 416–18**; **14** 458
Oshman's Sporting Goods, Inc., **16** 560; **17 368–70**; **27** 7
OSi Specialties, Inc., **16** 543; **36** 148–49
Osiris Holding Company, **16** 344
OSK. *See* Osaka Shosen Kaisha.
Osmonics, Inc., **18 399–401**
Oster. *See* Sunbeam-Oster.
Österreichische Brau-Beteiligungs AG. *See* BBAG Österreichische Brau-Beteiligungs AG.
Österreichische Bundesbahnen GmbH, **6 418–20**
Österreichische Creditanstalt-Wiener Bankverein, **IV** 230
Österreichische Elektrowerke, **IV** 230
Österreichische Industrieholding AG, **IV** 486–87
Österreichische Industriekredit AG, **IV** 230
Österreichische Länderbank, **II** 239; **23** 37
Österreichische Luftverkehrs AG. *See* Austrian Airlines AG.
Österreichische Mineralölverwaltung AG, **IV** 485
Österreichische Post- und Telegraphenverwaltung, **V 314–17**
Österreichische Stickstoffswerke, **IV** 486
Ostravar A.S., **38** 77
Ostschweizer Zementwerke, **III** 701
O'Sullivan Industries Holdings, Inc., **34 313–15**
Osuuskunta Metsäliito, **IV** 316
Oswald Tillotson Ltd., **III** 501; **7** 207
Otagiri Mercantile Co., **11** 95
Otake Paper Manufacturing Co., **IV** 327
OTC, **10** 492
Other Options, **29** 400
Otis Company, **6** 579
Otis Elevator Company, Inc., **I** 85, **III** 467, 663; **13 384–86**; **27** 267, 268; **29** 422; **39 311–15 (upd.)**
Otis Engineering Corp., **III** 498
Otis Spunkmeyer, Inc., **28 340–42**
Otosan, **I** 167, 479–80
OTR Express, Inc., **25 368–70**
Otsego Falls Paper Company, **8** 358
Ott and Brewer Company, **12** 312
Ottawa Fruit Supply Ltd., **II** 662
Ottaway Newspapers, Inc., **15 335–37**
Otter Tail Power Company, **18 402–05**; **37** 282
Otter-Westelaken, **16** 420; **43** 308
Otto-Epoka mbH, **15** 340
Otto Sumisho Inc., **V** 161
Otto Versand GmbH & Co., **V 159–61**; **10** 489–90; **15 338–40 (upd.)**; **27** 427, 429; **31** 188; **34 324–28 (upd.)**; **36** 177, 180
Ottumwa Daily Courier, **11** 251
Ourso Investment Corporation, **16** 344
Outback Steakhouse, Inc., **12 373–75**; **34 329–32 (upd.)**
Outboard Marine Corporation, **III** 329, **597–600**; **8** 71; **16** 383; **20 409–12 (upd.)**; **26** 494; **42** 45; **43** 287
The Outdoor Group Limited, **39** 58, 60
Outdoor Systems, Inc., **25 371–73**; **27** 278–80
Outdoor World. *See* Bass Pro Shops, Inc.
The Outdoorsman, Inc., **10** 216
Outlet, **6** 33
Outlet Retail Stores, Inc., **27** 286
Outlook Group Corporation, **37 294–96**
Outlook Window Partnership, **19** 446
Outokumpu Metals Group. *See* OM Group, Inc.
Outokumpu Oyj, **IV** 276; **38 335–37**
Ovako Oy, **III** 624
Ovation, **19** 285
OVC, Inc., **6** 313
Overhill Farms, **10** 382
Overland Energy Company, **14** 567
Overland Mail Co., **II** 380–81, 395; **10** 60; **12** 533
Overland Western Ltd., **27** 473
Overnite Transportation Co., **14 371–73**; **28** 492
Overseas Air Travel Ltd., **I** 95
Overseas Containers Ltd., **6** 398, 415–16
Overseas Petroleum and Investment Corp., **IV** 389
Overseas Shipholding Group, Inc., **11 376–77**
Overseas Telecommunications Commission, **6** 341–42
Overseas Telecommunications, Inc., **27** 304
Owatonna Tool Co., **I** 200; **10** 493
Owen Owen, **37** 8
Owen Steel Co. Inc., **15** 117
Owens & Minor, Inc., **10** 143; **16 398–401**
Owens Corning Corporation, **I** 609; **III** 683, **720–23**; **8** 177; **13** 169; **20 413–17 (upd.)**; **25** 535; **30** 283; **35** 98–99
Owens-Illinois Inc., **I 609–11**, 615; **II** 386; **III** 640, 720–21; **IV** 282, 343; **9** 261; **16** 123; **22** 254; **24** 92; **26 350–53 (upd.)**; **42** 438; **43** 188
Owens Yacht Company, **III** 443; **22** 115
Owensboro Municipal Utilities, **11** 37
Owosso Corporation, **29 366–68**
Oxdon Investments, **II** 664
Oxfam America, **13** 13
Oxford-AnsCo Development Co., **12** 18
Oxford Biscuit Fabrik, **II** 543
Oxford Bus Company, **28** 155–56
Oxford Chemical Corp., **II** 572
Oxford Financial Group, **22** 456
Oxford Health Plans, Inc., **16 402–04**
Oxford Industries, Inc., **8 406–08**; **24** 158
Oxford Instruments, **III** 491
Oxford Learning Centres, **34** 105
Oxford Paper Co., **I** 334–35; **10** 289
Oxford University Press, **23** 211
Oxirane Chemical Co., **IV** 456
OXO International, **16** 234
Oxy Petrochemicals Inc., **IV** 481
Oxy Process Chemicals, **III** 33
OxyChem, **11** 160
Oxygen Media, **28** 175
Ozalid Corporation, **I** 337–38; **IV** 563; **22** 226
Ozark Airlines, **I** 127; **12** 489
Ozark Automotive Distributors, **26** 347–48
Ozark Pipe Line Corp., **IV** 540
Ozark Utility Company, **6** 593
OZM. *See* OneZero Media, Inc.

P&C Foods Inc., **8 409–11**; **13** 95, 394
P&F Technologies Ltd., **26** 363
P&G. *See* Procter & Gamble Company.
P & M Manufacturing Company, **8** 386
P & O. *See* Peninsular & Oriental Steam Navigation Company.
P&O Nedlloyd, **26** 241, 243
P.A. Bergner & Company, **9** 142; **15** 87–88
P.A. Geier Company. *See* Royal Appliance Manufacturing Company.
P.A.J.W. Corporation, **9** 111–12
P.A. Rentrop-Hubbert & Wagner Fahrzeugausstattungen GmbH, **III** 582
P.C. Hanford Oil Co., **IV** 368
P.C. Richard & Son Corp., **23 372–74**
P. D'Aoust Ltd., **II** 651
P.D. Associated Collieries Ltd., **31** 369
P.D. Kadi International, **I** 580
P.D. Magnetics, **I** 330; **8** 153
P.E.C. Israel Economic Corporation, **24** 429
P.F. Chang's China Bistro, Inc., **37 297–99**
P.G. Realty, **III** 340
P.H. Glatfelter Company, **8 412–14**; **30 349–52 (upd.)**
P.Ink Press, **24** 430
P.L. Porter Co., **III** 580
P.R. Mallory, **9** 179
P.S.L. Food Market, Inc., **22** 549
P. Sharples, **III** 418
P.T. Bridgeport Perkasa Machine Tools, **17** 54
P.T. Dai Nippon Printing Indonesia, **IV** 599
P.T. Darya-Varia Laboratoria, **18** 180
P.T. Gaya Motor, **23** 290
P.T. Muaratewe Spring, **III** 581
P.T. Semen Nusantara, **III** 718
P.W. Huntington & Company, **11** 180
P.W.J. Surridge & Sons, Ltd., **43** 132
Pabst, **I** 217, 255; **10** 99; **18** 502
Pac-Am Food Concepts, **10** 178; **38** 102
Pac-Fab, Inc., **18** 161
PAC Insurance Services, **12** 175; **27** 258
PACCAR Inc., **I** 155, **185–86**; **10** 280; **26 354–56 (upd.)**; **40** 135
Pace-Arrow, Inc., **III** 484; **22** 206
Pace Companies, **6** 149; **26** 221
PACE Entertainment Corp., **36** 423–24
Pace Express Pty. Ltd., **13** 20
Pace Foods Ltd., **26** 58
Pace Management Service Corp., **21** 91
PACE Membership Warehouse, Inc., **V** 112; **10** 107; **12** 50; **18** 286; **40** 387
Pace Pharmaceuticals, **16** 439
Pacemaker Plastics, Inc., **7** 296
Pacer Technology, **40 347–49**
Pacer Tool and Mold, **17** 310
Pachena Industries Ltd., **6** 310
Pacific Advantage, **43** 253
Pacific Aero Products Co., **I** 47; **10** 162
Pacific Air Freight, Incorporated, **6** 345
Pacific Air Transport, **I** 47, 128; **6** 128; **9** 416
Pacific Alaska Fuel Services, **6** 383
Pacific and European Telegraph Company, **25** 99
Pacific Bell, **V** 318–20; **11** 59; **12** 137; **21** 285; **22** 19; **37** 126

Pacific Brick Proprietary, **III** 673
Pacific-Burt Co., Ltd., **IV** 644
Pacific Car & Foundry Company. *See* PACCAR Inc.
Pacific Cascade Land Co., **IV** 255
Pacific Coast Co., **IV** 165
Pacific Coast Condensed Milk Co., **II** 486
Pacific Coast Oil Co., **IV** 385
Pacific Communication Sciences, **11** 57
Pacific Dry Dock and Repair Co., **6** 382
Pacific Dunlop Limited, **10 444–46**
Pacific Electric Heating Co., **II** 28; **12** 194
Pacific Electric Light Company, **6** 565
Pacific Enterprises, **V 682–84**; **12** 477. *See also* Sempra Energy.
Pacific Express Co., **II** 381
Pacific Finance Corp., **I** 537; **9** 536; **13** 529; **26** 486
Pacific Fur Company, **25** 220
Pacific Gamble Robinson, **9** 39
Pacific Gas and Electric Company, **I** 96; **V 685–87**; **11** 270; **12** 100, 106; **19** 411; **25** 415. *See also* PG&E Corporation.
Pacific Guardian Life Insurance Co., **III** 289
Pacific Health Beverage Co., **I** 292
Pacific Home Furnishings, **14** 436
Pacific Indemnity Corp., **III** 220; **14** 108, 110; **16** 204
Pacific Lighting Corp., **IV** 492; **V** 682–84; **12** 477; **16** 496. *See also* Sempra Energy.
Pacific Linens, **13** 81–82
Pacific Link Communication, **18** 180
Pacific Lumber Company, **III** 254; **8** 348–50
Pacific Magazines and Printing, **7** 392
Pacific Mail Steamship Company, **6** 353
Pacific Manifolding Book/Box Co., **IV** 644
Pacific Media K.K., **18** 101
Pacific Metal Bearing Co., **I** 159
Pacific Monolothics Inc., **11** 520
Pacific National Bank, **II** 349
Pacific National Insurance Co. *See* TIG Holdings, Inc.
Pacific Natural Gas Corp., **9** 102
Pacific Northern, **6** 66
Pacific Northwest Bell Telephone Co., **V** 341; **25** 495
Pacific Northwest Laboratories, **10** 139
Pacific Northwest Pipeline Corporation, **9** 102–104, 540; **12** 144
Pacific Northwest Power Company, **6** 597
Pacific Pearl, **I** 417
Pacific Petroleums Ltd., **IV** 494; **9** 102
Pacific Platers Ltd., **IV** 100
Pacific Power & Light Company. *See* PacifiCorp.
Pacific Pride Bakeries, **19** 192
Pacific Recycling Co. Inc., **IV** 296; **19** 226; **23** 225
Pacific Refining Co., **IV** 394–95
Pacific Resources Inc., **IV** 47; **22** 107
Pacific Sentinel Gold Corp., **27** 456
Pacific-Sierra Research, **I** 155
Pacific Silver Corp., **IV** 76
Pacific Southwest Airlines Inc., **I** 132; **6** 132
Pacific Steel Ltd., **IV** 279; **19** 154
Pacific Sunwear of California, Inc., **28 343–45**
Pacific Telecom, Inc., **V** 689; **6 325–28**; **25** 101
Pacific Telesis Group, **V 318–20**; **6** 324; **9** 321; **11** 10–11; **14** 345, 347; **15** 125; **25** 499; **26** 520; **29** 387
Pacific Teletronics, Inc., **7** 15
Pacific Towboat. *See* Puget Sound Tug and Barge Company.
Pacific Trading Co., Ltd., **IV** 442
Pacific Trail Inc., **17** 462; **29** 293, 295–96
Pacific Western Extruded Plastics Company, **17** 441
Pacific Western Oil Co., **IV** 537
Pacific Wine Co., **18** 71
PacifiCare Health Systems, Inc., **III** 85; **11 378–80**; **25** 318
PacifiCorp, Inc., **V 688–90**; **6** 325–26, 328; **7** 376–78; **26 357–60 (upd.)**; **27** 327, 483, 485; **32** 372
Package Products Company, Inc., **12** 150
Packaged Ice, Inc., **21** 338; **26** 449
Packaging Corporation of America, **I** 526; **12 376–78**, 397; **16** 191
Packard Bell Electronics, Inc., **I** 524; **II** 86; **10** 521, 564; **11** 413; **13 387–89**, 483; **21** 391; **23** 471
Packard Motor Co., **I** 81; **8** 74; **9** 17
Packer's Consolidated Press, **IV** 651
Packerland Packing Company, **7** 199, 201
Pacolet Manufacturing Company, **17** 327
PacTel. *See* Pacific Telesis Group.
Paddington Corp., **I** 248
PAFS. *See* Pacific Alaska Fuel Services.
Page, Bacon & Co., **II** 380; **12** 533
Page Boy Inc., **9** 320
PageAhead Software, **15** 492
Pageland Coca-Cola Bottling Works, **10** 222
PageMart Wireless, Inc., **18** 164, 166
Paging Network Inc., **11 381–83**; **39** 24–25; **41** 266–67
Pagoda Trading Company, Inc., **V** 351, 353; **20** 86
Paid Prescriptions, **9** 346
Paige Publications, **18** 66
PaineWebber Group Inc., **I** 245; **II 444–46**, 449; **III** 409; **13** 449; **22** 352, **404–07 (upd.)**, 542; **25** 433
Painter Carpet Mills, **13** 169
Painton Co., **II** 81
PairGain Technologies, **36** 299
Paisley Products, **32** 255
La Paix, **III** 273
Pak-a-Sak, **II** 661
Pak-All Products, Inc., **IV** 345
Pak Arab Fertilizers Ltd., **IV** 364
Pak Mail Centers, **18** 316
Pak-Paino, **IV** 315
Pak Sak Industries, **17** 310; **24** 160
Pak-Well, **IV** 282; **9** 261
Pakhoed Holding, N.V., **9** 532; **26** 420; **41** 339–40
Pakkasakku Oy, **IV** 471
Paknet, **11** 548
Pakway Container Corporation, **8** 268
PAL. *See* Philippine Airlines, Inc.
Pal Plywood Co., Ltd., **IV** 327
Palace Station Hotel & Casino. *See* Station Casinos Inc.
Palais Royal, Inc., **24** 456
Palatine Insurance Co., **III** 234
Palco Industries, **19** 440
Pale Ski & Sports GmbH, **22** 461
Palestine Coca-Cola Bottling Co., **13** 163
Pall Corporation, **9 396–98**
Palm Beach Holdings, **9** 157
Palm Harbor Homes, Inc., **39 316–18**
Palm, Inc., **34** 441, 445; **36 355–57**; **38** 433
Palm Shipping Inc., **25** 468–70
Palmafina, **IV** 498–99
Palmer Communications, **25** 418
Palmer G. Lewis Co., **8** 135
Palmer Tyre Ltd., **I** 428–29
Palmolive Co. *See* Colgate-Palmolive Company.
Palo Alto Brewing, **22** 421
Palo Alto Products International, Inc., **29** 6
Palo Alto Research Center, **10** 510
Palomar Medical Technologies, Inc., **22 408–10**; **31** 124
PAM Group, **27** 462
Pamida Holdings Corporation, **15 341–43**
Pamour Porcupine Mines, Ltd., **IV** 164
Pampa OTT, **27** 473
The Pampered Chef, Ltd., **18 406–08**
Pamplemousse, **14** 225
Pan-Alberta Gas Ltd., **16** 11
Pan American Banks, **II** 336
Pan American Petroleum & Transport Co., **IV** 368–70
Pan American World Airways, Inc., **I** 20, 31, 44, 64, 67, 89–90, 92, 99, 103–04, 112–13, **115–16**, 121, 124, 126, 129, 132, 248, 452, 530, 547–48; **III** 536; **6** 51, 65–66, 71, 74–76, 81–82, 103–05, 110–11, 123, 129–30; **9** 231, 417; **10** 561; **11** 266; **12** 191, **379–81 (upd.)**, 419; **13** 19; **14** 73; **24** 397; **29** 189; **36** 52–53; **39** 120
Pan European Publishing Co., **IV** 611
Pan Geo Atlas Corporation, **18** 513
Pan Ocean, **IV** 473
Pan Pacific Fisheries, **24** 114
Panacon Corporation, **III** 766; **22** 545
Panagra, **I** 547–48; **36** 53
Panama Refining and Petrochemical Co., **IV** 566
PanAmSat, **18** 211, 213
Panarctic Oils, **IV** 494
Panasonic, **9** 180; **10** 125; **12** 470; **43** 427
Panatech Research & Development Corp., **III** 160
Panavia Aircraft GmbH, **24** 84, 86–87
Panavia Consortium, **I** 74–75
Panavision Inc., **24 372–74**; **28** 249; **38** 295
PanCanadian Petroleum Ltd., **27** 217
Panda Management Company, Inc., **35 327–29**
Pandair, **13** 20
Pandel, Inc., **8** 271
Pandick Press Inc., **23** 63
PanEnergy Corporation, **27** 128, 131
Panerai, **27** 489
Panhandle Eastern Corporation, **I** 377, 569; **IV** 425; **V 691–92**; **10** 82–84; **11** 28; **14** 135; **17** 21
Panhandle Oil Corp., **IV** 498
Panhandle Power & Light Company, **6** 580
Panhard, **I** 194
Panhard-Levassor, **I** 149
Panificadora Bimbo, **19** 191
AB Pankakoski, **IV** 274
Panmure Gordon, **II** 337
Pannill Knitting Company, **13** 531
Panocean Storage & Transport, **6** 415, 417
Panola Pipeline Co., **7** 228
Panosh Place, **12** 168

Pansophic Systems Inc., **6** 225
Pantepec Oil Co., **IV** 559, 570; **24** 520
Pantera Energy Corporation, **11** 27
Pantheon Books, **13** 429; **31** 376
Panther, **III** 750
Panther Express International Company, **6** 346
The Pantry, Inc., 36 358–60
Pantry Pride Inc., **I** 668; **II** 670, 674; **III** 56; **23** 407–08
Pants Corral, **II** 634
Papa John's International, Inc., 15 344–46; **16** 447; **24** 295
Pape and Co., Ltd., **10** 441
Papelera General, S.A. de C.V., **39** 188
Papelera Navarra, **IV** 295; **19** 226
Papeleria Calparsoro S.A., **IV** 325
Papeles Venezolanos C.A., **17** 281
Paper Direct, **37** 107–08
The Paper Factory of Wisconsin, Inc., **12** 209
Paper Magic Group, **35** 130–31
Paper Makers Chemical Corp., **I** 344
Paper Recycling International, **V** 754
Paper Software, Inc., **15** 322
Paper Stock Dealers, Inc., **8** 476
Paperituote Oy, **IV** 347–48
PaperMate, **III** 28; **23** 54
Paperwork Data Comm Services Inc., **11** 64
Papeterie de Pont Sainte Maxence, **IV** 318
Papeteries Aussedat, **III** 122
Papeteries Boucher S.A., **IV** 300
Les Papeteries de la Chapelle-Darblay, **IV** 258–59, 302, 337
Papeteries de Lancey, 23 366–68
Les Papeteries du Limousin, **19** 227
Papeteries Navarre, **III** 677; **16** 121
Papetti's Hygrade Egg Products, Inc., 25 332–33; **39 319–21**
Papierfabrik Salach, **IV** 324
Papierwaren Fleischer, **IV** 325
Papierwerke Waldhof-Aschaffenburg AG, **IV** 323–24
Papyrus Design Group, **IV** 336; **15** 455
Para-Med Health Services, **6** 181–82
Parachute Press, **29** 426
Parade Gasoline Co., **7** 228
Paradigm Entertainment, **35** 227
Paradise Creations, **29** 373
Paradise Island Resort and Casino. *See* Sun International Hotels Limited.
Paradise Music & Entertainment, Inc., 42 271–74
Paradyne, **22** 19
Paragon Corporate Holdings, Inc., **IV** 552; **28** 6, 8
Paragon Vineyard Company, **36** 114
Paragren Technologies Inc., **38** 432
Parallax Software Inc., **38** 70
Paramax, **6** 281–83
Parametric Technology Corp., 16 405–07
Parametrics Corp., **25** 134
Paramount Communications Inc., **16** 338; **19** 403–04; **28** 296
Paramount Fire Insurance Co., **26** 486
Paramount Oil Company, **18** 467
Paramount Paper Products, **8** 383
Paramount Pictures Corporation, I 451–52; **II** 129, 135, 146–47, **154–56**, 171, 173, 175, 177; **IV** 671–72, 675; **7** 528; **9** 119, 428–29; **10** 175; **12** 73, 323; **19** 404; **21** 23–25; **23** 503; **24** 327; **25** 88, 311, 327–29, 418; **31** 99; **35** 279
Parasitix Corporation. *See* Mycogen Corporation.
Parasole Restaurant Holdings, Inc., **38** 117
Paravision International, **III** 48; **8** 343
Parcelforce, **V** 498
PARCO Co., Ltd., **V** 184–85; **42** 341
Parcor, **I** 676
ParentWatch, **34** 105
Parfums Chanel, **12** 57
Parfums Christian Dior, **I** 272
Parfums Rochas, **I** 670; **III** 68; **8** 452
Parfums Stern, **III** 16
Pargas, **I** 378
Paribas. *See* Banque de Paris et des Pays-Bas, BNP Paribas Group *and* Compagnie Financiere de Paribas.
Paridoc and Giant, **12** 153
Paris Bourse, **34** 13
Paris Corporation, 22 411–13
Paris Group, **17** 137
Paris Playground Equipment, **13** 319
Parisian, Inc., 14 374–76; **19** 324–25; **41** 343–44
Park Acquisitions, Inc., **38** 308
Park Consolidated Motels, Inc., **6** 187; **14** 105; **25** 306
Park Corp., 22 414–16
Park Drop Forge Co. *See* Park-Ohio Industries Inc.
Park Hall Leisure, **II** 140; **24** 194
Park Inn International, **11** 178
Park-Ohio Industries Inc., 17 371–73
Park Ridge Corporation, **9** 284
Park View Hospital, Inc., **III** 78
Parkdale State Bank, **25** 114
Parkdale Wines, **I** 268; **25** 281
Parke-Bernet, **11** 453
Parke, Davis & Co. *See* Warner-Lambert Co.
Parker, **III** 33
Parker Appliance Co., **III** 601–02
Parker Brothers, **II** 502; **III** 505; **10** 323; **16** 337; **21** 375; **25** 489; **43** 229, 232
Parker Drilling Company, 28 346–48
Parker Drilling Company of Canada, **9** 363
Parker-Hannifin Corporation, III 601–03; **21** 108; **24 375–78 (upd.)**
Parker Pen Corp., **III** 218; **9** 326
Parker's Pharmacy, Inc., **15** 524
Parkinson Cowan, **I** 531
Parkmount Hospitality Corp., **II** 142
Parks-Belk Co., **19** 324
Parks Box & Printing Co., **13** 442
Parkway Distributors, **17** 331
Parr's Bank, **II** 334; **III** 724
Parson and Hyman Co., Inc., **8** 112
Parsons Brinckerhoff, Inc., 34 333–36
The Parsons Corporation, III 749; **8 415–17**
Parsons International Trading Business, **27** 195
Parsons Place Apparel Company, **8** 289
Partech, **28** 346, 348
Partek Corporation, **11** 312
Partex, **IV** 515
Parthénon, **27** 10
Parthenon Insurance Co., **III** 79
Participating Annuity Life Insurance Co., **III** 182; **21** 14
La Participation, **III** 210
Partlow Corporation, **7** 116
Partnership Pacific Ltd., **II** 389
Parts Industries Corp., **III** 494–95
Parts Plus, **26** 348
PartyLite Gifts, Inc., **18** 67, 69
Pascagoula Lumber Company, **28** 306
Pascale & Associates, **12** 476
Paschen Contractors Inc., **I** 585
Pasha Pillows, **12** 393
Pasminco, **IV** 61
Pasqua Inc., **28** 64
Pass & Seymour, **21** 348–49
Passive Power Products, Inc., **32** 41
Patagonia, **16** 352; **18** 376; **21** 193; **25** 206. *See also* Lost Arrow Inc.
Patak Spices Ltd., **18** 247
Pataling Rubber Estates Syndicate, **III** 697, 699
Patch Rubber Co., **19** 277–78
Patchoque-Plymouth Co., **IV** 371
PATCO. *See* Philippine Airlines, Inc.
Patent Arms Manufacturing Company, **12** 70
Patent Nut & Bolt Co., **III** 493
Patent Slip and Dock Co., **I** 592
La Paternelle, **III** 210
Paternoster Stores plc, **V** 108; **24** 269
Paterson Candy Ltd., **22** 89
Paterson, Simons & Co., **I** 592
Path-Tek Laboratories, Inc., **6** 41
Pathé Cinéma, **6** 374
Pathe Communications Co., **IV** 676; **7** 529; **25** 329
Pathé Fréres, **IV** 626; **19** 203
Pathé SA, 29 369–71. *See also* Chargeurs International.
Pathmark Stores, Inc., II 672–74; **9** 173; **15** 260; **18** 6; **19** 479, 481; **23 369–71**; **33** 436
PathoGenesis Corporation, **36** 119
Patience & Nicholson, **III** 674
Patient Care, Inc., **13** 150
Patil Systems, **11** 56
Patina Oil & Gas Corporation, 24 379–81
Patino N.V., **17** 380
Patrick Industries, Inc., 30 342–45
Patrick Raulet, S.A., **36** 164
Patricof & Company, **24** 45
Patriot American Hospitality, Inc., **21** 184
Patriot Co., **IV** 582
Patriot Life Insurance Co., **III** 193
PATS Inc., **36** 159
Patterson Dental Co., 19 289–91
Patterson Industries, Inc., **14** 42
Pattison & Bowns, Inc., **IV** 180
Patton Electric Company, Inc., **19** 360
Patton Paint Company. *See* PPG Industries, Inc.
Paul A. Brands, **11** 19
Paul Andra KG, **33** 393
Paul Boechat & Cie, **21** 515
Paul C. Dodge Company, **6** 579
Paul Davril, Inc., **25** 258
Paul H. Rose Corporation, **13** 445
Paul Harris Stores, Inc., 15 245; **18 409–12**
Paul, Hastings, Janofsky & Walker LLP, 27 357–59
Paul Koss Supply Co., **16** 387
Paul Marshall Products Inc., **16** 36
Paul Masson, **I** 285
Paul Ramsay Group, **41** 323
The Paul Revere Corporation, 12 382–83
Paul Revere Insurance, **34** 433

Paul Wahl & Co., **IV** 277
Paul Williams Copier Corp., **IV** 252; **17** 28
Paul Wurth, **IV** 25
Paulaner Brauerei GmbH & Co. KG, 35 330–33
Pauls Plc, **III** 699
Pavallier, **18** 35
Pavex Construction Company. *See* Granite Rock Company.
Pawnee Industries, Inc., **19** 415
Paxall, Inc., **8** 545
Paxson Communications Corporation, 33 322–26
Pay 'N Pak Stores, Inc., 9 399–401; 16 186–88
Pay 'n Save Corp., **12** 477; **15** 274; **17** 366
Pay Less, **II** 601, 604
Paychex, Inc., 15 347–49
Payless Cashways, Inc., 11 384–86; 13 274
Payless DIY, **V** 17, 19
PayLess Drug Stores, **12** 477–78; **18** 286; **22** 39
Payless ShoeSource, Inc., V 132, 135; **13** 361; **18 413–15**; **26** 441
PBF Corp. *See* Paris Corporation.
PBL. *See* Publishing and Broadcasting Ltd.
PBS. *See* Public Broadcasting Stations.
PC Connection, Inc., 37 300–04
PC Globe, Inc., **13** 114
PC Realty, Canada Ltd., **III** 340
PCA-Budafok Paperboard Ltd., **12** 377
pcBoat.com, **37** 398
PCI Acquisition, **11** 385
PCI/Mac-Pak Group, **IV** 261
PCI NewCo Inc., **36** 159
PCI Services, Inc. *See* Cardinal Health, Inc.
PCL Industries Ltd., **IV** 296; **19** 226
PCO, **III** 685
PCS. *See* Potash Corp. of Saskatchewan Inc.
PCS Health Systems Inc., **12** 333
PDA Engineering, **25** 305
PDA Inc., **19** 290
PDO. *See* Petroleum Development Oman.
PDQ Transportation Inc., **18** 226
PDV America, Inc., **31** 113
PDVSA. *See* Petróleos de Venezuela S.A.
Peabody Coal Company, I 559; **III** 248; **IV** 47, 169–71, 576; **7** 387–88; **10 447–49**
Peabody Holding Company, Inc., IV 19, **169–72**; **6** 487; **7** 209
Peabody, Riggs & Co., **II** 427
Peaches Entertainment Corporation, **24** 502
Peachtree Doors, **10** 95
Peachtree Federal Savings and Loan Association of Atlanta, **10** 92
Peachtree Software Inc., **18** 364
Peak Oilfield Service Company, **9** 364
The Peak Technologies Group, Inc., 14 377–80
Peakstone, **III** 740
Peapod, Inc., 22 522; **30 346–48**
Pearce-Uible Co., **14** 460
Pearl Health Services, **I** 249
Pearl Package Co., Ltd., **IV** 327
Pearle Vision, Inc., I 688; **12** 188; **13 390–92**; **14** 214; **23** 329; **24** 140; **34** 179
Pearson plc, IV 611, 652, **657–59**; **14** 414; **25** 283, 285; **32** 355; **38** 402
Peasant Restaurants Inc., **30** 330
Pease Industries, **39** 322, 324
Peat Marwick. *See* KPMG Peat Marwick.
Peaudouce, **IV** 339
Peavey Electronics Corporation, II 494; **12** 81; **16 408–10**
Peavey Paper Mills, Inc., **26** 362
Pebble Beach Corp., **II** 170
PEC Plastics, **9** 92
Pechelbronn Oil Company, **III** 616; **17** 416–17
Pechiney S.A., I 190, 341; **IV** 12, 59, 108, **173–75**, 560; **V** 605; **12** 253–54; **14** 216; **26** 403; **31** 11
Péchiney-Saint-Gobain, **I** 389; **III** 677; **16** 121
PECO Energy Company, 11 387–90
Pediatric Services of America, Inc., 31 356–58
Pedigree Petfoods, **22** 298
Peebles Inc., 16 411–13; 43 296–99 (upd.)
Peekskill Chemical Works. *See* Binney & Smith Inc.
Peel-Conner Telephone Works, **II** 24
Peerless, **III** 467; **8** 74; **11** 534
Peerless Gear & Machine Company, **8** 515
Peerless Industries, Inc., **III** 569; **20** 360; **39** 264
Peerless Paper Co., **IV** 310; **19** 266
Peerless Pump Co., **I** 442
Peerless Spinning Corporation, **13** 532
Peerless Systems, Inc., **17** 263
Peet's Coffee & Tea, Inc., 13 493; **18** 37; **38 338–40**
Pegulan, **I** 426–27; **25** 464
PEI. *See* Process Engineering Inc.
Peine, **IV** 201
Pekema Oy, **IV** 470–71
Peko-Wallsend Ltd., **13** 97
Pel-Tex Oil Co., **IV** 84; **7** 188
Pelican and British Empire Life Office, **III** 372
Pelican Homestead and Savings, **11** 107
Pelican Insurance Co., **III** 349
Pelican Life Assurance, **III** 371–72
Pelikan Holding AG, **18** 388
Pella Corporation, 10 95; **12 384–86**; **22** 346; **39 322–25 (upd.)**
Pelto Oil Company, **14** 455
PEM International Ltd., **28** 350
Pemex. *See* Petróleos Mexicanos.
Peñarroya, **IV** 107–08
Penda Corp., **19** 415
Pendexcare Ltd., **6** 181
Pendle Travel Services Ltd. *See* Airtours Plc.
Pendleton Woolen Mills, Inc., 42 275–78
Pengrowth Gas Corp., **25** 232
Penguin Publishing Co. Ltd., **IV** 585, 659
Penhaligon's, **24** 237
Peninsula Stores, Ltd. *See* Lucky Stores, Inc.
The Peninsular and Oriental Steam Navigation Company, II 296; **III** 521–22, 712; **V 490–93**; **22** 444; **26** 241, 243; **37** 137; **38 341–46 (upd.)**
Peninsular and Oriental Steam Navigation Company (Bovis Division), I 588–89
Peninsular Portland Cement, **III** 704
Peninsular Power, **6** 602
Peninsular Railroad Company, **17** 440
Penn Advertising, **27** 280
Penn-American Refining Co., **IV** 489
Penn Central Corp., **I** 435; **II** 255; **IV** 576; **10** 71, 73, 547; **17** 443
Penn Champ Co., **9** 72
Penn Controls, **III** 535–36; **26** 229
Penn Corp., **13** 561
Penn Cress Ice Cream, **13** 393
Penn Engineering & Manufacturing Corp., 28 349–51
Penn Fuel Co., **IV** 548
Penn Health, **III** 85
Penn National Gaming, Inc., 33 327–29
Penn Square Bank, **II** 248, 262
Penn-Texas Corporation, **I** 434; **12** 71
Penn Traffic Company, 8 409–10; **13** 95, **393–95**
Penn-Western Gas and Electric, **6** 524
Pennaco Hosiery, Inc., **12** 93
Pennington Drug, **III** 10
Pennroad Corp., **IV** 458
Pennsalt Chemical Corp., **I** 383
Pennsylvania Blue Shield, III 325–27
Pennsylvania Coal & Coke Corp., **I** 434
Pennsylvania Coal Co., **IV** 180
Pennsylvania Electric Company, **6** 535; **27** 182
Pennsylvania Farm Bureau Cooperative Association, **7** 17–18
Pennsylvania Gas and Water Company, **38** 51
Pennsylvania General Fire Insurance Assoc., **III** 257
Pennsylvania Glass Sand Co., **I** 464; **11** 198
Pennsylvania House, Inc., **10** 324; **12** 301
Pennsylvania International Raceway, **V** 494
Pennsylvania Life Insurance Company, **27** 47
Pennsylvania Power & Light Company, V 676, **693–94**; **11** 388
Pennsylvania Pump and Compressor Co., **II** 16
Pennsylvania Railroad, **I** 456, 472; **II** 329, 490; **6** 436; **10** 71–73; **26** 295
Pennsylvania Refining Co., **IV** 488–89
Pennsylvania Salt Manufacturing Co., **I** 383
Pennsylvania Steel Co., **IV** 35; **7** 48
Pennsylvania Steel Foundry and Machine Co., **39** 32
Pennsylvania Water & Power Company, **25** 44
Pennwalt Corporation, I 382–84; **IV** 547; **12** 18; **21** 205
Penny Curtiss Baking Co., Inc., **13** 395
Pennzoil Company, IV 488–90, 551, 553; **10** 190; **14** 491, 493; **20 418–22 (upd.)**; **23** 40–41; **25** 443, 445; **39** 330; **41** 391, 394
Penray, **I** 373
Penrod Drilling Corporation, **7** 228, 558
Pension Benefit Guaranty Corp., **III** 255; **12** 489
Penske Corporation, V 494–95; **19** 223, **292–94 (upd.)**; **20** 263
Penske Motorsports, **32** 440
Penske Truck Rental, **24** 445
Pentair, Inc., III 715; **7 419–21**; **11** 315; **26 361–64 (upd.)**
Pental Insurance Company, Ltd., **11** 523
Pentane Partners, **7** 518
Pentastar Transportation Group, Inc. *See* Dollar Thrifty Automotive Group, Inc.
Pentaverken A.B., **I** 209

Pentech International, Inc., **14** 217; **29** **372–74**
Pentes Play, Inc., **27** 370, 372
Pentland Group plc, **20** **423–25**; **35** 204, 206–07
Pentland Industries PLC, **V** 375; **26** 396–97
Penton Media, Inc., **9** 414; **27** **360–62**; **33** 335–36
People Express Airlines Inc., **I** 90, 98, 103, **117–18**, 123–24, 129–30; **6** 129; **21** 142; **22** 220
People That Love (PTL) Television, **13** 279
People's Bank of Halifax, **II** 210
People's Bank of New Brunswick, **II** 210
People's Drug Store, **II** 604–05; **22** 37–38
People's Ice and Refrigeration Company, **9** 274
People's Insurance Co., **III** 368
People's Natural Gas, **IV** 548; **6** 593
People's Radio Network, **25** 508
People's Trust Co. of Brooklyn, **II** 254; **9** 124
Peoples, **24** 315–16
Peoples Bancorp, **14** 529
Peoples Bank, **13** 467; **17** 302
Peoples Bank & Trust Co., **31** 207
Peoples Bank of Youngstown, **9** 474
Peoples Energy Corporation, **6** **543–44**
Peoples Finance Co., **II** 418
Peoples Gas Light & Coke Co., **IV** 169; **6** 529, 543–44
Peoples Gas Light Co., **6** 455; **25** 44
Peoples Jewelers of Canada, **16** 561; **40** 472
Peoples Life Insurance Co., **III** 218
Peoples National Bank, **41** 178–79
Peoples Natural Gas Company of South Carolina, **6** 576
Peoples Restaurants, Inc., **17** 320–21
Peoples Savings of Monroe, **9** 482
Peoples Security Insurance Co., **III** 219
PeopleServe, Inc., **29** 401
PeopleSoft Inc., **11** 78; **14** **381–83**; **33** **330–33 (upd.)**; **38** 432
The Pep Boys—Manny, Moe & Jack, **11** **391–93**; **16** 160; **26** 348; **36** **361–64 (upd.)**
PEPCO. *See* Portland Electric Power Company *and* Potomac Electric Power Company.
Pepe Clothing Co., **18** 85
Pepper Hamilton LLP, **43** **300–03**
Pepperell Manufacturing Company, **16** 533–34
Pepperidge Farm, **I** 29; **II** 480–81; **7** 67–68; **26** 56–57, 59
The Pepsi Bottling Group, Inc., **40** **350–53**
PepsiCo, Inc., **I** 234, 244–46, 257, 269, **276–79**, 281, 291; **II** 103, 448, 477, 608; **III** 106, 116, 588; **7** 265, 267, 396, 404, 434–35, 466, 505–06; **8** 399; **9** 177, 343; **10** 130, 199, 227, 324, **450–54 (upd.)**; **11** 421, 450; **12** 337, 453; **13** 162, 284, 448, 494; **15** 72, 75, 380; **16** 96; **18** 65; **19** 114, 221; **21** 143, 313, 315–16, 362, 401, 405, 485–86; **22** 95, 353; **23** 418, 420; **25** 91, 177–78, 366, 411; **28** 271, 473, 476; **31** 243; **32** 59, 114, 205; **36** 234, 237; **38** **347–54 (upd.)**; **40** 340–42, 350–52
Pepsodent Company, **I** 14; **9** 318
Perception Technology, **10** 500
Percy Bilton Investment Trust Ltd., **IV** 710
Percy Street Investments Ltd., **IV** 711
Perdue Farms Inc., **7** **422–24**, 432; **23** **375–78 (upd.)**; **32** 203
Perfect Circle Corp., **I** 152
Perfect Fit Industries, **17** 182–84
Perfect-Ventil GmbH, **9** 413
Performance Contracting, Inc., **III** 722; **20** 415
Performance Food Group Company, **31** **359–62**
Performance Technologies, Inc., **10** 395
Perfumania, Inc., **22** 157
Pergamon Holdings, **15** 83
Pergamon Press, **IV** 611, 641–43, 687; **7** 311–12
Perini Corporation, **8** **418–21**; **38** 481
Perisem, **I** 281
The Perkin-Elmer Corporation, **III** 455, 727; **7** **425–27**; **9** 514; **13** 326; **21** 123
Perkins, **I** 147; **12** 90
Perkins Bacon & Co., **10** 267
Perkins Cake & Steak, **9** 425
Perkins Engines Ltd., **III** 545, 652; **10** 274; **11** 472; **19** 294; **27** 203
Perkins Family Restaurants, L.P., **22** **417–19**
Perkins Oil Well Cementing Co., **III** 497
Perkins Products Co., **II** 531
Perl Pillow, **19** 304
Perland Environmental Technologies Inc., **8** 420
Permal Group, **27** 276, 513
Permaneer Corp., **IV** 281; **9** 259. *See also* Spartech Corporation.
Permanent General Companies, Inc., **11** 194
Permanent Pigments Inc., **25** 71
Permanente Cement Co., **I** 565
Permanente Metals Corp., **IV** 15, 121–22
Permian Corporation, **V** 152–53
PERMIGAN, **IV** 492
Permodalan, **III** 699
Pernod Ricard S.A., **I** 248, **280–81**; **21** **399–401 (upd.)**
Pernvo Inc., **I** 387
Perot Systems Corporation, **13** 482; **29** **375–78**
Perret-Olivier, **III** 676; **16** 120
Perrier, **19** 50
Perrier Corporation of America, **16** 341
Perrigo Company, **12** 218, **387–89**
Perrin, **IV** 614
Perrot Brake Co., **I** 141
Perrow Motor Freight Lines, **6** 370
Perry Brothers, Inc., **24** 149
Perry Capital Corp., **28** 138
Perry Drug Stores Inc., **12** 21; **26** 476
Perry Ellis International, Inc., **16** 37; **41** **291–94**
Perry Manufacturing Co., **16** 37
Perry Sports, **13** 545; **13** 545
Perry Tritech, **25** 103–05
Perry's Shoes Inc., **16** 36
Perscombinatie, **IV** 611
Pershing & Co., **22** 189
Personal Care Corp., **17** 235
Personal Performance Consultants, **9** 348
Personal Products Company, **III** 35; **8** 281, 511
Personnel Pool of America, **29** 224, 26–27
Perstorp A.B., **I** **385–87**
PERTAMINA, **IV** 383, 461, **491–93**, 517, 567
Pertec Computer Corp., **17** 49; **18** 434
Pertech Computers Ltd., **18** 75
Perusahaan Minyak Republik Indonesia, **IV** 491
Peruvian Corp., **I** 547
Pet Food & Supply, **14** 385
Pet Foods Plus Inc., **39** 355
Pet Incorporated, **I** 457; **II** 486–87; **7** **428–31**; **10** 554; **12** 124; **13** 409; **14** 214; **24** 140; **27** 196; **43** 217
Petco Animal Supplies, Inc., **29** **379–81**
Pete's Brewing Company, **18** 72, 502; **22** **420–22**
Peter Bawden Drilling, **IV** 570; **24** 521
Peter, Cailler, Kohler, Chocolats Suisses S.A., **II** 546; **7** 381
Peter Cundill & Associates Ltd., **15** 504
Peter Gast Shipping GmbH, **7** 40; **41** 42
Peter J. Schmitt Co., **13** 394; **24** 444–45
Peter J. Schweitzer, Inc., **III** 40; **16** 303; **43** 257
Peter Jones, **V** 94
Peter Kiewit Sons' Inc., **I** 599–600; **III** 198; **8** **422–24**; **15** 18; **25** 512, 514
Peter Norton Computing Group, **10** 508–09
Peter Paul/Cadbury, **II** 477, 512; **15** 221
Peterbilt Motors Co., **I** 185–86; **26** 355
Peters-Revington Corporation, **26** 100. *See also* Chromcraft Revington, Inc.
Peters Shoe Co., **III** 528
Petersen Publishing Company, **21** **402–04**
Peterson, Howell & Heather, **V** 496
Peterson Soybean Seed Co., **9** 411
Petit Bateau, **35** 263
La Petite Academy, **13** 299
Petite Sophisticate, **V** 207–08
Petoseed Co. Inc., **29** 435
Petrie Stores Corporation, **8** **425–27**
Petrini's, **II** 653
Petro-Canada Limited, **IV** 367, **494–96**, 499; **13** 557
Petro/Chem Environmental Services, Inc., **IV** 411
Petro-Coke Co. Ltd., **IV** 476
Petro-Lewis Corp., **IV** 84; **7** 188
Petroamazonas, **IV** 511
Petrobas, **21** 31
Petrobel, **IV** 412
Petrobrás. *See* Petróleo Brasileiro S.A.
Petrocarbona GmbH, **IV** 197–98
Petrocel, S.A., **19** 12
Petrochemical Industries Co., **IV** 451
Petrochemicals Company, **17** 90–91
Petrochemie Danubia GmbH, **IV** 486–87
Petrochim, **IV** 498
Petrocomercial, **IV** 511
Petrocorp. *See* Petroleum Company of New Zealand.
Petroecuador. *See* Petróleos del Ecuador.
Petrofertil, **IV** 501
PetroFina S.A., **IV** 455, 495, **497–500**, 576; **7** 179; **26** **365–69 (upd.)**
Petrogal. *See* Petróleos de Portugal.
Petroindustria, **IV** 511
Petrol, **IV** 487
Petrol Ofisi Anonim Sirketi, **IV** 564
Petrolane Properties, **17** 558
Petróleo Brasileiro S.A., **IV** 424, **501–03**
Petróleo Mecânica Alfa, **IV** 505
Petróleos de Portugal S.A., **IV** **504–06**

Petróleos de Venezuela S.A., **II** 661; **IV** 391–93, **507–09**, 571; **24** 522; **31** 113
Petróleos del Ecuador, **IV 510–11**
Petróleos Mexicanos, **IV 512–14**, 528; **19** 10, **295–98 (upd.)**; **41** 147
Petroleum and Chemical Corp., **III** 672
Petroleum Authority of Thailand, **IV** 519
Petroleum Company of New Zealand, **IV** 279; **19** 155
Petroleum Development (Qatar) Ltd., **IV** 524
Petroleum Development (Trucial States) Ltd., **IV** 363
Petroleum Development Corp. of the Republic of Korea, **IV** 455
Petroleum Development Oman LLC, **IV 515–16**
Petroleum Helicopters, Inc., **35 334–36**; **37** 288; **39** 8
Petroleum Projects Co., **IV** 414
Petroleum Research and Engineering Co. Ltd., **IV** 473
Petrolgroup, Inc., **6** 441
Petroliam Nasional Bhd. *See* Petronas.
Petrolite Corporation, **15 350–52**
Petrolube, **IV** 538
Petromex. *See* Petróleos de Mexico S.A.
Petromin Lubricating Oil Co., **17** 415
Petronas, **IV 517–20**; **21** 501
Petronor, **IV** 514, 528
Petropeninsula, **IV** 511
Petroproduccion, **IV** 511
Petroquímica de Venezuela SA, **IV** 508
Petroquimica Española, **I** 402
Petroquisa, **IV** 501
PETROSUL, **IV** 504, 506
Petrotransporte, **IV** 511
PETsMART, Inc., **14 384–86**; **27** 95; **29** 379–80; **41 295–98 (upd.)**
Petstuff, Inc., **14** 386; **41** 297
Pettibone Corporation, **19** 365
Petzazz, **14** 386
Peugeot S.A., **I** 163, **187–88**; **II** 13; **III** 508; **11** 104; **26** 11. *See also* PSA Peugeot Citroen S.A.
The Pew Charitable Trusts, **35 337–40**
Pez Candy, Inc., **38 355–57**
Pfaff-Pegasus of U.S.A. Inc., **15** 385
Pfaltz & Bauer, Inc., **38** 3
The Pfaltzgraff Co. *See* Susquehanna Pfaltzgraff Company.
Pfaudler Vacuum Co., **I** 287
Pfauter-Maag Cutting Tools, **24** 186
PFCI. *See* Pulte Financial Companies, Inc.
PFI Acquisition Corp., **17** 184
Pfizer, Hoechst Celanese Corp., **8** 399
Pfizer Inc., **I** 301, 367, **661–63**, 668; **9** 356, **402–05 (upd.)**; **10** 53–54; **11** 207, 310–11, 459; **12** 4; **17** 131; **19** 105; **38 358–67 (upd.)**
Pflueger Corporation, **22** 483
PG&E Corporation, **26 370–73 (upd.)**; **27** 131. *See also* Portland General Electric.
PGA. *See* The Professional Golfers' Association.
PGH Bricks and Pipes, **III** 735
Phaostron Instruments and Electronic Co., **18** 497–98
Phar-Mor Inc., **12** 209, **390–92**, 477; **18** 507; **21** 459; **22** 157
Pharma Plus Drugmarts, **II** 649–50
Pharmacia & Upjohn Inc., **25** 22, **374–78 (upd.)**; **34** 177, 179
Pharmacia A.B., **I** 211, **664–65**
Pharmaco Dynamics Research, Inc., **10** 106–07
Pharmacom Systems Ltd., **II** 652
Pharmacy Corporation of America, **16** 57
PharmaKinetics Laboratories, Inc., **10** 106
Pharmanex, Inc., **27** 352
Pharmaprix Ltd., **II** 663
Pharmazell GmbH, **IV** 324
Pharmedix, **11** 207
Pharos, **9** 381
Phelan & Collender, **III** 442
Phelan Faust Paint, **8** 553
Phelps Dodge Corporation, **IV** 33, **176–79**, 216; **7** 261–63, 288; **19** 375; **28 352–57 (upd.)**; **40** 411
Phenix Bank, **II** 312
Phenix Cheese Corp., **II** 533
Phenix Insurance Co., **III** 240
Phenix Mills Ltd., **II** 662
PHF Life Insurance Co., **III** 263; **IV** 623
PHH Corporation, **V 496–97**; **6** 357; **22** 55
PHI. *See* Pizza Hut, Inc.
Phibro Corporation, **II** 447–48; **IV** 80; **13** 447–48; **21** 67
Philadelphia and Reading Corp., **I** 440; **II** 329; **6** 377; **25** 165
Philadelphia Carpet Company, **9** 465
Philadelphia Coke Company, **6** 487
Philadelphia Company, **6** 484, 493
Philadelphia Drug Exchange, **I** 692
Philadelphia Eagles, **37 305–08**
Philadelphia Electric Company, **V 695–97**; **6** 450
Philadelphia Life, **I** 527
Philadelphia Smelting and Refining Co., **IV** 31
Philadelphia Suburban Corporation, **39 326–29**
Philco Corp., **I** 167, 531; **II** 86; **III** 604; **13** 402
Phildar, **37** 22
Philip Environmental Inc., **16 414–16**
Philip Morris Companies Inc., **I** 23, 269; **II** 530–34; **V** 397, 404, **405–07**, 409, 417; **6** 52; **7** 272, 274, 276, 548; **8** 53; **9** 180; **12** 337, 372; **13** 138, 517; **15** 64, 72–73, 137; **18** 72, **416–19 (upd.)**; **19** 112, 369; **20** 23; **22** 73, 338; **23** 427; **26** 249, 251; **29** 46–47; **32** 472, 476
Philip Smith Theatrical Enterprises. *See* GC Companies, Inc.
Philipp Abm. Cohen, **IV** 139
Philipp Brothers Chemicals, Inc., **II** 447; **IV** 79–0; **25** 82
Philipp Holzmann AG, **II** 279, 386; **14** 169; **16** 284, 286; **17 374–77**
Philippine Aerospace Development Corporation, **27** 475
Philippine Airlines, Inc., **I** 107; **6 106–08**, 122–23; **23 379–82 (upd.)**; **27** 464
Philippine American Life Insurance Co., **III** 195
Philippine Sinter Corp., **IV** 125
Philips, **V** 339; **6** 101; **10** 269; **22** 194
Philips Electronics N.V., **8** 153; **9** 75; **10** 16; **12** 475, 549; **13** 396, **400–03 (upd.)**; **14** 446; **23** 389; **26** 334; **27** 190–92; **32** 373; **34** 258; **37** 121
Philips Electronics North America Corp., **13 396–99**; **26** 334
N.V. Philips Gloeilampenfabriken, **I** 107, 330; **II** 25, 56, 58, **78–80**, 99, 102, 117, 119; **III** 479, 654–55; **IV** 680; **12** 454. *See also* Philips Electronics N.V.
Philips Medical Systems, **29** 299
Phillip Hawkins, **III** 169; **6** 285
Phillip Securities, **16** 14; **43** 8
Phillippe of California, **8** 16; **36** 24
Phillips & Drew, **II** 379
Phillips & Jacobs, Inc., **14** 486
Phillips Cables, **III** 433
Phillips Carbon Black, **IV** 421
Phillips Colleges Inc., **22** 442; **39** 102
Phillips Manufacturing Company, **8** 464
Phillips Petroleum Company, **I** 377; **II** 15, 408; **III** 752; **IV** 71, 290, 366, 405, 412, 414, 445, 453, 498, **521–23**, 567, 570–71, 575; **10** 84, 440; **11** 522; **13** 356, 485; **17** 422; **19** 176; **24** 521; **31** 457; **38** 407; **40 354–59 (upd.)**
Phillips Sheet and Tin Plate Co., **IV** 236
Phillips-Van Heusen Corporation, **24 382–85**
PHLCorp., **11** 261
PHM Corp., **8** 461
Phoenicia Glass, **25** 266–67
Phoenix Assurance Co., **III** 242, 257, 369, 370–74
Phoenix Financial Services, **11** 115
Phoenix Fire Office, **III** 234
Phoenix Insurance Co., **III** 389; **IV** 711
Phoenix Microsystems Inc., **13** 8
Phoenix Mutual Life Insurance, **16** 207
Phoenix Oil and Transport Co., **IV** 90
Phoenix-Rheinrohr AG, **IV** 222
Phoenix State Bank and Trust Co., **II** 213
Phoenix Technologies Ltd., **13** 482
Phone America of Carolina, **8** 311
Phonogram, **23** 389
Photocircuits Corp., **18** 291–93
PhotoDisc Inc., **31** 216, 218
PHP Healthcare Corporation, **22 423–25**
Phuket Air Catering Company Ltd., **6** 123–24; **27** 464
PhyCor, Inc., **36 365–69**
Physical Measurements Information, **31** 357
Physician Corporation of America, **24** 231
Physician Sales & Service, Inc., **14 387–89**
Physician's Weight Loss Center, **10** 383
Physicians Formula Cosmetics, **8** 512
Physicians Placement, **13** 49
Physio-Control International Corp., **18 420–23**; **30** 316
Physiotherapy Associates Inc., **29** 453
Piaget, **27** 487, 489
Piaggio & C. S.p.A., **17** 24; **20 426–29**; **36** 472; **39** 36–37
PIC International Group PLC, **24 386–88 (upd.)**
Pic 'N' Save, **17** 298–99
PIC Realty Corp., **III** 339
Picard Surgeles, **27** 93
Picault, **19** 50
Piccadilly Cafeterias, Inc., **19 299–302**
Pick, **III** 98
Pick-N-Pay, **II** 642; **9** 452
Pickands Mather, **13** 158
Picker International Corporation, **II** 25; **8** 352; **30** 314
Pickfords Ltd., **6** 412–14
Pickland Mather & Co., **IV** 409
PickOmatic Systems, **8** 135
Pickwick Dress Co., **III** 54

Pickwick International, **I** 613; **9** 360; **38** 315
Piclands Mather, **7** 308
Pico Ski Area Management Company, **28** 21
Picture Classified Network, **IV** 597
PictureTel Corp., 10 455–57; 27 363–66 (upd.)
Piece Goods Shops, **16** 198
Piedmont Airlines, Inc., **6** 132; **12** 490; **28** 507
Piedmont Coca-Cola Bottling Partnership, **10** 223
Piedmont Concrete, **III** 739
Piedmont Natural Gas Company, Inc., 27 367–69
Piedmont Pulp and Paper Co. *See* Westvaco Corporation.
Pier 1 Imports, Inc., 12 179, 200, **393–95; 34 337–41 (upd.)**
Pierburg GmbH, **9** 445–46
Pierce, **IV** 478
Pierce Brothers, **6** 295
Pierce Leahy Corporation, 24 389–92. *See also* Iron Mountain Inc.
Pierce National Life, **22** 314
Pierce Steam Heating Co., **III** 663
Piercing Pagoda, Inc., 29 382–84; 40 472
Pierre Foods, **29** 203
Pierre Frozen Foods Inc., **13** 270–72
Pierson, Heldring, and Pierson, **II** 185
Pietrafesa Corporation, **29** 208
Pietro's Pizza Parlors, **II** 480–81; **26** 56–57
Piezo Electric Product, Inc., **16** 239
Pig Improvement Co., **II** 500
Piggly Wiggly Southern, Inc., II 571, 624; **13** 251–52, **404–06; 18** 6, 8; **21** 455; **22** 127; **26** 47; **27** 245; **31** 406, 408; **32** 260
Pignone, **IV** 420
Pike Adding Machine, **III** 165
Pike Corporation of America, **I** 570; **8** 191
Pikrose and Co. Ltd., **IV** 136
Pilgrim Curtain Co., **III** 213
Pilgrim's Pride Corporation, 7 432–33; 23 383–85 (upd.); 39 229
Pilkington plc, I 429; **II** 475; **III** 56, 641–42, 676–77, 714–15, **724–27; 16** 7, 9, 120–21; **22** 434; **34 342–47 (upd.)**
Pillar Holdings, **IV** 191
Pilliod Furniture, Inc., **12** 300
Pillowtex Corporation, 19 303–05; 31 200; **41 299–302 (upd.)**
Pillsbury Company, II 133, 414, 493–94, 511, **555–57**, 575, 613–15; **7** 106, 128, 277, 469, 547; **8** 53–54; **10** 147, 176; **11** 23; **12** 80, 510; **13 407–09 (upd.)**, 516; **14** 212, 214; **15** 64; **16** 71; **17** 70–71, 434; **22** 59, 426; **24** 140–41; **25** 179, 241; **27** 196, 287; **29** 433; **32** 32, 67; **38** 100
Pillsbury Madison & Sutro LLP, 29 385–88
Pilot, **I** 531
Pilot Freight Carriers, **27** 474
Pilot Insurance Agency, **III** 204
Pinal-Dome Oil, **IV** 569; **24** 520
Pinault-Printemps-Redoute S.A., 15 386; **19 306–09 (upd.); 22** 362; **27** 513; **41** 185–86; **42** 171
Pincus & Co., **7** 305
Pine Tree Casting. *See* Sturm, Ruger & Company, Inc.
Pinecliff Publishing Company, **10** 357
Pinelands, Inc., **9** 119; **26** 33
Pineville Kraft Corp., **IV** 276
Pinewood Studios, **II** 157
Pininfarina, **I** 188
Pinkerton's Inc., 9 406–09; 13 124–25; **14** 541; **16** 48; **41** 77, 79. *See also* Securitas AB.
Pinnacle Art and Frame, **31** 436
Pinnacle Books, **25** 483
Pinnacle Fitness, **25** 42
Pinnacle West Capital Corporation, 6 545–47; 26 359
Pinsetter Corp., **III** 443
Pinto Island Metals Company, **15** 116
Pioneer Airlines, **I** 96; **21** 141
Pioneer Asphalt Co., **I** 404; **36** 146–47
Pioneer Asphalts Pty. Ltd., **III** 728
Pioneer Bank, **41** 312
Pioneer Concrete Services Ltd., **III** 728–29
Pioneer Cotton Mill, **12** 503
Pioneer Electronic Corporation, II 103; **III 604–06; 28 358–61 (upd.)**
Pioneer Federal Savings Bank, **10** 340; **11** 115
Pioneer Financial Corp., **11** 447
Pioneer Food Stores Co-op, **24** 528
Pioneer Hi-Bred International, Inc., 9 410–12; 17 131; **21** 387; **41 303–06 (upd.)**
Pioneer International Limited, III 687, **728–30; 28** 83
Pioneer Life Insurance Co., **III** 274
Pioneer Natural Gas Company, **10** 82
Pioneer Outdoor, **27** 280
Pioneer Plastics Corporation, **31** 399–400
Pioneer Readymixed Concrete and Mortar Proprietary Ltd., **III** 728
Pioneer Saws Ltd., **III** 598
Pioneer-Standard Electronics Inc., 13 47; **19 310–14**
Pipasa, **41** 329
Pipe Line Service Company. *See* Plexco.
Pipeline and Products Marketing Co., **IV** 473
Piper Aircraft Corp., **I** 482; **II** 403; **8** 49–50
Piper Jaffray Companies Inc., 22 426–30, 465. *See also* U.S. Bancorp.
Pirelli S.p.A., IV 174, 420; **V 249–51; 10** 319; **15 353–56 (upd.); 16** 318; **21** 73; **28** 262
Piscataquis Canal and Railroad Company, **16** 348
Pisces Inc., **13** 321
Pispalan Werhoomo Oy, **I** 387
The Piston Ring Company, **I** 199; **10** 492
Pitcairn Aviation, **I** 101
Pitney Bowes, Inc., III 156–58, 159; **19 315–18 (upd.)**
Pittman Company, **28** 350
Pittsburgh & Lake Angeline Iron Company, **13** 156
Pittsburgh & Lake Erie Railroad, **I** 472
Pittsburgh Aluminum Alloys Inc., **12** 353
Pittsburgh Brewing Co., **10** 169–70; **18** 70, 72
Pittsburgh Chemical Co., **IV** 573; **7** 551
Pittsburgh Consolidation Coal Co., **8** 346
Pittsburgh Corning Corp., **III** 683
Pittsburgh Life, **III** 274
Pittsburgh National Bank, **II** 317, 342; **22** 55
Pittsburgh National Corp., **II** 342
Pittsburgh Paint & Glass. *See* PPG Industries, Inc.
Pittsburgh Plate Glass Co. *See* PPG Industries, Inc.
Pittsburgh Railway Company, **9** 413
Pittsburgh Reduction Co., **II** 315; **IV** 9, 14
Pittsburgh Steel Company, **7** 587
Pittsburgh Trust and Savings, **II** 342
The Pittston Company, IV 180–82, 566; **10** 44; **19 319–22 (upd.)**
Pittway Corporation, 9 413–15; 27 361–62; **28** 133–34; **33 334–37 (upd.)**
Pixar Animation Studios, 34 348–51
Pixel Semiconductor, **11** 57
Pizitz, Inc., **19** 324
Pizza Dispatch. *See* Dominos's Pizza, Inc.
Pizza Hut Inc., I 221, 278, 294; **II** 614; **7** 152–53, 267, **434–35**, 506; **10** 450; **11** 50; **12** 123; **13** 336, 516; **14** 107; **15** 344–46; **16** 446; **17** 71, 537; **21** 24–25, 315, **405–07 (upd.); 22** 353; **24** 295; **25** 179–80, 227; **28** 238; **33** 388; **40** 340
Pizza Inn, **16** 447; **25** 179
PizzaCo, Inc., **7** 152
Pizzeria Uno, **25** 178
PJS Publications, **22** 442
PKbanken, **II** 353
Place Two, **V** 156
Placer Cego Petroleum Ltd., **IV** 367
Placer Development Ltd., **IV** 19
Placer Dome Inc., IV 571; **20 430–33; 24** 522; **36** 314
Placid Oil Co., **7** 228
Plaid Holdings Corp., **9** 157
Plain Jane Dress Company, **8** 169
Plainwell Paper Co., Inc., **8** 103
Planet Hollywood International, Inc., 18 424–26; 25 387–88; **32** 241, 243–44; **41 307–10 (upd.)**
Planet Insurance Co., **III** 343
Plank Road Brewery, **I** 269; **12** 337
Plankinton Packing Co., **III** 534
Plant Genetics Inc., **I** 266; **21** 320
Planters Company, **24** 287
Planters Lifesavers, **14** 274–75
Planters Nut & Chocolate Co., **I** 219; **II** 544
Plas-Techs, Inc., **15** 35
Plastic Coating Corporation, **IV** 330; **8** 483
Plastic Containers, Inc., **15** 129; **25** 512
Plastic Engineered Products Company. *See* Ballard Medical Products.
Plastic Parts, Inc., **19** 277
Plasticos Metalgrafica, **I** 231
Plastics, Inc., **13** 41
Plasto Bambola. *See* BRIO AB.
Plastrier. *See* Compagnie de Saint-Gobain S.A.
Plate Glass Group, **24** 450
Plateau Holdings, Inc., **12** 260; **13** 502
Platinum Entertainment, Inc., 35 341–44
PLATINUM Technology, Inc., 14 390–92
Platt & Co., **I** 506
Platt Bros., **III** 636
Platt's Price Service, Inc., **IV** 636–37
Play by Play Toys & Novelties, Inc., 26 374–76
Play It Again Sports, **18** 207–08
Playboy Enterprises, Inc., 18 427–30
PlayCore, Inc., 27 370–72
Players International, Inc., 16 263, 275; **19** 402; **22 431–33; 33** 41; **43** 226–27
Playland, **16** 389
Playmates Toys, 23 386–88

Playskool, Inc., **III** 504, 506; **12** 169; **13** 317; **16** 267; **25 379–81**; **43** 229, 232
Playtex Products, Inc., **II** 448, 468; **8** 511; **13** 448; **15 357–60**; **24** 480
Playworld, **16** 389–90
Plaza Coloso S.A. de C.V., **10** 189
Plaza Medical Group, **6** 184
Plaza Securities, **I** 170
PLC. *See* Prescription Learning Corporation.
Pleasant Company, **25** 314; **27 373–75**
Pleasurama PLC, **I** 248; **12** 228; **32** 243
Plessey Company, PLC, **II** 25, 39, **81–82**; **IV** 100; **6** 241; **33** 287–88
Plews Manufacturing Co., **III** 602
Plexco, **7** 30–31
Plexus Corporation, **35 345–47**
Plezall Wipers, Inc., **15** 502
Plitt Theatres, Inc., **6** 162; **23** 126
Plon et Juillard, **IV** 614
Plough Inc., **I** 684
Plum Associates, **12** 270
Plum Creek Timber Company, Inc., **43 304–06**
Pluma, Inc., **27 376–78**
Plumb Tool, **II** 16
Plus Development Corporation, **10** 458–59
Plus Mark, Inc., **7** 24
Plus System Inc., **9** 537
Plus-Ultra, **II** 196
Plus Vita, **36** 162
Pluto Technologies International Inc., **38** 72
Ply Gem Industries Inc., **12 396–98**; **23** 225
Plymouth County Electric Co., **14** 124
Plymouth Mills Inc., **23** 66
PMC Contract Research AB, **21** 425
PMC Specialties Group, **III** 745
PMI Corporation, **6** 140. *See also* Physical Measurements Information
PMI Mortgage Insurance Company, **10** 50
PMS Consolidated, **8** 347
PMT Services, Inc., **24 393–95**
PN Pertambangan Minyak Dan Gas Bumi Negara, **IV** 492
PNC Bank Corp., **13 410–12 (upd.)**; **14** 103; **18** 63
PNC Financial Corporation, **II** 317, **342–43**; **9** 476; **17** 114
Pneumo Abex Corp., **I** 456–58; **III** 512; **10** 553–54; **38** 293–94
Pneumo Dynamics Corporation, **8** 409
PNL. *See* Pacific Northwest Laboratories.
PNM. *See* Public Service Company of New Mexico.
PNP. *See* Pacific Northwest Power Company.
POAS, **IV** 563
POB Polyolefine Burghausen GmbH, **IV** 487
Pocahontas Foods USA, **31** 359, 361
Pocket Books, Inc., **10** 480; **13** 559–60
Poclain Company, **10** 380
Poe & Associates, Inc., **41** 63–64
Pogo Producing Company, **I** 441; **39 330–32**
Pohang Iron and Steel Company Ltd., **IV 183–85**; **17** 351
Pohjan Sellu Oy, **IV** 316
Pohjoismainen Osakepankki, **II** 302
Pohjola Voima Oy, **IV** 348
Pohjolan Osakepankki, **II** 303
Point Chehalis Packers, **13** 244
Polak & Schwarz Essencefabricken, **9** 290
Poland Spring Natural Spring Water Co., **31** 229
Polar Manufacturing Company, **16** 32
Polar Star Milling Company, **7** 241
Polaris Industries Inc., **12 399–402**; **35 348–53 (upd.)**; **40** 47, 50
Polaroid Corporation, **I** 30–31; **II** 412; **III** 475–77, 549, 584, **607–09**; **IV** 330; **7** 161–62, **436–39 (upd.)**; **12** 180; **28 362–66 (upd.)**; **36** 171–73; **41** 104, 106
Polbeth Packaging Limited, **12** 377
Polenghi, **25** 84
Policy Management Systems Corporation, **11 394–95**
Poliet S.A., **33** 175–77, **338–40**; **40** 108
Polioles, S.A. de C.V., **19** 10, 12
Politos, S.A. de C.V., **23** 171
Polk Audio, Inc., **34 352–54**
Pollenex Corp., **19** 360
Polo Food Corporation, **10** 250
Polo/Ralph Lauren Corporation, **9** 157; **12 403–05**; **16** 61; **25** 48
Polser, **19** 49, 51
Polskie Linie Lotnicze S.A. *See* LOT Polish Airlines.
Poly-Glas Systems, Inc., **21** 65
Poly-Hi Corporation, **8** 359
Poly P, Inc., **IV** 458
Poly Version, Inc., **III** 645
Polyblend Corporation, **7** 4
Polycell Holdings, **IV** 666; **17** 397
Polydesign België, **16** 421
Polydesign Nederland, **16** 421
Polydor B.V., **23** 389
Polydor KK, **23** 390
Polydress Plastic GmbH, **7** 141
Polygon Networks Inc., **41** 73
PolyGram N.V., **13** 402; **22** 194; **23 389–92**; **25** 411; **26** 152, 314, 394; **31** 269
Polyken Technologies, **11** 220
Polymer Technologies Corporation, **26** 287
Polysar Energy & Chemical Corporation of Toronto, **V** 674
Polysius AG, **IV** 89
Pomeroy Computer Resources, Inc., **33 341–44**
Pomeroy's, **16** 61
Pommersche Papierfabrik Hohenkrug, **III** 692
Pommery et Greno, **II** 475
Ponderosa Steakhouse, **7** 336; **12** 373; **14** 331; **15 361–64**
Ponderosa System Inc., **12** 199
Pont-à-Mousson S.A., **III** 675, 677–78, 704; **16** 119, 121–22; **21** 253
Pontiac, **III** 458; **10** 353
Pontificia, **III** 207
Ponto Frio Bonzao, **22** 321
Pony Express, **II** 380–81, 395
Poorman-Douglas Corporation, **13** 468
Pop.com, **43** 144
Pope and Talbot, Inc., **12 406–08**
Pope Cable and Wire B.V., **19** 45
Pope Tin Plate Co., **IV** 236; **26** 527
Popeye's/Church's, **23** 115, 117
Popeyes Famous Fried Chicken and Biscuits, Inc., **7** 26–28; **32** 13
Pophitt Cereals, Inc., **22** 337
Poppe Tyson Inc., **23** 479; **25** 91
Poppin' Fresh Pies, Inc., **12** 510
Popsicle, **II** 573; **14** 205
Popular Aviation Company, **12** 560
Popular Club Plan, **12** 280; **34** 232
Popular, Inc., **41 311–13**
Popular Merchandise, Inc., **12** 280
Pori, **IV** 350
Poron Diffusion, **9** 394
Poron, S.A., **42** 268–69
Porsche AG, **13** 28, 219, **413–15**; **31 363–366 (upd.)**; **36** 198
Port Arthur Finance Corp., **37** 309
Port Blakely Mill Company, **17** 438
Port Dickson Power Sdn. Bhd., **36** 435–36
Port Harcourt Refining Co., **IV** 473
Port Stockton Food Distributors, Inc., **16** 451, 453
Portage Industries Corp., **19** 415
Portals Water Treatment, **11** 510
Porter-Cable Corporation, **26** 361–63
Porter Chadburn plc, **28** 252
Porter Shoe Manufacturing Company, **13** 360
Portex, **25** 431
Portia Management Services Ltd., **30** 318
Portland General Corporation, **6 548–51**
Portland Heavy Industries, **10** 369
Portland Plastics, **25** 430–31
Portland-Zementwerke Heidelberg A.G., **23** 326
Portnet, **6** 435
Portsmouth & Sunderland, **35** 242, 244
Portways, **9** 92
Poseidon Exploration Ltd., **IV** 84; **7** 188
Posey, Quest, Genova, **6** 48
Positive Response Television, Inc., **27** 337–38
Post Office Counters, **V** 496
Post Office Group, **V 498–501**
Post Properties, Inc., **26 377–79**
PostBank, **II** 189
La Poste, **V 470–72**
Posti- Ja Telelaitos, **6 329–31**
PostScript, **17** 177
Postum Cereal Company, **II** 497, 523, 530–31; **7** 272–73; **13** 291
Potash Corporation of Saskatchewan Inc., **18** 51, **431–33**; **27** 318
Potlatch Corporation, **IV** 282; **8 428–30**; **9** 260; **19** 445; **34 355–59 (upd.)**
Potomac Edison Company, **38** 39–40
Potomac Electric Power Company, **6 552–54**; **25** 46
Potomac Insurance Co., **III** 257
Potomac Leasing, **III** 137
Potter & Brumfield Inc., **11 396–98**
Pottery Barn, **13** 42; **17** 548–50
Potts, **IV** 58
Poulan/Weed Eater. *See* White Consolidated Industries Inc.
Poulsen Wireless, **II** 490
PowCon, Inc., **17** 534
Powell Duffryn plc, **III** 502; **IV** 38; **31 367–70**
Powell Energy Products, **8** 321
Powell Group, **33** 32
Powell River Co. Ltd., **IV** 306–07
Powell's Books, Inc., **37** 181; **40 360–63**
Power Applications & Manufacturing Company, Inc., **6** 441
Power Corporation of Canada, **36 370–74 (upd.)**
Power Financial Corp., **III** 260–61
Power Jets Ltd., **I** 81
Power Parts Co., **7** 358
Power Products, **8** 515
Power Specialty Company, **6** 145

Power Team, **10** 492
Powercor. *See* PacifiCorp.
PowerFone Holdings, **10** 433
PowerGen PLC, **11 399–401**; **12** 349; **13** 458, 484
Powerhouse Technologies, Inc., **13** 485; **27 379–81**
Powers Accounting Machine Company, **6** 240
Powers Regulator, **III** 535
Powers-Samas, **6** 240
PowerSoft Corp., **11** 77; **15** 374
Pozzi-Renati Millwork Products, Inc., **8** 135
PP&L. *See* Pennsylvania Power & Light Company.
PPG Industries, Inc., **I** 330, 341–42; **III** 21, 641, 667, 676, 722, 725, **731–33**; **8** 153, 222, 224; **16** 120–21; **20** 415; **21** 221, 223; **22** 147, **434–37 (upd.)**; **37** 73; **39** 292
PPI. *See* Precision Pattern Inc.
PPL Corporation, **41 314–17 (upd.)**
PR Holdings, **23** 382
PR Newswire, **35 354–56**
Prac, **I** 281
Practical and Educational Books, **13** 105
Practical Business Solutions, Inc., **18** 112
Pragma Bio-Tech, Inc., **11** 424
Prairie Farmer Publishing Co., **II** 129
Prairie Holding Co., **IV** 571; **24** 522
Prairie Oil and Gas Co., **IV** 368
Prairielands Energy Marketing, Inc., **7** 322, 325
Prakla Seismos, **17** 419
Pratt & Whitney, **I** 47, 78, 82–85, 128, 434; **II** 48; **III** 482; **6** 128; **7** 456; **9** 14, 16–18, 244–46, **416–18**; **10** 162; **11** 299, 427; **12** 71; **13** 386; **14** 564; **24** 312; **25** 267; **39** 313
Pratt Holding, Ltd., **IV** 312; **19** 268
Pratt Hotel Corporation, **21** 275; **22** 438
Pratt Properties Inc., **8** 349
Pratta Electronic Materials, Inc., **26** 425
Praxair, Inc., **11 402–04**; **16** 462; **43** 265
Praxis Biologics, **8** 26; **27** 115
Praxis Corporation, **30** 499
Pre-Fab Cushioning, **9** 93
Pre-Paid Legal Services, Inc., **20 434–37**
PreAnalytiX, **39** 335
Precious Metals Development, **IV** 79
Precise Fabrication Corporation, **33** 257
Precise Imports Corp., **21** 516
Precision Castparts Corp., **15 365–67**
Precision Games, **16** 471
Precision Husky Corporation, **26** 494
Precision Interconnect Corporation, **14** 27
Precision LensCrafters, **13** 391
Precision Moulds, Ltd., **25** 312
Precision Optical Co., **III** 120, 575
Precision Optical Industry Company, Ltd. *See* Canon Inc.
Precision Pattern Inc., **36** 159
Precision Power, Inc., **21** 514
Precision Software Corp., **14** 319
Precision Studios, **12** 529
Precision Tube Formers, Inc., **17** 234
Precor, **III** 610–11
Predica, **II** 266
Predicasts Inc., **12** 562; **17** 254
Preferred Medical Products. *See* Ballard Medical Products.
Preferred Products, Inc., **II** 669; **18** 504
PREINCO Holdings, Inc., **11** 532
PREL&P. *See* Portland Railway Electric Light & Power Company.
Prelude Corp., **III** 643
Premark International, Inc., **II** 534; **III 610–12**; **14** 548; **28** 479–80
Premcor Inc., **37 309–11**
Premex A.G., **II** 369
Premier (Transvaal) Diamond Mining Co., **IV** 65–66
Premier & Potter Printing Press Co., Inc., **II** 37
Premier Brands Foods, **II** 514
Premier Consolidated Oilfields PLC, **IV** 383
Premier Cruise Lines, **6** 368; **27** 92
Premier Diamond Mining Company, **7** 122
Premier Health Alliance Inc., **10** 143
Premier Industrial Corporation, **9 419–21**; **19** 311
Premier Insurance Co., **26** 487
Premier Medical Services, **31** 357
Premier Milling Co., **II** 465
Premier One Products, Inc., **37** 285
Premier Parks, Inc., **27 382–84**
Premier Radio Networks, Inc., **23** 292, 294
Premier Rehabilitation Centers, **29** 400
Premier Sport Group Inc., **23** 66
Premiere Products, **I** 403
Premisteres S.A., **II** 663
Premium Standard Farms, Inc., **30 353–55**
PremiumWear, Inc., **30 356–59**
Prémontré, **III** 676; **16** 120
Prentice Hall Computer Publishing, **10** 24
Prentice Hall Inc., **I** 453; **IV** 672; **19** 405; **23** 503
Prescott Ball & Turben, **III** 271; **12** 60
Prescott Investors, **14** 303
Prescription Learning Corporation, **7** 256; **25** 253
Présence, **III** 211
La Preservatrice, **III** 242
Preserves and Honey, Inc., **II** 497
President Baking Co., **36** 313
President Casinos, Inc., **22 438–40**
President Riverboat Casino-Mississippi Inc., **21** 300
Presidential Airlines, **I** 117
Presidents Island Steel & Wire Company. *See* Laclede Steel Company.
Presidio Oil Co., **III** 197; **IV** 123
Press Associates, **IV** 669; **19** 334
Press Trust of India, **IV** 669
Presse Pocket, **IV** 614
Pressed Steel Car Co., **6** 395; **25** 169
Presses de la Cité, **IV** 614–15
Presstar Printing, **25** 183
Presstek, Inc., **33 345–48**
Pressware International, **12** 377
Prest-O-Lite Co., Inc., **I** 399; **9** 16, 516; **11** 402
Prestige et Collections, **III** 48
Prestige Fragrance & Cosmetics, Inc., **22** 158
The Prestige Group plc., **19** 171
Prestige International, **33** 284
Prestige Leather Creations, **31** 435–36
Prestige Properties, **23** 388
Presto Products, Inc., **II** 609–10; **IV** 187; **19** 348
Preston Corporation, **6 421–23**; **14** 566, 568
Prestone Products Corp., **22** 32; **26** 349
Prestwick Mortgage Group, **25** 187
Pretty Good Privacy, Inc., **25** 349
Pretty Neat Corp., **12** 216
Pretty Paper Inc., **14** 499
Pretty Polly, **I** 429
Pretzel Time. *See* Mrs. Fields' Original Cookies, Inc.
Pretzelmaker. *See* Mrs. Fields' Original Cookies, Inc.
Pretzels Incorporated, **24** 241
Preussag AG, **I** 542–43; **II** 386; **IV** 109, 201, 231; **17 378–82**; **21** 370; **28** 454; **42 279–83 (upd.)**
Preussenelektra Aktiengesellschaft, **I** 542; **V 698–700**; **39** 57
Preval, **19** 49–50
Previews, Inc., **21** 96
PreVision Marketing, Inc., **37** 409
Priam Corporation, **10** 458
Priba, **26** 158, 160
Pribina, **25** 85
Price Chopper Supermarkets. *See* The Golub Corporation.
Price Club, **V** 162–64
Price Co., **34** 198
Price Communications Corporation, **42 284–86**
Price Company Ltd, **II** 664; **IV** 246–47; **V 162–64**; **14** 393–94; **25** 11
Price Enterprises, Inc., **14** 395
Price, McCormick & Co., **26** 451
Price Rite, **25** 67
Price Waterhouse LLP, **III** 84, 420, 527; **9 422–24**; **14** 245; **26** 439. *See also* PricewaterhouseCoopers
PriceCostco, Inc., **14 393–95**
Pricel, **6** 373; **21** 103
PricewaterhouseCoopers, **29 389–94 (upd.)**
Prichard and Constance, **III** 65
Pride & Clarke, **III** 523
Pride Petroleum Services. *See* DeKalb Genetics Corporation.
Priggen Steel Building Co., **8** 545
Primadonna Resorts Inc., **17** 318
Primark Corp., **10** 89–90; **13 416–18**
Prime Care International, Inc., **36** 367
Prime Computer, Inc. *See* Computervision Corporation.
Prime Motor Inns Inc., **III** 103; **IV** 718; **11** 177; **17** 238
The Prime-Mover Co., **13** 267
Prime Service, Inc., **28** 40
Prime Telecommunications Corporation, **8** 311
PrimeAmerica, **III** 340
Primedex Health Systems, Inc., **25 382–85**
Primedia Inc., **7** 286; **12** 306; **21** 403–04; **22 441–43**; **23** 156, 158, 344, 417; **24** 274
Primergy Corp., **39** 261
Primerica Corporation, **I** 597, 599–602, 604, 607–09, **612–14**, 615; **II** 422; **III** 283 **8** 118; **9** 218–19, 360–61; **11** 29; **15** 464; **27** 47; **36** 202. *See also* American Can Co.
Primerica Financial Services, **30** 124
PriMerit Bank, **19** 412
Primes Régal Inc., **II** 651
PrimeSource, **26** 542
Primestar, **38** 176
PRIMESTAR Partners L.P., **28** 241
Primex Fibre Ltd., **IV** 328
Primo Foods Ltd., **I** 457; **7** 430

Prince Co., **II** 473
Prince Gardner Company, **17** 465; **23** 21
Prince Golf International, Ltd., **23** 450
Prince Holding Corporation, **26** 231
Prince Motor Co. Ltd., **I** 184
Prince of Wales Hotels, PLC, **14** 106; **25** 308
Prince Sports Group, Inc., **15 368–70**
Prince Street Technologies, Ltd., **8** 271
Prince William Bank, **II** 337; **10** 425
Princess Cruise Lines, **IV** 256; **22 444–46**
Princess Dorothy Coal Co., **IV** 29
Princess Hotel Group, **21** 353
Princess Metropole, **21** 354
Princeton Gas Service Company, **6** 529
Princeton Laboratories Products Company, **8** 84; **38** 124
The Princeton Review, Inc., **12** 142; **42** 210, **287–90**
Princeton Telecommunications Corporation, **26** 38
Princeville Airlines, **24** 22
Principal Mutual Life Insurance Company, **III 328–30**
Principles, **V** 21–22
Princor Financial Services Corp., **III** 329
Pringle Barge Line Co., **17** 357
Print Technologies, Inc., **22** 357
Printex Corporation, **9** 363
Printronix, Inc., **14** 377–78; **18 434–36**
Priority Records, **22** 194
Pripps Ringnes, **18** 394, 396–97
Prism Systems Inc., **6** 310
Prismo Universal, **III** 735
Prisunic SA, **V** 9–11; **19** 307–09
Prisunic-Uniprix, **26** 160
Pritchard Corporation. *See* Black & Veatch, Inc.
Pritzker & Pritzker, **III** 96–97
Privatbanken, **II** 352
Pro-Fac Cooperative, Inc., **7** 104–06; **21** 154–55, 157
Pro-Lawn, **19** 250
Pro-Line Corporation, **36** 26
Pro-optik AG, **31** 203
Probe Exploration Inc., **25** 232
Process Engineering Inc., **21** 108
Process Systems International, **21** 108
Processing Technologies International. *See* Food Ingredients Technologies.
Procino-Rossi Corp., **II** 511
Procor Limited, **16** 357
Procordia Foods, **II** 478; **18** 396
Procter & Gamble Company, **I** 34, 129, 290, 331, 366; **II** 478, 493, 544, 590, 684, 616; **III** 20–25, 36–38, 40–41, 44, **50–53**; **IV** 282, 290, 329–30; **6** 26–27, 50–52, 129, 363; **7** 277, 300, 419; **8** 63, 106–07, 253, 282, 344, 399, **431–35 (upd.)**, 477, 511–12; **9** 260, 291, 317–19, 552; **10** 54, 288; **11** 41, 421; **12** 80, 126–27, 439; **13** 39, 197, 199, 215; **14** 121–22, 262, 275; **15** 357; **16** 302–04, 440; **18** 68, 147–49, 217, 229; **22** 146–47, 210; **26 380–85 (upd.)**; **32** 208, 474–77; **35** 111, 113; **37** 270; **38** 365; **42** 51; **43** 257–58
Proctor & Collier, **I** 19
Proctor & Schwartz, **17** 213
Proctor-Silex. *See* Hamilton Beach/Proctor-Silex Inc.
Prodigy Communications Corporation, **10** 237–38; **12** 562; **13** 92; **27** 517; **34 360–62**
Product Components, Inc., **19** 415
Productos Ortiz, **II** 594
Produits Chimiques Ugine Kuhlmann, **I** 303; **IV** 547
Produits Jaeger, **27** 258
Profarmaco Nobel S.r.l., **16** 69
Professional Care Service, **6** 42
Professional Computer Resources, Inc., **10** 513
Professional Education Systems, Inc., **17** 272
The Professional Golfers' Association of America, **41 318–21**
Professional Health Care Management Inc., **14** 209
Professional Research, **III** 73
Proffitt's, Inc., **19 323–25**, 510, 512. *See also* Saks Holdings, Inc.
Profile Extrusion Company, **22** 337
Profimatics, Inc., **11** 66
PROFITCo., **II** 231
Progil, **I** 389
Progress Development Organisation, **10** 169
Progress Software Corporation, **15 371–74**
Progressive Bagel Concepts, Inc. *See* Einstein/Noah Bagel Corporation.
Progressive Corporation, **11 405–07**; **29 395–98 (upd.)**
Progressive Distributors, **12** 220
Progressive Grocery Stores, **7** 202
Progressive Networks, **37** 193
Progresso, **I** 514; **14** 212
Project Carriers. *See* Hansa Linie.
Projexions Video Supply, Inc., **24** 96
Projiis, **II** 356
Prolabo, **I** 388
Proland, **12** 139
Proler International Corp., **13** 98; **19** 380–81
Promarkt Holding GmbH, **24** 266, 270
Promigas, **IV** 418
Promodès Group, **24** 475; **26** 158, 161; **37** 21
Promotional Graphics, **15** 474
Promstroybank, **II** 242
Promus Companies, Inc., **III** 95; **9 425–27**; **15** 46; **16** 263; **22** 537; **38** 76–77; **43** 225–26
Pronto Pacific, **II** 488
Prontophot Holding Limited, **6** 490
Prontor-Werk Alfred Gauthier GmbH, **III** 446
Propaganda Films, Inc., **23** 389, 391
Prophet Foods, **I** 449
Propwix, **IV** 605
Prosim, S.A., **IV** 409
ProSource Distribution Services, Inc., **16** 397; **17** 475
Prospect Farms, Inc., **II** 584; **14** 514
The Prospect Group, Inc., **11** 188
Prospect Provisions, Inc. *See* King Kullen Grocery Co., Inc.
Prospectors Airways, **IV** 165
Protan & Fagertun, **25** 464
Protection One, Inc., **32 372–75**
Protective Closures, **7** 296–97
La Protectrice, **III** 346–47
Protek, **III** 633
Proto Industrial Tools, **III** 628
Protogene Laboratories Inc., **17** 288
Proventus A.B., **II** 303
Proventus Handels AB, **35** 362
Provi-Soir, **II** 652
Provi-Viande, **II** 652
Provibec, **II** 652
The Providence Journal Company, **28 367–69**; **30** 15
La Providence, **III** 210–11
Providence National Bank, **9** 228
Providence Steam and Gas Pipe Co. *See* Grinnell Corp.
Providencia, **III** 208
Provident Bank, **III** 190
Provident Institution for Savings, **13** 467
Provident Life and Accident Insurance Company of America, **III 331–33**, 404
Provident National Bank, **II** 342
Provident Services, Inc., **6** 295
Provident Travelers Mortgage Securities Corp., **III** 389
Provigo Inc., **II 651–53**; **12** 413
Provimi, **36** 185
Les Provinces Réunies, **III** 235
Provincetown-Boston Airlines, **I** 118
Provincial Bank of Ireland Ltd., **16** 13
Provincial Engineering Ltd, **8** 544
Provincial Gas Company, **6** 526
Provincial Insurance Co., **III** 373
Provincial Newspapers Ltd., **IV** 685–86; **28** 502
Provincial Traders Holding Ltd., **I** 437
Provinzial-Hülfskasse, **II** 385
Provost & Provost, **II** 651
PROWA, **22** 89
Proximity Technology, **23** 210
Prudential Assurance Company, **24** 314
Prudential Bache Securities, **9** 441
Prudential-Bache Trade Corporation, **II** 51; **21** 331
Prudential Corporation plc, **II** 319; **III 334–36**; **IV** 711; **8** 276–77
Prudential Insurance Company of America, **I** 19, 334, 402; **II** 103, 456; **III** 79, 92, 249, 259, 265–67, 273, 291–93, 313, 329, **337–41**; **IV** 410, 458; **10** 199; **11** 243; **12** 28, 453, 500; **13** 561; **14** 95, 561; **16** 135, 497; **17** 325; **22** 266; **23** 226; **25** 399; **30 360–64 (upd.)**; **36** 77–78; **42** 193, 196
Prudential Oil & Gas, Inc., **6** 495–96
Prudential Refining Co., **IV** 400
Prudential Steel, **IV** 74; **24** 143–44
PSA. *See* Pacific Southwest Airlines.
PSA Peugeot Citroen S.A., **7** 35; **28 370–74 (upd.)**
PSB Company, **36** 517
PSCCo. *See* Public Service Company of Colorado.
PSE, Inc., **12** 100
PSF. *See* Premium Standard Farms, Inc.
PSI. *See* Process Systems International.
PSI Resources, **6 555–57**
Psychiatric Institutes of America, **III** 87–88
Psychological Corp., **IV** 623; **12** 223
PT Components, **14** 43
PT PERMINA, **IV** 492, 517
PTI Communications, Inc. *See* Pacific Telecom, Inc.
PTT Nederland N.V., **27** 472; **30** 393–94
PTT Telecom BV, **V** 299–301; **6** 303
PTV. *See* Österreichische Post- und Telegraphenverwaltung.

Pubco Corporation, 17 383–85
Publi-Graphics, **16** 168
Public Broadcasting Stations, **29** 426
Public Home Trust Co., **III** 104
Public National Bank, **II** 230
Public Savings Insurance Co., **III** 219
Public Service Co., **14** 124
Public Service Company of Colorado, 6 558–60
Public Service Company of Indiana. *See* PSI Energy.
Public Service Company of New Hampshire, 21 408–12
Public Service Company of New Mexico, 6 561–64; **27** 486
Public Service Electric and Gas Company, **IV** 366; **V** 701–03; **11** 388
Public Service Enterprise Group Incorporated, V 701–03
Public Service Market. *See* The Golub Corporation.
Public Storage, Inc., **21** 476
Public/Hacienda Resorts, Inc. *See* Santa Fe Gaming Corporation.
Publicaciones Citem, S.A. de C.V., **39** 188
Publicis S.A., 13 204; **19 329–32**; **21** 265–66; **23** 478, 480; **25** 91; **33** 180; **39** 166, 168; **42** 328, 331
Publicker Industries Inc., **I** 226; **10** 180
Publishers Clearing House, 23 393–95; **27** 20
Publishers Group, Inc., 35 357–59
Publishers Paper Co., **IV** 295, 677–78; **19** 225
Publishers Press Assoc., **IV** 607; **25** 506
Publishing and Broadcasting Ltd., **19** 400–01
Publix Super Markets Inc., II 155, 627; **7 440–42**; **9** 186; **20** 84, 306; **23** 261; **31 371–374 (upd.)**
Puck Holdings, **35** 474, 476
Puck Lazaroff Inc. *See* The Wolfgang Puck Food Company, Inc.
Puente Oil, **IV** 385
Puerto Rican Aqueduct and Sewer Authority, **6** 441
Puerto Rican-American Insurance Co., **III** 242
Puget Mill Company, **12** 406–07
Puget Sound Alaska Van Lines. *See* Alaska Hydro-Train.
Puget Sound National Bank, **8** 469–70
Puget Sound Power And Light Company, 6 565–67
Puget Sound Pulp and Timber Co., **IV** 281; **9** 259
Puget Sound Tug and Barge Company, **6** 382
Pulaski Furniture Corporation, 33 349–52
Pulitzer Publishing Company, 15 375–77
Pullman Co., **II** 403; **III** 94, 744
Pullman Savings and Loan Association, **17** 529
Pullman Standard, **7** 540
Pulsar Internacional S.A., 21 413–15
Pulse Engineering, Inc., **29** 461
Pulte Corporation, 8 436–38; **22** 205, 207
Pulte Homes, Inc., 42 291–94 (upd.)
Puma AG Rudolf Dassler Sport, 35 360–63; **36** 344, 346
AB Pump-Separator, **III** 418–19
Punchcraft, Inc., **III** 569; **20** 360
Purdue Fredrick Company, **13** 367
Pure Milk Products Cooperative, **11** 24
Pure Oil Co., **III** 497; **IV** 570; **24** 521
Pure Packed Foods, **II** 525; **13** 293
Purex Corporation, **I** 450; **III** 21; **22** 146
Purex Pool Systems, **I** 13, 342; **18** 163
Purfina, **IV** 497
Purina Mills, Inc., 32 376–79
Puris Inc., **14** 316
Puritan-Bennett Corporation, 13 419–21
Puritan Chemical Co., **I** 321
Puritan Fashions Corp., **22** 122
Purity Stores, **I** 146
Purity Supreme, Inc., **II** 674; **24** 462
Purle Bros., **III** 735
Purnell & Sons Ltd., **IV** 642; **7** 312
Purodenso Co., **III** 593
Purolator Courier, Inc., **6** 345–46, 390; **16** 397; **18** 177; **25** 148
Purolator Products Company, III 593; **21 416–18**; **28** 263
Puros de Villa Gonzales, **23** 465
Push Records, Inc., **42** 271
Puss 'n Boots, **II** 559
Putnam Investments Inc., **25** 387; **30** 355
Putnam Management Co., **III** 283
Putnam Reinsurance Co., **III** 198
Putt-Putt Golf Courses of America, Inc., 23 396–98
PWA Group, IV 323–25; **28** 446
PWS Holding Corporation, **13** 406; **26** 47
PWT Projects Ltd., **22** 89
PWT Worldwide, **11** 510
PYA/Monarch, **II** 675; **26** 504
Pyramid Breweries Inc., 33 353–55
Pyramid Communications, Inc., **IV** 623
Pyramid Electric Company, **10** 319
Pyramid Electronics Supply, Inc., **17** 275
Pyramid Technology Corporation, **10** 504; **27** 448
Pytchley Autocar Co. Ltd., **IV** 722
Pyxis. *See* Cardinal Health, Inc.
Pyxis Resources Co., **IV** 182

Q Lube, Inc., **18** 145; **24** 339
Qantas Airways Limited, I 92–93; **6** 79, 91, 100, 105, **109–13**, 117; **14** 70, 73; **24 396–401 (upd.)**; **27** 466; **31** 104; **38** 24
Qatar General Petroleum Corporation, IV 524–26
Qiagen N.V., 39 333–35
Qintex Australia Ltd., **II** 150; **25** 329
QMS Ltd., **43** 284
QO Chemicals, Inc., **14** 217
QSP, Inc., **IV** 664
Qtera Corporation, **36** 352
Quad/Graphics, Inc., 19 333–36
Quail Oil Tools, **28** 347–48
Quaker Alloy, Inc., **39** 31–32
Quaker Fabric Corp., 19 337–39
Quaker Oats Company, I 30; **II 558–60**, 575, 684; **12** 167, 169, **409–12 (upd.)**; **13** 186; **22** 131, 337–38; **25** 90, 314; **27** 197; **30** 219; **31** 282; **34 363–67 (upd.)**; **38** 349; **43** 121, 218
Quaker State Corporation, 7 443–45; **21 419–22 (upd.)**; **25** 90; **26** 349
Qualcomm Inc., 20 438–41; **26** 532; **38** 271; **39** 64; **41** 289; **43** 312–13
Qualicare, Inc., **6** 192
QualiTROL Corporation, **7** 116–17
Quality Bakers of America, **12** 170
Quality Care Inc., **I** 249
Quality Courts Motels, Inc., **14** 105. *See also* Choice Hotels International, Inc.
Quality Dining, Inc., 18 437–40
Quality Food Centers, Inc., 17 386–88; **22** 271, 273
Quality Importers, **I** 226; **10** 180
Quality Inns International, **13** 363; **14** 105. *See also* Choice Hotels International, Inc.
Quality Markets, Inc., **13** 393
Quality Oil Co., **II** 624–25
Quality Paperback Book Club (QPB), **13** 105–07
Quality Products, Inc., **18** 162
Qualtec, Inc., **V** 623
Quanex Corporation, 13 422–24
Quantex Microsystems Inc., **24** 31
Quantum Chemical Corporation, 8 439–41; **11** 441; **30** 231, 441
Quantum Computer Services, Inc. *See* America Online, Inc.
Quantum Corporation, 6 230–31; **10** 56, 403, **458–59**, 463; **25** 530; **36** 299–300
Quantum Health Resources, **29** 364
Quantum Marketing International, Inc., **27** 336
Quantum Offshore Contractors, **25** 104
Quantum Overseas N.V., **7** 360
Quantum Restaurant Group, Inc., **30** 330
Quarex Industries, Inc. *See* Western Beef, Inc.
Quark, Inc., 36 375–79
Quarrie Corporation, **12** 554
Quasi-Arc Co., **I** 315; **25** 80
Quebec Bank, **II** 344
Quebéc Hydro-Electric Commission. *See* Hydro-Quebéc.
Quebecor Inc., 12 412–14; **19** 333; **26** 44; **29** 471
Queen Casuals, **III** 530
Queen City Broadcasting, **42** 162
Queen Insurance Co., **III** 350
Queens Isetan Co., Ltd., **V** 87
Queensborough Holdings PLC, **38** 103
Queensland Alumina, **IV** 59
Queensland and Northern Territories Air Service. *See* Qantas Airways Limited.
Queensland Mines Ltd., **III** 729
Queensland Oil Refineries, **III** 672
Queiroz Pereira, **IV** 504
Quelle Group, V 165–67
Quennessen, **IV** 118
Quesarias Ibéricas, **23** 219
Quesnel River Pulp Co., **IV** 269
Quest Aerospace Education, Inc., **18** 521
Quest Diagnostics Inc., 26 390–92
Quest Education Corporation, **42** 212
Quest Pharmacies Inc., **25** 504–05
Questar Corporation, 6 568–70; **10** 432; **26 386–89 (upd.)**
Questor Partners, **I** 332; **26** 185
The Quick & Reilly Group, Inc., 18 552; **20 442–44**; **26** 65
QUICK Corp., **IV** 656
Quick-Shop, **II** 619
Quicken.com. *See* Intuit Inc.
Quickie Designs, **11** 202, 487–88
Quik Stop Markets, Inc., **12** 112
Quiksilver, Inc., 18 441–43; **27** 329
QuikTrip Corporation, 36 380–83
QuikWok Inc., **II** 556; **13** 408
Quill Corporation, 28 375–77
Quillery, **27** 138
Quilter Goodison, **II** 260

Quimica Industrial Huels Do Brasil Ltda., **I** 350
Quimicos Industriales Penoles. *See* Industrias Penoles, S.A. de C.V.
Quincy Compressor Co., **I** 434–35
Quincy Family Steak House, **II** 679; **10** 331; **19** 287; **27** 17, 19
Quintana Roo, Inc., **17** 243, 245; **25** 42
Quintex Australia Limited, **25** 329
Quintiles Transnational Corporation, 21 423–25
Quinton Hazell Automotive, **III** 495; **IV** 382–83
Quintron, Inc., **11** 475
Quintus Computer Systems, **6** 248
Quixote Corporation, 15 378–80
Quixtar Inc., **30** 62
Quixx Corporation, **6** 580
The Quizno's Corporation, 32 444; **42 295–98**
Quoddy Products Inc., **17** 389, 390
Quotron Systems, Inc., **III** 119; **IV** 670; **9** 49, 125; **30** 127
QVC Network Inc., 9 428–29; **10** 175; **12** 315; **18** 132; **20** 75; **24** 120, 123
Qwest Communications International, Inc., 25 499; **26** 36; **32** 218; **36** 43–44; **37** 126, **312–17**
QwikSilver II, Inc., **37** 119

R & B Manufacturing Co., **III** 569; **20** 361
R&O Software-Technik GmbH, **27** 492
R. and W. Hawaii Wholesale, Inc., **22** 15
R-Anell Custom Homes Inc., **41** 19
R-B. *See* Arby's, Inc.
R-Byte, **12** 162
R-C Holding Inc. *See* Air & Water Technologies Corporation.
R.A. Waller & Co., **III** 282
R. Buckland & Son Ltd., **IV** 119
R.C. Bigelow, **16** 90
R.C. Willey Home Furnishings, **18** 60
R. Cubed Composites Inc., **I** 387
R.E. Funsten Co., **7** 429
R.G. Barry Corp., 17 389–91
R.G. Dun-Bradstreet Corp., **IV** 604–05
R. Griggs Group Limited, 23 399–402; **31** 413–14
R.H. Macy & Co., Inc., I 30; **V 168–70**; **8 442–45 (upd.)**; **10** 282; **11** 349; **13** 42; **15** 281; **16** 206–07, 328, 388, 561; **23** 60; **27** 60, 481; **30 379–83 (upd.)**; **31** 190, 192–93
R.H. Squire, **III** 283
R.H. Stengel & Company, **13** 479
R. Hoe & Co., **I** 602; **13** 189
R. Hornibrook (NSW), **I** 592
R.J. Brown Co., **IV** 373
R.J. Reynolds, **I** 259, 261, 363; **II** 542, 544; **III** 16; **IV** 523; **V** 396, 404–05, 407–10, 413, 415, 417–18; **7** 130, 132, 267, 365, 367; **9** 533; **13** 490; **14** 78; **15** 72–73; **16** 242; **18** 416; **19** 369; **21** 315; **27** 125; **29** 195; **32** 344. *See also* RJR Nabisco.
R.J. Reynolds Tobacco Holdings, Inc., 30 384–87 (upd.)
R.J. Tower Corporation. *See* Tower Automotive, Inc.
R.K. Brown, **14** 112
R.L. Crain Limited, **15** 473
R.L. Manning Company, **9** 363–64
R.L. Polk & Co., 10 460–62
R.N. Coate, **I** 216
R-O Realty, Inc., **43** 314
R.O. Hull Co., **I** 361
R.P.M., Inc., **25** 228
R.P. Scherer Corporation, I 678–80; **33** 145
R.R. Bowker Co., **17** 398; **23** 440
R.R. Donnelley & Sons Company, IV 660–62, 673; **9 430–32 (upd.)**; **11** 293; **12** 414, 557, 559; **18** 331; **19** 333; **38 368–71 (upd.)**
R.S.R. Corporation, **31** 48
R.S. Stokvis Company, **13** 499
R. Scott Associates, **11** 57
R. Stock AG, **IV** 198
R-T Investors LC, **42** 323–24
R.T. French USA, **II** 567
R.T. Securities, **II** 457
R.W. Beck, **29** 353
R.W. Harmon & Sons, Inc., **6** 410
R.W. Sears Watch Company, **V** 180
RABA PLC, **10** 274
Rabbit Software Corp., **10** 474
Rabobank Group, 26 419; **33 356–58**
Racal-Datacom Inc., 11 408–10
Racal Electronics PLC, II 83–84; **11** 408, 547; **42** 373, 376
Race Z, Inc. *See* Action Peformance Companies, Inc.
Rachel's Dairy Ltd., **37** 197–98
Racine Hardware Co., **III** 58
Racine Hidraulica, **21** 430
Racine Threshing Machine Works, **10** 377
Racing Champions. *See* Action Performance Companies, Inc.
Racing Champions Corporation, 37 318–20
Racing Collectables Club of America, Inc. *See* Action Performance Companies, Inc.
Rack Rite Distributors, **V** 174
Racket Store. *See* Duckwall-ALCO Stores, Inc.
Rada Corp., **IV** 250
Radian Group Inc., 42 299–301
Radiant Lamp Corp., **13** 398
Radiation Dynamics, **III** 634–35
Radiation, Inc., **II** 37–38
Radiation-Medical Products Corp., **I** 202
Radiator Specialty Co., **III** 570; **20** 362
Radio & Allied Industries, **II** 25
Radio & Television Equipment Company (Radio-Tel), **16** 200–01; **43** 168–69
Radio Austria A.G., **V** 314–16
Radio Cap Company. *See* Norwood Promotional Products, Inc.
Radio City Productions, **30** 102
Radio Corporation of America. *See* RCA Corporation.
Radio Flyer Inc., 34 368–70
Radio-Keith-Orpheum, **II** 32, 88, 135, 146–48, 175; **III** 428; **9** 247; **12** 73; **31** 99
Radio Receptor Company, Inc., **10** 319
Radio Shack, **II** 106–08; **12** 470; **13** 174
Radio Vertrieb Fürth. *See* Grundig AG.
Radiocel, **39** 194
Radiometer A/S, **17** 287
Radiometrics, Inc., **18** 369
RadioShack Canada Inc., **30** 391
RadioShack Corporation, 36 384–88 (upd.)
Radiotelevision Española, **7** 511
Radisson Hotels Worldwide, **22** 126–27
Radium Pharmacy, **I** 704
Radius Inc., 16 417–19
Radix Group, Inc., **13** 20
RadNet Managed Imaging Services, Inc., **25** 382–84
Radnor Venture Partners, LP, **10** 474
Raet, **39** 177
Raf, Haarla Oy, **IV** 349
Raffinerie Tirlemontoise S.A., **27** 436
Raffineriegesellschaft Vohburg/Ingolstadt mbH, **7** 141
RAG AG, 35 364–67
Rag Shops, Inc., 30 365–67
Ragan Outdoor, **27** 280
Ragazzi's, **10** 331
Ragnar Benson Inc., **8** 43–43
RAI, **I** 466
Rail Link, Inc., **27** 181
Railroad Enterprises, Inc., **27** 347
RailTex, Inc., 20 445–47
Railtrack, **39** 238
Railway Express Agency, **I** 456; **II** 382; **6** 388–89; **25** 146–48
Railway Maintenance Equipment Co., **14** 43
Railway Officials and Employees Accident Assoc., **III** 228
Railway Passengers Assurance Co., **III** 178, 410
Rainbow Crafts, **II** 502; **10** 323
Rainbow Home Shopping Ltd., **V** 160
Rainbow Production Corp., **I** 412
Rainbow Programming Holdings, **7** 63–64
Rainbow Resources, **IV** 576
RainbowBridge Communications, Inc., **25** 162
Raincoast Book Distribution, **34** 5
Rainer Pulp & Paper Company, **17** 439
Rainfair, Inc., **18** 298, 300
Rainforest Café, Inc., 25 386–88; **32** 241, 244
Rainier Brewing Company, 23 403–05
Rainier Pulp and Paper Company. *See* Rayonier Inc.
Rainy River Forest Products, Inc., **26** 445
Rajastan Breweries, Ltd., **18** 502
Raky-Danubia, **IV** 485
Ralcorp Holdings, Inc., **13** 293, 425, 427; **15** 189, 235; **21** 53, 56; **22** 337; **36** 238; **43** 438. *See also* Ralston Purina Company.
Raley's Inc., 14 396–98
Ralli International, **III** 502; **IV** 259
Rally's Hamburgers, Inc., 25 389–91
Rally's Inc., **14** 452; **15** 345; **16** 96–97; **23** 225
Rallye S.A., **12** 154. *See also* Casino.
Ralph & Kacoo's. *See* Piccadilly Cafeterias, Inc.
Ralph Lauren. *See* Polo/Ralph Lauren Corportion.
The Ralph M. Parsons Company. *See* The Parsons Corporation.
Ralph Wilson Plastics, **III** 610–11
Ralph's Industries, **31** 191
Ralphs Grocery Company, 35 368–70
Ralston Purina Company, I 608, **II** 544, 560, **561–63**, 617; **III** 588; **6** 50–52; **7** 209, 396, 547, 556; **8** 180; **9** 180; **12** 276, 411, 510; **13** 137, 270, 293, **425–27 (upd.)**; **14** 194–95, 558; **18** 312; **21** 56; **23** 191. *See also* Ralcorp Holdings, Inc.
Ram dis Ticaret, **I** 479
Ram Golf Corp., **III** 24; **32** 447
Ram's Insurance, **III** 370

Ramada International Hotels & Resorts, **II** 142; **III** 99; **IV** 718; **9** 426; **11** 177; **13** 66; **21** 366; **25** 309; **28** 258; **38** 320
Ramazotti, **I** 281
Rambol, **25** 84
Ramo-Woolridge Corp., **I** 539; **14** 510
Ramón Areces Foundation, **V** 52
Rampage Clothing Co., **35** 94
Ramsay Youth Services, Inc., **41 322–24**
Ranbar Packing, Inc. *See* Western Beef, Inc.
Ranchers Packing Corp. *See* Western Beef, Inc.
Rand American Investments Limited, **IV** 79; **21** 211
Rand Capital Corp., **35** 52–53
Rand Drill Co., **III** 525
Rand Group, Inc., **6** 247; **24** 234
Rand McNally & Company, **28 378–81**
Rand Mines Ltd., **I** 422; **IV** 22, 79, 94
Rand Selection Corp. Ltd., **IV** 79
Randall's Food Markets, Inc., **40 364–67**
Random House, Inc., **II** 90; **IV** 583–84, 637, 648; **13** 113, 115, 178, **428–30**; **14** 260; **18** 329; **19** 6, 285; **31 375–380 (upd.)**; **42** 287
Randon Meldkamer, **43** 307
Randstad Holding n.v., **16 420–22**; **43 307–10 (upd.)**
Randsworth Trust P.L.C., **IV** 703
Rank Organisation PLC, **II** 139, 147, **157–59**; **III** 171; **IV** 698; **6** 288; **12** 229; **14 399–402 (upd.)**; **24** 194; **26** 543, 546; **32** 241, 243–44; **34** 140; **40** 296, 298
Ranks Hovis McDougall Limited, **II** 157, **564–65**; **28 382–85 (upd.)**
Ransburg Corporation, **22** 282
Ransom and Randolph Company, **10** 271
Ransomes America Corp., **III** 600
Rapala-Normark Group, Ltd., **30 368–71**
Rapicom, **III** 159
Rapid American, **I** 440
Rapides Bank & Trust Company, **11** 107
Rapidforms, Inc., **35** 130–31
Rapifax of Canada, **III** 160
Rare Hospitality International Inc., **19 340–42**
RAS. *See* Riunione Adriatica di Sicurtà SpA.
Rascal House, **24** 243
Rassini Rheem, **III** 581
Rational GmbH, **22** 354
Rational Systems Inc., **6** 255; **25** 299
Ratti Vallensasca, **25** 312
Raufast et Fils, **35** 205
Rauland Corp., **II** 124; **13** 573
Rauma-Repola Oy, **II** 302; **IV** 316, 340, 349–50. *See also* Metso Corporation
Rauscher Pierce Refsnes, Inc., **15** 233
Raven Industries, Inc., **33 359–61**
Raven Press, **14** 555
Ravenhead, **16** 120
Ravenna Metal Products Corp., **12** 344
Ravenseft Properties Ltd., **IV** 696, 704–05
RAVIcad, **18** 20; **43** 17
Rawlings Sporting Goods Co., Inc., **7** 177; **23** 449; **24 402–04**
Rawlplug Co. Ltd., **IV** 382–83
Rawls Brothers Co., **13** 369
Rawson, Holdsworth & Co., **I** 464
Ray Industries, **22** 116
Ray Simon, **24** 94
Ray Strauss Unlimited, **22** 123
Ray's Printing of Topeka, **II** 624
Raychem Corporation, **III** 492; **8 446–47**
Raycom Sports, **6** 33
Raymar Book Corporation, **11** 194
Raymond International Inc., **28** 201
Raymond, Jones & Co., **IV** 647
Raymond, Trice & Company, **14** 40
Raynet Corporation, **8** 447
Rayonese Textile, Inc., **29** 140
Rayonier Inc., **24 405–07**
Rayovac Corporation, **13 431–34**; **17** 105; **23** 497; **24** 480; **39 336–40 (upd.)**
Raytheon Company, **I** 463, 485, 544; **II** 41, 73, **85–87**; **III** 643; **8** 51, 157; **11** 197, **411–14 (upd.)**; **12** 46, 247; **14** 223; **17** 419, 553, 564; **21** 200; **23** 181; **24** 88; **25** 223; **36** 190–91; **38 372–77 (upd.)**; **42** 373, 376
Razorback Acquisitions, **19** 455
Razorfish, Inc., **37 321–24**
RB&W Corp., **17** 372
RBC Dominion Securities, **25** 12
RCA Corporation, **I** 142, 454, 463; **II** 29–31, 34, 38, 56, 61, 85–86, **88–90**, 96, 102, 117–18, 120, 124, 129, 132–33, 151–52, 313, 609, 645; **III** 118, 122, 132, 149, 152, 165, 171, 569, 653–54; **IV** 252, 583, 594; **6** 164–66, 240, 266, 281, 288, 334; **7** 520; **8** 157; **9** 283; **10** 173; **11** 197, 318, 411; **12** 204, 208, 237, 454, 544, 548; **13** 106, 398, 429, 506, 573; **14** 357, 436; **16** 549; **17** 29; **20** 361; **21** 151; **22** 541; **23** 181; **26** 358, 511; **28** 349; **31** 376; **34** 186, 516; **38** 373
RCA Global Communications, Inc., **27** 304
RCG International, Inc., **III** 344
RCM Technologies, Inc., **34 371–74**
RCN Corp., **25** 107
RDO Equipment Company, **33 362–65**
REA. *See* Railway Express Agency.
Rea & Derick, **II** 605
Rea Construction Company, **17** 377
Rea Magnet Wire Co., **IV** 15
React-Rite, Inc., **8** 271
Read, R.L., **II** 417
Read-Rite Corp., **10** 403–04, **463–64**; **18** 250
The Reader's Digest Association, Inc., **IV 663–64**; **17 392–95 (upd.)**
Reader's Garden Inc., **22** 441
Reading and Bates, **III** 559
Reading Railroad, **9** 407
Ready Mixed Concrete, **III** 687, 737–40; **28** 82
Real Decisions, **21** 236
Real Estate Maintenance, **25** 15
Real Fresh, **25** 85
Real Goods Trading Company, **41** 177
Real-Share, Inc., **18** 542
RealCom Communications Corporation, **15** 196
Reale Mutuale, **III** 273
The Really Useful Group, **23** 390; **26 393–95**; **34** 422
Realty Development Co. *See* King Kullen Grocery Co., Inc.
Realty Investment Group, **25** 127
Realty Parking Properties II L.P., **18** 104
Réassurances, **III** 392
Recaro North America Inc., **26** 231
Reckitt & Colman plc, **II 566–67**; **15** 46, 360; **18** 556; **22** 148; **27** 69
Reckitt Benckiser plc, **42 302–06 (upd.)**
Reconstruction Bank of Holland, **IV** 707
Reconstruction Finance Bank, **II** 292
Reconstruction Finance Corp., **I** 67, 203; **II** 261; **IV** 10, 333
Record Bar / Licorice Pizza, **9** 361
Record Merchandisers. *See* Entertainment UK.
Record World Inc., **9** 361
Recoton Corp., **15 381–83**
Recoupe Recycling Technologies, **8** 104
Recovery Centers of America, **III** 88
Recovery Engineering, Inc., **25 392–94**
Recreational Equipment, Inc., **18 444–47**; **22** 173
Recticel S.A., **III** 581; **17** 182–84
Rectigraph Co., **III** 171
Recycled Paper Greetings, Inc., **21 426–28**
Red & White, **II** 682
The Red Adair Company, **37** 171
Red Ant Entertainment, **17** 14
Red Apple Group, Inc., **23 406–08**; **24** 528–29; **31** 231
Red Arrow, **II** 138
Red Ball, Inc., **18** 300
Red Brick Systems Inc., **30** 246
Red Bull, **31** 244
Red Carpet Food Systems, **39** 409
Red Food Stores, Inc., **19** 327–28
Red House Books Ltd., **29** 426
Red Kap, **V** 390–91
Red L Foods, **13** 244
Red Lion Entertainment, **29** 503
Red Lobster Inns of America, **16** 156–58
Red Lobster Restaurants, **II** 502–03; **6** 28; **10** 322–24; **19** 258
Red Oak Consulting, **42** 244
Red Owl Stores, Inc., **II** 670; **18** 506
Red Roof Inns, Inc., **13** 363; **18 448–49**; **21** 362
Red Rooster, **V** 35
Red Sea Insurance Co., **III** 251
Red Star Express, **14** 505
Red Star Milling Co., **II** 501; **6** 397; **10** 322
Red Storm, **41** 409
The Red Wing Co., Inc., **28** 382
Red Wing Shoe Company, Inc., **9 433–35**; **30 372–75 (upd.)**
Redactron, **III** 166; **6** 282
Redbook Florists Service, **28** 138
Redbook Publishing Co., **14** 460
Reddy Elevator Co., **III** 467
Reddy Ice, **II** 661
Redentza, **IV** 504
Redgate Communications, **26** 19
Redhill Tile Co., **III** 734
Redhook Ale Brewery, Inc., **31 381–84**
Redi, **IV** 610
Rediffusion, **II** 139; **24** 194
Reditab S.p.A., **12** 109
Redken Laboratories, **8** 131; **24** 251
Redland Plasterboard, **28** 83
Redland plc, **III** 495, 688, **734–36**; **14** 249, 739; **15** 154; **37** 205
Redlaw Industries Inc., **15** 247
Redman Industries, Inc., **17** 81, 83
Redmond & Co., **I** 376
La Redoute, S.A., **V** 11; **19** 306, 309
Redpath Industries, **II** 581–82
Redrow Group plc, **31 385–87**
Redwood Design Automation, **11** 47; **16** 520

Redwood Fire & Casualty Insurance Co., **III** 214
Reebok International Ltd., **V 375–77**; **8** 171, 303–04, 393; **9** 134–35, **436–38 (upd.)**; **11** 50–51, 349; **13** 513; **14** 8; **17** 244–45, 260; **18** 266; **19** 112; **22** 173; **25** 258, 352, 450; **26 396–400 (upd.)**; **36** 346
Reed & Ellis, **17** 439
Reed & Gamage, **13** 243
Reed Corrugated Containers, **IV** 249
Reed Elsevier plc, **19** 268; **23** 271, 273; **31 388–394 (upd.)**; **32** 354; **33** 263, 265–66, 458; **34** 438; **43** 92–93
Reed International PLC, **I** 423; **IV** 270, 642, **665–67**, 711; **7** 244–45, 343; **10** 407; **12** 359; **17 396–99 (upd.)**; **23** 350
Reed Tool Coompany, **III** 429; **22** 68
Reeder Light, Ice & Fuel Company, **6** 592
Reedpack, **IV** 339–40, 667; **28** 445
Reeds Jewelers, Inc., **22 447–49**
Reese Finer Foods, Inc., **7** 429
Reese Products, **III** 569; **11** 535; **20** 361
Reeves Banking and Trust Company, **11** 181
Reeves Brothers, **17** 182
Reeves Pulley Company, **9** 440
Refco, Inc., **10** 251; **22** 189
Reference Software International, **10** 558
Refined Sugars, **II** 582
Reflectone Inc., **24** 87
Reflex Winkelmann & Pannhoff GmbH, **18** 163
Reform Rt, **IV** 652; **7** 392
Refractarios Mexicanos, S.A. de C.V., **22** 285
Refrigeração Paraná S.A., **22** 27
Regal-Beloit Corporation, **18 450–53**
Regal Drugs, **V** 171
Regal Inns, **13** 364
Regal Manufacturing Co., **15** 385
Regency, **12** 316
Regency Electronics, **II** 101
Regency Health Services Inc., **25** 457
Regency International, **10** 196
Regenerative Environmental Equipment Company, Inc., **6** 441
Regeneron Pharmaceuticals Inc., **10** 80
Regent Canal Co., **III** 272
Regent Carolina Corporation, **37** 226
Regent Communications Inc., **23** 294
Regent Insurance Co., **III** 343
Regent International Hotels Limited, **9** 238; **29** 200
Régie Autonome des Pétroles, **IV** 544–46; **21** 202–04
Régie des Mines de la Sarre, **IV** 196
Régie des Télégraphes et Téléphones. *See* Belgacom.
Régie Nationale des Usines Renault, **I** 136, 145, 148, 178–79, 183, **189–91**, 207, 210; **II** 13; **III** 392, 523; **7** 566–67; **11** 104; **12** 91; **15** 514; **19** 50; **22** 331. *See also* Renault SA.
Regina Verwaltungsgesellschaft, **II** 257
Regional Bell Operating Companies, **15** 125; **18** 111–12, 373
Regis Corporation, **18 454–56**; **22** 157; **26** 475, 477
Register & Tribune Co. *See* Cowles Media Company.
Registered Vitamin Company, **V** 171
Regnecentralen AS, **III** 164
Rego Supermarkets and American Seaway Foods, Inc., **9** 451; **13** 237
Rehab Hospital Services Corp., **III** 88; **10** 252
RehabClinics Inc., **11** 367
REI. *See* Recreational Equipment, Inc.
Reich, Landman and Berry, **18** 263
Reichart Furniture Corp., **14** 236
Reichhold Chemicals, Inc., **I** 386, 524; **8** 554; **10 465–67**
Reichs-Kredit-Gesellschaft mbH, **IV** 230
Reichs-Kredit- und Krontrollstelle GmbH, **IV** 230
Reichswerke AG für Berg- und Hüttenbetriebe Hermann Göring, **IV** 200
Reichswerke AG für Erzbergbau und Eisenhütten, **IV** 200
Reichswerke Hermann Göring, **IV** 233
Reid Bros. & Carr Proprietary, **III** 672–73
Reid Dominion Packaging Ltd., **IV** 645
Reid Ice Cream Corp., **II** 471
Reid, Murdoch and Co., **II** 571
Reid Press Ltd., **IV** 645
Reidman Corporation, **41** 65
Reidsville Fashions, Inc., **13** 532
Reigel Products Corp., **IV** 289
Reimersholms, **31** 458–60
Reims Aviation, **8** 92; **27** 100
Rein Elektronik, **10** 459
Reinsurance Agency, **III** 204–05
Reisebüro Bangemann, **II** 164
Reisholz AG, **III** 693
Reisland GmbH, **15** 340
Reiue Nationale des Usines Renault, **7** 220
Rekkof Restart NV, **28** 327
Relational Courseware, Inc., **21** 235–36
Relational Database Systems Inc., **10** 361–62
Relational Technology Inc., **10** 361
Relationship Marketing Group, Inc., **37** 409
Release Technologies, **8** 484
Reliable Stores Inc., **14** 236
Reliable Tool, **II** 488
Reliance Electric Company, **IV** 429; **9 439–42**
Reliance Group Holdings, Inc., **II** 173; **III 342–44**; **IV** 642
Reliance Life Insurance Co., **III** 275–76
Reliance National Indemnity Company, **18** 159
Reliance Steel & Aluminum Co., **19 343–45**
ReLife Inc., **14** 233; **33** 185
Relocation Central. *See* CORT Business Services Corporation.
Rembrandt Group, **I** 289; **IV** 91, 93, 97; **V** 411–13; **19** 367–69; **24** 449
RemedyTemp, Inc., **20 448–50**
Remgro, **IV** 97
Remington Arms Company, Inc., **I** 329; **8** 152; **12 415–17**; **26** 125; **40 368–71 (upd.)**
Remington Products Company, L.L.C., **42 307–10**
Remington Rand, **III** 122, 126, 148, 151, 165–66, 642; **6** 251, 265, 281–82; **10** 255; **12** 416; **19** 430; **30** 337
Remmele Engineering, Inc., **17** 534
Rémy Cointreau S.A., **20 451–53**
REN Corp. USA, Inc., **13** 161
Renaissance Communications Corp., **22** 522
Renaissance Connects, **16** 394
Renaissance Cosmetics Inc. *See* New Dana Perfumes Co.
Renaissance Hotel Group N.V., **38** 321
Renaissance Learning Systems, Inc., **39 341–43**
Renal Systems, Inc. *See* Minntech Corporation.
Renault. *See* Régie Nationale des Usines Renault.
Renault S.A., **26** 11, **401–04 (upd.)**; **34** 303, 306
Rendeck International, **11** 66
Rendic International, **13** 228
René Garraud, **III** 68
Renfro Corp., **25** 167
Rengo Co., Ltd., **IV 326**
RENK AG, **37 325–28**
Rennies Consolidated Holdings, **I** 470; **20** 312
Reno Air Inc., **23 409–11**; **24** 400; **28** 25
Reno de Medici S.p.A., **41 325–27**
Réno-Dépôt Inc., **26** 306
Reno Technologies, **12** 124
Rent-A-Center, **22** 194; **24** 485; **33** 366, 368
Rent-Way, Inc., **33 366–68**
Rental Service Corporation, **28 386–88**
Rentokil Initial plc, **34** 43
Rentrak Corporation, **35 371–74**
Rentz, **23** 219
Reo Products. *See* Lifetime Hoan Corporation.
Repco Ltd., **15** 246
REPESA, **IV** 528
Replacement Enterprises Inc., **16** 380
Repligen Inc., **13** 241
Repola Ltd., **19** 465; **30** 325
Repola Oy, **IV** 316, 347, 350
Repsol S.A., **IV** 396–97, 506, 514, **527–29**; **16 423–26 (upd.)**
Repsol-YPF S.A., **40 372–76 (upd.)**
Repubblica, **IV** 587
Republic Aircraft Co., **I** 89
Republic Airlines, **I** 113, 132; **6** 104; **25** 421; **28** 265
Republic Aviation Corporation, **I** 55; **9** 205–07
Republic Broadcasting Corp., **23** 292
Republic Corp., **I** 447
Republic Engineered Steels, Inc., **7 446–47 26 405–08 (upd.)**
Republic Freight Systems, **14** 567
Republic Indemnity Co. of America, **III** 191
Republic Industries, Inc., **24** 12; **26 409–11**, 501
Republic Insurance, **III** 404
Republic National Bank, **19** 466
Republic New York Corporation, **11 415–19**
Republic Pictures, **9** 75
Republic Powdered Metals, Inc., **8** 454
Republic Realty Mortgage Corp., **II** 289
Republic Rubber, **III** 641
Republic Steel Corp., **I** 491; **IV** 114; **7** 446; **12** 353; **13** 169, 157; **14** 155; **24** 304. *See also* Republic Engineered Steels, Inc.
Republic Supply Co. of California, **I** 570
Res-Care, Inc., **29 399–402**
Research Analysis Corporation, **7** 15
Research Cottrell, Inc., **6** 441
Research Polymers International, **I** 321; **12** 103

Research Publications, **8** 526
Resem SpA, **I** 387
Reserve Mining Co., **17** 356
Reservoir Productions, **17** 150
Residence Inns, **III** 103; **9** 426
Residential Funding Corporation, **10** 92–93
Resin Exchange, **19** 414
Resinous Products, **I** 392
ResNet Communications Inc., **28** 241
Resolution Systems, Inc., **13** 201
Resolution Trust Corp., **10** 117, 134; **11** 371; **12** 368
Resorts International, Inc., **I** 452; **12** **418–20**; **19** 402; **26** 462
Resource America, Inc., **42** **311–14**
Resource Associates of Alaska, Inc., **7** 376
The Resource Club, **32** 80
Resource Electronics, **8** 385
Resource Group International, **25** 207
ReSource NE, Inc., **17** 553
reSOURCE PARTNER, INC., **22** 95
Response Oncology, Inc., **27** **385–87**
Rest Assured, **I** 429
The Restaurant Company, **22** 417
Restaurant Enterprises Group Inc., **14** 195
Restaurant Franchise Industries, **6** 200
Restaurant Property Master, **19** 468
Restaurants Les Pres Limitée, **II** 652
Restaurants Universal Espana S.A., **26** 374
Restaurants Unlimited, Inc., **13** **435–37**; **23** 127–29
Restoration Hardware, Inc., **30** **376–78**
Resurgens Communications Group, **7** 336; **8** 311; **27** 306
Retail Credit Company. *See* Equifax.
Retail Systems Consulting, Inc., **24** 395
Retail Ventures Inc., **14** 427; **24** 26
Retailers Commercial Agency, Inc., **6** 24
Retequattro, **19** 19
Retirement Care Associates Inc., **25** 457
Retirement Inns of America, Inc., **III** 16; **11** 282
Reuben H. Donnelley Corp., **IV** 605, 661; **19** 133
Reunion Properties, **I** 470; **20** 311–12
Reuters Holdings PLC, **IV** 259, 652, 654, 656, **668–70**; **10** 277, 407; **21** 68–70; **22** **450–53 (upd.)**; **34** 11, 227
Revco D.S., Inc., **II** 449; **III** 10; **V** **171–73**; **9** 67, 187; **12** 4; **13** 449; **16** 560; **19** 357; **32** 169–70
Revell-Monogram Inc., **16** **427–29**; **25** 71; **27** 14
Revere Copper and Brass Co., **IV** 32. *See also* The Paul Revere Corporation.
Revere Foil Containers, Inc., **12** 377
Revere Furniture and Equipment Company, **14** 105; **25** 307
Revere Ware Corporation, **22** **454–56**
Revlon Inc., **I** 29, 449, 620, 633, 668, 677, 693, 696; **II** 498, 679; **III** 29, 46, **54–57**, 727; **6** 27; **8** 131, 341; **9** 202–03, 291; **11** 8, 333–34; **12** 314; **16** 439; **17** 110, **400–04 (upd.)**; **18** 229; **22** 157; **25** 55; **26** 384; **28** 246–47; **30** 188–89
Revson Bros., **III** 54
Rewe Group, **37** 241
Rewe-Liebbrand, **28** 152
Rex Pulp Products Company, **9** 304
REX Stores Corp., **10** **468–69**; **19** 362
Rexall Drug & Chemical Co., **II** 533–34; **III** 610; **13** 525; **14** 547
Rexall Sundown, Inc., **37** 340, 342
Rexam PLC, **32** **380–85 (upd.)**
Rexel, Inc., **15** **384–87**
Rexene Products Co., **III** 760; **IV** 457
Rexham Inc., **IV** 259; **8** 483–84
Rexnord Corporation, **I** 524; **14** 43; **21** **429–32**; **37** 30
Reydel Industries, **23** 95–96
Reyes Holdings, Inc., **24** 388
Reymer & Bros., Inc., **II** 508; **11** 172
Reymersholm, **II** 366
Reynolds and Reynolds Company, **17** 142, 144
Reynolds Electric Co., **22** 353
Reynolds Metals Company, **II** 421–22; **IV** 11–12, 15, 59, **186–88**; **IV** 122; **12** 278; **19** **346–48 (upd.)**; **21** 218; **22** 455; **25** 22
RF Communications, **II** 38
RF Micro Devices, Inc., **43** **311–13**
RF Monolithics Inc., **13** 193
RHC Holding Corp., **10** 13; **13** 364; **27** 11
RHD Holdings, **23** 413
Rhee Syngman, **I** 516; **12** 293
Rheem Manufacturing, **25** 368
Rhein-Elbe Gelsenkirchener Bergwerks A.G., **IV** 25
Rheinelbe Union, **I** 542
Rheinisch Kalksteinwerke Wulfrath, **III** 738
Rheinisch Oelfinwerke, **I** 306
Rheinisch-Westfalische Bank A.G., **II** 279
Rheinisch-Westfälischer Sprengstoff AG, **III** 694
Rheinisch-Westfälisches Elektrizatätswerke AG, **I** 542–43; **III** 154; **IV** 231; **V** 744; **25** 102
Rheinische Aktiengesellschaft für Braunkohlenbergbau, **V** 708
Rheinische Creditbank, **II** 278
Rheinische Metallwaaren- und Maschinenfabrik AG, **9** 443–44
Rheinische Wasserglasfabrik, **III** 31
Rheinische Zuckerwarenfabrik GmbH, **27** 460
Rheinmetall Berlin AG, **9** **443–46**
Rheinsche Girozentrale und Provinzialbank, Düsseldorf, **II** 385
Rheinstahl AG, **IV** 222
Rheinstahl Union Brueckenbau, **8** 242
Rheintalische Zementfabrik, **III** 701
Rhenus-Weichelt AG, **6** 424, 426
RHI Entertainment Inc., **16** 257
Rhino Entertainment Company, **18** **457–60**; **21** 326
RHM. *See* Ranks Hovis McDougall.
Rhodes & Co., **8** 345
Rhodes Inc., **23** **412–14**
Rhodesian Anglo American Ltd., **IV** 21, 23; **16** 26
Rhodesian Development Corp., **I** 422
Rhodesian Selection Trust, Ltd., **IV** 17–18, 21
Rhodesian Sugar Refineries, **II** 581
Rhodia SA, **38** **378–80**
Rhodiaceta, **I** 388–89
Rhokana Corp., **IV** 191
Rhône Moulage Industrie, **39** 152, 154
Rhône-Poulenc S.A., **I** 303–04, 371, **388–90**, 670, 672, 692; **III** 677; **IV** 174, 487, 547; **8** 153, 452; **9** 358; **10** **470–72 (upd.)**; **16** 121, 438; **21** 466; **23** 194, 197; **34** 284; **38** 379
Rhymey Breweries, **I** 294
Rhymney Iron Company, **31** 369
Rhythm Watch Co., Ltd., **III** 454; **21** 121
La Riassicuratrice, **III** 346
Rica Foods, Inc., **41** **328–30**
Ricard, **I** 280
Riccar, **17** 124; **41** 114
Riccardo's Restaurant, **18** 538
Rice Broadcasting Co., Inc., **II** 166
Rice-Stix Dry Goods, **II** 414
Riceland Foods, Inc., **27** 390
Rich Products Corporation, **7** **448–49**; **38** **381–84 (upd.)**
Rich's Inc., **9** 209; **10** 515; **31** 191
Richard A. Shaw, Inc., **7** 128
Richard D. Irwin Inc., **IV** 602–03, 678
Richard Hellman Co., **II** 497
Richard Manufacturing Co., **I** 667
Richard P. Simmons, **8** 19
Richard Shops, **III** 502
Richard Thomas & Baldwins, **IV** 42
Richards & O'Neil LLP, **43** 70
Richards Bay Minerals, **IV** 91
Richardson Company, **36** 147
Richardson Electronics, Ltd., **17** **405–07**
Richardson-Vicks Company, **III** 53; **8** 434; **26** 383
Richardson's, **21** 246
Richfield Oil Corp., **IV** 375–76, 456
Richfood Holdings, Inc., **7** **450–51**
Richland Co-op Creamery Company, **7** 592
Richland Gas Company, **8** 349
Richmon Hill & Queens County Gas Light Companies, **6** 455
Richmond American Homes of Florida, Inc., **11** 258
Richmond Carousel Corporation, **9** 120
Richmond Cedar Works Manufacturing Co., **12** 109; **19** 360
Richmond Corp., **I** 600; **15** 129
Richmond Paperboard Corp., **19** 78
Richmond Pulp and Paper Company, **17** 281
Richton International Corporation, **39** **344–46**
Richway, **10** 515
Richwood Building Products, Inc., **12** 397
Richwood Sewell Coal Co., **17** 357
Ricils, **III** 47
Rickards, Roloson & Company, **22** 427
Rickel Home Centers, **II** 673
Ricky Shaw's Oriental Express, **25** 181
Ricoh Company, Ltd., **III** 121, 157, **159–61**, 172, 454; **6** 289; **8** 278; **18** 386, 527; **19** 317; **21** 122; **24** 429; **36** **389–93 (upd.)**
Ricolino, **19** 192
Riddell Inc., **33** 467
Riddell Sports Inc., **22** **457–59**; **23** 449
Ridder Publications, **IV** 612–13, 629; **7** 191
Ride, Inc., **22** **460–63**
Ridge Tool Co., **II** 19
Ridgewell's Inc., **15** 87
Ridgewood Properties Inc., **12** 394
Ridgway Co., **23** 98
Ridgway Color, **13** 227–28
Rieck-McJunkin Dairy Co., **II** 533
Riedel-de Haën AG, **22** 32; **36** 431
Riegel Bag & Paper Co., **IV** 344
Rieke Corp., **III** 569; **11** 535; **20** 361
The Riese Organization, **38** **385–88**
Rieter Holding AG, **42** **315–17**
Rieter Machine Works, **III** 638
Rig Tenders Company, **6** 383
Riggin & Robbins, **13** 244

Riggs National Corporation, **13 438–40**
Right Associates, **27** 21
Right Management Consultants, Inc., **42 318–21**
Right Source, Inc., **24** 96
RightSide Up, Inc., **27** 21
Rijnhaave Information Systems, **25** 21
Rike's, **10** 282
Riken Corp., **IV** 160; **10** 493
Riken Kankoshi Co. Ltd., **III** 159
Riken Optical Co., **III** 159
Riklis Family Corp., **9 447–50**; **12** 87; **13** 453; **38** 169; **43** 355
Riku-un Moto Kaisha, **V** 477
La Rinascente, **12** 153
Ring King Visibles, Inc., **13** 269
Ring Ltd., **43** 99
Ringier America, **19** 333
Ringköpkedjan, **II** 640
Ringling Bros., Barnum & Bailey Circus, **25** 312–13
Ringnes Bryggeri, **18** 396
Rini-Rego Supermarkets Inc., **13** 238
Rini Supermarkets, **9** 451; **13** 237
Rinker Materials Corp., **III** 688
Rio Grande Industries, Inc., **12** 18–19
Rio Grande Oil Co., **IV** 375, 456
Rio Grande Servaas, S.A. de C.V., **23** 145
Rio Grande Valley Gas Co., **IV** 394
Rio Sportswear Inc., **42** 269
Rio Sul Airlines, **6** 133
Rio Tinto plc, **19 349–53 (upd.)**; **27** 253; **42** 395
Rio Tinto-Zinc Corp., **II** 628; **IV** 56, 58–61, 189–91, 380; **21** 352
Rioblanco, **II** 477
Riordan Freeman & Spogli, **13** 406
Riordan Holdings Ltd., **I** 457; **10** 554
Riser Foods, Inc., **9 451–54**; **13** 237–38
Rising Sun Petroleum Co., **IV** 431, 460, 542
Risk Management Partners Ltd., **35** 36
Risk Planners, **II** 669
Rit Dye Co., **II** 497
Ritchie Bros. Auctioneers Inc., **41 331–34**
Rite Aid Corporation, **V 174–76**; **9** 187, 346; **12** 221, 333; **16** 389; **18** 199, 286; **19 354–57 (upd.)**; **23** 407; **29** 213; **31** 232; **32** 166, 169–70
Rite-Way Department Store, **II** 649
Riteway Distributor, **26** 183
Rittenhouse and Embree, **III** 269
Rittenhouse Financial Services, **22** 495
Ritter Co. *See* Sybron Corp.
Ritz Camera Centers, **18** 186; **34 375–77**
Ritz-Carlton Hotel Company L.L.C., **9 455–57**; **21** 366; **29 403–06 (upd.)**
Ritz Firma, **13** 512
Riunione Adriatica di Sicurtà SpA, **III** 185, 206, **345–48**
The Rival Company, **17** 215; **19 358–60**
Rivarossi, **16** 337
Rivaud Group, **29** 370
River Boat Casino, **9** 425–26
River City Broadcasting, **25** 418
River North Studios. *See* Platinum Entertainment, Inc.
River Oaks Furniture, Inc., **43 314–16**
River-Raisin Paper Co., **IV** 345
River Ranch Fresh Foods—Salinas, Inc., **41** 11
River Steam Navigation Co., **III** 522
River Thames Insurance Co., Ltd., **26** 487
Riverdeep Group plc, **41** 137
Riverside Chemical Company, **13** 502
Riverside Furniture, **19** 455
Riverside Insurance Co. of America, **26** 487
Riverside Iron Works, Ltd., **8** 544
Riverside National Bank of Buffalo, **11** 108
Riverside Press, **10** 355–56
Riverside Publishing Company, **36** 272
Riverwood International Corporation, **7** 294; **11 420–23**
Riviana Foods, **III** 24, 25; **27 388–91**
Riyadh Armed Forces Hospital, **16** 94
Rizzoli Publishing, **IV** 586, 588; **19** 19; **23** 88
RJMJ, Inc., **16** 37
RJR Nabisco Holdings Corp., **I** 249, 259, 261; **II** 370, 426, 477–78, 542–44; **V 408–10, 415**; **7** 130, 132, 277, 596; **9** 469; **12** 82, 559; **13** 342; **14** 214, 274; **17** 471; **22** 73, 95, 441; **23** 163; **24** 273; **30** 384; **32** 234; **33** 228; **36** 151, 153. *See also* R.J Reynolds Tobacco Holdings Inc., Nabisco Brands, Inc. *and* R.J. Reynolds Industries, Inc.
RKO. *See* Radio-Keith-Orpheum.
RKO-General, Inc., **8** 207
RKO Radio Sales, **6** 33
RLA Polymers, **9** 92
RM Marketing, **6** 14
RMC Group p.l.c., **III** 734, **737–40**; **34 378–83 (upd.)**
RMF Inc., **I** 412
RMH Teleservices, Inc., **42 322–24**
RMP International, Limited, **8** 417
Roadhouse Grill, Inc., **22 464–66**
Roadline, **6** 413–14
Roadmaster Industries, Inc., **16 430–33**; **22** 116
Roadmaster Transport Company, **18** 27; **41** 18
RoadOne. *See* Miller Industries, Inc.
Roadway Express, Inc., **25 395–98 (upd.)**
Roadway Services, Inc., **V 502–03**; **12** 278, 309; **14** 567; **15** 111
Roaman's, **V** 115
Roan Selection Trust Ltd., **IV** 18, 239–40
Roanoke Capital Ltd., **27** 113–14
Roanoke Fashions Group, **13** 532
Robb Engineering Works, **8** 544
Robbins & Myers Inc., **13** 273; **15 388–90**
Robbins Co., **III** 546
Robeco Group, **IV** 193; **26** 419–20
Roberds Inc., **19 361–63**
Roberk Co., **III** 603
Robert Allen Companies, **III** 571; **20** 362
Robert Benson, Lonsdale & Co. Ltd., **II** 232, 421–22; **IV** 191
Robert Bosch GmbH, **I 392–93**, 411; **III** 554, 555, 591, 593; **13** 398; **16 434–37 (upd.)**; **22** 31; **43 317–21 (upd.)**
Robert E. McKee Corporation, **6** 150
Robert Fleming Holdings Ltd., **I** 471; **IV** 79; **11** 495
Robert Gair Co., **15** 128
Robert Garrett & Sons, Inc., **9** 363
Robert Grace Contracting Co., **I** 584
Robert Half International Inc., **18 461–63**
Robert Hall Clothes, Inc., **13** 535
Robert Johnson, **8** 281–82
Robert McLane Company. *See* McLane Company, Inc.
Robert McNish & Company Limited, **14** 141
Robert Mondavi Corporation, **15 391–94**; **39** 45
Robert R. Mullen & Co., **I** 20
Robert Skeels & Company, **33** 467
Robert Stigwood Organization Ltd., **23** 390
Robert W. Baird & Co., **III** 324; **7** 495
Robert Warschauer and Co., **II** 270
Robert Watson & Co. Ltd., **I** 568
Robert Wood Johnson Foundation, **35 375–78**
Robertet SA, **39 347–49**
Roberts Express, **V** 503
Roberts, Johnson & Rand Shoe Co., **III** 528–29
Roberts Pharmaceutical Corporation, **16 438–40**
Robertson Building Products, **8** 546
Robertson-Ceco Corporation, **8** 546; **19 364–66**
Robertson, Stephens & Co., **22** 465
Robin Hood Flour Mills, Ltd., **7** 241–43; **25** 241
Robin International Inc., **24** 14
Robinair, **10** 492, 494
Robinson & Clark Hardware. *See* Clarcor Inc.
Robinson Clubs, **II** 163–64
Robinson-Danforth Commission Co., **II** 561
Robinson-Humphrey, **II** 398; **10** 62
Robinson Industries, **24** 425
Robinson Radio Rentals, **I** 531
Robinson Smith & Robert Haas, Inc., **13** 428
Robinson's Japan Co. Ltd., **V** 89; **42** 191
Robinsons Soft Drinks Limited, **38** 77
Robot Manufacturing Co., **16** 8
Robotic Vision Systems, Inc., **16** 68
ROC Communities, Inc., **I** 272; **22** 341
Roccade, **39** 177
Roch, S.A., **23** 83
Roche Biomedical Laboratories, Inc., **8** 209–10; **11 424–26**. *See also* Laboratory Corporation of America Holdings.
Roche Bioscience, **14 403–06 (upd.)**
Roche Holding AG, **30** 164; **32** 211, 213–14; **37** 113
Roche Products Ltd., **I** 643
Rochester American Insurance Co., **III** 191
Rochester Gas And Electric Corporation, **6 571–73**
Rochester German Insurance Co., **III** 191
Rochester Instrument Systems, Inc., **16** 357
Rochester Telephone Corporation, **6 332–34**; **12** 136; **16** 221
Röchling Industrie Verwaltung GmbH, **9** 443
Rock Bottom Restaurants, Inc., **25 399–401**
Rock Island Oil & Refining Co., **IV** 448–49
Rock Island Plow Company, **10** 378
Rock of Ages Corporation, **37 329–32**
Rock Systems Inc., **18** 337
Rock-Tenn Company, **IV** 312; **13 441–43**; **19** 268
Rockcor Inc., **I** 381; **13** 380
Rockcote Paint Company, **8** 552–53
Rockefeller & Andrews, **IV** 426; **7** 169
The Rockefeller Foundation, **34 384–87**

Rockefeller Group, **IV** 714
Rocket Chemical Company. *See* WD-40 Company.
Rockford Corporation, 43 322–25
Rockford Drilling Co., **III** 439
Rocking Horse Child Care Centers of America Inc. *See* Nobel Learning Communities, Inc.
Rockland Corp., **8** 271
Rockland React-Rite, Inc., **8** 270
Rockmoor Grocery, **II** 683
Rockower of Canada Ltd., **II** 649
Rockport Company, **V** 376–77; **26** 397
Rockresorts, Inc., **22** 166
RockShox, Inc., 26 412–14
Rockwell Automation, 43 326–31 (upd.)
Rockwell International Corporation, I 71, **78–80**, 154–55, 186; **II** 3, 94, 379; **6** 263; **7** 420; **8** 165; **9** 10; **10** 279–80; **11** 268, 278, **427–30 (upd.)**, 473; **12** 135, 248, 506; **13** 228; **18** 369, 571; **22** 51, 53, 63–64; **32** 81, 84–85; **33** 27; **35** 91; **36** 121–22; **39** 30
Rocky Mountain Bankcard, **24** 393
Rocky Mountain Financial Corporation, **13** 348
Rocky Mountain Pipe Line Co., **IV** 400
Rocky River Power Co. *See* Connecticut Light and Power Co.
Rocky Shoes & Boots, Inc., 26 415–18
Rod's Food Products, **36** 163
Rodale Press, Inc., 22 443; **23 415–17**
Rodamco N.V., IV 698; **26 419–21**
Rodel, Inc., **26** 425
Röder & Co., **34** 38, 40
Rodeway Inns of America, **II** 142; **III** 94; **11** 242; **25** 309
Rodgers Instrument Corporation, **38** 391
Rodney Square Management Corp., **25** 542
Rodven Records, **23** 391
Roederstein GmbH, **21** 520
Roegelein Co., **13** 271
Roehr Products Co., **III** 443
Roermond, **IV** 276
Roessler & Hasslacher Chemical Co., **IV** 69
Roger Cleveland Golf Company, **15** 462; **43** 375–76
Roger Williams Foods, **II** 682
Rogers & Oling, Inc., **17** 533
Rogers Bros., **I** 672
Rogers CanGuard, Inc., **32** 374
Rogers Communications Inc., 30 388–92 (upd.). *See also* Maclean Hunter Publishing Limited.
Rohde & Schwarz GmbH & Co. KG, 39 350–53
Rohe Scientific Corp., **13** 398
Röhm and Haas Company, I 391–93; **14** 182–83; **26 422–26 (upd.)**
ROHN Industries, Inc., 22 467–69
Rohölgewinnungs AG, **IV** 485
Rohr Gruppe, **20** 100
Rohr Incorporated, I 62; **9 458–60**; **11** 165
Roja, **III** 47
The Rokke Group, **16** 546; **32** 100
Rokuosha, **III** 547
Rol Oil, **IV** 451
Rola Group, **II** 81
Roland Berger & Partner GmbH, 37 333–36
Roland Corporation, 38 389–91
Roland Murten A.G., 7 452–53
Roland NV, **41** 340
Rolex. *See* Montres Rolex S.A.
Roll International Corporation, 37 337–39
Rollalong, **III** 502; **7** 208
Rollerblade, Inc., 15 395–98; **22** 202–03; **34 388–92 (upd.)**
Rolling Stones Records, **23** 33
Rollins Burdick Hunter Co., **III** 204
Rollins Communications, **II** 161
Rollins, Inc., 11 431–34
Rollins Specialty Group, **III** 204
Rollo's, **16** 95
Rolls-Royce Allison, 29 407–09 (upd.)
Rolls-Royce Motors Ltd., I 25–26, 81–82, 166, **194–96**; **III** 652; **9** 16–18, 417–18; **11** 138, 403; **21** 435
Rolls-Royce plc, I 41, 55, 65, **81–83**, 481; **III** 507, 556; **7 454–57 (upd.)**; **9** 244; **11** 268; **12** 190; **13** 414; **21 433–37 (upd.)**; **24** 85; **27** 495–96
Rolm Corp., **II** 99; **III** 149; **18** 344; **22** 51; **34** 512
Rolodex Electronics, **23** 209, 212
Rolscreen. *See* Pella Corporation.
Rombas, **IV** 226
Rome Cable and Wire Co., **IV** 15
Rome Network, Inc., **24** 95
Romper Room Enterprises, Inc., **16** 267
Rompetrol, **IV** 454
Ron Nagle, **I** 247
Ronco, Inc., 15 399–401; **21** 327
Rondel's, Inc., **8** 135
Ronel, **13** 274
Roni-Linda Productions, Inc., **27** 347
Ronnebyredds Trävaru, **25** 463
Ronningen-Petter, **III** 468
Ronzoni Foods Corp., **15** 221
Roombar S.A., **28** 241
Rooms To Go Inc., 28 389–92
Rooney Brothers Co., 25 402–04
Roots Canada Ltd., 27 194; **42 325–27**
Roots-Connersville Blower Corp., **III** 472
Roper Industries Inc., III 655; **12** 550; **15 402–04**; **25** 89
Ropert Group, **18** 67
Ropes & Gray, 40 377–80
RoProperty Services BV. *See* Rodamco N.V.
Rorer Group, I 666–68; **12** 4; **16** 438; **24** 257
Rosaen Co., **23** 82
Rosarita Food Company, **25** 278
Rose & Co., **26** 65
Rose Exterminator Company, **25** 15
Rose Foundation, **9** 348
Rose's Stores, Inc., 13 261, **444–46**; **23** 215
Rosebud Dolls Ltd., **25** 312
Rosefield Packing Co., **II** 497
Rosehaugh, **24** 269
RoseJohnson Incorporated, **14** 303
Rosemount Inc., II 20; **13** 226; **15 405–08**
Rosen Enterprises, Ltd., **10** 482
Rosenblads Patenter, **III** 419
Rosenbluth International Inc., 14 407–09
Rosenfeld Hat Company. *See* Columbia Hat Company.
Rosenmund-Guèdu, **31** 158
Rosenthal A.G., **I** 347; **18** 236; **34** 493, 496
Rosevear, **III** 690
Rosewood Financial, Inc., **24** 383
Roshco, Inc., **27** 288
Ross Carrier Company, **8** 115
Ross Clouston, **13** 244
Ross Gear & Tool Co., **I** 539; **14** 510
Ross Hall Corp., **I** 417
Ross Stores, Inc., 17 408–10; **43 332–35 (upd.)**
Rossendale Combining Company, **9** 92
Rossignol Ski Company, Inc. *See* Skis Rossignol S.A.
Rössing Uranium Ltd., **IV** 191
Rossville Union Distillery, **I** 285
Rostocker Brauerei VEB, **9** 87
Roswell Public Service Company, **6** 579
Rota Bolt Ltd., **III** 581
Rotadisk, **16** 7
Rotan Mosle Financial Corporation, **II** 445; **22** 406
Rotary International, 31 395–97
Rotary Lift, **III** 467–68
Rotax, **III** 555–56. *See also* Orbital Engine Corporation Ltd.
Rote. *See* Avery Dennison Corporation.
Rotelcom Data Inc., **6** 334; **16** 222
Rotex, **IV** 253
Roth Co., **16** 493
Roth Freres SA, **26** 231
Rothmans International BV, **33** 82
Rothmans International p.l.c., I 438; **IV** 93; **V 411–13**; **27** 488
Rothmans UK Holdings Limited, 19 367–70 (upd.)
Rothschild Financial Corporation, **13** 347
Rothschild Group, **6** 206
Rothschild Investment Trust, **I** 248; **III** 699
Roto-Rooter Corp., 13 149–50; **15 409–11**; **16** 387
Rotodiesel, **III** 556
Rotor Tool Co., **II** 16
Rotterdam Bank, **II** 183–85
Rotterdam Beleggings (Investment) Consortium. *See* Robeco.
Rotterdam Lloyd, **6** 403–04; **26** 241–42
The Rottlund Company, Inc., 28 393–95
Rouge et Or, **IV** 614
Rouge Steel Company, 8 448–50
Roughdales Brickworks, **14** 249
Rougier. *See* Groupe Rougier, SA.
Round Hill Foods, **21** 535
Round Table, **16** 447
Roundup Wholesale Grocery Company, **V** 55
Roundy's Inc., 14 410–12
The Rouse Company, II 445; **15 412–15**; **22** 406
Roussel Uclaf, I 669–70; **8 451–53 (upd.)**; **18** 236; **19** 51; **25** 285; **38** 379
Rousselot, **I** 677
Routh Robbins Companies, **21** 96
Roux Séguéla Cayzac & Goudard. *See* Euro RSCG Worldwide S.A.
Rover Group Ltd., I 186; **7 458–60**; **11** 31, 33; **14** 36; **21 441–44 (upd.)**; **24** 87–88; **38** 83, 85–86
Rowan Companies, Inc., 43 336–39
Rowe & Pitman, **14** 419
Rowe Bros. & Co., **III** 680
Rowe Price-Fleming International, Inc., **11** 495
Rowell Welding Works, **26** 433
Rowenta. *See* Groupe SEB.
Rowland Communications Worldwide, **42** 328, 331
Rowntree and Co., **27** 104

Rowntree Mackintosh PLC, **II** 476, 511, 521, 548, **568–70**; **7** 383; **28** 311
Roxana Petroleum Co., **IV** 531, 540
Roxell, N.V., **43** 129
Roxoil Drilling, **7** 344
Roy and Charles Moore Crane Company, **18** 319
Roy F. Weston, Inc., **33 369–72**
Roy Farrell Import-Export Company, **6** 78
Roy Rogers, **III** 102
Royal Ahold. *See* Koninklijke Ahold N.V.
Royal Aluminium Ltd., **IV** 9
Royal Appliance Manufacturing Company, **15 416–18**; **17** 233
Royal Baking Powder Co., **II** 544; **14** 17
Royal Bank of Australia, **II** 188
The Royal Bank of Canada, **II 344–46**; **21 445–48 (upd.)**
Royal Bank of Ireland Ltd., **16** 13
Royal Bank of Queensland, **II** 188
The Royal Bank of Scotland Group plc, **II** 298, 358; **10** 336–37; **12 421–23**; **38** 13, **392–99 (upd.)**; **42** 76
Royal Bankgroup of Acadiana, Inc., **37** 201
Royal Brewing Co., **I** 269; **12** 337
Royal Business Machines, **I** 207, 485; **III** 549
Royal Canada, **III** 349
Royal Canin S.A., **39 354–57**
Royal Caribbean Cruises Ltd., **6** 368; **22** 444–46; **470–73**; **27** 29, 91
Royal Copenhagen A/S, **9** 99
Royal Crown Company, Inc., **II** 468; **6** 21, 50; **8** 536–37; **14** 32–33; **23 418–20**
Royal Data, Inc. *See* King Kullen Grocery Co., Inc.
Royal Doulton plc, **IV** 659; **14 413–15**; **34** 497; **38 400–04 (upd.)**
Royal Dutch Harbour Co., **IV** 707
Royal Dutch Paper Co., **IV** 307
Royal Dutch Petroleum Company, **IV 530–32**, 657; **24** 496. *See also* Shell Transport and Trading Company p.l.c.
Royal Dutch/Shell Group, **I** 368, 504; **III** 616; **IV** 132–33, 378, 406, 413, 429, 434, 453–54, 460, 491–92, 512, 515, 517–18, 530–32, 540–45, 557–58, 569; **7** 56–57, 172–73, 481–82; **17** 417; **19** 73, 75; **21** 203; **22** 237; **24** 520; **32** 175, 180; **41** 356–57, 359
Royal Electric Company, **6** 501
Royal Exchange Assurance Corp., **III** 233–34, 278, 349, 369–71, 373
Royal Farms, **24** 528
Royal Food Distributors, **II** 625
Royal Food Products, **24** 528–29; **36** 163
Royal General Insurance Co., **III** 242
Royal Hawaiian Macadamia Nut Co., **II** 491
Royal Industries, Inc., **19** 371
Royal Insurance Holdings plc, **III 349–51**
Royal International, **II** 457; **III** 349
Royal Interocean Lines, **6** 404; **26** 243
Royal Jackson, **14** 236
Royal Jordanian, **6** 101
Royal KPN N.V., **30 393–95**, 461, 463
Royal London Mutual Insurance, **IV** 697
Royal Mail Group, **V** 498; **6** 416; **19** 198
Royal Nedlloyd. *See* Koninglijke Nedlloyd N.V.
Royal Nepal Airline Corporation, **41 335–38**
Royal Netherlands Steamship Company. *See* KNSM.
Royal Numico N.V., **33** 145, 147; **37 340–42**
Royal Orchid Holidays, **6** 122–23
Royal Ordnance plc, **13** 356; **24** 87–88
Royal Packaging Industries Van Leer N.V., **9** 305; **30 396–98**
Royal Pakhoed N.V., **9** 532
Royal PTT Post, **30** 463
Royal Re, **III** 349
Royal Sash Manufacturing Co., **III** 757
Royal Securities Company, **6** 585
Royal Securities Corp. of Canada, **II** 425
Royal Sporting House Pte. Ltd., **21** 483
Royal Trust Co., **II** 456–57; **V** 25
Royal Union Life Insurance Co., **III** 275
Royal USA, **III** 349
Royal Vopak NV, **41 339–41**
Royal Wessanen, **II** 527
Royale Belge, **III** 177, 200, 394
Royale Inns of America, **25** 307
Royalite, **I** 285
Royce Electronics, **III** 569; **18** 68; **20** 361
Royce Ltd., **I** 194
Royster-Clark, Inc., **13** 504
Rozes, **I** 272
RPC Industries, **III** 635
RPI. *See* Research Polymers International.
RPM Inc., **8 III** 598; **454–57**; **36 394–98 (upd.)**
RSC. *See* Rental Service Corporation.
RSI Corp., **8** 141–42; **30** 160
RSO Records, **23** 390
RSV, **26** 496
RTE Corp., **II** 17
RTL Group, **41** 29
RTL-Véeronique, **IV** 611
RTZ Corporation PLC, **IV 189–92**; **7** 261, 263; **27** 256
RTZ-CRA Group. *See* Rio Tinto plc.
Rubber Latex Limited, **9** 92
Rubbermaid Incorporated, **III 613–15**; **12** 168–69; **13** 317–18; **19** 407; **20** 262, **454–57 (upd.)**; **21** 293; **28** 479; **31** 160–61; **34** 369
Ruberoid Corporation, **I** 339; **22** 227
Rubicon Group plc, **32** 50
Rubio's Restaurants, Inc., **35 379–81**
Rubloff Inc., **II** 442
Rubo Lederwaren, **14** 225
Rubry Owen, **I** 154
Ruby, **III** 47
Ruby Tuesday, Inc., **18 464–66**
Rubyco, Inc., **15** 386
La Ruche Meridionale, **12** 153
Ruddick Corporation, **23** 260
Rudisill Printing Co., **IV** 661
Rudolf Wolff & Co., **IV** 165
Rudolph Fluor & Brother, **I** 569
Ruel Smith Transportation Services, Inc., **39** 66
Ruff Hewn, **25** 48
Rug Corporation of America, **12** 393
The Rugby Group plc, **31 398–400**; **34** 380
Ruger Corporation, **19** 431
Ruhr-Zink, **IV** 141
Ruhrgas AG, **V 704–06**; **7** 141; **18** 50; **38 405–09 (upd.)**; **42** 263
Ruhrkohle AG, **IV 193–95**. *See also* RAG AG.
Ruinart Père et Fils, **I** 272
Rumbelows, **I** 532
Runcorn White Lead Co., **III** 680
Runnymede Construction Co., **8** 544
Runo-Everth Treibstoff und Ol AG, **7** 141
Rural Bank, **IV** 279; **19** 155
Rural Cellular Corporation, **43 340–42**
Rural/Metro Corporation, **28 396–98**; **39** 22
Rurhkohle AG, **V** 747
Rush Communications, **33 373–75**
Rush Laboratories, Inc., **6** 41
Russ Berrie and Company, Inc., **12 424–26**
Russell & Co., **II** 296
Russell Corporation, **8 458–59**; **12** 458; **30 399–401 (upd.)**
Russell Electric, **11** 412
Russell Electronics, **II** 85
Russell Kelly Office Services, Inc. *See* Kelly Services Inc.
Russell, Majors & Waddell, **II** 381
Russell Reynolds Associates Inc., **38 410–12**
Russell Stover Candies Inc., **12 427–29**
Russwerke Dortmund GmbH, **IV** 70
Rust Craft Greeting Cards Incorporated, **12** 561
Rust International Inc., **V** 754; **6** 599–600; **11 435–36**
Rust-Oleum Corporation, **36** 396
Rustenburg Platinum Co., **IV** 96, 118, 120
Rütgerswerke AG, **IV** 193; **8** 81
Ruth's Chris Steak House, **28 399–401**; **37** 297
Ruti Machinery Works, **III** 638
Rutland Plastics, **I** 321; **12** 103
RWE Group, **V 707–10**; **33** 194, 196
RxAmerica, **22** 40; **25** 297
Ryan Aeronautical, **I** 525; **10** 522; **11** 428
Ryan Aircraft Company, **9** 458
Ryan Homes, Inc., **8** 401–02
Ryan Insurance Co., **III** 204
Ryan Milk Company of Kentucky, **7** 128
Ryan's Family Steak Houses, Inc., **15 419–21**; **19** 287; **22** 464
Ryanair Holdings plc, **35 382–85**
Rycade Corp., **IV** 365, 658
Rydelle-Lion, **III** 45
Ryder System, Inc., **V 504–06**; **13** 192; **19** 293; **24 408–11 (upd.)**; **25** 93, 144; **28** 3; **41** 37
Ryerson Tull, Inc., **19** 216; **40** 269, **381–84 (upd.)**
Rykoff-Sexton, Inc., **21** 497; **26** 503, 505
The Ryland Group, Inc., **8 460–61**; **19** 126; **37 343–45 (upd.)**
Ryobi Ltd., **I** 202
Ryohin Keikaku Co., Ltd., **36** 420
Rypper Corp., **16** 43
Rysher Entertainment, **22** 162; **25** 329
Ryukyu Cement, **III** 760
The Ryvita Company Limited, **II** 466; **13** 52; **41** 31

S&A Restaurant Corp., **7** 336; **10** 176; **14** 331; **15** 363; **38** 100–01
S&C Electric Company, **15 422–24**
S&H. *See* Sperry and Hutchinson Co.
S&H Diving Corporation, **6** 578
S&K Famous Brands, Inc., **23 421–23**
S&V Screen Inks, **13** 227–28
S. & W. Berisford, **II** 514, 528
S&W Fine Foods, **12** 105
S + T Gesellschaft fur Reprotechnik mbH, **29** 306

S.A. CARFUEL, **12** 152
S.A. Cockerill Sambre. *See* Cockerill Sambre Group.
S.A. de C.V., **29** 461
S.A. des Ateliers d'Aviation Louis Breguet. *See* Groupe Dassault Aviation SA.
s.a. GB-Inno-BM. *See* GIB Group.
S.A. Greetings Corporation, **22** 35
S.A. Innovation—Bon Marché N.V., **26** 160
S.A. Schonbrunn & Co., **14** 18
S.B. Irving Trust Bank Corp., **II** 218
S.B. Penick & Co., **I** 708; **8** 548
S.C. Johnson & Son, Inc., I 14; **III** 45, **58–59**; **8** 130; **10** 173; **12** 126–28; **17** 215; **21** 386; **28** 215, **409–12 (upd.)**
S-C-S Box Company, **8** 173
S.D. Cohn & Company, **10** 455; **27** 364
S.D. Warren Co., **IV** 329–30
S-E Bank Group, **II** 351–53
S.E. Massengill, **III** 66
S.E. Rykoff & Co., **26** 503
S.F. Braun, **IV** 451
S.G. Warburg and Co., **II** 232, 259–60, 422, 629; **14** 419; **16** 377. *See also* SBC Warburg.
S. Grumbacher & Son. *See* The Bon-Ton Stores, Inc.
S.H. Benson Ltd., **I** 25–26
S.H. Kress & Co., **17** 203–04
S.I.P., Co., **8** 416
S-K-I Limited, 15 457–59
S.K. Wellman, **14** 81
S. Kuhn & Sons, **13** 221
S.M.A. Corp., **I** 622
S Pearson & Son Ltd., **IV** 657–59; **38** 290
S.R. Dresser Manufacturing Co., **III** 470–71
S.S. Kresge Company. *See* Kmart Corporation.
S.S.V. Inc., **36** 420
S.S. White Dental Manufacturing Co., **I** 383
S. Smith & Sons. *See* Smiths Industries PLC.
S.T. Cooper & Sons, **12** 283
S.T. Dupont Company, **III** 28; **23** 55
S.W.M. Chard, **27** 259
SA Alliance Air, **28** 404
SA Express, **28** 404
Sa SFC NA, **18** 163
Sa SFC NV, **18** 162
SAA. *See* South African Airways.
SAA (Pty) Ltd., 28 402–04
SAAB. *See* Svenska Aeroplan Aktiebolaget.
Saab Automobile AB, 32 386–89 (upd.); **36** 242–43
Saab-Scania A.B., I 197–98, 210; **III** 556; **V** 339; **10** 86; **11 437–39 (upd.)**; **16** 322; **34** 117
Saarberg-Konzern, IV 196–99
Saarstahl AG, **IV** 228
Saatchi & Saatchi plc, I 21, 28, **33–35**, 36; **6** 53, 229; **14** 49–50; **16** 72; **21** 236; **22** 296; **33** 65, 67; **328–31 (upd.)**
SAB. *See* South African Breweries Ltd.
Sabah Timber Co., **III** 699
Saban Entertainment, **24** 171
Sabena S.A./N.V., 6 96; **18** 80; **33** 49, 51, **376–79**; **34** 398
Saber Energy, Inc., **7** 553–54
Saber Software Corp., **25** 348
Sabi International Ltd., **22** 464
Sabian Ltd., **38** 68
SABIM Sable, **12** 152
Sabine Corporation, **7** 229
Sabine Investment Co. of Texas, Inc., **IV** 341
SABO Maschinenfabrik AG, **21** 175
Sabratek Corporation, 29 410–12
SABRE Group Holdings, Inc., 25 144; **26 427–30**; **28** 22
Sacer, **31** 127–28
Sachs-Dolmer G.m.b.H., **22** 334
Sachsgruppe, **IV** 201
Sacilor, **IV** 174, 226–27
Sackett Plasterboard Co., **III** 762
Sacks Industries, **8** 561
OY Saco AB, **23** 268
SACOR, **IV** 250, 504–06
Sacramento Savings & Loan Association, **10** 43, 45
SADE Ingenieria y Construcciones S.A., **38** 435, 437
SAE Magnetics Ltd., **18** 250
Saeger Carbide Corp., **IV** 203
Saes, **III** 347
SAFECO Corporation, III 352–54; **10** 44
Safeguard Scientifics, Inc., 10 232–34, **473–75**; **27** 338
Safelite Glass Corp., 19 371–73
Safer, Inc., **21** 385–86
Safeskin Corporation, 18 467–70
Safety 1st, Inc., 24 412–15
Safety Fund Bank, **II** 207
Safety-Kleen Corp., 8 462–65
Safety Rehab, **11** 486
Safety Savings and Loan, **10** 339
Safeway Inc., II 424, 601, 604–05, 609–10, 628, 632, 637, **654–56**; **6** 364; **7** 61, 569; **9** 39; **10** 442; **11** 239, 241; **12** 113, 209, 559; **13** 90, 336, 340; **16** 64, 160, 249, 452; **22** 37, 126; **24** 273, **416–19 (upd.)**; **25** 296; **27** 292; **28** 510; **30** 24, 27; **33** 305; **40** 366
Saffa SpA, **41** 325–26
Safilo, **40** 155–56
Safmarine, **IV** 22
SAFR. *See* Société Anonyme des Fermiers Reúnis.
Safrap, **IV** 472
Saga Communications, Inc., II 608; **III** 103; **IV** 406; **27** 226, **392–94**
Saga Petroleum ASA, **35** 318
The Sage Group, 43 343–46
Sagebrush Sales, Inc., **12** 397
Sagebrush Steakhouse, **29** 201
SAGEM S.A., 37 346–48
Saginaw Dock & Terminal Co., **17** 357
Sagitta Arzneimittel, **18** 51
Sagittarius Productions Inc., **I** 286
Sahara Casino Partners L.P., **19** 379
Sahara Resorts. *See* Santa Fe Gaming Corporation.
SAI. *See* Stamos Associates Inc.
Sai Baba, **12** 228
Saia Motor Freight Line, Inc., **6** 421–23
Saibu Gas, **IV** 518–19
SAIC Velcorex, **12** 153; **27** 188
Saiccor, **IV** 92
Sainrapt et Brice, **9** 9
Sainsbury's. *See* J Sainsbury PLC.
St. Alban Boissons S.A., **22** 515
St. Alban's Sand and Gravel, **III** 739
St. Andrews Insurance, **III** 397
St. Charles Manufacturing Co., **III** 654
St. Clair Industries Inc., **I** 482
St. Clair Press, **IV** 570
St. Croix Paper Co., **IV** 281; **9** 259
St. George Reinsurance, **III** 397
Saint-Gobain. *See* Compagnie de Saint Gobain S.A.
St. Helens Crown Glass Co., **III** 724
St. Ives Laboratories Inc., **36** 26
St Ives plc, 34 393–95
St. James Associates, **32** 362–63
The St. Joe Company, 31 422–25
St. Joe Gold, **23** 40
St. Joe Minerals Corp., **I** 569, 571; **8** 192
St. Joe Paper Company, 8 485–88
St. John Knits, Inc., 14 466–68
St. John's Wood Railway Company, **6** 406
St. Joseph Co., **I** 286, 684
St. Jude Medical, Inc., 6 345; **11 458–61**; **43 347–52 (upd.)**
St. Laurent Paperboard Inc., **30** 119
St. Lawrence Cement Inc., **III** 702; **8** 258–59
St. Lawrence Corp. Ltd., **IV** 272
St. Lawrence Steamboat Co., **I** 273; **26** 303
St. Louis and Illinois Belt Railway, **6** 504
Saint Louis Bread Company, **18** 35, 37
St. Louis Concessions Inc., **21** 39
St. Louis Refrigerator Car Co., **I** 219; **34** 36
St. Louis Troy and Eastern Railroad Company, **6** 504
St. Martin's Press, **25** 484–85; **35** 452
St. Paul Bank for Cooperatives, 8 489–90
The St. Paul Companies, III 355–57; **15** 257; **21** 305; **22** 154, **492–95 (upd.)**
St. Paul Fire and Marine Insurance Co., **III** 355–56
St. Paul Venture Capital Inc., **34** 405–06
Saint-Quirin, **III** 676; **16** 120
St. Regis Corp., **I** 153; **IV** 264, 282; **9** 260; **10** 265; **20** 129
St. Regis Paper Co., **IV** 289, 339; **12** 377; **22** 209
Sainte Anne Paper Co., **IV** 245–46; **25** 10
Saipem, **IV** 420–22, 453
SAirGroup, **29** 376; **33** 268, 271; **37** 241
Saison Group, **V** 184–85, 187–89; **36** 417–18, 420; **42** 340–41
Saito Ltd., **IV** 268
Saiwa, **II** 543
Sako Ltd., **39** 151
Saks Fifth Avenue, **I** 426; **15** 291; **18** 372; **21** 302; **22** 72; **25** 205; **27** 329
Saks Holdings, Inc., 24 420–23
Saks Inc., 41 342–45 (upd.)
Sakura Bank, **39** 286
Sakurai Co., **IV** 327
Salada Foods, **II** 525; **13** 293
Salant Corporation, 12 430–32; **27** 445
Sale Knitting Company, **12** 501. *See also* Tultex Corporation.
Salem Broadcasting, **25** 508
Salem Carpet Mills, Inc., **9** 467
Salem Sportswear, **25** 167
Salen Energy A.B., **IV** 563
Salick Health Care, Inc., **21** 544, 546
Salim Group, **18** 180–81
Salinas Equipment Distributors, Inc., **33** 364
Sallie Mae. *See* SLM Holding Corp. *and* Student Loan Marketing Association.
Sally Beauty Company, Inc., **8** 15–17; **36** 23–26
Salmon Carriers, **6** 383

Salmon River Power & Light Company, **12** 265
Salomon Brothers Inc., **28** 164
Salomon Inc., **I** 630–31; **II** 268, 400, 403, 406, 426, 432, 434, 441, **447–49**; **III** 221, 215, 721; **IV** 80, 137; **7** 114; **9** 378–79, 386; **11** 35, 371; **13** 331, **447–50 (upd.)** Inc.; **18** 60, 62; **19** 293; **21** 67, 146; **22** 102; **23** 472–74; **25** 12, 125; **42** 34
Salomon Smith Barney, **30** 124
Salomon Worldwide, **20 458–60**; **33** 7. *See also* adidas-Salomon AG.
Salora, **II** 69; **17** 353
Salsåkers Ångsågs, **IV** 338
Salt River Project, **19 374–76**
Salton, Inc., **30 402–04**
Saltos del Sil, **II** 197
Salvagnini Company, **22** 6
The Salvation Army USA, **15** 510–11; **32 390–93**
Salzgitter AG, **IV** 128, 198, **200–01**; **17** 381
SAM. *See* Sociedad Aeronáutica de Medellín, S.A.
Sam & Libby Inc., **30** 311
Sam Ash Music Corporation, **30 405–07**
Sam Goody, **I** 613; **9** 360–61
Sam's Club, **V** 216–17; **8** 555–57; **12** 221, 335; **13** 548; **14** 393; **15** 470; **16** 64; **25** 235; **40 385–87**; **41** 254–56
Samancor Ltd., **IV** 92–93
Samaritan Senior Services Inc., **25** 503
Sambo's, **12** 510
Sambre-et-Moselle, **IV** 52
Samcor Glass, **III** 685
Samedan Oil Corporation, **11** 353
Sames, S.A., **21** 65–66
Samim, **IV** 422
Samkong Fat Ltd. Co., **III** 747
Samna Corp., **6** 256; **25** 300
Sampson's, **12** 220–21
Samson Technologies Corp., **30** 406
Samsonite Corporation, **6** 50; **13** 311, **451–53**; **16** 20–21; **38** 169; **43 353–57 (upd.)**
Samsung-Calex, **17** 483
Samsung Electronics Co., Ltd., **14 416–18**; **18** 139, 260; **41 346–49 (upd.)**
Samsung Group, **I 515–17**; **II** 53–54; **III** 143, 457–58, 517, 749; **IV** 519; **7** 233; **12** 211–12; **13** 387; **18** 124; **29** 207–08
Samuel Austin & Son Company, **8** 41
Samuel Meisel & Company, Inc., **11** 80–81; **29** 509, 511
Samuel Montagu & Co., **II** 319; **17** 324–25
Samuel Moore & Co., **I** 155
Samuel Samuel & Co., **IV** 530, 542
Samuel, Son & Co. Ltd., **24** 144
Samuels Jewelers Incorporated, **30 408–10**
Samwha Paper Co., **III** 748
San Antonio Public Service Company, **6** 473
San Diego Gas & Electric Company, **V 711–14**; **6** 590; **11** 272; **25** 416
San Francisco Mines of Mexico Ltd., **22** 285
San Gabriel Light & Power Company, **16** 496
San Giorgio Macaroni Inc., **II** 511
SAN-MIC Trading Co., **IV** 327
San Miguel Corporation, **I** 221; **15 428–30**; **23** 379
Sanborn Co., **III** 142; **6** 237
Sanborn Hermanos, S.A., **20 461–63**; **21** 259
Sanborn Manufacturing Company, **30** 138
Sandcastle 5 Productions, **25** 269–70
Sanders Associates, Inc., **9** 324; **13** 127–28
Sanderson & Porter, **I** 376
Sanderson Computers, **10** 500
Sanderson Farms, Inc., **15 425–27**
Sandoz Ltd., **I** 632–33, **671–73**, 675; **7** 315, 452; **8** 108–09, 215; **10** 48, 199; **11** 173; **12** 388; **15** 139; **18** 51; **22** 475; **27** 299. *See also* Novartis AG.
Sandoz Nutrition Corp., **24** 286
SandPoint Corp., **12** 562; **17** 254
Sandusky Plastics, Inc., **17** 157
Sandusky Portland Cement Company, **24** 331
Sandvik AB, **III** 426–27; **IV 202–04**; **32 394–98 (upd.)**
Sandwell, Inc., **6** 491
Sandwich Chef, Inc. *See* Wall Street Deli, Inc.
Sandy's Pool Supply, Inc. *See* Leslie's Poolmart, Inc.
SANFLO Co., Ltd., **IV** 327
Sanford-Brown College, Inc., **41** 419–20
Sangu Express Company, **V** 463
Sanichem Manufacturing Company, **16** 386
Sanitary Farm Dairies, Inc., **7** 372
Sanitas Food Co., **II** 523
Sanitation Systems, Inc. *See* HMI Industries.
Sanjushi Bank, **II** 347
Sanka Coffee Corp., **II** 531
Sankin Kai Group, **II** 274
Sanko Kabushiki Kaisha. *See* Marubeni Corporation.
Sankyo Company Ltd., **I** 330, **674–75**; **III** 760; **8** 153
Sanlam, **IV** 91, 93, 535
Sano Railway Company, **6** 430
Sanofi Group, **I** 304, **676–77**; **III** 18; **IV** 546; **7** 484–85; **21** 205; **23** 236, 238, 242; **35** 262–63, 265
Sanrio Company, Ltd., **38 413–15**
Sanseisha Co., **IV** 326
Santa Ana Savings and Loan, **10** 339
Santa Ana Wholesale Company, **16** 451
Santa Barbara Restaurant Group, Inc., **37 349–52**
The Santa Cruz Operation, Inc., **6** 244; **38 416–21**
Santa Cruz Portland Cement, **II** 490
Santa Fe Gaming Corporation, **19 377–79**
Santa Fe Gold Corporation, **38** 232
Santa Fe Industries, **II** 448; **12** 19; **13** 448; **28** 498
Santa Fe International Corporation, **IV** 451–52; **38 422–24**
Santa Fe Pacific Corporation, **V 507–09**; **24** 98. *See also* Burlington Northern Santa Fe Corporation.
Santa Fe Railway, **12** 278; **18** 4
Santa Fe Southern Pacific Corp., **III** 512; **IV** 721; **6** 150, 599; **9** 391; **22** 491
Santa Rosa Savings and Loan, **10** 339
Santal, **26** 160
Santiam Lumber Co., **IV** 358
Santone Industries Inc., **16** 327
Sanus Corp. Health Systems, **III** 317
Sanwa Bank, Ltd., **II** 276, 326, **347–48**, 442, 511; **III** 188, 759; **IV** 150–51; **7** 119; **15** 43, **431–33 (upd.)**; **24** 356, 358
Sanyo Chemical Manufacturing Co., **III** 758
Sanyo Electric Co., Ltd., **I** 516; **II** 55–56, **91–92**; **III** 569, 654; **6** 101; **14** 535; **20** 361; **36 399–403 (upd.)**
Sanyo Ethylene Co. Ltd., **IV** 476
Sanyo-Kokusaku Pulp Co., Ltd., **IV** 326, **327–28**
Sanyo Petrochemical Co. Ltd., **IV** 476
Sanyo Railway Co., **I** 506; **II** 325
Sanyo Semiconductor, **17** 33
SAP AG, **11** 78; **16 441–44**; **25** 34; **26** 496, 498; **43 358–63 (upd.)**
SAP America Inc., **38** 431–32
SAPAC. *See* Société Parisienne d'Achats en Commun.
Sapirstein Greeting Card Company. *See* American Greetings Corporation.
Sappi Ltd., **IV** 91–93
Sapporo Breweries Limited, **I 282–83**; **13 454–56 (upd.)**; **20** 28–29; **21** 319–20; **36 404–07 (upd.)**
Sara Lee Corporation, **I** 15, 30; **II 571–73**, 675; **7** 113 **8** 262; **10** 219–20; **11** 15, 486; **12** 494, 502, 531; **15** 359, **434–37 (upd.)**, 507; **19** 192; **25** 91, 125, 166, 523; **26** 325, 503; **29** 132; **38** 381
Saracen's Head Brewery, **21** 245
Saratoga Partners, **24** 436
Sarawak Trading, **14** 448
Sargent & Lundy, **6** 556
Sarget S.A., **IV** 71
SARL, **12** 152
Sarma, **III** 623–24; **26** 159–61
Sarmag, **26** 161
Saros Corp., **15** 474
Sarotti A.G., **II** 546
Sarpe, **IV** 591
Sarriò S.A., **41** 325–26
SAS. *See* Scandinavian Airlines System.
The SAS Group, **34 396–99 (upd.)**
SAS Institute Inc., **10 476–78**; **38** 432
Saseba Heavy Industries, **II** 274
Saskatchewan Oil and Gas Corporation, **13** 556–57
Sasol Limited, **IV 533–35**
Sason Corporation, **V** 187
SAT. *See* Stockholms Allmänna Telefonaktiebolag.
Satcom Group of Companies, **32** 40
Satellite Business Systems, **III** 182; **21** 14; **23** 135; **27** 304
Satellite Information Services, **II** 141
Satellite Software International, **10** 556
Satellite Television PLC, **IV** 652; **7** 391; **23** 135
Satellite Transmission and Reception Specialist Company, **11** 184
Säteri Oy, **IV** 349
Sato Yasusaburo, **I** 266
Saturday Evening Post Co., **II** 208; **9** 320
Saturn Corporation, **III** 593, 760; **7 461–64**; **21 449–53 (upd.)**; **22** 154; **36** 242
Saturn Industries, Inc., **23** 489
SATV. *See* Satellite Television PLC.
Saucona Iron Co., **IV** 35; **7** 48
Saucony Inc., **35 386–89**
Sauder Woodworking Co., **12 433–34**; **35 390–93 (upd.)**

Saudi Arabian Airlines, **6** 84, **114–16**; **27** 132, **395–98 (upd.)**
Saudi Arabian Oil Company, **IV 536–39**; **17 411–15 (upd.)**. *See also* Arabian American Oil Co.
Saudi Arabian Parsons Limited, **8** 416
Saudi British Bank, **II** 298
Saudi Consolidated Electric Co., **IV** 538; **17** 414
Saudi Refining Inc., **IV** 539; **17** 414
Saudia. *See* Saudi Arabian Airlines.
Sauer Motor Company, **I** 177; **22** 329
Saul Lerner & Co., **II** 450
Saunders Karp & Co., **26** 190
Saunders, Karp, and Megrue, LP, **28** 258
Saunders-Roe Ltd., **IV** 658
Sauza, **31** 92
Sav-on Drug, **II** 605; **12** 477
Sav-X, **9** 186
Sava Group, **20** 263
Savacentre Ltd., **II** 658; **13** 284
Savage, **19** 430
Savage Shoes, Ltd., **III** 529
Savannah Electric & Power Company, **38** 448
Savannah Foods & Industries, Inc., **7 465–67**; **32** 274, 277; **35** 178
Savannah Gas Company, **6** 448; **23** 29
Save & Prosper Group, **10** 277
Save-A-Lot, **II** 682; **11** 228
Save Mart, **14** 397; **27** 292
Save.com, **37** 409
Savia S.A. de C.V., **29** 435
Saviem, **III** 543
Savin, **III** 159; **26** 497
Savings of America, **II** 182
Savio, **IV** 422
Oy Savo-Karjalan Tukkuliike, **8** 293
Savon Sellu Mills, **IV** 315
Savory Milln, **II** 369
Savoy Group, **I** 248; **IV** 705; **24** 195
Savoy Industries, **12** 495
Savoy Pictures Entertainment Inc., **25** 214
Sawdust Pencil Company, **29** 372
Sawhill Tubular Products, **41** 3
Sawtek Inc., **43 364–66 (upd.)**
Sawyer Electrical Manufacturing Company, **11** 4
Sawyer Industries, Inc., **13** 532
Sawyer Research Products, Inc., **14** 81
Saxby, S.A., **13** 385
Saxon and Norman Cement Co., **III** 670
Saxon Oil, **11** 97
Saxon Petroleum, Inc., **19** 162
Sayama Sekiyu, **IV** 554
SBAR, Inc., **30** 4
Sbarro, Inc., **16 445–47**; **19** 435; **27** 146
SBC Communications Inc., **25** 498–99; **29** 62; **32 399–403 (upd.)**; **34** 362; **43** 447
SBC Warburg, **II** 369; **14 419–21**; **15** 197
Sberbank, **II** 242
SBK Entertainment World, Inc., **22** 194; **24** 485; **26** 187
SBS Technologies, Inc., **25 405–07**
SCA. *See* Svenska Cellulosa Aktiebolaget.
SCA Services, Inc., **V** 754; **9** 109
Scaldia Paper BV, **15** 229
Scali, McCabe & Sloves, **I** 27; **22** 200
Scan Screen, **IV** 600
Scana Corporation, **6 574–76**; **19** 499
Scanair, **34** 397–98
Scancem, **38** 437
Scandinavian Airlines System, **I** 107, **119–20**, 121; **6** 96, 122; **25** 159; **26** 113; **27** 26, 463, 474; **31** 305; **33** 50; **38** 105. *See also* The SAS Group.
Scandinavian Bank, **II** 352
Scandinavian Trading Co., **I** 210
ScanDust, **III** 625
Scania-Vabis. *See* Saab-Scania AB.
ScanSource, Inc., **29 413–15**
Scantron Corporation, **17** 266–68
Scarborough Public Utilities Commission, **9 461–62**
Scaturro Supermarkets, **24** 528
SCB Computer Technology, Inc., **29 416–18**
SCEcorp, **V** 713–14, **715–17**; **6** 590
Scenic Airlines, Inc., **25** 420, 423
Scenographic Designs, **21** 277
Schäfer, **31** 158
Schaffhausenschor Bankverein, **II** 281
Schaper Mfg. Co., **12** 168
Scharff-Koken Manufacturing Co., **IV** 286
Scharnow, **II** 163–64
Schaum Publishing Co., **IV** 636
Schauman Wood Oy, **IV** 277, 302
Schawk, Inc., **24 424–26**
Schein Pharmaceutical Inc., **13** 77
Schenker-Rhenus Ag, **6 424–26**
Schenley Industries Inc., **I** 226, 285; **9** 449; **10** 181; **24** 140
Scherer. *See* R.P. Scherer.
Schering A.G., **I 681–82**, 684, 701; **10** 214; **14** 60; **16** 543; **36** 92, 148
Schering-Plough Corporation, **I** 682, **683–85**; **II** 590; **III** 45, 61; **11** 142, 207; **14** 58, 60, **422–25 (upd.)**; **36** 91–92
Schiavi Homes, Inc., **14** 138
Schibsted ASA, **31 401–05**
Schicht Co., **II** 588
Schick Products, **41** 366
Schick Shaving, **I** 711; **III** 55; **38** 363, 365
Schieffelin & Co., **I** 272
Schindler Holding AG, **II** 122; **12** 546; **27** 267; **29 419–22**
Schlage Lock Co., **III** 526
Schleppschiffahrtsgesellschaft Unterweser, **IV** 140
Schlesischer Bankverein, **II** 278
Schlitz Brewing Co., **I** 218, 255, 268, 270, 291, 600; **10** 100; **12** 338; **18** 500; **23** 403
Schlotzsky's, Inc., **36 408–10**
Schlumberger Limited, **III** 429, 499, **616–18**; **13** 323; **17 416–19 (upd.)**; **22** 64, 68; **25** 191; **43** 91, 338
Schmalbach-Lubeca-Werke A.G., **15** 128
Schmid, **19** 166
Schmidt, **I** 255
Schmitt Music Company, **40 388–90**
Schneider Co., **III** 113
Schneider et Cie, **IV** 25; **22** 42
Schneider National, Inc., **36 411–13**
Schneider S.A., **II 93–94**; **18 471–74 (upd.)**; **19** 165–66; **37** 39
Schneiderman's Furniture Inc., **28 405–08**
Schnitzer Steel Industries, Inc., **19 380–82**
Schnoll Foods, **24** 528
Schober Direktmarketing, **18** 170
Schocken Books, **13** 429
Schoeller & Hoesch Group, **30** 349, 352
Schoenfeld Industries, **16** 511
Scholastic Corporation, **10 479–81**; **29** 143, **423–27 (upd.)**
Scholl Inc., **I** 685; **14** 424
Schöller, **27** 436, 439
Scholz Homes Inc., **IV** 115
Schott Glass Technologies Inc., **34** 94
Schott Glaswerke, **III** 445–47
Schott-Zwiesel-Glaswerke AG, **34** 94
Schottenstein Stores Corp., **14 426–28**; **19** 108; **24** 26; **38** 475. *See also* American Eagle Outfitters, Inc.
Schrader Bellows, **III** 603
Schreiber Foods, **26** 432
Schreiber Frères. *See* Groupe Les Echos.
Schrock Cabinet Company, **13** 564
Schroder Darling & Co., **II** 389
Schroders plc, **42 332–35**
Schroders Ventures, **18** 345
Schroeter, White and Johnson, **III** 204
Schroff Inc., **26** 361, 363
Schubach, **30** 408
Schubert & Salzer GmbH, **42** 316
Schuck's Auto Supply. *See* CSK Auto Corporation.
Schuff Steel Company, **26 431–34**
Schuitema, **II** 642; **16** 312–13
Schuler Chocolates, **15** 65
Schuller International, Inc., **11** 421
Schultz Sav-O Stores, Inc., **21 454–56**; **31 406–08**
Schumacher Co., **II** 624
Schuykill Energy Resources, **12** 41
Schwabe-Verlag, **7** 42
Schwabel Corporation, **19** 453
Schwan's Sales Enterprises, Inc., **7 468–70**; **26 435–38 (upd.)**
Schwartz Iron & Metal Co., **13** 142
Schwarze Pumpe, **38** 408
Schweitzer-Maudit International Inc., **16** 304; **43** 258
Schweiz Allgemeine, **III** 377
Schweiz Transport-Vericherungs-Gesellschaft, **III** 410
Schweizer Rück Holding AG, **III** 377
Schweizerische Bankgesellschaft AG, **II** 379; **V** 104
Schweizerische Kreditanstalt, **III** 375, 410; **6** 489
Schweizerische Nordostbahn, **6** 424
Schweizerische Post-, Telefon- und Telegrafen-Betriebe, **V 321–24**
Schweizerische Ruckversicherungs-Gesellschaft. *See* Swiss Reinsurance Company.
Schweizerische Unfallversicherungs-Actiengesellschaft in Winterthur, **III** 402
Schweizerische Unionbank, **II** 368
Schweizerischer Bankverein, **II** 368
Schweppe, Paul & Gosse, **II** 476
Schweppes Ltd. *See* Cadbury Schweppes PLC.
Schwinn Cycle and Fitness L.P., **16** 494; **19 383–85**; **26** 412
The Schwinn GT Co., **26** 185
Schwitzer, **II** 420
SCI. *See* Service Corporation International *or* Société Centrale d'Investissement.
SCI Systems, Inc., **9 463–64**; **12** 451
Scicon, **14** 317
SciCor Inc., **30** 152
Science Applications International Corporation, **15 438–40**
Scientific-Atlanta, Inc., **6 335–37**
Scientific Communications, Inc., **10** 97

Scientific Data Systems, **II** 44; **III** 172; **6** 289; **10** 365
Scientific Games Holding Corp., **III** 431; **20** 48
Scientific Materials Company, **24** 162
SciMed Life Systems, **III** 18–19; **37** 43
Scioto Bank, **9** 475
Scitex Corporation Ltd., **15** 148, 229; **24 427–32**; **26** 212; **43** 150
SCM Corp., **I** 29; **III** 502; **IV** 330; **7** 208; **8** 223–24; **17** 213
SCO. *See* Santa Cruz Operation, Inc.
SCOA Industries, Inc., **13** 260
Scopus Technology Inc., **38** 431
SCOR S.A., **III** 394; **20 464–66**
The Score Board, Inc., **19 386–88**
Score! Learning, Inc., **42** 211
Scot Bowyers, **II** 587
Scot Lad Foods, **14** 411
Scotch House Ltd., **19** 181
Scotia Securities, **II** 223
Scotiabank. *See* The Bank of Nova Scotia.
Scotsman Industries, Inc., **II** 420; **16** 397; **20 467–69**
Scott-Ballantyne Company. *See* Ballantyne of Omaha, Inc.
Scott Communications, Inc., **10** 97
Scott Fetzer Company, **III** 214; **12 435–37**, 554–55; **17** 233; **18** 60, 62–63; **42** 33
Scott, Foresman, **IV** 675
Scott Graphics, **IV** 289; **8** 483
Scott Health Care, **28** 445
Scott Holdings, **19** 384
Scott Lithgow, **III** 516; **7** 232
Scott-McDuff, **II** 107
Scott Paper Company, **III** 749; **IV** 258, 289–90, 311, 325, 327, **329–31**; **8** 483; **16** 302, 304; **17** 182; **18** 181; **19** 266; **22** 210; **29** 333; **31 409–412 (upd.)**; **43** 258
Scott Transport, **27** 473
Scotti Brothers, **20** 3
Scottish & Newcastle plc, **15 441–44**; **35 394–97 (upd.)**
Scottish Aviation, **I** 50; **24** 85–86
Scottish Brick, **14** 250
Scottish Electric, **6** 453
Scottish General Fire Assurance Corp., **III** 256
Scottish Hydro-Electric PLC, **13 457–59**
Scottish Inns of America, Inc., **13** 362
Scottish Land Development, **III** 501; **7** 207
Scottish Malt Distillers, **I** 240
Scottish Media Group plc, **32 404–06**; **41** 350–52
Scottish Mutual plc, **39** 5–6
Scottish Nuclear, Ltd., **19** 389
Scottish Radio Holding plc, **41 350–52**
Scottish Sealand Oil Services Ltd., **25** 171
Scottish Union Co., **III** 358
ScottishPower plc, **19 389–91**; **27** 483, 486
ScottishTelecom plc, **19** 389
The Scotts Company, **22 474–76**
Scotts Stores, **I** 289
Scotty's, Inc., **12** 234; **22 477–80**; **26** 160–61
Scovill Fasteners Inc., **IV** 11; **22** 364; **24 433–36**
SCP Pool Corporation, **39 358–60**
Scranton Corrugated Box Company, Inc., **8** 102
Scranton Plastics Laminating Corporation, **8** 359
Screen Gems, **II** 135–36; **12** 74; **22** 193
Screg Group, **I** 563; **24** 79; **31** 128
Scribbans-Kemp Ltd., **II** 594
Scriha & Deyhle, **10** 196
Scripps-Howard, Inc., **IV** 607–09, 628; **7** 64, 157–59. *See also* The E.W. Scripps Company.
Scrivner Inc., **17** 180
Scudder Kemper Investments. *See* Zurich Financial Services.
Scudder, Stevens & Clark, **II** 448; **13** 448
Scurlock Oil Co., **IV** 374
SD-Scicon plc, **24** 87
SDC Coatings, **III** 715
SDGE. *See* San Diego Gas & Electric Company.
SDK Health Care Information Systems, **16** 94
SDK Parks, **IV** 724
Sea-Alaska Products, **II** 494
Sea Containers Ltd., **29 428–31**
Sea Diamonds Ltd., **IV** 66; **7** 123
Sea Far of Norway, **II** 484
Sea Insurance Co. Ltd., **III** 220
Sea-Land Service Inc., **I** 476; **9** 510–11; **22** 164, 166
Sea Life Centre Aquariums, **10** 439
Sea Ray, **III** 444
Sea Star Line, **41** 399
Sea World, Inc., **IV** 623–24; **12** 224
Seabee Corp., **18** 276
Seaboard Air Line Railroad. *See* CSX Corporation.
Seaboard Corporation, **36 414–16**
Seaboard Finance Company, **13** 63
Seaboard Fire and Marine Insurance Co., **III** 242
Seaboard Life Insurance Co., **III** 193
Seaboard Lumber Sales, **IV** 307
Seaboard Oil Co., **IV** 552
Seaboard Surety Company, **III** 357; **22** 494
Seabourn Cruise Lines, **6** 368; **27** 90, 92
Seabrook Farms Co., **24** 527–28
Seabulk Offshore International. *See* Hvide Marine Incorporated.
Seabury & Smith, **III** 283
Seacat-Zapata Off-Shore Company, **18** 513
Seacoast Products, **III** 502
Seafield Capital Corporation, **27** 385, 387
Seafield Estate and Consolidated Plantations Berhad, **14** 448
Seafirst. *See* Seattle First National Bank, Inc.
SeaFirst Corp., **II** 228; **17** 462
Seagate Technology, Inc., **6** 230–31; **8 466–68**; **9** 57; **10** 257, 403–04, 459; **11** 56, 234; **13** 483; **18** 250; **25** 530; **34 400–04 (upd.)**
The Seagram Company Ltd., **I** 26, 240, 244, **284–86**, 329, 403; **II** 456, 468; **IV** 401; **7** 155; **18** 72; **21** 26, 401; **22** 194; **23** 125; **25** 266, 268, 366, **408–12 (upd.)**; **26** 125, 127, 152; **28** 475; **29** 196; **31** 269; **33** 375, 424, 432
Seagull Energy Corporation, **11 440–42**
Seahawk Services Ltd., **37** 289
Seal Products, Inc., **12** 264
Seal Sands Chemicals, **16** 69
Sealand Petroleum Co., **IV** 400
Sealectro, **III** 434
Sealed Air Corporation, **14 429–31**
Sealed Power Corporation, **I 199–200**; **10** 492–94
Sealright Co., Inc., **17 420–23**
SealRite Windows, **19** 446
Sealtest, **14** 205
Sealy Inc., **12 438–40**; **28** 416; **34** 407
Seaman Furniture Company, Inc., **28** 389; **32 407–09**
Seamless Rubber Co., **III** 613
Seaquist Manufacturing Corporation, **9** 413–14; **33** 335–36
Searle & Co. *See* G.D. Searle & Co.
Sears Canada Inc., **25** 221
Sears Logistics Services, **18** 225–26
Sears plc, **V 177–79**
Sears, Roebuck and Co., **I** 26, 146, 516, 556; **II** 18, 60, 134, 331, 411, 414; **III** 259, 265, 340, 536, 598, 653–55; **V 180–83**; **6** 12–13; **7** 166, 479; **8** 224, 287–89; **9** 44, 65–66 156, 210, 213, 219, 235–36, 430–31, 538; **10** 10, 50–52, 199, 236–37, 288, 304–05, 490–91; **11** 62, 349, 393, 498; **12** 54, 96–98, 309, 311, 315, 430–31, 439, 522, 548, 557; **13** 165, 260, 268, 277, 411, 545, 550, 562–63; **14** 62; **15** 402, 470; **16** 73, 75, 160, 327–28, 560; **17** 366, 460, 487; **18** 65, 168, 283, 445, **475–79 (upd.)**; **19** 143, 221, 309, 490; **20** 259, 263; **21** 73, 94, 96–97; **23** 23, 52, 210; **25** 221, 357, 535; **27** 30, 32, 163, 347–48, 416, 428–30; **33** 311–12; **36** 418
Sears Roebuck de México, S.A. de C.V., **20 470–72**; **21** 259; **34** 340
Seashore Transportation Co., **13** 398
Season-all Industries, **III** 735
SEAT. *See* Sociedad Española de Automoviles de Turismo.
Seatrain International, **27** 474
Seattle Brewing and Malting Company. *See* Rainier Brewing Company.
Seattle Coffee Company, **32** 12, 15
Seattle Electric Company, **6** 565
Seattle FilmWorks, Inc., **20 473–75**
Seattle First National Bank Inc., **8 469–71**
Seattle Times Company, **15 445–47**
Seaview Oil Co., **IV** 393
Seaway Express, **9** 510
Seaway Food Town, Inc., **9** 452; **15 448–50**
SeaWest, **19** 390
SEB-Fastigheter A.B., **II** 352
SEB S.A. *See* Groupe SEB.
Sebastiani Vineyards, Inc., **28 413–15**; **39** 421
SECA, **IV** 401
SECDO, **III** 618
SECO Industries, **III** 614
Seco Products Corporation, **22** 354
Secon GmbH, **13** 160
Second Bank of the United States, **II** 213; **9** 369
Second Harvest, **29 432–34**
Second National Bank, **II** 254
Second National Bank of Bucyrus, **9** 474
Second National Bank of Ravenna, **9** 474
Secoroc, **III** 427
Le Secours, **III** 211
SecPac. *See* Security Pacific Corporation.
Secure Horizons, **11** 378–79
Secure Networks, Inc., **25** 349
Securicor, **11** 547
Securitas AB, **41** 77, 80; **42** 165–66, **336–39**
Securitas Esperia, **III** 208

Securities Industry Automation Corporation, **9** 370
Securities International, Inc., **II** 440–41
Securities Management & Research, Inc., **27** 46
Security Bancorp, **25** 186–87
Security Capital Corporation, 17 424–27; **21** 476
Security Connecticut Life Insurance Co., **III** 276
Security Data Group, **32** 373
Security Engineering, **III** 472
Security Express, **10** 269
Security First National Bank of Los Angeles, **II** 349
Security Life and Annuity Company, **11** 213
Security Management Company, **8** 535–36
Security National Bank, **II** 251, 336
Security National Corp., **10** 246
Security Pacific Corporation, II 349–50, 422; **III** 366; **8** 45, 48; **11** 447; **17** 137
Security Trust Company, **9** 229, 388
Security Union Title Insurance Co., **10** 43–44
SED International Holdings, Inc., 43 367–69
Sedat Eldem, **13** 475
SEDCO, **17** 418
Sedgwick Group PLC, **I** 427; **III** 280, 366; **10** 38; **22** 318
Sedgwick Sales, Inc., **29** 384
SEDTCO Pty., **13** 61
See's Candies, Inc., III 213; **18** 60–61; **30 411–13**
Seeburg Corporation, **II** 22; **III** 430; **15** 538
Seed Restaurant Group Inc., **13** 321; **27** 145
Seed Solutions, Inc., **11** 491
Seeger-Orbis, **III** 624
Seeger Refrigerator Co., **III** 653; **12** 548
Seeman Brothers. *See* White Rose, Inc.
SEEQ Technology, Inc., **9** 114; **13** 47; **17** 32, 34
SEG, **I** 463
Sega Enterprises, Ltd., **28** 320
Sega of America, Inc., 7 396; **10** 124–25, 284–86, **482–85**; **18** 520
Sega of Japan, **24** 4
Segespar, **II** 265
Sego Milk Products Company, **7** 428
Seguros Comercial America, **21** 413
Seguros El Corte Inglés, **V** 52
Seguros Monterrey, **19** 189
Seguros Serfin S.A., **25** 290
Seibels, Bruce & Co., **11** 394–95
Seiberling Rubber Company, **V** 244; **20** 259
Seibu Allstate Life Insurance Company, Ltd., **27** 31
Seibu Department Stores, Ltd., II 273; **V 184–86**; **42 340–43 (upd.)**
Seibu Group, **36** 417–18
Seibu Railway Co. Ltd., V 187, **510–11**, 526
Seibu Saison, **6** 207
Seigle's Home and Building Centers, Inc., 41 353–55
Seijo Green Plaza Co., **I** 283
Seikatsu-Soko, **V** 210
Seiko Corporation, I 488; **III** 445, **619–21**; **11** 46; **12** 317; **13** 122; **16** 168, 549; **17 428–31 (upd.)**; **21** 122–23; **22** 413; **41** 72
Seiko Instruments USA Inc., **23** 210
Seine, **III** 391
Seino Transportation Company, Ltd., 6 427–29
Seismograph Service Limited, **II** 86; **11** 413; **17** 419
Seita, 23 424–27
Seiwa Fudosan Co., **I** 283
The Seiyu, Ltd., V 187–89; **36 417–21 (upd.)**
Seizo-sha, **12** 483
Sekisui Chemical Co., Ltd., III 741–43
SEL, **I** 193, 463
Selat Marine Services, **22** 276
Selden, **I** 164, 300
Select Comfort Corporation, 34 405–08
Select-Line Industries, **9** 543
Select Theatres Corp. *See* Shubert Organization Inc.
Selection Trust, **IV** 67, 380, 565
Selective Auto and Fire Insurance Co. of America, **III** 353
Selective Insurance Co., **III** 191
Selectronics Inc., **23** 210
Selectrons Ltd., **41** 367
Selena Coffee Inc., **39** 409
Selenia, **I** 467; **II** 86; **38** 374
Self Auto, **23** 232
The Self-Locking Carton Company, **14** 163
Self-Service Drive Thru, Inc., **25** 389
Self Service Restaurants, **II** 613
Selfridges Plc, V 94, 177–78; **34 409–11**
Seligman & Latz, **18** 455
Selkirk Communications Ltd., **26** 273
Selleck Nicholls, **III** 691
Sells-Floto, **32** 186
The Selmer Company, Inc., 19 392–94, 426, 428
Seltel International Inc., **6** 33; **35** 246
Semarca, **11** 523
Sematech, **18** 384, 481
Sembler Company, **11** 346
Semet-Solvay, **22** 29
Semi-Tech Global, **30** 419–20
Seminis, Inc., 21 413; **29 435–37**
Seminole Electric Cooperative, **6** 583
Seminole Fertilizer, **7** 537–38
Seminole National Bank, **41** 312
Semitic, Inc., **33** 248
Semitool, Inc., 18 480–82
Sempra Energy, 25 413–16 (upd.)
Semrau and Sons, **II** 601
Semtech Corporation, 32 410–13
SEN AG, **IV** 128
Sencel Aero Engineering Corporation, **16** 483
Seneca Foods Corporation, 17 432–34
Senelle-Maubeuge, **IV** 227
Senior Corp., **11** 261
Senshusha, **I** 506
Sensi, Inc., **22** 173
Sensormatic Electronics Corp., 11 443–45; **39** 77–79
Sensory Science Corporation, 37 353–56
Sentinel Foam & Envelope Corporation, **14** 430
Sentinel Group, **6** 295
Sentinel Savings and Loan, **10** 339
Sentinel-Star Company, **IV** 683; **22** 521
Sentinel Technologies, **III** 38
Sentrust, **IV** 92
Sentry, **II** 624
Sentry Insurance Company, **10** 210
Senyo Kosakuki Kenkyujo, **III** 595
Seohan Development Co., **III** 516; **7** 232
Sepa, **II** 594
Sepal, Ltd., **39** 152, 154
AB Separator, **III** 417–19
SEPECAT, **24** 86
SEPIC, **I** 330
Sept, **IV** 325
Sequa Corp., 13 460–63
Séquanaise, **III** 391–92
Sequel Corporation, **41** 193
Sequent Computer Systems Inc., **10** 363
Sequoia Athletic Company, **25** 450
Sequoia Insurance, **III** 270
Sequoia Pharmacy Group, **13** 150
Sera-Tec Biologicals, Inc., **V** 175–76; **19** 355
Seraco Group, **V** 182
Serck Group, **I** 429
SEREB, **I** 45; **7** 10
Sereg Valves, S.A., **17** 147
Serewatt AG, **6** 491
Sergeant Drill Co., **III** 525
Sero-Genics, Inc., **V** 174–75
Serta, Inc., 28 416–18
Serval Marketing, **18** 393
Servam Corp., **7** 471–73
Servel Inc., **III** 479; **22** 25
Service America Corp., 7 471–73; **27** 480–81
Service Bureau Corp., **III** 127
Service Control Corp. *See* Angelica Corporation.
Service Corporation International, 6 293–95; **16** 343–44; **37** 66–68
Service Corporation of America, **17** 552
Service Games Company, **10** 482
Service Master L.P., **34** 153
Service Merchandise Company, Inc., V 190–92; **6** 287; **9** 400; **19 395–99 (upd.)**
Service Partner, **I** 120
Service Pipe Line Co., **IV** 370
Service Q. General Service Co., **I** 109
Service Systems, **III** 103
ServiceMaster Inc., 23 428–31 (upd.)
Servicemaster Limited Partnership, 6 44–46; **13** 199
Services Maritimes des Messageries Impériales. *See* Compagnie des Messageries Maritimes.
ServiceWare, Inc., **25** 118
Servicios Financieros Quadrum S.A., **14** 156
Servisco, **II** 608
ServiStar Coast to Coast Corporation. *See* TruServ Corporation.
ServoChem A.B., **I** 387
Servomation Corporation, **7** 472–73
Servomation Wilbur. *See* Service America Corp.
Servoplan, S.A., **8** 272
SES Staffing Solutions, **27** 21
Sesame Street Book Club, **13** 560
Sespe Oil, **IV** 569; **24** 519
Sessler Inc., **19** 381
SET, **I** 466
SETCAR, **14** 458
Settsu Marine and Fire Insurance Co., **III** 367
Seven Arts Limited, **25** 328
Seven Arts Productions, Ltd., **II** 147, 176
7-Eleven, Inc., 32 414–18 (upd.); **36** 358

Seven-Eleven Japan Co., **41** 115. *See also* Ito-Yokado Co., Ltd.
Seven Generation, Inc., **41** 177
Seven Network Limited, **25** 329
Seven-Up Bottling Co. of Los Angeles, **II** 121
Seven-Up Co., **I** 245, 257; **II** 468, 477; **18** 418
Sevenson Environmental Services, Inc., 42 344–46
Severn Trent PLC, 12 441–43; 38 425–29 (upd.)
Seversky Aircraft Corporation, **9** 205
Sevin-Rosen Partners, **III** 124; **6** 221
Sewell Coal Co., **IV** 181
Sewell Plastics, Inc., **10** 222
Sextant In-Flight Systems, LLC, **30** 74
Seybold Machine Co., **II** 37; **6** 602
Seymour Electric Light Co., **13** 182
Seymour International Press Distributor Ltd., **IV** 619
Seymour Press, **IV** 619
Seymour Trust Co., **13** 467
SFIC Holdings (Cayman) Inc., **38** 422
SFIM Industries, **37** 348
SFNGR. *See* Nouvelles Galeries Réunies.
SFS Bancorp Inc., **41** 212
SFX Broadcasting Inc., **24** 107
SFX Entertainment, Inc., 36 422–25; 37 383–84
SGC. *See* Supermarkets General Corporation.
SGE. *See* Vinci.
SGI, 29 438–41 (upd.)
SGL Carbon AG, **40** 83
SGLG, Inc., **13** 367
SGS Corp., **II** 117; **11** 46
Shaffer Clarke, **II** 594
Shakespeare Company, 16 296; **22 481–84**
Shakey's Pizza, **16** 447
Shaklee Corporation, 12 444–46; 17 186; **38** 93; **39 361–64 (upd.)**
Shalco Systems, **13** 7
Shampaine Industries, Inc., **37** 399
Shamrock Advisors, Inc., **8** 305
Shamrock Broadcasting Inc., **24** 107
Shamrock Capital L.P., **7** 81–82
Shamrock Holdings, **III** 609; **7** 438; **9** 75; **11** 556; **25** 268
Shamrock Oil & Gas Co., **I** 403–04; **IV** 409; **7** 308
Shan-Chih Business Association, **23** 469
Shanghai Crown Maling Packaging Co. Ltd., **13** 190
Shanghai Hotels Co., **IV** 717
Shanghai International Finance Company Limited, **15** 433
Shanghai Kyocera Electronics Co., Ltd., **21** 331
Shanghai Petrochemical Co., Ltd., 18 483–85; 21 83
Shangri-La Asia Ltd., **22** 305
Shannon Aerospace Ltd., 36 426–28
Shannon Group, Inc., **18** 318, 320
Shansby Group, **27** 197; **43** 218
Share Drug plc, **24** 269
Shared Financial Systems, Inc., **10** 501
Shared Medical Systems Corporation, 14 432–34
Shared Technologies Inc., **12** 71
Shared Use Network Systems, Inc., **8** 311
Shari Lewis Enterprises, Inc., **28** 160
Sharon Steel Corp., **I** 497; **7** 360–61; **8** 536; **13** 158, 249
Sharon Tank Car Corporation, **6** 394; **25** 169
Sharp & Dohme, Incorporated, **I** 650; **11** 289, 494
Sharp Corporation, I 476; **II 95–96; III** 14, 428, 455, 480; **6** 217, 231; **11** 45; **12 447–49 (upd.); 13** 481; **16** 83; **21** 123; **22** 197; **40 391–95 (upd.)**
The Sharper Image Corporation, 10 486–88; 23 210; **26** 439; **27** 429
Sharples Co., **I** 383
Sharples Separator Co., **III** 418–20
Shasta Beverages. *See* National Beverage Corp.
Shaw Communications Inc., **26** 274; **35** 69
Shaw Industries, Inc., 9 465–67; 19 274, 276; **25** 320; **40 396–99 (upd.)**
Shaw's Supermarkets, Inc., **II** 658–59; **23** 169
Shawell Precast Products, **14** 248
Shawinigan Water and Power Company, **6** 501–02
Shawmut National Corporation, II 207; **12** 31; **13 464–68**
Shea's Winnipeg Brewery Ltd., **I** 268; **25** 280
Sheaffer Group, **23** 54, 57
Shearman & Sterling, 32 419–22; 35 467
Shearson Hammill & Company, **22** 405–06
Shearson Lehman Brothers Holdings Inc., I 202; **II** 398–99, 450, 478; **III** 319; **8** 118; **9 468–70 (upd.); 10** 62–63; **11** 418; **12** 459; **15** 124, 463–64
Shearson Lehman Hutton Holdings Inc., II 339, 445, **450–52; III** 119; **9** 125; **10** 59, 63; **17** 38–39
Shedd's Food Products Company, **9** 318
Sheepbridge Engineering, **III** 495
Sheffield Banking Co., **II** 333
Sheffield Exploration Company, **28** 470
Sheffield Forgemasters Group Ltd., **39** 32
Sheffield Motor Co., **I** 158; **10** 292
Sheffield Twist Drill & Steel Co., **III** 624
Shekou Container Terminal, **16** 481; **38** 345
Shelby Insurance Company, **10** 44–45
Shelby Steel Tube Co., **IV** 572; **7** 550
Shelby Williams Industries, Inc., 14 435–37
Shelco, **22** 146
Sheldahl Inc., 23 432–35
Shelf Life Inc. *See* King Kullen Grocery Co., Inc.
Shell. *See* Shell Transport and Trading Company p.l.c. *and* Shell Oil Company.
Shell Australia Ltd., **III** 728
Shell BV, **IV** 518
Shell Canada Limited, **32** 45
Shell Chemical Corporation, **IV** 410, 481, 531–32, 540; **8** 415; **24** 151
Shell Coal International, **IV** 532
Shell Forestry, **21** 546
Shell France, **12** 153
Shell Nederland BV, **V** 658–59
Shell Oil Company, I 20, 26, 569; **III** 559; **IV** 392, 400, 531, **540–41; 6** 382, 457; **8** 261–62; **11** 522; **14** 25, **438–40 (upd.); 17** 417; **19** 175–76; **21** 546; **22** 274; **24** 520; **25** 96, 232, 469; **26** 496; **41 356–60 (upd.)**, 395
Shell Transport and Trading Company p.l.c., I 605; **II** 436, 459; **III** 522, 735; **IV** 363, 378–79, 381–82, 403, 412, 423, 425, 429, 440, 454, 466, 470, 472, 474, 484–86, 491, 505, 508, **530–32**, 564; **31** 127–28. *See also* Royal Dutch Petroleum Company *and* Royal Dutch/Shell.
Shell Western E & P, **7** 323
Shell Winning, **IV** 413–14
Sheller-Globe Corporation, I 201–02; 17 182
Shells Seafood Restaurants, Inc., 43 370–72
Shelly Brothers, Inc., **15** 65
Shenley Laboratories, **I** 699
Shepard Warner Elevator Co., **III** 467
Shepard's Citations, Inc., **IV** 636–37
Shepherd Hardware Products Ltd., **16** 357
Shepherd Neame Limited, 30 414–16
Shepherd Plating and Finishing Company, **13** 233
Shepler Equipment Co., **9** 512
Sheraton Corp. of America, **I** 463–64, 487; **III** 98–99; **11** 198; **13** 362–63; **21** 91
Sherborne Group Inc./NH Holding Inc., **17** 20
Sherbrooke Paper Products Ltd., **17** 281
Sheridan Bakery, **II** 633
Sheridan Catheter & Instrument Corp., **III** 443
Sherix Chemical, **I** 682
Sherr-Gold, **23** 40
Sherritt Gordon Mines, **7** 386–87; **12** 260
The Sherwin-Williams Company, III 744–46; 8 222, 224; **11** 384; **12** 7; **13 469–71 (upd.); 19** 180; **24** 323; **30** 474
Sherwood Equity Group Ltd. *See* National Discount Brokers Group, Inc.
Sherwood Medical Group, **I** 624; **III** 443–44; **10** 70
SHI Resort Development Co., **III** 635
ShianFu Optical Fiber, **III** 491
Shibaura Seisakusho Works, **I** 533; **12** 483
Shieh Chi Industrial Co., **19** 508
Shields & Co., **9** 118
Shikoku Drinks Co., **IV** 297
Shikoku Electric Power Company, Inc., V 718–20
Shikoku Machinery Co., **III** 634
Shiley, Inc., **38** 361
Shillito's, **31** 192
Shimotsuke Electric Railway Company, **6** 431
Shimura Kako, **IV** 63
Shin-Nihon Glass Co., **I** 221
Shin Nippon Machine Manufacturing, **III** 634
Shinano Bank, **II** 291
Shinko Electric Co., Ltd., **IV** 129
Shinko Rayon Ltd., **I** 363; **V** 369–70
Shinriken Kogyo, **IV** 63
Shintech, **11** 159–60
Shinwa Tsushinki Co., **III** 593
Shiomi Casting, **III** 551
Shionogi & Co., Ltd., I 646, 651; **III 60–61; 11** 90, 290; **17 435–37 (upd.)**
Ship 'n Shore, **II** 503; **9** 156–57; **10** 324
Shipley Co. Inc., **26** 425
Shipowners and Merchants Tugboat Company, **6** 382
Shipper Group, **16** 344
Shipstad & Johnson's Ice Follies, **25** 313
Shiro Co., Ltd., **V** 96
Shirokiya Co., Ltd., **V** 199

Shiseido Company, Limited, **II** 273–74, 436; **III** 46, 48, **62–64**; **8** 341, 343; **22 485–88 (upd.)**
SHL Systemhouse Inc., **27** 305
Shochiku Company Ltd., **28** 461
Shockley Electronics, **20** 174
Shoe Carnival Inc., **14 441–43**
Shoe Corp., **I** 289
Shoe Supply, Inc., **22** 213
Shoe-Town Inc., **23** 310
Shoe Works Inc., **18** 415
Shohin Kaihatsu Kenkyusho, **III** 595
Shoman Milk Co., **II** 538
Shonac Corp., **14** 427
Shonco, Inc., **18** 438
Shoney's, Inc., **7 474–76**; **14** 453; **19** 286; **23 436–39 (upd.)**; **29** 290–91
Shop & Go, **II** 620
Shop 'n Bag, **II** 624
Shop 'n Save, **II** 669, 682; **12** 220–21
Shop Rite Foods Inc., **II** 672–74; **7** 105; **19** 479. *See also* Big V Supermarkets, Inc.
ShopKo Stores Inc., **II** 669–70; **18** 505–07; **21 457–59**
Shoppers Food Warehouse Corporation, **16** 159, 161
Shoppers World Stores, Inc. *See* LOT$OFF Corporation.
ShopRite, **24** 528. *See also* Foodarama Supermarkets, Inc.
Shopwell/Food Emporium, **II** 638; **16** 247, 249
Shore Manufacturing, **13** 165
Shorewood Packaging Corporation, **28 419–21**
Short Aircraft Co., **I** 50, 55, 92
Short Brothers, **24** 85
Shoseido Co., **17** 110
Shoshi-Gaisha, **IV** 320
Shotton Paper Co. Ltd., **IV** 350
Showa Aircraft Industry Co., **I** 507–08
Showa Aluminum Corporation, **8** 374
Showa Bank, **II** 291–92
Showa Bearing Manufacturing Co., **III** 595
Showa Cotton Co., Ltd., **IV** 442
Showa Denko, **I** 493–94; **II** 292; **IV** 61; **24** 324–25
Showa Marutsutsu Co. Ltd., **8** 477
Showa Paper Co., **IV** 268
Showa Photo Industry, **III** 548
Showa Products Company, **8** 476
Showa Shell Sekiyu K.K., **II** 459; **IV 542–43**
ShowBiz Pizza Time, Inc., **12** 123; **13 472–74**; **15** 73; **16** 447. *See also* CEC Entertainment, Inc.
Showboat, Inc., **19 400–02**; **43** 227
Showcase of Fine Fabrics, **16** 197
Showco, Inc., **35** 436
Showerings, **I** 215
Showscan Entertainment Inc., **34** 230
Showscan Film Corporation, **28** 206
Showtime, **II** 173; **7** 222–23; **9** 74; **23** 274–75, 391, 503; **25** 329–30
Shredded Wheat Co., **II** 543; **7** 366
Shreve and Company, **12** 312
Shreveport Refrigeration, **16** 74
Shrewsbury and Welshpool Old Bank, **II** 307
Shu Uemura, **III** 43
Shubert Organization Inc., **24 437–39**
Shubrooks International Ltd., **11** 65
Shueisha, **IV** 598
Shuford Mills, Inc., **14** 430
Shugart Associates, **6** 230; **8** 466; **22** 189
Shull Lumber & Shingle Co., **IV** 306
Shulman Transport Enterprises Inc., **27** 473
Shun Fung Ironworks, **IV** 717
Shunan Shigyo Co., Ltd., **IV** 160
Shurgard Storage Centers of Seattle, **21** 476
Shuttleworth Brothers Company. *See* Mohawk Industries, Inc.
Shuwa Corp., **22** 101; **36** 292
SHV Holdings N.V., **IV** 383; **14** 156
SI Holdings Inc., **10** 481; **29** 425
SIAS, **19** 192
SIAS-MPA, **I** 281
SIATA S.p.A., **26** 363
SIB Financial Services, **39** 382
Sibco Universal, S.A., **14** 429
Siboney Shoe Corp., **22** 213
SIBV/MS Holdings, **IV** 295; **19** 226
Sicard Inc., **I** 185
SICC. *See* Univision Communications Inc.
Sichuan Station Wagon Factory, **38** 462
Sick's Brewery, **26** 304
Siclet, **25** 84
Sicma Aero Seat, **36** 529
Siddeley Autocar Co., **III** 508
Sidel. *See* Groupe Sidel S.A.
Sidélor, **IV** 226
Siderbrás, **IV** 125
Siderca S.A.I.C., **41** 405–06
Sidermex, **III** 581
Sidérurgie Maritime, **IV** 26
Sidley Austin Brown & Wood, **40 400–03**
SIDMAR NV, **IV** 128
Siebe plc, **13** 235. *See also* BTR Siebe plc.
Siebel Group, **13** 544–45
Siebel Marketing Group, **27** 195
Siebel Systems, Inc., **38 430–34**
Siebert Financial Corp., **32 423–25**
Siegas, **III** 480; **22** 26
Siegler Heater Corp., **I** 481
Siemens AG, **I** 74, 192, 409–11, 462, 478, 542; **II** 22, 25, 38, 80–82, **97–100**, 122, 257, 279; **III** 139, 154–55, 466, 482, 516, 724; **6** 215–16; **7** 232; **9** 11, 32, 44; **10** 16, 363; **11** 59, 196, 235, 397–98, 460; **12** 546; **13** 402; **14** 169, **444–47 (upd.)**; **15** 125; **16** 392; **18** 32; **19** 166, 313; **20** 290; **22** 19, 373–74; **23** 389, 452, 494–95; **24** 88; **30** 11; **33** 225, 288
The Sierra Club, **28 422–24**
Sierra Designs, Inc., **10** 215–16
Sierra Health Services, Inc., **15 451–53**
Sierra Leone External Telegraph Limited, **25** 100
Sierra Leone Selection Trust, **IV** 66
Sierra On-Line, Inc., **13** 92, 114; **14** 263; **15 454–56**; **16** 146; **29** 75; **41 361–64 (upd.)**
Sierra Pacific Industries, **22 489–91**
Sierrita Resources, Inc., **6** 590
SIFCO Industries, Inc., **41**
Sight & Sound Entertainment, **35** 21
Sigma-Aldrich Corporation, **I 690–91**; **36 429–32 (upd.)**
Sigma Alimentos, S.A. de C.V., **19** 11–12
Sigma Coatings, **IV** 499
Sigma Network Systems, **11** 464
Sigmor Corp., **IV** 410; **31** 455
Signal Companies, Inc. *See* AlliedSignal Inc.
Signal Galaxies, **13** 127
Signal Oil & Gas Inc., **I** 71, 178; **IV** 382; **7** 537; **11** 278; **19** 175; **22** 331
Signalite, Inc., **10** 319
Signature Brands USA Inc., **28** 135; **30** 139
Signature Corporation, **22** 412–13
Signature Group, **V** 145
Signature Health Care Corp., **25** 504
Signet Banking Corporation, **11 446–48**
Signet Communications Corp., **16** 195
Signetics Co., **III** 684; **11** 56; **18** 383
Signode Industries, **III** 519; **22** 282
Sika Finanz AG, **28** 195
SIKEL NV, **IV** 128
Sikes Corporation, **III** 612
Sikorsky Aircraft Corporation, **I** 47, 84, 115, 530; **III** 458, 602; **9** 416; **10** 162; **18** 125; **24 440–43**; **41** 368
SIL&P. *See* Southern Illinois Light & Power Company.
SILA. *See* Swedish Intercontinental Airlines.
Silband Sports Corp., **33** 102
Silenka B.V., **III** 733; **22** 436
Silex. *See* Hamilton Beach/Proctor-Silex Inc.
Silgan Holdings Inc., **26** 59
Silicon Beach Software, **10** 35
Silicon Compiler Systems, **11** 285
Silicon Engineering, **18** 20; **43** 17
Silicon Graphics Inc., **9 471–73**; **10** 119, 257; **12** 323; **15** 149, 320; **16** 137, 140; **20** 8; **25** 96; **28** 320; **38** 69; **43** 151. *See also* SGI.
Silicon Microstructures, Inc., **14** 183
Silicon Systems Inc., **II** 110
Silo Electronics, **16** 73, 75
Silo Holdings, **9** 65; **23** 52
Silo Inc., **V** 50; **10** 306, 468; **19** 123
Silver & Co., **I** 428
Silver Burdett Co., **IV** 672, 675; **7** 528; **19** 405
Silver City Airways. *See* British World Airlines Ltd.
Silver City Casino, **6** 204
Silver Dollar Mining Company, **20** 149
Silver Dolphin, **34** 3, 5
Silver Furniture Co., Inc., **15** 102, 104
Silver King Communications, **25** 213
Silver King Mines, **IV** 76
Silver Screen Partners, **II** 174
Silver's India Rubber Works & Telegraph Cable Co., **I** 428
Silverado Banking, **9** 199
Silverado Partners Acquisition Corp., **22** 80
Silverline, Inc., **16** 33
Silvermans Menswear, Inc., **24** 26
SilverPlatter Information Inc., **23 440–43**
Silvershoe Partners, **17** 245
Silverstar Ltd. S.p.A., **10** 113
Silvertown Rubber Co., **I** 428
Silvey Corp., **III** 350
Simca, **I** 154, 162; **11** 103
Simco S.A., **37 357–59**
Sime Darby Berhad, **14 448–50**; **36 433–36 (upd.)**
Simeira Comercio e Industria Ltda., **22** 320
SIMEL S.A., **14** 27
Simer Pump Company, **19** 360
SIMEST, **24** 311
Simi Winery, Inc., **34** 89
Simicon Co., **26** 153

Simkins Industries, Inc., **8** 174–75
Simmons Co., **34** 407
Simms, **III** 556
Simon & Schuster Inc., II 155; **IV 671–72; 13** 559; **19 403–05 (upd.); 23** 503; **28** 158
Simon Adhesive Products, **IV** 253; **17** 30
Simon de Wit, **II** 641
Simon DeBartolo Group Inc., **26** 146; **27** 401
Simon Engineering, **11** 510
Simon Marketing, Inc., **19** 112, 114
Simon Property Group, Inc., 27 399–402
Simon Transportation Services Inc., 27 403–06
Simonius'sche Cellulosefabriken AG, **IV** 324
Simonize, **I** 371
Simons Inc., **26** 412
AB Simpele, **IV** 347
Simple Shoes, Inc., **22** 173
Simplex Industries, Inc., **16** 296
Simplex Technologies Inc., 21 460–63
Simplex Wire and Cable Co., **III** 643–45
Simplicity Pattern Company, **I** 447; **8** 349; **23** 98; **29** 134
Simpson Investment Company, 17 438–41
Simpson Marketing, **12** 553
Simpson Thacher & Bartlett, 27 327; **39 365–68**
Simpsons, **V** 80; **25** 221
Sims Telephone Company, **14** 258
Simsmetal USA Corporation, **19** 380
SimuFlite, **II** 10
Simula, Inc., 41 368–70
Sinai Kosher Foods, **14** 537
Sincat, **IV** 453
Sinclair Broadcast Group, Inc., 25 417–19
Sinclair Coal Co., **IV** 170; **10** 447–48
Sinclair Crude Oil Purchasing Co., **IV** 369
Sinclair Oil Corp., **I** 355, 569; **IV** 376, 394, 456–57, 512, 575
Sinclair Paint Company, **12** 219
Sinclair Petrochemicals Inc., **IV** 456
Sinclair Pipe Line Co., **IV** 368–69
Sinclair Research Ltd., **III** 113
Sindo Ricoh Co., **III** 160
Sing Tao Holdings Ltd., **29** 470–71
Singapore Airlines Ltd., 6 100, **117–18,** 123; **12** 192; **20** 313; **24** 399; **26** 115; **27** 26, **407–09 (upd.),** 464, 466; **29** 301; **38** 26
Singapore Alpine Electronics Asia Pte. Ltd., **13** 31
Singapore Candle Company, **12** 393
Singapore Cement, **III** 718
Singapore Petroleum Co., **IV** 452
Singapore Straits Steamship Company, **6** 117
Singapore Telecom, **18** 348
Singapour, **II** 556
Singareni Collieries Ltd., **IV** 48–49
Singer & Friedlander Group plc, I 592; **41 371–73**
Singer Company, **I** 540; **II** 9–11; **6** 27, 241; **9** 232; **11** 150; **13** 521–22; **19** 211; **22** 4; **26** 3; **29** 190. *See also* Bicoastal Corp.
The Singer Company N.V., 30 417–20 (upd.)
Singer Controls, **I** 155
Singer Hardware & Supply Co., **9** 542
Singer Sewing Machine Co., **12** 46
Singer Supermarkets, **25** 235
Single Service Containers Inc., **IV** 286
Singleton Seafood, **II** 494
Singular Software, **9** 80
Sinister Games, **41** 409
Sinkers Inc., **21** 68
Sinochem. *See* China National Chemicals Import and Export Corp.
Sintel, S.A., **19** 256
Sioux City Gas and Electric Company, **6** 523–24
SIP. *See* Società Italiana per L'Esercizio delle Telecommunicazioni p.A.
Siporex, S.A., **31** 253
Sir Speedy, Inc., 16 448–50; 33 231
SIRCOMA, **10** 375
SIREM, **23** 95
The Sirena Apparel Group Inc., **25** 245
Sirloin Stockade, **10** 331
Sirrine. *See* CRSS Inc.
Sirrine Environmental Consultants, **9** 110
Sirte Oil Co., **IV** 454
Sisters Chicken & Biscuits, **8** 564
Sisters of Bon Secours USA. *See* Bon Secours Health System, Inc.
SIT-Siemens. *See* Italtel.
Sitca Corporation, **16** 297
Sithe Energies, Inc., **24** 327
Sitmar Cruises, **22** 445
Sitzmann & Heinlein GmbH, **IV** 198–99
Six Companies, Inc., **IV** 121; **7** 355
Six Flags Theme Parks, Inc., III 431; **IV** 676; **17 442–44**
600 Fanuc Robotics, **III** 482–83
Six Industries, Inc., **26** 433
61 Going to the Game!, **14** 293
Sixt AG, 39 369–72
Sizes Unlimited, **V** 115
Sizzler International Inc., **15** 361–62
SJB Equities, Inc., **30** 53
The SK Equity Fund, L.P., **23** 177
Skånes Enskilda Bank, **II** 351
Skånska Ättiksfabriken, **I** 385
Skadden, Arps, Slate, Meagher & Flom, 10 126–27; **18 486–88; 27** 325, 327
Skaggs-Albertson's Properties, **II** 604
Skaggs Companies, **22** 37
Skaggs Drug Centers, Inc., **II** 602–04; **7** 20; **27** 291; **30** 25–27
Skagit Nuclear Power Plant, **6** 566
Skandia, **25** 85
Skandinaviska Enskilda Banken, II 351–53, 365–66; **IV** 203
Skanska AB, IV 204; **25** 463; **32** 396; **38 435–38**
Skanza Mammoet Transport Sdn Bhd, **26** 280
Skechers U.S.A. Inc., 31 413–15
Skelly Oil Co., **IV** 575
Sketchley plc, **19** 124
SKF. *See* Aktiebolaget SKF.
SKF Industries Inc. *See* AB Volvo.
Ski-Doo. *See* Bombardier Inc.
Skidmore, Owings & Merrill, 13 475–76
Skil-Craft Playthings, Inc., **13** 560
Skillern, **16** 560
Skillware, **9** 326
Skinner Macaroni Co., **II** 511
Skis Rossignol S.A., 15 460–62; 43 373–76 (upd.)
Skoda Auto a.s., 39 373–75
SKODA Group, **37** 399–400
Skönvik, **IV** 338
SKS Group, **20** 363
SKW Nature's Products, Inc., **25** 332
SKW-Trostberg AG, **IV** 232
Sky Channel, **IV** 652
Sky Chefs, Inc., **16** 397
Sky Climber Inc., **11** 436
Sky Courier, **6** 345
Sky Merchant, Inc., **V** 78
Sky Television, **IV** 652–53; **7** 391–92
Skyband, Inc., **IV** 652; **7** 391; **12** 359
SkyBox International Inc., **15** 72–73
Skylight, **25** 508
Skyline Corporation, 30 421–23
Skyline Homes, **17** 82
SkyMall, Inc., 26 439–41; 28 241
Skypak, **27** 474
Skyservice Airlines Inc., **42** 327
SkyTel Corp., **18** 349; **23** 212
Skywalker Sound, **12** 322
Skyway Airlines, **6** 78; **11** 299; **32** 335; **35** 293–94
SkyWest, Inc., 25 420–24
SL Holdings. *See* Finlay Enterprises, Inc.
Slade Gorton & Company, **13** 243
Slater Co. Foods, **II** 607
Slater Electric, **21** 349
Slater Systems, Inc., **13** 48
Sleepy's Inc., 32 426–28
Slick Airways, **6** 388; **25** 146
Slim-Fast Nutritional Foods International, Inc., 12 531; **18 489–91; 27** 196
Slim Jim, Inc. *See* GoodMark Foods, Inc.
Slingerland Drum Company, **16** 239
Slip-X Safety Treads, **9** 72
SLJFB Vedrenne, **22** 344
SLM Holding Corp., 25 425–28 (upd.)
SLM International Inc. *See* The Hockey Company.
SLN-Peñarroya, **IV** 108
Sloan's Supermarkets Inc. *See* Gristede's Sloan's, Inc.
Sloman Neptun Schiffahrts, **26** 279
Slope Indicator Company, **26** 42
Sloss Industries Corporation, **22** 544
Slots-A-Fun, **6** 204
Slough Estates plc, IV 722–25
AB Small Business Investment Co., Inc., **13** 111–12
Small Tube Products, Inc., **23** 517
SMALLCO, **III** 340
Smalley Transportation Company, **6** 421–23
SMAN. *See* Societe Mecanique Automobile du Nord.
Smart & Final, Inc., 12 153–54; **16 451–53**
Smart Communications, **18** 180, 182
Smart Shirts Ltd., **8** 288–89
Smart Talk Network, Inc., **16** 319
SmartCash, **18** 543
SmartForce PLC, 43 377–80
SmarTTarget Marketing, **36** 342
Smead Manufacturing Co., 17 445–48
Smed International, **39** 207
Smedley's, **II** 513
Smethwick Drop Forgings, **III** 494
SMH. *See* The Swatch Group SA.
SMI Industries, **25** 15
Smiles Holdings Ltd., **38** 501
Smirnoff, **14** 212; **18** 41
Smit International, **26** 241
Smith and Bell Insurance, **41** 178, 180
Smith & Butterfield Co., Inc., **28** 74

Smith & Hawken, **10** 215, 217
Smith & Nephew plc, 17 449–52; 41 374–78 (upd.)
Smith & Wesson Corporation, 30 424–27
Smith & Weston, **19** 430
Smith & Wollensky Operating Corp., **32** 362
Smith Barney Inc., I 614; **III** 569; **6** 410; **10** 63; **13** 328; **15 463–65**; **19** 385; **20** 360; **22** 406
Smith Bros., **I** 711
Smith Corona Corp., III 502; **7** 209; **13 477–80**; **14** 76; **23** 210
Smith-Higgins, **III** 9–10
Smith International, Inc., III 429; **15 466–68**
Smith Mackenzie & Co., **III** 522
Smith McDonell Stone and Co., **14** 97
Smith Meter Co., **11** 4
Smith New Court PLC, **13** 342; **40** 313
Smith Packaging Ltd., **14** 429
Smith Parts Co., **11** 3
Smith Transfer Corp., **II** 607–08; **13** 49
Smith Wall Associates, **32** 145
Smith's Food & Drug Centers, Inc., 8 472–74; **17** 558, 561; **24** 36; **26** 432
Smith's Stampings, **III** 494
Smithfield Foods, Inc., 7 477–78, 524–25; **22** 509, 511; **43** 25, **381–84 (upd.)**
SmithKline Beckman Corporation, I 389, 636, 640, 644, 646, 657, **692–94**, 696; **II** 331; **III** 65–66; **14** 46, 53; **26** 391; **30** 29–31
SmithKline Beecham plc, III 65–67; **8** 210; **9** 347; **10** 47, 471; **11** 9, 90, 337; **13** 77; **14** 58; **16** 438; **17** 287; **24** 88; **25** 82; **32** 212–13, **429–34 (upd.)**; **36** 91; **38** 362
Smiths Bank, **II** 333
Smiths Food Group, Ltd., **II** 502; **10** 323
Smiths Industries PLC, III 555; **25 429–31**
Smithsonian Institution, 27 410–13
Smithway Motor Xpress Corporation, 39 376–79
Smitty's Super Valu Inc., **II** 663–64; **12** 391; **17** 560–61
Smittybilt, Incorporated, **40** 299–300
SMP Clothing, Inc., **22** 462
SMS, **IV** 226; **7** 401
Smucker. *See* The J.M. Smucker Company.
Smurfit Companies. *See* Jefferson Smurfit Group plc.
Smurfit-Stone Container Corporation, 26 442–46 (upd.)
SN Repal. *See* Société Nationale de Recherche de Pétrole en Algérie.
Snack Ventures Europe, **10** 324; **36** 234, 237
Snake River Sugar Company, **19** 468
Snam Montaggi, **IV** 420
Snam Progetti, **IV** 420, 422
Snap-On, Incorporated, 27 414–16 (upd.); **32** 397
Snap-on Tools Corporation, III 628; **7 479–80**; **25** 34
Snapper, **I** 447
Snapple Beverage Corporation, 11 449–51; **12** 411; **24** 480; **27** 153; **31** 243; **34** 366; **39** 383, 386
Snapps Drive-Thru, **25** 389
Snappy Car Rental, Inc., **6** 393; **25** 142–43. *See also* Republic Industries, Inc.
SNE Enterprises, Inc., **12** 397
SNEA. *See* Société Nationale Elf Aquitaine.
Snecma Group, **17** 482
Snell & Wilmer L.L.P., 28 425–28
Snell Acoustics, **22** 99
SNET. *See* Southern New England Telecommunications Corporation.
SNMC Management Corporation, **11** 121
Snoqualmie Falls Plant, **6** 565
Snow Brand Milk Products Company, Limited, II 574–75
Snow King Frozen Foods, **II** 480; **26** 57
Snow White Dairies Inc. *See* Dairy Mart Convenience Stores, Inc.
Snowy Mountains Hydroelectric Authority, **IV** 707; **13** 118
SNPA, **IV** 453
Snyder Communications, **35** 462, 465
Snyder Oil Corporation, **24** 379–81
Snyder's of Hanover, **35** 213
SnyderGeneral Corp., **8** 321. *See also* AAF-McQuay Incorporated.
Soap Opera Magazine, **10** 287
Sobrom, **I** 341
Sobu Railway Company, **6** 431
Socal. *See* Standard Oil Company (California).
Socamel-Rescaset, **40** 214, 216
SOCAR, **IV** 505
Sochiku, **9** 30
Sociade Intercontinental de Compressores Hermeticos SICOM, S.A., **8** 515
La Sociale di A. Mondadori & C., **IV** 585
La Sociale, **IV** 585
Sociedad Aeronáutica de Medellín, S.A., **36** 53
Sociedad Alfa-Laval, **III** 419
Sociedad Bilbaina General de Credito, **II** 194
Sociedad Española de Automobiles del Turismo S.A. (SEAT), **I** 207, 459–60; **6** 47–48; **11** 550
Sociedad Financiera Mexicana, **19** 189
Sociedade Anónima Concessionária de Refinacao em Portugal. *See* SACOR.
Sociedade de Lubrificantes e Combustiveis, **IV** 505
Sociedade Nacional de Petróleos, **IV** 504
Sociedade Portuguesa de Petroquimica, **IV** 505
Società Anonima Fabbrica Italiana di Automobili, **I** 161
Società Anonima Lombarda Fabbrica Automobili, **13** 27
Società Azionaria Imprese Perforazioni, **IV** 419–20
Società Concessioni e Costruzioni Autostrade, **I** 466
Società Edison, **II** 86
Societa Esercizio Fabbriche Automobili e Corse Ferrari, **13** 219
Società Finanziaria Idrocarburi, **IV** 421
Società Finanziaria Telefonica per Azioni, I 465–66; **V 325–27**
Società Generale di Credito Mobiliare, **II** 191
Società Idrolettrica Piemonte, **I** 465–66
Societa Industria Meccanica Stampaggio S.p.A., **24** 500
Societa Italiana Gestione Sistemi Multi Accesso, **6** 69
Società Italiana per L'Esercizio delle Telecommunicazioni p.A., **I** 466–67; **V** 325–27
Società Italiana per la Infrastrutture e l'Assetto del Territoria, **I** 466
Società Italiana Pirelli, **V** 249
Società Italiana Vetro, **IV** 421
Società Nazionale Metanodotti, **IV** 419–21
Società Ravennate Metano, **IV** 420
Società Reale Mutua, **III** 207
Société Africaine de Déroulage des Ets Rougier, **21** 439
Société Air France, 27 417–20 (upd.). *See also* Groupe Air France.
Société Alsacienne de Magasins SA, **19** 308
Societe Anonima Italiana Ing. Nicola Romeo & Company, **13** 27
Societe Anonomie Alfa Romeo, **13** 28
Societe Anonyme Automobiles Citroen, **7** 35–36. *See also* PSA Peugeot Citroen S.A.
Société Anonyme Belge des Magasins Prisunic-Uniprix, **26** 159
Société Anonyme de la Manufactures des Glaces et Produits Chimiques de Saint-Gobain, Chauny et Cirey. *See* Compagnie de Saint-Gobain S.A.
Société Anonyme des Ciments Luxembourgeois, **IV** 25
Société Anonyme des Fermiers Reúnis, **23** 219
Société Anonyme des Hauts Fourneaux et Aciéries de Differdange-St. Ingbert-Rumelange, **IV** 26
Société Anonyme des Hauts Fourneaux et Forges de Dudelange, **22** 42
Société Anonyme des Mines du Luxembourg et des Forges de Sarrebruck, **IV** 24; **22** 42
La Societe Anonyme Francaise Holophane, **19** 211
Societe Anonyme Francaise Timken, **8** 530
Société Anonyme Telecommunications, **III** 164
Société, Auxiliaire d'Entrepreses SA, **13** 206
Société Belge de Banque, **II** 294–95
Société BIC, S.A., **III** 29; **8** 60–61; **23** 55–57
Société Calédonia, **IV** 107
Société Centrale d'Investissement, **29** 48
Société Centrale Union des Assurances de Paris, **III** 391, 393
Société Chimiques des Usines du Rhône, **I** 388
Société Civil des Mousquetaires. *See* ITM Entreprises SA.
Société Civile Valoptec, **21** 222
Societe Commerciale Citroen, **7** 36
Société Congolaise des Grands Magasins Au Bon Marché, **26** 159
Société d'Emboutissage de Bourgogne. *See* Groupe SEB.
Société d'Investissement de Travaux Publics, **31** 128
Société d'Ougrée-Marihaye, **IV** 51
Société de Collecte des Prodicteirs de Preval, **19** 50
Societe de Construction des Batignolles, **II** 93
Societé de Crédit Agricole, **II** 264

Société de Développements et d'Innovations des Marchés Agricoles et Alimentaires, **II** 576
Société de Diffusion de Marques, **II** 576
Société de Diffusion Internationale Agro-Alimentaire, **II** 577
Societé de garantie des Crédits à court terme, **II** 233
Société de l'Oléoduc de la Sarre a.r.l., **IV** 197
Société de Prospection Électrique, **III** 616; **17** 416
La Société de Traitement des Minerais de Nickel, Cobalt et Autres, **IV** 107
Société des Caves de Roquefort, **24** 444
Société des Caves et des Producteurs Reunis de Roquefort, **19** 49
Société des Ciments Français, **33** 339
Société des Eaux d'Evian, **II** 474
Société des Etablissements Gaumont. *See* Gaumont SA.
Société des Forges d'Eich–Metz et Cie, **IV** 24
Société des Forges et Aciéries du Nord-Est, **IV** 226
Société des Forges et Fonderies de Montataire, **IV** 226
Société des Grandes Entreprises de Distribution, Inno-France, **V** 58
Société des Hauts Fourneaux et Forges de Denain-Anzin, **IV** 226
Société des Immeubles de France, **37** 357, 359
Société des Mines du Luxembourg et de Sarrebruck, **IV** 25
Société des Pétroles d'Afrique Equatoriale, **IV** 545; **7** 482
Société des Usines Chimiques des Laboratoires Français, **I** 669
Société des Vins de France, **I** 281
Société du Louvre, **27 421–23**
Société Economique de Rennes, **19** 98
Société Électrométallurgique Francaise, **IV** 173
Société European de Semi-Remorques, **7** 513
Société Européenne de Brasseries, **II** 474–75
Société Européenne de Production de L'avion E.C.A.T. *See* SEPECAT.
Société Financiére Européenne, **II** 202–03, 233
Societe Financiere pour l caise pour l'Exploitation du Pétrole, **IV** 557
Société Gélis-Poudenx-Sans, **IV** 108
Société General de Banque, **17** 324
Société Générale, **II** 233, 266, 295, **354–56**; **9** 148; **13** 203, 206; **19** 51; **33** 118–19; **42 347–51 (upd.)**
Société Générale de Banque, **II** 279, 295, 319; **14** 169
Société Générale de Belgique S.A., **II** 270, 294–95; **IV** 26; **10** 13; **22** 44; **26** 368; **27** 11; **36** 456
Société Générale des Entreprises. *See* Vinci.
Société Générale du Telephones, **21** 231
Société Générale pour favoriser l'Industrie nationale, **II** 294
Societe-Hydro-Air S.a.r.L., **9** 27
Société Industrielle Belge des Pétroles, **IV** 498–99
Société Internationale Pirelli S.A., **V** 250
Société Irano-Italienne des Pétroles, **IV** 466
Société Laitière Vendômoise, **23** 219
Société Le Nickel, **IV** 107–08, 110
Societe Mecanique Automobile de l'Est/du Nord, **7** 37
Société Métallurgique, **IV** 25–26, 227
Société Minière de Bakwanga, **IV** 67
Société Minière des Terres Rouges, **IV** 25–26
Société Nationale de Programmes de Télévision Française 1. *See* Télévision Française 1.
Société Nationale de Recherche de Pétrole en Algérie, **IV** 545, 559; **7** 482
Société Nationale de Transport et de Commercialisation des Hydrocarbures, **IV** 423
Société Nationale des Chemins de Fer Français, **V 512–15**
Société Nationale des Pétroles d'Aquitaine, **21** 203–05
Société Nationale Elf Aquitaine, **I** 303–04, 670, 676–77; **II** 260; **IV** 174, 397–98, 424, 451, 453–54, 472–74, 499, 506, 515–16, 518, 525, 535, **544–47**, 559–60; **V** 628; **7 481–85 (upd.)**; **8** 452; **11** 97; **12** 153
Société Nationale pour la Recherche, la Production, le Transport, la Transformation et la Commercialisation des Hydrocarbures, **IV** 423–24
Société Nord Africaine des Ciments Lafarge, **III** 703
Société Nouvelle d'Achat de Bijouterie, **16** 207
Société Nouvelle des Etablissements Gaumont. *See* Gaumont SA.
Société Parisienne d'Achats en Commun, **19** 307
Societe Parisienne pour l'Industrie Electrique, **II** 93
Société Parisienne Raveau-Cartier, **31** 128
Société pour l'Eportation de Grandes Marques, **I** 281
Société pour l'Étude et la Realisation d'Engins Balistiques. *See* SEREB.
Société pour L'Exploitation de la Cinquième Chaîne, **6** 374
Société pour le Financement de l'Industrie Laitière, **19** 51
Société Samos, **23** 219
Société Savoyarde des Fromagers du Reblochon, **25** 84
Société Succursaliste S.A. d'Approvisonnements Guyenne et Gascogne. *See* Guyenne et Gascogne.
Société Suisse de Microelectronique & d'Horlogerie. *See* The Swatch Group SA.
Société Tefal. *See* Groupe SEB.
Societe Vendeenne des Embalages, **9** 305
Society Corporation, **9 474–77**
Society of Lloyd's, **III** 278–79
SOCO Chemical Inc., **8** 69
Socombel, **IV** 497
Socony. *See* Standard Oil Co. (New York).
Socony Mobil Oil Co., Inc., **IV** 465; **7** 353
Socony-Vacuum Oil Company. *See* Mobil Corporation.
Sodak Gaming, Inc., **9** 427; **41** 216
Sodastream Holdings, **II** 477
Sodexho Alliance SA, **23** 154; **29 442–44**
Sodiaal S.A., **II** 577; **19** 50; **36 437–39 (upd.)**
SODIMA. *See* Sodiaal S.A.
Sodiso, **23** 247
Sodyeco, **I** 673
Soekor, **IV** 93
Soffo, **22** 365
Soficom, **27** 136
SOFIL. *See* Société pour le Financement de l'Industrie Laitière.
Sofimex. *See* Sociedad Financiera Mexicana.
Sofiran, **IV** 467
Sofitam, S.A., **21** 493, 495
Sofitels. *See* Accor SA.
Sofrem, **IV** 174
Soft Lenses Inc., **25** 55
Soft Sheen Products, Inc., **31 416–18**
Soft*Switch, **25** 301
Softbank Corp., **12** 562; **13 481–83**; **16** 168; **27** 516, 518; **36** 523; **38 439–44 (upd.)**
Softimage Inc., **38** 71–72
SoftKat. *See* Baker & Taylor, Inc.
SoftKey Software Products Inc., **24** 276
Softsel Computer Products, **12** 334–35
SoftSolutions Technology Corporation, **10** 558
Software AG, **11** 18
Software Arts, **6** 254; **25** 299
Software Development Pty., Ltd., **15** 107
Software Dimensions, Inc. *See* ASK Group, Inc.
Software, Etc., **13** 545
The Software Group Inc., **23** 489, 491
Software International, **6** 224
Software Plus, Inc., **10** 514
Software Publishing Corp., **14** 262
Softwood Holdings Ltd., **III** 688
Sogara S.A., **23** 246–48
Sogebra S.A., **I** 257
Sogedis, **23** 219
Sogen International Corp., **II** 355
Sogexport, **II** 355
Soginnove, **II** 355–56
Sogo Co., **42** 342
Sohio Chemical Company, **13** 502
Sohken Kako Co., Ltd., **IV** 327
Soil Teq, Inc., **17** 10
Soilserv, Inc. *See* Mycogen Corporation.
Soinlahti Sawmill and Brick Works, **IV** 300
Sola Holdings, **III** 727
Solair Inc., **14** 43; **37** 30–31
La Solana Corp., **IV** 726
Solar, **IV** 614
Solar Electric Corp., **13** 398
Solaray, Inc., **37** 284–85
Solectron Corp., **12** 161–62, **450–52**; **38** 186, 189
Solel Boneh Construction, **II** 47; **25** 266–67
Soletanche Co., **I** 586
Solid Beheer B.V., **10** 514
Solid State Dielectrics, **I** 329; **8** 152
Solite Corp., **23** 224–25
Söll, **40** 96, 98
Sollac, **IV** 226–27; **24** 144; **25** 96
Solley's Delicatessen and Bakery, **24** 243
Solmer, **IV** 227
Solo Serve Corporation, **23** 177; **28 429–31**
Soloman Brothers, **17** 561
Solomon Smith Barney Inc., **22** 404
Solomon Valley Milling Company, **6** 592
Solon Automated Services, **II** 607
Solsound Industries, **16** 393

Soltam, **25** 266
Solutia Inc., **29** 330
Solvay & Cie S.A., I 303, **394–96,** 414–15; **III** 677; **IV** 300; **16** 121; **21** 254, **464–67 (upd.)**
Solvay Animal Health Inc., **12** 5
Solvent Resource Recovery, Inc., **9** 109
Solvents Recovery Service of New Jersey, Inc., **8** 464
SOMABRI, **12** 152
SOMACA, **12** 152
Somali Bank, **31** 220
Someal, **27** 513, 515
Somerville Electric Light Company, **12** 45
Somerville Packaging Group, **28** 420
Sommer-Allibert S.A., 19 406–09; **22** 49; **25** 462, 464
Sommers Drug Stores, **9** 186
SONAP, **IV** 504–06
Sonat, Inc., 6 577–78; **22** 68
Sonatrach. *See* Entreprise Nationale Sonatrach.
Sonecor Systems, **6** 340
Sonesson, **I** 211
Sonet Media AB, **23** 390
Sonic Corp., 37 14 451–53; **16** 387; **360–63 (upd.)**
Sonic Restaurants, **31** 279
Sonneborn Chemical and Refinery Co., **I** 405
Sonnen Basserman, **II** 475
SonnenBraune, **22** 460
Sonoco Products Company, 8 475–77; **12** 150–51; **16** 340
The Sonoma Group, **25** 246
Sonoma Mortgage Corp., **II** 382
Sonometrics Inc., **I** 667
Sony Corporation, I 30, 534; **II** 56, 58, 91–92, **101–03**, 117–19, 124, 134, 137, 440; **III** 141, 143, 340, 658; **6** 30; **7** 118; **9** 385; **10** 86, 119, 403; **11** 46, 490–91, 557; **12** 75, 161, 448, **453–56 (upd.)**; **13** 399, 403, 482, 573; **14** 534; **16** 94; **17** 533; **18** 18; **19** 67; **20** 439; **21** 129; **22** 194; **24** 4; **25** 22; **26** 188, 433, 489, 511; **28** 241; **30** 18; **31** 239; **40 404–10 (upd.)**; **43** 15
Sonzogno, **IV** 585
Soo Line, **V** 429–30; **24** 533
Soo Line Mills, **II** 631
Sooner Trailer Manufacturing Co., **29** 367
Soparind, **25** 83–85
Sope Creek, **30** 457
SOPEAL, **III** 738
Sophia Jocoba GmbH, **IV** 193
SOPI, **IV** 401
SOPORCEL, **34** 38–39
Sopwith Aviation Co., **III** 507–08
Soravie, **II** 265
Sorbents Products Co. Inc., **31** 20
Sorbus, **6** 242
Sorcim, **6** 224
Soreal, **8** 344
Sorenson Research Company, **36** 496
Sorg Paper Company. *See* Mosinee Paper Corporation.
Soriana. *See* Organización Soriana, S.A. de C.V.
Soros Fund Management LLC, 27 198; **28 432–34**; **43** 218
Sorrento, Inc., 19 51; **24 444–46**; **26** 505
SOS Co., **II** 531
SOS Staffing Services, 25 432–35
Sosa, Bromley, Aguilar & Associates, **6** 22
Soterra, Inc., **15** 188
Sotheby's Holdings, Inc., 11 452–54; **15** 98–100; **29 445–48 (upd.)**; **32** 164; **39** 81–84
Sound Advice, Inc., 41 379–82
Sound of Music Inc. *See* Best Buy Co., Inc.
Sound Trek, **16** 74
Sound Video Unlimited, **16** 46; **43** 60
Sound Warehouse, **9** 75
Souplantation Incorporated. *See* Garden Fresh Restaurant Corporation.
Source One Mortgage Services Corp., **12** 79
Source Perrier, **7** 383; **24** 444
Souriau, **19** 166
South African Airways Ltd., **6** 84, 433, 435; **27** 132
The South African Breweries Limited, I 287–89, 422; **24 447–51 (upd.)**; **26** 462
South African Coal, Oil and Gas Corp., **IV** 533
South African Railways, **6** 434–35
South African Torbanite Mining and Refining Co., **IV** 534
South African Transport Services, **6** 433, 435
South American Cable Co., **I** 428
South Asia Tyres, **20** 263
South Bend Toy Manufacturing Company, **25** 380
South Carolina Electric & Gas Company, **6** 574–76
South Carolina Industries, **IV** 333
South Carolina National Corporation, **16** 523, 526
South Carolina Power Company, **38** 446–47
South Central Bell Telephone Co. **V** 276–78
South Central Railroad Co., **14** 325
South China Morning Post (Holdings) Ltd., **II** 298; **IV** 652; **7** 392
South Coast Gas Compression Company, Inc., **11** 523
South Coast Terminals, Inc., **16** 475
South Dakota Public Service Company, **6** 524
South Fulton Light & Power Company, **6** 514
South Improvement Co., **IV** 427
South Jersey Industries, Inc., 42 352–55
South Manchuria Railroad Co. Ltd., **IV** 434
South of Scotland Electricity Board, **19** 389–90
South Penn Oil Co., **IV** 488–89
South Puerto Rico Sugar Co., **I** 452
South Puerto Rico Telephone Co., **I** 462
South Sea Textile, **III** 705
South Texas Stevedore Co., **IV** 81
South Wales Electric Company, **34** 219
South Western Electricity plc, **38** 448; **41** 316
South-Western Publishing Co., **8** 526–28
Southam Inc., 7 486–89; **15** 265; **24** 223; **36** 374
Southco, **II** 602–03; **7** 20–21; **30** 26
Southcorp Holdings Ltd., **17** 373; **22** 350
Southdown, Inc., 14 454–56
Southeast Bank of Florida, **11** 112
Southeast Banking Corp., **II** 252; **14** 103
Southeast Public Service Company, **8** 536
Southeastern Personnel. *See* Norrell Corporation.
Southeastern Power and Light Company, **6** 447; **23** 28
Southeastern Telephone Company, **6** 312
Southern and Phillips Gas Ltd., **13** 485
Southern Australia Airlines, **24** 396
Southern Bank, **10** 426
Southern Bearings Co., **13** 78
Southern Bell, **10** 202
Southern Biscuit Co., **II** 631
Southern Blvd. Supermarkets, Inc., **22** 549
Southern Box Corp., **13** 441
Southern California Edison Co., **II** 402; **V** 711, 713–15, 717; **11** 272; **12** 106; **35** 479
Southern California Financial Corporation, **27** 46
Southern California Fruit Growers Exchange. *See* Sunkist Growers, Inc.
Southern California Gas Co., **I** 569; **25** 413–14, 416
Southern Casualty Insurance Co., **III** 214
Southern Clay Products, **III** 691
Southern Clays Inc., **IV** 82
Southern Co., **24** 525
Southern Colorado Power Company, **6** 312
Southern Comfort Corp., **I** 227
The Southern Company, 38 445–49 (upd.)
Southern Connecticut Newspapers Inc., **IV** 677
Southern Cotton Co., **IV** 224; **24** 488
Southern Cotton Oil Co., **I** 421; **11** 23
Southern Cross Paints, **38** 98
Southern Discount Company of Atlanta, **9** 229
Southern Electric PLC, 13 484–86
Southern Electric Supply Co., **15** 386
Southern Electronics Corp. *See* SED International Holdings, Inc.
Southern Equipment & Supply Co., **19** 344
Southern Extract Co., **IV** 310; **19** 266
Southern Forest Products, Inc., **6** 577
Southern Gage, **III** 519; **22** 282
Southern Graphic Arts, **13** 405
Southern Guaranty Cos., **III** 404
Southern Idaho Water Power Company, **12** 265
Southern Illinois Light & Power Company, **6** 504
Southern Indiana Gas and Electric Company, 13 487–89
Southern Japan Trust Bank, **V** 114
Southern Kraft Corp., **IV** 286
Southern Lumber Company, **8** 430
Southern Manufacturing Company, **8** 458
Southern Minnesota Beet Sugar Cooperative, **32** 29
Southern National Bankshares of Atlanta, **II** 337; **10** 425
Southern Natural Gas Co., **III** 558; **6** 447–48, 577
Southern Nevada Power Company, **11** 343
Southern Nevada Telephone Company, **6** 313; **11** 343
Southern New England Telecommunications Corporation, 6 338–40
Southern Nitrogen Co., **IV** 123
Southern Oregon Broadcasting Co., **7** 15
Southern Pacific Communications Corporation, **9** 478–79

Southern Pacific Rail Corp., **12** 18–20. *See also* Union Pacific Corporation.
Southern Pacific Railroad, **I** 13; **II** 329, 381, 448; **IV** 625; **19** 202
Southern Pacific Transportation Company, V 516–18; **12** 278; **26** 235; **37** 312
Southern Peru Copper Corp.,
Southern Peru Copper Corporation, IV 3; **40** 220, 222, **411–13**
Southern Phenix Textiles Inc., **15** 247–48
Southern Pine Lumber Co., **IV** 341
Southern Power Company. *See* Duke Energy Corporation.
Southern Railway Company, **V** 484–85; **29** 359
Southern Science Applications, Inc., **22** 88
Southern States Cooperative Incorporated, 36 440–42
Southern States Trust Co., **II** 336
Southern Sun Hotel Corporation. *See* South African Breweries Ltd. and *Sun International Hotels Limited.*
Southern Surety Co., **III** 332
Southern Telephone Company, **14** 257
Southern Television Corp., **II** 158; **IV** 650; **7** 389
Southern Union Company, **12** 542; **27 424–26**
Southern Utah Fuel Co., **IV** 394
Southern Video Partnership, **9** 74
Southern Water plc, **19** 389–91
Southgate Medical Laboratory System, **26** 391
The Southland Corporation, **II** 449, 620, **660–61**; **IV** 392, 508; **V** 89; **7** 114, 374, **490–92 (upd.)**; **9** 178; **13** 333, 449, 525; **23** 406–07; **25** 125; **26** 447; **31** 115, 231; **42** 191. *See also* 7- Eleven, Inc.
Southland Mobilcom Inc., **15** 196
Southland Paper, **13** 118
Southland Royal Company, **27** 86
Southland Royalty Co., **10** 190
Southlife Holding Co., **III** 218
Southmark Corp., **11** 483; **33** 398
Southtrust Corporation, 11 455–57
Southview Pulp Co., **IV** 329
Southwest Airlines Co., **I** 106; **6** 72–74, **119–21**; **21** 143; **22** 22; **24 452–55 (upd.)**; **25** 404; **26** 308, 439–40; **33** 301–02; **35** 383
Southwest Airmotive Co., **II** 16
Southwest Convenience Stores, LLC, **26** 368
Southwest Converting, **19** 414
Southwest Enterprise Associates, **13** 191
Southwest Forest Industries, **IV** 287, 289, 334
Southwest Gas Corporation, 19 410–12
Southwest Hide Co., **16** 546
Southwest Potash Corp., **IV** 18; **6** 148–49
Southwestern Bell Corporation, V 328–30; **6** 324; **10** 431, 500; **14** 489; **17** 110; **18** 22. *See also* SBC Communications Inc.
Southwestern Bell Publications, **26** 520
Southwestern Electric Power Co., 21 468–70
Southwestern Gas Pipeline, **7** 344
Southwestern Illinois Coal Company, **7** 33
Southwestern Life Insurance, **I** 527; **III** 136
Southwestern Pipe, **III** 498
Southwestern Public Service Company, 6 579–81
Southwestern Refining Company, Inc., **IV** 446; **22** 303
Southwestern Textile Company, **12** 393
Southwire Company, Inc., 8 478–80; **12** 353; **23 444–47 (upd.)**
Souvall Brothers, **8** 473
Sovereign Corp., **III** 221; **14** 109; **37** 84
Sovran Financial, **10** 425–26
SovTransavto, **6** 410
Soyland Power Cooperative, **6** 506
SP Reifenwerke, **V** 253
SP Tyres, **V** 253
Space Control GmbH, **28** 243–44
Space Craft Inc., **9** 463
Space Data Corporation, **22** 401
Space Systems Corporation. *See* Orbital Sciences Corporation.
Space Systems/Loral, **9** 325
Spacehab, Inc., 37 364–66
Spacemakers Inc., **IV** 287
Spaghetti Warehouse, Inc., 25 436–38
Spagnesi, **18** 258
Spago. *See* The Wolfgang Puck Food Company, Inc.
Spalding & Evenflo, **24** 530
Spalding, Inc., **17** 243; **23** 449
Spanish Broadcasting System, Inc., 41 383–86
Spanish International Communications Corp. *See* Univision Communications Inc.
Spanish River Pulp and Paper Mills, **IV** 246; **25** 10
SPAO, **39** 184
Spar Aerospace Limited, 32 435–37
SPAR Handels AG, 35 398–401; **36** 296
Sparbanken Bank, **18** 543
SPARC International, **7** 499
Spare Change, **10** 282
Sparklets Ltd., **I** 315; **25** 80
Sparks Computerized Car Care Centers, **25** 445
Sparks Family Hospital, **6** 191
Sparks-Withington Company. *See* Sparton Corporation.
Sparrow Records, **22** 194
Sparta, Inc., **18** 369
Sparta Surgical Corporation, **33** 456
Spartan Communications, **38** 308–09
Spartan Insurance Co., **26** 486
Spartan Motors Inc., 14 457–59
Spartan Stores Inc., **I** 127; **II** 679–80; **8 481–82**; **10** 302; **12** 489; **14** 412
Spartech Corporation, **9** 92; **19 413–15**; **33** 78–79
Sparton Corporation, 18 492–95
SPCM, Inc., **14** 477
Spec's Music, Inc., 19 416–18
Spécia, **I** 388
Special Agent Investigators, Inc., **14** 541
Special Foods, **14** 557
Special Light Alloy Co., **IV** 153
Special Zone Limited, **26** 491
Specialized Bicycle Components Inc., **19** 384
Specialty Brands Inc., **25** 518
Specialty Coatings Inc., 8 483–84
Specialty Equipment Companies, Inc., 25 439–42
Specialty Foods Corporation, **29** 29, 31
Specialty Papers Co., **IV** 290
Specialty Products Co., **8** 386
Specialty Retailers, Inc., **24** 456
Spectra-Physics AB, **9** 380–81
Spectra Star, Inc., **18** 521
Spectradyne, **28** 241
Spectral Dynamics Corporation. *See* Scientific- Atlanta, Inc.
Spectron MicroSystems, **18** 143
Spectrum Club, **25** 448–50
Spectrum Communications Holdings International Limited, **24** 95
Spectrum Concepts, **10** 394–95
Spectrum Data Systems, Inc., **24** 96
Spectrum Dyed Yarns of New York, **8** 559
Spectrum Health Care Services, **13** 48
Spectrum Medical Technologies, Inc., **22** 409
Spectrum Technology Group, Inc., **7** 378; **18** 112
Spectrumedia, **21** 361
Speed-O-Lac Chemical, **8** 553
SpeeDee Marts, **II** 661
SpeeDee Oil Change and Tune-Up, 25 443–47
Speedway Motorsports, Inc., 32 438–41
Speedy Auto Glass, **30** 501
Speedy Muffler King, **10** 415; **24** 337, 339
Speidel Newspaper Group, **IV** 612; **7** 191
Spelling Entertainment, 14 460–62; **35 402–04 (upd.)**
Spencer & Spencer Systems, Inc., **18** 112
Spencer Beef, **II** 536
Spencer Gifts, Inc., **II** 144; **15** 464
Spencer Stuart and Associates, Inc., 14 463–65
Spenco Medical Corp., **III** 41; **16** 303; **43** 257
Sperry & Hutchinson Co., **12** 299; **23** 243–44
Sperry Aerospace Group, **II** 40, 86; **6** 283; **12** 246, 248
Sperry Corporation, **I** 101, 167; **III** 165, 642; **6** 281–82; **8** 92; **11** 139; **12** 39; **13** 511; **18** 386, 542; **22** 379; **36** 481. *See also* Unisys Corporation.
Sperry Milling Co., **II** 501; **10** 322
Sperry New Holland. *See* New Holland N.V.
Sperry Rand Corp., **II** 63, 73; **III** 126, 129, 149, 166, 329, 642; **6** 241, 261, 281–82; **16** 137
Sperry Top-Sider, Inc., **37** 377, 379
Sphere Inc., **8** 526; **13** 92
Sphere SA, **27** 9
Spicer Manufacturing Co., **I** 152; **III** 568; **20** 359; **23** 170–71
Spie Batignolles SA, **I** 563; **II** 93–94; **13** 206; **18** 471–73; **24** 79
Spiegel, Inc., **III** 598; **V** 160; **8** 56–58; **10** 168, **489–91**; **11** 498; **9** 190, 219; **13** 179; **15** 339; **27 427–31 (upd.)**; **34** 232, 324, 326; **36** 177, 180
Spillers, **II** 500
Spin Physics, **III** 475–76; **7** 163
SpinCircuit Inc., **38** 188
Spinnaker Industries, Inc., **43** 276
Spinnaker Software Corp., **24** 276
SPIRE Corporation, **14** 477
Spire, Inc., **25** 183
Spirella Company of Great Britain Ltd., **V** 356
Spirit Airlines, Inc., 31 419–21
Spirit Cruises, **29** 442–43
Spliethoff, **26** 280
Spoerle Electronic, **10** 113

Spokane Falls Electric Light and Power Company. *See* Edison Electric Illuminating Company.
Spokane Falls Water Power Company, **6** 595
Spokane Gas and Fuel, **IV** 391
Spokane Natural Gas Company, **6** 597
Spokane Street Railway Company, **6** 595
Spokane Traction Company, **6** 596
Spom Japan, **IV** 600
Spoor Behrins Campbell and Young, **II** 289
Spoornet, **6** 435
Sporis, **27** 151
Sporloisirs S.A., **9** 157
Sport Chalet, Inc., **16 454–56**
Sport Developpement SCA, **33** 10
Sport Supply Group, Inc., **22** 458–59; **23 448–50**; **30** 185
Sporting Dog Specialties, Inc., **14** 386
Sporting News Publishing Co., **IV** 677–78
Sportland, **26** 160
Sportmart, Inc., **15 469–71**. *See also* Gart Sports Company.
Sports & Co. *See* Hibbett Sporting Goods, Inc.
Sports & Recreation, Inc., **15** 470; **17 453–55**
The Sports Authority, Inc., **15** 470; **16 457–59**; **17** 453; **18** 286; **24** 173; **43 385–88 (upd.)**
The Sports Club Company, **25 448–51**
Sports Experts Inc., **II** 652
Sports Holdings Corp., **34** 217
Sports Inc., **14** 8; **33** 10
Sports-Tech Inc., **21** 300
Sports Traders, Inc., **18** 208
Sportservice Corporation, **7** 133–35
The Sportsman's Guide, Inc., **36 443–46**
Sportstown, Inc., **15** 470
Sportsystems Corporation, **7** 133, 135
Sprague Co., **I** 410
Sprague Devices, Inc., **11** 84
Sprague Electric Company, **6** 261
Sprague Electric Railway and Motor Co., **II** 27; **12** 193
Sprague Technologies, **21** 520
Sprague, Warner & Co., **II** 571
Spray-Rite, **I** 366
Sprayon Products, **III** 745
Spraysafe, **29** 98
Sprecher & Schub, **9** 10
Spreckels Sugar Company, Inc., **32** 274, 277
Spring Co., **21** 96, 246
Spring Forge Mill, **8** 412
Spring Industries, Inc., **V 378–79**
Spring Valley Brewery. *See* Kirin Brewery Company, Limited.
Springbok Editions, **IV** 621
Springer Verlag GmbH & Co., **IV** 611, 641
Springfield Bank, **9** 474
Springfield Gas Light Company, **38** 81
Springhouse Corp., **IV** 610
Springhouse Financial Corp., **III** 204
Springmaid International, Inc., **19** 421
Springs Industries, Inc., **19 419–22 (upd.)**; **29** 132; **31** 199
Sprint Communications Company, L.P., **9 478–80**; **10** 19, 57, 97, 201–03; **11** 183, 185, 500–01; **18** 32, 164–65, 569–70; **22** 19, 162; **24** 120, 122; **25** 102; **26** 17; **27** 365; **36** 167. *See also* US Sprint Communications.
Sprint PCS, **33** 34, 36–37; **38** 433
Sprout Group, **37** 121
Spruce Falls Power and Paper Co., **III** 40; **IV** 648; **16** 302, 304; **19** 284; **43** 256
SPS Technologies, Inc., **30 428–30**
Spun Yarns, Inc., **12** 503
Spur Oil Co., **7** 362
SPX Corporation, **10 492–95**
SPZ, Inc., **26** 257
SQ Software, Inc., **10** 505
SQL Solutions, Inc., **10** 505
Square D Company, **18** 473
Square Industries, **18** 103, 105
Squibb Beech-Nut. *See* Beech-Nut Nutrition Corp.
Squibb Corporation, **I** 380–81, 631, 651, 659, 675, **695–97**; **III** 17, 19, 67; **8** 166; **9** 6–7; **13** 379–80; **16** 438–39[see_ aslo]Bristol-Myers Squibb Company.
Squire Fashions Inc. *See* Norton McNaughton of Squire, Inc.
SR. *See* Southern Railway.
SR Beteilgungen Aktiengesellschaft, **III** 377
SRI International, **10** 139
SRI Strategic Resources Inc., **6** 310
SS Cars, Ltd. *See* Jaguar Cars, Ltd.
SSA. *See* Stevedoring Services of America Inc.
Ssangyong Cement Industrial Co., Ltd., **III 747–50**; **IV** 536–37, 539
Ssangyong Motor Company, **34** 132
SSC&B-Lintas, **I** 16–17; **14** 315
SSDS, Inc., **18** 537; **43** 433
SSI Medical Services, Inc., **10** 350
SSMC Inc., **II** 10
SSP Company, Inc., **17** 434
St. *See under* Saint
Staal Bankiers, **13** 544
Stackpole Fibers, **37** 427
Stadia Colorado Corporation, **18** 140
Stadt Corporation, **26** 109
Städtische Elecktricitäts-Werke A.G., **I** 410
Staefa Control System Limited, **6** 490
Staff International, **40** 157
StaffAmerica, Inc., **16** 50
Stafford-Lowdon, **31** 435
Stafford Old Bank, **II** 307
Stag Cañon Fuel Co., **IV** 177
Stage Stores, Inc., **24 456–59**
Stagecoach Holdings plc, **30 431–33**
Stags' Leap Winery, **22** 80
Stahl-Urban Company, **8** 287–88
Stahlwerke Peine-Salzgitter AG, **IV** 201
Stahlwerke Röchling AG, **III** 694–95
Stahlwerke Südwestfalen AG, **IV** 89
Stal-Astra GmbH, **III** 420
Staley Continental, **II** 582
Stamford Drug Group, **9** 68
Stamford FHI Acquisition Corp., **27** 117
Stamos Associates Inc., **29** 377
Stamps.com Inc., **34** 474
Stanadyne Automotive Corporation, **37 367–70**
Stanadyne, Inc., **7** 336; **12** 344
Standard & Poor's Corp., **IV** 29, 482, 636–37; **12** 310; **25** 542
Standard Accident Co., **III** 332
Standard Aero, **III** 509
Standard Aircraft Equipment, **II** 16
Standard Alaska, **7** 559
Standard Bank, **17** 324
Standard Bank of Canada, **II** 244
Standard Box Co., **17** 357
Standard Brands, **I** 248; **II** 542, 544; **7** 365, 367; **18** 538
Standard Car Truck, **18** 5
Standard Chartered PLC, **II** 298, 309, 319, **357–59**, 386; **10** 170
Standard Chemical Products, **III** 33
Standard Commercial Corporation, **12** 110; **13 490–92**; **27** 126
Standard Drug Co., **V** 171
Standard Electric Time Company, **13** 233
Standard Electrica, **II** 13
Standard Elektrik Lorenz A.G., **II** 13, 70; **17** 353
Standard Equities Corp., **III** 98
Standard Federal Bank, **9 481–83**
Standard Fire Insurance Co., **III** 181–82
Standard Fruit and Steamship Co. of New Orleans, **II** 491; **31** 168
Standard Gauge Manufacturing Company, **13** 233
Standard General Insurance, **III** 208
Standard Gypsum Corp., **19** 77
Standard Industrial Group Ltd., **IV** 658
Standard Insert Co., **28** 350
Standard Insulation Co., **I** 321
Standard Insurance Co. of New York, **III** 385
Standard Investing Corp., **III** 98
Standard Kollsman Industries Inc., **13** 461
Standard Life & Accident Insurance Company, **27** 47–48
Standard Life Assurance Company, **III 358–61**; **IV** 696–98
Standard Life Insurance Company, **11** 481
Standard Magnesium & Chemical Co., **IV** 123
Standard Metals Corp., **IV** 76
Standard Microsystems Corporation, **11 462–64**
Standard Milling Co., **II** 497
Standard Motor Co., **III** 651
Standard Motor Products, Inc., **40 414–17**
Standard of America Life Insurance Co., **III** 324
Standard of Georgia Insurance Agency, Inc., **10** 92
Standard Oil Co., **III** 470, 513; **IV** 46, 372, 399, 426–29, 434, 463, 478, 488–89, 530–31, 540, 542, 551, 574, 577–78, 657; **V** 590, 601; **6** 455; **7** 169–72, 263, 351, 414, 551; **8** 415; **10** 110, 289; **14** 21, 491–92; **25** 230; **27** 129. *See also* Exxon Corporation.
Standard Oil Co. (California), **II** 448; **IV** 18–19, 385–87, 403, 429, 464, 536–37, 545, 552, 560, 578; **6** 353; **7** 172, 352, 483; **13** 448
Standard Oil Co. (Illinois), **IV** 368
Standard Oil Co. (Indiana), **II** 262; **IV** 366, 368–71, 466–67; **7** 443; **10** 86; **14** 222
Standard Oil Co. (Minnesota), **IV** 368
Standard Oil Co. (New York), **IV** 428–29, 431, 460, 463–65, 485, 504, 537, 549, 558; **7** 171, 351–52
Standard Oil Co. of Iowa, **IV** 385
Standard Oil Co. of Kentucky, **IV** 387
Standard Oil Co. of New Jersey, **I** 334, 337, 370; **II** 16, 496; **IV** 378–79, 385–86, 400, 415–16, 419, 426–29, 431–33, 438, 460, 463–64, 488, 522, 531, 537–38, 544, 558, 565, 571; **V**

658–59; **7** 170–72, 253, 351; **13** 124; **17** 412–13; **24** 521
Standard Oil Co. of Ohio, **IV** 373, 379, 427, 452, 463, 522, 571; **7** 57, 171, 263; **12** 309; **21** 82; **24** 521
Standard Oil Development Co., **IV** 554
Standard Oil Trust, **IV** 31, 368, 375, 385–86, 427, 463
Standard Plastics, **25** 312
Standard Printing Company, **19** 333
Standard Process & Engraving, Inc., **26** 105
Standard Products Company, **19** 454
Standard Rate & Data Service, **IV** 639; **7** 286
Standard Register Co., 15 472–74
Standard Sanitary, **III** 663–64
Standard Screw Co., **12** 344
Standard Shares, **9** 413–14
Standard Steel Propeller, **I** 47, 84; **9** 416; **10** 162
Standard Telephone and Radio, **II** 13
Standard Telephones and Cables, Ltd., **III** 162–63; **6** 242
Standard Tin Plate Co., **15** 127
Standard-Vacuum Oil Co., **IV** 431–32, 440, 460, 464, 491–92, 554–55; **7** 352
Standex International Corporation, 16 470–71; **17 456–59**
Stanhome Inc., 9 330; **11** 94–96; **15 475–78**
Stanhome Worldwide Direct Selling, **35** 262, 264
STANIC, **IV** 419, 421
Stanko Fanuc Service, **III** 483
Stanley Electric Manufacturing Co., **II** 28; **12** 194
Stanley Furniture Company, Inc., 34 412–14
Stanley Home Products, Incorporated. *See* Stanhome Inc.
Stanley Mining Services, Ltd., **19** 247
The Stanley Works, III 626–29; **7** 480; **9** 543; **13** 41; **20 476–80 (upd.)**
StanMont, Inc., **24** 425
Stanolind Oil & Gas Co., **III** 498; **IV** 365, 369–70
Stant Corporation, **15** 503, 505
Staples, Inc., 8 404–05; **10 496–98**; **18** 24, 388; **20** 99; **22** 154; **23** 363, 365; **24** 270
Star, **10** 287–88
Star Air Service. *See* Alaska Air Group, Inc.
Star Alliance, **26** 113; **33** 51; **38** 36
Star Banc Corporation, 11 465–67; **13** 222; **31** 206. *See also* Firstar Corporation.
Star Building Systems, Inc., **19** 366
Star Engraving, **12** 471
Star Enterprise, **IV** 536, 539, 553
Star Enterprises, Inc., **6** 457
Star Finishing Co., **9** 465
Star Laboratories Inc., **24** 251
Star Markets Company, Inc., **23** 169
Star Medical Technologies, Inc., **22** 409; **31** 124
Star Paper Ltd., **IV** 300
Star Paper Tube, Inc., **19** 76–78
Star Sportwear Manufacturing Corp., **29** 294
Star Video, Inc., **6** 313
Starber International, **12** 181
Starbucks Corporation, 13 493–94; **18** 37; **22** 370; **25** 178, 501; **28** 63; **34 415–19 (upd.)**; **36** 156–57; **37** 181; **38** 340; **40** 152–53
Starcraft Corporation, III 444; **13** 113; **22** 116; **30 434–36**
Stardent Computer Inc., **III** 553; **26** 256
Starfish Software, **23** 212
Stark Record and Tape Service. *See* Camelot Music, Inc.
StarKist Foods, **II** 508; **11** 172; **36** 254–55
Starlawerken, **I** 527
Starlen Labs, Ltd., **31** 346
Starlight Networks, Inc., **27** 366
Starline Optical Corp., **22** 123
StarMed Staffing Corporation, **6** 10
Starpointe Savings Bank, **9** 173
Starrett Corporation, 21 471–74
Star's Discount Department Stores, **16** 36
Startech Semiconductor Inc., **14** 183
Startel Corp., **15** 125
Starter Corp., 12 457–458
Starwood Capital, **29** 508
Starwood Hotels and Resorts Worldwide Inc., **33** 217
State Bank of Albany, **9** 228
State Farm Insurance Companies, **27** 30; **29** 397; **39** 155
State Farm Mutual Automobile Insurance Company, III 362–64; **10** 50; **22** 266; **23** 286; **25** 155; **41** 313
State Finance and Thrift Company, **14** 529
State Leed, **13** 367
State Metal Works, **III** 647
State-o-Maine, **18** 357–59
State-Record Co., **IV** 630
State Savings Bank and Trust Co., **11** 180; **42** 429
State Street Boston Corporation, 8 491–93
State Trading Corp. of India Ltd., **IV** 143
Staten Island Advance Corp., **IV** 581–82; **19** 4
Staten Island Bancorp, Inc., 39 380–82
Stater Brothers, **17** 558
Statex Petroleum, Inc., **19** 70
Static, Inc., **14** 430
Station Casinos Inc., 25 452–54
Stationers Distributing Company, **14** 523
Stationers, Inc., **28** 74
Statler Hotel Co., **III** 92, 98; **19** 206
Statoil. *See* Den Norske Stats Oljeselskap AS.
StatScript Management Services, **26** 73
Statter, Inc., **6** 27
Staubli International, **II** 122; **12** 546
Stauffer Chemical Company, **8** 105–07; **21** 545
Stauffer Communications, Inc., **36** 339–41
Stauffer-Meiji, **II** 540
Stax Records, **23** 32
STC PLC, III 141, **162–64**; **25** 497; **36** 351
Stead & Miller, **13** 169
Steag AG, **IV** 193
Steak & Ale, **II** 556–57; **7** 336; **12** 373; **13** 408–09
The Steak n Shake Company, 14 130–31; **41 387–90**
Steam and Gas Pipe Co., **III** 644
Steam Boiler Works, **18** 318
Steamboat Ski and Resort Corporation, **28** 21
Stearman, **I** 47, 84; **9** 416; **10** 162
Stearns & Foster, **12** 439
Stearns Catalytic World Corp., **II** 87; **11** 413
Stearns Coal & Lumber, **6** 514
Stearns, Inc., 43 389–91
Stearns Manufacturing Co., **16** 297
Steaua-Romana, **IV** 557
Steego Auto Paints, **24** 160
Steel and Tube Co. of America, **IV** 114
Steel Authority of India Ltd., IV 205–07
Steel Ceilings and Aluminum Works, **IV** 22
Steel Co. of Canada Ltd., **IV** 208
Steel Dynamics, Inc., **18** 380; **26** 530
Steel Mills Ltd., **III** 673
Steel Products Engineering Co., **I** 169
Steel Stamping Co., **III** 569; **20** 360
Steelcase Inc., 7 493–95; **8** 251–52, 255, 405; **25** 500; **27 432–35 (upd.)**; **39** 205–07
Steelmade Inc., **I** 513
Steely, **IV** 109
Steenfabriek De Ruiterwaard, **14** 249
Steenkolen Handelsvereniging, **IV** 132; **39** 176
Steering Aluminum, **I** 159
Stefany, **12** 152
Stegbar Pty Ltd., **31** 398–400
Steger Furniture Manufacturing Co., **18** 493
Steiff. *See* Margarete Steiff GmbH.
Steil, Inc., **8** 271
Stein Mart Inc., 19 423–25
Stein Printing Company, **25** 183
Stein Robaire Helm, **22** 173
Steinbach Inc., **IV** 226; **14** 427
Steinbach Stores, Inc., **19** 108
Steinberg Incorporated, II 652–53, **662–65**; **V** 163
Steinberger, **16** 239
Steinheil Optronik GmbH, **24** 87
Steinman & Grey, **6** 27
Steinmüller Verwaltungsgesellschaft, **V** 747
Steinway & Sons, **16** 201; **43** 170
Steinway Musical Properties, Inc., 19 392, 394, **426–29**
Stelco Inc., IV 208–10; **24** 144
Stella Bella Corporation, **19** 436
Stella D'Oro Company, **7** 367
Stellar Systems, Inc., **III** 553; **14** 542
Stellenbosch Farmers Winery, **I** 288
Stelux Manufacturing Company, **13** 121; **41** 71
Stena AB, **25** 105; **29** 429–30
Stena Line AB, **38** 345
Stena-Sealink, **37** 137
Stensmölla Kemiska Tekniska Industri, **I** 385
Stentor Canadian Network Management, **6** 310
Stenval Sud, **19** 50
Stepan Company, 30 437–39
Stephen F. Whitman & Son, Inc., **7** 429
Stephens Inc., **III** 76; **16** 59; **18** 223
Stephenson Clarke and Company, **31** 368–69
Sterchi Bros. Co., **14** 236
Stericycle Inc., 33 380–82
STERIS Corporation, 29 449–52
Sterling Chemicals, Inc., 16 460–63; **27** 117
Sterling Drug Inc., I 309–10, **698–700**; **III** 477; **7** 163; **13** 76–77; **36** 173; **41** 45

Sterling Electronics Corp., **18 496–98**; **19** 311
Sterling Engineered Products, **III** 640, 642; **16** 9
Sterling Forest Corp., **III** 264
Sterling House Corp., **42** 4
Sterling Industries, **13** 166
Sterling Information Services, Ltd., **IV** 675; **7** 528
Sterling Manhattan, **7** 63
Sterling Oil, **I** 526
Sterling Oil & Development, **II** 490
Sterling Organics Ltd., **12** 351
Sterling Plastics, **III** 642
Sterling Plastics Inc., **16** 9
Sterling Products Inc., **I** 622; **10** 68
Sterling Remedy Co., **I** 698
Sterling Software, Inc., **11 468–70**; **31** 296
Sterling Stores Co. Inc., **24** 148
Sterling Winthrop, **7** 164; **36** 174
Stern & Stern Textiles, **11** 261
Stern-Auer Shoe Company, **V** 207
Stern Bros. Investment Bank, **V** 362–65; **19** 359
Stern Bros., LLC, **37** 224
Stern Publishing, **38** 478
Stern's, **9** 209
Sternco Industries, **12** 230–31
STET. *See* Società Finanziaria Telefonica per Azioni.
Steuben Glass, **III** 683
Stevcoknit Fabrics Company, **8** 141–43
Stevedoring Services of America Inc., **28 435–37**
Steven Madden, Ltd., **37 371–73**
Stevens Linen Associates, Inc., **8** 272
Stevens Park Osteopathic Hospital, **6** 192
Stevens Sound Proofing Co., **III** 706; **7** 291
Stevens, Thompson & Runyan, Inc. *See* CRSS Inc.
Steve's Ice Cream, **16** 54–55
Steward Esplen and Greenhough, **II** 569
Stewards Foundation, **6** 191
Stewart & Stevenson Services Inc., **11 471–73**
Stewart Bolling Co., **IV** 130
Stewart Cash Stores, **II** 465
Stewart Enterprises, Inc., **16** 344; **20 481–83**; **37** 67
Stewart P. Orr Associates, **6** 224
Stewart Systems, Inc., **22** 352–53
Stewart's Beverages, **39 383–86**
Steyr Walzlager, **III** 625
Stichting Continuiteit AMEV, **III** 202
Stieber Rollkupplung GmbH, **14** 63
Stihl Inc. *See* Andreas Stihl.
Stilecraft, **24** 16
Stimson & Valentine, **8** 552
Stinnes AG, **6** 424, 426; **8** 68–69, **494–97**; **23** 68–70, **451–54 (upd.)**; **33** 195
Stirling Readymix Concrete, **III** 737–38
STM Systems Corp., **11** 485
Stock, **IV** 617–18
Stock Clearing Corporation, **9** 370
Stock Yards Packing Co., Inc., **37 374–76**
Stockholder Systems Inc., **11** 485
Stockholm Southern Transportation Co., **I** 553
Stockholms Allmänna Telefonaktiebolag, **V** 334
Stockholms Enskilda Bank, **II** 1, 351, 365–66; **III** 419, 425–26
Stockholms Intecknings Garanti, **II** 366
Stockton and Hartlepool Railway, **III** 272
Stockton Wheel Co., **III** 450
Stoelting Brothers Company, **10** 371
Stokely Van Camp, **II** 560, 575; **12** 411; **22** 338
Stokvis/De Nederlandsche Kroon Rijwiefabrieken, **13** 499
Stoll-Moss Theatres Ltd., **34 420–22**
Stolt-Nielsen S.A., **42 356–59**
Stone & Webster, Inc., **13 495–98**
Stone and Kimball, **IV** 660
Stone-Consolidated Corporation, **25** 9, 12
Stone Container Corporation, **IV 332–34**; **8** 203–04; **15** 129; **17** 106; **25** 12. *See also* Smurfit-Stone Container Corporation.
Stone Exploration Corp., **IV** 83; **7** 187
Stone Manufacturing Company, **14 469–71**; **43 392–96 (upd.)**
Stonega Coke & Coal Co. *See* Westmoreland Coal Company.
Stoner Associates. *See* Severn Trent PLC.
Stonewall Insurance Co., **III** 192
Stonington Partners, **19** 318
StonyBrook Services Inc., **24** 49
Stoody Co., **19** 440
Stoof, **26** 278–79
Stoomvaart Maatschappij Nederland, **6** 403–04; **26** 241
The Stop & Shop Companies, Inc., **II 666–67**; **9** 451, 453; **12** 48–49; **16** 160, 314; **23** 169; **24 460–62 (upd.)**
Stop N Go, **7** 373; **25** 126
Stoppenbauch Inc., **23** 202
Stora Enso Oyj, **36** 128, **447–55 (upd.)**
Stora Kopparbergs Bergslags AB, **III** 693, 695; **IV 335–37**, 340; **12** 464; **28** 445–46
Storage Dimensions Inc., **10** 404
Storage Technology Corporation, **III** 110; **6 275–77**; **12** 148, 161; **16** 194; **28** 198
Storage USA, Inc., **21 475–77**
Storebrand Insurance Co., **III** 122
Storehouse PLC, **II** 658; **13** 284; **16 464–66**; **17** 42–43, 335; **24** 75
Storer Communications, **II** 161; **IV** 596; **7** 91–92, 200–1; **24** 122
Storer Leasing Inc., **I** 99; **6** 81
Storm Technology, **28** 245
Storz Instruments Co., **I** 678; **25** 56; **27** 115
Stouffer Corp., **I** 485; **II** 489, 547; **6** 40; **7** 382; **8 498–501**
Stouffer Foods Corporation, **28** 238
Stout Air Services, **I** 128; **6** 128
Stout Airlines, **I** 47, 84; **9** 416; **10** 162
Stout Metal Airplane Co., **I** 165
Stowe Machine Co., Inc., **30** 283
Stowe Woodward, **I** 428–29
STP, **19** 223; **26** 349
STRAAM Engineers. *See* CRSS Inc.
Straits Steamship Co. *See* Malaysian Airlines System.
Stran, **8** 546
Strata Energy, Inc., **IV** 29
StrataCom, Inc., **11** 59; **16 467–69**; **34** 113
Strategix Solutions, **43** 309
Stratford Corporation, **15** 103; **26** 100
Strathmore Consolidated Investments, **IV** 90
Stratos Boat Co., Ltd., **III** 600
Stratton Oakmont Inc., **37** 372–73
Stratton Ski Corporation, **15** 235
Stratus Computer, Inc., **6** 279; **10 499–501**
Straus-Frank Company, **29** 86, 88
Strauss Turnbull and Co., **II** 355
Strawberries, **30** 465
Strawbridge & Clothier's, **6** 243
Streamline Holdings, **39** 237–38
Street & Smith Publications, Inc., **IV** 583; **13** 178
The Stride Rite Corporation, **8 502–04**; **9** 437; **33** 244; **37 377–80 (upd.)**
Stroehmann Bakeries, **II** 631
Stroh and Co., **IV** 486
The Stroh Brewery Company, **I** 32, 255, **290–92**; **13** 10–11, 455; **18** 72, **499–502 (upd.)**; **22** 422; **23** 403, 405; **36** 14–15
Strömberg, **IV** 300; **27** 267, 268
Stromberg Carburetor Co., **I** 141
Stromberg-Carlson, **II** 82
Stromeyer GmbH, **7** 141
Strong Brewery, **I** 294
Strong Electric Corporation, **19** 211
Strong International, **27** 57
Stroock & Stroock & Lavan LLP, **40 418–21**
Strother Drug, **III** 9–10
Strouds, Inc., **33 383–86**
Structural Dynamics Research Corporation, **10** 257
Structural Fibers, Inc. *See* Essef Corporation.
Structural Iberica S.A., **18** 163
Struebel Group, **18** 170
Strydel, Inc., **14** 361
Stryker Corporation, **10** 351; **11 474–76**; **29 453–55 (upd.)**
Stuart & Sons Ltd., **34** 493, 496
Stuart Co., **I** 584
Stuart Entertainment Inc., **16 470–72**
Stuart Hall Co., **17** 445
Stuart Medical, Inc., **10** 143; **16** 400
Stuart Perlman, **6** 200
Stuckey's, Inc., **7** 429
Studebaker Co., **I** 141–42, 451; **8** 74; **9** 27
Studebaker-Packard, **9** 118; **10** 261
Studebaker Wagon Co., **IV** 660
Student Loan Marketing Association, **II 453–55**. *See also* SLM Holding Corp.
Studiengesellschaft, **I** 409
Studley Products Inc., **12** 396
Stuffit Co., **IV** 597
Stuller Settings, Inc., **35 405–07**
Sturbridge Yankee Workshop, Inc., **10** 216
Sturgeon Bay Shipbuilding and DryDock Company, **18** 320
Sturm, Ruger & Company, Inc., **19 430–32**
Stuttgart Gas Works, **I** 391
Stuttgarter Verein Versicherungs-AG, **III** 184
Stuyvesant Insurance Group, **II** 182
Stylus Writing Instruments, **27** 416
Stymer Oy, **IV** 470–71
SU214, **28** 27, 30
Suave Shoe Corporation. *See* French Fragrances, Inc.
Sub-Zero Freezer Co., Inc., **31 426–28**
Subaru, **6** 28; **23** 290
SubLogic, **15** 455

Submarine Boat Co., **I** 57
Submarine Signal Co., **II** 85–86; **11** 412
Suburban Cablevision, **IV** 640
Suburban Coastal Corporation, **10** 92
Suburban Cos., **IV** 575–76
Suburban Light and Power Company, **12** 45
Suburban Propane Partners, L.P., **I** 378; **30 440–42[ro**
Suburban Savings and Loan Association, **10** 92
Subway, **15** 56–57; **32 442–44**
Successories, Inc., **30 443–45[ro**
Suchard Co., **II** 520
Sud-Aviation, **I** 44–45; **7** 10; **8** 313
Sudbury Inc., **16 473–75**; **17** 373
Sudbury River Consulting Group, **31** 131
Suddeutsche Bank A.G., **II** 279
Süddeutsche Donau- Dampfschiffahrts-Gesellschaft, **6** 425
Süddeutsche Kalkstickstoffwerke AG, **IV** 229, 232
Sudler & Hennessey, **I** 37
Südpetrol, **IV** 421
Südzucker AG, **27 436–39**
Suez Bank, **IV** 108
Suez Canal Co., **IV** 530
Suez Lyonnaise des Eaux, **36 456–59 (upd.)**; **38** 321; **40** 447, 449; **42** 386, 388
Suez Oil Co., **IV** 413–14
Suffolk County Federal Savings and Loan Association, **16** 346
Sugar Land State Bank, **25** 114
Sugar Mount Capital, LLC, **33** 355
Sugarland Industries. *See* Imperial Holly Corporation.
SugarLoaf Creations, Inc. *See* American Coin Merchandising, Inc.
Sugarloaf Mountain Corporation, **28** 21
Suita Brewery, **I** 220
Suito Sangyo Co., Ltd. *See* Seino Transportation Company, Ltd.
Suiza Foods Corporation, **25** 512, 514; **26 447–50**; **37** 197; **38** 381
Sukhoi Design Bureau Aviation Scientific-Industrial Complex, **24 463–65**
Sullair Co., **I** 435
Sullivan & Cromwell, **26 451–53**; **27** 327
Sullivan-Schein Dental Products Inc., **31** 256
Sullivan, Stauffer, Colwell & Bayles, **14** 314
Sullivan Systems, **III** 420
Sulpetro Limited, **25** 232
Sulphide Corp., **IV** 58
Sulzbach, **I** 409
Sulzer Brothers Limited, **III** 402, 516, **630–33**, 638
Sumergrade Corporation, **19** 304; **41** 300
Suminoe Textile Co., **8** 235
Sumisei Secpac Investment Advisors, **III** 366
Sumisho Electronics Co. Ltd., **18** 170
Sumitomo Bank, Limited, **I** 587; **II** 104, 224, 273–74, 347, **360–62**, 363, 392, 415; **IV** 269, 726; **9** 341–42; **18** 170; **23** 340; **26 454–57 (upd.)**
Sumitomo Chemical Company Ltd., **I** 363, **397–98**; **II** 361; **III** 715; **IV** 432
Sumitomo Corporation, **I** 431–32, 492, 502, 504–05, 510–11, 515, **518–20**; **III** 43, 365; **V** 161; **7** 357; **11 477–80 (upd.)**, 490; **15** 340; **17** 556; **18** 170; **24** 325; **28** 288; **36** 420
Sumitomo Electric Industries, **I** 105; **II 104–05**; **III** 490, 684; **IV** 179; **V** 252
Sumitomo Heavy Industries, Ltd., **III** 533, **634–35**; **10** 381; **42 360–62 (upd.)**
Sumitomo Life Insurance Co., **II** 104, 360, 422; **III** 288, **365–66**
Sumitomo Marine and Fire Insurance Company, Limited, **III 367–68**
Sumitomo Metal Industries, Ltd., **I** 390; **II** 104, 361; **IV** 130, **211–13**, 216; **10** 463–64; **11** 246; **24** 302
Sumitomo Metal Mining Co., Ltd., **IV 214–16**; **9** 340; **23** 338
Sumitomo Realty & Development Co., Ltd., **IV 726–27**
Sumitomo Rubber Industries, Ltd., **V 252–53**; **20** 263
Sumitomo Trust & Banking Company, Ltd., **II** 104, **363–64**; **IV** 726
Sumitomo Wire Company, **16** 555
Summa Corporation, **9** 266; **17** 317
Summer Paper Tube, **19** 78
Summers Group Inc., **15** 386
The Summit Bancorporation, **14 472–74**
Summit Constructors. *See* CRSS Inc.
Summit Engineering Corp., **I** 153
Summit Family Restaurants Inc., **19** 89, 92, **433–36**
Summit Gear Company, **16** 392–93
Summit Management Co., Inc., **17** 498
Summit Screen Inks, **13** 228
Summit Technology Inc., **30** 485
Sun Aire, **25** 421–22
Sun Alliance Group PLC, **III** 296, **369–74**, 400; **37** 86
Sun Apparel Inc., **39** 247
Sun Chemical Corp. *See* Sequa Corp.
Sun Company, Inc., **I** 286, 631; **IV** 449, **548–50**; **7** 114, 414; **11** 484; **12** 459; **17** 537; **25** 126
Sun Country Airlines, **I** 114; **30 446–49**
Sun-Diamond Growers of California, **7 496–97**
Sun Distributors L.P., **12 459–461**
Sun Electric, **15** 288
Sun Electronics, **9** 116
Sun Equities Corporation, **15** 449
Sun-Fast Color, **13** 227
Sun Federal, **7** 498
Sun Federal Savings and Loan Association of Tallahassee, **10** 92
Sun Financial Group, Inc., **25** 171
Sun Fire Coal Company, **7** 281
Sun Fire Office, **III** 349, 369–71
Sun Foods, **12** 220–21
Sun Healthcare Group Inc., **25 455–58**
Sun International Hotels Limited, **12** 420; **26 462–65**; **37** 254–55
Sun Kyowa, **III** 43
Sun Life Assurance Co. of Canada, **IV** 165
Sun Life Group of America, **11** 482
Sun-Maid Growers of California, **7** 496–97
Sun Mark, Inc., **21** 483
Sun Media, **27** 280; **29** 471–72
Sun Men's Shop Co., Ltd., **V** 150
Sun Microsystems, Inc., **II** 45, 62; **III** 125; **6** 222, 235, 238, 244; **7 498–501**; **9** 36, 471; **10** 118, 242, 257, 504; **11** 45–46, 490–91, 507; **12** 162; **14** 15–16, 268; **15** 321; **16** 140, 195, 418–19; **18** 537; **20** 175, 237; **21** 86; **22** 154; **23** 471; **25** 348, 499; **26** 19; **27** 448; **30 450–54 (upd.)**; **36** 80–81; **38** 416, 418; **43** 238–40
Sun Newspapers, **III** 213–14
Sun Oil Co., **III** 497; **IV** 371, 424, 548–50; **7** 413–14; **11** 35; **18** 233; **19** 162; **36** 86–87. *See also* Sunoco, Inc.
Sun Optical Co., Ltd., **V** 150
Sun-Pat Products, **II** 569
Sun Pharmaceuticals, **24** 480
Sun Shades 501 Ltd., **21** 483
Sun Ship, **IV** 549
Sun Sportswear, Inc., **17 460–63**; **23** 65–66
Sun State Marine Services, Inc. *See* Hvide Marine Incorporated.
Sun Techno Services Co., Ltd., **V** 150
Sun Technology Enterprises, **7** 500
Sun Television & Appliances Inc., **10 502–03**; **19** 362
Sun Valley Equipment Corp., **33** 363
SunAir, **11** 300
SunAmerica Inc., **11 481–83**
Sunbeam-Oster Co., Inc., **9 484–86**; **14** 230; **16** 488; **17** 215; **19** 305; **22** 3; **28** 135, 246; **30** 136; **42** 309
Sunbelt Beverage Corporation, **32** 520
Sunbelt Coca-Cola, **10** 223
Sunbelt Nursery Group, Inc., **12** 179, 200, 394
Sunbelt Rentals Inc., **34** 42
Sunbird, **III** 600; **V** 150
Sunburst Hospitality Corporation, **26 458–61**
Sunburst Technology Corporation, **36** 273
Sunburst Yarns, Inc., **13** 532
Sunciti Manufacturers Ltd., **III** 454; **21** 122
Sunclipse Inc., **IV** 250
Sunco N.V., **22** 515
Suncoast Motion Picture Company, **9** 360
SunCor Development Company, **6** 546–47
Suncor Energy, **33** 167
Sundance Publishing, **IV** 609; **12** 559
Sunday Pictorial, **IV** 665–66; **17** 397
Sundheim & Doetsch, **IV** 189
Sunds Defibrator AG, **IV** 338–40, 350; **28** 444
Sundstrand Corporation, **7 502–04**; **21 478–81 (upd.)**
Sundt Corp., **24 466–69**
SunGard Data Systems Inc., **11 484–85**
Sunglass Hut International, Inc., **18** 393; **21 482–84**
Sunglee Electronics Co. Ltd., **III** 748–49
Sunila Oy, **IV** 348–49
Sunkiss Thermoreactors, **21** 65
Sunkist Growers, Inc., **7** 496; **25** 366; **26 466–69**
Sunkist Soft Drinks Inc., **I** 13
Sunkus Co. Ltd., **V** 150
Sunnybrook Farms, **25** 124
Sunoco, Inc., **28 438–42 (upd.)**
SunQuest HealthCare Corp. *See* Unison HealthCare Corporation.
Sunray DX Oil Co., **IV** 550, 575; **7** 414
The Sunrider Corporation, **26** 316, **470–74**; **27** 353
Sunrise Medical Inc., **11** 202, **486–88**
Sunrise Test Systems, **11** 491
Sunsations Sunglass Company, **21** 483
Sunshine Biscuit Co., **35** 181; **36** 313
Sunshine Bullion Co., **25** 542
Sunshine Jr. Stores, Inc., **17** 170
Sunshine Mining Company, **20** 149

SunSoft Inc., **7** 500; **43** 238
Sunstate, **24** 396
Sunsweet Growers, **7** 496
Suntory Ltd., **13** 454; **21** 320; **36** 404
SunTrust Banks Inc., 23 455–58; 33 293
Sunward Technologies, Inc., **10** 464
Supasnaps, **V** 50
Supelco, Inc., **36** 431
Super Bazars, **26** 159
Super D Drugs, **9** 52
Super Dart. *See* Dart Group Corporation.
Super 8 Motels, Inc., **11** 178
Super Food Services, Inc., 15 479–81; 18 8
Super Oil Seals & Gaskets Ltd., **16** 8
Super 1 Stores. *See* Brookshire Grocery Company.
Super-Power Company, **6** 505
Super Quick, Inc., **7** 372
Super Rite Foods, Inc., **V** 176; **19** 356
Super Sagless Spring Corp., **15** 103
Super Sol Ltd., **41** 56–57
Super Store Industries, **14** 397
Super Valu Stores, Inc., II 632, **668–71; 6** 364; **7** 450; **8** 380; **14** 411; **17** 180; **22** 126; **23** 357–58. *See also* Supervalu Inc.
SuperAmerica Group, Inc., **IV** 374
Superbrix, **14** 248
Supercomputer Systems, Inc., **III** 130; **16** 138
Supercuts Inc., 26 475–78
Superdrug plc, **V** 175; **24** 266, 269–70
Superenvases Envalic, **I** 231
Superior Bearings Company. *See* Federal-Mogul Corporation.
Superior Healthcare Group, Inc., **11** 221
Superior Industries International, Inc., 8 505–07
Superior Oil Co., **III** 558; **IV** 400, 465, 524; **7** 353
Superior Recycled Fiber Industries, **26** 363
Superior Transfer, **12** 309
Superior Uniform Group, Inc., 30 455–57
SuperMac Technology Inc., **16** 419
Supermarchés GB, **26** 159
Supermarchés Montréal, **II** 662–63
Supermarkets General Holdings Corporation, II 672–74; 16 160; **23** 369–70
Supermart Books, **10** 136
Supersaver Wholesale Clubs, **8** 555
Supersnaps, **19** 124
SuperStation WTBS, **6** 171
Supertest Petroleum Corporation, **9** 490
Supervalu Inc., 18 503–08 (upd.); 21 457–57; **22** 327. *See also* Super Valu Stores, Inc.
Supervalue Corp., **13** 393
Supervised Investors Services, **III** 270
SupeRx, **II** 644
Suprema Specialties, Inc., 27 440–42
Supreme International Corporation, 27 443–46; 30 358; **41** 291
Supreme Life Insurance Company of America, **28** 212
Supreme Sugar Co., **I** 421; **11** 23
Supron Energy Corp., **15** 129
Surety Life Insurance Company, **10** 51
SureWay Air Traffic Corporation, **24** 126
Surgical Health Corporation, **14** 233
Surgical Mechanical Research Inc., **I** 678
Surgical Plastics, **25** 430–31
Surgikos, Inc., **III** 35
Surgitool, **I** 628
Suroflex GmbH, **23** 300
Surpass Software Systems, Inc., **9** 81
Surplus Software, **31** 176
Surridge Dawson Ltd. *See* Dawson Holdings PLC.
Survey Research Group, **10** 360
SurVivaLink, **18** 423
Susan Bristol, **16** 61
Susan Kay Cosmetics. *See* The Cosmetic Center, Inc.
Susie's Casuals, **14** 294
Susquehanna Pfaltzgraff Company, 8 508–10
Sussex Group, **15** 449
Sussex Trust Company, **25** 541
Sutherland Lumber Co., **19** 233
Sutter Corp., **15** 113
Sutter Health, **12** 175–76
Sutter Home Winery Inc., 16 476–78
Sutton & Towne, Inc., **21** 96
Sutton Laboratories, **22** 228
Suunto Oy, **41** 14, 16
Suwa Seikosha, **III** 620
Suzaki Hajime, **V** 113–14
Suzannah Farms, **7** 524
Suze, **I** 280
Suzhou Elevator Company, **29** 420
Suzuki & Co., **I** 509–10; **IV** 129; **9** 341–42; **23** 340
Suzuki Motor Corporation, III 581, 657; **7** 110; **8** 72; **9 487–89; 23** 290, **459–62 (upd.); 36** 240, 243; **39** 38
Suzuki Shoten Co., **V** 380, 457–58
Suzy Shier, **18** 562
Svea Choklad A.G., **II** 640
Svensk Fastighetskredit A.B., **II** 352
Svensk Golvindustri, **25** 463
Svenska A.B. Humber & Co., **I** 197
Svenska Aeroplan Aktiebolaget. *See* Saab-Scania AB.
Svenska Cellulosa Aktiebolaget SCA, II 365–66; **IV** 295–96, 325, 336, **338–40,** 667; **17** 398; **19** 225–26; **28 443–46 (upd.)**
Svenska Centrifug AB, **III** 418
Svenska Elektron, **III** 478
A.B. Svenska Flaktfabriken, **II** 2; **22** 8
Svenska Flygmotor A.B., **I** 209; **26** 10
Svenska Handelsbanken, II 353, **365–67; IV** 338–39; **28** 443–44
Svenska Järnvagsverkstäderna A.B., **I** 197
Svenska Kullagerfabriken A.B., **I** 209; **III** 622; **7** 565; **26** 9. *See also* AB Volvo.
Svenska Oljeslageri AB, **IV** 318
Svenska Stålpressnings AB, **26** 11
Svenska Varv, **6** 367
Svenska Varv, **27** 91
Svenskt Stål AB, **IV** 336
Sverdrup Corporation, 14 475–78
Sverker Martin-Löf, **IV** 339
SVF. *See* Société des Vins de France.
SVIDO, **17** 250
Sviluppo Iniziative Stradali Italiene, **IV** 420
SVPW, **I** 215
Swallow Airplane Company, **8** 49; **27** 98
Swallow Sidecar and Coach Building Company, **13** 285
Swan, **10** 170
Swan Electric Light Co., **I** 410
Swan's Down Cake Flour, **II** 531
Swank Inc., 17 464–66
Swann Corp., **I** 366
Swarovski International Holding AG, 40 422–25
The Swatch Group SA, 7 532–33; **25** 481; **26 479–81**
Swearingen Aircraft Company, **9** 207
SwedeChrome, **III** 625
Swedish Ericsson Group, **17** 353
Swedish Furniture Research Institute, **V** 82
Swedish Intercontinental Airlines, **I** 119; **34** 396
Swedish Match AB, 39 387–90 (upd.)
Swedish Match S.A., IV 336–37; **9** 381; **12 462–64; 23** 55; **25** 464
Swedish Ordnance-FFV/Bofors AB, **9** 381–82
Swedish Telecom, V 331–33
Sweedor, **12** 464
Sweeney Specialty Restaurants, **14** 131
Sweeney's, **16** 559
Sweet & Maxwell, **8** 527
Sweet Life Foods Inc., **18** 507
Sweet Traditions LLC, **21** 323
Sweetheart Cup Company, Inc., 36 460–64
Swenson Granite Company, Inc., **37** 331
Swett & Crawford Group, **III** 357; **22** 494
Swift & Co., **II** 447, 550; **13** 351, 448; **17** 124; **41** 114
Swift Adhesives, **10** 467
Swift-Armour S.A., **II** 480
Swift-Armour S.A. Argentina, **25** 517; **26** 57
Swift-Eckrich, **II** 467
Swift Independent Packing Co., **II** 494; **13** 350, 352; **42** 92
Swift Textiles, Inc., **12** 118; **15** 247
Swift Transportation Co., Inc., 26 533; **33** 468; **42 363–66**
Swinerton Inc., 43 397–400
Swing-N-Slide, Inc. *See* PlayCore, Inc.
Swingline, Inc., **7** 3–5
Swire Group, **34** 100
Swire Pacific Ltd., I 469–70, **521–22; 6** 78; **16 479–81 (upd.); 18** 114; **20** 310, 312
Swisher International Group Inc., 14 17–19; **23 463–65; 27** 139
Swiss Air Transport Company Ltd., I 107, 119, **121–22; 24** 312; **27** 409; **33** 49, 51, 271
Swiss-American Corporation, **II** 267; **21** 145
Swiss Banca de Gottardo, **26** 456
Swiss Banca della Svizzera Italiano, **II** 192
Swiss Bank Corporation, II 267, **368–70,** 378–79; **14** 419–20; **21** 145–46
Swiss Cement-Industrie-Gesellschaft, **III** 701
Swiss Colony Wines, **I** 377
Swiss Drilling Co., **IV** 372; **19** 22
Swiss Federal Railways (Schweizerische Bundesbahnen), V 519–22
Swiss General Chocolate Co., **II** 545–46; **7** 380–81
Swiss Locomotive and Machine Works, **III** 631–32
Swiss Oil Co., **IV** 372–73
Swiss Reinsurance Company, III 299, 301, 335, **375–78; 15** 13; **21** 146
Swiss Saurer AG, **39** 39, 41
Swiss Time Australia Pty Ltd, **25** 461
Swiss Volksbank, **21** 146–47
Swissair Associated Co., **I** 122; **6** 60, 96, 117; **34** 397–98; **36** 426

Switchboard Inc., **25** 52
SXI Limited, **17** 458
Sybase, Inc., **6** 255, 279; **10** 361, **504–06**; **11** 77–78; **15** 492; **25** 96, 299; **27** **447–50 (upd.)**
SyberVision, **10** 216
Sybra, Inc., **19** 466–68
Sybron International Corp., **14** **479–81**; **19** 289–90
SYCOM, Inc., **18** 363
Sydney Electricity, **12** 443
Sydney Paper Mills Ltd., **IV** 248
Sydney Ross Co., **I** 698–99
Syfrets Trust Co., **IV** 23
Sylacauga Calcium Products, **III** 691
Syllogic B.V., **29** 376
Sylvan, Inc., **22** **496–99**
Sylvan Lake Telephone Company, **6** 334
Sylvan Learning Systems, Inc., **35** **408–11**
Sylvan Learning Systems Inc., **13** 299; **34** 439
Sylvania Companies, **I** 463; **II** 63; **III** 165, 475; **V** 295; **7** 161; **8** 157; **11** 197; **13** 402; **23** 181
Sylvia Paperboard Co., **IV** 310; **19** 266
Symantec Corporation, **10** **507–09**; **25** 348–49
Symbios Logic Inc., **19** 312; **31** 5
Symbiosis Corp., **10** 70
Symbol Technologies, Inc., **10** 363, 523–24; **15** **482–84**
Symington-Wayne, **III** 472
Symphony International, **14** 224
Syms Corporation, **29** **456–58**
Symtron Systems Inc., **37** 399–400
Symtronix Corporation, **18** 515
Syn-Optics, Inc., **29** 454
Synbiotics Corporation, **23** 284
Syncordia Corp., **15** 69
Syncrocom, Inc., **10** 513
Syncrude Canada Limited, **25** 232
Synercom Technology Inc., **14** 319
Synercon Corporation, **25** 538
Synergen Inc., **13** 241
Synergy Dataworks, Inc., **11** 285
Synergy Software Inc., **31** 131
Synetic, Inc., **16** 59
Synfloor SA, **25** 464
Synopsis, Inc., **11** **489–92**; **18** 20; **43** 17
SynOptics Communications, Inc., **10** 194, **510–12**; **11** 475; **16** 392; **22** 52
Synovus Financial Corp., **12** **465–67**; **18** 516–17
Syntax Ophthalmic Inc., **III** 727
Syntex Corporation, **I** 512, **701–03**; **III** 18, 53; **8** 216–17, 434, 548; **10** 53; **12** 322; **26** 384
Syntex Pharmaceuticals Ltd., **21** 425
Synthecolor S.A., **8** 347
Synthélabo, **III** 47–48
Synthetic Blood Corp., **15** 380
Synthetic Pillows, Inc., **19** 304
Syntron, Inc., **18** 513–15
SyQuest Technology, Inc., **18** **509–12**
Syracuse China, **8** 510
Syratech Corp., **14** **482–84**; **27** 288
Syrian Airways, **6** 85; **27** 133
Syroco, **14** 483–84
SYSCO Corporation, **II** **675–76**; **9** 453; **16** 387; **18** 67; **24** **470–72 (upd.)**, 528; **26** 504
Syscon Corporation, **38** 227
Sysorex Information Systems, **11** 62
SysScan, **V** 339
Systech Environmental Corporation, **28** 228–29
System Designers plc. *See* SD-Scicon plc.
System Development Co., **III** 166; **6** 282
System Fuels, Inc., **11** 194
System Integrators, Inc., **6** 279
System Parking West, **25** 16
System Software Associates, Inc., **10** **513–14**
Systematics Inc., **6** 301; **11** 131
Systembolaget, **31** 459–60
Systems & Computer Technology Corp., **19** **437–39**
Systems and Services Company. *See* SYSCO Corporation.
Systems Center, Inc., **6** 279; **11** 469
Systems Construction Ltd., **II** 649
Systems Development Corp., **25** 117
Systems Engineering and Manufacturing Company, **11** 225
Systems Engineering Labs (SEL), **11** 45; **13** 201
Systems Exploration Inc., **10** 547
Systems Magnetic Co., **IV** 101
Systems Marketing Inc., **12** 78
Systronics, **13** 235
Syufy Enterprises. *See* Century Theatres, Inc.
Szabo, **II** 608

T. and J. Brocklebank Ltd., **23** 160
T&N PLC, **26** 141
T-Fal. *See* Groupe SEB.
T.G.I. Friday's, **10** 331; **19** 258; **20** 159; **21** 250; **22** 127
T.J. Falgout, **11** 523
T.J. Maxx, **V** 197–98; **13** 329–30; **14** 62
T. Kobayashi & Co., Ltd., **III** 44
T.L. Smith & Company, **21** 502
T/Maker, **9** 81
T. Mellon & Sons, **II** 315
T. Rowe Price Associates, Inc., **10** 89; **11** **493–96**; **34** **423–27 (upd.)**
T.S. Farley, Limited, **10** 319
T-Shirt Brokerage Services, Inc., **26** 257
T-Tech Industries, **26** 363
T. Wear Company S.r.l., **25** 121
TA Associates Inc., **10** 382; **32** 146
TA Media AG, **15** 31
TAB Products Co., **17** **467–69**
Tabacalera, S.A., **V** **414–16**; **15** 139; **17** **470–73 (upd.)**
Table Supply Stores, **II** 683
Tabulating Machine Company. *See* International Business Machines Corporation.
TACA. *See* Grupo TACA.
Taco Bell Corp., **I** 278; **7** 267, **505–07**; **9** 178; **10** 450; **13** 336, 494; **14** 453; **15** 486; **16** 96–97; **17** 537; **21** 315, **485–88 (upd.)**; **25** 178; **37** 349, 351
Taco Cabana, Inc., **23** **466–68**
Taco John's International Inc., **15** **485–87**
Taco Kid, **7** 506
Tadiran Telecommunications Ltd., **II** 47; **25** 266–67
Taehan Cement, **III** 748
Taft Broadcasting Co. *See* Great American Broadcasting Inc.
TAG Heuer International SA, **7** 554; **25** **459–61**
TAG Pharmaceuticals, **22** 501
Taguchi Automobile. *See* Seino Transportation Company, Ltd.
Tahoe Joe's, Inc., **32** 102 **32** 249
TAI, Ltd., **34** 397
Taiba Corporation, **8** 250
Taiheiyo Bank, **15** 495
Taikoo Dockyard Co., **I** 521; **16** 480
Taikoo Sugar Refinery, **I** 521; **16** 480
Taio Paper Mfg. Co., Ltd. *See* Daio Paper Co., Ltd.
Taisho America, **III** 295
Taisho Marine and Fire Insurance Co., Ltd., **III** 209, 295–96
Taisho Pharmaceutical, **I** 676; **II** 361
Taittinger S.A., **27** 421; **43** **401–05**
Taiwan Aerospace Corp., **11** 279; **24** 88
Taiwan Auto Glass, **III** 715
Taiwan Power Company, **22** 89
Taiwan Semiconductor Manufacturing Company Ltd., **18** 20; **22** 197; **43** 17
Taiway, **III** 596
Taiyo Bussan, **IV** 225; **24** 489
Taiyo Fishery Company, Limited, **II** **578–79**
Taiyo Kobe Bank, Ltd., **II** 326, **371–72**
Taiyo Kogyo Corporation, **35** 98, 100
Taiyo Metal Manufacturing Co., **III** 757
Takada & Co., **IV** 151; **24** 358
Takanashi Milk Products Ltd., **37** 197
Takara, **25** 488
Takaro Shuzo, **III** 42
Takashimaya Co., Limited, **V** **193–96**; **41** 114
Takeda Chemical Industries Ltd., **I** **704–06**; **III** 760
Takeda Riken, **11** 504
Takeuchi Mining Co., **III** 545
Takihyo, **15** 145
Takkyubin, **V** 537
Tako Oy, **IV** 314
The Talbots, Inc., **II** 503; **10** 324; **11** **497–99**; **12** 280; **31** **429–432 (upd.)**
Talcott National Corporation, **11** 260–61
Talegen Holdings Inc., **26** 546
Taliq Corp., **III** 715
Talisman Energy, **9** **490–93**
TALK Corporation, **34** 48
Talk Radio Network, Inc., **23** 294
Talley Industries, Inc., **10** 386; **16** **482–85**
Tally Corp., **18** 434
Talmadge Farms, Inc., **20** 105
TAM Ceramics, **III** 681
Tamar Bank, **II** 187
Tamarkin Co., **12** 390
Tambrands Inc., **III** 40; **8** **511–13**; **12** 439; **15** 359–60, 501; **16** 303; **26** 384; **37** 394
Tamco, **12** 390; **19** 380
TAMET, **IV** 25
Tamglass Automotive OY, **22** 436
Tampa Electric Company, **6** 582–83
Tampax Inc. *See* Tambrands Inc.
Oy Tampella Ab, **II** 47; **III** 648; **IV** 276; **25** 266
Tampere Paper Board and Roofing Felt Mill, **IV** 314
Tampereen Osake-Pankki, **II** 303
Tampimex Oil, **11** 194
TAMSA. *See* Tubos de Acero de Mexico, S.A.
Tamura Kisan Co., **II** 552
Tanaka, **6** 71
Tanaka Kikinzoku Kogyo KK, **IV** 119

Tanaka Matthey KK, **IV** 119
Tandem Computers, Inc., 6 278–80; 10 499; **11** 18; **14** 318; **26** 93; **29** 477–79
Tandon, **25** 531
Tandy Corporation, II 70, **106–08; 6** 257–58; **9** 43, 115, 165; **10** 56–57, 166–67, 236; **12 468–70 (upd.); 13** 174; **14** 117; **16** 84; **17** 353–54; **24** 502; **25** 531; **26** 18; **34** 198. *See also* RadioShack Corporation.
Tandycrafts, Inc., 31 433–37
Tangent Industries, **15** 83
Tangent Systems, **6** 247–48
Tangiers International. *See* Algo Group Inc.
Tangram Rehabilitation Network, Inc., **29** 401
Tanjong Pagar Dock Co., **I** 592
Tanks Oil and Gas, **11** 97
Tanne-Arden, Inc., **27** 291
Tanner-Brice Company, **13** 404
Tantalum Mining Corporation, **29** 81
TAP Air Portugal. *See* Transportes Aereos Portugueses.
Tapiola Insurance, **IV** 316
Tapis-St. Maclou, **37** 22
Tappan. *See* White Consolidated Industries Inc.
Tara Exploration and Development Ltd., **IV** 165
Tara Foods, **II** 645
Target Rock Corporation, **35** 134–36
Target Stores, V 35, 43–44; **10** 284, **515–17; 12** 508; **13** 261, 274, 446; **14** 398; **15** 275; **16** 390; **17** 460–61; **18** 108, 137, 283, 286; **20** 155; **22** 328; **27** 315, **451–54 (upd.); 39** 269, 271
Tarkett Sommer AG, 12 464; **25 462–64**
Tarmac plc, III 734, **751–54; 14** 250; **28 447–51 (upd.); 36** 21
TarMacadam (Purnell Hooley's Patent) Syndicate Ltd., **III** 751
Tarragon Oil and Gas Ltd., **24** 522
Tarslag, **III** 752
TASC. *See* Analytical Sciences Corp.
Tashima Shoten, **III** 574
Tasman Pulp and Paper Co. Ltd. *See* Fletcher Challenge Ltd.
Tasman U.E.B., **IV** 249
Tasmanian Fibre Containers, **IV** 249
Tastee Freeze, **39** 234
Tasty Baking Company, 14 485–87; 35 412–16 (upd.)
TAT European Airlines, **14** 70, 73; **24** 400
Tata Airlines. *See* Air-India Limited.
Tata Enterprises, **III** 43
Tata Industries, **20** 313; **21** 74
Tata Iron and Steel Company Ltd., IV 48, 205–07, **217–19**
Tate & Lyle PLC, II 514, **580–83; 7** 466–67; **13** 102; **26** 120; **42 367–72 (upd.)**
Tatebayashi Flour Milling Co., **II** 554
Tateisi Electric Manufacturing, **II** 75
Tateisi Medical Electronics Manufacturing Co., **II** 75
Tatham Corporation, **21** 169, 171
Tatham/RSCG, **13** 204
Tati SA, 25 465–67
Tattered Cover Book Store, 43 406–09
Tatung Co., III 482; **13** 387; **23 469–71**
Taurus Exploration, **21** 208
Taurus Programming Services, **10** 196
Tax Management, Inc., **23** 92
Taylor Corporation, 36 465–67; 37 108
Taylor Diving and Salvage Co., **III** 499
Taylor-Evans Seed Co., **IV** 409
Taylor Made Golf Co., 23 270, **472–74; 33** 7
Taylor Material Handling, **13** 499
Taylor Medical, **14** 388
Taylor Nelson Sofres plc, 34 428–30; 37 144
Taylor Petroleum, Inc., **17** 170
Taylor Publishing Company, 12 471–73; 25 254; **36 468–71 (upd.)**
Taylor Rental Corp., **III** 628
Taylor Wines Co., **I** 234; **10** 227
Taylor Woodrow plc, I 590–91; III 739; **13** 206; **38 450–53 (upd.)**
Taylors and Lloyds, **II** 306
Tayto Ltd., **22** 515
Tazuke & Co., **IV** 151; **24** 358
TBC Corp., **20** 63
TBS. *See* Turner Broadcasting System, Inc.
TBWA Advertising, Inc., 6 47–49; 22 394
TBWA Worldwide, **42** 175; **43** 412
TBWA\Chiat\Day, 43 410–14 (upd.)
TC Advertising. *See* Treasure Chest Advertising, Inc.
TC Debica, **20** 264
TCA. *See* Air Canada.
TCBC. *See* Todays Computers Business Centers.
TCBY Enterprises Inc., 17 474–76
TCF. *See* Tokyo City Finance.
TCF Holdings, Inc., **II** 170–71
TCH Corporation, **12** 477
TCI. *See* Tele-Communications, Inc.
TCI Communications, **29** 39
TCI Inc., **33** 92–93
TCI International Inc., **43** 48
TCPL. *See* TransCanada PipeLines Ltd.
TCS Management Group, Inc., **22** 53
TCW Capital, **19** 414–15
TDK Corporation, I 500; **II 109–11; IV** 680; **17 477–79 (upd.)**
TDS. *See* Telephone and Data Systems, Inc.
Teaberry Electronics Corp., **III** 569; **20** 361
Teachers Insurance and Annuity Association, III 379–82; 22 268; **35** 75
Teachers Service Organization, Inc., **8** 9–10
Team America, **9** 435
Team Penske, **V** 494
Team Rental Group. *See* Budget Group, Inc.
Teams, Inc., **37** 247
Teamsters Central States Pension Fund, **19** 378
Teamsters Union, **13** 19
TearDrop Golf Company, 32 445–48
Tebel Maschinefabrieken, **III** 420
Tebel Pneumatiek, **III** 420
Tech Data Corporation, 10 518–19
Tech Pacific International, **18** 180; **39** 201, 203
Tech-Sym Corporation, 18 513–15
Tech Textiles, USA, **15** 247–48
Techalloy Co., **IV** 228
Technair Packaging Laboratories, **18** 216
Technical Ceramics Laboratories, Inc., **13** 141
Technical Coatings Co., **13** 85; **38** 96–97
Technical Materials, Inc., **14** 81
Technical Publishing, **IV** 605
Technicare, **11** 200
Technicolor Inc., **28** 246
Technicon Instruments Corporation, **III** 56; **11** 333–34; **22** 75
Technifax, **8** 483
Techniques d'Avant-Garde. *See* TAG Heuer International SA.
Technisch Bureau Visser, **16** 421
Technitrol, Inc., 29 459–62
Techno-Success Company, **V** 719
AB Technology, **II** 466
Technology Management Group, Inc., **18** 112
Technology Resources International Ltd., **18** 76
Technology Venture Investors, **11** 490; **14** 263
Technophone Ltd., **17** 354
TechTeam Europe, Ltd., **41** 281
Teck Corporation, 9 282; **27 455–58**
Tecnamotor S.p.A., **8** 72, 515
Tecneco, **IV** 422
Tecnifax Corp., **IV** 330
Tecnipublicaciones, **14** 555
Tecnost S.p.A., **34** 319
TECO Energy, Inc., 6 582–84
Tecom Industries, Inc., **18** 513–14
Tecstar, Inc., **30** 436
Tecumseh Products Company, 8 72, **514–16**
Ted Bates, Inc., **I** 33, 623; **10** 69; **16** 71–72
Teddy's Shoe Store. *See* Morse Shoe Inc.
Tedelex, **IV** 91–92
Teekay Shipping Corporation, 25 468–71
Tees and Hartlepool, **31** 367, 369
Tefal. *See* Groupe SEB.
TEFSA, **17** 182
TEIC. *See* B.V. Tabak Export & Import Compagnie.
Teijin Limited, I 511; **V 380–82**
Teikoku Bank, **I** 507; **II** 273, 325–26
Teikoku Hormone, **I** 704
Teikoku Jinken. *See* Teijin Limited.
Teikoku Sekiyu Co. Ltd., **IV** 475
Teikoku Shiki, **IV** 326
Teito Electric Railway, **V** 461
Teito Transport Co. Ltd., **V** 536
Tejas Gas Co., **41** 359
Tejon Ranch Company, 35 417–20
Tekmunc A/S, **17** 288
Teknekron Infoswitch Corporation, **22** 51
Teknika Electronics Corporation, **43** 459
Tekrad, Inc. *See* Tektronix, Inc.
Tekton Corp., **IV** 346
Tektronix, Inc., II 101; **8 517–21; 10** 24; **11** 284–86; **12** 454; **36** 331; **38** 71; **39** 350, 353; **41** 235
Tel-A-Data Limited, **11** 111
TelAutograph Corporation, **29** 33–34
Telcon. *See* Telegraph Construction and Maintenance Company.
Tele-Communications, Inc., II 160–62, 167; **10** 484, 506; **11** 479; **13** 280; **15** 264–65; **17** 148; **18** 64–66, 211, 213, 535; **19** 282; **21** 307, 309; **23** 121, 502; **24** 6, 120; **25** 213–14; **26** 33; **28** 241; **38** 120; **42** 114–15; **43** 433
Tele Consulte, **14** 555
Telebook, **25** 19
Telec Centre S.A., **19** 472
TeleCheck Services, **18** 542

TeleCheck Services, Inc., **11** 113
TeleChef, **33** 387, 389
Teleclub, **IV** 590
Teleco Oilfield Services Inc., **6** 578; **22** 68
TeleColumbus, **11** 184
Telecom Australia, 6 341–42
Telecom Canada. *See* Stentor Canadian Network Management.
Telecom Eireann, 7 508–10. *See also* eircom plc.
Telecom Italia S.p.A., **15** 355; **24** 79; **34** 316, 319; **43 415–19**
Telecom New Zealand, **18** 33
Telecom One, Inc., **29** 252
Telecom*USA, **27** 304
Telecommunications of Jamaica Ltd., **25** 101
Telecomputing Corp., **I** 544
Telecredit, Inc., **6** 25
Telectronic Pacing Systems, **10** 445
Teledyne Inc., **I** 486, **523–25**; **II** 33, 44; **10** 262–63, 365, **520–22 (upd.)**; **11** 265; **13** 387; **17** 109; **18** 369; **29** 400; **35** 136
Teleflora Inc., **28** 1 8–90; **19** 12; **21** 259
Teleflora LLC, **37** 337
Telefonaktiebolaget LM Ericsson, V 334–36
Telefónica de España, S.A., **V 337–40**; **43** 422
Telefonos de Mexico S.A. de C.V., **14 488–90**
Téléfrance, **25** 174
Telefunken Fernseh & Rundfunk GmbH., **I** 411; **II** 117
Telegate, **18** 155
Teleglobe Inc., **14** 512
Telegraph Condenser Co., **II** 81
Telegraph Construction and Maintenance Company, **25** 98–100
Telegraph Manufacturing Co., **III** 433
Telegraph Works, **III** 433
Telegraphic Service Company, **16** 166
Telekomunikacja S.A., **18** 33
Telelistas Editors Ltda., **26** 520
TeleMarketing Corporation of Louisiana, **8** 311
Telemarketing Investments, Ltd., **8** 311
Telematics International Inc., **18** 154, 156
Télémécanique, **II** 94; **18** 473; **19** 166
Telemundo Group, Inc., **III** 344; **24** 516
Telenet Communications, **18** 32
Telenor, **31** 221
Telenorma, **I** 193
Telenova, **III** 169; **6** 285
Teleos Communications Inc., **26** 277
Telephone and Data Systems, Inc., **9 494–96**, 527–529; **31** 449
Telephone Company of Ireland, **7** 508
Telephone Exchange Company of Indianapolis, **14** 257
Telephone Management Corporation, **8** 310
Telephone Utilities, Inc. *See* Pacific Telecom, Inc.
Telephone Utilities of Washington, **6** 325, 328
Telepictures, **II** 177
TelePizza S.A., 33 387–89
Teleport Communications Group, **14** 253; **24** 122
Teleprompter Corp., **II** 122; **7** 222; **10** 210; **18** 355
Telerate Systems Inc., **IV** 603, 670; **10** 276–78; **21** 68
Teleregister Corp., **I** 512
Telerent Europe. *See* Granada Group PLC.
TeleRep, **IV** 596
Telesat Cable TV, Inc., **23** 293
Telesis Oil and Gas, **6** 478
Telesistema, **18** 212
Telesistema Mexico. *See* Grupo Televisa.
Telesphere Network, Inc., **8** 310
Telesystems SLW Inc., **10** 524
Telettra S.p.A., **V** 326; **9** 10; **11** 205
Tele2 AB, **26** 331–33
Teletype Corp., **14** 569
Televimex, S.A., **18** 212
Television de Mexico, S.A., **18** 212
Television Española, S.A., **7 511–12**; **18** 211
Télévision Française 1, 23 475–77
Television Sales and Marketing Services Ltd., **7** 79–80
Teleway Japan, **7** 118–19; **13** 482
Telex Corporation, **II** 87; **13** 127
Telfin, **V** 339
Telia Mobitel, **11** 19; **26** 332
Telihoras Corporation, **10** 319
Telinfo, **6** 303
Telinq Inc., **10** 19
Telios Pharmaceuticals, Inc., **11** 460; **17** 288
Tellabs, Inc., **11 500–01**; **40 426–29 (upd.)**
Telmex. *See* Teléfonos de México S.A. de C.V.
Telpar, Inc., **14** 377
Telport, **14** 260
Telrad Telecommunications Ltd., **II** 48; **25** 266–67
Telxon Corporation, 10 523–25
Tembec, Inc., **IV** 296; **19** 226
Temco Electronics and Missile Co., **I** 489
Temenggong of Jahore, **I** 592
Temerlin McClain, **23** 479; **25** 91
TEMIC TELEFUNKEN, **34** 128, 133, 135
Temp Force, **16** 421–22; **43** 308
Temp World, Inc., **6** 10
Temple, Barker & Sloan/Strategic Planning Associates, **III** 283
Temple Frosted Foods, **25** 278
Temple Inks Company, **13** 227
Temple-Inland Inc., **IV** 312, **341–43**, 675; **8** 267–69; **19** 268; **31 438–442 (upd.)**
Temple Press Ltd., **IV** 294–95; **19** 225
Templeton, **II** 609
TEMPO Enterprises, **II** 162
Tempo-Team, **16** 420; **43** 307
Tempus Expeditions, **13** 358
TemTech Ltd., **13** 326
10 Sen Kinitsu Markets, **V** 194
Ten Speed Press, **27** 223
Tenacqco Bridge Partnership, **17** 170
Tenby Industries Limited, **21** 350
TenFold Corporation, 35 421–23
Tengelmann Group, **II** 636–38; **16** 249–50; **27 459–62**; **35** 401
Tengen Inc., **III** 587; **7** 395
Tennant Company, **13 499–501**; **33 390–93 (upd.)**
Tenneco Inc., **I** 182, **526–28**; **IV** 76, 152, 283, 371, 499; **6** 531; **10** 379–80, 430, **526–28 (upd.)**; **11** 440; **12** 91, 376; **13** 372–73; **16** 191, 461; **19** 78, 483; **21** 170; **22** 275, 380; **24** 358; **38** 325, 380; **40** 134
Tennessee Book Company, **11** 193
Tennessee Coal, Iron and Railroad Co., **IV** 573; **7** 550
Tennessee Eastman Corporation, **III** 475; **7** 161. *See also* Eastman Chemical Company.
Tennessee Electric Power Co., **III** 332
Tennessee Gas Pipeline Co., **14** 126
Tennessee Gas Transmission Co., **I** 526; **13** 496; **14** 125
Tennessee Insurance Company, **11** 193–94
Tennessee Paper Mills Inc. *See* Rock-Tenn Company.
Tennessee Restaurant Company, **9** 426; **30** 208–9
Tennessee River Pulp & Paper Co., **12** 376–77
Tennessee Trifting, **13** 169
Tennessee Valley Authority, **II** 2–3, 121; **IV** 181; **22** 10; **38** 447
Tennessee Woolen Mills, Inc., **19** 304
Tenngasco, **I** 527
Teollisuusosuuskunta Metsä-Saimaa, **IV** 315
TEP. *See* Tucson Electric Power Company.
Tequila Sauza, **31** 91
Tequilera de Los Altos, **31** 92
TeraBeam Networks Inc., **41** 261, 263–64
Teradata Corporation, **6** 267; **30** 339–40
Teradyne, Inc., 11 502–04
Terex Corporation, **7 513–15**; **8** 116; **40 430–34 (upd.)**
Teril Stationers Inc., **16** 36
Terminal Transfer and Storage, Inc., **6** 371
Terminix International, **6** 45–46; **11** 433; **23** 428, 430; **25** 16
Terra Industries, Inc., **13** 277, **502–04**
Terra Lycos, Inc., 43 420–25
Terrace Park Dairies, **II** 536
Terracor, **11** 260–61
Terragrafics, **14** 245
Terrain King, **32** 26
Terre Haute Electric, **6** 555
Terre Lune, **25** 91
Territorial Hotel Co., **II** 490
Territory Ahead, Inc., **29** 279
Territory Enterprises Ltd., **IV** 59
Terry Coach Industries, Inc., **III** 484; **22** 206
Terry's of York, **II** 594
Tesa, S.A., **23** 82
TESC. *See* The European Software Company.
Tesco PLC, **II** 513, **677–78**; **10** 442; **11** 239, 241; **24 473–76 (upd.)**
Tesoro Bolivia Petroleum Company, **25** 546
Tesoro Petroleum Corporation, 7 516–19
Tesseract Inc., **11** 78; **33** 331
Tessman Seed, Inc., **16** 270–71
Testor Corporation, **8** 455
TETI, **I** 466
Tetley Inc., **I** 215; **14** 18
Tetra Plastics Inc., **V** 374; **8** 393
Tetra Tech, Inc., 29 463–65
Teutonia National Bank, **IV** 310; **19** 265
Teva Pharmaceutical Industries Ltd., **22 500–03**
Tex-Mex Partners L.C., **41** 270
Tex-Star Oil & Gas Corp., **IV** 574; **7** 551
Texaco Canada Inc., **25** 232
Texaco Inc., **I** 21, 360; **II** 31, 313, 448; **III** 760; **IV** 386, 403, 418, 425, 429, 439, 461, 464, 466, 472–73, 479–80, 484, 488, 490, 510–11, 530–31, 536–39, 545, **551–53**, 560, 565–66, 570, 575; **7** 172, 280, 483; **9** 232; **10**

190; **12** 20; **13** 448; **14 491–94 (upd.)**; **17** 412; **18** 488; **41** 359, **391–96 (upd.)** **19** 73, 75, 176; **24** 521; **27** 481; **28** 47;
Texada Mines, Ltd., **IV** 123
Texas Air Corporation, **I** 97, 100, 103, 118, **123–24**, 127, 130; **6** 82, 129; **12** 489; **21** 142–43; **35** 427
Texas Almanac, **10** 3
Texas Bus Lines, **24** 118
Texas Butadiene and Chemical Corp., **IV** 456
Texas Co., **III** 497; **IV** 386, 400, 464, 536, 551–52; **7** 352
Texas Commerce Bankshares, **II** 252
Texas Eastern Corp., **6** 487; **11** 97, 354; **14** 126
Texas Eastern Transmission Company, **11** 28
Texas Eastman, **III** 475; **7** 161
Texas Electric Service Company, **V** 724
Texas Gas Resources Corporation, **IV** 395; **22** 166
Texas Gypsum, **IV** 341
Texas Homecare, **21** 335
Texas Industries, Inc., **8 522–24**; **13** 142–43
Texas Instruments Incorporated, **I** 315, 482, 523, 620; **II** 64, **112–15**; **III** 120, 124–25, 142, 499; **IV** 130, 365, 681; **6** 216, 221–22, 237, 241, 257, 259; **7** 531; **8** 157; **9** 43, 116, 310; **10** 22, 87, 307; **11** 61, 308, 490, 494, **505–08 (upd.)**; **12** 135, 238; **14** 42–43; **16** 4, 333; **17** 192; **18** 18, 436; **21** 123; **23** 181, 210; **25** 81, 96, 531; **38** 375; **43** 15
Texas International Airlines, **I** 117, 123; **II** 408; **IV** 413; **21** 142
Texas Life Insurance Co., **III** 293
Texas Metal Fabricating Company, **7** 540
Texas-New Mexico Utilities Company, **6** 580
Texas Oil & Gas Corp., **IV** 499, 572, 574; **7** 549, 551
Texas Overseas Petroleum Co., **IV** 552
Texas Pacific Coal and Oil Co., **I** 285–86
Texas Pacific Group Inc., **22** 80; **23** 163, 166; **30** 171; **34** 231; **36 472–74**
Texas Pacific Oil Co., **IV** 550
Texas Pipe Line Co., **IV** 552
Texas Power & Light Company, **V** 724
Texas Public Utilities, **II** 660
Texas Super Duper Markets, Inc., **7** 372
Texas Trust Savings Bank, **8** 88
Texas United Insurance Co., **III** 214
Texas Utilities Company, **V 724–25**; **12** 99; **25 472–74 (upd.)**; **35** 479
Texasgulf Inc., **IV** 546–47; **13** 557; **18** 433
Texboard, **IV** 296; **19** 226
Texize, **I** 325, 371
Texkan Oil Co., **IV** 566
Texstar Petroleum Company, **7** 516
Texstyrene Corp., **IV** 331
Textile Diffusion, **25** 466
Textile Paper Tube Company, Ltd., **8** 475
Textile Rubber and Chemical Company, **15** 490
Textron Inc., **I** 186, **529–30**; **II** 420; **III** 66, 628; **8** 93, 157, 315, 545; **9** 497, 499; **11** 261; **12** 251, 382–83, 400–01; **13** 63–64; **17** 53; **21** 175; **22** 32; **27** 100; **34 431–34 (upd.)**; **35** 350–51
Textron Lycoming Turbine Engine, **9 497–99**
Texwood Industries, Inc., **20** 363
TF-I, **I** 563
TFC. *See* Times Fiber Communications, Inc.
TFN Group Communications, Inc., **8** 311
TF1 **24** 79. *See also* Télévision Française 1
TGEL&PCo. *See* Tucson Gas, Electric Light & Power Company.
Th. Pilter, **III** 417
TH:s Group, **10** 113
Thai Airways International Ltd., **I** 119; **II** 442; **6 122–24**
Thai Airways International Public Company Limited, **27 463–66 (upd.)**
Thai Aluminium Co. Ltd., **IV** 155
Thai Union International Inc., **24** 116
Thalassa International, **10** 14; **27** 11
Thales S.A., **42 373–76**
Thalhimer Brothers, **V** 31
Thames Board Ltd., **IV** 318
Thames Television Ltd., **I** 532
Thames Trains, **28** 157
Thames Water plc, **11 509–11**; **22** 89
Thameslink, **28** 157
Tharsis Co., **IV** 189–90
Thatcher Glass, **I** 610
THAW. *See* Recreational Equipment, Inc.
Thayer Laboratories, **III** 55
Theatrical Syndicate, **24** 437
Theo H. Davies & Co., **I** 470; **20** 311
Theo Hamm Brewing Co., **I** 260
Théraplix, **I** 388
Therm-o-Disc, **II** 19
Therm-X Company, **8** 178
Thermacote Welco Company, **6** 146
Thermadyne Holding Corporation, **19 440–43**
Thermal Dynamics, **19** 441
Thermal Energies, Inc., **21** 514
Thermal Power Company, **11** 270
Thermal Snowboards, Inc., **22** 462
Thermal Transfer Ltd., **13** 485
Thermo BioAnalysis Corp., **25 475–78**
Thermo Electron Corporation, **7 520–22**; **11** 512–13; **13** 421; **24** 477; **25** 475–76
Thermo Fibertek, Inc., **24 477–79**
Thermo Instrument Systems Inc., **11 512–14**; **25** 475–77
Thermo King Corporation, **13 505–07**
Thermodynamics Corp., **III** 645
Thermoforming USA, **16** 339
Thermogas Co., **IV** 458–59; **35** 175
Thermolase Corporation, **22** 410
Thermoplast und Apparatebau GmbH, **IV** 198
Thermos Company, **16 486–88**
TheStreet.com, **34** 125
Thies Companies, **13** 270
Thiess, **III** 687
Thiess Dampier Mitsui, **IV** 47
Things Remembered, **13** 165–66
Think Entertainment, **II** 161
Think Technologies, **10** 508
Thiokol Corporation, **I** 370; **8** 472; **9** 358–59, **500–02 (upd.)**; **12** 68; **22 504–07 (upd.)**
Third National Bank. *See* Fifth Third Bancorp.
Third National Bank of Dayton, **9** 475
Third National Bank of New York, **II** 253
Third Wave Publishing Corp. *See* Acer Inc.
Thistle Group, **9** 365
Thom McAn, **V** 136–37; **11** 349
Thomas & Betts Corp., **II** 8; **11 515–17**; **14** 27
Thomas and Hochwalt, **I** 365
Thomas & Howard Co., **II** 682; **18** 8
Thomas and Judith Pyle, **13** 433
Thomas Barlow & Sons Ltd., **I** 288, 422; **IV** 22
Thomas Bros. Maps, **28** 380
Thomas Cook Group Ltd., **17** 325
Thomas Cook Travel Inc., **6** 84; **9 503–05**; **27** 133; **33 394–96 (upd.)**; **42** 282
Thomas Firth & Sons, **I** 573
Thomas H. Lee Co., **11** 156, 450; **14** 230–31; **15** 309; **19** 371, 373; **24 480–83**; **25** 67; **28** 134; **30** 219; **32** 362
Thomas Industries Inc., **29 466–69**
Thomas J. Lipton Company, **II** 609, 657; **11** 450; **14 495–97**; **16** 90; **32** 474
Thomas Jefferson Life Insurance Co., **III** 397
Thomas Kinkade Galleries. *See* Media Arts Group, Inc.
Thomas Linnell & Co. Ltd., **II** 628
Thomas Nationwide Transport. *See* TNT.
Thomas Nationwide Transport Limited. *See* TNT Post Group N.V.
Thomas Nelson Inc., **8** 526; **14 498–99**; **24** 548; **38 454–57 (upd.)**
Thomas Publishing Company, **26 482–85**
Thomas Tilling plc, **I** 429
Thomas Y. Crowell, **IV** 605
Thomaston Mills, Inc., **27 467–70**
Thomasville Furniture Industries, Inc., **III** 423; **12 474–76**; **22** 48; **28** 406; **31** 248; **39** 170, 174
Thompson and Formby, **16** 44
Thompson Aircraft Tire Corp., **14** 42
Thompson-Hayward Chemical Co., **13** 397
Thompson Medical Company. *See* Slim-Fast Nutritional Foods International Inc.
Thompson Nutritional Products, **37** 286
Thompson PBE Inc., **24** 160–61
Thompson Products Co., **I** 539
Thompson-Ramo-Woolridge, **I** 539
Thompson-Werke, **III** 32
Thomson BankWatch Inc., **19** 34
Thomson-Bennett, **III** 554
Thomson-Brandt, **I** 411; **II** 13, 116–17; **9** 9
The Thomson Corporation, **IV** 651, 686; **7** 390; **8 525–28**; **10** 407; **12** 361, 562; **17** 255; **22** 441; **34 435–40 (upd.)**
Thomson-CSF, **II** 116–17; **III** 556. *See also* Thales S.A.
Thomson-Houston Electric Co., **II** 27, 116, 330; **12** 193
Thomson International, **37** 143
Thomson-Jenson Energy Limited, **13** 558
Thomson-Lucas, **III** 556
THOMSON multimedia S.A., **18** 126; **36** 384; **42 377–80 (upd.)**
Thomson-Ramo-Woolridge. *See* TRW Inc.
Thomson S.A., **I** 411; **II** 31, **116–17**; **7** 9; **13** 402. *See also* THOMSON multimedia S.A.
Thomson T-Line, **II** 142
Thomson Travel Group, **27** 27
Thonet Industries Inc., **14** 435–36
Thor Industries, Inc., **39 391–94**
Thorn Apple Valley, Inc., **7 523–25**; **12** 125; **22 508–11 (upd.)**; **23** 203
Thorn EMI plc, **I** 52, 411, **531–32**; **II** 117, 119; **III** 480; **19** 390; **22** 27, 192–94; **24** 87, 484–85; **26** 151; **40** 105
Thorn plc, **24 484–87**

Thorncraft Inc., **25** 379
Thorndike, Doran, Paine and Lewis, Inc., **14** 530
Thornton, **III** 547
Thornton & Co., **II** 283
Thornton Stores, **14** 235
Thoroughgood, **II** 658
Thorsen Realtors, **21** 96
Thos. & Wm. Molson & Company. *See* The Molson Companies Limited.
Thousand Trails, Inc., **13** 494; **33 397–99**
Thousands Springs Power Company, **12** 265
THQ, Inc., **39 395–97**
Threadz, **25** 300
Three-Diamond Company. *See* Mitsubishi Shokai.
The 3DO Company, **43 426–30**
3 Guys, **II** 678, **V** 35
3-in-One Oil Co., **I** 622
3 Maj, **25** 469
Three Rivers Pulp and Paper Company, **17** 281
Three Score, **23** 100
3 Suisses International, **12** 281
3Com Corporation, **III** 143; **6** 238, 269; **10** 237; **11 518–21**; **20** 8, 33; **26** 276; **34 441–45 (upd.)**; **36** 122, 300, 357. *See also* Palm, Inc.
3D Planet SpA, **41** 409
3DO Inc., **10** 286
3M. *See* Minnesota Mining & Manufacturing Co.
3S Systems Support Services Ltd., **6** 310
Threlfall Breweries, **I** 294
Threshold Entertainment, **25** 270
Thrif D Discount Center, **V** 174
Thrift Drug, **V** 92
Thrift Mart, **16** 65
ThriftiCheck Service Corporation, **7** 145
Thriftimart Inc., **12** 153; **16** 452
Thriftway Food Drug, **21** 530
Thriftway Foods, **II** 624
Thrifty Corporation, **25** 413, 415–16
Thrifty PayLess, Inc., **V** 682, 684; ; **12 477–79**; **18** 286; **19** 357; **25** 297
Thrifty Rent-A-Car, **6** 349; **24** 10. *See also* Dollar Thrifty Automotive Group, Inc.
Throwing Corporation of America, **12** 501
Thrustmaster S.A., **41** 190
Thummel Schutze & Partner, **28** 141
Thunder Bay Press, **34** 3–5
Thuringia Insurance Co., **III** 299
Thurmond Chemicals, Inc., **27** 291
Thurston Motor Lines Inc., **12** 310
Thy-Marcinelle, **IV** 52
Thyssen AG, **II** 279; **III** 566; **IV** 195, **221–23**, 228; **8** 75–76; **14** 169, 328
Thyssen Krupp AG, **28** 104, **452–60 (upd.)**; **42** 417
Thyssen-Krupp Stahl AG, **26** 83
Thyssengas, **38** 406–07
TI. *See* Texas Instruments.
TI Corporation, **10** 44
TI Group plc, **17 480–83**
Tianjin Agricultural Industry and Commerce Corp., **II** 577
Tianjin Automobile Industry Group, **21** 164
Tianjin Bohai Brewing Company, **21** 230
Tibbals Floring Co., **III** 611
Tibbett & Britten Group plc, **32 449–52**
Tiber Construction Company, **16** 286
Tichenor Media System Inc., **35** 220
Ticino Societa d'Assicurazioni Sulla Vita, **III** 197
Ticketmaster Corp., **13 508–10**; **25** 214; **36** 423–24
Ticketmaster Group, Inc., **37 381–84 (upd.)**
Ticketron, **13** 508–09; **24** 438; **37** 381–82
Tichnor & Fields, **10** 356
Tickometer Co., **III** 157
Ticor Title Insurance Co., **10** 45
Tidel Systems, **II** 661; **32** 416
Tidewater Inc., **11 522–24**; **37 385–88 (upd.)**
Tidewater Oil Co., **IV** 434, 460, 489, 522
Tidi Wholesale, **13** 150
Tidy House Products Co., **II** 556
Tiel Utrecht Fire Insurance Co., **III** 309–10
Tien Wah Press (Pte.) Ltd., **IV** 600
Le Tierce S.A., **II** 141
Tierco Group, Inc., **27** 382
Tierney & Partners, **23** 480
Tiffany & Co., **III** 16; **12** 312; **14 500–03**; **15** 95; **19** 27; **26** 145; **27** 329; **41** 256
TIG Holdings, Inc., **26 486–88**
Tiger Accessories, **18** 88
Tiger International, Inc., **17** 505; **18** 178; **42** 141
Tiger Management Associates, **13** 158, 256
Tiger Oats, **I** 424
Tigon Corporation, **V** 265–68; **41** 288
Tilcon, **I** 429
Tilden Interrent, **10** 419
Tile & Coal Company, **14** 248
Tilgate Pallets, **I** 592
Tillie Lewis Foods Inc., **I** 513–14
Tillinghast, Nelson & Warren Inc., **32** 459
Tillotson Corp., **14** 64; **15 488–90**
Tim-Bar Corp., **IV** 312; **19** 267
Tim Horton's Restaurants, **23** 507
Timber Lodge Steakhouse, Inc., **37** 351–52
Timber Realization Co., **IV** 305
The Timberland Company, **11** 349; **13 511–14**; **17** 245; **19** 112; **22** 173; **25** 206
Timberline Software Corporation, **15 491–93**
TIMCO. *See* Triad International Maintenance Corp.
Time Distribution Services, **13** 179
Time Electronics, **19** 311
Time Industries, **IV** 294; **19** 225; **26** 445
Time-Life Books, Inc. *See* Time Warner Inc.
Time-O-Stat Controls Corp., **II** 41; **12** 247
Time Saver Stores, Inc., **12** 112; **17** 170
Time-Sharing Information, **10** 357
Time Warner Inc., **II** 155, 161, 168, 175–177, 252, 452; **III** 245; **IV** 341–42, 636, **673–76**; **6** 293; **7** 63, 222–24, 396, **526–30 (upd.)**; **8** 267–68, 527; **9** 119, 469, 472; **10** 168, 286, 484, 488, 491; **12** 531; **13** 105–06, 399; **14** 260; **15** 51, 54; **16** 146, 223; **17** 148, 442–44; **18** 66, 535; **19** 6, 336; **22** 52, 194, 522; **23** 31, 33, 257, 274, 276, 393; **24** 321–22; **25** 141, 498–99; **26** 33, 151, 441; **27** 121, 429–30; **43** 55
Timely Brands, **I** 259
Timeplex, **III** 166; **6** 283; **9** 32
Times Fiber Communications, Inc., **40** 35–36
Times Media Ltd., **IV** 22
The Times Mirror Company, **I** 90; **IV** 583, 630, **677–78**; **14** 97; **17 484–86 (upd.)**; **21** 404; **22** 162, 443; **26** 446; **35** 419
Times Newspapers, **8** 527
Times-Picayune Publishing Co., **IV** 583
TIMET. *See* Titanium Metals Corporation.
Timex Corporation, **25 479–82 (upd.)**
Timex Enterprises Inc., **III** 455; **7 531–33**; **10** 152; **12** 317; **21** 123; **25** 22
The Timken Company, **III** 596; **7** 447; **8 529–31**; **15** 225; **42 381–85 (upd.)**
Timothy Whites, **24** 74
Timpte Industries, **II** 488
Tioxide Group PLC, **III** 680
Tip Corp., **I** 278
Tip Top Drugstores plc, **24** 269
Tip Top Tailors, **29** 162
TIPC Network. *See* Gateway 2000.
Tiphook PLC, **13** 530
Tipton Centers Inc., **V** 50; **19** 123
Tiroler Hauptbank, **II** 270
Tishman Realty and Construction, **III** 248
Tissue Papers Ltd., **IV** 260
Tissue Technologies, Inc., **22** 409
The Titan Corporation, **36 475–78**
Titan Manufacturing Company, **19** 359
Titanium Metals Corporation, **10** 434; **21 489–92**
Titanium Technology Corporation, **13** 140
Titianium Enterprises, **IV** 345
TITISA, **9** 109
Title Guarantee & Trust Co., **II** 230
Titmus Optical Inc., **III** 446
Titmuss Sainer Dechert. *See* Dechert.
Tivoli Systems, Inc., **14** 392
TJ International, Inc., **19 444–47**
The TJX Companies, Inc., **V 197–98**; **13** 548; **14** 426; **19 448–50 (upd.)**; **29** 106
TKD Electronics Corp., **II** 109
TKM Foods, **II** 513
TKR Cable Co., **15** 264
TLC Associates, **11** 261
TLC Beatrice International Holdings, Inc., **22 512–15**
TLC Gift Company, **26** 375
TLC Group, **II** 468
TLO, **25** 82
TMB Industries, **24** 144
TMC Industries Ltd., **22** 352
TML Information Services Inc., **9** 95
TMP Worldwide Inc., **30 458–60**
TMS, Inc., **7** 358
TMS Marketing, **26** 440
TMS Systems, Inc., **10** 18
TMT. *See* Trailer Marine Transport.
TN Technologies Inc., **23** 479
TNT Crust, Inc., **23** 203
TNT Freightways Corporation, **IV** 651; **14 504–06**
TNT Limited, **V 523–25**; **6** 346
TNT Post Group N.V., **27 471–76 (upd.)**; **30** 393, **461–63 (upd.)**
Toa Airlines, **I** 106; **6** 427
Toa Fire & Marine Reinsurance Co., **III** 385
Toa Kyoseki Co. Ltd., **IV** 476
Toa Medical Electronics Ltd., **22** 75
Toa Nenryo Kogyo, **IV** 432
Toa Oil Co. Ltd., **IV** 476, 543
Toa Tanker Co. Ltd., **IV** 555
Toasted Corn Flake Co., **II** 523; **13** 291
Toastmaster, **17** 215; **22** 353
Tobacco Group PLC, **30** 231

Tobacco Products Corporation, **18** 416
Tobata Imaon Co., **I** 183
Tobias, **16** 239
Tobler Co., **II** 520–21
Tobu Railway Co Ltd, 6 430–32
TOC Retail Inc., **17** 170
Tocom, Inc., **10** 320
Today's Man, Inc., 20 484–87; **21** 311
Todays Computers Business Centers, **6** 243–44
Todays Temporary, **6** 140
The Todd-AO Corporation, 33 400–04. *See also* Liberty Livewire Corporation.
Todd Shipyards Corporation, **IV** 121; **7** 138; **14 507–09**
Todhunter International, Inc., 27 477–79
Todito.com, S.A. de C.V., **39** 194, 196
Todorovich Agency, **III** 204
Toei Co. Ltd., **9** 29–30; **28** 462
Tofas, **I** 479–80
Toggenburger Bank, **II** 378
Togo's Eatery, **29** 19
Toho Co., Ltd., **I** 363; **IV** 403; **24** 327; **28 461–63**
Tohoku Alps, **II** 5
Tohoku Pulp Co., **IV** 297
Tohokushinsha Film Corporation, **18** 429
Tohuku Electric Power Company, Inc., **V** 724, 732
Tojo Railway Company, **6** 430
Tokai Aircraft Co., Ltd., **III** 415
The Tokai Bank, Limited, **II 373–74**; **15 494–96 (upd.)**
Tokai Paper Industries, **IV** 679
Tokan Kogyo, **I** 615
Tokheim Corporation, 21 493–95
Tokio Marine and Fire Insurance Co., Ltd., **II** 323; **III** 248, 289, 295, **383–86**
Tokos Medical Corporation, **17** 306, 308–09
Tokushima Ham Co., **II** 550
Tokushima Meat Processing Factory, **II** 550
Tokushu Seiko, Ltd., **IV** 63
Tokuyama Soda, **I** 509
Tokuyama Teppan Kabushikigaisha, **IV** 159
Tokyo Broadcasting System, **7** 249; **9** 29; **16** 167
Tokyo Car Manufacturing Co., **I** 105
Tokyo City Finance, **36** 419–20
Tokyo Confectionery Co., **II** 538
Tokyo Corporation, **V** 199
Tokyo Dairy Industry, **II** 538
Tokyo Denki Kogaku Kogyo, **II** 109
Tokyo Dento Company, **6** 430
Tokyo Disneyland, **IV** 715; **6** 123, 176
Tokyo Electric Company, Ltd., **I** 533; **12** 483
Tokyo Electric Express Railway Co., **IV** 728
Tokyo Electric Light Co., **IV** 153
Tokyo Electric Power Company, **IV** 167, 518; **V 729–33**
Tokyo Electronic Corp., **11** 232
Tokyo Express Highway Co., Ltd., **IV** 713–14
Tokyo Express Railway Company, **V** 510, 526
Tokyo Fire Insurance Co. Ltd., **III** 405–06, 408
Tokyo Food Products, **I** 507
Tokyo Fuhansen Co., **I** 502, 506
Tokyo Gas and Electric Industrial Company, **9** 293
Tokyo Gas Co., Ltd., **IV** 518; **V 734–36**
Tokyo Ishikawajima Shipbuilding and Engineering Company, **III** 532; **9** 293
Tokyo Maritime Insurance Co., **III** 288
Tokyo Motors. *See* Isuzu Motors, Ltd.
Tokyo Sanyo Electric, **II** 91–92
Tokyo Shibaura Electric Company, Ltd., **I** 507, 533; **12** 483
Tokyo Steel Works Co., Ltd., **IV** 63
Tokyo Stock Exchange, **34** 254
Tokyo Tanker Co., Ltd., **IV** 479
Tokyo Telecommunications Engineering Corp. *See* Tokyo Tsushin Kogyo K.K.
Tokyo Trust & Banking Co., **II** 328
Tokyo Tsushin Kogyo K.K., **II** 101, 103
Tokyo Yokohama Electric Railways Co., Ltd., **V** 199
Tokyu Corporation, **IV** 728; **V** 199, **526–28**
Tokyu Department Store Co., Ltd., **V 199–202**; **32 453–57 (upd.)**
Toledo Edison Company. *See* Centerior Energy Corporation.
Toledo Milk Processing, Inc., **15** 449
Toledo Scale Corp., **9** 441; **30** 327
Toledo Seed & Oil Co., **I** 419
Toll Brothers Inc., 15 497–99
Tom Bowling Lamp Works, **III** 554
Tom Brown, Inc., 37 389–91
Tom Doherty Associates Inc., 25 483–86
Tom Huston Peanut Co., **II** 502; **10** 323
Tom Piper Ltd., **I** 437
Tom Snyder Productions, **29** 470, 472
Tom Thumb, **40** 365–66
Tom Thumb-Page, **16** 64
Tomakomai Paper Co., Ltd., **IV** 321
Toman Corporation, **19** 390
Tombstone Pizza Corporation, **13 515–17**
Tomei Fire and Marine Insurance Co., **III** 384–85
Tomen Corporation, **IV 224–25**; **19** 256; **24 488–91 (upd.)**
Tomen Transportgerate, **III** 638
Tomkins-Johnson Company, **16** 8
Tomkins plc, **11 525–27**; **28** 382, 384; **30** 424, 426
Tomlee Tool Company, **7** 535; **26** 493
Tommy Armour Golf Co., **32** 446–47
Tommy Hilfiger Corporation, **16** 61; **20 488–90**; **25** 258
Tomoe Trading Co., **III** 595
Tonami Transportation Company, **6** 346
Tone Brothers, Inc., 21 496–98
Tone Coca-Cola Bottling Company, Ltd., **14** 288
Tonen Corporation, **IV 554–56**; **16 489–92 (upd.)**
Tong Yang Group, **III** 304
Toni Co., **III** 28; **9** 413
Tonka Corporation, **12** 169; **14** 266; **16** 267; **25** 380, **487–89**; **43** 229, 232
Tonkin, Inc., **19** 114
Tony Lama Company Inc., **19** 233
Tony Roma's, A Place for Ribs Inc., **40** 340–41
Tony Stone Images, **31** 216–17
Toohey, **10** 170
Toolex International N.V., 26 489–91
Tootal Group, **V** 356–57
Tootsie Roll Industries Inc., **12 480–82**; **15** 323
Top End Wheelchair Sports, **11** 202
Top Green International, **17** 475
Top Man, **V** 21
Top Shop, **V** 21
Top Tool Company, Inc., **25** 75
Top Value Stamp Co., **II** 644–45; **6** 364; **22** 126
Topco Associates, **17** 78
Topkapi, **17** 101–03
Toppan Printing Co., Ltd., **IV** 598–99, **679–81**
Topps Company, Inc., **13 518–20**; **19** 386; **34 446–49 (upd.)**
Topps Markets, **16** 314
Tops Appliance City, Inc., 17 487–89
Topy Industries, Limited, **8** 506–07
Tor Books. *See* Tom Doherty Associates Inc.
Toray Industries, Inc., **V** 380, **383**; **17** 287
Torbensen Gear & Axle Co., **I** 154
Torchmark Corporation, **III** 194; **9 506–08**; **10** 66; **11** 17; **22** 540–43; **33 405–08 (upd.)**
Torfeaco Industries Limited, **19** 304
Torise Ham Co., **II** 550
Tornator Osakeyhtiö, **IV** 275–76
Toro Assicurazioni, **III** 347
The Toro Company, **III** 600; **7 534–36**; **26 492–95 (upd.)**
Toromont Industries, Ltd., 21 499–501
Toronto and Scarborough Electric Railway, **9** 461
Toronto-Dominion Bank, **II** 319, **375–77**, 456; **16** 13–14; **17** 324; **18** 551–53; **21** 447; **43** 7
Toronto Electric Light Company, **9** 461
Torpshammars, **IV** 338
Torrey Canyon Oil, **IV** 569; **24** 519
The Torrington Company, **III** 526, 589–90; **13 521–24**
Torrington National Bank & Trust Co., **13** 467
Torstar Corporation, **IV** 672; **7** 488–89; **19** 405; **29 470–73**
Tosa Electric Railway Co., **II** 458
Toscany Co., **13** 42
Tosco Corporation, **7 537–39**; **12** 240; **20** 138; **24** 522; **36** 359; **40** 358
Toshiba Corporation, **I** 221, 507–08, **533–35**; **II** 5, 56, 59, 62, 68, 73, 99, 102, 118, 122, 326, 440; **III** 298, 461, 533, 604; **6** 101, 231, 244, 287; **7** 529; **9** 7, 181; **10** 518–19; **11** 46, 328; **12** 454, **483–86 (upd.)**, 546; **13** 324, 399, 482; **14** 117, 446; **16** 5, 167; **17** 533; **18** 18, 260; **21** 390; **22** 193, 373; **23** 471; **40 435–40 (upd.)**; **43** 15
Toshin Kaihatsu Ltd., **V** 195
Toshin Paper Co., Ltd., **IV** 285
Tostem. *See* Toyo Sash Co., Ltd.
Total Audio Visual Services, **24** 95
Total Beverage Corporation, **16** 159, 161
Total Compagnie Française des Pétroles S.A., **I** 303; **II** 259; **III** 673; **IV** 363–64, 423–25, 466, 486, 498, 504, 515, 525, 544–47, **557–61**; **V** 628; **7** 481–84; **13** 557; **21** 203
Total Exploration S.A., **11** 537
Total Global Sourcing, Inc., **10** 498
Total Home Entertainment (THE), **39** 240, 242
Total Petroleum Corporation, **21** 500

TOTAL S.A., 24 492–97 (upd.), 522; **25** 104; **26** 369
Total System Services, Inc., 12 465–66; **18** 168, 170, **516–18**
Totem Resources Corporation, 9 509–11
Totino's Finer Foods, **II** 556; **13** 516; **26** 436
Toto Bank, **II** 326
TOTO LTD., III 755–56; **28 464–66 (upd.)**
Totsu Co., **I** 493; **24** 325
Touch America, **37** 127
Touch-It Corp., **22** 413
Touche Remnant Holdings Ltd., **II** 356
Touche Ross. *See* Deloitte Touche Tohmatsu International.
Touchstone Films, **II** 172–74; **6** 174–76; **30** 487
Tour d'Argent, **II** 518
Tourang Limited, **7** 253
Touristik Union International GmbH. and Company K.G., II 163–65
Touron y Cia, **III** 419
Touropa, **II** 163–64
Toval Japon, **IV** 680
Towa Nenryo Kogyo Co. Ltd., **IV** 554–55
Towa Optical Manufacturing Company, **41** 261–63
Tower Air, Inc., 28 467–69
Tower Automotive, Inc., 24 498–500
Tower Records, **9** 361; **10** 335; **11** 558; **30** 224. *See also* MTS Inc.
Towers, **II** 649
Towers Perrin, 32 458–60
Towle Manufacturing Co., **14** 482–83; **18** 69
Town & City, **IV** 696
Town & Country Corporation, 7 372; **16** 546; **19 451–53**; **25** 254
Town Investments, **IV** 711
Townsend Hook, **IV** 296, 650, 652; **19** 226
Toxicol Laboratories, Ltd., **21** 424
Toy Biz, Inc., 10 402; **18 519–21**
Toy Liquidators, **13** 541–43
Toy Park, **16** 390
Toyad Corp., **7** 296
Toymax International, Inc., 29 474–76
Toyo Bearing Manufacturing, **III** 595
Toyo Cotton Co., **IV** 224–25
Toyo Ink Manufacturing, **26** 213
Toyo Kogyo, **I** 167; **II** 361; **11** 139
Toyo Marine and Fire, **III** 385
Toyo Menka Kaisha Ltd. *See* Tomen Corporation.
Toyo Microsystems Corporation, **11** 464
Toyo Oil Co., **IV** 403
Toyo Pulp Co., **IV** 322
Toyo Rayon, **V** 381, 383
Toyo Sash Co., Ltd., III 757–58
Toyo Seikan Kaisha Ltd., I 615–16
Toyo Soda, **II** 301
Toyo Tire & Rubber Co., **V** 255–56; **9** 248
Toyo Toki Co., Ltd., **III** 755
Toyo Tozo Co., **I** 265; **21** 319
Toyo Trust and Banking Co., **II** 347, 371; **17** 349
Toyoda Automatic Loom Works, Ltd., I 203; **III** 591, 593, 632, **636–39**
Toyokawa Works, **I** 579
Toyoko Co., Ltd., **V** 199
Toyoko Kogyo, **V** 199
Toyomenka (America) Inc., **IV** 224
Toyomenka (Australia) Pty., Ltd., **IV** 224
Toyota Gossei, **I** 321
Toyota Industrial Equipment, **27** 294, 296
Toyota Motor Corporation, I 9–10, 174, 184, **203–05**, 507–08, 587; **II** 373; **III** 415, 495, 521, 523, 536, 579, 581, 591–93, 624, 636–38, 667, 715, 742; **IV** 702; **6** 514; **7** 111, 118, 212, 219–21; **8** 315; **9** 294, 340–42; **10** 353, 407; **11** 351, 377, 487, **528–31 (upd.)**; **14** 321; **15** 495; **21** 162, 273; **23** 289–90, 338–40; **25** 198; **34** 303, 305–06; **38 458–62 (upd.)**
Toyota Tsusho America, Inc., **13** 371
Toys 'R' Us, Inc., III 588; **V 203–06**; **7** 396; **10** 235, 284, 484; **12** 178; **13** 166; **14** 61; **15** 469; **16** 389–90, 457; **18 522–25 (upd.)**; **24** 412; **25** 314; **31** 477–78; **37** 129; **43** 385
Tozer Kemsley & Milbourn, **II** 208
TP Transportation, **39** 377
TPA. *See* Aloha Airlines Incorporated.
TPCR Corporation, **V** 163; **14** 394
TPG. *See* TNT Post Group N.V.
Trace International Holdings, Inc., **17** 182–83; **26** 502
Tracey Bros., **IV** 416
Tracey-Locke, **II** 660
Tracinda Corporation, **25** 329–30
Tracker Marine. *See* Bass Pro Shops, Inc.
Tracker Services, Inc., **9** 110
Traco International N.V., **8** 250; **32** 249
Tracor Inc., 10 547; **17 490–92**; **26** 267
Tractebel S.A., 20 491–93. *See also* Suez Lyonnaise des Eaux.
Tractor Supply Corp., **I** 446
Tradax, **II** 617; **13** 137
Trade Assoc. of Bilbao, **II** 194
Trade Development Bank, **11** 415–17
Trade Waste Incineration, Inc., **9** 109
Trade Winds Campers, **III** 599
TradeARBED, **IV** 25
Trader Joe's Co., 13 525–27; **41** 422
Trader Publications, Inc., **IV** 597
Trader Publishing Company, **12** 302
Traders & General Insurance, **III** 248
Traders Bank of Canada, **II** 344
Traders Group Ltd., **11** 258
Tradesmens National Bank of Philadelphia, **II** 342
The Trading Service, **10** 278
Traex Corporation, **8** 359
Trafalgar House Investments Ltd., **I** 248–49, 572–74; **IV** 259, 711; **20** 313; **23** 161; **24** 88; **36** 322
Trafiroad NV, **39** 239
Trailer Bridge, Inc., 41 397–99
Trailer Marine Transport, **6** 383
Trailways Lines, Inc., **I** 450; **9** 425; **32** 230
Trak Auto Corporation, **16** 159–62
TRAK Microwave Corporation, **18** 497, 513
Trammell Crow Company, IV 343; **8** 326–28, **532–34**
Tran Telecommunications Corp., **III** 110; **14** 14
Trane Company, **III** 663, 665; **10** 525; **21** 107; **22** 6; **26** 4; **30** 46, 48–49
Trans Air System, **6** 367; **27** 90
Trans-Arabian Pipe Line Co., **IV** 537, 552
Trans-Australia Airlines, **6** 110–12
Trans-Canada Air Lines. *See* Air Canada.
Trans Colorado, **11** 299
Trans-Continental Leaf Tobacco Company, (TCLTC), **13** 491
Trans Freight Lines, **27** 473–74
Trans International Airlines, **I** 537; **13** 529; **41** 402
Trans Louisiana Gas Company, **43** 56–57
Trans-Mex, Inc. S.A. de C.V., **42** 365
Trans-Natal Coal Corp., **IV** 93
Trans Ocean Products, **II** 578; **8** 510
Trans-Pacific Airlines, **22** 251. *See also* Aloha Airlines Incorporated.
Trans Rent-A-Car, **6** 348
Trans-Resources Inc., **13** 299
Trans Union Corp., **IV** 137; **6** 25; **28** 119
Trans Western Publishing, **25** 496
Trans World Airlines, Inc., I 58, 70, 90, 97, 99–100, 102, 113, 121, 123–24, **125–27**, 132, 466; **II** 32–33, 142, 425, 679; **III** 92, 428; **6** 50, 68, 71, 74, 76–77, 81–82, 114, 130; **9** 17, 232; **10** 301–03, 316; **11** 277, 427; **12** 381, **487–90 (upd.)**; **13** 341; **14** 73; **15** 419; **21** 141–42; **22** 22, 219; **26** 439; **29** 190; **35 424–29 (upd.)**
Trans-World Corp., **19** 456
Trans World Entertainment Corporation, 24 501–03
Trans World International, **18** 262–63
Trans World Life Insurance Company, **27** 46–47
Trans World Music, **9** 361
Trans World Seafood, Inc., **13** 244
Transaction Systems Architects, Inc., 29 477–79
Transaction Technology, **12** 334
TransAlta Utilities Corporation, 6 585–87
Transamerica—An AEGON Company, 41 400–03 (upd.)
Transamerica Corporation, I 536–38; **II** 147–48, 227, 288–89, 422; **III** 332, 344; **7** 236–37; **8** 46; **11** 273, 533; **13 528–30 (upd.)**; **21** 285; **25** 328; **27** 230. *See also* TIG Holdings, Inc.
Transamerica Pawn Holdings. *See* EZCORP Inc.
TransAmerican Waste Industries Inc., **41** 414
Transat. *See* Compagnie Générale Transatlantique (Transat).
Transatlantic Holdings, Inc., III 198; **11 532–33**; **15** 18
Transatlantische Dampfschiffahrts Gesellschaft, **6** 397
Transatlantische Gruppe, **III** 404
TransBrasil S/A Linhas Aéreas, 6 134; **29** 495; **31 443–45**
TransCanada PipeLines Limited, I 264; **V** 270–71, **737–38**; **17** 22–23
Transco Energy Company, IV 367; **V** 739–40; **6** 143; **18** 366
Transcontinental Air Transport, **I** 125; **9** 17; **11** 427; **12** 487
Transcontinental and Western Air Lines, **9** 416; **12** 487
Transcontinental Gas Pipe Line Corporation, **V** 739; **6** 447
Transcontinental Pipeline Company, **6** 456–57
Transcontinental Services Group N.V., **16** 207
TransCor America, Inc., **23** 154
Transelco, Inc., **8** 178
TransEuropa, **II** 164
Transflash, **6** 404; **26** 243
Transfracht, **6** 426
Transinternational Life, **II** 422

Transit Mix Concrete and Materials Company, **7** 541
Transitions Optical Inc., **21** 221, 223
Transitron, **16** 332
Transking Inc. *See* King Kullen Grocery Co., Inc.
Transkrit Corp., **IV** 640; **26** 273
Translite, **III** 495
Transmanche-Link, **13** 206–08; **37** 135
Transmedia Network Inc., 20 494–97
Transmedica International, Inc., **41** 225
Transmisiones y Equipos Mecanicos, S.A. de C.V., **23** 171
Transmitter Equipment Manufacturing Co., **13** 385
TransMontaigne Inc., 28 470–72
Transmontane Rod and Gun Club, **43** 435–36
Transnet Ltd., 6 433–35
TransOcean Oil, **III** 559
Transpac, **IV** 325
Transport Management Co., **III** 192
Transport- und Unfall-Versicherungs-Aktiengesellschaft Zürich, **III** 411
Transportacion Maritima Mexicana S.A. de C.V., **12** 279; **26** 236
Transportation Insurance Co., **III** 229
Transportes Aéreas Centro-Americanos. *See* Grupo TACA.
Transportes Aereos Portugueses, S.A., 6 125–27
Transportes Aeromar, **39** 188
Transrack S.A., **26** 363
Transtar, **6** 120–21; **24** 454
Transue & Williams Steel Forging Corp., **13** 302
Transvaal Silver and Base Metals, **IV** 90
Transway International Corp., **10** 369
Transworld Communications, **35** 165
Transworld Corp., **14** 209
Transworld Drilling Company Limited. *See* Kerr-McGee Corporation.
The Tranzonic Companies, 8 512; **15 500–02**; **37 392–95**
Trapper's, **19** 286
Trasgo, S.A. de C.V., **14** 516
Trausch Baking Co., **I** 255
Trävaru Svartvik, **IV** 338
Travel Air Manufacturing Company, **8** 49; **27** 97
Travel Automation Services Ltd., **I** 95
Travel Inc., **26** 309
Travel Information Group, **17** 398
Travel Ports of America, Inc., 17 493–95
Travelers Bank & Trust Company, **13** 467
Travelers Book Club, **13** 105
Travelers Corporation, I 37, 545; **III** 313, 329, **387–90**, 707–08; **6** 12; **15** 463 124. *See also* Citigroup Inc.
Travelers/Aetna Property Casualty Corp., **21** 15
Traveller's Express, **I** 449
TraveLodge, **III** 94, 104–06
Travenol Laboratories, **I** 627–28; **10** 141–43
Travers Morgan Ltd., **42** 183
Travis Boats & Motors, Inc., 37 396–98
Travis Perkins plc, 34 450–52
Travocéan, **25** 104
Trayco, **III** 570; **20** 362
Traylor Engineering & Manufacturing Company, **6** 395; **25** 169
TRC. *See* Tennessee Restaurant Company.
TRC Companies, Inc., 32 461–64
TRE Corp., **23** 225
Treadco, Inc., 16 39; **19** 38, **454–56**
Treasure Chest Advertising Company, Inc., 21 60; **32 465–67**
Treasure House Stores, Inc., **17** 322
Treatment Centers of America, **11** 379
Trebuhs Realty Co., **24** 438
Trechmann, Weekes and Co., **III** 669
Tredegar Industries, Inc., **10** 291
Tree of Life, Inc., II 528; **29 480–82**
Tree Sweet Products Corp., **12** 105; **26** 325
Tree Tavern, Inc., **27** 197
TrefilARBED, **IV** 26
Tréfimétaux, **IV** 174
Trefoil Capital Investors, L.P., **8** 305
Trek, **IV** 90, 92–93
Trek Bicycle Corporation, 16 493–95; **19** 384–85
Trelleborg A.B., **III** 625; **IV** 166
Tremec. *See* Transmisiones y Equipos Mecanicos, S.A. de C.V.
Tremletts Ltd., **IV** 294; **19** 225
Tremont Corporation, **21** 490
Trend International Ltd., **13** 502
Trend-Lines, Inc., 22 516–18
Trendwest Resorts, Inc., 12 439; **33 409–11**
Trent Tube, **I** 435
Trenton Foods, **II** 488
TrentonWorks Limited. *See* The Greenbrier Companies.
Tresco, **8** 514
Trethowal China Clay Co., **III** 690
Tri-City Federal Savings and Loan Association, **10** 92
Tri-City Utilities Company, **6** 514
Tri-County National Bank, **9** 474
Tri-Marine International Inc., **24** 116
Tri-Miller Packing Company, **7** 524
Tri-Sonics, Inc., **16** 202; **43** 170
Tri-State Improvement Company, **6** 465–66
Tri-State Publishing & Communications, Inc., **22** 442
Tri-State Recycling Corporation, **15** 117
Tri-State Refining Co., **IV** 372
Tri-Union Seafoods LLC, **24** 116
Tri Valley Growers, 32 468–71
Triad, **14** 224
Triad Artists Inc., **23** 514
Triad International Maintenance Corp., **13** 417
Triad Nitrogen, Inc., **27** 316, 318
Triad Systems Corp., **38** 96
Triangle Auto Springs Co., **IV** 136
The Triangle Group, **16** 357
Triangle Industries Inc., **I** 602, 607–08, 614; **II** 480–81; **14** 43
Triangle Manufacturing, **26** 57
Triangle Portfolio Associates, **II** 317
Triangle Publications, Inc., **IV** 652; **7** 391; **12** 359–60
Triangle Refineries, **IV** 446; **22** 302
Triarc Companies, Inc., 8 535–37; **13** 322; **14** 32–33; **34 453–57 (upd.)**; **39** 383, 385
Triathlon Leasing, **II** 457
Tribe Computer Works. *See* Zoom Telephonics.
Tribune Company, III 329; **IV 682–84**; **10** 56; **11** 331; **22 519–23 (upd.)**; **26** 17; **32** 358–59; **38** 306; **42** 133
Trical Resources, **IV** 84
Tricity Cookers, **I** 531–32
Trick & Murray, **22** 153
Trico Products Corporation, I 186; **15 503–05**
Tricon Global Restaurants, Inc., **21** 313, 317, 405, 407, 485; **40** 342
Tridel Enterprises Inc., 9 512–13
Trident NGL Holdings Inc., **18** 365, 367
Trident Seafoods, **II** 494
Trifari, Krussman & Fishel, Inc., **9** 157
Trigen Energy Corporation, 6 512; **42 386–89**
Trigon Industries, **13** 195; **14** 431
Trilan Developments Ltd., **9** 512
Trilogy Fabrics, Inc., **16** 125
Trilon Financial Corporation, II 456–57; **IV** 721; **9** 391
Trimac Ltd., **25** 64
TriMas Corp., III 571; **11 534–36**; **20** 359, 362; **39** 266
Trimble Navigation Limited, 40 441–43
Trinidad and Tobago External Telecommunications Company, **25** 100
Trinidad Oil Co., **IV** 95, 552
Trinidad-Tesoro Petroleum Company Limited, **7** 516, 518
Trinity Beverage Corporation, **11** 451
Trinity Broadcasting, **13** 279
Trinity Capital Opportunity Corp., **17** 13
Trinity Distributors, **15** 139
Trinity Industries, Incorporated, 7 540–41
Trinkaus und Burkhardt, **II** 319; **17** 324
TRINOVA Corporation, III 640–42, 731; **13** 8; **16** 7, 9
Trintex, **6** 158
Triology Corp., **III** 110
Triple P N.V., 26 496–99
Triplex, **6** 279
Triplex (Northern) Ltd., **III** 725
Trippe Manufacturing Co., **10** 474; **24** 29
Triquet Paper Co., **IV** 282; **9** 261
TriStar Pictures, **I** 234; **II** 134, 136–37; **6** 158; **10** 227; **12** 75, 455; **23** 275; **28** 462; **32** 114. *See also* Columbia TriStar Motion Pictures Companies.
Triton Bioscience, **III** 53; **26** 384
Triton Cellular Partners, L.P., **43** 341
Triton Energy Corporation, 11 537–39
Triton Group Ltd., **I** 447; **31** 287; **34** 339
Triton Oil, **IV** 519
Triton Systems Corp., **22** 186
Triumph-Adler, **I** 485; **III** 145; **11** 265
Triumph American, Inc., **12** 199
Triumph Films, **25** 174
Triumph, Finlay, and Philips Petroleum, **11** 28
Triumph Group, Inc., 21 153; **31 446–48**
Trivest, Inc., **II** 457; **21** 531–32
Trizec Corporation Ltd., 9 84–85; **10 529–32**
TrizecHahn, **37** 311
TRM Copy Centers Corporation, 18 526–28
Trojan, **III** 674
Troll, **13** 561
Trolley Barn Brewery Inc., **25** 401
Trona Corp., **IV** 95
Tropical Marine Centre, **40** 128–29
Tropical Oil Co., **IV** 415–16
Tropical Shipping, Inc., **6** 529, 531
Tropical Sportswear Int'l Corporation, **42** 120
Tropicana Products, Inc., II 468, 525; **13** 293; **25** 366; **28** 271, **473–77**; **38** 349

Trotter-Yoder & Associates, **22** 88
Troxel Cycling, **16** 53
Troy & Nichols, Inc., **13** 147
Troy Metal Products. *See* KitchenAid.
Troyfel Ltd., **III** 699
TRT Communications, Inc., **6** 327; **11** 185
Tru-Run Inc., **16** 207
Tru-Stitch, **16** 545
Tru-Trac Therapy Products, **11** 486
Truck Components Inc., **23** 306
Trudeau Marketing Group, Inc., **22** 386
True Form Boot Co., **V** 177
True North Communications Inc., **23 478–80**; **25** 91
True Temper Hardware Co., **30** 241–42
True Value Hardware Stores, **V** 37–38; **30** 168. *See also* TruServ Corporation.
Trugg-Hansa Holding AB, **III** 264
TruGreen, **23** 428, 430
Truitt Bros., **10** 382
Truman Dunham Co., **III** 744
Truman Hanburg, **I** 247
Trumball Asphalt, **III** 721
Trümmer-Verwertungs-Gesellschaft, **IV** 140
Trump Organization, **16** 262; **23 481–84**; **43** 225
Trunkline Gas Company, **6** 544; **14** 135
Trunkline LNG Co., **IV** 425
Trus Joist Corporation. *See* TJ International, Inc.
TruServ Corporation, **24 504–07**
Trussdeck Corporation. *See* TJ International, Inc.
Trust Company of the West, **19** 414; **42** 347
Trustcorp, Inc., **9** 475–76
Trusted Information Systems, Inc., **25** 349
Trustees, Executors and Agency Co. Ltd., **II** 189
Trusthouse Forte PLC, **I** 215; **III 104–06**; **16** 446
TRW Inc., **I 539–41**; **II** 33; **6** 25; **8** 416; **9** 18, 359; **10** 293; **11** 68, **540–42 (upd.)**; **12** 238; **14 510–13 (upd.)**; **16** 484; **17** 372; **18** 275; **19** 184; **23** 134; **24** 480; **26** 141; **28** 119; **32** 437; **33** 47; **34** 76; **43** 311, 313
TRW Vehicle Safety Systems Inc., **41** 369
Tryart Pty. Limited, **7** 253
TSA. *See* Transaction Systems Architects, Inc.
Tsai Management & Research Corp., **III** 230–31
TSB Group plc, **12 491–93**; **16** 14
TSI Inc., **38** 206
TSI Soccer Corporation, **29** 142–43
TSO. *See* Teacher's Service Organization, Inc.
TSO Financial Corp., **II** 420; **8** 10
Tsogo Sun Gaming & Entertainment, **17** 318
TSP. *See* Tom Snyder Productions.
TSR Inc., **24** 538
Tsuang Hine Co., **III** 582
Tsubakimoto-Morse, **14** 64
Tsukumo Shokai, **I** 502; **III** 712
Tsumeb Corp., **IV** 17–18
Tsurumi Steelmaking and Shipbuilding Co., **IV** 162
Tsurusaki Pulp Co., Ltd., **IV** 285
Tsutsunaka Plastic Industry Co., **III** 714; **8** 359
TSYS. *See* Total System Services, Inc.
TTK. *See* Tokyo Tsushin Kogyo K.K.
TTX Company, **6 436–37**
Tube Fab Ltd., **17** 234
Tube Forming, Inc., **23** 517
Tube Investments, **II** 422; **IV** 15
Tube Reducing Corp., **16** 321
Tube Service Co., **19** 344
Tubed Chemicals Corporation, **27** 299
Tuborg, **9** 99
Tubos de Acero de Mexico, S.A. (TAMSA), **41 404–06**
Tuboscope, **42** 420
Tucker, Lynch & Coldwell. *See* CB Commercial Real Estate Services Group, Inc.
TUCO, Inc., **8** 78
Tucson Electric Power Company, **V** 713; **6 588–91**; **42** 388
Tucson Gas & Electric, **19** 411–12
Tuesday Morning Corporation, **18 529–31**
Tuff Stuff Publications, **23** 101
TUI. *See* Touristik Union International GmbH. and Company K.G.
TUI Group, **42** 283
Tuileries et Briqueteries d'Hennuyeres et de Wanlin, **14** 249
TUJA, **27** 21
Tultex Corporation, **13 531–33**
Tumbleweed, Inc., **33 412–14**
Tunhems Industri A.B., **I** 387
Tupolev Aviation and Scientific Technical Complex, **24 58–60**
Tupperware Corporation, **I** 29; **II** 534; **III** 610–12;, **15** 475, 477; **17** 186; **18** 67; **28 478–81**
Turbinbolaget, **III** 419
Turbine Engine Asset Management LLC, **28** 5
Turcot Paperboard Mills Ltd., **17** 281
Turkish Engineering, Consultancy and Contracting Corp., **IV** 563
Turkish Petroleum Co. *See* Türkiye Petrolleri Anonim Ortakliği.
Türkiye Garanti Bankasi, **I** 479
Türkiye Petrolleri Anonim Ortakliği, **IV** 464, 557–58, **562–64**; **7** 352
Turnbull, **III** 468
Turner Broadcasting System, Inc., **II** 134, 149, 161 **166–68**; **IV** 676; **6 171–73 (upd.)**; **7** 64, 99, 306, 529; **23** 33, 257; **25** 313, 329, 498; **28** 71; **30** 100
The Turner Corporation, **8 538–40**; **23 485–88 (upd.)**; **25** 402; **33** 197
Turner Entertainment Co., **18** 459
Turner Glass Company, **13** 40
Turner Network Television, **21** 24
Turner's Turkeys, **II** 587
TURPAS, **IV** 563
Turtle Wax, Inc., **15 506–09**; **16** 43; **26** 349
Tuscarora Inc., **17** 155; **29 483–85**
Tussauds Group Ltd., **IV** 659
Tutt Bryant Industries PLY Ltd., **26** 231
Tuttle, Oglebay and Company. *See* Oglebay Norton Company.
TV & Stereo Town, **10** 468
TV Asahi, **7** 249
TV Azteca, S.A. de C.V., **39** 194–95, **398–401**
TV Food Network, **22** 522
TV Guide, Inc., **43 431–34 (upd.)**
TVA. *See* Tennessee Valley Authority.
TVE. *See* Television Española, S.A.
TVE Holdings, **22** 307
TVH Acquisition Corp., **III** 262, 264
TVI, Inc., **15 510–12**
TVN Entertainment Corporation, **32** 239
TVS Entertainment PLC, **13** 281
TVW Enterprises, **7** 78
TVX, **II** 449; **13** 449
TW Kutter, **III** 420
TW Services, Inc., **II 679–80**; **10** 301–03
TWA. *See* Trans World Airlines *and* Transcontinental & Western Airways.
Tweco Co., **19** 441
Tweeds, **12** 280
Tweeter Home Entertainment Group, Inc., **30 464–66**; **41** 379, 381
Twen-Tours International, **II** 164
Twentieth Century Fox Film Corporation, **II** 133, 135, 146, 155–56, **169–71**, 175; **IV** 652; **7** 391–92; **12** 73, 322, 359; **15** 23, 25, 234; **25** 327, **490–94 (upd.)**; **43** 173
Twentsche Bank, **II** 183
"21" International Holdings, **17** 182
21 Invest International Holdings Ltd., **14** 322
21st Century Food Products. *See* Hain Food Group, Inc.
21st Century Mortgage, **18** 28
Twenty-Second National Bank, **II** 291
TWI. *See* Trans World International.
Twin City Wholesale Drug Company, **14** 147
Twin Disc, Inc., **21 502–04**
Twining Crosfield Group, **II** 465; **13** 52
Twinings' Foods International, **II** 465–66; **III** 696
Twinings Tea, **41** 31
Twinlab Corporation, **34 458–61**
Twinpak, **IV** 250
Two Guys, **12** 49
2-in-1 Shinola Bixby Corp., **II** 497
21st Century Mortgage, **41** 18, 20
TWW Plc, **26** 62
TXEN, Inc., **18** 370
TXL Oil Corp., **IV** 552
TXP Operation Co., **IV** 367
TxPort Inc., **13** 8
Ty-D-Bol, **III** 55
Ty Inc., **33 415–17**
Tyco International Ltd., **21** 462; **28 482–87 (upd.)**; **30** 157
Tyco Laboratories, Inc., **III 643–46**; **13** 245–47
Tyco Submarine Systems Ltd., **32** 217
Tyco Toys, Inc., **12 494–97**; **13** 312, 319; **18** 520–21; **25** 314
Tyler Corporation, **23 489–91**
Tymnet, **18** 542
Tyndall Fund-Unit Assurance Co., **III** 273
Typhoo Tea, **II** 477
Typpi Oy, **IV** 469
Tyrolean Airways, **9** 233; **33** 50
Tyrvään Oy, **IV** 348
Tyskie Brewery, **24** 450
Tyson Foods, Inc., **II 584–85**; **7** 422–23, 432; **14 514–16 (upd.)**; **21** 535; **23** 376, 384; **26** 168; **39** 229

U.C.L.A.F. *See* Roussel-Uclaf.
U-Haul International Inc. *See* Amerco.
U.K. Corrugated, **IV** 296; **19** 226
U.S. Aggregates, Inc., **42 390–92**
U.S. Appliances, **26** 336

U.S. Bancorp, **12** 165; **14 527–29**; **36 489–95 (upd.)**
U.S. Bank of Washington, **14** 527
U.S. Banknote Company, **30** 43
U.S. Bearings Company. *See* Federal-Mogul Corporation.
U.S. Billing, Inc. *See* Billing Concepts Corp.
U.S. Biomedicals Corporation, **27** 69
U.S. Bioscience, Inc., **35** 286, 288
U.S. Borax, Inc., 42 393–96
U.S. Brass., **24** 151
U.S. Can Corporation, 30 474–76
U.S. Cellular Corporation, 31 449–452 (upd.)
U.S. Computer of North America Inc., **43** 368
U.S. Delivery Systems, Inc., **22** 153, **531–33**
U.S. Electrical Motors, **II** 19
U.S. Elevator Corporation, **19** 109–11
U.S. Envelope, **19** 498
U.S. Food Products Co., **I** 376
U.S. Foodservice, 26 503–06; **37** 374, 376
U.S.G. Co., **III** 762
U.S. Generating Company, **26** 373
U.S. Geological Survey, **9** 367
U.S. Graphite. *See* Wickes Inc.
U.S. Guarantee Co., **III** 220; **14** 108
U.S. Healthcare, Inc., **6 194–96**; **21** 16
U.S. Home Corporation, 8 541–43
U.S. Industries, Inc., **7** 208; **18** 467; **23** 296; **24** 150; **27** 288
U.S. Intec, **22** 229
U.S. International Reinsurance, **III** 264
U.S. Investigations Services Inc., **35** 44
U.S. Land Co., **IV** 255
U.S. Lawns, **31** 182, 184
U.S. Life Insurance, **III** 194
U.S. Lines, **I** 476; **III** 459; **11** 194
U.S. Lock Corporation, **9** 543; **28** 50–52
U.S. Long Distance Corp. *See* Billing Concepts Corp.
U.S. Marine Corp., **III** 444
U.S. News and World Report Inc., **30 477–80**
U.S. Office Products Company, **25 500–02**; **41** 69, 247
U.S. Overall Company, **14** 549
U.S. Plywood Corp. *See* United States Plywood Corp.
U.S. Realty and Improvement Co., **III** 98
U.S. RingBinder Corp., **10** 313–14
U.S. Robotics Inc., **9 514–15**; **20** 8, 69; **22** 17; **24** 212; **34** 444; **36** 122, 357
U.S. Rubber Company, **I** 478; **10** 388
U.S. Satellite Broadcasting Company, Inc., **20 505–07**
U.S. Satellite Systems, **III** 169; **6** 285
U.S. Shoe Corporation, **43** 98
U.S. Smelting Refining and Mining, **7** 360
U.S. Software Inc., **29** 479
U.S. Steel Corp. *See* United States Steel Corp.
U.S. Telephone Communications, **9** 478
U.S. Tile Co., **III** 674
U.S. Timberlands Company, L.P., **42 397–400**
U.S. Time Corporation, **13** 120
U.S. Trust Co. of New York, **II** 274
U.S. Trust Corp., **17 496–98**
U.S. Vanadium Co., **9** 517
U.S. Venture Partners, **15** 204–05
U.S. Vitamin & Pharmaceutical Corp., **III** 55
U S West, Inc., **V 341–43**; **11** 12, 59, 547; **25** 101, **495–99 (upd.)**; **32** 218; **36** 43; **37** 124–27
U.S. Windpower, **11** 222–23
U.S. Xpress Enterprises, Inc., **18** 159
U-Tote'M, **II** 620; **7** 372
UA. *See* Metro- Goldwyn-Mayer Inc., MGM/UA Communications Company, *and* United Artists Corp.
UAA. *See* EgyptAir.
UAL Corporation, 34 462–65 (upd.)
UAL, Inc. *See* United Airlines.
UAP. *See* Union des Assurances de Paris.
UARCO Inc., **15** 473–74
UAT. *See* UTA.
Ub Iwerks, **6** 174
Ube Industries, Ltd., **III 759–61**; **38 463–67 (upd.)**
Uberseebank A.G., **III** 197
Ubi Soft Entertainment S.A., **41** 188–89, **407–09**
Ubique Ltd, **25** 301
UBL Educational Loan Center, **42** 211
UBS. *See* Union Bank of Switzerland.
Ucabail, **II** 265
UCAR International, Inc., **40** 83
UCC-Communications Systems, Inc., **II** 38
Uccel, **6** 224
Uchiyama, **V** 727
UCI, **IV** 92; **25** 173
UCPMI, **IV** 226
Uddeholm and Bohler, **IV** 234
Udet Flugzeugwerke, **I** 73
Udo Fischer Co., **8** 477
UE Automotive Manufacturing, **III** 580
UETA Inc., **29** 510–11
Ugg Holdings, Inc., **22** 173
UGI. *See* United Gas Improvement.
UGI Corporation, 12 498–500
Ugine-Kuhlmann, **IV** 108, 174
Ugine S.A., **IV** 174; **20 498–500**
Ugine Steels, **IV** 227
Ugly Duckling Corporation, 22 524–27
Uhlmans Inc., **24** 458
UI International, **6** 444
UIB. *See* United Independent Broadcasters, Inc.
UICI, 33 418–21
Uinta Co., **6** 568
Uintah National Corp., **11** 260
UIS Co., **13** 554–55; **15** 324
Uitgeversmaatschappij Elsevier, **IV** 610
Uitzendbureau Amstelveen. *See* Randstad Holding n.v.
UJB Financial Corp., **14** 473
UK Paper, **IV** 279; **19** 155
UKF. *See* Unie van Kunstmestfabrieken.
Ukrop's Super Market's, Inc., 39 402–04
UL. *See* Underwriters Laboratories, Inc.
Ullrich Copper, Inc., **6** 146
Ullstein AV Produktions-und Vertriebsgesellschaft, **IV** 590
Ullstein Langen Müller, **IV** 591
Ullstein Tele Video, **IV** 590
ULN. *See* Union Laitière Normande.
ULPAC, **II** 576
Ulstein Holding ASA, **27** 494
Ulster Bank, **II** 334
Ultimate Electronics, Inc., **18 532–34**; **21** 33; **24** 52, 269
Ultra Bancorp, **II** 334
Ultra High Pressure Units Ltd., **IV** 66; **7** 123
Ultra Mart, **16** 250
Ultra Pac, Inc., **24 512–14**
Ultra Radio & Television, **I** 531
UltraCam. *See* Ultrak Inc.
UltraCare Products, **18** 148
Ultrak Inc., **24 508–11**
Ultralar, **13** 544
Ultramar Diamond Shamrock Corporation, 31 453–457 (upd.)
Ultramar PLC, IV 565–68
Ultrametl Mfg. Co., **17** 234
Ultronic Systems Corp., **IV** 669
UM Technopolymer, **III** 760
Umacs of Canada Inc., **9** 513
Umberto's of New Hyde Park Pizzeria, **16** 447
Umbro Holdings Ltd., **43** 392. *See also* Stone Manufacturing Company.
UMG. *See* Universal Music Group.
UMI Company, **29** 58
Umm-al-Jawabi Oil Co., **IV** 454
Umpqua River Navigation Company, **13** 100
Unadulterated Food Products, Inc., **11** 449
UNAT, **III** 197–98
Unbrako Socket Screw Company Ltd., **30** 429
Uncas-Merchants National Bank, **13** 467
Uncle Ben's Inc., **22 528–30**
Under Sea Industries, **III** 59
Underground Group, **6** 407
Underwood, **III** 145; **24** 269
Underwriters Adjusting Co., **III** 242
Underwriters Laboratories, Inc., **30 467–70**
Underwriters Reinsurance Co., **10** 45
Unefon, S.A., **39** 194, 196
UNELCO. *See* Union Electrica de Canarias S.A.
Unelec, Inc., **13** 398
Unfall, **III** 207
Ungermann-Bass, Inc., **6** 279
Uni-Cardan AG, **III** 494
Uni-Cast. *See* Sturm, Ruger & Company, Inc.
Uni-Charm, **III** 749
Uni Europe, **III** 211
Uni-Marts, Inc., **17 499–502**
Uni-Sankyo, **I** 675
Unibail SA, **40 444–46**
Unibank, **40** 336
Unic, **V** 63
Unicapital, Inc., **15** 281
Unicare Health Facilities, **6** 182; **25** 525
Unicco Security Services, **27** 22
Unicel. *See* Rural Cellular Corporation.
Unicer, **9** 100
Unichem, **25** 73
Unichema International, **13** 228
Unicoa, **I** 524
Unicom Corporation, 29 486–90 (upd.)
Unicomi, **II** 265
Unicon Producing Co., **10** 191
Unicoolait, **19** 51
UNICOR. *See* Federal Prison Industries, Inc.
Unicord, **24** 115
Unicorn Shipping Lines, **IV** 91
UniCorp, **8** 228
Unicorp Financial, **III** 248
Unicredit, **II** 265
Uniden, **14** 117

UniDynamics Corporation, **8** 135
Unie van Kunstmestfabrieken, **I** 326
Uniface Holding B.V., **10** 245; **30** 142
Unifi, Inc., **12 501–03**
Unified Management Corp., **III** 306
Unified Western Grocers, **31** 25
UniFirst Corporation, **16** 228; **21** 115, **505–07**
Uniforce Services Inc., **40** 119
Unigate PLC, **II 586–87**; **28 488–91 (upd.)**; **29** 150
Unigep Group, **III** 495
Unigesco Inc., **II** 653
Uniglory, **13** 211
Unigroup, **15** 50
UniHealth America, **11** 378–79
Unik S.A., **23** 170–171
Unilab Corp., **26** 391
Unilac Inc., **II** 547
Unilever PLC/Unilever N.V., **I** 369, 590, 605; **II** 547, **588–91**; **III** 31–32, 46, 52, 495; **IV** 532; **7** 382, **542–45 (upd.)**, 577; **8** 105–07, 166, 168, 341, 344; **9** 449; **11** 205, 421; **13** 243–44; **14** 204–05; **18** 395, 397; **19** 193; **21** 219; **22** 123; **23** 242; **26** 306; **28** 183, 185; **30** 396–97; **32 472–78 (upd.)**; **36** 237
Unilife Assurance Group, **III** 273
UniLife Insurance Co., **22** 149
Unilog SA, **42 401–03**
UniMac Companies, **11** 413
Unimat, **II** 265
Unimation, **II** 122
Unimetal, **IV** 227; **30** 252
Uninsa, **I** 460
Union, **III** 391–93
Union & NHK Auto Parts, **III** 580
Union Acceptances Ltd., **IV** 23
Unión Aérea Española, **6** 95
Union Aéromaritime de Transport. *See* UTA.
Union Assurance, **III** 234
Union Bag–Camp Paper Corp., **IV** 344–45
Union Bancorp of California, **II** 358
Union Bank. *See* State Street Boston Corporation.
Union Bank of Australia, **II** 187–89
Union Bank of Birmingham, **II** 318; **17** 323
Union Bank of California, **16 496–98**
Union Bank of Canada, **II** 344
Union Bank of England, **II** 188
Union Bank of Finland, **II** 302, 352
Union Bank of Halifax, **II** 344
Union Bank of London, **II** 235
Union Bank of New London, **II** 213
Union Bank of New York, **9** 229
Union Bank of Prince Edward Island, **II** 220
Union Bank of Scotland, **10** 337
Union Bank of Switzerland, **II** 257, 267, 334, 369, 370, **378–79**; **21** 146
Union Battery Co., **III** 536
Union Bay Sportswear, **17** 460
Union Camp Corporation, **IV 344–46**; **8** 102; **39** 291
Union-Capitalisation, **III** 392
Union Carbide Corporation, **I** 334, 339, 347, 374, 390, **399–401**, 582, 666; **II** 103, 313, 562; **III** 742, 760; **IV** 92, 374, 379, 521; **7** 376; **8** 180, 182, 376; **9** 16, **516–20 (upd.)**; **10** 289, 472; **11** 402–03; **12** 46, 347; **13** 118; **14** 281–82; **16** 461; **17** 159; **18** 235; **22** 228, 235; **43** 265–66
Union Cervecera, **9** 100
Union Colliery Company, **V** 741
Union Commerce Corporation, **11** 181
Union Commerciale, **19** 98
Union Corporation. *See* Gencor Ltd.
Union d'Etudes et d'Investissements, **II** 265
Union des Assurances de Paris, **II** 234; **III** 201, **391–94**
Union des Coopératives Bressor, **25** 85
Union des Cooperatives Laitières. *See* Unicoolait.
Union des Transports Aériens. *See* UTA.
Union Electric Company, **V** 741–43; **6** 505–06; **26** 451
Union Electrica de Canarias S.A., **V** 607
Union Equity Co-Operative Exchange, **7** 175
Union et Prévoyance, **III** 403
Union Fertilizer, **I** 412
Union Fidelity Corp., **III** 204
Union Financiera, **19** 189
Union Gas & Electric Co., **6** 529
Union Générale de Savonnerie, **III** 33
l'Union Générale des Pétroles, **IV** 545–46, 560; **7** 482–83
Union Glass Co., **III** 683
Union Hardware, **III** 443; **22** 115
Union Hop Growers, **I** 287
Union Laitière Normande, **19** 50. *See also* Compagnie Laitière Européenne.
Union Levantina de Seguros, **III** 179
Union Light, Heat & Power Company, **6** 466
Union Marine, **III** 372
Union Mutual Life Insurance Company. *See* UNUM Corp.
Union National Bank, **II** 284; **10** 298
Union National Bank of Wilmington, **25** 540
Union of European Football Association, **27** 150
Union of Food Co-ops, **II** 622
Union of London, **II** 333
Union Oil Associates, **IV** 569
Union Oil Co., **9** 266
Union Oil Co. of California, **I** 13; **IV** 385, 400, 403, 434, 522, 531, 540, 569, 575; **11** 271. *See also* Unocal Corporation.
Union Pacific Corporation, **I** 473; **II** 381; **III** 229; **V 529–32**; **12** 18–20, 278; **14** 371–72; **28 492–500 (upd.)**; **36** 43–44
Union Pacific Tea Co., **7** 202
Union Paper Bag Machine Co., **IV** 344
Union Petroleum Corp., **IV** 394
L'Union pour le Developement Régional, **II** 265
Union Power Company, **12** 541
Union Rückversicherungs-Gesellschaft, **III** 377
Union Savings, **II** 316
Union Savings and Loan Association of Phoenix, **19** 412
Union Savings Bank, **9** 173
Union Savings Bank and Trust Company, **13** 221
Union Steam Ship Co., **IV** 279; **19** 154
Union Steamship Co. of New Zealand Ltd., **27** 473
Union Steel Co., **IV** 22, 572; **7** 550
Union Sugar, **II** 573
Union Sulphur Co., **IV** 81; **7** 185
Union Supply Co., **IV** 573; **7** 550
Union Tank Car Co., **IV** 137
Union Telecard Alliance, LLC, **34** 223
Union Telephone Company, **14** 258
Union Texas Petroleum Holdings, Inc., **I** 415; **7** 379; **9 521–23**; **22** 31
Union-Transport, **6** 404; **26** 243
Union Trust Co., **II** 284, 313, 315–16, 382; **9** 228; **13** 222
The Union Underwear Company, **I** 440–41; **8** 200–01; **25** 164–66
Union Wine, **I** 289
Unionamerica, Inc., **16** 497
Unionamerica Insurance Group, **III** 243
UnionBay Sportswear Co., **27** 112
Unione Manifatture, S.p.A., **19** 338
Uniphase Corporation. *See* JDS Uniphase Corporation.
Uniplex Business Software, **41** 281
Unique Casual Restaurants, Inc., **27 480–82**
Uniroy of Hempstead, Inc. *See* Aris Industries, Inc.
Uniroyal Chemical Corporation, **36** 145
Uniroyal Corp., **I** 30–31; **II** 472; **V** 242; **8** 503; **11** 159; **20** 262
Uniroyal Goodrich, **42** 88
Uniroyal Holdings Ltd., **21** 73
Unishops, Inc. *See* Aris Industries, Inc.
Unison HealthCare Corporation, **25 503–05**
Unisource, **I** 413
Unistar Radio Networks, **23** 510
Unisys Corporation, **II** 42; **III 165–67**; **6 281–83 (upd.)**; **8** 92; **9** 32, 59; **12** 149, 162; **17** 11, 262; **18** 345, 386, 434, 542; **21** 86; **36 479–84 (upd.)**
The Unit Companies, Inc., **6** 394, 396; **25** 170
Unit Group plc, **8** 477
Unitech plc, **27** 81
United Acquisitions, **7** 114; **25** 125
United Advertising Periodicals, **12** 231
United Agri Products, **II** 494
United AgriSeeds, Inc., **21** 387
United Air Express. *See* United Parcel Service of America Inc.
United Air Fleet, **23** 408
United Aircraft and Transportation Co., **I** 48, 76, 78, 85–86, 96, 441, 489; **9** 416, 418; **10** 162, 260; **12** 289; **21** 140
United Airlines, **I** 23, 47, 71, 84, 90, 97, 113, 116, 118, 124, **128–30**; **II** 142, 419, 680; **III** 225; **6** 71, 75–77, 104, 121, 123, **128–30 (upd.)**, 131, 388–89; **9** 271–72, 283, 416, 549; **10** 162, 199, 301, 561; **11** 299; **12** 192, 381; **14** 73; **21** 141; **22** 199, 220; **24** 21, 22; **25** 146, 148, 421–23; **26** 113, 338–39, 440; **27** 20; **29** 507; **38** 105. *See also* UAL Corporation.
United Alaska Drilling, Inc., **7** 558
United Alkalai Co., **I** 351
United Alloy Steel Company, **26** 405
United-American Car, **13** 305
United American Insurance Company of Dallas, **9** 508; **33** 407
United American Lines, **6** 398
United Arab Airlines. *See* EgyptAir.
United Artists Corp., **I** 537; **II** 135, 146–48, 149, 157–58, 160, 167, 169; **III** 721; **IV** 676; **6** 167; **9** 74; **12** 13, 73; **13** 529; **14** 87, 399; **21** 362; **23** 389; **26** 487; **36** 47; **41** 402. *See also* MGM/UA Communications Company *and* Metro-Goldwyn-Mayer Inc.

United Artists Theatre Circuit, Inc., **37** 63–64
United Auto Group, Inc., 26 500–02
United Bank of Arizona, **II** 358
United Biscuits (Holdings) plc, II 466, 540, **592–94; III** 503; **26** 59; **36** 313; **42 404–09 (upd.)**
United Brands Company, II 595–97; III 28; **7** 84–85; **12** 215; **21** 110, 112; **25** 4
United Breweries Ltd. **I** 221, 223, 288; **24** 449. *See also* Carlsberg A/S.
United Broadcasting Corporation Public Company Ltd., **31** 330
United Cable Television Corporation, **II** 160; **9** 74; **18** 65; **43** 431
United California Bank, **II** 289
United Car, **I** 540; **14** 511
United Carbon Co., **IV** 373
United Central Oil Corporation, **7** 101
United Cigar Manufacturers Company, **II** 414. *See also* Culbro Corporation.
United Cities Gas Company, **43** 56, 58
United City Property Trust, **IV** 705
United Co., **I** 70
United Communications Systems, Inc. **V** 346
United Computer Services, Inc., **11** 111
United Consolidated Industries, **24** 204
United Corp., **10** 44
United County Banks, **II** 235
United Dairies, **II** 586–87
United Dairy Farmers, **III** 190
United Defense, L.P., 30 471–73
United Distiller & Vintners, **43** 215. *See also* Diageo plc.
United Distillers Glenmore, Inc., **34** 89
United Dominion Corp., **III** 200
United Dominion Industries Limited, IV 288; **8 544–46; 16 499–502 (upd.)**
United Drapery Stores, **III** 502; **7** 208
United Drug Co., **II** 533
United Electric Light and Water Co., **13** 182
United Engineering Steels, **III** 495
United Engineers & Constructors, **II** 86; **11** 413
United Express, **11** 299
United Factors Corp., **13** 534–35
United Features Syndicate, Inc., **IV** 607–08
United Federal Savings and Loan of Waycross, **10** 92
United Financial Corporation, **12** 353
United Financial Group, Inc., **8** 349
United 5 and 10 Cent Stores, **13** 444
United Foods, Inc., 21 508–11
United Fruit Co., **I** 529, 566; **II** 120, 595; **IV** 308; **7** 84–85; **21** 110–11
United Funds, Inc., **22** 540–41
United Gas and Electric Company of New Albany, **6** 555
United Gas and Improvement Co., **13** 182
United Gas Corp., **IV** 488–90
United Gas Improvement Co., **IV** 549; **V** 696; **6** 446, 523; **11** 388
United Gas Industries, **III** 502; **7** 208
United Gas Pipe Line Co., **IV** 489–90
United Geophysical Corp., **I** 142
United Graphics, **12** 25
United Grocers, **II** 625
United Guaranty Corp., **III** 197
United Health Maintenance, Inc., **6** 181–82
United HealthCare Corporation, 9 524–26; 24 229, 231. *See also* Humana Inc.
The United Illuminating Company, 21 512–14
United Image Entertainment, **18** 64, 66
United Independent Broadcasters, Inc., **II** 132
United Industrial Corporation, 37 399–402
United Industrial Syndicate, **8** 545
United Information Systems, Inc., **V** 346
United Insurance Co., **I** 523
Oy United International, **IV** 349
United International Holdings Inc., **28** 198
United International Pictures, **II** 155
United Investors Life Insurance Company, **22** 540; **33** 407
United Iron & Metal Co., **14** 156
United Jewish Communities, 33 422–25
United Kent Fire, **III** 350
United Kingdom Atomic Energy Authority, **6** 451–52
United Knitting, Inc., **21** 192, 194
United Liberty Life Insurance Co., **III** 190–92
United Life & Accident Insurance Co., **III** 220–21; **14** 109
United Life Insurance Company, **12** 541
United Light & Railway Co., **V** 609
United Light and Power, **6** 511
United Machinery Co., **15** 127
United Match Factories, **12** 462
United Media, **22** 442
United Medical Service, Inc., **III** 245–46
United Merchandising Corp., **12** 477
United Merchants & Manufacturers, Inc., 13 534–37; 31 160
United Meridian Corporation, **8** 350
United Metals Selling Co., **IV** 31
United Microelectronics Corporation, **22** 197
United Micronesian, **I** 97; **21** 142
United Molasses, **II** 582
United Mortgage Servicing, **16** 133
United Natural Foods, Inc., 32 479–82
United Natural Gas Company, **6** 526
United Netherlands Navigation Company. *See* Vereenigde Nederlandsche Scheepvaartmaatschappij.
United News & Media plc, 28 501–05 (upd.); 35 354
United Newspapers plc, IV 685–87
United of Omaha, **III** 365
United Office Products, **11** 64
United Oil Co., **IV** 399
United Optical, **10** 151
United Pacific Financial Services, **III** 344
United Pacific Insurance Co., **III** 343
United Pacific Life Insurance Co., **III** 343–44
United Pacific Reliance Life Insurance Co. of New York, **III** 343
United Packages, **IV** 249
United Paper Mills Ltd., II 302; **IV** 316, **347–50**
United Paramount Network, **25** 418–19; **26** 32; **31** 109
United Paramount Theatres, **II** 129
United Parcel Service of America Inc., V 533–35; 6 345–46, 385–86, 390; **11** 11; **12** 309, 334; **13** 19, 416; **14** 517; **17 503–06 (upd.); 18** 82, 177, 315–17; **24** 22, 133; **25** 148, 150, 356; **27** 471, 475; **34** 15, 17, 473; **39** 33; **41** 245; **42** 140
United Pipeline Co., **IV** 394
United Power and Light Corporation, **6** 473; **12** 541
United Presidential Life Insurance Company, **12** 524, 526
United Press International, Inc., IV 607, 627, 669–70; **7** 158–59; **16** 166; **19** 203; **22** 453; **25 506–09**
United Railways & Electric Company, **25** 44
United Refining Co., **23** 406, 408
United Rentals, Inc., 28 386, 388; **34 466–69**
United Resources, Inc., **21** 514
United Retail Group Inc., 33 426–28
United Retail Merchants Stores Inc., **9** 39
United Roasters, **III** 24; **14** 121
United Satellite Television, **10** 320
United Savings of Texas, **8** 349
United Servomation, **7** 471–72
United Shirt Shops, Inc. *See* Aris Industries, Inc.
United Skates of America, **8** 303
United Software Consultants Inc., **11** 65
United States Aluminum Co., **17** 213
United States Aviation Underwriters, Inc., **24** 176
United States Baking Co., **II** 542
United States Can Co., **15** 127, 129
United States Cellular Corporation, 9 494–96, **527–29**. *See also* U.S. Cellular Corporation.
United States Department of Defense, **6** 327
United States Distributing Corp., **IV** 180–82
United States Electric and Gas Company, **6** 447
United States Electric Light and Power Company, **25** 44
The United States Electric Lighting Company, **11** 387
United States Export-Import Bank, **IV** 55
United States Express Co., **II** 381, 395–96; **10** 59–60; **12** 534
United States Fidelity and Guaranty Co., **III** 395
United States Filter Corporation, I 429; **IV** 374; **20 501–04; 38** 168, 170
United States Foil Co., **IV** 186; **19** 346
United States Football League, **29** 347
United States Glucose Co., **II** 496
United States Graphite Company, **V** 221–22
United States Gypsum Co., **III** 762–64
United States Health Care Systems, Inc. *See* U.S. Healthcare, Inc.
United States Independent Telephone Company, **6** 332
United States Leasing Corp., **II** 442
United States Mail Steamship Co., **23** 160
United States Medical Finance Corp., **18** 516, 518
United States Mortgage & Trust Company, **II** 251; **14** 102
United States National Bancshares, **25** 114
United States National Bank of Galveston. *See* Cullen/Frost Bankers, Inc.
United States National Bank of Oregon, **14** 527
The United States National Bank of Portland, **14** 527–28
United States National Bank of San Diego, **II** 355

United States Pipe and Foundry Co., **III** 766; **22** 544–45
United States Plywood Corp., **IV** 264, 282, 341; **9** 260; **13** 100; **20** 128
United States Postal Service, **10** 60; **14** **517–20**; **34** **470–75 (upd.)**; **42** 140
United States Realty-Sheraton Corp., **III** 98
United States Satellite Broadcasting Company Inc., **24** 226; **38** 176
United States Security Trust Co., **13** 466
United States Shoe Corporation, **V** **207–08**; **17** 296, 390; **23** 328; **39** 301
United States Steel Corp., **I** 298, 491; **II** 129, 330; **III** 282, 326, 379; **IV** 35, 56, 110, 158, 572–74; **6** 514; **7** 48, 70–73, 401–02, 549–51; **10** 32; **11** 194; **12** 353–54; **17** 350, 356; **18** 378; **26** 405, 451. *See also* USX Corporation.
United States Sugar Refining Co., **II** 496
United States Surgical Corporation, **10** **533–35**; **13** 365; **21** 119–20; **28** 486; **34** **476–80 (upd.)**
United States Tobacco Company, **9** 533
United States Trucking Corp., **IV** 180–81
United States Trust Co. of New York. *See* U.S. Trust Corp.
United States Underseas Cable Corp., **IV** 178
United States Zinc Co., **IV** 32
United Stationers Inc., **14** **521–23**; **25** 13; **36** 508
United Steel, **III** 494
United Steel Mills Ltd., **25** 266
United Supers, **II** 624
United Technologies Automotive Inc., **15** **513–15**
United Technologies Corporation, **I** 68, **84–86**, 143, 411, 530, 559; **II** 64, 82; **III** 74; **9** 18, 418; **10** **536–38 (upd.)**; **11** 308; **12** 289; **13** 191, 384–86; **22** 6; **34** 371–72, 432, **481–85 (upd.)**; **39** 311, 313
United Telecommunications, Inc., **V** **344–47**; **8** 310; **9** 478–80; **10** 202; **12** 541
United Telephone Company, **7** 508; **14** 257
United Telephone Company of the Carolinas, **10** 202
United Telephone of Indiana, **14** 259
United Telephone System, Inc., **V** 346
United Telespectrum, **6** 314
United Television, Inc., **9** 119; **26** 32
United Television Programs, **II** 143
United Thermal Corp., **42** 388
United Transportation Co., **6** 382
United Truck Lines, **14** 505
United Utilities, Inc., **V** 344; **10** 202
United Van Lines, **14** 37; **15** 50
United Verde Copper Co., **IV** 178
United Video Satellite Group, **18** **535–37**. *See also* TV Guide, Inc.
United Vintners, **I** 243, 260–61
United Water Resources, Inc., **40** **447–50**
United Way of America, **36** **485–88**
United Westburne Inc., **19** 313
United Westphalia Electricity Co., **IV** 127
Unitek Corp., **III** 18
Unitel Communications, **6** 311
Unitika Ltd., **V** **387–89**
Unitil Corporation, **37** **403–06**
Unitog Co., **16** 228; **19** **457–60**; **21** 115
Unitransa, **27** 474
Unitrin Inc., **16** **503–05**
Unitron Medical Communications, **29** 412
Unity Cellular Systems, Inc. *See* Rural Cellular Corporation.
Unity Financial Corp., **19** 411
Unity Joint-Stock Bank, **II** 334
UNIVAC, **III** 133, 152, 313; **6** 233, 240, 266
Univar Corporation, **8** 99; **9** **530–32**; **12** 333; **41** 340
Univas, **13** 203 **23** 171
Univasa, **39** 229
Univel Inc., **38** 418
Universal Adding Machine, **III** 165
Universal American, **I** 452
Universal Atlas Cement Co., **IV** 573–74; **7** 550–51
Universal Belo Productions, **10** 5
Universal Cheerleaders Association. *See* Varsity Spirit Corp.
Universal Cigar Corp., **14** 19
Universal Consumer Products Group, **30** 123
Universal Containers, **IV** 249
Universal Controls, Inc., **10** 319
Universal Cooler Corp., **8** 515
Universal Corporation, **V** **417–18**
Universal Data Systems, **II** 61; **22** 17
Universal Electronics Inc., **39** **405–08**
Universal Foods Corporation, **7** **546–48**; **21** 498
Universal Footcare Products Inc., **31** 255
Universal Forest Products Inc., **10** **539–40**
Universal Frozen Foods, **23** 321
Universal Furniture, **III** 571; **20** 362
Universal Genève, **13** 121
Universal Guaranty Life Insurance Company, **11** 482
Universal Health Services, Inc., **6** **191–93**
Universal Highways, **III** 735
Universal Industries, Inc., **10** 380; **13** 533
Universal Instruments Corp., **III** 468
Universal International, Inc., **25** 353, 355, **510–11**
Universal Juice Co., **21** 55
Universal Leaf Tobacco Company. *See* Universal Corporation.
Universal Manufacturing, **I** 440–41; **25** 167
Universal Marking Systems, **25** 331
Universal Match, **12** 464
Universal Matchbox Group, **12** 495
Universal Matthey Products Ltd., **IV** 119
Universal Music Group, **22** 194; **26** 152; **37** 193
Universal Paper Bag Co., **IV** 345
Universal Pictures, **II** 102, 135, 144, 154–55, 157; **10** 196; **14** 399; **25** 271. *See also* Universal Studios, Inc.
Universal Press Syndicate, **10** 4; **40** 38
Universal Records, **27** 123
Universal Resources Corporation, **6** 569; **26** 388
Universal Shoes, Inc., **22** 213
Universal Stamping Machine Co., **III** 156
Universal Studios Florida, **14** 399
Universal Studios, Inc., **II** 143–44; **12** 73; **21** 23–26; **25** 411; **33** **429–33**
Universal Telephone, **9** 106
Universal Television, **II** 144
Universal Textured Yarns, **12** 501
Universal Transfers Co. Ltd., **IV** 119
University Computing Corp., **II** 38; **11** 468; **17** 320; **25** 87
University Microfilms, **III** 172; **6** 289
University of Phoenix, **24** 40
Univisa, **24** 516
Univision Communications Inc., **IV** 621; **18** 213; **24** **515–18**; **41** 150–52
Unix System Laboratories Inc., **6** 225; **25** 20–21; **38** 418
UNM. *See* United News & Media plc.
Uno Restaurant Corporation, **16** 447; **18** 465, **538–40**
Uno-Ven, **IV** 571; **24** 522
Unocal Corporation, **IV** 508, **569–71**; **24** **519–23 (upd.)**
UNR Industries, Inc. *See* ROHN Industries, Inc.
Unterberg Harris, **25** 433
UNUM Corp., **III** 236; **13** **538–40**
Uny Co., Ltd., **II** 619; **V** **209–10**, 154; **13** 545; **36** 419
UPI. *See* United Press International.
Upjohn Company, **I** 675, 684, 686, 700, **707–09**; **III** 18, 53; **6** 42; **8** **547–49 (upd.)**; **10** 79; **12** 186; **13** 503; **14** 423; **16** 440; **29** 363. *See also* Pharmacia & Upjohn Inc.
UPM-Kymmene Corporation, **19** **461–65**; **25** 12; **30** 325
UPN. *See* United Paramount Network.
Upper Deck Company, LLC, **34** 448; **37** 295
UPS. *See* United Parcel Service of America Inc.
UPSHOT, **27** 195
Upton Machine Company, **12** 548
Uraga Dock Co., **II** 361; **III** 634
Uraga Heavy Industries, **III** 634
Urbaine, **III** 391–92
Urban Investment and Development Co., **IV** 703
Urban Outfitters, Inc., **14** **524–26**
Urban Systems Development Corp., **II** 121
Urenco, **6** 452
Urwick Orr, **II** 609
US Airways Express, **32** 334; **38** 130
US Airways Group, Inc., **28** **506–09 (upd.)**; **33** 303
US Industrial Chemicals, Inc., **I** 377; **8** 440
US Industries Inc., **30** 231
US 1 Industries, **27** 404
US Order, Inc., **10** 560, 562
US Sprint Communications Company, **V** 295–96, 346–47; **6** 314; **8** 310; **9** 32; **10** 543; **11** 302; **12** 136, 541; **14** 252–53; **15** 196; **16** 318, 392; **25** 101; **29** 44; **43** 447. *See also* Sprint Communications Company, L.P.
US Telecom, **9** 478–79
US West Communications Services, Inc., **19** 255; **21** 285; **29** 39, 45, 478; **37** 312, 315–16. *See also* Regional Bell Operating Companies.
USA Cafes, **14** 331
USA Floral Products Inc., **27** 126
USA Networks Inc., **25** 330, 411; **33** 432; **37** 381, 383–84; **43** 422
USA Security Systems, Inc., **27** 21
USA Truck, Inc., **42** **410–13**
USAA, **10** **541–43**
USAir Group, Inc., **I** 55, **131–32**; **III** 215; **6** 121, **131–32 (upd.)**; **11** 300; **14** 70, 73; **18** 62; **21** 143; **24** 400; **26** 429; **42** 34. *See also* US Airways Group, Inc.
USANA, Inc., **27** 353; **29** **491–93**
USCC. *See* United States Cellular Corporation.

USCP-WESCO Inc., **II** 682
USF&G Corporation, **III 395–98**; **11** 494–95; **19** 190
USFL. *See* United States Football League.
USFreightways, **27** 475
USG Corporation, **III 762–64**; **26 507–10 (upd.)**
Usines de l'Espérance, **IV** 226
Usines Métallurgiques de Hainaut, **IV** 52
Usinor SA, **42 414–17 (upd.)**
Usinor Sacilor, **IV 226–28**; **22** 44; **24** 144; **26** 81, 84
USLD Communications Corp. *See* Billing Concepts Corp.
USLIFE, **III** 194
USM, **10** 44
Usource LLC, **37** 406
USPS. *See* United States Postal Service.
USSC. *See* United States Surgical Corporation.
USSI. *See* U.S. Software Inc.
UST Inc., **9 533–35**; **42** 79
UST Wilderness Management Corporation, **33** 399
USV Pharmaceutical Corporation, **11** 333
USWeb/CKS. *See* marchFIRST, Inc.
USX Corporation, **I** 466; **IV** 130, 228, **572–74**; **7** 193–94, **549–52 (upd.)**
UTA, **I** 119, 121; **6** 373–74, 93; **34** 397
Utag, **11** 510
Utah Construction & Mining Co., **I** 570; **IV** 146; **14** 296
Utah Federal Savings Bank, **17** 530
Utah Gas and Coke Company, **6** 568
Utah Group Health Plan, **6** 184
Utah International, **II** 30; **12** 196
Utah Medical Products, Inc., **36 496–99**
Utah Mines Ltd., **IV** 47; **22** 107
Utah Oil Refining Co., **IV** 370
Utah Power and Light Company, **9** 536; **12** 266; **27 483–86**. *See also* PacifiCorp.
UTI Energy Corp., **12** 500
Utilicom, **6** 572
Utilicorp United Inc., **6 592–94**
UtiliTech Solutions, **37** 88
Utilities Power & Light Corporation, **I** 512; **6** 508
Utility Constructors Incorporated, **6** 527
Utility Engineering Corporation, **6** 580
Utility Fuels, **7** 377
Utility Services, Inc., **42** 249, 253
Utility Supply Co. *See* United Stationers Inc.
AB Utra Wood Co., **IV** 274
Utrecht Allerlei Risico's, **III** 200
UUNET, **38 468–72**
UV Industries, Inc., **7** 360; **9** 440

V & V Cos., **I** 412
V&S Variety Stores, **V** 37
V.A.W. of America Inc., **IV** 231
V.L. Churchill Group, **10** 493
Vabis, **I** 197
Vacheron Constantin, **27** 487, 489
Vaco, **38** 200, 202
Vaculator Division. *See* Lancer Corporation.
Vacuum Metallurgical Company, **11** 234
Vacuum Oil Co., **IV** 463–64, 504, 549; **7** 351–52
Vadic Corp., **II** 83
Vadoise Vie, **III** 273
Vagnfabriks A.B., **I** 197
Vail Associates, Inc., **11 543–46**; **31** 65, 67
Vail Resorts, Inc., **43 435–39 (upd.)**
Val Corp., **24** 149
Val-Pak Direct Marketing Systems, Inc., **22** 162
Val Royal LaSalle, **II** 652
Valassis Communications, Inc., **8 550–51**; **37 407–10 (upd.)**
Valcambi S.A., **II** 268; **21** 145
Valcom, **13** 176
ValCom Inc. *See* InaCom Corporation.
Valdi Foods Inc., **II** 663–64
Valdosta Drug Co., **III** 9–10
Vale do Rio Doce Navegacao SA—Docenave, **43** 112
Vale Harmon Enterprises, Ltd., **25** 204
Vale Power Company, **12** 265
Valentine & Company, **8** 552–53
Valeo, **III** 593; **23 492–94**
Valero Energy Corporation, **IV** 394; **7 553–55**; **19** 140; **31** 119
Valhi, Inc., **10** 435–36; **19 466–68**
Valid Logic Systems Inc., **11** 46, 284
Valio-Finnish Co-operative Dairies' Assoc., **II** 575
Valke Oy, **IV** 348
Valley Bank of Helena, **35** 197, 199
Valley Bank of Nevada, **19** 378
Valley Crest Tree Company, **31** 182–83
Valley Deli Inc., **24** 243
Valley East Medical Center, **6** 185
Valley Falls Co., **III** 213
Valley Fashions Corp., **16** 535
Valley Federal of California, **11** 163
Valley Fig Growers, **7** 496–97
Valley Forge Life Insurance Co., **III** 230
Valley Media Inc., **35 430–33**
Valley National Bank, **II** 420
Valley-Todeco, Inc., **13** 305–06
Valley Transport Co., **II** 569
Valleyfair, **22** 130
Vallourec, **IV** 227
Valmac Industries, **II** 585
Valmet Corporation, **I** 198; **III 647–49**; **IV** 276, 350, 471
Valmet Oy. *See* Metso Corporation.
Valmont Industries, Inc., **13** 276; **19** 50, **469–72**
Valores Industriales S.A., **19** 10, 12, 189, **473–75**; **29** 219
The Valspar Corporation, **8 552–54**; **32 483–86 (upd.)**
Valtec Industries, **III** 684
Valtek International, Inc., **17** 147
Valtur, **6** 207
Value America, **29** 312
Value City Department Stores,
Value City Department Stores, Inc., **29** 311; **38 473–75**
Value Foods Ltd., **11** 239
Value Giant Stores, **12** 478
Value House, **II** 673
Value Investors, **III** 330
Value Line, Inc., **16 506–08**
Value Merchants Inc., **13 541–43**
Value Rent A Car, **9** 350; **23** 354
Valueland, **8** 482
ValueVision International, Inc., **22 534–36**; **27** 337
ValuJet, Inc. *See* AirTran Holdings, Inc.
Valvoline, Inc., **I** 291; **IV** 374
Valvtron, **11** 226
Van Ameringen-Haebler, Inc., **9** 290
Van Brunt Manufacturing Co., **III** 462; **21** 173
Van Camp Seafood Company, Inc., **II** 562–63; **7 556–57**; **13** 426. *See also* Chicken of the Sea International.
Van Cleef & Arpels Inc., **26** 145
Van de Kamp's, Inc., **II** 556–57; **7** 430; **32** 67
Van den Bergh Foods, **II** 588; **9** 319
Van der Horst Corp. of America, **III** 471
Van der Moolen Holding NV, **37** 224
Van Dorn Company, **13** 190
Van Dorn Electric Tool Co., **III** 435
Van Gend and Loos, **6** 404; **26** 241, 243
Van Houton, **II** 521
Van Houtte Inc., **39 409–11**
Van Kirk Chocolate, **7** 429
Van Kok-Ede, **II** 642
Van Leer Containers Inc., **30** 397
Van Leer Holding, Inc., **9** 303, 305
Van Leer N.V. *See* Royal Packaging Industries Van Leer N.V.
Van Mar, Inc., **18** 88
Van Munching & Company, Inc., **I** 256; **13** 257, 259; **34** 202
Van Nostrand Reinhold, **8** 526
Van Ommeren, **41** 339–40
Van Ryn Gold Mines Estate, **IV** 90
Van Schaardenburg, **II** 528
Van Sickle, **IV** 485
Van Waters & Rogers, **8** 99; **41** 340
Van Wezel, **26** 278–79
Van Wijcks Waalsteenfabrieken, **14** 249
Vanadium Alloys Steel Company (VASCO), **13** 295–96
Vanant Packaging Corporation, **8** 359
Vance International Airways, **8** 349
Vancouver Pacific Paper Co., **IV** 286
Vanderbilt Mortgage and Finance, **13** 154
Vanderlip-Swenson-Tilghman Syndicate, **IV** 81; **7** 185
Vanessa and Biffi, **11** 226
The Vanguard Group, Inc., **34 486–89 (upd.)**
The Vanguard Group of Investment Companies, **9** 239; **14 530–32**
Vanity Fair Mills, Inc., **V** 390–91
Vanity Fair Paper Mills, **IV** 281; **9** 259
Vans, Inc., **16 509–11**; **17** 259–61
Vansickle Industries, **III** 603
Vanstar, **13** 176
Vantage Analysis Systems, Inc., **11** 490
Vantive Corporation, **33** 333; **38** 431–32
Vantona Group Ltd., **V** 356
Vantress Pedigree, Inc., **II** 585
Vapor Corp., **III** 444
Varco International, Inc., **42 418–20**
Varco-Pruden, Inc., **8** 544–46
Vare Corporation, **8** 366
Vari-Lite International, Inc., **35 434–36**
Variable Annuity Life Insurance Co., **III** 193–94
Varian Associates Inc., **12 504–06**
Varibus Corporation, **6** 495
Variform, Inc., **12** 397
VARIG S.A. (Viação Aérea Rio-Grandense), **6 133–35**; **26** 113; **29 494–97 (upd.)**; **31** 443–45; **33** 19
Varity Corporation, **III 650–52**; **7** 258, 260; **19** 294; **27** 203, 251
Varlen Corporation, **16 512–14**
Varney Air Lines, **I** 47, 128; **6** 128; **9** 416
Varney Speed Lines. *See* Continental Airlines, Inc.

Varo, **7** 235, 237
Varsity Spirit Corp., **15 516–18**; **22** 459
Varta AG, **III** 536; **9** 180–81; **23 495–99**; **26** 230
Vasco Metals Corp., **I** 523; **10** 520, 522
Vascoloy-Ramet, **13** 295
VASP (Viaçao Aérea de Sao Paulo), **6** 134; **29** 495; **31** 444–45
Vasset, S.A., **17** 362–63
Vast Solutions, **39** 24
Vastar Resources, Inc., **24 524–26**; **38** 445, 448
Vaughan Harmon Systems Ltd., **25** 204
Vaughan Printers Inc., **23** 100
Vaungarde, Inc., **22** 175
Vauxhall, **19** 391
VAW Leichtmetall GmbH, **IV** 231
VBB Viag-Bayernwerk-Beteiligungs-Gesellschaft mbH, **IV** 232
VDM Nickel-Technologie AG, **IV** 89
VEB Londa, **III** 69
Veba A.G., **I** 349–50, **542–43**; **III** 695; **IV** 194–95, 199, 455, 508; **8** 69, 494–495; **15 519–21 (upd.)**; **23** 69, 451, 453–54; **24** 79; **25** 102; **26** 423; **32** 147
VECO International, Inc., **7 558–59**
Vector Automotive Corporation, **13** 61
Vector Casa de Bolsa, **21** 413
Vector Gas Ltd., **13** 458
Vector Group Ltd., **35 437–40 (upd.)**
Vector Video, Inc., **9** 74
Vedelectric, **13** 544
Vedior NV, **35 441–43**
Veeco Instruments Inc., **32 487–90**
Veeder-Root Company, **7** 116–17
Veit Companies, **43 440–42**
Vel-Tex Chemical, **16** 270
Velcarta S.p.A., **17** 281
Velcro Industries N.V., **19 476–78**
Velda Farms, Inc., **26** 448
Vellumoid Co., **I** 159
VeloBind, Inc., **10** 314
Velsicol, **I** 342, 440
Velva-Sheen Manufacturing Co., **23** 66
Vemar, **7** 558
Venator Group Inc., **35 444–49 (upd.)**
Vencemos, **20** 124
Vencor, Inc., **IV** 402; **14** 243; **16 515–17**; **25** 456
Vendex International N.V., **10** 136–37; **13 544–46**; **26** 160
Vendôme Luxury Group plc, **27 487–89**; **29** 90, 92
Vendors Supply of America, Inc., **7** 241–42; **25** 241
Venevision, **24** 516, 517
Vennootschap Nederland, **III** 177–78
Ventshade Company, **40** 299–300
Ventura, **29** 356–57
Venture Out RV, **26** 193
Venture Stores Inc., **V** 134; **12 507–09**
Venturi, Inc., **9** 72
Vepco. *See* Virginia Electric and Power Company.
Vera Cruz Electric Light, Power and Traction Co. Ltd., **IV** 658
Vera Imported Parts, **11** 84
Verafumos Ltd., **12** 109
Veragon Corporation. *See* Drypers Corporation.
Veratex Group, **13** 149–50
Veravision, **24** 510
Verbatim Corporation, **III** 477; **7** 163; **14 533–35**; **36** 173
Verbundnetz Gas AG, **38** 408
Verd-A-Fay, **13** 398
Vereenigde Nederlandsche Scheepvaartmaatschappij, **6** 404; **26** 242
Vereeniging Refractories, **IV** 22
Vereeniging Tiles, **III** 734
Verein für Chemische Industrie, **IV** 70
Vereinigte Aluminium Werke AG, **IV** 229–30, 232
Vereinigte Deutsche Metallwerke AG, **IV** 140
Vereinigte Elektrizitäts und Bergwerke A.G., **I** 542
Vereinigte Elektrizitätswerke Westfalen AG, **IV** 195; **V 744–47**
Vereinigte Energiewerke AG, **V** 709
Vereinigte Flugtechnische Werke GmbH., **I** 42, 55, 74–75
Vereinigte Glanzstoff Fabriken, **13** 21
Vereinigte Industrie-Unternehmungen Aktiengesellschaft, **IV** 229–30
Vereinigte Leichmetall-Werke GmbH, **IV** 231
Vereinigte Papierwarenfabriken GmbH, **IV** 323
Vereinigte Papierwerke Schickedanz AG, **26** 384
Vereinigte Stahlwerke AG, **III** 565; **IV** 87, 104–05, 132, 221; **14** 327
Vereinigte Versicherungsgruppe, **III** 377
Vereinigten Westdeutsche Waggonfabriken AG, **III** 542–43
Vereinsbank Wismar, **II** 256
Vereinte Versicherungen, **III** 377
Verenigde Bedrijven Bredero, **26** 280
N.V. Verenigde Fabrieken Wessanen and Laan, **II** 527
Verenigde Nederlandse Uitgeverijen. *See* VNU N.V.
Verenigde Spaarbank Groep. *See* VSB Groep.
Verienigte Schweizerbahnen, **6** 424
VeriFone, Inc., **15** 321; **18 541–44**; **27** 219–21; **28** 191
Verilyte Gold, Inc., **19** 452
Veritas Capital Partners, **26** 408
Veritus Inc., **27** 208–09
Verizon Communications, **43 443–49 (upd.)**
Verizon Wireless, Inc., **42** 284
Verlagsgruppe Georg von Holtzbrinck GmbH, **15** 158, 160; **25** 485; **35 450–53**
Vermeer Manufacturing Company, **17 507–10**
The Vermont Teddy Bear Co., Inc., **36 500–02**
Verneuil Holding Co, **21** 387
Vernitron Corporation, **18** 293
Vernon and Nelson Telephone Company. *See* British Columbia Telephone Company.
Vernon Graphics, **III** 499
Vernon Paving, **III** 674
Vernon Savings & Loan, **9** 199
Vernons, **IV** 651
Vernors, Inc., **25** 4
Vero, **III** 434
La Verrerie Souchon-Neuvesel, **II** 474
Verreries Champenoises, **II** 475
Versace. *See* Gianni Versace SpA.
Versatec Inc., **13** 128
Versatile Farm and Equipment Co., **22** 380
Versax, S.A. de C.V., **19** 12
Versicherungs-Verein, **III** 402, 410–11
Verson Allsteel Press Co., **21** 20, 22
Vert Baudet, **19** 309
Vertical Technology Industries, **14** 571
Verticom, **25** 531
Verve Records, **23** 389
Vessel Management Services, Inc., **28** 80
Vestar Capital Partners, **42** 309
Vestek Systems, Inc., **13** 417
Vestro, **19** 309
Vesuvius Crucible Co., **III** 681
Vesuvius USA Corporation, **8** 179
Veszpremtej, **25** 85
Veterinary Cos. of America, **III** 25
VEW AG, **IV** 234; **39 412–15**
Vexlar, **18** 313
VF Corporation, **V 390–92**; **12** 205; **13** 512; **17** 223, 225, **511–14 (upd.)**; **25** 22; **31** 261
VFW-Fokker B.V., **I** 41, 55, 74–75
VHA Long Term Care, **23** 431
VH1 Inc., **23** 503
VI-Jon Laboratories, Inc., **12** 388
VIA/Rhin et Moselle, **III** 185
Via-Générale de Transport et d'Industrie SA, **28** 155
Viacao Aerea Rio Grandense of South America. *See* VARIG, SA.
Viacom Enterprises, **6** 33; **7** 336
Viacom Inc., **23** 274–76, **500–03 (upd.)**; **24** 106, 327; **26** 32; **28** 295; **30** 101; **31** 59, 109; **35** 402. *See also* National Amusements Inc.
Viacom International Inc., **7** 222–24, 530, **560–62**; **9** 429; **10** 175; **19** 403
Viag AG, **IV 229–32**, 323; **25** 332; **32** 153; **43** 188–89
Viajes El Corte Inglés, S.A., **26** 129
VIASA, **I** 107; **6** 97; **36** 281
Viasoft Inc., **27 490–93**
Viatech Continental Can Company, Inc., **25 512–15 (upd.)**
Vichy, **III** 46
Vickers-Armstrong Ltd., **I** 50, 57, 82; **24** 85
Vickers Inc., **III** 640, 642; **13** 8; **23** 83
Vickers plc, **I** 194–95; **II** 3; **III** 555, 652, 725; **16** 9; **21** 435; **27 494–97**
Vicoreen Instrument Co., **I** 202
VICORP Restaurants, Inc., **12 510–12**
Vicra Sterile Products, **I** 628
Vicsodrive Japan, **III** 495
Victor Company, **10** 483
Victor Company of Japan, Ltd., **I** 411; **II** 55–56, 91, 102, **118–19**; **III** 605; **IV** 599; **12** 454; **26 511–13 (upd.)**
Victor Comptometer, **I** 676; **III** 154
Victor Equipment Co., **19** 440
Victor Manufacturing and Gasket Co., **I** 152
Victor Musical Industries Inc., **II** 119; **10** 285
Victor Talking Machine Co., **II** 88, 118
Victor Value, **II** 678
Victoria, **III** 308
Victoria & Co., **39** 247
Victoria & Legal & General, **III** 359
Victoria Coach Station, **6** 406
Victoria Creations Inc., **13** 536
VICTORIA Holding AG, **III 399–401**
Victoria Paper Co., **IV** 286
Victoria Sugar Co., **III** 686
Victoria Wine Co., **I** 216

Victoria's Secret, **V** 115–16; **11** 498; **12** 557, 559; **16** 219; **18** 215; **24** 237; **25** 120–22, 521
Victorinox AG, **21 515–17**
Victory Fire Insurance Co., **III** 343
Victory Insurance, **III** 273
Victory Oil Co., **IV** 550
Victory Refrigeration Company, **22** 355
Victory Savings and Loan, **10** 339
Victory Supermarket. *See* Big V Supermarkets, Inc.
Vidal Sassoon, **17** 110
Video Concepts, **9** 186
Video Independent Theatres, Inc., **14** 86
Video Library, Inc., **9** 74
Video News International, **19** 285
Video Superstores Master Limited Partnership, **9** 74
Videoconcepts, **II** 107
VideoFusion, Inc., **16** 419
Videotex Network Japan, **IV** 680
Videotron, **25** 102
VideV, **24** 509
La Vie Claire, **13** 103
Vielle Montaign, **22** 285
Vienna Sausage Manufacturing Co., **14 536–37**
Viessmann Werke GmbH & Co., **37 411–14**
View-Master/Ideal Group, **12** 496
Viewdata Corp., **IV** 630; **15** 264
Viewer's Edge, **27** 429
Viewlogic, **11** 490
ViewStar Corp., **20** 103
Viewtel, **14** 36
Vigilance-Vie, **III** 393
Vigilant Insurance Co., **III** 220; **14** 108; **37** 83
Vigoro, **22** 340
Vigortone, **II** 582
Viiala Oy, **IV** 302
Viking, **II** 10; **IV** 659
Viking Brush, **III** 614
Viking Building Products, **22** 15
Viking Computer Services, Inc., **14** 147
Viking Consolidated Shipping Corp, **25** 470
Viking Direct Limited, **10** 545
Viking Foods, Inc., **8** 482; **14** 411
Viking Industries, **39** 322, 324
Viking Office Products, Inc., **10 544–46**
Viking Penguin, **IV** 611
Viking Press, **12** 25
Viking Pump Company, **21** 499–500
Viking Star Shipping, Inc. *See* Teekay Shipping Corporation.
Viktor Achter, **9** 92
Village Inn. *See* VICORP Restaurants, Inc.
Village Super Market, Inc., **7 563–64**
Village Voice Media, Inc., **38 476–79**
Villager, Inc., **11** 216; **39** 244
Villazon & Co., **27** 139
Villeroy & Boch AG, **37 415–18**
VILPAC, S.A., **26** 356
Vin & Spirit AB, **31 458–61**
Vinci, **27** 54; **43 450–52**
Vine Products Ltd., **I** 215
Viner Bros., **16** 546
Vingaarden A/S, **9** 100
Vingresor A.B., **I** 120
Vining Industries, **12** 128
Viniprix SA, **10** 205; **19** 309; **27** 95
Vinland Web-Print, **8** 360
Vinson & Elkins L.L.P., **28** 48; **30 481–83**
Vintage Petroleum, Inc., **42 421–23**
Vintners International, **34** 89
Vinyl Maid, Inc., **IV** 401
Vipont Pharmaceutical, **III** 25; **14** 122
VIPS, **11** 113
Viratec Thin Films, Inc., **22** 347
Virco Manufacturing Corporation, **17 515–17**
Virgin Atlantic Airlines. *See* Virgin Group PLC.
Virgin Express, **35** 384
Virgin Group PLC, **12 513–15**; **14** 73; **18** 80; **22** 194; **24** 486; **29** 302; **32 491–96 (upd.)**
The Virgin Islands Telephone Co., **19** 256
Virgin Retail Group Ltd., **9** 75, 361; **37** 262
Virginia Eastern Shore Sustainable Development Corporation, **28** 307
Virginia Electric and Power Company, **V** 596–98
Virginia Fibre Corporation, **15** 188
Virginia Folding Box Company, **IV** 352; **19** 497
Virginia Laminating, **10** 313
Virginia Mason Medical Center, **41** 183
Virginia National Bankshares, **10** 426
Virginia Railway and Power Company (VR&P), **V** 596
Virginia Trading Corp., **II** 422
Viromedics, **25** 382
Visa. *See* Valores Industriales S.A.
Visa International, **II** 200; **9** 333–35, **536–38**; **18** 543; **20** 59; **26 514–17 (upd.)**; **41** 200–01
Visco Products Co., **I** 373; **12** 346
Viscodrive GmbH, **III** 495
Viscount Industries Limited, **6** 310
Vishay Intertechnology, Inc., **11** 516; **21 518–21**
VisiCorp, **6** 254; **25** 298
Vision Centers, **I** 688; **12** 188
Vision Technology Group Ltd., **19** 124
Visionware Ltd., **38** 419
Visionworks, **9** 186
Viskase Corporation, **17** 157, 159
Visking Co., **I** 400
Visnews Ltd., **IV** 668, 670
VisQueen, **I** 334
Vista Bakery Inc., **14** 306
Vista Chemical Company, **I 402–03**; **V** 709
Vista Concepts, Inc., **11** 19
Vista Resources, Inc., **17** 195
Vista 2000, Inc., **36** 444
Vistana, Inc., **22 537–39**; **26** 464
Visual Action Holdings plc, **24** 96, 374
Visual Information Technologies, **11** 57
Visual Technology, **6** 201
VISX, Incorporated, **30 484–86**
Vita-Achter, **9** 92
Vita Lebensversicherungs-Gesellschaft, **III** 412
Vita Liquid Polymers, **9** 92
Vitafoam Incorporated, **9** 93; **33** 78
Vital Health Corporation, **13** 150
Vital Processing Services LLC, **18** 516, 518
Vitalink Communications Corp., **11** 520; **34** 444
Vitalink Pharmacy Services, Inc., **15 522–24**; **25** 309–10
Vitalscheme, **38** 426
Vitamin World, **31** 346–48
Vitesse Semiconductor Corporation, **32 497–500**
Vitex Foods, **10** 382
Vitoria-Minas Railroad, **43** 111
Vitro Corp., **8** 178; **10 547–48**; **17** 492
Vitro Corporativo S.A. de C.V., **34 490–92**
Vitro S.A., **19** 189
VIVA, **23** 390
Viva Home Co., **III** 757
Vivendi SA, **29** 369, 371; **32** 52, 54; **33** 178, 181; **34** 83, 85; **38** 168, 170; **40** 408
Vivendi Universal Publishing, **41** 361
Vivendi Universal S.A., **43** 450, 452
Vivendia, **40** 449
Vivesvata Iron and Steel Ltd., **IV** 207
Viviane Woodard Cosmetic Corp., **II** 531
Vivra, Inc., **15** 119; **18 545–47**
VK Mason Construction Ltd., **II** 222
VKI Technologies Inc., **39** 409
Vlasic Foods International Inc., **II** 480–81; **7** 67–68; **25 516–19**; **26** 56, 59
VLN Corp., **I** 201
VLSI Technology, Inc., **11** 246; **16 518–20**; **31** 300
VMG Products. *See* Drypers Corporation.
VMX Inc., **14** 355; **41** 289
VND, **III** 593
Vnesheconobank, **II** 242
VNG. *See* Verbundnetz Gas AG.
VNS. *See* Vereenigde Nederlandsche Scheepvaartmaatschappij.
VNU N.V., **27** 361, **498–501**; **38** 8
VNU/Claritas, **6** 14
Vobis Microcomputer, **20** 103; **23** 311
VocalTec, Inc., **18** 143
Vodac, **11** 548
Vodafone Group Plc, **II** 84; **11 547–48**; **34** 85; **36 503–06 (upd.)**; **38** 296, 300
Vodapage, **11** 548
Vodata, **11** 548
Vodavi Technology Corporation, **13** 213
Voest-Alpine Stahl AG, **IV 233–35**; **31** 47–48
Vogel Peterson Furniture Company, **7** 4–5
Vogoro Corp., **13** 503
Voice Data Systems, **15** 125
Voice Powered Technology International, Inc., **23** 212
Voice Response, Inc., **11** 253
Voith, **II** 22
Voith Sulzer Papiermaschinen GmbH. *See* J.M. Voith AG.
Vokes, **I** 429
Volition, Inc., **39** 395
Volkert Stampings, **III** 628
Volkswagen Aktiengesellschaft, **I** 30, 32, 186, 192, **206–08**, 460; **II** 279; **IV** 231; **7** 8; **10** 14; **11** 104, **549–51 (upd.)**; **13** 413; **14** 169; **16** 322; **19** 484; **26** 12; **27** 11, 496; **31** 363–65; **32 501–05 (upd.)**; **34** 55, 130; **39** 373–74
Volt Information Sciences Inc., **26 518–21**
Volta Aluminium Co., Ltd., **IV** 122
Volume Distributors. *See* Payless ShoeSource, Inc.
Volume Service Company. *See* Restaurants Unlimited, Inc.
Volume Shoe Corporation. *See* Payless ShoeSource,Inc.

Voluntary Hospitals of America, **6** 45
Volunteer Leather Company, **17** 202, 205
Volunteer State Life Insurance Co., **III** 221; **37** 84
AB Volvo, **I** 186, 192, 198, **209–11; II** 5, 366; **III** 543, 591, 623, 648; **IV** 336; **7** **565–68 (upd.)**; **9** 283–84, 350, 381; **10** 274; **12** 68, 342; **13** 30, 356; **14** 321; **15** 226; **16** 322; **18** 394; **23** 354; **26 9–12 (upd.)**, 401, 403; **33** 191, 364; **39** 126. *See also* Ford Motor Company.
Volvo-Penta, **21** 503
von Roll, **6** 599
Von Ruden Manufacturing Co., **17** 532
von Weise Gear Co., **III** 509
Von's Grocery Co., **II** 419; **8** 474; **17** 559
The Vons Companies, Incorporated, **II** 655; **7 569–71**; **12** 209; **24** 418; **28** **510–13 (upd.)**; **35** 328
VOP Acquisition Corporation, **10** 544
Vornado Realty Trust, **20 508–10**; **39** 211
Voroba Hearing Systems, **25** 56
Vortex Management, Inc., **41** 207
Vorwerk & Co., **27 502–04**
Vosper Thornycroft Holding plc, **41** **410–12**
Votainer International, **13** 20
Vought Aircraft Co., **11** 364
Voxson, **I** 531; **22** 193
Voyage Conseil, **II** 265
Voyager Communications Inc., **24** 5
Voyager Energy, **IV** 84
Voyager Ltd., **12** 514
Voyager Petroleum Ltd., **IV** 83; **7** 188
Voyageur Travel Insurance Ltd., **21** 447
VR&P. *See* Virginia Railway and Power Company.
Vratislavice A.S., **38** 77
VRG International. *See* Roberts Pharmaceutical Corporation.
Vroom & Dreesmann, **13** 544–46
Vrumona B.V., **I** 257
VS Services, **13** 49
VSA. *See* Vendors Supply of America, Inc.
VSB Groep, **III** 199, 201
VSD Communications, Inc., **22** 443
VSEL, **24** 88
VSM. *See* Village Super Market, Inc.
VST. *See* Vision Technology Group Ltd.
Vtel Corporation, **10** 456; **27** 365
VTR Incorporated, **16** 46; **43** 60
Vulcan Materials Company, **7 572–75**; **12** 39; **25** 266; **41** 147, 149
Vulcan Ventures Inc., **32** 145; **43** 144
Vulcraft, **7** 400–02
VVM, **III** 200
VW&R. *See* Van Waters & Rogers.
VWR Textiles & Supplies, Inc., **11** 256
VWR United Company, **9** 531
Vycor Corporation, **25** 349
Vyvx, **31** 469

W&A Manufacturing Co., LLC, **26** 530
W&F Fish Products, **13** 103
W. & G. Turnbull & Co., **IV** 278; **19** 153
W & J Sloane Home Furnishings Group, **35** 129
W. & M. Duncan, **II** 569
W.A. Bechtel Co., **I** 558
W.A. Harriman & Co., **III** 471
W.A. Krueger Co., **19** 333–35
W. Atlee Burpee & Co., **II** 532; **11** 198; **27 505–08**
W.B. Constructions, **III** 672
W.B. Doner & Company, **10** 420; **12** 208; **28** 138
W.B. Saunders Co., **IV** 623–24
W.C. Bradley Company, **18** 516
W.C.G. Sports Industries Ltd. *See* Canstar Sports Inc.
W.C. Heraeus GmbH, **IV** 100
W.C. Norris, **III** 467
W.C. Platt Co., **IV** 636
W.C. Ritchie & Co., **IV** 333
W.C. Smith & Company Limited, **14** 339
W. Duke & Sons, **V** 395, 600
W. Duke Sons & Company, **27** 128
W.E. Andrews Co., Inc., **25** 182
W.E. Dillon Company, Ltd., **21** 499
W.F. Linton Company, **9** 373
W. Gunson & Co., **IV** 278; **19** 153
W. Gutzeit & Co., **IV** 274–77
W.H. Brady Co., **17 518–21**
W.H. Gunlocke Chair Co. *See* Gunlocke Company.
W.H. McElwain Co., **III** 528
W.H. Morton & Co., **II** 398; **10** 62
W.H. Smith & Son (Alacra) Ltd., **15** 473
W H Smith Group PLC, **V 211–13**
W.J. Noble and Sons, **IV** 294; **19** 225
W.L. Gore & Associates, Inc., **14** **538–40**; **26** 417
W.M. Bassett Furniture Co. *See* Bassett Furniture Industries, Inc.
W.M. Ritter Lumber Co., **IV** 281; **9** 259
W.O. Daley & Company, **10** 387
W.R. Bean & Son, **19** 335
W.R. Berkley Corp., **III** 248; **15 525–27**
W.R. Breen Company, **11** 486
W.R. Case & Sons Cutlery Company, **18** 567
W.R. Grace & Company, **I 547–50**; **III** 525, 695; **IV** 454; **11** 216; **12** 337; **13** 149, 502, 544; **14** 29; **16** 45–47; **17** 308, 365–66; **21** 213, 507, 526; **22** 188, 501; **25** 535; **35** 38, 40; **43** 59–60
W. Rosenlew, **IV** 350
W.S. Barstow & Company, **6** 575
W.T. Grant Co., **16** 487
W.T. Rawleigh, **17** 105
W.T. Young Foods, **III** 52; **8** 433; **26** 383
W. Ullberg & Co., **I** 553
W.V. Bowater & Sons, Ltd., **IV** 257–58
W.W. Cargill and Brother, **II** 616; **13** 136
W.W. Grainger, Inc., **V 214–15**; **13** 297; **26 537–39 (upd.)**
W.W. Kimball Company, **12** 296; **18** 44
W.W. Norton & Company, Inc., **28** **518–20**
Waban Inc., **V** 198; **13 547–49**; **19** 449. *See also* HomeBase, Inc.
Wabash National Corp., **13 550–52**
Wabash Valley Power Association, **6** 556
Wabtec Corporation, **40 451–54**
Wabush Iron Co., **IV** 73; **24** 143
Wachbrit Insurance Agency, **21** 96
Wachovia Bank of Georgia, N.A., **16** **521–23**
Wachovia Bank of South Carolina, N.A., **16 524–26**
Wachovia Corporation, **II** 336; **10** 425; **12** 16, **516–20**; **16** 521, 524, 526; **23** 455
The Wackenhut Corporation, **13** 124–25; **14 541–43**; **28** 255; **41** 80
Wacker-Chemie GmbH, **35 454–58**
Wacker Oil Inc., **11** 441
Waco Aircraft Company, **27** 98
Wacoal Corp., **25 520–24**
Waddell & Reed, Inc., **22 540–43**; **33** 405, 407
Wade Smith, **28** 27, 30
Wadsworth Inc., **8** 526
WaferTech, **18** 20; **43** 17
Waffle House Inc., **14 544–45**
Wagenseller & Durst, **25** 249
Waggener Edstrom, **42 424–26**
The Wagner & Brown Investment Group, **9** 248
Wagner Castings Company, **16** 474–75
Wagner Litho Machinery Co., **13** 369–70
Wagner Spray Tech, **18** 555
Wagonlit Travel, **22** 128
Wagons-Lits, **27** 11; **29** 443; **37** 250–52
Wah Chang Corp., **I** 523–24; **10** 520–21
AB Wahlbecks, **25** 464
Wahlstrom & Co., **23** 480
Waialua Agricultural Co., **II** 491
Waitaki International Biosciences Co., **17** 288
Waite Amulet Mines Ltd., **IV** 164
Waitrose Ltd. *See* John Lewis Partnership plc.
Wakefern Food Corporation, **II** 672; **7** 563–64; **18** 6; **25** 66, 234–35; **28** 143; **33 434–37**
Wako Shoji Co. Ltd. *See* Wacoal Corp.
Wakodo Co., **I** 674
Wal-Mart de Mexico, S.A. de C.V., **35** 322, **459–61 (upd.)**
Wal-Mart Stores, Inc., **II** 108; **V 216–17**; **6** 287; **7** 61, 331; **8** 33, 295, **555–57 (upd.)**; **9** 187, 361; **10** 236, 284, 515–16, 524; **11** 292; **12** 48, 53–55, 63–64, 97, 208–09, 221, 277, 333, 477, 507–08; **13** 42, 215–17, 260–61, 274, 332–33, 444, 446; **14** 235; **15** 139, 275; **16** 61–62, 65, 390; **17** 297, 321, 460–61; **18** 108, 137, 186, 283, 286; **19** 511; **20** 263; **21** 457–58; **22** 224, 257, 328; **23** 214; **24** 148, 149, 334; **25** 221–22, 254, 314; **26 522–26 (upd.)**, 549; **27** 286, 313, 315, 416, 451; **29** 230, 314, 318; **32** 169, 338, 341; **33** 307; **34** 198; **37** 64; **41** 61, 115
Walbridge Aldinger Co., **38 480–82**
Walbro Corporation, **13 553–55**
Walchenseewerk AG, **23** 44
Waldbaum, Inc., **II** 638; **15** 260; **16** 247, 249; **19 479–81**; **24** 528
Walden Book Company Inc., **V** 112; **10** 136–37; **16** 160; **17 522–24**; **25** 30
Waldes Truarc Inc., **III** 624
Oy Waldhof AB, **IV** 324
Wales & Company, **14** 257
Walgreen Co., **V 218–20**; **9** 346; **18** 199; **20 511–13 (upd.)**; **21** 186; **24** 263; **32** 166, 170
Walk Haydel & Associates, Inc., **25** 130
Walk Softly, Inc., **25** 118
Walker & Lee, **10** 340
Walker Cain, **I** 215
Walker Dickson Group Limited, **26** 363
Walker Interactive Systems, **11** 78; **25** 86
Walker Manufacturing Company, **I** 527; **19 482–84**
Walker McDonald Manufacturing Co., **III** 569; **20** 361
Walkers Parker and Co., **III** 679–80
Walki GmbH, **IV** 349
AB Walkiakoski, **IV** 347

Walkins Manufacturing Corp., **III** 571; **20** 362
Walkup's Merchant Express Inc., **27** 473
Wall Drug Store, Inc., **40 455–57**
Wall Paper Manufacturers, **IV** 666; **17** 397
Wall Street Deli, Inc., **33 438–41**
Wall Street Leasing, **III** 137
Wallace and Tiernan, **I** 383; **11** 361
The Wallace Berrie Company. *See* Applause Inc.
Wallace Computer Services, Inc., **36 507–10**
Wallace International Silversmiths, **I** 473; **14** 482–83
Wallace Murray Corp., **II** 420
Wallbergs Fabriks A.B., **8** 14
Wallens Dairy Co., **II** 586
Wallin & Nordstrom, **V** 156
Wallingford Bank and Trust Co., **II** 213
Wallis, **V** 177
Wallis Arnold Enterprises, Inc., **21** 483
Wallis Tin Stamping Co., **I** 605
Wallis Tractor Company, **21** 502
Walrus, Inc., **18** 446
Walsin-Lihwa, **13** 141
Walston & Co., **II** 450; **III** 137
Walt Disney Company, **II** 102, 122, 129, 156, **172–74**; **III** 142, 504, 586; **IV** 585, 675, 703; **6** 15, **174–77 (upd.)**, 368; **7** 305; **8** 160; **10** 420; **12** 168, 208, 229, 323, 495–96; **13** 551; **14** 260; **15** 197; **16** 143, 336; **17** 243, 317, 442–43; **21** 23–26, 360–61; **23** 257–58, 303, 335, 476, 514; **25** 172, 268, 312–13; **27** 92, 287; **30 487–91 (upd.)**; **34** 348; **43** 142, 447
Walt Disney World, **6** 82, 175–76; **18** 290
Walter Baker's Chocolate, **II** 531
Walter Bau, **27** 136, 138
Walter E. Heller, **17** 324
Walter Herzog GmbH, **16** 514
Walter Industries, Inc., **III 765–67**; **22 544–47 (upd.)**
Walter Kidde & Co., **I** 475, 524; **27** 287
Walter Pierce Oil Co., **IV** 657
Walter Wright Mammoet, **26** 280
Walton Manufacturing, **11** 486
Walton Monroe Mills, Inc., **8 558–60**
Wander Ltd., **I** 672
Wanderer Werke, **III** 154
Wang Global, **39** 176–78
Wang Laboratories, Inc., **II** 208; **III 168–70**; **6 284–87 (upd.)**; **8** 139; **9** 171; **10** 34; **11** 68, 274; **12** 183; **18** 138; **19** 40; **20** 237
Wanishi, **IV** 157; **17** 349
WAP, **26** 420
Waples-Platter Co., **II** 625
War Damage Corp., **III** 353, 356; **22** 493
War Emergency Tankers Inc., **IV** 552
Warbasse-Cogeneration Technologies Partnership, **35** 479
Warburg, Pincus Capital Corp., **6** 13; **9** 524; **14** 42; **24** 373
Warburg USB, **38** 291
Warburtons Bakery Cafe, Inc., **18** 37
Ward Manufacturing Inc., **IV** 101
Ward's Communications, **22** 441
Wardley Ltd., **II** 298
Wards. *See* Circuit City Stores, Inc.
Waring and LaRosa, **12** 167
The Warnaco Group Inc., **9** 156; **12 521–23**; **22** 123; **25** 122, 523. *See also* Authentic Fitness Corp.
Warner & Swasey Co., **III** 168; **6** 284; **8** 545
Warner Brothers, **25** 327–28; **26** 102
Warner Communications Inc., **II** 88, 129, 135, 146–47, 154–55, 169–70, **175–77**, 208, 452; **III** 443, 505; **IV** 623, 673, 675–76; **7** 526, 528–30 **8** 527; **9** 44–45, 119, 469; **10** 196; **11** 557; **12** 73, 495–96; **17** 65, 149, 442–43; **21** 23–25, 360; **22** 519, 522; **23** 23–24, 390, 501; **24** 373; **25** 418–19, 498; **26** 151. *See also* Time Warner Inc.
Warner Cosmetics, **III** 48; **8** 129
Warner Gear Co., **III** 438–39; **14** 63–64
Warner-Lambert Co., **I** 643, 674, 679, 696, **710–12**; **7** 596; **8** 62–63; **10 549–52 (upd.)**; **12** 480, 482; **13** 366; **16** 439; **20** 23; **25** 55, 366; **34** 284; **38** 366
Warner Records, **II** 177
Warner Sugar Refining Co., **II** 496
Warren Apparel Group Ltd., **39** 257
Warren Bank, **13** 464
Warren, Gorham & Lamont, **8** 526
Warren Oilfield Services, **9** 363
Warren Petroleum Company, **18** 365, 367
Warri Refining and Petrochemicals Co., **IV** 473
Warrick Industries, **31** 338
Warringah Brick, **III** 673
Warrington Products Ltd. *See* Canstar Sports Inc.
Warrior River Coal Company, **7** 281
Wartsila Marine Industries Inc., **III** 649
Warwick Chemicals, **13** 461
Warwick Electronics, **III** 654
Warwick International Ltd., **13** 462
Wasa, **I** 672–73
Wasag-Chemie AG, **III** 694
Wasatch Gas Co., **6** 568
Wascana Energy Inc., **13 556–58**
Washburn Crosby Co., **II** 501, 555; **10** 322
Washburn Graphics Inc., **23** 100
The Washington Companies, **33 442–45**
Washington Duke Sons & Co., **12** 108
Washington Federal, Inc., **17 525–27**
Washington Football, Inc., **35 462–65**
Washington Gas Light Company, **19 485–88**
Washington Inventory Service, **30** 239
Washington Mills Company, **13** 532
Washington Mutual, Inc., **17 528–31**
Washington National Corporation, **11** 482; **12 524–26**
Washington Natural Gas Company, **9 539–41**
The Washington Post Company, **III** 214; **IV 688–90**; **6** 323; **11** 331; **18** 60, 61, 63; **20 515–18 (upd.)**; **23** 157–58; **42** 31, 33–34, 209–10
Washington Railway and Electric Company, **6** 552–53
Washington Scientific Industries, Inc., **17 532–34**
Washington Specialty Metals Corp., **14** 323, 325
Washington Steel Corp., **14** 323, 325
Washington Water Power Company, **6** 566, **595–98**
Washtenaw Gas Company. *See* MCN Corporation.
Wassall Plc, **18 548–50**
Wasserstein Perella Partners, **II** 629; **III** 512, 530–31; **V** 223; **17** 366
Waste Control Specialists LLC, **19** 466, 468
Waste Holdings, Inc., **41 413–15**
Waste Management, Inc., **V** 749–51, **752–54**; **6** 46, 600; **9** 73, 108–09; **11** 435–36; **18** 10; **20** 90; **23** 430
Water Engineering, **11** 360
Water Pik Technologies, Inc., **I** 524–25; **34 498–501**
Water Products Group, **6** 487–88
Water Street Corporate Recovery Fund, **10** 423
The Waterbury Companies, **16** 482
Waterford Wedgwood Holdings PLC, **IV** 296; **12 527–29**
Waterford Wedgwood plc, **34 493–97 (upd.)**; **38** 403
Waterhouse Investor Services, Inc., **18 551–53**
Waterloo Gasoline Engine Co., **III** 462; **21** 173
Waterlow and Sons, **10** 269
Waterman Marine Corporation, **27** 242
The Waterman Pen Company. *See* BIC Corporation.
WaterPro Supplies Corporation, **6** 486, 488
Waters Corporation, **43 453–57**
Waterstone's, **42** 444
Waterstreet Inc., **17** 293
Watertown Insurance Co., **III** 370
Watkins-Johnson Company, **15 528–30**
Watkins Manufacturing Co., **I** 159
Watkins-Strathmore Co., **13** 560
Watmough and Son Ltd., **II** 594
Watney Mann and Truman Brewers, **I** 228, 247; **9** 99
Watson-Haas Lumber Company, **33** 257
Watson Pharmaceuticals Inc., **16 527–29**
Watson-Triangle, **16** 388, 390
Watson-Wilson Transportation System, **V** 540; **14** 567
Watson Wyatt Worldwide, **42 427–30**
Watt & Shand, **16** 61
Watt AG, **6** 491
Watt Electronic Products, Limited, **10** 319
The Watt Stopper, **21** 348, 350
Wattie Pict Ltd., **I** 437
Wattie's Ltd., **7 576–78**; **11** 173
Watts Industries, Inc., **19 489–91**
Watts/Silverstein, Inc., **24** 96
Waukesha Engine Servicenter, **6** 441
Waukesha Foundry Company, **11** 187
Waukesha Motor Co., **III** 472
Wausau Paper Mills, **15** 305
Wausau Sulphate Fibre Co. *See* Mosinee Paper Corporation.
Wavelength Corporate Communications Pty Limited, **24** 95
Waverly, Inc., **10** 135; **16 530–32**; **19** 358
Waverly Oil Works, **I** 405
Waverly Pharmaceutical Limited, **11** 208
Wawa Inc., **17 535–37**
Waxman Industries, Inc., **III** 570; **9 542–44**; **20** 362; **28** 50–51
Wayco Foods, **14** 411
Waycross-Douglas Coca-Cola Bottling, **10** 222
Wayne Home Equipment. *See* Scott Fetzer Company.
Wayne Oakland Bank, **8** 188
WB. *See* Warner Communications Inc.
WBI Holdings, Inc., **42** 249, 253
WCI Holdings Corporation, **V** 223; **13** 170; **41** 94

WCK, Inc., **14** 236
WCRS Group plc, **6** 15
WCT Live Communication Limited, **24** 95
WD-40 Company, **18 554–57**
Wear-Ever, **17** 213
WearGuard, **13** 48
Wearne Brothers, **6** 117
The Weather Department, Ltd., **10** 89
Weather Guard, **IV** 305
Weatherford International, Inc., **39 416–18**
Weathers-Lowin, Leeam, **11** 408
Weaver, **III** 468
Webb & Knapp, **10** 43
Webb Corbett and Beswick, **38** 402
Webber Gage Co., **13** 302
WeBco International LLC, **26** 530
Webco Securities, Inc., **37** 225
Weber, **16** 488
Weber Aircraft Inc., **41** 369
Weber Metal, **30** 283–84
Weber-Stephen Products Co., **40 458–60**
Webers, **I** 409
Weblock, **I** 109
WebLogic Inc., **36** 81
Webster Publishing Co., **IV** 636
Webtron Corp., **10** 313
Webvan Group Inc., **38** 223
Wedgwood. *See* Waterford Wedgewood Holdings PLC.
Week's Dairy, **II** 528
Wegert Verwaltungs-GmbH and Co. Beteiligungs-KG, **24** 270
Wegmans Food Markets, Inc., **9 545–46**; **24** 445; **41 416–18 (upd.)**
Weidemann Brewing Co., **I** 254
Weider Health and Fitness, Inc., **38** 238
Weider Nutrition International, Inc., **29 498–501**; **33** 146–47; **34** 459
Weider Sporting Goods, **16** 80
Weifang Power Machine Fittings Ltd., **17** 106
Weight Watchers Gourmet Food Co., **43** 218
Weight Watchers International Inc., **II** 508; **10** 383; **11** 172; **12 530–32**; **13** 383; **27** 197; **33 446–49 (upd.)**; **36** 255–56
Weiner's Stores, Inc., **33 450–53**
Weirton Steel Corporation, **I** 297; **IV 236–38**; **7** 447, 598; **8** 346, 450; **10** 31–32; **12** 352, 354; **26** 407, **527–30 (upd.)**
Weis Markets, Inc., **15 531–33**
The Weitz Company, Inc., **42 431–34**
Welbecson, **III** 501
Welbilt Corp., **19 492–94**; **27** 159
Welborn Transport Co., **39** 64, 65
Welch's, **25** 366
Welcome Wagon International Inc., **III** 28; **16** 146
Weldless Steel Company, **8** 530
Welex Jet Services, **III** 498–99
Wella Group, **III 68–70**
Wellby Super Drug Stores, **12** 220
Wellcome Foundation Ltd., **I** 638, **713–15**; **8** 210, 452; **9** 265; **10** 551; **32** 212
Wellcome Trust, **41** 119
Weller Electric Corp., **II** 16
Wellington, **II** 457
Wellington Management Company, **14** 530–31; **23** 226
Wellington Sears Co., **15** 247–48
Wellman, Inc., **8 561–62**; **21** 193
Wellmark, Inc., **10** 89
Wellness Co., Ltd., **IV** 716
WellPoint Health Networks Inc., **25 525–29**
Wells Aircraft, **12** 112
Wells Fargo & Company, **II 380–84**, 319, 395; **III** 440; **10** 59–60; **12** 165, **533–37 (upd.)**; **17** 325; **18** 60, 543; **19** 411; **22** 542; **25** 434; **27** 292; **32** 373; **38** 44, **483–92 (upd.)**; **41** 200–01. *See also* American Express Company.
Wells Fargo HSBC Trade Bank, **26** 203
Wells-Gardner Electronics Corporation, **43 458–61**
Wells Lamont, **IV** 136
Wells Rich Greene BDDP, **6** 48, **50–52**
Wells' Dairy, Inc., **36 511–13**
Wellspring Associates L.L.C., **16** 338
Wellspring Resources LLC, **42** 429
Welsbach Mantle, **6** 446
Welsh Associated Collieries Ltd., **31** 369
Welsh Water. *See* Hyder plc.
Weltkunst Verlag GmbH, **IV** 590
Wendy's International, Inc., **II** 614–15, 647; **7** 433; **8 563–65**; **9** 178; **12** 553; **13** 494; **14** 453; **16** 95, 97; **17** 71, 124; **19** 215; **23** 384, **504–07 (upd.)**; **26** 284; **33** 240; **36** 517, 519; **41** 114
Wenger S.A., **III** 419; **21** 515
Wenlock Brewery Co., **I** 223
Wenner Media, Inc., **32 506–09**
Wenstroms & Granstoms Electriska Kraftbolag, **II** 1
Werkhof GmbH, **13** 491
Werknet, **16** 420; **43** 308
Werner Enterprises, Inc., **26 531–33**
Werner International, **III** 344; **14** 225
Wernicke Co., **I** 201
Wertheim Schroder & Company, **17** 443
Weru Aktiengesellschaft, **18 558–61**
Wesco Financial Corp., **III** 213, 215; **18** 62; **42** 32–34
Wesco Food Co., **II** 644
Wescot Decisison Systems, **6** 25
Weserflug, **I** 74
Wesper Co., **26** 4
Wesray and Management, **17** 213
Wesray Capital Corporation, **6** 357; **13** 41; **17** 443
Wesray Corporation, **22** 55
Wesray Holdings Corp., **13** 255
Wesray Transportation, Inc., **14** 38
Wessanen. *See* Koninklijke Wessanen N.V.
Wessanen and Laan, **II** 527
Wessanen Cacao, **II** 528
Wessanen USA, **II** 528; **29** 480
Wessanen's Koninklijke Fabrieken N.V., **II** 527
Wesson/Peter Pan Foods Co., **17** 241
West Australia Land Holdings, Limited, **10** 169
West Bend Co., **III** 610–11; **14 546–48**; **16** 384; **43** 289
West Coast Entertainment Corporation, **29 502–04**
West Coast Grocery Co., **II** 670; **18** 506
West Coast Machinery, **13** 385
West Coast of America Telegraph, **I** 428
West Coast Power Company, **12** 265
West Coast Restaurant Enterprises, **25** 390
West Coast Savings and Loan, **10** 339
West Coast Telecom, **III** 38
West Corporation, **42 435–37**
West End Family Pharmacy, Inc., **15** 523
West Fraser Timber Co. Ltd., **IV** 276; **17 538–40**
West Georgia Coca-Cola Bottlers, Inc., **13** 163
West Group, **34** 438, **502–06 (upd.)**
West Ham Gutta Percha Co., **I** 428
West Harrison Gas & Electric Company, **6** 466
West India Oil Co., **IV** 416, 428
West Japan Heavy Industries, **III** 578–79; **7** 348
West Jersey Electric Company, **6** 449
West Lynn Creamery, Inc., **26** 450
West Marine, Inc., **17 541–43**; **37** 398
West Missouri Power Company. *See* UtiliCorp United Inc.
West Newton Savings Bank, **13** 468
West Newton Telephone Company, **14** 258
West of England, **III** 690
West of England Sack Holdings, **III** 501; **7** 207
West One Bancorp, **11 552–55**; **36** 491
West Penn Electric. *See* Allegheny Power System, Inc.
West Penn Power Company, **38** 38–40
West Pharmaceutical Services, Inc., **42 438–41**
West Point-Pepperell, Inc., **8 566–69**; **9** 466; **15** 247; **25** 20; **28** 218. *See also* WestPoint Stevens Inc. *and* JPS Textile Group, Inc.
West Publishing Co., **IV** 312; **7 579–81**; **10** 407; **19** 268; **33** 264–65. *See also* The West Group.
West Rand Consolidated Mines, **IV** 90
West Rand Investment Trust, **IV** 21; **16** 27
West Richfield Telephone Company, **6** 299
West Side Bank, **II** 312
West Side Printing Co., **13** 559
West Surrey Central Dairy Co. Ltd., **II** 586
West TeleServices Corporation. *See* West Corporation.
West Texas Utilities Company, **6** 580
West Union Corporation, **22** 517
West Virginia Bearings, Inc., **13** 78
West Virginia Pulp and Paper Co. *See* Westvaco Corporation.
West Witwatersrand Areas Ltd., **IV** 94–96
West Yorkshire Bank, **II** 307
West's Holderness Corn Mill, **II** 564
Westaff Inc., **33 454–57**
WestAir Holding Inc., **11** 300; **25** 423; **32** 336
Westamerica Bancorporation, **17 544–47**
Westbrae Natural, Inc., **27** 197–98; **43** 218
Westburne Group of Companies, **9** 364
Westchester County Savings & Loan, **9** 173
Westchester Specialty Group, Inc., **26** 546
Westclox Seth Thomas, **16** 483
Westcott Communications Inc., **22** 442
Westdeutsche Landesbank Girozentrale, **II** 257–58, **385–87**; **33** 395
Westec Corporation. *See* Tech-Sym Corporation.
Western Aerospace Ltd., **14** 564
Western Air Express, **I** 125; **III** 225; **9** 17
Western Air Lines, **I** 98, 100, 106; **6** 82; **21** 142; **25** 421–23
Western Alaska Fisheries, **II** 578
Western American Bank, **II** 383
Western Assurance Co., **III** 350

Western Atlas Inc., **III** 473; **12 538–40**; **17** 419
Western Australian Specialty Alloys Proprietary Ltd., **14** 564
Western Auto, **19** 223
Western Auto Supply Co., **8** 56; **11** 392
Western Automatic Machine Screw Co., **12** 344
Western Bancorporation, **I** 536; **II** 288–89; **13** 529
Western Bank, **17** 530
Western Beef, Inc., **22 548–50**
Western Bingo, **16** 471
Western California Canners Inc., **I** 513
Western Canada Airways, **II** 376
Western Coalfields Ltd., **IV** 48–49
Western Company of North America, **15 534–36**; **25** 73, 75
Western Condensing Co., **II** 488
Western Copper Mills Ltd., **IV** 164
Western Corrugated Box Co., **IV** 358
Western Crude, **11** 27
Western Dairy Products, **I** 248
Western Data Products, Inc., **19** 110
Western Digital Corp., **10** 403, 463; **11** 56, 463; **25 530–32**
Western Edison, **6** 601
Western Electric Co., **II** 57, 66, 88, 101, 112; **III** 162–63, 440; **IV** 181, 660; **V** 259–64; **VII** 288; **11** 500–01; **12** 136; **13** 57
Western Empire Construction. *See* CRSS Inc.
Western Equities, Inc. *See* Tech-Sym Corporation.
Western Federal Savings & Loan, **9** 199
Western Fire Equipment Co., **9** 420
Western Geophysical, **I** 485; **11** 265; **12** 538–39
Western Glucose Co., **14** 17
Western Grocers, Inc., **II** 631, 670
Western Hotels Inc. *See* Westin Hotels and Resorts Worldwide.
Western Illinois Power Cooperative, **6** 506
Western Inland Lock Navigation Company, **9** 228
Western International Communications, **35** 68
Western International Hotels, **I** 129; **6** 129
Western International Media, **22** 294
Western International University, **24** 40
Western Kentucky Gas Company, **43** 56–57
Western Kraft Corp., **IV** 358; **8** 476
Western Life Insurance Co., **III** 356; **22** 494
Western Light & Telephone Company. *See* Western Power & Gas Company.
Western Light and Power. *See* Public Service Company of Colorado.
Western Massachusetts Co., **13** 183
Western Medical Services, **33** 456
Western Merchandise, Inc., **8** 556
Western Merchandisers, Inc., **29** 229–30
Western Mining Corp., **IV** 61, 95
Western-Mobile, **III** 735
Western Mortgage Corporation, **16** 497
Western National Life Company, **10** 246; **14** 473
Western Natural Gas Company, **7** 362
Western New York State Lines, Inc., **6** 370
Western Newell Manufacturing Company. *See* Newell Co.
Western Nuclear, Inc., **IV** 179
Western Offset Publishing, **6** 13
Western Offshore Drilling and Exploration Co., **I** 570
Western Pacific, **22** 220
Western Pacific Industries, **10** 357
Western Paper Box Co., **IV** 333
Western Pioneer, Inc., **18** 279
Western Piping and Engineering Co., **III** 535
Western Platinum, **21** 353
Western Playing Card Co., **13** 559
Western Powder Co., **I** 379; **13** 379
Western Power & Gas Company. *See* Centel Corporation.
Western Printing and Lithographing Company, **19** 404
Western Public Service Corporation, **6** 568
Western Publishing Group, Inc., **IV** 671; **13** 114, **559–61**; **15** 455; **25** 254, 313; **28** 159; **29** 76
Western Reserve Bank of Lake County, **9** 474
Western Reserve Telephone Company. *See* Alltel Corporation.
Western Reserves, **12** 442
Western Resources, Inc., **12 541–43**; **27** 425; **32** 372–75
Western Rosin Company, **8** 99
Western Sizzlin', **10** 331; **19** 288
Western Slope Gas, **6** 559
Western Steel Group, **26** 407
Western Steer Family Restaurant, **10** 331; **18** 8
Western Sugar Co., **II** 582; **42** 371
Western Telegraph Company, **25** 99
Western Telephone Company, **14** 257
Western Union Corporation, **I** 512; **III** 644; **6** 227–28, 338, 386; **9** 536; **10** 263; **12** 9; **14** 363; **15** 72; **17** 345–46; **21** 25; **24** 515
Western Union Insurance Co., **III** 310
Western Vending, **13** 48; **41** 22
Western Veneer and Plywood Co., **IV** 358
Western Wireless Corporation, **36 514–16**
Westfair Foods Ltd., **II** 649
Westfalenbank of Bochum, **II** 239
Westfalia AG, **III** 418–19
Westfalia Dinnendahl Gröppel AG, **III** 543
Westfälische Transport AG, **6** 426
Westfälische Verbands- Elektrizitätswerk, **V** 744
Westgate House Investments Ltd., **IV** 711
Westimex, **II** 594
Westin Hotel Co., **I** 129–30; **6** 129; **9** 283, **547–49**; **21** 91
Westin Hotels and Resorts Worldwide, **29 505–08 (upd.)**
Westinghouse Air Brake Company. *See* Wabtec Corporation.
Westinghouse Brake & Signal, **III** 509
Westinghouse Cubic Ltd., **19** 111
Westinghouse Electric Corporation, **I** 4, 7, 19, 22, 28, 33, 82, 84–85, 524; **II** 57–58, 59, 80, 86, 88, 94, 98–99, **120–22**, 151; **III** 440, 467, 641; **IV** 59, 401; **6** 39, 164, 261, 452, 483, 556; **9** 12, 17, 128, 162, 245, 417, 439–40, 553; **10** 280, 536; **11** 318; **12** 194, **544–47 (upd.)**; **13** 230, 398, 402, 506–07; **14** 300–01; **16** 8; **17** 488; **18** 320, 335–37, 355; **19** 164–66, 210; **21** 43; **26** 102; **27** 269; **28** 69; **33** 253; **36** 327; **41** 366. *See also* CBS Corporation.
WestJet Airlines Ltd., **38 493–95**
Westland Aircraft Ltd., **I** 50, 573; **IV** 658; **24** 85
WestLB. *See* Westdeutsche Landesbank Girozentrale.
Westmark Mortgage Corp., **13** 417
Westmark Realty Advisors, **21** 97
Westmark Systems, Inc., **26** 268
Westmill Foods, **II** 466
Westminster Bank Ltd., **II** 257, 319, 320, 333–34; **17** 324
Westminster Press Ltd., **IV** 658
Westminster Trust Ltd., **IV** 706
Westmoreland Coal Company, **7 582–85**
Westmount Enterprises, **I** 286
Weston and Mead, **IV** 310
Weston Bakeries, **II** 631
Weston Foods Inc. *See* George Weston Limited.
Weston Pharmaceuticals, **V** 49; **19** 122–23
Weston Resources, **II** 631–32
Westpac Banking Corporation, **II 388–90**; **17** 285
Westphalian Provinzialbank-Hülfskasse, **II** 385
WestPoint Stevens Inc., **16 533–36**; **21** 194; **28** 219. *See also* JPS Textile Group, Inc.
Westport Woman, **24** 145
Westvaco Corporation, **I** 442; **IV 351–54**; **19 495–99 (upd.)**
The Westwood Group, **20** 54
Westwood One, Inc., **17** 150; **23 508–11**
Westwood Pharmaceuticals, **III** 19
Westwools Holdings, **I** 438
Westworld Resources Inc., **23** 41
Westwynn Theatres, **14** 87
The Wet Seal, Inc., **18 562–64**
Wetterau Incorporated, **II** 645, **681–82**; **7** 450; **18** 507; **32** 222
Wexpro Company, **6** 568–69
Weyco Group, Incorporated, **32 510–13**
Weyerhaeuser Company, **I** 26; **IV** 266, 289, 298, 304, 308, **355–56**, 358; **8** 428, 434; **9 550–52 (upd.)**; **19** 445–46, 499; **22** 489; **26** 384; **28 514–17 (upd.)**; **31** 468; **32** 91; **42** 397
Weyman-Burton Co., **9** 533
WGM Safety Corp., **40** 96–97
WH Smith PLC, **42 442–47 (upd.)**
Whalstrom & Co., **I** 14
Wharf Holdings Limited, **12** 367–68; **18** 114
Wheat, First Securities, **19** 304–05
Wheaton Industries, **8 570–73**
Wheatsheaf Investment, **27** 94
Wheel Horse, **7** 535
Wheel Restaurants Inc., **14** 131
Wheelabrator Technologies, Inc., **I** 298; **II** 403; **III** 511–12; **V** 754; **6 599–600**; **10** 32; **11** 435
Wheeled Coach Industries, Inc., **33** 105–06
Wheeler Condenser & Engineering Company, **6** 145
Wheeler, Fisher & Co., **IV** 344
Wheeling-Pittsburgh Corp., **7 586–88**
Wheelock Marden, **I** 470; **20** 312
Whemco, **22** 415
Whemo Denko, **I** 359
Wherehouse Entertainment Incorporated, **9** 361; **11 556–58**; **29** 350; **35** 431–32
WHI Inc., **14** 545
Whippet Motor Lines Corporation, **6** 370

Whippoorwill Associates Inc., **28** 55
Whirl-A-Way Motors, **11** 4
Whirlpool Corporation, **I** 30; **II** 80; **III** 572, 573, **653–55**; **8** 298–99; **11** 318; **12** 252, 309, **548–50 (upd.)**; **13** 402–03, 563; **15** 403; **18** 225–26; **22** 218, 349; **23** 53; **25** 261
Whirlwind, Inc., **6** 233; **7** 535
Whiskey Trust, **I** 376
Whistler Corporation, **13** 195
Whitaker-Glessner Company, **7** 586
Whitaker Health Services, **III** 389
Whitall Tatum, **III** 423
Whitbread PLC, **I** 288, **293–94**; **18** 73; **20 519–22 (upd.)**; **29** 19; **35** 395; **42** 247
Whitby Pharmaceuticals, Inc., **10** 289
White & Case LLP, **35 466–69**
White Automotive, **10** 9, 11
White Brand, **V** 97
White Brothers, **39** 83, 84
White Bus Line, **I** 448
White Castle System, Inc., **12 551–53**; **33** 239; **36 517–20 (upd.)**
White Consolidated Industries Inc., **II** 122; **III** 480, 654, 573; **8** 298; **12** 252, 546; **13 562–64**; **22** 26–28, 216–17, 349
White Discount Department Stores, **16** 36
White Eagle Oil & Refining Co., **IV** 464; **7** 352
White Fuel Corp., **IV** 552
White Industrial Power, **II** 25
White Miller Construction Company, **14** 162
White Motor Co., **II** 16
White Mountain Freezers, **19** 360
White-New Idea, **13** 18
White Oil Corporation, **7** 101
White Rock Corp., **I** 377; **27** 198; **43** 218
White-Rodgers, **II** 19
White Rose, Inc., **12** 106; **24 527–29**
White Star Line, **23** 161
White Stores, **II** 419–20
White Swan Foodservice, **II** 625
White Tractor, **13** 17
White Wave, **43 462–64**
White Weld, **II** 268; **21** 145
White-Westinghouse. *See* White Consolidated Industries Inc.
Whiteaway Laidlaw, **V** 68
Whitehall Canadian Oils Ltd., **IV** 658
Whitehall Company Jewellers, **24** 319
Whitehall Electric Investments Ltd., **IV** 658
Whitehall Labs, **8** 63
Whitehall Petroleum Corp. Ltd., **IV** 657–58
Whitehall Securities Corp., **IV** 658
Whitehall Trust Ltd., **IV** 658
Whitewater Group, **10** 508
Whitewear Manufacturing Company. *See* Angelica Corporation.
Whitman Corporation, **7** 430; **10** 414–15, **553–55 (upd.)**; **11** 188; **22** 353–54; **27** 196; **43** 217
Whitman Education Group, Inc., **41 419–21**
Whitman Publishing Co., **13** 559–60
Whitman's Chocolates, **I** 457; **7** 431; **12** 429
Whitmire Distribution. *See* Cardinal Health, Inc.
Whitney Communications Corp., **IV** 608
Whitney Group, **40** 236–38
Whitney Holding Corporation, **21 522–24**
Whitney National Bank, **12** 16
Whitney Partners, L.L.C., **40** 237
Whittaker Corporation, **I 544–46**; **III** 389, 444; **34** 275
Whittar Steel Strip Co., **IV** 74; **24** 143
Whitteways, **I** 215
Whittle Communications L.P., **IV** 675; **7** 528; **13** 403; **22** 442
Whittman-Hart Inc. *See* marchFIRST, Inc.
Whitworth Brothers Company, **27** 360
Whole Foods Market, Inc., **19** 501–02; **20 523–27**; **41** 422–23
Wholesale Cellular USA. *See* Brightpoint, Inc.
The Wholesale Club, Inc., **8** 556
Wholesale Depot, **13** 547
Wholesale Food Supply, Inc., **13** 333
Wholesome Foods, L.L.C., **32** 274, 277
Wholly Harvest, **19** 502
Whyte & Mackay Distillers Ltd., **V** 399; **19** 171
Wicat Systems, **7** 255–56; **25** 254
Wichita Industries, **11** 27
Wickes Companies, Inc., **I** 453, 483; **II** 262; **III** 580, 721; **V 221–23**; **10** 423; **13** 169–70; **15** 281; **17** 365–66; **19** 503–04; **20** 415; **41** 93
Wickes Inc., **25 533–36 (upd.)**
Wickman-Wimet, **IV** 203
Widows and Orphans Friendly Society, **III** 337
Wielkopolski Bank Kredytowy, **16** 14
Wien Air Alaska, **II** 420
Wienerwald Holding, **17** 249
Wiesner, Inc., **22** 442
Wifstavarfs, **IV** 325
Wiggins Teape Ltd., **I** 426; **IV** 290
Wild by Nature. *See* King Cullen Grocery Co., Inc.
Wild Leitz G.m.b.H., **23** 83
Wild Oats Markets, Inc., **19 500–02**; **29** 213; **41 422–25 (upd.)**
Wildlife Conservation Society, **31 462–64**
Wildwater Kingdom, **22** 130
Wiles Group Ltd., **III** 501; **7** 207
Wiley Manufacturing Co., **8** 545
Oy Wilh. Schauman AB, **IV** 300–02; **19** 463
Wilhelm Fette GmbH, **IV** 198–99
Wilhelm Weber GmbH, **22** 95
Wilhelm Wilhelmsen Ltd., **7** 40; **41** 42
Wilkins Department Store, **19** 510
Wilkinson, Gaddis & Co., **24** 527
Wilkinson Sword Co., **III** 23, 28–29; **12** 464; **38** 365
Willamette Falls Electric Company. *See* Portland General Corporation.
Willamette Industries, Inc., **IV 357–59**; **13** 99, 101; **16** 340; **28** 517; **31 465–468 (upd.)**
Willcox & Gibbs Sewing Machine Co., **15** 384
Willetts Manufacturing Company, **12** 312
William A. Rogers Ltd., **IV** 644
William B. Tanner Co., **7** 327
William Barnet and Son, Inc., **III** 246
William Barry Co., **II** 566
William Benton Foundation, **7** 165, 167
William Bonnel Co., **I** 334; **10** 289
The William Brooks Shoe Company. *See* Rocky Shoes & Boots, Inc.
William Burdon, **III** 626
William Byrd Press Inc., **23** 100
William Carter Company, **17** 224
William Colgate and Co., **III** 23
William Collins & Sons, **II** 138; **IV** 651–52; **7** 390–91; **24** 193
William Cory & Son Ltd., **6** 417
William Crawford and Sons, **II** 593
William Douglas McAdams Inc., **I** 662; **9** 403
William Duff & Sons, **I** 509
William E. Pollack Government Securities, **II** 390
William E. Wright Company, **9** 375
William Esty Company, **16** 72
William Gaymer and Son Ltd., **I** 216
William George Company, **32** 519
William Grant Company, **22** 343
William H. Rorer Inc., **I** 666
William Hancock & Co., **I** 223
William Hewlett, **41** 117
William Hodges & Company, **33** 150
William J. Hough Co., **8** 99–100
William Lyon Homes, **III** 664
William M. Mercer Cos. Inc., **III** 283; **32** 459
William Mackinnon & Co., **III** 522
William McDonald & Sons, **II** 593
William Morris Agency, Inc., **III** 554; **23 512–14**; **43** 235–36
William Morrow & Company, **19** 201
William Neilson, **II** 631
William Odhams Ltd., **7** 244
William P. Young Contruction, **43** 400
William Penn Cos., **III** 243, 273
William Penn Life Insurance Company of New York, **24** 285
William Press, **I** 568
William R. Warner & Co., **I** 710
William S. Kimball & Co., **12** 108
William Southam and Sons, **7** 487
William T. Blackwell & Company, **V** 395
William Underwood Co., **I** 246, 457; **7** 430
William Varcoe & Sons, **III** 690
William Zinsser & Co., **8** 456
Williams & Glyn's Bank Ltd., **12** 422
Williams & Wilkins. *See* Waverly, Inc.
Williams Brother Offshore Ltd., **I** 429
Williams Communications Group, Inc., **6** 340; **25** 499; **34 507–10**
The Williams Companies, Inc., **III** 248; **IV** 84, 171, **575–76**; **27** 307; **31 469–472 (upd.)**
Williams Deacon's Bank, **12** 422
Williams, Donnelley and Co., **IV** 660
Williams Electronics, **III** 431; **12** 419
Williams Electronics Games, Inc., **15** 539
Williams Gold Refining Co., **14** 81
The Williams Manufacturing Company, **19** 142–43
Williams/Nintendo Inc., **15** 537
Williams Oil-O-Matic Heating Corporation, **12** 158; **21** 42
Williams Printing Company. *See* Graphic Industries Inc.
Williams-Sonoma, Inc., **13** 42; **15** 50; **17 548–50**; **27** 225, 429
Williamsburg Gas Light Co., **6** 455
Williamson-Dickie Manufacturing Company, **14 549–50**
Willie G's, **15** 279
Willis Corroon Group plc, **III** 280, 747; **22** 318; **25 537–39**
Willis Stein & Partners, **21** 404

Williston Basin Interstate Pipeline Company, **7** 322, 324. *See also* WBI Holdings, Inc.
Willor Manufacturing Corp., **9** 323
Willys-Overland, **I** 183; **8** 74
Wilmington Coca-Cola Bottling Works, Inc., **10** 223
Wilmington Trust Corporation, 25 540–43
Wilsdorf & Davis, **13** 353–54
Wilshire Real Estate Investment Trust Inc., **30** 223
Wilshire Restaurant Group Inc., **13** 66; **28** 258
Wilson & Co., **I** 490
Wilson Brothers, **8** 536
Wilson Foods Corp., **I** 489, 513; **II** 584–85; **12** 124; **14** 515; **22** 510
Wilson, H.W., Company. *See* H.W. Wilson Company.
Wilson Jones Company, **7** 4–5
Wilson Learning Group, **17** 272
Wilson-Maeulen Company, **13** 234
Wilson Pharmaceuticals & Chemical, **I** 489
Wilson Sonsini Goodrich & Rosati, 34 511–13
Wilson Sporting Goods Company, I 278, 489; **13** 317; **16** 52; **23** 449; **24** 403, **530–32**; **25** 167; **41** 14–16
Wilson's Motor Transit, **6** 370
Wilson's Supermarkets, **12** 220–21
Wilsons The Leather Experts Inc., 21 525–27
WilTel Network Services, **27** 301, 307
Wilts and Dorset Banking Co., **II** 307
Wiltshire United Dairies, **II** 586
Wimpey International Ltd., **13** 206
Wimpey's plc, **I** 315, 556
Win-Chance Foods, **II** 508; **36** 255
Win Schuler Foods, **II** 480; **25** 517; **26** 57
Wincanton Group, **II** 586–87
Winchell's Donut Shops, **II** 680
Winchester Arms, **I** 379–81, 434; **13** 379
Wind River Systems, Inc., 37 419–22
Windmere Corporation, 16 537–39. *See also* Applica Incorporated.
Windmere-Durable Holdings, Inc., **30** 404
WindowVisions, Inc., **29** 288
Windsor Manufacturing Company, **13** 6
Windsor Trust Co., **13** 467
Windstar Sail Cruises, **6** 368; **27** 90–91
Windsurfing International, **23** 55
Windward Capital Partners, **28** 152, 154
The Wine Group, Inc., 39 419–21
Wine World, Inc., **22** 78, 80
Winfire, Inc., **37** 194
Wingate Partners, **14** 521, 523
Wings & Wheels, **13** 19
Wings Luggage, Inc., **10** 181
WingspanBank.com, **38** 270
Winkelman Stores, Inc., **8** 425–26
Winkler-Grimm Wagon Co., **I** 141
Winlet Fashions, **22** 223
Winmar Co., **III** 353
Winn-Dixie Stores, Inc., II 626–27, 670, **683–84**; **7** 61; **11** 228; **15** 178; **16** 314; **18** 8; **21 528–30 (upd.)**; **34** 269
Winnebago Industries Inc., 7 589–91; **22** 207; **27 509–12 (upd.)**
Winners Apparel Ltd., **V** 197
Winning International, **21** 403
Winschermann group, **IV** 198
WinsLoew Furniture, Inc., 21 531–33
Winston & Newell Company. *See* Supervalu Inc.
Winston & Strawn, 35 470–73
Winston Furniture Company, Inc., **21** 531–33
Winston Group, **10** 333
Winston, Harper, Fisher Co., **II** 668
WinterBrook Corp., **26** 326
Winterflood Securities Limited, **39** 89, 91
Wintershall AG, **I** 306; **IV** 485; **18** 49; **38** 408
Winterthur Insurance, **21** 144, 146–47
Winterthur Schweizerische Versicherungs-Gesellschaft, III 343, **402–04**
Winthrop Laboratories, **I** 698–99
Winthrop Lawrence Corporation, **25** 541
Winton Engines, **10** 273
Winton Motor Car Company, **V** 231
Wipro Limited, 43 465–68
Wire and Cable Specialties Corporation, **17** 276
Wire and Plastic Products PLC. *See* WPP Group PLC.
Wireless Hong Kong. *See* Hong Kong Telecommunications Ltd.
Wireless LLC, **18** 77
Wireless Management Company, **11** 12
Wireless Speciality Co., **II** 120
Wirtz Productions Ltd., **15** 238
Wisaforest Oy AB, **IV** 302
Wisconsin Bell, Inc., 14 551–53; **18** 30
Wisconsin Central Transportation Corporation, 12 278; **24 533–36**
Wisconsin Dairies, 7 592–93
Wisconsin Energy Corporation, 6 601–03, 605
Wisconsin Gas Company, **17** 22–23
Wisconsin Knife Works, **III** 436
Wisconsin Power and Light, **22** 13; **39** 260
Wisconsin Public Service Corporation, 6 604–06; **9 553–54**
Wisconsin Steel, **10** 430; **17** 158–59
Wisconsin Tissue Mills Inc., **8** 103
Wisconsin Toy Company. *See* Value Merchants Inc.
Wisconsin Wire and Steel, **17** 310; **24** 160
Wise Foods, Inc., **22** 95
Wiser's De Luxe Whiskey, **14** 141
Wishnick-Tumpeer Chemical Co., **I** 403–05
Wispark Corporation, **6** 601, 603
Wisser Service Holdings AG, **18** 105
Wisvest Corporation, **6** 601, 603
Witco Corporation, I 403, **404–06**; **16 540–43 (upd.)**
Wite-Out Products, Inc., **23** 56–57
Witech Corporation, **6** 601, 603
Withington Company. *See* Sparton Corporation.
Wittington Investments Ltd., **13** 51
The Wiz. *See* Cablevision Electronic Instruments, Inc.
Wizards of the Coast Inc., 24 537–40; **43** 229, 233
WizardWorks Group, Inc., **31** 238–39
WLR Foods, Inc., 14 516; **21 534–36**
WM Investment Company, **34** 512
Wm. Morrison Supermarkets PLC, 38 496–98
Wm. Underwood Company, **40** 53
Wm. Wrigley Jr. Company, 7 594–97
WMC, Limited, 43 469–72
WMS Industries, Inc., III 431; **15 537–39**; **41** 215–16
WMX Technologies Inc., 11 435–36; **17 551–54**; **26** 409
Woermann and German East African Lines, **I** 542
Wöhlk, **III** 446
Wolf Furniture Enterprises, **14** 236
Wolfe & Associates, **25** 434
Wolfe Industries, Inc., **22** 255
Wolff Printing Co., **13** 559
The Wolfgang Puck Food Company, Inc., 26 534–36
Wolohan Lumber Co., 19 503–05; **25** 535
Wolters Kluwer NV, IV 611; **14 554–56**; **31** 389, 394; **33 458–61 (upd.)**
Wolvercote Paper Mill, **IV** 300
Wolverine Die Cast Group, **IV** 165
Wolverine Insurance Co., **26** 487
Wolverine Tube Inc., 23 515–17
Wolverine World Wide Inc., 16 544–47; **17** 390; **32** 99
Womack Development Company, **11** 257
Women's Specialty Retailing Group. *See* Casual Corner Group, Inc.
Women's World, **15** 96
Wometco Coca-Cola Bottling Co., **10** 222
Wometco Coffee Time, **I** 514
Wometco Enterprises, **I** 246, 514
Wonderware Corp., **22** 374
Wong International Holdings, **16** 195
Wood Fiberboard Co., **IV** 358
Wood Gundy, **II** 345; **21** 447
Wood Hall Trust plc, I 438, **592–93**
Wood-Metal Industries, Inc. *See* Wood-Mode, Inc.
Wood-Mode, Inc., 23 518–20
Wood River Oil and Refining Company, **11** 193
Wood Shovel and Tool Company, **9** 71
Wood, Struthers & Winthrop, Inc., **22** 189
Wood Wyant Inc., **30** 496–98
Woodall Industries, **III** 641; **14** 303
Woodard-Walker Lumber Co., **IV** 358
Woodbury Co., **19** 380
Woodcock, Hess & Co., **9** 370
Woodfab, **IV** 295; **19** 225
Woodhaven Gas Light Co., **6** 455
Woodhill Chemical Sales Company, **8** 333
Woodland Publishing, Inc., **37** 286
Woodlands, **7** 345–46
Woods and Co., **II** 235
Woods Equipment Company, **32** 28
Woodside Travel Trust, **26** 310
Woodville Appliances, Inc., **9** 121
Woodward Corp., **IV** 311; **19** 267
Woodward Governor Co., 13 565–68
Woodworkers Warehouse, **22** 517
Woolco Department Stores, **II** 634; **7** 444; **V** 107, 225–26; **14** 294; **22** 242
Woolverton Motors, **I** 183
The Woolwich plc, 30 492–95
Woolworth Corporation, II 414; **6** 344; **V** 106–09, **224–27**; **8** 509; **14** 293–95; **17** 42, 335; **20 528–32 (upd.)**; **25** 22. *See also* Venator Group Inc.
Woolworth Holdings, **II** 139; **V** 108; **19** 123; **24** 194
Woolworth's Ltd., **II** 656. *See also* Kingfisher plc.
Wooster Preserving Company, **11** 211
Wooster Rubber Co., **III** 613
Worcester City and County Bank, **II** 307

Worcester Gas Light Co., **14** 124
Worcester Wire Works, **13** 369
Word, Inc., **14** 499; **38** 456
Word Processors Personnel Service, **6** 10
WordPerfect Corporation, **6** 256; **10** 519, **556–59**; **12** 335; **25** 300; **41** 281. *See also* Corel Corporation.
WordStar International, **15** 149; **43** 151. *See also* The Learning Company Inc.
Work Wear Corp., **II** 607; **16** 229
Working Assets Funding Service, **43 473–76**
Working Title Films, **23** 389
Workscape Inc., **42** 430
World Air Network, Ltd., **6** 71
World Airways, **10** 560–62; **28** 404
World Bank Group, **33 462–65**
World Book Group. *See* Scott Fetzer Company.
World Book, Inc., **IV** 622; **12 554–56**
World Championship Wrestling (WCW), **32** 516
World Color Press Inc., **12 557–59**; **19** 333; **21** 61
World Commerce Corporation, **25** 461
World Communications, Inc., **11** 184
World Duty Free Americas, Inc., **29 509–12 (upd.)**
World Duty Free plc, **33** 59
World Film Studio, **24** 437
World Financial Network National Bank, **V** 116
World Flight Crew Services, **10** 560
World Foot Locker, **14** 293
World Gift Company, **9** 330
World International Holdings Limited, **12** 368
World Journal Tribune Inc., **IV** 608
World Publishing Co., **8** 423
World Savings and Loan, **19** 412
World Service Life Insurance Company, **27** 47
World Trade Corporation. *See* International Business Machines Corporation.
World Trans, Inc., **33** 105
World-Wide Shipping Group, **II** 298; **III** 517
World Wrestling Federation Entertainment, Inc., **32 514–17**
World Yacht Enterprises, **22** 438
World's Finest Chocolate Inc., **39 422–24**
WorldCom, Inc., **14** 330, 332; **18** 33, 164, 166; **29** 227; **38** 269–70, 468. *See also* MCI WorldCom, Inc.
WorldCorp, Inc., **10 560–62**
WorldGames, **10** 560
WorldMark, The Club, **33** 409
Worlds of Fun, **22** 130
Worlds of Wonder, Inc., **25** 381; **26** 548
Worldview Systems Corporation, **26** 428
WorldWay Corporation, **16** 41
Worldwide Logistics, **17** 505
Worldwide Underwriters Insurance Co., **III** 218–19
Wormald International Ltd., **13** 245, 247
Worms et Cie, **27** 275–76, **513–15**
Wormser, **III** 760
Worth Corp., **27** 274
Wortham, Gus Sessions, **III** 193; **10** 65
Worthen Banking Corporation, **15** 60
Worthington & Co., **I** 223
Worthington Corp., **I** 142
Worthington Foods, Inc., **I** 653; **14 557–59**; **33** 170
Worthington Industries, Inc., **7 598–600**; **8** 450; **21 537–40 (upd.)**
Worthington Telephone Company, **6** 312
Woven Belting Co., **8** 13
WPL Holdings, **6 604–06**
WPM. *See* Wall Paper Manufacturers.
WPP Group plc, **I** 21; **6 53–54**; **22** 201, 296; **23** 480. *See also* Ogilvy Group Inc.
Wrather Corporation, **18** 354
Wrenn Furniture Company, **10** 184
WRG. *See* Wells Rich Greene BDDP.
Wright & Company Realtors, **21** 257
Wright Aeronautical, **9** 16
Wright Airplane Co., **III** 151; **6** 265
Wright and Son, **II** 593
Wright Company, **9** 416
Wright Engine Company, **11** 427
Wright Group, **22** 519, 522
Wright Manufacturing Company, **8** 407
Wright Plastic Products, **17** 310; **24** 160
Wright, Robertson & Co. *See* Fletcher Challenge Ltd.
Wright Stephenson & Co., **IV** 278
Wrightson Limited, **19** 155
Write Right Manufacturing Co., **IV** 345
WSGC Holdings, Inc., **24** 530
WSI Corporation, **10** 88–89
WSM Inc., **11** 152
WSMP, Inc., **29** 202
WTC Airlines, Inc., **IV** 182
WTD Industries, Inc., **20 533–36**
Wührer, **II** 474
Wunderlich Ltd., **III** 687
Wunderman, Ricotta & Kline, **I** 37
Wurlitzer Co., **17** 468; **18** 45
Württembergische Landes- Elektrizitäts AG, **IV** 230
WVPP. *See* Westvaco Corporation.
WWG Industries, Inc., **22** 352–53
WWTV, **18** 493
Wyandotte Chemicals Corporation, **18** 49
Wyandotte Corp., **I** 306
Wyant Corporation, **30 496–98**
Wycombe Bus Company, **28** 155–56
Wyeth-Ayerst Laboratories, **25** 477; **27** 69
Wyeth Laboratories, **I** 623; **10** 69
Wyle Electronics, **14 560–62**; **19** 311
Wyly Corporation, **11** 468
Wyman-Gordon Company, **14 563–65**; **30** 282–83; **41** 367
Wymore Oil Co., **IV** 394
Wynkoop Brewing Company, **43** 407
Wynn's International, Inc., **22** 458; **33 466–70**
Wynncor Ltd., **IV** 693
Wyoming Mineral Corp., **IV** 401
Wyse Technology, Inc., **10** 362; **15 540–42**

X-Acto, **12** 263
X-Chem Oil Field Chemicals, **8** 385
XA Systems Corporation, **10** 244
Xaos Tools, Inc., **10** 119
Xcelite, **II** 16
Xcor International, **III** 431; **15** 538
Xeikon NV, **26 540–42**
Xenia National Bank, **9** 474
Xenotech, **27** 58
Xerox Corporation, **I** 31–32, 338, 490, 693; **II** 10, 117, 157, 159, 412, 448; **III** 110, 116, 120–21, 157, 159, **171–73**, 475; **IV** 252, 703; **6** 244, **288–90 (upd.)**, 390; **7** 45, 161; **8** 164; **10** 22, 139, 430, 510–11; **11** 68, 494, 518; **13** 127, 448; **14** 399; **17** 28–29, 328–29; **18** 93, 111–12; **22** 411–12; **25** 54–55, 148, 152; **26** 213, 540, 542, **543–47 (upd.)**; **28** 115; **36** 171; **40** 394; **41** 197
Xiamen Airlines, **33** 99
Xilinx, Inc., **16** 317, **548–50**; **18** 17, 19; **19** 405; **43** 15–16
XMR, Inc., **42** 361
XP, **27** 474
Xpert Recruitment, Ltd., **26** 240
Xpress Automotive Group, Inc., **24** 339
XRAL Storage and Terminaling Co., **IV** 411
Xros, Inc., **36** 353
XTRA Corp., **18** 67
XTX Corp., **13** 127
Xynetics, **9** 251
Xytek Corp., **13** 127

Y & S Candies Inc., **II** 511
Yacimientos Petrolíferos Fiscales Sociedad Anónima, **IV** 578
Yageo Corporation, **16 551–53**
Yahoo! Inc., **25** 18; **27 516–19**; **38** 439
Yakovlev, **24** 60
Yale & Towne Manufacturing Co., **I** 154–55; **10** 279
Yamabun Oil Co., **IV** 403
Yamagata Enterprises, **26** 310
Yamaguchi Bank, **II** 347
Yamaha Corporation, **III** 366, 599, **656–59**; **11** 50; **12** 401; **16** 410, **554–58 (upd.)**; **17** 25; **18** 250; **19** 428; **22** 196; **33** 28; **40 461–66 (upd.)**
Yamaha Musical Instruments, **16** 202; **43** 170
Yamaichi Capital Management, **42** 349
Yamaichi Securities Company, Limited, **II** 300, 323, 434, **458–59**; **9** 377
Yamano Music, **16** 202; **43** 171
Yamanouchi Consumer Inc., **39** 361
Yamanouchi Pharmaceutical Co., Ltd., **12** 444–45; **38** 93
Yamatame Securities, **II** 326
Yamato Transport Co. Ltd., **V 536–38**
Yamazaki Baking Co., **II** 543; **IV** 152; **24** 358
Yanbian Industrial Technology Training Institute, **12** 294
Yangzhou Motor Coach Manufacturing Co., **34** 132
The Yankee Candle Company, Inc., **37 423–26**; **38** 192
Yankee Energy Gas System, Inc., **13** 184
YankeeNets LLC, **35 474–77**
Yankton Gas Company, **6** 524
Yarmouth Group, Inc., **17** 285
Yaryan, **I** 343
Yashica Co., Ltd., **II** 50–51; **21** 330
Yasuda Fire and Marine Insurance Company, Limited, **II** 292, 391; **III 405–07**, 408
Yasuda Mutual Life Insurance Company, **II** 292, 391, 446; **III** 288, 405, **408–09**; **22** 406–07; **39 425–28 (upd.)**
The Yasuda Trust and Banking Company, Limited, **II** 273, 291, **391–92**; **17 555–57 (upd.)**
Yates-Barco Ltd., **16** 8
Yates Circuit Foil, **IV** 26

Yawata Iron & Steel Co., Ltd., **I** 493, 509; **II** 300; **IV** 130, 157, 212; **17** 350; **24** 325
Year Book Medical Publishers, **IV** 677–78
Yearbooks, Inc., **12** 472
Yeargin Construction Co., **II** 87; **11** 413
Yellow Cab Co., **I** 125; **V** 539; **10** 370; **12** 487; **24** 118
Yellow Corporation, 14 566–68
Yellow Freight System, Inc. of Deleware, V 503, **539–41**; **12** 278
Yeomans & Foote, **I** 13
Yeomans & Partners Ltd., **I** 588
YES! Entertainment Corporation, 10 306; **26 548–50**
Yesco Audio Environments, **18** 353, 355
Yeti Cycles Inc., **19** 385
Yeung Chi Shing Estates, **IV** 717
YGK Inc., **6** 465, 467
Yhtyneet Paperitehtaat Oy. *See* United Paper Mills Ltd.
Yili Food Co., **II** 544
YKK, **19** 477
YMCA of the USA, 31 473–76
Ymos A.G., **IV** 53; **26** 83
Yogen Fruz World-Wide, Inc. *See* CoolBrands International Inc.
Yokado Clothing Store, **V** 88
Yokogawa Electric Corp., **III** 142–43, 536; **26** 230
Yokogawa Electric Works, Limited, **6** 237; **13** 234
Yokohama Bottle Plant, **21** 319
Yokohama Cooperative Wharf Co., **IV** 728
Yokohama Electric Cable Manufacturing Co., **III** 490
The Yokohama Rubber Co., Ltd., V 254–56; 19 506–09 (upd.)
Yokohama Specie Bank, **I** 431; **II** 224
Yokohama Tokyu Deppartment Store Co., Ltd., **32** 457
Yoosung Enterprise Co., Ltd., **23** 269
Yoplait S.A. *See* Sodiaal S.A.
York & London, **III** 359
The York Bank and Trust Company, **16** 14; **43** 8
York-Benimaru, **V** 88
York Corp., **III** 440
York Developments, **IV** 720
York International Corp., 13 569–71; **22** 6
York Research Corporation, 35 478–80
York Manufacturing Co $$York Manufacturing Co., **13** 385
York Safe & Lock Company, **7** 144–45; **22** 184
York Steak House, **16** 157
York Wastewater Consultants, Inc., **6** 441
Yorkshire and Pacific Securities Ltd., **IV** 723
Yorkshire Insurance Co., **III** 241–42, 257
Yorkshire Paper Mills Ltd., **IV** 300
Yorkshire Post Newspapers, **IV** 686; **28** 503
Yorkshire Television Ltd., **IV** 659
Yorkshire-Tyne Tees Television, **24** 194
Yorkville Group, **IV** 640
Yosemite Park & Curry Co., **II** 144
Yoshikazu Taguchi, **6** 428
Yoshitomi Pharmaceutical, **I** 704
Young & Co.'s Brewery, P.L.C., 38 499–502
Young & Rubicam Inc., I 9–11, 25, **36–38**; **II** 129; **6** 14, 47; **9** 314; **13** 204; **16** 166–68; **22 551–54 (upd.)**; **41** 89–90, 198
Young & Selden, **7** 145
Young & Son, **II** 334
Young Broadcasting Inc., 40 467–69; **42** 163
Young Readers of America, **13** 105
Young's Engineering Company Limited, **IV** 717; **38** 319
Young's Market Company, LLC, 32 518–20
Youngblood Truck Lines, **16** 40
Youngs Drug Products Corporation, **8** 85; **38** 124
Youngstown, **IV** 114
Youngstown Pressed Steel Co., **III** 763
Youngstown Sheet & Tube, **I** 490–91; **13** 157
Younkers, Inc., 19 324–25, **510–12**; **41** 343–44
Yount-Lee Oil Co., **IV** 369
Youth Centre Inc., **16** 36
Youth Services International, Inc., 21 541–43; **30** 146
Youthtrack, Inc., **29** 399–400
Yoxall Instrument Company, **13** 234
Yoyoteiki Cargo Co., Ltd., **6** 428
YPF Sociedad Anónima, IV 577–78. *See also* Repsol-YPF S.A.
Yside Investment Group, **16** 196
YTT. *See* Yorkshire-Tyne Tees Television.
Yuasa Battery Co., **III** 556
Yuba Heat Transfer Corp., **I** 514
The Yucaipa Cos., 17 558–62; **22** 39; **32** 222; **35** 369
Yukon Pacific Corporation, **22** 164, 166
Yurakucho Seibu Co., Ltd., **V** 185
Yutani Heavy Industries, Ltd., **IV** 130
Yves Rocher. *See* Laboratoires de Biologie Végétale Yves Rocher.
Yves Saint Laurent, **I** 697; **12** 37
Yves Soulié, **II** 266

Z.C. Mines, **IV** 61
Z-Spanish Media Corp., **35** 220; **41** 151
Zaadunie B.V., **I** 672
Zagara's Inc., **35** 190–91
Zahnfabrik Weinand Sohne & Co. G.m.b.H., **10** 271
Zahnradfabrik Friedrichshafen, **III** 415
Zale Corporation, 16 206, **559–61**; **17** 369; **19** 452; **23** 60; **40 470–74 (upd.)**
Zambezi Saw Mills (1968) Ltd., **IV** 241
Zambia Breweries, **25** 281
Zambia Industrial and Mining Corporation Ltd., IV 239–41
Zamboni. *See* Frank J. Zamboni & Co., Inc.
Zander & Ingeström, **III** 419
Zanders Feinpapiere AG, **IV** 288; **15** 229
Zanussi, **III** 480; **22** 27
Zany Brainy, Inc., 31 477–79; **36** 502
Zap, Inc., **25** 546
Zapata Corporation, 17 157, 160; **25 544–46**
Zapata Drilling Co., **IV** 489
Zapata Gulf Marine Corporation, **11** 524
Zapata Offshore Co., **IV** 489
Zapata Petroleum Corp., **IV** 489
Zaring Premier Homes, **41** 133
Zausner, **25** 83
Zayre Corp., **V** 197–98; **9** 20–21; **13** 547–48; **19** 448; **29** 106; **30** 55–56; **33** 198
ZCMI. *See* Zion's Cooperative Mercantile Institution.
ZDF, **41** 28–29
ZDNet, **36** 523
Zealand Mines S.A., **23** 41
Zebco, **22** 115
Zebra Technologies Corporation, 14 378, **569–71**
Zecco, Inc., **III** 443; **6** 441
Zehrmart, **II** 631
Zeiss Ikon AG, **III** 446
Zell Bros., **16** 559
Zell/Chilmark Fund LP, **12** 439; **19** 384
Zellers, **V** 80; **25** 221
Zellstoff AG, **III** 400
Zellstoffabrik Waldhof AG, **IV** 323–24
Zellweger Telecommunications AG, **9** 32
Zeneca Group PLC, 21 544–46
Zengine, Inc., **41** 258–59
Zenith Data Systems, Inc., II 124–25; **III** 123; **6** 231; **10 563–65**; **36** 299
Zenith Electronics Corporation, II 102, **123–25**; **10** 563; **11** 62, 318; **12** 183, 454; **13** 109, 398, **572–75 (upd.)**; **18** 421; **34 514–19 (upd.)**
Zenith Media, **42** 330–31
Zentec Corp., **I** 482
Zentralsparkasse und Kommerzialbank Wien, **23** 37
Zentronics, **19** 313
Zergo Holdings, **42** 24–25
Zero Corporation, 17 563–65
Zero Plus Dialing, Inc. *See* Billing Concepts Corp.
Zetor s.p., **21** 175
Zeus Components, Inc., **10** 113
Zewawell AG, **IV** 324
Zhongbei Building Material Products Company, **26** 510
Ziebart International Corporation, 30 499–501
The Ziegler Companies, Inc., 24 541–45
Ziff Communications Company, 7 239–40; **12** 359, **560–63**; **13** 483; **16** 371; **17** 152, 253; **25** 238, 240; **41** 12
Ziff Davis Media Inc., 36 521–26 (upd.)
Ziff-Davis Publishing Co., **38** 441
Zijlker, **IV** 491
Zilber Ltd., **13** 541
Zildjian. *See* Avedis Zildjian Co.
Zilkha & Company, **12** 72
Zilog, Inc., 15 543–45; **16** 548–49; **22** 390
Zimbabwe Sugar Refineries, **II** 581
Zimmer AG, **IV** 142
Zimmer Inc., **10** 156–57; **11** 475
Zimmer Manufacturing Co., **III** 18; **37** 110, 113
Zinc Corp., **IV** 58–59, 61
Zinc Products Company, **30** 39
Zion Foods, **23** 408
Zion's Cooperative Mercantile Institution, 33 471–74
Zions Bancorporation, 12 564–66; **24** 395
Zippo Manufacturing Company, 18 565–68
Zipps Drive-Thru, Inc., **25** 389
Zippy Mart, **7** 102
Zircotube, **IV** 174
Zivnostenska, **II** 282
Zodiac S.A., 36 527–30
Zody's Department Stores, **9** 120–22
Zoecon, **I** 673

Zoll Medical, **18** 423
Zoloto Mining Ltd., **38** 231
Zoltek Companies, Inc., 37 427–30
Zondervan Publishing House, 14 499; **24 546–49**
Zoom Telephonics, Inc., 18 569–71
Zortech Inc., **10** 508
Zotos International, Inc., **III** 63; **17** 110; **22** 487; **41** 228
ZPT Radom, **23** 427
ZS Sun Limited Partnership, **10** 502
Zuari Cement, **40** 107, 109
Zuid Nederlandsche Handelsbank, **II** 185
Zürcher Bankverein, **II** 368
Zurich Financial Services, 40 59, 61; **42 448–53 (upd.)**
Zurich Insurance Group, **15** 257; **25** 154, 156
Zürich Versicherungs-Gesellschaft, III 194, 402–03, **410–12.** *See also* Zurich Financial Services
Zurn Industries, Inc., **24** 150
Zwarovski, **16** 561
Zycad Corp., **11** 489–91
Zycon Corporation, **24** 201
Zygo Corporation, 42 454–57
Zymaise, **II** 582
ZyMOS Corp., **III** 458
Zytec Corporation, 19 513–15

INDEX TO INDUSTRIES

Index to Industries

ACCOUNTING

Andersen Worldwide, 29 (upd.)
Deloitte & Touche, 9
Deloitte Touche Tohmatsu International, 29 (upd.)
Ernst & Young, 9; 29 (upd.)
KPMG International, 33 (upd.)
L.S. Starrett Co., 13
McLane Company, Inc., 13
NCO Group, Inc., 42
Price Waterhouse, 9
PricewaterhouseCoopers, 29 (upd.)
Robert Wood Johnson Foundation, 35
Univision Communications Inc., 24

ADVERTISING & OTHER BUSINESS SERVICES

A.C. Nielsen Company, 13
ABM Industries Incorporated, 25 (upd.)
Ackerley Communications, Inc., 9
ACNielsen Corporation, 38 (upd.)
Adecco S.A., 36 (upd.)
Adia S.A., 6
Advo, Inc., 6
Aegis Group plc, 6
AHL Services, Inc., 27
American Building Maintenance Industries, Inc., 6
The American Society of Composers, Authors and Publishers (ASCAP), 29
Analysts International Corporation, 36
The Arbitron Company, 38
Armor Holdings, Inc., 27
Ashtead Group plc, 34
The Associated Press, 13
Barrett Business Services, Inc., 16
Bates Worldwide, Inc., 14; 33 (upd.)
Bearings, Inc., 13
Berlitz International, Inc., 13
Big Flower Press Holdings, Inc., 21
Bozell Worldwide Inc., 25
Bright Horizons Family Solutions, Inc., 31
Broadcast Music Inc., 23
Burns International Security Services, 13
Burns International Services Corporation, 41 (upd.)
Cambridge Technology Partners, Inc., 36
Campbell-Mithun-Esty, Inc., 16
Carmichael Lynch Inc., 28
Central Parking Corporation, 18
Chiat/Day Inc. Advertising, 11
Chicago Board of Trade, 41
Chisholm-Mingo Group, Inc., 41
Christie's International plc, 15; 39 (upd.)
Cintas Corporation, 21
COMFORCE Corporation, 40
Computer Learning Centers, Inc., 26
CORT Business Services Corporation, 26
Cox Enterprises, Inc., 22 (upd.)
Creative Artists Agency LLC, 38
Cyrk Inc., 19
Dale Carnegie Training, Inc., 28
D'Arcy Masius Benton & Bowles, Inc., 6; 32 (upd.)
Dawson Holdings PLC, 43
DDB Needham Worldwide, 14
Deluxe Corporation, 22 (upd.)
Dentsu Inc., I; 16 (upd.); 40 (upd.)
Deutsch, Inc., 42
Deutsche Post AG, 29
Earl Scheib, Inc., 32
EBSCO Industries, Inc., 17
Ecology and Environment, Inc., 39
Edison Schools Inc., 37
Education Management Corporation, 35
Employee Solutions, Inc., 18
Ennis Business Forms, Inc., 21
Equifax Inc., 6; 28 (upd.)
Equity Marketing, Inc., 26
ERLY Industries Inc., 17
Euro RSCG Worldwide S.A., 13
Fallon McElligott Inc., 22
Fiserv, Inc., 33 (upd.)
FlightSafety International, Inc., 29 (upd.)
Florists' Transworld Delivery, Inc., 28
Foote, Cone & Belding Communications, Inc., I
Frankel & Co., 39
Franklin Covey Company, 37 (upd.)
Gage Marketing Group, 26
The Gallup Organization, 37
Grey Advertising, Inc., 6
Group 4 Falck A/S, 42
Gwathmey Siegel & Associates Architects LLC, 26
Ha-Lo Industries, Inc., 27
Hakuhodo, Inc., 6; 42 (upd.)
Handleman Company, 15
Havas SA, 33 (upd.)
Hays Plc, 27
Headway Corporate Resources, Inc., 40
Heidrick & Struggles International, Inc., 28
Hildebrandt International, 29
Interep National Radio Sales Inc., 35
International Brotherhood of Teamsters, 37
International Management Group, 18
International Total Services, Inc., 37
The Interpublic Group of Companies, Inc., I; 22 (upd.)
Iron Mountain, Inc., 33
ITT Educational Services, Inc., 33
J.D. Power and Associates, 32
Japan Leasing Corporation, 8
Jostens, Inc., 25 (upd.)
JWT Group Inc., I
Katz Communications, Inc., 6
Katz Media Group, Inc., 35
Kelly Services Inc., 6; 26 (upd.)
Ketchum Communications Inc., 6
Kinko's Inc., 16; 43 (upd.)
Korn/Ferry International, 34
Labor Ready, Inc., 29
Lamar Advertising Company, 27
Learning Tree International Inc., 24
Leo Burnett Company Inc., I; 20 (upd.)
Lintas: Worldwide, 14
Mail Boxes Etc., 18; 41 (upd.)
Manpower, Inc., 30 (upd.)
marchFIRST, Inc., 34
Maritz Inc., 38
MAXIMUS, Inc., 43
National Media Corporation, 27
New England Business Services, Inc., 18
New Valley Corporation, 17
NFO Worldwide, Inc., 24
Nobel Learning Communities, Inc., 37
Norrell Corporation, 25
Norwood Promotional Products, Inc., 26
The Ogilvy Group, Inc., I
Olsten Corporation, 6; 29 (upd.)
Omnicom Group, I; 22 (upd.)
On Assignment, Inc., 20
1-800-FLOWERS, Inc., 26
Outdoor Systems, Inc., 25
Paris Corporation, 22
Paychex, Inc., 15
Pierce Leahy Corporation, 24
Pinkerton's Inc., 9
PMT Services, Inc., 24
Publicis S.A., 19
Publishers Clearing House, 23
Randstad Holding n.v., 16; 43 (upd.)
RemedyTemp, Inc., 20
Rental Service Corporation, 28
Right Management Consultants, Inc., 42
Ritchie Bros. Auctioneers Inc., 41
Robert Half International Inc., 18
Roland Berger & Partner GmbH, 37
Ronco, Inc., 15
Russell Reynolds Associates Inc., 38
Saatchi & Saatchi, I; 42 (upd.)
Securitas AB, 42
ServiceMaster Limited Partnership, 6
Shared Medical Systems Corporation, 14
Sir Speedy, Inc., 16
Skidmore, Owings & Merrill, 13
SmartForce PLC, 43
SOS Staffing Services, 25
Sotheby's Holdings, Inc., 11; 29 (upd.)
Spencer Stuart and Associates, Inc., 14
Superior Uniform Group, Inc., 30
Sylvan Learning Systems, Inc., 35
Taylor Nelson Sofres plc, 34
TBWA Advertising, Inc., 6
TBWA\Chiat\Day, 43 (upd.)
Thomas Cook Travel Inc., 33 (upd.)
Ticketmaster Group, Inc., 13; 37 (upd.)
TMP Worldwide Inc., 30
TNT Post Group N.V., 30
Towers Perrin, 32
Transmedia Network Inc., 20
Treasure Chest Advertising Company, Inc., 32
TRM Copy Centers Corporation, 18
True North Communications Inc., 23
Tyler Corporation, 23
U.S. Office Products Company, 25
UniFirst Corporation, 21
United News & Media plc, 28 (upd.)
Unitog Co., 19
Valassis Communications, Inc., 37 (upd.)
Vedior NV, 35
The Wackenhut Corporation, 14
Waggener Edstrom, 42

Wells Rich Greene BDDP, 6
Westaff Inc., 33
Whitman Education Group, Inc., 41
William Morris Agency, Inc., 23
WPP Group plc, 6
Young & Rubicam, Inc., I; 22 (upd.)

AEROSPACE

A.S. Yakovlev Design Bureau, 15
The Aerospatiale Group, 7; 21 (upd.)
Alliant Techsystems Inc., 30 (upd.)
Aviacionny Nauchno-Tehnicheskii Komplex im. A.N. Tupoleva, 24
Avions Marcel Dassault-Breguet Aviation, I
B/E Aerospace, Inc., 30
Banner Aerospace, Inc., 14
Beech Aircraft Corporation, 8
The Boeing Company, I; 10 (upd.), 32 (upd.)
Bombardier Inc., 42 (upd.)
British Aerospace plc, I; 24 (upd.)
Canadair, Inc., 16
Cessna Aircraft Company, 8
Cobham plc, 30
Daimler-Benz Aerospace AG, 16
DeCrane Aircraft Holdings Inc., 36
Ducommun Incorporated, 30
Empresa Brasileira de Aeronáutica S.A. (Embraer), 36
Fairchild Aircraft, Inc., 9
G.I.E. Airbus Industrie, I; 12 (upd.)
General Dynamics Corporation, I; 10 (upd.); 40 (upd.)
GKN plc, 38 (upd.)
Groupe Dassault Aviation SA, 26 (upd.)
Grumman Corporation, I; 11 (upd.)
Gulfstream Aerospace Corporation, 7; 28 (upd.)
HEICO Corporation, 30
N.V. Koninklijke Nederlandse Vliegtuigenfabriek Fokker, I; 28 (upd.)
Learjet Inc., 8; 27 (upd.)
Lockheed Corporation, I; 11 (upd.)
Lockheed Martin Corporation, 15 (upd.)
Martin Marietta Corporation, I
McDonnell Douglas Corporation, I; 11 (upd.)
Meggitt PLC, 34
Messerschmitt-Bölkow-Blohm GmbH., I
Moog Inc., 13
Northrop Corporation, I; 11 (upd.)
Orbital Sciences Corporation, 22
Pratt & Whitney, 9
Rockwell International Corporation, I; 11 (upd.)
Rolls-Royce Allison, 29 (upd.)
Rolls-Royce plc, I; 7 (upd.); 21 (upd.)
Sequa Corp., 13
Shannon Aerospace Ltd., 36
Sikorsky Aircraft Corporation, 24
Smiths Industries PLC, 25
Société Air France, 27 (upd.)
Spacehab, Inc., 37
Spar Aerospace Limited, 32
Sukhoi Design Bureau Aviation Scientific-Industrial Complex, 24
Sundstrand Corporation, 7; 21 (upd.)
Textron Lycoming Turbine Engine, 9
Thales S.A., 42
Thiokol Corporation, 9; 22 (upd.)
United Technologies Corporation, I; 10 (upd.)
Zodiac S.A., 36

AIRLINES

Aer Lingus Group plc, 34
Aeroflot Soviet Airlines, 6
Aeroflot—Russian International Airlines, 29 (upd.)
Aerolíneas Argentinas S.A., 33
Air Canada, 6; 23 (upd.)
Air New Zealand Limited, 14; 38 (upd.)
Air-India Limited, 6; 27 (upd.)
AirTran Holdings, Inc., 22
Alaska Air Group, Inc., 6; 29 (upd.)
Alitalia-Linee Aeree Italiana, S.p.A., 6; 29 (upd.)
All Nippon Airways Company Limited, 6; 38 (upd.)
Aloha Airlines, Incorporated, 24
America West Airlines, 6
America West Holdings Corporation, 34 (upd.)
American Airlines, I; 6 (upd.)
AMR Corporation, 28 (upd.)
Amtran, Inc., 34
Atlas Air, Inc., 39
Austrian Airlines AG (Österreichische Luftverkehrs AG), 33
Aviacionny Nauchno-Tehnicheskii Komplex im. A.N. Tupoleva, 24
Avianca Aerovías Nacionales de Colombia SA, 36
Banner Aerospace, Inc., 37 (upd.)
British Airways PLC, I; 14 (upd.); 43 (upd.)
British Midland plc, 38
British World Airlines Ltd., 18
Cathay Pacific Airways Limited, 6; 34 (upd.)
Chautauqua Airlines, Inc., 38
China Airlines, 34
China Eastern Airlines Co. Ltd., 31
China Southern Airlines Company Ltd., 33
Comair Holdings Inc., 13; 34 (upd.)
Continental Airlines, Inc., I; 21 (upd.)
Corporación Internacional de Aviación, S.A. de C.V. (Cintra), 20
Delta Air Lines, Inc., I; 6 (upd.); 39 (upd.)
Deutsche Lufthansa Aktiengesellschaft, I; 26 (upd.)
Eastern Airlines, I
easyJet Airline Company Limited, 39
EgyptAir, 6; 27 (upd.)
El Al Israel Airlines Ltd., 23
The Emirates Group, 39
Finnair Oy, 6; 25 (upd.)
Frontier Airlines, Inc., 22
Garuda Indonesia, 6
Groupe Air France, 6
Grupo TACA, 38
HAL Inc., 9
Hawaiian Airlines, Inc., 22 (upd.)
Iberia Líneas Aéreas de España S.A., 6; 36 (upd.)
Japan Air Lines Company Ltd., I; 32 (upd.)
Kitty Hawk, Inc., 22
Kiwi International Airlines Inc., 20
Koninklijke Luchtvaart Maatschappij, N.V. (KLM Royal Dutch Airlines), I; 28 (upd.)
Korean Air Lines Co., Ltd., 6; 27 (upd.)
Lan Chile S.A., 31
LOT Polish Airlines (Polskie Linie Lotnicze S.A.), 33
LTU Group Holding GmbH, 37
Malév Plc, 24
Malaysian Airlines System Berhad, 6; 29 (upd.)
Mesa Air Group, Inc., 32 (upd.)
Mesa Airlines, Inc., 11
Mesaba Holdings, Inc., 28
Midway Airlines Corporation, 33
Midwest Express Holdings, Inc., 35
Northwest Airlines Corporation, I; 6 (upd.); 26 (upd.)
Offshore Logistics, Inc., 37
Pan American World Airways, Inc., I; 12 (upd.)
People Express Airlines, Inc., I
Petroleum Helicopters, Inc., 35
Philippine Airlines, Inc., 6; 23 (upd.)
Preussag AG, 42 (upd.)
Qantas Airways Limited, 6; 24 (upd.)
Reno Air Inc., 23
Royal Nepal Airline Corporation, 41
Ryanair Holdings plc, 35
SAA (Pty) Ltd., 28
Sabena S.A./N.V., 33
The SAS Group, 34 (upd.)
Saudi Arabian Airlines, 6; 27 (upd.)
Scandinavian Airlines System, I
Singapore Airlines Ltd., 6; 27 (upd.)
SkyWest, Inc., 25
Southwest Airlines Co., 6; 24 (upd.)
Spirit Airlines, Inc., 31
Sun Country Airlines, 30
Swiss Air Transport Company, Ltd., I
Texas Air Corporation, I
Thai Airways International Public Company Limited, 6; 27 (upd.)
Tower Air, Inc., 28
Trans World Airlines, Inc., I; 12 (upd.); 35 (upd.)
TransBrasil S/A Linhas Aéreas, 31
Transportes Aereos Portugueses, S.A., 6
TV Guide, Inc., 43 (upd.)
UAL Corporation, 34 (upd.)
United Airlines, I; 6 (upd.)
US Airways Group, Inc., 28 (upd.)
USAir Group, Inc., I; 6 (upd.)
VARIG S.A. (Viação Aérea Rio-Grandense), 6; 29 (upd.)
WestJet Airlines Ltd., 38

AUTOMOTIVE

AB Volvo, I; 7 (upd.); 26 (upd.)
Adam Opel AG, 7; 21 (upd.)
Alfa Romeo, 13; 36 (upd.)
American Motors Corporation, I
Applied Power Inc., 32 (upd.)
Arvin Industries, Inc., 8
Automobiles Citroen, 7
Automobili Lamborghini Holding S.p.A., 34 (upd.)
Automobili Lamborghini S.p.A., 13
Bajaj Auto Limited, 39
Bayerische Motoren Werke AG, I; 11 (upd.); 38 (upd.)
Bendix Corporation, I
Blue Bird Corporation, 35
Bombardier Inc., 42 (upd.)
Borg-Warner Automotive, Inc., 14; 32 (upd.)
The Budd Company, 8
CARQUEST Corporation, 29
Chrysler Corporation, I; 11 (upd.)
CNH Global N.V., 38 (upd.)
Consorcio G Grupo Dina, S.A. de C.V., 36
CSK Auto Corporation, 38
Cummins Engine Company, Inc., I; 12 (upd.); 40 (upd.)
Custom Chrome, Inc., 16
Daihatsu Motor Company, Ltd., 7; 21 (upd.)
Daimler-Benz A.G., I; 15 (upd.)
DaimlerChrysler AG, 34 (upd.)
Dana Corporation, I; 10 (upd.)
Deere & Company, 42 (upd.)
Don Massey Cadillac, Inc., 37
Douglas & Lomason Company, 16
Ducati Motor Holding S.p.A., 30
Eaton Corporation, I; 10 (upd.)

Echlin Inc., I; 11 (upd.)
Edelbrock Corporation, 37
Federal-Mogul Corporation, I; 10 (upd.); 26 (upd.)
Ferrari S.p.A., 13; 36 (upd.)
Fiat S.p.A, I; 11 (upd.)
FinishMaster, Inc., 24
Ford Motor Company, I; 11 (upd.); 36 (upd.)
Ford Motor Company, S.A. de C.V., 20
Fruehauf Corporation, I
General Motors Corporation, I; 10 (upd.); 36 (upd.)
Gentex Corporation, 26
Genuine Parts Company, 9
GKN plc, 38 (upd.)
Harley-Davidson Inc., 7; 25 (upd.)
Hayes Lemmerz International, Inc., 27
The Hertz Corporation, 33 (upd.)
Hino Motors, Ltd., 7; 21 (upd.)
Honda Motor Company Limited (Honda Giken Kogyo Kabushiki Kaisha), I; 10 (upd.); 29 (upd.)
Insurance Auto Auctions, Inc., 23
Isuzu Motors, Ltd., 9; 23 (upd.)
Kelsey-Hayes Group of Companies, 7; 27 (upd.)
Kia Motors Corporation, 12; 29 (upd.)
Lear Seating Corporation, 16
Lithia Motors, Inc., 41
Lotus Cars Ltd., 14
Lund International Holdings, Inc., 40
Mack Trucks, Inc., I; 22 (upd.)
Masland Corporation, 17
Mazda Motor Corporation, 9; 23 (upd.)
Mel Farr Automotive Group, 20
Metso Corporation, 30 (upd.)
Midas International Corporation, 10
Mitsubishi Motors Corporation, 9; 23 (upd.)
Monaco Coach Corporation, 31
Monro Muffler Brake, Inc., 24
National R.V. Holdings, Inc., 32
Navistar International Corporation, I; 10 (upd.)
Nissan Motor Co., Ltd., I; 11 (upd.); 34 (upd.)
O'Reilly Automotive, Inc., 26
Officine Alfieri Maserati S.p.A., 13
Oshkosh Truck Corporation, 7
Paccar Inc., I
PACCAR Inc., 26 (upd.)
Pennzoil Company, 20 (upd.)
Penske Corporation, 19 (upd.)
The Pep Boys—Manny, Moe & Jack, 11; 36 (upd.)
Peugeot S.A., I
Piaggio & C. S.p.A., 20
Porsche AG, 13; 31 (upd.)
PSA Peugeot Citroen S.A., 28 (upd.)
Regie Nationale des Usines Renault, I
Renault S.A., 26 (upd.)
Republic Industries, Inc., 26
Robert Bosch GmbH., I; 16 (upd.); 43 (upd.)
RockShox, Inc., 26
Rockwell Automation, 43 (upd.)
Rolls-Royce plc, I; 21 (upd.)
Rover Group Ltd., 7; 21 (upd.)
Saab Automobile AB, 32 (upd.)
Saab-Scania A.B., I; 11 (upd.)
Safelite Glass Corp., 19
Saturn Corporation, 7; 21 (upd.)
Sealed Power Corporation, I
Sheller-Globe Corporation, I
Sixt AG, 39
Skoda Auto a.s., 39
Spartan Motors Inc., 14
SpeeDee Oil Change and Tune-Up, 25
SPX Corporation, 10
Standard Motor Products, Inc., 40
Superior Industries International, Inc., 8
Suzuki Motor Corporation, 9; 23 (upd.)
Tower Automotive, Inc., 24
Toyota Motor Corporation, I; 11 (upd.); 38 (upd.)
TRW Inc., 14 (upd.)
Ugly Duckling Corporation, 22
United Auto Group, Inc., 26
United Technologies Automotive Inc., 15
Valeo, 23
Volkswagen Aktiengesellschaft, I; 11 (upd.); 32 (upd.)
Walker Manufacturing Company, 19
Winnebago Industries Inc., 7; 27 (upd.)
Ziebart International Corporation, 30

BEVERAGES

A & W Brands, Inc., 25
Adolph Coors Company, I; 13 (upd.); 36 (upd.)
Allied Domecq PLC, 29
Allied-Lyons PLC, I
Anheuser-Busch Companies, Inc., I; 10 (upd.); 34 (upd.)
Asahi Breweries, Ltd., I; 20 (upd.)
Bacardi Limited, 18
Banfi Products Corp., 36
Baron Philippe de Rothschild S.A., 39
Bass PLC, I; 15 (upd.); 38 (upd.)
BBAG Osterreichische Brau-Beteiligungs-AG, 38
Beringer Wine Estates Holdings, Inc., 22
Boston Beer Company, 18
Brauerei Beck & Co., 9; 33 (upd.)
Brown-Forman Corporation, I; 10 (upd.); 38 (upd.)
Canandaigua Brands, Inc., 34 (upd.)
Canandaigua Wine Company, Inc., 13
Carlsberg A/S, 9; 29 (upd.)
Carlton and United Breweries Ltd., I
Casa Cuervo, S.A. de C.V., 31
Cerveceria Polar, I
The Chalone Wine Group, Ltd., 36
Coca Cola Bottling Co. Consolidated, 10
The Coca-Cola Company, I; 10 (upd.); 32 (upd.)
Corby Distilleries Limited, 14
D.G. Yuengling & Son, Inc., 38
Dean Foods Company, 21 (upd.)
Distillers Company PLC, I
Dr Pepper/Seven Up, Inc., 9; 32 (upd.)
E. & J. Gallo Winery, I; 7 (upd.); 28 (upd.)
Ferolito, Vultaggio & Sons, 27
Foster's Brewing Group Ltd., 7; 21 (upd.)
Fuller Smith & Turner P.L.C., 38
G. Heileman Brewing Company Inc., I
The Gambrinus Company, 40
General Cinema Corporation, I
Golden State Vintners, Inc., 33
Grand Metropolitan PLC, I
Green Mountain Coffee, Inc., 31
The Greenalls Group PLC, 21
Greene King plc, 31
Grupo Modelo, S.A. de C.V., 29
Guinness PLC, I
Guinness/UDV, 43 (upd.)
The Hain Celestial Group, Inc., 43 (upd.)
Hansen Natural Corporation, 31
Heineken N.V, I; 13 (upd.); 34 (upd.)
Heublein, Inc., I
Hiram Walker Resources, Ltd., I
Interbrew S.A., 17
Jacob Leinenkugel Brewing Company, 28
JD Wetherspoon plc, 30
Karlsberg Brauerei GmbH & Co KG, 41
Kendall-Jackson Winery, Ltd., 28
Kikkoman Corporation, 14
Kirin Brewery Company, Limited, I; 21 (upd.)
König Brauerei GmbH & Co. KG, 35 (upd.)
Labatt Brewing Company Limited, I; 25 (upd.)
Laurent-Perrier SA, 42
Maison Louis Jadot, 24
Marchesi Antinori SRL, 42
Marie Brizard & Roger International S.A., 22
MBC Holding Company, 40
Miller Brewing Company, I; 12 (upd.)
The Minute Maid Company, 28
Moët-Hennessy, I
The Molson Companies Limited, I, 26 (upd.)
National Beverage Corp., 26
National Grape Cooperative Association, Inc., 20
Ocean Spray Cranberries, Inc., 25 (upd.)
Odwalla, Inc., 31
Paulaner Brauerei GmbH & Co. KG, 35
Peet's Coffee & Tea, Inc., 38
The Pepsi Bottling Group, Inc., 40
Pepsico, Inc., I; 10 (upd.); 38 (upd.)
Pernod Ricard S.A., I; 21 (upd.)
Pete's Brewing Company, 22
Philip Morris Companies Inc., 18 (upd.)
Pyramid Breweries Inc., 33
Rainier Brewing Company, 23
Redhook Ale Brewery, Inc., 31
Rémy Cointreau S.A., 20
Robert Mondavi Corporation, 15
Royal Crown Company, Inc., 23
Sapporo Breweries Limited, I; 13 (upd.); 36 (upd.)
Scottish & Newcastle plc, 15; 35 (upd.)
The Seagram Company Ltd., I; 25 (upd.)
Sebastiani Vineyards, Inc., 28
Shepherd Neame Limited, 30
Snapple Beverage Corporation, 11
The South African Breweries Limited, I; 24 (upd.)
Starbucks Corporation, 13; 34 (upd.)
Stewart's Beverages, 39
The Stroh Brewery Company, 18 (upd.)
The Stroh Brewing Company, I
Sutter Home Winery Inc., 16
Taittinger S.A., 43
Todhunter International, Inc., 27
Triarc Companies, Inc., 34 (upd.)
Van Houtte Inc., 39
Vin & Spirit AB, 31
Whitbread and Company PLC, I
The Wine Group, Inc., 39
Young & Co.'s Brewery, P.L.C., 38

BIOTECHNOLOGY

Amgen, Inc., 10; 30 (upd.)
Biogen Inc., 14; 36 (upd.)
Centocor Inc., 14
Charles River Laboratories International, Inc., 42
Chiron Corporation, 10; 36 (upd.)
Covance Inc., 30
Delta and Pine Land Company, 33
Enzo Biochem, Inc., 41
Genentech, Inc., 32 (upd.)
Genzyme Corporation, 38 (upd.)
Howard Hughes Medical Institute, 39
Huntingdon Life Sciences Group plc, 42
IDEXX Laboratories, Inc., 23
Immunex Corporation, 14

Life Technologies, Inc., 17
Medtronic, Inc., 30 (upd.)
Millipore Corporation, 25
Minntech Corporation, 22
Mycogen Corporation, 21
Qiagen N.V., 39
Quintiles Transnational Corporation, 21
Seminis, Inc., 29
Sigma-Aldrich Corporation, 36 (upd.)
STERIS Corporation, 29
Waters Corporation, 43

CHEMICALS

A. Schulman, Inc., 8
Aceto Corp., 38
Air Products and Chemicals, Inc., I; 10 (upd.)
Akzo Nobel N.V., 13
AlliedSignal Inc., 22 (upd.)
American Cyanamid, I; 8 (upd.)
ARCO Chemical Company, 10
Atochem S.A., I
Baker Hughes Incorporated, 22 (upd.)
Balchem Corporation, 42
BASF Aktiengesellschaft, I; 18 (upd.)
Bayer A.G., I; 13 (upd.); 41 (upd.)
Betz Laboratories, Inc., I; 10 (upd.)
The BFGoodrich Company, 19 (upd.)
BOC Group plc, I; 25 (upd.)
Brenntag AG, 8; 23 (upd.)
Burmah Castrol PLC, 30 (upd.)
Cabot Corporation, 8; 29 (upd.)
Cambrex Corporation, 16
Celanese Corporation, I
Chemcentral Corporation, 8
Chemi-Trol Chemical Co., 16
Church & Dwight Co., Inc., 29
Ciba-Geigy Ltd., I; 8 (upd.)
The Clorox Company, 22 (upd.)
Crompton & Knowles, 9
Crompton Corporation, 36 (upd.)
Cytec Industries Inc., 27
Degussa-Hüls AG, 32 (upd.)
DeKalb Genetics Corporation, 17
The Dexter Corporation, I; 12 (upd.)
The Dow Chemical Company, I; 8 (upd.)
DSM, N.V, I
E.I. Du Pont de Nemours & Company, I; 8 (upd.); 26 (upd.)
Eastman Chemical Company, 14; 38 (upd.)
Ecolab Inc., I; 13 (upd.); 34 (upd.)
Elementis plc, 40 (upd.)
English China Clays Ltd., 40 (upd.)
English China Clays plc, 15 (upd.)
ERLY Industries Inc., 17
Ethyl Corporation, I; 10 (upd.)
Ferro Corporation, 8
First Mississippi Corporation, 8
Formosa Plastics Corporation, 14
Fort James Corporation, 22 (upd.)
G.A.F., I
The General Chemical Group Inc., 37
Georgia Gulf Corporation, 9
Givaudan SA, 43
Great Lakes Chemical Corporation, I; 14 (upd.)
H.B. Fuller Company, 32 (upd.)
Hawkins Chemical, Inc., 16
Henkel KGaA, 34 (upd.)
Hercules Inc., I; 22 (upd.)
Hoechst A.G., I; 18 (upd.)
Hoechst Celanese Corporation, 13
Huls A.G., I
Huntsman Chemical Corporation, 8
IMC Fertilizer Group, Inc., 8
Imperial Chemical Industries PLC, I
International Flavors & Fragrances Inc., 9; 38 (upd.)
Koppers Industries, Inc., I; 26 (upd.)
L'Air Liquide, I
Lawter International Inc., 14
LeaRonal, Inc., 23
Loctite Corporation, 30 (upd.)
Lubrizol Corporation, I; 30 (upd.)
M.A. Hanna Company, 8
MacDermid Incorporated, 32
Mallinckrodt Group Inc., 19
MBC Holding Company, 40
Melamine Chemicals, Inc., 27
Methanex Corporation, 40
Mississippi Chemical Corporation, 39
Mitsubishi Chemical Industries, Ltd., I
Mitsui Petrochemical Industries, Ltd., 9
Monsanto Company, I; 9 (upd.); 29 (upd.)
Montedison SpA, I
Morton International Inc., 9 (upd.)
Morton Thiokol, Inc., I
Nagase & Company, Ltd., 8
Nalco Chemical Corporation, I; 12 (upd.)
National Distillers and Chemical Corporation, I
National Sanitary Supply Co., 16
NCH Corporation, 8
NL Industries, Inc., 10
Nobel Industries AB, 9
Norsk Hydro ASA, 35 (upd.)
Novacor Chemicals Ltd., 12
NutraSweet Company, 8
Olin Corporation, I; 13 (upd.)
OM Group, Inc., 17
Pennwalt Corporation, I
Perstorp A.B., I
Petrolite Corporation, 15
Pioneer Hi-Bred International, Inc., 41 (upd.)
Praxair, Inc., 11
Quantum Chemical Corporation, 8
Reichhold Chemicals, Inc., 10
Rhodia SA, 38
Rhône-Poulenc S.A., I; 10 (upd.)
Robertet SA, 39
Rohm and Haas Company, I; 26 (upd.)
Roussel Uclaf, I; 8 (upd.)
RPM, Inc., 36 (upd.)
The Scotts Company, 22
SCP Pool Corporation, 39
Sequa Corp., 13
Shanghai Petrochemical Co., Ltd., 18
Sigma-Aldrich Corporation, 36 (upd.)
Solvay & Cie S.A., I; 21 (upd.)
Stepan Company, 30
Sterling Chemicals, Inc., 16
Sumitomo Chemical Company Ltd., I
Terra Industries, Inc., 13
Teva Pharmaceutical Industries Ltd., 22
TOTAL S.A., 24 (upd.)
Ube Industries, Ltd., 38 (upd.)
Union Carbide Corporation, I; 9 (upd.)
Univar Corporation, 9
The Valspar Corporation, 32 (upd.)
Vista Chemical Company, I
Witco Corporation, I; 16 (upd.)
Zeneca Group PLC, 21

CONGLOMERATES

Accor SA, 10; 27 (upd.)
AEG A.G., I
Alcatel Alsthom Compagnie Générale d'Electricité, 9
Alco Standard Corporation, I
Alexander & Baldwin, Inc., 40 (upd.)
Alfa, S.A. de C.V., 19
Allied Domecq PLC, 29
Allied-Signal Inc., I
AMFAC Inc., I
The Anschutz Corporation, 36 (upd.)
Aramark Corporation, 13
ARAMARK Corporation, 41
Archer-Daniels-Midland Company, I; 11 (upd.)
Arkansas Best Corporation, 16
BAA plc, 33 (upd.)
Barlow Rand Ltd., I
Bat Industries PLC, I
Berkshire Hathaway Inc., 42 (upd.)
Bond Corporation Holdings Limited, 10
BTR PLC, I
Bunzl plc, 31 (upd.)
Burlington Northern Santa Fe Corporation, 27 (upd.)
C. Itoh & Company Ltd., I
Cargill, Incorporated, 13 (upd.); 40 (upd.)
CDI Industries, Inc., 7
Chemed Corporation, 13
Chesebrough-Pond's USA, Inc., 8
CITIC Pacific Ltd., 18
Colt Industries Inc., I
The Connell Company, 29
CSR Limited, 28 (upd.)
Daewoo Group, 18 (upd.)
De Dietrich & Cie., 31
Deere & Company, 21 (upd.)
Delaware North Companies Incorporated, 7
Desc, S.A. de C.V., 23
The Dial Corp., 8
EBSCO Industries, Inc., 40 (upd.)
El Corte Inglés Group, 26 (upd.)
Elders IXL Ltd., I
Engelhard Corporation, 21 (upd.)
Farley Northwest Industries, Inc., I
Fimalac S.A., 37
First Pacific Company Limited, 18
Fisher Companies, Inc., 15
Fletcher Challenge Ltd., 19 (upd.)
FMC Corporation, I; 11 (upd.)
Fortune Brands, Inc., 29 (upd.)
Fuqua Industries, Inc., I
General Electric Company, 34 (upd.)
GIB Group, 26 (upd.)
Gillett Holdings, Inc., 7
Grand Metropolitan PLC, 14 (upd.)
Great American Management and Investment, Inc., 8
Greyhound Corporation, I
Grupo Carso, S.A. de C.V., 21
Grupo Industrial Bimbo, 19
Gulf & Western Inc., I
Hagemeyer N.V., 39
Hankyu Corporation, 23 (upd.)
Hanson PLC, III; 7 (upd.)
Hitachi, Ltd., I; 12 (upd.); 40 (upd.)
Hutchison Whampoa Ltd., 18
IC Industries, Inc., I
Ilitch Holdings Inc., 37
Inchcape plc, 16 (upd.)
Ingram Industries, Inc., 11
Instituto Nacional de Industria, I
International Controls Corporation, 10
International Telephone & Telegraph Corporation, I; 11 (upd.)
Istituto per la Ricostruzione Industriale, I
ITOCHU Corporation, 32 (upd.)
Jardine Matheson Holdings Limited, I; 20 (upd.)
Jason Incorporated, 23
Jefferson Smurfit Group plc, 19 (upd.)
The Jim Pattison Group, 37
Jordan Industries, Inc., 36
Justin Industries, Inc., 19
Kanematsu Corporation, 24 (upd.)
Kao Corporation, 20 (upd.)

Katy Industries, Inc., I
Kesko Ltd. (Kesko Oy), 8; 27 (upd.)
Kidde, Inc., I
KOC Holding A.S., I
Koninklijke Nedlloyd N.V., 26 (upd.)
Koor Industries Ltd., 25 (upd.)
K2 Inc., 16
The L.L. Knickerbocker Co., Inc., 25
Lancaster Colony Corporation, 8
Larry H. Miller Group, 29
Lear Siegler, Inc., I
Lefrak Organization Inc., 26
Leucadia National Corporation, 11
Litton Industries, Inc., I; 11 (upd.)
Loews Corporation, I; 12 (upd.); 36 (upd.)
Loral Corporation, 8
LTV Corporation, I
LVMH Moët Hennessy Louis Vuitton SA, 33 (upd.)
Marubeni Corporation, 24 (upd.)
Marubeni K.K., I
MAXXAM Inc., 8
McKesson Corporation, I
Menasha Corporation, 8
Metallgesellschaft AG, 16 (upd.)
Metromedia Co., 7
Minnesota Mining & Manufacturing Company (3M), I; 8 (upd.); 26 (upd.)
Mitsubishi Corporation, I; 12 (upd.)
Mitsubishi Heavy Industries, Ltd., 40 (upd.)
Mitsui & Co., Ltd., 28 (upd.)
Mitsui Bussan K.K., I
The Molson Companies Limited, I; 26 (upd.)
Montedison S.p.A., 24 (upd.)
NACCO Industries, Inc., 7
National Service Industries, Inc., 11
New World Development Company Limited, 38 (upd.)
Nichimen Corporation, 24 (upd.)
Nissho Iwai K.K., I
Norsk Hydro A.S., 10
Ogden Corporation, I
Onex Corporation, 16
Orkla A/S, 18
Park-Ohio Industries Inc., 17
Pentair, Inc., 7
Poliet S.A., 33
Powell Duffryn plc, 31
Power Corporation of Canada, 36 (upd.)
Preussag AG, 17
Pubco Corporation, 17
Pulsar Internacional S.A., 21
The Rank Organisation Plc, 14 (upd.)
Red Apple Group, Inc., 23
Roll International Corporation, 37
Rubbermaid Incorporated, 20 (upd.)
Samsung Group, I
San Miguel Corporation, 15
Sara Lee Corporation, 15 (upd.)
Schindler Holding AG, 29
Sea Containers Ltd., 29
Seaboard Corporation, 36
ServiceMaster Inc., 23 (upd.)
Sime Darby Berhad, 14; 36 (upd.)
Société du Louvre, 27
Standex International Corporation, 17
Stinnes AG, 23 (upd.)
Sudbury Inc., 16
Sumitomo Corporation, I; 11 (upd.)
Swire Pacific Ltd., I; 16 (upd.)
Talley Industries, Inc., 16
Tandycrafts, Inc., 31
Teledyne, Inc., I; 10 (upd.)
Tenneco Inc., I; 10 (upd.)
Textron Inc., I; 34 (upd.)
Thomas H. Lee Co., 24
Thorn Emi PLC, I
Thorn plc, 24
TI Group plc, 17
Time Warner Inc., IV; 7 (upd.)
Tomen Corporation, 24 (upd.)
Tomkins plc, 11
Toshiba Corporation, I; 12 (upd.); 40 (upd.)
Tractebel S.A., 20
Transamerica Corporation, I; 13 (upd.)
Transamerica–An AEGON Company, 41 (upd.)
The Tranzonic Cos., 15
Triarc Companies, Inc., 8
TRW Inc., I; 11 (upd.)
Unilever, 32 (upd.)
Unilever PLC, II; 7 (upd.)
United Technologies Corporation, 34 (upd.)
Universal Studios, Inc., 33
Valhi, Inc., 19
Valores Industriales S.A., 19
Veba A.G., I; 15 (upd.)
Vendôme Luxury Group plc, 27
Viacom Inc., 23 (upd.)
Virgin Group, 32 (upd.)
Virgin Group PLC, 12
W.R. Grace & Company, I
The Washington Companies, 33
Wheaton Industries, 8
Whitbread PLC, 20 (upd.)
Whitman Corporation, 10 (upd.)
Whittaker Corporation, I
WorldCorp, Inc., 10
Worms et Cie, 27
Yamaha Corporation, 40 (upd.)

CONSTRUCTION

A. Johnson & Company H.B., I
ABC Supply Co., Inc., 22
Abrams Industries Inc., 23
AMREP Corporation, 21
ASV, Inc., 34
The Austin Company, 8
Balfour Beatty plc, 36 (upd.)
Baratt Developments PLC, I
Beazer Homes USA, Inc., 17
Bechtel Group, Inc., I; 24 (upd.)
BFC Construction Corporation, 25
Bilfinger & Berger Bau A.G., I
Bird Corporation, 19
Black & Veatch LLP, 22
Boral Limited, 43 (upd.)
Bouygues S.A., I; 24 (upd.)
Brown & Root, Inc., 13
Bufete Industrial, S.A. de C.V., 34
CalMat Co., 19
Centex Corporation, 8; 29 (upd.)
Cianbro Corporation, 14
The Clark Construction Group, Inc., 8
Colas S.A., 31
Day & Zimmermann, Inc., 31 (upd.)
Dillingham Corporation, I
Dominion Homes, Inc., 19
The Drees Company, Inc., 41
Edw. C. Levy Co., 42
Eiffage, 27
Ellerbe Becket, 41
Empresas ICA Sociedad Controladora, S.A. de C.V., 41
Encompass Services Corporation, 33
Environmental Industries, Inc., 31
Eurotunnel PLC, 13
Fairclough Construction Group PLC, I
Fleetwood Enterprises, Inc., 22 (upd.)
Fluor Corporation, I; 8 (upd.); 34 (upd.)
George Wimpey PLC, 12
Gilbane, Inc., 34
Granite Rock Company, 26
Grupo Ferrovial, S.A., 40
Habitat for Humanity International, 36
Hillsdown Holdings plc, 24 (upd.)
Hochtief AG, 33
Horton Homes, Inc., 25
Hospitality Worldwide Services, Inc., 26
Hovnanian Enterprises, Inc., 29
J.A. Jones, Inc., 16
Jarvis plc, 39
John Brown PLC, I
John Laing PLC, I
Kajima Corporation, I
Kaufman and Broad Home Corporation, 8
Kitchell Corporation, 14
The Koll Company, 8
Komatsu Ltd., 16 (upd.)
Kraus-Anderson, Incorporated, 36
Kumagai Gumi Company, Ltd., I
L'Entreprise Jean Lefebvre, 23
Lennar Corporation, 11
Lincoln Property Company, 8
Lindal Cedar Homes, Inc., 29
Linde A.G., I
Mellon-Stuart Company, I
Michael Baker Corp., 14
Morrison Knudsen Corporation, 7; 28 (upd.)
New Holland N.V., 22
NVR L.P., 8
Ohbayashi Corporation, I
Opus Group, 34
The Peninsular & Oriental Steam Navigation Company (Bovis Division), I
Perini Corporation, 8
Peter Kiewit Sons' Inc., 8
Philipp Holzmann AG, 17
Post Properties, Inc., 26
Pulte Corporation, 8
Pulte Homes, Inc., 42 (upd.)
Redrow Group plc, 31
RMC Group p.l.c., 34 (upd.)
Rooney Brothers Co., 25
The Rottlund Company, Inc., 28
The Ryland Group, Inc., 8; 37 (upd.)
Sandvik AB, 32 (upd.)
Schuff Steel Company, 26
Shorewood Packaging Corporation, 28
Simon Property Group, Inc., 27
Skanska AB, 38
Sundt Corp., 24
Swinerton Inc., 43
Taylor Woodrow plc, I; 38 (upd.)
Thyssen Krupp AG, 28 (upd.)
Toll Brothers Inc., 15
Trammell Crow Company, 8
Tridel Enterprises Inc., 9
The Turner Corporation, 8; 23 (upd.)
U.S. Aggregates, Inc., 42
U.S. Home Corporation, 8
Veit Companies, 43
Walbridge Aldinger Co., 38
Walter Industries, Inc., 22 (upd.)
The Weitz Company, Inc., 42
Wood Hall Trust PLC, I

CONTAINERS

Ball Corporation, I; 10 (upd.)
BWAY Corporation, 24
Clarcor Inc., 17
Continental Can Co., Inc., 15
Continental Group Company, I
Crown Cork & Seal Company, Inc., I; 13 (upd.); 32 (upd.)
Gaylord Container Corporation, 8
Golden Belt Manufacturing Co., 16
Greif Bros. Corporation, 15

Grupo Industrial Durango, S.A. de C.V., 37
Inland Container Corporation, 8
Kerr Group Inc., 24
Keyes Fibre Company, 9
Liqui-Box Corporation, 16
The Longaberger Company, 12
Longview Fibre Company, 8
The Mead Corporation, 19 (upd.)
Metal Box PLC, I
National Can Corporation, I
Owens-Illinois, Inc., I; 26 (upd.)
Primerica Corporation, I
Reynolds Metals Company, 19 (upd.)
Royal Packaging Industries Van Leer N.V., 30
Sealright Co., Inc., 17
Smurfit-Stone Container Corporation, 26 (upd.)
Sonoco Products Company, 8
Thermos Company, 16
Toyo Seikan Kaisha, Ltd., I
U.S. Can Corporation, 30
Ultra Pac, Inc., 24
Viatech Continental Can Company, Inc., 25 (upd.)
Vitro Corporativo S.A. de C.V., 34

DRUGS/PHARMACEUTICALS

A.L. Pharma Inc., 12
Abbott Laboratories, I; 11 (upd.); 40 (upd.)
Akorn, Inc., 32
Alpharma Inc., 35 (upd.)
ALZA Corporation, 10; 36 (upd.)
American Home Products, I; 10 (upd.)
Amgen, Inc., 10
Astra AB, I; 20 (upd.)
Barr Laboratories, Inc., 26
Bayer A.G., I; 13 (upd.)
Block Drug Company, Inc., 8
Bristol-Myers Squibb Company, III; 9 (upd.); 37 (upd.)
C.H. Boehringer Sohn, 39
Carter-Wallace, Inc., 8; 38 (upd.)
Chiron Corporation, 10
Ciba-Geigy Ltd., I; 8 (upd.)
D&K Wholesale Drug, Inc., 14
Eli Lilly & Company, I; 11 (upd.)
F. Hoffmann-Laroche & Company A.G., I
Fisons plc, 9; 23 (upd.)
FoxMeyer Health Corporation, 16
Fujisawa Pharmaceutical Company Ltd., I
G.D. Searle & Co., I; 12 (upd.); 34 (upd.)
GEHE AG, 27
Genentech, Inc., I; 8 (upd.)
Genetics Institute, Inc., 8
Genzyme Corporation, 13
Glaxo Holdings PLC, I; 9 (upd.)
Heska Corporation, 39
Huntingdon Life Sciences Group plc, 42
Johnson & Johnson, III; 8 (upd.)
Jones Medical Industries, Inc., 24
Leiner Health Products Inc., 34
Marion Merrell Dow, Inc., I; 9 (upd.)
McKesson Corporation, 12
MedImmune, Inc., 35
Merck & Co., Inc., I; 11 (upd.)
Miles Laboratories, I
Monsanto Company, 29 (upd.)
Moore Medical Corp., 17
Murdock Madaus Schwabe, 26
Mylan Laboratories Inc., I; 20 (upd.)
National Patent Development Corporation, 13
Novartis AG, 39 (upd.)
Novo Industri A/S, I
Pfizer Inc., I; 9 (upd.); 38 (upd.)
Pharmacia & Upjohn Inc., 25 (upd.)
Pharmacia A.B., I
Quintiles Transnational Corporation, 21
R.P. Scherer, I
Roberts Pharmaceutical Corporation, 16
Roche Bioscience, 14 (upd.)
Rorer Group, I
Roussel Uclaf, I; 8 (upd.)
Sandoz Ltd., I
Sankyo Company, Ltd., I
Sanofi Group, I
Schering A.G., I
Schering-Plough Corporation, I; 14 (upd.)
Shionogi & Co., Ltd., 17 (upd.)
Sigma-Aldrich Corporation, I; 36 (upd.)
SmithKline Beckman Corporation, I
SmithKline Beecham plc, 32 (upd.)
Squibb Corporation, I
Sterling Drug, Inc., I
The Sunrider Corporation, 26
Syntex Corporation, I
Takeda Chemical Industries, Ltd., I
Teva Pharmaceutical Industries Ltd., 22
The Upjohn Company, I; 8 (upd.)
Vitalink Pharmacy Services, Inc., 15
Warner-Lambert Co., I; 10 (upd.)
Watson Pharmaceuticals Inc., 16
The Wellcome Foundation Ltd., I

ELECTRICAL & ELECTRONICS

ABB ASEA Brown Boveri Ltd., II; 22 (upd.)
Acer Inc., 16
Acuson Corporation, 10; 36 (upd.)
ADC Telecommunications, Inc., 30 (upd.)
Adtran Inc., 22
Advanced Micro Devices, Inc., 30 (upd.)
Advanced Technology Laboratories, Inc., 9
Agilent Technologies Inc., 38
Aiwa Co., Ltd., 30
Akzo Nobel N.V., 41 (upd.)
Alliant Techsystems Inc., 30 (upd.)
AlliedSignal Inc., 22 (upd.)
Alpine Electronics, Inc., 13
Alps Electric Co., Ltd., II
Altera Corporation, 18; 43 (upd.)
Altron Incorporated, 20
Amdahl Corporation, 40 (upd.)
American Power Conversion Corporation, 24
AMP Incorporated, II; 14 (upd.)
Amphenol Corporation, 40
Analog Devices, Inc., 10
Analogic Corporation, 23
Anam Group, 23
Anaren Microwave, Inc., 33
Andrew Corporation, 10; 32 (upd.)
Apple Computer, Inc., 36 (upd.)
Applied Power Inc., 32 (upd.)
Arrow Electronics, Inc., 10
Ascend Communications, Inc., 24
Astronics Corporation, 35
Atari Corporation, 9; 23 (upd.)
Atmel Corporation, 17
Audiovox Corporation, 34
Ault Incorporated, 34
Autodesk, Inc., 10
Avnet Inc., 9
Bang & Olufsen Holding A/S, 37
Benchmark Electronics, Inc., 40
Bicoastal Corporation, II
Bose Corporation, 13; 36 (upd.)
Boston Acoustics, Inc., 22
Bowthorpe plc, 33
Broadcom Corporation, 34
Bull S.A., 43 (upd.)
Burr-Brown Corporation, 19
C-COR.net Corp., 38
Cabletron Systems, Inc., 10
Canon Inc., 18 (upd.)
Carbone Lorraine S.A., 33
Carl-Zeiss-Stiftung, 34 (upd.)
CASIO Computer Co., Ltd., 16 (upd.); 40 (upd.)
Checkpoint Systems, Inc., 39
Cisco Systems, Inc., 34 (upd.)
Citizen Watch Co., Ltd., 21 (upd.)
Cobham plc, 30
Cobra Electronics Corporation, 14
Coherent, Inc., 31
Cohu, Inc., 32
Compagnie Générale d'Électricité, II
Conexant Systems, Inc., 36
Cooper Industries, Inc., II
Cray Research, Inc., 16 (upd.)
CTS Corporation, 39
Cubic Corporation, 19
Cypress Semiconductor Corporation, 20
Daktronics, Inc., 32
Dallas Semiconductor Corporation, 13; 31 (upd.)
De La Rue plc, 34 (upd.)
Dell Computer Corporation, 31 (upd.)
DH Technology, Inc., 18
Digi International Inc., 9
Discreet Logic Inc., 20
Dixons Group plc, 19 (upd.)
Dolby Laboratories Inc., 20
Dynatech Corporation, 13
E-Systems, Inc., 9
Electronics for Imaging, Inc., 15; 43 (upd.)
Emerson Electric Co., II
Emerson Radio Corp., 30
ENCAD, Incorporated, 25
ESS Technology, Inc., 22
Everex Systems, Inc., 16
Exabyte Corporation, 40 (upd.)
Exar Corp., 14
Exide Electronics Group, Inc., 20
Flextronics International Ltd., 38
Fluke Corporation, 15
Foxboro Company, 13
Fuji Electric Co., Ltd., II
Fujitsu Limited, 16 (upd.); 42 (upd.)
General Dynamics Corporation, 40 (upd.)
General Electric Company, II; 12 (upd.)
General Electric Company, PLC, II
General Instrument Corporation, 10
General Signal Corporation, 9
GenRad, Inc., 24
GM Hughes Electronics Corporation, II
Goldstar Co., Ltd., 12
Gould Electronics, Inc., 14
Grundig AG, 27
Guillemot Corporation, 41
Hadco Corporation, 24
Hamilton Beach/Proctor-Silex Inc., 17
Harman International Industries Inc., 15
Harris Corporation, II; 20 (upd.)
Hayes Corporation, 24
Herley Industries, Inc., 33
Hewlett-Packard Company, 28 (upd.)
Holophane Corporation, 19
Honeywell Inc., II; 12 (upd.)
Hubbell Incorporated, 9; 31 (upd.)
Hughes Supply, Inc., 14
Hutchinson Technology Incorporated, 18
Hypercom Corporation, 27
IEC Electronics Corp., 42
Imax Corporation, 28
In Focus Systems, Inc., 22
Indigo NV, 26
Intel Corporation, II; 10 (upd.)
International Business Machines Corporation, 30 (upd.)

International Rectifier Corporation, 31
Itel Corporation, 9
Jabil Circuit, Inc., 36
Jaco Electronics, Inc., 30
JDS Uniphase Corporation, 34
Juno Lighting, Inc., 30
Keithley Instruments Inc., 16
Kemet Corp., 14
Kent Electronics Corporation, 17
Kenwood Corporation, 31
Kingston Technology Corporation, 20
KitchenAid, 8
KnowledgeWare Inc., 9
Kollmorgen Corporation, 18
Konica Corporation, 30 (upd.)
Koor Industries Ltd., II
Koss Corporation, 38
Kulicke and Soffa Industries, Inc., 33
Kyocera Corporation, II
LaBarge Inc., 41
Lattice Semiconductor Corp., 16
LeCroy Corporation, 41
Legrand SA, 21
Linear Technology, Inc., 16
Littelfuse, Inc., 26
Loral Corporation, 9
Lowrance Electronics, Inc., 18
LSI Logic Corporation, 13
Lucent Technologies Inc., 34
Lucky-Goldstar, II
Lunar Corporation, 29
Mackie Designs Inc., 33
MagneTek, Inc., 15; 41 (upd.)
Marconi plc, 33 (upd.)
Marquette Electronics, Inc., 13
Matsushita Electric Industrial Co., Ltd., II
Maxim Integrated Products, Inc., 16
Merix Corporation, 36
Methode Electronics, Inc., 13
Mitel Corporation, 18
MITRE Corporation, 26
Mitsubishi Electric Corporation, II
Motorola, Inc., II; 11 (upd.); 34 (upd.)
National Instruments Corporation, 22
National Presto Industries, Inc., 16; 43 (upd.)
National Semiconductor Corporation, II; 26 (upd.)
NEC Corporation, II; 21 (upd.)
Nintendo Co., Ltd., 28 (upd.)
Nokia Corporation, II; 17 (upd.); 38 (upd.)
Nortel Networks Corporation, 36 (upd.)
Oak Technology, Inc., 22
Oki Electric Industry Company, Limited, II
Omron Corporation, 28 (upd.)
Omron Tateisi Electronics Company, II
Otter Tail Power Company, 18
Palm, Inc., 36
Palomar Medical Technologies, Inc., 22
The Peak Technologies Group, Inc., 14
Peavey Electronics Corporation, 16
Philips Electronics N.V., II; 13 (upd.)
Philips Electronics North America Corp., 13
Pioneer Electronic Corporation, 28 (upd.)
Pioneer-Standard Electronics Inc., 19
Pittway Corporation, 9
The Plessey Company, PLC, II
Plexus Corporation, 35
Polk Audio, Inc., 34
Potter & Brumfield Inc., 11
Premier Industrial Corporation, 9
Protection One, Inc., 32
Racal Electronics PLC, II
RadioShack Corporation, 36 (upd.)
Radius Inc., 16
Raychem Corporation, 8
Rayovac Corporation, 13
Raytheon Company, II; 11 (upd.); 38 (upd.)
RCA Corporation, II
Read-Rite Corp., 10
Reliance Electric Company, 9
Rexel, Inc., 15
Richardson Electronics, Ltd., 17
Ricoh Company, Ltd., 36 (upd.)
The Rival Company, 19
Rockford Corporation, 43
S&C Electric Company, 15
SAGEM S.A., 37
Sam Ash Music Corporation, 30
Samsung Electronics Co., Ltd., 14; 41 (upd.)
SANYO Electric Co., Ltd., 36 (upd.)
Sanyo Electric Company, Ltd., II
ScanSource, Inc., 29
Schneider S.A., II; 18 (upd.)
SCI Systems, Inc., 9
Scitex Corporation Ltd., 24
Seagate Technology, Inc., 34 (upd.)
Semtech Corporation, 32
Sensormatic Electronics Corp., 11
Sensory Science Corporation, 37
SGI, 29 (upd.)
Sharp Corporation, II; 12 (upd.); 40 (upd.)
Sheldahl Inc., 23
Siemens A.G., II; 14 (upd.)
Silicon Graphics Incorporated, 9
Smiths Industries PLC, 25
Solectron Corp., 12
Sony Corporation, II; 12 (upd.); 40 (upd.)
Sterling Electronics Corp., 18
Sumitomo Electric Industries, Ltd., II
Sun Microsystems, Inc., 30 (upd.)
Sunbeam-Oster Co., Inc., 9
SyQuest Technology, Inc., 18
Tandy Corporation, II; 12 (upd.)
Tatung Co., 23
TDK Corporation, II; 17 (upd.)
Tech-Sym Corporation, 18
Technitrol, Inc., 29
Tektronix, Inc., 8
Telxon Corporation, 10
Teradyne, Inc., 11
Texas Instruments Incorporated, II; 11 (upd.)
Thales S.A., 42
THOMSON multimedia S.A., 42 (upd.)
Thomson S.A., II
The Titan Corporation, 36
Tops Appliance City, Inc., 17
Toromont Industries, Ltd., 21
Trimble Navigation Limited, 40
Tweeter Home Entertainment Group, Inc., 30
Ultrak Inc., 24
Universal Electronics Inc., 39
Varian Associates Inc., 12
Veeco Instruments Inc., 32
Victor Company of Japan, Limited, II; 26 (upd.)
Vishay Intertechnology, Inc., 21
Vitesse Semiconductor Corporation, 32
Vitro Corp., 10
VLSI Technology, Inc., 16
Wells-Gardner Electronics Corporation, 43
Westinghouse Electric Corporation, II; 12 (upd.)
Wyle Electronics, 14
Yageo Corporation, 16
York Research Corporation, 35
Zenith Data Systems, Inc., 10
Zenith Electronics Corporation, II; 13 (upd.); 34 (upd.)
Zoom Telephonics, Inc., 18
Zytec Corporation, 19

ENGINEERING & MANAGEMENT SERVICES

AAON, Inc., 22
Aavid Thermal Technologies, Inc., 29
Alliant Techsystems Inc., 30 (upd.)
Analytic Sciences Corporation, 10
Arcadis NV, 26
Arthur D. Little, Inc., 35
The Austin Company, 8
Balfour Beatty plc, 36 (upd.)
Brown & Root, Inc., 13
Bufete Industrial, S.A. de C.V., 34
C.H. Heist Corporation, 24
CDI Corporation, 6
CH2M Hill Ltd., 22
The Charles Stark Draper Laboratory, Inc., 35
Coflexip S.A., 25
Corrections Corporation of America, 23
CRSS Inc., 6
Dames & Moore, Inc., 25
DAW Technologies, Inc., 25
Day & Zimmermann Inc., 9; 31 (upd.)
Donaldson Co. Inc., 16
EG&G Incorporated, 8; 29 (upd.)
Eiffage, 27
Essef Corporation, 18
Fluor Corporation, 34 (upd.)
Foster Wheeler Corporation, 6; 23 (upd.)
Framatome SA, 19
Gilbane, Inc., 34
Halliburton Company, 25 (upd.)
Harding Lawson Associates Group, Inc., 16
Harza Engineering Company, 14
ICF Kaiser International, Inc., 28
Jacobs Engineering Group Inc., 6; 26 (upd.)
JWP Inc., 9
Kvaerner ASA, 36
Layne Christensen Company, 19
The MacNeal-Schwendler Corporation, 25
Malcolm Pirnie, Inc., 42
McDermott International, Inc., 37 (upd.)
McKinsey & Company, Inc., 9
Ogden Corporation, 6
Opus Group, 34
Parsons Brinckerhoff, Inc., 34
The Parsons Corporation, 8
RCM Technologies, Inc., 34
Rosemount Inc., 15
Roy F. Weston, Inc., 33
Royal Vopak NV, 41
Rust International Inc., 11
Sandvik AB, 32 (upd.)
Science Applications International Corporation, 15
Stone & Webster, Inc., 13
Susquehanna Pfaltzgraff Company, 8
Sverdrup Corporation, 14
Tetra Tech, Inc., 29
Thyssen Krupp AG, 28 (upd.)
Towers Perrin, 32
Tracor Inc., 17
TRC Companies, Inc., 32
Underwriters Laboratories, Inc., 30
United Dominion Industries Limited, 8; 16 (upd.)
VECO International, Inc., 7
Vinci, 43

ENTERTAINMENT & LEISURE

A&E Television Networks, 32
Acclaim Entertainment Inc., 24
Activision, Inc., 32
AEI Music Network Inc., 35
Airtours Plc, 27
All American Communications Inc., 20

Alliance Entertainment Corp., 17
Amblin Entertainment, 21
AMC Entertainment Inc., 12; 35 (upd.)
American Skiing Company, 28
Ameristar Casinos, Inc., 33
AMF Bowling, Inc., 40
Anchor Gaming, 24
Applause Inc., 24
Aprilia SpA, 17
Argosy Gaming Company, 21
The Art Institute of Chicago, 29
Artisan Entertainment Inc., 32 (upd.)
Asahi National Broadcasting Company, Ltd., 9
Aspen Skiing Company, 15
Aston Villa plc, 41
Atlanta National League Baseball Club, Inc., 43
The Atlantic Group, 23
Autotote Corporation, 20
Aztar Corporation, 13
Baker & Taylor Corporation, 43 (upd.)
Baker & Taylor, Inc., 16
Bally Total Fitness Holding Corp., 25
Bertelsmann A.G., 15 (upd.); 43 (upd.)
Bertucci's Inc., 16
Blockbuster Entertainment Corporation, 9
Blockbuster Inc., 31 (upd.)
Boca Resorts, Inc., 37
Bonneville International Corporation, 29
Booth Creek Ski Holdings, Inc., 31
Boston Celtics Limited Partnership, 14
Boston Professional Hockey Association Inc., 39
The Boy Scouts of America, 34
British Broadcasting Corporation Ltd., 7; 21 (upd.)
British Sky Broadcasting Group Plc, 20
Cablevision Systems Corporation, 7
Canterbury Park Holding Corporation, 42
Capital Cities/ABC Inc., II
Carlson Companies, Inc., 22 (upd.)
Carmike Cinemas, Inc., 14; 37 (upd.)
Carnival Corporation, 27 (upd.)
Carnival Cruise Lines, Inc., 6
The Carsey-Werner Company, L.L.C., 37
CBS Inc., II; 6 (upd.)
Cedar Fair, L.P., 22
Central Independent Television, 7; 23 (upd.)
Century Theatres, Inc., 31
Championship Auto Racing Teams, Inc., 37
Chicago Bears Football Club, Inc., 33
Chris-Craft Industries, Inc., 31 (upd.)
Chrysalis Group plc, 40
Churchill Downs Incorporated, 29
Cinar Corporation, 40
Cineplex Odeon Corporation, 6; 23 (upd.)
Cinram International, Inc., 43
Cirque du Soleil Inc., 29
Cleveland Indians Baseball Company, Inc., 37
ClubCorp, Inc., 33
Columbia Pictures Entertainment, Inc., II
Columbia TriStar Motion Pictures Companies, 12 (upd.)
Comcast Corporation, 7
Continental Cablevision, Inc., 7
Corporation for Public Broadcasting, 14
Cox Enterprises, Inc., 22 (upd.)
Cruise America Inc., 21
Cunard Line Ltd., 23
Dallas Cowboys Football Club, Ltd., 33
Dave & Buster's, Inc., 33
Death Row Records, 27
The Detroit Pistons Basketball Company, 41
dick clark productions, inc., 16
DIRECTV, Inc., 38
Dover Downs Entertainment, Inc., 43
DreamWorks SKG, 43
E! Entertainment Television Inc., 17
Edwards Theatres Circuit, Inc., 31
Equity Marketing, Inc., 26
Esporta plc, 35
Euro Disneyland SCA, 20
Family Golf Centers, Inc., 29
Fédération Internationale de Football Association, 27
Feld Entertainment, Inc., 32 (upd.)
First Choice Holidays PLC, 40
First Team Sports, Inc., 22
Fisher-Price Inc., 32 (upd.)
Fox Entertainment Group, Inc., 43
Fox Family Worldwide, Inc., 24
Gaumont SA, 25
Gaylord Entertainment Company, 11; 36 (upd.)
GC Companies, Inc., 25
Geffen Records Inc., 26
Gibson Guitar Corp., 16
Girl Scouts of the USA, 35
Granada Group PLC, II; 24 (upd.)
Grand Casinos, Inc., 20
The Green Bay Packers, Inc., 32
Hallmark Cards, Inc., 40 (upd.)
Hanna-Barbera Cartoons Inc., 23
Hard Rock Cafe International, Inc., 32 (upd.)
Harpo Entertainment Group, 28
Harrah's Entertainment, Inc., 16; 43 (upd.)
Harveys Casino Resorts, 27
Hasbro, Inc., 43 (upd.)
Hastings Entertainment, Inc., 29
HIT Entertainment PLC, 40
HOB Entertainment, Inc., 37
Hollywood Casino Corporation, 21
Hollywood Entertainment Corporation, 25
Hollywood Park, Inc., 20
Home Box Office Inc., 7; 23 (upd.)
Imax Corporation, 28
Infogrames Entertainment S.A., 35
International Creative Management, Inc., 43
International Family Entertainment Inc., 13
International Game Technology, 41 (upd.)
International Speedway Corporation, 19
Interscope Music Group, 31
The Intrawest Corporation, 15
Irvin Feld & Kenneth Feld Productions, Inc., 15
Isle of Capri Casinos, Inc., 41
Iwerks Entertainment, Inc., 34
Jackpot Enterprises Inc., 21
Japan Broadcasting Corporation, 7
Jillian's Entertainment Holdings, Inc., 40
The Jim Henson Company, 23
Kampgrounds of America, Inc. (KOA), 33
King World Productions, Inc., 9; 30 (upd.)
Knott's Berry Farm, 18
Kuoni Travel Holding Ltd., 40
The Kushner-Locke Company, 25
Ladbroke Group PLC, II; 21 (upd.)
Lego A/S, 13; 40 (upd.)
Liberty Livewire Corporation, 42
Lionel L.L.C., 16
Lions Gate Entertainment Corporation, 35
LIVE Entertainment Inc., 20
LodgeNet Entertainment Corporation, 28
Lucasfilm Ltd., 12
Luminar Plc, 40
Manchester United Football Club plc, 30
Mandalay Resort Group, 32 (upd.)
The Marcus Corporation, 21
Mashantucket Pequot Gaming Enterprise Inc., 35
MCA Inc., II
Media General, Inc., 7
Metro-Goldwyn-Mayer Inc., 25 (upd.)
Metromedia Companies, 14
Métropole Télévision, 33
Metropolitan Baseball Club Inc., 39
Metropolitan Opera Association, Inc., 40
MGM Grand Inc., 17
MGM/UA Communications Company, II
Midway Games, Inc., 25
Mikohn Gaming Corporation, 39
Milwaukee Brewers Baseball Club, 37
Mizuno Corporation, 25
Mohegan Tribal Gaming Authority, 37
Motown Records Company L.P., 26
Movie Gallery, Inc., 31
Multimedia Games, Inc., 41
Muzak, Inc., 18
National Amusements Inc., 28
National Association for Stock Car Auto Racing, 32
National Broadcasting Company, Inc., II; 6 (upd.)
National Football League, 29
National Hockey League, 35
National Public Radio, 19
National Rifle Association of America, 37
Navarre Corporation, 24
Nintendo Co., Ltd., 28 (upd.)
O'Charley's Inc., 19
Orion Pictures Corporation, 6
Paradise Music & Entertainment, Inc., 42
Paramount Pictures Corporation, II
Pathé SA, 29
Penn National Gaming, Inc., 33
Philadelphia Eagles, 37
Pixar Animation Studios, 34
Platinum Entertainment, Inc., 35
Play by Play Toys & Novelties, Inc., 26
Players International, Inc., 22
PolyGram N.V., 23
Powerhouse Technologies, Inc., 27
Premier Parks, Inc., 27
President Casinos, Inc., 22
Preussag AG, 42 (upd.)
Princess Cruise Lines, 22
The Professional Golfers' Association of America, 41
Promus Companies, Inc., 9
Putt-Putt Golf Courses of America, Inc., 23
Rainforest Cafe, Inc., 25
Rank Organisation PLC, II
Rawlings Sporting Goods Co., Inc., 24
The Really Useful Group, 26
Rentrak Corporation, 35
Rhino Entertainment Company, 18
Ride, Inc., 22
Rollerblade, Inc., 34 (upd.)
Royal Caribbean Cruises Ltd., 22
Rush Communications, 33
S-K-I Limited, 15
Salomon Worldwide, 20
Santa Fe Gaming Corporation, 19
Schwinn Cycle and Fitness L.P., 19
Scottish Radio Holding plc, 41
Seattle FilmWorks, Inc., 20
Sega of America, Inc., 10
SFX Entertainment, Inc., 36
Showboat, Inc., 19
Shubert Organization Inc., 24
Six Flags Theme Parks, Inc., 17
Smithsonian Institution, 27
Sony Corporation, 40 (upd.)
Speedway Motorsports, Inc., 32
Spelling Entertainment Group, Inc., 14
The Sports Club Company, 25

Station Casinos Inc., 25
Stoll-Moss Theatres Ltd., 34
Stuart Entertainment Inc., 16
Tele-Communications, Inc., II
Television Española, S.A., 7
Thomas Cook Travel Inc., 9
The Thomson Corporation, 8
Thousand Trails, Inc., 33
THQ, Inc., 39
Ticketmaster Corp., 13
The Todd-AO Corporation, 33
Toho Co., Ltd., 28
The Topps Company, Inc., 34 (upd.)
Touristik Union International GmbH. and Company K.G., II
Toy Biz, Inc., 18
Trans World Entertainment Corporation, 24
Turner Broadcasting System, Inc., II; 6 (upd.)
Twentieth Century Fox Film Corporation, II; 25 (upd.)
Ubi Soft Entertainment S.A., 41
Universal Studios, Inc., 33
Univision Communications Inc., 24
Vail Associates, Inc., 11
Vail Resorts, Inc., 43 (upd.)
Viacom Inc., 7; 23 (upd.)
Walt Disney Company, II; 6 (upd.); 30 (upd.)
Warner Communications Inc., II
Washington Football, Inc., 35
West Coast Entertainment Corporation, 29
Wherehouse Entertainment Incorporated, 11
Wildlife Conservation Society, 31
Wilson Sporting Goods Company, 24
Wizards of the Coast Inc., 24
World Wrestling Federation Entertainment, Inc., 32
YankeeNets LLC, 35
YES! Entertainment Corporation, 26
YMCA of the USA, 31
Young Broadcasting Inc., 40

FINANCIAL SERVICES: BANKS

Abbey National plc, 10; 39 (upd.)
Abigail Adams National Bancorp, Inc., 23
Algemene Bank Nederland N.V., II
Allied Irish Banks, plc, 16; 43 (upd.)
American Residential Mortgage Corporation, 8
AmSouth Bancorporation, 12
Amsterdam-Rotterdam Bank N.V., II
Anchor Bancorp, Inc., 10
Australia and New Zealand Banking Group Ltd., II
Banc One Corporation, 10
Banca Commerciale Italiana SpA, II
Banco Bilbao Vizcaya, S.A., II
Banco Bradesco S.A., 13
Banco Central, II
Banco do Brasil S.A., II
Banco Espírito Santo e Comercial de Lisboa S.A., 15
Banco Itaú S.A., 19
Banco Santander Central Hispano S.A., 36 (upd.)
Bank Austria AG, 23
Bank Brussels Lambert, II
Bank Hapoalim B.M., II
Bank of Boston Corporation, II
Bank of Mississippi, Inc., 14
Bank of Montreal, II
Bank of New England Corporation, II
The Bank of New York Company, Inc., II
The Bank of Nova Scotia, II
Bank of Tokyo, Ltd., II
Bank of Tokyo-Mitsubishi Ltd., 15 (upd.)
Bank One Corporation, 36 (upd.)
BankAmerica Corporation, II; 8 (upd.)
Bankers Trust New York Corporation, II
Banque Nationale de Paris S.A., II
Barclays PLC, II; 20 (upd.)
BarclaysAmerican Mortgage Corporation, 11
Barings PLC, 14
Barnett Banks, Inc., 9
BayBanks, Inc., 12
Bayerische Hypotheken- und Wechsel-Bank AG, II
Bayerische Vereinsbank A.G., II
Beneficial Corporation, 8
BNP Paribas Group, 36 (upd.)
Boatmen's Bancshares Inc., 15
Canadian Imperial Bank of Commerce, II
Carolina First Corporation, 31
Casco Northern Bank, 14
The Chase Manhattan Corporation, II; 13 (upd.)
Chemical Banking Corporation, II; 14 (upd.)
Citicorp, II; 9 (upd.)
Citigroup Inc., 30 (upd.)
Citizens Financial Group, Inc., 42
Close Brothers Group plc, 39
Commercial Credit Company, 8
Commercial Federal Corporation, 12
Commerzbank A.G., II
Compagnie Financiere de Paribas, II
Continental Bank Corporation, II
CoreStates Financial Corp, 17
Countrywide Credit Industries, Inc., 16
Crédit Agricole, II
Crédit Lyonnais, 9; 33 (upd.)
Crédit National S.A., 9
Credit Suisse Group, II; 21 (upd.)
Credito Italiano, II
Cullen/Frost Bankers, Inc., 25
The Dai-Ichi Kangyo Bank Ltd., II
The Daiwa Bank, Ltd., II; 39 (upd.)
Dauphin Deposit Corporation, 14
Deposit Guaranty Corporation, 17
Deutsche Bank AG, II; 14 (upd.); 40 (upd.)
Dexia Group, 42
Dime Savings Bank of New York, F.S.B., 9
Donaldson, Lufkin & Jenrette, Inc., 22
Dresdner Bank A.G., II
Fifth Third Bancorp, 13; 31 (upd.)
First Bank System Inc., 12
First Chicago Corporation, II
First Commerce Bancshares, Inc., 15
First Commerce Corporation, 11
First Empire State Corporation, 11
First Fidelity Bank, N.A., New Jersey, 9
First Hawaiian, Inc., 11
First Interstate Bancorp, II
First Nationwide Bank, 14
First of America Bank Corporation, 8
First Security Corporation, 11
First Tennessee National Corporation, 11
First Union Corporation, 10
First Virginia Banks, Inc., 11
Firstar Corporation, 11; 33 (upd.)
Fleet Financial Group, Inc., 9
FleetBoston Financial Corporation, 36 (upd.)
Fourth Financial Corporation, 11
The Fuji Bank, Ltd., II
Generale Bank, II
German American Bancorp, 41
Glacier Bancorp, Inc., 35
The Governor and Company of the Bank of Scotland, 10
Grameen Bank, 31
Granite State Bankshares, Inc., 37
Great Lakes Bancorp, 8
Great Western Financial Corporation, 10
GreenPoint Financial Corp., 28
Grupo Financiero Serfin, S.A., 19
H.F. Ahmanson & Company, II; 10 (upd.)
Habersham Bancorp, 25
Hancock Holding Company, 15
Hibernia Corporation, 37
The Hongkong and Shanghai Banking Corporation Limited, II
HSBC Holdings plc, 12; 26 (upd.)
Hudson River Bancorp, Inc., 41
Huntington Bancshares Inc., 11
IBERIABANK Corporation, 37
The Industrial Bank of Japan, Ltd., II
J Sainsbury plc, 38 (upd.)
J.P. Morgan & Co. Incorporated, II; 30 (upd.)
J.P. Morgan Chase & Co., 38 (upd.)
Japan Leasing Corporation, 8
Kansallis-Osake-Pankki, II
KeyCorp, 8
Kredietbank N.V., II
Kreditanstalt für Wiederaufbau, 29
Lloyds Bank PLC, II
Long Island Bancorp, Inc., 16
Long-Term Credit Bank of Japan, Ltd., II
Manufacturers Hanover Corporation, II
MBNA Corporation, 12
Mellon Bank Corporation, II
Mercantile Bankshares Corp., 11
Meridian Bancorp, Inc., 11
Metropolitan Financial Corporation, 13
Michigan National Corporation, 11
Midland Bank PLC, II; 17 (upd.)
The Mitsubishi Bank, Ltd., II
The Mitsubishi Trust & Banking Corporation, II
The Mitsui Bank, Ltd., II
The Mitsui Trust & Banking Company, Ltd., II
N M Rothschild & Sons Limited, 39
National Bank of Greece, 41
National City Corp., 15
National Westminster Bank PLC, II
NationsBank Corporation, 10
NBD Bancorp, Inc., 11
NCNB Corporation, II
Nippon Credit Bank, II
Nordea AB, 40
Norinchukin Bank, II
Northern Rock plc, 33
Northern Trust Company, 9
NVR L.P., 8
Old Kent Financial Corp., 11
Old National Bancorp, 15
PNC Bank Corp., 13 (upd.)
PNC Financial Corporation, II
Popular, Inc., 41
Pulte Corporation, 8
Rabobank Group, 33
Republic New York Corporation, 11
Riggs National Corporation, 13
The Royal Bank of Canada, II; 21 (upd.)
The Royal Bank of Scotland Group plc, 12; 38 (upd.)
The Ryland Group, Inc., 8
St. Paul Bank for Cooperatives, 8
The Sanwa Bank, Ltd., II; 15 (upd.)
SBC Warburg, 14
Seattle First National Bank Inc., 8
Security Capital Corporation, 17
Security Pacific Corporation, II
Shawmut National Corporation, 13
Signet Banking Corporation, 11
Singer & Friedlander Group plc, 41
Skandinaviska Enskilda Banken, II

Société Générale, II; 42 (upd.)
Society Corporation, 9
Southtrust Corporation, 11
Standard Chartered PLC, II
Standard Federal Bank, 9
Star Banc Corporation, 11
State Street Boston Corporation, 8
Staten Island Bancorp, Inc., 39
The Sumitomo Bank, Limited, II; 26 (upd.)
The Sumitomo Trust & Banking Company, Ltd., II
The Summit Bancorporation, 14
SunTrust Banks Inc., 23
Svenska Handelsbanken, II
Swiss Bank Corporation, II
Synovus Financial Corp., 12
The Taiyo Kobe Bank, Ltd., II
The Tokai Bank, Limited, II; 15 (upd.)
The Toronto-Dominion Bank, II
TSB Group plc, 12
U.S. Bancorp, 14; 36 (upd.)
U.S. Trust Corp., 17
Union Bank of California, 16
Union Bank of Switzerland, II
Wachovia Bank of Georgia, N.A., 16
Wachovia Bank of South Carolina, N.A., 16
Wachovia Corporation, 12
Washington Mutual, Inc., 17
Wells Fargo & Company, II; 12 (upd.); 38 (upd.)
West One Bancorp, 11
Westamerica Bancorporation, 17
Westdeutsche Landesbank Girozentrale, II
Westpac Banking Corporation, II
Whitney Holding Corporation, 21
Wilmington Trust Corporation, 25
The Woolwich plc, 30
World Bank Group, 33
The Yasuda Trust and Banking Company, Ltd., II; 17 (upd.)
Zions Bancorporation, 12

FINANCIAL SERVICES: NON-BANKS

A.G. Edwards, Inc., 8; 32 (upd.)
ACE Cash Express, Inc., 33
ADVANTA Corp., 8
Advanta Corporation, 38 (upd.)
American Express Company, II; 10 (upd.); 38 (upd.)
American General Finance Corp., 11
Ameritrade Holding Corporation, 34
Arthur Andersen & Company, Société Coopérative, 10
Avco Financial Services Inc., 13
Bear Stearns Companies, Inc., II; 10 (upd.)
Bill & Melinda Gates Foundation, 41
Bozzuto's, Inc., 13
Carnegie Corporation of New York, 35
Cash America International, Inc., 20
Cetelem S.A., 21
The Charles Schwab Corporation, 8; 26 (upd.)
Citfed Bancorp, Inc., 16
Comerica Incorporated, 40
Commercial Financial Services, Inc., 26
Coopers & Lybrand, 9
Cramer, Berkowitz & Co., 34
Credit Acceptance Corporation, 18
CS First Boston Inc., II
Dain Rauscher Corporation, 35 (upd.)
Daiwa Securities Company, Limited, II
Datek Online Holdings Corp., 32
The David and Lucile Packard Foundation, 41
Dean Witter, Discover & Co., 12
Dow Jones Telerate, Inc., 10
Drexel Burnham Lambert Incorporated, II
E*Trade Group, Inc., 20
Eaton Vance Corporation, 18
Edward Jones, 30
Euronext Paris S.A., 37
Fair, Isaac and Company, 18
Federal National Mortgage Association, II
Fidelity Investments Inc., II; 14 (upd.)
First Albany Companies Inc., 37
First Data Corporation, 30 (upd.)
First USA, Inc., 11
FMR Corp., 8; 32 (upd.)
Forstmann Little & Co., 38
Fortis, Inc., 15
Franklin Resources, Inc., 9
Gabelli Asset Management Inc., 30
Goldman, Sachs & Co., II; 20 (upd.)
Grede Foundries, Inc., 38
Green Tree Financial Corporation, 11
Gruntal & Co., L.L.C., 20
H & R Block, Incorporated, 9; 29 (upd.)
Hoenig Group Inc., 41
Household International, Inc., II; 21 (upd.)
Instinet Corporation, 34
Inter-Regional Financial Group, Inc., 15
Istituto per la Ricostruzione Industriale S.p.A., 11
JB Oxford Holdings, Inc., 32
Jefferies Group, Inc., 25
John Hancock Financial Services, Inc., 42 (upd.)
The John Nuveen Company, 21
Kansas City Southern Industries, Inc., 26 (upd.)
Kleinwort Benson Group PLC, II
Kohlberg Kravis Roberts & Co., 24
KPMG Worldwide, 10
LaBranche & Co. Inc., 37
Lazard LLC, 38
Legg Mason, Inc., 33
London Stock Exchange Limited, 34
MacAndrews & Forbes Holdings Inc., 28
MasterCard International, Inc., 9
MBNA Corporation, 33 (upd.)
Merrill Lynch & Co., Inc., II; 13 (upd.); 40 (upd.)
Morgan Grenfell Group PLC, II
Morgan Stanley Dean Witter & Company, 33 (upd.)
Morgan Stanley Group Inc., II; 16 (upd.)
Mountain States Mortgage Centers, Inc., 29
National Association of Securities Dealers, Inc., 10
National Auto Credit, Inc., 16
National Discount Brokers Group, Inc., 28
Navy Federal Credit Union, 33
New Street Capital Inc., 8
New York Stock Exchange, Inc., 9; 39 (upd.)
The Nikko Securities Company Limited, II; 9 (upd.)
Nippon Shinpan Company, Ltd., II
Nomura Securities Company, Limited, II; 9 (upd.)
Orix Corporation, II
PaineWebber Group Inc., II; 22 (upd.)
The Pew Charitable Trusts, 35
Piper Jaffray Companies Inc., 22
The Prudential Insurance Company of America, 30 (upd.)
The Quick & Reilly Group, Inc., 20
Resource America, Inc., 42
Safeguard Scientifics, Inc., 10
Salomon Inc., II; 13 (upd.)
SBC Warburg, 14
Schroders plc, 42
Shearson Lehman Brothers Holdings Inc., II; 9 (upd.)
Siebert Financial Corp., 32
SLM Holding Corp., 25 (upd.)
Smith Barney Inc., 15
Soros Fund Management LLC, 28
State Street Boston Corporation, 8
Student Loan Marketing Association, II
T. Rowe Price Associates, Inc., 11; 34 (upd.)
Texas Pacific Group Inc., 36
Total System Services, Inc., 18
Trilon Financial Corporation, II
United Jewish Communities, 33
The Vanguard Group of Investment Companies, 14
The Vanguard Group, Inc., 34 (upd.)
VeriFone, Inc., 18
Visa International, 9; 26 (upd.)
Waddell & Reed, Inc., 22
Washington Federal, Inc., 17
Waterhouse Investor Services, Inc., 18
Watson Wyatt Worldwide, 42
Working Assets Funding Service, 43
Yamaichi Securities Company, Limited, II
The Ziegler Companies, Inc., 24
Zurich Financial Services, 42 (upd.)

FOOD PRODUCTS

Agway, Inc., 7
Ajinomoto Co., Inc., II; 28 (upd.)
The Albert Fisher Group plc, 41
Alberto-Culver Company, 8
Aldi Group, 13
Alpine Lace Brands, Inc., 18
American Crystal Sugar Company, 11; 32 (upd.)
American Foods Group, 43
American Italian Pasta Company, 27
American Maize-Products Co., 14
American Rice, Inc., 33
Amfac/JMB Hawaii L.L.C., 24 (upd.)
Archer-Daniels-Midland Company, 32 (upd.)
Archway Cookies, Inc., 29
Associated British Foods plc, II; 13 (upd.); 41 (upd.)
Associated Milk Producers, Inc., 11
Aurora Foods Inc., 32
B&G Foods, Inc., 40
The B. Manischewitz Company, LLC, 31
Balance Bar Company, 32
Baltek Corporation, 34
Barilla G. e R. Fratelli S.p.A., 17
Bear Creek Corporation, 38
Beatrice Company, II
Beech-Nut Nutrition Corporation, 21
Ben & Jerry's Homemade, Inc., 10; 35
Besnier SA, 19
Bestfoods, 22 (upd.)
Blue Bell Creameries L.P., 30
Blue Diamond Growers, 28
Bongrain SA, 25
Booker PLC, 13; 31 (upd.)
Borden, Inc., II; 22 (upd.)
Brach and Brock Confections, Inc., 15
Bridgford Foods Corporation, 27
Brothers Gourmet Coffees, Inc., 20
Broughton Foods Co., 17
Brown & Haley, 23
Bruce Foods Corporation, 39
BSN Groupe S.A., II
Burger King Corporation, 17 (upd.)
Bush Boake Allen Inc., 30
C.H. Robinson Worldwide, Inc., 40 (upd.)
Cadbury Schweppes PLC, II
Cagle's, Inc., 20

Calcot Ltd., 33
Campbell Soup Company, II; 7 (upd.); 26 (upd.)
Canada Packers Inc., II
Cargill Inc., 13 (upd.)
Carnation Company, II
Carvel Corporation, 35
Castle & Cooke, Inc., II; 20 (upd.)
Cattleman's, Inc., 20
Celestial Seasonings, Inc., 16
Central Soya Company, Inc., 7
Chelsea Milling Company, 29
Chicken of the Sea International, 24 (upd.)
Chiquita Brands International, Inc., 7; 21 (upd.)
Chock Full o'Nuts Corp., 17
Chocoladefabriken Lindt & Sprüngli AG, 27
Chupa Chups S.A., 38
The Clorox Company, 22 (upd.)
Coca-Cola Enterprises, Inc., 13
ConAgra Foods, Inc., 42 (upd.)
Conagra, Inc., II; 12 (upd.)
The Connell Company, 29
ContiGroup Companies, Inc., 43 (upd.)
Continental Grain Company, 10; 13 (upd.)
CoolBrands International Inc., 35
CPC International Inc., II
Cranswick plc, 40
Cumberland Packing Corporation, 26
Curtice-Burns Foods, Inc., 7; 21 (upd.)
Czarnikow-Rionda Company, Inc., 32
Dairy Crest Group plc, 32
Dalgery, PLC, II
Dannon Co., Inc., 14
Darigold, Inc., 9
Dawn Food Products, Inc., 17
Dean Foods Company, 7; 21 (upd.)
DeKalb Genetics Corporation, 17
Del Monte Corporation, 7
Del Monte Foods Company, 23 (upd.)
Di Giorgio Corp., 12
Diageo plc, 24 (upd.)
Dole Food Company, Inc., 9; 31 (upd.)
Domino Sugar Corporation, 26
Doskocil Companies, Inc., 12
Dreyer's Grand Ice Cream, Inc., 17
The Earthgrains Company, 36
Emge Packing Co., Inc., 11
Eridania Béghin-Say S.A., 36
ERLY Industries Inc., 17
Eskimo Pie Corporation, 21
Farmland Foods, Inc., 7
Fieldale Farms Corporation, 23
Fleer Corporation, 15
Fleury Michon S.A., 39
Florida Crystals Inc., 35
Flowers Industries, Inc., 12; 35 (upd.)
FoodBrands America, Inc., 23
Foster Poultry Farms, 32
Fresh America Corporation, 20
Fresh Foods, Inc., 29
Frito-Lay Company, 32
Fromageries Bel, 23
Fyffes Plc, 38
Gardenburger, Inc., 33
Geest Plc, 38
General Mills, Inc., II; 10 (upd.); 36 (upd.)
George A. Hormel and Company, II
George Weston Limited, 36 (upd.)
Gerber Products Company, 7; 21 (upd.)
Ghirardelli Chocolate Company, 30
Givaudan SA, 43
Gold Kist Inc., 17; 26 (upd.)
Golden Enterprises, Inc., 26
Gonnella Baking Company, 40
Good Humor-Breyers Ice Cream Company, 14
GoodMark Foods, Inc., 26
Gorton's, 13
Goya Foods Inc., 22
Grist Mill Company, 15
Groupe Danone, 32 (upd.)
Gruma, S.A. de C.V., 31
Grupo Herdez, S.A. de C.V., 35
H.J. Heinz Company, II; 11 (upd.); 36 (upd.)
The Hain Celestial Group, Inc., 43 (upd.)
Hain Food Group, Inc., 27
Hanover Foods Corporation, 35
The Hartz Mountain Corporation, 12
Hazlewood Foods plc, 32
Herman Goelitz, Inc., 28
Hershey Foods Corporation, II; 15 (upd.)
Hill's Pet Nutrition, Inc., 27
Hillsdown Holdings plc, II; 24 (upd.)
Horizon Organic Holding Corporation, 37
Hormel Foods Corporation, 18 (upd.)
Hudson Foods Inc., 13
Hunt-Wesson, Inc., 17
Iams Company, 26
IBP, Inc., II; 21 (upd.)
Iceland Group plc, 33
Imperial Holly Corporation, 12
Imperial Sugar Company, 32 (upd.)
Industrias Bachoco, S.A. de C.V., 39
International Multifoods Corporation, 7; 25 (upd.)
Interstate Bakeries Corporation, 12; 38 (upd.)
Itoham Foods Inc., II
J & J Snack Foods Corporation, 24
The J.M. Smucker Company, 11
J.R. Simplot Company, 16
Jacobs Suchard A.G., II
Jim Beam Brands Co., 14
John B. Sanfilippo & Son, Inc., 14
Just Born, Inc., 32
Kal Kan Foods, Inc., 22
Keebler Foods Company, 36
Kellogg Company, II; 13 (upd.)
Kerry Group plc, 27
Kikkoman Corporation, 14
The King Arthur Flour Company, 31
King Ranch, Inc., 14
Koninklijke Wessanen N.V., II
Kraft General Foods Inc., II; 7 (upd.)
Kraft Jacobs Suchard AG, 26 (upd.)
Krispy Kreme Doughnut Corporation, 21
La Choy Food Products Inc., 25
Lamb Weston, Inc., 23
Lance, Inc., 14; 41 (upd.)
Land O'Lakes, Inc., II; 21 (upd.)
Leprino Foods Company, 28
Lincoln Snacks Company, 24
Malt-O-Meal Company, 22
Maple Leaf Foods Inc., 41
Mars, Incorporated, 7; 40 (upd.)
Maui Land & Pineapple Company, Inc., 29
McCormick & Company, Incorporated, 7; 27 (upd.)
McIlhenny Company, 20
McKee Foods Corporation, 7; 27 (upd.)
Meiji Milk Products Company, Limited, II
Meiji Seika Kaisha, Ltd., II
Michael Foods, Inc., 25
Mid-America Dairymen, Inc., 7
Mike-Sell's Inc., 15
Monfort, Inc., 13
Mrs. Baird's Bakeries, 29
Murphy Family Farms Inc., 22
Nabisco Foods Group, II; 7 (upd.)
Nantucket Allserve, Inc., 22
Nathan's Famous, Inc., 29
National Presto Industries, Inc., 43 (upd.)
National Sea Products Ltd., 14
Nestlé S.A., II; 7 (upd.); 28 (upd.)
New England Confectionery Co., 15
Newhall Land and Farming Company, 14
Newman's Own, Inc., 37
Nippon Meat Packers, Inc., II
Nippon Suisan Kaisha, Limited, II
Nisshin Flour Milling Company, Ltd., II
Northern Foods PLC, 10
Northland Cranberries, Inc., 38
Nutraceutical International Corporation, 37
NutraSweet Company, 8
Ocean Spray Cranberries, Inc., 7; 25 (upd.)
Ore-Ida Foods Incorporated, 13
Oscar Mayer Foods Corp., 12
Otis Spunkmeyer, Inc., 28
Papetti's Hygrade Egg Products, Inc., 39
PepsiCo, Inc., 38 (upd.)
Perdue Farms Inc., 7; 23 (upd.)
Pet Incorporated, 7
Pez Candy, Inc., 38
Philip Morris Companies Inc., 18 (upd.)
PIC International Group PLC, 24 (upd.)
Pilgrim's Pride Corporation, 7; 23 (upd.)
Pillsbury Company, II; 13 (upd.)
Pioneer Hi-Bred International, Inc., 9
Premium Standard Farms, Inc., 30
The Procter & Gamble Company, III; 8 (upd.); 26 (upd.)
Purina Mills, Inc., 32
Quaker Oats Company, II; 12 (upd.); 34 (upd.)
Ralston Purina Company, II; 13 (upd.)
Ranks Hovis McDougall Limited, II; 28 (upd.)
Reckitt & Colman PLC, II
Reckitt Benckiser plc, 42 (upd.)
Rica Foods, Inc., 41
Rich Products Corporation, 7; 38 (upd.)
Riviana Foods Inc., 27
Roland Murten A.G., 7
Rowntree Mackintosh, II
Royal Numico N.V., 37
Russell Stover Candies Inc., 12
Sanderson Farms, Inc., 15
Sara Lee Corporation, II; 15 (upd.)
Savannah Foods & Industries, Inc., 7
Schlotzsky's, Inc., 36
Schwan's Sales Enterprises, Inc., 7
See's Candies, Inc., 30
Seminis, Inc., 29
Smithfield Foods, Inc., 7; 43 (upd.)
Snow Brand Milk Products Company, Limited, II
Sodiaal S.A., 36 (upd.)
SODIMA, II
Sorrento, Inc., 24
Stock Yards Packing Co., Inc., 37
Stolt-Nielsen S.A., 42
Stouffer Corp., 8
Südzucker AG, 27
Suiza Foods Corporation, 26
Sun-Diamond Growers of California, 7
Sunkist Growers, Inc., 26
Supervalu Inc., 18 (upd.)
Suprema Specialties, Inc., 27
Sylvan, Inc., 22
Taiyo Fishery Company, Limited, II
Tasty Baking Company, 14; 35 (upd.)
Tate & Lyle PLC, II; 42 (upd.)
TCBY Enterprises Inc., 17
Thomas J. Lipton Company, 14
Thorn Apple Valley, Inc., 7; 22 (upd.)
TLC Beatrice International Holdings, Inc., 22
Tombstone Pizza Corporation, 13
Tone Brothers, Inc., 21
Tootsie Roll Industries Inc., 12
Tri Valley Growers, 32

Tropicana Products, Inc., 28
Tyson Foods, Incorporated, II; 14 (upd.)
U.S. Foodservice, 26
Uncle Ben's Inc., 22
Unigate PLC, II; 28 (upd.)
United Biscuits (Holdings) plc, II; 42 (upd.)
United Brands Company, II
United Foods, Inc., 21
Universal Foods Corporation, 7
Van Camp Seafood Company, Inc., 7
Vienna Sausage Manufacturing Co., 14
Vlasic Foods International Inc., 25
Wattie's Ltd., 7
Wells' Dairy, Inc., 36
White Wave, 43
Wisconsin Dairies, 7
WLR Foods, Inc., 21
Wm. Wrigley Jr. Company, 7
World's Finest Chocolate Inc., 39
Worthington Foods, Inc., 14

FOOD SERVICES & RETAILERS

Advantica Restaurant Group, Inc., 27 (upd.)
AFC Enterprises, Inc., 32 (upd.)
Albertson's Inc., II; 7 (upd.); 30 (upd.)
Aldi Group, 13
Alex Lee Inc., 18
All Nippon Airways Co., Ltd., 38 (upd.)
America's Favorite Chicken Company, Inc., 7
American Stores Company, II
Applebee's International, Inc., 14; 35 (upd.)
ARA Services, II
Arby's Inc., 14
Arden Group, Inc., 29
Argyll Group PLC, II
Ark Restaurants Corp., 20
Asahi Breweries, Ltd., 20 (upd.)
Asda Group PLC, II
ASDA Group plc, 28 (upd.)
Associated Grocers, Incorporated, 9; 31 (upd.)
Association des Centres Distributeurs E. Leclerc, 37
Au Bon Pain Co., Inc., 18
Auchan, 37
Auntie Anne's, Inc., 35
Avado Brands, Inc., 31
Back Bay Restaurant Group, Inc., 20
Bashas' Inc., 33
Bear Creek Corporation, 38
Benihana, Inc., 18
Big Bear Stores Co., 13
Big V Supermarkets, Inc., 25
Blimpie International, Inc., 15
Bob Evans Farms, Inc., 9
Boston Chicken, Inc., 12
Brinker International, Inc., 10; 38 (upd.)
Brookshire Grocery Company, 16
Bruno's, Inc., 7; 26 (upd.)
Buca, Inc., 38
Buffets, Inc., 10; 32 (upd.)
Burger King Corporation, II
C.H. Robinson, Inc., 11
California Pizza Kitchen Inc., 15
Cargill, Inc., II
Caribou Coffee Company, Inc., 28
Carlson Companies, Inc., 22 (upd.)
Carr-Gottstein Foods Co., 17
Casey's General Stores, Inc., 19
CBRL Group, Inc., 35 (upd.)
CEC Entertainment, Inc., 31 (upd.)
Chart House Enterprises, Inc., 17
Checkers Drive-Up Restaurants Inc., 16
The Cheesecake Factory Inc., 17
Chi-Chi's Inc., 13
Chick-fil-A Inc., 23
Cinnabon Inc., 23
The Circle K Corporation, II
CKE Restaurants, Inc., 19
Coborn's, Inc., 30
Compass Group PLC, 34
Comptoirs Modernes S.A., 19
Consolidated Products Inc., 14
Controladora Comercial Mexicana, S.A. de C.V., 36
The Cooker Restaurant Corporation, 20
The Copps Corporation, 32
Cracker Barrel Old Country Store, Inc., 10
D'Agostino Supermarkets Inc., 19
Dairy Mart Convenience Stores, Inc., 7; 25 (upd.)
Darden Restaurants, Inc., 16
Dean & DeLuca, Inc., 36
DeMoulas / Market Basket Inc., 23
DenAmerica Corporation, 29
Diedrich Coffee, Inc., 40
Domino's Pizza, Inc., 7; 21 (upd.)
Eateries, Inc., 33
Edeka Zentrale A.G., II
Einstein/Noah Bagel Corporation, 29
El Chico Restaurants, Inc., 19
Elmer's Restaurants, Inc., 42
Embers America Restaurants, 30
Etablissements Economiques du Casino Guichard, Perrachon et Cie, S.C.A., 12
Famous Dave's of America, Inc., 40
Fazoli's Systems, Inc., 27
Flagstar Companies, Inc., 10
Fleming Companies, Inc., II
Food Lion, Inc., II; 15 (upd.)
Foodarama Supermarkets, Inc., 28
Foodmaker, Inc., 14
The Fred W. Albrecht Grocery Co., 13
Fresh Choice, Inc., 20
Fresh Foods, Inc., 29
Friendly Ice Cream Corp., 30
Frisch's Restaurants, Inc., 35
Fuller Smith & Turner P.L.C., 38
Furr's Supermarkets, Inc., 28
Garden Fresh Restaurant Corporation, 31
The Gateway Corporation Ltd., II
Genuardi's Family Markets, Inc., 35
George Weston Limited, II; 36 (upd.)
Ghirardelli Chocolate Company, 30
Giant Food Inc., II; 22 (upd.)
Godfather's Pizza Incorporated, 25
Golden Corral Corporation, 10
Golden State Foods Corporation, 32
The Golub Corporation, 26
Gordon Food Service Inc., 8; 39 (upd.)
The Grand Union Company, 7; 28 (upd.)
The Great Atlantic & Pacific Tea Company, Inc., II; 16 (upd.)
Gristede's Sloan's, Inc., 31
Ground Round, Inc., 21
Groupe Promodès S.A., 19
Guyenne et Gascogne, 23
H.E. Butt Grocery Co., 13; 32 (upd.)
Haggen Inc., 38
Hannaford Bros. Co., 12
Hard Rock Cafe International, Inc., 12
Harris Teeter Inc., 23
Harry's Farmers Market Inc., 23
Hickory Farms, Inc., 17
Holberg Industries, Inc., 36
Hooters of America, Inc., 18
Hughes Markets, Inc., 22
Hungry Howie's Pizza and Subs, Inc., 25
Hy-Vee, Inc., 36
ICA AB, II
Iceland Group plc, 33
IHOP Corporation, 17
Il Fornaio (America) Corporation, 27
In-N-Out Burger, 19
Ingles Markets, Inc., 20
Inserra Supermarkets, 25
International Dairy Queen, Inc., 10; 39 (upd.)
ITM Entreprises SA, 36
Ito-Yokado Co., Ltd., 42 (upd.)
J Sainsbury plc, II; 13 (upd.); 38 (upd.)
JD Wetherspoon plc, 30
Jerry's Famous Deli Inc., 24
Jitney-Jungle Stores of America, Inc., 27
John Lewis Partnership plc, 42 (upd.)
Johnny Rockets Group, Inc., 31
KFC Corporation, 7; 21 (upd.)
King Kullen Grocery Co., Inc., 15
Koninklijke Ahold N.V. (Royal Ahold), II; 16 (upd.)
Koo Koo Roo, Inc., 25
The Kroger Company, II; 15 (upd.)
The Krystal Company, 33
Kwik Save Group plc, 11
La Madeleine French Bakery & Café, 33
Landry's Seafood Restaurants, Inc., 15
Leeann Chin, Inc., 30
Levy Restaurants L.P., 26
Little Caesar Enterprises, Inc., 24 (upd.)
Little Caesars International, Inc., 7
Loblaw Companies Limited, 43
Logan's Roadhouse, Inc., 29
Long John Silver's Restaurants Inc., 13
Luby's Cafeteria's, Inc., 17
Luby's, Inc., 42 (upd.)
Lucky Stores, Inc., 27
Lund Food Holdings, Inc., 22
Marie Callender's Restaurant & Bakery, Inc., 28
Marsh Supermarkets, Inc., 17
Max & Erma's Restaurants Inc., 19
McDonald's Corporation, II; 7 (upd.); 26 (upd.)
Megafoods Stores Inc., 13
Meijer Incorporated, 7
Metromedia Companies, 14
Mexican Restaurants, Inc., 41
The Middleby Corporation, 22
Minyard Food Stores, Inc., 33
MITROPA AG, 37
Morrison Restaurants Inc., 11
Morton's Restaurant Group, Inc., 30
Mrs. Fields' Original Cookies, Inc., 27
Nash Finch Company, 8; 23 (upd.)
Nathan's Famous, Inc., 29
National Convenience Stores Incorporated, 7
New York Restaurant Group, Inc., 32
Noble Roman's Inc., 14
NPC International, Inc., 40
O'Charley's Inc., 19
Old Spaghetti Factory International Inc., 24
The Oshawa Group Limited, II
Outback Steakhouse, Inc., 12; 34 (upd.)
P&C Foods Inc., 8
P.F. Chang's China Bistro, Inc., 37
Panda Management Company, Inc., 35
Papa John's International, Inc., 15
Pathmark Stores, Inc., 23
Peapod, Inc., 30
Penn Traffic Company, 13
Performance Food Group Company, 31
Perkins Family Restaurants, L.P., 22
Piccadilly Cafeterias, Inc., 19
Piggly Wiggly Southern, Inc., 13
Pizza Hut Inc., 7; 21 (upd.)
Planet Hollywood International, Inc., 18; 41 (upd.)
Players International, Inc., 22

Ponderosa Steakhouse, 15
Provigo Inc., II
Publix Super Markets Inc., 31 (upd.)
Publix Supermarkets Inc., 7
Quality Dining, Inc., 18
Quality Food Centers, Inc., 17
The Quizno's Corporation, 42
Rally's Hamburgers, Inc., 25
Ralphs Grocery Company, 35
Randall's Food Markets, Inc., 40
Rare Hospitality International Inc., 19
Restaurants Unlimited, Inc., 13
Richfood Holdings, Inc., 7
The Riese Organization, 38
Riser Foods, Inc., 9
Roadhouse Grill, Inc., 22
Rock Bottom Restaurants, Inc., 25
Rubio's Restaurants, Inc., 35
Ruby Tuesday, Inc., 18
Ruth's Chris Steak House, 28
Ryan's Family Steak Houses, Inc., 15
Safeway Inc., 24 (upd.)
Safeway Stores Incorporated, II
Santa Barbara Restaurant Group, Inc., 37
Sbarro, Inc., 16
Schlotzsky's, Inc., 36
Schultz Sav-O Stores, Inc., 21
Schwan's Sales Enterprises, Inc., 26 (upd.)
Seaway Food Town, Inc., 15
Second Harvest, 29
See's Candies, Inc., 30
Seneca Foods Corporation, 17
Service America Corp., 7
Shells Seafood Restaurants, Inc., 43
Shoney's, Inc., 7; 23 (upd.)
ShowBiz Pizza Time, Inc., 13
Smart & Final, Inc., 16
Smith's Food & Drug Centers, Inc., 8
Sodexho Alliance SA, 29
Sonic Corporation, 14; 37 (upd.)
The Southland Corporation, II; 7 (upd.)
Spaghetti Warehouse, Inc., 25
SPAR Handels AG, 35
Spartan Stores Inc., 8
The Steak n Shake Company, 41
Steinberg Incorporated, II
The Stop & Shop Companies, Inc., II
Subway, 32
Super Food Services, Inc., 15
Super Valu Stores, Inc., II
Supermarkets General Holdings Corporation, II
Supervalu Inc., 18 (upd.)
SYSCO Corporation, II; 24 (upd.)
Taco Bell Corp., 7; 21 (upd.)
Taco Cabana, Inc., 23
Taco John's International Inc., 15
TelePizza S.A., 33
Tesco PLC, II
Trader Joe's Co., 13
Travel Ports of America, Inc., 17
Tree of Life, Inc., 29
Triarc Companies, Inc., 34 (upd.)
Tumbleweed, Inc., 33
TW Services, Inc., II
Ukrop's Super Market's, Inc., 39
Unique Casual Restaurants, Inc., 27
United Natural Foods, Inc., 32
Uno Restaurant Corporation, 18
Vail Resorts, Inc., 43 (upd.)
VICORP Restaurants, Inc., 12
Village Super Market, Inc., 7
The Vons Companies, Incorporated, 7; 28 (upd.)
Waffle House Inc., 14
Wakefern Food Corporation, 33
Waldbaum, Inc., 19
Wall Street Deli, Inc., 33
Wawa Inc., 17
Wegmans Food Markets, Inc., 9; 41 (upd.)
Weis Markets, Inc., 15
Wendy's International, Inc., 8; 23 (upd.)
Wetterau Incorporated, II
White Castle System, Inc., 12; 36 (upd.)
White Rose, Inc., 24
Wild Oats Markets, Inc., 19; 41 (upd.)
Winn-Dixie Stores, Inc., II; 21 (upd.)
Wm. Morrison Supermarkets PLC, 38
The Wolfgang Puck Food Company, Inc., 26
Young & Co.'s Brewery, P.L.C., 38
Yucaipa Cos., 17

HEALTH & PERSONAL CARE PRODUCTS

Akorn, Inc., 32
Alberto-Culver Company, 8
Alco Health Services Corporation, III
Allergan, Inc., 10; 30 (upd.)
American Safety Razor Company, 20
American Stores Company, 22 (upd.)
Amway Corporation, III; 13 (upd.)
Aveda Corporation, 24
Avon Products Inc., III; 19 (upd.)
Bally Total Fitness Holding Corp., 25
Bausch & Lomb Inc., 7; 25 (upd.)
Baxter International Inc., I; 10 (upd.)
BeautiControl Cosmetics, Inc., 21
Becton, Dickinson & Company, I; 11 (upd.)
Beiersdorf AG, 29
Big B, Inc., 17
Bindley Western Industries, Inc., 9
Block Drug Company, Inc., 8; 27 (upd.)
The Boots Company PLC, 24 (upd.)
Bristol-Myers Squibb Company, III; 9 (upd.)
C.R. Bard Inc., 9
Cardinal Health, Inc., 18
Carson, Inc., 31
Carter-Wallace, Inc., 8
Chattem, Inc., 17
Chesebrough-Pond's USA, Inc., 8
Chronimed Inc., 26
The Clorox Company, III
CNS, Inc., 20
Colgate-Palmolive Company, III; 14 (upd.); 35 (upd.)
Conair Corp., 17
Cordis Corp., 19
Cosmair, Inc., 8
Coty, Inc., 36
Datascope Corporation, 39
Del Laboratories, Inc., 28
Dentsply International Inc., 10
DEP Corporation, 20
DePuy, Inc., 30
The Dial Corp., 23 (upd.)
Drackett Professional Products, 12
Elizabeth Arden Co., 8
Elizabeth Arden, Inc., 40 (upd.)
Empi, Inc., 26
Enrich International, Inc., 33
The Estée Lauder Companies Inc., 9; 30 (upd.)
Ethicon, Inc., 23
Forest Laboratories, Inc., 11
Forever Living Products International Inc., 17
French Fragrances, Inc., 22
General Nutrition Companies, Inc., 11; 29 (upd.)
Genzyme Corporation, 13
The Gillette Company, III; 20 (upd.)
Groupe Yves Saint Laurent, 23
Guerlain, 23
Guest Supply, Inc., 18
Hanger Orthopedic Group, Inc., 41
Helen of Troy Corporation, 18
Helene Curtis Industries, Inc., 8; 28 (upd.)
Henkel KGaA, III
Henry Schein, Inc., 31
Herbalife International, Inc., 17; 41 (upd.)
Inter Parfums Inc., 35
Invacare Corporation, 11
IVAX Corporation, 11
John Paul Mitchell Systems, 24
Johnson & Johnson, III; 8 (upd.); 36 (upd.)
Kao Corporation, III
Kendall International, Inc., 11
Kimberly-Clark Corporation, III; 16 (upd.); 43 (upd.)
Kyowa Hakko Kogyo Co., Ltd., III
L'Oreal, III; 8 (upd.)
Laboratoires de Biologie Végétale Yves Rocher, 35
The Lamaur Corporation, 41
Lever Brothers Company, 9
Lion Corporation, III
Luxottica SpA, 17
Mannatech Inc., 33
Mary Kay Corporation, 9; 30 (upd.)
Maxxim Medical Inc., 12
Medco Containment Services Inc., 9
Medtronic, Inc., 8
Melaleuca Inc., 31
The Mentholatum Company Inc., 32
Mentor Corporation, 26
Merck & Co., Inc., 34 (upd.)
Merit Medical Systems, Inc., 29
Nature's Sunshine Products, Inc., 15
NBTY, Inc., 31
Neutrogena Corporation, 17
New Dana Perfumes Company, 37
Nikken Global Inc., 32
Nutrition for Life International Inc., 22
OEC Medical Systems, Inc., 27
Patterson Dental Co., 19
Perrigo Company, 12
Physician Sales & Service, Inc., 14
Playtex Products, Inc., 15
The Procter & Gamble Company, III; 8 (upd.); 26 (upd.)
Revlon Group Inc., III
Revlon Inc., 17 (upd.)
Roche Biomedical Laboratories, Inc., 11
S.C. Johnson & Son, Inc., III
Safety 1st, Inc., 24
Schering-Plough Corporation, 14 (upd.)
Shaklee Corporation, 39 (upd.)
Shionogi & Co., Ltd., III
Shiseido Company, Limited, III; 22 (upd.)
Slim-Fast Nutritional Foods International, Inc., 18
Smith & Nephew plc, 17
SmithKline Beecham PLC, III
Soft Sheen Products, Inc., 31
Sunrise Medical Inc., 11
Tambrands Inc., 8
The Tranzonic Companies, 37
Turtle Wax, Inc., 15
United States Surgical Corporation, 10; 34 (upd.)
USANA, Inc., 29
Utah Medical Products, Inc., 36
VISX, Incorporated, 30
Water Pik Technologies, Inc., 34
Weider Nutrition International, Inc., 29
Wella Group, III
West Pharmaceutical Services, Inc., 42

HEALTH CARE SERVICES

Acadian Ambulance & Air Med Services, Inc., 39
Alterra Healthcare Corporation, 42
The American Cancer Society, 24
American Medical Association, 39
American Medical International, Inc., III
American Medical Response, Inc., 39
American Red Cross, 40
AmeriSource Health Corporation, 37 (upd.)
Applied Bioscience International, Inc., 10
Assisted Living Concepts, Inc., 43
Beverly Enterprises, Inc., III; 16 (upd.)
Bon Secours Health System, Inc., 24
Caremark International Inc., 10
Children's Comprehensive Services, Inc., 42
Chronimed Inc., 26
COBE Laboratories, Inc., 13
Columbia/HCA Healthcare Corporation, 15
Community Psychiatric Centers, 15
CompDent Corporation, 22
CompHealth Inc., 25
Comprehensive Care Corporation, 15
Continental Medical Systems, Inc., 10
Express Scripts Incorporated, 17
Extendicare Health Services, Inc., 6
FHP International Corporation, 6
Genesis Health Ventures, Inc., 18
GranCare, Inc., 14
Group Health Cooperative, 41
Hazelden Foundation, 28
HCA - The Healthcare Company, 35 (upd.)
Health Care & Retirement Corporation, 22
Health Risk Management, Inc., 24
Health Systems International, Inc., 11
HealthSouth Corporation, 33 (upd.)
HealthSouth Rehabilitation Corporation, 14
Highmark Inc., 27
The Hillhaven Corporation, 14
Hooper Holmes, Inc., 22
Hospital Corporation of America, III
Howard Hughes Medical Institute, 39
Humana Inc., III; 24 (upd.)
Intermountain Health Care, Inc., 27
Jenny Craig, Inc., 10; 29 (upd.)
Kinetic Concepts, Inc. (KCI), 20
Laboratory Corporation of America Holdings, 42 (upd.)
Lincare Holdings Inc., 43
Manor Care, Inc., 6; 25 (upd.)
March of Dimes, 31
Matria Healthcare, Inc., 17
Maxicare Health Plans, Inc., III; 25 (upd.)
Mayo Foundation, 9; 34 (upd.)
Merit Medical Systems, Inc., 29
National Health Laboratories Incorporated, 11
National Medical Enterprises, Inc., III
NovaCare, Inc., 11
Orthodontic Centers of America, Inc., 35
Oxford Health Plans, Inc., 16
PacifiCare Health Systems, Inc., 11
Palomar Medical Technologies, Inc., 22
Pediatric Services of America, Inc., 31
PHP Healthcare Corporation, 22
PhyCor, Inc., 36
Primedex Health Systems, Inc., 25
Quest Diagnostics Inc., 26
Ramsay Youth Services, Inc., 41
Res-Care, Inc., 29
Response Oncology, Inc., 27
Rural/Metro Corporation, 28
Sabratek Corporation, 29
St. Jude Medical, Inc., 11; 43 (upd.)
Sierra Health Services, Inc., 15
Smith & Nephew plc, 41 (upd.)
The Sports Club Company, 25
Stericycle Inc., 33
Sun Healthcare Group Inc., 25
Twinlab Corporation, 34
U.S. Healthcare, Inc., 6
Unison HealthCare Corporation, 25
United HealthCare Corporation, 9
United Way of America, 36
Universal Health Services, Inc., 6
Vencor, Inc., 16
VISX, Incorporated, 30
Vivra, Inc., 18
WellPoint Health Networks Inc., 25

HOTELS

All Nippon Airways Co., Ltd., 38 (upd.)
Amerihost Properties, Inc., 30
Aztar Corporation, 13
Bass PLC, 38 (upd.)
Boca Resorts, Inc., 37
Boyd Gaming Corporation, 43
Bristol Hotel Company, 23
The Broadmoor Hotel, 30
Caesars World, Inc., 6
Candlewood Hotel Company, Inc., 41
Carlson Companies, Inc., 22 (upd.)
Castle & Cooke, Inc., 20 (upd.)
Cedar Fair, L.P., 22
Choice Hotels International Inc., 14
Circus Circus Enterprises, Inc., 6
Club Mediterranée S.A., 6; 21 (upd.)
Doubletree Corporation, 21
Extended Stay America, Inc., 41
Fibreboard Corporation, 16
Four Seasons Hotels Inc., 9; 29 (upd.)
Fuller Smith & Turner P.L.C., 38
Gaylord Entertainment Company, 36 (upd.)
Granada Group PLC, 24 (upd.)
Grand Casinos, Inc., 20
Grand Hotel Krasnapolsky N.V., 23
Helmsley Enterprises, Inc., 9
Hilton Hotels Corporation, III; 19 (upd.)
Holiday Inns, Inc., III
Hospitality Franchise Systems, Inc., 11
Howard Johnson International, Inc., 17
Hyatt Corporation, III; 16 (upd.)
ITT Sheraton Corporation, III
JD Wetherspoon plc, 30
John Q. Hammons Hotels, Inc., 24
The La Quinta Companies, 42 (upd.)
La Quinta Inns, Inc., 11
Ladbroke Group PLC, 21 (upd.)
Mandalay Resort Group, 32 (upd.)
Manor Care, Inc., 25 (upd.)
The Marcus Corporation, 21
Marriott International, Inc., III; 21 (upd.)
Mirage Resorts, Incorporated, 6; 28 (upd.)
Motel 6 Corporation, 13
Omni Hotels Corp., 12
Park Corp., 22
Players International, Inc., 22
Preussag AG, 42 (upd.)
Promus Companies, Inc., 9
Red Roof Inns, Inc., 18
Resorts International, Inc., 12
Ritz-Carlton Hotel Company L.L.C., 9; 29 (upd.)
Santa Fe Gaming Corporation, 19
The SAS Group, 34 (upd.)
Showboat, Inc., 19
Sun International Hotels Limited, 26
Sunburst Hospitality Corporation, 26
Trusthouse Forte PLC, III
Vail Resorts, Inc., 43 (upd.)
The Walt Disney Company, 30 (upd.)
Westin Hotel Co., 9
Westin Hotels and Resorts Worldwide, 29 (upd.)
Young & Co.'s Brewery, P.L.C., 38

INFORMATION TECHNOLOGY

Acxiom Corporation, 35
Adaptec, Inc., 31
Adobe Systems Incorporated, 10; 33 (upd.)
Advanced Micro Devices, Inc., 6
Agence France-Presse, 34
Agilent Technologies Inc., 38
Aldus Corporation, 10
AltaVista Company, 43
Amdahl Corporation, III; 14 (upd.); 40 (upd.)
America Online, Inc., 10 ; 26 (upd.)
American Business Information, Inc., 18
American Management Systems, Inc., 11
American Software Inc., 25
Amstrad PLC, III
Analytic Sciences Corporation, 10
Analytical Surveys, Inc., 33
Apollo Group, Inc., 24
Apple Computer, Inc., III; 6 (upd.)
The Arbitron Company, 38
Asanté Technologies, Inc., 20
AsiaInfo Holdings, Inc., 43
ASK Group, Inc., 9
AST Research Inc., 9
At Home Corporation, 43
AT&T Bell Laboratories, Inc., 13
AT&T Corporation, 29 (upd.)
AT&T Istel Ltd., 14
Autologic Information International, Inc., 20
Automatic Data Processing, Inc., III; 9 (upd.)
Autotote Corporation, 20
Avid Technology Inc., 38
Aydin Corp., 19
Baan Company, 25
Baltimore Technologies Plc, 42
Banyan Systems Inc., 25
Battelle Memorial Institute, Inc., 10
BBN Corp., 19
BEA Systems, Inc., 36
Bell and Howell Company, 9; 29 (upd.)
Billing Concepts Corp., 26
Bloomberg L.P., 21
Boole & Babbage, Inc., 25
Booz Allen & Hamilton Inc., 10
Borland International, Inc., 9
Bowne & Co., Inc., 23
Brite Voice Systems, Inc., 20
Broderbund Software, 29 (upd.)
Broderbund Software, Inc., 13
Bull S.A., 43 (upd.)
Business Objects S.A., 25
C-Cube Microsystems, Inc., 37
CACI International Inc., 21
Cadence Design Systems, Inc., 11
Caere Corporation, 20
Cahners Business Information, 43
CalComp Inc., 13
Cambridge Technology Partners, Inc., 36
Canon Inc., III
Cap Gemini Ernst & Young, 37
Caribiner International, Inc., 24
Catalina Marketing Corporation, 18
CDW Computer Centers, Inc., 16
Cerner Corporation, 16
Cheyenne Software, Inc., 12
CHIPS and Technologies, Inc., 9
Ciber, Inc., 18
Cincom Systems Inc., 15
Cirrus Logic, Incorporated, 11
Cisco Systems, Inc., 11

Citizen Watch Co., Ltd., 21 (upd.)
Commodore International Ltd., 7
Compagnie des Machines Bull S.A., III
Compaq Computer Corporation, III; 6 (upd.); 26 (upd.)
Complete Business Solutions, Inc., 31
CompuAdd Computer Corporation, 11
CompuCom Systems, Inc., 10
CompUSA, Inc., 35 (upd.)
CompuServe Incorporated, 10
CompuServe Interactive Services, Inc., 27 (upd.)
Computer Associates International, Inc., 6
Computer Data Systems, Inc., 14
Computer Sciences Corporation, 6
Computervision Corporation, 10
Compuware Corporation, 10; 30 (upd.)
Comshare Inc., 23
Conner Peripherals, Inc., 6
Control Data Corporation, III
Control Data Systems, Inc., 10
Corbis Corporation, 31
Corel Corporation, 15; 33 (upd.)
Corporate Software Inc., 9
Cray Research, Inc., III
CTG, Inc., 11
Cybermedia, Inc., 25
Dassault Systèmes S.A., 25
Data Broadcasting Corporation, 31
Data General Corporation, 8
Datapoint Corporation, 11
Dell Computer Corp., 9
Dialogic Corporation, 18
Digital Equipment Corporation, III; 6 (upd.)
The Dun & Bradstreet Corporation, IV; 19 (upd.)
Dun & Bradstreet Software Services Inc., 11
EarthLink, Inc., 36
ECS S.A, 12
Edmark Corporation, 14; 41 (upd.)
Egghead Inc., 9
El Camino Resources International, Inc., 11
Electronic Arts Inc., 10
Electronic Data Systems Corporation, III; 28 (upd.)
Electronics for Imaging, Inc., 43 (upd.)
EMC Corporation, 12
Encore Computer Corporation, 13
Evans & Sutherland Computer Corporation, 19
Exabyte Corporation, 12
First Financial Management Corporation, 11
Fiserv Inc., 11
FlightSafety International, Inc., 9
FORE Systems, Inc., 25
Franklin Electronic Publishers, Inc., 23
FTP Software, Inc., 20
Fujitsu Limited, III; 42 (upd.)
Fujitsu-ICL Systems Inc., 11
Future Now, Inc., 12
Gartner Group, Inc., 21
Gateway 2000, Inc., 10
Gateway, Inc., 27 (upd.)
GEAC Computer Corporation Ltd., 43
Getronics NV, 39
GT Interactive Software, 31
Guthy-Renker Corporation, 32
Hewlett-Packard Company, III; 6 (upd.)
Hyperion Software Corporation, 22
ICL plc, 6
Imation Corporation, 20
Information Access Company, 17
Information Builders, Inc., 22
Information Resources, Inc., 10
Informix Corporation, 10; 30 (upd.)
Infosys Technologies Ltd., 38
Ing. C. Olivetti & C., S.p.a., III
Inso Corporation, 26
Intel Corporation, 36 (upd.)
Intelligent Electronics, Inc., 6
Intergraph Corporation, 6; 24 (upd.)
International Business Machines Corporation, III; 6 (upd.); 30 (upd.)
Intuit Inc., 14; 33 (upd.)
Iomega Corporation, 21
IONA Technologies plc, 43
J.D. Edwards & Company, 14
Jack Henry and Associates, Inc., 17
Juniper Networks, Inc., 43
Juno Online Services, Inc., 38
KLA Instruments Corporation, 11
KnowledgeWare Inc., 31 (upd.)
Komag, Inc., 11
Kronos, Inc., 18
Lam Research Corporation, 11
Lason, Inc., 31
Lawson Software, 38
The Learning Company Inc., 24
Learning Tree International Inc., 24
Legent Corporation, 10
LEXIS-NEXIS Group, 33
Logica plc, 14; 37 (upd.)
Logicon Inc., 20
Logitech International SA, 28
Lotus Development Corporation, 6; 25 (upd.)
The MacNeal-Schwendler Corporation, 25
Madge Networks N.V., 26
MAI Systems Corporation, 11
Maxtor Corporation, 10
Mead Data Central, Inc., 10
Mecklermedia Corporation, 24
Mentor Graphics Corporation, 11
Merisel, Inc., 12
Metro Information Services, Inc., 36
Micro Warehouse, Inc., 16
Micron Technology, Inc., 11; 29 (upd.)
Micros Systems, Inc., 18
Microsoft Corporation, 6; 27 (upd.)
MITRE Corporation, 26
The Motley Fool, Inc., 40
National Semiconductor Corporation, 6
National TechTeam, Inc., 41
Navarre Corporation, 24
NCR Corporation, III; 6 (upd.); 30 (upd.)
Netscape Communications Corporation, 15; 35 (upd.)
Network Associates, Inc., 25
Nextel Communications, Inc., 10
NFO Worldwide, Inc., 24
Nichols Research Corporation, 18
Nimbus CD International, Inc., 20
Nixdorf Computer AG, III
Novell, Inc., 6; 23 (upd.)
Océ N.V., 24
Odetics Inc., 14
Oracle Corporation, 24 (upd.)
Oracle Systems Corporation, 6
Packard Bell Electronics, Inc., 13
Parametric Technology Corp., 16
PC Connection, Inc., 37
PeopleSoft Inc., 14; 33 (upd.)
Perot Systems Corporation, 29
Pitney Bowes Inc., III
PLATINUM Technology, Inc., 14
Policy Management Systems Corporation, 11
Primark Corp., 13
The Princeton Review, Inc., 42
Printronix, Inc., 18
Prodigy Communications Corporation, 34
Progress Software Corporation, 15
Quantum Corporation, 10
Quark, Inc., 36
Racal-Datacom Inc., 11
Razorfish, Inc., 37
RCM Technologies, Inc., 34
Renaissance Learning Systems, Inc., 39
Reuters Holdings PLC, 22 (upd.)
Ricoh Company, Ltd., III
SABRE Group Holdings, Inc., 26
The Sage Group, 43
The Santa Cruz Operation, Inc., 38
SAP AG, 16; 43 (upd.)
SAS Institute Inc., 10
SBS Technologies, Inc., 25
SCB Computer Technology, Inc., 29
Schawk, Inc., 24
Seagate Technology, Inc., 8
Siebel Systems, Inc., 38
Sierra On-Line, Inc., 15; 41 (upd.)
SilverPlatter Information Inc., 23
SmartForce PLC, 43
Softbank Corp., 13; 38 (upd.)
Standard Microsystems Corporation, 11
STC PLC, III
Sterling Software, Inc., 11
Storage Technology Corporation, 6
Stratus Computer, Inc., 10
Sun Microsystems, Inc., 7; 30 (upd.)
SunGard Data Systems Inc., 11
Sybase, Inc., 10; 27 (upd.)
Symantec Corporation, 10
Symbol Technologies, Inc., 15
Synopsis, Inc., 11
System Software Associates, Inc., 10
Systems & Computer Technology Corp., 19
Tandem Computers, Inc., 6
TenFold Corporation, 35
Terra Lycos, Inc., 43
The Thomson Corporation, 34 (upd.)
3Com Corporation, 11; 34 (upd.)
The 3DO Company, 43
Timberline Software Corporation, 15
Transaction Systems Architects, Inc., 29
Triple P N.V., 26
Ubi Soft Entertainment S.A., 41
Unilog SA, 42
Unisys Corporation, III; 6 (upd.); 36 (upd.)
UUNET, 38
Verbatim Corporation, 14
VeriFone, Inc., 18
Viasoft Inc., 27
Volt Information Sciences Inc., 26
Wang Laboratories, Inc., III; 6 (upd.)
West Group, 34 (upd.)
Western Digital Corp., 25
Wind River Systems, Inc., 37
Wipro Limited, 43
Wolters Kluwer NV, 33 (upd.)
WordPerfect Corporation, 10
Wyse Technology, Inc., 15
Xerox Corporation, III; 6 (upd.); 26 (upd.)
Xilinx, Inc., 16
Yahoo! Inc., 27
Zapata Corporation, 25
Ziff Davis Media Inc., 36 (upd.)
Zilog, Inc., 15

INSURANCE

AEGON N.V., III
Aetna Life and Casualty Company, III
Aetna, Inc., 21 (upd.)
AFLAC Incorporated, 10 (upd.); 38 (upd.)
Alexander & Alexander Services Inc., 10
Alleghany Corporation, 10
Allianz Aktiengesellschaft Holding, III; 15 (upd.)
The Allstate Corporation, 10; 27 (upd.)

American Family Corporation, III
American Financial Corporation, III
American General Corporation, III; 10 (upd.)
American International Group, Inc., III; 15 (upd.)
American National Insurance Company, 8; 27 (upd.)
American Premier Underwriters, Inc., 10
American Re Corporation, 10; 35 (upd.)
N.V. AMEV, III
Aon Corporation, III
Assicurazioni Generali SpA, III; 15 (upd.)
Axa, III
AXA Colonia Konzern AG, 27
B.A.T. Industries PLC, 22 (upd.)
Bâloise-Holding, 40
Berkshire Hathaway Inc., III; 18 (upd.)
Blue Cross and Blue Shield Association, 10
Brown & Brown, Inc., 41
Business Men's Assurance Company of America, 14
Capital Holding Corporation, III
Catholic Order of Foresters, 24
The Chubb Corporation, III; 14 (upd.); 37 (upd.)
CIGNA Corporation, III; 22 (upd.)
Cincinnati Financial Corporation, 16
CNA Financial Corporation, III; 38 (upd.)
Commercial Union PLC, III
Connecticut Mutual Life Insurance Company, III
Conseco Inc., 10; 33 (upd.)
The Continental Corporation, III
Empire Blue Cross and Blue Shield, III
Enbridge Inc., 43
The Equitable Life Assurance Society of the United States Fireman's Fund Insurance Company, III
Erie Indemnity Company, 35
Farm Family Holdings, Inc., 39
Farmers Insurance Group of Companies, 25
First Executive Corporation, III
Foundation Health Corporation, 12
Gainsco, Inc., 22
GEICO Corporation, 10; 40 (upd.)
General Accident PLC, III
General Re Corporation, III; 24 (upd.)
Great-West Lifeco Inc., III
Gryphon Holdings, Inc., 21
Guardian Royal Exchange Plc, 11
Harleysville Group Inc., 37
The Home Insurance Company, III
Horace Mann Educators Corporation, 22
Household International, Inc., 21 (upd.)
Jackson National Life Insurance Company, 8
Jefferson-Pilot Corporation, 11; 29 (upd.)
John Hancock Financial Services, Inc., 42 (upd.)
John Hancock Mutual Life Insurance Company, III
Johnson & Higgins, 14
Kemper Corporation, III; 15 (upd.)
Legal & General Group plc, III; 24 (upd.)
The Liberty Corporation, 22
Lincoln National Corporation, III; 25 (upd.)
Lloyd's of London, III; 22 (upd.)
The Loewen Group Inc., 40 (upd.)
Lutheran Brotherhood, 31
Marsh & McLennan Companies, Inc., III
Massachusetts Mutual Life Insurance Company, III
The Meiji Mutual Life Insurance Company, III
Mercury General Corporation, 25
Metropolitan Life Insurance Company, III
Mitsui Marine and Fire Insurance Company, Limited, III
Mitsui Mutual Life Insurance Company, III; 39 (upd.)
Munich Re (Münchener Rückversicherungs-Gesellschaft), III
The Mutual Benefit Life Insurance Company, III
The Mutual Life Insurance Company of New York, III
Nationale-Nederlanden N.V., III
New England Mutual Life Insurance Company, III
New York Life Insurance Company, III
Nippon Life Insurance Company, III
Northwestern Mutual Life Insurance Company, III
NYMAGIC, Inc., 41
Ohio Casualty Corp., 11
Old Republic International Corp., 11
The Paul Revere Corporation, 12
Pennsylvania Blue Shield, III
Principal Mutual Life Insurance Company, III
Progressive Corporation, 11
The Progressive Corporation, 29 (upd.)
Provident Life and Accident Insurance Company of America, III
Prudential Corporation PLC, III
The Prudential Insurance Company of America, III; 30 (upd.)
Radian Group Inc., 42
Reliance Group Holdings, Inc., III
Riunione Adriatica di Sicurtà SpA, III
Royal Insurance Holdings PLC, III
SAFECO Corporaton, III
The St. Paul Companies, Inc., III; 22 (upd.)
SCOR S.A., 20
The Standard Life Assurance Company, III
State Farm Mutual Automobile Insurance Company, III
Sumitomo Life Insurance Company, III
The Sumitomo Marine and Fire Insurance Company, Limited, III
Sun Alliance Group PLC, III
SunAmerica Inc., 11
Swiss Reinsurance Company (Schweizerische Rückversicherungs-Gesellschaft), III
Teachers Insurance and Annuity Association, III
Texas Industries, Inc., 8
TIG Holdings, Inc., 26
The Tokio Marine and Fire Insurance Co., Ltd., III
Torchmark Corporation, 9; 33 (upd.)
Transatlantic Holdings, Inc., 11
The Travelers Corporation, III
UICI, 33
Union des Assurances de Pans, III
Unitrin Inc., 16
UNUM Corp., 13
USAA, 10
USF&G Corporation, III
VICTORIA Holding AG, III
W.R. Berkley Corp., 15
Washington National Corporation, 12
Willis Corroon Group plc, 25
''Winterthur'' Schweizerische Versicherungs-Gesellschaft, III
The Yasuda Fire and Marine Insurance Company, Limited, III
The Yasuda Mutual Life Insurance Company, 39 (upd.)
The Yasuda Mutual Life Insurance Company, Limited, III
''Zürich'' Versicherungs-Gesellschaft, III

LEGAL SERVICES

Akin, Gump, Strauss, Hauer & Feld, L.L.P., 33
American Bar Association, 35
American Lawyer Media Holdings, Inc., 32
Arnold & Porter, 35
Baker & Hostetler LLP, 40
Baker & McKenzie, 10; 42 (upd.)
Baker and Botts, L.L.P., 28
Bingham Dana LLP, 43
Brobeck, Phleger & Harrison, LLP, 31
Cadwalader, Wickersham & Taft, 32
Chadbourne & Parke, 36
Cleary, Gottlieb, Steen & Hamilton, 35
Clifford Chance LLP, 38
Coudert Brothers, 30
Covington & Burling, 40
Cravath, Swaine & Moore, 43
Davis Polk & Wardwell, 36
Debevoise & Plimpton, 39
Dechert, 43
Fenwick & West LLP, 34
Foley & Lardner, 28
Fried, Frank, Harris, Shriver & Jacobson, 35
Gibson, Dunn & Crutcher LLP, 36
Heller, Ehrman, White & McAuliffe, 41
Hildebrandt International, 29
Holme Roberts & Owen LLP, 28
Hunton & Williams, 35
Jones, Day, Reavis & Pogue, 33
Kelley Drye & Warren LLP, 40
King & Spalding, 23
Latham & Watkins, 33
LeBoeuf, Lamb, Greene & MacRae, L.L.P., 29
Milbank, Tweed, Hadley & McCloy, 27
Morgan, Lewis & Bockius LLP, 29
O'Melveny & Myers, 37
Paul, Hastings, Janofsky & Walker LLP, 27
Pepper Hamilton LLP, 43
Pillsbury Madison & Sutro LLP, 29
Pre-Paid Legal Services, Inc., 20
Ropes & Gray, 40
Shearman & Sterling, 32
Sidley Austin Brown & Wood, 40
Simpson Thacher & Bartlett, 39
Skadden, Arps, Slate, Meagher & Flom, 18
Snell & Wilmer L.L.P., 28
Stroock & Stroock & Lavan LLP, 40
Sullivan & Cromwell, 26
Vinson & Elkins L.L.P., 30
White & Case LLP, 35
Wilson Sonsini Goodrich & Rosati, 34
Winston & Strawn, 35

MANUFACTURING

A.B.Dick Company, 28
A.O. Smith Corporation, 11; 40 (upd.)
A.T. Cross Company, 17
AAF-McQuay Incorporated, 26
AAON, Inc., 22
AAR Corp., 28
ABC Rail Products Corporation, 18
ACCO World Corporation, 7
Acme-Cleveland Corp., 13
Acuson Corporation, 36 (upd.)
Adams Golf, Inc., 37
AEP Industries, Inc., 36
Ag-Chem Equipment Company, Inc., 17
AGCO Corp., 13
Aisin Seiki Co., Ltd., III
AK Steel Holding Corporation, 41 (upd.)
Aktiebolaget Electrolux, 22 (upd.)
Aktiebolaget SKF, III; 38 (upd.)
Alamo Group Inc., 32

Alberto-Culver Company, 36 (upd.)
Alfa-Laval AB, III
Allen Organ Company, 33
Alliant Techsystems Inc., 8; 30 (upd.)
Allied Healthcare Products, Inc., 24
Allied Products Corporation, 21
Allied Signal Engines, 9
AlliedSignal Inc., 22 (upd.)
Allison Gas Turbine Division, 9
Alltrista Corporation, 30
Amer Group plc, 41
American Biltrite Inc., 43 (upd.)
American Business Products, Inc., 20
American Homestar Corporation, 18; 41 (upd.)
American Locker Group Incorporated, 34
American Standard Companies Inc., 30 (upd.)
American Tourister, Inc., 16
American Woodmark Corporation, 31
Ameriwood Industries International Corp., 17
AMETEK, Inc., 9
AMF Bowling, Inc., 40
Ampex Corporation, 17
Amway Corporation, 30 (upd.)
Analogic Corporation, 23
Anchor Hocking Glassware, 13
Andersen Corporation, 10
The Andersons, Inc., 31
Andreas Stihl, 16
Anthem Electronics, Inc., 13
Applica Incorporated, 43 (upd.)
Applied Materials, Inc., 10
Applied Micro Circuits Corporation, 38
Applied Power Inc., 9; 32 (upd.)
ARBED S.A., 22 (upd.)
Arctco, Inc., 16
Arctic Cat Inc., 40 (upd.)
Armor All Products Corp., 16
Armstrong World Industries, Inc., III; 22 (upd.)
Ashley Furniture Industries, Inc., 35
Astronics Corporation, 35
ASV, Inc., 34
Atlas Copco AB, III; 28 (upd.)
Avedis Zildjian Co., 38
Avery Dennison Corporation, 17 (upd.)
Avondale Industries, 41 (upd.)
Avondale Industries, Inc., 7
Badger Meter, Inc., 22
Baker Hughes Incorporated, III
Baldor Electric Company, 21
Baldwin Piano & Organ Company, 18
Baldwin Technology Company, Inc., 25
Balfour Beatty plc, 36 (upd.)
Ballantyne of Omaha, Inc., 27
Ballard Medical Products, 21
Bally Manufacturing Corporation, III
Baltek Corporation, 34
Barmag AG, 39
Barnes Group Inc., 13
Barry Callebaut AG, 29
Bassett Furniture Industries, Inc., 18
Bath Iron Works, 36 (upd.)
Bath Iron Works Corporation, 12
Beckman Coulter, Inc., 22
Beckman Instruments, Inc., 14
Becton, Dickinson & Company, 36 (upd.)
Beiersdorf AG, 29
Belden Inc., 19
Bell Sports Corporation, 16
Beloit Corporation, 14
Benjamin Moore & Co., 13; 38 (upd.)
Berry Plastics Corporation, 21
BIC Corporation, 8; 23 (upd.)
BICC PLC, III
Binks Sames Corporation, 21
Binney & Smith Inc., 25
Biomet, Inc., 10
BISSELL Inc., 9; 30 (upd.)
The Black & Decker Corporation, III; 20 (upd.)
Blount, Inc., 12
Blyth Industries, Inc., 18
BMC Industries, Inc., 17
Boral Limited, 43 (upd.)
Borden, Inc., 22 (upd.)
Borg-Warner Automotive, Inc., 14
Borg-Warner Corporation, III
Boston Scientific Corporation, 37
The Boyds Collection, Ltd., 29
Brass Eagle Inc., 34
Bridgeport Machines, Inc., 17
Briggs & Stratton Corporation, 8; 27 (upd.)
BRIO AB, 24
British Vita plc, 33 (upd.)
Brother Industries, Ltd., 14
Brown & Sharpe Manufacturing Co., 23
Brown-Forman Corporation, 38 (upd.)
Broyhill Furniture Industries, Inc., 10
Brunswick Corporation, III; 22 (upd.)
BTR Siebe plc, 27
Buckeye Technologies, Inc., 42
Bucyrus International, Inc., 17
Bugle Boy Industries, Inc., 18
Bulgari S.p.A., 20
Bulova Corporation, 13; 41 (upd.)
Bundy Corporation, 17
Burelle S.A., 23
Burton Snowboards Inc., 22
Bush Boake Allen Inc., 30
Bush Industries, Inc., 20
Butler Manufacturing Co., 12
C.F. Martin & Co., Inc., 42
Callaway Golf Company, 15
Cannondale Corporation, 21
Caradon plc, 20 (upd.)
The Carbide/Graphite Group, Inc., 40
Carbone Lorraine S.A., 33
Carl-Zeiss-Stiftung, III; 34 (upd.)
Carrier Corporation, 7
CASIO Computer Co., Ltd., III; 40 (upd.)
Catalina Lighting, Inc., 43 (upd.)
Caterpillar Inc., III; 15 (upd.)
Central Sprinkler Corporation, 29
Cessna Aircraft Company, 27 (upd.)
Champion Enterprises, Inc., 17
Chanel, 12
Chart Industries, Inc., 21
Chris-Craft Industries, Inc., 31 (upd.)
Christian Dalloz SA, 40
Christofle SA, 40
Chromcraft Revington, Inc., 15
Ciments Français, 40
Cincinnati Milacron Inc., 12
Cinram International, Inc., 43
Circon Corporation, 21
Citizen Watch Co., Ltd., III
Clarcor Inc., 17
Clark Equipment Company, 8
Clayton Homes Incorporated, 13
The Clorox Company, 22 (upd.)
CNH Global N.V., 38 (upd.)
Cobra Golf Inc., 16
Cockerill Sambre Group, 26 (upd.)
Cohu, Inc., 32
Colas S.A., 31
The Coleman Company, Inc., 30 (upd.)
Collins & Aikman Corporation, 41 (upd.)
Collins Industries, Inc., 33
Colt's Manufacturing Company, Inc., 12
Columbia Sportswear Company, 19
Columbus McKinnon Corporation, 37
Concord Camera Corporation, 41
Congoleum Corp., 18
Conso International Corporation, 29
Consorcio G Grupo Dina, S.A. de C.V., 36
Converse Inc., 9
The Cooper Companies, Inc., 39
Corrpro Companies, Inc., 20
Crane Co., 8; 30 (upd.)
Crown Equipment Corporation, 15
CTB International Corporation, 43 (upd.)
Cuisinart Corporation, 24
Culligan International Company, 12
Culligan Water Technologies, Inc., 38 (upd.)
Cummins Engine Company, Inc., 40 (upd.)
Curtiss-Wright Corporation, 10; 35 (upd.)
Cutter & Buck Inc., 27
Daewoo Group, III
Daikin Industries, Ltd., III
Danaher Corporation, 7
Daniel Industries, Inc., 16
Day Runner, Inc., 41 (upd.)
Decora Industries, Inc., 31
DeCrane Aircraft Holdings Inc., 36
Deere & Company, III; 42 (upd.)
Defiance, Inc., 22
Department 56, Inc., 14
DePuy Inc., 37 (upd.)
Detroit Diesel Corporation, 10
Deutsche Babcock A.G., III
Deutz AG, 39
Diebold, Incorporated, 7; 22 (upd.)
Diesel SpA, 40
Dixon Industries, Inc., 26
Dixon Ticonderoga Company, 12
Donnelly Corporation, 12; 35 (upd.)
Douglas & Lomason Company, 16
Dover Corporation, III; 28 (upd.)
Dresser Industries, Inc., III
Drew Industries Inc., 28
Drexel Heritage Furnishings Inc., 12
Drypers Corporation, 18
Ducommun Incorporated, 30
Duracell International Inc., 9
Durametallic, 21
Duriron Company Inc., 17
Eagle-Picher Industries, Inc., 8; 23 (upd.)
Eastman Kodak Company, III; 7 (upd.); 36 (upd.)
ECC International Corp., 42
Ecolab Inc., 34 (upd.)
Eddie Bauer Inc., 9
EG&G Incorporated, 29 (upd.)
Ekco Group, Inc., 16
Elano Corporation, 14
Electrolux Group, III
Eljer Industries, Inc., 24
Elscint Ltd., 20
Encompass Services Corporation, 33
Energizer Holdings, Inc., 32
Enesco Corporation, 11
English China Clays Ltd., 40 (upd.)
Escalade, Incorporated, 19
Essilor International, 21
Esterline Technologies Corp., 15
Ethan Allen Interiors, Inc., 12; 39 (upd.)
The Eureka Company, 12
Fabbrica D' Armi Pietro Beretta S.p.A., 39
Facom S.A., 32
Faiveley S.A., 39
Falcon Products, Inc., 33
Fanuc Ltd., III; 17 (upd.)
Farah Incorporated, 24
Fastenal Company, 42 (upd.)
Featherlite Inc., 28
Fedders Corporation, 18; 43 (upd.)
Federal Prison Industries, Inc., 34
Federal Signal Corp., 10
Fellowes Manufacturing Company, 28

Fender Musical Instruments Company, 16; 43 (upd.)
Figgie International Inc., 7
Firearms Training Systems, Inc., 27
First Alert, Inc., 28
First Brands Corporation, 8
Fisher Controls International, Inc., 13
Fisher Scientific International Inc., 24
Fisher-Price Inc., 12; 32 (upd.)
Fiskars Corporation, 33
Fisons plc, 9
Fleetwood Enterprises, Inc., III; 22 (upd.)
Flexsteel Industries Inc., 15; 41 (upd.)
Flextronics International Ltd., 38
Flint Ink Corporation, 41 (upd.)
Florsheim Shoe Company, 9
Flowserve Corporation, 33
Fort James Corporation, 22 (upd.)
Fountain Powerboats Industries, Inc., 28
Foxboro Company, 13
Framatome SA, 19
Frank J. Zamboni & Co., Inc., 34
Franklin Electric Company, Inc., 43
Freudenberg & Co., 41
Frigidaire Home Products, 22
Frymaster Corporation, 27
FSI International, Inc., 17
Fuji Photo Film Co., Ltd., III; 18 (upd.)
Fuqua Enterprises, Inc., 17
Furniture Brands International, Inc., 39 (upd.)
Furon Company, 28
The Furukawa Electric Co., Ltd., III
G.S. Blodgett Corporation, 15
The Gates Corporation, 9
GE Aircraft Engines, 9
GEA AG, 27
Gehl Company, 19
GenCorp Inc., 8; 9 (upd.)
General Cable Corporation, 40
General Dynamics Corporation, 40 (upd.)
General Housewares Corporation, 16
Gerber Scientific, Inc., 12
Gerresheimer Glas AG, 43
Giddings & Lewis, Inc., 10
The Gillette Company, 20 (upd.)
GKN plc, III; 38 (upd.)
Gleason Corporation, 24
The Glidden Company, 8
Glock Ges.m.b.H., 42
Goodman Holding Company, 42
Goody Products, Inc., 12
The Gorman-Rupp Company, 18
Goss Holdings, Inc., 43
Goulds Pumps Inc., 24
Graco Inc., 19
Griffon Corporation, 34
Grinnell Corp., 13
Groupe André, 17
Groupe Guillin SA, 40
Groupe Legis Industries, 23
Groupe SEB, 35
Grow Group Inc., 12
Grupo Cydsa, S.A. de C.V., 39
The Gunlocke Company, 23
H.B. Fuller Company, 8; 32 (upd.)
Hach Co., 18
Haemonetics Corporation, 20
Halliburton Company, III
Hallmark Cards, Inc., 40 (upd.)
Hanson PLC, 30 (upd.)
Hardinge Inc., 25
Harland and Wolff Holdings plc, 19
Harmon Industries, Inc., 25
Harnischfeger Industries, Inc., 8; 38 (upd.)
Harsco Corporation, 8
Hartmarx Corporation, 32 (upd.)
Hasbro, Inc., III; 16 (upd.)
Hawker Siddeley Group Public Limited Company, III
Haworth Inc., 8; 39 (upd.)
Health O Meter Products Inc., 14
Heekin Can Inc., 13
HEICO Corporation, 30
Heidelberger Druckmaschinen AG, 40
Henkel Manco Inc., 22
The Henley Group, Inc., III
Herman Miller, Inc., 8
Hermès International S.A., 34 (upd.)
Hillenbrand Industries, Inc., 10
Hillsdown Holdings plc, 24 (upd.)
Hitachi Zosen Corporation, III
Hitchiner Manufacturing Co., Inc., 23
HMI Industries, Inc., 17
Holnam Inc., 8
Holson Burnes Group, Inc., 14
HON INDUSTRIES Inc., 13
The Hoover Company, 12; 40 (upd.)
Huffy Corporation, 7; 30 (upd.)
Hunt Manufacturing Company, 12
Hunter Fan Company, 13
Hyster Company, 17
Hyundai Group, III; 7 (upd.)
Icon Health & Fitness, Inc., 38
Igloo Products Corp., 21
Illinois Tool Works Inc., III; 22 (upd.)
IMI plc, 9
Imo Industries Inc., 7; 27 (upd.)
Inchcape PLC, III; 16 (upd.)
Industrie Natuzzi S.p.A., 18
Ingalls Shipbuilding, Inc., 12
Ingersoll-Rand Company, III; 15 (upd.)
Insilco Corporation, 16
Interco Incorporated, III
Interface, Inc., 8
The Interlake Corporation, 8
International Controls Corporation, 10
International Flavors & Fragrances Inc., 38 (upd.)
International Game Technology, 10
Irwin Toy Limited, 14
Ishikawajima-Harima Heavy Industries Co., Ltd., III
J.I. Case Company, 10
J.M. Voith AG, 33
Jabil Circuit, Inc., 36
Jacuzzi Inc., 23
Jayco Inc., 13
Jenoptik AG, 33
Jervis B. Webb Company, 24
Johnson Controls, Inc., III; 26 (upd.)
Johnson Worldwide Associates, Inc., 28
Johnstown America Industries, Inc., 23
Jones Apparel Group, Inc., 11
Jostens, Inc., 7; 25 (upd.)
Kaman Corporation, 12; 42 (upd.)
Kasper A.S.L., Ltd., 40
Kawasaki Heavy Industries, Ltd., III
Kaydon Corporation, 18
KB Toys, 35 (upd.)
Kerr Group Inc., 24
Kewaunee Scientific Corporation, 25
Key Tronic Corporation, 14
Keystone International, Inc., 11
KHD Konzern, III
Kimball International, Inc., 12
Kit Manufacturing Co., 18
Knape & Vogt Manufacturing Company, 17
Knoll Group Inc., 14
Kobe Steel, Ltd., IV; 19 (upd.)
Koch Enterprises, Inc., 29
Kohler Company, 7; 32 (upd.)
Komatsu Ltd., III; 16 (upd.)
Kone Corporation, 27
Konica Corporation, III
Kubota Corporation, III; 26 (upd.)
Kuhlman Corporation, 20
Kyocera Corporation, 21 (upd.)
L.B. Foster Company, 33
LADD Furniture, Inc., 12
Ladish Co., Inc., 30
Lafarge Corporation, 28
Lafuma S.A., 39
Lam Research Corporation, 31 (upd.)
Lamson & Sessions Co., 13
Lancer Corporation, 21
The Lane Co., Inc., 12
Leggett & Platt, Incorporated, 11
Leica Camera AG, 35
Leica Microsystems Holdings GmbH, 35
Lennox International Inc., 8; 28 (upd.)
Lenox, Inc., 12
Lexmark International, Inc., 18
Linamar Corporation, 18
Lincoln Electric Co., 13
Lindal Cedar Homes, Inc., 29
Lindsay Manufacturing Co., 20
Little Tikes Co., 13
Loctite Corporation, 8
Logitech International SA, 28
The Longaberger Company, 12
Louis Vuitton, 10
Lucas Industries PLC, III
Lynch Corporation, 43
M&F Worldwide Corp., 38
MacAndrews & Forbes Holdings Inc., 28
Mail-Well, Inc., 28
Makita Corporation, 22
MAN Aktiengesellschaft, III
Manitou BF S.A., 27
Manitowoc Company, Inc., 18
Mannesmann AG, III; 14 (upd.)
Margarete Steiff GmbH, 23
Marisa Christina, Inc., 15
Mark IV Industries, Inc., 7; 28 (upd.)
The Marmon Group, 16 (upd.)
Marvin Lumber & Cedar Company, 22
Mary Kay, Inc., 30 (upd.)
Masco Corporation, III; 20 (upd.); 39 (upd.)
Mattel, Inc., 7; 25 (upd.)
Matthews International Corporation, 29
Maxco Inc., 17
Maxwell Shoe Company, Inc., 30
Maytag Corporation, III; 22 (upd.)
McDermott International, Inc., III
McKechnie plc, 34
Meade Instruments Corporation, 41
Meadowcraft, Inc., 29
Meggitt PLC, 34
Merck & Co., Inc., 34 (upd.)
Merillat Industries Inc., 13
Mestek Inc., 10
Metso Corporation, 30 (upd.)
Mettler-Toledo International Inc., 30
Michael Anthony Jewelers, Inc., 24
Microdot Inc., 8
Mikasa, Inc., 28
Mikohn Gaming Corporation, 39
Miller Industries, Inc., 26
Milton Bradley Company, 21
Mine Safety Appliances Company, 31
Minolta Camera Co., Ltd., III
Minolta Co., Ltd., 18 (upd.); 43 (upd.)
Mitsubishi Heavy Industries, Ltd., III; 7 (upd.)
Mity Enterprises, Inc., 38
Modine Manufacturing Company, 8
Moen Incorporated, 12
Mohawk Industries, Inc., 19
Molex Incorporated, 11
Montres Rolex S.A., 13; 34 (upd.)
Moulinex S.A., 22

Movado Group, Inc., 28
Mr. Coffee, Inc., 15
Mr. Gasket Inc., 15
Mueller Industries, Inc., 7
Nashua Corporation, 8
National Envelope Corporation, 32
National Gypsum Company, 10
National Picture & Frame Company, 24
National Standard Co., 13
NCR Corporation, 30 (upd.)
New Balance Athletic Shoe, Inc., 25
New Holland N.V., 22
Newcor, Inc., 40
Newell Co., 9
Newport News Shipbuilding and Dry Dock Co., 13
Newport News Shipbuilding Inc., 38 (upd.)
NHK Spring Co., Ltd., III
NIKE, Inc., 36 (upd.)
Nikon Corporation, III
Nintendo Co., Ltd., III; 7 (upd.)
Nippon Seiko K.K., III
Nippondenso Co., Ltd., III
NKK Corporation, 28 (upd.)
NordicTrack, 22
Nordson Corporation, 11
Nortek, Inc., 34
Norton Company, 8
Norton McNaughton, Inc., 27
Novellus Systems, Inc., 18
NTN Corporation, III
Nu-kote Holding, Inc., 18
O'Sullivan Industries Holdings, Inc., 34
Oak Industries Inc., 21
Oakwood Homes Corporation, 15
The Ohio Art Company, 14
Oil-Dri Corporation of America, 20
Oneida Ltd., 7; 31 (upd.)
Osmonics, Inc., 18
Otis Elevator Company, Inc., 13; 39 (upd.)
Outboard Marine Corporation, III; 20 (upd.)
Owens Corning Corporation, 20 (upd.)
Owosso Corporation, 29
Pacer Technology, 40
Pacific Dunlop Limited, 10
Pall Corporation, 9
Palm Harbor Homes, Inc., 39
Panavision Inc., 24
Park Corp., 22
Parker-Hannifin Corporation, III; 24 (upd.)
Patrick Industries, Inc., 30
Pella Corporation, 12; 39 (upd.)
Penn Engineering & Manufacturing Corp., 28
Pentair, Inc., 26 (upd.)
Pentech International, Inc., 29
The Perkin-Elmer Corporation, 7
Phillips-Van Heusen Corporation, 24
Physio-Control International Corp., 18
Pilkington plc, 34 (upd.)
Pioneer Electronic Corporation, III
Pitney Bowes, Inc., 19
Pittway Corporation, 33 (upd.)
PlayCore, Inc., 27
Playmates Toys, 23
Playskool, Inc., 25
Pleasant Company, 27
Ply Gem Industries Inc., 12
Polaris Industries Inc., 12; 35 (upd.)
Polaroid Corporation, III; 7 (upd.); 28 (upd.)
PPG Industries, Inc., 22 (upd.)
Precision Castparts Corp., 15
Premark International, Inc., III
Presstek, Inc., 33
Prince Sports Group, Inc., 15
Printronix, Inc., 18
Pulaski Furniture Corporation, 33
Puritan-Bennett Corporation, 13
Purolator Products Company, 21
Quixote Corporation, 15
R. Griggs Group Limited, 23
Racing Champions Corporation, 37
Radio Flyer Inc., 34
Rapala-Normark Group, Ltd., 30
Raven Industries, Inc., 33
Raychem Corporation, 8
Rayovac Corporation, 39 (upd.)
Recovery Engineering, Inc., 25
Red Wing Shoe Company, Inc., 9
Regal-Beloit Corporation, 18
Reichhold Chemicals, Inc., 10
Remington Arms Company, Inc., 12; 40 (upd.)
Remington Products Company, L.L.C., 42
RENK AG, 37
Revell-Monogram Inc., 16
Revere Ware Corporation, 22
Rexam PLC, 32 (upd.)
Rexnord Corporation, 21
RF Micro Devices, Inc., 43
Rheinmetall Berlin AG, 9
Riddell Sports Inc., 22
Rieter Holding AG, 42
River Oaks Furniture, Inc., 43
RMC Group p.l.c., 34 (upd.)
Roadmaster Industries, Inc., 16
Robbins & Myers Inc., 15
Robertson-Ceco Corporation, 19
RockShox, Inc., 26
Rockwell Automation, 43 (upd.)
Rohde & Schwarz GmbH & Co. KG, 39
ROHN Industries, Inc., 22
Rohr Incorporated, 9
Roland Corporation, 38
Rollerblade, Inc., 15; 34 (upd.)
Roper Industries Inc., 15
Royal Appliance Manufacturing Company, 15
Royal Canin S.A., 39
Royal Doulton plc, 14; 38 (upd.)
RPM, Inc., 8; 36 (upd.)
Rubbermaid Incorporated, III
Russ Berrie and Company, Inc., 12
S.C. Johnson & Son, Inc., 28 (upd.)
Safeskin Corporation, 18
Salant Corporation, 12
Salton, Inc., 30
Samsonite Corporation, 13; 43 (upd.)
Sandvik AB, 32 (upd.)
Sanrio Company, Ltd., 38
Sauder Woodworking Company, 12; 35 (upd.)
Sawtek Inc., 43 (upd.)
Schindler Holding AG, 29
Schlumberger Limited, III
Scotsman Industries, Inc., 20
Scott Fetzer Company, 12
The Scotts Company, 22
Scovill Fasteners Inc., 24
Sealed Air Corporation, 14
Sealy Inc., 12
Seiko Corporation, III; 17 (upd.)
Select Comfort Corporation, 34
The Selmer Company, Inc., 19
Semitool, Inc., 18
Sequa Corp., 13
Serta, Inc., 28
Shakespeare Company, 22
Shelby Williams Industries, Inc., 14
Shorewood Packaging Corporation, 28
SIFCO Industries, Inc., 41
Simula, Inc., 41
The Singer Company N.V., 30 (upd.)
Skis Rossignol S.A., 15; 43 (upd.)
Skyline Corporation, 30
Smead Manufacturing Co., 17
Smith & Wesson Corporation, 30
Smith Corona Corp., 13
Smith International, Inc., 15
Smiths Industries PLC, 25
Snap-on Tools Corporation, 7
Snap-On, Incorporated, 27 (upd.)
Sparton Corporation, 18
Specialty Equipment Companies, Inc., 25
SPS Technologies, Inc., 30
Stanadyne Automotive Corporation, 37
Standex International Corporation, 17
Stanley Furniture Company, Inc., 34
The Stanley Works, III; 20 (upd.)
Stearns, Inc., 43
Steelcase, Inc., 7; 27 (upd.)
Steinway Musical Properties, Inc., 19
Stewart & Stevenson Services Inc., 11
Stryker Corporation, 11; 29 (upd.)
Sturm, Ruger & Company, Inc., 19
Sub-Zero Freezer Co., Inc., 31
Sudbury Inc., 16
Sulzer Brothers Limited (Gebruder Sulzer Aktiengesellschaft), III
Sumitomo Heavy Industries, Ltd., III; 42 (upd.)
Susquehanna Pfaltzgraff Company, 8
Swank Inc., 17
Swarovski International Holding AG, 40
The Swatch Group SA, 26
Swedish Match AB, 39 (upd.)
Swedish Match S.A., 12
Sweetheart Cup Company, Inc., 36
Sybron International Corp., 14
Syratech Corp., 14
TAB Products Co., 17
TAG Heuer International SA, 25
Tarkett Sommer AG, 25
Taylor Made Golf Co., 23
TearDrop Golf Company, 32
Tecumseh Products Company, 8
Tektronix, Inc., 8
Tennant Company, 13; 33 (upd.)
Terex Corporation, 7; 40 (upd.)
Thales S.A., 42
Thermadyne Holding Corporation, 19
Thermo BioAnalysis Corp., 25
Thermo Electron Corporation, 7
Thermo Fibertek, Inc., 24
Thermo Instrument Systems Inc., 11
Thermo King Corporation, 13
Thiokol Corporation, 22 (upd.)
Thomas & Betts Corp., 11
Thomas Industries Inc., 29
Thomasville Furniture Industries, Inc., 12
Thor Industries, Inc., 39
Thyssen Krupp AG, 28 (upd.)
Timex Corporation, 25 (upd.)
Timex Enterprises Inc., 7
The Timken Company, 8; 42 (upd.)
TJ International, Inc., 19
Todd Shipyards Corporation, 14
Tokheim Corporation, 21
Tonka Corporation, 25
Toolex International N.V., 26
Topps Company, Inc., 13
The Toro Company, 7; 26 (upd.)
The Torrington Company, 13
TOTO LTD., 28 (upd.)
Town & Country Corporation, 19
Toymax International, Inc., 29
Toyoda Automatic Loom Works, Ltd., III
Trek Bicycle Corporation, 16
Trico Products Corporation, 15
TriMas Corp., 11
Trinity Industries, Incorporated, 7
TRINOVA Corporation, III

Triumph Group, Inc., 31
Tubos de Acero de Mexico, S.A. (TAMSA), 41
Tultex Corporation, 13
Tupperware Corporation, 28
Twin Disc, Inc., 21
Ty Inc., 33
Tyco International Ltd., 28 (upd.)
Tyco Laboratories, Inc., III
Tyco Toys, Inc., 12
U.S. Robotics Inc., 9
Ube Industries, Ltd., 38 (upd.)
United Defense, L.P., 30
United Dominion Industries Limited, 8; 16 (upd.)
United Industrial Corporation, 37
United States Filter Corporation, 20
Unitog Co., 19
Utah Medical Products, Inc., 36
Valmet Corporation (Valmet Oy), III
Valmont Industries, Inc., 19
The Valspar Corporation, 8
Vari-Lite International, Inc., 35
Varity Corporation, III
Varlen Corporation, 16
Varta AG, 23
Velcro Industries N.V., 19
Vermeer Manufacturing Company, 17
Vickers plc, 27
Victorinox AG, 21
Viessmann Werke GmbH & Co., 37
Villeroy & Boch AG, 37
Virco Manufacturing Corporation, 17
Vitro Corporativo S.A. de C.V., 34
Vorwerk & Co., 27
Vosper Thornycroft Holding plc, 41
W.H. Brady Co., 17
W.L. Gore & Associates, Inc., 14
W.W. Grainger, Inc., 26 (upd.)
Wabash National Corp., 13
Wabtec Corporation, 40
Walbro Corporation, 13
Washington Scientific Industries, Inc., 17
Wassall Plc, 18
Waterford Wedgwood Holdings PLC, 12
Waterford Wedgwood plc, 34 (upd.)
Waters Corporation, 43
Watts Industries, Inc., 19
WD-40 Company, 18
Weber-Stephen Products Co., 40
Welbilt Corp., 19
Wellman, Inc., 8
Weru Aktiengesellschaft, 18
West Bend Co., 14
Western Digital Corp., 25
Whirlpool Corporation, III; 12 (upd.)
White Consolidated Industries Inc., 13
Wilson Sporting Goods Company, 24
Windmere Corporation, 16
WinsLoew Furniture, Inc., 21
WMS Industries, Inc., 15
Wolverine Tube Inc., 23
Wood-Mode, Inc., 23
Woodward Governor Co., 13
Wyant Corporation, 30
Wyman-Gordon Company, 14
Wynn's International, Inc., 33
Yamaha Corporation, III; 16 (upd.)
York International Corp., 13
Zero Corporation, 17
Zippo Manufacturing Company, 18
Zodiac S.A., 36
Zygo Corporation, 42

MATERIALS

AK Steel Holding Corporation, 19
American Biltrite Inc., 16
American Colloid Co., 13
American Standard Inc., III
Ameriwood Industries International Corp., 17
Apogee Enterprises, Inc., 8
Asahi Glass Company, Limited, III
Bairnco Corporation, 28
Bayou Steel Corporation, 31
Blessings Corp., 19
Blue Circle Industries PLC, III
Boral Limited, III
British Vita PLC, 9
Cameron & Barkley Company, 28
Carborundum Company, 15
Carl-Zeiss-Stiftung, 34 (upd.)
Carlisle Companies Incorporated, 8
Cemex SA de CV, 20
CertainTeed Corporation, 35
Chargeurs International, 21 (upd.)
Chemfab Corporation, 35
Compagnie de Saint-Gobain S.A., III; 16 (upd.)
Cookson Group plc, III
Corning Incorporated, III
CSR Limited, III
Dal-Tile International Inc., 22
The David J. Joseph Company, 14
The Dexter Corporation, 12 (upd.)
Dyckerhoff AG, 35
ECC Group plc, III
Edw. C. Levy Co., 42
84 Lumber Company, 9; 39 (upd.)
English China Clays Ltd., 40 (upd.)
English China Clays plc, 15 (upd.)
Envirodyne Industries, Inc., 17
Feldmuhle Nobel A.G., III
Fibreboard Corporation, 16
Foamex International Inc., 17
Formica Corporation, 13
GAF Corporation, 22 (upd.)
The Geon Company, 11
Giant Cement Holding, Inc., 23
Gibraltar Steel Corporation, 37
Granite Rock Company, 26
Groupe Sidel S.A., 21
Harbison-Walker Refractories Company, 24
Harrisons & Crosfield plc, III
Heidelberger Zement AG, 31
Hexcel Corporation, 28
''Holderbank'' Financière Glaris Ltd., III
Holnam Inc., 39 (upd.)
Howmet Corp., 12
Ibstock Brick Ltd., 37 (upd.)
Ibstock plc, 14
Imerys S.A., 40 (upd.)
Joseph T. Ryerson & Son, Inc., 15
Lafarge Coppée S.A., III
Lafarge Corporation, 28
Lehigh Portland Cement Company, 23
Manville Corporation, III; 7 (upd.)
Matsushita Electric Works, Ltd., III; 7 (upd.)
Medusa Corporation, 24
Mitsubishi Materials Corporation, III
Nippon Sheet Glass Company, Limited, III
OmniSource Corporation, 14
Onoda Cement Co., Ltd., III
Owens-Corning Fiberglass Corporation, III
Pilkington plc, III; 34 (upd.)
Pioneer International Limited, III
PPG Industries, Inc., III
Redland plc, III
RMC Group p.l.c., III
Rock of Ages Corporation, 37
The Rugby Group plc, 31
Schuff Steel Company, 26
Sekisui Chemical Co., Ltd., III
Shaw Industries, 9
The Sherwin-Williams Company, III; 13 (upd.)
Simplex Technologies Inc., 21
Sommer-Allibert S.A., 19
Southdown, Inc., 14
Spartech Corporation, 19
Ssangyong Cement Industrial Co., Ltd., III
Sun Distributors L.P., 12
Tarmac PLC, III
Tarmac plc, 28 (upd.)
TOTO LTD., III; 28 (upd.)
Toyo Sash Co., Ltd., III
Tuscarora Inc., 29
U.S. Aggregates, Inc., 42
Ube Industries, Ltd., III
USG Corporation, III; 26 (upd.)
Vulcan Materials Company, 7
Wacker-Chemie GmbH, 35
Walter Industries, Inc., III
Waxman Industries, Inc., 9
Zoltek Companies, Inc., 37

MINING & METALS

A.M. Castle & Co., 25
Aggregate Industries plc, 36
Aktiebolaget SKF, 38 (upd.)
Alcan Aluminium Limited, IV; 31 (upd.)
Alleghany Corporation, 10
Allegheny Ludlum Corporation, 8
Altos Hornos de México, S.A. de C.V., 42
Aluminum Company of America, IV; 20 (upd.)
AMAX Inc., IV
Amsted Industries Incorporated, 7
Anglo American Corporation of South Africa Limited, IV; 16 (upd.)
ARBED S.A., IV, 22 (upd.)
Arch Mineral Corporation, 7
Armco Inc., IV
ASARCO Incorporated, IV
Ashanti Goldfields Company Limited, 43
Atchison Casting Corporation, 39
Barrick Gold Corporation, 34
Battle Mountain Gold Company, 23
Bethlehem Steel Corporation, IV; 7 (upd.); 27 (upd.)
Birmingham Steel Corporation, 13; 40 (upd.)
Boart Longyear Company, 26
Boral Limited, 43 (upd.)
British Coal Corporation, IV
British Steel plc, IV; 19 (upd.)
Broken Hill Proprietary Company Ltd., IV, 22 (upd.)
Brush Wellman Inc., 14
Buderus AG, 37
Carpenter Technology Corporation, 13
Chaparral Steel Co., 13
Christensen Boyles Corporation, 26
Cleveland-Cliffs Inc., 13
Coal India Limited, IV
Cockerill Sambre Group, IV; 26 (upd.)
Coeur d'Alene Mines Corporation, 20
Cold Spring Granite Company, 16
Cominco Ltd., 37
Commercial Metals Company, 15; 42 (upd.)
Companhia Vale do Rio Doce, 43
Companhia Vale do Rio Duce, IV
Corporacion Nacional del Cobre de Chile, 40
CRA Limited, IV
Cyprus Amax Minerals Company, 21
Cyprus Minerals Company, 7
Daido Steel Co., Ltd., IV

De Beers Consolidated Mines Limited/De Beers Centenary AG, IV; 7 (upd.); 28 (upd.)
Degussa Group, IV
Dofasco Inc., IV; 24 (upd.)
Echo Bay Mines Ltd., IV; 38 (upd.)
Engelhard Corporation, IV
Fansteel Inc., 19
Fluor Corporation, 34 (upd.)
Freeport-McMoRan Inc., IV; 7 (upd.)
Fried. Krupp GmbH, IV
Gencor Ltd., IV, 22 (upd.)
Geneva Steel, 7
Gold Fields of South Africa Ltd., IV
Grupo Mexico, S.A. de C.V., 40
Handy & Harman, 23
Hanson PLC, 30 (upd.)
Hecla Mining Company, 20
Hemlo Gold Mines Inc., 9
Heraeus Holding GmbH, IV
Hitachi Metals, Ltd., IV
Hoesch AG, IV
Homestake Mining Company, 12; 38 (upd.)
The Hudson Bay Mining and Smelting Company, Limited, 12
Hylsamex, S.A. de C.V., 39
IMCO Recycling, Incorporated, 32
Imerys S.A., 40 (upd.)
Imetal S.A., IV
Inco Limited, IV
Industrias Penoles, S.A. de C.V., 22
Inland Steel Industries, Inc., IV; 19 (upd.)
Intermet Corporation, 32
Ispat Inland Inc., 40 (upd.)
Ispat International N.V., 30
Johnson Matthey PLC, IV; 16 (upd.)
Kaiser Aluminum & Chemical Corporation, IV
Kawasaki Steel Corporation, IV
Kennecott Corporation, 7; 27 (upd.)
Kentucky Electric Steel, Inc., 31
Kerr-McGee Corporation, 22 (upd.)
Kinross Gold Corporation, 36
Klockner-Werke AG, IV
Kobe Steel, Ltd., IV; 19 (upd.)
Koninklijke Nederlandsche Hoogovens en Staalfabrieken NV, IV
Laclede Steel Company, 15
Layne Christensen Company, 19
Lonrho Plc, 21
The LTV Corporation, 24 (upd.)
Lukens Inc., 14
Magma Copper Company, 7
The Marmon Group, IV; 16 (upd.)
MAXXAM Inc., 8
Metaleurop S.A., 21
Metallgesellschaft AG, IV
Minerals and Metals Trading Corporation of India Ltd., IV
Minerals Technologies Inc., 11
Mitsui Mining & Smelting Co., Ltd., IV
Mitsui Mining Company, Limited, IV
National Steel Corporation, 12
NERCO, Inc., 7
Newmont Mining Corporation, 7
Niagara Corporation, 28
Nichimen Corporation, IV
Nippon Light Metal Company, Ltd., IV
Nippon Steel Corporation, IV; 17 (upd.)
Nisshin Steel Co., Ltd., IV
NKK Corporation, IV; 28 (upd.)
Noranda Inc., IV; 7 (upd.)
North Star Steel Company, 18
Nucor Corporation, 7; 21 (upd.)
Oglebay Norton Company, 17
Okura & Co., Ltd., IV
Oregon Metallurgical Corporation, 20
Oregon Steel Mills, Inc., 14
Outokumpu Oyj, 38
Park Corp., 22
Peabody Coal Company, 10
Peabody Holding Company, Inc., IV
Pechiney, IV
Peter Kiewit Sons' Inc., 8
Phelps Dodge Corporation, IV; 28 (upd.)
The Pittston Company, IV; 19 (upd.)
Placer Dome Inc., 20
Pohang Iron and Steel Company Ltd., IV
Potash Corporation of Saskatchewan Inc., 18
Quanex Corporation, 13
RAG AG, 35
Reliance Steel & Aluminum Co., 19
Republic Engineered Steels, Inc., 7; 26 (upd.)
Reynolds Metals Company, IV
Rio Tinto plc, 19 (upd.)
RMC Group p.l.c., 34 (upd.)
Rouge Steel Company, 8
The RTZ Corporation PLC, IV
Ruhrkohle AG, IV
Ryerson Tull, Inc., 40 (upd.)
Saarberg-Konzern, IV
Salzgitter AG, IV
Sandvik AB, IV
Schnitzer Steel Industries, Inc., 19
Southern Peru Copper Corporation, 40
Southwire Company, Inc., 8; 23 (upd.)
Steel Authority of India Ltd., IV
Stelco Inc., IV
Sumitomo Metal Industries, Ltd., IV
Sumitomo Metal Mining Co., Ltd., IV
Tata Iron and Steel Company Ltd., IV
Teck Corporation, 27
Texas Industries, Inc., 8
Thyssen AG, IV
The Timken Company, 8; 42 (upd.)
Titanium Metals Corporation, 21
Tomen Corporation, IV
U.S. Borax, Inc., 42
Ugine S.A., 20
Usinor SA, 42 (upd.)
Usinor Sacilor, IV
VIAG Aktiengesellschaft, IV
Voest-Alpine Stahl AG, IV
Walter Industries, Inc., 22 (upd.)
Weirton Steel Corporation, IV; 26 (upd.)
Westmoreland Coal Company, 7
Wheeling-Pittsburgh Corp., 7
WMC, Limited, 43
Worthington Industries, Inc., 7; 21 (upd.)
Zambia Industrial and Mining Corporation Ltd., IV

PAPER & FORESTRY

Abitibi-Consolidated, Inc., 25 (upd.)
Abitibi-Price Inc., IV
Amcor Limited, IV; 19 (upd.)
American Pad & Paper Company, 20
Arjo Wiggins Appleton p.l.c., 34
Asplundh Tree Expert Co., 20
Avery Dennison Corporation, IV
Badger Paper Mills, Inc., 15
Beckett Papers, 23
Bemis Company, Inc., 8
Bohemia, Inc., 13
Boise Cascade Corporation, IV; 8 (upd.); 32 (upd.)
Bowater PLC, IV
Bunzl plc, IV
Canfor Corporation, 42
Caraustar Industries, Inc., 19
Champion International Corporation, IV; 20 (upd.)
Chesapeake Corporation, 8; 30 (upd.)
Consolidated Papers, Inc., 8; 36 (upd.)
Crane & Co., Inc., 26
Crown Vantage Inc., 29
CSS Industries, Inc., 35
Daio Paper Corporation, IV
Daishowa Paper Manufacturing Co., Ltd., IV
Dillard Paper Company, 11
Domtar Inc., IV
Enso-Gutzeit Oy, IV
Esselte Pendaflex Corporation, 11
Federal Paper Board Company, Inc., 8
FiberMark, Inc., 37
Fletcher Challenge Ltd., IV
Fort Howard Corporation, 8
Fort James Corporation, 22 (upd.)
Georgia-Pacific Corporation, IV; 9 (upd.)
Groupe Rougier SA, 21
Guilbert S.A., 42
Honshu Paper Co., Ltd., IV
International Paper Company, IV; 15 (upd.)
James River Corporation of Virginia, IV
Japan Pulp and Paper Company Limited, IV
Jefferson Smurfit Group plc, IV
Jujo Paper Co., Ltd., IV
Kimberly-Clark Corporation, 16 (upd.); 43 (upd.)
Kruger Inc., 17
Kymmene Corporation, IV
Longview Fibre Company, 8; 37 (upd.)
Louisiana-Pacific Corporation, IV; 31 (upd.)
MacMillan Bloedel Limited, IV
The Mead Corporation, IV; 19 (upd.)
Metsa-Serla Oy, IV
Mo och Domsjö AB, IV
Monadnock Paper Mills, Inc., 21
Mosinee Paper Corporation, 15
Nashua Corporation, 8
National Envelope Corporation, 32
NCH Corporation, 8
Oji Paper Co., Ltd., IV
P.H. Glatfelter Company, 8; 30 (upd.)
Packaging Corporation of America, 12
Papeteries de Lancey, 23
Plum Creek Timber Company, Inc., 43
Pope and Talbot, Inc., 12
Potlatch Corporation, 8; 34 (upd.)
PWA Group, IV
Rayonier Inc., 24
Rengo Co., Ltd., IV
Reno de Medici S.p.A., 41
Rexam PLC, 32 (upd.)
Riverwood International Corporation, 11
Rock-Tenn Company, 13
St. Joe Paper Company, 8
Sanyo-Kokusaku Pulp Co., Ltd., IV
Scott Paper Company, IV; 31 (upd.)
Sealed Air Corporation, 14
Sierra Pacific Industries, 22
Simpson Investment Company, 17
Specialty Coatings Inc., 8
Stone Container Corporation, IV
Stora Enso Oyj, 36 (upd.)
Stora Kopparbergs Bergslags AB, IV
Svenska Cellulosa Aktiebolaget SCA, IV; 28 (upd.)
Temple-Inland Inc., IV; 31 (upd.)
TJ International, Inc., 19
U.S. Timberlands Company, L.P., 42
Union Camp Corporation, IV
United Paper Mills Ltd. (Yhtyneet Paperitehtaat Oy), IV
Universal Forest Products Inc., 10
UPM-Kymmene Corporation, 19
West Fraser Timber Co. Ltd., 17
Westvaco Corporation, IV; 19 (upd.)

Weyerhaeuser Company, IV; 9 (upd.); 28 (upd.)
Wickes Inc., 25 (upd.)
Willamette Industries, Inc., IV; 31 (upd.)
WTD Industries, Inc., 20

PERSONAL SERVICES

AARP, 27
ADT Security Systems, Inc., 12
American Retirement Corporation, 42
Arthur Murray International, Inc., 32
Berlitz International, Inc., 39 (upd.)
Carriage Services, Inc., 37
Childtime Learning Centers, Inc., 34
Corinthian Colleges, Inc., 39
Correctional Services Corporation, 30
CUC International Inc., 16
DeVry Incorporated, 29
Educational Testing Service, 12
The Ford Foundation, 34
Franklin Quest Co., 11
Goodwill Industries International, Inc., 16
The John D. and Catherine T. MacArthur Foundation, 34
Kaplan, Inc., 42
KinderCare Learning Centers, Inc., 13
The Loewen Group Inc., 16; 40 (upd.)
Management and Training Corporation, 28
Manpower, Inc., 9
Regis Corporation, 18
The Rockefeller Foundation, 34
Rollins, Inc., 11
Rosenbluth International Inc., 14
Rotary International, 31
The Salvation Army USA, 32
Service Corporation International, 6
SOS Staffing Services, 25
Stewart Enterprises, Inc., 20
Supercuts Inc., 26
Weight Watchers International Inc., 12; 33 (upd.)
Youth Services International, Inc., 21

PETROLEUM

Abu Dhabi National Oil Company, IV
Agway, Inc., 21 (upd.)
Alberta Energy Company Ltd., 16; 43 (upd.)
Amerada Hess Corporation, IV; 21 (upd.)
Amoco Corporation, IV; 14 (upd.)
Anadarko Petroleum Corporation, 10
ANR Pipeline Co., 17
Anschutz Corp., 12
Apache Corporation, 10; 32 (upd.)
Arctic Slope Regional Corporation, 38
Ashland Inc., 19
Ashland Oil, Inc., IV
Atlantic Richfield Company, IV; 31 (upd.)
Baker Hughes Incorporated, 22 (upd.)
Belco Oil & Gas Corp., 40
BJ Services Company, 25
The British Petroleum Company plc, IV; 7 (upd.); 21 (upd.)
British-Borneo Oil & Gas PLC, 34
Broken Hill Proprietary Company Ltd., 22 (upd.)
Burlington Resources Inc., 10
Burmah Castrol PLC, IV; 30 (upd.)
Caltex Petroleum Corporation, 19
Chevron Corporation, IV; 19 (upd.)
Chiles Offshore Corporation, 9
Chinese Petroleum Corporation, IV; 31 (upd.)
CITGO Petroleum Corporation, IV; 31 (upd.)
The Coastal Corporation, IV; 31 (upd.)
Compañia Española de Petróleos S.A., IV
Conoco Inc., IV; 16 (upd.)
Cooper Cameron Corporation, 20 (upd.)
Cosmo Oil Co., Ltd., IV
Crown Central Petroleum Corporation, 7
DeepTech International Inc., 21
Den Norse Stats Oljeselskap AS, IV
Deutsche BP Aktiengesellschaft, 7
Diamond Shamrock, Inc., IV
Egyptian General Petroluem Corporation, IV
Elf Aquitaine SA, 21 (upd.)
Empresa Colombiana de Petróleos, IV
Enbridge Inc., 43
Energen Corporation, 21
Enron Corporation, 19
Ente Nazionale Idrocarburi, IV
Enterprise Oil plc, 11
Entreprise Nationale Sonatrach, IV
Exxon Corporation, IV; 7 (upd.); 32 (upd.)
Ferrellgas Partners, L.P., 35
FINA, Inc., 7
Flying J Inc., 19
Forest Oil Corporation, 19
General Sekiyu K.K., IV
Giant Industries, Inc., 19
Global Industries, Ltd., 37
Global Marine Inc., 9
Grey Wolf, Inc., 43
Halliburton Company, 25 (upd.)
Helmerich & Payne, Inc., 18
Holly Corporation, 12
Hunt Consolidated, Inc., 27 (upd.)
Hunt Oil Company, 7
Idemitsu Kosan K.K., IV
Imperial Oil Limited, IV; 25 (upd.)
Indian Oil Corporation Ltd., IV
Kanematsu Corporation, IV
Kerr-McGee Corporation, IV; 22 (upd.)
King Ranch, Inc., 14
Koch Industries, Inc., IV; 20 (upd.)
Koppers Industries, Inc., 26 (upd.)
Kuwait Petroleum Corporation, IV
Libyan National Oil Corporation, IV
The Louisiana Land and Exploration Company, 7
Lyondell Petrochemical Company, IV
MAPCO Inc., IV
Maxus Energy Corporation, 7
McDermott International, Inc., 37 (upd.)
Meteor Industries Inc., 33
Mitchell Energy and Development Corporation, 7
Mitsubishi Oil Co., Ltd., IV
Mobil Corporation, IV; 7 (upd.); 21 (upd.)
Murphy Oil Corporation, 7; 32 (upd.)
Nabors Industries, Inc., 9
National Iranian Oil Company, IV
Neste Oy, IV
NGC Corporation, 18
Nigerian National Petroleum Corporation, IV
Nippon Oil Company, Limited, IV
Noble Affiliates, Inc., 11
OAO Gazprom, 42
OAO LUKOIL, 40
Occidental Petroleum Corporation, IV; 25 (upd.)
Oil and Natural Gas Commission, IV
ÖMV Aktiengesellschaft, IV
Oryx Energy Company, 7
Parker Drilling Company, 28
Patina Oil & Gas Corporation, 24
Pennzoil Company, IV; 20 (upd.)
PERTAMINA, IV
Petro-Canada Limited, IV
PetroFina S.A., IV; 26 (upd.)
Petróleo Brasileiro S.A., IV
Petróleos de Portugal S.A., IV
Petróleos de Venezuela S.A., IV
Petróleos del Ecuador, IV
Petróleos Mexicanos, IV; 19 (upd.)
Petroleum Development Oman LLC, IV
Petronas, IV
Phillips Petroleum Company, IV; 40 (upd.)
Pogo Producing Company, 39
Premcor Inc., 37
Qatar General Petroleum Corporation, IV
Quaker State Corporation, 7; 21 (upd.)
Repsol S.A., IV; 16 (upd.)
Repsol-YPF S.A., 40 (upd.)
Resource America, Inc., 42
Rowan Companies, Inc., 43
Royal Dutch Petroleum Company/ The "Shell" Transport and Trading Company p.l.c., IV
Santa Fe International Corporation, 38
Sasol Limited, IV
Saudi Arabian Oil Company, IV; 17 (upd.)
Schlumberger Limited, 17 (upd.)
Seagull Energy Corporation, 11
Shanghai Petrochemical Co., Ltd., 18
Shell Oil Company, IV; 14 (upd.); 41 (upd.)
Showa Shell Sekiyu K.K., IV
Société Nationale Elf Aquitaine, IV; 7 (upd.)
Suburban Propane Partners, L.P., 30
Sun Company, Inc., IV
Sunoco, Inc., 28 (upd.)
Talisman Energy, 9
Tesoro Petroleum Corporation, 7
Texaco Inc., IV; 14 (upd.); 41 (upd.)
Tidewater Inc., 37 (upd.)
Tom Brown, Inc., 37
Tonen Corporation, IV; 16 (upd.)
Tosco Corporation, 7
Total Compagnie Française des Pétroles S.A., IV
TOTAL S.A., 24 (upd.)
TransMontaigne Inc., 28
Travel Ports of America, Inc., 17
Triton Energy Corporation, 11
Türkiye Petrolleri Anonim Ortakliği, IV
Ultramar Diamond Shamrock Corporation, 31 (upd.)
Ultramar PLC, IV
Union Texas Petroleum Holdings, Inc., 9
Unocal Corporation, IV; 24 (upd.)
USX Corporation, IV; 7 (upd.)
Valero Energy Corporation, 7
Varco International, Inc., 42
Vastar Resources, Inc., 24
Vintage Petroleum, Inc., 42
Wascana Energy Inc., 13
Weatherford International, Inc., 39
Western Atlas Inc., 12
Western Company of North America, 15
The Williams Companies, Inc., IV; 31 (upd.)
YPF Sociedad Anonima, IV

PUBLISHING & PRINTING

A.B.Dick Company, 28
A.H. Belo Corporation, 10; 30 (upd.)
Advance Publications Inc., IV; 19 (upd.)
Advanced Marketing Services, Inc., 34
Affiliated Publications, Inc., 7
Agence France-Presse, 34
American Banknote Corporation, 30
American Greetings Corporation, 7, 22 (upd.)
American Media, Inc., 27
American Printing House for the Blind, 26
Andrews McMeel Universal, 40
The Antioch Company, 40

Arandell Corporation, 37
Arnoldo Mondadori Editore S.p.A., IV; 19 (upd.)
The Associated Press, 31 (upd.)
The Atlantic Group, 23
Axel Springer Verlag AG, IV; 20 (upd.)
Banta Corporation, 12; 32 (upd.)
Bauer Publishing Group, 7
Berlitz International, Inc., 13
Bernard C. Harris Publishing Company, Inc., 39
Bertelsmann A.G., IV; 15 (upd.); 43 (upd.)
Big Flower Press Holdings, Inc., 21
Blue Mountain Arts, Inc., 29
Book-of-the-Month Club, Inc., 13
Bowne & Co., Inc., 23
Broderbund Software, 29 (upd.)
Brown Printing Company, 26
Burda Holding GmbH. & Co., 23
The Bureau of National Affairs, Inc., 23
Butterick Co., Inc., 23
Cadmus Communications Corporation, 23
Cahners Business Information, 43
CCH Inc., 14
Central Newspapers, Inc., 10
Champion Industries, Inc., 28
The Chronicle Publishing Company, Inc., 23
Chrysalis Group plc, 40
CMP Media Inc., 26
Commerce Clearing House, Inc., 7
Concepts Direct, Inc., 39
The Condé Nast Publications Inc., 13
Consumers Union, 26
The Copley Press, Inc., 23
Courier Corporation, 41
Cowles Media Company, 23
Cox Enterprises, Inc., IV; 22 (upd.)
Crain Communications, Inc., 12; 35 (upd.)
Current, Inc., 37
Dai Nippon Printing Co., Ltd., IV
Daily Mail and General Trust plc, 19
Dawson Holdings PLC, 43
Day Runner, Inc., 14
DC Comics Inc., 25
De La Rue plc, 10; 34 (upd.)
Deluxe Corporation, 7; 22 (upd.)
Dorling Kindersley Holdings plc, 20
Dover Publications Inc., 34
Dow Jones & Company, Inc., IV; 19 (upd.)
The Dun & Bradstreet Corporation, IV; 19 (upd.)
Duplex Products Inc., 17
The E.W. Scripps Company, IV; 7 (upd.); 28 (upd.)
Edmark Corporation, 14
Electronics for Imaging, Inc., 43 (upd.)
Elsevier N.V., IV
EMAP plc, 35
EMI Group plc, 22 (upd.)
Encyclopaedia Britannica, Inc., 39 (upd.)
Encyclopedia Britannica, Inc., 7
Engraph, Inc., 12
Enquirer/Star Group, Inc., 10
Entravision Communications Corporation, 41
Essence Communications, Inc., 24
Farm Journal Corporation, 42
Farrar, Straus and Giroux Inc., 15
Flint Ink Corporation, 13
Follett Corporation, 12; 39 (upd.)
Forbes Inc., 30
Franklin Electronic Publishers, Inc., 23
Freedom Communications, Inc., 36
Gannett Co., Inc., IV; 7 (upd.); 30 (upd.)
Gibson Greetings, Inc., 12
Golden Books Family Entertainment, Inc., 28
Goss Holdings, Inc., 43
Graphic Industries Inc., 25
Gray Communications Systems, Inc., 24
Grolier Incorporated, 16; 43 (upd.)
Groupe de la Cite, IV
Groupe Les Echos, 25
Hachette, IV
Hachette Filipacchi Medias S.A., 21
Hallmark Cards, Inc., IV; 16 (upd.); 40 (upd.)
Harcourt Brace and Co., 12
Harcourt Brace Jovanovich, Inc., IV
Harcourt General, Inc., 20 (upd.)
HarperCollins Publishers, 15
Harris Interactive Inc., 41
Harte-Hanks Communications, Inc., 17
Havas SA, 10; 33 (upd.)
Hazelden Foundation, 28
The Hearst Corporation, IV; 19 (upd.)
Her Majesty's Stationery Office, 7
N.V. Holdingmaatschappij De Telegraaf, 23
Hollinger International Inc., 24
Houghton Mifflin Company, 10; 36 (upd.)
IDG Books Worldwide, Inc., 27
International Data Group, Inc., 7; 25 (upd.)
IPC Magazines Limited, 7
John Fairfax Holdings Limited, 7
John H. Harland Company, 17
John Wiley & Sons, Inc., 17
Johnson Publishing Company, Inc., 28
Johnston Press plc, 35
Jostens, Inc., 25 (upd.)
Journal Register Company, 29
Kaplan, Inc., 42
Kinko's, Inc., 43 (upd.)
Knight-Ridder, Inc., IV; 15 (upd.)
Kodansha Ltd., IV; 38 (upd.)
Krause Publications, Inc., 35
Landmark Communications, Inc., 12
Larry Flynt Publishing Inc., 31
Le Monde S.A., 33
Lee Enterprises, Incorporated, 11
LEXIS-NEXIS Group, 33
Maclean Hunter Publishing Limited, IV; 26 (upd.)
Macmillan, Inc., 7
Martha Stewart Living Omnimedia, L.L.C., 24
Marvel Entertainment Group, Inc., 10
Matra-Hachette S.A., 15 (upd.)
Maxwell Communication Corporation plc, IV; 7 (upd.)
McClatchy Newspapers, Inc., 23
The McGraw-Hill Companies, Inc., IV; 18 (upd.)
Mecklermedia Corporation, 24
Media General, Inc., 38 (upd.)
Meredith Corporation, 11; 29 (upd.)
Merrill Corporation, 18
The Miner Group International, 22
Mirror Group Newspapers plc, 7; 23 (upd.)
Moore Corporation Limited, IV
Morris Communications Corporation, 36
Multimedia, Inc., 11
National Audubon Society, 26
National Geographic Society, 9; 30 (upd.)
New York Daily News, 32
The New York Times Company, IV; 19 (upd.)
News America Publishing Inc., 12
News Corporation Limited, IV; 7 (upd.)
Newsquest plc, 32
Nihon Keizai Shimbun, Inc., IV
Ottaway Newspapers, Inc., 15
Outlook Group Corporation, 37
Pearson plc, IV
Penton Media, Inc., 27
Petersen Publishing Company, 21
Playboy Enterprises, Inc., 18
Pleasant Company, 27
PR Newswire, 35
Primedia Inc., 22
The Providence Journal Company, 28
Publishers Group, Inc., 35
Pulitzer Publishing Company, 15
Quad/Graphics, Inc., 19
Quebecor Inc., 12
R.L. Polk & Co., 10
R.R. Donnelley & Sons Company, IV; 9 (upd.); 38 (upd.)
Rand McNally & Company, 28
Random House Inc., 13; 31 (upd.)
The Reader's Digest Association, Inc., IV; 17 (upd.)
Recycled Paper Greetings, Inc., 21
Reed Elsevier plc, 31 (upd.)
Reed International PLC, IV; 17 (upd.)
Reuters Holdings PLC, IV; 22 (upd.)
Rodale Press, Inc., 23
Rogers Communications Inc., 30 (upd.)
St Ives plc, 34
Schawk, Inc., 24
Schibsted ASA, 31
Scholastic Corporation, 10; 29 (upd.)
Scott Fetzer Company, 12
Scottish Media Group plc, 32
Seattle Times Company, 15
The Sierra Club, 28
Simon & Schuster Inc., IV; 19 (upd.)
Sir Speedy, Inc., 16
SkyMall, Inc., 26
Softbank Corp., 13
Southam Inc., 7
Standard Register Co., 15
Taylor Corporation, 36
Taylor Publishing Company, 12; 36 (upd.)
Thomas Nelson, Inc., 14; 38 (upd.)
Thomas Publishing Company, 26
The Thomson Corporation, 8; 34 (upd.)
The Times Mirror Company, IV; 17 (upd.)
Tom Doherty Associates Inc., 25
Toppan Printing Co., Ltd., IV
The Topps Company, Inc., 34 (upd.)
Torstar Corporation, 29
Tribune Company, IV, 22 (upd.)
U.S. News and World Report Inc., 30
United News & Media plc, 28 (upd.)
United Newspapers plc, IV
United Press International, Inc., 25
Valassis Communications, Inc., 8
Value Line, Inc., 16
Verlagsgruppe Georg von Holtzbrinck GmbH, 35
Village Voice Media, Inc., 38
VNU N.V., 27
Volt Information Sciences Inc., 26
W.W. Norton & Company, Inc., 28
Wallace Computer Services, Inc., 36
The Washington Post Company, IV; 20 (upd.)
Waverly, Inc., 16
Wenner Media, Inc., 32
West Group, 34 (upd.)
West Publishing Co., 7
Western Publishing Group, Inc., 13
WH Smith PLC, 42 (upd.)
Wolters Kluwer NV, 14; 33 (upd.)
World Book, Inc., 12
World Color Press Inc., 12
Xeikon NV, 26
Zebra Technologies Corporation, 14
Ziff Communications Company, 12
Ziff Davis Media Inc., 36 (upd.)
Zondervan Publishing House, 24

REAL ESTATE

Amfac/JMB Hawaii L.L.C., 24 (upd.)
Associated Estates Realty Corporation, 25
Boston Properties, Inc., 22
Bramalea Ltd., 9
Canary Wharf Group Plc, 30
CapStar Hotel Company, 21
Castle & Cooke, Inc., 20 (upd.)
Catellus Development Corporation, 24
CB Commercial Real Estate Services Group, Inc., 21
Chateau Communities, Inc., 37
Cheung Kong (Holdings) Limited, IV; 20 (upd.)
Del Webb Corporation, 14
The Edward J. DeBartolo Corporation, 8
Fairfield Communities, Inc., 36
Forest City Enterprises, Inc., 16
Gecina SA, 42
Griffin Land & Nurseries, Inc., 43
Grubb & Ellis Company, 21
The Haminerson Property Investment and Development Corporation plc, IV
Hammerson plc, 40
Harbert Corporation, 14
Helmsley Enterprises, Inc., 39 (upd.)
Home Properties of New York, Inc., 42
Hongkong Land Holdings Limited, IV
Hyatt Corporation, 16 (upd.)
JMB Realty Corporation, IV
Kaufman and Broad Home Corporation, 8
Kerry Properties Limited, 22
Kimco Realty Corporation, 11
The Koll Company, 8
Land Securities PLC, IV
Lefrak Organization Inc., 26
Lend Lease Corporation Limited, IV; 17 (upd.)
Lincoln Property Company, 8
The Loewen Group Inc., 40 (upd.)
Mack-Cali Realty Corporation, 42
Manufactured Home Communities, Inc., 22
Maui Land & Pineapple Company, Inc., 29
Maxco Inc., 17
Meditrust, 11
Melvin Simon and Associates, Inc., 8
MEPC plc, IV
Meritage Corporation, 26
Mitsubishi Estate Company, Limited, IV
Mitsui Real Estate Development Co., Ltd., IV
The Nature Conservancy, 28
New Plan Realty Trust, 11
New World Development Company Ltd., IV
Newhall Land and Farming Company, 14
Olympia & York Developments Ltd., IV; 9 (upd.)
Park Corp., 22
Perini Corporation, 8
Post Properties, Inc., 26
Rodamco N.V., 26
The Rouse Company, 15
Shubert Organization Inc., 24
The Sierra Club, 28
Simco S.A., 37
Slough Estates PLC, IV
Starrett Corporation, 21
Storage USA, Inc., 21
Sumitomo Realty & Development Co., Ltd., IV
Taylor Woodrow plc, 38 (upd.)
Tejon Ranch Company, 35
Tokyu Land Corporation, IV
Trammell Crow Company, 8
Trendwest Resorts, Inc., 33
Tridel Enterprises Inc., 9
Trizec Corporation Ltd., 10
Trump Organization, 23
Unibail SA, 40
Vistana, Inc., 22
Vornado Realty Trust, 20

RETAIL & WHOLESALE

A.C. Moore Arts & Crafts, Inc., 30
Aaron Rents, Inc., 14; 35 (upd.)
ABC Appliance, Inc., 10
ABC Carpet & Home Co. Inc., 26
Abercrombie & Fitch Co., 15
Academy Sports & Outdoors, 27
Ace Hardware Corporation, 12; 35 (upd.)
Action Performance Companies, Inc., 27
Alba-Waldensian, Inc., 30
Alberto-Culver Company, 36 (upd.)
Allders plc, 37
Allou Health & Beauty Care, Inc., 28
Amazon.com, Inc., 25
American Coin Merchandising, Inc., 28
American Eagle Outfitters, Inc., 24
American Furniture Company, Inc., 21
American Stores Company, 22 (upd.)
AmeriSource Health Corporation, 37 (upd.)
Ames Department Stores, Inc., 9; 30 (upd.)
Amway Corporation, 13; 30 (upd.)
The Andersons, Inc., 31
Ann Taylor Stores Corporation, 13
AnnTaylor Stores Corporation, 37 (upd.)
Appliance Recycling Centers of America, Inc., 42
Arbor Drugs Inc., 12
Arcadia Group plc, 28 (upd.)
Army and Air Force Exchange Service, 39
Art Van Furniture, Inc., 28
ASDA Group plc, 28 (upd.)
Ashworth, Inc., 26
Au Printemps S.A., V
Audio King Corporation, 24
Authentic Fitness Corp., 20
Auto Value Associates, Inc., 25
AutoZone, Inc., 9; 31 (upd.)
AVA AG (Allgemeine Handelsgesellschaft der Verbraucher AG), 33
Aveda Corporation, 24
Aviation Sales Company, 41
B. Dalton Bookseller Inc., 25
Babbage's, Inc., 10
Baby Superstore, Inc., 15
Baccarat, 24
Bachman's Inc., 22
Banana Republic Inc., 25
Barnes & Noble, Inc., 10; 30 (upd.)
Barnett Inc., 28
Barney's, Inc., 28
Bass Pro Shops, Inc., 42
Bear Creek Corporation, 38
Bearings, Inc., 13
bebe stores, inc., 31
Bed Bath & Beyond Inc., 13; 41 (upd.)
Belk Stores Services, Inc., V; 19 (upd.)
Bergen Brunswig Corporation, V; 13 (upd.)
Bernard Chaus, Inc., 27
Best Buy Co., Inc., 9; 23 (upd.)
Bhs plc, 17
Big O Tires, Inc., 20
Birkenstock Footprint Sandals, Inc., 42 (upd.)
Black Box Corporation, 20
Blacks Leisure Group plc, 39
Blair Corporation, 25; 31 (upd.)
Bloomingdale's Inc., 12
Blue Square Israel Ltd., 41
Blyth Industries, Inc., 18
The Body Shop International PLC, 11
The Bombay Company, Inc., 10
The Bon Marché, Inc., 23
The Bon-Ton Stores, Inc., 16
Books-A-Million, Inc., 14; 41 (upd.)
The Boots Company PLC, V; 24 (upd.)
Borders Group, Inc., 15; 43 (upd.)
Boscov's Department Store, Inc., 31
Bozzuto's, Inc., 13
Bradlees Discount Department Store Company, 12
Brambles Industries Limited, 42
Broder Bros. Co., 38
Brooks Brothers Inc., 22
Brookstone, Inc., 18
The Buckle, Inc., 18
Buhrmann NV, 41
Burlington Coat Factory Warehouse Corporation, 10
The Burton Group plc, V
Buttrey Food & Drug Stores Co., 18
C&A, 40 (upd.)
C&A Brenninkmeyer KG, V
Cabela's Inc., 26
Cablevision Electronic Instruments, Inc., 32
Cache Incorporated, 30
Caldor Inc., 12
Camelot Music, Inc., 26
Campeau Corporation, V
Campo Electronics, Appliances & Computers, Inc., 16
Carrefour SA, 10; 27 (upd.)
Carson Pirie Scott & Company, 15
Carter Hawley Hale Stores, Inc., V
Cartier Monde, 29
Casual Corner Group, Inc., 43
Catherines Stores Corporation, 15
Cato Corporation, 14
CDW Computer Centers, Inc., 16
Celebrity, Inc., 22
Central Garden & Pet Company, 23
Chadwick's of Boston, Ltd., 29
Charlotte Russe Holding, Inc., 35
Charming Shoppes, Inc., 38
The Children's Place Retail Stores, Inc., 37
Christopher & Banks Corporation, 42
Cifra, S.A. de C.V., 12
The Circle K Company, 20 (upd.)
Circuit City Stores, Inc., 9; 29 (upd.)
Clinton Cards plc, 39
The Clothestime, Inc., 20
CML Group, Inc., 10
Coborn's, Inc., 30
Coinmach Laundry Corporation, 20
Coldwater Creek Inc., 21
Cole National Corporation, 13
Coles Myer Ltd., V; 20 (upd.)
Comdisco, Inc., 9
CompUSA, Inc., 10
Computerland Corp., 13
Concepts Direct, Inc., 39
The Container Store, 36
Controladora Comercial Mexicana, S.A. de C.V., 36
Corby Distilleries Limited, 14
Corporate Express, Inc., 22
The Cosmetic Center, Inc., 22
Cost Plus, Inc., 27
Costco Wholesale Corporation, V; 43 (upd.)
Cotter & Company, V
County Seat Stores Inc., 9
CPI Corp., 38
Crate and Barrel, 9
Croscill, Inc., 42
Crowley, Milner & Company, 19
Crown Books Corporation, 21
Cumberland Farms, Inc., 17
Daffy's Inc., 26
The Daiei, Inc., V; 17 (upd.); 41 (upd.)

The Daimaru, Inc., V; 42 (upd.)
Dairy Mart Convenience Stores, Inc., 25 (upd.)
Daisytek International Corporation, 18
Damark International, Inc., 18
Dart Group Corporation, 16
Darty S.A., 27
David's Bridal, Inc., 33
Dayton Hudson Corporation, V; 18 (upd.)
Deb Shops, Inc., 16
Debenhams Plc, 28
dELiA*s Inc., 29
Department 56, Inc., 34 (upd.)
Designer Holdings Ltd., 20
Deveaux S.A., 41
Diesel SpA, 40
Dillard Department Stores, Inc., V; 16 (upd.)
Dillon Companies Inc., 12
Discount Auto Parts, Inc., 18
Discount Drug Mart, Inc., 14
Dixons Group plc, V; 19 (upd.)
Do it Best Corporation, 30
Dollar Tree Stores, Inc., 23
The Dress Barn, Inc., 24
Drug Emporium, Inc., 12
Du Pareil au Même, 43
Duane Reade Holding Corp., 21
Duckwall-ALCO Stores, Inc., 24
Duty Free International, Inc., 11
Dylex Limited, 29
E-Z Serve Corporation, 17
Eagle Hardware & Garden, Inc., 16
eBay Inc., 32
Eckerd Corporation, 9; 32 (upd.)
Eddie Bauer, Inc., 36 (upd.)
Egghead.com, Inc., 31 (upd.)
El Corte Inglés Group, V
Elder-Beerman Stores Corporation, 10
Ellett Brothers, Inc., 17
EMI Group plc, 22 (upd.)
Ethan Allen Interiors, Inc., 39 (upd.)
EToys, Inc., 37
Euromarket Designs Inc., 31 (upd.)
Evans, Inc., 30
EZCORP Inc., 43
Family Dollar Stores, Inc., 13
Fastenal Company, 14; 42 (upd.)
Fay's Inc., 17
Federated Department Stores, Inc., 9; 31 (upd.)
Fielmann AG, 31
Fila Holding S.p.A., 20
Fingerhut Companies, Inc., 9; 36 (upd.)
The Finish Line, Inc., 29
Finlay Enterprises, Inc., 16
Fleming Companies, Inc., 17 (upd.)
Florsheim Shoe Company, 9
Florsheim Shoe Group Inc., 31 (upd.)
FNAC, 21
Follett Corporation, 12
Footstar, Incorporated, 24
Fortunoff Fine Jewelry and Silverware Inc., 26
Frank's Nursery & Crafts, Inc., 12
Fred Meyer, Inc., V; 20 (upd.)
Fred's, Inc., 23
Frederick Atkins Inc., 16
Fretter, Inc., 10
Friedman's Inc., 29
Funco, Inc., 20
G.I. Joe's, Inc., 30
Gadzooks, Inc., 18
Gaiam, Inc., 41
Galeries Lafayette S.A., V; 23 (upd.)
Gander Mountain, Inc., 20
Gantos, Inc., 17
The Gap, Inc., V; 18 (upd.)
Garden Ridge Corporation, 27
Gart Sports Company, 24
GEHE AG, 27
General Binding Corporation, 10
General Host Corporation, 12
Genesco Inc., 17
Genovese Drug Stores, Inc., 18
Gerald Stevens, Inc., 37
Giant Food Inc., 22 (upd.)
GIB Group, V; 26 (upd.)
The Good Guys!, Inc., 10
The Good Guys, Inc., 30 (upd.)
Goodwill Industries International, Inc., 16
Goody's Family Clothing, Inc., 20
Gottschalks, Inc., 18
GrandVision S.A., 43
The Great Universal Stores plc, V; 19 (upd.)
Griffin Land & Nurseries, Inc., 43
Grossman's Inc., 13
Groupe Castorama-Dubois Investissements, 23
Groupe DMC (Dollfus Mieg & Cie), 27
Groupe Go Sport S.A., 39
Groupe Lapeyre S.A., 33
Groupe Zannier S.A., 35
Grow Biz International, Inc., 18
Grupo Casa Saba, S.A. de C.V., 39
Grupo Elektra, S.A. de C.V., 39
Grupo Gigante, S.A. de C.V., 34
Gruppo Coin S.p.A., 41
GT Bicycles, 26
Guccio Gucci, S.p.A., 15
Guilbert S.A., 42
Guitar Center, Inc., 29
Hahn Automotive Warehouse, Inc., 24
Half Price Books, Records, Magazines Inc., 37
Hallmark Cards, Inc., 40 (upd.)
Hammacher Schlemmer & Company, 21
Hancock Fabrics, Inc., 18
Hankyu Department Stores, Inc., V
Hanover Direct, Inc., 36
Harold's Stores, Inc., 22
Hasbro, Inc., 43 (upd.)
Haverty Furniture Companies, Inc., 31
Hechinger Company, 12
Heilig-Meyers Company, 14; 40 (upd.)
Helzberg Diamonds, 40
Hennes & Mauritz AB, 29
Henry Modell & Company Inc., 32
Hertie Waren- und Kaufhaus GmbH, V
Hibbett Sporting Goods, Inc., 26
Hills Stores Company, 13
The Hockey Company, 34
Holiday RV Superstores, Incorporated, 26
Holt's Cigar Holdings, Inc., 42
The Home Depot, Inc., V; 18 (upd.)
Home Shopping Network, Inc., V; 25 (upd.)
HomeBase, Inc., 33 (upd.)
Hot Topic, Inc., 33
House of Fabrics, Inc., 21
Hudson's Bay Company, V; 25 (upd.)
The IKEA Group, V
IKEA International A/S, 26 (upd.)
InaCom Corporation, 13
Insight Enterprises, Inc., 18
Intimate Brands, Inc., 24
Isetan Company Limited, V; 36 (upd.)
Ito-Yokado Co., Ltd., V; 42 (upd.)
J&R Electronics Inc., 26
J. Baker, Inc., 31
The J. Jill Group, Inc., 35
J.C. Penney Company, Inc., V; 18 (upd.); 43 (upd.)
Jack Schwartz Shoes, Inc., 18
Jacobson Stores Inc., 21
Jalate Inc., 25
James Beattie plc, 43
Jay Jacobs, Inc., 15
Jennifer Convertibles, Inc., 31
Jetro Cash & Carry Enterprises Inc., 38
JG Industries, Inc., 15
JJB Sports plc, 32
John Lewis Partnership plc, V; 42 (upd.)
JUSCO Co., Ltd., V
Just For Feet, Inc., 19
K & B Inc., 12
K & G Men's Center, Inc., 21
K-tel International, Inc., 21
Karstadt Aktiengesellschaft, V; 19 (upd.)
Kash n' Karry Food Stores, Inc., 20
Kasper A.S.L., Ltd., 40
Kaufhof Holding AG, V
Kaufhof Warenhaus AG, 23 (upd.)
Kaufring AG, 35
Kay-Bee Toy Stores, 15
Kingfisher plc, V; 24 (upd.)
Kinney Shoe Corp., 14
Kmart Corporation, V; 18 (upd.)
Knoll Group Inc., 14
Kohl's Corporation, 9; 30 (upd.)
Kotobukiya Co., Ltd., V
Krause's Furniture, Inc., 27
L. Luria & Son, Inc., 19
L.A. T Sportswear, Inc., 26
L.L. Bean, Inc., 38 (upd.)
La-Z-Boy Chair Company, 14
Lamonts Apparel, Inc., 15
Lands' End, Inc., 9; 29 (upd.)
Laura Ashley Holdings plc, 37 (upd.)
Lazare Kaplan International Inc., 21
Lechmere Inc., 10
Lechters, Inc., 11; 39 (upd.)
LensCrafters Inc., 23
Lesco Inc., 19
Leslie's Poolmart, Inc., 18
Levitz Furniture Inc., 15
Lewis Galoob Toys Inc., 16
Lifetime Hoan Corporation, 27
Lillian Vernon Corporation, 12; 35
The Limited, Inc., V; 20 (upd.)
Linens 'n Things, Inc., 24
The Littlewoods Organisation PLC, V
Littlewoods plc, 42 (upd.)
Liz Claiborne, Inc., 25 (upd.)
Loehmann's Inc., 24
Lojas Arapuã S.A., 22
Longs Drug Stores Corporation, V; 25 (upd.)
Lost Arrow Inc., 22
LOT$OFF Corporation, 24
Lowe's Companies, Inc., V; 21 (upd.)
Mac Frugal's Bargains - Closeouts Inc., 17
MarineMax, Inc., 30
Marks and Spencer p.l.c., V; 24 (upd.)
Marks Brothers Jewelers, Inc., 24
Marshalls Incorporated, 13
Marui Co., Ltd., V
Maruzen Co., Limited, 18
Mary Kay, Inc., 30 (upd.)
Matsuzakaya Company Limited, V
The Maxim Group, 25
The May Department Stores Company, V; 19 (upd.)
Mayor's Jewelers, Inc., 41
Mazel Stores, Inc., 29
McLane Company, Inc., 13
MCSi, Inc., 41
Media Arts Group, Inc., 42
Meier & Frank Co., 23
Meijer Incorporated, 27 (upd.)
Melville Corporation, V
The Men's Wearhouse, Inc., 17
Menard, Inc., 34

Mercantile Stores Company, Inc., V; 19 (upd.)
Merry-Go-Round Enterprises, Inc., 8
Mervyn's, 10
Mervyn's California, 39 (upd.)
Michaels Stores, Inc., 17
Micro Warehouse, Inc., 16
MicroAge, Inc., 16
Mitsukoshi Ltd., V
Monsoon plc, 39
Montgomery Ward & Co., Incorporated, V; 20 (upd.)
Moore-Handley, Inc., 39
Morse Shoe Inc., 13
Mothers Work, Inc., 18
Mr. Bricolage S.A., 37
MTS Inc., 37
Musicland Stores Corporation, 9; 38 (upd.)
Nagasakiya Co., Ltd., V
National Intergroup, Inc., V
National Record Mart, Inc., 29
Natural Wonders Inc., 14
Navy Exchange Service Command, 31
Neff Corp., 32
Neiman Marcus Co., 12
New Look Group plc, 35
Next plc, 29
Nichii Co., Ltd., V
NIKE, Inc., 36 (upd.)
Nine West Group Inc., 11
99¢ Only Stores, 25
Noland Company, 35
Noodle Kidoodle, 16
Nordstrom, Inc., V; 18 (upd.)
Norelco Consumer Products Co., 26
The North West Company, Inc., 12
Norton McNaughton, Inc., 27
Nu Skin Enterprises, Inc., 27
Office Depot Incorporated, 8; 23 (upd.)
OfficeMax, Inc., 15; 43 (upd.)
Old America Stores, Inc., 17
One Price Clothing Stores, Inc., 20
Orchard Supply Hardware Stores Corporation, 17
Organización Soriana, S.A. de C.V., 35
The Orvis Company, Inc., 28
OshKosh B'Gosh, Inc., 42 (upd.)
Oshman's Sporting Goods, Inc., 17
Otto Versand (GmbH & Co.), V; 15 (upd.); 34 (upd.)
Owens & Minor, Inc., 16
P.C. Richard & Son Corp., 23
Pamida Holdings Corporation, 15
The Pampered Chef, Ltd., 18
The Pantry, Inc., 36
Parisian, Inc., 14
Paul Harris Stores, Inc., 18
Pay 'N Pak Stores, Inc., 9
Payless Cashways, Inc., 11
Payless ShoeSource, Inc., 18
Pearle Vision, Inc., 13
Peebles Inc., 16; 43 (upd.)
Peet's Coffee & Tea, Inc., 38
Petco Animal Supplies, Inc., 29
Petrie Stores Corporation, 8
PETsMART, Inc., 14; 41 (upd.)
Phar-Mor Inc., 12
Pier 1 Imports, Inc., 12; 34 (upd.)
Piercing Pagoda, Inc., 29
Pinault-Printemps Redoute S.A., 19 (upd.)
Pomeroy Computer Resources, Inc., 33
Powell's Books, Inc., 40
The Price Company, V
PriceCostco, Inc., 14
Proffitt's, Inc., 19
Purina Mills, Inc., 32
Quelle Group, V
QuikTrip Corporation, 36
Quill Corporation, 28
R.H. Macy & Co., Inc., V; 8 (upd.); 30 (upd.)
RadioShack Corporation, 36 (upd.)
Rag Shops, Inc., 30
Raley's Inc., 14
Rapala-Normark Group, Ltd., 30
RDO Equipment Company, 33
Reckitt Benckiser plc, 42 (upd.)
Recoton Corp., 15
Recreational Equipment, Inc., 18
Reeds Jewelers, Inc., 22
Rent-Way, Inc., 33
Restoration Hardware, Inc., 30
Revco D.S., Inc., V
REX Stores Corp., 10
Rhodes Inc., 23
Richton International Corporation, 39
Riklis Family Corp., 9
Rite Aid Corporation, V; 19 (upd.)
Ritz Camera Centers, 34
Roberds Inc., 19
Rocky Shoes & Boots, Inc., 26
Rogers Communications Inc., 30 (upd.)
Rooms To Go Inc., 28
Roots Canada Ltd., 42
Rose's Stores, Inc., 13
Ross Stores, Inc., 17; 43 (upd.)
Roundy's Inc., 14
S&K Famous Brands, Inc., 23
Saks Holdings, Inc., 24
Saks Inc., 41 (upd.)
Sam Ash Music Corporation, 30
Sam's Club, 40
Samuels Jewelers Incorporated, 30
Sanborn Hermanos, S.A., 20
Schmitt Music Company, 40
Schneiderman's Furniture Inc., 28
Schottenstein Stores Corp., 14
Schultz Sav-O Stores, Inc., 31
The Score Board, Inc., 19
Scotty's, Inc., 22
SCP Pool Corporation, 39
Seaman Furniture Company, Inc., 32
Sears plc, V
Sears Roebuck de México, S.A. de C.V., 20
Sears, Roebuck and Co., V; 18 (upd.)
SED International Holdings, Inc., 43
Seibu Department Stores, Ltd., V; 42 (upd.)
Seigle's Home and Building Centers, Inc., 41
The Seiyu, Ltd., V; 36 (upd.)
Selfridges Plc, 34
Service Merchandise Company, Inc., V; 19 (upd.)
7-Eleven, Inc., 32 (upd.)
Shaklee Corporation, 12
The Sharper Image Corporation, 10
Shoe Carnival Inc., 14
ShopKo Stores Inc., 21
SkyMall, Inc., 26
Sleepy's Inc., 32
Solo Serve Corporation, 28
Sound Advice, Inc., 41
Southern States Cooperative Incorporated, 36
Spec's Music, Inc., 19
Spiegel, Inc., 10; 27 (upd.)
Sport Chalet, Inc., 16
Sport Supply Group, Inc., 23
Sportmart, Inc., 15
Sports & Recreation, Inc., 17
The Sports Authority, Inc., 16; 43 (upd.)
The Sportsman's Guide, Inc., 36
Stage Stores, Inc., 24
Stanhome Inc., 15
Staples, Inc., 10
Starbucks Corporation, 34 (upd.)
Starcraft Corporation, 30
Stein Mart Inc., 19
Stinnes AG, 8
The Stop & Shop Companies, Inc., 24 (upd.)
Storehouse PLC, 16
Stride Rite Corporation, 8
Strouds, Inc., 33
Stuller Settings, Inc., 35
Successories, Inc., 30
Sun Television & Appliances Inc., 10
Sunglass Hut International, Inc., 21
Supreme International Corporation, 27
Swarovski International Holding AG, 40
Syms Corporation, 29
Takashimaya Co., Limited, V
The Talbots, Inc., 11; 31 (upd.)
Target Stores, 10; 27 (upd.)
Tati SA, 25
Tattered Cover Book Store, 43
Tech Data Corporation, 10
Tengelmann Group, 27
Tesco PLC, 24 (upd.)
Thrifty PayLess, Inc., 12
Tiffany & Co., 14
The TJX Companies, Inc., V; 19 (upd.)
Today's Man, Inc., 20
Tokyu Department Store Co., Ltd., V; 32 (upd.)
Tops Appliance City, Inc., 17
Toys "R" Us, Inc., V; 18 (upd.)
Travis Boats & Motors, Inc., 37
Travis Perkins plc, 34
Trend-Lines, Inc., 22
TruServ Corporation, 24
Tuesday Morning Corporation, 18
Tupperware Corporation, 28
TVI, Inc., 15
Tweeter Home Entertainment Group, Inc., 30
Ultimate Electronics, Inc., 18
Ultramar Diamond Shamrock Corporation, 31 (upd.)
Uni-Marts, Inc., 17
United Rentals, Inc., 34
The United States Shoe Corporation, V
United Stationers Inc., 14
Universal International, Inc., 25
Uny Co., Ltd., V
Urban Outfitters, Inc., 14
Valley Media Inc., 35
Value City Department Stores, Inc., 38
Value Merchants Inc., 13
ValueVision International, Inc., 22
Venator Group Inc., 35 (upd.)
Vendex International N.V., 13
Venture Stores Inc., 12
The Vermont Teddy Bear Co., Inc., 36
Viking Office Products, Inc., 10
Vorwerk & Co., 27
W. Atlee Burpee & Co., 27
W H Smith Group PLC, V
W.W. Grainger, Inc., V
Waban Inc., 13
Wacoal Corp., 25
Wal-Mart de Mexico, S.A. de C.V., 35 (upd.)
Wal-Mart Stores, Inc., V; 8 (upd.); 26 (upd.)
Walden Book Company Inc., 17
Walgreen Co., V; 20 (upd.)
Wall Drug Store, Inc., 40
Weiner's Stores, Inc., 33
West Marine, Inc., 17
Western Beef, Inc., 22
The Wet Seal, Inc., 18

Weyco Group, Incorporated, 32
WH Smith PLC, 42 (upd.)
Whole Foods Market, Inc., 20
Wickes Inc., V; 25 (upd.)
Williams-Sonoma, Inc., 17
Wilsons The Leather Experts Inc., 21
Wolohan Lumber Co., 19
Woolworth Corporation, V; 20 (upd.)
World Duty Free Americas, Inc., 29 (upd.)
The Yankee Candle Company, Inc., 37
Young's Market Company, LLC, 32
Younkers, Inc., 19
Zale Corporation, 16; 40 (upd.)
Zany Brainy, Inc., 31
Ziebart International Corporation, 30
Zion's Cooperative Mercantile Institution, 33

RUBBER & TIRE

Aeroquip Corporation, 16
Bandag, Inc., 19
The BFGoodrich Company, V
Bridgestone Corporation, V; 21 (upd.)
Carlisle Companies Incorporated, 8
Compagnie Générale des Établissements Michelin, V; 42 (upd.)
Continental Aktiengesellschaft, V
Continental General Tire Corp., 23
Cooper Tire & Rubber Company, 8; 23 (upd.)
Elementis plc, 40 (upd.)
General Tire, Inc., 8
The Goodyear Tire & Rubber Company, V; 20 (upd.)
The Kelly-Springfield Tire Company, 8
Myers Industries, Inc., 19
Pirelli S.p.A., V; 15 (upd.)
Safeskin Corporation, 18
Sumitomo Rubber Industries, Ltd., V
Tillotson Corp., 15
Treadco, Inc., 19
Ube Industries, Ltd., 38 (upd.)
The Yokohama Rubber Co., Ltd., V; 19 (upd.)

TELECOMMUNICATIONS

A.H. Belo Corporation, 30 (upd.)
Acme-Cleveland Corp., 13
ADC Telecommunications, Inc., 10
Adelphia Communications Corp., 17
Adtran Inc., 22
AEI Music Network Inc., 35
AirTouch Communications, 11
Alcatel S.A., 36 (upd.)
Alliance Atlantis Communications Inc., 39
Alltel Corporation, 6
American Telephone and Telegraph Company, V
American Tower Corporation, 33
Ameritech Corporation, V; 18 (upd.)
Arch Wireless, Inc., 39
ARD, 41
Ascom AG, 9
Aspect Telecommunications Corporation, 22
AT&T Bell Laboratories, Inc., 13
AT&T Corporation, 29 (upd.)
BCE Inc., V
Belgacom, 6
Bell Atlantic Corporation, V; 25 (upd.)
Bell Canada, 6
BellSouth Corporation, V; 29 (upd.)
BET Holdings, Inc., 18
BHC Communications, Inc., 26
Bonneville International Corporation, 29
Bouygues S.A., 24 (upd.)
Brightpoint, Inc., 18
Brite Voice Systems, Inc., 20
British Columbia Telephone Company, 6
British Telecommunications plc, V; 15 (upd.)
C-COR.net Corp., 38
Cable & Wireless HKT, 30 (upd.)
Cable and Wireless plc, V; 25 (upd.)
Cablevision Systems Corporation, 30 (upd.)
The Canadian Broadcasting Corporation (CBC), 37
Canal Plus, 10; 34 (upd.)
CanWest Global Communications Corporation, 35
Capital Radio plc, 35
Carlton Communications plc, 15
Carolina Telephone and Telegraph Company, 10
CBS Corporation, 28 (upd.)
Centel Corporation, 6
Centennial Communications Corporation, 39
Century Communications Corp., 10
Century Telephone Enterprises, Inc., 9
Chancellor Media Corporation, 24
Charter Communications, Inc., 33
Chris-Craft Industries, Inc., 9
Chrysalis Group plc, 40
Cincinnati Bell, Inc., 6
Citadel Communications Corporation, 35
Clear Channel Communications, Inc., 23
COLT Telecom Group plc, 41
Comcast Corporation, 24 (upd.)
Comdial Corporation, 21
Commonwealth Telephone Enterprises, Inc., 25
Comsat Corporation, 23
Comverse Technology, Inc., 15; 43 (upd.)
Cumulus Media Inc., 37
DDI Corporation, 7
Deutsche Bundespost TELEKOM, V
Dialogic Corporation, 18
Directorate General of Telecommunications, 7
DIRECTV, Inc., 38
Discovery Communications, Inc., 42
DSC Communications Corporation, 12
EchoStar Communications Corporation, 35
ECI Telecom Ltd., 18
eircom plc, 31 (upd.)
Electric Lightwave, Inc., 37
Electromagnetic Sciences Inc., 21
Entravision Communications Corporation, 41
EXCEL Communications Inc., 18
Executone Information Systems, Inc., 13
Fox Family Worldwide, Inc., 24
France Télécom Group, V; 21 (upd.)
Frontier Corp., 16
Gannett Co., Inc., 30 (upd.)
Gaylord Entertainment Company, 36 (upd.)
General DataComm Industries, Inc., 14
Geotek Communications Inc., 21
Getty Images, Inc., 31
Global Crossing Ltd., 32
Granite Broadcasting Corporation, 42
Gray Communications Systems, Inc., 24
Groupe Vidéotron Ltée., 20
Grupo Televisa, S.A., 18
GTE Corporation, V; 15 (upd.)
Guthy-Renker Corporation, 32
GWR Group plc, 39
Harmonic Inc., 43
Havas, SA, 10
Hispanic Broadcasting Corporation, 35
Hong Kong Telecommunications Ltd., 6
Hubbard Broadcasting Inc., 24
Hughes Electronics Corporation, 25
IDB Communications Group, Inc., 11
IDT Corporation, 34
Illinois Bell Telephone Company, 14
Indiana Bell Telephone Company, Incorporated, 14
Infinity Broadcasting Corporation, 11
IXC Communications, Inc., 29
Jacor Communications, Inc., 23
Jones Intercable, Inc., 21
Koninklijke PTT Nederland NV, V
LCI International, Inc., 16
LDDS-Metro Communications, Inc., 8
LIN Broadcasting Corp., 9
Lincoln Telephone & Telegraph Company, 14
LodgeNet Entertainment Corporation, 28
Mannesmann AG, 38 (upd.)
Martha Stewart Living Omnimedia, L.L.C., 24
MasTec, Inc., 19
McCaw Cellular Communications, Inc., 6
MCI Communications Corporation, V
MCI WorldCom, Inc., 27 (upd.)
McLeodUSA Incorporated, 32
Mercury Communications, Ltd., 7
Metrocall, Inc., 41
Metromedia Companies, 14
Métropole Télévision, 33
MFS Communications Company, Inc., 11
Michigan Bell Telephone Co., 14
MIH Limited, 31
MITRE Corporation, 26
Mobile Telecommunications Technologies Corp., 18
Modern Times Group AB, 36
Multimedia, Inc., 11
National Broadcasting Company, Inc., 28 (upd.)
NCR Corporation, 30 (upd.)
NetCom Systems AB, 26
Nevada Bell Telephone Company, 14
New Valley Corporation, 17
Nextel Communications, Inc., 27 (upd.)
Nippon Telegraph and Telephone Corporation, V
Norstan, Inc., 16
Nortel Networks Corporation, 36 (upd.)
Northern Telecom Limited, V
NYNEX Corporation, V
Octel Communications Corp., 14
Octel Messaging, 41 (upd.)
Ohio Bell Telephone Company, 14
Olivetti S.p.A., 34 (upd.)
Österreichische Post- und Telegraphenverwaltung, V
Pacific Telecom, Inc., 6
Pacific Telesis Group, V
Paging Network Inc., 11
Paxson Communications Corporation, 33
PictureTel Corp., 10; 27 (upd.)
Posti- ja Telelaitos, 6
Price Communications Corporation, 42
Qualcomm Inc., 20
QVC Network Inc., 9
Qwest Communications International, Inc., 37
RMH Teleservices, Inc., 42
Rochester Telephone Corporation, 6
Rogers Communications Inc., 30 (upd.)
Royal KPN N.V., 30
Rural Cellular Corporation, 43
Saga Communications, Inc., 27
Sawtek Inc., 43 (upd.)
SBC Communications Inc., 32 (upd.)
Schweizerische Post-, Telefon- und Telegrafen-Betriebe, V
Scientific-Atlanta, Inc., 6
Sinclair Broadcast Group, Inc., 25

Società Finanziaria Telefonica per Azioni, V
Southern New England Telecommunications Corporation, 6
Southwestern Bell Corporation, V
Spanish Broadcasting System, Inc., 41
Spelling Entertainment, 35 (upd.)
Sprint Communications Company, L.P., 9
StrataCom, Inc., 16
Swedish Telecom, V
SynOptics Communications, Inc., 10
Telecom Australia, 6
Telecom Eireann, 7
Telecom Italia S.p.A., 43
Telefonaktiebolaget LM Ericsson, V
Telefónica de España, S.A., V
Telefonos de Mexico S.A. de C.V., 14
Telephone and Data Systems, Inc., 9
Télévision Française 1, 23
Tellabs, Inc., 11; 40 (upd.)
The Titan Corporation, 36
TV Azteca, S.A. de C.V., 39
U.S. Satellite Broadcasting Company, Inc., 20
U S West, Inc., V; 25 (upd.)
U.S. Cellular Corporation, 31 (upd.)
United States Cellular Corporation, 9
United Telecommunications, Inc., V
United Video Satellite Group, 18
Verizon Communications, 43 (upd.)
Vodafone Group PLC, 11; 36 (upd.)
The Walt Disney Company, 30 (upd.)
Watkins-Johnson Company, 15
West Corporation, 42
Western Wireless Corporation, 36
Westwood One, Inc., 23
Williams Communications Group, Inc., 34
The Williams Companies, Inc., 31 (upd.)
Wipro Limited, 43
Wisconsin Bell, Inc., 14
Working Assets Funding Service, 43
Young Broadcasting Inc., 40

TEXTILES & APPAREL

Abercrombie & Fitch Co., 35 (upd.)
Adidas AG, 14
adidas-Salomon AG, 33 (upd.)
Alba-Waldensian, Inc., 30
Albany International Corp., 8
Algo Group Inc., 24
American Safety Razor Company, 20
Amoskeag Company, 8
Angelica Corporation, 15; 43 (upd.)
AR Accessories Group, Inc., 23
Aris Industries, Inc., 16
Authentic Fitness Corp., 20
Banana Republic Inc., 25
Benetton Group S.p.A., 10
Bill Blass Ltd., 32
Birkenstock Footprint Sandals, Inc., 12
Blair Corporation, 25
Brazos Sportswear, Inc., 23
Brooks Brothers Inc., 22
Brooks Sports Inc., 32
Brown Group, Inc., V; 20 (upd.)
Bugle Boy Industries, Inc., 18
Burberry Ltd., 41 (upd.)
Burberrys Ltd., 17
Burlington Industries, Inc., V; 17 (upd.)
Calcot Ltd., 33
Calvin Klein, Inc., 22
Candie's, Inc., 31
Canstar Sports Inc., 16
Carhartt, Inc., 30
Cato Corporation, 14
Chargeurs International, 21 (upd.)
Charming Shoppes, Inc., 8
Cherokee Inc., 18
Chic by H.I.S, Inc., 20
Chorus Line Corporation, 30
Christian Dior S.A., 19
Christopher & Banks Corporation, 42
Claire's Stores, Inc., 17
Coach Leatherware, 10
Coats Viyella Plc, V
Collins & Aikman Corporation, 13
Columbia Sportswear Company, 19; 41 (upd.)
Concord Fabrics, Inc., 16
Cone Mills Corporation, 8
Converse Inc., 31 (upd.)
Courtaulds plc, V; 17 (upd.)
Croscill, Inc., 42
Crown Crafts, Inc., 16
Crystal Brands, Inc., 9
Culp, Inc., 29
Cygne Designs, Inc., 25
Dan River Inc., 35
Danskin, Inc., 12
Deckers Outdoor Corporation, 22
Delta Woodside Industries, Inc., 8; 30 (upd.)
Designer Holdings Ltd., 20
The Dixie Group, Inc., 20
Dominion Textile Inc., 12
Donna Karan Company, 15
Donnkenny, Inc., 17
Duck Head Apparel Company, Inc., 42
Dyersburg Corporation, 21
Edison Brothers Stores, Inc., 9
Esprit de Corp., 8; 29 (upd.)
Evans, Inc., 30
Fab Industries, Inc., 27
Fabri-Centers of America Inc., 16
Fieldcrest Cannon, Inc., 9; 31 (upd.)
Fila Holding S.p.A., 20
Florsheim Shoe Group Inc., 31 (upd.)
Fossil, Inc., 17
Frederick's of Hollywood Inc., 16
French Connection Group plc, 41
Fruit of the Loom, Inc., 8; 25 (upd.)
Fubu, 29
G&K Services, Inc., 16
G-III Apparel Group, Ltd., 22
Galey & Lord, Inc., 20
Garan, Inc., 16
Gianni Versace SpA, 22
The Gitano Group, Inc. 8
Greenwood Mills, Inc., 14
Groupe DMC (Dollfus Mieg & Cie), 27
Groupe Yves Saint Laurent, 23
Guccio Gucci, S.p.A., 15
Guess, Inc., 15
Guilford Mills Inc., 8; 40 (upd.)
Gymboree Corporation, 15
Haggar Corporation, 19
Hampton Industries, Inc., 20
Happy Kids Inc., 30
Hartmarx Corporation, 8
The Hartstone Group plc, 14
Healthtex, Inc., 17
Helly Hansen ASA, 25
Hermès S.A., 14
The Hockey Company, 34
Hyde Athletic Industries, Inc., 17
I.C. Isaacs & Company, 31
Interface, Inc., 8; 29 (upd.)
Irwin Toy Limited, 14
Items International Airwalk Inc., 17
J. Crew Group, Inc., 12; 34 (upd.)
Jockey International, Inc., 12; 34 (upd.)
Johnston Industries, Inc., 15
Jones Apparel Group, Inc., 39 (upd.)
Jordache Enterprises, Inc., 23
Jos. A. Bank Clothiers, Inc., 31
JPS Textile Group, Inc., 28
K-Swiss, Inc., 33
Kellwood Company, 8
Kenneth Cole Productions, Inc., 25
Kinney Shoe Corp., 14
L.A. Gear, Inc., 8; 32 (upd.)
L.L. Bean, Inc., 10; 38 (upd.)
LaCrosse Footwear, Inc., 18
Laura Ashley Holdings plc, 13
Lee Apparel Company, Inc., 8
The Leslie Fay Companies, Inc., 8
The Leslie Fay Company, Inc., 39 (upd.)
Levi Strauss & Co., V; 16 (upd.)
Liz Claiborne, Inc., 8
London Fog Industries, Inc., 29
Lost Arrow Inc., 22
Maidenform Worldwide Inc., 20
Malden Mills Industries, Inc., 16
Marzotto S.p.A., 20
Milliken & Co., V; 17 (upd.)
Mitsubishi Rayon Co., Ltd., V
Mossimo, Inc., 27
Mothercare UK Ltd., 17
Movie Star Inc., 17
Nautica Enterprises, Inc., 18
New Balance Athletic Shoe, Inc., 25
Nike, Inc., V; 8 (upd.)
Nine West Group, Inc., 39 (upd.)
The North Face, Inc., 18
Oakley, Inc., 18
OshKosh B'Gosh, Inc., 9; 42 (upd.)
Oxford Industries, Inc., 8
Pacific Sunwear of California, Inc., 28
Pendleton Woolen Mills, Inc., 42
Pentland Group plc, 20
Perry Ellis International, Inc., 41
Pillowtex Corporation, 19; 41 (upd.)
Pluma, Inc., 27
Polo/Ralph Lauren Corporation, 12
PremiumWear, Inc., 30
Puma AG Rudolf Dassler Sport, 35
Quaker Fabric Corp., 19
Quiksilver, Inc., 18
R.G. Barry Corp., 17
Recreational Equipment, Inc., 18
Red Wing Shoe Company, Inc., 30 (upd.)
Reebok International Ltd., V; 9 (upd.); 26 (upd.)
Rieter Holding AG, 42
Rollerblade, Inc., 15
Russell Corporation, 8; 30 (upd.)
St. John Knits, Inc., 14
Saucony Inc., 35
Shaw Industries, Inc., 40 (upd.)
Shelby Williams Industries, Inc., 14
Skechers U.S.A. Inc., 31
Springs Industries, Inc., V; 19 (upd.)
Starter Corp., 12
Steven Madden, Ltd., 37
Stone Manufacturing Company, 14; 43 (upd.)
The Stride Rite Corporation, 8; 37 (upd.)
Sun Sportswear, Inc., 17
Superior Uniform Group, Inc., 30
Teijin Limited, V
Thomaston Mills, Inc., 27
The Timberland Company, 13
Tommy Hilfiger Corporation, 20
Toray Industries, Inc., V
Tultex Corporation, 13
Unifi, Inc., 12
United Merchants & Manufacturers, Inc., 13
United Retail Group Inc., 33
Unitika Ltd., V
Vans, Inc., 16
Varsity Spirit Corp., 15
VF Corporation, V; 17 (upd.)

Walton Monroe Mills, Inc., 8
The Warnaco Group Inc., 12
Wellman, Inc., 8
West Point-Pepperell, Inc., 8
WestPoint Stevens Inc., 16
Weyco Group, Incorporated, 32
Williamson-Dickie Manufacturing Company, 14
Wolverine World Wide Inc., 16

TOBACCO

American Brands, Inc., V
B.A.T. Industries PLC, 22 (upd.)
Brooke Group Ltd., 15
Brown & Williamson Tobacco Corporation, 14; 33 (upd.)
Culbro Corporation, 15
Dibrell Brothers, Incorporated, 12
DIMON Inc., 27
800-JR Cigar, Inc., 27
Gallaher Limited, V; 19 (upd.)
Holt's Cigar Holdings, Inc., 42
Imasco Limited, V
Japan Tobacco Incorporated, V
Philip Morris Companies Inc., V; 18 (upd.)
R.J. Reynolds Tobacco Holdings, Inc., 30 (upd.)
RJR Nabisco Holdings Corp., V
Rothmans International p.l.c., V
Rothmans UK Holdings Limited, 19 (upd.)
Seita, 23
Standard Commercial Corporation, 13
Swisher International Group Inc., 23
Tabacalera, S.A., V; 17 (upd.)
Universal Corporation, V
UST Inc., 9
Vector Group Ltd., 35 (upd.)

TRANSPORT SERVICES

Aéroports de Paris, 33
Air Express International Corporation, 13
Airborne Freight Corporation, 6; 34 (upd.)
Alamo Rent A Car, Inc., 6; 24 (upd.)
Alexander & Baldwin, Inc., 10
Amerco, 6
American Classic Voyages Company, 27
American President Companies Ltd., 6
Anschutz Corp., 12
Aqua Alliance Inc., 32 (upd.)
Atlas Van Lines, Inc., 14
Avis Rent A Car, Inc., 22 (upd.)
Avis, Inc., 6
BAA plc, 10
Bekins Company, 15
Boyd Bros. Transportation Inc., 39
Brambles Industries Limited, 42
British Railways Board, V
Broken Hill Proprietary Company Ltd., 22 (upd.)
Budget Group, Inc., 25
Budget Rent a Car Corporation, 9
Burlington Northern Inc., V
Burlington Northern Santa Fe Corporation, 27 (upd.)
C.H. Robinson Worldwide, Inc., 40 (upd.)
Canadian National Railway System, 6
Canadian Pacific Limited, V
Carey International, Inc., 26
Carlson Companies, Inc., 6
Carolina Freight Corporation, 6
Celadon Group Inc., 30
Central Japan Railway Company, 43
Chargeurs, 6
Chicago and North Western Holdings Corporation, 6
Coach USA, Inc., 24
Coles Express Inc., 15
Compagnie Générale Maritime et Financière, 6
Consolidated Delivery & Logistics, Inc., 24
Consolidated Freightways Corporation, V; 21 (upd.)
Consolidated Rail Corporation, V
Crowley Maritime Corporation, 6; 28 (upd.)
CSX Corporation, V; 22 (upd.)
Danzas Group, V; 40 (upd.)
Deutsche Bundesbahn, V
DHL Worldwide Express, 6; 24 (upd.)
Dollar Thrifty Automotive Group, Inc., 25
East Japan Railway Company, V
Emery Air Freight Corporation, 6
Emery Worldwide Airlines, Inc., 25 (upd.)
Enterprise Rent-A-Car Company, 6
Eurotunnel Group, 37 (upd.)
Evergreen Marine Corporation Taiwan Ltd., 13
Executive Jet, Inc., 36
Expeditors International of Washington Inc., 17
Federal Express Corporation, V
FedEx Corporation, 18 (upd.); 42 (upd.)
Fritz Companies, Inc., 12
Frozen Food Express Industries, Inc., 20
GATX Corporation, 6; 25 (upd.)
GE Capital Aviation Services, 36
Genesee & Wyoming Inc., 27
The Go-Ahead Group Plc, 28
The Greenbrier Companies, 19
Greyhound Lines, Inc., 32 (upd.)
Hankyu Corporation, V; 23 (upd.)
Hapag-Lloyd AG, 6
Harland and Wolff Holdings plc, 19
Harper Group Inc., 17
Heartland Express, Inc., 18
The Hertz Corporation, 9
Holberg Industries, Inc., 36
Hospitality Worldwide Services, Inc., 26
Hub Group, Inc., 38
Hvide Marine Incorporated, 22
Illinois Central Corporation, 11
International Shipholding Corporation, Inc., 27
J.B. Hunt Transport Services Inc., 12
John Menzies plc, 39
Kansas City Southern Industries, Inc., 6; 26 (upd.)
Kawasaki Kisen Kaisha, Ltd., V
Keio Teito Electric Railway Company, V
Kinki Nippon Railway Company Ltd., V
Kirby Corporation, 18
Koninklijke Nedlloyd Groep N.V., 6
Kuhne & Nagel International A.G., V
La Poste, V
Leaseway Transportation Corp., 12
London Regional Transport, 6
Maine Central Railroad Company, 16
Mammoet Transport B.V., 26
Mayflower Group Inc., 6
Mercury Air Group, Inc., 20
The Mersey Docks and Harbour Company, 30
Metropolitan Transportation Authority, 35
Miller Industries, Inc., 26
Mitsui O.S.K. Lines, Ltd., V
Moran Towing Corporation, Inc., 15
Morris Travel Services L.L.C., 26
Motor Cargo Industries, Inc., 35
National Car Rental System, Inc., 10
National Railroad Passenger Corporation, 22
NFC plc, 6
Nippon Express Co., Ltd., V
Nippon Yusen Kabushiki Kaisha, V
Norfolk Southern Corporation, V; 29 (upd.)
Ocean Group plc, 6
Odakyu Electric Railway Company Limited, V
Oglebay Norton Company, 17
Österreichische Bundesbahnen GmbH, 6
OTR Express, Inc., 25
Overnite Transportation Co., 14
Overseas Shipholding Group, Inc., 11
The Peninsular and Oriental Steam Navigation Company, V; 38 (upd.)
Penske Corporation, V
PHH Corporation, V
Post Office Group, V
Preston Corporation, 6
RailTex, Inc., 20
Roadway Express, Inc., 25 (upd.)
Roadway Services, Inc., V
Royal Vopak NV, 41
Ryder System, Inc., V; 24 (upd.)
Santa Fe Pacific Corporation, V
Schenker-Rhenus AG, 6
Schneider National, Inc., 36
Seibu Railway Co. Ltd., V
Seino Transportation Company, Ltd., 6
Simon Transportation Services Inc., 27
Smithway Motor Xpress Corporation, 39
Société Nationale des Chemins de Fer Français, V
Southern Pacific Transportation Company, V
Stagecoach Holdings plc, 30
Stevedoring Services of America Inc., 28
Stinnes AG, 8
Stolt-Nielsen S.A., 42
Sunoco, Inc., 28 (upd.)
Swift Transportation Co., Inc., 42
The Swiss Federal Railways (Schweizerische Bundesbahnen), V
Teekay Shipping Corporation, 25
Tibbett & Britten Group plc, 32
Tidewater Inc., 11; 37 (upd.)
TNT Freightways Corporation, 14
TNT Limited, V
TNT Post Group N.V., 27 (upd.); 30 (upd.)
Tobu Railway Co Ltd, 6
Tokyu Corporation, V
Totem Resources Corporation, 9
Trailer Bridge, Inc., 41
Transnet Ltd., 6
TTX Company, 6
U.S. Delivery Systems, Inc., 22
Union Pacific Corporation, V; 28 (upd.)
United Parcel Service of America Inc., V; 17 (upd.)
United States Postal Service, 14; 34 (upd.)
USA Truck, Inc., 42
Werner Enterprises, Inc., 26
Wisconsin Central Transportation Corporation, 24
Yamato Transport Co. Ltd., V
Yellow Corporation, 14
Yellow Freight System, Inc. of Delaware, V

UTILITIES

The AES Corporation, 10; 13 (upd.)
Air & Water Technologies Corporation, 6
Alberta Energy Company Ltd., 16; 43 (upd.)
Allegheny Energy, Inc., 38 (upd.)
Allegheny Power System, Inc., V
American Electric Power Company, Inc., V
American Water Works Company, 6
American Water Works Company, Inc., 38 (upd.)
Arkla, Inc., V
Associated Natural Gas Corporation, 11

Atlanta Gas Light Company, 6; 23 (upd.)
Atlantic Energy, Inc., 6
Atmos Energy Corporation, 43
Baltimore Gas and Electric Company, V; 25 (upd.)
Bay State Gas Company, 38
Bayernwerk AG, V; 23 (upd.)
Bewag AG, 39
Big Rivers Electric Corporation, 11
Black Hills Corporation, 20
Boston Edison Company, 12
Bouygues S.A., 24 (upd.)
British Gas plc, V
British Nuclear Fuels plc, 6
Brooklyn Union Gas, 6
Calpine Corporation, 36
Canadian Utilities Limited, 13
Carolina Power & Light Company, V; 23 (upd.)
Cascade Natural Gas Corporation, 9
Centerior Energy Corporation, V
Central and South West Corporation, V
Central Hudson Gas and Electricity Corporation, 6
Central Maine Power, 6
Centrica plc, 29 (upd.)
Chubu Electric Power Company, Incorporated, V
Chugoku Electric Power Company Inc., V
Cincinnati Gas & Electric Company, 6
CIPSCO Inc., 6
Citizens Utilities Company, 7
City Public Service, 6
Cleco Corporation, 37
CMS Energy Corporation, V, 14
The Coastal Corporation, 31 (upd.)
Cogentrix Energy, Inc., 10
The Coleman Company, Inc., 9
The Columbia Gas System, Inc., V; 16 (upd.)
Commonwealth Edison Company, V
Commonwealth Energy System, 14
Connecticut Light and Power Co., 13
Consolidated Edison Company of New York, Inc., V
Consolidated Natural Gas Company, V; 19 (upd.)
Consumers Power Co., 14
Consumers Water Company, 14
Consumers' Gas Company Ltd., 6
Destec Energy, Inc., 12
The Detroit Edison Company, V
Dominion Resources, Inc., V
DPL Inc., 6
DQE, Inc., 6
DTE Energy Company, 20 (upd.)
Duke Energy Corporation, 27 (upd.)
Duke Power Company, V
Eastern Enterprises, 6
El Paso Electric Company, 21
El Paso Natural Gas Company, 12
Electricité de France, V; 41 (upd.)
Elektrowatt AG, 6
Enbridge Inc., 43
ENDESA Group, V
Enron Corp., V
Enserch Corporation, V
Ente Nazionale per L'Energia Elettrica, V
Entergy Corporation, V
Equitable Resources, Inc., 6
Florida Progress Corporation, V; 23 (upd.)
Fortis, Inc., 15
Fortum Corporation, 30 (upd.)
FPL Group, Inc., V
Gaz de France, V; 40 (upd.)
General Public Utilities Corporation, V
Générale des Eaux Group, V
GPU, Inc., 27 (upd.)
Gulf States Utilities Company, 6
Hawaiian Electric Industries, Inc., 9
Hokkaido Electric Power Company Inc., V
Hokuriku Electric Power Company, V
Hongkong Electric Holdings Ltd., 6; 23 (upd.)
Houston Industries Incorporated, V
Hyder plc, 34
Hydro-Québec, 6; 32 (upd.)
Idaho Power Company, 12
Illinois Bell Telephone Company, 14
Illinois Power Company, 6
Indiana Energy, Inc., 27
IPALCO Enterprises, Inc., 6
The Kansai Electric Power Co., Inc., V
Kansas City Power & Light Company, 6
Kenetech Corporation, 11
Kentucky Utilities Company, 6
KeySpan Energy Co., 27
KU Energy Corporation, 11
Kyushu Electric Power Company Inc., V
LG&E Energy Corporation, 6
Long Island Lighting Company, V
Lyonnaise des Eaux-Dumez, V
Madison Gas and Electric Company, 39
Magma Power Company, 11
MCN Corporation, 6
MDU Resources Group, Inc., 7; 42 (upd.)
Midwest Resources Inc., 6
Minnesota Power & Light Company, 11
Minnesota Power, Inc., 34 (upd.)
Montana Power Company, 11
National Fuel Gas Company, 6
National Power PLC, 12
Nebraska Public Power District, 29
N.V. Nederlandse Gasunie, V
Nevada Power Company, 11
New England Electric System, V
New York State Electric and Gas, 6
Niagara Mohawk Power Corporation, V
NICOR Inc., 6
NIPSCO Industries, Inc., 6
North West Water Group plc, 11
Northeast Utilities, V
Northern States Power Company, V; 20 (upd.)
NorthWestern Corporation, 37
Nova Corporation of Alberta, V
Oglethorpe Power Corporation, 6
Ohio Edison Company, V
Oklahoma Gas and Electric Company, 6
ONEOK Inc., 7
Ontario Hydro, 6
Ontario Hydro Services Company, 32 (upd.)
Osaka Gas Co., Ltd., V
Otter Tail Power Company, 18
Pacific Enterprises, V
Pacific Gas and Electric Company, V
PacifiCorp, V; 26 (upd.)
Panhandle Eastern Corporation, V
PECO Energy Company, 11
Pennsylvania Power & Light Company, V
Peoples Energy Corporation, 6
PG&E Corporation, 26 (upd.)
Philadelphia Electric Company, V
Philadelphia Suburban Corporation, 39
Piedmont Natural Gas Company, Inc., 27
Pinnacle West Capital Corporation, 6
Portland General Corporation, 6
Potomac Electric Power Company, 6
PowerGen PLC, 11
PPL Corporation, 41 (upd.)
PreussenElektra Aktiengesellschaft, V
PSI Resources, 6
Public Service Company of Colorado, 6
Public Service Company of New Hampshire, 21
Public Service Company of New Mexico, 6
Public Service Enterprise Group Incorporated, V
Puget Sound Power and Light Company, 6
Questar Corporation, 6; 26 (upd.)
Rochester Gas and Electric Corporation, 6
Ruhrgas AG, V; 38 (upd.)
RWE Group, V
Salt River Project, 19
San Diego Gas & Electric Company, V
SCANA Corporation, 6
Scarborough Public Utilities Commission, 9
SCEcorp, V
Scottish Hydro-Electric PLC, 13
ScottishPower plc, 19
Sempra Energy, 25 (upd.)
Severn Trent PLC, 12; 38 (upd.)
Shikoku Electric Power Company, Inc., V
Sonat, Inc., 6
South Jersey Industries, Inc., 42
The Southern Company, V; 38 (upd.)
Southern Electric PLC, 13
Southern Indiana Gas and Electric Company, 13
Southern Union Company, 27
Southwest Gas Corporation, 19
Southwestern Electric Power Co., 21
Southwestern Public Service Company, 6
Suez Lyonnaise des Eaux, 36 (upd.)
TECO Energy, Inc., 6
Texas Utilities Company, V; 25 (upd.)
Thames Water plc, 11
Tohoku Electric Power Company, Inc., V
The Tokyo Electric Power Company, Incorporated, V
Tokyo Gas Co., Ltd., V
TransAlta Utilities Corporation, 6
TransCanada PipeLines Limited, V
Transco Energy Company, V
Trigen Energy Corporation, 42
Tucson Electric Power Company, 6
UGI Corporation, 12
Unicom Corporation, 29 (upd.)
Union Electric Company, V
The United Illuminating Company, 21
United Water Resources, Inc., 40
Unitil Corporation, 37
Utah Power and Light Company, 27
UtiliCorp United Inc., 6
Vereinigte Elektrizitätswerke Westfalen AG, V
VEW AG, 39
Washington Gas Light Company, 19
Washington Natural Gas Company, 9
Washington Water Power Company, 6
Western Resources, Inc., 12
Wheelabrator Technologies, Inc., 6
Wisconsin Energy Corporation, 6
Wisconsin Public Service Corporation, 9
WPL Holdings, Inc., 6

WASTE SERVICES

Allwaste, Inc., 18
Appliance Recycling Centers of America, Inc., 42
Azcon Corporation, 23
Brambles Industries Limited, 42
Browning-Ferris Industries, Inc., V; 20 (upd.)
Chemical Waste Management, Inc., 9
Copart Inc., 23
Ecology and Environment, Inc., 39
Philip Environmental Inc., 16
Roto-Rooter Corp., 15
Safety-Kleen Corp., 8
Sevenson Environmental Services, Inc., 42

Severn Trent PLC, 38 (upd.)
Stericycle Inc., 33
TRC Companies, Inc., 32
Veit Companies, 43
Waste Holdings, Inc., 41
Waste Management, Inc., V
WMX Technologies Inc., 17

GEOGRAPHIC INDEX

Geographic Index

Algeria

Entreprise Nationale Sonatrach, IV

Argentina

Aerolíneas Argentinas S.A., 33
YPF Sociedad Anonima, IV

Australia

Amcor Limited, IV; 19 (upd.)
Australia and New Zealand Banking Group Ltd., II
Bond Corporation Holdings Limited, 10
Boral Limited, III; 43 (upd.)
Brambles Industries Limited, 42
Broken Hill Proprietary Company Ltd., IV; 22 (upd.)
Carlton and United Breweries Ltd., I
Coles Myer Ltd., V; 20 (upd.)
CRA Limited, IV
CSR Limited, III; 28 (upd.)
Elders IXL Ltd., I
Foster's Brewing Group Ltd., 7; 21 (upd.)
John Fairfax Holdings Limited, 7
Lend Lease Corporation Limited, IV; 17 (upd.)
News Corporation Limited, IV; 7 (upd.)
Pacific Dunlop Limited, 10
Pioneer International Limited, III
Qantas Airways Limited, 6; 24 (upd.)
Telecom Australia, 6
Westpac Banking Corporation, II
WMC, Limited, 43

Austria

Austrian Airlines AG (Österreichische Luftverkehrs AG), 33
Bank Austria AG, 23
BBAG Osterreichische Brau-Beteiligungs-AG, 38
Glock Ges.m.b.H., 42
ÖMV Aktiengesellschaft, IV
Österreichische Bundesbahnen GmbH, 6
Österreichische Post- und Telegraphenverwaltung, V
Voest-Alpine Stahl AG, IV

Bahamas

Sun International Hotels Limited, 26
Teekay Shipping Corporation, 25

Bangladesh

Grameen Bank, 31

Belgium

Bank Brussels Lambert, II
Belgacom, 6
C&A, 40 (upd.)
Cockerill Sambre Group, IV; 26 (upd.)
Generale Bank, II
GIB Group, V; 26 (upd.)
Interbrew S.A., 17
Kredietbank N.V., II
PetroFina S.A., IV; 26 (upd.)
Sabena S.A./N.V., 33
Solvay & Cie S.A., I; 21 (upd.)
Tractebel S.A., 20
Xeikon NV, 26

Bermuda

Bacardi Limited, 18
Jardine Matheson Holdings Limited, I; 20 (upd.)
Sea Containers Ltd., 29
Tyco International Ltd., III; 28 (upd.)

Brazil

Banco Bradesco S.A., 13
Banco Itaú S.A., 19
Companhia Vale do Rio Doce, IV; 43 (upd.)
Empresa Brasileira de Aeronáutica S.A. (Embraer), 36
Lojas Arapua S.A., 22
Petróleo Brasileiro S.A., IV
TransBrasil S/A Linhas Aéreas, 31
VARIG S.A. (Viaçâo Aérea Rio-Grandense), 6; 29 (upd.)

Canada

Abitibi-Consolidated, Inc., V; 25 (upd.)
Abitibi-Price Inc., IV
Air Canada, 6; 23 (upd.)
Alberta Energy Company Ltd., 16; 43 (upd.)
Alcan Aluminium Limited, IV; 31 (upd.)
Algo Group Inc., 24
Alliance Atlantis Communications Inc., 39
Bank of Montreal, II
Bank of Nova Scotia, The, II
Barrick Gold Corporation, 34
BCE Inc., V
Bell Canada, 6
BFC Construction Corporation, 25
Bombardier Inc., 42 (upd.)
Bramalea Ltd., 9
British Columbia Telephone Company, 6
Campeau Corporation, V
Canada Packers Inc., II
Canadair, Inc., 16
Canadian Broadcasting Corporation (CBC), The, 37
Canadian Imperial Bank of Commerce, II
Canadian National Railway System, 6
Canadian Pacific Limited, V
Canadian Utilities Limited, 13
Canfor Corporation, 42
Canstar Sports Inc., 16
CanWest Global Communications Corporation, 35
Cinar Corporation, 40
Cineplex Odeon Corporation, 6; 23 (upd.)
Cinram International, Inc., 43
Cirque du Soleil Inc., 29
Cominco Ltd., 37
Consumers' Gas Company Ltd., 6
CoolBrands International Inc., 35
Corby Distilleries Limited, 14
Corel Corporation, 15; 33 (upd.)
Discreet Logic Inc., 20
Dofasco Inc., IV; 24 (upd.)
Dominion Textile Inc., 12
Domtar Inc., IV
Dylex Limited, 29
Echo Bay Mines Ltd., IV; 38 (upd.)
Enbridge Inc., 43
Extendicare Health Services, Inc., 6
Fortis, Inc., 15
Four Seasons Hotels Inc., 9; 29 (upd.)
GEAC Computer Corporation Ltd., 43
George Weston Limited, II; 36 (upd.)
Great-West Lifeco Inc., III
Groupe Vidéotron Ltée., 20
Hemlo Gold Mines Inc., 9
Hiram Walker Resources, Ltd., I
Hockey Company, The, 34
Hudson Bay Mining and Smelting Company, Limited, The, 12
Hudson's Bay Company, V; 25 (upd.)
Hydro-Québec, 6; 32 (upd.)
Imasco Limited, V
Imax Corporation, 28
Imperial Oil Limited, IV; 25 (upd.)
Inco Limited, IV
Intrawest Corporation, The, 15
Irwin Toy Limited, 14
Jim Pattison Group, The, 37
Kinross Gold Corporation, 36
Kruger Inc., 17
Labatt Brewing Company Limited, I; 25 (upd.)
Linamar Corporation, 18
Lions Gate Entertainment Corporation, 35
Loblaw Companies Limited, 43
Loewen Group, Inc., The, 16; 40 (upd.)
Maclean Hunter Publishing Limited, IV; 26 (upd.)
MacMillan Bloedel Limited, IV
Maple Leaf Foods Inc., 41
Methanex Corporation, 40
Mitel Corporation, 18
Molson Companies Limited, The, I; 26 (upd.)
Moore Corporation Limited, IV
National Sea Products Ltd., 14
Noranda Inc., IV; 7 (upd.)
Nortel Networks Corporation, 36 (upd.)
North West Company, Inc., The, 12
Northern Telecom Limited, V
Nova Corporation of Alberta, V
Novacor Chemicals Ltd., 12
Olympia & York Developments Ltd., IV; 9 (upd.)
Onex Corporation, 16
Ontario Hydro Services Company, 6; 32 (upd.)
Oshawa Group Limited, The, II
Petro-Canada Limited, IV
Philip Environmental Inc., 16
Placer Dome Inc., 20

Canada *(continued)*

Potash Corporation of Saskatchewan Inc., 18
Power Corporation of Canada, 36 (upd.)
Provigo Inc., II
Quebecor Inc., 12
Ritchie Bros. Auctioneers Inc., 41
Rogers Communications Inc., 30 (upd.)
Roots Canada Ltd., 42
Royal Bank of Canada, The, II; 21 (upd.)
Scarborough Public Utilities Commission, 9
Seagram Company Ltd., The, I; 25 (upd.)
Southam Inc., 7
Spar Aerospace Limited, 32
Steinberg Incorporated, II
Stelco Inc., IV
Talisman Energy, 9
Teck Corporation, 27
Thomson Corporation, The, 8; 34 (upd.)
Toromont Industries, Ltd., 21
Toronto-Dominion Bank, The, II
Torstar Corporation, 29
TransAlta Utilities Corporation, 6
TransCanada PipeLines Limited, V
Tridel Enterprises Inc., 9
Trilon Financial Corporation, II
Trizec Corporation Ltd., 10
Van Houtte Inc., 39
Varity Corporation, III
Wascana Energy Inc., 13
West Fraser Timber Co. Ltd., 17
WestJet Airlines Ltd., 38

Chile

Corporacion Nacional del Cobre de Chile, 40
Lan Chile S.A., 31

China

Asia Info Holdings, Inc., 43
China Eastern Airlines Co. Ltd., 31
China Southern Airlines Company Ltd., 33
Chinese Petroleum Corporation, IV; 31 (upd.)
Directorate General of Telecommunications, 7
Hongkong and Shanghai Banking Corporation Limited, The, II
Shanghai Petrochemical Co., Ltd., 18

Colombia

Avianca Aerovías Nacionales de Colombia SA, 36
Empresa Colombiana de Petróleos, IV

Czech Republic

Skoda Auto a.s., 39

Denmark

Bang & Olufsen Holding A/S, 37
Carlsberg A/S, 9; 29 (upd.)
Group 4 Falck A/S, 42
IKEA International A/S, V; 26 (upd.)
Lego A/S, 13; 40 (upd.)
Novo Industri A/S, I

Ecuador

Petróleos del Ecuador, IV

Egypt

EgyptAir, 6; 27 (upd.)
Egyptian General Petroluem Corporation, IV

El Salvador

Grupo TACA, 38

Finland

Amer Group plc, 41
Enso-Gutzeit Oy, IV
Finnair Oy, 6; 25 (upd.)
Fiskars Corporation, 33
Fortum Corporation, 30 (upd.)
Kansallis-Osake-Pankki, II
Kesko Ltd. (Kesko Oy), 8; 27 (upd.)
Kone Corporation, 27
Kymmene Corporation, IV
Metsa-Serla Oy, IV
Metso Corporation, 30 (upd.)
Neste Oy, IV
Nokia Corporation, II; 17 (upd.); 38 (upd.)
Outokumpu Oyj, 38
Posti- ja Telelaitos, 6
Stora Enso Oyj, 36 (upd.)
United Paper Mills Ltd. (Yhtyneet Paperitehtaat Oy), IV
UPM-Kymmene Corporation, 19
Valmet Corporation (Valmet Oy), III

France

Accor SA, 10; 27 (upd.)
Aéroports de Paris, 33
Aerospatiale Group, The, 7; 21 (upd.)
Agence France-Presse, 34
Alcatel Alsthom Compagnie Générale d'Electricité, 9
Alcatel S.A., 36 (upd.)
Association des Centres Distributeurs E. Leclerc, 37
Atochem S.A., I
Au Printemps S.A., V
Auchan, 37
Automobiles Citroen, 7
Avions Marcel Dassault-Breguet Aviation, I
Axa, III
Baccarat, 24
Banque Nationale de Paris S.A., II
Baron Philippe de Rothschild S.A., 39
Besnier SA, 19
BNP Paribas Group, 36 (upd.)
Bongrain SA, 25
Bouygues S.A., I; 24 (upd.)
BSN Groupe S.A., II
Bull S.A., 43 (upd.)
Burelle S.A., 23
Business Objects S.A., 25
Canal Plus, 10; 34 (upd.)
Cap Gemini Ernst & Young, 37
Carbone Lorraine S.A., 33
Carrefour SA, 10; 27 (upd.)
Cetelem S.A., 21
Chanel, 12
Chargeurs International, 6; 21 (upd.)
Christian Dalloz SA, 40
Christian Dior S.A., 19
Christofle SA, 40
Ciments Français, 40
Club Mediterranée S.A., 6; 21 (upd.)
Coflexip S.A., 25
Colas S.A., 31
Compagnie de Saint-Gobain S.A., III; 16 (upd.)
Compagnie des Machines Bull S.A., III
Compagnie Financiere de Paribas, II
Compagnie Générale d'Électricité, II
Compagnie Générale des Établissements Michelin, V; 42 (upd.)
Compagnie Générale Maritime et Financière, 6
Comptoirs Modernes S.A., 19
Crédit Lyonnais, 9; 33 (upd.)
Crédit National S.A., 9
Darty S.A., 27
Dassault Systèmes S.A., 25
De Dietrich & Cie., 31
Deveaux S.A., 41
Dexia Group, 42
Du Pareil au Même, 43
ECS S.A, 12
Eiffage, 27
Electricité de France, V; 41 (upd.)
Elf Aquitaine SA, 21 (upd.)
Eridania Béghin-Say S.A., 36
Essilor International, 21
Etablissements Economiques du Casino Guichard, Perrachon et Cie, S.C.A., 12
Euro Disneyland SCA, 20
Euro RSCG Worldwide S.A., 13
Euronext Paris S.A., 37
Facom S.A., 32
Faiveley S.A., 39
Fimalac S.A., 37
Fleury Michon S.A., 39
FNAC, 21
Framatome SA, 19
France Télécom Group, V; 21 (upd.)
Fromageries Bel, 23
G.I.E. Airbus Industrie, I; 12 (upd.)
Galeries Lafayette S.A., V; 23 (upd.)
Gaumont SA, 25
Gaz de France, V; 40 (upd.)
Gecina SA, 42
Générale des Eaux Group, V
GrandVision S.A., 43
Groupe Air France, 6
Groupe André, 17
Groupe Castorama-Dubois Investissements, 23
Groupe Danone, 32 (upd.)
Groupe Dassault Aviation SA, 26 (upd.)
Groupe de la Cite, IV
Groupe DMC (Dollfus Mieg & Cie), 27
Groupe Go Sport S.A., 39
Groupe Guillin SA, 40
Groupe Lapeyre S.A., 33
Groupe Legris Industries, 23
Groupe Les Echos, 25
Groupe Promodès S.A., 19
Groupe Rougier SA, 21
Groupe SEB, 35
Groupe Sidel S.A., 21
Groupe Yves Saint Laurent, 23
Groupe Zannier S.A., 35
Guerlain, 23
Guilbert S.A., 42
Guillemot Corporation, 41
Guyenne et Gascogne, 23
Hachette, IV
Hachette Filipacchi Medias S.A., 21
Havas, SA, 10; 33 (upd.)
Hermès International S.A., 34 (upd.)
Hermès S.A., 14
Imerys S.A., 40 (upd.)
Imetal S.A., IV
Infogrames Entertainment S.A., 35
ITM Entreprises SA, 36
L'Air Liquide, I
L'Entreprise Jean Lefebvre, 23
L'Oreal, III; 8 (upd.)
La Poste, V
Laboratoires de Biologie Végétale Yves Rocher, 35
Lafarge Coppée S.A., III
Lafuma S.A., 39
Laurent-Perrier SA, 42
Lazard LLC, 38
Le Monde S.A., 33

Legrand SA, 21
Louis Vuitton, 10
LVMH Möet Hennessy Louis Vuitton SA, 33 (upd.)
Lyonnaise des Eaux-Dumez, V
Maison Louis Jadot, 24
Manitou BF S.A., 27
Marie Brizard & Roger International S.A., 22
Matra-Hachette S.A., 15 (upd.)
Metaleurop S.A., 21
Métropole Télévision, 33
Moët-Hennessy, I
Moulinex S.A., 22
Mr. Bricolage S.A., 37
Papeteries de Lancey, 23
Pathé SA, 29
Pechiney, IV
Pernod Ricard S.A., I; 21 (upd.)
Peugeot S.A., I
Pinault-Printemps Redoute S.A., 19 (upd.)
Poliet S.A., 33
PSA Peugeot Citroen S.A., 28 (upd.)
Publicis S.A., 19
Regie Nationale des Usines Renault, I
Rémy Cointreau S.A., 20
Renault S.A., 26 (upd.)
Rhodia SA, 38
Rhône-Poulenc S.A., I; 10 (upd.)
Robertet SA, 39
Roussel Uclaf, I; 8 (upd.)
Royal Canin S.A., 39
SAGEM S.A., 37
Salomon Worldwide, 20
Sanofi Group, I
Schneider S.A., II; 18 (upd.)
SCOR S.A., 20
Seita, 23
Simco S.A., 37
Skis Rossignol S.A., 15; 43 (upd.)
Société Air France, 27 (upd.)
Société du Louvre, 27
Société Générale, II; 42 (upd.)
Société Nationale des Chemins de Fer Français, V
Société Nationale Elf Aquitaine, IV; 7 (upd.)
Sodexho Alliance SA, 29
Sodiaal S.A., 36 (upd.)
SODIMA, II
Sommer-Allibert S.A., 19
Suez Lyonnaise des Eaux, 36 (upd.)
Taittinger S.A., 43
Tati SA, 25
Télévision Française 1, 23
Thales S.A., 42
THOMSON multimedia S.A., 42 (upd.)
Thomson S.A., II
Total Compagnie Française des Pétroles S.A., IV
TOTAL S.A., 24 (upd.)
Ubi Soft Entertainment S.A., 41
Ugine S.A., 20
Unibail SA, 40
Unilog SA, 42
Union des Assurances de Pans, III
Usinor SA, 42 (upd.)
Usinor Sacilor, IV
Valeo, 23
Vinci, 43
Worms et Cie, 27
Zodiac S.A., 36

Germany

Adam Opel AG, 7; 21 (upd.)
Adidas AG, 14
adidas-Salomon AG, 33 (upd.)
AEG A.G., I
Aldi Group, 13
Allianz Aktiengesellschaft Holding, III; 15 (upd.)
Andreas Stihl, 16
ARD, 41
AVA AG (Allgemeine Handelsgesellschaft der Verbraucher AG), 33
AXA Colonia Konzern AG, 27
Axel Springer Verlag AG, IV; 20 (upd.)
Barmag AG, 39
BASF Aktiengesellschaft, I; 18 (upd.)
Bauer Publishing Group, 7
Bayer A.G., I; 13 (upd.); 41 (upd.)
Bayerische Hypotheken- und Wechsel-Bank AG, II
Bayerische Motoren Werke AG, I; 11 (upd.); 38 (upd.)
Bayerische Vereinsbank A.G., II
Bayernwerk AG, V; 23 (upd.)
Beiersdorf AG, 29
Bertelsmann A.G., IV; 15 (upd.); 43 (upd.)
Bewag AG, 39
Bilfinger & Berger Bau A.G., I
Brauerei Beck & Co., 9; 33 (upd.)
Brenntag AG, 8; 23 (upd.)
Buderus AG, 37
Burda Holding GmbH. & Co., 23
C&A Brenninkmeyer KG, V
C.H. Boehringer Sohn, 39
Carl-Zeiss-Stiftung, III; 34 (upd.)
Commerzbank A.G., II
Continental Aktiengesellschaft, V
Daimler-Benz A.G., I; 15 (upd.)
Daimler-Benz Aerospace AG, 16
DaimlerChrysler AG, 34 (upd.)
Degussa Group, IV
Degussa-Huls AG, 32 (upd.)
Deutsche Babcock A.G., III
Deutsche Bank AG, II; 14 (upd.); 40 (upd.)
Deutsche BP Aktiengesellschaft, 7
Deutsche Bundesbahn, V
Deutsche Bundespost TELEKOM, V
Deutsche Lufthansa Aktiengesellschaft, I; 26 (upd.)
Deutsche Post AG, 29
Deutz AG, 39
Dresdner Bank A.G., II
Dyckerhoff AG, 35
Edeka Zentrale A.G., II
Feldmuhle Nobel A.G., III
Fielmann AG, 31
Freudenberg & Co., 41
Fried. Krupp GmbH, IV
GEA AG, 27
GEHE AG, 27
Gerresheimer Glas AG, 43
Grundig AG, 27
Hapag-Lloyd AG, 6
Heidelberger Druckmaschinen AG, 40
Heidelberger Zement AG, 31
Henkel KGaA, III; 34 (upd.)
Heraeus Holding GmbH, IV
Hertie Waren- und Kaufhaus GmbH, V
Hochtief AG, 33
Hoechst A.G., I; 18 (upd.)
Hoesch AG, IV
Huls A.G., I
J.M. Voith AG, 33
Jenoptik AG, 33
Karlsberg Brauerei GmbH & Co KG, 41
Karstadt Aktiengesellschaft, V; 19 (upd.)
Kaufhof Holding AG, V
Kaufhof Warenhaus AG, 23 (upd.)
Kaufring AG, 35
KHD Konzern, III
Klockner-Werke AG, IV
König Brauerei GmbH & Co. KG, 35 (upd.)
Kreditanstalt für Wiederaufbau, 29
Leica Camera AG, 35
Leica Microsystems Holdings GmbH, 35
Linde A.G., I
LTU Group Holding GmbH, 37
MAN Aktiengesellschaft, III
Mannesmann AG, III; 14 (upd.); 38 (upd.)
Margarete Steiff GmbH, 23
Messerschmitt-Bölkow-Blohm GmbH., I
Metallgesellschaft AG, IV; 16 (upd.)
MITROPA AG, 37
Munich Re (Münchener Rückversicherungs-Gesellschaft), III
Nixdorf Computer AG, III
Otto Versand GmbH & Co., V; 15 (upd.); 34 (upd.)
Paulaner Brauerei GmbH & Co. KG, 35
Philipp Holzmann AG, 17
Porsche AG, 13; 31 (upd.)
Preussag AG, 17; 42 (upd.)
PreussenElektra Aktiengesellschaft, V
Puma AG Rudolf Dassler Sport, 35
PWA Group, IV
Qiagen N.V., 39
Quelle Group, V
RAG AG, 35
RENK AG, 37
Rheinmetall Berlin AG, 9
Robert Bosch GmbH, I; 16 (upd.); 43 (upd.)
Rohde & Schwarz GmbH & Co. KG, 39
Roland Berger & Partner GmbH, 37
Ruhrgas AG, V; 38 (upd.)
Ruhrkohle AG, IV
RWE Group, V
Saarberg-Konzern, IV
Salzgitter AG, IV
SAP AG, 16; 43 (upd.)
Schenker-Rhenus AG, 6
Schering AG
Siemens A.G., II; 14 (upd.)
Sixt AG, 39
SPAR Handels AG, 35
Stinnes AG, 8; 23 (upd.)
Südzucker AG, 27
Tarkett Sommer AG, 25
Tengelmann Group, 27
Thyssen Krupp AG, IV; 28 (upd.)
Touristik Union International GmbH. and Company K.G., II
Varta AG, 23
Veba A.G., I; 15 (upd.)
Vereinigte Elektrizitätswerke Westfalen AG, V
Verlagsgruppe Georg von Holtzbrinck GmbH, 35
VEW AG, 39
VIAG Aktiengesellschaft, IV
VICTORIA Holding AG, III
Viessmann Werke GmbH & Co., 37
Villeroy & Boch AG, 37
Volkswagen Aktiengesellschaft, I; 11 (upd.); 32 (upd.)
Vorwerk & Co., 27
Wacker-Chemie GmbH, 35
Wella Group, III
Weru Aktiengesellschaft, 18
Westdeutsche Landesbank Girozentrale, II

Ghana

Ashanti Goldfields Company Limited, 43

Greece

National Bank of Greece, 41

Hong Kong

Cable & Wireless HKT, 30 (upd.)
Cathay Pacific Airways Limited, 6; 34 (upd.)
Cheung Kong (Holdings) Limited, IV; 20 (upd.)
CITIC Pacific Ltd., 18
First Pacific Company Limited, 18
Hong Kong Telecommunications Ltd., 6
Hongkong Electric Holdings Ltd., 6; 23 (upd.)
Hongkong Land Holdings Limited, IV
Hutchison Whampoa Ltd., 18
Kerry Properties Limited, 22
New World Development Company Limited, IV; 38 (upd.)
Playmates Toys, 23
Singer Company N.V., The, 30 (upd.)
Swire Pacific Ltd., I; 16 (upd.)
Tommy Hilfiger Corporation, 20

Hungary

Malév Plc, 24

India

Air-India Limited, 6; 27 (upd.)
Bajaj Auto Limited, 39
Coal India Limited, IV
Indian Oil Corporation Ltd., IV
Infosys Technologies Ltd., 38
Minerals and Metals Trading Corporation of India Ltd., IV
Oil and Natural Gas Commission, IV
Steel Authority of India Ltd., IV
Tata Iron and Steel Company Ltd., IV
Wipro Limited, 43

Indonesia

Garuda Indonesia, 6
PERTAMINA, IV

Iran

National Iranian Oil Company, IV

Ireland

Aer Lingus Group plc, 34
Allied Irish Banks, plc, 16; 43 (upd.)
Baltimore Technologies Plc, 42
eircom plc, 31 (upd.)
Fyffes Plc, 38
Harland and Wolff Holdings plc, 19
IONA Technologies plc, 43
Jefferson Smurfit Group plc, IV; 19 (upd.)
Kerry Group plc, 27
Ryanair Holdings plc, 35
Shannon Aerospace Ltd., 36
Telecom Eireann, 7
Waterford Wedgwood plc, 34 (upd.)

Israel

Bank Hapoalim B.M., II
Blue Square Israel Ltd., 41
ECI Telecom Ltd., 18
El Al Israel Airlines Ltd., 23
Elscint Ltd., 20
Koor Industries Ltd., II; 25 (upd.)
Scitex Corporation Ltd., 24
Teva Pharmaceutical Industries Ltd., 22

Italy

Alfa Romeo, 13; 36 (upd.)
Alitalia-Linee Aeree Italiana, S.p.A., 6; 29 (upd.)
Aprilia SpA, 17
Arnoldo Mondadori Editore S.p.A., IV; 19 (upd.)
Assicurazioni Generali SpA, III; 15 (upd.)
Automobili Lamborghini Holding S.p.A., 34 (upd.)
Automobili Lamborghini S.p.A., 13
Banca Commerciale Italiana SpA, II
Barilla G. e R. Fratelli S.p.A., 17
Benetton Group S.p.A., 10
Bulgari S.p.A., 20
Credito Italiano, II
Diesel SpA, 40
Ducati Motor Holding S.p.A., 30
Ente Nazionale Idrocarburi, IV
Ente Nazionale per L'Energia Elettrica, V
Fabbrica D' Armi Pietro Beretta S.p.A., 39
Ferrari S.p.A., 13; 36 (upd.)
Fiat S.p.A, I; 11 (upd.)
Fila Holding S.p.A., 20
Gianni Versace SpA, 22
Gruppo Coin S.p.A., 41
Guccio Gucci, S.p.A., 15
Industrie Natuzzi S.p.A., 18
Ing. C. Olivetti & C., S.p.a., III
Istituto per la Ricostruzione Industriale S.p.A., I; 11
Luxottica SpA, 17
Marchesi Antinori SRL, 42
Marzotto S.p.A., 20
Montedison SpA, I; 24 (upd.)
Officine Alfieri Maserati S.p.A., 13
Olivetti S.p.A., 34 (upd.)
Piaggio & C. S.p.A., 20
Pirelli S.p.A., V; 15 (upd.)
Reno de Medici S.p.A., 41
Riunione Adriatica di Sicurtè SpA, III
Società Finanziaria Telefonica per Azioni, V
Telecom Italia S.p.A., 43

Japan

Aisin Seiki Co., Ltd., III
Aiwa Co., Ltd., 30
Ajinomoto Co., Inc., II; 28 (upd.)
All Nippon Airways Co., Ltd., 6; 38 (upd.)
Alpine Electronics, Inc., 13
Alps Electric Co., Ltd., II
Asahi Breweries, Ltd., I; 20 (upd.)
Asahi Glass Company, Limited, III
Asahi National Broadcasting Company, Ltd., 9
Bank of Tokyo-Mitsubishi Ltd., II; 15 (upd.)
Bridgestone Corporation, V; 21 (upd.)
Brother Industries, Ltd., 14
C. Itoh & Company Ltd., I
Canon Inc., III; 18 (upd.)
CASIO Computer Co., Ltd., III; 16 (upd.); 40 (upd.)
Central Japan Railway Company, 43
Chubu Electric Power Company, Incorporated, V
Chugoku Electric Power Company Inc., V
Citizen Watch Co., Ltd., III; 21 (upd.)
Cosmo Oil Co., Ltd., IV
Dai Nippon Printing Co., Ltd., IV
Dai-Ichi Kangyo Bank Ltd., The, II
Daido Steel Co., Ltd., IV
Daiei, Inc., The, V; 17 (upd.); 41 (upd.)
Daihatsu Motor Company, Ltd., 7; 21 (upd.)
Daikin Industries, Ltd., III
Daimaru, Inc., The, V; 42 (upd.)
Daio Paper Corporation, IV
Daishowa Paper Manufacturing Co., Ltd., IV
Daiwa Bank, Ltd., The, II; 39 (upd.)
Daiwa Securities Company, Limited, II
DDI Corporation, 7
Dentsu Inc., I; 16 (upd.); 40 (upd.)
East Japan Railway Company, V
Fanuc Ltd., III; 17 (upd.)
Fuji Bank, Ltd., The, II
Fuji Electric Co., Ltd., II
Fuji Photo Film Co., Ltd., III; 18 (upd.)
Fujisawa Pharmaceutical Company Ltd., I
Fujitsu Limited, III; 16 (upd.); 42 (upd.)
Furukawa Electric Co., Ltd., The, III
General Sekiyu K.K., IV
Hakuhodo, Inc., 6; 42 (upd.)
Hankyu Corporation, V; 23 (upd.)
Hino Motors, Ltd., 7; 21 (upd.)
Hitachi Ltd., I; 12 (upd.)
Hitachi Metals, Ltd., IV
Hitachi Zosen Corporation, III
Hitachi, Ltd., 40 (upd.)
Hokkaido Electric Power Company Inc., V
Hokuriku Electric Power Company, V
Honda Motor Company Limited, I; 10 (upd.); 29 (upd.)
Honshu Paper Co., Ltd., IV
Idemitsu Kosan K.K., IV
Industrial Bank of Japan, Ltd., The, II
Isetan Company Limited, V; 36 (upd.)
Ishikawajima-Harima Heavy Industries Co., Ltd., III
Isuzu Motors, Ltd., 9; 23 (upd.)
Ito-Yokado Co., Ltd., V; 42 (upd.)
ITOCHU Corporation, 32 (upd.)
Itoham Foods Inc., II
Japan Airlines Company, Ltd., I; 32 (upd.)
Japan Broadcasting Corporation, 7
Japan Leasing Corporation, 8
Japan Pulp and Paper Company Limited, IV
Japan Tobacco Incorporated, V
Jujo Paper Co., Ltd., IV
JUSCO Co., Ltd., V
Kajima Corporation, I
Kanematsu Corporation, IV; 24 (upd.)
Kansai Electric Power Co., Inc., The, V
Kao Corporation, III; 20 (upd.)
Kawasaki Heavy Industries, Ltd., III
Kawasaki Kisen Kaisha, Ltd., V
Kawasaki Steel Corporation, IV
Keio Teito Electric Railway Company, V
Kenwood Corporation, 31
Kikkoman Corporation, 14
Kinki Nippon Railway Company Ltd., V
Kirin Brewery Company, Limited, I; 21 (upd.)
Kobe Steel, Ltd., IV; 19 (upd.)
Kodansha Ltd., IV; 38 (upd.)
Komatsu Ltd., III; 16 (upd.)
Konica Corporation, III; 30 (upd.)
Kotobukiya Co., Ltd., V
Kubota Corporation, III; 26 (upd.)
Kumagai Gumi Company, Ltd., I
Kyocera Corporation, II; 21 (upd.)
Kyowa Hakko Kogyo Co., Ltd., III
Kyushu Electric Power Company Inc., V
Lion Corporation, III
Long-Term Credit Bank of Japan, Ltd., II
Makita Corporation, 22
Marubeni Corporation, I; 24 (upd.)
Marui Co., Ltd., V
Maruzen Co., Limited, 18
Matsushita Electric Industrial Co., Ltd., II
Matsushita Electric Works, Ltd., III; 7 (upd.)
Matsuzakaya Company Limited, V
Mazda Motor Corporation, 9; 23 (upd.)
Meiji Milk Products Company, Limited, II
Meiji Mutual Life Insurance Company, The, III

Meiji Seika Kaisha, Ltd., II
Minolta Co., Ltd., III; 18 (upd.); 43 (upd.)
Mitsubishi Bank, Ltd., The, II
Mitsubishi Chemical Industries, Ltd., I
Mitsubishi Corporation, I; 12 (upd.)
Mitsubishi Electric Corporation, II
Mitsubishi Estate Company, Limited, IV
Mitsubishi Heavy Industries, Ltd., III; 7 (upd.); 40 (upd.)
Mitsubishi Materials Corporation, III
Mitsubishi Motors Corporation, 9; 23 (upd.)
Mitsubishi Oil Co., Ltd., IV
Mitsubishi Rayon Co., Ltd., V
Mitsubishi Trust & Banking Corporation, The, II
Mitsui & Co., Ltd., 28 (upd.)
Mitsui Bank, Ltd., The, II
Mitsui Bussan K.K., I
Mitsui Marine and Fire Insurance Company, Limited, III
Mitsui Mining & Smelting Co., Ltd., IV
Mitsui Mining Company, Limited, IV
Mitsui Mutual Life Insurance Company, III; 39 (upd.)
Mitsui O.S.K. Lines, Ltd., V
Mitsui Petrochemical Industries, Ltd., 9
Mitsui Real Estate Development Co., Ltd., IV
Mitsui Trust & Banking Company, Ltd., The, II
Mitsukoshi Ltd., V
Mizuno Corporation, 25
Nagasakiya Co., Ltd., V
Nagase & Company, Ltd., 8
NEC Corporation, II; 21 (upd.)
NHK Spring Co., Ltd., III
Nichii Co., Ltd., V
Nichimen Corporation, IV; 24 (upd.)
Nihon Keizai Shimbun, Inc., IV
Nikko Securities Company Limited, The, II; 9 (upd.)
Nikon Corporation, III
Nintendo Co., Ltd., III; 7 (upd.); 28 (upd.)
Nippon Credit Bank, II
Nippon Express Co., Ltd., V
Nippon Life Insurance Company, III
Nippon Light Metal Company, Ltd., IV
Nippon Meat Packers, Inc., II
Nippon Oil Company, Limited, IV
Nippon Seiko K.K., III
Nippon Sheet Glass Company, Limited, III
Nippon Shinpan Company, Ltd., II
Nippon Steel Corporation, IV; 17 (upd.)
Nippon Suisan Kaisha, Limited, II
Nippon Telegraph and Telephone Corporation, V
Nippon Yusen Kabushiki Kaisha, V
Nippondenso Co., Ltd., III
Nissan Motor Company Ltd., I; 11 (upd.); 34 (upd.)
Nisshin Flour Milling Company, Ltd., II
Nisshin Steel Co., Ltd., IV
Nissho Iwai K.K., I
NKK Corporation, IV; 28 (upd.)
Nomura Securities Company, Limited, II; 9 (upd.)
Norinchukin Bank, II
NTN Corporation, III
Odakyu Electric Railway Company Limited, V
Ohbayashi Corporation, I
Oji Paper Co., Ltd., IV
Oki Electric Industry Company, Limited, II
Okura & Co., Ltd., IV
Omron Corporation, II; 28 (upd.)
Onoda Cement Co., Ltd., III
Orix Corporation, II
Osaka Gas Co., Ltd., V
Pioneer Electronic Corporation, III; 28 (upd.)
Rengo Co., Ltd., IV
Ricoh Company, Ltd., III; 36 (upd.)
Roland Corporation, 38
Sankyo Company, Ltd., I
Sanrio Company, Ltd., 38
Sanwa Bank, Ltd., The, II; 15 (upd.)
SANYO Electric Company, Ltd., II; 36 (upd.)
Sanyo-Kokusaku Pulp Co., Ltd., IV
Sapporo Breweries, Ltd., I; 13 (upd.); 36 (upd.)
Seibu Department Stores, Ltd., V; 42 (upd.)
Seibu Railway Co. Ltd., V
Seiko Corporation, III; 17 (upd.)
Seino Transportation Company, Ltd., 6
Seiyu, Ltd., The, V; 36 (upd.)
Sekisui Chemical Co., Ltd., III
Sharp Corporation, II; 12 (upd.); 40 (upd.)
Shikoku Electric Power Company, Inc., V
Shionogi & Co., Ltd., III; 17 (upd.)
Shiseido Company, Limited, III; 22 (upd.)
Showa Shell Sekiyu K.K., IV
Snow Brand Milk Products Company, Limited, II
Softbank Corp., 13; 38 (upd.)
Sony Corporation, II; 12 (upd.); 40 (upd.)
Sumitomo Bank, Limited, The, II; 26 (upd.)
Sumitomo Chemical Company Ltd., I
Sumitomo Corporation, I; 11 (upd.)
Sumitomo Electric Industries, Ltd., II
Sumitomo Heavy Industries, Ltd., III; 42 (upd.)
Sumitomo Life Insurance Company, III
Sumitomo Marine and Fire Insurance Company, Limited, The, III
Sumitomo Metal Industries, Ltd., IV
Sumitomo Metal Mining Co., Ltd., IV
Sumitomo Realty & Development Co., Ltd., IV
Sumitomo Rubber Industries, Ltd., V
Sumitomo Trust & Banking Company, Ltd., The, II
Suzuki Motor Corporation, 9; 23 (upd.)
Taiyo Fishery Company, Limited, II
Taiyo Kobe Bank, Ltd., The, II
Takashimaya Co., Limited, V
Takeda Chemical Industries, Ltd., I
TDK Corporation, II; 17 (upd.)
Teijin Limited, V
Tobu Railway Co Ltd, 6
Toho Co., Ltd., 28
Tohoku Electric Power Company, Inc., V
Tokai Bank, Limited, The, II; 15 (upd.)
Tokio Marine and Fire Insurance Co., Ltd., The, III
Tokyo Electric Power Company, Incorporated, The, V
Tokyo Gas Co., Ltd., V
Tokyu Corporation, V
Tokyu Department Store Co., Ltd., V; 32 (upd.)
Tokyu Land Corporation, IV
Tomen Corporation, IV; 24 (upd.)
Tonen Corporation, IV; 16 (upd.)
Toppan Printing Co., Ltd., IV
Toray Industries, Inc., V
Toshiba Corporation, I; 12 (upd.); 40 (upd.)
TOTO LTD., III; 28 (upd.)
Toyo Sash Co., Ltd., III
Toyo Seikan Kaisha, Ltd., I
Toyoda Automatic Loom Works, Ltd., III
Toyota Motor Corporation, I; 11 (upd.); 38 (upd.)
Ube Industries, Ltd., III; 38 (upd.)
Unitika Ltd., V
Uny Co., Ltd., V
Victor Company of Japan, Limited, II; 26 (upd.)
Wacoal Corp., 25
Yamaha Corporation, III; 16 (upd.); 40 (upd.)
Yamaichi Securities Company, Limited, II
Yamato Transport Co. Ltd., V
Yasuda Fire and Marine Insurance Company, Limited, The, III
Yasuda Mutual Life Insurance Company, The, 39 (upd.)
Yasuda Mutual Life Insurance Company, Limited, The, III
Yasuda Trust and Banking Company, Ltd., The, II; 17 (upd.)
Yokohama Rubber Co., Ltd., The, V; 19 (upd.)

Korea

Anam Group, 23
Daewoo Group, III; 18 (upd.)
Electronics Co., Ltd., 14
Goldstar Co., Ltd., 12
Hyundai Group, III; 7 (upd.)
Korean Air Lines Co., Ltd., 6; 27 (upd.)
Lucky-Goldstar, II
Pohang Iron and Steel Company Ltd., IV
Samsung Group, I
Ssangyong Cement Industrial Co., Ltd., III

Kuwait

Kuwait Petroleum Corporation, IV

Luxembourg

ARBED S.A., IV; 22 (upd.)

Lybia

Libyan National Oil Corporation, IV

Malaysia

Malaysian Airlines System Berhad, 6; 29 (upd.)
Petronas, IV
Sime Darby Berhad, 14; 36 (upd.)

Mexico

Alfa, S.A. de C.V., 19
Altos Hornos de México, S.A. de C.V., 42
Bufete Industrial, S.A. de C.V., 34
Casa Cuervo, S.A. de C.V., 31
Cemex SA de CV, 20
Cifra, S.A. de C.V., 12
Consorcio G Grupo Dina, S.A. de C.V., 36
Controladora Comercial Mexicana, S.A. de C.V., 36
Corporación Internacional de Aviación, S.A. de C.V. (Cintra), 20
Desc, S.A. de C.V., 23
Empresas ICA Sociedad Controladora, S.A. de C.V., 41
Gruma, S.A. de C.V., 31
Grupo Carso, S.A. de C.V., 21
Grupo Casa Saba, S.A. de C.V., 39
Grupo Cydsa, S.A. de C.V., 39
Grupo Elektra, S.A. de C.V., 39
Grupo Financiero Serfin, S.A., 19
Grupo Gigante, S.A. de C.V., 34
Grupo Herdez, S.A. de C.V., 35
Grupo Industrial Bimbo, 19

Mexico *(continued)*

Grupo Industrial Durango, S.A. de C.V., 37
Grupo Mexico, S.A. de C.V., 40
Grupo Modelo, S.A. de C.V., 29
Grupo Televisa, S.A., 18
Hylsamex, S.A. de C.V., 39
Industrias Bachoco, S.A. de C.V., 39
Industrias Penoles, S.A. de C.V., 22
Organización Soriana, S.A. de C.V., 35
Petróleos Mexicanos, IV; 19 (upd.)
Pulsar Internacional S.A., 21
Sanborn Hermanos, S.A., 20
Sears Roebuck de México, S.A. de C.V., 20
Telefonos de Mexico S.A. de C.V., 14
Tubos de Acero de Mexico, S.A. (TAMSA), 41
TV Azteca, S.A. de C.V., 39
Valores Industriales S.A., 19
Vitro Corporativo S.A. de C.V., 34
Wal-Mart de Mexico, S.A. de C.V., 35 (upd.)

Nepal

Royal Nepal Airline Corporation, 41

New Zealand

Air New Zealand Limited, 14; 38 (upd.)
Fletcher Challenge Ltd., IV; 19 (upd.)
Wattie's Ltd., 7

Nigeria

Nigerian National Petroleum Corporation, IV

Norway

Den Norse Stats Oljeselskap AS, IV
Helly Hansen ASA, 25
Kvaerner ASA, 36
Norsk Hydro ASA, 10; 35 (upd.)
Orkla A/S, 18
Schibsted ASA, 31

Oman

Petroleum Development Oman LLC, IV

Peru

Southern Peru Copper Corporation, 40

Philippines

Philippine Airlines, Inc., 6; 23 (upd.)
San Miguel Corporation, 15

Poland

LOT Polish Airlines (Polskie Linie Lotnicze S.A.), 33

Portugal

Banco Espírito Santo e Comercial de Lisboa S.A., 15
Petróleos de Portugal S.A., IV
Transportes Aereos Portugueses, S.A., 6

Qatar

Qatar General Petroleum Corporation, IV

Russia

A.S. Yakovlev Design Bureau, 15
Aeroflot--Russian International Airlines, 6; 29 (upd.)
Aviacionny Nauchno-Tehnicheskii Komplex im. A.N. Tupoleva, 24
OAO Gazprom, 42
OAO LUKOIL, 40
Sukhoi Design Bureau Aviation Scientific-Industrial Complex, 24

Saudi Arabia

Saudi Arabian Airlines, 6; 27 (upd.)
Saudi Arabian Oil Company, IV; 17 (upd.)

Scotland

Distillers Company PLC, I
General Accident PLC, III
Governor and Company of the Bank of Scotland, The, 10
Royal Bank of Scotland Group plc, The, 12
Scottish & Newcastle plc, 15
Scottish Hydro-Electric PLC, 13
Scottish Media Group plc, 32
ScottishPower plc, 19
Stagecoach Holdings plc, 30
Standard Life Assurance Company, The, III

Singapore

Flextronics International Ltd., 38
Singapore Airlines Ltd., 6; 27 (upd.)

South Africa

Anglo American Corporation of South Africa Limited, IV; 16 (upd.)
Barlow Rand Ltd., I
De Beers Consolidated Mines Limited/De Beers Centenary AG, IV; 7 (upd.); 28 (upd.)
Gencor Ltd., IV; 22 (upd.)
Gold Fields of South Africa Ltd., IV
SAA (Pty) Ltd., 28
Sasol Limited, IV
South African Breweries Limited, The, I; 24 (upd.)
Transnet Ltd., 6

South Korea

Kia Motors Corporation, 12; 29 (upd.)
Samsung Electronics Co., Ltd., 41 (upd.)

Spain

Banco Bilbao Vizcaya, S.A., II
Banco Central, II
Banco do Brasil S.A., II
Banco Santander Central Hispano S.A., 36 (upd.)
Chupa Chups S.A., 38
Compañia Española de Petróleos S.A., IV
El Corte Inglés Group, V; 26 (upd.)
ENDESA Group, V
Grupo Ferrovial, S.A., 40
Iberia Líneas Aéreas de España S.A., 6; 36 (upd.)
Instituto Nacional de Industria, I
Repsol S.A., IV; 16 (upd.)
Repsol-YPF S.A., 40 (upd.)
Tabacalera, S.A., V; 17 (upd.)
Telefónica de España, S.A., V
TelePizza S.A., 33
Television Española, S.A., 7
Terra Lycos, Inc., 43

Sweden

A. Johnson & Company H.B., I
AB Volvo, I; 7 (upd.); 26 (upd.)
Aktiebolaget Electrolux, 22 (upd.)
Aktiebolaget SKF, III; 38 (upd.)
Alfa-Laval AB, III
Astra AB, I; 20 (upd.)
Atlas Copco AB, III; 28 (upd.)
BRIO AB, 24
Electrolux Group, III
Hennes & Mauritz AB, 29
ICA AB, II
Mo och Domsjö AB, IV
Modern Times Group AB, 36
NetCom Systems AB, 26
Nobel Industries AB, 9
Nordea AB, 40
Perstorp A.B., I
Saab Automobile AB, 32 (upd.)
Saab-Scania A.B., I; 11 (upd.)
Sandvik AB, IV; 32 (upd.)
SAS Group, The, 34 (upd.)
Scandinavian Airlines System, I
Securitas AB, 42
Skandinaviska Enskilda Banken, II
Skanska AB, 38
Stora Kopparbergs Bergslags AB, IV
Svenska Cellulosa Aktiebolaget SCA, IV; 28 (upd.)
Svenska Handelsbanken, II
Swedish Match AB, 39 (upd.)
Swedish Telecom, V
Telefonaktiebolaget LM Ericsson, V
Vin & Spirit AB, 31

Switzerland

ABB ASEA Brown Boveri Ltd., II; 22 (upd.)
Adecco S.A., 36 (upd.)
Adia S.A., 6
Arthur Andersen & Company, Société Coopérative, 10
Ascom AG, 9
Bâloise-Holding, 40
Barry Callebaut AG, 29
Chocoladefabriken Lindt & Sprüngli AG, 27
Ciba-Geigy Ltd., I; 8 (upd.)
Credit Suisse Group, II; 21 (upd.)
Danzas Group, V; 40 (upd.)
De Beers Consolidated Mines Limited/De Beers Centenary AG, IV; 7 (upd.); 28 (upd.)
Elektrowatt AG, 6
F. Hoffmann-Laroche & Company A.G., I
Fédération Internationale de Football Association, 27
Givaudan SA, 43
Holderbank Financière Glaris Ltd., III
Jacobs Suchard A.G., II
Kraft Jacobs Suchard AG, 26 (upd.)
Kuhne & Nagel International A.G., V
Kuoni Travel Holding Ltd., 40
Logitech International SA, 28
Mettler-Toledo International Inc., 30
Montres Rolex S.A., 13; 34 (upd.)
Nestlé S.A., II; 7 (upd.); 28 (upd.)
Novartis AG, 39 (upd.)
Rieter Holding AG, 42
Roland Murten A.G., 7
Sandoz Ltd., I
Schindler Holding AG, 29
Schweizerische Post-, Telefon- und Telegrafen-Betriebe, V
Sulzer Brothers Limited (Gebruder Sulzer Aktiengesellschaft), III
Swarovski International Holding AG, 40
Swatch Group SA, The, 26
Swedish Match S.A., 12
Swiss Air Transport Company, Ltd., I
Swiss Bank Corporation, II

Swiss Federal Railways (Schweizerische Bundesbahnen), The, V
Swiss Reinsurance Company (Schweizerische Rückversicherungs-Gesellschaft), III
TAG Heuer International SA, 25
Union Bank of Switzerland, II
Victorinox AG, 21
Winterthur Schweizerische Versicherungs-Gesellschaft, III
Zurich Financial Services, 42 (upd.)
Zürich Versicherungs-Gesellschaft, III

Taiwan

Acer Inc., 16
China Airlines, 34
Evergreen Marine Corporation Taiwan Ltd., 13
Formosa Plastics Corporation, 14
Tatung Co., 23
Yageo Corporation, 16

Thailand

Thai Airways International Public Company Limited, 6; 27 (upd.)

The Netherlands

AEGON N.V., III
Akzo Nobel N.V., 13; 41 (upd.)
Algemene Bank Nederland N.V., II
Amsterdam-Rotterdam Bank N.V., II
Arcadis NV, 26
Baan Company, 25
Buhrmann NV, 41
CNH Global N.V., 38 (upd.)
DSM, N.V, I
Elsevier N.V., IV
Getronics NV, 39
Grand Hotel Krasnapolsky N.V., 23
Hagemeyer N.V., 39
Heineken N.V., I; 13 (upd.); 34 (upd.)
Indigo NV, 26
Ispat International N.V., 30
Koninklijke Ahold N.V. (Royal Ahold), II; 16 (upd.)
Koninklijke Luchtvaart Maatschappij, N.V. (KLM Royal Dutch Airlines), I; 28 (upd.)
Koninklijke Nederlandsche Hoogovens en Staalfabrieken NV, IV
Koninklijke Nedlloyd N.V., 6; 26 (upd.)
Koninklijke PTT Nederland NV, V
Koninklijke Wessanen N.V., II
KPMG International, 33 (upd.)
KPMG Worldwide, 10
Mammoet Transport B.V., 26
MIH Limited, 31
N.V. AMEV, III
N.V. Holdingmaatschappij De Telegraaf, 23
N.V. Koninklijke Nederlandse Vliegtuigenfabriek Fokker, I; 28 (upd.)
N.V. Nederlandse Gasunie, V
Nationale-Nederlanden N.V., III
New Holland N.V., 22
Océ N.V., 24
Philips Electronics N.V., II; 13 (upd.)
PolyGram N.V., 23
Qiagen N.V., 39
Rabobank Group, 33
Randstad Holding n.v., 16; 43 (upd.)
Rodamco N.V., 26
Royal Dutch Petroleum Company/ The Shell Transport and Trading Company p.l.c., IV
Royal KPN N.V., 30
Royal Numico N.V., 37
Royal Packaging Industries Van Leer N.V., 30
Royal Vopak NV, 41
TNT Post Group N.V., V, 27 (upd.); 30 (upd.)
Toolex International N.V., 26
Triple P N.V., 26
Unilever N.V., II; 7 (upd.); 32 (upd.)
Vedior NV, 35
Velcro Industries N.V., 19
Vendex International N.V., 13
VNU N.V., 27
Wolters Kluwer NV, 14; 33 (upd.)

Turkey

KOC Holding A.S., I
Türkiye Petrolleri Anonim Ortakliği, IV

United Arab Emirates

Abu Dhabi National Oil Company, IV
Emirates Group, The, 39

United Kingdom

Abbey National plc, 10; 39 (upd.)
Aegis Group plc, 6
Aggregate Industries plc, 36
Airtours Plc, 27
Albert Fisher Group plc, The, 41
Allders plc, 37
Allied Domecq PLC, 29
Allied-Lyons PLC, I
Amstrad PLC, III
Arcadia Group plc, 28 (upd.)
Argyll Group PLC, II
Arjo Wiggins Appleton p.l.c., 34
ASDA Group plc, II; 28 (upd.)
Ashtead Group plc, 34
Associated British Foods plc, II; 13 (upd.); 41 (upd.)
Aston Villa plc, 41
AT&T Istel Ltd., 14
B.A.T. Industries PLC, I; 22 (upd.)
BAA plc, 10; 33 (upd.)
Balfour Beatty plc, 36 (upd.)
Barclays PLC, II; 20 (upd.)
Barings PLC, 14
Barratt Developments PLC, I
Bass PLC, I; 15 (upd.); 38 (upd.)
Bat Industries PLC, I; 20 (upd.)
Bhs plc, 17
BICC PLC, III
Blacks Leisure Group plc, 39
Blue Circle Industries PLC, III
BOC Group plc, I; 25 (upd.)
Body Shop International PLC, The, 11
Booker plc, 13; 31 (upd.)
Boots Company PLC, The, V; 24 (upd.)
Bowater PLC, IV
Bowthorpe plc, 33
British Aerospace plc, I; 24 (upd.)
British Airways PLC, I; 14 (upd.); 43 (upd.)
British Broadcasting Corporation Ltd., 7; 21 (upd.)
British Coal Corporation, IV
British Gas plc, V
British Midland plc, 38
British Nuclear Fuels plc, 6
British Petroleum Company plc, The, IV; 7 (upd.); 21 (upd.)
British Railways Board, V
British Sky Broadcasting Group Plc, 20
British Steel plc, IV; 19 (upd.)
British Telecommunications plc, V; 15 (upd.)
British Vita plc, 9; 33 (upd.)
British World Airlines Ltd., 18
British-Borneo Oil & Gas PLC, 34
BTR PLC, I
BTR Siebe plc, 27
Bunzl plc, IV; 31 (upd.)
Burberry Ltd., 41 (upd.)
Burberrys Ltd., 17
Burmah Castrol PLC, IV; 30 (upd.)
Burton Group plc, The, V
Cable and Wireless plc, V; 25 (upd.)
Cadbury Schweppes PLC, II
Canary Wharf Group Plc, 30
Capital Radio plc, 35
Caradon plc, 20 (upd.)
Carlton Communications plc, 15
Cartier Monde, 29
Central Independent Television, 7; 23 (upd.)
Centrica plc, 29 (upd.)
Christie's International plc, 15; 39 (upd.)
Chrysalis Group plc, 40
Clifford Chance LLP, 38
Clinton Cards plc, 39
Close Brothers Group plc, 39
Coats Viyella Plc, V
Cobham plc, 30
COLT Telecom Group plc, 41
Commercial Union PLC, III
Compass Group PLC, 34
Cookson Group plc, III
Courtaulds plc, V; 17 (upd.)
Cranswick plc, 40
Daily Mail and General Trust plc, 19
Dairy Crest Group plc, 32
Dalgety, PLC, II
Dawson Holdings PLC, 43
De La Rue plc, 10; 34 (upd.)
Debenhams Plc, 28
Diageo plc, 24 (upd.)
Dixons Group plc, V; 19 (upd.)
Dorling Kindersley Holdings plc, 20
easyJet Airline Company Limited, 39
ECC Group plc, III
Elementis plc, 40 (upd.)
EMAP plc, 35
EMI Group plc, 22 (upd.)
English China Clays Ltd., 40 (upd.)
English China Clays plc, 15 (upd.)
Enterprise Oil plc, 11
Esporta plc, 35
Eurotunnel Group, 37 (upd.)
Eurotunnel PLC, 13
Fairclough Construction Group PLC, I
First Choice Holidays PLC, 40
Fisons plc, 9; 23 (upd.)
French Connection Group plc, 41
Fuller Smith & Turner P.L.C., 38
Gallaher Limited, V; 19 (upd.)
Gateway Corporation Ltd., The, II
Geest Plc, 38
General Electric Company PLC, II
George Wimpey PLC, 12
GKN plc, III; 38 (upd.)
Glaxo Holdings PLC, I; 9 (upd.)
Go-Ahead Group Plc, The, 28
Granada Group PLC, II; 24 (upd.)
Grand Metropolitan PLC, I; 14 (upd.)
Great Universal Stores plc, The, V; 19 (upd.)
Greenalls Group PLC, The, 21
Greene King plc, 31
Guardian Royal Exchange Plc, 11
Guinness PLC, I
Guinness/UDV, 43 (upd.)
GWR Group plc, 39
Hammerson plc, 40
Hammerson Property Investment and Development Corporation plc, The, IV

United Kingdom *(continued)*

Hanson PLC, III; 7 (upd.); 30 (upd.)
Harrisons & Crosfield plc, III
Hartstone Group plc, The, 14
Hawker Siddeley Group Public Limited Company, III
Hays Plc, 27
Hazlewood Foods plc, 32
Her Majesty's Stationery Office, 7
Hillsdown Holdings plc, II; 24 (upd.)
HIT Entertainment PLC, 40
HSBC Holdings plc, 12; 26 (upd.)
Huntingdon Life Sciences Group plc, 42
Ibstock Brick Ltd., 37 (upd.)
Ibstock plc, 14
ICL plc, 6
IMI plc, 9
Imperial Chemical Industries PLC, I
Inchcape PLC, III; 16 (upd.)
IPC Magazines Limited, 7
J Sainsbury plc, II; 13 (upd.); 38 (upd.)
James Beattie plc, 43
Jarvis plc, 39
JD Wetherspoon plc, 30
JJB Sports plc, 32
John Brown PLC, I
John Laing PLC, I
John Lewis Partnership plc, V; 42 (upd.)
John Menzies plc, 39
Johnson Matthey PLC, IV; 16 (upd.)
Johnston Press plc, 35
Kennecott Corporation, 7; 27 (upd.)
Kingfisher plc, V; 24 (upd.)
Kleinwort Benson Group PLC, II
Kvaerner ASA, 36
Ladbroke Group PLC, II; 21 (upd.)
Land Securities PLC, IV
Laura Ashley Holdings plc, 13; 37 (upd.)
Legal & General Group plc, III; 24 (upd.)
Littlewoods Organisation PLC, The, V
Littlewoods plc, 42 (upd.)
Lloyd's of London, III; 22 (upd.)
Lloyds Bank PLC, II
Logica plc, 14; 37 (upd.)
London Regional Transport, 6
London Stock Exchange Limited, 34
Lonrho Plc, 21
Lotus Cars Ltd., 14
Lucas Industries PLC, III
Luminar Plc, 40
Madge Networks N.V., 26
Manchester United Football Club plc, 30
Marconi plc, 33 (upd.)
Marks and Spencer p.l.c., V; 24 (upd.)
Maxwell Communication Corporation plc, IV; 7 (upd.)
McKechnie plc, 34
Meggitt PLC, 34
MEPC plc, IV
Mercury Communications, Ltd., 7
Mersey Docks and Harbour Company, The, 30
Metal Box PLC, I
Midland Bank PLC, II; 17 (upd.)
Mirror Group Newspapers plc, 7; 23 (upd.)
Monsoon plc, 39
Morgan Grenfell Group PLC, II
Mothercare UK Ltd., 17
N M Rothschild & Sons Limited, 39
National Power PLC, 12
National Westminster Bank PLC, II
New Look Group plc, 35
Newsquest plc, 32
Next plc, 29
NFC plc, 6
North West Water Group plc, 11
Northern Foods PLC, 10
Northern Rock plc, 33
Ocean Group plc, 6
Pearson plc, IV
Peninsular & Oriental Steam Navigation Company (Bovis Division), The, I
Peninsular and Oriental Steam Navigation Company, The, V; 38 (upd.)
Pentland Group plc, 20
PIC International Group PLC, 24 (upd.)
Pilkington plc, III; 34 (upd.)
Plessey Company, PLC, The, II
Post Office Group, V
Powell Duffryn plc, 31
PowerGen PLC, 11
R. Griggs Group Limited, 23
Racal Electronics PLC, II
Rank Organisation Plc, The, II; 14 (upd.)
Ranks Hovis McDougall Limited, II; 28 (upd.)
Really Useful Group, The, 26
Reckitt & Colman PLC, II
Reckitt Benckiser plc, 42 (upd.)
Redland plc, III
Redrow Group plc, 31
Reed Elsevier plc, 31 (upd.)
Reed International PLC, IV; 17 (upd.)
Reuters Holdings PLC, IV; 22 (upd.)
Rexam PLC, 32 (upd.)
Rio Tinto plc, 19 (upd.)
RMC Group p.l.c., III ; 34 (upd.)
Rolls-Royce Motors Ltd., I
Rolls-Royce plc, I; 7 (upd.); 21 (upd.)
Rothmans International p.l.c., V
Rothmans UK Holdings Limited, 19 (upd.)
Rover Group Ltd., 7; 21 (upd.)
Rowntree Mackintosh, II
Royal Bank of Scotland Group plc, The, 38 (upd.)
Royal Doulton plc, 14; 38 (upd.)
Royal Dutch Petroleum Company/ The Shell Transport and Trading Company p.l.c., IV
Royal Insurance Holdings PLC, III
RTZ Corporation PLC, The, IV
Rugby Group plc, The, 31
Saatchi & Saatchi PLC, I
Sage Group, The, 43
SBC Warburg, 14
Schroders plc, 42
Scottish & Newcastle plc, 35 (upd.)
Scottish Radio Holding plc, 41
Sea Containers Ltd., 29
Sears plc, V
Selfridges Plc, 34
Severn Trent PLC, 12; 38 (upd.)
Shepherd Neame Limited, 30
Singer & Friedlander Group plc, 41
Slough Estates PLC, IV
Smith & Nephew plc, 17;41 (upd.)
SmithKline Beecham plc, III; 32 (upd.)
Smiths Industries PLC, 25
Southern Electric PLC, 13
St Ives plc, 34
Standard Chartered PLC, II
STC PLC, III
Stoll-Moss Theatres Ltd., 34
Stolt-Nielsen S.A., 42
Storehouse PLC, 16
Sun Alliance Group PLC, III
Tarmac plc, III; 28 (upd.)
Tate & Lyle PLC, II; 42 (upd.)
Taylor Nelson Sofres plc, 34
Taylor Woodrow plc, I; 38 (upd.)
Tesco PLC, II; 24 (upd.)
Thames Water plc, 11
Thorn Emi PLC, I
Thorn plc, 24
TI Group plc, 17
Tibbett & Britten Group plc, 32
Tomkins plc, 11
Travis Perkins plc, 34
Trusthouse Forte PLC, III
TSB Group plc, 12
Ultramar PLC, IV
Unigate PLC, II; 28 (upd.)
Unilever PLC, II; 7 (upd.); 32 (upd.)
United Biscuits (Holdings) plc, II; 42 (upd.)
United News & Media plc, 28 (upd.)
United Newspapers plc, IV
Vendôme Luxury Group plc, 27
Vickers plc, 27
Virgin Group, 12; 32 (upd.)
Vodafone Group PLC, 11; 36 (upd.)
Vosper Thornycroft Holding plc, 41
W H Smith Group PLC, V
Wassall Plc, 18
Waterford Wedgwood Holdings PLC, 12
Watson Wyatt Worldwide, 42
Wellcome Foundation Ltd., The, I
WH Smith PLC, 42 (upd.)
Whitbread PLC, I; 20 (upd.)
Willis Corroon Group plc, 25
Wm. Morrison Supermarkets PLC, 38
Wood Hall Trust PLC, I
Woolwich plc, The, 30
WPP Group plc, 6
Young & Co.'s Brewery, P.L.C., 38
Zeneca Group PLC, 21

United States

A & E Television Networks, 32
A & W Brands, Inc., 25
A. Schulman, Inc., 8
A.B.Dick Company, 28
A.C. Moore Arts & Crafts, Inc., 30
A.C. Nielsen Company, 13
A.G. Edwards, Inc., 8; 32
A.H. Belo Corporation, 10; 30 (upd.)
A.L. Pharma Inc., 12
A.M. Castle & Co., 25
A.O. Smith Corporation, 11; 40 (upd.)
A.T. Cross Company, 17
AAF-McQuay Incorporated, 26
AAON, Inc., 22
AAR Corp., 28
Aaron Rents, Inc., 14; 35 (upd.)
AARP, 27
Aavid Thermal Technologies, Inc., 29
Abbott Laboratories, I; 11 (upd.); 40 (upd.)
ABC Appliance, Inc., 10
ABC Carpet & Home Co. Inc., 26
ABC Rail Products Corporation, 18
ABC Supply Co., Inc., 22
Abercrombie & Fitch Co., 15; 35 (upd.)
Abigail Adams National Bancorp, Inc., 23
ABM Industries Incorporated, 25 (upd.)
Abrams Industries Inc., 23
Academy Sports & Outdoors, 27
Acadian Ambulance & Air Med Services, Inc., 39
Acclaim Entertainment Inc., 24
ACCO World Corporation, 7
ACE Cash Express, Inc., 33
Ace Hardware Corporation, 12; 35 (upd.)
Aceto Corp., 38
Ackerley Communications, Inc., 9
Acme-Cleveland Corp., 13
ACNielsen Corporation, 38 (upd.)
Action Performance Companies, Inc., 27
Activision, Inc., 32
Acuson Corporation, 10; 36 (upd.)
Acxiom Corporation, 35
Adams Golf, Inc., 37
Adaptec, Inc., 31

ADC Telecommunications, Inc., 10; 30 (upd.)
Adelphia Communications Corp., 17
Adobe Systems Inc., 10; 33 (upd.)
Adolph Coors Company, I; 13 (upd.); 36 (upd.)
ADT Security Systems, Inc., 12
Adtran Inc., 22
Advance Publications Inc., IV; 19 (upd.)
Advanced Marketing Services, Inc., 34
Advanced Micro Devices, Inc., 6; 30 (upd.)
Advanced Technology Laboratories, Inc., 9
ADVANTA Corp., 8
Advanta Corporation, 38 (upd.)
Advantica Restaurant Group, Inc., 27 (upd.)
Advo, Inc., 6
AEI Music Network Inc., 35
AEP Industries, Inc., 36
Aeroquip Corporation, 16
AES Corporation, The, 10; 13 (upd.)
Aetna, Inc., III; 21 (upd.)
AFC Enterprises, Inc., 32
Affiliated Publications, Inc., 7
AFLAC Incorporated, 10 (upd.); 38 (upd.)
Ag-Chem Equipment Company, Inc., 17
AGCO Corp., 13
Agilent Technologies Inc., 38
Agway, Inc., 7; 21 (upd.)
AHL Services, Inc., 27
Air & Water Technologies Corporation, 6
Air Express International Corporation, 13
Air Products and Chemicals, Inc., I; 10 (upd.)
Airborne Freight Corporation, 6; 34 (upd.)
AirTouch Communications, 11
AirTran Holdings, Inc., 22
AK Steel Holding Corporation, 19; 41 (upd.)
Akin, Gump, Strauss, Hauer & Feld, L.L.P., 33
Akorn, Inc., 32
Alamo Group Inc., 32
Alamo Rent A Car, Inc., 6; 24 (upd.)
Alaska Air Group, Inc., 6; 29 (upd.)
Alba-Waldensian, Inc., 30
Albany International Corp., 8
Alberto-Culver Company, 8; 36 (upd.)
Albertson's Inc., II; 7 (upd.); 30 (upd.)
Alco Health Services Corporation, III
Alco Standard Corporation, I
Aldus Corporation, 10
Alex Lee Inc., 18
Alexander & Alexander Services Inc., 10
Alexander & Baldwin, Inc., 10; 40 (upd.)
All American Communications Inc., 20
Alleghany Corporation, 10
Allegheny Energy, Inc., 38 (upd.)
Allegheny Ludlum Corporation, 8
Allegheny Power System, Inc., V
Allen Organ Company, 33
Allergan, Inc., 10; 30 (upd.)
Alliance Entertainment Corp., 17
Alliant Techsystems Inc., 8; 30 (upd.)
Allied Healthcare Products, Inc., 24
Allied Products Corporation, 21
Allied Signal Engines, 9
AlliedSignal Inc., I; 22 (upd.)
Allison Gas Turbine Division, 9
Allou Health & Beauty Care, Inc., 28
Allstate Corporation, The, 10; 27 (upd.)
Alltel Corporation, 6
Alltrista Corporation, 30
Allwaste, Inc., 18
Aloha Airlines, Incorporated, 24
Alpharma Inc., 35 (upd.)
Alpine Lace Brands, Inc., 18
AltaVista Company, 43
Altera Corporation, 18; 43 (upd.)
Alterra Healthcare Corporation, 42
Altron Incorporated, 20
Aluminum Company of America, IV; 20 (upd.)
ALZA Corporation, 10; 36 (upd.)
AMAX Inc., IV
Amazon.com, Inc., 25
Amblin Entertainment, 21
AMC Entertainment Inc., 12; 35 (upd.)
Amdahl Corporation, III; 14 (upd.); 40 (upd.)
Amerada Hess Corporation, IV; 21 (upd.)
Amerco, 6
America Online, Inc., 10 ; 26 (upd.)
America West Airlines, 6
America West Holdings Corporation, 34 (upd.)
America's Favorite Chicken Company, Inc., 7
American Airlines, I; 6 (upd.)
American Banknote Corporation, 30
American Bar Association, 35
American Biltrite Inc., 16; 43 (upd.)
American Brands, Inc., V
American Building Maintenance Industries, Inc., 6
American Business Information, Inc., 18
American Business Products, Inc., 20
American Cancer Society, The, 24
American Classic Voyages Company, 27
American Coin Merchandising, Inc., 28
American Colloid Co., 13
American Crystal Sugar Company, 9; 32 (upd.)
American Cyanamid, I; 8 (upd.)
American Eagle Outfitters, Inc., 24
American Electric Power Company, Inc., V
American Express Company, II; 10 (upd.); 38 (upd.)
American Family Corporation, III
American Financial Corporation, III
American Foods Group, 43
American Furniture Company, Inc., 21
American General Corporation, III; 10 (upd.)
American General Finance Corp., 11
American Greetings Corporation, 7; 22 (upd.)
American Home Products, I; 10 (upd.)
American Homestar Corporation, 18; 41 (upd.)
American International Group, Inc., III; 15 (upd.)
American Italian Pasta Company, 27
American Lawyer Media Holdings, Inc., 32
American Locker Group Incorporated, 34
American Maize-Products Co., 14
American Management Systems, Inc., 11
American Media, Inc., 27
American Medical Association, 39
American Medical International, Inc., III
American Medical Response, Inc., 39
American Motors Corporation, I
American National Insurance Company, 8; 27 (upd.)
American Pad & Paper Company, 20
American Power Conversion Corporation, 24
American Premier Underwriters, Inc., 10
American President Companies Ltd., 6
American Printing House for the Blind, 26
American Re Corporation, 10; 35 (upd.)
American Red Cross, 40
American Residential Mortgage Corporation, 8
American Retirement Corporation, 42
American Rice, Inc., 33
American Safety Razor Company, 20
American Skiing Company, 28
American Society of Composers, Authors and Publishers (ASCAP), The, 29
American Software Inc., 25
American Standard Companies Inc., III; 30 (upd.)
American Stores Company, II; 22 (upd.)
American Telephone and Telegraph Company, V
American Tourister, Inc., 16
American Tower Corporation, 33
American Water Works Company, 6
American Water Works Company, Inc., 38 (upd.)
American Woodmark Corporation, 31
Amerihost Properties, Inc., 30
AmeriSource Health Corporation, 37 (upd.)
Ameristar Casinos, Inc., 33
Ameritech Corporation, V; 18 (upd.)
Ameritrade Holding Corporation, 34
Ameriwood Industries International Corp., 17
Ames Department Stores, Inc., 9; 30 (upd.)
AMETEK, Inc., 9
AMF Bowling, Inc., 40
Amfac/JMB Hawaii L.L.C., I; 24 (upd.)
Amgen, Inc., 10; 30 (upd.)
Amoco Corporation, IV; 14 (upd.)
Amoskeag Company, 8
AMP Incorporated, II; 14 (upd.)
Ampex Corporation, 17
Amphenol Corporation, 40
AMR Corporation, 28 (upd.)
AMREP Corporation, 21
AmSouth Bancorporation, 12
Amsted Industries Incorporated, 7
Amtran, Inc., 34
Amway Corporation, III; 13 (upd.); 30 (upd.)
Anadarko Petroleum Corporation, 10
Analog Devices, Inc., 10
Analogic Corporation, 23
Analysts International Corporation, 36
Analytic Sciences Corporation, 10
Analytical Surveys, Inc., 33
Anaren Microwave, Inc., 33
Anchor Bancorp, Inc., 10
Anchor Gaming, 24
Anchor Hocking Glassware, 13
Andersen Corporation, 10
Andersen Worldwide, 29 (upd.)
Andersons, Inc., The, 31
Andrew Corporation, 10; 32 (upd.)
Andrews McMeel Universal, 40
Angelica Corporation, 15; 43 (upd.)
Anheuser-Busch Companies, Inc., I; 10 (upd.); 34 (upd.)
Ann Taylor Stores Corporation, 13
AnnTaylor Stores Corporation, 37 (upd.)
ANR Pipeline Co., 17
Anschutz Corporation, The, 12; 36 (upd.)
Anthem Electronics, Inc., 13
Antioch Company, The, 40
Aon Corporation, III
Apache Corporation, 10; 32 (upd.)
Apogee Enterprises, Inc., 8
Apollo Group, Inc., 24
Applause Inc., 24
Apple Computer, Inc., III; 6 (upd.); 36 (upd.)
Applebee's International Inc., 14; 35 (upd.)
Appliance Recycling Centers of America, Inc., 42
Applica Incorporated, 43 (upd.)
Applied Bioscience International, Inc., 10
Applied Materials, Inc., 10
Applied Micro Circuits Corporation, 38

United States *(continued)*
Applied Power, Inc., 9; 32 (upd.)
Aqua Alliance Inc., 32 (upd.)
AR Accessories Group, Inc., 23
ARA Services, II
Aramark Corporation, 13
ARAMARK Corporation, 41
Arandell Corporation, 37
Arbitron Company, The, 38
Arbor Drugs Inc., 12
Arby's Inc., 14
Arch Mineral Corporation, 7
Arch Wireless, Inc., 39
Archer-Daniels-Midland Company, I; 11 (upd.); 32 (upd.)
Archway Cookies, Inc., 29
ARCO Chemical Company, 10
Arctco, Inc., 16
Arctic Cat Inc., 40 (upd.)
Arctic Slope Regional Corporation, 38
Arden Group, Inc., 29
Argosy Gaming Company, 21
Aris Industries, Inc., 16
Ark Restaurants Corp., 20
Arkansas Best Corporation, 16
Arkla, Inc., V
Armco Inc., IV
Armor All Products Corp., 16
Armor Holdings, Inc., 27
Armstrong World Industries, Inc., III; 22 (upd.)
Army and Air Force Exchange Service, 39
Arnold & Porter, 35
Arrow Electronics, Inc., 10
Art Institute of Chicago, The, 29
Art Van Furniture, Inc., 28
Arthur D. Little, Inc., 35
Arthur Murray International, Inc., 32
Artisan Entertainment Inc., 32 (upd.)
Arvin Industries, Inc., 8
Asanté Technologies, Inc., 20
ASARCO Incorporated, IV
Ascend Communications, Inc., 24
Ashland Inc., 19
Ashland Oil, Inc., IV
Ashley Furniture Industries, Inc., 35
Ashworth, Inc., 26
ASK Group, Inc., 9
Aspect Telecommunications Corporation, 22
Aspen Skiing Company, 15
Asplundh Tree Expert Co., 20
Assisted Living Concepts, Inc., 43
Associated Estates Realty Corporation, 25
Associated Grocers, Incorporated, 9; 31 (upd.)
Associated Milk Producers, Inc., 11
Associated Natural Gas Corporation, 11
Associated Press, The, 13; 31 (upd.)
AST Research Inc., 9
Astronics Corporation, 35
ASV, Inc., 34
At Home Corporation, 43
AT&T Bell Laboratories, Inc., 13
AT&T Corporation, 29 (upd.)
Atari Corporation, 9; 23 (upd.)
Atchison Casting Corporation, 39
Atlanta Gas Light Company, 6; 23 (upd.)
Atlanta National League Baseball Club, Inc., 43
Atlantic Energy, Inc., 6
Atlantic Group, The, 23
Atlantic Richfield Company, IV; 31 (upd.)
Atlas Air, Inc., 39
Atlas Van Lines, Inc., 14
Atmel Corporation, 17
Atmos Energy Corporation, 43
Au Bon Pain Co., Inc., 18
Audio King Corporation, 24
Audiovox Corporation, 34
Ault Incorporated, 34
Auntie Anne's, Inc., 35
Aurora Foods Inc., 32
Austin Company, The, 8
Authentic Fitness Corp., 20
Auto Value Associates, Inc., 25
Autodesk, Inc., 10
Autologic Information International, Inc., 20
Automatic Data Processing, Inc., III; 9 (upd.)
Autotote Corporation, 20
AutoZone, Inc., 9; 31 (upd.)
Avado Brands, Inc., 31
Avco Financial Services Inc., 13
Aveda Corporation, 24
Avedis Zildjian Co., 38
Avery Dennison Corporation, IV; 17 (upd.)
Aviation Sales Company, 41
Avid Technology Inc., 38
Avis Rent A Car, Inc., 6; 22 (upd.)
Avnet Inc., 9
Avon Products Inc., III; 19 (upd.)
Avondale Industries, 41 (upd.)
Avondale Industries, Inc., 7
Aydin Corp., 19
Azcon Corporation, 23
Aztar Corporation, 13
B&G Foods, Inc., 40
B. Dalton Bookseller Inc., 25
B. Manischewitz Company, LLC, The, 31
B/E Aerospace, Inc., 30
Babbage's, Inc., 10
Baby Superstore, Inc., 15
Bachman's Inc., 22
Back Bay Restaurant Group, Inc., 20
Badger Meter, Inc., 22
Badger Paper Mills, Inc., 15
Bairnco Corporation, 28
Baker & Hostetler LLP, 40
Baker & McKenzie, 10; 42 (upd.)
Baker & Taylor Corporation, 43 (upd.)
Baker & Taylor, Inc., 16
Baker and Botts, L.L.P., 28
Baker Hughes Incorporated, III; 22 (upd.)
Balance Bar Company, 32
Balchem Corporation, 42
Baldor Electric Company, 21
Baldwin Piano & Organ Company, 18
Baldwin Technology Company, Inc., 25
Ball Corporation, I; 10 (upd.)
Ballantyne of Omaha, Inc., 27
Ballard Medical Products, 21
Bally Manufacturing Corporation, III
Bally Total Fitness Holding Corp., 25
Baltek Corporation, 34
Baltimore Gas and Electric Company, V; 25 (upd.)
Banana Republic Inc., 25
Banc One Corporation, 10
Bandag, Inc., 19
Banfi Products Corp., 36
Bank of Boston Corporation, II
Bank of Mississippi, Inc., 14
Bank of New England Corporation, II
Bank of New York Company, Inc., The, II
Bank One Corporation, 36 (upd.)
BankAmerica Corporation, II; 8 (upd.)
Bankers Trust New York Corporation, II
Banner Aerospace, Inc., 14; 37 (upd.)
Banta Corporation, 12; 32 (upd.)
Banyan Systems Inc., 25
BarclaysAmerican Mortgage Corporation, 11
Barnes & Noble, Inc., 10; 30 (upd.)
Barnes Group Inc., 13
Barnett Banks, Inc., 9
Barnett Inc., 28
Barney's, Inc., 28
Barr Laboratories, Inc., 26
Barrett Business Services, Inc., 16
Bashas' Inc., 33
Bass Pro Shops, Inc., 42
Bassett Furniture Industries, Inc., 18
Bates Worldwide, Inc., 14; 33 (upd.)
Bath Iron Works, 12; 36 (upd.)
Battelle Memorial Institute, Inc., 10
Battle Mountain Gold Company, 23
Bausch & Lomb Inc., 7; 25 (upd.)
Baxter International Inc., I; 10 (upd.)
Bay State Gas Company, 38
BayBanks, Inc., 12
Bayou Steel Corporation, 31
BBN Corp., 19
BEA Systems, Inc., 36
Bear Creek Corporation, 38
Bear Stearns Companies, Inc., II; 10 (upd.)
Bearings, Inc., 13
Beatrice Company, II
BeautiControl Cosmetics, Inc., 21
Beazer Homes USA, Inc., 17
bebe stores, inc., 31
Bechtel Group, Inc., I; 24 (upd.)
Beckett Papers, 23
Beckman Coulter, Inc., 22
Beckman Instruments, Inc., 14
Becton, Dickinson & Company, I; 11 (upd.); 36 (upd.)
Bed Bath & Beyond Inc., 13; 41 (upd.)
Beech Aircraft Corporation, 8
Beech-Nut Nutrition Corporation, 21
Bekins Company, 15
Belco Oil & Gas Corp., 40
Belden Inc., 19
Belk Stores Services, Inc., V; 19 (upd.)
Bell and Howell Company, 9; 29 (upd.)
Bell Atlantic Corporation, V; 25 (upd.)
Bell Sports Corporation, 16
BellSouth Corporation, V; 29 (upd.)
Beloit Corporation, 14
Bemis Company, Inc., 8
Ben & Jerry's Homemade, Inc., 10; 35 (upd.)
Benchmark Electronics, Inc., 40
Bendix Corporation, I
Beneficial Corporation, 8
Benihana, Inc., 18
Benjamin Moore & Co., 13; 38 (upd.)
Bergen Brunswig Corporation, V; 13 (upd.)
Beringer Wine Estates Holdings, Inc., 22
Berkshire Hathaway Inc., III; 18 (upd.); 42 (upd.)
Berlitz International, Inc., 13; 39 (upd.)
Bernard C. Harris Publishing Company, Inc., 39
Bernard Chaus, Inc., 27
Berry Plastics Corporation, 21
Bertucci's Inc., 16
Best Buy Co., Inc., 9; 23 (upd.)
Bestfoods, 22 (upd.)
BET Holdings, Inc., 18
Bethlehem Steel Corporation, IV; 7 (upd.); 27 (upd.)
Betz Laboratories, Inc., I; 10 (upd.)
Beverly Enterprises, Inc., III; 16 (upd.)
BFGoodrich Company, The, V; 19 (upd.)
BHC Communications, Inc., 26
BIC Corporation, 8; 23 (upd.)
Bicoastal Corporation, II
Big V Supermarkets, Inc., 25
Big B, Inc., 17
Big Bear Stores Co., 13
Big Flower Press Holdings, Inc., 21

Big O Tires, Inc., 20
Big Rivers Electric Corporation, 11
Bill & Melinda Gates Foundation, 41
Bill Blass Ltd., 32
Billing Concepts Corp., 26
Bindley Western Industries, Inc., 9
Bingham Dana LLP, 43
Binks Sames Corporation, 21
Binney & Smith Inc., 25
Biogen Inc., 14; 36 (upd.)
Biomet, Inc., 10
Bird Corporation, 19
Birkenstock Footprint Sandals, Inc., 12; 42 (upd.)
Birmingham Steel Corporation, 13; 40 (upd.)
BISSELL Inc., 9; 30 (upd.)
BJ Services Company, 25
Black & Decker Corporation, The, III; 20 (upd.)
Black & Veatch LLP, 22
Black Box Corporation, 20
Black Hills Corporation, 20
Blair Corporation, 25
Blair Corporation, 31
Blessings Corp., 19
Blimpie International, Inc., 15
Block Drug Company, Inc., 8; 27 (upd.)
Blockbuster Entertainment Corporation, 9
Blockbuster Inc., 31 (upd.)
Bloomberg L.P., 21
Bloomingdale's Inc., 12
Blount, Inc., 12
Blue Bell Creameries L.P., 30
Blue Bird Corporation, 35
Blue Cross and Blue Shield Association, 10
Blue Diamond Growers, 28
Blue Mountain Arts, Inc., 29
Blyth Industries, Inc., 18
BMC Industries, Inc., 17
Boart Longyear Company, 26
Boatmen's Bancshares Inc., 15
Bob Evans Farms, Inc., 9
Boca Resorts, Inc., 37
Boeing Company, The, I; 10 (upd.); 32 (upd.)
Bohemia, Inc., 13
Boise Cascade Corporation, IV; 8 (upd.); 32 (upd.)
Bombay Company, Inc., The, 10
Bon Marché, Inc., The, 23
Bon Secours Health System, Inc., 24
Bon-Ton Stores, Inc., The, 16
Bonneville International Corporation, 29
Book-of-the-Month Club, Inc., 13
Books-A-Million, Inc., 14; 41 (upd.)
Boole & Babbage, Inc., 25
Booth Creek Ski Holdings, Inc., 31
Booz Allen & Hamilton Inc., 10
Borden, Inc., II; 22 (upd.)
Borders Group, Inc., 15; 43 (upd.)
Borg-Warner Automotive, Inc., 14; 32 (upd.)
Borg-Warner Corporation, III
Borland International, Inc., 9
Boscov's Department Store, Inc., 31
Bose Corporation, 13; 36 (upd.)
Boston Acoustics, Inc., 22
Boston Beer Company, 18
Boston Celtics Limited Partnership, 14
Boston Chicken, Inc., 12
Boston Edison Company, 12
Boston Professional Hockey Association Inc., 39
Boston Properties, Inc., 22
Boston Scientific Corporation, 37
Bowne & Co., Inc., 23
Boy Scouts of America, The, 34
Boyd Bros. Transportation Inc., 39
Boyd Gaming Corporation, 43
Boyds Collection, Ltd., The, 29
Bozell Worldwide Inc., 25
Bozzuto's, Inc., 13
Brach and Brock Confections, Inc., 15
Bradlees Discount Department Store Company, 12
Brass Eagle Inc., 34
Brazos Sportswear, Inc., 23
Bridgeport Machines, Inc., 17
Bridgford Foods Corporation, 27
Briggs & Stratton Corporation, 8; 27 (upd.)
Bright Horizons Family Solutions, Inc., 31
Brightpoint, Inc., 18
Brinker International, Inc., 10; 38 (upd.)
Bristol Hotel Company, 23
Bristol-Myers Squibb Company, III; 9 (upd.); 37 (upd.)
Brite Voice Systems, Inc., 20
Broadcast Music Inc., 23
Broadcom Corporation, 34
Broadmoor Hotel, The, 30
Brobeck, Phleger & Harrison, LLP, 31
Broder Bros. Co., 38
Broderbund Software, Inc., 13; 29 (upd.)
Brooke Group Ltd., 15
Brooklyn Union Gas, 6
Brooks Brothers Inc., 22
Brooks Sports Inc., 32
Brookshire Grocery Company, 16
Brookstone, Inc., 18
Brothers Gourmet Coffees, Inc., 20
Broughton Foods Co., 17
Brown & Brown, Inc., 41
Brown & Haley, 23
Brown & Root, Inc., 13
Brown & Sharpe Manufacturing Co., 23
Brown & Williamson Tobacco Corporation, 14; 33 (upd.)
Brown Group, Inc., V; 20 (upd.)
Brown Printing Company, 26
Brown-Forman Corporation, I; 10 (upd.); 38 (upd.)
Browning-Ferris Industries, Inc., V; 20 (upd.)
Broyhill Furniture Industries, Inc., 10
Bruce Foods Corporation, 39
Bruno's, Inc., 7; 26 (upd.)
Brunswick Corporation, III; 22 (upd.)
Brush Wellman Inc., 14
Buca, Inc., 38
Buckeye Technologies, Inc., 42
Buckle, Inc., The, 18
Bucyrus International, Inc., 17
Budd Company, The, 8
Budget Group, Inc., 25
Budget Rent a Car Corporation, 9
Buffets, Inc., 10; 32 (upd.)
Bugle Boy Industries, Inc., 18
Bulova Corporation, 13; 41 (upd.)
Bundy Corporation, 17
Bureau of National Affairs, Inc.,The 23
Burger King Corporation, II; 17 (upd.)
Burlington Coat Factory Warehouse Corporation, 10
Burlington Industries, Inc., V; 17 (upd.)
Burlington Northern Santa Fe Corporation, V; 27 (upd.)
Burlington Resources Inc., 10
Burns International Security Services, 13
Burns International Services Corporation, 41 (upd.)
Burr-Brown Corporation, 19
Burton Snowboards Inc., 22
Bush Boake Allen Inc., 30
Bush Industries, Inc., 20
Business Men's Assurance Company of America, 14
Butler Manufacturing Co., 12
Butterick Co., Inc., 23
Buttrey Food & Drug Stores Co., 18
BWAY Corporation, 24
C-COR.net Corp., 38
C-Cube Microsystems, Inc., 37
C.F. Martin & Co., Inc., 42
C.H. Heist Corporation, 24
C.H. Robinson Worldwide, Inc., 40 (upd.)
C.H. Robinson, Inc., 11
C.R. Bard Inc., 9
Cabela's Inc., 26
Cabletron Systems, Inc., 10
Cablevision Electronic Instruments, Inc., 32
Cablevision Systems Corporation, 7; 30 (upd.)
Cabot Corporation, 8; 29 (upd.)
Cache Incorporated, 30
CACI International Inc., 21
Cadence Design Systems, Inc., 11
Cadmus Communications Corporation, 23
Cadwalader, Wickersham & Taft, 32
Caere Corporation, 20
Caesars World, Inc., 6
Cagle's, Inc., 20
Cahners Business Information, 43
CalComp Inc., 13
Calcot Ltd., 33
Caldor Inc., 12
California Pizza Kitchen Inc., 15
Callaway Golf Company, 15
CalMat Co., 19
Calpine Corporation, 36
Caltex Petroleum Corporation, 19
Calvin Klein, Inc., 22
Cambrex Corporation, 16
Cambridge Technology Partners, Inc., 36
Camelot Music, Inc., 26
Cameron & Barkley Company, 28
Campbell Soup Company, II; 7 (upd.); 26 (upd.)
Campbell-Mithun-Esty, Inc., 16
Campo Electronics, Appliances & Computers, Inc., 16
Canandaigua Brands, Inc., 34 (upd.)
Canandaigua Wine Company, Inc., 13
Candie's, Inc., 31
Candlewood Hotel Company, Inc., 41
Cannondale Corporation, 21
Canterbury Park Holding Corporation, 42
Capital Cities/ABC Inc., II
Capital Holding Corporation, III
CapStar Hotel Company, 21
Caraustar Industries, Inc., 19
Carbide/Graphite Group, Inc., The, 40
Carborundum Company, 15
Cardinal Health, Inc., 18
Caremark International Inc., 10
Carey International, Inc., 26
Cargill, Incorporated, II; 13 (upd.); 40 (upd.)
Carhartt, Inc., 30
Caribiner International, Inc., 24
Caribou Coffee Company, Inc., 28
Carlisle Companies Incorporated, 8
Carlson Companies, Inc., 6; 22 (upd.)
Carmichael Lynch Inc., 28
Carmike Cinemas, Inc., 14; 37 (upd.)
Carnation Company, II
Carnegie Corporation of New York, 35
Carnival Corporation, 27 (upd.)
Carnival Cruise Lines, Inc., 6
Carolina First Corporation, 31
Carolina Freight Corporation, 6
Carolina Power & Light Company, V; 23 (upd.)

United States *(continued)*
Carolina Telephone and Telegraph Company, 10
Carpenter Technology Corporation, 13
CARQUEST Corporation, 29
Carr-Gottstein Foods Co., 17
Carriage Services, Inc., 37
Carrier Corporation, 7
Carsey-Werner Company, L.L.C., The, 37
Carson Pirie Scott & Company, 15
Carson, Inc., 31
Carter Hawley Hale Stores, Inc., V
Carter-Wallace, Inc., 8; 38 (upd.)
Carvel Corporation, 35
Cascade Natural Gas Corporation, 9
Casco Northern Bank, 14
Casey's General Stores, Inc., 19
Cash America International, Inc., 20
Castle & Cooke, Inc., II; 20 (upd.)
Casual Corner Group, Inc., 43
Catalina Lighting, Inc., 43 (upd.)
Catalina Marketing Corporation, 18
Catellus Development Corporation, 24
Caterpillar Inc., III; 15 (upd.)
Catherines Stores Corporation, 15
Catholic Order of Foresters, 24
Cato Corporation, 14
Cattleman's, Inc., 20
CB Commercial Real Estate Services Group, Inc., 21
CBI Industries, Inc., 7
CBRL Group, Inc., 35 (upd.)
CBS Corporation, II; 6 (upd.); 28 (upd.)
CCH Inc., 14
CDI Corporation, 6
CDW Computer Centers, Inc., 16
CEC Entertainment, Inc., 31 (upd.)
Cedar Fair, L.P., 22
Celadon Group Inc., 30
Celanese Corporation, I
Celebrity, Inc., 22
Celestial Seasonings, Inc., 16
Centel Corporation, 6
Centennial Communications Corporation, 39
Centerior Energy Corporation, V
Centex Corporation, 8; 29 (upd.)
Centocor Inc., 14
Central and South West Corporation, V
Central Garden & Pet Company, 23
Central Hudson Gas and Electricity Corporation, 6
Central Maine Power, 6
Central Newspapers, Inc., 10
Central Parking Corporation, 18
Central Soya Company, Inc., 7
Central Sprinkler Corporation, 29
Century Communications Corp., 10
Century Telephone Enterprises, Inc., 9
Century Theatres, Inc., 31
Cerner Corporation, 16
CertainTeed Corporation, 35
Cessna Aircraft Company, 8; 27 (upd.)
Chadbourne & Parke, 36
Chadwick's of Boston, Ltd., 29
Chalone Wine Group, Ltd., The, 36
Champion Enterprises, Inc., 17
Champion Industries, Inc., 28
Champion International Corporation, IV; 20 (upd.)
Championship Auto Racing Teams, Inc., 37
Chancellor Media Corporation, 24
Chaparral Steel Co., 13
Charles River Laboratories International, Inc., 42
Charles Schwab Corporation, The, 8; 26 (upd.)
Charles Stark Draper Laboratory, Inc., The, 35
Charlotte Russe Holding, Inc., 35
Charming Shoppes, Inc., 8; 38
Chart House Enterprises, Inc., 17
Chart Industries, Inc., 21
Charter Communications, Inc., 33
Chase Manhattan Corporation, The, II; 13 (upd.)
Chateau Communities, Inc., 37
Chattem, Inc., 17
Chautauqua Airlines, Inc., 38
Checkers Drive-Up Restaurants Inc., 16
Checkpoint Systems, Inc., 39
Cheesecake Factory Inc., The, 17
Chelsea Milling Company, 29
Chemcentral Corporation, 8
Chemed Corporation, 13
Chemfab Corporation, 35
Chemi-Trol Chemical Co., 16
Chemical Banking Corporation, II; 14 (upd.)
Chemical Waste Management, Inc., 9
Cherokee Inc., 18
Chesapeake Corporation, 8; 30 (upd.)
Chesebrough-Pond's USA, Inc., 8
Chevron Corporation, IV; 19 (upd.)
Cheyenne Software, Inc., 12
Chi-Chi's Inc., 13
Chiat/Day Inc. Advertising, 11
Chic by H.I.S, Inc., 20
Chicago and North Western Holdings Corporation, 6
Chicago Bears Football Club, Inc., 33
Chicago Board of Trade, 41
Chick-fil-A Inc., 23
Chicken of the Sea International, 24 (upd.)
Children's Comprehensive Services, Inc., 42
Children's Place Retail Stores, Inc., The, 37
Childtime Learning Centers, Inc., 34
Chiles Offshore Corporation, 9
CHIPS and Technologies, Inc., 9
Chiquita Brands International, Inc., 7; 21 (upd.)
Chiron Corporation, 10; 36 (upd.)
Chisholm-Mingo Group, Inc., 41
Chock Full o' Nuts Corp., 17
Choice Hotels International Inc., 14
Chorus Line Corporation, 30
Chris-Craft Industries, Inc., 9; 31 (upd.)
Christensen Boyles Corporation, 26
Christopher & Banks Corporation, 42
Chromcraft Revington, Inc., 15
Chronicle Publishing Company, Inc., The, 23
Chronimed Inc., 26
Chrysler Corporation, I; 11 (upd.)
CH2M Hill Ltd., 22
Chubb Corporation, The, III; 14 (upd.); 37 (upd.)
Church & Dwight Co., Inc., 29
Churchill Downs Incorporated, 29
Cianbro Corporation, 14
Ciber, Inc., 18
CIGNA Corporation, III; 22 (upd.)
Cincinnati Bell, Inc., 6
Cincinnati Financial Corporation, 16
Cincinnati Gas & Electric Company, 6
Cincinnati Milacron Inc., 12
Cincom Systems Inc., 15
Cinnabon Inc., 23
Cintas Corporation, 21
CIPSCO Inc., 6
Circle K Company, The, II; 20 (upd.)
Circon Corporation, 21
Circuit City Stores, Inc., 9; 29 (upd.)
Circus Circus Enterprises, Inc., 6
Cirrus Logic, Incorporated, 11
Cisco Systems, Inc., 11; 34 (upd.)
Citadel Communications Corporation, 35
Citfed Bancorp, Inc., 16
CITGO Petroleum Corporation, IV, 31 (upd.)
Citicorp, II; 9 (upd.)
Citigroup Inc., 30 (upd.)
Citizens Financial Group, Inc., 42
Citizens Utilities Company, 7
City Public Service, 6
CKE Restaurants, Inc., 19
Claire's Stores, Inc., 17
Clarcor Inc., 17
Clark Construction Group, Inc., The, 8
Clark Equipment Company, 8
Clayton Homes Incorporated, 13
Clear Channel Communications, Inc., 23
Cleary, Gottlieb, Steen & Hamilton, 35
Cleco Corporation, 37
Cleveland Indians Baseball Company, Inc., 37
Cleveland-Cliffs Inc., 13
Clorox Company, The, III; 22 (upd.)
Clothestime, Inc., The, 20
ClubCorp, Inc., 33
CML Group, Inc., 10
CMP Media Inc., 26
CMS Energy Corporation, V, 14
CNA Financial Corporation, III; 38 (upd.)
CNS, Inc., 20
Coach Leatherware, 10
Coach USA, Inc., 24
Coastal Corporation, The, IV, 31 (upd.)
COBE Laboratories, Inc., 13
Coborn's, Inc., 30
Cobra Electronics Corporation, 14
Cobra Golf Inc., 16
Coca Cola Bottling Co. Consolidated, 10
Coca-Cola Company, The, I; 10 (upd.); 32 (upd.)
Coca-Cola Enterprises, Inc., 13
Coeur d'Alene Mines Corporation, 20
Cogentrix Energy, Inc., 10
Coherent, Inc., 31
Cohu, Inc., 32
Coinmach Laundry Corporation, 20
Cold Spring Granite Company, 16
Coldwater Creek Inc., 21
Cole National Corporation, 13
Coleman Company, Inc., The, 9; 30 (upd.)
Coles Express Inc., 15
Colgate-Palmolive Company, III; 14 (upd.); 35 (upd.)
Collins & Aikman Corporation, 13; 41 (upd.)
Collins Industries, Inc., 33
Colt Industries Inc., I
Colt's Manufacturing Company, Inc., 12
Columbia Gas System, Inc., The, V; 16 (upd.)
Columbia Pictures Entertainment, Inc., II
Columbia Sportswear Company, 19; 41 (upd.)
Columbia TriStar Motion Pictures Companies, 12 (upd.)
Columbia/HCA Healthcare Corporation, 15
Columbus McKinnon Corporation, 37
Comair Holdings Inc., 13; 34 (upd.)
Comcast Corporation, 7; 24 (upd.)
Comdial Corporation, 21
Comdisco, Inc., 9
Comerica Incorporated, 40
COMFORCE Corporation, 40
Commerce Clearing House, Inc., 7

Commercial Credit Company, 8
Commercial Federal Corporation, 12
Commercial Financial Services, Inc., 26
Commercial Metals Company, 15; 42 (upd.)
Commodore International Ltd., 7
Commonwealth Edison Company, V
Commonwealth Energy System, 14
Commonwealth Telephone Enterprises, Inc., 25
Community Psychiatric Centers, 15
Compaq Computer Corporation, III; 6 (upd.); 26 (upd.)
CompDent Corporation, 22
CompHealth Inc., 25
Complete Business Solutions, Inc., 31
Comprehensive Care Corporation, 15
CompuAdd Computer Corporation, 11
CompuCom Systems, Inc., 10
CompUSA, Inc., 10; 35 (upd.)
CompuServe Interactive Services, Inc., 10; 27 (upd.)
Computer Associates International, Inc., 6
Computer Data Systems, Inc., 14
Computer Learning Centers, Inc., 26
Computer Sciences Corporation, 6
Computerland Corp., 13
Computervision Corporation, 10
Compuware Corporation, 10; 30 (upd.)
Comsat Corporation, 23
Comshare Inc., 23
Comverse Technology, Inc., 15; 43 (upd.)
ConAgra Foods, Inc., 42 (upd.)
Conagra, Inc., II; 12 (upd.)
Conair Corp., 17
Concepts Direct, Inc., 39
Concord Camera Corporation, 41
Concord Fabrics, Inc., 16
Condé Nast Publications Inc., The, 13
Cone Mills Corporation, 8
Conexant Systems, Inc., 36
Congoleum Corp., 18
Connecticut Light and Power Co., 13
Connecticut Mutual Life Insurance Company, III
Connell Company, The, 29
Conner Peripherals, Inc., 6
Conoco Inc., IV; 16 (upd.)
Conseco, Inc., 10; 33 (upd.)
Conso International Corporation, 29
Consolidated Delivery & Logistics, Inc., 24
Consolidated Edison Company of New York, Inc., V
Consolidated Freightways Corporation, V; 21 (upd.)
Consolidated Natural Gas Company, V; 19 (upd.)
Consolidated Papers, Inc., 8; 36 (upd.)
Consolidated Products Inc., 14
Consolidated Rail Corporation, V
Consumers Power Co., 14
Consumers Union, 26
Consumers Water Company, 14
Container Store, The, 36
ContiGroup Companies, Inc., 43 (upd.)
Continental Airlines, Inc., I; 21 (upd.)
Continental Bank Corporation, II
Continental Cablevision, Inc., 7
Continental Can Co., Inc., 15
Continental Corporation, The, III
Continental General Tire Corp., 23
Continental Grain Company, 10; 13 (upd.)
Continental Group Company, I
Continental Medical Systems, Inc., 10
Control Data Corporation, III
Control Data Systems, Inc., 10
Converse Inc., 9; 31 (upd.)
Cooker Restaurant Corporation, The, 20
Cooper Cameron Corporation, 20 (upd.)
Cooper Companies, Inc., The, 39
Cooper Industries, Inc., II
Cooper Tire & Rubber Company, 8; 23 (upd.)
Coopers & Lybrand, 9
Copart Inc., 23
Copley Press, Inc., The, 23
Copps Corporation, The, 32
Corbis Corporation, 31
Cordis Corp., 19
CoreStates Financial Corp, 17
Corinthian Colleges, Inc., 39
Corning Incorporated, III
Corporate Express, Inc., 22
Corporate Software Inc., 9
Corporation for Public Broadcasting, 14
Correctional Services Corporation, 30
Corrections Corporation of America, 23
Corrpro Companies, Inc., 20
CORT Business Services Corporation, 26
Cosmair, Inc., 8
Cosmetic Center, Inc., The, 22
Cost Plus, Inc., 27
Costco Wholesale Corporation, V; 43 (upd.)
Cotter & Company, V
Coty, Inc., 36
Coudert Brothers, 30
Countrywide Credit Industries, Inc., 16
County Seat Stores Inc., 9
Courier Corporation, 41
Covance Inc., 30
Covington & Burling, 40
Cowles Media Company, 23
Cox Enterprises, Inc., IV; 22 (upd.)
CPC International Inc., II
CPI Corp., 38
Cracker Barrel Old Country Store, Inc., 10
Crain Communications, Inc., 12; 35 (upd.)
Cramer, Berkowitz & Co., 34
Crane & Co., Inc., 26
Crane Co., 8; 30 (upd.)
Crate and Barrel, 9
Cravath, Swaine & Moore, 43
Cray Research, Inc., III; 16 (upd.)
Creative Artists Agency LLC, 38
Credit Acceptance Corporation, 18
Crédit Agricole, II
Crompton & Knowles, 9
Crompton Corporation, 36 (upd.)
Croscill, Inc., 42
Crowley Maritime Corporation, 6; 28 (upd.)
Crowley, Milner & Company, 19
Crown Books Corporation, 21
Crown Central Petroleum Corporation, 7
Crown Crafts, Inc., 16
Crown Equipment Corporation, 15
Crown Vantage Inc., 29
Crown, Cork & Seal Company, Inc., I; 13; 32 (upd.)
CRSS Inc., 6
Cruise America Inc., 21
Crystal Brands, Inc., 9
CS First Boston Inc., II
CSK Auto Corporation, 38
CSS Industries, Inc., 35
CSX Corporation, V; 22 (upd.)
CTB International Corporation, 43 (upd.)
CTG, Inc., 11
CTS Corporation, 39
Cubic Corporation, 19
CUC International Inc., 16
Cuisinart Corporation, 24
Culbro Corporation, 15
Cullen/Frost Bankers, Inc., 25
Culligan International Company, 12
Culligan Water Technologies, Inc., 38 (upd.)
Culp, Inc., 29
Cumberland Farms, Inc., 17
Cumberland Packing Corporation, 26
Cummins Engine Company, Inc., I; 12 (upd.); 40 (upd.)
Cumulus Media Inc., 37
Cunard Line Ltd., 23
Current, Inc., 37
Curtice-Burns Foods, Inc., 7; 21 (upd.)
Curtiss-Wright Corporation, 10; 35 (upd.)
Custom Chrome, Inc., 16
Cutter & Buck Inc., 27
Cybermedia, Inc., 25
Cygne Designs, Inc., 25
Cypress Semiconductor Corporation, 20
Cyprus Amax Minerals Company, 21
Cyprus Minerals Company, 7
Cyrk Inc., 19
Cytec Industries Inc., 27
Czarnikow-Rionda Company, Inc., 32
D&K Wholesale Drug, Inc., 14
D'Agostino Supermarkets Inc., 19
D'Arcy Masius Benton & Bowles, Inc., VI; 32 (upd.)
D.G. Yuengling & Son, Inc., 38
Daffy's Inc., 26
Dain Rauscher Corporation, 35 (upd.)
Dairy Mart Convenience Stores, Inc., 7; 25 (upd.)
Daisytek International Corporation, 18
Daktronics, Inc., 32
Dal-Tile International Inc., 22
Dale Carnegie Training, Inc., 28
Dallas Cowboys Football Club, Ltd., 33
Dallas Semiconductor Corp., 13
Dallas Semiconductor Corporation, 31
Damark International, Inc., 18
Dames & Moore, Inc., 25
Dan River Inc., 35
Dana Corporation, I; 10 (upd.)
Danaher Corporation, 7
Daniel Industries, Inc., 16
Dannon Co., Inc., 14
Danskin, Inc., 12
Darden Restaurants, Inc., 16
Darigold, Inc., 9
Dart Group Corporation, 16
Data Broadcasting Corporation, 31
Data General Corporation, 8
Datapoint Corporation, 11
Datascope Corporation, 39
Datek Online Holdings Corp., 32
Dauphin Deposit Corporation, 14
Dave & Buster's, Inc., 33
Davey Tree Expert Company, The, 11
David and Lucile Packard Foundation, The, 41
David J. Joseph Company, The, 14
David's Bridal, Inc., 33
Davis Polk & Wardwell, 36
DAW Technologies, Inc., 25
Dawn Food Products, Inc., 17
Day & Zimmermann Inc., 9; 31 (upd.)
Day Runner, Inc., 14; 41 (upd.)
Dayton Hudson Corporation, V; 18 (upd.)
DC Comics Inc., 25
DDB Needham Worldwide, 14
Dean & DeLuca, Inc., 36
Dean Foods Company, 7; 21 (upd.)
Dean Witter, Discover & Co., 12
Death Row Records, 27
Deb Shops, Inc., 16
Debevoise & Plimpton, 39
Dechert, 43
Deckers Outdoor Corporation, 22
Decora Industries, Inc., 31

United States *(continued)*

DeCrane Aircraft Holdings Inc., 36
DeepTech International Inc., 21
Deere & Company, III; 21 (upd.); 42 (upd.)
Defiance, Inc., 22
DeKalb Genetics Corporation, 17
Del Laboratories, Inc., 28
Del Monte Foods Company, 7; 23 (upd.)
Del Webb Corporation, 14
Delaware North Companies Incorporated, 7
dELiA*s Inc., 29
Dell Computer Corporation, 9; 31 (upd.)
Deloitte Touche Tohmatsu International, 9; 29 (upd.)
Delta Air Lines, Inc., I; 6 (upd.); 39 (upd.)
Delta and Pine Land Company, 33
Delta Woodside Industries, Inc., 8; 30 (upd.)
Deluxe Corporation, 7; 22 (upd.)
DeMoulas / Market Basket Inc., 23
DenAmerica Corporation, 29
Dentsply International Inc., 10
DEP Corporation, 20
Department VVI, Inc., 14; 34 (upd.)
Deposit Guaranty Corporation, 17
DePuy Inc., 30; 37 (upd.)
Designer Holdings Ltd., 20
Destec Energy, Inc., 12
Detroit Diesel Corporation, 10
Detroit Edison Company, The, V
Detroit Pistons Basketball Company, The, 41
Deutsch, Inc., 42
DeVry Incorporated, 29
Dexter Corporation, The, I; 12 (upd.)
DH Technology, Inc., 18
DHL Worldwide Express, 6; 24 (upd.)
Di Giorgio Corp., 12
Dial Corp., The, 8; 23 (upd.)
Dialogic Corporation, 18
Diamond Shamrock, Inc., IV
Dibrell Brothers, Incorporated, 12
dick clark productions, inc., 16
Diebold, Incorporated, 7; 22 (upd.)
Diedrich Coffee, Inc., 40
Digi International Inc., 9
Digital Equipment Corporation, III; 6 (upd.)
Dillard Department Stores, Inc., V; 16 (upd.)
Dillard Paper Company, 11
Dillingham Corporation, I
Dillon Companies Inc., 12
Dime Savings Bank of New York, F.S.B., 9
DIMON Inc., 27
DIRECTV, Inc., 38
Discount Auto Parts, Inc., 18
Discount Drug Mart, Inc., 14
Discovery Communications, Inc., 42
Dixie Group, Inc., The, 20
Dixon Industries, Inc., 26
Dixon Ticonderoga Company, 12
Do it Best Corporation, 30
Dolby Laboratories Inc., 20
Dole Food Company, Inc., 9; 31 (upd.)
Dollar Thrifty Automotive Group, Inc., 25
Dollar Tree Stores, Inc., 23
Dominion Homes, Inc., 19
Dominion Resources, Inc., V
Domino Sugar Corporation, 26
Domino's Pizza, Inc., 7; 21 (upd.)
Don Massey Cadillac, Inc., 37
Donaldson Co. Inc., 16
Donaldson, Lufkin & Jenrette, Inc., 22
Donna Karan Company, 15
Donnelly Corporation, 12; 35 (upd.)
Donnkenny, Inc., 17
Doskocil Companies, Inc., 12
Doubletree Corporation, 21
Douglas & Lomason Company, 16
Dover Corporation, III; 28 (upd.)
Dover Downs Entertainment, Inc., 43
Dover Publications Inc., 34
Dow Chemical Company, The, I; 8 (upd.)
Dow Jones & Company, Inc., IV; 19 (upd.)
Dow Jones Telerate, Inc., 10
DPL Inc., 6
DQE, Inc., 6
Dr Pepper/Seven Up, Inc., 9; 32 (upd.)
Drackett Professional Products, 12
DreamWorks SKG, 43
Drees Company, Inc., The, 41
Dress Barn, Inc., The, 24
Dresser Industries, Inc., III
Drew Industries Inc., 28
Drexel Burnham Lambert Incorporated, II
Drexel Heritage Furnishings Inc., 12
Dreyer's Grand Ice Cream, Inc., 17
Drug Emporium, Inc., 12
Drypers Corporation, 18
DSC Communications Corporation, 12
DTE Energy Company, 20 (upd.)
Duane Reade Holding Corp., 21
Duck Head Apparel Company, Inc., 42
Duckwall-ALCO Stores, Inc., 24
Ducommun Incorporated, 30
Duke Energy Corporation, 27 (upd.)
Duke Power Company, V
Dun & Bradstreet Corporation, The, IV; 19 (upd.)
Dun & Bradstreet Software Services Inc., 11
Duplex Products Inc., 17
Duracell International Inc., 9
Durametallic, 21
Duriron Company Inc., 17
Duty Free International, Inc., 11
Dyersburg Corporation, 21
Dynatech Corporation, 13
E! Entertainment Television Inc., 17
E*Trade Group, Inc., 20
E. & J. Gallo Winery, I; 7 (upd.); 28 (upd.)
E.I. Du Pont de Nemours & Company, I; 8 (upd.); 26 (upd.)
E.W. Scripps Company, The, IV; 7 (upd.); 28 (upd.)
Eagle Hardware & Garden, Inc., 16
Eagle-Picher Industries, Inc., 8; 23 (upd.)
Earl Scheib, Inc., 32
Earthgrains Company, The, 36
EarthLink, Inc., 36
Eastern Airlines, I
Eastern Enterprises, 6
Eastman Chemical Company, 14; 38 (upd.)
Eastman Kodak Company, III; 7 (upd.); 36 (upd.)
Eateries, Inc., 33
Eaton Corporation, I; 10 (upd.)
Eaton Vance Corporation, 18
eBay Inc., 32
EBSCO Industries, Inc., 17; 40 (upd.)
ECC International Corp., 42
Echlin Inc., I; 11 (upd.)
EchoStar Communications Corporation, 35
Eckerd Corporation, 9; 32 (upd.)
Ecolab, Inc., I; 13 (upd.); 34 (upd.)
Ecology and Environment, Inc., 39
Eddie Bauer, Inc., 9; 36 (upd.)
Edelbrock Corporation, 37
Edison Brothers Stores, Inc., 9
Edison Schools Inc., 37
Edmark Corporation, 14; 41 (upd.)
Education Management Corporation, 35
Educational Testing Service, 12
Edw. C. Levy Co., 42
Edward J. DeBartolo Corporation, The, 8
Edward Jones, 30
Edwards Theatres Circuit, Inc., 31
EG&G Incorporated, 8; 29 (upd.)
Egghead Inc., 9
Egghead.com, Inc., 31 (upd.)
84 Lumber Company, 9; 39 (upd.)
800-JR Cigar, Inc., 27
Einstein/Noah Bagel Corporation, 29
Ekco Group, Inc., 16
El Camino Resources International, Inc., 11
El Chico Restaurants, Inc., 19
El Paso Electric Company, 21
El Paso Natural Gas Company, 12
Elano Corporation, 14
Elder-Beerman Stores Corporation, 10
Electric Lightwave, Inc., 37
Electromagnetic Sciences Inc., 21
Electronic Arts Inc., 10
Electronic Data Systems Corporation, III; 28 (upd.)
Electronics for Imaging, Inc., 15; 43 (upd.)
Eli Lilly & Company, I; 11 (upd.)
Elizabeth Arden Co., 8
Elizabeth Arden, Inc., 40 (upd.)
Eljer Industries, Inc., 24
Ellerbe Becket, 41
Ellett Brothers, Inc., 17
Elmer's Restaurants, Inc., 42
Embers America Restaurants, 30
EMC Corporation, 12
Emerson Electric Co., II
Emerson Radio Corp., 30
Emery Worldwide Airlines, Inc., 6; 25 (upd.)
Emge Packing Co., Inc., 11
Empi, Inc., 26
Empire Blue Cross and Blue Shield, III
Employee Solutions, Inc., 18
ENCAD, Incorporated, 25
Encompass Services Corporation, 33
Encore Computer Corporation, 13
Encyclopaedia Britannica, Inc., 39 (upd.)
Encyclopedia Britannica, Inc., 7
Energen Corporation, 21
Energizer Holdings, Inc., 32
Enesco Corporation, 11
Engelhard Corporation, IV, 21 (upd.)
Engraph, Inc., 12
Ennis Business Forms, Inc., 21
Enquirer/Star Group, Inc., 10
Enrich International, Inc., 33
Enron Corporation, V, 19
Enserch Corporation, V
Entergy Corporation, V
Enterprise Rent-A-Car Company, 6
Entravision Communications Corporation, 41
Envirodyne Industries, Inc., 17
Environmental Industries, Inc., 31
Enzo Biochem, Inc., 41
Equifax Inc., 6; 28 (upd.)
Equitable Life Assurance Society of the United States, III
Equitable Resources, Inc., 6
Equity Marketing, Inc., 26
Erie Indemnity Company, 35
ERLY Industries Inc., 17
Ernst & Young, 9; 29 (upd.)
Escalade, Incorporated, 19
Eskimo Pie Corporation, 21
Esprit de Corp., 8; 29 (upd.)
ESS Technology, Inc., 22
Essef Corporation, 18
Esselte Pendaflex Corporation, 11
Essence Communications, Inc., 24

Estée Lauder Companies Inc., The, 9; 30 (upd.)
Esterline Technologies Corp., 15
Ethan Allen Interiors, Inc., 12; 39 (upd.)
Ethicon, Inc., 23
Ethyl Corporation, I; 10 (upd.)
EToys, Inc., 37
Eureka Company, The, 12
Euromarket Designs Inc., 31 (upd.)
Evans & Sutherland Computer Corporation, 19
Evans, Inc., 30
Everex Systems, Inc., 16
Exabyte Corporation, 12; 40 (upd.)
Exar Corp., 14
EXCEL Communications Inc., 18
Executive Jet, Inc., 36
Executone Information Systems, Inc., 13
Exide Electronics Group, Inc., 20
Expeditors International of Washington Inc., 17
Express Scripts Incorporated, 17
Extended Stay America, Inc., 41
Exxon Corporation, IV; 7 (upd.); 32 (upd.)
EZCORP Inc., 43
E-Systems, Inc., 9
E-Z Serve Corporation, 17
Fab Industries, Inc., 27
Fabri-Centers of America Inc., 16
Fair, Isaac and Company, 18
Fairchild Aircraft, Inc., 9
Fairfield Communities, Inc., 36
Falcon Products, Inc., 33
Fallon McElligott Inc., 22
Family Dollar Stores, Inc., 13
Family Golf Centers, Inc., 29
Famous Dave's of America, Inc., 40
Fansteel Inc., 19
Farah Incorporated, 24
Farley Northwest Industries, Inc., I
Farm Family Holdings, Inc., 39
Farm Journal Corporation, 42
Farmers Insurance Group of Companies, 25
Farmland Foods, Inc., 7
Farrar, Straus and Giroux Inc., 15
Fastenal Company, 14; 42 (upd.)
Fay's Inc., 17
Fazoli's Systems, Inc., 27
Featherlite Inc., 28
Fedders Corporation, 18; 43 (upd.)
Federal Express Corporation, V
Federal National Mortgage Association, II
Federal Paper Board Company, Inc., 8
Federal Prison Industries, Inc., 34
Federal Signal Corp., 10
Federal-Mogul Corporation, I; 10 (upd.); 26 (upd.)
Federated Department Stores Inc., 9; 31 (upd.)
FedEx Corporation, 18 (upd.); 42 (upd.)
Feld Entertainment, Inc., 32 (upd.)
Fellowes Manufacturing Company, 28
Fender Musical Instruments Company, 16; 43 (upd.)
Fenwick & West LLP, 34
Ferolito, Vultaggio & Sons, 27
Ferrellgas Partners, L.P., 35
Ferro Corporation, 8
FHP International Corporation, 6
FiberMark, Inc., 37
Fibreboard Corporation, 16
Fidelity Investments Inc., II; 14 (upd.)
Fieldale Farms Corporation, 23
Fieldcrest Cannon, Inc., 9; 31 (upd.)
Fifth Third Bancorp, 13; 31 (upd.)
Figgie International Inc., 7
FINA, Inc., 7
Fingerhut Companies, Inc., 9; 36 (upd.)
Finish Line, Inc., The, 29
FinishMaster, Inc., 24
Finlay Enterprises, Inc., 16
Firearms Training Systems, Inc., 27
Fireman's Fund Insurance Company, III
First Albany Companies Inc., 37
First Alert, Inc., 28
First Bank System Inc., 12
First Brands Corporation, 8
First Chicago Corporation, II
First Commerce Bancshares, Inc., 15
First Commerce Corporation, 11
First Data Corporation, 30 (upd.)
First Empire State Corporation, 11
First Executive Corporation, III
First Fidelity Bank, N.A., New Jersey, 9
First Financial Management Corporation, 11
First Hawaiian, Inc., 11
First Interstate Bancorp, II
First Mississippi Corporation, 8
First Nationwide Bank, 14
First of America Bank Corporation, 8
First Security Corporation, 11
First Team Sports, Inc., 22
First Tennessee National Corporation, 11
First Union Corporation, 10
First USA, Inc., 11
First Virginia Banks, Inc., 11
Firstar Corporation, 11; 33 (upd.)
Fiserv Inc., 11; 33 (upd.)
Fisher Companies, Inc., 15
Fisher Controls International, Inc., 13
Fisher Scientific International Inc., 24
Fisher-Price Inc., 12; 32 (upd.)
Flagstar Companies, Inc., 10
Fleer Corporation, 15
Fleet Financial Group, Inc., 9
FleetBoston Financial Corporation, 36 (upd.)
Fleetwood Enterprises, Inc., III; 22 (upd.)
Fleming Companies, Inc., II; 17 (upd.)
Flexsteel Industries Inc., 15; 41 (upd.)
FlightSafety International, Inc., 9; 29 (upd.)
Flint Ink Corporation, 13; 41 (upd.)
Florida Crystals Inc., 35
Florida Progress Corporation, V; 23 (upd.)
Florists' Transworld Delivery, Inc., 28
Florsheim Shoe Company, 9
Florsheim Shoe Group Inc., 31 (upd.)
Flowers Industries, Inc., 12; 35 (upd.)
Flowserve Corporation, 33
Fluke Corporation, 15
Fluor Corporation, I; 8 (upd.); 34 (upd.)
Flying J Inc., 19
FMC Corporation, I; 11 (upd.)
FMR Corp., 8; 32 (upd.)
Foamex International Inc., 17
Foley & Lardner, 28
Follett Corporation, 12; 39 (upd.)
Food Lion, Inc., II; 15 (upd.)
Foodarama Supermarkets, Inc., 28
FoodBrands America, Inc., 23
Foodmaker, Inc., 14
Foote, Cone & Belding Communications, Inc., I
Footstar, Incorporated, 24
Forbes Inc., 30
Ford Foundation, The, 34
Ford Motor Company, I; 11 (upd.); 36 (upd.)
Ford Motor Company, S.A. de C.V., 20
FORE Systems, Inc., 25
Forest City Enterprises, Inc., 16
Forest Laboratories, Inc., 11
Forest Oil Corporation, 19
Forever Living Products International Inc., 17
Formica Corporation, 13
Forstmann Little & Co., 38
Fort Howard Corporation, 8
Fort James Corporation, 22 (upd.)
Fortune Brands, Inc., 29 (upd.)
Fortunoff Fine Jewelry and Silverware Inc., 26
Fossil, Inc., 17
Foster Poultry Farms, 32
Foster Wheeler Corporation, 6; 23 (upd.)
Foundation Health Corporation, 12
Fountain Powerboats Industries, Inc., 28
Fourth Financial Corporation, 11
Fox Entertainment Group, Inc., 43
Fox Family Worldwide, Inc., 24
Foxboro Company, 13
FoxMeyer Health Corporation, 16
FPL Group, Inc., V
Frank J. Zamboni & Co., Inc., 34
Frank's Nursery & Crafts, Inc., 12
Frankel & Co., 39
Franklin Covey Company, 37 (upd.)
Franklin Electric Company, Inc., 43
Franklin Electronic Publishers, Inc., 23
Franklin Quest Co., 11
Franklin Resources, Inc., 9
Fred Meyer, Inc., V; 20 (upd.)
Fred W. Albrecht Grocery Co., The, 13
Fred's, Inc., 23
Frederick Atkins Inc., 16
Frederick's of Hollywood Inc., 16
Freedom Communications, Inc., 36
Freeport-McMoRan Inc., IV; 7 (upd.)
French Fragrances, Inc., 22
Fresh America Corporation, 20
Fresh Choice, Inc., 20
Fresh Foods, Inc., 29
Fretter, Inc., 10
Fried, Frank, Harris, Shriver & Jacobson, 35
Friedman's Inc., 29
Friendly Ice Cream Corp., 30
Frigidaire Home Products, 22
Frisch's Restaurants, Inc., 35
Frito-Lay Company, 32
Fritz Companies, Inc., 12
Frontier Airlines, Inc., 22
Frontier Corp., 16
Frozen Food Express Industries, Inc., 20
Fruehauf Corporation, I
Fruit of the Loom, Inc., 8; 25 (upd.)
Frymaster Corporation, 27
FSI International, Inc., 17
FTP Software, Inc., 20
Fubu, 29
Fujitsu-ICL Systems Inc., 11
Funco, Inc., 20
Fuqua Enterprises, Inc., 17
Fuqua Industries, Inc., I
Furniture Brands International, Inc., 39 (upd.)
Furon Company, 28
Furr's Supermarkets, Inc., 28
Future Now, Inc., 12
G&K Services, Inc., 16
G-III Apparel Group, Ltd., 22
G. Heileman Brewing Company Inc., I
G.A.F., I
G.D. Searle & Company, I; 12 (upd.); 34 (upd.)
G.I. Joe's, Inc., 30
G.S. Blodgett Corporation, 15
Gabelli Asset Management Inc., 30
Gadzooks, Inc., 18
GAF Corporation, 22 (upd.)
Gage Marketing Group, 26
Gaiam, Inc., 41
Gainsco, Inc., 22

United States *(continued)*
Galey & Lord, Inc., 20
Gallup Organization, The, 37
Gambrinus Company, The, 40
Gander Mountain, Inc., 20
Gannett Co., Inc., IV; 7 (upd.); 30 (upd.)
Gantos, Inc., 17
Gap, Inc., The, V; 18 (upd.)
Garan, Inc., 16
Garden Fresh Restaurant Corporation, 31
Garden Ridge Corporation, 27
Gardenburger, Inc., 33
Gart Sports Company, 24
Gartner Group, Inc., 21
Gates Corporation, The, 9
Gateway XX00, Inc., 10
Gateway, Inc., 27 (upd.)
GATX Corporation, 6; 25 (upd.)
Gaylord Container Corporation, 8
Gaylord Entertainment Company, 11; 36 (upd.)
GC Companies, Inc., 25
GE Aircraft Engines, 9
GE Capital Aviation Services, 36
Geffen Records Inc., 26
Gehl Company, 19
GEICO Corporation, 10; 40 (upd.)
GenCorp Inc., 8; 9
Genentech, Inc., I; 8 (upd.); 32 (upd.)
General Binding Corporation, 10
General Cable Corporation, 40
General Chemical Group Inc., The, 37
General Cinema Corporation, I
General DataComm Industries, Inc., 14
General Dynamics Corporation, I; 10 (upd.); 40 (upd.)
General Electric Company, II; 12 (upd.); 34 (upd.)
General Host Corporation, 12
General Housewares Corporation, 16
General Instrument Corporation, 10
General Mills, Inc., II; 10 (upd.); 36 (upd.)
General Motors Corporation, I; 10 (upd.); 36 (upd.)
General Nutrition Companies, Inc., 11; 29 (upd.)
General Public Utilities Corporation, V
General Re Corporation, III; 24 (upd.)
General Signal Corporation, 9
General Tire, Inc., 8
Genesco Inc., 17
Genesee & Wyoming Inc., 27
Genesis Health Ventures, Inc., 18
Genetics Institute, Inc., 8
Geneva Steel, 7
Genovese Drug Stores, Inc., 18
GenRad, Inc., 24
Gentex Corporation, 26
Genuardi's Family Markets, Inc., 35
Genuine Parts Company, 9
Genzyme Corporation, 13; 38 (upd.)
Geon Company, The, 11
George A. Hormel and Company, II
Georgia Gulf Corporation, 9
Georgia-Pacific Corporation, IV; 9 (upd.)
Geotek Communications Inc., 21
Gerald Stevens, Inc., 37
Gerber Products Company, 7; 21 (upd.)
Gerber Scientific, Inc., 12
German American Bancorp, 41
Getty Images, Inc., 31
Ghirardelli Chocolate Company, 30
Giant Cement Holding, Inc., 23
Giant Food Inc., II; 22 (upd.)
Giant Industries, Inc., 19
Gibraltar Steel Corporation, 37
Gibson Greetings, Inc., 12
Gibson Guitar Corp., 16
Gibson, Dunn & Crutcher LLP, 36
Giddings & Lewis, Inc., 10
Gilbane, Inc., 34
Gillett Holdings, Inc., 7
Gillette Company, The, III; 20 (upd.)
Girl Scouts of the USA, 35
Gitano Group, Inc., The, 8
Glacier Bancorp, Inc., 35
Gleason Corporation, 24
Glidden Company, The, 8
Global Crossing Ltd., 32
Global Industries, Ltd., 37
Global Marine Inc., 9
GM Hughes Electronics Corporation, II
Godfather's Pizza Incorporated, 25
Gold Kist Inc., 17; 26 (upd.)
Golden Belt Manufacturing Co., 16
Golden Books Family Entertainment, Inc., 28
Golden Corral Corporation, 10
Golden Enterprises, Inc., 26
Golden State Foods Corporation, 32
Golden State Vintners, Inc., 33
Goldman, Sachs & Co., II; 20 (upd.)
Golub Corporation, The, 26
Gonnella Baking Company, 40
Good Guys, Inc., The, 10; 30 (upd.)
Good Humor-Breyers Ice Cream Company, 14
Goodman Holding Company, 42
GoodMark Foods, Inc., 26
Goodwill Industries International, Inc., 16
Goody Products, Inc., 12
Goody's Family Clothing, Inc., 20
Goodyear Tire & Rubber Company, The, V; 20 (upd.)
Gordon Food Service Inc., 8; 39 (upd.)
Gorman-Rupp Company, The, 18
Gorton's, 13
Goss Holdings, Inc., 43
Gottschalks, Inc., 18
Gould Electronics, Inc., 14
Goulds Pumps Inc., 24
Goya Foods Inc., 22
GPU, Inc., 27 (upd.)
Graco Inc., 19
GranCare, Inc., 14
Grand Casinos, Inc., 20
Grand Union Company, The, 7; 28 (upd.)
Granite Broadcasting Corporation, 42
Granite Rock Company, 26
Granite State Bankshares, Inc., 37
Graphic Industries Inc., 25
Gray Communications Systems, Inc., 24
Great American Management and Investment, Inc., 8
Great Atlantic & Pacific Tea Company, Inc., The, II; 16 (upd.)
Great Lakes Bancorp, 8
Great Lakes Chemical Corporation, I; 14 (upd.)
Great Western Financial Corporation, 10
Grede Foundries, Inc., 38
Green Bay Packers, Inc., The, 32
Green Mountain Coffee, Inc., 31
Green Tree Financial Corporation, 11
Greenbrier Companies, The, 19
GreenPoint Financial Corp., 28
Greenwood Mills, Inc., 14
Greif Bros. Corporation, 15
Grey Advertising, Inc., 6
Grey Wolf, Inc., 43
Greyhound Lines, Inc., I; 32 (upd.)
Griffin Land & Nurseries, Inc., 43
Griffon Corporation, 34
Grinnell Corp., 13
Grist Mill Company, 15
Gristede's Sloan's, Inc., 31
Grolier Incorporated, 16; 43 (upd.)
Grossman's Inc., 13
Ground Round, Inc., 21
Group Health Cooperative, 41
Grow Biz International, Inc., 18
Grow Group Inc., 12
Grubb & Ellis Company, 21
Grumman Corporation, I; 11 (upd.)
Gruntal & Co., L.L.C., 20
Gryphon Holdings, Inc., 21
GT Bicycles, 26
GT Interactive Software, 31
GTE Corporation, V; 15 (upd.)
Guccio Gucci, S.p.A., 15
Guess, Inc., 15
Guest Supply, Inc., 18
Guilford Mills Inc., 8; 40 (upd.)
Guitar Center, Inc., 29
Gulf & Western Inc., I
Gulf States Utilities Company, 6
Gulfstream Aerospace Corporation, 7; 28 (upd.)
Gunlocke Company, The, 23
Guthy-Renker Corporation, 32
Gwathmey Siegel & Associates Architects LLC, 26
Gymboree Corporation, 15
H & R Block, Incorporated, 9; 29 (upd.)
H.B. Fuller Company, 8; 32 (upd.)
H.E. Butt Grocery Company, 13; 32 (upd.)
H.F. Ahmanson & Company, II; 10 (upd.)
H.J. Heinz Company, II; 11 (upd.); 36 (upd.)
Ha-Lo Industries, Inc., 27
Habersham Bancorp, 25
Habitat for Humanity International, 36
Hach Co., 18
Hadco Corporation, 24
Haemonetics Corporation, 20
Haggar Corporation, 19
Haggen Inc., 38
Hahn Automotive Warehouse, Inc., 24
Hain Celestial Group, Inc., The, 43 (upd.)
Hain Food Group, Inc., 27
HAL Inc., 9
Half Price Books, Records, Magazines Inc., 37
Halliburton Company, III; 25 (upd.)
Hallmark Cards, Inc., IV; 16 (upd.); 40 (upd.)
Hamilton Beach/Proctor-Silex Inc., 17
Hammacher Schlemmer & Company, 21
Hampton Industries, Inc., 20
Hancock Fabrics, Inc., 18
Hancock Holding Company, 15
Handleman Company, 15
Handy & Harman, 23
Hanger Orthopedic Group, Inc., 41
Hanna-Barbera Cartoons Inc., 23
Hannaford Bros. Co., 12
Hanover Direct, Inc., 36
Hanover Foods Corporation, 35
Hansen Natural Corporation, 31
Happy Kids Inc., 30
Harbert Corporation, 14
Harbison-Walker Refractories Company, 24
Harcourt Brace and Co., 12
Harcourt Brace Jovanovich, Inc., IV
Harcourt General, Inc., 20 (upd.)
Hard Rock Cafe International, Inc., 12; 32 (upd.)
Harding Lawson Associates Group, Inc., 16
Hardinge Inc., 25
Harley-Davidson Inc., 7; 25 (upd.)
Harleysville Group Inc., 37
Harman International Industries Inc., 15
Harmon Industries, Inc., 25

Harmonic Inc., 43
Harnischfeger Industries, Inc., 8; 38 (upd.)
Harold's Stores, Inc., 22
Harper Group Inc., 17
HarperCollins Publishers, 15
Harpo Entertainment Group, 28
Harrah's Entertainment, Inc., 16; 43 (upd.)
Harris Corporation, II; 20 (upd.)
Harris Interactive Inc., 41
Harris Teeter Inc., 23
Harry's Farmers Market Inc., 23
Harsco Corporation, 8
Harte-Hanks Communications, Inc., 17
Hartmarx Corporation, 8; 32 (upd.)
Hartz Mountain Corporation, The, 12
Harveys Casino Resorts, 27
Harza Engineering Company, 14
Hasbro, Inc., III; 16 (upd.); 43 (upd.)
Hastings Entertainment, Inc., 29
Haverty Furniture Companies, Inc., 31
Hawaiian Airlines, Inc., 22 (upd.)
Hawaiian Electric Industries, Inc., 9
Hawkins Chemical, Inc., 16
Haworth Inc., 8; 39 (upd.)
Hayes Corporation, 24
Hayes Lemmerz International, Inc., 27
Hazelden Foundation, 28
HCA - The Healthcare Company, 35 (upd.)
Headway Corporate Resources, Inc., 40
Health Care & Retirement Corporation, 22
Health O Meter Products Inc., 14
Health Risk Management, Inc., 24
Health Systems International, Inc., 11
HealthSouth Corporation, 33 (upd.)
HealthSouth Rehabilitation Corporation, 14
Healthtex, Inc., 17
Hearst Corporation, The, IV; 19 (upd.)
Heartland Express, Inc., 18
Hechinger Company, 12
Hecla Mining Company, 20
Heekin Can Inc., 13
HEICO Corporation, 30
Heidrick & Struggles International, Inc., 28
Heilig-Meyers Company, 14; 40 (upd.)
Helen of Troy Corporation, 18
Helene Curtis Industries, Inc., 8; 28 (upd.)
Heller, Ehrman, White & McAuliffe, 41
Helmerich & Payne, Inc., 18
Helmsley Enterprises, Inc., 9; 39 (upd.)
Helzberg Diamonds, 40
Henkel Manco Inc., 22
Henley Group, Inc., The, III
Henry Modell & Company Inc., 32
Henry Schein, Inc., 31
Herbalife International, Inc., 17; 41 (upd.)
Hercules Inc., I; 22 (upd.)
Herley Industries, Inc., 33
Herman Goelitz, Inc., 28
Herman Miller, Inc., 8
Hershey Foods Corporation, II; 15 (upd.)
Hertz Corporation, The, IX; XXXIII (upd.)
Heska Corporation, 39
Heublein, Inc., I
Hewlett-Packard Company, III; 6 (upd.); 28 (upd.)
Hexcel Corporation, 28
Hibbett Sporting Goods, Inc., 26
Hibernia Corporation, 37
Hickory Farms, Inc., 17
Highmark Inc., 27
Hildebrandt International, 29
Hill's Pet Nutrition, Inc., 27
Hillenbrand Industries, Inc., 10
Hillhaven Corporation, The, 14
Hills Stores Company, 13
Hilton Hotels Corporation, III; 19 (upd.)
Hispanic Broadcasting Corporation, 35
Hitchiner Manufacturing Co., Inc., 23
HMI Industries, Inc., 17
HOB Entertainment, Inc., 37
Hoechst Celanese Corporation, 13
Hoenig Group Inc., 41
Holberg Industries, Inc., 36
Holiday Inns, Inc., III
Holiday RV Superstores, Incorporated, 26
Hollinger International Inc., 24
Holly Corporation, 12
Hollywood Casino Corporation, 21
Hollywood Entertainment Corporation, 25
Hollywood Park, Inc., 20
Holme Roberts & Owen LLP, 28
Holnam Inc., 8; 39 (upd.)
Holophane Corporation, 19
Holson Burnes Group, Inc., 14
Holt's Cigar Holdings, Inc., 42
Home Box Office Inc., 7; 23 (upd.)
Home Depot, Inc., The, V; 18 (upd.)
Home Insurance Company, The, III
Home Properties of New York, Inc., 42
Home Shopping Network, Inc., V; 25 (upd.)
HomeBase, Inc., 33 (upd.)
Homestake Mining Company, 12; 38 (upd.)
HON INDUSTRIES Inc., 13
Honda Motor Company Limited, I; 10 (upd.); 29 (upd.)
Honeywell Inc., II; 12 (upd.)
Hooper Holmes, Inc., 22
Hooters of America, Inc., 18
Hoover Company, The, 12; 40 (upd.)
Horace Mann Educators Corporation, 22
Horizon Organic Holding Corporation, 37
Hormel Foods Corporation, 18 (upd.)
Horton Homes, Inc., 25
Hospital Corporation of America, III
Hospitality Franchise Systems, Inc., 11
Hospitality Worldwide Services, Inc., 26
Hot Topic, Inc., 33
Houghton Mifflin Company, 10; 36 (upd.)
House of Fabrics, Inc., 21
Household International, Inc., II; 21 (upd.)
Houston Industries Incorporated, V
Hovnanian Enterprises, Inc., 29
Howard Hughes Medical Institute, 39
Howard Johnson International, Inc., 17
Howmet Corp., 12
Hub Group, Inc., 38
Hubbard Broadcasting Inc., 24
Hubbell Incorporated, 9; 31 (upd.)
Hudson Foods Inc., 13
Hudson River Bancorp, Inc., 41
Huffy Corporation, 7; 30 (upd.)
Hughes Electronics Corporation, 25
Hughes Markets, Inc., 22
Hughes Supply, Inc., 14
Humana Inc., III; 24 (upd.)
Hungry Howie's Pizza and Subs, Inc., 25
Hunt Consolidated, Inc., 27 (upd.)
Hunt Manufacturing Company, 12
Hunt Oil Company, 7
Hunt-Wesson, Inc., 17
Hunter Fan Company, 13
Huntington Bancshares Inc., 11
Hunton & Williams, 35
Huntsman Chemical Corporation, 8
Hutchinson Technology Incorporated, 18
Hvide Marine Incorporated, 22
Hy-Vee, Inc., 36
Hyatt Corporation, III; 16 (upd.)
Hyde Athletic Industries, Inc., 17
Hypercom Corporation, 27
Hyperion Software Corporation, 22
Hyster Company, 17
I.C. Isaacs & Company, 31
Iams Company, 26
IBERIABANK Corporation, 37
IBP, Inc., II; 21 (upd.)
IC Industries, Inc., I
ICF Kaiser International, Inc., 28
Icon Health & Fitness, Inc., 38
Idaho Power Company, 12
IDB Communications Group, Inc., 11
IDEXX Laboratories, Inc., 23
IDG Books Worldwide, Inc., 27
IDT Corporation, 34
IEC Electronics Corp., 42
Igloo Products Corp., 21
IHOP Corporation, 17
Il Fornaio (America) Corporation, 27
Ilitch Holdings Inc., 37
Illinois Bell Telephone Company, 14
Illinois Central Corporation, 11
Illinois Power Company, 6
Illinois Tool Works Inc., III; 22 (upd.)
Imation Corporation, 20
IMC Fertilizer Group, Inc., 8
IMCO Recycling, Incorporated, 32
Immunex Corporation, 14
Imo Industries Inc., 7; 27 (upd.)
Imperial Holly Corporation, 12
Imperial Sugar Company, 32 (upd.)
In Focus Systems, Inc., 22
In-N-Out Burger, 19
InaCom Corporation, 13
Indiana Bell Telephone Company, Incorporated, 14
Indiana Energy, Inc., 27
Infinity Broadcasting Corporation, 11
Information Access Company, 17
Information Builders, Inc., 22
Information Resources, Inc., 10
Informix Corporation, 10; 30 (upd.)
Ingalls Shipbuilding, Inc., 12
Ingersoll-Rand Company, III; 15 (upd.)
Ingles Markets, Inc., 20
Ingram Industries, Inc., 11
Inland Container Corporation, 8
Inland Steel Industries, Inc., IV; 19 (upd.)
Inserra Supermarkets, 25
Insight Enterprises, Inc., 18
Insilco Corporation, 16
Inso Corporation, 26
Instinet Corporation, 34
Insurance Auto Auctions, Inc., 23
Intel Corporation, II; 10 (upd.); 36 (upd.)
Intelligent Electronics, Inc., 6
Inter Parfums Inc., 35
Inter-Regional Financial Group, Inc., 15
Interco Incorporated, III
Interep National Radio Sales Inc., 35
Interface, Inc., 8; 29 (upd.)
Intergraph Corporation, 6; 24 (upd.)
Interlake Corporation, The, 8
Intermet Corporation, 32
Intermountain Health Care, Inc., 27
International Brotherhood of Teamsters, 37
International Business Machines Corporation, III; 6 (upd.); 30 (upd.)
International Controls Corporation, 10
International Creative Management, Inc., 43
International Dairy Queen, Inc., 10; 39 (upd.)
International Data Group, Inc., 7; 25 (upd.)
International Family Entertainment Inc., 13
International Flavors & Fragrances Inc., 9; 38 (upd.)
International Game Technology, 10; 41 (upd.)
International Management Group, 18
International Multifoods Corporation, 7; 25 (upd.)
International Paper Company, IV; 15 (upd.)
International Rectifier Corporation, 31

United States *(continued)*
International Shipholding Corporation, Inc., 27
International Speedway Corporation, 19
International Telephone & Telegraph Corporation, I; 11 (upd.)
International Total Services, Inc., 37
Interpublic Group of Companies, Inc., The, I; 22 (upd.)
Interscope Music Group, 31
Interstate Bakeries Corporation, 12; 38 (upd.)
Intimate Brands, Inc., 24
Intuit Inc., 14; 33 (upd.)
Invacare Corporation, 11
Iomega Corporation, 21
IPALCO Enterprises, Inc., 6
Iron Mountain, Inc., 33
Irvin Feld & Kenneth Feld Productions, Inc., 15
Isle of Capri Casinos, Inc., 41
Ispat Inland Inc., 40 (upd.)
Itel Corporation, 9
Items International Airwalk Inc., 17
ITT Educational Services, Inc., 33
ITT Sheraton Corporation, III
IVAX Corporation, 11
Iwerks Entertainment, Inc., 34
IXC Communications, Inc., 29
J & J Snack Foods Corporation, 24
J&R Electronics Inc., 26
J. Baker, Inc., 31
J. Crew Group Inc., 12; 34 (upd.)
J. Jill Group, Inc., The, 35
J.A. Jones, Inc., 16
J.B. Hunt Transport Services Inc., 12
J.C. Penney Company, Inc., V; 18 (upd.); 43 (upd.)
J.D. Edwards & Company, 14
J.D. Power and Associates, 32
J.I. Case Company, 10
J.M. Smucker Company, The, 11
J.P. Morgan & Co. Incorporated, II; 30 (upd.)
J.P. Morgan Chase & Co., 38 (upd.)
J.R. Simplot Company, 16
Jabil Circuit, Inc., 36
Jack Henry and Associates, Inc., 17
Jack Schwartz Shoes, Inc., 18
Jackpot Enterprises Inc., 21
Jackson National Life Insurance Company, 8
Jaco Electronics, Inc., 30
Jacob Leinenkugel Brewing Company, 28
Jacobs Engineering Group Inc., 6; 26 (upd.)
Jacobson Stores Inc., 21
Jacor Communications, Inc., 23
Jacuzzi Inc., 23
Jalate Inc., 25
James River Corporation of Virginia, IV
Jason Incorporated, 23
Jay Jacobs, Inc., 15
Jayco Inc., 13
JB Oxford Holdings, Inc., 32
JDS Uniphase Corporation, 34
Jefferies Group, Inc., 25
Jefferson-Pilot Corporation, 11; 29 (upd.)
Jennifer Convertibles, Inc., 31
Jenny Craig, Inc., 10; 29 (upd.)
Jerry's Famous Deli Inc., 24
Jervis B. Webb Company, 24
Jetro Cash & Carry Enterprises Inc., 38
JG Industries, Inc., 15
Jillian's Entertainment Holdings, Inc., 40
Jim Beam Brands Co., 14
Jim Henson Company, The, 23
Jitney-Jungle Stores of America, Inc., 27
JMB Realty Corporation, IV
Jockey International, Inc., 12; 34 (upd.)
John B. Sanfilippo & Son, Inc., 14
John D. and Catherine T. MacArthur Foundation, The, 34
John H. Harland Company, 17
John Hancock Financial Services, Inc., 42 (upd.)
John Hancock Mutual Life Insurance Company, III
John Nuveen Company, The, 21
John Paul Mitchell Systems, 24
John Q. Hammons Hotels, Inc., 24
John Wiley & Sons, Inc., 17
Johnny Rockets Group, Inc., 31
Johnson & Higgins, 14
Johnson & Johnson, III; 8 (upd.); 36 (upd.)
Johnson Controls, Inc., III; 26 (upd.)
Johnson Publishing Company, Inc., 28
Johnson Worldwide Associates, Inc., 28
Johnston Industries, Inc., 15
Johnstown America Industries, Inc., 23
Jones Apparel Group, Inc., 11; 39 (upd.)
Jones Intercable, Inc., 21
Jones Medical Industries, Inc., 24
Jones, Day, Reavis & Pogue, 33
Jordache Enterprises, Inc., 23
Jordan Industries, Inc., 36
Jos. A. Bank Clothiers, Inc., 31
Joseph T. Ryerson & Son, Inc., 15
Jostens, Inc., 7; 25 (upd.)
Journal Register Company, 29
JPS Textile Group, Inc., 28
Juniper Networks, Inc., 43
Juno Lighting, Inc., 30
Juno Online Services, Inc., 38
Just Born, Inc., 32
Just For Feet, Inc., 19
Justin Industries, Inc., 19
JWP Inc., 9
JWT Group Inc., I
K & B Inc., 12
K & G Men's Center, Inc., 21
K-Swiss, Inc., 33
K-tel International, Inc., 21
Kaiser Aluminum & Chemical Corporation, IV
Kal Kan Foods, Inc., 22
Kaman Corporation, 12; 42 (upd.)
Kampgrounds of America, Inc. 33
Kansas City Power & Light Company, 6
Kansas City Southern Industries, Inc., 6; 26 (upd.)
Kaplan, Inc., 42
Kash n' Karry Food Stores, Inc., 20
Kasper A.S.L., Ltd., 40
Katy Industries, Inc., I
Katz Communications, Inc., 6
Katz Media Group, Inc., 35
Kaufman and Broad Home Corporation, 8
Kay-Bee Toy Stores, 15
Kaydon Corporation, 18
KB Toys, 35 (upd.)
Keebler Foods Company, 36
Keithley Instruments Inc., 16
Kelley Drye & Warren LLP, 40
Kellogg Company, II; 13 (upd.)
Kellwood Company, 8
Kelly Services Inc., 6; 26 (upd.)
Kelly-Springfield Tire Company, The, 8
Kelsey-Hayes Group of Companies, 7; 27 (upd.)
Kemet Corp., 14
Kemper Corporation, III; 15 (upd.)
Kendall International, Inc., 11
Kendall-Jackson Winery, Ltd., 28
Kenetech Corporation, 11
Kenneth Cole Productions, Inc., 25
Kent Electronics Corporation, 17
Kentucky Electric Steel, Inc., 31
Kentucky Utilities Company, 6
Kerr Group Inc., 24
Kerr-McGee Corporation, IV; 22 (upd.)
Ketchum Communications Inc., 6
Kewaunee Scientific Corporation, 25
Key Tronic Corporation, 14
KeyCorp, 8
Keyes Fibre Company, 9
KeySpan Energy Co., 27
Keystone International, Inc., 11
KFC Corporation, 7; 21 (upd.)
Kidde, Inc., I
Kimball International, Inc., 12
Kimberly-Clark Corporation, III; 16 (upd.); 43 (upd.)
Kimco Realty Corporation, 11
KinderCare Learning Centers, Inc., 13
Kinetic Concepts, Inc. (KCI), 20
King & Spalding, 23
King Arthur Flour Company, The, 31
King Kullen Grocery Co., Inc., 15
King Ranch, Inc., 14
King World Productions, Inc., 9; 30 (upd.)
Kingston Technology Corporation, 20
Kinko's, Inc., 16; 43 (upd.)
Kinney Shoe Corp., 14
Kirby Corporation, 18
Kit Manufacturing Co., 18
Kitchell Corporation, 14
KitchenAid, 8
Kitty Hawk, Inc., 22
Kiwi International Airlines Inc., 20
KLA Instruments Corporation, 11
Kmart Corporation, V; 18 (upd.)
Knape & Vogt Manufacturing Company, 17
Knight-Ridder, Inc., IV; 15 (upd.)
Knoll Group Inc., 14
Knott's Berry Farm, 18
KnowledgeWare Inc., 9; 31 (upd.)
Koch Enterprises, Inc., 29
Koch Industries, Inc., IV; 20 (upd.)
Kohl's Corporation, 9; 30 (upd.)
Kohlberg Kravis Roberts & Co., 24
Kohler Company, 7; 32 (upd.)
Koll Company, The, 8
Kollmorgen Corporation, 18
Komag, Inc., 11
Koo Koo Roo, Inc., 25
Koppers Industries, Inc., I; 26 (upd.)
Korn/Ferry International, 34
Koss Corporation, 38
Kraft General Foods Inc., II; 7 (upd.)
Kraus-Anderson, Incorporated, 36
Krause Publications, Inc., 35
Krause's Furniture, Inc., 27
Krispy Kreme Doughnut Corporation, 21
Kroger Company, The, II; 15 (upd.)
Kronos, Inc., 18
Krystal Company, The, 33
K2 Inc., 16
KU Energy Corporation, 11
Kuhlman Corporation, 20
Kulicke and Soffa Industries, Inc., 33
Kushner-Locke Company, The, 25
L. Luria & Son, Inc., 19
L.A. Gear, Inc., 8; 32 (upd.)
L.A. T Sportswear, Inc., 26
L.B. Foster Company, 33
L.L. Bean, Inc., 10; 38 (upd.)
L.L. Knickerbocker Co., Inc., The, 25
L.S. Starrett Co., 13
La Choy Food Products Inc., 25
La Madeleine French Bakery & Café, 33
La Quinta Companies, The, 42 (upd.)

La Quinta Inns, Inc., 11
La-Z-Boy Chair Company, 14
LaBarge Inc., 41
Labor Ready, Inc., 29
Laboratory Corporation of America Holdings, 42 (upd.)
LaBranche & Co. Inc., 37
Laclede Steel Company, 15
LaCrosse Footwear, Inc., 18
LADD Furniture, Inc., 12
Ladish Co., Inc., 30
Lafarge Corporation, 28
Lam Research Corporation, 11; 31 (upd.)
Lamar Advertising Company, 27
Lamaur Corporation, The, 41
Lamb Weston, Inc., 23
Lamonts Apparel, Inc., 15
Lamson & Sessions Co., 13
Lancaster Colony Corporation, 8
Lance, Inc., 14; 41 (upd.)
Lancer Corporation, 21
Land O'Lakes, Inc., II; 21 (upd.)
Landmark Communications, Inc., 12
Landry's Seafood Restaurants, Inc., 15
Lands' End, Inc., 9; 29 (upd.)
Lane Co., Inc., The, 12
Larry Flynt Publishing Inc., 31
Larry H. Miller Group, 29
Lason, Inc., 31
Latham & Watkins, 33
Lattice Semiconductor Corp., 16
Lawson Software, 38
Lawter International Inc., 14
Layne Christensen Company, 19
Lazare Kaplan International Inc., 21
LCI International, Inc., 16
LDDS-Metro Communications, Inc., 8
Lear Seating Corporation, 16
Lear Siegler, Inc., I
Learjet Inc., 8; 27 (upd.)
Learning Company Inc., The, 24
Learning Tree International Inc., 24
LeaRonal, Inc., 23
Leaseway Transportation Corp., 12
LeBoeuf, Lamb, Greene & MacRae, L.L.P., 29
Lechmere Inc., 10
Lechters, Inc., 11; 39 (upd.)
LeCroy Corporation, 41
Lee Apparel Company, Inc., 8
Lee Enterprises, Incorporated, 11
Leeann Chin, Inc., 30
Lefrak Organization Inc., 26
Legent Corporation, 10
Legg Mason, Inc., 33
Leggett & Platt, Incorporated, 11
Lehigh Portland Cement Company, 23
Leiner Health Products Inc., 34
Lennar Corporation, 11
Lennox International Inc., 8; 28 (upd.)
Lenox, Inc., 12
LensCrafters Inc., 23
Leo Burnett Company Inc., I; 20 (upd.)
Leprino Foods Company, 28
Lesco Inc., 19
Leslie Fay Companies, Inc., The, 8; 39 (upd.)
Leslie's Poolmart, Inc., 18
Leucadia National Corporation, 11
Lever Brothers Company, 9
Levi Strauss & Co., V; 16 (upd.)
Levitz Furniture Inc., 15
Levy Restaurants L.P., 26
Lewis Galoob Toys Inc., 16
LEXIS-NEXIS Group, 33
Lexmark International, Inc., 18
LG&E Energy Corporation, 6
Liberty Corporation, The, 22
Liberty Livewire Corporation, 42
Life Technologies, Inc., 17
Lifetime Hoan Corporation, 27
Lillian Vernon Corporation, 12; 35 (upd.)
Limited, Inc., The, V; 20 (upd.)
LIN Broadcasting Corp., 9
Lincare Holdings Inc., 43
Lincoln Electric Co., 13
Lincoln National Corporation, III; 25 (upd.)
Lincoln Property Company, 8
Lincoln Snacks Company, 24
Lincoln Telephone & Telegraph Company, 14
Lindal Cedar Homes, Inc., 29
Lindsay Manufacturing Co., 20
Linear Technology, Inc., 16
Linens 'n Things, Inc., 24
Lintas: Worldwide, 14
Lionel L.L.C., 16
Liqui-Box Corporation, 16
Lithia Motors, Inc., 41
Littelfuse, Inc., 26
Little Caesar Enterprises, Inc., 7; 24 (upd.)
Little Tikes Co., 13
Litton Industries, Inc., I; 11 (upd.)
LIVE Entertainment Inc., 20
Liz Claiborne, Inc., 8; 25 (upd.)
Lockheed Corporation, I; 11 (upd.)
Lockheed Martin Corporation, 15 (upd.)
Loctite Corporation, 8; 30 (upd.)
LodgeNet Entertainment Corporation, 28
Loehmann's Inc., 24
Loews Corporation, I; 12 (upd.); 36 (upd.)
Logan's Roadhouse, Inc., 29
Logicon Inc., 20
London Fog Industries, Inc., 29
Long Island Bancorp, Inc., 16
Long Island Lighting Company, V
Long John Silver's Restaurants Inc., 13
Longaberger Company, The, 12
Longs Drug Stores Corporation, V; 25 (upd.)
Longview Fibre Company, 8; 37 (upd.)
Loral Corporation, 8; 9
Lost Arrow Inc., 22
LOT$OFF Corporation, 24
Lotus Development Corporation, 6; 25 (upd.)
Louisiana Land and Exploration Company, The, 7
Louisiana-Pacific Corporation, IV; 31 (upd.)
Lowe's Companies, Inc., V; 21 (upd.)
Lowrance Electronics, Inc., 18
LSI Logic Corporation, 13
LTV Corporation, The, I; 24 (upd.)
Lubrizol Corporation, I; 30 (upd.)
Luby's Cafeteria's, Inc., 17
Luby's, Inc., 42 (upd.)
Lucasfilm Ltd., 12
Lucent Technologies Inc., 34
Lucky Stores, Inc., 27
Lukens Inc., 14
Lunar Corporation, 29
Lund Food Holdings, Inc., 22
Lund International Holdings, Inc., 40
Lutheran Brotherhood, 31
Lynch Corporation, 43
Lyondell Petrochemical Company, IV
M&F Worldwide Corp., 38
M.A. Hanna Company, 8
Mac Frugal's Bargains - Closeouts Inc., 17
MacAndrews & Forbes Holdings Inc., 28
MacDermid Incorporated, 32
Mack Trucks, Inc., I; 22 (upd.)
Mack-Cali Realty Corporation, 42
Mackie Designs Inc., 33
Macmillan, Inc., 7
MacNeal-Schwendler Corporation, The, 25
Madison Gas and Electric Company, 39
Magma Copper Company, 7
Magma Power Company, 11
MagneTek, Inc., 15; 41 (upd.)
MAI Systems Corporation, 11
Maidenform Worldwide Inc., 20
Mail Boxes Etc., 18; 41 (upd.)
Mail-Well, Inc., 28
Maine Central Railroad Company, 16
Malcolm Pirnie, Inc., 42
Malden Mills Industries, Inc., 16
Mallinckrodt Group Inc., 19
Malt-O-Meal Company, 22
Management and Training Corporation, 28
Mandalay Resort Group, 32 (upd.)
Manitowoc Company, Inc., 18
Mannatech Inc., 33
Manor Care, Inc., 6; 25 (upd.)
Manpower, Inc., 9; 30 (upd.)
Manufactured Home Communities, Inc., 22
Manufacturers Hanover Corporation, II
Manville Corporation, III; 7 (upd.)
MAPCO Inc., IV
March of Dimes, 31
marchFIRST, Inc., 34
Marcus Corporation, The, 21
Marie Callender's Restaurant & Bakery, Inc., 28
MarineMax, Inc., 30
Marion Laboratories, Inc., I
Marisa Christina, Inc., 15
Maritz Inc., 38
Mark IV Industries, Inc., 7; 28 (upd.)
Marks Brothers Jewelers, Inc., 24
Marmon Group, The, IV; 16 (upd.)
Marquette Electronics, Inc., 13
Marriott International, Inc., III; 21 (upd.)
Mars, Incorporated, 7; 40 (upd.)
Marsh & McLennan Companies, Inc., III
Marsh Supermarkets, Inc., 17
Marshalls Incorporated, 13
Martha Stewart Living Omnimedia, L.L.C., 24
Martin Marietta Corporation, I
Marvel Entertainment Group, Inc., 10
Marvin Lumber & Cedar Company, 22
Mary Kay Corporation, 9; 30 (upd.)
Masco Corporation, III; 20 (upd.); 39 (upd.)
Mashantucket Pequot Gaming Enterprise Inc., 35
Masland Corporation, 17
Massachusetts Mutual Life Insurance Company, III
MasTec, Inc., 19
MasterCard International, Inc., 9
Matria Healthcare, Inc., 17
Mattel, Inc., 7; 25 (upd.)
Matthews International Corporation, 29
Maui Land & Pineapple Company, Inc., 29
Max & Erma's Restaurants Inc., 19
Maxco Inc., 17
Maxicare Health Plans, Inc., III; 25 (upd.)
Maxim Group, The, 25
Maxim Integrated Products, Inc., 16
MAXIMUS, Inc., 43
Maxtor Corporation, 10
Maxus Energy Corporation, 7
Maxwell Shoe Company, Inc., 30
MAXXAM Inc., 8
Maxxim Medical Inc., 12
May Department Stores Company, The, V; 19 (upd.)
Mayflower Group Inc., 6
Mayo Foundation, 9; 34 (upd.)
Mayor's Jewelers, Inc., 41

United States *(continued)*

Maytag Corporation, III; 22 (upd.)
Mazel Stores, Inc., 29
MBC Holding Company, 40
MBNA Corporation, 12; 33 (upd.)
MCA Inc., II
McCaw Cellular Communications, Inc., 6
McClatchy Newspapers, Inc., 23
McCormick & Company, Incorporated, 7; 27 (upd.)
McDermott International, Inc., III; 37 (upd.)
McDonald's Corporation, II; 7 (upd.); 26 (upd.)
McDonnell Douglas Corporation, I; 11 (upd.)
McGraw-Hill Companies, Inc., The, IV; 18 (upd.)
MCI Communications Corporation, V
MCI WorldCom, Inc., 27 (upd.)
McIlhenny Company, 20
McKee Foods Corporation, 7; 27 (upd.)
McKesson Corporation, I; 12
McKinsey & Company, Inc., 9
McLane Company, Inc., 13
McLeodUSA Incorporated, 32
MCN Corporation, 6
MCSi, Inc., 41
MDU Resources Group, Inc., 7; 42 (upd.)
Mead Corporation, The, IV; 19 (upd.)
Mead Data Central, Inc., 10
Meade Instruments Corporation, 41
Meadowcraft, Inc., 29
Mecklermedia Corporation, 24
Medco Containment Services Inc., 9
Media Arts Group, Inc., 42
Media General, Inc., 7; 38 (upd.)
MedImmune, Inc., 35
Meditrust, 11
Medtronic, Inc., 8; 30 (upd.)
Medusa Corporation, 24
Megafoods Stores Inc., 13
Meier & Frank Co., 23
Meijer Incorporated, 7; 27 (upd.)
Mel Farr Automotive Group, 20
Melaleuca Inc., 31
Melamine Chemicals, Inc., 27
Mellon Bank Corporation, II
Mellon-Stuart Company, I
Melville Corporation, V
Melvin Simon and Associates, Inc., 8
Men's Wearhouse, Inc., The, 17
Menard, Inc., 34
Menasha Corporation, 8
Mentholatum Company Inc., The, 32
Mentor Corporation, 26
Mentor Graphics Corporation, 11
Mercantile Bankshares Corp., 11
Mercantile Stores Company, Inc., V; 19 (upd.)
Merck & Co., Inc., I; 11 (upd.); 34 (upd.)
Mercury Air Group, Inc., 20
Mercury General Corporation, 25
Meredith Corporation, 11; 29 (upd.)
Meridian Bancorp, Inc., 11
Merillat Industries Inc., 13
Merisel, Inc., 12
Merit Medical Systems, Inc., 29
Meritage Corporation, 26
Merix Corporation, 36
Merrell Dow, Inc., I; 9 (upd.)
Merrill Corporation, 18
Merrill Lynch & Co., Inc., II; 13 (upd.); 40 (upd.)
Merry-Go-Round Enterprises, Inc., 8
Mervyn's, 10
Mervyn's California, 39 (upd.)
Mesa Air Group, Inc., 11; 32 (upd.)
Mesaba Holdings, Inc., 28
Mestek Inc., 10
Meteor Industries Inc., 33
Methode Electronics, Inc., 13
Metro Information Services, Inc., 36
Metro-Goldwyn-Mayer Inc., 25 (upd.)
Metrocall, Inc., 41
Metromedia Co., 7; 14
Metropolitan Baseball Club Inc., 39
Metropolitan Financial Corporation, 13
Metropolitan Life Insurance Company, III
Metropolitan Opera Association, Inc., 40
Metropolitan Transportation Authority, 35
Mexican Restaurants, Inc., 41
MFS Communications Company, Inc., 11
MGM Grand Inc., 17
MGM/UA Communications Company, II
Michael Anthony Jewelers, Inc., 24
Michael Baker Corp., 14
Michael Foods, Inc., 25
Michaels Stores, Inc., 17
Michigan Bell Telephone Co., 14
Michigan National Corporation, 11
Micro Warehouse, Inc., 16
MicroAge, Inc., 16
Microdot Inc., 8
Micron Technology, Inc., 11; 29 (upd.)
Micros Systems, Inc., 18
Microsoft Corporation, 6; 27 (upd.)
Mid-America Dairymen, Inc., 7
Midas International Corporation, 10
Middleby Corporation, The, 22
Midway Airlines Corporation, 33
Midway Games, Inc., 25
Midwest Express Holdings, Inc., 35
Midwest Resources Inc., 6
Mikasa, Inc., 28
Mike-Sell's Inc., 15
Mikohn Gaming Corporation, 39
Milbank, Tweed, Hadley & McCloy, 27
Miles Laboratories, I
Miller Brewing Company, I; 12 (upd.)
Miller Industries, Inc., 26
Milliken & Co., V; 17 (upd.)
Millipore Corporation, 25
Milton Bradley Company, 21
Milwaukee Brewers Baseball Club, 37
Mine Safety Appliances Company, 31
Miner Group International, The, 22
Minerals Technologies Inc., 11
Minnesota Mining & Manufacturing Company (3M), I; 8 (upd.); 26 (upd.)
Minnesota Power & Light Company, 11
Minnesota Power, Inc., 34 (upd.)
Minntech Corporation, 22
Minute Maid Company, The, 28
Minyard Food Stores, Inc., 33
Mirage Resorts, Incorporated, 6; 28 (upd.)
Mississippi Chemical Corporation, 39
Mitchell Energy and Development Corporation, 7
MITRE Corporation, 26
Mity Enterprises, Inc., 38
Mobil Corporation, IV; 7 (upd.); 21 (upd.)
Mobile Telecommunications Technologies Corp., 18
Modine Manufacturing Company, 8
Moen Incorporated, 12
Mohawk Industries, Inc., 19
Mohegan Tribal Gaming Authority, 37
Molex Incorporated, 11
Monaco Coach Corporation, 31
Monadnock Paper Mills, Inc., 21
Monfort, Inc., 13
Monro Muffler Brake, Inc., 24
Monsanto Company, I; 9 (upd.); 29 (upd.)
Montana Power Company, 11
Montgomery Ward & Co., Incorporated, V; 20 (upd.)
Moog Inc., 13
Moore Medical Corp., 17
Moore-Handley, Inc., 39
Moran Towing Corporation, Inc., 15
Morgan Stanley Dean Witter & Company, 33 (upd.)
Morgan Stanley Group Inc., II; 16 (upd.)
Morgan, Lewis & Bockius LLP, 29
Morris Communications Corporation, 36
Morris Travel Services L.L.C., 26
Morrison Knudsen Corporation, 7; 28 (upd.)
Morrison Restaurants Inc., 11
Morse Shoe Inc., 13
Morton International Inc., 9 (upd.)
Morton Thiokol, Inc., I
Morton's Restaurant Group, Inc., 30
Mosinee Paper Corporation, 15
Mossimo, Inc., 27
Motel 6 Corporation, 13
Mothers Work, Inc., 18
Motley Fool, Inc., The, 40
Motor Cargo Industries, Inc., 35
Motorola, Inc., II; 11 (upd.); 34 (upd.)
Motown Records Company L.P., 26
Mountain States Mortgage Centers, Inc., 29
Movado Group, Inc., 28
Movie Gallery, Inc., 31
Movie Star Inc., 17
Mr. Coffee, Inc., 15
Mr. Gasket Inc., 15
Mrs. Baird's Bakeries, 29
Mrs. Fields' Original Cookies, Inc., 27
MTS Inc., 37
Mueller Industries, Inc., 7
Multimedia Games, Inc., 41
Multimedia, Inc., 11
Murdock Madaus Schwabe, 26
Murphy Family Farms Inc., 22
Murphy Oil Corporation, 7; 32 (upd.)
Musicland Stores Corporation, 9; 38 (upd.)
Mutual Benefit Life Insurance Company, The, III
Mutual Life Insurance Company of New York, The, III
Muzak, Inc., 18
Mycogen Corporation, 21
Myers Industries, Inc., 19
Mylan Laboratories Inc., I; 20 (upd.)
Nabisco Foods Group, II; 7 (upd.)
Nabors Industries, Inc., 9
NACCO Industries, Inc., 7
Nalco Chemical Corporation, I; 12 (upd.)
Nantucket Allserve, Inc., 22
Nash Finch Company, 8; 23 (upd.)
Nashua Corporation, 8
Nathan's Famous, Inc., 29
National Amusements Inc., 28
National Association for Stock Car Auto Racing, 32
National Association of Securities Dealers, Inc., 10
National Audubon Society, 26
National Auto Credit, Inc., 16
National Beverage Corp., 26
National Broadcasting Company, Inc., II; 6 (upd.); 28 (upd.)
National Can Corporation, I
National Car Rental System, Inc., 10
National City Corp., 15
National Convenience Stores Incorporated, 7
National Discount Brokers Group, Inc., 28
National Distillers and Chemical Corporation, I
National Envelope Corporation, 32

National Football League, 29
National Fuel Gas Company, 6
National Geographic Society, 9; 30 (upd.)
National Grape Cooperative Association, Inc., 20
National Gypsum Company, 10
National Health Laboratories Incorporated, 11
National Hockey League, 35
National Instruments Corporation, 22
National Intergroup, Inc., V
National Media Corporation, 27
National Medical Enterprises, Inc., III
National Patent Development Corporation, 13
National Picture & Frame Company, 24
National Presto Industries, Inc., 16; 43 (upd.)
National Public Radio, 19
National R.V. Holdings, Inc., 32
National Railroad Passenger Corporation, 22
National Record Mart, Inc., 29
National Rifle Association of America, 37
National Sanitary Supply Co., 16
National Semiconductor Corporation, II; VI, 26 (upd.)
National Service Industries, Inc., 11
National Standard Co., 13
National Steel Corporation, 12
National TechTeam, Inc., 41
NationsBank Corporation, 10
Natural Wonders Inc., 14
Nature Conservancy, The, 28
Nature's Sunshine Products, Inc., 15
Nautica Enterprises, Inc., 18
Navarre Corporation, 24
Navistar International Corporation, I; 10 (upd.)
Navy Exchange Service Command, 31
Navy Federal Credit Union, 33
NBD Bancorp, Inc., 11
NBTY, Inc., 31
NCH Corporation, 8
NCNB Corporation, II
NCO Group, Inc., 42
NCR Corporation, III; 6 (upd.); 30 (upd.)
Nebraska Public Power District, 29
Neff Corp., 32
Neiman Marcus Co., 12
NERCO, Inc., 7
Netscape Communications Corporation, 15; 35 (upd.)
Network Associates, Inc., 25
Neutrogena Corporation, 17
Nevada Bell Telephone Company, 14
Nevada Power Company, 11
New Balance Athletic Shoe, Inc., 25
New Dana Perfumes Company, 37
New Plan Realty Trust, 11
New Street Capital Inc., 8
New UK Business Services, Inc., 18
New UK Confectionery Co., 15
New UK Electric System, V
New UK Mutual Life Insurance Company, III
New Valley Corporation, 17
New York Daily News, 32
New York Life Insurance Company, III
New York Restaurant Group, Inc., 32
New York State Electric and Gas, 6
New York Stock Exchange, Inc., 9; 39 (upd.)
New York Times Company, The, IV; 19 (upd.)
Newcor, Inc., 40
Newell Co., 9
Newhall Land and Farming Company, 14
Newman's Own, Inc., 37
Newmont Mining Corporation, 7
Newport News Shipbuilding and Dry Dock Co., 13
Newport News Shipbuilding Inc., 38 (upd.)
News America Publishing Inc., 12
Nextel Communications, Inc., 10; 27 (upd.)
NFO Worldwide, Inc., 24
NGC Corporation, 18
Niagara Corporation, 28
Niagara Mohawk Power Corporation, V
Nichols Research Corporation, 18
NICOR Inc., 6
NIKE, Inc., V; 8 (upd.); 36 (upd.)
Nikken Global Inc., 32
Nimbus CD International, Inc., 20
Nine West Group, Inc., 11; 39 (upd.)
99¢ Only Stores, 25
NIPSCO Industries, Inc., 6
NL Industries, Inc., 10
Nobel Learning Communities, Inc., 37
Noble Affiliates, Inc., 11
Noble Roman's Inc., 14
Noland Company, 35
Noodle Kidoodle, 16
NordicTrack, 22
Nordson Corporation, 11
Nordstrom, Inc., V; 18 (upd.)
Norelco Consumer Products Co., 26
Norfolk Southern Corporation, V; 29 (upd.)
Norrell Corporation, 25
Norstan, Inc., 16
Nortek, Inc., 34
North Face, Inc., The, 18
North Star Steel Company, 18
Northeast Utilities, V
Northern States Power Company, V; 20 (upd.)
Northern Trust Company, 9
Northland Cranberries, Inc., 38
Northrop Corporation, I; 11 (upd.)
Northwest Airlines Corporation, I; 6 (upd.); 26 (upd.)
NorthWestern Corporation, 37
Northwestern Mutual Life Insurance Company, III
Norton Company, 8
Norton McNaughton, Inc., 27
Norwood Promotional Products, Inc., 26
NovaCare, Inc., 11
Novell, Inc., 6; 23 (upd.)
Novellus Systems, Inc., 18
NPC International, Inc., 40
Nu Skin Enterprises, Inc., 27
Nu-kote Holding, Inc., 18
Nucor Corporation, 7; 21 (upd.)
Nutraceutical International Corporation, 37
NutraSweet Company, 8
Nutrition for Life International Inc., 22
NVR L.P., 8
NYMAGIC, Inc., 41
NYNEX Corporation, V
O'Charley's Inc., 19
O'Melveny & Myers, 37
O'Reilly Automotive, Inc., 26
O'Sullivan Industries Holdings, Inc., 34
Oak Industries Inc., 21
Oak Technology, Inc., 22
Oakley, Inc., 18
Oakwood Homes Corporation, 15
Occidental Petroleum Corporation, IV; 25 (upd.)
Ocean Spray Cranberries, Inc., 7; 25 (upd.)
Octel Communications Corp., 14
Octel Messaging, 41 (upd.)
Odetics Inc., 14
Odwalla, Inc., 31
OEC Medical Systems, Inc., 27
Office Depot Incorporated, 8; 23 (upd.)
OfficeMax, Inc., 15; 43 (upd.)
Offshore Logistics, Inc., 37
Ogden Corporation, I; 6
Ogilvy Group, Inc., The, I
Oglebay Norton Company, 17
Oglethorpe Power Corporation, 6
Ohio Art Company, The, 14
Ohio Bell Telephone Company, 14
Ohio Casualty Corp., 11
Ohio Edison Company, V
Oil-Dri Corporation of America, 20
Oklahoma Gas and Electric Company, 6
Old America Stores, Inc., 17
Old Kent Financial Corp., 11
Old National Bancorp, 15
Old Republic International Corp., 11
Old Spaghetti Factory International Inc., 24
Olin Corporation, I; 13 (upd.)
Olsten Corporation, 6; 29 (upd.)
OM Group, Inc., 17
Omni Hotels Corp., 12
Omnicom Group, I; 22 (upd.)
OmniSource Corporation, 14
On Assignment, Inc., 20
One Price Clothing Stores, Inc., 20
1-800-FLOWERS, Inc., 26
Oneida Ltd., 7; 31 (upd.)
ONEOK Inc., 7
Opus Group, 34
Oracle Corporation, 6; 24 (upd.)
Orbital Sciences Corporation, 22
Orchard Supply Hardware Stores Corporation, 17
Ore-Ida Foods Incorporated, 13
Oregon Metallurgical Corporation, 20
Oregon Steel Mills, Inc., 14
Orion Pictures Corporation, 6
Orthodontic Centers of America, Inc., 35
Orvis Company, Inc., The, 28
Oryx Energy Company, 7
Oscar Mayer Foods Corp., 12
OshKosh B'Gosh, Inc., 9; 42 (upd.)
Oshkosh Truck Corporation, 7
Oshman's Sporting Goods, Inc., 17
Osmonics, Inc., 18
Otis Elevator Company, Inc., 13; 39 (upd.)
Otis Spunkmeyer, Inc., 28
OTR Express, Inc., 25
Ottaway Newspapers, Inc., 15
Otter Tail Power Company, 18
Outback Steakhouse, Inc., 12; 34 (upd.)
Outboard Marine Corporation, III; 20 (upd.)
Outdoor Systems, Inc., 25
Outlook Group Corporation, 37
Overnite Transportation Co., 14
Overseas Shipholding Group, Inc., 11
Owens & Minor, Inc., 16
Owens Corning Corporation, III; 20 (upd.)
Owens-Illinois, Inc., I; 26 (upd.)
Owosso Corporation, 29
Oxford Health Plans, Inc., 16
Oxford Industries, Inc., 8
P&C Foods Inc., 8
P.C. Richard & Son Corp., 23
P.F. Chang's China Bistro, Inc., 37
P.H. Glatfelter Company, 8; 30 (upd.)
Paccar Inc., I; 26 (upd.)
Pacer Technology, 40
Pacific Enterprises, V
Pacific Gas and Electric Company, V
Pacific Sunwear of California, Inc., 28
Pacific Telecom, Inc., 6
Pacific Telesis Group, V
PacifiCare Health Systems, Inc., 11
PacifiCorp, V; 26 (upd.)
Packaging Corporation of America, 12

United States *(continued)*
Packard Bell Electronics, Inc., 13
Paging Network Inc., 11
PaineWebber Group Inc., II; 22 (upd.)
Pall Corporation, 9
Palm Harbor Homes, Inc., 39
Palm, Inc., 36
Palomar Medical Technologies, Inc., 22
Pamida Holdings Corporation, 15
Pampered Chef, Ltd., The, 18
Pan American World Airways, Inc., I; 12 (upd.)
Panavision Inc., 24
Panda Management Company, Inc., 35
Panhandle Eastern Corporation, V
Pantry, Inc., The, 36
Papa John's International, Inc., 15
Papetti's Hygrade Egg Products, Inc., 39
Paradise Music & Entertainment, Inc., 42
Parametric Technology Corp., 16
Paramount Pictures Corporation, II
Paris Corporation, 22
Parisian, Inc., 14
Park Corp., 22
Park-Ohio Industries Inc., 17
Parker Drilling Company, 28
Parker-Hannifin Corporation, III; 24 (upd.)
Parsons Brinckerhoff, Inc., 34
Parsons Corporation, The, 8
Pathmark Stores, Inc., 23
Patina Oil & Gas Corporation, 24
Patrick Industries, Inc., 30
Patterson Dental Co., 19
Paul Harris Stores, Inc., 18
Paul Revere Corporation, The, 12
Paul, Hastings, Janofsky & Walker LLP, 27
Paxson Communications Corporation, 33
Pay 'N Pak Stores, Inc., 9
Paychex, Inc., 15
Payless Cashways, Inc., 11
Payless ShoeSource, Inc., 18
PC Connection, Inc., 37
Peabody Coal Company, 10
Peabody Holding Company, Inc., IV
Peak Technologies Group, Inc., The, 14
Peapod, Inc., 30
Pearle Vision, Inc., 13
Peavey Electronics Corporation, 16
PECO Energy Company, 11
Pediatric Services of America, Inc., 31
Peebles Inc., 16; 43 (upd.)
Peet's Coffee & Tea, Inc., 38
Pella Corporation, 12; 39 (upd.)
Pendleton Woolen Mills, Inc., 42
Penn Engineering & Manufacturing Corp., 28
Penn National Gaming, Inc., 33
Penn Traffic Company, 13
Pennsylvania Blue Shield, III
Pennsylvania Power & Light Company, V
Pennwalt Corporation, I
Pennzoil Company, IV; 20 (upd.)
Penske Corporation, V; 19 (upd.)
Pentair, Inc., 7; 26 (upd.)
Pentech International, Inc., 29
Penton Media, Inc., 27
People Express Airlines, Inc., I
Peoples Energy Corporation, 6
PeopleSoft Inc., 14; 33 (upd.)
Pep Boys--Manny, Moe & Jack, The, 11; 36 (upd.)
Pepper Hamilton LLP, 43
Pepsi Bottling Group, Inc., The, 40
Pepsico, Inc., I; 10 (upd.); 38 (upd.)
Perdue Farms Inc., 7; 23 (upd.)
Performance Food Group Company, 31
Perini Corporation, 8
Perkin-Elmer Corporation, The, 7
Perkins Family Restaurants, L.P., 22
Perot Systems Corporation, 29
Perrigo Company, 12
Perry Ellis International, Inc., 41
Pet Incorporated, 7
Petco Animal Supplies, Inc., 29
Pete's Brewing Company, 22
Peter Kiewit Sons' Inc., 8
Petersen Publishing Company, 21
Petrie Stores Corporation, 8
Petroleum Helicopters, Inc., 35
Petrolite Corporation, 15
PETsMART, Inc., 14; 41 (upd.)
Pew Charitable Trusts, The, 35
Pez Candy, Inc., 38
Pfizer Inc., I; 9 (upd.); 38 (upd.)
PG&E Corporation, 26 (upd.)
Phar-Mor Inc., 12
Pharmacia & Upjohn Inc., I; 25 (upd.)
Phelps Dodge Corporation, IV; 28 (upd.)
PHH Corporation, V
Philadelphia Eagles, 37
Philadelphia Electric Company, V
Philadelphia Suburban Corporation, 39
Philip Morris Companies Inc., V; 18 (upd.)
Philips Electronics North America Corp., 13
Phillips Petroleum Company, IV; 40 (upd.)
Phillips-Van Heusen Corporation, 24
PHP Healthcare Corporation, 22
PhyCor, Inc., 36
Physician Sales & Service, Inc., 14
Physio-Control International Corp., 18
Piccadilly Cafeterias, Inc., 19
PictureTel Corp., 10; 27 (upd.)
Piedmont Natural Gas Company, Inc., 27
Pier 1 Imports, Inc., 12; 34 (upd.)
Pierce Leahy Corporation, 24
Piercing Pagoda, Inc., 29
Piggly Wiggly Southern, Inc., 13
Pilgrim's Pride Corporation, 7; 23 (upd.)
Pillowtex Corporation, 19; 41 (upd.)
Pillsbury Company, II; 13 (upd.)
Pillsbury Madison & Sutro LLP, 29
Pinkerton's Inc., 9
Pinnacle West Capital Corporation, 6
Pioneer Hi-Bred International, Inc., 9; 41 (upd.)
Pioneer-Standard Electronics Inc., 19
Piper Jaffray Companies Inc., 22
Pitney Bowes Inc., III; 19
Pittston Company, The, IV; 19 (upd.)
Pittway Corporation, 9; 33 (upd.)
Pittway Corporation, 9
Pixar Animation Studios, 34
Pizza Hut Inc., 7; 21 (upd.)
Planet Hollywood International, Inc., 18; 41 (upd.)
Platinum Entertainment, Inc., 35
PLATINUM Technology, Inc., 14
Play by Play Toys & Novelties, Inc., 26
Playboy Enterprises, Inc., 18
PlayCore, Inc., 27
Players International, Inc., 22
Playskool, Inc., 25
Playtex Products, Inc., 15
Pleasant Company, 27
Plexus Corporation, 35
Plum Creek Timber Company, Inc., 43
Pluma, Inc., 27
Ply Gem Industries Inc., 12
PMT Services, Inc., 24
PNC Bank Corp., II; 13 (upd.)
Pogo Producing Company, 39
Polaris Industries Inc., 12; 35 (upd.)
Polaroid Corporation, III; 7 (upd.); 28 (upd.)
Policy Management Systems Corporation, 11
Polk Audio, Inc., 34
Polo/Ralph Lauren Corporation, 12
PolyGram N.V., 23
Pomeroy Computer Resources, Inc., 33
Ponderosa Steakhouse, 15
Pope and Talbot, Inc., 12
Popular, Inc., 41
Portland General Corporation, 6
Post Properties, Inc., 26
Potlatch Corporation, 8; 34 (upd.)
Potomac Electric Power Company, 6
Potter & Brumfield Inc., 11
Powell's Books, Inc., 40
Powerhouse Technologies, Inc., 27
PPG Industries, Inc., III; 22 (upd.)
PPL Corporation, 41 (upd.)
PR Newswire, 35
Pratt & Whitney, 9
Praxair, Inc., 11
Pre-Paid Legal Services, Inc., 20
Precision Castparts Corp., 15
Premark International, Inc., III
Premcor Inc., 37
Premier Industrial Corporation, 9
Premier Parks, Inc., 27
Premium Standard Farms, Inc., 30
PremiumWear, Inc., 30
President Casinos, Inc., 22
Presstek, Inc., 33
Preston Corporation, 6
Price Communications Corporation, 42
Price Company, The, V
Price Waterhouse, 9
PriceCostco, Inc., 14
PricewaterhouseCoopers, 29 (upd.)
Primark Corp., 13
Primedex Health Systems, Inc., 25
Primedia Inc., 22
Primerica Corporation, I
Prince Sports Group, Inc., 15
Princess Cruise Lines, 22
Princeton Review, Inc., The, 42
Principal Mutual Life Insurance Company, III
Printronix, Inc., 18
Procter & Gamble Company, The, III; 8 (upd.); 26 (upd.)
Prodigy Communications Corporation, 34
Professional Golfers' Association of America, The, 41
Proffitt's, Inc., 19
Progress Software Corporation, 15
Progressive Corporation, The, 11; 29 (upd.)
Promus Companies, Inc., 9
Protection One, Inc., 32
Providence Journal Company, The, 28
Provident Life and Accident Insurance Company of America, III
Prudential Insurance Company of America, The, III; 30 (upd.)
PSI Resources, 6
Pubco Corporation, 17
Public Service Company of Colorado, 6
Public Service Company of New Hampshire, 21
Public Service Company of New Mexico, 6
Public Service Enterprise Group Incorporated, V
Publishers Clearing House, 23
Publishers Group, Inc., 35
Publix Supermarkets Inc., 7; 31 (upd.)
Puget Sound Power and Light Company, 6
Pulaski Furniture Corporation, 33
Pulitzer Publishing Company, 15

Pulte Corporation, 8
Pulte Homes, Inc., 42 (upd.)
Purina Mills, Inc., 32
Puritan-Bennett Corporation, 13
Purolator Products Company, 21
Putt-Putt Golf Courses of America, Inc., 23
Pyramid Breweries Inc., 33
Quad/Graphics, Inc., 19
Quaker Fabric Corp., 19
Quaker Oats Company, The, II; 12 (upd.); 34 (upd.)
Quaker State Corporation, 7; 21 (upd.)
Qualcomm Inc., 20
Quality Dining, Inc., 18
Quality Food Centers, Inc., 17
Quanex Corporation, 13
Quantum Chemical Corporation, 8
Quantum Corporation, 10
Quark, Inc., 36
Quest Diagnostics Inc., 26
Questar Corporation, 6; 26 (upd.)
Quick & Reilly Group, Inc., The, 20
Quiksilver, Inc., 18
QuikTrip Corporation, 36
Quill Corporation, 28
Quintiles Transnational Corporation, 21
Quixote Corporation, 15
Quizno's Corporation, The, 42
QVC Network Inc., 9
Qwest Communications International, Inc., 37
R.G. Barry Corp., 17
R.H. Macy & Co., Inc., V; 8 (upd.); 30 (upd.)
R.J. Reynolds Tobacco Holdings, Inc., 30 (upd.)
R.L. Polk & Co., 10
R.P. Scherer, I
R.R. Donnelley & Sons Company, IV; 9 (upd.); 38 (upd.)
Racal-Datacom Inc., 11
Racing Champions Corporation, 37
Radian Group Inc., 42
Radio Flyer Inc., 34
RadioShack Corporation, 36 (upd.)
Radius Inc., 16
Rag Shops, Inc., 30
RailTex, Inc., 20
Rainforest Cafe, Inc., 25
Rainier Brewing Company, 23
Raley's Inc., 14
Rally's Hamburgers, Inc., 25
Ralphs Grocery Company, 35
Ralston Purina Company, II; 13 (upd.)
Ramsay Youth Services, Inc., 41
Rand McNally & Company, 28
Randall's Food Markets, Inc., 40
Random House, Inc., 13; 31 (upd.)
Rapala-Normark Group, Ltd., 30
Rare Hospitality International Inc., 19
Raven Industries, Inc., 33
Rawlings Sporting Goods Co., Inc., 24
Raychem Corporation, 8
Rayonier Inc., 24
Rayovac Corporation, 13; 39 (upd.)
Raytheon Company, II; 11 (upd.); 38 (upd.)
Razorfish, Inc., 37
RCA Corporation, II
RCM Technologies, Inc., 34
RDO Equipment Company, 33
Read-Rite Corp., 10
Reader's Digest Association, Inc., The, IV; 17 (upd.)
Recoton Corp., 15
Recovery Engineering, Inc., 25
Recreational Equipment, Inc., 18
Recycled Paper Greetings, Inc., 21
Red Apple Group, Inc., 23
Red Roof Inns, Inc., 18
Red Wing Shoe Company, Inc., 9; 30 (upd.)
Redhook Ale Brewery, Inc., 31
Reebok International Ltd., V; 9 (upd.); 26 (upd.)
Reeds Jewelers, Inc., 22
Regal-Beloit Corporation, 18
Regis Corporation, 18
Reichhold Chemicals, Inc., 10
Reliance Electric Company, 9
Reliance Group Holdings, Inc., III
Reliance Steel & Aluminum Co., 19
RemedyTemp, Inc., 20
Remington Arms Company, Inc., 12; 40 (upd.)
Remington Products Company, L.L.C., 42
Renaissance Learning Systems, Inc., 39
Reno Air Inc., 23
Rent-Way, Inc., 33
Rental Service Corporation, 28
Rentrak Corporation, 35
Republic Engineered Steels, Inc., 7; 26 (upd.)
Republic Industries, Inc., 26
Republic New York Corporation, 11
Res-Care, Inc., 29
Resorts International, Inc., 12
Resource America, Inc., 42
Response Oncology, Inc., 27
Restaurants Unlimited, Inc., 13
Restoration Hardware, Inc., 30
Revco D.S., Inc., V
Revell-Monogram Inc., 16
Revere Ware Corporation, 22
Revlon Inc., III; 17 (upd.)
REX Stores Corp., 10
Rexel, Inc., 15
Rexnord Corporation, 21
Reynolds Metals Company, IV; 19 (upd.)
RF Micro Devices, Inc., 43
Rhino Entertainment Company, 18
Rhodes Inc., 23
Rica Foods, Inc., 41
Rich Products Corporation, 7; 38 (upd.)
Richardson Electronics, Ltd., 17
Richfood Holdings, Inc., 7
Richton International Corporation, 39
Riddell Sports Inc., 22
Ride, Inc., 22
Riese Organization, The, 38
Riggs National Corporation, 13
Right Management Consultants, Inc., 42
Riklis Family Corp., 9
Riser Foods, Inc., 9
Rite Aid Corporation, V; 19 (upd.)
Ritz Camera Centers, 34
Ritz-Carlton Hotel Company L.L.C., 9; 29 (upd.)
Rival Company, The, 19
River Oaks Furniture, Inc., 43
Riverwood International Corporation, 11
Riviana Foods Inc., 27
RJR Nabisco Holdings Corp., V
RMH Teleservices, Inc., 42
Roadhouse Grill, Inc., 22
Roadmaster Industries, Inc., 16
Roadway Express, Inc., V; 25 (upd.)
Robbins & Myers Inc., 15
Roberds Inc., 19
Robert Half International Inc., 18
Robert Mondavi Corporation, 15
Robert Wood Johnson Foundation, 35
Roberts Pharmaceutical Corporation, 16
Robertson-Ceco Corporation, 19
Roche Biomedical Laboratories, Inc., 11
Roche Bioscience, 14 (upd.)
Rochester Gas and Electric Corporation, 6
Rochester Telephone Corporation, 6
Rock Bottom Restaurants, Inc., 25
Rock of Ages Corporation, 37
Rock-Tenn Company, 13
Rockefeller Foundation, The, 34
Rockford Corporation, 43
RockShox, Inc., 26
Rockwell Automation, 43 (upd.)
Rockwell International Corporation, I; 11 (upd.)
Rocky Shoes & Boots, Inc., 26
Rodale Press, Inc., 23
Rohm and Haas Company, I; 26 (upd.)
ROHN Industries, Inc., 22
Rohr Incorporated, 9
Roll International Corporation, 37
Rollerblade, Inc., 15; 34 (upd.)
Rollins, Inc., 11
Rolls-Royce Allison, 29 (upd.)
Ronco, Inc., 15
Rooms To Go Inc., 28
Rooney Brothers Co., 25
Roper Industries Inc., 15
Ropes & Gray, 40
Rorer Group, I
Rose's Stores, Inc., 13
Rosemount Inc., 15
Rosenbluth International Inc., 14
Ross Stores, Inc., 17; 43 (upd.)
Rotary International, 31
Roto-Rooter Corp., 15
Rottlund Company, Inc., The, 28
Rouge Steel Company, 8
Roundy's Inc., 14
Rouse Company, The, 15
Rowan Companies, Inc., 43
Roy F. Weston, Inc., 33
Royal Appliance Manufacturing Company, 15
Royal Caribbean Cruises Ltd., 22
Royal Crown Company, Inc., 23
RPM, Inc., 8; 36 (upd.)
Rubbermaid Incorporated, III; 20 (upd.)
Rubio's Restaurants, Inc., 35
Ruby Tuesday, Inc., 18
Rural Cellular Corporation, 43
Rural/Metro Corporation, 28
Rush Communications, 33
Russ Berrie and Company, Inc., 12
Russell Corporation, 8; 30 (upd.)
Russell Reynolds Associates Inc., 38
Russell Stover Candies Inc., 12
Rust International Inc., 11
Ruth's Chris Steak House, 28
Ryan's Family Steak Houses, Inc., 15
Ryder System, Inc., V; 24 (upd.)
Ryerson Tull, Inc., 40 (upd.)
Ryland Group, Inc., The, 8; 37 (upd.)
S&C Electric Company, 15
S&K Famous Brands, Inc., 23
S-K-I Limited, 15
S.C. Johnson & Son, Inc., III; 28 (upd.)
Saatchi & Saatchi, 42 (upd.)
Sabratek Corporation, 29
SABRE Group Holdings, Inc., 26
SAFECO Corporaton, III
Safeguard Scientifics, Inc., 10
Safelite Glass Corp., 19
Safeskin Corporation, 18
Safety 1st, Inc., 24
Safety-Kleen Corp., 8
Safeway Inc., II; 24 (upd.)
Saga Communications, Inc., 27
St. Joe Company, The, 31
St. Joe Paper Company, 8
St. John Knits, Inc., 14
St. Jude Medical, Inc., 11; 43 (upd.)

United States *(continued)*

St. Paul Bank for Cooperatives, 8
St. Paul Companies, Inc., The, III; 22 (upd.)
Saks Holdings, Inc., 24
Saks Inc., 41 (upd.)
Salant Corporation, 12
Salomon Inc., II; 13 (upd.)
Salt River Project, 19
Salton, Inc., 30
Salvation Army USA, The, 32
Sam Ash Music Corporation, 30
Sam's Club, 40
Samsonite Corporation, 13; 43 (upd.)
Samuels Jewelers Incorporated, 30
San Diego Gas & Electric Company, V
Sanderson Farms, Inc., 15
Santa Barbara Restaurant Group, Inc., 37
Santa Cruz Operation, Inc., The, 38
Santa Fe Gaming Corporation, 19
Santa Fe International Corporation, 38
Santa Fe Pacific Corporation, V
Sara Lee Corporation, II; 15 (upd.)
SAS Institute Inc., 10
Saturn Corporation, 7; 21 (upd.)
Saucony Inc., 35
Sauder Woodworking Company, 12; 35 (upd.)
Savannah Foods & Industries, Inc., 7
Sawtek Inc., 43 (upd.)
Sbarro, Inc., 16
SBC Communications Inc., 32 (upd.)
SBS Technologies, Inc., 25
SCANA Corporation, 6
ScanSource, Inc., 29
SCB Computer Technology, Inc., 29
SCEcorp, V
Schawk, Inc., 24
Schering-Plough Corporation, I; 14 (upd.)
Schlotzsky's, Inc., 36
Schlumberger Limited, III; 17 (upd.)
Schmitt Music Company, 40
Schneider National, Inc., 36
Schneiderman's Furniture Inc., 28
Schnitzer Steel Industries, Inc., 19
Scholastic Corporation, 10; 29 (upd.)
Schottenstein Stores Corp., 14
Schuff Steel Company, 26
Schultz Sav-O Stores, Inc., 21; 31 (upd.)
Schwan's Sales Enterprises, Inc., 7; 26 (upd.)
Schwinn Cycle and Fitness L.P., 19
SCI Systems, Inc., 9
Science Applications International Corporation, 15
Scientific-Atlanta, Inc., 6
Score Board, Inc., The, 19
Scotsman Industries, Inc., 20
Scott Fetzer Company, 12
Scott Paper Company, IV, 31 (upd.)
Scotts Company, The, 22
Scotty's, Inc., 22
Scovill Fasteners Inc., 24
SCP Pool Corporation, 39
Seaboard Corporation, 36
Seagate Technology, Inc., 8; 34 (upd.)
Seagull Energy Corporation, 11
Sealed Air Corporation, 14
Sealed Power Corporation, I
Sealright Co., Inc., 17
Sealy Inc., 12
Seaman Furniture Company, Inc., 32
Sears, Roebuck and Co., V; 18 (upd.)
Seattle FilmWorks, Inc., 20
Seattle First National Bank Inc., 8
Seattle Times Company, 15
Seaway Food Town, Inc., 15
Sebastiani Vineyards, Inc., 28
Second Harvest, 29
Security Capital Corporation, 17
Security Pacific Corporation, II
SED International Holdings, Inc., 43
See's Candies, Inc., 30
Sega of America, Inc., 10
Seigle's Home and Building Centers, Inc., 41
Select Comfort Corporation, 34
Selmer Company, Inc., The, 19
Seminis, Inc., 29
Semitool, Inc., 18
Sempra Energy, 25 (upd.)
Semtech Corporation, 32
Seneca Foods Corporation, 17
Sensormatic Electronics Corp., 11
Sensory Science Corporation, 37
Sequa Corp., 13
Serta, Inc., 28
Service America Corp., 7
Service Corporation International, 6
Service Merchandise Company, Inc., V; 19 (upd.)
ServiceMaster Inc., 6; 23 (upd.)
7-11, Inc., 32 (upd.)
Sevenson Environmental Services, Inc., 42
SFX Entertainment, Inc., 36
SGI, 29 (upd.)
Shakespeare Company, 22
Shaklee Corporation, 12; 39 (upd.)
Shared Medical Systems Corporation, 14
Sharper Image Corporation, The, 10
Shaw Industries, 9
Shaw Industries, Inc., 40 (upd.)
Shawmut National Corporation, 13
Shearman & Sterling, 32
Shearson Lehman Brothers Holdings Inc., II; 9 (upd.)
Shelby Williams Industries, Inc., 14
Sheldahl Inc., 23
Shell Oil Company, IV; 14 (upd.); 41 (upd.)
Sheller-Globe Corporation, I
Shells Seafood Restaurants, Inc., 43
Sherwin-Williams Company, The, III; 13 (upd.)
Shoe Carnival Inc., 14
Shoney's, Inc., 7; 23 (upd.)
ShopKo Stores Inc., 21
Shorewood Packaging Corporation, 28
ShowBiz Pizza Time, Inc., 13
Showboat, Inc., 19
Shubert Organization Inc., 24
Sidley Austin Brown & Wood, 40
Siebel Systems, Inc., 38
Siebert Financial Corp., 32
Sierra Club, The, 28
Sierra Health Services, Inc., 15
Sierra On-Line, Inc., 15; 41 (upd.)
Sierra Pacific Industries, 22
SIFCO Industries, Inc., 41
Sigma-Aldrich Corporation, I; 36 (upd.)
Signet Banking Corporation, 11
Sikorsky Aircraft Corporation, 24
Silicon Graphics Incorporated, 9
SilverPlatter Information Inc., 23
Simon & Schuster Inc., IV; 19 (upd.)
Simon Property Group, Inc., 27
Simon Transportation Services Inc., 27
Simplex Technologies Inc., 21
Simpson Investment Company, 17
Simpson Thacher & Bartlett, 39
Simula, Inc., 41
Sinclair Broadcast Group, Inc., 25
Sir Speedy, Inc., 16
Six Flags Theme Parks, Inc., 17
Skadden, Arps, Slate, Meagher & Flom, 18
Skechers USA Inc., 31
Skidmore, Owings & Merrill, 13
Skyline Corporation, 30
SkyMall, Inc., 26
SkyWest, Inc., 25
Sleepy's Inc., 32
Slim-Fast Nutritional Foods International, Inc., 18
SLM Holding Corp., 25 (upd.)
Smart & Final, Inc., 16
SmartForce PLC, 43
Smead Manufacturing Co., 17
Smith & Wesson Corporation, 30
Smith Barney Inc., 15
Smith Corona Corp., 13
Smith International, Inc., 15
Smith's Food & Drug Centers, Inc., 8
Smithfield Foods, Inc., 7; 43 (upd.)
SmithKline Beckman Corporation, I
Smithsonian Institution, 27
Smithway Motor Xpress Corporation, 39
Smurfit-Stone Container Corporation, 26 (upd.)
Snap-on Tools Corporation, 7
Snap-On, Incorporated, 27 (upd.)
Snapple Beverage Corporation, 11
Snell & Wilmer L.L.P., 28
Society Corporation, 9
Soft Sheen Products, Inc., 31
Solectron Corp., 12
Solo Serve Corporation, 28
Sonat, Inc., 6
Sonic Corp., 14; 37 (upd.)
Sonoco Products Company, 8
Soros Fund Management LLC, 28
Sorrento, Inc., 24
SOS Staffing Services, 25
Sotheby's Holdings, Inc., 11; 29 (upd.)
Sound Advice, Inc., 41
South Jersey Industries, Inc., 42
Southdown, Inc., 14
Southern Company, The, V; 38 (upd.)
Southern Indiana Gas and Electric Company, 13
Southern New UK Telecommunications Corporation, 6
Southern Pacific Transportation Company, V
Southern States Cooperative Incorporated, 36
Southern Union Company, 27
Southland Corporation, The, II; 7 (upd.)
Southtrust Corporation, 11
Southwest Airlines Co., 6; 24 (upd.)
Southwest Gas Corporation, 19
Southwestern Bell Corporation, V
Southwestern Electric Power Co., 21
Southwestern Public Service Company, 6
Southwire Company, Inc., 8; 23 (upd.)
Spacehab, Inc., 37
Spaghetti Warehouse, Inc., 25
Spanish Broadcasting System, Inc., 41
Spartan Motors Inc., 14
Spartan Stores Inc., 8
Spartech Corporation, 19
Sparton Corporation, 18
Spec's Music, Inc., 19
Specialty Coatings Inc., 8
Specialty Equipment Companies, Inc., 25
SpeeDee Oil Change and Tune-Up, 25
Speedway Motorsports, Inc., 32
Spelling Entertainment, 14; 35 (upd.)
Spencer Stuart and Associates, Inc., 14
Spiegel, Inc., 10; 27 (upd.)
Spirit Airlines, Inc., 31
Sport Chalet, Inc., 16
Sport Supply Group, Inc., 23
Sportmart, Inc., 15

Sports & Recreation, Inc., 17
Sports Authority, Inc., The, 16; 43 (upd.)
Sports Club Company, The, 25
Sportsman's Guide, Inc., The, 36
Springs Industries, Inc., V; 19 (upd.)
Sprint Communications Company, L.P., 9
SPS Technologies, Inc., 30
SPX Corporation, 10
Squibb Corporation, I
Stage Stores, Inc., 24
Stanadyne Automotive Corporation, 37
Standard Commercial Corporation, 13
Standard Federal Bank, 9
Standard Microsystems Corporation, 11
Standard Motor Products, Inc., 40
Standard Register Co., 15
Standex International Corporation, 17
Stanhome Inc., 15
Stanley Furniture Company, Inc., 34
Stanley Works, The, III; 20 (upd.)
Staples, Inc., 10
Star Banc Corporation, 11
Starbucks Corporation, 13; 34 (upd.)
Starcraft Corporation, 30
Starrett Corporation, 21
Starter Corp., 12
State Farm Mutual Automobile Insurance Company, III
State Street Boston Corporation, 8
Staten Island Bancorp, Inc., 39
Station Casinos Inc., 25
Steak n Shake Company, The, 41
Stearns, Inc., 43
Steelcase, Inc., 7; 27 (upd.)
Stein Mart Inc., 19
Steinway Musical Properties, Inc., 19
Stepan Company, 30
Stericycle Inc., 33
STERIS Corporation, 29
Sterling Chemicals, Inc., 16
Sterling Drug, Inc., I
Sterling Electronics Corp., 18
Sterling Software, Inc., 11
Stevedoring Services of America Inc., 28
Steven Madden, Ltd., 37
Stewart & Stevenson Services Inc., 11
Stewart Enterprises, Inc., 20
Stewart's Beverages, 39
Stock Yards Packing Co., Inc., 37
Stone & Webster, Inc., 13
Stone Container Corporation, IV
Stone Manufacturing Company, 14; 43 (upd.)
Stop & Shop Companies, Inc., The, II; 24 (upd.)
Storage Technology Corporation, 6
Storage USA, Inc., 21
Stouffer Corp., 8
StrataCom, Inc., 16
Stratus Computer, Inc., 10
Stride Rite Corporation, The, 8; 37 (upd.)
Stroh Brewery Company, The, I; 18 (upd.)
Stroock & Stroock & Lavan LLP, 40
Strouds, Inc., 33
Stryker Corporation, 11; 29 (upd.)
Stuart Entertainment Inc., 16
Student Loan Marketing Association, II
Stuller Settings, Inc., 35
Sturm, Ruger & Company, Inc., 19
Sub-Zero Freezer Co., Inc., 31
Suburban Propane Partners, L.P., 30
Subway, 32
Successories, Inc., 30
Sudbury Inc., 16
Suiza Foods Corporation, 26
Sullivan & Cromwell, 26
Summit Bancorporation, The, 14
Summit Family Restaurants, Inc. 19
Sun Company, Inc., IV
Sun Country Airlines, 30
Sun Distributors L.P., 12
Sun Healthcare Group Inc., 25
Sun Microsystems, Inc., 7; 30 (upd.)
Sun Sportswear, Inc., 17
Sun Television & Appliances Inc., 10
Sun-Diamond Growers of California, 7
SunAmerica Inc., 11
Sunbeam-Oster Co., Inc., 9
Sunburst Hospitality Corporation, 26
Sundstrand Corporation, 7; 21 (upd.)
Sundt Corp., 24
SunGard Data Systems Inc., 11
Sunglass Hut International, Inc., 21
Sunkist Growers, Inc., 26
Sunoco, Inc., 28 (upd.)
Sunrider Corporation, The, 26
Sunrise Medical Inc., 11
SunTrust Banks Inc., 23
Super Food Services, Inc., 15
Super Valu Stores, Inc., II
Supercuts Inc., 26
Superior Industries International, Inc., 8
Superior Uniform Group, Inc., 30
Supermarkets General Holdings Corporation, II
Supervalu Inc., 18 (upd.)
Suprema Specialties, Inc., 27
Supreme International Corporation, 27
Susquehanna Pfaltzgraff Company, 8
Sutter Home Winery Inc., 16
Sverdrup Corporation, 14
Swank Inc., 17
Sweetheart Cup Company, Inc., 36
Swift Transportation Co., Inc., 42
Swinerton Inc., 43
Swisher International Group Inc., 23
Sybase, Inc., 10; 27 (upd.)
Sybron International Corp., 14
Sylvan Learning Systems, Inc., 35
Sylvan, Inc., 22
Symantec Corporation, 10
Symbol Technologies, Inc., 15
Syms Corporation, 29
Synopsis, Inc., 11
SynOptics Communications, Inc., 10
Synovus Financial Corp., 12
Syntex Corporation, I
SyQuest Technology, Inc., 18
Syratech Corp., 14
SYSCO Corporation, II; 24 (upd.)
System Software Associates, Inc., 10
Systems & Computer Technology Corp., 19
T. Rowe Price Associates, Inc., 11; 34 (upd.)
TAB Products Co., 17
Taco Bell Corp., 7; 21 (upd.)
Taco Cabana, Inc., 23
Taco John's International Inc., 15
Talbots, Inc., The, 11; 31 (upd.)
Talley Industries, Inc., 16
Tambrands Inc., 8
Tandem Computers, Inc., 6
Tandy Corporation, II; 12 (upd.)
Tandycrafts, Inc., 31
Target Stores, 10; 27 (upd.)
Tasty Baking Company, 14; 35 (upd.)
Tattered Cover Book Store, 43
Taylor Corporation, 36
Taylor Made Golf Co., 23
Taylor Publishing Company, 12; 36 (upd.)
TBWA Advertising, Inc., 6
TBWA\Chiat\Day, 43 (upd.)
TCBY Enterprises Inc., 17
Teachers Insurance and Annuity Association, III
TearDrop Golf Company, 32
Tech Data Corporation, 10
Tech-Sym Corporation, 18
Technitrol, Inc., 29
TECO Energy, Inc., 6
Tecumseh Products Company, 8
Tejon Ranch Company, 35
Tektronix, Inc., 8
Tele-Communications, Inc., II
Teledyne, Inc., I; 10 (upd.)
Telephone and Data Systems, Inc., 9
Tellabs, Inc., 11; 40 (upd.)
Telxon Corporation, 10
Temple-Inland Inc., IV; 31 (upd.)
TenFold Corporation, 35
Tennant Company, 13; 33 (upd.)
Tenneco Inc., I; 10 (upd.)
Teradyne, Inc., 11
Terex Corporation, 7; 40 (upd.)
Terra Industries, Inc., 13
Tesoro Petroleum Corporation, 7
Tetra Tech, Inc., 29
Texaco Inc., IV; 14 (upd.); 41 (upd.)
Texas Air Corporation, I
Texas Industries, Inc., 8
Texas Instruments Incorporated, II; 11 (upd.)
Texas Pacific Group Inc., 36
Texas Utilities Company, V; 25 (upd.)
Textron Inc., I , 34 (upd.)
Textron Lycoming Turbine Engine, 9
Thermadyne Holding Corporation, 19
Thermo BioAnalysis Corp., 25
Thermo Electron Corporation, 7
Thermo Fibertek, Inc., 24
Thermo Instrument Systems Inc., 11
Thermo King Corporation, 13
Thermos Company, 16
Thiokol Corporation, 9; 22 (upd.)
Thomas & Betts Corp., 11
Thomas Cook Travel Inc., 9; 33 (upd.)
Thomas H. Lee Co., 24
Thomas Industries Inc., 29
Thomas J. Lipton Company, 14
Thomas Nelson, Inc., 14; 38 (upd.)
Thomas Publishing Company, 26
Thomaston Mills, Inc., 27
Thomasville Furniture Industries, Inc., 12
Thor Industries, Inc., 39
Thorn Apple Valley, Inc., 7; 22 (upd.)
Thousand Trails, Inc., 33
THQ, Inc., 39
3Com Corporation, 11; 34 (upd.)
3DO Company, The, 43
Thrifty PayLess, Inc., 12
Ticketmaster Group, Inc., 13; 37 (upd.)
Tidewater Inc., 11; 37 (upd.)
Tiffany & Co., 14
TIG Holdings, Inc., 26
Tillotson Corp., 15
Timberland Company, The, 13
Timberline Software Corporation, 15
Time Warner Inc., IV; 7 (upd.)
Times Mirror Company, The, IV; 17 (upd.)
Timex Corporation, 7; 25 (upd.)
Timken Company, The, 8; 42 (upd.)
Titan Corporation, The, 36
Titanium Metals Corporation, 21
TJ International, Inc., 19
TJX Companies, Inc., The, V; 19 (upd.)
TLC Beatrice International Holdings, Inc., 22
TMP Worldwide Inc., 30
TNT Freightways Corporation, 14
Today's Man, Inc., 20
Todd Shipyards Corporation, 14
Todd-AO Corporation, The, 33
Todhunter International, Inc., 27

United States *(continued)*

Tokheim Corporation, 21
Toll Brothers Inc., 15
Tom Brown, Inc., 37
Tom Doherty Associates Inc., 25
Tombstone Pizza Corporation, 13
Tone Brothers, Inc., 21
Tonka Corporation, 25
Tootsie Roll Industries Inc., 12
Topps Company, Inc., The, 13; 34 (upd.)
Tops Appliance City, Inc., 17
Torchmark Corporation, 9; 33 (upd.)
Toro Company, The, 7; 26 (upd.)
Torrington Company, The, 13
Tosco Corporation, 7
Total System Services, Inc., 18
Totem Resources Corporation, 9
Tower Air, Inc., 28
Tower Automotive, Inc., 24
Towers Perrin, 32
Town & Country Corporation, 19
Toy Biz, Inc., 18
Toymax International, Inc., 29
Toys 'R'' Us, Inc., V; 18 (upd.)
Tracor Inc., 17
Trader Joe's Co., 13
Trailer Bridge, Inc., 41
Trammell Crow Company, 8
Trans World Airlines, Inc., I; 12 (upd.); 35 (upd.)
Trans World Entertainment Corporation, 24
Transaction Systems Architects, Inc., 29
Transamerica Corporation, I; 13 (upd.)
Transamerica–An AEGON Company, 41 (upd.)
Transatlantic Holdings, Inc., 11
Transco Energy Company, V
Transmedia Network Inc., 20
TransMontaigne Inc., 28
Tranzonic Companies, The, 37
Tranzonic Cos., The, 15
Travel Ports of America, Inc., 17
Travelers Corporation, The, III
Travis Boats & Motors, Inc., 37
TRC Companies, Inc., 32
Treadco, Inc., 19
Treasure Chest Advertising Company, Inc., 32
Tree of Life, Inc., 29
Trek Bicycle Corporation, 16
Trend-Lines, Inc., 22
Trendwest Resorts, Inc., 33
Tri Valley Growers, 32
Triarc Companies, Inc., 8; 34 (upd.)
Tribune Company, IV; 22 (upd.)
Trico Products Corporation, 15
Trigen Energy Corporation, 42
TriMas Corp., 11
Trimble Navigation Limited, 40
Trinity Industries, Incorporated, 7
TRINOVA Corporation, III
Triton Energy Corporation, 11
Triumph Group, Inc., 31
TRM Copy Centers Corporation, 18
Tropicana Products, Inc., 28
True North Communications Inc., 23
Trump Organization, 23
TruServ Corporation, 24
TRW Inc., I; 11 (upd.); 14 (upd.)
TTX Company, 6
Tucson Electric Power Company, 6
Tuesday Morning Corporation, 18
Tultex Corporation, 13
Tumbleweed, Inc., 33
Tupperware Corporation, 28
Turner Broadcasting System, Inc., II; 6 (upd.)
Turner Corporation, The, 8; 23 (upd.)
Turtle Wax, Inc., 15
Tuscarora Inc., 29
TV Guide, Inc., 43 (upd.)
TVI, Inc., 15
TW Services, Inc., II
Tweeter Home Entertainment Group, Inc., 30
Twentieth Century Fox Film Corporation, II; 25 (upd.)
Twin Disc, Inc., 21
Twinlab Corporation, 34
Ty Inc., 33
Tyco Toys, Inc., 12
Tyler Corporation, 23
Tyson Foods, Incorporated, II; 14 (upd.)
U S West, Inc., V; 25 (upd.)
U.S. Aggregates, Inc., 42
U.S. Bancorp, 14; 36 (upd.)
U.S. Borax, Inc., 42
U.S. Can Corporation, 30
U.S. Cellular Corporation, 31 (upd.)
U.S. Delivery Systems, Inc., 22
U.S. Foodservice, 26
U.S. Healthcare, Inc., 6
U.S. Home Corporation, 8
U.S. News and World Report Inc., 30
U.S. Office Products Company, 25
U.S. Robotics Inc., 9
U.S. Satellite Broadcasting Company, Inc., 20
U.S. Timberlands Company, L.P., 42
U.S. Trust Corp., 17
UAL Corporation, 34 (upd.)
UGI Corporation, 12
Ugly Duckling Corporation, 22
UICI, 33
Ukrop's Super Market's, Inc., 39
Ultimate Electronics, Inc., 18
Ultra Pac, Inc., 24
Ultrak Inc., 24
Ultramar Diamond Shamrock Corporation, 31 (upd.)
Uncle Ben's Inc., 22
Underwriters Laboratories, Inc., 30
Uni-Marts, Inc., 17
Unicom Corporation, 29 (upd.)
Unifi, Inc., 12
UniFirst Corporation, 21
Union Bank of California, 16
Union Camp Corporation, IV
Union Carbide Corporation, I; 9 (upd.)
Union Electric Company, V
Union Pacific Corporation, V; 28 (upd.)
Union Texas Petroleum Holdings, Inc., 9
Unique Casual Restaurants, Inc., 27
Unison HealthCare Corporation, 25
Unisys Corporation, III; 6 (upd.); 36 (upd.)
United Airlines, I; 6 (upd.)
United Auto Group, Inc., 26
United Brands Company, II
United Defense, L.P., 30
United Dominion Industries Limited, 8; 16 (upd.)
United Foods, Inc., 21
United HealthCare Corporation, 9
United Illuminating Company, The, 21
United Industrial Corporation, 37
United Jewish Communities, 33
United Merchants & Manufacturers, Inc., 13
United Natural Foods, Inc., 32
United Parcel Service of America Inc., V; 17 (upd.)
United Press International, Inc., 25
United Rentals, Inc., 34
United Retail Group Inc., 33
United States Cellular Corporation, 9
United States Filter Corporation, 20
United States Postal Service, 14; 34 (upd.)
United States Shoe Corporation, The, V
United States Surgical Corporation, 10; 34 (upd.)
United Stationers Inc., 14
United Technologies Automotive Inc., 15
United Technologies Corporation, I; 10 (upd.); 34 (upd.)
United Telecommunications, Inc., V
United Video Satellite Group, 18
United Water Resources, Inc., 40
United Way of America, 36
Unitil Corporation, 37
Unitog Co., 19
Unitrin Inc., 16
Univar Corporation, 9
Universal Corporation, V
Universal Electronics Inc., 39
Universal Foods Corporation, 7
Universal Forest Products Inc., 10
Universal Health Services, Inc., 6
Universal International, Inc., 25
Universal Studios, Inc., 33
Univision Communications Inc., 24
Uno Restaurant Corporation, 18
Unocal Corporation, IV; 24 (upd.)
UNUM Corp., 13
Upjohn Company, The, I; 8 (upd.)
Urban Outfitters, Inc., 14
US Airways Group, Inc., 28 (upd.)
USA Truck, Inc., 42
USAA, 10
USAir Group, Inc., I; 6 (upd.)
USANA, Inc., 29
USF&G Corporation, III
USG Corporation, III; 26 (upd.)
UST Inc., 9
USX Corporation, IV; 7 (upd.)
Utah Medical Products, Inc., 36
Utah Power and Light Company, 27
UtiliCorp United Inc., 6
UUNET, 38
Vail Associates, Inc., 11
Vail Resorts, Inc., 43 (upd.)
Valassis Communications, Inc., 8; 37 (upd.)
Valero Energy Corporation, 7
Valhi, Inc., 19
Valley Media Inc., 35
Valmont Industries, Inc., 19
Valspar Corporation, The, 8; 32 (upd.)
Value City Department Stores, Inc., 38
Value Line, Inc., 16
Value Merchants Inc., 13
ValueVision International, Inc., 22
Van Camp Seafood Company, Inc., 7
Vanguard Group of Investment Companies, The, 14
Vanguard Group, Inc., The, 34 (upd.)
Vans, Inc., 16
Varco International, Inc., 42
Vari-Lite International, Inc., 35
Varian Associates Inc., 12
Varlen Corporation, 16
Varsity Spirit Corp., 15
Vastar Resources, Inc., 24
VECO International, Inc., 7
Vector Group Ltd., 35 (upd.)
Veeco Instruments Inc., 32
Veit Companies, 43
Venator Group Inc., 35 (upd.)
Vencor, Inc., 16
Venture Stores Inc., 12
Verbatim Corporation, 14
VeriFone, Inc., 18
Verizon Communications, 43 (upd.)
Vermeer Manufacturing Company, 17

Vermont Teddy Bear Co., Inc., The, 36
VF Corporation, V; 17 (upd.)
Viacom Inc., 7; 23 (upd.)
Viasoft Inc., 27
Viatech Continental Can Company, Inc., 25 (upd.)
VICORP Restaurants, Inc., 12
Vienna Sausage Manufacturing Co., 14
Viking Office Products, Inc., 10
Village Super Market, Inc., 7
Village Voice Media, Inc., 38
Vinson & Elkins L.L.P., 30
Vintage Petroleum, Inc., 42
Virco Manufacturing Corporation, 17
Visa International, 9; 26 (upd.)
Vishay Intertechnology, Inc., 21
Vista Chemical Company, I
Vistana, Inc., 22
VISX, Incorporated, 30
Vitalink Pharmacy Services, Inc., 15
Vitesse Semiconductor Corporation, 32
Vitro Corp., 10
Vivra, Inc., 18
Vlasic Foods International Inc., 25
VLSI Technology, Inc., 16
Volt Information Sciences Inc., 26
Vons Companies, Incorporated, The, 7; 28 (upd.)
Vornado Realty Trust, 20
Vulcan Materials Company, 7
W. Atlee Burpee & Co., 27
W.H. Brady Co., 17
W.L. Gore & Associates, Inc., 14
W.R. Berkley Corp., 15
W.R. Grace & Company, I
W.W. Grainger, Inc., V; 26 (upd.)
W.W. Norton & Company, Inc., 28
Waban Inc., 13
Wabash National Corp., 13
Wabtec Corporation, 40
Wachovia Bank of Georgia, N.A., 16
Wachovia Bank of South Carolina, N.A., 16
Wachovia Corporation, 12
Wackenhut Corporation, The, 14
Waddell & Reed, Inc., 22
Waffle House Inc., 14
Waggener Edstrom, 42
Wakefern Food Corporation, 33
Wal-Mart Stores, Inc., V; 8 (upd.); 26 (upd.)
Walbridge Aldinger Co., 38
Walbro Corporation, 13
Waldbaum, Inc., 19
Walden Book Company Inc., 17
Walgreen Co., V; 20 (upd.)
Walker Manufacturing Company, 19
Wall Drug Store, Inc., 40
Wall Street Deli, Inc., 33
Wallace Computer Services, Inc., 36
Walt Disney Company, The, II; 6 (upd.); 30 (upd.)
Walter Industries, Inc., II; 22 (upd.)
Walton Monroe Mills, Inc., 8
Wang Laboratories, Inc., III; 6 (upd.)
Warnaco Group Inc., The, 12
Warner Communications Inc., II
Warner-Lambert Co., I; 10 (upd.)
Washington Companies, The, 33
Washington Federal, Inc., 17
Washington Football, Inc., 35
Washington Gas Light Company, 19
Washington Mutual, Inc., 17
Washington National Corporation, 12
Washington Natural Gas Company, 9
Washington Post Company, The, IV; 20 (upd.)
Washington Scientific Industries, Inc., 17
Washington Water Power Company, 6
Waste Holdings, Inc., 41
Waste Management, Inc., V
Water Pik Technologies, Inc., 34
Waterhouse Investor Services, Inc., 18
Waters Corporation, 43
Watkins-Johnson Company, 15
Watson Pharmaceuticals Inc., 16
Watson Wyatt Worldwide, 42
Watts Industries, Inc., 19
Waverly, Inc., 16
Wawa Inc., 17
Waxman Industries, Inc., 9
WD-40 Company, 18
Weatherford International, Inc., 39
Weber-Stephen Products Co., 40
Wegmans Food Markets, Inc., 9; 41 (upd.)
Weider Nutrition International, Inc., 29
Weight Watchers International Inc., 12; 33 (upd.)
Weiner's Stores, Inc., 33
Weirton Steel Corporation, IV; 26 (upd.)
Weis Markets, Inc., 15
Weitz Company, Inc., The, 42
Welbilt Corp., 19
Wellman, Inc., 8
WellPoint Health Networks Inc., 25
Wells Fargo & Company, II; 12 (upd.); 38 (upd.)
Wells Rich Greene BDDP, 6
Wells' Dairy, Inc., 36
Wells-Gardner Electronics Corporation, 43
Wendy's International, Inc., 8; 23 (upd.)
Wenner Media, Inc., 32
Werner Enterprises, Inc., 26
West Bend Co., 14
West Coast Entertainment Corporation, 29
West Corporation, 42
West Group, 34 (upd.)
West Marine, Inc., 17
West One Bancorp, 11
West Pharmaceutical Services, Inc., 42
West Point-Pepperell, Inc., 8
West Publishing Co., 7
Westaff Inc., 33
Westamerica Bancorporation, 17
Western Atlas Inc., 12
Western Beef, Inc., 22
Western Company of North America, 15
Western Digital Corp., 25
Western Publishing Group, Inc., 13
Western Resources, Inc., 12
Western Wireless Corporation, 36
Westin Hotels and Resorts Worldwide, 9; 29 (upd.)
Westinghouse Electric Corporation, II; 12 (upd.)
Westmoreland Coal Company, 7
WestPoint Stevens Inc., 16
Westvaco Corporation, IV; 19 (upd.)
Westwood One, Inc., 23
Wet Seal, Inc., The, 18
Wetterau Incorporated, II
Weyco Group, Incorporated, 32
Weyerhaeuser Company, IV; 9 (upd.); 28 (upd.)
Wheaton Industries, 8
Wheelabrator Technologies, Inc., 6
Wheeling-Pittsburgh Corp., 7
Wherehouse Entertainment Incorporated, 11
Whirlpool Corporation, III; 12 (upd.)
White & Case LLP, 35
White Castle System, Inc., 12; 36 (upd.)
White Consolidated Industries Inc., 13
White Rose, Inc., 24
Whitman Corporation, 10 (upd.)
Whitman Education Group, Inc., 41
Whitney Holding Corporation, 21
Whittaker Corporation, I
Whole Foods Market, Inc., 20
Wickes Inc., V; 25 (upd.)
Wild Oats Markets, Inc., 19; 41 (upd.)
Wildlife Conservation Society, 31
Willamette Industries, Inc., IV; 31 (upd.)
William Morris Agency, Inc., 23
Williams Communications Group, Inc., 34
Williams Companies, Inc., The, IV; 31 (upd.)
Williams-Sonoma, Inc., 17
Williamson-Dickie Manufacturing Company, 14
Wilmington Trust Corporation, 25
Wilson Sonsini Goodrich & Rosati, 34
Wilson Sporting Goods Company, 24
Wilsons The Leather Experts Inc., 21
Wind River Systems, Inc., 37
Windmere Corporation, 16
Wine Group, Inc., The, 39
Winn-Dixie Stores, Inc., II; 21 (upd.)
Winnebago Industries Inc., 7; 27 (upd.)
WinsLoew Furniture, Inc., 21
Winston & Strawn, 35
Wisconsin Bell, Inc., 14
Wisconsin Central Transportation Corporation, 24
Wisconsin Dairies, 7
Wisconsin Energy Corporation, 6
Wisconsin Public Service Corporation, 9
Witco Corporation, I; 16 (upd.)
Wizards of the Coast Inc., 24
WLR Foods, Inc., 21
Wm. Wrigley Jr. Company, 7
WMS Industries, Inc., 15
WMX Technologies Inc., 17
Wolfgang Puck Food Company, Inc., The, 26
Wolohan Lumber Co., 19
Wolverine Tube Inc., 23
Wolverine World Wide Inc., 16
Wood-Mode, Inc., 23
Woodward Governor Co., 13
Woolworth Corporation, V; 20 (upd.)
WordPerfect Corporation, 10
Working Assets Funding Service, 43
World Bank Group, 33
World Book, Inc., 12
World Color Press Inc., 12
World Duty Free Americas, Inc., 29 (upd.)
World Wrestling Federation Entertainment, Inc., 32
World's Finest Chocolate Inc., 39
WorldCorp, Inc., 10
Worthington Foods, Inc., 14
Worthington Industries, Inc., 7; 21 (upd.)
WPL Holdings, Inc., 6
WTD Industries, Inc., 20
Wyant Corporation, 30
Wyle Electronics, 14
Wyman-Gordon Company, 14
Wynn's International, Inc., 33
Wyse Technology, Inc., 15
Xerox Corporation, III; 6 (upd.); 26 (upd.)
Xilinx, Inc., 16
Yahoo! Inc., 27
Yankee Candle Company, Inc., The, 37
YankeeNets LLC, 35
Yellow Corporation, 14
Yellow Freight System, Inc. of Delaware, V
YES! Entertainment Corporation, 26
YMCA of the USA, 31
York International Corp., 13
York Research Corporation, 35
Young & Rubicam, Inc., I; 22 (upd.)
Young Broadcasting Inc., 40

United States (*continued*)

Young's Market Company, LLC, 32
Younkers, Inc., 19
Youth Services International, Inc., 21
Yucaipa Cos., 17
Zale Corporation, 16; 40 (upd.)
Zany Brainy, Inc., 31
Zapata Corporation, 25
Zebra Technologies Corporation, 14
Zenith Data Systems, Inc., 10
Zenith Electronics Corporation, II; 13 (upd.); 34 (upd.)
Zero Corporation, 17
Ziebart International Corporation, 30
Ziegler Companies, Inc., The, 24
Ziff Communications Company, 12
Ziff Davis Media Inc., 36 (upd.)
Zilog, Inc., 15
Zion's Cooperative Mercantile Institution, 33
Zions Bancorporation, 12
Zippo Manufacturing Company, 18
Zoltek Companies, Inc., 37
Zondervan Publishing House, 24
Zoom Telephonics, Inc., 18
Zygo Corporation, 42
Zytec Corporation, 19

Venezuela

Cerveceria Polar, I
Petróleos de Venezuela S.A., IV

Wales

Hyder plc, 34
Iceland Group plc, 33
Kwik Save Group plc, 11

Zambia

Zambia Industrial and Mining Corporation Ltd., IV

NOTES ON CONTRIBUTORS

Notes on Contributors

ALLEN, Jerod L. Seattle-based writer and musician.

AMOROSINO, Chris John. Connecticut-based freelance writer.

BAXTER, Melissa Rigney. Indiana-based freelance writer.

BIANCO, David P. Freelance writer, editor, and publishing consultant.

BRYNILDSSEN, Shawna. Freelance writer and editor based in Bloomington, Indiana.

CASON, Rebecca Rayko. Business editor of the *Northwest Florida Daily News* and contributor to *Flight International*; former editor of AeroWorldNet.com and U.S. editor of *Commercial Aviation Report.*

COHEN, M. L. Novelist and freelance writer living in Paris.

COVELL, Jeffrey L. Freelance writer and corporate history contractor.

CULLIGAN, Susan B. Minnesota-based freelance writer.

DeVAULT, Kerri. Seattle-based freelance writer.

DINGER, Ed. Freelance writer and editor based in Brooklyn, New York.

FEDER, Michelle. Seattle-based writer and editor who covers such areas as food, business, and social trends.

FIERO, John W. Freelance writer, researcher, and consultant.

GWILYM, Linda M. Seattle-based writer, editor, and movie reviewer.

INGRAM, Frederick C. Utah-based business writer who has contributed to *GSA Business, Appalachian Trailway News, Encyclopedia of Business, Encyclopedia of Global Industries, Encyclopedia of Consumer Brands,* and other regional and trade publications.

MALLETT, Daryl F. Freelance writer and editor; actor; contributing editor and series editor at The Borgo Press; series editor of SFRA Press's *Studies in Science Fiction, Fantasy and Horror;* associate editor of Gryphon Publications and for *Other Worlds Magazine.*

MARL, Emma. Writer and editor.

POTTER, Anne L. Policy analyst and writer based in Portland, Oregon.

RHODES, Nelson. Freelance editor, writer, and consultant in the Chicago area.

ROTHBURD, Carrie. Freelance writer and editor specializing in corporate profiles, academic texts, and academic journal articles.

ROWE, Suzanne L. Writer and editor based in Seattle.

SALAMIE, David E. Part-owner of InfoWorks Development Group, a reference publication development and editorial services company.

SELVAGGI, Suzanne P. Seattle-based writer and marketing specialist.

SHÉ, Elizabeth. Novelist and poet.

TRADII, Mary. Freelance writer based in Denver, Colorado.

UHLE, Frank. Ann Arbor-based freelance writer; movie projectionist, disc jockey, and staff member of *Psychotronic Video* magazine.

WALDEN, David M. Freelance writer and historian in Salt Lake City; adjunct history instructor at Salt Lake City Community College.

WHIPPLE, Lisa. Freelance writer living in Seattle, Washington; writings include reviews, technical documentation, and poetry for such companies as Amazon.com, Microsoft, AOL Time Warner, and Hasbro; her articles have appeared in several publications, including *McSweeney's* and *Arcade.*

WILLIAMS, Genevieve. Seattle-based freelance writer and fact-finder; former content editor at Amazon.com.

WRIGHTSMAN, Heidi. Seattle-based writer, editor, and researcher.